The
Victoria Cross
1856–1920

THE
VICTORIA CROSS
1856–1920

A COMPLETE RECORD OF THE RECIPIENTS OF THE
VICTORIA CROSS FROM ITS INSTITUTION IN 1856, TO THE
29TH OCTOBER, 1920 WITH DESCRIPTIONS OF THE DEEDS
AND SERVICES FOR WHICH THE AWARD WAS GIVEN AND
WITH MANY BIOGRAPHICAL AND OTHER DETAILS

*Compiled from official publications and despatches, letters from
Commanding Officers and other contemporary accounts, and from
information from private sources*

EDITED BY

**The Late SIR O'MOORE CREAGH, V.C., G.C.B., G.C.S.I.
(until 1920)**

AND

E. M. HUMPHRIS

WITH A FOREWORD BY
Admiral of the Fleet EARL BEATTY, O.M., G.C.B., G.C.V.O., K.C.B.
General The EARL OF CAVAN, G.C.M.G., G.C.V.O., K.C.B.
AND
Air Chief Marshal SIR H. M. TRENCHARD, K.C.B., D.S.O.

With 722 Illustrations

J. B. Hayward & Son
The Medal Specialists
The Old Rectory · Polstead
Suffolk

Originally published in 1920 as Volume I
'The V.C. and D.S.O.'

ISBN 0 903754 22 3

©J. B. Hayward & Son 1985

Printed in Great Britain by
Short Run Press Ltd
Bittern Road
Sowton Industrial Estate
Exeter

FOREWORD

THIS publication should prove very acceptable to the vast public of the British Empire, being a complete and authentic record of the deeds of their sons which have won for them such coveted Distinctions.

Embracing the finest episodes in British Naval and Military History and the gallant exploits of the Royal Air Force—deeds which will for ever live in the memory of man— it should prove a powerful incentive to uphold the honour of the Flag for generations to come.

Edited until 1920 by the late General Sir O'Moore Creagh, V.C., G.C.B., G.C.S.I. (who unfortunately never lived to see his work completed), with the assistance of a literary staff actively engaged from 1918, compiling the immense amount of necessary detail, the work stands as an Individual Record and " Who's Who " of thousands of Acts of Valour and of the men who performed them.

Striking, as it does, the personal note, it is in our opinion a unique work of reference for the home, library, school, club, etc., and will doubtless be treasured by the families of those whose names are honoured therein.

PREFACE

SIR O'MOORE CREAGH made out a rough draft of the preface which he meant to write for the three volumes of this book.

It reads :

" In notifying the completion of the V.C. and D.S.O. book I would state that it gives the particulars of deeds of valour and services of individual officers and soldiers for which decorations have been awarded in all wars since the Crimea, and it is further an epitome of these wars themselves. In compiling this account I have been assisted by many distinguished officers, and so the correctness of events described may be relied on. I am also indebted to the War Office for the facilities which have been accorded to me."

Sir O'Moore Creagh did not live to finish this preface. He was greatly interested in the book, and one day, after he had read a good many of the lives of V.C.s, he told me he liked them so much that he had read them all a second time, for he said they were a personal history of all the wars.

Many of the officers and non-commissioned officers and men were known to Sir O'Moore, and he was specially interested in the accounts of the Indian V.C.s, for I think it was by his recommendation that the Victoria Cross was given to our Indian fellow subjects whom Sir O'Moore loved so well. He and his friend the late Sir Pertab Singh were at a reception given to one of the Indian V.C.s some years ago, and there was a charming picture of them in one of the illustrated papers.

The book has many mistakes and faults, no doubt, as is almost unavoidable in dealing with such an immense mass of material, but it was a labour of love with Sir O'Moore and the rest of us.

The different arrangement of the third volume of the book was found to be necessary by the publishers on account of the difficulty of getting information of the later and younger D.S.O.s and the great number of entries, which made it needful to save space and avoid further delay as much as possible. We had had many troubles over the earlier part of the work, and when they were at their worst Mr. Alfred Spencer, the Editor of the famous " Memoirs of William Hickey," had most kindly come to our assistance. For more than two years he devoted a vast amount of his time to helping us, finally planning this third volume, preparing the MS. of it for the printers, correcting the proofs and generally seeing it through the press.

Sir Evelyn Wood had the MSS. of the lives of the Crimean Naval V.C.s back from the printers, and he went through them all and made additions and corrections, particularly to the life of his beloved Captain, Sir William Peel, V.C., K.C.B.,

R.N. Afterwards he came one morning and told me about the storming of the Redan, at which, as an invalid midshipman, he was present without leave. Later on Sir Evelyn would always correct or read any of the lives we cared to submit to him, and I think he liked the book as much as Sir O'Moore did, but, like him, he did not live to see it finished.

Sir Evelyn Wood's other favourite V.C. was Sapper Hackett, who let himself be buried alive to save his badly injured fellow soldier. Sir O'Moore said the best thing in the book was Gunner Lodge's description of the adventures of his battery in the South African War.

Sir James Hills Johnes went through the lives of Lord Roberts and Sir Harry Tombs and Herbert Harington and the other Bengal Horse Artillery V.C.s, who were his friends. He asked his friend General Saward to help us, which he did.

Sir Henry Geary corrected some of the R.A. V.C.s' lives. He asked the R.A. Institution to help us and they did so. Colonel Boileau also searched the R.A. records for us.

Colonel Kendal Coghill rounded up the Mutiny V.C.s and sent out circulars himself *commanding* them to order books.

Mrs. Harris, one of Colonel Coghill's friends, was the widow of General Harris, who formerly commanded the Munster Fusiliers, and she nursed a lot of the officers through an outbreak of cholera, so they gave her a gold V.C. for Valour. Colonel Coghill asked Mrs. Harris's brother, Mr. Matthews, of Grindlay's, to look up particulars of officers in Indian regiments who were not well known and were difficult to get at, and Mr. Matthews most kindly went through lists of names and got hold of information and photographs for us.

There were Sir Edward Thackeray and Colonel Cadell, who sent information, and also Colonel A. S. Jones, who was temporarily so disfigured by his wounds that, he said, Queen Victoria winced and pricked him through his tunic when she pinned on his Cross at, I think, the second investiture at Southsea, of which we could never find an account in the newspapers.

Major Daniell, the Captain of the Invalids at Chelsea, was a friend of Colonel Coghill's and of little Tommy Butler's, the steeplechasing V.C., whom they both loved, and he and Colonel Johnston searched out the records of all the Munsters' V.C.s.

The late Lord Lichfield turned out details of his uncle's old services, and Colonel Jourdain told us a lot about the Connaught Rangers' V.C.s.

The late Duke of Northumberland and Lord Algernon Percy sent particulars about their uncle, and Lord Peel of Sir Evelyn Wood's handsome captain.

Sir Ernest Pollock lent us the photograph of his cousin Lieutenant Pollock Hamilton, and sent us some details.

Mr. Laughton, then of the Admiralty Library, went through the early Naval V.C.s to see that we did not sin technically, and told us of old records in the MS. Room of the British Museum and Naval and Military newspapers in the branch of the British Museum then, I think, at Henley, and, of course, in the Admiralty Library. We were shown a great deal of kindness by War Office officials. I was allowed to go through some of the Scots Guards' records at Buckingham Gate, and they and the Coldstream Guards lent us pictures. The officers commanding the Lincolnshire, D.C.L.I. and other regimental depôts helped us.

Mr. Walter Hutchinson wrote up a lot of records of V.C.s; lent us several books and worked at the V.C. volume in many ways.

Sir Ian Hamilton gave us a very great deal of help and wrote some of the records, both of V.C.s and D.S.O.s, and Lord Ailesbury's knowledge of military history was a great advantage to the book.

Major Burnham, the famous American scout, asked us to use the late Colonel J. W. Yardley's book, "With the Inniskilling Dragoons in South Africa," in writing up his record, and Colonel Yardley helped us in other ways too, as did Sir Willoughby Maycock.

Miss Dolores Grenfell lent us records, and so did Lord Desborough, and Lord Burnham allowed us to quote from some of his fine writings.

Captain and Mrs. Basil Taylour worked a great deal at the records, and their help spread over some years, and Colonel J. J. Porteous wrote a good many of the lives. Major H. R. S. Brown also worked on the third volume.

Sir Aylmer Hunter-Weston asked Messrs. Swaine and also Mr. Hay Wrightson to lend us photographs, and helped us in other ways. We put in the whole of his recruiting speech because at the time it seemed advantageous to publish it as much as possible.

The difficulties of getting information about some of the recipients of decorations in the Great War have been enormous, particularly with a number of them who came from the outposts of the Empire. Many were young and comparatively unknown, and their names were not even in the Army List. The book was begun in August, 1916, when there were not, I believe, more than about 3,600 D.S.O.s and about 600 V.C.s, and now there are close upon 13,000 D.S.O.s and nearly 1,200 V.C.s. To search out particulars of awards of the Decoration and Bars and details of services of this large number of recipients has, of course, occupied an infinite amount of time, and to get some 10,000 records within the scope of one volume has brought about the form in which the last volume now appears. The first D.S.O. volume has longer lives, it is true, but it is in many cases a record of Field-Marshals and Generals and Admirals who have long lists of war services. Had time and opportunity permitted, we could not have written long lives of these boys fresh from school. Wherever we have written the life of a General or Admiral, especially one who commanded in any campaign where decorations have been won, we have tried to give an account of that campaign so that the story of the commanding officer's services is, to a great extent, the story of the younger men whom he commanded.

Miss Hallowes did a great deal of work on the book, and Miss Ethel Deaville worked at it for several years and gave the most invaluable help.

Messrs. Swaine, Russell, Elliott and Fry, Hay Wrightson, and the *Canadian Gazette* kindly lent us many photographs.

Mr. Philip Wilkins, the author of the delightful "History of the Victoria Cross," lent us records and many photographs, and helped us greatly, and Mr. Flatman, of Diss, Norfolk, lent us the whole of his magnificent collection of photographs of V.C.s—I think nearly 300—which added vastly to the value and interest of the work. Mr. Toomey, who has written a very interesting book on the Victoria Cross, also very kindly lent us some photographs.

E. M. HUMPHRIS.

Volumes II and III of the original work have been reprinted by J. B. Hayward & Son as 'The Distinguished Service Order 1886–1926'

ISBN 0 903754 12 6

CONTENTS

ERRATA

The record of William Leefe Robinson indexed as appearing on page 118 was accidentally omitted. It will be found below.

The concluding portion of the record of W. Williams on page 246 commencing with the words "Surgeon P. Burrowes Kelly, R.N., D.S.O., writes," and ending with the words "he had ever met," should be omitted. It is part of the record of W. C. Williams on page 184 and will be found in that record.

In the 29th line of the record of F. A. de Pass on page 160, the words "English Corps in France" should read "Indian Corps in France," and in the 39th and 40th lines of the same record the words "The Indian Corps in India" should read "The Indian Corps in France."

THE FOLLOWING ARE THE CORRECT INDEX REFERENCES TO THE UNDERMENTIONED NAMES

ALTERATIONS TO BE MADE IN NAMES IN THE INDEX

NAMES TO BE ADDED TO THE INDEX

NAMES TO BE STRUCK OUT OF THE INDEX

OMITTED FROM CORRECT POSITION ON PAGE 118

ROBINSON, WILLIAM LEEFE, Lieut., was born at Tollidetta, South Coory, in Southern India, 14 July, 1895, son of Horace Robinson and grandson of W. C. Robinson, R.N., Chief Naval Constructor at Portsmouth Dockyard. He was educated at St. Bees School, Cumberland, and after travelling in France and Russia, entered Sandhurst in August, 1914. In December, 1914, he was gazetted to the Worcestershire Regiment. He joined the Royal Flying Corps in France as an observer in March, 1915, and on May 9th received a shrapnel bullet in his right arm while over Lille. A few weeks later he had recovered and was learning to fly at Farnborough. He took his pilot's certificate on September 15, and was appointed a flying officer in the R.F.C. three days later. He was from that time attached to various stations for night flying, and was up on every occasion of a raid in the neighbourhood of London during the seven months before his great exploit at Cuffley, when he was the first airman to bring down a Zeppelin in England. For this he won great fame and various honours and rewards, and was awarded the Victoria Cross [London Gazette, 5 September, 1916]: "War Office, 5 September, 1916. His Majesty the King has been gra-

ciously pleased to award the Victoria Cross to the undermentioned officer, Lieutenant William Leefe Robinson, Worcestershire Regiment and Royal Flying Corps. For most conspicuous bravery. He attacked an enemy airship under circumstances of great difficulty and danger, and sent it crashing to the ground as a flaming wreck. He had been in the air for more than two hours and had previously attacked another airship during his flight."

Captain Robinson was subsequently taken prisoner by the Germans in April, 1917, and after three or four attempts to escape he was put into solitary confinement in a small cell and only returned from captivity on December 14th, 1918. After his repatriation he suffered severely as the result of his imprisonment in Germany, and for over a week was ill with influenza, to which his death at Harrow Weald on 31 December, 1918, was attributed. Captain Robinson was engaged to Joan, widow of Captain H. C. Whipple, of the Devon Regiment, who was killed in action in December, 1914.

The
Victoria Cross
1856–1920

THE VICTORIA CROSS WARRANTS

The V.C. was instituted on 29th January, 1856

VICTORIA R.

WHEREAS WE, taking into Our Royal consideration that there exists no means of adequately rewarding the individual gallant services either of officers of the lower grades in Our naval and military service, or of warrant and petty officers, seamen and marines in Our navy, and non-commissioned officers and soldiers in Our army, And whereas the third class of Our most Honourable Order of the Bath is limited, except in very rare cases, to the higher ranks of both services, and the granting of medals, both in Our navy and army, is only awarded for long service or meritorious conduct, rather than for bravery in action or distinction before an enemy, such cases alone excepted where a general medal is granted for a particular action or campaign or a clasp added to the medal for some special engagement, in both of which cases all share equally in the boon, and those who by their valour have particularly signalised themselves remain undistinguished from their comrades. Now, for the purpose of attaining an end so desirable as that of rewarding individual instances of merit and valour, We have instituted and created, and by these presents, for Us, Our heirs and successors, institute and create a new naval and military decoration, which We are desirous should be highly prized and eagerly sought after by the officers and men of Our naval and military services, and are graciously pleased to make, ordain and establish the following rules and ordinances for the government of the same, which shall from henceforth be inviolably observed and kept.

Firstly.—It is ordained that the distinction shall be styled and designated the " Victoria Cross," and shall consist of a Maltese Cross of Bronze with Our Royal Crest in the centre, and underneath which an escroll bearing this inscription, " For Valour."

Secondly.—It is ordained that the Cross shall be suspended from the left breast by a blue riband for the navy, and by a red riband for the army.

Thirdly.—It is ordained that the names of those upon whom We may be pleased to confer the decoration shall be published in the *London Gazette*, and a registry thereof kept in the office of Our Secretary of State for War.

Fourthly.—It is ordained that anyone who, after having received the Cross, shall again perform an act of bravery, which, if he had not received such Cross, would have entitled him to it, such further act shall be recorded by a Bar attached to the riband by which the Cross is suspended, and for every additional act of bravery an additional Bar may be added.

Fifthly.—It is ordained that the Cross shall only be awarded to those officers or men who have served Us in the presence of the enemy, and shall have then performed some signal act of valour or devotion to their country.

Sixthly.—It is ordained, with a view to place all persons on a perfectly equal footing in relation to eligibility for the decoration, that neither rank, nor long service, nor wounds, nor any other circumstance or condition whatsoever, save the merit of conspicuous bravery, shall be held to establish a sufficient claim to the honour.

Seventhly.—It is ordained that the decoration may be conferred on the spot where the act to be rewarded by the grant of such decoration has been performed under the following circumstances :

I. When the fleet or army in which such act has been performed, is under the eye and command of an admiral or general officer commanding the forces.

II. Where the naval or military force is under the eye and command of an admiral or commodore commanding a squadron or detached naval force, or of a general commanding a corps, or division or brigade on a distinct and detached service, when such admiral, commodore, or general officer shall have the power of conferring the decoration on the spot, subject to confirmation by Us.

Eighthly.—It is ordained, where such act shall not have been performed in sight of a commanding officer as aforesaid, then the claimant for the honour shall prove the act to the satisfaction of the captain or officer commanding his ship, or to the officer commanding the regiment to which the claimant belongs, and such captain or such commanding officer shall report the same through the usual channel to the admiral or commodore commanding the force employed on the service, or to the officer commanding the forces in the field, who shall call for such description and attestation of the act as he may think requisite, and on approval shall recommend the grant of the decoration.

Ninthly.—It is ordained that every person selected for the Cross, under Rule Seven, shall be publicly decorated before the naval or military force or body to which he belongs, and with which the act of bravery for which he is to be rewarded shall have been performed, and his name shall be recorded in a General Order, together with the cause of his especial distinction.

Tenthly.—It is ordained that every person selected under Rule Eight shall receive his decoration as soon as possible, and his name shall likewise appear in a General Order as above required, such General Order to be issued by the naval or military commander of the forces employed on the service.

Eleventhly.—It is ordained that the General Orders above referred to shall from time to time be transmitted to Our Secretary of State for War, to be laid before Us, and shall be by him registered.

Twelfthly.—It is ordained that as cases may arise not falling within the rules above specified, or in which a claim, though well founded, may not have been established on the spot, We will, on the joint submission of Our Secretary of State for War, and of Our Commander-in-chief of Our army, or on that of Our Lord High Admiral or Lords Commissioners of the Admiralty in the case of the navy, confer the decoration, but never without conclusive proof of the performance of the act of bravery for which the claim is made.

Thirteenthly.—It is ordained that, in the event of a gallant and daring act having been performed by a squadron, ship's company, a detached body of seamen and marines, not under fifty in number, or by a brigade, regiment, troop, or company, in which the admiral, general or other officer commanding such forces, may deem that all are equally brave and distinguished, and that no special selection can be made by them, then in such case the admiral, general, or other officer commanding may direct that for any such body of seamen and marines, or for every troop or company of soldiers, one officer shall be selected by the officers engaged for the decoration ; and in like manner one petty officer or non-commissioned officer shall be selected by the petty officers and non-commissioned officers engaged ; and two seamen or private soldiers or marines shall be selected by the seamen, or private soldiers, or marines engaged respectively for the decoration ; and the names of those selected shall be transmitted by the senior officer in command of the naval force, brigade, regiment, troop, or company, to the admiral or general officer commanding, who shall in due manner confer the decoration as if the acts were done under his own eye.

Fourteenthly.—It is ordained that every warrant officer, petty officer, seaman, or marine, or non-commissioned officer or soldier, who shall have received the Cross, shall, from the date of the act by which the decoration has been gained, be entitled to a special pension of Ten Pounds a year, and each additional Bar conferred under Rule Four on such warrant or petty officers or non-commissioned officers or men shall carry with it an additional pension of Five Pounds per annum.

Fifteenthly.—In order to make such additional provision as shall effectually preserve pure this most honourable distinction, it is ordained that if any person on whom such distinction shall be conferred, be convicted of treason, cowardice, felony, or of any infamous crime, or if he be accused of any such offence and doth not after a reasonable time surrender himself to be tried for the same, his name shall forthwith be erased from the registry of individuals upon whom the said decoration shall have been conferred by an especial warrant under Our Royal Sign Manual, and the pension conferred under Rule Fourteen shall cease and determine from the date of such warrant. It is hereby further declared that We, Our heirs and successors, shall be the sole judges of the circumstance demanding such expulsion ; moreover, We shall at all times have power to restore such persons as may at any time have been expelled both to the enjoyment of the decoration and pension.

Given at Our Court at Buckingham Palace, this twenty-ninth day of January, in the nineteenth year of Our reign, and in the year of our Lord one thousand eight hundred and fifty-six.
By Her Majesty's Command,
PANMURE.

From the *London Gazette*, August 10th, 1858.

BY a Warrant under Her Royal Sign Manual August 10, 1858, Her Majesty was pleased to direct that the Victoria Cross should be conferred subject to the rules and ordinances already made on officers and men of Her Majesty's Naval and Military Services who may perform acts of conspicuous courage and bravery under circumstances of extreme danger, such as the occurrence of a fire on board ship, or the foundering of a vessel at sea, or under any other circumstances in which, through the courage and devotion displayed, life or public property might be saved.

From the *London Gazette*, July 8th, 1859.

War Office, July 6th, 1859.

THE Queen, having been graciously pleased by a warrant under Her Royal Sign Manual, bearing date December 13, 1858, to declare that Non-Military Persons who, as Volunteers, have borne arms against the Mutineers, both at Lucknow and elsewhere, during the late operations in India, shall be considered as eligible to receive the Decoration of the Victoria Cross, subject to the rules and ordinances already made and ordained for the government thereof, provided that it be established in any case that the person was serving under the orders of a General or other Officer in Command of Troops in the Field when he performed the Act of Bravery for which it is proposed to confer the decoration; Her Majesty has accordingly been pleased to signify Her intention to confer this high distinction on, etc., etc. (names following).

———————

VICTORIA R.

WHEREAS, by a Warrant under Our Royal Sign Manual, countersigned by one of Our Principal Secretaries of State, and bearing date at Our Court at Buckingham Palace, the twenty-ninth day of January, one thousand eight hundred and fifty-six, in the nineteenth year of Our reign, We did constitute and create a new naval and military decoration, to be styled and designated the Victoria Cross, which decoration We expressed Our desire should be highly prized and eagerly sought after by the officers and men of Our naval and military services, and did also make, ordain and establish the rules and ordinances therein set forth for the government of the same to be thenceforth inviolably observed and kept.

And whereas, during the progress of the operations which We have undertaken against the Insurgent native tribes in Our Colony of New Zealand, it has happened that persons serving in the Local Forces of Our said Colony have performed deeds of gallantry, in consideration of which they are not, according to the strict provisions of Our said recited Warrant, eligible for this high distinction.

Now know ye, that We, of Our especial grace, certain knowledge, and mere motion, have thought fit hereby to signify Our Royal Will and Pleasure, that the said decoration may be conferred on such persons aforesaid, who may be qualified to receive the same in accordance with the rules and ordinances made, ordained and established by Us for the government thereof, by Our said recited Warrant, and we do by these presents for Us, Our heirs and successors, ordain and appoint that it shall be competent for such persons aforesaid to obtain the said decoration, in the manner set forth in the rules and ordinances referred to, or in accordance with such further rules and ordinances as may hereafter be made and promulgated by Us, Our heirs and successors, for the government of the said decoration, provided that it be established in any case that the person was serving with Our Troops, under the orders of a general or other officer, under circumstances which would entitle an officer or soldier of Our army to be recommended for the said decoration, in accordance with the rules and ordinances prescribed in Our said recited Warrant, and provided also that such person shall be recommended for it by such General or other Officer.

And We do further, for Us, Our heirs and successors, ordain and appoint that the said decoration may also be conferred, in accordance with the rules and ordinances prescribed in Our said recited Warrant, and subject to the provisos aforesaid, on such persons as may be qualified to receive the same in accordance with the said rules and ordinances who may hereafter be employed in the Local Forces raised, or which may be raised, in Our Colonies and their dependencies, and who may be called upon to serve in co-operation with Our Troops, in military operations which it may be necessary to undertake for the suppression of rebellion against Our authority, or for repelling invasion by a Foreign enemy.

Given at Our Court at Osborne House, Isle of Wight, this first day of January, one thousand eight hundred and sixty-seven, in the thirtieth year of Our reign.
By Her Majesty's Command,
J. PEEL.

———————

VICTORIA R.

WHEREAS doubts have arisen as to the qualification required for the decoration of the Victoria Cross, and whereas the description of such qualification in Our Royal Warrant of twenty-ninth day of January, one thousand eight hundred and fifty-six, is not uniform, Our Will and Pleasure is that the qualification shall be " conspicuous bravery or devotion to the country in the presence of the enemy ; " and that Our Royal Warrant of the twenty-ninth day of January, one thousand eight hundred and fifty-six, shall be read and interpreted accordingly.

It is Our further Will and Pleasure that officers and men of Our Auxiliary and Reserve Forces (naval and military), shall be eligible for the decoration of the Victoria Cross, under the conditions of Our said Warrant, as amended by this, Our Warrant.

Given at Our Court at Osborne, this twenty-third day of April, one thousand eight hundred and eighty-one, in the forty-fourth year of Our reign.
By Her Majesty's Command,
HUGH C. E. CHILDERS.

———————

VICTORIA R.

VICTORIA, by the Grace of God, of the United Kingdom of Great Britain and Ireland, Queen, Defender of the Faith, Empress of India, to all to whom these presents shall come, greeting.

WHEREAS, by a Warrant under Our Royal Sign Manual, countersigned by one of Our Principal Secretaries of State, and bearing date at Our Court at Buckingham Palace, the twenty-ninth day of January, one thousand eight hundred and fifty-six, in the nineteenth year of Our reign, We did constitute and create a new naval and military decoration, to be styled and designated the " Victoria Cross," which decoration We expressed Our desire should be highly prized and eagerly sought after by the officers and men of Our naval and military services, and did also make, ordain and establish the rules and ordinances therein set forth for the government of the same to be thenceforth inviolably observed and kept.

And whereas, by another Warrant under Our Royal Sign Manual, countersigned by one of Our Principal Secretaries of State, and bearing date at Our Court at Windsor, the twenty-ninth day of October, one thousand eight hundred and fifty-seven, in the twenty-first year of Our reign, We thought fit to signify Our Royal Will and Pleasure, that the said decoration shall be conferred on the officers and men of the naval and military services of the East India Company, who may be qualified to receive the same in accordance with the rules and ordinances made, ordained and established by Us, for the government thereof, by Our first recited Warrant, aforesaid.

And whereas it has been represented to Us that the Members of the Indian Ecclesiastical Establishments, although not receiving military commissions, are liable to be attached to an army in the field, and are then required to perform the same duties as the commissioned chaplains of Our army, who are eligible for this decoration.

Now know ye that We of Our especial grace, certain knowledge and mere motion have thought fit hereby to signify Our Royal Will and Pleasure, that the said decoration shall be conferred on such persons as aforesaid, who may be qualified to receive the same in accordance with the rules and ordinances made, ordained and established by Us, for the government thereof, by Our said first recited Warrant, and We do by these presents for Us, Our heirs and successors, ordain and appoint that it shall be competent for such persons as aforesaid to obtain the said decoration in the manner set forth in the rules and ordinances referred to, or in accordance with such further rules and ordinances as may hereafter be made and promulgated by Us, Our heirs and successors, for the government of the said decoration, provided that it be established in any case that the person was serving, for the time being, under the orders of a general or other officer in command of troops in the field.

Given at Our Court at Osborne House, Isle of Wight, this sixth day of August, one thousand eight hundred and eighty-one, in the forty-fifth year of Our reign.
By Her Majesty's Command,
HUGH C. E. CHILDERS.

———————

From the *London Gazette*, August 8th, 1902.

THE King has been graciously pleased to approve of the Decoration of the Victoria Cross being given to the representatives of the undermentioned officers, non-commissioned officers and men who fell during the recent operations in South Africa in the performance of acts of valour, which would, in the opinion of the Commander-in-Chief of the Forces in the Field, have entitled them to be recommended for that distinction had they survived. (Here follow names.)

———————

GEORGE R. & I.

GEORGE, by the Grace of God, of the United Kingdom of Great Britain and Ireland, and of the British Dominions beyond the Seas, King, Defender of the Faith, Emperor of India, to all to whom these presents shall come, Greeting.

WHEREAS Her Majesty, Queen Victoria, by a Warrant under Her Royal Sign Manual, countersigned by one of Her Principal Secretaries of State, and bearing date at Her Court at Buckingham Palace, the twenty-ninth day of January, one thousand eight hundred and fifty-six, in the nineteenth year of Her reign, did institute and create a new naval and military decoration, to be styled and designated the " Victoria Cross," which decoration She expressed Her desire should be highly prized and eagerly sought after by the officers and men of Her Naval and Military Services, and did also make, ordain, and establish the rules and ordinances therein set forth for the government of the same, to be thenceforward inviolably observed and kept.

And whereas for divers reasons Us thereunto moving, We are desirous of rewarding the individual gallant services of native officers, non-commissioned officers and men of Our Indian Army by the bestowal of the said decoration, which We are desirous shall be highly prized and eagerly sought after by the said native officers, non-commissioned officers and men.

Now know ye that We, of Our especial grace, certain knowledge, and mere motion, have thought fit hereby to signify Our Royal Will and Pleasure that the said decoration shall be conferred on the native officers, non-commissioned officers and men of Our Indian Army who may be qualified to receive the same, in accordance with the rules and ordinances made, ordained and established for the government thereof by the said recited Warrant, and We do by these Presents, for Us, Our Heirs and Successors, ordain and appoint that it shall be competent for the native officers, non-commissioned officers and men of Our Indian Army to obtain the said decoration in the manner set forth in the rules and ordinances referred to, or in accordance with any further rules and ordinances which may hereafter be made and promulgated by Us, Our Heirs and Successors, for the government of the said decoration.

And We do further, for Us, Our Heirs and Successors, ordain and appoint that in place of the special pension conferred by the fourteenth rule of the said recited Warrant, every native officer who shall have received the Cross shall from the date of the act by which such decoration has been gained be entitled to a special pension of five hundred and twenty-five rupees a year, and each additional bar conferred under the fourth rule on such native officer shall carry with it an additional pension of one hundred and fifty rupees a year. In the case of a warrant or non-commissioned officer or soldier the special pension shall be one hundred and fifty rupees, with seventy-five rupees additional for each additional bar. On the death of a recipient of the Cross these pensions shall be continued to his widow until her death or remarriage.

Given at Our Court at St. James's this 21st day of October, in the second year of Our Reign, and in the year of Our Lord one thousand nine hundred and eleven.

By His Majesty's Command,
HALDANE OF CLOAN.

GEORGE R. & I.

WHEREAS Her late Majesty Queen Victoria, by a Warrant under Her Royal Sign Manual dated 29th January, 1856, did create a Naval and Military Decoration to be styled and designated "The Victoria Cross," and did express Her desire that this decoration should be highly prized and eagerly sought after by the Officers and Men of Her Naval and Military Services.

AND WHEREAS by divers subsequent Warrants other Officers and Men were admitted to and made eligible for the decoration, and certain amendments were made to the Rules and Ordinances attaching thereto.

AND WHEREAS We deem it expedient that the said Warrant and subsequent Warrants before referred to, as also the Rules and Ordinances affecting the same, shall be consolidated, varied and extended.

Now, THEREFORE, We do hereby declare that the said Warrants, and the Rules and Ordinances heretofore in force for the Government of the said Decoration, shall for that purpose be amended, varied, modified and extended ; and in substitution thereof We by these presents, for Us, Our Heirs and Successors, are graciously pleased to make, ordain and establish the following Rules and Ordinances for the Government of the same which shall from henceforth be inviolably observed and kept :—

Firstly : It is ordained that the distinction shall as heretofore be styled and designated " The Victoria Cross," and shall consist of a Maltese Cross of bronze with our Royal Crest in the centre and underneath it an escroll bearing this inscription : " For Valour."

Secondly : It is ordained that the Cross shall be suspended from the left breast by a red riband, and on those occasions when only the riband is worn a replica of the Cross in miniature shall be affixed to the centre of the riband.

Thirdly : It is ordained that the Cross shall only be awarded for most conspicuous bravery or some daring or pre-eminent act of valour or self-sacrifice or extreme devotion to duty in the presence of the enemy.

Fourthly : It is ordained that the Cross may be awarded posthumously.

Fifthly : It is ordained that the names of all those persons upon or on account of whom We may be pleased to confer or present the decoration shall be published in the *London Gazette*, and a Registry thereof kept in the Office of Our Secretary of State for War.

Sixthly : It is ordained that :—

(1) Officers, Warrant Officers and subordinate Officers hereinafter referred to as Officers, Chief Petty Officers and Petty Officers hereinafter referred to as Petty Officers, men and boys hereinafter referred to as Seamen, serving in—(a) our Navy or in ships of any description for the time being under Naval Command ; (b) our Indian Marine Service ; (c) Navies or Marine Services of our Dominions, Colonies, Dependencies or Protectorates ; and (d) our Mercantile Marine whilst serving under Naval or Military Authority, or who in the course of their duties may become subject to enemy action ;

(2) Officers, Warrant Officers, Non-Commissioned Officers, men and boys hereinafter referred to as Marines, serving in our Marines ;

(3) Officers, Warrant Officers (Classes I. and II.), Non-Commissioned Officers, men and boys hereinafter referred to as Privates, of all ranks serving in our Army, our Army Reserve, our Territorial or other forces, and the Forces of our Dominions, Colonies, Dependencies or Protectorates ;

(4) Officers, Warrant Officers, Non-Commissioned Officers, and Airmen in the ranks of Our Air Force, or the Air Forces of our Dominions, Colonies, Dependencies or Protectorates ;

(5) British and Indian Officers and men of all ranks of Our Indian Army, the Imperial Service Troops of Native States of India, or any other Forces there serving under the Command, guidance, or direction of any British or Indian Officer, or of a Political Officer attached to such Forces on Our behalf, and

(6) Matrons, sisters, nurses and the staff of the Nursing Services and other Services pertaining to Hospitals and Nursing, and Civilians of either sex serving regularly or temporarily under the Orders, direction or supervision of any of the above mentioned Forces

shall be eligible for the decoration of the Cross.

Seventhly : It is ordained that if any recipient of the Cross shall again perform such an act of bravery, as would have made him or her eligible to receive the Cross, such further act of bravery shall be recorded by a Bar to be attached to the Riband by which the Cross is suspended, and for every such additional act of bravery, an additional Bar shall be added, and any such Bar or Bars may be awarded posthumously. For every Bar awarded a replica of the Cross in miniature shall be added to the riband when worn alone.

Eighthly : It is ordained that every recommendation for the Award of the decoration of the Cross shall be made and reported through the usual channel to the Senior Naval, Military or Air Force Officer Commanding the Force, who shall call for such description, conclusive proof as far as the circumstances of the case will allow, and attestation of the act as he may think requisite, and if he approve he shall recommend the grant of the decoration to Our Lords Commissioners of the Admiralty, Our Secretary of State for War and the Royal Air Force as the case may be, who shall submit to Us the names of every one so recommended whom they shall consider worthy : in the case of there being no British or Indian Officer, then the Political Officer attached to the Force shall, after obtaining conclusive proof of the act of bravery as far as is possible, if he approve, submit the recommendation to Us through the proper channels.

Ninthly : It is ordained that in the event of any unit of our Naval, Military or Air Forces, consisting in the case of our Navy of a squadron, flotilla or ship's company, or of a detached body of seamen or marines ; or in the case of our Army of a regiment, squadron, battery or company, or of a detached body of soldiers ; or in the case of our Air Force of a Squadron or other body of airmen, having distinguished itself collectively by the performance of an act of heroic gallantry or daring in the presence of the enemy in such a way that the Admiral, General or other Officer in Command of the Force to which such an unit belongs is unable to single out any individual as specially pre-eminent in gallantry or daring, then one or more of the officers, warrant officers, petty officers, non-commissioned officers, seamen, marines, private soldiers or airmen in the ranks comprising the unit shall be selected to be recommended to Us for the award of the Victoria Cross in the following manner :—

(a) When the total personnel of the unit does not exceed 100, then one officer shall be selected for the decoration by the officers engaged ; and in like manner one warrant officer or petty officer or non-commissioned officer of the unit shall be selected by the warrant officers, petty officers or non-commissioned officers engaged, and one seaman, marine, private soldier, or airman in the ranks shall be selected by the seamen, marines, private soldiers or airmen in the ranks engaged.

(b) When the total personnel of the unit exceeds 100 but does not exceed 200, then the number of seamen, marines, private soldiers or airmen in the ranks to be selected in the manner described in (a) shall be increased to two.

(c) When the total personnel of the unit exceeds 200 in number, the number of Crosses to be awarded in accordance with these provisions shall be the subject of special consideration by Our Lords Commissioners of the Admiralty or by one of Our Secretaries of State for submission to Us.

(d) The selection to be by a secret ballot in such manner as shall be determined in accordance with the foregoing provisions by the Officer directing the selection to be made.

(e) The death of any person engaged shall not be a bar to his selection.

(f) The names of the persons recommended in accordance with these provisions shall be submitted to Us in the manner laid down in Rule 8.

Tenthly : It is ordained that every recipient of the Cross, not being nor ranking as a Commissioned Officer nor, in the case of Our Navy, being or ranking with a warrant officer, nor coming within Rule 11, shall from the date of the act by which the decoration has been gained, be entitled to a special pension of Ten Pounds a year, and each additional Bar conferred under Rule 7 on such recipient shall carry with it an additional pension of Five Pounds per annum.

Eleventhly : Every Indian Officer of Our Indian Army of rank junior to that of Second Lieutenant who shall have received the Cross shall, from the date of the act by which such decoration has been gained, be entitled to a special pension of Five hundred and twenty-five rupees a year, and each additional Bar conferred on such Indian Officer shall carry with it an additional pension of One hundred and fifty rupees a year. In the case of a Warrant or Non-Commissioned Officer or soldier of Our Indian Army aforesaid We ordain and award a special pension of One hundred and fifty rupees, with Seventy-five rupees additional for each additional Bar. On the death of these recipients of the Cross these pensions shall be continued to his widow until her death or remarriage.

Twelfthly : In order to make such additional provision as shall effectually maintain pure this most honourable distinction, it is ordained that if any person on whom such distinction shall be conferred be convicted of treason, cowardice, felony, or of any infamous crime, or if he or she be accused of any such offence and doth not after a reasonable time surrender himself or herself to be tried for the same, his or her name shall by an especial Warrant under Our Royal Sign Manual forthwith be erased from the registry of individuals upon whom the said decoration shall have been conferred and the pension conferred under Rules 10 and 11 shall cease and determine from the date of such Warrant. It is hereby further declared that We, Our Heirs and Successors, shall be the sole judges of the circumstance demanding such expulsion ; moreover, We shall at all times have power to restore such persons as may at any time have been expelled, both to the enjoyment of the decoration and pension, and notice thereof of expulsion or restoration in every case shall be published in the *London Gazette*.

Given at Our Court at St. James's this 22nd day of May, in the eleventh year of Our reign, and in the year of Our Lord one thousand nine hundred and twenty.

By His Majesty's Command,
WINSTON S. CHURCHILL.

The Victoria Cross

London Gazette, 24th Feb. 1857.

" The Queen has been graciously pleased to signify Her intention to confer the Decoration of the Victoria Cross on the undermentioned officers and men of Her Majesty's Navy and Marines, and officers, non-commissioned officers and men of Her Majesty's Army, who have been recommended to Her Majesty for that Decoration in accordance with the rules laid down in Her Majesty's Warrant of the 29th Jan. 1856, on account of Acts of Bravery performed by them before the enemy during the late War, as recorded against their several names."

BUCKLEY, CECIL WILLIAM, Commander, Royal Navy ; *b.* in 1830, and entered the Royal Navy in 1843.

Cecil William Buckley.

He served as Mate in the Daedalus and Royal George ; promoted Lieut. 11 Jan. 1850 ; appointed to the Miranda, Capt. E. M. Lyons, 24 May, 1850, and was in the latter ship in 1854, assisting in the capture of Kola, the capital of Russian Lapland. In the Sea of Azoff he was present, 28 May, 1855, in the attack on the Fort of Arabat. Next day he was with the boats of the Miranda and Swallow, under the command of Lieut. J. F. C. Mackenzie, and helped to set fire to 73 ships, and to the corn stores of Genitchi. Lieut. Buckley and his companions were subsequently awarded the Victoria Cross [London Gazette, 24 Feb. 1857] : " Cecil William Buckley, Commander, Royal Navy. Date of Act of Bravery : 29 May, 1855. Lord Lyons reports that : ' Whilst serving as Junior Lieut. of the Miranda, this officer landed in presence of a superior force, and set fire to the Russian stores at Genitchi,' and he also performed a similar desperate service at Taganrog. The first service referred to occurred after the shelling of the town of Genitchi 29 May, 1855. After mentioning that the stores were in a very favourable position for supplying the Russian Army, and that, therefore, their destruction was of the utmost importance, Capt. Lyons writes : ' Lieut. Cecil W. Buckley, Lieut. Hugh T. Burgoyne, and Mr. John Roberts, Gunner, volunteered to land alone and fire the stores, which offer I accepted, knowing the imminent risk there would be in landing a party in presence of such a superior force, and out of gunshot of the ships. This very dangerous service they most gallantly performed, narrowly escaping the Cossacks, who all but cut them off from their boat.' (Despatch from Admiral Lord Lyons, 2 June, 1855 ; No. 419). The second volunteer service was performed while the town of Taganrog was being bombarded by the boats of the Fleet, and is thus recorded by Capt. Lyons : ' Lieut. Cecil Buckley, in a four-oared gig, accompanied by Mr. Henry Cooper, Boatswain, and manned by volunteers, repeatedly landed and fired the different stores and Government buildings. This dangerous, not to say desperate, service (carried out in a town containing upwards of 3,000 troops constantly endeavouring to prevent it, and only checked by the fire of the boats' guns) was most effectually performed.' (Despatch from Admiral Lord Lyons, 6 June, 1855 ; No. 429)." Another account of these services reads as follows : " The ships accordingly resumed their fire upon the town, and the boats proceeded. Lieut. Cecil W. Buckley, Lieut. Hugh T. Burgoyne, of the Swallow, and Mr. John Robarts, Gunner of the Ardent, volunteered to land alone and fire the stores, as there would be imminent risk in landing a party in presence of such a superior force and out of gunshot of the ships. This very daring service they most gallantly performed, narrowly escaping the Cossacks, who all but cut them off." The second service is thus described : " The Recruit, as well as the boats which took up a position in line for this purpose under the command of Commander Cowper Coles, opened fire upon the stores. This proved so effective that the enemy made repeated efforts to get down to the houses lining the beach, so as to save the long ranges of store-houses from destruction ; they never succeeded in doing so in sufficient numbers. Lieut. Buckley landed and set fire to several stores and Government buildings, a dangerous service in the presence of 3,000 troops, who were duly kept in check by the fire of the boats' guns. By 3 p.m. the long ranges of stores of grain and timber, and all the vessels on the stocks were in a blaze," and the boats moved off. Kinglake says that the immunity from serious loss of life in the successful operations in the Sea of Azoff was largely owing to the superb seamanship of young Lyons, and also to the well-applied daring of particular men. " Thus, when Lieut. Buckley and John Robarts, Gunner, at Genitchi, and Lieut. Buckley again, with Henry Cooper, Boatswain, at Taganrog, volunteered to take special service of a hazardous kind, they effectually compassed their objects, but they did something more. By dispensing with the aid of numbers, they plainly averted the evil of having to risk many lives." Though Lieut. Lucas was the first man to actually win the Victoria Cross, Lieut. Buckley's decoration was the first to be gazetted. His was the first also of the nine Crosses given for the Sea of Azoff. Lieut. Buckley assumed command of the Snake soon after the events recorded in the Gazette, and was engaged in operations in the Kertch Strait. On 27 April, 1856, he became Commander. Besides the Victoria Cross he received the Medal with clasps for Sebastopol and Azoff. On 24 May, 1857, he was appointed to the Merlin steam vessel of 6 guns and 312 h.p., fitting for the West Coast of Africa, whence he returned to England. Commander Buckley later served for some time on the Cape Station, and was later in the Forte. He had been advanced to the rank of Captain on 18 April, 1862. During the years 1868–1870 he commanded the Pylades on the Pacific Station. In Dec. 1871, he was appointed to the command of the Valiant coastguard ship in the Shannon, but failing health compelled him to retire in the following Oct. Capt. Buckley died at Funchal, Madeira, 7 Dec. 1872, aged 42. He was married, and left behind him a son and a daughter.

BURGOYNE, HUGH TALBOT, Commander, Royal Navy ; *b.* 19 July, 1833, in Dublin, only *s.* of Field-Marshal Sir John Fox Burgoyne (Colonel Commandant, Royal Engineers, Inspector General of Fortifications, and at that time Chairman of the Board of Public Works in Dublin), and Charlotte, dau. and co-heiress of Lieut.-Colonel Hugh Rose, of Holme, Nairn, N.B., a brother-in-law of the Hon. George Wrottesley, President of the Royal Society, who wrote the life of Sir John Burgoyne. Hugh Burgoyne entered the Royal Navy in 1847. Field-Marshal Sir Evelyn Wood says that Burgoyne was serving in H.M.S. Queen in 1852, and adds :

Hugh Talbot Burgoyne.

" Many of the younger officers were above the average in ability and efficiency, the most striking personality being Hugh (commonly called Billy) Burgoyne, a son of the Field-Marshal whose statue stands in Waterloo Place. Mr. Burgoyne was as brave as a lion, as active as a cat, and a very Mark Tapley in difficulties." On page 221 of " The Crimea in 1854 and 1894," Sir Evelyn Wood says : " Whenever I was not on trench or transport duty I was sent to Balaklava or to Kamiesh to buy food for our Mess, and at the latter place I called in Kazatch Bay to see my friend Hewett (afterwards Admiral Sir W. N. W. Hewett, V.C.), of H.M.S. Beagle, who had been ordered home. I stayed on board for the night, greatly appreciating not only the good food, but unlimited ablutions. When I was leaving next morning, Lieut. Burgoyne, H.M.S. Swallow, who had dined with Hewett in order to meet me, asked me to carry a letter for his father, General Sir John Burgoyne, up to Head-quarters, and I gladly assented, although to del.ver it would take me some way round. Burgoyne and I had served together in H.M.S. Queen the previous year, when he was Mate of the Maintop, of which I was Mid-shipman. While at sea in half a gale of wind we were ordered to send down our top-gallant masts, and during the operation he showed a courage and power of bearing pain I have seldom seen equalled. For the sake of my readers who are not acquainted with the mysteries of nautical terms, I may explain that to ' send up ' a topmast, it is placed alongside the lower mast, and is pulled up into its position by a rope running over a pulley at the top of the topmast. In the lower end of the top-gallant mast is a hole corresponding with the hole in the top of the topmast ; and when as the mast rises the two holes coincide, a wedge-shaped piece of iron called a fid, being slipped in, takes and supports the weight of the top-gallant mast. The man at the top mast-head, whose duty it was to pull out the fid, was afraid to put both hands on to the grummet which ran through the end of the iron wedge, for the ship was rolling so heavily in the trough of the seas as to render it difficult for anyone to retain his position aloft without holding on : and Burgoyne, using strong language at the man for his want of nerve, ran nimbly aloft, and pushing him out of the way, put both his hands on to the fid and attempted to pull it out. The wood, however, after several hours' rain, had swollen, enclosing the fid so tightly that it required considerable effort to move it. During the half-hearted efforts of the man, who only exerted the force of one arm, the marines on deck had got tired of the strain of holding the weight, and just as Burgoyne. getting the fingers of both hands inside the hole, had succeeded in slightly moving the fid, the marines ' coming up ' (i.e., slacking their hold) let down the top-gallant mast, weighing three-quarters of a ton, on to Bur-goyne's hand, and it caught the tips of two fingers, which were crushed. Burgoyne felt that his hand was jammed beyond any effort he could make to extricate it. If he had screamed or shouted, the fifty men on the top-gallant fall (hoisting rope) would have looked up, and he would have remained pinned by the tips of his fingers, but with extraordinary self-command, placing his disengaged hand to his mouth, he hailed the deck in a voice which rang clear amidst the howling wind, shouting, ' On deck there ? '—' Ay, ay ! '—' Sway again.' And the marines ' falling back ' (i.e., throwing all their weight on to the rope), lifted the mass from off my friend's fingers, who managed to withdraw his hand, though he fainted immediately, and we had to send him down on deck slung in the bight of a rope." Burgoyne passed his examination on 18 Jan. 1853 ; served at the Cape of Good Hope as Mate of the Peregrine, and later of the Dolphin ; was promoted to Lieut. 11 Jan. 1854, and appointed to the Boscawen, and afterwards to the Swallow, attached to the Black Sea Fleet, and entered the Sea of Azoff with the Flotilla under Capt. Lyons, where Lieut. Burgoyne was detached with the Wrangler to Genitchi, there to watch the entrance of the Putrid Sea. While a heavy column of the enemy was retreating the Lancaster guns of the Wrangler kept up an effective fire on them from an extraordinary distance. Lieut. Burgoyne became Commander 10 July, 1856, and was on its institution awarded the Victoria Cross [London Gazette, 24 Feb. 1857] : " John Talbot Burgoyne, Commander, Royal Navy. Date of Act of Bravery : 29 May, 1855. Lord Lyons writes, ' As Senior Lieut. of the Swallow, this officer landed with Lieut. Buckley and Mr. J. Roberts, Gunner, in presence of a superior force, and set fire to the stores at Genitchi, a service of imminent risk ' (Despatch from Admiral Lord Lyons, 2 June, 1855; No. 419). N.B. This service is described in the preceding notice of Lieut. Buckley's services." The London Gazette 13 March, 1857, says: "Erratum:—'For John Talbot Burgoyne, Commander, Royal Navy,' in the London Gazette 24 Feb. 1857, read 'Hugh Talbot Burgoyne.'" Besides the Victoria Cross, Commander Burgyone received the Legion of Honour and the Crimean Medal with the Azoff clasp. On 13 June, he obtained command of the Wrangler schooner, of 4 guns and 130 h.p., and assisted on July 16th in a successful attack made by the Allied Fleet under Capt. S. Osborn on the Fort and Batteries of Petrovski. In Jan. 1857, he was serving as Commander of the Ganges in the Pacific, and when that vessel was paid off he was advanced to be Capt. 15 May, 1861. In 1863 he accompanied Capt. Sherard Osborn to China, as second in command of the Anglo-Chinese Flotilla, and when Osborn threw up the command in consequence of a disagreement with the Chinese Government, the appointment was offered to Burgoyne with very liberal pay. He, however, declined it, as did the other officers, and eventually the flotilla was broken up. Capt. Burgoyne married in 1864, Evelyn Laure, dau. of Admiral Sir Baldwin Wake Walker. On 27 Sept. 1865, he was appointed to the Wyvern, a small turret ship, in which he continued for the next two years, after which he commanded the Constance frigate on the North American Station. In the following year he superintended the building and fitting out of the Captain, an experimental ship, full-rigged, with turrets, and a low free-board, which the Admiralty had determined to try on a very large scale. But the ship, with 490 officers and men on board, foundered in a squall off Cape Finisterre, on the 7th of Sept. 1870, and only 18 men were saved. It is said that Capt. Burgoyne was last seen encouraging the men to save themselves in the boats. "Jump, men, jump," he said, but he did not jump himself. Either he thought that the boats were over-manned, or he preferred not to survive his ship. With him and the rest perished Capt. Coles, whose ideas were embodied in the ship's design, and who had been given carte-blanche for her construction. Admiral Milne said in his report on the loss of the Captain that Capt. Burgoyne was a thoroughly practical sailor. He added: "I had thorough confidence in him, and it is impossible that the Captain could have been better commanded. The Service will regret the loss of an officer of much ability and promise." Sir Evelyn Wood says in "Winnowed Memories" (page 46): "The loss of the Captain was very sad, for not only had Billy Burgoyne, a son of the General who fought through the Peninsular War and was Lord Raglan's trusted adviser in the Crimean War, been especially selected for the new experiment in armoured batteries on board ship, but several officers of repute and a son of the First Lord of the Admiralty were all drowned." And with the ship of which so much had been expected went down all the hopes of poor old Sir John Burgoyne. All his interests had been centred in this his only son, and he felt that now indeed he had little left to live for. He died a year afterwards at 5, Pembridge Gardens, on 7 Oct. 1871. A brass tablet in St. Paul's Cathedral commemorates Capt. Burgoyne and the officers and crew of the ill-fated Captain. Besides his other decorations, Capt. Burgoyne held the Order of the Medjidie, 5th class.

ROBARTS, JOHN, Gunner, Royal Navy, served in the Crimean War and was the companion of Lieuts. Buckley and Burgoyne in the expedition which won the Victoria Cross for all three of them. Kinglake says (Volume VIII., page 67): "The service of landing on a part of the beach out of gunshot of the squadron, and there re-firing the corn-stores in the teeth of the Russians there seen to be gathered, seemed to be one of a desperate kind; and supposing the enterprise to be attempted by a considerable body of men, it promised to involve a painful sacrifice of life; but three fearless officers—Lieut. Buckley, of the Miranda, Lieut. Burgoyne, of the Swallow, and Mr. John Robarts, Gunner of the Ardent—volunteered to achieve the object with their own unaided hands; and Capt. Lyons accepted the offer. They not only accomplished the task, but then happily made good their way back, in spite of all the Cossacks endeavouring to cut them off from their boats. That day 90 merchant-vessels and corn-stores supposed to be worth £100,000 were destroyed." The stores fired by Buckley, Burgoyne and Robarts might, owing to a shift in the wind, easily have escaped. Kinglake says (Volume VIII., page 67): "By a skilful manœuvre of his vessel, the Ardent, in deep water found near the shore, Lieut. Horton proved able to land, from Kiten Bay, Mr. Robarts, the Gunner, and he, with but two men to aid him, destroyed sacks of flour collected for embarkation." For his services in the Crimean War Mr. Robarts was made a Knight of the Legion of Honour, and was awarded the Victoria Cross [London Gazette, 24 Feb. 1857]: "John Roberts, Gunner, Royal Navy. This warrant officer landed with Lieuts. Buckley and Burgoyne at Genitchi, in presence of a superior force, and set fire to the stores, a service of imminent risk. (Despatch from Admiral Lord Lyons, 2 June, 1855; No. 419)." This service is more fully described in the Gazette of Lieut. Buckley's Victoria Cross. Mr. John Robarts was decorated by Queen Victoria at the first Investiture in Hyde Park 26 June, 1857. The "Times" of 8 Oct. 1888, says: "Our Portsmouth correspondent says: 'The death is announced of Mr. John Robarts, V.C., a retired gunner in the Navy, at his residence at Southsea.'" The "Naval and Military Record" for 25 Oct. 1888, says: "The death is announced of Mr. John Robarts, a retired Chief Gunner, Royal Navy, who won the Victoria Cross for his bravery in the Black Sea during the Crimean War. The deceased, who has resided at Southsea, was just over 68 years of age."

John Robarts.

COOPER, HENRY, Boatswain, Royal Navy. The Naval and Military Record says of Henry Cooper: "His career was of a very exciting and stirring character. Entering the Navy in the year 1841, he served as boatswain for 23 years, and received for his gallant services at different times the much coveted Victoria Cross, as well as the Legion of Honour, the Black Sea, Turkish and Baltic Medals, with clasps for Sebastopol and the Sea of Azoff. Prior to the Crimean War he had been engaged in some exciting adventures in other parts of the world. In the year 1848, while serving in the Philomel, under Commander Wood, he was engaged in a boat action against a piratical slaver on the West Coast of Africa. The boat was riddled with grape-shot from stem to stern—one man was killed and nine others wounded, but notwithstanding this and a desperate resistance on the part of the pirates, the slaver was captured and her crew of sixty men were made prisoners. Before the Miranda left Plymouth for the Black Sea she was saluting the Port Admiral when an explosion occurred, and a seaman named John Selvey was thrown overboard. Mr. Cooper at once jumped in after him, and succeeded in keeping him afloat till a boat put out and rescued them. Selvey's hands had been blown off. In the year 1854 Mr. Cooper served in the White Sea, and assisted in the destruction of the town and forts of Kola, the capital of Russian Lapland, and also at the destruction of the forts of Salonika. He was present also at the attack on the fort of Arabat in the Sea of Azoff on the 28th May, 1855. The fort, which mounted 30 guns, was captured and the magazine blown up. Next day he formed one of a boat expedition under Lieut. Mackenzie, and took an active part in setting fire to 73 vessels and the corn stores at Genitchi, a town at the entrance to the Putrid Sea, where the enemy had six pieces of cannon and 200 men, in addition to a battalion of infantry and Cossacks. In this expedition Capt. Lyons gave him the command of the 2nd cutter and all the combustibles for setting fire to the enemy's shipping. This dangerous and desperate task was successfully accomplished and the boats got safely away, although in doing so they had to run the gauntlet of a heavy fire of grape and canister from the enemy. On the 3rd of June, 1855, Mr. Cooper took part in the expedition against Taganrog. Under the command of Lieut. Buckley he landed in a four-oared gig and fired the stores, the Government buildings, and the shipping in a town containing 3,000 troops." Kinglake thus describes the deed for which Mr. Cooper received not only the Victoria Cross but also the Legion of Honour: "With a separate division of light boats, carrying rockets and guns on board, Lieut. Mackenzie covered the approach of Lieut. Buckley, who, in a four-oared gig, accompanied by Mr. Henry Cooper, Boatswain, and manned by volunteers, landed and repeatedly fired the stores and Government buildings. By three o'clock in the afternoon all the long ranges of grain, planks and tar and the vessels on the stocks were in a blaze, as were also the Customs House and other Government buildings." ("History of the Crimean War," Vol. VIII., page 71.) Henry Cooper's Victoria Cross was gazetted 24 Feb. 1857: "Henry Cooper, Boatswain, Royal Navy. Date of Act of Bravery: 3 June, 1855. Performed the desperate service of landing at Taganrog in presence of a large force, to set fire to the Government stores. See memoir of Commander Buckley. (Despatch from Admiral Lord Lyons, 6 June, 1855; No. 429)." [See preceding memoir of Commander Buckley.] The Naval and Military Record continues: "While engaged in two night attacks at Sebastopol, Capt. Lyons was mortally wounded, and Mr. Cooper with great bravery caught up the wounded officer and carried him out of range of the enemy. As Boatswain of the Miranda, he was present at an attack on the forts opposite Kertch He had charge of the boats, and after landing and driving the Russians from their position, he was the first to plant the British colours on the enemy's ground." Mr. Cooper received his Victoria Cross at the hands of Queen Victoria, at the first presentation in Hyde Park, 26 June, 1857. He lived for many years after his retirement, quietly and unobtrusively, at Tor Point in Cornwall, where he was held in universal esteem. He died on Saturday, 15 July, 1893, at the age of 68 years. "At the inquest, which was held at Tor Point on Monday, relative to the death of Mr. Henry Cooper, V.C., R.N., who died suddenly on Saturday morning, the jury, of whom Mr. C. Selley was foreman, returned a verdict of 'Death from natural causes.'" "On 29 Nov. 1907, at Sotheby's, Mr. Baldwin, of Concannon Street, bought for £70 a rare group of naval decorations, won in the Crimea by Boatswain Henry Cooper, consisting of the Victoria Cross, the Cross of the Légion d'Honneur, the Crimean, Baltic and Turkish Medals, along with a green Russian flag, bearing the white cross of St. Andrew."

Henry Cooper.

TREWAVAS, JOSEPH, Seaman, Royal Navy; *b.* 14 Dec. 1835, at Mousehole, co. Cornwall, *s.* of Joseph and Ann Trewavas; educ. at the National School, Paul, near Penzance. Joined H.M.S. Agamemnon at Devonport 15 Oct. 1853, and served in the Crimean Campaign 1854–55, taking part in the bombardment of Sebastopol 17 Oct. 1854. He landed on 23 Oct. with the Naval Brigade. On 3 July, 1855, in the Straits of Genitchi, the shore being completely lined with the enemy's troops, and the adjacent houses filled with riflemen, Seaman Trewavas (one of the crew of H.M.S. Beagle) went forward under a heavy fire from only 80 yards' distance, and with great heroism cut the hawsers of the floating bridge. He was hit in the body in the moment of success, but he attained his object, and a means of carrying stores to the enemy was completely destroyed. Lieut. Hewett (afterwards Admiral Hewett, V.C., who was then only 21) had given orders that the pontoon must be destroyed at all costs. The first attempt, which was made at night, was unsuccessful. On the return of the party to the ship Hewett swore it should be done, if not by night, then by day. Under the cover of a little paddle-steamer with one gun, Trewavas started again in a four-oared boat. The paddle-steamer fired one round, then the gun collapsed, remaining useless for the rest of the time. Rowing up to the pontoon, Trewavas leapt on to it and cut the hawsers. The Russians then realized what the small party of British soldiers were doing, upon which they opened a terrific fire on them. " By coolness and pulling for dear life," said Mr. Trewavas, " and by the Russians' shocking aim, we got back to the ships, the boat completely riddled and up to the thwarts in water." For these services Trewavas was awarded the Victoria Cross [London Gazette, 24 Feb. 1857]: " Joseph Trewavas, Seaman, Royal Navy. Particularly mentioned as having cut the hawsers of the floating bridge in the Straits of Genitchi, under a heavy fire of musketry, on which occasion he was wounded. This service was performed by the crews of the Captain's gig and of one of the paddle-box boats of the Beagle, under a heavy fire of musketry, at about a distance of 80 yards; the beach was completely lined with troops, and the adjacent houses filled with riflemen. Joseph Trewavas is especially mentioned in the Despatches as having been the person who cut the hawser. (Despatch from Admiral Lord Lyons, 10 July, 1855. No. 546)." The destruction of the ferry between Genitchi and the Arabat Spit by Lieut. Hewett in the Beagle is detailed by that officer as follows: " July 4th, 1855. On my arrival at this place—off Genitchi—I at once proceeded to examine the communication between the town and the Arabat Spit, and found it to be by means of its large flats and hawsers, which I determined to destroy, if possible. I accordingly despatched my gig, under Mr. John Hayles, Acting Gunner of this ship, and paddle-box boat, under Mr. Martin Tracy, Midshipman. They succeeded entirely in destroying it by cutting the hawsers and casting the boats adrift, which was done under a very heavy fire of musketry from about 80 yards; the troops completely lined the beach, the adjacent houses being filled with riflemen. Great credit is due to Mr. Hayles for his activity and zeal in destroying the same, and to Mr. Tracy for the effective fire he kept up in covering his retreat; the firing from the ship and paddle-box boats at the same time causing great confusion and loss among the enemy. Mr. Hayles speaks in the highest possible terms of the boats's crew, especially of Joseph Trewavas, Ordinary Seaman—lent from the Agamemnon—who cut the hawsers." For the same services, in the performance of which he was slightly wounded, Mr. Trewavas was made a Knight of the Legion of Honour. He also received the Crimean Medal, with bars for Inkerman and Sebastopol, and the Turkish Crimean Medal. His was one of the nine Victoria Crosses given for the Sea of Azoff. Mr. Trewavas was personally decorated by Queen Victoria, 26 June, 1857. He had become Able Seaman on 12 July, 1855; became Leading Seaman, and retired from the Service on 22 May, 1857. He was well known for many years as a fisherman at Penzance, and was a hale and hearty old man, despite his wounds received from the Russians, though for some time before his death advancing years prevented him from going to sea so often as before. Mr. Trewavas married, 15 Jan. 1866, at Paul Church, Margaret, dau. of Benjamin and Sarah Harry, and they had three children: Joseph, *b.* 14 Dec. 1866; Elizabeth and Sarah. He died 20 July, 1905, at Mousehole.

Joseph Trewavas.

KELLAWAY, JOSEPH, Boatswain, Royal Navy, served in the Crimean War, and was awarded the Victoria Cross [London Gazette, 24 Feb. 1857]: " Joseph Kellaway, Boatswain, Royal Navy. Whilst Boatswain of the Wrangler, in the Sea of Azoff, was taken prisoner after a stout resistance, whilst endeavouring to rescue Mr. Odevaine, Mate. This gallant service was performed on shore, near Marioupol. A detachment consisting of Mr. Odevaine, Mate, Mr. Kellaway, Boatswain, and three seamen, had been despatched from the Wrangler to endeavour to burn some boats, fishing stations and haystacks on the opposite side of a small lake. They had nearly reached the spot when they were fired upon by a party of 50 Russian soldiers, who suddenly rushed from their ambush and endeavoured to cut off their retreat. One man fell into the enemy's hands, but Mr. Kellaway and the two other seamen had continued to make good their escape, when Mr. Odevaine accidentally fell. Mr. Kellaway, apparently imagining him to be wounded, without a moment's hesitation returned to his rescue, risking his own life to succour his commanding officer. Unfortunately, while lifting up Mr. Odevaine, they were surrounded by the enemy, and notwithstanding a gallant but hopeless resistance by Mr. Kellaway, they were both made prisoners. Commander Burgoyne, who has furnished these particulars, observes: ' I was myself an observer of the zeal, gallantry, and self-devotion that characterized Mr. Kellaway's conduct.' (Despatches from Admiral Lord Lyons, 8 Sept. 1855; No. 746; and 22 Sept. 1855, No. 796)." Mr. Kellaway was decorated with the Victoria Cross by Queen Victoria in Hyde Park on 26 June, 1857. He was given the Legion of Honour by the French. This gallant seaman died at Chatham on 10 Oct. 1880.

Joseph Kellaway.

DAY, GEORGE FIOTT, Commander, Royal Navy; *b.* in June, 1820; 4th *s.* of Charles Day, of Bobis Hill, Southampton, and had two brothers, a brother-in-law, and other relatives in the Service. This officer entered the Royal Navy from the Royal Naval College in Aug. 1833, as a First Class Volunteer on board the Challenger (28 guns, Captain M. Seymour), in which vessel he sailed for the Pacific, and was wrecked off the coast of Patagonia 19 May, 1835. He next served on the Conway, and later under Captain the Hon. H. Keppel on the coast of Spain during the Carlist Wars. In June, 1837, on the West Coast of Africa, he volunteered to join the Childers, at the time a prey to yellow fever, which had carried off nearly all the officers and crew. In an open boat, with only five men, Mr. Day captured a schooner, mounting a large 18-pounder on a pivot, with a complement of 30 men, well-armed, and a cargo of 230 slaves. After the Childers was paid off, in Aug. 1838, he completed his time on board the Racer and Orestes sloops, fitting at Portsmouth, and passed his examination, 10 Nov. 1838; after which he was employed six and a half years in the Mediterranean as Mate in the Benbow, Queen and Formidable respectively. He was present in the Benbow (Captain Houston Stewart), and commanded the barge of his ship in the attack on the town of Tortosa, on the coast of Syria, and he also took part in the bombardment of St. John d'Acre (Syrian and St. John d'Acre Medals). On 13 Dec. 1845, Mr. Day was promoted Lieut., and was appointed to the Bittern, on the African Station; on 31 March, 1847, to the Excellent, and on 3 Aug. 1848, as Gunnery-Lieut. to the Southampton, first at the Cape of Good Hope, and then off the coast of Brazil; on 12 Nov. 1851, he was appointed Commander of H.M.S. Locust, a steamer of three guns and 100 h.p., employed up the Rivers Plate and Paraguaya during the hostilities between Buenos Ayres and the Argentine Confederation. For his services he received the thanks of both the British Ministers stationed in that quarter, and of the British Plenipotentiary, Captain Sir C. Hotham, whom he conveyed to Asunçion, which had never before been visited by a steamer or man-of-war. While on the latter service he prepared a running track-chart of the river, the first ever executed, for which he received the thanks of the Admiralty, under Rear-Admiral Sir C. Napier. In 1854 the Locust was sent to the Baltic, and took part in the capture of Bomarsund, herself seizing two large troop-boats full of men. In 1854 Lieut. Day proceeded to join the Fleet in the Mediterranean, and was appointed Lieut.-Commander of the Recruit. In her he sailed with the Weser gun-vessel, 4 April, 1855, under orders for the Black Sea. On the 24th the Weser caught fire, struck on a rock at the entrance to the Dardanelles, and was beached to avoid sinking. After some days of exertion she was got off by the Recruit and taken, lashed head and stern alongside the latter, and with 19 holes in her bottom, to Constantinople. The Recruit took part in the expedition to Kertch, where Commander Day rendered important service in the disembarkation of troops, forced the entrance into the Sea of Azoff, under Captain E. M. Lyons, and was engaged in the attack upon the Fort of Arabat. Before the attack upon Taganrog, Lieut. Day discovered during the night a passage which enabled Captain Lyons to reconnoitre the town successfully. This he did on board the Recruit. While serving in the Sea of Azoff under the direction of Captain S. Osborn, Lieut. Day was entrusted in the following September with the duty of watching the Strait of Genitchi, where he achieved the desperate undertaking which won him his Cross and the Legion of Honour. In the north-east of the Crimea is a low-lying, marshy chain of lakes and inlets called the Putrid Sea. The Strait of Genitchi leads into it from the Sea of Azoff, forming the only entrance. Across this swampy tract the Russians brought their stores, mostly across the Bridge of Chingan, which the Naval Expedition was out to destroy at all costs. The Spit of Arabat lies along the Sea of Azoff—a tongue of land 70 miles long and varying in width from half a mile to three miles, its nose forming one side of the Strait. Behind the Spit were the Russian stores, and opposite to the town of Genitchi itself four gunboats, which commanded the channel. The Spit was strongly garrisoned by Cossacks and horse artillery. Lieut. Day resolved to cross this tongue of land and reconnoitre the position of the bridge, batteries and gunboats. Day was stationed off the entrance to the Strait in the Recruit, a paddle-steamer with two white funnels, the first iron vessel built for our Navy in 1846. He thought the enemy's forces were less numerous than usual; sent two gunboats to explore, and found that he was right. At night he was pulled by two bluejackets towards the land, landed, and told them to pull out of gunshot and wait till he hailed them. He crept past the Cossack outposts, reconnoitred, was seven hours on his return journey, and was taken on board the boat. This he did on a second night, and this time was so long on shore that the seamen gave him up for lost and returned without him. Mr. Parker, however, came to look again, and found Day lying exhausted, and took him back to the ship. Captain Osborn visited him next day. He recovered from the exposure, was thanked in a letter from the Admiralty, and later given the Victoria Cross [London Gazette, 24 Feb. 1857]: " George Fiott Day, Commander, Royal Navy. ' With great enterprise and gallantry, landed and successfully carried out a reconnaissance within the enemy's lines at Genitchi. This service was performed by Commander Day, with the view to ascertaining the practicability of reaching the enemy's gun-vessels, which lay within the Straits of Genitchi, close to the town. It was performed by Commander Day alone on a dark but fine night, with the assistance of a pocket compass. After traversing four or five miles of low, swampy ground, occasionally up to his knees in water, he at length advanced to within about 200 yards of the vessel. From the perfect silence on board then it was his conviction

George Fiott Day.

that they were without crews, and when he returned it was with the full impression that the expedition was a feasible one. This opinion, however, he was induced to change on the following day, in consequence of the increasing activity which was apparent in the direction of the vessels, and therefore he determined on making a second visit to the spot. On this occasion the night was a squally one, and the journey longer and more difficult than before. On reaching the spot, finding the vessels manned, and their crews apparently on the alert, he decided that the effort to surprise them was out of the question.' (Despatch from Admiral Lord Lyon 9 Oct. 1855; No. 844). N.B.—It was while attempting a reconnaissance on the same ground, that Captain l'Allemand, of the French steam-vessel Mouette, lost his life." These Acts of Bravery took place on 17 and 29 Sept. 1855. He was promoted Commander with seniority dating from 19 Nov. 1855. On 15 Oct. his left foot was severely injured in an accident, notwithstanding which he landed at Glofira from the westward with two other officers in order to co-operate with a party landing from the eastward. During this winter he was engaged with the Turkish contingent, and for his services throughout the Crimean War was further rewarded with the Crimean Medal with the Azoff clasp, the Turkish Medal and the Order of the Medjidie. He next returned to England, and was appointed 26 May, 1857, to the command of the Firefly steamer, four guns and 220 h.p., employed on the West Coast of Africa, with which vessel he captured two slavers. He brought the Firefly home and paid her off in Aug. 1858. On 19 Oct. 1858, Captain Day married Mary, third dau. of the late James R. Todd, of 33, Portland Place, London, W., and of Ballyragget, in Ireland, and for many years M.P. for Honiton. Shortly afterwards he sailed for China in charge of two gunboats. For his services on this Station he received the China Medal. He was promoted Captain in Aug. 1861, but in consequence of impaired health was obliged to decline active employment, and in Feb. 1867, was placed on the Captains' Retired List. In further recognition of his services he was nominated a C.B. in May, 1875. He died at Weston-super-Mare after a long illness,18 Dec. 1876, aged 55.

COMMERELL, EDMUND JOHN, Commander, Royal Navy; *b.* at Park Street, Grosvenor Square, London, W., 13 Jan. 1829; 2nd *s.* of John William Commerell, Esq., of Strood Park, Horsham, and of Sophia, dau. of Jacob William Bosanquet, Banker, of Harley Street, W. He was educ. at Naval Schools and at Clifton, and entered the Royal Navy 8 March, 1842, when 12 years of age. He served in the Agincourt; in the Cornwallis, on the China Station, and in the Firebrand, under Captain (afterwards Admiral Sir James) Hope, on the south-east coast of America, during the operations in Parana, including the engagement with the batteries at Obbligado on 20 Nov. 1845, when the chain was cut by the boats of the Firebrand, under Hope's immediate supervision, an act for which many people thought that Hope well deserved the Victoria Cross. Mr. Commerell passed his examination in seamanship 16 May, 1848, and was acting Mate in the Comus, (14 guns, Captain E. C. Tennyson D'Eyncourt), until the following autumn, when he returned to England, and on passing at the Royal Naval College, was presented with a Lieutenant's commission, dated 28 Dec. 1848. On 18 April, 1849, he was appointed to the Dragon, on the Home Station; then served in the Mediterranean. On 13 Oct. 1853, at St. Peter's, Eaton Square, S.W., he married Matilda, dau. of J. Bushby Esq., of 3, Halkin Street, Belgrave Square, London, S.W. On 15 Feb. 1854, he was appointed to the Vulture, and served in the Baltic until 20 Feb. 1855, when he was promoted Commander and given the command of the Weser, a small steam-vessel of 6 guns and 160 h.p., and in the following April he sailed with her for the Black Sea. On 24 April, near the Dardanelles, the Weser caught fire, struck on a rock and had to be beached to avoid sinking. She was eventually towed off, and at length she reached the scene of hostilities and assisted on the night of 16 June in discharging a heavy fire on the town and sea-defences of Sebastopol, preparatory to the unsuccessful land attack on the 18th on the Redan and Malakoff. After this Lieut. Commerell took her into the Sea of Azoff and the Putrid Sea, where she formed part of the squadron under the command of Captain S. Osborn, which harassed the enemy at Genitchi, cutting off all communication along the Spit. Here he won his Cross under circumstances described by Admiral Sir Sydney Eardley Wilmot in his "Life of Lord Lyons": "Lieutenant Commerell, in the Weser, had already performed good service, and this active officer now obtained permission from Captain Osborn—lately deservedly promoted—to attempt to burn the stores collected at the mouth of the Salghir River. This runs into the lower part of the Putrid Sea, nearly opposite to the middle of the Arabat Spit. A reconnaissance of this part some time previously had shown that a considerable amount of forage and grain was stored there. Accordingly Lieut. Commerell, Mr. N. D. Lillingston, mate, and three seaman—Rickard, Milestone and Hoskins—left their ship in a small boat at half-past two in the morning of October 11th. Hauling their skiff across the Spit, they pulled through the Putrid Sea. About four o'clock they reached the other side, and, as the water was too shallow for the boat to get close in, Commerell, with two of the men, Rickard and Milestone, went on shore, leaving Mr. Lillingston and Hoskins in the boat. Striking a course by aid of a pocket-compass, in the direction they thought the stores were situated, they walked for about two miles, and then waited till it was lighter to discover the object of their search. After lying hid for half an hour, day began to break, and then they observed the stores about a mile off, with a large red building close to a Cossack station and signal-post.

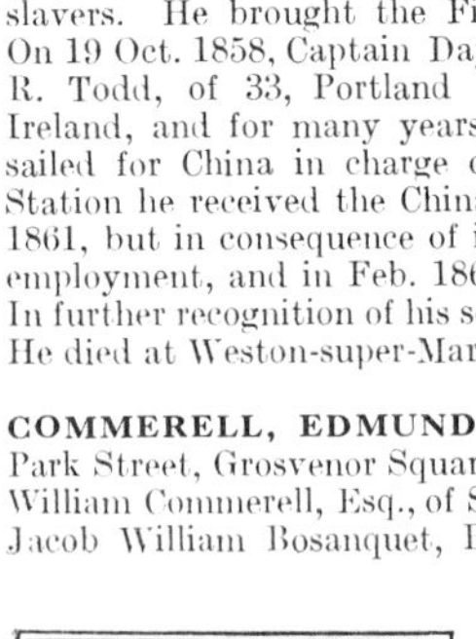

Edmund J. Commerell.

The small party at once made for this point, having to wade across two canals up to their necks. On arrival they soon set fire to the stores; but as regards the red house, Commerell came to the conclusion it would take too long to ignite, and give no chance for escape. As it was, the Cossacks were fully aroused before the three men had finished their incendiary work with the forage; but some time elapsed before the enemy realized the cause of the blaze and who had effected it. So Commerell and his companions managed to get the start of a mile before they were discovered. But double that distance had to be traversed before they reached the boat, and one of them—Milestone—was almost done up. He had to be helped along by the other two, and though he begged them to leave him, this they were determined not to do. The sight of their boat about a mile off on the right cheered their spirits, but at the same time they observed a party of Cossacks in their front. It was a question of which would get to the boat first. Milestone was now so exhausted that they had to take his boots off. This delay lessened the distance of their pursuers, and the Cossacks began to get unpleasantly close. When the three men got within 200 yards of the boat the enemy were only 60 yards behind. Milestone then became almost helpless, and fell several times. The Russians, who had already opened fire, thinking he was wounded, raised a shout of delight. The position of the party at this moment seemed almost perilous; but the Cossacks were checked by the fire of Lillingston and Hoskins from the boat, and Commerell with his revolver stopped the leading horseman. At last, by dint of half-carrying, half-dragging Milestone, they got him to the boat, and pushing her off, got clear of their pursuers. They reached the ship without further incident, and had the satisfaction of observing from her mast-head that the fire consumed everything." For these services he received the Victoria Cross [London Gazette, 24 Feb. 1857]: "John Edmund Commerell, Commander, Royal Navy. When commanding the Weser in the Sea of Azoff, crossed the Isthmus of Arabat and destroyed large quantities of forage on the Crimean shore of the Siwash. This enterprise was performed by Commander Commerell at night, accompanied by William Rickard, Quartermaster, and George Milestone, Able Seaman. Having hauled their small boat across the Spit of Arabat, they traversed the Siwash to the Crimean shore of the Putrid Sea. The magazine of corn of which they were in search lay about two miles and a half off, and to reach it they had to ford two rivers, the Karu-su and the Salghir. The forage and corn, amounting to 400 tons, were stacked on the banks of the latter river, in the vicinity of a guard-house, and close to from 20 to 30 mounted Cossacks, who were encamped in the neighbouring village. Commander Commerell and his two companions contrived to ignite the stacks, the rapid blazing of which alarmed the guards, who pursued them to the shore with a heavy fire of musketry, and very nearly succeeded in taking them prisoners. (Despatch from Admiral Lord Lyons, 6 Nov. 1855; No. 899)." "William Rickard, Quartermaster, Royal Navy. Accompanied his Commander, Lieut. Commerell of the Weser, to the Crimean shore of the Siwash, and whilst under a heavy fire of musketry, remained to assist George Milestone, who had fallen. (Despatch from Admiral Lord Lyons, 6 Nov. 1855; No. 899)." The French gave him the Legion of Honour, and he also received the Baltic and Sebastopol Medals (1854) and the Crimean Medal with two clasps (1855). He resigned command of the Weser after the fall of Kimburn, and was appointed to command the Snake, with which vessel he was in the Mediterranean until the summer of 1857. On 4 Oct. 1858, he was in command of the Fury on the East Indies and China Stations, and on 25 June commanded a division of seamen landed for the attack on the Taku Forts. The attack was repulsed with great loss, for 64 officers and men were killed and 252 wounded. His Commander was disabled, and the command devolved upon Commander Commerell, to whom Rear-Admiral Hope, the Commander-in-Chief, expressed his warmest thanks. Notwithstanding the disastrous losses incurred, the courage and persistence displayed by the landing-party were considered both officially and by the general public to be honourable in the highest degree. He received illuminated votes of thanks from the Houses of Lords and Commons, also the China Medal. Commander Commerell was promoted Captain 18 July, 1859. In 1866, in command of the Terrible, he assisted in laying the Atlantic Cable, for which service he was rewarded by a Civil C.B. In 1869 he received the more appropriate Military Order, and in 1868 and 1869 he commanded the turret-ship Monarch—an experiment on a large scale—and in her in Dec. 1869, took across to the United States the body of the philanthropist, George Peabody. In Feb. 1871, Captain Commerell was Commodore and Commander-in-Chief on the West Coast of Africa and at the Cape of Good Hope. While reconnoitring up the River Prah in 1873 to discover the position of the Ashantis, he was dangerously wounded by a musket-shot in the lungs, which compelled him to go back to the Cape and eventually to invalid to England. From 1872 to 1879 Captain Commerell was A.D.C. to Her Majesty Queen Victoria, and from 1874 to 1879 he was a Groom-in-Waiting. On 31 March, 1874, he was nominated a K.C.B., and 12 Nov. 1876, became a Rear-Admiral. The following year he was sent out to the Mediterranean as Second in Command, under, and at the special request of, Sir Geoffrey Hornby, with whom he worked most happily, not only on active service but for the welfare and comfort of the men. Admiral Hornby wrote home: "Commerell has made friends with the Vali of Smyrna." He went on to relate how his Second in Command had discovered that a Greek was selling bad wine and had threatened to hang him, and how, owing to his friendship with the Vali, Commerell might have easily carried his threat into execution. "If we could but hang all the Greeks, the Eastern question might soon be happily settled." Rear-Admiral Commerell was mentioned in Despatches by Sir Geoffrey Hornby. From 1879 to 1880 he was a Lord of the Admiralty; on 19 Jan. 1881, he became a Vice-Admiral, and in November of that year he went out as Commander-in-Chief on the North American and West Indian Station. He returned to England in the autumn of 1885, and at the General Election of that year was returned to Parliament as Member for Southampton, as also in the General Election of 1886. "At this time and for the next two years he endeavoured to hammer some sense

of the needs of the Navy into a careless and unsympathetic public, and he may be credited with a large share in calling up that feeling which produced Lord George Hamilton's Naval Defence Act of 1889. But Sir Edmund Commerell had resigned his seat some months before on being appointed, in July, 1888, Commander-in-Chief at Portsmouth." (The "Times," 25 May, 1901). He had attained, on 2 April, 1886, the rank of Admiral, and on the Queen's Jubilee, 21 June, 1887, was given a G.C.B. As Commander-in-Chief at Portsmouth at the time of the Kaiser's visit and the Naval Review of 1889, he was necessarily thrown much into close correspondence with that monarch, who presented him with a sword, accompanied by an autograph letter. During the Kaiser's visits to England Sir Edmund was always in waiting on him, also on Prince Henry of Prussia and Princess Charlotte of Saxe-Meiningen. He was promoted, nominated to the rank of Admiral of the Fleet, on 14 Feb. 1892, in the vacancy caused by the death of Admiral Wallis. Sir Edmund was placed on the retired list in Jan. 1899, and from 1891 was Groom-in-Waiting to Queen Victoria, in which capacity he was acting not long before his death at the Court of King Edward. He was J.P. for Hampshire. Admiral Commerell died at his residence, 45, Rutland Gate, Hyde Park, W., on 21 May, 1901, and was buried in Folkestone Cemetery, where his daughter had also been interred. Wreaths were sent by the Kaiser and by Prince Henry of Prussia, and from the Staff of Messrs. Vickers, Sons & Maxim. A Memorial Service was held at All Saints', Ennismore Gardens, S.W. (the church which the Admiral attended), at which the King, the German Emperor, the Duke of Cornwall and York, the Duke of Connaught and Princess Henry of Battenberg were all represented. Sir Edmund and Lady Commerell had three daughters, of whom only one survives. Admiral Commerell was a Knight of Grace of the Order of St. John of Jerusalem.

RICKARD, WILLIAM, Quartermaster, Royal Navy, served in the Crimean Campaign and was given the Victoria Cross for his services with Commander Commerell in that campaign [London Gazette, 24 Feb. 1857]: "John Edmund Commerell, Commander, Royal Navy: 'When commanding the Weser in the Sea of Azoff, crossed the Isthmus of Arabat and destroyed large quantities of forage on the Crimean shore of the Siwash. This enterprise was performed by Commander Commerell at night, accompanied by William Rickard, Quartermaster, and George Milestone, Able Seaman. Having hauled their small boat across the Spit of Arabat, they traversed the Siwash to the Crimean shore of the Putrid Sea. The magazine of corn of which they were in search lay about two miles and a half off, and to reach it, they had to ford two rivers, the Karu-su and the Salghir. The forage and corn, amounting to 400 tons, were stacked on the banks of the latter river, in the vicinity of a guard-house, and close to from 20 to 30 mounted Cossacks, who were encamped in the neighbouring village. Commander Commerell and his two companions contrived to ignite the stacks, the rapid blazing of which alarmed the guard, who pursued them to the shore with a very heavy fire of musketry, and very nearly succeeded in taking them prisoners.' (Despatch from Admiral Lord Lyons, 6 Nov. 1855; No. 899). 'William Rickard, Quartermaster, Royal Navy. Accompanied his Commander, Lieut. Commerell, of the Weser, to the Crimean shore of the Siwash, and whilst under a heavy fire of musketry, remained to assist George Milestone, who had fallen.' (Despatch from Admiral Lord Lyons, 6 Nov. 1855; No. 899). The service performed by William Rickard is thus mentioned by Commander Commerell in his despatch: 'I must bring to notice the excellent conduct of the small party that accompanied me, more especially that of William Rickard, Quartermaster, who, though much fatigued himself, remained to assist the other seaman, who, from exhaustion, had fallen in the mud and was unable to extricate himself, notwithstanding the enemy were keeping up a heavy fire upon us at the distance of 30 or 40 yards as we crossed the mud.' (Despatch from Admiral Lord Lyons, 6 Nov. 1855; No. 899)." William Rickard was given the Legion of Honour for the same services which gained him the Cross. He died on 21 Feb. 1905.

William Rickard.

THE NAVAL BRIGADE

PEEL, WILLIAM, Captain, Royal Navy; *b.* 2 Nov. 1824, 3rd *s.* of the great statesman, Sir Robert Peel (2nd Bart., 1788–1850), and of Julia, yst. dau. of General Sir John Ffloyd, Bart. Besides William Peel, three of Sir Robert's five sons attained to considerable eminence, viz.: Sir Robert Peel (3rd Bart.), politician; Sir Frederick Peel, K.C.M.G., Chief Railway Commissioner, and Arthur Wellesley Peel, created Viscount Peel, Speaker of the House of Commons. An entry in the Harrow Register is as follows: "Peel, William (The Park); entered, 1837. Son of Sir R. Peel (O.H.), 2nd Bart. Left in 1838." William Peel entered the Royal Navy on 7 April, 1838, as Midshipman, Princess Charlotte (Captain Arthur Fanshawe), bearing the flag in the Mediterranean of the Hon. Sir Robert Stopford. There is an interesting letter from Captain Peel to Mr. O'Byrne among the O'Byrne Manuscripts in the British Museum, which were the material from which Mr. O'Byrne wrote his Lives of Naval Officers. "I was present," Captain Peel says in this letter to Mr. O'Byrne, "at Acre, and served in China throughout the year 1842, but was not present at any of the actions up the river, my ship being employed elsewhere." After being present in several operations on the coast of Syria, he was further employed on the Mediterranean Station in the Monarch (84 guns, Captain Sam Chambers); after which he successively joined the William and Mary yacht (Captain Phipps Hornby) and the Cambrian (36 guns, Captain H. Ducie Chads). He returned to England in the Belleisle troopship with Captain J. Kingcome in Sept. 1843, and was received on board the Camperdown (104 guns), bearing the flag of Sir Edward Brace, at the Nore, and in the following Nov. he joined the Excellent gunnery-ship at Portsmouth. He passed his examination in May, 1844, "with a brilliance that called forth a flattering eulogium from Sir Thomas Hastings and a very flattering notice from Sir Charles Napier in the House of Commons" (O'Byrne—Hansard, 16 May), and a week later, 13 May, was promoted to be Lieut. of the Winchester, flagship of Rear-Admiral Sir Josceline Percy, at the Cape of Good Hope. He does not appear, however, to have actually joined that vessel, and was appointed on 13 June as additional to the Cormorant steam-sloop (Captain George Thomas Gordon) in the Pacific. Thence he was removed to the Thalia, and next, O'Byrne thinks, to the America (50 guns, Captain the Hon. John Gordon), by whom he was sent in charge of despatches from San Blas to Vera Cruz—and thence to England. After a brief interval of half-pay he was appointed 27 Feb. 1846, to the Devastation steam-sloop (Captain Edward Crouch), equipping at Woolwich, and on 15 May to the Constance (50 guns, Captain Sir Baldwin Wake Walker), lying at Devonport. He attained the rank of Commander 27 June, 1846, and on 11 Feb. 1847, assumed command of the Daring (12 guns), on the North American and West India Station. On 10 Jan. 1849, he was promoted to be Captain. As he expected to be on half pay for some time, he made up his mind to explore Central Africa, with the idea of doing something to improve the condition of the negro. With this object in view he studied Arabic for some months under Joseph Chuni, a Maronite, educated at Rome; and in Sept. 1850, he proposed to Chuni that they should make a short tour together and visit Egypt, Mount Sinai, Jerusalem, Nazareth and Syria. Chuni agreed, and they left England on 20 Oct. and were back by Feb. 1851. On 20 Aug. they started on their African explorations, and went up the Nile and across the desert to Khartoum and on to El Obeid, where both travellers had a severe attack of fever and ague. Peel returned to England early in January, and published an account of the journey under the title of "A Ride through the Nubian Desert" (1852). In Oct. 1852, Peel commissioned the Diamond frigate, attached to the fleet in the Mediterranean, and afterwards in the Black Sea. Field-Marshal Sir Evelyn Wood, in "The Crimea in 1854 and 1894," says: "Our Captain, acting as Commodore, signalled H.M.S. Diamond, to carry in our letters for the English mail, and her Captain, William Peel, came on board for orders. All our officers were anxious to see one who had already a service reputation as not only our youngest Post Captain, but as one of the best. William Peel . . . was then thirty years of age. . . . In Aug. 1854, I had no idea I was to spend months with this man of highly-strung, nervous temperament, whom I learnt to love and esteem more and more daily as 'the bravest of the brave,' till we were separated; both wounded and invalided to England. I was evidently much impressed, however, for I recorded in boyish language, 'Captain Peel—very intelligent, sharp as a needle, never saw a more perfect gentleman.' His looks and bearing were greatly in his favour, for he had a singularly striking appearance, showing both in face and figure what is described in well-bred horses as 'quality.' His height was about medium; head gracefully set on broad, well-turned shoulders; he was light in lower body, with dignified yet easy deportment. His dark brown, wavy hair was carefully brushed back, disclosing a perfectly oval face, a high square forehead and deep blue-grey eyes, which flashed when he was talking eagerly, as he often did. He had a somewhat austere face, smooth and chiselled in outline, with a firm-set mouth, which was the more noticeable from his being clean-shaved at that time; such was the man, quick in movement and brave in spirit, as shown in the first bombardment when he lifted a live shell!

"'And as it burned
From the rent breach the fiery death returned.'"

When the Naval Brigade was landed for the Siege of Sebastopol, under Captain Stephen Lushington, Peel was one of the first to be landed with it. "Captain Peel," says Kinglake, "undertook a battery with a number of his men from the Diamond." Of the deed which won Peel his Cross the Crimean historian says: "There occurred on this day one of those incidents of war which show how instantaneous in heroic natures is the process of both the thought and the resolve from which brave actions spring. The horses which were drawing the ammunition waggon for the Diamond Battery having refused to face the fire, some volunteers went to the waggon to clear it, and they succeeded in bringing in their load, but before the powder could be stored away in the magazine, a shell came into the middle of it, while the volunteers were still close to the heap. A voice cried, 'The fuse is burning!' Then instantly and, as the narrator says, 'with one spring,' Captain Peel darted upon the live shell and threw it over the parapet. The shell burst about four yards from his hands without hurting anyone." Field-Marshal Sir Evelyn Wood lately said: "I was on the 21-gun battery before Sebastopol sixty-one years ago when Captain Sir William Peel, R.N., picked up from amongst a number of powder-cases and carried, resting on his chest, a 42-pounder live Russian shell, which burst as he threw it over the parapet." Of the incident for which the second date was engraved upon Peel's Cross, Kinglake again gives a graphic account. He says that during the Battle of Inkerman, the Duke of Cambridge, with the surviving officers of his staff, including Captain Higginson and about 100 men, were grouped around the colours of the Grenadier Guards, and, unknown to themselves, were cut off by a force interposed in their rear. Also, two other battalions were coming up to attack them in the direction of their left front. Some of

William Peel.

the officers were beginning to think that their own people were firing upon them. "At this moment, with a midshipman on a pony beside him, there came up on foot a ship's captain, no other than Peel of the Diamond. With the field-glass he carried, the seaman's calm gaze had enabled him to speak as one certain, and he instinctively saw how advantageous it would be if the ugly truth could become known to so able an officer as Captain Higginson a few minutes before its discovery by the men. Therefore, speaking so as to be heard by the Captain and none other, he pointed by a slight gesture to Mount Head and said that the body thence firing were Russians. It was owing in part to this thoughtfulness of Captain Peel's that the discovery, when it came, caused no confusion. The men had scarce learnt that they were cut off when already the voice of authority was telling them what to do." (Kinglake's "Crimean War," Vol. V., page 274). Sir George Higginson says in "Seventy-one Years of a Guardsman's Life" (page 199): "Again hurled back from their little Sandbag Battery or Redoubt (for it is difficult to give it a name, inasmuch as it had never been armed, and was not much more than thirty feet wide, with embrasures for two guns), our Grenadiers formed a compact body around the colours, while I limped off a short distance to the left, hoping to descry through the mist and fog the approach of reinforcements; but I found the gap increasing, and, as it was afterwards proved, the remainder of our comrades, with the Scots Fusiliers, were encountering another heavy column of the enemy, threatening the left of our position. It was at this moment that I saw a figure in naval uniform, rendered more distinctive by a tall, glazed hat, coming towards me. The new arrival proved to be Captain Peel of the Diamond, one of the most adventurous and daring of that Naval Brigade which had been landed to take part in the siege operations. On my expressing astonishment at seeing him amongst us at such a moment, he simply remarked, 'Oh, there was nothing going on at my little battery on the hill behind; and as I heard you fellows had plenty to do, I thought I would come and have a look at you.' I replied with some gravity of manner that we were in a tight place awaiting supply of ammunition and long-expected support. While this conversation was going on, I felt a bullet pass from behind through my bearskin cap, causing me, for the moment, to stoop forward. I exclaimed, 'This is rather hard lines! here are our fellows mistaking us for the enemy, and firing upon us, instead of coming to our relief.' He turned his field-glass in the direction I pointed, and said in a subdued voice, 'No, by heaven! it is the enemy getting round our rear.' I moved at once to our sturdy group rallied round the colours, and explained to Charles Lindsay, the only officer that at the moment I could find, our new danger, and then began our ever-to-be-remembered retreat." The midshipman on the pony was, of course, the heroic boy, Edward St. John Daniel, who won his Cross that day for his devotion to his adored Captain. Peel led seven charges in the Battle of Inkerman. He and Midshipman Daniel were amongst the first to be awarded the Victoria Cross after the institution of the decoration. [London Gazette, 24 Feb. 1857]: "William Peel, Captain, Royal Navy. Sir Stephen Lushington recommends this officer: Firstly, for having on 18 Oct. 1854, at the greatest possible risk, taken up a live shell, with the fuse still burning, from among several powder-cases, outside the magazine, and thrown it over the parapet (the shell bursting as it left his hands), thereby saving the magazine and the lives of those immediately round it. (Despatch from Sir Stephen Lushington, enclosed in letter from Admiral Lord Lyons, 10 May, 1856). Secondly: On 5 Nov. 1854, at the Battle of Inkerman, for joining the officers of the Grenadier Guards, and assisting in defending the colours of that regiment, when hard-pressed at the Sandbag Battery. (Sir Stephen Lushington is authorized to make the statement by the Lieut.-General commanding the Division, His Royal Highness the Duke of Cambridge, who is ready to bear testimony to the fact). Thirdly: On 18 June, 1855, for volunteering to lead the Ladder Party at the Assault on the Redan, and carrying the first ladder until wounded." For his services in this campaign Peel was also given a C.B., 5 July; 1855. On the morning of the assault on the Redan Midshipman Evelyn Wood was ill in bed with dysentery. He was awakened by Able Seaman Michael Hardy, who said: "If ye miss this day's divarsion ye'll regret it to the day of your death." The night before Captain Peel had told Mr. Wood he was to be sure to stay in bed and not take part in the assault. Wood had said: "Is Daniel going?" and Captain Peel said "Yes." So Hardy pulled on Mr. Wood's trousers and put on the rest of his clothes, and propped him up against the bed-post while he went to look for his pony. He gave him some brandy and helped him on, and held on to his leg as they went up to join the rest so that he should not fall off. On the way Mr. Wood began to feel better, but he thought he would like a strong man near him, so he said to Hardy: "You keep by me, and I'll keep near the Captain." Hardy said: "I'll keep near him if he keeps in front; not unless." When they got there, Mr. Wood tied up his pony to a gun of the 21-gun battery. Captain Peel was very angry when he saw Mr. Wood appearing on the scene and sent him off on sundry futile errands as a pretext for keeping him out of danger, as he was so young and so ill. Wood went on the errands and walked slowly back across the line of fire, and Peel saw he meant business and let him come. In spite of being ill, because he was seventeen and Peel was thirty-six, he got ahead of him. He had a flag in his hand, and suddenly was shot in the hand, and his arm felt as if it had been paralysed. He fell down—but soon picked himself up and found a bit had been shot out of his thumb, but there was only a little bit of blood on it, and he went on. Hardy had gone ahead of him, and he wondered that he had not kept near him, but he soon knew why, for the seaman's dead body was found next day under an embrasure of the Redan, the only man, so far as Mr. Wood knew, who crossed the Abatis and ditch. Midshipman Daniel was Captain Peel's first aide-de-camp; he belonged to his ship and Wood didn't, and was only second aide-de-camp. Wood had had all the long watches given him in his ship, and had got rather punished generally, and Peel had heard him well spoken of and took him for his aide-de-damp. Daniel was eighteen at this time and he was as brave as a lion and didn't know what fear meant. Captain Peel was very handsome. Sir Evelyn Wood says that most of us have to be touched up by portrait-painters and made look as our best girls see us, but Peel didn't need that at all; he was just as handsome as his pictures. He was a very clean-minded man, and very clean-mouthed; though he did *occasionally* use bad language. On 13 Sept. 1856, Captain Peel commissioned for service in China Her Majesty's screw steam frigate Shannon (51 guns, 600 h.p., and 2,667 tons), at Portsmouth, at the time the finest frigate afloat, first of a very new and powerful class, calculated to obtain great speed under sail or steam. She was ordered to China, and left England on 17 March, 1857. She anchored in Simon's Bay on 7 May, and sailed again on the 11th, and on 11 June was anchored off Singapore, when news was received of the outbreak of the Mutiny in India. On the 23rd Lord Elgin embarked with his staff, and the Shannon sailed for Hong-Kong on 2 July. On the 16th, hearing that things in India looked very black, Lord Elgin re-embarked. The Shannon took on board a detachment of Royal Marines and of the 90th Regt. and sailed from Hong-Kong for Calcutta, touching at Singapore *en route*. On 6 Aug. she anchored off the Mouths of the Ganges, and on nearing Calcutta was repeatedly cheered by the people on the shore at Garden Reach. At Calcutta Lord Elgin disembarked. Captain Peel offered to the Governor-General the services of the bluejackets of the Shannon, with their ship's guns, to form a Naval Brigade. His offer was accepted, and preparations were immediately made for service on shore. The dress of the men was not altered, but their straw hats were covered with white cotton and provided with curtains to protect the backs of their necks. On 14 Aug. 1857, the river steamer China came alongside the frigate and Captain Peel embarked with the following officers: Lieuts. Young, Wilson, Hay and Salmon; Captain Gray and Lieut. Stirling, R.M., Lieut. Lind-af-Hageby, of the Swedish Navy; the Rev. E. L. Bowman, Dr. Flanagan, Mr. Comerford, Assistant Paymaster; Messrs. M. Daniel, Garvey, E. Daniel, Lord Walter Kerr (now Admiral of the Fleet), Lord Arthur Clinton, and Mr. Church, Midshipman; Messrs. Brown, Bone and Henry, engineers; Mr. Thompson, gunner; Mr. Boyce, carpenter; Mr. Staunton, assistant clerk, and Messrs. Watson and Lascelles, naval cadets. Four hundred and fifty-four men, with their arms and ammunition, embarked in the flat, which was taken in tow by the Chunar. Captain Peel also took up a launch and cutter belonging to the frigate. Captain Vaughan was left in charge of the Shannon, but on 18 Sept. he embarked with reinforcements for the Shannon Brigade, on the river steamer Benares, with Lieut. Wrenston, Mr. Heney, Mate; Mr. Way, Midshipman, and Mr. Richards, naval cadet; 120 men in the flat, with ammunition. The frigate was left under the command of Mr. Waters, Master, with about 140 men. Captain Vaughan joined Peel on 20 Oct. at Allahabad. From that time the Shannon's Brigade was present at nearly all the operations of the Army. Kaye and Malleson, in their "History of the Sepoy Mutiny," say of Peel, in Vol. IV., page 90, that he was "a man who would have made his mark in any age. To an energy that nothing could daunt, a power that seemed never to tire, he added a freshness of intellect, a fund of resources. . . . Bright and joyous in the field, with a kind word for every comrade, he caused the sternest duty ordered by him to be looked upon as a pleasant pastime. . . . Starting from Calcutta on an expedition unprecedented in Indian warfare, he conquered every obstacle, he succeeded to the very utmost of the power to succeed. He showed eminently all the qualities of an organizer and leader of men. Not one single speck of failure marred the brightness of his ermine." Peel was everywhere remarkable for his imperturbable coolness, and his powerful battery did great execution, for he worked and manœuvred the huge guns as though they had been light field pieces. He had strange armoured cars, too, with a mast in the middle. On 21 Jan. 1858, Captain Peel was created a K.C.B., and the news of this reached the Brigade about 2 March, 1858. They heard also that he had been appointed A.D.C. to the Queen. In the second Relief of Lucknow he was badly wounded in the thigh by a musket ball, which was cut out from the opposite side of his leg. He recovered enough to be taken out for exercise in a dhoolie, and Lieut. Verney procured a carriage and made it as comfortable as he could ready for Captain Peel to travel in it from Lucknow to Cawnpore. This, however, he refused to do, saying that he would sooner travel in a dhoolie, like one of his bluejackets, and it is supposed that the dhoolie must have been previously used for a small-pox patient. Lord Roberts says in his "Forty-one Years in India" (page 230): "I marched to Cawnpore with Army Headquarters. Sir William Peel, who was slowly recovering from his wounds, was of the party. We reached Cawnpore on the 17th. . . . Peel and I dined together on the 19th, when to all appearances he was perfectly well, but on going to his room on the next morning I found him in a high fever, and had some suspicious-looking spots about his face. I went off at once in search of a doctor, and soon returned with one of the surgeons of the 5th Fusiliers, who, to my horror—for I had observed that Peel was nervous about himself—exclaimed, with brutal frankness, the moment he entered the room, 'You have got small-pox!' It was only too true. On being convinced that this was the case, I went to the Chaplain, the Rev. Thomas Moore, and told him of Peel's condition. Without an instant's hesitation he decided that the invalid must come to his house to be taken care of. That afternoon I had the poor fellow carried over, and there I left him in the kind hands of Mrs. Moore, the padre's wife, who had, as a special case, been allowed to accompany her husband to Cawnpore. Peel died on the 27th." The news of his death was brought to the Shannon's Brigade at Lucknow by an officer passing through on his way down to Calcutta. "I cannot say," writes Lieut. E. H. Verney, in "The Shannon's Brigade in India" (page 139), "what a sad loss we all feel this to be, and how deeply his death is felt and regretted by every officer and man; the mainspring that worked the machinery is gone; we never felt ourselves to be the *Shannon's* Naval Brigade, or even the *Admiralty* Naval Brigade, but always *Peel's* Naval Brigade. He it was who first originated the idea of sailors going one thousand four hundred miles away from the sea, and afterwards carried it out in such an able and judicious manner. I do not doubt that his worth will be appreciated and his death deeply lamented by the people of England." Lord Canning, in a General Order issued 30 April, wrote: "The loss of his daring but thoughtful courage, joined with eminent abilities, is a heavy one to this country; but it is not more to be deplored than the loss of that influence which his earnest character, admirable temper and gentle, kindly bearing exercised on all within his reach—an influence that was exerted unceasingly for the public good, and of which the Governor-General believes that it may with truth be said that there is not a man of any rank or profession who, having been associated with William Peel in these times of anxiety and danger, has not felt and acknowledged it." "The memory of his great name and of his great deeds still survives," wrote Colonel Malleson. "In the Eden Gardens of Calcutta a statue in white marble recalls to the citizens by whom these gardens are nightly thronged, the form and fashion of him who was indeed the noblest volunteer of this or any age; who was successful because he was really great, and who, dying early, left a reputation without spot, the best inheritance he could bequeath to his country." Sir William Peel's portrait by John Lucas is in the Painted Hall at Greenwich. An extract from the London Gazette of 25 May, 1858, runs as follows: "No. 17 Nominal Roll of Officers of Her Majesty's Ship Shannon's Brigade, serving under Captain Peel, K.C.B., who are deemed worthy of promotion and of honourable mention for their services during the campaign and on the capture of Lucknow, March, 1858: Lieut. Thomas J. Young, gunnery officer of Her Majesty's Ship Shannon.—This officer has been distinguished in every engagement by his cool courage and active skill as a gunnery officer; has been specially employed on all critical occasions and has been recommended for the Victoria Cross.—Recommended for promotion. Lieut. Nowell Salmon.—An excellent officer, distinguished himself in the Shannon Brigade at the Relief of Lucknow; was severely wounded and named for the Victoria Cross.—Recommended for promotion. Mr. Edmund H. Verney, Senior Acting Mate, zealous and well-conducted.—Recommended for promotion. Officers not eligible for promotion but worthy of honourable mention:—Lord Walter T. Kerr, Midshipman: Has had an independent command. Is very highly recommended. Lord A. P. Clinton and Mr. E. J. Church, Midshipmen. Have behaved admirably and are very promising officers.—William Peel, Captain, R.N., Commanding Shannon's Naval Brigade, Lucknow, 31 March, 1858." Commander Vaughan, R.N., of the Shannon's Naval Brigade, was created a C.B., an honour never before given to any officer below the rank of Captain. Lieut. Young, V.C., was promoted to Captain, and so was Lieut. Salmon, V.C. The Indian Medal with the Lucknow clasp was given to each of the men, and Lieuts. Young and Salmon and Mr. E. St. J. Daniel received also the Relief of Lucknow clasp for the Relief of Lucknow on 17 Nov. 1857.

DANIEL, EDWARD ST. JOHN, Midshipman, Royal Navy; served in the Crimean campaign of 1854–55, and was "the midshipman on a pony," who is described as having been present at the Battle of Inkerman as Aide-de-camp to Capt. William Peel, Royal Navy. Field-Marshal Sir Evelyn Wood says in "The Crimea in 1854 and 1894," in describing the Battle of Inkerman: "When our officers and non-commissioned officers were shot down, groups of privates, banding together under some natural and self-elected leader of men, would rush forward on the foe, and in the Naval Brigade we heard next day that Captain Peel had led seven such separate attacks." Of these charges Sir Evelyn says that one may fairly say that Mr. Daniel was close to Capt. Peel all the time. Midshipman Evelyn Wood also became an Aide-de-camp to Capt. Peel, to whom the two boys were devoted, while Capt. Peel, who was so reckless of his own life, tried hard to keep them out of unnecessary danger. He wrote to his brother, later Sir Frederick Peel: "I really sometimes thought it rather inconvenient having two such spirits with me as Messrs. Daniel and Wood." Sir Evelyn Wood describes the Assault on the Redan in "From Midshipman to Field Marshal," and he says: "My brother aide-de-camp (Mr. Daniel) kindly came to see if I was up" (on the morning of the assault). "We had fully made up our minds that our chief would be killed in the assault, and had agreed to stand by him or to bring in his body." Capt. Peel was struck half-way up the glacis by a bullet, which penetrated his left arm, and he fell half fainting, but was caught by Mr. Daniel, who coolly rendered first-aid in the face of the enemy, and put a tourniquet on his captain's arm. Sir Evelyn Wood says that at this time "The senior lieutenant had been slightly wounded, and my friend Dalyell had loss his left arm, shattered by a grape shot. Capt. Peel was also struck when about half-way up the glacis by a bullet, which passed through his left arm, and he became so faint that he reluctantly came back, attended by Mr. Daniel, who was the only unwounded naval officer out with our column. He escaped injury, although his pistol case was shot through in two places and his clothes were cut several times. Thus before our party got half way I was the sole officer remaining effective." Admiral Lord Lyons said, in his speech at the Mansion House on 15 Feb. 1858: "All behaved well, but I doubt whether there is anything in the annals of chivalry that surpasses the conduct of Capt. Peel's Aides-de-camp, Messrs. Daniel and Wood, one of whom (Mr. Wood), when wounded, placed a scaling ladder against the Redan." Sir Stephen Lushington's first three recommendations for the Victoria Cross were that it should be awarded to Capt. Peel and to Midshipmen Daniel and Wood. Mr. Wood, however, was not given the Victoria Cross, the First Lord holding that the decoration should be treated, not only as a reward, but as an incentive to others; he left the Navy in 1855. Mr. Wood joined the Army and won the Victoria Cross later on in the Indian Mutiny Campaign. The London Gazette of 24 Feb. 1857, says that "the Victoria Cross has been awarded to Edward St. John Daniels, Midshipman, Royal Navy. Sir Stephen Lushington recommends this officer: (1) For answering the call for volunteers to bring in powder to the battery from a waggon in a very heavy fire, a shot having disabled the horses. (This was reported by Capt. Peel, commanding the battery, at the time.) (2) For accompanying Capt. Peel at the Battle of Inkerman as Aide-de-camp. (3) For devotion to his leader, Capt. Peel, on 18 June, 1855, in tying a tourniquet on his arm on the glacis of the Redan, whilst exposed to a very heavy fire. (Despatch from Sir Stephen Lushington, enclosed in a letter from Admiral Lord Lyons, 10 May, 1856)." The London Gazette of 13 March, 1857, says: "Erratum.—'For Edward St. John Daniels, Midshipman,' in the London Gazette of 24 Feb. 1857, read, 'Edward St. John Daniel.'" Of the first act of bravery, the date of which is inscribed on Mr. Daniel's Victoria Cross, Sir Evelyn Wood says in "The Crimea in 1854 and 1894": "Mr. Daniel, of H.M.S. Diamond, Aide-de-camp to Capt. Peel, went to carry one" (of the boxes of powder) "with me, slinging the box on a fascine; but the box held 112 lbs. of powder, had interior cases of thick zinc, and solid wooden outer coverings, and the weight was too great." After this Mr. Daniel seems to have carried some of the contents of the boxes loose, for he "brought in the cartridges and powder without receiving a scratch, and the battery cheered to a man as the plucky little chap scrambled over the parapet with his last armful." Capt. Peel asked Lieut. Ridge and Midshipman Daniel, of the Diamond, and Lieut. Douglas and Midshipman Wood, of the Queen, to always walk slowly and with their heads erect when under fire, as an example to the rest. This they invariably did. Mr. Daniel served in the Indian Mutiny with the Shannon's Brigade, and Lieut. E. H. Verney says (in "The Shannon's Brigade in India") in the entry in his Diary for 22 Oct. 1857: "Mr. E. Daniel, who received the V.C. when serving under Capt. Peel in the Crimea, has already been sent on to Cawnpore, as an artillery officer was telegraphed for." For his services in this campaign he received the Indian Medal with the Lucknow clasp, and also the clasp for the Relief of Lucknow on 17 Nov. He was promoted to Lieut. 15 Sept. 1859, is said to have served in the Mars, was on half-pay in 1860, was appointed to the Victor Emanuel, serving in the Mediterranean, on 26 Jan. 1861, and left the Navy towards the end of the same year. His Victoria Cross is in the collection belonging to Lord Cheylesmore in the United Service Museum.

HEWETT, WILLIAM NATHAN WRIGHTE, Lieut., Royal Navy, *b.* at Brighton on 12 Aug. 1834; *s.* of Dr. William Wrighte Hewett and Susan Moore, dau. of Dr. John Maddy. He entered the Royal Navy 26 March, 1847; served as a Midshipman in the Burmese War of 1851, and with the Naval Brigade in China (Burmese and China Medals). In 1854–55, while acting Mate of the Beagle gun-vessel, he was attached to the Naval Brigade in the Crimea, and on 26 Oct. was in command of a Lancaster gun in the battery before Sebastopol. Kinglake, when describing the Battle of Inkerman, says: "When at last he had fled clear of his pursuers, the enemy again incurred fire; for Mr. Hewett (the naval officer then acting in the Lancaster Battery) threw down the part of the parapet which intercepted the fire he had planned, slewed round his Lancaster gun, and was presently hurling its missiles into the midst of the retreating force. The effect in this part of the field was decisive." Field Marshal Sir Evelyn Wood, in "The Crimea in 1854 and 1894," gives a graphic account of Lieut. Hewett's deed of daring: "The order . . . reached Mr. Hewett at a critical moment, for Russians were just then coming out of the Careenage Ravine from somewhat behind the battery. Hewett had been firing at and keeping back some of the enemy, who had attempted to approach on the ridge in his right front; but now one or more of them who had ascended the Careenage Ravine, out of sight of the battery, were advancing by, and had got to within 300 yards of the right flank of, the battery. The gun could not be trained to reach them, as the embrasure confined its 'field' of fire; but Hewett was quick of resource, and after one more round, as the gun was being reloaded, he gave the word, 'Four handspikes, muzzle to the right' (in artillery language, 'Trail left'), and trained the gun so that its muzzle rested against the earthen flank wall of his battery. Turning to a messenger who was repeating the order to fall back, he shouted, 'Retire!—Retire be damned—Fire!' A mass of earth, stones and gabions was driven forward by the projectile and 16 lbs. of powder, forming a wide-spreading extemporized shell. Then the Russians fell back, and our infantry pursued them, being led most gallantly by Lieut. Conolly, the only man just then in red, the others wearing great-coats." A few days after this, Hewett's daring conduct was again reported by Capt. Lushington, and he was immediately promoted to be Lieut., with seniority of 26 Oct., and was given command of the Beagle, in which he served during the war, especially in the operations against Kertch and Yenikale and in the Sea of Azoff, and which he held after the peace till the summer of 1857. Kinglake tells us how Sherard Osborn and Hewett "completed the work of destruction, and obtained control of the Arabit Spit, that singular natural causeway thrown up between the two seas, which, with scarce room for anything else, still carried the Imperial post road a distance of some 80 miles, and therefore seemed precious to the Russians." For these services Lieut. Hewett received the Legion of Honour, the Crimean Medal with Azoff and Sebastopol clasps, the Turkish and Sardinian Medals, and the Order of the Medjidie, 5th Class, and the Victoria Cross on its institution. [London Gazette, 24 Feb. 1857]: "William Nathan Wrighte Hewett, Lieut., Royal Navy: (1st) On the occasion of a repulse of a sortie of Russians by Sir De Lacy Evans' Division, on 26 Oct. 1854, Mr. Hewett, then Acting Mate of Her Majesty's Ship Beagle, was in charge of the Right Lancaster Battery before Sebastopol. The advance of the Russians placed the gun in great jeopardy, their skirmishers advancing within 300 yards of the battery and pouring in a sharp fire from their Minie rifles. By some misapprehension, the word was passed to spike the guns and retreat; but Mr. Hewett, taking upon himself the responsibility

William N. W. Hewett.

of disregarding the order, replied that 'Such order did not come from Capt. Lushington, and he would not do it till it did.' Mr. Hewett then pulled down the parapet of the battery, and with the assistance of some soldiers, got his gun round, and poured upon the advancing column of Russians a most destructive and effectual fire. For the gallantry exhibited on this occasion, the Board of Admiralty promoted him to the rank of Lieut. (2) On 5 Nov. 1854, at the Battle of Inkerman, Capt. Lushington again brought before the Commander-in-Chief the services of Mr. Hewett, saying, 'I have much pleasure in bringing Mr. Hewett's conduct to your notice.' (Sir Stephen Lushington to Vice-Admiral Sir J. D. Dundas, enclosed in Despatches of 1 Nov. 1854, and 5 Nov. 1854.)" Lieut. Hewett was decorated by Queen Victoria at the Review in Hyde Park, 26 June, 1857, being fifth in order of those then decorated. In May, 1857, at Patras, Mr. Hewett *m.* Jane Emily Blackadder, dau. of Mr. Thomas Wood, late Consul at Patras. Their children were Hugh Miller, William Warrington, Edward Watson, Charles Byng, Jane and Evelyn. In 1857 he had to pass his rather belated examination at Portsmouth, for his rank all through the war had been only provisional. He was appointed to the Royal Yacht, from which he was promoted to the rank of Commander 13 Sept. 1858. He then commanded the Viper on the West Coast of Africa, and the Rinaldo on the North American and West Indian Station. He was made Capt. on 24 Nov. 1862, and afterwards commanded the Basilisk on the China Station from 1865 to 1869. He was Flag-Captain to Sir H. Kellett in the Ocean on the China Station from 1870 to 1872, and from Oct. 1873, to Oct. 1876; was Commodore and Commander-in-Chief on the West Coast of Africa in charge of the naval operations during the Ashanti War, being present at Amoaful and at the capture of Coomassie. For his services in this campaign he was given a K.C.B. 31 March, 1874, and the Ashanti Medal with the Coomassie clasp. In May, 1877, Lieut. Hewett was appointed to the Achilles, and commanded her in the Mediterranean and in the Sea of Marmora under Sir G. Hornby. He attained his Flag rank on 21 March, 1878, and in April, 1882, he was appointed Commander-in-Chief in the East Indies. In the Egyptian War of 1882 he was placed at the head of the naval forces guarding the Suez Canal, and he conducted all the operations in the Red Sea, especially in the occupation of Suez and the seizure of the Canal in Aug. For these services he received the thanks of Parliament and a K.C.S.I. He became Vice-Admiral in 1884. He was again in the Red Sea for the war in the Eastern Sudan. After the defeat of the Egyptians at El Teb, Hewett landed with a force of seamen and marines for the defence of Suakim on 6 Feb. 1884, and on the 10th he was formally appointed by Baker Pasha as representative of the Khedive. On the 29th he was present, unofficially, as it seems, at the Second Battle of El Teb. In April he went on a mission to King John of Abyssinia to ensure his aid in the relief of the garrison at Kassala (Abyssinian Order of Solomon), and on his return he was nominated for office as a Junior Lord of the Admiralty; but the defeat of Mr. Gladstone's Government prevented his taking up the appointment. On 13 March, 1886, he assumed command of the Channel Squadron, and he hauled down his flag on board the Northumberland on 17 April, 1888, his health having for some time noticeably failed. After his retirement from his command he became rapidly worse, and at last was so ill at his residence at Southsea that his brother, Sir Prescott Hewett, was sent for, and, under his directions, with the concurrence of the physicians in attendance, the Admiral was conveyed to Haslar Hospital, where he died on 13 May, 1888. On 15 May the "Times" correspondent telegraphed that the Roman Press generally expressed regret at the death of Sir William Hewett, and recalled his recent visit to Genoa with the Channel Fleet. On the 17th he was buried at the Highland Road Cemetery, Southsea. The funeral procession left Haslar at 1.30. The body was preceded by the band of the Royal Marine Light Infantry, and was placed on board the Magnet, the departure of which was signalized by the firing of 13 minute-guns from the Duke of Wellington. The coffin was landed at the dockyard railway jetty, and conveyed thence by rail to the new station at Southsea, where it was received by the personal friends of the deceased and by a large number of naval and military officers. The station was occupied by the massed bands and men of the Channel Squadron. The road leading to the cemetery was lined on both sides by the troops and seamen from the Fleet, whilst at the cemetery there was a detachment of the Royal Marine Artillery and a Guard of Honour from the Northumberland. The Queen sent a laurel wreath, and wreaths were sent by the Empress of Germany, Lord Wolseley, and many others. Sir John Cowell represented the Queen, and Col. the Hon. W. Colville the Duke of Edinburgh, whilst the Admiralty was represented by Vice-Admiral Hoskins. Amongst the immense gathering were Admirals Commerell and Lord Charles Beresford, M.P., and Mr. Chiddle, the last survivor of the Lancaster gun-crew who were with Sir W. N. W. Hewett when he won his Victoria Cross.

John Sullivan.

SULLIVAN, JOHN, Boatswain's Mate, Royal Navy. Admiral Sir Sydney Eardley Wilmot says in his "Life of Lord Lyons": "When the Naval Brigade was formed, John Sullivan, a young boatswain's mate of H.M.S. Rodney, was selected for duty on shore. He was appointed Capt. of one of the guns lent by the Terrible, and had the honour of making the first breach in the Malakoff Battery, and also of blowing up the magazine at the commencement of the siege. After attracting the attention of Sir Stephen Lushington by their great gallantry, Sullivan and his crew were, with their gun, removed to the Greenhill Battery. On 10 April, 1855, a volunteer was asked for to take out a flagstaff, and place it on a mound which hid a well-known battery from the view of the sentries. Sullivan, feeling that as captain of the gun any specially dangerous duty ought to be performed by him, at once offered his services. On reaching the mound, he looked both ways to make sure that he was on direct line between the British guns and the Russian battery. Being at length satisfied, he proceeded to scrape with his hands to make a hole for the flagstaff, and to collect stones and sods with which to bank it up. During this operation he was exposed to a continuous fire from some Russian sharpshooters posted not far off. One in particular attracted Sullivan's attention. He fired three shots in quick succession, but Sullivan saw that the movements of the man were too rapid and excited to cause much fear. Still, the continual whistling of bullets all round him convinced Sullivan that his position was dangerous. He was, however, resolved to die rather than to retire without having accomplished his task, and he stuck to his work until the flag was fixed. This was not the only occasion on which he distinguished himself." He received the Victoria Cross on its institution [London Gazette, 24 Feb. 1857]: "John Sullivan, Boatswain's Mate, Royal Navy. Recommended by Sir Stephen Lushington, for having on or about 10 April, 1855, deliberately placed a flag on a mound, in a most exposed position, under a heavy fire, to enable Battery 5 to open fire upon a concealed Russian battery that was doing great execution on one of our advanced works. This was reported by Commander Kennedy, commanding the battery. Commander Kennedy speaks of this act in high terms of praise, and observes that John Sullivan's gallantry was always conspicuous. (Despatch from Admiral Lord Lyons, 5 Dec. 1855, and 10 May, 1856.)" "Mr. Sullivan was later for many years a boatswain in Portsmouth Dockyard, and bore on his breast, in addition to the Victoria Cross thus gallantly won, the Legion of Honour for a special service rendered to the French, a Medal for conspicuous gallantry, the Sardinian Medal, the Royal Humane Society Medal, besides the Turkish Medal and the Crimean Medal with clasps for Inkerman and Sebastopol." (Page 110, "The Victoria Cross—by Whom it was Won," Lieut.-Colonel W. W. Knollys and Major W. J. Elliott.)

SHEPHEARD, JOHN, Boatswain, Royal Navy, served in the Crimean Campaign. Capt. Peel was much interested in a scheme for capturing Russian men-of-war. John Shepheard, Boatswain's Mate of the St. Jean d'Acre, got bitten with the same idea, and, says Sir Evelyn Wood, in "The Crimea in 1854 and 1894," invented and constructed a small boat suitable for carrying one man and a powerful explosive. This duck-like structure floated only three inches above water, and in it, after giving notice, he visited in succession several ships of our squadron without being discovered. He then conceived the idea of launching his boat in the harbour and paddling it under one of the Russian men-of-war, to which he proposed to fix an explosive and retire before the fuse acted. On 15 July, 1855, in the presence of the officers commanding the Naval Brigade, Shepheard launched his little craft under protection of the French sentries, in Careening Bay, and paddled westwards until his progress was stopped by a number of boats conveying troops from the Inner Harbour to the North Side. No one appears to have noticed him, but he could not venture through the string of boats, and eventually retired in safety back to Careening Bay shortly before daybreak. General Sir George Higginson says, in "Seventy-one Years of a Guardsman's Life" (page 176): "The daring exploit of a certain petty officer in the St. Jean d'Acre, Capt. Harry Keppel's ship, deserves to be recorded. Immediately after their defeat on the Alma, the Russians, anticipating an attempt by the allied fleet to force an entrance into Sebastopol harbour, sank several of their ships of war across the mouth. But they kept some of their best ships afloat further up the harbour, where they were nearly out of range of our batteries. The petty officer aforesaid offered to blow up any one of these ships by means of his own devising if given a free hand to use a special kind of canoe he had constructed. Being allowed to explain his purpose, he declared that, if allowed to choose his own time, he would place a bag containing one hundredweight of explosive powder in such a position against the forefront of any ship in the allied fleet as would, when exploded, sink it. He was allowed to try the experiment 'in dummy' on the British fleet. Sharp look-out was kept by patrol-boats, despite which there was found at daylight one morning a dummy bag, large enough to hold one hundredweight of explosive, screwed to the forefoot of the British Admiral's flagship! It appeared that, clothing himself entirely in white, his canoe being covered all over with white canvas, this adventurous youth started by night noiselessly from his own ship, unseen except by a confederate, with the bag attached to a large auger. He then paddled noiselessly through the fleet, and slipping close past the side of the flagship, with two turns of the auger fastened the bag to the forefoot of the Admiral's ship and adjusted what would represent a fuse. It was clear that, if by any means the canoe could be floated from some unseen spot at the upper part of the harbour, a successful attempt might be made to send the Russian flagship, the Twelve Apostles, to the bottom, though the ultimate fate of the daring seaman would be very doubtful. However, no part of our siege-works approached so near to the harbour as to afford a starting point; moreover, as my informant specially told me, neither the Admiral nor Lord Raglan appear to have approved of the proposal, because, as neither the torpedo nor submarine had at that time been invented, it was hardly thought to be 'cricket.'" The French,

John Shepheard.

however, heard of the idea, and obtained leave from the British to make the attempt, borrowing the man and his canoe for that purpose. A mixed party of French and English sailors carried the canoe to the chosen starting-place, and the gallant adventurer set forth. He returned late in the evening of the next day, and reported that he had been stopped by a bridge of boats, and had had to be concealed all night and till dark next day. He brought back much valuable information, though he had not succeeded in blowing up the Russian flagship. Shepheard was awarded the Victoria Cross [London Gazette, 24 Feb. 1857]: " John Shepheard, Boatswain, Royal Navy. Date of Act of Bravery: 15 July, 1855. Recommended by Capt. Keppel for, on 15 July, 1855, while serving as Boatswain's Mate of the St. Jean D'Acre (attached to the Naval Brigade), proceeding in a punt with an exploding apparatus into the harbour of Sebastopol, to endeavour to blow up one of the Russian line-of-battle ships. This service, which was twice attempted, is described by Lord Lyons ' as a bold one, and gallantly executed.' On the first occasion Mr. Shepheard proceeded past the enemy's steamboats at the entrance of Careening Bay ; but was prevented penetrating further by the long string of boats that were carrying troops from the south to the north side of Sebastopol. The second attempt was made on 16 Aug. 1855, from the side of Careening Bay in the possession of the French. (Despatches by Capt. the Hon. H. Keppel in Admiral Lord Lyons' letter, 10 May, 1856, and Admiral Lord Lyons, 4 Oct. 1855.)" John Shepheard died on 7 Dec. 1884.

REEVES, THOMAS, Seaman, Royal Navy ; served in the Crimean War, and was awarded the Victoria Cross on its institution, for services described in the London Gazette of 24 Feb. 1857 : " Thomas Reeves, Seaman, James Gorman, Seaman and Mark Scholefield, Seaman, Royal Navy. At the Battle of Inkerman, 5 Nov. 1854, when the Right Lancaster Battery was attacked, these three seamen mounted the Banquette, and under a heavy fire made use of the disabled soldiers' muskets, which were loaded for them by others under the parapet. They are the survivors of five who performed the above action. (Letter from Sir Stephen Lushington, 7 June, 1856.)" Thomas Reeves was presented with his Victoria Cross by Queen Victoria at the inauguration of the new decoration at a military parade in Hyde Park 26 June, 1857.

GORMAN, JAMES, Seaman, Royal Navy, served in the Crimean Campaign, and for his services was awarded the Victoria Cross on its institution [London Gazette, 24 Feb. 1857]: " James Gorman, Seaman, Mark Scholefield, Seaman, and Thomas Reeves, Seaman, Royal Navy. At the Battle of Inkerman, 5 Nov. 1854, when the Right Lancaster Battery was attacked, these three seamen mounted the Banquette, and under a heavy fire, made use of the disabled soldiers' muskets, which were loaded for them by others under the parapet. They are the survivors of five who performed the above action. (Letter from Sir Stephen Lushington, 7 June, 1856.)" Mr. Gorman died on 27 Dec. 1889.

SCHOLEFIELD, MARK, Seaman, Royal Navy, served in the Crimean War, and for his services was given the Victoria Cross on its institution [London Gazette, 24 Feb. 1857]: " Thomas Reeves, Seaman, James Gorman, Seaman, and Mark Scholefield, Seaman, Royal Navy. At the Battle of Inkerman, 5 Nov. 1854, when the Right Lancaster Battery was attacked, these three seamen mounted the Banquette, and under a heavy fire made use of the disabled soldiers' muskets, which were loaded for them by others under the parapet. They are the survivors of five who performed the above action. (Letter from Sir Stephen Lushington, 7 June, 1856.)"

RABY, HENRY JAMES, Commander, Royal Navy, was *b.* 26 Sept. 1827 ; the *s.* of the late Arthur Turnour Raby, Esq., of Llanelly, co. Carmarthen. He was educ. at Sherborne School, and entered the Royal Navy in 1842 as a first-class Volunteer, H.M.S. Monarch. In 1848 he was rated Mate, and two years later received his commission as Lieut. In this grade he served for some time in the Wasp on the West Coast of Africa, and on the outbreak of war with Russia in 1854 was sent to the Black Sea. There he landed with the Naval Brigade, and served in the trenches from 23 Oct. 1854, until 16 Sept. 1855. As Second in Command of a ladder-party on the Redan, he performed the act of gallantry which won him the Victoria Cross on its institution, and which is thus described in the London Gazette, 24 Feb. 1857: " Henry James Raby, Commander ; John Taylor, Capt. of the Forecastle ; Henry Curtis, Boatswain's Mate, Royal Navy. ' On 18 June, 1855, immediately after the assault on Sebastopol, a soldier of the 57th Regt., who had been shot through both legs, was observed sitting up and calling for assistance. Climbing over the breastwork of the advanced sap, Commander Raby and the two seamen proceeded upwards of seventy yards across the open space towards the salient angle of the Redan, and, in spite of the heavy fire which was still continuing, succeeded in conveying the wounded soldier to a place of safety, at the imminent risk of their own lives.' (Letter from Sir Stephen Lushington, 7 June, 1856.)" For service in the trenches he was, in Sept. 1855, promoted to be Commander, and received the ribbon of the Legion of Honour, the Crimean, Sardinian and Turkish Medals, with the clasps for Sebastopol and Inkerman, and the Order of the Medjidie, 5th Class. Commander Raby was the first officer to be decorated by Queen Victoria at the first presentation when the new decoration was inaugurated in Hyde Park, 26 June, 1857. His

Henry James Raby.

next appointment was to the command of the Alecto on the West Coast of Africa in 1859–62, during which time he commanded the boats of the squadron at the capture of Port Nova, when he was wounded, and for this and other services in the suppression of the slave trade was repeatedly mentioned in Despatches. He received his promotion to the rank of Capt. in Nov. 1862, for his services on the West Coast. In 1863 Capt. Raby married Judith, dau. of the late Colonel Watkin Forster, of Holt Manor, Trowbridge. He next commanded the Adventure on the China Station from 1868 to 1871. In 1877 he retired from the Active List, and his subsequent step was gained in retirement in 1878. He had in 1875 been made a C.B. (Military), and in 1875 was granted a Good Service pension. Admiral Raby spent his latter days in Southsea, where he took a great interest in the Royal Seamen and Marines' Orphanage, the Royal Sailors' Home, and in various other philanthropic institutions in the town. He died on the morning of 13 Feb. 1907, at his residence, 8, Clarence Parade, Southsea.

TAYLOR, JOHN, Capt. of the Forecastle, Royal Navy, served in the Crimean War, and was awarded the Victoria Cross for his services in that campaign [London Gazette, 24 Feb. 1857]: " Henry James Raby, Commander, Royal Navy ; John Taylor, Captain of the Forecastle, Royal Navy ; Henry Curtis, Boatswain's Mate, Royal Navy. ' On 18 June, 1855, immediately after the assault on Sebastopol, a soldier of the 57th Regt., who had been shot through both legs, was observed sitting up and calling for assistance. Climbing over the breastwork of the advanced sap, Commander Raby and the two seamen proceeded upwards of seventy yards across the open space towards the salient angle of the Redan, and in spite of a heavy fire which was still continuing, succeeded in conveying the wounded soldier to a place of safety, at the imminent risk of their own lives.' (Letter from Sir Stephen Lushington, 7 June, 1855.)" Mr. Taylor never lived to wear his Victoria Cross, for he died on 24 Feb. 1857, the very day on which his name appeared in the Gazette.

CURTIS, HENRY, Boatswain's Mate, Royal Navy, served in the Crimean War, and for his services in that campaign was awarded the Victoria Cross [London Gazette, 24 Feb. 1857]: " Henry James Raby, Commander ; John Taylor, Capt. of the Forecastle ; Henry Curtis, Boatswain's Mate, Royal Navy. ' On 18 June, 1855, immediately after the assault on Sebastopol, a soldier of the 57th Regt., who had been shot through both legs, was observed sitting up and calling for assistance. Climbing over the breastwork of the advanced sap, Commander Raby and the two seamen proceeded upwards of seventy yards across the open space towards the salient angle of the Redan, and in spite of the heavy fire which was still continuing, succeeded in conveying the wounded soldier to a place of safety, at the imminent risk of their own lives.'

Henry Curtis.

(Letter from Sir Stephen Lushington, 7 June, 1856.)" He was decorated by Queen Victoria at the first Presentation in Hyde Park, 26 June, 1857. Mr. Curtis died at Buckland, Portsmouth, on 23 Nov. 1896.

THE BALTIC

INGOUEVILLE, GEORGE, Capt. of the Mast, Royal Navy, served in the Crimean Campaign, and was awarded the Victoria Cross on its institution [London Gazette, 24 Feb. 1857]: " George Ingouville, Capt. of the Mast, Royal Navy. On 13 July, 1855, while the boats of the Arrogant were engaged with the enemy's gunboats and batteries off Viborg, her second cutter was swamped by the blowing up of her magazine, and drifted under a battery. Notwithstanding that he was wounded in the arm, and that the boat was under a very heavy fire, Ingoueville, without any order to do so, jumped overboard, caught hold of her painter, and saved her. (Despatches from Capt. Yelverton, 18 Nov. 1855, and Rear-Admiral Hon. Sir R. T. Dundas, 12 Dec. 1855, No. 759.)" " While the boats were still under fire an explosion took place in the Arrogant's second cutter, killing Mr. Story, the Midshipman in charge of her, and half swamping the boat, which drifted under the battery. All remaining in her would probably have been killed or taken, had not George Ingoueville, one of her crew, though wounded, jumped overboard with the painter in his hand, and turned her off. Her condition was then seen from the Ruby, whereupon Lieut. George Dare Dowell, R.M.A., of the Magicienne, who happened to be on board, calling for volunteers, jumped into the Ruby's gig, was joined by Lieut. Henry Vachell Haggard (promoted Commander 24 July, 1855, for this service), of the Arrogant, and two men, and pulled off under an increasingly heavy fire to the rescue. The gallant little party saved the boat and her crew, but the whole affair cost the loss of two killed and ten wounded. Ingoueville and Lieut. Dowell received the Victoria Cross for their bravery and initiative " (" History of the Royal Navy," by William Laird Clowes). George Ingoueville was decorated by Queen Victoria in Hyde Park 26 June, 1857. He died 13 Jan. 1869.

BYTHESEA, JOHN, Lieut., Royal Navy, was *b.* 15 June, 1827 ; fifth and yst. *s.* of the Rev. G. Bythesea, of Grosvenor, Bath, Rector and Patron of Freshford, Somerset, and Mary, dau. of Francis Glossop, of Glossop-dale, co. Derby. The Bytheseas are an ancient family, long resident in Somerset and Wiltshire. The first Mayor of Axbridge, 1598, created by Queen Elizabeth, was a Bythesea of Week House. The family residence is a mile from Trowbridge, co. Wilts, and the Bytheseas resided there for many years, intermarrying with the Vyners, Scropes and Longs. John Bythesea entered the Royal Navy in 1841, and passed his examination 6 Jan. 1848. He was appointed to the Arrogant, and served in the Crimean campaign. "The British Fleet lay off the Island of Wardo, in the Baltic, on 7 Aug., Lieut. Bythesea being an officer of the watch on board H.M.S. Arrogant, the senior flagship, commanded by Capt. Yelverton. After paying an official visit to Sir Charles Napier one day, the Capt. came back to the ship and said to young Bythesea that Sir Charles had through him administered a gentle rebuke to the whole fleet. 'He has learned,' said Capt. Yelverton, 'that important despatches from the Czar are constantly being landed on the island (Wardo), and then forwarded to the Commanding Officer at Bomarsund. And Sir Charles is surprised rather that no officer has had sufficient enterprise to put a stop to this kind of thing.' This was more than enough for this young lieutenant, who there and then resolved to emulate the exploits of Dick Turpin. The moment his 'turn' on deck was over, he asked at the ship's office whether any man on board spoke Swedish. Yes. Stoker Johnstone did, having been born in that country; and Stoker Johnstone found the adventure after his own heart. When Capt. Yelverton heard of Bythesea's intention, he suggested a stronger force than two men for so perilous a mission. He was overruled, however, on the ground that a large party would be likely to attract attention, and so spoil the whole affair. On 9 Aug. Johnstone and his officer landed in a small bay and strolled along to a farmhouse close by. Here the gallant stoker got into conversation with the Finnish farmer, whose language was painful and frequent and free. This was because the Russians had 'hired' all his horses, so he couldn't gather his crops. Sympathy with these grievances brought valuable information and hospitality to the 'expedition.' Johnstone, prompted by his officer, remarked casually, 'I hear that mails and despatches are carried through Wardo to Bomarsund; they'd be important, I suppose?' 'Important!' echoed the farmer. 'I should think so, indeed. Why, the Russians repaired nine miles of the road to facilitate their transport.' This was conclusive enough, for when the Russians take to road-repairing they are usually actuated by something more urgent than the mere well-being of the community. The farmer promised his visitors food and lodging in an out-house, if not in the farm itself. It soon became known, however, that a party had landed from the British Fleet, and the Russians made searching inquiries in every direction, even going as far as domiciliary visits. One night the very farmhouse in which Bythesea and his companion slept was surrounded by soldiers, and the adventurous twain had given up all hope, when they were skilfully saved by their host's young daughters, who disguised them beautifully as Finnish peasants. After this came several other narrow escapes of capture and certain death. One day these daring fellows met a Russian search-party, whereupon they slouched down to the beach, put off in a small boat, and rowed out to sea, this time masquerading as fishermen. On the morning of 12 Aug., the twelfth day of the adventure, Lieut. Bythesea learned from his farmer friend that the Russian mails were landed, and that these, as well as the usual despatches, would be sent on to the fortress that night in charge of the Emperor's Aide-de-camp. 'The escort will number four or five men,' continued the farmer, 'and will start as soon as the moon rises. They proceed until they reach that part of the island nearest the British Fleet, and then they lie low until the moon has disappeared.' Now by this time the young officer knew every inch of the route traversed, so at midnight he and his companion took up positions close to the spot selected as a hiding-place by the mail-carriers and their escort. In a few minutes the whole Russian party came along quietly, and concealed themselves at the roadside, one man almost touching the English officer. Suddenly up jumped the latter, his pistol covering the soldier nearest him; Johnstone did the same. Three of the five men were overcome with terror, thinking that a large force was upon them, but two of the carriers dropped their bags and took to their heels. The remaining three were quickly disarmed, and sternly ordered to get into the big boat close by, taking the mail bags and despatches with them. The moment the boat was launched the prisoners were compelled to row, Bythesea steering, while the chuckling stoker sat in the bow, pistol in hand. The adventurers were only just in time. Soon after their boat had glided away in the darkness, the Russian Guard came along to see whether the mails had been got through safely. Seeing nothing of the carriers, they went back, singing, to report that all was well. When the prisoners had been put on board the Arrogant, the mails and despatches were taken to Sir Charles Napier, whose surprise and admiration were unbounded. The senior officer, General Baraguay d'Hilliers, could not at first credit the story; but his scepticism gave way to enthusiasm on beholding the valuable papers in his own cabin." Mrs. Bythesea says that the only weapon Lieut. Bythesea used was a flint pistol. Stoker Johnstone was unarmed. For this service both Lieut. Bythesea and Stoker Johnstone received the Victoria Cross, theirs being the second and third crosses actually to be won, though they were the 22nd and 23rd to be gazetted [London Gazette, 24 Feb. 1857]: "John Bythesea, Commander, Royal Navy. On 9 Aug. 1854, having discovered that the aide-de-camp of the Emperor of Russia had landed on the Island of Wardo, in charge of a mail and despatches for the Russian General, Commander Bythesea obtained permission for himself and William Johnstone, a stoker, to proceed on shore with a view to intercept them. Being disguised, they concealed themselves till the night of the 12th, when the mail bags were landed close to the spot where they lay secreted in the bushes. The mails were accompanied by a military escort, which passed close to them, and which, as soon as it was ascertained that the road was clear, took its departure. Availing themselves of this opportunity, Commander Bythesea and the stoker attacked the five men in charge of the mail, took three of them prisoners, and brought them in their own boat on board the Arrogant. The despatches were carried to General Baraguay d'Hilliers, who expressed himself in the highest terms of approval. (Despatch from Capt. Yelverton, enclosed in a letter from Vice-Admiral Sir C. Napier, 14 Jan. 1856.)" The decoration was presented to Commander Bythesea by Queen Victoria 26 June, 1857, and he was the second officer to receive the decoration at Her Majesty's hands. Lieut. Bythesea obtained command of the Locust steam vessel, of three guns and 100 horse-power, having previously served some time in the Baltic and the Freemantle. He was present at the Fall of Bomarsund, and commanded the Locust at the bombardment of Sveaborg in Aug. 1855. He received the Baltic and Crimean medals. He was promoted Commander 10 May, 1856, and assumed command of the Cruiser on the East India and China Station (1858–60), and was present at the taking of the Peiho Forts and forcing the Nankin Forts with Lord Elgin's Expedition to Hankow (Medal and clasp). He afterwards took the Cruiser to the south-east coast of America; was on the Royal Defence Commission of 1862, and afterwards became Naval Attaché at Washington (1865). In March, 1874, at Bath, Capt. Bythesea married Fanny Belinda, third dau. of Col. George Nelson Prior and Maria Louisa, dau. of Lieut.-Colonel Benjamin Way, commanding the Buckinghamshire Militia, of Denham Place, co. Buckingham. From 1874 to 1880 Rear-Admiral Bythesea was Consulting Naval Officer to the Government of India, and he remodelled the Royal Indian Marine out of the old Indian Navy. He was created a C.B. (Military) in 1877, and a C.I.E. in 1878. He travelled a great deal, and to the end of his life displayed great keenness in service matters. He died in London, 18 May, 1906, and was buried at Bath.

John Bythesea.

JOHNSTONE, WILLIAM, Stoker, Royal Navy, served in the Crimean Campaign, and was awarded the Victoria Cross on its institution. His was the third Cross to be actually won, and the twenty-third to be gazetted [London Gazette, 24 Feb. 1857]: "John Bythesea, Commander (now Capt.), Royal Navy. On 9 Aug. 1854, having ascertained that an Aide-de-camp of the Emperor of Russia had landed on the Island of Wardo, in charge of a mail and despatches for the Russian General, Commander Bythesea obtained permission for himself and William Johnstone, a stoker, to proceed on shore, with a view to intercept them. Being disguised and armed, they concealed themselves till the night of the 12th, when the mail bags were landed, close to the spot where they lay secreted in the bushes. The mails were accompanied by the military escort, which passed close to them, and which, as soon as it was ascertained that the road was clear, took its departure. Availing themselves of this opportunity, Commander Bythesea and the stoker attacked the five men in charge of the mail, took three of them prisoners, and brought them in their own boat to the Arrogant. The despatches were carried to General Baraguay d'Hilliers, who expressed himself in the highest terms of approval. (Despatch from Capt. Yelverton, enclosed in a letter from Vice-Admiral Sir C. Napier, 31 Jan. 1856.)" "William Johnstone, Stoker. This person was the companion of Commander Bythesea in that officer's enterprise mentioned above. (Despatch from Capt. Yelverton, enclosed in a letter from Vice-Admiral Sir C. Napier, 31 Jan. 1856.)" Mrs. Bythesea says that Commander Bythesea, on the night of 12 Aug., hid in the hedge of the main road, and put Johnstone on the opposite side of the road some yards further down. The Gazette says they were "armed," and so they were—with *one* flint pistol. When the five men in charge of the mail came up, Commander Bythesea gave a low whistle, and Johnstone came running up the road. He had a rope in his pocket, which he threw round the Russians, and though they struggled a bit, they soon became quiet. Commander Bythesea then ordered the prisoners to their own boat, and told them to row back to the Arrogant. He covered them with the pistol while Johnstone steered.

LUCAS, CHARLES DAVIS, Lieut., Royal Navy, was *b.* at Drumargole, co. Armagh, Ireland, on 19 Feb. 1834; *s.* of Davis Lucas, of Clontibret, co. Monaghan (who belonged to the family of Lucas, of Castle Shane). Charles Lucas joined the Royal Navy in 1847, and served in the Burmese War of 1852 and 1853, taking part in the capture of Rangoon, Dalta Pegu, Prome, etc. For his services in this campaign he received the Pegu Medal. He served in the Crimean War. At the age of 18, he performed the Act of Bravery which gained for him the first of that most coveted of all decorations. "I was serving," says Sir Evelyn Wood, in "Winnowed Memories" (page 277), "in the Royal Navy when Lieut. Lucas, H.M.S. Hecla, earned the first Victoria Cross . . . for having thrown overboard a live shell." On 20 June the British Fleet was bombarding Bomarsund, a fort in the Aland Islands, Gulf of Bothnia. Capt. Hall, of the Hecla, had a plan of his own, and resolved to attack the fortress independently. Under his orders were the Valorous (Capt. Buckle) and the Odin (Capt. Scott), and with these, next morning at ten o'clock, he steamed into position and at once opened fire on the principal fort, which mounted the formidable armament of 80 guns. The fire was at once returned, and the action became pretty general, for the other forts soon opened on the Hecla. The range was only 500

Charles Davis Lucas.

yards, and almost every shot told. It was then that Mr. Lucas hurled a live shell into the sea, which, almost before reaching the water, exploded with a terrific roar, but there spent itself harmlessly. He was specially and immediately promoted Lieut., received the Baltic Medal, and, on the institution of the Victoria Cross (29 Jan. 1856), he was strongly recommended by Sir Charles Napier for " the new Naval and Military decoration." The London Gazette of 24 Feb. 1857, says : " Charles Davis Lucas, Lieut. (now Commander), Royal Navy. This officer was promoted to his present rank on 21 June, 1854, for his gallantry in throwing overboard a live shell at the first attack on the batteries at Bomarsund. Capt. Hall writes to Sir Charles Napier : ' With regard to Mr. Lucas, I have the pleasure to report a remarkable instance of coolness and presence of mind in action, he having taken up and thrown overboard a live shell thrown on board by the enemy, while the fuse was burning.' (Letter of Capt. Hall to Sir Charles Napier, 22 June, 1854.) Sir Charles Napier, in forwarding Capt. Hall's letter, remarks : ' Their lordships will observe in Capt. Hall's letter the great courage of Mr. C. D. Lucas in taking up a live shell and throwing it overboard, and I trust their lordships will mark their sense of it by promoting him.' (Sir Charles Napier to Secretary of Admiralty, 28 June, 1854.)" He was decorated by Queen Victoria 26 June, 1857. In 1879, Capt. Lucas married Frances Russell Hall, the daughter of his old Captain, who was later Admiral Sir William Hutcheson Hall, K.C.B., F.R.S., and of his wife, the Honourable Lady Hall, dau. of the sixth Viscount Torrington. Admiral Lucas was awarded the Royal Humane Society's Medal for saving life. He was a J.P. for co. Kent and co. Argyll, and died, leaving a widow and three daughters, on 7 Aug. 1914, at Great Culverdon, Tunbridge Wells.

THE ROYAL MARINES

DOWELL, GEORGE DARE, Lieut., Royal Marine Artillery, s. of the late George Dowell, Paymaster, R.N., and of Anne Tulman ; b. 15 Feb. 1831, at Chichester. He was educated at the Royal Naval School, New Cross, S.E., and entered the Royal Marine

George Dare Dowell.

Artillery as 2nd Lieut. 26 July, 1848, and in June, 1849, joined the artillery, to which branch of the Service he remained attached. He was promoted Lieut. 6 Oct. 1851, and on 29 Nov. 1852, he was appointed to the Magicienne steam vessel (16 guns, Capts. Thomas Fisher and Nicholas Vansittart). On 22 May, 1854, Lieut. Dowell was in action with the batteries at Hango Head, and afterwards was repeatedly in action, helping on 11 Jan. to destroy a Cossack battery at Portsoiki. Next day the boats of the Magicienne and Arrogant advanced with a gunboat, towards Witog, the party opening fire on a Russian war-steamer with two large gunboats in tow. As they came within sight of Witog, the British found themselves unexpectedly faced by a barrier and exposed to the fire of a masked battery. They therefore returned to the Strait of Stralsund, and it was there that young Dowell won his decoration. The cutter mentioned in the Gazette as having been swamped was commanded by Mr. George Story, a Midshipman, who was killed. Lieut. G. D. Dowell hardly missed a single action in the Baltic during the two years our fleet occupied that sea. Early on Friday, 13 June, 1855, the boats of H.M.S. Arrogant engaged the Russian gunboats, together with the fortress of Viborg, in the Gulf of Finland. During the action a shell exploded the magazine of one of our cutters, which was used as a rocket-boat. The boat did not sink, but immediately swamped, and then drifted slowly away under the batteries. One of the seamen on board (George Ingoueville), although severely wounded, jumped into the sea, swam round to the boat's painter, and then commenced to tow her off, so as to prevent her falling into the enemy's hands as a prize. At this time many of the crew were clinging helplessly to the boat, and were in imminent danger of being drowned or killed by the showers of grape and small shot poured by the Russian gunners into the helpless craft. Seeing this, Lieut. Dowell, who was on board the Ruby, jumped into one of the ship's boats with a few volunteers, seized the stroke oar, and pulled with might and main towards the disabled cutter. The risk was terrible, as the gunboats were concentrating their fire on the one cutter. Notwithstanding this, Lieut. Dowell rescued three of the half-drowned crew and placed them safely on board the Ruby. Once more Dowell and his companions advanced fearlessly towards the belching batteries, this time rescuing poor Ingoueville and taking the cutter in tow. Finally, amid the ringing cheers, not only of our own comrades, but also of the Russians, Lieut. Dowell's party drew out of range, and placed in safety the rescued boat and disbanded crew. In the following Aug. Lieut. Dowell was present at the bombardment of Sveaborg. He left the Magicienne in Dec. of the same year. He was present at the actions of 18, 23 and 30 June, 1855, on which latter date 30 vessels were destroyed ; at Lovisa, 5 July, when the Government houses were burnt, and at the shelling of a Cossack encampment and destruction of their barracks on 10 and 12 July respectively. Lieut. Dowell received the Victoria Cross on its institution, for services described in the London Gazette of 24 Feb. 1857 : " George Dare Dowell, Lieut., Royal Marine Artillery. Date of Act of Bravery, 13 July, 1855. An explosion having occurred in one of the rocket-boats of the Arrogant during the attack on some forts near Viborg, Lieut. Dowell (who was on board the Ruby gunboat, while his own boat was receiving a small supply of rockets) was the first to jump into the quarter-boat of the Ruby, and with three volunteers, himself pulling the stroke oar, proceeded instantly, under

a heavy fire of grape and musketry, to the assistance of the cutter's crew. The Russians endeavoured to prevent his object of saving the men and the boat, but Lieut. Dowell succeeded in taking up three of the boat's crew and placing them on board the Ruby, and, on his returning to the spot, was mainly instrumental in keeping afloat, and bringing off the sunken cutter. (Despatches from Rear-Admiral Sir R. S. Dundas, 17 July, 1855, and letter from Colonel Wesley, Deputy-Adjutant-General of Royal Marines.)" Lieut. Dowell was decorated by Queen Victoria, 26 June, 1857. He was given the Brevets of Major (17 Sept. 1861) and Lieut.-Colonel, and became an Instructor of Musketry. He m. at Alverstoke, co. Hants, Mary, dau. of Colonel Robert and Mrs. Mansel. Their sons are George Cecil Dowell, C.M.G., Colonel, Royal Artillery, b. 28 July, 1862 ; Clement Coltman, Robert Arthur, Ernest and James Alaric. Their daus. are Mary Constance, Clara Josephine, Gertrude Annie and Lucy Violet. Brevet Lieut.-Colonel Dowell died 3 Aug. 1910, aged 79, at The Haven, Remuera, Auckland, New Zealand.

WILKINSON, THOMAS, Bombardier, Royal Marine Artillery, served in the Crimean campaign, and was awarded

Thomas Wilkinson.

the Victoria Cross on its institution [London Gazette, 24 Feb. 1857]: " Thomas Wilkinson, Bombardier, Royal Marine Artillery. ' Specially recommended for gallant conduct in the advanced batteries 7 June, 1855, in placing sandbags to repair the work under a galling fire, his name having been sent up on the occasion as worthy of special notice, by the Commanding Officer of the Artillery of the Right Attack.' (Letter from Colonel Wesley, Deputy-Adjutant-General, Royal Marines.)" Wilkinson was given the Legion of Honour when he gained his Cross. He was decorated by the Queen 26 June, 1857. Thomas Wilkinson died at York on 22 Sept. 1887.

PRETTYJOHN, JOHN, Corpl., Royal Marines, was b. at Dean Prior, near Ashburton. He enlisted in the Plymouth Division of the Royal Marines on 10 Dec. 1844, and was present at the Battle of Balaklava and the Battle of Inkerman. He was also present at the capture of Sebastopol, and served in the trenches. Corpl. Prettyjohn was given the Crimean Medal, with clasps for Balaklava, Inkerman and Sebastopol, the Turkish Crimean Medal and the Sardinian Military Medal, and was awarded the Victoria Cross on its institution, for gallantry at the Battle of Inkerman [London Gazette, 24 Feb. 1857]: " John Prettyjohn, Corpl., Royal Marines. ' Reported for gallantry at the Battle of Inkerman, having placed himself in an advanced position, and noticed as having himself shot four Russians.'

John Prettyjohn.

(Despatch from Lieut.-Colonel Hopkins, Senior Officer of Marines engaged at Inkerman, and letter from Colonel Wesley, Deputy-Adjutant-General.)" He later served in China, and was present at the assault and capture of Canton. Colour-Sergt. Prettyjohn held the China Medal with Canton clasp, and the Medal bestowed for Meritorious Conduct in the Field. He was discharged on pension on 16 June, 1865, having completed 21 years and six days' service. Colour-Sergt. John Prettyjohn died at Manchester on Thursday, 20 Jan. 1887, at the age of 63. The " Naval and Military Record " for 27 Jan. 1887, says : " After church parade on Sunday, at the Royal Marine Barracks, Plymouth, Colonel-Commandant F. G. Le Grand presented medals for long service and distinction. He said it was with deep regret that he announced to the division that information had just been received of the death of Colour-Sergt. Prettyjohn, V.C." " The funeral of the late Colour-Sergt. Prettyjohn, V.C., R.M.L.I., took place yesterday (26 Jan.) at Manchester. Instructions were given for the non-commissioned officers on the recruiting service in the Manchester district to attend the funeral, and Colonel-Commandant F. G. Le Grand, of the Stonehenge Division, forwarded a wreath to be placed on the coffin, along with a letter of condolence to the family of the deceased."

THE ARMY

GRIEVE, JOHN, Sergt.-Major. " As a young man ran through a small fortune, and then enlisted in the ' Greys,' and rose to the rank of Sergt.-Major during the Crimean War. He was offered a commission, and, coming into more money, accepted it, and, I believe, died Adjutant of his old regiment, to which he was appointed on 18 Feb. 1859. He was a first cousin of my father's. I much regret that I can give no further information as to the career of John Grieve. I never saw him, and my father lost sight of him for many years." (Mr. Charles Grieve, 31, Grosvenor Road, Richmond, S.W.) Of John Grieve's heroic deed Charles Dickens wrote in an early number of " All the Year Round ": " It is not a thing that should be suffered to die away. When he cut off a soldier's head at a blow, and disabled and dispersed several others, he had no very exciting motives of self-devotion. Pay, promotion, or popularity could not well enter his head, for he knew the rules of the Service about rising from the ranks, and he knew, too, that the British public rarely asks the names of the poor privates and non-commissioned officers who fall. What John Grieve did, then, was an act of the purest and most unselfish heroism ; but I daresay, when the Queen pinned the Cross to his breast in Hyde Park that day, he felt he was more than rewarded for what to him was a very ordinary matter-of-fact bit of duty. Yet, had he been an old Greek or Roman, with not too much clothing and a very burnished helmet, the world would have rung with his name two thousand years after." He was awarded the Victoria Cross [London Gazette, 24 Feb. 1857] : " John Grieve, No. 774, Sergt.-Major, 2nd Dragoons. Saved the life of an officer in the Heavy Cavalry Charge at Balaklava, who was surrounded by Russian cavalry, by his gallant conduct of riding up to his rescue and cutting off the head of one Russian, disabling and dispersing the others." He was decorated by Queen Victoria 26 June, 1857. Grieve became Cornet from Sergt.-Major, without purchase, 4 Dec. 1857 ; Adjutant, 15 Feb. 1859 ; Lieut. 30 Jan. 1863 ; was Adjutant 2nd Dragoons until 26 May, 1865, and died before the year 1870.

PARKES, SAMUEL, Private, served in the Crimean War. Colonel W. W. Knollys, in " The Victoria Cross in the Crimea," says : " In the 4th Hussars, Trumpet-Major Crawford's horse, apparently during the retreat, fell. The rider was dismounted and lost his sword. Two Cossacks, seeing a helpless victim, rode at him. But help was at hand. Private Samuel Parkes, of the same regiment, whose horse had been killed, happened to be near. Seeing his comrade's danger, he, banishing all thoughts of his own escape, and heedless of the swarms of Cossacks near, rushed to Crawford's assistance and drove the cowardly pair away. The two comrades then hastened on foot along the valley, but were soon attacked by six Russians at once. So dauntlessly and skilfully, however, did Parkes use his sword, that he succeeded in keeping off the foes. After fighting and retreating for some distance, a shot dashed Parkes's sword out of his hand. Probably this shot came from the Russian artillery, which was firing indiscriminately on foe and friend, and induced the six of the enemy who had beset the two comrades to retire. At all events, the latter escaped." He was awarded the Victoria Cross [London Gazette, 24 Feb. 1857] : " Samuel Parkes, No. 635, Private, 4th Light Dragoons. In the charge of the Light Cavalry Brigade at Balaklava, Trumpet-Major Crawford's horse fell, and dismounted him, and he lost his sword ; he was attacked by two Cossacks, when Private Samuel Parkes (whose horse had been shot), saved his life by placing himself between them and the Trumpet-Major, and drove them away by his sword. In attempting to follow the Light Cavalry Brigade in the retreat, they were attacked by six Russians, whom Parkes kept at bay, and retired slowly, fighting and defending the Trumpet-Major for some time, until deprived of his sword by a shot." Private Parkes was decorated with the Victoria Cross by Queen Victoria, 26 June, 1857. He died on 14 Nov. 1864.

DUNN, ALEXANDER ROBERTS, Lieut., was the 2nd *s.* of the late Hon. John Henry Dunn, formerly Receiver-General of Upper Canada. He entered the 11th Hussars in 1852 ; served in the Crimean War, and

won his Victoria Cross under the following circumstances : The 11th Hussars were returning at a hand-gallop under a galling rifle fire from the Fedioukine Hills on their right, when Sergt. Bentley's worn-out mount refused to keep up with the rest, and his comrades saw the fair-haired lieutenant, six foot two in height, turn his charger, one of the most notorious kickers in the regiment, and ride back towards the sergeant, who was trying to defend himself against three Russian Dragoons. He sabred the first dragoon out of his saddle, allowing Bentley time to get to his feet, and although his horse became almost unmanageable, he and the remaining Russians ' closed and hacked and circled round and round,' until he had killed them both.

Alexander Roberts Dunn.

He later killed a Russian Hussar who was attacking Private Levett, also of the 11th, lost his charger, and escaped on foot to our lines. The Victoria Cross was conferred upon him for these two deeds, given by the unanimous vote of his fellow-soldiers, who saw his gallant bearing in the peril whith they shared with him. He was the only officer to win this decoration in the Valley of Death, but he thus won it twice over. He served in the Battles of Alma, Balaklava and Inkerman, and the Siege of Sebastopol, and received the Crimean Medal with clasps and the Turkish Medal. His Victoria Cross was gazetted 24 Feb. 1857 : " Alexander Roberts Dunn, Lieut. (late 11th Hussars). For having, in the Light Cavalry Charge of 25 Oct. 1854, saved the life of Sergt. Bentley, 11th Hussars, by cutting down two or three Russian Lancers, who were attacking him from the rear, and afterwards cutting down a Russian Hussar, who was attacking Private Levett, 11th Hussars." Lieut. Dunn was decorated by Queen Victoria, 26 June, 1857. A wealthy man, after this campaign he sold out and retired to his estates in Canada : but, on the outbreak of the Indian Mutiny, he raised the 100th Regt. in Canada and was appointed its Lieut.-Colonel. He became Major 29 June, 1858, and Lieut.-Colonel of the regiment he had raised 29 June, 1861. In 1868 he was commanding the 33rd (Duke of Wellington's) Regt. in the Abyssinian War, and was the youngest colonel in the Army. Though a strict disciplinarian, he was greatly beloved by his soldiers and all under him, and " his career," says the " Times " of 20 Feb. 1868, " had already given sufficient promise of distinction to justify the belief of his friends that the highest military appointments were within his reach." The " Times " special correspondent, in describing the advance into Abyssinia, describes the tragedy which on 25 Jan. 1868, cut short this brilliant career : " I found Serape, on my arrival yesterday, full of a terrible tragedy which

has cast a gloom over all the camp. One of the most popular and promising officers attached to the Abyssinian Force, Colonel Dunn, of the 33rd Regt., had two days before accidentally shot himself. He had gone out with his rifle after game, and, from the account of his native servant, who was the only person with him when the accident happened, it seems that he was stooping forward over a ditch to get some water, both barrels went off, and lodged their contents in his right side. His death must have been instantaneous. He was just able to say, ' Run for a doctor,' and then dropped dead. There is not an officer of the same rank in this force whose loss would have been more severely felt. Indeed, the whole army has sustained a heavy loss in the death of Colonel Dunn. . . . The servant who was with him when the accident occurred—one of a race which rarely allows itself to be betrayed into the outward display of any violent emotion—was so overcome that in the first frenzy of grief he broke to pieces the rifle which had killed his master, and even those who did not know Colonel Dunn well enough to appreciate his good qualities, cannot but feel a pang of regret at the thought that so gallant a soldier, in the prime of manhood and with fresh hopes of distinction just dawning upon him, should have died thus."

BERRYMAN, JOHN, Troop Sergt.-Major, *b.* 28 July, 1825. He served

with the 17th Lancers throughout the Eastern Campaign of 1854, including the affair of Bulgarrac, Mackenzie's Farm, the night attack on the Russian outposts on 19 Feb. 1855, the Battles of the Alma, Balaklava, Inkerman, Tchernaya, and the Siege and Fall of Sebastopol. He received the Medal with four clasps, and was awarded the Victoria Cross [London Gazette, 24 Feb. 1857] : " John Berryman, Troop Sergt.-Major, 17th Lancers. Served with his regiment the whole of the war ; was present at the Battle of the Alma, and also engaged in the pursuit at Mackenzie's Farm, where he succeeded in capturing three Russian prisoners, when they were within reach of their own guns. Was present, and charged at the Battle of Balaklava, where, his horse being shot

John Berryman.

under him, he stopped on the field with a wounded officer (Capt. Webb), amidst a shower of shot and shell, although repeatedly told by that officer to consult his own safety and leave him ; but he refused to do so, and, on Sergt. Farrell coming up, with his assistance, carried Capt. Webb out of range of the guns. He has also a clasp for Inkerman." When Berryman and Farrell were carrying Capt. Webb, the celebrated French General Morris met them, and said to Berryman : " Ah ! and you, sergeant : if you were in the French service I would make you an officer on the spot." It was this General who said the Charge of the Light Brigade was magnificent but it was not war. Sergt. Berryman served with the 17th Lancers in the Indian Mutiny, and also in the Zulu War of 1879. He was present at Ulundi. On 12 April, 1864, he became Quartermaster, and in 1881 received the honorary rank of Capt., and in 1883 the honorary rank of Major. Major Berryman was for years a conspicuous figure at the Balaklava dinner. He died on Saturday, 27 June, 1896.

HENRY, ANDREW, Sergt.-Major, entered the Royal Artillery ; was promoted to Sergt.-Major, and served in the Crimean War, including the Battles of Alma, Balaklava and Inkerman, and the Siege of Sebastopol.

For his services at the Battle of Inkerman he was given a commission in the Land Transport Corps on 15 May, 1855, and became Second Capt. 28 Nov. 1855. He received the Medal and four clasps and the Turkish Medal, and was awarded the Victoria Cross [London Gazette, 24 Feb. 1857] : " Andrew Henry, Capt., Land Transport Corps (late Royal Artillery). For defending the guns of his battery against overwhelming numbers of the enemy at the Battle of Inkerman, and continuing to do so until he had received twelve bayonet wounds. He was at the time Sergt.-Major of the G Battery, 2nd Division." He was decorated by Queen Victoria in Hyde Park, 26 June,

Andrew Henry.

1857. Kinglake says, in his " Invasion of the Crimea " (Vol. VI., page 318) : " The troops of the enemy vanguard were not moving on a front so closely connected and straight as to be in the order for making an absolutely single attack along their whole line, but at nearly, if not quite the same time, they might burst upon the threatened hillside in several waves, and the onset now first to be witnessed is one which broke over the western extremity of the Home Ridge. It was there, as we saw, that a demi-battery under Second Capt. Boothby, which formed part of Capt. Turner's command, had been placed by Colonel Fitzmayer. For want of room on the crest, the leftmost of the three pieces—the one under Sergt.-Major Henry—had been placed on the westward slope of the ridge, where it not only stood lower down than the rest of the demi-battery, but upon ground encompassed by tall brushwood, which, indeed, at the first, reached so close to the mouth of the gun that, until the oak boughs had been some of them lopped, it could not be brought into action. The assailants were advancing in strength against both the front and the right-front of Boothby's guns ; but it was from another direction that the enemy delivered his home thrust, for one of his columns, which had made a bend round by its right, in order to approach unobserved, now all at once flooded in from the west upon this half battery, and in an instant Henry's gun was surrounded by Russians. From the other part of the half battery men found time to fire a round of case, but not, it would seem, with any great result, for the weight of the attack was in the flank. I cannot undertake so broad a statement as to assert that no English infantry were witnesses of this attack, but it is certain that none came up in time to avert the capture. An order was given to limber up, but the drivers, it then appeared, had already retreated with all the limbers and teams ; and Russian troops then breaking in upon the two upper guns, the officers and artillerymen present with part of the demi-battery then fell back several paces, or rather moved up by their right to a higher part of the ridge. When the foremost of the enemy's troops had so closely surrounded Henry's gun as to be actually but a few paces off, they charged in with loud shouts, undertaking to bayonet the gunners, but by Henry himself, and one at least of his people, they were encountered with a desperate valour. Henry called upon his men to defend the gun. He and a valiant gunner named James Taylor drew their swords and stood firm. The throng of the Russians came flowing in, very many of them for some reason bareheaded, and numbers of men, in the words of a victim, howling like dogs. Henry, with his left hand, wrested a bayonet from one of the Russians, and found means to throw the man down, fighting hard all the time with his sword arm against some of his other assailants. Soon both Henry and Taylor were closed in upon all sides and bayoneted again and again, Taylor then receiving his death wounds. Henry received in his chest the upthrust of a bayonet delivered with such power as to lift him almost from the ground, and at the same time he was stabbed in the back and stabbed in the arms. Then, from loss of blood, he became unconscious, but the raging soldiery, inflamed by religion, did not cease from stabbing his heretic body. He received 12 wounds, yet survived." Though the guns were captured, they did not remain long in the Russians' possession. Capt. Henry was Capt. Royal Artillery in 1859, and Capt. Coast Brigade of Artillery in 1860. He was for many years stationed in the Western District, and commanded the 4th Division of the Coast Brigade, and was greatly liked and respected. He died suddenly on Friday night, 14 Oct. 1870, and was buried with full military honours in Plymouth Cemetery on 19 Oct. His funeral was a most imposing ceremony ; there was a large attendance of officers of the Royal Artillery from the garrison and from Her Majesty's ships in the port. An obituary notice and an account of Capt. Henry's funeral appeared in the " Times " of 15 Oct. and 20 Oct. 1870.

DIXON, MATTHEW CHARLES, Capt., was *b.* at Avranches, Brittany, in 1821 ; *s.* of Col. Matthew Charles Dixon, Royal Engineers ; and gdson. of Sir Manley Dixon, K.C.B., Admiral of the Fleet. He was educated at the R.M.A., Woolwich ; joined the Royal Artillery on 19 March, 1839 ; became Lieut. 11 April, 1841, Capt. 30 June, 1848, Major 17 June, 1855, and Lieut.-Colonel 2 Nov. 1855. Major-General C. H. Owen says : " Major-General Matthew Dixon I knew well in the Crimea, and we were together in the eight-gun battery, right attack, for several months. A magazine was exploded by a shell one day, and seven of the eight guns were so buried that only one gun could be used. Although so dilapidated, we went on firing that one gun. For this M. Dixon, being the senior in command, got the V.C." His Victoria Cross was gazetted

Matthew Charles Dixon.

24 Feb. 1857 : " Matthew Charles Dixon, Brevet Lieut.-Colonel, Royal Artillery. On 17 April, 1855, about 2 p.m., when the battery he commanded was blown up by a shell which burst in the magazine, destroyed the parapets, killed and wounded ten men, disabled five guns and covered a sixth with earth, for most gallantly reopening fire with the remaining gun before the enemy had ceased cheering from their parapets (on which they had mounted), and fighting it till sunset, despite the heavy concentrated fire of the enemy's batteries and the ruined state of his own." Besides receiving the Victoria Cross, Brevet Lieut.-Colonel Dixon was made a Knight of the Legion of Honour by the French. He had already received the Brevets of Major and Lieut.-Colonel for his services in this campaign, and was given the Medal with clasp, the 5th Class of the Medjidie and the Turkish Medal. He was decorated by Queen Victoria at the first Investiture in Hyde Park, 26 June, 1857. On 28 June, 1862, he was promoted Colonel, and retired from the Royal Artillery on 19 March, 1869, with the honorary rank of Major-General. He died at Woodsgate, Pembury, Tunbridge Wells, on Saturday, 7 Jan. 1905, aged 84. A funeral service was held at Pembury Upper Church, and he was buried at Kensal Green Cemetery. Major-General Dixon married Henrietta, dau. of Admiral Charles John Bosanquet, of Wildswood, Middlesex.

ARTHUR, THOMAS, Gunner and Driver, Royal Artillery, served in the Crimean War. Colonel Knollys says of Arthur, in describing how he won the Victoria Cross : " His duty was to remain at the magazine in question, but he saw he could be useful by quitting his post and heeding neither the responsibility nor the danger." The Colonel of the Infantry (W. L. Yea, The Fusiliers), Arthur left his post to help, was watching him through his field-glasses, and he fortunately came up in the nick of time when there was a question of a court-martial. Arthur was given the Victoria Cross on its institution. The official notice in the London Gazette of 24 Feb. 1857, reads : " Thomas Arthur, Gunner and Driver, Royal Artillery. When in charge of the magazine in one of the left advanced batteries of the right attack on 7 June, when the

Quarries were taken, he, of his own accord, carried barrels of infantry ammunition for the 7th Fusiliers several times during the evening across the open. Volunteered for, and formed one of the spiking party of artillery

Thomas Arthur.

at the assault on the Redan on 18 June, 1855. Devoted heroism in sallying out of the trenches on numerous occasions and bringing in wounded officers and men." He was decorated by Queen Victoria at the first presentation of the new decoration in Hyde Park, 26 June, 1857. Arthur fought in the China War in 1860, and died at Savernake on 2 March, 1902. His Victoria Cross was sold on 17 July of that year for £47.

GRAHAM, GERALD, Lieut.; *b.* 27 June, 1831; the only survg. *s.* of the late Robert Hay Graham (who died in 1859), of Edenbrows, Cumberland, and of Frances (who died in 1878), dau. of Richard Oakley, of Oswald Kirk, Yorkshire, and afterwards of Pen Park, Bristol. He was *b.* at Acton, Middlesex ; educ. Dresden, Wimbledon, Edinburgh, and the Royal Military College, Woolwich, being gazetted to the Royal Engineers 19 June, 1850 ; promoted to Lieut. 17 Feb. 1854, and on 24 Feb. of that year embarked for Turkey to take part in the war with Russia. It was three years later to the very day of the month that his Victoria Cross was gazetted, when he was amongst the first recipients of the new decoration. Lieut. Graham was employed with his company at Gallipoli on the defensive works of Boulair ; went to Varna in May, and was engaged in the engineering preparations for the expedition to the Crimea. He was present at the Battle of the Alma 20 Sept. 1854, and at the Battle of Inkerman 5 Nov. ;

Gerald Graham.

was employed both in the left and right attack at the siege of Sebastopol, and attracted much attention throughout the operations by his coolness under fire. He was slightly wounded 13 April, 1855, in No. 7 Battery. He led the ladder-party of Sir John Campbell's column in the unsuccessful attack on the right flank of the Redan 18 June, and after the first check made a second attempt. He was lying for some time under fire waiting in vain for the storming party. " The vast stature of the young engineer," says Kinglake, " made him strangely conspicuous in the field. . . . The sailors eagerly wished—making an exception only for Graham—to dispense with the aid of all soldiers. They had lost their naval commanders (Lieut. Kidd killed and Lieut. Cave gravely wounded), but Mr. Kennedy, Mate, still remained to them ; and delighted with their pilot—Gerald Graham, a giant intent on his work, as though proof against grape-shot—they wanted, if he would lead them, to go and attack and take the Redan without asking any one other landsman to share the bliss of the enterprise." " I wish," wrote Lord West, " I wish I could do justice to the daring and intrepid conduct of the party of sailors. Lieut. Graham, of the Engineers, who led the ladder-party, evinced a coolness and readiness to expose himself to personal risk which does him the greatest possible credit." When Graham came out of action his friend Charles Gordon (afterwards General Gordon) met him and inquired what was the duty awaiting him. Graham answered lightly that the engagement had ceased and there was nothing more to do. Gordon was much annoyed at having missed the affair, and at Graham's want of sympathy, and there was a coolness between the two for some days afterwards. For his services on this occasion Lieut. Graham was awarded the Victoria Cross [London Gazette, 24 Feb. 1857] : " Gerald Graham, Lieut., Royal Engineers. Determined gallantry at the head of a ladder-party, at the assault of the Redan, on 18 June 1855. Devoted heroism in sallying out of the trenches on numerous occasions, and bringing in wounded officers and men." One of the occasions mentioned in the Gazette was when Graham, in company with Sapper Perie (who also received the Victoria Cross), went to help a naval officer to carry a man in from the open. He was wounded for a second time 9 July, 1855, and had to go to Therapia, but returned in time for the final operations 8 Sept. After the fall of Sebastopol he was employed on the destruction of the docks, when he, with Major (later Colonel) Nicholson, made a gallant attempt to rescue a man who had been poisoned by the foul air from the bottom of a shaft. Besides the Victoria Cross, Graham was given the Brevet of Major in 1859. He also received the Medal and three clasps, the Legion of Honour, the Turkish Medal and the Fifth Class Medjidie, and was twice mentioned in Despatches, viz., on 21 Dec. 1855, and 15 Feb. 1856. Lieut. Graham returned to England in May, 1856, and was decorated with the Victoria Cross by the Queen at the first Investiture in Hyde Park 26 June, 1857. He was next employed in Scotland and then at Aldershot, and went out to India in Aug. 1858, to take command of the 23rd Coy., Royal Engineers, becoming Capt. 28 Oct. 1858. The Indian Mutiny was then practically over, and in 1859 he took his company to Canton, at that time in British occupation, and in the spring of 1860 joined Sir Hope Grant's force to take part in the Anglo-French Expedition against China. Capt. Graham was seriously wounded 21 Aug. 1860, whilst directing the bombing party at the successful attack on the Taku Forts, but he recovered in time to be present at the entry into Pekin. He was mentioned in Despatches 4 Nov. 1860 ; received the Medal and clasp, and was given the Brevet of Colonel, returning to England in May, 1861. He *m.* at St. Peter's, Eaton Square, 29 April, 1862, Jane, dau. of George Durrant, Esq., of South Elmham Hall, Suffolk, and widow of the Rev. V. S. B. Blacker, Rector of East and West Rudham, Norfolk. He was Commandant, Royal Engineers, at Shorncliffe, and later at Aldershot, and from May, 1866, was for three years Commandant, Royal Engineers, in Montreal (Military C.B. and Brevet of Colonel). On his return home he was quartered at Chatham and then at Manchester, and in 1871 in York, where he remained for six years. In 1877 he attended the Army Manœuvres in Germany, and the following year in Switzerland. He was Assistant Director of Bombing at the War Office from Dec. 1877, to Oct. 1881, when he became Major-General. In 1882 he commanded the Second Infantry Brigade in Egypt throughout the campaign under Sir Garnet Wolseley, and he was in command at the Battle of Kassassin 23 Aug. 1882. In a Despatch written the day after this victory Sir Garnet Wolseley said that General Graham's dispositions "were all that they should have been, and his operations were carried out with that coolness for which he has always been so well known." In another Despatch Sir Garnet remarked that the brunt of the fighting had always fallen to Graham's lot, and that it could not have been in better hands. To that coolness and gallantry for which he had always been well known, he added the power of leading and commanding others. He was frequently mentioned in Despatches (3, 19 and 21 Sept.; 6 Oct. and 2 Nov. 1882), was thanked by both Houses of Parliament, received the Medal and clasp, the Bronze Star, the Second Class Medjidie, and was created a K.C.B. At the end of Jan. 1884, Graham accompanied Gordon from Cairo as far as Korosko, on the latter's last journey to Khartoum, and returned to Cairo to find that he had been appointed to command an expedition to the Eastern Sudan, with the object of relieving Tokar and destroying the power of Osman Digna. On 2 Oct. he fought the Second Battle of El Teb; he occupied the whole position of the Arabs, and the next day entered Tokar. He then moved his force back by sea to Suakin, fought the Second Battle of Tamai, burned the village and destroyed a great deal of ammunition. General Graham was most anxious to open up the Suakin-Berber route, and so reach out a hand to help Gordon. He afterwards greatly regretted that he had not done this on his own responsibility instead of asking permission. He was mentioned in Despatches 27 March, 3, 11 and 29 April, and 6 May, 1884; was thanked by both Houses of Parliament, received two clasps to the Egyptian Medal, the Grand Cordon of the Medjidie, and was promoted to be Lieut.-General. In Feb. 1885, when the Expedition had failed to relieve Khartoum, it was resolved to put an end to the power of the Mahdi. Graham was told off to destroy Osman Digna's force and push forward the railway. He occupied Handoub 8 April, and Olao on the 16th, and completed the railway for 19 miles. On account of complications in the East, the Government now resolved to abandon the proposed advance on Khartoum. A garrison was left at Suakin, and Graham returned to England, where he received for the third time the thanks of both Houses of Parliament, and was created a G.C.M.G. He received another clasp to the Egyptian Medal. In 1888 he declined the Governorship of Bermuda, and 14 June, 1890, in accordance with regulations, he was placed on the Retired List. He was created a G.C.B. on 20 May, 1896, and was appointed a Colonel Commandant of the Royal Engineers in 1899. Sir Gerald Graham died after a few days' illness at Springfield, Bideford, 17 Dec. 1899. The Mayor and Corporation of Bideford were present at his funeral, as were representatives of the Navy and Army, and particularly of his own Corps, the Royal Engineers. His portrait was painted for the Royal Engineers and now hangs in the Royal Engineers' Mess at Chatham. Sir Gerald Graham was of a retiring and reserved disposition, and Lord Wolseley said of him that he was "a man with the heart of a lion and the modesty of a young girl." He also said that Graham was perhaps the bravest man he had ever met.

LENNOX, WILBRAHAM OATES, Lieut.; *b.* 4 May, 1830, at Molecomb House, Goodwood, Chichester; *s.* of the late Colonel Lord John George Lennox, M.P. for West Sussex (2nd *s.* of General Charles Lennox, 4th Duke of Richmond, K.G.), and Louisa Fredrica, dau. of Capt. the Hon. George John Rodney, M.P. He entered the Royal Military Academy, Woolwich, 6 July, 1846; joined the Royal Engineers as a second lieutenant 27 July, 1848; passed some years in Ceylon, where he shot 100 elephants, and was promoted Lieut. 7 Feb. 1854. He landed in the Crimea 30 Sept. 1854, and served continuously till the British re-embarked, in June, 1856. He was present at the Battle of Inkerman; "was also present at the capture of Tryon's rifle pits 20 Nov. 1854, which the Russians had established in front of the Greenhill attack within 250 yards of our second parallel. They thus seriously impeded our advance, and were most gallantly driven out by Lieut. Tryon, of the Rifle Brigade (who was killed), and 200 of his men. Lieuts. Lennox and Phillips, with a working party of 100 men, threw themselves into the rifle pits, where under extreme exposure they entrenched themselves, and repulsed the attempts of the enemy to dislodge them during the night." The following is an extract from a letter dated 22 Nov., from Lieut. Lennox, on the subject: "At 4 p.m. 200 of the Rifle Brigade, under Tryon, Bourchier and Cunningham, paraded at our park, and were conducted by self and Phillips, Royal Engineers, to the advanced trench, where Tryon made his arrangements. He and Bourchier, with a hundred men, were to sneak round by the right, and Cunningham, with the rest, was to remain as a reserve and advance when the pits were taken. Tryon's party got within about 80 yards of the Russians before being twigged, and then they went forward with a rush, the Russians bolting away; they rallied about 100 yards off, and then commenced a sharp musketry fire. In the meantime the forts of Sebastopol opened with shot and shell as Phillips and I brought up our working party of 100 men in rear of Cunningham's rifles out of the left of the advanced trench. We found Bourchier's party (poor Tryon was shot dead while leading) in possession of the pits, and we were only annoyed once more by the Russians advancing, but a few rounds sent them back, and as the rifles were short of ammunition, I extended some of my working party and set the rest to work to make a trench to connect the pits we had taken, and to convert them into English instead of Russian ones. I also sent to the field officer of the trenches for rifle ammunition and a support. We worked hard all night, and in the morning had the satisfaction of having provided cover for the Rifles to hold the ground during the day, and keep the Russians well away from us—altogether a good night's work, and one which pleased, I hear, General Canrober much." For his services on this occasion Lieut. Lennox was awarded the Victoria Cross on its institution [London Gazette, 24 Feb. 1857]: "W. O. Lennox, Lieut. Royal Engineers: Cool and gallant conduct in establishing a lodgment in Tryon's Rifle Pit, and assisting to repel the assaults of the enemy. This brilliant operation drew forth a special order from General Canrobert." He was at first erroneously gazetted as "Lieut. 'D.' Lennox." On Sunday, 17 June, 1855, Lieut. Lennox writes in his diary: "Sir Richard England's third Division was divided into two brigades, one under Barnard to advance up the Woronzoff Road, with Neville and Penn; the other brigade under Eyre to make a feint at the creek battery, Chapman and I as his A.D.C. to accompany Sir. R. England. What with having to look after the tools and carry messages for Sir R. England and Colonel Wyndham, I did not get to bed till one o'clock." For his services in this campaign, besides being given the Victoria Cross, Lieut. Lennox was mentioned in Despatches in the London Gazette, 21 Dec. 1855, and received the Crimean Medal with two clasps (for Inkerman and the Siege and Fall of Sebastopol), the Fifth Class Medjidie and the Sardinian and Turkish Medals. In 1857 Lieut. Lennox was Senior Subaltern of the 23rd (Capt. Clarke's) Coy., Royal Engineers, with Lieuts. Malcolm and Pritchard, and embarked for the expected war in China. While on the way the Indian Mutiny suddenly broke out, and when they stopped at Singapore the Company was ordered to India. On the march to Cawnpore it was in action at Khnjwa 1 Nov., when, among other casualties, Capt. Clarke was severely wounded, and the command of the Company devolved on Lennox. Capt. Peel, R.N., commanded on the occasion, and in his official report, referring to a critical incident in the fight, he mentioned he was "assisted principally by Lieut. Lennox, Royal Engineers." On 25 Nov. 1857, Lennox became 2nd Captain. Proceeded with the company to Lucknow, where he commanded the Brigade of Engineer Companies and where he was acting Commander Royal Engineers in the relief of the Residency under Sir Colin Campbell. General Sir Richard Harrison said that one evening afterwards he dined in Simla with Sir William Mansfield (the Chief of the Staff); the latter told him that when the Commander-in-Chief and himself had arrived in Lucknow and had before them the difficult task of relieving the beleaguered garrison he cast about for an officer who would suggest a plan for doing the work. . . . Lieut. Lennox . . . asked for half an hour to consider the question, and at the end of that time came back with a plan; the plan was approved, was carried out in the letter, and the Residency was relieved. For his services at Lucknow Lieut. Lennox was mentioned in Despatches and thanked by the Governor-General in Council. He and the 23rd Coy were afterwards engaged with the Gwalior Contingent, which was defeated at Cawnpore 6 Dec. 1857, and at the action of Futtegurh, on both occasions under Sir Colin Campbell. The company was joined by a detachment under Lieut. R. Harrison at Cawnpore in Feb. 1858, soon after which it marched to the Alumbagh under General Outram, where the C.R.E. was assisted by Lennox as Field Engineer. Sir R. Harrison says: "As soon as Sir John Campbell had collected sufficient troops for the purpose, and brought up a siege train, the Siege took place. Brigadier-General Napier was now C.R.E., and Colonel Harness, with Lennox as his assistant, was put in charge of the main attack on the city, and it was a sight that I shall never forget. The old Colonel, with somewhat bent figure but clear brain, engaged in his first fight, and the Lieutenant who had won the V.C. in the Crimea, and already acquired considerable experience of Indian warfare, side by side, at the head of the sap, apparently never tired, with little or no food, until the Kaiser Bagh was won and the Siege was over." During the Siege Capt. Clarke was killed, and the command of the 23rd Coy. again fell to Lennox. About this time he became Capt., and was made a Brevet Major for his previous services in the Crimea. After the Fall of Lucknow, Lennox was C.R.E., with Sir R. Walpole's force sent to subjugate Rohilcund. In Sept. 1858, he was C.R.E. of the Column with which his company served, under the immediate direction of the Commander-in-Chief, in the operations against Oudh. On the way to Allahabad he was ordered by Lord Clive to come and live with him till his company arrived. The 23rd Coy., Royal Engineers, took part also in the last campaign of the Mutiny, called the Trans-Gagra Campaign. Three brigades were formed under the direction of the Commander-in-Chief, and again Lennox was C.R.E. of the field force. Afterwards the company went to Lucknow. He was four times mentioned in Despatches for his services in the Mutiny; was given the Brevet of Lieut.-Colonel. He sailed from Calcutta for England 25 March, 1859. He *m.* first, in 1861, Mary Harriet, dau. of Mr. Robert Harrison, of Plas Gough, co. Dalkeith. She died in 1863. Their children were: Gerald Wilbraham Stuart, *b.* 29 April, 1872, and Lilian Emily, who died in infancy. In the Franco-Prussian War of 1870 he was sent officially to accompany the German Armies in France from Nov. 1870, to March, 1871. He was present at the Siege of Paris, when he was at Army Headquarters; of

Wilbraham Oates Lennox.

Mezières, of Belfort, of Schletstadt, of New Breisch, and of Strassburg. "The specific lesson of 1871, to be confirmed in 1877 in another theatre, was the extraordinary increase of the retaining power of the entrenched infantry armed with breech-loading rifles." In Nov. 1876, Colonel Lennox went to Montenegro as British Military Attaché with the armistice on the Montenegrin Frontier. Thence he was sent into Turkey, via Vienna, Bucharest and Giurgevo, reaching Constantinople. He *m.* secondly, his second cousin, Susan Hay (Lady Lennox Sinclair from Nov. 1910), of Stevenson, co. Haddingdon, and Murkle and Achnarasdal, co. Caithness, youngest dau. of Admiral Sir John Gordon Sinclair, 8th Baronet, of the same places. Their children were : Charles Gordon Sinclair, *b.* 9 July, 1868 (deceased) ; Cecil George Pelham (now Lennox Sinclair, of above places), *b.* 2 April, 1872 ; Claud Henry Maitland, *b.* 20 April, 1873 ; Louisa Edith, *b.* 1 Sept. 1869 (deceased), and Cecilia Georgina Susan. Colonel Lennox served in the Russo-Turkish War of 1868 as Military Attaché with the Turkish troops, and received the Turkish War Medal in Dec. 1876. He next proceeded to Bulgaria, and remained there during and after the Turco-Russian War from 1876 to 1878 as Military Attaché. From 1884 to 1887 (Turkish War Medal) he commanded the garrison of Alexandria, and during the Nile Campaign of 1884–1885 he organized the landing and despatch of the troops, and the transmission of the Nile boats, stern-wheelers, etc., for the expedition. While in the East he visited the Holy Land, and after leaving Egypt in 1887, commanded the troops in Ceylon till 1888, returning home via Australia and America. He was created a K.C.B. in 1891. General Sir W. O. Lennox was Director of Military Education from 1893–1895. Sir W. O. Lennox died 7 Feb. 1897. A most interesting memoir of the late Sir W. O. Lennox was written by his friend, General T. Fraser. Mr. C. W. P. Lennox-Sinclair says : "My father has told me that Moltke sent for him several times during the entry of the German Army into Paris, and wished my father to be near him, but my father being British Military Attaché kept on falling behind. I believe he started the Royal Engineers' Charitable Fund with money he found in the Indian Mutiny. He was the first European to climb the Sigur rock fortress in Ceylon, and also climbed and sat astride the weather-cock on the top of Chichester Cathedral. I have a large piece of plate given to Colonel W. O. Lennox in 1868 by the Duke of Connaught."

ROSS, JOHN, Corpl., served in the Crimean War, and for his services received the Victoria Cross on its institution [London Gazette, 24 Feb. 1857]: "John Ross, No. 997, Corpl., Royal Engineers. Recommended for distinguished conduct 21 July, 1855, in connecting the 4th parallel right attack with an old Russian rifle-pit in front. Extremely creditable conduct 23 Aug. 1855, in charge of the advance from the 5th parallel right attack on the Redan in placing and filling 25 gabions under a very heavy fire, whilst annoyed by the presence of light balls. Intrepid and devoted conduct in creeping to the Redan in the night of the 8th Sept. 1855, and reporting its evacuation, on which its occupation by the British took place." Ross had three dates engraved on his Cross. For the first act of bravery General Simpson gave him £2. He crept out

John Ross.

at night with a working-party of 200 men, each carrying an entrenching tool and a gabion, and before morning a long line of perfect cover was revealed to the enemy, extending from the parallel to the rifle-pit. On the second occasion commemorated on Ross's Cross, Ross worked under the eye of Capt. Wolseley, of the 90th Perthshire Light Infantry, afterwards Field-Marshal Lord Wolseley, who was in charge of the advance works. This time General Simpson rewarded him with £3. The third deed was when Ross discovered the evacuation of the Redan and carried back a wounded man. Corpl. Ross was decorated by Queen Victoria at the Military Parade in Hyde Park 26 June, 1857. Besides the Victoria Cross, Ross received the French War Medal. He was afterwards promoted Sergt. Sergt. Ross died 23 Oct. 1879.

LENDRIM, WILLIAM, Corpl., served in the Crimean War, and for his services in that campaign received the Victoria Cross on its institution [London Gazette, 24 Feb. 1857]: "No. 1078, William J. Lendrim, Corpl., Royal Engineers. Recommended for intrepidity—getting on the top of a magazine and extinguishing sand-bags which were burning, and making good the breach under fire 11 April, 1855. For courage and praiseworthy example in superintending 150 French Chasseurs 14 Feb. 1855, in building No. 9 Battery, left attack, and replacing the whole of the capsized gabions under a heavy fire. Was one of four volunteers for destroying the farthest rifle-pit on 20 April." Corpl. Lendrim thus had three dates engraved upon the Victoria Cross which he was awarded for the above-mentioned exploits. Corpl. James Knight joined Corpl. Lendrim in the deed of gallantry 11 April, but not having the same claim for other services did not receive the Victoria Cross. Colonel Knollys, in his "The Victoria Cross in the Crimea," says : "On 14 Feb. 1855, L.-Corpl. William Lendrim, Royal Engineers, was told off as Sapper Superintendent of the 8-gun Battery being

William Lendrim.

constructed in rear of the right advanced parallel, the French finding the working-party. A heavy fire from the Russians knocked over several gabions, thus making a series of small breaches in the parapet. 'To fill up these gaps was,' says the author of 'The History of the Royal Sappers and Miners,' 'a species of forlorn hope. As two of the Frenchmen were killed and four others wounded in the trench, Corpl. Lendrim, an intrepid and skilful man, accustomed to lead, zealously pushed on from gap to gap, and by his exertions every gabion was firmly replaced. The French officer in charge of the Chasseurs witnessed with admiration the Corporal's coolness and good example, and applauded them to the British Engineer.' 'On the 12th April,' says Colonel Knollys, 'Corpl. Lendrim was in the batteries of the left attack. The second bombardment was going on and the fire was heavy. A sand-bag in one of the embrasures took fire, and Lendrim was about to enter the embrasure to remove it, when a petty officer of the Naval Brigade begged him to wait till he had fired his gun, as it was already loaded. Just then a young Midshipman came up and asked Lendrim why he was waiting. Lendrim explained, on which the Middy sprang into the embrasure and threw down the burning sand-bag. Piqued at thus being interfered with, Lendrim told the Middy that he did not thank anyone for doing a duty for which he was responsible, finishing with the insubordinate remark, ' Since you have done so much, you had better finish the job.' The Middy, being a good-natured fellow, made allowances for Lendrim's irritation, and took no notice of the remark. Lendrim then went into the embrasure, quenched another burning sand-bag, and, getting the better of his temper, repaired the damage. On finishing this hazardous duty, the Middy said, ' I would not have touched the bag if I had known that you were one of the old Sappers.' This observation completely appeased the sensitive Corporal. On the 20th April, Corpl. Lendrim was one of four sappers who volunteered for destroying the screen which the Russians had erected to conceal their advanced rifle-pits." There is another exploit recorded of Corpl. Lendrim, which, though not mentioned in the Official Chronicle of the Victoria Cross, is so much to his credit that we will briefly describe it. After the repulse of a sortie on 22 March, he heard the groans of a wounded man out in the open. Clambering over the parapet, he, accompanied by two other men of the line, proceeded amidst a hail of bullets to the spot where the man was lying, which was about 30 yards in front. On arriving they found he was a Russian, but humanity knows no distinction between friend and foe, and, lifting him up, the gallant trio carried the poor wretch to the parapet. Laying him gently down when they reached the parapet, they were just about to lift him into the trench when the Russian expired. For his first Victoria Cross exploit Corpl. Lendrim was given the French War Medal, as the French officer had reported that he had saved the Battery from destruction. He also received the Legion of Honour. Corpl. Lendrim was decorated by Queen Victoria in Hyde Park 26 June, 1857. He was later Quartermaster-Sergt. at the Royal Military College, Sandhurst, and he died 28 Nov. 1891. The "Evening Standard" of 23 April, 1915, says that Sergt.-Major William Lendrim, Royal Engineers (late of the Staff College, Camberley), had the Victoria Cross with three dates on it.

PERIE, JOHN, Sapper, served in the Crimean War, and for his services in that campaign was awarded the Victoria Cross on its institution [London Gazette, 24 Feb. 1857]: "No. 854, John Perie, Sapper, Royal Engineers. Conspicuous valour in leading the sailors with the ladders to the storming of the Redan 18 June, 1855. He was invaluable on that day. Devoted conduct in rescuing a wounded man from the open, although he himself had just been wounded by a bullet in the side." When Lieut. Murray, of the Engineers, fell mortally wounded, Lieut. Gerald Graham took his place. He had previously sent Perie out to Murray with a message, and afterwards saw how fearlessly the man disappeared into the thick of the fire and returned miraculously unharmed. Wherever Graham exposed himself to danger, Perie was always at hand to help him. At last Graham realized the hopelessness of the attempt and ordered the storming party back. While sheltering in a trench, an officer in the Naval Brigade heard a wounded sailor lying out in front calling for help. He asked for another volunteer to help bring the man in. " I'm with you ! " cried Graham. " And I too," added John Perie, though he was suffering with a musket-shot wound in the side. Fortune favoured the brave, they rescued the wounded man and returned with him without being hit. Both were awarded the Victoria Cross for their heroism on that day, and Perie in addition received the French War Medal. He received his Victoria Cross at the hands of Queen Victoria in Hyde Park 26 June, 1857. Sapper John Perie died on 17 Sept. 1874. His Victoria Cross and French War Medal were sold in London 26 Sept. 1911.

RUSSELL, SIR CHARLES, Bart., Brevet Major ; *b.* Sothern Hill, near Reading, 22 June, 1826 ; the second surviv. *s.* of Sir Henry Russell, Bart., by his wife, Marie Clotilde, dau. of Baron Benoit Mottet de la Fontaine ; educ. Eton ; joined the 35th Regt. in 1846, when it was quartered in Ireland, and later he went with it to Mauritius. In 1848 the Great Duke of Wellington, who was a personal friend of Sir Henry Russell's, gave Charles Russell his commission in the Grenadier Guards. He became Lieut. and Capt. in 1853, accompanying his regiment to the Crimea. He took part in the Battles of Alma, Balaklava and Inkerman, and in the Siege and Capture of Sebastopol, serving as D.A.Q.M.G. to the 1st Division. On his return to England he was one of the first on whom Her Majesty pinned the Cross " For Valour," 26 June, 1857. His decoration was

Charles Russell.

gazetted in the London Gazette 24 Feb. 1857: "Sir Charles Russell, Baronet, Brevet Major, Grenadier Guards. Offered to dislodge a party of Russians from the Sand-bag Battery if anyone would follow him. Sergt. Norman, Privates Anthony Palmer and Bailey (who was killed) volunteered the first. The attack succeeded." The following is an account taken from Kinglake's "Crimea" and other sources as to how Sir Charles Russell won his Victoria Cross: "On 7 Nov. 1854, after the Russians had retaken the Sand-bag Battery and were pouring from it a steady fire, some man said: 'If any officer will lead, we will charge!' Sir Charles Russell then jumped into the embrasure, and, waving his revolver, said: 'Come on, my lads, who will follow me?' Sergt. Norman and Privates Anthony Palmer and Bailey at once volunteered, and their example was soon followed. Sir Charles began by firing his revolver at a Russian who barred the way. The pistol snapped, but pulling again, Sir Charles killed the man. At this moment a Grenadier tapped him on the shoulder and said, 'You was near done for.' 'Oh, no,' replied Sir Charles, 'he was some way from me.' The Grenadier rejoined: 'His bayonet was all but into you when I clouted him on the head.' Looking round, Sir Charles saw that the Guardsman had spoken truly, and had saved him from an attack of which he was only then aware. 'Well,' said Sir Charles, 'if I live through this you shall not be forgotten. What is your name?' 'Anthony Palmer,' was the reply; and he was not forgotten. He was publicly made a Corpl. on parade next day and ultimately received the Victoria Cross. Again and again the little band was hemmed in by apparently overwhelming numbers, and seemed on the point of being annihilated, but the valour of our men and their superior skill with the bayonet would not be denied, and after superhuman toil they wrested the triumph from their stubborn foes. Sir Charles himself performed prodigies of valour, and—in single combat—wrenched the rifle out of the grasp of a powerful Russian; a trophy which he carried out of action, and which is still at Swallowfield Park." For his services in the Crimean Campaign (1854 to 1856), Sir Charles Russell received—besides the Victoria Cross—the Brevet of Major, the Crimean Medal with four clasps, the Turkish Medal, the Legion of Honour and the Medjidie. In 1855 he was promoted Major, and in 1858 Lieut.-Colonel. He retired from the Service in 1868, having been in 1865 elected M.P. for Berkshire in the Conservative interest, and he sat for this county till 1868. In 1874 he became one of the Members for Westminster, and in 1877 he was appointed Colonel, 4th Middlesex Volunteers. Kinglake wrote to Sir Charles Russell in 1872, asking for the loan for the second time of his Crimean Journal, and in writing to him afterwards said, "It has been my fate to see a great many journals, but I can say most truly that I have never seen anything so terse as yours. For me—with my knowledge of the collateral circumstances—there is a volume almost of interesting narrative in less than one page of the Journal." Sir Charles Russell died unmarried 14 April, 1883, and was succeeded in the baronetcy by his brother, Sir George Russell, father of the present Baronet.

PALMER, ANTHONY, Private, served in the Crimean War, and for his services in that campaign was awarded the Victoria Cross on its institu-

Anthony Palmer.

tion [London Gazette, 24 Feb. 1857]: "No. 3571, Anthony Palmer, Private, 3rd Battn. Grenadier Guards. Brevet Major Sir Charles Russell, Bart., Grenadier Guards, offered to dislodge a party of Russians from the Sand-bag Battery if anyone would follow. Sergt. Norman, Privates Anthony Palmer and Bailey (who was killed) volunteered the first. The attack succeeded. No. 3571, Private Anthony Palmer, 3rd Battn. Grenadier Guards. Present when the charge was made in defence of the Colours, and also charged singly upon the enemy, as witnessed by Sir Charles Russell; is said to have saved Sir C. Russell's life." Kinglake says, when describing the Battle of Inkerman (Vol. VI., page 237): "They were chafing at the obstacle interposed by a benchless parapet, which condemned them almost to inaction, without giving them the slightest security against overwhelming disasters. On the left of the work some man said, 'If any officer will lead we will follow!' Sir Charles Russell, of the Grenadier Guards, having chanced to be the only one who had heard this appeal, was moved to accept the challenge. Crying, 'Follow me, lads,' he sprang out through the left embrasure, and the next instant was busy with his revolver amongst numbers of the Russians standing clustered about on that part of the ridge. But he had been followed by only one man, a private soldier named Anthony Palmer. Palmer quickly shot down an assailant who was in the act of bayoneting Sir Charles; and somehow the two—the Captain and the brave Grenadier —not only found means to defend themselves for the moment, but even made good their way, fighting, to a part of the ledge where they saw a few more of the bearskins. Russell was a man of slight build, not disclosing great bodily strength, yet, in one of his struggles for the mastery—which were also struggles for life—he was able to tear a rifle from the hands of a Russian soldier, and he kept it till the end of the day." Kinglake is, of course, mistaken in saying that only one man followed Sir Charles. Sergt. Norman and Private Bailey were also with him, and the latter would almost certainly have been nowadays awarded the Victoria Cross posthumously. Palmer was also one of the small band which, by a desperate charge against overwhelming numbers, saved the Colours of the battalion from capture. He was made a Corporal on Parade the morning after the battle, and on its institution was awarded the Victoria Cross. He was decorated by Her Majesty in Hyde Park 26 June, 1857. Sir Charles Russell's valiant man

later became a Captain in the 3rd Essex Volunteer Regt. His Victoria Cross is now in the United Service Institute, London. Capt. Palmer died 12 Dec. 1892.

ABLETT, ALFRED, Sergt., enlisted in the Grenadier Guards, and served

Alfred Ablett.

in the Crimean War. During the Siege of Sebastopol a burning shell fell into the trench where two cases of ammunition were placed, and a soldier of the Grenadier Guards, by name Ablett, of the 6th Coy., at once realized the imminent danger to which all were exposed. He seized the shell in his hands with the burning fuse, and threw it over the parapet, when it immediately exploded as it touched the ground, but not a man was touched. It is said that as he pulled the shell away it actually rolled between Ablett's legs, knocking him over and covering him with stones and gravel before he hurled it out of the trench. "For this act of prompt courage," says Colonel Knollys in his "Victoria Cross in the Crimea" (page 66), "Ablett was promoted Corpl., and then Sergt., and received at the hands of his Chief a silk necktie made by Her Majesty, who personally gave him the Victoria Cross at the first Presentation 26 June, 1857. He was also awarded the Medal for Distinguished Conduct in the Field." Private Ablett received a gratuity of £5 in money. His Victoria Cross was gazetted 24 Feb. 1857: "Alfred Ablett, No. 5872, Sergt., 3rd Battn. Grenadier Guards. On 2 Sept. 1855, seeing a shell fall in the centre of a number of ammunition cases and powder, he instantly seized it and threw it outside the trench; it burst as it touched the ground." In later life Sergt. Ablett held the appointment of Inspector of Police, Millwall Docks, London. He died there 12 March, 1897. His Victoria Cross was sold in London 20 March, 1903, for £62.

GOODLAKE, GERALD LITTLEHALES, Brevet Major, *s.* of T. Goodlake, Esq., of Wadley, co. Berks; was *b.* on 14 May, 1832. He entered the Royal Welsh Fusiliers in 1848, exchanging into the Coldstream Guards

Gerald L. Goodlake.

14 June, 1850, with whom he served through the Crimean Campaign, and was present at Alma, Balaklava, Inkerman, Tchernaya, and the Siege and Fall of Sebastopol. He became Lieut. 27 June, 1851, Capt. 14 July, 1854, and Major 14 June, 1856. Kinglake says (Vol. IV., page 299, note): "An appeal for volunteer sharpshooters brought about the formation of that little body of about 60 men of the Guards, which, under Cameron of the Grenadiers, Goodlake of the Coldstreams, and Baring of the Scots Fusiliers, became afterwards famous for extraordinary exploits and adventures. . . . At Careenage Ravine, a picket of the Light Division (which, however, was quickly drawn in), and 60 volunteers of the Guards, under Capt. Goodlake (but these last were joined towards the close of the combat—26 Oct.—by some men of the Rifles under Capt. Markham), completed the enemy's discomfiture, and took an officer and several men prisoners. . . . To assure himself against any ambush, Capt. Goodlake (taking with him Sergt. Ashton) had gone up to examine the caves, leaving the rest of his sixty men halted across the bed of the chasm, and partly, too, on each bank. Whilst thus left for a moment without their commander, Goodlake's men were suddenly confronted by the sight of the Russian column thronging up round the corner below. The hostile force seemed like a mob, numbering about 600 or 800 hundred men, and was pressing forward along the bed of the ravine and also along each of its banks. Goodlake's people were retreating, firing. Goodlake himself, with Sergt. Ashton at his side, was still by the caves. Hemmed in by assailants and debarred by the craggy and difficult ground from any possibility of effectual retreat, he thought that he and the sergeant must needs submit to be made prisoners. Sergt. Ashton, however, suggested that if the captain and he were made prisoners, they would assuredly be put to death in revenge for one of their recent exploits (referring to the fact that the little force under Goodlake had lately attacked a Russian picket, taking an officer and some of the men prisoners), and all notion of surrender being thereupon discarded, the alternative was, of course, resistance. The Russians, whilst closing in upon their two adversaries, fired at them a number of shots, which all, however, proved harmless. On the other hand, Goodlake and the sergeant fired, each of them once, into the nearest clump of Russians, and then with the butt-ends of their rifles knocked away the foremost of their assailants, and ran down the foot of the bank. There, however, they were in the midst of a mob of Russians advancing up the ravine. To their great surprise no one seized them, and it was evident that, owing to the grey cloaks and plain caps they both wore, the enemy was mistaking them for his own fellow-countrymen. Shielded by this illusion, and favoured, too, by the ruggedness of the ground and obstructive thickets of brushwood, which enabled them to be constantly changing their neighbours without exciting attention, they moved unmolested into the midst of their foes; and, though strange, it is none the less true, that this singular march was continued along a distance of more than half a mile. At length, with its two interlopers, the Russian throng came to a halt, and not without reason, for it was confronted by the sixty men of the Guards, who, after the lengthened

retreat they had made when their chief was cut off from them, were now plainly making a stand, and had posted themselves some thirty miles off, behind a little trench, which there seamed the bed of the gorge. Goodlake, with his trusty sergeant, soon crossed the intervening space which divided the Russians from the English, and found himself once more amongst his own people." For his exploits in command of the sharpshooters Brevet Major Goodlake was highly praised in General Orders, received the Legion of Honour, and—on its institution—was awarded the Victoria Cross [London Gazette, 24 Feb. 1857]: "Gerald Littlehales Goodlake, Brevet Major, Coldstream Guards. For distinguished gallantry whilst in command of the sharpshooters furnished by the Coldstream Guards on 28 Oct. 1854, on the occasion of the powerful sortie on the 2nd Division, when he held Windmill Ravine, below the Picquet House, against a much larger force of the enemy. The party of sharpshooters under his command killed 38 (one an officer), and took three prisoners of the enemy (of the latter one an officer), Major Goodlake being the sole officer in command. Also for distinguished gallantry on the occasion of a surprise of a picquet of the enemy in Nov. at the bottom of the Windmill Ravine, by the sharpshooters under his sole leading and command, when the knapsacks and rifles of the enemy's party fell into his hands." He received the Victoria Cross at the first Investiture in Hyde Park 26 June, 1857. On 6 June, 1856, he became a Major, and Lieut.-Colonel 29 Nov. 1859, and in 1869 he was appointed A.D.C. to Her Majesty Queen Victoria. He was Major-General to the Land Forces in 1879, and retired in 1881 with the rank of Lieut.-General. General Goodlake died on Saturday, 5 April, 1890, at Denham Fishery, Uxbridge, at the age of 57, and was buried at Harefield Church.

STANLACK, WILLIAM, Private, was *b*. in the parish of Halwell, Okehampton, co. Devon, and joined the Coldstream Guards at the age of 19 years, at Totnes, on 27 July, 1852. He served in the Crimean War, and was awarded the Victoria Cross on its institution, for his services in this campaign [London Gazette, 24 Feb. 1857]: "William Stanlack, No. 3968, Private, Coldstream Guards. For having volunteered, when employed as one of the sharpshooters in Oct. 1854, for reconnoitring purposes, to crawl up within six yards of a Russian sentry, and so enabled the officer in command to effect a surprise; Private Stanlack having been warned beforehand of the imminent risk which he would run in the adventure." Kinglake says that: "At Inkerman the venturesome Goodlake was present on the morning of the action with 30 men of the Guards," in advance of the 2nd Division pickets. The venturesome captain had some equally venturesome followers. He stole one night upon a picket of the foe in a ravine. "Private William Stanlack, Coldstream Guards," says Colonel Knollys, "one of Goodlake's sharpshooters, had distinguished himself, and earned the Victoria Cross when the Russian picket was surprised. He on that occasion volunteered to reconnoitre, though warned of the imminent danger which he was encountering, crawled up to within six yards of a Russian sentry, and brought back such information that his party was enabled to effect its object." Stanlack, in addition to earning the Victoria Cross, was in possession of the Crimean Medal with four clasps, the Turkish Medal, and Medal for Distinguished Conduct in the Field. He served in the Coldstream Guards from 29 July, 1852, until 28 Jan. 1863. During his services in the Coldstream Guards he received no promotion whatever. He died on 24 April, 1904, and his widow died on 8 May, 1917.

William Stanlack.

STRONG, GEORGE, Private, was *b*. in the parish of Odenrube, Yeovil, co. Somerset, and joined the Coldstream Guards at Plymouth, at the age of 19 years, on 27 Nov. 1854. He served in that regiment until 29 Nov. 1864. During his service he did not receive any promotion, but for his services in the Crimean Campaign he was awarded the Crimean Medal with one clasp, the Turkish War Medal, and the Victoria Cross [London Gazette, 24 Feb. 1857]: "George Strong, No. 4787, Private, Coldstream Guards. For having, when on duty in the trenches, in the month of Sept. 1855, removed a live shell from the place where it had fallen." Private Strong was decorated by Queen Victoria at the first Investiture in Hyde Park, 26 June, 1857. Private Strong died on 25 Aug. 1888. His Cross was sold in London 17 April, 1907.

George Strong.

LINDSAY, ROBERT JAMES, Capt. and Brevet Major, was *b*. 16 April, 1832; the 2nd *s*. of the late Lieut.-General James Lindsay, of Balcarres, co. Fife, and of his wife, Anne, eldest dau. of Sir Coutts Trotter, Baronet. His elder brother was Sir Coutts Lindsay; one of his sisters married her cousin, the late Earl of Crawford (then Lord Lindsay), the well-known historian of Art, and another sister married the late Mr. Holford, of Dorchester House. He was educated at Eton, and entered the Scots Fusilier Guards as Ensign 13 Dec. 1850, and became Capt. 6 Nov. 1854. On the outbreak of the war with Russia he embarked for the Crimea on 28 Feb. 1854, and in March, 1854, became Aide-de-

Camp to General Simpson; but gave up the appointment 14 Aug. 1855, in order to become Adjutant 1st Battn. Scots Guards. He held the Adjutancy until 29 April, 1858. A writer in the "Times" says that "the tall, handsome young officer distinguished himself very brilliantly at the Alma." The Records of the Scots Guards say that Lindsay "carried the Queen's Colour at the Battle of the Alma. In that engagement, when the Light Division, misled by an unauthorized order, temporarily fell back, they carried with them part of the Scots Fusilier Guards. Lindsay—with a group of other officers, including Adjutant Drummond, whose horse had been killed —rallied a party of non-commissioned officers and men round the Colours, and held their ground against an overwhelming force until the enemy retired on the battalion coming up the hill." Capt. Lindsay is mentioned by Kinglake as one of those who, "springing forward, opposed themselves singly and in knots to the thickening flakes of the Russian infantry" at Inkerman. For his conduct on these two occasions he was awarded the Victoria Cross [London Gazette, 24 Feb. 1857]: "Robert James Lindsay, Capt. and Brevet Major, Scots Fusilier Guards. When the formation of the line of the regiment was disordered at the Alma, Capt. Lindsay stood firm with the Colours, and by his example and energy tended to restore order. At Inkerman, at a most trying moment, he, with a few men, charged a party of Russians, driving them back and running one through the body himself." For his services in this campaign he also received the Brevet of Major, the Legion of Honour, the Medal with clasp, and the Turkish Medal. He received the Victoria Cross at the first presentation 26 June, 1857. He was promoted Major 26 Dec. 1856, and Lieut.-Colonel in 1859, and was Equerry to the Prince of Wales in 1858 and 1859. In 1858 Colonel Lindsay married the Honourable Harriet Sarah Loyd, only dau. and heiress of Lord Overstone, the head of the banking firm of Jones, Loyd & Company. Just before his marriage he assumed (23 Oct. 1858) the name of Loyd in conjunction with his own. He retired from the Army 16 Sept. 1859, and became the first Lieut.-Colonel commanding the 1st Volunteer Battn. Princess Charlotte of Wales's (Royal Berkshire) Regt. 1 June, 1860. At the General Election of 1865 Colonel Lindsay was elected one of the three Members for Berkshire, and he held this seat until he was given a peerage in 1885. He was Lieut.-Colonel Commandant Honourable Artillery Company from 1866 to 1881, and it was during his tenure of this office that the company successfully resisted the claims made by other City Volunteers for the use of their ground for training purposes. He realized the extreme importance of the Volunteer movement. Colonel Lindsay was Financial Secretary to the War Office 1877 to 1880. He was created a K.C.B. 4 May, 1881, and was raised to the peerage with the title of Baron Wantage of Lockinge in the County of Berkshire, creation 23 July, 1885. He was one of the first Brigadiers appointed when, in 1888, the Volunteer battalions were organized into 34 infantry brigades, being appointed (11 July, 1888) to the command of the Home Counties Brigade, which has its Headquarters at Reading. He was also one of the earliest and most active members of the National Rifle Association, which was formed in 1860; served on its council for many years, was its president in 1887, and when the association received its charter on 25 Nov. 1891, Lord Wantage was the chairman of the council, a post which he held up to the time of his death. His name will always be associated by the general public with the Loyd-Lindsay Prize, which was first given by him in 1873, to be competed for at the Wimbledon meetings and subsequently at Bisley by teams from the Yeomanry Cavalry, the Volunteer Light Horse, Mounted Rifles, or troops of Mounted Infantry. In 1886 Lord Wantage was made Lord-Lieutenant of Berkshire. He was an extensive landowner, and possessed over 18,000 acres in that county and 28,000 acres in Northamptonshire, besides property in the counties of Buckingham, Oxford and Huntingdon. He took a great interest in farming; was a most generous landlord, and cultivated about 4,000 acres himself. He instituted a profit-sharing system among his labourers, and did all he could to improve the conditions under which they lived, especially in the matter of housing accommodation. Lord Wantage was president of the Shire Horse Society in 1889. He was chairman of the Committee on Recruiting for the Army in 1890. A letter written on 22 July, 1870, to the "Times" by Colonel Loyd-Lindsay resulted in the formation of the National Society for Aid to the Sick and Wounded, which subsequently became the British Red Cross Society. Besides being one of its founders, he was a most energetic promoter of the work of the Red Cross Society, of which he was chairman from the time of the Franco-Prussian War, and devoted much time and energy to the advancement of its interests until his death. In connection with the work of the society he was allowed through the German lines and in beleaguered Paris in 1870. In the difficult office of chairman of the society he did laborious service, of which others are now reaping the fruits. "In person," say the Records of the Scots Guards, "Lindsay was tall and handsome, with an almost perfect figure, and was for many years a brilliant ornament of society during the golden age of Queen Victoria. His wide and unostentatious charity was the outcome of a naturally affectionate and generous disposition. 'He was most kind-hearted,' says a contemporary writer, 'not only to men in the aggregate, but to men individually.'" He was much liked and respected, and a high military authority described him as "the best fellow in the world and the straightest man in the Army." His knowledge of pictures was considerable, and he made many notable additions to the fine collection of pictures which came to him and Lady Wantage from her father. Amongst these were Turner's "Sheerness" and "Walton Bridges," and the pair

Robert James Lindsay.

of pictures from the Torriciani Palace in Florence. Lord Wantage died, after a long illness, on 10 June, 1901, at his residence, Lockinge House, Berkshire.

M'KECHNIE, JAMES, Sergt., was *b.* in the town of High Church, in or

James M'Kechnie.

near the town of Paisley, in the county of Renfrew. He was by trade a tinsmith, and enlisted in the Scots Fusilier Regt. of Foot Guards on 11 Feb. 1845. He was attested to the said regiment at Edinburgh on 11 Feb. 1845, at the age of 18 years and five months. He was promoted Corpl. 12 Sept. 1847, and Sergt. 12 Jan. 1853. Sergt. M'Kechnie is described as being five feet nine and three-quarter inches in height, of fresh complexion, with blue eyes and brown hair. He served abroad in the East from 28 Feb. 1854, to 4 July, 1856, at the Alma, Balaklava and Sebastopol, and for his services at the Alma was awarded the Victoria Cross [London Gazette, 24 Feb. 1857]: " James M'Kechnie, No. 3234, Sergt., Scots Fusilier Guards. When the formation of the regiment was disordered at Alma, for having behaved gallantly and rallied the men round the Colours." When the shot and shell from the batteries just in front of his battalion threw it into momentary disorder, it was forced out of its formation, and became something like a huge triangle, with one corner pointing towards the foe, and at that angle Capt. Robert Lindsay was waving the Queen's Colour, which had the pole smashed and twenty bullet holes through the silk. Sergt. M'Kechnie held up his rifle and dashed for the Colours, calling out, as if advancing in line on parade, " By the centre, Scots, by the centre; look to the Colours and march by them." Sergt. M'Kechnie was wounded (contusion of the side) at the Alma. He served in Canada from 20 Dec. 1861, to 18 Sept. 1864. On 4 Sept. 1865, he was receiving Good Conduct pay at fourpence, and he was discharged at his own request to pension at the age of 39 years nine months, making a total service of 21 years and three days. He intended to reside at Glasgow. His character was reported by the Regimental Board to be that of " a very good and sober soldier. He is in possession of four Good Conduct badges and the Victoria Cross. Pension awarded, one shilling for life." Sergt. M'Kechnie died on 5 July, 1886.

REYNOLDS, WILLIAM, Private, was *b.* in the parish of St. Stephen's,

William Reynolds.

near the town of Edinburgh, in the County Edinburgh, and was by trade a mason. He is described as having a fresh complexion, grey eyes and black hair. He was five feet eleven inches in height, and " tattoo'd with an anchor on the left arm." He enlisted for the Scots Fusilier Regt. of Foot Guards on 2 April, 1846; was attested for the same regiment at Edinburgh on 4 April, 1846, aged eighteen years and eight months. He served in the East from 28 Feb. 1854, to 4 July, 1856, at the Alma, Balaklava, Inkerman and Sebastopol, and was awarded the Victoria Cross [London Gazette, 24 Feb. 1857]: " William Reynolds, No. 3368, Private, Scots Fusilier Guards. When the formation of the line was disordered at Alma, for having behaved in a conspicuous manner in rallying the men round the Colours." On 4 April, 1857, he was getting one penny per diem Good Conduct pay, and he was discharged on 15 Oct. 1867, at his own request, to pension, at the age of forty years and two months, having completed twenty-one years' service. His character was reported by the Regimental Board to be that of " a good and efficient soldier, trustworthy and sober; he is in possession of two Good Conduct badges. Pension, tenpence per diem for life. Intends to reside at London." Private Reynolds died on 20 Oct. 1869.

PROSSER, JOSEPH, Private, joined the Royal Regt.; served in the Crimean War, and was—on its institution—awarded the Victoria Cross [London Gazette, 24 Feb. 1857]: " Joseph Prosser, No. 1672, Private, 1st Regt. The Royal Scots. On 16 June, 1855, when on duty in the trenches before Sebastopol, for pursuing and apprehending (whilst exposed to two cross-fires) a soldier in the act of deserting to the enemy. 2nd.—On 11 Aug. 1855, before Sebastopol, for leaving the most advanced trench, and assisting to carry in a soldier of the 95th Regt. who lay severely wounded and unable to move. This gallant and humane act was performed under a very heavy fire from the enemy." Private J. Prosser died either in 1869 or in 1870.

MAUDE, FREDERICK FRANCIS, Major, *b.* 20 Dec. 1821; was 4th *s.* of the late Rev. the Honourable J. C. Maude. On 13 March, 1840, he joined the Buffs, and became a Lieut. on 27 Aug. 1841. He served through the Gwalior Campaign of 1843-44 as Adjutant of the Buffs, and was present at the Battle of Punniar on 29 Dec. 1843, in which he had his horse shot under him, and for which he received the Bronze Star. In 1853 he married Catherine, dau. of the Very Rev. Sir George Bisshopp, eighth baronet. Lady Maude died in 1892. He served in the Crimean Campaign from April, 1855, including both the assaults on the Redan, on 18 June, in reserve, and 8 Sept., and the Siege and Fall of Sebastopol. He commanded the Buffs from 3 Aug. to 8 Sept., on which

date he commanded the covering and ladder party of the 2nd Division, furnished by his regiment, at the final assault of the Redan. He was dangerously wounded; was mentioned in Despatches; received the

Frederick F. Maude.

brevet rank of Lieut.-Colonel, the Medal with clasp, the C.B., the Fifth Class of the Medjidie and the Turkish Medal; was made a Knight of the Legion of Honour, and—on its institution—was awarded the Victoria Cross [London Gazette, 24 Feb. 1857]: " Frederick Francis Maude, Brevet Lieut.-Colonel, the 3rd Regt. Date of Act of Bravery, 8 Sept. 1855. For conspicuous and most devoted bravery on 8 Sept. 1855, when in charge of the covering and ladder party of the 2nd Division, in the assault of the Redan, to which he gallantly led his men. Having entered the Redan, he, with only nine or ten men, held a position between traverses, and only retired when all hope of support was at an end, himself dangerously wounded." He became Lieut.-Colonel on 2 Nov. 1855, and Colonel on 30 May, 1861. Colonel Maude served as A.A.G. at Gibraltar from 1861 to 1866, and was Inspector-General of Irish Militia from 1867 to 1873. He became a Major-General on 6 March, 1868, and commanded a division in India from 1875 to 1880, including the 2nd command of the 2nd Division Peshawar Valley Field Force during the campaign of 1878-79 in Afghanistan. For the latter service he was mentioned in Despatches, received the thanks of both Houses of Parliament, and was made a K.C.B. He was placed on the Retired List as General in 1885, and was created a G.C.B. in 1886. General Sir F. F. Maude died at his residence, Sutherland Tower, Torquay, on Sunday morning, 20 June, 1897. He was the father of the late Lieut.-General Sir Stanley Maude, late Commander-in-Chief of the Army in Mesopotamia.

CONNORS, JOSEPH, Private, served in the Crimean Campaign, and for his services was, on its institution, awarded the Victoria Cross [London Gazette, 24 Feb. 1857]: " Joseph Connors, Private, No. 2649, 3rd Regt. Distinguished himself most conspicuously at the assault on the Redan 8 Sept. 1855, in personal conflict with the Russians; rescued an officer of the 30th Regt., who was surrounded by Russians, by shooting one and bayoneting another, and was observed inside the Redan in personal conflict with the Russians for some time. Was selected by his company for the French War Medal."

HUGHES, MATTHEW, Private, served in the Crimean War, and for

Matthew Hughes.

his services in that campaign was awarded the Victoria Cross on its institution [London Gazette, 24 Feb. 1857]: " Matthew Hughes, Private, No. 1879, 7th Royal Fusiliers. Was noticed by Colonel Campbell, 90th Light Infantry, on 7 June, 1855, at the storming of the Quarries, for twice going for ammunition, under a heavy fire, across the open ground; he also went to the front, and brought in Private John Hampton, who was lying severely wounded; and on 18 June, 1855, he volunteered to bring in Lieut. Hobson, 7th Royal Fusiliers, who was lying severely wounded, and in the act of doing so was severely wounded himself." Private Hughes was presented with his Victoria Cross at the first Investiture in Hyde Park 26 June, 1857. He died on 9 Jan. 1882.

NORMAN, WILLIAM, Private, joined the Royal Fusiliers; served in the Crimean War, and was, on its institution, awarded the Victoria Cross for his services in that campaign [London Gazette, 24 Feb. 1857]: " William Norman, Private, 7th Regt. On the night of 19 Dec. 1854, he was placed on single sentry, some distance in front of the advanced sentries of an outlying picket in the White Horse Ravine, a post of much danger, and requiring great vigilance; the Russian picquet was posted about 300 yards in his front; three Russian soldiers advanced, under cover of the brushwood, for the purpose of reconnoitring. Private William Norman, single-handed, took two of them prisoners, without alarming the Russian picquet." Private Nor-

William Norman.

man was decorated by Queen Victoria at the first presentation in Hyde Park, 26 June, 1857. He died 13 March, 1896.

MOYNIHAN, ANDREW, Ensign, *b.* 1 Jan. 1867. He served in the Crimean War. This gallant officer greatly distinguished himself in the trenches before Sebastopol, and earned for himself, by his daring gallantry at the last bloody assault on the Redan, where he received twelve wounds, the much coveted distinction of the Victoria Cross [London Gazette, 24 Feb. 1857]: " Andrew Moynihan, Ensign, 8th Regt. When

Segt., 90th Light Infantry, at the assault on the Redan 8 Sept. 1855, personally encountered and killed five Russians, and rescued from near the Redan a wounded officer under a heavy fire."

Andrew Moynihan.

"Soon afterwards," says the "Army and Navy Gazette" of 1 June, 1867, " his services were still further rewarded by promotion to the rank of Ensign. At the termination of the Crimean War he proceeded to join the 8th Regt., then engaged in suppressing the great Indian Mutiny, and was present at the defeat of the rebels in several actions during the campaigns of 1857, 1858 and 1859. The following *résumé* of his services is taken from 'Hart's Quarterly Army List': 'Capt. Moynihan served with the 90th Light Infantry in the Crimea from 5 Dec. 1854, including the Siege and Fall of Sebastopol, capture of the Quarries on 7 June, attack of the Redan on 18 June, and assault of the Redan on 8 Sept., with the storming party, being the first man to enter, and was made prisoner when rescuing the body of Lieut. Swift from a party of Russians inside the Redan, but was released by an advance of the British after having been twice bayoneted. He held a position inside the Redan for a considerable time, and was again wounded in several places. After all the men had retired into the trenches from the assault, he recrossed the open ground under a terrific fire, and rescued from near the Redan a wounded officer. Mentioned in Despatches (Medal and clasp, Victoria Cross, Turkish Medal and French War Medal). Served in the Indian Campaign from Nov. 1857, and was present at the defeat of the rebels in the ravines of the Chumbal, attack and capture of Bhugah and Sevrale; also served in the Oude campaign of 1858–59, including the attack and capture of the fort and town of Sandee (Medal).' This is a brief statement of the services performed in the field by this distinguished officer; they are such as might be expected from a man who possessed in a very high degree all those physical and moral qualities which constitute the beau-ideal of a model British soldier. He was powerfully built, capable both of undergoing prolonged fatigue, and of making the most vigorous exertion. His intelligence was quick and penetrating, his character was decided and energetic, and his habits exceedingly simple and temperate. He possessed a minute knowledge of everything connected with the exercises and management of infantry soldiers. To perfect the training and promote the welfare of the men under his command was an object which absorbed every other interest, and to which he devoted all his time and all his thoughts. There is, we venture to say, no company in the British Army more perfect in all its arrangements than that which now mourns the premature loss of its distinguished captain—Andrew Moynihan. His body was interred with military honours in the Ta Braxia Cemetery on Monday, the 20th instant, and was followed to the grave by all the officers of both battalions of his regiment, and by Major-General Atherley, and the staff of the garrison, and very many of the other officers of the division, and of the Royal Navy." The "Army and Navy Gazette" of 1 June, 1867, says also : " We much regret having to announce the death of Capt. A. Moynihan, V.C., of the 2nd Battn. 8th (The King's) Regt., Acting Inspector of Musketry, Malta, which melancholy event took place on Sunday last, the 19th inst. at his residence, Floriana, after a short but severe attack of fever." Sir Berkeley Moynihan, C.B., is a son of Capt. Moynihan's.

SMITH, PHILIP, Corpl., joined the Leicestershire Regt. ; served in the Crimean War, and was, on its institution, awarded the Victoria Cross [London Gazette, 24 Feb. 1857]: " Philip Smith, Corpl. (L.-Sergt.), 17th Regt. For repeatedly going out in front of the advanced trenches against the Great Redan on 18 June, 1855, under a heavy fire, after the column had retired from the assault, and bringing in wou ded comrades." Corpl. Smith died on 16 Jan. 1906.

LYONS, JOHN, Private, served in the Crimean War, and was, on its institution, awarded the Victoria Cross [London Gazette, 24 eb. 1857]: " John Lyons, No. 1051, Private, 19th Regt. For, on 10 June, 1855, taking up a live shell which fell among the guard of the trenches, and throwing it over the parapet." Private Lyons was decorated by Queen Victoria at the first presentation in Hyde Park, 26 June, 1857.

BELL, EDWARD WILLIAM DERRINGTON, Brevet Lieut.-Colonel, was *b.* 18 May, 1824 ; *s.* of Lieut.-General Edward Wells Bell, late of the 7th Royal Fusiliers, who fought at Vittoria and Salamanca, and later

Edward W. D. Bell.

was Governor of Jamaica. He was educated at Sandhurst from the age of 14, and joined the Army in April, 1842, going out to Canada. He became Capt. in Dec. 1848. He served in the Crimean War, including the Battles of the Alma and Inkerman and the Siege of Sebastopol. At the Battle of the Alma, 20 Sept. 1854 : " Some Englishmen—or many, perhaps, at the same moment—looking keen through the smoke, saw teams of artillery horses moving, and there was a sound of ordnance wheels. Our panting soldiery broke from their silence : ' By all that is holy ! he is limbering up !' ' He is carrying off his guns !' ' Stole away ! Stole away !' The glacis of the Great Redoubt had come to sound more joyous than the covert's side in England. The embrasures were empty, and in rear of the work, long artillery teams—eight-horse and ten-horse teams—were rapidly dragging off the guns " (Kinglake's " Invasion of the Crimea," Vol. II., pp. 333 and 334). When the redoubt was taken by our troops, " There was only one piece of ordnance remaining in the work. This was a brass 24-pound howitzer. . . . But there was a better prize than this within the reach of a nimble soldier, for of the guns moving off towards the rear there was one which, dragged by only three horses, had scarcely yet gained the rear of the redoubt. Capt. Bell, of the Royal Welsh, ran up, overtook it, and pointing his capless pistol at the head of the driver, ordered him, or rather signed to him, to stop instantly and dismount. The driver sprang from his saddle and fled. Bell seized the bridle of the near horse, and he had already turned the gun round, when, Sir George Brown riding up angry, and ordering him to go to his company, he of course obeyed, yet not until he had effectually started the horses in the right direction, for they drew the gun down the hill, and the capture became complete. Bell went back to his corps, and, in truth, his services were soon about to be needed, for already Colonel Chester, commanding the regiment, had been killed," and Capt. Campbell, who next took command, being wounded and having to fall to the rear, the honour of bringing the 23rd Royal Welsh Fusiliers out of action devolved upon Capt. Bell. This was the first and only effective field gun captured from the enemy. It was afterwards known as Bell's gun, and was brought to England, and in 1885 was sent to the brigade depot at Wrexham, where it now stands, in front of the officers' mess. The horses were afterwards used in the Black Battery. He was awarded the Victoria Cross [London Gazette, 24 Feb. 1857]: " Edward William Derrington Bell, Lieut.-Colonel, Royal Welsh Fusiliers. Date of Act of Bravery 20 Sept. 1854. Recommended for his gallantry, more particularly at the Battle of the Alma, where he was the first to seize upon and capture one of the enemy's guns, which was limbered up and being carried off. He, moreover, succeeded to the command of that gallant reigment, which he brought out of action, all his senior officers having been killed or wounded." For his services in this campaign Capt. Bell received, in addition to the Victoria Cross, the Brevets of Major (April, 1854) and Lieut.-Colonel, and the British Crimean Medal with three clasps (Alma, Inkerman and Sebastopol), and was mentioned in Despatches. He was given the Legion of Honour by the French, and the Turkish War Medal. Major R. Broughton–Mainwaring says, in the " Historical Records of the Royal Welsh Fusiliers," that in 1857 that regiment left England for China in three divisions. The 3rd Division, under the command of Lieut.-Colonel Bell, V.C., embarked on 23 June in H.M.S. Melville. When the news came of the outbreak of the Indian Mutiny, the troops were ordered to India. Delayed by adverse winds, H.M.S. Melville did not arrive at Calcutta until 18 Nov., when Lieut.-Colonel Bell's division at once disembarked and proceeded up country to join headquarters. On 12 Dec. three companies, under Lieut.-Colonel Bell, V.C., joined the headquarters at the Alambagh. He was present at the Siege and Capture of Lucknow. He crossed the Goomtee under Sir James Outram, who mentioned him in two Despatches. For his services in this campaign he received the Indian Mutiny Medal with the clasp for Lucknow. Lieut.-Colonel Bell was appointed to the command of the 2nd Battn. 14th Regt., but returned to his old corps, raising the 2nd Battn. at Malta, and commanded it for twelve years, afterwards going on half-pay until 1872, when he was given the command of the Regimental Depot at Wrexham, just formed. In 1866 orders were received for the 2nd Battn. Royal Welsh Fusiliers to proceed to British North America (Canada), and it embarked under the command of Colonel Bell, V.C., on board H.M.S. Orontes, and sailed on 23 July, 1866. On the voyage the ship touched at Fayal, where the band was landed and played in the public gardens. The battalion arrived at Quebec on 11 July, when it was ordered to Montreal. It arrived there on 13 July. He attained the rank of Major-General in 1868, and was in command of the Belfast Division from Feb. 1875, up to the time of his death, which occurred on 10 Nov. 1879, at his residence, Lisbreen, Fort William Park, Belfast. An obituary notice of Major-General E. W. D. Bell, V.C., C.B., appeared in the " Times " of 11 Nov. 1879. He was in receipt of a reward for distinguished service, and was mentioned seven times in Despatches. He held the Order of the Medjidie. He married on 3 Aug. 1869, Charlotte Wadsworth, *née* Bartell, widow of John Davies, Surgeon, at St. Mary's Church, Cheltenham, by whom he had four children : Caroline Mary Ann, Margaret Derrington, William Edward Derrington, born in 1874, and Katharine Annabella. Lieut.-General Bell (Major-General Bell's father) married a sister of Sir Thomas Chapman, Bart., of Killua Castle, co. Westmeath, she having previously married Capt. Battersby, R.N., who was in command of the ship which took Napoleon to St. Helena.

O'CONNOR, LUKE, Sergt. ; *b.* 21 Feb. 1831, at Elphin, co. Roscommon,

Luke O'Connor.

and enlisted in the Royal Welsh Fusiliers in 1849, at the age of 17, becoming Sergt. in 1850. With his Regt. he landed in the Crimea, 14 Sept. 1854, and soon came under fire afterwards on the heights of the Alma, where the closely contested battle had begun. The 23rd had just come within range of fire, when, says Kinglake, " a small, childlike youth ran forward before the throng, carrying a Colour ; this was young Anstruther. He carried the Queen's Colour of the Royal Welsh." On his falling mortally wounded, the Colour was picked up by Private Evans, who gave it to Corpl. Luby, an Irishman, who afterwards received the Distinguished Service Medal. Corpl. Luby in his turn gave the Colour to Sergt. Luke O'Connor, who rushed forward in face of a withering fire and planted the Colour on the Redoubt before those of the enemy who were near at hand could realize their perilous position. The effect on the advancing battalion was instantaneous. The gallant 23rd saw what the heroism of one man, Sergt. O'Connor, had accomplished, and pressed onwards to his support. Within a few seconds the position had been carried at the point of the bayonet. When this was accomplished, O'Connor was urged to put himself in the doctor's hands, but he pleaded so hard to be allowed to go through with it that he had his way. Thus he carried the Colour till the battle was over, received the praise and thanks of Sir George Brown and Col. Codrington on the field, before his assembled comrades, and was told that he would be recommended for a commission. "His own simple comment on his exploit in later years was that he ' only did a soldier's duty.' " He was appointed to an ensigncy whilst in hospital, but he was to receive a greater honour than this, for, when the new decoration was created, the Victoria Cross was awarded to him [London Gazette, 24 Feb. 1857]: "Luke O'Connor, Lieut., 23rd Regt. Dates of Acts of Bravery : 20 Sept. 1854, and 8 Sept. 1855. Was one of the centre sergeants at the Battle of the Alma, and advanced between the officers carrying the Colour. When near the Redoubt, Lieut. Anstruther, who was carrying the Colour, was mortally wounded, and he was shot in the breast at the same time, and fell, but recovered himself, snatched the Colour from the ground, and continued to carry it to the end of the action, although urged by Capt. Granville to relinquish it on account of his wound ; was recommended for and received his commission for his services at the Alma. Also behaved with great gallantry at the assault on the Redan, 8 Sept. 1855, where he was shot through both thighs." The Cross was pinned on his breast by Queen Victoria at the great military parade in Hyde Park on 26 June, 1857. O'Connor had become Lieut. in Feb. 1855, and had returned to duty in time to be present at the Siege and Fall of Sebastopol, the attack on the Quarries, and the assaults of 18 June and 8 Sept. On the latter occasion he again distinguished himself by what was described as "his cool heroism and the splendid example he set to all about him." For his services in the Crimea in addition to the Victoria Cross, he received the Medal with two clasps, the Sardinian and Turkish Medals, and the 5th Class of the Medjidie. On the outbreak of the Mutiny in 1857, the 23rd—which had returned home at the end of the Crimean War—at once embarked for China, but was ordered to India, and there O'Connor saw service under Sir Colin Campbell in the operations for the Second Relief of Lucknow. He was present at the defeat of the Gwalior Contingent at Cawnpore, at the Siege and Fall of Lucknow, the operations across the Coomtee, under Outram, and in several minor affairs. He was promoted to Captain in Aug. 1858, and received the Mutiny Medal with clasp. At the end of 1873, after several uneventful years, he took part in Sir Garnet Wolseley's expedition to Kumasi, having then attained his Majority. For this campaign he received a brevet Lieut.-Colonelcy and the Medal with clasp. On 24 June, 1884, he succeeded to the command of the 2nd Battn. The Royal Welsh Fusiliers, and in 1886 he went on half-pay with the rank of Colonel. He was granted the Distinguished Service Reward, and retired on 2 March, 1887, with the rank of Major-General ; was created a C.B. in 1900, and a K.C.B. in 1913, and in 1914 was appointed honorary Colonel of his old regiment. Sir Luke O'Connor became ill, and, after lingering in a critical condition for some time, died in London on 1 Feb. 1915, in his 84th year.

SHIELDS, ROBERT, Corpl., joined the Royal Welsh Fusiliers, served in the Crimea, and for his services was awarded the Victoria Cross, on its institution [London Gazette, 24 Feb. 1857]: "Robert Shields, No. 2945, Corpl., 23rd Regt. For volunteering on 8 Sept. 1855, to go out to the front from the 5th parallel, after the attack on the Redan, to bring in Lieut. Dyneley, who was wounded, and found afterwards to be mortally so."

COFFEY, WILLIAM, Private, served in the Crimean Campaign, and for his services was awarded the Victoria Cross on its institution [London Gazette, 24 Feb. 1857]: "William Coffey, No. 3837, Private, 34th Regt. For having, on 29 March, 1855, thrown a lighted shell, that fell into a trench, over the parapet." Private Coffey was decorated by Queen Victoria at the first Investiture in Hyde Park, 26 June, 1857.

John J. Sims.

SIMS, JOHN J., Private, served in the Crimean Campaign, and was awarded the Victoria Cross on its institution [London Gazette, 24 Feb. 1857]: "John J. Sims, No. 3482, Private, 34th Regt. For having, on 18 June, 1855, after the Regiment had retired into the trenches from the assault on the Redan, gone out into the open ground under a heavy fire, in broad daylight, and brought in wounded soldiers outside the trenches." Private Sims was presented with his Victoria Cross at the inauguration of the new decoration in Hyde Park, 26 June, 1857.

ROWLANDS, HUGH, Brevet Major ; b. in 1829, s. of John Rowlands, Esq., J.P., D.L. (Carnarvonshire), and Elizabeth Hartwell. He obtained his first commission at the age of 20 as Ensign in the 41st Foot, becoming Captain in Aug. 1854. In the latter year, he proceeded with his regiment to the Crimea and was present at the Battle of the Alma, the repulse of the Russian sortie of 26 Oct., and for his gallantry at the Battle of Inkerman—where he was severely wounded—was awarded the Victoria Cross [London Gazette, 24 Feb. 1857]: "Hugh Rowlands, Brevet Major, 41st Regt. For having rescued Col. Haly, of the 47th Regt., from Russian soldiers, Col. Haly having been wounded and surrounded by them, and for gallant exertions in holding the ground occupied by his advance picquet against the enemy at the commence-

ment of the Battle of Inkerman." His name appeared in the first list of recipients of the new decoration. On recovering from his wounds he rejoined his regiment and took part in the work of the Siege of Sebastopol, including the attack on the Quarries, 7 June, two attacks on the Rifle Pits, and also the two attacks on the Redan on 18 June and 8 Sept., being again wounded. In addition to the Victoria Cross, he received the Medal with three clasps, was promoted Major by brevet, appointed a Knight of the Legion of Honour, awarded the 5th Class of the Medjidie and the Turkish Medal, and nominated a Companion of the Bath (1875). In 1866 he succeeded to the command of his regiment, and from May, 1875, to 1878 he also commanded the 34th Regt., attaining in the meantime the rank of Colonel. In 1867, he m. Isabella Jane, the dau. of T. J. R. Barrow, Esq., R.N., of Ryelands, Gloucestershire. In 1878 he was employed on special service at Luneberg, South Africa, and commanded the troops in action

Hugh Rowlands.

with the Kaffirs at Tolako Mountain, for which service he was mentioned in Despatches and received the Medal and clasp. He was promoted Major-General in 1881, Lieut.-General in 1890, and General in 1894, and filled in succession various appointments both at home and in India, the more important being the command of a 1st Class District in Madras from 1884 to 1889, the office for a few months of Lieutenant of the Tower of London, and the command of the Scottish district from 1894 to 1896, when he retired from the active list. In 1897 he was appointed Colonel of the West Riding Regt., and the following year created a K.C.B. General Sir Hugh Rowlands died on Sunday, 1 Aug., 1909, at Plas Tirion, his birthplace, near Carnarvon, in his 82nd year.

MADDEN, AMBROSE, Sergt.-Major, joined the Welsh Regiment ; served in the Crimean War, and for his services in that campaign was awarded the Victoria Cross [London Gazette, 24 Feb. 1857]: " Ambrose Madden, Sergt.-Major, 41st Regt. For having headed a party of men of the 41st Regt., and having cut off and taken prisoners one Russian officer and fourteen privates, three of whom he, personally and alone, captured." Sergt.-Major A. Madden was appointed an Ensign in the West India Regt. on 24 Dec. 1858.

McWHEENEY, WILLIAM, Sergt., served in the Crimean War, and for his services was awarded the Victoria Cross [London Gazette, 24 Feb. 1857]: "William McWheeney, Sergt., 44th Foot. Volunteered as a sharp-shooter at the commencement of the siege, and was in charge of the party of the 44th Regt. ; was always vigilant and active, and signalized himself on 20 Oct. 1854, when one of his party, Private John Keane, 44th Regt., was dangerously wounded on the Woronzoff Road, at the time the sharp-shooters were repulsed from the Quarries by overwhelming numbers. Sergt. McWheeney, on his return, took the wounded man on his back, and brought him to a place of safety. This was under a very heavy fire. He was also the means of saving the life of Corpl. Courtney. This man was one of the sharp-shooters, and was severely wounded in the head, 5 Dec. 1854. Sergt. McWheeney brought him in from under the fire, and dug up a slight cover with his bayonet, where the two remained until dark, when they retired. Sergt. McWheeney volunteered for the advanced guard of General Eyre's Brigade in the Cemetery on 18 June, 1855, and was never absent from duty during the war." He died 17 May, 1866.

William McWheeney.

M'DERMOND, JOHN, Private, served in the Crimean Campaign, and was awarded the Victoria Cross on its institution [London Gazette, 24 Feb. 1857]: "John M'Dermond, No. 2040, Private, 47th Regt. For saving the life of Col. Haly, on 5 Nov. 1854, by his intrepid conduct in rushing up to his rescue when lying on the ground, disabled and surrounded by a party of Russians, and killing the man who disabled him." This heroic action is also described in the Gazette of Brevet Major Hugh Rowlands's Victoria Cross : " For rescuing Col. Haly, of the 47th Regt., from Russian soldiers, Col. Haly having been wounded and surrounded by them, and for gallant exertions in holding the ground occupied by his advanced picket against the enemy at the commencement of the Battle of Inkerman." He was promoted to Corpl. Corpl. M'Dermond died 22 July, 1868.

John M'Dermond.

WALTERS, GEORGE, Sergt., served in the Crimean Campaign, and was awarded the Victoria Cross [London Gazette, 24 Feb. 1857]: "George Walters, Sergt., 49th Regt. Highly distinguished himself at the Battle of Inkerman, in having rescued Brigadier-General Adams, C.B., when surrounded by Russians, one of whom he bayoneted." Sergt. Walters was decorated by Queen Victoria at the first presentation of the new decoration, 26 June, 1857. He joined the London Police Force, and died on 3 June, 1872. His Cross was sold with six others in Nov. 1910, for £72.

James Owens.

OWENS, JAMES, Corpl., enlisted in the 49th Regt. (now the 1st Battn. The Royal Berkshire Regt.), and served in the Crimea. He was present at the Alma, Inkerman and Sebastopol, and was awarded the Victoria Cross [London Gazette, 24 Feb. 1857]: "James Owens, Corpl., 49th Regt. Greatly distinguished himself on 30 Oct. 1854, in personal encounter with the Russians, and nobly assisted Major Conolly, Coldstream Guards." Queen Victoria presented Corpl. Owens with his Victoria Cross at the first Investiture in Hyde Park, 26 June, 1857. He also received the Medal with clasps for the Alma, Inkerman and Sebastopol. He was promoted to Sergt. Owens died on Tuesday night, 20 Aug. 1901, at Romford, aged 75. An obituary notice of him appeared in the "Times" of 22 Aug. 1901.

BEACH, THOMAS, Private, served in the Crimean Campaign, and for his services was awarded the Victoria Cross [London Gazette, 24 Feb. 1857]: "Thomas Beach, Private, 55th Regt. For conspicuous gallantry at the Battle of Inkerman, 5 Nov. 1854, when on picquet, in attacking several Russians who were plundering Lieut.-Colonel Carpenter, 41st Regt., who was lying wounded on the ground. He killed two of the Russians, and protected Lieut.-Colonel Carpenter until the arrival of some men of the 41st Regt." He died 24 Aug. 1864.

ELTON, FREDERICK COCKAYNE, Brevet Major, joined the 55th Regt. 19 Jan. 1849 ; became Lieut. 30 April, 1852, and served throughout the Eastern Campaign of 1854 and 1855, being present at the Battle of Inkerman, the memorable Siege and Fall of Sebastopol, the sortie of Oct. 26, the attack on the Quarries, and the assault on the Redan. For his gallant services during the attack on the Quarries he was mentioned in Despatches. He had succeeded to the command of his regiment, and brought it out of action in such a skilful manner that he was again mentioned in Despatches, and was afterwards present at an action in the trenches, where he was wounded. For his services in this campaign he received the Crimean Medal with two clasps, the 5th Class of the Medjidie and the Turkish Medal. He was also created a Knight of the Legion of Honour and given the brevet of Major and subsequently awarded the Victoria Cross [London Gazette, 24 Feb. 1857]:

Frederick C. Elton.

" Frederick Cockayne Elton, Brevet Major, 55th Regt. Dates of Acts of Bravery : 4 Aug. 1855 ; March, 1855, and 7 June, 1855. For distinguished conduct on the night of the 4 Aug. 1855, when in command of a working party in the advanced trenches in front of the Quarries, in encouraging and inciting his men, by his example, to work under a dreadful fire ; and when there was some hesitation shown in consequence of the severity of the fire, going into the open and working with pick and shovel —thus showing the best possible example to the men. In the words of one of them, ' There was not another officer in the British Army who would have done what Major Elton did that night.' In the month of March, 1855, Major Elton volunteered with a small party of men, to drive off a body of Russians who were destroying one of our new detached works, and succeeded in doing so, taking prisoner one of the enemy with his own hands. On the night of the 7th of June, 1855, Major Elton was the first of the party to leave our trenches leading his men ; when in the Quarries, he several times rallied his men around him." He became Major 2 Nov. 1855, and was afterwards Lieut.-Colonel, 21st Fusiliers. Lieut.-Colonel F. C. Elton died 24 March, 1888, and an obituary notice in the "Times" of 28 March says : " By the death of Lieut.-Colonel Frederick C. Elton, V.C. (late of the 21st Royal Scots Fusiliers and the 55th (Border) Regt.), which occurred in London on the 24th inst., at the age of 55, the Army has lost one of its bravest officers. . . . The death of Lieut.-Colonel Elton will be regretted by all who knew him, and has deprived the Queen and country of an officer distinguished by his gallantry and devotion to the Service."

McCURRIE, CHARLES, Private, served in the Crimean War, and for his services was awarded the Victoria Cross [London Gazette, 24 Feb. 1857]: " Charles McCurrie, No. 1971, Private, 57th Regt. On the night of 23 June, 1855, he threw over the parapet a live shell which had been thrown from the enemy's battery." Private McCurrie died 8 April, 1857, less than two months after his Victoria Cross was gazetted.

HAMILTON, THOMAS DE COURCY, Capt., b. 20 July, 1825 ; second s. of the late T. T. Hamilton, of Ballymacoll, County Meath ; and a gdson. on his mother's side of the twenty-sixth Baron Kingsale. He joined the 90th Light Infantry 30 Sept. 1842, and served with this regiment in South Africa during the Kaffir Wars of 1846–47. It was, however, in the Crimea that he established his reputation as a soldier. He went to South Russia with the 68th Light Infantry, and served with it throughout the campaign. He took part in the action of the Alma,

the Battles of Balaklava and Inkerman, and the siege operations before Sebastopol. It was in the trenches as a Captain that he won his Victoria Cross, which was awarded to him on the institution of the decoration [London Gazette, 24 Feb. 1857]: " Thomas De Courcy Hamilton, Captain, 68th Regt. Date of Act of Bravery : 11 May, 1855. For having on the night of 11 May, 1855, during a most determined sortie, boldly charged the enemy, with a small force, from a battery of which they had obtained possession in great numbers, thereby saving the works from falling into the hands of the enemy. He was conspicuous on this occasion for his gallantry and daring conduct." Besides the Victoria Cross, Capt. Hamilton received the Crimean Medal with four clasps, the Turkish decoration, and was made a Knight of the Legion of Honour. On his return from the Crimea he was appointed a Brigade Major at Colchester. It was about this time that he married a daughter of the late Sir William Baynes, and accepted a Staff appointment in the Ionian Isles, which he held from 1857 to 1862. He was given his Majority in the 8th Regt. 10 March, 1857, and on promotion five years later was transferred to command the 64th Regt. He became Colonel 20 May, 1873, and retired in 1874 on full pay, with the honorary rank of Major-General. He spent the last twenty-seven years of his life in Cheltenham, where he was very well known, and took a great interest in the formation of the Gordon Boys' Brigade. He died 3 March, 1908, at his residence, Dunboyne, Cheltenham.

Thomas De C. Hamilton.

BYRNE, JOHN, Private, served in the Crimean War, and on its institution was awarded the Victoria Cross [London Gazette, 24 Feb. 1857]: " John Byrne, Private, 68th Regt. At the Battle of Inkerman, when the Regt. was ordered to retire, Private John Byrne went back at the risk of his own life and brought in a wounded soldier under fire. On 11 May, 1855, he, having engaged in a hand-to-hand conflict with one of the enemy on a parapet of the work he was defending, prevented the entrance of the enemy, killed his antagonist and captured his arms." Private Byrne died 6 Dec. 1872.

PARK, JOHN, Sergt., served during the Crimean War, and for his services was awarded the Victoria Cross [London Gazette, 24 Feb. 1857]: " John Park, No. 2100, Sergt., 77th Regt. For conspicuous bravery at the Battles of Alma and Inkerman. Highly distinguished himself at the taking of the Russian Rifle Pits on the night of 19 April, 1855. His valour during that attack called forth the approbation of the late Colonel Egerton. He was severely wounded. Remarked for determined resolution at both attacks on the Redan." Sergt. Park died 18 May, 1863.

WRIGHT, ALEXANDER, Private, served in the Crimean Campaign, and on its institution was awarded the Victoria Cross [London Gazette, 24 Feb. 1857]: " Alexander Wright, Private, No. 2239, 77th Regt. For conspicuous bravery through the whole Crimean War. Highly distinguished on the night of 22 March, 1855, in repelling a sortie. Highly distinguished at the taking of the Rifle Pits on the night of 19 April, 1855 ; remarked for the great encouragement he gave the men while holding the Pits under a terrible fire. He was wounded. Highly distinguished on 30 Aug. 1855." Private A. Wright died 28 July, 1858.

ALEXANDER, JOHN, Private, served in the Crimean War, and was awarded the Victoria Cross for his services in this campaign [London Gazette, 24 Feb. 1857]: " John Alexander, Private, No. 2932, 90th Regt. After the attack on the Redan, 18 June, 1855, went out of the trenches under a very heavy fire, and brought in several wounded men. Also when with a working party in the most advanced trench on 6 Sept. 1855, went out in front of the trenches under a very heavy fire, and assisted in bringing in Capt. Buckley, Scots Fusilier Guards, being dangerously wounded." Private Alexander never lived to receive the Victoria Cross he had deserved so well, for he was killed 24 Sept. 1857, during the Relief of the Rendary of Lucknow.

LUMLEY, CHARLES, Capt. and Brevet Major, joined the Army 30 Aug. 1844 ; became Lieut. 18 Feb. 1848 ; Capt. 29 Dec. 1854, and Brevet Major 2 Nov. 1855. He served in the Crimean War, and for his services in this campaign was awarded the Victoria Cross [London Gazette, 24 Feb. 1857]: " Charles Lumley, Capt. and Brevet Major, 97th Regt. For having distinguished himself highly by his bravery at the assault on the Redan 8 Sept. 1855, being amongst the first inside the work, where he was immediately engaged with three Russian gunners, reloading a field piece, who attacked him ; he shot two of them with his revolver, when he was knocked down by a stone which stunned him for the moment, but on recovery he drew his sword, and was in the act of cheering his men on, when he received a ball in his mouth, which wounded him most severely." He received the Victoria Cross from Queen Victoria at the first presentation in Hyde Park 26 June, 1857. He was promoted to Major 4 Dec. 1857 ; was Major, unattached, in 1858, and died in that year.

COLEMAN, JOHN, Sergt., served in the Crimean Campaign, and for his services was awarded the Victoria Cross [London Gazette, 24 Feb. 1857]: " John Coleman, Sergt., 97th Regt. Conspicuous for great bravery and coolness on the night of 30 Aug. 1855, when the enemy attacked ' New Sap,' and drove the working party in ; he remained in the open, perfectly exposed to the enemy's rifle pits, until all around him had been killed or wounded. He finally carried one of his officers, who was mortally wounded, to the rear." He was personally decorated by Queen Victoria at the first presentation in Hyde Park 26 June, 1857. Sergt. Coleman died 4 June, 1882.

CLIFFORD, HENRY HUGH, Brevet Major The Honourable; *b.* in 1826; *s.* of the 7th Baron Clifford of Chudleigh, by Mary Lucy, dau. of Thomas Weld, of Lulworth. He entered the Rifle Brigade 5 Aug. 1846; became Lieut. 13 April, 1849, and Capt. 29 Dec. 1854, and served in the Caffre War. He next saw active service in the Crimea, and was awarded the Victoria Cross [London Gazette, 24 Feb. 1857]: " The Honourable Henry Hugh Clifford, Brevet Major, 1st Battn. The Rifle Brigade. For conspicuous courage at the Battle of Inkerman in leading a charge and killing one of the enemy with his sword, disabling another, and saving the life of a soldier." He was personally decorated by Queen Victoria at the first Investiture in Hyde

The Hon. Henry H. Clifford. Park 26 June, 1857. For his services in this campaign he also received the Medal and clasp, the Order of the Medjidie, the Legion of Honour and the Brevet of Major. He became Major 17 July, 1855, and Lieut.-Colonel in 1858. Lieut.-Colonel the Honourable H. H. Clifford served in the China War (Medal), and became Major-General in 1877. He was created a C.B. and a K.C.M.G. He died on Thursday 12 April, 1888, at Ugbrook, near Chudleigh.

CUNINGHAME, WILLIAM JAMES MONTGOMERY, Capt.; *b.* in 1834; the only surv. *s.* of the eighth baronet, Sir Thomas Montgomery Cuninghame, of Corse Hill, Ayrshire (who died in 1870); educ. at Harrow, and entered the Army in 1854. Two years later he was promoted to Capt. in the Rifle Brigade, with the 1st Battn. of which he served throughout the Crimean War, being present at the Battles of the Alma, Balaklava, Inkerman and at the Siege and Fall of Sebastopol. For his services in this campaign he received the Medal with four clasps, the 5th Class of the Medjidie and the Turkish Medal, and was one of the earliest recipients of the Victoria Cross. The decoration was gazetted 24 Feb. 1857: " William James Montgomery Cuninghame, Capt., 1st Battn. Prince Consort's Own Rifle Brigade. Highly distinguished himself at the capture of the Rifle Pits 20 Nov. 1854. His gallantry was recorded in the French

William J. M. Cuninghame. General Orders." Capt. Cuninghame was promoted to Major, and was transferred to the 4th Battn. Royal Scots Fusiliers, in which regiment he was Major and Honorary Lieut.-Colonel. In 1869 he *m.* Elizabeth, dau. of Edward Bourchier Hartopp, Esq., of Dalby Hall, near Melton Mowbray. Their surv. children are : Thomas Andrew Alexander, *b.* 30 March, 1877; Edward, *b.* 1878; Edith Honoria (Mrs. J. A. G. Tilley); Marjory Eva Charlotte; Violet Jessie; Bridget Ann (Mrs. Smith-Rewse). Lieut.-Colonel W. J. Cuninghame succeeded his father as 9th Baronet in 1870. As representative of the male line of the Cuninghame family, he claimed the dormant Earldom of Glencairn. Sir William Cuninghame was elected Conservative Member of Parliame .t for Ayr Burghs in Feb. 1874, and represented the district until April, 1880, when he was defeated in the election. He unsuccessfully contested the College Division of Glasgow in 1885. After his retirement from the Army he took a great interest in the Volunteer Movement, and commanded the Inns of Court Rifles from 1868 (when he succeeded Lieut.-General J. N. Sargent, C.B.) until 1870. He was also Brigadier commanding the Glasgow Infantry Volunteer Brigade from 1888 until not long before his death. He was an Archer of the Royal Body Guard of Scotland. Sir William Cuninghame died 11 Nov, 1897, at Gunton Old Hall, Lowestoft, and was succeeded by the present holder of the title, Sir Thomas Cuninghame, Major in the Rifle Brigade, Lieut.-Colonel on the General Staff, who served in the South African War of 1899-1902; was wounded at Vaalkrantz, and was awarded the Distinguished Service Order. He subsequently served as Military Attaché to the Courts of Vienna and Cettinje (1912-1914) and Athens (1915). In the European War he served from 1914 on the staff of the British Expeditionary Force (Battles of Marne, Aisne, Ypres) and in the Dardanelles. Sir William Cuninghame's second son, Lieut.-Colonel Edward Cuninghame, Royal Artillery, served in the South African War of 1899-1902, and in the European War at Le Cateau, the Marne, Aisne, Ypres, and afterwards in Palestine.

BOURCHIER, CLAUDE THOMAS, Brevet Major, obtained his first commission in the Rifle Brigade in the spring of 1849, and eminently distinguished himself by his gallantry. He served with the Rifle Brigade in the Caffre War of 1852-53, also in the Eastern Campaign of 1854, including the Battles of the Alma, Balaklava and Inkerman (in the latter as Aide-de-Camp to General Torrens), and at the Siege of Sebastopol. Sir William Cope says in his " History of the Rifle Brigade " (pages 323-327): " The Russian riflemen having established themselves in some rifle pits in front of the left attack along some rising ground, annoyed our working parties, as well as those on the other side of the ravine, by their fire. Lord Raglan determined to drive them back and to take possession of the pits. These pits, caverns, or ' ovens,' as they were called by the men, are formed by the decay of softer portions of the rock between the harder strata, leaving caves in the side of the hill. The duty of driving the Russians from them was confided to the 1st Battn., and on 20 Nov. a party, con-

sisting of Lieut. Henry Tryon in command, with Lieuts. Bourchier and Cuninghame, four sergeants and 200 rank and file, was detailed to carry it into execution. It was kept a secret what the service was to be till the party fell in about four o'clock in the afternoon. Then Tryon wheeled them round him and told the men what they were wanted for. He said he intended to drive the Russians out, and that he was sure that they could do it, and right well they did it. Marching down to the trenches, they lay down till dark. They then advanced stealthily, creeping along the broken ground which led first down a slight incline, and then up towards the enemy, who were completely surprised by the attack. Fifty men under Tryon formed the storming column, 50 the supports under Bourchier, and 100 the reserve under Cuninghame. Eventually these parties became practically one. They quickly drove the Russian riflemen from their cover, though supported by a heavy column of Russian infantry. The occupants of the pit were evidently surprised. But soon the pits poured grape and canister on the Riflemen, who had no cover, for the pits were open on the enemy's side. In the moment of taking possession of the pits, the gallant Tryon fell, shot in the head; Bourchier, who succeeded to the command of the party, maintained his advantage, and Cuninghame greatly distinguished himself by the energy with which he repulsed an attempt to turn the left flank of the advanced party, and thereby ensure the success of the capture. Repeatedly during that long night did the Russians attempt to retake the pits; sometimes by sending forward strong columns, sometimes by creeping up a few at a time, and when they got near making signals for their companions to come on. But this handful of Riflemen under the command of these two young officers bravely withstood them and held the position until relieved next day by another party of the battalion. In this affair Lieut. Tryon and nine men were killed, and 17 men were wounded." This gallant exploit was thus described in the Despatch addressed by Lord Raglan to the Duke of Newcastle : " Before Sebastopol, 23 Nov. 1856. My Lord Duke,—The Russian advanced posts in front of our left attack having taken up a position which incommoded our troops in the trenches, and occasioned not a few casualties, and at the same time took in reverse the French troops working on their lines, a representation of which was made to me both by our own officers and by General Canrobert, a detachment of the 1st Battn. The Rifle Brigade, under Lieut. Tryon, was directed on the night of the 20th to dislodge the enemy, and this service was performed most gallantly and effectively, but at some cost both in killed and wounded, and at the cost of the life of Lieut. Tryon, who rendered himself conspicuous on the occasion. He was considered a most promising officer, and held in the highest estimation by all. The Russians attempted several times to re establish themselves on the ground before daylight on the 21st, but they were instantly repulsed by Lieut. Bourchier, the senior surviving officer of the party, and it now remains in our possession. Brigadier Sir John Campbell speaks highly of the conduct of the detachment, and of Lieut. Bourchier and Lieut. Cuninghame, and he laments the death of Lieut. Tryon, who so ably led them in the first instance. This little incident was so highly prized by General Canrobert that he instantly published an ' Ordre Général,' announcing it to the French Army, and combining, with a just tribute to the gallantry of the troops, the expression of his deep sympathy in the regret felt at the loss of a young officer of so much distinction.—(Signed) Raglan." The following is the order referred to, issued by the French General, a most honourable and unusual distinction " Ordre Général. Dans la nuit du 20 ou 21, sur la demande de concours que j'avais addressée au Commandant de l'Armée Anglaise, en lui faisan observer que les tirailleurs Russes s'établissaient à couvert en avant de ses lignes pour prendre à revers nos travailleurs, ces riflemen Anglais ont tourné par la gauche les positions occupées par l'ennemi, et les on enlevées après l'avoir débusqué. Les Russes, formés en colonnes profondes ont tenté trois fois de les reprendre à la baïonnette, après avoir fait pleuvoi la mitraille sur le détachement Anglais. Nos alliés ont tenu ferme ave l'énergie que nous leur connaissons et sont restés maîtres de la position où nous pouvons les apercevoir ce matin. J'ai voulu rendre hommag devant vous à la vigueur avec laquelle s'est accompli ce hardi coup de main qui a malheureusement coûté la vie du vaillant Capitaine Tryon. Nou lui donnerons les regrets dus à sa fin glorieuse. Elle resserrera les liens d loyale confraternité d'armes qui nous unissent à nos alliés.—Au quartie général, devant Sébastopol, le 21 Novembre, 1854. Le Général en Chef (Signed) Canrobert. Pour ampliation, Le Général Chef d'Etat-Majo Général, E. de Martimprey." Sir W. Cope says : " I am indebted t Marshal Canrobert for a copy of this order, which conferred so unusua and marked a distinction on the regiment. In the letter which accom panied the transcript the Marshal expresses his appreciation of ' la mag nifique conduite du détachement de la Rifle Brigade commandé par l Capitaine Tryon.' " The following is the translation of the precedin General Order, which was appended to Lord Raglan's orders on the occa sion : " Camp before Sebastopol, 21 Nov. 1854. On the night of th 20th or 21st, on a request made by me to Lord Raglan, Commander-in Chief of the English Army, pointing out to him that the Russian riflemen had placed themselves under cover in front of the lines, from whence the could enfilade our workmen, one hundred Riflemen, under the command o Lieut. Tryon, left the English trenches, and turning the flank of the enemy charged and dispersed them. The Russians, formed in deep column attempted three times during the night to retake the place, after pourin in grape and canister on the English detachment. With that energ belonging to our allies, they held firmly their ground, and we can now se them where the enemy once stood. I wish before you all to render th homage due to so gallant an act, which unfortunately cost the life of th brave officer, Lieut. Tryon. We will give him all the regrets so glorious a end deserves. It will be an additional link to the loyal fraternity of arm which unites us to our allies.—(Signed) General Canrobert." The follow ing General Order from Lord Raglan was also issued : " General Orde 24 Nov. 1854. The Commander of the Forces cannot pass unnoticed th attack on the night of the 20th instant, of a detachment of the 1st Battn. The Rifle Brigade, under Lieut. Tryon, upon the advanced posts of the enemy, which had been pushed forward so as to enfilade the English trenches and to take in reverse those of the French troops. The advance was made in the most spirited and determined manner, and was completely successful. And though several vigorous attempts were afterwards made by the enemy to dislodge the gallant band, they utterly failed, and the ground remains in our possession. Lieut. Tryon, whose conduct was most conspicuous, was unfortunately killed, and several valuable soldiers shared the same fate. The General in Chief of the French Army so highly prized the achievement that he published a General Order eulogizing the conduct of the detachment, and paying a just tribute to the officer who led it. —(Signed) J. B. B. Estcourt, Adjutant-General." The valiant captors of the pits were relieved a little before daylight on the 21st by a party of the 1st Battn., under the command of Lieut. Flower, and accompanied by Lieut. the Hon. G. B. Legge. Colour-Sergt. Hicks, who had volunteered for this duty, and was close to Tryon when he fell, obtained the French War Medal. For his gallantry in the Crimea, Bourchier was given the brevet of Major. He also received the Medal with four clasps, was made a Knight of the Legion of Honour, received the Fifth Class of the Order of the Medjidie, the Turkish Medal and was awarded the Victoria Cross [London Gazette, 24 Feb. 1857]: "Claude Thomas Bourchier, Brevet Major, 1st Battn. The Rifle Brigade. Date of Act of Bravery: 20 Nov. 1854. Highly distinguished at the capture of the rifle-pits, 20 Nov. 1854. His gallant conduct was recorded in the French General Orders." He was decorated by Her Majesty Queen Victoria at the first Investiture in Hyde Park 26 June, 1857. In the Indian Mutiny he served in the Campaign of 1857–59, including the siege and capture of Lucknow, Battle of Nawabgunge, attack and capture of Fort Oomerea, for which he received the Medal and clasp. He served also on the Afghan frontier, near Peshawar, during the disturbance among the native tribes in the winter of 1863. Colonel Bourchier was appointed Aide-de-Camp to the Queen in April, 1869, having retired on full pay as Colonel the same year. He died on Monday, 19 Nov. 1877, at 38, Brunswick Road, Brighton, and an obituary notice in the "Times," of 23 Nov. says: "The Army has lost a distinguished officer by the death of Colonel Claude Thomas Bourchier, who died after a protracted illness on Monday last at Brighton, at the comparatively early age of 46 years." Sir W. Cope's and Colonel Willoughby Verner's Histories of the Rifle Brigade have been consulted in compiling this account.

WHEATLEY, FRANCIS, Private, served in the Crimean Campaign of 1854–55, and for his services was awarded the Victoria Cross on its institution [London Gazette, 24 Feb. 1857]: "F. Wheatley, Private, 2nd Battn. The (Prince Consort's Own) Rifle Brigade. For throwing a live shell over the parapet of the trenches before Sebastopol." In the trenches, as related above, Private Wheatley tackled a live shell that fell in the midst of the riflemen. He first tried to knock out the burning fuse with the butt of his rifle; but as he was unsuccessful in this, he deliberately picked up the shell and threw it over the parapet, where it at once exploded. Private Wheatley was decorated by Queen Victoria at the first Investiture in Hyde Park, 26 June, 1857. Wheatley became a lodge-keeper at Bramshill Park, Winchfield, co. Hants, the residence of the late Sir William Cope, Bart., a former officer of the Rifle Brigade, and died there on 21 May, 1865.

KNOX, JOHN SIMPSON, Lieut., was *b.* in King Street, Calton, Glasgow, on 30 Sept. 1828; a member of a yeoman family. Major Knox's father, Mr. John Knox, was *b.* at Inverkeithing in Nov. 1772. He served in the 90th Light Infantry from 10 Feb. 1794, till 24 Dec. 1802, after which he joined the 28th, a Stirlingshire Regiment of Militia, under His Grace the Duke of Montrose, in Capt. Maxwell's Company, and served eleven years, being discharged in 1814. After his discharge he lived in King Street, Glasgow. He married twice, Major Knox being a child of the second marriage. While serving in the 90th Light Infantry, Mr. John Knox was employed as compounder and dispenser of medicines for the sick soldiers. He frequently assisted in the hospital under the doctors, and was a very well-educated man. Major Knox ran away from an unhappy home, and, being very tall for his age, enlisted in Glasgow in the Scots Fusilier Guards 15 May, 1843, at the age of fourteen and a half. He never told his family much about his early life, but they believe he was bought out and re-enlisted. He kept an old scrap-book, into which he pasted any interesting letters, cuttings or pictures, and from this may be gleaned many particulars about his career. He was promoted Acting Corpl. 28 July, 1845, Corpl. 11 June, 1846, Drill Corpl. 16 Nov. 1846, Acting Sergt. 11 Dec. 1850, Sergt. 9 July, 1851, and Drill Sergt. 7 July, 1853. A letter in Major Knox's old book is from the late General Lord Rokeby, and is dated "The Deanery, Windsor, 7 Dec." He wrote: "I have watched your career with great interest since in 1853 I recommended you for promotion to the rank of Sergt. The ability and activity with which immediately afterwards in the camp at Chobham you performed the duties of Quartermaster caused me to select you for a Drill Sergt., and your gallantry both at the Alma and Inkerman justified your selection for promotion to the adjutancy of the Rifle Brigade." Young Knox had developed into a man of magnificent physique, and seemed marked out for promotion. He was one of the youngest non-commissioned officers which his gallant regiment has had. In June, 1891, he pasted into his scrap-book an announcement of the death of Major-General Drake, C.B., late Royal Engineers. Underneath this notice Major Knox has written: "In April, 1853, I was sent from Windsor to Chobham with 40 soldiers, 1st Battn. Scots Guards, to prepare the ground for the encampment, and to act under the command of Lieut. Drake, then a young officer of Engineers. We formed at that time a friendship which lasted the remainder of his life." General Sir W. Knollys, K.C.B., says, in a letter dated 21 Feb. 1872: "I have known Capt. Knox since he entered the Army in 1843, having served in the same regiment of Guards till he went to the Crimea." He had been a soldier a little under ten years when the great war against Russia broke out. John Knox, according to the records at the Scots Guards' Headquarters, "served in the Eastern Campaign of 1854–55 (from 24 Feb. 1854), including the Battles of Alma, Balaklava, Inkerman, the Siege of Sebastopol, repulse of the ladder-party on the Redan on 18 June and 8 Sept." "At 7 a.m. on 28 Feb. 1854, the day on which she issued her Declaration of War, the Queen with the Prince Consort came out upon the middle balcony of Buckingham Palace to bid 'God-speed' to the Scots Fusiliers as they marched through the courtyard. It was a fine morning, and the sun shone brightly over the towers of Westminster Abbey when the gallant fellows formed line, presented arms to their Sovereign, and went off, cheering loudly" ("Victoria, Queen and Empress," by J. C. Jeaffreson, Vol. II., chapter X., page 71). Major Knox used to write to his brother-in-law in after years, and his daughter has copied the old letters into his old book. One runs as follows: "Landed in the Crimea 14 Sept.; appointed Colour-Sergt. 18 Sept. Commenced march to Sebastopol 19 Sept.; fired first shot at half-past 3 p.m. same day. The retiring enemy fired a village, directly in front of the Light Division and Guards. After a time the L.D. dashed through the burning village, closely followed by Guards; the grape and canister shot fell like hail around us—and numbers of our men were wounded. After passing the village, we passed through a running stream, the depth of which varied from hip to shoulder. We had a difficulty in reforming, as the banks were steep, and the enemy gallantly came to the top . . . and gave us a warm reception. However, we soon formed and drove them back, the Light Dragoons following close and the Guards and Highlanders moving in support. In advancing up the hill there opened a strong fire from a field battery, which caused great loss of officers and men. Many retired, and, in doing so, forced the Fusilier Guards back about 100 yards. The enemy, seeing this, came out of the battery, bringing their right shoulders forward a little. We faced round about and opened a strong fire, all the while advancing, and made no more halts until the place was carried at the point of the bayonet and the enemy in full retreat. As the Guards and Highlanders advanced, the Light Division formed behind them, and soon came up to our support. The 2nd Regt. of the Light Division, after the action, had only four or five officers untouched. My regiment suffered much. On mustering after the action there were 11 sergeants, 14 corporals and 149 privates missing. Several of these have since rejoined." "On landing in the Crimea, on 14 Sept. 1854, we had a short march from the beach to the ground where we remained for the night and in camp until the 19th. The first night we were visited by heavy rain. Fortunately I had collected a quantity of branches from trees and covered them thickly with weeds, making myself a fairly good bed, so thick as to keep me dry. The rain flowing underneath in the morning, the only part of me wet was my knees. The hot sun soon dried them. Early in the day (15th) I started with two or three kindred spirits to visit a Tartar village, about two miles to the left rear of the army, guarded by a strong party of the 2nd Battn. The Rifle Brigade, under command of Major Norcote. By barter and money we got some poultry and returned to camp to enjoy it. Shortly after my return I was sent for by the Commanding Officer and appointed Colour-Sergt. On the 18th we started for the Alma, passing over large tracts of open ground. My water-supply failed, and I was all but done up and going to lie down when Colonel Ridley gave me a spoonful of brandy. This kept me going till we reached the ground where we had to pass the night. Several of our men died from cholera during the night, and were buried before continuing our march. The night passed quietly. Early next morning we stood to our arms, and after much delay the Army moved on and came within sight of the enemy's forces, posted on the high ground beyond the Alma. Our division formed here and were ordered to lie down. After some delay the division was ordered to advance to support the Light Division. We had to cross a number of cultivated gardens, enclosed in stone walls from three to four feet high. The walls, being of loose stones, were easily pushed down. The Russians fired heavily, but did little execution. At last we reached the river, and on my part got over without any difficulty and with very little wetting. On reaching the path on the opposite side, running parallel with the river, the battalion, still in line, began to reform their ranks. My chief exertions at the time were exercised in getting our men together. Repeated and pressing requests came several times from the Light Division, asking us to hurry on to their support. Before the ranks were properly reformed, Sir Charles Hamilton ordered the battalion to advance, and away they went, leaving, to my surprise, many of our men under the shelter of the bank. I did all I could to clear them out and send them on to glory. I then passed over myself, and to my surprise found our battalion retiring, mixed up with the men of the Light Division. Capt. Scarlett was frantic, flourishing his sword and violently exerting himself to stop the retreat. He asked me to help him. By good fortune, at that moment old Bill Douglas was near us. I called upon him to stand

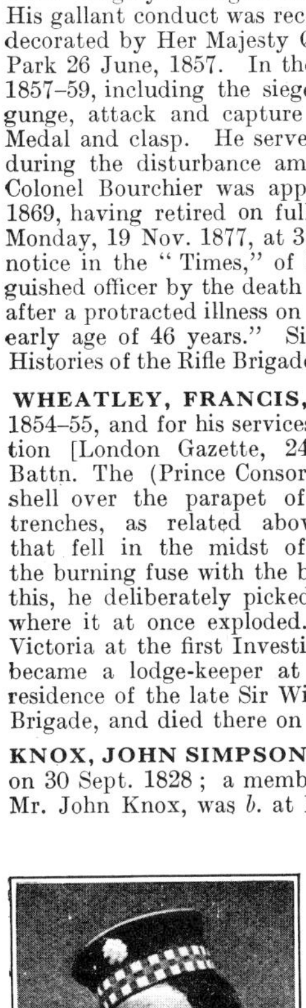

John Simpson Knox.

still, face the enemy and fire. Without any hesitation the old soldier obeyed my order. I got others to join him, and, about the same time, order was restored in the ranks, line reformed, and file-firing opened on the enemy. This fire, combined with cross-fire from the left company of the Grenadier Guards, quickly settled the enemy and enabled us without any loss to capture the battery. During the time our men were firing, an order was passed down the line for us to retire, and some of the companies had actually faced about, when I persuaded Colonel Dalrymple that we were making a blunder, our interests urgently requiring an advance and not a retreat. Colonel D. took the same view and stopped it. After capturing the battery there was no more fighting; we remained in possession of the field, the enemy's troops retiring. My meeting Capt. Scarlett early in the fight was a most fortunate thing for Bill Douglas and myself. The former was appointed full corporal next day and a sergeant a few months later, with the advantage of a sergeant's pension instead of a private's when discharged, and the regiment made good the public money he lost when on recruiting service. When the time came, Capt. Scarlett recommended me for the V.C., and I got it. I believe I told you long ago about the cowardice displayed both there (Alma) and at Inkerman, by ——; I will not repeat it now. At the close of the battle I was sent with a party of men to move in our wounded to the field hospitals. I recollect seeing Sergt. Robbie lying on his back with a bullet through his head near the redoubt. On finishing with the wounded it was dark; the army had moved on and in what direction I did not know. Fortunately we hit off our army on the heights, and the party rejoined the battalion about eleven o'clock at night. With my usual good fortune I procured some straw to sleep on, and felt none the worse next day for the fatigue and want of food of the day of battle. Two or three days after the battle Colonel Walker, direct from home, assumed command of the battalion. He was a very good, energetic officer, holding strong opinions in favour of the wisdom of the Duke of Wellington. On the march to Balaklava nothing very exciting occurred except our coming in contact by accident with the rearguard of the Russians returning from Sebastopol into the interior. Some of the men and a portion of their luggage was captured. The next day we reached Balaklava and the following laughable affair occurred between the Colonel and his Junior Drill-Sergt.: The battalion was ordered to pile arms and fall out for a time. J. S. K., standing in the open, saw an old barndoor fowl picking up a living. The act of piling arms brought many other eyes upon the bird. J. S. K., from his position, had a good start of his comrades and shied a stick; missed his prey; the delay in recovering the stick led to other sportsmen obtaining the lead; the fowl was captured and soon disappeared. J. S. K., in a disconsolate state, musing over his bad luck, was told by the Sergt.-Major the Colonel wished to see him. He went to the Colonel, and, saluting, said: 'Do you wish to see me, sir?' 'See you, sir! I never witnessed such a disgraceful act in the whole course of my service, and I am surprised that a man in your position should set such a bad example to those under you. I've a good mind to try you by drumhead court-martial.' (All this time I had no idea what I had done.) 'But I will overlook it in consequence of your gallantry in the late battle if you will promise me never to repeat it again.' 'Thank you, sir; but before I promise, may I, with all due respect, ask what crime I have committed?' This caused the cup to run over; he became very angry, and told me he had last seen me running after an old hen. I restrained, the best way I could, my wounded feelings, expressed my regret, thinking how quickly the experience of camp life would change his tone." In a letter to Lord Roden, dated 2 Oct. 1895, Major Knox relates an incident which took place during the Battle of Inkerman: "After the death of Sir G. Cathcart our troops were hard pressed, and barely able to hold their ground against the enemy. Our leaders deemed it necessary, and wisely so, to get all the men together that they could lay their hands on. The three regiments of the Guards managed to gather some three companies, more or less, in line. The Duke, placing himself in the centre, drew his sword and called out: 'Come along, my brave fellows, I will lead you.' And we steadily followed him until we reached the ridge of the Ink, near the camp of the 2nd Division. We were then ordered to lie down. Accident brought me close to you, and you spoke to me several times about the events going on round us. The enemy's fire of shot and shell was very heavy at the time, and many of our comrades were killed and wounded by bursting shells. During a short lull in the firing you remarked, 'I am very hungry.' I replied, 'I have some ration pork and biscuits in my haversack to spare. Will you accept them?' You said, 'Thank you. Are you sure you don't want them yourself?' I then turned round, raised myself on my knees, took the haversack from my shoulders and handed it over to you. You, on receiving it, raised yourself. At that instant a round shot bounded over our heads, and one of the men who was a short distance from us, called out, 'That was a narrow shave, sir.' 'What do you mean?' I said. The answer was, 'Look at your feet, sir.' On doing so, I saw the headless body of a drummer of the 20th Regt., who, it appeared, had been sitting eating with his back to the enemy. The shot had struck him between the head and the shoulders and smashed him in pieces. I fear the event made little impression upon me. Nothing makes men so selfish as war as long as oneself is safe. One cares nothing for anyone else. I think this event took place somewhere after noon. We remained together until the close of the fight. . . . It is forty-one years to-day since the battalion marched up the heights of Sebastopol. Little did any of us foresee on that day the trials we were to endure. As far as I can learn, I am now the last of the Battalion Staff in the ranks on that day. Time is dealing gently with me." Lord Roden replied to Major Knox: "The circumstances you mention are now perfectly well recalled to my mind, and I recollect that it was the end of the action at Inkerman, when the few of us left were ordered to lie down in rear of a French battery that was pitching into a Russian battalion in retreat." In a letter written 24 Nov. 1869, Lieut.-General Sir E. W. J. Walker, K.C.B., said: "Capt. Knox, V.C. (then Drill-Sergt. in the Scots Fusilier Guards), served under my command in the Crimea; he was present with his regiment in all the engagements, and at the Siege of Sebastopol his conduct was conspicuous for gallantry, and in every way he set an example to those around him; so much so that I determined to recommend him for a commission should the opportunity occur." Knox became Colour-Sergt. 13 Sept. 1854. The splendid behaviour of the three battalions of Foot Guards, and particularly the valour displayed by them at Inkerman, so delighted the Prince Consort, that—to mark a sense of their courage under trying conditions—he placed a commission in his own regiment, the Rifle Brigade, at the disposal of General Lord Rokeby, whose selection of Sergt. Knox for the high honour gave widespread satisfaction among his colleagues. Colonel Walker's letter recommending Sergt. Knox for the commission is in Major Knox's book:

"Camp before Sebastopol,
"February 26th, 1855.

"Sir,—

"In obedience to the command of His Royal Highness Prince Albert, I have now the honour to lay before you for His Royal Highness's approval the name of Sergt. John Knox, Scots Fusilier Guards, who has been for some time Assistant Drill-Sergt., and has given me great satisfaction.

"I therefore wish to recommend him to His Royal Highness for the commission in the Rifles to which you allude in your letter of the 8th inst. A proud position I think him well qualified to fill.

"I have the honour to be, Sir,
"Your obedient servant,
"E. W. J. Walker,
"Colonel in Charge Commanding 1st Battn. S.F. Guards.

This letter was written on a sheet of ordinary notepaper, and under it Major Knox has written: "The original letter in which my name was placed, recommending me for a commission. The letter was returned because it was not on foolscap paper—a fact."

Before his promotion to a Lieutenancy, Sergt. Knox had achieved a reputation for conspicuous bravery among the many thousands of the allied forces. Sergt. Knox, then, received the Inkerman commission awarded to the Scots Guards. A similar honour in the Grenadier Guards passed to Sergt. James Cross, who was made Adjutant of the 46th Regt., but was lost sight of after his retirement at the end of the war. The Coldstream Adjutancy went to Sergt. James Ashton, Goodlake's right hand in the famous "volunteer party of sharpshooters selected from the Brigade of Guards." He sold out, and historians have also lost all trace of him. Early in Nov. 1893, a banquet was given in Cardiff to veterans of the Crimea and Indian Mutiny. Lord Tredegar and Sir James Hills-Johnes, V.C., G.C.B., were amongst those invited, and so was Major Knox, who wrote a letter expressing his regret that his old body was not equal to the fatigue of being present. He added: "When I became a soldier, now over fifty years ago, little interest was taken in soldiers by the British public. The war of 1854 broke the spell of night, and brought to light the pluck, self-denial and endurance of our Army—men all anxious to win the favourable opinions of their country. Often have I heard my old comrades say after the stout fight of Inkerman: 'I wonder what they will say at home about our doings out here?' Delighted, indeed, were we all to learn, weeks after the battle, how pleased you all were with our conduct." There is a letter from the late Lord Abinger in Major Knox's book which says:

"Dear Mr. Knox,—

"I have written to Colonel Walker stating that you were with my company when our ranks were broken by a brigade of the Light Division; that I desired you to assist me in reforming the ranks, which I consider you did in a very cool, gallant and admirable manner, and that I was much indebted to you for your assistance.

"I only hope you will obtain your Cross, and I am sure if you do, very few will wear it who can say they have done more to deserve it.

"Believe me,
"Yours truly,
"W. F. Scarlett.

"Guards Club, October 4th, 1856."

Sergt. Knox was discharged 5 Nov. 1854, on being appointed Ensign in the Rifle Brigade, March, 1855, and was appointed Lieut. in April. His Ensigncy was antedated to 5 Nov. 1854, and Lieutenancy to 29 Dec. 1854. Lieut. Knox was the volunteer officer in charge of the ladder-party at the unsuccessful attack on the Redan in June, 1855, when his brother officer, Capt. Foreman, was killed and he himself lost his left arm. In a letter written by Major Knox to H. Gale, written 17 June, 1895, he says: "All my actions of 39 years ago come clearly before me as I write: my volunteering for the ladder-party, Sir William Codrington thanking me for undertaking so dangerous a duty, then making my will, marching off to the trenches on a nice summer Sunday night, helping Capt. Blackett to arrange our men, with the ladders in the advance trench. His sending me back to Colonel Yea to await final orders—then squatting on the ground near the 21st Gun Battery, and listening to him giving his instructions to the different officers on their arrival. He (Colonel Yea) was killed leading the attack, a most promising commander. About midnight I received his finishing instructions, and rejoined Blackett as soon as possible. At daybreak the French began the attack, the English waiting for the signal to advance. The Russians were all the time preparing to receive us warmly. At last, about 5 a.m., the flag was hoisted, and away we went, meeting a powerful fire, sweeping us down in all directions. At starting we were only a short two hundred yards from the

Redan ; on leaving the trench, I met Blackett with a smashed leg moving back on his hips and hands. The command then fell to me, but not a dozen men were left to lead. These I led up to the Abattis ; then taking a rifle from a dead Rifleman, I fired several shots at the enemy, all the time talking to Capt. Foreman, in command of the sharpshooters, about what ought to be done, both deciding there was nothing for it but to remain until shot over. My rifle was aimed at a Russian when I was struck in the left arm, the weapon falling to the ground, upon which poor Foreman remarked, ' You are wounded.' I replied, ' I fancy I am.' He offered me some brandy ; this I declined. Having a stout handkerchief ready for the work, he took it, and by chance placed himself in front of me and bound up the wound. At that instant a shower of grape-shot passed ; he was struck dead, falling on my feet speechless, the spirit gone. I remained standing, strange to say. Having had enough I retired. A short distance off a grape-shot caught the broken arm and lodged in the arm. Still I kept my feet and walked on into our trenches, there tumbling over through loss of blood. Four soldiers of the 23rd placed me on a stretcher and bore me along, until Lord Raglan stopped them, inquiring in a most kind manner if I was hurt. At the same time one of his Staff offered me brandy, which I declined. The men then moved on to the mule ambulance, and I was placed in a litter, but from the mules' motion causing the bone to grit, the pain became so great I made them let me down. Nature, however, was not equal to the wish. I had to return to the stretcher, and so reached my tent. Walking out of the battle got me back before the doctors had any of them work to do. They were waiting for a job, soon removed the arm from the socket under chloroform, without any pain or trial to me. Seven days after I was out of bed, walking about none the worse man, although only one arm left. Poor Foreman, who lost his life trying to help me, only married a few days before leaving home. Had he lived, he would have been owner of Hensal Castle and a large estate near Cardiff." A letter from Capt. (afterwards Sir Edward) Blackett, dated "Sandhurst, 10 Oct.," says : " I wrote to Colonel Hill, stating what I considered to be your claims to the decoration. Hill writes to say that he will not fail to bring your name to notice, so that I consider the thing as done. I am much pleased to think that my recommendation may have been of service to you." For his services in the Crimean campaign, Lieut. Knox received the Crimean Medal with four bars and the Turkish Medal. He used to say that a ship was sunk which was bringing the Turkish Medals destined for some of the British regiments. The Turkish Government was too poor to provide a second free consignment, but the British soldiers were given to understand that the decoration would be awarded to those who paid for it ! He was also awarded the Legion of Honour, and the Warrant is in his book :

" Grande Chancellerie,
No. 80917.
Ordre Impérial de la Légion d'Honneur.
Nomination de Chevalier.
S.M. l'Empereur,
par decret du Seize Juin,
Mil huit cent cinquante six, a nommé Chevalier
de l'Ordre Impérial de la Légion d'Honneur,
M. Le Lieutenant
JOHN SIMPSON KNOX,
pour prendre rang à dater
du même jour.
Paris, le 21 Juin, 1856.
Le Grand Chancelier
de la Légion d'Honneur,
Duc de Plaisance."

" Aldershot, 27 April, 1856.

" MY DEAR CHALMERS,
" So peace is concluded at last, and our Army is about to quit the scene of their miseries and triumphs, and return, some to the Colonies and others, more fortunate, to their native land. I daresay your feelings join with mine in envying those how have gone through all and are now about to return. My Commanding Officer has informed me that he has submitted my name for the Legion of Honour. I will feel proud of the decoration if I get it, and I fancy I have a claim, for I was in every engagement, great and small, during the campaign, except the final attack on 8 Sept., and I volunteered for the ladder-party on 18 June. I shall feel dissatisfied if passed over. G. Knowles is trying to get me the Order of ' Merit,' so I make sure of it. Her Majesty did me the honour of noticing me at her inspection of the troops. After marching past, G. Knowles called me out and introduced me to H.M., who spoke as only Royalty can speak. The Prince made some flattering allusion to my conduct in the East. I returned to the ranks gratified at the honourable mark of distinction conferred on me by my Sovereign. I attended a Levee and kissed hands on my appointment. Altered days ! I thought so when I got out of the carriage at the Queen's Guard and saw the sentries walking up and down on the posts that I had often occupied as one of themselves. H.M. paid a visit to the camp last week and inspected the troops. In passing down the line I was honoured with a bow, and the Duke of Cambridge spoke to me, so, my dear Chalmers, you see there are many advantages attached to the loss of an arm. The battalion returns immediately in time for the review in Hyde Park. I will then be relieved from my duties, which don't at all suit. Militia officers and bands have been ordered to confine themselves to regulation dress. High time they were, for they are the most preposterous dressers in camp that brain of man ever invented.
" Yours, etc.,
" J. S. K."

He was awarded the Victoria Cross [London Gazette, 24 Feb. 1857 : " John Knox, Lieut., 2nd Battn. The Scots Fusilier Guards. While

serving as a Sergt. in the Scots Fusilier Guards, Lieut. Knox was conspicuous in his exertions in reforming the ranks of the Guards at the Battle of the Alma. Subsequently, when in the Rifle Brigade, he volunteered for the ladder-party in the attack on the Redan on 18 June, and (in the words of Capt. Blackett, under whose command he was) behaved admirably, remaining on the field until twice wounded." Lieut. Knox received his decoration at the first Investiture. He says in his scrapbook : " The Queen, on 26 June, 1857, in Hyde Park, London, fastened the Cross on the left breast of each recipient, before a large crowd of the public. Her Majesty was on horseback, dressed in a Field-Marshal's uniform. Colonel Lord Henry Percy, Grenadier Guards, was in command of the men who received the Cross. Lieut. Knox, Rifle Brigade, acted as his Adjutant. The weather was lovely. Mrs. Knox's father and her brother Godwin witnessed the ceremony from the grand stand. I afterwards lunched at Holford House, Park Lane, and in the evening dined with Lord Carington in Whitehall Yard." It is said that just before the Investiture it was decided that Her Majesty could not pin on the Crosses through the thick cloth of the recipients' tunics. Lieut. Knox was therefore told he had better get some ribbon, which was to be cut in little bits and fastened on to each man's tunic. " Who's going to pay for it ? " asked Knox. He was informed that he was to pay for it, and that the money would be refunded. But it never was. A newspaper published in 1871 says : " It is a common remark in the German Army that the Imperial Crown Prince has a remarkable memory for faces. Of this faculty he gave a striking proof to-day at one of the firing points. Capt. Knox, V.C., Rifle Brigade, is acting as one of the range brigadiers, and was met casually by the Prince, who, greeting him, observed : ' I saw that Cross ' (pointing to the Victoria Cross worn by the gallant Captain) ' pinned on your breast by the Queen at the back of the Horse Guards after the Crimean War.' Capt. Knox had no difficulty in owning that he was right ; but it is not given to every man to remember ten years after a face seen so casually at a military parade. Capt. Knox is emphatically one of the Queen's good bargains. He earned his commission, as he did the Victoria Cross at Alma, by conspicuous valour at Inkerman, and has risen step by step by dint of sheer merit." " Punch," 4 July, 1857, has the following lines :

THE STAR OF VALOUR.
Distributed by the Queen's Own Hand,
June 26th, 1857.

A rift is made in that dark shade
Which o'er our soldiers flung its blight,
And through the shroud of its cold cloud,
The Star of Valour throws a light.

Low-born and noble, side by side,
Colonel and private stand to-day,
Their comrades' boast, their country's pride,
When all were brave, the bravest they !

The fount of Honour, sealed till now
To all save claims of rank and birth,
Makes green the laurel on the brow
Ennobled but by soldier's worth.

The Queen's own hand on each brave breast—
Beat it 'neath serge or superfine—
Hangs the plain cross, whose bronze so prest
Beameth with more than diamond's shine.

That bronze, cast from the steadfast guns
Which blazed along the red Redan,
Whose maddening music, while it stuns
The coward, only wakes the man.

From whose hot muzzles was plucked forth,
The fame their metal now rewards
In these plumed warriors of the North,
These Sailors, Rifles, Linesmen, Guards.

These Heavy Horsemen who rode out,
Stern and sedate, though one to ten,
Then, through the Russian line in rout,
Stern and sedate rode back again.

And these Light Horse—of deathless name,
Who charged, unquestioning of their doom,
Through those long miles all fire and flame,
And at the end, a soldier's tomb !

Of these the bravest and the best
Who 'scaped the chance of shot and sword,
England doth, by her Queen, invest
With Valour's Cross—their great reward !

Marking her sense of something, still,
A central nobleness that lies
Deeper than rank which royal will,
Or birth, or chance, or wealth supplies.

Knighthood that girds all valiant hearts,
Knighthood that crowns each fearless brow,
The knighthood this bronze cross imparts—
Let Fleece and Bath and Garter bow !

Lieut. Knox was appointed Acting Paymaster, Depot, 2nd Battn. Rifle Brigade, 1 Jan. 1886. He obtained a First Class Certificate in Musketry: " No. 157.—This is to certify that Lieut. John Knox, of the 4th Battn. Rifle Brigade, underwent a course of training at the School of Musketry, Hythe, and that he is perfectly qualified to instruct in the Art and Practice of Musketry.—Hythe, the 8th day of January, 1858.—Charles Kay, Commandant, School of Musketry." Lieut. Knox was appointed Instructor of Musketry, 4th Battn. Rifle Brigade, 7 Jan. 1858 ; was promoted to Capt. 30 April, 1858, and was appointed Instructor of Musketry at Gibraltar 2 Feb. 1862. In Major Knox's book there is a copy of a letter from Colonel Maude, afterwards Major-General Sir F. F. Maude, at the time Inspector-General of Irish Militia, dated " Dublin Castle, 4 Oct. 1869." In it Colonel Maude says : " Capt. Knox, V.C., Rifle Brigade, was District Inspector of Musketry at Gibraltar during the years 1862–63–64–65, when I was there as Assistant Adjutant-General. He performed his duties most correctly, being energetic, punctual, painstaking, and having a good name with both officers and men. Capt. Knox was a thorough, good, practical soldier.—(Signed) F. F. Maude, Colonel, Inspector-General of Irish Militia." On 30 July, 1862, Capt. Knox was married in Holy Trinity Church, Winchester, to Harriet Louisa Gale, daughter of R. C. Gale, Esq., of Winchester, and their children are : Lucy (died at Gibraltar, 18 Jan. 1865) ; Harriet Margaret ; Emily Louisa ; John Abercromby, born 20 Aug. 1869 (died 27 Jan. 1880) ; Edith Mary ; Gladys Fairfield, and Winifred. Mrs. Knox died on 4 Jan. 1890. Capt. Knox was appointed Inspector of Musketry at Portsmouth 13 Dec. 1865. He was elected Governor of Cardiff Prison 8 April, 1872; was appointed Brevet Major for gallantry in the field 7 June, 1872; retired from the Army 8 June, 1872. He writes to Capt. Chalmers from Cardiff, 23 Jan. 1878, telling him of his election as Governor of Cardiff Prison and retirement from the Army : " They gave me the full market value of my commission, £2,500. The Duke of Cambridge stood my friend. I attended his Levee to say good-bye and asked for the rank of Major. He told me I was a badly-treated officer ; that eleven years ago he had recommended me for a Majority, and he could not understand how it was refused, but he would try again, and so I got it. On my leaving his room, he said, ' The Queen is losing a devilish fine soldier, sir.' I replied it was the highest compliment I ever had paid me." The result of Capt. Knox's interview with the Duke of Cambridge is seen in the following letter :

" 5999   " Horse Guards, War Office,
—   " 5 June, 1872.
9

" SIR,
" With reference to the interview which you had with the Field-Marshal Commanding-in-Chief on the 29th April last, as well as your memorial of the same date, I have the satisfaction to acquaint you that in consideration of your Service, particularly in the Field, His Royal Highness will recommend to Her Majesty that you be granted a step of Brevet Rank on your retirement from the Service.
" I have the honour to be, Sir,
" Your obedient Servant,
" K. S. QUENTIN.
" Capt. J. S. Knox, Rifle Brigade."

Major Knox became very popular in Cardiff. A stern disciplinarian, he maintained perfect order, and at the same time showed the utmost kindness to the prisoners. He was transferred to Kirkdale Prison as Governor in Sept. 1886, and on 24 Oct. 1891, he was appointed Governor of Hull Prison. On 15 Jan. 1892, he retired from the Prison Service owing to failing health, and on 25 April, 1892, left Kirkdale and arrived in Cheltenham. " On 29 April myself and children occupied 6, Oriel Terrace." Major Knox died at this house on 8 Jan. 1897, at 4.5 p.m., and was buried in the Cheltenham Cemetery on Tuesday, 12 Jan.

McGREGOR, R., Private, served in the Crimean War, and was awarded the Victoria Cross on its institution [London Gazette, 24 Feb. 1857]: " R. McGregor, No. 2074, Private, 1st Battn. The Prince Consort's Own Rifle Brigade. For courageous conduct when employed as a sharpshooter in the advanced trenches before Sebastopol, in the month of July, 1855. A rifle-pit was occupied by two Russians, who annoyed our troops by their fire. Private McGregor crossed the open space under fire, and, taking cover under a rock, dislodged them and occupied the pit." On 22 April a bandsman of the 2nd Battn., named Wright, who was on duty in the trenches, going to fetch water from a well in front of the advanced trench near the Quarries, was killed, it being impossible to throw up any cover near the well in consequence of the rockiness of the soil. This man being a great favourite of his comrades, a number of them rushed out, determined to drive out the Russian riflemen, by whose fire he had fallen, from the pits which they occupied. Three men, Bradshaw, Humpston and McGregor, were the first to reach them, and drove the Russians out, killing some, while a few escaped. For this gallant deed these three Riflemen received the Victoria Cross, Bradshaw being also decorated with the French War Medal. " In the official notice of the grant of the Victoria Cross, McGregor is said to have performed this act in the month of July ; but I have been frequently assured by Bradshaw," says Sir William Cope, " that he, Humpston and McGregor were together, and won their Crosses on this occasion." (Page 222, " History of the Rifle Brigade," by Sir William Cope, Bart.) Private McGregor was decorated by Queen Victoria at the first Investiture held in Hyde Park on 26 Jan. 1857. He died on 10 Aug. 1888.

HUMPSTON, ROBERT, Private, entered the 2nd Battn. The Prince Consort's Own Rifle Brigade, and served through the Crimean War. For his services in this campaign he was awarded the Victoria Cross

on its institution [London Gazette, 24 Feb. 1857]: " Robert Humpston, No. 2638, Private, 2nd Battn. The Prince Consort's Own Rifle Brigade. A Russian rifle-pit, situated among the rocks overhanging the Woronzoff Road, between the 3rd parallel, right attack, and the Quarries (at that period in the possession of the enemy), was occupied every night by the Russians, and their riflemen commanded a portion of the left attack, impeding the work in a new battery then being erected on the extreme right front of the 2nd parallel, left attack. It was carried in daylight on 22 April, 1855, by two riflemen, one of whom was Private Humpston ; he received a gratuity of £5, and was promoted. The rifle-pit was subsequently destroyed, on further support being obtained." Besides being awarded the Victoria Cross, Private Humpston received the Crimean Medal. He received his Victoria Cross from Queen Victoria at the first Investiture in Hyde Park, 26 June, 1857.

Robert Humpston.

BRADSHAW, JOSEPH, Private, entered the 2nd Battn. The Prince Consort's Own Rifle Brigade. He served through the Crimean War of 1854–55, and for his services in that campaign was awarded the Victoria Cross on its institution [London Gazette, 24 Feb. 1857]: " Joseph Bradshaw, Private, 2nd Battn. The Prince Consort's Own Rifle Brigade. A Russian rifle-pit, situated among some rocks overhanging the Woronzoff Road, between the 3rd parallel, right attack, and the Quarries (at that period in the possession of the enemy), was occupied every night by the Russians, and their riflemen commanded a portion of the left attack, impeding the work in a new battery then being erected on the extreme right front of the 2nd parallel, left attack. It was carried in daylight on 22 April, 1855, by two riflemen, one of whom was Private Bradshaw. He has since received the French War Medal. The rifle-pit was subsequently destroyed, on fresh support being obtained." Besides the Victoria Cross, French War Medal, and the Crimean War Medal with clasps, Bradshaw received a gratuity of £5. On 9 Feb. 1858, the object of the day's work was to drive the rebels out of the Yellow Bungalow, the key of their position. Lieutenant Cooper and the Riflemen went at it with a rush. Lieutenant Cooper and Corporal Bradshaw, V.C., were the first over the wall of the compound surrounding it. Private Bradshaw received his Victoria Cross at the first Investiture in Hyde Park, 26 June, 1857. He died on 21 March, 1875, and his Victoria Cross and Medals were afterwards for sale in London.

Joseph Bradshaw.

War Office, 5 May, 1857.—The Queen has been graciously pleased to signify her intention to confer the decoration of the Victoria Cross on the undermentioned Officers of Her Majesty's Army, who have been recommended to Her Majesty for that Decoration, in accordance with the rules laid down in Her Majesty's Warrant of 29 Jan. 1856, on account of acts of bravery performed by them before the enemy in the late war, as recorded against their several names :—

PERCY, HENRY HUGH MANVERS, Colonel the Honourable (afterwards Lord Henry Percy); b. 22 Aug. 1817, at Burwood House, Cobham, Surrey ; 3rd s. of George, Lord Lovaine, later 5th Duke of Northumberland, and of Louisa Harcourt, 3rd dau. of the Hon. Stuart-Wortley Mackenzie. He obtained his commission in the Grenadier Guards, as an Ensign, on 1 July, 1836, and was present during the Insurrection in Canada in 1838, having sailed for Canada in April of that year—arriving at Quebec 9 May, and after some severe experiences, owing to the severity of the weather and poor accommodation during the Rebellion, returned with his Battn. in Sept. 1842. He was appointed Adjutant for the 1st Battn. in 1847. As Captain and Lieut.-Col. in his Regt. he served during the Eastern Campaign of 1854–55, including the Battle of the Alma (where he was wounded), at Balaklava, Inkerman (where he was again wounded), and at the Siege and Fall of Sebastopol. At Inkerman, Nov. 5, 1854, he won his Victoria Cross [London Gazette, 5 May, 1857]: " The Hon. Henry Hugh Manvers Percy, Colonel, Grenadier Guards. Date of Act of Bravery : 5 Nov. 1854. At a moment when the Guards were at some distance from the Sand-bag Battery, at the Battle of Inkerman, Col. Percy charged singly into the Battery, followed immediately by the Guards ; the embrasure of the Battery, as also the parapet, were held by the Russians, who kept up a most severe fire of musketry. At the Battle of Inkerman Col. Percy found himself, with many men of various regiments who had charged too far, nearly surrounded by Russians, and

The Hon. H. H. M. Percy.

without ammunition. Col. Percy, by his knowledge of the ground, although wounded, extricated these men, and passing under a heavy fire of the Russians, then in the Sand-bag Battery, brought them safe to where ammunition was to be obtained, thereby saving some 50 men and enabling them to renew the combat. He received the approval of His Royal Highness the Duke of Cambridge for this action on the spot. Col. Percy also engaged with and put *hors de combat* a Russian soldier." Col. W. W. Knollys, in "The Victoria Cross in the Crimea," says: "Lieut.-Col. the Hon. Henry Percy displayed at Inkerman an intrepidity worthy of his name. When his Battn. was advancing to replace the Sand-bag Battery, he ran out in front and dashed ahead of all into the mass of Russians. Either then or afterwards, he engaged in single combat with and disabled a Russian soldier. When the Battery was recaptured the Russians only got down the hill far enough to obtain cover, and soon began to surge up again under the parapet. From this position some men fired through the embrasure at the Grenadiers, while others were so venturesome as to climb up on top of the parapet, and to fire down from thence into the mass of Guardsmen at their feet. Col. Percy, being of a fiery disposition, could not submit to this, as it seemed to him impertinence, and himself climbed up to the top of the parapet, only to be knocked back into the work again by a stone thrown at him by a Russian. Mounting the parapet again, notwithstanding that he thus became a mark for a hundred muskets only a few yards off, he was once more knocked backwards by a stone, and this time fell senseless to the ground. He lay some time, bleeding, disabled, and half-blinded, when suddenly hearing the word "Charge!" he rose to his feet and joined in the torrent which drove the Russians down the hill into the Valley of the Tchernaya. Finding after he had gone some distance, together with a small party of men, that two battalions of Russians had passed his flank, and cut him off from his comrades, he prepared to open a way by force. His men, however, saying that they had no ammunition, he managed by a path through the brushwood to bring his party back unperceived to the higher ground." For his personal bravery on this occasion, then Lieut.-Col. the Hon. H. H. M. Percy received the Victoria Cross, with which he was decorated by Her Majesty in Hyde Park 26 June, 1857. For his gallantry throughout the whole campaign he was given the Brevet of Colonel and was appointed an Aide-de-Camp to H. M. Queen Victoria (29 June, 1855, to 10 Feb. 1865). The French made him a Knight of the Legion of Honour; the Turks gave him the Order of the Medjidie, 4th Class. He had also the Crimean Medal with four clasps, and the Turkish Medal. Col. Percy was later appointed to the command of the British-Italian Legion, with the local rank of Brigadier-General. On the occurrence of the Trent misunderstanding with the United States in Dec. 1861, he was sent to New Brunswick in charge of the 1st Battn. of the Grenadier Guards. Lord Henry Percy was in command at Colchester in 1863, and from 19 July, 1865, until 11 Nov. 1868, he sat in Parliament as Conservative Member for North Northumberland, in conjunction with the late Sir Matthew White Ridley, 4th Bart. On 10 Feb. 1865, he obtained the rank of Major-General, and on 29 May, 1873, that of Lieut.-General. He had been created a K.C.B. on 24 May. In June, 1874, he was appointed Colonel of the 89th (Princess Victoria's) Foot. On 1 Oct. 1877, under the new Army Scheme, Lord Henry Percy was promoted General. He died very suddenly of angina pectoris at his residence, 40, Eaton Square, London, S.W., on 3 Dec. 1877, and was buried in the family vault in Westminster Abbey at noon on Friday, 17 Dec. "On the pall were placed the plumed hat, sash and sword of the deceased, and the decoration of the Victoria Cross and the Order of the Bath. Dr. Bridge, the organist, played Mendelssohn's Funeral March as the body was received at the entrance to the Nave. The funeral procession passed to the Choir, the body being placed under the lantern in front of the Sacrarium. The chief mourners took their seats on the south side of the Choir, the seats on the opposite side being occupied by personal friends—among whom were Col. Burnaby, commanding the Grenadier Guards, representing the Regiment, and Major-General Brownrigg. . . . The 90th Psalm was read by the Rev. S. Flood Jones, the lesson being read by Canon Prothero from his stall the Choir, after which the body was removed to the South Transept to the vault in St. Nicholas's Chapel, adjoining that of Henry VII."

HOPE, WILLIAM, Lieut., *b.* 12 April, 1834, in Edinburgh. He was the only survg. *s.* of the late Right Hon. John Hope, Lord Chief Justice Clerk of Scotland, and of his wife, Jessie Scott Irving; educ. at a Preparatory School at Hatfield, by private tutors, and at Trinity College, Cambridge, and entered the 7th Regt., The Royal Fusiliers (City of London Regt.) 12 April, 1855, and served through the Crimean War of 1855–1856. In the attack on the Redan the 7th Regt. The Royal Fusiliers, charged three times, and were so decimated that William Hope and seven men were all who came back unwounded. He heard that the Adjutant was missing, and instantly went out again to look for him under a very heavy fire. He found the Adjutant so shattered that he dared not attempt to carry him for fear of increasing his sufferings, so he fetched a stretcher-party to bring him in. The Adjutant subsequently died of his wounds, but Hope was awarded the Victoria Cross for the attempt to save life under enemy fire. [Victoria Cross, London Gazette, 5th May, 1857]: "William Hope, Lieut., the 7th Regt. (The Royal Fusiliers) City of London Regt. Date of Act of Bravery: 18 June, 1855. After the troops had retreated on the morning of the 18th June, 1855, Lieut. W. Hope, being informed by the late Sergt.-Major William Bacon, who was himself wounded, that Lieut. and Adjutant Hobson was lying outside the trenches, badly wounded, went out to look for him, and found him lying in the old Agricultural Ditch running towards the left flank of the Redan. He then returned and got four men to bring him in. Finding, however, that Lieut. Hobson could not be removed without a stretcher, he then ran back across the open to Egerton's Pit, where he procured one, and carried it to where Lieut. Hobson was lying. All this was done under a very heavy fire from the Russian batteries." Lieut. Hope was decorated by Queen Victoria at the first Presentation in Hyde Park 26 June, 1857. In Nov. 1855, occurred the great explosion which was described by the War Correspondent of the "Daily News" as follows: "Over an area of nearly half a mile the air was one huge column of powder-smoke and cast-up earth, up into and athwart which, ignited or exploding balls and rockets ever and anon darted and flashed by hundreds, spreading destruction to nearly everything, animate and inanimate, within a radius of more than a thousand yards. Heavy siege-guns were wrenched from their carriages and thrown many perches away from where they had been standing, whilst the carriages themselves—torn asunder—were flung high into the air. Both within our enclosures and those of the French, great heaps of firewood, old gabions and other combustible materials had been collected; and these speedily ignited. As night came on, the whole broke into great sheets of fire, firing the separate piles of ammunition as it rolled along. . . . Immediately after the first great explosion, when it was ascertained that the windmill itself—which forms our main magazine in that part of the camp—had escaped, General Straubenzee, who commands the Brigade, hurried up to the tents of the 7th Fusiliers, and asked if any of the men would volunteer to mount the wall of the mill and cover the wall with wet tarpauline and blankets, as a precaution against the thickly flying sparks and burning wood. Now the concussion had literally thrown the roof off the old building, and there it stood in the very centre of the spreading flames, exposed every minute to a thousand chances of destruction. Hardly anything could exceed the danger attending such a labour as the General proposed; notwithstanding, Lieut. Hope and twenty-five men at once responded to the Brigadier's appeal, and proceeded to the powder-crammed building. A sergeant and some men of the Rifles, with also a party of the 34th Regt., were induced to accompany them; and within ten minutes from the first great blow Mr. Hope was on the walls of the mill, piling the wet coverings over the exposed powder-boxes, exploding shells and burning wood flying through the air in perfect streams the while. Whilst the officer and some half-dozen of the men were thus employed, the remainder carried water to throw upon the blankets and bare rafters of the mill, and in little more than half an hour this vast pile of powder was as well-protected from the thickly-flying sparks and rockets as it could be, short of entire removal from the scene of the conflagration. . . . For the most perilous service which he had so bravely and efficiently rendered, Lieut. Hope was publicly thanked by General Straubenzee and the Colonel of his regiment on Thursday on parade; and I, one of many, sincerely hope that his daringly meritorious conduct will not be allowed to pass without further reward. Had the contents of the windmill exploded, we should not now be reckoning our killed and wounded by tens but by hundreds, for experienced Engineer officers declare that hardly a living thing in the whole division could have escaped destruction." The only reward, however, that he received, was the Sardinian Medal for Military Valour, conferred by Victor Emmanuel. He received neither thanks nor promotion for saving the windmill, and left the Army on his marriage in April, 1857. He received the Crimean Medal with one clasp, and the Turkish Medal. His wife was Margaret Jane Cunninghame Graham, and their children were: the late Adrian Charles Francis (for twenty years Secretary to the Great Ormond Street Hospital for Sick Children); John Archibald Graham; Charles Douglas (Head Master of the College, Potchefstroom, South Africa); Jessie Margaret (Graham Hope, a well-known novelist); Laura Charlotte (Mrs. Allen), and Margaret Elizabeth Horatia (Mrs. Napier). After leaving the Army, Lieut. Hope invented the shrapnel shell for rifled guns, and many other improvements. He commanded the 1st City of London Artillery Volunteers for several years. A letter from Colonel Hope appeared in the "Daily Telegraph" of 3 July, 1908: "Sir,—It is doubtless to that wonderful man, the doyen of war correspondents, my friend—if he will allow me to call him so—Mr. Bennet Burleigh, that I owe my exhumation from the tomb in your list of Crimean V.C.'s still living. It is with a sharp pain that I find the list is so terribly shrunk, and think of my comrades who have passed away. But at all events I am truly thankful to be able to add one more to the list, namely, 'Alma Jones,' shot through the jaw carrying the Queen's Colours at the Alma, shot in the shoulder during the six assaults during the night of 7–8 June, 1855, on the 'Quarries,' which we had to deliver, or attacks which we had to repel, before we could hold the work. We had attacked at dusk—a forlorn hope of 600—and Lord Raglan's excellent orders provided for our being supported, if we effected a lodgement, by 1,800, to be followed again by a working-party of 1,000 to 'turn' the work. But the Headquarter Staff did not carry out Lord Raglan's orders, and our 'supports' only came to relieve us—at least, the remains of us—at about nine on the morning of the 8th. But to come back to 'Alma Jones.' He was again wounded in the chest on 8 Sept. (final assault on the Redan), being struck by a large shell splinter on the glacis of the work. He is, I am happy to say, still alive and wonderfully well. I expect to see him shortly on a flying visit to London. Thus the list of survivors is increased by six, and it is not a little remarkable that half of these were Royal Fusiliers. We began the war with twenty-nine officers, and had fifty-six casualties, the entire staff of the regiment being swept away on 7 and 18 June, 1855. 'Alma Jones' and I were both killed by the War Office many years ago, when it was discovered that neither of us had any pension, and, therefore, no right to live; so the young gentleman told off to keep the list in the War Office promptly killed us both. —I am, Sir, Yours faithfully, W. Hope, Colonel, formerly commanding No. 1 Coy., The Royal Fusiliers." A little more than a year after he

William Hope.

wrote this letter, and a week after the death of his wife, Colonel Hope died on 17 Dec. 1909, at a nursing home in London, aged 75. He was buried at Brompton with military honours, and among those at the funeral were Private Lewis, a Chelsea pensioner, who had served with him in the Crimea, and a young neighbour who had joined the Army in a boyish spirit of hero-worship. Of his grandsons, four were of military age at the outbreak of the European War : Archibald Napier, a Lieut. in the Cheshires, lost a leg at La Bassée in Oct. 1914, but returned to France in the Royal Air Force ; Laurence Napier, a Lieut. in the Royal Navy ; two others, Adrian and James Hope, came over from South Africa to Sandhurst, and have passed out, one into a Scotch Regt., the other into the King's Own Scottish Borderers ; a fifth, Henry Hope, sailed from South Africa in 1918 to join the Flying Corps.

HALE, THOMAS EGERTON, M.D., Assistant Surgeon, 7th Regt. ;

Thomas E. Hale.

educated at St. Andrews University (M.D., St. Andrews, 1856, and M.R.C.S., England, 1854). He entered the Army in 1854 ; served in the Crimean War, and was awarded the Victoria Cross [London Gazette, 5 May, 1857]: " Thomas Egerton Hale, M.D., Assistant Surgeon, 7th Regt. Date of Act of Bravery : 8 Sept. 1855. 1. For remaining with an officer who was dangerously wounded (Capt. H. M. Jones, 7th Regt.) in the fifth parallel on 8 Sept. 1855, when all the men in the immediate neighbourhood retreated, excepting Lieut. W. Hope and Dr. Hale ; and for endeavour-ing to rally the men, in conjunction with Lieut. W. Hope, 7th Regt. The Royal Fusiliers. 2. For having on 8 Sept. 1855, after the regiment had retired into the trenches, cleared the most advanced

sap of the wounded, and carried into the sap, under a heavy fire, several wounded men from the open ground, being assisted by Sergt. Charles Fisher, 7th Regt. The Royal Fusiliers." He received the Medal with clasp, and the Turkish Medal. Major Hale retired from the Army in 1876. He was created a C.B. He died at Botterley Hill, Nantwich, 25 Dec. 1909, aged 77.

CONOLLY, JOHN AUGUSTUS, Brevet Major, b. in 1829 ; s. of Edward Michael Conolly, Esq., of Castletown and Cliff, Lieut.-Colonel Donegal Militia, and M.P. for County Donegal, and of his wife, Catherine Jane,

John Augustus Conolly.

dau. of Chambre Brabazon Ponsonby-Barker, by the Lady Henrietta Taylor, his wife, dau. of Thomas, Earl of Bective. John Augustus Conolly joined the 49th (now the Royal Berkshire) Regt. ; served in the Eastern Campaign of 1854, and was present at the Battle of the Alma, the Siege of Sebastopol, and also at the repulse of the powerful sortie 26 Oct., where he was dangerously wounded, being shot through the chest, and gallantly dis-tinguished himself. On this occasion the Russians attacked Shell Hill, and were met by the fire of our guns as they appeared on its crest, which speedily repulsed them. They retired precipitately, pursued by the picquets and under the fire of the Lan-caster Battery. Field-Marshal Sir Evelyn Wood relates that the Russians " fell back,

and our infantry pursued them, being led most gallantly by Lieut. Conolly, the only man just then in red, the others wearing great coats." For his gallantry on this occasion Conolly was subsequently awarded the Victoria Cross. He, of course, won the decoration in the 49th Regt., but the decora-tion was gazetted after he had been transferred to the Coldstream Guards [London Gazette, 5 May, 1857]: " John Augustus Conolly, Brevet Major, Coldstream Guards (late 49th Regt). Date of Act of Bravery : 26 Oct. 1854. In the attack by the Russians against the position held by the 2nd Division on the 26 Oct. 1854, Major Conolly, then a Lieut. in the 49th Regt., while in command of a company of that regiment, on outlying picquets, made himself most conspicuous by the gallantry of his behaviour. He came particularly under the observation of the late Field-Marshal Lord Raglan, while in personal encounter with several Russians in defence of his post. He ultimately fell dangerously wounded. Lieut. Conolly was highly praised in General Orders, and promoted into the Coldstream Guards, as a reward for his exemplary behaviour on this occasion." Corpl. Owens, V.C., is described in the Gazette of his Victoria Cross as having " greatly distinguished himself in personal encounter with the Russians, and nobly assisted Major Conolly, Coldstream Guards." Brevet Major Conolly was personally decorated by Queen Victoria at the first Investiture after the institution of the Victoria Cross, which was held in Hyde Park 26 June, 1857. He m. 4 Aug. 1864, Ida Charlotte (who died in 1886), dau. of Edwin Burnaby, of Baggrave Hall, Leicestershire, and their children were : John Richard Arthur (b. in 1869) ; Alice Geta Katherine (m. Eustace Abel Smith, of Longhills, Lincoln) ; Conagh Edwina (m. John McNeill, Cold-stream Guards) ; Louisa Augusta, and Irene Beatrice. Major Conolly was promoted to Lieut.-Colonel, and retired from the Army in 1863 ; became Sub-Commissioner, Dublin Metropolitan Police, and later Resident Magistrate for the Curragh of Kildare. Lieut.-Colonel Conolly died in Jan. 1889, and an obituary notice of him appeared in the " Times " of Friday, 18 Jan. of that year.

London Gazette, 23 June, 1857.—The Queen has been graciously

pleased to signify her intention to confer the Decoration of the Victoria Cross on the undermentioned Officers, Non-commissioned Officer and men of Her Majesty's Army, who have been recommended to her for that decora-tion, on account of Acts of Bravery performed by them before the enemy during the late war as recorded against their several names :—

GRADY, THOMAS, Private, joined the 4th (Royal Lancaster) Regt.,

Thomas Grady.

and served in the Crimean Campaign of 1854–55, and was awarded the Victoria Cross [London Gazette, 23 June, 1857]: " Thomas Grady, Private, 4th Regt. Dates of Acts of Bravery, 18 Oct. 1854 ; 22 Nov. 1854. For having on 18 Oct. 1854, volunteered to repair the embrasures of the Sailors' Battery on the Left Attack, and effected the same under a very heavy fire from a line of batteries. For gallant conduct on 22 Nov. 1854, in the repulse of the Russian attack on the advanced trench of the Left Attack, when, on being severely wounded, he refused to quit the front, encouraging by such determined bearing the weak force engaged with the enemy to maintain its position." Private Grady was decorated by Queen Victoria at

the first Presentation in Hyde Park 26 June, 1857. He was promoted to Sergt. ; emigrated to Australia, and died there 18 May, 1891, and was interred with full military honours.

EVANS, SAMUEL, Private, joined the 26th Cameronians in 1839,

Samuel Evans.

serving with that regiment in China in 1842 (China Medal). He was transferred to the 1st Yorkshires, and, as related in the Gazette, entered an embrasure and repaired a breach under very heavy fire in one of our batteries before Sebastopol. Our gunners had been most of them killed, and while others were being brought to take their place, Evans and Callaghan went into the Battery and leapt into the embrasure, where they persevered until the breach was mended. Callaghan fell during the war, but Evans was one of the sixty-two who received the Victoria Cross from the hands of Her Majesty the Queen 26 June, 1857. Besides the Victoria Cross, Evans also received for this campaign the Crimean Medal with three clasps, the

French War Medal and the Turkish Medal. The award of his Victoria Cross is notified in the London Gazette of 23 June, 1857 : " Samuel Evans, Private, 19th Regt. Date of Act of Bravery : 13 April, 1855. For volunteering to go into an embrasure, thereby render-ing very great assistance in repairing damage, under the very heavy fire from the enemy, 13 April, 1855." He died at Edinburgh in his eightieth year, in Oct. 1901.

DICKSON, COLLINGWOOD, Brevet Lieut.-Colonel, b. 20 Nov. 1817 ; 3rd s. of the late Major-General Sir Alexander Dickson, G.C.B., R.A., and a gdson. of the late Admiral William Dickson, Admiral of the Blue, by his

Collingwood Dickson.

marriage with Jane, dau. of Mr. Alexander Collingwood, of Unthank, Northumber-land ; educ. at the Royal Military Academy, Woolwich and entered the Royal Artillery as 2nd Lieut. on 18 Dec. 1835, getting his first step in Nov. 1837, and being made Capt. and Brevet Major in 1846. At the time of Sir Collingwood Dickson's death a most interesting letter from his old friend and comrade-in-arms, Major-General C. H. Owen, appeared in the " Army and Navy Gazette," in which the latter wrote : " In all the accounts of his (Sir C. Dickson's) services in the different newspapers, I have not seen one that mentions his having served under Sir De Lacy Evans in the Carlist War in Spain. I think I shall be right in stating

that it was for this service that he got his brevet rank of Major. There were only two or three Brevet Majors in the Royal Artillery before the Crimean War, and there had been few oppor-tunities for officers of that arm seeing active service during the long peace succeeding the Waterloo Campaign. For this service in Spain he got, I suppose, the Order of Charles III." He had also the Orders of San Fernando and Isabella la Catolica. On 14 Jan. 1847, he m. Harriet, dau. of the Rev. Thomas Burnaby, Vicar of Blakesley, Northamptonshire. Lady Dickson died in Feb. 1894. He was promoted to Major in 1848, and in 1854 became Lieut.-Colonel. He served on the staff of Lord Raglan in the Crimea 1854–55, and was present at the affairs of Balganac and Mackenzie's Farm, the Battles of Alma and Inkerman, capture of Balaklava, the expedi-tion to Kertch, and the Siege of Sebastopol. During the Siege he commanded the Right Siege Train, and was present at the bombardments of 17 Oct., 9 April and 17 June. Major-General C. H. Owen says : " As to the services of Sir Collingwood Dickson in the Siege Train, those who, like myself, served in the Right Attack before Sebastopol, well know their great value.

He was to the gunners what Capt. Peel, R.N., was to the sailors. He was one of the coolest men under fire I ever saw, full of energy and interest in all the siege work, including the comfort of the artillery in this attack, among other things organizing a comfortable kitchen for the use of all the companies, and so economizing also the scanty amount of fuel that could be procured, and making some rough cooking and a supply of hot water for coffee possible. As to his directing the unloading of an ammunition wagon behind the 21–gun battery, 17 Oct. 1854, I have a pretty vivid memory of that dangerous service, for when we of the second relief reached the spot, Sir Collingwood Dickson picked me out and ordered me to go on with the unloading of the wagon and sending the ammunition-boxes on hand-barrows up to the battery. We were under the apparent shelter of the hill on which the battery was placed, but practically in the open, as the shot and shell from the Russian guns passing over the battery ranged along at about three feet above the rear slope and pretty parallel to it. A round shot cut down two horses in the wagon, and continued its course as if it had done nothing ; and I must confess that we of the party were not sorry when a Russian shell plunged into the mass of boxes of ammunition in the wagon and blew them up, so that I could withdraw the men into the 21–gun battery. Sir Collingwood Dickson's example was an encouragement to all to do their duty, and socially he was most pleasant and genial." For his services in this campaign Colonel Dickson received the Medal with four clasps, was created a Companion of the Bath, was given the Brevet of Colonel, appointed A.D.C. to Queen Victoria, and awarded the Victoria Cross [London Gazette, 24 Feb. 1857] : " Collingwood Dickson, C.B., Brevet Colonel, Royal Artillery. Date of Act of Bravery : 17 Oct. 1854. For having on 17 Oct. 1854, when the batteries of the right attack had run short of powder, displayed the greatest coolness and contempt of danger in directing the unloading of several wagons of the field battery which were brought up to the trenches to supply the want, and having personally assisted in carrying the powder-barrels under a severe fire from the enemy." Colonel Dickson also received the foreign decorations of the Legion of Honour, the Second Class of the Medjidie, and the Turkish Medal. From 1856 to 1862 he was Assistant Adjutant-General for Royal Artillery in Ireland, and was promoted to the rank of substantive Colonel 5 April, 1866, and Major-General in the same year. From 1870 to 1875 he was the Inspector-General of Artillery ; was created a K.C.B. in 1871, and was promoted Lieut.-General 8 June, 1876, having been made Colonel-Commandant of the Royal Regiment of Artillery in the previous year. The date of his commission as General was 1 Oct. 1877, and that of his retirement from the active list was 20 Nov. 1884, in which year he received the Grand Cross of the Bath. From 1881 to 1885 he was President of the Ordnance Committee at the War Office. General Sir Collingwood Dickson died at his residence, 79, Claverton Street, S.W., 28 Nov. 1904, aged 87.

DAVIS, GRONOW, Capt., joined the Royal Artillery 18 Dec. 1837 ; became Lieut. 11 April, 1841, and Capt. 30 March, 1848. He served in the Crimean War, and was awarded the Victoria Cross [London Gazette, 23 June, 1857] : " Gronow Davis, Capt., Royal Artillery. Date of Act of Bravery : 8 Sept. 1855. For great coolness and gallantry in the attack on the Redan 8 Sept. 1855, on which occasion he commanded the spiking party, and after which he saved the life of Lieut. Sanders, 39th Regt., by jumping over the parapet of a sap, and proceeding twice some distance across the open, under a murderous fire, to assist in conveying that officer, whose leg was broken and who was otherwise severely wounded, under cover, and repeated this act in the conveyance of other wounded soldiers from the same exposed position." He also received the Brevet of Major and the Medjidie for his gallant conduct. Capt. Davis was decorated by Queen Victoria at the first Presentation in Hyde Park 26 June, 1857. He became Major 28 Aug. 1857 ; Lieut.-Colonel 29 Aug. 1868 ; Colonel 1 Oct. 1876, and Major-General 29 Oct. 1881. Major-General Gronow Davis retired from the Army in 1881, and died at 5, Royal Park, Clifton, in his 64th year, on Sunday, 18 Oct. 1891. His *s.* is Lieut.-Colonel Gronow Davis, D.S.O.

CAMBRIDGE, DANIEL, Sergt., entered the Royal Artillery ; served in the Crimean Campaign of 1854–55. For his services in this war he received the Crimean Medal with clasps, and was awarded the Victoria Cross [London Gazette, 23 June, 1857 : " Daniel Cambridge, Sergt., Royal Artillery. Date of Act of Bravery, 8 Sept. 1855. For having volunteered for the spiking party at the assault on the Redan 8 Sept. 1855, and continuing therewith, after being severely wounded ; and for having in the after part of the same day gone out in front of the advanced trench, under a heavy fire, to bring in a wounded man, in performing which service he was himself severely wounded a second time." Sergt. Cambridge was decorated by Her Majesty at the first Investiture in Hyde Park, 26 June, 1857. Cambridge lost his Cross, and a duplicate one was supplied to him.

Daniel Cambridge.

Subsequently both came into the market, and the duplicate one was the subject of police-court proceedings, but eventually came into the possession of the purchaser of the original Cross. In later years Cambridge became one of the Yeomen of the Guard.

London Gazette, 25 Sept. 1857.—War Office, 25 Sept. 1857. The Queen has been graciously pleased to signify her intention to confer the Victoria Cross on the undermentioned Officers and Non-commissioned Officer of Her Majesty's Army, who have been recommended to Her Majesty for that Decoration, in accordance with the rules laid down in Her Majesty's Warrant of 29 Jan. 1856, on account of Acts of Bravery performed by them before the enemy during the late war, as recorded against their several names, viz. :—

TEESDALE, CHRISTOPHER CHARLES, Lieut., *b.* in 1833, and joined the Royal Artillery. During the Crimean War he acted as Aide-de-Camp to the celebrated Sir Fenwick Williams at Kars, and was shut up there during the blockade of that place. He was awarded the Victoria Cross [London Gazette, 25 Sept. 1857] : " Christopher Charles Teesdale, C.B., Lieut. Royal Artillery. Date of Act of Bravery : 29 Sept. 1855. For gallant conduct in having, while acting as Aide-de-Camp to Major-General Sir William Fenwick Williams, Bart., K.C.B., at Kars, volunteered to take command of the force engaged in the defence of the most advanced part of the works—the key of the position—against the attack of the Russian Army ; when by throwing himself into the midst of the enemy, who had penetrated into the above redoubt, he encouraged the garrison to make an attack so vigorous as to drive out the Russians therefrom and prevent its capture ; also for having during the hottest part of the action, when the enemy's fire had driven the Turkish artillerymen from their guns, rallied the latter, and by his intrepid example induced them to return to their post ; and further, after having led the final charge, which completed the victory of the day, for having at the greatest personal risk saved from the fury of the Turks a considerable number of the disabled among the enemy, who were lying wounded outside the works, an action witnessed and acknowledged gratefully before the Russian Staff by General Mouravieff." He was created a K.C.M.G. in 1887, and was for ten years A.D.C. to the Queen ; was Equerry to the Prince of Wales, and was later Master of the Ceremonies to Her Majesty. In 1893 Major-General Sir C. Teesdale went on a ten weeks' visit to Germany, where he had a slight paralytic attack, from which no serious consequences were anticipated. On Sunday, 29 Nov., he went to church, and next day was seized with an attack of paralysis, dying 1 Dec. at his residence, The Ark, South Bersted, Bognor. Sir Christopher Teesdale was unmarried.

MALONE, JOSEPH, Sergt., enlisted in the 13th Light Dragoons in 1851 ; was promoted to L.-Sergt. without having been Corpl., and served in the Crimea 1854–55. It was for remaining with Capt. Webb after the Charge of the Light Brigade that Sergt. Malone won his Cross. The award is recorded in the London Gazette of 25 Sept. 1857 : " Joseph Malone, Sergt., 13th Light Dragoons. Date of Act of Bravery : 25 Oct. 1854. For having stopped under a very heavy fire to take charge of Capt. Webb, 17th Lancers, until others arrived to assist him in removing that officer, who was (as it was afterwards proved) mortally wounded. Sergt. Malone performed this act of bravery while returning on foot from the Charge at the Battle of Balaklava, in which his horse had been shot." He was made Riding Master in the 6th

Joseph Malone.

Dragoons ; Capt. in 1881. With them he served in South Africa from Nov. 1882, until his death at Pinetown in June, 1883. There is a very good portrait of him in the " Records of the 13th Hussars."

JONES, HENRY MITCHELL, Capt., entered the Army in April, 1849, as an Ensign in the 18th Foot. In 1854 he exchanged into the 7th Fusiliers, with whom he served in the Crimea. He was severely wounded at the Battle of the Alma 20 Sept. 1854, and slightly wounded at the assault of the Quarries 7 June, 1855, on which day he won the Victoria Cross [London Gazette, 25 Sept. 1857] : " Henry Mitchell Jones, Capt., The Royal Fusiliers. Date of Act of Bravery : 7 June, 1855. For having distinguished himself while serving with the party which stormed and took the Quarries before Sebastopol, he repeatedly leading on his men to repel the continual assaults of the enemy during the night. Although wounded early in the evening, Capt. Jones remained un-flinchingly at his post until after daylight the following morning." He had become

Henry Mitchell Jones.

Captain in 1855 ; was again wounded 8 Sept. at the assault of the Redan. Capt. Jones, who retired from the Army in 1857, subsequently entered the Diplomatic Service (1858), and was Acting Vice-Consul at Bosna Seraj and Skutari. In 1863 he was appointed Consul for the Fiji and Tonga, and five years later was promoted to be Consul-General at Tabreez. He became Consul-General at Christiania in 1875, and for Eastern Rumelia in 1880. " The death has taken place," says the " Times " of 26 Dec. 1916, " at 25, Gildredge Road, Eastbourne, at the age of 85, of Capt. Henry M. Jones, V.C. (late of the Royal Fusiliers, King's Dragoon Guards and the Diplomatic Service)."

ESMONDE, THOMAS, Capt., was *b.* at Pembrokestown, County Waterford, Ireland, on 25 Aug. 1829 ; *s.* of Capt. James Esmonde, Royal Navy, and of Anne Maria Murphy, of Ringmahon, County Cork. He was the younger brother of the late Sir John Esmonde, 10th baronet, M.P. The seat of the Esmonde family is Ballynastragh, Gorey, County Wexford. They were seated in Wexford as far back as the tenth century, and are descended from Henry Esmonde, who was Seneschal of Wexford in 1294. John Esmonde, a member of this ancient family, was Bishop of Ferns in 1340. In the reign of Queen Elizabeth the head of the house was Sir Laurence Esmonde, who abandoned the creed of his ancestors, took up arms in the cause of Queen Elizabeth, professed himself a Protestant, and was subsequently raised to the peerage as Lord Esmonde of Lymbrick, County Wexford. He married a Roman Catholic lady, Margaret, daughter of O'Flaherty, Dynast of Iar (Connaught), husband of the celebrated Grace O'Malley. They had a son, and Lady Esmonde, fearing that her son would be brought up as a Protestant, ran off with him to her own people in Connaught and brought him up as a strict Roman Catholic. Her husband disowned them both, on the plea that a marriage between a Catholic and a Protestant was voidable in law. The child, Thomas Esmonde, however, eventually obtained possession of the Wexford estate, and would probably have had the peerage, too, but for the confusion wrought by the Civil War. He served in the armies of the King of Sweden, and afterwards commanded a regiment in the Siege of La Rochelle. He raised a troop of horse for the service of Charles I., by whom he was created a baronet (1628). He was attainted in 1642 by the Cromwellian Parliament, and his estates confiscated. His son, Sir Laurence Esmonde, the second baronet, served in the French Army, and was created a Privy Councillor by James II. One of his descendants, Maurice, took service in the Austrian Army, and attained the rank of Baron. His daughter married Count Kavanagh. Sir John Esmonde, 5th Baronet, served in the Spanish Army, and took part in the Siege of Naples in 1736. Sir James Esmonde, 7th Baronet, served in the French Army, as did his son, Sir Thomas Esmonde, the 8th Baronet. Thomas Esmonde was educated at Clongowes Wood College, Ireland. "The Clongonian" of Christmas, 1898, says: "'The late Sir John Esmonde and his brothers were at Clongowes with me. Tommy, afterwards "Esmonde of the Redan," was a general favourite.' These words of an old Clongonian, Mr. John Cullin of Enniscorthy, introduced to our notice one of the most brilliant officers ever sent to the Army from Clongowes. Thomas Esmonde came to Clongowes after his brothers John and James, in 1840; and he left the College in 1846, having 'done' Rhetoric. In the 'Annual Academic Exercises, 1846,' we find him heading the list with an 'Introductory Latin Oration,' and it may be noted that lower down is the item, 'French Dialogue Scene from Molière's *Fourberies de Scapin*,' in which Lee O'Connor (Port of Spain, Trinidad) plays Scapin, and Christopher Pallas (Chief Baron, 1898) takes the part of Argante." After leaving school, young Esmonde joined the 18th Royal Irish Regt. as Ensign on 22 Nov. 1851, and saw service in India and in the Burmese Campaign of 1852–53, receiving the Medal and clasp for Pegu, and became Lieut. 7 June, 1853. Lieut. Esmonde took part in the Crimean War 1854–55, being present at the Siege and Capture of Sebastopol from 30 Dec. 1854, to 27 July, 1855, including the well-known assault on the Cemetery on the fortieth anniversary of Waterloo. We are told by Colonel O. Le M. Gretton, in his "History of the Royal Irish Regiment" (page 141), that—before the attack on the Redan—the Irish Regt. was in the wildest high spirits at the prospect of the coming fight. "Though it was almost day," he says, "the Russians had not yet detected the presence of Eyre's troops, and the General took an opportunity of addressing the Royal Irish, telling them that he knew that they would prove themselves good soldiers, and 'this day do something that will ring in every cabin in Ireland.' Then he added: 'Now, men, above all things, you must be quiet or you'll get peppered!' In answer to this very reasonable appeal a shout arose from the ranks: 'All right, your Honour, we'll get in. Three cheers for the General!' Before the officers could stop them the men had given three lusty cheers. Eyre remonstrated, but the Royal Irish were far too eager for the fray to be sensible, and in response to his reiterated entreaties for silence they burst forth into stentorian cheering, this time for Old Ireland. 'Let them go in and attack,' cried the General in despair; 'they will only draw fire upon us.'" Before the attack also, two parties of the Royal Irish—one of them under Capt. Esmonde—occupied for several hours some houses from which they drove out the Russians, who were just going to have some breakfast. A newspaper cutting says of this exploit: "The Irish public are well acquainted with the soldierly qualities of Major Esmonde and proud of the distinction he had won in the Crimean War, especially within Sebastopol, long before that great fortress had fallen, when as the commander of a party of the Royal Irish he had, through the fortune of war, to hold his ground within the Russian lines for several hours, and ultimately he succeeded in conducting back into safety the gallant band who had followed him." It is a tradition in the regiment that Esmonde and his companions thoroughly enjoyed the feast spread for them by their involuntary hosts. Mr. Cullin says: "On the occasion of the famous assault on the Redan, Capt. Esmonde's company was the first to enter Sebastopol. The attack failed, and the main body of the assailants retired to the trenches, leaving Capt. Esmonde and his men in the Russian works. They maintained their position until nightfall, and then withdrew under cover of darkness. To show that he had been undoubtedly in Sebastopol, Capt. Esmonde took back two Russian books found in one of the houses held by his men. These he fastened to his sword-belt. In the retreat at nightfall the Irishmen were discovered by the Russians, and a heavy fire was at once opened on the little party. A rifle bullet lodged in one of the books, the one that is now in the library of the Jesuit residence at Gardiner Street, Dublin. The other is in Sir Thomas Esmonde's library at Ballynastragh." One of the results of the attack on the Redan was that Capt. Esmonde was one of the first to receive the Victoria Cross on its institution, being the third officer to win it. His Victoria Cross was gazetted 25 Sept. 1857: "Thomas Esmonde, Capt., 18th Regt. Dates of Acts of Bravery, 18 June, 1855, and 20 June, 1855. For having, after being engaged in the attack on the Redan, repeatedly assisted at great personal risk, under a heavy fire of shell and grape, in rescuing wounded men from exposed situations; and also, while in command of a covering party two days after, for having rushed with the most prompt and daring gallantry to the spot where a fireball from the enemy had just lodged, which he effectually extinguished before it had betrayed the position of the working party under his protection, thus saving it from a murderous fire of shell and grape which was immediately opened upon the spot where the fireball had fallen." He had been promoted to Capt. 6 April, 1855. Besides the Victoria Cross he received the Crimean Medal with a clasp for Sebastopol, and the Turkish Medal, and was given the Brevet of Major in his regiment. Colonel Edwards wrote in a letter describing the attack on the Redan: "Our brigade was more than successful, and have received great praise, especially the Royal Irish Regt." "When the war was over," writes Father Joseph Dalton, S.J., in his "Reminiscences of Clongowes Sixty Years Ago," "Tommy Esmonde came down and spent a few days with us at Clongowes, where he endeared himself to his old masters, and to all the house." Capt. Esmonde was devoted to sports of all sorts, a keen sportsman, winning the Grand Military of 1857, at Punchestown, on his own horse, Archimedes. He was promoted to Major on 29 Dec. 1857. In Nov. 1858, he married, at Gardiner Street, Dublin, Matilda O'Kelly, daughter of De Pentony O'Kelly, Esq., of Barrettstown, County Kildare, and "rarely," says Father Joseph Dalton, "was there a brighter prospect of a long and happy union. Happy indeed it was, but ere the gallant soldier reached the prime of life, a great sorrow cut short the happiness for ever." Colonel and Mrs. Esmonde had five children: (a) Thomas Louis Esmonde, Esq., of Ballycowcey, County Wexford, who married Mary, daughter of George Mansfield, Esq., D.L., of Morristown, Lattin, County Kildare. (b) Eva Mary, married James Comerford, Esq., of Ardavon, County Wexford. Their son, Thomas Comerford, served in the Royal Munster Fusiliers at Gallipoli, was favourably mentioned, and later joined an Indian Cavalry regiment. (c) Matilda Mary Josephine, married Arthur Westropp Dawson, Esq., of Old Court, County Tipperary. (d) Frances. (e) Georgiana Helen Mary. He became Lieut.-Colonel and A.D.C. to the Lord Lieutenant of Ireland on 2 Dec. 1868, and retired on that date by the sale of his commission. On leaving the service, Lieut.-Colonel Esmonde was appointed by the Lord-Lieutenant of the day (Ireland), Lord Carlisle, who had taken a great fancy to him, Deputy-Inspector-General of the Royal Irish Constabulary, in which situation he gave the greatest satisfaction, both to the public and to those under him, by his affable and gentle manners. He was in command of the Royal Irish Constabulary. "When following the Kildares one day in 1872, Mr. Cullin tells us, a branch struck him (Colonel Esmonde) in the eye severely as he cleared a thorn fence. The injured eye became badly inflamed, and the other shortly after became affected. Brain fever followed, and soon death came to close the sufferings of a brave Irishman and an ever-loyal son of Clongowes." Colonel Esmonde died at Bruges, Belgium, on Sunday, 14 Jan. 1873, aged 45.

Thomas Esmonde.

The London Gazette, 20 Nov. 1857.—War Office, 18 Nov. 1857. The Queen has been most graciously pleased to signify her intention to confer the Decoration of the Victoria Cross on the undermentioned Officers and Non-commissioned Officer of Her Majesty's Army, who have been recommended to Her Majesty for that Decoration, in accordance with the rules laid down in Her Majesty's Warrant of 29 Jan. 1856, on account of Acts of Bravery performed by them before the enemy during the late war, as recorded against their several names :—

FARRELL, JOHN, Sergt., served in the Crimean War of 1854–55, and for his services in that campaign was awarded the Victoria Cross [London Gazette, 18 Nov. 1857]: "John Farrell, Quartermaster-Sergt., 17th Lancers. Date of Act of Bravery: 25 Oct. 1854" (subsequently corrected to 6 June, 1854). "For having remained amidst a shower of shot and shell, with Capt. Webb, who was severely wounded, and whom he and Sergt.-Major Berryman had carried as far as the pain of his wounds would allow, until a stretcher was procured, when he assisted the sergeant-major and a private of the 13th Dragoons (Malone) to carry that officer off the field. This took place on 25 Oct. 1854, after the charge at the Battle of Balaklava, in which Farrell's horse was killed under him." Quartermaster-Sergt Farrell, V.C., died at Secunderabad on 3 Aug. 1865.

SYMONS, GEORGE, Lieut., served in the Crimean War of 1854–55, and for his services in that campaign was awarded the Victoria Cross [London Gazette, 20 Nov. 1857]: "George Symons, Lieut., Military Train, 5th Battn. (late Sergt. Royal Artillery). Date of Act of Bravery: 18 Oct. 1854. For conspicuous gallantry on 18 Oct. 1854, in having volunteered to unmask the embrasures of a five-gun battery in the advanced Right Attack, and when so employed, under a terrific fire, which the enemy commenced immediately on the opening of the first embrasure, and increased on the unmasking of each additional one, in having overcome the great difficulty of uncovering the last by boldly mounting the parapet, and throwing down the sand-bags, when a shell from the enemy burst and wounded him severely." Erratum in the London Gazette of 20 Nov. Corrected 1 Dec. 1857: "The date of G. Symons's Act of Bravery is 6 June, 1855, and not 18 Oct. 1854." Lieut. Symons's Victoria Cross is in the United Service Institute, London, S.W.

CRAIG, JAMES, Ensign and Adjutant, was *b.* in the parish of St. Martin's, in or near the town of Perth, in the county of Perth. His calling, before he joined the Army, was that of a labourer, and he was five feet eight and a quarter inches in height, and had blue eyes and fair hair. He enlisted in the Scots Fusilier Regt. of Foot Guards on 25 Aug. 1843, and was attested to the said regiment at Perth on 26 Aug. 1843, at the age of eighteen years and three months. He served as a Private (No. 3075) in the Scots Fusilier Guards from 26 Aug. 1843, to 10 June, 1846 (two years and 289 days); Corpl. 11 June, 1846, to 21 July, 1851 (five years and 41 days); Sergt. 22 July, 1851, to 26 June, 1855 (three years and 340 days), and Colour-Sergt. 27 June, 1855, to 25 June 1856 (213 days). His service abroad with the Scots Guards was in the East from 28 Feb. 1854, to 15 Jan. 1855, and he was present at the Battles of Balaklava and Inkerman, the Siege and Fall of Sebastopol, and at the sortie of 26 Oct. He was wounded at the Battle of Inkerman—a severe gunshot wound through both legs—and was awarded the Victoria Cross [London Gazette, 18 Nov. 1857]: " James Craig, Ensign and Adjutant, Military Train (late Scots Fusilier Guards). For having volunteered and personally collected other volunteers to go out under a heavy fire of grape and small arms on the night of 6 Sept. 1855, when in the right advanced sap in front of the Redan, to look for Capt. Buckley, Scots Fusilier Guards, who was supposed to be wounded. Sergt. Craig brought in, with the assistance of a drummer, the body of that officer, whom he found dead, in the performance of which act he was wounded." Sergt. Craig received the Crimean Medal with three clasps, and was appointed Cornet and Adjutant in the Land Transport Corps on 26 Jan. 1856. In 1859 he was Lieut. and Adjutant in the 10th (Lincolnshire) Regt., and his name disappears from the Army List in 1862.

SYLVESTER, HENRY THOMAS, Assistant Surgeon, is M.D., L.R.C.S.

Edinburgh, L.S.A. He served in the Crimean War; was present at the Siege and Fall of Sebastopol, 1856; was mentioned in Despatches; received the Medal with clasp; was created a Knight of the Legion of Honour, and was awarded the Victoria Cross [London Gazette, 20 Nov. 1857]: " Assistant Surgeon Henry Thomas Sylvester, 23rd Regt. Date of Act of Bravery: 8 Sept. 1855. For going out on 8 Sept, 1855, under a heavy fire, in front of the fifth parallel Right Attack, to a spot near the Redan, where Lieut. and Adjutant Dyneley was lying, mortally wounded, and for dressing his wounds in that dangerous and exposed situation. (N.B.—This officer was mentioned in General Sir James Simpson's Despatch of 18 Sept. 1855, for his courage in

Henry T. Sylvester.

going to the front, under a heavy fire, to assist the wounded.)" He served in the Indian Mutiny Campaign of 1857-58, including the Relief of Lucknow (Medal with two clasps), and retired in 1861.

The London Gazette, 15 Jan. 1858.—War Office, 15 Jan. 1858. The Queen has been graciously pleased to signify her intention to confer the Decoration of the Victoria Cross on the undermentioned Officers and men of Her Majesty's Army, who have been recommended to Her Majesty for that Decoration, in accordance with the rules laid down in Her Majesty's Warrant of 29 Jan. 1856, on account of Acts of Bravery performed by them in India as recorded against their several names :—

CROWE, JOSEPH, Lieut., joined the 78th Highlanders (Ross-shire Buffs) as Ensign in 1846; became Lieut. in 1850, and served in the Persian Campaign of 1856 (Medal and clasp). Also in the Indian Mutiny Cam-

paign, and was present at the actions of Futtehpore, Pandoo Nuddee, Cawnpore, Oonao, Buseerutgunge, Boorzeke Chowkee, and other actions, and received the Medal and two clasps, and " for distinguished and gallant conduct " was awarded the Victoria Cross [London Gazette, 15 Jan. 1858: " Joseph P. H. Crowe, Lieut. 78th Regt. (now Capt. 10th Regt.). For being the first to enter the redoubt at Boorzeke Chowkee, the entrenched village in front of the Busherutgunge, on 12 Aug. (Telegram from the late Major-General Havelock to the Commander-in-Chief in India. Dated Cawnpore, 18 Aug. 1857)." In the race to enter the redoubt, Lieut. H. D. Campbell was neck and neck with him, but died of cholera the next

Joseph Crowe.

day. A paragraph appeared in the papers on 16 Aug. 1917: " Sixth Decimal Notice. Campbell. On 16 Aug. 1857, at Cawnpore (having been selected with Lieut. Crowe for the V.C. given 12 Aug. to the regiment by Havelock) died Capt. Howard Douglas Campbell, 78th Highlanders (Ross-shire Buffs), son of Admiral Donald Campbell, of Barbeck, Argyll. Death robbed him of his well-earned distinction. D. A. Campbell, Lieut.-Colonel, Clare, Suffolk." In 1858 Crowe was promoted Capt. into the 10th (Lincolnshire) Regt., and in 1859 was given the Brevet of Major. He became Major in 1867, was given the Brevet of Lieut.-Colonel in 1871, and was for some years in command of a battalion of the Lincolnshire Regt. In 1875 he was promoted to Lieut.-Colonel, and attained the command of the 2nd Battn. He retired in 1876, and died in February of that year.

HAVELOCK, HENRY MARSHMAN, Lieut., was *b.* at Chinsurah on 6 Aug. 1830; eldest *s.* of (then) Lieut. Henry Havelock, 13th Foot (Major-General Sir Henry Havelock, K.C.B.), and Hannah, youngest daughter

of the Rev. Dr. Marshman. He was appointed Ensign, 39th Regt. of Foot (The Dorsetshire Regt.) 31 March, 1846, when he was little more than fifteen. He became Lieut. (by purchase) 86th Regt. of Foot (The Royal County Down Regt.) 23 June, 1848; (by exchange) 10th Regt. of Foot (The North Lincolnshire Regt.) 13 Feb. 1852, and Adjutant of the regiment on the same date, and which post he was permitted, although on the Staff, in the latter part of the Mutiny. He saw service in the Persian Gulf, while acting (22 Jan. to 25 May, 1857) as D.A.Q.M.G. on the Staff of his father, who commanded the second division. He was present at the bombardment and capture of Mohummerah (Despatches [London Gazette, 18 Aug.

Henry M. Havelock.

1857]; Medal). He proceeded to India as A.D.C. to Brigadier-General Havelock, Bengal (23 June to 29 Nov. 1857), and served throughout the Mutiny Campaign of 1857–59, being present at the Battles of Futtehpore, Aoung, Pandoo-Nuddee, Cawnpore (where he won his Victoria Cross), Oonao, Busseerat Gunge (where his horse was shot under him), Nawabgunge, Boorbeake, Chowkee, Bithoor, Mungarwaar and Alumbagh, and at the Relief of Lucknow (dangerously wounded by a musket ball through the left elbow, and horse shot), defence of the Residency, and Second Relief of Lucknow (severely wounded). On 9 Oct. 1857, Lieut. Havelock was promoted Capt. into the Royal Irish Regt. (18th Regt. of Foot). He served with the Jounpore Field Force under General Franks, as D.A.A.G., and was present at the actions of Meerutpore, Chanda, Umeerpore, Sultanpore (where the force joined the Commander-in-Chief) and Dowraha, and at the Siege and Capture of Lucknow, where he again attracted attention by his extreme gallantry; and it is related that at the capture of Alumbagh Lieut. Havelock twice saved General Outram's life, who again recommended him for the Victoria Cross. The decoration was, however, subsequently awarded to him for the services described in the first recommendation [London Gazette, 15 Jan. 1858]: " Henry Marshman Havelock, Lieut., 10 Regt. 'In the combat at Cawnpore Lieut. Havelock was my aide-de-camp. The 64th Regt. had been much under artillery fire, from which it had severely suffered. The whole of the infantry was lying down in line, when, perceiving that the enemy had brought out the last reserved gun, a 24-pounder, and was rallying round it, I called up the regiment to rise and advance. Without any other word from me, Lieut. Havelock placed himself on his horse in front of the centre of the 64th—opposite the muzzle of the gun. Major Stirling, commanding the regiment, was in front, dismounted, but the lieutenant continued to move steadily on in front of the regiment at a foot pace on his horse. The gun discharged shot until the troops were within a short distance, when it fired grape. In went the corps, led by the lieutenant, who still steered steadily on the gun's muzzle, until it was mastered by a rush of the 64th.' (Extract from a telegram from the late Major-General Sir Henry Havelock to the Commander-in-Chief in India, dated Cawnpore, 18 Aug. 1857)." He was also present at the relief of Azimghur, the action at the Matehi and skirmishes in the Jugdespur jungles (wounded). His next appointment was that of D.A.G. to General Luard's Field Force in the Behar and Ghazeepore districts, including operations in the latter district, with the relief of Russoorah and the campaign in Shahabad. He commanded a flying column of cavalry in pursuit of the Jugdespur rebels into the Kymore Hills, and commanded the 1st Regt. of Hodson's Horse during the campaign in Oudh, including the action at Burgedia, capture of Musjeedia, and action on the Raptee. In addition to the Brevet of Major, he was, on 26 April, 1859, given the Brevet of Lieut.-Colonel, when he was barely thirty years of age. He was, as has been related, awarded the Victoria Cross, and received one year's service for Lucknow and the Medal with two clasps. He was mentioned in Despatches [London Gazettes, 13 Oct. 1857, 17 Feb., 31 March, 25 May, 17 July, 31 Aug., 15 Nov. 1858; 31 Jan., 22 Feb. and 24 March, 1859]. In 1858 he was created a baronet, his father, for whom the honour was originally intended, having died before it could be conferred on him. On his return to England he was, on 1 Oct. 1861, appointed D.A.A.G. at Aldershot; but two years later was again on active service in the New Zealand War (25 Oct. 1863, to Jan. 1865) as D.A.Q.M.G. to the troops, and was present at the actions of Rangariri, Paterangi, Rangiawhia and Orakan. He was in command of the troops at the skirmish at Waiari, when the enemy's loss fell altogether upon that tribe which had brought about the war. He was mentioned in Despatches [London Gazettes, 19 Feb. and 14 May, 1864]; received the New Zealand Medal, and was created a C.B. 10 Aug. 1886. He was Major, half-pay, unattached, 23 June, 1864. In 1865 Sir Henry Havelock married Lady Alice Moreton, daughter of the second Earl of Ducie, and they had two sons, Henry Spencer Moreton, the present baronet, and Allan, and a daughter, Ethel, who married in 1886 Mr. Joseph Albert Pease, M.P., who became Lord Gainford in 1916. From 13 March, 1867, until 31 March, 1869, he served in Canada as A.Q.M.G.; he was given the Brevet of Colonel on 17 June, 1865; was A.A.Q.M.G. in Ireland 1 Aug. 1869, till 30 Sept. 1872. It was during this tour of duty that, on obtaining leave of absence, he proceeded to France as a war correspondent, and was present on 2 Sept. 1870, at the surrender of the Emperor Napoleon III. and the French Army at Sedan. In 1873 Sir Henry became Parliamentary candidate for Stroud, but was defeated; in the following year, however, he was elected Member for Sunderland as an advanced Liberal. In 1877 he employed what leisure politics allowed him in acting as war correspondent for several months. Attached to the Russian Army, he was present at the operations in the Shipka Pass and at the Siege of Plevna. He retained his seat as M.P. for Sunderland till April, 1881, when he was appointed to command the 3rd Brigade at Aldershot; but ill-health compelled his retirement on half-pay with the honorary rank of Lieut.-General in Dec. of that year. He had been promoted to Major-General on 18 March, 1880, and on 23 March, 1880, had assumed the additional name of Allan, in compliance with the desire of his cousin, Mr. R. H. Allan, of Blackwell Hall, Darlington, co. Durham. In 1882 he was at Ismailia, where Sir Garnet Wolseley had his Headquarters, and he was unofficially present at the engagement at Tel-el-Kebir. He "went over the top," as we would say nowadays, with the Highland Brigade, commanded by Sir Archibald Alison, one of the battalions of which—the 74th, now the 2nd Battn. the Highland Light Infantry—had been under his command in the 3rd Brigade at Aldershot. Tradition says that he rode at the earthworks behind which Arabi Pasha's infantry were waiting the assault, as if riding at a fence out hunting, and that his horse missed his footing. He must, however, have eventually succeeded in surmounting the obstacle, for it is said that he rode through to Cairo that evening with the Cavalry Brigade. Tradition lies, however, when it says that he was armed only with a hunting-crop; he knew better—he carried a revolver. His gallantry on this occasion coming to the ears of an insurance company interested in the length of his days, they forthwith cancelled his policy. In 1884 Sir Henry was returned as Liberal M.P. for South-East Durham. When the Home Rule question seemed to him to threaten the integrity of the Empire he became a Unionist. His great personal popularity enabled him to retain his seat at the election of 1886, and although in 1892 he lost his seat by a small majority, 1895 saw him back at Westminster as a representative of the Durham miners till his death in 1897. He was Honorary Colonel, Northern Division, 2nd Brigade Royal Artillery (late Durham Militia Artillery) 7 May, 1887; Officer Commanding the Tyne and Tees Volunteer Infantry Brigade 17 Oct. 1888; was created K.C.B. 21 June, 1887. On 27 Nov. of that year he was appointed Colonel-in-Chief of the Royal Irish Regt. Of all his honours and distinctions he valued this one, perhaps, the most highly. On 22 June, 1897, he was created a G.C.B. Sir Henry Havelock-Allan went to India at the end of 1897, to inquire into the justice, or otherwise, of certain criticisms which had been made on the state of discipline in the 2nd Battn. Royal Irish Regt. Whilst in India he was attached to Sir William Lockhart's punitive expedition, and was provided with an escort by that General, whom he promised to run no unnecessary risks. But habit was too strong for him; he constantly rode ahead of his escort, and on 30 Dec. 1897, was reported missing. His dead body was discovered later—on it his diary, the last entry in which ran as follows: "A lovely morning—got them all up—as fit as a fiddle." He had been shot by the Afridis. At the special request of the Royal Irish Regt. the body was taken to Rawal Pindi, where that regiment was quartered. Sir Henry was a man of infinite versatility; he loved books, pictures and horses; but what he probably loved most was danger, for its own sake. Lord Wolseley once described him as the "bravest man in the British Army." But besides this dowry of heroism, he had other gifts: the "pen of a ready writer." His "Three Great Military Questions of the Day," which appeared in 1867, and which contained exhaustive accounts of Sheridan's operations in the American War of Secession, might serve even to-day as a practical manual on mounted infantry tactics. The gift of tongues also—French and German he spoke like a native, and used to a good purpose during the campaigns of 1870 and 1877–78, when he was in constant and intimate touch with the Headquarters of the King of Prussia and the Czar Alexander. As a platform speaker he was unsurpassed; the Durham miners still talk of his ready and mordant wit, and many of the older ones believe him to be still alive. His tenants, one and all, worshipped him. An extraordinarily brilliant, but yet an unfortunate man, for he never enjoyed any of the higher prizes of a profession which he adored.

HANCOCK, THOMAS, Private, served in the Indian Mutiny, and for his services in that campaign was awarded the Victoria Cross [London Gazette, 15 Jan. 1858]: "Thomas Hancock and John Purcell, Privates, 9th Lancers. 'The guns, I am happy to say, were saved, but a wagon of Major Scott's battery was blown up. I must not fail to mention the excellent conduct of a sowar of the 4th Irregular Cavalry and two men of the 9th Lancers, Privates Thomas Hancock and John Purcell, who, when my horse was shot down, remained with me throughout. One of these men and the sowar offered me their horses, and I was dragged out by the sowar's horse. Private Hancock was severely wounded and Private Purcell's horse was killed under him. The sowar's name is Roopur Khan.' (Extract from a letter from Brigadier J. H. Grant, C.B., to the Deputy-Assistant-Adjutant-General of Division. Dated, Camp, Delhi, 22 June, 1857)." Private T. Hancock died on 12 March, 1871.

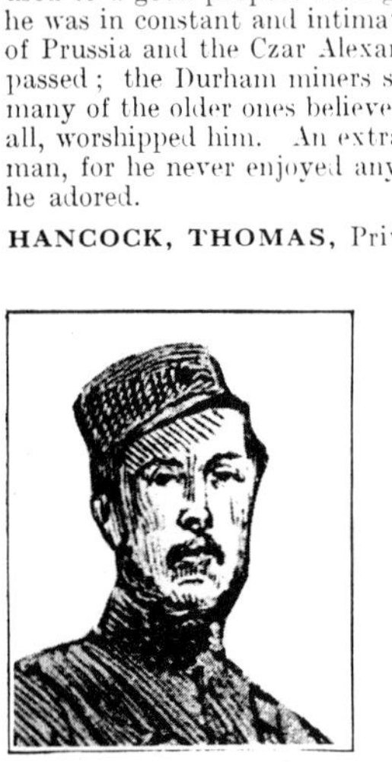

Thomas Hancock.

PURCELL, JOHN, Private, served in the Indian Mutiny, and was awarded the Victoria Cross for his services in that campaign [London Gazette, 15 Jan. 1858]: "Thomas Hancock and John Purcell, Privates, 9th Lancers. 'The guns, I am happy to say, were saved, but a wagon of Major Scott's battery was blown up. I must not fail to mention the excellent conduct of a sowar of the 4th Irregular Cavalry and two men of the 9th Lancers, Privates Thomas Hancock and John Purcell, who, when my horse was shot down, remained by me throughout. One of these men and the sowar offered me their horses, and I was dragged out by the sowar's horse. Private Hancock was severely wounded and Private Purcell's horse was killed under him. The sowar's name is Roopur Khan' (Extract from a letter from Brigadier J. H. Grant, C.B., Commanding Cavalry Brigade of the Field Force, to the Deputy-Assistant-Adjutant-General of Division. Dated, Camp, Delhi, 22 June, 1857)." Private Purcell was killed before Delhi at a later period.

London Gazette, 27 April, 1858.—War Office, 24 April, 1858. The Queen has been graciously pleased to signify her intention to confer the Decoration of the Victoria Cross on the undermentioned Officers, Non-commissioned Officers and men of Her Majesty's and of the East India Company's Armies, who have been recommended to Her Majesty for that Decoration, in accordance with the rules laid down in Her Majesty's Warrant instituting the same, on account of Acts of Bravery performed by them in India, as recorded against their several names, viz.:—

TOMBS, HENRY, Lieut.-Colonel, C.B., was *b.* on 10 Nov. 1825, in India; *s.* of Major-General John Tombs and Mary, younger daughter of Mr. John Remington, of Barton End House, Stroud, co. Gloucester. General John Tombs was an excellent soldier, full of initiative and resource, and a sound disciplinarian, and was beloved by his family and respected by his comrades. He commanded the 3rd Bengal Cavalry at the Siege of Bhurtpore 1824–25, and received the Medal with clasp for that campaign. He died at Malta 30 Oct. 1848, aged 71. General John Tombs's widow lived until 27 Dec. 1876, and was 84 years old when she died. She was extremely practical, and brought up a family of one daughter and seven sons; but her force of character enabled her to train them with tactful firmness and loving discretion, and at the same time to win their entire devotion. Henry Tombs, the seventh son, was christened at Calcutta on 10 Jan. 1825. He joined the Royal Military College, Sandhurst, on 12 Feb. 1839, at the age of fourteen years and three months, where he remained until 30 June, 1839; he went to Addiscombe from 9 Aug. 1839, until 11 June, 1841, when he was gazetted to the Bengal Artillery as 2nd Lieut. He reached Calcutta on 18 Nov. 1841, and in Nov. 1843, joined the Army of Gwalior; was present at the action of Punniar with the 16th Light Field Battery, and was mentioned in Despatches for having "done good service by firing with effect on the enemy" when commanding two guns on rearguard. He received the Bronze Star for the campaign. In Jan. 1844, he was promoted to Lieut., and in March of the same year was appointed to the 1st Troop, 1st Brigade, Bengal Horse Artillery. He served in the Sutlej Campaign of 1845–46, and was present at the actions of Moodki, Ferozeshah and Buddiwal. He acted as A.D.C. to General Sir Harry Smith at Buddiwal and Aliwal, and was mentioned in Despatches and received the Medal with two clasps for this campaign. Lieut. Tombs served in the Punjab Campaign of 1848–49 as D.A.Q.M.G. to all the artillery commanded by Brigadier James Tennant, Bengal Artillery. He was present at the action of Ramnugger, at the passage of the Chenab, at the fight at Sadulapur and the Battle of Chillianwallah, and at Gujerat, when Lord Gough completely routed the Sikhs. Tombs was mentioned in Despatches for Chillianwallah and Gujerat; was recommended for a Brevet Majority on promotion to Capt., and received the Punjab Medal with two clasps. On 30 Oct. 1850, he was appointed Adjutant of the 2nd Brigade, Bengal Horse Artillery, which post he held until 30 Nov. 1853, when he was transferred to the Field Artillery on proceeding on furlough. He became Capt. 25 July, 1854; Brevet-Major, for his services during the Punjab Campaign, on 1 Aug. 1854; reappointed to the Bengal Horse Artillery 27 Nov. 1855, and was given command of the 2nd Troop, 1st Brigade, at Jullundur in 1856. This troop became famous under Tombs during the Indian Mutiny, but its previous record had been a distinguished one. It was raised by Capt. Roderick Roberts at Cawnpore on 24 June, 1825. On transfer to the Royal Artillery in 1861 it became B Battery, 2nd Brigade, Royal Horse Artillery, later C Battery, C Brigade, Royal Horse Artillery, and is now represented by No. 56 Battery, Royal Field Artillery. The 2nd Troop, 1st Brigade, marched from Jullundur to Meerut, arriving there on 16 March, 1857. At one of the encamping grounds near Delhi, Major Tombs was told by the "Tehsildar" (Native Executive Revenue Official) there was a prophecy that the whole country would be running in blood; that British rule would be nearly destroyed, but that it would recover itself and be stronger than ever. The Indian Mutiny broke out at Meerut on 10 May, 1857, when the native cavalry and infantry stationed there revolted and murdered their officers, with their wives and many other Europeans also. Tombs's troop was the first to respond to the alarm. With the 60th Rifles and Carabiniers it moved down to the blazing lines of the native regiments. At their approach the rebels moved off to Delhi. Tombs's troop bivouacked for the night on the open ground between the lines of the artillery and 60th Rifles. On 27 May four of the guns of the troop, under Major Tombs, Lieuts. Perkins and Wilson, and 2nd Lieut. James Hills, accompanied Brigadier Archdale Wilson on his march towards Delhi, while the remaining two guns were left under Lieut. T. P. Smith for the protection of Meerut. On 30 and 31 May were fought the actions on the Hindun. On the 30th Tombs's horse was shot. On the 31st the enemy unexpectedly attacked near the Hindun. Tombs's troop crossed the river, took the rebels in flank and silenced their guns. Other troops co-operated, and

Henry Tombs.

after a severe fight of two hours the enemy was routed and Lieut. Perkins killed. The splendid behaviour of Tombs's troop was the admiration of all. On 7 June General Archdale Wilson's column joined the force under the Commander-in-Chief, General Sir H. Barnard, at Alipur, which on the 8th completely defeated the rebels in the Battle of Badli-ke-Serai. On the same day the heights before Delhi were occupied by the Commander-in-Chief, and from that time until the final capture of the city on 20 Sept. the troop took part in almost daily fights. For some days after reaching the ridge Tombs helped to defend the post at Hindu Rao's House. After the heavy guns were in position the troop was on picquet duty (two guns at a time) at "The Mound," in rear of the right flank of the camp. Tombs greatly distinguished himself in the events of 17, 19 and 23 June, and he took a prominent part in the destruction of a battery which the enemy was constructing near a Mohammedan mosque, called the Idgah, which Lord Roberts thus describes: "On 17 June, 1857, we were attacked from almost every direction—a manœuvre intended to prevent our observing a battery which was being constructed close to the Idgah situated on a hill to our right, from which to enfilade our position on the ridge. As it was very important to prevent the completion of this battery, Barnard ordered it to be attacked by two small columns, one commanded by Tombs of the Bengal Horse Artillery, the other by Reid. Tombs, with 400 of the 60th Rifles and 1st Bengal Fusiliers, 30 of the Guides Cavalry, 20 Sappers and Miners, and his own troop of Horse Artillery, moved towards the enemy's left. . . . Tombs drove the rebels through a succession of gardens, till they reached the Idgah, where they made an obstinate but unavailing resistance. The gates of the mosque were blown open and thirty-nine of its defenders were killed. Tombs himself was slightly wounded, and had two horses killed, making five which had been shot under this gallant soldier since the commencement of the campaign. . . . Henry Tombs, of the Bengal Horse Artillery . . . an unusually handsome man and a thorough soldier. His gallantry in the attack in the Idgah was the talk of the camp. I had always heard of Tombs as one of the best officers in the regiment, and it was with feelings of respectful admiration that I made his acquaintance a few days later. As a cool, bold leader of men Tombs was unsurpassed; no fire, however hot, and no crisis, however unexpected, could take him by surprise. He grasped the situation in a moment and issued his orders without hesitation, inspiring all ranks with confidence in his power and capacity. He was something of a martinet, and was more feared than liked by his men until they realized what a grand leader he was, when they gave him their entire confidence and were ready to follow him anywhere and everywhere." The men got to worship him. Tombs was publicly commended by the Commander-in-Chief, who described his conduct as "glorious." On 19 June Tombs's guns were saved from capture by Daly with his Guides, who had come up after their magnificent march from Hoti Mardan to Delhi. On 23 June Major Tombs was in command of the artillery during heavy fighting in scorching heat. Early on 9 July the rebels made a sudden attack on the English camp, and for their gallantry on this occasion Tombs and Hills were awarded the Victoria Cross [London Gazette, 24 April, 1858]: "Henry Tombs, C.B., Lieut.-Colonel, and James Hills, 2nd Lieut. For very gallant conduct on the part of Lieut. Hills before Delhi in defending the position assigned to him in case of alarm, and for noble behaviour on the part of Lieut.-Colonel Tombs in twice coming to his subaltern's rescue, and on each occasion killing his man. (See Despatch of Lieut.-Colonel Mackenzie, Commanding 1st Brigade of Horse Artillery, dated Camp near Delhi, 10 July, 1857, published in the Supplement to the London Gazette of 16 Jan. 1858)." The official record of his gallantry when he won the Victoria Cross is set forth at length in "Despatch No. 40, Lieut.-Colonel M. Mackenzie, Commanding 1st Brigade, Horse Artillery, to Brigadier Wilson, Commandant of Artillery":

"Camp near Delhi,
"July 10th, 1857.

"Sir,

"It is with great pleasure that I submit for the information of the Brigadier-Commandant the following account of James Hills, of the 2nd Troop, 1st Brigade Horse Artillery, and the noble behaviour of his Commanding Officer, Major H. Tombs, in twice coming to his subaltern's rescue and on each occasion killing his man. Yesterday, the 9th inst., 2nd Lieut. J. Hills was on picquet duty with two guns at The Mound to the right of the camp. About eleven o'clock a.m. there was a rumour that the enemy's cavalry were coming down upon this post. Lieut. Hills proceeded to take up the position assigned in case of alarm, but before he reached the spot he saw the enemy close upon his guns before he had time to form up. To enable him to do this, Lieut. Hills boldly charged single-handed the head of the enemy's column, cut down the first man, struck the second, and was then ridden down horse and all. On getting up and searching for his sword, three more men came at him (two unmounted). The first man he wounded with his pistol; he caught the lance of the second with his left hand, and wounded him with his sword. The first man then came on again and was cut down; the third man (on foot) then came up and wrenched the sword from the hand of Lieut. Hills (who fell in the struggle), and the enemy was about to cut him down when Major Tombs (who had gone up to visit his two guns) saw what was going on, rushed in and shot the man and saved Lieut. Hills. By this time the enemy had passed by, and Major Tombs and Lieut. Hills observed one of the enemy passing with his (Lieut. Hills') pistol. They walked up to him. The man began flourishing his sword and dancing about. He first cut at Lieut. Hills, who parried the blow, and he then turned on Major Tombs, who received the blow in the same manner. His second attack on Lieut. Hills was, I regret to say, more successful, as he was cut down by a bad sword-cut on the head, and would have been no doubt killed had not Major Tombs rushed in and put his sword through the man. I feel convinced that such gallant conduct on the part of these two officers has only to be brought properly forward to meet with an appreciative reward. Major Tombs was saved from a severe sword-cut on the head by the wadded headdress he wore.

"(Signed) M. Mackenzie, Lieut.-Colonel."

The Commander-in-Chief, when forwarding the above, stated: "It is unnecessary for me to make any further comment on Lieut.-Colonel Mackenzie's Report than to observe that the conduct of these officers has always been conspicuous for distinguished gallantry . . . and that in recommending them to the most favourable consideration of the Governor-General in Council, I consider them to be worthy of the highest distinction that can be awarded for valour and heroism." And the Right Honourable the Governor-General of India, in a General Order dated 4 Dec. 1857, remarked: "The readiness and coolness, as well as gallantry, evinced by Major Tombs of the Bengal Artillery, on various occasions recorded in these papers, and the signal daring of Lieut. Hills, who alone and unsupported charged a body of the enemy's cavalry and saved his battery, commanded the admiration of the Governor-General in Council." At the Battle of Najafgarh, on 25 Aug. 1857, Major Tombs commanded the artillery, and Lieut. Wilson commanded Tombs's troop. Brigadier-General John Nicholson mentioned Tombs in Despatches for his services in this engagement [London Gazette, 24 Nov. 1857]. For the assault on Delhi, 14 Sept. 1857, No. 10 Battery, under the command of Major H. Tombs, "was erected near the Kudsia Bagh and, armed with four 10-inch and six 8-inch mortars, commenced firing on the night of the 10th. Its task was to assist in silencing the guns in the Kashmir and Water Bastions and in the Curtain between." On the day of the assault the troop suffered so heavily during the Siege of Delhi, that it was not fit to accompany the column despatched to the south after the fall of that place. In Oct. it was ordered to Meerut to refit, and in Jan. 1858, joined the force under Sir Colin Campbell at Cawnpore, and took part in the operations before Lucknow and in subsequent actions in Oudh and Rohilcund. From 16 to 19 March, 2/1 Horse Artillery accompanied a column under Brigadier Campbell in pursuit of the rebels, and then joined Major-General Walpole's force in the Western Oudh; was present at the taking of Fort Rooiya 15 April, 1858, and at the affair of Allygunge. Tombs and his troop took part in the Battle of Bareilly, under the Commander-in-Chief, and in the Relief of Shahjehanpore 18 May, 1858. He next commanded the artillery of a column which proceeded to Mohumdee on 24 to 29 May, and also of a force which was sent to Shahabad on 31 May. The troop returned to Meerut in Aug. 1858, and was specially mentioned in General Orders, 4 Dec. 1858, by the Commander-in-Chief, while Tombs himself was highly praised in Despatches on every occasion. He was also eulogized by the Government and in the House of Lords by the Secretary of State. He was twice wounded, had five horses shot under him, was promoted to Brevet Colonel 20 July, 1858, was awarded the Victoria Cross for repeated acts of gallantry and for twice saving Lieut. Hills' life, and was created a C.B. [London Gazette, 22 Jan. 1858]. On 29 April, 1861, Tombs was promoted to Regtl. Lieut.-Colonel, and relinquished the command of his troop. He was appointed to the 2nd Brigade Royal Horse Artillery, and to the command of the artillery at Meerut. On 16 May, 1863, he was appointed Brigadier-General to command the Gwalior district, and from Feb. to April, 1865, he was selected by the Commander-in-Chief, Sir Hugh Rose, to command the right column of the Bhutan Field Force for the purpose of recapturing Dewangiri. It was under his command at this time that the Victoria Cross was so splendidly won by Trevor and Dundas. General Tombs was thanked by Government for his distinguished services in the capture and destruction of Dewangiri, received the Medal and clasp for the campaign, and was appointed A.D.C. to Queen Victoria, and given a Good Service Reward in 1865. He was awarded the K.C.B. on 14 March, 1868. On promotion to Major-General 11 March, 1867, he relinquished the command of the Gwalior district and proceeded to England. In 1869 Sir Henry Tombs married Georgina Janet, youngest daughter of Admiral Sir James Stirling, K.C.B., Knight Grand Cross of the Redeemer of Greece, and Ellen, daughter of James Mangles, Esq., M.P. for Guildford. They had three children: Dorothea Gwladys, now Countess of Lanesborough; Mabel, who married Major Boyce Combe, 11th Hussars, and Henry Edwin Stirling, who was born at Lucknow 27 Oct. 1873, and died at Suez 2 Dec. 1874. In Aug. 1871, Sir H. Tombs was appointed to the command of the Allahabad Division, and on 1 April, 1872, was transferred to the Oudh Division. From Dec. 1871, to Jan. 1872, he commanded the 3rd Division at the Army Manœuvres near Delhi, under Lord Napier of Magdala, and in the following cold weather he commanded the 1st Division at the Camp of Exercise at Hussan Abdal, in Attock District. At the termination of this camp on 11 Feb. 1873, Sir Henry was cheered again and again by the rest of the officers as he came out of the Durbar Tent after the Commander-in-Chief's Levee. About Christmas, 1873, Sir Henry Tombs became ill, and in Feb. 1874, he left Lucknow on sick leave, and by the time he reached Marseilles his illness had become so serious that he underwent an operation in Paris. On reaching England he was told that his illness was incurable, and he bore this crushing blow with the utmost fortitude and resignation, and went to Newport, Isle of Wight, to end his days. His sufferings became more intense, but he endured them without hope of relief and without complaining, in the true spirit of a brave Christian soldier, and on Sunday, 2 Aug. 1874, died before he was fifty, the humble trusting servant of God. He was buried in the Cemetery at Carisbrooke. Her Majesty Queen Victoria during his last illness constantly inquired after him, and on his death expressed much sorrow at the great loss which Her Majesty, the Army and his family had sustained. The Commander-in-Chief in India issued the following General Order: "General Orders by the Right Honourable the Commander-in-Chief. Headquarters, Simla, 14 Aug. 1874.—The Army in India will share with the Right Honourable the Commander-in-Chief the deep regret with which he has received the intelligence of the death in England of Major-General

Sir Henry Tombs, K.C.B., V.C., of the Royal, late Bengal, Artillery. The career of this distinguished officer is identified with the history of this country for the last thirty years. The decorations which he wore on his breast, for Gwalior, the Sutlej campaign, the campaign of the Punjab, the Siege of Delhi, and recapture of Lucknow, and for the recapture of Dewangiri in Bhootan under his independent command, bore testimony to the conspicuous part he took in nearly all the more important military events that have taken place during that period. Appointed to the command of a division of the Army in 1871, Sir Henry Tombs displayed all those attributes of a General of which his early career had given promise, and fully justified his selection for the high trust which had been confided to him. Firm in the maintenance of discipline, courteous in his demeanour, strict and impartial in the exercise of his command, he acquired in a remarkable degree the respect, confidence and affection of all with whom he was associated. His premature death, which Lord Napier of Magdala so greatly deplores, has deprived the Government and the country of an accomplished and devoted servant, the Commander-in-Chief of a valued friend and trusted lieutenant, and the Army of a gallant comrade and one of its most brilliant ornaments.—By order of the Right Honourable the Commander-in-Chief in India, E. B. Johnson, Major-General, Adjutant-General in India." Kaye and Malleson, in their "History of the Sepoy Mutiny," describe Tombs as "a man of noble presence, tall, strong, of robust frame and handsome countenance, dark-haired, dark-bearded, and of swarthy complexion; he was in all outward semblance the model of a Faringhi warrior; and the heroic aspect truly expressed the heroic qualities of the man. There was no finer soldier in the camp." Lord Roberts wrote: "Tombs was marked out from the beginning of his career for success. He was gifted with a bright and cheerful nature, great charm of manner, good looks, and a fine soldierly bearing, which all contributed to make Harry Tombs the attractive and remarkable figure we knew and loved." Sir George Cowper, Bart., C.B., who had known Tombs since they were boys together at Sandhurst, said of him that: "In the eyes of all those who had watched his career from its brilliant and joyous commencement to its most sad and untimely end, he was the very type of Spartan fortitude, of chivalrous valour and of every manly grace . . . one who united in himself all the attributes of a heroic martyr, of a splendid soldier, and of a knightly gentleman." Sir James Hills Johnes wrote: "I am only too glad to do anything I can to help to make public Sir Harry Tombs's good name. He was the finest commander I ever served under, and that is saying a great deal, as I have served under Sir Donald Stewart and Lord Roberts, and other good men. It was splendid the way Tombs used to lead his men into action—just as if on an ordinary field day—the troops advancing in line with him a few yards in front, so steady at all paces, walk, trot, or gallop. Whenever I speak or write of Tombs his splendid leading always comes before me." A fund was collected in India and in England, and a memorial was placed in the Garrison Church at Woolwich, and with the remainder of the money "the Tombs Memorial Scholarship" was founded, to be awarded to the Senior Cadet who is periodically commissioned to the Royal Artillery from the Royal Military Academy at Woolwich. Lady Tombs, on 19 Dec. 1877, married Capt. Herbert Stewart, 3rd Dragoon Guards, who afterwards became Major-General Sir Herbert Stewart, K.C.B., and commanded the Desert Column despatched from Korti for the relief of General Gordon. Sir Herbert Stewart died on 16 Feb. 1885, and Lady Stewart died at Plymouth on 4 April, 1910. They had one son, Geoffrey, who served in the Coldstream Guards during the South African War, and who was killed in action in France.

HILLS, JAMES, 2nd Lieut., was *b.* at Neechindipore, Bengal, India, on 20 Aug. 1833. He was the *s.* of James Hills, Esq., a well-known indigo-planter, whose name is a household word in that part of India, and of his wife, Charlotte, daughter of Signor Angelo Savi, Moisgunge, Bengal. He was educated at the Academy and Military Academy, Edinburgh, and at Addiscombe, and received his commission as 2nd Lieut. Bengal Artillery on 11 June, 1853. He served throughout the Indian Mutiny, 1857–58, as Subaltern, 2nd (Tombs's) Troop, 1st Brigade, Bengal Horse Artillery, being present at the actions of the Hindun River (30 and 31 May, 1857); at the Battle of Badli-ke-Serai (8 June) and occupation of the Delhi Ridge, after which—for some days—the troop helped to defend the post at Hindoo Rao's House, where there was almost daily fighting. After the heavy guns were placed in position, the troop was on picquet duty (two guns at a time) at "The Mound," in rear of the right flank of the camp. Kaye and Malleson publish a MS. Memorandum in their "History of the Sepoy Mutiny," which says: "The Mound was about half-way between the Ridge and the Canal which protected the Birtish rear. It was on the right rear flank of the camp, and overlooked Sabzimandi. Between the Mound and the Canal there were several clumps of trees, and the Canal bank also being fringed with them, their view in that direction was confused and interrupted, and for this reason a cavalry picquet was thrown out on the Canal bank, somewhat in advance of the Mound, from which, however, the videttes of the cavalry picquets were visible. . . . The guns and the Carabiniers were not stationed on the Mound, but at the foot of, and on the right flank of it, so that facing to their proper front, the Sabzimandi, the Mound was on their left hand and the Canal on their right. To their front was a small breast-work, to which it was ordered that the guns should be run up and fought behind in case of an attack, and until the picquet could be reinforced." The Mound was a favourite place of gathering in the camp, and it often happened that many officers went there to see how things were progressing below, and to talk over the operations of the siege. But the heavy rain of the 9th had driven most of them to the shelter of their tents. Major Tombs was in one of the cheeriest places in camp—the artillery mess-tent. Lord Roberts says, on page 102 of his "Forty-one Years in India": "We were not long left in peace, for on the morning of 9 July the enemy moved out of the city in great force, and for several hours kept up an incessant cannonade on our right and front flanks. The picquet below the General's Mound happened to be held this day by two guns of Tombs's troop, commanded by 2nd Lieut. James Hills, and by thirty-men of the Carabiniers under Lieut. Stillman. A little beyond, and to the right of this picquet, a native officer's party of the 9th Irregular Cavalry had been placed to watch the Trunk Road. These men were still supposed to be loyal, the regiment to which they belonged had a good reputation, and as Christie's Horse had done good service in Afghanistan, where Neville and Crawford Chamberlain had served with it as subalterns. It was therefore believed at the Mound Picquet that ample warning would be given of any enemy coming from the direction of the Trunk Road, so that the approach of some horsemen dressed like the men of the 9th Irregulars attracted little notice. Stillman and Hills were breakfasting together when a sowar from the native officer's party rode up and reported that a body of the enemy's cavalry were in sight. Hills told the man to gallop on to headquarters with the report, and to warn Tombs as he passed his tent. Hills and Stillman then mounted their horses, neither of them having the remotest idea that the news of the enemy's advance had been purposely delayed until there was not time to turn out the troops. They imagined that the sowar was acting in good faith, and had given them sufficient notice, and while Hills moved his guns towards the position from which he could command the Trunk Road, Stillman proceeded to the top of the Mound in order to get a better view of the ground over which the enemy were supposed to be advancing. The troop of the Carabiniers was thus left by itself to receive the first rush of the rebel cavalry; it was composed of young soldiers, some of them quite untrained, who turned and broke. The moment Hills saw the enemy he shouted 'Action front!' In the hope of giving his men time to load and fire a round of grape, he gallantly charged the head of the column single-handed, cut down the leading man, struck the second, and then was ridden down himself. It had been raining heavily, so Hills wore his cloak, which probably saved his life, for it was cut through in many places, as were his jacket and even his shirt. As soon as the body of the troops had passed on (Sir James Hills-Johnes has here struck out the word 'on' and put in the words 'over him'!), Hills . . . got up and searched for his sword, which he had lost in the mêlée. He had just found it when he was attacked by three men, two of whom were mounted; he fired and wounded the first man, then caught the lance of the second in his left hand, and ran him through the body with his sword. The first assailant coming on again, Hills cut him down, upon which he was attacked by the third man on foot, who succeeded in wrenching his sword from him. Hills fell in the struggle and must have been killed if Tombs, who had been duly warned by the sowar, had not come to the rescue and saved his plucky subaltern's life." One of the troopers of the 9th Irregular Cavalry, in a state of great excitement, had ridden up to the Artillery Mess-tent and asked the way to the General's Headquarters. In reply to a question from Tombs, he said that the enemy were showing in front of our picquets. The man's words did not seem to account for his excitement, and Tombs hurried to his own tent, took his sword and revolver, and ordering his horse to be brought after him, walked down to the Mound picquets. As he came near the post he saw the Carabiniers drawn up in mounted array and our guns getting ready for action. "In a minute" (write Kaye and Malleson) "there was a tremendous rush of Irregular Horse, the troopers brandishing their swords and vociferating lustily; then there was to be seen the sad spectacle of our Dragoons, broken and flying in the rear, whilst one of our guns went right about, some of the horses mounted and some riderless, and galloped towards our camp. Tombs was now in the midst of the enemy; who were striking at him from all sides, but with no effect. . . ." Kaye and Malleson's history here describes what Tombs saw from the Mound, but Sir James Hills-Johnes says: "He did not go up the Mound until he had shot the man who had got me down, and thus saved my life." He had seen Hills lying on the ground, apparently entangled in his cloak, with a dismounted sowar standing over him, evidently about to kill him. At this time Tombs was about thirty paces from his friend, and he could not reach the enemy in time to cut him down with the sabre. So he rested his revolver on his left arm and took steady aim at the trooper, who was facing him, and shot him through the body. They were not yet out of the wood, but the immediate danger was passed. Tombs helped Hills to his feet, and they climbed up the slope of the Mound. As they were watching the movements of the enemy, they saw a little way beneath them a dismounted sowar, who was making off with Hills's revolver. They made for him at once. He was a young, strong and active trooper, and when he turned and attacked them they found that he was a good swordsman. Hills parried his first blow; then he struck at Tombs, who likewise guarded the cut. But the despairing energy of his third blow broke down Hills's guard and went through his skull to the brain. A fresh blow at Tombs broke down his guard and cut through the cap he was wearing, but did not hurt him, and the next moment he drove his sword through the trooper's body. Notwithstanding Hills's gallant attempt to stop the sowars, his men had not time to fire a single shot before the enemy was upon them. The rebels' object, however, was not to capture these two guns, but to induce the Native Horse Artillery to join them. They galloped past the picquet and made straight for the troop, calling on the men to bring away their guns. The Native Artillerymen behaved splendidly. They not only refused to join the mutineers, but they begged the men of the European troop which was unlimbered close by to fire through them on the rebels.

James Hills.

Second Lieut. Hills was severely and dangerously wounded on this occasion. He was promoted to Lieut. 8 Sept. 1857, and the gallantry of Tombs and his subaltern was reported by Lieut.-Colonel Mackenzie, who tore up Tombs's report in which he had said nothing about his own part in the affair. They were especially commended by the Commander-in-Chief and by the Governor-General, and recommended for the Victoria Cross, which was awarded them [London Gazette, 27 April, 1858]: "Henry Tombs, C.B., Lieut.-Colonel, and James Hills, Lieut., The Bengal Artillery. Date of Act of Bravery : 9 July, 1857. 'For very gallant conduct on the part of Lieut. Hills before Delhi in defending the position assigned to him in case of alarm, and for notable behaviour on the part of Lieut.-Colonel Tombs in twice coming to his subaltern's rescue, and on each occasion killing his man.' (See Despatch of Lieut.-Colonel Mackenzie, Commanding 1st Brigade of Horse Artillery, dated Camp near Delhi, 10 July, 1857, published in the Supplement to the London Gazette of 16 Jan. 1858.)" Lieut. Hills was present with Tombs's Troop at the Battle of Nujeefghar 25 Aug. 1857, and at the assault on Delhi and the fall of that city on 20 Sept. He took part in the Siege and Capture of Lucknow (2 to 16 March, 1858); was present at the taking of Fort Rooiya (15 April); at the Battle of Bareilly (5 May); the Relief of Shahjehanpur (18 May). He was favourably mentioned in Despatches and received the Mutiny Medal with two clasps. From the time when 2nd Lieut. Hills so greatly distinguished himself whilst serving with 2/1 B.H.A., under Major Tombs, the two men became lifelong friends, and Hills was present at all the actions with Tombs's troop throughout 1857 and 1858. Lord Roberts says, in "Forty-one Years in India" (page 96): "Jemmy Hills, one of the subalterns in Tombs's troop was an old Addiscombe friend of mine; he delighted in talking of his commander, in dilating on his merits as a soldier and his skill in handling each arm of the service." A portrait of Sir James Hills-Johnes faces this page of Lord Roberts's book. Lieut. Hills was Aide-de-Camp to the Governor-General of India (Lord Canning) from Sept. 1859, to March, 1862. Lord Roberts says that at Delhi: "Lord Canning was anxious to understand all about the siege and visit the different positions. . . . There were two Delhi men besides myself to explain everything to him, Sir Edward Campbell and Jemmy Hills, who had now become Viceroy's Aide-de-Camp." Lieut. Hills was promoted to Capt. 24 Nov. 1862, and was given the Brevet of Major 19 Jan. 1864. He was Assistant Resident of Nepal from April, 1862, to March, 1863. In April, 1863, he rejoined the Horse Artillery as Capt. Bengal Artillery, Royal Horse Artillery (Major Bunny's). He was appointed Brigade Major, Royal Artillery, Northern Division, Bengal, from Sept. 1864, to 1869, and held this appointment for five years, with a break whilst serving in the Abyssinian Expedition of 1867 to 1868. We get another glimpse of Capt. Hills in Lord Roberts's book when the latter describes how the expedition set out: "On 9 Jan. 1868, Stewart and his Staff left Calcutta in the P. and O. Steamer Golconda. The officers and men of the Mountain Battery were also on board, Capt. Boyle in command, my friend Jemmy Hills in my place as 2nd Capt., and Collen and Disney as subalterns." Capt. Hills commanded an 8-inch Mortar Battery throughout this campaign, and was present at the Capture of Magdala. He was mentioned in Despatches, received the Medal, and was given the Brevet of Lieut.-Colonel 15 Aug. 1868. He was appointed Commandant of the Peshawar Mountain Battery in Oct. 1869, and whilst quartered at Kohat commanded the district and garrison from Feb. 1870, till April, 1871. He commanded the Peshawar Mountain Battery throughout the Lushai Campaign of 1871 to 1872; was favourably mentioned in Despatches, created a C.B., and received the Medal and clasp. He was appointed to the command of C Battery, F Brigade, Royal Horse Artillery, 1 Aug. 1872, and held this appointment until 1875. On 14 Feb. 1876, he was given the Brevet of Colonel. From July, 1876, to Aug. 1879, he was Assistant-Adjutant-General, Lahore Division. On 12 Oct. 1878, he joined the Kandahar Field Force as Assistant-Adjutant-General, and served in that capacity throughout the first phase of the Afghan War of 1878–80. He was mentioned in Lieut.-General Sir Donald Stewart's Despatches 24 June, 1879, and 22 July, 1879, and vacated his appointment on promotion to Major-General in Aug. 1879. He joined Sir F. S. Roberts's Force in the Kurram Valley Sept. 1879, and in order to do this made a record journey. He left Kandahar at 3.30 p.m. on 9 Sept., and rode 26 miles. He then rested till one a.m. on the 10th; rode alone, in excessive heat on any animal obtainable, 341 miles to Jacobahad, arriving 7 a.m. on the 13th. By Tonga to Thull, whence he rode 96 miles to Alikeyl in time to accompany the force to Kabul. On 27 Sept. Lord Roberts says he set out for Kushi. "Just before I started I had the pleasure of welcoming my old friend and brother officer, Major-General J. Hills, V.C., C.B., who had been with Sir Donald Stewart as Assistant-Adjutant-General from the beginning of the campaign, and who had, the moment he heard there was to be an advance on Kabul, come with all speed to place his services at my disposal. Although I had no employment for Hills at the time, there would be plenty for all to do at Kabul, and I was delighted to have such a good soldier with me." Major-General Hills then accompanied the column to Kabul, and was present at the Battle of Charasiah and occupation of the city of Kabul. He held no position in the force during these operations, but assisted the Commissariat to obtain supplies, for which service he was favourably mentioned by Sir F. Roberts in his first Kabul Despatch 20 Nov. 1879 [London Gazette, 16 Jan. 1880]. He was appointed Military Governor, City of Kabul, 13 Oct. 1879, holding this appointment till its abolition 17 Jan. 1880, with a break of ten days whilst the troops were confined in the Sherpur Cantonment 14 to 23 Dec. 1879, during which time he commanded a section of the line of defence. Major-General Hills received the thanks of the Governor-General, and was favourably mentioned in Despatches. From 18 Jan. till 15 May, 1880, he was out of official employment, but his services were utilized on committee duties, assessing compensation for losses sustained by friendly Sirdars, etc., at the hands of the Ghazis; in assisting the Commissariat Department to obtain supplies and in getting information for the Commander of the Forces. On 16 May, 1880, he was appointed, and assumed command of the 3rd Division, Northern Afghanistan Field Force; remained in command till the dissolution of the division on its return to Peshawar Sept. 1880. He was mentioned in Despatches; created a K.C.B.; thanked by both Houses of Parliament 5 May, 1881, and received the Medal and clasp for the campaign. He received a Good Service Pension 15 Dec. 1881. Sir James Hills married Miss Elizabeth Johnes in Westminster Abbey 16 Sept. 1882, and added her name to his own. She was of an ancient Welsh family, co-heiress with her elder sister, Mrs. Johnes, daughter of the late John Johnes, Esq., of Dolaucothy, Carmarthenshire. He was promoted Lieut.-General 26 Jan. 1886, and retired on special pension in 1888. General Hills-Johnes was appointed Honorary Colonel, Carmarthenshire Artillery, Western Division, Royal Artillery, in . . . 1891, and was created a G.C.B. in 1893. He accompanied Lord Roberts in a private capacity from Kronstadt to Diamond Hill during the war in South Africa. He was appointed Honorary Colonel of the 4th Welsh Regt., and was chairman of the Territorial Force Association, Carmarthenshire, and of the three counties, Cardigan, Carmarthen and Pembroke, since the formation of the force. Sir James Hills-Johnes died on 3 Jan. 1919.

KERR, WILLIAM ALEXANDER, Lieut., was *b.* at The Holmes, near Melrose, Roxburgh, North Britain, on 18 July, 1831. He was the son of Loraine McDowell Kerr, Esq., and of Marianne White, daughter of Admiral White. He was educated at Loretto, near Musselburgh, North Britain, and joined the 24th Bombay Native Infantry in June, 1849. He served through the Indian Mutiny 1857–58–59, and his exploits attracted an extraordinary amount of attention. "On 8 July, 1857, the officers of the South Mahratta Horse stationed at Sattara were at mess. The conversation turned on the Mutiny, and a young officer, Lieut. W. A. Kerr, expressed the opinion that, come what might, the loyalty and courage of his men were to be relied upon. He had scarcely finished speaking when a telegram was delivered to the Commanding Officer announcing that the 27th Bombay Native Infantry at Kolapore had mutinied. It went on to say that European officers and residents had taken refuge in the Residency, where they were protected by a few faithful native troops. The garrison was, however, destitute of food, and could not therefore hold out long. The Commanding Officer hesitated for a moment as to what was to be done, for it was doubtful whether, if he sent a party to the relief of Kolapore his men would prove true. Kerr expressed full faith in them, and volunteered for the dangerous service. Only fifty horsemen could be spared him, and at the head of these he half an hour later started for Kolapore, seventy-five miles distant. It was in the middle of the rainy season, several swollen rivers had to be crossed, and the country was almost impassable from mud. All difficulties were, however, overcome; three large, two small rivers and seven ravines filled with water were swum, and at the end of twenty-six hours' toilsome marching Kerr reached his destination. He found the Sepoys posted in a fort. What was to be done? He had no guns, and a couple which a neighbouring rajah lent him proved to be useless. His men were worn out and night was at hand. He resolved, therefore, to attack before the ardour of his troopers had subsided. Dismounting his men, he selected seventeen for the storming party. The garrison consisted of thirty-four Sepoys, who, having taken part in the murder of some of their officers, despaired of mercy. The entrance was by a succession of massive teak doors, six feet high, and backed with large stones and earth. Kerr's most trusted follower was, singularly enough, named Gumpunt Rao Deo Kur. The Lieutenant and this man provided themselves with crowbars, and heedless of the enemy's fire, soon made in the front door an opening large enough to admit one man at a time on his hands and knees. Kerr, followed by Gumpunt Rao, unhesitatingly crept through. As they appeared, twenty Sepoys fired a volley at them; but as they were stooping the bullets whistled harmlessly over their heads. Kerr then rushed on to the enemy, sword in hand, followed by his men. A fierce hand-to-hand encounter followed, but notwithstanding their superiority in numbers, some of the Sepoys were slain and the remainder driven into a loop-holed house which covered the second door. Kerr attacked the house on the side where there were no loopholes, and contrived to set it on fire. Several of the enemy perished in the flames. The survivors escaped through the door into an inner court of the fort, and were joined by the rest of the garrison. Kerr, assisted by Gumpunt Rao with crowbars, effected a small opening in the second door amidst a storm of bullets. Creeping through this opening, they again were greeted by a volley and again escaped untouched. Before the Sepoys had time to reload, Kerr and his Mahrattas were among them. Driven into a corner, the rebels fought hard. One of their bullets cut the chain of Kerr's helmet; another struck his sword. A musket discharged close to Kerr's face for a moment blinded him, but the man who fired it was the next moment struck through the body by Kerr's sword. Such was the force of the thrust that Kerr could not at once withdraw his weapon, and while thus helpless he was struck on the head by the butt-end of a musket. He staggered, almost lost consciousness, and was on the point of being bayoneted, when Gumpunt Rao snatched up a musket and shot his officer's adversary dead. As the man fell, Kerr cut down another Sepoy. At length the few surviving Sepoys took refuge in an old temple, and, barricading the door, kept up a hot fire on the assailants, who now mustered only eight, ten having been killed or disabled. Once more the crowbar was tried, but this time nothing could be effected by

William Alexander Kerr.

it. Some hay was, however, lying near, and Kerr and his men, piling it against a door, set fire to it. In a few minutes the expedient had succeeded, the door fell in, and through the flame and smoke the gallant little band rushed into the building. The clashing of weapons, the sound of swords cleaving flesh and bone, the brief, fierce sounds of men engaged in mortal strife, the groans of the wounded ensued, and then all was over. Kerr had slain, disabled or captured the whole of the mutineers. He had accomplished his perilous undertaking, he had saved Kolapore, and had arrested the rising tide of rebellion in the Bombay Presidency. The price, however, had been large: Kerr himself had been wounded, eight of his followers had been slain on the spot, four died subsequently of their wounds, and of the remaining five troopers, not one escaped unhurt." Thus the late Colonel Knollys graphically described the Act of Bravery by which Kerr won the Victoria Cross, and Gumpunt Rao surely deserved it. Colonel Knollys concludes with these words: "A more gallant deed, and one more fittingly rewarded by the Victoria Cross had never been performed." In the defeat of Tantia Topi in Dec. 1858, by General Parke, we are told that "Tantia first endeavoured to turn the British right; but Kerr, changing his front, charged with great impetuosity, and driving the rebels from the field, pursued them for a considerable distance, laying sixty of them low. . . . This engagement was fatal to Tantia's hopes regarding Barodah." The "Times" says: "It is to Capt. Kerr and the Southern Mahratta Horse that credit is due for turning Tantia Topee from the plunder of Bhilsa." On 6 Dec. 1858, the "Times of Central India" says: "Tantia Topee sent in a message to him" (Capt. Kerr), "asking on what terms he would be allowed to surrender. Kerr replied that he would preserve his life until he had conferred with the competent authorities for instructions, but warned him that if he caught him in the field he would certainly have him hanged. When you consider that Kerr had with him but six hundred men, natives, but well known throughout India for their boldness in action, you will be convinced, as I am, that if the intelligence I have now given is confirmed, we will have nothing to fear from this notorious freebooter." Capt. Kerr also put down a rising at Hulgulee, and a contemporary writer remarked: "A little delay and hesitation such as that manifested in Bengal in May might have set the Southern Mahratta country in a blaze. With promptitude such as Colonel Jacob and Lieut. Kerr displayed, how much of the misery of the Bengal insurrection might have been saved." Capt. Kerr says: "I always hold my operations in Central India to have been my best 'bit.' . . . We turned the tide of invasion from the Deccan. At that period the whole of that part of the country, the Southern Mahratta States and the greater part of the Nizam's territory were ready to join hands with Tantia, whose forces were composed chiefly of men from the Gwalior Contingent which had handled General Wyndham so severely outside Cawnpore. When we turned the enemy into the hills he had eleven guns. The most of these he had to abandon in the jungle, and shed his last piece after crossing the Hoosingabad Road. From Huttipore I was enabled to warn Sir Robert Hamilton, the Viceroy's Agent, and also the Bombay Government. Thus the authorities had time to hurry up troops from the south. Finding himself baffled and this road to the Deccan closed, Tantia turned westwards on debouching from the hills on the south-western flank, making for Ahamadabad. At Chota Oodipore, we having joined Parke's Brigade, the enemy was broken up into three divisions and severely defeated, rendering his force useless for offence. For this prolonged march I received the high commendations of the Bombay Government." "This was the one moment of great peril for us. If Tantia, with even a broken force of seven thousand men, entered the Deccan, he would in a week have been at the head of one hundred thousand men. The Government was really alarmed, but as the danger was greater, so were the means of pacifying it greater, since Lord Elphinstone had pushed up a large force of European and Native Cavalry to render the hunt after Tantia more effective, while from Kamptie in Nagpore to the Gulf of Cambay there was a great stir of troops and a readiness to move at the slightest notice to guard the passes and fords and great roads southwards. And the measures adopted proved to be effective. Tantia found he could not get further than the hills of Sindwarra, but out of these he was forced by Lieut. Kerr" ("Cassell's Illustrated History of England"). The newspapers were full of Lieut. Kerr's adventure, which caused a stir even in such stirring times. For his services in this campaign Lieut. Kerr received the Mutiny Medal with a bar for Central India. He was frequently mentioned in Despatches, and was awarded the Victoria Cross [London Gazette, 27 April, 1858]: "William Alexander Kerr, Lieut., 24th Bombay Native Infantry. Date of Act of Bravery: 10 July, 1857. On the breaking out of a mutiny in the 27th Bombay Native Infantry in July, 1857, a party of the mutineers took up a position in the stronghold, or paga, near the town of Kolapore, and defended themselves to extremity. 'Lieut. Kerr, of the Southern Mahratta Irregular Horse, took a prominent share of the attack on the position, and at the moment when its capture was of great public importance, he made a dash at one of the gateways with some dismounted horsemen, and forced an entrance by breaking down the gate. The attack was completely successful, and the defenders were either killed, wounded or captured, a result that may with perfect justice be attributed to Lieut. Kerr's dashing and devoted bravery.' (Letter from the Political Superintendent at Kolapore to the Adjutant-General of the Army, dated 10 Sept. 1857)." The following General Order was issued by His Excellency the Commander-in-Chief:

"Headquarters, Bombay Army, Poona,
18 Sept. 1858.

"Reverting to the Extract from the London Gazette, dated 27 April last, and republished in G.G.O. 6 Sept. 1858, No. 896, the Commander-in-Chief has much pleasure in notifying to the Army that Lieut. William Alexander Kerr, of the 24th Regt. Native Infantry, and Second-in-Command of the Southern Mahratta Irregular Horse, has been decorated with the Victoria Cross, which the Queen has been pleased to confer on him, to commemorate an Act of Bravery, as recorded in the Gazette above mentioned.

"Taking into consideration the distance that officer was from Army Headquarters, the weather peculiar to this season of the year, the disturbed and uncertain times, and the important position of the outpost which Lieut. Kerr had then charge of, his absence from which would have been inconvenient to the public service, Sir Henry Somerset was constrained, on these grounds, to forgo the intention of ordering Lieut. Kerr to Army Headquarters, that His Excellency might have the gratification of presenting, in person, the decoration awarded to Lieut. Kerr.

"The important duty was therefore delegated to the Major-General Lester, Commanding Southern Division of the Army, who was directed to carry it out in the manner best adapted to evince Her Majesty's sense of the noble daring displayed by Lieut. Kerr before the enemy, to testify her wish that a distinction, in which the officer or private soldier may equally share, may be highly prized and eagerly sought after by all, of whatever rank or degree, in Her Majesty's Naval and Military Services, omitting nothing which could tend to redound to Lieut. Kerr's honour, and enhance the value of this decoration.

"The sudden and much lamented death of Major-General Lester caused, for some time, a delay (to) in carrying out His Excellency's commands; but Sir Henry Somerset has now had the pleasure of receiving from Major-General Farrell, Commanding Southern Division of the Army, a report that the Victoria Cross was presented by the Major-General to Lieut. Kerr on 4 Sept.; and, from the Major-General's report, hereto annexed, in a manner which cannot fail to be flattering to Lieut. Kerr, and gratifying not only to him but to all who witnessed the ceremony, as doing honour to a deserving and gallant officer thus publicly receiving the acknowledgment of his Sovereign for good service rendered to Her Most Gracious Majesty and the country in times when rebellion was rife, and imminent danger threatened the State:

"'No. 267.

"'Headquarters, S.D.A.,
"'Belgaum, 6 Sept. 1858.

"'From the Major-General Commanding Southern Division of the Army.

"'To the Adjutant-General of the Army, Poona.

"'SIR,—

"'Agreeably to the instructions conveyed in your letter No. 2577, of 2nd ultimo, I have the honour to report that Lieut. Kerr, of the Southern Muratha Irregular Horse, having reported his arrival on the 3rd, I directed the whole of the troops at Belgaum to parade in Review Order at 5 p.m. on the 4th, and in communication with Mr. Seton Kerr, invited the attendance of all the Civil Officers at the stations to witness the ceremony.

"'Agreeably to the instructions contained in paragraph 4 of your letter No. 1846, of 28 June, I caused the Native portion of the Troops to be previously informed of the object of the Parade by their respective Commanding Officers. The Troops were formed up in three sides of a square in contiguous columns at close order. Having summoned Lieut. Kerr to my side, I personally read out your letter No. 1846, and its accompaniments, to the whole Troops assembled, and then addressed a few words to Lieut. Kerr, expressive of the great pleasure and honour I felt that the gratifying duty of presenting him with the Victoria Cross had been deputed to me by His Excellency the Commander-in-Chief, and that I trusted he might live many years to enjoy the high honour conferred to him by our Beloved Sovereign. The Troops then presented Arms, and afterwards marched past, Lieut. Kerr being on my right hand.

"'I have the honour to be, etc.,

"'(Signed) F. T. FARRELL, Major-General,
"'Commanding S.D.A.'

"By order of His Excellency the Commander-in-Chief,
"EDWARD GREEN, Colonel.
"Adjutant-General of the Army."

Capt. Kerr rose to be Second-in-Command of the Southern Mahratta Horse, and resigned in 1860 on hearing that the Southern Mahratta Horse was to be disbanded. On 4 Jan. 1860, Capt. Kerr married at Rugby Parish Church, Harriet, daughter of Major James Atty, D.L., late 52nd Light Infantry, of Rosemount, Rugby. One of their wedding presents was the bracelet found on the body of the Rani of Jhansi. It was given to Mrs. Kerr by Colonel Battingel, 24th Regt. Bombay Native Infantry. (Capt. Kerr had been at Gwalior and Jhansi.) Since his retirement he had written several books on horsemanship, which were splendidly reviewed. Capt. Kerr died on 19 May, 1919, and an obituary notice of him appeared in the "Times" of 27 May.

SMITH, JOHN, Sergt., Bengal Engineers (or Sappers and Miners), served in the Indian Mutiny Campaign. In Kaye and Malleson's "Sepoy War," Sergt. John Smith's account of the blowing in of the Cashmere Gate is given: "The party for blowing in the gate, the 60th Rifles leading, went off at the double from Ludlow Castle, until they arrived at the cross-road leading to the Customs, and they opened out right and left, the Sappers going to the gate led by Lieut. Home and one bugler (Hawthorne), Lieut. Salkeld with the party carrying the powder a few paces behind, three European non-commissioned officers, and nine natives with twelve bags of twenty pounds each. My duty was to bring up the rear, and see that none of them remained behind. Lieut. Salkeld had passed through the temporary Burn Gate with Sergts. Carmichael and Burgess, but four of the natives had stopped behind the above gate and refused to go on. I had to put down my bag and take my gun, and threatened to shoot them, when Lieut. Salkeld came running back, and said, 'Why the —— don't you come on?' I told him that there were four men behind the gate, and that I was going to shoot them. He said, 'Shoot them, d—n their eyes, shoot them!' I said, 'You hear the orders, and I will shoot you,' raising the gun slowly to 'present' to give fair time, when two men went on. Lieut. Salkeld said, 'Do not shoot; with your own bag it will be enough.' I went on, and only Lieut. Salkeld and Sergt. Burgess were there; Lieut. Home and the bugler had jumped into the ditch, and Sergt. Carmichael was killed as he went up with his powder on his shoulder, evidently having been shot from the wicket while crossing the broken part of the bridge along one of the beams. I placed my bag, and then at great risk reached Carmichael's bag from in front of the wicket, placed it, arranged the fuse for the explosion and reported all ready to Lieut. Salkeld, who held the slow match (*not a port-fire*, as I have seen stated). In stooping down to light the quick match, he put out his foot, and was shot through the thigh from the wicket, and in falling had the presence of mind to hold out the slow match, and told me to fire the charge. Burgess was next him and took it. I told him to fire the charge and keep cool. He turned round and said, 'It won't go off, sir; it has gone out, sir' (not knowing that one officer had fallen into the ditch). I gave him a box of lucifers, and as he took them, he let them fall into my hand, he being shot through the body at the wicket also, and fell over after Lieut. Salkeld. I was then left alone, and keeping close to the charge, seeing from where the others were shot, I struck a light, when the port-fire in my fuse went off in my face, the light not having gone out as we thought. I took up my gun and jumped into the ditch, but before I had reached the ground the charge went off, and filled the ditch with smoke so that I saw no one. I turned while in the act of jumping, so that my back would come to the wall to save me from falling. I stuck close to the wall, and by that I escaped being smashed to pieces, only getting a severe bruise on the leg, the leather helmet saving my head. I put my hands along the wall and touched someone, and asked who it was. 'Lieut. Home,' was the answer. I said, 'Has God spared you? Are you hurt?' He said, 'No,' and asked the same from me. As soon as the dust cleared a little, we saw Lieut. Salkeld and Burgess covered with dust; their lying in the middle of the ditch had saved them from being smashed to pieces and covered by the debris from the top of the wall, the shock only toppling the stones over, which fell between where we stood and where they lay. I went to Lieut. Salkeld and called the bugler to help me to remove him under the bridge as the fire had covered upon us, and Lieut. Salkeld's arm was broken. . . . Lieut. Salkeld would not let us remove him, so I put a bag of powder under his arm for a pillow, and with the bugler's puggery bound up his arms and thigh, and I left the bugler to look to him, and went to Burgess, took off his sword, which I put on, and did [*sic*] what I could for him. I got some brandy from Lieut. Home, and gave to both, also to a Havildar (Pelluck Singh), who had his thigh shot through, and was under the bridge by a ladder which had been put into the ditch by mistake by the Rifles. . . . I then went to the rear for three stretchers and brought them, one of which was taken from me by an officer of the Rifles. I had to draw my sword and threaten to run anyone through who took the other two. I put them into the ditch, and with the bugler's assistance got Lieut. Salkeld into one, and sent him with him, charging him strictly not to leave him until he had placed him in the hands of a surgeon, and with the assistance of a Naick who had come to the Havildar, got Burgess into one, and sent the Havildar and the Naick with him, I being scarcely able to walk, and in a few minutes he returned to say that he was dead, and asked for further orders. I told him to take him to the hospital. After assisting to clear away the gate and make the roadway again, I went on to the front to see what was going on." For these services Sergt. Smith was awarded the Victoria Cross [London Gazette, 27 April, 1858]: "John Smith, Sergt., Bengal Sappers and Miners. Date of Act of Bravery: 14 Sept. 1857. 'For conspicuous gallantry, in conjunction with Lieuts. Home and Salkeld, in the performance of the desperate duty of blowing in the Cashmere Gate of the fortress of Delhi in broad daylight, under a heavy and destructive fire of musketry, on the morning of the 14 Sept. 1857, preparatory to the assault.' (General Order of Major-General Sir Archdale Wilson, Bart., K.C.B., dated Headquarters, Delhi City, 21 Sept. 1857)."

HAWTHORN, ROBERT, Bugler, was an Irishman from Moghera, near Londonderry, who enlisted in the 52nd Foot (now 2nd Battn. The Oxfordshire and Buckinghamshire Light Infantry) 15 Feb. 1853, and served in the Mutiny Campaign. Lord Roberts says in "Forty-one Years in India" (page 126): "No. 3 Column had advanced towards the Kashmir Gate and halted. Lieuts. Home and Salkeld, with eight Sappers and Miners, and a Bugler of the 52nd Foot, went forward to blow the gate open. The enemy were apparently so astounded at the audacity of this proceeding that for a minute or two they offered but slight resistance. They soon, however, discovered how small the party was and the object for which it had come, and forthwith opened a deadly fire upon the gallant little band from the top of the gateway, from the city wall and through the open wicket. The bridge over the gateway had been destroyed, and it was with some difficulty that the single beam which remained could be crossed. Home, with the men carrying the powder-bags, got over first. As the bags were being attached to the gate, Sergt. Carmichael was killed, and Havildar Madhoo wounded; the rest then slipped into the ditch to allow the firing party which had come up under Salkeld to carry out its share of the duty. While endeavouring to fire the charge, Salkeld, being shot through the leg and arm, handed the slow-match to Corpl. Burgess, who fell mortally wounded, but not till he had successfully performed his task. As soon as the explosion had taken place, Bugler Hawthorn sounded the regimental call of the 52nd. Meeting with no response, he sounded it twice again. The noise of the firing and shouting was so great that neither the sound of the bugle nor that of the explosion reached the column, but Campbell, after allowing the firing party what he thought was a sufficient time, gave the order to advance. Capt. Crosse, of the 52nd, was the first to reach the gate, followed closely by Corpl. Taylor of his own company, and Capt. Synge of the same regiment, who was Campbell's Brigade Major. In single file along the narrow plank, they crossed the ditch in which lay the shattered remnant of the gallant little band; they crept through the wicket, which was the only part blown in, and found the interior of the gateway blocked up by an 18-pounder gun, under which were lying the scorched bodies of two or three sepoys, who had evidently been killed by the explosion. The rest of the column advanced as rapidly as the precarious crossing would admit, and when Campbell got inside he found himself face to face with both Nicholson's and Jones's columns, which, after mounting the three breaches, poured in a mingled crowd into the open space between the Kashmir Gate and the church." Hawthorn was awarded the Victoria Cross [London Gazette, 27 April, 1858]: "Robert Hawthorn, Bugler, 52nd Regt. Date of Act of Bravery: 14 Sept. 1857. 'Bugler Hawthorn, who accompanied the explosion party, not only performed the dangerous duty on which he was employed, but previously attached himself to Lieut. Salkeld, of the Engineers, when dangerously wounded, bound up his wounds under a heavy musketry fire, and had him removed without further injury.' (General Order of Major-General Sir Archdale Wilson, Bart., K.C.B., dated Headquarters, Delhi City, 21st Sept. 1857)." Robert Hawthorn died 2 Feb. 1879. His Victoria Cross was purchased in 1909 by the officers of the 52nd Regt., at the sale of Mr. J. B. Gaskell's medal collection. Colonel Mockler-Ferryman says that there is a portrait sketch of Hawthorn in the Records of the Regiment, a fancy drawing by Simkin, made twelve years after the man's death, from what people remembered him to be like! There is also a picture—also "fancy," in the Officers' Mess of the Bengal Sappers and Miners, at Rorki, India. Official rolls omit the "e" from the end of Hawthorn's name. It is uncertain if "Hawthorn" or "Hawthorne" is correct.

Robert Hawthorn.

SMITH, HENRY, L.-Corpl., enlisted in the 52nd Foot (now 2nd Battn. The Oxfordshire and Buckinghamshire Light Infantry) at Ditton, Surrey, 9 Feb. 1853, and served in the Indian Mutiny Campaign. While Number 3 Column was fighting its way towards the far-famed Chandni Chauk (Silver Bazaar), it met with such resistance that Colonel Campbell retired and held the Bagam Bagh for an hour and a half, after which he fell back to the church and posted his sadly diminished force in the church itself and in the houses round it, with guns pointing up the two streets that led to the interior of the city. It was during this temporary retirement that L.-Corpl. Henry Smith won the Victoria Cross [London Gazette, 14 Sept. 1857]: "Henry Smith, L.-Corpl., 52nd Foot. Date of Act of Bravery, 14 Sept. 1857. 'L.-Corpl. Smith most gallantly carried away a wounded comrade under a heavy fire of grape and musketry on the Chaundee Chouch, in the City of Delhi, on the morning of the assault on the 14th Sept. 1857.' (General Order of Major-General Sir Archdale Wilson, Bart., K.C.B., dated Headquarters, Delhi City, 21 Sept. 1857)." He was promoted to Sergeant. Sergt. Smith's Victoria Cross and Mutiny Medal were sold in July, 1896, for £70, at Sotheby and Wilkinson's auction rooms, and purchased by the officers of the 52nd Regt.

DIAMOND, BERNARD, Sergt., served in the Indian Mutiny Campaign. He was awarded the Victoria Cross [London Gazette, 24 April, 1858]: "Bernard Diamond, Sergt., and Richard Fitzgerald, Gunner. Date of Act of Bravery, 28 Sept. 1857. 'For an act of valour performed in action against the rebels and mutineers at Boolundshuhur on the 28th Sept. 1857, when these two soldiers evinced the most determined bravery in working their gun under a very heavy fire of musketry, whereby they cleared the road of the enemy, after every other man belonging to it had been either killed or disabled by wounds.' (Despatch of Major Turner, Bengal Horse Artillery, dated Boolundshuhur, 2 Oct. 1857)." Sergt. B. Diamond died 24 Jan. 1892.

Bernard Diamond.

FITZGERALD, RICHARD, Gunner, served in the Indian Mutiny Campaign, and for his services was awarded the Victoria Cross [London Gazette, 27 April, 1858]: "Bernard Diamond, Sergt., and Richard Fitzgerald, Gunner, Bengal Horse Artillery. Date of Act of Bravery: 28 Sept. 1857. 'For an act of valour performed in action against the rebels and mutineers at Boolundshuhur on the 28th Sept. 1857, when these two soldiers evinced the most determined bravery in working their gun under a very heavy fire of musketry, whereby they cleared the road of the enemy, after every other man belonging to it had been either killed or disabled by wounds.' (Despatch of Major Turner, Bengal Horse Artillery, dated Boolundshuhur, 2 Oct. 1857)."

London Gazette, 4 June, 1858. "War Office, 2 June, 1858.—The Queen has been graciously pleased to signify her intention to confer the Decoration of the Victoria Cross on the undermentioned Officers and Non-commissioned Officers of Her Majesty's Army, who have been recommended to Her Majesty for that Decoration in accordance with the rules laid down in Her Majesty's Warrant of the 29th Jan. 1856, on account of Acts of Bravery performed by them in the Crimea during the late war, as recorded against their several names."

RAMAGE, HENRY, Sergt., served in the Indian Mutiny, and for his services in this campaign was awarded the Victoria Cross [London Gazette, 4 June, 1858]: " Henry Ramage, Sergt., 2nd Dragoons (Scots Greys). Date of Act of Bravery : 25 Oct. 1854. For having at the Battle of Bala-klava galloped out to the assistance of Private M'Pherson, of the same regiment, on perceiving him surrounded by seven Russians, when by his gallantry he dispersed the enemy and saved his comrade's life ; for having on the same day, when the Heavy Brigade was rallying, and the enemy retiring, finding his horse would not leave the ranks, dismounted and brought in a prisoner from the Russian lines ; also for having dismounted on the same day when the Heavy Brigade was covering the retreat of the Light Cavalry, and lifted from his horse Private Gardiner, who was dis-abled from a severe fracture of the leg by a round shot. Sergt. Ramage then carried him to the rear under a very heavy cross-fire, thereby saving his life, the spot where he must inevitably have fallen having been imme-diately afterwards covered by the Russian Cavalry." Sergt. Ramage died 29 Dec. 1859, at Newbridge, Curragh of Kildare, Ireland.

WALKER, MARK, Brevet Major, *b.* 24 Nov. 1827 ; *s.* of Capt. Alexander Walker, of Gore Port, a distinguished officer who served in the Peninsular War ; educ. at Portarlington, and was gazetted to the 30th Foot as Ensign

25 Sept. 1846. He served throughout the Crimean Campaign as Adjutant 30th Regt. (30 Dec. 1854, to 14 May, 1855); was present at the Battle of the Alma (wounded, horse shot), at Inkerman, and at the Siege of Sebastopol 9 June, including the sortie of 20 Oct. (severely wounded, right arm amputated). At the Battle of Inkerman he greatly distinguished himself. When the alarm was given by the picquets, the 30th Regt. advanced in two batta-lions, the right under Colonel Mauleverer, the left under Colonel Patullo. Lieut. Walker was with Colonel Mauleverer's battalion, which moved towards a low wall and lay down. Suddenly, from out the thick fog which had hung over them since daylight, two heavy columns of Russian Infantry appeared close upon them, and the

Mark Walker.

command was given to open fire. In those days it was customary to pile arms at night before the men's tents, and the stoppers of the rifles had been lost, which caused the arms to become wet and useless. The Russians came nearer and nearer, and the position grew desperate. There was a possibility of the men getting nervous and out of hand. But Lieut. Walker seized the psychological moment and jumped over the low wall, calling to the men to follow him with the bayonet. He led them straight at the Russians, who were paralysed at the appearance of our men and the suddenness of the attack. They could not see how small was Lieut. Walker's following across country, and they were panic-stricken. Despite the exhortations of the Russian officers, their men turned and fairly bolted, pursued for some distance by Walker. Soon after winning the Victoria Cross he won fresh distinction by volunteering and leading a party which took and destroyed a Russian rifle-pit. For this service he was promoted into the Buffs (1854), but almost immediately afterwards was dangerously wounded in the trenches, and his right arm was amputated. He was mentioned in Despatches [London Gazette, 7 May, 1855], received the Crimean Medal with three clasps, the 5th Class of the Order of the Medjidie and the Turkish Medal ; was given the Brevet of Major, and awarded the Victoria Cross [London Gazette, 4 June, 1858]: " Mark Walker, Brevet Major, 3rd Regt., late of the 30th Regt. Date of Act of Bravery : 5 Nov. 1854. For having at Inkerman distinguished himself in front of his regiment by jumping over a wall in face of two battalions of Russian Infantry, which were marching towards it, for the purpose of encouraging his comrades by his example to advance against such heavy odds—which they did, and succeeded in driving back both battalions." He became Captain 15 May, 1855, and Brevet Major 6 June, 1856. Major Walker served in the China War from 30 March, 1860, to 15 Nov, 1860, as Brigade Major, being present at the Battle of Sinho, the capture of the Taku Forts, Shanken Wan, Tientsein, Ting Chin and Pekin. He was mentioned in Despatches, received the Medal with two clasps, and was given the Brevet of Lieut.-Colonel 15 Feb. 1861. He was also given the Brevet of Colonel 15 Feb. 1869 ; became Major 3rd Foot 3 Aug. 1870, and Lieut.-Colonel 45th Foot 10 Dec. 1873. In 1875 he was created a C.B., and from 4 Aug. 1875, to 4 Nov. 1879, he commanded a brigade at Kamptu, Madras. He was Lieut.-Colonel on half-pay 17 March, 1877, and was promoted to Major-General 11 Nov. 1878. In 1881, Major-General Walker *m.* Catherine, dau. of Robert Bruce Chichester, Esq., of Arlington, Devon. From 1 April, 1883, to 31 March, 1884, he commanded a brigade at Alder-shot, and he was Major-General, Gibraltar, from 1 April, 1884, to 31 March, 1888. On the 16th Dec. 1888, he was promoted to Lieut.-General, and on the 27th Sept. 1900, became Colonel, Derbyshire Regt. In 1893 he was created a K.C.B. (Military). He became General 15 Feb. 1893, and retired 1 April of the same year. Sir Mark Walker lived for many years at 10, Castle Avenue, Folkestone, and he died at Arlington Rectory, near Barnstaple, on Friday, 18 July, 1902, and was buried at Folkestone. In May, 1913, Lady Walker left her husband's Victoria Cross and medals (miniatures only), and watch and the grey overcoat he wore at Inkerman to the 1st Battn. The East Lancashire Regt. She also endowed a bed at the Union Jack Club to his memory. Major E. R. Collins, D.S.O., writes : " I was serving with the 1st Battn. The East Lancashire Regt. when we

received the miniature medals and decorations, also a portrait from Lady Walker. This portrait is an enlarged photograph in General's uniform, and far better than the one you have attached ; it is at present in store with the rest of the Mess property. The actual medals were left to the East Kent Regt. (The Buffs), I believe. As regards the account of the 30th Foot at Inkerman, our records state as follows :—' For a moment the men—baffled by the failure of their muskets to fire in the close presence of the enemy—seemed to waver, but Colonel Mauleverer, who was on foot, was equal to the emergency. He caused his men to advance to the main picket and lie down behind it for a moment. The enemy's masses approached, and the head of the column was within a few yards, when the Colonel, Lieut. Walker, his Adjutant, and the rest of the officers, jumped upon the wall. A moment's pause, and then they leapt down upon the enemy. In an instant the men were up and over the wall, and—giving up the cartridges, useless to them—charged down the hill with the bayonet,' etc., etc. In the regiment we always consider Colonel Mauleverer as leader of this charge, and Lieut. Walker as receiving the V.C. for personal bravery during the action. Your account rather points to Lieut. Walker as leader in this action."

GARDINER, GEORGE, Colour-Sergt., served in the Indian Mutiny, and was awarded the Victoria Cross [London Gazette, 2 June, 1858]: " George Gardiner, Colour-Sergt., 57th Regt. Dates of Acts of Bravery : 22 March and 18 June, 1855. For distinguished coolness and gallantry upon the occasion of a sortie by the enemy, and when he was acting as Orderly-Sergt. to the Field Officer of the trenches—left attack upon Sebastopol—in having rallied the covering parties which had been driven in by the Russians, thus regaining and keeping possession of the trenches ; also for unflinching and devoted courage in the attack on the Redan 18 June, 1855, in having remained, and encouraging others to remain, in the holes made by the explosions of the shells, from whence, by making parapets of the dead bodies of their comrades, they kept

George Gardiner.

up a continuous fire until their ammunition was exhausted, thus clearing the enemy away from the parapet of the Redan. This was done under a fire in which nearly half the officers and a third of the rank and file of the party of the regiment were placed *hors de combat.*" Colour-Sergt. G. Gardiner died 17 Nov. 1891.

MOUAT, JAMES, Surgeon, C.B., *b.* in 1815 ; *s.* of the late James Mouat, Esq., M.D. ; educ. at University College and Hospital, London (F.R.C.S., 1852). He entered the Medical Department of the Army as Assistant-

Surgeon in 1838 ; was Surgeon to the 6th Dragoons, and had medical charge of the General Field Hospital of the 3rd Division until the fall of Sebastopol, being present at the Battles of Balaklava, Inkerman and Tchernaya. For his services in the Crimean Campaign Surgeon Mouat received the Medal with three clasps, the Legion of Honour, and was awarded the Victoria Cross [London Gazette, 2 June, 1858]: " James Mouat, C.B., Surgeon, 6th Dragoons, now Deputy Inspector-General of Hospitals. Date of Act of Bravery : 26 Oct. 1854. For having voluntarily proceeded to the assistance of Lieut.-Colonel Morris, C.B., 17th Lancers, who was lying dangerously wounded in an exposed position after the retreat of Light Cavalry at the Battle of Balaklava, and

James Mouat.

having dressed that officer's wounds in the presence and under a heavy fire of the enemy. Thus, by stopping a severe hæmorrhage, he assisted in saving that officer's life." Capt. Morris, when returning wounded out of the Valley of Death, had fallen at the feet of his dead friend, Capt. Nolan, that brilliant cavalry officer and writer on military subjects, who was born before his time, the Aide-de-Camp who was—to a great extent unjustly—blamed for the charge of the Light Brigade. Sergt. Wooden —a German—helped Dr. Mouat to bind up Colonel Morris's wounds, and together these good Samaritans carried him to a place of safety. Morris only survived the Mutiny to die in India, in 1858, having been promoted to Colonel and given a C.B. Had he lived he would perhaps have been able to re-establish the military reputation of his friend, Capt. Nolan. Dr. Mouat served throughout the Maori Wars, and received the thanks of the New Zealand Government for the special and very valuable services which he rendered to the colony. In 1858 he was appointed Deputy Inspector-General, and in 1864 Inspector-General of Hospitals. In 1868 the good service pension vacant by the death of Inspector-General Mahoney was conferred upon him. In 1888 he was appointed Honorary Surgeon to the Queen, and in 1894 was created a K.C.B. He died on Wednesday, 4 Jan. 1899, at his residence, 1, Palace Gate Gardens, Kensington.

ELPHINSTONE, HOWARD CRAUFORD, Lieut., *b.* 12 Dec. 1829, at Wattram, in Livonia ; 4th *s.* of Capt. Alexander Francis Elphinstone, R.N. ; educ. abroad, and at Woolwich, and received his first commission in the Royal Engineers 18 Dec. 1847, at the age of eighteen, becoming

Lieut. 11 Nov. 1851. In 1853 he attended the Military Reviews in Prussia in an official capacity, and up to March, 1854, was employed in Ordnance Survey in Scotland. He then went to Malta, Bulgaria

Howard C. Elphinstone.

and the Crimea, and on the 29 Sept. 1854, reached Balaklava, and served in the trenches of the Right Attack, being 81 days and 91 nights on trench duty. He was conspicuous in the assault on the Quarries before the Redan 18 June, and took part in the final assault on Sebastopol 8 Sept., where he was wounded in the left eye by a splinter and lost the sight of that eye. For his services in this campaign he was mentioned in Despatches in the London Gazettes of 21 June, and 21 Dec. 1855, receiving the Medal and clasps; was given the Brevet of Major; was made a Knight of the Legion of Honour; awarded the Medjidie of the fifth class, and the Turkish Medal. He also received a pension for wounds, and on its institution was awarded the Victoria Cross [London Gazette, 2 June, 1858]: "Howard Crauford Elphinstone, Lieut., Royal Engineers. Date of Act of Bravery: 18 June, 1855. For fearless conduct in having, on the night of the successful attack on the Redan, volunteered to command a party of volunteers. He proceeded to search for and bring back the scaling ladders left behind after the repulse; and while successfully performing this task of rescuing trophies from the Russians, Capt. Elphinstone conducted a persevering search, close to the enemy, for wounded men, twenty of whom he rescued and brought back to the trenches." He became Second Captain; and Captain 20 April, 1856; Brevet Major 26 Dec. 1856; Major 5 July, 1862, and on 23 Aug. 1865, he was created a Military C.B. He was given the Brevet of Lieut.-Colonel 9 April, 1868; on 28 July, 1870, he was created C.M.G., and on 3 July, 1871, a Civil K.C.B. He was promoted to Colonel on 23 May, 1873. A great favourite with Her Majesty, Major-General Sir Howard Elphinstone had been entrusted by Queen Victoria with the training of the Duke of Connaught from the time when Prince Arthur was eight years old. Up to the very last Sir Howard was Treasurer and Comptroller of the Duke of Connaught's Household; was in command of Royal Engineer Troops at Aldershot in Aug. 1873, to March, 1874, and the troops and companies to Dec. 1881. On 1 Oct. 1877, he was given the Brevet of Colonel, and on 31 Oct. 1877, was appointed A.D.C. to the Queen. He was Commanding Engineer at Aldershot 31 Dec. 1881, to 31 Dec. 1886; was temporary Military Attaché at Berlin during some of this period, and was very well known in that city. He was promoted to Colonel 2 May, 1884, and to Major-General 29 Jan. 1887. From 1 April, 1889, he was in command of the Western District, and with Lady Elphinstone and one of his daughters he was a passenger to New Zealand on one of the New Zealand Shipping Company's steamers. He was swept overboard and drowned on the night of the 8th March, 1890, and his body was never found. The "Times" of 4 March, 1890, says that the General's death "robbed the Western District of one of the best Generals who ever commanded it, and the Service of one of its brightest ornaments. . . . By his quiet and unobtrusive bearing, to say nothing of his fair-mindedness, he had won the respect of all in his important command." There is a brass tablet to his memory in Devonport Chapel. Sir Howard Elphinstone was survived by Lady Elphinstone and four young daughters.

MACDONALD, HENRY, Colour-Sergt., served in the Crimean War of 1854–55, and for his services in that campaign was awarded the Victoria Cross [London Gazette, 2 June, 1858]: "Henry Macdonald, Colour-Sergt., Royal Engineers. Date of Act of Bravery: 19 April, 1855. For gallant conduct when engaged in effecting a lodgement in the enemy's rifle-pits in front of the left advance of the right attack on Sebastopol, and for subsequent valour when, by the Engineer Officer being disabled from wounds, the command devolved upon him, and he determinately persisted in carrying on the sap, notwithstanding the repeated attacks of the enemy." The rifle-pits are described as having been complete little batteries for riflemen. Colour-Sergt. Macdonald became Garrison Quartermaster, Gibraltar, and was promoted Captain. He died in Glasgow 15 Feb. 1893, aged 70.

Henry Macdonald.

Peter Leitch.

LEITCH, PETER, Colour-Sergt., served in the Crimean War, and for his services in that campaign was awarded the Victoria Cross [London Gazette, 2 June, 1858]: "Peter Leitch, Colour-Sergt., Royal Engineers. Date of Act of Bravery: 18 June, 1855. For conspicuous gallantry in the assault on the Redan, when, after approaching it with the leading ladders, he formed a caponnière across the ditch, as well as a ramp, by fearlessly tearing down gabions from the parapet, and placing and filling them until he was disabled from wounds." Leitch had previously in 1854, at Bomarsund, been

noticed for his conspicuous gallantry, and besides the Victoria Cross and the Crimean Medal with clasps, he was given the Legion of Honour. Colour-Sergt. P. Leitch died 6 Dec. 1892.

London Gazette, 18 June, 1858.—War Office, 18 June, 1858. The Queen has been graciously pleased to confirm the grant of the Victoria Cross to the undermentioned Officers, Non-commissioned Officers and men of Her Majesty's and of the East India Company's Armies, which Decoration had been provisionally conferred upon them by Major-General Sir James Outram, G.C.B., and by the late Major-General Sir Henry Havelock, K.C.B., on account of the Acts of Bravery performed by them in India, as recorded against their several names, in virtue of that power delegated to Generals commanding Corps, Divisions or Brigades by Her Majesty's Warrant of the 29th Jan. 1856:—

MAUDE, FRANCIS CORNWALLIS, Capt., b. 28 Oct. 1828; s. of the Honourable Francis Maude, Capt., Royal Navy, and of Fanny, dau. of A. H. Brooking, Esq.; educ. at Rugby, and at the Royal Military Academy, Woolwich. Colonel F. C. Maude says in

Francis Cornwallis Maude.

his "Memories of the Mutiny" (page 408): "One morning at the time of the advance on Lucknow, a tallish man with yellow hair, a pale, smooth face, heavy moustache and large, unforgiving eyes, came into my room at Duncan's. He looked at me in a stony way, and then relaxing his features with a laugh, said: 'I have a job for you.' It was William Hodson. I had met him in India, but not since the days of his celebrity; and the joke about the 'job' was in reference to years before, when I was his 'fag' at Rugby, and had to brush his study out and make his coffee by the time he was back from first lesson. (This was my second 'situation;' I had previously been valet to the late Bishop of Madras.) Besides this relation, I had known him also in family circles, for his Archdeacon father belonged to a school of religionists amongst whom my people also took their part. Willie Hodson of the yellow hair—not great in cricket or football, but distinguished for running and athletic feats of endurance—was a soldier almost by an afterthought, for he had to get into the Army through the Jersey Militia on account of age, finding his true throne at last on an Irregular Cavalry saddle." Francis Maude joined the Royal Artillery as 2nd Lieut. 1 Oct. 1847, and became Lieut. on the 30th June, 1848, and Captain on the 13th Dec. 1854. He went to Trincomalee, Ceylon, early in 1855, in command of a battery of Royal Artillery, and writes in his "Memories of the Mutiny" (page 4): "In the afternoon of 6 June, 1857, our lotus-eating life was suddenly disturbed by the arrival in Back Bay, Trincomalee, of the Semiramis, a frigate belonging to the East India Company, which brought the astonishing news that the Sepoy Mutiny had broken out, and that every European soldier was to proceed immediately to British India." Maude and his battery arrived in Calcutta on the 13th June, and on the 18th started up country to join Havelock's flying column at Allahabad, where that General was preparing to take the field with the object and hope of relieving General Wheeler's force at Cawnpore. Just, however, as the column was ready to start, came the news of the surrender and massacre of the British garrison at Cawnpore. The slaughter of the remaining women and children did not take place till some time later. On the march to Cawnpore a body of enemy cavalry was encountered, and Capt. Maude brought his guns into action. He laid a nine-pounder himself at 700 yards range, and knocked over an elephant said to have been ridden by Tantia Topi, who unfortunately survived his fall. Capt. Maude became Major on the 19th Jan. 1858. He was with Outram's force at Alumbagh from Jan. to March, 1858. He thus describes the action at the Alumbagh in his "Memories of the Mutiny" (page 292): "As we were by this time (9 o'clock a.m.) supported by the remainder of the column, the enemy abandoned the Yellow House and neighbouring gardens, at the same time retiring two of their guns down the lane, a little to the right of the house. As will be seen from the map, this lane also takes a bend to the left at this point, nearly at right angles to the Alumbagh Road. The distance from the Bridge was under three hundred yards. Soon after we turned the corner. I will here quote the words of General Fred. A. Willis, C.B., in a letter to the 'Times,' dated 23 March, 1890: 'Maude's battery followed the 84th to the Char Bagh (Four Gardens), and I shall never forget seeing the two leading guns unlimber, and come into action on the road at very close range (150 yards) opposite the Char Bagh Bridge, under a murderous fire from the enemy's guns in position on the further side of the bridge. . . . The first discharge from one of the enemy's guns disabled one of Maude's guns, the greater portion of the detachment serving it being killed or wounded. It was then I offered to assist him, by calling for volunteers from the regiments, many men of which, for some time, whilst lying inactive in Cawnpore, had by order been instructed in gun-drill. Private Joel Holmes was the first man of the Gun Regiment to respond, and his example was followed by others.' (Amongst whom were Lieuts. Pearson and Aitken.) 'The gun was again served, the men remaining with it the remainder of the day. The gallantry displayed by Private Holmes throughout the day caused me to recommend him for the Victoria Cross, which he received. . . . A portion of the Madras Fusiliers came up to the Char Bagh in support, and they, with the 84th, charged across the bridge, and captured the four (there were five) guns in position; and I well remember during this charge the leading officer of the Madras Fusiliers (Lieut. Groom) had his foot shot off at the ankle, by my side, and I myself was wounded by the last discharge from the guns in position at the Char Bagh Bridge. When these guns were captured the leading portion of the column was halted for the main body to join it, and I recall with pride the fact that General Outram, when he came up, complimented the 84th and Madras Fusiliers for the dash and gallantry displayed in the capture of these guns. At this point the enemy had five guns . . . two being 24-pounders. They were behind a cleverly-constructed earthwork, while we had two 9-pounders in the open. Our men were fatigued and disheartened by a severe action, in which we had lost twenty-one of the finest of our little band. Yet we held our own for half an hour against these tremendous odds, and although the range was only 150 yards, we really lost comparatively few men, keeping the enemy's fire down, if we did not exactly silence all their guns.' The following is an extract from a letter written by Major-General Sir James Outram, G.C.B., etc., to Brigadier-General Havelock, C.B., etc.:

'Lucknow,
'October 12th, 1857.

'Sir,

'It is my pleasing duty to recommend to you as deserving the high distinction of the Victoria Cross, two officers of whose heroic gallantry on the 25th ultimo I was an admiring witness, but who, having on that occasion been under your own command, can only through yourself receive the reward they so justly merit. The officers I refer to are Capt. Maude, of the Royal Artillery, and Lieut. Havelock, Assistant Adjutant-General. The former of these, as you are aware, with his bullock battery, and supported by a small party of the 5th Fusiliers, formed the advance guard when the troops moved on from the Alum Bagh. The enemy had on that occasion flanked his road under cover of long, high grass, and a murderous fire was poured on the column from a double-storied house, full of musketeers, and from loop-holed walls of the large surrounding gardens, from two guns that raked the road from the right flank, and another that commanded his front. But steadily and cheerfully Capt. Maude pressed on with his brave men, and in the face of this desperate opposition did he bring them through, though not without the loss of nearly one third of his artillery force. This was no reckless or foolhardy daring; but the calm heroism of a true soldier, who fully appreciated the difficulties and the dangers of the task he had undertaken.

'(Signed) J. Outram,
'Major-General Commanding Cawnpore and Dinapore Divisions.'"

For his services in this campaign, Maude was three times recommended for the Victoria Cross, which was awarded to him [London Gazette, 18 June, 1858]: "Francis Cornwallis Maude, C.B., Captain (now Major), Royal Artillery. This officer steadily and cheerfully pushed on with his men, and bore down the desperate opposition of the enemy, though with the loss of one-third of his artillerymen. Sir James Outram adds, 'that this attack appeared to him to indicate no reckless or foolhardy daring, but the calm heroism of a true soldier who fully appreciates the difficulties and dangers of the task he has undertaken; and that, but for Capt. Maude's nerve and coolness on this trying occasion, the Army could not have advanced.' (Extract from Field Force Orders of the late Major-General Havelock, 17 Oct. 1857)." Maude had three or four batteries under his charge at the Siege of Lucknow, one of which was the "Redan" Battery, immediately below the Residency Tower at Lucknow. This had five guns in it, one of which had been dismounted by the rebels' fire. "There was a provoking little battery of the enemy's just across the river, under a mosque, which did a lot of damage, firing on the slope which led to the water's edge, and which was crowded with soldiers, horses, bullocks, hackeries and natives. One day, as I was passing, a shot took off both the legs of a British soldier who was by my side. . . . I resolved to avenge him and try and silence the gun. It was protected by heavy shutters. . . . One night I mounted an 18-pounder iron gun in the embrasure of our dismantled piece. I also had an 8-inch mortar brought into the battery. . . . We fired the usual four guns at the Mosque Battery, and then treated them to the novelty of a well-timed shell from the 8-inch mortar. While the latter missile was distracting their attention, I carefully laid the new 18-pounder. Shortly after the mortar shell had burst the enemy opened the protecting shutters." Maude at once fired his reserve gun, and, "as luck would have it, the shot went clean into the enemy's embrasure, and knocked the gun over. They never fired from that place again. About an hour afterwards Outram and one or two of his Staff came down to see the spot, the news having quickly reached Headquarters. The Bayard of India said with his genial smile: 'I have heard of your feat of arms, Maude, and I now give you the highest reward it is in my power to bestow!' at the same time handing me a Manilla cheroot. A most seasonable gift it was, and I heartily and laughingly thanked the good General for it." (Cheroots were sixpence each at the time in Lucknow.) For his services in the Mutiny Campaign, Capt. Maude received—besides the Victoria Cross—the Brevet of Major and Lieut.-Colonel, a year's service, and the Mutiny Medal with clasps, and was created a C.B. He was repeatedly mentioned in Despatches. On 20 July, 1858, he became Lieut.-Colonel. In 1860, at Colombo, he *m.* Paulina S. Sterling, dau. of the Honourable Paul Ivy Sterling, Judge of the Supreme Court, Ceylon, and three daus. and one son survived them. He became Colonel on the 20th July, 1866, and was placed on half-pay on the 29th Aug. 1869. He was Her Britannic Majesty's Consul-General at Warsaw, Poland, 1876–1886; was appointed a Military Knight of Windsor in 1895. He died at Windsor (a Military Knight of the Upper Foundation) 19 Oct. 1900.

OLPHERTS, WILLIAM, Capt., *b.* 8 March, 1822; *s.* of the late William Olpherts, Esq., J.P., of Dartrey, co. Armagh; educ. at Gracehill and Dungannon Schools, and at Addiscombe, and entered the Bengal Artillery 11 June, 1839. He commanded four guns on service in Burmah in 1841, and two guns at the action of Jhirnaghat, during the insurrection of 1842, in the Sangor and Nerbudda Territory. In 1843 and 1844 he commanded a light field battery in the Gwalior Campaign; was present at Panmar, and mentioned in Despatches by Sir Hugh (Lord) Gough. He also received the bronze star. In 1844 he raised and commanded the Artillery in Bundelcund, and commanded it during the operations—against the hill tribes of Sindh—under Sir Charles Napier in 1844–45. In 1852 he served under Sir Colin Campbell in operations in the Peshawar Valley (Medal with clasp). In the following year he attained the rank of Captain. When the Crimean War commenced, Capt. Olpherts was employed in Kars and Erzeroum in Armenia, under Sir Fenwick Williams. As soon as he could, "ever greedy of fighting," he hastened to Turkey and served in that country and in Armenia (1854–55) till the Peace (Medal with clasps). At the outbreak of the Mutiny, "Hell-fire Jack" at once became known as a daring and able officer. His first exploit was to take part in the defeat by Colonel Neill of three native regiments at Benares, the entire British force being only 200 Horse. He afterwards joined Havelock's force at Cawnpore, and was present at the actions of Bithour, Mungulwar and Alumbagh, and in the First Relief of the Residency at Lucknow. On the 25th, when Havelock's force fought their way through the city, Capt. Olpherts charged with the 90th Regt. "It was before the Charbagh Bridge had been carried that William Olpherts performed the gallant feat which gained for him the Victoria Cross. The 90th Light Infantry, led by Colonel Campbell, had been ordered to charge and carry a battery of two guns, strongly posted at the end of a street. They charged and carried it. Whilst they held back the guns, Olpherts, who had charged with them, galloped back under a severe fire of musketry, and brought up the limbers and horses to carry off the captured ordnance. This was, in round numbers, the thirtieth time that this gallant officer had deserved the Cross he so nobly wears!" (Kaye and Malleson's "Sepoy War," Vol. III., page 364). He was elected by his comrades for the Victoria Cross. For his assistance in another of Olphert's exploits Private Duffy was awarded the same decoration. His Victoria Cross was gazetted 18 June, 1858: "William Olpherts, Capt. (now Lieut.-Colonel), Bengal Artillery. Date of Act of Bravery: 25 Sept. 1857. 'For highly distinguished conduct on the 25th Sept. 1857, when the troops penetrated into the city of Lucknow, in having charged on horseback with Her Majesty's 90th Regt., when, gallantly headed by Colonel Campbell, it captured two guns in the face of a heavy fire of grape, and having afterwards returned, under a severe fire of musketry, to bring up limbers and horses to carry off the captured ordnance, which he accomplished.' (Extract from Field Force Orders of the late Major-General Havelock, dated 17 Oct. 1857)." He was also given the Brevets of Major and Lieut.-Colonel, and in 1858 was created a C.B. He also received the Medal with two clasps; was mentioned in Despatches, and wounded. An Artilleryman—also a V.C. man—related an anecdote which "though apocryphal, shows what was thought of Olpherts." The story was that Olpherts, seeing a rebel battery in his front, did not wait to fire, but charged with the limbers and mounted detachments, the enemy at once abandoning his guns. Till the Relief of Lucknow, Olpherts commanded the Artillery in the Residency, was wounded and mentioned in Despatches. He served throughout the Mutiny Campaign. Olpherts "revelled in danger, and possessed the *coup d'œil* of a dashing leader," says Colonel Malleson, who again remarks that the deed for which he was gazetted was "in round numbers, the thirtieth time that this gallant officer had deserved the Cross he so nobly wears." Lord Wolseley vividly described Olpherts: "His battery was a sort of military curiosity in every way. His gun-carriages were old, and always on the verge of absolute dissolution; and as for his harness, it seemed to be tied together with pieces of string. First came dear old Billy himself, clad in garments he had used in the Crimean War, a fez cap and a Turkish grego, the latter tied round his waist with a piece of rope. About fifty yards behind him came his well-known battery sergeant-major, in a sort of shooting coat made from the green baize of a billiard-table; then a gun, every driver flogging as hard as he could; then another a long distance in the rear. . . . Some of the spokes had gone; they all rattled." Lord Napier of Magdala said of Olpherts: "I have often seen him in action, but never without his deserving the Victoria Cross." General Olpherts is said to have once described himself as "an old smooth-bore muzzle-loader, hopelessly behind the times." He was a splendid type of the fire-eating officer of the old school. His last campaign was against the Wuzerees in 1859 and 1860, when he served as a Volunteer under Sir N. Chamberlain. In 1861 he *m.* Alice Maria, dau. of Major-General George Cautley, Bengal Cavalry. In 1864 he was promoted Colonel, and in 1868 received a Sword of Honour from the County and City of Armagh. From 1870 to 1875 he was Major-General Commanding the Gwalior and Rohilkund Districts and the Sirkind and Oudh Districts. In 1877 Major-General Olpherts became Lieut.-General, and in 1883 General. In 1886 he was created a K.C.B. (military). In 1888 Sir William Olpherts became Colonel Commandant of the Royal Artillery. He died at his residence at Upper Norwood 30 April, 1902, in his 81st year, and was carried to his grave in Richmond Cemetery on a gun-carriage, escorted by a detachment of X Battery, Royal Horse Artillery, during a thunderstorm.

William Olpherts.

MACPHERSON, HERBERT TAYLOR, Lieut., *b.* 27 Jan. 1827; *s.* of the late Colonel Duncan Macpherson, of Ardersier, Inverness-shire, N.B. Herbert Macpherson entered the Army in 1845; and one of his first regiments was his father's, the 78th Ross-shire Buffs. He became Lieut. in 1847, and saw his first military service in the Expedition to Persia, and was present in the night attack on and Battle of Kooshab, and the bombardment of Mohummerah 1856-7. In the Indian Mutiny he was one of Havelock's force which was hurriedly assembled and pushed forward to the relief of Cawnpore and Lucknow. He was present in all the battles fought with the Oudh Mutineers and the followers of Nana Sahib. He was wounded at the Battle of Oonao, but this was no obstacle to his presence in the encounters of Buseerutgunge, Boorbeake-Chowkee and Bithoor. He served with Outram's force in Alumbagh after the reinforcement of the Lucknow Garrison, and acted as Brigade-Major during the general attack by Sir C. Campbell on that city. Lieut. Macpherson was twice wounded in this campaign, received the Medal and clasps, and was awarded the Victoria Cross [London Gazette, 18 June, 1858]: "Herbert Taylor Macpherson, Lieut. (now Capt.), the 78th Regt. Date of Act of Bravery: 25 Sept. 1857. For distinguished conduct at Lucknow on 25 Sept. 1857, in setting an example of heroic gallantry to the men of the regiment at the period of the action in which they captured two brass 9-pounders at the point of the bayonet." He became Capt. at the end of Dec. 1857. After the Mutiny he returned to England, and *m.* in 1859 a daughter of Lieut.-General James Eckford. He was next on active service in the Hazara or Black Mountain Campaign of 1868, and three years later he took part in the Lushai Expedition on the opposite frontier. The credit of the Second Battle of Charasiah fell to Sir H. Macpherson. And in the Battle of Kandahar the 1st Brigade led the advance and broke the enemy in one charge. Two years later General Macpherson commanded the Indian Contingent sent to Egypt, at the time of Arabi's revolt, and won much credit for his rapid advance on Cairo after Tel-el-Kebir. He held the Madras Command in 1885. Sir H. Macpherson was fortunate in being able to use in other fields the experience gained in his Indian campaigns. It was considered that an excellent appointment had been made when he was appointed to the direction of the campaign on the Irrawaddy. He won great popularity in Burma, and great regret was shown when his distinguished career was brought, on 20 Oct. 1886, to a sudden and premature close at Prome, by fever caught in the Palace at Mandalay. The " Times " said in an obituary notice that : " After Sir Frederick Roberts alone, he realized in the eyes of the Anglo-Indian Army the beau-ideal of what a leader of men should be. Frank and daring, convinced of the courage of his troops, and believing that all the direction they required was an example to follow, his influence over the Anglo-Indian Army—and in the phrase we include natives as well as Englishmen accustomed to Eastern service—was as marked under the depressing circumstances of the fighting round Kabul as it was under the more favourable surroundings of the Egyptian Campaign of 1882." Major-General Sir H. T. Macpherson, K.C.B., died 1 July, 1882.

Herbert T. Macpherson.

M'MASTER, VALENTINE MUNBEE, Assistant Surgeon, served with the 78th Regt. in Persia, and also during the Mutiny Campaign, and for his services was awarded the Victoria Cross [London Gazette, 18 June, 1858]: "Valentine Munbee M'Master, Assistant-Surgeon, 78th Regt. Date of Act of Bravery: 25 Sept. 1857. For the intrepidity with which he exposed himself to fire of the enemy, in bringing in and attending to the wounded on 25 Sept., at Lucknow.' (Extract from Field Force Orders of the late Major-General Havelock, dated 17 Oct. 1857)." In 1864, at Mhow, he was in medical charge of the 6th Inniskilling Dragoons, which at that period had two other V.C. officers on its muster-roll, viz., Wooden, Quartermaster, and Malone, Riding Master. He died at Belfast, in Jan. 1872, when again with the old 78th Ross-shires.

Valentine M. M'Master.

LAMBERT, GEORGE, Sergt.-Major, served with Havelock's Column in the actions of Oonao, Buseerutgunge (1st and 2nd), Boorbeake-Chowkee, Bithoor, Nungana, second Relief of Lucknow (severely wounded), and storming of Hiran Khana (Victoria Cross), and with Outram's force at the Alumbagh, also at the Assault and Capture of Lucknow and Relief of Azimghur. For his services in this campaign he received the Medal, was promoted to Ensign 12 Dec. 1857, and was awarded the Victoria Cross for his distinguished bravery in three of Havelock's battles, namely, at Oonao on 29 July, at Bithoor on 11 Aug., when the rebels were driven at the point of the bayonet out of a strong position, and at the passage through Lucknow to the Residency on 25 Sept. His Victoria Cross was gazetted 18 June, 1858 : " George Lambert, Sergt.-Major (now Ensign), 84th Regt. Dates of Acts of Bravery : 29 July, 16 Aug., and 25 Sept. 1857. 'For distinguished conduct at Oonao on 29 July ; at Bithoor on 16 Aug. ; and at Lucknow on 25 Sept.' (Extract from Field Force Orders of the late Major-General Havelock, dated 17 Oct. 1857.)" Sergt.-Major G. Lambert was promoted to Lieut. 17 Dec. 1858, and was Adjutant, 84th Regt., 12 Dec. 1857, to 17 Sept. 1858.

MAHONEY, PATRICK, Sergt., served in the Indian Mutiny War. " When Havelock marched from Allahabad there was a great dearth of cavalry with his little force. He had only thirty irregular cavalry and eighteen volunteer cavalry, commanded by Capt. Barrow. These volunteers were composed of officers whose regiments had mutinied, of civil servants, of two young men waiting for commissions—the two Goldsworthys —and one or two European soldiers. Among the latter was Sergt. Patrick Mahoney of the 1st Munster Fusiliers." For his services in this campaign he was awarded the Victoria Cross [London Gazette, 18 June, 1858]: " Patrick Mahoney, Sergt., 1st Madras Fusiliers. Date of Act of Bravery : 21 Sept. 1857. 'For distinguished gallantry (whilst doing duty with the Volunteer Cavalry) in aiding in the capture of the Regimental Colour of the 1st Regt. Native Infantry at Mungulwar on 21 Sept. 1857.' (Extract from Field Force Orders of the late Major-General Havelock, dated 17 Oct. 1857.)"

BOULGER, ABRAHAM, L.-Corpl., entered the 84th Regt., and served through the Indian Mutiny, 1857-59. " This gallant soldier " (says Colonel Knollys) " was one of the party which stormed the bridge over the canal on the occasion of Havelock's Relief of the Residency, and shot a gunner who was in the act of firing a 68-pounder in the face of our troops. He was also the first man to enter a masked battery. This feat was mentioned in General Orders. In the subsequent defence of the Residency he was severely wounded." He received the Medal with two clasps and was awarded the Victoria Cross [London Gazette, 18 June, 1858]: " Abraham Boulger, L.-Corpl., 84th Regt. Dates of Acts of Bravery : from 12 July to 25 Sept. 1857. ' For distinguished bravery and forwardness, as a skirmisher, in all the twelve actions fought between 12 July and 25 Sept., 1857.' (Extract from Field Force Orders of the late Major-General Havelock, dated 17 Oct. 1857.)." He became Quartermaster of his regiment in 1872, and took part in the storming of Tel-el-Kebir. He became honorary Lieut.-Colonel, and retired in Nov. 1887. Lieut.-Colonel Boulger died in Ireland, his native country, 23 Jan. 1900.

Abraham Boulger.

HOLMES, JOEL, Private, served in the Indian Mutiny Campaign, and was awarded the Victoria Cross [London Gazette, 18 June, 1858]: " Joel Holmes, Private, 84th Regt. For distinguished conduct in volunteering to assist in working a gun of Capt. Maude's battery under a heavy fire, from which nearly all the artillerymen had been shot away. (Extract from Field Force Orders of the late Major-General Havelock, dated 17 Oct. 1857)." Private Holmes died 27 July, 1872.

HOLLOWELL, JAMES, Private, served in the Indian Mutiny Campaign, and for his services at that time was awarded the Victoria Cross [London Gazette, 18 June, 1858]: " James Hollowell, Private, 2nd Battn. 78th Regt. Date of Act of Bravery : 26 Sept. 1857. ' A party on 26 Sept. 1857, was shut up and besieged in a house in the city of Lucknow by the rebel sepoys. Private James Hollowell, one of the party, behaved throughout the day in a most admirable manner : he directed, encouraged and led the others, exposing himself fearlessly, and by his talent in persuading and cheering, prevailed on nine dispirited men to make a successful defence in a burning house, with the enemy firing through four windows.' (Extract from Divisional Orders of Major-General Sir James Outram, G.C.B., dated 17 Oct. 1857)." (See McManus and Ryan.) Private Hollowell died 12 April, 1876.

James Hollowell.

McMANUS, PETER, Private, entered the 5th Regt. (Northumberland Fusiliers), and served throughout the Indian Mutiny Campaign. For his valour on the occasion related below he received the Victoria Cross. He also was given the Mutiny Medal with clasps. His Victoria Cross was gazetted 18 June, 1858 : " Peter McManus, Private, 5th Regt. 'On the occasion when a party, on the 26th Sept. 1857, was shut up and besieged in a house in the city of Lucknow by the rebel sepoys, Private McManus kept outside the house until he himself was wounded, and, under the cover of a pillar, kept firing on the sepoys and prevented their rushing on the house. He also, in conjunction with Private John Ryan, rushed into the street, and took Captain Arnold out of a dhooly, and brought him into the house, in spite of a heavy fire, in which Captain Arnold was again wounded.' (Extract from Divisional Orders of Major-General Sir James Outram, G.C.B., dated 14 Oct. 1857)." [See gazettes of Hollowell and Ryan.] Sergt. McManus died at Allahabad of small-pox, on 27 April, 1859.

RYAN, JOHN, Private, enlisted in the 1st Madras Fusiliers (now the 1st Battn. 102nd Foot, The Royal Dublin Fusiliers). He served in the Indian Mutiny, and for his gallant efforts to save the wounded under the charge of Surgeon Home from the rebel sepoys, he was awarded the Victoria Cross [London Gazette, 18 June, 1858]: " John Ryan, Private, 1st Madras Fusiliers. Date of Act of Bravery : 26 Sept. 1857. A party on the 26th Sept. 1857, was shut up and besieged in a house in the city of Lucknow by the rebel sepoys. Private Ryan, in conjunction with Private McManus, of the 5th Regt., rushed into the street and took Capt. Arnold, of the 1st Madras Fusiliers, out of a dhooly, and brought him into the house, in spite of a heavy fire, in which Capt. Arnold was again wounded. In addition to the above act Private Ryan distinguished himself throughout the day by his intrepidity, and especially devoted himself to rescuing the wounded in the neighbourhood from being massacred. He was most anxious to visit every dhooly." Mr. D. H. Parry gives a splendid account of how Ryan's and other Victoria Crosses were won, in Chapter XVIII. of his book, " The V.C. : Its Heroes and their Valour " (Cassell). He tells how the devoted Surgeon, afterwards Sir Anthony Home, V.C., K.C.B., and the survivors of the party with him had almost given up hope. " Most of them cared little whether they lived or died, until, soon after dawn had flushed the domes and cupolas of the city, more firing was heard, and Private Ryan shouted : 'Boys, them's our own chaps!' 'Cheer together, men!' exclaimed Surgeon Home, as they distinguished the well-known ring of the Enfield rifles, and they cheered together—a cheer with more than one sob in it—but a cheer that was answered by another, as our fellows charged into that ghastly 'Dhoolie Square,' and swept it of its rebel garrison, the rescued handful also firing their remaining shots as they rushed out to join their deliverers. Of the four officers who saw that morning break, three died of their wounds ; but Home, McManus, Hollowell and Ryan won the Cross for their never exceeded heroism."

DUFFY, THOMAS, Private, served in the Indian Mutiny with his regiment, the 1st Madras Fusiliers, and for his services was awarded the Victoria Cross [London Gazette, 18 June, 1858] : " Thomas Duffy, Private, 1st Madras Fusiliers. 'For his cool intrepidity and daring skill, whereby a 24-pounder gun was saved from falling into the hands of the enemy.' (Extract from Divisional Orders of Major-General Sir James Outram, G.C.B., dated 16 Oct. 1857)." " It now became a great object to extricate from the exposed position in which it had been left on the 26th, a 24-pounder gun, used the previous day against the enemy. It was scarcely possible to approach the gun, so heavy was the fire maintained on it. The attempt, however, was made by three daring men, Olpherts of the Bengal Artillery, Crump of the Madras Artillery, and Private Duffy of the Madras Fusiliers ; but Duffy, by a display of combined daring and ingenuity, managed to fasten a rope to the gun in such a manner as to ensure its withdrawal. The gun having been recaptured, earnest endeavours were made to open out a road for the whole of the ordnance through the palaces to the Residency. . . . By the 1st Oct. every gun and wagon was safely lodged in the Residency. . . . For this act, Duffy, on the recommendation of Olpherts, received the Victoria Cross." (Kaye and Malleson's "Sepoy Mutiny," Vol. III., page 266.) Private T. Duffy died on 23 Dec. 1868. His Victoria Cross was sold in London on 28 Oct. 1902, for £53, and on 21 March, 1910, for £60.

WARD, HENRY, Private, served in the Indian Mutiny, and for his services with his Regt., the Seaforth Highlanders (Ross-shire Buffs), was awarded the Victoria Cross [London Gazette, 18 June, 1858] : " Henry Ward, Private, 78th Regt. Dates of Acts of Bravery : 25 and 26 Sept. 1857. For his gallant and devoted conduct in having, on the night of the 25th and morning of the 26th Sept. 1857, remained by the dhooly of Lieut. H. M. Havelock, 10th Foot, Deputy-Assistant-Adjutant-General, Field Force, who was severely wounded, and on the morning of the 26th Sept. escorted that officer and Private Thomas Pilkington, 78th Highlanders, who was also wounded and had taken refuge in the same dhooly, through a very heavy cross-fire of ordnance and musketry. This soldier remained by the side of the dhooly, and by his example and exertions kept the dhooly-bearers from dropping their double load through the heavy fire, with the same steadiness as if on parade, thus saving the lives of both and bringing them safely to the Baillie Guard. (Extract from Divisional Orders of Major-General Sir James Outram, G.C.B., dated 27 Oct. 1857)." He later became Quartermaster-Sergeant, and died in 1859 or 1860.

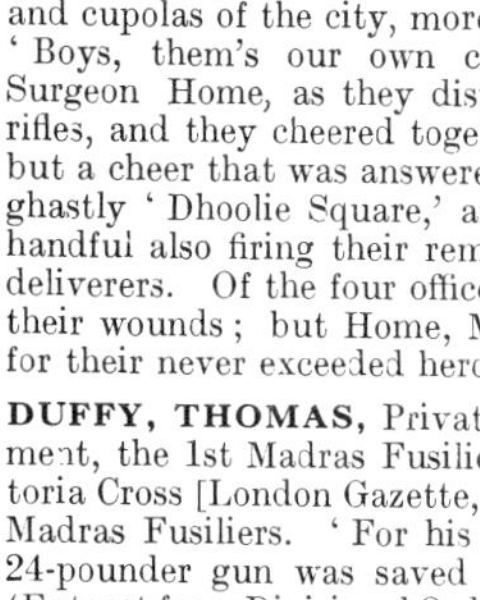

Henry Ward.

HOME, ANTHONY DICKSON, Surgeon, was born 30 Nov. 1826 ; the son of the late George Home, Esq. He took the degrees of M.R.C.S., England, and M.D., St. Andrews, in 1847, and entered the Army Medical Department as Assistant Surgeon in 1848. He served in the Eastern Campaign, 1854–5, with the 8th and 13th Hussars (Medal with two clasps) ; in the Indian Mutiny, 1857–8, with the 90th Light Infantry, when he received the Mutiny Medal with two clasps, and was awarded the Victoria Cross [London Gazette, 18 June, 1858] : " Anthony Dickson Home, Surgeon, 90th Regt. Date of Act of Bravery : 26 Sept. 1857. For persevering bravery and admirable conduct in charge of the wounded men left behind the column, when the troops under the late Major-General Havelock forced their way into the Residency of Lucknow, on the 26th Sept. 1857. The escort left with the wounded had, by casualties, been reduced to a few stragglers, and being entirely separated from the column, this small party with the wounded, were forced into a house, in which they defended themselves till it was set on fire. They then retreated to a shed a few yards from it, and in this place continued to defend themselves for more than 22 hours, till relieved. At last only six men and Mr. Home remained to fire. Of four officers who were with the party, all were badly wounded, and three subsequently died. The conduct of the defence during the latter part of the time therefore devolved on Mr. Home, and to his active exertions, previously to his being forced into the house, and his good conduct throughout, the safety of any of the wounded, and the successful defence, is mainly to be attributed." In 1858 Surgeon Home married Jessey, daughter of T. P. L. Hallett, Esq., and they had two sons and six daughters. He served in the China War of 1860 (Medal) ; in the New Zealand War of 1863–5 (Medal). In 1865 he was created a C.B. In the Ashanti Expedition of 1873–4 (Medal). He was created a Military K.C.B. in the latter year ; was Principal Medical Officer. Field-Marshal Sir Evelyn Wood says in " Winnowed Memories " : " The sanitary and medical arrangements for the Ashanti Expedition, 1873–4, left nothing to be desired, but the circumstances were exceptional. The two European battalions were only on shore for seven weeks, and in the best sense the General in Command was a military genius. His first and very capable Medical Officer was a former brother-officer in the 90th Light Infantry (2nd Scottish Rifles), and enjoyed the General's confidence. Dr. Anthony Home, V.C., C.B., preceded the expedition by four months. He studied closely the pestilential climate of the Gold Coast, and had matured his plans for the prevention of sickness when Sir Garnet Wolseley arrived and approved of them. Later, when Dr. Home, struck down by fever, was invalided, he was replaced by another selected and capable officer, Surgeon W. Mackinnon, C.B." From 1878 to 1879 Dr. Home was P.M.O., with the local rank of Surgeon-General, at Cyprus. In 1880 he was promoted Surgeon-General. From 1881 to 1885, he was Principal Medical Officer to the British Forces in India. From 1885 to 1886, Sir Anthony Home was P.M.O. in the Southern District. He retired in 1886. The late Sir Anthony Home lived for many years at 7, Palace Gardens, Kensington, W., where he died on 10 Aug. 1914, three days after the first V.C., Admiral C. D. Lucas.

Anthony D. Home.

BRADSHAW, WILLIAM, Assistant-Surgeon, became L.R.C.S., Ireland, in 1854 ; served in the Indian Mutiny, and was awarded the Victoria Cross [London Gazette, 18 June, 1858] : " William Bradshaw, Assistant-Surgeon, 90th Regt. Date of Act of Bravery : 26 Sept. 1857. For intrepidity and good conduct when ordered with Surgeon Home, 90th Regt., to remove the wounded men left behind the column that forced its way into the Residency of Lucknow, on the 26th Sept. 1857. The dhooly-bearers had left the dhoolies, but by great exertions, and notwithstanding the close proximity of the sepoys, Surgeon Home and Assistant-Surgeon Bradshaw got some of the bearers together, and Assistant-Surgeon Bradshaw, with about twenty dhoolies, becoming separated from the rest of the party, succeeded n reaching the Residency in safety by the river bank."

FORREST, GEORGE, Capt., served in the Mutiny. For his services in this campaign he was awarded the Victoria Cross [London Gazette, 18 June, 1858] : " George Forrest, Capt., Bengal Veteran Establishment. Date of Act of Bravery : 11 May, 1857. For gallant conduct in the defence of the Delhi Magazine, on the 11th May, 1857." The account in Kaye and Malleson's " Sepoy Mutiny " (Vol. II., pages 66–69) of the blowing up of the Delhi Magazine is as follows : " The great Delhi Magazine, with all its vast supplies of munitions of war, was in the city, at no great distance from the Palace. It was in charge of Lieut. George Willoughby, of the Bengal Artillery, with whom were associated Lieuts. Forrest and Raynor, officers of the Ordnance Commissariat Department, and European Conductors and Commissariat Sergeants. All the rest of the establishment was Native. Early morning work is a condition of Anglo-Indian life, and Willoughby was at the Magazine, superintending the accustomed duties of his department, and little dreaming what the day would bring forth, when Forrest came in, accompanied by the magistrate, Sir Theophilus Metcalfe, and informed him that the Mirath mutineers were streaming across the river. It was Metcalfe's object to obtain from the Magazine a couple of guns wherewith to defend the bridge. But it was soon apparent that the time for such defence had passed. The troopers had crossed the river, and had found ingress at the Palace Gate. A brave and resolute man, who, ever in the midst of danger, seemed almost to bear a charmed life, Metcalfe then went about other work, and Willoughby braced himself up for the defence of the Magazine. He knew how much depended on its safety. He knew that not only the mutinous soldiery, but the dangerous classes of Delhi, would pour down upon the Magazine, some eager to seize its accumulated munitions of war, others greedy only for plunder. If, he thought, he could hold out but a little while, the white regiments at Mirath would soon come to his aid, and a strong guard of English riflemen, with guns manned by British artillerymen, would make the Magazine secure against all comers. It was soon plain that the Native establishment of the Magazine was not to be trusted. But there were nine resolute Englishmen who calmly prepared themselves to face the tremendous odds which threatened them, and, if the sacrifice were required, to die beneath the ruins of the Magazine. Cheered by the thought of the approaching succour from Mirath, these brave men began their work. The outer gates were closed and barricaded. Guns were then brought out, loaded with double charges of grape, and posted within the gates. One of the nine, with port-fire in hand, stood ready to discharge the contents of the six-pounder full upon the advancing enemy if they should find their way into the enclosure. These arrangements completed, a train was laid from the powder-magazine, and on a given signal from Willoughby, if further defence should be hopeless, a match was to be applied to it, and the Magazine blown into the air. Whilst in this attitude of defence, a summons to surrender came to them in the name of the King. It was treated with contemptuous silence. Again and again messengers came from the Palace saying that His Majesty had ordered the gates to be opened and the stores given up to the Army. If not, ladders would be sent, and the Magazine carried by escalade. Unmoved by these menaces, Willoughby and Forrest answered nothing, but looked to their

defences, and presently it was plain that the scaling-ladders had arrived. The enemy were swarming over the walls. At this point all the Natives in the Magazine, the gun-lascars, the artificers and others, whose defection had been expected, threw off their disguise, and, ascending some sloping sheds, joined the enemy on the side. The time for vigorous action had now arrived. As the enemy streamed over the walls, round after round of murderous grape-shot from our guns, delivered with all the coolness and steadiness of a practice-parade, riddled the advancing multitudes ; but still they poured on, keeping up a heavy fire of musketry from the walls. Yet, hoping against hope to hear the longed-for sound of coming help from Mirath, the devoted Englishmen held their ground until their available ammunition was expended. Then further defence was impossible ; they could not leave the guns to bring up shot from the Magazine, and there were none to help them. Meanwhile the Mutineers were forcing their way at other unprotected points into the great enclosure, and it was plain that the nine—two among them wounded, though not disabled, for the strong will kept them at their posts—could no longer hold the great storehouse from the grasp of the enemy. So the signal was given. Conductor Scully fired the train. In a few seconds there was a tremendous explosion. The Magazine had been blown into the air. Not one of the gallant band had expected to escape with his life. But four of the nine, in the confusion which ensued, though at first stunned and bewildered, shattered and bruised, made good their escape from the ruins. Willoughby and Forrest escaped to the main guard. Raynor and Buckley took a different direction, and eventually reached Mirath. Scully and his gallant comrades were never seen alive again. But the lives thus nobly sacrificed were dearly paid for by the enemy. Hundreds perished in that great explosion, and others at a distance were struck down by the fragments of the building, or by bullets ignited from the cartridges in store. But it was not possible that by any such explosion as this the immense material resources of the great Delhi Magazine should be so destroyed as to be unserviceable to the enemy. The effects of the heroic deed which had given to those devoted Nine a cherished place in history, can never be exactly computed. But the grandeur of the conception is not to be measured by its results. From one end of India to another it filled men's minds with enthusiastic admiration ; and when news reached England that a young artillery officer named Willoughby had blown up the Delhi Magazine, there was a burst of applause that came from the deep heart of the nation. It was the first of many intrepid acts which have made us proud of our countrymen in India ; but its brilliancy has never been surpassed." A miniature of Forrest was destroyed at Delhi in 1857. A son of Capt. Forrest is Sir G. W. Forrest, C.I.E.

RAYNOR, WILLIAM, Lieut., served in the Indian Mutiny, and for his services in that campaign was awarded the Victoria Cross [London Gazette, 18 June, 1858]: " William Raynor, Bengal Veteran Establishment. For gallant conduct in the defence of the Magazine at Delhi, on the 11th May, 1857." Of the gallant nine only four escaped. When the Magazine was blown into the air, five of them died with it—and with them died also a thousand Mutineers. Willoughby and Forrest joined a party of Europeans at the Main Guard at Delhi, so blackened as to be almost unrecognizable. Willoughby was shortly afterwards killed in an encounter with the Mutineers in a village on the way to Kurnaul. At the attack on the Fort of Rooya, Lieut. Edward Willoughby (brother of Willoughby of the Powder Magazine), though on the sick-list, left his dhooly to join in the fight, and was killed in a daring attempt to scale the parapet. Captain Cafe and Private Thomson brought in his body, and won the Victoria Cross. The two other men of the nine who escaped were Raynor and Buckley, who, taking different directions, eventually reached Meerut in safety. The Victoria Cross was awarded to the three men who survived to be decorated, and a memorial tablet was erected over the gate of the old Magazine, with the following inscription :

" On 11 May, 1857,
Nine Resolute Englishmen,
George Dobree Willoughby, Bengal Artillery,
in Command,
Lieut. William Raynor, Lieut. George Forrest, Conductor G. William Shaw, Conductor John Buckley, Conductor John Scully, Sub-Conductor William Crow, Sergt. Bryan Edwards, Sergt. Peter Stewart, defended the Magazine of Delhi for more than five hours against large numbers of rebels and mutineers, until, the wall being scaled, and all hope of succour gone, these brave men fired the Magazine. Five of the gallant band perished in the explosion, which at the same time destroyed many of the enemy.
This tablet,
marking the former entrance gate to the Magazine, is placed here by the Government of India."

BUCKLEY, JOHN, Deputy Assistant Commissary of Ordnance, served in the Indian Mutiny, and for his services in blowing up the powder-magazine at Delhi was awarded the Victoria Cross [London Gazette, 18 June, 1858]: " John Buckley, Deputy Assistant Commissary of Ordnance, Commissariat Department, Bengal Establishment. Date of Act of Bravery: 11 May, 1857. For gallant conduct in the defence of the Magazine of Delhi, on the 11th May, 1857." Mr. John Buckley died in the borough of Poplar, E., where he had long resided, some three decades ago.

John Buckley.

BLAIR, ROBERT, Lieut., was born in Ayrshire, Scotland, about the year 1837. He entered the 9th Queen's Royal Lancers on 16 Dec. 1853, as a Cornet (by purchase), from the 16th Lancers, and became Lieutenant (also by purchase) 2 Nov. 1855. He was living with his friend Jones in the same bungalow at Umballa in 1855–6, when they read of the Order, V.C., being issued. Both resolved to get it if possible by exchanging into some regiment serving in the Crimea, but their Colonel, Hope Grant, would not let them go, and was very savage with Jones for appealing to the General Commanding at Umballa. In Jan. 1857, Lieut. Blair exchanged with Lieut. J. De Heley Chadwick into the 2nd Dragoon Guards, but either had not joined the regiment or was temporarily attached to the 9th Lancers. For on the day he won his Victoria Cross (28 Sept. 1857) he was in charge of a party of ten men of the 9th Lancers, which was sent to bring in an abandoned ammunition wagon. In the " Life of Sir Hope Grant " by Colonel Knollys (Vol. I., page 241), Sir Hope Grant says in his Diary : " In consequence of numerous casualties and sickness which had reduced the strength of our artillery, I had been requested by General Wilson to furnish some men from the cavalry to assist in the trenches. Consequently ten of the Carabiniers and 60 of the 9th Lancers were sent, under Lieuts. Blair and Evans, of the latter regiment, who volunteered their services for this duty. The way in which the men vied with each other, day and night, in the performance of this arduous task, was beyond all praise." Major-General Wilson, in his Despatches, wrote : " I should neither be fulfilling the repeatedly expressed wishes of the artillery officers attached to the force, nor following the dictates of my own inclination, if I failed to acknowledge the valuable assistance which has throughout the operations before Delhi been most cheerfully given by the non-commissioned officers and men of Her Majesty's 9th Lancers and the 6th Dragoon Guards in working the batteries. Without it, owing to the comparatively small number of artillerymen, I should have been quite unable to man the batteries efficiently, or keep up the heavy fire which, aided by these men, I have been happily able to do." Lieuts. Jones and Blair both carried out their plans, and won the Victoria Cross. " Jones won it first " (as related in the account of Colonel A. S. Jones, V.C.). " Now Lieut. Blair on several occasions volunteered to leave his squadron during the siege, for like enterprise, and finally—at Bulandshahr—got leave with a dozen men to capture a hackerry carrying off treasure under a Mutineer guard of some 60 Sowars, which he accomplished, killing four men with his own sword, but receiving a sabre-cut which nearly severed his left shoulder. He received the Cross like his comrade, and as they had both resolved to try for it a year or so before the Mutiny, this is somewhat singular." Sir Hope Grant says in his Diary : " I heard here (at Meerut) that the movable column, which had been sent out from Delhi under Colonel Greathed, had had a severe fight at Bulandshahr, where their success was due to the magnificent conduct of the cavalry, especially of the 9th Lancers, who advanced and charged into the town, cleared the streets and captured a number of guns. I was grieved to learn, however, that four of my best officers had been wounded. . . . Lieut. Blair, who had behaved so gallantly at Delhi, had been sent some little distance in advance, with the men of the 9th Lancers, to bring in an abandoned ammunition wagon. They rode up to it, supposing none of the enemy to be at hand, when 50 or 60 Sowars suddenly galloped out upon them from behind some adjacent houses and surrounded the little party. Blair saw that his only chance was to dash at them and cut his way through. He gave the order to his men, and bravely they obeyed him, killing nine rebels. The only one of our detachment who was injured was Blair himself, who, when in the act of running a man through the body, received a severe sword-cut from his antagonist on the top of the shoulder, severing the joint. I saw the poor boy in the Meerut Hospital on my way down, to which place he had been sent, full of spirits and on a fair way to recovery. I obtained the Victoria Cross for him, which made him quite happy, but he died some time afterwards from consumption, brought on, in all probability, by his wound." Lieut. Blair was awarded the Victoria Cross [London Gazette, 18 June, 1858 : " Robert Blair, Lieut., 2nd Dragoon Guards. Date of Act of Bravery : 28 Sept. 1857. ' A most gallant feat was performed by Lieut. Blair, who was ordered to take a party of one sergeant and twelve men, and bring in a deserted ammunition wagon. As his party approached, a body of fifty or sixty of the enemy's horse came down upon him from a village, where they had remained unobserved ; without a moment's hesitation he formed up his men, and, regardless of the odds, gallantly led them on, dashing through the rebels. He made good his retreat without losing a man, leaving nine of them dead on the field. Of these he killed four himself, but to my regret, after having run a native officer through the body with his sword, he was severely wounded, the joint of his shoulder being nearly severed.' (Despatch from Major-General Sir James Hope Grant, C.B., dated 10 Jan. 1858)." Lieut. Blair was promoted Captain, 2nd Dragoon Guards (without purchase), 7 July, 1858. He died in Nov. 1858, in consequence of wounds received at Bulandshahr.

JONES, ALFRED STOWELL, Lieut., was born in Liverpool, 24 Jan. 1832 ; the son of the late Archdeacon John Jones and of his wife, Hannah, daughter of the late John Pares, of Hopwell Hall, Derbyshire, and founder of Pares' Bank, Leicester. He was educated at Liverpool College and at Sandhurst, and entered the 9th Lancers on 9 July, 1852, as a Cornet, by purchase. He became Lieutenant 21 Sept. 1855. He served throughout the Siege of Delhi as D.A.Q.M.G. of the Cavalry. In the first engagement, 8 June, 1857, at Budli-ka-Serai, Mr. Jones, leading the right troop of the 4th Squadron, 9th Lancers, which was galloping in line after a cloud of dust which had been pointed out by a Staff Officer as enemy guns, saw a 9-pounder with six horses and drivers on the left flank of his squadron, galloping to the left front.

Alfred Stowell Jones.

He pulled up short, and, when clear of the ranks, started his Arab charger after the gun, while the squadron kept on its course after the cloud of dust. The six Mutineer drivers kept flogging their horses—looking back over their shoulders, until Jones came alongside the off-wheeler and cut his rider over the shoulders, whereupon the driver fell between the wheel horses, and clinging to his bridle, stopped the whole team. Then the Regimental Sergeant-Major, Thonger, stopped two or three men from rear rank, and this party, who, riding as serrefile, in rear of the squadron, had alone seen Jones bolt away, attacked the drivers of the four lead gun-horses. The drivers all fell among the horses' feet and were killed instantly, while Jones' whole attention was engaged in getting ready to render the gun useless (with one or two steel spikes which had been served out to Cavalry officers the previous night, because on the open plains were straggling Mutineers and no friend in sight). Presently the whole squadron, having failed to overtake the cloud of dust, rejoined their Regimental Troop Leader, and then the other three squadrons—under Colonel Yule, 9th Lancers—turned up, as the main force with which they had acted were following the defeated Mutineers. Colonel Yule found ammunition on the gun-limber and fired a few rounds against a fortified village. Then Jones was allowed to take his prize, which had belonged to Captain De Tessier's Field Battery, which had mutinied at Delhi a month before. When looking round, Jones found that all the four lead horses had been hurt about the fetlocks, from his men's excitement in shooting the drivers with their pistols, instead of striking them with their lances, so he borrowed a pair of horses from the Artillery and mounted his men on the sound wheel-horses to draw the gun to the camp, which was being formed behind the ridge at Delhi. He there handed over the gun to the Artillery, but kept the two wheel-horses with his troop, and found them a most useful addition to his chargers all through the siege. Colonel Hope Grant reported the above facts as "a well-conceived act, gallantly executed," for the Victoria Cross, which bears the date, "8 June, 1857." Jones felt he could not stop the squadron or get across to the gun, which—looking to the left, to keep his dressing—he alone saw, and could not let it escape to Delhi. Colonel Jones remarked: "It is questionable if the V.C. does not interfere with discipline, which might have demanded a trial by court-martial if I had been riding a slower horse, and so had failed to reach my prey." Lord Roberts says, in "Forty-one Years in India" (page 152): "The 9th Lancers made a series of brilliant charges. One troop especially distinguished itself by recovering Blunt's captured gun; the Captain (French) was killed, and the subaltern (Jones), covered with wounds, was left on the ground for dead." On this occasion (10 Oct. 1857), Lieut. Jones had a bullet through the bridle-arm and 22 sabre-cuts. Sir Hope Grant wrote in his diary: "The troops fell in as they best could, many of them in their shirt-sleeves. The 9th Lancers were soon in the saddle, with gallant Drysdale at their head. Poor French was shot through the body at the head of his squadron, and died before he could be carried to the town. Jones was struck down from his horse by a shot, and when on the ground was fearfully hacked about by some rebel Sowars with their tulwars; he had twenty-two wounds about him. The squadron to which these two officers belonged met a large force of the enemy's cavalry, charged, drove them away, and retook one of our guns which had been captured by one of the rebels." For his services in the Mutiny Campaign Lieut. Jones received the Mutiny Medal with two clasps, was promoted to Captain and Brevet Major, and thrice mentioned in Despatches. He was also awarded the Victoria Cross [London Gazette, 18 June, 1858]: "Alfred Stowell Jones, Lieut. (now Captain), 9th Lancers. Date of Act of Bravery: 8 June, 1857. The Cavalry charged the rebels and rode through them. Lieut. Jones with his squadron captured one of their guns, killing the drivers, and with Lieut.-Colonel Yule's assistance, turned it upon a village occupied by the rebels, who were quickly dislodged. This was a well-conceived act, gallantly executed. (Despatch from Major-General Hope Grant, K.C.B., dated 10 Jan. 1858.)" Colonel Jones writes: "I was startled by the date, June 18th, of the London Gazette, and began with my blue pencil, because in these days it seems ridiculous that I should not have known anything about it for more than a month. But I was very busy breaking in horses and teaching recruits to ride for the 18th Hussars, then being raised at Leeds, and I distinctly remember my surprise at receiving an order at Mess dinner to go down to Portsmouth one day at the very end of July, or nearly in August, for a Parade on Southsea Common, when twelve V.C.'s were to be presented by Queen Victoria, and that was the first intimation I had that I had been recommended for the Cross. A young horse I was riding in the School at Leeds a few days before, had thrown up his head and bruised my blind eye-brow, so my appearance was shocking, and made the Queen so nervous that she pricked me in pinning the Cross through my tunic." Later, when Grant became Brigadier-General, he appointed Jones D.A.Q.M.G. to the Cavalry, and Lieut. F. Roberts, R.A., secured the like Staff appointment to the Artillery of the Delhi Field Force, never meeting again until—some fifty years later—these two old comrades settled down in Berkshire (1907) as happy neighbours. In Lord Roberts' "Forty-one Years in India" is a full account of the sanitary work during the Siege of Delhi, which arose from Lieut. Jones having studied Parkes' "Military Hygiene"—a then new book, which Dr. Clifford, Assistant-Surgeon, 9th Lancers, brought out from Netley Hospital when he joined in 1856. Thus his attention was drawn to the subject in time for his duties as D.A.Q.M.G. at Delhi, "and," says Colonel Jones, "twenty years later I left the Army to become a Civil Engineer and one of the Founders of the Royal Sanitary Institute." Major Jones graduated at the Staff College in 1860. In 1863 he married Emily, youngest daughter of the late John Back, of Aldershot Place, Surrey, and they had five sons and one daughter. One son, a Lieutenant in the 11th Hussars, was killed in a polo accident in India, in 1895. Lieut. Tertius Jones, R.H.A., died at Meerut in 1896. The eldest son, the late Capt. Harry Jones, R.N., commanding H.M. Battleship "Africa," died of Bright's disease in 1914. Capt. Owen Jones, R.N.R., the 2nd son, is now living at Woking, an Elder Brother of Trinity House, and Captain Percy Jones (4th son), an indigo planter of Tirhoot, India, was with the 13th Lancers, Mesopotamian Field Force; killed in action 2 Nov. 1917, at Samara, Mesopotamia. The daughter married Major, now Major-General, W. Arthur Watson, C.B., eldest son of General Sir John Watson, G.C.M.G., a comrade of Colonel Jones at Delhi, and now his neighbour at North Court, Finchampstead. He served on the Staff at the Cape of Good Hope as D.A.Q.M.G., 1861–67, and retired in 1872. Lieut.-Colonel Jones was Manager of all Sewage Works of the 1st Army Corps, Aldershot, 1895–1912; retired, 1912. He has published the following books: "Will a Sewage Farm Pay?" (three editions, 1874–87); "Natural and Artificial Sewage Treatment" (1902), and also has written many papers in professional journals. He has been a Member of the Institution of Civil Engineers since 1878, and latterly a J.P. for Berks. The 9th Lancers obtained 14 V.C.'s in the Mutiny, and got one V.C. in the very first engagement both in the Mutiny and in the Great War with Germany. Colonel Jones has a letter from Captain Grenfell, V.C., in which the latter says: "It is a great honour to me to receive congratulations from you, who received the first V.C. in the Delhi Campaign."

PROBYN, DIGHTON MACNAGHTEN, Capt., was born on 21 Jan. 1833; son of the late Capt. G. Probyn and Alicia, daughter of the late Sir F. Workman Macnaghten, 1st Bart. He joined the Bengal Cavalry, Indian Army, in 1849. From 1852 to 1857 he served in the 2nd Punjab Cavalry on the Trans-Indus Frontier, and was engaged in the operations in the Bozdar Hills and other fights on that frontier (Medal with clasps). He served in the Indian Mutiny, 1857–58; was at Delhi during the Siege, and fought in the Battles of Bolundshuhar, Allighur and Agra, in the Battle of Kanuje and Relief of Lucknow, under Sir Colin Campbell, and the Battle of Cawnpore, Dec. 1857, and the Storming of Lucknow in March, 1858. Lord Roberts tells us in his "Forty-one Years in India" how he had the dying Nicholson conveyed to the hospital. Continuing his ride, he fell in with Hope Grant's column and met Hodson, some officers of the 9th Lancers, and Probyn, Watson and Younghusband. "Probyn was in great spirits, having fallen temporarily into the command of his squadron, owing to Charles Nicholson (John Nicholson's younger brother) having been selected to take Cole's place with the 1st Punjab Infantry. Probyn retained his command throughout the Campaign, for Charles Nicholson was wounded that very morning while gallantly leading his regiment. His right arm was being amputated when his brother was carried mortally wounded into the same hospital and laid on the bed beside him." Lord Roberts later remarks on "the great delight of his many friends in the column" when Probyn was awarded the Victoria Cross. When a column was sent to Cawnpore, detachments of three Punjab Cavalry Regiments (the 1st, the 2nd and the 5th), formed part of it, and these were commanded by Lieuts. John Watson, Dighton Probyn and George Younghusband. Lord Roberts says that "under their gallant young leaders . . . the three squadrons of Punjab Cavalry . . . showed of what good stuff they were made." Lieut. Probyn was promoted Captain in 1857, and Major in 1858. During this Campaign he was seven times mentioned in Despatches, was thanked by Lord Canning, the Governor-General, awarded the Victoria Cross, created a C.B., and received the Mutiny Medal with three clasps. His Victoria Cross was gazetted 18 June, 1858: "Dighton Macnaghten Probyn, Captain (now Major), 2nd Punjab Cavalry. Has been distinguished for gallantry and daring throughout this Campaign. At the Battle of Agra, when his squadron charged the rebel Infantry, he was sometimes separated from his men and surrounded by five or six Sepoys. He defended himself from the various cuts made at him, and, before his own men had joined him, had cut down two of his assailants. At another time, in single combat with a Sepoy, he was wounded in the wrist by the bayonet, and his horse also slightly wounded; but, though the Sepoy fought desperately, he cut him down. The same day he singled out a standard-bearer, and, in the presence of a number of the enemy, killed him and captured the standard. These are only a few of the gallant deeds of this brave young officer. (Despatch from Major-General James Hope Grant, K.C.B., dated 10 Jan. 1858)." He served in the China Campaign in 1860 (Medal with two clasps, mentioned in Despatches). In 1861 Major Probyn was promoted Lieutenant-Colonel, and he served in the Umbeyla Expedition, in which he was mentioned in Despatches and received the Medal with clasp. In 1866 he became Colonel, and in 1870 Major-General. In 1872 he married Letitia Maria (who died in 1900), daughter of the late Thomas Roberts Thelluson. In 1876 Major-General Probyn was created a K.C.S.I. From 1872 to 1877 he was Equerry to King Edward VII. (then Prince of Wales), and as such accompanied His Royal Highness in his Indian tour (1875–6). In 1877, Sir Dighton Probyn became Lieutenant-General, and was also created a K.C.B. (civil). From 1877 to 1891 he was Comptroller and Treasurer to King Edward, when Prince of Wales. He was promoted General in 1888, and in 1896 he was created a K.C.V.O., and in 1901 became a P.C., in 1902 a G.C.B. (civil), and in 1903, I.S.O. From 1902 to 1910 Sir Dighton Probyn was Keeper of the Privy Purse and Extra Equerry to H.M. King Edward VII., a Member of the Council of the Duchy of Lancaster, and Secretary and Registrar to the Royal Victorian Order. In 1904 he was appointed Colonel of the 11th (King Edward's Own) Lancers (Probyn's Horse). In 1909 he was created a K.C.B. (military), and in 1910 a G.C.B. (military). Since 1910 Sir Dighton Probyn has been Comptroller of the Household to H.M. Queen Alexandra and an Extra Equerry to H.M. King George V. In 1911 he was created a G.C.S.I. He is a Governor of W[illegible]gton College.

Dighton M. Probyn.

WATSON, JOHN, Lieut., was born 6 Sept. 1829, the son of William George Watson, Esq., of Chigwell, Essex, and Harriett, daughter of Hugh Atkins. He entered the Bombay Army in 1848, and was shortly afterwards

John Watson.

posted to the Bombay Fusiliers, familiarly known as the Bombay Buffs, now the 2nd Battn. of the Royal Dublin Fusiliers. With this regiment he served in the Punjab Campaign of 1848–49. He carried the Regimental Colour up the breach at the Siege of Multan, and was present afterwards at the Battle of Gujerat and occupation of Peshawar (Medal with two clasps). After this campaign he was transferred to the 28th Bombay Infantry, and then to the 1st Baluchis; but he served a very short time in these battalions. The opening of his career as a cavalry soldier occurred a little later, when he joined the 1st Punjab Cavalry. He shortly became Adjutant of this regiment, and before long was regarded as one of the most promising officers of the Punjab Frontier Force. It was some years, however, before he was employed again on active service. At the beginning of 1857 he served in the Bozdar Campaign and the forcing of the Kahn Bund Pass. A few months later the Mutiny broke out at Meerut and Delhi was besieged by a British Army. Amongst the many units which John Lawrence, sent down from the Punjab to the assistance of the Commander-in-Chief before Delhi were three squadrons of the Punjab Frontier Force, one each from the 1st, 2nd and 5th Punjab Cavalry, commanded respectively by Lieuts. John Watson, Dighton Probyn and George Younghusband. All these three officers distinguished themselves greatly during the fighting which ensued. After the fall of Delhi a column of all arms, under the command of Colonel Greathead, who was shortly afterwards succeeded by Brigadier-General Hope Grant, was dispatched to Lucknow. At Bulandshahr the column came in contact with an enemy force. "The work fell," says Lord Roberts in his "Forty-One Years in India," "chiefly on the Cavalry and Horse Artillery. . . . The three squadrons of Punjab Cavalry, under their gallant young leaders . . . showed of what good stuff they were made." At Agra Lieuts. Roberts, Watson and others, who had just marched in with the column, were at breakfast in the fort when they heard firing, and discovered that an action was taking place. It was, indeed, the Battle of Agra. They rushed out, and mounting their horses, were soon in the thick of the mêlée. To continue to quote from Lord Roberts: "Watson, Probyn and Younghusband, with their three squadrons, cleared the enemy's flank, capturing two guns and some standards." At Cawnpore, some days later, the column was again engaged with the enemy. "On we flew," says Lord Roberts, "Probyn's and Watson's squadrons leading the way in parallel lines about a mile apart. I was with the latter, and we had a running fight till we reached the Ganges, into which plunged those of the enemy whom we had not been able to overtake. We reined up. . . . Watson had the fore-finger of his right hand badly cut in an encounter with a young sowar. I chaffed him at allowing himself to be nearly cut down by a mere boy, upon which he laughingly retorted: 'Well, boy or not, he was bigger than you.' During one of Watson's many reconnaissances he received a cut on the face from a sabre. One of the 2nd Punjab Cavalrymen, seeing what had happened, rushed to Probyn and said: 'Watson sahib has got a wound worth a lakh of rupees.'" At Lucknow Lieut. Watson greatly distinguished himself. The infantry having driven the enemy out of the Martiniere, the cavalry pursued them as far as the canal. A long way ahead of his squadron, he suddenly came on a squadron of the enemy. Knowing that if he returned to his men to give them orders they would misunderstand his movement, and probably go back themselves, he charged the enemy entirely alone, and was at once engaged with the leader and six or seven of the front men. The leader's pistol missed his mark, and Watson ran him through with his sabre. The remainder of the squadron then attacked him; but Probyn, who was not far off with his own and Watson's squadrons, galloped up to the rescue, and the enemy fled. For this, and for gallantry on other occasions, Watson received the Victoria Cross. The London Gazette of 18 June, 1858, described the incident as follows: "John Watson, Lieutenant, 1st Punjab Cavalry. Date of Act of Bravery, 14 Nov. 1857. Lieut. Watson, on 14 Nov., with his own squadron, and that under Captain, then Lieut. Probyn, came upon a body of the rebel cavalry. The Ressaldar in command of them—a fine specimen of the Hindustani Mussalman—and backed up by some half-dozen equally brave men, rode out to the front. Lieut. Watson singled out this fine-looking fellow and attacked him. The Ressaldar presented his pistol at Lieut. Watson's breast at a yard's distance and fired, but most providentially without effect; the ball must have by accident previously fallen out. Lieut. Watson ran the man through with his sword and dismounted him; but the native officer, nothing daunted, drew his tulwar, and with his sowars renewed his attack upon Lieut. Watson, who bravely defended himself until his own men joined in the mêlée, and utterly routed the party. In this rencontre Lieut. Watson received a blow on the head from a tulwar, another on the left arm, which severed his chain gauntlet glove, a tulwar cut on his right arm, which fortunately only divided the sleeve of his jacket, but disabled the arm for some time; a bullet also passed through his coat, and he received a blow on his leg which lamed him for some days afterwards. (Despatch from Major-General Sir James Hope Grant, K.C.B., dated 10 Jan. 1858.)" In the Mutiny Campaign Lieut. Watson was three times wounded. He received the Medal with three clasps and the Victoria Cross. In 1860 he married Eliza Jesser, daughter of John Davis, Esq., of Cranbrook Park, Essex. In 1861 he was promoted Captain. His fourth campaign was with the Eusofzai Field Force in 1863. In this year he was created a C.B.,

and in 1864 he was promoted Major. In 1869 he was promoted Lieutenant-Colonel, and in 1873 Colonel. He commanded the Cavalry Brigade which formed part of the force that occupied Cyprus in 1878. In 1879–80 occurred the Afghan War, his fifth and last campaign. During the first phase he was in command of the Punjab Chiefs' Contingent, and during the second of the Kurram Field Force. For his services in this campaign Sir John Watson received the thanks of both Houses of Parliament. In 1881 he was promoted Major-General, and from 1881 to 1886 was Governor-General's Agent at Baroda. In 1886 he was created a K.C.B. In 1887 he was promoted Lieutenant-General, and in 1891 General. In 1902 he was created a G.C.B. Sir John Watson's eldest son, Major-General W. A. Watson, C.B., C.M.G., C.I.E., married in 1897, Marguerite Audrey, daughter of Lieut.-Colonel Alfred Stowell Jones, V.C., of Ridge Cottage, Finchampstead, the officer who, as a Cornet of the 9th Lancers, gained his Victoria Cross before Delhi, and during the Battle of Agra received twenty-five sabre wounds and was left for dead on the ground, though he still survives to tell the story. Sir John Watson had two other sons serving in the present war: Major-General H. D. Watson, C.B., C.M.G., C.I.E., M.V.O., and Major J. H. Watson, 13th Lancers (Watson's Horse). Sir J. Watson died on 23 Jan. 1919.

HOME, DUNCAN CHARLES, Lieut., Bengal Engineers, volunteered for the dangerous duty of blowing up the Kashmir Gate before the great assault on the city of Delhi. He was

Duncan Charles Home.

promised the Victoria Cross on the field by General Wilson, and the award was confirmed after his death [London Gazette, 18 June, 1858]: "Duncan Charles Home, Lieutenant; Philip Salkeld, Lieutenant; Bengal Engineers. Date of Act of Bravery, 14 Sept. 1857. (Upon whom the Victoria Cross was provisionally conferred by Major-General Sir Archdale Wilson, Bart., K.C.B.) For their conspicuous bravery in the performance of the desperate duty of blowing in the Cashmere Gate of the Fortress of Delhi in broad daylight, under a heavy fire of musketry, on the morning of 14 Sept. 1857, preparatory to the assault. Would have been recommended to Her Majesty for confirmation in that distinction had they survived." Lieut. Home, indeed, escaped with his life when he blew in the Kashmir Gate, 14 Sept. 1857, but he was killed in the following Oct. from the effects of the premature explosion of a mine, after the capture of the Fort of Malagurh. All had been got ready, and the slow match was lighted, but as no explosion followed in the ordinary time, Lieut. Home went forward to light the match, which had, as he thought, gone out. Thus this gallant soldier met his death after having previously come safely through such terrible danger.

SALKELD, PHILIP, Lieut., was born at Fontmell Magna, Dorsetshire, on 13 Oct. 1830, son of the late Rev. Robert Salkeld, of Fifehead Neville, and Rector of Fontmell Magna, Dorsetshire. He passed into

Philip Salkeld.

the Bengal Engineers from Addiscombe, and went out to India in 1851, taking part in the Siege of Delhi. He volunteered for the duty of blowing up the Cashmere Gate, which was carried out in the early morning of 14 Sept. 1857. Through some delay it was broad daylight when this was done. A great deal depended upon the success of the attack on the city of Delhi on 14 Sept. 1857. Had this failed, a great many more lives would have been lost. The late Colonel Thomas Adair Butler, V.C., who was present at the Siege of Delhi, wrote as follows: "As soon as the rear of No. 1 Column cleared the road leading to the Cashmere Gate, the party of Engineers who were told off to blow it in rushed up. This little band of heroes consisted of Lieuts. Salkeld and Home, Sergts. Smith and Carmichael and Corpl. Burgess (all of the Bengal Engineers), with three Sikh sappers, Havildars Mahore and Tillah Sing, and Sepoy Ramloll; Bugler Hawthorne, of the 52nd Light Infantry, was also attached to the party. They reached the gateway unhurt, and found that part of the drawbridge had been destroyed, but passing along the precarious footway supplied by the remaining beams, they proceeded to lodge their powder-bags against the gate. Sergt. Carmichael was killed while laying his bag, and Havildar Mahore at the same time severely wounded; Lieut. Home, having seen the powder-bags properly placed, jumped down into the ditch to allow Lieut. Salkeld and the firing party to advance. While endeavouring to fire the charge Lieut. Salkeld was mortally wounded. He, however, notwithstanding his wound, handed the slow match to Corpl. Burgess, who was shot dead just as he had accomplished the duty. Sepoy Ramloll was also killed, and Havildar Tellah Sing wounded. The explosion was completely successful, but Sergt. Smith was severely injured by the falling debris. Bugler Hawthorne then sounded the advance, which was the signal for the third column to come up and enter the city at the Cashmere Gate. The fire that the Engineers were exposed to came from the city wall that runs at right angles to the Cashmere Gate. It is an error, as stated in some accounts, that "they were exposed to a fire through the gateway and from both flanks," for No. 1 Column was in possession of the wall to the left and the space inside the gate when the explosion took place. Lieut. Salkeld died of his wounds afterwards. The Victoria Cross was promised to him by General Wilson on the field. This is the first occasion on which the decoration was gazetted and actually presented after its recipient's death. It was sent to Lieut. Salkeld's father, and was gazetted 18 June, 1858 : " Duncan Charles Home, Lieutenant ; Philip Salkeld, Lieutenant, Bengal Engineers. Date of Act of Bravery : 14 Sept. 1857. (Upon whom the Victoria Cross was provisionally conferred by Major-General Sir Archdale Wilson, Bart, K.C.B.) For their conspicuous bravery in the performance of the desperate duty of blowing in the Cashmere Gate of the Fortress of Delhi, in broad daylight, under a heavy fire of musketry, on the morning of 14 Sept. 1857, preparatory to the assault. Would have been recommended to Her Majesty for confirmation in that distinction had they survived." Lieut. Salkeld was a brother of Mr. Charles Salkeld, of Stour House, Blandford, Dorset. Mr. C. Salkeld's second son, Philip D'Oyley Salkeld, also volunteered for a desperate duty during the Boer War in South Africa, and was killed in action at Carter's Ridge, under Major Turner, near Kimberley, when a sortie was made, intended to help General Methuen during the fight at Magersfontein. His name is on the monument at Kimberley put up to the memory of the defenders of that place, and his father also erected a marble cross to his memory in the Cemetery there.

London Gazette, 24 Aug. 1858.—" War Office, 24 Aug. 1858. The Queen has been graciously pleased to signify her intention to confer the Decoration of the Victoria Cross on the undermentioned Officer and Non-commissioned Officers, who have been recommended to Her Majesty for that Decoration on account of Acts of Bravery performed by them in India, as recorded against their several names."

TYTLER, JOHN ADAM, Lieut., was born in Bengal 29 Oct. 1825 ; the third son of John Tytler (Surgeon, Honourable East India Company's Service), and of his wife, a daughter of W. Gillies, Esq., of

London. He was sent home from India when only five years of age, to the care of his mother's sisters, with whom he lived until his parents returned from India in 1835. The family stayed for a year in London, and then went to Jersey, where John Tytler attended a day school near St. Heliers, kept by a Mr. de Joux. In March, 1837, his father died, and Mrs. Tytler went to live in Edinburgh, where John attended the Academy and won several prizes. He then went for a year to a school at Lisle. In 1843, his father's old friend, Sir Jeremiah Bryant, gave him a commission in the Company's service, and in the autumn of that year he proceeded to India. In Dec. 1844,

John Adam Tytler.

John Tytler was posted to the 66th Native Infantry, and he first saw active service on the Peshawar Frontier, under Sir Colin Campbell, in 1851. He was detained in the hills, and so was present at none of the great sieges of the Mutiny Campaign. In Feb. 1858, at the action of Churpara, his men showed signs of wavering, somewhat staggered by the heavy fire of grape with which they were received on approaching the enemy's position. Lieut. Tytler at once dashed on ahead, and alone attacked the rebel gunners ; for a few seconds he was personally engaged in a hand-to-hand fight, and before his men reached him had been dangerously wounded in three places. He recovered enough, however, to take part in the closing scenes of the suppression of the Mutiny, and to receive the Victoria Cross for his valour at Churpara. He also received the Medal, and was mentioned in Despatches. His Victoria Cross was gazetted 24 Aug. 1858 : " Tytler, Lieut. John Adam, 66th Bengal Native Infantry. Date of Act of Bravery : 10 Feb. 1858. On the attacking parties approaching the enemy's position under a heavy fire of round shot, grape and musketry, on the occasion of the action at Choorpoorah on 10 Feb., Lieut. Tytler dashed on horseback ahead of all, and alone, up to the enemy's guns, where he remained engaged hand-to-hand, until they were carried by us, and where he was shot through the left arm, had a spear-wound in his chest, and had a ball through the right sleeve of his coat. (Letter from Capt. C. C. C. Ross, commanding 66th (Goorkha) Regt., to Capt. Brownlow, Major of Brigade, Kenaon Field Force.)" In April, 1859, he was promoted to Captain. In the Umbeyla Expedition of 1863 Capt. Tytler commanded his regiment, the 4th Gurkhas, with marked distinction, and was prominently mentioned in Despatches, and was promoted Major in 1864. Four years later he led the same gallant regiment (one of the model corps of the Bengal Army) in the Hazara Expedition, under Sir Alfred Wilde, and again he was mentioned in Despatches. In 1870 he was promoted Colonel. In 1872 he served through the Lushai Expedition, and for his services was created a C.B. On the outbreak of the Afghan War Colonel Tytler was given command of a brigade, and after the fall of Ali Musjid (at which he commanded one of the flanking brigades) he was entrusted with the task of maintaining communications between Sir Samuel Browne's force and Peshawar. " Here he acted with rare skill and sagacity : twice he led his brigade into the Afridi Hills in order to chastise certain sections of the turbulent clans who were harassing convoys in the neighbourhood of the Khyber. Later on, he defeated the Shinwaris in a sharp engagement. After the Treaty of Gandamak, General Tytler was placed in command of the troops between Landi Kotal and the old frontier ; but ill-health compelled him to resign his brigade before the outbreak of last September." (" Times," 23 Feb. 1880.) On learning of the massacre at the Embassy, General Tytler—though by no means recovered—could not bear to be idle, and he was given command of the troops destined to act against the hostile Zaimushts. These

operations were conducted with consummate skill, and swept the Zaimushts from their rocky fastnesses, hitherto deemed impregnable. " Never physically a strong man, the exposure and hardship of the two winter campaigns must naturally have told on a frame enfeebled by dangerous wounds ; and just as he was about to reap the rewards of a distinguished career, pneumonia—that fell disease on the Punjab Frontier—had claimed him," says the " Times," " as its last and most valued victim. Modest and unassuming as all brave men are, few who did not know General Tytler would recognize in him a man who had won the Victoria Cross for an act which onlookers deemed a ride to certain death ; still less would they consider him one capable of converting raw Gurkha levies into one of the smartest regiments in the Indian Army. A long record of hard service has been closed by a death no less honourable than if won on the battlefield. He will be mourned, not merely by the few who knew and loved him well, but by the many who admired his daring gallantry, his earnest perseverance, and the patience with which he bore what most men would have deemed official neglect ; for though General Tytler commanded his regiment on three separate campaigns and earned the earnest praise of all the Generals under whom he served, he never received Brevet promotion for his distinguished services in the field. Even his brilliant conduct in the late Afghan War was unrewarded by riband or professional advancement. His death " (which occurred at Thal, Punjab, on 14 Feb. 1880) " deprives the Queen of the services of one of the best and bravest men who have ever won her Cross, and the Indian Army of a General whose place it will not be easy to fill. He was an officer of the old school, and one of its best and most valued representatives."

ROSAMUND, M., Sergt.-Major, was born either at Swallow Cliffe, in Wiltshire, or Seaton Town, Luton, Bedfordshire ; anyway, his early years were spent in the latter. He was the son and grandson of a soldier, and

was originally sent to India in the early forties, served in the Sikh War, and was present at Chilianwallah and Gujerat. In the Mutiny he was with Neil when he disarmed the Indian troops. He was awarded the Victoria Cross [London Gazette, 24 Aug. 1858]: " M. Rosamund, Sergeant-Major, 37th Bengal Native Infantry. Date of Act of Bravery : 4 June, 1857. This non-commissioned officer volunteered to accompany Lieut.-Colonel Spottiswoode, commanding the 37th Regt. of Bengal Native Infantry, to the right of the lines, in order to set them on fire, with the view of driving out the sepoys, on the occasion of the outbreak at Benares, on the evening of 4 June, 1857 ; and also volunteered, with Sergt.-

M. Rosamund.

Major Gill, of the Loodiana Regt., to bring off Capt. Brown, Pension Paymaster, his wife and infant, and also some others, from a detached bungalow, into the barracks. His conduct was highly meritorious, and he has been since promoted." Sergt.-Major Rosamund's Cross was sold in London on 25 Nov. 1903, for £54. He received a commission, and was appointed Ensign on 16 April, 1858 ; Lieutenant, 6 Sept. 1864, and was Barrack Master at Barrackspore and Dundurn in 1863, and at Fort William, Calcutta, 1865. He came to England in 1860, and was presented to the Queen by Sir Charles Woods at a Levee. Lieut. Rosamund died in the Red Sea 14 July, 1866, and was buried at sea. Much of the above information was given to Mr. Philip Wilkins by Mrs. Parmiter, 30 Radipole Road, Fulham, S.W.

GILL, PETER, Sergt.-Major, served in the Indian Mutiny, and for his services was awarded the Victoria Cross [London Gazette, 24 Aug. 1858]: " Peter Gill, Sergt.-Major, Loodiana Regt. Date of Act of Bravery : 4 June, 1857. This non-commissioned officer conducted himself with gallantry at Benares on the night of 4 June, 1857. He volunteered with Sergt.-Major Rosamund, of the 37th Regt. of the Bengal Native Infantry, to bring in Capt. Brown, Paymaster, and his family, from a detached bungalow to the barracks, and saved the life of the Quartermaster-Sergeant of the 25th Regt. of Bengal Native Infantry, in the early part of the evening, by cutting off the head of the sepoy who had just bayoneted him. Sergt.-Major Gill states that on the same night he faced a guard of twenty-seven men, with only a sergeant's sword, and it is also represented that he twice saved the life of Major Barrett, 27th Regt. of Bengal Native Infantry, when attacked by sepoys of his own regiment."

GARDNER, WILLIAM, Colour-Sergt., served in the Indian Mutiny, and was awarded the Victoria Cross [Lon-

don Gazette, 23 Aug. 1858]: " William Gardner, Colour-Sergt., 42nd Regiment. Date of Act of Bravery : 5 May, 1858. For his conspicuous and gallant conduct on the morning of the 5th May, in having saved the life of Lieut.-Colonel Cameron, his Commanding Officer, who during the action of Bareilly on that day had been knocked from his horse when three fanatics rushed upon him. Colour-Sergt. Gardner ran out, and in a moment bayoneted two of them, and was in the act of attacking the third when he was shot down by another soldier of the regiment. (Letter from Capt. Macpherson, 42nd Regiment, to Lieut.-Colonel Cameron, commanding that regiment)." William

William Gardner

Gardner died in Nov. 1897. He was the last of the eight men of his regiment who were awarded the Victoria Cross for services during the Indian Mutiny.

London Gazette, 3 Sept. 1858.—"War Office, 3 Sept. 1858. The Queen has been graciously pleased to signify her intention to confer the Decoration of the Victoria Cross on the undermentioned Officers and Non-commissioned Officers, who have been recommended to Her Majesty for that Decoration on account of Acts of Bravery performed by them in India, as recorded against their several names."

AIKMAN, FREDERICK ROBERTSON, Lieut., was the son of the late Capt. George Robertson Aikman, of Ross, Broomelton, Lanarkshire, Scotland. He joined the 4th Bengal Native Infantry, took part in the Sutlej Campaign of 1845 and 1846, and also at the Battle of the Sobraon, receiving for his services at the latter a medal. He served throughout the Punjab Campaign of 1848 and 1849 with General Wheeler's Field Force, receiving another medal. In the Indian Mutiny Campaign of 1857 and 1858 he was present at the Siege and Capture of Delhi, at the action of Bolandshuhur and the Siege of Lucknow, and for his services received the Medal with two clasps, and was awarded the Victoria Cross [London Gazette, 3 Sept. 1858]: "Frederick Robertson Aikman, Lieut., 4th Bengal Native Infantry. Date of Act of Bravery: 1 March, 1858. This officer commanding the 3rd Sikh Cavalry on the advanced picket, with one hundred of his men, having obtained information, just as the force marched on 1 March, 1858, of the proximity, three miles off the high road, of a body of five hundred rebel infantry, two hundred horse and guns, under Moosahib Ali Chuckbdar, attacked and utterly routed them, cutting up more than one hundred men, capturing two guns, and driving the survivors into and over the Goomtee. This feat was performed under every disadvantage of broken ground, and partially under the flanking fire of an adjoining fort. Lieut. Aikman received a severe sabre-cut in the face in a personal encounter with the enemy." This wound ultimately compelled him to retire on half-pay. The late Colonel F. R. Aikman was a Member of the Honourable Corps of Gentlemen-at-Arms from 13 May, 1865, until his death. He was Commandant for many years of the Royal East Middlesex Militia. On 5 Oct. 1888, he dropped dead while attending a ball. The "Times" of 8 Oct. had an obituary notice, and also the following announcement: "On the 5th inst., suddenly, at Hamilton, N.B., Colonel F. R. Aikman, V.C., of 7, Queen's Gate, son of the late Captain George Robertson Aikman, of Ross, Broomelton, Lanarkshire."

CONNOLLY, WILLIAM, Gunner, served in the Indian Mutiny, and was awarded the Victoria Cross [London Gazette, 3 Sept. 1858]: "William Connolly, Gunner, Bengal Horse Artillery. Date of Act of Bravery: 7 July, 1857. This soldier is recommended for the Victoria Cross for his gallantry in action with the enemy at Khelum on 7 July, 1857. Lieut. Cookes, Bengal Horse Artillery, reports that 'About daybreak on that day I advanced my half-troop at a gallop, and engaged the enemy within easy musket-range. The sponge-man of one of my guns having been shot during the advance, Gunner Connolly assumed the duties of second sponge-man, and he had barely assisted in two discharges of his gun when a musket-ball through the left thigh felled him to the ground; nothing daunted by pain and loss of blood, he was endeavouring to resume his post, when I ordered a movement in retirement, and, though severely wounded, he was mounted on his horse in the gun-team, and rode to the next position which the guns took up, and manfully declined going to the rear when the necessity of his doing so was represented to him. About eleven o'clock a.m., when the guns were still in action, the same gunner, whilst sponging, was again knocked down by a musket-ball striking him on the hip, thereby causing great faintness and partial unconsciousness, for the pain appeared excessive and the blood flowing fast. On seeing this, I gave directions for his removal out of action, but this brave man, hearing me, staggered to his feet, and said, "No, sir, I'll not go there whilst I can work here," and shortly afterwards he resumed his post as sponge-man. Late in the afternoon of the same day my three guns were engaged at one hundred yards from the walls of a village with the defenders, viz., the 14th Native Infantry, mutineers, amidst a storm of bullets which did great execution. Gunner Connolly, though suffering severely from his two previous wounds, was wielding his sponge with an energy and courage which attracted the admiration of his comrades, and while cheerfully encouraging a wounded man to hasten in bringing up the ammunition, a musket-ball tore through the muscles of his left leg; but with the most undaunted bravery he struggled on, and not till he had loaded six times did this man give way, when, through loss of blood, he fell in my arms, and I placed him on a wagon, which shortly afterwards bore him in a state of unconsciousness from the fight.'"

Patrick Carlin.

London Gazette, 26 Oct. 1858.—"War Office, 26 Oct. 1858. The Queen has been graciously pleased to confirm and grant the Decoration of the Victoria Cross to the undermentioned Private Soldiers of Her Majesty's Army, which Decoration has been provisionally conferred upon them by the Commander-in-Chief in India, and by Major-General James Hope Grant, K.C.B."

CARLIN, PATRICK, Private, served in the Indian Mutiny, and was awarded the Victoria Cross [London Gazette, 26 Oct. 1858]: "Patrick Carlin, Private, 13th Regiment. Date of Act of Bravery: 6 April, 1858. For the act of bravery recorded in a General Order issued by the Commander-in-Chief in India, of which the following is a copy: 'General Order.

—Headquarters, Allahabad, 29 June, 1858.—The Commander-in-Chief in India directs that the undermentioned soldier of the 13th Foot be presented, in the name of Her Most Gracious Majesty, with a Medal of the Victoria Cross for Valour and daring in the field, viz., Private Patrick Carlin, No. 3611, of the 13th Foot, for rescuing, on 6 April, 1858, a wounded Naick, of the 4th Madras Rifles, in the field of battle, after killing with the Naick's sword a mutineer sepoy who fired at him while bearing off his wounded comrade on his shoulders.—(Signed) C. Campbell, Commander-in-Chief, East Indies.'" The Victoria Cross was awarded to Carlin almost on the spot, by the Commander-in-Chief in India, Sir Colin Campbell. Sir Colin did this also in the case of Patrick Green. In no other case has it ever been done. Private Carling died on 11 May, 1895, in the Union Infirmary, Belfast. His Cross was sold on 25 Nov. 1903, for £63.

GREEN, PATRICK, Private, served in the Indian Mutiny, and was

Patrick Green.

awarded the Victoria Cross [London Gazette, 26 Oct. 1858]: "Patrick Green, Private, 75th Regiment. Date of Act of Bravery: 11 Sept. 1857. For the act of bravery recorded in a General Order issued by the Commander-in-Chief in India, of which the following is a copy: 'General Order.—Headquarters, Allahabad, 28 July, 1858.—The Commander-in-Chief in India is pleased to approve that the undermentioned soldier is presented, in the name of Her Most Gracious Majesty, with a Medal of the Victoria Cross, for Valour and daring in the field, viz., Private Patrick Green, Her Majesty's 75th Foot, for having, on 11 Sept. 1857, when the picket at Koodsia Baugh, at Delhi, was hotly pressed by a large body of the enemy, successfully rescued a comrade who had fallen wounded as a skirmisher.—(Signed) C. Campbell, General, Commander-in-Chief, East Indies.'" Patrick Green was later promoted to Colour-Sergeant. He died on 19 July, 1889.

SHAW, SAME, Private, served in the Indian Mutiny, and was awarded the Victoria Cross [London Gazette, 26 Oct. 1858]: "Same Shaw, Private, 3rd Battn. Rifle Brigade. Date of Act of Bravery: 13 June, 1858. For the act of bravery recorded in a despatch from Major-General Sir James Hope Grant, K.C.B., commanding the Lucknow Field Force, to the Deputy-Adjutant-General of the Army, of which the following is an extract: 'Nawabgunge, 17 June, 1858.—I have to bring to notice the conduct of Private Same Shaw, of the 3rd Battn. Rifle Brigade, who is recommended by the Commanding Officer for the Victoria Cross. An armed rebel had been seen to enter a tope of trees. Some officers and men ran into the tope in search of him. This man was a Ghazee. Private Shaw drew his short sword, and with that weapon rushed single-handed on the Ghazee. Shaw received a severe tulwar-wound, but after a desperate struggle he killed the man. I trust His Excellency will allow me to recommend this man for the Victoria Cross, and that he will approve of my having issued a division order stating that I have done so.'" Private Shaw's death is said to have occurred in 1869 or 1870. There seems to be some doubt as to whether his Christian name was Same or John.

London Gazette, 26 Oct. 1858.—"War Office, 26 Oct. 1858. Her Majesty has been graciously pleased to confer the Decoration of the Victoria Cross on the undermentioned Non-commissioned Officer of Her Majesty's Army, who has been recommended to Her Majesty for that Decoration on account of an Act of Bravery performed by him in the Crimea during the late war, as recorded against his name."

WOODEN, CHARLES, Sergt.-Major, was a German with a ginger beard, and was nicknamed, in the 17th Lancers, "Tish me—the Devil," from a broken English exclamation one night when the sentry on the gate did not recognize him. He was awarded the Victoria Cross for his services in the Crimean Campaign of 1854-55 [London Gazette, 26 Oct. 1858]: "Charles Wooden, Sergeant-Major, 17th Lancers. Date of Act of Bravery: 26 Oct. 1854. For having, after the retreat of the Light Cavalry, at the Battle of Balaklava, been instrumental, together with Dr. James Mouat, C.B., in saving the life of Lieut.-Colonel Morris, C.B., of the 17th Lancers, by proceeding under a heavy fire to his assistance, when he was lying very dangerously wounded in an exposed situation." Charles Wooden became Quartermaster. He is said to have shot himself years ago at Dover.

Charles Wooden.

London Gazette, 24 Dec. 1858.—"War Office, 24 Dec. 1858. The Queen has been graciously pleased to confirm the grant of the Decoration of the Victoria Cross to the undermentioned Officers, Non-commissioned Officers and Privates of Her Majesty's Forces and Indian Military Forces, which Decoration has been provisionally conferred upon them by the Commander-in-Chief in India, in accordance with the rules laid down in Her Majesty's Warrant, instituting the same, on account of Acts of Bravery performed by them in that country, during operations under his command, as recorded against their several names."

ROBINSON, EDWARD, Able Seaman, Naval Brigade, served in the Indian Mutiny, and was awarded the Victoria Cross [London Gazette, 24 Dec. 1858]: " Edward Robinson, Able Seaman, Royal Navy. Date of Act of Bravery : 13 March, 1858. For conspicuous bravery in having at Lucknow, on the 13th March, 1858, under a heavy musketry fire, within 50 yards, jumped on the sand-bags of a battery, and extinguished a fire among them. He was dangerously wounded while performing this service." Edward Robinson died at Windsor, 2 Oct. 1896.

Edward Robinson.

HARRISON, JOHN, Naval Brigade, served in the Indian Mutiny, and was awarded the Victoria Cross [London Gazette, 24 Dec. 1858]: " John Harrison, Naval Brigade, and Nowell Salmon, Lieut. (now Commander). Date of Act of Bravery : 16 Nov. 1857. For conspicuous gallantry at Lucknow, on the 16th Nov. 1857, in climbing up a tree touching the angle of the Shah Nujjiff, to reply to the fire of the enemy, for which most dangerous service the late Capt. William Peel, K.C.B., had called for volunteers." Mr. Harrison died on the 25th Dec. 1865.

SALMON, NOWELL, Lieut., Royal Navy, was born on 20 Feb. 1835 ; the son of the late Rev. Henry Salmon, Rector of Swarraton, in Hampshire, and of Emily, daughter of Admiral Nowell, of Iffley, Oxford ; an officer who had served with the highest distinction as a Lieutenant in the Battle of Dominica, and as a Commander in the opening years of the Revolutionary War, but had been incapacitated for further active employment by the partial loss of sight, which resulted from a wound in the head. Nowell Salmon received his early education at Marlborough, and entered the Royal Navy in May, 1847. As Midshipman and Mate he was in the Baltic in 1854–5, throughout the Russian War (Medal), and was promoted to Lieutenant in Jan. 1856. A few months later he was appointed to the Shannon, commanded by Capt. (afterwards Sir William) Peel, and in her went out to India, where he went up country with the famous Shannon Brigade.

Nowell Salmon.

At the Second Relief of Lucknow, during the attack on the Residency, the attack on the Shah Najaf Mosque had proceeded for three hours, and the day was drawing to a close. The prospect seemed gloomy when Sir Colin Campbell placed himself at the head of the 93rd and called on them to follow him. " They moved off," says Lord Roberts in " Forty-one Years in India " (page 184), " followed by Peel's guns dragged by sailors and some of the Madras Fusiliers, the advance of the party being covered by Middleton's Field Battery, which dashed to the front and opened with grape. . . . On reaching the wall of the Shah Najaf enclosure, it was found to be 20 feet high ; no entrance could be seen, and there were no scaling-ladders available, so there was nothing for it but to breach the massive wall. Lieut. Salmon, R.N. (now Admiral Sir Nowell Salmon, K.C.B.) climbed up a tree overhanging this wall, in order to see what was going on behind it ; he succeeded in obtaining useful information, but, on being perceived, was fired at and badly wounded. He received the V.C. The 24-pounders hammered away at the wall for some time, but made no impression whatever, and the order was given to retire, when Capt. Allgood, Adrian Hope and a Sergeant of the 93rd found an opening, and soon the formidable position was in our possession. It was getting dark when at length we occupied the Shah Najaf." Another account says : " The sailors were suffering great loss from one of the enemy's sharpshooters, who, from a point of vantage on the wall, shot down all that came within reach. A neighbouring tree commanded his hiding-place, but the attempt to climb it was fatal to several. Salmon, however, succeeded, and from it killed the sepoy." For this service Lieut. Salmon was promoted to the rank of Commander, 22 March, 1858, for the Indian Mutiny Campaign, 1857–8, he received the Medal with the Lucknow clasp, and he was awarded the Victoria Cross [London Gazette, 24 Dec. 1858]: " John Harrison, R.N., Nowell Salmon, Lieut., R.N., Naval Brigade. Date of Act of Bravery : 16 Nov. 1857. For conspicuous gallantry at Lucknow, on the 16th Nov. 1857, in climbing up a tree, touching the angle of the Shah Nujeeff, to reply to the fire of the enemy, for which most dangerous service the late Capt. William Peel, K.C.B., had called for volunteers." From 1859 to 1863 he commanded the Icarus in the Mediterranean and in the West Indies. In 1860 he captured and made an end of the American filibuster, Walker, on the coast of Honduras.

" Here lies Walker, W.W.,
Who never more will trouble you, trouble you,"

is said to have been the epitaph written for himself by that daring leader of freebooters before he faced the firing-party. On 12 Dec. 1863, Lieut. Salmon was promoted to be Post-Captain. In that rank he commanded the Defence in the West Indies and Mediterranean ; the Valiant, guardship in the Shannon, and the Swiftsure in the Mediterranean. On the 11th Jan. 1866, at Upwey, Dorsetshire, Capt. Salmon married Emily Augusta, daughter of Erasmus Saunders, Esq., of Westbrook, and they had one son, now Lieut.-Colonel Geoffrey Nowell Salmon, C.M.G., D.S.O., and one

daughter, Eleanor Nowell Salmon. Capt. Salmon was A.D.C. to the Queen from 1874 to 1879. He was created a C.B. in 1876. On 2 Aug. 1879, he became a Rear-Admiral, and from 1882 to 1885 was Commander-in-Chief at the Cape of Good Hope. He was made a Vice-Admiral on the 1st July, 1885, and a K.C.B. (addition Military) on the occasion of Queen Victoria's Jubilee, 21 June, 1887. In that year he was appointed a Member of the Royal Commission to inquire into the system under which patterns of warlike stores were adopted, and the stores obtained and passed into Her late Majesty's service. From Dec. 1887, to Jan. 1891, he was Commander-in-Chief in China ; he became Admiral on the 10th Sept. 1891, and was Commander-in-Chief at Portsmouth from June, 1894, to Aug. 1897, his term being extended for two months in order that he might command at the Review held at Spithead in commemoration of the Queen's Diamond Jubilee, 26 June, 1897. On this occasion, 22 June, he was nominated a G.C.B. With reference to that review the First Lord of the Admiralty said : " While compliments are being paid to the display at Spithead, we should not forget the Commander-in-Chief at Portsmouth, Sir Nowell Salmon, and his staff. The perfect mooring of that 25 miles of ships reflected the greatest credit upon all the Portsmouth officials." From Aug. 1897, Sir Nowell was the Queen's First and Principal Naval Aide-de-Camp till 18 Jan. 1899, when he was promoted to the rank of Admiral of the Fleet. He was retired from the active list in Feb. 1905. He held the Jubilee and two Coronation Medals. Sir Nowell Salmon died at six o'clock on Wednesday morning, 14 Feb. 1912, in his 77th year, at 44, Clarence Parade, Southsea. He had been in frail health for some years, and had been suffering from bronchitis for a few days before his death. He was buried at Curdridge, Hampshire. Lady Salmon died on the same date three years later.

GOAT, WILLIAM, L.-Corpl., served in the Crimean War, and was awarded the Victoria Cross [London Gazette, 24 Dec. 1858]: " W. Goat, L.-Corpl., 9th Lancers. Date of Act of Bravery : 6 March, 1858. For conspicuous gallantry at Lucknow, on the 6th March, 1858, in having dismounted, in the presence of a number of the enemy, and taken up the body of Major Smyth, 2nd Dragoon Guards, which he attempted to bring off the field, and after being compelled to relinquish it, being surrounded by the enemy's cavalry, he went a second time under a heavy fire to recover the body. (Despatch from Major-General Sir James Hope Grant, K.C.B., dated 8 April, 1858)." William Goat's Cross, with his Mutiny Medal, was sold in London in May, 1902, for £85.

William Goat.

NEWELL, R., Private, served in the Indian Mutiny, and was awarded the Victoria Cross [London Gazette, 24 Dec. 1858]: " R. Newell, Private, 9th Lancers. Date of Act of Bravery : 19 March, 1858. For conspicuous gallantry at Lucknow, on the 19th March, 1858, in going to the assistance of a comrade whose horse had fallen on bad ground, and bringing him away, under a heavy fire of musketry, from a large body of the enemy. (Despatch from Major-General Sir James Hope Grant, K.C.B., dated 8 April, 1858)."

SPENCE, DAVID, Troop Sergt.-Major, served in the Indian Mutiny, and was awarded the Victoria Cross [London Gazette, 24 Dec. 1858]: " D. Spence, Troop Sergt.-Major, 9th Lancers. Date of Act of Bravery : 17 Jan. 1858. For conspicuous gallantry on the 17th Jan. 1858, at Shumshabad, in going to the assistance of Private Kidd, who had been wounded and his horse disabled, and bringing him out from a large quantity of rebels." He died 17 April, 1877.

RUSHE, DAVID, Troop Sergt.-Major, served in the Indian Mutiny, and was awarded the Victoria Cross [London Gazette, 24 Dec. 1858]: " — Rushe, Troop Sergt.-Major, 9th Lancers. On the 19th March, 1858, this non-commissioned officer displayed conspicuous bravery near Lucknow in having, with one other soldier, attacked eight mutineers posted in a nullah, and killed three of them." He died 6 Nov. 1886.

David Rushe.

FFRENCH, ALFRED KIRKE, Capt., was born 25 Feb. 1835, at Meerut ; son of Lieut.-Colonel Ffrench, 53rd Regt. He was educated privately, and he entered the Army by purchase at Sandhurst in 1854, joining the 53rd (Shropshire) Regt. as Ensign on the 10th Feb. 1854, and became Lieutenant on the 21st Oct. 1855. He served in the Indian Campaign of 1857–59, including the Relief of Lucknow by Lord Clyde ; the Battle of Cawnpore on the 6th Dec. ; the pursuit of the Gwalior Contingent to Serai Ghat ; the action of Khodagunge and entry into Futtehghur, the storming and capture of Meangunge,

Alfred Kirke Ffrench.

the Siege of Lucknow, affair of Koorsie ; passage of the Goomtee and occupation of Sultanpore, passage of the Gagra at Fyzabad on the 25th Nov. ; action of Toolsepore and minor affairs. For his services in the Mutiny Campaign he received the Medal and clasps, a year's service for Lucknow, and was awarded the Victoria Cross [London Gazette, 24 Dec. 1858] : " Alfred Kirke Ffrench, Lieut., the 53rd Regt. Date of Act of Bravery : 16 Nov. 1857. For conspicuous bravery on the 16th Nov. 1857, at the taking of the Secundra Bagh, Lucknow, when in command of the Grenadier Company, being one of the first to enter the building. His conduct was highly praised by the whole company. Elected by the officers of the regiment." He was promoted to Captain.

PYE, CHARLES COLQUHOUN, Sergt.-Major (now Ensign), served with the 40th Regt. at the Battle of Maharajpore, on the 29th Dec. 1843 (Bronze Star). With the 21st Regt. during the Sutlej Campaign of 1845–46, including the Battles of Moodkee, Aliwal and Sobraon (Medal and clasps). Served with the 53rd Regt. in the Punjab Campaign of 1848–49 (Medal) ; Campaign in 1852 against the Hill tribes on the Peshawar frontier ; Indian Campaign of 1857–59, including the action of Khujwah, Relief of Lucknow by Lord Clyde (severely wounded), Battle of Cawnpore on the 6th Dec., and pursuit of the Gwalior Contingent to Serai Ghat, action of Khodagunge and entry into Futtehghur, affair of Shumshabad, storming and capture of Meangunge, siege and capture of Lucknow, affair of Koorsie, passage of the Goomtee and occupation of Sultanpore. He received the Medal and clasps ; was promoted to Ensign 2 July, 1858, and awarded the Victoria Cross [London Gazette, 24 Dec. 1858] : "Charles Pye, Sergt.-Major (now Ensign), 53rd Regt. Date of Act of Bravery : 17 Nov. 1857. For steadiness and fearless conduct under fire at Lucknow on the 17th Nov. 1857, when bringing up ammunition to the Mess House, and on every occasion when the regiment had been engaged. Elected by the non-commissioned officers of the regiment." He was promoted to Lieutenant on the 9th April, 1861, and was Adjutant 53rd Regt.

KENNY, J., Private, served in the Indian Mutiny, and was awarded the Victoria Cross [London Gazette, 24 Dec. 1858] : " J. Kenny, Private, 53rd Regt. Elected by the private soldiers of his regiment for his gallant conduct and fearless bravery at the assault on the Secundra Bagh, Lucknow, on the 16th Nov. 1857, when, in spite of a most heavy cross-fire, he volunteered to bring up fresh ammunition to his company."

IRWIN, CHARLES, Private, joined the 53rd Foot ; served in the Indian Mutiny, and was awarded the Victoria Cross [London Gazette, 24 Dec. 1858] : " C. Irwin, Private, 53rd Regt. Date of Act of Bravery : 16 Nov. 1857. For conspicuous bravery at the taking of the Secundra Bagh, at Lucknow, on the 16th Nov. 1857. Although severely wounded through the right shoulder, he was one of the first men who entered the buildings under a very severe fire. Elected by the private soldiers of the regiment." He died 29 March, 1873.

BAMBRICK, VALENTINE, Private, joined the 1st Battn. 60th Foot (King's Royal Rifle Corps) ; served in the Indian Mutiny, and was awarded the Victoria Cross [London Gazette, 24 Dec. 1858] : " V. Bambrick, Private, 60th Regt. 1st Battn. Date of Act of Bravery : 6 May, 1858. For conspicuous bravery at Bareilly, on the 6th May, 1858, when in a Serai, he was attacked by three Ghazees, one of whom he cut down. He was wounded twice on this occasion." Private Bambrick afterwards joined the 87th Foot.

Charles Irwin.

MYLOTT, PATRICK, Private, joined the 84th (York and Lancaster) Regt. ; served in the Indian Mutiny, and was awarded the Victoria Cross [London Gazette, 24 Dec. 1858] : " P. Mylott, Private, 84th Regt. For being foremost in rushing across a road, under a shower of balls, to take an opposite enclosure ; and for gallant conduct at every engagement at which he was present with his regiment from the 12th July, 1857, to the relief of the Lucknow garrison. Elected by the private soldiers of the regiment." Private Mylott died on the 7th Dec. 1877.

ANSON, AUGUSTUS HENRY ARCHIBALD, Capt. the Honourable, was born on the 5th March, 1835. He was the 3rd son of the 1st Earl of Lichfield and Louisa Catherine, youngest daughter of Nathaniel Phillips, Esq., of Slebech Hall, co. Pembroke. He entered the Rifle Brigade on the 27th May, 1853, and became Lieutenant 8 Dec. 1854. On the 8th Jan. 1855, he went out to the Crimea. In a letter from Colonel Somerset, commanding the Rifle Brigade in the Crimea, is the following : " On the 12th, volunteers were called for to man some rifle-pits next day. Young Anson and 75 men came out. They only took him and 18 men. He is quite a boy. The Engineers had constructed the parapet and cover so badly that although they fired for some time without being taken much notice of, when once they began to annoy the enemy seriously, they opened such a fire of round shot and shell that they knocked the place all to pieces. However, they remained in it till dark, though he had one sergeant and four men killed, and several wounded. He escaped himself, and seems to have acted and done everything in the

Hon. Aug. H. A. Anson.

most perfect manner, quite as well as if he had risen from the ranks and were 35 years of age." For his services in this campaign Lieut. Anson received the Crimean Medal with clasp for Sebastopol, the Medjidie and the Sardinian Medal. He was promoted Captain 6 July, 1855 ; exchanged into the 84th Regt., and was appointed A.D.C. to his uncle, General the Hon. G. Anson, Commander-in-Chief in India. On the outbreak of the Mutiny, General Anson was hurrying to Delhi when he died of cholera. Before Delhi in June, 1857, Sir Hope Grant says in his journal that he had as yet no A.D.C. : " One day I received a note from Capt. the Hon. Richard Curzon, who had been Military Secretary to General Anson before his death, asking me if I would take young Augustus Anson, who had lost his appointment as A.D.C. to his uncle. I at once agreed to do so, and the young gentleman accordingly came to my tent to introduce himself to me. He was an intelligent, good-looking young fellow, with a look of honest determination in his countenance which pleased me greatly ; but as he felt a natural diffidence on his first appearance, and looked rather pale and worn-out, I proceeded to my bed, drew out from beneath a bottle of sparkling beer, and gave him a tumbler of the delicious elixir. He had scarcely quaffed it when the change appeared marvellous—his diffidence departed from him, his countenance brightened up with a rosy hue, and a great friendship was soon established between us." At Bulandshahr the enemy occupied a very strong position in the gaol and a walled serai at the entrance to the town, their left being covered by the enclosed gardens and ruined houses of the deserted civil station. From this they were driven by the 75th Foot, who captured two 9-pounder guns, while a third was taken by the Cavalry. " The rebels now began to retreat," says Lord Roberts, in " Forty-one Years in India." " We soon became entangled in narrow streets, but at last found ourselves in a gateway leading out of the town. . . . Anson was surrounded by mutineers, and performed prodigies of valour, for which he was rewarded with the Victoria Cross." [London Gazette, 24 Dec. 1858] : " The Hon. Augustus Henry Archibald Anson, Capt., the 84th (York and Lancaster) Regt. (now of the 7th Hussars). Dates of Acts of Bravery : 28 Sept. and 16 Nov. 1857. For conspicuous bravery at Bulandshahr on the 28th Sept. and 16 Nov. 1857. The 9th Light Dragoons had charged through the town and were reforming in the Serai ; the enemy had attempted to close the entrance by drawing their carts across it, so as to shut in the cavalry and form a cover from which to fire upon them. Capt. Anson, taking a lance, dashed out of the gateway, and knocked the drivers off their carts. Owing to a wound in his left hand, received at Delhi, he could not stop his horse, and rode into the middle of the enemy, who fired a volley at him, one ball passing through his coat. At Lucknow, at the assault of the Secundra Bagh on the 16th Nov. 1857, he entered with the storming party on the gates being burst open. He had his horse killed, and was himself slightly wounded. He had shown the greatest gallantry on every occasion, and has slain many enemies in the fight. (Despatch from Major-General Sir James Hope Grant, K.C.B., dated 12 Aug. 1858)." Sir Hope Grant writes in his journal that when on his way to Agra he had again no A.D.C., " For Augustus Anson, my former A.D.C., who was a regular fire-eater, had been allowed to march with the 9th Lancers." In 1896 Lord Wolseley told Lord Wemyss that he and Augustus Anson lived together in India during the Mutiny in the same tent. That Anson kept a list of his hand-to-hand fights—of these combats he had 34—and had killed 28 men. Mr. Kavanagh, in " How I Won the Victoria Cross," describes how Capt. Anson " fearlessly rode through woods and lanes far in advance of the skirmishers," and remarks, " I trembled for his safety." Lord Wolseley writes in his " Story of a Soldier's Life," about the charge of the 7th Hussars at Nawabgunj : " Augustus Anson was riding a big, flea-bitten, greyish Gulf Arab that had belonged to his uncle, General Anson, who died when Commander-in-Chief, at the beginning of the Mutiny. Augustus, an indifferent horseman and a bad swordsman, never lost a chance of taking part in any cavalry charge that was going on in his neighbourhood. So of course he also charged with Fraser and joined in this mêlée to his heart's content. When I saw him after the charge, his flea-bitten grey was bleeding from many a sabre-cut. During the course of the Mutiny he had had a large number of hand-to-hand encounters with individual Sowars, in which he had generally killed his man. I can see him now in my mind's-eye, with his mouth firmly closed and determination marked on every feature of his face. He was in every sense a soldier, absolutely indifferent to danger ; he revelled in these hand-to-hand encounters. His family should revere his memory, for he was a relative to be remembered ; I know that I am proud to have been his friend."

Capt. Anson was mentioned in Despatches with monotonous frequency :

Services for which mentioned.	By whom mentioned.	Reference to Authority.
Operations near Delhi.	Major Gaitskell.	Calcutta Gazette, 24 Feb. 1857.
Siege of Delhi.	Major Gaitskell.	Calcutta Gazette, 7 Nov. 1857.
Siege of Delhi.	Brigadier-General Hope Grant.	Calcutta Gazette, 5 Dec. 1857.
Second Relief of Lucknow.	Sir C. Campbell.	11 Dec. 1857
Battle of Bulandshahr.	Major Ouvry.	24 Dec. 1857
Operations at Agra.	Colonel Greathead and Colonel Cotton.	
Attack on Cawnpore by the Gwalior Mutineers.	Sir C. Campbell.	
Action at Serai Ghaut.	Brigadier-General Hope Grant	
Capture of Meeangunje.	Sir J. Hope Grant	24 March, 1858.
Capture of Lucknow	,, ,, ,,	14 April, 1858.
Action at Koorsee	,, ,, ,,	21 April, 1858.

Services.	*By whom mentioned.*	*Reference to Authority.*
Action at Barree	Sir J. Hope Grant	26 May, 1858.
Action near Nawabgunje.	,, ,, ,,	10 July, 1858.
Passage of the Goomtee.	,, ,, ,,	13 Oct. 1858.

For his services in this campaign Capt. Anson received the Victoria Cross, and the Mutiny Medal with three clasps (for Delhi, the Relief of Lucknow, and Lucknow). Capt. Anson served in the China War of 1860 as A.D.C. to General Sir J. Hope Grant, Commander-in-Chief in China. Soon after the Mutiny he had been transferred to the 7th Light Dragoons. On the occasion of the storming of the North Taku Fort he was the first to cross the ditch and enter it. Sir Hope Grant says in his Diary: At the storming of the Taku Forts, "My Aide-de-Camp, Anson, gallantly succeeded in clambering across a drawbridge which had been hauled up over the ditch in front of my force, and with his sword cut the supporting ropes. In this operation he was nobly aided by Lieut.-Colonel Mann, of the Royal Engineers. The bridge fell into its proper position, and afforded our men the means of crossing." To mark his appreciation of Anson, Sir Hope Grant entrusted him with the conveyance of his Despatches home announcing the Capture of Pekin. For his services in this campaign he received the China Medal with two clasps (for Pekin and Taku Forts). Colonel Anson was Member of Parliament for Lichfield from 1859 to 1868, and for Bewdley from 1868 to 1872. He married in 1859, Amelia, daughter of the Right Rev. Thomas Legh Claughton, D.D., Bishop of St. Albans, and niece of William, Earl of Dudley. After Colonel Anson's death, which took place on the 17th Dec. 1877, his widow married the 8th Duke of Argyll, K.G. The following inscription is in Lichfield Cathedral: "This monument is erected in memory of Lieut.-Colonel the Hon. A. H. A. Anson, V.C., 3rd son of the 1st Earl of Lichfield, who died the 17th Dec. 1877; greatly regretted. He is buried at Cannes, in France. He served with great distinction in the Crimea, India and China. He sat in Parliament for some time as Representative of the Borough of Bewdley. An intrepid soldier. An enlightened politician. He was highly esteemed in the Army. He was respected in the Senate. In perpetual record of his worth his comrades and friends have instituted the *Anson Memorial Sword*. Which by permission of the Sovereign will be annually awarded to the most deserving Cadet at the Royal Military College, Sandhurst." The following is an extract from Standing Orders of the Royal Military College, Sandhurst: "At the end of each Christmas term the 'Anson Memorial Sword' will be given to the Cadet who passes out first at the final examination." The photograph reproduced was lent by the late Earl of Lichfield. It was taken in China.

SINNOTT, JOHN, L.-Corpl., was born in Wexford, in 1829; enlisted on the 24th Oct. 1849, at Dublin, in the 84th (York and Lancaster) Regt.; served in the Indian Mutiny, and was awarded the Victoria Cross [London Gazette, 24 Dec. 1858]: "Sinnott, L.-Corpl., 84th Regt. Date of Act of Bravery: 6 Oct. 1858. For conspicuous gallantry at Lucknow, on the 6th Oct., in going out with Sergts. Glynn and Mullins, and Private Mullins, to rescue Lieut. Ghibaut, who, in carrying out water to extinguish a fire in the breastwork, had been mortally wounded, and lay outside. They brought in the body under a heavy fire. L.-Corpl. Sinnott was twice wounded. His comrades unanimously elected him for the Victoria Cross as the most worthy. He had previously repeatedly accompanied Lieut. Ghibaut when he carried out water to extinguish the fire. (Despatch from Lieut.-General Sir James Outram, Bart., G.C.B., dated 2 Dec. 1857)." John Sinnott was elected by his fellow-soldiers to received the Victoria Cross under Rule 13 of the Warrant. He was later promoted Corporal. He was twice wounded 6 Oct. 1857. He also received the Mutiny Medal with two clasps, the Good Conduct Medal, and a gratuity of £10. He served in India from 1850 to 1859; in Malta in 1868, and Jamaica in 1870, and was discharged on the 22nd March, 1870, being granted a pension of two shillings per day.

John Sinnott.

GUISE, JOHN CHRISTOPHER, Major, was born on the 27th July, 1823; son of General Sir John Guise, 3rd Baronet, G.C.B., of Highnam, Gloucestershire, and of Charlotte Diana Vernon. He joined the Scottish Rifles as an Ensign on the 6th June, 1843; became Lieutenant, and was promoted to Captain on the 9th Nov. 1846. He served in the Crimean War from 5 Dec. to 24 Dec. 1854, being present at the Siege of Sebastopol (Medal with clasp and Turkish Medal). On the 20th July, 1855, he was promoted to Major. He took part in the Indian Mutiny Campaign of 1857–8, including the Siege and Capture of Lucknow, where he led the attack on the Secundra Bagh. When the attack was made on the Mess House at Lucknow, —"a double-storied building, situated on slightly rising ground, surrounded by a ditch 12 feet broad, and beyond that at some little distance by a loop-holed wall. . . . Peel's guns were brought to bear on it, and kept up a continued fire until 3 p.m., when the enemy seemed to think they had had enough, their musketry fire slackened off, and the Commander-in-Chief, considering the assault might safely be made, gave the order to advance. The attacking party was commanded by Brevet-Major Wolseley, of the 90th Light Infantry, and consisted of a company of his own regiment, a picquet of the 53rd Foot, under Capt. Hopkins, and a few men of the 2nd Punjab Infantry, under Capt. Powlett, supported by Barnston's Detachments, under Capt. Guise of the 90th." (Lord Roberts's "Forty-one Years in India," page 187.) Capt. Guise was elected for the Victoria Cross by the officers of the Scottish Rifles—some thirty-five or forty in number, and among them was the late F.M. Lord Wolseley. His Victoria Cross was gazetted 24 Dec. 1858: "John Christopher Guise, Major (now Brevet Lieut.-Colonel), 90th Regt., Perthshire Light Infantry. Dates of Acts of Bravery: 16 and 17 Nov. 1857. For gallant conduct on the 16th and 17 Nov. 1857, at the storming of the Secundra Bagh at Lucknow, in saving the life of Capt. Irby, warding off with his firelock a tulwar-cut made at his head by a sepoy, and in going out under a heavy fire to help two wounded men. Also for general gallant conduct throughout the operations for the Relief of the Lucknow garrison. Elected by the officers of the regiment." In 1890, forty-five years after he had first joined the Army, he became Colonel of the Leicestershire Regt. Lieut.-General Sir John Christopher Guise, Bart., V.C., C.B., died on Thursday, 5 Feb. 1895, at St. Waleran, Gorey, Ireland, the same day as Major-General Montresor Rogers, V.C., who had served with him before Sebastopol.

John Christopher Guise.

HILL, SAMUEL, Sergt., enlisted in the 90th Foot, and served in the Indian Mutiny. He was awarded the Victoria Cross [London Gazette, 24 Dec. 1858]: "S. Hill, Sergt., 90th Regt. Dates of Acts of Bravery: 16 and 17 Nov. 1857, at the storming of the Secundra Bagh at Lucknow, in saving the life of Capt. Irby, warding off with his firelock a tulwar-cut made at his head by a sepoy, and in going out under a heavy fire to help two wounded men. Also for general gallant conduct throughout the operations for the relief of the Lucknow garrison. Elected by the officers of the regiment." Sergt. Hill died on the 21st Feb. 1863.

GRAHAME, PATRICK, Private, enlisted in the 90th Regt. (Scottish Rifles) Perthshire Volunteer Light Infantry; served in the Indian Mutiny, and was awarded the Victoria Cross [London Gazette, 24 Dec. 1858]: "P. Graham, Private, 90th Regt. Date of Act of Bravery: 17 Nov. 1857. For bringing in a wounded comrade under a very heavy fire, on the 17th Nov. 1857. Elected by the private soldiers of the regiment." Private P. Grahame died on the 3rd June, 1875.

STEUART, WILLIAM GEORGE DRUMMOND, Capt., was the only son of Sir William Steuart, Bart., of Grantully and Murthly, co. Perth (formerly of the 15th Hussars), and of his wife, Christina Mary Steuart; was born in 1831, and entered the Army in 1848 as an Ensign in the 93rd Highland Regt., and after four years' home service obtained his promotion as Lieutenant, becoming a Captain two years later. In Feb. 1854, on the outbreak of the war with Russia, the 93rd Highlanders embarked for the Crimea, where they were destined to see much fighting and to win great renown. Steuart was present in the Battle of Alma, and at Balaclava was one of the famous "thin red line" which, unsupported, repulsed the charge of a large body of the enemy's cavalry. He also served in the Siege of Sebastopol, and remained in the Crimea until July, 1856, when his regiment returned to England. For his services in the Campaign he received the Crimean Medal with clasp for Alma, Balaclava and Sebastopol, the Turkish Medal and the Order of the Medjidie. The following summer found the 93rd on its way to India, where the laurels gained in the Crimea were to be more than doubled. The regiment reached Calcutta in Sept. 1857, just in time to join Sir Colin Campbell's advance to the Relief of Lucknow. The heroic achievements of Sir Colin's little force are matters of history, foremost among them stand the operations of the 16th Nov. —the Capture of the Sikandarbagh and Shaf Najaf—deeds with which the name of the 93rd will ever be associated. While the artillery was being brought to bear on the Sikandarbagh, Capt. Steuart, with some Highlanders and a few of the 53rd Foot, advanced towards two of the enemy's guns, which were maintaining a heavy flanking fire and which covered the approach to the barracks—a large cross-shaped building surrounded by outhouses. Steuart captured the guns in a most gallant manner, and by this means his little force was able to gain possession of the barracks—an action which Lord Roberts says (to quote "Forty-one Years in India," Vol. I., page 323), "was as serviceable as it was heroic, for it silenced the fire most destructive to the attacking force." The possession of this building secured the left of the British advance, and greatly facilitated the ultimate withdrawal of the garrison of Lucknow. Six Victoria Crosses in all were bestowed on the 93rd Highlanders for their gallantry on the 16th Nov., but it was decreed that only one of these should be given to the officers. Votes were therefore taken, and Capt. Steuart was chosen by his brother officers to receive the much prized honour. After the withdrawal of the Lucknow garrison Sir Colin's army was hurried back to Cawnpore, and Steuart took part in the great battle which ensued there on the 6th Dec. On this occasion his regiment was once more in the thick of the fighting and two days later it formed part of the force under Sir Hope Grant, which completed the destruction of the Gwalior rebels, as they were attempting to cross the Ganges into Oude. After two months of minor operations the 93rd once more fought its way into Lucknow under Sir Colin Campbell, and it distinguished itself no whit less than on the previous occasion. Steuart took part in the storming of the Mogum's Palace on the 11th March, 1858, and with characteristic daring led a small party beyond the building in pursuit of the mutineers. Lucknow captured, the 93rd was sent into Rohilkand under Brigadier-General Walpole, helped to defeat the enemy at Alaganj, and fought under Sir Colin Campbell at Bareilly. There the regiment remained throughout the hot weather, and in the following winter took part in the pacification of Oude, which was finally accomplished by the beginning of 1859. For his services in this campaign, besides the Victoria Cross, Capt. Steuart received the Mutiny Medal with clasps for Lucknow and the Relief of Lucknow. His Victoria Cross was gazetted

24 Dec. 1858 : " William George Drummond Steuart, Capt., 93rd Highlanders. Date of Act of Bravery : 16 Nov. 1857. In leading an attack upon and capturing two guns, by which the position of the Mess House was secured. Elected by the officers of the regiment." A year later William Steuart left the service, having attained the rank of Major. On his return home the tenants on his father's estate presented him with a sword of honour in recognition of his gallantry. He died on the 26th Oct. 1868, when not more than 37 years of age. Many of the details given above are taken from " Military History of Perthshire," edited by the Duchess of Athol.

PATON, JOHN, Sergt., joined the Argyll and Sutherland Highlanders, and served in the Campaigns of Turkey, the Crimea and India, from Feb. 1854, to July, 1856. Before the Crimean War, the 42nd, 79th and 93rd Highlanders were formed into the Highland Brigade. They landed in the Crimea on the 8th Sept. 1854, and on the 18th marched for the Alma, fighting the battle of that name on the 20th. Marched to Balaklava on the 22nd, being left there in charge of the harbour-shipping and stores. The rest of the troops marched to attack Sebastopol. On the 25th the Highland Brigade formed part of the historic " thin red line " which faced the whole of the Russian Cavalry at Balaklava. On the 7th Sept. 1855, the Brigade marched to the front to take part in the storming of Sebastopol. It returned home at the beginning of 1856, and early in 1857 was ordered to proceed to China, but on reaching the Cape found orders to proceed as quickly as possible to India as the Mutiny had broken out. The Brigade arrived in Calcutta at the end of Oct., and at once marched on Lucknow, reached it on the 15th Nov., and on the same day took part in some hard fighting with the enemy's outposts. Next day the Secundra Bagh was stormed, 2,000 sepoys being killed. The Shah Nujjiff was then attacked, when Paton won his Cross. He went through all the hard fighting at Cawnpore, and Lucknow and Bareilly, and the last of his long list of services in this campaign is the Storming of Dilkusha Bagh. His Victoria Cross was gazetted 24 Dec. 1858 : " J. Paton, Sergt., 93rd Foot. Date of Act of Bravery : 16 Nov. 1857. For distinguished personal gallantry at Lucknow on the 16th Nov. 1857, in proceeding alone round the Shah Nujjiff, and under an extremely heavy fire, discovering a breach in the opposite side, to which he afterwards conducted the regiment, by which means that important position was taken." He left the Army in 1861, and went out to Australia, where he became Governor of the Goulburn Gaol, retiring in 1896. Sergt. Paton died on the 1st April, 1914, in Australia.

DUNLEY, J., L.-Corpl., enlisted in the 93rd Foot (Argyll and Sutherland Highlanders) ; served in the Indian Mutiny, and was awarded the Victoria Cross [London Gazette, 24 Dec. 1858] : " J. Dunley, L.-Corpl., 93rd Regt. Date of Act of Bravery : 16 Nov. 1857. For being the first man, now surviving, of the regiment, who, on the 16th Nov. 1857, entered one of the breaches in the Secundra Bagh, at Lucknow, with Capt. Burroughs, whom he most gallantly supported against superior numbers. Elected by the private soldiers of the regiment." He died on the 17th Oct. 1890, aged 57, in South Infirmary, Cork, from injuries received in an accident. His proper name was Dunlea.

McKAY, DAVID, Private, enlisted in the 93rd Foot (Argyll and Sutherland Highlanders) ; served in the Indian Mutiny, and was awarded the Victoria Cross [London Gazette, 24 Dec. 1858] : " D. McKay, Private, 93rd Regt. Date of Act of Bravery : 16 Nov. 1857. For great personal gallantry in capturing an enemy's Colour, after a most obstinate resistance at the Secundra Bagh, Lucknow, on the 16th Nov. 1857. He was severely wounded afterwards at the capture of the Shah Nujjiff. Elected by the private soldiers of the regiment." Private D. McKay died on the 18th Dec. 1880.

Peter Grant.

William M'Bean.

GRANT, PETER, Private, enlisted in the 93rd Foot (Argyll and Sutherland Highlanders) ; served in the Indian Mutiny, and was awarded the Victoria Cross [London Gazette, 24 Dec. 1857] : " P. Grant, Private, 93rd Regt. Date of Act of Bravery : 16 Nov. 1857. For great personal gallantry, on 16 Nov. 1857, at the Secundra Bagh, in killing five of the enemy with one of their own swords, who were attempting to follow Lieut.-Col. Ewart, when that officer was carrying a Colour which he had captured. Elected by the private soldiers of the regiment." Private Grant was drowned on the 10th Jan. 1868.

M'BEAN, WILLIAM, Lieut. and Adjutant, was an Inverness-shire ploughman until he enlisted in the Argyll and Sutherland Highlanders, and at that time he is said to have walked with a rolling gait, about which the drill corporal made disparaging remarks and at length became so unbearable that a fellow-recruit proposed to M'Bean (who was a very powerfully-built lad) that they should get the corporal behind the canteen in the barrack yard and give him a good hiding. " Toots, toots, man," replied M'Bean, " that would never do. I am going to command this regiment before I leave it, and it would be an ill beginning to be brought before the Colonel for thrashing the drill corporal." He was given a commission as Ensign on the 10th Aug. 1854, and was promoted to Lieutenant on

the 8th Dec. of the same year. He served in the Crimean Campaign from 25 Dec. 1854, including the Siege and Fall of Sebastopol and assaults of the 18th June and 8th Sept., also the Expedition to the Sea of Azoff and the capture of Kertch and Yenikale. For his services in this campaign he received the Medal and clasp, the 5th Class of the Medjidie and the Turkish Medal. Lieut. M'Bean served in the Indian Mutiny Campaign from the 25th Dec. 1854, including the Relie of Lucknow by Lord Clyde, the defeat of the Gwalior Contingent at Cawnpore and pursuit to Seraighat, the affair of Kalee Nuddee, siege and capture of Lucknow, affair of Alligunge, battle of Bareilly, actions of Pusgaor and Russulpore, and evacuation of the forts of Mithowli. Forbes-Mitchell (in his " Reminiscences of the Great Mutiny ") tells us how Lieut. M'Bean, with Sergt. Hutchinson and Drummer Ross, a boy of about twelve years of age, climbed to the top of the dome of the Shah Nujjiff by means of a rude rope-ladder which was fixed on it. This was during the Relief of Lucknow, and they did it in order to signal the position of the Relieving Force to the Garrison of the Residency. They were seen by the enemy on the Badshahibagh, who turned their guns on them. Forbes-Mitchell describes the assault on Begum's Kothee in which Lieut. M'Bean won his Cross. After the assault the men were broken up into small parties in a series of separate fights all over the detached buildings of the palace. M'Bean (who was called " Willie " by the officers and " Paddy " by the men) encountered a Havildar, a aick and nine Sepoys at one gate, and killed the whole eleven, one after the other. The Havildar was the last, and by the time he got through the narrow gate, several men came to M'Bean's assistance. But he called out to them not to interfere, and he and the Havildar set to with their swords. At length M'Bean made a feint cut, but gave the point instead, and put his sword through his adversary's chest. When commended for his achievement the Lieutenant remarked, " It didna tak me twenty minutes." He became Captain on the 16th Aug. 1858. For his services in the Mutiny he received the Medal and two clasps, was given the Brevet of Major, and was awarded the Victoria Cross [London Gazette, 24 Dec. 1858] : " William M'Bean, Lieut. and Adjutant (now Captain), 93rd Regt. For distinguished personal bravery in killing eleven of the enemy with his own hand in the main breach of the Begum Bagh at Lucknow, on the 11th March, 1858." M'Bean kept his word, and rose to command his regiment, and he went through every rank from private to Major-General.

WILMOT, HENRY, Capt., was born in 1831 ; the second son of Sir Henry Sacheverel Wilmot, Bart., of Chaddesden, co. Derby (a magistrate and Deputy-Lieutenant for Derbyshire : High Sheriff in 1852, and a Lieutenant,

Henry Wilmot.

Royal Navy, on reserved half-pay), and of Maria, eldest daughter of Edward Miller Mundy, Esq., of Shipley, co. Derby. He was educated at Rugby ; joined the 43rd Light Infantry in 1841. In 1851—on obtaining his company—he was transferred to the 2nd Battn. of the Rifle Brigade (Jan. 1856), and took part in the Crimean War. In July, 1857, he sailed for India, and won his Victoria Cross at Lucknow. It was gazetted 24 Dec. 1858 : " Henry Wilmot, Capt., 2nd Battn. The Rifle Brigade ; W. Nash, Corpl., and David Hawkes, Private. Date of Act of Bravery : 11 March, 1858. For conspicuous gallantry at Lucknow on the 11th March, 1858. Capt. Wilmot's company was engaged with a large body of the enemy near the Iron Bridge. That officer found himself at the end of a street with only four of his men, opposed to a considerable body. One of the four was shot through both legs and became utterly helpless ; the two men lifted him up, and although Private Hawkes was severely wounded, he carried him for a considerable distance, exposed to the fire of the enemy, Capt. Wilmot firing with the men's rifles, and covering the retreat of the party. (Despatches of Brigadier-General Walpole, C.B., dated 20 March, 1858)." After this he served on the staff of Sir J. Hope Grant as Deputy-Judge-Advocate-General in Oudh. His last active service was when—as Judge-Advocate-General of the Expeditionary Force—he took part in the campaign in China. He succeeded his father, and died at his residence at Chaddesden, 7 April, 1901.

NASH, WILLIAM, Corpl., enlisted in the Rifle Brigade, and served in the Indian Mutiny, and was awarded the Victoria Cross [London Gazette, 24 Dec. 1858] : " Henry Wilmot, Capt., 2nd Battn. The Rifle Brigade ; W. Nash, Corpl., and David Hawkes, Private. Date of Act of Bravery : 11 March, 1858. For conspicuous gallantry at Lucknow on the 11th March, 1858. Capt. Wilmot's company was engaged with a large body of the enemy near the Iron Bridge. That officer found himself at the end of a street with only four of his men, opposed to a considerable body. One of the four was shot through both legs and became utterly helpless ; the two men lifted him up, and although Private Hawkes was severely wounded, he carried him for a considerable distance, exposed to the fire of the enemy, Capt. Wilmot firing with the men's rifles, and covering the retreat of the party. (Despatches of Brigadier-General Walpole, C.B., dated 20 March, 1858)." Corpl. Nash died on the 29th April, 1875.

William Nash.

HAWKES, DAVID, Private, enlisted in the Rifle Brigade ; served in the Indian Mutiny, and was awarded the Victoria Cross [London Gazette, 24 Dec. 1858] : " Henry Wilmot, Capt., 2nd Battn. The Rifle Brigade ; W. Nash, Corpl., and David Hawkes, Private. Date of Act of Bravery : 11 March, 1858. For conspicuous gallantry at Lucknow on the 11th March, 1858. Capt. Wilmot's company was engaged with a large body of the enemy near the Iron Bridge. That officer found himself at the end of a street with only four of his men, opposed to a considerable body. One of the four was shot through both legs and became utterly helpless ; the two men lifted him up, and although Private Hawkes was severely wounded, he carried him for a considerable distance, exposed to the fire of the enemy, Capt. Wilmot firing with the men's rifles, and covering the retreat of the party. (Despatches of Brigadier-General Walpole, C.B., dated 20 March, 1858)." Private D. Hawkes died on the 14th Aug. 1858.

SMITH, J., Private, served in the 1st Madras Fusiliers (Royal Dublin Fusiliers) in the Indian Mutiny Campaign, and was awarded the Victoria Cross [London Gazette, 24 Dec. 1858] : " J. Smith, Private, 1st Madras Fusiliers. Date of Act of Bravery : 16 Nov. 1857. For having been one of the first to try and enter the gateway on the north side of Secundra Bagh. On the gateway being burst open, he was one of the first to enter, and was surrounded by the enemy. He received a sword-cut on the head, a bayonet-wound on the left side, and a contusion from the butt-end of a musket on the right shoulder, notwithstanding which he fought his way out, and continued to perform his duties for the rest of the day. Elected by the private soldiers of the regiment, 1st Madras Fusiliers."

HARINGTON, HASTINGS EDWARD, Lieut., was born in 1835 ; son of the Rev. John Harington, and is said to have entered Addiscombe College in his seventeenth year. In the autumn of 1852 he proceeded to

Hastings E. Harington.

India as Second Lieutenant in the Bengal Artillery. His first station was Peshawar, and he afterwards went to Sialkote, and he was absent from that station on a short leave in the spring of 1857. Having learned at Cashmere some particulars as to the disaffection, he hastened by rapid journeys to rejoin his battery. He arrived in time to take part with General Nicholson in his engagement with the Sialkote rebels at Trimmoo Ghat. He was wounded in the right foot. Lieut. Harington took part in the siege and assault of Delhi, where he behaved with great gallantry. He was next attached to the movable column under Colonel Greathed, and was present at the action of Bulandshahr, and afterwards in the decisive engagement near Agra. The column under Sir Hope

Grant reached Cawnpore on the 27th Oct. Crossing the Ganges into Oudh, it joined on the 12th Nov. the force of Sir Colin Campbell assembled at the Alambagh, and in the operations connected with the Siege of Lucknow he displayed extraordinary heroism, and was awarded the Victoria Cross [London Gazette, 24 Dec. 1858] : " Hastings Edward Harington, Lieut. ; Edward Jennings, Rough-rider ; T. Laughnan, Gunner ; H. McInnes, Gunner, Bengal Artillery. Dates of Acts of Bravery : from 14 Nov. 1857, to 22 Nov. 1857 Elected respectively, under the thirteenth clause of the Royal Warrant of the 29th Jan. 1856, by the officers and non-commissioned officers generally, and by the private soldiers of each troop or battery, for conspicuous gallantry at the Relief of Lucknow, from the 14th to the 22nd Nov. 1857." Colonel F. C. Maude wrote, in his " Memories of the Mutiny," that on the 26th Oct. 1857, he met, entering Cawnpore, the well-known flying column (now commanded by Hope Grant) that had such strange adventures at Agra under Greathed. He " saw three men riding abreast, two of them being Harington, of the Legislative Council, and Herbert Harington, telegraphist. These were relatives of mine, and, of course, the meeting was pleasant enough ; we had all of us been through trials, but we were all well and hearty, and looked forward, not behind. . . . My especial Harington was at the hotel, and we had plenty to talk of ; indeed, everywhere the conversation was most interesting : stories of Delhi, stories of Agra, stories of the march—all full of romance. . . . The career of Herbert Harington so well illustrates the temper of the times that I may be excused for briefly noticing it. He was at Oxford pursuing his studies ; the Crimean War came—studies seemed derogatory at such a crisis, and he volunteered for service, but the authorities would not let him go out in the transport. He went out and worked hard at Kertch and other places, came home through Hungary, and landed at Dover with sixpence in his pocket. Bought rolls, drank water, slept under a haystack, and reached at last the old parsonage where he had been bred. Then he returned to Oxford, and took a Second, which, considering all interruptions, was very fair. But the crumbs of adventure had been tasted, and the quiet academical career seemed impossible. He must go somewhere. ' To India,' said O'Shaughnessy, ' in my telegraph service, the finest service in the world.' . . . So in the telegraph he came, arriving at Agra in the cold weather, and taking his sword off the roof of the dak carriage with the expression : ' My old Crimean sword ; I shall not want that again.' However, the summer found him in the Volunteer Cavalry—only too glad to possess the old Crimean sword. And so here he had turned up as a telegraphist." " Herbert Harington," when Maude met him, " was with his brother Hastings, the young artillery officer to whom his brother gunners by acclamation assigned the Victoria Cross for siege operations at Delhi. There was a Cross to be given, and the officers were allowed to choose the recipient. This was a double honour : ' for valour ' from the Queen, ' for worth ' from his corps. The column stayed a very short time in Oudh. . . Harington went down to Calcutta to take his

seat in the Legislative Council, Herbert went on towards Lucknow." On the 20th Nov. Hastings was dangerously wounded. Transferred to the Horse Artillery, he served under Colonel Turner in Sir Hope Grant's flying column, and was again before Lucknow with Sir Colin Campbell in March, 1858. At the storming of the Secundrabagh he was struck in the right thigh by a spent ball, but did not report himself as wounded. On the fall of Lucknow he accompanied Brigadier Walpole's column into Rohilcund. At the attack on the fort of Rooyah, on the 15th April, he received a severe wound in the left thigh. In the following January he landed in England, and in June was decorated with the Victoria Cross by the Queen, returning to India in the Colombo. From Calcutta he was sent up the country to join the expedition to Sikhim. At Sinchal, a ridge of the Himalayas, where he was some time stationed, he suffered much from the intense cold. " I wish," he wrote to his friends at home, " you could see those glorious mountains, surpassing my wildest imagination ; the highest so close and distinct (awfully so) as to carry one's thoughts, and almost one's self, right up into the presence of the high and holy One that inhabits Eternity." From the camp at Sikhim Harington is said to have been posted to the Horse Artillery troops at Muttra. He had only been a few weeks at that station when he heard that he had been promoted to Second Captain and had received the Adjutancy at Agra. He entered on his duties as Adjutant in June, 1861. On Friday, the 19th July, he became ill with cholera, and his sufferings were very severe. " Whom the Lord loveth He chasteneth," he said to Mr. Ross, the Presbyterian, who prayed beside him. " Rest, rest," were his last faint words before his gallant spirit returned to God who gave it. So died a very gallant soldier at the age of twenty-six. His brother officers loved him, and raised a monument over his grave, and his men, too, esteemed him very highly, though he was a strict disciplinarian.

JENNINGS, EDWARD, Rough-rider, Bengal Artillery, served in the Mutiny, and was awarded the Victoria

Edward Jennings.

Cross [London Gazette, 24 Dec. 1858] : " Hastings Edward Harington, Lieut. ; Edward Jennings, Rough-rider ; J. Park, Gunner ; T. Laughnan, Gunner ; H. McInnes, Gunner, Bengal Artillery. Dates of Acts of Bravery : from 14 Nov. 1857, to 22 Nov. 1857. Elected respectively, under the thirteenth clause of the Royal Warrant of the 29th Jan. 1856, by the officers and non-commissioned officers generally, and by the private soldiers of each troop or battery, for conspicuous gallantry at the Relief of Lucknow, from the 14th to the 22nd Nov. 1857." Jennings worked for many years as a Corporation labourer at Shields, and died some years ago at the age of 74.

PARK, J., Gunner, Bengal Artillery, served in the Mutiny Campaign, and was awarded the Victoria Cross [London Gazette, 24 Dec. 1858] : " Hastings Edward Harington, Lieut. ; Edward Jennings, Rough-rider ; J. Park, Gunner ; T. Laughnan, Gunner ; H. McInnes, Gunner, Bengal Artillery. Dates of Acts of Bravery : from 14th Nov. 1857, to 22 Nov. 1857. Elected respectively, under the thirteenth clause of the Royal Warrant of the 29th Jan. 1856, by the officers and non-commissioned officers generally, and by the private soldiers of each troop or battery, for conspicuous gallantry at the Relief of Lucknow, from the 14th to the 22nd Nov. 1857."

LAUGHNAN, T., Gunner, served in the Indian Mutiny, and was awarded the Victoria Cross : [London Gazette, 24 Dec. 1857] : " Hastings Edward Harington, Lieut. ; Edward Jennings, Rough-rider ; J. Park, Gunner ; T. Laughnan, Gunner ; H. McInnes, Gunner, Bengal Artillery. Dates of Acts of Bravery : from 14 Nov. 1857, to 22 Nov. 1857. Elected respectively, under the thirteenth clause of the Royal Warrant of the 29th Jan. 1857, by the officers and non-commissioned officers generally, and by the private soldiers of each troop or battery, for conspicuous gallantry at the Relief of Lucknow, from the 14th to the 22nd Nov. 1857."

McINNES, H., Gunner, Bengal Artillery, served in the Indian Mutiny, and was awarded the Victoria Cross [London Gazette, 24 Dec. 1858] : " Hastings Edward Harington, Lieut. ; Edward Jennings, Rough-rider ; J. Park, Gunner ; T. Laughnan, Gunner ; H. McInnes, Gunner, Bengal Artillery. Dates of Acts of Bravery : from 14 Nov. 1857, to 22 Nov. 1857. Elected respectively, under the thirteenth clause of the Royal Warrant of the 29th Jan. 1856, by the officers and non-commissioned officers generally, and by the private soldiers of each troop or battery, for conspicuous gallantry at the Relief of Lucknow, from the 14th to the 22nd Nov. 1857."

GOUGH, HUGH HENRY, Lieut., was the third son of Mr. George Gough, of Rathronan House, County Tipperary ; he was born on 14 Nov. 1833 ; was gazetted a Lieutenant in the 3rd Bengal Cavalry in Aug. 1853, and served throughout the Indian Mutiny. He was present at the siege, storm and capture of Delhi, and in the action at Rohtuk ; was wounded and his horse shot under him. He took part in the Battles of Bolundshuhur and Futtehghur, as well as in the relief and capture of Lucknow, where he was severely wounded and had two horses shot under him. Lord Roberts says in " Forty-one Years in India " that on the march from Lucknow, near the old fort of Jalalabad, " Hugh Gough pushed on with his squadron of cavalry to see if he

Hugh Henry Gough.

could find a way through the apparently impassable swamp to the enemy's right and rear. Bourchier's battery coming up in the nick of time, the hostile guns were soon silenced, and Gough, having succeeded in getting through, made a most plucky charge, in which he captured two guns and killed a number of the enemy. For his gallant conduct on this occasion he was awarded the Victoria Cross, the second of two brothers to win this much coveted distinction." For his services in the Mutiny, Lieut. Gough was five times mentioned in Despatches [London Gazette, Dec. 1857, and Jan. 1859]; he was twice thanked by the Governor-General in Council, received a Brevet Majority and the Medal with three clasps, and was awarded the Victoria Cross [London Gazette, 24 Dec. 1858]: "Hugh Henry Gough, Lieut., 1st Bengal European Light Cavalry. Dates of Acts of Bravery: 15 Nov. 1857, and 25 Feb. 1858. Lieut. Gough, when in command of a party of Hodson's Horse, near Alumbagh, on the 12th Nov. 1857, particularly distinguished himself by his forward bearing in charging across a swamp and capturing two guns, although defended by a vastly superior body of the enemy. On this occasion he had his horse wounded in two places and his turban cut through by sword-cuts, whilst engaged in combat with three sepoys. Lieut. Gough also particularly distinguished himself near Jellalabad, Lucknow, on the 25th Feb. 1858, by showing a brilliant example to his regiment when ordered to charge the enemy's guns, and by his gallant and forward conduct he enabled them to effect their object. On this occasion he engaged himself in a series of single combats, until at length he was disabled by a musket ball through the leg, while charging two sepoys with fixed bayonets. Lieut. Gough on that day had two horses killed under him, a shot through his helmet and another through his scabbard, besides being severely wounded." He married in Sept. 1863, Annie Margaret, daughter of Mr. Edward Eustace Hill and Lady Georgiana Keppel, and they had four sons and four daughters. His next active service was in the Abyssinian Expedition, when he commanded the 12th Bengal Cavalry, of which regiment he in 1904 became the honorary Colonel. He was present at the capture of Magdala; was twice mentioned in Despatches [London Gazette, 16 and 30 June, 1868]; received the Medal, and was created a C.B. He was promoted to Colonel in Oct. 1877, and in the following year, as a Brigadier-General, took part in the Afghan War. He was the first to reach the crest at the forcing of the Peiwar Kotal, and with his cavalry pursued the fleeing enemy along the Alikhel Road. At the action of Maturi, in command of the cavalry division, he succeeded—by dismounted fire and by several bold charges, notwithstanding the difficult nature of the ground—in driving the enemy to the highest ridges, from which they were dislodged by the artillery. Later he was given charge of the lines of communication, and at the fighting at and around Kabul in Dec. 1879, he was wounded. In the march from Kabul to Kandahar he commanded the Cavalry Brigade, and took part in the battle fought on 1 Sept. 1880. For his services in this campaign he was six times mentioned in Despatches [London Gazette, Feb., March and Nov. 1879, May and 3 and 31 Dec. 1880]; received the Medal with four clasps, and the bronze star, and was created a K.C.B. This was his last war service. In Feb. 1887 he was made a Major-General, and he commanded a division of the Bengal Army from that year to 1892. Two years later he was promoted to General; in 1896 he was created a G.C.B., and in 1897 retired. In 1898, in recognition of his long and distinguished service, Sir Hugh Gough was made Keeper of the Crown Jewels in the Tower of London, where he died on Wednesday, 12 May, 1909. He was buried with military honours in Kensal Green Cemetery, the pall-bearers being Earl Roberts, V.C., Viscount Gough, Admiral Sir Henry Stephenson, Lieut.-General Sir J. Hills Johnes, V.C., General Sir W. G. Nicholson (Chief of the General Staff), Major-General H. S. Gough, and Lieut.-Colonel H. de la P. Gough. A squadron of the 2nd Life Guards and a battery of the Royal Horse Artillery escorted the body through the streets of the City from the Tower in the East to its last resting-place in the West. Sir Hugh Gough was the author of a book called "Old Memories."

Frederick Sleigh Roberts.

ROBERTS, FREDERICK SLEIGH, Lieut., was born on the 30th Sept. 1832, at Cawnpore. He was the son of Major-General Sir Abraham Roberts, G.C.B., who belonged to a family well known in County Waterford, and had a trace of Huguenot blood through his father's mother. She was a daughter of Major Francis Sautelle, who fought under William of Orange at the Battle of the Boyne. Frederick Roberts's mother was Isabella, daughter of Major Abraham Bunbury, 62nd Foot, of Kilfeacle, County Tipperary. When he was two years old he was taken home by his parents and left at Clifton when they returned to India. He was educated at Eton, Sandhurst and Addiscombe; was gazetted to the Bengal Artillery on 12 Dec. 1851, and joined his regiment at Dum Dum on the 2nd April, 1852. In the following autumn he joined his father, who was at the time in command of the Lahore Division. Second Lieut. Roberts did double duty for twelve months as A.D.C. and Battery Officer. At Cherat he met for the first time John Nicholson, who, he said, impressed him more than anyone he had ever met before, or ever met afterwards. "I have never seen anyone like him. He was the beau-ideal of a soldier and a gentleman." At the end of 1853 Sir Abraham Roberts went home on account of ill health. On the occurrence of a vacancy in the Horse Artillery, Frederick Roberts was selected for it, and became Lieutenant on 31 May, 1857. The news of the outbreak of the Mutiny reached Peshawar, where he was then, on the 27th May, 1857. Sir James Hills Johnes says that to the best of his recollection Lieut. Roberts joined the Delhi Field Force at Delhi with Nicholson's column, some little time after the Siege began, and was then appointed to the Headquarters Staff as D.A.Q.M.G. On the capture of Delhi he accompanied a column which was sent from there to Cawnpore, where Roberts and his comrades gazed with horror on the place where their unfortunate countrywomen with their little children had been murdered just as the sound of Havelock's avenging guns was heard. From there, in reply to an urgent call for assistance, he marched with a force to Agra, reaching that place on the 10th Oct. The force crossed the River Jamna by a bridge of boats, passing under the walls of the picturesque old fort built by the Emperor Akbar nearly 300 years before. On the 30th Oct. the column left Cawnpore and crossed the Ganges into Oudh, accompanied by the 93rd Highlanders. On the 9th Nov., at the Alambagh, Sir Colin Campbell joined the column and marched into Lucknow, via the Dilkusha and the Martinière. Sir Colin Campbell made the Martinière his Headquarters, and thence he sent Lieut. Roberts back to the Alambagh for more ammunition. It was a dangerous undertaking, and as Roberts on his return rode up to the Martinière, "I could see," he says, "old Sir Colin only partially dressed, in evident anxiety over my non-arrival." At eight o'clock next morning the troops moved off, and the Sikanderbagh was stormed. Campbell now moved on towards the Residency, occupying the Shah Najaff. The next day Peel's guns opened a heavy fire on the Mess-house, and the building was carried by an attacking party under Brevet Major Wolseley. Before sunset the Moti Mahal was in British hands, "the last position which separated the relieved from the relieving force." Sir Colin Campbell told Roberts to hoist a Colour on a turret, and on the ground sloping down from the Mess-house, Sir Colin met Outram and Havelock. After a fight with the Gwalior Contingent and Mutineers from Bundelkand, and a short stay in Cawnpore, Lieut. Roberts was attached to Hope Grant's Cavalry Division. When Sir Colin Campbell attacked Khudaganj, he rode in the cavalry charge with Younghusband's Squadron. "We overtook a batch of the Mutineers, who faced about and fired into the Squadron at close quarters. I saw Younghusband fall, but I could not go to his assistance, as at that moment one of his sowars was in dire peril from a sepoy who was attacking him with his fixed bayonet, and had I not helped the man and disposed of his opponent, he must have been killed. The next moment I descried in the distance two sepoys making off with a standard which I determined must be captured, so I rode off after the rebels and overtook them, and while wrenching the staff out of the hands of one of them, whom I cut down, the other fired his musket close to my body; fortunately for me it missed fire, and I carried off the standard. For these two acts I was awarded the Victoria Cross." And now, to Roberts's and everyone else's great grief, Tyrrell Rose, the doctor, came up and pronounced Younghusband's wound to be mortal. Roberts remained with Hope Grant until the capture of Lucknow and that of Delhi had convinced the rebels that their cause was hopeless. Khansi, the rest of Oudh, Rohilkand and the greater part of Central India had still to be conquered, but the subjugation of the enemy was only a question of time. In the Mutiny Campaign Lieut. Roberts served throughout the Siege of Delhi (wounded 14 July, horse shot 14 Sept. 1857). He was present at the actions of Bulandshahr (horse shot), Aligarh, Agra, Kanavj (horse wounded), and Bantharra, etc., and throughout all the operations connected with the Relief of Lucknow. He took part in the Battle of Cawnpore, resulting in the defeat of the Gwalior Contingent; was present at the action of Khudaganj and at the reoccupation of Fatigarh; at the storming of Miangarif and at the operations connected with the Siege of Lucknow. He received the Medal with clasps; was given the Brevet of Major on attaining the rank of Captain, and was awarded the Victoria Cross [London Gazette, 24 Dec. 1858]: "Frederick Sleigh Roberts, Lieut., The Bengal Artillery. Date of Act of Bravery: 2 Jan. 1858. Lieut. Roberts' gallantry had on every occasion been most marked. On following up the retreating enemy on the 2nd Jan. 1858, at Khodagunge, he saw in the distance two sepoys going away with a standard. Lieut. Roberts put spurs to his horse, and overtook them just as they were about to enter a village. They immediately turned round and presented their muskets at him, and one of the men pulled the trigger, but fortunately the caps snapped, and the standard-bearer was cut down by this gallant young officer and the standard taken possession of by him. He also, on the same day, cut down another sepoy who was standing at bay with musket and bayonet keeping off a sowar. Lieut. Roberts rode to the assistance of the horseman, and rushing at the sepoy with one blow of his sword cut him across the face, killing him on the spot." After the Fall of Lucknow the doctors ordered Roberts, whose health had suffered from exposure to the climate and hard work, home to England. He had been serving as Deputy-Assistant-Quartermaster-General on Hope Grant's Staff, and on the 1st April, 1858, the sixth anniversary of his own arrival in India, he handed over this office to Wolseley, and soon afterwards left Lucknow *en route* for England. On the 17th May, 1859, in the parish church of Waterford, Lieut. Roberts married Miss Nora Bews. Their children who lived to grow up were the late Lieut. the Hon. Frederick Roberts, V.C., killed in action in the South African War; Lady Eileen Roberts (now Countess Roberts), and Lady Edwina Roberts, who married Major Lewin, and has a son. While on his wedding tour in Scotland Lieut. Roberts was commanded to be present at Buckingham Palace on the 8th June, when he was decorated with the Victoria Cross by Queen Victoria. On the 27th he and his wife started for India, where he was to take up an appointment in the Quartermaster-General's office. On 12 Nov. 1860, Lieut. Roberts was promoted Second Captain, and the next day was given the Brevet Majority he had been promised on attaining the rank of Captain. In 1863 Major Roberts served in the Umbeyla Expedition. In 1867 he was again Q.M.G. with the Abyssinian Force, and was sent to England afterwards as the bearer of Sir Robert Napier's final Despatches. For his services in this campaign he received a Medal; was given the Brevet of Lieutenant-Colonel [London Gazette, 14 Aug. 1868], and was promoted Lieutenant-Colonel next day. He took part in the Lushai Expedition of 1871–72; was created a C.B. in Sept. 1872.

He became Quartermaster-General in 1874, and Brevet Colonel and Quarter-master-General and temporary Major-General in Jan. 1875; Colonel on 30 Jan. 1875, and was given command of the Punjab Frontier Force in 1878. On the outbreak of the first phase of the Afghan War in 1878, he was given command of a column which moved up the Kurram Valley, won the Peiwar Kotal and pushed on to Shutargardan. On 26 May the new Amir of Afghanistan signed the Treaty of Gandamak. The Afghans, however, did not consider themselves beaten, and Roberts considered the peace so insecure that it was with much misgiving that he bade farewell to Sir Louis Cavagnari and his mission on the summit of the Shutargardan. On 5 Sept. the news reached Simla that all the members of the mission except a few soldiers of the escort had been murdered. Roberts's force was the only one available for a hurried march on Kabul, twelve miles south of which he fought the Battle of Charasia, and captured Kabul. In Dec. he had—after a couple of days' fighting with many thousands of Afghans—to retire into Sherpur Cantonments; was fiercely attacked at the end of a week, and finally repulsed and drove off the attacking force. The troops coming to his assistance arrived the day after the defeat. On the receipt of the news of the disaster at Maiwand he set out on his famous march from Kabul to Kandahar, and dispersed Ayub Khan's army on the 31st Aug. He became Major-General 31 Dec. 1878. For his services during the Afghan War he received the thanks of Parliament and a baronetcy, and was created a G.C.B. He was given the command in Madras, but had to take a trip home on account of his health, and had been in England three months when he was sent to South Africa, after Majuba, but arrived just as a peace had been arranged, and in 24 hours was on his way back to England. In 1881 he returned to India and held the command at Madras to the end of 1885, when he succeeded Sir Donald Stewart as Commander-in-Chief in India. He had become Lieutenant-General on 26 July, 1883. In 1890 he was offered the appointment of Adjutant-General, and accepted it, but three months afterwards it was found that he could not be spared from India. He became General, 29 Nov. 1890. On 1 Jan. 1892, a further extension of the command was offered to him, and he was given a peerage. On 25 May, 1895, he was made a Field-Marshal, and in Oct. of that year became Commander-in-Chief in Ireland. It is well known to everyone how Lord Roberts's only son was killed in the South African War at the action of Colenso, and not long afterwards Lord Roberts himself went out to South Africa and assumed command of the Forces there, with Lord Kitchener as his Chief of the Staff. On 27 Feb. 1900 (Majuba Day), Cronje surrendered; on the 17th Mafeking was relieved, and on the 31st Lord Roberts entered Johannesburg. Lord Roberts was to succeed Lord Wolseley as Commander-in-Chief, and was wanted in England. So on 2 Jan. 1901, Lord Roberts landed in England, leaving Lord Kitchener to finish his work in South Africa. He was in time to receive the thanks of Queen Victoria, who made him a Knight of the Garter and gave him an Earldom. Three weeks later he was called upon to superintend the arrangements for her funeral. On 18 Feb. 1903, the office of Commander-in-Chief was abolished, and Lord Roberts retired. King Edward publicly expressed his thanks to the Field-Marshal for his services of more than 50 years, in India, Africa, and at home. "During that long time," the King wrote, "he had performed every duty entrusted to him with unswerving zeal and unfailing success." Lord Roberts still retained his seat on the Committee of National Defence, but in Dec. 1905 he sent in his resignation, and became President of the National Service League, and spent practically the rest of his life in preparing for the great war he felt sure was at hand. In Aug. 1914, the storm burst of which he had so truly read the signs of the times. Lord Roberts was Colonel-in-Chief of the Irish Guards, and he inspected them at Wellington Barracks before the departure for the front. He said to his countrymen: "I cannot be with you in person, having passed the years allotted to man, but I shall be at the head of the battalion in spirit; my thoughts will ever be with you, and I shall look out eagerly for reports of you." On Wednesday, the 11th Nov. 1914, Lord Roberts went to France to visit the Indian troops, which he did on Thursday, and was received by the Maharajah of Bikanir and Sir Pertab Singh. He caught a chill, and on Saturday, the 14th, the great soldier died among the Indian and British troops he loved so well. "A thousand miles of cannon spoke when the Master Gunner died."—(Kipling.) Lord Roberts was buried amid universal mourning, and his body was carried to the grave on the gun-carriage which had been presented to him after the South African War. It belonged to the gun his son had lost his life in trying to save. Lord Roberts was a Knight of the Garter; Knight of St. Patrick; Knight Grand Commander of the Bath; had the Order of Merit; was Knight Grand Commander of the Indian Empire; had the Volunteer Decoration; was Knight of Justice of St. John of Jerusalem; Colonel Commandant, Royal Artillery (7 Oct. 1896); Colonel of the Irish Guards (17 Oct. 1900).

War Office, 24 Dec. 1858.—The Queen has been graciously pleased to signify her intention to confer the Decoration of the Victoria Cross on the undermentioned Officers, Non-commissioned Officers and Soldiers of Her Majesty's Army and Indian Military Forces, whose claims to the same have been submitted for Her Majesty's approval, on the recommendation of the Commander-in-Chief in India, on account of Acts of Bravery performed by them in that country, as recorded against their several names, viz. :—

DONOHUE, PATRICK, Private, served in the Mutiny, and was awarded the Victoria Cross [London Gazette, 24 Dec. 1858]: " P. Donohue, Private, 9th Lancers. Date of Act of Bravery: 28 Sept. 1857. For having, at Bolundshuhur, on the 28th Sept. 1857, gone to the support of Lieut. Blair, who had been severely wounded, and, with a few other men, brought that officer in safety through a large body of the enemy's cavalry. (Despatch from Major-General Sir James Hope Grant, K.C.B., dated 8 April, 1858)." Lieut. Blair himself won the Victoria Cross. Private Donohue died on the 16th Aug. 1876.

FREEMAN, JOHN, Private, served in the Indian Mutiny, and was awarded the Victoria Cross [London Gazette, 24 Dec. 1858]: " J. Freeman, Private, 9th Lancers. Date of Act of Bravery: 10 Oct. 1857. For conspicuous gallantry on the 10th Oct. 1857, at Agra, in having gone to the assistance of Lieut. Jones who had been shot, killing the leader of the enemy's cavalry, and defending Lieut. Jones against several of the enemy. (Despatch from Major-General Sir James Hope Grant, K.C.B., dated 8 April, 1858)." His Cross is in the United Service Institute, London.

ROBERTS, JAMES REYNOLDS, Private, served in the Indian Mutiny, and was awarded the Victoria Cross [London Gazette, 24 Dec. 1858]: " J. R. Roberts, Private, 9th Lancers. Date of Act of Bravery: 28 Sept. 1857. For conspicuous gallantry at Bolundshuhur on the 28th Sept. 1857, in bringing a comrade, mortally wounded, through a street under heavy musketry fire, in which service he was himself wounded. (Despatch from Major-General Sir James Hope Grant, K.C.B., dated 8 April, 1858)." Private Roberts died on the 1st Aug. 1859.

KELLS, ROBERT, L.-Corpl., served in the Indian Mutiny, and was awarded the Victoria Cross [London Gazette, 24 Dec. 1858]: " Robert Kells, L.-Corpl., 9th Lancers. Date of Act of Bravery: 28 Sept. 1857. For conspicuous bravery at Bolunshuhur on the 28th Sept. 1857, in defending, against a number of the enemy, his Commanding Officer, Capt. Drysdale, who was lying in a street with his collar-bone broken, his horse having been disabled by a shot, and remaining with him till out of danger. (Despatch from Major-General Sir James Hope Grant, K.C.B., dated 8 April, 1858)." He also received the Mutiny Medal with clasps for Delhi and Lucknow. He became a Yeoman of the Guard in July, 1901; was presented with the Royal Victor an Medal by H.M. King Edward. Trumpet-Major R. Kells died on the 14th April, 1905.

Robert Kells.

LEITH, JAMES, Lieut., was the third son of the late General Sir Alexander Leith, K.C.B., of Freefield and Glenkendie, Aberdeenshire, N.B. He was gazetted to the 14th Light Dragoons (now 14th Hussars) as Cornet on 4 May, 1849, and became Lieutenant 27 May, 1853. He served in the Persian Expedition of 1857 with the 14th Hussars (Medal). Lieut. Leith also took an active part in the suppression of the Mutiny at Aurungabad; served with the Malwa Field Force at the Siege and Capture of Dhal, and was present at the actions before Mundesore (wounded), in the Battle of Gooravia and Relief of Neemuch. He next served with the Central India Field Force under Sir Hugh Rose, and was present at the Siege and Capture of Rathghur, Relief of Saugor, Capture of Gurrakota and pursuit across the Beas, forcing of the Muddenpore Pass, Siege and Capture of Jhamsi, action of the Betwa, and all the affairs during the advance on Calpee. In recognition of his gallant services he was twice mentioned in Despatches, received the Medal, was given the Brevet of Major 20 July, 1858, and was awarded the Victoria Cross [London Gazette, 24 Dec. 1858]: " James Leith, Lieut. (now Brevet Major), 14th Light Dragoons (now of the 6th Dragoons). Date of Act of Bravery: 1 April, 1858. For conspicuous bravery at Betwa on the 1st April, 1858, in having charged alone, and rescued Capt. Need of the same regiment, when surrounded by a large number of rebel infantry. (Despatch from Sir Hugh Henry Rose, G.C.B., 28 April, 1858)." He became Captain 27 July, 1853. Major Leith was put on the Half-pay List on the 31st Dec. 1861, and retired in 1864. He died on Thursday morning, the 13th May, 1869, at 35, Gloucester Place, Hyde Park, at the age of 42.

James Leith.

NAPIER, WILLIAM, Sergt., enlisted in the 13th Foot (The Prince Consort's Own Somerset Light Infantry) on 10 Dec. 1846. He served in the Indian Mutiny, and was awarded the Victoria Cross [London Gazette, 24 Dec. 1858]: " W. Napier, Sergt., 1st Battn. 13th Foot. Date of Act of Bravery: 6 April, 1858. For conspicuous gallantry near Azimghur, on the 6th of April, 1858, in daving defended and finally rescued Private Benjamin Milnes, of the same regiment, when severely wounded on the Baggage Guard. Sergt. Napier remained with him at the hazard of his own life. When surrounded by sepoys, bandaged his wound under fire, and then carried him in safety to the convoy. (Despatch from Colonel Lord Mark Kerr, C.B., dated 2 Aug. 1858)." Sergt. William Napier was discharged on his own request on 10 Dec. 1862. He died on the 2nd June, 1908.

William Napier.

Richard Wadeson.

WADESON, RICHARD, Lieut., was gazetted to the 75th (Gordon) Highlanders, and served in the Indian Mutiny, taking part in the Battle of Badlu Keserai, the siege operations before Delhi and the repulse of sorties, and also in the repulse of the night attacks on the camp in the months of June and July. He was severely wounded during the Siege and Capture of Delhi, and received the Medal and clasp, and was awarded the Victoria Cross [London Gazette, 24 Dec. 1858]: "Richard Wadeson, Lieut., 75th Regt. Date of Act of Bravery: 18 July, 1857. For conspicuous bravery at Delhi on the 18th July, 1857, when the regiment was engaged in the Subjee Mundee, in having saved the life of Private Michael Farrell, when attacked by a sowar of the enemy's cavalry, and killed the sowar. Also on the same day for rescuing Private John Barry, of the same regiment, when, wounded and helpless, he was attacked by a cavalry sowar, whom Lieut. Wadeson killed." He had been promoted to a Lieutenancy in Sept. 1857; became Captain in 1864, Major in 1872, Lieutenant-Colonel in 1877; commanded the 75th Regt., and became Colonel in 1880, in which year he was placed on half-pay. Colonel Wadeson was Lieut.-Governor of Chelsea Hospital until his death, which occurred at his residence there on Saturday, 24 Jan. 1885, at the age of 58 years.

COCHRANE, HUGH STEWART, Lieut., was born 4 Aug. 1829; was gazetted to the 86th (the Royal County Down) Regt., now the 2nd Royal Irish Rifles, as Ensign, 13 April, 1849; was Adjutant 86th Regt. from

Hugh Stewart Cochrane.

1856 to 1858, and as such served in the Indian Mutiny 1857–59, in the campaign under Sir Hugh Rose. He was present at the storm and capture of the hill fort of Chandairee (slightly wounded); Battle of Betwa (three horses shot under him); siege, and storm and capture of the city and fortress of Jhansi, where, under a tremendous fire from the fort, he placed the British flag on the top of the palace. He was present at the battle and capture of Koonch; various actions before Calpee from 15 to 21 May, 1858; Battle of Gowlowlee; capture of the city of Gwalior. He was Second in Command of Meade's Horse, Central India, from 1858 to 1859, and commanded the Irregular Cavalry under Sir Robert Napier in the pursuit of Tantia Topi and Ferozeshah in the jungles of Central India. Capt. W. A. Kerr, V.C. (late Second in Command of the Southern Mahratta Horse), has in his possession the following account of the Warrior Queen of Jhansi, who, with Tantia Topi, resisted Sir Hugh Rose so strenuously during the campaign in Central India: "The most heroic figure upon either side in the final campaign was a woman and a rebel, and the career and death of the Rani of Jhansi are not surpassed in passionate daring and chivalry by the story of Joan of Arc herself. . . . The sex, the personality, the fate of the Mahratta Princess, the superb audacity of her last success, the lost battle and the quenched life under that huge encampment of the rock-fortress of Gwalior, which the very genius of tragedy might have chosen as a fitting background for this last flash of an unconquerable resistance—all these elements combined to make for ever a sombre and fascinating drama, thrilling with action, yet almost intolerably touched by the sense of tears in mortal things." The territory of the dead Rajah of Jhansi had been annexed by the East India Company, and his young widow had been treated with meanness. When the Mutiny broke out the Rani made secret preparations, and at her swift attack the handful of Christians in the cantonments threw themselves into the fort, but were short of food and water and ammunition. The Rani lured them to surrender—after a gallant defence—with promises of a safe conduct, but slaughtered them all, a ruthless action which has left a stain on her meteoric career. She in her turn was besieged by Sir Hugh Rose, and her ally, Tantia Topi, tried to raise the siege. Sir Hugh Rose struck with vigour; the force which had hoped to raise the siege of Jhansi was swept out of the field, and Sir Hugh Rose turned to close upon the fortress with a grip of iron. The British stormed the city, but the enemy fought like demons. The Palace was carried room by room, and at the last moment the Rani was lowered from a window and swung into the saddle. She escaped to another fortress of Kalpe—out of which she was again driven. Sir Hugh Rose now thought that he had broken the back of the existing Central Indian disaffection, and made preparations to break up the force under him and to distribute its units, rather with an eye to police than to military requirements. Sir Colin Campbell was rapidly restoring order around Lucknow. Just then the Viceroy issued a proclamation announcing the wholesale confiscation of the estates of the Talukdars, or semi-princely families of Oudh, and thus blew again upon the smouldering embers of the Mutiny. The news came that the Rani of Jhansi had captured Gwalior itself. The Queen's career was finally ended outside Gwalior, when she was fleeing, pursued by Irregular Cavalry, and was struck down by a soldier who mistook her for one of her own troopers. It was during the Siege of Jhansi that Lieut. Cochrane won his Victoria Cross: "Date of Act of Bravery: 1 April, 1858. For conspicuous gallantry near Jhansi on the 1st April, 1858, when No. 1 Company of the regiment was ordered to take a gun, in dashing forward at a gallop, under a heavy musketry and artillery fire, driving the enemy from the gun, and

keeping possession of it until the company came up. Also for conspicuous gallantry in attacking the rearguard of the enemy, when he had three horses shot under him in succession. (Despatch from Major-General Sir Hugh Rose, G.C.B., dated 23 April, 1858)." Lieut. Cochrane also received the Medal and clasp. He was transferred to the 7th Fusiliers and promoted Captain. Later he became Lieutenant-Colonel in the 43rd Light Infantry, which he commanded in India from Feb. 1878, until his retirement. Besides winning the Victoria Cross, Capt. Cochrane was twice mentioned in Despatches, received the Medal with clasp and the Brevet of Major 19 Jan. 1864. He became Captain 24 Aug. 1858; was transferred as Captain to the 7th Royal Fusiliers 21 March, 1859. Capt. Cochrane served as Major of Brigade with the Eusofzye Field Force; was present at the action of Umbeyla Pass, and received the Medal and clasp. He became Major 7th Fusiliers 28 Oct. 1871; Brevet Lieutenant-Colonel 7 Jan. 1874; was Commandant at Khandala 1874 to 1875; Commandant, Deolali Depot, 1875 to 1877; transferred to the 43rd Light Infantry to command that regiment 16 Feb. 1878. He commanded the 43rd Light Infantry in India 1878–81; was given the Brevet of Colonel 7 Jan. 1881. Colonel Cochrane retired on account of ill health on 27 July, 1881, receiving the value of his commission. He died in 1884, and the "Times" of Monday, 21 April, 1884, says that his death is announced and gives an account of his services.

RENNIE, WILLIAM, Lieut. and Adjutant, served with the 73rd Regt. in Monte Videa during its blockade in 1846. He served also in the Kaffir War of 1846–47, and throughout that of 1850–53 (Medal), being

William Rennie.

present at many engagements, including the Battle of Berea, and was promoted to Ensign for his gallant conduct in the field 11 Aug. 1854. He served with the 90th Light Infantry throughout the Indian Campaign of 1857–59; entered Lucknow with Havelock's column (wounded); took part in the relief and defence of Lucknow. He became Lieutenant on the 24th Feb. 1857. For his services in the Mutiny Campaign, Lieut. Rennie received the Medal and two clasps, a year's service, and was awarded the Victoria Cross [London Gazette, 24 Dec. 1858]: "William Rennie, Lieut. and Adjutant, 90th Regt. Dates of Acts of Bravery: 21 Sept. 1857, and 25 Sept. 1857. For conspicuous gallantry in the advance upon Lucknow, under the late Major-General Havelock, on the 21st Sept. 1857, in having charged the enemy's guns in advance of the skirmishers of the 90th Light Infantry, under a heavy musketry fire, and prevented them dragging off one gun, which was consequently captured. For conspicuous gallantry at Lucknow, on the 25th Sept. 1857, in having charged in advance of the 90th Column, in the face of a heavy fire of grape, and forced the enemy to abandon their guns." Sir Evelyn Wood, in "From Midshipman to Field-Marshal" (Vol. I., page 247), tells how he joined his new battalion, the 90th Light Infantry, at Glasgow, and went to pay his respects to the colonel. He met four or five officers there who had just breakfasted, among them one named Arthur Eyre. Sir E. Wood told some of the officers a story of this young man's father, Sir W. Eyre—a very strict disciplinarian, who, in June, 1852 (mid-winter), made a forced march during the Kaffir War with his battalion, the 73rd Perthshire. They marched from King William's Town to the Dohne, Kabourie Nek—carrying "their packs: two blankets and greatcoats, seven days' biscuits, and groceries and 70 rounds. There was much complaining among the men, who said they could not march further carrying all this load. So Sir Wm. Eyre burnt the blankets of sixty of the worst grumblers!" As Sir E. Wood finished speaking, "a deep voice came from an elderly captain on the sofa, who had not previously spoken, 'It's tr-r-rue, every wur-r-rd, for I was there as a Pr-r-rivate in the regiment.' The officer who corroborated my story was Capt. Rennie, who, promoted into the 90th from the 73rd, gained his V.C. at Lucknow." Lieut. Rennie was promoted to Captain on the 9th Jan. 1863, Major 10 Dec. 1873, Lieutenant-Colonel 28 March, 1874, and retired in 1875. He died at Elgin in Aug. 1896, aged 75 years.

INNES, JOHN JAMES M'LEOD, Lieut., was born at Baghulpur, Bengal, on 5 Feb. 1830; the son of Surgeon James Innes, of the Honourable East India Company's Civil Service and Bengal Army, and of Jane Alicia Innes (née M'Leod). He was

John James M'L. Innes.

educated at Edinburgh University and at Addiscombe Academy. At Edinburgh he greatly distinguished himself in his classes, and was awarded the Mathematical Medal for his year; at Addiscombe he carried off the Pollock Medal. He graduated from Addiscombe in 1848, and joined the Bengal Engineers on 8 Dec. of the same year. He had specialized in subjects which disposed him to take up a civil career, and in 1851 he was transferred to the Public Works Department, Bengal. On the 1st Aug. 1854, he was promoted Lieutenant, and when the Mutiny broke out he returned to military duty, and he was one of the most gallant and enterprising of the young engineer officers engaged in the defence of Lucknow. He later wrote one of the most just and accurate accounts of this great achievement in military defence in his book, "Lucknow and Oude," published in

1895. In it he wrote of the work in which he had been engaged : " But the mining warfare that was now certain, and which immediately ensued, involved the most deadly peril to the garrison, whose means of labour were small, while those of the enemy were unlimited. A simultaneous effort on their part at several points could hardly fail to result in success at some of them. Fortunately, however, the besiegers did not adopt these tactics of simultaneous efforts all round the position." Lord Roberts says, in his " Forty-one Years in India," that at Lucknow he was shown " Innes's advanced post, named after M'Leod Innes, a talented engineer officer, who also subsequently gained that coveted reward " (the Victoria Cross). After the Relief of Lucknow Lieut. Innes was promoted to Captain 27 Aug. 1858, and Brevet Major next day, and joined General Franks's force as a field engineer. He accompanied this force in the march through Oudh, and was present at the actions of Chanda, Amirpur and Soltanpur, and for his distinguished gallantry in the last-mentioned engagement he was awarded the Victoria Cross [London Gazette, 24 Dec. 1858] : " John James M'Leod Innes, Lieut., Bengal Engineers. Date of Act of Bravery : 23 Feb. 1858. At the action of Sultanpore Lieut. Innes, far in advance of the leading skirmishers, was the first to secure a gun which the enemy were abandoning. Retiring from this, they rallied round another gun farther back, from which the shot would in an instant have ploughed through our advancing columns, when Lieut. Innes rode up unsupported, shot the gunner who was about to apply the match, and, remaining undaunted at his post, the mark for a hundred matchlock men who were sheltered in some adjoining huts, kept the artillerymen at bay until assistance reached him. (Letter from Major-General Thomas Harte Franks, K.C.B., of 12 March, 1858)." Later on, at the attack of the fort at Dhowarah, Capt. Innes was severely wounded. He was three times mentioned in Despatches, and received—besides the Victoria Cross—the Medal and two clasps, the Brevet of Major, and a year's service for the defence of Lucknow. In 1855 he had married at Jalander (Punjab), Lucy Jane Macpherson, daughter of Professor Hugh Macpherson, of Aberdeen. Their children were: James Edgeworth, born 17 March, 1859 (died 1881); Hugh McLeod, born 22 March, 1862 ; Arthur Donald, born 15 Sept. 1863, and Alicia Sibella. After the Mutiny Major Innes returned to civil employment, and was in turn Accountant-General, Public Works Department Commissioner, the Bombay Bank, Inspector-General of Military Works, and served on the India Defence Committee Inquiry. He retired in 1886. Lieut.-General Innes died at 5, Pemberton Terrace, Cambridge, on the 13th Dec. 1907. Besides " Lucknow and Oude," he published in 1897, " The Sepoy Revolt," and in 1898, " Sir Henry Lawrence." He also edited a Memoir of General Sir James Browne, R.E.

THOMAS, J., Bombardier, served in the Indian Mutiny, and was awarded the Victoria Cross [London Gazette, 24 Dec. 1858] : " J. Thomas, Bombardier, Bengal Artillery. Date of Act of Bravery : 27 Sept. 1857. For distinguished gallantry at Lucknow on the 27th Sept. 1857, in having brought off on his back, under a heavy fire, under circumstances of considerable difficulty, a wounded soldier of the Madras Fusiliers, when the party to which he was attached was returning to the Residency from a sortie, whereby he saved him from falling into the hands of the enemy."

M'GUIRE, JAMES, Sergt., was a native of Enniskillen, and a labourer by trade. He enlisted at Enniskillen for ten years in the Honourable East India Company's Service on the 29th March, 1849. He sailed for India in the troopship Ellenborough, where he arrived on the 10th Oct. 1849. He served in the Burmese War, 1852–53, receiving the Medal with clasp for Pegu. He again saw active service in the Indian Mutiny. The late Major T. A. Butler, V.C. (Royal Munster Fusiliers), wrote : " With Nicholson's fall all attempt at storming the Burn Bastion that day was abandoned, and the men retired to the Kabul Gate. . . . Whilst the troops were waiting at the Kabul Gate, the reserve ammunition was carried up on to the ramparts to be put into a small magazine, which had been built to hold the expense ammunition of the battery close by ; but before it could all be safely stowed away, three boxes were exploded and two set on fire by a shot from the enemy. Sergt. M'Guire and Drummer Ryan, of the 1st Fusiliers, who formed part of the ammunition guard, seeing the danger of the fire extending to the remaining boxes, seized the two that were alight, and threw them over the ramparts into the canal which flowed below ; this gallant action no doubt saved many lives, and it is satisfactory to be able to relate that both these men were awarded the Victoria Cross." His decoration was gazetted on 24 Dec. 1858 : " J. M'Guire, No. 1863, Sergt., and M. Ryan, No. 1874, Drummer, 1st European Bengal Fusiliers. Date of Act of Bravery : 14 Sept. 1857. At the assault on Delhi on the 14th Sept. 1857, when the brigade had reached the Cabul Gate, the 1st Fusiliers and 75th Regt. and some Sikhs were waiting for orders, and some of the regiments were getting ammunition served out (three boxes of which exploded from some cause not clearly known, and two others were in a state of ignition), when Sergt. M'Guire and Drummer Ryan rushed into the burning mass, and, seizing the boxes, threw them, one after the other, over the parapet into the water. The confusion subsequent on the explosion was very great, and the crowd of soldiers and native followers, who did not know where the danger lay, were rushing into certain destruction, when Sergt. M'Guire and Drummer Ryan, by their coolness and personal daring, saved the lives of many at the risk of their own." Sergt. M'Guire was discharged to a pension of one shilling a day on 16 May, 1859, and it is thought that he died at Londonderry 22 Dec. 1862. The 1st Bengal European Fusiliers later became the 1st Royal Munster Fusiliers.

RYAN, MILES, Drummer, was a native of Londonderry and a blacksmith by trade. He enlisted in the Company's service for ten years at Bambridge on the 29th Sept. 1848, and sailed for India on the troopship Ellenborough. The official records at the India Office say he arrived on the 14th Oct. 1849, but Sergt. M'Guire is said to have arrived on the 10th Oct., and evidently he and Ryan went out together and arrived on the same day. Drummer Ryan served in the Burmese War, 1852–53, receiving the Medal and clasp for Pegu ; and again during the Indian Mutiny, for which he gained the Medal with clasps for Delhi and Lucknow, besides the Victoria Cross, which was gazetted 24 Dec. 1858 : " J. M'Guire, No. 1863, Sergt., and M. Ryan, No. 1874, Drummer. Date of Act of Bravery : 14 Sept. 1857. At the assault on Delhi on the 14th Sept. 1857, when the brigade had reached the Cabul Gate, the 1st Fusiliers and 75th Regt. and some Sikhs were waiting for orders, and some of the regiments were getting ammunition served out (three boxes of which exploded from some cause not clearly known, and two others were in a state of ignition), when Sergt. M'Guire and Drummer Ryan rushed into the burning mass, and, seizing the boxes, threw them, one after the other, over the parapet into the water. The confusion consequent on the explosion was very great, and the crowd of soldiers and native followers, who did not know where the danger lay, were rushing into certain destruction, when Sergt. M'Guire and Drummer Ryan, by their coolness and personal daring, saved the lives of many at the risk of their own." Drummer Ryan was discharged to pension of one shilling a day on 16 May, 1859. He lived till the early part of the year 1887, as his name appears in the list of recipients of the Victoria Cross in the quarterly Army List for Jan. 1887. The 1st Bengal European Fusiliers afterwards became the 1st Royal Munster Fusiliers.

London Gazette, 26 Jan. 1859.—" The Queen has been graciously pleased to confirm the grant of the Decoration of the V.C. to the undermentioned Officer, Non-commissioned Officer, Farrier, and Private of Her Majesty's 8th Hussars, which Decoration has been provisionally conferred upon them by Major-General Sir Hugh Henry Rose, G.C.B., Commanding the Central India Field Force, in accordance with the rules laid down in Her Majesty's Warrant instituting the same, on account of an Act of Bravery performed by them in India, as recorded against their several names."

HENEAGE, CLEMENT WALKER, Capt., was born 6 March, 1831, the son of George Heneage Walker-Heneage, of Compton Bassett, M.P., for Devizes, and of his wife, Harriet, daughter of William Webber, of Haldon, Exeter. He was educated at Eton, and Christchurch, Oxford, and was gazetted to the 8th Hussars as a Cornet on the 10th Aug. 1851, becoming Lieutenant on the 3rd Sept. 1854, and Second Captain 28 Nov. 1855. He served throughout the Eastern Campaign of 1854–55, being present at the Battles of Alma, Balaklava, Inkerman and Tchermaya, and at the action at Mackenzie's Farm, at the Siege and Fall of Sebastopol, and in the Kenteh Expedition, and for his services in this campaign he received the Crimean Medal with four clasps and the Turkish Medal. Proceeding to India immediately after the Crimean War, he was promoted Captain on the 12th May, 1857 ; served throughout the Indian Mutiny Campaign, and was engaged on the suppression of the rebels in Rajputana and Central India. He was present at the capture of Kolah, the reoccupation of Chundaree, the Battle of Kotah-ka (? Ra) Serai, the capture of Gwalior and subsequent actions. Sir Hugh Rose had just taken Calpe when the news came that the Rani of Jhansi had captured Gwalior itself ! She had ensconced herself in safety upon the summit of the Gibraltar of India, the rock-fortress which dominated the surrounding plain. Sir Hugh Rose retraced his steps, and it was in the battle fought at Gwalior that Capt. Heneage, Sergt. Ward, Trooper Hollis and Private Pearson won the Victoria Cross. The rebels were retreating towards Lashkar, a garden suburb of Gwalior, when the sudden appearance on their flank of a squadron of the 8th Hussars completed their discomfiture. " There was no pretence of resistance any longer except from a slight, fully-armed figure that was helplessly whirled along in this cataract of men and horses. Again and again this one leader, gesticulating and vociferating, attempted to stem the torrent of routed rebels, but all in vain. There was no possibility of holding up the broken Mahrattas, and at last a chance shot struck down, across his horse's neck, this one champion of the retreating force. A moment later the swaying figure was overtaken, and one stroke from a Hussar's sabre ended the whole matter. There was no time to halt, for the victory had to be pressed home ; but as the squadron returned, it was discovered that it was the Rani of Jhansi herself who had thus ended her meteoric career." For this charge, and for his services in the Mutiny Campaign, Capt. Heneage received the Indian Mutiny Medal with the Central India clasp, was given the Brevet of Major 20 July, 1858, and was awarded the Victoria Cross [London Gazette, 26 Jan. 1859] : " Clement Walker Heneage, Capt. ; Joseph Ward, No. 1584, Sergt. ; George Hollis, No. 1298, Farrier ; John Pearson, No. 861, Private, 8th Hussars. Date of Acts of Bravery : 17 June, 1858. Selected for the Victoria Cross by their companions in the gallant charge made by a squadron of the regiment at Gwalior on the 17th June, 1858, when, supported by a division of the Bombay Horse Artillery and H.M. 95th Regt., they routed the enemy who were advancing against Brigadier Smith's position, charged through the rebel camp into two batteries, capturing and bringing into their camp two of the enemy's guns, under a heavy and converging fire from the fort and town. (Field Force Orders by Major-General Hugh Henry Rose, G.C.B., Commanding Central India Field Force, dated Camp, Gwalior, 28 June, 1858)." Capt. Heneage became Major in Nov. 1860. On the 7th Dec. 1865, at St. Paul's Church, Sketty, South Wales, Major Heneage married Henrietta Letitia Victoria Vivian, daughter of J. H. Vivian, Esq.,

Clement Walker Heneage.

of Singleton, M.P. for Swansea, and a brother of the first Lord Vivian. Their children were Godfrey Clement Walker, born 17 May, 1868, Major, late Grenadier Guards, D.S.O., M.V.O.; John Vivian Walker, born 27 May, 1869; Algernon Walker, born 4 Feb. 1871, Rear-Admiral, R.N., C.B., M.V.O.; Claud Walker, born 24 April, 1875, B.A., Barrister-at-Law, and Aline Dulcie Walker, born 18 Aug. 1877. Major Heneage retired from the Army in 1868, and died at Compton Bassett, Calne, Wiltshire, on 9 Dec. 1901.

WARD, JOSEPH, Sergt., served in the Mutiny, and was awarded the Victoria Cross [London Gazette, 26 Jan. 1859]: " Clement Walker Heneage, Capt., the 8th Hussars ; No. 1584, Joseph Ward, Sergt. ; No. 1298, George Hollis, Farrier ; No. 861, John Pearson, Private. Date of Act of Bravery : 17 June, 1858. Selected for the Victoria Cross by their companions. In the gallant charge made by a squadron of the regiment at Gwalior on the 17th June, 1858, when, supported by a division of the Bombay Horse Artillery and H.M. 95th Regt., they routed the enemy who were advancing against Brigadier Smith's position, charged through the rebel camp into two batteries, capturing and bringing into their camp two of the enemy's guns, under a heavy and converging fire from the fort and town. (Field Force Orders by Major-General Sir Hugh Henry Rose, G.C.B., Commanding Central India Field Force, dated Camp, Gwalior, 28 June, 1858)." Sergt. Ward died in 1873 or 1874.

HOLLIS, GEORGE, Farrier, 8th Hussars, served in the Mutiny, and was awarded the Victoria Cross [London Gazette, 26 Jan. 1859]: " Clement Walker Heneage, Capt., 8th Hussars ; No. 1584, Joseph Ward, Sergt. ; No. 1298, George Hollis, Farrier ; No. 861, John Pearson Private. Date of Acts of Bravery : 17 June, 1858. Selected for the Victoria Cross by their companions. In the gallant charge made by a squadron of the regiment at Gwalior on the 17th June, 1858, when, supported by a division of the Bombay Horse Artillery and her Majesty's 95th Regt., they routed the enemy, who were advancing against Brigadier Smith's position, charged through the rebel camp into two batteries, capturing and bringing into their camp two of the enemy's guns, under a heavy and converging fire from the fort and town. (Field Force Orders by Major-General Sir Hugh Henry Rose, G.C.B., Commanding Central India Field Force, dated, Camp, Gwalior, 28 June, 1858)." Farrier Hollis died on the 16th May, 1879.

PEARSON, JOHN, Private, served in the Mutiny, and was awarded the Victoria Cross [London Gazette, 26 Jan. 1859]: " Clement Walker Heneage, Capt., 8th Hussars ; No. 1584, Joseph Ward, Sergt. ; No. 1298, George Hollis, Farrier ; No. 861, John Pearson, Private. Date of Acts of Bravery : 17 June, 1858. Selected for the Victoria Cross by their companions. In the gallant charge made by a squadron of the regiment at Gwalior on the 17th June, 1858, when, supported by a division of the Bombay Horse Artillery and Her Majesty's 95th Regt., they routed the enemy, who were advancing against Brigadier Smith's position, charged through the rebel camp into two batteries, capturing and bringing into their camp two of the enemy's guns, under a heavy and converging fire from the fort and town. (Field Force Orders by Major-General Sir Hugh Henry Rose, G.C.B., Commanding Central India Field Force, dated Camp, Gwalior, 28 June, 1858)." Private John Pearson later joined the 19th Hussars. He died 18 April 1892.

John Pearson.

" War Office, 1 Feb. 1859.—The Queen has been graciously pleased to signify her intention to confer the Decoration of the Victoria Cross on the undermentioned Officer and Seaman of Her Majesty's Navy, who have been recommended to Her Majesty for that Decoration for their gallantry whilst serving in the Naval Brigade in India under the orders of the late Capt. William Peel, K.C.B."

YOUNG, THOMAS JAMES, Lieut., Royal Navy, served in the Mutiny Campaign. Lord Elgin, as described in the account of Sir William Peel, set off to Calcutta with 1,500 sailors and marines, chiefly belonging to the steamers Pearl and Shannon. These were formed into brigades to act on shore, just as had been done in the Crimea. Capt. Peel started up the Ganges with ten huge 68-pounders and 400 bluejackets, known officially as the Shannon Brigade—but usually called Peel's. Progress was terribly slow, and it was not until the 30th Sept. that he reached Benares with 286, and arrived at Allahabad three days later. There they found, to their horror, that the big guns must be left, as they could not be transported across country. Peel therefore remained until the 28th, organizing siege-trains of 24-pounders and sending them on to Cawnpore. He finally started for the front—and for his last campaign—with hunting-spurs peeping from beneath his white trousers and the three gold bands that denoted his rank of Post-Captain on the cuffs of his undress uniform. From Cawnpore, after a considerable amount of fighting, the Naval Brigade, reduced to 250 men, accompanied Sir Colin Campbell on his march to Lucknow ; and Peel's fiddlers played the 93rd

Thomas James Young.

Highlanders into the camp at the Alumbagh. Peel had invented some " rocket cars " : " Though on your own side, the very sight of the little car, with the mast slipped into the centre, makes your hair stand on end. Reader, if you ever see it coming (Peel will probably be whistling or telling some amusing anecdote—in fact, as much unconcerned as if going to an evening party), and you are trying to snooze off the effects of a hard day's work, quietly move off as far as possible ; your rest is gone. A more diabolical apparatus for rousing an army from its repose was never invented ; but, abominable as is the disturbance they make, their effect, as Peel used them, must have been terrific in a crowded city." (Colonel G. Bourchier, C.B.) After pounding away at the walls of the Secundrabagh, Peel's guns were ordered on to the Shah Nujjiff Mosque, and, although covered by the Highlanders, the sailors were exposed to a rattling fire from the mob over the wall. Sir Colin Campbell said that " Capt. Peel behaved very much as if he had been laying the Shannon alongside an enemy's frigate." Hand grenades fell among them, but Lieut. Young and William Hall, A.B., a negro, ran the 24-pounder which the sailors called the " Shannon," close to the masonry; and fired round after round point-blank at it. Both were awarded the Victoria Cross [London Gazette, 1 Feb. 1859]: " Thomas James Young, Lieut., late Gunnery Officer of H.M.S. Shannon ; William Hall, Captain of the Foretop of H.M.S. Shannon. Recommended by the late Capt. Peel for their gallant conduct at a 24-pounder gun, brought up to the angle of the Shah Nujjiff at Lucknow on the 10th Nov. 1857." Lieut. Young became Commander. He died at Caen on the 20th March, 1869.

HALL, WILLIAM, Captain of the Foretop, Royal Navy, was born at Avonport, Horton, Nova Scotia. He was educated at Avonport, and served as an ordinary seaman with the Naval Brigade at Lucknow and Calcutta in 1857. He was decorated with the Victoria Cross on the recommendation of Capt. Peel, of H.M.S. Shannon [London Gazette, 1 Feb. 1859]: " Thomas James Young, Lieut., late Gunnery Officer of H.M.S. Shannon ; William Hall, Captain of the Foretop of H.M.S. Shannon. Recommended by the late Capt. Peel for their gallant conduct at a 24-pounder gun, brought up to the angle of the Shah Nujjiff at Lucknow on the 10th Nov. 1857." William Hall is one of the three negroes who have been awarded the Victoria Cross ; the others were Samuel Hodge and W. J. Gordon. In describing the scene at the Shah Nujjiff, " I remem-

William Hall.

ber," said Hall, " that after firing each round we ran our gun forward, until at last my gun's crew were actually in danger of being hit by splinters of brick and stone torn by the round shot from the walls we were bombarding. Our Lieutenant, Mr. Thomas Young, moved from gun to gun with a quiet smile and a word of encouragement ; and when at last the gunner next to me fell dead, Mr. Young at once took his place." William Hall afterwards retired to his native place, and became a farmer at Avonport, King's County, Nova Scotia. His favourite recreation as given in " Who's Who " was " shooting crows." He died about 1900.

London Gazette, 12 April, 1859.—" The Queen has been most graciously pleased to confirm the grant of the Decoration of the Victoria Cross to the undermentioned Officer and Private of Her Majesty's Army, which Decoration has been provisionally conferred on them by the Commander-in-Chief in India, in accordance with the rules laid down in Her Majesty's Warrant instituting the same, on account of Acts of Bravery performed by them during the operations under his personal command, as recorded against their names."

HACKETT, THOMAS BERNARD, Lieut., was born in 1836 ; son of the late Mr. Thomas Hackett, of Moor Park and Riverstown, co. Tipperary, by his marriage with Jane Bernard, youngest daughter of the late Mr. Bernard Shaw, of Monkstown Castle, co. Cork, and a niece of the late Sir Robert Shaw, of Bushy Park, co. Dublin. He entered the Army on the 7th June, 1854, as an Ensign in the 23rd Regt. (the Royal Welsh Fusiliers), and became Lieutenant on the 9th Feb. 1855. He served with his regiment in the Crimea from the 5th June to the 6th Sept. 1855, including the Siege of Sebastopol and assault on the Redan on the 18th June (Medal with clasp and Turkish Medal). He served in the Indian Campaign of 1857–58, including the Relief of Lucknow by Lord Clyde, the defeat of the Gwalior Contingent at Cawnpore on the 6th Dec., the operations across the Goomtee, Siege and Capture of Lucknow. He was present with the left wing of the regiment in the Biaswarrah District, including the affairs of Jubrowlie, Poornab and Doondiakiara. For his services in this campaign he received the Medal with two clasps, and was awarded the Victoria Cross [London Gazette, 12 April, 1859]: " Thomas Bernard Hackett, Lieut. (now Capt.), 23rd Regt. For daring gallantry at Secunda Bagh, Lucknow, on the 18th Nov. 1857, in having, with others, rescued a Corporal of the 23rd Regt., who was lying wounded and exposed to very heavy fire. Also for conspicuous bravery in having, under a heavy fire, ascended the roof and cut

Thomas B. Hackett.

down the thatch of a bungalow to prevent its being set on fire. This was a most important service at the time." He was promoted Captain 26 Jan. 1858, and Major 3 Sept. 1870. He retired from the Army 1 April, 1874, by the sale of his commission, with the rank of Lieutenant-Colonel.

Lieut.-Colonel Thomas Hackett, of Riverstown, was a Magistrate for the County Tipperary. He was killed on the 5th Oct. 1880, at Arrabeg, at the age of 46, by the explosion of his own gun. An obituary notice of Colonel Hackett appeared in the "Times" of the 29th Oct. 1880.

MONGER, GEORGE, Private, enlisted in the 23rd Regt. (Royal Welsh Fusiliers); served in the Indian Mutiny, and was awarded the Victoria Cross [London Gazette, 12 April, 1859]: "George Monger, Private, 23rd Regt. For daring gallantry at Secundra Bagh, Lucknow, on the 18th Nov. 1857, in having volunteered to accompany Lieut. Hackett, whom he assisted in bringing in a Corporal of the 23rd Regt., who was lying wounded in an exposed position." He died on the 9th Aug. 1887.

George Monger.

London Gazette, 12 April, 1859.—" Her Majesty has also been graciously pleased to signify her intention to confer the Decoration of the Victoria Cross on the undermentioned Officers and Soldiers of Her Majesty's Army and Indian Military Forces, whose claims to the same have been submitted for Her Majesty's approval, on account of Acts of Bravery performed by them in India, as recorded against their several names."

RENNY, GEORGE ALEXANDER, Lieut., was born in 1827. He was educated at Addiscombe, obtaining his commission in the Bengal Horse Artillery 7 June, 1844, becoming Lieutenant 6 Oct. 1846. He served through the Sutlej Campaign, and was present at the Battle of Sobraon and through the Mutiny Campaign (1857–58); received the Medal with clasps; was mentioned in Despatches at Delhi, and awarded the Victoria Cross [London Gazette, 12 April, 1859]: "George Alexander Renny, Lieut., Bengal Horse Artillery. Date of Act of Bravery: 16 Sept. 1857. Lieut.-Colonel Farquhar, commanding the 1st Belooch Battn., reports that he was in command of the troops stationed in the Delhi Magazine after its capture on the 16th Sept. 1857. Early in the prenoon of that day a vigorous attack was made on the post by the enemy, and was kept up with great violence for some time, without the slightest chance of success. Under cover of a heavy cross-fire from the high houses on the right flank of the Magazine, and from Selinghur and the Palace, the enemy advanced to the high wall of the Magazine and endeavoured to set fire to a thatched roof. The roof was partially set fire to, which was extinguished at the spot by a sepoy of the Belooch Battn., a soldier of the 61st Regt. having in vain attempted to do so. The roof having been again set on fire, Capt. Renny, with great gallantry, mounted to the top of the wall of the Magazine and flung several shells with lighted fuzes into the midst of the enemy, which had an almost immediate effect, as the attack at once became feeble at that point, and soon after ceased there." He became Captain on the 27th April, 1858, and Major on the 20th July, 1858. He commanded "D" Battery and Brigade, Royal Horse Artillery, through the Hazara Campaign of 1868. Major-General Renny died at Bath on 5 Jan. 1887.

RODDY, PATRICK, Ensign, was born 17 March, 1827, and received a commission as Ensign in the Bengal Artillery. During the Indian Mutiny he served under Sir James Outram in the First Relief of Lucknow, at the Siege of the Bailey Guard, the Defence of the Alambagh, Capture of Lucknow, and in almost every subsequent engagement up to the suppression of the rebels on the Oudh Frontier in 1860. He received the Mutiny Medal with clasp; was frequently mentioned in Despatches; received the thanks of the Indian Government, and was awarded the Victoria Cross [London Gazette, 12 April, 1859]: "Patrick Roddy, Ensign, Bengal Army (unattached). Date of Act of Bravery: 27 Sept. 1858. Major-General Sir James Hope Grant, K.C.B., commanding Oudh Force, bears testimony to the gallant conduct of Lieut. Roddy on several occasions. One instance is particularly mentioned. On the return from Kuthirga of the Kupperthulla Contingent on the 27th Sept. 1858, this officer, when engaged with the enemy, charged a rebel (armed with a percussion musket), when the cavalry were afraid to approach, as each time they attempted to do so the rebel knelt and covered his assailant; this, however, did not deter Lieut. Roddy, who went boldly in, and when within six yards, the rebel fired, killing Lieut. Roddy's horse, and before he could get disentangled from the horse the rebel attempted to cut him down. Lieut. Roddy seized the rebel until he could get at his sword, when he ran him through the body. The rebel turned out to be a scubardar of the late 8th Native Infantry—a powerful man and a most determined character." He served in the Abyssinian War of 1868; was mentioned in Despatches; received the Brevet of Major, and Medal; and in the Afghan War of 1878–79 was mentioned in Despatches and received the Afghan Medal with clasp for Ali Musjid. He retired as a Colonel in 1887, having been thirty-nine years in the Bengal Service. Colonel Roddy died in Jersey on 21 Nov. 1895.

Patrick Roddy.

McPHERSON, STEWART, Colour-Sergt., served with his regiment, The Seaforth Highlanders (Ross-shire Buffs), in the Indian Mutiny, and was awarded the Victoria Cross [London Gazette, 12 April, 1859]: "Stewart McPherson, Colour-Sergt., 78th Regt. For daring gallantry in the Lucknow Residency on the 26th Sept. 1857, in having rescued at great personal risk a wounded private of his company, who was lying in a most exposed situation, under a very heavy fire. Colour-Sergt. McPherson was also distinguished on many occasions by his coolness and gallantry in action." He died on the 7th Dec. 1892.

Stewart McPherson.

FLINN, THOMAS, Drummer, enlisted in the 64th (North Staffordshire) Regt., and served in the Indian Mutiny. He was awarded the Victoria Cross [London Gazette, 12 April, 1859]: "Thomas Flinn, Drummer, 64th Regt. Date of Act of Bravery: 28 Nov. 1857. For conspicuous bravery in the charge on the enemy's (India) guns on the 28th Nov. 1857, when, being himself wounded, he engaged in a hand-to-hand encounter with two of the rebel artillerymen." Drummer Flinn died on the 10th Aug. 1892.

Thomas Flinn.

MILLER, FREDERICK, Major, was educated at the Royal Military Academy, Woolwich, becoming a Cadet on the 28th Jan. 1847. He was gazetted to the Royal Artillery as 1st Lieutenant, 19 Dec. 1848 at the age of 17 years; served in the Crimean Campaign, and was present at the Battles of Alma and Balaklava, at the sortie of the 26th Oct., at the Battle of Inkerman and the Siege of Sebastopol. He was mentioned in Despatches; received the Medal and four clasps; was made a Knight of the Legion of Honour; received the Order of the Medjidie; was given his Brevet Majority, and awarded the Victoria Cross [London Gazette, 6 May, 1859]: "Frederick Miller, Brevet Major, Royal Artillery. Date of Act of Bravery: 5 Nov. 1854. For having at the Battle of Inkerman personally attacked three Russians, and with the gunners of his division of the battery prevented the Russians from doing mischief to the guns which they had surrounded. Part of a regiment of English Infantry had previously retired through the battery in front of this body of Russians." He became 2nd Captain 13 April, 1855, Brevet Major 2 Nov. 1855, Captain 11 Dec. 1861, Brevet Lieut.-Colonel 2 Feb. 1867, and Regimental Lieut.-Colonel 9 Aug. 1873. Lieut.-Colonel F. Miller died at the Cape of Good Hope on 17 Feb. 1874.

BUTLER, THOMAS ADAIR, Lieut., was born in 1836, most likely at Soberton, Hampshire, where his father was Curate from 1826 to 1848. He was baptized at Soberton on 10 July, 1836. His father was the Rev. Stephen Butler, son of Thomas Butler, Esquire, of Bury Lodge, Hambledon, Hampshire, and his mother was Mary Anne, daughter of Thomas Thistlethwayte, Esquire, of Southwick Park, Hampshire. The present Vicar of Soberton, the Rev. W. H. Morley, says of Stephen Butler: "I came here in 1874, and I used to hear much of him. The old people who knew him are now dead. He was a very tall, handsome man, said his old clerk, and a splendid preacher, and had a great influence over men. He was much interested in the old 'Poor Laws' of his time, and I believe he was called up to London on the subject by the authorities, and gave useful help. Mr. Stephen Butler was beloved by his people, and also filled his church. We still have the clock which measured the length of his sermons. He could watch it from the pulpit. He and the Roman Catholic priest were considered the two finest men in Hampshire. 'Why are the clergy not beloved like they used to be?' said a lady the other day to me. 'Look at this book, "From our dear Clergyman, Stephen Butler."' On Sunday he used to walk to the School (two-thirds of a mile) in his surplice, and bring the children to the morning service himself, by the Church Meadow. He had a very powerful voice. There was no stove in the church in those days." Stephen Butler became Incumbent of Holy Trinity Church, Southampton, in 1848, and, as such, his name occurs in the Clergy List up till 1855. He died at Guildford 5 Nov. 1855, aged 53, and was buried at Soberton 10 Nov. Thomas A. Butler's mother died when she was 31 years old, and was buried at Soberton 26 May, 1838. He was educated at Mr. Burney's School, Gosport, and gazetted to the 1st Bengal European Fusiliers as Ensign 9 June, 1854, becoming Lieutenant 23 Nov. 1856, and afterwards Instructor of Musketry to the regiment. He served in the Indian Mutiny Campaign from 10 June, 1857. James Peter Brougham, Esq., M.D., says, in "The 1st Bengal Fusiliers in the Delhi Campaign": "Lieut. Butler joined from leave on the 9th, having ridden in from Missourie, 110 miles

Thomas Adair Butler.

in three days. As this was done on one horse, it was pretty good travelling for the season; but the young soldier is partial to equestrian exercise, and his powers of adhesion are very great." Lieut. Butler used to ride a good deal in steeplechases, and Major Daniell, who speaks of him as "a fellow-jockey," says they rode at the same race meetings in India, often got up among themselves. Major J. W. Daniell, who is one of the Delhi survivors, left the 1st Bengal Fusiliers in 1859. He made a great name when with the regiment as a successful jockey, and as backing him was found to be more successful than backing any horse, the wise ones found out which horse he was riding before they made their "investments." He went on sick half-pay in 1864. Lieut. Butler was in all the engagements under the walls of Delhi; was galloper to General Nicholson at the action of Nugafshot, and took part in the storming of the Moghul Capital, being wounded in that action. He took part in the actions of Gunjaree Puttialee and Mynpoorie, and was present at the storming of Lucknow, where he won the Victoria Cross. At the storming of Delhi on 14 Sept. 1857, "after taking the church," wrote Major Butler, "some thirty men, with Lieut. Butler of the 1st Fusiliers, and about fifty Ghoorkas under Lieut. Davidson, followed up the retreating sepoys, and not only drove them right through the college, but actually advanced as far as the gate of the arsenal, and occupied it without knowing the important position they had taken. Butler, however, being aware that his regiment was to advance along the walls to the right, told Davidson he must proceed in that direction, and Davidson, not being strong enough to hold so advanced a position, retired to the church. Butler's party passed along through the compound of Skinner's house (a large brick, double-storied building, a little in rear of the Morie Bastion), and here they found some bottles of brandy, laid about, no doubt, to tempt the British soldiers. The officers called on the men to smash the bottles with the butt of their muskets, telling them that they were poisoned, and most of them were in this way destroyed, till an old soldier (in every sense of the word) took up one, carefully examined the neck, and then said, 'This has never been poisoned; the capsule is the same as when it was corked,' and the bottle went into his haversack. Very slight opposition was offered between the Morie Bastion and Cabul Gate; the enemy were on the run, and the flying sepoys carried the others along with them; had the pursuit been continued, the Burn Bastion and Lahore Gate would probably have been captured without very heavy loss; but there was a fatal delay of about two hours on account of the non-arrival of No. 4 Column from Kissengunge, and Nos. 1 and 2 Columns were halted at the Cabul Gate till Reid should appear advancing on the Lahore Gate from outside. During this time the enemy, finding they were not pressed, rallied in large numbers at the Burn Bastion, and on the tops of houses in rear of it; they also brought up two 6-pounder field guns to a spot half-way down the lane between the Burn Bastion and the Cabul Gate, placing one on the road and the other on the ramparts; a heavier gun (an 18-pounder) was also placed in position at the extreme end of the lane by the Lahore Gate (it was this gun that afterwards killed General Nicholson). As soon as the General found that Reid's Column (for reason then unknown) was not advancing, he ordered the wing of the 1st Fusiliers (now greatly reduced in numbers), and two very weak companies of the 75th Regt. in support, to storm the Burn Bastion and seize the Lahore Gate. This little force came under a heavy fire the moment they showed themselves in the lane from the two 6-pounder guns and an ever-increasing crowd of sepoys on the house-tops, for as the enemy came back from Kissengunge they collected at this spot. The two 6-pounders were taken with a rush. Colour-Sergt. Jordan and three men of the 1st Fusiliers ran up the slope on to the ramparts and spiked the one there by breaking off the tip of a ramrod into the vent-hole, and throwing the remaining part down to Capt. Greville, that officer spiked the gun in the lane in the same way. Sergt. Jordan escaped untouched, but the three men with him were all killed. The force now came under the fire of the 18-pounder at the far end of the lane, which poured round after round of grape into it with terrible effect. Major Jacob fell mortally wounded, Capt. Greville shot through the right shoulder; Lieut. Wemyss, the Adjutant, got a bullet through the leg, and in a very few minutes Lieuts. Butler and Speke were the only two officers left unwounded. Wemyss now called out to Butler to take the command, as he was the senior officer, and these two led the few men left as far as the Burn Bastion. Here a gigantic garzie (fanatic)—he must have been quite seven feet high—with a two-handed sword in his hands, rushed out on the soldiers. He struck at the nearest man with all his tremendous strength; but fortunately the sword twisted in his hands, and he only delivered the blow with the flat of the blade. This sent the soldier staggering against the wall, but before the garzie could recover himself he had four bayonets in his chest, and was still fighting when a bullet from the officer's pistol put an end to the struggle. Our men were now immediately in rear of the Burn Bastion, the floor of which was about twelve feet above the lane, on a level with the ramparts, and closed with a stone wall eight feet high at the gorge, all but a gateway of about ten feet wide, and loopholed onwards. There was a small recess below, where the men could obtain some shelter from the 18-pounder, and after a hasty consultation with Speke, Butler determined to take ten men up some stone steps just opposite, which led to the ramparts, and see if an entrance to the Burn Bastion could be effected from there, Speke remaining as much as possible under cover with the rest of the men till wanted; but when this small party reached the rampart, they found an iron-faced, bullet-proof door, used for closing the Bastion completely at the gorge, swung back right across the rampart, and as it protruded two feet beyond the wall, it was impossible to get round it. Butler now ordered the men to run down the steps as quickly as possible, for they were perceived by the enemy, and already a heavy fire of musketry was directed on them from the neighbouring house-tops; but when he himself went to move he found a bayonet thrust through the loopholes on each side of him; behind each bayonet was, of course, a loaded musket, so that to move either way seemed certain death, besides which the bullets were splashing against the wall like rain. Just at this moment he was felled to the ground by a heavy blow on the left side of the head from a large stone. Looking up, he saw a native standing on the wall above him in the act of receiving another large stone from a man inside the Bastion; but Butler pulled out his pistol and shot the native through the body before he could do any more mischief. This, however, did not remove the bayonets, so he jerked his pistol into the loophole on the left and fired. The bayonet disappeared and Butler ran down the steps. On arriving at the lane below, he found poor Speke mortally wounded, nearly half the men either killed or wounded, and feeling himself very sick from the effects of the blow on his head, he was on the point of giving the order to fall back on the Cabul Gate when he saw General Nicholson coming up the lane; so he ran down and hastily explained to him the position of affairs. Nicholson would not hear of retiring, and called on a few men who were sheltering in some shallow arches to advance, saying, 'I never knew British soldiers required to be told more than once to advance against the enemy,' but the next instant he was mortally wounded by a grape-shot which entered between his shoulders. With Nicholson's fall all attempt at storming the Burn Bastion that day was abandoned, and the men retired to the Cabul Gate. Eight or nine men of the 1st Fusiliers who went up this lane were either killed or wounded. Major Jacob's death was a terrible loss to the 1st Fusiliers; he was a man of extraordinary coolness under fire, as brave as a lion, yet as gentle as a woman, beloved by all the officers and men of his regiment, who would have done anything in the world for him, and followed him anywhere." In an account of the 1st Bengal Fusiliers in the Delhi Campaign, James Peter Brougham, Esq., M.D., says of this affair at the Burn Bastion: "At this place Lieut. Butler greatly distinguished himself, doing his utmost to encourage the men; and how he escaped with his life is a perfect marvel." Colonel P. R. Innes, in his "History of the Royal Munster Fusiliers," says that, at Lucknow, on 9 March, 1858, "General Outram now gave orders for a party of the 1st Bengal Fusiliers (now 1st Battn. Royal Munster Fusiliers) to retrograde along the river bank with some heavy guns, and, having reached the junction of the Gumti and the canal, to enfilade the enemy's batteries, which formed their first defence on the city side of the canal. The expedition was commanded by Major Nicholson of the Engineers. The infantry was under Capt. F. O. Salusbury." Here Dr. Brougham gives an account of Lieut. Butler's heroism: "They soon came to that part of the enemy's batteries which touched upon the river. Here the pandies had made a deep cut, communicating with the Goomtee and the canal, for a little below this point the Lucknow Canal runs into the river. The heavy guns were unloaded, and Major Nicholson, of the Royal Engineers, commenced his work, observing at the same time that the lines seemed deserted. Capt. Salusbury proposed getting boats and crossing a party of the 1st, but as Major Nicholson considered it might be hazardous to leave the guns, this was not done. Lieut. Butler, 1st Fusiliers, and four men, however, volunteered to go down to the river and call to the Highlanders, who were about six hundred yards on the other side. They reached the bank, but being unable to make the infantry hear, Lieut. Butler took off his coat and entered the stream, which runs there strongly, and is perhaps sixty yards wide, swam across, and entered the works from their rear; then, mounting the parapet, quickly attracted the attention of our troops. After a short delay a staff officer rode down to where Butler stood, and was informed as to the state of matters, and urged at once to send men to occupy the deserted batteries; he, however, seemed to consider that this would not be correct without having received orders, so cantered off for instructions. Meanwhile Butler began to feel rather uncomfortable; first, he was wet and cold, and next, he saw some natives, who, though distant, might return, and who, in fact, fired at him twice; lastly, although he had taken his fort, yet a garrison of one is rather a small force to hold even a strong place; moreover, he had no arms; he therefore began to telegraph again. This time a Highland officer advanced. He at once saw the importance of securing the fort, and ordered his company on without delay—the rest of the Highlanders and Sikhs following. Lieut. Butler, having thus delivered over his fort, again entered the river and swam safely to our side. This act speaks for itself, had a great object in view, and was well performed. It must not be fancied that because Butler was only fired at from a distance he therefore ran no risk; whoever has been at Lucknow knows the danger of entering seemingly deserted places. The party under Capt. Salusbury returned at night to the place where it bivouacked." Lord Roberts says, in "Forty-one Years in India" (page 223), of Butler's feat, that it was "successfully performed by the plucky young volunteer; he found the enemy had retired, and, on giving the information to Hope, the brigade advanced, and before nightfall the whole of the enemy's first line was in our possession—a success which had been achieved with but slight loss to us, the chief casualty during the day being William Peel, the gallant commander of the Naval Brigade, who had been seriously wounded while in command of a battery near the Dilkusha." In a letter written 11 Aug. 1857, by Major J. W. Daniell, Royal Munster Fusiliers, from the Camp, Delhi, is the following: "My chum Butler had a narrow escape; he was some way in front of his company when they charged, when all of a sudden two sepoys came upon him (not more than ten paces from him). One of them quietly raised his musket to take a shot at him, when Butler quietly pulled out his revolver and shot one through the heart." Major Daniell provided nearly all the material for this account of Major Butler. They were great chums and used to live together. The late Colonel Kendal Coghill, C.B., asked Major Daniell to help with this short biography of "dear little Tommy Butler, a great pal of mine." Colonel Coghill, C.B., who died 15 July, 1919, was in the Munster Fusiliers, and was transferred to the 19th (Queen Alexandra's Own) Hussars, of which regiment he became the Colonel. He helped a great deal with this book, and all his friends, who loved him very much, were glad to help with it for his sake, if for no other reason. Colonel David Johnston wrote out a great deal about the V.C.'s of the Royal Munster Fusiliers, and in many cases Colonel Innes's invaluable history of the regiment has been quoted. Lieut. Butler took part in the siege and capture of Lucknow, and for his services at that time, was awarded the Victoria Cross [London Gazette, 6 May, 1859]: "Thomas Adair Butler, Lieut., 1st Bengal European Fusiliers. Date of Act of Bravery: 9 March, 1858. Of which success the skirmishers on the other side of the river were subsequently apprised by Lieut. Butler, of the Bengal Fusiliers, who swam across the Goomtee, and, climbing the parapet, remained in that position for a considerable time under a heavy fire of musketry until the work was occupied." (Extract from Lieut.-General Sir James Outram's Memorandum of Operations at the Siege of Lucknow.) Lieut. Butler also took part in the subsequent operations in Oudh. He became Captain 16 Jan. 1863, and served in the North-West Frontier Campaign of that year, being present at the attack on the Crag Picket, Conical Hill and Umbeyla, and received the Medal with clasp for Umbeyla. In an old book of cuttings Major Daniell has an account of " The Deposition of the Colours of the 101st Regt. in Winchester Cathedral." The newspaper from which it is taken is dated 22 July, 1871: " Last Tuesday," says this newspaper, " our ancient city witnessed a novel and imposing ceremony—that of depositing the shot-torn colours of the 101st Regt. (Royal Bengal Fusiliers) within that magnificent pile which the citizens of no mean city delight to glory in. The question was naturally asked ' How came the regiment to select Winchester as a place to erect a memorial to its officers who had fallen in battle, and as a resting-place for their shredded banners ? ' We cannot answer this question thoroughly, but we have heard that Colonel Lambert and Capt. Butler, V.C., are both connected with the county. Indeed, the father of the latter was a well-known clergyman of the diocese, his mother belonged to an old county family, and his grandfather was fifty years a magistrate. But, if chance has brought these trophies here, surely no worthier place could be found for them, nor could more earnest desire to improve and render the occasion impressive have been shown. The guard of honour was under the command of Capt. T. A. Butler, V.C. The escort for the colours was formed and marched to the colours, the band preceding it playing ' The British Grenadiers.' It was halted a short distance from the colours, which were handed to the Sergt.-Major by General Warren (an officer who has seen the severest service and who has been wounded times almost innumerable), and Colonel Salusbury, C.B., who gave them to the ensigns (who saluted), and the escort and sentries then presented arms, the band playing ' God Save the Queen.' Arrived at the cathedral, the form of asking permission to deposit the colours was gone through; the two ensigns—Knight and Johnston—were most courteously received by the Rev. Canon Carus and the authorities and the Dean and Corporation. The Venerable Dean and the Vice-Dean received the colours, and Canon Carus preached the sermon. Among the officers connected with these colours, and was severely wounded while leading the storming party at Chusnee; Colonel Salusbury, C.B., who was shot while carrying the Queen's colour at Ferozeshuhur; Colonel Brown, severely wounded at Delhi; Colonel Lambert, then commanding the regiment; Major St. George, wounded at Lucknow; Major Parsons, Capt. Daniell and Capt. Ellis, who served with distinction at Delhi, and Capt. Butler, V.C. at Delhi." He retired with the rank of Honorary Major 30 Sept. 1874. Miss Butler says that he was of the most cheerfull and genial temperament and had many devoted friends. Another cousin, Capt. Sir Thomas Butler, K.C.V.O., says of Major Butler: " He wrote an account of the exploits of his regiment (not his own) in the ' United Service Magazine ' for Feb. 1893. Though I knew him very well, I never once heard him speak of what he had done himself. He was very fond of all sports." Thomas Adair Butler died at Yorktown on the 17th May, 1901, after a long illness, heart-disease, contracted in his younger days by strain from diving. His funeral took place at St. Michael's on the 20th of the month. The coffin was covered with the Union Flag, and among the many floral tributes was a wreath tied with the regimental colours, sent by the officers of his old battalion, who were represented by Lieut.-Colonel C. M. de Longueville (formerly of the regiment), Major S. T. Banning and Capt. E. D. Macpherson, who were at the time instructors at the Royal Military College.

" War Office, 27 May, 1859.—The Queen has been graciously pleased to signify her intention to confer the Decoration of the Victoria Cross on the undermentioned Non-commissioned Officers and Privates of Her Majesty's Army, whose claims to the same have been submitted for Her Majesty's approval, on account of Acts of Bravery performed by them in India, as recorded against their several names."

MURPHY, MICHAEL, Private (Farrier), served in the Indian Mutiny, and was awarded the Victoria Cross [London Gazette, 27 May, 1859]: " Michael Murphy, Private (Farrier), 2nd Battn. Military Train. Date of Act of Bravery: 15 April, 1858. For daring gallantry on the 15th April, 1858, when engaged in the pursuit of Koer Sing's army from Azimghur, in having rescued Lieut. Hamilton, Adjutant of the 3rd Sikh Cavalry, who was wounded, dismounted and surrounded by the enemy. Farrier Murphy cut down several men, and, although himself severely wounded, he never left Lieut. Hamilton's side until support arrived." Michael Murphy was afterwards Farrier-Major, 7th Hussars. He is thought to have died on the 5th March, 1872.

Alexander Thompson.

THOMPSON, ALEXANDER, L.-Corpl., served in the Mutiny, and was awarded

the Victoria Cross [London Gazette, 27 May, 1859]: " Alexander Thompson, L.-Corpl., 42nd Regt. Date of Act of Bravery: 15 April, 1858. For daring gallantry on the 15th April, 1858, when at the attack on the fort of Ruhya, in having volunteered to assist Capt. Cafe, commanding the 4th Punjab Rifles, in bringing in the body of Lieut. Willoughby, of that corps, from the top of the glacis, in a most exposed situation, under a heavy fire." Four men of the 42nd helped Capt. Cafe to bring in Lieut. Willoughby's body: L.-Corpl. Thompson and Private Cook (who were awarded the Victoria Cross), Private Spence, who was mortally wounded and was posthumously awarded the Victoria Cross many years afterwards, and Private Crowie, who possibly died soon afterwards; in any case, he did not receive the Cross. He was promoted to Sergeant. Sergt. Thompson died on the 29th March, 1880, at Perth.

SIMPSON, JOHN, Quartermaster-Sergt. (now Quartermaster), served with his regiment, the Black Watch (Royal Perth Rifles), in the Mutiny, and was awarded the Victoria Cross [London Gazette,

John Simpson.

27 May, 1859]: " John Simpson, Quartermaster-Sergt. (now Quartermaster), 42nd Regt. Date of Act of Bravery: 15 April, 1858. For conspicuous bravery at the attack on the fort of Ruhya on the 15th April, 1858, in having volunteered to go to an exposed point within forty yards of the parapet of the fort under a heavy fire, and brought in, first, Lieut. Douglas, and afterwards a private soldier, both of whom were dangerously wounded." He died at Perth on the 27th Oct. 1883.

James Davis.

DAVIS, JAMES, Private, was born in Edinburgh. He served in the Indian Mutiny, and was awarded the Victoria Cross [London Gazette, 27 May, 1859]: " James Davis, Private, 42nd Regt. Date of Act of Bravery: 15 April, 1858. For conspicuous gallantry at the attack on the fort of Ruhya, when, with an advanced party to point out the gate of the fort to the Engineer officer, Private Davis offered to carry the body of Lieut. Bramley, who was killed at this point, to the regiment. He performed the duty of danger and affection under the very walls of the fort." Private Davis also received the Crimean Medal, with clasps for Alma, Balaklava and Sebastopol. Private Davis died at Edinburgh early in March, 1893.

" War Office, 18 June, 1859.—The Queen has been graciously pleased to confirm the grant of the Victoria Cross to the undermentioned Officer of Her Majesty's Army, which Decoration has been provisionally conferred on him by the Commander-in-Chief in India, in accordance with the rules laid down in Her Majesty's Warrant instituting the same, for an Act of Bravery performed by him in that country, when serving under his personal command, as recorded against his name."

FARQUHARSON, FRANCIS EDWARD H., Lieut., was gazetted to the 42nd (the Royal Highland) Regt. of Foot, as Ensign, 19 Jan. 1855; became Lieutenant 24 April, 1855; served in the Siege of Sebastopol from 14 July, 1855 (Medal and clasp). He served in the Indian Mutiny, and was awarded the Victoria Cross [London Gazette, 21 June, 1859]: " Francis Edward Henry Farquharson, Lieut., 42nd Regt. Date of Act of Bravery: 9 March, 1858. For conspicuous bravery when engaged before Lucknow, on the 9th March, 1858, in having led a portion of his company, stormed a bastion mounting two guns, and spiked the guns, by which the advanced positions held during the night of the 9th March were rendered secure from the fire of artillery. Lieut. Farquharson was severely wounded while holding an advanced position on the morning of the 10th March." He also received the Medal and clasp for his services in the Mutiny Campaign, which included the actions of Kudygunge and Shumsabad, Siege and Fall of Lucknow, and Assault of the Martiniere and Banks's Bungalow. Lieut. Farquharson became Captain on the 28th June, 1862.

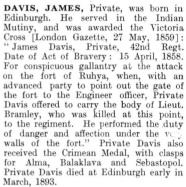

F. E. H. Farquharson.

London Gazette, 18 June, 1859.—" Her Majesty has been graciously pleased to signify her intention to confer the Decoration of the Victoria Cross on the undermentioned Officers and Privates of Her Majesty's Army and Indian Military Forces, whose claims to the same have been submitted for Her Majesty's approval, on account of Acts of Bravery performed by them in India, as recorded against their several names."

COOK, WALTER, Private, served with his regiment, the Black Watch, in the Mutiny, and was awarded the Victoria Cross [London Gazette, 21

June, 1859]: " Walter Cook, Private, 42nd Regt. Date of Act of Bravery : 15 Jan. 1859. At the action at Maylah Ghaut, on the 15th Jan. 1859, Brigadier-General Walpole reports that the conduct of Privates Cook and Miller deserves to be particularly pointed out. At the time the fight was the severest, and the few men of the 42nd Regt. were skirmishing so close to the enemy (who were in great numbers) that some of the men were wounded by sword-cuts, and the only officer of the 42nd was carried to the rear, severely wounded, and the colour-sergeant was killed, these soldiers went to the front, took a prominent part in directing the company, and displayed a courage, coolness and discipline which was the admiration of all who witnessed it."

MILLAR, DUNCAN, Private, served in the Indian Mutiny Campaign, and was awarded the Victoria Cross [London Gazette, 21 June, 1859] : " Walter Cook and Duncan Miller, Privates. Date of Act of Bravery : 15 Jan. 1859. In the action at Maylah Ghaut, on the 15th Jan. 1859, Brigadier-General Walpole reports that the conduct of Privates Cook and Miller deserves to be particularly pointed out. At the time the fight was the severest, and the few men of the 42nd Regt. were skirmishing so close to the enemy (who were in great numbers) that some of the men were wounded by sword-cuts, and the only officer of the 42nd was carried to the rear, severely wounded, and the colour-sergeant was killed, these men went to the front, took a prominent part in directing the company, and displayed a courage, coolness and discipline which was the admiration of all who witnessed it." Private D. Millar died on the 7th July, 1881.

Duncan Millar.

CUBITT, WILLIAM GEORGE, Lieut., was born on 19 Oct. 1836 ; the son of Major William Cubitt, the Hon. East India Company's Service, and Harriet Harcourt. He was educated privately, and entered the 13th Bengal Native Infantry (now the 16th Lucknow Regt.) in 1853. He served in the Santhal Campaign, after which he went through the Mutiny. He took part in the defence of the Residency, was wounded, mentioned in Despatches, and received the Medal with clasp, and was awarded the Victoria Cross for saving the lives of three men of the Duke of Cornwall's Light Infantry, during the retreat after the action of Chinhut [London Gazette, 21 June, 1859] : " William George Cubitt, Lieut., 13th Bengal Native Infantry. Date of Act of Bravery : 30 June, 1857. For having on the retreat from Chinhut, on the 30th June, 1857, saved the lives of three men of the 32nd Regt. at the risk of his own." He was promoted Captain in 1865 ; served in the Duffla Expedition of 1874, and was mentioned in Despatches. In 1879 he became Lieutenant-Colonel ; served in the Afghan War of 1878-80, but was invalided from Ali Musjid in the hot weather of 1880, and nearly succumbed to a very serious illness, the result of blood-poisoning, while quartered at Ali Musjid. He was promoted to Colonel in 1883 ; served in the Akka Expedition of 1885 (Despatches). Colonel Cubitt served through the Burma War of 1887, and for his services in this campaign was created a Companion of the Distinguished Service Order [London Gazette, 11 Sept. 1903] : " William George Cubitt, V.C., Lieut.-Colonel, Bengal Staff Corps." Colonel Cubitt married, in Fort William, Calcutta, Miss Charlotte Isabella Hills, daughter of James Hills, Esq., of Neechindapur, Bengal, whose second son was General Sir James Hills-Johnes, V.C., G.C.B. Their surviving children are : Major William Martin Cubitt, born 13 June, 1864 ; James Edward Cubitt, born 6 Oct. 1865 : Ethel Mary (married), and Helen Anne Thomas (married). Lewis Hills Cubitt, born 20 Sept. 1872, died 1 July, 1911. Colonel Cubitt retired from the Army in 1891. He died at Camberley on the 23rd Jan. 1903, and was buried at Frimley.

William George Cubitt.

SPENCE, EDWARD, Private (deceased), 42nd Regt., would have been recommended to Her Majesty for the Decoration of the Victoria Cross had he survived. He and L.-Corpl. Thompson of that regiment volunteered at the attack on the fort of Ruhya, on the 15th April, 1858, to assist Capt. Cafe, commanding the 4th Punjab Rifles, in bringing in the body of Lieut. Willoughby from the top of the glacis. Private Spence dauntlessly placed himself in an exposed position, so as to cover the party bearing away the body. He died on the 17th of the same month from the effects of the wound which he received on the occasion [London Gazette, 18 June, 1859].

Hanson C. T. Jarrett.

JARRETT, HANSON CHAMBERS TAYLOR, Lieut., was born on 2 March, 1837, in Madras, India ; son of Thomas Jarrett, Esq., Barrister, and Eliza Julia Chambers, daughter of Capt. Chambers, 86th Foot. He was educated at Prior Park College, near Bath, and joined the 26th Bengal Infantry, the Honourable East India Company's Army, as Ensign 10 June, 1854, becoming Lieutenant on the 27th Aug. 1857. He served in the Indian Mutiny, and received the Medal and the Victoria Cross [London Gazette, 18 June, 1859]: " Hanson Chambers Taylor Jarrett, Lieut., 26th Bengal Native Infantry. Date of Act of Bravery : 14 Oct. 1858. For an act of daring bravery at the village, of Baroun on the 14th Oct. 1858, on an occasion when about seventy sepoys were defending themselves in a brick building, the only approach to which was up a very narrow street, in having called on the men of his regiment to follow him, when, backed by only some four men, he made a dash at the narrow entrance, where, though a shower of balls were poured on him, he pushed his way up to the wall of the house, and beating up the bayonets of the rebels with his sword, endeavoured to get in." He was promoted to Captain, Bengal Staff Corps, 10 June, 1866, and Major 10 June, 1874, and subsequently Colonel Jarrett married on the 26th March, 1890, in Allahabad Cathedral, India, Nina Louise, daughter of Théfield Joseph de Dombasle, of Nancy, and of Margaret Ellen Turner, of London. He died on the 11th April, 1890. Colonel Jarrett was a very great sportsman and big-game hunter, and kept a record of all his kills, and it was owing to his love of sport that he joined the Forest Department a few years before his death.

M'GOVERN, JOHN, Private, was a native of Templeport, County Cavan, and a labourer by trade. He enlisted at Limerick for the Company's service for ten years on the 18th Nov. 1845, and sailed for India in the troopship Cressy, where he arrived on the 11th Sept. 1846. M'Govern was " always in trouble " until he won the Victoria Cross. This tempestuous Irishman served in the Burmese War, 1852–53, receiving the Medal with a clasp for Pegu. He served in the Indian Mutiny, " and," says the " Munster Fusiliers' Regimental Annual " for 1912 (page 44), " really won the V.C. twice over, as at the Battle of Narkoul, on 16 Dec. 1857, three sepoys took refuge in a small turret, and there was much difficulty in dislodging them, and orders were given to the sergeant-major to do this. Private M'Govern was standing near when this order was given, and volunteered to go himself, and went up the staircase. The sergeant-major was then told to send at least half a dozen men, but replied, ' Never mind, sir ; he'll be no loss.' M'Govern heard this, and determined to do the work himself. He mounted the narrow staircase, and reached the top of the wall, where the sepoys were waiting for him. They fired at once, but M'Govern, jumping down a couple of steps, escaped unhurt, and then, before they could reload, shot the man in front, and rushing upon the other two, bayoneted them without giving them time to recover." " Jock " M'Govern's Victoria Cross was gazetted on 18 June, 1859 : " John M'Govern, No. 95, Private, 1st Bengal Fusiliers. Date of Act of Bravery : 23 June, 1857. For gallant conduct during the operations before Delhi, but more especially on the 23rd June, 1857, when he carried into camp a wounded comrade under heavy fire from the enemy's battery at the risk of his own life." Afterwards M'Govern was a changed man, and did not get into trouble for drinking and fighting in camp, and one thing and another, as he had done before. He " wouldn't disgrace the Victoria Cross." For his services in the Indian Mutiny Private M'Govern also gained the Medal, with clasps for Delhi and Lucknow. He transferred to the 101st Fusiliers on the 1st Bengal Fusiliers being transferred to Her Majesty's service in 1861, but remained " local in India." When one of the officers asked him if he meant to go into the line or remain " local in India," M'Govern replied that he was going to stay in India. " I should have thought," said the officer, " that you'd have been one of the first to go." No," said Jock, " what'd I be doing in the line with this arm ? " He had had his arm badly wounded some time before. He lived till the early part of the year 1891, for his name appears in the list of surviving holders of the V.C. in the Quarterly Army List for January of that year, but not in the list for the April quarter. M'Govern's name is spelt M'Gauran in the regimental roll at the India Office and in the Army List. The accepted pronunciation of his patronymic seems to have been " Maggoverran." Colonel David Johnston, late Royal Munster Fusiliers, writes : " Private M'Govern was known for his bravery all through the Army in India, and performed many deeds for which, had he not already possessed it, he would have won the soldier's most coveted decoration. His deeds are described in Colonel Munro's beautiful history of the regiment. Private M'Govern, who had already won the Victoria Cross for distinguished bravery on 23 June, 1859, was a well-known character in his regiment, his reckless, dare-devil acts being the talk of the Army. Only about five years ago this man's Cross and War Medals and discharge certificate, which at some time or other were no doubt pawned for a mere song, were sold by public auction, and purchased for eighty pounds by the officers of the regiment. They are now exhibited in a case in the officers' mess, and treasured with this grand soldier's memory. I hope, when Colonel Munro's interesting book is read, people will not be unjust, but will remember that the noblest men have their failings, and that M'Govern joined in days when drinking to excess was much resorted to, and not alone by one class. Did I know where this man was buried and if it were within reach, I should deem it an honour to place flowers on his grave."

" War Office, 6 July, 1859.—The Queen, having been graciously pleased by warrant under Her Royal Sign Manual bearing date 13 Dec. 1858, to declare that Non-Military persons who, as Volunteers, have borne arms against Mutineers, both at Lucknow and elsewhere, during the late operations in India, shall be considered eligible to receive the Decoration of the Victoria Cross, subject to rules and ordinances already made and ordained for the government thereof, provided that it be established in any case that the person was serving under the orders of a General or other officer in command of Troops in the Field when he performed the Act of Bravery for which it is proposed to confer the Decoration, Her Majesty has accordingly been pleased to signify her intention to confer this high distinction on the undermentioned Gentlemen, whose claims to the same have been submitted for Her Majesty's approval, on account of Acts of Bravery performed by them in India, as recorded against their names."

KAVANAGH, THOMAS HENRY, was born at Mullingar, County Westmeath, on 15 July, 1821. He was educated in Ireland and joined the Indian Civil Service about 1849; went out to Oudh in 1849 with Sir Henry Lawrence; became a member of the Punjab Commission; went to Lucknow with Sir Henry Lawrence, and was there at the time of the Indian Mutiny. He had married Agnes Mary Courtney. Mr. Kavanagh wrote in his diary: "My family were staying in Cawnpore, and it was arranged they should spend the summer there with some friends, as houses were difficult to get in Lucknow then; but Providence willed that my wife should differ with some people under the same roof, and she at once came to me at Lucknow. Thank God she did." Mrs. McMinn, Mr. Kavanagh's daughter, writes: "My father had fourteen children, and my mother and the four eldest children were in the Residency—Baron, Blanche, Kathleen and Cecil (who died in the Residency as a baby). My mother was also wounded by a shell in the Residency and had wound-money." Kathleen (Mrs. Haynes) was at the time about two and a half to three years old. The Residency at Lucknow was besieged from the 30th June, 1857, by mutineers and rebels in the proportion of thirty to one of the defenders. Generals Outram and Havelock, with over 2,000 troops, fought their way through the city on the 26th Sept., intending to rescue the garrison and return to Cawnpore. But they, too, were surrounded, and obliged to defend themselves in places adjoining the Residency Entrenchment, and on reduced rations both forces subsisted on the provisions of the original garrison, as the Generals had brought none. The situation had become very critical by November, and if the relief coming down from Cawnpore was to be successful, it must be sure and speedy, as provisions and ammunition would have run out in a few days. Mr. Kavanagh was at the time thirty-six years old, a tall man, with a fair complexion and blue eyes. His hair was auburn in colour, and he wore a short beard. He thought over the state of affairs, and decided in his own mind that the early success of the relieving force would be assured if the Commander-in-Chief had a guide in whom he could repose confidence and who was conversant with the city and its environment. He therefore volunteered, on 9 Nov., to leave the defences to convey information to Sir Colin Campbell and help him as his guide. Mr. Kavanagh wrote himself: "Sir James Outram and Colonel Napier were much against my going, but Sir James Outram—as I disclosed my reasons for wishing to go out, and figuratively placed them in one hand and my life in the other, and asked whether the advantages were not weighty enough to overbalance his scruple to adventure a single life—was not less astonished than Colonel Napier; but in the true spirit of chivalry he at once conceived and appreciated the motives of my proposition, and reasoned with me upon the probability of success. He frankly confessed he thought it of the utmost importance that a European officer acquainted with the localities and buildings intervening between Dilkooshah and the Residency should be provided to guide the relieving force, should its commander determine on advancing by that route; but that the impossibility of any European being able to escape through the city undetected, deterred him from ordering any officer to go, or even seeking volunteers for such a duty. He observed that my services as a guide would be very valuable, and that he, therefore, with difficulty resisted the temptation to accept my disinterested offer, of which he thought he ought to avail himself. I was, however, so earnest in my entreaties to be allowed to go, that he yielded, provided he was satisfied with the disguise and that I was of the same mind when the hour for departure arrived. After Sir James had explained to me his plans and the course which he advised Sir Colin Campbell to follow, he pressed me not to hesitate to abandon the adventure if I wished to do so on further consideration. The friends of that able officer will understand how his chivalrous and generous heart suffered while doubtful of the fate of 'the guide' who deemed it no small honour to be engaged in executing his plan for the relief of the Lucknow garrison. Next came the parting from my dear wife and children (they did not then know what I was going to do). I was accustomed to kiss my family at six o'clock and go on duty in the mines, and I told them I might be detained till late in the morning. I carried my bundle of clothes that I had collected from different natives to a small room in the slaughter-fold, and was then dressed by that good, steady young man, Mr. Quieros, whom I enjoined to keep it a secret for the present. I was amused at my own ugliness, as I carefully surveyed each feature in the glass to see that the colouring was well spread, a dye I had procured. I did not think the shade of black quite natural, and I felt somewhat uneasy about it till we talked over the chances of detection, and came to the conclusion that the darkness of the night was favourable to me. 'Kanonjee Lal,' my native guide, now joined me, and seemed to chuckle at the ridiculous appearance of the metamorphosed Sahib as we walked over together to the quarters of Sir James Outram. Natives are not permitted to go into the house of a European with shoes on, nor to take a seat uninvited. In order to draw particular attention to myself I did both, and the eyes of the officers, who sat at the General's table, were at once turned angrily and inquiringly upon the queer man who did such impudent things. Questions and answers were exchanged without detecting the disguise, although my plain features were known to every one of the outraged officers, who called in the General, and he took some time to recognize me. I regarded this first step in the adventure as presaging success, and was glad to lay hold on any little thing to keep up my confidence. I was daubed once more by the General himself with a burnt cork and oil, and considering where I was going to there was extraordinary hilarity in the whole proceeding, which was most beneficial to my nerves. My turban was readjusted, my habiliments subjected to a close inspection, and my waistband adorned by a loaded double-barrelled pistol (belonging to the gallant, amiable Capt. Sitwell, A.D.C.), which was intended for myself should there be no possibility of escaping death at the hands of the mutineers, who would have done it in their own particular way. At half-past eight o'clock our gaiety ceased, for that was the time appointed to leave. The kind-hearted and chivalrous Sir James and my good friend Colonel Napier pressed my hand, with a few encouraging words. The rest, with many earnest prayers for my success, shook hands, and I started with Kanonjee Lal in the company of brave Capt. Harding, who came down to the picquet on the River Goomtee to pass me out. As I parted from him he tightly squeezed my hand, as if much affected, and slowly observed that he would give his life to perform what I was doing." Mr. Kavanagh left the Residency after dark on 9 Nov., and walked nearly fifteen miles past houses and through fields. He was accompanied by Misqua Kanonjee Lal, a Brahmin, and Mr. Kavanagh attributed much of the success of the exploit to the courage and intelligence of this devoted servant of the Government. They were twice stopped by mutineers, but managed to satisfy their curiosity without exciting their suspicions. By midday on 10 Nov. a message was sent to Sir James Outram from the Alambagh (a fortified garden nearly two miles outside the city) by a semaphore on the roof of the garden-house, informing him of the safe arrival of Mr. Kavanagh, and his wife was then, for the first time, told of his escape. On the afternoon of 17 Nov. Mr. Kavanagh ran alone in advance of the relieving force to the nearest post of the Residency, and led over Sir James Outram, through the fire of the enemy, to Sir Colin Campbell, when the two Generals met for the first time in their lives and in the din of war, and the besieged were saved. Sir Colin Campbell acknowledged Mr. Kavanagh's services thus: "This escape at a time when the entrenchment was closely invested by a large army and communication, even through natives, was almost impossible, is, in Sir Colin Campbell's opinion, one of the most daring feats ever attempted, and the result was most beneficial, for in the immediate subsequent advance on Lucknow of a force under the Commander-in-Chief's directions, the thorough acquaintance with the localities possessed by Mr. Kavanagh and his knowledge of the approaches to the British position were of the greatest use; and his Excellency desires to record his obligations to this gentleman, who accompanied him throughout the operations, and was ever present to afford valuable information." He was awarded the Victoria Cross [London Gazette, 6 July, 1859]: "Thomas Henry Kavanagh, Assistant Commissioner, in Oudh, Bengal Civil Service. Date of Act of Bravery: 9 Nov. 1857. On the 9th Nov. 1857, Mr. Kavanagh, then serving under the orders of Lieut.-General Sir James Outram, in Lucknow, volunteered on the dangerous duty of proceeding through the city to the camp of the Commander-in-Chief, for the purpose of guiding the relieving force to the beleaguered garrison in the Residency—a task which he performed with the most chivalrous gallantry and devotion." A water-colour drawing of Mr. Kavanagh in his disguise was presented to the N.W.P. and Oudh Museum at Lucknow by his son, Hope Kavanagh, Esq., District Superintendent of Allahabad. The Victoria Cross was presented to Mr. Kavanagh by Queen Victoria on 4 Jan. 1860. He had also the Medal for the Relief and Siege of Lucknow—two bars. He died at Gibraltar on the 11th Nov. 1882.

Thomas H. Kavanagh.

MANGLES, ROSS LOWIS, was born at Calcutta 14 April, 1833; the son of R. D. Mangles, Esq. (Member of the Bengal Civil Service, and after his retirement M.P. for Guildford, and a Director of the Old East India Company). He was educated at Bath Grammar School, and at Haileybury College, entering the Bengal Civil Service in 1853. In 1857 he was Assistant Magistrate at Patna, accompanying the 45th (Rattray's) Sikhs in quelling a disturbance in Patna City, subsequently joining the Arrah Relief Force as a volunteer. Fifteen Europeans and fifty of Rattray's Sikhs were holding out in Arrah against 4,000 mutineers. The Relief Force fell into an ambush on the night of 29 July, 1857, and lost 300 of the 450 men. A retreat was made next morning in blazing sunshine and under a terrible fire from the sepoys. At the first attack Mr. Mangles was wounded, but, regardless of that, he helped the surgeon to look after the injured men, and fetched water for them. "In the flower of his youth" ("Kaye's Sepoy War"), "a man of fine presence, with a long stride and a firm hand on his two-barrel, our men looked to him as one, who, though without official command, had natural right to be obeyed." He was a splendid shot, and from his post he kept up a hot fire on the enemy while several men kept him supplied with loaded muskets. During the retreat Richard Taylor, a soldier of the 37th, had been wounded, and implored Mangles not to leave him to the tender mercies of the enemy. Under a hail of lead the civilian bound up the soldier's wounds, and for six miles he carried him over swampy ground, harassed by the pursuing enemy, until at last he got him into a boat. The soldier told the surgeon who attended to him, and more than a year afterwards Sir James Outram told Lord Canning about it, and finally Mr. Mangles was given the Victoria Cross, after the Warrant of the decoration had been altered to include

Ross Lowis Mangles.

civilians [London Gazette, 6 July, 1859]: "Mr. Ross Lewis Mangles, of the Bengal Civil Service, Assistant Magistrate at Patna. Date of Act of Bravery : 30 July, 1857. Mr. Mangles volunteered and served with the force consisting of detachments of Her Majesty's 10th and 37th Regts. and some native troops, despatched to the Relief of Arrah, in July, 1857, under the command of Capt. Dunbar, of the 10th Regt. The force fell into an ambuscade on the night of the 29th July, 1857, and during the retreat on the next morning Mr. Mangles, with signal gallantry and general self-devotion, and notwithstanding that he had himself been previously wounded, carried for several miles out of action a wounded soldier of Her Majesty's 37th Regt., after binding up his wounds under a murderous fire, which killed or wounded almost the whole detachment, and he bore him in safety to the boat." He received his Cross from Queen Victoria, at Windsor Castle, on 4 Jan. 1860. Immediately after the retreat the sepoys were driven out of Arrah and Behar by Sir Vincent Eyre. Mr. Mangles was then appointed Magistrate in the Chumparan District, North Behar, being engaged there in procuring supplies and carriage for the Gurkhas under Jung Bahadur, who had marched down from Nepal to our assistance. Early in 1858 Mr. Mangles held the station of Jenan in the Churpah District until the sepoys under the Koer Singh returned to Behar, upon which, having only a guard of a few native police armed with swords, he escaped from one end of the station as the rebels came in at the other, and after a ride of forty miles reached Churpah in safety. He later held the appointments of Commissioner of Revenue and Circuit in several districts of Bengal ; Judicial Commissioner of Mysore and Coorg in Madras ; Secretary to the Government of Bengal and Member of the Board of Revenue, Lower Provinces. Mr. Mangles died at Pirbright, 28 Feb. 1905, aged 71. His eldest surviving son is Major Walter James Mangles, D.S.O.

London Gazette, 2 Sept. 1859.—" The Queen has been graciously pleased to signify her intention to confer the Victoria Cross on the undermentioned Officer and Private of Her Majesty's Army, whose claims to the same have been submitted for Her Majesty's approval, on account of Acts of Bravery performed by them in India, as recorded against their names."

BOGLE, ANDREW CATHCART, Lieut., was born 20 Jan. 1829 ; the son of Archibald Bogle, Esq., of Gilmore Hill, Glasgow, N.B. He was educated at Cheltenham College, where he was Head of the Modern Side in June, 1847, and was in the Cricket Eleven in 1845–46–47. He entered the 78th Highlanders as an Ensign on 28 Dec. 1849, and was transferred to the 78th Regt. in 1850. On 18 March, 1853, he was promoted Lieutenant. Lieut. Bogle served in the Persian War of 1856–57, including the bombardment of Mohumrah. For his services in this campaign he received the Persian Medal with clasp. Lieut. Bogle served in Bengal with Havelock's Column from its first taking the field in 1857, including the actions of Futtehpore, Aoung, Pandoo-Nuddee, Cawnpore, Oonao and Buseerut. He was present at Cawnpore under Windham when attacked by the Gwalior Mutineers ; served as Adjutant to the regiment in the force under Outram at Alumbagh, including the repulse

Andrew Cathcart Bogle.

of the numerous attacks, and also in the operations ending in the final capture of Lucknow. He served in Rohilcund in 1858, under Lord Clyde, and at the action of Bareilly. The gates of Oonao were blown in under Havelock by the 78th Regt., and it was then that Lieut. Bogle got together a few men and stormed a contested passage. He thus opened the way for the force to advance, being himself severely wounded. He was mentioned in Despatches ; was shortly afterwards promoted Captain, and subsequently received the Victoria Cross [London Gazette, 2 Sept. 1859] : " Bogle, Lieut. (now Capt.) Andrew Cathcart, The 78th Regt. (Seaforth Highlanders), now of the 2nd Battn. 73rd Regt. Date of Act of Bravery : 29 July, 1857. For conspicuous gallantry on the 29th July, 1857, in the attack on Oonao, in leading the way into a loopholed house, strongly occupied by the enemy, from which a heavy fire harassed the advance of his regiment. Capt. Bogle was severely wounded in this important service." He received the Mutiny Medal with clasp. Lieut. Bogle became Captain 31 Aug. 1858, and Adjutant in the same year, and was transferred to the 13th Foot, and in 1859 to the 10th Foot. He became Major 25 April, 1865, and was Major on half-pay in 1865 ; was appointed to the 23rd Foot in 1868, and retired from the Army in 1868. After twenty-five years' retirement, Major Bogle died at Sherborne House, Dorset, on 11 Dec. 1890, after a long illness.

ADDISON, HENRY, Private, enlisted in the 43rd (Monmouthshire) Light Infantry (now the 1st Battn. The Oxford-shire and Buckinghamshire Light Infantry), and served in the Indian Mutiny. In 1858 the rebel Rajput Chief, Koer Singh, though defeated, made his way with a small force towards Rewah. He hoped to make his way to Upper India, or even Delhi, and render assistance to the besieged. The Political Agent at this time was Lieut. Willoughby Osborne, and he and Lieut.-Colonel Hinde, who commanded the Rewah Contingent, so influenced the Rajah of Rewah that he refused to allow

Henry Addison.

the rebel force to traverse the country, and Koer Singh had to abandon the attempt. It was in the following year that Private H. Addison was awarded the Victoria Cross [London Gazette, 2 Sept. 1859] : " Henry Addison, Private, The 43rd Regt. Date of Act of Bravery : 2 Jan. 1859. Near Kurrereah, in defending against a large force and saving the life of Lieut. Osborne, Political Agent, who had fallen on the ground wounded. Private Addison received two dangerous wounds and lost a leg in this gallant service."

London Gazette, 21 Oct. 1859.—" The Queen has been graciously pleased to signify her intention to confer the Decoration of the Victoria Cross on the undermentioned Officers and Private Soldier of Her Majesty's Indian Military Forces, whose claims to the same have been submitted for Her Majesty's approval, on account of Acts of Bravery performed by them in India, as recorded against their several names."

GOUGH, CHARLES JOHN STANLEY, Major, belonged to a family whose name has long held a place of honour in the annals of the British Army. His grandfather was Thomas Bunbury Gough, Dean of Derry

Charles John S. Gough.

(brother of the first Viscount Gough), who married Charlotte, daughter of Mr. John Bloomfield and sister of Lieut.-General Lord Bloomfield. He was thus a brother of the late General Sir Hugh Gough, V.C., and a second cousin of Viscount Gough. Charles John Stanley Gough was born on 28 Jan. 1832, and at the age of 16 he went to India, where he was posted to the 8th Bengal Cavalry. He was fortunate enough to arrive in time to take part in the Punjab Campaign of 1848–49, in which he served throughout, including the action of Ram-nuggur, the passage of the Chenab, and the battles of Sadoolapur, Chillianwalla and Goojerat. For these services he received the Medal with two clasps ; but it was eight years later, on the outbreak of the Indian Mutiny, that he was destined to come prominently into notice. Proceeding with the Indian Corps to join the Army which had been hastily gathered together to effect the capture of Delhi, " he and his brother were immediately recognized as two of the most brilliant of the younger generation of cavalry leaders, of which Hodson, of Hodson's Horse, became the best known." In the continual actions in which his regiment was engaged before the stronghold of the Mutineers was successfully assaulted, Charles Gough's reputation increased day by day, and his name often appeared in Despatches. Transferred to Hodson's Irregular Horse, he accompanied, a few weeks later, Sir Colin Campbell's Force in the Second Relief of Lucknow, and, mentioned three times more in Despatches, his services were acknowledged in General Orders by the Governor-General in Council. He returned to Cawnpur ; he was present in the operations in that district, whence his regiment was sent to reinforce Sir James Outram at the Alambagh, and during one of the many attacks on this position he was wounded, but not seriously enough to prevent him from taking part in the final siege and capture of Lucknow. For his gallant and distinguished services rendered during the campaign he received the Medal with two clasps, a Brevet Majority, and the Victoria Cross [London Gazette, 21 Oct. 1859] : " Charles John Stanley Gough, Major, 5th Bengal European Cavalry. Dates of Acts of Bravery : 15 Aug. 1857 ; 18 Aug. 1857 ; 27 Jan, 1858 ; 23 Feb. 1858. First, for gallantry in an affair at Khurkowdah, near Rohtuck, on the 15th Aug. 1857, in which he saved his brother, who was wounded, and killed two of the enemy. Secondly, for gallantry on the 18th Aug., when he led a troop of the Guide Cavalry in a charge and cut down two of the enemy's sowars, with one of whom he had a desperate hand-to-hand combat. Thirdly, for gallantry on the 27th Jan. 1858, at Shumshahbad, where, in a charge, he attacked one of the enemy's leaders, and pierced him with his sword, which was carried out of his hand in the mêlée. He defended himself with his revolver, and shot two of the enemy. Fourthly, for gallantry on the 23rd Feb., at Meangunge, where he came to the assistance of Brevet Major O. H. St. George Anson, and killed his opponent, immediately afterwards cutting down another of the enemy in the same gallant manner." Except that he took part in the Expedition to Bhootan in 1864 (Medal and clasp), Major Gough had no further opportunity for distinguishing himself until the outbreak of the Afghan War in 1878, by which time he had reached the rank of Colonel. During the first phase of the campaign which ended with the peace of Gandamak, he commanded a cavalry brigade in the Peshawar Valley Field Force, under Lieut.-General Sir Samuel Browne, and took part in the operations in this area, including the attack on Ali Musjid. He was in command at the engagement at Futteabad, and was subsequently mentioned in Despatches. After the massacre of the British Mission at Kabul, hostilities were resumed, and Colonel Gough was given command of the 1st Brigade of the force with which Major General R. O. Bright held the Khyber lines of communication, and from his position in advance it fell to his share to join hands with General Macpherson, who was operating from Kabul. When this was accomplished Colonel Gough returned to Gandamak, and took part in the subsequent fighting under Sir Frederick Roberts until he was ordered in Dec. 1879, to advance once more to Kabul, which he did, and thus effected a junction between the Khyber and Kurram divisions. For the rest of the winter and until the end of the campaign he took part in the continuous fighting round Kabul. For his services in this campaign he received the Medal with two clasps and a K.C.B. Soon after his return to India he was given command of the Hyderabad Contingent, which he held until his promotion to Major-

General in 1885, after which for the next five years he commanded a first-class district in Bengal, which brought to a close his active career. He became Lieut.-General in 1889, and General two years afterwards, and in 1895 he was placed on the Unemployed Supernumerary List, in which year he was also created a G.C.B. He had also a reward for distinguished service; was Honorary Colonel of the 5th Cavalry (Indian Army) and of the Tipperary Royal Field Reserve Artillery. After his retirement Sir Charles Gough lived in Ireland the life of a country gentleman, and until his health broke down he hunted regularly. He sometimes wrote letters to the "Times" on national defence and on Indian affairs, and in 1897, with Mr. Arthur Innes as a collaborator, he published a book called "The Sikhs and the Sikh Wars." It described the rise, conquest and annexation of the Punjab State. His ability and personal knowledge of the subject received added weight from his access to the diary and memoranda of the first Lord Gough, which dealt more especially with the campaigns of 1846 and 1848. Sir Charles married, in 1869, Harriette, daughter of the late Mr. J. W. Power, M.P., and he was survived by two sons: General H. de la P. Gough and the late General J. E. Gough, V.C. He died on 6 Sept. 1912, at Innislonagh, Clonmel, in his 81st year.

SHEBBEARE, ROBERT HAYDON, Brevet Capt., served in the Indian Mutiny, and was awarded the Victoria Cross [London Gazette, 21 Oct. 1859]: "Robert Haydon Shebbeare, Brevet Capt., 60th Bengal Native Infantry. Date of Act of Bravery: 14 Sept. 1857. For distinguished gallantry at the head of the Guides with the 4th Column of Assault at Delhi on the 14th Sept. 1857, when, after twice charging beneath the wall of the loopholed serai, it was found impossible, owing to the murderous fire, to attain the breach. Capt. (then Lieut.) Shebbeare endeavoured to reorganize the men, but one-third of the Europeans having fallen, his efforts to do so failed. He then conducted the rearguard of the retreat across the canal most successfully. He was most miraculously preserved through the affair, but yet left the field with one bullet through his cheek and a bad scalp-wound along the back of the head from another." Capt. Shebbeare was killed in the China War of 1860.

CLOGSTOUN, HERBERT MACKWORTH, Capt., served in the Indian Mutiny, and was awarded the Victoria Cross [London Gazette, 21 Oct. 1859]: "Herbert Mackworth Clogstoun, Capt., 19th Madras Native Infantry. Date of Act of Bravery: 15 Jan, 1859. For conspicuous bravery in charging the rebels into Chichumbah with only eight men of his regiment (the 2nd Cavalry Hyderabad Contingent), compelling them to re-enter the town, and finally to abandon their plunder. He was severely wounded himself, and lost seven out of the eight men who accompanied him." Major Clogstoun died in 1861. His daughter Mary married, in 1881, Sir Elwin M. Palmer, K.C.B., K.C.M.G., Governor of the National Bank of Egypt.

LYSTER, HARRY HAMMON, Lieut., was born at Blackrock, County Dublin, 25 Dec. 1830, and baptized at Monkstown. He was the son of Anthony Lyster, Esq., of Stillorgan Park, Dublin, and Marcia Deborah Tate, 6th daughter of James Tate, Esq., of Ballintaggart, County Wicklow, by his wife, Maria Stratford, of Belan, County Kildare, whose father was John, 3rd Earl of Aldborough. Harry Hammon Lyster served as a Special Constable in 1847 in London during the time of the Chartist Riots. At the age of seventeen and nine months he entered the Army, receiving a commission in the Honourable East India Company's Army 20 Sept. 1848. Before he sailed for India his father took him to Wilkinson's in London to buy a sword. They could not make up their minds which one they would have, when a gentleman who was in the shop stepped forward and said to Mr. Lyster: "I think I can assist you in the choice of your son's sword. I am a good judge of swords." They took the sword chosen by the stranger, who turned out to be the Prince Napoleon, afterwards the Emperor Napoleon III. Lyster arrived in India 9 Nov. 1848, and was posted to do duty with the 48th Native Infantry. After a few months he was appointed to the 72nd Bengal Native Infantry, then on active service in the Punjab, at the Siege of Mooltan, but he was made to stay at Meerut by the General in command there, because young officers were not permitted to join a regiment on active service. He was therefore not allowed to join his regiment till it returned from service. He served with the 72nd Bengal Native Infantry for seven years, becoming Lieutenant 23 Nov. 1856, afterwards dated 13 Nov. 1854. He served on the staff of General Sir Hugh Rose (afterwards Lord Strathnairn), commanding the Central India Field Force, as Interpreter and A.D.C. throughout the whole of the Central India Campaign, from Dec. 1857, to June, 1858. He took part in the siege and capture of the fort of Rathgurh and the repulse of the rebels when attacking the camp during the siege in the action of Baroda. In the last-named affair the native cavalry were commanded by the nephew of Mahomed Fazie Khan. Sir Hugh Rose had a bodyguard of a troop of Hyderabad Cavalry, and as they had no European officer with them, he ordered Lieut. Lyster to take command and to advance against the enemy, who were by this time retreating. Lyster ordered the cavalry to charge, leading them himself, but except for a native officer no man charged. Lyster dashed through the enemy's rearguard, killed three men, and had his horse wounded by a sword-cut on the off side and his bridle cut through on that side. He called to the native officer and told him to charge through, but the latter stopped to fight, and was cut to pieces. Then Lyster saw the enemy's cavalry at some distance off and stopped, when the rebel commander advanced, brandishing his sword, and left his men at the halt. As Lyster took this to be a challenge to single combat he advanced also; they both met at a gallop, and Lyster thrust his sword through his adversary's body, killing him, himself receiving a wound in the right arm. The enemy's cavalry then turned and fled. Lyster rode back, had his wound dressed, and rejoined Sir H. Rose. This fight was specially mentioned by Sir Hugh Rose in his Despatches. Lyster was present at the taking of Baroda and at the forcing of Muddinpoor. In the spring of 1858 Sir Hugh Rose prepared to storm the town of Jhansi, when the Rani of Jhansi was holding out against the British. He said to Lieut. Lyster, "It will be necessary to have the place reconnoitred and situations chosen for the batteries, but the task is so dangerous that I do not like to order anyone to undertake it." "If you will allow me, sir," replied Lyster, "I will undertake it, if I can do it my own way, and without a guard." Accordingly he set off, dressed in an old shooting suit and accompanied by a boy on a pony. When they got near Jhansi he left his horse with the boy, and told him to conceal himself and to come when he whistled for him. He then crept through the scrub, across the level space which surrounded the walls, marked suitable positions for the artillery, and at last actually went up to the gate of the town, put his ear against it and listened to the conversation of the guard inside. Then he turned back, but was soon discovered, fired at and pursued. The boy came up with his horse and they managed to escape. When the siege took place batteries were erected upon all the positions selected by Lyster. "Nothing could be more conclusive proof of the skill of this officer." ("Life of Sir Hugh Rose, Lord Strathnairn.") When the town was stormed on 4 April, 1858, Lyster took part in the action. The Rani escaped out of Jhansi, and after the town was taken Lieut. Lyster discovered her jewels hidden in a casket, but he never received a penny of prize-money for this. He took part in the Battle of Betwa, and in the action of Koonch 11 May, 1858, and the capture of that town. His charger received one bayonet and two tulwar wounds. The Battle of Koonch was "one of the most hard-fought in the history of the Mutiny, and nothing but the most resolute courage on the part of our troops gave us complete victory instead of a crushing defeat." "When the enemy retreated, worsted from the conflict, they fell back in good order, covered by skirmishers. General Rose had sent Lieut. Lyster with an order to the cavalry to charge. Threatened by cavalry, some of the rebels formed themselves into a rallying square, when they were charged, not by a squadron, not by a troop, not even by a sergeant's party, but by one horseman, who, driving in among them, broke the square and slew two or three of the sepoys, himself escaping without a wound. That single horseman was Lieut. Harry Hammon Lyster." It was on this occasion that he won the Victoria Cross [London Gazette, 21 Oct. 1859]: "Harry Hammon Lyster, the 72nd Bengal Native Infantry. Date of Act of Bravery: 23 May, 1858. For gallantly charging and breaking singly, a skirmishing square of the retreating rebel army from Calpee, and killing two or three sepoys in the conflict. Major-General Sir Hugh Rose reports that this act of bravery was witnessed by himself and by Lieut.-Colonel Gall, C.B., of the 14th Light Dragoons." Lieut. Lyster took part subsequently in this campaign in the repulse of the attack on the camp of the 2nd Brigade at the village of Mutra, and of that on the camp of the 1st Brigade at Gookowlee, in the taking of the town and fort of Calpee, the capture of the Morar cantonments, the storming of Lushkar and of the Fort at Gwalior 19 June, 1858. He was mentioned in Despatches five times, twice specially mentioned for gallant conduct in the field, and received the Medal and clasp. From July, 1860, to Aug. 1863, he was A.D.C. to His Excellency the Commander-in-Chief; Captain, 72nd Bengal Native Infantry, 23 Dec. 1862, afterwards dated 18 Feb. 1861; Staff Corps Communications 12 Sept. 1866; Brevet Major, 3rd Gurkhas, 19 Jan. 1864; Major 20 Sept. 1868; Brevet Lieut.-Colonel 18 March, 1870; Lieut.-Colonel 20 Sept. 1874; Brevet Colonel 27 May, 1879; Officer, Second in Command, 8 April, 1872; Second in Command 23 June, 1873; Commandant 1 Dec. 1879. "The Englishman" said at this time: "We do not know exactly whether to congratulate Colonel Lyster on being appointed to the command of the 3rd Gurkhas or not; it rather becomes a doubtful point when the officer ought at least to be commanding a Brigade, if not a Division, to congratulate him on commanding a regiment. . . . Few officers can show a more brilliant record of service to the State." Colonel Lyster commanded the 3rd (Queen Alexandra's Own) Gurkhas in the first Afghan Campaign, 1878–9, and in the second Afghan Campaign, 1879–80, under General Sir Donald Stewart. On the 19th April, 1880, the enemy were encountered at Ahmed Khel, and it is said that in the great victory which was gained "Colonel Lyster contributed mainly to the success of the action." Ghuzni was entered without firing a shot. Colonel Lyster also commanded the 3rd Gurkhas at the Battle of Urzoo, near Ghuzni. He was given a C.B., "for his distinguished conduct in repelling with his regiment, in diamond squares and well posted, a sudden rush of the enemy made on Sir Donald Stewart's Force." ("Life of Sir Hugh Rose.") He was mentioned in Despatches; received the Medal and clasp, and received the Good Service Pension of £100 a year. He commanded, during the absence of the Duke of Connaught, the troops at Camp of Exercise, some 7,000 men, at Meerut, in 1883–4. After the Afghan War he was appointed to the command of the Viceroy's escort at Lahore, consisting of cavalry, artillery and infantry. He was gazetted Lieut.-General in Sept. 1891, and placed on the Unemployed Supernumerary List of the Indian Army in July, 1892. General Lyster married, 1st, 12 Dec. 1865, at Calcutta, Mrs. Caroline Matilda Underdown, daughter of J. Davies, Esq. He married, secondly, 25 July, 1901, Ada Emily Cole, daughter of John Cole, Esq. A good deal of the information given above is taken from "Memoirs of an Ancient House," by the Rev. H. L. Lyster-Denny, M.A.

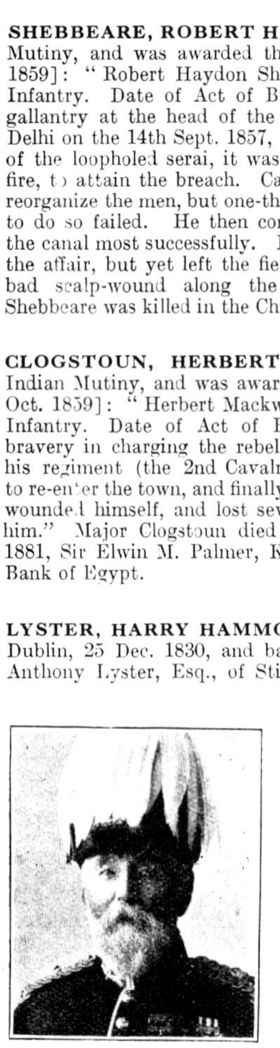

Harry Hammon Lyster.

PRENDERGAST, HARRY NORTH DALRYMPLE, Lieut., was born in Madras on 15 Oct. 1834; the son of Thomas Prendergast, Esq., of the Madras Civil Service (and afterwards of Meldon Lodge, Cheltenham), and of Lucy Caroline, daughter of Martin Dalrymple, Esq., of Cleland and Fordell (related to the Earl of Stair). He was educated at a private school at Cheam; at Brighton College, and at Addiscombe, and entered the Royal Engineers as a 2nd Lieutenant in 1854; Captain and Major in 1863. He served in the Persian War of 1856–7, the bombardment of the redoubts and batteries, and the defeat of the Persian Army (Medal with clasp); with the Malwa Field Force in 1857; present at the Relief of Mhow, the Siege and Capture of Dhar, and the Battle of Mundisore; twice recommended for the Victoria Cross; mentioned in Despatches, severely wounded; with the Central India Field Force in 1858, under Sir Hugh Rose, at the Battle of Bhooina (horse shot under him), the Siege and Capture of Gorakota, the affair of Baradia, the forcing of Muddinpore Passes, the Siege of Jhansi, the Battle of the Betwa (severely wounded); present on the sick-list at the capture of Calpee (Despatches, Medal with clasp and Victoria Cross). He received the Mutiny Medal with clasp, and the Victoria Cross [London Gazette, 21 Oct. 1859]: "Harry North Dalrymple Prendergast, Lieut., Madras Engineers. Dates of Acts of Bravery: 21 Nov. 1857, and other occasions. For conspicuous bravery on the 21st Nov. 1857, at Mundisore, in saving the life of Lieut. G. Dew, 14th Light Dragoons, at the risk of his own, by attempting to cut down a Velaitee who covered him (Lieut. Dew) with his piece, from only a few yards to the rear. Lieut. Prendergast was wounded in this affair by the discharge of the piece, and would probably have been cut down had not the rebel been killed by Major Orr. He also distinguished himself by his gallantry in the actions at Ratgurh and Betwa, when he was severely wounded." Major-General Sir Hugh Rose, in forwarding his recommendation of this officer, states: "Lieut. Prendergast, Madras Engineers, was specially mentioned by Brigadier (now Sir Charles) Stuart, for the gallant action at Mundisore, when he was severely wounded; secondly, he was 'specially mentioned' by me when acting voluntarily as my aide-de-camp in the action before Nesilging Ratgurh, on the Beena River, for gallant conduct. His horse was killed on that occasion. Thirdly, at the action of Betwa, he again voluntarily acted as my aide-de-camp and distinguished himself by his bravery in the charge which I made with Capt. Need's troop, Her Majesty's 14th Light Dragoons, against the left of the so-called Peishwa's Army under Tantia Topee. He was severely wounded on that occasion." General Prendergast's own account of the action at Mundisore is as follows: "I had been ordered to reconnoitre around Mundisore, being then Second Lieutenant and Assistant Engineer in the Malwa Field Force. But before leaving the outpost, the enemy's cavalry became visible on a hill to the left front, and presently large masses of infantry appeared in front of the pickets. Having reported the circumstances to General Sir Charles Stewart, commanding the column, I rode to the front and met Lieuts. Clark and Dew, whose pickets had been driven in by the enemy's infantry. The British Force was falling in, but was not ready to receive the enemy. Clark, Dew and myself, with a handful of cavalry, charged into the thick of the enemy's infantry, thereby causing some hesitation on their part. When the cavalry charged, the artillery, not to be left behind, charged with their guns. I rode right into the centre of the enemy's forces—as a matter of fact, between their standard-bearers. Dew and I then found ourselves charging with the 3rd Hyderabad Contingent Cavalry, and afterwards passing through the first lot, we came across various bodies of the enemy, whom we charged one after the other. At one place where I happened to be leading, my horse refused a brook, and a party of the enemy who had taken up a position on a hillock commanding this brook fired on me. I floundered through the water and engaged the enemy on the hillock. In the mêlée on the top, I came upon a water-carrier, but did not strike him, and shouted to a dragoon who was going to cut him down, that he was a water-carrier, but the dragoon struck at him. Some time after this, Lieut. Dew was leading, and a splendid man—one of the enemy—was about to fire on him. I shouted to warn Dew and divert the attention of the man who had covered him, when he turned round and covered me with the piece. I rode for him, but he reserved his fire till I was so close that the gunpowder of the charge was ingrained in my hand. The bullet passed through my body on the left side, and the man was cut down by Major Orr. I was sent to the rear, and was escorted back to the main body by two orderlies with lame horses. When we came to the place where I had seen the water-carrier, one of the soldiers said, 'It was here some fool of an officer told me not to strike at a water-carrier, but I had half his head off.' But before we got back to the camp we were fired on by straggling portions of the enemy, and once I had to draw my pistol. . . . On the 31st March, 1858, Sir Hugh Rose, to whom I was acting as aide-de-camp, was besieging Jhansi. That evening, Tantia Topi, one of the great rebel leaders, having marched from Calpee, attempted to raise the siege. Early on the 1st April commenced the Battle of Betwa. A brigade under General Stewart was holding the pass two miles from Jhansi, on the Jhansi-Calpee road. The Irregular Cavalry Corps had twice charged the enemy's left, when Sir Hugh Rose led a squadron of dragoons to charge the artillery and infantry of the enemy's left flank. Topi's guns and foot soldiers were drawn up behind a ridge of rocks. The order to charge was given, and when nearing the battery, the General drew rein, and I made for the enemy's heavy guns. It was necessary to jump the rocks after having passed through a terrific musketry fire. After a severe fight in the battery, during which I received some deep cuts on the left arm, the enemy retired, excepting those who were cut to pieces, and the guns were seized by the 86th Regt., which followed the Cavalry charge." He also received the Brevet of Major. In 1863 Lieut. Prendergast became Captain and Major. In 1864 he married Emilie, daughter of Frederick Simpson, Esq., and their children were: Amy L. C., who became the wife of Hugh Gough, Esq., and died; Fanny B.; Ella T. D., who in 1913 married Kaid Sir Harry Maclean, K.C.M.G.; Maude D. J., who has been Commandant of the V.A.D. Hospital on Richmond Green, and was made a Member of the Order of British Empire in Sept. 1914; Harry Y. D., who was in the Uganda Civil Service, and died; George W. Y. (deceased); Herbert H. L., who was a Civil Engineer, and now is a Captain in the Royal Engineers, and served on the Western Front and then in Egypt and Asia Minor, and was twice wounded; Arthur F. C. V., a Captain in the Hampshire Regt., who served from Aug. 1914, at the Western Front and was four times wounded. Major Prendergast served through the Abyssinian War of 1867 and 1868, and was present at the Battle of Arrogi and at the capture of Magdala (mentioned in Despatches, Medal and Brevet of Lieutenant-Colonel). He became Lieutenant-Colonel in 1868; was created a C.B. in 1875, and promoted Colonel in 1875. In 1878 he was in command of the Sappers with the Indian Expedition to the Mediterranean. From 1869 to 1880 he commanded the Madras Sappers and Miners. In 1880 he was appointed Honorary A.D.C. to the Viceroy and became Brigadier-General. He acted as Quartermaster-General of the Madras Army and as Secretary to the Government in the Military Department; he commanded the Western District in 1880 and the Ceded Districts in 1881, when he received the Distinguished Service Pension. He was promoted Major-General in 1882, and Lieutenant-General in 1885. He held appointments in the Department of Public Works and in the Railway Department. He commanded the Madras Sappers and Miners for 10 years; he commanded the British Burma Division in 1883 and the Hyderabad Subsidiary Force in 1884. He commanded the Burma Expeditionary Force in the campaign of 1885–6, which resulted in the dethronement of King Theebaw and the annexation of Burma. He was present at the attack on Nyaung-ben-Maw, at the capture of the Forts of Guegzam-Kaimzo and Muhla, at the taking of Pagan, the bombardment and occupation of Nyungzam, the disarmament of Ceva and Sazina, the advance on Mandalay. He dethroned and deported King Theebaw. When General Prendergast told Theebaw he must embark for India, that monarch asked for a delay of three months, and was told he must be ready to start in ten minutes. Theebaw then begged that General Prendergast would allow him to keep his ruby ring and the most precious of his wives. The General smiled in a way which brought despair into the King's demeanour, and he exclaimed, "Then, Great Commander, take my wife, but, oh! spare me my ring!" General Prendergast delivered Theebaw and his family to the captain of a steamer, and was given a receipt for "One King, three Queens, one Prime Minister, three Councillors, and so many Maids of Honour." For his services in this campaign General Prendergast was thanked by the Queen and by the Government of India, and was created a K.C.B. In one of the congratulatory letters, the Viceroy, the Marquis of Dufferin, wrote: "History will record that in the course of ten days you conquered a kingdom and overthrew a dynasty, and this in consequence of the VIGOUR, the celerity and the judicious character of your operations." Sir Harry Prendergast became General in 1887. He afterwards acted as officiating Resident in Travancore and Cochin, then Resident of Mysore and Chief Commissioner of Coorg from Oct. 1887, to Jan. 1889. He was Governor-General's Agent at Baroda in Jan. 1889, then acted as officiating Governor-General's Agent in Baluchistan, afterwards officiating Resident in Mysore and Chief Commissioner of Coorg from Aug. 1891, to April, 1892. He retired from India at 57, when he still had so many years of full vigour and activity before him; settling at Richmond, he became a hard-working servant of his country, a strong supporter of National Service from the initial stages; was President of the Richmond Division, and Member of the Executive Committee for Surrey from the beginning of the movement, and did much splendid work. As a Chairman, his immense popularity, bred of admiration for the fearless, single-hearted soldier who added Upper Burma to the British Crown, coupled with a magnetic personal influence, ensured large audiences willing to rely on his considered judgment, and when it was known that the National Service League was especially the work of his later life an undoubted impetus was given to the movement in Surrey. He urged upon the people: "The absolute necessity for public interest and participation in the defence of the country," and again: "That an Army cannot be raised suddenly, and that England, if she desires Peace, must stand prepared for WAR." This was said in Oct. 1898. In a speech at a banquet in Dublin in 1898, he appealed for an "efficient fighting Army which should be our first line of *offence*." "Two ways of getting this, either an increase of the Regulars and Auxiliary Forces, or compulsory enlistment not only of the inhabitants of Great Britain, but also of Greater Britain, for there is no reason why the latter should not be enrolled for the defence of the EMPIRE." Sir Harry was a Colonel-Commandant of the Royal Engineers and Colonel of the 2nd (Queen's Own) Madras Sappers and Miners, being received in audience of King Edward for the purpose of presenting an album of photographs on behalf of the regiment. He was created a G.C.B. in 1902. On 13 Dec. 1904, Sir Henry received the Freedom of the City of London. He had the Distinguished Service Reward. Sir H. Prendergast was made a G.C.B., and his Banner and Brass are to be seen in the Chapel of that Order at Westminster Abbey. For the Golden Commemoration of the Indian Mutiny Veterans, which took place at the Royal Albert Hall on 23 Dec. 1907, Sir Henry was on the Committee, which was headed by Earl Roberts, K.G., V.C. General Prendergast died at his residence, 2, Heron Court, Richmond, on 24 July, 1913. In his younger days Sir Harry was very fond of boxing, fencing, polo, hunting, cricket, football, and, in fact, almost every kind of sport.

Harry N. D. Prendergast.

WHIRLPOOL, FREDERICK, Private, enlisted in the 3rd Bombay European Regiment (now the 109th Leinster Regiment), and served in the Mutiny Campaign. He was awarded the Victoria Cross [London Gazette, 21 Oct. 1859]: "Frederick Whirlpool, Private, 3rd Bombay European Regt. Dates of Acts of Bravery: 3 April and 2 May, 1858. For gallantly volunteering on the 3rd April, 1858, in the attack on Jhansi, to return and carry away several killed and wounded, which he did twice under a very heavy fire from the wall; also for devoted bravery at the assault on Lohari on the 2nd May, 1858, in rushing to the rescue of Lieut. Donne, of the regiment, who was dangerously wounded. In this service Private Whirlpool received seventeen desperate wounds, one of which nearly severed his head from his body. The gallant example shown by this man is considered to have greatly contributed to the success of the day." Private Whirlpool died in New South Wales on the 24th June, 1899.

London Gazette, 21 Oct. 1859.—" Ensign Everard Aloysius Lisle Phillips, of the 11th Regt. of Bengal Native Infantry, would have been recommended to Her Majesty for the Decoration of the Victoria Cross had he survived, for many gallant deeds which he performed during the Siege of Delhi, during which he was wounded three times. At the assault of that city he captured the Water Bastion, with a small party of men, and was finally killed in the streets of Delhi on the 18th Sept."

London Gazette, 11 Nov. 1859.—" The Queen has been graciously pleased to signify her intention to confer the Decoration of the Victoria Cross on the undermentioned Officers and Private Soldiers of Her Majesty's Army, whose claims to the same have been submitted for Her Majesty's approval, on account of Acts of Bravery performed by them in India, as recorded against their several names."

JEROME, HENRY EDWARD, Capt. and Brevet Major, was born 2 Feb. 1830, at Antigua, West Indies; son of Joseph Jerome, Esq., and Mrs. Jerome, née Walker. He was educated at Sandhurst, and was gazetted to

the 86th Regt. on the 21st Jan. 1848, becoming Lieutenant on the 30th April, 1852. He served with his regiment in the Indian Mutiny, and at Calpee had part of his head torn away. He took part in the storming and capture of Chandairee, the siege and capture of Jhansi and the action of Koonch, and was several times mentioned in Despatches, given the Brevet of Major, and was on five separate occasions recommended for the Victoria Cross, which is believed to constitute a record. The Decoration was awarded to him [London Gazette, 11 Nov. 1859]: "Henry Edward Jerome, Capt. (now Brevet Major), 86th Regt. (now of the 19th Regt.). Date of Acts of Bravery: 3 April and 28 May, 1858. For conspicuous gallantry at Jhansi, on the 3rd April and 28th May, 1858, in having, with the assistance of Private Byrne, removed under a very heavy fire Lieut. Sewell, of the 86th Regt., who was severely wounded, at a very exposed point of the attack upon the Fort; also for gallant conduct at the capture of the fort of Chandairee, the storming of Jhansi, and in action with a superior rebel force on the Jumna on the 28th May, 1858, when he was severely wounded." His Victoria Cross has three dates on it. Having been transferred to the West Riding Regt. he served in the Hazara Campaign, an expedition against the tribes of the Black Mountain, for which he received the Medal and clasp. He became Major on the 1st July, 1868. From 1876 to 1884 he served on the Staff in England, and in 1885 retired with the rank of Major-General and received the reward for distinguished and meritorious service. Major-General Jerome died at his residence at Bath on Monday night, 25 Feb. 1901, at the age of 71. He had been ill for a month, but his death was quite sudden, and his son says : "He died of the shock it gave him when *his* regiment surrendered to the Boers." Mr. Jerome further says that his father "was not popular in the Army, as he was inclined to tell people what he thought, and, well——" Major-General Jerome married, in London, Inez Temple Frances Cowper, daughter of Henry Augustine Cowper, late H.B.M.'s Consul-General, Havana, and their only child is Mr. Lucien Joseph Jerome, who became H.B.M.'s Consul-General at Ecuador in 1913, and later held the same appointment in Seville.

Henry Edward Jerome.

CAMERON, AYLMER SPICER, Lieut., was born 12 Aug. 1833, the son of the late Lieut.-Col. William Gordon Cameron, K.H., of the Grenadier Guards, who served in the Peninsular War, and was severely wounded there,

and who lost his right arm at Waterloo, where he was A.D.C. to the Duke of Wellington in the battle; and grandson of General Neville Cameron, R.E., who was at the storming and capture of Gwalior, India. He entered the 72nd Highlanders in 1852, and served in the Crimean Campaign 1854–6, including both assaults on the Redan (Medal with clasp and Turkish Medal), and in the Indian Mutiny Campaign 1857–8. At Kotah, " after occupying the bastions, the troops proceeded to clear the houses. Many a mortal tussle took place. Lieut. Cameron, 72nd Highlanders, led a forlorn hope up a narrow entrance of a house, defended by a party of desperate men, two of whom he slew and was himself desperately wounded." (Account by an officer.) Lieut. Cameron

Aylmer S. Cameron.

was reported " desperately wounded " at Kotah, and had three wounds the same day. He was twice mentioned in Despatches, and received the Victoria Cross and the Mutiny Medal with clasp. His Victoria Cross was gazetted 11 Nov. 1859: " Aylmer Spicer Cameron, Lieut., 72nd Regt. (Seaforth Highlanders). Date of Act of Bravery: 30 March, 1858. For conspicuous bravery on the 30th March, 1858, at Kotah, in having headed a small party of men, and attacked a body of armed fanatic rebels, strongly posted in a loopholed house, with one narrow entrance. Lieut. Cameron stormed the house, and killed three rebels in single combat. He was severely wounded, having lost half of one hand by a stroke from a tulwar." He was Chief Instructor in Bengal 1874–6; Assistant Adjutant-General in Canada 1879–81; in command of the King's Own Scottish Borderers 1881–3; Chief of the Intelligence Branch, Headquarters, 1883–5. He was created a C.B. in 1886, and from 1886 to 1888 he was Commandant of the Royal Military College, Sandhurst. He received the Distinguished Service Reward. His four brothers and five sons have all held commissions in the Navy and Army. Colonel Cameron died 11 June, 1908. His brothers were : General Sir W. G. Cameron, G.C.B.; Lieut. G. Cameron, Coldstream Guards (Page of Honour to H.M. Queen Victoria); Capt. H. Cameron, 19th Regt., who died in the Ashantee War, and Capt. O. Cameron, R.N., who was present at the taking of Taku Fort, China. Colonel Cameron married Arabella Piercy Henderson, of Park Hill, Perthshire, in 1869, and had eight children : Lieut. Aylmer Cameron, R.N., died of fever in Malta ; Amy, married A. Cookson, Esq.; Rose, married Lieut.-Col. Bingham, C.M.G., D.S.O., A.Q.M.G.; she served with the Y.M.C.A. in France, 1915 and 1916 ; Neville Cameron, died in Australia, and his son served in the European War in the Marines on H.M.S. Neptune ; Lieut.-Col. Orford Cameron, D.S.O., serving abroad ; Captain Cyril Cameron, R.N., who served in the Dardanelles; Esmé, married Capt. Henley, R.N., Flag Captain on H.M.S. Emperor of India, and Major Cecil Cameron, D.S.O., serving at home.

SLEAVON, MICHAEL, Corpl., served in the Indian Mutiny, and was awarded the Victoria Cross [London Gazette, 11 Nov. 1859]: " Michael Sleavon, Corpl., Royal Engineers. For determined bravery at the attack of the fort of Jhansi on the 3rd April, 1858, in maintaining his position at the head of a sap, and continuing the work under a heavy fire with a cool and steady determination." Sleavon died on the 14th Aug. 1902. His Victoria Cross was sold in London on 22 Jan. 1903, for £53.

Michael Sleavon.

BRENNAN, JOSEPH, Bombardier, served in the Indian Mutiny, and was awarded the Victoria Cross [London Gazette, 11 Nov. 1859]: " Joseph Brennan, Bombardier, Royal Artillery. For marked gallantry at the assault of Jhansi on the 3rd April, 1858, in bringing up two guns of the Hyderabad Contingent, manned by natives, laying each under a heavy fire from the walls, and directing them so accurately as to compel the enemy to abandon his battery." He was promoted Sergeant. He died on the 23rd Sept. 1872.

RICHARDSON, GEORGE, Private, joined the Border Regt.; served in the Indian Mutiny, and was awarded the Victoria Cross [London Gazette, 11 Nov. 1859]: " George Richardson, Private, 34th Regt. Date of Act of Bravery : 27 April, 1859. At Kewarie Trans-Gogra, on the 27th April, 1859, for determined courage in having, though severely wounded—one arm being disabled—closed with and secured a rebel sepoy armed with a broad revolver."

M'QUIRT, BERNARD, Private, joined the 95th (The Derbyshire) Regt., and served in the Indian Mutiny, and was awarded the Victoria Cross [London Gazette, 11 Nov. 1859]: " Bernard M'Quirt, Private, 95th Regt. Date of Act of Bravery : 6 Jan. 1858. For gallant conduct on the 6th Jan. 1858, at the capture of the entrenched town of Rowa, when he was severely and dangerously wounded in a hand-to-hand fight with three men, of whom he killed one and wounded another. He received five sabre-cuts and a musket-shot in this service." Private M'Quirt died on the 5th Oct. 1888.

BYRNE, JAMES, Private, enlisted in the 86th Regt. (The Royal Irish Rifles), and served in the Indian Mutiny. He was awarded the Victoria Cross [London Gazette, 11 Nov. 1859]: " James Byrne, Private, 86th Regt. For gallant conduct on the 3rd April, 1858, in the attack on the fort at Jhansi, in carrying Lieut. Sewell, who was lying badly wounded, to a place of safety under a very heavy fire, assisted by Capt. Jerome, in the performance of which act he was wounded by a sword-cut." He was promoted to Sergeant. Sergt. Byrne died on the 6th Dec. 1872, and his Victoria Cross was sold by auction by Messrs. Sotheby in June, 1903, for £35.

RODGERS, GEORGE, Private, enlisted in the 71st Regt. (The Highland Light Infantry), and served in the Indian Mutiny. He was awarded the Victoria Cross [London Gazette, 11 Nov. 1859]: " George Rodgers, Private, the 71st Regt. For daring conduct at Marar, Gwalior, on the 16th June, 1858, in attacking by himself a party of seven rebels, one of whom he killed. This was remarked as a valuable service, the party of rebels being well armed and strongly posted in the line of advance of a detachment of the 71st." Private Rodgers died on the 9th March, 1870.

London Gazette, 21 Nov. 1859.—" The Queen has been graciously pleased to signify her intention to confer the Decoration of the Victoria Cross on the undermentioned Officer, Non-commissioned Officer and Private of Her Majesty's 32nd Regiment of Foot, whose claims to the same have been submitted for her Majesty's approval on account of Acts of Bravery performed by them at Lucknow in India, as recorded against their several names."

LAWRENCE, SAMUEL HILL, Lieut., was gazetted to the 32nd Foot (Duke of Cornwall's Light Infantry) as Ensign 12 Dec. 1847. He served with his regiment in the Punjab Campaign of 1848–49, including the second siege operations before Mooltan, including the storming and capture of the city and surrender of the fortress; also at the surrender of the fort and garrison at Cheniste and battle of Gujerat (Medal and clasps). He became Lieutenant on the 22nd Feb. 1850. Lieut. Lawrence served during the Indian Mutiny in 1857–58; commanded the Headquarters of the 32nd Regt. at the evacuation of Fort Muchee Bhawan on 1 July, 1857, and from that date was engaged in the defence of the Residency of Lucknow until its final relief on the 24th Nov. by Lord Clyde, during the greater part of which he commanded the Redan Battery; led a sortie on the 7th July, and a division of another on the 26th Sept., when his company captured a 9-pounder gun at the point of the bayonet. He was mentioned in Despatches by Sir John Inglis and the Governor-General, and was given the Brevet of Major, Medal, and clasp, and awarded the Victoria Cross [London Gazette, 22 Nov. 1859]: "Samuel Hill Lawrence, Lieut., now Brevet Major, 32nd Foot. Dates of Acts of Bravery: 7 July and 26 Sept. 1857. For distinguished bravery in a sortie on the 7th July, 1857, made, as reported by Major Wilson, late Deputy-Assistant-Adjutant-General of the Lucknow Garrison, 'for the purpose of examining a house strongly held by the enemy, in order to discover whether or not a mine was being driven from it.' Major Wilson states that he saw the attack and was an eye-witness to the great personal gallantry of Major Lawrence on the occasion, he being the first person to mount the ladder and enter the window of the house, in effecting which he had his pistol knocked out of his hand by one of the enemy. Also for distinguished gallantry in a sortie on the 26th Sept. 1857, in charging with two of his men in advance of his company, and capturing a 9-pounder gun." Lord Roberts says that he had the pleasure at Lucknow of renewing an acquaintance with many of the garrison whom he had known before; "amongst these was Sam Lawrence, of the 32nd Foot, a friend of Peshawar days." Lieut. Lawrence became Captain on the 1st July, 1857, and was given the Brevet of Major 24 March, 1858. His name appeared in the Army List until 1874.

OXENHAM, WILLIAM, Corpl., enlisted in the 32nd Foot (Duke of Cornwall's Light Infantry); served in the Indian Mutiny, and was awarded the Victoria Cross [London Gazette, 22 Nov. 1859]: "William Oxenham, Corpl., 32nd Regt. Date of Act of Bravery: 30 June, 1857. For distinguished bravery in saving the life of Mr. Capper, of the Bengal Civil Service, by extricating him from the ruins of a verandah which had fallen on him, Corpl. Oxenham being for ten minutes exposed to a heavy fire while doing so." Mr. Capper evidently thought that Capt. Anderson ought to have had the Victoria Cross as well as Oxenham. A first consequence of the defeat of Chinhat was the occupation of Lakhnao by the rebels. They began to loophole many of the houses, and brought a six-pounder to bear on the outer verandah of the post afterwards known as Anderson's Post. "The post, however, was so important that orders were sent to its garrison to hold it to the last extremity. . . . The house which was thus being defended was the residence of Mr. Capper, C.S. Mr. Capper had volunteered to aid in its defence, and was standing for that purpose under the verandah, behind one of the pillars, when the enemy's fire brought down the verandah and buried him under six feet of wood and masonry. Capt. Anderson, 25th Native Infantry, though not the senior officer present, at once called upon the garrison to assist in rescuing the buried gentleman. The work was one of no ordinary danger, for there was no protection against the concentrated fire of the enemy, and one at least of those present expressed the opinion that the act would be useless, as Mr. Capper would probably be dead. Anderson was not discouraged by these doubts. Announcing his intention to rescue Capper at all risks, he called on those around to aid him, and set to work with a will. He was speedily joined by Corporal Oxenham, 32nd Foot, Monsieur Geoffroi, a Frenchman, Signor Barsatelli, an Italian, and two Englishmen, Lincoln and Chick, from the Post Office Garrison. The enemy's round shot continued to pour over the place where Capper lay, and to be able to work the six men I have mentioned were forced to lie on their stomachs and grub away in that position. At length they succeeded in extricting Capper's body, but his legs still remained buried. The situation for him was now replete with danger, for to stand up was almost certain death. In this dilemma, Oxenham, obeying a signal from Anderson, who was supporting the head, dashed round to the other side, and extricated, by a supreme effort, the buried legs. This done, Capper was hauled in by the other five men, and was saved. For this act Oxenham received the Victoria Cross; but Mr. Capper ever considered that he owed his life mainly to Anderson, who alike suggested the attempt and by his example carried it to a successful issue. Anderson was recommended for the Cross in 1868, but it was not bestowed upon him. On this occasion Mr. Capper wrote as follows: 'My former letters clearly acknowledge that it was to the gallantry of Colonel Anderson that I owe my life; that had he not, by word and example, shamed the others to action, no effort would have been made to save me. . . . It is clear that Colonel Anderson must have voluntarily exposed himself to imminent danger for the long period of three-quarters of an hour—contrary to the advice of his superior officer—with the object of rescuing a comrade from a terrible and lingering death. At the moment when Corpl. Oxenham (at the call of Colonel Anderson) went forward to extricate my legs and feet, Colonel Anderson was supporting my head and shoulders; and whilst all three of us were exposed to the cannonade, the head and upper part of Anderson's body must have been exposed to the same heavy musketry-fire as was risked by Oxenham. The risk of life accepted by Anderson was continuous; and if the question is, to whom (under God) I am chiefly indebted for the preservation of my life, the answer is—Colonel Anderson.'" (Kaye and Malleson, Vol. III., page 277.) Corpl. Oxenham died on the 29th Dec. 1874. His Victoria Cross was sold with six others in Nov. 1910, for £77.

DOWLING, WILLIAM, Private, enlisted in the 32nd Foot (Duke of Cornwall's Light Infantry); served in the Indian Mutiny, and was awarded the Victoria Cross [London Gazette, 22 Nov. 1859]: "William Dowling Private, 32nd Regt. Dates of Acts of Bravery: 4th and 9th July and 27th Sept. 1857. For distinguished gallantry on the 4th July, 1857, in going out with two other men, since dead, and spiking two of the enemy's guns. He killed a subadar of the enemy by one of the guns. Also for distinguished gallantry on the 9th of the same month, in going out again with three men, since dead, to spike one of the enemy's guns. He had to retire, the spike being too small, but was exposed to the same danger. Also for distinguished bravery on the 27th Sept. 1857, in spiking an 18-pounder gun during a sortie, he being at the same time under a most heavy fire from the enemy." Private Dowling died on the 17th Feb. 1887.

London Gazette, 20 Jan. 1860.—"The Queen has been graciously pleased to signify her intention to confer the Decoration of the Victoria Cross on the undermentioned Officer and Soldiers of Her Majesty's Army, whose claims to the same have been submitted for Her Majesty's approval, on account of Acts of Bravery performed by them in India, as recorded against their several names."

HEATHCOTE, ALFRED SPENCER, Lieut., was born in 1833, at Winchester. He joined the 2nd Battn. 60th Royal Rifles, as Ensign, 16 May, 1856; became Lieutenant 60th Royal Rifles (King's Royal Rifle Corps) 22 June, 1858, and served in the campaign of 1857–58, against the Mutineers in India, including the actions on the Hindun, Battle of Budli-Re-Serai and taking the heights before Delhi. Lord Roberts says in "Forty-one Years in India" (page 136): "Home of the Engineers, the hero of the Kashmir Gate exploit, first advanced with some sappers and blew in the outer gate. At this, the last struggle for the capture of Delhi, I wished to be present, so attached myself for the occasion to a party of the 60th Rifles, under the command of Ensign Alfred Heathcote. As soon as the smoke of the explosion cleared away, the 60th, supported by the 4th Punjab Infantry, sprang through the gateway; but we did not get very far, for there was a second door beyond, chained and barred, which was with difficulty forced open, and the whole party rushed in. The recesses in the long passage which led to the palace buildings were crowded with wounded men, but there was very little opposition; only a few fanatics still held out. One of these—a Mahomedan sepoy in the uniform of a Grenadier of the 37th Native Infantry—stood quietly about thirty yards up the passage, with his musket on his hip. As we approached he slowly raised his weapon and fired, sending a bullet through McQueen's hemlet. The brave fellow then advanced at the charge and was—of course—shot down. So ended the 20th Sept., a day I am never likely to forget." This was the last day of Alfred Heathcote's services in the Siege of Delhi, which were so great that the duration of the whole siege is given as the date of his Act of Bravery. He received the Mutiny Medal and the Victoria Cross [London Gazette, 30 Jan. 1860]: "Alfred Spencer Heathcote, Lieut., 60th Rifles. For highly gallant and daring conduct at Delhi, throughout the siege, from June to Sept. 1857, during which he was wounded He volunteered for services of extreme danger, especially during the six days of severe fighting in the streets after the assault. Elected by the officers of his regiment." Lieut. Heathcote took part in the campaign in Rohilcund, including the actions of Bugawalla and Nugena, the relief of Moradabad, the action on the Dogma, assault and capture of Bareilly; attack and bombardment of Shahjehanpore, defeat of the rebels and relief of the garrison; capture of the town and fort of Bunnaif, pursuit of the enemy to the left bank of the Goomtee, and action at the Shahabad. The following is an extract from a memorandum, dated "14 March, 1862, Cambridge Barracks, Portsmouth," by the Lieutenant-Colonel commanding the 2nd Battn. 60th Royal Rifles: "It is a source of great pleasure to me to have the opportunity of expressing the admiration I have always felt for Lieut. Alfred Heathcote. No one ever better deserved the Victoria Cross; he obtained it not only for one act, but for many acts during his active service, commencing with the march on Delhi. On one occasion an advanced post in Delhi was retained by his declaring to the officer in command, who wished to retire, that he could do so with his own men, but that he, Lieut. Heathcote, would endeavour to hold the post with six riflemen he had with him. On another occasion he made his way to the front with six men, supported by fourteen under my own command. He and his party killed eight or ten of the enemy. This was the first forward step taken after the Army had been three days in the portion of Delhi first occupied by it." He also received the Medal and clasp. Lieut. Heathcote served in the China Campaign, for which he received the China Medal. He married Mary Harriet Thompson. He died at Bowral, New South Wales, on the 21st Feb. 1912, aged seventy-nine. His daughter, Miss Beatrice Heathcote, lives at Katcoomba, New South Wales.

Alfred S. Heathcote.

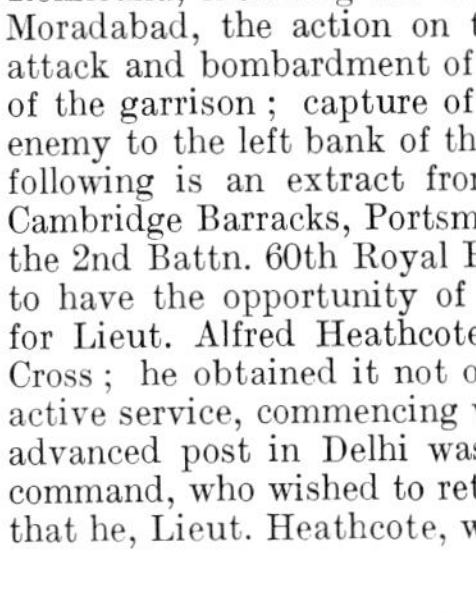

James Champion.

CHAMPION, JAMES, Troop Sergt.-Major, enlisted in the 8th Hussars, was promoted to Troop Sergeant-Major, and

was awarded the Victoria Cross [London Gazette, 20 Jan. 1860]: " James Champion, Troop Sergt.-Major, 8th Hussars. For distinguished bravery at Beejapore on 8 Sept. 1858, when both the officers attached to the troop were disabled, and himself severely wounded at the commencement of the action by a ball through his body, in having continued at his duty forward throughout the pursuit, and disabled several of the enemy with his pistol. Also recommended for distinguished conduct at Gwalior." Troop Sergt.-Major Champion died on the 4th May, 1904.

WALLER, GEORGE, Colour-Sergt., served in the Indian Mutiny, and was awarded the Victoria Cross [London Gazette, 20 Jan. 1860]: " George Waller, Colour-Sergt., 1st Battn. 25th Bombay Light Infantry. Dates of Acts of Bravery : 14 and 18 Sept. 1857. For conspicuous bravery at Delhi on 14 Sept. 1857, in charging and capturing the enemy's guns near the Cabul Gate ; and again on 18 Sept. 1857, in the repulse of a sudden attack made by the enemy on a gun near the Chaudney Chouk. Elected by the non-commissioned officers of the regiment." Colour-Sergt. Waller died on the 16th Jan. 1877.

GARVIN, STEPHEN, Colour-Sergt., enlisted in the 60th Rifles (King's Royal Rifle Corps), was promoted to Colour-Sergeant, served in the Indian Mutiny Campaign, and was awarded the Victoria Cross [London Gazette, 20 Jan. 1860]: " Stephen Garvin, Colour-Sergt., 60th Rifles (1st Battn.). Date of Act of Bravery : 23 June, 1857. For daring and gallant conduct before Delhi on the 23rd June, 1857, in volunteering to lead a small party of men, under a heavy fire, to the 'Sammy House,' for the purpose of dislodging a number of the enemy in position there, who kept up a destructive fire on the advanced battery of heavy guns, in which, after a sharp contest, he succeeded. Also recommended for gallant conduct throughout the operations before Delhi." Colour-Sergt. Garvin died on the 23rd Nov. 1874.

SUTTON, WILLIAM, Bugler, enlisted in the 1st Battn. 60th Rifles (King's Royal Rifle Corps), served in the Indian Mutiny, and was awarded the Victoria Cross [London Gazette, 20 Jan. 1860]: " William Sutton, Bugler, 1st Battn. 60th Rifles. Date of Act of Bravery : 13 Sept. 1857. For gallant conduct at Delhi on the 13th Sept. 1857, the night previous to the assault, in volunteering to reconnoitre the breach. This soldier's conduct was conspicuous throughout the operations, especially on the 2nd Aug. 1857, on which occasion, during an attack by the enemy in force, he rushed over the trenches and killed one of the enemy's buglers, who was in the act of sounding. Elected by the privates of the regiment." Bugler Sutton died on the 16th Feb. 1888.

William Sutton.

DIVANE, JOHN, Private, enlisted in the 1st Battn. 60th Rifles (King's Royal Rifle Corps), served in the Mutiny, and was awarded the Victoria Cross [London Gazette, 20 Jan. 1860]: " John Divane, Private, 1st Battn. 60th Rifles. Date of Act of Bravery : 10 Sept. 1857. For distinguished gallantry in heading a successful charge made by the Beeloochee and Sikh troops on one of the enemy's trenches before Delhi on the 10th Sept. 1857. He leaped out of our trenches, closely followed by the native troops, and was shot down from the top of the enemy's breastworks. Elected by the privates of the regiment." Private Divane died on the 1st Dec. 1888.

John Divane.

THOMPSON, JAMES, Private, enlisted in the 60th Rifles (King's Royal Rifle Corps), served in the Indian Mutiny Campaign, and was awarded the Victoria Cross [London Gazette, 20 Jan. 1860]: " James Thompson, Private, 60th Rifles (1st Battn.). Date of Act of Bravery : 9 July, 1857. For gallant conduct in saving the life of his Captain (Capt. Wilton), on the 9th July, 1857, by dashing forward to his relief, when that officer was surrounded by a party of Ghazees, who made a sudden rush on him from a serai, and killing two of them before further assistance could reach. Also recommended for conspicuous conduct throughout the Siege. Wounded. Elected by the privates of the regiment." Private Thompson died on the 5th Dec. 1891. His Victoria Cross is in the possession of Alexander Duncan, Esq., of Penarth.

James Thompson.

TURNER, SAMUEL, Private, enlisted in the 60th Rifles (King's Royal Rifle Corps), served in the Mutiny Campaign, and was awarded the Victoria Cross [London Gazette, 20 Jan. 1860]: " Samuel Turner, Private, 60th Rifles (1st Battn.). Date of Act of Bravery : 19 June, 1857. For having at Delhi, on the night of the 19th June, 1857, during a severe conflict with the enemy, who attacked the rear of the camp, carried off on his shoulders, under a heavy fire, a mortally wounded officer, Lieut. Humphreys, of the

Indian Service. During this service Private Turner was wounded by a sabre-cut in the right arm. His gallant conduct saved the above-named officer from the fate of others, whose mangled remains were not recovered until the following day." Private Turner died on the 13th June, 1868.

KIRK, JOHN, Private, enlisted in the 10th (Lincolnshire) Regt. and served in the Indian Mutiny. The " History of the 10th Foot " (Vol. II., page 162), says : " At Benares on 4 June, 1857, Kirk happened to hear that Capt. Brown, Pensions Paymaster, his wife and little child, were shut in and surrounded in a detached bungalow. Kirk made at once for the place, meeting Sergt.-Major Rosamund, of the mutinous 37th, and Sergt.-Major Gill, of the Loodiana Regt., who had also volunteered to make an attempt to save Brown and his party. On reaching the bungalow they forced their way in, in spite of the fact that the rebels were firing on them and on the house. Joining those who were shut in thus, the three soldiers opened fire on the rebels, and to such purpose that they retired, so that the Europeans were brought out and conducted to the lines. For this service all three soldiers were awarded the V.C." Private Kirk's Victoria Cross was gazetted [London Gazette, 20 Jan. 1860]: " John Kirk, Private, the 10th Regt. Date of Act of Bravery : 4 June, 1857. For daring gallantry at Benares, on the 4th June, 1857, at the outbreak of the mutiny of the native troops at that station, in having volunteered to proceed with two non-commissioned officers to rescue Capt. Brown, Pension Paymaster, and his family, who were surrounded by rebels in the compound of their house, and having, at the risk of his own life, succeeded in saving them." In Nov. 1860, Private Kirk went down to Windsor, and received at the hands of his Sovereign his Victoria Cross for the gallant deed done by him during the Indian Mutiny. Private Kirk died on the 30th Aug. 1865.

London Gazette, 17 Feb. 1860.—" The Queen having been graciously pleased, by a Warrant under Her Royal Sign Manual, bearing date 13 Dec. 1858, to declare that Non-Military Persons who, as Volunteers, have borne arms against the Mutineers, both at Lucknow and elsewhere, during the late operations in India, shall be considered as eligible to receive the Decoration of the Victoria Cross, subject to the rules and ordinances already made and ordained for the government thereof, provided that it be established in any case that the person was serving under the orders of a General or other Officer in Command of Troops in the field when he performed the Act of Bravery for which it is proposed to confer the distinction. Her Majesty has accordingly been pleased to signify her intention to confer this high distinction on the undermentioned gentlemen, whose claim to the same has been submitted for Her Majesty's approval, on account of an Act of Bravery performed by him in India, as recorded against his name."

McDONELL, WILLIAM FRASER, was born 17 Dec. 1829 ; the son of Æneas Ranald McDonell, Esq., Madras Civil Service, and Juliana Charlotte Wade, who lived at Pittville House, Cheltenham. William Fraser McDonell entered Cheltenham College on its foundation in 1841, and completed his education at the Honourable East India Company's College at Haileybury (1847–1849—First Class, Highly Distinguished). He entered the Bengal Civil Service in 1849 ; became Assistant-Magistrate and Collector, Sarun, 1852–1855, and Magistrate of Sarun 1855–1859. In that district, with the exception of a few months in Champarun, he remained till the outbreak of the Mutiny found him there as Joint-Magistrate with his lifelong friend, Mr. R. J. Richardson, as Collector. When the Civil Officers of the outlying districts were called to Patna, Mr. McDonell was then without definite employment, and eagerly embraced the opportunity of volunteering to accompany the expedition for the relief of Arrah which started from Dinapur on the 29th July, 1857. At Arrah a little garrison of 70 souls, mostly composed of Rattray's Sikhs, was making a gallant stand in a small house, where it was besieged by an army of sepoy rebels. The Relief Column was surprised when within a mile of its destination by an overwhelming force of the sepoys, who attacked it as it was marching along the length of a dense mango grove at dead of night. In the first volley Capt. Dunbar and several officers were shot dead, and only the presence of mind of an officer saved the column—surrounded as it was by invisible foes—from the confusion which would have ended in a massacre. He caused the " assembly " to be sounded in an enclosed field a short distance from the grove. The men at once rallied to the bugle call, and in the hollow of a disused tank found to a certain extent protection from the enemy's fire, which they returned as best they could, but with little effect. There is an account in Kaye and Malleson's " History " : " Under these difficult circumstances the * * * officers held a council of war. They felt that with their dispirited and diminished forces it would be impossible to reach Arrah ; that they would be fortunate if they could fall back upon Sone. They resolved then to commence a retrograde movement as soon as the not then distant dawn would enable them to find the road. As soon as it was daylight the men formed up in order and marched out on the Arrah road. But the enemy had been as vigilant as they. Every point on their route—the ditches, the jungles, the houses—had been occupied in force. The British force marched straight onwards, returning in a desultory manner the fire which was poured upon them, but intent only on reaching the Sone. The power of driving back the enemy was denied them by the fact that no enemy was in sight. They were sheltered behind the trees, the copses, the bushes, the ditches, and the jungle. Occasionally, indeed, maddened by the sight of their comrades falling around them, the men constituting by accident the rear-guard formed up, faced about and tried to charge. But there was no enemy to receive the charge.

William F. McDonell.

Five or six thousand men, the revolted sepoys and levies of Kunwar Singh, kept themselves under the shelter offered by the natural obstacles of the country. At last, after losing many of their comrades, the main body of the British force reached the banks of the rivulet, to cross which the previous night they had found boats ready to their hand. The boats were still there. During the night, however, the water had run down, and of all the boats only two were floating. These were promptly seized by the men in advance and pushed off. Then ensued a scene which it is impossible to paint in living words. It was a scene to which the imagination only could do justice. There were the stranded boats on the bank of the river, the defeated soldiers rushing at them to push them further into the stream, the musket-fire from the victorious sepoys, the cries of the wounded and dying, the disorder and confusion naturally associated with a military disaster. It was a scene to call forth all that was manly and heroic, all that was mean and selfish. But whilst the first-named qualities were markedly visible the latter were conspicuous only by their absence. The difficulties already numerated were added to by the fact that some of the boats caught fire. The losses of the British troops here sustained probably exceeded those they had suffered during the retreat. Order was impossible. To push a boat into the stream, to climb into it, to help others in, was the aim of every man's exertions. But when the boats would not be moved the chance of drowning was preferred to the tender mercies of the sepoys. Many stripped and rushed in, until at last the majority of the survivors found themselves on the opposite bank. Many acts of daring were performed during the retreat and crossing. . . . Another of the volunteers, McDonell, of the Civil Service, received the Victoria Cross for cutting the lashings of one of the boats, full of men, amid a storm of bullets to which he was exposed from the opposite bank. Lieut. Ingelby, who had volunteered to command the Sikhs, was the last man to leave the shore. He plunged into the water and was shot in the act of crossing. These are a few among the many instances which occurred of combined courage and humanity." Kaye's account of an act of daring self-devotion done by Mr. McDonell is as follows: "It was in no small measure owing to his representations and to his offer to act as guide to the relieving force, for he knew the country well, that General Lloyd consented to send the European detachment into Shahabad. Always in the front, always in the thick of the battle, he did excellent service, as I have said before, on the march. Many a Mutineer sank beneath the fire of his rifle. He was beside Dunbar when he fell, and was sprinkled with the blood of the luckless leader. Wounded himself, he still fought on gallantly during the retreat, and reached the nullah with a stiffened limb, but with no abatement of vigorous courage. There, having done his best to assist others more helpless than himself, he entered the last of the boats and deliverance seemed to be at hand. But the insurgents had taken away the oars and had lashed the rudder, and though the breeze was favourable for the escape of our people, the current carried the boat back to the river bank, and fast and furious came the shower of musket balls from the pieces of the enemy. The boats were the large covered boats—'the floating haystacks' of the country, which afforded excellent shelter to those who huddled together beneath the clumsy thatch. There were thirty-five European soldiers on board the boat, and McDonell, seeing the difficulty and danger which the impossibility of steering the vessel brought upon them, called upon the men to cut the lashings of the rudder. But no man stirred, so McDonell went out from the shelter, and climbing on to the roof of the boat, perched himself on the rudder and cut the lashings amidst a storm of bullets from the contiguous bank. It was truly a providential deliverance that he escaped instant death. Coolly and steadily he went about his perilous work, and though some balls passed through his hat not one did him any harm. Thus the rudder was loosened, the boat answered to the helm, and by McDonell's gallant act the crew were saved from certain destruction." Captain Medhurst, of the 60th Rifles (formerly of the 10th Foot), in his official account, says: "After assisting some wounded men into the farthest boat and being myself pulled in, I saw that Mr. McDonell, who was one of our number, was exerting himself with a sergeant to move the boat into the stream. It being discovered that the boat was bound to the bank, one or two men jumped out and loosened the rope and the boat moved. Assisted by the less exhausted of my party, I was keeping up a fire of Enfields on the enemy, whose musketry was very galling. Whilst so employed I heard Mr. McDonell call out for a knife to cut away some rope which bound the rudder to the right, causing the lumbering boat to veer round into the right shore again, and for a time causing it to stick fast. On looking round I saw him seated on the stern extremity of the boat, in full view of the enemy and quite exposed to their fire. He cut away the before-mentioned rope, and guiding the rudder himself, a fortunate breeze carried our boat across the stream, grounding at about ten yards from the left bank, whereby all those who were alive were enabled to jump out and reach the steamer in safety. The number of men thus saved was about 35, and during the passage across three men were shot dead, one was mortally and two or three slightly wounded. I may safely assert that it was owing to Mr. McDonell's presence of mind and at his personal risk that our boat got across on that day." For this deed Mr. McDonell received the Victoria Cross [London Gazette, 20 Jan. 1860]: "Mr. William Fraser McDonell, of the Bengal Civil Service, Magistrate of Sarun. Date of Act of Bravery: 30 July, 1857. During the retreat from Arrah, in having climbed, under an incessant fire, outside the boat in which he and several soldiers were, up to the rudder, and with considerable difficulty cut through the lashing which secured it to the side of the boat. On the lashing being cut, the boat obeyed the helm, and thus thirty-five European soldiers escaped certain death." On the collapse of the Mutiny in Behar Mr. McDonell was entrusted with the task of settling the confiscated estates of the rebel leader, Koer Singh, till in June, 1860, he proceeded on three years' furlough to Europe. Returning to India in 1863, he was posted in Nadia, and remained in that district almost without intermission, first as Magistrate and Collector and afterwards as Judge, till he again took furlough in July, 1870. On the conclusion of his leave he was posted to Patna as Judge, an appointment which he held till promoted to the High Court, temporarily in 1874 and permanently in Aug. 1878. He finally resigned the Service and his seat on the Bench on the 29th April, 1886. Mr. McDonell was greatly beloved in India. He was a keen sportsman, and as a young man was known as a brilliant pig-sticker, a fearless rider to hounds and an excellent gentleman rider. When his age and health made these pursuits no longer possible, he devoted much of his leisure to upholding the best traditions of the Indian Turf. "As a steward of the Calcutta Turf Club and of the Calcutta races, his judicial mind, his hatred of wrong, and his gentle, kindly nature enabled him to render services to both institutions which it is difficult to overrate. To mention the qualities just named is indeed to strike the keynote of his whole life; a heart as tender as a woman's, a most equal and genial temper, a generous hand were combined in him with a careful and well-balanced mind, a resolute courage and hatred of all that was false, sordid, or dishonourable." ("The Englishman," Calcutta, 3 Aug. 1894.) After his retirement Mr. McDonell lived in London for some time, where he was a familiar figure at the Oriental Club. He subsequently went to live in Cheltenham, where he became a member of the Council (1890–94) and one of the Governors of the College. His health failed a good deal in 1893, and he spent the winter in Malta. In 1894 he caught a chill on the East Gloucester Cricket Ground at Cheltenham, and died of pneumonia, 31 July, after a short illness. He was buried in Leckhampton churchyard. Mr. McDonell married Annie Louisa Duff, who survived him many years. A memorial tablet has been erected to him in the Cheltenham College Chapel, and in Calcutta a memorial drinking fountain and horse-trough with a suitable inscription has been erected opposite the High Court by his many friends, both official and non-official.

London Gazette, 17 Feb. 1860.—"Her Majesty has also been graciously pleased to signify Her intention to confer the Decoration of the Victoria Cross on the undermentioned Officers and Private Soldier, whose claims to the same have been submitted for Her Majesty's approval, on account of Acts of Bravery performed by them in India, as recorded against their several names."

CAFE, WILLIAM MARTIN, Capt., was born on the 23rd March, 1826; entered the Army as Ensign 11 June, 1842; became Lieutenant 12 April, 1843; was present at the Battle of Marajpore in Dec. 1842, and received the Bronze Star for his services. He became Captain 27 Jan. 1849, and took an active part throughout the operations of the Punjab Campaign of that year, being present at the actions of Sadoolapore, Chilianwallah and Gujerat, and the pursuit of the Sikhs and Afghans, receiving a Medal and two clasps. He also served during the Indian Mutiny in 1857 and 1858, and was present during the engagement at Meangunge, the siege and capture of Lucknow, and the action at Rooyah, being severely wounded. For his services in these engagements he was awarded the Victoria Cross [London Gazette, 17 Feb. 1860]: "William Martin Cafe, Capt., 56th Bengal Native Infantry (late). Date of Act of Bravery: 15 April, 1858. For bearing away under a heavy fire, with the assistance of Privates Thompson, Crowie, Spence and Cook, the body of Lieut. Willoughby, lying near the ditch of the Fort at Ruhya, and for running to the rescue of Private Spence, who had been severely wounded." Lieut. Willoughby was the brother of Capt. Willoughby, one of the nine who blew up the Magazine at Delhi. He became Major 29 Aug. 1861; Lieutenant-Colonel 26 July, 1864; Colonel 21 March, 1873, and retired with the rank of General. General Cafe died at 16, Wetherby Place, South Kensington, S.W., on Monday, 6 Aug. 1906, and an obituary notice of him appeared in the "Times" of the following Saturday.

BROWN, FRANCIS DAVID MILLETT, Lieut., was born 7 Aug. 1837, and was gazetted Ensign, Bengal Army, 8 Dec. 1855; Second Lieutenant, 1st Bengal European Fusiliers, 7 March, 1856; Lieutenant 7 June, 1857. He served in the Indian Mutiny, received the Medal with clasps for Delhi and Lucknow, and was awarded the Victoria Cross [London Gazette, 17 Feb. 1860]: "Francis David Millett Brown, Lieut., 1st Bengal European Fusiliers. Date of Act of Bravery, 16 Nov. 1857. For great gallantry at Narrioul, on the 16th Nov. 1857, in having, at the imminent risk of his own life, rushed to the assistance of a wounded soldier of the 1st European Bengal Fusiliers, whom he carried off under a heavy fire from the enemy, whose cavalry were within forty or fifty yards of him at the time." When the 1st Bengal Fusiliers were transferred to Her Majesty's service in 1861, Major Brown remained "local in India" and did not go into the line. He served in the North-West Frontier of India Campaign in 1863, and was present at the forcing of the Umbeyla Pass, receiving the Medal with clasp for Umbeyla. He became Captain, 101st European Fusiliers, 23 Aug. 1864; was transferred to the Bengal Staff Corps 14 Sept. 1865. He became Major 8 Dec. 1875, and Lieutenant-Colonel 8 Dec. 1881. He was placed on the Unemployed Supernumerary List 9 Aug. 1894, and died on the 21st Nov. 1895. His eldest son, Lieut. Frank Russell Brown, was gazetted to the regiment on the 21st Dec. 1892; joined the 1st Battn. in Dublin, and went out with them to the South African War, and was serving with the Munster Infantry when he died on the 4th April, 1900, of wounds received in the action at Sanna's Post. His second son, Major Claude Russell Brown, joined the Royal Engineers in 1892, and was severely wounded in the South African War; he was Professor at the Royal Military College, Canada, from 28 Sept. 1905, to 31 July, 1910; became temporary Lieutenant-Colonel, R.E., 2 Oct. 1915.

DEMPSEY, DENIS, Private, enlisted in the 10th (Lincolnshire) Regt. and served in the Indian Mutiny. "The History of the 10th Foot" (Vol. II., pages 126–137 and 138), says of Private Dempsey: "He belonged to the Grenadier Company. In the attempt to relieve Arrah on 29 July, 1857, Ensign Erskine fell mortally wounded. Dempsey went to him, in spite of the bullets that were whistling past him, and taking him in his arms, carried him out of danger. Erskine was so badly wounded that he died the next day. It was during the fight on 14 Nov. that Dempsey again distinguished himself. On the same day on which the regiment and the Sikhs took the

Imanbarrah and the Kaiserbagh, the sepoys erected batteries of guns in the streets. One of these stopped the progress of the 10th, and the only way of getting through was to breach it. An engineer asked for a volunteer to carry a bag of gunpowder to the breach, and lay a fuse to it and blow it up. The mere suggestion seemed madness, but Dempsey immediately volunteered. Taking the bag of powder, he kept on the side of the street where the guns could not play on him, exposed, however, to the fire of any marksman who might be with the battery. His movements were covered by the fire of his comrades, and hurrying up the street, he threw down the powder-bag, and, although wounded, laid the fuse and blew up the front of the battery." He was awarded the Victoria Cross [London Gazette, 17 Feb. 1860]: " Denis Dempsey, Private, 1st Battn. 10th Regt. Dates of Acts of Bravery: 12 Aug. 1857; 14 March, 1858. For having at Lucknow, on the 14th March, 1858, carried a powder-bag through a burning village, with great coolness and gallantry, for the purpose of mining a passage in rear of the enemy's position. This he did, exposed to a very heavy fire from the enemy behind loopholed walls, and to an almost still greater danger from the sparks which flew in every direction from the blazing houses. Also for having been first man who entered the village of Jugdispore, on the 12th Aug. 1857, under a most galling fire. Private Dempsey was likewise one of those who helped to carry Ensign Erskine, of the 10th Regt., in the retreat from Arrah in July, 1857." The two men carried Ensign Erskine, who was mortally wounded, for five miles. In Nov. 1860, Privates Dempsey and Kirk, both of the 10th Regt., went down to Windsor and received at the hands of their Sovereign their Victoria Crosses, for the gallant deeds done by them during the Indian Mutiny. Private Dempsey died in Canada on the 10th Jan. 1896.

London Gazette, 27 April, 1860.—" War Office, 27 April, 1860.—The Queen having been graciously pleased, by a Warrant under Her Royal Sign Manual, bearing the date the 13th Dec. 1858, to declare that Non-Military Persons who, as Volunteers, have borne arms against the Mutineers, both at Lucknow and elsewhere, during the late operations in India, shall be considered eligible to receive the Decoration of the Victoria Cross, subject to the rules and ordinances already made and ordained for the government thereof, provided that it be established in any case that the person was serving under the orders of a General or other Officer in Command of Troops in the Field when he performed the Act of Bravery for which it is proposed to confer the decoration: Her Majesty has accordingly been pleased to signify Her intention to confer this high distinction on the undermentioned Gentleman, whose claim to the same has been submitted for Her Majesty's approval on account of an Act of Bravery performed by him in India, as recorded against his name."

CHICKEN, GEORGE BELL, joined the Indian Navy, and served with the Naval Brigade in the Indian Mutiny. " In the Jagdispur jungles Lieut. Carew (Indian Navy), serving under Colonel Corfield, did excellent service. Several of the Indian Navy soldiers died of exposure, and the same cause compelled Carew to resign his command to Mr. Midshipman Cotgrave. Lieutenant, afterwards Commander, Batt did splendid service in the same district. Batt had distinguished himself by his activity in the Ganges, between Allahabad and Kanhpur, in July and Aug. 1857, by shelling the rebels out of their position in the fort of Kali Kanki. Subsequently he commanded at Baksar, where he repaired the fort, made gun-carriages, and trained his men. Later on, in the autumn of 1858, he assisted in the measures taken to drive the followers of Kunwar Singh from the jungles of Jagdispur, being always to the front. On one of the many occasions when he was in action, an officer serving under him, Acting-Master George Chicken, gained the Victoria Cross. The force to which Chicken was attached was engaged with, and had driven back, the rebels near Piru on the 4th Sept. 1858. In the pursuit Chicken suddenly came alone upon a group of twenty preparing to rally and open fire on their scattered pursuers. He at once charged them. Surrounded on all sides, Chicken fought most desperately and killed five of the rebels. He would, however, have succumbed had not four native troopers arrived in the nick of time to his rescue. He escaped with a severe wound." (" Kaye and Malleson," Vol. VI., page 172.) He was awarded the Victoria Cross [London Gazette, 27 April, 1860]: " Mr. George Bell Chicken, Indian Naval Brigade. Date of Act of Bravery: 27 Sept. 1858. For great gallantry on the 4th Sept. 1858, at Suhejnee, near Peroo, in having charged into the middle of a considerable number of the rebels, who were preparing to rally and open fire upon the scattered pursuers. They were surrounded on all sides, but, fighting desperately, Mr. Chicken succeeded in killing five before he was cut down himself. He would have been cut to pieces had not some of the men of the 1st Bengal Police and 3rd Sikhs Irregular Cavalry dashed into the crowd to his rescue, and routed it, after killing several of the enemy." Two officers of the Indian Navy won the Victoria Cross, of whom one (Mr. Mayo) survives, and it is said that the other (Mr. Chicken) " found a sailor's grave with his ship and all hands."

London Gazette, 28 April, 1860.—" The Queen has been graciously pleased to signify Her intention to confer the decoration of the Victoria Cross on the undermentioned Soldier, whose claim to the same has been submitted for Her Majesty's approval, on account of an Act of Bravery performed by him in India, as recorded against his name."

PEARSON, JAMES, Private, enlisted in the 86th (Royal County Down) Regt., served in the Mutiny, and was awarded the Victoria Cross [London Gazette, 1 May, 1860]: " James Pearson, No. 1882, Private, 86th Regt. (now of the 56th Regt.). Date of Act of Bravery: 3 April, 1858. For having gallantly attacked a number of armed rebels on the occasion of the storming of Jhansi, on the 3rd April, 1858, one of whom he killed, and bayoneted two others. He was himself wounded in the attack. Also for having brought into Calpee, under a heavy fire, Private Michael Burns, who afterwards died of his wounds."

London Gazette, 19 June, 1860.—" The Queen has been graciously pleased to signify her intention to confer the Decoration of the Victoria Cross on the undermentioned Soldiers of Her Majesty's Army, whose claims to the same have been submitted for Her Majesty's approval, on account of Acts of Bravery performed by them in India, as recorded against their several names."

HARTIGAN, H., Pensioned Sergt., served in the Indian Mutiny, and was awarded the Victoria Cross [London Gazette, 19 June, 1860]: " H. Hartigan, Pensioned Sergt., 9th Lancers. For daring and distinguished gallantry in the following instances: At the Battle of Budle-ke-Serai, near Delhi, on 8 June, 1857, in going to the assistance of Sergt. H. Helstone, who was wounded, dismounted and surrounded by the enemy, and at the risk of his own life carrying him to the rear. On 10 Oct. 1857, at Agra, in having run unarmed to the assistance of Sergt. Crews, who was attacked by four rebels. Hartigan caught a tulwar with his right hand from one of them, and with the other hit him on the mouth, and then defending himself against the other three, killing one and wounding two, when he was himself disabled from service by severe and dangerous wounds." " At the end of the year 1857 the want of native troopers and orderlies at Agra had been greatly felt, and a corps of cavalry was raised which was subsequently known as Meade's Horse. As there were in the fort officers whom the Mutiny had deprived of employment, it was decided to raise it on a military footing, and the task was entrusted to Capt. R. J. Meade. He had been for some years Brigade-Major of the Gwalior Contingent, knew the language of the people, and was much esteemed by the officers under whom he served. A hundred Sikhs and Punjabi Mohammedans formed the nucleus of this new regiment, and to them Meade added some forty Eurasians and native Christians, chiefly drummers and bandsmen taken from the disbanded native regiments. None of them had ever been on a horse's back before! In January, 1858, forty-five mounted Jats were added to the corps, under a native officer of good family, who soon induced a neighbouring chief to raise seventy more horsemen. Thus the regiment was formed, and Meade was in a short time able to divide it into six class troops. The labour of drilling the men and teaching many of them to ride may be imagined when it is considered that none of the men had served in the cavalry or as soldiers at all. Working incessantly himself, and aided by such men as Sergt. Hartigan, V.C., of the 9th Lancers, and who subsequently obtained a commission in the 16th; by Cockburn, . . . and by others, Meade was able, in the beginning of March, to show a fair proportion of his regiment fit for service." Hartigan, as has been said, was commissioned into the 16th Lancers. He died on the 29th Oct. 1886.

GRANT, ROBERT, Sergt., enlisted in the Northumberland Fusiliers; served in the Indian Mutiny, and was awarded the Victoria Cross [London Gazette, 19 June, 1860]: " Ewart, Sergt. Robert, 1st Battn. 5th Regt. Date of Act of Bravery: 24 Sept. 1857. For conspicuous devotion at Alumbagh, on 24 Sept., in proceeding under a heavy and galling fire to save the life of Private E. Deveney, whose leg had been shot away, and eventually carrying him safe into camp, with the assistance of the late Lieut. Brown and some comrades." The London Gazette of 2 Oct. reads: " For 1st Battn. 5th Regt., Sergt. Robert Ewart, read 1st Battn. 5th Regt., Sergt. Robert Grant. Erratum in London Gazette of Tuesday, 19 June, 1860." Sergt. Robert Grant died on the 23rd Nov. 1874, when a constable of " Y " Division.

M'HALE, PATRICK, Private, enlisted in the 5th Fusiliers on 18 Dec. 1847. He was then twenty-one years old, and joined the depôt at Parkstone Barracks, Isle of Wight. He sailed on the 8th May, 1848, on board the Lady Edmondsbury, for the island of Mauritius. He was a sandyhaired, freckled man, standing about six feet two inches, with a broad chest and square shoulders. He could neither read nor write. He served nine years at Mauritius, and in 1857 arrived at the headquarters of the regiment in India, and proceeded with his company to the relief of Arrah and the operations in the Jugdespore district. He served with Havelock's column and was present at the Battle of Mungulwar, at the capture of Alambagh, and the first Relief of Lucknow on 25 Sept. During the period when the regiment was besieged for nearly two months in the Residency M'Hale was much to the fore. After the relief by Sir C. Campbell in Nov. the regiment was encamped at the Alambagh, and was attached to the 1st Brigade of Sir J. Outram's force. It was in a night attack by Outram on the village of Guilee that M'Hale specially distinguished himself. He was at the final Relief of Lucknow, and also in Oudh in 1858-59, and through the whole of the campaign, without a scratch, for his services in which, besides the Victoria Cross, he received the Medal with clasps for the Defence of Lucknow and Lucknow, the Good Conduct Medal and the Regimental Medal of Merit. His Victoria Cross was gazetted 19 June, 1860: " Patrick McHale, Private, 1st Battn. 5th Regt. Dates of Acts of Bravery: 2 Oct. 1857, and 22 Dec. 1857. For conspicuous bravery at Lucknow on the 2nd Oct. 1857, when he was the first man at the capture of one of the guns at the Cawnpore Battery; and again, on the 22nd Dec. 1857, when, by a bold rush, he was the first to take possession of one of the enemy's guns, which had sent several rounds of grape through his company, which was skirmishing up to it. On every occasion of attack, Private McHale has been the first to meet the foe, amongst whom he caused such consternation by the boldness of his rush as to leave little work for those who followed to his support. By his habitual coolness and daring, and sustained bravery in action, his name has become a household word for gallantry among his comrades." On his return to England in 1861 he served with the regiment until it embarked for India in 1866, when he was sent with the other old soldiers to Shorncliffe to form the regimental depôt. He died at Shorncliffe on the 29th Oct. 1866, and a stone was erected over his grave by his comrades.

London Gazette, 3 Aug. 1860.—" The Queen has been graciously pleased to signify her intention to confer the Decoration of the Victoria Cross on the undermentioned Officers of Her Majesty's Indian Forces, whose claims to the same have been submitted for Her Majesty's approval, in consideration of their gallantry and distinguished conduct during the operations of the Expeditionary Force in Persia in 1856–57, as recorded against their several names."

WOOD, JOHN AUGUSTUS, Capt., joined the 20th Bombay Native Infantry (now the 120th Rajputana Infantry) in 1839 ; served in the Persian Expedition of 1856–57, and was awarded the Victoria Cross [London Gazette, 3 Aug. 1860]: " John Augustus Wood, Capt., 20th Bombay Native Infantry. Date of Act of Bravery : 9 Dec. 1856. On the 9th Dec. 1856, Capt. Wood led the Grenadier Company which formed the head of the assaulting column sent against Bushire. He was the first man on the parapet of the fort, where he was instantly attacked by a large number of the garrison, who suddenly sprang on him from a trench cut in the parapet itself. These men fired a volley at Capt. Wood and the head of the storming party, when only a yard or two distant from that officer but although Capt. Wood was struck by no less than seven musket-balls, he at once threw himself upon the enemy, passed his sword through the body of their leader, and being closely followed by the men of his company, speedily overcame all opposition, and established himself in the place. Capt. Wood's decision, energy and determined valour undoubtedly contributed in a high degree to the success of the attack. His wounds compelled him to leave the force for a time ; but with the true spirit of a good soldier he rejoined his regiment, and returned to his duty at Bushire before the wounds were properly healed."

MOORE, ARTHUR THOMAS, Lieut. and Adjutant, was born on the 20th Sept. 1830 ; the son of Edward Francis Moore, Esquire, of Carlingford, formerly of the 45th Regt., and belonged to an old family in County Louth. He entered the 3rd Bombay Light Cavalry, Bombay Army, on the 29th July, 1850, as Second Lieutenant, and became Lieutenant 28 Aug. 1855. With this regiment, of which he was Adjutant, he saw much service. He fought through the Persian Campaign of 1856–57, and was present at the Battle of Khoosh-ab (Persia), and for his gallantry on that occasion was awarded the Victoria Cross [London Gazette, 3 Aug. 1860]: " Arthur Thomas Moore, Lieut. and Adjutant ; John Grant Malcolmson, Lieut., 3rd Bombay Light Cavalry. Dates of Acts of Bravery : 8 Feb. 1857. On the occasion of an attack on the enemy on the 8th Feb. 1857, led by Lieut.-Col. Forbes, C.B., Lieut. Moore, the Adjutant of the regiment, was perhaps the first of all by a horse's length. His horse leapt into the square, and instantly fell dead, crushing down his rider and breaking his sword as he fell amid the broken ranks of the enemy. Lieut. Moore speedily extricated himself, and attempted with his broken sword to force his way through the press ; but he would assuredly have lost his life had not the gallant young Lieut. Malcolmson, observing his peril, fought his way to his dismounted comrade through a crowd of enemies, to his rescue, and giving him his stirrup, safely carried him through everything out of the throng. The thoughtfulness for others, cool determination, devoted courage, and ready activity shown in extreme danger by this young officer, Lieut. Malcolmson, appear to have been most admirable, and to be worthy of the highest honour." We are told elsewhere that in this battle Lieut. Moore charged an infantry square of 500 Persians at the head of his regiment and jumped his horse over the bayonets of the enemy. He stood with shattered sabre astride his dead charger until Lieut. Malcolmson came to his assistance and got him safely away. Lieut. Malcolmson also received the Victoria Cross. He became Captain and died a few years before General Moore. Lieut. Moore afterwards served in the Indian Mutiny Campaign, under Sir Hugh Rose, and was present at the siege and capture of Ratghur, the action at Barodia, the relief of Sangor, the siege and capture of Garakota, the affairs on the Junna, the capture of Calpe, the advance on and capture of Gwalior, the action at Morar, the Battle of Jowra, Alipore, and the action of Khow–Mohoni. He was mentioned in Despatches and received the Medal and clasp. He became Captain 29 July, 1862 ; Major 29 July, 1870 ; Lieutenant-Colonel 1 July, 1881 ; was created a C.B. in 1887 ; was placed on the Retired List 26 Sept. 1888, and was given the honorary rank of Major-General 13 June, 1891. Major-General Moore married Annie, daughter of Henry Leslie Prentice, Esq., J.P., D.L., of Ennislare, County Armagh, and Caledon, County Tyrone. He died of heart failure after influenza, at his residence, 18, Waterloo Place, Dublin, on Friday, 25 April, 1913.

MALCOLMSON, JOHN GRANT, Lieut., was born in 1835, the son of the late James Malcolmson, of Muchrach, Inverness-shire. He entered the 3rd Bombay Light Cavalry, served in the Persian War, and was present at the capture of Reshire and surrender of Bushire in the Persian War (V.C., Medal with clasp). He served in the Indian Mutiny Campaign, and was present at the Central India operations from the siege of Ratghur to the fall of Calpe. He served in the Persian Expedition of 1856–57, and was awarded the Victoria Cross [London Gazette, 3 Aug. 1860]: " Arthur Thomas Moore, Lieut. and Adjutant, and John Grant Malcolmson, Lieut., 3rd Bombay Native Cavalry. Date of Acts of Bravery : 8 Feb. 1857. On the occasion of an attack on the enemy on the 8th Feb. 1857, led by Lieut.-Colonel Forbes, C.B., Lieut. Moore, the Adjutant of the regiment, was perhaps the first of all by a horse's length. His horse leaped into the square and instantly fell dead, crushing down his rider and breaking his sword as he fell amid the broken ranks of the enemy. Lieut. Moore speedily extricated himself, and attempted with his broken sword to force his way through the press ; but would assuredly have lost his life had not the gallant young Lieut. Malcolmson, observing his peril, fought his way to his dismounted comrade through a crowd of enemies, to his rescue, and giving him his stirrup, safely carried him through everything out of the throng. The thoughtfulness for others, cool determination and

ready activity shown in extreme danger by this young officer, Lieut. Malcolmson, appear to have been most admirable, and to be worthy of the highest honour." Lieut. Malcolmson became a Gentleman-at-Arms in 1870, and died suddenly at 29, Bramham Gardens, S.W., on 14 Aug. 1902.

London Gazette, 3 Aug. 1860.—" Her Majesty has also been graciously pleased to signify her intention to confer the Decoration of the Victoria Cross on the undermentioned Seaman of the Royal Navy, whose claim to the same has been submitted for Her Majesty's approval, in consideration of an Act of Bravery which he performed in the recent operations against Rebel Natives in New Zealand, as recorded against his name."

ODGERS, WILLIAM, Leading Seaman, Royal Navy, served in New Zealand in 1860, and was awarded the Victoria Cross [London Gazette, 3 Aug. 1860]: " William Odgers, Leading Seaman, of Her Majesty's Ship Niger. On the 28th March, 1860, William Odgers displayed conspicuous gallantry at the storming of a pass during operations against the rebel natives in New Zealand, having been the first to enter it under a heavy fire, and having assisted in hauling down the enemy's colours." He died on the 20th Dec. 1873.

London Gazette, 7 Aug. 1860.—" The Queen has been graciously pleased to signify her intention to confer the Decoration of the Victoria Cross on the undermentioned Soldier of Her Majesty's Army, whose claim to the same has been submitted for Her Majesty's approval, on account of an Act of Bravery performed by him in India, as recorded against his name."

Samuel Morley.

MORLEY, SAMUEL, Private, No. 201, served in the Military Train (now A.S.C.) in the Indian Mutiny, and was awarded the Victoria Cross [London Gazette, 7 Aug. 1860]: " Samuel Morley, No. 201, Private, 2nd Battn. Military Train. Date of Act of Bravery : 15 April, 1858. On the evacuation of Azinghur by Koer Singh's Army, on the 15th April, 1858, a squadron of the military train and half a troop of horse artillery were sent in pursuit. Upon overtaking them, and coming into action with their rearguard, a squadron of the 3rd Sikh Cavalry (also detached in pursuit), and one troop of the military train were ordered to charge, when Lieut. Hamilton, who commanded the Sikhs, was unhorsed, and immediately surrounded by the enemy, who commenced cutting and hacking him whilst on the ground. Private Samuel Morley, seeing the predicament that Lieut. Hamilton was in, although his (Morley's) horse had been shot from under him, immediately and most gallantly rushed up, on foot, to his assistance, and in conjunction with Farrier Murphy, who has already received the Victoria Cross for the same thing, cut down one of the sepoys, and fought over Lieut. Hamilton's body, until further assistance came up, and thereby was the means of saving Lieut. Hamilton from being killed on the spot."

London Gazette, 4 Sept. 1860.—" The Queen has been graciously pleased to signify her intention to confer the Decoration of the Victoria Cross on the undermentioned Officer of Her Majesty's Army, whose claim to the same has been submitted for Her Majesty's approval, on account of Acts of Bravery performed by him in India as recorded against his name."

WOOD, HENRY EVELYN, Lieut., was born at the Vicarage, Cressing, near Braintree, Essex, on the 9th Feb. 1838. He was the youngest son of Sir John Page Wood, 2nd Baronet, Clerk in Holy Orders and Rector of St. Peter's, Cornhill, in the City of London, and formerly Chaplain and Private Secretary to Queen Caroline ; and of Emma Carolina Michell, daughter of Admiral Sampson Michell, of Croft West, Cornwall. He was educated at Marlborough, from Feb. 1847, till Feb. 1849, in the Grammar School, and from Feb. 1849, till Feb. 1852, at the College. On 15 April, 1852, he passed the examination, and entered the Royal Navy, joining H.M.S. Queen, commanded by Capt. Charles Wise, then in the Channel Fleet. In 1853 H.M.S. Queen, now commanded by Capt. F. Michell, joined the Fleet at Constantinople towards the end of 1853, and in January 1854, proceeded to Sinope in the Black Sea. On 15 April, 1854, Mr. Wood passed the examination for Midshipman on completing two years' service. On 22 April, 1854, he was present in H.M.S. Queen while the steamers bombarded the military works of Odessa, and in May, June and July, 1854, was cruising in H.M.S. Queen off Sebastopol ; on 14 and 15 Sept. 1854, employed in landing the army in the Crimea. On 20 Sept. 1854, H.M.S Queen anchored off the mouth of the Alma River, as the army attacked the Russian position. On 1 Oct. 1854, Mr. Wood was sent to Balaklava for service with the Naval Brigade, and on 17 Oct. 1854, he volunteered with Mr. Daniels to lead a working party, and brought under cover from an exposed position a quantity of powder under a heavy fire. On 18 Oct. Capt. William Peel, R.N., Commanding the Naval Brigade in the 21-gun battery, thanked Mr. Wood

Henry Evelyn Wood.

before the guns' crews for having mounted and extinguished, under a very heavy fire from the Malakhoff and Redan, the roof of a magazine which had been set on fire by shells. On the 9th April, Mr. Wood was commended on parade before the sailors for having, on the opening of the second bombardment, repeatedly repaired the parapet at the angle of the 21-gun battery under the very heavy fire which destroyed it. In May, 1855, Mr. Wood was appointed aide-de-camp to Capt. Peel, who wrote of him and of Mr. Daniels, his other A.D.C.: "The names of these two heroes are known throughout the whole army, and I almost thought it inconvenient having two such spirits under me." He wrote also of Evelyn Wood that "Not only did he show the most beautiful courage, but his conduct and manners are as exemplary as his courage." Capt. Peel informed Mr. Wood that he had reported two acts to His Excellency Lord Raglan, commanding the Army, and Lord Raglan referred to them later in the winter when presenting Mr. Wood to Marshal Neil. On the 18th June, 1855, Mr. Wood served in the ladder-party of the right storming party; was twice wounded; carried a ladder to the abatis, and was the only Naval officer with the right column to reach the Redan. Capt. William Peel, R.N., wrote to Frederic Peel, Esq., M.P.: "Would you let Sir Page Wood know that his gallant son behaved with great intrepidity. He was, or is, my A.D.C., and received a severe wound from a grape-shot, but will not lose his arm. I can assure you I thought more of that boy than of anything else, and tried in vain to plead some excuse for getting him out of the way; but he *would* be my A.D.C., and it would have been a worse blow to have denied him. Thank God! He is safe, and it was such a relief to me." Sir Evelyn Wood says of Sir William Peel that he was not only a great sailor, a "first-class fighting man," but also "one of the most noble of creation." The following is an extract from a letter from Lord Raglan to Capt. Michell, R.N., of H.M.S. Queen:

"Before Sebastopol, 21 June, 1855.

"I am very pleased to have had the opportunity of being in any the smallest degree useful to your nephew, Mr. E. Wood, whose distinguished career cannot fail to enlist everybody in his favour."

Extract from the Despatch of Lord Raglan to Lord Panmure:

"Before Sebastopol, 23 June, 1855.

"I must not omit to mention the following officers of the Royal Navy who particularly distinguished themselves on the 18th June: Messrs. Wood (severely wounded) and Daniels, who have been through the whole siege."

Extract from a speech of Admiral Sir Edmund (late Lord Lyons) at a banquet given to him by the Lord Mayor, 13 Feb. 1856: "All behaved well, but I doubt if in the whole history of chivalry we could find anything finer than the conduct of Capt. Peel and his two gallant A.D.C.'s, one of whom" (Mr. Wood), "when wounded, placed the scaling ladders against the walls of the Redan." Extract certificate: "I can strongly recommend this young officer for his gallantry and good conduct during the whole time he was under my command; he was severely wounded on the 18th June while carrying the ladders." On 18 June Mr. Wood served in the ladder-party of the right storming column; was twice wounded; carried a ladder to the abatis, and was the only Naval officer with the right column who reached the Redan. On 18 June, Lord Raglan, on hearing Mr. Wood was wounded, at once sent a Staff officer to inquire at what time Mr. Wood would like to have his lordship's carriage to go to the anchorage. In June, 1855, Admiral Lushington informed Mr. Wood on parade that he had been recommended for the Victoria Cross, his name standing third in order of merit. Extract from a letter from Admiral Sir Stephen Lushington to Lieut. E. Wood:

"Brighton, 18 Sept. 1856.

". . . You have no one in the world to thank for the Legion of Honour but your own gallant conduct throughout the war, from the day you made me a saucy speech when acting as my guide, to the last crowning act when you walked up from the Redan with a huge piece of grape-shot sticking out of your arm, and which, by the way, I took for the bone protruding. I still hope to see the Victoria Cross on your breast, although it does look as though the said Cross had died a natural death. With that I had something to do."

Mr. Wood had acted as A.D.C. to Capt. Peel from the 1st Jan. 1855, to June 29, 1855, and served through part of the Siege of Sebastopol; was recommended for the Victoria Cross, and received the Legion of Honour (1 Aug. 1856); the Medjidie (April, 1858); the Crimean Medal with two clasps (Inkerman and Sebastopol), and the Turkish Medal. He was twice mentioned in Despatches [London Gazette [2 and 24 July, 1855]. On 10 July, 1855, Mr. Wood's wound not improving, he was sent to Therapia Hospital on the Bosphorus, and later thence to England. On 20 June, 1855, Mr. Wood was sent on board H.M.S. Queen, after nearly nine months service in the Crimea, during which time he had never missed a day's duty. Mr. Wood resigned his commission in Her Majesty's Navy 7 Sept. 1855, and for his services in the Crimea was granted a commission of Cornet without purchase in the 13th Light Dragoons, 8 Sept. 1855. On 1 Oct. 1855, he joined the Depôt at Dorchester, and on 20 Dec. he sailed for Constantinople, and proceeded with the regiment to Scutari, but was stricken down by typhoid and pneumonia. On 1 Feb. 1856, Mr. Wood was promoted to be Lieutenant without purchase, and on 16 May, 1856, he returned invalided to England, after spending five months in bed. In June, 1857, on the outbreak of the Mutiny becoming known, Lieut. Wood tried to arrange an exchange in India. Failing to effect this, he was transferred, at his own request, to the 17th Lancers, and in October, 1857, sailed for Bombay, arriving shortly before Christmas, the regiment being mounted at Kirkee. In May, 1858, he proceeded with the 1st Squadron of his regiment to Mhow, acting as

interpreter in Hindustani. During the month the native commissariat officer deserted, and Lieut. Wood performed his duties. In Aug. 1858 the officer commanding the 3rd Bombay Native Infantry having applied for his services, Lieut. Wood left Mhow with a force marching against Tantia Topi. In Sept., after being continually employed in outpost duties, Lieut. Wood commanded the advanced guard squadron at the action of Rajghur, when twenty-six guns were taken by it from the enemy. On 19 Oct. he commanded a squadron 3rd Bombay Cavalry at Sindwaho, and again on 25 Oct. at Kurai. For his services at Sindwaho he was mentioned in General Orders by His Excellency the Viceroy and Governor-General, 16 Jan. 1859, and he was also mentioned in Brigadier-General Somerset's Despatch of 15 April, 1859, for his gallantry, zeal and intelligence and facility in the management of Indian troops, "quite unusual in one so lately arrived in the country."

From Brigadier Somerset, commanding Field Brigade, to the Assistant-Adjutant-General, M.D.A.:

"Camp, Pachore, 15 April, 1859.

"In the various duties that have devolved upon Lieut. Wood, as my only Staff Officer, while under my command he has shown the most unvaried zeal, particularly on occasions of the rapid pursuit of the enemy—calling for the utmost exertions from all—especially from one whose position did not admit of his taking advantage of the few short hours that others had to rest, as well as high intelligence and facility in the management of native Indians, quite unusual in one so lately arrived in the country."

His gallantry at Sindwaho had been brought specially to notice by Colonel de Salis of the 17th Lancers, who said he had "come up and attacked almost single-handed a body of the enemy. In May, 1859, Lieut. Wood was ordered to Bombay to receive and train recruits for the 17th Lancers. He, on passing through Mhow, was ordered on the 15th June to proceed to join, as Brigade Major, General Beatson's Brigade of Irregular Horse at Aurungabad (Nov. 1858, to 5 April, 1859). He raised and commanded the 2nd Regt. of Central India Horse. On 28 Dec. 1859, he attacked a band of seventy robbers with twelve natives, and released two loyal natives about to be hanged.

From Colonel Shakespeare to Cecil Beadon, Esq., Secretary to the Government of India, with the Governor-General, Indore Presidency Camp:

"Kulookeera, 9 Jan., 1860.

"SIR,

"(1) I have the honour to forward copies of letters noted in the margin, from the Political Agent, Bhopal, and the officer commanding the 1st Regt. of Beatson's Horse.

"(2) A band of robbers has for some time infested the jungles between Beora and Muksudnuggar. They have committed several depredations in the Barseah District, and have been frequently attacked by different parties.

"(3) A Potail, of the name of Chemmum Singh, has incurred their enmity by giving information regarding their movements. They continued to capture this man, and carried him off to the jungle, where they intended to hang him. Lieut. Wood, after a long march, arrived at Sindhora, a port held by his regiment, and there he heard of Chemmum Singh's capture. He immediately started with a Duffadar and four sepoys of his own regiment and a Naick and six Sowars of the Bareilly Levy.

"(5) After proceeding twelve miles from Sindhora, a fire was perceived in a dense jungle.

"(6) Lieut. Wood dismounted, and leaving three Sowars to hold the horses, advanced through the jungle on foot with the rest of the party. After walking three miles through a very thick jungle, they found themselves at 1 a.m. within twenty-six feet of the rebels.

"(7) Four or five were awake, but all the rest, to the number of seventy, were asleep.

"(8) Lieut. Wood fired a volley, and rushed forward into the nullah amongst the rebels, followed by the Duffadar and Sowar of his regiment, keeping well up with him. Several rebels were killed, the remainder fled, leaving their arms, and the Potail, Chemmum Singh, was released.

"(9) Had the Naick and six sepoys (Bareilly Levy) kept close to Lieut. Wood, a greater number of rebels would doubtless have been killed, but to have released Chemmum Singh under such circumstances will have an excellent effect, and Lieut. Wood deserves the highest credit for his noble conduct in releasing him.

"(10) I feel sure that the conduct of Lieut. Wood, and that of the Duffadar and Sowar who accompanied him, will be noticed and remembered by His Excellency the Viceroy."

Lieut. Wood was recommended for the Victoria Cross, and Duffadar Burmadeen Singh, who accompanied Lieut. Wood on the 28th Dec. 1859, received the Order of Merit. Lieut. Wood had been present at the actions of Rajghur, Sindwaho, Kurai and Baroda. He was mentioned in Despatches [London Gazette, 24 March and 5 May, 1859], and received the Mutiny Medal and the Victoria Cross [London Gazette, 4 Sept. 1860]: "Henry Evelyn Wood, Lieut., 17 Lancers. For having, on the 19th Oct. 1858, during an action at Sindwaho, when in command of a troop of the 3rd Light Cavalry, attacked with much gallantry, almost single-handed, a body of rebels who had made a stand, whom he routed; also for having subsequently, near Sindhora, gallantly advanced with a Duffadar and Sowar of Beatson's Horse, and rescued from a band of robbers, a Potail, Chemmum Singh, whom they had captured and carried off to the jungles, where they intended to hang him." On the 24th Nov. 1860, Lieut. Wood being invalided, sailed from Calcutta to England. He was promoted Captain 1 April, 1861, and in 1862 was given a Brevet Majority in the 17th

Lancers for his services in Central India 19 Aug. 1862 ; exchanged into the 73rd Foot 21 Oct. 1862, and passed the Staff College in 1864 ; was A.D.C. in Dublin 22 Jan. 1865, to 31 March, 1865. He exchanged into the 17th Foot 10 Nov. 1865 ; was Brigade-Major at Aldershot 31 July, 1866, to 14 Nov. 1868. In 1867 he married the Hon. Mary Paulina Southwell (died in 1891), sister of the 4th Viscount Southwell. Their children were : Lieut.-Colonel Evelyn Fitzmaurice Wood, D.S.O., born in 1869, Secretary City of London Territorial Force Association, married, 1st, L. Hutton ; she died, leaving three daughters ; 2ndly, Alla Wood, widow of Hatherley Wood, and has two sons ; Lieut.-Colonel Charles Michell Wood, D.S.O., born in 1873, married Olive Miles ; Major Arthur Wood, R.F.A. Reserve, married Ethel Duncan ; Anna Paulina, married General Sir H. D. Farnham, K.C.B. ; Mareela, married Major R. E. G. Blount ; Victoria (god-daughter of Queen Victoria), married H. Balfour. In 1870 he became Major (unattached), and from 14 Nov. 1868, to 25 Nov. 1871, was D.A.A.G. at Aldershot. On 19 Jan. 1873, Major Wood received the Brevet of Lieutenant-Colonel. On 27 Aug. 1873, Lieut.-Colonel Wood left Cannock Chase (where he had been appointed D.A.Q.M.G. to the Army Corps assembled there for manœuvres), having been named for service on the Gold Coast, Africa. On 12 Sept. he sailed for the West Coast of Africa, and on 2 Oct. landed at Elmina on the Gold Coast. He organized and commanded a Transport ; commanded Wood's Regiment throughout the campaigns, and commanded a column which marched into the bush and routed the enemy at Essaman (15 Oct.). Lord Wolseley congratulated him on the very able manner in which everything was carried out on this occasion, and said that all Lieut.-Colonel Wood's previous arrangements were admirable. On 27 Nov. 1873, Lieut.-Colonel Wood, with between 200 and 300 natives, drove in the enemy's rear-guard near Faisowah and engaged a large force of Ashantis, till, being nearly surrounded, he retired, followed for five miles by the enemy. The Ashantis were then seized with a panic and retired, scarcely stopping till they reached the Prah. A week later they were all over the river, and the British Protectorate was freed from the invaders. In Dec. 1873, Lieut.-Colonel Evelyn Wood, having cleared the ground at Prahsu, then collected materials for the Europeans' huts, who, on their march from the coast to the Prah River, found regularly built huts at every stage constructed by the native troops and labourers. On 31 Jan., at the action of Anoaful, Lieut.-Colonel Wood led the right column until he was wounded in the chest by a slug. He was mentioned in Sir Garnet Wolseley's Despatch, dated 1 Feb. 1874. In March, 1874, he returned to England. For his services in this campaign Lieut.-Colonel Wood was mentioned in Despatches [London Gazettes of 18 and 25 Nov. 1873, and 7 and 31 March, 1874] ; was created a C.B. [London Gazette, 31 March, 1874], and given the Brevet of Colonel (31 March, 1874). In 1874 he became a Barrister-at-Law. From 10 Sept. 1874, to 27 March, 1876, he was Superintending Officer of Garrison Instruction. From 28 March, 1876, to Feb. 1878, he was Assistant-Quartermaster-General at Aldershot, and in Dec. 1877, the 90th Light Infantry, of which Colonel Wood was the senior but supernumerary Major, proceeded to South Africa. He resigned his Aldershot appointment, and proceeded to South Africa on special service with orders to assume command of his battalion on the 1st of April. Lieut.-Colonel Wood served throughout the South African War of 1878 and 1881. In the Kaffir Campaign he commanded the force in clearing the Buffalo Poort and Perie Bush, and at the attack on the Tutu Bush ; was at the attack on Intaba Ka Edoda Bush, and in the operations on the Buffalo Range. Lieut.-General Thesieger wrote, 26 June, 1878, to the Secretary of State for War, of Lieut.-Colonel Wood : " I cannot speak too highly of the good service rendered by this officer. He has exercised his command with marked ability and tact. I am of opinion that his indefatigable exertions and personal influence have been mainly instrumental in bringing the war to a speedy close." Lord Chelmsford wrote to Colonel Evelyn Wood from Natal :

"Maritzburg, 10 Dec. 1878.
" You have done wonders with the Dutchmen, and I am quite sure that the High Commissioner will be as much obliged to you from a political point of view as I am from a military one."

Sir Bartle Frere wrote to the Secretary of State for the Colonies :

"Maritzburg, 23 Dec. 1878.
" I have little doubt but that the firm, conciliatory and judicious treatment of these gentlemen by Colonel Evelyn Wood will have an excellent effect, not only locally, but generally throughout the South-Eastern Transvaal District."

Sir B. Frere wrote to the Secretary of State for the Colonies, 16 Jan. 1879 : " Colonel Wood has been instructed to act altogether independently. He will take up a position covering Utrecht and the adjacent Transvaal frontier wherever he considers his force can be most usefully employed." Colonel Wood served in the Zulu War, and on 24 June, 1878, assumed command of a column ordered to march by Pondoland to Natal (ten miles). On 17 Sept. he assumed the command at Utrecht, and in October took two companies of the 90th Light Infantry to Luneberg, in order to protect the settlers from Cetewayo. On 16 Dec. he was appointed to command No. 4 Column, and on 12 Jan. he met Lord Chelmsford near Rorke's Drift. On 20 Jan. he halted near the Umvolusi River, moving his force to the east of the Zunguin Nek, where he defeated the Zulus on 22 Jan. On hearing of the disaster at Isandlhwana, the column returned to the Umvolusi River. On 26 Jan. Colonel Wood moved northwards to obtain firewood, and on 31 Jan. No. 4 Column recrossed the Umvolusi River to the eastward, and encamped on a spur named Kambula, a lower feature of the Ngabe-ka-Hawane River. There he severely defeated the Amaqulosi Regiment, and at Inhlobane Mountain dispersed some Zulus and took 500 head of cattle. His horse was shot. At Kam-

bula the Zulu army, 23,500 strong, attacked Colonel Wood's column for five and a half hours. Though all the natives, 2,000 strong, of Wood's regiment deserted, the 1,800 white men utterly defeated the Zulu army, and pursued until dark. It is of interest that the Zulu army never recovered that, to them, disastrous day. The affair at Kambula is considered to have saved Natal. He commanded a column at the Battle of Ulundi, and was thanked by Lord Chelmsford. Colonel Wood was frequently mentioned in Despatches [London Gazettes of 17 May, 11 and 15 June, 1878, and 21 Feb., 5, 15, 21 and 28 March, 4, 14 and 21 April, 7 and 10 May, and 21 Aug. 1879. General Sir G. Wolseley wrote in 1879 about Colonel Wood's " genius for war," and he wrote to Colonel Wood on the 9th July, 1879 : " You and Buller have been the bright spots in this miserable war." Colonel Wood was given the local rank of Brigadier-General 8 April, 1879, and was nominated a K.C.B. (Military) 23 June, 1879. He also received the Medal and clasp. On the 17th July, 1879, Brigadier-General Wood left the Army to return to England. He received a silver shield from the Cape Colony and a piece of plate from the inhabitants of Natal. He was promoted Major-General 12 Aug. 1881, and was created a G.C.M.G. He was on special service in South Africa 25 Feb. 1878, to 2 April, 1879 ; Brigadier-General, South Africa, 3 April, 1879, to 5 Aug. 1879. In 1878 he become Honorary Colonel 2nd Battn. Essex Rifle Volunteers ; Brigadier-General at Belfast and Chatham 15 Dec. 1879, to 14 Jan. 1881 ; Local Major-General in South Africa 15 Jan. 1881, to 27 Feb. 1881 ; Major-General in South Africa 28 Feb. 1881, to 16 Feb. 1882 ; Brigadier-General, Chatham, 1 Nov. to 20 Dec. 1882. In the Transvaal Campaign he conducted negotiations and concluded peace with the Boers 12 Aug. 1881. In the Egyptian Campaign of 1882 Major-General Sir Evelyn Wood commanded the 4th Brigade, 2nd Division. Operations near Alexandria and surrender of Kafr Dowar and Damietta. He was mentioned in Despatches [London Gazette, Nov. 1882] ; was thanked by both Houses of Parliament, received the Egyptian Medal, the Khedive's Bronze Star and the Order of the Medjidie, Second Class. As the Sirdar, he raised and commanded an Egyptian Army. He commanded on the Lines of Communication of the Nile 15 Sept. 1884, to 14 June, 1885, and in the Sudan Expedition 1884–85 (Despatches). Lord Granville wrote to the Secretary of State for War :

" Foreign Office, 10 May, 1885.
" Her Majesty's Government fully appreciate the services of their officers, but their thanks are especially due to Sir Evelyn Wood himself, for the energy, zeal and ability with which he has devoted himself to a task in itself arduous, increased by the difficult circumstances in which it has been undertaken."

Lord Wolseley said in his Despatch of 25 Aug. 1885 : " Our line of communication by rail, river and desert from Alexandria to Gubat was about 1,500 miles in length. The responsibility of supervising it was great, but thanks to Sir Evelyn's ability and energy . . . the Army operating at the front was well fed and provided with all it required." From 1 April, 1886, to 31 Dec. 1888, Sir Evelyn Wood was Major-General, Eastern District. General Lord Wolseley and the Adjutant-General wrote, 24 Oct. 1886, to Sir Evelyn Wood : " Yours is our model district in every respect." From 1 Jan. 1889, to 8 Oct. 1893, he was Lieutenant-General Commanding at Aldershot. He became Lieutenant-General 1 April, 1890 ; Quartermaster to the Forces 1 Oct. 1897, to 30 Sept. 1907. Sir Evelyn Wood became General 26 March, 1895. He became Honorary Colonel 14th Middlesex (Inns of Court) Volunteers in 1900 ; G.C.B. in 1901 ; Field-Marshal 8 April, 1903 ; Grand Cross Imperial Leopold Order in 1904, and was General Commanding 2nd Army Corps, later Southern Command, 1 Oct. 1901, to 31 Dec. 1904. He has published : " The Crimea," 1854–94 ; " Cavalry at Waterloo," 1896 ; " Achievements of Cavalry ; " " From Midshipman to Field-Marshal," 1906 ; " The Revolt in Hindustani," 1908 ; " Our Fighting Services " and " Winnowed Memories," 1917.

London Gazette, 8 Nov. 1860.—" The Queen has been graciously pleased to signify Her intention to confer the Decoration of the Victoria Cross on the undermentioned Officers and Soldier of Her Majesty's Army, whose claims to the same have been submitted for Her Majesty's approval, on account of Acts of Bravery performed by them in India, as recorded against their names."

FRASER, CHARLES CRAUFORD, Major, was born 31 Aug. 1829 ; joined the 7th Hussars and served in the Mutiny. He received the Mutiny Medal with clasp, and was awarded the Victoria Cross [London Gazette,

Charles Crauford Fraser.

8 Nov. 1860] : " Charles Crauford Fraser, Major, 7th Hussars (now of the 11th Hussars). Date of Act of Bravery : 31 Dec. 1858. For conspicuous and cool gallantry on the 31st Dec. 1858, in having volunteered, at great personal risk, and under a sharp fire of musketry, to swim to the rescue of Capt. Stisted and some men of the 7th Hussars, who were in imminent danger of being drowned in the River Raptee, while in pursuit of the rebels. Major Fraser succeeded in this gallant service, although at the same time partially disabled, not having recovered from a severe wound received while leading a squadron in a charge against some fanatics in the action of Nawab-Gunge on the 13th June, 1858." He was afterwards transferred to the 11th Hussars. Major Fraser received the Gold Medal of the Royal Humane Society, in addition to the Victoria Cross, for the deed which is thus described by Mr. G. W. Forrest in his " History of the Indian Mutiny " :

In the action of Nawabgunj the enemy were posted upon a large plateau surrounded on three sides by a stream, which was crossed by a fine old stone bridge at a little distance from Nawabgunj. On the fourth side was a jungle. To turn their right and to interpose between them and the jungle was Sir Hope Grant's desire." He determined to cross the stream about two miles further up, which he did, and surprised the enemy, who, however, fought desperately and broke the formation of Hodson's Horse. They had brought up two guns, and the attacking force with the two guns were in great jeopardy. Then Hope Grant ordered up the 7th Hussars and the other four guns belonging to the battery. They soon arrived and opened a fire of grape on the enemy, which mowed them down. Two squadrons of the 7th Hussars, under Sir William Russell, now came up, and forced the survivors to abandon their two guns, leaving 125 corpses on the ground. "The Hussars twice charged upon them. Captain Charles Fraser, a daring and brilliant cavalry leader, got right in among some of the enemy's horse and foot, and there was many a fierce hand-to-hand encounter." He served in the Abyssinian War of 1868 (Medal); was A.D.C. to H.R.H. the Duke of Cambridge 1873–77. Was Inspector-General of Cavalry 1880–84. In 1882 Major-General C. C. Fraser, V.C., C.B., was commanding the Curragh Brigade. He sat in Parliament as Conservative Member for North Lambeth 1884–92. General Sir C. C. Fraser, V.C., C.B., died in London 7 June, 1895, aged 66.

JEE, JOSEPH, Surgeon, was the son of the late Christopher Preston Jee, Esq., of Hartshill, Atherstone, Warwickshire. He was educated at the Universities of London and Edinburgh, and at the Ecole de Médecine, Paris; M.R.C.S. England, 1841. He entered the Army as Assistant Surgeon in the 15th Hussars in 1842, and was promoted Surgeon into the 78th (Seaforth) Highlanders in 1854. He served with that regiment in the Persian Campaign, 1857, being present at the Battle of Koosh-ab and at the bombardment of Mohammen (Medal with clasp), and throughout the Indian Mutiny Campaign, 1857 and 1858, and accompanied Generals Havelock's and Outram's Force to the relief of the Residency of Lucknow, where they became besieged for two months, and took part in the operations at Rohil Kund and capture of Bareilly. He received the Medal with clasps, one year's service for Lucknow, was created a C.B. 1858, and awarded the Victoria Cross [London Gazette, 9 Nov. 1860]: "Joseph Jee, Surgeon, 78th Regt. Date of Act of Bravery: 25 Sept. 1857. For most conspicuous gallantry and important services on the entry of the late Major-General Havelock's relieving force into Lucknow, on the 25th Sept. 1857, in having, during action (when the 78th Highlanders, then in possession of the Char Bagh, captured two 9-pounders at the point of the bayonet), by great exertion and devoted exposure, attended to the large number of men wounded in the charge, whom he succeeded in getting removed on cots and the backs of their comrades, until he had collected the dhooly-bearers. who had fled. Subsequently, on the same day, in endeavouring to reach the Residency with the wounded men, Surgeon Jee became besieged by an overwhelming force in the Mote Mehal, where he remained during the whole night and the following morning, voluntarily and repeatedly exposing himself to a heavy fire in proceeding to dress the wounded men who fell while serving a 24-pounder in a most exposed position. He eventually succeeded in taking many of the wounded through a cross-fire of ordnance and musketry safely into the Residency, by the river bank, although repeatedly warned not to make the perilous attempt." He was transferred to the Royal Dragoons in 1864, and became Deputy Inspector-General of Army Hospitals (n.p.), 1868. He married in 1880, Norah Carola, daughter of the late Charles Riley, Esq., Barrister-at-Law, of 55, Queensborough Terrace, W. After many years of retirement, he died at Queensborough Hall, Leicestershire, 17 March, 1899.

Joseph Jee.

MUNRO, JAMES, Colour-Sergt., enlisted in the 93rd Regt. (Argyll and Sutherland Highlanders), was promoted to Colour-Sergeant, and was awarded the Victoria Cross [London Gazette, 9 Nov. 1860]: "James Munro, Colour-Sergt., 93rd Regt. (late). Date of Act of Bravery: 16 Nov. 1857. For devoted gallantry at Secundra Bagh on the 16th Nov. 1857, in having promptly rushed to the rescue of Capt. E. Walsh, of the same corps, when wounded and in danger of his life, whom he carried to a place of comparative safety, to which place the sergeant was brought in very shortly afterwards, badly wounded." Colour-Sergt. J. Munro died on the 15th Feb. 1871. His Victoria Cross is now in the United Service Institute, London.

James Munro.

London Gazette, 5 Feb. 1861.—"War Office, 5 Feb. 1861. The Queen has been graciously pleased to signify Her intention to confer the Decoration of the Victoria Cross on the undermentioned Officer of Her Majesty's Army, whose claim to the same has been submitted for Her Majesty's approval, on account of Acts of Bravery performed by him in India, as recorded against his name."

Herbert Taylor Reade.

READE, HERBERT TAYLOR, Surgeon, was born in 1828, the son of the late Colonel G. H. Reade, Canadian Militia. He joined the Army, became Surgeon, 61st (Gloucester) Regt., served in the Indian Mutiny, and was awarded the Victoria Cross [London Gazette, 5 Feb. 1861]: "Herbert Taylor Reade, Surgeon, 61st Regt. Dates of Acts of Bravery: 14 and 16 Sept. 1857. During the Siege of Delhi, and on the 14th Sept. 1857, while Surgeon Rendle was attending to the wounded at the end of one of the streets of the city, a party of rebels advanced from the direction of the Bank, and, having established themselves in the houses of the street, commenced firing from the roofs. The wounded were thus in very great danger, and would have fallen into the hands of the enemy, had not Surgeon Reade drawn his sword, and calling upon the few soldiers who were near to follow, succeeded, after a very heavy fire, in dislodging the rebels from their position. Surgeon Reade's party consisted of about ten in all, of whom two were killed and five or six wounded. Surgeon Reade also accompanied the regiment at the assault of Delhi, and on the morning of the 16th Sept. 1857, was one of the first up at the breach in the magazine, which was stormed by the 61st Regt. and Belooch Battalion, on which occasion he, with a sergeant of the 61st Regt., spiked one of the enemy's guns." He was Principal Medical Officer, Southern District, 1886, retiring in 1887. He died at Bath in June, 1897, aged 68.

London Gazette, 1 March, 1861.—"The Queen has been graciously pleased to signify Her intention to confer the Decoration of the Victoria Cross on the undermentioned Officers of Her Majesty's Indian Forces, whose claims to the same have been submitted for Her Majesty's approval, on account of Acts of Bravery performed by them in India, as recorded against their several names."

TRAVERS, JAMES, Colonel, was born on 6 Oct. 1820, the son of Major-General Sir Robert Travers, and was educated at Addiscombe. He served in Afghanistan, 1840–42, at the operations at Zamindanar, capture of Ghuzni, action of Mydan. Served in Bhopal and at Kulla Karee, 1846. In 1856 he served against the rebel Sunker Singh, and received the thanks of the Agent to the Governor-General of Central India for his services. For his services in the Indian Mutiny he was awarded the Victoria Cross [London Gazette, 1 March, 1861]: "James Travers, Colonel, late 2nd Bengal Native Infantry. Date of Act of Bravery: July, 1857. For a daring act of bravery, in July, 1857, when the Indore Presidency was suddenly attacked by Holkar's troops, in having charged the guns with only five men to support him, and driven the gunners from the guns, thereby creating a favourable diversion, which saved the lives of many persons, fugitives to the Residency. It is stated that officers who were present considered the effect of the charge was to enable many Europeans to escape from actual slaughter, and time was gained which enabled the faithful Bhopal Infantry to man their guns. Colonel Travers' horse was shot in three places, and his accoutrements were shot through in various parts. He commanded the Bhopal Levy."

James Travers.

BROWNE, SAMUEL JAMES, Lieut.-Col., C.B., son of the late Dr. John Browne, H.E.I.C.S., of Alnwick, N.B., was born in India, 3 Oct. 1824. He entered the Indian Army in 1840; served throughout the Punjab Campaign of 1848-9, being present at Chillianwallah and Gujerat (Medal and two clasps); commanded the 2nd Punjab Cavalry and the Corps of Guides; served on the Derejat and Peshawar Frontier, in the operations against the Omerzale Wuzerees (1851-2), 1850-69 (Medal with clasp), and, in command 2nd Punjab Cavalry, was through the Bozdar Belooch Expeditions in March, 1857; through many other tribal campaigns, including the attacks on Narinjee in July and August, 1857. In the Indian Mutiny he was dangerously wounded twice and lost his arm, and was present at the capture of Lucknow and at the actions of Roorsee, Rooyah, Aligunge, Mohunpore, Seerporah, and at the capture of Ali Masjid. He was promoted to Major in 1858, and Lieut.-Col. in 1859. For his services in the Indian Mutiny Lieut.-Col. Browne was three times mentioned in Despatches, received the thanks of the Commander-in-Chief and of the Government, and was given the Brevets of Major and Lieut.-Col., the Medal with clasps, and the Victoria Cross [London Gazette, 1 March, 1861]: "Samuel James Browne, Lieut.-Col., C.B., (late) 46th Bengal Native Infantry. Date of Act of Bravery: 31 Aug. 1858. For having

Samuel James Browne.

at Seerporah, in an engagement with the Rebel Forces under Khan Ali Khan, on the 31st Aug., 1858, whilst advancing upon the enemy's position at daybreak, pushed on with one orderly sowar upon a 9-pounder gun that was commanding one of the approaches to the enemy's position, and attacked the gunners, thereby preventing them from reloading and firing upon the infantry, who were advancing to the attack. In doing this a personal conflict ensued, in which Captain (now Lieut.-Col.) Samuel James Browne, Commandant of the 2nd Punjab Cavalry, received a severe sword-cut wound on the left knee, and shortly afterwards another sword-cut wound which severed the left arm at the shoulder, not, however, before Lieut.-Col. Browne had succeeded in cutting down one of his assailants. The gun was prevented from being reloaded, and was eventually captured by the Infantry, and the gunner slain." For 19 years, 1850–69, he was in command of the Punjab Cavalry and the Guides Corps, and he was the inventor of the "Sam Browne" belt, known throughout the British Army. In 1860 he married Lucy, daughter of R. C. Sherwood, Esq., and in 1861 he received a C.B. He became Colonel in 1864 and Major-General in 1870. In 1875 and 1876 he was on special duty in India with H.R.H. the Prince of Wales. In 1876 he was given a K.C.S.I., and in 1877 was promoted Lieut.-General. He commanded the 1st Division of the Peshawar Field Force at the capture of the Fort of Ali Masjid and 24 pieces of artillery, and at the forcing of the Khyber Pass in Nov. 1858, and throughout the subsequent operations of the Afghan Campaign of 1879-80 until the signing of the Treaty and return of the troops. Sir Samuel Browne was for his services in this war thanked by the Government of India and by both Houses of Parliament, and given a K.C.B. (1879). He became General in 1888, and in 1891 was created a G.C.B. (Military). General Sir Samuel Browne, G.C.B., K.C.S.I., V.C., died at Ryde 14 March, 1901. Not long after the death of this gallant soldier a tablet and monument were unveiled in St. Paul's Cathedral by Earl Roberts of Kandahar, and four of his contemporaries, each wearing the Victoria Cross, were present to pay respect to his memory. The monument was placed close to that of the great Duke of Wellington, and is of pure white marble, carved in low relief, with the figure of a Punjab cavalryman holding a scroll, on which are the words: "To the glory of God and in perpetual memory of General Sir Samuel Browne, V.C., G.C.B., K.C.S.I., a distinguished soldier of the Indian Army. This tablet is erected by friends who loved, and comrades who trusted him." On this occasion Lord Roberts said that there never was "a truer man, a firmer friend, a braver soldier, or one more worthy of a memorial in that venerable cathedral than Sir Samuel Browne." A replica of the memorial was set up in Lahore Cathedral.

London Gazette, 17 July, 1861.—" The Queen has been graciously pleased to signify Her intention to confer the Decoration of the Victoria Cross on the undermentioned Non-commissioned Officer, whose claim to the same has been submitted for Her Majesty's approval, in consideration of an Act of Bravery which he has performed in New Zealand, as recorded against his name."

LUCAS, JOHN, Colour-Sergt., served in the Maori War with his Regiment, the 40th (South Lancashire), and was awarded the Victoria Cross [London Gazette, 19 July, 1861]: " John Lucas, Colour-Sergt., 40th Regt. Date of Act of Bravery: 18th March, 1861. On the 18th March, 1861, Colour-Sergt. Lucas acted as sergeant of a party of the 40th Regt., employed as skirmishers to the right of No. 7 Redoubt, and close to the Huirangi Bush, facing the left of the positions occupied by the natives. At about 4 p.m. a very heavy and well-directed fire was suddenly opened upon them from the bush and the high ground on the left. Three men being wounded simultaneously, two of them mortally, assistance was called for in order to have them carried to the rear; a file was immediately sent, but had scarcely arrived when one of them fell, and Lieut. Rees was wounded at the same time. Colour-Sergt. Lucas, under a very heavy fire from the rebels, who were not more than thirty yards distant, immediately ran up to the assistance of this officer, and sent one man with him to the rear. He then took charge of the arms belonging to the killed and wounded men, and maintained his position until the arrival of supports under Lieuts. Gibson and Whelan." He was promoted to Sergt.-Major. Sergt.-Major J. Lucas died in Dublin 29 Feb. 1892.

London Gazette, 13 Aug. 1861.—" The Queen has been graciously pleased to signify Her intention to confer the Decoration of the Victoria Cross on the undermentioned Officers and Soldiers, whose claims to the same have been submitted for Her Majesty's approval, on account of Acts of Bravery performed by them in China, on the occasion of the assault and capture of North Taku Fort on the 21st of Aug. 1860, as recorded against their several names."

ROGERS, ROBERT MONTRESOR, Lieut., was born 4 Sept. 1834, and joined the 44th Regt. in Feb., 1855. He became Lieut. in Aug. 1855, and served in the Crimean War from 27 Aug. 1855, and was present at the siege and fall of Sebastopol (Medal and clasp). He served in the China Campaign of 1860, being present at the action at Sinho, where he was severely wounded at the storming of the Taku Forts. Together with Private John M'Dougall, 44th Foot, and Lieut. C. H. Lenon, 67th Foot, he was awarded the Victoria Cross for distinguished gallantry in swimming the ditches and entering the North Taku Fort by an embrasure during the assault. They were the first of the English established on the walls of the fort, which they entered in the order in which their names are here recorded, each one

Robt. Montresor Rogers.

being assisted by the others to mount the embrasure. He received the China Medal with clasp, was promoted Captain in Nov. 1860, and was awarded the Victoria Cross [London Gazette, 13 Aug. 1861]: " Robert Montresor Rogers, Lieut. (now Captain), 44th Regt. (now of the 90th Regt.), and No. 220, John M'Dougall, Private. For distinguished gallantry in swimming the ditches and entering the North Taku Fort by an embrasure during the assault. They were the first of the English established on the walls of the Fort, which they entered in the order in which their names are here recorded." He became Major in April, 1873. He commanded the 90th Light Infantry throughout the Zulu War of 1879; was present at the engagement at Zunyin Nek and Kambula. He was created a C.B. Major-General Rogers died at Maidenhead on Tuesday, 5 Feb. 1895.

M'DOUGALL, JOHN, Private, No. 220, enlisted in the Essex Regiment, served in the China Campaign of 1860, and was awarded the Victoria Cross [London Gazette, 13 Aug. 1861]: " Robert Montresor Rogers, Lieut., 44th Regt. (now of the 90th Regt.), and John M'Dougall, No. 220, Private, 44th Regt. Date of Acts of Bravery: Aug. 1860. For distinguished gallantry in swimming the ditches and entering the North Taku Fort by an embrasure during the assault. They were the first of the English established on the walls of the Fort, which they entered in the order in which their names are here recorded, each one being assisted by the others to mount the embrasure. (Note.—The third being Lieut. Henry Lenon, of the 67th Regt.)." Private M'Dougall died on 10 March, 1869.

LENON, EDMUND HENRY, Lieut., joined the 67th Foot (The Hampshire Regt.), and served in the China Campaign of 1860. He was awarded the Victoria Cross [London Gazette, 13 Aug. 1861]: " Edmund Henry Lenon, Lieut., the 67th Regt. For distinguished gallantry in swimming the ditches and entering the North Taku Fort by an embrasure during the assault. He was one of the first of the English established on the walls of the Fort."

Edmund Henry Lenon.

BURSLEM, NATHANIEL, Lieut., joined the Army as Ensign, 12 Feb. 1858, and served throughout the China Campaign with his regiment, the 67th Foot (Hampshire Regt.), including the storming of the Taku Fort—being about the first Englishman who entered the fort—and was badly wounded in three places, and mentioned in Despatches. He was also present at the surrender of Pekin. For his services in this Campaign he received the Medal and clasp, and was awarded the Victoria Cross [London Gazette, 13 Aug. 1861]. The official notice in the London Gazette of 13 Aug. 1861, reads: " Nathaniel Burslem, Lieut. (now Captain), and No. 612, Thomas Lane, Private, the 67th Regt. For distinguished gallantry in swimming the ditches of the North Taku Fort, and persevering in attempting during the assault, and before the entrance of the Fort had been effected by anyone, to enlarge an opening in the wall, through which they eventually entered, and in doing so were both severely wounded." Afterwards, on attaining his company, Captain Burslem exchanged into the 60th Rifles. He became Captain 20 Nov. 1860, and retired by the sale of his commission in 1864.

Nathaniel Burslem.

LANE, THOMAS, Private, No. 612, enlisted in the 67th Foot (The Hampshire Regt.), and served in the China Campaign of 1860. He was awarded the Victoria Cross [London Gazette, 13 Aug. 1861]: " Nathaniel Burslem, Lieut., 67th Regt. (now of the 60th Regt.), and Thomas Lane, No. 612, Private, 67th Regt. For distinguished gallantry in swimming the ditches of the North Taku Fort, and persevering in attempting during the assault, and before the entrance of the Fort had been effected by anyone, to enlarge an opening in the wall, through which they eventually entered, and in doing so were both severely wounded." Private Lane's gallantry is mentioned in the Gazette of Lieut. J. W. Chaplin's Victoria Cross.

CHAPLIN, JOHN WORTHY, Ensign, was born 23 July, 1840; son of William James Chaplin, M.P. for Salisbury, and Elizabeth Alston; was educated a Harrow, and entered the 67th (South Hampshire) Regt. on 13 April, 1858. He served in the China Campaign of 1860; was present at the action of Sinho, taking of Tongho and the storming of the Taku Forts (wounded); was mentioned in Despatches [London Gazette, 4 Nov. 1860]; promoted to Lieut. and awarded the Victoria Cross [London Gazette, 13 Aug. 1861]: " John Worthy Chaplin, Ensign (now Lieut.), 67th Regt. (now of the 100th Regt.). For distinguished gallantry at the North Taku Fort. This officer was carrying the Queen's Colours of the Regiment, and first planted the Colours on the breach made by the storming

John Worthy Chaplin.

party, assisted by Private Lane, and subsequently on the cavalier of the fort, which he was the first to mount. In doing this he was severely wounded." He became Captain in the 8th Hussars in 1864, and Major in 1878. From 1869 to 1874 he was an extra A.D.C. to the Lord-Lieutenant of Ireland. On 22 Aug. 1871, at Bishopsthorpe in Yorkshire, Major Chaplin married Isabel, daughter of J. Thompson, Esq. They have two children: Reginald Spencer, born 21 Nov. 1872, and Muriel Gladys. He was promoted Lieut.-Col. in 1879. Lieut.-Col. Chaplin commanded the 8th King's Royal Irish Hussars in the Afghanistan Campaign of 1879-80, in the Lines of Communication (Afghanistan Medal). In 1883 he became a Colonel on half-pay, and in 1887 was created a C.B. He retired in 1888.

FITZGIBBON, ARTHUR, Hospital Apprentice, served in China, and was awarded the Victoria Cross [London Gazette, 13 Aug. 1861]: " Arthur Fitzgibbon, Hospital Apprentice, Indian Medical Establishment. For having behaved with great coolness and courage at the capture of the North Taku Fort, on the 21st Aug. 1860. On the morning of that day he accompanied a wing of the 67th Regt. when it took up a position within 500 yards of the fort. Having quitted cover, he proceeded, under a very heavy fire, to attend to a dhoolie-bearer, whose wound he had been directed to bind up ; and while the regiment was advancing under the enemy's fire, he ran across the open to attend to another wounded man, in doing which he was himself severely wounded."

London Gazette, 25 Feb. 1862.—" The Queen has been graciously pleased to signify Her intention to confer the Decoration of the Victoria Cross on the undermentioned Officers and Non-commissioned Officer, whose claims to the same have been submitted for Her Majesty's approval, on account of Acts of Bravery performed by them in India, as recorded against their several names."

KEATINGE, RICHARD HARTE, Major, was born in 1825 ; the son of the late Right Honourable Richard Keatinge. He entered the Bombay Artillery in June, 1842, became Lieutenant in 1845, and Captain in 1857. He served as Political Officer with the Mhow Field Force and the 1st Brigade Central Field Force, 1857-58 ; was dangerously wounded ; received the Medal, and was awarded the Victoria Cross [London Gazette, 25 Feb. 1862]: " Richard Harte Keatinge, Major, Bombay Artillery (now of the Staff Corps). Date of Act of Bravery : 17 March, 1858. For having rendered most efficient aid at the assault of Chundairee, in voluntarily leading the column through the breach, which was protected by a heavy cross-fire. He was one of the foremost to enter, and was severely wounded in the breach. The column was saved from a serious loss that would probably have resulted but for Major Keatinge's knowledge of the small path leading across the ditch, which had been examined during the night by himself and a servant, who declined, when required, to lead the column without his master. Having cleared the breach, he led into the fort, where he was struck down by another dangerous wound. The Commander-in-Chief in India states that the success at Chundairee was mainly owing to this officer, whose gallantry, really brilliant, he considers was equalled by his ability and devotion. Major Keatinge was at the time a Political Officer with the 2nd Brigade of the Central Indian Field Force." He became Major in 1858 ; commanded a force of irregular troops against Seeta Ram Holkar, in Sathpoora Hills, in Oct. 1858 ; served with Brigadier Parke's Brigade in pursuit of Tantia Topi in Nov. 1858 ; commanded the irregular troops against insurgents in the Sathpoora Hills in 1859, and field detachments in Kattywar against rebel Wagheers in 1865. He was promoted Lieutenant-Colonel in 1866, and in the same year was created a C.S.I. He was Governor-General's Agent in the Rajputana States from 1867 to 1870 ; Chief Commissioner of the Central Provinces from 1870 to 1872 ; became Colonel in 1873, and was Chief Commissioner from 1878 to 1880. He became Major-General in 1884, being placed at the same time on the Unemployed Supernumerary List ; Lieutenant-Colonel in 1887, and General in 1894. Major-General R. H. Keatinge was twice married ; first to a daughter of Mr. Thomas Pottinger, of Mount Pottinger, County Down ; and secondly, in 1882, to the widow of Mr. E. C. Fox, a daughter of the late J. Alderson, Esq. (43rd Light Infantry), of Gannowhill, Derbyshire. He died on Wednesday, 25 May, 1904, at his residence, Lynwood, Horsham. An obituary notice appeared in the " Times " of the following day.

BLAIR, JAMES, Capt., was born on 27 Jan. 1828 ; the son of the late Capt. E. M. Blair, Bengal Cavalry. He entered the Bombay Cavalry in 1844 served throughout the Indian Mutiny, 1857-9 (twice severely wounded) ; mentioned in Despatches ; Medal with clasp, and Victoria Cross [London Gazette, 25 Feb. 1862]: " James Blair, Capt., 2nd Bombay Light Cavalry. Dates of Acts of Bravery : 12 Aug. and 23 Oct. 1857. For having on two occasions distinguished himself by his gallant and daring conduct. First on the night of the 12th Aug. 1857, at Neemuch, in volunteering to apprehend seven or eight armed mutineers, who had shut themselves up for defence in a house, the door of which he burst open. He then rushed in among them, and forced them to escape through the roof ; in this encounter he was severely wounded. In spite of his wounds he pursued the fugitives, but was unable to come up to them in consequence of the darkness of the night. Secondly, on the 23rd Oct. 1857, at Jeerum, in fighting his way most gallantly through a body of rebels who had literally surrounded him. After breaking the end

James Blair.

of his sword on one of their heads, and receiving a severe sword-cut on his right arm, he rejoined his troops. In this wounded condition, and with no other weapon than the butt of his broken sword, he put himself at the head of his men, charged the rebels most effectually, and dispersed them." He became Captain in 1857, Major in 1864, Lieutenant-Colonel in 1870, Colonel in 1875. He married Frances B. E. Halhed, daughter of the late N. J. Halhed, Esq., B.C.S., of Gately Hall, Hampshire. He was Political Resident and Brigadier-General at Aden (1882-5). He became Major-General in 1885 ; Lieutenant-General and was created a C.B. (Military) in 1889. In 1894 he became General. He died at Melrose, 14 Jan. 1905, aged 77.

BAKER, CHARLES GEORGE, Lieut., started life in the service of the P. & O. Company. When the S.S. Duro was wrecked on the Paracel Shoal, in 1854, he volunteered with six others to make a voyage of over 500 miles in an open boat, with very little food and water, and in rough weather with Chinese pirates about, to obtain succour, which was done. He then joined the Bengal Police, and won great distinction during the Mutiny. He performed his V.C. exploit with only 123 men of all ranks of Irregular Cavalry and 3rd Sikhs. He served under Colonel Gawler in Sikkim in 1861, and won high praise. His Victoria Cross was gazetted 25 Feb. 1862 : " Charles George Baker, Lieut., Bengal Police Battn. Date of Act of Bravery : 27 Sept. 1858. For gallant conduct on the occasion of an attack on the rebels at Suhejnee, near Peroo, on the 27th Sept. 1858, which is thus described in this officer's own words : ' The enemy (at the time supposed to have mustered from 900 to 1,000 strong in infantry, with 50 cavalry) advanced. Without exchanging a shot, I at once retired slowly, followed up steadily by the rebel line for 100 yards clear of village or jungle, when, suddenly wheeling about my divisions into line, with a hearty cheer, we charged into and through the centre of the enemy's line ; Lieut. Broughton, with his detachment, immediately following up the movement, with excellent effect, from his position upon the enemy's left. The rebel right wing, of about 300 men, broke at once, but the centre and left, observing the great labour of the horses in crossing the heavy ground, stood, and, receiving the charge with repeated volleys, were cut down or broke only a few yards ahead of the cavalry. From this moment the pursuit was limited to the strongest and best horses of the force, numbering some sixty of all ranks, who, dashing into and swimming a deep and wide nullah, followed the flying enemy through the village of Russowlee and its sugar-cane khets, over two miles of swamp, and 500 yards into the thick jungles near Peroo, when, both men and horses being completely exhausted, I sounded the halt and assembly, and, collecting my wounded, returned to the camp at Munjhaen about 6 p.m.' The charge ended in the utter defeat of the enemy, and is referred to by Lord Clyde ' as deserving of the highest encomium, on account both of conception and execution.' It is also described as having been as gallant as any during the war." In 1863 he was appointed Officiating Deputy-Inspector-General of Military Police for the Dacca Circle of Bengal. His health broke down ; he left India and took service with the Sultan of Turkey. Serving under Valentine Baker Pasha in the Balkan Campaigns, he was taken prisoner by the Russians. He afterwards went with him to Egypt, and succeeded him in the command of the Egyptian Police. He was made " lena Pasha," or Major-General, and Chief of the Public Security Department of the Egyptian Ministry of the Interior, which post he held until his retirement in 1885. He died on the 19th Feb. 1906, aged 76, at Southbourne-on-Sea, Hants.

Charles George Baker.

WALLER, WILLIAM FRANCIS FREDERICK, Lieut., was born in 1840. He entered the service in 1857, and in the following year saw considerable service in India, including the siege and storming of Chandaree and Jhansi, the battle of the Betwa and capture of Jhansi, and for his gallantry at the capture and storming of the fortress of Gwalior, he was awarded the Victoria Cross [London Gazette, 25 Feb. 1862]: " William Francis Frederick Waller, Lieut. (now Major), 25th Bombay Light Infantry. Date of Act of Bravery : 20 June, 1858. For great gallantry at the capture by storm of the fortress of Gwalior on the 20th June, 1858. He and Lieut. Rose, who was killed, were the only Europeans present, and with a mere handful of men, they attacked the fortress, climbed on the roof of a house, shot the gunners opposed to them, carried all before them, and took the fort, killing every man in it." Colonel Waller died on 29 Jan. 1885. The " Times " of 4 Feb. 1885, says that it has to record the death of another Victoria Cross Officer in the person of Colonel W. F. F. Waller, V.C., Bombay Staff Corps, and late of the 25th Bombay Native Infantry, in his 45th year.

William F. F. Waller.

DAUNT, JOHN CHARLES CAMPBELL, Lieut., served in the Mutiny, and was awarded the Victoria Cross [London Gazette, 25 Feb. 1862]: " John Charles Campbell Daunt, Lieut., 11th (late 70th) Bengal Native Infantry. Date of Acts of Bravery : 2 Oct. 1857. For conspicuous gallantry in action on the 2nd Oct. 1857, with the mutineers of the Ramgurh Battn. at Chota Behar, in capturing two guns, particularly the last, when he, in conjunction with Sergt. Dynon,

John Charles C. Daunt.

of the 53rd Foot, rushed at and captured it by pistolling the gunners, who were mowing the detachment down with grape, one-third of which was *hors de combat* at the time. Lieut. Daunt is also recommended for chasing, on the 2nd Nov. following, the mutineers of the 32nd Bengal Native Infantry across a plain into a rich cultivation, into which he followed them with a few of Rattray's Sikhs. He was dangerously wounded in the attempt to drive out a large body of these mutineers from an inclosure, the preservation of many of his party on the occasion being attributed to his gallantry."

DYNON, DENIS, Sergt., served in the Mutiny with his regiment, the 53rd (Shropshire Light Infantry), and was awarded the Victoria Cross [London Gazette, 25 Feb. 1862]: "Denis Dynon, No. 2165, Sergt., 53rd Regt. Date of Act of Bravery : 2 Oct. 1857. Lieut. Daunt, 11th Bengal Native Infantry, and Sergt. Dynon are recommended for conspicuous gallantry in action, on the 2nd Oct. 1857, with the mutineers of the Ramgurh Battn. at Chota Behar, in capturing two guns, particularly the last, when they rushed at and captured it by pistolling the gunners, who were mowing the detachment down with grape, one-third of which was *hors de combat* at the time." Sergt. Dynon died on the 16th Feb. 1863.

London Gazette, 29 April, 1862.—"War Office, 29 April, 1862. The Queen has been graciously pleased to signify Her intention to confer the Decoration of the Victoria Cross on the undermentioned Officers of Her Majesty's Indian forces, whose claims to the same have been submitted for Her Majesty's approval on account of Acts of Bravery performed by them in India, as recorded against their several names."

MILLER, JAMES, Conductor, Ordnance Department, Bengal, served in the Mutiny, and was awarded the Victoria Cross [London Gazette, 25 Feb. 1862]: "James Miller, Conductor, Ordnance Department, Bengal. Date of Act of Bravery : 28 Oct. 1857. For having, on the 28th Oct. 1857, at great personal risk, gone to the assistance of, and carried out of action, a wounded officer, Lieut. Glubb, of the late 38th Regt. of Bengal Native Infantry. He was himself subsequently wounded and sent to Agra. Conductor Miller was at the time employed with heavy howitzers and ordnance stores attached to a detachment of troops commanded by the late Colonel Cotton, C.B., in the attack on the above-mentioned date on the rebels who had taken up their position on the Serai at Futtehpore Sikra, near Agra."

MAYO, ARTHUR, Midshipman, Indian Navy, was born 18 May, 1840, at Oxford ; son of Herbert Mayo, F.G.S., Cheshunt, Herts, and his wife, Sarah (*née* Harman), of Theobalds, Cheshunt. He was educated at Berkhampstead School, Herts (1847–54). Mr.

Arthur Mayo.

Mayo says : "The years from late in 1854 to early 1857 require being accounted for, as a voyage to India in the Wellesley (1855–6), as Midshipman, was of great value to me, and it included my finding out the existence of the Indian Navy." Mr. Mayo joined the Indian Navy on 19 Feb. 1857. He served first in the steam frigate Punjaub, and afterwards in the No. 4 Indian Naval Brigade from June, 1857, to Jan. 1860. The 64th Regt. reached Bombay from Persia—the Persian War being finished in May, 1857—and were immediately sent off to Calcutta. "The Panjaub took round from Bombay to Calcutta, the Headquarters of the old 64th Regt., which, with the 78th, went up country and were with Havelock at Lucknow. I remember the battered-looking band instruments (I am musical), as well as the kindness of the officers, and the benefit to the Mids of the soldiers' porter. The battering of the instruments must have been done in the Persian War. The steam frigate Punjaub sent part of the Naval Brigade—called then No. 4 Detachment—ashore in June, 1857, from Calcutta. This Brigade went first to Dacca. (The Zenobia also supplied men for our Punjaub Brigade, so we were not all Punjaubs)." A Despatch from Lieut. T. E. Lewis, Indian Navy, commanding detachment, Dacca, to the Senior Indian Naval Officer, Calcutta, describes the disarming of the Bengal Artillery (Native) and the 73rd Native Infantry at Dacca. It is dated 22 Nov. 1857 (the 73rd Native Infantry was the chief factor at Dacca in point of numbers):

" SIR,

" I have the honour to report for your information that, in compliance with the orders of the civil authorities at Dacca, I proceeded on Sunday to disarm the sepoys stationed at Dacca. The Treasury, Executive Engineers and Commissariat Guards were disarmed without resistance. We then marched down to the Lall Bagh ; on entering the lines, the sepoys were found drawn up by their magazine, with two 6-pounders in the centre. Their hospital and numerous buildings in the Lall Bagh, together with the barracks, which are on the top of the hill, and are built of brick and loopholed, were also occupied by them in great force. Immediately we

deployed into line, they opened fire on us from front and left flank, with canister and musketry. We gave them one volley, and then charged with the bayonet up the hill, and carried the whole of the barracks on the top of it, breaking the doors with our musket-butts, and bayoneting the sepoys inside. As soon as this was done, we charged down hill, and taking them in flank, carried both their guns and all the buildings, driving them into the jungle. While we were thus employed with the small-arm men, the two mountain train howitzers, advancing within 150 yards, took up a position to the right, bearing on the enemy's guns in rear of their magazine, and, unlimbering, kept up a steady and well-directed fire. Every one, both officers and men, behaved most gallantly, charging repeatedly, in face of a most heavy fire, without the slightest hesitation for a moment. I beg particularly to bring to notice the conduct of Mr. Midshipman Mayo, who led the last charge on their guns most gallantly, being nearly 20 yards in front of the men. I regret to say that our loss has been severe, but not more, I think, than could have been expected from the strength of the position and the obstinacy of the defence. Forty-one sepoys were counted by Mr. Boatswain Brown dead on the ground, and eight have since been brought in desperately wounded. Three also were drowned or shot in attempting to escape across the river. I enclose a list of killed and wounded. Dr. Best being ill, Dr. Green, Civil Surgeon, accompanied the detachment into action, and was severely wounded. I was most ably seconded by Mr. Conner, my Second in Command. We were also accompanied by Messrs. Carnac, C. S. Macpherson and Bainbridge and Lieut. Hitchins, Bengal Native Infantry, who rendered great assistance with their rifles, and to whom my thanks are due. Our Force consisted of five officers and 85 men ; and the enemy's 200 in the lines.

" I have, etc.,

" T. E. LEWIS."

A Despatch dated 4 Dec. 1857, from the Secretary to the Government of India to the Senior Officer of the Indian Navy, states that the Governor-General in Council . . . " desires me to request that you will convey to Lieut. Lewis, and to the officers and men under his command, the thanks of the Government of India for the gallant manner in which they performed their duty. His Lordship in Council notices, with approbation, the conduct of Mr. Midshipman Mayo in leading a charge against the enemy's guns." For these services Mr. Mayo was awarded the Victoria Cross, which he won when he was just seventeen and a half years of age. He also received the Indian Medal. After the charge at Dacca, in which Mr. Mayo won his Victoria Cross, and for which he was mentioned twice in Despatches, No. 4 Detachment, Indian Naval Brigade, went to Sylhet, and afterwards to Debrooghur, which it left on the 14th Feb. 1859, on an expedition into the Abor Hills with a force of Native Infantry and Artillery, the whole under command of Lieut.-Colonel Hannay, of the 1st Assam Infantry. For his services in this expedition, Mr. Mayo was twice mentioned in Despatches, by Lieut.-Colonel Hannay, 28th Feb. 1859, and by Lieut. Lewis, Indian Navy, 28 Feb. 1859. He received the Indian Medal, and was awarded the Victoria Cross [London Gazette, 25 Feb. 1862]: " Arthur Mayo, Midshipman, Indian Navy. Date of Act of Bravery : 22 Nov. 1857. For having headed the charge on the 22nd Nov. 1857, in the engagement between the Indian Naval Brigade and the mutineers of the 73rd Native Infantry and Bengal Native Artillery, when the former was ordered to charge two 6-pounders which were keeping up a heavy fire. Mr. Mayo was nearly twenty yards in front of anyone else during the advance." He was invalided home in 1860, matriculated at Magdalen Hall (now Hertford College), Oxford, in May, 1862. He married, 18 July, 1865, at Oxford, Ellen H., daughter of the late Mr. and Mrs. Joseph Baker, and they have had six children : Mary A. E. Mayo, born 20 April, 1866 (Dominican Nun, now of North Adelaide, South Australia); Arthur J. Mayo, born 9 May, 1867, died 23 Nov. 1867 ; the Rev. Edward A. A. Mayo, born 6 Nov. 1868 (Priest, S.J., Beaumont College) ; the Rev. Francis X. M. Mayo, born 3 Sept. 1870 (Priest, S.J., Georgetown, British Guiana); the Rev. Raymund Mayo, born 5 Dec. 1871 (Priest, S.J., St. Ignatius, Preston), and Margaret Mary, born 18 March, 1880. In Feb. 1866, Mr. Mayo was ordained Deacon by Bishop Hamilton, of Salisbury, for Exeter Diocese. He served as Curate at St. Peter's, Plymouth, till Oct. 1867 and was received into the Roman Catholic Church by Father Peter Gallwey, S.J., at Farm Street, on 5 Nov. of that year.

CADELL, THOMAS, Lieut., was born 5 Sept. 1835, at Cockenzie House, East Lothian, N.B. ; son of Hew Francis Cadell, of Cockenzie, and of Janet, daughter of Francis Buchan Sydserff, of Ruchlaw, East Lothian. His

Thomas Cadell.

brothers were the late General Sir Robert Cadell, K.C.B., of the Royal Artillery, and Capt. Francis Cadell, the Explorer, who navigated the sources of the Murray River, Australia. He was educated at Edinburgh Academy ; the Grange, Sunderland, and abroad. He received his commission on April 17, 1854, and was gazetted to the 2nd European Bengal Fusiliers (now the Royal Munster Fusiliers), and was promoted Lieutenant 23 Nov. 1856. He greatly distinguished himself during the Siege of Delhi, and received the Victoria Cross [London Gazette, 29 April, 1862]: " Thomas Cadell, Lieut., late 2nd Bengal European Fusiliers. Date of Act of Bravery : 12 June, 1857. For having, on the 12th June, 1857, at the flag-staff picquet of Her Majesty's 75th Regt. and 2nd European Bengal Fusiliers were driven in by a large body of the enemy, brought in from amongst the enemy a wounded bugler of his own regiment, under a most severe fire, who would otherwise have been cut up by the rebels. Also, on the same day, when the Fusiliers were retiring, by order, on Metcalfe's house, on its being reported that there was a wounded man left behind, Lieut. Cadell went back of his own accord towards the enemy, accompanied by three men, and brought in a man of the 75th Regt., who was severely wounded, under a most heavy fire from the advancing enemy." He served throughout the Oudh Campaign (1858-9) with the 4th Irregular Cavalry, and commanded a Flying Column in Bundlekhund against the Bheels (1859-60), being mentioned in Despatches, and receiving the thanks of Government for his services. He became Captain 17 April, 1866, and Major 17 April, 1874. He entered the Political Department, and held various political appointments in Central India and Rajputana. From 1879 till 1892, when he retired, he held the appointment of Chief Commissioner of the Andaman and Nicobar Islands. Colonel Cadell was created a C.B. in 1907 for his services in the Indian Mutiny. He married in 1867, Anna Catherine, daughter of Patrick Dalmahoy, Esq., of Bourhouse, East Lothian, and has two daughters and two surviving sons: Major Hew Francis Cadell, the Lothians and Border Horse, and Patrick Robert Cadell, C.I.E., of the Indian Civil Service, Chief Secretary to the Government, Bombay. Colonel Cadell died on 6 April, 1919.

THACKERAY, EDWARD TALBOT, 2nd Lieut., was born 19 Oct. 1836, at Broxbourne, Herts; son of the late Rev. Francis St. John Thackeray, M.A., of Broxbourne, and of Mary Anne, daughter of John Shakespear, of Singleton, Essex. Sir Edward Thackeray is William Makepeace Thackeray's first cousin. He was educated at Marlborough College, and at the Honourable East India Company's Military College, Addiscombe, and entered the Royal Engineers on the 9th Dec. 1854. Second Lieut. E. T. Thackeray served throughout the Indian Mutiny Campaign; was mentioned in the Despatch of General Sir Archdale Wilson, G.C.B., commanding the Delhi Field Force, dated 20 Sept. 1857, and for his services during the Siege of Delhi was awarded the Victoria Cross [London Gazette, 29 April, 1862]: "Edward Talbot Thackeray, 2nd Lieut., Bengal Engineers. Date of Act of Bravery: 16 Sept. 1857. For cool intrepidity and characteristic daring in extinguishing a fire in the Delhi Magazine enclosure, on the 16th Sept. 1857, under a close and heavy musketry-fire from the enemy, at the imminent risk of his life from the explosion of combustible stores in the shed in which the fire occurred." He married, first, in 1862, Amy Mary Anne (she died in 1865), daughter of Eyre Evans Crowe, by whom he had two daughters: Amy Margaret Ritchie and Anne Wynne Thackeray. In 1865 Lieut. Thackeray was promoted to Captain. He married secondly, on 2 Dec. 1869, Elizabeth, daughter of the late Major T. B. Pleydell, and they have four sons: Lieut.-Colonel E. F. Thackerary, C.M.G., D.S.O. (who holds the Croix de Guerre), born 2 Nov. 1870; Richmond Clive Thackerary, born 19 Sept. 1873; Lieut.-Colonel Charles Bouverie Thackeray, D.S.O., R.F.A., born 20 Dec. 1875, and H. St. J. P. Thackeray, born 6 Oct. 1879. He served in the Afghan Campaign, 1879-80, and was in command of Jugdulak Fort when the fort was attacked by a large force of Ghilzais, who were repulsed with heavy losses. The fort was defended by two companies of Sappers and a company of the 24th Native Infantry. Major Thackeray was severely wounded; mentioned in Despatches, and received the Medal, and subsequently (in 1886) was created a C.B. (Military Division). He was Commandant of the Bengal Sappers and Miners from 1879 to 1885. In 1880 he became Lieutenant-Colonel, and in 1884, Colonel, and he retired from the Army in 1888. From 1893 Colonel Thackeray was Chief Commissioner of the Ambulance Brigade of the Order of St. John of Jerusalem, and he is a Knight of Grace of the Order. He was made a K.C.B. (Civil) in 1897. His published works are: "Two Indian Campaigns," "Biographies of Officers of the Bengal Engineers," and "Reminiscences of the Indian Mutiny and Afghanistan." During the war with Germany he was Vice-President of the Bordighera Branch of the British Red Cross in Italy, and was mentioned in the Despatch of General the Earl of Cavan [London Gazette, 3 June, 1919].

Edward T. Thackeray.

London Gazette, 20 June, 1862.—"The Queen has been graciously pleased to signify Her intention to confer the Decoration of the Victoria Cross on the undermentioned Officer of Her Majesty's Army, whose claim to the same has been submitted for Her Majesty's approval, for his conspicuous bravery during the Siege of Lucknow, as recorded against his name."

GORE-BROWNE, HENRY GEORGE, Capt., was a son of the late Mr. Arthur Browne, of Newtown, Roscommon; was born in 1830; educated at Trinity College, Dublin, and at the age of 25 was gazetted to the 32nd Light Infantry in 1855. He served through the Mutiny Campaign, and took part in the defence of the Lucknow Residency, when he was awarded the Victoria Cross [London Gazette, 20 June, 1862]: "Henry George Browne, Capt., 32nd Regt. Date of Act of Bravery: 21 Aug. 1857. For conspicuous bravery in having, on the 21st Aug. 1857, during

Henry G. Gore-Browne.

the Siege of the Lucknow Residency, gallantly led a sortie, at great personal risk, for the purpose of spiking two heavy guns, which were doing considerable damage to the defences. It appears from the statements of the non-commissioned officers and men who accompanied Capt. Browne on the occasion, that he was the first person who entered the battery, which consisted of the two guns in question, protected by high palisades, the embrasures being closed with sliding shutters. On reaching the battery Capt. Browne removed the shutters and jumped into the battery. The result was that the guns were spiked, and it is supposed that about 100 of the enemy were killed." In the following year he served with Maxwell's Force. For his services in the Indian Mutiny, besides being given the Victoria Cross, he was thanked in General Orders by Sir James Outram, Sir John Inglis and the Governor-General; received the Medal and clasp, a year's service for Lucknow, and special promotion to the rank of Captain. Captain Browne was twice wounded in this campaign, once severely. He was not fortunate enough to see any more active service, and retired from the Army comparatively early, as a Major, with the brevet rank of Lieutenant-Colonel. Lieut.-Colonel Browne married in 1882, Jane Anne, sister of Sir Charles Bravely, and his only son died two years before him. He managed Sir Charles Seeley's estate in the Isle of Wight, and was a keen and practical agriculturist, being President of the Isle of Wight Agricultural Society, of which the King is Patron. Colonel Browne also supported the Isle of Wight Hunt. He was a Magistrate for the county of Southampton, and often presided at the Ryde Court. For some years he served on the Isle of Wight Board of Guardians; he was a Highway Commissioner, and a great supporter of the work of the Island Life-boat Board. He was a member of the Isle of Wight Conservative Association and Chairman of the Shanklin Conservative Club. He did his utmost for the Territorial units and National Reserves in the island, and was much to the fore in all patriotic movements. In May, 1912, he was appointed Deputy Governor of the Island. Brevet Lieut.-Colonel and Honorary Colonel Henry George Browne, V.C., late retired pay, by deed of poll changed his name to Gore-Browne. He died 15 Nov. 1912, at Shanklin. Colonel Gore-Browne was very proud of the fact that he was the great-grandson of Arthur Browne, in whose arms Wolfe is said to have died at Quebec. He had a great reverence for Wolfe's memory.

London Gazette, 11 Nov. 1862.—"The Queen has been graciously pleased to signify Her intention to confer the Decoration of the Victoria Cross on the undermentioned Officers of the Army, whose claims to the same have been submitted for Her Majesty's approval, on account of Acts of Bravery performed by them in India, as recorded against their several names."

COGHLAN, CORNELIUS, Colour-Sergt., was born in June, 1828; the son of Edward and Catherine Coghlan. He was educated at Eyrecourt, County Galway, and entered the 75th (Stirlingshire) Regt., now the 1st Battn. the Gordon Highlanders, serving in it for 21 years. For his services in the Mutiny Campaign, 1857-8, he received the Victoria Cross and the Indian Mutiny Medal with two clasps for Delhi and the Relief of Lucknow. He was wounded on the left knee 8 June, 1857. His Victoria Cross was gazetted 11 Nov. 1862: "Cornelius Coghlan, Sergt., 75th Regt. Dates of Acts of Bravery: 8 June, 1857; 18 July, 1857. For gallantly venturing, under a heavy fire, with three others, into a serai occupied by the enemy in great numbers, and removing Private Corbett, 75th Regt., who lay severely wounded. Also for cheering and encouraging a party which hesitated to charge down a lane in Subjee Mundee, at Delhi, lined on each side with huts, and raked by a cross-fire; then entering with the said party into an enclosure filled with the enemy, and destroying every man. For having, also, on the same occasion, returned under a cross-fire to collect dhoolies and carry off the wounded; a service which was successfully performed, and for which this man received great praise from the officers of his regiment." He served 13 years in India; four years as Sergeant-Major; 10 years as Colour-Sergeant; two years as Private. He also served as Sergeant-Major for 21 years in the 3rd Connaught Rangers, Permanent Staff. His favourite recreation was angling. Sergt.-Major Coghlan died 14 Feb. 1915.

Cornelius Coghlan.

ANDERSON, CHARLES, Corpl., enlisted in the Queen's Bays, served in the Mutiny Campaign, and was awarded the Victoria Cross [London Gazette, 11 Nov. 1862]: "No. 875, Charles Anderson, Corpl. (then Private); No. 1158, Thomas Monaghan, Trumpeter, 2nd Dragoon Guards. Date of Acts of Bravery: 8 Oct. 1858. For saving the life of Lieut.-Colonel Seymour, C.B., commanding the regiment, in an attack made on him on the 8th Oct., 1858, by mutinous sepoys, in a dense jungle of sugar-canes, from which an attempt was made to dislodge them. The mutineers were between 30 and 40 in number. They suddenly opened fire on Lieut.-Colonel Seymour and his party at a few yards' distance, and immediately afterwards rushed in upon them with drawn (native) swords. Pistolling a

Charles Anderson

man cutting at him, and emptying with deadly effect at arm's length every barrel of his revolver, Lieut.-Colonel Seymour was cut down by two sword-cuts, when the two men above recommended rushed to his rescue, and the Trumpeter shooting a man with his pistol in the act of cutting at him, and both the Trumpeter and Dragoon driving at the enemy with their swords, enabled him to arise and assist in defending himself again, when the whole of the enemy were despatched. The occurrence took place near Sundeela, Oudh, on the date above mentioned." Anderson's Cross is now in the United Service Museum, London. He seems to have spent his later years at Waterford.

MONAGHAN, THOMAS, Trumpeter, No. 1158, joined the 2nd Dragoon Guards (Queen's Bays), served in the Indian Mutiny, and was awarded the Victoria Cross [London Gazette, 11 Nov. 1862]: "Charles Anderson, No. 875, Private, and Thomas Monaghan, No. 1158, Trumpeter, 2nd Dragoon Guards. Date of Acts of Bravery: 8 Oct. 1858. For saving the life of Lieut.-Colonel Seymour, C.B., commanding the regiment, in an attack made on him on the 8th Oct. 1858, by mutinous sepoys, in a dense jungle of sugar-canes, from which an attempt was made to dislodge them. The mutineers were between 30 and 40 in number. They suddenly opened fire on Lieut.-Colonel Seymour and his party at a few yards' distance, and immediately afterwards rushed in upon them with drawn (native) swords. Pistolling a man cutting at him, and emptying with deadly effect every barrel of his revolver, Lieut.-Colonel Seymour was cut down by two sword-cuts, when the two men above recommended rushed to his rescue, and the Trumpeter shooting a man with his pistol in the act of cutting at him, and both the Trumpeter and Dragoon driving at the enemy with their swords, enabled him to arise and assist in defending himself again, when the whole of the enemy were despatched. The occurrence took place soon after the action fought near Sundeela, Oudh, on the date above mentioned." He died on the 10 Nov. 1895. Monaghan's Victoria Cross was sold in London on 5 Nov. 1903, for £43.

Thomas Monaghan.

London Gazette, 6 Feb. 1863.—" War Office, 6 Feb. 1863. The Queen has been graciously pleased to signify Her intention to confer the Decoration of the Victoria Cross on the undermentioned Seaman of the Royal Navy, whose claim to the same has been submitted for Her Majesty's approval, for his gallant conduct at the capture of Fung-wha, in China, as recorded against his name."

HINCKLEY, GEORGE, Able Seaman, Royal Navy, was born at Liverpool, and joined the Royal Navy. He served in China, in 1863, and was awarded the Victoria Cross [London Gazette, 6 Feb. 1863]: "George Hinckley, Able Seaman, of Her Majesty's Ship Sphinx. For volunteering while under the east gate of the city of Fung-wha, to carry to a Joss-house one hundred and fifty yards distant, under a heavy and continuous fire of musketry, gingalls and stink-pots, Mr. Coker, Master's Assistant of the Sphinx, who had been wounded in the advance to the gate, in which object Hinckley succeeded. On his return to the gate under a similar fire he again volunteered, and succeeded in carrying the Joss-house Mr. Bremen, an officer of Ward's forces, who had also been wounded in the advance on the gate, and he again returned to his post under the gate." Quartermaster George Hinckley died at Plymouth, 31 Dec. 1904, aged 85. Colonel Chaplin, V.C., is now the only surviving recipient of the Victoria Cross in the China Campaign in 1862.

George Hinckley.

London Gazette, 17 April, 1863.—" War Office, 16 April, 1863. The Queen has been graciously pleased to signify Her intention to confer the Decoration of the Victoria Cross on the undermentioned Officers, whose claims to the same have been submitted for Her Majesty's approval, on account of Acts of Bravery performed by them in India, as recorded against their several names."

AITKEN, ROBERT HOPE MONCRIEFF, Lieut., was born on 14 April, 1828 ; the son of J. Aitken, Esq., of Cupar, Fife. He went to India in 1847, and entered the Honourable Company's 13th Regt. of Bengal Native Infantry as Ensign in 1847, serving in the Punjab Campaign of 1848-9. He was present at the action of Ramnugger, at the passage of the Chenab, Battle of Goojerat, and with the column which, under Major General Sir Walter Gilbert, pursued the Sikh and Afghan Army (Medal and clasp). He served with the 13th Regt. Bengal Infantry in the Santhal Rebellion of 1855 ; was present in some skirmishes with the Santhals, and, assisted by Lieut. Loughnan, 13th Native Infantry, personally took prisoner Koulea, a Santhal chief, for whose capture a reward of Rs. 5,000 was offered. (This reward was not paid to the captors on the ground that soldiers were not entitled to it.) Lieut. Aitken served throughout the Indian Mutiny in 1857-8. He was engaged (1) in action against the mutineers in Lucknow Cantonments on 30 and 31 May, 1857. (2) In the Battle of Chunhut, on 30 June, 1859. (3) Commanded throughout the defence of Lucknow the whole of the Hindustani sepoys of the 13th Bengal Native Infantry, who

remained faithful ; and, with them alone, held the Baillie Guard Post stated by Sir John Inglis to be perhaps the most important position in the whole of the defences. (4) Commanded in two sorties, and was present in two others. (5) Commanded the remains of the 13th Native Infantry (both Hindustanis and Sikhs) in the movement of retreat from the Residency on the night of 22 Nov., under General Sir Colin Campbell, G.C.B., Commander-in-Chief. Lieut. Aitken was present (as Paymaster of the Army under Sir Colin Campbell) in the fighting against the Gwalior Contingent in Cawnpore from 29 Nov. to 5 Dec. 1857, and at the defeat of the rebels on 6 Dec. in the Battle of Cawnpore. He raised the Cawnpore Levy, and commanded it in Futtehpore District in support of the troops engaged under Sir Colin Campbell in the Baiswarah Campaign (Oudh) in 1858. Lieut. Aitken was mentioned ten times in the Despatches connected with the Defence of Lucknow, and received the thanks of the Governor-General in Council. He was awarded the Victoria Cross [London Gazette, 17 April, 1863]: "Robert Hope Moncrieff Aitken, Lieut. (now Capt.), the late 13th Bengal Native Infantry (now of the Bengal Staff Corps). For various acts of gallantry performed during the defence of the Residency of Lucknow, from the 30th June to the 22nd Nov. 1857. On three different occasions Lieut. Aitken went into the garden under the enemy's loopholes in the 'Captain's Bazaar.' On two of these occasions he brought out a number of bullocks which had been left in the garden. Subsequently, on the 3rd July, the enemy having set fire to the Bhoosa Stock in the garden, and it being apprehended that the fire would reach the powder-magazine which had been left there, Lieut. Aitken, accompanied by other officers, went into the garden and cut down all the tents, which might have communicated the fire to the powder. This was done close to the enemy's loopholes, under a bright light from the flames. It was a most dangerous service. (2) On the night of the 20th Aug., the enemy having set fire to the Baillie Guard Gate, Lieut. Aitken was the first man in the gateway, and assisted by some sepoys and a water-carrier of his regiment, he partially opened the gate under a heavy fire of musketry, and, having removed the burning wood and straw, saved the gate. (3) On the evening of the 25 Sept., this officer led on twelve sepoys of his regiment for the purpose of attacking two guns opposite the gate referred to, in order to prevent their being turned on the late Major-General Havelock's second column. Having captured them, he attacked and took Teree Kotee with a small force. (4) On the morning of the 26th Sept., with a small party of his regiment, he assaulted and captured the barricaded gateway of the Fureed Buksh Palace and the palace itself. On this occasion he sprang up against a small wicket-gate on the right, and prevented the enemy from shutting it, until, with assistance, it was forced open and the assaulting party were thus enabled to rush in. The complete success of the attack was solely owing to this officer's distinguished bravery. (5) In a subsequent sortie, on the 29th Sept., Lieut. Aitken volunteered to take a gun which still continued firing, taking with him four soldiers through the houses and lanes to the gun. The enemy fired on this party from the houses, but they held their ground until, a stronger party coming up, the gun was upset from its carriage and taken into the Residency. Another gun was subsequently taken." Sir Hugh Rose gave an address in presenting the Victoria Cross to Lieut. Aitken, in the midst of scenes to which, he said, Aitken and his gallant companions in arms had imparted a celebrity which could never pass away. In April, 1871, Colonel Aitken was recommended for the C.B. by H.E. Lord Napier, G.C.B., Commander-in-Chief of the Indian Army, and by H.E. Lord Mayo, G.C.B., Governor-General of India. Colonel Aitken died in Sept. 1887.

GOODFELLOW, CHARLES AUGUSTUS, Lieut., entered the Bombay Engineers in 1855, and served throughout the Mutiny Campaign, being present at the Sieges of Rhatghur, Gorakolta and Jhansi, and receiving mention in Despatches in July, 1858. In the following year he was awarded the Victoria Cross [London Gazette, 16 April, 1863]: "Charles Augustus Goodfellow, Lieut., The Late Bombay Engineers, now of the Royal Engineers. For gallant conduct at the attack on the Fort of Beyt, on 6 Oct. 1859. On that occasion a soldier of the 28th Regt. was shot under the walls, under a sharp fire of matchlocks, and he bore off the body of the soldier who was then dead, but whom he at first supposed to be wounded only." His was the last Victoria Cross granted for the Mutiny, and the place of action seems to have been where the last stand was made, at Beyt, in Kattiwar, Western India. This officer served in Abyssinia in 1868, and was again mentioned in Despatches. He attained the rank of Lieutenant-General in 1892. The "Times" of the 2nd Sept. 1915, says : "Lieut.-General John Augustus Goodfellow, V.C., C.B., of Leamington, died yesterday in his 80th year."

Charles A. Goodfellow.

London Gazette, 19 Jan. 1864.—" War Office, 16 Jan. 1864. The Queen has been graciously pleased to signify Her intention to confer the Decoration of the Victoria Cross on the undermentioned Officer and Non-commissioned Officer of Her Majesty's Army, whose claims to the same have been submitted for Her Majesty's approval, on account of Acts of Bravery performed by them in New Zealand, as recorded against their several names."

McKENNA, EDWARD, Colour-Sergt. (now Ensign), a wire-worker by trade, enlisted in the 65th Regt. of Foot on the 15th Jan. 1854, at Leeds, at the age of 17 years and 11 months. He was 5 feet 6 inches in height, of a sallow complexion, and with grey eyes and brown hair. On the 1st

March, 1860, he was promoted Corporal ; on the 1st July, 1862, Sergeant, and on the 15th May, 1863, Colour-Sergeant. He served abroad in Australia and New Zealand from the 18th May, 1846, to the 7th Sept. 1863. On the 9th June, 1853, at Wellington, New Zealand, he was married. He served in the Maori War in New Zealand, and for his services in that campaign was promoted to the rank of Ensign 8 Sept. 1863, and was awarded the Victoria Cross [London Gazette, 16 Jan. 1864] : " Edward McKenna, Colour-Sergt. (now Ensign), 65th Regt. For gallant conduct at the engagement near Cameron Town, New Zealand, on the 7th Sept. 1863, after both his Officers, Capt. Smith and Lieut. Butler, had been shot, in charging through the position of an enemy heavily outnumbering him, and drawing off his small force, consisting of two sergeants, one bugler, and thirty-five men, through a broken and rugged country, with the loss of one man killed and another missing. Lieut.-General Cameron, C.B., commanding Her Majesty's forces in that colony, reports that in Colour-Sergt. McKenna the detachment found a commander whose coolness, intrepidity and judgment justified the confidence placed in him by the soldiers brought so suddenly under his command." Ensign McKenna's total amount of service was 18 years and 206 days. By Ensign McKenna's request, his widow presented to the Auckland Museum his Victoria Cross, Medals and the revolver given to him by his wounded officer.

RYAN, JOHN, L.-Corpl., No. 261, enlisted in the 65th (York and Lancaster) Regt. ; was promoted to Lance-Corporal ; served in the Maori War in New Zealand, and was awarded the Victoria Cross [London Gazette, 16 Jan. 1864] : " John Ryan, L.-Corpl., 65th Regt. Date of Act of Bravery : 7 Sept. 1863. For gallant conduct at the engagement—near Cameron Town, above referred to. This non-commissioned officer, with Privates Bulford and Talbot, of the same regiment, who have been recommended for the Medal for distinguished conduct in the field for their behaviour on the same occasion, removed the body of the late Capt. Smith from the field of action after he had been mortally wounded, and remained with it all night in a bush surrounded by the enemy." Privates Bulford and Talbot were both awarded the Medal for Distinguished Conduct, and Ryan was awarded the Victoria Cross, but he did not live very long afterwards. He was drowned near Tuakan on the 29th Dec. 1863, while trying to rescue a comrade. His Victoria Cross was sold in London on 17 April, 1902, for £58.

London Gazette, 19 July, 1864.—"War Office, 16 July, 1864. The Queen has been graciously pleased to signify Her intention to confer the Decoration of the Victoria Cross on the undermentioned Officer of Her Majesty's Indian Forces, whose claim to the same has been submitted for Her Majesty's approval, for his gallant conduct during operations at Umbeyla, on the North-Western Frontier of India, as recorded against his name."

PITCHER, HENRY WILLIAM, Lieut., served on the North-Western Frontier of India in 1863, and was awarded the Victoria Cross [London Gazette, 16 July, 1864] : " Henry William Pitcher, Lieut., Bengal Staff Corps ; Adjutant, 4th Punjab Infantry. Dates of Acts of Bravery : 30 Oct. 1863 ; 16 Nov. 1863. For the daring and gallant manner in which, in the course of the recent operations against the Frontier tribes, on the 30th Oct. 1863, he led a party of his regiment to recapture the Crag Picquet, after its garrison had been driven in by the enemy, on which occasion sixty of them were killed in desperate hand-to-hand fighting. From the nature of the approach to the top of the Crag, amongst the large rocks, one or two men only could advance at one time. ' Whilst I ascended one path,' relates Major Keyes, commanding the 1st Punjab Infantry, ' I directed Lieut. Fosbery, of the late 4th European Regt., to push up another, at the head of a few men. He led this party with the greatest coolness and intrepidity, and was the first man to gain the top of the Crag on his side of the attack. Lieut. Pitcher, equally cool and daring, led a party of men up to the last rock, until he was knocked down and stunned by a large stone thrown from above, within a few yards of him.' Lieut. Pitcher also displayed great gallantry in leading on a party of his regiment to endeavour to recover the Crag Picquet, when it again fell into the enemy's hands, on the 13th Nov., as related in the following extract from Major Keyes's report of the 16th of that month : ' The duty of leading the first charge devolved upon Lieut. Pitcher, and I beg to bring to the special notice of the Brigadier-General commanding the admirable manner in which he performed this important duty. He was by many yards the foremost of his party, and the gallant bearing of this excellent young officer was the admiration of all spectators. It is impossible to say too much or to overrate his services on this occasion. Lieut. Pitcher was severely wounded, and was obliged to be carried back.' " Lieut. Pitcher was later promoted to Captain.

Samuel Mitchell.

London Gazette, 26 July, 1864.—"War Office, 23 July, 1864. The Queen has been graciously pleased to signify Her intention to confer the Decoration of the Victoria Cross on the undermentioned Seaman of the Royal Navy, whose claim to the same has been submitted for Her Majesty's approval, for his gallant conduct in New Zealand, as recorded against his name."

MITCHELL, SAMUEL, Captain of the Foretop, Royal Navy, served in the New Zealand War, and was awarded the Victoria Cross [London Gazette, 26 July, 1864] : " Samuel Mitchell, Capt. of the Foretop of Her Majesty's Ship Harrier. For his gallant conduct in the attack of Te Papa, Tauranga, on the 29th April, 1864, in entering the pah with

Commander Hay, and when that officer was mortally wounded, bringing him out, although ordered by Commander Hay to leave him and seek his own safety. This man was at the time Captain of the Foretop of the Harrier, doing duty as Captain's Coxswain ; and Commodore Sir William Wiseman brings his name to special notice for this act of gallantry." Samuel Mitchell died 16 March, 1894. His Victoria Cross was sold 20 Nov. 1908, for £50.

London Gazette, 16 Aug. 1864.—" War Office, 16 Aug. 1864. The Queen has been graciously pleased to signify Her intention to confer the Decoration of the Victoria Cross on the undermentioned Officer, whose claim to the same has been submitted for Her Majesty's approval, for his gallant conduct in New Zealand, as recorded against his name."

M'NEILL, JOHN CARSTAIRS, Lieut.-Colonel, was born 29 March, 1831 ; the son of the late Capt. Alexander M'Neill, and of the daughter and heiress of Mr. Cairstairs, of an old Fifeshire family. He was a

John Carstairs M'Neill.

nephew of Lord Colonsay and of Sir John M'Neill, G.C.B. John M'Neill was educated at the College, St. Andrews, and at Addiscombe. On leaving Addiscombe he was gazetted to the 12th Bengal Native Infantry, which regiment mutinied. Then he was A.D.C. to General Sir E. Lugard (Mutiny Medal and clasp). Then after the Mutiny some additional regiments were created, and he was gazetted to the 107th, which, however, he never joined, but exchanged into the 48th Northamptonshire Regt., and, as Captain and Brevet Lieutenant-Colonel, commanded the Tipperary Flying Column. He became Captain 31 Aug. 1860, Major 8 Oct. 1861, and Lieutenant-Colonel 1 March, 1864. He served (2) in the New Zealand Campaign of 1864-5 ; received the Medal, and was awarded the Victoria Cross [London Gazette, 16 July, 1864] : " John Carstairs M'Neill, Lieut.-Colonel, 107th Regt. Date of Act of Bravery : 30 March, 1864. For the valour and presence of mind which he displayed in New Zealand on the 30th March, 1864, which is thus described by Private Vosper, of the Colonial Defence Force. Private Vosper states that he was sent on that day with Private Gibson, of the same force, as an escort to Major (now Lieut.-Colonel) M'Neill, Aide-de-Camp to Lieut.-General Sir Duncan Cameron. Lieut.-Colonel M'Neill was proceeding to Te Awamutu on duty at the time. On returning from that place and about a mile on this side of Ohanpu, this officer, having seen a body of the enemy in front, sent Private Gibson back to bring up Infantry from Ohanpu, and he and Private Vosper proceeded leisurely to the top of a rise to watch the enemy. Suddenly they were attacked by about fifty natives, who were concealed in the fern close at hand. Their only chance of escape was by riding for their lives, and as they turned to gallop Private Vosper's horse fell and threw him. The natives thereupon rushed forward to seize him, but Lieut.-Colonel M'Neill, on perceiving that Private Vosper was not following him, returned, caught his horse, and helped him to mount. The natives were firing sharply at them, and were so near that, according to Private Vosper's statement, it was only by galloping as hard as they could that they escaped. He says he owes his life entirely to Lieut.-Colonel M'Neill's assistance, for he could not have caught his horse alone, and in a few minutes must have been killed." (3) He was in command of the Tipperary Flying Column during the Fenian disturbance of 1866-7 (thanked in General Orders). (4) As Military Secretary to Lord Lisgar, Governor-General of Canada, 1868-72, being on the Staff of the Red River Expedition from Canada (created a C.M.G., 1870) ; became Colonel 25 April, 1872. (5) Served as Colonel on the Staff and second in command of Ashanti Expedition, 1873, until severely wounded (mentioned in Despatches, Medal and C.B.). (6) In 1874 he was appointed Equerry to Her Majesty, and A.D.C. to H.R.H. The Commander-in-Chief. In 1880 he accompanied H.R.H. Prince Leopold to Canada. He served in the Egyptian Campaign of 1882 (Medal with clasp and 2nd Class Medjidie). He became Major-General in 1882, and in that year acccompanied H.R.H. the Duke of Connaught to Egypt. He was created a G.C.V.O., and a K.C.M.G., and was an Extra Equerry to H.M. King Edward, and Bath King at Arms. Sir John M'Neill was a J.P., and D.L. for Argyllshire. He died in St. James's Palace, 25 April, 1904, aged 75.

London Gazette, 23 Sept. 1864.—" War Office, 22 Sept. 1864. The Queen has been graciously pleased to signify Her intention to confer the Decoration of the Victoria Cross on the undermentioned Officers and Drummer of Her Majesty's Army, whose claims to the same have been submitted for Her Majesty's approval, on account of Acts of Bravery performed by them in New Zealand, as stated against their names."

MANLEY, WILLIAM GEORGE NICHOLAS, Assistant-Surgeon, was born in Dublin in 1831, the son of the Rev. William Nicholas Manley. He became M.R.C.S. (England) in 1851 ; joined the Army Medical Staff in 1855, and served during the Crimean Campaign of 1855 and 1856 (Medal with clasp, Turkish Medal). He served throughout the New Zealand War 1864-67 ; was twice wounded ; mentioned in Despatches, and given R.H.S. Medal for saving a man of the R.A. who had fallen overboard in the Waitotara River, New Zealand, on the 21st July, 1865. He was also promoted Staff Surgeon, and was awarded the Victoria Cross [London Gazette, 22 Sept. 1864] : " William George Manley, Assistant-Surgeon, Royal Artillery. Date of Act of Bravery : 29 April, 1864. For his conduct during the assault on the Rebel Pah, near Tauranga, New Zealand, on the 29th April last, in most nobly risking his own life, according to the testimony of Commodore Sir William Wiseman, Bart., C.B., in his endeavour to save that of the late Commander Hay, of the Royal Navy, and others. Having volunteered to accompany the storming party into the Pah, he attended on that officer when he was carried away mortally wounded, and then volunteered to return, in order to see if he could find any more wounded. It is stated that he was one of the last officers to leave the Pah." During the Franco-Prussian War of 1870–71 he accompanied the British Ambulance, and received the thanks of the Prussian General in command of the division to which he was attached. For his courage and devotion during the action at Châteauneuf and Bretoncelles and at Orleans and Cracaut, he was granted the Steel War Medal, Second Class of the Iron Cross, and the Bavarian Order of Merit. He served through the Afghan War of 1878–79 (mentioned in Despatches ; thanked by the Viceroy, and the Government of India ; Medal). He served in the Egyptian War of 1882, taking part in the Battle of Tel-el-Kebir (mentioned in Despatches ; Medal with clasp ; Bronze Star ; Third Class Osmanieh ; promoted Deputy-Surgeon-General). He was promoted Surgeon-General and retired in 1884. Surgeon-General Manley was created a C.B. (Military) in 1884. He died on the 16th Nov. 1891.

TEMPLE, WILLIAM, Assistant-Surgeon, was born on 7 Nov. 1833, son of the late William Temple, M.D., of Monaghan, and of Anne, daughter of Hugh Hammill, of Rooskey, County Monaghan. He was educated privately at Rev. John Bleckley's School,

Monaghan, and at Trinity College, Dublin. He entered the Army 1 Nov. 1858. He served in the Taranaki Campaign (New Zealand) of 1860–61. On 21 Oct. 1862, at Auckland, New Zealand, Assistant-Surgeon Temple married Anne Theodosia (who died in 1914), fourth daughter of the late Major-General T. R. Mould, C.B., R.E. Their children were William Arthur Mould Temple, Capt., The Gloucestershire Regt., died of wounds 22 Oct. 1914 ; Brevet Lieut.-Colonel Reginald Cecil Temple, R.M.A. ; Bertram Henry Temple ; Brevet Lieut.-Colonel, and Temporary Brigadier-General Frank Valiant Temple, R.M.L.I. ; Annie Georgina Temple ; Elizabeth Alice Hickman ; Mabel Eva

William Temple.

Sanders ; Ethel Kate Morphy Beames, and Eleanor Thompson. Assistant-Surgeon Temple served in the later New Zealand Campaign, in which he won his Victoria Cross. He was present at the actions of Teairei, Rangiriri, and Rangiawhia. " Where the Royal Artillery displayed great daring and intrepidity in the assault on the Central Redoubt. The enemy kept up a deadly fire through a narrow opening in the parapet of the redoubt, and prevented the wounded who were lying close to the work from being removed, amongst them Capt. Mercer, R.A. Assistant-Surgeon Temple here performed an act of courage and devotion to his duty worthy of record, by passing this opening for the purpose of attending to the wounded, although the extreme danger of his doing so was pointed out to him ; every man but one (Lieut. Pickard) who had previously attempted to cross having been killed or wounded." (Extract from Lieut.-General Sir Duncan Cameron, K.C.B.'s, Despatch of 26 Nov. 1863.—Commanding the Forces in the Australian Colonies and in New Zealand.) The award of his Victoria Cross was gazetted 22 Sept. 1864 : " William Temple, Assistant-Surgeon, and Arthur Frederick Pickard, Lieut., Royal Artillery. For gallant conduct during the assault of the enemy's position at Rangiriri, in New Zealand, on the 20th Nov. 1863, in exposing their lives to imminent danger, in crossing the entrance of the Maori Keep at a point upon which the enemy had concentrated their fire, with a view to render assistance to the wounded, and more especially to the late Capt. Mercer, of the Royal Artillery. Lieut. Pickard, it is said, crossed and recrossed the parapet to procure water for the wounded when none of the men could be induced to perform this service, the space over which he traversed being exposed to a cross-fire, and testimony is borne to the calmness displayed by him and Assistant-Surgeon Temple under the trying circumstances to which they were exposed." During his second term of service in India Lieut.-Colonel Temple was Secretary to the Surgeon-General of H.M. Forces from 1884 to 1889, and Honorary Surgeon to H.E. the Viceroy of India from 1886 to 1889. Lieut.-Colonel Temple died on 13 Feb. 1919, after a long illness.

PICKARD, ARTHUR FREDERICK, Lieut., served in the Maori Campaign in New Zealand, and was awarded the Victoria Cross [London Gazette, 22 Sept. 1864] : " Assistant-Surgeon William Temple ; Lieut. Arthur Frederick Pickard, Royal Artillery. Date of Acts of Bravery : 20 Nov. 1863. For gallant conduct during the assault on the enemy's position a Rangiriri, in New Zealand, on the 20th Nov. last, in exposing their lives to imminent danger, in crossing the entrance of the Maori Keep at a point upon which the enemy had concentrated their fire, with a view to render assistance to the wounded, and more especially to the late Capt. Mercer, of the Royal Artillery. Lieut. Pickard, it is stated, crossed and recrossed the parapet to procure water for the wounded, when none of the men could be induced to perform this service, the space over which he traversed being exposed to a cross-fire, and testimony is borne to the coolness displayed by him and Assistant-Surgeon Temple. under the trying circumstances to which they were exposed." He later became Colonel, and was created a C.B. Colonel Pickard was Equerry to H.R.H. the Duke of Connaught, and later Equerry to Her Majesty Queen Victoria. He died of consumption at Cannes early in the 'nineties.

DOWN, JOHN THORNTON, Ensign, joined the 57th Regt., the Duke of Cambridge's Own, served in the Maori Campaign in New Zealand, and was awarded the Victoria Cross [London Gazette, 22 Sept. 1864]: "John Thornton Down, Ensign, and Dudley Stagpoole, Drummer, 57th Regt. Date of Acts of Bravery : 2 Oct. 1863. For their conduct at Pontoko, on the 2nd Oct. 1863, in rescuing a wounded comrade from the rebel Maoris. They

John Thornton Down.

succeeded in bringing in the wounded man, who was lying at about fifty yards from the bush, although the enemy kept up a very heavy fire from the bush, at short range, and also from behind fallen logs close at hand. The man had been wounded during an engagement with rebel natives, and Ensign Down and Drummer Stagpoole responded to the call of the officer commanding the detachment of the regiment for volunteers to bring him in. The Medal for Distinguished Conduct had already been conferred on Drummer Stagpoole for the energy and devotion which he displayed on the 25th Sept. 1863, at the affair near Kaipakopako, in having, though wounded in the head, twice volunteered and brought in wounded men." John Thornton Down died of fever in New Zealand in 1866. A brass tablet was erected in St. Paul's Cathedral to the memory of the officers of the 57th Regt. who fell in action or died during the New Zealand campaigns, amongst whom he is included.

STAGPOOLE, DUDLEY, Drummer, joined the 57th (West Middlesex) Regt. (The Duke of Cambridge's Own), and served in the Maori War in New Zealand. He was awarded the Victoria Cross [London Gazette, 22 Sept. 1864] : " John Thornton Down, Ensign ; Dudley Stagpoole, Drummer, 57th Regt. Date of Acts of Bravery : 2 Oct. 1863. For their conduct

Dudley Stagpoole.

at Pontoko, on the 2nd Oct. 1863, in rescuing a wounded comrade from the rebel Maoris. They succeeded in bringing in the wounded man, who was lying at about fifty yards from the bush, although the enemy kept up a very heavy fire from the bush at short range, and also from behind fallen logs close at hand. The man had been wounded during an engagement with rebel natives, and Ensign Down and Drummer Stagpoole responded to the call of the officer commanding the detachment of the regiment for volunteers to bring him in. The Medal for Distinguished Conduct in the Field has already been conferred on Drummer Stagpoole for the energy and devotion which he displayed on the 25th Sept. 1863, at the affair near Kaipakopako, in having, though wounded in the head, twice volunteered and brought in wounded men." Dudley Stagpoole died on the 1st Aug. 1911.

London Gazette, 4 Nov. 1864.—" War Office, 4 Nov. 1864. The Queen has been graciously pleased to signify Her intention to confer the Decoration of the Victoria Cross on the undermentioned Officer and Non-commissioned Officer of Her Majesty's Navy, whose claims to the same have been submitted for Her Majesty's approval, on account of Acts of Bravery performed by them in New Zealand, as stated against their names."

SMITH, FREDERICK AUGUSTUS, Capt., became Ensign, 1st Foot, 1 Jan. 1849 ; Lieutenant, 1st Foot, 30 April, 1852 ; Captain, 1st Foot, 30 March, 1855. Served in the Crimea, 1854–55, including Alma, Inkerman and Sebastopol. Medal with three clasps, and Turkish Medal. Exchanged as Captain to the 43rd Light Infantry (now 1st Battn. Oxfordshire and Buckinghamshire) 9 April, 1861. He served with the 43rd in the New Zealand War, and was present at the actions of Maketu and Tauranga, and was awarded the Victoria Cross [London Gazette, 4 Nov. 1864]: " Frederick Augustus Smith, Capt., the 43rd Regt. For his distinguished conduct during the engagement at Tauranga on the 21st June. He is stated to have led his company in the most

Frederick Augustus Smith. gallant manner at the attack on the Maoris' position, and, although wounded previously to reaching the rifle pits, to have jumped down into them, when he commenced a hand-to-hand encounter with the enemy, thereby giving his men great encouragement, and setting them a fine example." He was given the Brevet of Major in 1865 ; became Major, 1868 ; was given the Brevet of Lieutenant-Colonel in 1874 ; became Lieutenant-Colonel in 1875, and retired in 1878. Lieut.-Colonel F. A. Smith died on the 22nd July, 1887.

MURRAY, JOHN, Sergt., joined the 68th Regt., and served in the Maori War in New Zealand. He was awarded the Victoria Cross [London Gazette, 4 Nov. 1864]: " John Murray, No. 2918, Sergt., 68th Regt. Date of Act of Bravery : 2 June, 1864. For his distinguished conduct during the engagement at Tauranga, on the 21st June, when the enemy's position was being stormed, in running up to a rifle-pit containing from eight to ten of the enemy, and, without any assistance, killing and wounding every one of them. He is stated to have afterwards proceeded up the works fighting desperately, and still continuing to bayonet the enemy." Sergt. Murray died on the 7th Nov. 1911.

London Gazette, 21 April, 1865.—" War Office, 21 April, 1865. The Queen has been graciously pleased to signify Her intention to confer the Decoration of the Victoria Cross on the undermentioned Midshipman and Seamen of the Royal Navy, whose claims to the same have been submitted for Her Majesty's approval, on account of the gallantry displayed by them during the operations in the Straits of Simono Seki, Japan, as recorded against their names."

John Murray.

BOYES, DUNCAN GORDON, Midshipman, R.N., was born on 5 Nov. 1846, the son of John Boyes, Esq., 3, Paragon Buildings, Cheltenham. He entered Cheltenham College in Jan. 1859, and joined the Royal Navy; served during the operations in the Straits of Simono Seki, Japan, and was awarded the Victoria Cross [London Gazette, 21 April, 1865]: " Duncan Gordon Boyes, Royal Navy, Midshipman of Her Majesty's Ship Euryalus. For the conspicuous gallantry, which, according to the testimony of Capt. Alexander, C.B., at that time Flag Captain to Vice-Admiral Sir Augustus Kuper, K.C.B., Mr. Boyes displayed in the capture of the enemy's stockade. He carried a Colour with the leading company, kept it in advance of all, in the face of the thickest fire, his colour-sergeants having fallen, one mortally, the other dangerously wounded, and he was only detained from proceeding yet further by the orders of his superior officer. The Colour he carried was six times pierced by musket-balls." He died about 1869 in New Zealand.

PRIDE, THOMAS, Captain of the After-Guard, Royal Navy, joined the Royal Navy, and served during the operations in the Straits of Simono Seki, Japan, and was associated with Mr. Boyes in the gallant deed described in the Gazette of that officer's Victoria Cross. Thomas Pride was awarded the Victoria Cross [London Gazette, 21 April, 1865]: " Thomas Pride, R.N., Captain of the After-Guard, H.M.S. Euryalus. The survivor of the two colour-sergeants who supported Mr. Boyes in the gallant rush which he made, in advance of the attack, was recommended for the Victoria Cross for his conduct on this occasion." Thomas Pride died at Parkstone 16 July, 1893.

Thomas Pride.

SEELEY, WILLIAM, Seaman, R.N., served in the Straits of Simono Seki, Japan, and was awarded the Victoria Cross [London Gazette, 21 April, 1865]: " William Seeley, Ordinary Seaman, Royal Navy, of Her Majesty's Ship Euryalus. For the intelligence and daring which, according to the testimony of Lieut. Edwards, commanding the third company, he exhibited in ascertaining the enemy's position, and for continuing to retain his position in front, during the advance, after he had been wounded in the arm."

London Gazette, 7 July, 1865.—" War Office, 7 July, 1865. The Queen has been graciously pleased to signify Her intention to confer the Decoration of the Victoria Cross on the undermentioned Officer of Her Majesty's Indian Forces, whose claim to the same has been submitted for Her Majesty's approval, for his gallant conduct during the operation at Umbeyla, on the North-Western Frontier of India, as recorded against his name."

FOSBERY, GEORGE VINCENT, Lieut., was born at Sturt, near Devizes, the eldest son of the late Rev. T. V. Fosbery, a member of a family seated at Fosbery in Wiltshire in the reign of William the Conqueror, one of whom, John, was Forester to King Edward I., and his son a ward of King Edward II. A descendant settled in Ireland in 1090. He was educated at Eton, and entered the Bengal Army in 1852. He was attached by Sir Hugh Rose, the Commander-in-Chief, to the Umbeyla Expedition (N.W. India) in 1863, in which he took part in every important action, and commanded a body of marksmen of the 71st and 101st Regts. armed with rifles firing explosive bullets of his own invention. He was awarded the Victoria Cross [London Gazette, 7 July, 1865]: " George Vincent Fosbery, Lieut. (now Capt.), late 4th Bengal European Regt. Date of Act of Bravery : 30 Oct. 1863. For the daring and gallant manner in which, on the 30th Oct. 1863, acting as a

George Vincent Fosbery.

volunteer at the time, he led a party of his regiment to recapture the Crag Picquet, after its garrison had been driven in by the enemy, on which occasion sixty of them were killed in desperate hand-to-hand fighting. From the nature of the approach to the top of the Crag, amongst the large rocks, one or two men only could advance at one time. ' Whilst I ascended one path,' relates Lieut.-Colonel Keyes, C.B., commanding the 1st Punjab Infantry, ' I directed Lieut. Fosbery, of the late 4th European Regt., to push up another at the head of a few men. He led this party with great coolness and intrepidity, and was the first man to gain the top of the Crag on his side of the attack.' Subsequently Lieut.-Colonel Keyes being wounded, Lieut. Fosbery assembled a party, with which he pursued the routed enemy in the direction of the Lalloo Ridge, inflicting on them further loss and confirming possession of the post." He was promoted Captain in 1864, Major in 1866, and Lieutenant-Colonel in 1876. Lieut.-Colonel Fosbery retired from the Army in 1877, and devoted himself to the perfecting of machine guns, being the first to introduce them to the British Government. He invented the " Paradox Gun," and the automatic revolver which bears his name. He also introduced an explosive bullet, as a means of ascertaining range for infantry and mountain guns. Lieut.-Colonel Fosbery, V.C., died at Bath, 8 May, 1907.

London Gazette, 28 Nov. 1865.—" War Office, 28 Nov. 1865. The Queen has been graciously pleased to signify Her intention to confer the Decoration of the Victoria Cross on the undermentioned Officer of Her Majesty's Army, whose claim to the same has been submitted for Her Majesty's approval, on account of an Act of Bravery performed by him in New Zealand, as stated against his name."

SHAW, HUGH, Capt., was born 4 Feb. 1839, in India ; son of Mr. James Shaw, Inspector-General of Hospitals, Madras, and Mrs. James Shaw. He was educated at Sandhurst, and joined the 18th Foot (now the Royal Irish Regt.) as an Ensign on 10 May, 1855. He served in the Crimea after the fall of Sebastopol, from Dec. 1855, until the conclusion of the war ; received the Crimean Medal, and became Lieutenant in 1857. He served also in the Indian Mutiny. Mrs. Shaw says that General Shaw did not receive the Crimean and Mutiny Medals. He told her that his regiment had been awarded the former, but that they had been taken from them to give to the French. He was Adjutant of his regiment from 1859 to 1864, when he obtained his company. He took part in the War in New Zealand in 1864–66, and was present in the engagements at Nukumam, for which he obtained mentions in Despatches, received the Medal, and was awarded the Victoria Cross [London Gazette, 28 Nov. 1865]: " Hugh Shaw, Capt., 18th Regt. Date of Act of Bravery : 24 Jan. 1865. For his gallant conduct at the skirmish near Nukumam, in New Zealand, on the 24th Jan. 1865, in proceeding under a heavy fire with four privates of the regiment, who volunteered to accompany him, to within thirty yards of the bush occupied by the rebels, in order to carry off a comrade who was badly wounded. On the afternoon of that day Capt. Shaw was ordered to occupy a position about half a mile from the camp. He advanced in skirmishing order, and when about thirty yards from the bush, he deemed it prudent to retire to a palisade about sixty yards from the bush, as two of his party had been wounded. Finding that one of them was unable to move, he called for volunteers to advance to the front, to carry the man to the rear, and the four privates referred to accompanied him, under a heavy fire, to the place where the wounded man was lying, and they succeeded in bringing him to the rear." On 21 June, 1870, he married Emily Grace Sheffield, daughter of Mr. W. Sheffield, East India Company's Service, and their children are Nina Jane, Dolores Evangeline and Mabel Annie From June, 1873, till Feb. 1878, he was employed on Staff Service, as Adjutant of the North Tipperary Militia and as a Major, which rank he obtained by brevet on the issue of the Royal Warrant on 1 Oct. 1887, and in the Royal Irish Regt. on 22 May, 1878. He was engaged in the Afghan Campaign in 1880, with the Khyber Line Field Force, and received the Medal. He became Lieutenant-Colonel in Sept. 1881, and served in the Sudan Expedition to the Nile in 1884–85, in command of his regiment (which, with the 2nd East Surrey Regt., had been brought from India) during the march for the Relief of Gordon. His command on this occasion won the £100 prize offered by Lord Wolseley for the quickest and smartest voyage on the whale boats between Sarras and Korti (16 Dec. 1884, to 24 Jan. 1885), from which point it marched on foot through the Bayuda Desert, 175 miles, to Metemneh, in eleven days. He was again mentioned in Despatches, was created a C.B., and received the Medal and clasp and the Khedive's Bronze Star. He became substantive Colonel in Sept. 1885 ; retired from the command of his battalion in May, 1887, and was placed on the Retired List with the rank of Major-General, having been granted a distinguished service reward in the preceding month. Major-General Shaw died in Sept. 1904.

Hugh Shaw.

London Gazette, 1 Jan. 1867.—" War Office, 1 Jan. 1867. The Queen has been graciously pleased by a Warrant under Her Royal Sign Manual, bearing date 10 Aug. 1858, to direct that the Decoration of the Victoria Cross shall be conferred, subject to rules and ordinances already made and ordained for the government thereof, on Officers and Men of Her Majesty's Naval and Military Services who may perform acts of conspicuous courage and bravery under circumstances of extreme danger, such as the occurrence of a fire on board ship, or of foundering of a vessel at sea, or under any other circumstances in which, through the courage and devotion displayed, life or public property may be saved. Her Majesty has accordingly been pleased to signify Her intention to confer this high distinction on the undermentioned Private Soldier, whose claim to the same has been submitted for Her Majesty's approval, for his courageous conduct in Canada, as recorded against his name."

O'HEA, TIMOTHY, Private, was serving with his regiment in Canada when he was awarded the Victoria Cross [London Gazette, 1 Jan. 1867]: "Timothy O'Hea, Private, 1st Battn. The Prince Consort's Own Rifle Brigade. For his conspicuous conduct on the occasion of a fire which occurred in a railway car, containing ammunition, between Quebec and Montreal, on the 19th June, 1866. The sergeant in charge of the escort states that when, at Danville Station, on the Grand Trunk Railway, the alarm was given that the car was on fire, it was immediately disconnected, and, whilst considering what was best to be done, Private O'Hea took the keys from his hand, rushed to the car, opencd it, and called out for water and a ladder. It is stated that it was due to his example that the fire was suppressed." Under Rule 5 of the Victoria Cross Warrant, the Decoration could not originally be awarded except for acts performed in the presence of the enemy. On 10 Aug. 1858, however, a new clause was inserted in the Order, and under that rule Private O'Hea was—eight years later—awarded the Decoration. He is the only man who has so far received the Victoria Cross under this new clause. Private O'Hea was (about 1876) lost in the Australian Bush, and no trace of him could ever be found.

London Gazette, 4 Jan. 1867.—" War Office, 4 Jan. 1867. The Queen has been graciously pleased to signify Her intention to confer the Decoration of the Victoria Cross on the undermentioned Private Soldier, whose claim to the same has been submitted for Her Majesty's approval, for his gallant conduct at the Siege and Capture of Tubabecolong, Gambia River, as recorded against his name."

HODGE, SAMUEL, Private, served in West Africa, and was awarded the Victoria Cross [London Gazette, 4 Jan. 1867]: "Samuel Hodge, Private, 4th West India Regt. Date of Act of Bravery: 30 June, 1866. For his bravery at the storming and capture of the stockaded town of Tubabecolong, in the kingdom of Barra, River Gambia, on the evening of the 30th June last. Colonel D'Arcy, of the Gambia Volunteers, states that this man and another, who was afterwards killed—pioneers in the 4th West India Regt.—answered his call for volunteers, with axes in hand, to hew down the stockade. Colonel D'Arcy having effected an entrance, Private Hodge followed him through the town, opening with his axe two gates from the inside, which were barricaded, so allowing the supports to enter, who carried the place from east to west at the point of the bayonet. On issuing to the glacis through the west gate, Private Hodge was presented by Colonel D'Arcy to his comrades as the bravest soldier of their regiment, a fact which they acknowledged with loud acclamations." Hodge was terribly wounded on this occasion. He is one of the three men of negro descent who won the Victoria Cross. The two others were William Hall, of Peel's Naval Brigade, who won the Cross in the Mutiny, and W. J. Gordon (West India Regt.), who was decorated for his gallantry at Toniatebe, West Africa, in 1892.

London Gazette, 8 Feb. 1867.—" War Office, 8 Feb. 1867. The Queen having been graciously pleased, by an instrument under Her Royal Sign Manual, bearing the date the 1st Jan. 1867, to direct that the Decoration of the Victoria Cross may be conferred on persons serving with the Local Forces of New Zealand, who have performed deeds of gallantry during the progress of the operations undertaken against the insurgent native tribes in the Colony—Her Majesty has accordingly been pleased to signify Her intention to confer this high distinction on the undermentioned Officer of the Local Forces of that Colony, whose claim to the same has been submitted for Her Majesty's approval."

HEAPHY, CHARLES, Major, served in New Zealand, and was awarded the Victoria Cross [London Gazette, 1 Jan. 1867]: "Charles Heaphy, Major, Auckland Militia. For his gallant conduct at the skirmish on the banks of the Mangapiko River, in New Zealand, on the 11th Feb. 1864, in assisting a wounded soldier of the 40th Regt., who had fallen into a hollow among the thickest of the concealed Maories. Whilst doing so he became the target for a volley at a few feet distant. Five balls pierced his clothes and cap, and he was wounded in three places. Although hurt, he continued to aid the wounded until the end of the day. Major Heaphy was at the time in charge of a party of soldiers of the 40th and 50th Regts., under the orders of Lieut.-Colonel Sir Henry Marshman Havelock, Bart., C.B., V.C., the senior officer on the spot, who had moved rapidly down to the place where the troops were hotly engaged and pressed." He is said to have died in 1898.

London Gazette, 17 Dec. 1867.—" War Office. 17 Dec. 1867. The Queen has been graciously pleased to signify Her intention to confer the Decoration of the Victoria Cross on the undermentioned Officer and Private Soldiers of Her Majesty's Army, whose claims to the same have been submitted for Her Majesty's approval, for their gallant conduct at Little Andaman Island, as recorded against their names."

DOUGLAS, CAMPBELL MILLIS, Assistant Surgeon, was the son of Dr. George M. Douglas; was born in Quebec, and educated at St. John's, Canada; Laval University, and at Edinburgh (became M.D. and L.R.C.S., Edinburgh, in 1861), and joined the 24th Regt. (South Wales Borderers) in 1873. He won his Victoria Cross while serving as Medical Officer to the Expedition to Little Andaman Island in 1867 [London Gazette, 17 Dec. 1867]: "Campbell Millis Douglas, M.D., Assistant Surgeon, 2nd Battn.; Thomas Murphy, Private; James Cooper, Private; David Bell, Private, and William Griffiths, Private, 24th Regt. For the very gallant and daring manner in which they risked their lives in manning a boat and proceeding through a dangerous surf to the rescue of some of their comrades who formed part of an expedition which had been sent to the Island of Andaman, by order of the Chief Commissioner of British Burmah, with the view of ascertaining the fate of the commander and seven of the crew of the ship Assam Valley, who had landed there, and were supposed to have been murdered by the natives. The officer who commanded the troops on the occasion reports: 'About an hour later in the day Dr. Douglas, 2nd Battn. 24th Regt., and the four privates referred to, gallantly manning the second gig, made their way through the surf almost to the shore, but finding their boat was half filled with water, they retired. A second attempt made by Dr. Douglas and party proved successful, five of us being safely passed through the surf to the boats outside. A third and last trip got the whole of the party left on shore safe to the boats.' It is stated that Dr. Douglas accomplished these trips through the surf to the shore by no ordinary exertion. He stood in the bows of the boat, and worked her in an intrepid and business-like manner, cool to a degree, as if what he was then doing was an ordinary act of everyday life. The four privates behaved in an equally cool and collected manner, rowing through the roughest surf, when the slightest hesitation or want of pluck on the part of any one of them would have been attended by the gravest results. It is reported that seventeen officers and men were thus saved from what must otherwise have been a fearful risk, if not certainty, of death." Dr. Douglas, Privates Cooper, Murphy, Bell and Griffiths were the first of the "Old Green Howards" to receive the Victoria Cross. In 1904 the famous regiment had sixteen Crosses to its credit, of which seven were gained at Rorke's Drift in the Zulu War of 1879. He was Medical Officer in Charge of the Field Hospital during the 2nd Riel Expedition of 1885. He published a pamphlet relating to Boat Service of Vessels, papers on "The Recruit Nervous Degeneration," etc. Brigade Surgeon Douglas married Eleanor Annie M'Master, niece of the late Sir Edward Belcher, R.M. His favourite recreations were cycling and boating. He died 31 Dec. 1909, at Wells, Somerset, aged 69.

MURPHY, THOMAS, Private, enlisted in the 24th (2nd Warwickshire) Regt., South Wales Borderers; served on the Andaman Islands, and was awarded the Victoria Cross [London Gazette, 17 Dec. 1867]: "Campbell Millis Douglas, M.D., Assistant Surgeon; Thomas Murphy, Private; James Cooper, Private; David Bell, Private; William Griffiths, Private, 2nd Battn. 24th Regt. Date of Acts of Bravery: 7 May, 1867. For the very gallant and daring manner in which, on the 7th May, 1867, they risked their lives in manning a boat, and proceeding through a dangerous surf to the rescue of some of their comrades, who formed part of an expedition which had been sent to the Island of Andaman, by order of the Chief Commissioner of British Burmah, with the view of ascertaining the fate of the commander and seven of the crew of the ship Assam Valley, who had landed there and were supposed to have been murdered by the natives. The officer who commanded the troops on the occasion reports: 'About an hour later in the day Dr. Douglas, 2nd Battn. 24th Regt., and the four privates referred to, gallantly manned the second gig, made their way through the surf almost to the shore, but finding their boat was half filled with water, they retired. A second attempt made by Dr. Douglas and the party proved successful, five of us being safely passed through the surf to the boats outside. A third and last trip got the whole of the party left on shore safe to the boats.' It is stated that Dr. Douglas accomplished these trips through the surf to the shore by no ordinary exertion. He stood in the bows of the boat, and worked her in an intrepid and seamanlike manner, cool to a degree, as if what he was doing then was an ordinary act of everyday life. The four privates behaved in an equally cool and collected manner, rowing through the roughest surf when the slightest hesitation or want of pluck on the part of any of them would have been attended with the gravest results. It is reported that seventeen officers and men were thus saved from what must otherwise have been a fearful risk, if not certainty, of death." He is said to have gone to Philadelphia, U.S.A., and died on the 22nd March, 1900.

COOPER, JAMES, Private, enlisted in the 24th (2nd Warwickshire) Regt., South Wales Borderers; served in the Andaman Islands, and was awarded the Victoria Cross [London Gazette, 17 Dec. 1867]: "Campbell Millis Douglas, M.D., Assistant Surgeon; Thomas Murphy, Private; James Cooper, Private; David Bell, Private; William Griffiths, Private, 2nd Battn. 24th Regt. Date of Acts of Bravery: 7 May, 1867. For the very gallant and daring manner in which, on the 7th May, 1867, they risked their lives in manning a boat, and proceeding through a dangerous surf to the rescue of some of their comrades who formed part of an expedition which had been sent to the island of Little Andaman, by order of the Chief Commissioner of British Burmah, with the view of ascertaiinng the fate of the commander and seven of the crew of the ship Assam Valley, who had landed there and were supposed to have been murdered by the natives. The officer who commanded the troops on the occasion reports: 'About an hour later in the day Dr. Douglas, 2nd Battn. 24th Regt., and the four privates referred to, gallantly manned the second gig, made their way through the surf almost to the shore, but finding their boat was half filled with water, they retired. A second attempt made by Dr. Douglas and party proved successful, five of us being safely passed through the surf to the boats outside. A third and last trip got the whole of the party left on shore safe to the boats.' It is stated that Dr. Douglas accomplished these trips through the surf to the shore by no ordinary exertion. He stood in the bows of the boat, and worked her in an intrepid and seamanlike manner, cool to a degree, as if what he was doing then was an ordinary act of everyday life. The four privates behaved in an equally cool and collected manner, rowing through the roughest surf when the slightest hesitation or want of pluck on the part of any of them would have been attended with the gravest results. It is reported that seventeen officers and men were thus saved from what must otherwise have been a fearful risk, if not certainty, of death." James Cooper died on the 9th Aug. 1882; it is said in Birmingham.

BELL, DAVID, Private, enlisted in the 24th (2nd Warwickshire) Regt., South Wales Borderers; served in the Andaman Islands, and was awarded the Victoria Cross [London Gazette, 17 Dec. 1867]: "Campbell Millis Douglas, M.D., Assistant Surgeon; Thomas Murphy, Private; James Cooper, Private; David Bell, Private; William Griffiths, Private, 2nd Battn. 24th Regt. Date of Acts of Bravery: 7 May, 1867. For the very gallant and daring manner in which, on the 7th May, 1867, they risked their lives in manning a boat, and proceeding through a dangerous surf to the rescue of some of their comrades who formed part of an expedition which had been sent to the island of Little Andaman, by order of the Chief Commissioner of British Burmah, with the view of ascertaining the fate of the commander and seven of the crew of the ship Assam Valley, who had landed there, and were supposed to have been murdered by the natives. The officer who commanded the troops on the occasion reports: 'About an hour later in the day Dr. Douglas, 2nd Battn. 24th Regt., and the four privates referred to, gallantly manned the second gig, made their way through the surf almost to the shore, but finding their boat was half filled with water, they retired. A second attempt made by Dr. Douglas and party proved successful, five of us being safely passed through the surf to the boats outside. A third and last trip got the whole of the party left on shore safe to the boats.' It is stated that Dr. Douglas accomplished these trips through the surf to the shore by no ordinary exertion. He stood in the bows of the boat, and worked her in an intrepid and seamanlike manner, cool to a degree, as if what he was doing then was an ordinary act of everyday life. The four privates behaved in an equally cool and collected manner, rowing through the roughest surf when the slightest hesitation or want of pluck on the part of any of them would have been attended with the gravest results. It is reported that seventeen officers and men were thus saved from what must otherwise have been a fearful risk, if not certainty, of death." He later became Sergeant.

GRIFFITHS, WILLIAM, Private, No. 1702, 2nd Battn. The 24th (2nd Warwickshire) Regt., South Wales Borderers. The official notice in the London Gazette of 17 Dec. 1867, reads: "Campbell Millis Douglas, M.D., Assistant Surgeon; Thomas Murphy, Private; James Cooper, Private; David Bell, Private; William Griffiths, Private, 2nd Battn. 24th Regt. Date of Acts of Bravery: 7 May, 1867. For the very gallant and daring manner in which, on the 7th May, 1867, they risked their lives in manning a boat, and proceeding through a dangerous surf to the rescue of some of their comrades who formed part of an expedition which had been sent to the island of Little Andaman, by order of the Chief Commissioner of British Burmah, with the view of ascertaining the fate of the commander and seven of the crew of the ship Assam Valley, who had landed there, and were supposed to have been murdered by the natives. The officer who commanded the troops on the occasion reports: 'About an hour later in the day Dr. Douglas, 2nd Battn. 24th Regt., and the four privates referred to, gallantly manned the second gig, made their way through the surf, almost to the shore, but finding their boat was half filled with water, they retired. A second attempt made by Dr. Douglas and party proved successful, five of us being safely passed through the surf to the boats outside. A third and last trip got the whole of the party left on shore safe to the boats.' It is stated that Dr. Douglas accomplished these trips through the surf to the shore by no ordinary exertion. He stood in the bows of the boat, and worked her in an intrepid and seamanlike manner, cool to a degree, as if what he was doing then was an ordinary act of everyday life. The four privates behaved in an equally cool and collected manner, rowing through the roughest surf when the slightest hesitation or want of pluck on the part of any of them would have been attended by the gravest results. It is reported that seventeen officers and men were thus saved from what must otherwise have been a fearful risk, if not certainty, of death." Private William Griffiths was killed at Isandhlwana, 22 Jan. 1879.

London Gazette, 31 Dec. 1867.—" The Queen has been graciously pleased to signify Her intention to confer the Decoration of the Victoria Cross on the undermentioned Officers, whose claims to the same have been submitted for Her Majesty's approval, for their gallant conduct in Bhootan, as recorded against their names."

TREVOR, WILLIAM SPOTTISWOODE, Major, was the second son of Capt. Robert Salusbury Trevor, of the Bengal Cavalry, who was murdered at Kabul at the time of the assassination of the British Envoy, Sir William MacNaghton, by Akhbar Khan, in Dec. 1841. As a boy of ten, he, with his mother and her six other children, was among the captives detained by Akhbar Khan, and released after nine months' captivity by the force sent under Sir George Pollock to avenge the murder of the Envoy and the destruction of the Army of Occupation, and remembered vividly to the end of his days the events of that time. He had learned to write Hindustani and Persian, and used to relate how Akhbar Khan tried to avail himself of this knowledge to find out what was being talked about among the prisoners, and to persuade him to translate letters received from India. A favourite amusement of Akhbar's was to get up fights between Trevor and the Afghan boys, offering legs of mutton as prizes. It may well be that these experiences of the captivity helped to form the character which distinguished him in after life. After the return of the family to England he was one of three of the brothers who obtained cadetships to Addiscombe, where he did well, passing out third of his year, and gaining his first commission, dated 11 Dec. 1849, in the Bengal Engineers. After the usual period of training at the Royal Engineer Establishment at Chatham, in the course of which he was employed on special duty under the Commissioners of the Great Exhibition of 1851, he proceeded to India, where he arrived on the 5th Feb. 1852, and was almost immediately detailed for active service with "the Army of Ava," under General Godwin. He served through the Second Burmese War; was mentioned in Despatches by General Godwin for his conduct at the storming of the White House Picket Stockade at Rangoon on the 12th April, 1852, where he was with the escalading party, pushed on, after his arm had been shattered by a bullet from wrist to elbow, to the foot of the wall, and was "first on the ladder"—when he fell, disabled by his wound. After some months in hospital he recovered sufficiently to be present at several minor engagements in the vicinity of Prome, and to take part in the Expedition under Sir John Cheape to Donabew, where a noted leader had taken up a strong position, and had repulsed a party of sailors sent to dislodge him, with the loss of two of the naval guns. The advance from the river to Donabew lay for several miles through thick jungle, the Burmese from the shelter of the trees bringing a heavy fire to bear on the advancing force. Their main position was a strongly-placed parapet protected by a deep wet ditch, the only causeway across which was defended by the two captured guns. As the storming parties advanced, the head of the column was twice swept away by the fire of these guns. A third column was then formed, to which Ensign (afterwards F.M. Lord) Wolseley, Trevor and other officers were attached, and which succeeded, though not without futher heavy loss, in carrying the position. In Sir John Cheape's Despatch on this engagement Lieut. Trevor was mentioned as "having nobly seconded" Lieut. Mullins, of the Madras Engineers, in command of the party of sappers and pioneers, to whose laborious work, and "the zeal and talent with which their energies were directed," it was mainly due that "the troops were enabled to reach the enemy's position"—and as having been "the first, with Corpl. Livingston and Private Preston, of the 51st K.O.L.I., to enter the enemy's breastwork, the two former" (Trevor and Livingston) "each shooting down one of the enemy opposing their entrance. The lead devolved on them . . . when Lieut. Taylor, Ensign Wolseley, and Colour-Sergt. Donnahoe fell in the advance." For his services on this occasion Trevor, who had again been wounded, received the thanks of Government. Active operations practically ended with the taking of Donabew, but Trevor remained in Burmah employed on various important and often hazardous duties till Oct. 1857, when he was transferred to Bengal. While employed at Darjeeling in constructing barracks for European soldiers on a site at Senchal, selected under the orders of Colonel (afterwards Lord) Robert Napier, he had his only opportunity of taking part in the operations connected with the Mutiny, when he accompanied the Darjeeling Field Force, under Capt. The Honourable E. Curzon, H.M.'s 52nd Regt., sent to intercept the mutineers of the 75th N.I. from Decca, who were endeavouring to join their comrades at Nilfigorie, and was present at an engagement with them at Cherabunder on the Bhutan Frontier by which the junction was prevented. After the completion of the barracks at Senchal, he was employed on the construction of the Ganges and Darjeeling Road, until April, 1861, when he was appointed Garrison Engineer at Fort William, and in that capacity left his mark on Calcutta by designing and partly carrying out the conversion of a tract of waste land on the bank of the Hoogly into the well-known Eden Gardens, one of the chief attractions of the city. This work was completed by his brother, Capt. S. T. Trevor, also of the Bengal Engineers, who succeeded him as Garrison Engineer. In Feb. 1862, he was appointed to officiate as Superintending Engineer of the Northern Circle, and under his supervision the Ganges and Darjeeling Road, on which he had been employed as Executive Engineer, was completed to the foot of the mountains, and the mountain road in continuation up to Darjeeling was laid out and partly executed. It was during his employment in this and other appointments that he began to criticize the methods of the Public Works Accounts Department, which he held to be at once ineffective as a check on undue expenditure and needlessly harassing to the Executive Staff. At the expense of some odium he overcame the opposition of those responsible for the system, and being appointed, in May, 1863, to be Controller of Accounts, was enabled to give effect to his views, to the admittedly great improvement of the working of the Department. In Feb. 1865, he was attached to the Bhutan Field Force. For his services on this and on previous occasions he received promotion, under date 2 June, 1866, to the rank of Brevet Major, and later the Victoria Cross, the deed by which the Cross was earned being described in the London Gazette of 2 June, 1866, in the following terms: "William Spottiswoode Trevor, Major, and James Dundas, Lieut., Royal (late Bengal) Engineers. For their gallant conduct at the attack on the Blockhouse at Dewan-Giri, in Bhootan, on the 30th April, 1865. Major-General Tombs, C.B., V.C., the officer in command at the time, reports that a party of the enemy, from 180 to 200 in number, had barricaded themselves in the blockhouse in question, which they continued to defend after the rest of the position had been carried, and the main body was in retreat. The blockhouse, which was loopholed, was the key of the enemy's position. Seeing no officer of the storming party near him, and being anxious that the place should be taken immediately, as any protracted resistance might have caused the main body of the Bhooteas to rally, the British force having been fighting in a broiling sun on very steep and difficult ground for upwards of three hours, the General in command ordered these two officers to show the way into the blockhouse. They had to climb up a wall which was fourteen feet high, and then to enter a house occupied by some 200 desperate men, head foremost through an opening not more than two feet wide between the top of the wall and the roof of the blockhouse. Major-General Tombs states that on speaking

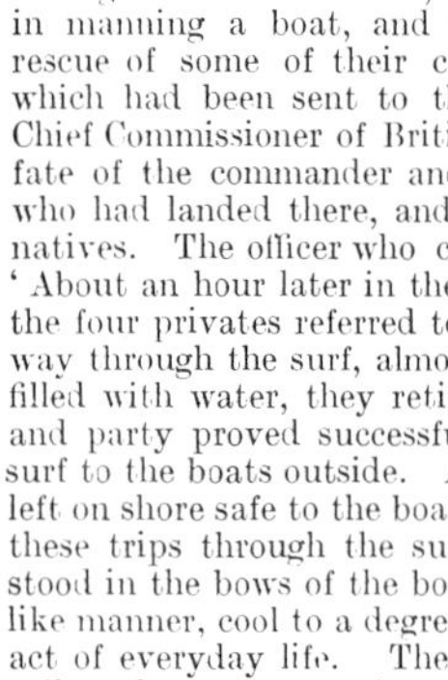

William S. Trevor.

to the Sikh soldiers around him, and telling them in Hindoostani to swarm up the wall, none of them responded to the call until these two officers had shown them the way, when they followed with the greatest alacrity. Both of them were wounded." In quoting this description in his book, "Addiscombe and its Heroes and Men of Note," Colonel Vibart remarks: "How Trevor and Dundas escaped death was a marvel; perhaps the restricted space at the point of entry had something to do with their success, the defenders being unable to use their swords effectively . . . while the officers used their revolvers with fatal effect till they cleared the gallery and enabled the storming party to effect a lodgment." The most severe of several injuries sustained by Capt. Trevor, who, it may be noted, was ill at the time, was from a spear-thrust delivered from below, through the bamboo flooring of the gallery. As the result of this illness and his injuries Trevor had to take sick leave, on his return from which he became Superintending Engineer, Presidency Division. In 1870 he again took leave, in the course of which he managed to see a good deal of the earlier phases of the Franco-Prussian War, and had many amusing stories to tell of his experiences in that connection. On 15 Aug. 1874, he was promoted to Lieutenant-Colonel, and in the same year was made Special Chief Engineer for Famine Relief Works north of the Ganges, under Sir Richard Temple, when he bore an important part in laying the first foundations of the system which in its further developments has met with so large a measure of success in subsequent famines. For his services on this occasion he again received the thanks of Government. He was then for a time Inspector-General of Military Works. In Jan. 1873, he was transferred as Chief Engineer to Central India, and in Dec. 1875, was appointed Chief Engineer, British Burmah, which post he held till 1880. While he was in Burmah his services were demanded by the Government of India for help in the preparation of a scheme for the reorganization of the Engineer Establishment, for which he once more received the thanks of Government. On 19 Aug. 1879, he was made Brevet Colonel. In 1880 he succeeded his brother, Major-General J. S. Trevor, C.S.I., R.E., as Director-General of Railways, and in Feb. 1882, was appointed Secretary to the Government of India in the Public Works Department. This post he held for five years, retiring from the service on 27 Feb. 1887, with the rank of Major-General. He settled in London, and died at his residence, 11, Queen's Mansions, Victoria Street, on the 2nd Nov. 1907, at the age of 76. He married in 1858, Miss Eliza Fisher, daughter of the Rev. H. Fisher, of the Indian Ecclesiastical Establishment, and left one daughter, Florence Mary, who married Colonel M. C. Brackenbury, C.S.I., R.E., and was left a widow on 18 March, 1915. It was said of General W. S. Trevor that "no man had more or truer hearted friends, and it may safely be asserted that he never made an enemy." His two most prominent contemporaries and special rivals at Addiscombe, Generals Craster and Brownlow, wrote of him, the former, who served with him in Burmah, that "He was a firm friend, always ready to uphold the right regardless of any consequences to himself, with a clear brain which enabled him to see clearly to the bottom of a subject and to detect all fallacies that enveloped it;" and the latter, that "Morally and intellectually he was a grand man—upright, fearless, broad-minded and modest." The "Pioneer Mail," of 15 Nov. 1907, in an obituary notice published on receipt in India of the news of his death, after giving a sketch of his career, went on to say: "Had fortune allowed him to be with the Delhi or Lucknow forces during the Mutiny, he would no doubt have made his reputaiton as a soldier rapidly, having every qualification for eminence in the profession of arms—strong mental capacity, decision of character, a daring spirit and a robust frame; but he was employed in Lower Bengal when the rebellion broke out, and could not succeed in getting to the front." And apropos of these remarks, Colonel J. P. Steel, R.E., another lifelong friend, in a memoir published in the "Royal Engineers' Journal," from which the materials for this notice have been largely derived, takes occasion to observe: "This is indeed true, for he had all the instincts of a soldier and—under an unassuming manner—rare courage and determination. He was a deadly shot with a revolver—to which on several occasions he owed his life—and an expert swordsman. More than once in his young days it occurred that someone who fancied himself with either foil or sword learnt from Trevor the lesson he thought to teach. The Calcutta Tent Club knew him as a daring rider, even among men of lighter weight and better mounted than himself. But his was a many-sided character, and in more ways than one will William Trevor be remembered. Those who served under him, and whom he inspired to a remarkable degree with a feeling of affectionate loyalty, will recall his readiness to give advice or assistance to help anyone whose heart was in his work, and the chivalry of his nature in awarding praise that he might have appropriated to himself. Those associated with him later in public life in his own immediate profession will remember his unerring judgment; his determination to uphold the right fearless of any consequences to himself, and his desire to combine the lessons of experience with the deductions of scientific inquiry. Those in the wider circle of administration will remember him as a man whose opinions were always worth having, and whose contribution on such different subjects as the reorganization of the Indian Army, the Public Works Department, the currency, the defence of our frontier and the purchase of guaranteed railways by the State were always interesting, and in some cases helped to shape the policy of the Government. To the friends of his later years the most pleasing reminiscences will perhaps be the extent of his knowledge, the charm of his conversation and the warmth of his friendships, and they will note with a sense of personal injury that the Government he served so well allowed him to go to his grave without any other decoration than that which he earned at the cost of a lifelong injury."

DUNDAS, JAMES, Lieut., eldest son of the late George Dundas, one of the Judges of the Court of Session in Scotland, by Elizabeth, daughter of Colin Mackenzie, of Portmore, Peeblesshire, was born on 12 Sept. 1842. He was educated at the Edinburgh Academy, Trinity College Glenalmond, and Addiscombe College, from which he was appointed Lieutenant in the Royal (late Bengal) Engineers on 8 June, 1860. After the usual course of study at Chatham he sailed for India in March, 1862, and on arrival was posted to the Sappers and Miners at Rurki. In due course he was appointed to the Public Works Department in Bengal, and was soon promoted to be Executive Engineer of one of the most responsible Divisions in that Presidency. In 1865 Dundas was appointed to the right brigade of the Force employed in Bhootan, and so distinguished himself as to be recommended by Major-General Tombs, V.C., C.B., for the Victoria Cross. The official report [London Gazette, 31 Dec. 1867] is as follows: "William Spottiswoode Trevor, Major; James Dundas, Lieut., Royal (late Bengal) Engineers. Date of Acts of Bravery: 30 April, 1865. For their gallant conduct at the attack on the Blockhouse at Dewan-Giri, in Bhootan, on the 30th April, 1865. Major-General Tombs, V.C., C.B., the officer in command at the time, reports that a party of the enemy, from 180 to 200 in number, had barricaded themselves in the blockhouse in question, which they continued to defend after the rest of the position had been carried and the main body was in retreat. The blockhouse, which was loopholed, was the key of the enemy's position. Seeing no officer of the storming party near him, and being anxious that the place should be taken immediately, as any protracted resistance might have caused the main body of the Bhooteas to rally, the British force having been fighting in a broiling sun on very steep and difficult ground for upwards of three hours, the General in command ordered these two officers to show the way into the blockhouse. They had to climb up a wall which was 14 feet high, and then to enter a house occupied by some 200 desperate men, head foremost through an opening not more than two feet wide between the top of the wall and the roof of the blockhouse. Major-General Tombs states that on speaking to the Sikh soldiers around him, and telling them in Hindoostani to swarm up the wall, none of them responded to the call until these two officers had shown them the way, when they followed with the greatest alacrity. Both of them were wounded." At the end of the campaign Lieut. Dundas rejoined the Public Works Department, and went to England on leave in 1870, and again in 1877, having succeeded by the death of his uncle, the Right Honourable Sir David Dundas, to the estate of Ochtertyre, in Stirlingshire; rejoining his appointment in India early in 1878. In the summer of that year—at the risk of his own life—he saved a native from death in a burning house in the Simla Bazaar. For many years Capt. Dundas worked with the late General Sir Alexander Taylor, K.C.B., R.E. In the spring of 1879 he was specially selected for transfer to the Secretariat of the Government of India in the Public Works Department, but he preferred service in the field, and in the summer of 1879 he found his way to the front on the fresh outbreak of war in Afghanistan. When General Roberts advanced on Kabul in the autumn of 1879 he selected Dundas to accompany the Field Force as Commanding Royal Engineer, believing that Colonel Perkins had left Kuram; but the latter subsequently rejoined the Division. The manner in which the Engineers carried out the duty of providing shelter for the troops after the retirement into the Sherpur Cantonments at the close of the year received the warm acknowledgments of the General. On the afternoon of 23 Dec. 1879, Capt. Dundas, with Lieut. Nugent, was ordered to join General Macpherson's Force to aid in the destruction of the line of forts held by the enemy on the south side of the British position at Sherpur. It was while carrying out this duty, through a premature mine explosion, which has been attributed to the use of a home-made fuse in lieu of an unserviceable one which had been supplied, that he lost his life. His body was recovered by his comrades on the same day. Sir Alexander Taylor wrote soon afterwards: "In him the Corps has lost one of its 'very best.' A man of high abilities, well cultivated—a modest, high-minded English gentleman, brave, gentle and courteous, I do not know that he ever gave offence to anyone; far less do I believe that he ever had an enemy. To me he was an invaluable professional assistant, and I owe much to his varied and accurate engineering knowledge, to his trustworthy character and universal popularity." The first part of this account was written by Major Broadfoot, R.E., specially for this book, and many of the facts given afterwards were taken from a notice in the "Royal Engineers' Journal," of the 2nd Feb. 1880, written by Major Broadfoot, R.E., who was one of Capt. Dundas's oldest friends. Other particulars were gleaned from "The Afghan Campaigns of 1879–1880," by Sydney H. Shadbolt.

James Dundas.

London Gazette, 28 July, 1868.—"War Office, 28 July, 1868. The Queen has been graciously pleased to signify Her intention to confer the Decoration of the Victoria Cross on the undermentioned Soldiers, whose claims to the same have been submitted for Her Majesty's approval, for their gallant conduct in Abyssinia, as recorded against their several names."

Michael Magner.

MAGNER, MICHAEL, Drummer, enlisted in the West Riding Regt., served in Abyssinia, and was awarded the Victoria Cross [London Gazette, 28 July, 1868]: "No. 3691, Michael Magner, Drummer, and No. 949, James Bergin,

Private. Date of Act of Bravery : 13 April, 1868. For their conspicuous gallantry in the assault of Magdala on the 13th April, 1868. Lieut.-General Lord Napier reports that, whilst the head of a column of attack was checked by the obstacles at the gate, a small stream of officers and men of the 33rd Regt., and an officer of the Royal Engineers, breaking away from the main approach to Magdala and climbing up a cliff, reached the defences, and forced their way over the wall and through the strong and thorny fence, thus turning the defenders of the gateway. The first two men to enter, and the first in Magdala, were Drummer Magner and Private Bergin, of the 33rd Regt." Drummer Magner died on the 6th Feb. 1897.

James Bergin.

BERGIN, JAMES, Private, enlisted in the West Riding Regt., served in Abyssinia, and was awarded the Victoria Cross [London Gazette, 13 April, 1868]: " Michael Magner, No. 3691, Drummer, and James Bergin, No. 949, Private, 33rd Regt. Date of Act of Bravery : 13 April, 1868. For their conspicuous gallantry in the assault on Magdala on the 13th April last. Lieut.-General Lord Napier reports that, whilst the head of the column of attack was checked by the obstacles at the gate, a small stream of officers and men of the 33rd Regt., and an officer of Engineers, breaking away from the main approach to Magdala and climbing up a cliff, reached the defences, and forced their way over the wall and through the strong and thorny fence, thus turning the defenders of the gateway. The first two men to enter, and the first in Magdala, were Drummer Magner and Private Bergin, of the 33rd Regt." James Bergin was born at Killbricken, Queen's County, Ireland, on 29 June, 1845. He enlisted in the 10th Regt. in 1862, and the following year volunteered into the 108th, with which regiment he sailed for India in 1863. In 1867 he was transferred to the 33rd Regt., with which he served in the Abyssinian War. He later joined the 78th Highlanders. Private Bergin died at Poona, 1 Dec. 1880.

London Gazette, 27 Sept. 1872.—" War Office, 27 Sept. 1872. The Queen has been graciously pleased to signify Her intention to confer the Decoration of the Victoria Cross on the undermentioned Officer, whose claim to the same has been submitted for Her Majesty's approval, for an Act of Bravery performed by him when serving with the Looshai Expeditionary Force, as recorded against his name."

MACINTYRE, DONALD, Major, was born in 1831, at Kincraig, Ross-shire, N.B., educated at Addiscombe, and entered the Army on 14 June, 1850, and became Lieutenant 23 Nov. 1856. When still a junior subaltern he served with the 66th Gurkhas with both Expeditions of 1852, under Sir Colin Campbell, afterwards Lord Clyde, against the hill tribes on the Peshawar Frontier, including the destruction of the fort and village of Pranghur and the action at Ishkakot. A year later he was engaged with the Expeditionary Force against the Boree Afridis. In 1856 he served with the 66th Gurkhas in the Expedition, under Sir Neville Chamberlain, to the Kurram Valley, Afghanistan. He became Captain 14 June, 1862, and served in 1864 with the Doaba Field Force in the Peshawar Valley. During 1857–58, while engaged in raising what is now the 4th Gurkha Regt., he was employed on several occasions in protecting the hill tribes on the Kale Kumaon Frontier from the Rohilcund Rebels, and in maintaining order in the district. It was for services with the Lushai Expedition (North East India), 1872, that Major Macintyre was subsequently awarded the Victoria Cross [London Gazette, 27 Sept. 1872]: " Donald Macintyre, Major (now Lieutenant-Colonel), Bengal Staff Corps. For his gallant conduct at the storming of the stockaded village of Lalgnoora on the 4th Jan. 1872. Colonel Macpherson, C.B., V.C., commanding the 2nd Gurkha Regt., in which Lieut.-Colonel Macintyre was serving, at the time as Second in Command, reports that this officer, who led the assault, was the first to reach the stockade (on this side from eight to nine feet high) ; and that to climb over and disappear among the flames and smoke of the burning village was the work of a very short time. The stockade, he adds, was successfully stormed by this officer under fire, the heaviest the Looshais delivered that day." He became Major 14 June, 1870. At the close of the operations Major Macintyre, who had been several times mentioned in Despatches, received, in addition to the Victoria Cross, the Brevet of Lieutenant-Colonel and the thanks of the Governor-General of India in Council. He was promoted to Lieutenant-Colonel 11 Sept. 1872, and Colonel 1 Oct. 1877. His last active service was in the Afghan Campaign of 1878–79, when he commanded the 2nd Gurkhas the Khaibar Column, and was with both Expeditions to the Bazar Valley. He retired from the Bengal Staff Corps 24 Dec. 1880, with the rank of Major-General. General Macintyre died on Wednesday, 15 April, 1903, at his residence, Fortrose, aged 71. An obituary notice appeared in the " Times " of 17 April, 1903.

London Gazette, 31 March, 1874.—" War Office, 31 March, 1874 The Queen has been graciously pleased to signify Her intention to confer the Decoration of the Victoria Cross on the undermentioned Officer and Non-commissioned Officer, whose claims to the same have been submitted for Her Majesty's approval, for Acts of Bravery performed by them in the recent Ashanti War, as recorded against their names."

GIFFORD, LORD (The Honourable Edric Frederick Gifford), Lieut., was born 5 July, 1849 ; the eldest son of Robert Francis, 2nd Baron Gifford, and of the Honourable Frederica Charlotte Fitzhardinge, eldest daughter of the 1st Baron Fitzhardinge. He was educated at Harrow, and entered the Army in 1869. He became Lieutenant in the 63rd Regt.

in 1872. In 1872 he succeeded his father as the 3rd Baron Gifford. In 1873 he was transferred to the 24th Regt. (The South Wales Borderers) ; won his Victoria Cross in the Ashanti Campaign of 1873–4 in the operations before the taking of Becquah, and was decorated by Her Majesty Queen Victoria at the review in Windsor Park in April, 1874. His Victoria Cross was gazetted 28 March, 1874: " Lord Gifford, Lieut., 24th Regt.

Lord Gifford.

For his gallant conduct during the operations and especially at the taking of Becquah. The officer commanding the Expeditionary Force reports that Lord Gifford was in charge of the scouts after the army crossed the Prah, and that it is no exaggeration to say that since the Adansi Hills were passed, he daily carried his life in his hand in the performance of his most dangerous duties. He hung upon the rear of the enemy, discovering their position, and ferreting out their intentions. With no other man with him, he captured numerous prisoners ; but Sir Garnet Wolseley brings him forward for this mark of Royal favour most especially for his conduct at the taking of Becquah, into which place he penetrated with his scouts before the troops carried it, when his gallantry and courage were most conspicuous." He became Captain in the 57th Regt. in 1876. In 1879 at the close of the Zulu War, Lord Gifford nearly captured Cetewayo. He had been searching for the Zulu King for fifteen days, and when at last he found out his whereabouts Lord Gifford's scouts were utterly worn out, and he decided to wait until night before attempting the capture. Meanwhile Major Marter found out Cetewayo's hiding-place, marched straight to it and captured the King. In 1880 Lord Gifford became Brevet Major in the 1st Battn. The Middlesex Regt. He was Colonial Secretary for West Australia and Senior Member of the Legislative Council from 1880 to 1883. From 1883 to 1888 he was Colonial Secretary at Gibraltar. Lord Gifford died at Old Park, Chichester, 5 June, 1911, and was buried with military honours. Boy Scouts lined the path to Bosham Church, and a bugler of the Royal Sussex Regt. sounded the " Last Post."

M'GAW, SAMUEL, L.-Sergt., enlisted in The Black Watch, served in Ashanti, and was awarded the Victoria Cross [London Gazette, 28 March, 1874]: " Samuel M'Gaw, L.-Sergt., 42nd Regt. Date of Act of Bravery : 21 Jan. 1874. For having, at the Battle of Amoaful, led his section through the bush in the most excellent manner, continuing to do so throughout the whole day, although badly

Samuel M'Gaw.

wounded early in the engagement." When landing at Cyprus four years later, on the 7th July, 1878, L.-Sergt. M'Gaw dropped dead from sunstroke.

London Gazette, 27 Oct. 1874.—" War Office, 26 Oct. 1874. The Queen has been graciously pleased to signify Her intention to confer the Decoration of the Victoria Cross on the undermentioned Officer, whose claim to the same has been submitted for Her Majesty's approval, for an Act of Bravery which he performed during the late Ashanti War, as recorded against his name."

SARTORIUS, REGINALD WILLIAM, Major, was born 8 May, 1841, son of Admiral Sir George Rose Sartorius, G.C.B. He entered the Army on 20 Jan. 1858, and in the following May he was promoted to Lieutenant.

Reginald W. Sartorius.

Lieut. Sartorius served in the Indian Mutiny in 1858 and 1859, and was present at the Relief of Azimghur, where he volunteered to carry Despatches through the encircling enemy. He succeeded, but had his cap shot through and his head grazed, also his heel ; and he was thanked on parade by his General. He also took part in the operations in the Goruckpore district. He received the Mutiny Medal. In 1864 he served in the Bhootan Expedition and received the Medal with clasp. In 1868 he was promoted Captain. He served in the Ashanti War of 1873–4, and the " Daily Telegraph " of 9 August, 1907, speaks of his " vigorous personality, which at one dramatic moment of his life attracted the attention of all Britain and even of the world. The time was that of the war against Coffee Calcoli, the King of Ashantee, in which the then Sir Garnet Wolseley had just captured, and, after fruitless efforts to induce the King to come into the town to sign a treaty, burnt, as he had threatened to do, the capital city of Coomassie, the centre of a vast system of cruel slaughter, under the religious forms of fetish rites, of all the neighbouring tribes. At home it was the very period of that General Election which resulted in the overthrow of Mr. Gladstone's first administration and the seating, for the first time, of Mr. Disraeli in real power, though not for the first time in the Premiership. It was February, 1874. A Despatch from

Sir Garnet Wolseley had reached London, announcing his capture of Coomassie. It was published during the heat of the elections, and received with the utmost scepticism as too convenient for the Government to be believed. The fact that for some days previous to its being sent off all trace of the expedition had been lost, because Sir Garnet had plunged forward into the forest, cutting himself off both from his regular line of supplies and from his connection with the coast, had created no little anxiety, and even when the news came those who believed it were not altogether satisfied, because, as the natives themselves put it, the British had behaved like a little boy who sets fire to a house and then runs away. Yet a few days, and a strange sequel followed. Sir Garnet had halted on the Adansi Hills, prior to leading his little army back to the coast, when Capt. Sartorius, with twenty men, each having only forty rounds, rode into the camp. He had been sent on ahead of an expedition commanded by Capt. Glover, of the Navy. This had been working along the River Volta, a line independent of that followed by the forces which had captured Coomassie. He had travelled for fifty-five miles through the heart of the Ashantee Kingdom, and then passed through the burnt streets of the town. His safety was due to the fact that all the aggressive party had been completely cowed. This was made the more evident shortly afterwards when the King sent in hot haste men with full authority to give all the guarantees required by Sir Garnet, and to accept all the terms of the treaty which he had till then refused. Not any hope of further successful resistance, but the fear of treachery such as he would himself have used towards an enemy under similar circumstances, had hitherto prevented his accepting the conditions dictated to him. He now only prayed that Sir Garnet would stop Capt. Glover's further advance towards him. In fact, it would have still required some time for the Volta Expedition to reach Coomassie, and the very effective part which it actually played in the final catastrophe was entirely due to the audacious note of Sartorius, whom Glover had sent ahead to communicate with Wolseley as soon as he had heard that he (Wolseley) had reached the capital. Meeting with no opposition, Sartorius was not the man to conjure up imaginary dangers, and accordingly, having at first approached the town under the impression that it was still held by our troops, he, finding it deserted, had tracked his way by the ample tracks left behind it by the little force of 1,000 men which had left the town. When he joined the headquarter camp his ride had all the influence of a second seizure of the town. Simple as the story is, it illustrates one of the most important of all the factors that go to ensure victory. Physically, Sartorius had no strength with him whatever. His seizure or destruction would have been supremely easy for the still potent forces of Ashantee warriors, but he came in unexpectedly, just at the moment when all the old organisation had been so completely shattered that no one was ready to take the responsibility of ordering fresh effort of even the slight kind that would have been required to annihilate him and his little band. The moral forces, such as they were, of the great ' charnel house,' as Sir Garnet justly called it in one of his Despatches, were, for the time at least, dead." For his services in the Ashanti Campaign he was twice mentioned in Despatches, was given the Brevet of Major, created a C.M.G., and awarded the Victoria Cross [London, Gazette, 26 Oct. 1874]: " Reginald William Sartorius, C.M.G., Major, 6th Bengal Cavalry. Date of Act of Bravery: 17 Jan. 1874. For having during the attack on Abogoo, on the 17th Jan. last, removed under a heavy fire Sergt.-Major Braimah, Doctor, a Houssa non-commissioned officer, who was mortally wounded, and placed him under cover." He was on the staff of King Edward VII. when, as Prince of Wales, he visited India in the two following years, and afterwards he took part in the Afghan Campaigns of 1879 and 1880, and received the Medal. Major Sartorius became Colonel in 1886, and Major-General in 1895, and retired in 1897. He married in 1887, Agnes, daughter of Dr. J. Kemp and granddaughter of General Sir Francis Wheler. He was a member of the Royal Yacht Squadron. Major-General R. W. Sartorius died suddenly at Cowes on Wednesday, 8 Aug. 1907, aged 66.

London Gazette, 20 Nov. 1874.—" War Office, 20 Nov. 1874. The Queen has been graciously pleased to signify Her intention to confer the Decoration of the Victoria Cross on the undermentioned Officer, whose claim to the same has been submitted for Her Majesty's approval, for his gallant and distinguished conduct during the late Ashantee War, as recorded against his name."

BELL, MARK SEVER, Capt., was born at Sydney, New South Wales, 15 May, 1843, the second son of the late Hutchinson Bell, Esq., of Leconfield, Yorkshire. He was educated privately and at King's College, London (Fellow, 1890); entered the R.E. in 1862. He served with the Bhutan Expedition, commanding the R.E. and Bengal Sappers and Miners 1865–66 (Medal with clasp); commanded R.E. as Assistant Field Engineer in the Hazara Expedition, 1868 (specially mentioned in Despatches for his forced march of 600 miles; clasp). During the Ashanti War of 1873–74 he was Adjutant to the R.E., Brigade and Special Service Officer. He received the Medal; was mentioned in Despatches for other acts than that for which he was awarded the Victoria Cross [London Gazette, 20 Nov. 1874]: " Mark Sever Bell, Capt., Royal Engineers. For distinguished bravery and zealous, resolute and self-devoted conduct at the Battle of Ordashu on the 4th Feb. 1874, whilst serving under the immediate orders of Colonel Sir John Chetham McLeod, K.C.B., of the 42nd Regt., who commanded the advanced Guard. Sir John McLeod was an eye-witness of his gallant and distinguished conduct on the occasion, and considers that this officer's fearless and resolute bearing, being always in the front, urging on and encouraging an unarmed working party of Fantee labourers, who were exposed not only to the fire of the enemy, but to the wild and irregular fire of the native troops in the rear, contributed very materially to the success of the day. By his example he made these men do what no European party was ever required to do in warfare, namely, to work under fire in the face of the enemy without a covering party." He married—1st, in 1875, Angelina Helen (died 1879), daughter of Capt. H. B. F. Dickenson, 15th Regt. He became Major in 1882; was Intelligence Officer during the Burma Campaign of 1886–87 (clasp). He was A.Q.M.G. for Intelligence 1880–85; promoted Brevet Lieutenant-Colonel in 1883 and Brevet Colonel in 1887; A.D.C. to H.M. Queen Victoria, 1887; D.Q.M.G., 1885–88. Colonel Bell was Colonel on the Staff, and commanding R.E., Western District, from 1894 to 1898. He married—2ndly, in 1890, Nora Margaret, daughter of Hext Roger, Esq., of Inceworth, South Devon. In 1893 he was created a C.B. (Military), and in 1898 was placed on half-pay on account of ill-health. He was well known as a great traveller in the East, and had traversed over 12,000 miles in generally unknown parts of Central Asia, China and the East. He was an author of military and geographical articles, and was the first MacGregor Gold Medallist of U.S. Institute, India. Colonel Bell died at Earlywood Lodge, Sunninghill, on the 26th June, 1906, aged 63. His eldest son, Anthony Harley Mark Bell, 3rd (K.O.) Hussars, served in France from August, 1914; M.C. and 1914 Star; mentioned in Despatches. His youngest son, Robert de Hougham Mark Bell, K.R.R.C., was killed in action 3 Sept. 1916; mentioned in Despatches 1 Jan. 1916.

Mark Sever Bell.

London Gazette, 15 April, 1876.—" War Office, 14 April, 1876. The Queen has been graciously pleased to confer the Decoration of the Victoria Cross on the undermentioned Officer, whose claim to the same has been submitted for Her Majesty's approval for his gallant conduct during the recent operations against the Malays in Perak."

CHANNER, GEORGE NICOLAS, Brevet Major, the son of Colonel George Girdwood Channer, and his wife, Susan Kendall, daughter of the Rev. Nicolas Kendall, Vicar of Lanlivery, Cornwall, was born 7 Jan. 1843, at Allahabad, India. Educated at Truro Grammar School and Cheltenham College, he entered the Service as an Ensign in the Bengal Infantry. Promoted Lieutenant in 1861, he served in the Umbeyla Expedition on the N.W. Frontier of India, 1863–64 (Medal and clasp); Lushai Expedition, N.E. Frontier, 1870–71; Malay Peninsula, 1875–76; capture of Bukit Pass and stockades, being mentioned in Despatches, thanked by the Government of India and Colonial Office. For his services he was awarded the V.C. and Brevet of Major, and received the clasp " Perak " to his Frontier Medal. His Victoria Cross was gazetted 12 April, 1876: " George Nicolas Channer, Brevet Major, Bengal Staff Corps. Date of Act of Bravery: 20 Dec. 1875. For having, with the greatest gallantry, been the first to jump into the enemy's stockade, to which he had been despatched with a small party of the 1st Ghurka Light Infantry, on the afternoon of the 20th Dec. 1875, by the officer commanding the Malacca column, to procure the intelligence as to its strength, position, etc. Capt. Channer got completely in rear of the enemy's position, and finding himself so close that he could hear the voices of the men inside, who were cooking at the time and keeping no look-out, he beckoned to his men, and the whole party then came up and entered the stockade, which was of a most formidable nature, surrounded by a bamboo palisade; about seven yards within was a log house, loopholed, with two narrow entrances, and trees laid latitudinally to the thickness of two feet. The officer commanding reports that if Capt. Channer, by his foresight, coolness and intrepidity, had not taken this stockade, a great loss of life must have occurred, as from the fact of his being unable to bring the guns to bear on it, from the steepness of the hill and the density of the jungle, it must have been taken at the point of the bayonet." He next saw service in the Jowaki Afridi Expedition in 1877–78, for which he obtained another clasp. He served in the Afghan War of 1878–80, being present at the capture of Peiwar Kotal and in other minor affairs. Mentioned in Despatches, Brevet of Lieutenant-Colonel, Medal and clasp. He again saw fighting on the Frontier in 1888, when he commanded the 1st Brigade in the Black Mountain Expedition. Mentioned in Despatches, received the C.B. and clasp to Medal. In the Chitral Campaign, 1895, General Channer commanded the Reserve Brigade. Awarded a Good Service Pension in 1893, he was promoted Major-General the same year, Lieutenant-General in 1896, and General in 1899. He married 29 June, 1878, Annie Isabella, daughter of J. W. Watson, Esq., of Shooter's Hill, by whom he had six sons (two of whom died young), and four daughters. General Channer, V.C., C.B., died at Westward Ho! North Devon, on the 13th Dec. 1905, aged 62 years. He was an excellent revolver shot and an enthusiastic big game hunter and explorer in Thibet and unknown parts of the Himalayas.

George Nicolas Channer.

London Gazette, 18 Jan. 1878.—" War Office, 16 Jan. 1878. The Queen has been graciously pleased to signify Her intention to confer the Decoration of the Victoria Cross on the undermentioned Officer, whose claim to the same has been submitted for Her Majesty's approval, for his gallant conduct at Quetta, in the East Indies, as recorded against his name."

SCOTT, ANDREW, Capt., joined the Army 4 March, 1860; was promoted Lieutenant 1 Jan. 1862, and Captain 4 March, 1872; joined the Bengal Staff Corps; served in Baluchistan, and was awarded the Victoria Cross [London Gazette, 16 Jan. 1878]: "Andrew Scott, Capt., Bengal Staff Corps. For his gallant conduct at Quetta, on the 26th July, 1877, whilst serving in the 4th Sikh Infantry, on the occasion of an attack by some coolies on Lieuts. Hewson and Kunhardt, of the Royal Engineers. On the evening of that day, Capt. Scott, whilst on duty at the regimental parade ground of the 4th Sikh Infantry at Quetta, hearing an alarm that British officers were being killed, spontaneously rushed to the rescue, and finding Lieut. Hewson cut down and Lieut. Kunhardt retiring hard pressed and wounded, and only protected by sepoy Ruchpul Singh, of the above-mentioned regiment, fell on the assailants, and with his own hand bayoneted two men and closed with a third, who fell with him to the ground and was killed by sepoys of the regiment. This act of courage and devotion saved the life of Lieut. Kunhardt." He became Major, 4th Sikhs.

London Gazette, 18 March, 1879.—"War Office, 18 March, 1879. The Queen has been graciously pleased to signify Her intention to confer the Decoration of the Victoria Cross on the undermentioned Officer, whose claim to the same has been submitted for Her Majesty's approval, for his gallant conduct at the Peiwar Kotal, in the East Indies, as recorded against his name."

COOK, JOHN, Capt., was born at Edinburgh in Aug. 1843, and was the second son of Alexander Shank Cook, a well-known Scottish Advocate and Sheriff, and grandson of George Cook, D.D., who was for many years leader of the moderate party in the Church of Scotland. He was educated at Edinburgh Academy and Addiscombe. When John Cook was eleven years old his father received a nomination for him for Addiscombe. He was one of the last of the cadets who entered the college under the old nomination system. When he was seventeen he went to India, and soon after his arrival he was posted to the 3rd Sikhs, with which regiment he went through the Umbeyla Campaign. He was mentioned in Despatches, and was specially thanked by his colonel for his gallantry in leading a very effectual bayonet charge. In 1868 he took part in the Hazara Expedition. For these services he received the India Medal with two clasps. After ten years' service he took the furlough to which he

John Cook.

was entitled, and spent a year at home, returning to India in 1871. In 1872 he was promoted Captain, and in 1873 was transferred to the 5th Gurkhas as Wing Commander. When the Afghan War broke out the 5th Gurkhas joined the Kurram Field Force under General Roberts, and led the attack at the Battle of Peiwar Kotal 2 Dec. 1878. Here Capt. Cook won the Victoria Cross [London Gazette, 18 March, 1879]: "John Cook, Capt., Bengal Staff Corps. For a signal act of valour at the action of the Peiwar Kotal on the 2nd Dec. 1878, in having, during a very heavy fire, charged out of the entrenchments with such impetuosity that the enemy broke and fled. When perceiving at the close of the mêlée the danger of Major Galbraith, Assistant Adjutant-General Kurram Column Field Force, who was in personal conflict with an Afghan soldier, Capt. Cook distracted his attention to himself, and aiming a sword-cut, which the Douranee avoided, sprang upon him, and, grasping his throat, grappled with him. They both fell to the ground. The Douranee, a most powerful man, still endeavouring to use his rifle, seized Capt. Cook's arm in his teeth, until the struggle was ended by the man being shot through the head." When the Kabul insurrection broke out in 1879, the 5th Gurkhas accompanied General Roberts in his march to the scene of the massacre. Capt. Cook was given the Brevet of Major, 1879. He was wounded in the left leg 12 Dec. 1879, while leading an attack on a high conical hill, the Takht-i-Shah peak, about three miles from Kabul. Mortification set in and he died on the 19th Dec. 1879. The following Divisional Order was issued by the Lieutenant-General Commanding: "It is with deep regret that the Lieutenant-General announces to the Cabul Field Force the death from a wound received 12 Dec. of Major John Cook, V.C., 5th Gurkhas. While yet a young officer, Major Cook served at Umbeyla in 1863, where he distinguished himself, and in the Black Mountain Campaign in 1868. Joining the Kurram Field Force on its formation, Major Cook was present at the capture of the Peiwar Kotal, his conduct on that occasion earning for him the admiration of the whole force and the Victoria Cross. In the return in the Monghyr Pass he again brought himself prominently to notice by his cool and gallant bearing. In the capture of the heights at Sang-i-Nawishta, Major Cook again distinguished himself, and in the attack on the Takht-i-Shah Peak 12 Dec. he ended a noble career in a manner worthy even of his great name for bravery. By Major Cook's death Her Majesty has lost the services of an officer who would, had he been spared, have risen to the highest honours of his profession, and Sir F. Roberts feels sure the whole Cabul Field Force will share in the pain his loss has occasioned him." Lieut.-Colonel W. Cook, Indian Army, writes of the above account of Major Cook: "The only error occurs in the official 'record' of this act by which my brother received the V.C. This record cannot, of course, now be altered, and I only mention the fact, as I have heard my brother refer to it humorously on more than one occasion. I think you knew him. He was an immensely powerful man, and laughingly objected to the wording of this 'record': 'They both fell to the ground.' What really happened was that my brother cross-buttocked the Afghan, and would undoubtedly have

succeeded in strangling him had not somebody else—quite unnecessarily—interfered by shooting the man through the head."

Supplement, London Gazette.—"War Office, 2 May, 1879. The Queen has been most graciously pleased to signify Her intention to confer the Decoration of the Victoria Cross on the undermentioned Officers and Soldiers of Her Majesty's Army, whose claims to the same have been submitted for Her Majesty's approval for their gallant conduct in defence of Rorke's Drift, on the occasion of the attack by Zulus as recorded against their names."

"Memorandum (London Gazette). Lieut. Melvill, of the 1st Battn. 24th Foot, on account of the gallant efforts made by him to save the Queen's Colour of his Regiment after the disaster at Isandhlwana, and also Lieut. Coghill, 1st Battn. 24th Foot, on account of his heroic conduct in endeavouring to save his brother officer's life,—would have been recommended to Her Majesty for the Victoria Cross had they survived."

CHARD, JOHN ROUSE MARRIOTT, Lieut., was born in 1847. He was the son of Mr. W. W. Chard, of Pathe, Somerset, and Mount Tamar, Devon. He was educated at Plymouth New Grammar School, Cheltenham, and Woolwich, and entered the Royal Engineers in 1868. He was stationed for some time at Bermuda, and went to South Africa at the outbreak of the Zulu War. For his services at the defence of Rorke's Drift he was promoted Captain and Brevet Major, and given the Victoria Cross [London Gazette, 2 May, 1879]: "J. M. R. Chard, Lieut. (now Capt. and Brevet Major), and G. Bromhead, Lieut. (now Capt. and Brevet Major), 2nd Battn. 24th Regt. For their gallant conduct at the defence of Rorke's Drift, on the occasion of the attack by the Zulus, on the 22nd and 23rd Jan. 1879. The Lieut.-General commanding the troops reports that had

John Rouse M. Chard.

it not been for the fine example and excellent behaviour of these two officers under the most trying circumstances, the defence of Rorke's Drift post would not have been conducted with that intelligence and tenacity which so essentially characterized it. The Lieut.-General adds that its success must, in a great degree, be attributed to the two young officers who exercised the chief command on the occasion in question." Queen Victoria caused the names of Lieuts. Chard and Bromhead, together with those of Lieuts. Melvill and Coghill, to be inscribed on the colour pole of the 24th Regt. Soon after the defence of Rorke's Drift he became ill of fever, and went to Ladysmith to recover. He was well enough to take part in the Battle of Ulundi. Towards the end of 1879 he was ordered home, and was met at Plymouth by a telegram from Queen Victoria, who received him at Balmoral. Colonel Chard retired from the Army in Aug. 1897, and died at Hatch Beauchamp Rectory, near Taunton, Somerset, 1 Nov. 1897.

BROMHEAD, GONVILLE, Lieut., was born 29 Aug. 1844, at Versailles, France, the third son of Sir Edmund de Gonville Bromhead, Bart., of Thurlby, Lincolnshire (Major, retired), and Judith Christine, daughter of James Wood, Esq., of Woodville, Sligo. He was educated at Newark, and joined the South Wales Borderers as an Ensign 20 April, 1867. He served in the South African War of 1877–78–79. Lieut. Gonville Bromhead received the Victoria Cross for the defence of Rorke's Drift on the night of the 22nd–23rd Jan. 1879. After the Zulus had surprised the camp left at Isandhlwana and practically annihilated it, they marched on to Rorke's Drift, a post guarding the crossing on the Buffalo River on the road to Natal. Lord Chelmsford's Column having returned from its march too late to save Isandhlwana, followed up the Zulu Army to Rorke's Drift, which it was feared must also have fallen, especially when heavy smoke was

Gonville Bromhead.

seen to be rising from the spot, and Zulus retiring from it; but, in the words of Lord Chelmsford's despatch: "To our intense relief, however, the waving of hats was seen from the inside of a hastily erected entrenchment, and information soon reached me that the gallant garrison of this post, some eighty men of the 2nd Battn. 24th Regt., under Lieut. Bromhead, and a few volunteers and departmental officers, the whole under Lieut. Chard, Royal Engineers, had for twelve hours made the most gallant resistance I have ever heard of, against the determined attack of some three thousand Zulus, three hundred and seventy of whose bodies surrounded the post." For his services in this campaign, and especially in the defence of Rorke's Drift, Lieut. Bromhead was mentioned in Despatches published in the London Gazette of 1 March and 15 March, 1879. He was promoted Captain and given the Brevet of Major. He also received the South African Medal with clasp, and was awarded the Victoria Cross [London Gazette, 2 May, 1879]: "Lieut. Chard, Royal Engineers, and Lieut. Gonville S. Bromhead, 2nd Battn. 24th Regt. For their gallant conduct at the defence of Rorke's Drift, on the occasion of the attack by the Zulus, on the 22nd and 23rd Jan. 1879. The Lieut.-General commanding the troops reports that, had it not been for the fine example and excellent behaviour of these two officers under the most trying circumstances, the defence of Rorke's Drift post would not have been conducted with that intelligence and tenacity which so essentially characterized it. The Lieut.-General adds that its success must in a great degree be attributable to the two young officers who exercised the chief command on the occasion in question." Major Bromhead served in the Burmese Expeditions of 1885 and 1887–89 (Medal with two clasps). He died in Lucknow, India, 10 Feb. 1891.

WILLIAMS, JOHN, Private, No. 1395, was born at Abergavenny 24 May, 1857. He enlisted in the South

John Williams.

Wales Borderers at Brecon 27 May, 1877, and joined the 2nd Battn. at Chatham in June, 1877. He served in the Zulu War, and was awarded the Victoria Cross for his services at Rorke's Drift [London Gazette, 2 May, 1879]: " John Williams, Private, and Henry Hook, Private, 2nd Battn. 24th Regt. Private John Williams was posted with Private Joseph Williams and Private William Horrigan, 1st Battn. 24th Regt., in a distant room of the hospital, which they held for more than an hour, so long as they had a round of ammunition left. As communication was for the time cut off, the Zulus were enabled to advance and burst open the door ; they dragged out Private Joseph Williams and two of the patients and assegaied them. Whilst the Zulus were occupied with the slaughter of these men a lull took place, during which Private John Williams, who, with two patients, were the only men now left alive in this ward, succeeded in knocking a hole in the partition, and in taking the two patients into the next ward, where he found Private Hook (Henry Hook, Private, 2nd Battn.). These two men together, one man working whilst the other fought and held the enemy at bay with his bayonet, broke through three more partitions, and were thus enabled to bring eight patients through a small window into the inner line of defence." He was discharged from the Army Reserve on the 22nd May, 1893, but rejoined for the duration of the war, serving at the Depôt at Brecon.

HOOK, ALFRED HENRY, Private, was born at Churcham, near Gloucester, and served for five years in

Alfred Henry Hook.

the Monmouthshire Militia before joining the 24th Regt. He served through the Kaffir War of 1877–78. He served in the Zulu War of 1879, and won the Victoria Cross for the part he took in the defence of Rorke's Drift. It was presented to him by Lord Wolseley on 3 Aug. 1879. His Victoria Cross was gazetted 2 May, 1879 : " John Williams, Private ; Henry Hook, Private, 2nd Battn. 24th Regt. Private John Williams was posted with Private Joseph Williams and Private William Horrigan, 1st Battn. 24th Regt., in a distant room of the hospital, which they held for more than an hour, so long as they had a round of ammunition left. As communication was for the time cut off, the Zulus were able to advance and burst open the door : they dragged out Private Joseph Williams, with two of the patients, and assegaied them. Whilst the Zulus were occupied with the slaughter of these men a lull took place, during which Private John Williams, who, with two patients, were the only men now left alive in this ward, succeeded in knocking a hole in the partition, and in taking the patients into the next ward, where he found Private Hook. These two men together, one man working whilst the other fought and held the enemy at bay with his bayonet, broke through three more partitions, and were thus enabled to bring eight patients through a small window into the inner line of defence." He served in the Volunteers as a Sergeant in the 1st Volunteer Battn. Royal Fusiliers, and was in later years one of the staff at the British Museum. He died at Gloucester 12 March, 1905, and was buried at Churcham.

JONES, WILLIAM, Private, No. 804, enlisted in the 24th Regt. (South Wales Borderers) ; served in the Zulu War, and was awarded the Victoria Cross for his services at Rorke's Drift [London Gazette, 2 May, 1879]: " William Jones and Robert Jones, Privates, 2nd Battn. the 24th Regt. In another ward, facing the hill, Private William Jones and Private Robert Jones defended the post to the last until six out of the seven patients it contained had been removed. The seventh, Sergt. Maxwell, 2nd Battn. 24th Regt., was delirious from fever. Although they had previously dressed him, they were unable to induce him to move. When Private Robert Jones returned to endeavour to carry him away, he found him being stabbed by the Zulus as he lay on his bed." Private William Jones was discharged from the Army Reserve on the 26th Jan. 1888.

William Jones.

JONES, ROBERT, Private, No. 716, was born 19 Aug. 1857, at Raglan, Monmouthshire, and enlisted in the 24th Regt. about Aug. 1875, joining the 2nd Battn. at Dover at the end of 1876. He served in the Zulu War, and was awarded the Victoria Cross [London Gazette, 2 May, 1879]: " William Jones, Private ; Robert Jones, Private, 2nd Battn. 24th Regt. At the hospital, in a ward facing the hill, Private William Jones and Private Robert Jones defended the post to the last, until six out of the seven patients it contained had been removed. The seventh, Sergt. Maxwell, was delirious through fever. Although they had previously dressed him, they were unable to induce him to move. When Private Robert Jones returned to to endeavour to carry him away, he found him being stabbed by the Zulus as he lay in his bed." Private R. Jones died at Madley, Hereford, on the 6th Sept. 1898.

Robert Jones.

ALLEN, WILLIAM, Corpl., No. 1240, served in the South Wales Borderers in the Zulu War, and was awarded the Victoria Cross [London Gazette, 2 May, 1879]: " William Allen Corporal, and Frederick Hitch, Private, 2nd Battn. 24th Regt. It was chiefly due to the courageous conduct of these men that communication with the hospital was kept up at all. Holding together at all costs a most dangerous post, raked in reverse by the enemy's fire from the hill, they were both severely wounded, but their determined conduct enabled the patients to be withdrawn from the hospital ; and when incapacitated by their wounds from fighting, they continued, as soon as their wounds had been dressed, to serve out ammunition to their comrades during the night." William Allen was afterwards Sergt. Instructor of Musketry.

William Allen.

He died on the 12th March, 1890. Mr. Philip Wilkins bought his Victoria Cross and Medal on the 21st June, 1906.

HITCH, FREDERICK, Private, No. 1362, enlisted in the South Wales Borderers, served in the Zulu War, and for his services at Rorke's Drift was awarded the Victoria Cross [London Gazette, 2 May, 1879]: " William Allen, Corpl., and Frederick Hitch, Private, 2nd Battn. 24th Regt. It was chiefly due to the courageous conduct of these men that communication with the hospital was kept up at all. Holding together at all costs a most dangerous post, raked in reverse by the enemy's fire from the hill, they were both severely wounded, but their determined conduct enabled the patients to be withdrawn from the hospital, and when incapacitated by their wounds from fighting, they continued, as soon as their wounds were dressed, to serve out ammunition to their comrades during the night." While employed at the R.U.S.

Frederick Hitch.

Institute, Hitch's Cross was stolen from his coat, but King Edward ordered another to be made, and it was presented to him by Lord Roberts. Hitch in later life became a cab proprietor, and later still drove a taxicab. He was so unassuming and modest that few of his mates knew until after his death that they had been working with one of the heroes of Rorke's Drift. He died on the 7th Jan. 1913, at 62, Cranbrook Road, Chiswick, and had a fine military funeral. His old regiment mustered strong, including the Colonel and many officers, and among the followers were more than 1,500 taxi-drivers, with whom Hitch had been working when on strike when he died. A monument was erected to his memory in Chiswick Cemetery.

London Gazette, 10 June, 1879.—" War Office, 10 June, 1879. The Queen has been graciously pleased to signify Her intention to confer the Decoration of the Victoria Cross on the undermentioned Officer of Her Majesty's Army, whose claim has been submitted for Her Majesty's approval, for his gallant conduct in rescuing a wounded Sowar of the 13th Bengal Lancers, on the 31st Jan. 1879, as recorded in the accompanying statement."

HART, REGINALD CLARE, Lieut., was born on the 11th June, 1848, at Scarif, County Clare, Ireland. He is the last surviving son of the late Lieut.-General Henry George Hart (son of Lieut.-Colonel William Hart, of Netherbury, Dorset), and of Frances Alicia, daughter of the Rev. Holt Okes, D.D. He was educated at Marlborough and Cheltenham Colleges ; was in the Football XV. at Cheltenham, 1864–65 ; passed into the Royal Military Academy in June, 1866, and was commissioned a Lieutenant in the Royal Engineers on the 13th Jan. 1869, and did duty for three years in England. He was given the Silver Medal of the Royal Humane Society, a Medallion from the Mayor, in the name of the city of Boulogne, and a Medal of Honour of the First Class presented by the President of the French Republic, for saving the life of a Frenchman who was drowning in the harbour of Boulogne-sur-

Mer, on the 27th July, 1869. In doing this, Lieut. Hart received several severe wounds in the head and face, from striking, in leaping from the pier, some sunken piles or rocks. He was present at the Siege of Paris during the Commune War of 1871. In 1872 Lieut. Hart married Charlotte Augusta, daughter of Mark Seton Synnot, Esq., D.L., of Ballymoyer, County Armagh, Ireland. They have surviving three sons and one daughter. Lieut. Hart obtained First Class Extra Hythe Musketry Certificate in 1879, and he passed the final examination at the Staff College in 1880, without having gone through the two years' course of instruction at the College (mention and special mention in several subjects), and passed a good examination in French and a very good in Geology as Voluntary Subjects. He embarked in Oct. 1872, for India, and was posted to the Bengal Sappers and Miners. From Sept. 1874, to March, 1878, he was Assistant Garrison Instructor at Umballa, subsequently returning to England on sick leave. In Dec. 1878, Lieut. Hart proceeded a second time to India, and served with the Khyber Field Force in the Afghan War. He was at first attached as a regimental officer to the 24th Punjab Infantry, a unit of the 2nd Division. In this capacity he took part in the 2nd Bazar Valley Expedition against the Zaka Khel Afridis, and for his distinguished conduct on the 31st Jan. 1879, while on convoy duty, was awarded the Victoria Cross [London Gazette, 10 June 1879]: "Reginald Clare Hart, Lieut., The Royal Engineers. For his gallant conduct in risking his own life to save the life of a private soldier. The Lieut.-General commanding the 2nd Division, Peshawar Field Force, reports that when on convoy duty with that force on 31 Jan. 1879, Lieut. Hart, of the Royal Engineers took the initiative in running some 1,200 yards to the rescue of a wounded sowar of the 13th Bengal Lancers in a river-bed exposed to the fire of the enemy, of unknown strength, from both flanks, and also from a party in the river-bed. Lieut. Hart reached the wounded sowar, drove off the enemy, and brought him under cover with the aid of some soldiers who accompanied him on the way." For his services in the Afghan War he also received the Afghan Medal, and was mentioned in Despatches. He was decorated with the Victoria Cross by Queen Victoria at Windsor Castle, 9 Dec. 1879. He afterwards served in the 1st Division of the Force, and was several times employed by the Quartermaster-General's Department in making reconnaissances. In Feb. 1881, it was reported that the Ashantis had declared war and invaded the Gold Coast Colony. Lieut. Hart, receiving his orders only a few hours before starting, accompanied Sir Samuel Rowe, the Governor and Commander-in-Chief, to the West Coast of Africa, and served on the Special Service Staff of that officer from Feb. to June. In the succeeding month he received his promotion. ("The Afghan Campaigns," S. H. Shadbolt.) Promoted Brevet Major 18 Jan. 1882. He served in the Egyptian War of 1882 (twice mentioned in Despatches, Brevet of Lieut.-Colonel, Medal with clasp, Fourth Class Osmanieh and Khedive's Star). In 1881–82 for a time he was employed on special duty at the Intelligence Department, Horse Guards. He returned to India in 1884. Colonel Hart was awarded the Silver Clasp of the Royal Humane Society for saving, on the 15th Dec. 1884, a gunner who had been knocked off a pontoon bridge into the Ganges Canal at Roorkee. From 1885 to 1888 he was Garrison Instructor. From 1888 to 1896, Director of Military Education in India. In 1886 he was given the Brevet of Colonel. From 1896 to 1899 he commanded a 2nd Class District in India, with the rank of Brigadier-General. From 1899 to 1902 he commanded a 1st Class District, with the rank of Major-General. From 1897 to 1898 Brigadier-General Hart commanded the 1st Brigade, Tirah Campaign (twice mentioned in Despatches, K.C.B., 1898, Medal and two clasps). From 1899 to 1902 he commanded the Quetta District with the temporary rank of Major-General. Sir Reginald Hart served on the N.W. Frontier of India, 1901–2 (clasp). He became substantive Major-General in 1902. From 1902 to 1906 he was G.O.C. Thames District. From 1902 to 1905 he was also Commandant of the School of Military Engineering. In 1904 he was created a K.C.V.O. He commanded Cape Colony District from 1907 to 1909. In 1908 he became Lieut.-General. Sir Reginald Hart was Commander-in-Chief in South Africa from 1912 to 1914. In 1914 he became General. He was Lieut.-Governor of Guernsey, 1914–18, and on relinquishing the appointment he received the thanks of His Majesty's Government for his services "during a very critical and difficult period." Sir R. Hart is fond of all games; won several prizes for athletics, and was successful in big game shooting and fishing. He has written "Reflections on the Art of War," "Sanitation and Health," and various magazine articles.

Reginald Clare Hart.

London Gazette, 17 June, 1879.—"War Office, 17 June, 1879. The Queen has been graciously pleased to signify Her intention to confer the Decoration of the Victoria Cross on the undermentioned Officers and Soldier of Her Majesty's Army whose claims have been submitted for Her Majesty's approval, for their gallant conduct during the recent operations in South Africa, as recorded against their names."

BULLER, REDVERS HENRY, Capt. and Brevet Lieut.-Colonel, was born at Downes, Devon, 1839; the son of John Wentworth Buller and Charlotte, daughter of Lord Henry Howard. He was educated at Eton. On 23 May, 1858, Redvers Buller was gazetted Ensign in the 60th Rifles (2nd Battn.), and thus began an exceptionally brilliant military career. In 1860 he served in the China Campaign, and was present at the taking of the Taku Forts and at the advance upon Pekin. He received the Chinese Medal with two clasps. In 1870 he took part in the Red River Expedition, being gazetted Captain, and recommended for promotion to Brevet Major by Lord Wolseley, who once declared him to be the bravest man he had ever known. In 1873 he sailed with the Expeditionary Force to Ashanti as Deputy Assistant Quartermaster-General. He was frequently mentioned in Lord Wolseley's Despatches. On his return he was appointed Deputy Assistant Adjutant-General at Headquarters. In 1878 Major Buller served through the Kaffir War. Commanded Frontier Light Horse. After Taba-ka-Udoda recommended for repeated acts of gallantry by Lord Chelmsford. Received the Brevet of Lieut.-Colonel. In 1879 he served in the Zulu War, and won the Victoria Cross at Inhlobana. Sir Evelyn Wood said he had "recommended him for the V.C. for having saved three lives, but he had really won it a dozen times." Sir Evelyn Wood gives the following account of how Colonel Buller won his V.C.: "When the last of the troops had left the plateau, Buller was heard to say to Commandant Piet Uys, who was in command of thirty Dutchmen, 'You go down, Piet; I'll stop here. And when you get to the bottom, halt some men to cover us as we come down.' Turning then to Lieut. Everitt, of the Frontier Light Horse, he ordered him to halt ten men, who, as a covering party, were to descend last of all. Mr. Everitt could only collect seven men, but these kept the Zulus back for some time, descending later with the enemy close upon them. Four of the little party were almost immediately killed, and Lieut. Everitt's horse was assegaied. Buller, now seizing Mr. Everitt, who was exhausted, by the collar of the coat, pulled him out of the way of the pursuing Zulus, who were themselves greatly impeded by the rugged nature of the cliffs, and standing over his breathless lieutenant, received from him a carbine and ammunition. Then, with the three men remaining alive out of the rear-guard seven, Buller covered the retreat of the last of those descending the cliff. Buller was ubiquitous, and to my knowledge rescued four men that day, three of whom lived for years afterwards; the fourth man whom he pulled out of the middle of a struggling crowd of Zulus, and carried, holding on to his stirrup, down the hill, was eventually wounded much lower down, and lost his life. Trooper Randal, Frontier Light Horse, told me, five days later, that in the retreat his horse was completely exhausted, when he was overtaken by Colonel Buller, who was falling back with the rearmost men, and that the colonel put him up on his own horse and carried him for some distance; then, dropping him, returned again to the fight, this time picking up Capt. D'Arcy, also of the Frontier Light Horse. This officer had lost both his horses, and when panting along on foot, with the Zulus less than a hundred yards behind him, was rescued by Colonel Buller, who took him up on his horse." His Victoria Cross was gazetted 11 June, 1879: "Redvers Henry Buller, Capt. and Brevet Lieut.-Colonel, C.B., 60th Rifles (King's Royal Rifle Corps). For his gallant conduct at the retreat at Inhlobana on the 28th March, 1879, in having assisted, while hotly pursued by the Zulus in rescuing Capt. D'Arcy of the Frontier Light Horse, who was retiring on foot, and carrying him on his horse until he overtook the rearguard; also for having, on the same date, and under the same circumstances, conveyed Lieut. Everitt, of the F.L.H., whose horse had been killed under him, to a place of safety. Later on Colonel Buller in the same manner saved a trooper of the F.L.H., whose horse was completely exhausted, and who would otherwise have been killed by the Zulus, who were within eighty yards of him." In 1885 he was in command of the Desert Column. He was created a K.C.M.G. (Medal and clasp). In 1886 Major-General Sir R. Buller was sent to Ireland to reorganize the Constabulary. From 1887 to 1890 he was Quartermaster-General of the Forces. In 1890 he was appointed Adjutant-General in succession to Lord Wolseley. In 1891 he became Lieut.-General, and was created a G.C.B. In 1898 he was in command at Aldershot, and on the outbreak of the Boer War was appointed Commander-in-Chief in South Africa. In 1900 he won the Battle of Colenso and occupied Spion Kop. In 1901 he personally conducted the Relieving Force across the Tugela, and on the 28th Feb. relieved Ladysmith. He then commenced a forward move, occupied Newcastle, forced Alleman's Nek, and reached Lydenburg In 1902 Sir Redvers Buller resumed the command at Aldershot. He died at his home, Downes, near Crediton, on the 2nd June, 1908. At Exeter a beautiful equestrian statue of him was erected by his admirers at home and abroad, and there is a magnificent recumbent effigy of Sir Redvers Buller in Winchester Cathedral, also a very fine Memorial in Crediton Church. At Winchester the words of the memorial are: "A great Leader—Beloved of his men."

Redvers Henry Buller.

LEET, WILLIAM KNOX, Major, was born 3 Nov. 1833. During the Indian Mutiny Lieut. Leet served with marked distinction, both with his battalion under Lord Mark Kerr and as a Staff Officer to several columns towards the close of the campaign (twice mentioned in General Orders; Medal). In 1878 he served in South Africa against Sekukuni. In 1879 Major Leet served in the Zulu War. Sir Evelyn Wood says, in "From Midshipman to Field-Marshal" (Vol. II., page 46): "In the forenoon of the 27th March, the two columns which were to attack the Inhlobane at daylight next morning marched. I followed in the evening, intending to lie down five miles under the western edge of the Inhlobane. The more important part of the operation was entrusted to Colonel Buller, under whose orders I placed the two battalions of Wood's Regt. The 1st Battn., under Major Leet, bivouacking near the White Umvolusi, where Vryheid now stands, was intended to ascend the western end of the mountain; both columns were to get as high up as they could before daylight on the 28th. So far as I know, the only officer who got down the western end of the Inhlobane on horseback was Major Leet, who commanded the 1st Battn. Wood's Irregulars. Six weeks earlier, at the athetic sports, we had a tug-of-war between the officers of the 13th and 90th Light Infantry, captained by Leet and myself, and as the 90th pulled over the 13th, Leet wrenched his knee out of joint, and I had told him to remain in camp on the 27th. This, however, he did not do, and as he could only hobble, he tried, and successfully, to ride down the mountain. I believe he got down before the counter-attack ; but while on the Lower Plateau, and being followed up closely by the enemy, he showed distinguished courage in going back to help a dismounted officer, for which he received the Victoria Cross." [London Gazette, 17 June, 1879] : " William K. Leet, Major, 1st Regt. 13th Regt. For his gallant conduct on the 28th March, 1879, in rescuing from the Zulus, Lieut. A. M. Smith, of the Frontier Light Horse, during the retreat from Inhlobane. Lieut. Smith, whilst on foot, his horse having been shot, was closely pursued by the Zulus, and would have been killed, had not Major Leet taken him upon his horse, and rode with him under the fire of the enemy to a place of safety." In 1886 and 1887 he served in the Expedition to Mandalay (mentioned in Despatches and created a C.B.). Major-General Leet died 27 June, 1898, aged 65.

REYNOLDS, JAMES HENRY, Surgeon-Major, was the son of Mr. L. Reynolds, J.P., of Dalyston House, Granard, Ireland. He was born at Kingstown, Dublin, on 3 Feb. 1844, and was educated at Castle Knock

James Henry Reynolds.

and at Trinity College Dublin (B.A., and LL.D., hon.). He entered the Medical Staff Corps as Assistant Surgeon 31 March, 1868, and joined the 36th Regt. in 1869 as Medical Officer. He received the thanks of the Commander-in-Chief, Lord Sandhurst, for his services during a severe outbreak of cholera in the 36th Regt. in India. He became Surgeon 1 March, 1873. He served in the Kaffir War of 1877–78, and was present at the engagement with Galeckasat Impetu. And in the Zulu War he was present at the Battle of Ulundi, besides winning his Victoria Cross at Rorke's Drift, when he was specially promoted Surgeon-Major for distinguished field service 23 Jan. 1879. The British Medical Association gave him their Gold Medal for his services at Rorke's Drift. His Victoria Cross was gazetted 17 June, 1879 : " James Henry Reynolds, Surgeon-Major, Army Medical Department. For the conspicuous bravery during the attack at Rorke's Drift, on the 22nd and 23rd Jan. 1879, which he exhibited in his constant attention to the wounded under fire, and in his voluntarily conveying ammunition from the store to the defenders of the hospital, whereby he exposed himself to a cross-fire from the enemy both in going and returning." He has the South African Medal with three dates, 1887–88–89, equal to three clasps. In 1880 Surgeon-Major Reynolds married Elizabeth, daughter of Dr. M'Cormick. He was promoted Lieutenant-Colonel 1 April, 1887, and obtained his substantive step, Brigade-Surgeon Lieutenant-Colonel, 25 Dec. 1892. He retired from the Army in 1896, and was later in Medical Charge of the Royal Army Clothing Factory, London.

Edward S. Browne.

BROWNE, EDWARD S., Lieut., entered the 24th Regt. (The South Wales Borderers) in 1871 ; served in the Zulu war, 1879 ; was mentioned in Despatches, received the Medal, and was awarded the Victoria Cross [London Gazette, 17 June, 1879] : " Edward S. Browne, Lieut., 1st Battn. 24th Regt. For his gallant conduct on the 29th March, 1879, when the mounted infantry were being driven in by the enemy at Inhlobana, in galloping back and twice assisting on his horse (under heavy fire and within a few yards of the enemy) one of the mounted men, who must otherwise have fallen into the enemy's hands." From 1902 he commanded the 5th Army Corps at York. Brigadier-General E. S. Browne, V.C., C.B., died in Switzerland on the 16th July, 1907.

Samuel Wassall

WASSALL, SAMUEL, Private, enlisted in the 80th (South Staffordshire) Regt. ; served in the Zulu War, and was awarded the Victoria Cross [London Gazette, 17 June, 1879] : " Samuel Wassall, Private, 80th Regt. For his gallant conduct in having, at the imminent risk of his own life, saved that of Private Westwood, of the same regiment. On the 22nd Jan. 1879, when the camp at Isandhlwana was taken by the enemy, Private Wassall retreated towards the Buffalo River, in which he saw a comrade struggling and apparently drowning. He rode to the bank, dismounted, leaving his horse on the Zulu side, rescued the man from the stream, and again mounted his horse, dragging Private Westwood across the river under a heavy shower of bullets."

London Gazette, 27 June, 1879.—" War Office, 27 June, 1879. The Queen has been graciously pleased to signify Her intention to confer the Decoration of the Victoria Cross upon the undermentioned Officer of Her Majesty's Army, whose claim has been submitted for Her Majesty's approval, for his courageous conduct in attempting the rescue of Private Giese, Frontier Armed Mounted Police, on the 29th Dec. 1877, as recorded in the accompanying statement."

MOORE, HANS GARRETT, Brevet Major, was born at Richmond Barracks, Dublin, son of Capt. Garrett Moore, 88th Connaught Rangers, Richmond Barracks, Dublin, and of Charlotte Butler, of Drum, County

Hans Garrett Moore.

Tipperary. His great-grandfather was G. Moore, brother of The O'Moore of Cloghan Castle. Colonel Moore's family are representatives in the male line of the O'Moores of Cloghan Castle, descendants of Rory O'Moore, the famous Irish Prince who fought with Henry VIII., and made a treaty with him on equal terms, as one Sovereign with another. He broke out again in the time of Queen Elizabeth, and Her Majesty of blessed memory, who was nothing if not drastic in her methods, annexed Rory O'Moore's Principality of Leix, which became Queen's County, and cut off the head of her own General, Essex. Garrett Moore was educated at the Royal School, Banagher, and at Trinity College, Dublin, which he entered at the age of sixteen. He volunteered and obtained a commission without purchase from the Commander-in-Chief, on account of the war services of his family, especially in the Crimea, and was gazetted to the 59th Regt. as Ensign on first appointment, 7 June, 1855, and was transferred to the 88th Foot as Ensign 13 July, 1855, becoming Lieutenant on 6 Oct. of the same year. Lieut. Moore served with his regiment in the Indian Mutiny Campaign from Dec. 1857, including the affair of Bhognapore, the siege of Lucknow in March, the siege of Calpee, action of Selimpore (slightly wounded) and Jamoo, storming and capture of the Birwah Forts (slightly wounded). It is said by an old comrade that " at Selimpore the 8's were shot off his forage-cap, and at Birwah his revolver broken at his side, while in the same action he made a furious onslaught alone on a party of three of the enemy in a native house, the result of which we should never have known from him had we not, on missing him, ascertained that, armed only with his regulation sword, he had disposed of the party single-handed. Yet to show what a chivalrous nature was his, I saw him not long afterwards risk his own life to save a poor native coolie, who was one of our beaters in a shooting party in Oudh, and who, on missing his footing and falling into the Goomti River, then in rapid flood, was rescued by Moore at once plunging in, clothes and all, and bringing him almost lifeless to the bank. Would to heaven that help as effectual had been near him when his own gallant life was taken in the same element." The late Colonel Kendal Coghill, C.B. (late commanding the 19th (Queen Alexandra's Own) Hussars), wrote : " A thought flashed across me that when last I wrote I omitted to answer about Colonel ' Garry ' Moore. Yes, I knew him intimately, and always looked on him as one of the bravest of the brave and a man hard as nails. He earned his Cross well in South Africa, but was sadly drowned in the dark when trying to rescue his yacht on a lake during a violent storm one night. I saw him break his collar-bone once at Delhi or Cawnpore in the 'fifties, when he was thrown out of his dogcart on a plain, but held on to the reins of his bolting horse, being dragged along the ground until he stopped the runaway. His regiment (88th) and mine (Bengal European Fusiliers, now Royal Munster Fusiliers) were quartered together at Delhi and Cawnpore, and I am rather hazy as to which of the two it was where the accident occurred, but I think Delhi." For his services in the Mutiny Campaign he was mentioned in Despatches [London Gazette, 31 Jan. 1858], and received the Medal and clasp for Central India. He was Adjutant, 88th Foot, from 18 Aug. 1863, to 18 June, 1872, and was promoted to Captain 19 June, 1872. Capt. Moore volunteered and was employed on special service in the Ashanti War of 1873–74 ; was employed in raising a force in the Wassawand and Denkera country on the left flank of the main line of advance, and on the return of the troops to the coast was employed in the Transport Service. For his services in this campaign he was given the Brevet of Major (1 April, 1874), and received the Medal with clasp. He served in the South African War of 1877–78, in the Kaffir Campaign served in the 1st Galeka Campaign from 22 Nov. to 3 Dec. 1877 ; commanded at the affair near Draaibosch on 29 Nov. 1877 (severely wounded ; horse wounded). Also commanded at the action at the same place on 30 Dec. (horse wounded three times) ; commanded small columns in the subsequent operations in the Komgha, Chichaba and Transkei districts, and engaged in the Transkei in pursuit of Kreli and his followers in Aug. 1878. The " Eastern Province Herald," Port Elizabeth, 29 Jan. 1877, has an account of Major Moore's gallantry on two occasions when he commanded troops at Draaibosch : " The actions referred to in the despatches are those which occurred on the 29th and 30th ult., between a patrol of the Connaught Rangers, accompanied by Mounted Police, and a large force of Gaikas, many of whom were mounted. The Europeans were on both occasions led by Major Moore, and the encounters were desperate and well sustained. The Gaikas exhibited their traditional valour, and are described as ' advancing rapidly and in perfect order.' Shots were exchanged at thirty yards, and fighting was frequently pursued within ' assegai distance.' In the first engagement 32 Europeans, chiefly Police, routed 300 Gaikas with the loss of one man (Private Giese). On the day following, 61 men of the 88th and Police, assisted by three volunteers or civilians, met and defeated 600 of the enemy with the loss of two killed and 'missing.' Major Moore's horse was thrice shot under him and had to be destroyed. The conduct of that officer is described by his immediate superior, Colonel Lambert, in terms of warm commendation. 'I cannot,' he says, 'close my report without directing special attention to the bravery and gallant conduct of Major Moore. On the 29th he rallied a few men of the F.A.M.P., and made a desperate attempt to save Policeman Giese. He was wounded severely in the arm with an assegai, and his horse also received a wound. On the 30th the conduct of this officer was beyond all praise, and is the theme of high commendation with everyone. I am of opinion that the mere handful of young soldiers with Major Moore could only have been made to stand as firmly as they did by such conspicuous courage and cool daring; the least wavering would have been fatal.' Similar testimony is borne by Colonel Bellairs, commanding the Eastern Frontier, who states that the affairs of the 29th and 30th Dec., at Draaibosch, were well carried out by Major Moore, 'who exhibited conspicuous bravery on both occasions, setting a fine example to his men, and materially contributing to the successful issue of the engagements.' Sir Arthur Cunynghame is equally explicit, and declares that the Major's 'conspicuous gallantry would have been more fully brought to light had he not been himself the reporting officer on his own deeds.' It is thus placed beyond all question that Major Moore has proved himself the bravest of the brave, and, withal, a prudent and experienced commander. . . . We have now before us the published despatches of Lieut.-Colonel Lambert and Brevet Major Moore, 88th Regt., reporting the 'affairs of the 29th and 30th Dec.,' at Draaibosch, in which Major Moore greatly distinguished himself by the manner in which he held a perilous position in the face of overhwelming odds. On the 29th Dec. last the post riders carrying the mail to Kei Road Station had been fired at and forced to return to Komgha. Major Moore, then under orders from Colonel Lambert, started with a patrol of thirty-two officers and men of the F.A.M.P., under Sub-Inspector Mitchell, in the direction of Draaibosch. After some brushes with the enemy, the patrol came upon a body of three hundred Kaffirs. The troop of Police, after firing a few shots, retired, and were followed by the Kaffirs, who overtook and killed Private Giese, despite a brave attempt on the part of Major Moore and others to rescue him. Subsequently the enemy retired and the patrol returned to Komgha." It was for his gallantry during this first action at Draaibosch that Major Moore eventually received the Victoria Cross. Lieut.-Colonel H. F. N. Jourdain, C.M.G., says of Colonel H. G. Moore that he was "a splendid soldier and a splendid adjutant, and his name lasted long in the 88th for gallantry. He came back after Draaibosch, when he won the V.C., with an assegai sticking in his arm, through the muscle of the biceps. He would not let them take it out before, as he would have bled profusely. He sat down on a stump of a tree, and let the doctor cut out the assegai-head while he smoked a black pipe." At the time of his death a brother officer wrote to a newspaper: "Many of your military readers learned with regret of the untimely death of Colonel Hans Garrett Moore, V.C.—'Bould Moore,' as he was called by the men of his old regiment, the Connaught Rangers. A more intrepid soldier never lived. I remember during the last Kaffir War, when he was wounded trying to save a man who had fallen into the hands of the Kaffirs, and for which he got the V.C. When the doctor was trying to take the bent assegai-head out of his arm, some anxious bystander attempted to cut open the sleeve of his patrol jacket, when, with perfect coolness, he said, 'Hold on, this is my only coat; rip it up the seam.' The next morning he went out to look for the Kaffirs, and found them twenty to one, and, after three hours' fighting, defeated them. He was the only officer who rode his horse out of action, all the others having been killed or captured. He said to me, 'Where is my horse wounded?' and on examination I found three distinct bullets had entered, but the poor animal carried him home that night and then died." At the time of Colonel Moore's death the following letter, giving an account of the second action at Draaibosch, appeared in the "Cape Times":

"Cape Town, 18 Nov. 1889.

"*To the Editor of the Cape Times.*

"Sir,—The brief notice that has appeared in the newspapers respecting that gallant soldier, Colonel Moore, whose untimely death is so deplored, has been supplemented by a letter written to the 'Irish Times' by an old Connaught Ranger, in which he bears testimony (were testimony needed) to the splendid qualities of the deceased officer, whom he rightly terms 'as intrepid a soldier as ever lived.' The writer mentioned that Colonel Moore admitted to him that he 'was in a funk' on one occasion,—and that was in the action at Draaibosch, on the 30th Dec. 1877. May I, as one who had the privilege of serving with Colonel Moore on that day, tell your readers in what kind of a way that 'funk' displayed itself. Our men, some fifty of the Connaught Rangers, about thirty of the F.A.M. Police (who were dismounted for the action), and five or six volunteers, were in line on the crest of the hill above the Draaibosch Hotel and facing the Komgha Road, towards which, and from the direction of Sandilli's Kraal, on the banks of the Kabousie, the whole force of the enemy, some 1,000 foot and 600 horse, were advancing. Suddenly, and when within about 350 yards of us, they deployed, one half sweeping round to our left flank, and the remainder to our right, whilst the horse went at a canter to our rear. It was a critical moment. Colonel Moore, who was mounted, told Capt. Acklom to move the men at the double to the crest of the hill, facing Savage's Shop, as the force of the enemy flanking our position in that direction were nearest, and were then charging up the hill with loud cries. Before the movement could be completed the enemy were upon us—some of the F.A.M. Police flung themselves on their horses and rode hard away (I may here mention that others of that force remained and did gallant service afterwards), and the young soldiers of the Rangers, mere boys for the most part, showed signs of wavering. What, at this moment, was Colonel Moore doing? He was sitting immovably, calm, on his horse, facing the hordes of the enemy, and issuing the words of command to his forces as if he had been on parade. One indecision on his part—even, I verily believe, had he turned his horse's head from the enemy—and our little force would have been annihilated. But there he was: there his young soldiers saw him, the grim, stern personification of the warrior undaunted in the very face of what to all seemed certain death. And the men in a moment reassured, halted at the entreaties of their officers, and with ringing cheers charged with the bayonet, and for the moment checked the rush of the savages. Colonel Moore throughout the day (on which he held the hill to his last cartridge, and during which he had his horse three times shot under him) displayed the same perfect coolness and calm courage, and by those qualities, I am persuaded, saved the Colony from the devastation which would have followed a defeat of his force in that first and the most remarkable action of the campaign, an action in which, moreover, the natives for the first and only time in their history, charged our soldiers to the very point of the bayonet. Remember, too, that only thirty-six hours previously Colonel Moore had been dangerously wounded by an assegai whilst endeavouring to protect the body of Private Giese against a horde of assailants. This was the 'funk' displayed by Colonel Moore on the one occasion on which he owned to it.

"I am, etc.,

W. J. J. W."

The "Eastern Province Herald," of 29 Jan. 1877, says: "It is to the engagement of the 30th Dec. that we wish to direct special attention. On that day Major Moore, though severely wounded by an assegai on the previous day, left Komgha with forty men of the 88th Regt., under Capt. Acklom, and twenty-one men of the F.A.M. Police, under Sub-Inspector White, for the purpose of escorting the mail from the Transkei past Draaibosch, the post riders of the previous day having made three unsuccessful attempts to carry it through to Gray's Farm. As this small party of sixty-one men, and three or four others who went as volunteers, approached Savage's Shop, about six miles from Komgha, the enemy was seen to be collecting in force and forming an attack. Major Moore selected a good defensive position on the crown of a hill about half a mile beyond Savage's Shop and close to the road, and now began a fight which lasted an hour and a half, such as is rarely seen in Kaffir warfare, in which 'frequent bayonet charges' were made by the colonial forces. It is seldom, indeed, that Kaffirs give them the chance, and the only matter for regret, in this instance, is that the defensive force did not consist of older and more experienced men. The forty men of the 88th Regt.—the Connaught Rangers—we are told, were mere boys, 'not one of whom had ever seen an enemy before, and their firing was very wild.' Their courage is not questioned for a moment, and they charged with a cheer when called upon, every time repulsing the enemy. . . . It is a wonder that this small force, under such circumstances, was not completely cut up. The bayonet charges, no doubt, were their salvation. . . . The fight lasted from 2.15 p.m. to 3.45 p.m., say an hour and a half." For his services in this campaign Brevet Major H. G. Moore was mentioned in Despatches [London Gazette, 26 Feb. 1878], and on two other occasions; was promoted Major, half-pay, given the Brevet of Lieutenant-Colonel 9 March 1878; received the Medal with clasp, and was awarded the Victoria Cross [London Gazette, 27 June, 1879]: "Hans Garrett Moore, Major, 88th Foot. For his gallant conduct in risking his own life in endeavouring to save the life of Private Giese of the Frontier Armed Mounted Police, on the occasion of the action with the Gaikas near Komgha, on the 29th Dec. 1877. It is reported that when a small body of Mounted Police were forced to retire before overwhelming numbers of the enemy, Major Moore observed that Private Giese was unable to mount his horse, and was thereby left at the mercy of the Kaffirs. Perceiving the man's danger, Major Moore rode back alone into the midst of the enemy, and did not desist in his endeavour to save the man until the latter was killed, Major Moore having shot two Kaffirs and received an assegai in the arm during this gallant attempt." A contemporary newspaper says: "The new colonial regiment which is being raised in South Africa for the defence of the Cape Colony will bear the name of its predecessor, the Cape Mounted Rifles, and is to be placed under the command of Brevet Lieut.-Colonel H. Garrett Moore, late of the Connaught Rangers. Capt. R. G. Southey, late of the 2nd Battn. 10th Regt., who recently went out to the Cape as special officer, will act for the present as Second in Command, and Capt. E. G. Brabant, who was for many years connected with the old Cape Regt., and has distinguished himself on several occasions during the late campaign, has been asked to connect himself with the new corps." Brevet Major Moore had been put on half-pay previous to joining the Cape Mounted Police, and bought in as a Major into the Argyll and Sutherland Highlanders 15 March, 1879. He was—as has been said—given the Brevet of Lieutenant-Colonel, and he became Colonel (Army) 29 April, 1882. He resigned the command of the Cape Mounted Rifles in order to serve once more under his old chief, Sir Garnet Wolseley, in the Egyptian Campaign of 1882, as Provost Marshal (A.A. and Q.M.G.) at Headquarters. He was present at the second action at Kassassin and at the Battle of Tel-el-Kebir (Despatches [London Gazette, 2 Nov. 1882]; Medal with clasp; C.B.; Third Class Osmanieh: Khedive's Star). This was Colonel Moore's last active service, for after commanding his regiment, the 93rd Sutherland Highlanders, now the 2nd Battn. The Argyll and Sutherland Highlanders, he retired, on retired pay as Colonel, having been offered, and refused, the rank of Major-General on retired pay. Colonel Moore belonged to a family of great horsemen. His nephew—another Garrett Moore—was the celebrated gentleman rider who won the Grand National in 1879 on his own horse Liberator—a magnificent race. Liberator was third in the Grand National, ridden by Mr. Thomas, in 1877. In 1880 he was second to Empress, and was ridden by Garrett Moore. He fell in 1881 and 1882. Liberator was quite a character, a cunning old horse, who thought a good deal. He would sort of brush through the fences on the racecourses round London, but he knew he could take no liberties with those at Aintree. Colonel Garrett Moore's family owned many good horses, among others, Rory of the Hills. Colonel Moore, when in India, was Master of the Connaught Rangers' pack of hounds, and he was a good steeplechase rider and the winner of many races. He was also an expert swimmer and yachtsman, and it was owing to his fondness for the last-named pastime that he met his death. On the 6th Oct. 1889, Colonel Moore left Portumna Bay in his steam launch, the Foam, accompanied by his stoker, Patrick Byrne, of Banagher. They both went on shore, and Byrne returned to the launch at about half-past nine o'clock. After some time he took in the punt for Colonel Moore, who had dined with General Cooper, and came back with him to the launch at about half-past twelve o'clock. Colonel Moore, however, rowed off in a tremendous gale to secure the rope which fastened the launch to a buoy. He could not row back against the wind and drifted out into Dromineer Bay. His body was found on Sunday in fourteen feet of water at the Buggaun Island, Urrow Shore. His features were quite unchanged, and he seemed as if he was peacefully asleep. He had never known fear by sight in his life or in his death. He was buried in Mount Jerome Cemetery. The Connaught Rangers have among their regimental plate twenty-five silver goblets, a large number of which were given by officers on St. Patrick's Day, 1876. On one of them is inscribed : " Presented by Brevet Major H. G. Moore, 17 March, 1876." They have also a silver inkstand which was presented by Colonel H. G. Moore on leaving the regiment at Cape Town on 7 June, 1878. On it is the following inscription : " To the officers of the 88th, The Connaught Rangers. From Brevet Lieut.-Colonel H. G. Moore, in Grateful Remembrance of 23 Happy Years' Service in the Regiment. Cape Town, 7 June, 1878." Colonel Moore was drowned in October, 1889, by the capsizing of a boat on a stormy night. Many of the above details are taken from " A History of the Mess Plate of the 88th Connaught Rangers," 1904, by Lieut.-Colonel H. F. N. Jourdain, C.M.G., and most of the rest are supplied by Colonel Moore's niece, Miss Bird. The Marquis of Dufferin, when replying, a short time before Colonel Moore's death, to an address of welcome on his return from India, " took occasion to enumerate the names of Irishmen who had distinguished themselves, and mentioned two military men who took precedence of all others— *Colonel Moore was one of these.*

London Gazette, 9 Sept. 1879.—" War Office, 23 Aug. 1879. The Queen has been graciously pleased to signify Her intention to confer the Decoration of the Victoria Cross upon the undermentioned Officer of Her Majesty's Army, whose claim has been submitted for Her Majesty's approval, for an Act of Bravery performed by him during the War against the Zulus, as recorded against his name."

BERESFORD, LORD WILLIAM LESLIE DE LA POER, Capt., was born on 20 July, 1847, at Mullaghbragh, Ireland ; 3rd son of the 4th Marquis of Waterford and of Christiana, daughter of the late Colonel Charles Powell

Leslie, of Glaslough, County Monaghan. He was educated at Eton and entered the 9th Lancers in 1867, as a Cornet, and became Lieutenant in 1870. The regiment was then stationed at Island Bridge Barracks, Dublin. He soon became known as a successful amateur rider and was a prominent member of the regimental polo team. In the autumn of 1874 he sailed with his regiment for India. In 1874 he was appointed A.D.C. on the Staff of the retiring Viceroy, Lord Northbrook, who was being succeeded by Lord Lytton, to whom Lord William later became Military Secretary, and remained in this capacity with four successive Viceroys until the spring of 1894. He became Captain in 1876. His first active service was with General Keyes in the Jowaki Expedition

Lord William Beresford.

of 1877–8, when Lord Lytton gave him leave of absence. For his services he received the Medal and clasp. In the second phase of the Afghan War Lord William again obtained leave of absence and served with his regiment under the late General Sir Samuel Browne, V.C. ; was mentioned in Despatches and received the Afghan Medal with clasp. A third time, for the news of Isandhlwana had made him determined to get to South Africa if possible, he was given leave of absence by Lord Lytton and arrived at Durban in April, 1879, where he served in the Zulu War. He won the Victoria Cross for rescuing Sergt. Fitzmaurice against the will of the latter, who thought it impossible that two could escape and begged Lord William to leave him and escape. By dint of the powerful vocabulary which was his at command, and the exercise of much bodily strength, he got the Sergeant on his horse, and—just when the horse and its riders were nearly done—Sergt. O'Toole saw their danger and rode out to the rescue, shooting several Zulus and helping him with the now helpless Fitzmaurice. For this service Lord William was awarded the Cross—as has been said—but he said he ought not to have it unless it was awarded to Sergt. O'Toole as well. This was done. His Victoria Cross was gazetted 23 Aug. 1879 : " Lord William Leslie de la Poer Beresford, Capt., 9th Lancers. For gallant conduct in having at great personal risk, during the retirement of the reconnoitring party across the ' White Umvolosi River ' on the 3rd July last, turned to assist Sergt. Fitzmaurice, 1st Battn. 24th Foot (whose horse had fallen with him), mounted him behind him on his own horse, and brought him away in safety under the close fire of the Zulus, who were in great force and coming on quickly. Lord William Beresford's position was rendered most dangerous from the fact that Sergt. Fitzmaurice twice nearly pulled him from his horse." He spent the last eighteen days of his leave in England, and was personally decorated by the Queen at Windsor. Lord William took the

greatest interest in racing in India, and was very successful both as a rider and owner. His tact, kindness and charm of manner made him excessively popular in India, and before he left for England in 1894 he was given a farewell banquet in the Calcutta Town Hall by a large number of friends, with Mr. C. H. Moore in the chair. In returning thanks Lord William said : " With regard to the allusion he " (Mr. Moore) " made to the straightness of the nose—(laughter)—that he recollects . . . he is not quite correct, and there is a gentleman, Mr. J. J. Allan, among my hosts here to-night, that can testify to the fact that, owing to a slight disagreement he and I had many years ago, not actually in the playing fields of Eton, but close by, he made a little arrangement that prevented that particular nose referred to being worn straight by its owner for the rest of his life." On 30 April, 1895, at St. George's, Hanover Square, Lord William married Lilian Warren, daughter of Cicero Price, Commodore, United States Navy, and widow of the 8th Duke of Marlborough. They had one son, William Warren de la Poer, born 4 Feb. 1897. In Oct. 1895, King Edward (then Prince of Wales) stayed with Lord William and his wife at Deepdene, Dorking. At the end of 1895, Lord William entered into partnership in a racing stable with Mr. Pierre Lorillard, and shared with him some good horses, the most successful being Paris III., bought from the widow of the Hon. James White. When the doctors advised Mr. Lorillard to give up racing, Lord William bought his interest in the stable. In Dec. 1896, while out with the Warnham Stag Hounds, Lord William met with a frightful accident, from the effects of which he only partially recovered. In 1897 he introduced Tod Sloan to the British public, and that and the three following years were great ones for the Beresford stable. " In 1898," says Mrs. Stuart-Menzies, in her " Memories of Lord William Beresford," " Lord William owned many winners entered in the name of one or other of the two partners. Caiman as a two-year-old won the Middle Park Plate, value £2,775, Sloan riding ; beating the Duke of Westminster's Flying Fox, ridden by Mornington Cannon. . . . The chief races won in 1898 were the Clearwell Stakes and Middle Park Plate by Caiman, Esher Stakes by Diakka, Thirty-fifth Biennial at Ascot, by Sandia, Exeter Stakes, by Dominie. Mykka won the Lancaster Nursery First October Two Year Old Stakes, Prendergast Stakes, and Sandown Great Sapling Plate. On 30 Sept., Sloan won the Bretby Welter on Draco for Lord William by six lengths, the next race, the Scurry Nursery, on Manatee, the next race again, the Rous Memorial Stakes, on Landrail, by three lengths, another on Libra, by two lengths, the Newmarket St. Leger on Galashiels, by a head, making five wins and a second out of seven mounts, not a bad day for one stable." In 1899 Democrat came on the scene, and won the Coventry Stakes, Ascot, the Hurst Park Foal Plate, Hurst Park, the National Breeders' Produce Stakes, Sandown Park, the Champagne Stakes, Doncaster, the Rous Memorial Stakes, Newmarket, the Middle Park Plate, Newmarket and the Dewhurst Plate, Newmarket. As a three-year-old, Democrat secured the Royal Stakes at Newmarket, his last win. He was subsequently given by Mr. Richard Marsh to Lord Kitchener, who rode him at the Delhi Durbar and in King Edward's Coronation Procession. A statue of Lord Kitchener, mounted on Democrat, was erected in Calcutta in 1913. Huggins trained for Lord William Beresford and Mr. Lorillard at Heath House, the old home of Matthew Dawson and of Fred Archer, who had had the mount on Iroquois (the only American horse that ever won the Derby)—owned by Mr. Lorillard and trained by Huggins. Lieut.-Colonel Lord William Beresford, V.C., died of peritonitis on 28 Dec. 1900, universally mourned. He was buried in the family vault at Clonagam Church. The late Robert Martin (Ballyhooley) wrote the following lines about him :

" The old grey year is stricken down and lying
(The days are dark, the trees stand gaunt and bare),
Stretches its hand, and takes from us—while dying—
One whom we ill could spare.

" Soldier and sportsman, no fond hand could save you
From the old robber bearing you away ;
England who once the Cross for Valour gave you,
Honours you with tears to-day.

" What is the epitaph which shall be found him ?
Let this story of his lost life tell,
All hearts that knew him to-day around him
Whisp'ring, ' Kind friend, farewell.'

" Erin, a vigil o'er her dead son keeping,
Now takes him softly, sadly to her breast,
Under her grassy mantle hides him sleeping,
And gives him his long rest."

London Gazette, 7 Oct. 1879.—" War Office, 1 Sept. 1879. The Queen has been graciously pleased to signify Her intention to confer the Decoration of the Victoria Cross upon the undermentioned Officer of Her Majesty's Army, whose claim has been submitted for Her Majesty's approval, for his gallant conduct at the action of Futtehabad, on the 2nd April, 1879, as recorded against his name."

HAMILTON, WALTER RICHARD POLLOCK, Lieut., was the 4th son of Alexander Hamilton, Esq., J.P., of Inistioge, Ireland, and Emma, his wife, daughter of the late Right Hon. Sir Frederick Pollock, Bart., for twenty-two years Lord Chief Baron of Her Majesty's Court of Exchequer, and was great-grandson of the Right Reverend Hugh Hamilton, D.D., Lord Bishop of Ossory. He was born on the 18th Aug. 1856, and was educated at Eagle House, Wimbledon, and Felsted School, Essex. In Jan. 1874, he obtained twenty-first place in the open examination for the Army, and was gazetted to the 70th Regt. He served a few months at the Depôt, and then embarked for India in Oct. 1874.

On arrival he joined the Headquarters at Rawal Pindi. On being promoted Lieutenant, Hamilton was offered, and accepted, a commission in the Corps of Guides. Within three months of joining that famous regiment, he passed the higher standard examination in languages, and was detailed to the Cavalry. He served throughout the Itwaki-Afridi Expedition of 1877–8. He served as A.D.C. to the Commanding Officer, General Keyes. On the 14th March, 1878, he was present at the operations against the Ranizai village of Skhakat. In Oct. 1878, in view of the threatened hostilities with Afghanistan, the Corps of Guides was removed to Jamrud at the mouth of the Khyber, and for a period of six weeks was engaged in reconnoitring the mountains about the Pass. In the first of the two ensuing campaigns, Hamilton participated throughout in the Cavalry of the Corps, on which much of the heavy work fell. He was present at the capture of Ali Musjid. In March, 1879, he commanded a troop on escort duty with a surveying party under Lieut. Leach, R.E., which succeeded in beating off an attack of the Ghinwari tribe. In the last days of March, 1879, Lieut. Hamilton took part in the advance of General C. Gough's Brigade to Futtehabad, and was present at the engagement in that place, in which his dear friend Battye met his death, and Hamilton himself won the Victoria Cross. He was recommended for the decoration, but at first the War Office refused to grant it. When at last Lieut. Hamilton's gallantry was recognized he was already dead. The Victoria Cross was sent to his father after his death. His decoration was gazetted 7 Oct. 1879: "Walter Richard Pollock Hamilton, Lieut., Bengal Staff Corps. For conspicuous gallantry during the action at Futtehabad on the 2nd April, 1879, in leading on the Guide Cavalry in a charge against very superior numbers of the enemy, and particularly at a critical moment, when his commanding officer (Major Wigram Battye) fell. Lieut. Hamilton—then the only officer left with the regiment—assumed command and cheered on his men to avenge Major Battye's death. In this charge Lieut. Hamilton, seeing Sowar Dowlut Ram down, and attacked by three of the enemy, whilst entangled with his horse (which had been killed), rushed to the rescue, and followed by a few of his men, cut down all three and saved the life of Sowar Dowlut Ram." When it was determined to send an Embassy to Kabul, and Sir Louis Cavagnari was selected to act as Minister and Plenipotentiary, he chose Lieut. Hamilton for his political Assistant as well as to command his escort of seventy men of the Corps of Guides. The entire Embassy and escort—except one or two men of the Corps of Guides—was foully murdered after a six weeks' residence in the capital on the 3rd Sept. 1879. The official account of the tragedy says "that at his final charge to silence a gun which he did silence, Lieut. Hamilton fell where he said he would fall, killing on his way to inevitable death three men with his pistol and two with his sword." Eight days before his own death Walter Hamilton sent home his own prophetic verses on the Kabul disaster of 1841. He wrote :

Walter R. P. Hamilton.

"How England's fame shone brighter as she fought,
And wrenched lost laurels from their funeral pile,
And rose at last from out misfortune's tide
Supreme—for God and right were on her side."

There is a statue of him in Dublin in the Museum in Kildare Street.

London Gazette, 10 Oct. 1879.—"War Office, 9 Oct. 1879. The Queen has been graciously pleased to signify Her intention to confer the Decoration of the Victoria Cross upon the undermentioned Officer and Non-commissioned Officer of Her Majesty's Army, whose claims have been submitted for Her Majesty's approval, for their several Acts of Valour in endeavouring to save lives of soldiers during the reconnaissance made before Ulundi on the 3rd July, 1879, as recorded against their names."

D'ARCY, CECIL, Capt., was the son of Major D'Arcy, C.M.R.; served in Zululand with the Frontier Light Horse. He was awarded the Victoria Cross [London Gazette, 9 Oct. 1879]: "Cecil D'Arcy, Capt. (now Commandant), Cape Frontier Light Horse. For his gallant conduct on the 3rd July, 1879, during the reconnaissance made before Ulundi by the Mounted Corps, in endeavouring to rescue Trooper Raubenheim, of the Frontier Light Horse, who fell from his horse as the troops were retiring. Capt. D'Arcy, though the Zulus were quite close upon them, waited for the man to mount behind him. The horse kicked them both off, and though much hurt by the fall and quite alone, Capt. D'Arcy coolly endeavoured to lift the trooper, who was stunned, on to the horse, and it was only when he found that he had not strength to do so that he mounted and rode off. His escape was miraculous, as the Zulus had actually closed upon him." Colonel Hartley, V.C., C.M.G., says that Capt. Cecil D'Arcy was "awarded the V.C. for rescuing a wounded trooper at Zlobane Mountain, Zululand, 1879, and was also rescued himself by Major Redvers Buller (General Buller, V.C.). I am not sure about this, nor whether the incidents took place on the same day. Capt. D'Arcy was the son of Major D'Arcy, C.M.R., and was given a squadron in the Cape Mounted Rifles for his services in Zululand. His end was a tragic one. Whilst suffering from delirium after illness, he wandered into the bush and apparently lost himself. Although most diligent search was made, his body was not discovered for three months afterwards in the forest. We, the Cape Mounted Rifles, were very proud of having five V.C.'s in the regiment at one time : Sergt. Scott, Private P. Brown (deceased), Surgeon-Major McCrea (deceased), Capt. Cecil D'Arcy (deceased), and E. B. Hartley. Alas ! I don't think there is one in the regiment now."

O'TOOLE, EDMUND, Sergt., served in the Zulu War, and was awarded the Victoria Cross [London Gazette, 9 Oct. 1879]: "Edmund O'Toole, Sergt., Cape Frontier Light Horse. For his conspicuous courage and bravery on several occasions during the campaign, and especially for his conduct on the 3rd July, 1879, at the close of the reconnaissance before Ulundi, in assisting to rescue Sergt. Fitzmaurice, 1st Battn. 24th Mounted Infantry, whose horse fell and rolled on him, as the troops retired before great numbers of the enemy. When lifted up behind him by Lord William Beresford, the man, half stunned by the fall, could not hold on, and he must have been left had not Sergt. O'Toole, who was keeping back the advancing Zulus, given up his carbine and assisted to hold Sergt. Fitzmaurice on the horse. At the time the Zulus were rapidly closing on them, and there was no armed man between them and Sergt. O'Toole." When Lord William Beresford had rescued Sergt. Fitzmaurice from the Zulus and got him away on his own horse, the enemy pursued them hotly, and just when Lord William was beginning to feel he could not support Fitzmaurice any longer, "help came" (says Mrs. Stuart-Menzies, in her "Recollections of Lord William Beresford") "in the shape of Sergt. O'Toole, who had seen their danger and rode out in hot haste to the rescue, shooting Zulu after Zulu with his revolver as they came within measurable distance. He then assisted Lord William Beresford with his helpless burden. It is interesting to note that both these brave men, Lord William Beresford and Fitzmaurice" (who at first refused to be helped, fearing that Lord William would sacrifice his own life), "were Irishmen, O'Toole, who came to the rescue, was Irish, and the horse which bore them into safety was Irish, each so splendid in their several parts : Lord William risking his life to save his countryman, he in his turn refusing to jeopardize his officer's life, then the plucky Irish horse straining every nerve in response to his master's bidding, though carrying a double burden of swaying riders. Again, the Irishman that grasped the situation and, without waiting for any word of command, lost not a moment in riding to their rescue, no precious time being lost in wondering what had happened, and if there had been a disaster."

London Gazette, 18 Nov. 1879.—"War Office, 17 Nov. 1879. The Queen has been graciously pleased to signify Her intention to confer the Decoration of the Victoria Cross upon the undermentioned Officers, whose claims to the same have been submitted for Her Majesty's approval, for their gallant and courageous conduct during the recent operations in Afghanistan and South Africa, as recorded against their respective names."

CREAGH, (GARRETT) O'MOORE, Capt., was born 2 April, 1848, at Cahirbane, County Clare, Ireland ; son of Captain James Creagh, R.N., of Cahirbane, and Grace Emily, daughter of The O'Moore, Cloghan Castle, King's County, Ireland. He was educated at a private school, and at the Royal Military College, Sandhurst ; was gazetted to an Ensigncy by purchase in the 95th Regt. on the 2nd Oct. 1866, and, after serving at the Depôt at Pembroke Dock till Jan. 1869, embarked for India and joined the service companies of his regiment at Mhow. In June, 1870 he entered the Bombay Staff Corps and was promoted Lieutenant. He served for a short time with the Marine Battalion and with the 25th Bombay Light Infantry, and was then appointed Officiating Adjutant of the Deoli Irregular Force and Station Staff Officer at Deoli. In June, 1871 he was selected as Adjutant to the Merwara Battalion on its transfer from the Civil to the Military Establishment. He married—1st, 1874, Mary Letitia Longfield, daughter of John Brereton, of Old Court, County Tipperary (she died, 1876). In 1878—while still holding the post of Adjutant—he was appointed Officiating Commandant. In Oct. of the same year he was promoted Captain in the Bombay Staff Corps. When the Merwara Battalion volunteered for service on the outbreak of the Afghan War, Lieut. Creagh was the only European officer present with it. He commanded it through its subsequent march from Ajmere, Rajputana, to Hassan Abdal, Punjab. Since its establishment in 1822 the Corps had not till now moved more than thirty miles from its headquarters. Capt. Creagh took part as Second in Command in the subsequent operations of the battalion in Afghanistan, serving in the Peshawar Valley Field Force at Ali Musjid till March, 1879, when the regiment was ordered to garrison Daka Fort. His services in the first Afghan Campaign, included the Bazar Valley expedition, action at Kam Daka, and other affairs in the Khyber Pass. Before the regiment went to Daka, Capt. Creagh, accompanied by two Afridi tribesmen, surveyed the route through Bourg to the Bazar Valley, for which he received the special thanks of the General Commanding, and took part in the first expedition into that district. On the 20th he was sent with a detachment of his regiment to Kam Daka, and for the services he rendered there he was recommended for the Victoria Cross. "I consider the cool determination of Capt. Creagh to do his duty," wrote Lieut.-General Maude, V.C., "his self-possession, and the gallant example he set to his little band, were most conspicuous." While Major Barnes, commanding at Daka Fort, says in his report : "In this miserable position, fully commanded by the surrounding hills, he (Capt. Creagh) made a noble defence and deserves the highest praise I can afford him." For his services in the campaign Capt. Creagh received the Medal, and the Brevet of Major, and was awarded the Victoria Cross [London Gazette, 18 Nov. 1879]: "O'Moore Creagh, Capt., Bombay Staff Corps. On the 21st April, Capt. Creagh was detached from Daka with two companies of his battalion, to protect the village of Kam Daka, on the Cabul River, against a threatened incursion of the Mohmands, and reached that place the same night. On the following morning, the detachment (150 men)

O'Moore Creagh.

was attacked by the Mohmands in overwhelming numbers (about 1,500); and the inhabitants of the Kam Daka having themselves taken part with the enemy, Capt. Creagh found himself under the necessity of retiring from the village. He took up a position in a cemetery not far off, which he made as defensible as circumstances would admit of, and this position he held against all the efforts of the enemy, repeatedly repulsing them with the bayonet until three o'clock in the afternoon, when he was relieved by a detachment sent for the purpose from Daka. The enemy were then finally repulsed, and being charged by a troop of the 10th Bengal Lancers, under the command of Capt. D. M. Strong, were routed and broken, and great numbers of them driven into the river. The Commander-in-Chief in India has expressed his opinion that, but for the coolness, determination, and gallantry of the highest order, and the admirable conduct which Capt. Creagh displayed on this occasion, the detachment under his command would, in all probability, have been cut off and destroyed." When peace was signed at Gandamak he returned to Ajmer with the battalion. On the renewal of hostilities in the autumn of 1879, Major Creagh volunteered for service and was ordered to Ali Khel as Orderly Officer to Brigadier-General Gordon. On arrival there, he was appointed Deputy Assistant Quartermaster-General to the Kurram Force, and subsequently Assistant Quartermaster-General. He served in Kurram from Sept. 1879, to Nov. 1880, and was Senior Officer with the force in his department. He was present when the attack on Ali Khel on 14 Oct. was repulsed, and served in the Zaimusht and Cham Kanni Expeditions. When peace was again concluded Major Creagh, who had been promoted Brigade Major, rejoined the Merwara battalion. From 1882 to 1886 he was in command of the 44th Merwara Infantry, when he was transferred to the command of the 2nd Baluchis. In 1890 he served with the Zhob Valley Expedition (Despatches), and with Kidarzai Expedition (Despatches). In 1891 he married Lilah, daughter of the late E. Read, of Kilverton, Bucks, Lady of Grace of the Order of St. John of Jerusalem. He has one daughter, M. G., married to H. Williams, Esq., C.E., and one son, Capt. D. V. Creagh, M.C. 7th (Queen's Own) Hussars, who has served throughout this war with the British Expeditionary Force in France, and is now Brigade Major of the Lancer Brigade of the Army of the Rhine. In 1895 he was appointed Adjutant-General of Division, and in 1896 Assistant Quartermaster, Bombay Command. From 1898 to 1900 he was Political Resident and General Officer Commanding at Aden. In 1900 he was appointed General Officer Commanding a Brigade and subsequently to the command of the China Field Force 1900 (Medal and Despatches) till 1903. In 1901 he was created a C.B., and the year following a K.C.B. In 1903 he was appointed Colonel of the 129th (Duke of Connaught's Own) Baluchis. In 1903 he received the Order of the Rising Sun of Japan. From 1903 to 1907 he commanded a Division, and in that year he was appointed Secretary to the Military Department at the India Office. In 1909 he was created a G.C.B. (Military), and from 1909 to 1914 he was Commander-in-Chief in India. In 1911 he was created a G.C.S.I. Sir O'Moore Creagh has been five times mentioned in Despatches, and has received the thanks of the Secretaries of State for Foreign Affairs and India. He was for twenty-eight years a regimental officer, and retired from the Army in 1914, after forty-eight and a half years' service. He was A.D.C. General to H.M. the King, and is a Knight of Grace of St. John of Jerusalem.

DALTON, JAMES, Acting-Assistant-Commissary, Commissariat and Transport Corps (now Army Service Corps), enlisted in the British Army and became Sergeant-Major before he entered the Commissary and Transport Department. Pressure of public opinion was brought to bear on the War Office, who had quite overlooked his splendid gallantry at Rorke's Drift. The facts were laid before Parliament, and many months after the Defence of the Hospital—in Nov. 1879—James Dalton was awarded the Victoria Cross [London Gazette, 17 Nov. 1879]: "James Langley Dalton, Acting-Assistant-Commissary (now Sub-Assistant), Commissariat and Transport Corps. Date of Act of Bravery: 22 Jan. 1879. For his conspicuous gallantry during the attack on Rorke's Drift Post by the Zulus on the night of the 22nd Jan. 1879, when he actively superintended the work of defence, and was amongst the foremost of those who received the first attack at the corner of the hospital, where the deadliness of his fire did great execution, and the mad rush of the Zulus met with its first check, and where, by his cool courage, he saved the life of a man of the Army Hospital Corps, by shooting the Zulu who, having seized the muzzle of the man's rifle, was in the act of assegaing him. This officer, to whose energy much of the defence of the place was due, was severely wounded during the contest, but still continued to give the same example of cool courage." He died at Portsmouth in April, 1887.

James Dalton.

London Gazette, 2 Dec. 1879.—"War Office, 29 Nov. 1879. The Queen has been graciously pleased to signify Her intention to confer the Decoration of the Victoria Cross upon the undermentioned Non-commissioned Officer of the Natal Native Contingent, whose claim has been submitted for Her Majesty's approval, for his gallant conduct during the recent operations in South Africa, as recorded against his name."

SCHIESS, F. C., Corpl., served in the Zulu War, and for his services at Rorke's Drift was awarded the Victoria Cross [London Gazette, 29 Nov. 1879]: "Schiess, Corpl., Natal Native Contingent. For conspicuous gallantry in the defence of Rorke's Drift Post on the night of the 22nd Jan. 1879, when, in spite of his having been wounded in the foot a few days previously, he greatly distinguished himself when the garrison were repulsing, with the bayonet a series of desperate assaults made by the Zulus, and displayed great activity and devoted gallantry throughout the defence. On one occasion, when the garrison had retired to the inner line of defence, and the Zulus occupied the wall of mealie bags which had been abandoned, he crept along the wall, without any order, to dislodge a Zulu who was shooting better than usual, and succeeded in killing him and two others before he, the Corporal, returned to the inner defences."

London Gazette, 9 Dec. 1879.—"War Office, 6 Dec. 1879. The Queen has been graciously pleased to signify Her intention to confer the Decoration of the Victoria Cross upon the undermentioned Officer of Her Majesty's Army, whose claim has been submitted for Her Majesty's approval, for his gallant conduct at Afghanistan, as recorded against his name."

LEACH, EDWARD PEMBERTON, Capt., was the 2nd son of Lieut.-Colonel Sir George Archibald Leach, K.C.B. (who, after serving many years in the Royal Engineers, joined the Civil Service, and eventually became Secretary to the Board of Agriculture), and of Emily Leigh, eldest daughter of Edward Leigh Pemberton, of 29, Eaton Place, and Torry Hill, Sittingbourne Kent. He was born on 2 April, 1847, at Londonderry, and educated at Highgate School and the Royal Military Academy, Woolwich He was gazetted to the Royal Engineers on 17 April, 1866, and served at Chatham till Oct. 1868, sailing for India in the following Nov. From March, 1869, to Feb. 1870, he commanded a detachment of the Bengal Sappers at Rawal Pindi, and subsequently joined the Public Works Department in Central India. In Oct. 1871, he was appointed to the Indian Survey, and served in his new capacity with the Cachar Column of the Lushai Expeditionary Force. In Nov. 1877, he went on furlough to England, but returned in 1878 as Private Secretary to Sir James Caird, K.C.B., Famine Commissioner. On the Second Afghan War breaking out, he joined the Khyber Survey Party, and, while making a survey reconnaissance in the Shinwari country with detachments of the Guides Cavalry and the 45th Sikhs, was attacked by the enemy. The following description of this encounter is given in the London Gazette of 6 Dec. 1879, when the award of his Victoria Cross was published: "Edward Pemberton Leach, Capt. (now Major), Royal Engineers. For having in action with the Shinwaris near Maidanak, Afghanistan, on the 17th March, 1879, when covering the retirement of the Survey Escort, who were carrying Lieut. Barclay, 45th Sikhs, mortally wounded, behaved with the utmost gallantry in charging, with some men of the 45th Sikhs, a very much larger number of the enemy. In this encounter Capt. Leach killed two or three of the enemy himself, and received a severe wound from an Afghan knife in the left arm. Capt. Leach's determination and gallantry in this affair, in attacking and driving back the enemy from the last position, saved the whole party from annihilation." At the end of 1879 he was invalided to England, but returned to India in the following March and joined the Kandahar Field Force, under Major-General Primrose, for survey work. In June, 1880, he made a successful reconnaissance with 150 men to Giriskht, on the Helmund, 35 miles west of Kandahar, and on the 4th July he left again for Giriskht with the force under Brigadier-General Burrows, to whom he acted as galloper at the Battle of Maiwand (horse wounded) and in the subsequent retreat to Kandahar. On his return to the latter place he was appointed Brigade Major, Royal Engineers, and was present at the final defeat of the enemy by Sir Frederick Roberts. During the course of the campaign he was four times mentioned in Despatches, and in addition to receiving the thanks of the Government was given the Brevets of Major and Lieutenant-Colonel. In 1885 he took part in the operations at Suakim; was twice mentioned in Despatches and received the C.B. for his gallantry at Tofrek Zareba, subsequently commanding a Brigade at Korosko and afterwards at Assouan (1885–86). After serving as C.R.E. in England and Halifax, he was appointed to the command of the 9th Division, 3rd Army Corps, at Belfast, and shortly after the completion of his tenure of that appointment he became Commander-in-Chief in Scotland, which post he held for four years. In 1906 he was made a K.C.V.O., and in 1909 a K.C.B. He married, in 1883, Elizabeth Mary, eldest daughter of Sir Thomas Bazley, Bart., of Hatherop Castle, Fairford, by whom he had one son and two daughters. He was promoted Lieutenant-General on 3 April, 1905; General on 31 Aug. 1910; retired on 4 Sept. 1912, and died on the 27th April, 1913, at Cadenabbia, on Lake Como, in his 67th year.

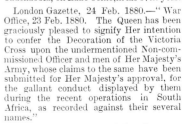

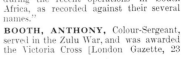

Edward P. Leach.

London Gazette, 24 Feb. 1880.—"War Office, 23 Feb. 1880. The Queen has been graciously pleased to signify Her intention to confer the Decoration of the Victoria Cross upon the undermentioned Non-commissioned Officer and men of Her Majesty's Army, whose claims to the same have been submitted for Her Majesty's approval, for the gallant conduct displayed by them during the recent operations in South Africa, as recorded against their several names."

BOOTH, ANTHONY, Colour-Sergeant, served in the Zulu War, and was awarded the Victoria Cross [London Gazette, 23

Anthony Booth.

Feb. 1880] : " Anthony Booth, Colour-Sergt., 80th Regt. Date of Act of Bravery : 12 March, 1879. For his gallant conduct, on the 12th March, 1879, during the Zulu attack on the Intombi River, in having, when considerably outnumbered by the enemy, rallied a few men on the south bank of the river, and covered the retreat of fifty soldiers and others for a distance of three miles. The officer commanding the 80th Regt. reports that, had it not been for the coolness displayed by this non-commissioned officer, not one man would have escaped."

FLAWN, THOMAS, Private, was born at Irthlingborough, Northampton-shire, on the 22nd Dec. 1857 ; son of Thomas Flawn, farm hand, and Fanny

Thomas Flawn.

Flawn. He was educated at the Church School at Finedon Northamptonshire, and enlisted on 27 Oct. 1876, at Leeds, York-shire, into the 25th King's Own Scottish Borderers. Private Flawn writes : " I volunteered to the 108th Regt., when under orders in case trouble should come with Russia in 1877. As it all passed off quietly, I volunteered to the 26th Cameronians for the Zulu War. Owing to so many young officers, General Steel, commanding at Aldershot, stopped the 26th from going—as far as the ordinary soldier knew ; I cannot say if it was so—but 600 volunteered to nine different regiments. I still meant going if possible, so I volunteered to the 94th Regt., went through the latter part of the ZuluWar and then, under the command of Sir Garnet Wolseley, to the Sekukuni Campaign, and Fitzpatrick and I saved Lieut. Dewar, of the 1st King's Dragoon Guards, who was attached to our Mounted Infantry, and we were both awarded the Victoria Cross, both of us, for the deed." Private Flawn's Victoria Cross was gazetted 23 Feb. 1880 : " Thomas Flawn, Private, 94th Foot ; Francis Fitzpatrick, Private, 94th Foot. Date of Acts of Bravery : 28 Nov. 1879. In recognition of their gallant conduct during the attack on Sekukuni's Town, on the 28th Nov. last, in carrying out of action Lieut. Dewar, 1st Dragoon Guards, when badly wounded. At the time he received his wound Lieut. Dewar had with him only Privates Flawn and Fitzpatrick, and six of the Native Contingent, and being incapable of moving without assistance, the natives proceeded to carry him down the hill, when about thirty of the enemy appeared in pursuit, about forty yards in the rear, whereupon the men of the Native Contingent deserted Lieut. Dewar, who must have been killed but for the devoted gallantry of Privates Flawn and Fitzpatrick, who carried him alternately, one covering the retreat and firing on the enemy." Private Flawn says : " Fitzpatrick and I went through the Boer War of 1881, and returned to this country in 1882, and my time came to an end—six years with the Colours." He married, 1st—the daughter of William Barley, Northamptonshire, and 2ndly—the daughter of Richard Oakley, of Eversholt, Bedfordshire.

FITZPATRICK, FRANCIS, Private, joined the 94th Regt. (2nd Battn. The Connaught Rangers), served in the Zulu War and was awarded the Victoria Cross [London Gazette, 23 Feb. 1880] : " Thomas Flawn, Private ;

Francis Fitzpatrick

Francis Fitzpatrick, Private, 94th Foot. Date of Acts of Bravery : 28 Nov. 1879. In recognition of their gallant conduct during the attack on Sekukuni's Town, on the 28th Nov. last, in carrying out of action Lieut. Dewar, 1st Dragoon Guards, when badly wounded. At the time when he received his wound Lieut. Dewar had with him only Privates Flawn and Fitzpatrick, and six of the Native Contingent, and, being incapable of moving without assist-ance, the natives proceeded to carry him down the hill, when about thirty of the enemy appeared in pursuit, about forty yards in the rear, whereupon the men of the Native Contingent deserted Lieut. Dewar, who must have been killed but for the devoted gallantry of Privates Flawn and Fitzpatrick, who carried him alter-nately, one covering the retreat and firing on the enemy." Sekukuni's Town was the stronghold of a Native Chief in South Africa. It caused us much trouble until it was reduced long after the Zulu War was ended. Private Fitzpatrick served through the Boer War of 1881, and returned to England in 1882. He was discharged from the Duke of Cornwall's Light Infantry on the 10th May, 1888.

London Gazette, 13 April, 1880.—" War Office, 12 April, 1880. The Queen has been graciously pleased to signify Her intention to confer the Decoration of the Victoria Cross upon the undermentioned Soldier of Her Majesty's Army, whose claim has been submitted for Her Majesty's approval, for his meritorious conduct at Moirosi's Mountain on the 8th April, 1879, as recorded against his name."

BROWN, PETER, Trooper, served in the Zulu War, and was awarded the Victoria Cross [London Gazette, 12 April, 1880] : " Peter Brown, Trooper, Cape Mounted Rifles. Trooper P. Brown, during the assault on Moirosi's Mountain on the 8th April, 1879, whilst lying under cover waiting for the order to recommence the advance, heard two men, who had been wounded some time before, crying out for water. Trooper Brown carried a water-bottle to these men under a heavy fire, to an adjacent rock to which they had crept for shelter. Whilst giving the first man water he was wounded severely in the right thigh, and immediately afterwards a bullet shattered

his right arm, the use of which he has never recovered." Colonel E. B. Hartley, V.C., says : " Private Peter Brown was awarded the Victoria Cross for most conspicuous bravery at the unsuccessful attack on Moirosi's Moun-tain, Basutoland, South Africa, on 8 April, 1879. He was all day carrying water to his wounded comrades, who were lying about among the rocks, during which he was wounded in the forearm, smashing the bone ; he was also wounded in the leg, and did not cease his efforts until his water-bottle became useless through being shot through. All this took place within a couple of hundred yards of the enemy, who were briskly firing from redoubts up the sides of the mountain. Private Brown had to retire on pension on account of his wounds, but unfortunately did not live many years to enjoy it." Sir Evelyn Wood tells us, in " From Midshipman to Field-Marshal," how he sent Trooper Brown, V.C., with the Zulu who had assegaied Captain Barton, to find the body of the latter, and the savage went straight to the spot fourteen months after he had killed Captain Barton. Trooper Brown buried the body." Peter Brown died on the 11th Sept. 1894. His Victoria Cross was sold in Aug. 1895. The following is an extract from the " Argus " (Cape), Aug. 1895 : " At a recent Parade Sale, Trooper Brown's Victoria Cross, together with the '77, '78 and '79 War Medal and clasp, were put up to auction and knocked down to a bidder at twenty-five shillings. Twenty-five shillings was the exact price of the rarest distinction that can be con-ferred on a Briton for doing his duty on the field of battle. The purchaser—a Captain in the Cape Town Highlanders, who says he would give his own right hand for such a distinction—purposes presenting the Cross and Medal to the Commanding Officer of the Cape Mounted Rifles, and in so doing he is taking the only right and proper course. The little story is its own moral, and we leave our readers to follow out the reflections which it may awaken. Of one thing we may be certain, that the dead Trooper's Cross and Medal will not again come beneath the hammer of the auctioneer. The Com-manding Officer of the Cape Mounted Rifles will see to that."

London Gazette, 11 May, 1880.—" War Office, 8 May, 1880. The Queen has been graciously pleased to signify Her intention to confer the Decora-tion of the Victoria Cross upon the undermentioned Officer, whose claim to the same has been submitted for Her Majesty's approval, for his gallant conduct at Konoma, on the Eastern Frontier of India, as recorded against his name."

RIDGEWAY, RICHARD KIRBY, Capt., was born at Oldcastle, County Meath, Ireland, 18 Aug. 1848 ; 2nd son of R. Ridgeway, Esq., F.R.C.S., and Annette, daughter of R. Adams, Esq., of Cavanagh, County Cavan. He

Richard K. Ridgeway

was educated at a private school, and at the Royal Military College, Sandhurst, and was gazetted to the 96th Regt. as Ensign on 8 Jan. 1868, and became Lieu-tenant 14 Feb. 1870. In 1871 he married Emily Maria (Amy), daughter of S. W. Fallan. She died in July, 1917. He was transferred to the Indian Staff Corps in 1872, and was Adjutant, 44th Gurkha Rifles, from 1874 to 1880. In 1875 he served in the Naga Hills Expedition (Despatches), and in 1879 and 1880 in the Second Naga Hills Expedition ; was severely wounded and mentioned in Despatches ; received the Medal and clasp, and was awarded the Victoria Cross [Lon-don Gazette, 11 May, 1880] : " Richard Kirby Ridgeway, Capt., Bengal Staff Corps. For conspicuous gallantry through-out the attack on Konoma, on the 22nd Nov. 1879, more especially in the final assault, when, under a heavy fire from the enemy, he rushed up to a barricade and attempted to tear down the planking surrounding it, to enable him to effect an entrance, in which act he received a very severe rifle-shot wound in the left shoulder." He had become Captain, Indian Staff Corps, 8 Jan. 1880. Captain Ridgeway passed the Staff College in 1883 ; became D.A.Q.M.G. 1884 ; Major, 1888 ; A.Q.M.G., Army Head-quarters, India, 1889-90 ; commanded the 44th Gurkha Rifles 1891-95 ; took part in the Manipur Expedition 1891 (clasp ; Despatches) : was promoted to Lieutenant-Colonel in 1894 ; was A.Q.M.G., Army Headquar-ters, India, 1895-98, and became Colonel in 1898 ; served in the Tirah Campaign as A.A.G., 2nd Division, 1897 (Medal and three clasps) ; was A.A.G., Peshawar, 1898-1900. Colonel Ridgeway was created a C.B. in 1905 ; he retired in 1906.

London Gazette, 1 Oct. 1880.—" War Office, 1 Oct. 1880. The Queen has been graciously pleased to signify Her intention to confer the Decoration of the Victoria Cross upon the undermentioned Officer of the Cape Mounted Riflemen,whose claim has been submitted for Her Majesty's approval, for his gallant conduct during the recent operations in South Africa, as recorded against his name."

SCOTT, ROBERT GEORGE, Sergt., was born at Whittlesea, near Peterborough, on 22 April, 1857. He was the son of the late Robert Charles Scott, Fleet-Surgeon, Royal Navy, and of the late Mary Eliza-beth Scott, daughter of the late Rev. Richard Sinclair. He was educated at Epsom College and Aberdeen Grammar School, and joined the Cape Mounted Rifles on the 26th Sept. 1876. He served as a

Robert George Scott.

Cape Mounted Rifleman in 1876, 1877, 1878 and 1879, in the regular South African forces, but afterwards always as a volunteer, and raised corps as required. He served in the Zulu War, received the Medal, and was awarded the Victoria Cross [London Gazette, 1 Oct. 1880]: Robert George Scott, Sergt., Cape Mounted Rifles. For conspicuous gallantry and devotion during an attack on Moirosi's Mountain, on the 8th April, 1879, in volunteering to throw time-fuse shells as hand grenades over a line of stone barricades from behind which the enemy were bringing a heavy fire to bear on the colonial troops, and which it was impossible effectually to return. After causing all the men of his party to retire under cover—lest the shell burst prematurely—by which precaution many lives were in all probability saved, Sergt. Scott advanced in the most deliberate manner under a heavy fire, and, having got under the wall, made two attempts to throw shells over it. At the second attempt, owing to some defect in the fuse which he had just lighted, the shell exploded almost in Sergt. Scott's hands, blowing his right hand to pieces and wounding him severely in the left leg." On 8 April, 1884, at Kimberley, South Africa, he married Constance Mary, daughter of the late Lieut.-Colonel C. A. Daniell, and their children are Dulcie Mary ; John Dayrell Sinclair ; Robert Falkines Sinclair, born 1893, and Guy Sinclair, born 1896. Sergt. Scott became Lieutenant, Cape Mounted Rifles, in Sept. 1879. Major Scott served in the South African War of 1899–1902, with the Kimberley Light Horse ; was mentioned in Despatches ; received the Queen's Medal with three clasps, the King's Medal with two clasps, and was created a Companion of the Distinguished Service Order [London Gazette, 27 Sept. 1901]: " Robert George Scott, Major, Kimberley Light Horse." Lieut.-Colonel Scott said : " I have no knowledge of anything I did to deserve this honour, but think it was for general services during the South African War. It was awarded to me after the declaration of peace." In the European War Lieut.-Colonel Scott commanded the Kimberley Commando on the borders of German South-West Africa during the Cape Rebellion, and later commanded the Veteran Regiment. These latter services were in 1914 and 1915. He died at Cape Town on 3 Oct. 1917.

London Gazette, 17 May, 1881.—" War Office, 16 May, 1881. The Queen has been graciously pleased to signify Her intention to confer the Decoration of the Victoria Cross upon the undermentioned Officer, Non-commissioned Officer and Soldiers of Her Majesty's Army, whose claims have been submitted for Her Majesty's approval, for their gallant conduct during the recent operations in Afghanistan and South Africa, as recorded against their names."

SARTORIUS, EUSTON HENRY, Capt., was born at Cintra, Portugal, in 1884 ; the third son of the late Admiral of the Fleet Sir G. Sartorius, G.C.B. He was educated at Woolwich, and at the Royal Military College,

Euston H. Sartorius.

Sandhurst, and was gazetted to an Ensigncy in the 59th Foot. He became Lieutenant in July, 1865. On 29 June, 1869, Lieut. Sartorius received the Humane Society's Medal for saving the lives of three girls at Broadstairs. In Dec. 1870 he passed the examination at the Staff College, and subsequently for a period of four years served as Instructor in Military Surveying at the Royal Military College, Sandhurst. In 1874 he married Emily (died Jan. 1915), daughter of Sir F. Cook, 1st Bart. He has two daughters, and his only son died from wounds in April, 1915. When proceeding in 1874 to join his regiment in India, Capt. Sartorius travelled for a year, *en route*, in Persia, where he added largely to his experiences and gained much valuable information. In the Afghan War he com-

manded the company of the 59th which escorted the guns of Battery D/2, Royal Artillery, from Quetta to Kandahar, and afterwards served with the regiment in the advance to and capture of Kalat-i-Ghilzai in Jan. 1879. He was present—when acting as Assistant Field Engineer—at the subsequent occupation of that place in Oct. 1879. Major Sartorius was in command of the company which took part in the advance of Brigadier-General Hughes' force in Tazi. At the action of Shahjui on the 24th Oct. 1879, he commanded the detachment of his regiment which was present, and for his services in leading an attack on and taking a hill in the possession of the Ghilzais on that day received the Victoria Cross, as described in the London Gazette of 17 May, 1881 : " Euston Henry Sartorius, Capt. (now Brevet Major), 59th Regt. Date of Act of Bravery : 24 Oct. 1879. For conspicuous bravery, during the action at Shahjui, on the 24th Oct. 1879, in leading a party of five or six men of the 59th Regt. against a body of the enemy, of unknown strength, occupying an almost inaccessible position on the top of a precipitous hill. The nature of the ground made any sort of regular formation impossible, and Capt. Sartorius had to bear the first brunt of the attack from the whole body of the enemy, who fell upon him and his men as they gained the top of the precipitous pathway ; but the gallant and determined bearing of this officer, emulated as it was by his men, led to the most perfect success, and the surviving occupants of the hill-top, seven in number, were all killed. In this encounter Capt. Sartorius was wounded by sword-cuts in both hands, and one of his men was killed." In addition to being twice mentioned in Despatches, Major Sartorius was specially commended for his " excellent work and gallant conduct " in connection with the Survey Department, in the Report of the Proceedings of the Government of India in the Home Revenue and Agricultural Department, bearing date 17 May, 1880, and was thanked by the Indian Government. From the wounds he received in the action of Shahjui he partially lost the use of his left hand. He was D.A.A.G. and D.A.Q.M.G. at Aldershot in 1880 ; served in the

Egyptian Campaign in 1882 as D.A.A.G., was mentioned in Despatches, received the Order of the Osmanieh and the Brevet of Lieutenant-Colonel. He was C.S.O., Portsmouth ; Military Attaché, Japan, and was created a C.B. in 1896. Colonel Sartorius was attached to the Crown Prince of Siam at the celebration of Her Majesty's Jubilee and at the Coronation of King Edward. Major-General Sartorius was attached to Prince Chaterabhong of Siam at the Coronation of King George. While in Portugal he bears the title of Conde di Penhafirme.

MULLANE, PATRICK, Sergt., served in the Afghan War, and was awarded the Victoria Cross [London Gazette, 17 May, 1881]: " Patrick Mullane, Sergt., Royal Horse Artillery. Date of Act of Bravery : 27 July, 1880. For conspicuous bravery during the action of Maiwand, on the 27th July, 1880, in endeavouring to save the life of Driver Pickwell Istead. This non-commissioned officer, when the battery to which he belonged was on the point of retiring, and the enemy were within ten or fifteen yards, unhesitatingly ran back about two yards and picked up Driver Istead, placed him on the limber, where, unfortunately, he died almost immediately. Again, during the retreat, Sergt. Mullane volunteered to procure water for the wounded, and suc-

Patrick Mullane.

ceeded in doing so by going into one of the villages in which so many men lost their lives." He became Sergeant-Major and was discharged on pension.

COLLIS, JAMES, Gunner, was born at Cambridge in 1860 ; enlisted in the Royal Horse Artillery ; served in the Afghan War, and was awarded the Victoria Cross [London Gazette, 17 May, 1881]: " James Collis, Gunner, Royal Horse Artillery. Date of Act of Bravery : 28 July, 1880. For conspicuous bravery during the retreat from Maiwand to Kandahar, on the 28th July, 1880, when the officer commanding the battery was endeavouring to bring in a limber, with wounded men, under a cross-fire, in running forward and drawing the enemy's fire on himself, thus taking off their attention from the limber." Collis's Victoria Cross was presented to him on Poona Race Course by Sir Frederick Roberts. He remained in the Royal Horse Artillery, C Battery, B Brigade, until 1881, when he joined the Bombay Police ; returned to England and remained there until 1888, when he re-enlisted and went to India. He was invalided home and discharged at Netley Hospital. In 1893 he entered Charing Cross Hospital with rheumatic fever ; spent three months there, and until 1907 was employed as a carman.

FARMER, JOSEPH JOHN, L.-Corpl., served in the Transvaal Campaign, in 1881, and was awarded the Victoria Cross [London Gazette, 17 May, 1881]: " Joseph John Farmer, Provisional L.-Corpl., Army Hospital Corps. Date of Act of Bravery : 27 Feb. 1881. For conspicuous bravery during the engagements with the Boers at the Majuba Mountain, on the 27th Feb. 1881, when he showed a spirit of self-abnegation and an example of cool courage which cannot be too highly commended. While the Boers closed with the British troops near the Wells, Corpl. Farmer held a white flag over the wounded, and when the arm holding the flag was shot through, he called out that he had ' another.' He then raised the flag with the other arm, and continued to do so until that also was shot through." Joseph John Farmer was born in London 5 May, 1854. His Cross was presented to him by Queen Victoria at Osborne on 9 Aug. 1881. Owing to his wounds he left the Service and later followed the occupation of a house-painter in London.

London Gazette, 3 June, 1881.—" War Office, 2 June, 1881. The Queen has been graciously pleased to signify Her intention to confer the Decoration of the Victoria Cross upon the undermentioned Officer of Her Majesty's Army, whose claim has been submitted for Her Majesty's approval, for his gallant conduct in Afghanistan, as recorded against his name."

WHITE, GEORGE STUART, Major, was born 6 July, 1835, at Rock Castle, Portstewart, County Antrim, Ireland ; son of James Robert White, Esq., of Whitehall, Broughshane, County Antrim, and Frances Stuart, of

George Stuart White.

Dinaghy, County Tyrone. He was educated at King William's College, Isle of Man, and at Sandhurst, and was gazetted to Ensign into the 27th Inniskilling Fusiliers in Nov. 1853, with which regiment he served in the Indian Mutiny, 1857–9, and was actively employed on the North West Frontier (Medal) ; having become Lieutenant in Jan. 1855. He was promoted Captain into the Gordon Highlanders in 1863, and became Major in 1873. Major White married in Simla, on 31 Oct. 1874, Amy, daughter of the Ven. Joseph Baly, Archdeacon of Calcutta, and their children were : Rose Frances ; James Robert (born 1879) ; May Constance ; Amy Gladys Stuart, and Georgina Mary. Miss Gladys White married, in 1917, the Hon. A. E. A. Napier, son of the late Field-

Marshal Lord Napier of Magdala. Major White took part with his regiment, the 92nd Highlanders, in Oct. 1879, in the advance of the Division on Kabul, and commanded the right attack at the action of Charasiah on the 6th of the month, for his gallantry on which occasion he was awarded the Victoria Cross [London Gazette, 3 June, 1881]: " George Stuart White,

Major (now Brevet Lieutenant-Colonel), 92nd Regt. (Gordon Highlanders). Date of Act of Bravery: 6 Oct. 1879. For conspicuous bravery during the engagement at Charasiah, on the 6th Oct. 1879, when, finding that the artillery and rifle fire failed to dislodge the enemy from a fortified hill which it was necessary to capture, Major White led an attack on it in person. Advancing with two companies of his regiment, and climbing from one steep ledge to another, he came upon a body of the enemy strongly posted and outnumbering his force by about eight to one. His men being much exhausted and immediate action being necessary, Major White took a rifle and, going on by himself, shot the leader of the enemy. This act so intimidated the rest that they fled round the side of the hill, and the position was won. Again, on the 1st Sept. 1880, at the Battle of Kandahar, Major White, in leading the final charge under a heavy fire from the enemy, who held a strong position and were supported by two guns, rode straight up to within a few yards of them, and seeing the guns, dashed forward and secured one, immediately after which the enemy retired." He was present at the pursuit of the enemy on the 8th Oct., and the occupation of the capital; commanded the regiment in the expedition to Niardan, under Brigadier-General Baker in Nov.; served in the operations round Kabul in Dec., commanding four companies of the 92nd in the brilliant assault and capture of the Takht-i-Shah, and being present at the action on the 23rd; again at the action of Childuktean on the 25th April, 1880, commanding a wing of the regiment; and after taking part in the memorable march of the relieving force from Kabul to Kandahar was present at the reconnaissance on the 31st Aug. and the crowning defeat in Sept. (Shadbolt's "Afghan Campaigns"). His brilliant services in the Afghan War caused him to be frequently singled out for commendation in Despatches, and he received the Brevet of Lieutenant-Colonel (1881), and was awarded a C.B. (Medal with three clasps, and Kabul-Kandahar Bronze Star). In 1881 he was Military Secretary to the Viceroy of India; took part in the Nile Expedition, 1884. He was A.Q.M.G. in Egypt during the Khartoum Relief Expedition; became Colonel 1885; in command of a brigade in Burma 1885–6, being promoted Major-General for his distinguished services, and thanked by the Indian Government. He was in command of the Zhob Expedition, and subsequently Commander-in-Chief in India from 1893–8; became Lieutenant-General 1895; Q.M.G. to the Forces 1898–9. During the Boer War, about from the outbreak of hostilities until the Relief by General Sir Redvers Buller, he commanded the Garrison of Ladysmith, holding out against terrific odds, heavier armaments, and the privations and disease of a severe siege of 119 days (2 Nov. 1899, to 1 March, 1900). Just before the war he had had an accident to his leg, and Lord Wolseley told him that he was afraid his lameness must keep him from the front. "I beg your pardon, sir," was the reply, "my leg is well enough for anything except running away." He said after the Relief, "Thank God we kept the flag flying!" In 1900 he became Governor of Gibraltar, and in 1903 was promoted to the rank of Field-Marshal. Field-Marshal Sir George Stuart White, V.C., G.C.B., O.M., G.C.S.I., G.C.M.G., G.C.I.E., G.C.V.O., Colonel, Gordon Highlanders, died on 24 June, 1912, at Chelsea Hospital, of which he was Governor. The funeral procession passed from Chelsea to Euston amidst signs of universal sorrow. Among the regiments that escorted the gun-carriage was the Gordon Highlanders, of which he was Colonel, and the 27th Inniskilling Fusiliers, in which he held his first commission.

London Gazette, 28 June, 1881.—"The Queen has been graciously pleased to signify Her intention to confer the Decoration of the Victoria Cross upon the undermentioned Officer, whose claim has been submitted for Her Majesty's approval, for his conspicuous bravery in South Africa, as recorded against his name."

McCREA, JOHN FREDERICK, Surgeon, was born at St. Peter's Port, Guernsey. He became M.R.C.S., England, 1878, and M.R.C.S., Edinburgh, 1878; joined the 1st Regt., Cape Yeomanry, in Aug. 1880, as Surgeon, and marched with it to Basutoland. He was one of the few who escaped from the unexpected attack of the Basuto Cavalry on his regiment whilst proceeding to relieve Colonel Carrington (afterwards Major-General Sir F. Carrington, K.C.B.), who with 200 Cape Mounted Rifles had been besieged for six weeks at Mafeteng. In the early part of Jan. 1881, Colonel Carrington was again heavily engaged by the Basutos at Tweefontein, and there were numerous casualties. Surgeon McCrea was the only doctor present, and notwithstanding a serious wound on the breast-bone, which he plugged himself with lint, he most gallantly took into shelter the wounded, and throughout the rest of the day dressed all the men who required attention. He was awarded the V.C., promoted Surgeon-Major and transferred to the Cape Mounted Rifles. His Victoria Cross was gazetted, 28 June, 1881: "John Frederick McCrea, Surgeon, 1st Regt., Cape Mounted Infantry. For his conspicuous bravery during the severely contested engagement with the Basutos, on the 14th Jan. 1881, at Tweefontein, near Thaba Tsen, when after the enemy had charged the burghers in the most determined manner, forcing them to retire with a loss of sixteen killed and twenty-one wounded, Surgeon McCrea went out for some distance, under a heavy fire, and, with the assistance of Capt. Buxton, of the Mafeteng Contingent, conveyed a wounded burgher named Aircamp to the shelter of a large ant-heap, and, having placed him in a position of safety, returned to the ambulance for a stretcher. Whilst on his way thither Surgeon McCrea was severely wounded in the right breast by a bullet, notwithstanding which he continued afterwards to attend the wounded during the remainder of the day, and scarcely taking time to dress his own wound, which he was obliged to do himself, there being no other medical officer in the field. Had it not been for this gallantry and devotion to his duty on the part of Surgeon McCrea, the sufferings of the wounded would undoubtedly have been much aggravated and greater loss of life might very probably have ensued." He died in 1894 of heart failure at Kokstad, East Griqualand, whilst performing his regimental duties. There is probably a unique incident in the case of Surgeon-Major McCrea's V.C., as it was the only decoration or medal he wore, the Basuto War Medal not being issued until twenty years after the termination of the war.

London Gazette, 26 Aug. 1881.—"War Office, 24 Aug. 1881. The Queen having been graciously pleased, by Warrant under Her Royal Sign Manual, bearing date the 6th Aug. 1881, to direct that the Decoration of the Victoria Cross shall be conferred on the Members of the Indian Ecclesiastical Establishments who may be qualified to receive the same, in accordance with rules and ordinances made and ordained for the Government thereof, provided that it may be established in any case that the person was serving under the orders of a General or other Officer in Command of Troops in the Field when he performed the Act of Bravery for which it is proposed to confer the Decoration—Her Majesty has accordingly been pleased to signify Her intention to confer this high distinction on the undermentioned gentleman, whose claim has been submitted for Her Majesty's approval, on account of his conspicuous bravery in Afghanistan, as recorded against his name."

ADAMS, JAMES WILLIAMS, The Rev. was born at Cork in 1839, son of Thomas O'Brion Adams, J.P., of Cork, and Elizabeth Williams (who belonged to a Scotch family). He was educated at Hamlin and Porter's School, Cork, and at Trinity College, Dublin, where he took his B.A. degree. Colonel Vibart says in a Memoir of Mr. Adams: "He always was considered the strongest man in Ireland, excelled in all forms of athletics and vied with his friend, Colonel Fred Burnaby, in his gymnastic feats. He was also a fine horseman. Was ordained deacon in 1863 and priest in 1864, and was curate to the Rev. J. Warren at Hyde, Hampshire, till 1866, when he made up his mind to go out to India, and became Chaplain of the Bengal Establishment, under Bishop Milman, in Oct. 1866, at Calcutta. Here he had a very severe attack of fever and was sent on sick leave to Ceylon. On his recovery he was appointed to Peshawar, always his favourite station, and he did much work among the large number of troops stationed there and on the frontier. He was indefatigable in visiting the out-stations at Nowshera and Kohat, and after the Sunday duty at Peshawar would ride out at night to one or other of these stations and take the service there next morning. He did much in restoring and beautifying the church and the cemetery at Peshawar, and he received the thanks of the Government for his exertions in the cholera camps during the terrible outbreaks. He was moved to Allahabad in March, 1870, and returned to Peshawar in Dec. of that year, and then was appointed to the Camp of Exercise at Hassan Abdul, Army Headquarters (Dec. 1872, to March, 1873), and was later sent to Kashmir on special duty in March, 1874. Here he built, in great part with his own hands, a much-needed church of pine logs, where services were frequently held for the numerous visitors to Gulmerg and Soonamerg. Some years later permission was given to some travellers to stable their horses in the church, with the result that the syces' fires burnt the building down. Mr. Adams was appointed in Jan. 1876, to Meerut, and in Dec. of that year was summoned to take charge of the Cavalry and Artillery Camp for the Delhi Durbar assemblage, on the occasion of the Prince of Wales' visit. He was Chaplain of Chakrata in Jan. 1877, and of Jubbulpore and Allahabad in 1878. In Nov. of that year he was summoned to join the Kurram Field Force, and he accompanied the Kabul Field Force under Sir Donald Stewart and Sir Frederick Roberts. He took part in the march of the latter from Kabul to Kandahar, and was present at the engagements of Kandahar, Kabul, Charasia and Peiwar Kotal. Mrs. Adams writes: "I have heard Lord Roberts speak of the invaluable help rendered him in the Peiwar Kotal action by my husband, acting as an A.D.C., in recovering a large body of troops, who had gone astray in the forest, at a very critical time." Lord Roberts describes this incident in his "Forty-one Years in India." He risked his life at Killa Kazi, 11 Dec. 1879, to rescue some of the 9th Lancers who were struggling beneath their horses in a nullah, and succeeded, though up to his waist in water, in dragging them free, the Afghans having meanwhile advanced quite close to the spot. For this Sir Frederick Roberts recommenced him for the Victoria Cross, but it was pronounced to be an impossibility that it should be given him, as it was a decoration for the Army and Navy only. But in the London Gazette of 24 Aug. 1881, it was announced that "the Queen had been pleased by Royal Warrant to direct that the Victoria Cross should be conferred on members of the Indian Ecclesiastical Establishments who might be qualified, etc., etc., etc., and accordingly to signify Her intention to confer this high distinction on the Rev. J. W. Adams, whose claim had been submitted for her approval, on account of conspicuous bravery in Afghanistan, etc." He was accordingly awarded the Victoria Cross [London Gazette, 26 Aug. 1881]: "The Reverend James Williams Adams, (late) Chaplain to the Kabul Field Force. Date of Act of Bravery: 11 Dec. 1879. During the action at Killa Kazi, on the 11th Dec. 1879, some men of the 9th Lancers having fallen, with their horses, into a wide and deep 'nullah,' or ditch, and the enemy being close upon them, the Rev. J. W. Adams rushed into the water (which filled the ditch), dragged the horses from off the men, upon whom they were lying, and extricated them, he being at the time under a heavy fire and up to his waist in water. At this time the Afghans were pressing on very rapidly, the leading men getting within a few yards of Mr. Adams, who, having let go his horse in order to render more effectual assistance, had eventually to escape on foot." Besides the Victoria Cross, Mr. Adams received the Bronze Star for the Kabul to Kandahar March, and the Afghan Medal with four clasps for Kandahar, Kabul, Charasia and Peiwar Kotal. Mr. Adams was

James W. Adams.

personally decorated with the Victoria Cross by Queen Victoria just before his return to India, at the end of his first and only furlough home, during which he had (16 Aug. 1881, at Iver Heath, Bucks), married Alice Mary, daughter of the late General Sir Thomas Willshire, G.C.B., District Commissioner, British East Africa. Mr. Adams was appointed on reaching India to Lucknow Cantonments, and remained there a year, during which, on 10 Aug., his only child, Edith Juliet Mary, was born. She married on 27 Oct. 1910, Geoffrey A. Stafford Northcote, District Commissioner, British East Africa. In Feb. 1883, he was sent up to Naini Tal, a two years' appointment, and was instrumental there in the erection of the beautiful east window and alabaster and gold mosaic reredos, put up in memory of those who had perished in the great landslip. At the petition of the station, he was given an additional year at Naini Tal, and then sent to Meerut, but trouble having arisen in Burma, Lord Roberts applied for him to accompany the Field Force sent up the country, and he took part in the operations there, receiving the Medal with one clasp. In 1886 his term of 20 years' service in India having come to an end, he returned to England, and was given by Lord Rosebery the living of Postwick, near Norwich, where he remained till 1894, when, his health having failed, he had to resign the living, and went abroad, to Jersey, for two years' rest. He then accepted the living of Stow Bardolph with Wimbotsham, near Downham Market, offered him by Sir Thomas Hare, and spent several happy years there; but he suffered more and more from the effects of habitual overwork, which nothing would induce him to relax, even after a long attack of illness. At the age of 60 he was holding five services and preaching three sermons every Sunday, as he hired a schoolroom in the Fen district of the parish, where he held a service in the afternoon for those at a distance from either of the other two churches. In 1902 he was obliged to resign, and left Stow for a small living of Lord Downe's, Ashwell, near Oakham, where there was only one church. But it was too late. Neuritis attacked him in the muscles of both arms, and caused him most acute suffering for the remainder of his life—all remedies proving unavailing, till it ended in partial paralysis, and after lingering a month, conscious, and most patient and calm, he died 20 Oct. 1903. He received from King Edward a most kind autograph letter, and from the Queen, then in Denmark, a long telegram of sympathy, and His Majesty was represented at the funeral at Ashwell, on 24 Oct., by Canon Hervey. Lord Roberts was also present. Mr. Adams was appointed in 1900 Honorary Chaplain to Queen Victoria, and King Edward made him Chaplain in Ordinary in 1901. As Chaplain he took part in the Coronation ceremonial of June, 1902, and walked in the Procession. On the 30th June, 1903, his University had conferred on him—at the same time as on Lord Roberts—the honorary degree of M.A. Three brass tablets have been erected in memory of him, one by Sir Thomas Hare, in Stow Bardolph Church; another by Lord Roberts in the little church built in the Fens as a memorial in place of the schoolroom that he used to hire for services; and the third is a large brass in Peshawar Church, put up in 1910 by surviving friends who had known "Padre Adams" in Peshawar or during the Afghan War. Mr. W. Lane wrote of Mr. Adams: "His generous, kindly, and benevolent disposition endeared him to all who knew him. He was the idol of the soldiers among whom he worked, and worked well, for many years, and who always looked on him as their best friend and counsellor. Cork has had many distinguished sons; to none of their memories can she point with more pride than to that of 'Parson Adams.'"

London Gazette, 7 Oct. 1881.—"War Office, 4 Oct. 1881. The Queen has been graciously pleased to signify Her intention to confer the Decoration of the Victoria Cross upon the undermentioned Officers and Soldier, whose claims have been submitted for Her Majesty's approval, for their conspicuous gallantry during the recent operations in South Africa (Basutoland), and in Afghanistan, as recorded against their names."

HARTLEY, EDMUND BARON, Major, was born at Ivybridge, South Devon, the eldest son of the late Dr. Edmund Hartley, and received his medical education at St. George's Hospital, London, where he took the Diplomas of M.R.C.S., England, and L.R.C.P., Edinburgh. Previous to this, from 1867 to 1869, he was a clerk in H.M. Inland Revenue, but resigned his appointment to take up the medical profession. In the year 1874 Mr. Hartley went to South Africa, and was soon appointed District Surgeon of British Basutoland, being the first English medical man in that country. His experiences among the natives and the Boer farmers were very interesting and uncommon, the country being little known in those days and little understood. He remained there until 1877, when native wars broke out on the south-eastern frontiers of the Cape Colony, and he immediately volunteered for service, and was appointed Surgeon of the Frontier Armed Mounted Police; the title of the Corps was changed to Cape Mounted Riflemen in Aug. 1878, and it has been again changed to South African Mounted Riflemen, and is the only regular corps—as it has always been—belonging to the Cape. Surgeon Hartley's first experience of warfare was as medical officer of a column composed of Naval Brigade, 1/24th Regt. and Connaught Rangers (88th Regt.), operating against the Galeeka tribe. In the next year, 1878, came the Gaika campaign, when Hartley was appointed Principal Medical Officer of the Cape Colonial Forces, and continued as such until his retirement in 1903. In 1879 occurred the Moirosi Rebellion, when Surgeon Hartley was mentioned in Despatches, received the Medal and clasps, and was awarded the Victoria Cross [London Gazette, 7 Oct. 1881]: "Edmund Baron Hartley, Surgeon-Major, Cape Mounted Rifles. For conspicuous gallantry displayed by him in attending the wounded, under fire, at the unsuccessful attack on Moirosi's Mountain, in Basutoland, on the 5th June, 1879; and for having proceeded into the open ground, under a heavy fire, and carried in his arms, from an exposed position, Corpl. A. Jones, of the Capt Mounted Riflemen, who was wounded. The Surgeon-Major then returned, under the severe fire of the enemy, in order to dress the wounds of other men of the storming party." Sergt. R. Scott (now Lieut.-Colonel Scott, D.S.O.) and Private Peter Brown, both of the Capt Mounted Rifles, had already gained the Victoria Cross at the same mountain, two months earlier and on the same ground. In 1880 and 1881 Surgeon-Major Hartley served in the Basuto Campaign (twice mentioned in Despatches). In 1882–3, during the ten months General C. E. Gordon (Khartoum) commanded the Colonial Forces, Colonel Hartley was his Principal Medical Officer, and received many acts of great kindness from him. In 1897 he served in the Bechuanaland Rebellion, where he was slightly wounded whilst dressing a mortally wounded officer (Despatches and Medal). He served throughout the Boer War 1899–1900–1901–1902. He was, first, in command of the Bearer Company of the Highland Brigade at the Battle of Magersfontein, and of the affair at Enslin. Later he was Principal Medical Officer of the Colonial Division (Despatches, Queen's and King's Medals and clasps, and C.M.G.). Colonel Hartley was founder and late Colonel Commanding Cape Medical Corps (now South African Medical Corps and lately engaged in its fourth campaign: Bechuanaland, Boer, South-West Africa, France), and is a Knight of Grace of St. John of Jerusalem, and has given much time and labour to ambulance work both at the Cape and in England. He was Commandant of six Voluntary Aid Detachments in Somersetshire in 1910–11–12, and served as Secretary, Voluntary Aid Hospital, Seaton, Devon, during the European war. Colonel Hartley died on 20 March, 1919.

Edmund B. Hartley.

CHASE, WILLIAM ST. LUCIEN, Lieut., was born at St. Lucia, West Indies, eldest son of the late Capt. R. H. Chase, Commissary of Ordnance (died, 1873) and Susan Ifill, daughter of John Buhott. He was educated privately, and entered the Army in 1875, being gazetted in the month of Sept. of that year to Her Majesty's 15th Foot. He did duty with the Headquarters of his regiment in India for two years, passed with distinction the necessary examinations, and was admitted to the Bombay Staff Corps. He did duty successively at Poona, Almadabad, Baroda and Surat. In the Afghan War he served with the 28th Bombay Native Infantry and accompanied the Headquarters of that regiment—a constituent of the Kandahar Field Force—in Jan. 1888, to Chaman, from whence, after the massacre of Major Waudby and his party in May, 1880, he was subsequently detached to the command of the post of Gatai. He was present with the 28th Native Infantry throughout the defence of Kandahar, and took part with the four companies in that ill-fated sortie to Deh Khwaja, when the casualties of the regiment included Lieut.-Col. Newport and thirty rank and file killed, and Lieut.-Col. Nimmo (commanding) and twenty rank and file wounded. "Many gallant deeds," wrote the late Lieut.-Col. A. G. Daubeny, 7th Fusiliers, giving in a private letter a thrilling account of the affair, "were done on that day. Thus, while holding our ground to cover the retreat of the stragglers or wounded, an officer, Lieut. Chase, was suddenly seen coming towards us from the block-house, with a wounded soldier on his back, and attended by a fusilier. The enemy had also seen him, and turned their fire on him. A few yards and he is down, and all thought he was done for. Not so; he only wanted breath; and, jumping up, he brought his man in amid a shower of bullets and the cheers of our men." The Rev. A. G. Cane, late Chaplain to the Force, says: "I soon had my attention directed to a man leaving one of the Ziarets with another on his back. He was then, I suppose, about 400 yards off, and running as fast as possible towards the walls. There was a fearfully heavy fire directed on him from the villages (Kairabad and Deh Khawaja) on both sides. After running for about a hundred yards I saw both fall and lie flat on the ground, the bullets all the time striking the ground, and raising the dust where they struck all round them. I, of course, was under the impression that they had been hit. Soon, however, I noticed Mr. Chase get up again, and again take the man on his back for another stage of the same distance, and again lie down for a rest. Again he got up and carried his burden for a third stage, and again lay down. By this time he had got close to the walls. Only those who saw the terrific fire that was brought to bear on these two coming in can realize how marvellous was their escape untouched. At the time they came in they were almost the only object on which the enemy were directing their fire, as the rest of the fugitives had already reached shelter." For this act Lieut. Chase was awarded the Victoria Cross [London Gazette, 7 Oct. 1881]: "William St. Lucien Chase, Lieut., Bombay Staff Corps. Date of Act of Bravery: 16 Aug. 1880. For conspicuous gallantry on the occasion of the sortie from Kandahar, on the 16th Aug. 1880, against the village of Deh Khoja, in having rescued and carried for a distance of over 200 yards, under the fire of the enemy, a wounded soldier, Private Massey, of the Royal Fusiliers, who had taken shelter in a block-house. Several times they were compelled to rest, but they persevered in bringing him to a place of safety. Private Ashford rendered Lieut. Chase every assistance, and remained with him throughout." After the regiment had left Kandahar, Lieut. Chase was given the command of the Killa Abdulla Post, and continued in the tenure of the appointment until relieved in the month of Nov. In Jan. 1881, he was again sent to command the post of Gatai, on the

William St. L. Chase.

lines of communication, and remained there until all the troops of the Kandahar Evacuating Force had passed through it *en route* to India. For his services in this campaign Lieut. Chase received the Victoria Cross and the Afghan Medal. In 1884 he served in the Zhob Campaign, in the Chin Lushai Expedition, and the advance on Fort Haka. In 1893 he took part in the Naga Hills Campaign and Manipur; in 1897 in the Mohmand Expedition; in 1897 and 1898 in the Tirah Campaign, and was present at the actions of Sampagha Pass; occupation of Maiden and Bagh Valley, and operations in Dwatoi Defile, Rajghul Valley and Bara Valley. He was continually mentioned in Despatches. Lieut.-Col. Chase was subsequently in command of the 28th Bombay Pioneers. Brevet Colonel Chase, C.B., died in India in July, 1908.

ASHFORD, THOMAS, Private, served in the Afghan War, and was awarded the Victoria Cross [London Gazette, 7 Oct. 1881]: "Thomas Ashford, Private, The Royal Fusiliers. Date of Act of Bravery: 16 Aug. 1880. For conspicuous gallantry on the occasion of the sortie from Kandahar, on the 16th Aug. 1880, against the village of Deh Khoja, in having rescued and carried for a distance of over 200 yards, under the fire of the enemy, a wounded soldier, Private Massey, of the Royal Fusiliers, who had taken shelter in a block-house. Several times they were compelled to rest, but they persevered in bringing him to a place of safety. Private Ashford rendered Lieut. Chase every assistance, and remained with him throughout." Ashford was the only V.C. Postman, and he daily walked twenty miles when delivering letters in the Whitwick district, Leicestershire. He died at Whitwick on 21 Feb. 1913, of bronchitis.

Thomas Ashford.

The London Gazette, 18 Oct. 1881.—" War Office, 15 Oct. 1881. The Queen has been graciously pleased to signify Her intention to confer the Decoration of the Victoria Cross on the undermentioned Officers and Soldiers, whose claims have been submitted for Her Majesty's approval, for their gallant conduct in Afghanistan, as recorded against their names."

VOUSDEN, WILLIAM JOHN, Capt., was born at Perth, Scotland, on 20 Sept. 1845, the only son of the late Captain Vousden, of the 51st (N.B.) Fusiliers. He was educated at Dr. Hill's Establishment at Woolwich, and King's School, Canterbury. Entering the Army in 1864, he was gazetted in the month of Jan. of that year to an Ensigncy in the 35th Regt. In Oct. 1867, he was promoted Lieutenant, and transferred to the 5th Punjab Cavalry, and in due course was admitted to the Bengal Staff Corps. His commission as Captain bears date 8 Jan. 1876. He served in the two Afridi Campaigns on the Staff, and in both phases of the Afghan War he participated with his regiment in the arduous and important work which fell to its share. Besides being employed in numerous minor operations, he served in the Khort Valley Expedition in Jan. 1879, including the action at Matun on the 7th of the month. He took part in the second campaign in the advance of the Division under Sir Frederick Roberts on the capital, was present on the 27th Sept. 1879, at the skirmish at Karatiga, in which his charger was shot; at the action at Charasiah on the 6th Oct.; the capture of Kabul on the 8th, and the cavalry pursuit of the enemy on the 9th idem; was with General Baker's Brigade in the flank march on the 9th to the 12th Dec.; was present at the actions in the neighbourhood of Kabul on the two succeeding days—it was on the 14th that he won the Victoria Cross. He formed one of the beleaguered force in Sherpur from the 15th to the 23rd Dec., and was present at the action of the 23rd, and in the succeeding cavalry pursuit. In the cavalry affair on the 14th Dec. in which Capt. Vousden won his Cross, the squadron of the 5th Punjab Cavalry, under Capt. Carr, with which he was employed, was acting as escort to Battery G/3, Royal Artillery. At midday, Capt. Vousden, with about a dozen men, came across on the Bala Hissar Road, and in open and level country, a body of Kohistanis, numbering from three to four hundred, making for the bridge over the Kabul River. It is a significant fact and one which speaks of itself for the gallantry displayed in encountering such terrific odds, and of the undaunted spirit in which the encounter was sustained, that, in the charge which ensued, six men of Capt. Vousden's little band of twelve were wounded, of whom three subsequently died, and that when the enemy dispersed they left no fewer than thirty of their number on the ground, all killed by the sword—of whom Capt. Vousden had himself cut down five. For the services he rendered in the war Capt. Vousden was three times mentioned in Despatches, and received, besides the Victoria Cross, a Brevet Majority and the Afghan Medal with two clasps. His Victoria Cross was gazetted 18 Oct. 1881: " William John Vousden, Capt. now Brevet Major, Bengal Staff Corps. For the exceptional gallantry displayed by him on the 14th Dec. 1879, on the Koh Asmai Heights, near Kabul, in charging, with a small party, into the centre of the line of the retreating Kohistani Force, by whom they were greatly outnumbered, and who did their utmost to close round them. After rapidly charging through and through the enemy, backwards and forwards, several times, they swept off round the opposite side of the village, and joined the rest of the troops." His subsequent active service was in the Miranzai Expedition, Tochi Field Force, and Tirah Campaign, and in the fighting on the North-West of India 1897–8. In every one of these campaigns he was specially mentioned in Despatches, and three times in the Afghan War. When Capt. Vousden won his Victoria Cross he was armed with an ordinary cavalry sword, and in each case he first parried the blow aimed at him, and then cut back as he passed. According to his own account, had he given the point, his sword would have been entangled and the next Afghan would have "got" him before he could have extricated it. His experience was quoted in an interesting discussion to illustrate the value of the " cut " as well as of the " thrust " for mounted work. From 1901 Major-General W. J. Vousden, V.C., C.B., commanded the Punjab Frontier Force and District, India. He had married, in 1891, the daughter of Major-General Drummond. He died at Lahore, India, 29 Jan. 1902.

HAMMOND, ARTHUR GEORGE, Capt., was born 28 Sept. 1843, the son of Major Thomas John Hammond, H.E.I.C.S., and his wife, Anne Hammond (*née* Warren). He was educated at King Edward VI. School, Sherborne, Dorset, and at Addiscombe College, which he entered in Feb. 1861, and on 7 June of the same year obtained his commission, gaining 2nd place in the examination and taking four prizes. He landed at Calcutta on the 31st Dec. 1861, and was attached to Her Majesty's 82nd Regt., then quartered at Delhi. On the 17th Oct. 1862, he joined the 12th (Kalat-i-Ghilzai) Native Infantry, and having passed the P.H. examination in Hindustani, was posted in Sept. 1863, to the Corps of Guides, which regiment he joined 17 Sept. at Mardan. The Guides formed part of the army then being assembled for the Umbeyla Campaign, and Lieut. Hammond was placed in command of a detachment of the corps which was left to hold the fort at Mardan. In May, 1864, he was appointed Quartermaster of his regiment; in Nov. 1865, Wing-Commander; in June, 1867, he was admitted to the Bengal Staff Corps, and in April, 1875, he passed in Military Surveying and Field Engineering at the Rurki College by " the Higher Standard with great credit." Capt. Hammond served with the Q.V.O. Corps of Guides as Wing-Commander through the whole of the Jowaki Campaign of 1877–1878, including the capture of Payah and Jammu, and the forcing of the Naru-Kula Pass. Twice he was mentioned in Despatches and " specially thanked for gallant conduct " by General Keyes (G.O. 738), 9 Aug. 1878 (North-West Frontier Medal and two clasps). In 1878 he was with his regiment in the operations against the Ranizai village of Skhakat, 14 Sept., and in the attack on the Utman Khel villages on the 21st of the same month. He served with the Guide Infantry throughout the whole of the Afghan Campaign of 1878–79–80. Besides taking part in many minor affairs, he was present at the storming of the Takht-i-Shah on the 13th and the Asmai Heights on the 14th of December, the march into Koh-i-Damon, and the second action at Charasiah on the 25th April, 1880. He was mentioned in Despatches (23 Jan. 1880) by Sir F. Roberts, who says: " Another officer who greatly distinguished himself on this occasion was Capt. A. G. Hammond, Queen's Own Corps of Guides. He had been very forward during the storming of the Asmai Heights, and now, when the enemy were crowding up the western slopes, he remained with a few men on the ridge until the Afghans were within thirty yards of them. During the retirement, one of the men of the Guides was shot. Capt. Hammond stopped and assisted in carrying him away, though the enemy were at the time close by and firing heavily." (G.O.C.C. No. 137.) For his services on this day Capt. Hammond was awarded the Victoria Cross. He also received the Afghan Medal and two clasps. His Victoria Cross was gazetted 18 Oct. 1881: " Arthur George Hammond, Capt. (now Major), Bengal Staff Corps. For conspicuous coolness and gallantry at the action on the Asmai Heights, near Kabul, on the 14th Dec. 1879, in defending the top of the hill, with a rifle and fixed bayonet, against large numbers of the enemy, while the 72nd Highlanders and Guides were retiring; and again, on the retreat down the hill, in stopping to assist in carrying away a wounded sepoy, the enemy being not 60 yards off, firing heavily all the time." On 2 June, 1886, at St. George's, Campden Hill, London, he married Edith Jane, daughter of the late Major H. J. Wright, M.S. Corps, Indian Army. They have three children: Edith Amber; Veronica Ruth, and Arthur Verney, born 16 Oct. 1892, now in the Cavalry Corps of Guides (Queen Victoria's Own). During the Hazara Campaign of 1888, he commanded the 3rd Sikhs; was mentioned in Despatches, received a clasp to the North-West Frontier Medal and was created a Companion of the Distinguished Service Order [London Gazette, 12 April, 1889]: " Arthur George Hammond, Bengal Staff Corps." Was Commandant Queen's Own Corps of Guides from 1 Feb. 1891, to 28 Sept. 1895. In the Hazara Campaign of 1891 Brigadier-General Hammond commanded the Right Column up to 17 July, 1891, and commanded the Hazara Field Force 17 July, 1891, to 2 Dec. 1891. He was thus mentioned in Despatches by General Elles: " Brigadier-General Hammond in his detached operations exhibited an energy and resource worthy of all praise." (G.O.D., 28 Aug. 1891.) Brigadier-General Hammond received a clasp to the North-West Frontier Medal, and was created a C.B. In 1892, in the Isazai Expedition, he was Brigadier-General Commanding the 2nd Brigade Communications and the 4th Brigade. In the Relief of Chitral he was Brigadier-General Commanding Communications and the 4th Brigade, and was mentioned in Despatches (G.O.D., 998, dated 27 Sept. 1895), Medal and clasp. In 1897 he was Brigadier-General Commanding the Assam Brigade. He commanded the Peshawar Column and later the 3rd Brigade, Khyber Field Force, in the Tirah Campaign of 1897–98. He was mentioned in Despatches and received two clasps to India Medal of 1895. From 1890 to 1898 he was A.D.C. to H.M. Queen Victoria from Colonelcy. In 1903 he was created a K.C.B. In 1907 he received the Jubilee Medal. In 1898 Colonel A. G. Hammond was awarded a Good Service Pension. Hawking was the great sport at Mardan, both of antelope and bustard; he took up that keenly, and had one tiger shoot in Rewah, getting as his share a bag of seven tigers.

Arthur G. Hammond.

He was very fond of cricket and racquets and lawn tennis. He died on 20 April, 1919, and is buried in St. Michael's Churchyard, Camberley.

DICK-CUNYNGHAM, WILLIAM HENRY, Lieut., was born on 16 June, 1851, the youngest son of the late Sir William Hamner Dick-Cunyngham, Bart., of Prestonfield and Lambrughton, and Susan, 3rd daughter of the late Major James Alston Stewart, of Urrard, County Perth. He was educated at Trinity College, Glenalmond, N.B., and at the Royal Military College, Sandhurst. Gazetted to an Ensigncy in the 92nd Highlanders in Feb. 1872, he was successively promoted Lieutenant in Feb. 1873, and Captain in Oct. 1881. His services with the 92nd included a term of years (Jan. 1873, to Jan. 1881) spent in India, during which time he was Adjutant of a wing of the regiment from Jan. 1877, to April, 1878. Capt. Dick-Cunyngham served over a wide extent of territory and in various capacities throughout the Afghan War. He was detailed in the first instance to the Transport Department of the Quetta Field Force, and took part in the advance of Sir Donald Stewart's Division on Kandahar. In the forward movement on Kalat-i-Ghilzai he was attached to the Headquarters Staff, and on the return of General Biddulph's Column by the Thal-Chotiah route to India, he accompanied it in the capacity of Transport Officer. He rejoined his regiment—which had meantime been sent to the Kurram Front—and served with it in nearly all its diverse operations in the second phase of the campaign from the renewal to the cessation of hostilities. Besides taking part in numerous minor affairs, he was present at the action with the hill tribes at Ali Khel, on the 14th Oct. 1879, in the expedition to Mardan in Nov., and in the operations in the neighbourhood of Kabul from the 8th to the 23rd Dec. It was at the assault on the Takht-i-Shah that Lieut. Dick-Cunyngham won the Victoria Cross [London Gazette, 18 Oct. 1881]: "William Henry Dick-Cunyngham, Capt., the Gordon Highlanders. Date of Act of Bravery : 13 Dec. 1879. For the conspicuous gallantry and bravery displayed by him on the 13th Dec. 1879, at the attack on the Sherpur Pass, in Afghanistan, in having exposed himself to the full fire of the enemy, and by his example and encouragement rallied the men who, having been beaten back, were at the moment wavering at the top of the hill." "After the fall of the officer and colour-sergeant," wrote Sir. F. Roberts, with reference to the deaths of Lieut. St. John Forbes and Colour-Sergeant James Drummond, in describing in his Despatch of 23 Jan. 1880, the brilliant manner in which the commanding position held by the enemy was carried by the 92nd Highlanders on the 13th Dec, " there was a momentary waver, when Lieut. W. H. Dick-Cunyngham rushed forward and, gallantly exposing himself to the full fire poured upon this point, rallied the men by his example and cheering words, and, calling upon those near to follow him, charged into the middle of the enemy." Lieut. Dick-Cynyngham was also present at the action on the 23rd of the month. As Adjutant of a wing of the 92nd he was present on the 25th April, 1880, at the action at Childukhtean, and for his services on this occasion he was mentioned in Despatches. He took part with the regiment in the march of General Roberts' Column to the relief of Kandahar, and was present at the reconnaissance of the 31st Aug., and at the crowning victory on the 1st Sept., for his services on which occasion he was again mentioned in Despatches. Besides the Victoria Cross he received the Afghan Medal with two clasps, and the Kabul-Kandahar Bronze Star. In Oct. 1880, he was selected to fill the regimental Adjutancy, and in this capacity Capt. Dick-Cunyngham accompanied the 92nd to South Africa, and served with it in the Transvaal Campaign of 1881. On the Declaration of War against the Boers in 1899 Lieut.-Colonel Dick-Cunyngham went to the front in command of the 2nd Battn. of his gallant regiment, and led it into action, at the Battle of Elandslaagte, where he was wounded in the leg. This wound incapacitated him during the early part of the Siege of Ladysmith. On 6 Jan. 1900, almost the first day on which he resumed his active duties, while the great attack on the town was going on, he was killed by a chance shot at nearly 3,000 yards' range.

SELLAR, GEORGE, L.-Corpl., served in the Afghan War. General Roberts saw him through his glass, leading the stormers at Asmai Heights, Kabul, where he was severely wounded by a Ghazi. He was awarded the Victoria Cross [London Gazette, 18 Oct. 1881]: "George Sellar, L.-Corpl., Seaforth Highlanders. Date of Act of Bravery : 14 Dec. 1879. For conspicuous gallantry displayed by him at the assault on the Asmai Heights, round Kabul, on the 14th Dec. 1879, in having in a marked manner led the attack, under a heavy fire, and, dashing on in front of the party up a slope, engaged in a desperate conflict with an Afghan who sprang out to meet him. In this encounter L.-Corpl. Sellar was severely wounded." He died on the 1st Nov. 1889.

George Sellar.

London Gazette, 14 March, 1882.—" War Office, 13 March, 1882. The Queen has been graciously pleased to signify Her intention to confer the Decoration of the Victoria Cross upon the undermentioned Officer and men, whose claims have been submitted for Her Majesty's approval, in recognition of their conspicuous bravery during the recent operations in South Africa, as recorded against their names."

HILL-WALKER, ALAN RICHARD, Major, was born 12 July, 1859 ; the eldest son of the late Capt. Hill (Chief Constable, North Riding of Yorkshire), and Frances Mirriam, daughter of T. Walker, Maunby Hall, Thirsk. He was educated at Richmond, Yorkshire, and privately ; joined the North York Rifles, 1877, and the 58th Regt. in 1879, with which regiment he served throughout the Zulu War of 1879 (Medal) and the Boer War of 1881. In the last-mentioned campaign he took part in the Battles of Ingogo, Majuba

Hill, where he was severely wounded, Laing's Nek, for his services in which engagement he was mentioned in Despatches, 10 March, 1881, and awarded the Victoria Cross [London Gazette, 14 March, 1882] : " Alan Richard Hill, Lieut., 2nd Battn. 58th (The Northamptonshire) Regt. Date of Act of Bravery : 28 Jan. 1881. For gallant conduct at the action of Laing's Nek on the 28th Jan. 1881, in having, after the retreat was ordered, remained behind and endeavoured to carry out of action Lieut. Baillie, of the same corps, who was lying on the ground severely wounded. Being unable to lift that officer into the saddle, he carried him in his arms until Lieut. Baillie was shot dead. Lieut. Hill then brought a wounded man out of action on his horse, after which he returned and rescued another, all these acts being performed under a heavy fire." The Northamptons were the last regiment to carry British Colours into action. This was at the fight at Laing's Nek, when, although we were repulsed, the regiment covered itself with glory. In 1883 and 1885 he served in Natal, Cape Town and South Africa ; he was Adjutant, 3rd and 4th Battns. Northampton Militia, 1887 to 1892. During the next three years he was Station Staff Officer at Bangalore ; officiating A.A.G. in Mandalay in 1897. In 1897 he took part in the Tirah Campaign, and the march down the Bara Valley, 1897 (Medal and two clasps). Major Hill married Lilias Oliphant, daughter of the late T. S. Walker, of Maunby Hall, Thirsk, and assumed the additional name of Walker in 1902. They have two sons. Major Hill-Walker is very fond of hunting, shooting and sport of all kinds.

DOOGAN, JOHN, Private, served in South Africa in 1881, and was awarded the Victoria Cross [London Gazette, 14 March, 1882] : " John Doogan, Private, late 1st Dragoon Guards. Date of Act of Bravery : 28 Jan. 1881. During the charge of the mounted men, Private Doogan, servant to Major Brownlow, 1st Dragoon Guards, seeing that officer (whose horse had been shot) dismounted and among the Boers, rode up and (though himself severely wounded) dismounted and pressed Major Brownlow to take his horse, receiving another wound while trying to induce him to accept it." Private Doogan was discharged on pension.

MURRAY, JAMES, L.-Corpl., served in South Africa in 1881, and was awarded the Victoria Cross [London Gazette 14 March, 1882] : " James Murray, L.-Corpl., 94th Regt. Date of Act of Bravery : 16 Jan. 1881. For gallant conduct (with Trooper Danagher, of Nourse's Horse) during an engagement with the Boers at Elandsfontein on the 16th Jan. 1881, in advancing for 500 yards, under a very heavy fire from a party of about sixty Boers, to bring out of action a private of the 21st Foot, who had been severely wounded ; in attempting which L.-Corpl. Murray was himself severely wounded." It was at Elandsfontein, near Pretoria that L.-Corpl. Murray and Trooper Danagher advanced 500 yards into the open, under heavy fire, to rescue two men of the 2nd Royal Scots Fusiliers, Byrne and Davis, who had been badly wounded.

James Murray.

They had no sooner started forward than Murray's horse was shot under him. Nevertheless, he went on on foot. In a letter dated Dublin, 25 March, 1891, L.-Corpl. Murray says : " We both reached them together, and, on stooping to raise Byrne's head, I was shot through the body, the ball entering my right side and passing out near the spine. Seeing how useless it was for Danagher to remain, I ordered him to secure my carbine and escape. Byrne breathed his last by my side soon after. Davis and I were taken prisoners, and, together with Byrne's body, carried in a bullock-hide to the Boer camp on the mountain-top, where we were well treated. By the courtesy of the Boer commandant, we were then permitted to return to Pretoria under a flag of truce, bringing with us the body of our poor comrade. Davis died five days afterwards."

DANAHER, JOHN, Trooper, Nourse's Horse, was born 25 June, 1860, at Limerick, Ireland. He was educated by the Christian Brothers at Edward Street, Limerick, and joined the Connaught Rangers on 25 April, 1881. Trooper John Danagher was awarded the Victoria Cross [London Gazette, 14 March, 1882] : " John Danagher, Trooper, Nourse's Horse, afterwards 2nd Battn. The Connaught Rangers. For gallant conduct (with L.-Corpl. James Murray, 2nd Battn. The Connaught Rangers) during an engagement with the Boers at Elandsfontein on the 16th Jan. 1881, in advancing for 500 yards, under a very heavy fire from a party of about sixty Boers, to bring out of action a private of the 21st Foot who had been severely wounded ; in attempting which L.-Corpl. Murray was himself severely wounded." He subsequently joined the Connaught Rangers. On 23 Aug. 1882, the whole of the troops at the Curragh and Newbridge were paraded in accordance with a General Order issued on 20 Aug. by the Deputy Adjutant-General, and with Brigade Orders issued by Major-General C. C. Fraser, V.C., C.B., commanding the Curragh Brigade : " As strong as possible at 11 a.m. . . . at the Curragh, for the purpose of witnessing the presentation " of the Victoria Cross to Private Danaher by the Viceroy. Brigade Orders issued from the Curragh Camp, 24 Aug. 1882, were as follows : " Victoria Cross.—His Excellency Earl Spencer, K.G., in presenting by Her Majesty's Command the Victoria

John Danaher.

Cross to Private Danaher, 2nd Connaught Rangers, made the following remarks: 'Private Danaher, the Queen has been pleased to signify Her intention to confer on you the decoration of the Victoria Cross. Her Majesty has done this to mark Her appreciation of the conspicuous bravery displayed by you during the military operations in South Africa. You then, under heavy fire, advanced a distance of 500 yards, with a comrade from your present regiment, to bring out of action a Private who had been seriously wounded. I now, before your Regiment and the troops encamped at Curragh, have the pleasure, as Her Majesty's representative, to give you this decoration. It is given only for conspicuous valour in the Field. It is open to every soldier of the Queen, Officers as well as Privates. You see it on the breast of the distinguished General under whose immediate orders you now serve: you see it on the breast of other Officers and men of the Forces now before you. You will now wear it yourself. You may well be proud of this honour, and of the sharing it with such distinguished men. I am sure that as you have done in the past, so in the future you will do honour by your conduct to your Queen, to your country, and the gallant Regiment to which you belong. May the distinction which I now confer upon you, encourage other men to deeds as noble as yours, so worthy of Queen Victoria and the ancient fame of her gallant Army.' *Note.*—General Sir Thomas Steele, K.C.B., General Commanding the Forces in Ireland, was present on the Parade. Private John Danaher, V.C., 2nd Battn. Connaught Rangers, was called to stand by the Viceroy at the Flagstaff during the March Past.—By Order, H. G. L. Crichton, Major, Brigade Major." Sergt. Danaher received, besides the Victoria Cross, the Long Service and Good Conduct Medal. He was recommended for Meritorious Service by General Sir Archibald Hunter. He is now discharged on pension. Sergt. Danaher had six sons in His Majesty's Forces during the European War. One son died of wounds received in action whilst serving with the 5th Connaught Rangers of the 10th (Irish) Division in Gallipoli, 23 Aug. 1915. Another son was a Prisoner of War and a third has been wounded. Sergt. Danaher died on 9 Jan. 1919.

OSBORNE, JAMES, Private, served in South Africa in 1881, with the Northamptonshire Regt., and was awarded the Victoria Cross [London Gazette, 14 March, 1882]: "James Osborne, Private, 2nd Battn. 58th Regt. Date of Act of Bravery: 22 Feb. 1881. For his gallant conduct at Wesselstroom, on the 22nd Feb. 1881, in riding, under a heavy fire, towards a party of forty-two Boers, picking up Private Mayes, who was lying wounded, and carrying him safely into camp."

London Gazette, 7 April, 1882.—"The Queen has been graciously pleased to signify Her intention to confer the Decoration of the Victoria Cross upon the undermentioned Officer and Soldier of Her Majesty's Army, whose claims have been submitted for Her Majesty's approval, for their conspicuous bravery at the assault of the Inhlobane Mountain, in Zululand, as recorded against their names."

LYSONS, HENRY, Lieut., was born at Morden, Surrey, on 13 July, 1858. He was the son of the late Sir Daniel Lysons, of Crimean fame, and was educated at Wellington College. He joined the 90th Light Infantry in 1878, serving through the Zulu War as A.D.C. to Sir Evelyn Wood, V.C. He took part in the affairs of Zungen Nek and the Inhlobane Mountain and the Battles of Kambula and Ulundi. He was twice mentioned in Despatches, and received the Medal and clasp, and the Victoria Cross [London Gazette, 7 April, 1880]: "Henry Lysons, Lieut., 2nd Battn. The Cameronians (Scottish Rifles). Date of Act of Bravery: 28 March, 1879. On the 28th March, 1879, during the assault of the Inhlobane Mountain, Sir Evelyn Wood ordered the dislodgment of certain Zulus (who were causing the troops much loss) from strong natural caves commanding the position in which some of the wounded were lying. Some delay occurring in the execution of the orders issued, Capt. the Hon. Ronald Campbell, Coldstream Guards, followed by Lieut. Lysons, Aide-de-Camp, and Private Fowler, ran forward in the most determined manner, and advanced over a mass of fallen boulders and between walls of rock, which led to a cave in which the enemy lay hidden. It being impossible for two men to walk abreast, the assailants were consequently obliged to keep in single file, and as Capt. Campbell was leading, he arrived first at the mouth of the cave, from which the Zulus were firing, and there met his death. Lieut. Lysons and Private Fowler, who were following close behind him, immediately dashed at the cave, from which led several subterranean passages, and firing into the chasm below, succeeded in forcing the occupants to forsake their stronghold. Lieut. Lysons remained at the cave's mouth for some minutes after the attack, during which time Capt. Campbell's body was carried down the slope." He served through the Soudan Campaign of 1884–5, with the Egyptian Army (Medal, clasp and Bronze Star). He married Vanda, daughter of C. E. Treffry, of Place, Fowey. Colonel Lysons, V.C., C.B. (late Colonel 1st Bedfordshire Regt.), died 24 July, 1907.

Edmund Fowler.

FOWLER, EDMUND, Private, was born in 1861, at Waterford, Ireland, the son of John and Bridget Fowler. He joined the 2nd Battn. The Scottish Rifles, and served in the Zulu Campaign. On 28 March, 1879, Sir Evelyn Wood ordered the storming of the Zlobane Mountain, where the Zulus were strongly posted. To effect their overthrow it was necessary to dislodge them from strong natural caves, which they were holding high up the mountain side. From this splendid position the Zulus, armed with guns and rifles, were doing considerable damage to our troops. At all costs, however, they had to be hunted out of the caves. Huge boulders lay between the enemy and our lines, and the path was so narrow that men advancing against them would be obliged to keep in single file. For some reason there was a delay in carrying out the order to advance, and at once a couple of officers with Private Fowler dashed forward. These three, therefore, were in advance of the others, and practically unsupported, but they dashed on till, as the path grew narrower, they were compelled to advance in single file under a heavy fire, and Capt. Campbell, who was in command, was the first to arrive, and as, sword in hand, he leapt into the mouth of the cave, the Zulus fired a volley point-blank at him, and he fell dead on the spot. But the next moment his subaltern and Private Fowler reached the cave, and springing forward, undismayed by the death of their leader, soon cleared the cave. For this magnificent act of bravery Private Fowler and his officer were awarded the Victoria Cross, and Sir Evelyn Wood said it was the bravest deed he ever saw performed in his life. The official notice in the London Gazette of 7 April, 1882, reads: "Edmund Fowler, Private, 2nd Battn. The Cameronians (Scottish Rifles) (since discharged). Date of Act of Bravery: 28 March, 1879. On the 28th March, 1879, during the assault of the Onhlobane Mountain, Sir Evelyn Wood ordered the dislodgment of certain Zulus (who were causing the troops much loss) from strong natural caves commanding the position in which some of the wounded were lying. Some delay occurring in the execution of the orders issued, Capt. the Hon. Ronald Campbell, Coldstream Guards, followed by Lieut. Lysons, Aide-de-Camp, and Private Fowler, ran forward in the most determined manner, and advanced over a mass of fallen boulders and between walls of rock, which led to a cave in which the enemy lay hidden. It being impossible for two men to walk abreast, the assailants were consequently obliged to keep in single file, and as Capt. Campbell was leading he arrived first at the mouth of the cave, from which the Zulus were firing, and there met his death. Lieut. Lysons and Private Fowler, who were following close behind him, immediately dashed into the cave, from which led several subterranean passages, and firing into the chasm below, succeeded in forcing the occupants to forsake their stronghold. Lieut. Lysons remained at the cave's mouth for some minutes after the attack, during which time Capt. Campbell's body was carried down the slope." Sir Evelyn Wood tells us how he succeeded in killing a Zulu Chief: "Private Fowler, one of my personal escort, who was lying in the ditch of the fort, had asked me, 'Would you kindly take a shot at that Chief, sir? It's a quarter of an hour I am shooting him, and cannot hit him at all!'" Private Fowler served in the Egyptian Campaign and received the Medal and Bronze Star. He later became Colour-Sergeant. Colour-Sergt. Fowler married Miss Mary Maguire, of County Donegal, Ireland.

London Gazette, 15 Sept. 1882.—"War Office, 15 Sept. 1882. The Queen has been graciously pleased to signify Her intention to confer the Decoration of the Victoria Cross upon the undermentioned Warrant Officer of the Royal Navy, whose claim has been submitted for Her Majesty's approval, for an act of gallant conduct performed by him during the Naval Attack of 11 July last, on the batteries of Alexandria, in Egypt, as recorded against his name."

HARDING, ISRAEL, Gunner, Royal Navy, served at the Bombardment of Alexandria by Lord Alcester in July, 1882, when one of the shells from Arabi Pasha's batteries entered the side of H.M.S. Alexandria. With great coolness and courage, Mr. Harding seized the shell and, plunging it into a tub of water, extinguished the fuse. He was awarded the Victoria Cross [London Gazette, 15 Sept. 1882]: "Mr. Israel Harding, Gunner, Royal Navy. At about nine o'clock on the morning of the 11th July, 1882, whilst Her Majesty's Ship Alexandria was engaging the Forts of Alexandria, a 10-inch spherical shell passed through the ship's side and lodged on the main deck. Mr. Harding, hearing the shout, 'There is a live shell just above the hatchway,' rushed up the ladder from below, and, observing that the fuse was burning, took some water from a tub standing near and threw it over the projectile, then picked it up and put it into the tub. Had the shell burst it would probably have destroyed many lives." The "Pall Mall Gazette" of 24 May, 1917, says: "Mr. Israel Harding, V.C., of Portsmouth, formerly a Chief Gunner in the Royal Navy, has died while on a visit to Billingshurst, Sussex." He was about eighty-six years of age.

The London Gazette, 13 Feb. 1883.—"War Office, 13 Feb. 1883. The Queen has been graciously pleased to signify Her intention to confer the Decoration of the Victoria Cross upon the undermentioned Officer, whose claim has been submitted for Her Majesty's approval, for his conspicuous bravery during the battle of Tel-el-Kebir, in Egypt, on the 13th Sept. last as recorded against his name."

EDWARDS, WILLIAM MORDAUNT MARSH, Lieut., was born at Hardingham Hall, Norfolk, on 7 May, 1855, son of William Henry Bartholomew Edwards, of Hardingham Hall, Norfolk, and of Caroline Marsh, of Gaynes Park, Epping, Essex. He was educated at a private school at Rottingdean, at Eton and at Trinity College, Cambridge. He was gazetted Sub-Lieutenant (unattached) on 22 March, 1876, and joined the 74th Highlanders in 1877. He served in the Straits Settlements and Hong Kong, and in Egypt in 1882. For his services in this last campaign he received the Tel-el-Kebir Medal and clasp, the Medjidie, and Victoria Cross [London Gazette, 13 Feb. 1883]: "William Mordaunt Marsh Edwards, Lieut., 2nd Battn. The Highland Light Infantry. Date of Act of Bravery: 13 Sept. 1882. For the conspicuous bravery displayed by

William M. M. Edwards.

him during the Battle of Tel-el-Kebir, on the 13th Sept. 1882, in leading a party of the Highland Light Infantry to storm a redoubt. Lieut. Edwards, who was in advance of his party, with great gallantry rushed alone into the battery, killed the artillery officer in charge, and was himself knocked down by a gunner with a rammer, and only rescued by the timely arrival of three men of his regiment." He served in India from 1884 to 1887, and was five years Adjutant of the 3rd Battn. Highland Light Infantry. On 1 Nov. 1889, at Peshawar, India, he married Alice, 3rd daughter of General Edward Nugent Norton, Indian Staff Corps. Their son, Barth Mordaunt Marsham Edwards, was born 30 March, 1891. Major Edwards retired in Nov. 1896. In 1899 he was appointed to H.M. Honourable Corps of Gentlemen-at-Arms. He died at Hardingham Hall, 17 Sept. 1912, aged 57. He held the Coronation Medals of King Edward VII. and King George.

London Gazette, 16 Feb. 1883.—" The Queen has been graciously pleased to signify Her intention to confer the Decoration of the Victoria Cross upon the undermentioned Soldier, whose claim has been submitted for Her Majesty's approval, for his conspicuous bravery during the recent campaign in Egypt, as recorded against his name."

Frederick Corbett.

CORBETT, FREDERICK, Private, was awarded the Victoria Cross [London Gazette, 16 Feb. 1883]: " Frederick Corbett, Private, 3rd Battn. The King's Royal Rifle Corps. During the reconnaissance upon Kafr Dowar, on the 5th Aug. 1882, the Mounted Infantry, with which Private Corbett was serving, came under a hot fire from the enemy, and suffered some loss, including Lieut. Howard Vyse, mortally wounded. This officer fell in the open, and there being then no time to move him, Private Corbett asked and obtained permission to remain by him, and though under a constant fire, he sat down and endeavoured to stop the bleeding of this officer's wounds, until the Mounted Infantry received orders to retire, when he rendered valuable assistance in carrying him off the field." Frederick Corbett's real name was David Embleton.

London Gazette, 20 May, 1884.—" War Office, 21 May, 1884. The Queen has been graciously pleased to signify Her intention to confer the Decoration of the Victoria Cross upon the undermentioned Officers, Non-commissioned Officer and Private Soldier, whose claims have been submitted for Her Majesty's approval, for their conspicuous bravery during the recent operations in the Soudan, as recorded against their names."

WILSON, ARTHUR KNYVET, Capt., was born 4 March, 1842, son of the late Rear-Admiral George Knyvet Wilson, and nephew of the late Major-General Sir Archdale Wilson, Bart., of Delhi. His elder brother is Sir R.- K. Wilson, 2nd Bart. Arthur Wilson served in the Crimean War of 1854-5 ; the China War of 1858 ; the Egyptian Campaign of 1882, and the Sudan Campaign in 1884. At the Battle of El Teb in the Red Sea Littoral, Capt. Wilson won his Victoria Cross. His sword was broken during the fight, and he attacked the Arabs with his fists. Thus one of the comparatively few Naval V.C.'s won his Victoria Cross not on sea but on land. His Victoria Cross was gazetted 21 May, 1884 : " Arthur Knyvet Wilson, Capt., Royal Navy. This officer, on the Staff of Rear-Admiral Sir William Hewett, at the Battle of El Teb on the 29th Feb. 1884, attached himself during the advance to the right half-battery, Naval Brigade, in the place of Lieut. Royds, Royal Navy, mortally wounded.

Arthur K. Wilson.

As the troops closed on the enemy's Krupp battery the Arabs charged out on the corner of the square, and on the detachment who were dragging the Gardner gun. Capt. Wilson then sprang to the front and engaged in single combat with some of the enemy, thus protecting his detachment till some men of the York and Lancaster Regt. came to his assistance with their bayonets. But for the action of this officer, Sir Redvers Buller thinks that one or more of his detachments must have been speared." He was A.D.C. to the Queen 1892-95, and a Lord Commissioner of the Admiralty and Comptroller of the Navy 1897-1901. He was created a K.C.B. 1902, and a G.C.B. 1903. From 1901 to 1903 he was in command of the Channel Squadron, and from 1903 to 1907 was Commander-in-Chief of the Home and Channel Fleets. In 1905 he was created a G.C.V.O., and in 1907 he became Admiral of the Fleet. From 1909 to 1912 he was First Sea Lord of the Admiralty. Admiral Sir A. K. Wilson, V.C., G.C.B., G.C.V.O., retired in 1912, and in that year he received the Order of Merit.

MARLING, PERCIVAL SCROPE, Lieut., eldest son of Sir William Henry Marling, Baronet, of Stanley Park, Stroud, Gloucestershire, was born 6 March, 1861,

Percival Scrope Marling.

and educated at Harrow and the R.M.C., Sandhurst. On 11 Aug. 1880, he was gazetted to a 2nd Lieutenancy in the 3rd Battn. 60th Rifles, and served with that regiment throughout the Boer War of 1880–81, being present at Sir George Colley's disastrous attack on Laing's Nek, and the severe conflict on the Ingogo River. Having obtained promotion to Lieutenant on 1 July, 1882, he participated in the fighting round Alexandria, the affair at Tel-el-Mahuta, the brilliant action at Kassassin on 9 Sept., and the total defeat of Arabi's army at Tel-el-Kebir on the 13th Sept., for which he received the Medal with clasp and the Khedive's Star. In 1884 Lieut. Marling served with the Mounted Infantry in the Soudan Expedition, and was again actively engaged, taking part in Sir Gerald Graham's fine victory at El Teb on 29 Feb., the relief of Tokar, the battle of Tamai and the affair at Tamanib. For his gallant conduct he was twice mentioned in Despatches, received two more clasps to his Medal, and was awarded the Victoria Cross for an act of gallantry at Tamai [London Gazette, 6 May, 1884]: " Percival Scrope Marling, Lieut., 3rd Battn. 60th Rifles (Mounted Infantry). For conspicuous bravery at the battle of Tamai on the 13th March, 1884, in risking his life to save that of Private Morley, Royal Sussex Regt., who, having been shot, was lifted and placed in front of Lieut. Marling on his horse. He fell off immediately, when Lieut. Marling dismounted, and gave up his horse for the purpose of carrying Private Morley, the enemy pressing close on to them, until they succeeded in carrying him to a place of comparative safety." Later in 1884 and in part of 1885, he took part with the Camel Corps in the Nile Expedition for the relief of General Gordon, and was present at the fighting in the Bayuda Desert, the actions near the Abu Klea Wells (where the intrepid Burnaby lost his life), and at Abu Kru ; the engagements at El Gubat and Metammeh, the second action at Abu Klea, and, in fact, all the Desert operations under the late Sir Herbert Stewart, for which he received two further clasps, making five in all. In Oct. 1885, Lieut. Marling was made a local Captain, and given the command of a company of Mounted Infantry in Egypt, which he commanded till Feb. 1887. For his services in Egypt H.R.H. The Duke of Cambridge specially promoted him to a troop in the 18th Hussars, which he joined in March, 1887. In 1889 Capt. Marling proceeded to India with the 18th Hussars, and, except for a year, when he was Adjutant of the West Somerset Yeomanry, he served in India till 1895. On 12 Aug. 1896, Capt. Marling received his Majority. In 1896 he was selected for the command of Regimental Depôt at Canterbury which post he held till 1898. Colonel Marling married on 18 May, 1890, Beatrice Caroline, eldest daughter of F. H. Beaumont, Esq., J.P., D.L., C.A., of Buckland Court, Surrey. Colonel Marling is fond of cricket, shooting, hunting, golf and polo. In June, 1899, he proceeded to Africa to rejoin his regiment, and was present with the 18th Hussars at the battle of Talana Hill, the retirement from Dundee to Ladysmith, the action at Lombard's Kop, the defence of Ladysmith, including the reconnaissance of 8 Dec. In June, 1900, he was invalided home with enteric fever, but returned to South Africa again in Feb. 1901. Major Marling had command of his regiment in the field from 10 April, 1901, to 31 May, 1902, during the operations in the Transvaal, the Orange River Colony, and on the Zulu Frontier of Natal, and was twice mentioned in Despatches, and promoted to the command of the 18th Hussars 2 Feb. 1902, awarded the C.B. [London Gazette, 17 July, 1902], and the Queen's Medal with five clasps and the King's Medal with two clasps. In 1905 Colonel Marling was promoted Brevet Colonel, and appointed to the command of the York Garrison and District. On 2 Feb. 1906, he completed four years in command of his regiment. In 1909 he was made a temporary Brigadier-General in South Africa, and retired in 1910 owing to injuries received by his horse falling on him while on duty. In 1914 he volunteered for active service, and went to France in Sept. 1914, and served at the front on the Headquarters Staff, Indian Army Corps, till 1915, when he was invalided home with congestion of the lungs. He has been awarded the Mons Star for 1914. Colonel Marling's seat is Sedbury Park, Tidenham, Gloucestershire, where he owns some 6,000 acres. He is a J.P. and D.L. and County Councillor for Gloucestershire, and a J.P. for Monmouthshire and D.L. for the City and County of Bristol.

MARSHALL, WILLIAM THOMAS, Quartermaster-Sergt., was born 5 Dec. 1854, at Newark, Nottinghamshire, son of John Richard Marshall. He was educated privately, and joined the 19th Hussars on the 20th July, 1873. He served in the Egyptian War 1882-84, was present at the battle of Tel-el-Kebir (Medal with clasp and Khedive's Star), and in the Sudan Expedition in 1884, being present in the engagements at El Teb and Tamai ; was mentioned in Despatches, received two clasps, and was awarded the Victoria Cross [London Gazette, 21 May, 1884]: " William Marshall, Quartermaster-Sergt., 19th Hussars. Date of Act of Bravery : 29 Feb. 1884. For his conspicuous bravery during the cavalry charge at El Teb, on the 29th Feb. 1884, in bringing Lieut.-Colonel Barrow, 19th Hussars, out of action. That officer, having been severely wounded and his horse killed, was on the ground surrounded by the enemy, when Quartermaster-Sergt. Marshall, who stayed behind with him, seized his hand and dragged him through the enemy back to the regiment. Had Lieut.-Colonel Barrow been left behind he must have been killed." He was commissioned as Quartermaster 20 Jan. 1885 ; served in the South African War from 1899 to 1900, and took part in the operations in Natal, including the actions at Lombard's Kop, the defence of Ladysmith, Laing's Nek, and received the Queen's Medal with four clasps. He married 24 Oct. 1900, at Ipswich, Louisa Wiseman, third daughter of Capt. C. S. Wiseman, Indian Army, and they have a daughter, Violet Wiseman Marshall. Lieut.-Colonel Marshall was Camp Quartermaster at Aldershot 1905, and retired 20 Jan. 1907. He became Secretary, Fife County Territorial Force Association, 1 March, 1908. Mentioned in Despatches 7 Aug. 1917, for valuable services rendered in connection with the war. Promoted Lieut.-Colonel 1 Jan. 1919. His favourite recreations are riding, tennis and skating.

Thomas Edwards.

EDWARDS, THOMAS, Private, 1st Battn. 42nd Regt. (The Black Watch) Royal Highlanders, was awarded the Victoria Cross [London Gazette, 21 May, 1884]: "Thomas Edwards, Private, 1st Battn. 42nd Regt. Royal Highlanders. Date of Act of Bravery: 13 March, 1884. For the conspicuous bravery displayed by him in the defence of one of the guns of the Naval Brigade, at the Battle of Tamai, on the 13th March, 1884. This man (who was attached to the Naval Brigade as Mule Driver) was beside the gun with Lieut. Almack, R.N., and a bluejacket. Both the latter were killed, and Edwards, after bayoneting two Arabs and himself receiving a wound with a spear, rejoined the ranks with his mules, and subsequently did good service in remaining by his gun throughout the action." Private Edwards was discharged from the Army Reserve on the 1st Dec. 1892.

London Gazette, 12 May, 1885.—"War Office, 12 May, 1885. The Queen has been graciously pleased to signify Her intention to confer the Decoration of the Victoria Cross upon the undermentioned Soldier of Her Majesty's Army, whose claim has been submitted for Her Majesty's approval, for conspicuous bravery at the action of Abu Klea on the 17th Jan. 1885, as recorded against his name."

SMITH, ALBERT, Gunner, R.A., was awarded the Victoria Cross for services in the Sudan [London Gazette, 12 May, 1885]: "Albert Smith, Gunner, Royal Artillery. Date of Act of Bravery: 17 Jan. 1885. At the action of Abu Klea, on the 17th Jan. 1885, when the enemy charged, the square fell back a short distance, leaving Lieut. Guthrie, Royal Artillery, with his gun in a comparatively unprotected position. At this moment a native rushed at Lieut. Guthrie with a spear, and would in all probability have killed that officer, who had no weapon in his hand at the time (being engaged in superintending the working of his gun), when Gunner Smith, with a gun handspike, warded off the thrust, thus giving Lieut. Guthrie time to draw his sword, and with a blow bring the assailant to his knees, but as the latter fell he made a wild thrust at the officer with a long knife, which Gunner Smith again warded off, not, however, before the native had managed to inflict a wound in Lieut. Guthrie's thigh. Before the Soudani could repeat the thrust, Gunner Smith killed him with the handspike, and thus for a time saved the life of his officer, though the latter unfortunately died some days afterwards of his wound." Gunner Smith was discharged from the Army Reserve on the 4th Dec. 1889.

London Gazette, 17 Sept. 1889.—"War Office, 17 Sept. 1889. The Queen has been graciously pleased to signify Her intention to confer the Decoration of the Victoria Cross upon the undermentioned Officer of the Bombay Medical Service, whose claim has been submitted for Her Majesty's approval, for his conspicuous bravery in action near Lwekaw, Eastern Karenni, on the 1st Jan. 1889, as recorded against his name."

John Crimmin.

CRIMMIN, JOHN, Surgeon, was born 19 March, 1859, and entered the I.M.S. in 1882. He is L.R.C.P., L.R.C.S., and D.P.H., Ireland. He served in Burma, 1886–89, with the Karene Field Force as Senior Medical Officer; was mentioned in Despatches [London Gazette, 15 Nov. 1889]; received the Medal and clasp, and was awarded the Victoria Cross [London Gazette, 17 Sept. 1889]: "John Crimmin, Surgeon, Bombay Medical Service. Lieut. Tighe, 27th Bombay Infantry (to the mounted infantry of which corps Surgeon Crimmin was attached), states that in the action near Lwekaw, Eastern Karenni, on the 1st Jan. 1889, four men charged with him into the midst of a large body of the enemy who were moving off from the Karen left flank, and two men fell to the ground wounded. He saw Surgeon Crimmin attending one of the men about two hundred yards to the rear. Karens were round the party in every direction, and he saw several fire at Surgeon Crimmin and the wounded man. A sepoy then galloped up to Surgeon Crimmin, and the latter joined the fighting line, which then came up. Lieut. Tighe further states that very shortly afterwards they were engaged in driving the enemy from small clumps of trees and bamboo, in which the Karens took shelter. Near one of these clumps he saw Surgeon Crimmin attending a wounded man. Several Karens rushed out at him. Surgeon Crimmin thrust his sword through one of them and attacked a second; a third Karen then dropped from the fire of a sepoy, upon which the remaining Karens fled." It was said that Surgeon Crimmin was as capable in the hospital as on the battle-field. "His arrangements for the disposal of the sick and wounded," said Brigadier-General Collett, "were as perfect as the circumstances of the time permitted." He became Major on 30 Sept. 1894, and Lieut.-Colonel in 1902, and was created a C.I.E. in 1901. He was Civil Surgeon at Rutnagherry; Health Officer of the Port of Bombay. He was created a C.B. in 1913, and promoted to Colonel 1 Oct. 1913, and later became Assistant Director of Medical Services, Kohat Brigade, India.

London Gazette, 29 Oct. 1889.—"War Office, 29 Oct. 1889. The Queen has been graciously pleased to signify Her intention to confer the Decoration of the Victoria Cross upon the undermentioned Officer of her Majesty's Army, whose claim has been submitted for Her Majesty's approval, for his conspicuous bravery during the attack on the village of Tartan, Upper Burma, by a column of the Chin Field Force, on the 4th May, 1889, as recorded against his name."

LE QUESNE, FERDINAND SIMEON, Surgeon, was born at Jersey 25 Dec. 1863, the third son of the late Lieut.-Colonel Giffard N. Le Quesne, Royal Jersey Artillery, and Augusta W., daughter of the late Admiral Charles Simeon. He was educated in the Channel Islands and at King's College Hospital, London. He served in the Burma Expedition of 1889. In the Expedition against the Chins he was severely wounded, mentioned in Despatches, and, for his services in this campaign, received the Victoria Cross [London Gazette, 29 Oct. 1889]: "Ferdinand Simeon Le Quesne, Surgeon, Medical Staff. Date of Act of Bravery: 4 May, 1889. Displayed conspicuous bravery and devotion to duty during the attack on the village of Tartan, by a column of the Chin Field Force, on the 4th May, 1889, in having remained for the space of about ten minutes in a very exposed position (within five yards of the loopholed stockade from which the enemy were firing), dressing with perfect coolness and self-possession the wounds from which Second Lieut. Michel, Norfolk Regt., shortly afterwards died. Surgeon Le Quesne was himself severely wounded later on whilst attending to the wounds of another officer." He also received the Medal and clasp. He served with the Chin Lushai Field Force, 1890 (clasp); with the Wuntho Field Force, 1891 (clasp). In 1898 he became Major. In 1901–2 Major Le Quesne served in the South African War (Queen's Medal, Cape Colony, 1901–2, three clasps). He became Lieut.-Colonel in 1906, and retired Dec. 1918. His recreations are shooting and lawn tennis.

London Gazette, May, 1891.—"War Office, 26 May, 1891. The Queen has been graciously pleased to signify Her intention to confer the Decoration of the Victoria Cross upon the undermentioned Officer of Her Majesty's Army, whose claim has been submitted for Her Majesty's approval, for the conspicuous bravery displayed by him during the recent operations in Manipur, Assam, commencing on 27 March, 1891, as recorded against his name."

GRANT, CHARLES JAMES WILLIAM, Lieutenant, was born at Bourtie, Aberdeenshire, 14 Oct. 1861, the son of Lieut.-General P. C. S. St. J. Grant, and Helen, daughter of Colonel William Birset; was educated

Charles J. W. Grant.

privately and at the R.M.C., Sandhurst. He joined the Suffolk Regt. on 10 May, 1882, and the Madras Staff Corps two years later, 10 May, 1884, taking part in the Burma Expedition, 1885–87 (Medal and clasp). He volunteered and went to the assistance of the Chief Commissioner's defeated escort 27 March, 1891, in command of eighty Punjabis and Gurkhas. He stormed and held Thobal 21 March (slightly wounded), till relieved 9 April. His horse was shot 13 April; he was severely wounded 25 April. For these services he received the clasp to the Burma Medal; was promoted Captain 10 May, 1891, and Brevet Major 11 May, 1891; granted two years' service; mentioned in Despatches 14 Aug. 1891, and decorated with the Victoria Cross. All his surviving men received the Order of Merit for devotion and heroism. His Victoria Cross was gazetted 26 May, 1891: "Charles James William Grant, Lieut., Indian Staff Corps. For the conspicuous bravery and devotion to his country displayed by him in having, upon hearing, on the 27th March, 1891, of the disaster at Manipur, at once volunteered to attempt the relief of the British captives, with eighty native soldiers, and having advanced with the greatest intrepidity, captured Thobal, near Manipur, and held it against a large force of the enemy. Lieut. Grant inspired his men with equal heroism and ever-present example of personal daring and resource." In 1891 he was A.D.C. to Lieut.-General Sir J. C. Dormer, Commander-in-Chief in Madras. In the same year he married Mary, daughter of T. Denton Scholes and widow of J. W. Langlois. He became Lieut.-Colonel 1 June, 1904, and Brevet Colonel 11 June, 1907, and retired 22 Oct. 1913. During the European War he was D.C.O., attached 3rd Royal Scots. Colonel Grant's recreations are fishing and shooting.

London Gazette, 12 July, 1892.—"War Office, 12 July, 1892. The Queen has been graciously pleased to signify Her intention to confer the Decoration of the Victoria Cross upon the undermentioned Officers of Her Majesty's Army, whose claims have been submitted for Her Majesty's approval, for the conspicuous bravery displayed by them during the recent operations in the Hunza and Nagar country on the Gilgit frontier in Dec. 1891, as recorded against their names."

AYLMER, FENTON JOHN, Capt., was born at Hastings 5 April, 1862, second son of the late Capt. F. J. Aylmer, 97th Regt.; was educated privately, and joined the Royal Engineers in 1880. He served in the Burma Expedition 1886–87 (Despatches, Medal and clasp); in the Hazara Expedition of 1891 (Despatches, clasp); in the Hunza Expedition of 1891–92, in which he was mentioned in Despatches, given a clasp and a Brevet Majority, and was awarded the Victoria Cross. The expedition sent into the Hunza-Nagar country had arrived at the Nilt Fort. Our force consisted of about a thousand men, mostly Kashmir, Imperial Service Troops, and sixteen British officers. The fort which was to be attacked stood at the extremity of a ledge which overhung the Nilt Nullah, and was protected by a precipice, while the only approach to the gate had been strongly defended by abattis of branches. It was impossible to bring the mountain guns to bear on this part, owing to the impracticability of dragging them up the cliffs which overlooked it, and for a long time a hot rifle fire was kept up by the British, which was replied to with equal severity by the enemy from their loopholed stronghold. At length it was resolved to take the fort by storm and to blow the great gate in, in order to effect an entrance. This dangerous duty was entrusted to Capt. Aylmer, in command of the Engineers, and he was supported by a hundred Gurkhas under Lieuts. Boisragon (V.C.) and Badcock. While the Gurkhas hacked at the branches of the abattis to make an entrance, the three officers with a few men got through the opening and forced the gate of the outer wall. Capt. Aylmer, with the utmost coolness, then advanced under heavy fire and placed the charge of gun-cotton against the main gate and lighted the fuse, when he was shot in the left leg. He then retired to await the explosion. For some reason the charge did not ignite, upon which he returned, rearranged the charge and relit the fuse. He was again severely injured in the hand from a rock hurled from above. The explosion now took place and blew in the gate, the officers and men dashed through, and a terrific hand-to-hand combat took place with the defenders, who were driven, after a most desperate resistance, from the fort. Capt. Aylmer, though again severely wounded, fired nineteen shots with his revolver, killed several of the enemy, and fought until, fainting from loss of blood, he had to be carried out of action. He was awarded the Victoria Cross [London Gazette, 12 July, 1892]: " Fenton John Aylmer, Capt., Royal Engineers. For his conspicuous bravery in the assault and capture of the Nilt Fort on 2 Dec. 1891. This officer accompanied the storming party, burst open the inner gate with gun-cotton, which he had placed and ignited, and though severely wounded, once in the leg and twice in the right hand, fired nineteen shots with his revolver, killing several of the enemy, and remained fighting, until, fainting from loss of blood, he was carried out of action." Capt. C. J. and E. E. Younghusband write in their " Relief of Chitral ": " During the construction, a very prompt and plucky act on Major Aylmer's part saved the life of a soldier. About a mile up stream, where the first floating bridge had been constructed, a flying bridge and rafts were still working backwards and forwards to supply the Guides with their wants on the other bank. One of these rafts, on which were two men of the Devonshire Regt. Maxim Gun Detachment, got accidentally overturned, and the boatmen and oars were all washed away. The two soldiers managed to climb on the raft and were carried down stream at a great pace. General Gatacre, seeing the accident, immediately galloped down to the site of the new bridge, to give warning in the hope of saving the men. Meanwhile, one of them had made an attempt to jump on shore and had been swept away and drowned, and the survivor on the raft came flying down the torrent. With the greatest presence of mind Major Aylmer immediately slipped down a slack wire that was across the river and just managed to grab the soldier as he shot past. The raft was immediately after dashed on the rocks below. With considerable difficulty they were both hauled on shore, and it was then found that the Major was badly bruised and cut by the wire. The Royal Humane Society's Medal has been given for many a less distinguished act of bravery, yet I do not think that, in the stir of passing events, it actually occurred to any of the spectators to send the recommendation home." In 1892 Major Aylmer served in the Isazai Expedition and in the Chitral Expedition of 1895 (Despatches, Medal and clasp, and Brevet Colonecy). He served in India from 1883; has been A.A.G. and acted as A.Q.M.G. and D.Q.M.G., Army Headquarters, and as A.Q.M.G., Madras Command (Ootacamund). He was created a C.B. in 1907, and a K.C.B. in 1916. Sir Fenton Aylmer became Lieut.-General.

BOISRAGON, GUY HUDLESTON, Colonel, was born at Kohat, Punjab, on 5 Nov. 1864, eldest son of Major-General Henry M. Boisragon, late Commandant of the 4th Sikhs, Punjab Frontier Force, and Anna, daughter of the late William Hudleston, of the Madras Civil Service. He was educated at Charterhouse and the R.M.C., Sandhurst, and joined the 10th (Lincolnshire) Regt. in 1885, and the 5th Gurkhas 1887. In 1888 he served in the Hazara Expedition (Medal and clasp), and in 1891 in the 2nd Hazara Expedition (clasp). He also served with the two Miranzai Expeditions in 1891, with the first expedition as Orderly Officer to the General Officer in Command (clasp). From 1891 to 1892 he served in the operations in the Hunza-Nagar country, including the capture of the Nilt Fort. It was here that, with Capt. Aylmer and Lieut. Badcock, Lieut. Boisragon took a prominent part in the reduction of the fort. He was mentioned in Despatches and received a clasp, and was awarded the Victoria Cross [London Gazette, 12 July, 1892]: " Guy Hudleston Boisragon, Lieut., Indian Staff Corps (ex Lincoln Regt.). For his conspicuous bravery in the assault and capture of the Nilt Fort on 2 Dec. 1891. This officer led the assault with dash and determination, and forced his way through difficult obstacles to the inner gate, when he returned for reinforcements, moving intrepidly to and fro, under a heavy cross-fire, until he had collected sufficient men to drive the enemy from the fort." He served in the Waziristan Expedition under Sir William Lockhart, 1894–95 (clasp). From 1894 to 1895 he was A.D.C. to the Lieut.-General Punjab Command. In 1896 he was promoted Captain, and in 1897 and 1898 took part in the operations in the Samana and Kurrum Valley, 1897 (Medal with two clasps). He served in the Tirah Expedition, 1897–98, in the reconnaissance of the Kharmana defile, and was present at the action of 7 Nov. 1897. Capt. Boisragon took part in the operations against the Khani Khel Chamkhannis (clasp). He became Major in 1903, Brevet Colonel, and later Colonel, Frontier Force. He served in the European War from 1914, and was wounded (Order of the Nile, Fourth Class).

SMITH, JOHN MANNERS, Lieut., was born at Lahore 30 Aug. 1864, the fifth son of the late Charles Manners Smith, F.R.C.S. (Surgeon-General, I.M.S.), and was educated at Trinity College, Stratford-on-Avon, at King Edward VI. School, Norwich, and at the Royal Military College, Sandhurst. He became a Lieutenant in the Norfolk Regiment in 1883, and in 1885 joined the Indian Staff Corps, and served with the 3rd Sikhs (Infantry) and the 5th Gurkha Rifles 1885–87. He was appointed Military Attaché to the Foreign Office, Government of India, and admitted to the Political Department in 1887. He accompanied Sir Mortimer Durand on his Missions to Sikkim, 1888, and Kabul, 1893. Lieut. Manners Smith won the Victoria Cross in the forcing of the Nilt position in the Hunza-Nagar Expedition of 1891, and received the Indian Frontier Medal with clasp. His Victoria Cross was gazetted 12 July, 1892: " John Manners Smith, Lieut., Indian Staff Corps. For his conspicuous bravery when leading the storming party at the attack and capture of the strong position occupied by the enemy near Nilt, in the Hunza-Nagar country, on the 20th Dec. 1891. The position was, owing to the nature of the country, an extremely strong one, and had barred the advance of the force for seventeen days. It was eventually forced by a small party of fifty rifles, with another of equal strength in support. The first of these parties was under the command of Lieut. Smith, and it was entirely owing to his splendid leading, and the coolness, combined with dash, he displayed while doing so, that a success was obtained. For nearly four hours on the face of the cliff, which was almost precipitous, he steadily moved his handful of men from point to point, as the difficulties of the ground and showers of stones from above gave him the opportunity, and during the whole of this time he was in such a position as to be unable to defend himself from any attack the enemy might choose to make. He was the first man to reach the summit, within a few yards of one of the enemy's sangars, which was immediately rushed, Lieut. Smith pistolling the first man." In 1896 he married Bertha Mabel, eldest daughter of the late Philip Arderne Latham. Lieut.-Colonel Smith has held political appointments in Kashmir, Bundhelkand, Baluchistan, Rajputana, Central India and Nepal, 1889 to 1919. He served in the Punjab Frontier and Tirah Expedition, 1897–98 (Medal with three clasps). He became a Political Resident, First Class, Political Department, Government of India, and Agent to the Governor-General in Rajputana and Chief Commissioner Ajmer-Mewara in 1917.

John Manners Smith.

London Gazette, 9 Dec. 1892.—" War Office, 9 Dec. 1892. The Queen has been graciously pleased to signify Her intention to confer the Decoration of the Victoria Cross upon the undermentioned Soldier of Her Majesty's Army, whose claim has been submitted for Her Majesty's approval, for the conspicuous bravery displayed by him during the attack on the stockaded town of Toniataba, Gambia River, on the 13th March, 1892, as recorded against his name."

GORDON, WILLIAM JAMES, Corpl., was awarded the Victoria Cross [London Gazette, 9 Dec. 1892]: " William James Gordon, No. 2829, Corpl., The West Indian Regt. During the attack on the town of Toniataba, Major G. C. Madden, West India Regt., who was in command of the troops, was superintending a party of twelve men who were endeavouring with a heavy beam to break down the south gate of the town, when suddenly a number of musket-muzzles were projected through a double row of loopholes which had been masked. Some of these were within two or three yards of that officer's back, and before he realized what had happened, L.-Corpl. Gordon threw himself between Major Madden and the muskets, pushing that officer out of the way, and exclaiming, 'Look out, sir!' At the same moment L.-Corpl. Gordon was shot through the lungs. By his bravery and self-devotion on this occasion the lance-corporal probably saved the life of his commanding officer." William James Gordon was the third man of colour to whom the Victoria Cross has been awarded. He was discharged on pension 18 April, 1902. The late Lieut.-Colonel G. C. Madden, C.B., D.S.O., whose life Gordon saved, died on 20 April, 1912.

William James Gordon.

London Gazette, 2 Jan. 1894.—" War Office, 2 Jan. 1894. The Queen has been graciously pleased to signify Her intention to confer the Decoration of the Victoria Cross upon the undermentioned Officer of Her Majesty's Army, whose claim has been submitted for Her Majesty's approval, for his conspicuous bravery during the attack on the Sima Post by Kachins, on the 6th Jan. last, as recorded against his name."

LLOYD, OWEN EDWARD PENNEFATHER, Surgeon-General, was born 1 Jan. 1854, son of the late Major M. Pennefather Lloyd, 59th Regt., of County Roscommon; was educated at Fermoy College, Cork, and Queen's University, Cork; is a Member of the Royal Irish University, and had the degrees of L.R.C.S., L.R.C.P., and L.M., Edinburgh. He joined the Army Medical Service in 1878; went through the

Zulu War in 1879; was present at the attack and capture of Seku-kuni's stronghold as Assistant Instructor to the Bearer Column in the Transvaal War of 1881–82. He was in Standerton during the siege.

Owen E. P. Lloyd.

Surgeon Lloyd took part in the Kachin Expedition of 1892–93, and was present at the attack on Fort Sima, where he won his Victoria Cross [London Gazette, 2 Jan. 1894]: "Owen Pennefather Lloyd, Surgeon, Army Medical Staff (Royal Army Medical Corps). Date of Act of Bravery: 6 Jan. 1893. During the attack on the Sima Post by Kachins, on the 6th Jan. 1893, Surgeon-Major Lloyd, on hearing that the Commanding Officer, Capt. Morton (who had left the fort to visit a picket about eighty yards distant), was wounded, at once ran out to his assistance under a close and heavy fire, accompanied by Suba-dar Matab Singh. On reaching the wounded officer, Surgeon-Major Lloyd sent Subadar Matab Singh back for further assistance, and remained with Capt. Morton till the Subadar returned with five men of the Magwe Battn. of Military Police, when he assisted in carrying Capt. Morton back to the fort, where that officer died in a few minutes afterwards. The enemy were within ten or fifteen paces, keeping up a heavy fire, which killed three men of the picket, and also Bugler Purna Singh. This man accompanied Capt. Morton from the fort, showed great gallantry in supporting him in his arms when wounded, and was shot while helping to carry him back to the fort. (The native officer and five sepoys above alluded to have been awarded the Order of Merit.)" He took command of the fort after the death of Capt. Morton, officer commanding. He married Florence, daughter of the late Capt. and Lady Louisa Morgan, of Bridestown House, County Cork, and has one son and one daughter. He was Medical Officer to the Franco–British Boundary Commission on the Burma Frontier, 1898–99; acted as H.B.M.'s Commissioner during the absence of Sir G. Scott; was Principal Medical Officer, Bareilly Brigades, India, and Hon. Surgeon to the Viceroy. He was P.M.O. in South Africa. He was created a C.B. in 1910, and retired in 1913. Surgeon-General Lloyd is very fond of all kinds of field sports, especially big game shooting; he was well known as a Shikari in Burma, killing in the year 1897 150 head of big game, including six tusker elephants.

London Gazette, 16 July, 1895.—"War Office, 16 July, 1895. The Queen has been graciously pleased to signify Her intention to confer the Decoration of the Victoria Cross upon the undermentioned Officer, whose claim has been submitted for Her Majesty's approval for his conspicuous bravery during the sortie from Chitral Fort, on the 3rd March last, as recorded against his name."

WHITCHURCH, HARRY FREDERICK, Capt., was born 22 Sept. 1866, the son of F. Whitchurch, Esq., of Sandown, Isle of Wight. He was educated in England, France and Germany; entered St. Bartholomew's Hospital in 1883, and the Indian Army in 1888. He served in the Lushai Expedition in 1892, and in the relief of Aijal and Changsil (Medal and clasp), and in the relief of Chitral, 1895; was mentioned in Despatches, received the Medal and clasp, and was awarded the Victoria Cross [London Gazette, 16 July, 1895]: "Harry Frederick Whitchurch, Surgeon-Capt., Indian Medical Service. During the sortie from Chitral Fort on the 3rd March last, at the commencement of the siege, Surgeon-Capt. Whitchurch went to the assistance of Capt. Baird, 24th Bengal Infantry, who was mortally wounded, and brought him back to the fort under a heavy fire from the enemy. Capt. Baird was on the right

Harry F. Whitchurch.

of the fighting line, and had only a small party of Gurkhas and men of the 4th Kashmir Rifles. He was wounded on the heights at a distance of a mile and a half from the fort. When Surgeon-Capt. Whitchurch proceeded to his rescue, the enemy, in great strength, had broken through the fighting line; darkness had set in, and Capt. Baird, Surgeon-Capt. Whitchurch and the sepoys were completely isolated from assistance. Capt. Baird was placed in a dhooly by Surgeon-Capt. Whitchurch, and the party then attempted to return to the fort. The Gurkhas bravely clung to the dhooly until three were killed and a fourth was severely wounded. Surgeon-Capt. Whitchurch then put Capt. Baird upon his back and carried him some distance with heroic courage and resolution. The little party kept diminishing in numbers, being fired at the whole way. On one or two occasions Surgeon-Capt. Whitchurch was obliged to charge walls, from behind which the enemy kept up an incessant fire. At one place particularly the whole party was in imminent danger of being cut up, having been surrounded by the enemy. Surgeon-Capt. Whitchurch gallantly rushed the position, and eventually succeeded in getting Capt. Baird and the sepoys into the fort. Nearly all the party were wounded, Capt. Baird receiving two additional wounds before reaching the fort." "Major Whitchurch's name recalls one of the many deeds of valour performed by the small garrison under Dr. (later Sir George) Scott Robertson, M.P., which defended Chitral Fort during its investment from 3 March to 18 April, 1895. During the sortie from the fort at the beginning of the siege, Major, then Surgeon-Capt., Whitchurch went to the assistance of Capt. Baird, of the 24th Bengal

Infantry, who was mortally wounded, and brought him back to the fort under a heavy fire from the enemy. In an account of the defence reprinted from the 'Pioneer,' Sir George Robertson is quoted as saying of the dying Baird: 'Characteristically he has urged me not to forget Whitchurch, and has told me how Whitchurch had to charge walls and small sangars on the road. On one occasion the party was surrounded, and must have been cut to pieces, Baird says, but for a splendid charge by Whitchurch, who lost four of his own men in hand-to-hand fighting, but inflicted such loss on the enemy that they did not again come within reach of the bayonets.' It is difficult to write temperately about Whitchurch." He took part in the defence of the Malakand, and in the relief of Chakdara, and the engagement of Landakai, N.W. Frontier of India, 1897–98 (Despatch of Major-General Sir Brandon Blood: "Surgeon-Capt. H. F. Whitchurch, V.C., attended to the wounded under fire throughout the fighting"). He served in China in 1901, taking part in the relief of the Chinese Legation. Surgeon-Major Whitchurch died of enteric 16 Aug. 1907, aged 40, at Dharmsala, Punjab, where his regiment, the 1st Prince of Wales's Own Gurkha Rifles (the Malaun Regt.), was stationed.

London Gazette, 7 May, 1897.—"War Office, 7 May, 1897. The Queen has been graciously pleased to signify Her intention to confer the Decoration of the Victoria Cross on the undermentioned Officer and Soldier, whose claims have been submitted for Her Majesty's approval, for their gallant conduct during the recent operations in South Africa, as recorded against their names."

NESBITT, RANDOLPH COSBY, Capt., was born at Queenstown in Cape Colony on 20 Sept. 1867, the son of Major C. A. Nesbitt; was educated at St. Paul's School, London, and joined the Cape Mounted Rifles

Randolph Cosby Nesbitt.

on the 10th Aug. 1885. He served through the Mashona Expedition of 1890, being promoted Lieutenant (Police) in Sept. 1891. He was Chief Constable at Fort Peddie, in the Cape, from March, 1892, till April, 1893. At the end of that year he returned to Mashonaland, and became an Inspector of the Mounted Police there. In 1895 he was appointed J.P. He served in Gazaland on special service in 1894. On 1 June, 1895, he was promoted a Captain in the British South Africa Police. He served in Mashonaland in 1896. In the native insurrection in Mashonaland in 1896, many of the homesteads were sacked and the settlers and their families murdered before help could be sent to them. For they lived—in many instances —in isolated parts of the country, miles from their nearest neighbours. In June, 1896, Mr. Judson, Director of Telegraphs at Salisbury, had ridden out with a patrol to the assistance of the miners at the Alice Mine in the Mazoe Valley. On reaching them, however, he found it quite impossible to bring them away through the hordes of savages, and was compelled to remain in laager with them. On the 19th Sept. Nesbitt was out with a patrol of thirteen men, and came across a runner from Mr. Judson, who had a note to Judge Vincent saying that a hundred men and a maxim gun would be needed in order to relieve them. Capt. Nesbitt read the note to his thirteen men, and asked them if they would come with him and try to rescue the beleaguered party. They readily agreed to do so, and the party set off at once. They fought their way through the enemy to the laager, put the three women who were with the miners into an armoured waggon, and began the return journey amidst heavy fighting. They steadily made their way through the masses of savages who barred their way, though the enemy often crept through the long grass and—when quite close—fired at the waggon. At length Capt. Nesbitt arrived at Salisbury, with the loss of only three men killed and five wounded, and eight horses killed and seven wounded. [London Gazette, 7 May, 1897]: "Randolph Cosby Nesbitt, Capt., Mashonaland Mounted Police. This officer, on the 19th June, 1896, led the Mazoe rescue patrol, consisting of only thirteen men, fought his way through the rebels to get to Salthouse's party, and succeeded in bringing them back to Salisbury, with heavy fighting, in which three of his small force were killed and five wounded, and fifteen horses killed and wounded." During the Boer War of 1899–1902, Major Nesbitt was in command of a squadron of the B.S.A.P., under Generals Plumer and Baden-Powell in the Transvaal. He became Native Commissioner, B.S.A. Police, in 1909.

HENDERSON, HERBERT STEPHEN Trooper, was born at Hillhead, Glasgow, 30 March, 1870, fourth son of William Henderson, Bishop Street Engineering Works, Glasgow, and grandson of James Henderson, shipbuilder, Glasgow. He was educated at Kelvinside Academy, Hillhead, Glasgow, and served a five years' apprenticeship with J. and J. Thomson, engineers, Glasgow, being afterwards connected with Workman, Clark and Company, Belfast, and with Harland and Wolff. In 1892 Mr. Henderson left Belfast for the Rand, and he was connected professionally with the Langlaagte, Primrose, Crœsus and George and May Gold Mines. In 1894 he left the Rand for Rhodesia, as engineer to Queen's Mine, etc. When the rebellion broke out he joined the Rhodesia Horse as a Scout, under Capt. M'Farlane. On the 28th March (Sunday) he left Buluwayo, and when about thirty-five miles from town, Celliers and himself, who formed the advance guard, were fired at and cut off by rebels. Celliers's horse was shot in five places, ran two hundred yards, and then dropped, while Celliers himself was shot through the knee. Henderson put him on his own pony, and by dint of dodging the Matabele, reached Buluwayo, but only on Wednesday. They had had nothing to eat from Sunday morning till Wednesday morning, and Mr. Henderson said he never wished to spend another birthday like it. For his gallantry on his occasion he was awarded the Victoria Cross [London Gazette, 7 May, 1897]: "Herbert Stephen Henderson, Trooper, Buluwayo Field Force. On the morning of the 30th March, 1896, just before daylight, Capt. M'Farlane's party was surprised by the natives. Troopers Celliers and Henderson, who formed part of the advanced guard, were cut off from the main body, and Celliers was shot through the knee. His horse also was badly wounded, and eventually died. Henderson then placed Celliers on his own horse, and made the best of his way to Buluwayo. The country between Campbell's Store, where they were cut off, and Buluwayo, a distance of about thirty-five miles, was full of natives fully armed, and they had, therefore, to proceed principally by night, hiding in the bush in the daytime. Celliers, who was weak from loss of blood and in great agony, asked Henderson to leave him, but he would not, and brought him in, after passing two days and one night in the veldt without food." Trooper Henderson was decorated by Lord Milner at the opening of the Buluwayo railway. He was later promoted to Lieutenant. His favourite recreations are yachting, riding, shooting and gymnastics.

"Memorandum, 7 May, 1897.—Trooper Frank William Baxter, of the Buluwayo Field Force, on account of his gallant conduct in having, on the 22nd April, 1896, dismounted and given up his horse to a wounded comrade, Corpl. Wiseman, who was being closely pursued by an overwhelming force of the enemy, would have been recommended to Her Majesty for the Victoria Cross had he survived."

London Gazette, 9 Nov. 1897.—"War Office, 9 Nov. 1897. The Queen has been graciously pleased to signify Her intention to confer the Decoration of the Victoria Cross on the undermentioned Officers, whose claims have been submitted for Her Majesty's approval, for their conspicuous bravery during the operations on the North-West Frontier of India, as recorded against their names."

ADAMS, ROBERT BELLEW, Major and Brevet Lieut.-Colonel, was born 26 July, 1856, at Murree, Punjab, India, the son of Major Robert Roy Adams, Bengal Staff Corps, and of Frances Charlotte C. Adams, daughter of Capt. F. Bellew, H.E.I.C.S. Major Adams served in the Honourable East India Company's Army; was present at the Battle of Maharajpur in 1843 (Maharajpur Star); served as Brigade-Major, Punjab Irregular Force, in Expeditions against the North-West Frontier Tribes in 1855-6 (Medal); Indian Mutiny, 1857-8 (Medal). He was assassinated by a fanatic when Deputy Commissioner of Peshawar in 1865. His son was educated at private schools and by tutors, and at Forest School, Walthamstow, Essex, and became a Sub-Lieutenant, in the 1st Battn. 12th Foot, on 11 Sept. 1876, and served with it in India till May, 1879. He served in the 3rd Punjab Cavalry in 1879, and in Queen Victoria's Own Corps of Guides from 1879-1904.

Robert Bellew Adams.

Lieut. R. B. Adams served with the Corps of Guides with the Afghanistan Field Force, 1879-80, joining Headquarters at Jagdalak in Nov. 1879. He marched with the Corps to Kabul, and was present with the Infantry in all the subsequent operations, including the storming of the Takht-i-Shah Heights, and Asmai Heights, the defence of Sherpur, and the second action of Charasiah. He became Officiating Adjutant of the Corps on 22 July, 1880, was mentioned in Despatches, and received the Afghan Medal with Kabul clasp. He was promoted Captain in 1887. In 1895 Capt. Adams served with the Chitral Relief Force in command of Guides Cavalry, and, after death in action at Panjkora of Lieut.-Colonel Battye, commanded the Corps of Guides (Infantry). He was present at the storming of the Malakand Pass, at the action near Khar (horse wounded), at the Passage of the Swat River, and at the action near Mamugai. He was mentioned in Despatches twice, and received the Brevet of Lieutenant-Colonel on attaining substantive rank as Major, Sept. 1896, and the India Medal with clasp (Chitral Relief Expedition). In 1897 he served with the Malakand Field Force, being present at the Defence of Malakand (horse shot). Mentioned in Despatches : " I also wish to bring the name of Lieut.-Colonel R. B. Adams of the Guides to His Excellency's notice. The prompt way in which the Guides mobilized and their grand march, reflects great credit on him and the Corps. Since arrival at the Malakand on the 27th July and till the morning of the 1st Aug., Lieut.-Colonel Adams was in command of the Lower Camp, i.e., that occupied by central and left position, and in the execution of this command and the arrangements he made for improving the defences, he gave me every satisfaction. I have also to express my appreciation of the way in which he conducted the cavalry reconnaissance on the 1st Aug., his horse being shot under him." He took part in the Relief of Chakdarra ; at the action of Landakai (horse wounded), and at the operations in the Mahmund Valley. He was mentioned in Despatches four times, received clasps for the Punjab Frontier, 1897-8, and for Malakand, 1897. He was awarded the Victoria Cross. His Victoria Cross was gazetted 9 Nov. 1897 : " Robert Bellew Adams, Major and Brevet Lieut.-Colonel, Indian Staff Corps. During the fighting at Nawa Kili, in Upper Swat, on the 17th Aug. 1897, Lieut.-Colonel R. B. Adams proceeded with Lieut. H. L. S. MacLean and Viscount Fincastle, and five men of the Guides, under a heavy and close fire, to the rescue of Lieut. R. T. Greaves, Lancashire Fusiliers, who was lying disabled by a bullet-wound, and surrounded by the enemy's swordsmen. In bringing him under cover, he (Lieut. Greaves) was struck by a bullet and killed,

Lieut. MacLean was mortally wounded, whilst the horses of Lieut.-Colonel Adams and Lieut. Viscount Fincastle were shot, as well as two troop horses." During a cavalry pursuit in the Swat Valley, Lieut. Greaves, who was acting as a War Correspondent, was carried by an impetuous pony to a low range of hills where the enemy had collected in large numbers after their flight across the plain, and had opened a heavy fire on the scattered pursuing cavalry. He was severely wounded, and fell from his horse disabled. As he was thus lying out in the open, some enemy swordsmen rushed down to attack him. Seeing this, Colonel Adams, who was near, galloped forward to the rescue, closely followed by Lord Fincastle, whose horse was shot on the way. The two officers tried to lift the half-conscious wounded man on to Colonel Adams' horse. Almost simultaneously Lieut. MacLean (Adjutant), quickly taking in the situation, rapidly collected some of his men, and dismounted them in a clump of trees close by, on a flank, to check by their fire the advance of the enemy down from the hill. He then dashed out, accompanied by two or three men of the Guides Cavalry, to assist in the rescue. While Lieut. Greaves was being lifted on to Lieut. MacLean's horse, Colonel Adams remained mounted, facing the enemy, to stop their rushing the party. During this time the small group was under an extremely hot fire at short range. Lieut. Greaves was hit again and killed, and Lieut. MacLean was mortally wounded. Colonel Adams' horse and two troop horses were also hit. Colonel Adams and Lord Fincastle received the Victoria Cross, and later a posthumous award of the Cross was made to Lieut. MacLean. Jemadar Bahadur Singh and the men of the Guides Cavalry were decorated with the Indian Order of Merit for their gallant behaviour under very trying circumstances. In 1898 Colonel Adams served with the Buner Field Force. He commanded a column invading Buner through the Pirsai Pass, was created a C.B., and mentioned in the Despatch of Major-General Sir B. Blood, K.C.B., dated 19th Jan. 1898 : " The movement thus successfully carried out by Lieut.-Colonel Adams, V.C., was of very great value, as the sudden appearance of five squadrons and two battalions in the middle of the Buner country helped most effectually to prevent the enemy from being encouraged to make fresh resistance " In April, 1899, he was appointed Commandant of the Queen's Own Corps of Guides, and in Sept, 1901, was appointed A.D.C. to the King, and given the Brevet of Colonel. In 1902 he became substantive Lieutenant-Colonel ; Brigadier-General in 1904 ; and in 1906 Major-General. In Jan. 1904, he was appointed Colonel on the Staff, commanding at Nowshera, and in Dec. 1904, Commander of the Cavalry Brigade at Ambala. He commanded the Derajat Brigade from April, 1906, till compelled to resign by illness, the result of an accident in Nov. 1908. He retired in Dec. 1911, having been awarded a Good Service Pension in 1910. In 1912 he was created a K.C.B. Sir R. B. Adams has the King Edward Coronation Medal.

FINCASTLE, VISCOUNT, ALEXANDER EDWARD MURRAY, Lieut., was born 22 April, 1871, son of the 7th Earl of Dunmore and Lady Gertrude Coke, 3rd daughter of the 2nd Earl of Leicester. He was educated at Eton, and joined the Army 30 May, 1891, becoming Lieutenant 1 Sept. 1894. He was A.D.C. to the Viceroy of India, 1895-97, and served in the Dongola Expedition, 1896 (two Medals). In 1897 he served in the Frontier War, Malakand, with the Guides Cavalry, took part in the action of Landakai, had his horse shot under him ; served with the Buner Field Force on the Staff, was mentioned in Despatches [London Gazette, 5 Nov. 1897 ; 11 Jan. and 22 April, 1898]. He became Captain 17 Oct. 1899, and served on the Staff in the South African War, 1899-1902, with the 6th (Inniskilling) Dragoons and 16th Lancers, and later with the Imperial Yeomanry, being present at the relief of Kimberley ; operations in the Orange Free State, Feb. to May, 1900, including operations at Paardeberg, actions

Viscount Fincastle.

at Poplar Grove and Karee Siding. Operations in the Transvaal, east of Pretoria, July to 29 Nov. 1900. Operations in the Transvaal, west of Pretoria, July to 29 Nov. 1900. Operations in Orange River Colony (May to 29 Nov. 1900). Operations in Cape Colony, south of Orange River, 1899-1900, including actions at Colesberg. Operations in Cape Colony, north of Orange River. He was afterwards in command of an Imperial Yeomanry Battalion (from 22 Jan. 1902). Lord Fincastle was mentioned in Despatches [London Gazette, 10 Sept. 1901], and received the Queen's Medal with 4 clasps. On 4 Jan. 1904, in London, he married Lucinda Dorothea, eldest daughter of Horace Kemble, Knock, Isle of Skye, and they have one son, Edward David Murray Viscount Fincastle (born 3 April, 1908), and two daughters, Lady Marjorie Murray, and Lady Elizabeth Murray. He succeeded his father in 1907 as 8th Earl of Dunmore. Lord Dunmore served in the European War from 1914, was wounded, and was created a Companion of the Distinguished Service Order for services on the General Staff, on the Somme, as G.S.O.2. He was created an M.V.O., and was four times mentioned in Despatches. Lord Dunmore is Lieutenant-Colonel (Reserve), 16th Lancers.

COSTELLO, EDMOND WILLIAM, Lieut., belongs to an Irish family, and was born on 7 Aug. 1873, at Sheikhbudin, North-

Edmond W. Costello.

West Frontier Province, India, the son of the late Colonel C. P. Costello, I.M.S., and Mrs. Costello, *née* Harkan. He was educated at Beaumont College, and Stonyhurst, and joined the West Yorkshire Regt. on 19 Nov. 1892. In 1894 he joined the 22nd Punjab Infantry. In 1897 he had been appointed to the Indian Staff Corps, and served with the Malakand Field Force, 1897, under Sir William Lockhart. He won the Victoria Cross as described in the London Gazette of 9 Nov. 1897: " Edmond William Costello, Lieut., Indian Staff Corps. On the night of the 26th July, 1897, at the Malakand, Lieut. Costello went out from the hospital enclosure, and, with the assistance of two sepoys, brought in a wounded lance-havildar, who was lying 60 yards away in the open on the football-ground. This ground was at the time overrun with swordsmen, and swept by a heavy fire from both the enemy and our own men, who were holding the sapper lines." He was twice wounded, 27th and 30th July, 1897; was mentioned in Despatches, and, besides the Victoria Cross, received the North-West Frontier Medal and clasps. " Lieut. E. W. Costello, 22nd Punjab Infantry, temporarily attached to the 24th Punjab Infantry, has behaved exceedingly well, and is the subject of a separate recommendation." In 1902 he married Elsie Maud Lang, daughter of Charles Lang Huggins, of Hadlow Grange, Buxted, and they have one daughter, "Kitty" (Elsie Maud) Costello. In 1908 he took part in the operations in the Mohmand country (Medal and clasp). Major Costello served in the European War, in Mesopotamia, continuously from 1914 to 1919. He was Second in Command, 22nd Punjabis, from Nov. 1914, to March, 1915, when he was appointed to the General Staff, becoming G.S.O.1., 15th Division, in 1916, He served on the Tigris, Lower Euphrates, as Chief Staff Officer to General Brooking, in the operations including the Battles of Ramedi and Khan Baghdadi on the Upper Euphrates, Mesopotamia. He was six times mentioned in Despatches, receiving a Brevet Lieutenant-Colonelcy in 1916, and a Brevet Colonelcy in 1919. He was created a Companion of the Distinguished Service Order [London Gazette, Aug. 1917]: " Edmond William Costello, Major, General Staff." In Sept. 1917 he was awarded the Croix de Guerre with palms, and in Jan. 1918, was created a C.M.G. He was promoted to Brigadier-General in May, 1918, commanding the 12th Brigade.

London Gazette, 9 Nov. 1897—*" During the fighting at Nawa Kili, in Upper Swat, on the 17th Aug. 1897, Lieut.-Colonel R. B. Adams proceeded with Lieuts. H. L. S. MacLean and Viscount Fincastle, and five men of the Guides, under a very heavy and close fire, to the rescue of Lieut. Greaves, Lancashire Fusiliers, who was lying disabled by a bullet-wound, and surrounded by the enemy's swordsmen. In bringing him under cover, he (Lieut. Greaves) was struck by a bullet and killed—*Lieut. MacLean* was mortally wounded—whilst the horses of Lieut.-Colonel Adams and Lieut. Viscount Fincastle were shot, as well as two troop horses.

Memorandum.—" Lieut. Hector Lachlan Stewart MacLean, Indian Staff Corps, on account of his gallant conduct as recorded above,* would have been recommended to Her Majesty for the Victoria Cross had he survived."

London Gazette, 20 May, 1898.—" War Office, 20 May, 1898. The Queen has been graciously pleased to signify Her intention to confer the Decoration of the Victoria Cross on the undermentioned Officers and Soldiers, whose claims have been submitted for Her Majesty's approval, for their gallant conduct during the recent operations on the North-West Frontier of India, as recorded against their names."

WATSON, THOMAS COLCLOUGH, Lieut., was born at Velsen, Holland, on 11 April, 1867, the son of Thomas Colclough Watson and Eliza Holmes Watson (*née* Reed). He was educated at Louth, Lincolnshire, and abroad, and entered the Royal Engineers on 18 Feb. 1888. On 16 Jan. 1892, at Meerut, India, he married Edythe, daughter of the late Major-General John Whateley Welchman, C.B., and Harriet Alzelea Welchman. Their only child, Gerald Thomas Colclough Watson, was born 24 Oct. 1892. Mrs. Watson has the Royal Red Cross, which was awarded to her after the Black Mountain Expedition in 1888. Lord and Lady Roberts and Colonel and Mrs. Watson were the only two British officers and their wives who held the V.C. and the R.R.C. Lieut.-Colonel (then Lieut.) Watson's Victoria Cross was gained at the village of Bilot, North-West Frontier, India, on 16 Sept. 1897. A Mountain Battery, half a company of the 4th Bengal Sappers and Miners, of which Lieut. Watson was in command, and a few men of the Buffs, were cut off by the enemy when returning to camp. They entrenched themselves as well as they could in the darkness and rain, and were heavily attacked by the enemy. After a time, as the ammunition was running short both for the guns and troops, only a few rounds being left, Lieut. Watson saw an opportunity for making a counter-attack, and, calling for volunteers, and eight men of the Buffs having responded, he led them against the enemy. He was soon wounded, both in the leg and the arm, and also several of his men. He retired to the main body for help to bring in the casualties, and again went out shortly afterwards, when he was badly wounded in the left hand, his thumb being shattered, and, owing to the artery being cut, he lost so much blood that he had to return to the main body in a fainting condition. Nevertheless, owing to his foresight in grasping the fact that at one spot the enemy could be held, he, in all probability, saved the whole force from being wiped out. His action kept the enemy at bay until they were relieved by a force from the Camp at dawn. Through his report a man of the Buffs was awarded the Victoria Cross. Lieut. Watson received the Indian Frontier War Medal, was mentioned in Despatches, and awarded the Victoria Cross [London Gazette, 20 May, 1898]: " Thomas Colclough Watson, Lieut., Royal Engineers. This officer, on the 16th Sept. 1897, at the village of Bilot, in the Mamund Valley, collected a few men of the Buffs (East Kent Regt.), and of No. 4 Company, Bengal Sappers and Miners, and led them into the dark and burning village to dislodge some of the enemy who were inflicting loss on our troops. After being wounded and driven back, he made a second attempt to clear the village, and only desisted after a second repulse and being again hit and severely wounded." Sir Bindon Blood's summary of Brigadier-General Jeffreys' Report of action of 16 Sept.: " Brigadier Jeffreys further refers in the strongest terms of commendation to the gallant conduct of Lieuts. T. C. Watson and J. M. C. Colvin, R.E., and of the handful of men of the Buffs and No. 4 Company, Bengal Sappers and Miners, who spent the night of the 16th–17th with him in the village of Bilot. The conduct of these officers and men entering the village several times in the dark in face of a heavy fire directed upon them at close quarters, seems deserving of the highest recognition, and I have consequently made a special communication to you on the subject." " Lieuts. Watson and Colvin, with their sappers and the twelve men of the Buffs, forced their way into the village, and tried to expel the enemy with the bayonet. The village was too large for so small a party to clear. The tribesmen moved from one part to another, repeatedly firing. They killed and wounded several of the soldiers, and a bullet smashed Lieut. Watson's hand. He, however, continued his efforts and did not desist until again shot, this time so severely as to be unable to stand. His men carried him from the village, and it was felt that it would be useless to try again. The attention of the reader is directed to the endurance of this officer. After a long day's marching and fighting in the dark, without food and with small numbers, the man who will go on, unshaken and unflinching, after he has received a severe and painful wound, has in respect of personal courage few equals and no superior in the world. It is perhaps as high a form of valour to endure as it is to fight. The combination of both is sublime." (" The Malakand Field Force," by Winston Churchill, page 204.) Lieut.-Colonel Watson served in the Mesopotamia Campaign of 1915, and was invalided home from there in June of that year. He died on 15 June, 1917. Lieut.-Colonel Watson held the Indian Durbar Medal. The " Times " of 18 June says: " The death has occurred in London, from illness contracted in Mesopotamia in 1915, of Lieut.-Colonel Thomas Colclough Watson, V.C., Royal Engineers. Colonel Watson was the youngest son of the late Thomas Colclough Watson, of Dovercourt, Essex, and was born in 1867. He joined the Royal Engineers early in 1888. His V.C. was won on the North-West Frontier of India in 1897. Brigadier-General Jeffreys had entered the Mahmund Valley to punish the tribesmen. The powerful resistance offered compelled the retirement of the force to its entrenched camp. When night closed in a severe thunderstorm broke, and the guns with a handful of troops were still outside the camp, and were compelled to entrench just outside a village which swarmed with tribesmen, who opened fire from two sides at about 30 yards' range. The enemy threw burning bhoosa, a species of chopped straw, into the midst of the little force, and by its light poured in its fire. Lieut. Watson, as he then was, called for volunteers, and with a party of the Buffs and his own sappers made a gallant bayonet rush into the village. He had his hand smashed by a bullet, but would not give in until he was again severely wounded, and had to be carried back to the little entrenchment. His comrade, Lieut. Colvin, continued the attempt, and Corpl. Smith, of the Buffs, also displayed the greatest courage. In the opinion of the officers in charge of the guns, the gallantry of the Buffs, the Engineer officers, and the sappers saved the battery and the detached party. Lieuts. Watson and Colvin were both awarded the Victoria Cross, and Corpl. Smith was also awarded the honour, but not until 19 months after the event. Colonel Watson married in 1892, Edythe (Royal Red Cross), younger daughter of the late Major-General John Whateley Welchman, C.B., Indian Army, who, with one son, survives him."

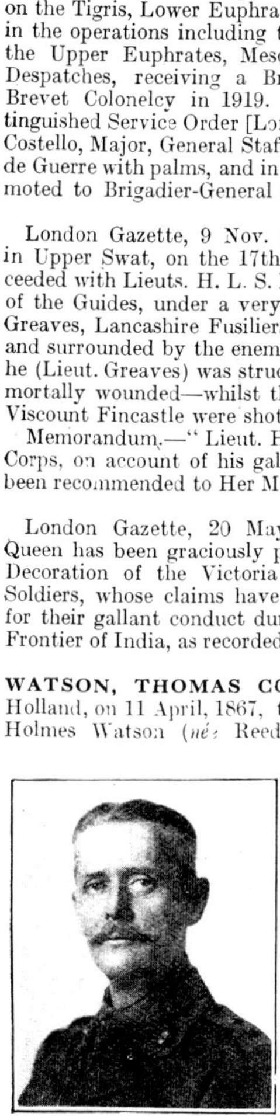

Thomas C. Watson.

COLVIN, JAMES MORRIS COLQUHOUN, Lieut., was born 26 Aug. 1870, at Bijnor, United Provinces, India, son of the late J. C. Colvin, Bengal Civil Service, of the Manor House, Sutton Veny, Wilts (one of the defenders of the house at Arrah), and of the late Camilla Fanny Marie Morris, eldest daughter of the Rev. Edward Morris. He was educated at Charterhouse, and at the Royal Military Academy, Woolwich, (Pollock Gold Medal), and joined the Royal Engineers on the 27th July, 1889. He served in the Chitral Relief Force in 1895, with the 4th Company, Bengal Sappers and Miners (India Medal, 1895, with clasp, Chitral Relief Force, 1895); on the North-West Frontier of India, with the Malakand Field Force, 1897–98, taking part in the operations in Bajaur, and in the Mohmand country and in Buner, with the 4th Company, Bengal Sappers and Miners. He was mentioned in Despatches [London Gazette, 11 Jan. 1898], received a clasp (Punjab Frontier, 1897–98), and was awarded the Victoria Cross [London Gazette, 20 May, 1898]: " James Morris Colquhoun Colvin, Lieut., Royal Engineers. Date of Act of Bravery: 16 Sept. 1897. On the same occasion, after Lieut. Watson had been incapacitated by his wounds from further effort, Lieut. Colvin continued the fight and persisted in two more attempts to clear the enemy out of the dark and still burning village. He was conspicuous during the whole night for his devotion to his men in the most exposed positions, under a heavy fire from the enemy." He served in 1901 and 1902 in South Africa, as Special

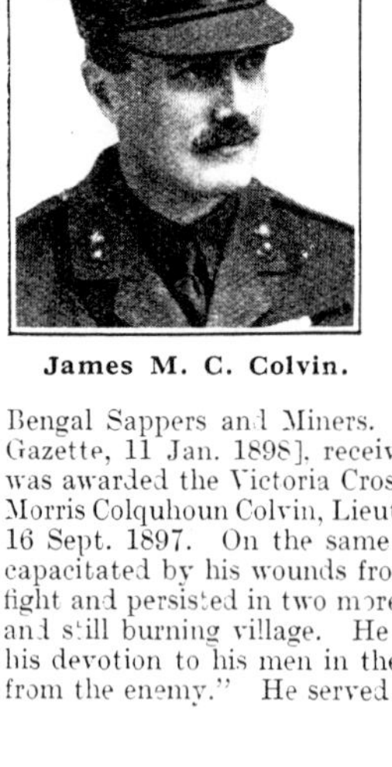

James M. C. Colvin.

Service Officer, and also on the Staff, was mentioned in Despatches [London Gazette, 22 Aug. 1902]; was given the Brevet of Major; his name was noted for as qualified for Staff employment, and he received the Queen's Medal with three clasps (Transvaal, South Africa, 1901, and South Africa 1902). On 23 Jan. 1904, at Simla, India, he married Katharine, youngest daughter of the late Colonel George Augustus Way, C.B., and their children are Katharine Camilla, James Bazett, and John Alexander (born 9 July, 1913). He passed the Staff College, Camberley, in 1909; was Staff Captain, Army Headquarters, Simla, 11 April, 1903, to 15 March, 1906; General Staff Officer, 2nd Grade, Quetta Division, 7 May, 1911, to 2 Nov. 1915. He became Lieutenant-Colonel 18 Jan. 1917, and Commandant, 3rd Sappers and Miners, Kirkey, India.

PENNELL, HENRY SINGLETON, Capt., was born on the 18th June, 1874; son of Mr. Edwin Pennell, of Daw-

Henry S. Pennell.

lish, Devonshire, and Henrietta, daughter of Henry Copeland. He was educated at Eastbourne College, and joined the Sherwood Foresters in 1893, being promoted Lieutenant in 1896. He accompanied his battalion with the Tirah Field Force (1897-98), was mentioned in Despatches, and awarded the Victoria Cross [London Gazette, 20 May, 1898]: "Henry Singleton Pennell, Lieut., Nottinghamshire and Derbyshire Regt. This officer, during the attack on the Dargai Heights, on the 20th Oct. 1897, when Capt. W. E. G. Smith, Derbyshire Regt., was struck down, ran to his assistance and made two distinct attempts, under a perfect hail of bullets, to carry and drag him back to cover, and only desisted when he found that he was dead." Lieut. Pennell's Victoria Cross was presented to him by Colonel Dowse at Bareilly, North-West India, on the 2nd Sept. 1898. He took part in the affair at Dargai, was present at Sampagha Pass, Arhanga Pass, and at the operations in Kanki, Waran and Bazar Valley, receiving two Medals and two clasps. In 1899 he was again on active service, attached to the West Yorkshire Regt. with the Natal Field Force. During the operations for the relief of Ladysmith he was present at all the chief operations, including Colenso, Spion Kop, Vaal Krantz, and the severe fighting on the Tugela, which culminated in the capture of Pieter's Hill, and he was severely wounded. He served on to 1900, received the Medal with five clasps, and was twice mentioned in Despatches. In 1900 he was promoted to the command of a company, and he was specially selected for the Staff College Course, graduated and posted to a Staff appointment, which he held up to the time of his death, which occurred at St. Moritzdorf, Switzerland, on the 19th Jan. 1907, as the result of an accident on the Cresta toboggan run.

FINDLATER, GEORGE, Piper, The Gordon Highlanders, was awarded the Victoria Cross [London Gazette, 20 May, 1898]: "George Findlater, Piper, The Gordon Highlanders. Date of Act of Bravery: 20 Oct. 1897. During the attack on the Dargai Heights on the 20th Oct. 1897, Piper Findlater, after being shot

George Findlater.

through both feet, and unable to stand, sat up, under a heavy fire, playing the regimental march to encourage the charge of the Gordon Highlanders." Piper Findlater was decorated by H.M. Queen Victoria at Netley Hospital.

LAWSON, EDWARD, Private, was awarded the Victoria Cross [London Gazette, 20 May, 1898]: "Edward Lawson, Private, The Gordon Highlanders. Date of Act of Bravery: 20 Oct. 1897. During the attack on the Dargai Heights on the 20th Oct. 1897, Private Lawson carried Lieut. K. Dingwall, the Gordon Highlanders (who was wounded and unable to move), out of a heavy fire, and subsequently returned and brought in Private McMillan, being himself wounded in two places." Private Lawson was discharged on the 31st Oct. 1902.

VICKERY, S., Private, enlisted in the 1st Battn. the Dorsetshire Regt., and was awarded the Victoria Cross [London Gazette, 20 May, 1898]: "S. Vickery, Private, the Dorsetshire Regt. During the attack on the Dargai Heights, on the 20th Oct. 1897, Private Vickery ran down the slope and rescued a wounded comrade under a heavy fire, bringing him back to cover. He subsequently distinguished himself with Brigadier-General Kempster's Column, in the Waran Valley, killing three

S. Vickery.

of the enemy who attacked him when separated from his company." Vickery became a Lance-Corporal.

London Gazette, 15 Nov. 1898.—"War Office, 15 Nov. 1898. The Queen has been graciously pleased to signify Her intention to confer the Decoration of the Victoria Cross on the undermentioned Officers and Private

Soldier, whose claims have been submitted for Her Majesty's approval, for their conspicuous bravery during the recent operations in the Soudan, as recorded against their names."

KENNA, PAUL ALOYSIUS, Brevet Major, was born on 16 Aug. 1862, at Oakfield House, Lancashire, son of James Kenna, Esq., and nephew of Matthew Kearney, of The Ford, Durham. He was educated at Stonyhurst

Paul A. Kenna.

and Sandhurst, and received his first commission with the 2nd West India Regt., serving with that unit for two years in the West Indies and West Africa. In 1889 he was transferred to the 21st Hussars, now the 21st (Empress of India's) Lancers. He served with his Regiment in the Egyptian Campaign of 1898, and won the Victoria Cross at the Battle of Omdurman [London Gazette, 15 Nov. 1898]: "Paul Aloysius Kenna, Capt., 21st Lancers. At the Battle of Omdurman, on the 2nd Sept. 1898, Capt. P. A. Kenna assisted Major Crole Wyndham, of the same regiment, by taking him on his horse, behind the saddle (Major Wyndham's horse having been killed in the charge), thus enabling him to reach a place of safety; and after the charge of the 21st Lancers, Capt. Kenna returned to assist Lieut. de Montmorency, who was endeavouring to recover the body of Lieut. R. G. Grenfell." The "Liverpool Daily Post" thus describes the actions for which Capt. Kenna won the decoration: "They had galloped but a short distance when the horse, under the unaccustomed weight, plunged, reared and threw off both officers. However, Capt. Kenna was soon upon his horse again," and "observing Lieut. de Montmorency riding back to seek his troop sergeant among the dervishes, he rode back with Corporal Swarbrick to his aid. De Montmorency had just found the body of Lieut. Grenfell, whom he supposed to be still alive. Whilst he was endeavouring to place Grenfell's body on his own horse the animal bolted, and he was left alone with his revolver some fifty yards from 300 dervishes. It was at this stage that Kenna returned, and along with Swarbrick, caught de Montmorency's horse, when all three answered the dervishes' fire with their revolvers, and then retreated to their own line untouched." General Kenna served in the South African Campaign of 1899-1902, firstly as Assistant Provost-Marshal on General French's Staff. He was appointed Brigade Major in 1900, and later, in 1901, was given command of a column. He took part in the Relief of Kimberley, in Orange Free State, Feb. to May, 1900, including operations at Paardeberg (17th to 20th Feb.); actions at Poplar Grove, Dreifontein, Karee Siding, Vet River (5th and 6th May), and Zand River. In the Transvaal, in May and June, 1900, including actions near Johannesburg, Pretoria and Diamond Hill (11th and 12th June). In the Transvaal, East of Pretoria, July to 29 Nov. 1900, including actions at Reit River and Belfort; Orange River, 1899 to 1900, including actions at Colesburg (1 Jan. to 12 Feb.). Also in the Transvaal and Orange River Colony, 30 Nov. 1900, to 31 May, 1902. Took part in the operations on the Zululand Frontiers of Natal (Sept. and Oct. 1901). Mentioned in Despatches (4 May and 10 Sept. 1901). Received the Brevet of Major, Queen's Medal with six clasps, and King's Medal with two clasps, and was created a Companion of the Distinguished Service Order [London Gazette, 23 Aug. 1902]: "Paul Aloysius Kenna, V.C., Capt. and Brevet Major, 21st Lancers." He was promoted substantive Major 7 Sept. 1902, and exactly two months later was selected for special service with the Somaliland Field Force. He commanded the Mounted Troops throughout the operations in Somaliland, and took part in the action of "Jidballi," receiving mentions in Despatches [London Gazette, 7 Aug. 1903; 30 May and 2 Sept. 1904]. On 7 Sept. 1904, he was promoted Brevet Lieutenant-Colonel, and he received the Medal and two clasps. On the conclusion of the campaign in June, 1904, he returned to duty with his regiment in England. He was appointed Brigade Major to the 1st Cavalry Brigade at Aldershot on 1 Oct. 1905, and held that appointment until gazetted to command the 21st Lancers on 7 Sept. 1906. He was promoted Brevet Colonel on 1 Dec. 1906, and on the following day was appointed A.D.C. to the King, and continued to perform that duty until his death in 1915. His period of Command of his Regiment terminated on 7 Sept. 1910, when he became a substantive Colonel. On 1 April, 1911, he was appointed to command the Notts and Derby Mounted Brigade. On 4 Aug. 1914, he was promoted Brigadier-General. In the spring of 1915 he took his Brigade to Egypt, and later to Gallipoli. During the operations culminating in the Battle of Chocolate Hill he was in command of the Division of which his Brigade formed part. On 30 Aug., whilst making a tour of inspection of his front-line trenches, General Kenna was severely wounded by a shot from a Turkish "sniper." This happened about 8 p.m. He was carried to the beach, and lived for seven hours, during which he was attended by two priests of the Church of which he was such a devoted son. Brigadier-General Kenna lies buried at Suvla Bay. In 1895 he received the Royal Humane Society's Certificate for going off the Liffey Embankment and saving a drowning man. Many friends wrote of him that he was "a man of surpassing courage, rigid, upright and simple, and he had the love and respect of all who knew him." He married (1st) Lady Cecil Bertie (who died in 1895), daughter of the 7th Earl of Abingdon. He married (2nd) Angela Mary, youngest daughter of the late Hubert Tichborne Hibbert, Esq., and they had two daughters, Kathleen Mary Pauline, and Cecilia Mary Ethel. General Kenna was a great sportsman. In 1893 and 1894 he headed the list of gentlemen riders in India, and in Egypt also from 1893 for some years. "It was a sheer delight," says an old school-fellow, "to watch him . . . jumping at the Military Tournament in competition with the best horsemen of all the European Armies. He was certainly first, but also easily first, I should say." He played for ten years and more in the regimental polo team, and did a good deal of big game shooting and hunting. A consummate horseman, he rode many winners on the flat, and across country and in " The Ring." Amongst his best remembered successes are on " Moonshine " (in India), " Sandy " on whom he won the Grand Military at Pretoria, " Dandy," " Twister," " Harmony," won him many Point-to-Points, and the latter with " Deliberation " were all known at the International Horse Shows. It was on " Harmony " that he won the King's Cup at Olympia. " Of course he had many a toss, chasing, hunting, and playing polo, but there never was anyone who took them more cheerily. He entered into every sport or game with the heart of a schoolboy, and was always out to win—in fact, he was a thorough sportsman, in the best sense of the word. With his natural seat and perfect ' hands ' he was always happiest on the top of a horse. There was nothing, indeed, he did not know about them, and he was equally good as horseman and horse-master. Always popular, wherever he went, he will be sorely missed by his many friends and fellow-competitors, whether in hunting-field, on polo ground, or in the Ring."

DE MONTMORENCY, THE HON. RAYMOND HANNAY LODGE JOSEPH, Lieut., was born on 5 Feb.1867, son of the late General Viscount Frankfort de Montmorency. He entered the 21st Lancers in Sept. 1887, and became Lieutenant in 1889,

and Adjutant, 21st Lancers, in 1893. In 1898 at the Battle of Khartoum, he won the Victoria Cross, when serving in the Khartoum Expedition [London Gazette, 15 Nov. 1898]: " The Honourable Raymond Hannay Lodge Joseph de Montmorency, Lieut., the 21st (Empress of India's) Lancers. At the Battle of Khartoum, on the 2nd Sept. 1898, Lieut. de Montmorency, after the charge of the 21st Lancers, returned to assist Second Lieut. R. G. Grenfell, who was lying surrounded by a large body of Dervishes. Lieut. de Montmorency drove the Dervishes off, and finding Lieut. Grenfell dead, put the body on his

Hon. R. H. de Montmorency. horse, which then broke away. Capt. Kenna and Corpl. Swarbrick then came to his assistance and enabled him to rejoin the regiment, which had begun to open a heavy fire on the enemy." Mr. Steevens, in " With Kitchener to Khartoum," says: " Lieut. de Montmorency missed his troop sergeant, and rode back among the slashes to look for him. There he found the hacked body of Lieut. Grenfell. He dismounted and put it upon his horse, not seeing in his haste that the life had drained out long since by a dozen channels. The horse bolted under the slackened muscles, and de Montmorency was left alone with his revolver and 3,000 screaming fiends. Capt. Kenna and Corpl. Swarbrick rode out, caught his horse and brought it back ; the three answered the fire of the 3,000 at fifty yards, and got quietly back to their own line untouched." He served in the South African Campaign of 1899–1900. Sir A. Conan Doyle (" The Great Boer War," page 203) says : " Scouting and raiding expeditions, chiefly organized by Capt. de Montmorency—whose early death cut short the career of one who possessed every quality of a partisan leader—broke the monotony of inaction." Sir A. Conan Doyle is here describing the doings of General Gatacre's force between Stormberg and the final general advance. In 1899 he was promoted Captain. Sir A. Conan Doyle later (page 356) describes his death, which occurred Feb. 23, 1900 : " During the long period which had elapsed since the repulse at Stormberg, General Gatacre had held his own at Sterkstroom, under orders not to attack the enemy, repulsing them easily upon the only occasion when they ventured to attack him. Now it was his turn also to profit by the success Lord Roberts had won. On 23 Feb. he reoccupied Molteno, and on the same day sent out a force to reconnoitre the enemy's position at Stormberg. The incident is memorable as having been the cause of the death of Capt. de Montmorency, one of the most promising of the younger officers of the British Army. He had formed a corps of scouts, consisting originally of four men, but soon expanding to seventy or eighty. At the head of these men he confirmed the reputation for desperate valour which he had won in the Soudan, and added to it proof of the enterprise and judgment which go to make a leader of light cavalry. In the course of the reconnaissance he ascended a small kopje, accompanied by three companions, Colonel Hoskier, a London volunteer soldier, Vice, a civilian, and Sergt. Howe. ' They are right on the top of us,' he cried to his comrades, as he reached the summit, and dropped next instant with a bullet through his heart. Hoskier was shot in five places, and Vice was mortally wounded, only Howe escaping. The rest of the scouts, being farther back, were able to get cover and to keep up a fight until they were extricated by the remainder of the force. Altogether our loss was formidable rather in quality than in quantity, for not more than a dozen were hit, while the Boers suffered considerably from the fire of our guns . . . de Montmorency had established a remarkable influence over his rough followers. To the end of the war they could not speak of him without tears in their eyes. When I asked Sergt. Howe why his captain went almost alone up the hill, his answer was, ' Because the Captain knew no fear.' Byrne, his soldier servant (an Omdurman V.C., like his master), galloped madly off next morning with a saddled horse to bring back his captain alive or dead, and had to be forcibly seized and restrained by our cavalry." The Rev. H. B. de Montmorency C.B., writes : " A day or so before the Battle of Omdurman, Raymond de Montmorency's horse was wounded, or somehow put out of action for the time being. In place of it, then, he rode a small white Arab polo pony, ' Baba,' through the famous charge, and it was it that bolted when Grenfell's

body was put on it. I think this adds slightly to the glory of de Montmorency's return into the Dervish hordes. After his death ' Baba ' became the regimental pet of the 21st Lancers, under the care of Farrier-Sergt. Pollock. When the regiment was afterwards stationed at the Marlborough Barracks, Dublin, I often saw the pony there, and have a photograph of it, in which the tribal (Arab) mark shows very clearly. ' Baba ' was afterwards presented to Miss K. de Montmorency and her sister, and drew them about in a phaeton. I do not know if it is still alive." Mr. de Montmorency also wrote : " One of Raymond de Montmorency's men whom I came across on the Karroo, shortly after his death, told me he was not killed outright by the first Boer volley, but as he lay wounded kept on firing at the enemy for a minute or two till he died."

BYRNE, THOMAS, Private, was born in Dec. 1866, at St. Thomas, Dublin, and when 20 years of age he enlisted into the 8th Hussars, and served with that regiment for over twelve months, when he was transferred

to the 21st Hussars, now the 21st (Empress of India's) Lancers. He served over 22 years abroad with this regiment ; eight years in India, two in Egypt, and one in South Africa. It was at Omdurman in 1898 that the 21st Lancers made the historic charge in which Byrne and two of his comrades won their Victoria Crosses in about as many minutes. When the hordes of the Dervishes had been driven back by the murderous fire of our troops and the Egyptian Infantrymen, under Sir Hector MacDonald, the cavalry were sent out to prevent the fugitives from taking up a position in a native village some distance off. Midway lay some low sandhills,

Thomas Byrne. and as a number of Sudanese were seen on the ridge it was decided to clear them out. " The Squadrons opened out into line and galloped up the slope. As they gained the summit a volley of musketry emptied many a saddle, as horses and riders went crashing to the ground. It was then discovered, to their astonishment, that nearly three thousand Dervishes were concealed in the dip of the hills and the Lancers had ridden into a veritable death-trap, instead of having to deal with a few hundred fugitives. To hesitate would have been fatal ; there was but one thing to do : ' Charge ! ' And the thin line of lances dropped forward as the troopers, bending low, rode like a whirlwind into the dense mass of Soudanese. Cutting, stabbing and thrusting, the 21st fought against the fierce Dervishes, who outnumbered them by ten to one, and finally they cut a passage through, lances and sword-blades dripping red. Many were killed in the charge, and many gallant deeds and rescues were performed." (" Military Mail," Friday, 20 Oct. 1911.) Lieut. Molyneux was wounded and thrown from his horse, and when attempting to rejoin the squadron he was pursued by three spearmen. Byrne had been shot through the right shoulder, but he immediately rode to the assistance of his officer. He tried to use his sword, but the weapon was too heavy for his wounded arm, and he got a spear-wound in the chest. He, however, created a diversion by riding the Dervishes down, and Lieut. Molyneux was able to get out of danger. When Byrne saw he was safe, he rode off to his own troop and managed to reach it without further injury. Mr. Winston Churchill, who rode in the charge, and was an eye-witness of the incident, said it was the bravest act he had ever seen performed. Trooper Byrne was awarded the Victoria Cross [London Gazette, 15 Nov. 1898] : " Thomas Byrne, Private, 21st Lancers. At the Battle of Khartoum, on the 2nd Sept. 1898, Private Byrne turned back in the middle of the charge of the 21st Lancers and went to the assistance of Lieut. the Hon. R. F. Molyneux, Royal Horse Guards, who was wounded, dismounted, disarmed, and being attacked by several Dervishes. Private Byrne, already severely wounded, attacked these Dervishes, received a second severe wound, and by his gallant conduct enabled Lieut. Molyneux to escape."

SMYTH NEVILL MASKELYNE, Capt., was born on 14 Aug. 1868, second son of the late Sir Warington Smyth, F.R.S., of Marazion, Cornwall. He was educated at Sandhurst (honours), and became a Second Lieut. in the

Queen's Bays in 1888. He served in the Zhob Valley in 1890, and in the Dongola Expedition of 1896 he was employed on special service with the Intelligence Department. He was Orderly Officer to the Officer Commanding the Mounted Forces in the Battle of Firket and pursuit to Suarda ; was on the Staff passing the flotilla up the Cataracts and acted as Orderly Officer to the Chief of the Staff in the action of Hafir and the occupation of Dongola. He rode through the retreating Dervishes with a Despatch to the Sirdar with the flotilla at Debba. Capt. Smyth was Staff Officer to Colonel Tudway, D.S.O., commanding the Camel Corps. For his services in this campaign he received the Medal with two clasps, the 4th Class Medjidieh, and was mentioned in

Nevill M. Smyth. Despatches. In the Sudan Campaign of 1897 he acted as Staff Officer to Sir Leslie Rundle, Commanding Dongola Province (bar) ; was D.A.A.G.1, and commanded the advanced posts on the Atbara ; commanded infantry and machine-guns at the gunboat bombardment of Metemmeh, 1 Jan. 1898, on board Admiral (then Commander) Beatty's gunboat. Reconnaissance and Battle of Atbara (Despatches, bar); Battle of Omdurman, as Orderly and Intelligence Officer to General Sir Archibald Hunter, commanding the Egyptian Division. In this battle he was severely wounded, was mentioned in Despatches, subsequently received the British Medal for Khartoum, and was awarded the Victoria Cross [London Gazette, 15 Nov. 1898]: "Nevill Maskelyne Smyth, Capt., 2nd Dragoon Guards. At the Battle of Khartoum, on the 2nd Sept. 1898, Capt. Smyth galloped forward and attacked an Arab who had run amok among some camp followers. Capt. Smyth received the Arab's charge, and killed him, being wounded with a spear in so doing. He thus saved the life of one at least of the camp followers." He was the first to enter the "Sair" or Citadel of Omdurman, with the force led by General Sir Archibald Hunter. In the Sudan Campaign of 1899 he suppressed Khalifa Sherif's rising on the Blue Nile; was present at the preliminary operations and final defeat and death of the two remaining Khalifas at Gedid. Awarded the 4th Class Osmanieh and four bars to the Egyptian Medal. He assisted in the Sudan Surveys, charted the Nile Cataracts from Wadi Halfa to Abyssinia, and established the fact of the existence of South African horse sickness in the Sudan. Employed on Abyssinian frontier delimitation. In the South African War, in 1902, he served as A.P.M. and D.A.A.G.1, in Lawley's Column, and for his services received the Medal with three clasps and the Brevet of Major. He was promoted Major into the Carabiniers in 1903, and Colonel in 1912. Aviator's Certificate in 1913; Commandant of the Khartoum District, 1913–14. Brigadier-General Smyth served in the European War, commanding the 1st Australian Infantry Brigade at the Dardanelles operations, from 20 May, 1915, including the assault of the Lone Pine position on 6 Aug. Created a C.B. in 1916. He was present at the First Battle of the Somme, including the capture of Pozières, 23 July, 1916. Advance to Bapaume and capture of the Hindenburg Line at Bullecourt, 1917 (Commander of the Order of Leopold). Third Battle of Ypres, Sept.–Oct. 1917 (Belgian Military Cross). Operations east of Amiens, May, 1918. Major-General Smyth was mentioned in Despatches eight times. Commanded 58th (London) Division, 1918, and the 59th Division, 1918–19, including the command of Portuguese Artillery and Infantry, the liberation of the City of Lille, Oct. 17 1918; the crossing of the River Scheldt 20 Oct. K.C.B. 9 June, 1919.

London Gazette, 2 Dec. 1898.—"War Office, 2 Dec. 1898. The Queen has been graciously pleased to signify Her intention to confer the Decoration of the Victoria Cross on the undermentioned Officer, whose claim has been submitted for Her Majesty's approval, for his conspicuous bravery during the outbreak at Candia on the 6th Sept. 1898, as recorded against his name."

MAILLARD, WILLIAM JOB, Surgeon, Royal Navy, was educated at Kingswood School, Bath, at Dunheved College, Launceston, and at Guy's Hospital, London (1882–89). He had the degrees M.D. (London University), M.R.C.S. and L.R.C.P., and qualified for the Gold Medal in Medicine. On 22 Aug. 1889, he entered the Royal Navy. In 1898 there were disturbances in Crete, brought about altogether by Turkish misrule. There were about 70,000 Moslems and 300,000 Christians in Crete. A tithe was granted to the Assembly on the export revenue, and its collection was made the excuse for an insurrection by the Mohammedan refugees in Candia on the 6th Sept. 1898. Nearly a hundred British soldiers and a thousand of the Christian inhabitants were killed, the British Vice-Consul was burned in his house, and the town was set on fire. It was bombarded by the British Fleet under Admiral Noel. The ringleaders were given up, and seven Mohammedans were hanged on the 18th Oct. for the murder of two privates of the Highland Light Infantry. Surgeon Maillard won his Victoria Cross for his gallant services at Crete, described below, was promoted Staff-Surgeon on 2 June, 1899, as well as awarded the Victoria Cross [London Gazette, 2 Dec. 1898]: "Maillard, M.D., Surgeon, Royal Navy. On the 6th Sept. 1898, during the landing of seamen from Her Majesty's Ship Hazard, Surgeon Maillard, who had disembarked and reached a place of safety, returned through a perfect deluge of bullets to the boat, and endeavoured to bring into safety Arthur Stroud, Ordinary Seaman, who had fallen back wounded into the boat as the other men jumped ashore. Surgeon Maillard failed to bring Stroud in only through the boat being cut adrift, and it being beyond his strength to lift the man (who was almost dead) out of so unstable a platform. Surgeon Maillard returned to his post with his clothes riddled with bullets, though he himself was unhurt." He was decorated by Queen Victoria at Windsor on 5 Dec. 1898. Staff-Surgeon Maillard retired in 1902, and died on the 12th Sept. 1903, at "Ville d'Eu," Shelburne Road, Bournemouth, aged forty.

William Job Maillard.

London Gazette, 28 Feb. 1899.—"War Office, 28 Feb. 1899. The Queen has been graciously pleased to signify Her intention to confer the Decoration of the Victoria Cross on the undermentioned Officer, whose claim has been submitted for Her Majesty's approval, for his conspicuous bravery during the attack on the Baggage Guard at the action of Gedarif, on the 22nd Sept. 1898, as recorded against his name."

HORE-RUTHVEN, THE HON. ALEXANDER GORE ARKWRIGHT, Capt., was born at Windsor 6 July, 1872, son of the 8th Baron Ruthven and Lady Caroline Annesley-Gore (died 1915), daughter of the

4th Earl of Arran, K.P. He was educated at Eton, and joined the Army 17 May, 1899. He served as Captain in the 3rd (Militia) Battn. Highland Light Infantry, attached to the Egyptian Army in the

Hon. A. G. A. Hore-Ruthven.

Sudan Campaign of 1898; commanded the Camel Corps Detachment at the Battle of Gedarif, and subsequent operations in the Sudan in 1899, including the final defeat of the Khalifa; won the Victoria Cross, being the first Militia officer to receive the decoration, as described in the London Gazette 13 Feb. 1899: "The Hon. Alexander Gore Arkwright Hore-Ruthven, Capt., 3rd (Militia) Battn. the Highland Light Infantry. Date of Act of Bravery: 22 Sept. 1898. On the 22nd Sept. 1898, during the action of Gedarif, Capt. Hore-Ruthven, seeing an Egyptian officer lying wounded within fifty yards of the advancing Dervishes, who were firing and charging, picked him up and carried him towards the 16th Egyptian Battn. He dropped the wounded officer two or three times, and fired upon the Dervishes, who were following, to check their advance. Had this officer been left where he first dropped, he must have been killed." He also received for his services in this campaign the Fourth Class Osmanieh, English and Egyptian Sudan Medals with three clasps. He was three times mentioned in Despatches. "On the 17th May (1899) Capt. the Hon. A. G. A. Hore-Ruthven, V.C. (from the 3rd Battn. Highland Light Infantry (Militia), attached to the Egyptian Army), was gazetted to the regiment." (Records of the Cameron Highlanders, page 341.) He became Lieutenant, Cameron Highlanders, 14 Dec. 1900; from 1903 to 1904 he was Special Service Officer in Somaliland, being present at the action of Jidballi (Medal and two clasps). From 1905 to 1908 was Military Secretary and A.D.C. to the Viceroy of Ireland. He was promoted into the 1st Dragoons as Captain 11 April, 1908, and on the 1st June in the same year married, at St. George's, Hanover Square, Zara, daughter of the late John Pollock, of Lismany, County Galway. They have one son, Alexander Hardinge Patrick (born 30 Aug. 1912). From 10 July, 1908, to 13 June, 1910, he was Military Secretary to the Earl of Dudley, then Governor-General of the Commonwealth of Australia; he was Brigade Major 20 Nov. 1914, to 23 March, 1915. On 2 April, 1915, he became Major in the Welsh Guards. From 9 June, 1915, to 9 Sept. 1915, he was G.S.O., Second Grade. Major Hore-Ruthven was created a Companion of the Distinguished Service Order, for services in Gallipoli [London Gazette, Aug. 1915]: "Hon. Alexander Gore Arkwright Hore-Ruthven, Major (Temp. Lieutenant-Colonel), Welsh Guards." "The first casualty of the new Welsh Guards Regt., Major Hore-Ruthven, V.C., who is unofficially reported wounded in the Gallipoli Campaign, is a son of the aged Lord Ruthven (pronounced 'Rivven'). These Ruthvens are a daring race, renowned in Scottish history and in military annals. Lord Ruthven, a soldier's son, fought in the Indian Mutiny, the Crimea and in Abyssinia. His martial example was followed by his four sons. The eldest, the Master of Ruthven, was mentioned in Despatches during the Boer War, and received the D.S.O. Two other sons, one of whom is dead, also fought in South Africa and won distinctions for bravery. Major Hore-Ruthven wears the V.C. for valour in saving the life of a brother officer under heavy fire in Egypt. He saw the officer, an Egyptian, lying within fifty yards of the charging Dervishes, and picking him up, he carried him to shelter, stopping repeatedly to fire at the nearest pursuers. Although only twenty-six at the time, the then Lieut. Ruthven commanded the Camel Corps, and in that capacity he was three times mentioned in Despatches. Since then he has seen service in Somaliland, and has been on the staff of two Lords-Lieutenant of Ireland and of the Governor-General of the Australian Commonwealth." He became Temporary Lieutenant-Colonel 18 Jan. 1916; was G.S.O.1. Jan. 1916, to Dec. 1917, and in July, 1917, was serving in France; became Brigadier-General, General Staff, Dec. 1917; C.M.G. 7 March, 1918, Commanding 26th Infantry Brigade; Staff College, 1913; Bar to D.S.O. [London Gazette, 2 April, 1919]; C.B. June, 1919.

London Gazette, 20 April, 1899.—"War Office, 21 April, 1899. The Queen has been graciously pleased to signify Her intention to confer the Decoration of the Victoria Cross on the undermentioned Non-commissioned Officer, whose claim has been submitted for Her Majesty's approval, for his conspicuous bravery during an engagement at Bilot, on the North-West Frontier of India, on the night of the 16th-17th Sept. 1897."

SMITH, JAMES, Corpl., was awarded the Victoria Cross [London Gazette. 21 April, 1899]: "James Smith, Corpl., The Buffs, East Kent Regt. Date of Act of Bravery: night of 16th-17th Sept. 1897. On the night of the 16th to 17th Sept. 1897, Corpl. Smith, with a party of the Buffs, responded to Lieut. Watson's call for volunteers, and followed that officer into the burning village of Bilot, driving off the enemy with the bayonet. Afterwards, although wounded, he continued firing steadily and coolly, and also helped to carry the wounded to the place prepared for them. When Lieut. Watson left, in order to fetch assistance for the wounded, Corpl. Smith held the position till that officer's return, exposing his life freely in watching the enemy and directing the fire of his men." Corpl.

James Smith.

Smith's decoration was not gazetted until nineteen months after the services for which he was awarded the Victoria Cross. He was promoted to Sergeant.

London Gazette, 3 Feb. 1900.—" War Office, 3 Feb. 1900. The Queen has been graciously pleased to signify Her intention to confer the Decoration of the Victoria Cross on the undermentioned Officers and Non-commissioned Officer, whose claims have been submitted for Her Majesty's approval, for their conspicuous bravery at the Battle of Colenso, as stated against their names."

CONGREVE, WALTER NORRIS, Capt., was born 20 Nov. 1862, son of the late William Congreve, J.P., D.L., of Congreve, Staffs, and Burton Hall, Cheshire, and Fanny Emma, daughter of Lee Porcher Townshend, of Wincham Hall, Chester. He was edu-

Walter Norris Congreve.

cated at Harrow, and entered the Rifle Brigade in 1885. He became Captain in 1893. He served in the Boer War of 1899–1902. Was mentioned in Despatches twice, received the Queen's Medal with seven clasps, the King's Medal with two clasps, the Brevet of Lieut.-Colonel, and the Victoria Cross [London Gazette, 7 Feb. 1900]: " Walter Norris Congreve, Capt., The Rifle Brigade. Date of Act of Bravery : 15 Dec. 1899. At Colenso, on the 15th Dec. 1899, the detachments serving the guns of the 14th and 66th Batteries, Royal Field Artillery, had all been either killed, wounded, or driven from their guns by infantry fire at close range, and the guns were deserted. About 500 yards behind the guns was a donga, in which some of the ew horses and drivers left alive were sheltered. The intervening space was swept with shell and rifle fire. Capt. Congreve, Rifle Brigade, who was in the donga, assisted to hook a team into a limber, went out and assisted to limber up a gun. Being wounded, he took shelter, but seeing Lieut. Roberts fall badly wounded, he went out and brought him in. Capt. Congreve was shot through the leg, the toe of his boot, grazed on the elbow and shoulder, and his horse shot in three places." He won the Victoria Cross with several others in an attempt to save Colonel Long's guns at Colenso. Capt. Congreve served on the Staff in South Africa, as A.M.S. and Private Secretary to Lord Kitchener. In 1900 he married Celia, daughter of the late Capt. C. B. La Touche, and they have three sons, one of whom was the late Major Congreve, V.C., D.S.O., M.C. He was promoted Major, and Lieutenant-Colonel on 21 Dec. 1901. In Dec. 1902, he became Assistant Military Secretary and A.D.C. to H.R.H. the Duke of Connaught in Ireland, being made a Member of the Royal Victorian Order by His Majesty the King when on a visit to that country in 1903. He became Major-General in 1915, and Lieutenant-General 1918, and was created a K.C.B. in 1917. General Sir W. N. Congreve is a Commander of the Legion of Honour and holds the Order of St. Anne of Russia, First Class.

ROBERTS, THE HONOURABLE FREDERICK SHERSTON, Lieut., was born at Umballa, India, 8 Jan. 1872. He entered the King's Royal Rifle Corps on 10 June, 1891, and during the four following years

The Hon. F. S. Roberts.

was on active service on the North-West Frontier of India, including Chitral, receiving the Medals and clasps and being mentioned in Despatches. He served in the Boer War of 1899–1902, and lost his life at the Battle of Colenso in an attempt (described in the account of Capt. Congreve) to save the guns of the 14th and 66th Batteries, R.F.A., which had dashed forward, far in advance of their flank supports, and opened fire on the Boer position. Without shelter of any description, and in full view of a strongly entrenched enemy, they became the object of a fearful storm of bullets and shells, which tore the horses to pieces and strewed the gunners on the ground around the guns. At last there were hardly enough men left to serve the guns, and it seemed impossible to bring relief from the donga five hundred yards to the rear. Soon the batteries had no one to serve them, and they were abandoned. But Colonel Long had said as they removed him from the gun by which he had fallen, " Abandon be damned ! We don't abandon guns." Others were of the same opinion, and Lieut. Roberts was one of those who answered General Buller's appeal for volunteers, and was mortally wounded in trying to save a gun, which was presented to Lord Roberts by the War Office authorities. On it, years afterwards, the great soldier's coffin was carried at his funeral. The following is an extract from a letter written by an officer at this time to a friend : " I was galloper to General Clery, who rode all day with Sir Redvers Buller. About ten o'clock two batteries, which had advanced too close, ran short of ammunition. Their limbers were about 800 yards behind. Horses and men were sheltering in a deep narrow nullah. General Buller told them to take the limbers up to the battery, but directly they emerged a storm of bullets and shells fell all around. . . . Generals Clery and Buller stood out in it, and said, ' Some of you go and help.' Schofield (A.D.C.), Roberts (Lord Roberts's son) and myself, with the help of a corporal and six gunners, went to the limbers, and got two of them horsed. I have never seen, even at field firing, the bullets fly thicker. All one could see was little tufts of dust all

over the ground, a whistling noise—' phux,' where they bit, and an increasing rattle of musketry, somewhere in front. My first bullet went through my left sleeve, and just made the joint of my elbow bleed, next a clod of earth caught me smack on the right arm ; then my horse got one, then my right leg one, my horse another, and that settled us, for he plunged, and I fell about a hundred yards short of the guns we were going to." The fury of that lea len storm can be imagined from the fact that one gunner was found with sixty-four wounds in his body. In the meantime Capt. Reed, of the 7th Battery, had arrived with three spare teams of horses, and he made another desperate effort to save the remaining guns, but five of his thirteen men were hit and one killed, and thirteen out of his twenty-one horses killed before he could get half-way to the guns. For his gallantry on this occasion he was afterwards awarded the Victoria Cross, as were Schofield, Congreve and Roberts. The Honourable Frederick Roberts's Victoria Cross was gazetted 2 Jan. 1900: " The Honourable Frederick Sherston Roberts (since deceased), Lieut., King's Royal Rifle Corps. At Colenso, on the 15th Dec. 1899, the detachments serving the guns of the 14th and 66th Batteries, Royal Field Artillery, had all been either killed, wounded, or driven from their guns by infantry fire at close range, and the guns were deserted. About 500 yards behind the lines was a donga, in which some of the few horses and drivers left alive were sheltered. The intervening space was swept with shell and rifle fire. Capt. Congreve, Rifle Brigade, who was in the donga, assisted to hook a team into a limber, went out, and assisted to limber up a gun. Being wounded, he took shelter ; but seeing Lieut. Roberts fall badly wounded, he went out again and brought him in. With him went the gallant Major Babtie, of the R.A.M.C., who had ridden across the donga amid a hail of bullets, and had done what he could for the wounded men. Capt. Congreve was shot through the leg, through the toe of his boot, grazed on the elbow and the shoulder, and his horse shot in three places. Lieut. Roberts assisted Capt. Congreve. He was wounded in three places."

NURSE, GEORGE EDWARD, Corpl., was born at Enniskilling, Ireland, son of Charles Nurse and Jane Nurse, of Cobo Hotel, Guernsey. After a course of higher class education at the Chamberlain Academy, Guernsey,

George Edward Nurse.

George Nurse joined the Royal Artillery, enlisting at St. George's Barracks, London, on 6 Jan. 1892. He served in London till May, 1897, and proceeded to South Africa in Dec. 1899. His unit was commanded by Major W. Foster, under Colonel Long, with General Hildyard in brigade command. Besides the first battle on the Tugela, he fought through almost the whole four colonies, from Durban on the east to Mafeking (Relief) on the northwest. He was awarded the Victoria Cross [London Gazette, 2 Feb. 1900]: " George Edward Nurse, Corpl., 66th Battery, Royal Field Artillery. At Colenso, on the 15th Dec. 1899, the detachments serving the guns of the 14th and 66th Batteries, Royal Field Artillery, had either been killed, wounded, or driven from their guns by infantry fire at close range, and the guns were deserted. About 500 yards behind the guns was a donga, in which some of the few horses and drivers left alive were sheltered. The intervening space was swept with shell and rifle fire. Capt. Congreve, Rifle Brigade, who was in the donga, assisted to limber up a gun. Being wounded he took shelter, but seeing Lieut. Roberts fall badly wounded, he went out again and brought him in. Capt. Congreve was shot through the leg, through the toe of his boot, grazed on the elbow and the shoulder, and his horse shot in three places. Lieut. Roberts, King's Royal Rifle Corps, assisted Capt. Congreve. He was wounded in three places. Corpl. Nurse also assisted." " I got hold of some loose horses and hooked them into the limbers, Lieut. Roberts holding my horse meanwhile. Just after we started Lieut. Roberts was shot. When we got to the guns, through a tornado of rifle bullet and shell, one gun had the spade clamping gear jammed. I ran to another gun, and with Capt. Schofield's help limbered it up, then ran back to the former gun, found the pin, and managed to limber it up myself. When we were out of bullet-range I met Capt. Reed and four teams, but they were bowled over at the drift at 500 yards' range." The " Times " of 23 Sept. 1915, says : " The London Gazette announces the appointment as Temporary Second Lieutenant of George Edward Nurse, V.C." His wife is Kathleen A. Nurse, and they have one son, Charles T. Colenso Nurse.

REED, HAMILTON LYSTER, Capt. was born on the 23rd of May, 1869, son of the late Sir Andrew Reed, K.C.B., C.V.O., Inspector-General, Royal Irish Constabulary, and of the late Elizabeth Mary, daughter of Hamilton Lyster, Esq., of Croghan, Parsonstown. He was educated at the Royal Military Academy, Woolwich, and was gazetted into the Royal Field Artillery, 16 Feb. 1888, becoming Capt. in 1898. In the South African War of 1899–1902, he was at first Captain, 7th Battery, R.F.A., later Adjutant, R.F.A., and D.A.A.G. on the Staff of the G.O.C., Orange River Colony. He took part in the operations in Natal (1899), was at the relief of Ladysmith, and the action at Colenso (where he gained the Victoria Cross, and was slightly wounded) ; operations of 17–24 Jan. 1900

Hamilton Lyster Reed.

and action at Spion Kop; operations of 5–7 Feb. 1900, and actions at Vaal Krantz; and during operations on Tugela Heights (14–24 Feb. 1900), and action at Pieter's Hill. In Natal, March to June, 1900, including actions at Laing's Nek (6–9 June). In the Transvaal, east of Pretoria, July to Oct. 1900, including actions at Belfast (26 and 27 Aug.) and Lydenburg (5–8 Sept.). Also during the operations in Orange River Colony (30 Nov. 1900, to 31 May, 1902). For his services in this campaign he was three times mentioned in Despatches [London Gazette, 26 Jan. 1900, 8 Feb. and 10 Sept. 1901]. He received the Queen's Medal with six clasps, the King's Medal with two clasps, and was awarded the Victoria Cross [London Gazette, 2 Feb. 1900]: "Hamilton Lyster Reed, Capt., 7th Battery, Royal Field Artillery. Date of Act of Bravery: 15 Dec. 1899. Capt. Reed, who had heard of the difficulty, shortly afterwards brought down three teams from his battery to see if he could be of any use. He was wounded, as were five of the thirteen men who rode with him. One was killed, and thirteen (including his own) out of twenty-one horses were killed before he got half-way to the guns, and he was obliged to retire." Capt. Reed's Victoria Cross was presented to him by Sir Redvers Buller at Ladysmith on 4 March, 1900. He was promoted to Major, 1904; passed the Staff College in 1905; was on the General Staff, Army Headquarters, from 1906 to 1910, and from 1910 to 1911 was Staff Officer to the Inspector-General, Overseas Force. In 1911 he married Marjorie Eleanor, younger daughter of A. Theodore Olive, Esq., of The Cedars, Datchet, and they have one son and two daughters. He was additional Military Attaché with Turkish Army, 1912 to 1913, during Balkan War. Colonel Reed served in the European War from 1914; was mentioned in Despatches 7 times; created a C.M.G. 10 April, 1916; was wounded; Brevet Colonel 13 May, 1916; C.B. 1 Jan. 1918; appointed Temporary Brigadier-General June, 1915, and Temporary Major-General whilst in command of a division Oct. 1917; promoted Major-General 3 June, 1919.

London Gazette, 20 April, 1900.—"War Office, 20 April, 1900. The Queen has been graciously pleased to signify Her intention to confer the Decoration of the Victoria Cross on the undermentioned Officer, whose claim has been submitted for Her Majesty's approval for his conspicuous bravery at the Battle of Colenso, as stated against his name."

BABTIE, WILLIAM, Major, was born in Scotland 7 May 1859, the eldest son of the late John Babtie, J.P., of Dumbarton. He was educated at the University of Glasgow, and took his M.B. degree in 1880, entering the Army Medical Service on 30 July 1881. He served during the international occupation of Crete as Senior Medical Officer 1897–98, and was created a C.M.G. (1899), also in South Africa on the Staff of the Natal Army, when he was present at all the actions for the relief of Ladysmith and the subsequent operations in Natal and Eastern Transvaal. When describing the battle of Colenso, Sir A. Conan Doyle says: "For two hours the little knot of heart-sick humiliated officers and men lay in the precarious shelter of the donga, and looked out at the bullet-swept plain and the line of silent guns. Many of them were wounded. Their chief lay among them, still calling out in his delirium for his guns. They had been joined by the gallant Babtie, a brave surgeon, who rode across to the donga amid a murderous fire and did what he could for the injured men." Later in the day we are told how Major Babtie went out with Capt. Congreve to bring in Lieut. Roberts. For his services in this campaign Major Babtie was mentioned in Despatches, promoted Lieut.-Colonel, received the Medal with five clasps, and the Victoria Cross. The London Gazette, 20 April, 1900, states: "William Babtie, C.M.G., Major, Royal Army Medical Corps. At Colenso, on the 15th Dec. 1899, the wounded of the 14th and 66th Batteries, Royal Field Artillery, were lying in an advanced donga close to the rear of the guns, without any medical officer to attend to them; and when a message was sent back asking for assistance, Major W. Babtie, R.A.M.C., rode up under a heavy rifle-fire, his pony being hit three times. When he arrived at the donga, where the wounded were lying in a sheltered corner, he attended to them all, going from place to place exposed to the heavy rifle-fire which greeted anyone who showed himself. Later on in the day Major Babtie went out with Capt. Congreve to bring in Lieut. Roberts, who was lying wounded on the veldt. This also was under a heavy fire." In 1903 Lieut.-Colonel Babtie married Edith Mary, daughter of the late W. H. Barry, Esq., of Ballyadam, County Cork, and widow of Major P. A. Hayes, A.M.S. They have one daughter. From 1901 to 1906 he was Assistant Director-General Army Medical Service, War Office; from 1907 to 1910, Inspector of Medical Services; from 1910 to 1914, Deputy Director-General, and in 1912 he was created a C.B. During the Great War he served from 1914 to 1915 as Director of Medical Services in India, and from 1915 to 1916 as Principal Director of Medical Services in the Mediterranean, during the operations in Egypt, the Dardanelles and Salonika. For his services in connection with the Expeditionary Forces in that area he was mentioned in Despatches and created a K.C.M.G. on 1 Jan. 1916. In 1916 he became a Director and in 1918 Inspector of Medical Services at the War Office, retiring with the rank of Lieut.-General in 1919, and was created a K.C.B. on 3 June of that year. General Babtie was an Honorary Surgeon to His Majesty from 1914 to 1919, and is a Knight of Grace of the Order of St. John of Jerusalem in England and an LL.D. of the University of Glasgow.

William Babtie.

London Gazette, 26 June, 1900.—"War Office, 26 June, 1900. The Queen has been graciously pleased to confirm the grant of the Decoration of the Victoria Cross to the undermentioned Officer, Non-commissioned Officer and Soldiers, which Decoration has been provisionally conferred upon them by the Field-Marshal Commanding-in-Chief in South Africa, in accordance with the rules laid down in Her Majesty's Warrant instituting the Decoration, for their conspicuous bravery during the action at Korn Spruit, on the 31st March, 1900, as stated against their names."

PHIPPS-HORNBY, EDMUND JOHN, Major, was born at Lordington, Emsworth, Hants, on 31 Dec. 1857, the second son of Admiral of the Fleet Sir Geoffrey Thomas Phipps-Hornby, G.C.B., and Emily Frances, daughter of the Rev. Richard Cowper Coles, of Ditcham, Petersfield, Hants. He was educated at a private school and at the Royal Military Academy, Woolwich, and entered the Royal Artillery in May, 1878. He served in Sir Charles Warren's Bechuanaland Expedition in 1884 and 1885, in the 2nd Mounted Rifles, commanded by Colonel Carrington, and became Captain in 1886. On 31 Jan. 1895, at St. Stephen's Church, Gloucester Road, S.W., Capt. Phipps-Hornby married Anna, eldest daughter of Mr. and Mrs. Jay, of Blendon Hall, Bexley, Kent, and they have two daughters, Irene and Betty. He was promoted to Major in 1895, served in the South African War of 1899–1902, was mentioned in Despatches and given the Brevet of Lieutenant-Colonel on 30 Nov. 1899; was A.D.C. to Lord Roberts, 1901 to 1903, and won the Victoria Cross as described later in the Gazette. Brigadier-General Phipps-Hornby writes: "On the night of 30–31 March, 1900, the 2nd Cavalry Brigade, with Q and U Batteries, R.H.A., retired from Tabanchu on Bloemfontein, followed by a superior force of Boers. By 4 a.m. the force was across the Modder River at the Waterworks, inside its own line of outposts. At daylight the heavy rifle-fire commenced and a few shells fell short. Soon afterwards the shells came over our heads and fell among the transport. The mules were at once inspanned, and each waggon moved off as soon as it was ready along the road to Bloemfontein. The two R.H.A. batteries were ordered to cross the Korn Spruit and cover the retirement. When nearing the drift it was noticed that all the transport was halted at the drift and had spread out fan-like. U Battery was ordered to trot on. When I got about 150 yards from the tail of the transport, a man ran out to me and said, 'We are prisoners. The Boers are all round us.' I ordered the battery to wheel about and gallop away. As it did so a heavy fire was opened on it from the spruit and upset one gun and stopped another waggon. After galloping back about half a mile I saw the Cavalry Brigade moving towards us. I blew my whistle and brought the battery into action by the tin huts of the railway station. The battery remained in action till ordered out by General Broadwood, Commanding the Cavalry Brigade. There were only myself, Captain Humphreys (wounded), and eight N.C.O.'s and men left with the guns then. We had to man-handle them back and get infantry to help us." He was awarded the Victoria Cross [London Gazette, 26 June, 1900]: "Edmund John Phipps-Hornby, Major, Q Battery, Royal Horse Artillery. Date of Act of Bravery: 31 March, 1900. On the occasion of the action at Korn Spruit on the 31st March, 1900, a British force, including two batteries of the Royal Horse Artillery, was retiring from Thabanchu, towards Bloemfontein. The enemy had formed an ambush at Korn Spruit, and, before their presence was discovered by the main body, had captured the greater portion of the baggage column and five out of the six guns of the leading battery. When the alarm was given, Q Battery, Royal Horse Artillery, was within three hundred yards of the spruit. Major Phipps-Hornby, who commanded it, at once wheeled about and moved off at a gallop under a very heavy fire. One gun was upset when the wheel horse was shot, and had to be abandoned with another waggon, the horses of which were killed. The remainder of the battery reached a position close to some unfinished railway buildings, and came into action 1,150 yards from the spruit, remaining in action until ordered to retire. When the order to retire was received, Major Phipps-Hornby ordered the guns and their limbers to be run back by hand to where the teams of uninjured horses stood behind the unfinished buildings. The few remaining gunners, assisted by a number of officers and men of a party of mounted infantry, and directed by Major Phipps-Hornby and Capt. Humphreys, the only remaining officers of the battery, succeeded in running back four of the guns under shelter. One or two of the limbers were similarly withdrawn by hand, but the work was most severe and the distance considerable. In consequence, all concerned were so exhausted that they were unable to drag in the remaining limbers of the fifth gun. It now became necessary to risk the horses, and volunteers were called for from among the drivers, who readily responded. Several horses were killed and men wounded, but at length only one gun and one limber were left exposed. Four separate attempts were made to rescue these, but when no more horses were available the attempt had to be given up and the gun and limber were abandoned. Meanwhile the other guns had been sent on one at a time, and after passing within seven or eight hundred yards of the enemy, in rounding the head of a donga and crossing two spruits, they eventually reached a place of safety, where the battery was reformed. After full consideration of the circumstances of the case, the Field-Marshal Commanding-in-Chief in South Africa formed the opinion that the conduct of all ranks of 'Q' Battery, Royal Horse Artillery, was conspicuously gallant and daring, but that all were equally brave and devoted in their behaviour. He therefore decided to treat the case of the battery as one of collective gallantry, under Rule 13 of the Victoria Cross Warrant, and directed that one officer should be selected for the decoration of the Victoria

E. J. Phipps-Hornby.

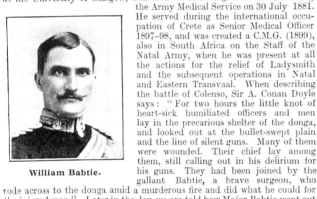

Cross by the officers, one non-commissioned officer by the non-commissioned officers, and two gunners or drivers by the gunners and drivers. A difficulty arose with regard to the officer, owing to the fact that there were only two officers—Major Phipps-Hornby and Capt. Humphreys—available for the work of saving the guns, and both of these had been conspicuous by their gallantry and by the fearless manner in which they exposed themselves, and each of them nominated the other for the decoration. It was ultimately decided in favour of Major Phipps-Hornby, as having been the senior concerned. Charles Parker, Sergt., was elected by the non-commissioned officers, as described above. Isaac Lodge, Gunner, and Horace Harry Glasock, Driver, were elected by the gunners and drivers as described above." From 1901 to 1903 Major Phipps-Hornby was A.D.C. to Lord Roberts. For his services in this campaign he was mentioned in Despatches, and received the Brevet of Lieutenant-Colonel. He became Lieutenant-Colonel in 1903, and was given command of the 4th R.H.A. Brigade at Woolwich and Aldershot till 1903, when he was promoted Colonel. In 1909 he was appointed Brigadier-General to command the artillery of the 4th Division, and remained in command of it till 1913. In 1911 he was created a C.B. On the outbreak of the European War Brigadier-General Phipps-Hornby was appointed to the command of the Artillery 3rd Corps, and went with it to France in Aug. 1914, and commanded the artillery of the Southern Army in England from April, 1916, to Dec. 1918. He was mentioned in Despatches four times during the Great War, and was created a C.M.G. in 1916. Brigadier-General E. J. Phipps-Hornby retired on 27 Dec. 1918.

PARKER, CHARLES, Sergt., son of George Parker (a Crimean veteran), who died 19 June, 1899), was born at St. John's, Kent, on 11 March, 1870, and entered the Royal Horse Artillery in Feb. 1885, serving in India from 1889 to 1895. He took part in the South African War from 1899 to 1900; received the Queen's Medal with clasps for Kimberley, Dreifontein, Diamond Hill and Wittebergen; was promoted to Sergt. by Lord Roberts for gallantry on 1 April, 1900, and was awarded the Victoria Cross [London Gazette, 26 June, 1900]: " Charles Parker, Sergt., Royal Horse Artillery. Date of Act of Bravery: 31 March, 1900. On the occasion of the action at Korn Spruit on the 31st March, 1900, a British force, including two batteries of the Royal Horse Artillery, was retiring from Thabanchu towards Bloemfontein. The enemy had formed an ambush at Korn Spruit, and before their presence was discovered by the main body had captured the greater portion of the baggage column and five out of the six guns of the leading battery. When the alarm was given, Q Battery, Royal Horse Artillery, was within three hundred yards of the spruit. Major Phipps-Hornby, who commanded it, at once wheeled about and moved off at a gallop under a very heavy fire. One gun was upset when the wheel horse was shot, and had to be abandoned, with another waggon, the horses of which were killed. The remainder of the battery reached a position close to some unfinished railway buildings, and came into action 1,150 yards from the spruit, remaining in action until ordered to retire. When the order to retire was received, Major Phipps-Hornby ordered the guns and their limbers to be run back by hand to where the team of uninjured horses stood behind the unfinished buildings. The few remaining gunners, assisted by a number of officers and men of a party of mounted infantry, and directed by Major Phipps-Hornby and Capt. Humphreys, the only remaining officers of the battery, succeeded in running back four of the guns under shelter. One or two of the limbers were similarly withdrawn by hand, but the work was most severe and the distance considerable. In consequence all concerned were so exhausted that they were unable to drag in the remaining limbers or the fifth gun. It now became necessary to risk the horses, and volunteers were called for from among the drivers, who readily responded. Several horses were killed and men wounded, but at length only one gun and one limber were left exposed. Four separate attempts were made to rescue these, but when no more horses were available the attempt had to be given up and the gun and limber were abandoned. Meanwhile the other guns had been sent on one at a time, and after passing within seven or eight hundred yards of the enemy, in rounding the head of a donga and crossing two spruits, they eventually reached a place of safety, where the battery was reformed. After full consideration of the circumstances of the case, the Field-Marshal Commanding-in-Chief in South Africa formed the opinion that the conduct of all ranks of Q Battery, Royal Horse Artillery, was conspicuously gallant and daring, but that all were equally brave and devoted in their behaviour. He therefore decided to treat the case of the battery as one of collective gallantry, under Rule 13 of the Victoria Cross Warrant, and directed that one officer should be selected for the decoration of the Victoria Cross by the officers, one non-commissioned officer by the non-commissioned officers, and two gunners or drivers by the gunners and drivers. A difficulty arose with regard to the officer, owing to the fact that there were only two officers—Major Phipps-Hornby and Capt. Humphreys—available for the work of saving the guns, and both of these had been conspicuous by their gallantry and by the fearless manner in which they exposed themselves, and each of them nominated the other for the decoration. It was ultimately decided in favour of Major Phipps-Hornby, as having been the senior concerned. Charles Parker, Sergt., was elected by the non-commissioned officers as described above. Isaac Lodge, Gunner, and Horace Harry Glasock, Driver, were elected by the gunners and drivers as described above." Sergt. Parker had two brothers serving in the same Battery, R.H.A. He died on 9 Aug. 1918.

Charles Parker.

LODGE, ISAAC, Gunner. " We most of us seem to have been named out of the Bible; my father's name was Elijah Lodge, my mother's was Rhoda. She was the daughter of William Ward, who lived at the farm down by the gates of Easton Park, where Lord Warwick lives. I was born at Great Canfield, near Dunmow, in Essex, and went to Great Canfield School. When I was eleven years old I was out at work; first on a farm, doing milking, and then I did various other things, tanning the barks of trees, and later on I was a gamekeeper, and my employer gave me two woods. It was a good job, but I *had* to be a soldier. Nothing put it into my head; it was there. And if I had my time over again I should be a soldier again. If I weren't so deaf I should be in it now. I enlisted in with the Royal Garrison Artillery on the 29th Dec. 1888, at Warley Barracks; that was the way you got into the Royal Horse Artillery in those days; and after a few weeks was transferred to the R.H.A., and came to St. John's Wood into a service battery, and then went to India with B Battery. We were at Meerut in Mount Rocket lines, and then marched up to Rawalpindi, and were there two years. I was transferred from B Battery to Q Battery. General Brunker that is now, made Q Battery efficient. He worked very hard at it; not a pin could be out of place nor a round of ammunition, and every man had to know where everything was and how much there was of everything. The horses were trained over jumps, singly and in pairs. If he ordered a parade at ten o'clock he was there to the second, and he expected everyone else to be there too. General Fanshawe was just the same. A Staff officer came to inspect us one day, and he asked one man how many shells there were in a portable magazine, and the gunner just held up three fingers and that was all the answer he got. He laughed and asked Major Brunker if that was how he trained his men, and he said, ' Something like that, sir.' Everything in Q Battery had to be ready and there, as I said. Once in Sialkot the alarm went like it does when there is a mutiny. Our horses were half harnessed, so we were out a few minutes before the Major could get up, and he was up to time. It was a treat to see the way the guns went out that day, here and there, where they were wanted, and all at full gallop. I used to sometimes sit on the end of the gun because my horse couldn't keep up. Q Battery came home from India to Ireland to Newbridge Barracks, and from there to Aldershot, and then to the South African War. We were thirty-eight days on the voyage. The propeller broke, and I began to think that we were looking for Boers on the water. They got the guns off first, of course; we were a bit late and they were wanted. U Battery marched across the Karn. We were on guard at De Aar, and then at Modder River. The Cavalry Brigade moved off in the middle of the night and outflanked Cronje's position at Magersfontein, and went on to the Relief of Kimberley, and then to Paardeberg, and then headed off Cronje into the river-bed. I was laying my gun on his laager when the order came that he'd surrendered. After that we had to go and outflank De Wet at Poplar Grove. He led us a dance like that one that's in London now, General Smuts. From Poplar Grove we went to Dreifontein, where we were in a place shaped like a horse-shoe. It was there they fought the fight for Bloemfontein. The order came to go and take Bloemfontein. Next morning we chased De Wet from his position and out of it altogether. The cavalry manœuvred through Bloemfontein and the battery kept working all the time. We went to Thaa'-Banchu, and were there some time till the order was given for the convoy to move off to the Waterworks and for us to stand fast till 7.30. No matches to be lit, no pipes, no smokes. We marched twenty-five miles from Thaa' Banchu to the Waterworks in the night, rested our horses by taking the saddles off till daybreak, when the guns opened fire. The convoy moved off at once; the order was given to harness up. The battery moved off in sections; then when Major Phipps-Hornby was told the Boers were in the spruit, he ordered ' Subsections left about wheel,' and ' Gallop.' The range was under 1,000 yards. No. 6 gun was brought down in the mouth of the donga, and one of my horses out of No. 5 was shot. I jumped off and unhooked it and threw it out, and then went up to where Major Phipps-Hornby had brought his guns into action. No. 4 gun joined in to make the section, which was commanded by Lieut. Ashmore and was firing at 1,500 yards. Lieut. Ashmore was lying down observing, and was shot in the shoulder, and Senior Sergt. Armstrong took his place. He got shot, and Sergt. Shimmons took his place. He was shot, and then there was me and that Norfolk fellow left by ourselves. Before long we ran short of ammunition, so I went to the old galvanized iron shed where our waggons were under cover. I go some ammunition and brought it back and served the guns with it. Of course, when I went there were two of us, but the other man got shot, so I was the only one left in my section in action who stuck to the guns. Major Phipps-Hornby was in the middle all the time, very cool and collected, giving orders. He now gave the order to get the guns out. Glasock, a plucky little lad, who came in to help try to get the guns out, had one horse shot from him. He went by the tin hut and got another horse from somewhere. I have sometimes wondered where he got it. Anyhow, he came in and tried again to get the guns out of action. We got them out by hand and with a pair of wheeler horses and limbers. Then Glasock—who was sitting on his horse—said, ' I'm shot.' I said, ' Where ? ' It had gone in behind the saddle, and he said, ' I guess they've got me in a soft place.' I went up to the old tin shed to see if there were

Isaac Lodge.

any orders, and saw a mounted orderly escort some of the Mounted Infantry, though one of his people said they were Roberts's Horse, and one officer said they were commanded by Major Pack-Beresford, my old officer in India. But they were Mounted Infantry, and though Major Pack-Beresford was somewhere about, he was not there. If he had been I should have gone and spoken to him, firing or no firing. Then we came up out of the donga. After getting clear of the trap, Major Phipps-Hornby collected his layers and gunners together and came into action again. The firing was then taken from him on the extreme left by the reinforcement. After that he watered the horses, and General Broadwood had what was left of us formed up, and said he was very pleased with the way the Major had commanded us, and then he said : 'Major Phipps-Hornby, you ought to be proud of the men that you have got working under you.' After that we got our orders to go into Bloemfontein and there get refitted, men, horses, guns, and whatever old things were smashed up, and then started out again on the road towards Kroonstadt. I greased my gun and waggon before going into Kroonstadt, and then was made go sick because I had ague and fever. We were in a sort of school, or church, lying on the floor, and Lord Roberts came and got mattresses for us to lie on. When I was better I went to Cape Town, and then back up to Bloemfontein. I took charge of the 'luxuries,' and smuggled them in to Pretoria, and then got a span of bullocks and took them from Pretoria to the battery. They were forbidden things, but the boys were smoking tea leaves. It was tobacco and smokes and Quaker oats, and a few little things like that, but perhaps you'd better say nothing about it. General Phipps-Hornby and the rest of us were given our V.C.'s by Lord Roberts at Pretoria in October. After that we were holding the Nek at Pretoria, and then from Rustenburg to Ollivant's Nek, fought our way on to Wolverdene Station, and from there to Potchefstroom, where we fought De La Rey. From Potchefstroom we came up in the New Year and joined in a big trek under Lord French. Lord French commanded one force and Sir Ian Hamilton another under him, so they had the Boers on two sides, and what one General couldn't do the other could. For nineteen days we lived on maize, and the cavalry on outpost duty had to eat it raw. We found three guns all in a bog and dug them out, and kept one ourselves and gave the others to the other section. We came back round by Dundee and Glencoe Heights, and one section went to the Springs and the other to Johannesburg to get refitted. After that at Calfontein we drove off the Boer attack, and then went on with Bindon Blood on another big trek. After that we came up to Amsterdam, Carolina, above Middelburg in the Transvaal. Then from Middelburg in trucks and down to Cape Colony. Centre section went to Naauport and left section to De Aar. We refitted with Scotch carts and marched from De Aar to Beaufort West, cut across Beaufort West to Aberdeen, from Aberdeen to Willowmoor. At Willowmoor the 10th Hussars got ambushed. The 12th Lancers and our section of guns went out into Long Kloof, where they made a charge and we fired, and got them back. They were pleased to see us at Houtsburn. We were fighting all along and cleared the bank of Scheeper's Mob ; we were all round them, Major Kavanagh's lot and others, and after a forty-five mile chase we ran them into another column. Then I finished up by Schwellendam and Naaupoort—the Headquarters, and when I came from Naaupoort I brought ordnance down to Cape Town and waited at Green Point till there was a boat from home. Major Humphreys saw me there, and I said I'd as soon wait and come home with the battery. He said, 'You get off now, and get a month's leave till the battery comes home, and then another month's leave with the battery.' . . . I have the Long Service Medal and King George's Coronation Medal, and, of course, the Queen's Medal with five clasps. I had eighteen months more service and was a Corporal, and they asked me would I be a Sergeant and drill recruits at the Depôt. I said, No, I'd finished my time with the battery." (For Gazette of Lodge's V.C. see account of Major Phipps-Hornby, etc.)

GLASOCK, HORACE HENRY, Driver, served in the South African Campaign of 1899–1902, and was awarded the Victoria Cross [London Gazette, 26 June, 1900]: "Horace Henry Glasock, Driver, Q Battery, Royal Horse Artillery. Date of Act of Bravery : 31 March, 1900. On the occasion of the action at Korn Spruit on the 31st March, 1900, a British force, including two batteries of the Royal Horse Artillery, was retiring from Thabanchu towards Bloemfontein. The enemy had formed an ambush at Korn Spruit, and before their presence was discovered by the main body had captured the greater portion of the baggage column and five out of the six guns of the leading battery. When the alarm was given, Q Battery, Royal Horse Artillery, was within three hundred yards of the spruit. Major Phipps-Hornby, who commanded it, at once wheeled about, and moved off at a gallop under a very heavy fire. One gun was upset when the wheel horse was shot, and had to be abandoned, with another waggon, the horses of which were killed. The remainder of the battery reached a position close to some unfinished railway buildings, and came into action 1,150 yards from the spruit, remaining in action until ordered to retire. When the order to retire was received, Major Phipps-Hornby ordered the guns and their limbers to be run back by hand to where the team of uninjured horses stood behind the unfinished buildings. The few remaining gunners, assisted by a number of officers and men of a party of mounted infantry, and directed by Major Phipps-Hornby and Capt. Humphreys, the only remaining officers of the battery, succeeded in running back four of the guns under shelter. One or two of the limbers were similarly withdrawn by hand, but the work was most severe and the distance considerable. In consequence all concerned were so exhuausted that they were unable to drag in the remaining limbers or the fifth gun. It now became necessary to risk the horses, and volunteers were called for from among the drivers, who readily responded. Several horses were killed and men wounded, but at length only one gun and one limber were left exposed. Four separate attempts were made to rescue these, but when no more horses were available, the attempt had to be given up and the gun and limber were abandoned. Meanwhile the other guns had been sent on one at a time, and after passing within seven or eight hundred yards of the enemy, in rounding the head of a donga and crossing two spruits, they eventually reached a place of safety, where the battery was reformed. After full consideration of the circumstances of the case, the Field-Marshal Commanding-in-Chief in South Africa formed the opinion that the conduct of all ranks of Q Battery, Royal Horse Artillery, was conspicuously gallant and daring, but that all were equally devoted in their behaviour. He therefore decided to treat the case of the battery as one of collective gallantry, under Rule 13 of the Victoria Cross Warrant, and directed that one officer should be selected for the decoration of the Victoria Cross by the officers, one non-commissioned officer by the non-commissioned officers, and two gunners or drivers by the gunners and drivers. A difficulty arose with regard to the officer, owing to the fact that there were only two unwounded officers—Major Phipps-Hornby and Capt. Humphreys—available for the work of saving the guns, and both of these had been conspicuous by their gallantry and by the fearless manner in which they exposed themselves, and each of them nominated the other for the decoration. It was ultimately decided in favour of Major Phipps-Hornby as having been the senior concerned. Charles Parker, Sergt., was elected by the non-commissioned officers as described above. Isaac Lodge, Gunner, and Horace Henry Glasock, Driver, were elected by the gunners and drivers as described above." Glasock's name was at first spelt "Glassock." This was corrected in the London Gazette, 6 July, 1900. "MEMORANDUM, 6 July, 1900.—The name of Driver Horace Harry Glasock, Q Battery, Royal Horse Artillery, the grant to whom of the Victoria Cross was notified in the London Gazette of the 26th June, 1900, is as now, and not as therein stated." He was discharged from the Royal Horse Artillery 25 Jan. 1911.

Horace Henry Glasock.

London Gazette, 6 July, 1900.—" War Office, 6 July, 1900. The Queen has been graciously pleased to signify Her intention to confer the Decoration of the Victoria Cross on the undermentioned Officers, Non-commissioned Officer and Trooper, whose claims have been submitted for Her Majesty's approval, for their conspicuous bravery in South Africa, as stated against their names."

TOWSE, ERNEST BEACHCROFT BECKWITH, Capt., was born 23 April, 1864, and educated at Wellington College. He was gazetted to the Wiltshire Regt. 16 Dec. 1885, and was posted to the Gordon Highlanders 2 Jan. 1886. In 1892 Capt. Towse married Gertrude, younger daughter of the late John Christie. He served with the Chitral Relief Force, 1895, including Malakand (Medal with clasp). He also served on the N.W. Frontier of India and at Tirah, 1897–98 (two clasps), and in South Africa, 1899–1900. In this campaign he was mentioned in Despatches twice, received the Queen's Medal with three clasps, and was dangerously wounded. He was awarded the Victoria Cross for the services described in the London Gazette, 6 July, 1900: "Ernest Beachcroft Beckwith Towse, Capt., Gordon Highlanders. Dates of Acts of Bravery : 11 Dec. 1899 ; 30 April, 1900. On the 11th Dec. 1899, at the action of Magersfontein, Capt. Towse was brought to notice by his commanding officer for his gallantry and devotion in assisting the late Colonel Downman, when mortally wounded, in the retirement, and endeavouring, when close up to the front of the firing-line, to carry Colonel Downman on his back ; but finding this not possible, Capt. Towse supported him till joined by Colour-Sergt. Nelson and L.-Corpl. Hodgson. On the 30th April, 1900, Capt. Towse, with twelve men, took up a position on the top of Mount Thaba, far away from support. A force of about 150 Boers attempted to seize the same plateau, neither party appearing to see the other until they were but one hundred yards apart. Some of the Boers then got within forty yards of Capt. Towse and his party, and called on him to surrender. He at once caused his men to open fire, and remained firing himself until severely wounded (both eyes shattered), thus succeeding in driving off the Boers. The gallantry of this officer in vigorously attacking the enemy (for he not only fired, but charged forward) saved the situation, notwithstanding the numerical superiority of the Boers." Capt. Towse was decorated by Queen Victoria, by whom in 1900 he was appointed Sergeant-at-Arms. In 1902 he was reappointed Sergeant-at-Arms by King Edward, and in 1903 became one of the Hon. Corps of Gentlemen-at-Arms. He is now Sergeant-at-Arms in Ordinary to His Majesty King George V., and has been appointed to the Hon. Corps of Gentlemen-at-Arms. Capt. Towse is a Knight of Grace of the Order of St. John of Jerusalem. Capt. Towse became an expert typist, and when the European War broke out he went to the front to type letters for wounded soldiers, and was mentioned in Sir Douglas Haig's Despatch in June, 1916. In 1915 he was promoted Staff Captain of Base Hospitals without pay and allowances. Chairman of the Grand Council of the Comrades of the Great War.

Ernest B. B. Towse.

FITZCLARENCE, CHARLES, Capt., was the grandson of George, 1st Earl of Munster, eldest son of King William IV. His father was the Honourable George Fitzclarence, Capt., Royal Navy, and his mother was Lady Maria Henriette, *née* Scott, eldest daughter of the 4th Earl of Clonmel. Capt. George Fitzclarence was one of four brothers who served either in the Navy or Army, the youngest dying of wounds received in the attack on the Redan in the Crimean War. A twin brother of Brigadier-General Charles Fitzclarence's, Edward, served in the Egyptian Army, and was killed at Abu Hamed in 1897. Charles Fitzclarence was born on 8 May, 1865, at Bishopscourt, County Kildare, and was educated at Eton and Wellington. He was gazetted Lieutenant from the Militia into the Royal Fusiliers 10 Nov. 1886. During Kitchener's Khartum Campaign he was Adjutant of the Mounted Infantry in Egypt. But to his grievous disappointment, when the other troops went up the Nile, the Mounted Infantry was left behind. He was promoted to Captain in the Royal Fusiliers 6 April, 1898, and, on the formation of the Irish Guards, was transferred to that regiment 6 Oct. 1900. Capt. Fitzclarence went to South Africa on special service in July, 1899, and was present throughout the siege of Mafeking, when his gallantry and daring gained for him the sobriquet of "The Demon." He was awarded the Victoria Cross [London Gazette, 6 July, 1900], having been recommended three times for it: "Charles Fitzclarence, Capt., The Royal Fusiliers (City of London Regt.). Dates for Acts of Bravery: 14 Oct. 1899, and 27 Oct. 1899. On the 14th Oct. 1899, Capt. Fitzclarence went with his squadron of the Protectorate Regt., consisting of only partially trained men, who had never been in action, to the assistance of an armoured train which had gone out from Mafeking. The enemy were in greatly superior numbers, and the squadron was for a time surrounded, and it looked as if nothing could save them from being shot down. Capt. Fitzclarence, however, by his personal coolness and courage, inspired the greatest confidence in his men, and by his bold and efficient handling of them, not only succeeded in relieving the armoured train, but inflicted a heavy defeat on the Boers, who lost fifty killed and a large number of wounded; his own losses being two killed and fifteen wounded. The moral effect of this blow had a very important bearing on subsequent encounters with the Boers. On the 27th Oct. 1899, Capt. Fitzclarence led his squadron from Mafeking across the open, and made a night attack with the bayonet on one of the enemy's trenches. A hand-to-hand fight took place in the trench, while a heavy fire was concentrated on it from the rear. The enemy was driven out with heavy loss. Capt. Fitzclarence was the first man into the position, and accounted for four of the enemy with his sword. The British lost six killed and nine wounded. Capt. Fitzclarence was himself slightly wounded. With reference to these two actions Major-General Baden-Powell states that had this officer not shown an extraordinary spirit and fearlessness, the attacks would have been failures, and we should have suffered heavy loss both in men and prestige. On the 26th Dec. 1899, during the action of Game Tree, near Mafeking, Capt. Fitzclarence again distinguished himself by his coolness and courage, and was again wounded severely through the leg." From Aug. 1900, to Feb. 1901, Capt. Fitzclarence was Brigade Major in South Africa. He was mentioned in Despatches [London Gazette, 8 Feb. 1901], for his services in the South African Campaign, and besides the Victoria Cross, with the dates 14 and 27 Oct. 1899, was given the Brevet of Major 29 Nov. 1900, and received the Queen's Medal with three clasps. From April, 1903, to March, 1906, he was Brigade Major of the 5th Brigade at Aldershot. He became Major in May, 1904, and succeeded to the command of the 1st Battn. Irish Guards in July, 1909. In 1913 he was appointed to the command of the regiment and regimental district, and this post he held until the outbreak of the European War, when he took over command of the 29th Brigade, 10th Division, at the Curragh, until 22 Sept. On the 27th Sept. he took command of the 1st Guards' Brigade with the Expeditionary Force in France, and he held this command until his death on 11 Nov., when he was killed in action leading the 1st Guards' Brigade against the Prussian Guard. The 1st Guards' Brigade consisted of the 1st Battn. of the Coldstream Guards, the 1st Battn. Scots Guards, a battalion of the Black Watch, and a battalion of Cameron Highlanders. "Not long after Fitzclarence's arrival in France," says Capt. Valentine Williams, M.C., writing under the pseudonym of "X" in "Blackwood's Magazine," "the British Expeditionary Force did its great swing round to the north, the 1st Corps detraining at St. Omer, and on 20 Oct. raking over the line north of Ypres from Bixschoote to Zonnebeke to support the weakened Belgian Army against the great northern attack which was known to be impending. Two days later the enemy attacked heavily at Pilkem, where the 1st Guards' Brigade was in position, and drove in the front of the Camerons; but a brilliant counter-attack by the 2nd Brigade the next day restored the line. On the night of the 23rd the French relieved the 1st Division, which went back to Ypres in reserve, but on the 25th was sent up again to take over a line from Reutel to the Menin Road. The Coldstream and Scots Guards' battalions of Fitzclarence's brigade, in trenches north of Gheluvelt, suffered terribly in a German attack, delivered in a dense mist on the morning of the 27th along the Menin road. The odds against the British were crushing, for on that day some 24,000 Germans were arrayed against about 5,000 exhausted British troops. In two days the Scots Guards lost 10 officers and 370 men killed and wounded. But the result of the day's fighting was that the British line stood firm and unbroken, while the Germans had sustained enormous losses." On the 31st Oct. 1914, the Germans had broken the line of the 1st Division and taken the village of Gheluvelt. Sir John French, in his Despatch published on the 30th Nov. 1914, described the fighting at this time: "Perhaps," he said, "the most important and decisive attack (except that of the Prussian Guard on the 10th Nov.) made against the 1st Corps during the whole of its arduous experiences in the neighbourhood of Ypres took place on the 31st Oct. After several attacks and counter-attacks during the course of the morning along the Menin–Ypres Road, south-east of Gheluvelt, an attack against that place developed in great force, and the line of the 1st Division was broken. Meantime, on the Menin Road, a counter-attack delivered by the left of the 1st Division against the right flank of the German line was completely successful, and the 2nd Worcester Regt. was to the fore in this. I was present with Sir Douglas Haig, at Hooge, between two and three o'clock on this day, when the 1st Division was retiring. I regard it as the most critical moment in the whole of this great battle. The rally of the 1st Division and the recapture of the village of Gheluvelt at such a time was fraught with momentous consequences. If any one unit can be singled out for special praise it is the Worcesters." Sir John French made a speech to the Worcesters on the 26th Nov. 1914, which appeared in the "Times" of the 14th Dec. 1914. In it he praised the Worcesters for what they had done on the 31st Oct., and he further said: "I have made repeated inquiries as to what officer was responsible for the conduct of this counter-attack on the 31st Oct., but have never so far been able to find out." It has since been made known and officially confirmed that it was Brigadier-General C. Fitzclarence who gave the order for the counter-attack. Later on, in a letter, Sir John French said: "During the first battle of Ypres, at the crisis of the fight on the 31st Oct., the situation was saved by the Worcesters. For many weeks and months afterwards I tried to ascertain who was responsible for this attack upon which so much depended. It was only late in 1915 that I obtained absolute proof that it was Brigadier-General C. Fitzclarence, V.C., who rallied the troops and directed the successful onslaught." In General Fitzclarence's diary, under the date of 31 Oct. 1914, he wrote: "Enemy shelled the 'Welsh' and the Queen's out of their trenches. I sent Worcesters with Thorne, ordering them to counter-attack and retake village and trenches. Worcesters did very well. Situation critical, and our line brought back to Veldhoek." It is all described in an admirable article by "X" (Capt. Valentine Williams) in "Blackwood's Magazine" for Aug. 1917, how Capt. Andrew Thorne (then Staff Capt. to the 1st Guards' Brigade, later Lieut.-Colonel A. Thorne, D.S.O., commanding a battalion of Grenadier Guards) was sent to guide Major Hankey with the 2nd Battn. Worcestershire Regt., who had been ordered by General Fitzclarence to put his battalion in to counter-attack against Gheluvelt. Statements by various officers are given in "Blackwood's," ending by one from Major (now Lieut.-Colonel) E. B. Hankey himself: "We were in Corps Reserve on the 31st Oct., and about 1.30 p.m. I was ordered to General Fitzclarence's Headquarters, which were about 300 yards from the corner of Polygon Wood, whereabout we were waiting. He personally gave me orders to counter-attack and try and retake the village of Gheluvelt and mend the line, and he pointed me out the church in the distance to give me the line. The General gave me a Staff officer (I forget his name), who went some distance to give me the direction of the right flank of the South Wales Borderers. I should like to add that I feel perfectly certain that by shoving us in at the time and place he did, the General saved the day. If he had waited any longer, I don't think I could have got the battalion up in time to save the South Wales Borderers and fill up the gap." On 2 Nov. the enemy attacked again along the Menin Road, and the 1st Guards' Brigade lost some ground, but held a line of trenches to the rear until it grew dark. The Germans gained about 300 yards, with casualties out of all proportion to their success. On 8 Nov. the Germans again attacked along the Menin Road, and again Fitzclarence's Brigade suffered heavily. The Scots Guards had their flank exposed and suffered accordingly. On the morning of 11 Nov. the Prussian Guard—a division strong—hurled themselves against the centre of the British troops along the Menin Road. Thirteen battalions of them came on, contemptuous equally of death and of the little Army in their way. The British machine-guns and the deadly fire of our infantry strewed the fields round Ypres with the flower of the Kaiser's hosts, and only in three places did the Prussian Guard break through. The 1st Guards' Brigade was forced out of its trenches and fell back. On the following morning it was ordered to counter-attack, with a view to recovering the lost ground. It had by this time suffered so severely that General Fitzclarence was lent several battations, including the 1st Battn. Irish Guards, which he himself had once commanded, and the 2nd Battn. Grenadier Guards. The counter-attack had for its objective the recovery of some trenches taken by the enemy in Polygon Wood, and the operation was to be carried out by the Grenadier Guards, who were already in position, and by the Irish Guards, who were unacquainted with the ground. The General himself decided to show his old regiment the way, and paid for the decision with his life. It was an awful night, and in the pitchy darkness the Irish Guards moved off along a country road and then struck across the open country. Suddenly the moon emerged from drifting clouds, and in the momentary brightness the Germans fired from the trenches a little way ahead. General Fitzclarence flung up his hands and fell dead, and Capt. Harding, an Irish Guards' officer behind him, was wounded. Neither Fitzclarence himself, nor Sir John French, nor the British nation then knew how well he had served his country at Gheluvelt. In his Despatch of the 20th Nov. 1914, Sir John French said of General Fitzclarence: "Another officer whose name was particularly mentioned to me was Brigadier-General Fitzclarence, V.C., commanding the 1st Guards' Brigade. He was unfortunately killed in the night attack of the 11th Nov. His loss will be severely felt." He married, 20 April, 1898, at the Ciddidal Church, Cairo, Violet, youngest daughter of the late Lord Alfred Spencer Churchill, M.P., and granddaughter of John, 6th Duke of Marlborough, and they had two children: Edward Charles, born 3 Oct. 1899, and Joan Harriet.

Charles Fitzclarence.

Sir John P. Milbanke.

MILBANKE, SIR JOHN PENISTON, Major, was born 9 Oct. 1872, at 30, Eccleston Street, London, S.W., the son of Sir Peniston Milbanke, 9th Baronet, J.P., D.L., Sussex, and Elizabeth, daughter of the Hon. Richard Denman. He was educated at Castlemount, Dover, and at Harrow, and joined the 10th Hussars on 26 Nov. 1892. He succeeded his father in Nov. 1899. He served in the South African War of 1899–1902, as A.D.C. to General French; was mentioned in Despatches; received the South African Medal with six clasps; was promoted Capt. (1900); awarded the Victoria Cross for the services thus described by a newspaper correspondent: " Another gallant act was that performed by Sir John Milbanke, A.D.C. to General French. It was on the day of the Suffolk abortive charge. Sir John asked to be allowed to patrol for the purpose of reconnoitring a hill, and for this took a corporal of the 10th Hussars and three men with him. They came in for an exceptionally heavy fire, during which the corporal's horse was shot underneath him, and Sir John Milbanke, turning round in a perfect hail of bullets, found the rider was lying on the veldt some distance in the rear; notwithstanding the fierce fusilade, moreover that he himself was wounded, the aide-de-camp turned right about, galloped up to the corporal and rescued him. The return journey was performed safely, and none other of the enemy's missiles taking effect. Viewed from Coles Kop, our informant said they regarded it as impossible to return alive after exposure to such a fearful shower of bullets." A letter says : " He was unconscious when he got back. Had he been able to deliver his message the Suffolks would not have been captured." Sir John Milbanke received the South African Medal with clasps. His Victoria Cross was gazetted 6 July, 1900 : " Sir John Peniston Milbanke Baronet, 10th Hussars. Date of Act of Bravery : 5 Jan. 1900. On the, 5th Jan. 1900, during a reconnaissance near Colesburg, Sir John Milbanke when retiring under fire with a small patrol of the 10th Hussars, notwithstanding the fact that he had been severely wounded in the thigh, rode back to the assistance of one of the men whose pony was exhausted, and who was under fire from some Boers who had dismounted. Sir John Milbanke took the man up on his own horse under a most galling fire, and brought him safely back to camp." On 6 Dec. 1901, at St. Peter's, Eaton Square, Sir John Milbanke married Leila, only daughter of Colonel the Hon. Charles Crichton (son of the 3rd Earl of Erne) and of Lady Madeline Taylour (daughter of the 3rd Marquis of Headfort). Their children are John Charles Peniston, born 9 Jan. 1902, and Ralph Mark, born 11 April, 1907. In 1910 Sir John Milbanke retired from the Army. In Aug. 1914, he rejoined. In Oct. 1914, he was appointed Lieut.-Colonel of the Nottinghamshire Yeomanry (Sherwood Foresters), and went to Egypt in command of the regiment in April, 1915. Major Sir John Milbanke was killed in action 21 Aug. 1915, in the Dardanelles, in charge at Hill 70. The following account is taken from part of an article by Mr. Ashmead Bartlett in the " Globe " of 4 Sept. 1915 : " The Yeomanry moved forward in a solid mass, forming up under the lower western and northern slopes. It was now almost dark and the attack seemed to hang fire, when suddenly the Yeomanry leapt to their feet, and as a single man charged right up the hill. They were met by a withering fire, which rose to a crescendo as they neared the northern crest, but nothing could stop them. They charged at amazing speed without a single halt from the bottom to the top, losing many men and many of their chosen leaders, including gallant Sir John Milbanke. It was a stirring sight, watched by thousands in the ever-gathering gloom. One moment they were below the crest, the next on top. A moment after many had disappeared inside the Turkish trenches, bayoneting all the defenders who had not fled in time, while others never stopped at trench-line, but dashed in pursuit down the reverse slopes. From a thousand lips a shout went up that Hill 70 was won. But night now was rapidly falling, the figures became blurred, then lost all shape, and finally disappeared from view. The battlefield had disappeared completely, and as one left Chocolate Hill one looked back on a vista of rolling clouds of smoke and huge fires, from the midst of which the incessant roar of the rifle-fire never for a moment ceased. This was ominous, for although Hill 70 was in our hands, the question arose could we hold it throughout the night in the face of determined counter-attacks? In fact, all through the night the battle raged incessantly, and when morning broke Hill 70 was no longer in our possession. Apparently the Turks were never driven off a knoll on the northern crest, from which they enfiladed us with machine guns and artillery fire, while those of the Yeomanry who had dashed down the reverse slopes in pursuit were counter-attacked and lost heavily and had been obliged to retire. In the night it was decided it would be impossible to hold the hill in daylight, and the order was given for the troops to withdraw to their original positions. Nothing, however, will lessen the glory of that final charge of England's Yeomen." The picture of Sir J. Milbanke reproduced here is from a painting by his brother, Mr. Mark Milbanke.

Horace R. Martineau.

MARTINEAU, HORACE ROBERT, Sergt., was born 31 Oct. 1874, in Bayswater, London, fifth son of Mr. William Martineau, of Hornsey. He was educated at University College School, and went out to South Africa, where he served under Sir Robert Baden-Powell in the successful campaign against the Matabele. He became first a Volunteer in the Cape Police and later in the Protectorate Regt., which he joined in 1889. With this regiment he served in the South African Campaign of 1899–1902, and took part in the defence of Mafeking. He was mentioned in Despatches, received the South African Medal, and was awarded the Victoria Cross [London Gazette, 6 July, 1900] : " Horace Robert Martineau, Sergt., the Protectorate Regt. On the 26th Dec. 1899, during the fight at Game Tree, near Mafeking, when the order to retire had been given, Sergt. Martineau stopped and picked up Corpl. Le Camp, who had been struck down about ten yards from the Boer trenches, and half dragged, half carried him towards a bush about 150 yards from the trenches. In doing this Sergt. Martineau was wounded in the side, but paid no attention to it, and proceeded to stanch and bandage the wounds of his comrade, whom he afterwards assisted to retire. The firing while they were retiring was very heavy, and Sergt. Martineau was again wounded. When shot the second time he was absolutely exhausted from supporting his comrade, and sank down unable to proceed farther. He received three wounds, one of which necessitated the amputation of his arm near the shoulder." He subsequently gave up soldiering and engaged in business in the African Boating Company, a large concern in Durban. When the European War broke out he joined up again, and served as Lieutenant in the Transport Service with the Anzacs at Suez and Gallipoli. He fell ill and was invalided back to New Zealand. The " Times " of 8 May, 1916, says : " Lieut. Horace Robert Martineau, V.C., of the Transport Section, New Zealand Force, died at Dunedin on 8 April, as the result of fever contracted in Gallipoli. He served in the second Matabele War and in Natal during the last native rising, and won the Victoria Cross for an act of heroism in the South African War."

RAMSDEN, H. E., Trooper, Protectorate Regt., was awarded the Victoria Cross for services in the South African War of 1899–1902 [London Gazette, 6 July, 1900] : " H. E. Ramsden, Trooper, Protectorate Regt. On the 26th Dec. 1899, during the fight at Game Tree, near Mafeking, after the order to retire was given, Trooper H. E. Ramsden picked up his brother, Trooper A. E. Ramsden, who had been shot through both legs and was lying about ten yards from the Boer trenches, and carried him about 600 or 800 yards under a heavy fire (putting him down from time to time to rest), till they met some men who helped to carry him to a place of safety." This is the second Victoria Cross awarded to a soldier for saving his own brother's life; the first was awarded to Sir C. J. S. Gough.

H. E. Ramsden.

London Gazette, 20 July, 1900.—" War Office, 20 July, 1900. The Queen has been graciously pleased to signify Her intention to confer the Decoration of the Victoria Cross on the undermentioned Officers, whose claims have been submitted for Her Majesty's approval for their conspicuous bravery in South Africa, as stated against their names."

MEIKLEJOHN, MATTHEW FONTAINE MAURY, Capt., was born on 27 Nov. 1870, son of the late Professor Meiklejohn, of St. Andrew's University, and was educated at Fettes College, Edinburgh. He joined the Gordon Highlanders in India on 17 June, 1891, and four years later saw his first active service with his regiment when Sir Robert Low's Field Force advanced to the relief of Chitral, by way of the Swat Valley. Two years later the Gordons were again actively employed on the Indian Frontier, and young Meiklejohn was slightly wounded when his regiment gallantly cleared the heights of Dargai of an Afridi lashkar. He saw much more fighting during the campaign in Tirah, especially in the Bara Valley. He received the Indian Medal with three clasps. On the outbreak of the South African War the Gordons came with the Infantry Brigade sent from India, and Meiklejohn was still with them. He was wounded early in the campaign at the battle of Elandslaagte, where he won the decoration of the Victoria Cross, and was desperately wounded. Brought back into Ladysmith, which was shortly afterwards invested by the Boers, he there shared the privations of a close and exhausting siege. It was wonderful, considering the hardships the garrison of Ladysmith suffered before they were relieved, that Capt. Meiklejohn survived his severe wounds, which entailed the loss of his right arm. It was for gallantry in this advance that Capts. Mullins and Johnstone, of the Imperial Light Horse, as well as Capt. Meiklejohn, received the Victoria Cross. His own decoration was gazetted on the 20th July, 1900, for the following act of bravery : " Matthew Fontaine Maury Meiklejohn, Capt., Gordon Highlanders. Date of Act of Bravery : 21 Oct. 1899. At the battle of Elandslaagte, on the 21st Oct. 1899, after the main Boer position had been captured, some of the men of the Gordon Highlanders, when about to advance, were exposed to a heavy cross-fire, and, having lost their leaders, commenced to waver. Seeing this, Capt. Meiklejohn rushed to the front and called on the Gordons to follow him. By his conspicuous bravery and fearless example he rallied the men and

M. F. M. Meiklejohn.

led them against the enemy's position, where he fell, desperately wounded in four places." Capt. Meiklejohn was mentioned in Despatches and received the Queen's Medal. In 1901 he was Garrison Adjutant at St. Helena, whence he returned to enter the Staff College. In 1904 he married Vèra Marshall, daughter of the late Lieut.-Colonel Lionel Marshall. They had one son and two daughters. Capt. Meiklejohn was later on the General Staff at Army Headquarters, during which service he was promoted to his majority. Major Meiklejohn died on 4 July, 1913, in the Middlesex Hospital, from the effects of an accident in Hyde Park on 28 June. His horse bolted. Major Meiklejohn, handicapped by the loss of his right arm, just managed to steer him into the rails bordering Rotten Row, opposite Knightsbridge Barracks, in order to avoid some children and their nurse, who probably would otherwise have been killed or seriously injured. The mother of these children wrote to the " Times " of July 7, 1913 : " As my nurse was the only eye-witness of the tragic accident which led to Major Meiklejohn's death, I think it right to acquaint the public with her story. She and my children were in Hyde Park on Saturday afternoon, 28 June. They had reached a spot opposite to Knightsbridge Barracks, and, as they were walking along the path, Major Meiklejohn on his runaway horse suddenly came upon them from between the trees. In order to avoid danger to the children, he turned his horse against the railings of Rotten Row, which he must have known he could not clear. He thus gave his life for theirs, and added one more to the long roll of his brave and unselfish deeds."

NORWOOD, JOHN, Lieut., was the son of J. Norwood, Esq., of Pembury Lodge, near Beckenham. He was educated at Abbey School, Beckenham, at Rugby and at Oxford, and entered the 5th (Princess Charlotte of Wales's) Dragoon Guards on 8 Feb. 1899. He served in the Boer War from 1899 to 1900, and was awarded the Victoria Cross [London Gazette, 27 July, 1900] : " John Norwood, Lieut., 5th Dragoon Guards. Date of Act of Bravery : 30 Oct. 1899. On the 30th Oct. 1899, this officer went out from Ladysmith in charge of a small patrol of the 5th Dragoon Guards. They came under a heavy fire from the enemy, who were posted on a ridge in great force. The patrol, which had arrived within about 600 yards of the ridge, then retired at full

John Norwood.

speed. One man dropped, and Second Lieut. Norwood galloped back about 300 yards through heavy fire, dismounted, and picking up the fallen trooper, carried him out of fire on his back, at the same time leading his horse with one hand. The enemy kept up an incessant fire during the whole time that Second Lieut. Norwood was carrying the man until he was quite out of range." He became Captain, 5th Dragoon Guards, and joined the Reserve of Officers 1 Feb. 1911. Capt. J. Norwood, 2nd County of London Yeomanry (Captain, Reserve of Officers), attached 5th Dragoon Guards, was killed in action while serving in the European War on 8 Sept. 1914.

ROBERTSON, WILLIAM, Lieut., was born at Dumfries, 27 Feb. 1865, the son of John M. and Janet Robertson. He was educated at Dumfries, and joined the Army on 1 Dec. 1884. He married, 29 March, 1891, in Belfast, Sara J. Ferris, daughter of Mr. and Mrs. S. Ferris, of Belfast, and their children are : William J. Robertson, born 18 Feb. 1892 (now Captain, R.A.M.C.) ; Marion M. Robertson ; Ian Gordon Robertson, born 18 Aug. 1897 (Second Lieut. The Gordon Highlanders ; killed at Beaumont Hamel), and Hector E. Robertson. William Robertson served for some years in India. He landed in South Africa on 8 Oct. 1899, two days before the Boer ultimatum to Great Britain, and proceeded to Ladysmith. During the defence of that town he fought and was wounded in the Battle of Elandslaagte, where he won the Victoria Cross. The following is the account from the London Gazette of 20 July, 1900: " William Robertson, Sergt.-Major (now Quartermaster and Honorary Lieut.) The

William Robertson.

Gordon Highlanders. Date of Act of Bravery : 21 Oct. 1899. At the Battle of Elandslaagte, on the 21st Oct. 1899, during the final advance on the enemy's position, this Warrant Officer led each successive rush, exposing himself fearlessly to the enemy's artillery and rifle fire to encourage the men. After the main position had been captured, he led a small party to seize the Boer Camp. Though exposed to a deadly cross-fire from the enemy's rifles, he gallantly held the position captured, and continued to encourage the men until he was wounded in two places." The recommendation was endorsed by the Brigadier (Ian Hamilton), who was an eye-witness to the second part of the Sergeant-Major's feat of arms. He writes now to say that no better V.C. was ever won than William Robertson's. There was no vainglory about it, but the danger was incurred in a cool and reasoned spirit for a military end of real importance. On his return from South Africa the Freedom of the Royal Burgh of Dumfries was conferred upon him. Lieut. Robertson was decorated with the Victoria Cross by Queen Victoria at Osborne. For his services in this campaign he also received the Queen's Medal with clasps for Ladysmith, Elandslaagte and Cape Colony. During the Great War he was Recruiting Staff Officer, at

Edinburgh, for which he was promoted Lieutenant-Colonel and made an Officer of the Order of the British Empire.

London Gazette, 10 Aug. 1900.—" War Office, 10 Aug. 1900. The Queen has been graciously pleased to confer the Decoration of the Victoria Cross on the undermentioned Non-commissioned Officer, whose claim has been submitted for Her Majesty's approval for his conspicuous bravery in South Africa, as stated against his name."

MACKAY, JOHN FREDERICK, University student, joined the 1st Gordon Highlanders. He served with the 1st Battn. Gordon Highlanders in the campaign on the North-West Frontier, India, and with the Tirah Expeditionary Force 1897–98, taking part in all the principal engagements, including Dargai, Tirah Maidan, Warran Valley, Bara River, and operations in Dwatoi country. For these services he received the Tirah Medal and the Punjab Frontier Medal with two clasps. He served with the 1st Battn. Gordon Highlanders, and afterwards with the King's Own Scottish Borderers in the South African War of 1899–1901. He was present in the advance on Kimberley, 1899, including the action at Magersfontein ; the operations in the Orange Free State, including the actions at Paardeberg and Zand River ; the operations in the Transvaal, including the actions of Johannesburg, Pretoria and Belfast, 1900 ; the operations in the east

John Frederick Mackay.

of the Transvaal in 1901. For these services he received the Queen's Medal with five clasps, the King's Medal with two clasps, was twice mentioned in Despatches, and was awarded the Victoria Cross in connection with the action at Doornkop, near Johannesburg, South Africa, 28 May, 1900, the particulars of which are given in the London Gazette of 10 Aug. 1900. His Victoria Cross was gazetted 10 Aug. 1900: " John Frederick MacKay, Gordon Highlanders. Date of Act of Bravery : 20 May, 1900. On the 20th May, 1900, during the action at Doornkop, near Johannesburg, MacKay repeatedly rushed forward, under a withering fire at short range, to attend to wounded comrades, dressing their wounds whilst he himself was without shelter, and in one instance carrying a wounded man from the open under a heavy fire to the shelter of a boulder." His name was again submitted for the Victoria Cross in connection with an act of gallantry in the action at Wolverkrantz, near Krugersdorp, on 11 July, 1900. Capt. MacKay was seconded for service May, 1903, with the Southern Nigeria Regt. He accompanied the expeditions to the Ime River, Cross River and Ibibio Country, 1904 and 1905. He accompanied the Bende Hinterland Expedition in 1905 and 1906. He also served with the Northern Nigeria Regt. in 1907, in command of the Ogumi Patrol. He received the West African General Service Medal with four clasps, and was twice mentioned in Despatches. He was transferred on promotion in 1907 from the King's Own Scottish Borderers to the Argyll and Sutherland Highlanders. In the European War he served in France in 1915 and 1916. Returning in 1916, he was promoted to the command of the 2/6th Battn. Highland Light Infantry, which appointment he held until the battalion was disbanded. Lieut.-Colonel MacKay was, in Aug. 1919, serving with his regiment, the 1st Battn. Argyll and Sutherland Highlanders, which unit is under orders to proceed to Bangalore.

London Gazette, 27 July, 1900.—" War Office, 27 July, 1900. The Queen has been graciously pleased to confer the Decoration of the Victoria Cross on the undermentioned Officer, whose claim has been submitted for Her Majesty's approval, for his conspicuous bravery in South Africa, as stated against his name."

MANSEL-JONES, CONWYN, Capt., was born at Beddington, Surrey, on 14 June, 1871, youngest son of the late Herbert Riversdale Mansel-Jones, Judge of County Courts, and Emilia, daughter of John Davis, of Cranbrook Park, Essex. He was educated at Haileybury and the Royal Military College, Sandhurst, and obtained his commission in The Prince of Wales's Own West Yorkshire Regt. 8 Oct. 1890. He served with his regiment in the Ashanti Expedition of 1895–96, and in British Central Africa in 1898–99, and he took part in the Expedition against Quamba in Aug. and Sept. 1899, under the Foreign Office. He became Captain 20 March, 1899. On the outbreak of the South African War he rejoined his regiment in Natal, and was awarded the Victoria Cross [London Gazette, 27 July, 1900] : " Conwyn Mansel-Jones, Capt., West Yorkshire Regt. On the 27th Feb. 1900, during the assault on Terrace Hill, north of the Tugela, in Natal, the companies of the West Yorkshire Regt. on the northern

Conwyn Mansel-Jones.

slope of the hill met with a severe shell, Vickers-Maxim and rifle fire, and their advance was for a few minutes checked. Capt. C. Mansel-Jones, however, by his strong initiative, restored confidence, and in spite of his falling very seriously wounded, the men took the whole ridge without further check ; this officer's self-sacrificing devotion to duty at a critical moment having averted what might have proved a serious check to the whole assault." He was D.A.A.G. for Recruiting at Headquarters from 1901 to 1906 ; Recruiting Staff Officer, London Area, 1903 to 1910, and was placed on retired pay on account of ill-health, caused by wounds, 9 March, 1910. In 1913 he married Marion, daughter of the late William Barton-Wright and Janet, daughter of the late General Forlonge, and he was called to the Bar of Lincoln's Inn in 1914. On the outbreak of the Great War he was mobilized and proceeded with the Expeditionary Force to France as D.A.A.G. at General Headquarters (3rd Echelon), becoming A.A.G. and temporary Lieutenant-Colonel in the Army in Dec. 1915. He served throughout the war in France. He was created a Companion of the Distinguished Service Order on 3 June, 1915. In 1917 he was promoted to Lieutenant-Colonel by brevet; and created Officier de la Légion d'Honneur by the President of the French Republic. In 1918 he was awarded the C.M.G., and he was six times mentioned in Despatches.

London Gazette, 14 Sept. 1900.—" War Office, 14 Sept. 1900. The Queen has been graciously pleased to signify Her intention to confer the Decoration of the Victoria Cross on the undermentioned Non-commissioned Officer, whose claim has been submitted for Her Majesty's approval, for his conspicuous bravery at the action at Wolve Spruit, as stated against his name."

RICHARDSON, ARTHUR HERBERT LINDSAY, Sergt., served in South Africa, and was the first Colonial whose Victoria Cross was gazetted during the Boer War [London Gazette, 14 Sept. 1900]: " Arthur Herbert Lindsay Richardson, Sergt., Lord Strathcona's Horse. On the 5th July, 1900, at Wolve Spruit, about fifteen miles north of Standerton, a party of Lord Strathcona's Corps, only thirty-eight in number, came into contact and was engaged at close quarters with a force of eighty of the enemy. When the order to retire had been given, Sergt. Richardson rode back under a very heavy cross-fire and picked up a trooper whose horse had been shot and who was wounded in two places, and rode with him out of fire. At the time when this act of gallantry was performed Sergt. Richardson was within 300 yards of the enemy, and was himself riding a wounded horse."

London Gazette, 28 Sept. 1900.—" War Office, 28 Sept. 1900. The Queen has been graciously pleased to signify Her intention to confer the Decoration of the Victoria Cross on the undermentioned Officer and Non-commissioned Officer and Private Soldier, whose claims have been submitted for Her Majesty's approval, for their conspicuous bravery in South Africa, 1900, as stated against their names."

GORDON, WILLIAM EAGLESON, Capt., was born on 4 May, 1866, son of the late W. E. Gordon, Esq., M.D., of Homehill, Bridge-of-Allan, Stirlingshire, and joined the 1st Gordon Highlanders, then in Malta, as

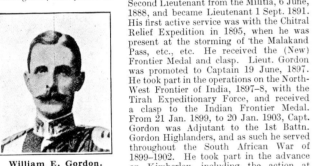

William E. Gordon.

Second Lieutenant from the Militia, 6 June, 1888, and became Lieutenant 1 Sept. 1891. His first active service was with the Chitral Relief Expedition in 1895, when he was present at the storming of the Malakand Pass, etc., etc. He received the (New) Frontier Medal and clasp. Lieut. Gordon was promoted to Captain 19 June, 1897. He took part in the operations on the North-West Frontier of India, 1897-8, with the Tirah Expeditionary Force, and received a clasp to the Indian Frontier Medal. From 21 Jan. 1899, to 20 Jan. 1903, Capt. Gordon was Adjutant to the 1st Battn. Gordon Highlanders, and as such he served throughout the South African War of 1899-1902. He took part in the advance on Kimberley, including the action at Magersfontein (dangerously wounded); operations in the Orange Free State, Feb. to May, 1900, including operations at Paardeberg, 17 to 28 Feb. 1900 (slightly wounded); actions at Poplar Grove, Dreifontein, Houtnek (Thobamount), Vet River (5 and 6 May), and Zand River; operations in the Transvaal in May and June, 1900, including actions near Johannesburg and Pretoria; operations in the Tranvsaal east of Pretoria, July to 29th Nov. 1900, including actions at Belfast (26 and 27 Aug.), and Lydenberg (5 to 8 Sept.); operations in the Transvaal west of Pretoria, July to 29 Nov. 1900; operations in Cape Colony south of Orange River 1899-1900; operations in Cape Colony north of Orange River; operations in the Transvaal 30 Nov. 1900 to 31 May, 1902. Three times mentioned in Despatches; Queen's Medal with five clasps; King's Medal with two clasps; Brevet of Lieutenant-Colonel on attaining rank of Major. He was awarded the Victoria Cross [London Gazette, 28 Sept. 1900]: " William Eagleson Gordon, Capt., Gordon Highlanders. Date of Act of Bravery: 11 July, 1900. On the 11th July, 1900, during the action near Leehoehoek (or Doornboschfontein, near Krugersdorf), a party of men, accompanied by Captains Younger and Allan, having succeeded in dragging an artillery waggon under cover when its horses were unable to do so by reason of the heavy and accurate fire of the enemy, Capt. Gordon called for volunteers to go out with him to try and bring in one of the guns. He went out alone to the nearest gun under a heavy fire, and with the greatest coolness fastened the drag-rope to the gun, and then beckoned to the men, who immediately doubled out to join him, in accordance with his previous instructions. While moving the gun Capt. Younger and three men were hit. Seeing that further attempts would only result in further casualties, Capt. Gordon ordered the remainder of the party under cover of the kopje again, and, having seen the wounded safely away, himself retired. Capt. Gordon's conduct under a particularly heavy and most accurate fire at only 600 yards' range was most admirable, and his manner of handling his men most masterly; his devotion on every occasion that his battalion has been under fire has been remarkable." Capt. Gordon was presented with his Victoria Cross by Lord Kitchener at Pretoria, on Peace Thanksgiving Day, June, 1902. He was Staff Captain, Highland

Grouped Regimental District, 6 June, 1905, to 31 March, 1908; was promoted to Major on 1 Jan. 1907, and gazetted Brevet Lieutenant-Colonel 2 Jan. 1907. From April, 1908, to 5 June, 1909, he was D.A.A. and Q.M.G., Highland Division, Scottish Command, and on 9 Oct. 1913, he was appointed A.D.C. to the King, with Brevet of Colonel. Colonel Gordon served in the European War from 1914; he was taken prisoner, and was released by exchange, unconditionally, in 1916. From 15 Sept. 1917, he commanded No. 1 (Midland) District, Scottish Command.

WARD, CHARLES, Private, was born 10 July, 1877, at Leeds, the son of Mr. George Ward. He was educated at Primrose Hill School, Leeds. On 29 April, 1897, he enlisted in the 1st Battn. Yorkshire Light Infantry (the old 51st Regt.), and served with this battalion for two years, joining the 2nd Battn. at Wynberg, Cape Colony. Owing to the severe wound he received, he has only two clasps to his South African Medal, for Cape Colony and Free State. When he won the Victoria Cross his company and commanding officers were Capt. Wittycombe and Lieut.-Colonel Barter, C.B., with Major-General A. H. Paget, C.V.O., as Chief. On his discharge from the service the citizens of Leeds presented him with a testimonial and £600, together with a commemorative medal in gold by Mr. William Owen. His Victoria Cross was gazetted 28 Sept. 1900:

Charles Ward.

" Charles Ward, Private, 2nd Battn. King's Own Yorkshire Light Infantry Date of Act of Bravery: 26 June, 1900. On the 26th June, 1900, at Lindley, a picquet of the Yorkshire Light Infantry was surrounded on three sides by about 500 Boers at close quarters. The two officers were wounded, and all but six of the men were killed or wounded. Private Ward then volunteered to take a message asking for reinforcements to the signalling station, about 150 yards in the rear of the post. His offer was at first refused, owing to the practical certainty of his being shot; but on his insisting, he was allowed to go. He got across untouched through a storm of shots from each flank, and having delivered his message, he voluntarily retired from a place of absolute safety and re-crossed the fire-swept ground to assure his commanding officer that the message had been sent. On this occasion he was severely wounded. But for this gallant action the post would certainly have been captured."

SHAUL, JOHN DAVID FRANCIS, Corpl., son of Sergt. John Shaul, late 2nd Battn. Royal Scots (veteran of the Crimean and China (1860) Campaigns), was born at King's Lynn, Norfolk, on 11 Sept. 1873, and educated at the Duke of York's School, Chelsea. At the age of fifteen he joined the 1st Battn. Highland Light Infantry, and served in Crete during the fighting in 1898. He served throughout the Boer War, receiving the Queen's and King's Medals with five clasps, besides the Victoria Cross. His commanding officers at Magersfontein were Lieut.-Colonel H. R. Kelham, C.B., and Major T. Richardson, D.S.O. Corpl. Shaul was decorated with the Victoria Cross by H.R.H. the Duke of York at Pietermaritzburg, 14 Aug. 1901. The decoration was gazetted 28 Sept. 1900: " J. Shaul, Corpl., Highland Light Infantry. Date of Act of Bravery: 11 Dec. 1899. On the 11th Dec. 1899, during the Battle of Magersfontein, Corpl. Shaul was observed, not only by the officers of his own battalion, but by several officers of other regiments, to perform several specific acts of bravery. Corpl. Shaul was in charge of stretcher-bearers; but at one period of the battle he was seen encouraging men to advance across the open. He was most conspicuous during the day in dressing men's wounds, and in one case he came, under a heavy fire, to a man who was lying wounded in the back, and with the utmost coolness and deliberation sat down beside the wounded man and proceeded to dress his wound. Having done this, he got up and went quietly to another part of the field. This act of gallantry was performed, under a continuous and heavy fire, as coolly and quietly as if there had been no enemy near." He became Band Sergeant.

London Gazette, 28 Sept. 1900.—" Memorandum.—Capt. David Reginald Younger, The Gordon Highlanders, in recognition of the conspicuous bravery displayed by him on the same occasion (11 June, 1900), would have been recommended to Her Majesty for the Victoria Cross had he survived."

London Gazette, 5 Oct. 1900.—" War Office, 5 Oct. 1900. The Queen has been graciously pleased to signify Her intention to confer the Decoration of the Victoria Cross on the undermentioned Non-commissioned Officers, whose claims have been submitted for Her Majesty's approval, for their conspicuous bravery in South Africa, 1900, as stated against their names."

H. Engleheart.

ENGLEHEART, H., Sergt., was born on 14 Nov. 1864, son of the late Mr. Francis Engleheart, formerly a member of the Stock Exchange, and grandson of N. B. Engleheart, Esq., of Blackheath, S.E., the last of the Queen's Proctors. He joined the 10th (The Prince of Wales's Own) Royal Hussars, and served with his regiment in the South African War of 1899-1902. He was one of the party, under Brevet Major Aylmer

Hunter Weston, that successfully destroyed the railway north of Bloemfontein. They had to charge through a Boer piquet, besides getting over four deep spruits, in order to creep back through the Boer lines. At the last of these spruits Sapper Webb's horse fell, and consequently he was left in a very dangerous position. Sergt. Engleheart went back to his assistance, through a deadly storm of shot and shell. He had to lose some time in getting Webb and his horse out of the spruit, and every moment the position became worse, owing to the rapid advance of the Boers. At last he succeeded in getting Webb back to the party. Just before this Sergt. Engleheart had shown great gallantry in dashing into the first spruit, which could only be approached in single file, and was still held by a party of Boers. He was awarded the Victoria Cross, [London Gazette, 5 Oct. 1900]: "H. Engleheart, Sergt., 10th Hussars." Sergt. Engleheart was the centre man of the last five of her soldiers to whom Queen Victoria personally presented the Victoria Cross, on 15 Dec. 1900.

KIRBY, FRANK HOWARD, Corpl., was born at Thame, Oxfordshire, on 12 Nov. 1871, the son of Mr. William Henry Kirby, of that town, and Ada Kirby. He was educated at Alleyn's School, Dulwich, S.E., and entered the Royal Engineers at St. George's Barracks, London, on 8 Aug. 1892, and proceeded to South Africa with Field Troops, Royal Engineers, on mobilization in 1899. He served in the South African War of 1899–1902, and gained the Distinguished Conduct Medal for blowing up the Bloemfontein Railway, at action of Bloemfontein, in March, 1900. He won his Victoria Cross in a raid north of Kronstadt with General Hunter Weston. He was mentioned several times in Despatches, and in July, 1900, was promoted Troop Sergeant-Major (from Corporal), on the field, by Lord Roberts. Sergt.-Major Kirby was decorated with the Victoria Cross by His Royal Highness the Duke of Cornwall and York at Cape Town on 19 Aug. 1901. His Victoria Cross was gazetted 8 Oct. 1900: "Frank Howard Kirby, Corpl., Royal Engineers. On the morning of the 2nd June, 1900, a party sent to try to cut the Delagoa Bay Railway were retiring, hotly pressed by very superior numbers. During one of the successive retirements of the rearguard, a man whose horse had been shot was seen running after his comrades. He was a long way behind the rest of his troop, and was under a brisk fire. From among the retiring troops Corpl. Kirby turned and rode back to the man's assistance. Although by the time he reached him they were under a heavy fire at close range, Corpl. Kirby managed to get the dismounted man up behind him and to take him clear off over the next rise held by our rearguard. This is the third occasion on which Corpl. Kirby has displayed gallantry in the face of the enemy." In Dec. 1906, he became a warrant officer. In 1909 he married Miss Kate Jolly, and they have two sons and two daughters. In April, 1911, he was commissioned from the ranks. Lieut. and Quartermaster F. H. Kirby was posted to the Air Battalion, Royal Engineers, at Farnborough, and in 1912 was gazetted to the Royal Flying Corps, in which he became a Squadron-Commander. He served in the European War in France in 1916 and 1917, and was given his Captaincy for services in the field, 1 Jan. 1917. He became temporary Lieutenant-Colonel.

Frank Howard Kirby.

London Gazette, 13 Nov. 1900.—"War Office, 13 Nov. 1900. The Queen has been graciously pleased to signify Her intention to confer the Decoration of the Victoria Cross on the undermentioned Private, whose claim has been submitted for Her Majesty's approval, for his conspicuous bravery in South Africa, as stated against his name."

BISDEE, JOHN HUTTON, Trooper, was born at Hutton Park, Tasmania, 28 Sept. 1869, son of John Bisdee, pastoralist (who died in 1891), and Ellen Jane Bisdee (*née* Butler), who died in 1905. Both his parents were born in Tasmania, and his grandfather, John Bisdee, and his grandmother, came from Hutton, Somersetshire, England. He was educated at Hutchin's School, Hobart, Tasmania, and lived on the estate of Hutton Park until 1900, when he enlisted in the ranks of the 1st Tasmanian Imperial Bushmen in the South African War; served in that campaign from 1899 to 1902. On 1 Sept. 1900, at Warm Baths, north of Pretoria, Major Eardley Wilmot Brooke was directed to proceed in command of a mounted reconnaissance composed partly of a troop of Tasmanian Imperial Bushmen and partly of men of the mounted branch of the Army Service Corps, then doing duty as mounted fighting troops. The former were under the command of Lieut. Wylly, Tasmanian Imperial Bushmen. Major Brooke's instructions were to proceed to a place north-west of Warm Baths, to drive off some Boer cattle supposed to be there, and to find out if there were any Boers in the neighbourhood. The only way through the mountains north of Warm Baths lay through a narrow pass, and the party proceeded westward until, at the mouth of the pass, they came upon a Kaffir Kraal. Here they ascertained that there were supposed to be Boers in the direction in which they had to go. The pass was narrow, with high precipitous cliffs on either side, and Major Brooke had so few men that he could not hope to hold it effectively. A deep formation was therefore adopted, and the small force was divided into an advanced party support, main body, and rear-guard, with connecting files. They went up the pass at a gallop, and, on reaching a wide open space between hills beyond, the advanced party opened as a screen. They then proceeded across a plain dotted with trees, till they came to some thickly wooded hills. There Major Brooke decided to turn back, as nothing could be seen of the cattle they were looking for. Except for some goats on the hills there was no sign of life anywhere. The advanced party were watering their horses at a stream before turning back, when a very heavy rifle-fire was opened from the scrub about a hundred yards in front. Major Brooke's horse took fright at the crack of the bullets on the hard ground and reared up, dragging the reins from his hand, and before he could draw his carbine from the bucket, she had galloped away with it, back towards the pass. Major Brooke ran back to some rocks, behind which were some of the men, including Trooper Bisdee. As he ran one bullet passed through his leg and another through his helmet. The Boers were now working round them, so there was nothing for it but to leave the rocks. The others, including a wounded man whom they had bound up, were on horseback, and Major Brooke on foot. When they got into the open his wounded leg was almost out of action, so Trooper Bisdee pulled up and asked him to get on his horse. This Major Brooke could not do, and he told him to go on. This the Tasmanian refused to do, and, though the bullets were knocking up the dust all around them, he dismounted, drew up his horse alongside an ant-bear heap, and helped his commanding officer into the saddle, getting up himself behind him. The fire was at short range, rapid and concentrated. On arriving at the main body Major Brooke borrowed a rifle and retained the horse, for though his own had been caught by the rear-guard he was not able to change on account of his wound. He then went back to look for any who might have been left behind, and met Lieut. Wylly, who was wounded, and carrying a man on his horse. He had been in the scrub some way to the right of the road, and for some time had returned the fire. At length he came away, with a man who had lost his horse. As Major Brooke found no more men, he sent the Tasmanians down the pass and formed a rear-guard of the A.S.C. men. He tried to drive off some cattle which they found, with the help of three men of the A.S.C. who volunteered to stay and help, but,as the Boers were reaching the top of the cliffs, they had to abandon the attempt. Major Brooke found his way back to Warm Baths with difficulty, owing to considerable loss of blood. The Boers, estimated at about 3,000, soon afterwards attacked Warm Baths with guns. Lieut.-Colonel Bisdee says of this affair: "On 1 Sept. a party of one officer and about 20 men of the A.S.C. were sent out from Warm Bad to forage for supplies of live-stock. Twenty men from the 1st Tasmanian Imperial Bushmen, under Lieut. Wylly, were sent to escort them. Marching up a narrow valley, the two officers being in front with the screen, evidence was seen that the place had been recently occupied. Shortly afterwards heavy fire at short range opened on us from concealed positions. The screen were all killed or wounded. Lieut. Wylly was wounded, and Major Brooke, the A.S.C. officer, had his horse shot, and was also wounded. The order to retire at the gallop was given. Seeing the officer without a horse, I put him on mine, and ran alongside until out of range and then mounted behind him, and rejoined the escort. (Note.—The official account is slightly different as to details, but the above is correct.) Lieut. Wylly was also awarded the V.C. at the same time, and several men the D.C.M. It was decidedly 'hot' while it lasted, but fortunately it was soon over." For the services described above the two gallant Tasmanians received the Victoria Cross. Trooper Bisdee's was the first Victoria Cross awarded to a Colonial. He also received the Queen's Medal with two clasps, and the King's Medal. Private Bisdee was awarded the Victoria Cross [London Gazette, 13 Nov. 1900]: "John Hutton Bisdee, Trooper, Tasmanian Imperial Bushmen. On the 1st Sept. 1900, Trooper Bisdee was one of an advanced scouting party passing through a rocky defile near Warm Bad, Transvaal. The enemy, who were in ambuscade, opened a sudden fire at close range, and six out of the party of eight were hit, including two officers. The horse of one of the wounded officers broke away and bolted. Finding that the officer was too badly wounded to go on, Trooper Bisdee dismounted, placed him on his horse, mounted behind him, and conveyed him out of range. This act was performed under a very hot fire, and in a very exposed place." He received a commission in the 2nd Tasmanian Imperial Bushmen in March, 1901; returned to Australia in 1902, and again took up pastoral pursuits. On 11 April, 1904, at New Town, Tasmania, he married Georgiana Theodosia, daughter of the late Right Rev. Bishop Hale, of Gloucester, England, and late of Queensland and West Australia. In 1906 he became Lieutenant in the 12th Australian Light Horse; promoted Captain in 1908. Commanded 26th Light Horse Regt., Tasmania, in 1912. Joined Australian Imperial Force for service overseas on 26 July, 1915, and posted to 12th Australian Light Horse. Promoted Major 16 Aug. 1915. Served with Australian Composite Regt. in Nov. and Dec. 1915, Senoussi Campaign, Egypt. Seconded as A.P.M. Anzac Mounted Division, 24 May, 1916. Seconded to command Australian Provost Corps, Egyptian Section, 20 Jan. 1918, and appointed A.P.M. Australian Imperial Force in Egypt. Promoted Lieutenant-Colonel 2 Feb. 1918. Awarded O.B.E. (Military Division) 3 June, 1919. Lieut.-Colonel Bisdee is fond of sports, especially football. Also hunting with the Hutton Park Beagles, Hutton Park, Tasmania.

John Hutton Bisdee.

London Gazette, 20 Nov. 1900.—"War Office, 20 Nov. 1900. The Queen has been graciously pleased to signify Her intention to award the Decoration of the Victoria Cross to the undermentioned Officer, whose claim has been submitted for Her Majesty's approval, for his conspicuous bravery during the engagement at Paardeberg, as stated against his name."

PARSONS, FRANCIS NEWTON, Lieut., was born 23 March, 1875, at Dover, son of Charles Parsons, M.D., and Venetia Digby Parsons. He was educated at King's College School, Cambridge; at Dover College, and at Sandhurst, and joined the 1st Battn. (44th)

Essex Regt. 29 Feb. 1896, being promoted to Lieutenant 1 March, 1898. He was awarded the Victoria Cross [London Gazette, 20 Nov. 1900]: "Francis Newton Parsons, Lieut., The Essex Regt. (since deceased). Date of Act of Bravery:

18 Feb. 1900. On the morning of the 18th Feb. 1900, at Paardeberg, on the south bank of the Modder River, Private Ferguson 1st Battn. Essex Regt., was wounded and fell in a place devoid of cover. While trying to crawl under cover, he was again wounded, in the stomach. Lieut. Parsons at once went to his assistance, dressed his wound, under heavy fire, went down twice (still under heavy fire) to the bank of the river to get water for Private Ferguson, and subsequently carried him to a place of safety. This officer was recommended for the Victoria Cross by Lieut.-General Kelly-Kenny, C.B., on the 3rd March last. Lieut. Parsons was killed on the 10th March, in the engagement at Dreifontein, on which occasion he again displayed conspicuous gallantry." He was again noticed for his conspicuous bravery on 10 March, 1900, in the fight at Dreifontein, on which occasion he met his death. His name is recorded, together with those of seven officers, one warrant officer, and 198 non-commissioned officers and men, on a tablet placed there in memory of the officers, non-commissioned officers and men of the Essex Regt. who gave their lives for their country in the Boer War. Sir Evelyn Wood unveiled this tablet in 1903.

Francis Newton Parsons.

London Gazette, 23 Nov. 1900.—" War Office, 23 Nov. 1900. The Queen has been graciously pleased to signify Her intention to confer the Decoration of the Victoria Cross on the undermentioned Officer, whose claim has been submitted for Her Majesty's approval, for his conspicuous bravery at Warm Bad, as stated against his name."

WYLLY, GUY GEORGE EGERTON, Lieut., was born 17 Feb. 1880, at Hobart, Tasmania, son of Major Edward Arthur Egerton Wylly (H.M. 109th Regt. and Madras Staff Corps) and Henrietta Mary, daughter of

Robert Clerk, Esq. (of West Holme, Somerset, and Sergeant-at-Arms to the House of Assembly, Hobart, Tasmania). He was educated at Hutchins' School, Tasmania, and at St. Peter's College, Adelaide, South Australia, and became a Lieutenant in the Tasmanian Imperial Bushmen on 26 April, 1900, serving in the South African War; was twice wounded, once slightly and once dangerously; received the Queen's Medal with three clasps, and was awarded the Victoria Cross [London Gazette, 23 Nov. 1900]: "Guy G. E. Wylly, Lieut., Tasmanian Imperial Bushmen. On the 1st Sept. 1900, near Warm Bad, Lieut. Wylly was with the advanced scouts of a foraging party. They were passing through a narrow gorge, very rocky and thickly wooded, when the enemy in force suddenly opened fire at short range from hidden cover, wounding six out of the party of eight, including Lieut. Wylly. That officer, seeing that one of his men was badly wounded in the leg, and that his horse was shot, went back to the man's assistance, made him take his (Lieut. Wylly's) horse, and opened fire from behind a rock to cover the retreat of the others, at the imminent risk of being cut off himself. Colonel T. E. Hickman, D.S.O., considers that the gallant conduct of Lieut. Wylly saved Corpl. Brown from being killed or captured, and that his subsequent action in firing to cover the retreat was 'instrumental in saving others of his men from death or capture.' "
He was gazetted Second Lieutenant, The Royal Berkshire Regt., dated 19 May, 1900; was transferred and gazetted Second Lieutenant, The South Lancashire Regt., dated 5 Nov. 1900; joined the 2nd Battn. The South Lancashire Regt. at Jubbulpore, India, 4 Dec. 1901; was transferred to the Indian Army and gazetted to the 46th Punjabis 1 Oct. 1902; transferred to the Queen's Own Corps of Guides 11 Feb. 1904. He was A.D.C. to Lord Kitchener, Commander in Chief in India, from Dec. 1904, to Sept. 1909; officiated as A.D.C. to Lieut.-General Sir James Willcocks, Commanding the Northern Army, India, Sept. 1915, to Feb. 1916; was nominated to the Staff College, Quetta, in 1914, by Sir O'Moore Creagh, Commander-in-Chief in India. He was appointed Staff Captain, Mhow Cavalry Brigade, 11 Nov. 1914; appointed Brigade Major, Mhow Cavalry Brigade, 15 Sept. 1915; appointed G.S.O.2., 4th Division, B.E.F., 20 June, 1916; appointed G.S.O.2., 3rd Australian Division, 19 July, 1916; appointed G.S.O.2., 1st Anzac Corps, in Feb. 1917. Major Wylly was wounded at Authoille in Aug. 1915; was mentioned in Despatches in June, 1916, and June, 1917. He has the Delhi Durbar Medal (1911).

Guy G. E. Wylly.

London Gazette, 1 Jan. 1901.—" War Office, 1 Jan. 1901. The Queen has been graciously pleased to signify Her intention to confer the Decoration of the Victoria Cross upon the undermentioned Officer of the Royal Marine Forces and Midshipman of the Royal Navy, whose claims have been submitted for Her Majesty's approval, for acts of gallantry performed by them during the recent disturbances in China, as recorded against their names."

HALLIDAY, LEWIS STRATFORD TOLLEMACHE, Lieut.-Colonel, was born 14 May, 1870, at Medstead, Hants, the eldest son of Lieut.-Colonel Stratford C. Halliday, R.A. He was educated at Elizabeth College,

Guernsey, and entered the Royal Marine Light Infantry on 1 Sept. 1889. In 1898 he was promoted Captain. On 29 May, 1900, he landed at Taku from H.M.S. Orlando, in command of 50 men of the Royal Marine Light Infantry, and proceeded to Pekin as Legation Guard. In the Defence of Pekin he won his Victoria Cross, as described in the London Gazette of 1 Jan. 1900: "Lewis Stratford Tollemache Halliday, Capt. (now Brevet Major), Royal Marine Light Infantry. Date of Act of Bravery: 24 June, 1900. On the 24th June, 1900, the enemy, consisting of Boxers and Imperial Troops, made a fierce attack on the west wall of the British Legation, setting fire to the West Gate of the South Stable quarters, and taking cover in the buildings which adjoined the wall.
The fire, which spread to part of the stables, and through which and the smoke a galling fire was kept up by the Imperial troops, was with difficulty extinguished, and as the presence of the enemy in the adjoining building was a grave danger to the Legation, a sortie was organised to drive them out. A hole was made in the Legation wall, and Capt. Halliday, in command of twenty Marines, led the way into the buildings and almost immediately engaged a party of the enemy. Before he could use his revolver, however, he was shot through the left shoulder at point-blank range, the bullet fracturing the shoulder and carrying away part of the lung. Notwithstanding the extremely severe nature of his wound, Capt. Halliday killed three of his assailants, and telling his men to ' carry on and not mind him,' walked back unaided to the hospital, refusing escort and aid, so as not to diminish the number of men engaged in the sortie." He also received the China Medal with clasp, inscribed " Defence of Legation," and received the Brevet of Major for Distinguished Service in the Field 12 Sept. 1900. He was mentioned in Despatches and dangerously wounded. In 1904 he was commanding the unit of his corps on board the " Empress of India." In 1908 he married Florence Clara, eldest daughter of the late Brigadier-General W. Budgen, D.S.O., and they have one son. From 1908 to 1911 he was Commander of a Company of Gentlemen Cadets at the Royal Military College, Sandhurst, and G.S.O., 2nd Grade. In 1912 he was appointed to serve on the Staff of the Royal Naval War College, and also on the Royal Naval War Staff, and in 1914 he was created a C.B. In 1916 Lieut.-Colonel Halliday married, 2ndly, Violet, daughter of Major Victor Blake, Hayling Island, Hants.

Lewis S. T. Halliday.

GUY, BASIL JOHN DOUGLAS, Midshipman, Royal Navy, was born 9 May, 1882, at Bishop Auckland, County of Dublin, son of the Rev. Douglas Sherwood Guy, M.A., Clerk in Holy Orders, Vicar of Christchurch, Harro-

gate, and of Mrs. Mary Guy. He was educated at Aysgarth School, Yorkshire; at Llandaff Cathedral School, and in H.M.S. Britannia, passing out to the Barfleur on 15 July, 1898. His services from that time were for a long time entirely in the East. He was landed and served ashore during the Boxer outbreak in China, in the course of which he was awarded the Victoria Cross [London Gazette, 8 Nov. 1900]: " Basil John Douglas Guy, Midshipman, Royal Navy. Of Her Majesty's Ship Barfleur. On 13 July, 1900, during the attack on Tientsin city, a very heavy cross fire was brought to bear on the Naval Brigade, and there were casualties. Among those who fell was one Able Seaman, T. McCarthy, shot about fifty yards short of cover. Mr. Guy stopped with him, and after seeing what the injury was, attempted to lift him up and carry him in, but was not strong enough, so after binding up the wound, Mr. Guy ran to get assistance. In the meantime the remainder of the company had passed in under cover, and the entire fire from the city wall was concentrated on Mr. Guy and McCarthy. Shortly after Mr. Guy had got in under cover the stretchers came up, and again Mr. Guy dashed out and assisted in placing McCarthy on the stretcher and carrying him in. The wounded man was, however, shot dead just as he was being carried into safety. During the whole time a very heavy fire had been brought to bear upon Mr. Guy, and the ground around him was absolutely ploughed up." Lieut. Guy received the Victoria Cross from the hands of H.M. the King on 8 March, 1902, at Keyham Barracks. His was the first Cross presented in the Navy after the accession of King Edward VII., and the 41st of those awarded to members of the Senior Service since the institution of the Decoration. He also received the China Medal. On 15 July, 1903, he was promoted to Lieutenant for his services in China. Lieut.-Commander Guy was created a Companion of the Distinguished Service Order [London Gazette, 24 May, 1917]: " Basil John Douglas Guy, V.C., Lieut.-Commander, Royal Navy. In recognition of his gallant and skilful conduct on 11 March, 1917, when in command of a decoy ship, H.M.S. Wonganella, in action with an enemy submarine." He was promoted to Commander on 30 June, 1918. Commander Guy holds King Edward VII.'s Coronation Medal (Guard of Honour at Westminster Abbey), and the 1914–15 Star, and General Service Medal for the Great War. On 8 Aug. 1917, at Christ

Basil J. D. Guy.

Church, High Harrogate, Yorkshire, Commander Guy married Elizabeth Mary Arnold, eldest daughter of the late William Sayles Arnold, of Doncaster and Harrogate.

London Gazette, 4 Jan. 1901.—" War Office, 4 Jan. 1901. The Queen has been graciously pleased to signify Her intention to confer the Decoration of the Victoria Cross on the undermentioned Non-commissioned Officer, whose claim has been submitted for Her Majesty's approval, for his conspicuous bravery during the operations near Van Wyk's Vlei, as stated against his name."

KNIGHT, H. J., Corpl., was awarded the Victoria Cross for services in South Africa [London Gazette, 4 Jan. 1901]: " H. J. Knight, Corpl., 1st Battn. The Liverpool Regt., No. 1 Company, 4th Division, Mounted Infantry. On the 21st Aug. during the operations near Van Wyk's Vlei, Corpl. Knight was posted in some rocks with four men, covering the right rear of a detachment of the same company, who, under Capt. Ewart, were holding the right of the line. The enemy, about fifty strong, attacked Capt. Ewart's right and almost surrounded, at short range, Corpl. Knight's small party. That non-commissioned officer held his ground, directing his party to retire one by one to better cover, while he maintained his position for nearly an hour, covering the withdrawal of Capt. Ewart's force, and losing two of his four men. He then retired, bringing with him two wounded men. One of these he left in a place of safety, the other he carried for nearly two miles. The party were hotly engaged during the whole time." He became a Sergeant. " Capt. H. J. Knight was a Corporal in the Liverpool Regt. when he won his V.C. in South Africa." (" Sketch," 12 March, 1915.)

H. J. Knight.

London Gazette, 15 Jan. 1901.—" War Office, 15 Jan. 1901. The Queen has been graciously pleased to confer the Decoration of the Victoria Cross on the undermentioned Officer and Non-commissioned Officer, whose claims have been submitted for Her Majesty's approval, for their conspicuous bravery in Ashanti, as stated against their names."

MELLISS, CHARLES JOHN, Capt., was born in 1862, the son of Lieut.-General G. J. Melliss, I.S.C. He was educated at Wellington College and Sandhurst, entered the Army (East Yorks Regt.) in 1882, and joined the Indian Army in 1884. He served in East Africa in 1896, in the operations against the Mazrui rebels (Medal, 2nd Class Order of the Brilliant Star of Zanzibar), in 1897 and 1898, on the North-West Frontier of India. He was present at the operations in the Kurram Valley in Aug. and Sept. 1897. He served in the Tirah Campaign in 1897 and 1898, taking part in the action of Dargai, and in the operations in the Bara Valley. For his services on the North-West Frontier he received the Medal with three clasps. Capt. Melliss served with the Northern Nigeria Regt. with the West African Frontier Force from 1898 to 1902. In the Ashanti Campaign of 1900 he was present at the Relief of Kumasi; was twice mentioned in Despatches, received the Brevet of Lieutenant-Colonel, the Medal and clasp. In Sir John Willcocks's Despatch of 25 Dec. 1900, he says : " Although this officer (Capt. Melliss) has been awarded the Victoria Cross for valour, his work throughout the Campaign has been so valuable and conspicuous that I sincerely trust he will be noted for higher promotion, on attaining the rank of Major, which he is now near. He has eighteen years' service, but is held back by the rules for promotion in the Indian Staff Corps." He was awarded the Victoria Cross [London Gazette, 15 Jan.1901] : " Charles John Melliss, Capt. (local Major), Indian Staff Corps. On the 30th Sept. 1900, at Obassa, Major Melliss, seeing that the enemy were very numerous, and intended to make a firm stand, hastily collected all stray men and any that he could get together, and charged at their head into the dense bush where the enemy were thick. His action carried all along with him ; but the enemy were determined to have a hand-to-hand fight. One fired at Major Melliss, who put his sword through the man, and they rolled over together. Another Ashanti shot him through the foot, the wound paralysing the limb. His wild rush had, however, caused a regular panic among the enemy, who were at the same time charged by the Sikhs, and killed in numbers. Major Melliss also behaved with great gallantry on three previous occasions." In 1901, Major Melliss married Kathleen, youngest daughter of the late General J. M. Walter, C.B. From 1902 to 1904 he served in East Africa, and took part in the operations in Somaliland. He was mentioned in Despatches and received the Medal with clasp. From 1906 to 1910 he commanded the 53rd Sikhs Frontier Force. From 1907 to 1912 he was A.D.C. to the King. In 1911 he was created a C.B. Major-General Melliss served in the European War, 1914–1916, in Mesopotamia, was mentioned in Despatches five times, and created a K.C.B. (1915) ; K.C.M.G. (1918). He commanded at the Battle of Shaiba, near Basra, on 13–14 April, 1915, where a Turkish Arab Force estimated at 25,000 to 30,000 was defeated by an Anglo-Indian force numbering some 7,500 men. He also took part in two subsequent operations on the

Charles John Melliss.

Kurkeh River, under Major-General Gorringe, in command of the 30th Brigade, Indian Expeditionary Force. Took part in the prolonged operations before Nasariyeh, in command of the 30th Brigade. Carried the Turkish entrenchments on the right bank of the Euphrates at the Battle of Nasariyeh in July, 1915. Was in command of the Flying Column at the Battle of Ctesiphon on 23 Nov. 1915. Took part in the Retreat on Kut-el-Amara, and in the defence of that place from 5 Dec. 1915 to 29 April, 1916. After the fall of Kut was a prisoner of war with the Turks for two and a half years.

MACKENZIE, JOHN, Sergt., was born in 1869, and enlisted in Aug. 1887, into the Seaforth Highlanders, at the Depôt, Fort George, Inverness. On 8 Dec. 1887, he was posted to the 1st Battn. (72nd), then stationed at Edinburgh Castle. He became Corporal in May, 1891, but on joining the 2nd Battn. the 78th Highlanders, he gave up his stripe and remained for nearly a year a Private, taking part in the Relief of Chitral in the spring of 1895 (Medal and clasp). He became Corporal in May, 1897, and was awarded the Distinguished Service Medal, in Nov. of which year he was posted to the Lagos Regt. on the West Coast of Africa. He was promoted to Sergeant in his Regt. in March, 1899. During his service in West Africa he took part in three distinct campaigns. In each of them he was mentioned in Despatches. He was badly wounded at the Relief of Kumasi and in the Ashanti Campaign, during which he won the Victoria Cross [London Gazette, 15 Jan. 1901]: " John Mackenzie, Sergeant, Seaforth Highlanders (Ross-shire Buffs, the Duke of Albany's Own), employed with the West African Field Force. Date of Act of Bravery : 6 June, 1900. On the 6th June, 1900, at Dompoassi, in Ashanti, Sergt. Mackenzie, after working two Maxim guns under a hot fire, and being wounded while doing so, volunteered to clear the stockades of the enemy, which he did in the most gallant manner, leading the charge himself, and driving the enemy headlong into the bush." On this occasion he was wounded, mentioned in Despatches, promoted Second Lieutenant, and received the Medal with clasp. In the next year he was again mentioned in Despatches for services with the Aro Expedition, as also in 1906, when he was Staff Officer of No. 2 Column of the Munster Field Force, and between these years he had further taken part in the Kano-Sokoto Campaign. " Truth," 2 June, 1915, says : " Major John Mackenzie, V.C., of the 2nd Battn. Bedfordshire Regt., who was reported last week to have been killed in action (date and place not stated), was one of the best known fighting soldiers in the Army, having been given a commission after thirteen years' service in the ranks, on the occasion of his gallant conduct in the Ashanti Expedition of 1900, when at a critical moment during the action of Dompoassi he charged at the head of a company into the enemy's stockades, and drove them into the bush. Previous to the present war he had served in seven campaigns, and had been four times mentioned in Despatches. A man of dauntless courage, he is said to have been absolutely fearless under fire, and inspired everyone round him with the fighting spirit which never failed him."

John Mackenzie.

London Gazette, 15 Jan. 1901.—" War Office, 15 Jan. 1901. The Queen has been graciously pleased to signify Her intention to confer the Decoration of the Victoria Cross on the undermentioned Officers and Non-commissioned Officers, whose claims have been submitted for Her Majesty's approval for their conspicuous bravery in South Africa, 1900, as stated against their names."

BROWNE-SYNGE-HUTCHINSON EDWARD DOUGLAS, Major, was born 6 March, 1861, son of the late Major David Philip Browne, 7th (Queen's Own) Hussars, and Frances Dorothy (daughter of Francis Synge-Hutchinson, Esq., and his wife, Lady Louisa Hely-Hutchinson, and sister of Sir Edward Synge-Hutchinson, 4th Baronet, of Castle Sallagh, County Wicklow). He was educated at Edinburgh Academy, Windermere College, and at the United Services College, Westward Ho ! and entered the Army, receiving a commission as Lieutenant in the 18th Hussars 7 Nov. 1883, and became Captain in less than five years, 8 Aug. 1888. On the 27th March, 1889, he exchanged into the 14th Hussars. From the 1st Jan. 1890, to the 31st Dec. 1894, he was Commandant of the Aldershot School of Instruction for Yeomanry. He became Major 28 Jan. 1899. Major Browne served in South Africa from 1899 to 1902, and at the action of Geluk he won the Victoria Cross for saving the lives of three men, one after the other. He says his age at that time was 37 years 8 months, which was then, he believes, about the limit of antiquity for this decoration. His Victoria Cross was gazetted 15 Jan. 1901 : " Edward Douglas Brown, Major, 14th Hussars. Date of Act of Bravery : 13 Oct. 1900. On the 13th Oct. 1900, at Geluk, when the enemy were within 400 yards, and bringing a heavy fire to bear, Major Brown, seeing that Sergt. Hersey's horse was shot, stopped behind the last squadron, as it was retiring, and helped Sergt. Hersey to mount behind him, carrying him for about three quarters of a mile to a place of safety.

E. D. Browne-Synge-Hutchinson.

He did this under a heavy fire. Major Brown afterwards enabled Lieut. Browne, 14th Hussars, to mount, by holding his horse, which was very restive under the heavy fire. Lieut. Browne could not otherwise have mounted. Subsequently Major Brown carried L.-Corpl. Trumpeter Leigh out of action." It was not mentioned in the official account that the horses of three other men were held by Major Browne, as they were in difficulties with them, and one of the animals, having run away, had to be caught and brought back. Major Browne was the last officer of the British Regular Army to win the Victoria Cross in the life-time of Queen Victoria, as she died on the 22nd Jan. 1901 (Lieut. Doxat, of the Imperial Yeomanry, won his Victoria Cross on 20 Oct. 1900). He was decorated by King George V. (then Duke of Cornwall and York) at Pietermaritzburg, Natal, on the 14th Aug. 1901. In the London Gazette of 1 Dec. 1901, by Sir John French, K.C.B. (2) By Lord Roberts and by Lord Kitchener. He was mentioned regimentally during the Boer War: (1) For service during the retirement at Thaba N'chu. (2) For leading to the most advanced position at the Battle of Diamond Hill under heavy fire. (3) For saving life at the Second Action of Geluk 13 Oct. 1900. (4) For General Distinguished Service during the war. (5) Brevet of Lieutenant-Colonel 17 June, 1902 (ante-dated to 29 Nov. 1900). He received the Queen's South African Medal with seven clasps, and the King's South African Medal with two clasps. He commanded the 14th Hussars for seven and a half months during the Boer War. In 1906 he was given the Brevet of Colonel, and in 1911 he became Substantive Colonel. In the same year he was made a Knight of Grace of the Order of St. John of Jerusalem in England and a Member of the Central Executive Committee of the St. John's Ambulance Association 1911 to 1919. He was also made a Freeman and Liveryman of the Worshipful Company of Spectacle Makers of the City of London, and Freeman of the City of London, 1911. He was created a C.B. in 1911. On 30 March, 1917, Colonel Browne-Synge-Hutchinson was promoted to be Knight of Justice of the Order of St. John of Jerusalem.

INKSON, EDGAR THOMAS, Lieut., was born 5 April, 1872, at Naini Tal, India, the son of the late Surgeon-General J. Inkson, Army Medical Service (Battle of Baltic, Indian Mutiny and Afghan Medals; died Sept.

Edgar Thomas Inkson.

1898), and of Mrs. Inkson, of Eastbourne. He was educated at Edinburgh Collegiate School, and received his medical education at University College Hospital, London. He is M.R.C.S. (England) and L.R.C.P. (London), and joined the Army in April, 1899, as Surgeon on probation; was gazetted Surgeon-Lieutenant 28 July, 1899, just ten weeks before the Boer War of 1899–1902, and proceeded to South Africa, as Medical Officer in Charge of the 7th, 14th and 66th Batteries R.F.A. in Oct. 1899. He was present with these batteries at Colenso on 15 Dec. 1899, when ten guns were lost. Shortly afterwards Surgeon-Lieut. Inkson was transferred as Medical Officer in Charge to the 27th Royal Inniskilling Fusiliers (Hart's Brigade), and served with this regiment at Vaalkrantz, Spion Kop, Pieter's Hill, and at the relief of Ladysmith. He rejoined the Artillery (28th, 78th and 66th Batteries) in April, 1900, when the brigade was with Hunter's Division at the battle of Roydam 5 May, 1900, and then with Ian Hamilton's Column. He rejoined the Inniskilling Fusiliers in April, 1901, and was with this regiment for about a year, part of the time with Allenby's Column. He was mentioned in Despatches three times, received the Queen's Medal with five clasps and the King's Medal with two clasps, and was awarded the Victoria Cross [London Gazette, 15 Jan. 1901]: "Edgar Thomas Inkson, Lieut., Royal Army Medical Corps. On the 24th Feb. 1900, Lieut. Inkson carried 2nd Lieut. Devenish (who was severely wounded and unable to walk) for three or four hundred yards, under a very heavy fire, to a place of safety. The ground over which Lieut. Inkson had to move was much exposed, there being no cover available." In the European War Lieut.-Colonel Inkson commanded No. 2 Field Ambulance, 1st Division, from Jan. 1915, to Nov. 1916, and was present with that unit in all the operations in which the division took part during the above period. He was mentioned in Despatches twice, awarded the Distinguished Service Order [London Gazette, 1 Jan. 1917]: "Edgar Thomas Inkson, Lieut.-Colonel, R.A.M.C." He was promoted Lieut.-Colonel 1 March, 1915, and in Jan. 1917, assumed command of No. 1 General Hospital, which post he held till July, 1917, and in Aug. 1917, he was given command of No. 4 Stationary Hospital.

DOXAT, ALEXIS C., Lieut., was born at Surbiton, Surrey, on 9 April, 1867, the son of Mr. Edmund Doxat, of Wood Green Park, Hertfordshire, and was educated at Norwich Grammar School and Philberd's, Maidenhead. He was a Captain in the Dalston Militia under Colonel Somerset, C.B., and Lieut.-Colonel Bowles, M.P., and passed the Auxiliary School of Instruction and the Hythe Musketry School. He became a member of the Stock Exchange, but left it on the outbreak of the Boer War to proceed to South Africa with Lord Scarbrough's detachment. He took part in Lord Methuen's advance from Boshof in May, 1900, and in September joined General Douglas's Column as personal A.D.C., acting chiefly as reconnaissance officer. He won the Victoria Cross near Zeerust for the services described in the Gazette, and was decorated by King Edward VII. at Marlborough House on 17 Dec. 1901. His V.C. was gazetted 15 Jan. 1901: "Alexis C. Doxat, Lieut., 3rd Battn. The Imperial Yeomanry. Date of Act of Bravery: 20 Oct. 1900. On the 20th Oct. 1900, near Zeerust, Lieut. Doxat proceeded with a party of mounted infantry to

reconnoitre a position held by 100 Boers on a ridge of kopjes. When within 300 yards of the position the enemy opened a heavy fire on Lieut. Doxat's party, which then retired, leaving one of their number who had lost his horse. Lieut. Doxat, seeing the dangerous position in which the man was placed, galloped back under a very heavy fire, and brought him on his horse to a place of safety." Lieut. Doxat married Mrs. Hugh Mair.

LAWRENCE, TOM, Sergt., served in the Boer War of 1899–1901, and

Tom Lawrence.

was awarded the Victoria Cross [London Gazette, 15 Jan. 1901]: "T. Lawrence, Sergt., 17th Lancers. Date of Act of Bravery: 7 Aug. 1900. On the 7th Aug. 1900, when on patrol duty near Essenbosch Farm, Sergt. Lawrence and a Private (Hayman) were attacked by twelve or fourteen Boers. Private Hayman's horse was shot, and the man was thrown, dislocating his shoulder. Sergt. Lawrence at once came to his assistance, extricated him from under the horse, put him on his own horse, and sent him on to the picket. Sergt. Lawrence took the soldier's carbine, and with his own carbine as well, kept the Boers off until Private Hayman was safely out of range. He then retired for some two miles on foot, followed by the Boers, and keeping them off till assistance arrived." Sergt. Lawrence was decorated by King Edward on 12 Aug. 1902, in London. He became Sergeant and Riding Master in the 18th Hussars, and was promoted Honorary Lieutenant and later Captain.

CURTIS, A. E., Private, won the Victoria Cross at Onderbank Spruit, during the Boer War of 1899–1902. He was decorated at Pietermaritzburg on 14 Aug. 1901, by the present King, then Duke of York. His Victoria Cross was gazetted 15 Jan. 1901: "A. E. Curtis, Private (now Corpl.), 2nd Battn. The East Surrey Regt. Date of Act of Bravery: 23 Feb. 1900. On the 23rd Feb. 1900, Colonel Harris lay all day long in a perfectly open space under close fire of a Boer breastwork. The Boers fired all day at any man who moved, and Colonel Harris was wounded eight or nine times. Private Curtis, after several attempts, succeeded in reaching the Colonel, bound his wounded arm, and gave him his flask, all under heavy fire. He then tried to carry him away, but was unable, on which he called for assistance, and Private Morton came out at once. Fearing that the men would be killed, Colonel Harris told them to leave him, but they declined, and after trying to carry the Colonel on their rifles, they made a chair with their hands and so carried him out of the fire." He later became a Sergeant.

London Gazette, 18 Jan. 1901.—" War Office, 18 Jan. 1901. The Queen has been graciously pleased to signify Her intention to confer the Decoration of the Victoria Cross on the undermentioned Soldier, whose claim has been submitted for Her Majesty's approval, for his conspicuous bravery in South Africa, on the 23rd Aug. 1900, as recorded against his name."

HEATON, WILLIAM, Private, won his Victoria Cross at the action of Geluk [London Gazette, 18 Jan. 1901]: "William Heaton, Private, 1st Battn. 8th (The King's Liverpool) Regt. On the 23rd Aug. 1900, the company to which Private Heaton belonged, advancing in front of the general line held by the troops, became surrounded by the enemy and was suffering severely. At the request of the officer commanding, Private Heaton volunteered to take a message back to explain the position of the company. He was successful, though at the imminent risk of his own life. Had it not been for Private Heaton's courage, there can be little doubt that the remainder of the company, which suffered very severely, would have had to surrender." He was later promoted Sergeant.

William Heaton.

London Gazette, 12 Feb. 1901.—" The King has been graciously pleased to signify His intention to confer the Decoration of the Victoria Cross on the undermentioned Officers and Non-commissioned Officers, whose claims have been submitted for His Majesty's approval, for their conspicuous bravery in South Africa, as stated against their names."

NICKERSON, WILLIAM HENRY SNYDER, Lieut., was born 27 March, 1875, at New Brunswick, Canada, son of the Rev. D. Nickerson, M.A., Chaplain to H.M.'s Forces (retired), and Catherine Snyder, daughter of the late Rev. W. H. Snyder, M.A. He was educated at Portsmouth Grammar School, and at Owens College, Manchester University (M.B., Ch.B., 1896), and entered the Royal Army Medical Corps on 27 July, 1898, serving in South Africa during every day of the Boer War from

William H. S. Nickerson.

11 Aug. 1899, to 31 May, 1902, attached to the Mounted Infantry. Brigadier-General Sitwell says that one of the two Victoria Crosses won the day he seized Bwab's Hill, near Dewetsdorp, was that "awarded to Lieut. Nickerson, R.A.M.C., for going out under shell and rifle fire and stitching up a man's stomach whose entrails were protruding, thereby saving his life. The man belonged to the Worcestershire Regt." and was lying in the open, and the enemy were concentrating their fire on this spot to prevent reinforcements from coming up to support the Mounted Infantry, who had been busily engaged all day. The man could not be moved and stretcher-bearers could not reach him until the fire slackened. For his services in the South African War Lieut. Nickerson was mentioned in Despatches April, 1901; promoted Capt., and awarded the Victoria Cross [London Gazette, 12 Feb. 1901]: "William Henry Snyder Nickerson, Lieut., Royal Army Medical Corps. At Wakkerstroom on the evening of the 20th April, 1900, during the advance of the infantry to support the mounted troops, Lieut. Nickerson went in a most gallant manner, under a heavy shell and rifle fire, to attend a wounded man, dressed his wounds, and remained with him until he had him conveyed a place of safety." He became Major 25 July, 1909. Major Nickerson served in the European War from 1914, with Cavalry during the retreat from Antwerp, first and second battles of Ypres, Neuve Chapelle, in the trenches at Ypres, and on other occasions; on the Somme from Sept. to Nov. 1915, and in Salonika from Dec. 1915. During the latter part of the war he held the appointment of A.D.M.S., 2nd Division. He was promoted to Lieutenant-Colonel, 1st March, 1915, and was created a C.M.G. in 1916; was three times mentioned in Despatches: 16 Feb. 1915; 1 Jan. 1916, and Oct. 1916.

BEET, HARRY CHURCHILL, Corpl., was born on 1 April, 1873, at Brackendale Farm, near Bingham, Notts, the son of Mr. J. A. Beet, Sculptor. He joined the Sherwood Foresters on 18 Feb. 1892, and sailed for India in Jan. 1894, where he served throughout the fighting on the Punjab Frontier, 1897 and 1898 (Medal and two clasps). He served in the South African War of 1899–1902, and won the Victoria Cross while under immediate command of Capt. P. Leveson-Gower. He was once wounded in this campaign on 9 Dec. 1901. He was promoted Sergeant by Lord Kitchener for service in the field. The Victoria Cross was presented to him at the capital of Natal on 14 Aug. 1901, by H.R.H. the Duke of York, now King George V. His Victoria Cross was gazetted 12 Feb. 1901: "Harry Churchill Beet, Corpl., 1st Battn. Mounted Infantry. At Wakkerstroom, on the 22nd April, 1900, No. 2 Mounted Infantry Company, 1st Battn. Derbyshire Regt., with two squadrons Imperial Yeomanry, had to retire from near a farm, under a ridge held by Boers. Corpl. Burnett, Imperial Yeomanry, was left on the ground wounded, and Corpl. Beet, on seeing him, remained behind and placed him under cover, bound up his wounds, and by firing prevented the Boers from coming down to the farm till dark, when Dr. Wilson, Imperial Yeomanry, came to the wounded man's assistance. The retirement was carried out under a very heavy fire, and Corpl. Beet was exposed to fire during the whole afternoon." The "Times," of 22 Feb. 1916, says: "The appointment of H. C. Beet, V.C., 32nd Reserve Canadian Infantry Battn., to be temporary Lieutenant was gazetted last night."

MULLINS, CHARLES HERBERT, Capt., was born in 1869, at Grahamstown, Cape Colony, son of the Rev. Canon Mullins. He was educated at St. Andrew's College, Grahamstown, and at Keble College, Oxford, and was called to the Bar at the Inner Temple in 1893. He served in the South African Campaign of 1899 to 1902, and was awarded the Victoria Cross [London Gazette, 12 Feb. 1901]: "Charles Herbert Mullins, Capt., Imperial Light Horse. On the 21st Oct. 1899, at Elandslaagte, at a most critical moment, the advance being momentarily checked by a severe fire at point-blank range, these two officers very gallantly rushed forward under this heavy fire and rallied the men, thus enabling the flanking movement which decided the day to be carried out. On this occasion Capt. Mullins was wounded." He was also created a C.M.G. (1900). Capt. Mullins was wounded at Elandslaagte, when he won the V.C., and a second time later on in the war, when he was literally riddled with bullets, and it seemed an even chance whether he would live or die. His pluck and his magnificent physique pulled him through at last, but his spine had been injured, and he remained a cripple on crutches to the day of his death. He married in 1902, Norah Gertrude, third daughter of S. Haslam, Esq., Brooklands, Uppingham, and they had two sons. Crippled and handicapped by constant illnesses, Capt. Mullins faced his life as he had before faced death, and "resolutely resumed his place in the life of the Rand. He took up his broken practice at the Bar, employed himself in various schemes of development, was an indefatigable supporter of the Church as it gradually revived after the war under Bishop Carter and Bishop Furse, and maintained a constant interest in his old corps, the I.L.H., which he had helped to found and to make famous. It was unthinkable, after all that he had suffered, that his life should be a long one, but he made the very utmost of it, not only in the glorious days of the war, but in the dull and often difficult times that followed." He died in the spring of 1916, and the "Times" of 29 April, 1916, said that his death was a real loss to South Africa, which could ill spare men of his sterling character, and that there were many of his old comrades in England and in the field at that time who would find time in the midst of a greater struggle to honour a gallant soldier and an unfailing friend.

Charles H. Mullins.

JOHNSTON, ROBERT, Capt., was born 13 Aug. 1872, son of Robert Johnston, Q.C., of Laputa, County Donegal. He was educated at King William's College, Isle of Man, and joined the 5th Battn. Royal Inniskilling Fusiliers 1890–94. He served in S. Africa 1899–1901, and was dangerously wounded in the Siege of Ladysmith. He won the Victoria Cross at Elandslaagte, and also received the Queen's Medal and bars and King's Medal for his services in this campaign. The Imperial Light Horse was recruited mostly from men from the gold mines of the Rand, and was commanded by Colonel Chisholm and Majors Karri Davis and Sampson, the last two being well known in connection with the Jameson Raid. His Victoria Cross was gazetted 12 Feb. 1901: "Robert Johnston, Capt., Imperial Light Horse. On the 21st Oct. 1899, at Elandslaagte, at a most critical moment, the advance being momentarily checked by a very severe fire at point-blank range, these two officers very gallantly rushed forward under this heavy fire and rallied the men, thus enabling the flanking movement which decided the day to be carried out. On this occasion Capt. Mullins was wounded." In 1902 he was Commandant at a concentration camp at Middelburg. In 1903 he was District Commissioner on the Eastern Transvaal. In 1911 he joined the Irish Prison Service. He was Commandant of the Prisoners of War at Oldcastle 1914–15, and was appointed Governor of His Majesty's Convict Prison at Maryborough in 1915, but again seconded for prison service in 1916 to resume duty at Oldcastle. Appointed a Resident Magistrate, Ireland, 1918. Major Johnston was in the Irish Rugby XV. in 1893, and in the English Rugby XV. in South Africa in 1897. He is very fond of fishing and golf.

London Gazette, 8 March, 1901.—"War Office, 8 March, 1901. The King has been graciously pleased to signify His intention to confer the Decoration of the Victoria Cross on the undermentioned Officer, whose claim has been submitted for His Majesty's approval, for his conspicuous bravery at Korn Spruit, as stated against his name."

MAXWELL, FRANCIS AYLMER, Lieut., was born on the 7th Sept. 1871, son of Surgeon-Major Thomas Maxwell, The Grange, Guildford. He was gazetted to the Royal Sussex Regt. on 24 Nov. 1893; joined the Indian Staff Corps on the 15th Dec. 1893, and served in Waziristan in 1895 (Medal with clasp), and in Chitral 1895 (Medal and clasp); on the North-West Frontier as A.D.C. to the G.O.C. Tirah Expeditionary Force from the 23rd Dec. 1897, to 1898; was mentioned in Despatches; was created a Companion of the Distinguished Service Order [London Gazette, 20 May, 1898]: "Francis Aylmer Maxwell, Lieut., Indian Staff Corps." The insignia was presented to him by the Queen at Windsor 25 June, 1898. He served in South Africa with Roberts's Horse, and as A.D.C. to Lord Kitchener, Chief of Staff, South Africa, 1 Nov. 1900, to 28 Nov. 1900, and as A.D.C. to Lord Kitchener, General Officer Commanding in Chief the Forces in South Africa, 29 Nov. 1900 to 12 July, 1902. For his services in this campaign he received the Queen's Medal with six clasps, the King's Medal with two clasps, a Brevet Majority 22 Aug. 1902, and was awarded the Victoria Cross [London Gazette, 6 March, 1901]: "Francis Aylmer Maxwell, Lieut., Indian Staff Corps (attached to Roberts's Light Horse). Lieut. Maxwell was one of three officers, not belonging to Q Battery, Royal Horse Artillery, specially mentioned by Lord Roberts as having shown the greatest gallantry and disregard of danger in carrying out the self-imposed duty of saving the guns of that battery during the affair of Korn Spruit on the 31st March, 1900. This officer went out on five different occasions, and assisted to bring in two guns and three limbers, one of which he, Capt. Humphreys, and some gunners dragged in by hand. He also went out with Capt. Humphreys and Lieut. Stirling to try and get the last gun in, and remained there till the last gun was abandoned. During a previous campaign (the Chitral Expedition of 1895) Lieut. Maxwell displayed gallantry in the removal of the body of Lieut.-Colonel F. D. Battye, Corps of Guides, under fire, for which, though recommended, he received no reward." Lieut. Maxwell became Captain, Indian Army, 10 July, 1901. On the 28th Nov. 1902, he was given the appointment of A.D.C. to Lord Kitchener, Commander in-Chief, East Indies. In 1905 he went to the Staff College, Camberley, and in 1906 married Charlotte Alice Hamilton, third daughter of the late P. H. Osborne of Currandooley, New South Wales, and they had two daughters. He attained his Majority in the Indian Army 7 Nov. 1909; served as Brigade-Major from the 7th Nov. 1909, to the 3rd March, 1910, and as Major, Australian Commonwealth Military Forces from the 4th March, 1910. From the 23rd Dec. 1910, until 1916, he was Military Secretary to Lord Hardinge, Governor-General of India. He was created a C.S.I. in 1911, and became Brevet Lieut.-Colonel 29 Nov. 1915. In the European War he commanded the 12th Battn. of the Middlesex Regt. from June to Oct. 1916, and on the 25th Nov. 1916, he was awarded a bar to the Distinguished Service Order: "Francis Aylmer Maxwell, V.C., C.S.I., D.S.O., Major and Brevet Lieut.-Colonel (temporary Lieut.-Colonel), 18th Lancers, Indian Army. He led his battalion with the greatest courage and initiative. Later he reorganized three battalions and consolidated the position under very heavy fire. He has previously done very fine work." For his services in the taking of Thiépval on 26 Sept. he was appointed to the command of the 18th (K.G.O.) Lancers, Indian Army, in Oct. 1916, but he continued serving with the 12th Middlesex. Brigadier-General F. A. Maxwell was killed in action near Ypres on 21 Sept. 1917. "Many will have seen with a pang the name of Brigadier-General F. A. Maxwell,

Francis Aylmer Maxwell.

The Victoria Cross

125

V.C., on the roll of honour. The third of several brothers, his brilliant military career is well known. Before he was thirty he had the V.C. (for which he was twice recommended), the D.S.O., and the Medals of the Chitral and South African campaigns. Later he was given the Order of the Star of India, and during this war he had been given a bar to his D.S.O. for ' conspicuous bravery and leadership.' He served on Lord Kitchener's Staff in South Africa and India, and later was Military Secretary to the Viceroy, Lord Hardinge. But those who knew him best and loved him most know that they have lost more than a brilliant soldier and charming companion. It seems impossible to believe that that gallant spirit and intense vitality have passed beyond this world. He could ever be counted on for encouragement and sympathy—once a friend always a friend—and only those who knew him intimately could appreciate his wonderful capacity for friendship. His great appreciation of others was as marked as his intense modesty and reserve about himself. It is impossible to think of Frank Maxwell as dead. He assuredly, with all that gallant band who have passed on, must ' come transfigured back secure from change in their high-hearted ways.' And in the possession of his endless friendship those who mourn for him will rest content."

London Gazette, 29 March, 1901.—" War Office, 29 March, 1901. The King has been graciously pleased to signify His intention to confer the Decoration of the Victoria Cross on the undermentioned Officer, whose claim has been submitted for His Majesty's approval, for his conspicuous bravery in South Africa, as stated against his name."

DOUGLAS, HENRY EDWARD MANNING, Lieut., was born 11 July, 1875, son of George Alexander Douglas, of Kingston, Jamaica. He entered the Medical Branch of the Service on 28 July, 1899, served in South Africa 1899–1901, was mentioned in Despatches, received the Queen's Medal with two clasps, was created a Companion of the Distinguished Service Order, and awarded the Victoria Cross [London Gazette, 29 March, 1901]: " Henry Edward Manning Douglas, Lieut., Royal Army Medical Corps. On the 11th Dec. 1899, during the action at Magersfontein, Lieut. Douglas showed great gallantry and devotion, under a very severe fire, in advancing in the open and attending to Capt. Gordon, Gordon Highlanders, who was wounded, and also attending to Major Robinson and other wounded men under a fearful fire. Many similar acts of devotion and gallantry were performed by Lieut. Douglas on the same day." He was promoted Captain 27 July, 1902, and on his return to England he did duty for a time at St. George's Barracks, London. In Oct. 1903, he again saw active service in Africa, with General Egerton's command in Somaliland, 1903–4, was present at the Battle of Jidballi, and received the Medal and two clasps. He became Major in 1911 ; served in the European War from 1914, was promoted to Lieut.-Colonel 1915, and created a C.M.G. 1916, and received the Order of St. Sava, Serbia, in 1916.

London Gazette, 12 April, 1901.—" War Office, 12 April, 1901. The King has been graciously pleased to signify His intention to confer the Decoration of the Victoria Cross on the undermentioned Non-commissioned Officer, whose claim has been submitted for His Majesty's approval, for his conspicuous bravery in South Africa, as stated against his name."

FARMER, DONALD, Sergt., joined the Cameron Highlanders on the 29th March, 1892, and served with the 1st Battn. in the Sudan Campaign, 1898, and was present at the battles of Atbara and Khartoum (British Medal and Khedive's Medal with two clasps); served with the Mounted Infantry Company of the 1st Battn. throughout the South African War, 1900–2 (twice mentioned in Despatches, Queen's Medal with four clasps and King's Medal with two clasps); awarded the Victoria Cross [London Gazette, 12 April, 1901]: " Donald Farmer, Sergt., 1st Battn. Cameron Highlanders. Date of Act of Bravery : 13 Dec. 1900. During the attack on General Clements' camp at Nooitgedacht, on the 13th Dec. 1900, Lieut. Sandilands, Cameron Highlanders, with fifteen men, went to the assistance of a picquet which was heavily engaged, most of the men having been killed or wounded. The enemy, who were hidden by trees, opened fire on the party at a range of about twenty yards, killing

Donald Farmer.

two and wounding five, including Lieut. Sandilands. Sergt. Farmer at once went to the officer, who was perfectly helpless, and carried him away under a very heavy and close fire to a place of comparative safety, after which he returned to the firing line, and was eventually taken prisoner." " In the first moments of the Boer attack Lieut. Murdoch was killed. He had previously been wounded at Vredefort, and throughout the campaign had displayed singular courage and devotion to duty. Lieut. Sandilands was also dangerously wounded. In this helpless condition he was assisted off the field by Sergt. Donald Farmer, who, displaying the greatest bravery under a heavy fire at close range, earned for himself the distinction of being the first Cameron Highlander to win the Victoria Cross." (Records of the Cameron Highlanders, page 358.) " On the 14th Sept (1901) the (1st) Battn. (Cameron Highlanders) once more returned to Pretoria. During its absence two officers (Lieut. A. B. Robertson and 2nd Lieut. Lord James Stewart-Murray) and fifty men of the Commander-in-Chief's escort had accompanied Lord Kitchener in his journey to Natal to meet Their Royal Highnesses the Duke and Duchess of York, who were visiting South Africa. This detachment was present on parade at Pietermaritzburg on 15 Aug., when the Duke of York presented fifty V.C.'s and D.S.O.'s to officers, non-commissioned officers and men who had distinguished them-

selves during the war. Amongst the recipients of the V.C. upon this occasion was Sergt. Donald Farmer." (Records of the Cameron Highlanders, page 366.) He became Colour-Sergeant 22 Feb. 1905, and he was promoted to Lieutenant.

London Gazette, 19 April, 1901.—" Memorandum. Lieut. Robert James Thomas Digby-Jones, Royal Engineers, and No. 459, Trooper H. Albrecht, Imperial Light Horse, would have been recommended to His Majesty for the Victoria Cross had they survived, on account of their having during the attack on Waggon Hill (Ladysmith) of 6 Jan. 1900, displayed conspicuous bravery and gallant conduct in leading the force which reoccupied the top of the hill at a critical moment just as the three foremost Boers reached it, the leader being shot by Lieut. Jones, and the two others by Trooper Albrecht."

London Gazette, 23 April, 1901.—" War Office, 23 April, 1901. The King has been graciously pleased to signify His intention to confer the Decoration of the Victoria Cross on the undermentioned Officers and Non-commissioned Officer, whose claims have been submitted for His Majesty's approval, for their conspicuous bravery during the defence at Komati River on the 7th Nov. 1900, as stated against their names."

COCKBURN, HAMPDEN ZANE CHURCHILL, Major, the son of Mr. George Ralph Richardson Cockburn (a Director of the Ontario Bank at Toronto, and for many years M.P. for that city, as well as Principal of Upper Canada College); was born on 19 Nov. 1857 ; was educated at Upper Canada College (Toronto), and Rugby School, England. On 20 Nov. 1891, he entered the Governor-General's Body-guard as 2nd Lieut. On 20 Sept. 1897, at great risk to himself he saved the lives of two brothers, Robert and James Harris, who were drowning in Lake Rousseau, Canada, and was awarded the Royal Canadian Humane Society's Medal. Early in 1900 he volunteered for service in the Boer War of 1899–1902, and won the Victoria Cross as described in the London Gazette of 23 April, 1901: " Hampden Zane Churchill Cockburn, Lieut., Royal Canadian Dragoons. Date of Act of Bravery : 7 Nov. 1900. Lieut. Cockburn, with a handful of men, at a most critical moment, held off the Boers to allow the guns to get away. To do so he had to sacrifice himself and his party, all of whom were killed, wounded, or taken prisoners, he himself being slightly wounded." Lieut. Cockburn, Lieut. Turner and Sergt. Holland won the Victoria Cross in a very gallant defence of the guns at Komati River. General Smith-Dorrien, by a wide turning movement, compelled the enemy to vacate a very strong position. The Boers were very strongly reinforced during the night and tried to recover their position next day ; but Colonel Evans, with the Canadian Mounted Rifles and two guns of the 84th Battery, forestalled them, after a gallop of two miles. On the returning march, the rearguard consisted of the Canadian Dragoons and two Canadian 12-pounders, under Colonel Lessard. After some heavy fighting they were unexpectedly charged in the afternoon by 200 mounted Boers, who got within seventy yards before they were stopped by the Canadian Dragoons. Lieut. Cockburn held them off at a most critical moment and deliberately sacrificed himself and his party to let the guns get away. He was slightly wounded himself, and his men were all either killed, wounded, or taken prisoners. Later in the day Lieut. Turner, who had already been twice wounded, dismounted, and deploying his men at close quarters, drove off the enemy. Sergt. Holland worked a Colt gun with most deadly effect, until at last he found the enemy almost on top of him, and the horse attached to the carriage much blown. He then lifted the gun off the carriage, mounted his horse, and rode away with the gun under his arm. Besides the Victoria Cross he also received the Queen's Medal, with clasps for Cape Colony, Diamond Hill, Johannesburg and Orange Free State. He commanded a troop of the Royal Canadian Dragoons in all these actions, and during the regiment's entire service in this campaign, when it marched 1,700 miles and took part in forty-five engagements. He won the Victoria Cross under the command of Colonel Lessard, commanding the unit, and Major-General Smith-Dorrien, General Officer Commanding. He was decorated by H.R.H. the Duke of Cornwall and York at Toronto on 11 Oct. 1901, and on the same occasion a sword of honour, voted to him by the council of that city, was presented to him. Major Cockburn later belonged to the Canadian Reserve of Officers. He was killed by his horse on his ranch at Maple Creek, Canada, July, 1913.

Hampden Z. C. Cockburn.

TURNER, RICHARD ERNEST WILLIAM. Lieut., Royal Canadian Dragoons. The official notice in the London Gazette of 23 April, 1901, reads : " Date of Act of Bravery : 7 Nov. 1900. Later in the day, when the Boers again threatened seriously to capture the guns, Lieut. Turner, although twice previously wounded, dismounted and deployed his men at close quarters, and drove off the Boers, thus saving the guns." Richard Ernest William Turner was born 25 July, 1871, the eldest son of Richard Turner, M.L.C. He was educated at Quebec, Canada, and entered the Royal Canadian Dragoons, serving as a Lieutenant with that regiment in the South African War of 1899–1902. He won the Victoria Cross, together with Lieut. Cockburn and Sergt. Holland, for actions of the most devoted heroism. He was three times mentioned in Despatches, given the Brevet of Lieutenant-Colonel, and created a Companion of the Distinguished Service Order [London Gazette, 19 April, 1901]: " Richard Ernest William Turner, Lieut., Royal Canadian Dragoons," and received the Queen's

Medal with six clasps for his services in this campaign. In 1900 he married Harriet Augusta, eldest daughter of Horace George Gooday, of London. They have one son and one daughter. He was in command of the Canadian Brigade of Infantry in the European War in 1914; has been mentioned in Despatches, and created a C.B. and a K.C.M.G. (1917). Major-General Sir R. E. W. Turner was recalled to England in 1917 and appointed General Officer commanding the Canadian Forces in Great Britain.

HOLLAND, E. Z., Sergt., served in the South African War of 1899–1902, and was awarded the Victoria Cross [London Gazette, 23 April, 1901]: " E. Holland, Sergt., Royal Canadian Dragoons. Date of Act of Bravery: 7 Nov. 1900. Sergt. Holland did splendid work with his Colt-gun, and kept the Boers off the two 12-pounders by its fire at close range. When he saw the enemy were too near for him to escape with the carriage, as the horse was blown, he calmly lifted the gun off and galloped away with it under his arm." He became Major, 13th Canadian Dragoons, Canadian Military Forces.

London Gazette, 4 June, 1901.—" War Office, 4 June, 1901. The King has been graciously pleased to signify His intention to confer the Decoration of the Victoria Cross on the undermentioned Officers, Non-commissioned Officers and Soldiers, for their conspicuous bravery in South Africa, as stated against their names."

HOWSE, NEVILLE REGINALD, Capt., was born at Stogursey, Somerset, on 26 Oct. 1863, the second surviving son of the late Alfred Howse, M.R.C.S. (England), and of the late Lucy Elizabeth, daughter of the late

John Hugh Claudius Beresford Conroy, of Rosevale, Raheny. He was educated at Fulland's School, Taunton; entered the London Hospital as a student in 1882, and took his diploma of M.R.C.S. (England) and L.R.C.P. (London) in 1886. He went to Australia in 1889, and practised at Taree, Manning River, until 1895, when he returned to England, devoting himself to surgery for a period of four years. He obtained his F.R.C.S. (England) in 1897. In 1899 he returned to Australia and settled at Orange, New South Wales. After a few months he went to South Africa as Lieutenant in New South Wales Army Medical Corps; promoted Captain; mentioned in Despatches 4 June, 1901;

Neville Reginald Howse.

received Queen's Medal with six clasps, and King's Medal with two clasps, and was awarded the Victoria Cross [London Gazette, 4 June, 1900]: " Neville Reginald Howse, Capt., New South Wales Medical Staff Corps. During the action at Vredefort on the 24th July, 1900, Capt. Howse went out under a very heavy cross-fire, and picked up a wounded man and carried him to a place of shelter. He was invalided to Australia, and in 1902 returned to South Africa as Major in Command of the 1st Australian Commonwealth Bearer Company. After the war he returned to Orange, and in 1905 married Evelyn, eldest daughter of C. de Vial Pilcher, of Newstead, Orange, and has two sons and three daughters: Everil Marjorie; Neville Charles, born in 1909; Evelyn Elizabeth; John Brooke, born in 1913; Alison Neville. When war broke out in 1914 he was promoted Lieutenant-Colonel; appointed R.M.O. of Australian Naval and Military Expeditionary Force, embarking at Sydney on 10 Aug. for Rabaul. He returned from Rabaul in Oct. 1914, and sailed with the first Expeditionary Force. Appointed A.D.M.S. 28 Dec. 1914, and promoted Colonel. Landed in Gallipoli on 25 April, 1915; appointed D.D.M.S., A.N.Z.A.C., on 11 Sept. 1915; mentioned in Despatches; created a C.B. 5 Aug. 1915. After evacuation proceeded to Egypt; promoted Surgeon-General in Dec. 1915, and appointed to D.M.S., A.I.F. After organizing the A.A.M.C. in Egypt, he was attached to Headquarters, A.I.F., London. He became a K.C.B. in Jan. 1917, and K.C.M.G. in June, 1919.

MASTERSON, JAMES EDWARD IGNATIUS, Lieut., was born on 20 June, 1862. He was educated by the Marist Brothers, and entered the Royal Irish Fusiliers in 1881. He served in Egypt in 1882, including Tel-el-Kebir, and received the Medal with clasp and the Khedive's Star. He was commissioned into the 2nd Devonshire Regt. in 1891. He served in Burmah from 1891 to 1902, and received the Burma Medal and clasp. He served on the North-West Frontier of India from 1897 to 1898, including operations in the Khankia Valley, the Battle of Gunda Kai and the action in the Sampagha Pass. For his services in this campaign he received the Medal with two clasps. He became Captain in 1900. He served in the Boer War of 1899–1902, and was present at the Battle of Elandslaagte and at the actions of Reitfontein and Lombard's Kop, and at the Defence of Ladysmith, including the action of Waggon Hill. During this campaign he was wounded, and was mentioned in Despatches three times. He received the Brevet of Major, the Queen's Medal with two clasps, and the Victoria Cross [London Gazette, 4 June, 1901]: " James Masterson, Lieut., 1st Battn. The Devonshire Regt. Date of Act of Bravery: 6 Jan. 1900. During the action at Waggon Hill, on the 6th Jan. 1900, Lieut. Masterson commanded, with the greatest gallantry and dash, one of the three companies of his regiment which charged a ridge held by the enemy, and captured their position. The companies were then exposed to a most heavy and galling fire from the right and left front. Lieut. Masterson undertook to give a message to the Imperial Light Horse, who were holding a ridge some hundred yards behind, to fire to the left front and endeavour to check the enemy's fire. In taking this message he crossed an open space of a hundred yards which was swept by a most heavy cross-fire, and, although badly wounded in both thighs, managed to crawl in and deliver his message before falling exhausted into the Imperial Light Horse trench. His unselfish heroism was undoubtedly the means of saving lives." In 1911 he

was promoted Major into the King's Own Royal Lancashire Regt., and in 1912 he was placed on retired pay. It was a Sergt. Patrick Masterson of the 87th who captured the first French Eagle taken during the Peninsular War, and Major Masterson, V.C., played his namesake's part in the Army pageant of 1910 at Fulham Palace. He served in the European War in 1914 and 1915 as Transport Officer. His favourite recreation is golf.

CLEMENTS, J. J., Corpl., " was," says Colonel M. F. Rimington, " South African born, of splendid physique, a good boxer and always ready for a ' scrap.' " He served in the South African War, and was awarded the Victoria Cross, while serving under Major Rimington, of the Inniskilling Dragoons, with Rimington's Guides, who were called Rimington's " Tigers " from the strip of spotted skin round their hats. Corpl. Clements was decorated in London on 1 July, 1902, at the same time as Lieut. F. E. Bell, V.C. [London Gazette, 4 June, 1901]: " J. J. Clements, Corpl., Rimington's Guides. On the 24th Feb. 1901, near Strijdenburg, when dangerously wounded through the lungs, and called upon to surrender, Corpl. Clements threw himself into the midst of a party of five Boers, shooting three of them with his revolver, and thereby causing the whole party to surrender to himself and two unwounded men of Rimington's Guides."

RAVENHILL, GEORGE, Private (at first gazetted as Charles), is the son of Mr. T. Ravenhill, Warren Road, Washwood, and was born at Birmingham on 21 Feb. 1872. In May, 1889, he joined the 1st Battn. of the Royal Scots Fusiliers, and served in India for nearly six years, and with the 2nd Battn. for two years in the South African Campaign of 1899–1902. He was awarded the D.C.M. for the action at Fredrickstad; the Medal was, however, cancelled when he won the Victoria Cross. He also received the Queen's and King's Medals with clasps for the Relief of Ladysmith, Transvaal and Cape Colony. He won his Victoria Cross under the command of Colonel E. E. Carr, C.B., and in General Geoffrey Barton's Brigade. The decoration was presented to him by H.R.H. the Duke of York (now King George V.) at Pietermaritzburg on 4 June, 1901. His Victoria Cross was gazetted 4 June, 1901: " C. Ravenhill, Private, 2nd Battn. Royal Scots Fusiliers. At Colenso, on the 15th Dec. 1899, Private Ravenhill went several times, under a heavy fire, from his sheltered position as one of the escort to the guns to assist the officers and drivers who were trying to withdraw the guns of the 14th and 66th Batteries, The Royal Field Artillery, when the detachments serving them had all been killed, wounded, or driven from them by infantry fire at close range, and helped to limber up one of the guns that were saved."

FIRTH, JAMES, Sergt., was born 15 Jan. 1874, at Wincobank, Sheffield,

son of Charles Firth, steel smelter, of Jarrow-on-Tyne, and Mrs. Charles Firth. He was educated at Swalwell, near Newcastle-on-Tyne, and joined the Army 29 July, 1889, being promoted to Sergeant, and serving in the South African War of 1899–1902. For his services in this campaign Sergt. Firth received the Queen's Medal with one clasp, and was awarded the Victoria Cross [London Gazette, 11 June, 1901]: " James Firth, 1st Battn. Duke of Wellington's West Riding Regt. During the action at Plewman's Farm, near Arundel, Cape Colony, on the 24th Feb. 1900, L.-Corpl. Blackman having been wounded and lying exposed to a hot fire at a range of from 400–500 yards, Sergt. Firth picked him up and carried him to

James Firth.

cover. Later in the day, when the enemy had advanced to within a short distance of the firing-line, Second Lieut. Wilson being dangerously wounded and in a most exposed position Sergt. Firth carried him over the crest of the ridge, which was being held by the troops, to shelter, and was himself shot through the nose and eye whilst doing so." He was at first wrongly gazetted as " W." Sergt. Firth married, on 6 June, 1897, at Emmanuel Church, Attercliffe, Sheffield, Mary Florence, only daughter of Thomas Edwards, of Swineshead, Lincolnshire, and they have two children: Alleyne G. Firth, born 25 June, 1903, and Cecil J. Firth, born 18 Dec. 1907.

London Gazette, 26 July, 1901.—" The King has been graciously pleased to signify His intention to confer the Decoration of the Victoria Cross on the undermentioned Soldiers, whose claims have been submitted for His Majesty's approval, for their conspicuous bravery in South Africa, as stated against their names."

SCOTT, ROBERT, Private, was born at Haslingden, Lancashire, on 4 June, 1874. On 2 Feb. 1895, he entered

the Manchester Regt., with which he was serving in Natal when the Boer War broke out in Oct. 1899. He went through the whole Siege of Ladysmith without being once absent from duty. He won the Victoria Cross, with which he was decorated by Lord Kitchener on 8 June, 1902, at Pretoria. He was serving under Lieut. R. Hunt-Grubbe during the great attack on Ladysmith on 6 Jan. 1900, when he won his Cross, which was gazetted 26 July, 1901: " R. Scott, Private, and J. Pitts, Private, 1st Battn. The Manchester Regt. During the attack on Cæsar's Camp, in Natal, on the 6th Jan. 1900, these two men occupied a sangar, on the left of which all our men had been shot down

Robert Scott.

and their positions occupied by Boers, and held their post for fifteen hours without food or water, all the time under an extremely heavy fire, keeping up their fire and a smart look-out, though the Boers occupied some sangars on their immediate left rear. Private Scott was wounded." Robert Scott became a Quartermaster-Sergeant (retired).

PITTS, J., Private, served in the South African War of 1899–1902, and was awarded the Victoria Cross [London Gazette, 26 July, 1901]: " J. Pitts, Private, 1st Battn. The Manchester Regt. Private R. Scott and Private J. Pitts. During the attack on Cæsar's Camp, in Natal, on the 6th Jan. 1900, these two men occupied a sangar, on the left of which all our men had been shot down and their positions occupied by Boers, and held their post for fifteen hours without food or water, all the time under an extremely heavy fire, keeping up their fire and a smart look-out, though the Boers occupied some sangars on their immediate left rear. Private Scott was wounded." Private Pitts became a Lance-Corporal, Army Reserve.

London Gazette, 30 Aug. 1901.—" War Office, 30 Aug. 1901. The King has been graciously pleased to signify His intention to confer the Decoration of the Victoria Cross upon the undermentioned Officer, whose claim has been submitted for His Majesty's approval, for his conspicuous bravery in South Africa, as stated against his name."

SCHOFIELD, HARRY NORTON, Capt., was born on 29 Jan. 1865, son of the late Christopher James Schofield, J.P., Lancashire. He entered the Royal Artillery from the Royal Military Academy, Woolwich, as Lieutenant, in Feb. 1884, and became Captain in Feb. 1893. Capt. Schofield served in the South African War in 1899 and 1900, as Aide-de-Camp to General Sir Redvers Buller, V.C., G.C.B., G.C.M.G. He was present at the Relief of Ladysmith, including the action at Colenso ; at the operations of 17 to 24 Jan. 1900, and the action at Spion Kop. Operations of 5 to 7 Feb. 1900, and action at Vaal Krantz ; operations on Tugela Heights (14 to 27 Feb.) and action at Pieter's Hill. Operations in Natal (March to June, 1900), including action at Laing's Nek (6 to 9 June). Operations in the Transvaal, East of Pretoria (July to Oct. 1900), including the action at Belfast (26 and 27 Aug.) and Lydenburg (5 to 8 Sept.). At the Battle of Colenso General Buller had ordered Colonel Long to take two batteries of Field Artillery and six naval guns to support the main attack. The 14th and 66th Field Batteries were accompanied by six naval guns (two of 4.7-inch and four 12-pounders), under Lieut. Ogilvy of the Terrible. At an early stage in the action, Long's field guns unlimbered within a thousand yards of the enemy's trenches. From this position he opened fire upon Fort Wylie, which was the centre of that portion of the Boer position which faced him. The two batteries were without shelter of any sort, and in full view of the strongly-entrenched and invisible enemy, and a fearful storm of bullets broke over them. After some time, owing to the ammunition running out, it was thought advisable to retire the officers and men to a small donga behind the guns, to which the wounded (including Colonel Long) had been taken. About 800 yards to the rear of the guns was a deep donga or nullah, in which the drivers and teams were taking cover ; along this Capt. Schofield was riding with Sir Redvers Buller, who expressed a wish to try and get some of the guns away ; so Gerard (the late Lord Gerard) and Schofield rode their horses into the donga and got some men and two teams out. Congreve, Schofield and Roberts, three aides-de-camp of the Generals, were the leaders in this forlorn hope, the latter being the only son of Lord Roberts. As soon as the teams were hooked in to the limbers on the bank of the donga, Capt. Schofield gave the order to gallop for the guns, and, as they got nearer, directed them on to the two on the right, as they appeared to be clear of dead horses. Corpl. Nurse galloped out with Schofield, and Roberts joined them, and was galloping along on Capt. Schofield's left. Congreve, after helping to hook a team in a limber, got his horse and came after them. On going about 400 yards, Roberts was shot and fell backwards. Congreve fell wounded when about 100 yards away from the guns, on reaching which Capt. Schofield and Corpl. Nurse jumped off their horses and hooked in the two guns, with which they returned. The drivers, Henry Taylor, Young, Petts, Rockall, Lucas and Williams, of the 66th Battery, all received the D.C.M. For his services in this campaign Capt. Schofield was mentioned in Despatches [London Gazette, 26 Jan. 1900, and London Gazette, 8 Feb. 1901 (Sir Redvers Buller, 30 March and 9 Nov. 1900)]. He received the Queen's Medal with six clasps, and was created a Companion of the Distinguished Service Order [London Gazette, 19 April, 1901]: " Harry Norton Schofield, Major, Royal Artillery. In recognition of services during the recent campaign in South Africa." The award was cancelled nearly two years after the Battle of Colenso, when he was awarded the Victoria Cross instead of the D.S.O. [London Gazette, 30 Aug. 1901]: " The King has been graciously pleased to signify His intention to confer the decoration of the Victoria Cross upon the undermentioned Officer, whose claims have been submitted for His Majesty's approval, for his conspicuous bravery in South Africa, as stated against his name : Harry Norton Schofield, Capt., Royal Field Artillery. Date of Act of Bravery : at Colenso on the 15th Dec. 1899. When the detachments serving the guns of the 14th and 66th Batteries, Royal Field Artillery, had all been killed, wounded or driven from them by infantry fire at close range, Capt. Schofield went out when the first attempt was made to extricate the guns, and assisted in withdrawing the two that were saved. Note.—In consequence of the above, the appointment of this Officer to the Distinguished Service Order, which was notified in the London Gazette of the 19th April, 1901, is cancelled." Capt. Schofield had been promoted to Major in 1900. Major Schofield retired in Dec. 1905. He is one of His Majesty's Honourable Corps of Gentlemen-at-Arms. Major Schofield was re-employed, 1914–1918, firstly on the British Remount Commission in Canada and America, and afterwards as Commandant on Lines of Communication, B.E.F. He was temporary Lieutenant-Colonel, 1915 to 1918, and retired in 1918 with the rank of Lieutenant-Colonel. In June, 1917, he married Dorothy Evelyn Vere, eldest daughter of the late Arthur Charles Isham.

Harry Norton Schofield.

London Gazette, 17 Sept. 1901.—"War Office, 17 Sept. 1901. The King has been graciously pleased to signify His intention to confer the Decoration of the Victoria Cross on the undermentioned Officer and Non-commissioned Officer, whose claims have been submitted for His Majesty's approval, for their conspicuous bravery in South Africa, as stated against their names."

DUGDALE, FREDERIC BROOKS, Lieut., was born on 21 Oct. 1877, the third son of Colonel James Dugdale, V.D., of Ivy Bank, Lancashire, and of Sezincot, Gloucestershire. He was educated at Marlborough, and Christ Church, Oxford, and entered the Army in Oct. 1899, being gazetted as 2nd Lieutenant to the 5th (Royal Irish) Lancers. He immediately left England to join his regiment, which on his arrival in South Africa was taking part in the Defence of Ladysmith. He served with the relieving force under Sir Redvers Buller, and was promoted Lieutenant in May, 1900. He served under Sir John French in Cape Colony. He won the Victoria Cross, as described in the Gazette, and also received the Queen's and King's Medals with clasps, also clasps for Tugela Heights, Orange Free State, Relief of Ladysmith, Laing's Nek, and Belfast, Cape Colony. He was decorated on 24 Oct. 1902, by His Majesty King Edward VII. His Victoria Cross was gazetted 17 Sept. 1901 : " Frederic Brooks Dugdale, Lieut., 5th Royal Irish Lancers. On 3 March, 1901, Lieut. Dugdale, who was in command of a small outpost near Derby, having been ordered to retire, his patrol came under a heavy fire at a range of about 250 yards, and a sergeant, two men, and a horse were hit. Lieut. Dugdale dismounted and placed one of the wounded men on his own horse ; he then caught another horse, galloped up to a wounded man and took him up behind him, and brought both men safely out of action." On the 13 Nov. of the same year, whilst hunting with the North Cotswold, his horse fell at a fence and crushed him so severely that he died within two hours, without regaining consciousness.

TRAYNOR, WILLIAM BERNARD, Sergt., was born on 31 Dec. 1870, at 29, Moxon Street, Hull, the son of Francis Traynor, Flax Dresser, of County Monaghan, Ireland, and Rebecca Traynor, formerly of Hull. He was educated at Pryme Street (Roman Catholic) School, Hull, and entered the 2nd Battn. West Yorkshire Regt. on 14 Nov. 1888. He served for some years in India, and from 1899 to 1901 in South Africa, where he won the Victoria Cross when serving under Lieut. G. L. Crossman, D.S.O., and Lieut.-Colonel W. Fry, C.B. Sergt. Traynor took part in the following operations in South Africa : Willow Grange (22 and 23 Nov. 1899); Colenso; Spion Kop; Vaal Krantz; operations in Natal from 14 to 27 Feb., ending at Pieter's Hill; Northern Natal and Orange River Colony, including action at Laing's Nek, and East and West Transvaal; severely wounded 6 Feb. 1901 ; arrived at hospital 15 Feb. For his services in this campaign Sergt. Traynor received also, besides the Victoria Cross, the Queen's Medal and clasps for Tugela Heights, Relief of Ladysmith, Laing's Nek, Transvaal and Orange River Colony Clasp for 1901. Owing to his state of health he was unable to travel to London to receive his decoration from King Edward, therefore his Victoria Cross was presented to him on 2 July, 1902, at York, by Colonel Edward Stevenson Browne, V.C., who had won his own Victoria Cross in the Zulu War of 1879. Corpl. Lintott, who so splendidly answered his comrade's call for assistance, was awarded the Distinguished Conduct Medal, and promoted Sergeant by Lord Kitchener. Sergt. Traynor's V.C. was gazetted 17 Sept. 1901 : " William Bernard Traynor, Sergt., 2nd Battn. The Prince of Wales' Own, West Yorkshire Regt. During the night attack on Bothwell Camp, on the 6th February, 1901, Sergt. Traynor jumped out of a trench and ran out under an extremely heavy fire to the assistance of a wounded man. While running out he was severely wounded, and being unable to carry the man by himself, he called for assistance. L.-Corpl. Lintott at once came to him, and between them they carried the wounded soldier into shelter. After this, although severely wounded, Sergt. Traynor remained in command of his section, and was most cheerful in encouraging his men till the attack failed." The following is an extract from Orders by Major-General Smith, Dorrien : " The G.O.C. compliments most highly the steadiness of all Infantry Battalions in the outpost line during the heavy attack last night. The conduct of the West Yorkshires, on whom the brunt of the battle fell, was especially fine, and their heavy losses are to be deplored. The casualties were very heavy, owing to the Boers getting through two picquets, having followed up a mob of 200 stampeded cavalry horses. These two picquets were practically wiped out." Sergt. Traynor's wound was so serious that he had to be invalided home in 1901, and discharged medically unfit from the Service 29 Sept. 1901, and was given a post as Barrack Warden at Dover on 8 Sept. 1902, in which capacity he was mentioned for valuable

William B. Traynor.

services in connection with the Great War 2 Sept. 1918. On 12 June, 1897, at Hunton, near Maidstone, Kent, Sergt. Traynor married Jane Elizabeth Martin, daughter of Elizabeth and James Martin. Their children are: Alice Kathleen, born 5 May, 1898 (deceased); Francis Bernard Redvers, born 7 Dec. 1899 (deceased); Cecil Robert, born 4 May, 1903; William Bothwell and Victor Charles, born 5 April, 1905, and Eileen May, born 20 July, 1910.

The London Gazette, 4 Oct. 1901.—" The King has been graciously pleased to signify His intention to confer the decoration of the Victoria Cross on the undermentioned Officers and Non-commissioned Officer, whose claims have been submitted for His Majesty's approval, for their conspicuous bravery in South Africa, as stated against their names."

BELL, FREDERICK WILLIAM, Lieut., served in the Boer War of 1899–1902, and won the Victoria Cross. He was decorated by King George V., then Prince of Wales, in London, on 11 July, 1902. His V.C. was gazetted 4 Oct. 1901: " Frederick William Bell, Lieut., West Australian Mounted Infantry. At Brakpan, on the 16th May, 1901, when retiring through a heavy fire after holding the right flank, Lieut. Bell noticed a man dismounted, and returned and took him up behind him. The horse, not being equal to the weight, fell with them. Lieut. Bell then remained behind, and covered the man's retirement till he was out of danger." He became temporary Captain while in command of a Rest Camp in 1915.

ENGLISH, WILLIAM JOHN, Lieut., was born 6 Oct. 1882, and served in the ranks. He served with the Scottish Horse in South Africa in the Boer War of 1899 to 1902, and was promoted Lieutenant in 1901. He won the Victoria Cross, and also received the Queen's Medal with five clasps. His V.C. was gazetted 4 Oct. 1901: " William John English, Lieut., 2nd Scottish Horse. This officer, with five men, was holding the right of the position at Vlakfontein, on the 3rd July, 1901, during an attack by the Boers. Two of his men were killed and two wounded, but the position was still held, largely owing to Lieut. English's personal pluck. When the ammunition ran short he went over to the next party and obtained more; to do this he had to cross some fifteen yards of open ground under a heavy fire at a range of from twenty to thirty yards." He became Lieut. Army Service Corps, 1907, and Captain in 1914.

William John English.

HARDHAM, WILLIAM JAMES, Farrier-Major, was born 31 July, 1876, at Wellington, New Zealand, son of George Hardham (of Surrey, England) and of Ann Hardham (of Sussex, England). He joined the Cadets in 1891, and the Volunteers in 1894, serving with the New Zealand Contingent in the South African War, 1900–1902, taking part in the operations in the Transvaal, west of Pretoria, Aug. to 29 Nov. 1900; and in the operations in the Transvaal, 30 Nov. 1900, to May, 1901, and May, 1902. He was mentioned in Despatches [London Gazette, 4 Oct. 1901], and was awarded the Victoria Cross [London Gazette, 4 Oct. 1901]: " W. J. Hardham, Farrier-Major, 4th New Zealand Contingent. On the 28th Jan. 1901, near Naauwpoort, this non-commissioned officer was with a section which was extended and hotly engaged with a party of about twenty Boers. Just before the force commenced to retire Trooper McCrae was wounded and his horse killed. Farrier-Major Hardham at once went under a heavy fire to his assistance, dismounted, and placed him on his own horse, and ran alongside until he had guided him to a place of safety." He was decorated with the Victoria Cross by H.M. King Edward VII., in London, on 1 July, 1902, and also received the Queen's Medal with five clasps, and King Edward's Coronation Medal. Capt. Hardham served with the New Zealand Mounted Rifles in Gallipoli, and was invalided 30 May, 1915. He later became Military Commandant of the Queen Mary Hospital for Sick and Wounded Returned Soldiers, at Hanmer Springs, New Zealand. At Rugby Football he represented Wellington Province from 1897 to 1910 (except three years' absence in South Africa on service); on many occasions as captain. He also played against the All England Team (Harding's) in 1904. He plays cricket, tennis, etc. He married, 11 March, 1916, at Wellington, New Zealand, Constance Evelyn Parsonstown, daughter of John and Elizabeth Parsonstown, of Doncaster, England.

Wm. James Hardham.

London Gazette, 18 Oct. 1901.—" War Office, 18 Oct. 1901. The King has been graciously pleased to signify His intention to confer the Decoration of the Victoria Cross on the undermentioned Non-commissioned Officer and Soldiers, whose claims have been submitted for His Majesty's approval, for their conspicuous bravery in South Africa, as stated against their names."

HAMPTON, HARRY, Sergt., was born at Crown Terrace, Richmond, Surrey, on 14 Dec. 1870, son of Mr. Samuel Hampton; entered the 1st Battn. The King's Liverpool Regt. at Aldershot 10 March, 1889, and became Corporal exactly two years later. He served in the West Indies, and also in Nova Scotia, between 1891 and 1897, in South Africa in 1897, and throughout the Boer War of 1899–1902, almost to its close, with the 1st Mounted Infantry Company of his regiment, the King's Liverpool Regt. He was present at the Siege of Ladysmith, when his regiment acted on the 6th Jan. 1900, as support to the defenders of Wagon Hill, and were under a very heavy shell and rifle fire the whole day. After the siege, as part of the 4th Division Mounted Infantry, they took part in the advance through Natal and the Eastern Transvaal, and were almost continuously engaged with the enemy. On the 21st Aug. 1900, at Van Wyk's Vlei, the unit was opposed by a very superior force of Boers, and a portion of it was only able to withdraw from the position it had taken up through the cool and gallant conduct of Sergt. Hampton and Corpl. H. J. Knight. Sergt. H. Hampton was in command of a small detached party of Mounted Infantry, and when he saw the men being driven back by the superior force of the Boers, held on to his position—a most important one—for some considerable time, in the face of large numbers of the enemy. When he found that his position was untenable he was compelled to retire, and the withdrawal was carried out in a most skilful manner. He saw all his men into safety and—although himself wounded in the head—supported L.-Corpl. Walsh (who was badly wounded and unable to walk) until the latter was again hit by a bullet and killed. Sergt. Hampton was again wounded shortly afterwards. For these services Sergt. Hampton was awarded the Victoria Cross, as related in the London Gazette, and was decorated by the late King Edward VII. at St. James's Palace. His Victoria Cross was gazetted 18 Oct. 1901: " Harry Hampton, Sergt., 2nd Battn. The King's (Liverpool) Regt. On the 21st Aug. 1900, at Van Wyk's Vlei, Sergt. Hampton, who was in command of a small party of Mounted Infantry, held an important position for some time against heavy odds, and when compelled to retire saw all his men into safety, and then, although he had himself been wounded in the head, supported L.-Corpl. Walsh, who was unable to walk, until the latter was again hit and apparently killed, Sergt. Hampton himself being again wounded some time after." He became Colour-Sergeant; was Sergeant Instructor in Musketry, and was discharged on pension. His was one of three Victoria Crosses won by his regiment in as many days.

Harry Hampton.

CRANDON, HARRY GEORGE, Private, was born 9 Feb. 1874, at Wells, Somerset, son of William Crandon (now deceased) and of Ellen Crandon (née Hewlett). Private Crandon wrote to Sir O'Moore Creagh: " Sir, I respectfully beg to state that I went to India in Oct. 1894, and from there to Ladysmith, South Africa, in 1898, where I served through the whole of the Boer War, and was in the Siege of Ladysmith. I gained the V.C. on the 4th of July, 1901, at Springboks Laagte, near Ermelo. Eastern Transvaal, for saving Private Berry, 18th Hussars. We were both advanced scouts together, and suddenly came upon a party of the Boers. Private Berry's horse got killed, and he himself was wounded in two places. I gave my horse to him and lifted him on to it, and sent him to an ambulance station, and got out of it the best way I could, and was not wounded myself. Had the V.C. presented by Lord Kitchener at Pretoria, 8 June, 1902." Private Crandon received the Queen's Medal with five clasps, and was awarded the Victoria Cross [London Gazette, 18 Oct. 1901]: " Henry George Crandon, Private, 18th Hussars. On the 4th July, 1901, at Springbok Laagte, Private Berry's horse fell and became disabled, and he was himself shot in the right hand and left shoulder. Private Crandon at once rode back under a heavy fire to his assistance, gave up his horse to the wounded man, to enable him to reach shelter, and followed him on foot, having to run for 1,100 yards, all the time under fire." Private Crandon writes: " I joined this war in Oct. 1914, in South Africa. I was wounded in the left foot at Ypres, 13 May, 1915. After I was convalescent I was sent to the Balkans and was there two years, and went from there to Egypt, and came home to England lastly from Jerusalem, Palestine."

Harry George Crandon.

KENNEDY, CHARLES THOMAS, Private, served in the South African War, 1899–1902, and was awarded the Victoria Cross [London Gazette, 18 Oct. 1901]: " C. Kennedy, Private, 2nd Battn. Highland Light Infantry. At Dewetsdorp, on the 22nd Nov. 1900, Private Kennedy carried a comrade, who was dangerously wounded and bleeding to death, from Gibraltar Hill to the hospital, a distance of three-quarters of a mile, under a very hot fire. On the following day, volunteers having been called for to take a message to the Commandant across a space over which it was almost certain death to venture, Private Kennedy at once stepped forward. He did not, however, succeed in delivering the message, as he was severely wounded before he had gone twenty yards." He was killed in Edinburgh,

24 April, 1907. A horse attached to a contractor's cart had bolted in Leith Walk, and in making a plucky attempt to stop it, he was knocked down, and the wheels passed over him. He was so seriously injured that he died on his way to the Royal Infirmary.

Edward Durrant.

DURRANT, EDWARD, Private, served in the South African War of 1899–1902, and was awarded the Victoria Cross [London Gazette, 18 Oct. 1901]: "E. Durrant, Private, 2nd Battn. The Rifle Brigade. Date of Act of Bravery: 27 Aug. 1900. At Bergendal, on the 27th Aug. 1900, Acting-Corpl. Wellar, having been wounded and being somewhat dazed, got up from his prone position in the firing line, exposing himself still more to the enemy's fire, and commenced to run towards them. Private Durrant rose, and, pulling him down, endeavoured to keep him quiet, but finding this impossible, he took him up and carried him back for 200 yards under a heavy fire to shelter, returning immediately to his place in the line." He became Lance-Corporal.

London Gazette, 8 Nov. 1901.—"War Office, 8 Nov. 1901. The King has been graciously pleased to signify His intention to confer the Decoration of the Victoria Cross on the undermentioned Non-commissioned Officer, whose claim has been submitted for His Majesty's approval, for his conspicuous bravery in South Africa, as stated against his name."

YOUNG, ALEXANDER, Sergt.-Major, was born on 27 Jan. 1873, at Ballinana, Clarinbridge, County Galway, son of William and Annie Young, and younger brother of Joseph Young, Esq., J.P., of Corrib House, Galway. He was educated at the Model School Galway. On 22 May, 1890, he joined the Queen's Bays at Renmore, where his superior horsemanship quickly brought him to notice. He served for a time in India, and became a Riding Instructor. In the Sudanese Campaign, under Kitchener, he first saw active service. He was for a time at Shorncliffe, and was transferred to the Cape Police as Instructor. Two other soldiers from Galway have described him in these days: Private James O'Heir, late of the 2nd Connaught Rangers, said of the late Lieut. A. Young, V.C., who fell fighting in France, "God bless his memory; he was a gallant hero, and may he and every brave soldier who fought for his King and country, and to whom the men who loved him have said their last 'Good-night,' rest in peace! I knew him as a boy in Galway; I knew his father and mother, and all his relatives. I first saw him abroad in Egypt. He was a Rough-Riding Sergeant-Major of the 2nd Dragoon Guards, and the battalion in which I served was placed under him for a course of mounted infantry drill. He was a wonderful horseman, and had the reputation of being the best rough-rider in the British Army, and also in Egypt; and he was a brave and high-minded man, distinguished by the natural traits of generous, open-hearted good nature, which popularized him with everyone, of every station in life, and endeared him especially to the Irish people then in Egypt. . . . All the Irish soldiers in Egypt were very proud that one of their countrymen should hold the high position of first horseman, and at the same time maintain in so high and unblemished a manner the national reputation for bravery, generosity and the manly virtues which often distinguish the Irish character under the stress and trial of the soldier's life. Mr. Young was a central figure in all Egyptian tournaments and public amusements, in which exhibitions of horsemanship took a foremost place. In every tournament in Cairo in which he competed Mr. Young was the victor, and ringing Irish cheers always welcomed him to the arena, and enthusiastic outbursts cheered his prowess, and inspired his genius for daring feats of horsemanship to wonderful achievements which excelled anything ever beheld there on these great public occasions. He never knew defeat in any contests of horsemanship! . . . Not only every Irishman, but every Britisher was proud of Mr. Young on these occasions. To the Irish private soldier he was always very friendly, and particularly so to a Galwayman, who could always reckon on his kind-hearted friendship; and, with the generosity which was characteristic of him on every occasion, he contributed the money prizes won by him to the Soldiers' Mess. At Aldershot, in 1897, Mr. Young performed wonderful feats of horsemanship before Queen Victoria, and later before King Edward. Mr. Young's control over a horse was supreme. The wild horses lassoed in the Arabian desert he broke in and trained to become the most manageable of animals, in his own way. It was usual with the rough-rider of the period to train the wild horses with sand-bags and dummy men on their backs, but Mr. Young would not use these things, mounting the horse's back and remaining there, despite every effort of the animal to throw him, or even to roll over or dislodge him. On such an occasion Mr. Young declared his maxim: 'I will either break him in, or he will break my neck.' Mr. Young left the 2nd Dragoon Guards in Egypt for the Headquarters in Canterbury, and from there to India, to teach horse-riding; and, after completing his period there, he returned to Canterbury in charge of the Riding School. There he got a severe kick from a horse, and shortly after he retired from the Army. He then came back to Galway, and resided here with his sister; but again, after about six months, he went out and joined the Cape Mounted Police, with the rank of Sergeant-Major. That was about two months before the outbreak of the South African War, when the authorities, knowing his extensive experience of the country, and of the Boers, put him in charge of a force over a large district. It was while in Basutoland he won the V.C., by his gallantry in a skirmish in which he risked his life under very dangerous circumstances. He was the only Galwayman who won the V.C. in the South African War." Also Private O'Heir said: "Mr. Young held the highest record as a rough-rider in the British Army: he competed for this honour with many men, including the best riders of the 17th and 21st Lancers and the 18th Hussars, and with Sergt. Bishop, a notorious rough-rider of the Egyptian Cavalry; but he beat all these very easily, and in no one did he find a close competitor, except in Mr. Michael Kelly, a native of the town of Kilkenny. At Aldershot Mr. Young won the Army Championship in a contest in which it was necessary to ride with a threepenny-piece on each stirrup-iron under the ball of the foot. Lieut.-Colonel Lambert, of Castle Lambert, was in command of the 2nd Dragoon Guards (Queen's Bays) while Mr. Young was in the regiment in Egypt; and everyone there knew that he greatly regretted the loss of so gallant a soldier when Mr. Young retired from that corps." Stephen O'Heir, late of the Connaught Rangers, brother of the above, said: "I went through a course of Mounted Infantry Drill in 1896, as a Private in the Connaught Rangers, attached to Mr. Young's regiment at Cairo. When I was put under him in the school he told me that I should very soon be nearly as good a rider as himself if I could claim to be a Galwayman. . . . I always admired his easy and graceful seat on horseback. No man seemed to be able to handle a horse like him. A dozen Arab ponies were brought in wild from the desert, and I watched him breaking them in. One threw itself on the ground, and Mr. Young still sat on him till he sprang to his feet, the rider on his back. . . . I last saw him in South Africa 1901, at a place called Burgess Dorp, and then he went down to Capetown, and I saw him no more until one day I beheld him in Galway. . . . It was a great pleasure to Galwaymen in the Army to see him the victor. No matter who contested them with him, the laurels still remained on the brow of Mr. Young. . . . In the Bengal Presidency it has always been a pleasure to Galwaymen to read of his daring feats of horsemanship, which were always so excellent of achievement. His name was famous, and he was spoken of as 'The Terror.'" Alexander Young was at Williamstown when the South African War broke out, and he "was with Gatacre on that tragic night when, against the advice of his staff, he tried to outflank the Boers by a movement between the hills. Young was wounded in the leg, but he managed to ride back to hospital. He was within a few yards of Capt. Montmorency, V.C., when that gallant officer fell mortally wounded in the attack on Schooman's Copje." For his services in this campaign he received the Queen's Medal with clasps; the King's Medal with clasps, and was awarded the Victoria Cross [London Gazette, 18 Nov. 1901]: "Alexander Young, Sergt.-Major, Cape Police. Towards the close of the action at Ruiter's Kraal on the 13th Aug. 1901, Sergt.-Major Young, with a handful of men, rushed some kopjes which were being held by Commandant Erasmus and about twenty Boers. On reaching these kopjes, the enemy were seen galloping back to another kopje held by the Boers. Sergt.-Major Young then galloped on some 50 yards ahead of his party, and, closing with the enemy, shot one of them and captured Commandant Erasmus, the latter firing at him three times at point-blank range before being taken prisoner." After the war Sergt.-Major Young returned to his position with the Cape Mounted Police, and left them once more in 1906, for service in the native rebellion, when he was wounded for the second time, and received a medal. A soldier's letter says: "Lieut. Young did for the Germans in a week what they had failed to do for themselves in three years. The Herero Rebellion broke out in German territory, and Lieut. Young was serving in the Cape Police on the border, and although the Germans quelled the rebellion they could not capture its leader. But Young did so, and was specially decorated by the Kaiser. This decoration he publicly burned at Capetown during the war with Germany." Later he served in the Zululand Rebellion, when he was once more wounded. For four years after this he farmed in Natal. The "Connacht Tribune" thus writes about the fair-haired, blue-eyed, fresh-complexioned Irishman: "There is always a breezy manliness about the man who has lived a strenuous, open-air life. Vast fields and plains, the freedom of the high-road, an occasional brush with danger, create a breadth of outlook and a natural zest for life as it used to be lived before civilization imposed its restrictions and its duties. Since 1890, when Alexander Young took the Queen's shilling at Renmore, and entered upon a new life as a Trooper in the Queen's Bays, he has lived after the manner of a soldier and a sportsman. . . . For four years . . . he 'ran' a farm in Natal. 'After such a life as I have led,' said he, with a smile, 'a man is only good for farming or soldiering.' The present war once more found him joining the colours, when De Wet's Rebellion broke out, this time as Regimental Sergeant-Major of the Cape Mounted Police. He served under Commandant Britz, who is to-day" (27 Nov. 1915) "taking the new column to German East Africa with Colonel Royston. The story of that march across the arid desert to Windhoek reads like a romance. The desert, with its poisoned wells (the Germans there, as elsewhere, outraged the rules of warfare), presented greater terrors than any brush with the enemy. After serving under Botha until the outbreak was successfully accounted for, Lieut. Young for the first time took on the responsibilities of commissioned rank. He was transferred and promoted into the 4th South African Mounted Rifles as 1st Lieutenant, and once more crossed the Veldt and fought under General Smuts in German East Africa until the Hun outpost in that part of the world was demolished and their flag hauled down. The Germans blew up every rail, and forced marches across the desert were resorted to. Nevertheless, he" (Lieut. Young) "said, the men were cheerful—as fine a lot of soldiers as one ever served with. The younger men found it hard

Alexander Young.

to stand up against the conditions imposed. After Gibeon, where the desert ends, had been passed, however, there was plenty of sport and wild game, and, moreover, victory was near, so that life took on brighter tints." Alexander Young told the writer of this most interesting article that: "The men got demobilized at Durban, after a march that ranks as one of the finest in history. 'We had occasional scraps with the enemy, but the long marches were the worst part of it all, and it was this that brought about such speedy victory. The Dutch South Africans are loyal. The rebellion was got up by a few agitators such as one will find in every country. When those men they led learned the real facts, they surrendered at every opportunity they could get.'" After demobilization, when General Smuts called for 10,000 volunteers for the British Forces in France, he was one of the first to come forward, and was accepted by Colonel Jones for a commission in the South African Scottish, and came to England with them. It was at this time that Lieut. Young revisited his old home. The South African Scottish were then camped near Aldershot, "whose bivouac," said the "Connacht Tribune" of 27 Nov. 1915, "very soon will be in the lines where danger lies, and where the battle for freedom and civilization is being waged. The South African Scottish will very likely eat their plum puddings (if they are lucky enough to get any) in the trenches. What has touched Lieut. Young most during his visit to Galway is the numerous friendly handshakes from the mothers of men at the front. 'You meet them everywhere,' he said, 'and there is no doubting their sincerity.' The manly heart of the man who won the soldier's blue riband has its human side." The "Galway Express" then takes up its parable and describes how Lieut. Young paid a visit to its office while he was staying with his brother in his native town. "He was full of hope, and spoke to us of some of his extraordinary experiences during the South African War." Although Lieut. Young had been in the Colonies for many years, he had many friends in Galway, and during his visit to Galway a few weeks before he left for the front he gained popularity among all classes. "Shortly afterwards," says the "Galway Express" of 28 Oct. 1916, "the young Galway hero was with his regiment on board a transport for the land of the Pharaohs, under Sir John Maxwell. He fought in Egypt against the Soudanese and Turks, who were quickly accounted for, their last lap in this campaign taking them among the ferocious Senussi tribe, who captured the crew of the S.S. Tara a year ago, after the vessel was sunk by a German submarine; the recapture of the crew by motor transports being one of the epic incidents of the war. Lieut. Young then returned to England again, but once more found himself sailing for the sunny coast of France in time to participate in the 'Big Push' on 1 July last. He was but fifteen days in the Somme fight when he received a wound at what Tommy calls 'The Devil's Wood,' and he was invalided home to England." A Press Association War Special runs as follows: "A special correspondent of Reuter's Agency, who has visited one of the South African hospitals, and conversed with a number of wounded men who have just returned from France, writes: 'Now that the fact that the South African Brigade has been engaged in the British offensive has been published in the Press and passed by the Censor, and that the South African casualties have appeared in the list, there can be no harm in dwelling on some of the deeds of gallantry performed by men from the Union. The first batch of South African wounded have reached London. All were in the cheeriest mood. About 60 per cent. had been through the South-West African Campaign. Many had served in Egypt, while a number of veterans had fought also in the Matabele, Bechuana and Boer Wars. They declare that the South-West African Campaign was a thirsty jaunt, while the fighting in France was hell. All the wounded were enthusiastic about the magnificent progress of our troops. One stalwart South African engineer, with shattered hand, who got his V.C. in the Boer War, was engaged in repairing signalling apparatus, when he saw lying under the enemy fire a French officer with a shattered leg. In spite of the terrific fire he picked up the officer and carried him out of the danger-zone, whereupon the officer took the Legion of Honour from his tunic, and pinned it on his gallant rescuer, who himself had his right hand shattered by a "whiz-bang."'" After being wounded this time Lieut. Young was in hospital at Brighton for some time, and returned to the firing-line in Sept., and, says the "Galway Express," "with the hardy boys from the veldt, now well inured to war, he kept the Hun on the move until the 19th of this month" (Sept.), "when he was killed. But he and his men had fought the stern and noble fight of men fighting for an ideal, and, unfortunately, as reports in the papers show, their ranks were sadly depleted." Lieut. Young was killed on the 19th Oct. 1916. "Only last week," continues the "Galway Express," "our representative had a chat with Private Lynch, Loughrea, who fought under Lieut. Young in two continents and was wounded on the same day as he, and he spoke in the most enthusiastic and eulogistic terms of the gallant officer who now lies beneath the cold soil of an alien clime. As a soldier and a man, too much cannot be said of Lieut. Young; gallant to rashness, sincere to a fault, honourable in all his dealings, imbued with a fraternal spirit which makes man and officer one, he has sealed with his life's blood a career that all may envy and few rival." On Saturday, Oct. 28, 1916, the Galway Urban Council adjourned their weekly meeting in sympathy with "their valued brother member, a distinguished Galwayman and an esteemed member of their Council" (Mr. Joseph S. Young, J.P.), on the death of his brother, Lieut. A. Young, V.C. The "Connacht Tribune" of Saturday, 28 Oct. 1916, said: "There has been but one Galway V.C., and, in the free, colonial parlance that he loved, he has 'gone West.' He has died as he has lived—on the battlefield, facing the foe. What more fitting grave than on the rolling plains of Flanders, where he has gone to rest amongst so many of the manly, fearless souls? No flower of the forest that has been 'wide awae' had in its fulness attained more manly, robust bloom than poor Sandy Young. His was a different outlook on life to that of most of us. It was not circumscribed by narrow boundaries or hemmed in by local institutions. Begot of the plains, it was wide and spacious and natural and free as they. No alloy of cheap conventionalism, no tinsel of empty form, held it to the things that do not matter. It brushed all these things aside and looked out on life as it is. Neither alloy of pettiness nor self-created idealism hindered its gaze. So much of the man, whose grave a little flower-woven cross marks in Flanders to-day. Of his life? His manly character, his great good nature were evolved from his life. Know these, and you perceive that he had communed with nature and faced danger without flinching. The great test of a man is that he lives in a town amongst minor interests, and yet preserves a bigness of outlook, and does not lose touch with the essentials. A greater test is that a man wins through hard experience in the battle of life, and does not achieve the crabbed soul of the cynic. Young stood this test mentally, as he stood every physical test that duty put on him. At home he learned horsemanship; abroad he excelled in it. From the Queen's Bays to the Cape Mounted Police; from that to the South African Scottish. And in between, he ran a bachelor's bungalow and a farm in Natal. When the war trumpets called, he obeyed, for he had learned to obey and to be obeyed. I can imagine the kilted veterans of the veldt loving Sandy Young, and following him to death. And I can imagine them taking the war-shattered body reverently to its resting-place amongst the silent companionship of the fallen. I can see the platoon trudging back to duty over the mud-flats, having paid the tribute of brave men's tears to the robust manliness that had ceased to lead them to action. . . . He was of striking contrast to his brother, and of a different school—the school that far-flung freedom and rude and natural conditions beget. His faith in humanity remained undimmed by the flight of time and soul-revealing experience; his own humanity was held in the secure chalice of that faith. He was not of those who achieve greatness by scholarly gifts, or by stolid steadfastness. He won his qualities from the free kingdoms of far-flung plains; he wore them without consciousness. It is good in these days to see the candour of a manly heart revealed. It is thrice sad to think that now that heart is stilled. Such hearts are needed amongst the pioneers that will rebuild the shattered fabric of the kingdoms of this world after the war. But now this noble spirit roams in other kingdoms; the body that bore it has for its kingdom 'a little, little grave.' May the flowers of the forest press lightly o'er!"

London Gazette, 29 Nov. 1901.—"War Office, 29 Nov. 1901. The King has been graciously pleased to signify His intention to confer the Decoration of the Victoria Cross on the undermentioned Officer, whose claim has been submitted for His Majesty's approval, for his conspicuous bravery in South Africa, as stated against his name."

PRICE-DAVIES, LLEWELYN ALBERIC EMILIUS, Lieut., was born 30 June, 1878, third son of the late Lewis Richard Price, of Marrington Hall, Chirbury, Salop. He was educated at Marlborough and Sandhurst, and entered the Army 23 Feb. 1898, serving throughout the South African War of 1899–1902. For his services in this campaign he was twice mentioned in Despatches, received the Queen's Medal with five clasps, the King's Medal with two clasps, and was created a Companion of the Distinguished Service Order [London Gazette, 19 April, 1901]: "Llewelyn Alberic Emilius Price-Davies, Lieut., King's Royal Rifle Corps. For services in S. Africa." He was also awarded the Victoria Cross [London Gazette, 29 Nov. 1901]: "Llewelyn Alberic Emilius Price-Davies, Lieut., King's Royal Rifle Corps. At Blood River Poort, on the 17th Sept. 1901, when the Boers had overwhelmed the right of the British column, and some four hundred of them were galloping round the flank and rear of the guns, riding up to the drivers (who were trying to get the guns away) and calling upon them to surrender, Lieut. Price-Davies, hearing an order to fire upon the charging Boers, at once drew his revolver and dashed in among them, firing at them in a most gallant and desperate attempt to rescue the guns. He was immediately shot and knocked off his horse, but was not mortally wounded, although he had ridden to what seemed to be almost certain death without a moment's hesitation." He was promoted to Captain 2 Jan. 1902. In 1906 Capt. Price-Davies married Eileen Geraldine Edith, daughter of the late James Wilson, D.L., of Currygrane, Edgeworthstown, Ireland. From the 22nd March, 1906, to the 31st July, 1906, he was Adjutant and Quartermaster, Mounted Infantry, Irish Command, and from Oct. 1906, to Nov. 1907, was Adjutant, 5th Battalion Mounted Infantry, South Africa. He was a student at the Staff College, Camberley, from 1908 to 1909; and from 1 Nov. 1910, to 17 June, 1912, was Brigade Major, 13th Brigade, Irish Command. From the 18th June, 1912, to the 4th Aug. 1914, he was G.S.O.3., War Office; and from the 5th Aug. 1914, to the 24th Sept. 1914, G.S.O.3, 2nd Div. He was G.S.O.2, G.H.Q., from the 2nd Oct. 1914, to the 11th March, 1915; G.S.O.2, 4th Div., from 12 March, 1915 to 24 Nov. 1915. He became Major 1 Sept. 1915, and commanded a Brigade in England from the 25th Nov. 1915, to the 29th Nov. 1915; in France from the 1st Dec. 1915, to the 7th Nov. 1917; Brevet Lieutenant-Colonel 1 Jan. 1916. He commanded a Brigade in England from the 8th Nov. 1917, to the 2nd April, 1918; was created a C.M.G. in Jan. 1918; commanded a Brigade in France from the 3rd April, 1918, to the 15th April, 1918, and was specially employed in Italy, with rank of temporary Major-General, from the 16th April 1918, to the 31st Dec. 1918; was given the Brevet of Colonel 3 June, 1918.

Lt. A. E. Price-Davies.

London Gazette, 17 Dec. 1901.—"War Office, 17 Dec. 1901. The King has been graciously pleased to signify His intention to confer the Decoration of the Victoria Cross on the undermentioned Soldier, whose claim has been submitted for His Majesty's approval, for his conspicuous bravery in South Africa, as stated against his name."

William Bees.

BEES, WILLIAM, Private, was born on 12 Sept. 1872 at Loughborough, Leicestershire, son of William and Jane Bees. He was educated at the Board School, and joined the Derbyshire Regt. on 7 March, 1890. He served on the Indian Frontier in 1897–98, taking part in the Tirah Campaign, 1897–98 (Medal). He again saw active service in the South African War of 1899–1902. For his services in this campaign (1899–1901), he received the Queen's Medal with three bars, the King's Medal with two bars, was made Corporal on the field of battle on winning the V.C., and was awarded the Victoria Cross [London Gazette, 17 Dec. 1901]: "W. Bees, Private, 1st Battn. The Derbyshire Regt. Private Bees was one of the Maxim-gun detachment which, at Moedwil, on the 30th Sept. 1901, had six men hit out of nine. Hearing his wounded comrades asking for water, he went forward, under a heavy fire, to a spruit held by Boers, about 500 yards ahead of the gun, and brought back a kettle full of water. In going and returning he had to pass within 100 yards of some rocks, also held by Boers, and the kettle which he was carrying was hit by several bullets." He was discharged on the 18th Sept. 1902. In Oct. 1914, he joined Kitchener's Army, but was discharged through sickness. He rejoined again, 6 April, 1915 (Sherwood Foresters), and was at Whitburn, Sunderland, until transferred to the Durham Light Infantry at Blythe and South Shields. He was transferred to Class W., for mining after serving for 1 year and 133 days with the Colours (character good). He enlisted again in the Royal Army Service Corps on 30 Jan. 1918, and was transferred to the Army Reserve in consequence of Demobilization on 6 Feb. 1919. He is now discharged. Private Bees was married at All Saints' Church, Loughborough, on 25 April, 1903. His wife's name is Sarah; and they have two children : Charles William, who was fifteen on the 25th March, 1919, and Lilian Elizabeth, twelve years on the 28th June, 1919.

London Gazette, 27 Dec. 1901.—"War Office, 27 Dec. 1901. The King has been graciously pleased to signify His intention to confer the Decoration of the Victoria Cross on the undermentioned Soldier, whose claim has been submitted for His Majesty's approval, for his conspicuous bravery in South Africa, as stated against his name."

BRADLEY, H. G., Driver, Royal Field Artillery, was born 27 Sept. 1876, at 5, Huntingdon Street, Kingsland, son of Edward Thomas Bradley, of Barnet. He entered the Royal Field Artillery as Driver, and served in the Boer War of 1899 to 1902. He displayed great gallantry at Itala, when Major Chapman and his little garrison made their splendid defence against Botha. Sixteen hundred Boers attacked in the early morning, and our men—mostly Mounted Infantry—held their ground for nineteen hours, inflicting a loss of five hundred killed, wounded, or taken prisoners. Lieut. Kane, of the South Lancashires, died at his post, shouting : " No surrender, men ! " and we lost heavily, but we kept our position against overwhelming odds. During the fight ammunition ran short at the top of a steep hill, one hundred and fifty yards from the main body, and Major Chapman, of the Dublin Fusiliers, called for volunteers to carry some up. It was then that

H. G. Bradley.

Driver Bradley won the Victoria Cross, and Driver Lancashire and Gunners Bull, Rabb and Boddy the Distinguished Conduct Medal. Bradley's Victoria Cross was gazetted 27 Dec. 1901 : " H. G. Bradley, Driver, Royal Field Artillery. Date of Act of Bravery : 26 Sept. 1901. During the action at Itala, Zululand, on the 26th Sept. 1901, Major Chapman called for volunteers to carry ammunition up the hill ; to do this a space of about 150 yards, swept by a heavy cross-fire, had to be crossed. Driver Lancashire and Gunner Bull at once came forward and started, but half-way across Driver Lancashire fell wounded ; Driver Bradley and Gunner Bull, without a moment's hesitation, ran out and caught Driver Lancashire up, and Gunner Rabb carried him under cover, the ground being swept by bullets the whole time. Driver Bradley then, with the aid of Gunner Boddy, succeeded in getting the ammunition up the hill." He was promoted to Bombardier, received the Queen's Medal with five clasps, and the King's Medal with two clasps. His Victoria Cross was presented to him by Lord Kitchener at Pretoria on Peace Thanksgiving Day.

London Gazette, 11 Feb. 1902.—"War Office, 11 Feb. 1902. The King has been graciously pleased to signify His intention to confer the Decoration of the Victoria Cross on the undermentioned Officers, whose claims have been submitted for His Majesty's approval, for their conspicuous bravery in South Africa, as stated against their names."

CREAN, THOMAS JOSEPH, Surgeon-Captain, was born in Dublin in 1873, 2nd son of the late Michael Theobald Crean, Barrister, and his wife, Emma (née Dunne) ; was educated at Clongowes, and the Royal College of Surgeons in Dublin, and joined the Imperial Light Horse as a trooper on the outbreak of hostilities in the Boer War, and was appointed Captain in March, 1900, but gave up Squadron Command in June, 1901, and became Surgeon-Captain. The Victoria Cross was presented to him by H.M. the

King, in St. James's Palace on 13 March, 1902, and was gazetted 11 Feb. 1902 : " Thomas Joseph Crean, Surgeon-Captain, 1st Imperial Light Horse. During the action with De Wet at Tygerskloof on the 18th Dec. 1901, this officer continued to attend to the wounded in the firing line, under a heavy fire at only 150 yards' range, after he had himself been wounded, and only desisted when he was hit a second time, and, as it was first thought, mortally wounded." He married Victoria, daughter of Señor Don Tomas Heredia, of Malaga, and has one son and one daughter. Major Crean is well known as an athlete, and played in the Irish International Rugby Fifteen in 1894 and 1896, and was one of the English team in South Africa in 1896. In the European War he served with the 1st Cavalry Brigade in 1915, and was twice mentioned in Despatches, and created a Companion of the Distinguished Service Order [London Gazette, 3 June, 1915] : " Thomas Joseph Crean, Major, Royal Army Medical Corps." In 1916 he commanded the 44th Field Ambulance, British Expeditionary Force, in France. Major Crean is Medical Officer in Charge, Hospital, Royal Enclosure, Ascot ; is Clinical Assistant, Sa Manten Hospital for Women, London, and a Member of the Irish Twentieth Club. He is L.R.C.P. and S.I., Hon. F.R.C.S. (Ireland), L.M., Rotunda Hospital, Dublin ; late Assistant Master, Lying-in Hospital, Dublin. He holds the Arnott Gold Medal, 1902, and the Royal Humane Society Testimonial for saving life at sea, and is a Member of the Council of the Irish Graduate Society.

MAYGAR, LESLIE CECIL, Lieut., was born on the 26th May, 1871, at The Dean Station, Victoria, New South Wales, son of the late Mr. Edwin Willis Maygar, formerly of Bristol, and of Helen Maygar. He was educated

Leslie Cecil Maygar.

privately, and entered the Victorian Mounted Rifles, 1 March, 1891, becoming Lieutenant in July, 1900, and serving in South Africa from 1 Feb. 1901, to 31 July, 1902, under Major Daly, O.C., 5th V.M.R., and Colonel Pulteney. For his services in this campaign in the Transvaal, Orange River Colony and Cape Colony, he received the Queen's Medal with four clasps, and was awarded the Victoria Cross [London Gazette, 11 Feb. 1902] : " Leslie Cecil Maygar, Lieut., 5th Victorian Mounted Rifles. At Geelhoutboom, on the 23rd Nov. 1901, Lieut. Maygar galloped out and ordered the men of a detached post, which was being outflanked, to retire. The horse of one of them being shot under him, when the enemy were within 200 yards, Lieut. Maygar dismounted and lifted him on to his own horse, which bolted into boggy ground, causing both of them to dismount. On extricating the horse and finding that it could not carry both, Lieut. Maygar again put the man on its back, and told him to gallop for cover at once, he himself proceeding on foot. All this took place under a very heavy fire." His Victoria Cross was presented to him at Pretoria on 8 June, 1902, by Lord Kitchener. He joined the Australian Imperial Force 20 Aug. 1914, and served with the 8th Australian Light Horse Regt., 3rd A.L.H. Brigade, arriving in Egypt with the 1st Division, Australian Imperial Force, in Dec. 1914. He served with his command in the field continuously without being wounded or a day away from his command on sick leave, so he said when he sent particulars of his services for this book. For his services in Palestine he was created a Companion of the Distinguished Service Order, and was promoted to Lieutenant-Colonel in June, 1917. He also received the Volunteer Decoration in July, 1917. Lieut.-Colonel Maygar was mortally wounded on 31 Oct. 1917, during the fighting at Beersheba. A newspaper account runs as follows : " Particulars of the death of Colonel Maygar, V.C., who was mortally wounded by an aeroplane bomb near Beersheba on 31 Oct., have been received by his brother, Mr. A. E. Maygar, of Longwood. Major A. W. G. McLaurin wrote : ' We were in the firing-line all day, and were relieved by the 11th Regt. about 4 o'clock in the afternoon. We were then retired to near Desert Corps Headquarters, where we arrived just about dusk. Your brother went to headquarters to report, and I took the regiment on some little distance to await him. We had dismounted, and he had just joined us, and was talking to some of the men in the rear of the regiment, when an enemy aeroplane came up and bombed some transport in our rear. The Colonel at once galloped forward, and was extending us when he was hit, and his horse bolted with him. That was the last I saw of him, although I sent out men to look for him. A man brought his horse back, and said he was severely wounded, and had been taken to a field ambulance. The regiment had immediate orders to go out to a certain position, and I was unable to see him. We were then attached to another brigade, and were fighting for two days and a night, and when we got back I inquired at the Beersheba Hospital, and was told that he was sent back to Karm ; we went back there a couple of days later, and on arrival was told he had died. I was told that his arm had been amputated, and that he was getting on well ; in fact, a little before his death he was laughing and joking with the men in the hospital, when a sudden hæmorrhage set in, and he died shortly afterwards (17 Nov. 1917). He was buried near the hospital at Karm.' "

London Gazette, 18 April, 1902.—"War Office, 18 April, 1902. The King has been graciously pleased to signify his intention to confer the Decoration of the Victoria Cross on the undermentioned Non-commissioned Officer, whose claim has been submitted for His Majesty's approval, for his conspicuous bravery in South Africa, as stated against his name."

ROGERS, JAMES, Sergt., was born in Riverina, New South Wales, Australia, on 2 June, 1875. He served in the South African War of 1899–1902, and was awarded the Victoria Cross [London Gazette, 18 April, 1902] : " James Rogers, Sergt., South African Constabulary. On the 15th June,

1901, during a skirmish near Thaba 'Nchu, a party of the rear-guard of Capt. Sitwell's Column, consisting of Lieut. F. Dickinson, Sergt. James Rogers, and six men of the South African Constabulary, was suddenly attacked by about sixty Boers. Lieut. Dickinson's horse having been shot, that officer was compelled to follow his men on foot. Sergt. Rogers, seeing this, rode back, firing as he did so, took Lieut. Dickinson up behind him, and carried him for half a mile on his horse. The sergeant then returned to within 400 yards of the enemy, and carried away, one after the other, two men who had lost their horses, after which he caught the horses of two other men, and helped the men to mount. All this was done under a very heavy rifle fire. The Boers were near enough to Sergt. Rogers to call upon him to surrender; his only answer was to continue firing." He joined the Australian Expeditionary Force on 6 Dec. 1914, and was attached to the same Brigade as the late Lieut.-Colonel Maygar in the early days of the European War. He was wounded 4 Aug. 1915, at Gallipoli, and returned invalided to Australia on 10 June, 1916. Lieut. Rogers' appointment terminated in Australia 31 Dec. 1916.

London Gazette, 13 May, 1902.—" War Office, 13 May, 1902. The King has been graciously pleased to signify His intention to confer the Decoration of the Victoria Cross on the undermentioned Officer, whose claim has been submitted for His Majesty's approval, for his conspicuous bravery in South Africa, as stated against his name."

MARTIN-LEAKE, ARTHUR, Surgeon-Captain. A bar to the Victoria Cross has been awarded on two occasions—both during the recent war. The first to gain the distinction was Lieut. A. Martin-Leake, the second was Capt. N. G. Chavasse, who unfortunately did not live to receive the reward which he had earned with such great gallantry. Both officers belonged to the Medical Profession. Arthur Martin-Leake, fifth son of Stephen Martin-Leake, of Thorpe Hall, Essex, and Marshalls, Ware, Herts, was born at Marshalls, on 4 April, 1874. He was educated at Westminster School, and University College, London, and qualified for the Medical Profession in 1898. When the South African War of 1899–1902 broke out he had recently been given charge of the District Hospital at Hemel Hempstead. As soon as it was settled to form the Imperial Yeomanry for service in South Africa he left the hospital and joined the Hertfordshire Company as a Trooper. Leake remained with this Company during its year's service in South Africa, taking part in several important engagements, notably Princeloo's surrender and the relief of Hoar's laager. When the Company went home he remained in South Africa, and was employed with the Army as a civil surgeon. Later, when the South African Constabulary was formed by General Baden-Powell, he joined that force in the rank of Surgeon-Captain, and served with it until he was invalided home on account of wounds. The following account of the action during which Surgeon-Captain Martin-Leake won his first V.C. is taken in an abbreviated form from a report by the Inspector-General, South African Constabulary. On the 8th Feb. 1902, a line of posts held by the C Division, South African Constabulary, near Van Tonders Hoek, in the Transvaal, was to be moved forward, as a force of Boers was known to be at that place. At 3.30 a.m. a reconnoitring party, consisting of 130 mounted men, under Capt. Capell, moved out and took up a position overlooking Van Tonders Hoek At daybreak Capt. Capell found himself within 400 yards of the Boer laager, and opened a heavy fire on it. The Boers were in strong force, replied by a determined attack on his front and left flank, and succeeded in rushing that flank, having come close up under cover of a donga in superior numbers. Capt. Capell withdrew a portion of his centre to a second position, whence he was able to cover the retirement of his left flank. Seeing that he was largely outnumbered by the enemy, he endeavoured to withdraw his extreme right flank, which, under Lieut. Swinburne, was holding a strong position, but the orderly conveying the message was shot while on his way, so that it never reached Lieut. Swinburne, and consequently he did not leave his post. The Boers attacked him in a determined way, but he drove them off with loss. They then sent him a message advising him to surrender, otherwise they would give him no quarter; this he declined, and held his post the whole day, up to nightfall, and then withdrew his party safely in the dark. Capt. Capell, meanwhile, being pressed by overwhelming numbers of Boers, withdrew the remainder of his force with great skill and coolness, and retired, contesting the ground, back to his line of block-houses, some seven miles distant. Capt. Capell says, in his report: " I cannot speak too highly of every officer and man, the latter being cool and splendid while in the firing line. Cases of gallantry were numerous; Capt. Leake, Medical Officer, was wounded in three places while attending Lieut. Abraham under murderous fire; Sergt. Hoffe and 2nd Class Trooper Marks distinguished themselves by their good work with Lieut. Swinburne; Corpl. Reeves, No. 4 Troop, during the retirement rode back under heavy fire, picking up a man whose horse had been shot, and was riding away with him when his own horse was shot dead; he and the other man were captured, resisting to the end; Hospital Orderly Odell, No. 5 Troop, did good service in carrying a message to Lieut. Swinburne while under fire. Our losses were heavy, viz.: 2 officers and 6 men killed; 1 officer and 10 men wounded; 24 horses killed and missing. The Boers admit they were 800 strong, and had 12 casualties. I deeply regret the loss that the Corps has sustained in the death of Lieut. D. O. P. Abraham, Lieut. A. C. Blackett, Sergt. G. Robinson, 1st Class Trooper M. H. Hutchins, Trooper McLarity, Trooper A. E. Scott, Trooper C. Morton, Trooper A. Pearl. But by their gallant self-sacrifice they have added another honour to the many which the South African Constabulary has gained for itself. I am highly pleased with the gallant and steady conduct of all ranks in this particularly trying engagement, especially as a large number of them were under fire for the first time, and I congratulate them all upon their very complete vindication of their action. The gallant conduct of Leake in tending wounded under murderous fire, and that of Corpl. Reeves, in going back under heavy fire to rescue a comrade, will be the subject of special report to the Commander-in-Chief." Surgeon-Captain A. M. Leake's name appeared in the War Office list of Casualties of 12 Feb. 1902, as " Severely wounded, right arm and left thigh." His wounds necessitated his return to England, where his right arm was very successfully operated on by the late Sir Victor Horsley. On 13 May, 1902, the following notice appeared in the London Gazette: " The King has been graciously pleased to signify His intention to confer the Decoration of the Victoria Cross on the undermentioned officer, whose claims have been submitted for His Majesty's approval, for his conspicuous bravery in South Africa, as stated against his name: Arthur Martin-Leake, Surgeon-Captain, South African Constabulary. For great devotion to duty and self-sacrifice at Vlakfontein, 8 Feb. 1902, when he went out into the firing-line to dress a wounded man under very heavy fire from about forty Boers only 100 yards off. When he had done all he could for him, he went over to a badly wounded officer, and while trying to place him in a more comfortable position he was shot three times. He only gave up when thoroughly exhausted, and then he refused water until other wounded men had been served." The Victoria Cross was presented to Surgeon-Captain Leake by King Edward VII. at St. James's Palace on 2 June, 1902. As soon as he was able to do so he resumed his professional studies, and having passed the necessary examination, was admitted a Fellow of the Royal College of Surgeons in June, 1903. In the autumn of 1903 he went to India to take up an appointment as Administrative Medical Officer of the Bengal-Nagpur Railway—an appointment which he still holds, and one which is eminently suited to his taste for all descriptions of sport and his devotion to his profession. With his headquarters at Calcutta and the facilities of a railway extending through the Central Provinces from east to west almost across India, he is able to employ much of his spare time in big game shooting, and has collected many fine trophies; as the Chief Medical Officer of the line he has under his charge a fine hospital and unlimited practice in surgery; the railway personnel provides two battalions of Infantry Volunteers, of which he is the Medical Officer. The Balkan War of 1912–13 commenced on the 8th Oct. 1912, by Montenegro declaring war on Turkey, Leake was then at home on leave from India. The formation by the British Red Cross Society of a unit for service with the Montenegran Army afforded him another opportunity for seeing active service. He managed to see a great deal of the fighting, which took place round Scutari and Tarabosh Mountain, and was awarded the Montenegran Red Cross decoration by King Nicholas. On the morning of 5 Aug. 1914, the declaration of war against Germany was known in Calcutta. Leake obtained leave of absence from his railway duties, and by good fortune found a companion—Capt. Benson, A.D.C. to the Viceroy—who was also anxious to be in time to break a lance with the Hun. They left Calcutta together on the following afternoon, and, after a few days' delay in Bombay, caused by the report that a German cruiser was in the vicinity, sailed for Europe in the P. & O. S.S. " Caledonia " on 22 Aug. 1914. As this ship was not to call at Marseilles, they landed at Malta. The question of a passage onward to Marseilles proved a difficult one. The French fleet was at Malta, and the Admiral promised to take them, but, unfortunately, just then the Fleet was ordered to the Adriatic. The authorities at Malta began to think that the procedure was irregular, and threatened shipment to England; but fortune smiled again, and an agreement with the Captain of the S.S. " Queen Eugénie," bound for Marseilles with a cargo of wheat, solved the problem. The journey came to an end at the Hôtel Bristol, Paris, on 30 Aug. 1914. This informal method of joining the Army must have taken the authorities rather by surprise; it was, however, the most critical period of the war, and not the time to make difficulties; Leake was appointed to the 5th Field Ambulance, 2nd Division, with the rank of Lieutenant. By the time he joined his unit the Germans were in full retreat from the Marne to the position which they subsequently held on the Aisne plateau. Then followed the extension northward of the French left flank, and the move of the British Army into Belgium to cover the Channel Ports. The German advance in that direction was stopped by the first battle of Ypres, which continued from 19 Oct. 1914, to 17 Nov. 1914. It was during this battle that Leake won the bar to his V.C. He was mentioned by Sir John French in his Despatch of the 14th Jan. 1915; and the London Gazette of 18 Feb. 1915, contained the following notice: " His Majesty the King has been graciously pleased to approve of the grant of the Victoria Cross to the undermentioned officers and men for conspicuous acts of bravery and devotion to duty whilst serving with the Expeditionary Force: . . . Clasp to the Victoria Cross.—Lieut. Arthur Martin-Leake, Royal Army Medical Corps, who was awarded the Victoria Cross on 13 May, 1902, is granted a clasp for conspicuous bravery in the present campaign. For most conspicuous bravery and devotion to duty throughout the campaign, especially during the period 29 Oct. to 8 Nov. 1914, near Zonnebeke, in rescuing, whilst exposed to constant fire, a large number of the wounded who were lying close to the enemy's trenches." The clasp was presented by His Majesty the King to Lieut. Martin-Leake at Windsor Castle on 24 July, 1915. He continued to serve with the Expeditionary Force, and was promoted Captain on 5 March, and Major on 27 Nov. 1915. Owing to his previous experience in the Balkans, he was selected to accompany the " Adriatic Mission " which was being despatched to assist the Serbians, then hard pressed by the Austrian invasion of their country, with supplies and medical assistance. The Mission left towards the end of Nov., but owing to the rapidity of the Serbian retreat was not able to be of much assistance. After spending some time in Italy and visiting Corfu, where numbers of refugees and sick and wounded were collected,

Arthur Martin-Leake.

Leake came home on 6 March, 1916, and returned to France on 20 March, 1916. On 3 April, 1917, he was given command of a Field Ambulance, and promoted to the temporary rank of Lieutenant-Colonel; and subsequently he commanded a Casualty Clearing Station with the 1st Army. He was mentioned by Sir Douglas Haig in his Despatch of 7 May, 1918. At the termination of his contract in Sept. 1918, Leake left the Service, and, after a short period of leave in England, returned to his appointment with the Bengal-Nagpur Railway. The British Medical Association at a meeting in June, 1915, awarded to him the Gold Medal of the Institution.

London Gazette, 8 Aug. 1902.—" The King has been graciously pleased to approve of the Decoration of the Victoria Cross being delivered to the representatives of the undermentioned Officers, Non-commissioned Officer, and men who fell during the recent operations in South Africa in the performance of Acts of Valour which would, in the opinion of the Commander-in-Chief of the Forces in the Field, have entitled them to be recommended for that distinction had they survived."

YOUNGER, DAVID REGINALD, Capt., was born 17 March, 1871, and served as an officer in the Duke of Edinburgh's Edinburgh Artillery. He was then commissioned as a 2nd Lieutenant into the Gordon Highlanders on 23 Dec. 1893. He took part in the fighting at Chitral and on the Punjab Frontier in 1895–1897 and 1898, and was present at the assault and capture of the Dargai Heights in Oct. 1897. For his services in these campaigns he received the Medal and three clasps, and after his death, in accordance with the regulations approved by H.M. King Edward VII. on 8 Aug. 1902, he was awarded the Victoria Cross, which was delivered to his relatives. [London Gazette, 28 Sept. 1900]: " (The late) David Reginald Younger, Capt., The Gordon Highlanders. In recognition of the conspicuous bravery displayed by him on the same occasion (11 July, 1900), would have been recommended to Her Majesty for the Victoria Cross had he survived." A later notice in the London Gazette of 8 Aug. 1902, reads: " Date of Act of Bravery: 11 July, 1900. This officer, during the action near Krugersdorp on the 11th July, 1900, volunteered for and took out the party which successfully dragged a Royal Artillery waggon under cover of a small kopje, though exposed to a very heavy and accurate fire at only 850 yards' range. He also accompanied the second party of volunteers who went out to try and bring in one of the guns. During the afternoon he was mortally wounded, dying shortly afterwards. His cool and gallant conduct was the admiration of all who witnessed it, and, had Capt. Younger lived, the Field-Marshal Commanding-in-Chief in South Africa would have recommended him for the high award of the Victoria Cross, at the same time as Capt. W. E. Gordon, of the same regiment."

DIGBY JONES, ROBERT JAMES THOMAS, Lieut., was born 27 Sept. 1876, son of Charles Digby Jones and Aimee Susanna Digby Jones (*née* Christie). He was educated first at Alnmouth, Northumberland, and afterwards at Sedbergh School, Yorkshire. A notice in " Rouge et Noir " (the Wilson's House periodical, published at Sedbergh) for Feb. 1900, says: " The death of R. J. T. Digby Jones . . . will have been received by all Wilsonites, past and present, with deep regret, though doubtless mingled with a certain sense of pride for an old schoolfellow who gave up his life in his country's cause; for the fact that he died the best of all deaths, fighting with conspicuous bravery for the Queen and the Flag, brings unbounded honour to Serbergh and to the House, which will always, we feel sure, be justly proud of him. He was a member of this House from May, 1890, till Dec. 1893. He was in the House Eleven for two, and the Fifteen for three, years, gaining his 1st Twelve Colours before he left. He was also a member of the House Eight, a strong swimmer and an excellent skater, and gained his 2nd Eleven Cap for his bowling in 1893. He also obtained the Sedgwick Mathematical Prize in the same year. In a word, he was a capital all-round athlete; twice in succession he won the boys' Scratch Gold Medal at North Berwick. He passed into Woolwich in 1894, thirty-fourth in order of merit, and was fifth when bifurcating for the Royal Engineers; passing out sixth in the Royal Engineer Division, and obtaining his commission on 5 Aug. 1896. After a course of instruction at Chatham he was posted to the 23rd Field Company, Royal Engineers. While at Chatham he was Secretary of the Royal Engineers' Football Club, and one of its foremost players. He was also Secretary of the Royal Engineers' Golf Club, forming one of the team in the annual inter-regimental matches with the Royal Artillery in the years 1897, 1898 and 1899, and doing the best round for the Sappers in 1899. He was promoted to Lieutenant in 1899. He accompanied the 23rd Field Company, Royal Engineers (under the command of Major S. R. Rice, R.E.) to Natal in June, 1899, proceeding straight to Ladysmith, where he was employed in the construction of a hospital in the Camp (afterwards abandoned when the siege began), and afterwards on the defences of the town. At Ladysmith, he speedily made a name for himself by blowing up with gun-cotton a 4.7 howitzer mounted on Surprise Hill, which threw a 40 lb. shell and had been causing much annoyance to the garrison. Early on the morning of the 11th Dec., five companies of the 2nd Battn. Rifle Brigade, under Colonel Metcalfe, and some Sappers and Engineers under Lieut. Digby Jones, marched out, and reached the foot of the slope before being challenged, when the order was given to fix bayonets and charge, and, under a heavy fire, the rifles moved up the slope with admirable steadiness. The Boers did not wait for the cold steel, but fled, removing the howitzer before they went, which caused a short delay. It was, however, soon found on the crest of a hill ten yards distant. Protected by a ring of rifles, Lieut. Digby Jones and his Engineers fixed charges of gun-cotton to the muzzle and breach of the howitzer and applied the fuse. Two minutes—the length of the fuse—three minutes, five minutes passed, and there was no explosion. Something must have happened to the fuse. Lieut. Digby Jones went back and lighted another. Two minutes later the muzzle of the howitzer split into fragments with a roar and a brilliant flame. The work was done, and with a loud cheer the companies of the Rifle Brigade began their march back to camp. Their return was, however, barred by the Boers, who had had plenty of time to reinforce their beaten comrades. But, using the bayonet freely, they burst through, losing 2 killed, 25 wounded, and the same number missing. The Boers admitted they had lost 28 men killed; so their actual losses must have been heavier than ours." The following account of the enemy's attack on Wagon Hill is contained in a report from Major S. R. Rice, Officer Commanding 23rd Field Company, to the Chief Engineer, Natal: " At 6.30 p.m., on the 5th Jan. 1900, a party of 33 N.C.O.'s and men of the 23rd Company left our camp at Ladysmith for night work on Wagon Hill, W. Lieut. R. J. T. Digby Jones was the Officer in Charge. Their duties were to make a second (or upper) emplacement for a naval 12-pr. gun; to assist in mounting a 4.7-inch gun, which was coming that night from Junction Hill, in the sunken emplacement already prepared; and to fix a platform in the lower 12-pr. emplacement. A working party of 50 Infantry was also provided for Lieut. Digby Jones. They joined at Wagon Hill without arms, and left at 2.30 a.m. on the 6th on completion of the work required of them. A party of 10 R.N. under Mr. Sim, R.N., assisted by a working party of 100 infantry, was detailed for the movement of the 4.7-inch gun. In addition, an escort of 70 infantry was provided. The permanent garrison of that end of Wagon Hill consisted of 25 Imperial Light Horse, with 2 officers. At about 5 a.m. on the 6th a report reached our camp that the enemy were on Wagon Hill, and that Lieut. Jones's detachment had been captured. This was the first intimation we (R.E.) had of any attack. The firing of guns had been heard for some time previously, but at that period of the siege this was not an unusual occurrence. In case of attack the orders were for the C.R.A., C.R.E., etc., to proceed to headquarters. But in view of the report I thought it best to ascertain personally what had occurred, so I rode out as quickly as possible, meeting Lieut. Digby Jones on the top of Wagon Hill at 5.45 a.m. Our men were then lining the front ridge of the plateau (Wagon Hill, W.), exchanging a hot fire with the enemy on their front and left flank; and Major Miller-Wallnutt, Gordon Highlanders, was present and in charge. Second Lieut. G. B. B. Denniss, the R.E. officer detailed by me for duty with that section of the defences, had already arrived. Lieut. Digby Jones gave me a very clear and full report of what had occurred within his observation up to the time of my arrival. I have also heard the statements of various N.C.O.'s and men of his party. In the following brief account of what occurred throughout the day I have relied on these reports in connection with anything recorded that did not come within my personal observation. On the arrival of the various parties at Wagon Hill, W., on the night of the 5th, work proceeded as usual until 2.45 a.m. on the 6th, when, without previous warning, musketry fire was opened on them from the outer crest-line of Wagon Hill proper, on their left flank, at a distance of about 150 yards. At that time Lieut. Digby Jones and about 25 of his party were working at the upper 12-pr. emplacement. The remaining 8 were fixing the platform in the lower 12-pr. emplacement at the W. extremity of the hill, distant about 70 yards. Digby Jones at once ordered the party to stand to their arms, which were piled by them; kicked over the lanterns, which were evidently attracting the enemy's fire; extended his men from right to left, and opened fire in return on the place whence they were being fired upon. The R.N. who were near the 4.7-inch emplacement also stood to their arms, under Mr. Sim. The party of Imperial Light Horse also fell in with their officers. Some of the Gordon Highlanders fell in with Digby Jones' party. Naturally a good deal of hurry and confusion occurred at first; but none of the parties mentioned above ever left, or were driven off, the top of the hill. Both I.L.H. officers were wounded almost at once, and Lieut. Digby Jones took command, remaining in charge of the various parties until 5.15 a.m., when reinforcements (I.L.H. and Gordon Highlanders, under Major Miller-Wallnutt) commenced to arrive. Shortly after the action opened Digby Jones pushed his men forward about 40 yards, with bayonets fixed, and occupied the outer crest of the hill; the I.L.H. also moved forward; and the R.N. party, with 8 sappers, occupied the lower 12-pr. emplacement and the outer crest of the right flank. The reinforcements, on arrival, took up practically the same positions, and absorbed the original defenders. In my official report to the Chief Staff Officer I brought to notice the steadiness of the men and the great coolness and resource shown by Lieut. Digby Jones in the trying circumstances in which he was suddenly called upon to act. I think I may draw attention, too, in this account to the value of the rule, which obtains in this unit, of never allowing the men, under any circumstances, to leave their camp for work without taking their arms with them, and of insisting on the arms being piled close to them whilst at work. Firing on both sides continued heavily before and after my arrival on the spot. We (R.E.) had several casualties at this time, principally from the fire of a small party of the enemy (about 15, I was told) who were lying among the rocks on our left flank, on the outer slopes of Wagon Hill proper, about 200 yards off. Other units suffered equally. At about 9 a.m. it was decided to attempt to turn out these men by a bayonet charge by the troops on Wagon Hill proper, and at Major Miller-Wallnutt's request, I formed a section of R.E. and R.N. at the lower 12-pr. emplacement, to support the charge by firing volleys on a knoll about 900 yards on our left front, whence the enemy were protecting by their rifle-fire their comrades above mentioned. I placed Mr. Sim, R.N., in charge of this party. The attempt was made and failed, Lieut. Todd, King's Royal Rifles, being killed. Shortly afterwards firing on both sides slackened, and at about 10.15 a.m. ceased almost entirely. The situation then appeared to be that the attack had been completely beaten off. I was informed that it had been decided to

R. J. T. Digby Jones.

leave the small party of the enemy on the outer slopes of Wagon Hill proper until nightfall, when they could be effectually dealt with. They were considered to be cut off from the rest of their force. This assumption afterwards proved to be wrong, as they could be, and were, reinforced under cover of the banks of a donga which ran almost up to the position they occupied. At about 11.15 a.m. I rode into Ladysmith to report myself to headquarters. Before leaving, I told Lieut. Digby Jones that if Major Miller-Wallnutt had no objection, he might collect his men near the 4.7-inch emplacement, and give them some food which I had sent for. This he did, and fortunately so, as the party was reformed in time for the attack made shortly afterwards. After reporting at headquarters, I returned to Wagon Hill, arriving there about 1.30 p.m. Near the 4.7-inch emplacement I met some of my men. The senior N.C.O. reported to me that both Digby Jones and Denniss were killed, and that they had had several other casualties. It appears that about midday the attack was renewed. A small party of Boers suddenly appeared within a few yards of the men on the outer crest, about fifteen yards from the 4.7-inch emplacement, evidently having ascended unperceived from the lower part of the outer slope. After a few rounds a panic seized the defenders, and they retired in disorder and confusion to the rear crest, and in some cases down the rear slope of the hill. Two Boers (Field Cornets de Villiers and de Jagers, I believe) then advanced to the 4.7-inch emplacement, in and around which Digby Jones and his detachment were resting and having some food. Apparently the retirement of the infantry defenders had been unnoticed by them, and the first intimation they had of the enemy being on the top of the hill was a shot, delivered over the parapet at a distance of a few feet, which killed Second Corpl. Hunt, R.E. In a moment Digby Jones picked up a rifle, dashed round the end of the epaulement, and killed de Villiers. L.-Corpl. Hockaday, R.E., at the same time shot de Jagers dead. Digby Jones was then heard to say, 'What's up? The infantry have gone.' A man replied: 'There is an order to retire, sir.' Jones said: 'I have had no order to retire.' A sergeant of the I.L.H. who was near him said: 'Don't let's retire, sir; let's give them Elandslaagte again.' I think this sergeant's name was Howard; he was killed afterwards. Digby Jones at once ordered bayonets to be fixed, and, calling on his men to follow him, led them (with Denniss) at the charge, reoccupying the firing-line in front of the 4.7-inch emplacement. Some Boers were seen by our men disappearing down the slope as they advanced. Heavy firing recommenced on both sides. After a short time the men who had been driven from the front were reinforced and moved forward into their places again. I think it was then that Major Miller-Wallnutt was unfortunately killed, but I am not sure as regards this point. At all events, the sappers were ordered back to the 4.7-inch emplacement, and were gradually withdrawn as the infantry came up. These latter had no officer with them (owing to casualties, I believe), and Digby Jones, acting under orders, went out to the centre of the ridge with the object of moving the men well forward at that point to their proper firing position. While performing this duty he was struck by a bullet in the throat, which killed him immediately. Shortly afterwards Denniss was heard to say, 'I hear Mr. Digby Jones is hit; I am going to see to him.' He was afterwards seen moving about on the sky-line carrying a stretcher. I found the bodies of these two most brave and promising young officers lying close to each other, about fifteen yards in front of the upper 12-pounder emplacement. At about 6.30 p.m., with the approval of General Ian Hamilton, I sent into Ladysmith for a fresh detachment of 33 N.C.O.'s and men with two officers; they were brought out by Lieut. Turner. On their arrival I took what remained of Lieut. Digby Jones's party back to camp, which they reached at 10.30 p.m. after 28 hours' continuous work and fighting. I returned to Wagon Hill at midnight in anticipation of further fighting, but none occurred. The names of several N.C.O.'s and men were specially mentioned by me in my official report; and I think it will be admitted that all of Lieut. Digby Jones's party did their duty in a way that reflects credit on themselves and their corps. The following were our losses: Killed—Lieut. R. J. T. Digby Jones, 2nd Lieut. G. B. B. Denniss, Sergt. C. Jackson, 2nd Corpl. R. Hunt, L.-Corpl. H. Bailey, and Sappers Simmons, Bland and Cox. Wounded—Sappers McCarron, Powell, Catchpole, Hudson and Rutt." Sir Arthur Conan Doyle says of the fighting on Wagon Hill: "There fought the gallant De Villiers, while Ian Hamilton rallied the defenders and led them in repeated rushes against the enemy's line. Continually reinforced from below, the Boers fought with extraordinary resolution. Never will anyone who witnessed that Homeric contest question the valour of our foes. It was a murderous business on both sides. Edwardes of the Light Horse was struck down. In a gun emplacement a strange encounter took place at point-blank range between a group of Boers and of Britons. De Villiers of the Free State shot Miller-Wallnutt dead. Ian Hamilton fired at De Villiers with his revolver and missed him. Young Albrecht of the Light Horse shot De Villiers. A Boer named De Jaeger shot Albrecht. Digby Jones of the Sappers shot De Jaeger. Only a few minutes later the gallant lad, who had already won fame enough for a veteran, was himself mortally wounded, and Denniss, his comrade in arms and in glory, fell by his side." The "South African Review" (24 Feb. 1900), in a paragraph on Lieut. Digby Jones, says: "So far as can be humanly judged, it was this officer who saved Ladysmith and the British arms from the mortification of a defeat and its incalculable consequences." General Ian Hamilton, who had witnessed Lieut. Digby Jones's gallant and resourceful conduct throughout the day, decided to recommend him for the Victoria Cross, which recommendation was fully approved by Sir George White and brought forward in his despatch. The London Gazette of 8 Aug. 1902 says: "Robert James Thomas Digby Jones, Royal Engineers; H. Albrecht, No. 459, Trooper, Imperial Light Horse. Would have been recommended for the Victoria Cross had they survived, on account of their having during the attack on Wagon Hill (Ladysmith), on 6 Jan. 1900, displayed conspicuous bravery and gallant conduct in leading the force which reoccupied the top of the hill at a critical moment just as the three foremost attacking Boers reached it, the leader being shot by Lieut. Jones and the two others by Albrecht." The Victoria Cross was given to Lieut. Digby Jones's relatives in accordance with the regulations of 8 Aug. 1902. The writer in "Rouge et Noir" remarks that it is rather a striking circumstance that his younger brother, O. G. Digby Jones, obtained his commission in the R.E. on the very day on which his brother was killed."

ALBRECHT, H., Trooper, "was," says Sir Ian Hamilton, "a very fine young fellow and very good looking at that. His uncle was in command of the artillery of the Orange Free State." "The Times History of the War in South Africa" (Vol. III., page 197) says: "Ian Hamilton, Wallnutt, Capt. Fitzgerald, Sergt. Lindsay, and Trooper Albrecht, I.L.H., Gunner Sims, R.N., and others threw themselves against the stream of panic-stricken men and checked their flight. Then they sprang forward to the crest. A dozen Boers had leapt on to the summit. But in the teeth of a hail of bullets from the Imperial Light Horse fort, 200 yards away, all but three hung back. The three, De Villiers, De Jager and Gert Wessels, rushed forward. There was a wild race for the gun-pits. Hamilton reached the 4.7 emplacement first, and, leaning his arm on the sandbag parapet, fired his revolver at the nearest Boer. Almost immediately Albrecht fired from outside the pit, while, at the same moment, from the other gun-pit rose the head and shoulders of Digby Jones and of Corpl. Hockaday, R.E., each firing at his man. De Villiers and De Jager fell dead against the wall of the 4.7 gun-pit, Wessels at the lower emplacement. Miller-Wallnutt fell, shot through the head, as he reached the 4.7 gun-pit; the brave Albrecht a second later." Sir A. Conan Doyle says, in his "Great Boer War" (page 228): "There has been no better fighting in our time than that upon Waggon Hill on that January morning, and no better fighters than the Imperial Light Horsemen who joined the centre of the defence. Here, as at Elandslaagte, they proved themselves worthy to stand in line with the crack regiments of the British Army." Trooper Albrecht was awarded the Victoria Cross by King Edward, for which he would have been recommended had he lived. London Gazette, 8 Aug. 1902: "Robert James Thomas Digby Jones, Lieut., Royal Engineers, and No. 459, Trooper H. Albrecht, Imperial Light Horse. Would have been recommended for the Victoria Cross had they survived, on account of their having during the attack on Waggon Hill (Ladysmith) on 6 Jan. 1900, displayed conspicuous bravery and gallant conduct in leading the force which reoccupied the top of the hill at a critical moment just as the three foremost attacking Boers reached it, the leader being shot by Lieut. Jones and the two others by Albrecht." The Victoria Cross was given to Sergt. Albrecht's representatives in accordance with the regulations of 8 Aug. 1902.

COULSON, GUSTAVUS HAMILTON BLENKINSOPP, Lieut. and Adjutant, was born at Wimbledon, Surrey, on 1 April, 1879, the only son of H. J. W. Coulson, of Newbrough Hall, Northumberland, and of Caroline Unwin, daughter of Henry Unwin, Esq., Bengal Civil Service. He was a great-grandson of Colonel Blenkinsopp Coulson, of Blenkinsopp Castle, Northumberland, one of a family of distinguished soldiers. He joined the 4th Battn. (Princess of Wales's Own) Yorkshire Regt., but left it in his twenty-first year to enter the King's Own Scottish Borderers in July, 1899. In Jan. 1900, he went on active service to South Africa, and for his services in this campaign he was mentioned in Despatches by Lords Roberts and Kitchener, received the Medal with five clasps, and was created a Companion of the Distinguished Service Order [London Gazette, 27 Sept. 1901]: "Gustavus Hamilton Blenkinsopp Coulson, Lieut., King's Own Scottish Borderers." He was also awarded the Victoria Cross after his death by King Edward, for his gallantry near Lambrechtfontein, when he rallied his men and saved the guns in a rearguard action, as well as saving his servant's life. He was mortally wounded on this occasion. The decoration was handed to Lieut. Coulson's representative, and was gazetted 8 Aug. 1902: "Gustavus Hamilton Blenkinsopp Coulson, D.S.O., Lieut. and Adjutant, King's Own Scottish Borderers, 7th Mounted Infantry. Date of Act of Bravery: 18 May, 1901. This officer, during a rearguard action near Lambrechtfontein, on the 18th May, 1901, seeing Corpl. Cranmer, 7th Mounted Infantry, dismounted, his horse having been shot, remained behind and took him up on his own horse. He rode a short distance, when the horse was shot, and both Lieut. Coulson and the corporal were brought to the ground. Lieut. Coulson told Corpl. Cranmer to get along with the wounded horse as best he could, and he would look after himself. Corpl. Cranmer got on the horse and rode away to the column. No. 4792, Corpl. Shaw (Lincolns), 7th Mounted Infantry, seeing Lieut. Coulson's position of danger, rode back through the rearguard and took him up on his horse. A few minutes later Corpl. Shaw was shot through the body, and there is reason to believe that Lieut. Coulson was wounded also, as he fell off his horse. Corpl. Shaw fell off a few minutes later. This officer on many occasions throughout the campaign displayed great coolness and gallantry under fire." The act for which the Victoria Cross was awarded to Lieut. Coulson was performed under the immediate command of Major F. C. Lloyd (of the Lincolns) and Colonel T. D. Pilcher, C.B., A.D.C. (late of the 2nd Bedfordshire Regt.). Lieut. Coulson was killed at Lambrechtfontein, Orange River Colony, on 18 May, 1901, aged 22. The following is a copy of a letter written by Colonel (now Major-General) T. D. Pilcher, C.B.:

Gustavus H. B. Coulson.

"Bloemfontein,
"24/5/01.

"DEAR MR. COULSON,

"You will doubtless have received news of the death of Lieut. Coulson, and I write in the name of all the officers and men of the column which I command to tell you how sincerely we feel his loss and how much we admire the way in which he died. It may also be some poor consolation to you to know that before I heard of his death I recommended him for the Victoria Cross. On 19 May Lieut. Coulson, as Adjutant of the 7th M.I., about 300 strong (which with a pompom was acting independently under Major Lloyd), went back to see that the camp they were leaving at Lambrechtfontein, about fifteen miles south of Bothaville, was clear of ammunition, etc. At this time the rearguard were attacked, and the enemy pressed on them. Lieut. Coulson rallied some men, and by his action saved a Maxim gun from falling into the enemy's hands. He afterwards galloped closer under the enemy's fire and got a wounded man on to his horse; the horse was shot. Corpl. Shaw, Lincoln Regt., helped Lieut. Coulson on to his own horse, but after galloping a short distance felt himself hit through the back and felt Lieut. Coulson fall off. Corpl. Shaw managed to get to our carts, though severely wounded. Colonel Godfray is giving me your address. I am asking Major Lloyd, commanding 7th M.I., to write to you. Lieut. Coulson's body was buried on the scene of action by Dr. May, whom I sent back with an ambulance. The enemy suffered more severely than Major Lloyd and party, for six dead Boers were found in one place, and the enemy did not succeed in taking any of our convoy. Please accept my sincerest sympathy in the loss of one whom I knew as a gallant, capable and hard-working officer, and believe me,

"Yours sincerely,

"T. D. PILCHER."

ATKINSON, ALFRED, Sergt., was born at Leeds, the son of Farrier-Major James Atkinson, H Battery, 4th Brigade, Royal Artillery (who is said to have been one of the party who captured the original cannon from which the Victoria Cross is now cast). He rejoined the Colours from the Reserve at the outbreak of the South African Campaign in 1899–1902, and five months before his death in the heroic service recorded below. Besides the Victoria Cross (which was given to him in accordance with the regulation of 8 Aug. 1902), Sergt. Alfred Atkinson was entitled to the Queen's Medal with clasps for Kimberley (Relief) and Paardeberg, where he fell. His Victoria Cross was gazetted 8 Aug. 1902: "A. Atkinson, No. 3264, Sergt., 1st Battn. The Yorkshire Regt. Date of Act of Bravery: 18 Feb. 1900. During the Battle of Paardeberg, 18 Feb. 1900, Sergt. A. Atkinson, 1st Battn. Yorkshire Regt., went out seven times, under heavy and close fire, to obtain water for the wounded. At the seventh attempt he was wounded in the head, and died a few days afterwards."

BARRY, J., Private, was born at St. Mary's Kilkenny, 1 Feb. 1873; entered the Royal Irish Regt. 1 Dec. 1890, and saw active service in India, receiving the India Medal, 1895, with clasps for services on the North-West Frontier, Sawana, 1897, and Punjab, 1897–98. He served in the South African Campaign, received the South African Medal with clasps for Belfast, Cape Colony and Winterbergen, and was killed in action at Monument Hill 8 Jan. 1901. For his gallantry in this action he was subsequently awarded the Victoria Cross, which was delivered to his representatives by order of King Edward VII., and in accordance with the regulation of 8 Aug. 1902: "J. Barry (the late), No. 3733, Private, 1st Battn. The Royal Irish Regt. During the night attack on the 7th–8th Jan. 1901, on Monument Hill, Private Barry, although surrounded and threatened by the Boers at the time, smashed the breach of the Maxim gun, thus rendering it useless to its captors, and it was in doing this splendid act for his country that he met his death."

London Gazette, 15 Aug. 1902.—"War Office, 15 Aug. 1902. The King has been graciously pleased to signify His intention to confer the Decoration of the Victoria Cross on the undermentioned Soldier, whose claim has been submitted for His Majesty's approval, for his conspicuous bravery in South Africa, as stated against his name."

IND, ALFRED ERNEST, Shoeing-Smith, is the son of Mr. George Ind, of Tetbury, Gloucestershire, where he was born on 16 Sept. 1872. He entered the Royal Horse Artillery on 19 Feb. 1901; served in the South African War of 1899–1901, and was awarded the Victoria Cross [London Gazette, 15 Aug. 1902]: "Alfred Ernest Ind, Shoeing Smith, Royal Horse Artillery, 11th Section Pompoms. Date of Act of Bravery: 20 Dec. 1901. During the action near Tafelkop, Orange River Colony, on the 20th Dec. 1901, Shoeing-Smith A. E. Ind, 11th Section Pompoms, stuck to his gun under a very heavy fire, when the whole of the remainder of the pompom team had been shot down, and continued to fire into the advancing Boers till the last possible moment. Capt. Jeffcoat, who was mortally wounded on this occasion, requested that Shoeing-Smith Ind's gallant conduct in this, and in every other action since he joined the Pompom Section should be brought to notice." He was mentioned in Despatches and promoted Corporal after Tafelkop, and was once wounded and mentioned in Despatches on three other occasions. Corpl. Shoeing-Smith Ind was decorated with the Victoria Cross by King Edward VII. at Buckingham Palace on 26 Nov. 1902. He was later a member of the celebrated battery known as the "Chestnut Troop," and is now discharged on pension.

London Gazette, 7 Oct. 1902.—"War Office, 7 Oct. 1902. The King has been graciously pleased to signify His intention to confer the Decoration of the Victoria Cross on the undermentioned Soldier, whose claim has been submitted for His Majesty's approval, for conspicuous bravery in South Africa, as stated against his name."

HOUSE, WILLIAM, Private, was born on 7 Oct. 1879, at Park Lane, Thatcham, Berkshire, the son of Mr. Thomas House, of that place. He entered into the Royal Berkshire Regt. on 3 Nov. 1896. His Victoria Cross was gazetted on his twenty-third birthday, 7 Oct. 1902,

William House.

and he was decorated by King Edward VII. on 24 Oct. 1902, in London. He also received both the Queen's and King's Medals, with clasps. [London Gazette, 7 Oct. 1902]: "William House, Private, 2nd Battn. The Royal Berkshire Regt. Date of Act of Bravery: 2 Aug. 1900. During the attack on Mosilikatse Nek, on the 2nd Aug. 1900, when a sergeant, who had gone forward to reconnoitre, was wounded, Private House rushed out from cover (though cautioned not to do so, as the fire from the enemy was very hot), picked up the wounded sergeant, and endeavoured to bring him into shelter, in doing which Private House was himself severely wounded. He, however, warned his comrades not to come to his assistance, the fire being so severe. The grant of the Medal for Distinguished Conduct in the Field to Private House, which was notified in the London Gazette of the 27th Sept. 1901, is hereby cancelled." He died by his own hand at Dover, when apparently cleaning his rifle, 28 Feb. 1912, shooting himself through the head, in which he had been already twice wounded at the time when he won the Victoria Cross.

London Gazette, 20 Jan. 1903.—"War Office, 20 Jan. 1903. The King, has been graciously pleased to signify His intention to confer the Decoration of the Victoria Cross on the undermentioned Officer, whose claim has been submitted for His Majesty's approval, for conspicuous bravery in Somaliland, as stated against his name."

COBBE, ALEXANDER STANHOPE, Lieut.-Colonel, was born 5 June, 1870, the son of the late Lieut.-General Sir A. H. Cobbe. He was educated at Wellington, and entered the South Wales Borderers (24th Regt.) as 2nd Lieutenant in 1889. He became Lieutenant in 1892; was transferred to the Indian Staff Corps in the same year, and served in the Chitral Relief Force in 1895; was mentioned in Despatches and received the Medal with clasp. He served in the Angoniland Expedition in 1898 (Medal with clasp); in the Expedition against Kwamba in 1899 (mentioned in Despatches). In 1900 he served in Ashanti, was severely wounded, was mentioned in Despatches twice, and received the Brevet of Lieut.-Colonel, and was created a Companion of the Distinguished Service Order. His Victoria Cross was gazetted 20 Jan. 1903: "Alexander Stanhope Cobbe, Capt. (local Lieut.-Colonel), D.S.O., 1st Central Africa Battn. King's African Rifles, Indian Army. During the action at Erego, on the 6th Oct. 1892, when some of the companies had retired, Lieut.-Colonel Cobbe was left by himself in front of the line with a Maxim gun. Without assistance he brought in the Maxim, and worked it at a most critical time. He then went out under an extremely hot fire from the enemy about twenty yards in front of him, from his own men (who had retired about the same distance behind), and succeeded in carrying in a wounded orderly. Colonel Swayne, who was in command of the force, personally witnessed this officer's conduct, which he described as most gallant." The decoration was presented to him by General Mannering on 22 Feb. 1903, at Obbia. In 1910 he married Winifred, eldest daughter of A. E. Bowen, Coleworth, Bedfordshire. He has been a General Staff Officer, 1st Grade, India, since 1910. He has served in the European War since 1914, been mentioned in Despatches three times, and created a C.B., and been promoted Major-General, and appointed a Temporary Lieutenant-General. In Lieut.-General Sir S. Maude's Despatch [London Gazette, 10 July, 1917] he describes the capture of Baghdad, and specially mentions Lieut.-General Cobbe's services: "While crossing at Shumran was proceeding, Lieut.-General Cobbe had secured the third and fourth line at Sannaiyat. . . . While these events were happening at Shumran, Lieut.-General Cobbe cleared the enemy's sixth line at Sannaiyat, the Nakhailat and Suwada positions, and the left bank as far as Kut, without much opposition. The pursuit was broken off at Aziziyeh (fifty miles from Kut and half-way to Baghdad), where the gunboats, cavalry and Lieut.-General Marshall's infantry were concentrated during the pause necessary to reorganize our extended line of communication preparatory to a further advance. Lieut.-General Cobbe's force closed to the front, clearing the battle-fields and protecting the line of march." Sir S. Maude says later that the British flag was hoisted over the city. "In the afternoon the gunboat flotilla, proceeding up stream in line ahead formation, anchored off the British Residency, and the two forces under Lieut.-Generals Marshall and Cobbe provided for the security of the approaches to the city, being disposed one on either bank of the river." A brief account is given of the pursuit of the Turks which followed the occupation of the city. On the right bank of the Tigris the retreating enemy had entrenched a strong position south of Mushaidie railway station, some twenty miles from Baghdad. A force under Lieut.-General Cobbe carried this on 14 March, after a brilliant charge by the Black Watch and Gurkhas. Lieut.-General A. S. Cobbe was created a K.C.B. in 1917.

London Gazette, 7 Aug. 1903.—"War Office, 7 Aug. 1903. The King has been graciously pleased to signify His intention to confer the Decoration of the Victoria Cross on the undermentioned Officers, whose claims have been submitted for His Majesty's approval, for their conspicuous bravery in Somaliland, as stated against their names."

WALKER, WILLIAM GEORGE, Capt., was born at Naina Tal, India, 29 May, 1863, son of Deputy-Surgeon-General W. Walker, I.M.S. He was educated at Haileybury, and St. John's College, Oxford (M.A. Oxford), and was gazetted to the Suffolk Regt. on 29 Aug. 1885, becoming Lieutenant, Indian Staff Corps, 28 May, 1887. He became Captain 29 Aug. 1896. He served in the Miranzai (2nd) Expedition, 1891, receiving the Medal and clasp, and in the Waziristan Expedition in 1895 (clasp). In 1903 and 1904 he served in East Africa, taking part in the operations in Somaliland. He was present at the actions at Daratoleh and Jidballi; was mentioned in Despatches [London Gazette, 7 Aug. 1903], and Despatches (Brigadier-General Manning, 17 Aug. 1903, and Sir C. C. Egerton, 30 May, 1904) [London Gazette, 2 Sept. 1904]; was given the Brevet of Lieut.-Colonel 7 Sept. 1904; received the Medal with two clasps, and was awarded the Victoria Cross [London Gazette, 7 Aug. 1903]: "William George Walker, Capt., Indian Army, and George Murray Rolland, Capt., Indian Army, Berbera Bohottle Flying Column. During the return of Major Gough's column to Donop on the 22nd April last, after the action at Daratoleh, the rearguard got considerably in rear of the column, owing to the thick bush, and to having to hold their ground while wounded men were being placed on camels. At this time Capt. Bruce was shot through the body from a distance of about twenty yards, and fell on the path unable to move. Capts. Walker and Rolland, two men of the 2nd Battn. King's African Rifles, one Sikh, and one Somali of the Camel Corps were with him when he fell. In the meantime the column, being unaware of what had happened, were getting farther away. Capt. Rolland then ran back some 500 yards, and returned with assistance to bring off Capt. Bruce, while Capt. Walker and the men remained with that officer, endeavouring to keep off the enemy, who were all round in the thick bush. This they succeeded in doing, though not before Capt. Bruce was hit a second time, and the Sikh wounded. But for the gallant conduct displayed by these officers and men, Capt. Bruce must have fallen into the hands of the enemy." The London Gazette of 7 Aug. 1903, also says: "The King has also been pleased to approve of the grant of the medal for Distinguished Conduct in the Field to the undermentioned soldiers in recognition of their gallant conduct in assisting Capts. Walker and Rolland to save Capt. Bruce from falling into the enemy's hands: No. 66, Sergt. Nderamani, 2nd Battn. King's African Rifles; No. 87, Corpl. Surmoni, 2nd Battn. King's African Rifles; Sowar Umar Ismail, Somali Camel Corps, 6th Battn. King's African Rifles. The services of the Sikh, Lance-Naik Maieya Singh, 24th Beluchistan Regt., Indian Contingent, British Central Africa (who also assisted), have been brought to the notice of the Government of India." Capt. Walker was promoted to Major, 29 Aug. 1903. He became Lieut.-Colonel, Indian Army, 6 Jan. 1904. He became Commandant, 1st Battn. 4th Gurkhas in 1910, and was promoted to Colonel 1 Jan. 1911. Colonel Walker served in the European War from 1914 to 1917; was Temporary Brigadier-General from 3 Jan. 1915, to 5 Nov. 1915, and Temporary Major-General 5 Nov. 1915, to 31 Dec. 1915. He became Major-General on 1 Jan. 1916. He was created a C.B. in 1914 (mentioned in Despatches three times). On 23 Feb. 1907, in Melbourne, Australia, he married Alice Elaine Molesworth, daughter of Judge Molesworth, and they have a son, George Anthony Gilbert, born 7 March, 1909, and a daughter, Lynette Alice Estree.

William George Walker.

ROLLAND, GEORGE MURRAY, Capt., was born at Wellington, India, 12 May, 1869, son of Major Patrick Murray Rolland, R.A., and Albinia Crofton. (Mrs. Murray Rolland wrote several successful novels.) He was educated at Harrow and Sandhurst, and on 9 Nov. 1889, joined the 2nd Battn. Bedfordshire Regt. as Second Lieutenant, becoming Lieutenant in 1891, and Captain 9 Nov. 1900. In August, 1901, he joined the Indian Army. He was Adjutant of the 1st Bombay Grenadiers from 1894 to 1901, and was with the Somaliland Field Force from Oct. 1902, to June, 1903, acting as Intelligence Officer to the Berbera Bohottle Flying Column, and Staff Officer to Major J. E. Gough's Column. A letter written by Capt. G. M. Rolland gives an account of the Battle of Daratoleh: "It was a grand fight, and for four hours our little band of 200 stood shoulder to shoulder in a tiny little square, being thirty yards on each side, with a hail of bullets falling all round us. Our ammunition was running short, so at 2.30 a.m. (the action began at 10.30 a.m.) Major Gough decided to retire. A horde of savages followed us for three more hours, coming to within fifteen to thirty yards of us. It was a tight corner. Major Gough is a splendid soldier, so cool and calm; he is a grand fellow. Poor Capt. Bruce and I were on the rearguard together—both Harrow boys. The bush was so dense we could hardly see a yard in it. We were left behind with four men, so Bruce called out, 'Rolland, come along with those men,' and we retired slowly, firing as we went. A savage crept up close to the path along which we were marching; owing to the dense grass and bush we did not notice it. Poor Capt. Bruce suddenly threw up his arms and fell on his face, shot through the body. The bullet entered his right side and passed out by the left. I saw the savage moving off; my carbine was on him in a second, and he rolled over. I can't tell whether he was actually the man who shot Capt. Bruce, but I saw no other, so think it must have been him. I ran to Capt. Bruce and raised him up, turning him on his back. He was bleeding terribly, and I saw at a glance that it was a mortal wound. I dragged him a little out of the path, which was much exposed to the enemy's fire, and undid his collar, taking off his bandolier, revolver and belt, while the four brave men covered me with their fire and kept the enemy in check, who were yelling with delight as they saw one white man dying and another close to him, and they kept calling out to each other. (I was told after by the Somali who fought by me that they were saying that they had got us all, and to come on and spear us.) Capt. Bruce was a very heavy man, of nearly fourteen stone, and I am only nine stone, so I could not lift him. None of the men could stop firing to help me, or the enemy would have been on us, so I shouted to the disappearing column, 'Halt in front!' It was then out of sight, slowly retiring along the winding path, and we were practically cut off. It was a moment of great despair, as I thought my shout had not been heard. The enemy were now pressing us very hard, so I had to stop attending to poor Capt. Bruce, and emptied the magazine of my carbine at them. Then I fired off my revolver and emptied that too. Suddenly Capt. Bruce stood up, and I rushed to hold him up. He walked two steps forward and fell on his face again. I tried to break his fall, and he brought me down too, as he was too heavy for me. I again turned him on his back. He opened his eyes and spoke to me (his last words): 'They have done for me this time, old man!' From now to his death he was practically unconscious. To my infinite relief I then saw Capt. Walker trekking towards me. He and I tried to carry Capt. Bruce, but it was no use, so then I left them and ran back 400 yards or more to where the rearguard was, to fetch help. It was a terribly long run, and I thought I must get hit every moment, as the bullets fell splashing round me. I seized a Bikanir camel, and was running back with it, when Major Gough came up and asked what was the matter. I told him, and he rushed back to Capt. Bruce. I followed slower, as the led camel refused to step out, and I could not induce mine to hurry up—in fact, he was frightened, and did not like to leave his friends. I reached the little group, and made the camel sit down, and we lifted up Capt. Bruce, Major Gough at his head, and Capt. Walker and I at his feet. While doing so three bullets struck the ground between us. One went through poor Capt. Bruce's leg, but he was too far gone to feel it. Then the Sikh, who had done his duty nobly, had his arm smashed by a fourth bullet. We had to throw Capt. Bruce on the camel anyhow, and as we did so the poor fellow died. The two Yaos (Africans), the Somali and the Sikh made up the four who helped us, and they did their work well. It was a wonder to me that out of our little group only the Sikh was wounded. I thought all the time that not one of us would escape, and that we should have fallen. However, we saved Capt. Bruce's body, and we could only regret that we could not save his life; but I knew when he fell that he had received his death-wound, and that all that we could save from falling into the enemy's hands would be his body, and I thank God we were able to do that, for he would have been mutilated had those savages got hold of him. He was a dear chap, a great friend of mine, and an old Harrow chum.—R.I.P. Well, we were not left alone till 5.30 p.m., and then the enemy drew off. It was the hardest day of my life. I fired and fired in that fight, till my rifle was boiling hot; even the woodwork felt on fire. Up to 3 a.m. a few biscuits and cocoa, then a twenty-five mile ride, a seven hours' fight, and twenty-five miles back to the camp—i.e., fifty miles that day; twenty-five hours without food of any kind, between the 3 a.m. biscuits and cocoa on the 22nd to the 4 a.m. dinner on the 23rd. Oh, the thirst of that day! I had two water-bottles on my camel, and drained them both. Hunger I did not feel. That march home was a terrible one! The smell of the dead bodies and the blood on our empty stomachs made us feel so sick, and as I rode up and down from the front to the rear of the column and back I passed the bodies of Capts. Bruce and Godfrey tied on to camels, and swaying about helplessly. Oh, it was a heartrending sight to me to see all that remained of two strong healthy men, who only that morning were so full of life and spirits! We reached Donop again at 2 a.m., and when I got off my camel I reeled from tiredness, which up to then I had not felt. However, I was given brandy and water, and then I had to go off and arrange for the dead to be laid out and placed under a guard for that night, to prevent hyænas attacking them. The wounded had to be looked to and made comfortable. Next morning, at 8 a.m., we buried Capts. Bruce and Godfrey side by side, just as they were, in their khaki uniforms. Major Gough read the service, and we all stood round. It was a most impressive funeral—a soldier's always is—but this one was unusually so. Not one of us could have spoken after it was over without breaking down, and we all walked away from the grave with silent, bowed heads. Half an hour later we were ourselves again, for there is not time in a soldier's life for grief. We were one and all busy with our respective work. I had only one suit of khaki with me, so, as it was covered with blood, I had to go and have it washed and dried, and went about practically naked while it took place." For his services on this occasion Capt. Rolland was awarded the Victoria Cross [London Gazette, 7 Aug. 1903]: "George Murray Rolland, Capt., Indian Army, Berbera Bohottle Flying Column. During the return of Major's Gough column to Donop on the 22nd April last, after the action at Daratoleh, the rearguard got considerably in rear of the column, owing to the thick bush, and to having to hold their ground while wounded men were being placed on camels. At this time Capt. Bruce was shot through the body from a distance of about twenty yards, and fell on the path unable to move. Capts. Walker and Rolland, two men of the 2nd Battn. King's African Rifles, one Sikh, and one Somali of the Camel Corps were with him when he fell. In the meantime the column, being unaware of what had happened, were getting farther away. Capt. Rolland then ran back some 500 yards, and returned with assistance to

George Murray Rolland.

bring off Capt. Bruce, while Capt. Walker and the men remained with that officer, endeavouring to keep off the enemy, who were all round in the thick bush. This they succeeded in doing, though not before Capt. Bruce was hit a second time and the Sikh wounded. But for the gallant conduct displayed by these officers and men, Capt. Bruce must have fallen into the hands of the enemy." In 1906 Major Rolland joined the Nagpur Volunteer Rifles as Adjutant, and he did much towards promoting the strength and proficiency of the corps. He died at Nagpur, Central Provinces, India, in 1910, from the effects of a fall. His funeral, we are told, was one of the grandest ever witnessed in Nagpur, and "testified to the esteem and regard in which the deceased officer was held by all classes, to whom he was always easily accessible. The coffin, which was covered with the Union Jack, was placed on a gun-carriage. In addition to the Nagpur Volunteers, who mustered strong, two companies of the Manchesters with band from Kamptee, arrived by special train. The Honourable the Chief Commissioner and all the principal civil and military officers of the station were present. The deceased officer . . . will long be remembered with affectionate regard by the Nagpur Volunteer Rifles, whom he so faithfully served. The funeral service was conducted by the Lord Bishop of Nagpur, assisted by the Venerable the Archdeacon. The Manchesters formed the firing party, and as the remains were lowered to their last resting-place three volleys were fired. Thus passed away a good man, whose untimely death is sincerely deplored by a large section of the public." Mrs. Murray Rolland erected a memorial brass to the memory of her only son in St. Stephen's Church, South Kensington.

London Gazette, 11 Sept. 1903.—" War Office, 11 Sept. 1903. The King has been graciously pleased to signify His intention to confer the Decoration of the Victoria Cross on the undermentioned Officer, whose claim has been submitted for His Majesty's approval, for conspicuous bravery during the Kano-Sokoto Expedition in West Africa, as stated against his name."

WRIGHT, WALLACE DUFFIELD, Lieut., was born at Gibraltar on 20 Sept. 1875, son of the late Mr. James Sykes Wright. He was gazetted to the 1st Battn. The Queen's Regt. on 9 Dec. 1896, and served on the

Wallace Duffield Wright.

North-West Frontier of India with the Malakand Field Force and Tirah Expeditionary Force in 1897 and 1898 ; was severely wounded, and received the Indian Medal (1895) with clasps for Punjab Frontier and Tirah. He was promoted to Lieutenant on 13 Sept. 1898. From 30 Oct. 1901, to 27 May, 1904, he was employed with the West African Frontier Force, under the Colonial Office, in Northern Nigeria. He was again wounded, received the African General Service Medal, and was awarded the Victoria Cross for services performed when under the command of Colonel Morland, C.B., D.S.O. The decoration was gazetted [London Gazette, 11 Sept. 1903] : "Wallace Duffield Wright, Lieut., Northern Nigeria Regt. Date of Act of Bravery : 24

March, 1903. On the 24th March, 1903, Lieut. Wright, with only one officer and forty-four men, took up a position in the path of the advancing enemy, and sustained the determined charges of 1,000 horse and 2,000 foot for two hours. and when the enemy, after heavy losses, fell back in good order, Lieut. Wright continued to follow them up till they were in full retreat. The personal example of this officer, as well as his skilful leadership, contributed largely to the brilliant success of this affair. He in no way infringed his orders by his daring initiative, as, though warned of the possibility of meeting large bodies of the enemy, he had been purposely left a free hand." The Victoria Cross was presented to Capt. Wright on 5 Nov. 1903. He had been promoted to Capt. on the 22nd Jan. 1903. He passed the Staff College, and was General Staff Officer, 3rd Grade, War Office, from 2 April, 1909, to 15 Aug. 1911. From 16 Aug. 1911, to 1 April, 1913, he was Brigade Major, 3rd Brigade, Aldershot Command. From 28 Jan. 1914, Capt. Wright became General Staff Officer, 2nd Grade, and was again employed with the West African Frontier Force. He served in the European War, in the Cameroons, from 1914, and on the Western Front in France from 1916 to 1919, when he held in turn the following appointments : G.S.O.2, 55th Division ; G.S.O.1., 18th Division ; Brigadier-General, Staff, 17th Army Corps ; Brigadier-General in command of the 89th Infantry Brigade. He married on 9 Aug. 1919, in Paris, Flora MacDonald Bewick, daughter of the late Richard Henry Bewick, and of Mrs. Edward I. Donnelly, of Atlanta, Georgia, U.S.A. He was given the Brevet of Major 24 July, 1915 ; became Major, Royal West Surrey Regt. 1 Sept. 1915 ; was given the Brevet of Lieut.-Colonel 1 Jan. 1916, and became Colonel by Brevet on 1 Jan. 1919. He was created a Companion of St. Michael and St. George in 1916, and was created a Companion of the Distinguished Service Order in 1918. Brigadier-General W. D. Wright was mentioned in Despatches five times.

London Gazette, 15 Jan. 1904.—" War Office, 15 Jan. 1904. The King has been graciously pleased to signify His intention to confer the Decoration of the Victoria Cross on the undermentioned Officer, whose claim has been submitted for His Majesty's approval, for conspicuous bravery in Somaliland, as stated against his name."

GOUGH, JOHN EDMUND, Capt. and Brevet Major, was the younger son of the late Sir Charles Gough, V.C., and nephew of the late General Sir Hugh Gough, V.C. This was the only instance when three members of the same family won the Victoria Cross. He first saw active service in British Central Africa in 1896–97, with the Expedition against Chitsusi and

Chilwa. In 1898 he was present at the Battle of Khartoum, and afterwards served through the South African War, taking part in the defence of Ladysmith, and in the actions of Laing's Nek, Belfast and Lydenburg.

John Edmund Gough.

He was three times mentioned in Despatches, received the Brevet of Major, and the Queen's and King's Medals with five clasps. In 1902 and 1903 he again saw service in Somaliland, when he won the Victoria Cross [London Gazette, 15 Jan. 1904] : "John Edmund Gough, Capt. and Brevet Major, The Rifle Brigade. Date of Act of Bravery : 22 April, 1903. During the action at Daratoleh, on the 22nd April, 1903, Major Gough assisted Capts. Walker and Rolland in carrying back the late Capt. Bruce (who had been mortally wounded), and prevented that officer from falling into the hands of the enemy. Capts. Walker and Rolland have already been awarded the Victoria Cross for their gallantry on this occasion, but Major Gough (who was in command of the

column) made no mention of his own conduct, which has only recently been brought to notice." Lieut. Bruce had been mortally wounded during the retreat of 200 men who were short of ammunition and exhausted by want of food and water, before a large force of Somali. They rode back with four native soldiers through a hail of bullets, and, being cut off from the retreating column, fought through the enemy and succeeded in mounting Lieut. Bruce on a camel. Eventually they brought him and Capt. Godfrey, who was mortally wounded, into camp. Gough saw much service as a Staff officer. From 1907 to 1909 he was Inspector-General of the King's African Rifles, and after four years as a General Staff Officer, 1st Grade, at the Staff College, he was appointed Brigadier-General, General Staff, Aldershot Command. Brigadier-General J. E. Gough, V.C., C.B., C.M.G., A.D.C., died on 22 Feb. 1915, at Estaires, of wounds received two days earlier, aged 43 years. An obituary notice of him appeared in the " Times " of 24 Feb. 1915.

London Gazette, 7 June, 1904.—" War Office, 7 June, 1904. The King has been graciously pleased to signify His intention to confer the Decoration of the Victoria Cross on the undermentioned Officer, whose claim has been submitted for His Majesty's approval, for conspicuous bravery in Somaliland, as stated against his name."

SMITH, CLEMENT LESLIE, Lieut., was born on 17 Jan. 1878, son of the Rev. Canon Clement Smith, M.V.O., M.A., Rector of Whippingham and Chaplain in Ordinary to the King, and of Mary Eliza, daughter

Clement Leslie Smith.

of the late Stephen Spurling. He was gazetted to the Duke of Cornwall's Light Infantry, from the Volunteers, on 5 May, 1900, and served on the Staff in the South African War in 1901 and 1902, receiving the Queen's Medal and five clasps. On 9 Aug. 1902, he was promoted to Lieutenant. In 1904 he served in Somaliland, 15 May, 1903, to 12 June, 1904, on the Staff, as Special Service Officer, being present at the action at Jidballi ; was mentioned in Despatches ; received the Medal and two clasps, and was awarded the Victoria Cross [London Gazette, 7 June, 1904] : "Clement Leslie Smith, Lieut., 2nd Battn. The Duke of Cornwall's Light Infantry. Date of Act of Bravery : 10 Jan. 1904. At the commencement of the fight at Jid-

balli, on the 10th Jan. 1904, the enemy made a very sudden and determined rush on the 5th Somali Mounted Infantry from under cover of bushes close at hand. They were supported by rifle-fire, advanced very rapidly, and got right amongst our men. Lieut. Smith, Somali Mounted Infantry, and Lieut. J. R. Welland, M.D., Royal Army Medical Corps, went out to the aid of Hospital Assistant Rahamat-Ali, who was wounded, and endeavoured to bring him out of action on a horse, but the rapidity of the enemy's advance rendered this impossible, and the hospital assistant was killed. Lieut. Smith then did all that any man could do to bring out Dr. Welland, helping him to mount a horse, and when that was shot, a mule. This also was hit, and Dr. Welland was speared by the enemy. Lieut. Smith stood by Dr. Welland to the end, and when that officer was killed, was within a few paces of him, endeavouring to keep off the enemy with his revolver. At that time the Dervishes appeared to be all round him, and it was marvellous that he escaped with his life." He was employed with the Egyptian Army from 15 Nov. 1905 ; served in the Sudan in 1910, and received the Medal and clasp. He was promoted to Captain 8 Jan. 1916. Capt. Smith served in the European War from 1914 ; was employed with the Egyptian Army 14 Nov. 1915, to 17 Jan. 1916 ; became Major, Duke of Cornwall's Light Infantry, 8 Jan. 1916. The London Gazette of 25 April, 1916, says : " The Nuba Mountains.—The King has conferred the Military Cross on the following officers in recognition of their distinguished service in the field from April to June, 1915, during the operations against Jebel Miri, Kadugli District, Nuba Mountain, Province of the Sudan : Capt. (now Major) Clement Leslie Smith, V.C., Duke of Cornwall's Light Infantry, and commanding the Camel Corps. . . ." Major Smith was given the Brevet of Lieutenant.-Colonel. He became Temporary Lieutenant.-Colonel, April, 1916, and in Dec. 1916, was appointed to command the Imperial Camel

Brigade, with the rank of Temporary Brigadier-General. He was transferred from the Imperial Camel Brigade to the command of the 24th Infantry Brigade, 10th Division, on the disbandment of the Imperial Camel Brigade, June, 1918. In June, 1919, he was given the Brevet of Colonel.

London Gazette, 9 Dec. 1904.—" The King has been graciously pleased to signify His intention to confer the Decoration of the Victoria Cross upon the undermentioned Officer, whose claim has been submitted for His Majesty's approval, for his conspicuous bravery in Somaliland, as stated against his name."

CARTER, HERBERT AUGUSTINE, Lieut., was born 26 May, 1874, at Exeter, second son of the late Rev. Conway R. D. Carter, Vicar of St. Erth, Cornwall, and of Mrs. Conway Carter. He was educated by private

Herbert A. Carter.

tuition, and obtained his first commission in the Duke of Cornwall's Light Infantry in May, 1897. He served throughout the operations against the Zakka Khel (Tirah Campaign), 1897–98, under General Sir William Lockhart, K.C.B., K.C.S.I., and received the Medal and two clasps. In 1899 he was transferred to the Indian Army, and joined the Indian Staff Corps, and in 1901 was seconded for active service in Somaliland with the King's African Rifles, and went in pursuit of the Mullah's raiding party to Adadhero. He served during the operations in Somaliland, 1902–4, under Lieut.-General C. C. Egerton, C.B., D.S.O., and was present at the action of Jidballi. For his services in this campaign he was first gazetted to a Companionship of the Distinguished

Service Order, and this was cancelled when Lieut. Carter was awarded the Victoria Cross [London Gazette, 9 Dec. 1904] : " Herbert Augustine Carter, Lieut., Indian Army, No. 6 Company, Indian Mounted Infantry. During a reconnaissance near Jidballi, on the 19th Dec. 1903, when the two sections of the Poona Mounted Infantry and the Tribal Horse were retiring before a force of Dervishes, which outnumbered them by thirty to one, Lieut. Carter rode back alone, a distance of 400 yards, to the assistance of Private Jai Singh, who had lost his horse and was closely pursued by a large number of the enemy, and taking the sepoy up behind him, brought him safely away. When Lieut. Carter reached Private Jai Singh, the sections were several hundred yards off. In consequence of the above, the appointment of this officer to the Distinguished Service Order, which was notified in the London Gazette of 7 June, 1904, is cancelled." The sepoy was so badly wounded that it was only after three attempts that Lieut. Carter was able to get him up on to his horse. Lieut. Carter also received the Medal with clasps and was mentioned in Despatches. In 1908 he was appointed O.C., Indian Contingent, King's African Rifles ; proceeded to India to raise a new Indian Contingent, and returned to Somaliland with the same in 1909. He served through the East African Campaign in 1908–10 in Somaliland, under Colonel J. E. Gough, V.C., in command of the Indian Contingent, taking part in the operations against the Mullah and the action of Tigra. On the 19th Oct. 1909, he was mentioned in Despatches by the Secretary of State for the Colonies, by whom the following report was sent to the India Office :

" Colonial Office,
" Downing Street,
" London, S.W.
" 19 Dec. 1909.
" Sir,—I am directed by the Earl of Crewe to transmit to you, for the information of the Secretary for India in Council, a copy of (From Commission 26 Oct. to Commmission 19 Nov.) Correspondence, with the Commissioner of Somaliland on the subject of a Dervish attack on the transport of the Indian Camel Company of the 6th Battn. King's African Rifles, and to request you to call attention of Lord Morley to the commendation of Capt. H. A. Carter, V.C., Indian Army.
" I am, etc.
(Sd.) " G. W. Fiddes.
" The Under-Secretary of State, India Office."

The Officer Commanding Troops, Somaliland Protectorate, also wrote his appreciation of the manner Capt. Carter dealt with the situation. The 1908–10 Somaliland operations were of a very exceptional nature, and he controlled the advanced Line of Communications—Indian Contingent—and Camel Corps while commanding at Burao, at one and the same time. In 1910 he was appointed to the Egyptian Army ; attached to the 15th Sudanese, and posted to the Blue Nile District as Commandant of Roseires and Kurnak. During that time he commanded the Soda Patrol, fighting in the action of Jebel Ferri. Major Carter was a fine big game shot, as the number of his trophies testifies. Upon one occasion when after big game in Somaliland, a lion, which had been badly wounded, sprang out of the jungle upon Capt. H. O'Neill, and got him down on to the ground. Seeing this, Capt. Carter immediately went up quite close to it, and shot it dead with his last cartridge. On 2 Feb. 1911, at St. James's, Piccadilly, he married Helen Lilian Wilmot Ware, youngest daughter of the late Rev. Canon Wilmot Ware, Rector of Barnborough, Yorkshire, and of Mrs. Wilmot Ware. After his marriage he resigned his appointment in the Egyptian Army, and rejoined the 101st Grenadiers for duty in Bangalore. In 1913 he went as an Attaché to Army Headquarters Staff, Simla. H.E. the Viceroy having presented new Colours to the 101st Grenadiers at Bangalore in Nov. 1913, Major (then Capt.) Carter, in March, 1914, pro-

ceeded to Poona with a Colour party of the regiment for the laying up of the old Colours in St. Mary's Church, Poona—to be placed over the tablet to the memory of the late Major Rolland, V.C., of the regiment. This was to prove to be his last military duty in India, as a few days afterwards he left India on leave for England, never to return. At the outbreak of the war Major Carter, who had obtained his Majority on 15 May, 1914, was on leave in England, and, being retained, was posted to the New Army and did much useful work with the 10th and 16th Service Battns. of the Durham Light Infantry. During that time he was recommended for the command of the 2/7th Service Battn. West Yorkshire Regt. by the County Association, with rank of Lieut.-Colonel ; but his services were not considered to be available on account of officers of the Indian Army not being allowed at that time to accept any permanent appointment which might prevent them from returning at any moment to an Indian regiment. Shortly afterwards he was ordered to join the Indian Expeditionary Force in France, and was attached to the 40th Pathans, proceeding with them later to British East Africa. Immediately upon arrival at Mombassa, although suffering from fever—at what ultimately proved to be the cost of his life—he took command of a relief column of the 40th Pathans on a forced march under great heat and difficulties, ordered to the relief of Mwele Mdogo. His unflinching determination and stern sense of duty triumphed over his physical state, and exhausted though he was through fever and severe trials on account of lack of water and dense bush—and with several bad fever cases on stretchers—he successfully reached his objective on the second day ; but the effort was more than an exhausted nature could withstand, and he breathed his last on 13 Jan. 1916. Ever ready for self-sacrifice at the call of duty, he thus died an heroic death. In connection with this, the following extracts from letters received are interesting as indicating the arduousness of the duty :

" EXTRACT FROM BATTALION ORDERS,

By Colonel E. S. V. Grimshawe,
Commanding 16th (2nd Res.) Battn. The Durham L.I.,
Rugeley Camp, Tuesday, May 9th, 1916.

" NOTICE.

" The Commanding Officer regrets to announce the death of Major H. A. Carter, V.C., late of the 101st Grenadiers, Indian Army, and of this Battalion, which occurred in East Africa on 13 Jan. last, from exhaustion.
" Major Carter, immediately on landing at Mombassa, was ordered on a forced march under great heat, with a company of the 40th Pathans, to relieve a post up country, which he successfully accomplished, and he died a gallant officer, whose devotion to duty will always remain an example to all ranks, to whom his personality had so endeared him."

General Tighe, Commanding the Troops in British East Africa, wrote as follows : " The post was seriously threatened, and the Arab garrison quite demoralized after their defeat and the death of Major Wavell. I know only too well the hardships your gallant husband and his men must have endured in marching to the relief of Mwele across that burning waterless tract of country, and how it must have been torture to a man not in the best of health. It shows what a splendid spirit he possessed."
Capt. E. Segar, of the 40th Pathans, wrote : " We also know that we have lost a thoroughly good leader, and I am sure that this is a serious loss to the Empire, as he was such a wonderful example to us all. I have already learned what a good example can do. During all the march, Major Carter, though probably as tired (at least) as anyone, was the most energetic and determined of us all, and he never rested at any halt until he had seen everything done that was to be done. I know that his experience of war would have been most useful out here, and he was most anxious to attack and turn out the Germans. All ranks feel his loss acutely, and he will certainly be remembered." Lieut. R. Thornton (now Capt. Thornton, M.C.), of the 40th Pathans, wrote as follows : " He seemed buoyed up with the thought that in spite of all, he had done what he had been told to do, in spite of the stupendous difficulties of having unfit men straight off a ship, and unacclimatized to the heat. We could never have done it without his indomitable courage forging ahead of the column, and just making us follow him. He seemed to imbue us all with his bravery, and, as I say, without him to lead us we could never have got there." Colonel P. H. Cunningham, the Officer Commanding, the 101st Grenadiers, wrote as follows : " To lose one's best and dearest is a dreadful thing. But we all think that the loss is softened by the splendid way your husband carried out the orders given to him without any regard for his own feelings, although really quite ill. We have in the Mess a photograph of himself wearing his V.C., and, when in conjunction with his last march, the regiment will remember with pride how he carried out his duty and more." Colonel W. Mitchell, the Officer Commanding the 40th Pathans, wrote : " For myself, I feel that I have lost a friend for whom, for many years, I have always had the greatest esteem and admiration. I had known him so well in Somaliland, where he had always shown such dash and bravery, that I had welcomed his coming to the regiment with the very greatest pleasure, and I was full of confidence that he would have been of the greatest help to me in this new country with his great experience as a soldier. He always inspired the greatest affection in his comrades and those under his command, as I know well from my experience with him in Somaliland. You will, I know, be glad to hear that the Pathans of his Double Company, with whom he had endeared himself during the short time he commanded them, insisted on carrying him to his last resting-place. You may be sure we all condole with you in your sorrow, and in our loss of a very gallant comrade." Major Carter's body was brought home and buried in St. Erth Churchyard, Cornwall. The following is an account of the landing of his body at Plymouth :

"HONOUR TO THE HEROIC DEAD."

(Extracts from the "Western Daily Mercury," Saturday, 6 May, 1916.)

"There was an impressive scene in the Great Western Docks at Plymouth upon the occasion of the landing of the mortal remains of a Cornish hero, a soldier who nearly thirteen years ago won the glorious and much-prized V.C. With all the pomp and ceremonial associated with such an occasion, all that is mortal of Major H. A. Carter, V.C., formerly of the Duke of Cornwall's Light Infantry, but afterwards of the 101st Grenadiers, was brought ashore. When the body of Major Carter was landed, the troops gravely and solemnly saluted in traditional form, but the majority of them knew that they had assembled to honour the final home-coming of one who years before had won the greatest distinction in the profession of arms, and now had made the great sacrifice for his King and country. How Major Carter won the V.C. is one of the thrilling stories of the Army. It was at Jidballi, when he was a Lieutenant, that he rode back alone and saved the life of a wounded sepoy—and it can be relied that the example he set that day in Somaliland has borne good fruit among the troops of the Indian Army. Such deeds of heroism and gallantry explain in a large measure the devotion of the Indian troops who fought so well and sacrificed so much in Flanders in the early days of the war, and in other spheres of activity in the days that have followed. Since then native soldiers have won the V.C. for risking their lives to save British officers, and, maybe, the Cornish soldier who is to be laid in a few days' time in a hero's grave in the soil that he loved, has done much to inspire that feeling of self-sacrifice and devotion to duty that has characterized our Indian troops."

A War Memorial Shrine was erected at St. Erth, Cornwall, to his memory —and to the memory of the Fallen from that Parish—by his widow, and was unveiled by Capt. Sir Hugh Molesworth St. Aubyn, Bart., representing the Duke of Cornwall's Light Infantry—this being Major Carter's first regiment. His widow also erected to his memory a bronze Relief by Mr. Bertram MacKennal, M.V.O., A.R.A., in York Minster, with the following inscription:

"Major Herbert Augustine Carter, V.C.,
The 101st Grenadiers, Indian Army.
He successfully led a Relief Column of the 40th Pathans on a forced march of two days under great heat and difficulties to the Relief of Mwele Mdogo, sacrificing his life in this glorious devotion to duty, 13 Jan. 1916."

The unveiling ceremony took place on 13 July, 1917, when the Memorial (which portrays Major Carter on his last march) was dedicated by the Dean of York, and unveiled by General Horatio Mends, C.B. Upon the occasion of the unveiling of the memorial in York Minster, General Mends spoke as follows: "In this glorious Minster there are many memorials to gallant warriors, and now another has been added, which is in itself a notable adornment, but which also signifies an addition to the roll of those whose lives are honourably commemorated as an example to the living as well as a memento of the past. Herbert Augustine Carter, in his all too short a life, was indeed an example of all that a soldier should be. Obtaining his commission in the Duke of Cornwall's Light Infantry in May, 1897, within a year he had served in the Tirah Campaign, receiving the Medal and two clasps. In 1899 he transferred to the Indian Army, and in 1902 proceeded on active service in Somaliland with the King's African Rifles, winning the Medal and clasps and the crowning honour of the Victoria Cross under the following circumstances: During a reconnaissance of the 19th Dec. 1903, two sections of the Poona Mounted Infantry and Tribal Horse were retiring before a force of Dervishes outnumbering them by 30 to 1. A wounded Sikh soldier had lost his horse and was being closely pursued by a number of the enemy. Lieut. Carter rode back some three hundred yards, charged and scattered the enemy, and, after three attempts, succeeded in getting the wounded man on his horse and bringing him in. He was mentioned in Despatches, as he was again in those of the campaign of 1908–10, in which he commanded the Indian Contingent. In 1910 he was appointed to the Egyptian Army, and again saw fighting in the Soudan. In 1911, having married, he rejoined his regiment, the 101st Grenadiers, in India. In May, 1914, he obtained his majority, and being in England at the beginning of the war, was attached to the 10th and the 16th Service Battns. of the Durham Light Infantry. From the latter he went to France. He there joined the 40th Panthans, and went with them to East Africa once more. Although suffering from fever, he went in command of a relief column of the regiment to Mwele Mdogo, by forced marches, and in great heat. The garrison, composed of Arabs, was demoralized by defeat and the death of Major Wavell, and the long march across a burning, waterless desert would have been trying to a man in robust health. How much more to one weakened by fever? An officer of the column wrote: 'He was such a wonderful example to us all. . . . During the march, Major Carter, though probably as tired (at least) as anyone, was the most energetic and determined of us all, and he never rested at any halt until he had seen to everything that was to be done.' One of the officers of the relieved garrison wrote: 'At five o'clock the column was seen wending its way down from the hills, and half an hour later we greeted Major Carter with an advance party of about fifty men. He was obviously quite done up, though bearing himself strongly, and quite cheerful. His first thoughts were of the enemy, and he asked eagerly of their positions, strength and other details.' He wished to attack at once, but was dissuaded. That was the end of the story. From sheer exhaustion he sank down, and passed away within a few hours. Strong and powerful as was his frame, it was too weak for such a heart. Another officer writing home, said: 'He seemed buoyed up by the thought that, in spite of all, he had done what he was told to do, in spite of the stupendous difficulties of having unfit men straight off a ship and unacclimatized. We could never have done it without his indomitable courage forging ahead of the column, and just making us follow him. He seemed to imbue us all with his bravery.' These extracts from letters by soldiers, so simply telling the tale of great heroism and leadership, give with unmatchable eloquence the nature of the man. Quiet, determined, brave to a fault, he possessed that sympathy and consideration for those under his command that ensured the ready gift of all their strength, energy, and even life itself. In letting their minds dwell on the loss to the nation of such an officer, they could not but think of what it meant to his devoted wife, who had given that Memorial. She followed him to East Africa to be near him who was her pride and everything in the world to her, and she underwent great peril by the ship she was on being sunk by the enemy. Rescued after being nineteen hours in an open boat, and joining her husband in Egypt, they went together to Mombassa, from whence Major Carter started on his last expedition. To his widow they could only hope that time would lessen the sorrow, with which all must sympathize, though the pride would ever remain undiminished. The flag which covered his remains during his long journey home to England veiled the beautiful memorial, which is now committed to you, Mr. Dean. It is by a great artist, to the memory of a great gentleman and valiant soldier, who gave his life for his country, and was an example of all that was best in the qualities of those who have made it great. God grant that it will ever find its sons ready to keep it so, and to follow in the footsteps of him whom we now commemorate by this memorial."

London Gazette, 24 Jan. 1905.—"War Office, 24 Jan. 1905. The King has been graciously pleased to signify His intention to confer the Decoration of the Victoria Cross upon the undermentioned Officer, whose claim has been submitted for His Majesty's approval, for his conspicuous bravery in Thibet, as stated against his name."

GRANT, JOHN DUNCAN, Lieut., was born at Roorkee, India, on the 28th Dec. 1877, the son of Colonel Suene Grant, R.E. He was educated at Manor House School, Hastings; Cheltenham College, and Sandhurst, and entered the Army 22 Jan. 1898, as 2nd Lieutenant, unattached, but he joined the Indian Staff Corps, 1899; was Lieutenant, Indian Army, in 1900. He served in Tibet in 1903 and 1904; was wounded; mentioned in Despatches; received the Medal and won the Victoria Cross [London Gazette, 24 Jan. 1905]: "John Duncan Grant, Lieut., 8th Gurkha Rifles. On the occasion of the storming of the Gyantse Jong on the 6th July, 1904, the storming company, headed by Lieut. Grant, on emerging from the cover of the village, had to advance up a bare, almost precipitous rock-face, with little or no cover available, and under a heavy fire from the curtain, flanking towers on both sides of the curtain, and other buildings higher up the Jong. Showers of rock and stones were at the time being hurled down the hillside by the enemy from above. One man could only go up at a time, crawling on hands and knees, to the breach in the curtain. Lieut. Grant, followed by Havildar Karbir Pun, 8th Gurkha Rifles, at once attempted to scale it, but on reaching near the top he was wounded and hurled back, as was also the Havildar, who fell down the rock some thirty feet. Regardless of their injuries, they again attempted to scale the breach, and, covered by the fire of the men below, were successful in their object, the Havildar shooting one of the enemy on gaining the top. The successful issue of the assault was greatly due to the splendid example shown by Lieut. Grant and Havildar Karbir Pun. The latter has been recommended for the Indian Order of Merit." On 19 Jan. 1907, at All Saints' Church, Margaret Street, London, he married Kathleen Mary Freyer, daughter of Lieut.-Colonel P. J. Freyer, C.B., M.D., I.M.S. They have two children: Hugh Duncan, born 3 June, 1908, and Madeline. In 1907 he was promoted Captain. He was Brigade-Major, 35th Brigade, I.E.F. "D.," 30 Nov. 1915, to 13 Jan. 1916; was wounded at Orah (Mesopotamia) 13 Jan. 1916, and mentioned in Despatches.

London Gazette, 15 Jan. 1907.—"War Office, 15 Jan. 1907. The King has been graciously pleased to approve of the Decoration of the Victoria Cross being delivered to the representatives of the undermentioned Officers and men who fell in the performance of Acts of Valour, and with reference to whom it was notified in the London Gazette that they would have been recommended to Her late Majesty for the Victoria Cross had they survived."

SPENCE, EDWARD, Private, served in the Indian Mutiny, and was awarded the Victoria Cross by King Edward [London Gazette, 15 Jan. 1907]: "Edward Spence (deceased), Private, 42nd Regt. Date of Act of Bravery: 15 April, 1858. Private Edward Spence, 42nd Regt., would have been recommended to Her Majesty for the decoration of the Victoria Cross had he survived. He and L.-Corpl. Thompson of that regiment, volunteered at the attack of the fort of Ruhya, on the 15th April, 1858, to assist Capt. Cafe, commanding the 4th Punjab Rifles, in bringing in the body of Lieut. Willoughby from the top of the glacis. Private Spence dauntlessly placed himself in an exposed position, so as to cover the party bearing away the body. He died on the 17th of the same month, from the effects of the wound which he received on the occasion." The above account formerly appeared in the Gazette of 21 Oct. 1859. The Victoria Cross was given to Private Spence's representatives.

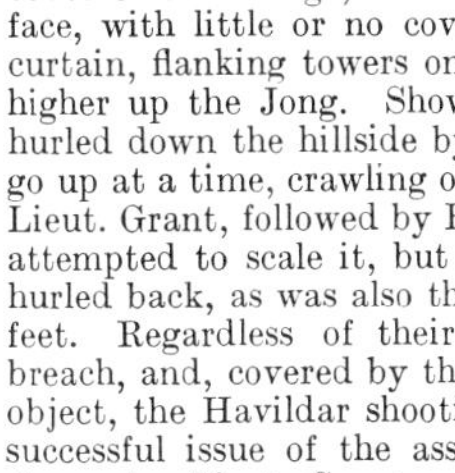

E. A. Lisle Phillipps.

LISLE PHILLIPPS, EVERARD ALOYSIUS, Ensign, was born in 1835, at Garendon Park, Leicestershire, being the second son of Ambrose Lisle March

Phillipps de Lisle, J.P., D.L. for Leicestershire, of Garendon Park and Gracedieu Manor, and of his wife, Laura Mary, daughter of the Honourable Thomas Clifford and his wife, Baroness Philipina von Lützow. Thomas Clifford was the fourth son of Hugh, fourth Lord Clifford of Chudleigh. Of Everard Lisle Phillipps's eight brothers, two still survive: Edwin Joseph Lisle March Phillipps de Lisle, formerly of Charnwood Lodge, Leicestershire, the last Conservative and Unionist M.P. for Mid-Leicestershire, who sat from 1886 to 1892, and Gerard Lisle March Phillipps de Lisle, of Garendon Farm, near Lloydminster, Saskatchewan, Canada; and of his seven sisters, the Honourable Mrs. Arthur Strutt, of Milford, Bournemouth. His nephew, Lieut.-Colonel Everard March Phillipps de Lisle, is the present proprietor of Garendon Park and Gracedieu Manor. The subject of this notice was educated at St. Edmund's College, Old Hall Green, near Ware, and at Oscott College, near Birmingham, and having learned Hindustani in Paris, joined the Company's Army (11th Regt., Bengal Infantry) in India in 1855. He reached Meerut on 4 May, 1857, and on the 10th of May, when the Mutiny broke out, his regiment joined it, and "Colonel Finnis was killed by his side; but he remained unhurt, though he had been called upon to read the address in Hindustani." He was given a commission in the Royal Army, in the 60th Rifles, as a reward for gallantry, the rigid rule of purchase of commissions notwithstanding. This was done on the application of Colonel Jones, who made him his orderly officer. In the "Life and Letters of Ambrose Phillipps de Lisle," by E. S. Purcell and Edwin de Lisle, is quoted a letter from Dr. (afterwards Cardinal) Newman, written from the Oratory at Birmingham on 30 July, 1857, in which he said: "We are praying here for your dear son. How anxious you must be." Everard was at that time fighting with the Queen's forces in the Indian Mutiny, and six weeeks after this letter was written he was killed in the streets of Delhi, on the last day of the siege. The London Gazette of the 21st Oct. 1859, contained the following notice: "Everard Aloysius Lisle Phillipps (deceased), 11th Regt. Bengal Infantry. Memorandum.—Ensign Everard Aloysius Lisle Phillipps, of the 11th Regt. of Bengal Infantry, would have been recommended to Her Majesty for the decoration of the Victoria Cross had he survived, for many gallant deeds which he performed during the Siege of Delhi, during which he was wounded three times. At the assault of that city he captured the Water Bastion, with a small party of men; and was finally killed in the streets of Delhi on the 18th Sept." This posthumous honour was finally awarded to him by King Edward VII., as is recorded in the London Gazette of 15 Jan. 1907, and his Victoria Cross was given to the elder of his two surviving brothers, Mr. Edwin de Lisle, F.S.A., in 1907, exactly fifty years after his death. In the charming memoir of his brother, Lieut. Rudolph de Lisle, R.N. (written by the late Rev. Henry Nutcombe Oxenham, M.A., who was killed at the Battle of Abu Klea, serving in the Naval Brigade, in the heroic attempt to relieve General Gordon and Khartoum, reference is made to Everard's many gallant deeds, for the two brothers were much alike in their martial characteristics, as well as for the domestic qualities which endeared them, not only to their own families and friends, but also to all who came in contact with them. Lord Beresford said of Rudolph: "A finer officer never stepped on board one of Her Majesty's ships," and the same might have been said of Everard, *mutatis mutandis*. Everard's untimely but glorious death made a great sensation in Leicestershire, and a fine Gothic tower of rough-hewn granite was built to perpetuate his memory on the top of one of the rocks in High Cadman Wood in Charnwood Forest, overlooking Gracedieu and the villages of Whitwick and Coalville, and can be seen from miles around. Few soldiers in England have such a fine and enduring monument. There is also a handsome brass to his memory in the beautiful chapel at Oscott College. A very appreciative article was published in the French "Correspondent" soon after his death. He was known in Paris, together with his elder brother Ambrose, as friends of the celebrated Count de Montalembert, religious writer and politician, and they used to attend the brilliant parties given by the Emperor Napoleon III. and Empress Eugénie, when their Court at the Tuileries was the centre of European gallantry and fashion. But it was as a young man of energy and sterling character that he was esteemed the most. Mr. Edwin de Lisle (who supplies much of the material for this short biography) says of his gallant brother that he was "a very keen sportsman and cricketer, a most affable and sympathetic friend, very energetic in all that he undertook, and a devout and sincere Roman Catholic Christian." Everard's picture, standing by his favourite charger, King David, which he left to his friend Hugh Gough (afterwards General Sir Hugh Gough, V.C., G.C.B.), was painted for the first Victoria Cross Exhibition by Des Anges, and now hangs in the dining-room at Garendon over the Gothic chimney-piece Both the brothers died in contests with the powerful forces of Islam, and it is interesting to note that their father, Ambrose L. M. Phillipps de Lisle, a fierce denouncer of Turkish misgovernment, author of "Mahomedanism in its relation to Prophecy," the ardent advocate of the Reunion of Christendom, and promoter of the Catholic Revival in the Established Anglican Church, erected the first wayside crucifix in England since the Reformation on Tullylog Rocks, near Thringstone, and placed the first cross on a Communion table in an Established Church since the Commonwealth. This was done at Shepshed, Leicestershire, in 1835, shortly before he joined the Roman Catholic Communion. The cross, a plain black one, with a white line running round it, was removed by the Bishop of Peterborough, "as savouring of Popery," and is still preserved at Garendon; but the movement thus begun has fructified to such an extent that now scarce anyone objects; memorial crosses mark the graves of Catholic and Protestant soldiers alike, and Holy Roods are found in many Anglican churches, from St. Paul's Cathedral downwards. In the great war just concluded, two of Everard Lisle Phillipps's nephews and some forty cousins have laid down their lives for King and country. Among other newspapers the "Tablet" had an admirable obituary notice of him, wherein mention was made of "Colonel Jones's and Capt. Owen's letters, and Father Sisk's oration."

MELVILL, TEIGNMOUTH, Lieut., was the younger son of Philip Melvill, Esq., late Secretary in the Military Department to the East India Company, by his marriage with Eliza, daughter of Colonel Sandy, of Helston. He was born in London on the 8th Sept. 1842; was educated at Harrow, Cheltenham and Cambridge, where he graduated B.A. in Feb. 1865. He entered the Army in 1865, and on 2 Dec. was gazetted to a Lieutenancy in the 1st Battn. of the 24th Regt. He joined the Corps in Ireland, and afterwards proceeded to Malta and Gibraltar, where he was appointed Adjutant 1/24th Regiment in Jan. 1875; and to the Cape. Whilst in South Africa he passed the examination for entrance into the Staff College, and in Jan. 1878, was ordered home to join that establishment. On hearing of the outbreak of fresh hostilities among the native tribes in Cape Colony, Lieut. Melvill immediately expressed his willingness to rejoin his regiment; he was ordered out accordingly,

Teignmouth Melvill.

and arrived in King William's Town at the Feb. He served with his corps through the whole of the suppression of the Saleka outbreak, performing many arduous and important duties. Immediately prior to the outbreak of the Zulu War, Lieut. Melvill proceeded with his regiment to join the Headquarters Column, which was then in course of formation on the Natal Frontier. Taking part in its subsequent advance into Zululand, he was present at the reduction of Sireyo's Stronghold in the Bashee Valley on the 13th Jan. 1879. The following account of the manner in which he met with his death on the day of the fatal attack on the camp at Isandhlwana, is taken from a Special Despatch written by General Glyn, describing the saving the Colours of the 24th Regt., bearing the date 21 Feb. 1879: "It would appear that, when the enemy had got into the camp, and when there was no longer any hope of saving it, the Adjutant of the 1st Battn. of the 24th Regt., Lieut. Teignmouth Melvill, departed from the camp on horseback, carrying the Colour with him, in hope of being able to save it. The only road to Rorke's Drift being already in possession of the enemy, Lieut. Melvill and the few others who still remained alive struck across country for the Buffalo River, which it was necessary to cross to reach a point of safety. In taking this line, the only one possible, ground had to be gone over which from its ruggedness and precipitous nature would under ordinary circumstances, it is reported, be deemed almost utterly impassable for mounted men. During a distance of about six miles Lieut. Melvill and his companions were closely pursued, or, more properly speaking, accompanied by a large number of the enemy, who, from their well-known agility in getting over rough ground, were able to keep up with our people, though the latter were mounted; so that the enemy kept up a constant fire on them, and sometimes even got close enough to assegai the men and horses. Lieut. Melvill reached the bank of the Buffalo, and at once plunged in, horse and all; but being encumbered with the Colour, which is an awkward thing to carry even on foot, and the river being full and running rapidly, he appears to have got separated from his horse when he was about half-way across. He still, however, held on resolutely to the Colour, and was being carried down stream when he was washed against a large rock in the middle of the river. Lieut. Higginson, of the Natal Native Contingent, who had also lost his horse in the river, was climbing to this rock, and Lieut. Melvill called to him to lay hold of the Colour. This Lieut. Higginson did, but the current was so strong that both officers with the Colour were again washed away into still water. In the meantime Lieut. Coghill, 1st Battn. 24th Regt., my Orderly Officer, who had been left in left camp that morning when the main body of the force moved out on account of a severe injury to his knee which rendered him unable to move without assistance, had also succeeded in gaining the river bank in company with Lieut. Melvill. He, too, had plunged at once into the river, and his horse had carried him safely across; but on looking round for Lieut. Melvill, and seeing him struggling to save the Colour in the river, he at once turned his horse and rode back into the stream again to Lieut. Melvill's assistance. It would appear that now the enemy had assembled in considerable force along their own banks, and had opened a heavy fire on our people, directing it more especially on Lieut. Melvill, who wore a red patrol jacket,; so that when Lieut. Coghill got into the river again, his horse was almost immediately killed by a bullet. Lieut. Coghill was then cast loose in the stream also, and notwithstanding the exertions of both these gallant officers, the Colour was carried off from them, and they themselves gained the bank in a state of extreme exhaustion. It would appear that they now attempted to move up the hill from the river-bank towards Helpmakas, but must have been too much exhausted to go on, as they were seen to sit down and rest again. That, I sorely regret to say, was the last time that these two gallant officers were seen alive. It was not for some days after the 22nd that I could gather any information as to the probable fate of these officers, but immediately I discovered in what direction those who had escaped from Isandhlwana had crossed the Buffalo, I sent under Major Blacke, 22nd Battn. 24th Regt., a mounted party who volunteered for this service, to search for any trace that could be found of them. This search was successful, and both bodies were found where they were last seen as above indicated. Several dead bodies of the enemy were found about them, so they must have sold their lives dearly at the last. I cannot conclude this report without drawing the attention of His Excellency the Lieutenant-General Commanding in the most impressive manner which words can command to the noble and heroic conduct of Lieutenant and Adjutant Melvill, who did not hesitate to encumber himself with the Colour of the regiment, in his resolve to save it, at a time when the camp was in the hands of the enemy, and its gallant defenders killed to the last man in its defence; and when there appeared but little prospects that any exertion Lieut. Melvill could make would enable him to save his own life—also later on to the noble perseverance with which, when struggling between life and death in the river, his chief thoughts were bent on the saving of the Colour. In conclusion I would add that both these officers gave up their lives in the truly noble task of endeavouring to save from the enemy's hands the Queen's Colour of their regiment; and greatly though their sad end is to be deplored, their deaths could not have been more noble or more full of honour. The two bodies were buried where they were found, and a stone cross was erected over the spot by Sir Bartle Frere and the members of his Staff, bearing the following inscription: 'In memory of Lieut. and Adjutant Teignmouth Melvill and Lieut. Nevill J. A. Coghill, 1st Battn. 24th Regt., who died on this spot 22 Jan. 1879, to save the Queen's Colour of their Regiment.' On the other face is inscribed, 'For Queen and Country—Jesu, Mercy.'" Immediately after Colonel Glyn's despatch to England, an official letter was sent to Mrs. Melvill from the Horse Guards, expressing the sympathy of the Field-Marshal Commanding-in-Chief, and intimating that the Victoria Cross would have been conferred on Lieut. Melvill had he survived his noble effort. The following notification appeared in a supplement to the London Gazette, 1 May, 1879: "Memorandum.—Lieut. Melvill, of the 1st Battn. 24th Foot, on account of the gallant efforts made by him to save the Queen's Colour of his Regiment after the disaster of Isandhlwana, and also Lieut. Coghill, 1st Battn. 24th Foot, on account of his heroic conduct in endeavouring to save his brother officer's life, would have been recommended to Her Majesty for the Victoria Cross had they survived." The Victoria Cross was awarded to Lieut. Coghill by King Edward [London Gazette, 15 Jan. 1907]: "Teignmouth Melvill, Lieut., 24th Regt. Memorandum.—Lieut. Melvill of the 1st Battn, 24th Foot, on account of gallant efforts made by him to save the Queen's Colour of his Regiment after the disaster at Isandhlwana, and also Lieut. Coghill, 1st Battn. 24th Foot, on account of his heroic conduct in attempting to save his brother officer's life, would have been recommended to Her Majesty for the Victoria Cross had they survived." The Victoria Cross was given to Lieut. Melvill's widow. Lieut. Melvill married in Feb. 1876, Sarah Elizabeth, daughter of George Thomas Reed, Esq., of Port Elizabeth, South Africa, and leaves two sons: the elder son, Teignmouth Philip, Lieut.-Colonel, D.S.O., 17th Lancers, and the younger son, Charles William, Brigadier-General, C.B., C.M.G., D.S.O., 1st New Zealand Infantry Brigade.

COGHILL, NEVILL JOSIAH AYLMER, Lieut., was born in Dublin, 25 Jan. 1852, son of Sir John Joscelyn Coghill, Baronet, and Katherine, daughter of Lord Plunket. He joined the 1st Battn. 24th Regt., and when the Zulu War broke out was serving as Aide-de-Camp to Sir Bartle Frere, the High Commissioner for South Africa, who, at young Coghill's earnest request, granted him leave to rejoin his regiment and go on active service with it. He won the Victoria Cross, and lost his own life at Isandhlwana. Lieut. Coghill's uncle, the late Colonel Kendal Coghill, C.B., late Commanding Queen Alexandra's Own 19th Hussars, wrote as follows: "The real story was that Nevill had a twisted knee which prevented him walking, so he was allowed to be mounted. When the débâcle occurred, the Colonel asked him and the only other mounted officer, Adjutant Melvill, to make their way through the Impi, if possible, and save the Colour. This they did till they reached the river, where Melvill's horse at first

Nevill Josiah A. Coghill.

refused to enter. Nevill got across under heavy fire, and, on landing, found Melvill wounded and surrounded. He then re-entered the river and cleared the way for Melvill to land. They were surrounded, and after a good fight were killed, and when found they had a lot of dead Zulus round them." Andrew Lang wrote a poem called "Melvill and Coghill: The Place of the Little Hand." It was published on page 12 of "Grass of Parnassus," which he dedicated to Sir Ian Hamilton. The lines are given here by permission of Messrs. Longmans, Green and Company.

"Dead with their eyes to the foe,
Dead with the foe at their feet,
Under the sky laid low
Truly their slumber is sweet,
Though the wind from the camp of the slain men blow
And the rain on the wilderness beat.

"Dead, for they chose to die
When that wild race was run;
Dead, for they would not fly,
Deeming their work undone,
Nor cared to look on the face of the sky,
Nor loved the light of the sun.

"Honour, we give them, and tears,
And the flag they died to save,
Rent from the rain of the spears,
Wet from the war and the wave,
Shall waft men's thoughts through the dust of the years,
Back to their lonely grave!"

Colonel Kendal Coghill had also some lines which were sent to Nevill Coghill's family, written on a deep mourning-edged card, unsigned:

"Lieuts. Melvill and Coghill, killed 23 Jan. 1879.
"They died,
Their glory won:
Honour was satisfied
And duty done.

"We found them with the Colour of their land
Untarnished by the murderous Zulu's hand,
And England's mighty bosom glows with pride
To know how well our gallant striplings died.
Why weep?—we all must die,
And in the dreamless sleep of destiny
Those who should rest the calmest sure are they
Whom duty unto death hath called away,
Whose glorious deeds through fame's emblazoning pen
Inspire the minds and touch the hearts of men."

The Victoria Cross was posthumously awarded to Lieut. Coghill by King Edward VII. [London Gazette, 15 Jan. 1907]: "Nevill Josiah Aylmer Coghill, Lieut., 24th Foot." A Memorandum had been published in the London Gazette of 2 May, 1879: "Lieut. Melvill, of the 1st Battn. 24th Foot, on account of the gallant effort to save the Queen's Colour of his Regiment after the disaster at Isandhlwana, and also Lieut. Coghill, 1st Battn. 24th Foot, on account of his heroic conduct in endeavouring to save his brother officer's life, would have been recommended to Her Majesty for the Victoria Cross had they survived." The following extract was sent to Lieut. Coghill's relations by Queen Victoria. It is taken from a letter from the Empress Eugénie to the Queen, dated:

"Maritzburg, 20 June, 1880.
"Nous avons placé les couronnes dont nous étions chargées sur la tombe des Lieutenants Coghill et Melvill. Si, comme je le crois, les morts voient ce qu'on fait pour eux, ils seront heureux de ne pas être oubliés par leur souveraine, eux qui ont donné leur vie pour sauver son Drapeau."

BAXTER, FRANK WILLIAM, Trooper, Buluwayo Field Force, showed great gallantry, as described by the late Capt. F. C. Selous in "Sunshine and Storm in Rhodesia" (page 164): "When the scouts were recalled and commenced to retire from the Umguza, after having driven a body of natives from its shelter, as I have already related, they were suddenly fired upon by a party of Matabele who had taken up a position amongst some bush to the left of their line of retreat. The foremost among the scouts galloped past their ambush, but Capt. Grey, with a few of those in the rear, halted and returned the enemy's fire. Trooper Wise was the first man hit, and seems to have received his wounds from behind, just as he was mounting his horse, as the bullet struck him high in the back, and, travelling up the shoulder-blade, came out near the collar-bone. At this instant Wise's horse stumbled, and then, recovering itself, broke away from its rider, galloping straight back to town, and leaving the wounded man on the ground. A brave fellow named Baxter at once dismounted and put Wise on his horse, thus saving the latter's life, but, as it proved, thereby sacrificing his own. Capt. Grey and Lieut. Hook at once went to Baxter's assistance, and they got him along as fast as they could, but the Kaffirs had now closed on them, and were firing out of the bush at very close quarters. Lieut. Hook was shot from behind, the bullet entering right buttock and coming out near the groin, but most likely, though severing the sciatic nerve, just missing the thigh bone and the femoral artery. Nearly at the same time, too, a bullet just grazed Capt. Grey's forehead, half-stunning him for an instant. 'Texas' Long, a well-known member of the scouts, then went to Baxter's assistance, and was helping him along, when a bullet struck the dismounted man in the side, and he at once let go of Long's stirrup-leather and fell to the ground. No further assistance was then possible, and poor Baxter was killed by the Kaffirs immediately afterwards." Trooper Baxter was awarded the Victoria Cross by King Edward [London Gazette, 15 Jan. 1907]: "The late Frank William Baxter, Trooper, Buluwayo Field Force. Trooper Frank William Baxter, of the Buluwayo Field Force, on account of his gallant conduct in having, on the 22nd April, 1896, dismounted and given up his horse to a wounded comrade, Trooper Wise, who was being closely pursued by an overwhelming force of the enemy, would have been recommended to Her Majesty for the Victoria Cross had he survived." The first notice appeared in the London Gazette of 7 May, 1897. Trooper Baxter's Victoria Cross was sold in London on the 17th March, 1909, for £45.

MACLEAN, HECTOR LACHLAN STEWART, Lieut., was born at Sheikh Budin Sanatorium, Bannu, North-West Frontier of India 13 Sept. 1870. He was the eldest son of Major-General Charles Smith MacLean, Indian Staff Corps, and Margaret MacQueen Bairnsfather, of Dumbarrow, Forfarshire. He was educated at St. Salvator's, St. Andrews, and Fettes College, Edinburgh, and joined the Northumberland Fusiliers as 2nd Lieutenant 24 April, 1889; became Probationer for Indian Staff Corps 17 Feb. 1891, and joined the Queen's Own Corps of Guides at Mardan 30 March, 1891. He took part in the Black Mountains Hazarah Expedition of 1891 (Medal and clasp); the Chitral Expedition of 1895 (Punjab Frontier Medal, 1907–8); Relief of Chitral, 1895 (clasp); during the Chitral Campaign he distinguished himself by swimming across the Panjkhora to join and encourage a detachment who had been cut off by the rapid rising of the river. He became Adjutant, Guides

Hector L. S. MacLean.

Cavalry, in 1896; served in the Malakand Campaign (Victoria Cross and clasps) in 1897, and was killed in the 27th year of his age, when still suffering from the severe wound he had received at the Defence of the Malakand a few days previously. Colonel Adams gives the following account of how Lieut. MacLean met his death and won the Victoria Cross, on the 17th Aug. 1897. Colonel Adams wrote: "All but a very few of the enemy had reached a spur of the hills before we could get up with them, and opened a very hot fire on all of us as we approached. What we should then have done, and what I intended to do, was to collect the scattered men behind the nearest available cover, and, with dismounted men, to open fire. Unfortunately, at this moment Lieut. Greaves, who was out with us as a Press correspondent, was run away with by his pony, and carried up to the foot of the spur amongst the enemy, one of whom shot him; and on his falling from his horse, others proceeded to hack at him with swords. Several of us who were nearest at once rushed to the rescue. Immediately as this happened, your son arrived—with Lieut. Norman, 11th Bengal Lancers, who was attached to us—at the corner of the village, where I had thought of dismounting the men. He at once said to Norman, 'We must get some men together,' and collecting about a dozen or so, who arrived at the same time, he brought them into the nearest point of cover, and left them, under the orders of Norman, to open fire on the enemy. He himself came out into the open in front at once, where we were struggling to get poor Greaves's body on to a horse, in order to carry it away. As he approached us he dismounted, and said, 'Here, put him on my horse,' and he himself assisted largely in lifting the body and placing it across the saddle. We had all started to return with the body to the nearest cover, and had carried it about fifteen yards when your son exclaimed that he had been hit in the thigh. He was unable to mount his horse, and so two of our men, who had come out after him and were alongside him at the moment, seized each an arm, and brought him along in that way for about twenty or thirty yards, to the corner of the wooded graveyard, where he had placed the dismounted men, and which was the nearest point of cover. He then sank unconscious, and had to be lifted up and carried in front of three men on their saddles, back to where Dr. Macnab was met, whose pony, being far back in passing the causeway, was delayed, and was at that moment only just nearing the scene of the fight. From the first, however, it was, I deeply regret to say, a hopeless case, and Dr. Macnab could do nothing to save him, and, without recovering consciousness, he very shortly afterwards expired. But for his action in placing those dismounted men at once in the graveyard, where their fire checked the enemy, the small party round Lieut. Greaves's body would most certainly have been rushed; and but for his coming out so readily to our assistance we should have had great difficulty in lifting and carrying away Lieut. Greaves, and would have been so much the longer delayed under the hot fire the enemy were pouring down upon us from the hill close by, when every additional moment increased the risk of further loss." Lord Fincastle wrote: "The enemy kept up a hot fire, and unfortunately killed the best soldier and most popular officer in the whole force, and I need not say how he is missed by his brother officers and all his friends." Dr. Macnab wrote to General MacLean: "It is very far from being an empty expression when I write that all who knew him grieve his loss as a friend, admire his character, example and devotion to duty, and are in deep sympathy with you all." The London Gazette of 9 Nov. 1897, says: "During the fighting at Nawa Kili, in Upper Swat, on the 17th Aug. 1897, Lieut.-Colonel R. B. Adams proceeded with Lieut. H. L. S. MacLean and Viscount Fincastle, and five men of the Guides, under a very heavy and close fire, to the rescue of Lieut. R. T. Greaves, Lancashire Fusiliers, who was lying disabled by a bullet-wound and surrounded by the enemy's swordsmen. In bringing him under cover, he (Lieut. Greaves) was struck by a bullet and killed. Lieut. MacLean was mortally wounded, whilst the horses of Lieut.-Colonel Adams and Lieut. Viscount Fincastle were shot, as well as two troop horses. Lieut. Hector Lachlan Stewart MacLean, Indian Staff Corps, on account of his gallant conduct as recorded above, would have been recommended for the Victoria Cross had he survived." The London Gazette of 15 Jan. 1907, announces that the King (Edward VII.) has approved of the Decoration of the Victoria Cross being delivered to the representatives of the undermentioned men and officers who fell in the performance of Acts of Valour, and with reference to whom it was notified in the London Gazette that they would have been recommended for the Victoria Cross to Her late Majesty had they survived: "Lieut. Hector Lachlan Stewart MacLean, Indian Staff Corps, etc., etc., mortally wounded in Swat at Landakai, on 17 Aug. 1897." Lieut. MacLean was a keen Shikari, and was Captain of the Guides' Polo Team.

London Gazette, 13 Nov. 1914.—"War Office, 16 Nov. 1914. His Majesty the King has been graciously pleased to approve of the grant of the Victoria Cross to the undermentioned Officers, Non-commissioned Officers and Men for their conspicuous bravery whilst serving with the Expeditionary Force."

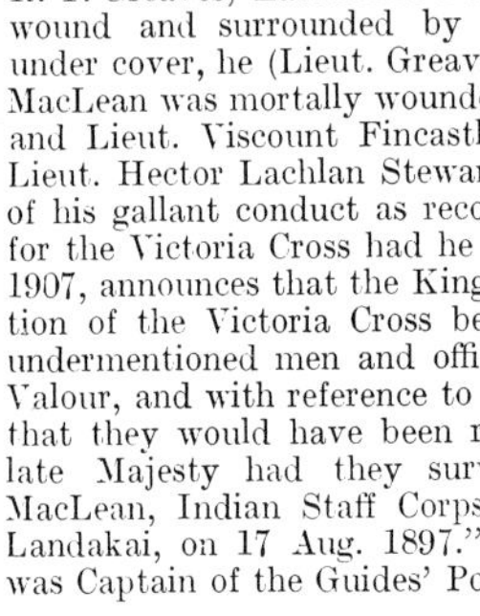

Francis Octavus Grenfell.

GRENFELL, FRANCIS OCTAVUS, Capt., and his twin brother, Riversdale Nonus, were born at Hatchlands, near Guildford, 4 Sept. 1880; sons of Pascoe du Pre Grenfell, who had married his cousin, Sofia, daughter of Admiral John Grenfell. The twins entered Eton in 1894. Francis became Master of the Beagles in 1898, and was in the Eton XI. in 1899, and in the Eton and Harrow match, in a critical part of the game, he made 81 runs, and helped to make a record for Eton when he and Longman made 170 for no wickets. The "Illustrated Sporting and Dramatic News" said of him: "It was during the Eton and Harrow match, 14–15 July, 1899, that this one of two famous twins first made a mark on the records of sport. Eton had made in the first innings 274 against 283 of Harrow, when F. O. Grenfell began Eton's second innings with H. K. Longman (now a Captain in the Gordons). The first wicket fell at 167, when H. J. Wyld bowled Longman. At 184 the same bowler, slow left arm, bowled Grenfell. Both batsmen made 81 runs, and both got out throwing their wickets away in trying to get runs fast, so that Eton might put Harrow in. Prior to this game the two elevens used to sit opposite to each other at lunch in comparative silence. F. O. Grenfell, though not captain, changed all this. The rival players were split up in twos and threes, and chaff, chat and banter became general where an awkward silence had reigned. A year later we find Longman, the Eton captain, going across to the rival dressing-room to shake hands with and congratulate the Harrow captain on the victory of his team. The example of F. O. Grenfell led to this desirable state of affairs." The above is quoted as an example of that extraordinary flair for doing and saying the right thing at the right moment which characterized Capt. Grenfell from his earliest youth onwards. The kennels for the beagles at Eton were built about the year 1898 by funds which the twins raised, and of which "Rivy" was chief organizer and administrator. The inseparables were first of all in the house of A. C. Benson, and afterwards in Walter Durnford's house. They were two of the five boys known as "The Old Firm," the other three being C. H. M. Ebden, the Cambridge Cricket Blue; W. Findlay, captain of Oxford and a renowned Lancashire wicket-keeper, and H. R. Pape. O. C. S. Gilliat was also one of the Eton XI. in the above-mentioned match, and he, like the Grenfells, was destined to fall in action in the European War. The brothers played an outstanding part in the modern development of polo, and between them they formed the Old Etonians side, which so often covered itself with glory. When Francis and Riversdale Grenfell had fallen in the European War, "W. D." wrote in the "Eton Chronicle": "So the twins, even in death, are not separated for long, and after six short months that gay and gallant pair sleep together as they would have wished, in the land where so many of Eton's best and bravest sons have found their last resting-place. 'His amor unus erat, pariterque in bella ruebant.' The words in which Virgil tells the story of the fate of the two soldier friends can very well be applied to the Grenfell twins. For indeed it is impossible to think of one without the other, and the record of Rivy's death could be applied to Francis without a single change. As the elder, Francis to some extent took the lead at Eton. He was Master of the Beagles while his brother was Whip; he was the better cricketer, and obtained a place in the XI. in his last year, 1899. But there was never the smallest jealousy between them, and the successes of Francis were an abiding glory to Rivy. So they passed, hand in hand as it were, through that enchanted land, the last Summer Half, and when the House broke up on the retirement of their Tutor in July, 1899, they went away to face the world, with the good wishes of hosts of friends and the high hopes of those who knew them best. For there were some who knew that under that gay and almost reckless demeanour there lay deep stores of affection, of love for the weak and suffering, of genuine religious faith, and so, when we read of their deaths, amid our tears, amid the heart-breaking sorrow for noble lives so early lost, we can hold fast with unclouded recollection and undying love, the memory of Francis and Rivy Grenfell." Another writer says of Francis: "At a school which turns out ready-made courtiers at the age of twenty he stood out among his fellows for his charming manner and general power of being at his ease in any company, and not only that, but also of putting others at their ease." On leaving Eton in 1899, he joined the 3rd (Militia) Battn. Seaforth Highlanders, and served with them over a year, going to Cairo in 1900. In May, 1901, he was gazetted Second Lieutenant in the 60th Rifles, and saw service in the Boer War, 1901–2, including operations in Orange River Colony, Cape Colony, and the Transvaal. He received for his services the Queen's Medal with five clasps. At the close of the war he went to India with his regiment; was promoted Lieutenant 5 Jan. 1905, and in May of the same year exchanged into the 9th Lancers. He worked hard to improve himself in his profession, and also did his best to train his men for war, leaving no stone unturned to raise enthusiasm in the men under him for their regiment and its splendid traditions. He was a careful student of military history, especially devoting himself to reading up the biographies of eminent soldiers and mastering the details of their campaigns. He had the highest possible ideals of a soldier's duty and acted up to them. He passed for Interpretership in Hindustani and French, and in 1909 he qualified for every subject for the Staff College. While in India he was, as usual, much taken up with sport. He and his (then) civilian brother Rivy greatly distinguished themselves at the Kadir Cup Meeting, the great Indian pig-sticking carnival, in 1905. That year it was held at Sherpur. Rivy Grenfell won the cup, which then left India for the first time. Miss Grenfell has a photograph of her brother—the only civilian—sitting among his fellow-competitors, both Indian and British. And another photograph shows him and Francis, with Rivy's pony, "Barmaid," and his splintered spear, taken just after his victory. These pictures are out of the "Illustrated Sporting and Dramatic News." At the same meeting Francis won the Hog Hunters' Cup for horses, three miles over a pig-sticking country, and in 1906 he won the Regimental Race Cup in India. In 1909 they played polo in America and Canada and in October Francis went big-game shooting in Central Africa. After Capt. Grenfell's death the polo correspondent of the "Daily Telegraph" wrote: "Eight or ten years have passed since Capt. Francis Grenfell came home on leave, and proved himself at the London clubs scarcely less brilliant a polo player than his twin brother 'Rivy.' He had learnt the game with that splendid polo regiment, the 9th Lancers, and when they returned to England Capt. Grenfell played for them in the semi-final round of the Inter-Regimental Tournament in 1911, in which they were beaten after a good game by the Royal Horse

Guards. His accident at steeplechasing kept him out of much polo in the following year, but when he had properly recovered he took his place as one of the finest players in London, his handicap being advanced last year to eight points, this placing him on the same mark as his brother. Both the Grenfells were, as a rule, magnificently mounted. They took great trouble in trying and schooling their ponies, and always had them fit in the first few weeks of the season. The brothers were never seen to so much advantage as when they were playing together at No. 1 and No. 2. Their combination, strong hitting, and tremendous vigour were delightful to watch. By their deaths polo loses two of its most dashing and enthusiastic players." In Jan. 1910, Francis was home at Woolwich, and gave very good lectures. In April, 1911, the twins spent Easter playing polo with the King of Spain. The Old Etonians side offered to go to America and try to recover the Cup, which has since then been brought back to England. The scheme, however, fell through because in Dec. 1911, Francis had a bad accident when riding Knight of Avon in a selling steeplechase at Kempton Park, from which he did not really recover till June, 1912, when he went to Berlin to learn German for the Staff College Examination. Francis Grenfell was greatly interested in steeplechasing, though his injuries at Kempton Park kept him from taking an active part in National Hunt racing for some time. In 1914 he had the satisfaction of seeing his colours win the Past and Present Handicap Steeplechase at the Grand Military Meeting, his brother officer, Mr. G. Phipps Hornby, being in the saddle. He became Adjutant in Sept. 1912, and was promoted to Captain in November. In 1913 and 1914 he was studying for the Staff College, and he was Adjutant for only eighteen months, as he gave it up in the spring of 1914, in order to give all the time he could to working up for the Staff College. When war broke out against Germany in Aug. 1914, he and his twin brother, who was attached to the 9th Lancers, left with the regiment on the 15th Aug. for France. On the first day of the war, 23 Aug., he did a reconnaissance early in the morning, when his horse was shot under him. Later in the day the regiment was in action, and on the 24th Francis Grenfell took part in the charge of cavalry against massed German infantry, when, as they were subjected to a severe fire from three sides, grievous losses occurred. They began by a dismounted action with the enemy's infantry at a range of over a thousand yards, close to the village of Andregnies. Then De Lisle ordered the 9th Lancers, with the other regiments as supports, to charge the flank of the advancing masses. " The charge of the 9th Lancers was as futile and as gallant as the other attempts in history on unbroken infantry and guns in position. To the opposing armies it proved that the spirit which had inspired the Light Brigade at Balaclava and Von Bredow's Todtenritt at Mars-La-Tour, was still alive in the cavalry of to-day. The ground had been poorly reconnoitred, and the Lancers found themselves brought up against double lines of wire within five hundred yards of the enemy. They simply galloped like rabbits in front of a line of guns, says one account, ' Men and horses falling in all directions.' There was no question of reaching the enemy ; the tornado of shell and rifle fire was too fierce and incessant. A moment's shelter was found behind a house, but the house was speedily blown to pieces. Capt. Francis Grenfell, who had kept his squadron together by giving the order to trot, found himself the senior officer in command." (See Nelson's " History of the War.") He was shot through the coat and boot. He rallied part of the regiment under a railway embankment, which afforded some shelter from the shells, but on the embankment Grenfell was hit in the hand and thigh and severely wounded. The Commander of the 119th Battery, Royal Field Artillery, now appealed to him to save the guns, for all the gunners were killed and the guns still under very heavy fire, and asked him if any exit could be found to get the guns away. Capt. Francis Grenfell at once responded, though his wounds had not been dressed, left the embankment and rode out to where the guns were. He found where they could be got out of fire, and then rode through a " perfect inferno of shells " slowly back to his men to give them confidence, and called for volunteers. He told them that the 9th Lancers helped to save the guns at Maiwand, and that these guns must be saved. The whole of the remainder, every man and officer of his squadron, volunteered and stepped forward to go to what looked like certain destruction. They and the survivors of the battery, the Commandant and some dozen gunners, then ran across two fields and manhandled and pushed the guns and limbers out of fire. This meant that the guns had to be slowly turned round, lifted over the dead gunners, and it required more than one journey under a hail of bullets to effect their object. A shell came right under one of the guns Capt. Grenfell and his men were lifting, and knocked them down. Luckily it did not explode, though he was slightly wounded in the face. The horses and drivers, who had fortunately been under cover, were then able to gallop the guns out of fire, and thus the battery was saved. Despite his wounds and weariness, Capt. Grenfell rode nearly ten miles back with the squadron before he had to give in from exhaustion. But he had been fighting since 4 a.m., and only gave in at 7 p.m. For these services he was awarded the first Victoria Cross of the European War [London Gazette, 16 Nov. 1914]: " Francis Octavus Grenfell, Capt., 9th Lancers. For gallantry in action against unbroken infantry at Andregnies, Belgium, on the 24th Aug. 1914, and for gallant conduct in assisting to save the guns of the 119th Battery, Royal Field Artillery, near Doubon the same day." Colonel A. S. Jones, V.C., late 9th Lancers, wrote to congratulate him on his Victoria Cross, and received the following letter :

" DEAR COLONEL JONES,
" Words fail me to thank you for your kind letter you sent me. It is a great honour for me to receive congratulations from you who received the first V.C. in the Delhi Campaign. You will be glad to hear that the regiment has, if it were possible, added to the great traditions of the past, and up to date has never failed to carry out what it has been asked to do. We have suffered severely, but have now refitted and are ready for the big campaign, which will soon be started, and I hope, if there is a race for

Berlin, that the old 9th will be there first. I hope you will forgive a typewritten letter, but I have received so many letters that it is impossible for me to answer them except in this manner before I return to France, which I hope will be very soon. Again thanking you,
" Yours sincerely,
" FRANCIS GRENFELL."

At Messines, on Friday, the 30th Oct., the 9th Lancers expected to have a rest at Neuve Eglise in billets, but at 11 a.m. received orders to saddle up immediately, and at 12 orders to march. They marched to Wulverghem, where, in a field, they dismounted and left their horses. During this time the 1st Cavalry Corps, about a mile in front, was holding Messines and being heavily shelled. Capt. Grenfell was told to take his squadron towards Wytschaete to prepare trenches, and while there, at 4.30 received further orders to hurry up to Messines. They marched through the town, which was under severe shelling, and on the way Grenfell told the General that the left—i.e., the north of Messines—was very weakly held. He then went on through Messines to trenches to relieve the 11th Hussars, took over the trench, and saw he had far too few men to hold it. So he made them make traverses in it, rather difficult under fire the whole time. Darkness now came on. On their extreme left in the dark they could see the Germans moving about. Some of the Germans shouted : " We surrender," but a moment later fired at the trench. Carefully looking round, Capt. Grenfell could see that his front trench was exposed to being enfiladed, and if anything happened to any of the troops near there, his trench made a salient and would be untenable, the trenches near his being so placed that his men could not fire properly. A Maxim gun was sent him, which he placed on the extreme left of the trench. He and his men were under fire all night. On Saturday, 31 Oct., after a very anxious night with no rest, they were heavily attacked at daybreak, and he was ordered to send troops to support the right, which weakened his force still more. All of a sudden he found that the troops on his left had given way and his trench was surrounded, as he expected it would be. The Germans were firing straight down the trench, and had also got right behind it. Troops on the other side had to withdraw, so Grenfell had to retire his men to some mined houses close by, being very distressed at leaving the trench. Then he heard a machine gun at the other end of the trench, so went to see, and found Corpl. Seaton firing at Germans who were twenty yards off. He stayed there firing his revolver while Corpl. Seaton undid the gun and took away the ammunition, for the gun had got damaged. They were being shot at from the front, flank and rear, but as the trench had not been taken he collected his squadron and they again occupied the trench. Corpl. Seaton got the D.C.M., and says he owes his life to Capt. Grenfell. Thus by the tenacity of two men the trench was regained, but soon after a shell burst in the middle of it, killed the officer next to Grenfell and badly wounded several of the men. He himself was hit in the thigh and soon found he couldn't move. Luckily a brother officer lifted him out and got him to a dressing station ; then he had himself carried to the General to tell him the serious situation that existed. He was taken to a cellar full of wounded men in the town, and from there to Bailleul. There he was told that he and a brother officer (whose stretcher oddly enough was put next to his) were the only two to escape ; the rest had been surrounded and taken prisoners. Seven officers wounded, two missing, one killed. Out of his squadron four out of five officers were killed or wounded. That evening he was put in an ambulance train, where he heard of the attacks all along the line. After a short time in a field hospital he came home. It took him some time to recover from this second wound, but as soon as possible he left again for the front, leaving home on Thursday night, 17 April. He had had his Victoria Cross from the King on the 21st Feb. He went through all the severe fighting at and near Ypres in April and May, and on the 18th May he wrote home : " Julian Grenfell did splendidly ; he is badly wounded, but will be all right. Whatever is in store in the future, I shall never be nearer death than I was on the 13th." On the 23rd May Francis's squadron and half a battalion of the Yorkshire Regt. took over the line previously held by the 18th and 19th Hussars at Hooge, on the Menin Road. After fighting all day and all night, their trenches had a gas attack at 4 a.m. on the 24th May, from which all suffered more or less, and later in the morning they were severely shelled. He was mortally wounded, and died a few minutes later. His last words were : " I die happy. Tell the men I loved my squadron." Nine officers and thirty-five N.C.O.'s and men— all that was left of the 9th Lancers that day—went back when relieved at dawn on the 25th May, and took with them their dead comrades, Capt. Francis Grenfell and a brother officer, and buried them at Vlamertinghe. One of them wrote : " We carried him back the five miles ; he looked so calm and peaceful in the moonlight. I shall never forget that walk back —everybody done to a turn. We buried him in Vlamertinghe churchyard next evening, General Mullen and all that was left of us being present. I can't tell you what his loss means to the regiment which had the honour of numbering Francis amongst its officers." An extract from a letter says : " Francis Grenfell has left a memory which will never fade, a braver soul never stepped ; his high ideals and boundless enthusiasm for the regiment and the cause for which we are fighting was an example we shall never forget, and the regiment is indeed proud to think it numbered Francis Grenfell in its ranks." He left his Victoria Cross and medals to the 9th Lancers—he said he owed his decoration entirely to them. Lord French says in his book " 1914," of the deed by which Capt. Grenfell won his Victoria Cross : " I noticed in particular one artillery brigade, some of whose guns had been saved from capture on the previous day by the cavalry. The Brigade Commander broke down with emotion as he recounted to me the glorious bravery displayed by Francis Grenfell and the 9th Lancers." In a sermon at the Temple Church, All Saints' Day, 1915, the Bishop of Kingston-on-Thames said : " Was there ever an army in which men followed their officers in more unquestioning devotion ? It is to the credit of both alike, but it began with a confidence in those who would not drive but knew how to lead; who gave orders for no hard task they were not themselves ready or foremost to face; who cared out of their hearts for those who looked up to them, who could say with that brave officer, Capt. Francis Grenfell, in his last words: ' Tell them I die happy; I loved my squadron.' " (The " Church Times," 5 Nov. 1915.) Lord Burnham wrote in the " Daily Telegraph " of 31 May, 1915: " Our Young Officers. The record of young lives, willingly given with such intense bravery and chivalrous devotion to King and Country, will never be forgotten in our history. It is a record of which every family suffering at this moment the anguish of deep sorrow, may truly be proud. And how many these families are! Day by day the long list lengthens, and those who sigh as they read know that till the very end of the war the scroll must be perpetually unrolled. The thought of so much bereavement would be almost unendurable but for the great glory of those who so simply lay down their lives, and the certainty that so much valour is not spent in vain. We recorded on Saturday the death of Capt. Francis Grenfell, V.C., Captain and Adjutant of the 9th Lancers, and there are many reasons which make it singularly appropriate to take his career as a shining example of the glorious company of regimental officers who are giving all they have to give for England at this hour. Capt. Francis Grenfell won the first V.C. of the Great War. The brief official record simply speaks of his ' gallantry in action against unbroken infantry,' and describes how on the self-same day he helped to save the guns of a battery of Royal Field Artillery whose horses had all been struck down. The guns were safely man-handled out of action amid a storm of shell, and in an episode where all were brave, Capt. Grenfell displayed a high heroic courage which gained him the crown of every soldier's ambition. He did not escape unscathed. He was severely wounded and returned to England. But at the earliest moment he was back again with his regiment, and a little later was wounded even more dangerously than before. A second time he fought his way laboriously back to recovery, only to receive a third and mortal wound a week ago. Thus he has joined after a few months' interval his gallant twin-brother, Capt. ' Rivy ' Grenfell. Few British officers were better known or better liked than these two Grenfells, whose younger brother had lit the way for them down to dusty death years before in the brilliant charge of the 12th Lancers at Omdurman. In the happy days before the war they were two of the best-known Eton men of their generation, and for several seasons their polo was the delight of Ranelagh and many another festive ground. As types of the British regimental officer, as soldiers, gentlemen and sportsmen, these two brothers had no superiors, and their memories will be treasured long. What is the ideal of these and many thousands more? What is the secret which makes them so beloved? There are many types of gallant officer, but there is a peculiarly British type, which is different in many subtle ways from all others, and the secret of the difference is best found in the British public-school spirit, which Sir Henry Newbolt has interpreted in verse:

> " ' To set the Cause above renown,
> To love the game beyond the prize,
> To honour, while you strike him down,
> The foe that comes with fearless eyes;
> To count the life of battle good,
> And dear the land that gave you birth,
> And nearer yet the brotherhood
> That binds the brave of all the earth.'

" In these noble lines we may detect the secret of the impulse which has moved so many thousand young officers to offer themselves in response to their country's call. The public schools of England no doubt have their faults. But they are gloriously redeemed at this moment by their shining virtues. No need of conscription or compulsion there. Those who learned to play the game at school rushed to play it on the fields of Flanders. We do not wish to exalt one class above another; nothing is further from our thoughts. To each its own conspicuous merits and equal honour. But no one who reads the brief obituary notices in the papers—necessarily brief, when all there is to tell is the name of school, college and regiment, and the military record is so often one of a few months only—can fail to feel a pang when he pictures to himself the bright young English faces and the boyish forms of the fallen, and then remembers what he has read of them in the simple untutored letters of their men. It is the rule and not the exception for the British regimental officer to be adored by his men, who know that he is ready to do himself all that he asks of them, and that he thinks more of their comfort and safety than of his own. Though he is their officer, they are all members of the same side, all in the same team, a band of brothers in face of the enemy. We find no thought among British regimental officers of belonging to an ' Officers' Corps.' The fierce, exclusive, haughty pride of the German ' Officers' Corps ' has no counterpart here, and one of many consequences is that British officers have no need to carry the knotted whips which appear to be part of the Prussian officer's regulation outfit. Let those, therefore, who will shake their heads over metaphors drawn from games and sports; it is just that sporting spirit which differentiates the British Army from all others in the world, and makes it a joyous company of high-spirited heroes. Gallant, boyish souls; perfect knights of modern chivalry; the very mirror of loyalty and courage, cheerfully stepping down into the dark, though none have ever loved more than they the bright sunshine and the open breath of heaven, not their friends alone mourn their untimely end in mingled sorrow and pride. Their country, too, will not forget.

> " ' What hath he lost that so great grace hath won?
> Young years for endless years, and hope unsure
> Of Fortune's gifts for wealth that still shall dure.
> Oh! happy race with so great praises run!' "

REYNOLDS, DOUGLAS, Capt., was born 20 Sept. 1882, at Clifton, Gloucestershire. His father was the late Lieut.-Colonel H. C. Reynolds, R.E. (son of the late General Reynolds, 11th Hussars), and his mother, Eleanor, daughter of Wildman Goodwyn, Esq., Indian Civil Service. He was educated at Cheltenham College, which he entered in Sept. 1892, as a day boy, entering the junior department, and subsequently going into the Military and Civil Side. He passed into the Royal Military Academy, Woolwich, in 1898, and was gazetted to the Royal Field Artillery at the end of 1899. Directly the Boer War commenced he volunteered for it, but was not sent out until about four months before the end of the campaign, during which time he served with the mounted infantry attached to the artillery. Capt. Reynolds spent most of the interval between the Boer War and the European War in India, where he was in command of an ammunition column at Nowshera,

Douglas Reynolds.

and was commended by the General for his services. He was a keen sportsman and an excellent shot, and he spent all his leave in Kashmir and the mountains of Baltistan. He was afterwards in Ireland, and in Aug. 1914, he went abroad directly war was declared with the 37th Howitzer Battery. From this time he fought incessantly, and was in the Retreat from Mons. He was mentioned in Sir John French's Despatches in 1914, for conspicuous gallantry during the operations between the 21st and 30th Aug., and again in 1915. He was awarded the Victoria Cross [London Gazette, 16 Nov. 1914]: " Douglas Reynolds, Capt., 37th Battery, Royal Field Artillery. At Le Cateau, on 26 Aug., he took up two teams to recapture two British guns, and limbered up two guns under heavy artillery and infantry fire, and though the enemy was within one hundred yards he got one gun away safely. At Pysloup, on the 9th Sept., he reconnoitred at close range, discovered a battery which was holding up the advance and silenced it." There were two dates inscribed on his V.C.—one for the reconnaissance under fire at Pysloup on 9 Sept., and the other for recapturing guns at Le Cateau on 26 Aug. 1914. In a private report of his share in the incidents of the battle of Le Cateau, Capt. Reynolds spoke with the warmest admiration and gratitude of the gallant support volunteered by Lieut. Earle (since awarded the D.S.O.) and the N.C.O.'s and men of the 37th Battery in his effort to recapture the British guns. It was a happy moment for their young leader when he heard that Driver Luke and Driver Drain had also won the coveted honour—making a record of three V.C.'s in our battery. During the Battle of the Aisne on 15 Sept. 1914, Capt. Reynolds was severely wounded in the side by a shrapnel bullet, which passed up to his breast and remained there. It could not be extracted. After recovery Major Reynolds was employed in training a new howitzer battery which he eventually took into action and commanded. Just before Christmas, 1915, he and several of his men suffered a good deal from heart weakness, after the bursting of an asphyxiating bomb near the battery, but they all apparently recovered, and Major Reynolds stuck to his guns until a few days before his death, which took place at Le Touquet on 23 Feb. 1916. The R.A.M.C. diagnosis was " Septicæmia from gas poisoning." He was buried at Etaples, France, among his comrades. Major Reynolds married Doris, daughter of W. Petersen, Esq., of Heronsghyll, Sussex, and his infant son, William Petersen Douglas Sinclair, was four weeks old the day his father died.

WRIGHT, THEODORE, Capt., was born at Brighton 15 May, 1883, son of the late William Walter Wright and of Mrs. Arabella Wright, of Albury, near Guildford. He was educated at Clifton College, and at the Royal Military Academy, Woolwich, where he was in the first Cricket XI., and in the Hockey team. He also played cricket for the Army v. Hampshire. He passed out of the Royal Military Academy, and was gazetted to the Royal Engineers in Oct. 1902, subsequently serving at Gibraltar and Cairo. He was promoted Lieutenant in June, 1905, and Captain in Oct. 1913. Capt. Wright served in the European War. He accompanied the British Expeditionary Force to France in Aug. 1914. A chauffeur said of Capt. Wright: " He was the officer who got wounded in the head while I was driving him at Mons. When I was under fire there I took a wounded soldier to the hospital and returned into the fire for the Captain. It was a bit risky, with eight cases of dynamite

Theodore Wright.

on the car. But he was a brave man." He was decorated for his gallantry in the very early part of the war. Corpl. Jarvis, who was on the same duty as Capt. Wright, said: " The work on the bridge was done under fire from three sides. Near the bridge I found Capt. Theodore Wright, V.C., wounded in the head. I wished to bandage him, but he said: ' Go back to the bridge.' It must be done—and so I went. The British infantry were posted behind barricades, and I had to make quite a detour to get round where I had to start operations." Capt. Wright was awarded the Victoria Cross [London Gazette, 16 Nov. 1914: " Theodore Wright, Capt., Royal Engineers. Date of Act of Bravery, 23 Aug. 1914. Gallantry at Mons on the 23rd Aug., in attempting to connect up the lead to demolish a bridge under heavy fire; although wounded in the head, he made a second attempt. At Vailly, on the 14th Sept., he assisted the passage of the 5th Cavalry Brigade over the pontoon bridge, and was mortally wounded whilst assisting wounded men into shelter." Colonel Wilson, of his corps, in writing to Capt. Wright's mother, said of him: "No one has earned a V.C. better, and I am truly glad they have given it to him. I have known him so long, and have always been very fond of him. He was one of the finest officers I have ever had, and I feel his loss every day. I enclose a cutting that you may not have seen from a letter of one of the Scots Greys officers, and I can endorse every word of it." The following is the account given by the cavalry officer referred to by Colonel Wilson: "We got across the river at . . . . the day before yesterday, a bit before our time, and had to go back over a pontoon bridge considerably quicker than was pleasant—under a very unpleasant fire, too. At the head of the bridge was a gallant Engineer officer, repairing bits blown off and putting down straw as cool as a cucumber—the finest thing I have ever seen. The poor fellow was killed just after my troops got across. No man ever earned a better V.C." Mrs. Wright received a letter from His Majesty the King, dated 5 Oct. 1915, from Buckingham Palace, which said: "It is a matter of sincere regret to me that the death of Capt. Theodore Wright deprived me of the pride of personally conferring upon him the Victoria Cross, the greatest of all military distinctions.—Sgd. GEORGE R.I."

DEASE, MAURICE JAMES, Lieut., was born at Gaulstown, Coole, County Westmeath, 28 Sept. 1889, son of Edmund Fitzlawrence Dease, J.P., of Levington, Mullingar, County Westmeath, and grandson of James Arthur Dease, of Turbotston, J.P., D.L., Vice-Lieutenant of Cavan. He was educated at Frognal Park, Hampstead, Stonyhurst College (1903), the Army College, Wimbledon, and Royal Military College, Sandhurst, joining the 4th Battn. Royal Fusiliers as Second Lieutenant 27 May, 1910, being promoted to Lieutenant 19 April, 1912. On the outbreak of war he proceeded with his regiment to France. An account of how he won the Victoria Cross is given in "Deeds that thrill the Empire" (published by Messrs. Hutchinson) (page 317): "On reaching Mons on 22 Aug. 1914, the part assigned to the British force was that of extending the French line in a north-westerly direction. The position taken extended along the line of the canal from Condé on the west through Mons and Binche on the east. From Condé to Mons inclusive was held by the 2nd Corps, and on the right of the 2nd Corps from Mons the 1st Corps was posted, while the 5th Cavalry Brigade was at Binche. The forward reconnaissance was entrusted to Brigadier-General Sir Philip Chetwode, with the 5th Cavalry Brigade, and with the assistance of a few squadrons, sent forward by General Allenby, most useful work was done. Several encounters took place, in which the British showed to great advantage, and some of the squadrons penetrated as far as Soignies. It was evident from the start that the area which covered the loop of the canal had been marked down by the enemy as the weakest point in the defence. If they succeeded in crossing the canal close to the British salient, the British would perforce have to abandon the line of defence along the straight road to Condé. For the time being, therefore, it was resolved to confine all efforts to the salient. With dawn on Sunday, 23 Aug., came the first shell in the great battle of Mons. The bombardment increased as the morning advanced, and when at 8 a.m. fresh batteries came into action, the first infantry attack was launched against the Nimy bridge, at the north-west corner of the canal loop. The northern side of the canal, throughout the entire length covered by the attack, is dotted with small fir plantations, and, screened by these, the enemy poured a deadly fire from machine guns on our troops, besides massing infantry attacks at whatever point they chose. With superior numbers Von Kluck could afford to throw away life freely, and about nine o'clock four battalions were suddenly flung at the head of the Nimy bridge. It was only defended by a single company of the Royal Fusiliers, under Capt. Ashburner, and a machine gun in charge of Lieut. Dease. As the enemy advanced in close column their front sections collapsed under the deadly fire poured into them by the British machine guns and rifles. They fell back in haste to one of the plantations, and then after about half an hour advanced in extended order. The attack was checked, but not stopped. As Capt. Ashburner was hard pressed on the Nimy bridge, 2nd Lieut. Mead was sent with a platoon to support him. He was at once badly wounded in the head, but, after being dressed, returned to the firing line, where in a few minutes he was shot through the head and killed. Capt. Bowden-Smith and Lieut. Smith then came up with another platoon, but within ten minutes they were both badly wounded. The position was now growing very desperate. Lieut. Dease had been hit three times while working his machine gun; Capt. Ashburner was wounded in the head, and Capt. Forster, in a trench to the right, had been shot through the right arm and stomach. Towards midday the attack against the straight reach of the canal became general, and the German infantry, coming out from the cover of the fir plantations, worked their way to within a few hundred yards of the water, and from the cover of the trees kept up a continuous rifle and machine-gun fire. They made no real advance, but when the Nimy salient was abandoned, the retirement of the troops to the left of it became imperative. This, however, was no easy matter. Before they reached cover they had to cross two hundred and fifty yards of flat open ground, which was swept by a storm of shrapnel and machine-gun fire. Lieut. Dease, who had stood by his gun all through, was now quite unable to move, having been hit no less than five times. Lieut. Steele, who alone of the whole section was neither killed nor wounded, caught him up and carried him from the fire zone to a place of safety, and here he subsequently succumbed to his wounds." For the most gallant part he took in the defence of the Nimy bridge a posthumous award of the V.C. was made [London Gazette, 16 Nov. 1914]: "Maurice Dease, Lieut., 4th Battn. Royal Fusiliers. Date of Act of Bravery, 23 Aug. 1914. Though two or three times badly wounded, he continued to control the fire of his machine guns at Mons on the 23rd Aug. until all his men were shot. He died of his wounds." Lieut. Dease was also mentioned in Field-Marshal Sir John French's Despatch of 7 Sept. 1914. His Commanding Officer wrote: "Lieut. Dease was wounded and man after man of his detachment was hit. He appears to have received a second wound after neglecting a first wound in the leg; taking a little time to recover, he managed to return to the gun and kept it in action. He was then incapacitated by a third wound. Thus his conduct was heroic indeed, and of the greatest service in delaying the crossing of the enemy, which it was our object, in accordance with orders, to effect. . . . I have brought his conspicuous gallantry to notice."

Maurice James Dease.

RANKEN, HARRY SHERWOOD, Capt., was born in Glasgow 3 Sept. 1883, elder son of the Rev. Henry Ranken, B.D., Minister of Irvine, and Helen, daughter of Mathew Morton. He was educated at Irvine Royal Academy, where he was dux boy, and at Glasgow University, where he graduated M.B., Ch.B., "with commendation," in 1905. In an 'Appreciation,' written of Capt. Ranken by Andrew Balfour, C.M.G., M.D., occurs the following passage: "That he was highly esteemed by his teachers there (at Glasgow University) is shown by the fact that he was appointed House Physician and House Surgeon to the Western Infirmary, Glasgow. At a later date he acted as assistant medical officer to the Brook Fever Hospital, London." He entered the Royal Army Medical Corps on the 30th Jan. 1909. "He showed himself keenly interested in bacteriology," continues Dr. Andrew Balfour, "and more especially in the problems presented by tropical medicine. He took first place in the entrance examination, and gained the Tulloch Medal, the medal for Military Medicine, the medal and prize for Tropical Medicine, the De Chaumont prize in Hygiene, and the prize of twenty pounds for grand aggregate marks in all examinations during the probationary course, open to the Royal Army Medical Corps and the Indian Medical Service. His bent was towards research. He worked with Sir William Leishman, and also assisted Mr. H. G. Plimmer in his investigations on the experimental treatment of Trypanosomiasis. Mr. Plimmer was wont to testify to his zeal, enthusiasm and carefulness." In 1910 he became a Member of the Royal College of Physicians, London. He passed his examination for Captain in 1911, with "special certificate," and was promoted to that rank on 30 July, 1912. Dr. Andrew Balfour says that "he finally entered the Egyptian Army, being selected by the late Colonel H. B. Mathias for special work in connection with Sleeping Sickness. He was made a member of the Sudan Sleeping Sickness Commission, and sent to the remote station of Yei, in what was until recently the Lado Enclave, and is now known as Western Mongalia. In the Sleeping Sickness camp there he was made responsible for the treatment of patients, and was soon busy testing the effects of various new remedies, and more especially of Salvarsan and Metallic Antimony. He worked under considerable difficulties, but he had the dour strain of the Scot in him, and laboured indefatigably. Further, he arranged and equipped a little laboratory, where he spent many hours of research in connection both with Sleeping Sickness and Yaws. His native patients, of many tribes and speaking many dialects, liked and trusted him. He learned to converse with some of them in their own tongues, and soon gained their confidence. Though so far from any medical centre and from sources of information, his pen was by no means idle. Considering his age, his contributions to literature were considerable, and were all characterized by care and accuracy. They were as follows: 'Reports on Experimental Treatment of Trypanosomiasis' (with H. G. Plimmer and W. B. Fry) ('Proceedings of the Royal Society, 1910–11'); 'A Note on Granule-Shedding in Treponema pertenne' ('British Medical Journal,' 29 June, 1912); 'Note on the Occurrence of a Spirochaete in Cercopithecus Ruber' ('British Medical Journal,' 29 June, 1912); 'Further Researches on the Extrusion of Granules by Tryponosomes, and on their Further Development' (Fry, Ranken and Plimmer) ('Proceedings of the Royal Society,' Series B, Vol. LXXXVI., 1913; also 'Journal of the Royal Army Medical Corps,' Vol. XXI., No. 3, Sept. 1913). At Yei he found the 'Sleeping Sickness Bulletins' and, later, the 'Bulletin of the Tropical Diseases Bureau' invaluable, and was always glad when the post-runners brought in a new number. Capt. Ranken was a great favourite with all who knew him. He was modest and unassuming, but he had a fund of quiet humour, and a most kindly and generous nature. The writer will not readily forget the hospitality shown him and Colonel Mathias at Yei in 1912, both by Capt. Ranken and his brother officer, Capt. R. J. C. Thompson. As we met in the forest, some miles from the post, two of us, with one accord, raised our helmets and exclaimed: 'Dr. Livingstone, I presume!' having, unknown to each other, determined to employ this historic greeting. One remembers how Capt. Ranken laughed heartily over this little episode. At Yei there was a special Glossina Palpatis which used to lie in wait for the traveller at the ferry across the river, and follow him for a mile or so through the cleared area. Capt. Ranken had a special nickname for this fly, which was exceedingly wary and always evaded capture. He was a keen shikari,

Harry Sherwood Ranken.

and every year succeeded in obtaining his two elephants; but he was a good sportsman, and never allowed his work to suffer by reason of his love for the chase." He came home in July, 1914, on leave, and on the outbreak of the European War he at once volunteered for active service, and was restored to the British establishment Aug. 1914. He went to the front 12 Aug. 1914, attached to the 1st King's Royal Rifle Corps, with the first part of the British Expeditionary Force. Dr. Andrew Balfour continues: "He died gallantly and nobly, serving his country, doing his duty fearlessly, and as a result of tending, under fire, the wounded committed to his care. His loss is a grievous one to the cause of Tropical Medicine, for good research workers are few. He was on leave at the time the war broke out, and having volunteered, was amongst the first of his distinguished corps to go to the front." The following extract from a private letter, which we have been privileged to reproduce, tells of Capt. Ranken's heroism and devotion: "Only last night I amputated poor Ranken's leg above the knee-joint, a terrible shell wound it was, but he will probably get a V.C. for his behaviour. Although the leg was only hanging on by very little, he continued to dress his wounded in the firing line." Capt. Ranken was mentioned in Despatches; was given the Croix de Chevalier of the Legion of Honour by the French, "for gallant conduct from 21st to 30th Aug. 1914," and was awarded the Victoria Cross. But he had died at Braisne 25 Sept. 1914, of his wounds received at Soupir on the 20th, before these honours could be conferred upon him. His Victoria Cross was gazetted 16 Nov. 1914, and was in the first list for the European War: "Harry Sherwood Ranken, Capt., Royal Army Medical Corps. Dates of Acts of Bravery: 19 and 20 Sept. 1914. For tending wounded in the trenches under rifle and shrapnel fire, at Hautvesnes on the 19th, and 20th Sept., continuing to attend to wounded after his thigh and leg had been shattered. (He has since died of his wounds.)." The "Times History of the War" (Part XLI., page 44) says: "It is a safe statement to make that no man ever won the Victoria Cross more nobly than did Capt. Harry Sherwood Ranken, R.A.M.C. Capt. Ranken was severely wounded in the leg whilst attending to his duties on the battlefield. He arrested the bleeding from this, and bound it up, and then continued to dress the wounds of his men, sacrificing his chances of salvation to their needs. When finally he permitted himself to be carried to the rear, his case had become almost desperate.. He died within a short period." Colonel Northey, commanding the 1st Battn. King's Royal Rifle Corps, wrote to his parents of his personal loss and the loss the whole battalion had sustained, and several other officers wrote in the same strain. The P.M.O. of the Egyptian Army regarded his death as a great loss to science. Sir William Leishman mourned the loss of a friend, and said he was a man who thought nothing of doing three men's work. And Dr. Andrew Balfour concludes his appreciation thus: "The Society (of Tropical Medicine) has lost a valued Fellow, but he has left behind him a record of work well, faithfully, and bravely accomplished even unto the end." Capt. Ranken was a big-game hunter, elephant, buffalo, etc., a member of the Automobile Club, and a scratch golfer."

DORRELL, GEORGE THOMAS, Battery Sergt.-Major, served in the European War. He greatly distinguished himself in what Lord Ernest Hamilton, in "The First Seven Divisions," calls "a very heroic little action at Nery." He describes it, and says that on the 31st Oct. 1914, the 1st C.B. and L Battery, R.H.A., which was attached to the brigade, had billeted in this little village. Lord Ernest says: "The village lies low in a broken and hilly country. To the south and east of it the ground rises suddenly and very steeply, forming a long ridge, which juts out into the plains from the north. Along these heights Lieut. Tailby, of the 11th Hussars, was patrolling in the early morning, and in a very thick fog, when he suddenly bumped right into a column of German cavalry. He had hardly time to gallop back and warn the brigade before shot and shell began to fly thickly into the village. The German force, as it afterwards turned out, consisted of no less than six cavalry regiments, with two batteries of six guns attached; and there is reason to believe that they were just as surprised at the encounter as was the 1st C.B. However that may be, the advantage in position, as well as in numbers, was greatly on the side of the Germans, who, from the heights they were on, completely dominated the ground below. Even the sun favoured them, for when that broke through at about five o'clock, it was at the backs of the enemy and full on the faces of the defenders. The lifting of the fog soon cleared up any doubts in the minds of all concerned as to how matters stood. On the heights above, with the sun behind them, were the six German regiments, dismounted, with their twelve guns. Down below, in an open orchard on the western side of the village, were the Bays and L Battery R.H.A. They were still in the position in which they had bivouacked the night previous. Beyond them were the 5th Dragoon Guards. The 11th Hussars were on the south-east side of the village nearest the enemy, but more or less hidden from view and protected from the enemy's fire by the lie of the land. Then began one of those rare episodes which will live for ever in history and romance. The position of L Battery had not been chosen with a view to action. Except for the fog, it would never have been caught there; but having been caught there, it accepted the situation. Owing to the broken nature of the ground, only three of its guns could be brought to bear on the enemy's position, but these three were quickly at work. The Bays, who were the regiment chiefly in the line of fire, got their horses into safety, and then joined in with rifle and machine-gun fire, taking what shelter they could; but this did not amount to much, and the sun was in their eyes. None of these disadvantages made themselves felt in the case of the 11th Hussars, who, from their sheltered position, were able to bring a most effective machine-gun fire to bear on the flank of the Germans. Their doings, however, we may pass by. The focus-point of German attention was the little Horse Artillery battery down in the apple orchard. This now became the target for a perfect tornado of shot and shell, and at a range of only 400 yards. Two of the three guns were quickly knocked out, and the fire of batteries, rifles and Maxims became concentrated on the one that remained. Men and officers combined to serve the guns. Capt. Bradbury, in command, had one leg taken off by a shell, but he propped himself up, and continued to direct the fire till he fell dead. Lieut. Campbell died beside him, as did also Brigade-Major Cawley, who came up with orders from Headquarters. Lieut. Gifford and Lieut. Mundy both fell wounded, and Sergt.-Major Dorrell took over command. With the support of Sergt. Nelson, Gunner Darbyshire and Driver Osborne, he cheerfully continued this absurd and unequal duel. In the meantime the 5th Dragoon Guards had been ordered to work round to the north-east, in order to make a diversion from that flank. This they were able to do to a certain extent, though at some cost, Colonel Ansell being killed at the outset. The regiment, however, was not strong enough, single-handed, to make more than a demonstration, and the whole situation was far from promising, when, by the mercy of Providence, the 4th C.B. most unexpectedly arrived on the scene from the direction of Compiègne. These lost no time in dismounting and joining up with the 5th Dragoon Guards, the four combined regiments pouring a steady fire into the flank of the enemy. This new development entirely changed the aspect of affairs, and, finding the situation getting rather too hot for them, the Germans made off hurriedly in the direction of Verrines, abandoning eight of their guns and a Maxim. They tried in this instance to man-handle their guns out of action, but the steady fire of the cavalry on their flank, supplemented now by a frontal fire from the Bays, who had by this time installed their machine gun in the sugar factory to the west of the village, proved too much for them, and they abandoned the attempt. The whole affair had so far lasted little over an hour; but the last word had yet to be said, for the 11th Hussars jumped on to their horses, galloped off in pursuit, and captured fifty horses and a number of prisoners. The German casualties in killed and wounded were also considerable, and on our side the troops in the open orchard suffered very severely. The Bays had shown great daring and activity throughout, Mr. de Crespigny particularly distinguishing himself. They lost seven officers, and out of L Battery only three men emerged unwounded. To the survivors of this battery, however, it must for ever be a source of gratification to reflect that the last shot in that preposterous duel was fired by the battered and bloodstained thirteen-pounder down in the apple orchard, and that it was fired at the backs of the enemy. Capt. Bradbury, Sergt.-Major Dorrell and Sergt. Nelson were awarded the Victoria Cross, the former posthumously. The last two named were also given their commissions. Lieut. Gifford got the Cross of the Legion of Honour, and the entire battery earned a name which will live as long as history." Sergt. Dorrell's Victoria Cross was gazetted 16 Nov. 1914: "G. T. Dorrell, Brigade Sergt.-Major, L Battery, Royal Horse Artillery. Date of Act of Bravery: 1 Sept. 1914. For continuing to serve a gun until all the ammunition was expended, after all officers were killed or wounded, in spite of concentrated fire from machine guns, at a range of 600 yards, at Nery, on the 1st Sept." Sergt. Dorrell was given a commission, as has been said, and became Major, R.H.A.

George Thomas Dorrell.

The following is taken from the official record of Capt. George Thomas Dorrell, V.C., R.F.A.: He was born 2 July, 1876; promoted Second Lieutenant, R.F.A., from the ranks, for service, 1 Oct. 1914; promoted Lieutenant, R.F.A., 9 June, 1915; promoted Captain, R.F.A., 18 May, 1918; appointed Temporary Lieutenant, 7 March, 1915; appointed Temporary Captain, 2 May, 1915; appointed Acting Major, whilst commanding A/122nd Brigade, R.F.A., 25 Sept. 1916; appointed Acting Major, whilst commanding B/190th Brigade, F.R.A., 19 March, 1917. He served overseas in the South African Campaign, 27 Oct. 1899, to 6 Nov. 1902; in India, 7 Nov. 1902, to 7 March, 1906; with the B.E.F., France, Aug. 1914, to May, 1917. He received the Queen's South African Medal (six clasps); the King's South African Medal (two clasps); the Victoria Cross [London Gazette, 16 Nov. 1914]; was mentioned in Despatches, 18 May, 1917. He served previously in the ranks: was attested Gunner, Royal Horse Artillery, 2 Dec. 1895; promoted Bombardier, Royal Horse Artillery, 2 Jan. 1900; promoted Corporal, R.H.A., 31 May, 1900; promoted Sergeant, R.H.A., 18 June, 1900; promoted B.Q.M.S., R.H.A., 2 Dec. 1908; promoted B.S.M., R.H.A., 29 Nov. 1911.

NELSON, DAVID, Sergt., served in the European War, and was awarded the Victoria Cross [London Gazette, 16 Nov. 1914]: "David Nelson, No. 33419, Sergt., L Battery, Royal Horse Artillery. Date of Act of Bravery: 1 Sept. 1914. Helping to bring the guns into action under heavy fire at Nery on the 1st Sept., and, while severely wounded, remaining with them until all the ammunition was expended, although he had been ordered to retire to cover." After describing some of the deeds which won the first Victoria Crosses of 1914, the "Times History of the War" (Vol. X., part 118), says: "Seven of the first batch of nine awards have been dealt with; two remain to be described, and this pair concern a

David Nelson.

deed which thrilled the Empire—the heroic stand of L Battery, Royal Horse Artillery, an act which may well be compared with the famous affair of Q Battery at Sanna's Post on 31 March, 1900, for which four Victoria Crosses were given: L Battery had greatly distinguished itself at Mons, and in helping to cover the retreat, fought a heavy rearguard action. On 1 Sept. 1914, the last day of the retirement, in a morning mist, the battery, at close range, unexpectedly came into action with a vastly superior German force. A fire was brought to bear on the battery which was so destructive that only one British gun was left in action, and this was served until all the ammunition was expended by Battery Sergt.-Major George Thomas Dorrell, Sergt. David Nelson, Gunner H. Darbyshire and Driver Osborne; all the rest of the men and officers of the battery having been killed or wounded. The Queen's Bays and I Battery came to the rescue at the close of the terrible artillery duel, and what was left of L Battery came out of action. Dorrell and Nelson received the Victoria Cross and commissions; Darbyshire and Osborne were awarded the Médaille Militaire of France." In the London Gazette of 26 Nov. 1914, the award of a posthumous Victoria Cross to Capt. Edward Kinder Bradbury was announced. "Deeds that thrill the Empire" (Vol. II., page 585) says: "Having discussed the situation with General Joffre, Sir John French renewed the retreat of his army on the afternoon of Saturday, 29 Aug. 1914. To meet present circumstances, the original plans of General Joffre had to be modified, and the British now moved towards the line of the river Aisne, from Soissons to Compiègne, and then in the direction of the Marne about Meaux. On the night of 31 Aug. the Bays and L Battery of the Royal Horse Artillery bivouacked in an open orchard on the west side of the village of Nery. The village lies in the midst of broken and hilly country. To the south and east the ground rises suddenly and very steeply, and on the heights Lieut. Tailby, of the Hussars, was patrolling in the early morning of 1 Sept. A thick fog hung over the ground, and besides shutting out the view, it muffled every sound. Nevertheless, he groped along, stopping every now and again to listen, but neither hearing the enemy nor seeing any signs of them. Then, all of a sudden, a whole column of German cavalry loomed out of the fog. Lieut. Tailby was seen, and turning his horse abruptly round, he galloped off to warn the brigade. He had just time enough to dash in and raise the alarm, and then the shot and shell began to fall thickly upon the village. About five o'clock the fog cleared, and away on the heights could be seen the six German regiments, dismounted, with their twelve guns. The advantage in an engagement would be greatly on the side of the Germans, both as regards numbers and the position which they held. But the British gallantly resolved to fight. Three only of the battery's guns could be brought into action, and these quickly opened fire. After getting their horses into safety, the Bays, who were in the line of fire, joined in with the rifles and machine guns. The three guns kept up their fire amidst a storm of shot and shell, but the range was only four hundred yards, and two of them were quickly knocked out of action. Capt. Bradbury, who was in command, had a leg blown off by a shell, but with the utmost bravery he propped himself up and continued to direct the fire till he fell dead. Both Lieut. Campbell and Brigade-Major Cawley died beside him, the latter after bringing up orders from Headquarters. Lieuts. Gifford and Mundy were both wounded, and then, amidst a storm of fire from field-guns, Maxims and rifles, Sergt.-Major Dorrell took command. He was supported by Sergt. Nelson, who, though severely wounded, refused to retire, and also by Gunner Darbyshire and Driver Osborne. While they kept the last gun in action, the 5th Dragoon Guards worked round to the north-east, to make a diversion from that flank. They succeeded to a certain extent, but Colonel Ansell fell, shot through the head, at the very commencement. Without reinforcements they could do no more than make a demonstration, and for a time the situation was doubtful. But the 4th Cavalry Brigade suddenly arrived on the scene. Dismounting from their horses, they at once joined up with the 5th Dragoon Guards, and the combined regiments then poured a steady fire into the enemy's flank. Finding that their position was getting rather hot, the Germans attempted to man-handle their guns out of action. A steady fire, however, was poured into their flank by the cavalry, and the Bays, who had mounted a machine gun in a sugar factory to the west of the village, attacked them with a frontal fire. This proved too much for them, and abandoning eight guns and a Maxim, they made off towards Verrines. The engagement had now been in progress a little over an hour, but to cap the victory the 11th Hussars sprang on to their horses and dashed off in pursuit. Fifty horses and a number of prisoners were brought back, and the German casualties in killed and wounded proved to be considerable. Of just over two hundred officers and men of L Battery, Royal Horse Artillery, only forty survived; but their magnificent courage and tenacity saved a serious situation, and, later, greatly helped towards the enemy's defeat." Sergt. Nelson was given a commission for his gallantry on this occasion, and later became a Major in the R.H.A. An obituary notice in 1918 says: "NELSON.—On the 8th April, of wounds received 7th April, Major D. Nelson, V.C., R.F.A., husband of Jessie Nelson, and son of the late Mr. G. Nelson, Deraghland, County Monaghan, aged 31."

The following is taken from the official record of the services of Lieut. and Acting Major David Nelson, V.C., R.F.A. (deceased): He was born in 1886; promoted Second Lieutenant, R.F.A., from the ranks, 15 Nov. 1914; promoted Lieutenant, R.F.A., 9 June, 1915; appointed Captain Instructor in Gunnery, 1 March, 1915; appointed Temporary Lieutenant, 3 June, 1915; appointed Temporary Captain, 12 Oct. 1916; appointed Acting Major, whilst commanding D Battery, 59th Brigade, R.F.A., 1 March, 1918. He served overseas: B.E.F., France, Aug. 1914, to Oct. 1918; B.E.F., France, Dec. 1917, to April, 1918; was wounded, G.H.Q., List, X73094, 8 April, 1918; died of wounds, List X73094, 8 April, 1918. He served previously in the ranks: attested Gunner, Royal Field Artillery, 27 Dec. 1904; promoted Bombardier, L Battery, R.H.A., 18 May, 1910; promoted Corporal, L Battery, R.H.A., 7 Jan. 1911; promoted Serjeant, L Battery, R.H.A., 5 Aug. 1914; awarded the Victoria Cross [London Gazette, 16 Nov. 1914]. Major Nelson died at No. 58 Casualty Clearing Station. He was buried in Lillers Communal Cemetery, N.W. of Bethune.

GARFORTH, CHARLES ERNEST, Corpl., was born at Willesden Green, London N.W., on 23 Oct. 1891. He was educated at Green Hill School, Harrow. On leaving school he returned to his home, his father being a house builder and decorator. As soon as Garforth was old enough, he joined the Territorial Force, in the 9th Battn. Middlesex Regt., and transferred in 1911 to the 15th (The King's) Hussars, and after doing his recruit's course at Aldershot, he joined the regiment in Potchefstroom, South Africa, returning home to England with the 15th in 1913. Garforth was promoted a Corporal just before the outbreak of war, and sailed with A Squadron, 15th Hussars, on 16 Aug. 1914. A Squadron was Divisional Cavalry to the 3rd Division. Garforth took part in the Battle of Mons, and fought throughout the retreat, the Battles of the Marne and Aisne, and, when the British Armies moved north, took part in the preliminary conflicts which took place before the Battle of Ypres; he was taken prisoner near Laventie on 13 Oct. 1914. Corpl. Garforth was recommended three times for the V.C., for the following acts of gallantry: On 23 Aug. 1914, his troop was fighting a rear-guard action near Harmignies; the troop was nearly surrounded, and was held up by a wire fence. Corpl. Garforth cut this wire fence, in spite of the fact that the Germans had turned machine-gun fire on to the fence, with the express purpose of preventing it being cut. This action allowed the troop to make a gallop for safety. Again on 6 Sept. 1914, near Dammartin, Corpl. Garforth was out on patrol. The patrol came under heavy fire and was forced to retire. Sergt. Scatterfield's horse was shot, and the Sergeant was lying under his horse. Garforth went forward under heavy fire and pulled the Sergeant from under his horse, and took him to a place of safety. Again on the following day, 7 Sept., when on patrol, Sergt. Lewis had his horse shot, and was on foot under machine-gun fire. Garforth drew the fire of the machine guns on to himself, and engaged the machine gun with his rifle fire, thus enabling the Sergeant to get away under cover. He was awarded the Victoria Cross [London Gazette, 16 Nov. 1914]: "Charles Ernest Garforth, No. 7368, Corpl., 15th Hussars. Date of Act of Bravery: 23 Aug. 1914. At Harmignies, on 23 Aug., volunteered to cut wire under fire, which enabled his squadron to escape. At Dammartin he carried a man out of action. On 3 Sept., when under Maxim fire, he extricated a Sergeant whose horse had been shot, and by opening fire for three minutes enabled the sergeant to get away safely." When the British Armies were moving on to the line La Bassée–Ypres, Corpl. Garforth was on patrol with Capt. Bradshaw, near Laventie; the patrol was surrounded, the Officer and seven men were killed. Corpl. Garforth held out until all his ammunition was expended; at that time Divisional Cavalry had not been given bayonets, and Corpl. Garforth was thus unarmed, and was taken prisoner on 13 Oct. 1914. He was first sent to Hamelin-on-Weser, and transferred from there to Bohmte; from this latter place he made three attempts to escape, and on each occasion reached the German-Dutch frontier, but was always recaptured on the frontier line, as each time his food ran out, and he was too weak and exhausted to avoid the frontier guards. On one occasion he was six days without food. He was punished by three weeks' solitary confinement in a dark cell on bread and water for these attempts to escape. He was finally sent to Holland on 19 March, 1918, repatriated to England on 18 Nov. 1918, and rejoined his regiment in Kerpen, near Cologne, on 4 Aug. 1919. He returned with the 15th Hussars to Kilkenny in Sept. 1919, where he is now serving with the Regt. as a Sergeant.

Chas. Ernest Garforth.

JARVIS, CHARLES ALFRED, L.-Corpl., served in the European War, and was awarded the Victoria Cross [London Gazette, 16 Nov. 1914]: "Charles Alfred Jarvis, L.-Corpl., No. 3976, 57th Field Coy., Royal Engineers. Date of Act of Bravery: 23 Aug. 1914. For great gallantry at Jemappes on 23 Aug. in working for one and a half hours under heavy fire in full view of the enemy, and in successfully firing charges for the demolition of a bridge." Lord Ernest Hamilton describes in "The First Seven Divisions" (pages 19 and 20) how the withdrawal of the troops to the left of the Nimy salient became necessary when its abandonment was decided on. "In the evening the 5th Division received the order to retire. This was not till long after the 3rd Division had abandoned the Nimy salient. The three brigades of this latter division, after putting up an heroic defence and suffering many casualties, got the order to retire at 3 p.m., whereupon the Royal Fusiliers fell slowly back through Mons to Hyon, and the Royal Scots Fusiliers, who had put up a great fight at Jemappes, through Flenn. The blowing up of the Jemappes bridge gave a lot of trouble. Corpl. Jarvis, Royal Engineers, worked at it for one and a half hours, continuously under fire, before he eventually managed to get it destroyed under the very noses of the Germans. He got a private of the Royal Scots Fusiliers, named Heron, to help him, who got the D.C.M. Jarvis got the Victoria Cross." "The Sapper," for Feb.

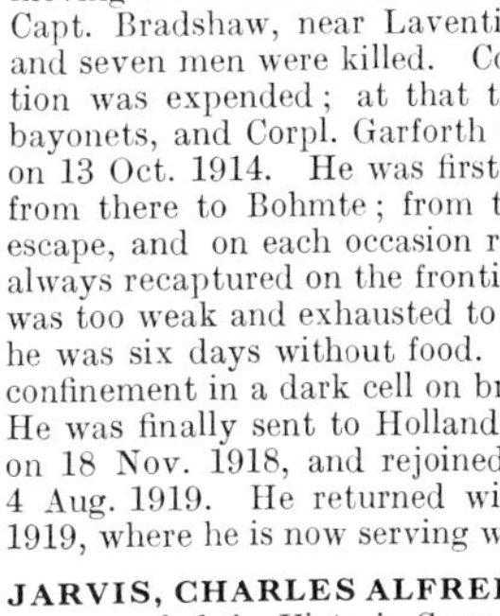

Charles Alfred Jarvis.

1915 (pages 172–173) says : " His Majesty the King presented nine Victoria Crosses at Buckingham Palace on the 13th Jan. 1915, amongst the recipients being L.-Corpl. Jarvis, late of the 57th Coy., Royal Engineers. After pinning on the Cross, His Majesty shook hands with L.-Corpl. Jarvis, and said : 'A very brave deed. Thank you very much for your gallant conduct, for which the V.C. is awarded you, and may you live long to do similar noble deeds.'

" Particulars of the award of the Victoria Cross appeared in ' The Sapper ' for Dec. 1914. The following further details will doubtless be read with much interest :

" The 57th (Field) Coy. were at Cuismes and Jemappes on the 22nd Aug. 1914, and assisted in preparing the defensive positions held by the infantry on the bank of the Mons Canal. Over this canal are a number of bridges, which can be raised to let the traffic on the canal pass. The roadway of each bridge is borne on three light steel girders. On the morning of the 23rd Aug. 1914, the company was detailed to positions on the canal. L.-Corpl. Jarvis and Sapper Neary were detailed with B Coy. Royal Scots Fusiliers, and ordered to prepare one of the bridges for demolition in case of a retirement. A small boat was procured, and two privates of the R.S.F. were detailed to hold the boat in position. The three girders needing separate charges, required in all 22 slabs of guncotton, which had to be securely fixed to the girders and tamped with clay.

" During the work of placing the charges the fire of the enemy gradually increased in violence. L.-Corpl. Jarvis sent the two infantrymen back to their company, and despatched Sapper Neary to obtain the exploder and leads, which were in the possession of another party under 2nd Corpl. Wiltshire. After some considerable time the amount of fire increased, so that reinforcements had to be sent for. Capt. Traill, R.S.F., who was wounded in the knee, procured a pony and went to fetch them, and also ammunition. By this time the firing on the position had become so violent and the casualties were so numerous that a retirement had been decided on. Corpl. Jarvis was then called upon to destroy the bridge, but was still without the exploder and leads, as the sapper had not returned. He pulled along the lock to a position where no fire was being directed, crawled out over the bank, and got into a street, where he commandeered a bicycle from a Belgian, and was riding toward the market square to find the exploder himself, when he met Capt. F. Wright, V.C., R.E., the Adjutant of the R.E. Companies, 3rd Division, who was then wounded in the head. Capt. Wright told L.-Corpl. Jarvis to go back to the bridge and be prepared to connect up the leads, as he would fetch them in a motor car, and taking the bicycle from Jarvis, went off to fetch the necessary articles. Jarvis returned to his former position to await the return of Capt. Wright. By this time the infantry had been terribly cut up, and the general order to retire came, which practically meant every man for himself.

" L.-Corpl. Jarvis gives the following account of succeeding events :

" ' When I got out of my position I saw civilians and soldiers running for their lives, and dropping to the volleys from the Germans. I got into another street, where I found Sapper Neary. The Uhlans by this time were well in pursuit of us. Finding a party of the R.S.F., we kept together until we were joined by Lieut. Boulnois, R.E., 2nd Corpl. C. Wiltshire, and Sapper Farmer. The officer decided we should make for Frameries, a suburb of Jemappes.

" ' When we got to Frameries we were joined by our section forage cart, with Sapper Carver and a mounted N.C.O. and driver. In pursuit of them were about twenty Uhlans. Owing to their erratic fire, we got safely away. Those who had no bicycles got on the cart, and we then made for the open country towards Genly, where we took up a position behind a hedge to await our pursuers, who disappointed us by remaining in Frameries. That night we slept in a barn on the main road. After being served with a meal of coffee, eggs and bread and jam by the farmer's wife, we barricaded ourselves in and slept among the straw till 2.30 a.m., when we got up and marched back to find our company at Frameries. We started pulling up the stone setts in the streets and forming barricades. By 9 o'clock in the morning we were shelled out by shrapnel, and we then made our way with the column to a place called Feignies, where we billeted in a small theatre. Finding a few instruments behind the stage, a cornet, bassoon, trombone, and big drum, we had an entertainment, having talent amongst us to manage each instrument. I'll never forget that band, nor Sapper Morton and his card juggling !

" ' On the evening of the 25th Aug. we went on the march again, and after doing about 30 miles on the heel and toe, got to Le Cateau and Bertry, where we started with the infantry getting trenches ready and providing overhead cover. Our artillery were in position in a dip behind us, and there were also two 120–pounders in a position just 200 yards to our rear. This was at about 10 o'clock on the morning of the 26th Aug. The battle started as an artillery duel. Part of my section were left in the trenches to improve them and the overhead cover. By about 12 o'clock the German infantry had gained a village at our front, and the sport began. Second Corpl. Wiltshire and I were at one side of a traverse keeping up the supply of ammunition to the Lincolns and R.S.F., who were manning the trenches. We were having a grand day as we thought,, as every time we saw the Germans rush to a position, our infantry saw them, and *our 120–pounders saw them too*, and we were so nicely under cover that we lost only one man in the trenches.

" ' At about 4 o'clock in the afternoon, to our consternation, a brigade-major came over to our lines of trenches shouting the order, " Retire to your left rear ! " We had to cross a field of clover and then a field of sugar-beet. We heard many shout " I'm hit ! " but we had to run on to evade capture. We ran on till we came to the position of our guns, which were in a dip and close to a village. From this point we started our great Retreat to the Marne, doing in some instances 64 miles in two days, with a column six miles long.' "

London Gazette, 19 Nov. 1914.—" War Office, 19 Nov. 1914. His Majesty the King has been graciously pleased to approve of the grant of the Victoria Cross to the undermentioned Officer for conspicuous bravery whilst serving with the Expeditionary Force."

DIMMER, JOHN HENRY STEPHEN, Lieut., was born in Oct. 1883, son of Mr. John Dimmer, late Royal Navy. He was educated at Merton School, Surrey, and Rutlish Science School, Merton, Surrey. He enlisted in 1902, and the following year was promoted Corporal for reconnaissance work in the Orange River Colony. He was made Lance-Sergeant in 1905 for scouting and signalling in the Mounted Infantry, and in 1906 he was sent to study the military systems of Belgium and Germany. In Nov. 1907, he visited a foreign country on behalf of the Intelligence Department, and for his work received a special letter of thanks from the Army Council. In Jan. 1908, Lord Methuen recommended him for a commission as Second Lieutenant, and from then until the outbreak of the present war, he was doing special work in West Africa. On the outbreak of the European War he went with the first Expeditionary Force to France. He rejoined the 2nd Battn. King's Royal Rifle Corps, and was thus in the First Division. He was present in the action at Klein Zillebeke on 12 Nov. 1914, and for his services was awarded the Victoria Cross and promoted Captain. In his own account of the affair he tells how the Prussian Guards suddenly attacked them, and besides shelling them, sent a hail of bullets at a range of about 100 yards. After smashing up one of Dimmer's guns almost at once, the Germans concentrated their attention on the gun Dimmer himself was with. He says : " My face is spattered with pieces of my gun and pieces of shell, and I have a bullet in my face and four small holes in my right shoulder. It made rather a mess of me at first, but now that I am washed and my wounds dressed, I look quite all right." He was awarded the Victoria Cross [London Gazette, 19 Nov. 1914] : " John Henry Stephen Dimmer, Lieut., 2nd Battn. King's Royal Rifle Corps. Date of Act of Bravery : 12 Nov. 1914. This officer served his machine-gun during the attack, on the 12th Nov., at Klein Zillebeke, until he had been shot five times—three times by shrapnel and twice by bullets—and continued at his post until his gun was destroyed."

John H. S. Dimmer.

" Deeds that thrill the Empire " (Vol. I., page 270) says : " On the morning of 10 Nov. 1914, the King's Royal Rifles, who had been attached to the sorely-shattered 4th (Guards') Brigade, relieved the London Scottish in the section of the trenches at Klein Zillebeke which the Territorials had held so gallantly in the face of heavy and persistent shelling. The machine-gun section, which was in charge of Lieut. Dimmer, took over from the Scots about noon, and that officer lost no time in placing his two Vickers machine-guns in position. The German trenches opposite to ours had been dug behind a bank on the edge of a wood, known to our men as the Brown Road Wood, and the trees of which, though it was already the second week in November, were still well covered with leaves. A great number of the trees had, however, been broken down by the fire of our artillery ; indeed, as viewed from the British trenches, the wood appeared almost impassable. The No Man's Land between the hostile lines presented a curious and gruesome spectacle, being covered with shell-holes and littered with the unburied bodies of fallen Germans—in heaps and singly—many of which had probably lain there since the desperate and sanguinary fighting of the last days of October. During the afternoon of the 10th the new arrivals were very badly shelled, and also much annoyed by the attention of the German snipers, a corporal of the King's Royal Rifles, named Cordingley, being shot dead by one of these gentry, while Lieut. Dimmer had two narrow escapes, the bullet on each occasion passing through his cap. On the 11th they were shelled all day, the bombardment being particularly severe in the afternoon. On the 12th, on which day the enemy began a series of attacks on the Klein Zillebeke positions, and along the whole of our line towards Messines, all was quiet until noon, when the German artillery started a violent bombardment of the ' Green Jackets' ' trenches. This continued for about half an hour, when it slackened, and the enemy's machine-guns began to pour a torrent of bullets through the gaps in the British parapet made by their artillery fire. Then, at 1 p.m., the Prussian Guard, in mass formation, advanced from the wood, the men marching shoulder to shoulder, in perfect order, as though they were on parade. At once the British machine-guns began to spit death amongst them, Lieut. Dimmer firing one of the guns himself, and the storm of bullets tore through their serried ranks, mowing them down as corn falls before the sickle. But still they came on, and presently the lieutenant's gun jammed, owing to the belt getting wet. In a moment he had climbed on to the emplacement, a large adjustable spanner in his hand, and got the deadly weapon again in working order ; but, as he did so, a rifle bullet struck him in the right jaw. Heedless of the pain, he began to pour a fresh stream of lead into the advancing masses, but he had not fired many rounds when the gun stuck when traversing. Reaching up to remedy the stoppage, he was again hit by a rifle bullet, this time in the right shoulder. But he got his gun going again for all that, and before the blast of death the Huns fell in swathes. Then a shrapnel shell burst above him, and he was hit for the third time, three bullets lodging in his injured shoulder. But, with the blood streaming from his wounds, the heroic officer went on firing his gun, until, when within fifty yards of our trenches, the Germans suddenly broke and ran for cover. Their artillery covered their retreat with a rain of shrapnel, and Lieut. Dimmer's gun was hit and destroyed, and his face spattered with splinters of broken metal. Exhausted with pain and loss of blood, he lost consciousness for a time, but, on coming to, insisted on proceeding to Brigade Headquarters to report in person to the Earl of Cavan, commanding the 4th (Guards') Brigade. Scarcely, however, had he made his report than his strength gave out, and he collapsed and was taken to the dressing-station. Happily, this most gallant officer, whose magnificent courage and tenacity were recognized by the award of the Victoria Cross, has since made a complete recovery, and after being attached for a time to the 6th Battn. of the King's Royal Rifle Corps at Sheerness, he was sent to Serbia." He was awarded the Military Cross [London Gazette, 1 Jan. 1915] (New Year's Honours List). Was given the command of a battalion of the Royal Berkshire Regt. in Oct. 1917. Twice mentioned in Despatches. Gained Observer's Wing while in Salonica, attached to the Flying Squadron. On the 19th Jan. 1918, at Moseley, Birmingham, he married Dora, daughter of W. Bayley-Parker, Esq., and of Mrs. Bayley-Parker, of The Oaklands, Moseley, Birmingham. He was killed on 21 March of the same year, leading his men into action.

London Gazette, 23 Nov. 1914.—" War Office, 23 Nov. 1914. His Majesty the King has been graciously pleased to approve of the grant of the Victoria Cross to the undermentioned Non-commissioned Officer for conspicuous bravery whilst serving with the Expeditionary Force."

FULLER, WILLIAM, L.-Corpl., was born at Laugharne, Carmarthenshire, son of William and Mary Fuller. He was educated at Swansea, and joined the Army in 1902, serving in the European War from 1914 to 31 Dec.

William Fuller.

1915. The way in which Sergt. Fuller's Victoria Cross was won is described in "Deeds that thrill the Empire" (page 526): "On Sunday, 13 Sept. 1914, the greater part of the British Expeditionary Force crossed the Aisne, and by the evening our men had dug themselves in well up on the farther slopes; and early next morning, while our engineers were busily strengthening the new bridges and repairing some of the old, which the Germans partially destroyed, so as to enable them to bear the weight of heavy traffic, a general advance was begun along the whole western section of the Allied front. On the part of the British, the real offensive was entrusted to the 1st Corps, under Sir Douglas Haig, which had bivouacked on the northern bank of the river, between

Chavonne and Moulins. Its objective was the Chemin des Dames, or Ladies' Road, four miles to the north, the possession of which would give us command of the southern part of the Craonne Plateau from Soissons to Berry-au-Bac. The 2nd Brigade, supported by the 25th Artillery Brigade, was to push forward from Moulins on the extreme right, and seize a spur east of the hamlet of Troyon, just south of the Ladies' Road, while the remaining two brigades of the 1st Division advanced up the Vendesse Valley. The 6th Brigade, in the 2nd Division, was to occupy the Ladies' Road south of Courtacon, while the rest of the division advanced up the Braye glen, and the 4th (Guards') Brigade, on its left, supported by the 36th Artillery Brigade, took the heights east of Ostel. The movement began just before dawn, and the Northamptons captured the spur east of Troyon at the point of the bayonet. But a desperate resistance was encountered at Troyon itself, where there was a sugar factory held in strong force by the enemy, and it was not until midday that it was carried by the North Lancashires, when the 1st and 2nd Brigades were drawn up on the line just south of the Ladies' Road. The 3rd Brigade continued the line west of Vendesse, and linked up with the 2nd Division, which had met with such fierce opposition that its right was hung up south of Braye, while its left was still some way from the Ostel ridge. About four in the afternoon a general advance of the 1st Corps was ordered, and by nightfall, though we had not succeeded in occupying the Ladies' Road, we had, in the words of Viscount French, 'gained positions which alone have enabled me to maintain my position for more than three weeks of very severe fighting on the north bank of the river.' But this success was not won without heavy losses, especially among the commissioned ranks of the 1st Corps, the Colonels of four of its twelve battalions—those of the Black Watch, Royal Sussex, North Lancashires and West Surreys—being all killed. The 3rd Brigade, in capturing the village of Chivy, had a particularly severe task, the enemy being in immensely superior force and very strongly posted. As the Welsh, in the centre, advancing by sections, neared the crest of the hill, behind which lay the village, Capt. Mark Haggard, a nephew of Sir Rider Haggard, ordered his men to lie down, and advanced alone to reconnoitre the German position. Then he turned and shouted, ' Fix bayonets, boys!' and the Welshmen, rising to their feet, dashed forward, to be met by a withering machine-gun and rifle fire. Calling on his men to follow him, Capt. Haggard, who carried, like them, rifle and bayonet, rushed forward to capture a Maxim gun, which was doing considerable damage. But just before he reached it, he was struck by several bullets, and fell to the ground, mortally wounded. ' Near me,' writes a private of the Welsh, who had himself been struck down almost at the same moment, ' was lying our brave captain, mortally wounded. As the shells burst over us, he would occasionally open his eyes between the spasms of pain, and call out weakly : " Stick it, Welsh ! " ' Seeing Capt. Haggard fall, L.-Corpl. William Fuller ran forward under tremendous fire, and, lifting him up, carried him back about one hundred yards, until he gained the shelter of the ridge, where he laid him down and dressed his wounds. Capt. Haggard begged him to fetch his rifle, which he had dropped where he fell, so that the Germans should not get possession of it ; and this Fuller succeeded in doing without getting hit. He then, with the assistance of a private named Snooks and

Lieut. Melvin, the officer in charge of the machine-gun section of the Welsh, carried Capt. Haggard to a barn adjoining a farmhouse some distance to the rear, which was being used as a dressing-station. Here he did what he could to relieve his sufferings, until the evening, when the unfortunate officer expired, his last words being ' Stick it, Welsh !' He was buried close to the farmhouse where he died. Capt. Mark Haggard, whose bravery on the occasion cost him his life, was the third son of Bayell Michael Haggard, of Kirby Cain, Norfolk, and was born in 1876. On the outbreak of the Boer War he joined the City of London Imperial Volunteers, and went with them to South Africa, and in 1900 received a commission in the Welsh. He became Captain in 1911. He was immensely popular in his regiment. ' We were prepared to follow him anywhere,' writes a private of his company. After Capt. Haggard's death, Sergt. Fuller attended to two officers of the South Wales Borderers, Lieut. the Hon. Fitzroy Somerset and Lieut. Richards, who were both lying wounded in the same barn, until the ambulance came to remove them. The barn was during this time exposed to very heavy shell fire, and the following day, after all our wounded officers and men had been got away, was blown to pieces by the German guns. He had also under his charge about sixty women and children of the neighbourhood, who had taken refuge in the cellar of an adjoining house, and whose wants he supplied until wagons were sent to fetch them away. This house, and, in fact, all the neighbouring buildings, were subsequently levelled to the ground by the enemy's shell fire. L.-Corpl. Fuller escaped unhurt on 14 Sept. About six weeks later (29 Oct.), during the desperate fighting near Gheluvelt, he was severely wounded by a piece of shrapnel, while dressing the wounds of a comrade named Private Tagge, who had been hit in both legs during the counter-attack by which we recovered most of the trenches from which our first division had been driven earlier in the day. The shrapnel entered the right side, travelled nearly twelve inches up under the shoulder-blade, and rested on the right lung. Sergt. Fuller was sent home to Wales, and was operated on at Swansea Hospital, where the shrapnel was extracted. On his recovery he was employed for some months on recruiting duties in Wales, in which he was most successful."

London Gazette, 25 Nov. 1914.—" War Office, 25 Nov. 1914. His Majesty the King has been graciously pleased to approve of the grant of the Victoria Cross to the undermentioned Officers, Non-commissioned Officers and men for conspicuous bravery whilst serving with the Expeditionary Force."

GODLEY, SYDNEY FRANK, Private, was born 14 Aug. 1889, at East

Sydney Frank Godley.

Grinstead, Sussex, son of Frank Godley. He was educated at Sidcup National Schools, and joined the Army 13 Dec. 1909. Private Godley was a noted sportsman in the battalion, being a good cross-country runner, also footballer and cricketer. He served in the European War from 1914, and was awarded the Victoria Cross, 23 Aug. 1914, for the defence of Nimy Bridge, for coolness and gallantry in fighting with a machine-gun under a very heavy fire for two hours after being severely wounded, and holding up the enemy advance single-handed, and thus allowing the Royal Fusiliers to retire. He was assisted for a time by Lieut. Pease, of the Royal Fusiliers, who was killed and was awarded the Victoria Cross. His Victoria Cross was gazetted, 25 Nov. 1914 :

" Sydney Frank Godley, No. 13814, 4th Battn. The Royal Fusiliers. Date of Act of Bravery : 23 Aug. 1914. For coolness and gallantry in fighting his machine-gun under a hot fire for two hours, after he had been wounded at Mons on the 23rd Aug." Private Godley married, 2 Aug. 1919, at St. Mark's Church, Harlesden, Helen Eliza, daughter of George Norman. He has the 1914 Star, etc.

DRAIN, JOB HENRY CHARLES, Driver, served in the European

Job H. C. Drain.

War. He won his Victoria Cross in the early days of the war, when the Germans —lavish of human life—hurled repeated assaults against the English batteries. On the " most critical day of all " (according to Sir John French's Despatch), 26 Aug. 1914, at Le Cateau, the day of " the glorious stand of the British troops," the artillery, although " outmatched by at least four to one," fought with unsurpassed gallantry, and wrought much havoc among the Boches. So determined were some of the German assaults that they actually succeeded in getting to within a hundred yards of our batteries, one of these being the 37th Battery, Royal Field Artillery. The Germans swept in dense formation towards the guns of the 37th, which seemed likely to fall into their hands, and be carried off as trophies. It seemed as if only by the aid of a miracle could the guns be saved. Capt. Douglas Reynolds and volunteers rushed up with two teams, and in spite of the withering German fire and the enemy's desperate attempts to prevent them, limbered up two guns and managed to save one of them. The risk was terrible, and the desperate valour of the British was all the more remarkable because they were worn out by protracted fighting and fatigue. The splendour of their achievement was marked by the award of the Victoria Cross to Reynolds, who was afterwards severely wounded, and to two members of the Battery, Driver J. H. C. Drain and Driver F. Luke—three in all, the same as the number of Crosses bestowed on L Battery. Driver Drain's Victoria Cross was gazetted 25 Nov. 1914: "Job Henry Charles Drain, No. 69960, Driver; Frederick Luke, No. 71787, Driver, 37th Battery, Royal Field Artillery. Date of Acts of Bravery: 1 Sept. 1914. At Le Cateau, on the 26th Aug., as volunteers, helping to save guns under fire from hostile infantry, who were 100 yards away."

LUKE, FREDERICK, Driver, served in the European War, and was awarded the Victoria Cross [London Gazette, 25 Nov. 1914]: "Job Henry Charles Drain, No. 69960, Driver; Frederick Luke, No. 71787, Driver, 37th Battery, Royal Horse Artillery. At Le Cateau, on the 26th Aug., as volunteers, helping to save guns under fire from hostile infantry, who were 100 yards away." "Deeds that thrill the Empire" (page 35) says: "On the morning of the 24th Aug. 1914, the retreat of the British from Mons began, and on the 26th Sir Horace Smith-Dorrien fought his famous action at Le Cateau, which saved the left wing of the Army from being enveloped and cut off. Smith-Dorrien had little time to entrench his position before the grey masses of the enemy's infantry were seen advancing, supported by the fire of some six hundred guns, on a front of about twelve miles. He had no reserves available, and could only strengthen a threatened part of his line by taking the risk of weakening another part of it. Heavy, indeed, was our men's task that day, and that of the artillery was the heaviest of all. Opposed to four times their number of guns—and guns for the most part of much heavier calibre than their own—their losses in horses and men were appalling. In one battery, towards the end of the fight, only a lieutenant and one gunner remained, still heroically contriving to keep a single gun in action. Several pieces were disabled by the huge shells from the German field howitzers, while the carriages of others were smashed to atoms. As the day wore on, Von Kluck began to use his superior numbers in a great enveloping movement on both flanks, and between three and four o'clock in the afternoon the British received orders to retire. The movement was covered by our artillery with the most splendid courage, but at a terrible cost, and it was at this moment that the incident we are about to relate occurred. Capt. Douglas Reynolds, of the 37th Battery, Royal Field Artillery, perceiving that the horses attached to several guns had all been killed or disabled, brought up two teams, driven by men who had volunteered their services, in a desperate attempt to save a couple of them. Though exposed to a very heavy shell and rifle fire—the advancing German infantry were scarcely a hundred yards distant—these brave men contrived to limber up two guns. But the next moment one entire team was shot down, while Driver Godley, the driver of the centre pair of the other team, fell dead from his saddle. Captain Reynolds, however, rode alongside the unguided pair, and kept them in hand, and with driver Luke driving the leaders and Driver Drain the wheelers, the gun was brought safely out of action. Each of these three heroes was awarded the Victoria Cross, and one of them, Capt. Reynolds, had the satisfaction of distinguishing himself again a fortnight later at the Battle of the Marne, when, reconnoitring at close range, he located a battery which was holding up our advance and silenced it. Unhappily, he was severely wounded at the Aisne on 15 Sept. 1914."

Frederick Luke.

YATE, CHARLES ALLIX LAVINGTON, Major, belonged to a Berkshire family, a branch of which had settled at Madeley Hall in Shropshire, in the time of his great-great-grandfather, that is, about the middle of the 18th century. He was the son of Prebendary George Edward Yate, who was vicar of Madeley from 1859 to 1908. Major Yate was born on 14 March, 1872. He was educated at Weymouth College. It had been his father's intention that he should be educated at Shrewsbury School, but, as a boy, Major Yate was delicate, and he was sent to Weymouth in the hope that the mild climate and sea air would benefit his health. This hope was fulfilled, and he remained at Weymouth College till Dec. 1890. In the following year he entered the Royal Military College at Sandhurst, passing in ninth out of 1,100 candidates, a number much above the average. On leaving Sandhurst he was gazetted on 13 Aug. 1892 to the King's Own (Yorkshire Light Infantry), and joined the 2nd Battn., which was then at Bombay. He first saw active service in the Tirah Expedition of 1897–8, and gained the Medal and clasp. His rank at that time was Lieutenant. He was promoted to the rank of Captain in 1899. From India the regiment was sent to Mauritius, and while there Major Yate passed the examination for entrance to the Staff College, taking a high place. Almost immediately afterwards the Boer War broke out. H.M.S. Powerful happened to be returning from the China seas, and received orders to call at Mauritius and convey the King's Own (Yorkshire Light Infantry) to South Africa. It was thus one of the first regiments to reach Cape Town. Major Yate was very dangerously wounded at the Battle of Graspan, and was unable to return to active service till the war was drawing to a close. He was one of the party who were sent with the white flag to General Botha to arrange the preliminaries for peace negotiations. He received for his services in this war the Queen's Medal with four clasps, and was mentioned by Lord Roberts in his Despatch of 10 Sept. 1901. He returned to England after this war, and graduated at the Staff College. Major Yate was sent in the autumn of 1903 on a special mission to Japan, with three other officers representing different branches of the British Army. Major Yate represented the Infantry. He was one of the officers chosen to report on the military tactics of the Japanese during the war between Russia and Japan, and served as Military Attaché with the Japanese Army throughout the siege of Port Arthur. He was one of the first to enter that stronghold with the Japanese. The Emperor of Japan decorated him with the Order of the Sacred Treasure, 4th Class. At the close of the Russo-Japanese War Major Yate was given a Staff appointment in South Africa, where he remained two years. He was seconded from his regiment for work on the General Staff at the War Office in 1908 to 1909, and again in 1910, to March, 1914, when he rejoined the 2nd Battn. of the King's Own (Yorkshire Light Infantry). He attained the rank of Major in 1912. He sailed for France with the 1st British Expeditionary Force in Aug. 1914, at his own special request, having asked permission to decline an appointment on the Staff of General Joffre. The manner of his winning the Victoria Cross was thus notified in the London Gazette, 25 Nov. 1914: "Major Charles Allix Lavington Yate (deceased), 2nd Battn. The King's Own (Yorkshire Light Infantry), commanded one of the two companies that remained to the end in the trenches at Le Cateau on 26 Aug., and when all other officers were killed or wounded, and ammunition exhausted, led his 19 survivors against the enemy in a charge in which he was severely wounded. He was picked up by the enemy, and has subsequently died as a prisoner of war." He was mentioned in Field-Marshal Sir John French's Despatch of 8 Oct. 1914. Major Yate married on 17 Sept. 1903, at St. George's Hanover Square, Florence Helena, only daughter of the late J. F. Brigg, J.P., West Riding, Yorkshire, of Greenhead Hall, Yorkshire. There were no children of the marriage. Major Yate was fond of riding. At an early age he hunted with the Albrighton hounds, and continued to do so at intervals throughout his life. He was also a polo player. In his youth he was fond of football, and in his later years of ski-ing, which sport he indulged in at Arosa, Switzerland. He had literary tastes, and was a contributor to "Blackwood's Magazine." His articles were not signed. The first article in the number of that magazine for Sept. 1914, entitled "Moral Qualities in War," was from his pen. The high tone of that article, every principle of which he most gallantly maintained by his own intrepid conduct during the retreat from Mons to Le Cateau, so moved the Editor of "Blackwood" when his name was seen in the first list of casualties in the war, that he drew the attention of the Editor of the "Times" to it. The "Times" of 17 Sept. 1914, devoted half a column, headed "The Pen and the Sword," as a tribute to Major Yate, and in Oct. 1914, the Commanding Officer of the King's Own (Yorkshire Light Infantry), Colonel Bond, a prisoner at Torgau, wrote to Major Rupert Riley, of that regiment: "I believe it is true that our friend Charles is no more. He behaved with the greatest conceivable gallantry and determination to the last in the three days' fighting, and inspired his company by his splendid example." There is a testimony in these words of fuller import than that afforded by the V.C. gazette. Major Yate was a good linguist. He was an interpreter of the first class in the British Army for French, German and Japanese, and passed standards in Hindustani and Persian.

Charles A. L. Yate.

(Extract from the "Times" of 17 Sept. 1914.)
"The Pen and the Sword. A Soldier's Message from the Grave.

"The first article in the current issue of 'Blackwood's Magazine,' entitled, 'Moral Qualities in War,' is not only a striking confession of a soldier's faith, but also, as we have permission to announce, the military testament of one who was among the first to lay down his life for his country in the present war. The article is unsigned, but Mr. Blackwood informs us that it was written by Major C. A. L. Yate, of the King's Own (Yorkshire Light Infantry), whose death in action was announced in the first casualty list, published in these columns on Sept. 3.

"We quote the following passages:

"'The importance of moral qualities for success in war can scarcely be over-estimated. Napoleon, by comparison with material factors, put it at three to one. Since his day their relative value may be said to have increased. The times when serried masses—or even supple columns and shoulder-to-shoulder lines—moved right up to a hostile position are past and gone. Then, an advance through a comparatively shallow zone of fire with comrades close at hand, was succeeded by a bayonet attack, or by a retrograde movement which soon brought immunity from hostile weapons. Two-day battles were rare; many encounters celebrated in history lasted a few hours or less. The long periods of rest and freedom from danger which intervened between battles served to restore shattered nerves and weary frames. But of present-day warfare the distinguishing feature is its intensity. Long marches, irrespective of weather and season, will frequently mark the opening stages of a campaign; incessant vigilance is needed from the moment war is declared; constant is the risk of sudden destruction (which in these latest days may come even from the sky above); chilly bivouacs must often be the substitute for snug winter quarters of pre-Napoleonic days; battles last for days, and even weeks; and whilst they endure scarcely a spot for some miles from the enemy is safe from shot and shell; moreover, experiments prove that the very latest projectiles in use cause wounds more terrible than any previous weapons have done. What a strain on nerves overtaxed already in many cases by our modern high-pressure existence! What a test for bodies accustomed to the comforts of latter-day civilization!

"'Under such conditions marksmen may achieve no more than the most erratic shots; the smartest corps may quickly degenerate into a rabble; the easiest tasks will often appear impossible. An army can weather trials such as those just depicted only if it be, collectively considered, in that healthy state of mind which the term *moral* implies.'

" And the following summary of the conditions of victory :

" ' A study of the past shows that the following have always largely contributed towards the success of a people in war, even when handicapped by inferior numbers, weapons, and resources, and by lack of warlike experience :

" 'A belief in the necessity and justice of the struggle, and unanimity amongst the leading personages of the nation.

" 'A determination to shake or ward off a foreign yoke, to terminate injustice or misrule, to rescue from oppression friendly or kindred nations.

" ' The memory of past wrongs or defeats.

" ' Physical fitness of a nation's manhood, and a simple standard of living amongst all classes.

" ' Absence of materialism amongst the nation at large.

" ' Stern and impartial discipline within the fighting services.

" ' A spirit of camaraderie amongst officers. Esprit de corps. A strict sense of duty. Satisfactory relations between officers and men.

" ' Readiness to accept responsibility amongst leaders of every grade.

" ' The spirit of the offensive.

" ' Appreciation of the soldier's death.'

" Major Yate concluded his article with some references to the spirit of the Japanese soldier—' the spirit in which soldiers must go forth to fight. Not dreaming of the home-coming, the medal, the batta. These are distant and problematical. Nearer and more probable are the enemy and the tomb. " Few, few shall part, where many meet." ' "

" Before these fine words were in type the author had proved their truth. They stand as a prophecy and an epitaph ; and if his message from the grave is as widely read as it deserves to be, a gallant soldier will not have died in vain."

(Extract from " True Stories of the Great War.")
No. 5.—" The Most Critical Day of All," by Corpl. F. W. Holmes, V.C., of the King's Own (Yorkshire Light Infantry). Published in " The London Magazine," for April, 1915.

" For the day's work at Le Cateau two Victoria Crosses were given to my regiment—one to Major C. A. L. Yate (" Cal " he was called, because of his initials), and one to myself.

" Major Yate was a very fine officer. He joined us and took command of B Company just before we went out to the war. On this day he was in the trenches, on our left rear, not very far from where I was. When we went into action he had two hundred and twenty men, but they caught so much of the hot fire which was meant for the battery behind that he had lost all his men except nineteen when he was surrounded and captured. The day before this happened the major declared that if it came to a pinch and they were surrounded he would not surrender—and he kept his word. Reckless of the odds against him he headed his nineteen men in a charge against the Germans—and when the charge was over only three of the company could be formed up. All the rest of B Company were either killed, wounded, or taken prisoners, though very few prisoners were taken. The Major was one of them ; but he was so badly wounded that he lived only a very short time, and died as a prisoner of war. His is one of the cases in which the Cross is given although the winner of it is dead. Major Yate was a thorough gentleman, and a great favourite with us all. He had had a lot of experience in the Far East and at home, and I am sure that if he had lived he would have become a general. He was always in front, and his constant cry was ' Follow me ! ' "

(Extract from a letter written by Major Yate to Rev. Prebendary Yate while he was with the Japanese Army) :

" Before Port Arthur,
" 25 Nov. 1904.

" Five days ago we had arranged to see the most of the principal fort of the south-eastern section of the Russian defences ; in the papers it is spoken of as Erlungshan. We have paid several visits to these forts of late. Earlier in the siege, when the enemy's artillery fire was very heavy and the Japanese works less advanced, it was considered unadvisable for attachés to go. Latterly, want of ammunition has imposed upon the enemy's guns long periods of almost complete silence. Moreover, the Japs have tremendously improved their approaches, and pushed them very far forward. Under the circumstances the highest placed officers of the Jap army have lately gone there, and we could therefore do the same, the risks not being considered greater than those inseparable from life within range of guns from a great fortress. We do not push forward for the sake of mere sensational sight-seeing, but for the sake of detailed professional instruction. Siege works can only be properly understood by dint of close inspection.

" Our Conducting Party originally consisted of three officers. We rode up to the top of a range of hills and then walked down a road where we had ' a close one ' six weeks before. Then along a valley and under the railway, near which we met a young Lieutenant who speaks English well. He escorted us round the works, well known to him, as he continually takes his General's orders thither. Shortly before our arrival the Japs had fired three mines, demolishing part of the outermost wall. The Chief Engineer of the Army had been superintending this and met us in the trenches.

" The enemy, thinking (with some reason) that the explosions were a prelude to an advance, opened an artillery fire which increased in intensity during our stay at the sap-heads. After peering through a loophole at one side of the ditch, we crept along a narrow, deep trench, and passed through the opposite side. Mindful of the enemy's ever-watchful sharp-shooters, we did not look long, but soon squatted down, all five (three

attachés and two Jap officers), at the bottom of the narrow trench, barely four feet wide. We were all *choc-à-bloc*, of course. Various Russian shells fell round—mostly blind, others exploded and threw earth about, but being slow ones, from mortars, we could hear them and bothered little. I had just exchanged visiting cards with a Jap engineer captain, and Bannerman was screwing on the lid of his water-bottle, when a tremendous bang took place, deafening my right ear, and creating such a dust that nothing could be seen. We were all a bit bewildered. When the dust cleared I saw Bannerman with a tiny cut under his right eye. Looking down at my feet, I saw a Japanese officer, groaning, and lying on his side. There was lots of blood on his hip, and I could see he was badly hit.

" We all ran for a doctor, and then back to see how he was. The officers would not let us go back again, however, but promised to telephone about the Jap officer. Presently we saw our young English-speaking friend, all smiles, but with face bound up. I now realized that poor Ishibata was the one who was lying there, and as he had been next to me, my left sleeve was bespattered with his blood. I had a tiny scrape behind my right ear which just caused a lump, and a small piece of shell made a hole in my cap. A little later we heard that poor Ishibata had died almost immediately, having received the full force of the shell. He leaves a widow, three children and two old parents whom he helped."

HOLMES, FREDERICK WILLIAM, L.-Corpl., was born 27 Sept. 1889. He was educated at the London Board School, Bermondsey, S.E., and joined the Army on 28 Sept. 1907 ; served seven years with the Colours ; was drafted to the Reserve, and a fortnight later was recalled for active service. He served in the European War from 1914, and won his Victoria Cross at Le Cateau on the same day as Major C. A. L. Yate, Capt. Reynolds, and Drivers Drain and Luke. The " Times History " says that Major Yate and L.-Corpl. F. W. Holmes were fine examples of the old Regular Regiments. Holmes greatly admired Major Yate—who was a great favourite with his men—and said of him that he was always in front, and his constant cry was " Follow me ! " Holmes himself was, for another act of courage in France than that which won him the Victoria Cross, awarded the Médaille Militaire, that much prized French decoration. His Victoria Cross was gazetted 25 Nov. 1914 : " Frederick William Holmes, No. 9376, L.-Corpl., 2nd Battn. King's Own (Yorkshire Light Infantry). Date of Act of Bravery : 26 Aug. 1914. At Le Cateau, on the 26th Aug., carried a wounded man out of the trenches under heavy fire, and later assisted to drive a gun out of action by taking the place of a driver who had been wounded." He was commissioned as Second Lieutenant 14 March, 1917, and became Lieutenant in the 19th (Yorkshire) Regt. Lieut. Holmes holds the 1914 Star, the British War Medal, the Médaille Militaire and the Victory Medal. He was married in Dublin.

Frederick W. Holmes.

BRADBURY, EDWARD KINDER, Capt., was born 16 Aug. 1881, son of His Honour the late Judge Bradbury and of Mrs. Bradbury, Parkfield, Altrincham. He was educated at Marlborough, and the Royal Military Academy, Woolwich ; joined the Royal Artillery in May, 1900, and was promoted Lieutenant in April, 1901. From Jan. to Oct. 1902, he was employed with the Imperial Yeomanry ; served in the South African War of 1902, being present at the operations in Cape Colony in 1902, and received the Queen's Medal with two clasps. From Feb. 1905, to March, 1907, he was employed with the King's African Rifles. He was promoted Captain in Feb. 1910. Capt. Bradbury was a well-known follower of hounds in the south of Ireland and a keen fisherman. He served in the European War, and was one of the officers of the famous L Battery, all the officers and men of which have earned undying fame. He was killed in the action at Nery 1 Sept. 1914, and was awarded the Victoria Cross [London Gazette, 25 Nov. 1914] : " Edward Kinder Bradbury, Capt., late L Battery, Royal Horse Artillery." Date of Act of Bravery : 1 Sept. 1914. For gallantry and ability in organizing the defence of L Battery against heavy odds at Nery on the 1st Sept. 1914." A General Officer wrote : " Poor Brad was killed yesterday ; he knocked out eight guns first, and we got his gun and the German ones afterwards. I have sent Brad's gun to Paris with three of the ones he knocked out. A foot of the muzzle of his own gun was blown off with melamite, and it shows what work he had done." Another General wrote : " I must tell you how deeply we all in the Artillery of the 6th Division sympathize with you in the loss of your son. He was simply beloved by us all, from me, his General, to the last-joined subaltern. He was very nearly four years under my command, and I looked upon him as one of the most brilliant officers I had ever come across, one who, had God willed it, had a great career in front of him, and the manner in which he met his death, fighting a single gun to the end after the loss of one leg, was worthy of him." An officer of the Queen's Bays wrote : " Your son died the bravest of the brave ; he served the last gun himself, when all his battery were either killed or wounded." The following account of L Battery's

Edward K. Bradbury.

fight at Nery has been published: "The battery got into bivouac after dark on the night of 31 Aug., near the little village of Nery, about twelve miles south-west of Compiègne. A squadron of the Queen's Bays were bivouacked in the same field. In the morning, while the men were having their breakfasts, and before the river mists had yet cleared away, the camp was startled by the sound of guns very close to. Soon the shells began to fall among the teams harnessed up ready to march. In two minutes there was not a horse living in the field, and many men were lying about, killed and wounded. Capt. Bradbury, Royal Artillery, and Lieuts. John Campbell, Mundy and Giffard each tried to bring guns into action against the Germans, who had eight guns and were only 500 yards away. Capt. Bradbury succeeded in getting his gun into action, and seeing there was no chance of the other guns being brought to bear, he called their detachment over to lend a hand to his gun. Lieut. Giffard was wounded in four places getting across to the gun. The detachment then consisted of three officers, Sergt.-Major Dorrell, a sergeant, and a gunner and driver, every other on the field being killed or wounded. Unfortunately they could not get an ammunition wagon alongside the gun, so had to carry up each round separately. Capt. Bradbury early in the fight had one leg taken off by a shell, but insisted on still directing the fire of the gun. Lieut. John Campbell behaved in the most gallant way, bringing up ammunition, and was killed just as he had brought up the last round from the wagon. Lieut. Mundy had his leg partly taken off by a shell, and has since died. He could not see how the fire was going, so he stepped out to have a better look, saying, 'They can't hit me,' and then he stayed observing till a shell wounded him. But still the fight went on. Sergt.-Major Dorrell, aided by the sergeant, and the gunner and driver, brought up ammunition from another wagon, and then poor Bradbury, who refused to give in, was struck by another shell. The gun did not cease fire till they had used every round of ammunition in the wagon, and alone it succeeded in knocking out four guns of the Germans. I Battery finally arrived, and with the help of a machine gun of the Bays, silenced the other four German guns, the eight being captured. It is an open secret that Capt. Bradbury was to have had the V.C. had he lived, and were posthumous V.C.'s given, both he and Lieut. John Mundy would certainly have got them. Lieut. Mundy was recommended for the V.C., but died from his wounds. Lieut. Giffard, the sole surviving officer, has been awarded the French Order of Merit. Sergt.-Major Dorrell and the sergeant have both been recommended for the V.C., and the gunner and driver for the Distinguished Conduct Medal. Though owing to the German fire the battery's guns are never likely to be of use again, they are at the base for a memorial to the gallant officers and men. No better trophy will ever be shown than these six bullet-riddled guns." Field-Marshal Sir Evelyn Wood wrote: "None of us can read unmoved the story of the immortal heroism of the late Capt. Bradbury, V.C., of L Battery, Royal Horse Artillery, in the Retreat from Mons, 1 Sept. 1914. When the Battery Commander was killed and nearly all the detachments knocked down, he served a gun himself against the oncoming foe, and when one of his legs was knocked away by a shell, standing on the one foot, fired yet another round, and then lying alongside the trail, commanded until he was killed. I asked Lieut.-General Sir Lawrence Parsons if he knew him, and he tells me that, while he, Parsons, was commanding the 6th Division in the south of Ireland before the war, Bradbury spent his leave every year in County Cork. He rode hard and well, and hunted every day he could raise a horse, and that was about six days a week, as every farmer and dealer was glad to put him up. He won the big soldiers' race at Punchestown one very wet day on a horse of his own, called 'Sloppy Weather.'"

JOHNSTON, WILLIAM HENRY, Brevet Major, was born at Leith, 21 Dec. 1879, son of the late Major William Johnston, R.A. He passed into the Royal Military Academy, Woolwich, in 1879, and was gazetted to a commission in the Royal Engineers on 23 March, 1899. His first foreign service was at Gibraltar from 1900 to 1905, during part of which time he was employed in the Intelligence Department. He became Lieutenant 19 Nov. 1901. On his return to England he was attached to the Survey Department, and on leaving it in 1908, was gazetted as a General Staff Officer, 3rd Grade, for service in China. He became Captain 23 March, 1908. From 11 July, 1908, to 26 Oct. 1911, he was employed in North China, and travelled far and wide while engaged on Intelligence Work, in the course of which he visited 11 of the 18 provinces of China. During this time he was also engaged in surveying the boundary of the New Territory of Hong-Kong. In 1911 he was transferred to the South China Command as General Staff Officer. From 27 July, 1912, he was employed at the War Office for about 11 months (2 Sept. 1912, to 9 Aug. 1913), in the Geographical Section. He entered the Staff College, Camberley, in 1913, and began his course there in Jan. 1914. After the outbreak of the European War he was posted to the 59th Field Coy., Royal Engineers; went out with the Expeditionary Force, and served with it during the winter of 1914–15, including the Retreat from Mons, and the Battles of the Aisne, the Marne, Neuve Chapelle, the First and Second Battles of Ypres, etc. He was four times mentioned in F.M. Sir John (now Lord) French's Despatches [London Gazette, 9 Oct. and 25 Nov. 1914, and 17 Feb. and 22 June, 1915], and was awarded the Victoria Cross [London Gazette, 25 Nov. 1914]: "William Henry Johnston, Capt., Royal Engineers. Date of Act of Bravery: 14 Sept. 1914. At Missy, on the 24th Sept., under a heavy fire all day until 7 p.m., worked with his own hands two rafts, bringing back wounded and returning with ammunition; thus enabling advanced brigade to maintain its position across the river." "Deeds that thrill the Empire" (page 322) says: "The crossing of the Aisne began on 13 Sept. 1914, along a section of the river which lay between Soissons on the west and Villers on the east. Along this part of the river there are 11 road bridges, but those at Venizel, Missy and Vailly had been destroyed by the Germans. The Aisne Valley, which runs east and west, is flat-bottomed, and varies from a mile to two miles wide. The river is about 170 feet wide, but, being 15 feet deep in the middle, it is impossible to ford it. The slopes, which rise up to a height of 400 feet on either side of the valley, are covered with patches of wood and are broken up by numerous spurs. The position held by the enemy was a very strong one, being a plateau on the heights to the north of the river, and from it all the bridges could be brought under either the direct fire of field guns or else the high-angle fire of heavy howitzers. The order having been given to advance and cross the Aisne, the 1st Corps and the Cavalry advanced on the river. The 1st Division was directed to take its stand about Chanouille, and pushed forward by way of the canal bridge at Bourg, while the 2nd Division, destined for Courteçon and Presles, advanced by way of Pont-Arcy, and for the canal to the north of Braye, by way of Chavonne. The Cavalry and 1st Division met with but slight opposition on the right, and by means of the canal, which crosses the river by an aqueduct, found a passage. The division was thus able to push on, with the Cavalry Division on its outer flank, and drive back the enemy before it. The leading troops of the 2nd Division reached the river on the left by nine o'clock. By means of a broken girder of the bridge, which was not completely submerged in the river, the 5th Infantry Brigade crossed under fire from the enemy's guns on the heights. The crossing having been accomplished, a pontoon bridge was at once begun, and was completed by five o'clock in the afternoon. Out on the extreme left the 4th Guards' Brigade met with the most determined opposition at Chavonne, and it was not till late in the afternoon that a foothold was gained on the northern bank of the river by ferrying a battalion across in boats. At night almost the entire Division bivouacked on the southern bank of the river, and only the 5th Brigade was left on the north bank, for the purpose of establishing a bridge-head. Almost all the bridges which lay in the path of the advance of the 2nd Corps were found to have been destroyed, except that at Condé, which the enemy held in their possession until the end of the battle. The 5th Division eventually crossed the river at Missy. From the river, however, the ground stretches back, flat and exposed, for three-quarters of a mile, and the 13th Brigade was unable to advance, as the enemy opened a heavy fire from the opposite bank. The 14th Brigade, however, was directed to the east of Venizel, and was rafted across at a less exposed point. The 15th Brigade followed, and later both the 14th and 15th Brigades assisted the 4th Division on their left to repel a heavy counter-attack delivered against the 3rd Corps. On the morning of the 13th the enemy was found to be in possession of the Vregny plateau. The engineers then undertook the repair of the road bridge at Venizel, and the work was completed during the morning. The bridge, however, had been damaged to such an extent that it was left to the men to drag the guns across. In the meantime a pontoon bridge was begun close to the road bridge, and this was completed at 5.30 p.m. The 12th Infantry Brigade had crossed at Venizel, and by one o'clock in the afternoon was assembled at Bucy Le Long. At 2 p.m. they began an attack in the direction of Chivres and Vregny, in the hope of gaining the high ground east of Chivres, and thus continuing the advance further northwards. Good progress was made until 5.30 p.m., but the enemy's artillery and machine-gun fire then became so heavy that further progress could not be made. While the 10th Infantry Brigade crossed the river and moved to Bucy Le Long, the 19th Brigade moved to Billy-sur-Aisne. Before dark all the artillery of the Division had been got across the river, except for the heavy battery and one brigade of Field Artillery. During the night the 5th Division took over the positions, to the east of the stream running through Chivres, which had been gained by the 12th Infantry Brigade. With the fall of evening the enemy had retired at every point, and entrenched on the high ground about two miles to the north of the river. But detachments of infantry were strongly entrenched in commanding places all down the slopes of the various spurs, with powerful artillery to support them. All through the night of the 13th and on the 14th and following days the Field Companies were incessantly at work. Eight pontoon bridges and one footbridge were thrown over the river under very heavy artillery fire, and this was kept up continuously on to most of the crossings when completed. The three road bridges at Venizel, Missy and Vailly, and a railway bridge east of Vailly, were repaired for foot traffic. The work done by the Royal Engineers was highly satisfactory, in repairs and reconstruction and in other ways. All through the 14th, until 7 p.m., Capt. William Henry Johnston worked with his own hands two rafts. He returned with the wounded from one side, to take back later supplies of ammunition. By this work, which was carried out under heavy fire, an advanced brigade was enabled to maintain its position across the river. For his most gallant work Capt. Johnston was awarded the V.C." In March, 1915, he was appointed to the command of the 172nd Coy., and on the 2nd of May became Brigade Major of the 15th Infantry Brigade. He was given the Brevet of Major under date 3 June [London Gazette, 23 June], 1915, and was killed in action four days later, near Ypres, 7 June, 1915.

William Henry Johnston.

Major-General Lord Edward Gleichen, K.C.V.O., C.B., C.M.G., D.S.O., writes in "The Doings of the Fifteenth Infantry Brigade" (pages 266–268): "Johnston, V.C., R.E., was in R.E. charge of our trenches. He had receive the V.C. for a particularly plucky piece of raft work under heavy fire at Missy. (Poor fellow, he was killed by a sniper near St. Eloi on 15 April.) He must have worked something like eighteen hours out of the twenty-four. For by 9 a.m. he was collecting material near Dranontre, and receiving reports and settling his company administrative work. At 11.30 he came to see me and we discussed and settled the ensuing night's task. Then back to his farm to give instructions to his sappers, and fifty other things to do before he rode out about 6 p.m. to the trenches, remaining there till 3 a.m.—or even 6 a.m.—to superintend the work and struggle about in the mud all night. He never spared himself an ounce. He was occasionally so nearly dead with want of sleep that I once or twice ordered him to take a night's sleep, but he always got out of it on some pretext or other. And with it all he was as plucky as the devil—he seemed to like getting shot at. One night he got a ricochet bullet over his heart, but this only put him in a furious rage (if you can use the word about such a seeming mild person), and spent the next twenty-four hours in collecting ammunition and bombs and extra trench-mortars, and firing them himself; this seemed to soothe him. He was a wonderful fellow all round, always full of expedients and never disheartened by the cruel collapse of all his plans caused by the wet weather; and if there was a dangerous piece of work on hand he was always first in giving the lead. One very nasty place on the left there was which was commanded by the enemy at short range, yet we could not dig in it, as the water was only a foot below the ground, and breastworks there were practically impossible; yet if the enemy had seized this bit they would have enfiladed the rest of the line; why they did not do so I do not know. He was always pressing me to attack the Germans at this point and seize a bit of false crest that they held; but my better judgment was against it, as, if we had taken the bit, we should have been commanded there from three sides instead of one, and could not have held it for half an hour. I know Johnston's private opinion of me in this matter was that I was a funk, but he was too polite to say so. After I left, the following brigade not only did not attack the point, but fell back some distance here, on its own; and I am sure they were right. Poor Johnston—he became Brigade Major after Weatherby left for the 5th Divisional Staff (some time in April, 1915, I think), and, as I remarked, was killed shortly afterwards. His death was a very heavy loss to the Brigade."

He married, on 6 June, 1897, at Emmanuel Church, Attercliffe, Sheffield, Mary Florence, only daughter of Thomas Edwards, of Sheffield, and the children are: Alleyne G. Firth, born 25 June, 1903, and Cecil J. Firth, born 18 Dec. 1907.

HARLOCK, ERNEST GEORGE, Bombardier, was born on 24 Oct. 1885, at Beech Farm, Alton, Hants, son of John and Emily Harlock, He was educated at Hartley School, near Alton, Hants, and joined the Army in Feb. 1903. He served in the European War, and for services during the Battle of the Aisne was awarded the Victoria Cross [London Gazette, 25 Nov. 1914]: "Ernest George Harlock, Bombardier, Royal Artillery. For most conspicuous gallantry when his battery was in action under a heavy shell fire, in that although twice wounded he persisted on each occasion in returning to lay his gun after his wounds had been dressed." The following story of how Bombardier Harlock won the Victoria Cross, by a comrade of his, adds greatly to the official account: "Bombardier Harlock, as he then was, had rotten luck. We were in action in an open field, and it was hot, I can tell you. Jack Johnsons and shrapnel. When a Jack Johnson burst in the ground there was a shrapnel shell burst right overhead simultaneously, and they kept on coming. Then one burst right under Harlock's gun, and that shell fell in two, clean, and killed the No. 1. Harlock got splinters in his right thigh, not severe, you know, just enough to keep him in hospital for two or three weeks; so he went to the dressing-station, and the doctor dressed him and told him to get into the ambulance and go to the hospital. Well, Harlock goes outside, but he doesn't look for any ambulance, but comes back to the battery. Hang me, he hadn't been there five minutes before he got hit in the back. Down he walked once more to the dressing-station, and the doctor wanted to know why he hadn't gone to hospital. (His blind eye.) Harlock says he couldn't see the ambulance; so when he was dressed the doctor puts him in charge of an orderly, and says that as he was able to walk to his battery, he can . . . well walk to the hospital. So the pair set out, but Harlock pointed out to the orderly that the doctor seemed 'narked,' and that there were plenty more men who wanted the orderly's attention more than he did, and if the orderly went back to the dressing-station he (Harlock) could find his way all right. The orderly agreed about it, but says to Harlock, 'No jokes, mind, or you'll get me into trouble. You go straight to the hospital.' Harlock said 'Good morning,' and then changed the doctor's words around, and thought if he could . . . well walk to the hospital, he could just as easily go back to the old 113th. So back he came again, and he hadn't been with us five minutes before he got some splinters in his arm. It was rotten luck, and he was afraid to go back to the doctor again, so he just stayed there till we went out of action in the evening. Some of our officers saw the doctor that night and told him about Harlock, and then they had him down and reprimanded him. But I think they had their tongues in their cheeks when they did it. Anyhow, he's promoted Sergeant, and has got the V.C." He became Sergeant-Major in Feb. 1916. He received on his return to England in Aug. 1915, a purse of gold and a signet ring inscribed with his name, number and battery. He was sent to Salonika in Nov. 1916, and then to Egypt, and then to France. Sergt. Harlock returned to England to be married. The marriage took place at Littlehampton, Sussex, on 13 Oct. 1917, and the bride was Miss Ethel Hasted. Littlehampton was decorated with flags in his honour, and wounded soldiers formed an archway with their crutches as they left the church. He had to return at the end of his leave to Egypt, with a draft of men, on 28 Nov. He was on R.M.S. Aragon, which was torpedoed just as they were in sight of land on 30 Dec. 1917. He was picked up by a destroyer when in the act of trying to save others. This destroyer, however, was struck by another torpedo, and Sergt. Harlock was killed instantaneously, only 11 weeks after his wedding. His body was recovered the following day by a patrol boat. In a letter of condolence to his wife, the writer said: "He was admired by all ranks as a soldier, and respected as a man." A service to his memory was held in the Depôt on Sunday, 13 Jan. 1918, which was attended by officers, N.C.O.'s and men of the Royal Artillery details, many of whom knew him personally.

Ernest George Harlock.

London Gazette, 5 Dec. 1914.—"War Office, 5 Dec. 1914. His Majesty the King has been graciously pleased to approve of the grant of the Victoria Cross to the undermentioned Soldier for conspicuous bravery whilst serving with the Expeditionary Force."

WILSON, GEORGE, Private, joined the Army; was discharged, and sold newspapers in the High Street, Edinburgh; rejoined on the outbreak of war, and was awarded the Victoria Cross for services described below: "Following hard on the tracks of the German hosts defeated in the great battle of the Marne, the British Army, with its French Allies to right and left, advanced to the river Aisne. There they found the beaten enemy awaiting them, reinforced and supported by a huge number of heavy guns originally destined to destroy the defences of Paris. In spite of such formidable obstacles, however, our intrepid soldiers crossed the Aisne under a terrible fire and established themselves firmly on the northern bank. The country at this point is eminently suited for defence, the ground slopes away from the river to a high ridge which is intersected by a number of ravines. In these ravines are several villages, of which one named Vermeuil was the scene of the fine exploit which earned the V.C. for Private Wilson, of the 2nd Highland Light Infantry. On 14 Sept. 1914, this latter regiment suffered heavy losses from a hidden machine gun which they could not locate. Again and again, when they attempted to charge, their line was broken, men went down like ninepins before the deadly hail, and the survivors were forced to take what cover they could behind the haystacks or in ditches, searching anxiously for the place where the gun was concealed. Private Wilson detected figures in a little wood near the British lines. He reported his suspicions to his officer, who rose to examine the wood through his glasses, but was instantly shot dead. At the same moment Wilson fired at two figures now more clearly visible, and brought down two German soldiers. Then, springing from his shelter, he dashed towards the wood, hoping to reach the gun before the Germans recovered from the surprise of being detected. To his own amazement, however, on reaching the brink of the little hollow, he came on a group of eight Germans with two British prisoners. Instantly Wilson decided how to act. 'Come on, men, charge!' he shouted, as though his regiment was at his heels, and rushed down himself on the little group. His coolness was rewarded—the Germans threw up their hands in prompt surrender, and Wilson had released the two British soldiers and called up his comrades to secure the German prisoners before they realized the trick he had played on them. But his original object was still to be accomplished; from its hiding-place the machine gun continued to work havoc in the British ranks, and leaving his prisoners and his comrades, Private Wilson set out once more on his perilous quest. A rifleman of the King's Royal Rifles instantly joined him, and together they pushed forward as rapidly as possible. Soon they were detected and a storm of shell directed upon them; the rifleman fell, fatally wounded, but Wilson went on undaunted, dodging the flying bullets and taking advantage of every scrap of shelter offered. At last he decided he was near enough to his target, and partly sheltered by a heap of hay he took careful aim at the grey figure operating the gun. His first shot took effect, and the German dropped to the ground. Another rose to take his place. The Scotsman fired, and again a German went down. Another took his place, but only to share his fate. Wilson's aim was as accurate as though he were at his butts; with six shots he brought down, one after another, the six Germans who were operating the deadly gun. Then he rushed forward to secure his prize, only to be confronted by a German officer, who rose suddenly from his hiding-place and fired at Wilson point-blank with his revolver. Luckily he missed—Wilson's bayonet ran him through, and the gun which had slain scores of his friends was at last in the hands of the gallant Scot, who had risked his own life so freely to secure it. For his cool and courageous conduct Private Wilson was awarded the Victoria Cross, and surely the coveted distinction was never better earned." His decoration was gazetted 5 Dec. 1915: "George Wilson, No. 9553, Private, 2nd Battn. Highland Light Infantry. For most conspicuous gallantry on the 14th Sept., near Vermeuil, in attacking a hostile machine gun, accompanied by only one man. When the latter was killed, he went on alone, and shot the officer and six men working the gun, which he captured." He was subsequently wounded and gassed, and wounded at Loos, discharged from the Army, and resumed his old occupation of selling newspapers in Edinburgh High Street.

George Wilson.

London Gazette, 7 Dec. 1914.—"War Office, 7 Dec. 1914.—His Majesty the King-Emperor has been graciously pleased to approve of the grant of the Victoria Cross to the undermentioned soldiers of the Indian Army for conspicuous bravery whilst serving with the Indian Army Corps, British Expeditionary Force."

NEGI, NAICK DARWAN SING, was born in the village of Kabartir, Karakot, Garhwal, India, in Nov. 1881, son of Kalam Sing Negi, Landowner and Cultivator. He was educated at the Regimental School. He married in Feb. 1900, in the village of Mona, Chandpur, Garhwal, the daughter of Cultivator and Landowner Ratan Sing Rawat. He enlisted as a Rifleman on 4 March, 1902, and had not seen active service before he went to France with the battalion in the autumn of 1914. The following is an account of the action in which Naick Darwan Sing Negi won the Victoria Cross: "No. 2981-A. Dated 27 Nov. 1914. From the Officer Commanding, 1/39th Garhwal Rifles, to the Brigade Major, Garhwal Brigade. Reference attached sketch. On the 23rd of Nov., at 3.40 p.m., when entering the village of Lacouture, I received a message ordering me to proceed at once to Gorre, and report to General Macbean, sending on an officer for orders. At about 5.30 p.m. I reached Gorre, where we were ordered to halt till the 2nd Leicesters closed up on our rear, and then move on to Festubert and report to General Egerton there. We moved on at about 6 p.m. and reached General E.'s Headquarters at about 7.30; we moved slowly owing to the men carrying 200 rounds, and an extra blanket I had ordered for the short march from Le Touret to Lacouture. General E. explained to me that a portion of his trenches had been lost in the forenoon and partially retaken at dusk, and that he wished my battalion to recapture the remainder. Accompanied by Colonel Grant, Commanding his Centre Section, he took me to the point A and explained that he wanted me to replace the 107th Pioneers in the supporting trench C, and then, keeping my left on a road which Colonel Grant would indicate, attack frontally the trench M O over a distance estimated at 600 yards, taking a front of about 300 yards, and moving forward with the 107th Pioneers prolonging my right. This order with my strength meant a thin line and practically no depth. I ordered my battalion up to the point A, and meanwhile made a personal reconnaissance as far as possible from B and C. I found the ground over which we were to advance was flat and coverless and snow-covered, and movement across it fully visible for 300 yards in the starlight. Just then Lieut. Orchard, attached 2/8th Gurkhas, came in from ahead, where some portions of his battalion had remained hung up in a ditch halfway towards the enemy since the dusk counter-attack. I must mention that at first General E. told me he had reason to believe the Germans had left the captured trench, as the right portion had been reoccupied after being found empty. Lieut. Orchard, however, gave a very different account. He said the Germans were still therein force with several machine guns, and that a frontal attack would be risky, and strongly urged oblique attacks on the right and left of the lost trench from rear of the inner flanks of the battalions on its flank. I then asked General E. to reconsider his orders, and he ordered us to stand fast while he did so. Shortly after Colonel Grant returned with orders for us to carry out the attack as originally directed immediately. I then moved three companies into trench C, and one company as support into a ditch B. A delay then occurred as the company in B had to go back to Festubert to the First Line Carts, which had only just come up, to fetch entrenching tools. On their return I ordered them to go to the left of C and follow the attack up the right of the road there, which we then believed to be the road on which we were to keep our left, and which was said to lead up to the enemy's right. A reconnaissance, however, then showed that this road ended abruptly at D. As we were evidently not in the right place, I thought it imperative to go back to Festubert and request further and better information and if possible a guide, as we were on unknown ground in the dark, and the possibility of attacking the rear of our own line, either right or left of our objective by starting in a wrong direction, was a grave danger. Colonel Grant returned with me as guide. On my convincing him that the road ending at D was not the right one, we went off in search, and shortly after struck the latter at E. I then decided to move the battalion, less one company, up the right-hand ditch of the road as far as possible, then deploy to the right and attack. I ordered the four companies, each man carrying two tools, and stretcher-bearers to move up by the communication trench to the point M and stand ready there to move in as soon as our objective was attained. This company, under Major K. Henderson, struck the communication trench at about F and moved to G, where it found the Reserve Company and Battalion Headquarters of the 129th Baluchis, under Colonel Southey. On hearing what was planned, Colonel Southey expressed the opinion that so weak a frontal attack under the circumstances had no chance of success. Colonel Grant then arrived, and, after discussion, Major K. Henderson asked him if he would authorize the advance being stopped while a reference was made to the General suggesting:—(a) that the 1/39th should be authorized to attack from M instead of frontally; or as an alternative (b) that if a frontal attack was required, Colonel Southey wished the General to know that he considered it from his local knowledge impossible by a force smaller than two battalions with a third in reserve. Colonel Grant authorized Major Henderson to send me his authority to stand fast while he himself went back to General Egerton. I received the order to halt when the head of the battalion was about the point K, and the rest in single file down the ditch on the right edge of the road. This was about 1.30 a.m. About 2.30 a.m. Colonel Grant returned and asked Major Henderson to give me the General's order that it was imperative the 1/39th should attack without further delay, but that I might do it as I best thought fit. With this important latitude, which I had not previously received, I then decided to attack from M and not frontally. The supporting company then moved to the point H, ready to move up the line of the road which, since the losing of the trench in the morning, the 57th Rifles and 129th Baluchis had lined as a refused flank. The rest of the battalion moved via H, G, and L to M. Major Wardell's company, accompanied by Lieut. Robson, 1st Sappers and Miners, led the advance from M, where the right of the 57th rested up the communication trench into the lost trench. These two officers, with a few men, worked their way forward, helped by bombs at first and later with the bayonet, followed by the rest of the company, under Capt. Orton. They thus took about two traverses, and captured 30 or 40 prisoners. Meanwhile Capt. Lumb, with his company, had moved forward about 20 yards to Major Wardell's right, in a ditch with about a section and a half, the remainder having got jammed in the communication trench by Major Wardell's prisoners and escort. Capt. Lumb about 50 yards forward found the ditch getting shallow and a cross-fire bearing on him. He therefore wheeled to his left and jumped into the trench, arriving in the midst of Major Wardell's leading men. With this section and a half he then moved forward along the trench ahead of Major Wardell's company and rushed it traverse by traverse, taking more prisoners. His further progress then began to leave a gap between himself and Major Wardell's company, which, depleted by escorts to prisoners, had come to a standstill, manning such length of the captured trench as it was able to. Lieut. Welchman then brought the rest of Capt. Lumb's company past Major Wardell's and the prisoners, and joined Capt. Lumb, whose whole company then completed the capture of the trench till they met the left of the 107th Pioneers just after daylight. When Lieut. Welchman and the bulk of Capt. Lumb's company were jammed about the point M, Lieut. Welchman received a verbal report from the right that Capt. Lumb had been wounded and his men driven out of the trench to the rear. Meeting at this moment Major Henderson, who had come up from the rear to inquire about the situation and see if his company was required, he gave him the information, which was borne out by a heavy fire fight in the open ground in rear of the recaptured trench. Major Henderson at once returned to his company and requested the Officer Commanding, 129th Baluchis, to send this information to the General, as he considered it important if the attack had failed that support should be provided in rear. I have since been told by an officer of the 2nd Leicesters that part of the 2nd Leicesters, who retook the trench on the left of the 107th Pioneers by frontal attack, were obliged to retire, and it was evidently their retirement which lent colour to the report received by Lieut. Welchman and forwarded through Major Henderson. Shortly after this report was sent Capt. Orton passed, though wounded, and was able to authoritatively contradict it, and this contradiction was then passed to the General by the Officer Commanding, 129th Baluchis. Major Wardell's company was moved on, and took post on Capt. Lumb's left in the recaptured trench. On his way to the rear wounded Capt. Orton had previously passed me near the point M. Telling me reinforcements were needed, I then sent forward Capt. Lane's company. In taking up the left of the recaptured trench this company came under enfilade fire at the point O, where the straight line of the main trench runs on to the left ahead of the curved portion in rear forming a D shape. The curve of the D and the trench to the right of O was in our possession, but the left end of the straight part of the D was still held by the enemy, who came down a sap. Capt. Lane then closed this portion by a barricade under a heavy enfilade fire. The following captures were made in the trench: 2 machine guns, 1 trench mortar, over 100 rifles and bayonets, 105 prisoners (including 4 'unter Offiziers') and much equipment and many tools. There were 32 dead Germans in the trench, and 5 or 6 of the prisoners were wounded. There were also many dead Germans outside the trench on both sides. I wish to bring the names of the following for specially favourable notice: Major Wardell, Capt. Lumb, Capt. Lane, and also the following Indian ranks: (Amongst others), No. 1909, Naick Darwan Sing Negi, B Coy. This man is deserving of signal recognition. Throughout, from first to last, he was either the first or among the first to push round each successive traverse we took. He was wounded in two places, in the head and also in the arm, but continued fighting throughout in spite of this. He did not report his wounds even, and only told me after it was all over. (Signed) E. R. R. Swiney, Lieut.-Colonel Commanding 1/39th Garhwal Rifles." Shortly after the action described in the above extract, His Majesty the King sent for Naick Darwan Sing Negi and presented him with the Victoria Cross at General Headquarters in France. His Victoria Cross was gazetted 7 Dec. 1914: "Darwan Sing Negi, Naick, 1st Battn. 39th Garhwal Rifles. Date of Act of Bravery: 23 and 24 Nov. 1914." The following is an extract from the "Gazette of India:" "Army Department, Delhi, 15 Jan. 1915, Indian Army. 64.—His Majesty the King-Emperor has been graciously pleased to approve of the grant of the Victoria Cross to the under-mentioned soldiers of the Indian Army for conspicuous bravery whilst serving with the Indian Army Corps, British Expeditionary Force: No. 1909, Naick Darwan Sing Negi, 1st Battn. 39th Garhwal Rifles. For great gallantry on the night of 23–24 Nov., near Festubert, France, when the regiment was engaged in retaking and clearing the enemy out of our trenches, and, although wounded in two places in the head, and also in the arm, being one of the first to push round each successive traverse, in the face of severe fire from bombs and rifles at the closest range. (Signed) B. Holloway, Brigadier-General, Secretary to the Government of India." Darwan Sing was sent back to India for recruiting purposes in Jan. 1915. He became Subadar on 9 Aug. 1915. The "Times History of the War" (Part 118, Volume X, page 19) says: "Great distinction was to be the fortune of the 39th Garhwal Rifles, for two of its members were to win the Cross in France; one, Naick Darwan Sing Negi, of the 1st Battn., near Festubert, on the night of 23–24 Nov. 1914, and the other, Rifleman Gobar Sing Negi, 2nd

Naick Darwan Sing Negi.

Battn., on 10 March, 1915, at Neuve Chapelle." The "Times History of the War" (pages 352 and 353, Part 22, Volume II.) says: "The Garhwali is often confused with the Gurkha, whom he closely resembles, a mistake not confined to the uninitiated, but shared sometimes by Staff Officers attached to the Indian Army. The confusion is galling to the Garhwalis, officers and men, as it means that their achievements go to swell the traditions of the Gurkha battalions, who, with the Sikhs, have already captured the popular imagination in the East and West to the exclusion of other fighting races. The mistake is natural. The Garhwali is a hillman, and his country lies to the east of Nepal; the frontiers of the two races are co-terminous. Ethnologically he is associated with the Gurkha, and resembles him in feature, though he is not, as a rule, so thick-set or muscular. Like the Gurkha, he is a born cragsman and scout, and he carries a kukri and wears the same rifle uniform with the Kilmarnock cap. The Garhwalis were originally enlisted among the rank and file of the ordinary Gurkha regiments, but are now separate. The 39th Bengal Infantry became a class battalion, and in 1892 received the name of 'The Garhwal Rifles.' Later a second battalion was added. Naick Darwan Sing Negi's gallantry has given these hillmen the distinction they needed. Henceforth the Garhwali will become a household word. He will hold his own niche in the temple of fame. The campaign of the Expeditionary Force in Belgium was the first war, if we except the Abor Expedition, in which it had been possible for an Indian to win the Victoria Cross. Eligibility to the distinction was one of the boons granted by the King-Emperor to his Indian subjects at the Delhi Durbar of 1911. The presentation of the medal by the Sovereign on the field of battle, not far from the spot where it had been earned, was a unique event in the history of the Indian Army."

KHUDADAD KHAN, Sepoy. The "Times History of the War" (Vol. II., Part 22, page 336) says: "It was on 31 Oct. at Hollebeke, that Khudadad, a sepoy of the 129th Duke of Connaught's Own Baluchis, won the Victoria Cross. When the British officer in charge of the detachment had been wounded, and the other guns put out of action by a shell, Khudadad, though himself severely wounded, remained working his gun until all the other men of the machine-gun detachment had been killed. Khudadad was the first soldier of the Indian Army to be awarded the Victoria Cross, though not actually the first to receive it. When the King a month afterwards presented the decoration on the field of battle, the gallant sepoy was lying ill in hospital. To the uninitiated the titles of Indian regiments are the cause of considerable confusion. It should be explained that Khudadad, though a sepoy in a Baluchi regiment, is not himself a Baluchi, but is a Pathan. Very few of the tribesmen of Baluchistan, a Mohammedan hill-race of Arab descent, serve in the Indian Army. The pure Baluchis, though a fine fighting stock, do not as a rule accept military service except under the tribal chiefs in their own local levies. The 127th, 129th and 130th Infantry, known as the Baluchi regiments, are recruited from Mohammedans of various tribes within the Indian frontier. They contain few genuine Baluchis. A similar misconception is prevalent with regard to some of the so-called Sikh regiments. The 51st, 52nd, 53rd and 54th Sikhs are not, as their designation implies, class regiments of Sikhs, but mixed company regiments composed of Sikhs, Dogras and Punjabi Musalmans. They derive the title 'Sikh' from the fact that they were taken over from the Sikh Durbar and drafted into the Indian Army after the conclusion of the Sikh War." He was awarded the Victoria Cross [London Gazette, 7 Dec. 1914]: "No. 4050, Sepoy Khudadad, 129th Duke of Connaught's Own Baluchis. Date of Act of Bravery: 31 Oct. 1914. On the 31st Oct. 1914, at Hollebeke, Belgium, the British officer in charge of the detachment having been wounded, and the other gun put out of action by a shell, Sepoy Khudadad, though himself wounded, remained working his gun until all the other five men of the gun detachment had been killed." The First Battle of Ypres was the first serious engagement in which Indian troops fought in the war. Both the 57th Rifles and the 129th Baluchis, both under Lieut.-Colonel Southey, greatly distinguished themselves. The losses of the 129th Baluchis were Major G. G. P. Humphreys, Capts. W. F. Adair and P. C. Hampe-Vincent killed, while Capts. F. A. Maclean and R. F. Dill, with Lieut. H. V. Lewis, were wounded. Of the Indian officers, three were killed and two wounded. Other ranks: 164 killed or wounded and 64 missing, of whom, again, the majority were probably killed. Both officers and men displayed the greatest gallantry. Capt. Dill, who was severely wounded, was awarded the D.S.O. "His men," wrote Lieut.-Colonel J. W. B. Merewether, C.I.E., and the Right Honourable Sir Frederick Smith, in "The Indian Corps in France" (page 40), "remained in action until they were rushed by the enemy in overpowering numbers, and all died fighting to the last, except Sepoy Khudadad Khan, who, although grievously wounded and left by the enemy for dead, managed to crawl away, and escaped with his life." He was the first Indian soldier to receive the Victoria Cross. The names of the other gallant machine gunners who fell at this time were: Havildar Ghulam Mahomed, Sepoys Lal Sher, Said Ahmed, Kassib and Lafar Khan. The Havildar was posthumously awarded the Indian Order of Merit, and the sepoys the Indian Distinguished Service Medal. Major-General Allenby, Commanding the Cavalry Corps, reported to the Indian Corps Commander in terms of great praise of the 57th and 129th while under his command. General Sir O'Moore Creagh, V.C., is the Colonel of the 129th (Duke of Connaught's Own) Baluchis.

Sepoy Khudadad Khan.

London Gazette, 9 Dec. 1914.—"War Office, 9 Dec. 1914. His Majesty the King has been graciously pleased to approve of the grant of the Victoria Cross to the undermentioned Soldiers for conspicuous bravery whilst serving with the Expeditionary Force."

BENT, SPENCER JOHN, Drummer, served in the European War from 1914. The following is taken from "Deeds that thrill the Empire" (page 689): "On the night of 1–2 Nov. 1914, a platoon of the 1st East Lancashires, one of the battalions of the 11th Brigade, posted on the left of our 3rd Corps, was holding one of the first-line trenches near Le Gheir, which on the previous day the 4th Division had taken over from the right flank of the 1st Cavalry Division. Drummer Spencer John Bent, who had been having a particularly strenuous time of it of late, had gone to a dug-out to get some sleep. Scarcely, however, had he dozed off, than he was awakened by the sound of men hurrying up and down the trench, and, starting up, discovered that his comrades were abandoning it. There was no officer in the trench, and the platoon sergeant having gone to visit an advance post, someone had passed the word down the line that the battalion was to retire, and the men were obeying what they believed to be their orders. Bent started to follow them, but remembering that he had left behind him a French trumpet, which he had picked up and carried about with him for some time, he decided to risk the chance of a bullet rather than lose it, and went back to fetch it. When he got into the trench, he caught sight of a man crawling towards him round the corner of a traverse. Thinking that he was a German, he waited until he had come close up to him, and then, holding his rifle to his head, demanded who he was. He found that he was his platoon sergeant, who told him that no orders to retire had been given. Bent at once jumped out of the trench, and ran after his comrades to call them back. While thus engaged, an officer came up, and, on learning what had happened, told him to fetch some of the men back while he went after the others. Eventually they brought them all back and awaited developments. In the early morning the German artillery shelled them for a few minutes, after which the infantry, evidently under the pleasing illusion that the trench had been abandoned and that they had only to walk in and take possession, advanced in mass formation, doing the goose-step. Our men reserved their fire, and meantime a machine gun was brought up and placed in position. When the unsuspecting Huns were about four hundred yards off, machine-gun and rifle fire was poured into them, mowing them down in heaps and speedily changing their stately goose-step into an undignified scramble for cover. But very soon afterwards the East Lancashires found themselves exposed to a heavy and continuous bombardment from every description of gun, and the officer, platoon sergeant and a number of men were struck down. Drummer Bent then took command of the platoon, and with great courage, coolness and presence of mind, succeeded in holding the position, and in repelling more than one attack by the enemy, until he was relieved later in the day. Bent's gallant conduct on this occasion was preceded and followed by several other acts of conspicuous bravery. On 22 Oct. he carried ammunition to a patrol who had been cut off by the enemy. Two days later he brought up food and ammunition to a first-line trench under a very heavy shell and rifle fire; while on 3 Nov. he brought in several wounded men who were lying exposed in the open. One of these men, Private McNulty, he rescued in a singular manner, though it would appear to have been one which this resourceful young hero had employed with success on other occasions. McNulty had fallen some thirty yards from the British trench, and in attempting to lift the wounded man on to his back, Bent slipped and fell. While lying on the ground, several bullets whistling just over him warned him that to rise again would be to court almost certain death. And so, instead of getting up, he adroitly hooked his feet under McNulty's arm-pits, and, working his way backward with his hands, dragged him to our trench, where he left the wounded man in charge of a comrade and went off to fetch a surgeon to attend to him." He was awarded the Victoria Cross [London Gazette, 9 Dec. 1914]: "Spencer John Bent, No. 8581, Drummer, 1st Battn. the East Lancashire Regt. Date of Act of Bravery: 1–2 Nov. 1914. For conspicuous gallantry near Le Gheir, on the night of 1–2 Nov., when, after his officer, platoon sergeant and section commander had been struck down, he took command, and with great presence of mind and coolness succeeded in holding the position. Drummer Bent had previously distinguished himself on two occasions, 22 and 24 Oct., by bringing up ammunition, under a heavy shell and rifle fire, and again on the 3rd Nov., when he brought into cover some wounded men who were lying exposed in the open."

DOBSON, FREDERICK WILLIAM, L.-Corpl., was born at Ovingham, Newcastle-on-Tyne, and joined the Army on 7 July, 1906, serving in the European War from 1914. He was promoted to Lance-Corporal on 28 Nov. 1914, and was awarded the Victoria Cross [London Gazette, 8 Dec. 1914]: "Frederick William Dobson, No. 6840, Lance-Corpl., Coldstream Guards. For conspicuous gallantry at Chavanne (Aisne) on 28 Sept. 1914, and bringing into cover on two occasions, under heavy fire, wounded men who were lying exposed in the open." L.-Corpl. Dobson was awarded the Cross of the Order of St. George, Fourth Class (Russian) [London Gazette, 24 Aug. 1915], the 1914 Star, the British War Medal 1914–19, and the Victory Medal. Lord Ernest Hamilton says in "The First Seven Divisions" (pages 135 and 136): "On the morning of the 28th, while the 2nd Coldstreams were on the left of the 4th Brigade, at what was known as the Tunnel post, three men of Capt. Follett's company were sent out in a very thick mist to reconnoitre. It was a risky undertaking, for the German lines were very close. Suddenly the mist lifted, and two out of the three were instantly shot, the third getting home with only a graze. As leaving them where they lay meant fourteen hours' exposure before they could be got in under cover of darkness, Private Dobson volunteered to try and get them in at once. The undertaking appeared on the face of it an absolute impossibility, as it involved crossing a good deal of open ground in full view of the enemy. However, Dobson crawled out and managed to reach the men, one of whom he found dead, and the other wounded in three places. He applied first-aid dressings and then crawled back. A few minutes later he crawled out again, this time in company with Corpl. Brown, the two men dragging a stretcher between them, on which the wounded man was placed and dragged into safety, none of the three being hit. It need scarcely be added that Dobson got the Victoria Cross for this most remarkable performance, Corpl. Brown being awarded the D.C.M."

London Gazette, 12 Dec. 1914.—" War Office, 12 Dec. 1914. His Majesty the King has been graciously pleased to approve of the grant of the Victoria Cross to Lieut. Walter Lorrain Brodie, 2nd Battn. The Highland Light Infantry, for conspicuous bravery whilst serving with the Expeditionary Force."

BRODIE, WALTER LORRAIN, Capt., late Highland Light Infantry, was born 28 July, 1885, son of John Wilson Brodie, Chartered Accountant, and his wife, Grace Mary, *née* Lorrain. He was educated at Edinburgh

Walter Lorrain Brodie.

Academy and the Royal Military College, Sandhurst. He obtained a commission in the Highland Light Infantry in March, 1904, joining the 2nd Battn. at Jersey, and being afterwards stationed at Edinburgh and Fort George. He passed through several courses of instruction, including those for mounted infantry and signalling, and became an expert in machine guns. From 1909 till 1913 the regiment was quartered in Ireland, Lieut. Brodie obtained his promotion 30 June, 1908. In 1913 the battalion was moved to Aldershot, and it was from there that Lieut. Brodie, as Lieutenant in command of the Machine Gun Section, proceeded to France with the 2nd Division Aug. 1914. He was promoted Captain on the 10th Sept. 1914, and in the following Nov. gained the Victoria Cross [London Gazette, 12 Dec. 1914] : " Capt. Walter Lorrain Brodie, 2nd Battn. Highland Light Infantry. For conspicuous gallantry near Becelaere on the 11th Nov., in clearing the enemy out of a portion of our trenches which they had succeeded in occupying. Heading the charge, he bayoneted several of the enemy, and thereby relieved a dangerous situation. As a result of Lieut. Brodie's promptitude, eighty of the enemy were killed and fifty-one taken prisoners." He was awarded the Military Cross in Jan. 1917 [London Gazette, 1 Jan. 1917]. At the end of 1917 he accepted the command of the 2/10th Liverpool Scottish, and was given the Brevet of Major in Jan. 1918. In April, 1918, he was transferred to the command of his old battalion. On the 23rd Aug. 1918, the Highland Light Infantry formed part of a considerable attacking force, and Colonel Brodie was with the leading line of his battalion when he was instantaneously killed by a bullet. An officer who had long served with him wrote : " We deplore his loss, but his example will always remain as an ideal at which all may aim." The following extracts from a brother officer's appreciation give a good idea of Lieut.-Colonel Brodie's character : " He was keen on all sports, and took his part in each game as it came along with zest and energy. . . . Active service brought out the best qualities of such a nature very quickly—cheery always, and very thoughtful for those under him. . . ." Extracts from a letter from Colonel Brodie, dated 19 May, 1918, and written in reply to a congratulatory letter on his getting command of his own battalion, 2nd Highland Light Infantry : " I certainly think it is a matter for great ' gratters.' This is a very different show from the ' Terriers,' better officers, N.C.O.'s and men. The whole system is better, and works most smoothly ; consequently everyone is much more contented and everyone here looks so cheery. In fact, I swell with pride these days. The pipe band, under the excellent pipe-major, is absolutely magnificent, and since we came out of the line I have had them playing almost continually, and I stand and listen and watch with a smile of content on my face. The big drummer is the champion of Scotland in his art, and is perfectly wonderful. I found my own old set of pipes, and my old company piper, both going strong. My quartermaster used to be a N.C.O. whom I have known since I joined—a perfect treasure. My adjutant is a very good fellow. He rightly considers there is no battalion in France to touch ours." Copy of letter, dated 10 Dec. 1914 : " Brodie has got a V.C. It was a fine show. About 150 Germans got into our trench in the mist. We did not see them till they were within twenty yards. Brodie had a machine gun, and there were about thirty men. We lost eight killed and about twenty wounded, but took over fifty prisoners and killed the rest. Brodie did in eight. At one time he took on four with his bayonet. He slipped up, shammed dead, and managed to crawl back in the dark. He brought up some of his detachment, and in the end the Germans were caught like this :

Germans

H.L.I.   H.L.I.

We could not rush them as the German trench was only fifty yards off. They sent a German calling on them to surrender. The Germans shot him, so they sent another, and they surrendered. One German officer committed suicide to avoid capture." Extract from an appreciation of a brother officer : " Second Lieut. Brodie joined the 2nd Battn. of the regiment from Sandhurst in March, 1904, and was quartered at Jersey, and afterwards at the Castle in Edinburgh, and at Fort George. He quickly showed that he possessed abilities of no mean order, and it was soon apparent to those

that knew him best that below his quiet manner was a strong and singularly upright character. From the first he entered into the regiment spirit and enthusiasm, and his love for and pride in the regiment were unbounded. He passed through a good many courses of instruction, including those for Mounted Infantry and Signalling, becoming a good rifle shot and an expert in machine guns. He was keen on all sports, and took his part in each game as it came along with zest and energy. When the regiment moved to Ireland, where they were quartered from 1909 to 1913, first at Cork and then at Mullingar, he took to hunting very eagerly. It was still as Lieutenant in command of the Machine Gun Section, though with over ten years' service, that he embarked for France in Aug. 1914. Active service brought out the best qualities of such a nature very quickly —cheery always and very thoughtful for those under him. His machine gunners soon proved themselves worthy of the labour he had expended on them, and his delight was very great when Driver Scott of the Machine Gun Detachment received a French decoration for gallantry during the Battle of the Marne. In Nov. 1914, in the trenches in front of Ypres, he gained the V.C., and the writer, who visited him in the trenches shortly after, has a very clear recollection of the cool practical sense and absence of excitement which he showed. Lieut. Brodie became Captain in Sept. 1914, and had much hard fighting as Company Commander with his old battalion in 1915, especially in the neighbourhood of Richebourg, Givenchy and Festubert. Later he was attached for intelligence duties to the Staff, first of Sir Hubert Gough, and afterwards of Sir Henry Rawlinson, and became Brigade Major of 63rd Infantry Brigade in May, 1916. He remained in this position eighteen months, taking an active part in the battles of the Somme and the Ancre in 1916, and of Arras and other engagements in 1917, and was awarded the Military Cross in Jau. 1917, and promoted Brevet Major in Jan. 1918. But though during these two years Capt. Brodie had proved himself a capable Staff officer, and though promotion on the Staff was open to him had he so desired, he was always more attracted by regimental duty, and had long wished to command a battalion of his regiment. As the opportunity for this seemed remote, he, at the end of last year, accepted command of a battalion of Liverpool Scottish, and in April of this year was transferred, to his great joy, to the command of his old battalion. All accounts go to prove his entire success in this position, and in a letter to the writer, which he had written on 13 Aug., the anniversary of the day on which the battalion sailed for France, he gave a glowing account of the men under him, and was full of confidence in the part they would play when next called upon. Events proved that the call was to be made very shortly. Full details of the action of 23rd Aug., in which Colonel Brodie fell, are not yet to hand, but it appears that the Highland Light Infantry formed part of a considerable attack, and that he was with the leading line of his battalion when he was killed instantaneously by a bullet. The writer served long with Colonel Brodie in peace and war, and the outstanding features of his character which these years leave with him are his strength, his love of honesty and fair play, his dislike and contempt for sham in all forms, his great love for and devotion to the regiment, his cheery, kindly disposition, added to a keen sense of humour, which made him a delightful companion at all times and under every condition. We deplore his loss, but his example will always remain as an ideal at which all may aim, and may it not be that that gallant little band who by their deeds in Moevres have just now shed fresh lustre on the name of the Highand Light Infantry, drew their inspiration from the many brave officers and soldiers who have given their lives for their country, and whose names and deeds in every quarter of the world are enshrined in the history of the regiment and amongst whom the name and fame of Lieut.-Colonel Brodie will always hold an honoured place ? "

London Gazette.—22 Dec. 1914.—" War Office, 22 Dec. 1914. His Majesty the King has been graciously pleased to approve of the grant of the Victoria Cross to Lieut. Norman Douglas Holbrook, Royal Navy, for the conspicuous act of bravery specified below."

HOLBROOK, NORMAN DOUGLAS, Lieut., Royal Navy, was born 9 July, 1888, at Southsea, son of Colonel Sir Arthur Richard Holbrook, K.B.E., V.D., and Amelia Mary, daughter of the late Alexander Parks,

Norman D. Holbrook.

of Southsea and Constantinople. He was educated privately, and joined the Royal Navy. He served in the European War from 1914, and, when in command of Submarine B 11, dived under five rows of mines in the Dardanelles on 13 Dec. 1914, and torpedoed the Turkish battleship Messoudieh. " Deeds that thrill the Empire " (page 457) says of this officer : " Lieut. Norman Douglas Holbrook, commanding Submarine B 11, was the first of our ' underground specialists' to demonstrate and overcome the difficulties with which our submarines had to contend in routing the enemy. The B 11 was stationed at Malta in the beginning of the war, and went down to the Eastern Mediterranean when hostilities were begun against Turkey. She belonged to one of the oldest groups of our submarines, having been launched in 1905 as a more or less experimental craft ; but much fame awaited her. At three o'clock in the morning of 13 Dec. 1914, she left her parent ship to attempt the passage of the Dardanelles and to do what damage she could before returning. So perilous was the undertaking that before she left everyone on board left a farewell letter to his friends to be posted if the writer never returned ; for it was known not only that the Straits were well defended by mine-fields and other obstructions, but that the natural difficulties of navigation were almost as threatening as these artificial dangers. A current sometimes runs through the passage of the Sea of Marmora to the Mediterranean at a rate of five knots, and as the B 11 could do no more than six when submerged, her advance was going to be deadly slow, and her withdrawal made full of jeopardy by the onward sweeping current. But off she went, first on the surface, and then sinking lower and lower as she crept along between the hostile shores. Down to sixty feet of water she went, and so, blindfold, almost felt her way along the treacherous passage. In this fashion, risking rocks and shoals, she crept along under five rows of submerged mines laid by the Turks for the defence of the Straits, any one of which could have blown the B 11 to pieces and her crew to eternity. But fortune favoured them. Torpedo craft there were—in the distance. Much more important at the moment was an old tub of a battleship, the Messoudieh, which had been anchored on the inner side of the mine-field in order to prevent any attempt to interfere with it. As soon as the battleship was sighted the B 11 dived again, while the men at the torpedo tubes in the bows made ready for discharge, and then the submarine slowly rose until Lieut. Holbrook was able once more to sight the battleship through the periscope and to get his little craft in line for firing. Then came the word 'Fire!' Out leapt the torpedo from its tube, making a bee-line for the Messoudieh, and at the same instant the periscope was detected by the enemy, and ships and forts opened a furious cannonade. But the submarine was too quick for them. She dived—and found herself grating along the bottom at a depth of only thirty feet. Luckily the bottom shelved rapidly, and she was soon in deep water again and heading for the Straits' mouth, forced onward by the current and pursued by torpedo craft, whose attentions were so insistent that she had to remain submerged for nine hours in order to escape them. Escape she did, however, and one of the first things her crew read when they reached their headquarters was the official Turkish statement that on 13 Dec. the battleship Messoudieh 'sank at her anchorage as the result of a leak!' Lieut. Holbrook and his little band of heroes had demonstrated in the most convincing manner that if the enemy were too timid to give them opportunities, the officers and men of our submarine service could make them for themselves. The Commanding Officer was awarded the Victoria Cross for his gallant exploit; his second in command, Lieut. Sydney Winn, received the D.S.O., and each member of the crew who had shared the common danger was given the Distinguished Service Medal. Later on, many submarines of a newer and more powerful type succeeded in getting right through the Dardanelles, and in doing great damage to the enemy in the Sea of Marmora; but as the first submarine to sink a battleship the B 11 deserves a special niche in history." Lieut. Holbrook's Victoria Cross was gazetted 22 Dec. 1914: "Norman Douglas Holbrook, Lieut., Royal Navy. Date of Act of Bravery: 13 Dec. 1914. For most conspicuous bravery on the 13th Dec., when, in command of the Submarine B 11, he entered the Dardanelles, and, notwithstanding the very difficult current, dived his vessel under five rows of mines, and torpedoed the Turkish battleship Messudiyeh, which was guarding the mine-field. Lieut. Holbrook succeeded in bringing the B 11 safely back, although assailed by gun-fire and torpedo boats, having been submerged on one occasion for nine hours." Lieut. Holbrook was subsequently slightly wounded when on patrolling duties. He returned to England in Sept. 1915, and then served in F 3, V 4 and E 41 (did twelve months' mine-laying in this vessel and was mentioned in Despatches in July, 1917), and served with the Grand Fleet submarine flotilla in J 2 till Aug. 1918. Left submarine service, and went out to North Russia as Lieut.-Commander of the Russian cruiser Askold. He married, on Saturday, 21 June, 1919, at Holy Trinity, Kensington Gore, Viva, widow of Frank Everard Dixon, of Stoke Lodge, Hyde Park Gate, S.W., and daughter of the late Frederick Woodin and Mrs. Woodin, of 23, Lewes Crescent, Brighton.

London Gazette, 22 Dec. 1914.—"War Office, 22 Dec. 1914. His Majesty the King has been graciously pleased to approve of the grant of the Victoria Cross to Second Lieut. James Leach, and to No. 9016, Sergt. John Hogan, 2nd Battn. The Manchester Regt., for their conspicuous bravery, specified below."

LEACH, JAMES, Second Lieut., lived as a boy in Manchester. He joined the 1st Northamptonshire Regt.; served in France from the outbreak of war, and on 1 Oct. 1914, was gazetted Second Lieutenant in the 2nd Manchesters, and was awarded the Victoria Cross [London Gazette, 22 Dec. 1914]: "James Leach, Second Lieut.; John Hogan, No. 9016, Sergt., 2nd Battn. The Manchester Regt. Date of Act of Bravery: 29 Oct. 1914. For conspicuous bravery near Festubert, on the 29th Oct., when, after their trench had been taken by the Germans, and after two attempts at recapture had failed, they voluntarily decided the same day to recover the trench themselves, and, working from traverse to traverse at close quarters with great bravery, they gradually succeeded in regaining possession, killing eight of the enemy, wounding two, and making sixteen prisoners." "Deeds that thrill the Empire" (page 754) says: "By the end of the third week in Oct. 1914, our 2nd Corps, which had crossed the Bethune–La Bassée Canal some days previously, had fought their way through the difficult country to the north-east of it until they held a line pivoting on Givenchy on the south, and then running east in a salient north of the La Bassée road to the village of Herlies, whence it bent westwards to Aubers. The 5th Division, which included the 14th Brigade, in which were the 2nd Manchesters, was on the right; the 3rd Division to the north of it. The strength of the two divisions amounted to some 30,000 men. Sir Horace Smith-Dorrien's aim had been to get astride the La Bassée–Lille road in the neighbourhood of Fournes, and so, with the help of the French 10th Army, to isolate the enemy on the high ground south of a La Bassée. But he was not then aware how over whelming were the forces opposed to him, and he was soon obliged to forgo this plan, and to devote all his energies to holding his ground. On the morning of the 22nd, the enemy made a determined attack on the southern part of the British line held by the 5th Division, and drove us out of the village of Violaines, between Givenchy and Lorgies; but a dashing counter-attack, in which the Manchesters greatly distinguished themselves, prevented their advancing further. That night, however, Smith-Dorrien withdrew to a new line running from just east of Givenchy, by Neuve Chapelle to Fauquissart. The Manchesters were posted near Festubert. On the 24th the enemy attacked heavily all along this new line, and fierce and obstinate fighting continued with little intermission during the remainder of the month. On the 27th the Germans, coming on in great force, got into Neuve Chapelle, from the greater part of which, however, they were ejected on the following day, after desperate hand-to-hand fighting, by three native battalions of the Lahore Division of the Indian Corps, which had been brought up to support the exhausted British. Next morning, on our right at Festubert, the 24th Brigade were fiercely attacked, the trenches of the Manchesters being assailed with especial violence. Second Lieut. James Leach, a lad of twenty recently promoted to a commission in the Manchesters from the 1st Northamptons, occupied with thirty-four men in an advanced trench, which, after being subjected to a very heavy shelling, was attacked by between two and three hundred of the enemy. The Manchesters put up a right gallant fight, and received the advancing Huns with so withering a fire that before the latter reached the parapet fully half of them must have fallen. But the odds against our men were still too great to be denied, and, by sheer weight of numbers, the remainder of the Germans succeeded in carrying the position, and forcing them to retire down the communication trench to the support trenches, with the loss of about a dozen men. The position was very important, and the men who had been forced to retire were determined to make every effort to recover it. Headed by Lieut. Leach and Sergt. John Hogan, a veteran of the South African War, they made with this object two gallant counter-attacks; but the Germans had brought up machine guns, and each attempt failed. Two brave failures against a much superior force, strongly posted and assisted by machine guns, would have left any regiment with its honour intact, but that kind of negative glory did not satisfy Lieut. Leach. He had made up his mind to retake the position at all costs. He waited until night fell, and then crept up cautiously to ascertain what the Germans were doing. The result of his reconnaissance was not exactly encouraging, since he found the enemy in the occupation of three out of the four traverses. He therefore decided to do nothing for the moment, and crept back as quietly as he had come. At eleven o'clock the young officer made another journey of inspection, and on this occasion he found the Germans occupying all the traverses. Thereupon he decided upon action, and sending for Sergt. Hogan, called for ten volunteers. They were readily forthcoming, and the little party of twelve set out on their perilous enterprise. Lieut. Leach conducted his men along the communication trench which led into the right of the advance trench. They had to crawl all the way, for fear of alarming the Germans. His plan was to push the enemy as far to the left as he could, and entrap them in the cul-de-sac formed by the traverse on the left. The Germans were completely taken by surprise, and, after some stern bayonet work, the little band succeeded in pushing the enemy into the next traverse. The lieutenant and the sergeant now went forward alone. They had reached a point where the captured trench turned sharply at right angles. Leach was armed with a revolver, and was able to reach his hand round the corner and fire along the sections without exposing himself. The Germans, being armed only with rifles, could not shoot without exposing part of their bodies. Meanwhile Hogan watched the parapet to ward off attacks from above, since it was quite possible that the Germans might climb over from the section and shoot the two men from above, or take them in the rear; but nothing untoward happened, and they advanced to the next section. Taking their stand at the next corner, they repeated the manœuvre, Leach now being obliged to fire with his left hand. Another section was won, and then came the advance to the third. During their progress Hogan put his cap on the end of his rifle and raised it above the parapet, with the object of letting his comrades behind know how far they had progressed, so that they would not sweep that part of the trench which had been retaken with their fire. All the while the Germans kept up 'an inferno of bullets'—to borrow Hogan's own expression—and at places fierce hand-to-hand encounters between them and the two heroes occurred. But they all ended in the discomfiture of the Huns, who were finally driven along the left traverse until they could get no farther, and Leach and Hogan had them at their mercy. Then the Germans decided to surrender. Leach was surprised to hear a voice calling in English: 'Don't shoot, sir!' The speaker turned out to be one of his own men who had been taken prisoner in the morning. He had been sent by the German officer to say that they wished to surrender. Proceeding round the corner of the traverse, the young lieutenant found the officer and about fourteen Huns on their knees, with their hands raised in supplication. At sight of him a chorus of 'Mercy' arose—the word these gentry usually employ when cornered by the British. Leach told them to take off their equipment and run into the British main trench. This they did with all speed, being evidently in fear of being shot down by their comrades in the German trenches. Leach then learned that two more of his own men had been captured by the Germans that morning, and that the officer who had just surrendered, and who could speak English, had promised them 'a good time' when they were sent to Berlin as prisoners. In all, Leach and Hogan killed eight of the enemy, wounded two, and made

James Leach.

sixteen prisoners, besides regaining possession of an important advance trench. For this magnificent work they were each subsequently awarded the Victoria Cross, and well did they deserve the coveted bronze medal. They had been brave as few men have been, and had risked their lives freely at the call of duty."

HOGAN, JOHN, Sergt., served in the South African War, was discharged and rejoined his regiment. He served in the European War. The Manchester Regt., when in occupation of Festubert, held its difficult position with splendid determination. Sergt. Hogan was awarded the Victoria Cross [London Gazette, 22 Dec. 1914]; James Leach, Second Lieut.; John Hogan, Sergt., 2nd Battn. The Manchester Regt. Date of Acts of Bravery: 29 Oct. 1914. For conspicuous bravery near Festubert, on the 29th Oct., when, after their trench had been taken by the Germans, and after two attempts at recapture had failed, they voluntarily decided the same day to recover the trench themselves, and, working from traverse to traverse at close quarters with great bravery, they gradually succeeded in regaining possession, killing eight of the enemy, wounding two, and making sixteen prisoners."

John Hogan.

London Gazette, 11 Jan. 1915.—"His Majesty the King has been graciously pleased to approve of the grant of the Victoria Cross to No. 7079, Bandsman Thomas Edward Rendle, 1st Battn. The Duke of Cornwall's Light Infantry, for his conspicuous bravery, specified below."

RENDLE, THOMAS EDWARD, Bandsman, was born 30 Nov. 1884, at 4, Mead Street, Bedminster, Bristol, son of James Rendle, Painter and Decorator, and of Charlotte Rendle, who died 4 Oct. 1898, leaving a family of three sons (all of whom served in the war) and four daughters. He was educated at St. Luke's School, New Cut, Bedminster, and joined the Army 5 Sept. 1902, being sent with a draft to join the 1st Battn. Duke of Cornwall's Light Infantry at Stellenbosch, Cape Colony, 3 Jan. 1903. The battalion later moved to Middelburg, and in July, 1904, were moved to Wynberg, Cape Colony, remaining there until 12 March, 1906. They then embarked for England on H.M.T. Soudan, landing at Plymouth 5 April, 1906, and proceeding to Crowshill. On the 7th Feb. 1906, in South Africa, he married Lilian, daughter of Bandsman W. Crowe (late 60th Rifles, Kandahar Star and Afghan Medal), and they have two children: Ruby Lilian Jessie, born 23 May, 1907, and Edward William Wootton, born 10 Oct. 1909. Sergt. Rendle writes: "I have been a bandsman since enlistment; was sent to South Africa in Jan. 1903, arrived in England April, 1906; served in various stations in the United Kingdom since, and in March, 1914, moved with the battalion to Newry, North Ireland, owing to Home Rule troubles. We returned to the Curragh the end of July, 1914, and marched out for the front 13 Aug. I was mentioned in Despatches early in the war, for good work in the field, was also mentioned in Sir John French's Despatches on the First Battle of Ypres, in conjunction with winning the Victoria Cross." The following is an account of an interview with Rendle, given by a newspaper correspondent: "Another hero of the war, Bandsman Thomas Edward Rendle, No. 7079, 1st Battn. Duke of Cornwall's Light Infantry, who has now been promoted Lance-Corporal, has been awarded the Victoria Cross for conspicuous bravery on 20 Nov., near Wulverghem. According to the Gazette, Rendle attended to the wounded under very heavy shell and rifle fire, and rescued men from the trenches in which they had been buried by the blowing in of the parapets by the fire of the enemy's heavy howitzers. Rendle is now a patient at No. 1 Military Hospital—better known as the Eye Infirmary at Exeter. He was born in Bristol thirty years ago, and educated there. The fact that he was attached to the Duke of Cornwall's Light Infantry was, to use his own words 'just a chance.' While he has been serving his wife has made her home at Monks Road, Exeter. When it was sought to obtain an interview with Rendle he first refused point-blank to be seen, much less interviewed. This was because he has been embarrassed by the fuss which has been made of him in consequence of the honour he has earned. At last, however, he consented to give an account of the incident which led to the award of the Victoria Cross. His impression of the events of 20 Nov. were not at all clear, and as he modestly put it 'there is really nothing in it.' Sights he had seen in the trenches, he said, were 'enough to move the heart of a stone.' Near Wulverghem he was in the trenches eight days, and he made up his mind to assist in the removal of the wounded at whatever cost. In the midst of shell and rifle fire, he took his wounded comrades out of the trench one after the other. He was warned again and again to 'come down,' but paid no heed to the danger. Men had been buried by the blowing in of the parapets by the German howitzers, and they would undoubtedly have perished had they not been carried away. He was acting as stretcher-bearer when Lieut. Colebrook was wounded. The German trenches were about 200 yards away, and our trenches were under a heavy fire of big guns, machine-guns, and rifles. Several sections of our trenches were blown in, and spaces, which were swept by fire and were without shelter, were left between the trenches which remained. 'After Lieut. Colebrooke was hit,' he said, 'Lieut. Wingate crawled over the gap to his assistance, and asked me to go with him. Together we bound up his wounds. An artery in his right thigh was severed, and he was bleeding rather badly. The Germans were popping at us all the time. To get the wounded officer back I started to make a shallow burrow across the open space with my hands. Every time I threw up the dirt I had scraped loose I suppose my head bobbed up, and the Germans took pot shots at it. I had two or three narrow escapes. I have no recollection of how long I was exposed to the fire. I didn't take much notice of it at the time; one gets used to that sort of thing. I had to make several burrows in order to get cover of any kind. Fortunately, neither Mr. Colebrooke nor I got hit on the way back. I had to crawl, of course, and carry him as best I could.' Rendle was invalided through sickness. He had been at the front since the beginning of the war, and although he had several narrow escapes he was never hit. He was glad to hear that Lieut. Colebrook was now convalescent, and mentioned that the officer had since thanked him for his help. Full justice was done to the bandsman's bravery in a letter written by Lieut. R. R. Wingate to his mother, Mrs. Wingate, The Court, Cullompton. In this letter Mr. Wingate said: 'We have had a terrible time in the trenches, getting well shelled.' Then followed the description of the incident in which Rendle distinguished himself, and the circumstances leading up to it: 'Two of the shells pitched into the trench only about 30 yards from me, and blew ten men to pieces. They also blew down all the front part of our trench, and the earth filled up the dug-out part. This was very annoying, as it divided our trench into two parts, and made it impossible to get from one half to the other without running across this open piece of ground, about five or six yards. Of course, the Germans realized this, and put a machine gun covering this space, so that anyone who crossed carried his life very much in his hands. A subaltern in my company (Colebrook) got shot that afternoon in that part of the trench without a communicating trench. He asked for me. So I went along to him; this meant that I had to cross this gap, but luckily they failed to hit me. We decided it was quite impossible to move him until dark, as there was no way of getting him across the gap, so I sat down to chat with him, when suddenly the Germans started again with their shells. The first two went over the trench, but the next one pitched just short, and that buried me with mud. This, I thought, was a bit too much, so I said that Colebrook must be got away. Just then I got called away to the other end of the trench for a few minutes. In the meantime, one of the stretcher-bearers (Rendle) lay on his stomach in the gap and under fire, and tried to clear the earth out of the original trench to get a safe path to get Colebrooke past the gap. But another shell came, and he decided to risk it. Rendle, the stretcher-bearer, took Colebrook on his back and wormed his way across the open gap on his stomach, thus getting him into the right half of the trench, where it was plain sailing. . . . We have Rendle's name in for distinction, so that if you see his name amongst the V.C.'s or D.C.M.'s you will know what he got it for.'" He was awarded the Victoria Cross [London Gazette, 11 Jan. 1915]: "Thomas Edward Rendle, No. 7079, 1st Battn. Duke of Cornwall's Light Infantry. Date of Act of Bravery: 20 Nov. 1914. For conspicuous bravery, on the 20th Nov. near Wulverghem, when he attended to the wounded under very heavy shell and rifle fire, and rescued men from the trenches in which they had been buried by the blowing in of the parapets by the fire of the enemy's heavy howitzers." He was promoted to Lance-Corporal, and received the 4th Class Russian Order of St. George. He was later promoted to Sergeant. It was a red-letter day at St. Luke's, Bedminster, when Sergt. Rendle made his appearance to fulfil his promise to visit his old school. Teachers and scholars were highly delighted, and showed their joy and enthusiasm in a thoroughly patriotic spirit. The gallant V.C., who looked in the best of health, highly appreciated the warm welcome accorded to him. He was interested to learn that the undermentioned Old Boys had also been honoured by their King and country: Corpl. F. Glanville (D.C.M.); Corpl. H. Glanville (D.C.M.) (brothers); Sergt. Frampton (M.M.), and Sapper T. E. Cockle (M.M.).

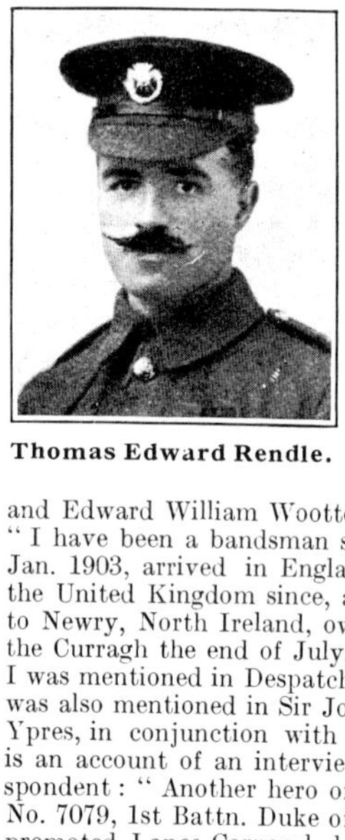

Thomas Edward Rendle.

London Gazette, 18 Feb. 1915.—"His Majesty the King has been graciously pleased to approve of the grant of the Victoria Cross to the undermentioned Officers and Men for their conspicuous bravery and devotion to duty whilst serving with the Expeditionary Force."

ALEXANDER, ERNEST WRIGHT, Lt.-Col., was born at Liverpool 2 Oct. 1870, son of Robert Alexander (Shipowner and Director, Suez Canal), and of Annie Alexander, daughter of James Cramton Gregg, of Belfast. He received his education at Cherbourg House, Malvern, and at Harrow, and entered the Royal Military Academy direct from Harrow in 1880, accelerated one term. Lord Ernest Hamilton, in "The First Seven Divisions," gives the following account of Major Alexander's act of bravery: "The dismounted men were gradually withdrawn. During the course of one of these withdrawals, Capt. Francis Grenfell, 9th Lancers, noticed Major Alexander, of the 119th Battery, in difficulties with regard to the withdrawal of his guns. All his horses had been killed, and almost every man in the detachment was either killed or wounded. Capt. Grenfell offered assistance, which was gladly accepted, and presently he returned with eleven officers of his regiment, and some forty men. The ground was very heavy, and the guns had to be run back by hand under a ceaseless fire, but they were all saved, Major Alexander, Capt. Grenfell, and the rest of the officers working as hard as the men. Capt. Grenfell was already wounded when he arrived, and was again hit while manhandling one of the guns, but he declined to retire till they were all saved. For this fine performance Major Alexander and Capt. Grenfell were each awarded the Victoria Cross, Sergts. Turner and Davids getting the D.C.M. The award was announced in the London Gazette [London Gazette, 18 Feb. 1915]: "Ernest Wright Alexander, Lieut.-Colonel, 119th Battery, Royal Field Artillery. Date of Act of Bravery: 24 Aug.

1914. For conspicuous bravery and great ability at Elouges on the 24th Aug. 1914, when the flank guard was attacked by a German corps, in handling his battery against overwhelming odds with such conspicuous success that all his guns were saved, notwithstanding that they had to be withdrawn by hand by himself and three other men. This enabled the retirement of the 5th Division to be carried out without serious loss. Subsequently Lieut.-Colonel Alexander (then Major) rescued a wounded man under a heavy fire with the greatest gallantry and devotion to duty." The following is taken from the official record of services of Colonel (Temporary Major-General) Ernest Wright Alexander, V.C., C.B., C.M.G., R.A.: He was born at Liverpool, 2 Oct. 1870; appointed Second Lieutenant, R.A., 27 July, 1889; promoted Captain, R.F.A., 26 Dec. 1899; promoted Major, R.A., 25 April, 1906; promoted Lieutenant-Colonel, R.H. and R.F.A., 30 Oct. 1914; promoted Colonel (Army), 2 June, 1919. He commanded the 22nd Brigade, R.F.A., France, 5 Oct. 1914; commanded the 27th Brigade, R.F.A., France; commanded Royal Artillery, 15th Division, France, and was Temporary Brigadier-General whilst so employed, 25 Aug. 1915; G.O.C., R.A., 15th Army Corps, and Temporary Brigadier-General whilst so employed, 24 April, 1916. He held the above appointment till 22 March, 1917; commanded Royal Artillery, 11th Corps, and was Temporary Brigadier-General whilst so employed, 31 May, 1917; vacated the above appointment, 9 April, 1918; was appointed Major-General, R.A., H.Q., 1st Army, and was Temporary Major-General whilst so employed, 9 April, 1918; commanded Royal Artillery, Southern Area, Aldershot Command, with the temporary rank of Brigadier-General (List dated 5 June, 1919). His service overseas was: in India, 23 Sept. 1892, to 13 Nov. 1900, and 1 Oct. 1903, to 25 June, 1906; with the B.E.F., France, Oct. 1914, to March, 1917, and May, 1917, to 1919. He was mentioned in Despatches [London Gazette, 19 Oct. 1914; 17 Dec. 1914; 22 June, 1915; 1 Jan. 1916; 15 June, 1916; 2 Jan. 1917; 30 May, 1918; 20 Dec. 1918, and 5 July, 1919]. He was awarded the Victoria Cross [London Gazette, 18 Feb. 1915]; created a C.M.G. [London Gazette, 23 June, 1915]; received the Military Order of Savoy (Cavalier) [London Gazette, 12 Sept. 1918]; was created a C.B. [London Gazette, 1 Jan. 1919]; received the Croix de Guerre [London Gazette, 21 Aug. 1919]; was created Grand Officer, Military Order of Avis, 21 Aug. 1919. He married, 1 Sept. 1903, at Aldershot Manor, Hants, Rose, daughter of the late Major H. G. Newcome, R.A. (retired), H.M. Bodyguard. There are four children: Annie, Robert (born 7 June, 1905), George William (born 30 June, 1911) and Mary.

KENNY, WILLIAM, Drummer, joined the Gordon Highlanders, served in the European War, and was awarded the Victoria Cross [London Gazette, 18 Feb. 1915]: "William Kenny, No. 6535, Drummer, 2nd Battn. The Gordon Highlanders. Date of Act of Bravery: 23 Oct. 1914. For conspicuous bravery on 23 Oct. near Ypres, in rescuing wounded men on five occasions under very heavy fire in the most fearless manner, and for twice previously saving machine guns by carrying them out of action. On numerous occasions Drummer Kenny conveyed urgent messages under very dangerous circumstances over fire-swept ground."

William Kenny.

BROOKE, JAMES ANSON OTHO, Capt., was born 3 Feb. 1884, son of Capt. Harry Vesey Brooke, J.P., D.L., late 92nd Gordon Highlanders, and his wife, Patricia, daughter of James Gregory Moir Eyres, Esquire, and grandson of the late Sir Arthur Bringley Brooke, Bart., M.P., of Colebrooke, co. Fermanagh. He was educated at Wellington, and the Royal Military College, Sandhurst, where he was captain of the Shooting Eight, tied for the Saddle, was in the football team, was Senior Colour-Sergeant of the College, and won the Sword of Honour. He received his commission as Second Lieutenant in the Gordon Highlanders 11 Oct. 1905, and joined the 1st Battn. at Cork in Nov. He was promoted Lieutenant on 5 Aug. 1907, and transferred to the 2nd Battn. in India, where he was soon recognized as one of the smartest young officers in his regiment, and the best of sportsmen. He was a splendid shot, and killed many

James A. O. Brooke.

head of large game, including ibex, markhor, leopards, bears and bisons. He was present at the Delhi Durbar, where he, as senior subaltern, received the new Regimental Colours from the King, and was awarded the Durbar Medal. He left India in 1913, and was serving with his regiment in Egypt when war broke out, and in Oct. 1914, proceeded to Belgium, landing at Zeebrugge, and taking part in severe fighting for several days. On the morning of 29 Oct. the 7th Division was attacked by a greatly superior force at Gheluvelt. His Colonel wrote: "On this occasion Lieut. Brooke, who was Assistant Adjutant, had been sent at a critical moment by his Colonel with a message from one end of the line to the other. On his way, noticing that the Germans were breaking through part of the line, he, with the greatest promptitude and bravery, gathered together all the men he could get hold of (about a hundred in number), and led them in a glorious charge against the advancing Germans, driving them back and thus saving the

situation and an enormous amount of valuable lives. But unfortunately shortly after this he was killed." An account taken from a newspaper says: "The British line was saved. During all this long-drawn-out agony Capt. Brooke was the undoubted hero of the hour. Not only had he grasped the terrible danger which threatened our positions, but he had acted with quickness and valour, gathering the men together, and, finally, leading them straight and sure to the enemy's lair. Once there, he saw to the consolidation of the newly-acquired trenches, and time and again exposed himself to the most fearful risks in order to bring up supports and have the defences strengthened against the Hun assaults. It was while so acting that he fell. His death, after such dearly won and splendid triumphs, was a tragic blow to officers and men alike, for on that great day he had been the bravest of the brave." He was posthumously awarded the Victoria Cross [London Gazette, 18 Feb. 1915]: "James Anson Otho Brooke, Lieut., Gordon Highlanders. Date of Act of Bravery: 29 Oct. 1914. For most conspicuous bravery and great ability near Gheluvelt, on the 29th Oct., in leading two attacks on the German trenches under heavy rifle and machine-gun fire, regaining a lost trench at a very critical moment. He was killed on that day. By his marked coolness and promptitude on this occasion, Lieut. Brooke prevented the enemy from breaking through our line at a time when a general counter-attack could not have been organized." Some eloquent and beautiful tributes have been paid to the memory of this right gallant Gordon. One officer, describing the scenes in which he had figured so heroically, wrote: "After terrible fighting, being attacked by very superior numbers, our men were beginning to feel the very hard strain when Otho took charge of the whole line, and we began to think that things were going to turn out all right. He went from right to left of the line, absolutely regardless of any danger, and at last gave the order for a general advance. Just after we got on the move he told me to swing half the line and make for some support trenches which had been made by the Grenadiers. We did this. We found, meantime, that Otho had captured the trench with about sixty men under his command. The parapet was too high for the men to use their rifles, but we found spaces and scooped away till I think most of them could fire fairly easy. We found the Germans were occupying the fire trench about 200 yards on our front. It wasn't a very nice position, and I saw Otho, who was on the left of the trench, twice leave it and double behind a house to send a message for some supports to come up on our right. He had about twenty-five yards in the open to cover, and each time, going out and coming in, I saw dozens of bullets spluttering red dust off the walls of the cottage he had to pass. There was a Lieutenant of the Grenadiers near me in the trench, and his words to me were: 'My God! Who is that? He is a plucky fellow!' I told him it was Otho, and that he was our assistant adjutant. 'Well,' he said, "he is a devilish brave fellow!' And so he was. Poor Otho was perfectly splendid. Shortly after this, word was passed to me that he was killed—practically instantaneously, and he had no pain, which is one thing to be thankful for. I can only add that he died the death of a brave man, and was a first-class fellow. His last words to me were: 'If they charge us, get out of the trench and wait for them.' " The Colonel also sent a letter to his mother, in which he said: "I write to tell you that Otho has given his life for his country and regiment. His actions on this day, which brought us all so much grief at his loss, were up to the very highest traditions of the British Army. All who saw him on that day wondered at his pluck, and were certain that had he not been there and done what he did so well and so gallantly, we should have suffered enormously. He saved the situation. I cannot tell you what Otho's death means to all of us, for we all loved him beyond the expression of words. Thank God he himself knew nothing. His death was instantaneous." Lieut. Brooke was promoted to Captain after his death, antedated to the previous Sept., and was also mentioned in Despatches.

VALLENTIN, JOHN FRANKS, Capt., was born on the 14th May, 1882, son of the late Grimble Vallentin and Mrs. Grimble Vallentin. He was a grandson of Colonel Finnis, the first victim of the Indian Mutiny, and a nephew of Major Vallentin, who was killed in action in the Boer War. He was educated at Wellington College; joined the 6th (Militia) Battn. Rifle Brigade, in Aug. 1899, and became Lieutenant in July, 1900. That battalion was embodied at the Curragh Camp, Kildare, from the beginning of the Boer War, for nearly a year, and on its disembodiment, Lieut. Vallentin was attached to the 3rd (Militia) Battn. Royal Sussex Regt., and served with it in the South African War of 1899–1902; took part in operations in the Orange River Colony from April to Dec. 1901, and in the Transvaal from the latter date till May, 1902 (Queen's Medal and five clasps). In July, 1903, he received his commission in the Royal Garrison Regt. (formed during the Boer War), being transferred to the South Staffordshire Regt. as Second Lieutenant in June, 1905. He became Lieutenant in Sept. 1907, and Captain in June, 1909. Capt. Vallentin served in the European War, when the 1st Battn. South Staffordshire Regt. formed part of the 7th Division, which landed at Zeebrugge on 7 Oct., and took part in all the fighting in the First Battle of Ypres. Its losses were so heavy that the day before Capt. Vallentin was killed his battalion and the 2nd Battn. Royal Warwickshire Regt. were formed into one small battalion, under the command of Capt. Vallentin. There were no officers of higher rank in either battalion. He led his command so well that he was awarded the Victoria Cross [London Gazette, 18 Feb. 1915]: " John Franks Vallentin, Capt., 1st Battn. The South

John Franks Vallentin.

Staffordshire Regt. Date of Act of Bravery : 7 Nov. 1914. For con-spicuous bravery on the 7th Nov. at Zillebeke. When leading the attack against the Germans under a very heavy fire he was struck down, and on rising to continue the attack was immediately killed. The capture of the enemy's trenches which followed was in a great measure due to the confi-dence which the men had in their Captain, arising from his many previous acts of great bravery and ability." Capt. Vallentin was mentioned in Sir John French's Despatch of 14 Jan. 1915. He was a keen polo player, and captain of the Regimental Polo Club. He was specially qualified in musketry.

DE PASS, FRANK ALEXANDER, Lieut., was born in London on the 26th of April, 1887, son of Eliot Arthur and Beatrice de Pass, of 23, Queen's Gate Terrace, London, S.W. He was educated at the Abbey School, Beckenham, and at Rugby School, which

Frank A. de Pass.

he entered in 1901, and passed direct into the Royal Military Academy, Woolwich, being third on the list of successful candi-dates in 1904. He was commissioned in the Royal Field Artillery in Jan. 1906, and was promoted to Lieutenant in March, 1909. In this year his battery was sta-tioned in India, and Lieut. de Pass applied for—and obtained—a commission in the 34th Poona Horse, Prince Albert Victor's Own, having, by his natural talent for linguistics, succeeded in passing the necessary standards in Hindustani within a period of six months. He also subse-quently passed in Persian. In Nov. 1913, he was appointed Orderly Officer, with the local rank of Captain, to Sir Percy Lake, K.C.M.G., C.B., Chief of the Staff in India. Lieut. de Pass was a successful rider, both on the flat and across country, and won several regimental races in India. He played polo, and was a good shot. On the outbreak of war he rejoined his regiment and accompanied it to the front in Sept. 1914. He was killed in action at the age of 27, near Festubert, in French Flanders, on 25 Nov. 1914, under cir-cumstances which are described in an extract, quoted below, from "The English Corps in France," which is based on the report written on the 27th of Nov. by the Captain in Command, who concluded the same thus : "I consider that Lieut. de Pass's conduct throughout was most intrepid, and that his actions were a magnificent example to the men of the Detachment." Lieut. Elphinstone, of the same regiment—in conveying to the parents of Lieut. de Pass the news of his death—wrote : "He had been behaving in the most gallant way possible ever since he went out to the trenches. . . . It is just what was to be expected of him. I have been with him pig-sticking and have played polo regularly with him, and I have no hesitation in saying he was quite the most gallant fellow it has ever been my good fortune to meet." The following is the account given in "The Indian Corps in India" (Lieut.-Colonel I. W. B. Merewether, C.I.E., and Sir Frederick E. Smith, Bart.) : "On the 23rd Nov. a detachment of the 34th Poona Horse, under the command of Capt. Grimshaw, took over a portion of the trenches of the Ferozepore Brigade. On arrival, at 4 a.m., it was found that the enemy had driven a sap right up to the parapet, which had been blown in, a breach of some eight feet in breadth being created, which exposed our trench to fire from the sap. As soon as it was daylight, Capt. Grimshaw inspected the breach, which had been guarded by a party under Lieut. F. de Pass, and called for a volunteer to reconnoitre along the sap towards the German line. Sowar Abdulla Khan at once came forward and proceeded to crawl out. On his return he reported that the enemy had erected a sand-bag traverse at a distance of about ten yards from our trench at the first bend in the sap. The traverse was loopholed and a German was on guard, a fact which Abdulla Khan ascertained by being fired at and missed. At 8 a.m. the enemy began to throw bombs into our trench from their side of the traverse. This went on all day, and caused several casualties. Early in the morning of the 24th, Lieut. de Pass determined at all costs to put an end to this state of affairs, and, accompanied by Sowars Fateh Khan and Firman Shah, he entered the sap and crawled along it until he reached the enemy's traverse. With the utmost coolness, he proceeded to place a charge of gun-cotton in the loophole, and fired it, with the result that the traverse was completely demolished, and the bend of the sap was rounded off to such an extent as to expose some thirty yards to our fire. While this was going on, the enemy threw a bomb at our little party, but by good luck it exploded behind Lieut. de Pass and did no damage, the trio return-ing to our trench in safety. All bombing on the part of the enemy was put a stop to during the remainder of the 24th, and there was only one casualty, compared with six on the previous day and nine on the 25th, by which time, under cover of darkness, the Germans had managed to replace their tra-verse. On the 24th Lieut. de Pass visited the neighbouring trench, which was occupied by the 7th Dragoon Guards. On his way he observed a sepoy of the 58th Rifles lying wounded outside our trench. Accompanied by Private C. Cook, of the 7th, he at once went out in broad daylight and brought the sepoy in, although exposed to the enemy's fire for a distance of about 200 yards. De Pass then again volunteered to enter the enemy's sap and attempt to blow up the traverse, but as this meant almost certain death permission was refused. On the 25th the enemy's bombing in-creased in violence, and de Pass went to the sap-head to superintend the repair of our parapet, which had again been seriously damaged. Observing a sniper at work behind the traverse, he tried to shoot him, but was himself shot through the head and killed. Many brave deeds have been performed during this war, but there are few instances of gallantry more conspicuous than that displayed by this heroic young soldier. He was the very perfect type of the British officer. He united to singular personal beauty a charm of manner and a degree of valour which made him the idol of his men. He

was honoured in death by the Victoria Cross. No one in the war earned it better. Sowars Abdullah Khan, Fateh Khan and Firman Shah, who so gallantly seconded their officer, received the Indian Distinguished Service Medal, while Private Cook was awarded the Distinguished Conduct Medal." Lieut. de Pass's Victoria Cross was gazetted 18 Feb. 1915 : "Frank Alexander de Pass, Lieut., late 34th Poona Horse. Date of Act of Bravery : 24th Nov. 1914. For conspicuous bravery near Festubert, on 24 Nov. 1914, in entering a German sap and destroying a traverse in the face of the enemy's bombs ; and for subsequently rescuing, under heavy fire, a wounded man who was lying exposed in the open. Lieut. de Pass lost his life on this day in a second attempt to capture the aforementioned sap, which had been reoccupied by the enemy."

ROBSON, HENRY HOWEY, Private, was born at South Shields, son of Mr. and Mrs. Robson, of Shotton Bridge, Durham. He joined the Army and served in the European War. Private Robson writes : "I

Henry Howey Robson.

took part in Mons and Cambrai, and was in the retirement until I got to the Marne, in which battle I took part, and then was on the River Aisne at Veilly (?). We were there holding it for 13 days, and afterwards we marched for La Bassée. I took part in the four days' advance, and afterwards we went to Kemmel, at which place I earned my Victoria Cross. I was severely wounded, and I did not take part in any-thing else until the 13th of Nov. 1916, when I was wounded at Serres-on-Ancre, which wound, up to the present, has left me useless." He was awarded the Victoria Cross [London Gazette, 18 Feb. 1915] : "Henry Howey Robson, Private, 2nd Battn. The Royal Scots (Lothian Regt.). For most conspicuous bravery near Kem-mel, on 14 Dec. 1914, during an attack on the German position, when he left his trench under a very heavy fire and rescued a wounded non-commissioned officer, and subsequently he tried during an attack to bring another wounded man into cover, whilst exposed to severe fire. In this attack he was at once wounded, but per-severed in his effort until rendered helpless by being shot a second time. He was again severely wounded on 13 Nov. 1916, at Serres-on-Ancre."

MACKENZIE, JAMES, Private, was born at West Glen, New Abbey, Kirkcudbrightshire, 2 April, 1889, son of the late Alexander Mackenzie, and Marion, daughter of Hugh Miller, of Meikle, Bern-cleugh, Irongray, Dumfries, Farmer. He was educated at Laurieknowe Public School, Maxwelltown ; enlisted in the 2nd Battn. Scots Guards, 16 Feb. 1912, and was awarded the Victoria Cross [London Gazette, 18 Feb. 1915] : "James Mac-kenzie, Private, No. 8185, Scots Guards. For conspicuous bravery at Rouges Bancs, 19 Dec., in rescuing a severely wounded man from the front of the German trenches, under a very heavy fire, and after a stretcher-bearer party had been com-pelled to abandon the attempt. Private Mackenzie was subsequently killed on that day, whilst in performance of a similar act of gallant conduct." Private Mackenzie

James Mackenzie.

was killed at 2 p.m. on 19 Dec. 1914. A comrade wrote : "He was return-ing to the trenches along with me and another stretcher-bearer when it occurred. We had only two or three cases that morning, so the last one was taken by us three. After we took the wounded soldier to hospital we returned to see if there were any more. There was a very dangerous place to pass. I went first, followed by another, then James came behind, which caused his death. He was shot in the heart by a sniper, and only lived five minutes." A memorial tablet erected by friends in the Burgh of Maxwelltown and parishioners of Trogneer was placed in the east vestibule of Trogneer Parish Church. A portrait has also been hung in his old school.

NEAME, PHILIP, Lieut., was born 12 Dec. 1888, at Macknade, Faversham, Kent, son of Frederick Neame, Esq., and of Kathleen Neame. He was educated at St. Michael's School, Westgate, and at Cheltenham College, and

Philip Neame

joined the Army 29 July, 1908. He served in the European War, going to France with the 8th Division at the begin-ning of Nov. 1914, as a subaltern (section officer) of 15th Field Company, Royal Engineers. He was promoted to Captain in Feb. 1915 (dated 30 Oct. 1914), and was present at the attack, north of Neuve Chapelle, on 18 Dec. 1914. He was men-tioned in Despatches in Feb. 1915, and was awarded the Victoria Cross [London Gazette, 18 Feb. 1915] : "Philip Neame, Lieut., Royal Engineers. For conspicuous bravery on the 19th Dec., near Neuve Chapelle, when, notwithstanding the very heavy rifle fire and bomb-throwing by the enemy, he succeeded in holding them back and in rescuing all the wounded men whom it was possible to move." On this occasion he says : " I had a bombing fight single-handed against the Germans, who were making a counter-attack, covered by rifle and machine-gun fire and heavy bomb-throwing, against the trenches captured from the Germans the night before. Our improvised bombs worked well, exploding violently amongst the German bombers, killing and wounding them, and checked their advance for about three-quarters of an hour." Capt. Neame was present at the Battle of Neuve Chapelle, 10–14 March, 1915. He became Adjutant, Royal Engineers, 8th Division, 30 March, 1915 ; was present at the Battle of Fromelles-Festubert, 9 May, 1915, and at the attack on the 25th Sept. 1915, between Neuve Chapelle and Armentières. He was created a Companion of the Distinguished Service Order [London Gazette, Jan. 1916] : " Philip Neame, Capt., Royal Engineers." He was also again mentioned in Despatches. On 11 Oct. 1915, he became G.S.O.3, 8th Division, and on 13 Feb. 1916, Capt. Neame became Brigade Major, 168th Infantry Brigade, 56th (London) Division. He was present at the assault on Gommecourt, 1 July, 1916. From 5 Sept. to 10 Oct. 1916, he took part in the Battle of the Somme, including attacks at Ginchy, Combles and Les Bœufs. He became General Staff Officer, 2nd Grade, 29 Nov. 1916, and joined 15th Corps Headquarters. On 1 Jan. 1917, he was given his Brevet Majority and mentioned in Despatches for work in the Somme Battle as Brigade Major of an Infantry Brigade. He took part in the advance to the Hindenburg Line just north of the River Somme in March and April, 1917, and in the operations round Nieuport during the Third Battle of Ypres. He was there awarded by the French the Legion of Honour (Chevalier) and Croix de Guerre. He was mentioned in Despatches in Dec. 1917. Major Neame joined 1st Army Headquarters as G.S.O.2 in Dec. 1917, and was with them during the great attacks of March, 1918, and the Battle of the Lys in April, 1918. He became General Staff Officer, 1st Grade, 30th Division, and was promoted Lieutenant-Colonel in June, 1918. With this Division he took part in the British attacks in Flanders during Sept., Oct. and Nov., advancing from Mont Kemmel, across the Rivers Lys and Scheldt, to the River Dendre, 25 miles from Brussels, where the Division halted on Armistice Day. He was awarded the Belgian Croix de Guerre. He was mentioned in Despatches and received a Brevet Lieutenant-Colonelcy in June, 1919.

ACTON, ABRAHAM, Private, was born 17 Dec. 1892, at Whitehaven, co. Cumberland, son of Mr. and Mrs. Robert Acton. He was educated at Crosthwaite Memorial School, and joined the Army as a unit of the 5th

Battn. Border Regt. (T.F.) ; transferred to the 2nd Battn. Border Regt. 17 Jan. 1914. Private Acton served in the European War from 25 Nov. 1914, and was awarded the Victoria Cross [London Gazette, 18 Feb. 1915] : " Abraham Acton, No. 10694, 2nd Battn. Border Regt. ; James Smith, No. 6423, Private, 3rd Battn. (attached 2nd Battn.) Border Regt. Date of Act of Bravery, 21 Dec. 1914. For conspicuous bravery on 21 Dec. 1914, at Rouges Bancs, in voluntarily going out from their trench and rescuing a wounded man who had been lying exposed against the enemy's trenches for seventy-five hours, and on the same day again leaving their trench voluntarily, under heavy fire, to bring into cover another wounded man. They were under fire for sixty

Abraham Acton.

minutes whilst conveying the wounded men into safety." Private Acton was a most devoted son, and wrote home whenever he could to his father and mother. He wrote from Shoeburyness : " We are guarding the . . . Thames and Medway defences. God help the Kaiser ! If he sends his Zeppelins up to London, this is the way he is going to come. You don't see us through the day. We're only out at nights, looking for Kaiser Bill's gas-bags. We have some nice little pills here for him if he sends them here. He will get both rifles and air-ship guns. We have also coast-guards on the watch with us. . . ."

In letters to his father which he wrote from France he said :

" I only received your parcel the day before we went into the trenches, and therefore I had no time. We are all enjoying ourselves out here, only it is rather cold, but we are well looked after, plenty of good clothes, mufflers, and Balaclava caps. One feels just like being at home. Our regiment has a fine name out here. You will have seen it in the ' Adver-tiser.' That little bit in the paper was all right. I think there was more than one saw it, as the Sergeant-Major of our company saw it as well. He was telling me about it. We have had another casualty in our regiment. A chap called L.-Corpl. Dent, from Westmorland, was killed on the 24th Jan. He was shot in the head. I heard he lived five and a half hours after. I suppose he would get a soldier's grave, like many another poor chap. It would nearly make the young fellows at home cry to see these graves of poor chaps who have died defending their King and country while they are idling their time away at home doing nothing. They will have to remember sooner or later. Poor little Belgium ! Think of the fate they received from the hands of the enemy, and the wilful damage they have done, both in this country and Belgium. But they will make everything good, as sure as the British bull-dogs guard our coast and also Tommy Atkins fights his country's battles. I think I have told you all. . . ."

" . . . Have you got any more news about going in the patrol boat yet ? I think it will be more in your own line, better than being a swaddy. I wish I was only with you when you go on it. I suppose you will miss a few pals from there when you go to sea. We will be having all the Border Regt. out here soon, as I hear our 1st Battn. is in England, and come home from India. We are going to have a fine crush out here soon. They "

(the Germans) " are the most unruly set of men ever I saw. They are always singing and shouting. The other night they were singing a song just like the song of the Fatherland. We do not take any heed to them. They always think they are winning. The Indian troops are the boys for them. They don't half dread them when they see them coming. They have no mercy for one when they get him. It is only right, for the way they do with our troops.

" The Kaiser made a big mistake when he said he would be in Calais on 10 Dec., and have his Xmas dinner in London. He did not know that 'the Border Regt. was helping to hold the road to Calais, a regiment that defied his crack soldiers at Ypres when they surrounded the Border Regt. there.

" Do you remember when you were at Barrow talking in a letter to me about coming home with a V.C. or a D.C.M. across my chest ? You did not know how soon these words would come true.

" We have had some queer times out here, with rain and snow enough to kill you, but the British can stick anything. It is well known the dis-comforts the soldiers have to put up with. . . ."

" . . . We have had a bit of a scrap with the Germans. We took 300 prisoners, but we had a few casualties, but they are not serious, best part of them. Private Smith, that V.C. chap, that mate of mine, was hit by a bullet in the hand. He is now in hospital.

" We have got a fine name, as our regiment out here is the talk of the country. Well, it does not do to brag too much, but it deserves it for Ypres and other places.

" Tell Charlie when he grows up he has got to be a soldier in Abraham's lot, the good old 5th Borders.

" I have a little bit of good news for you. On 21 Dec. we had word from the General there were two of our men lying outside the German trenches, so he asked to pass the word for two volunteers ; so me and another chap went out and brought them back ; they were both wounded in the thigh, they could not walk, so we had to crawl on and drag them with us. It was a very risky job, although we got through safe."

In his last letter home Private Acton said :

" We are most likely going in to another big attack by the time you receive this letter, so if you do not receive any letters for about a fortnight or so, don't get anxious, as I will write as soon as possible.

" . . . I hope everyone at home is in the best of health, and may they do so by God's help, so that if I am spared so long I may see them well."

When his father sent him a picture post-card photograph, he said :

" I see you have got the old smile on your face. Well, it's no use having a wry face ; we all must be happy whatever comes or goes. We all have our little bit to do."

Private Acton was killed in action at the Battle of Festubert, 16 May, 1915.

SMITH, JAMES, Private, served in the European War, and was awarded the Victoria Cross [London Gazette, 18 Feb. 1915] : " James Smith, No. 6423, Private, 3rd Battn. Border Regt. Date of Act of Bravery : 21 Dec. 1914. For conspicuous bravery on the 21st Dec., at Rouges Bancs, in volun-tarily going from their trench and rescuing a wounded man who had been lying exposed against the enemy's trenches for seventy-five hours, and on the same day again leaving their trench voluntarily, under heavy fire, to bring into cover another wounded man. They were under fire for sixty minutes whilst conveying the wounded men into safety."

O'LEARY, MICHAEL, L.-Corpl., was born at Inchigeela, near Macroom, County Cork, in 1890. " Deeds that thrill the Empire " (pages 165–168) says : " Before the Great War was a month old the critics and all the experts

had formally decided that men had ceased to count. They were never tired of telling us that it was purely an affair of machines of scientific destruction, and that personal courage was of no avail. Gone were the days of knightly deeds, of hair's-breadth adventures, of acts of individual prowess They told us so often and with such per-sistence that we all began to believe them, and then one day the world rang with the story of Michael O'Leary's great exploit, and we knew that the age of heroes was not yet past. Once more science had been dominated and beaten by human nerve and human grit. The school for heroes is not a bed of roses, and O'Leary's was no excep-tion. He was in the Navy, and then he served his time in the Irish Guards, and

Michael O'Leary.

after his seven years he went to Canada and joined the North-West Mounted Police. By the time he was twenty-five he had sampled most hardships that this soft age still offers to the adventurous, and given proof of the qualities which were to make him one of the outstanding figures of the ' Great Age.' A long and desperate fight with a couple of cut-throats in the Far West had revealed him to himself and shown his calibre to his friends. The ' Hun-tamer ' was in the making. On mobilization in August O'Leary hastened to rejoin his old regiment, and by November he found himself in France with the rank of Lance-Corporal. His splendid health, gained in the open-air life in the North-West, stood him in good stead during the long and trying winter ; but the enemy, exhausted by their frantic attempt to ' hack a way ' through to Calais, gave little trouble, and O'Leary had no chance to show his metal. With the spring, however, came a change, and there was considerable ' liveliness ' in that part of the line held by the Irish Guards. The regiment was holding important trenches at Cuinchy, a small village in the dull and dreary country dotted with brick-fields which lies south of the Bethune-

La Bassée Canal. On the last day of January the Germans attempted a surprise against the trenches neighbouring those of the Irish Guards. The position was lost, and had to be retaken, so that the line could be re established. There was much friendly rivalry between the Irish Guards and the Coldstreamers, who had lost the ground, but at length it was decided that the latter should lead the attack, while the Irish followed in support. The morning of 1 Feb., a day destined to be a red-letter day in the history of the British soldier, broke fine and clear, and simultaneously a storm of shot and shell descended on the German trenches which were marked down for recapture. For the wretched occupants there was no escape, for as soon as a head appeared above the level of the sheltering parapet it was greeted by a hail of fire from the rifles of our men. O'Leary, however, was using his head as well as his rifle. He marked down the spot where a German machine gun was to be found, and registered an inward resolve that that gun should be his private and peculiar concern when the moment for the rush came. After a short time the great guns ceased as suddenly as they had begun, and with a resounding cheer the Coldstreams sprang from the trenches and made for the enemy with their bayonets. The Germans, however, had not been completely annihilated by the bombardment, and the survivors gallantly manned their battered trenches and poured in a heavy fire on the advancing Coldstreams. Now was the turn of the Irish, and as quick as a flash they leapt up with a true Irish yell. Many a man bit the dust, but there was no holding back that mighty onslaught which swept towards the German lines. O'Leary, meanwhile, had not forgotten his machine gun. He knew that it would have been dismantled during the bombardment to save it from being destroyed, and it was a matter of life and death to perhaps hundreds of his comrades that he should reach it in time to prevent its being brought into action. He put on his best pace, and within a few seconds found himself in a corner of the German trench on the way to his goal. Immediately ahead of him was a barricade. Now a barricade is a formidable obstacle, but to O'Leary, with the lives of his company to save, it was no obstacle, and its five defenders quickly paid with their lives the penalty of standing between an Irishman and his heart's desire. Leaving his five victims, O'Leary started off to cover the eighty yards that still separated him from the second barricade, where the German machine gun was hidden. He was literally now racing with death. His comrades' lives were in his hand, and the thought spurred him on to super-human efforts. At every moment he expected to hear the sharp burr of the gun in the action. A patch of boggy ground prevented a direct approach to the barricade, and it was with veritable anguish that he realized the necessity of a detour by a railway line. Quick as thought he was off again. A few seconds passed, and then, the Germans working feverishly to remount their machine gun and bring it into action against the oncoming Irish, perceived the figure of Fate in the shape of Lance-Corpl. O'Leary, a few yards on their right with his rifle levelled at them. The officer in charge had no time to realize that his finger was on the button before death squared his account. Two other reports followed in quick succession, and two other figures fell to the ground with barely a sound. The two survivors had no mind to test O'Leary's shooting powers further, and threw up their hands. With his two captives before him, the gallant Irishman returned in triumph, while his comrades swept the enemy out of the trenches, and completed one of the most successful local actions we have ever undertaken. O'Leary was promoted Sergeant before the day was over. The story of his gallant deed was spread over the regiment, then over the brigade, then over the army. Then the official 'Eye-witness' joined in, and told the world, and finally came the little notice in the Gazette, the award of the Victoria Cross, and the homage of all who know a brave man when they see one." His decoration was gazetted [London Gazette, 18 Feb. 1915]: "Michael O'Leary, No. 3556, L.-Corpl., 1st Battn. Irish Guards. For conspicuous bravery at Cuinchy on 1 Feb. 1915. When forming one of the storming party which advanced against the enemy's barricades, he rushed to the front and himself killed five Germans who were holding the first barricade. After which he attacked a second barricade, although 60 yards further on, which he captured, after killing three of the enemy and making prisoners of two more. L.-Corpl. O'Leary thus practically captured the enemy's position by himself, and prevented the rest of the attacking party from being fired upon." He was mentioned in Despatches in 1914 and 1915, and promoted Second Lieutenant, Connaught Rangers. Lieut. O'Leary also received the Cross of St. George (Russia).

LEAKE, ARTHUR MARTIN, Lieut., is here awarded a Clasp to his V.C. [London Gazette, 18 Feb. 1915]: "War Office, 18 Feb. 1915. Clasp to Victoria Cross. Lieut. Arthur Martin Leake, Royal Army Medical Corps, who was awarded the Victoria Cross on 13 May, 1902, is granted a clasp for conspicuous bravery in the present campaign. For most conspicuous bravery and devotion to duty throughout the campaign, especially during the period 29 Oct. to 8 Nov. 1914, near Zonnebeke, in rescuing, whilst exposed to constant fire, a large number of the wounded who were lying close to the enemy's trenches."

London Gazette, 10 April, 1915.—"Admiralty, 10 April, 1915. The King has been graciously pleased to approve of the grant of the Victoria Cross to Commander Henry Peel Ritchie, Royal Navy, for the conspicuous act of bravery specified below."

RITCHIE, HENRY PEEL, Commander, Royal Navy, served in East Africa in 1914 and 1915, during the European War, was severely wounded, and for the operations at Dar-es-Salaam was awarded the Victoria Cross [London Gazette, 10 April, 1915]: "Henry Peel Ritchie, Commander, Royal Navy, of H.M.S. Goliath. Date of Act of Bravery: 29 Nov. 1914. For most conspicuous bravery on the 29th Nov. 1914, when in command of the searching and demolition operations at Dar-es-Salaam, East Africa. Though severely wounded several times, his fortitude and resolution enabled him to continue to do his duty, inspiring all by his example, until at his eighth wound he became unconscious. The interval between his first and last severe wound was between twenty and twenty-five minutes." "Deeds that thrill the Empire" (page 727) says: "It is significant of the broad range of British naval power that although 11 Victoria Crosses had been won by officers and men of the fleet in the first two years of the war, the only one earned within 2,000 miles of the British Isles was that of the unfortunate Flight Sub-Lieut. Warneford, for destroying a Zeppelin single-handed at Brussels. The very first naval V.C. of the war—the first, that is, in point of winning, though not in the date of award—was won in the tropical East African port of Dar-es-Salaam, where operations against the most prosperous of Germany's colonial possessions, exceeding in area the whole of the German Empire in Europe, were begun at an early stage in the conflict. The hero of this notable exploit, so typical of the breed of men who man our fighting ships, was Commander Henry Peel Ritchie, a gunnery officer of some distinction and second in command of the battleship Goliath—which vessel, it may be recalled, was torpedoed and sunk by a Turkish destroyer in the Dardanelles in May, 1915. During the closing months of 1914 the Goliath was employed on the East Coast of Africa as a support for the cruisers employed in rounding up the German commerce-raider Königsberg, and a detachment of her crew, under Lieut.-Commander Paterson, was actually present when that vessel was at last located and barricaded in the lower reaches of the Rufigi River. When this work had been accomplished, Commander Ritchie was detached from the Goliath and put in independent command of the armed auxiliary vessel Duplex, with instructions to proceed to Dar-es-Salaam and destroy any enemy vessels that might be found there. It was known, not only that the craft operating from this port had been used to keep the Königsberg supplied with fuel and provisions while she was at sea, but also that they might be employed for running supplies down the coast to her now that she was interned. The destruction of the Königsberg has already been fully detailed in this work, and it may be remembered that although she was successfully 'bottled up' in Nov. 1914, it was not till the following July that there arrived from England the special shallow-draught monitors required for dealing with her in her concealed position. Having arrived in the neighbourhood of the German port, Commander Ritchie at once set about the execution of his task. It was impossible for such a large vessel as the Duplex to go into the harbour and examine the many creeks that led into it, and the Commander therefore fitted out a small steam-boat with a Maxim gun, protected her sides as best he could with the material at his disposal, and on 28 Nov. made his way into the hostile haven and proceeded about his business, accompanied by two other tiny craft in support. It was a day worthy in every respect of the name of the place—which means 'Abode of Peace'—for not only was the weather perfect, but save for those three invading steamboats, there was not a sign of life to be seen. This was a reception for which Commander Ritchie and his men were altogether unprepared. They had expected to have to fight every inch of the way, and it is still a secret in possession of the enemy why they were allowed to steam uninterruptedly round the harbour, sinking or irreparably damaging every floating thing they came across. Nevertheless, that is what happened. Not a shot was fired while the work of destruction and demolition was in progress, although the pinnaces had to make their way into narrow creeks in which they might easily have been ambushed and enfiladed from either side. Commander Ritchie, however, was not for taking any chances. The absence of opposition struck him as altogether uncanny, and he scented a trap. Therefore, when he had thoroughly scoured the main creek running into the harbour and sunk nearly everything in it, he appropriated two steel lighters which he found there, and had them firmly lashed to the steamboat, one on either side. The real effect of this was to convert the boat into a miniature armed craft. Besides that, the barges lay deeper in the water than the steam-boat itself, and this, too, was a most useful circumstance. The character of the inner recesses of the harbour and of the creeks was by no means well known, and by lashing the boat between lighters of greater draught than itself it was assured that if the exploring party got into shallow water they would be the first to strike the bottom, leaving it possible for the steamboat to get safely away by cutting the lashings. Slowly and deliberately the strange and ungainly triptych made its way down the creek again and into the open harbour; and it was not until then that the troubles of the cutting-out expedition began. Why the defenders held themselves back so long we do not know, but at all events they began to make up for lost time as soon as Commander Ritchie's queer-looking craft passed out of the creek into the open. A heavy fire was opened from every point of the compass. From huts and houses, from wooded groves, from the hills surrounding the town, and even from the cemetery, came a hail of bullets and shells from rifles, machine guns and field pieces. Had it not been for Commander Ritchie's foresight in appropriating those two lighters for the protection of his little craft, it is certain that none of the party would have got back to the Duplex, and even as it was the defence proved hopelessly inadequate. The enemy's positions were cunningly concealed, and, even if they could have been located, the little Maxim would have been useless against them. Under the heavy fire many men were wounded more or less severely. Commander Ritchie himself was one of the first to be hit, though not badly enough to have to give over the direction of operations; and when, shortly after, first Petty Officer Clark and then Able Seaman Upton were so severely injured that they had to leave their

Henry Peel Ritchie.

places at the steering-wheel, the Commander himself took charge of it until his eighth wound knocked him out altogether. As the steamboat crossed the open waters of the harbour the enemy's fire redoubled in intensity. The single gun had long ago been disabled ; Commander Ritchie was wounded in half a dozen places ; Sub-Lieut. Loyd had been placed *hors de combat* by a bullet that missed his heart only by a quarter of an inch, and most of the petty officers and men were injured more or less severely by rifle and Maxim fire and flying splinters. Nevertheless, the strange little craft stood gallantly on, and it was not until she was nearing the mouth of the harbour that the Commander was compelled to give in, rendered unconscious through loss of blood, As he fell from his post at the wheel, Petty Officer Clark, whose wound had been roughly bandaged, stepped into it, and successfully piloted the steamboat out of the enemy's fire and into the safety of the open sea. For his ' most conspicuous bravery ' Commander Ritchie was worthily awarded the Victoria Cross. . . . He was . . . wounded in the forehead, in the left hand (near the thumb, which is shortened in consequence), in the left arm (twice), the right arm and the right hip, while the hits that finally bowled him over were two bullets through the right leg, which had been broken in two places five years before by an accident on service. He was six weeks in Zanzibar Hospital, and then, rapidly recovering his fitness, returned to service in May, 1915. Petty Officer Thomas James Clark received the Conspicuous Gallantry Medal for gallantly returning to the wheel after being wounded, and Able Seaman George Edward Upton, who was the first to relieve him after he was injured, was awarded the Distinguished Service Medal. The last-named, unfortunately, was lost when the Goliath was sunk. Many other brave deeds were done in the course of these operations, in which the small armed vessel Helmuth and a steam cutter from the cruiser Fox were also engaged. On one occasion the Fox's cutter came under fire from both sides, and a stoker was mortally wounded. In such a small craft the loss of a stoker means the loss of the only man appointed to keep the fires going, and if she had come to a standstill in her then precarious position there is little doubt that everyone on board would have been killed. In spite of the very heavy fire, therefore, Lieut. Eric Corson crept forward from the stern sheets, and, seizing the dying stoker's shovel, proceeded to tend the fires, and so brought the boat safely out of action. He was awarded the Distinguished Service Cross, and so also were Lieut. Herbert Walter Julian Orde (severely wounded on this occasion, and subsequently lost in the Goliath), and Sub-Lieut. Clement James Charlewood, of the Royal Naval Reserve, who extricated the Helmuth from a dangerous position. A second Conspicuous Gallantry Medal went to Leading Seaman Thomas Arthur Gallagher, coxswain of the Fox's steam cutter, who, in the words of the official report, ' when twice wounded, and under galling fire, remained at the tiller, and with the utmost coolness steered the boat through the danger zone.' "

London Gazette. 19 April, 1915.—" War Office, 19 April, 1915. His Majesty the King has been graciously pleased to approve of the grant of the Victoria Cross to the undermentioned Officer, Non-commissioned Officer and Men for their conspicuous acts of bravery and devotion to duty whilst serving with the Expeditionary Force."

BARBER, EDWARD, Private, was born at Tring, Herts, son of Mrs. William Barber. He was educated at the National Schools, Tring, and lived at home before he enlisted in the Grenadier Guards in Oct. 1911. Private Barber served in the European War, and was awarded the Victoria Cross [London Gazette, 19 April, 1915] : " Edward Barber, No. 15518, Private, 1st Battn. Grenadier Guards. Date of Act of Bravery : 12 March, 1915. For most conspicuous bravery on the 12th March, 1915, at Neuve Chapelle. He ran speedily in front of the grenade company to which he belonged and threw bombs on the enemy with such effect that a very great number of them at once surrendered. When the grenade party reached Private Barber they found him quite alone and unsupported, with the enemy surrendering all about him." The regiment was " incomparable in the final position in front of Ypres. After the battle and victory Sir Douglas Haig, in an order, said that the troops had been assailed by the Prussian Guard, 2nd, 23rd, 26th, 27th, and 15th Corps, each of which was beaten and Calais saved. ' No general could ask for finer troops.' At Neuve Chapelle the battalions rushed grandly, lost heavily, and both commanders, Lieut.-Colonels Fisher-Rowe and W. R. A. Smith, died of their wounds. Private Barber and L.-Corpl. Fuller won the V.C. At Loos the Guards' Division restored the line and made a brilliant attack on Hill 70, driving the Germans off the crest. The Germans could do nothing with the Guards at the Hohenzollern Redoubt." Private Barber was killed in action 19 March, 1915.

FULLER, WILFRED DOLBY, L.-Corpl, joined the Grenadier Guards, and was promoted to Lance-Corporal. He served in the European War. L.-Corpl. Fuller was awarded the Victoria Cross [London Gazette, 19 April, 1915] : " Wilfred Dolby Fuller, No. 15624, L.-Corpl., 1st Battn. Grenadier Guards. Date of Act of Bravery : 12 March, 1915. For most conspicuous bravery at Neuve Chapelle on the 12th March, 1915. Seeing a party of the enemy endeavouring to escape along a communication trench, he ran towards them and killed the leading man with a bomb ; the remainder (nearly 50), finding no means of evading his bombs, surrendered to him. L.-Corpl. Fuller was quite alone at the time."

MARTIN, CYRIL GORDON, Lieut., was born at Foochow, China, on 19 Dec. 1891, son of the Rev. John Martin, Vicar of Grandborough, near Rugby, late C.M.S. Missionary in China, and of Mrs. Martin, daughter of Judge Goldie, Indian Civil Service. He was educated at Hamilton House, Bath ; at Bath College and Clifton College, and joined the Army on 23 Dec. 1911, becoming Lieutenant 15 July, 1914, and serving

Cyril Gordon Martin.

in the European War. He was created a Companion of the Distinguished Service Order [London Gazette, 9 Nov. 1914] : " Cyril Gordon Martin, Lieut., 56th Coy. Royal Engineers. At Le Cateau on the 26th of Aug. he held with his section a post from which infantry had been driven, and remained there under a very heavy fire until the infantry relieved him." His was one of the first decorations to be gazetted during the war. " Deeds that thrill the Empire " (page 98) says : " At 7.30 on the morning of 10 March, 1915, the Battle of Neuve Chapelle began with perhaps the most terrific artillery preparation in the history of modern warfare, and by the evening of that day the village was ours, and on a front of three miles we had advanced more than a mile. But our ultimate objective—the driving of a great wedge into the enemy's line by the capture of the ridge south of Aubers —still remained to be accomplished ; and it was to this task, which was to prove, unfortunately, beyond the capacity of our troops, that the two following days were devoted. Simultaneously a number of movements were undertaken all along the British front, with the object of preventing any sudden massing of reinforcements, and it was during one of these attacks—that upon the German position at Spanbroek Molen—that a young officer of the 56th Field Coy. Royal Engineers, Lieut. Cyril Gordon Martin, performed the gallant action that gained him the Victoria Cross. Lieut. Martin had already won the Distinguished Service Order by his gallantry in the first weeks of the war, during the Retreat from Mons, when, at the head of his platoon, he had captured a German trench and held it until reinforcements arrived. On this occasion he was twice wounded, and invalided home for some months ; indeed, he had only recently returned to the front. Early in the action at Spanbroek Molen, Lieut. Martin was again wounded ; but he made light of his hurt, and volunteered to lead a little party of six bombers against a section of the enemy's trenches. So effectively did they discharge their deadly missiles that the Germans were quickly driven out in rout and confusion, when the Lieutenant and his men proceeded to transfer the parapet of the trench and to strengthen their position with sandbags, in readiness for the inevitable counter-attack. This was not long in coming, but, inspired by the splendid example of their leader, the little band of heroes drove their assailants back, and though the attack was again and again renewed in apparently overwhelming numbers, they succeeded in holding the enemy at bay for two and a half hours, when orders arrived for them to abandon the captured post and retire. By their gallant defence they had rendered most valuable service by holding up German reinforcements, who were unable to advance until this section of their trenches had been retaken." Lieut. Martin was twice mentioned in Despatches for his services during the Great War. He was promoted to Captain, and was later attached to the Egyptian Army Public Works Department. On 20 Aug. 1917, at Chatham Parish Church, he married Mabel, only daughter of the late Major Edward Hingston, R.E., and Mrs. Hingston.

MAY, HENRY, Private, was born 29 July, 1885, in Glasgow, son of William Henry May and Mrs. W. H. May. He was educated at Dalmarnock Public School, Glasgow, and joined the Army on 29 Aug. 1902. He served in the European War, and was awarded the Victoria Cross [London Gazette, 19 April, 1915] : " Henry May, No. 7504, Private, 1st Battn. Cameronians (Scottish Rifles). Date of Act of Bravery : 22 Oct. 1914. For most conspicuous bravery, near La Boutillerie, on the 22nd Oct. 1914, in voluntarily endeavouring to rescue, under very heavy fire, a wounded man, who was killed before he could save him ; and subsequently, on the same day, in carrying a wounded officer a distance of 300 yards into safety whilst exposed to very severe fire." Private May writes : " The following are the particulars as well as I can remember them : At daybreak of 22 Oct. 1914, my platoon, under command of Lieut. D. A. H. Graham, were sent out in advance at La Boutillerie, to hold the enemy in check whilst the main body entrenched themselves. We advanced about 700 or 800 yards, and took up positions in a ditch. Shortly afterwards the enemy engaged us ; they were many times our number. We managed to stop them until the main body had finished the trench-digging, and then we commenced to retire. As soon as we left the ditch one of my comrades was wounded away on the extreme right, about 100 yards away. As soon as I saw him drop, I ran across the firing line, through a hail of lead, followed by two of my chums, namely, L.-Corpl. James McCall and Private James Bell. When I got to the wounded man I pulled off his equipment and pulled him to his feet. L.-Corpl. J. McCall took one arm and I the other, with the intention of carrying him back to safety ; but the Huns had no respect for the wounded, but continued to fire, with the result that the wounded man was killed in my arms, and L.-Corpl. McCall was also knocked unconscious. I then flattened myself on the ground, determined to fire my last cartridge, when I saw Lieut. Graham go down with a bullet in the leg. I then jumped up and called to Private Bell to follow, and between the two of us we managed to carry the lieutenant

Henry May.

about 300 yards, when Bell got two bullet-wounds in hand and foot. I managed to drag the lieutenant still nearer safety, when a corporal came to my aid, and I lifted Lieut. Graham on his shoulders ; but no luck, the corporal was shot dead with the lieutenant on his shoulders. I then clenched my teeth and made a supreme effort, and I dragged Lieut. Graham into safety. I was wounded on 2 Nov. 1914 ; discharged 28 Aug. 1915."

TOLLERTON, ROSS, Private, served in the European War, and was awarded the Victoria Cross [London Gazette, 19 April, 1915]: " Ross Tollerton, No. 7281, Private, 1st Battn. Cameron Highlanders. Date of

Ross Tollerton.

Act of Bravery : 14 Sept. 1914. For most conspicuous bravery and devotion to duty on the 14th Sept. 1914, at the Battle of the Aisne. He carried a wounded officer under heavy fire, as far as he was able, into a place of greater safety ; then, although himself wounded in the head and hand, he struggled back to the firing line, where he remained until his battalion retired, when he returned to the wounded officer, and lay beside him for three days until they were both rescued." " Deeds that thrill the Empire " (page 80) says : " On Sunday, 13 Sept. 1914, the British, in the face of the fiercest and most determined opposition from the enemy, forced the passage of the Aisne, and before nightfall the bulk of our three army corps had crossed the river and entrenched themselves well up on the farther slopes. Early on the following morning a general advance was begun along the whole western section of the Allied front, the most important offensive movement being that entrusted to our 1st Corps, under Sir Douglas Haig, which lay between Chavonne and Moulins. Its objective was an important highway called the Chemin des Dames, or Ladies' Road, four miles to the northward, the possession of which would enable us to command the country between Soissons and Berry-au-Bac. At 4 a.m. the 1st Battn. Cameron Highlanders, who, with the 1st Coldstreams, 1st Scots Guards and 2nd Black Watch, composed the 1st Brigade, had their breakfasts served out to them ; and at dawn—the dawn of a wet misty morning—the historic red tartans began moving up the Vendresse valley. Among the Camerons was a young Ayrshire man, Private Ross Tollerton, to whom the impending action was to bring the crown of a soldier's ambition. Passing through the valley, the Camerons mounted the steep ascent to the north, and immediately deployed for action, the company to which Tollerton belonged being in reserve. Presently, however, it advanced and joined up with another company under Major Maitland, close to the famous three haystacks, south of the village of Troyon. Here the mist lifted somewhat, and they began marching in a north-westerly direction to the support of the 2nd Brigade, which was already heavily engaged, the 1st Scots Guards reinforcing their right. As they advanced they came under a very heavy shell and machine-gun fire, and Capt. Matheson fell severely wounded. Tollerton raised the wounded officer, and lifting him on his back, carried him into an adjoining corn-field, where he laid him down under cover of a small corn-stack, and then returned to the firing line. Scarcely had he rejoined his comrades than he was hit in both the right hand and the right temple. Nevertheless, when presently the Camerons received orders to retire, the brave fellow, without a thought for himself, made his way back to the wounded officer, and lay down beside him, to await a favourable opportunity to carry him back to our lines. He dared not raise his head, for they were surrounded by the enemy, and their snipers would very quickly have picked him off ; but he did all he could for his helpless comrade. Night came on, and he soon recognized that, even under cover of the darkness, it would be impossible to make his way with the wounded man through the German lines undetected, and they were therefore obliged to remain where they were. It was a miserable night, cold and wet, and they had nothing to eat ; but, by good fortune, Tollerton's water-bottle was nearly full, so they did not suffer from thirst. Towards dawn Tollerton saw a strong force of Germans forming up directly in front of where they lay, with the evident intention of making a counter-attack upon the British, and he was in dread lest they should deploy through the corn-field, in which event he and Capt. Matheson would most certainly be discovered But, to his great relief, they took the road down the valley. The enemy bombarded our lines nearly all day, and delivered a succession of desperate counter-attacks against our right, all of which were repulsed. However, the fact that the British were obliged to remain on the defensive and did not attempt any further advance, deprived the two Camerons in the corn-field of all chance of getting away for the present. The day had been fine and less cold than the preceding one ; but towards evening rain came on and continued intermittently until about nine o'clock on the 16th, with the result that they were soaked to the skin and passed a wretched night. By this time Tollerton was so weak from loss of blood, exposure and hunger—he had eaten nothing since his early breakfast on the 14th—that even if the road to safety had been open he would have had difficulty in reaching the British lines himself ; while to have carried the wounded officer so far would have been beyond his strength. Happily, towards the afternoon the Germans in that quarter retired, and between four and five o'clock he caught sight of a party of our men digging a trench some distance off. Although so weak that he could hardly keep his feet, he managed to make his way to them, and the officer in charge had a stretcher fetched for Capt. Matheson, and sent Tollerton to the nearest dressing-station." Private Ross Tollerton, as recorded above, received the Victoria Cross for his splendid gallantry and devotion. He was at the time twenty-six years of age, and his home is at Irvine, Ayrshire. Capt.

Matheson, whose life he saved, obtained his commission in the Camerons in 1900, and served with distinction in the South African War, for which he received the Queen's Medal and five clasps.

London Gazette, 23 April, 1915.—" His Majesty the King has been graciously pleased to approve of the award of the Victoria Cross to the undermentioned Officer, Non-commissioned Officer and Men for their conspicuous acts of bravery and devotion to duty whilst serving with the Expeditionary Force."

DANIELS, HARRY, Company Sergt.-Major, was born at Wymondham, Norfolk, 13 Dec. 1885, son of William Daniels (Baker and Confectioner, of Wymondham and Norwich) and Elizabeth Daniels. He was educated

Harry Daniels.

in Norwich, and joined the Army on 31 Jan. 1903, serving in various stations in India from 1905 till the outbreak of war. He won several boxing tournaments and contests while in India, and his chief pastimes are gymnastics, boxing and all outdoor sports. He was promoted to Corporal on 19 July, 1909 ; to Sergeant 21 Dec. 1910 ; to C.Q.M.-Sergeant 10 Oct. 1914 ; to Company Sergt.-Major 12 Dec. 1914. He married, in Calcutta, India, on 21 Jan. 1914, Kathleen Mary Perry, daughter of a warrant officer in the Manchester Regt. He was awarded the Victoria Cross [London Gazette, 28 April, 1915]: " Harry Daniels, No. 9665, Company Sergt.-Major, 2nd Battn. Rifle Brigade (The Prince Consort's Own). For most conspicuous gallantry on 12 March, 1915, at Neuve Chapelle. When their battalion was impeded in the advance to the attack by the wire entanglements and subjected to a very severe machine-gun and rifle fire, voluntarily rushed in front and succeeded in cutting the wire, being wounded then." He was granted a commission as Second Lieutenant 21 July, 1915, and became Lieutenant 23 Aug. 1916, and was awarded the Military Cross for services on 2 March, 1916, at Fromelles : " Harry Daniels, Lieut., Temporary Capt., Rifle Brigade. When a man of his patrol was wounded on the edge of the enemy's wire, he carried him in some 300 yards under very heavy fire. On another occasion, when two successive patrols had failed to find a wounded corporal, Second Lieut. Daniels volunteered to take out a third patrol, and brought in the corporal's body."

NOBLE, CECIL REGINALD, Corpl., was born at Bournemouth, son of the late Frederick Noble, Decorator. He was educated at St. Clement's Schools. He joined the Army about the early part of the year 1910.

Cecil Reginald Noble.

" Deeds that thrill the Empire " (pages 19-23) says : " There has been no more cruel spectacle in the present war than that of dauntless courage baffled and rendered impotent by mechanical contrivances ; of brave men advancing to the assault of the enemy's position in full confidence of victory, suddenly held up by barbed-wire entanglements which they had fondly imagined would have been completely swept away by their own artillery preparations, and, while thus checked, exposed to murderous fire from their entrenched foes. For, however heavy and long-continued the bombardment preceding an attack may have been, there will always be places here and there where high-explosive shells have failed to do their work, and where the wire entanglements still hold firm ; and cruel is the fate of the regiment which finds itself obliged to cut a way through such an obstacle while rifle and machine gun plays upon it at close range. If it escapes practical annihilation, it will be more than fortunate. From such a fate was the 2nd Battn. of the Rifle Brigade saved, on 12 March, 1915, at the Battle of Neuve Chapelle, by the heroism and devotion of two of its non-commissioned officers. When the ' green-jackets ' approached that section of the second-line German trenches which they had been ordered to take, they saw to their consternation that the wire entanglements protecting them were still practically intact, and that to force them would entail the most appalling loss. It was at this most critical moment that Acting Corpl. Noble and Company Sergt.-Major Daniels resolved to sacrifice themselves for their comrades. While the others threw themselves on the ground to take what cover they might from the withering fire beneath which they were falling fast, the two heroes ran towards the entanglements and began to cut away at them like men possessed. Well they knew that they were courting certain death ; that already a hundred rifles and half a score of machine guns were trained upon them. But they recked not that ; one thought alone possessed their minds—to make a way for their comrades before they were shot down. And they succeeded ; for though both speedily fell dangerously wounded, it was not before great lengths of the barbed wire had been cut through and the path to victory stood open. With resounding cheers the Riflemen rushed through the breach in the entanglements like a living tide ; the bayonet soon did its deadly work, and the trenches were won. Both of these gallant men were awarded the V.C. ' for most conspicuous bravery,' but it is sad to relate that Corpl. Noble never lived to receive the coveted distinction which he had so richly merited, as he died of his wounds shortly after the action. His decoration was gazetted with that of Company Sergt.-Major Daniels [London Gazette, 28 April, 1915]: "Harry Daniels, No. 9665, Company Sergt.-Major, 2nd Battn. Rifle Brigade; Cecil Reginald Noble, No. 3697, Acting Corpl. (late) 2nd Battn. Rifle Brigade. For most conspicuous bravery on the 12th March, 1915, at Neuve Chapelle. When their battalion was impeded in the advance to the attack by wire entanglements, and subjected to a very severe machine-gun fire, these two men voluntarily rushed in front and succeeded in cutting the wires. They were both wounded at once, and Corpl. Noble has since died." His Victoria Cross was presented to his mother by the King at Buckingham Palace.

BUCKINGHAM, WILLIAM, Private, was born in 1886, son of Leicester parents. When six years of age he entered the Countesthorpe Cottage Homes, as did also a brother, who later joined the Royal Navy. After William Buckingham won the Victoria Cross it came out that he had a mother living. But the Cottage Homes were his real home, where he was brought up. Mrs. Harrison, wife of the superintendent, said he was one of the nicest lads they had ever had. She would not say he was an angel, for he had a strong will of his own, and strong-willed persons occasionally came in contact with authority, but they had very pleasant memories of him. He left the homes in Nov. 1901, and with several other boys was keen on entering the Army. He joined the 2nd Battn. of the Leicestershire Regt., and was in many parts of the world with that battalion. He came with the first batch which came from India in Oct. 1914, and served in France. When on leave he always proudly returned to the Cottage Homes, and when leaving for the front in Feb. 1915, he said to Mr. Harrison: "Well, good-bye, sir; I'll win the V.C. or get killed." He was wounded at the Battle of Neuve Chapelle, and would probably have been killed, but for a packet of field postcards which he had in his pocket. He had been at the Cottage Homes for about three weeks recovering from his wound when he heard that he had won the Victoria Cross. When the news came a journalist wrote: "It was easy to find the place where the proudest people in Leicestershire lived this morning. The parish was Countesthorpe, and the particular place the Cottage Homes where Private Buckingham lived from his sixth to his fifteenth year, and where he is now spending the few remaining days of his furlough. He is rather a big 'boy' now, and it is pathetic to think that he has no other home in the world. The only other relative he knows of is his brother, who is in the Navy, and whom he has not seen for some years. There have been people in the past, and there are, it is to be feared, a few now who think that such places as the Cottage Homes are too luxurious for the children of the poor. The fact that one of these children has grown up to win the greatest reward for bravery that the Empire can give may give these good people cause to reconsider their opinions. When I went over this morning the excitement had simmered down a little. There was, however, a sense of bubbling-over enthusiasm in the air, which made it irksome to carry on the daily routine. Down in the village there was an air of pride that the first V.C. for Leicestershire should come to the neighbourhood; but in the little colony of houses which form the Cottage Homes everybody who had any recollection of Private Buckingham when he was a boy was most enthusiastic, and the others who had only known him recently were but little behind. It came as a great surprise to the colony. The news was conveyed in the morning newspapers. The foster-father, in the cottage nearest the entrance gate, saw the name, and ran down to where the V.C. was staying to learn if the number given corresponded with his, and then the news spread rapidly. The recipient was almost as much surprised as anyone; having been on furlough, he had not been officially notified of the recommendation, as he would have been if he had remained in the trenches." He received letters of congratulation from several officers, among them one from his Commanding Officer, Lieut.-Colonel H. Gordon. His decoration was gazetted 28 April, 1915: "William Buckingham, No. 6276, Private, 2nd Battn. The Leicestershire Regt. For conspicuous acts of bravery and devotion to duty in rescuing and rendering aid to the wounded whilst exposed to heavy fire, especially at Neuve Chapelle, on the 10th and 12th March." Buckingham was a very modest soldier, and he could not be got to say much about his experiences. By the promptings of Mr. Harrison he was led to repeat the story of the wounded German at Neuve Chapelle. "During the battle," he said, "I came upon a badly wounded German soldier. One of his legs had been blown off. He was lying right in the fire zone. His piteous appeal for help—well, I rendered first-aid as well as I could, and just carried him to a place of safety. Of course, I did what I could for others too, but really it's not worth talking about." Before Buckingham left Countesthorpe he went to a garden-party given to wounded soldiers by Mrs. Abel Smith, of Coleorton Hall. There he met a wounded corporal, who told the other guests that he was one of the men whom Buckingham had carried out of the firing line under a heavy fire, when wounded, and thus saved his life. Buckingham went up to town to receive his Victoria Cross from the King, and a picture in a scrap-book belonging to Mrs. Harrison shows the V.C. showing his decoration afterwards to Mr. and Mrs. Harrison, who had accompanied him to London. Another charming picture shows Buckingham walking through the village with the hero-worshipping little boys from the Cottage Homes holding on to his hands and his tunic, and getting as close to him as they could. Another photograph is of Buckingham with his fellow-convalescent whom he had rescued, Corpl. Tarry. Buckingham was, says a newspaper cutting, "Leicester's own V.C. He was, indeed, in more than the normal sense, a possession of the town, for the town had the signal honour of bringing him up and educating him." He had various presentations made to him, and among others was a purse of gold and a certificate showing that £100 had been invested for him, from his fellow towns-people. On that occasion the hero, soldier-fashion, returned thanks by smartly saluting. He afterwards wrote saying: "As a soldier not used to speaking in public, I regret I could not publicly return thanks at Countesthorpe for the handsome gift you were good enough to make me on behalf of the citizens of Leicester; but I can assure you that I value it most highly, and if I am spared to return to my native town after the war, I shall come back to it with feelings of warm affection." Among other things, he went on to say in this letter: "What I owe to Mr. and Mrs. Harrison, the superintendent and matron, I cannot properly express. Had they been my own parents, they could not have looked after my upbringing with greater care and more affectionate interest, and it was like going home to go there for my leave, and after recovering from my wounds." Private Buckingham was kept at home in Leicester for some time after he recovered from his wounds to help with recruiting. Afterwards he went to a training camp and got promoted, but gave up his stripes in order that he might go again to the front. There he acted as orderly to Capt. F. W. Mosse, who wrote to the Leicester Board of Guardians to announce Private Buckingham's death in action on the 15th Sept. 1916. Capt. Mosse added that it would be "impossible to replace him." In "An Appreciation" of him a friend said: "The thing which struck one most about the Leicester V.C., whose death in action we all mourn, was that the attention and honours lavished upon him left him entirely unspoilt. He remained what in obscurity he had always been—just a quiet, simple-minded soul, to whom the word 'duty' meant a great deal more than obeying military orders, or doing something bravely venturesome on the battle-field. Splendid soldier as he was, he had a great regard for human life and deep sympathy with suffering."

William Buckingham.

RIVERS, JACOB, Private, served in the European War, and was awarded the Victoria Cross [London Gazette, 28 April, 1915]: "Jacob Rivers, No. 6016, Private, late 1st Battn. Nottinghamshire and Derbyshire Regt. Date of Act of Bravery: 12 March, 1915. For most conspicuous bravery at Neuve Chapelle, on the 12th March, 1915, when he, on his own initiative, crept to within a few yards of a very large number of the enemy who were massed on the flank of an advanced company of his battalion, and hurled bombs on them. His action caused the enemy to retire, and so relieved the situation. Private Rivers performed a second act of great bravery on the same day, similar to the first-mentioned, again causing the enemy to retire. He was killed on this occasion." "Deeds that thrill the Empire" (page 242) says: "It is pathetic to reflect how many honours in the present war have been conferred posthumously, the brave fellows whose heroic deeds had so richly earned them having either been killed in the very action in which they were performed, or almost immediately afterwards. Private Rivers, who was thirty-four years of age and unmarried, was a native of Derby. He had already done twelve years' service in the Army, having been seven years in India with the Royal Scots Fusiliers, and afterwards five years with the Army Reserve. At the time when war broke out, however, he was free, and was in the employ of the Midland Railway Company at Derby, working as a labourer on a ballast train. But the old fighting spirit was there, and when his country needed his services he was not the man to stay at home. He was, indeed, one of the first to volunteer, and was accepted by the 1st Battn. Sherwood Foresters. Being an experienced soldier, he was ready for service at once, and went to France with one of the earliest drafts. The letters he wrote home appear to have been few and confined to news of a purely personal character. Certainly he made no attempt to describe his experiences, and the greatest of all he never lived to tell. This occurred on 12 March, 1915, at the Battle of Neuve Chapelle. Observing a large number of Germans massed on the flank of an advanced company of his battalion, Private Rivers, on his own initiative, crept up to within a few yards of the enemy and hurled bomb after bomb among them, throwing them into utter confusion and forcing them to retire. This most gallant action he repeated later on the same day, again causing the enemy to retire, but, unhappily, not before a bullet had cut short the career of one of Britain's bravest sons. 'The only personal effects belonging to the late Private Rivers which have been sent home to his mother,' says a writer in the 'Derby Daily Telegraph,' 'are the metal box containing Princess Mary's Christmas gift to the soldiers and a postcard which he had recently received. The box has a tragic interest, for it has been pierced by a bullet. It is the habit of soldiers to carry this box in their breast pocket, less as a shield against a possible bullet than as a convenient means of carrying their tobacco, and the fact that there is a hole right through it clearly indicates that Private Rivers was shot through the heart.'"

Jacob Rivers.

NEGI, GOBAR SING, Rifleman, served in the European War, and was awarded the Victoria Cross [London Gazette, 28 April, 1915]: "Gobar Sing Negi, No. 1685, Rifleman, 2nd Battn. 39th Garhwal Rifles. Date of Act of Bravery: 10 March, 1915. For most conspicuous bravery on the 10th March, 1915, at Neuve Chapelle. During our attack on the German position he was one of a bayonet party with bombs who entered their main trench, and was the first man to go round each traverse, driving back the enemy until they were eventually forced to surrender. He was killed during this engagement." In describing the attack on the German trenches west of Neuve Chapelle the authors of "With the Indian Corps in France" say: "The moment the guns lifted, the brigade swarmed over the parapet, and moving at a steady double over the intervening space of from one hundred to two hundred yards, reached (except as regards one battalion) their first objective without a check. The effect of the accurate and intense fire of our artillery was at once evident. The German wire had in nearly every place simply ceased to exist, while the trenches were practically blotted out, burying in their ruins numbers of the defenders. Such of the enemy as were still unhurt were either in a state of stupefaction or half delirious, while everywhere lay the mangled bodies of the dead and wounded. The 2/39th Garhwalis met with some rifle and machine-gun fire from trenches further in rear, but pressed on through the first trench and took the second with a rush, capturing a machine gun and some prisoners." After further describing the assault and the gallant conduct of the Indians, the authors go on to say: "During the assault on the main trench, Rifleman Gobar Sing Negi behaved with very distinguished courage. He was one of the bayonet party accompanying the bombers, and was the first man to go round each traverse in face of a most determined resistance by the enemy, of whom he killed several, driving the rest back until they surrendered. This brave soldier was afterwards unfortunately killed, but for his most conspicuous gallantry he was posthumously awarded the Victoria Cross."

London Gazette, 21 May, 1915.—"Admiralty, 21 May, 1915. The King has been graciously pleased to approve of the grant of the Victoria Cross to Lieut.-Commander Edward Courtenay Boyle, Royal Navy, for the conspicuous act of bravery specified below."

BOYLE, EDWARD COURTENAY, Commander, Royal Navy, served in the European War. "One of the earliest of the 'E' boats to win distinction was the E 14, a vessel completed by Messrs. Vickers soon after the outbreak of war, and despatched at once to the Eastern Mediterranean under the orders of Lieut.-Commander Edward Courtenay Boyle. This officer had already been mentioned in Despatches for his observation work off the German coast in the opening days of the war, his command then being Submarine D 3; but he was to do far greater things with E 14. On 27 April, 1915, he left the main body of the Fleet and made for the Dardanelles. In the four months that had elapsed since the B 11 had achieved such a brilliant coup, the Turks had greatly improved the anti-submarine defences of the narrow channel. The submerged mine-fields had been increased in number and efficiency; in certain parts of the Straits old hulks had been sunk in order to impede the progress of our submarines, while guns had been mounted in favourable positions ashore for covering any vessel that happened by this means to be compelled to rise to the surface. The enemy had also organized a system of patrols, a number of such vessels being apportioned to each two or three units of the channel to guard it against the passage of submarines. Appropriately enough, it was one of these very ships that E 14 secured as her first victim. The Dardanelles are so very narrow and the current that sweeps through them from the Sea of Marmora to the Mediterranean so strong, that a submarine is bound to rise at more or less frequent intervals in order to verify her course and avoid running into the banks either side. Lieut.-Commander Boyle had set out with the intention of first getting into the Sea of Marmora, and then settling down to work when he got there, but, coming up on one occasion to take his bearings, he saw, by the use of the periscope, the reflected image of a Turkish gunboat not many hundreds of yards distant. Now a periscope was the very thing that the gunboat had been set to look out for, and the Turks who failed to see it had no one but themselves to blame for what followed. Lieut.-Commander Boyle, intently studying the surrounding area of water reflected on the screen below, gently edged his vessel round until she was aiming straight at the hapless Turkish gunboat. A couple of brisk orders and three hundred pounds of guncotton was tearing towards the enemy at the rate of thirty-five miles an hour, eight or nine feet beneath the surface of the water. In a few seconds the submarine rocked to a terrific explosion as the torpedo reached its target. Those of the British vessel's crew who could be spared from their stations hurried along for a periscope-glance at the sinking gunboat; and then, remaining only long enough to assure himself of the enemy's fate, Lieut.-Commander Boyle dived his vessel and waited at a safe depth until the hubbub on the surface had subsided. Then he proceeded on his journey, leaving the Turkish Navy poorer by a vessel—either the Berk-i-Satvet or a sister ship—of 740 tons, built in Germany in 1907, and carrying a crew of 120 men. This was an excellent beginning, but more important successes were yet to be achieved. Entering the Sea of Marmora, Lieut.-Commander Boyle was compelled to use the utmost caution, for the news of his coming had preceded him, and the anti-submarine patrol, maintained by destroyers, sometimes compelled the E 14 to remain totally submerged for twelve hours at a stretch. On 29 April she 'bagged' her second victim—this time a Turkish transport, though whether she had troops on board at the time, or was returning more or less empty after carrying them across to the Asiatic side is not known. Four days later she repeated her success of 27 April, stalking and sinking one of the vessels specially deputed to get rid of her. The Turkish fleet comprised such a miscellaneous collection of ships of all ages and sizes that this was one of the many that our officers were unable to identify, and in the case of a submarine it is, of course, quite impossible for the attacking vessel to stand by and pick up survivors and learn the vessel's name that way. After this, the hunt became so hot that the E 14 had to make herself scarce, though she was still able to cruise about in the less frequented parts of the sea and pick up a good deal of useful information. For a week no favourable opportunity for using her torpedoes presented itself, but on 10 May came the greatest success of all. What the Admiralty described as "a very large transport, full of troops," was sighted not very long after she had left Constantinople. The sinking of transports laden with more or less helpless soldiers is not one of the nicest refinements of twentieth-century warfare, but it stands in principle on the same basis as the mining of an enemy trench, and its legitimacy is, of course, fully recognized by those who most deplore it. Consequently, when Lieut.-Commander Boyle found this transport, without convoy, carrying soldiers into the fighting line against British, French and Russian troops, he had no doubts whatever as to his duty. He took up his position at right angles to the course of the transport and waited, and when the right moment came, the torpedo was released. As there were no other hostile ships in sight, E 14 came to the surface. The transport was already settling down when our men emerged from the hatch of the conning tower on to the deck, and doubtless a large number of men had been killed by the torpedo's explosion. Others, however, had succeeded in launching boats and rafts, and these, of course, were not interfered with, though German submarines in similar circumstances had not hesitated to fire on innocent civilians. The submarine remained for some time on the surface, and when the approach of hostile torpedo craft warned her that it was time to submerge the transport had already disappeared. How many men went down with her only the Turks know. The E 14 remained in the Sea of Marmora another eight days after this, and on 13 May, while cruising on the surface, forced a small enemy steamer—probably carrying munitions of war—to run ashore, in order to avoid being torpedoed. On 18 May the submarine slipped back again into the Dardanelles, and within a few hours was past all dangers and back in the open Mediterranean. As a mere record of work done, her performance was a great one; but we shall fail to realize it to the full unless we remember that for three weeks she had been operating single-handed in an area only seventy-five miles long and fifty miles across at its widest part; its waters constantly scouted by hostile warships in search of submarines and every inch of its shores in the possession of the enemy. Within a few days after the E 14's return it was announced that the King had been pleased to award the Victoria Cross to her Commanding Officer, that the Distinguished Service Cross was awarded to Lieut. E. G. Stanley, and to Acting Lieut. R. W. Lawrence, of the Royal Naval Reserve, and that each member of the crew had been granted the Distinguished Service Medal. The official statement issued by the Admiralty recorded the report of Vice-Admiral de Robeck, Commander-in-Chief in the Eastern Mediterranean, that it was 'impossible to do full justice to this great achievement, and that His Majesty the King's appreciation and reward for these services have throughout the Allied Fleets given universal satisfaction.'" ("Deeds that thrill the Empire," pages 49 to 54.) His Victoria Cross was gazetted 21 May, 1915: "Edward Courtenay Boyle, Lieut.-Commander, Royal Navy. For most conspicuous bravery in command of Submarine E 14, when he dived his vessel under the enemy mine-fields and entered the Sea of Marmora on 27th April, 1915. In spite of great navigational difficulties from strong currents, of the continual neighbourhood of hostile patrols and of hourly danger of attack from the enemy, he continued to operate in narrow waters of the Straits, and succeeded in sinking two Turkish gunboats and one large military transport." Commander Boyle was given the decoration of Chevalier of the Legion of Honour.

Edward Courtenay Boyle.

London Gazette, 22 May, 1915.—"The King has been graciously pleased to approve of the grant of the Victoria Cross to the undermentioned Officers, Non-commissioned Officer and Men for their conspicuous acts of bravery and devotion whilst serving with the Expeditionary Force."

ANDERSON, WILLIAM, Corpl., was born in Nov. 1884, at Dallas, Elgin. His parents are both dead. He joined the 2nd Battn. Yorkshire Regt., and attained the rank of Corporal. He is assumed to have died on or since 13 March, 1915, the day after he won the Victoria Cross [London Gazette, 22 May, 1915]: "Anderson, William, No. 8191, Corpl., 2nd Battn. Yorkshire Regt. Date of Act of Bravery: 12 March, 1915. For most conspicuous bravery at Neuve Chapelle on the 12th March, 1915, when he led three men with bombs against a large party of the enemy who had entered our trenches, and by his prompt and determined action saved what might otherwise have become a serious situation. Corpl. Anderson first threw his own bombs, then those in possession of his three men (who had been wounded) amongst the Germans, after which he opened rapid rifle fire upon them with great effect, notwithstanding that he was at the time quite alone."

Edward Dwyer.

DWYER, EDWARD, Private, was a greengrocer's assistant of 16 when he joined the Army, putting on his age a couple of years to ensure acceptance. He went to the front with the Expeditionary Force, fought in the Mons Retreat and won the Victoria Cross, as is described in "Deeds that thrill the Empire" (pages 133–140): "About three miles south-east of Ypres and just east of the hamlet of Zwartleben, where our dismounted Household Cavalry

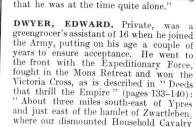

made their decisive charge on the night of 6 Nov. 1914, lies an earth heap from the cutting of the Ypres–Lille railway, some 250 yards long by 200 yards deep, which is known to fame by the name of Hill 60. Desperate, indeed, was the fighting of which Hill 60 was the scene towards the end of April, 1915. Its importance to the British consisted in the fact that it afforded an artillery position from which the whole German front from the neighbourhood of the Hollebeke Château could be commanded, and we were determined to get possession of it. Accordingly, about seven o'clock in the evening of 17 April, we exploded seven mines on the Hill, which played havoc with the defences, blowing up a trench line and 150 of the enemy with it, and enabled our men to win the top of the hill, where they entrenched themselves in the shell-craters and brought up machine guns. Next day the enemy delivered a series of the most determined counter-attacks, which resulted in desperate fighting at close quarters. But they were all repulsed, and by the evening the Germans had been driven from the slopes of the hill, and the glacis was littered with their dead. However, the position was of far too much importance to the enemy for them to desist from their efforts to recover it, and during the next three days our troops had no respite. All through the 19th and 20th they were subjected to a terrific bombardment from three sides, and lived through a veritable inferno; while on the evening of the latter day they were called on to withstand another fierce infantry attack. The 1st East Surreys were terribly hard pressed, and Lieut. George Roupell won the Victoria Cross. But he was not the only member of his battalion to gain the crown of the British soldier's ambition. A lad of nineteen, Private Edward Dwyer, who earlier in the day had displayed great gallantry in going out into the open, under heavy shell fire, to bandage the wounded, found himself alone in his trench, from which his comrades had been driven by a strong party of German bomb-throwers. The Germans were in a trench only some fifteen or twenty yards distant, so close that Dwyer could hear them talking; and the brave lad, aware that if they took his trench the trenches behind would be at their mercy, resolved to hazard his own life to save his comrades. Collecting all the grenades he could find, he climbed on to the parapet of the trench and began throwing them at the Germans. His appearance in this exposed position was, of course, the signal for a hail of bombs; but happily the Germans' aim was bad, while his own throwing was most accurate and effective. In fact, he succeeded single-handed in keeping the enemy at bay until reinforcements arrived, and the trench he had so heroically defended was saved. Dwyer was wounded on 27 April, and sent to the military hospital at Etretat, and it was not till nearly a month later that he learned that he had been awarded the Victoria Cross. He was decorated by the King himself at Buckingham Palace, 28 June, 1915, His Majesty shaking hands with him very cordially and complimenting him on his performance." Private Dwyer's Victoria Cross was gazetted 22 May, 1915: "Edward Dwyer, No. 10523, Private, 1st Battn. East Surrey Regt. Date of Act of Bravery: 20 April, 1915. For most conspicuous bravery and devotion to duty at Hill 60, on the 20th of April, 1915. When his trench was heavily attacked by German grenade-throwers, he climbed on to the parapet, and although subjected to a hail of bombs at close quarters, succeeded in dispersing the enemy by the effective use of his hand-grenades. Private Dwyer displayed great gallantry earlier in this day in leaving his trench, under heavy shell-fire, to bandage his wounded comrades." He is said to have been the youngest soldier who ever won the Victoria Cross. He was promoted to Corporal. On 4 Sept. 1916, he was killed in action at Guillemont. The "Daily Telegraph" said: "The sad news was conveyed to his parents at their home at Lintaine Grove, Fulham, S.W., by a letter which arrived from his Colonel on Saturday, and which told them that 'the little Corporal' had fallen while gallantly leading his men. London, and particularly his own borough of Fulham, was eager to fête this stripling of 19 when he won the greatest of all military decorations, but he turned his thoughts to more serious matters. It was in April, 1915, and we needed men for the Army. The 'little Corporal' threw himself whole-heartedly into the work of getting them. Any recruiting platform could command his services, and his ready Irish tongue—with an eloquence of pleading or scorn which astonished his most intimate friends—taught many a man his duty. Just before Christmas Corpl. Dwyer was quietly married to Miss Freeman, a Red Cross nurse whom he had met while lying wounded in a French hospital. The wedding took place at St. Thomas's, Fulham, to which church Dwyer, an earnest Catholic, was devotedly attached. After he had received his decoration from the King he addressed the scholars in the day school, and, pointing to his old seat, said: 'That is the first place where I learned discipline, and discipline is the mainstay of our Army.' 'Almost his last words to us here,' said Father Brown to a representative of the 'Daily Telegraph,' 'were sadly prophetic. "I'm going to the front again in a few days, and the general rule is that a V.C. gets knocked out the second time."' The Dwyer family has a proud record of service. The father, although 50 years of age, joined the Army Service Corps, and served in the Eastern Campaign. He has been invalided out of the Army. The eldest son is at Salonika, and the youngest lying in hospital, wounded. At the church of St. Thomas of Canterbury, Fulham, a high mass was celebrated yesterday for the repose of the soul of Corpl. Edward Dwyer, East Surrey Regt., the youngest V.C. in the Army, who was killed on 4 Sept., leading his platoon in the Big Push. Corpl. Dwyer was a native of Fulham. At the age of eighteen he won his Cross 'for conspicuous bravery and devotion to duty at Hill 60, on 20 April, 1915.' Father Crowley delivered a short address. He expressed to Corpl. Dwyer's parents, his widow and relations the heartfelt sympathy of the congregation and of the people of Fulham. Corpl. Dwyer was baptized in the church and had been educated in their schools. On the day that he received his V.C., Corpl. Dwyer said to the boys at the school where he was educated: 'This is the most eventful day of my life, and it makes me feel I should like to do something more for my country and my religion.' 'This wish has been gratified,' added Father Crowley, 'for he has given all—he has given his life.'"

MORROW, ROBERT, Private, was born at Lessia, Newmills, Tyrone, Ireland, son of Hugh Morrow and Margaret J. Morrow. He was educated at Carland Nationalist School, and joined the Army in 1912 in the 1st Battn. Royal Irish Fusiliers as a Private. He served in the European War, and was awarded the Victoria Cross [London Gazette, 22 May, 1915]: "Private Robert Morrow, 1st Battn. Princess Victoria's (Royal Irish Fusiliers). For most conspicuous bravery near Messines on 12 April, 1915, when he rescued and carried to places of comparative safety several men who had been buried in the debris of trenches wrecked by shell fire. Private Morrow carried out this gallant work on his own initiative, and under heavy shell fire from the enemy." He was killed in action on 25 April, 1915. The Cross was sent to his mother, who is a widow, and she took it to London, where she received it from the King's hands at an Investiture at Buckingham Palace. He also held the Medal of St. George, 3rd Class, conferred on him by the Emperor of Russia. This is the first Victoria Cross won by the regiment—The Faugh-a-Ballaghs—though they are a renowned fighting regiment. Private Morrow is being included in a large commemoration painting which is being executed for the French Government by M. Cairier-Bellew.

Robert Morrow.

RHODES-MOORHOUSE, WILLIAM BARNARD, Second Lieut., was born in London, 26 Sept. 1887, elder son of Edward Moorhouse, of Parnham House, Beaminster, Dorsetshire, and Mary Anne, daughter of the Hon. William Barnard Rhodes, M.L.C., New Zealand. He was educated at The Golden Parsonage, Hertfordshire; at Harrow, and at Trinity College, Cambridge. After leaving Cambridge he was engaged in monoplane experiments at Huntingdon in 1909 and 1910, and has been truthfully described as "one of the pioneers of aviation in England." He made many long flights before he took his pilot's certificate in Oct. 1911, and was then considered "probably the finest cross-country flier in this country, and quite the equal of anyone abroad." He finished third in the Aerial Derby for 1912, and the same year established a record in aviation as the first pilot to make a Channel-crossing with two passengers, one of whom was his wife. Soon after joining the Royal Flying Corps in Aug. 1914, he was placed in charge of workshops at Aircraft Park, South Farnborough, and remained there till 20 March, 1915, when he was sent out to the front to join the No. 2 Squadron, No. 1 Wing, at Merville, as a flying officer. His promotion to the rank of Lieutenant was gazetted after his death, to rank as from 24 April, 1915. On Monday, 26 April, during the Second Battle of Ypres, an urgent message came through from Headquarters, ordering the immediate destruction of the railway line at Courtrai Junction to prevent the bringing up of German reinforcements, and he was detailed for this important task, his instructions being "to use his own discretion as to the height at which he would drop his bomb." He left Merville flying ground at 3.5 p.m., and returned again mortally wounded at 4.15, having piloted his machine over 35 miles under conditions of extreme difficulty after receiving his first serious wound. He made a full report before he was taken to hospital, so that Sir John French was able to record the destruction of Courtrai Junction in his Report from Headquarters despatched the same evening. He died of his wounds next day, but before his death received the following message: "But for pressure of urgent work the Field-Marshal Commanding-in-Chief would have visited Second Lieut. Moorhouse himself to express his admiration of his courage and the way he carried out his duties yesterday." The Battle of Ypres was then in progress, and Merville was over 30 miles from General Headquarters. The following are extracts from the official report of his exploit: From Sir John French's Report from Headquarters, 26 April: "One of our airmen bombed Courtrai Station this afternoon and destroyed the junction. Although wounded, he brought his machine back to our lines." Extract from the Daily Bulletin issued to the troops (first issued by request to the Indian Corps), who "had seen him flying back, and were so impressed by his astounding courage" that they asked for further details and translated them into Hindustani, and it was afterwards circulated among all our troops at the Front. Dated 29 April, 1915: "British Air Raid on Courtrai. Details are now to hand of the successful air raid carried out on the 26th instant and mentioned in yesterday's bulletin. It is a story of amazing gallantry and heroism, and is worthy of special notice. The aviator, Second Lieut. W. B. Rhodes-Moorhouse, left Merville at 3.5 in the afternoon, alone in a biplane, to drop a heavy bomb on the railway junction at Courtrai. Arriving at his destination, he vol-planed down to a height of 300 feet, and successfully dropped the bomb on his objective, the effect of the explosion being felt by the aviator at a height of 300 feet. While at this low altitude he was subject to a tornado of fire from thousands of rifles, machine guns and shell fire. He was severely wounded in the thigh (part of which was torn away), but instead of descending into the German lines, where his life might have been saved, and to prevent his machine from falling into the hands of the Germans, he turned and made for the British lines. To increase his speed he descended a further 200 feet, and crossed the Ger-

W. B. Rhodes-Moorhouse.

man lines at a height of 100 feet only. He was again severely wounded by a bullet which ripped open his abdomen. Instead of landing at Ypres, he flew the whole way back to the flying ground at Merville, and made his report. We regret to say that he succumbed to his wounds 24 hours later. He was an aviator who had already performed several daring feats, and was the first man to do the 'tail slide,' and also the only man who had flown across the Channel with two passengers. This would appear worthy to be ranked among the most heroic stories of the world's history." The following is an extract from Eye-Witness's communication, dated 30 April: "The raid on Courtrai unfortunately cost the nation a very gallant life, but it will live as one of the most heroic episodes of the war. The aviator started on the enterprise alone in a biplane. On arrival at Courtrai he glided down to a height of 300 feet, and dropped a large bomb on the railway junction. While he did this he was the target of hundreds of rifles, of machine guns, and of anti-aircraft armament, and was severely wounded in the thigh. Though he might have saved his life by at once coming down in the enemy's lines, he decided to save his machine at all costs, and made for the British lines. Descending to a height of only 100 feet, in order to increase his speed, he continued to fly and was again wounded, this time mortally. He still flew on, however, and without coming down at the nearest of our aerodromes, went all the way back to his own base, where he executed a perfect landing and made his report. He died in hospital not long afterwards." He was mentioned in Field-Marshal Sir John (now Lord) French's Despatch of 3 May, 1915. At his own request, and by special permission of Sir John French, his body was sent home and was interred, on 5 May, 1917, in the park at Parnham House, Beaminster, Dorest, his home. "The airmen, too, did great work during this engagement" (the Second Battle of Ypres), "bombarding Steenstraate, Langemarck, Poelcapelle, and Passchendaele. In so short an account of so huge an operation it is difficult to descend to the individual, but no finer deed could be chronicled in the whole war than that of Lieut. Rhodes-Moorhouse, who, having been mortally wounded in the execution of his duty, none the less steered his machine home, delivered her at the hangar, and made his report before losing consciousness for ever." ("The British Campaign in France and Flanders in 1915," by Sir A. Conan Doyle, page 73.)

A leading article in the "Times" said:

"Let us begin with the bare facts. On 26 April, during the hottest of the fighting around Ypres, Lieut. Rhodes-Moorhouse, of the Royal Flying Corps, was ordered to drop bombs on the railway junction at Courtrai. He achieved his purpose. Gliding down to a height of 300 feet, to make sure of his aim, he became the target for hundreds of rifles, machine-guns, and anti-aircraft armament. He was severely wounded in the thigh. He might have saved his life by losing his machine and descending among the enemy. Instead, he headed for the British lines, tearing alone, in order to get the maximum of speed, below the level of many a London house-top, and was again, and this time mortally, wounded. But he still flew on over the British trenches, past the nearest aerodromes, back to his own base, where 'he executed a perfect landing and made his report.' The next day he died in hospital, and this week his body has been laid to rest in his native Dorset. The story is too simple and too splendidly complete in itself to need any artifice of narrative or comment; it speaks to us all. . . .

"'A Soldier,' whose letter we published yesterday, took the true soldier's line in this connexion. He asked whether 'Eye-Witness,' in simply stating that the anonymous airman, mortally stricken, had yet 'made his report,' had not written 'the finest epitaph that can be desired for a soldier dying in his devotion to duty.' Was not this 'better than to be trumpeted as a hero'? We entirely understand his point of view. It is that of the best officers of both Services, who live for their work, despise 'the sudden shining of splendid names,' and would gladly banish the word hero from the dictionary, and pass into oblivion like the brave men who lived before Agamemnon. But that spirit, indispensable as it is, and the root of all military virtues, is yet inadequate to some of the needs of the many-sided enterprise that modern warfare has become. The individual may care nothing for the reward of fame; but to his friends and relatives it is a precious possession and to his countrymen an example and a spur. The present policy of secrecy that refuses to link a Rhodes-Moorhouse with his achievement, that suppresses the names of regiments, and makes of the war an affair of asterisks in a land of blanks and dashes, is doing us incredible harm in many ways. . . ."

Mr. Beach Thomas wrote of him in the "Daily Mail," for 1 July, 1915:

"Such endurance is enough to make all of us ashamed of ever again complaining of any pain whatever. He was one of those who have never 'done their bit' till they have done the impossible."

The two following letters are from the Officers Commanding the First Wing and No. 2 Squadron of the Royal Flying Corps respectively, to Mrs. Rhodes-Moorhouse:

Lieut.-Col. Trenchard, commanding 1st Wing, R.F.C., wrote on 27 April, 1915:

"It is with the greatest sorrow that I write to tell you of the death of your gallant husband. He carried out a very important bombing expedition, and in order to thoroughly do the work he descended to a height of only three hundred feet, and was completely successful. He was then hit, and though suffering very acutely, he flew his machine all the way back to our lines at a very low altitude. He showed really marvellous endurance and pluck to do it. He was an officer for whom I had the greatest admiration and liking, and would have gone far had he been spared. He was one of the most popular officers in the 1st Wing. I fear he will not be able to be replaced. The only consolation that I can offer is that he died a very gallant death, fighting to the last."

Major T. I. Webb-Bowen, commanding No. 2 Squadron, R.F.C., wrote on 29 April:

". . . I feel that I should be doing your late husband's memory an injustice if I did not tell you how greatly we feel his loss in No. 2 Squadron. Although he had been with us but a short time he had endeared himself to everyone by his never-failing good spirits and ability. His last act has now set a standard of courage which others may hope to equal but never excel."

WOOLLEY, GEOFFREY HAROLD, Capt., was born at St. Peter's Vicarage, Bethnal Green, E., on the 14th of May, 1892, son of the Rev. George Herbert Woolley (who had been working in the East End of London for over twenty-five years), and of Sarah Woolley (*née* Cathcart). He was educated at St. John's, Leatherhead, and at Queen's College, Oxford, and joined the Army on 4 Aug. 1914, as a Second Lieutenant in the 5th Battn. The Essex Regt. When the Essex Territorial Brigade was split up in Sept. 1914, he was transferred to the 9th Battn. The London Regt. (Queen Victoria's Rifles), and went out to France with them in Nov. 1914. Sir Arthur Conan Doyle wrote in "The British Campaign in France and Flanders in 1915" (page 40): "Tuesday, 20 April, was another day of furious shell fire. A single shell upon that morning blew in a parapet and buried Lieut. Watson with twenty men of the Surreys. The Queen Victoria's, under Colonel Shipley, upheld the rising reputation of the Territorial troops by their admirable steadiness. Major Lees, Lieut. Summerhayes, and many others died an heroic death; but there was no flinching from that trench, which was so often a grave. As already explained, there was only one trench and room for a very limited number of men on the actual crest, while the rest were kept just behind the curve, so as to avoid a second Spion Kop. At one time upon this eventful day a handful of London Territorials, under a boy officer, Woolley of the Victoria's, were the only troops upon the top, but it was in safe keeping none the less. This officer received the Victoria Cross" [London Gazette, 22 May, 1915]: "Date of Act of Bravery, 20–21 April, 1915. Geoffrey Harold Woolley, 9th (County of London) Battn. The London Regt., Territorial Force. For most conspicuous bravery on Hill 60 during the night of 20–21 April, 1915. Although the only officer on the hill at the time, and with very few men, he successfully resisted all attacks on his trench, and continued throwing bombs and encouraging his men till relieved. His trench during all this time was being heavily shelled and bombed, and was subjected to heavy machine-gun fire by the enemy." He was also mentioned in Despatches. "Deeds that Thrill the Empire" (page 873) says: "Early in the eventful August of 1914, a young undergraduate of Queen's College, Oxford, the son of a clergyman, and who, but for the outbreak of war, would have been by this time a clergyman himself, joined the 5th Battn. Essex Regt., and went with them to Drayton, near Norwich, where that unit was to undergo its training under the command of Colonel J. M. Welch. His stay with the 5th Essex was very brief, however, for on 26 Aug. he was transferred to the Queen Victoria's Rifles. This young man was Second Lieut. Geoffrey Harold Woolley, who was to have the honour of being the first Territorial officer to win the Victoria Cross. The Queen Victoria's Rifles crossed the Channel in Nov. 1914, and in due course proceeded to take their turn in the trenches with the regular battalions of the 5th Division, to which they were attached, when they came in on occasion for some pretty severe shelling. But they were not employed in attack until the affair at Hill 60 in the following April, which was an experience none of them is ever likely to forget. Hill 60—hill, by the way, only by courtesy, since it is, in point of fact, merely an earth-heap from the cutting of the Ypres–Lille railway—lies a little to the west of Klein Zillebeke and just east of the hamlet of Zwartleben, the scene of the famous charge of our Household Cavalry on the night of 6 Nov. 1914. Its importance was that it afforded an artillery position from which the whole German front in the neighbourhood of Château Hollebeke could be commanded. At seven o'clock in the evening of 17 April, the British exploded seven mines on the hill, which played havoc with the defences, blowing up a trench line and 150 men, after which, under cover of heavy artillery fire, the position was stormed by the 1st West Kents and the 2nd King's Own Scottish Borderers, who entrenched themselves in the shell craters and brought up machine guns. During the night several of the enemy's counter-attacks were repulsed with heavy loss, and fierce hand-to-hand fighting took place; but in the early morning the Germans succeeded in forcing back the troops holding the right of the hill to the reverse slope, where, however, they hung on throughout the day. In the evening the West Kents and the King's Own Scottish Borderers were relieved by the 2nd West Ridings and the 2nd Yorkshire Light Infantry, who again stormed the hill, under cover of heavy artillery fire, and drove the enemy off with the bayonet. But Hill 60 was of vital importance to the enemy if they intended to maintain their Hollebeke ground, and on the 19th another fierce attack was made on it, with the support of artillery and asphyxiating bombs. It was repulsed, but the hill formed a salient, which exposed our men to fire from three sides, and all through the 19th and 20th a terrific cannonade was directed against them. In the evening of the latter day came another determined infantry attack, while all the night parties of the enemy's bomb-throwers kept working their way up to our trenches. At 9.30 that night two companies of the Queen Victoria's, under Major Rees and Capt. Westby, received orders to advance from their trenches and take up a position close to the top of the hill. Although the distance to be traversed was only some 200 yards, so terrible was the fire to which they were exposed that it took them two hours to reach the post assigned to them, where they dug themselves in close to a huge crater made by one of the British mines which had been exploded on the 17th. Towards midnight Sergt. E. H. Pulleyn was ordered to take sixteen men up to the very crest of the hill, some twenty yards away, to

Geoffrey H. Woolley.

fill a gap in our trench-line there. A withering fire was immediately opened upon the party by the enemy, who were not thirty yards distant, and only the Sergeant and eleven of his men reached the position, while of the survivors five fell almost immediately. Pulleyn and the remaining six maintained their ground for a few minutes, when, recognizing, the impossibility of holding it longer, they retired and rejoined their comrades, carrying their wounded with them. Both Major Rees and Capt. Westby had already been killed, and of 150 riflemen who had followed them up the fatal hill, two-thirds had fallen. The remainder held on stubbornly, however, and so accurate was their fire that the Germans did not dare to advance over the crest. But the cross-fire to which our men were exposed was terrible; never for a moment did it slacken, and man after man went down before it. When day began to break there were but thirty left. It was at this critical moment that an officer was seen making his way up the hill towards them. The men in the trench held their breath; it seemed to them impossible that anyone could come alive through the midst of the fearful fire which was sweeping the slope; every instant they expected to see him fall to rise no more. But on he came, sometimes running, sometimes crawling, while bullets buzzed past his head and shells burst all about him, until at last he climbed the parapet and stood amongst them, unharmed. Then they saw that he was Second Lieut. Woolley, who, learning that their officers had been killed, had left the security of his own trench and run the gauntlet of the enemy's fire to take charge of that gallant little band. His arrival put fresh heart into the Queen Victoria's, and there in that trench, choked with their dead and wounded comrades, shelled and bombed and enfiladed by machine guns, this Oxford undergraduate, the two brave N.C.O.'s, Pulleyn and Peabody, and their handful of Territorials, held the German hordes at bay, hour after hour, repelling more than one attack, in which the young Lieutenant rendered excellent service by the accuracy of his bomb-throwing, until at last relief came. Of four officers and 150 N.C.O.'s and men who had ascended the hill the previous night, only two N.C.O.'s and one man answered the roll-call. But, though they had suffered grievously, the battalion had gained great honour, both for themselves and the whole Territorial Force. Second-Lieut. Woolley had the proud distinction of being the first Territorial officer to be awarded the Victoria Cross, while Sergt. Pulleyn and Corpl. Peabody each received the Distinguished Conduct Medal for 'the great gallantry and endurance displayed, and for the excellent service rendered, in the fight for the possession of Hill 60.' Other decorations which had fallen to the share of the Queen Victoria's Rifles up to the end of 1915, were: Lieut.-Colonel R. B. Shipley—C.M.G.; Capt. S. J. Sampson—Military Cross; Sergt. E. G. Burgess—D.C.M." He returned to England on sick leave in June, 1915, and assisted for two months as Instructor at Cambridge School of Instruction. In Oct. 1915, he rejoined his unit in France. He was promoted to Captain 26 April, 1915. In March, 1916, he was appointed Instructor at the Third Army Infantry School. In Aug. 1916, he was appointed G.S.O.3 at Third Army Headquarters. In Dec. 1916, he returned to the 3rd Army Infantry School. On the opening of the German Offensive in March, 1918, he served for a month with the Headquarters, 17th Division, and was then reappointed G.S.O.3 at 3rd Army Headquarters, where he served till after the Armistice, doing liaison work with the troops of the 4th Corps. He was mentioned in Despatches 23 Dec. 1918, and awarded the Military Cross [London Gazette, 3 June, 1919]. He married Mrs. Janet Beatrix Culme-Seymour, widow of Capt. George Culme-Seymour, 60th Rifles, and daughter of the late C. L. Orr Ewing, M.P., of Dunskey, Portpatrick.

London Gazette, 10 June, 1915.—" The King has been graciously pleased to approve of the grant of the Victoria Cross to Flight Sub-Lieut. Reginald Alexander John Warneford, Royal Naval Air Service, for the conspicuous act of bravery specified below."

WARNEFORD, REGINALD ALEXANDER JOHN, Flight Sub-Lieut., was born at Darjeeling, Bengal, India, son of Reginald William Henry Warneford, and of Alexandra Warneford (*née* Campbell). He was educated at the Grammar School, Stratford-on Avon; entered the Merchant Service at the age of 13, and joined the Royal Naval Air Service in Feb. 1915, as a probationer. " Within four months," says " Deeds that thrill the Empire," " he had worthily earned the highest award 'For Valour' that the King can bestow. It was the German custom to send their huge Zeppelin airships on short cruises over the North Sea, in order to get their crews into training for raids on England. In the early morning of 7 June, 1915, one of these monsters was returning from such a cruise when she was sighted by Flight Sub-Lieut. Warneford, who was out on a lonely scouting expedition in a fast Morane monoplane. The intrepid airman, with nothing in sight to help him against the 600-foot ship, did not hesitate a moment, but immediately set off in pursuit. As he approached nearer and nearer, the Zeppelin opened fire on him with machine guns and heavier weapons; but still he kept on in his one-man machine, aiming always to get above his enemy, so that he might be able to drop his bombs—the only weapons he carried. The Zeppelin was flying her hardest to reach her shed at Gontrode, a trifle to the south of Ghent; but as she saw the little British monoplane gaining upon her, unharmed by the fusillade from her guns, she made that manœuvre which is one of the Zeppelin's best forms of defence. She dropped a quantity of ballast, and shot suddenly to a height of six thousand feet. The aeroplane is a slow climber compared with a gas-filled airship, but it was not in young Warneford to give up the chase. He set the nose of his machine into the air and doggedly followed his quarry. At that moment he could hardly help thinking that his efforts would be in vain; but suddenly, as they neared Ghent, the airship began to glide towards the earth. Her station was almost in sight, where she would find herself ringed by friends to protect her from her still silent pursuer. This anxiety for safety spelt her doom. As the Zeppelin dipped earthwards, so Warneford flew on and higher, until at last he was racing along fair above the German ship. It was just the position he had been praying for, and, very methodically and carefully, he began to drop his bombs. [His sister writes of his attack on the Zeppelin: " The first five bombs merely dropped through the Zeppelin and burst beneath her. Lieut. Warneford then rose higher and dropped his last bomb, which burst as it struck her and set her on fire."] Her crew of twenty-eight officers and men were all killed in the fall, or burned to death in the flames, and by a great misfortune the flaring ruin fell upon a convent in the Ghent suburb of Mont St. Amand, causing the loss of several innocent lives. Warneford had accomplished his task magnificently; but his own perils were not yet ended. The violence of the explosion caused by his last attack on the Zeppelin had been so great as to throw his aeroplane upside down in mid-air; but, with a coolness almost beyond belief, he succeeded in righting her, only to find that his petrol tanks had been drained dry while his machine hung reversed in the skies. There was nothing for it but to plane to earth—in the midst of territory thickly occupied by hostile troops. Choosing his landing-place with deliberation, he came down perfectly, and leaping from his seat, proceeded to fill his tanks from the reserve tins of petrol he carried. The British reports say the task took him fifteen minutes; the French say thirty-five; but, however that may be, he accomplished it in safety, and was able to soar into the air and away into safety just as hurrying Boches of the enemy opened fire on him with their rifles and machine guns. He got back to his base unharmed, the first airman in history to destroy a Zeppelin in flight. This was not the only 'record' he made. Within thirty-six hours of the airship's destruction he had received the following telegram from the King: 'I most heartily congratulate you upon your splendid achievement of yesterday, in which you, single-handed, destroyed an enemy Zeppelin. I have much pleasure in conferring upon you the Victoria Cross for this gallant act. George, R.I.' Never had the Cross been awarded so quickly after the deed that earned it; never had the recipient been advised of his distinction by a telegram from the reigning Sovereign. The whole nation applauded both the award and the King's promptness in making it; and our Allies, the French, showed their appreciation by making the gallant officer a Chevalier of the Legion of Honour." His Victoria Cross was gazetted 11 June, 1915: " Reginald Alexander John Warneford, Flight Sub-Lieut., Royal Naval Air Service. Date of Act of Bravery: 7 June, 1915. For most conspicuous bravery on the 7th of June, 1915, when he attacked, and single-handed completely destroyed, a Zeppelin in mid-air. This brilliant achievement was accomplished after chasing the Zeppelin from the coast of Flanders to Ghent, where he succeeded in dropping his bombs on to it from a height of only one or two hundred feet. One of these bombs caused a terrific explosion, which set the Zeppelin on fire from end to end but at the same time overturned his aeroplane and stopped his engine. In spite of this, he succeeded in landing safely in hostile country, and after fifteen minutes started his engine and returned to his base without damage." But Warneford's crowded hour of glorious life was drawing towards its close. On 17 June, while flying with Mr. Henry Needham, an American writer, at Buc Aerodrome, Paris, he and his passenger were killed; Warneford had been ordered to fly back to Dunkirk, where he was to resume duty. He had risen to about 700 feet, when the machine, after wobbling violently, overturned and threw out the two men, both of whom were killed instantly. It is said that on the day before his death Warneford had been given a bunch of roses in a restaurant, and someone said to him, " What rejoicings there will be when you return to Paris and see your mother again!" To this the young officer answered sadly, " I feel that I shall die before I return home." He was buried in Brompton Cemetery, the mourners including Mrs. Corkery, his mother. To her, on 5 Oct. 1915, the King wrote saying that it was to him a matter of sincere regret that the death of the officer had " deprived him of the pride of personally conferring upon him the Victoria Cross, the greatest of all naval distinctions."

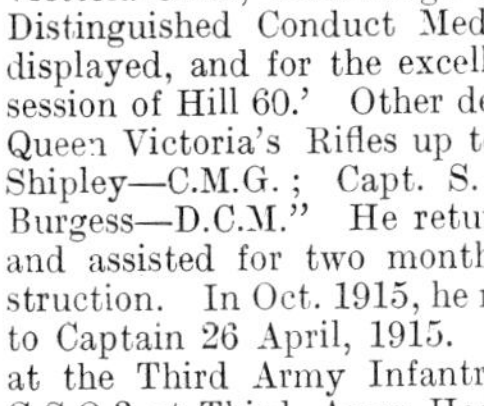

Reginald A.J.Warneford.

London Gazette, 23 June, 1915.—" The King has been graciously pleased to approve of the grant of the Victoria Cross to the undermentioned Officers and Men for most conspicuous bravery and devotion to duty."

DOUGHTY-WYLIE, CHARLES HOTHAM MONTAGU, Lieut.-Colonel, was born 23 July, 1868, elder son of Henry Montagu Doughty, of Theberton Hall, Suffolk, J.P., formerly R.N., and his wife, Edith Rebecca, only child of David Cameron, Chief Justice of Vancouver Island. He was educated at Winchester and Sandhurst (1888–89); was gazetted Second Lieutenant, Royal Welsh Fusiliers, 21 Sept. 1889, and promoted to Lieutenant 23 Sept. 1891. He served (1) in the Black Mountain Expedition, in 1891, and was severely wounded (Medal with Hazara clasp); (2) with the Chitral Relief Force as Transport Officer on the Staff of General Gatacre in 1895 (Medal with clasp). He became Captain 9 Sept. 1896; served (3) with the Nile Expedition 1898–99, being employed with the Egyptian Army 22 May, 1898, to 1 March, 1900; was Brigade-Major, Infantry Brigade, Flying Column; took part in the Battle of Khartoum, and in the operations resulting in the final defeat of the Khalifa

C. H. M. Doughty-Wylie.

(twice mentioned in Despatches [London Gazette, 30 Sept. 1898, and 30 Jan. 1900); Sudan Medal, Egyptian Medal with three clasps, Order of the Medjidie; (4) in the South African War 1899–1900; in command of a battalion of Mounted Infantry; took part in the operations in the Orange Free State, May to 29 Nov. 1900, including actions at Wittebergen (1 to 29 July), and Fredefort (severely wounded; Queen's Medal with three clasps); (5) at Tien Tsin, where he raised a regiment of Mounted Infantry, and (6) as Special Service Officer with the Somaliland Field Force 14 Jan. 1903, to June, 1904 (Medal with clasps). Capt. Doughty married, 1 June, 1904, Lilian Oimara, widow of Charles Henry Adams-Wylie, Lieut., Indian Medical Service, and eldest daughter of the late John Wylie, of West Clyffe Hall, Hampshire. He assumed the additional name of Wylie by Deed Poll in 1904. From 26 Sept. 1906, to 3 Dec. 1909, he was acting Vice-Consul at Mersina and Konia, Asia Minor, and during his tenure of this appointment occurred the massacre by the Turks of Armenians at Adana. Of his services on this occasion a correspondent wrote: "On his own responsibility he assumed practical command of the city of Adana, and by his courage and capacity saved the lives of hundreds—indeed, it was believed by those best able to judge, thousands of many nationalities" (there were 22,000 Armenians). "Wearing his military uniform, he rode through the town with a half-company of Turkish troops, compelling the raging mob to stop the killing, and posting guards over particular houses. His right arm was broken by a bullet, but this did not prevent him from riding out again, and in the second and worst outbreak of massacre again saving more hundreds of lives." The then British Ambassador at the Porte, Sir Gerard Lowther, afforded him a generous meed of support and encouragement, and Major Doughty-Wylie's services were recognized by the award of a C.M.G. He also received the warm thanks of many foreign Governments and public bodies. He afterwards organized a system of relief to the destitute—22,000 persons, exclusive of refugees in his own house, and exclusive also of the inmates of three hospitals, which were managed by Mrs. Doughty-Wylie. He had been promoted to Major on 21 Aug. 1907. On the 4th of Dec. 1909, he was appointed Consul at Adis Ababa, Abyssinia, where he rendered important services, acting as Chargé d'Affaires for considerable periods. Being home on leave in 1912, he was, with the consent of the Government, appointed Director-in-Chief of the Red Cross Units with the Turkish Forces during the Balkan War, and from 29 Aug. to 21 Dec. 1913, was British Representative on the International Commission for the delimitation of the Southern Frontier of Albania, of which commission he was elected President. For his services he received the Companionship of the Bath, and the Second Class of the Medjidie from the Sultan. On his return to England he was appointed to the General Staff (2nd Grade). He was made temporary Lieutenant-Colonel in 1913, when he was with the Commission in Albania, and was allowed to retain the rank on his return to Abyssinia in 1914. He got his Staff appointment after war broke out; served in the European War, and in 1915 went to the Dardanelles on the Staff of Sir Ian Hamilton. During the landings at the Beaches 25 and 26 April, 1915, he represented the Staff (Colonel Doughty-Wylie should have been in H.M.S. Queen at this landing; he asked special permission to be in the River Clyde as he had a presentiment that the landing from the first-named ship would not succeed) in the steamship River Clyde, which had been specially prepared for running on shore at V Beach, and which carried 2,200 troops of the 29th Division. This landing had almost failed, owing to the raking Turkish fire from the Castle and village, and on both sides of the bay, and no progress was made on the 25th, in spite of the desperate valour of the Munster and Dublin Fusiliers and the Hampshire Regt., but on the 26th Colonel Doughty-Wylie landed on his own initiative, and collecting the gallant survivors of the above-named regiments, with the assistance of Capt. Walford, organized an attack, and in some hours' fighting took the Castle and village of Sedd-el-Bahr, and finally led his handful of troops in a bayonet charge up Hill 141, since known as Colonel Doughty-Wylie's Hill. The Turks flew before them, and they occupied the Old Fort on the Crest, but Colonel Doughty-Wylie fell in the moment of victory. An eye-witness wrote: "All he carried was a small cane, and from a band he wore round his arm the men gathered he was a Staff Officer. He walked about in the open under a continuous fire, talking to the men, cheering them up, and rallying them together. Then when all was ready for the bayonet charge, he placed himself in front of them all, and armed simply with a small cane, led them in a great charge up the hill. No braver man ever lived. He had no business to be there as a Staff Officer, but the losses among officers in landing had been so great and the necessity for making headway quickly was so essential, that he felt his duty lay in leading the men, so he went forth fearlessly to his death, and the hill will be a lasting monument to his self-sacrifice and great valour. The magic of his personality and example infused the men with new resolution, and they pressed the attack home." General Hamilton stated that Colonel Doughty-Wylie saved the situation. For his services on this occasion he was awarded the Victoria Cross [London Gazette, 23 June, 1915]: "Charles Hotham Montagu Doughty-Wylie, Lieut.-Colonel, C.B., C.M.G., Headquarters Staff, Mediterranean Expeditionary Force. Date of Act of Bravery: 26 April, 1915. On the 26th April, 1915, subsequent to a landing having been effected on the beach at a point on the Gallipoli Peninsula, during which both Brigadier-General and Brigade-Major had been killed, Lieut.-Colonel Doughty-Wylie and Capt. Walford organized and led an attack through and on both sides of the village of Sedd-el-Bahr, on the Old Fort at the top of the hill inland. The enemy's position was very strongly held and entrenched, and defended with concealed machine guns and pompoms. It was mainly due to the initiative, skill and great gallantry of these two officers that the attack was a complete success. Both were killed in the moment of victory." Mrs. Doughty-Wylie writes: "Capt. Walford fell just outside the Castle of Sedd-el-Bahr, at the bottom of the village, and Colonel Doughty-Wylie in the Fort itself, after it was taken and while his men were actually cheering. I saw both graves myself on 17 Nov. 1915. The Fort and the Castle of Sedd-el-Bahr are not the same. The Castle is close to the sea; the Fort, which was taken about 4 p.m. on 26 April, after fighting had been going on all day, was at the top of the hill, and the village lay between it and the Castle." Surgeon Burroughes Kelly, R.N., D.S.O., wrote in his diary: "Lieut.-Colonel Doughty-Wylie, V.C., Royal Welsh Fusiliers. This officer belonged to G.H.Q., and accompanied us on River Clyde with his friend, Lieut.-Colonel Williams, also of G.H.Q., and his interpreter, Second Lieut. Hoyland. He possessed a most intimate knowledge of the Turks and their country, and was attached to Turkish Army during late Balkan Wars. During the day of landing, 25 April, he was everywhere assisting the wounded and doing the work of officers who had fallen. On the death of our Brigadier—Napier—Colonel Carrington Smith, of Hampshires, assumed command on River Clyde and 'V' Beach, and when he was shot dead on our lower fore bridge, Colonel Tizzard, of the Munsters, assumed command, and when he went there was no one left to do so. Early on the morning of the 26th, Doughty-Wylie left the River Clyde for the beach. He was prominent there throughout the forenoon, and about 11 a.m. he returned and drank a cup of tea. I had a chat of about a quarter of an hour with him, and he seemed depressed about the whole affair. Several times he remarked that something must be done. He then left us, and I recall vividly his walking-stick. The surviving troops had gradually got into Sedd-el-Bahr fort and up towards the main street of the village, and from where we were these places were well to the right or starboard side of Hill 141, our objective. About 1 p.m. Doughty-Wylie placed himself at the head of the ever dwindling Dublins, Munsters and Hampshires, and waving his walking-stick and calling on the men to follow him, he led a gallant charge on the old fort at 141. This charge carried the objective. As they entered, Doughty-Wylie, ever encouraging the men, fell to rise no more. He was shot through the head. With him fell Major Grimshaw, of the Dublins. Doughty-Wylie's last request was said to have been that someone bring to the notice of the authorities the 'gallant Capt. Unwin and the boy Drewry.' We buried him at midnight where he fell, and the River Clyde's carpenter made a simple wooden cross for his grave. The only woman to land in Gallipoli during our occupation was his widow, Mrs. Doughty-Wylie. She had a reception from the French, and it is interesting to note that on that day the enemy fired neither bullet nor shell."

WALFORD, GARTH NEVILLE, Capt., served in the European War with the Mediterranean Expeditionary Force. "Deeds that thrill the Empire" (page 58) says: "About one o'clock on the morning of Sunday, 25 April, 1915, the transports containing our Mediterranean Expeditionary Force dropped anchor at a point five miles from the shores of the Gallipoli Peninsula, and by the time the first streaks of dawn—the dawn of the last day which many a brave man was ever to see—appeared in the eastern sky, boats and destroyers crowded with troops were stealing in towards the land. Fierce was the resistance of the Turks from each of the six landing-places—from Gaba Tepe, on the north side of the peninsula, to Beach S in Morto Bay—but at Beach V, which at its southern extremity is commanded by the Castle and village of Sedd-el-Bahr, and where our men were exposed to every type of converging fire, it was the fiercest of all. Here fell Brigadier-General Napier, Capt. Costeker, his Brigade-Major, Lieut.-Colonel Carrington Smith, commanding the Hampshire Regt., and many other distinguished officers. Here a whole company of the Munsters was practically wiped out and a half company of the Dublin Fusiliers reduced by midday to twenty-five effectives; and when the morning of the 26th dawned the disembarkation was still in its first stage, and the remnant of the landing-party—the survivors of the Dublin and Munster Fusiliers, and of two companies of the Hampshires—had been crouching for many hours behind a steep sandy bank at the top of the beach, the cover afforded by which had alone preserved them from being annihilated. But cramped and stiff though they were, tormented by thirst, and subjected to a heavy and unceasing fire, our men were still full of fight, for with them were brave and devoted officers: Lieut.-Colonels Doughty-Wylie and Williams, of the Headquarters Staff, and Capt. Walford, Brigade-Major, R.A., who, with sublime indifference to their own danger, had been striving all through that day and night of ceaseless peril to keep their comrades in good heart. And now, when it was daylight once more, these officers proceeded to organize an attack against the hill above the beach. Fortunately it happened that at about this same time arrangements had been made for the warships to begin a heavy bombardment of the Old Fort, the village of Sedd-el-Bahr, the Old Castle, north of the village, and of the ground leading up from the beach, under cover of which our men, most gallantly led by Lieut.-Colonel Doughty-Wylie and Capt. Walford, succeeded by 10 a.m. in gaining a footing in the village. They had to encounter a most stubborn resistance, and suffered heavy losses from the fire of cleverly-concealed riflemen and machine guns. But though many fell, their comrades, supported by the terrific fire from the huge naval guns, continued to press on, breaking in the doors of the houses with the butts of their rifles, and routing the snipers out of their hiding-places at the point of the bayonet; and soon after midday they penetrated to the northern edge of the village, whence they were in a position to attack the Old Castle and Hill 141. Brave Capt. Walford had already fallen; and now, when, owing so largely to his inspiring example and splendid courage, the position had been almost won, Lieut.-

Garth Neville Walford.

Colonel Doughty-Wylie, who, with a little cane in his hand, had led the attack all the way up from the beach through the west side of the village, under a galling fire, was shot through the brain while leading the last assault. But our men, undeterred by the fall of their leaders, pushed resolutely forward, and fighting their way across the open in the most dashing manner, before 2 p.m. had gained the summit and occupied the Old Castle and Hill 141. Both Lieut.-Colonel Doughty-Wylie and Capt. Walford were awarded the Victoria Cross, the official announcement stating that it was mainly owing to the initiative, skill and great gallantry of these two officers that the attack was a complete success." The London Gazette for 23 June, 1915, says: "Garth Neville Walford, Capt., Brigade-Major, Royal Artillery, Mediterranean Expeditionary Force. Date of Act of Bravery: 26 April, 1915. On the 26th April, 1915, subsequent to a landing having been effected on the beach at a point on the Gallipoli Peninsula, during which both Brigadier-General and Brigade-Major had been killed, Lieut.-Colonel Doughty-Wylie and Capt. Walford organized and led an attack through and on both sides of the village of Sedd-el-Bahr on the Old Castle at the top of the hill inland. The enemy's position was very strongly held and entrenched and defended with concealed machine guns and pompoms. It was mainly due to the initiative, skill and great gallantry of these two officers that the attack was a complete success. Both were killed in the moment of victory."

SCRIMGER, FRANCIS ALEX. CARON, Capt., was born 8 Feb. 1880, in Montreal, Canada, the son of the late Rev. John Scrimger, M.A., D.D., Principal of the Presbyterian College, Montreal (who was much beloved and respected; was one of the leading clergymen of his denomination in Canada, and a strong advocate of Church union), and of Mrs. John Scrimger, of 83, Redpath Crescent, Montreal. He was educated at the Montreal High School, and is a graduate and member of the Teaching Staff of McGill University (Medical School), and on the Staff of the Royal Victoria Hospital, Montreal. "It is an interesting coincidence that Capt. (now Major) Scrimger is the only one of his family to bear the ancestral name of Alexander Carron, who, under Alexander II. of Scotland, in a critical moment in battle carried the King's Standard across a ford, thereby winning the battle for his King, and for himself and his descendants the honour and office of Hereditary Standard Bearer of Scotland, and the name Skirmisher (Scrymgeour or Scrimger), or hardy fighter, with the privilege of using the Scottish arms, reversed." Prior to the outbreak of war in Europe, Capt. Scrimger was Medical Officer to the Montreal Heavy Brigade. He joined the Canadian Expeditionary Force, and sailed with Canada's Army of 30,000 men, serving as Medical Officer, 14th Battn. Canadians. He landed at Plymouth. He served on the Western Front in Flanders, and was awarded the Victoria Cross [London Gazette, 23 June, 1915]: "Francis Alexander Caron Scrimger, Capt., Medical Officer, 14th Battn. Royal Montreal Regt. Dates of Acts of Bravery: between 22 and 25 April, 1915. On the afternoon of 25 April, 1915, in the neighbourhood of Ypres, when in charge of an advanced dressing station in some farm buildings, which were being heavily shelled by the enemy, he directed under heavy fire the removal of the wounded, and he himself carried a severely wounded officer out of a stable in search of a place of greater safety. When he was unable alone to carry this officer farther, he remained with him under fire till help could be obtained. During the very heavy fighting between 22 and 25 April, Capt. Scrimger displayed continuously day and night the greatest devotion to his duty among the wounded at the front."

Francis A. C. Scrimger.

Extract from a letter in the "Montreal Star," by Mr. H. G. Brewer, Saturday, 26 June, 1915:

"I would also like to tell you about the heroic work done by our Medical Officer, Capt. Scrimger, and his staff of first-aid men and stretcher-bearers, Capt. Scrimger during the first days' fighting replacing Capt. Boyd, who was wounded. He was doubtless glad to get back to his old regiment, from which owning to sickness he had been separated before we left England. The doctor had his work cut out for him, as our dressing-station was right up on the line, near Brigade Headquarters, and the wounded men were pouring in from several different battalions. Three nights and days Capt. Scrimger, assisted by Sergt. Bethell and the stretcher-bearer section, worked unceasingly, caring for the wounded from Canadian, British and even French regiments. They came in such numbers that time could not be spared to tag each man. The wounded were placed in rows on the floor of a big barn, and when darkness came, a fleet of silent motor-ambulances stole up and carried them away to the hospitals. In one afternoon and evening more than four hundred wounded passed through this dressing-station, and each man received skilled and thorough treatment, for, no matter what the emergency may be, our M.O. never allows himself to be rushed. And bear in mind that all this time the farm in which the dressing-station was situated was under constant shell and rifle fire.

"On the third day it was thought advisable to move the station further back, and all but fifteen badly wounded were removed to safety, when the enemy concentrated a furious fire on the group of farm buildings, throwing over incendiary bombs, which soon had the dressing-station and barn in a mass of flames. It was then that Capt. Scrimger and staff showed their metal, and accomplished the seemingly impossible feat of rescuing the fifteen helpless men from their new danger. For half an hour they toiled, assisted by volunteers, carrying the wounded out on their backs, and crossing a shell-swept field to cover. And these men were already exhausted from their superhuman efforts during the past three days.

"In tending wounded on the field and carrying them to safety, our stretcher-bearers have performed deeds of valour and endurance which in any other war than this would have entitled every mother's son of them to a V.C. Some were struck down while performing their humane duty; others worked till they dropped and were sent, babbling incoherently, to a nerve specialist in the hospital.

"All through the remaining days at Ypres, when we lost from ten to thirty men in a day, Capt. Scrimger was with us, as he still is, in and out of the trenches, invariably cool, and always just where he was needed most. He is immensely popular with the men, who place the utmost confidence in him."

Extracts from the "Canadian Medical Association Journal," April, 1916:

"It is nearly a year since the heroic action of our troops at Ypres and Langemarck won for the name of Canadians a dignity and a sacrificial lustre undimmed by comparison with the greatest deeds of history. As is well known, the fiercest part of the struggle and the heaviest casualties were shared by the 13th and 14th Battns., units raised in Montreal, numbering among their officers Major E. C. Norsworthy and Capts. Guy Drummond, C. N. Williamson, W. C. Brotherhood, and C. F. Stacey.

"Some two months later the news reached Canada that the opportunities for the exercise of skill and devotion which the terrible occasion offered, had brought to the Medical Officer of the 14th Battn., himself a Canadian, the high honour of the Victoria Cross. A wounded officer, Capt. MacDonald, of London, Ontario, whose life Capt. Scrimger saved under circumstances of peculiar physical strain, made the facts known, and on 21 July the doctor was summoned to Windsor, and received the decoration, pinned on by the King's own hand.

"The event was mentioned at the time in the 'Journal,' but the full details have not reached our readers. Capt. MacDonald's own account, given to Windermere, was published in the 'Montreal Star' on 16 July, 1915, as follows: 'I was in the front of the Canadian Headquarters Staff on 25 April, which was the third day of the terrific St. Julien fighting, when I was hit on the neck and shoulder. I was dragged into a building where Capt. Scrimger dressed my wounds. A few minutes later German shells found the building and set it on fire. The staff were forced to abandon the building and left me there as an apparently hopeless case. But Capt. Scrimger carried me out and down to a moat fifty feet in front, where we lay half in the water. Capt. Scrimger curled himself round my wounded head and shoulder to protect me from the heavy shell fire, at obvious peril of his own life. He stayed with me till the fire slackened, then got the stretcher-bearers and had me carried to the dressing-station. This, however, is only one of many incidents of Capt. Scrimger's heroism in those awful three days. No man ever better deserved the soldier's highest honour.'

"The following additional details are taken from a full account recently published in the 'British War Weekly' for 22 Jan. last: 'Of the three Canadian V.C. heroes, Capt. Francis Alexander Carron Scrimger, alone lives to wear the bronze medal. Throughout the fierce fighting of 22 to 25 April, at St. Julien, Capt. Scrimger displayed continuously day and night the greatest devotion to duty among the wounded. On the afternoon of the 25th, the fighting was very fierce, and the brave Canadian doctor had his hands full attending to the wounded. He was in charge of an advance dressing-station in some farm buildings. The enemy commenced a very heavy bombardment of the temporary hospital, and the inmates were in imminent risk of being killed. Capt. Scrimger remained perfectly cool, and was able to quiet the fears of his wounded charges. He gave orders for their removal and went about apparently wholly unconcerned amid the falling shells assisting the orderlies. A Canadian officer, Capt. MacDonald, was standing in front of a stable when he was hit on the neck and shoulder. Capt. Scrimger saw him fall, and promptly dragged him into the building, where he dressed his wounds, which were serious. Rather than leave the officer to die there, the gallant doctor carried him out and down to a moat in front, where they lay half under water (on the side of an earth bank), where he protected the wounded officer from falling earth which threatened to bury them. They were under heavy shell fire all the time. When the fire slackened he went out to find the stretcher-bearers and brought them back, and they removed Capt. MacDonald to the safety of a dressing-station.'"

Capt. Scrimger was invalided to England; served on the staff of the Canadian Hospital at Ramsgate, and was for a time Consultant Surgeon in hospitals in England. He was promoted to Major, and returned to France, serving in No. 3 Canadian Casualty Station, France. He married on 5 Sept. 1918, at St. Columba's (Church of Scotland), Pont Street, London, S.W., Ellen Emerson Carpenter, late C.A.M.C. Major Scrimger is a keen golfer and an ardent fencer. His brother, the Rev. J. Tudor Scrymgeour (who has adopted the usage in Scotland for spelling the name), was also in France during the European War, serving as Chaplain and hut worker under the Y.M.C.A., and having charge of a Headquarters Hut for a certain area.

The following is taken from "Thirty Canadian V.C.'s," published by Messrs. Skeffington:

"During the terrible days from April 22nd till April 25th, 1915, the Canadian troops had their mettle tested to a supreme degree. In those four days the second battle of Ypres was fought and the German drive held up where its authors had thought it irresistible. Even the deluge of gas—the first used in the war—gained them less benefit than they expected. That battle of Ypres was decidedly a Canadian victory. Captain F. A. C.

Scrimger, of the Canadian Army Medical Corps, was attached at the time to the 14th (Royal Montreal) Battalion. On April 22nd he was in charge of an advanced dressing-station situated in an old farm building near the battered city of Ypres. The house was surrounded by a moat over which there was only one road; and that afternoon, during the heavy fighting, the German artillery found the lonely house and began to shell it. For three days and nights Scrimger worked among the wounded, heedless of the pandemonium of the battle, in a situation which was perilous in the extreme. The Germans, in their forward rush, brought the farm within rifle range, but still Scrimger and his staff went about their work. On the afternoon of the 25th the German artillery sent over incendiary shells, and one of these, landing on the farm, set the place alight. The staff were at last forced to move. The single road was almost impassable owing to a heavy German shrapnel barrage, but the wounded were nevertheless taken back to places of comparative safety. Some of the staff, and some of the less badly wounded patients, swam the moat. They were all removed except one badly injured officer; for him swimming was out of the question. Scrimger took upon himself the task of saving this patient, but, as he was preparing to move, several direct hits were made on the house by the German artillery. Shrapnel burst through the rafters. Scrimger bent over his patient, protecting him with his body as the splinters fell around them, and finally, during a lull, carried him out of the blazing house on his back. But in the open there was not even the protection of the shaky walls of the farm, and Scrimger had not gone far with his burden when he saw that the officer was too severely wounded to bear this kind of journeying. There was no shelter in sight, nothing but the shrapnel-swept wastes and the torn, shuddering earth. Laying his patient down, Scrimger remained beside him, shielding him again with his own body, till help arrived later in the day."

ROUPELL, GEORGE ROWLAND PATRICK, Lieut., was born 7 April, 1892, at Tipperary, Ireland, son of Colonel F. F. F. Roupell and of Mrs. E. M. Roupell (*née* Bryden). He was educated at Rossall, and Sandhurst, and was gazetted to the East Surrey Regt. as Second Lieutenant 2 March, 1912, becoming Lieutenant 29 April, 1914. He went to France with the original Expeditionary Force, with the 1st Battn. East Surrey Regt.; fought at Mons, Le Cateau, The Retreat, Marne, Aisne, and the First Battle of Ypres. He commanded a platoon until on the Aisne he obtained command of a company, which he kept until wounded on Hill 60, where he won the Victoria Cross in April, 1915. "Deeds that thrill the Empire" (pages 550 to 557) describes how Lieut. Roupell, of the 1st Battn. East Surrey Regt., won the V.C., and Company Sergt.-Major Alexander John Reid, of the same battalion, won the D.C.M.: "There has been no more obstinate and sanguinary fighting on the blood-soaked soil of Flanders than that which took place towards the end of April, 1915, for the possession of the coveted position known as Hill 60, two miles east of Ypres; and in that desperate conflict there is no more stirring episode than the heroic defence of one of the forward trenches by a company of the 1st Battn. East Surreys, during the night of 20–21 April. That the East Surreys were enabled to hold the post against overwhelming numbers and in the face of the greatest difficulties was mainly due to the splendid gallantry and devotion of two men, Lieut. George Rowland Patrick Roupell and Company Sergt.-Major Alexander John Reid, the first of whom was stationed on the left of the position, and the second on the right. Except for the discharge of a few shells from the batteries on either side, the forenoon of 20 April had been very quiet; but about four o'clock in the afternoon the German artillery began a terrific bombardment of our position, which was only too evidently the prelude to a determined counter-attack to regain possession of the Hill. For several hours shells of every description rained upon the British trenches; but, though some battalions suffered severely, the East Surreys had but few casualties. Their comparative immunity did not continue long, however, for at dusk the counter-attack commenced, the method employed by the enemy being to send forward strong parties of bomb-throwers through a series of communication trenches which ran from their trenches to ours. The trench occupied by the East Surreys was assailed in the most desperate manner, and though the bombers were received with a heavy rifle fire, they continued to advance with the utmost courage and determination, and hurled their deadly missiles with great effect. Some of the bombs fell on the parapet, portions of which they completely demolished, and others fell into the trench itself, causing great havoc. On the right flank, where Sergt.-Major Reid was stationed, the position of affairs soon became most critical, for not only were the men falling fast, but ammunition was running short. Unless reinforcements and a fresh supply of cartridges could be brought up, it would be impossible to stem the advancing tide of Germans much longer. But how was help to be summoned? The communication trench leading to our reserve trenches had been so badly damaged that it afforded little or no shelter, while in places it was quite impassable; and the German shells seemed to be searching every yard of the open. A man must needs bear a charmed life to cross it in safety. Darkness fell—the intense darkness of a night unrelieved by moon or stars, and the obscurity was rendered the more profound by the smoke from the bursting shells. This made matters even worse for our men, for they had no Very-light pistol with them. There they stood, firing only when they felt certain that a cartridge would not be wasted, and waiting for the rush which they knew must overwhelm them, no matter how gallantly they might struggle. It was then that Company Sergt.-Major Reid resolved to take the fearful risk of crossing the zone of fire to our reserve trenches. Leaving the trench, he started at a run across the open, which was so torn up by the terrific shelling to which it was being subjected that it was fast becoming a mass of huge holes, and negotiating these craters successfully, a fall into one of which might have entailed a sprained ankle or even a more serious injury, reached our supports, hastily explained the critical situation of affairs, and hurried back with what men and ammunition he could obtain, and a promise that further reinforcements should be sent for. He regained the trench in safety, and not a moment too soon, for the East Surreys were falling fast, and but few cartridges remained in their bandoliers. He posted the men he had brought with him in the places where they were most needed and distributed the ammunition, but he very soon perceived that, unless further aid could be obtained, it would be impossible to hold the trench. He therefore again made the hazardous journey to our supports, and returned with a party of the Bedfords. By this time the trench was reduced almost to ruins and littered with dead and wounded. But the arrival of the Bedfords, who brought with them a Very-light pistol and Very lights, as well as a further supply of ammunition, put fresh heart into the survivors of the gallant little band. With the aid of the Very lights, they were now able to estimate the strength of the enemy, who, they saw, outnumbered them by two or three to one; and towards dawn, after consultation with the officer in charge of the Bedfords, the brave Sergt.-Major for the third time ran the gauntlet of the enemy's fire, and guided a party of the Queen Victoria Rifles to the assistance of his hard-pressed comrades. The arrival of these last reinforcements probably saved the situation, for, as day was breaking, the Germans made a most determined attempt to carry the trench, only, however, to be repulsed with considerable loss. While the right of the East Surreys was being so hard pressed, their comrades on the left were in equally desperate case. But here again the heroism of one man saved the situation. During the terrific bombardment of our position which preceded the German counter-attack, Lieut. Roupell was wounded in several places; nevertheless, he refused to quit his post, and led his men in repelling a determined assault by the enemy. During a lull in the bombardment he retired to have his wounds dressed, when the surgeon who attended him did everything possible to dissuade him from returning to the firing-line. He insisted on going back, however, and when towards evening he saw that it was impossible for his men to hold their ground unless assistance could be procured, he, though faint from loss of blood, made his way, like Sergt.-Major Reid, across the shell-swept open to the reserve trenches, and brought up reinforcements; with the aid of these he held the position throughout the night. At two o'clock in the morning of the 21st, the East Surreys were relieved by the Devons, when it was found that only a mere handful of them had come through that terrible ordeal. Two of their officers had been killed and three wounded, while one hundred and twenty N.C.O.'s and men were either killed, wounded or missing. In short that gallant company, as a fighting unit, had ceased to exist." Lieut. Roupell was awarded the Victoria Cross, while Company Sergt.-Major Reid (a Londoner, then twenty-nine years of age) received the D.C.M., for "conspicuous gallantry and valuable service." Elsewhere "Deeds that thrill the Empire" says: "Desperate indeed was the fighting of which Hill 60 was the scene towards the end of April, 1915. . . . All through the 19th and 20th our troops were subjected to a terrific bombardment from three sides, and lived through a veritable inferno; while on the evening of the latter day they were called upon to withstand another fierce infantry attack. The 1st East Surreys were terribly hard pressed, and Lieut. Roupell won the Victoria Cross . . . for the splendid tenacity with which he held his post with the remnants of his company until help came. But he was not the only man of his battalion to gain the crown of the British soldier's ambition. A lad of nineteen, Private Edward Dwyer, who earlier in the day had displayed great gallantry in going out into the open under heavy shell-fire to bandage the wounded found himself alone in his trench." As described in the account of Dwyer in this book, the lad held this trench single-handed, and won the Victoria Cross for his gallant behaviour throughout the day. The career of Capt. G. R. P. Roupell's father and his connection with the 1st Battn. East Surrey Regt. was described by a newspaper correspondent at the time of Colonel F. F. F. Roupell's death: "Born in July, 1848, he was appointed ensign in October, 1867, to the 70th Foot, which later was incorporated with the 31st to form the East Surrey Regiment. At the time of his death he was Chairman of the East Surrey Old Comrades Association, a member of the Council of the Army Rifle Association, Vice-President of the Kingston and Surbiton Rifle Club, and a life member of the Bengal-Punjab Rifle Association. Throughout his service he had taken the keenest interest in rifle shooting, and, besides winning numerous trophies, he captained the Army Rifle Team in India in 1898. When war broke out, although in his sixty-seventh year, he offered his services to the War Office as an instructor in musketry, and after going through a course at Bisley he was gazetted to the General Staff of the 22nd Division as divisional musketry instructor. The strenuous nature of this position during the winter of 1914 brought on the breakdown which, after an illness of over a year, was the cause of his death. Previously Colonel Roupell served on the Staff in the Khyber Pass during the Afghan War, 1878–80 (Medal), was afterwards appointed Chief of Staff to General T. G. Kennedy on the Mahsoud Waziri Expedition of 1880–81 (mentioned in Despatches), subsequently holding various Staff appointments in India, notably as D.A.A.G. for Musketry to the Old Frontier Force. Later he commanded the 1st Battalion (31st) East Surrey Regiment, and during the Boer War the Royal Lancaster Reserve Regiment, being subsequently appointed to the command of the 31st Regimental District at Kingston-on-Thames. The improvement of the standard of shooting in the Army had always been one of his chief interests, and it was while working for this object that he unquestionably gave his life for his country by his untiring zeal with the 22nd Division at Seaford under the very trying weather conditions of the winter of 1914. Of his three sons two have Regular com-

George R. P. Roupell.

missions in the Army—the elder, Capt. F. L. L. F. Roupell, in the R.G.A.; the younger, Capt. G. R. P. Roupell, who has already distinguished himself by gaining the V.C. and the Russian Order of St. George, in the East Surrey Regt. The youngest son would by now have followed his brothers, but had the misfortune to be interned in Germany on the outbreak of war whilst studying for Sandhurst. Colonel Roupell was loved and respected by all who knew him either in his military career or in his private life, and will be deeply mourned." Lieut. Roupell's Victoria Cross was gazetted 23 June, 1915: "George Rowland Patrick Roupell, Lieut. 1st Battn. The East Surrey Regt. Date of Act of Bravery: 20 April, 1915. For most conspicuous gallantry and devotion to duty on the 20th April, 1915, when he was commanding a company of his battalion on Hill 60, which was subjected to a most severe bombardment throughout the day. Though wounded in several places, he remained at his post and led his company in repelling a strong German assault. During a lull in the bombardment he had his wounds hurriedly dressed, and then insisted on returning to his trench, which was again being subjected to a severe bombardment. Towards evening, his company being dangerously weakened, he went back to his battalion headquarters, represented the situation to his commanding officer, and brought up reinforcements, passing backwards and forwards over ground swept by heavy fire. With these reinforcements he held his position throughout the night, and until his battalion was relieved next morning." After recovering from his wounds at Hill 60, Lieut. Roupell returned to the front as Adjutant to the 1st Battn., till promoted G.S.O.3 to XVIIth Army Corps. He was appointed G.S.O.3, Third Army, in Sept. 1916, and Brigade-Major, 105th Brigade, in Dec. 1916. Capt. Roupell was given the Order of St. George of Russia, and was twice mentioned in Despatches.

HALL, FREDERICK WILLIAM, Company Sergt.-Major, served in the European War with the Canadians, and was awarded the Victoria Cross [London Gazette, 23 June, 1915]: "Frederick William Hall, No. 1539, Company Sergt.-Major, 8th Canadian Infantry Battn. On the 24th April, 1915, in the neighbourhood of Ypres, when a wounded man who was lying some fifteen yards from the trench called for help, Company Sergt.-Major Hall endeavoured to reach him in the face of a heavy enfilade fire which was being poured in by the enemy. The first attempt failed, and a non-commissioned officer and private soldier, who were attempting to give assistance, were both wounded. Company Sergt.-Major Hall then made a second most gallant attempt, and was in the act of lifting up the wounded man to bring him in when he fell mortally wounded in the head." He died of his wounds on the following day.

The following is taken from "Thirty Canadian V.C.'s" published by Messrs. Skeffington:

"In the lesser wars of the past the Victoria Cross was more frequently awarded for demonstrations of valour in connection with the rescuing of wounded under fire than for courageous acts designed and carried out with more material and purely military advantages in view. To risk one's life, perhaps to lose it, in a successful or vain attempt to save the life of a disabled comrade was—granting favourable circumstances and conditions—to be recommended for that crowning award. When we consider the nature of those lesser wars we appreciate the admirable spirit in which those recommendations were made. Those were days of small armies, long marches and short battles. The fate of the Empire, say even of the world's freedom, never hung upon the turn of any one engagement. A soldier was something more romantic then than a unit of man-power. The length, the unrelieved ferocity and the stupendous proportions of this war, have somewhat altered the spirit in which recommendations for awards are made. The deed of valour must show material rather than sentimental results; the duty that inspires the deed must show a military rather than a humane intention. The spirit of our heroes is the same to-day as it was yesterday, whether the courageous act results in the holding of a position, the killing of a score of Germans, or the saving of one comrade's life. Only the spirit of official appreciation has changed; but this new spirit is logical. F. W. Hall was recommended for his Cross in the old spirit. The deed of valour for which Company Sergeant-Major Hall, of the 8th Canadian Infantry Battalion, was awarded the Victoria Cross was performed on the morning of the day following the great achievement and death of Lance-Corporal Fisher. Hall, too, lost his life in the very act of self-sacrifice by which he won immortality. During the night of April 23rd the 8th Battalion of our 2nd Infantry Brigade relieved the 15th Battalion of the 3rd Brigade, in a section of our front line. In moving up to our fire-trench the relieving troops had to cross a high bank which was fully exposed to the rifle and machine-gun fire of the enemy in the positions opposite. This bank lay about fifteen yards in rear of our forward position at this point. Its crest was continuously swept by bullets while the relief was taking place, and the incoming battalion suffered a number of casualties. In the darkness and the confusion of taking over a new trench under such adverse conditions, the exact extent of the casualties was not immediately known; but Sergeant-Major Hall missed a member of his company on two separate occasions and on two separate occasions left the trench and went back to the top of the bank, under cover of the dark, returning each time with a wounded man. At nine o'clock in the morning of the 24th, the attention of the occupants of the trench was attracted to the top of the bank by groans of suffering. Hall immediately suggested a rescue, in spite of the fact that it was now high daylight, and Corporal Payne and Private Rogerson as promptly volunteered to accompany him. The three went over the parados, with their backs to the enemy, and instantly drew a heavy fire. Before they could reach the sufferer, who lay somewhere just beyond their view on the top of the bank, both Payne and Rogerson were wounded. They crawled and scrambled back to the shelter of the trench, with Hall's assistance. There the Sergeant-Major rested for a few minutes, before attempting the rescue again. He refused to be accompanied the second time, knowing that as soon as he left the trench he would become the target for the excellent shooting that had already put Payne and Rogerson out of action. It was his duty as a non-commissioned officer to avoid making the same mistake twice. He had already permitted the risking of three lives in the attempt to save one life and had suffered two casualties; but doubtless he felt free to risk his own life again in the same adventure as he had already successfully accomplished two rescues over the same ground. He may be forgiven, I think, for not pausing to reflect that his own life was of more value to the cause than the life of the sufferer lying out behind the trench. The fire from the hostile positions in front and on the flanks of this point in our line was now hot and accurate. It was deliberate, aimed fire, discharged in broad daylight over adjusted sights at an expected target. Hall knew all this; but he crawled out of the trench. He moved slowly, squirming along very close to the ground. The bullets whispered past him and over him, cut the earth around him, pinged and thudded upon the face of the bank before him. Very low shots, ricocheting off the top of the parados in his rear, whined and hummed in erratic flight. He reached and crawled up the slope of the bank without being hit. He quickly located and joined the wounded man, guided straight by the weakening groans of suffering. He lay flat and squirmed himself beneath the other's helpless body. Thus he got the sufferer on his back, in position to be moved; but in the act of raising his head slightly to glance over the way by which he must regain the shelter of the trench, he received a bullet in the brain. Other bullets immediately put an end to the sufferings of the man on his back. Hall had been born in Belfast, Ireland, but Winnipeg was his Canadian home."

BELCHER, DOUGLAS WALTER, L.-Sergt., is employed by Messrs. Waring and Gillow. He served in the European War, and was awarded the Victoria Cross [London Gazette, 23 June, 1915]: "Douglas Walter Belcher, No. 9539, L.-Sergt., 1/5th (City of London) Battn. The London Regt. (London Rifle Brigade). Date of Act of Bravery: 13 May, 1915. On the early morning of 13th May, 1915, when in charge of a portion of an advanced breastwork south of the Wieltje–St. Julien Road, during a very fierce and continuous bombardment by the enemy, which frequently blew in the breastwork, L.-Sergt. Belcher, with a mere handful of men, elected to remain and endeavour to hold his position after the troops near him had been withdrawn. By his skill and great gallantry he maintained his position during the day, opening rapid fire on the enemy, who were only 150 to 200 yards distant, whenever he saw them collecting for an attack. There is little doubt that the bold front shown by L.-Sergt. Belcher prevented the enemy breaking through on the Wieltje Road, and averted an attack on the flank of one of our divisions." "Deeds that thrill the Empire" (page 517) says: "By a singular coincidence, the Second Battle of Ypres lasted almost exactly as long as the first, namely, three weeks. It began on the evening of Thursday, 22 April, 1915, when the Germans discharged their poison-gas against the French trenches between the Yser Canal and the Menin Road, and it may be said to have terminated on Thursday, 13 May, with the attack on our cavalry front, preceded by one of the most terrific bombardments our men had yet experienced, and that upon the infantry on their left, when Sergt. Douglas Belcher, of the London Rifle Brigade, with four survivors of his battalion and two Hussars, made the gallant stand which saved the right of the 4th Division."

Douglas Walter Belcher.

FISHER, FREDERICK, L.-Corpl., was born at St. Catherine's, Ontario, Canada, son of Mr. W. H. Fisher, and joined the Army in Valcartier, Canada, on the 23rd Sept. 1914. He served in the European War; was promoted to Lance-Corporal 22 Dec. 1914, and awarded the Victoria Cross [London Gazette, 23 June, 1915]: "Frederick Fisher, No. 24066, L.-Corpl., 13th Canadian Battn. Date of Act of Bravery: 23 April, 1915. On 23 April, 1915, in the neighbourhood of St. Julien he went forward with the machine gun of which he was in charge, under heavy fire, and most gallantly assisted in covering the retreat of a battery, losing four of his gun-team. Later, after obtaining four more men, he went forward again to the firing line, and was himself killed while bringing his machine gun into action under very heavy fire, in order to cover the advance of supports."

The following is taken from "Thirty Canadian V.C.'s" published by Messrs. Skeffington:

"In March, 1915, Canadian guns took part in the Battle of Neuve Chapelle and a Canadian regiment, the Princess Patricia's Light Infantry, fought well at St. Eloi; but it was not until April that the infantry of the 1st Canadian Division came to grips with the enemy. The Canadian Division moved into the Ypres Salient about a week before the Germans commenced their terrific and wanton bombardment of the unfortunate city of Ypres. They relieved troops of the 11th Division of the French Army in five thousand yards of undeveloped trenches. Fisher, a lance-corporal of the 13th Canadian Infantry Battalion, performed the deed of valour (at the cost of his life) for which he was granted the Victoria Cross, on the 23rd of April, 1915. He was our first V.C., in this war, by one day. On the afternoon of the 22nd of April the Germans projected their first attack of asphyxiating gas against a point of our Allies' front. Turcos and Zouaves fell back, strangled, blinded and dismayed. The British left was exposed. A four-mile gap—a way to Calais—lay open to the enemy. The 1st Canadian Division, the only Canadian Division in the field in those early days, held the British left. It blocked the four-mile gap and held up Germany, gas and all. There were no such things as gas masks in those days; but the Canadians were undismayed by that new and terrific form of murder.

They had left their offices and shops, their schools and farms and mills, with the intention of fighting the Hun, and, in return, of suffering the worst he could do to them. They did not expect him to fight like a sportsman, or even like a human being. So they accepted the gas as part of the day's work. It was the last day's work for hundreds of those good workmen. A battery of Canadian 18-pounders, commanded by Major W. B. M. King, C.F.A., maintained its original position well into the second day of the battle—the 23rd of April. The gunners were supported by a depleted Company of the 14th (Royal Montreal) Battalion, and kept up their fire on the approaching Germans until their final rounds were crashed into 'the brown' of the massed enemy at a range of less than two hundred yards. This is a class of performance which seems to make a particular appeal to the hearts of gunners. It calls for more than steadiness and desperate courage, for technical difficulties in the matter of timing the fuses to a fraction of a second must be overcome under conditions peculiarly adverse to the making of exact mathematical calculations. But this sort of thing is frequently done—always with gusto and sometimes with the loss of the guns and the lives of their crews. The gunner then feels all the primitive excitement of the infantryman in a bayonet charge. He claps his gun, that complicated, high-priced and prodigious weapon, at the very head of the enemy, as if it were no more than a pistol. On this occasion the guns were not lost. They were extricated from beneath the very boots and bayonets of the enemy and withdrawn to open fire again from a more secure position and at a more customary range. They were 'man-handled' out and back by the survivors of their own crews and of the supporting company of infantry; but all those heroic and herculean efforts would have availed nothing if Corporal Fisher had not played his part. Fisher was in command of a machine-gun and four men of his battalion—the 13th. He saw and understood the situation of Major King's battery and instantly hastened to the rescue. He set up his gun in an exposed position and opened fire on the advancing Germans, choosing for his target the point of the attack which most immediately menaced the battery of field-guns. His four men were put out of action. They were replaced, as they fell, by men of the 14th, who were toiling near-by at the stubborn guns. Fisher and his Colt remained unhit. The pressure of his finger did not relax from the trigger, nor did his eyes waver from the sights. Eager hands passed along the belts of ammunition and fed them into the devouring breech. So the good work was continued. The front of the attack was sprayed and ripped by bullets. Thus it was held until the 18-pounders were dragged back to safety. Not satisfied with this piece of invaluable work, Fisher advanced again, took up a yet more exposed position, and, under the combined enemy fire of shrapnel, H.E., machine-guns and rifles, continued to check and slay the Germans. The men who went up with him from his former firing position fell, one by one, crawled away or lay still in death. But the Lance-Corporal continued to fire. The pressure of his finger did not relax from the trigger until he was shot dead."

MARINER, WILLIAM, Private, was born at 12, Wellington Street, Chorley, Preston, Lancashire, son of Mrs. A. Wignall, and was educated at the Parochial School, Chorley, joining the 2nd King's Royal Rifle Corps about 1902. He served seven years in India with the Colours, and five years afterwards in the Reserve, and was discharged on the termination of his engagement. On 26 Aug. 1914, he re-enlisted with his old battalion, the 2nd King's Royal Rifles, and proceeded to France 29 Nov. 1914. He was invalided to the United Kingdom 24 Aug. 1915, and again went to France 12 Oct. 1915. He was awarded the Victoria Cross [London Gazette, 23 June, 1915]: "William Mariner, No. 2052, Private, 2nd Battn. King's Royal Rifle Corps. Date of Act of Bravery: 22 May, 1915. During a violent thunderstorm on the night of the 22nd May, 1915, he left his trench near Cambrin, and crept out through the German wire entanglements till he reached the emplacement of a German machine gun which had been damaging our parapets and hindering our working parties. After climbing on the top of the German parapet, he threw a bomb in under the roof of the gun emplacement, and heard some groaning and the enemy running away. After about a quarter of an hour he heard some of them coming back again, and climbed up on the other side of the emplacement and threw another bomb am ng them left-handed. He then lay still while the guns opened a heavy fire on the wire entanglement behind him, and it was only after about a quarter of an hour that he was able to come back to his own trench. Before starting out he had requested a sergeant to open fire on the enemy's trenches as soon as he had thrown his bombs. Rifleman Mariner was out alone for one and a half hours carrying out this gallant work." "Deeds that thrill the Empire" (pages 148–149) says: "Under circumstances of great daring, Private William Mariner, of the 2nd Battn. The King's Royal Rifles, left his trench near Cambrin on the night of 22 May, 1915. A violent thunderstorm was raging at the time, and this covered the sound of his movements as he crept towards the enemy's entanglements. When opposite the emplacement of a machine gun which had damaged the parapet of his trench and hindered working parties, Mariner climbed to the top of the enemy's parapet. Flinging a bomb under the emplacement of the gun, he knew his purpose was achieved on hearing groans and the sound of men dispersing. After a quarter of an hour, Mariner, who remained on the parapet, heard some of the enemy come back. With great daring he climbed up on the other side of the emplacement, and then threw a second bomb among them. The Germans thereupon brought a heavy fire to bear upon the wire entanglements where they expected Mariner would be. For an hour, however, he lay still out of sight, and when all was quiet, crawled back to the shelter of his trench after an absence of an hour and a half." Another writer says of Mariner: "The machine gun had been inflicting heavy casualties on his battalion. He volunteered for this mission, knowing full well that the chances were a hundred to one against his coming back. But he won through." Private Mariner was still serving in France when he was killed in action 1 July, 1916.

William Mariner.

London Gazette, 25 June, 1915.—"Admiralty, 25 June, 1915. The King has been graciously pleased to approve of the grant of the Victoria Cross to Lieut.-Commander Martin Eric Nasmith, R.N., for the conspicuous bravery specified below."

NASMITH, MARTIN ERIC, Lt.-Commander, was born 1 April, 1883, son of Martin Arthur Nasmith and of Caroline Nasmith. He was educated at Eastman's, Winchester, and joined the Royal Navy in May, 1898. He served in the European War. "Deeds that thrill the Empire" (page 86) says: "The spring of 1915 found the E11 attached to the Fleet in the Mediterranean, and, with Lieut.-Commander Martin Eric Nasmith in charge, she proceeded to make history at a rapid rate. It was in the middle of May that she left for her perilous passage through the Dardanelles, and before she was through them she ran across her first patch of excitement. When the Narrows had been successfully negotiated, and the submarine rose to get fresh bearings, two battleships were seen to be lying a little further on. Such an opportunity was not to be let slip without an effort, and, necessarily keeping the periscope above water, Lieut.-Commander Nasmith at once proceeded to put his boat in a suitable position for launching a torpedo. Unfortunately the Turks sighted the periscope a minute or two too soon, and instantly the battleships began blazing away with their light guns as hard as they could. At the same time they 'upped anchor' and got under way, so there was nothing for it for the E11 but to dive and hide herself until the furore had subsided. She was far too slow to catch the battleships if she ran submerged, and if she rose to the surface she would almost certainly have been breached by a shell. So she pushed on submerged, and entered the Sea of Marmora during the afternoon, where for several days she alternately rested and cruised about without finding anything that was worth the expenditure of a torpedo. Lieut.-Commander Nasmith made Constantinople the centre of his operations during the whole of this raid, and his first reward came one Sunday morning, just before half-past six, when a big gunboat was seen at anchor off the port. The submarine was ready for instant action, and in a brief space the fatal torpedo was under way. At 6.25 the gunbaat was hit; at 6.30 she had sunk, but not without giving the E11 something of a shock. A shot was fired from the sinking gunboat that went clean through the submarine's periscope, carrying away about four inches of the diameter a few feet from the top, and leaving the rest standing. Had the shot struck about six feet lower, it would very probably have made a breach in the conning tower, and so placed the submarine in an awkward predicament in such waters. The very next day brought an adventure which, if it was not so exciting, at any rate did not lack in interest. A big steamer was sighted making her way from Constantinople towards the Dardanelles, and the E11 came to the surface a short distance ahead, fired a shot across her bows, and brought her to a standstill. There happened to be a facetious American newspaper correspondent on board, and when Lieut.-Commander Nasmith hailed 'Who are you?'—meaning of course to inquire what the ship was and what was her business—this gentleman replied by giving his own name and that of the paper for which he was working. This was not good enough for the E11. A few more questions elicited the fact that the ship was a Turkish transport, the Nagara, and when he got as far as that, Nasmith promptly replied: 'Right, I am going to sink you.' 'May we have time to get off?' queried the newspaper man, by this time rather subdued. 'Yes,' came the answer from the submarine, 'but be d—— quick about it.' The Turks were so quick that they upset two of their boats in lowering them, and capsized several men into the water, though all of them managed to get into safety again. Then Lieut. D'Oyly-Hughes, from submarine E11, went on board the ship to see what she carried. There was a six-inch gun destined to strengthen the forts on the Dardanelles; there were several sets of mountings for weapons of large calibre, and there was a great quantity of ammunition for heavy guns on its way to the Dardanelles. The ship was, in fact, loaded from keel to upper-deck with war material, and when the crew, and the American correspondent, had withdrawn to a safe distance, the submarine drew off, having placed a bomb among the ammunition which sent the ship to the bottom. The most audacious act of the E11 was her raid on Constantinople itself. Early one morning, while she was slowly cruising off the mouth of the harbour, she sighted a Turkish merchantman through the morning haze making for the harbour. E11 set off in hot pursuit, but was unable to catch her. It may have been this incident that gave Nasmith his inspiration, but, however that may be, the E11 found herself early one morning lying actually within the port of Constantinople itself. Observations were cautiously taken, and it was seen that a number of enemy transports were lying alongside the wharves, and that some of them actually had troops on board. The harbour of Constantinople is traversed by tricky currents, and although the E11 fired two torpedoes, neither of them hit the object at which it was aimed. Nasmith's intention was, of

Martin Eric Nasmith.

course, to sink the transports, and although the first torpedo did not do that, it blew up a barge with such force that the transport Stamboul, lying close by, was so badly damaged that she had to be run ashore in order to save herself from sinking. The second torpedo did not hit a ship, but it exploded against the quayside and destroyed a considerable length of it. In the Turkish capital itself the moral effect of this attack was tremendous. Hearing the explosion of the two torpedoes and the noise of the guns which the Turkish batteries went on firing long after the E11 was safely out of sight, the civil population jumped to the conclusion that the Allied Fleet had arrived before their city. Thousands of them fled to the hills behind the town; most of the shops put up their shutters, and after the Turkish officers had vainly attempted to control the panic-stricken soldiers on board the transports with their swords and revolvers, all the men were marched ashore, and the transports left empty. It was several days before the capital settled down again. This by no means ended the thrilling experiences of the E11. Before she set out on her return journey from the Sea of Marmora, she had sunk in all one large gunboat, two transports, three storeships and the ammunition ship (the Nagara), and had forced another ship to run ashore, and when half-way through the Dardanelles, on her way back, she gave up hope of again meeting the battleships which had previously escaped her, Lieut.-Commander Nasmith returned a distance of some miles to sink a transport with a torpedo which had been reserved for a chance meeting with a battleship. In all, the E11 destroyed eleven ships—no bad record for a small vessel with a crew of thirty officers and men, who had to face the gravest perils single-handed from the time they entered the Dardanelles until they left them. On the way out these perils were encountered in a most alarming form. As the E11 was making her way seawards beneath the surface, those on board became aware of a resistance which was not of the sea, and every now and then a faint scraping of chain was heard against the vessel's side. Instinctively and instantly everyone on board realized what had happened. The submarine had fouled the cable by which a floating mine was chained to its anchor on the sea-bed, and the cable, instead of slipping past the smooth hull, had somehow become entangled in the forward hydroplanes. Any bump between submarine and mine might suffice to explode the latter, and send the submarine to the bottom like a log. It was impossible for Nasmith to manœuvre his boat in an effort to get rid of the thing, for he was passing through the most thickly-mined area of the whole Straits, and any deviation from the set course would almost certainly have taken the boat straight to destruction. Nor could he rise to the surface and send a man out to detach the machine, for the churning screws of the patrol boats could be heard overhead. There was nothing for it but to carry on as slowly and as carefully as possible and to trust to Providence. For eleven miles the submarine crept on with sudden death dangling from her bows—a death from which those on board were saved only by the buoyancy of the mine keeping it above the submarine's hull. A sharp blow would have detonated it. One can imagine what feelings of relief there were when the boat at last reached an area where she could 'break surface' in safety. This was carried out by going full speed astern and bringing the stern to the surface first, thus allowing the mine to clear itself, which it did. His splendid services brought Lieut.-Commander Nasmith the award of the Victoria Cross, while the two other officers on board, Lieut. Guy D'Oyly-Hughes and Lieut. Robert Brown (R.N.R.), received the Distinguished Service Cross. All the petty officers and men were granted the D.S.M." He was awarded the Victoria Cross [London Gazette, 25 June, 1915]: "Martin Eric Nasmith, Lieut.-Commander, Royal Navy. For most conspicuous bravery in command of one of His Majesty's submarines while operating in the Sea of Marmora. In the face of great danger he succeeded in destroying one large Turkish gunboat, two transports, one ammunition ship, and three store ships, in addition to driving one store ship ashore. When he had safely passed the most difficult part of his homeward journey, he returned again to torpedo a Turkish transport." He was promoted Commander 30 June, 1915, and was made a Chevalier of the Legion of Honour. Promoted Captain 30 June, 1916.

London Gazette, 29 June, 1915.—"His Majesty the King has been graciously pleased to approve of the grant of the Victoria Cross to the undermentioned Officer, Non-commissioned Officers and Men."

SMYTH, JOHN GEORGE, Lieut., was born at Teignmouth, South Devon, 25 Oct. 1893, son of William John Smyth, of the Indian Civil Service, and of Lilian May Smyth (*née* Clifford), and was educated at Oxford Preparatory School, at Repton School, and at Sandhurst. He joined the Indian Army as Second Lieutenant, Unattached, 24 Aug. 1912, and the 15th Ludhiana Sikhs, Indian Army, 5 Nov. 1913, becoming Lieutenant 24 Nov. 1914, and serving in France, with the Lahore Division, from Sept. 1914, to Aug. 1915, during which time he greatly distinguished himself. "Deeds that thrill the Empire" (pages 35–40) says: "There are no finer fighting men in our Indian Army than the Sikhs, the descendants of those fierce long-haired warriors who fought so stubbornly against us at Firozshah and Chilianwala, and afterwards stood so loyally by the British Raj in the dark days of the Mutiny. And there are no finer officers in the world than the men who lead them, for no youngster stands a chance of being gazetted to a Sikh regiment who has not shown that he possesses in a marked degree all the qualities which are likely to ensure the confidence and devotion of those whom he aspires to command. When the first Indian Contingent disembarked at Marseilles in the early autumn of 1914 there were some arm-chair critics who expressed doubts as to whether, under conditions of warfare so totally different from those with which he was familiar, the native soldier might not be found wanting. But these sceptics were speedily confounded, for, however strange and terrifying might be the sight of the destruction wrought by hand-grenades and high-explosive shells, however trying the long vigils in the trenches, knee-deep in mud and water, the Sepoy accepted it all with Oriental stoicism, and wherever his officer led, he cheerfully followed, though it was into the very jaws of death. And on many a desperate enterprise, on many a forlorn hope, did these officers lead him, but surely on none more so than that on which Lieut. Smyth, of the 15th Sikhs, led his little band of dark-skinned heroes on 18 May, 1915! On the previous night a company of the 15th, under Capt. Hyde Cates, had relieved a part of the 2nd Battn. Highland Light Infantry in a section of a trench known as the 'Glory Hole' near the Ferme du Bois, on the right front of the Indian Army Corps. Here for some time fighting of a peculiarly fierce and sanguinary character had been in progress, and the position of affairs at the moment when the Sikhs replaced the Highlanders was that our men were in occupation of a section of a German trench, the remaining portion being still held by the enemy, who had succeeded in erecting a strong barricade between themselves and the British. Towards dawn Capt. Cates observed that the Germans were endeavouring to reinforce their comrades in the trench, as numbers of men were seen doubling across the open towards its further extremity. He immediately ordered the Sikhs to fire upon them, but in the dim light they presented exceedingly difficult targets, and when morning broke it was ascertained that the German trench was packed with men, who were evidently meditating an attack. Shortly afterwards, in fact, a perfect hail of bombs began to fall among the Indians, who replied vigorously, and, to judge from the shrieks and curses which came from the other side of the barricade, with considerable effect, until towards noon their supply of bombs began to fail, many of them having been so damaged by the rain which had fallen during the night as to be quite useless. The situation was a critical one; only the speedy arrival of a bombing party from the reserve trenches could enable them to hold out. The reserve trenches were some 250 yards distant, and the ground between so exposed to the fire of the enemy as to render the dispatch of reinforcements a most desperate undertaking. Twice had the Highland Light Infantry made the attempt, and on both occasions the officer in command had been killed and the party practically wiped out. Nevertheless, the Sikhs were resolved to take their chance, and, on volunteers being called for, such was the magnificent spirit of the regiment that every man stepped forward, though no one doubted, if his services were accepted, almost certain death awaited him. The men were selected and placed under the command of Lieut. Smyth, a young officer of one-and-twenty, who had already distinguished himself on more than one occasion by his dashing courage. The names of those ten heroes deserve to be remembered. They were: Sepoys Fatteh Singh, Ganda Singh, Harnam Singh, Lal Singh, Naik Mangal Singh, Sarain Singh, Sapooram Singh, Sucha Singh, Sunder Singh and Ujagar Singh. At two o'clock in the afternoon Lieut. Smyth and his little band set out on their perilous enterprise, taking with them two boxes containing ninety-six bombs. The ground which they had to traverse was absolutely devoid of all natural cover. The only approach to shelter from the terrific fire which greeted them the moment they showed their heads above the parapet of our reserve trenches was an old partially demolished trench, which at the best of times was hardly knee-deep, but was now in places literally choked with the corpses of Highland Light Infantry, Worcesters, Indians and Germans. Dropping over the parapet, they threw themselves flat on the ground and painfully wriggled their way through the mud, pulling and pushing the boxes along with them, until they reached the scanty shelter afforded by the old trench, where they commenced a progress which for sheer horror can seldom have been surpassed. By means of pagris attached to the boxes, the men in front pulled them along over and through the dead bodies that encumbered the trench, while those behind pushed with all their might. The danger was enough to have appalled the stoutest heart. Rifle and machine-gun bullets ripped up the ground all around them, while the air above was white with the puffs of shrapnel. If a single bullet, a single fragment of shell, penetrated one of the boxes of explosives, the men propelling it would infallibly be blown to pieces. Before they had advanced a score of yards on their terrible journey, Fatteh Singh fell, severely wounded; in another hundred, Sucha Singh, Ujagar Singh and Sunder Singh were down, leaving only Lieut. Smyth and six men to get the boxes along. However, spurred on by the thought of the dire necessity of their comrades ahead, they, by superhuman efforts, succeeded in dragging them nearly to the end of the trench, when, in quick succession, Sarain Singh and Sapooram Singh were shot dead, while Ganda Singh, Harnam Singh and Naik Mangal Singh were wounded. The second box of bombs had therefore to be abandoned, and for the two remaining men to haul even one box along in the face of such difficulties appeared an impossible task. But nothing was impossible to the young lieutenant and the heroic Lal Singh, and presently the anxious watchers in the trench ahead saw them wriggling their way yard by yard into the open, dragging with them the box upon the safe arrival of which so much depended. As they emerged from the comparative shelter of the trench a veritable hail of lead burst upon them, but, escaping it as though by a miracle, they crawled on until they found themselves confronted by a small stream, which at this point was too deep to wade. They had, therefore, to turn aside and crawl along the bank of the stream until they came to a place which was just fordable. Across this they struggled with their precious burden, the water all about them churned into foam by the storm of bullets, clambered up the further bank, and in a minute more were amongst their cheering comrades. Both were unhurt, though their clothes were perforated by bullet holes; but it is sad to relate that scarcely had they reached the

John George Smyth.

trench than the gallant Lal Singh was struck by a bullet and killed instantly. For his 'most conspicuous bravery,' Lieut. Smyth received the Victoria Cross, and each of the brave men who accompanied him the Indian Distinguished Service Medal, and we may be very certain that 'ne'er will their glory fade' from the proud records of our Indian Army. It is, we may mention, the universal opinion of the men of the 15th Sikhs that Smyth Sahib bears a charmed life, since again and again he has escaped death by a hair's-breadth; on one occasion a match with which he was lighting a cigarette being taken out of his fingers by a bullet." "The Indian Corps in France" (pages 363–366), in describing the Battle of Festubert, relates how, on the morning of the 17th May, Capt. K. Hyde-Cates, with a company of the 15th Sikhs, relieved the 2nd Highland Light Infantry in a section of the captured trench known as the "Glory Hole." "The situation became very critical, and on the 18th, at 3.30 p.m., Lieut. J. G. Smyth, 15th Sikhs, was ordered to attempt to take bombs and a bombing party from the support trench (our former front line) to Capt. Hyde-Cates. The distance to be covered was about 250 yards over open ground. The only means of communication was a shallow trench, half full of mud and water, and in many places exposed to the enemy's snipers and machine guns. The trench was crammed with the dead bodies of British and Indian soldiers, as well as Germans. Lieut. Smyth took with him ten bombers from No. 4 Company, selected from the crowd of volunteers who at once responded to the call. The names of these heroes deserve to be put on mention. They were Lance-Naik Mangal Singh, Sepoys Lal Singh, Sucha Singh, Sapuram Singh, Sarain Singh, Sundur Singh, Ganda Singh, Harnam Singh (the last four being all of the 19th Punjabis), Fateh Singh and Ujagar Singh, both of the 45th Sikhs. The party took with them two boxes of bombs containing forty-eight each. For the first fifty yards the trench gave cover from the enemy's view, but on emerging from this portion the men came under enfilade shrapnel fire from the German field guns, which was so severe as to force them to crawl off to the right and take refuge in a small stream where the water reached chest-high. Here the first man was hit. Our men waited until the shelling slackened, and then, returning to the trench, continued their laborious progress. But now man after man was killed or wounded, for it was necessary to crawl over the top of the dead bodies, and the sides of the trench had been in many places broken down, exposing the party to the full view of the enemy, who, well aware of the object of the enterprise, pumped torrents of bullets into the trench. By the time Lieut. Smyth had arrived within thirty yards of Capt. Hyde-Cates' position, he had only three men left, and the slightest attempt to rise from a lying-down position brought a shower of bullets. Up to this point the boxes had been pushed or pulled along by means of pagris attached to them, but with the few men left, this was no longer possible. Lieut. Smyth now gave orders for the boxes to be opened, and for each man to carry two bombs in his hands. While opening a box another man was shot through the head and killed. There was nothing for it but to leave the bombs in the communication trench to be brought in after dark. The officer, Lance-Naik Mangal Singh, and one sepoy managed by crawling through the mud and water to reach Capt. Hyde-Cates' trench, being the sole survivors of the little band of eleven. So ended one of the most gallant episodes of the war. For his most conspicuous bravery Lieut. Smyth was awarded the Victoria Cross, and later the Fourth Class of the Order of St. George. Lance-Naik Mangal Singh received the Second Class Indian Order of Merit, while the Indian Distinguished Service Medal was conferred on all the sepoys of the party." On the 19th May, Capt. Waterfield, of the 15th Sikhs, was mortally wounded by a shell while talking to Capt. Finnis and Lieut. Smyth of his plans for his next leave. His loss was greatly felt by the officers and men of the regiment. Lieut. Smyth's Victoria Cross was gazetted 29 June, 1915: "John George Smyth, Lieut., 15th Ludhiana Sikhs. Date of Act of Bravery: 18 May, 1915. With a bombing party of ten men, who voluntarily undertook the duty, he conveyed a supply of ninety-six bombs to within twenty yards of the enemy's position, over exceptionally dangerous ground, after the attempts of two other parties had failed. Lieut. Smyth succeeded in taking the bombs to the desired position with the aid of two of his men (the other eight having been killed or wounded), and to effect his purpose he had to swim a stream, being exposed the whole time to howitzer, shrapnel, machine-gun and rifle fire." Lieut Smyth. was mentioned in Despatches, 22 June, 1915, and was awarded the Russian Order of St. George, Fourth Class. He was promoted to Captain, and became Brigade-Major, 43rd Brigade, Lahore. He served in Egypt (1) (Canal Defence) Aug. 1915, to Nov. 1915, and (2) in the Senussi Campaign on the Western Frontier Nov. 1915, to Feb. 1916. In India he took part in the Mohmand Blockade, Oct. 1916, to Dec. 1916. Capt. Smyth married Evelyn Monica, daughter of Lionel Robertson, P.W.D., and Mrs. Robertson, Lahore.

DAST, MIR, Jemadar, I.O.M., served in the European War in France, and was awarded the Victoria Cross [London Gazette, 29 June, 1915]: "Mir Dast, I.O.M., Subadar Bahadur, 55th Coke's Rifles (Frontier Force), attached 57th Wilde's Rifles (Frontier Force). Date of Act of Bravery: 26 April, 1915. For most conspicuous bravery and great ability at Ypres on 26 April, 1915, when he led his platoon with great gallantry during the attack, and afterwards collected various parties of the regiment (when no British officers were left) and kept them under his command until the retirement was ordered. Jemadar Mir Dast subsequently on this day displayed remarkable courage in helping to carry eight British and Indian officers into safety, while exposed to very heavy fire."

Mir Dast.

ANGUS, WILLIAM, L.-Corpl., was born at Carluke, Lanarkshire, N.B., son of Mr. and Mrs. Angus. He joined the Territorials; served in the European War, and greatly distinguished himself. "Deeds that thrill the Empire" (pages 466–473) says: "Before the war broke out there was, as will readily be remembered, a decided disinclination in certain quarters to take our Territorial forces quite seriously, and even our old friend 'Mr. Punch' could not resist the temptation of occasionally making their supposed ignorance of their duties the object of his genial satire. No one, of course, doubted their pluck or their patriotic spirit, but there were many who contended that their brief period of annual training was far too short to be of any real value, and that, in the event of war, many months of strenuous work would be required to fit them to take their place in the field by the side of seasoned troops. Never were critics more speedily confounded. For though, at the outset, necessarily much inferior in such matters as marksmanship, quickness in taking cover, and reconnoitring to the regular soldier with months or sometimes years of continuous training behind him, the intelligence and dash of the young man from the office or shop enabled him to master his duties with astonishing rapidity, while in courage and tenacity he very quickly showed that he had little or nothing to learn from his professional comrade. Indeed, it was a Scottish Territorial who was the hero of what in the opinion of one who witnessed it must be regarded as one of the most magnificent acts of gallantry and devotion that the modern battle-field has ever seen. On the night of 11–12 June, 1915, during the engagement at Givenchy, a party of the Lanarkshire Territorials (8th Battn. Highland Light Infantry), under the command of Lieut. Martin a young officer, whose unfailing good humour and pluck had made him exceedingly popular, was sent out for the purpose of destroying a German barricade. Some sharp fighting ensued, and while this was at its height a powerful German mine was fired, either intentionally or by accident. When the Scotsmen returned to the British trenches, it was found that Lieut. Martin was missing, and though several of his men volunteered to go back and search for him, and crawled about in all directions in the darkness, they could discover no trace of him. When day broke, however, one of the British sentries caught sight of someone moving in the midst of a mass of loose earth close to the parapet of the German trench. It was the missing officer, who had been wounded and stunned by the explosion of the mine, and half buried by the debris which it had raised, and who now, having recovered consciousness, was endeavouring to work his way clear of the earth which was pinning him down. There he lay, right at the foot of the German parapet, only some ten feet of earth between him and the most pitiless enemy that ever waged an unholy war. His very nearness to them hid him from their view, but already they must have heard him moving, for presently, when the sun was a little higher, the ugly head of a periscope, with its ghoulish eye, was thrust up from the German trench, and leered at the wounded officer below. A rifle rang out from the British lines, and a well-aimed bullet smashed the periscope to pieces, and though the Germans essayed repeatedly by the same means to ascertain Lieut. Martin's exact position, our marksmen shattered each periscope the moment it appeared. For the British had been fighting the unspeakable Hun too long to entertain the idea that the enemy wished to discover where the wounded man lay with any idea of throwing him a rope and drawing him in. They did not even expect them to be kind and merciful and kill him. No; they intended to leave him there in the cruel glare of a cloudless June sky, to serve as a bait to draw some gallant British soldier to his death; and it was to ascertain the spot upon which their bombs might most effectively be thrown that they had used the periscope. And, meantime, the lieutenant's company volunteered to a man to rush the German trench at dusk, cost what it might. But it was feared that before dusk fell the wounded officer, if left all day in the scorching sun, might be beyond human aid; and so, towards midday, when the suspense had become almost unendurable, permission was obtained by one of the brave Scotsmen to attempt the apparently impossible task of bringing him in—only one, for the commanding officer refused to consent to any more of his men throwing their lives away. There were many eager volunteers, but, after some discussion, L.-Corpl. William Angus, a young man born and bred in the Lanarkshire town of Carluke, where Lieut. Martin lived, was chosen. Angus was warned by an officer that he was going to certain death, but he was not dismayed. 'It does not matter much, sir, whether sooner or later,' was his firm reply. But before recounting this act of truly superb heroism, it may be as well to describe more fully the scene of it. The Germans were entrenched on a bare dry knoll, some seventy yards from the British, their trench having a high, irregular parapet, beneath which lay Lieut. Martin, now perfectly still. In front of our lines, for a distance of some thirty paces, there grew the self-sown corn of the previous year's harvest, rank with weeds and affording good cover. But for the remainder of the distance between the trenches every square inch of the ground was commanded by the enemy's fire, and there was no shelter whatever. Arrangements had been made for a heavy covering fire, which, it was hoped, would prevent a single German raising his head above the parapet; the trench was lined by our best riflemen, and on a ridge behind, and perhaps six feet higher, a machine-gun had been mounted. But, however accurate this fire might be, it could not interfere with the marksmen behind the steel shield or with the bomb-throwers. At two o'clock in the afternoon Angus slipped over the British parapet, and, flattened to earth, began to work his way towards the hostile trench, using

William Angus.

every precaution that training and skill have given to the soldier. No finer tribute, indeed, could have been paid to the way in which the young Territorial had been taught his business than the fact that he reached the German parapet without drawing the enemy's fire. Quickly, but coolly, he did his work. He was seen to touch the lieutenant's arm and whisper to him. Then he raised him up and placed a flask of brandy between his teeth, and together they sat at the base of the parapet for a few moments to gather strength for the fearful ordeal before them. The enemy had heard their movements by now, but the storm of bullets from the British trenches kept all German heads under cover. However, at that moment, one of the Huns lobbed a bomb just over the parapet. There was a loud explosion, a cloud of dust, and Angus and the wounded officer, realizing that it must be now or never, made their dash for safety, the strong man supporting the weak and guiding his faltering footsteps. And then the Germans made their mistake. The fastest sprinter in the world would have had but one chance in a thousand of crossing that open space alive if only they had been content to leave the work of murder to their snipers. Instead, they threw more bombs, raising great pillars of smoke and dust, which made it impossible for their riflemen to see where to aim, though they emptied their magazines at random. Suddenly, from out of the midst of a cloud of dust, there emerged two figures, which stumbled painfully towards the British lines, falling, rising, and falling again. Lieut. Martin managed to crawl in; L.-Corpl. Angus, rising sore wounded to his feet, became separated from the officer. A dozen bombs burst around him as he made for the trench at a different point; but he left the line of fire clear, and rifles and machine guns poured in a torrent of bullets, under cover of which he got in. He was wounded in no less than forty places, while his fellow-townsman, to save whom he had so gallantly faced almost certain death, was wounded in three places. Happily, neither was dangerously hurt, and both eventually recovered. The heroic young Territorial received the Victoria Cross, 'for most conspicuous bravery and devotion to duty,' at the hands of the King himself." L.-Corpl. Angus's Victoria Cross was gazetted 29 June, 1915: "William Angus, No. 7709, L.-Corpl., 8th (Lanark) Battn. (Territorial Force) Highland Light Infantry. Date of Act of Bravery: 12 June, 1915. For most conspicuous bravery and devotion to duty at Givenchy, on the 12th June, 1915, in voluntarily leaving his trench under very heavy bomb and rifle fire, and rescuing a wounded officer who was lying within a few yards of the enemy's position. L.-Corpl. Angus had no chance whatever in escaping the enemy's fire when undertaking this very gallant action, and in effecting the rescue he sustained about forty wounds from bombs, some of them being very serious."

BARTER, FREDERICK, Company Sergt.-Major, was born in Cardiff 17 Jan. 1891, son of Mr. and Mrs. Samuel Barter. He was educated in Cardiff, and having served his time with the Colours, he joined the Special Reserve, and was working for the Cardiff Gas Company at the time of the outbreak of the European War. He was called up as a Special Reservist. "Deeds that thrill the Empire" (pages 694–697) says: "At daybreak on 16 May, 1915, after very effective artillery preparation, which swept away the German wire entanglements as though they had been matchwood, and in places almost obliterated their trenches, the British infantry attacked the enemy's position immediately east of Festubert, where their front showed a pronounced salient. Two brigades of the 7th Division—the 20th and 22nd—and part of the Indian Corps, were the troops to which the movement was entrusted. The latter attacked on the left near Richebourg l'Avoué; the 20th Brigade moved from Rue du Bois south-eastward; while the 22nd Brigade advanced to the south-east of Festubert against the Rue d'Ouvert. The most successful movement was that of the 22nd Brigade on our right, composed of the 2nd Queen's, 1st Royal Welsh Fusiliers and the 1st South Staffords, with the 2nd Warwicks and the 8th Royal Scots in support, which advanced for more than a mile, and succeeded in obliterating the enemy's main communication trench near the Rue d'Ouvert. The German entrenchments in the Festubert area were curiously complicated, forming, in fact, a veritable network, and this circumstance naturally put a premium on bomb-throwing, the old eighteenth-century weapon being the most efficient we possessed for close-quarter fighting. Brilliant work was done by the bombers of the 1st Grenadiers, in the 20th Brigade, and by a party of the Post Office Rifles, on the following day, the four survivors being awarded the Distinguished Conduct Medal. But these feats were surpassed by those performed by a party of the 1st Welsh Fusiliers, led by Company Sergt.-Major Barter. When his battalion reached the first line of German trenches, Barter called for bomb-throwers to enable him to extend our line. With the eight volunteers who responded, he proceeded to deal out death and mutilation on so wholesale a scale that in a very short time he had cleared five hundred yards of hostile trenches and captured three officers and one hundred and two men, besides finding and cutting eleven mine leads, situated about twenty yards apart. For this most splendid exploit, worthy to rank with that of Sergt. Michael O'Leary at Cuinchy, Company Sergt.-Major Barter was awarded the Victoria Cross, whilst subsequently he was promoted to the rank of Second Lieutenant." For his services in the European War he was awarded the Victoria Cross [London Gazette, 29 June, 1915]: "Frederick Barter, No. 3902, Company Sergt.-Major, Special Reserve, attached 1st Battn. The Royal Welsh Fusiliers. Date of Act of Bravery: 16 May, 1915. For most conspicuous bravery and marked ability at Festubert, on the 16th May, 1915. When in the first line of German trenches, Company Sergt.-Major Barter called for volunteers to enable him to extend our line, and with eight men who responded he attacked the German position with bombs, capturing three German officers and 102 men, and 500 yards of their trenches. He subsequently found and cut eleven of the enemy's mine leads, situated about twenty yards apart." One of the eight men who assisted Sergt.-Major Barter in this exploit was a private of the 2nd Queen's, who went by the name of Thomas Hardy, but he had told Barter in confidence that this was not his real name, which he was only to disclose in the event of his death. He said that his real name was Smart, and that he had been a captain in the 53rd Sikhs. He was in India when the war broke out, came home on sick leave, and joined the Queen's Royal West Surrey Regt. as a private, in order to make sure of getting to the front. He was a splendid-looking man, obviously a gentleman, and much beloved by all his comrades. "In the bomb attack Private Hardy showed such splendid courage that, in Lieut. Barter's opinion, he would, had he survived, have certainly been awarded the Distinguished Conduct Medal. 'He was,' said he, in conversation with a representative of a London paper, 'about ten yards from the first German trench when he got wounded. It was a terrible blow in the right shoulder. Some of our men bound up the wound, and I shouted "Hardy, go back!" I could see, however, that he was determined to go at the enemy. Hardy answered: "It's all right, for I am left-handed." The next thing I saw was "Hardy" rushing off to our right, and, with a bravery that seemed his characteristic, he commenced to slam bombs at the enemy. He carried on like that for about twenty or thirty yards, and he was eventually shot through the head, half of which was blown off. He died a hero's death, and no one regretted his end more than I did, for I was probably attached to him more than anyone else, and was afforded opportunities of seeing his sterling worth. . . . "Hardy" was a man of splendid physique—I should say he was quite six feet high, and there can be no doubt of this, that he was six feet of real manhood. A more fearless fellow it would have been impossible to find. We all loved him. I have never seen a happier man. He seemed to live to beat the Germans.'" Lieut. Barter later was appointed Instructor to Western Command Grenade School, Prees Heath, Salop. Later, 1916, went back to France. Left France Feb. 1917; joined the Indian Army, sailed for India March, 1917; arrived India May, 1917; posted to 4/3rd Q.A.D. Gurkha Rifles stationed at Kohat, N.W.F.P. Appointed Brigade Bombing Officer. Left for service in Palestine Dec. 1917, and posted the 2/3rd Q.A.O. Gurkha Rifles. Won Military Cross in March, 1918; later made Acting Captain (present rank); invalided home with fever Jan. 1919.

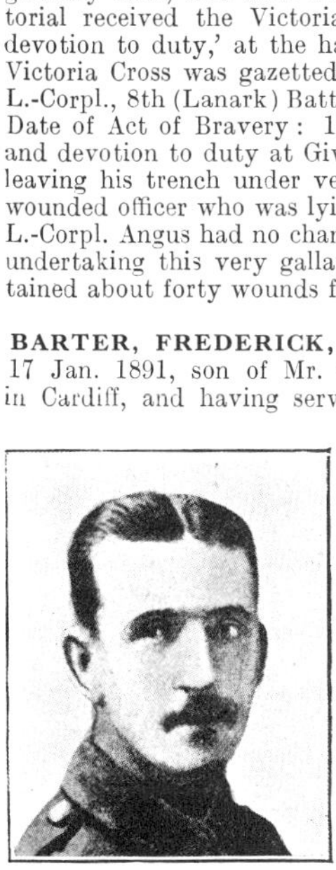
Frederick Barter.

FINLAY, DAVID, L.-Corpl., joined the Army and served in the European War. He was awarded the Victoria Cross [London Gazette, 29 June, 1915]: "David Finlay, No. 1780, L.-Corpl., 2nd Battn. Black Watch (Royal Highlanders). Date of Act of Bravery: 9 May, 1915. For most conspicuous bravery and devotion to duty, on the 9th May, 1915, near Rue du Bois, when he led a bombing party of twelve men with the greatest gallantry in the attack until ten of them had fallen. L.-Corpl. Finlay then ordered the two survivors to crawl back, and he himself went to the assistance of a wounded man, and carried him over a distance of one hundred yards of fire-swept ground into cover, quite regardless of his own personal safety. "Deeds that thrill the Empire" (pages 478–482) says of Finlay's exploit: "On Sunday, 9 May, 1915, the French began their great attack on the German position between La Targette and Carency, the advance of the infantry being preceded by the most terrific bombardment yet seen in Western Europe, which simply ate up the countryside for miles. On the same day, chiefly as an auxiliary to the effort of our Allies in the Artois, the British took the offensive in the Festubert area, the section selected being that between Festubert and Bois Grenier. The 8th Division, on our left, advanced from Rouges Bancs, on the upper course of the River des Layes, towards Fromelles and the northern part of the Aubers Ridge; while on our right, part of the 1st Corps and the Indian Corps advanced from the Rue du Bois, south of Neuve Chapelle, towards the Bois du Biez. The 8th Division captured the first line of German trenches about Rouges Bancs, and some detachments carried sections of their second and even their third line. But the violence of the enemy's machine-gun fire from fortified posts on the flanks rendered the captured trenches untenable, and practically all the ground the valour of our men had won had to be abandoned. South of Neuve Chapelle, the 1st Corps and the Indian Corps met with no greater success, though they displayed the utmost gallantry in the face of a most murderous fire, and many acts of signal heroism were performed, notably that which gained L.-Corpl. Finlay the Victoria Cross. The Bareilly Brigade, of which the 2nd Black Watch formed part, attacked early in the afternoon; but while our artillery preparation was still in progress, L.-Corpl. Finlay advanced at the head of a bombing party of ten men, with the object of getting as near the enemy's trenches as they could under cover of the bombardment. It was a desperate enterprise, for the German parapet bristled with machine guns, and each one of the party knew that his chance of returning in safety was slight indeed. About fifteen or twenty yards from our trenches, which were separated by some one hundred and fifty yards from the Germans, was a ditch full of water, ten to twelve feet wide and between four and five feet deep, spanned by three bridges. The party had got as far as the ditch before the enemy realized that they were advancing, when a fierce rifle and machine-gun fire was at once

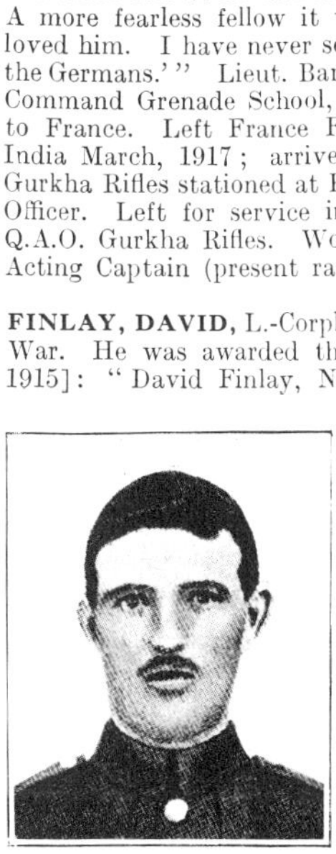
David Finlay.

opened upon them, and eight out of Finlay's ten men were put out of action, as all made for one of the bridges. Two were shot dead while crossing the bridge, and the others killed immediately upon reaching the other side. Undismayed by the fate of their comrades, Finlay and the two survivors rushed on, and had covered about eighty yards when a shell burst just behind Finlay. He was uninjured, but so violent was the concussion that it knocked him flat on his back, and he lost consciousness for some ten minutes. When he recovered his senses, he saw one of his two men lying on the ground about five paces to his left, and, crawling to him, he found that he had been wounded in two places. He opened his field-dressing and bandaged him up, and then, quite regardless of his own safety, half carried and half dragged him back to the British trench. L.-Corpl.—now Sergt.—David Finlay, who was awarded the Victoria Cross 'for most conspicuous bravery and devotion to duty,' is twenty-two years of age, and his home is in Fifeshire."

LYNN, JOHN, Private, was born in 1887, foster-son of John Harrison, of 20, Hindsley Place, Forest Hill, S.E., and of Elizabeth Harrison, having adopted him from three days old. He was educated at Christ Church Schools, Forest Hill, and joined the Army at the outbreak of war. He served in the European War, in all battles, until his death, and was awarded the Victoria Cross [London Gazette, 29 June, 1915]: "John Lynn, No. 1272, Private, 2nd Battn. Lancashire Fusiliers. Date of Act of Bravery: 2 May, 1915. For most conspicuous bravery near Ypres, on the 2nd May, 1915. When the Germans were advancing behind their wave of asphyxiating gas, Private Lynn, although almost overcome by the deadly fumes, handled his machine gun with very great effect against the enemy, and when he could not see them, he moved his gun higher upon the parapet, which enabled him to bring even more effective fire to bear, and eventually checked any further advance. The great courage displayed by this soldier had a fine effect on his comrades in the very trying circumstances. He died the following day from the effects of gas poisoning." "Deeds that thrill the Empire" (pages 7–11) says: "Private Lynn, of the Lancashire Fusiliers, might almost be said to have been born a hero. From the moment the Great War broke out and the British Expeditionary Force landed in France, he attracted the attention of his officers and comrades by his cheerfulness in adversity and his utter contempt of danger. Indeed, he might almost be said to have set up his own standard of courage, for the magnificent exploit which brought him a hero's death and the Victoria Cross was but the crowning act of a life of heroism, and merely an eclipse of his own previous records. He was not destined to be fêted and acclaimed, to hear his name become a household word, to see himself the idol of admiring thousands. Indeed, death robbed him of the knowledge that his supreme act of self-sacrifice had not passed unnoticed. But wherever the English language is spoken, the name of Lynn will be held in honoured remembrance, for his life and death added a new page to the long chapter of our national glory. The campaign had not been a month old when Lynn made his mark. The regiment was strenuously engaged in the region of the river Aisne, and the Germans were on the point of delivering one of their massed attacks when his machine gun jammed, a habit to which even the best of machine guns is addicted. The situation was critical, for a machine gun is worth a thousand men at such a moment. Quick as thought Lynn dismounted his gun, carried it to the rear under a heavy fire, repaired it with the calm precision of a boy playing in his nursery, and returned in time to annihilate the attacking column. For so valuable a service he was awarded the Distinguished Conduct Medal. No one was more surprised than he when the good news was announced, for to himself he pictured his deed as a simple act of duty, neither requiring nor deserving any special recognition. Of such stuff are heroes made. The long winter passed, and with it the period of cheerless days and sleepless nights in the welter of Flemish mud. The spring dried the ground. The weather became warmer, and even the professional grumbler, who flourishes in every British regiment, found himself becoming moderately contented. And then, as the end of April was approaching, the enemy showed that he had lost none of his cunning. What he had lost was his sense of chivalry, even of soldierly decency, and in a moment he told the world that there was no level to which he would not stoop if military advantage might be snatched thereby. He started out to poison his foes with the most virulent gases his chemists and scientists could find. All the world knows the story of the Second Battle of Ypres, how for three weeks our men, surprised and unprepared, held their ground round the ruined city while the poisonous fumes rolled over them, enveloped them, choked and killed them. On one of the most critical days of that most critical period the Lancashire Fusiliers were peacefully making their tea in the trenches. Some six hundred yards away was the enemy's line. There was a lull in the awful storm of shelling which had raged incessantly for a week. Suddenly the sentries called attention to a greenish-yellow smoke which was rising from the German trenches. The regiment had not had practical experience of the gas before, as they had only just arrived at that part of the front. Respirators of a sort had been issued to them the day before, but their efficiency was uncertain, and, indeed, they were replaced by a new pattern immediately afterwards. In ignorance of what was happening, the men watched the advancing cloud with no little curiosity. The Germans were seen retiring from their front trench, and immediately Lynn got his machine gun on to them with great effect. In a few moments, however, the poisonous vapour was rolling over the parapet, filling every hollow in the ground, and sinking to the bottom of the trench. There was no escape. The men, choked and blinded, fell writhing on the ground, and almost immediately came the order to retire to reserve trenches. Within a few seconds the trench was left to the dead, the dying, and a mere handful of British soldiers, among them Private Lynn. In the agony and confusion of that crisis Lynn realized that behind that cloud of gas the enemy were advancing, and that the trench was as good as lost. He made up his mind that the trench should not be lost. There was no time to fix his respirator, though his eyes and lungs were full of the poisonous fumes, and his efforts to breathe brought the blood to his mouth. One by one his comrades succumbed and dropped, and soon he was alone. The advancing Germans were near now, confident that their new weapon had delivered their enemies into their hands. They expected a trench empty except for corpses. They were mistaken. The very might and majesty of Britain stood waiting for them in the person of a simple private soldier. With a bound Lynn was on the parapet, and had trained his machine gun straight ahead through the gas. The Germans could not see him, and they fell in heaps, until the remnant lost heart and retired defeated. No German soldier set foot in the trench which the valour of one man had saved. Meanwhile reinforcements had been brought up, and the Lancashire Fusiliers prepared to charge and recover the trench which they had given up for lost. What was their amazement on discovering it tenanted, not by the enemy, but by Lynn, now in the last stage of exhaustion, but still fighting his gun from the top of the parapet. They lifted him up and tenderly carried him away to a dug-out. Not even then did the hero's spirit fail him. A short time after the alarm was given for a second attack. Lynn left the dug-out at once, and made a frantic effort to reach his gun. It was too late. The deadly poison had done its work. Only those who have seen the sufferings caused by gas-poisoning can realize the agonies he endured before death, more merciful than the Germans, released him from his pain twenty-four hours later. 'Somewhere in France' Lynn sleeps his last sleep, but he has a place in our hearts and memories, in the imperishable records of our fighting race."

John Lynn.

The following extracts were sent from Forest Hill:

"Glorious and heroic deeds in the field of battle are, during this terrible world conflict, chronicled almost daily; but of all the wonderful acts of heroism that have so far been recorded, none exceed in pluck and daring the one that secured for a Forest Hill hero that most coveted of honours, the award of a Victoria Cross. The pity is that this local hero was foully done to death by the Germans, not by the ordinary methods of warfare, to which the enemy had agreed at International Conference, but by poison. His memory will be revered by all patriots, and by none more than those who live in the district in which the heroic soldier was bred and born. His name will surely never be forgotten. To read of the great deed which secured for him the highest of all earthly awards, is in itself exalting. In the Borough of Lewisham's Roll of Honour the name of Private John Lynn will occupy a noble place. Although Lynn was this brave soldier's name really, he was more generally known by the name of his foster-parents, Mr. and Mrs. Harrison, of Malham Road, Forest Hill. He was adopted by them when only three days old, and they have worthily fulfilled the obligations they laid upon themselves. John Lynn, was to them, as it were, their own son, and the affection and care showered upon him has not been wasted efforts. No parents could be more proud of a son than Mr. and Mrs. Harrison of their foster-child, and, naturally enough, their grief is great to think that he is no more; that in performing this great deed he gave his life for his country, the noblest action that can fall to the lot of any man or woman. Among his old associates in Forest Hill he will always be affectionately remembered as 'Johnny Harrison,' more particularly by his old school chums who attended Christ Church School, Forest Hill, and they will read with pride of the way in which he distinguished himself, although this will be tinged with sorrow at his untimely death at the age of 27. But the deed which brought him the V.C. was not the only brave one that he had accomplished since he had been out at the front, for he had already been awarded the Distinguished Conduct Medal, a fact which only demonstrates the pluck, nerve and high sense of patriotism and duty, which Private John Lynn possessed. He had been in the Army for some time, but before joining the Lancashire Fusiliers was a sailor on the Exmouth. On joining the Fusiliers he became a member of the band, and had already served with his regiment in Malta and India. The Lancashire Fusiliers had been hotly engaged in fighting round Ypres, and the following is a description of the battle in which Private Lynn so nobly won the V.C. There had been a brief lull after the struggle, but early the next morning the Germans advanced, and began to envelop the Durham Regt. In these circumstances a retirement was ordered, but none of the brave men engaged lost spirit for a moment, but showed stubborn courage all the way through. Although their casualties were heavy, a stand was made which lasted several days. The Germans then 'gassed' that part of the line which the Lancashire Fusiliers and the Essex Regt. were holding. Most of the men had respirators, but they were not very effective on this occasion. In some of the trenches the men withdrew before the gas, and when it had passed over the trench, charged through it and reoccupied their positions. It was at this stage that Private John Lynn distinguished himself. As soon as he saw the greenish cloud rolling towards the British trenches, Lynn, without stopping to put on his respirator, turned his machine gun on the advancing gas, also on to the German trenches beyond it. Even when the gas reached him he would not stop, but kept up a fierce fire. When the Germans began to leave their trenches to attack the half-unconscious but still determined line of British, Lynn, with 'superhuman' effort—for he was almost choked and coughing badly by this time—lifted his gun right on to the parapet of the trench, and from there continued to play upon the advancing enemy. This extraordinary act—daring as it was, and actuated by the greatest pluck—was the means of preventing the Germans making any further advance, for so hot and withering was the fire which Lynn poured upon them that they were compelled to seek a hurried retreat, and finally sought cover behind their own line after losing many of their men. Even then, however, Lynn was not satisfied, but had to be literally dragged away from his gun. He was removed on an ambulance, and died the same day.

" A chum of our young hero soldier describes the incident in the following language : ' We were in the trenches at " Suicide Corner "—that is what we call Ypres. My chum, with his machine gun and four men of the section, were at the end of the trench. It was a fierce fight ; they came on in hundreds. After about an hour and a half, and we were getting plenty of losses, we were told of another big attack coming. I noticed that he was alone with the gun, and it was then that Jackie saved us. He lifted his gun from its hole right on to the top of the parapet, and in full view of the advancing Germans. He was feeling the gas very badly. But he never flinched, although bullets whistled by his head and the enemy came along in hundreds. When he got his gun in the open, he was able to swing it round into the Germans, who were getting closer and closer at each rush, and our fellows were dropping out. He stuck it with his gun until he collapsed, gasping for breath and black in the face with the awful pain of the gas in him. But he had saved us, for we got no more German attacks. The way he mowed 'em down was a sight. No one could have advanced under his fire. Then we found him lying there black in the face. We lifted him up, and then he said, " This is the last carry, Flash." That's my nickname, and not long afterwards he died.' Such is the plain, unvarnished story, which redounds to the credit of the whole British Army. Glorious it was, and it must surely be the regret of all who read this graphic description that Private Lynn did not live, in order that the people of Lewisham might have had the opportunity of doing him public honour. To his foster-parents the deepest sympathy will be extended, but, though dead, his example will live and be an incentive for others to copy.

" In the long Despatch from Sir John French on Monday, Lynn's act of heroism is mentioned ; in fact, his is the only name given in that part of the Despatch referring to individual deeds of gallantry. The words are those of Sir Herbert Plumer, who was entrusted with the work of retirement to a new line during the Second Battle of Ypres : ' There had been many cases of individual gallantry. As instances may be given the following : During one of the heavy attacks made against our infantry gas was seen rolling forward from the enemy's trenches. Private Lynn, of the 2nd Lancashire Fusiliers, at once rushed to the machine gun, without waiting to adjust his respirator. Single-handed, he kept his gun in action the whole time the gas was rolling over, actually hoisting it on a parapet to get a better field of fire. Although nearly suffocated with the gas, he poured a stream of lead into the advancing enemy, and checked their attack. He was carried to his dug-out, but hearing another attack was imminent, he tried to get back to his gun. Twenty-four hours later he died in great agony from the effects of the gas.' "

RIPLEY, JOHN, Corpl., served in the European War, and was awarded the Victoria Cross [London Gazette, 29 June, 1915] : " John Ripley, No. 2832, Corpl., 1st Battn. The Black Watch. Date of Act of Bravery : 9 May, 1915. For most conspicuous bravery at Rue du Bois, on the 9th May, 1915. When leading his section on the right of the platoon in the assault, he was the first man of the battalion to ascend the enemy's parapet, and from there he directed those following him to the gaps in the German wire entanglements. He then led his section through a breach in the parapet to a second line of trench, which had previously been decided upon as the final objective in this part of our line. In that position, Corpl. Ripley, with seven or eight men, established himself, blocking both flanks and arranging a fire position,

John Ripley.

which he continued to defend until all his men had fallen and he himself had been badly wounded in the head."

SHARPE, CHARLES, Corpl., joined the Army, and served in the European War. He was awarded the Victoria Cross [London Gazette, 29 June, 1915] : " Charles Sharpe, No. 7942, Acting Corpl., 2nd Battn. Lincolnshire Regt. Date of Act of Bravery : 9 May, 1915. For most conspicuous bravery, near Rouges Bancs, on the 9th May, 1915. When in charge of a blocking party sent forward to take a portion of the German trench, he was the first to reach the enemy's position, and, using bombs with great determination and effect, he himself cleared them out of a trench fifty yards long. By this time all his party had fallen, and he was then joined by four other men, with whom he attacked the enemy with bombs, and captured a further trench 250 yards long." Private Dunderdale, of the 2nd Battn.

Charles Sharpe.

Lincolnshire Regt., was decorated on 9 May, 1915, for rushing across the open at a time when the enemy's machine-gun and rifle fire was too strong to enable our men to advance over the parapet in open order. Private Dunderdale crawled through a hole in full view of the enemy, and went to the assistance of Corpl. Sharpe, who

was bombing the Germans alone. He forced his way along the enemy's trenches, and succeeded in clearing about two hundred and fifty yards, which was held the whole day.

UPTON, JAMES, Corpl., was born in the year 1888 at Meadows, Nottingham, and joined the Army on 24 July, 1906, at Derby, serving from 24 July, 1906, to 29 March, 1919 ; in France 4 Nov. 1914, to 7 Feb. 1918—three years ninety-six days. He was demobilized 30 March, 1919. He was awarded the Victoria Cross [London Gazette, 29 June, 1915] : " James Upton, No. 10082, Corpl., 1st Battn. Sherwood Foresters (Nottinghamshire and Derbyshire Regt.). Date of Act of Bravery : 9 May, 1915. For most conspicuous bravery, near Rouges Bancs, on the 9th May, 1915. During the whole of this day Corpl. Upton displayed the greatest courage in rescuing the wounded while exposed to very heavy rifle and artillery fire, going close to the enemy's parapet, regardless of his own personal safety. One wounded man was killed by a shell while this non-commissioned officer was carrying him. When Corpl. Upton was not actually carrying in the wounded,

James Upton.

he was engaged in bandaging and dressing the serious cases in front of our parapet, exposed to the enemy's fire." An account of his heroic deed is given in " Deeds that thrill the Empire " (page 129) : " On Sunday, 9 May, 1915, in conjunction with a forward movement of the French troops between the right of our line and Arras, our 1st Corps and the Indian Corps attacked the German position between Neuve Chapelle and Givenchy, while the 8th Division of the 4th Corps attacked the enemy's trenches in the neighbourhood of Rouges Bancs, to the north-west of Fromelles. Our artillery preparation at Rouges Bancs began shortly before 5 a.m., and half an hour later our infantry advanced to the assault of the German trenches, which were separated from ours by a distance of some 250 yards, the intervening ground being destitute of every vestige of cover. The attack was started by the East Lancashires and two companies of the 1st Sherwood Foresters ; but the artillery preparation had been altogether inadequate, and our men came up against unbroken wire and parapets. Many casualties occurred during the advance, and many more during the subsequent retirement. About 7 a.m., after a second bombardment of the enemy's position, the remaining two companies of the 1st Sherwood Foresters scaled the parapet and lined up about thirty yards in front of it, where they lay down in a shallow trench, to await the order to advance. With them was a young Lincolnshire man, Corpl. James Upton, who on that day was destined to win the most coveted distinction of the British soldier. The ground in front of the Sherwoods was strewn with the wounded, some of them terribly mutilated, and their cries for help were heart-rending. At last Corpl. Upton could listen to them no longer ; come what might, he was resolved to go to their succour. Crawling out of the trench, he made his way towards the enemy's lines, and had not gone far when he came upon a sergeant of the Worcesters who was wounded in the thigh, the leg being broken. Upton bandaged him up as well as he could with an old flag, and put his leg into splints, which done, he carried him on his back to our trench, and consigned him to the care of some of his comrades. Then, discarding the pack and rest of his equipment, which included a couple of jam-tin bombs, he went out again, and found another man, who had been hit in the stomach. As this man was too big and heavy to carry, he unrolled his waterproof sheet, placed him on it, and dragged him in. Going out for the third time, he was proceeding to carry in a man with both legs shattered, and had got within ten yards of the trench, when a high-explosive shell burst close to them. A piece of it struck the wounded man in the back, killing him instantaneously, and giving Upton, though he escaped unhurt, a bad shock. This obliged him to rest for a while, but as soon as he felt better the heroic non-commissioned officer resumed his work of mercy, and venturing out again and again into the fire-swept open, succeeded in rescuing no less than ten more wounded men. During the remainder of the day until eight at night he was engaged in dressing the serious cases in front of our trenches, exposed the whole time to a heavy artillery and rifle fire, from which, however, he emerged without a scratch." Corpl. Upton, who was awarded the Victoria Cross, was at the time about twenty-six years of age. His home is in Lincoln. His decoration was gazetted 29 June, 1915 : " James Upton, No. 10082, Corpl., 1st Battn. The Sherwood Foresters (Nottinghamshire and Derbyshire Regt.). Date of Act of Bravery : 9 May, 1915. For most conspicuous bravery near Rouges Bancs on the 9th of May, 1915. During the whole of this day Corpl. Upton displayed the greatest courage in rescuing the wounded while exposed to very heavy rifle and artillery fire, going close to the enemy's parapet, regardless of his own personal safety. One wounded man was killed by a shell while this non-commissioned officer was carrying him. When Corpl. Upton was not actually carrying in the wounded he was engaged in bandaging and dressing the serious cases in front of our parapet, exposed to the enemy's fire." Corpl. Upton married, on 20 July, 1915, at Lincoln, Mary Jane Chambers, and they have a son, Thomas Herbert, born 10 May, 1918.

Edward Warner.

WARNER, EDWARD, Private, joined the Army, and served in the European War.

He was awarded the Victoria Cross [London Gazette, 29 June, 1915]: " Edward Warner, No. 7602, Private, 1st Battn. Bedfordshire Regt. Date of Act of Bravery : 1 May, 1915. For most conspicuous bravery, near Hill 60, on the 1st May, 1915. After Trench No. 46 had been vacated by our troops, consequent on a gas attack, Private Warner entered it single-handed, in order to prevent the enemy taking possession. Reinforcements were sent to Private Warner, but could not reach him owing to the gas. He then came back and brought up more men, by which time he was completely exhausted, but the trench was held until the enemy's attack ceased. This very gallant soldier died shortly afterwards from the effects of gas poisoning."

London Gazette, 3 July, 1915.—" War Office, 3 July, 1915. His Majesty the King has been graciously pleased to approve of the award of the Victoria Cross to No. 3026, L.-Corpl. Leonard James Keyworth, 24th (County of London) Battn. The London Regt. (The Queen's), Territorial Force."

KEYWORTH, LEONARD JAMES, L.-Corpl., was born at Lincoln 12 Aug. 1893, and joined the 24th London Regt. at the beginning of the war ; served in France, and was promoted Lance-Corporal. This young

Leonard J. Keyworth.

Territorial of twenty-two took part in the British attack on the enemy's position at Givenchy on the night of 25–26 May, 1915. " Deeds that thrill the Empire" (page 69) says : " Keyworth's battalion having already made a successful assault on a part of the German line, determined to follow up this success by a bomb attack. The bomb-throwers, to the number of seventy-five, advanced to the attack from a small British trench situated on a slight hill, less than forty yards from the enemy's first-line trenches ; but though the distance was short, the ground between had been so badly cut up by shell fire that they could not progress very rapidly, and before they were half-way across the majority of them had already fallen beneath the withering fire from rifle and machine gun which was opened upon them. But the rest, undismayed by the fate of their comrades, came bravely on, and among them was L.-Corpl. Keyworth. Halting a few yards from the parapet, Keyworth began to throw his bombs. Then, springing on to the top of the parapet itself, he took a deliberate aim at the Germans beneath him, and rained his deadly missiles upon them with the most murderous effect. When his stock was exhausted, he leaped down, replenished it from the bag of some dead or dying comrade, and then returned to the attack. For two hours he continued thus, hurling, it is computed, 150 bombs on the panic-stricken Huns, until the trench was a veritable shambles, choked with the bodies of the dead and of shrieking, mutilated wretches, and presented an easy prey. And, marvellous to relate, though out of his seventy-four comrades no less than fifty-eight were either killed or wounded, and though he was continually standing fully exposed on the top of the parapet, so near to the Germans they could well-nigh have touched him with the muzzles of their rifles, Keyworth escaped without a scratch, which goes to show that dare-devil bravery such as he displayed on this occasion is often its own justification, creating as it does in the minds of an enemy a degree of amazement which renders him quite incapable of opposing it with his usual coolness and courage." He was awarded the Victoria Cross [London Gazette, 3 July, 1915]: " Leonard James Keyworth, No. 3026, L.-Corpl., 24th (County of London) Battn. The London Regt. (The Queen's). For most conspicuous bravery at Givenchy on the night of 25–26 May, 1915. After the successful assault on the German position by the 24th Battn. London Regt., efforts were made by that unit to follow up their success by a bomb-attack, during the progress of which fifty-eight men out of a total of seventy-five became casualties. During this very fierce encounter L.-Corpl. Keyworth stood fully exposed for two hours on the top of the enemy's parapet, and threw about 150 bombs amongst the Germans, who were only a few yards away."

London, Gazette, 24 July, 1915.—" His Majesty the King has been graciously pleased to award the Victoria Cross to the undermentioned Officers and Non-commissioned Officers."

JOTHAM, EUSTACE, Capt., was born 28 Nov. 1883, at Kidderminster, son of Frederick Charles Jotham, and of Mary C. A. Jotham (née Laxton). He was educated at Bromsgrove School and at Sandhurst, and joined

Eustace Jotham.

the 51st Sikhs ; served in the European War on the North-West Frontier of India, and was awarded the Victoria Cross [London Gazette, 24 July, 1915]: " Eustace Jotham, Capt., 51st Sikhs, Frontier Force. Date of Act of Bravery : 7 Jan. 1915. For most conspicuous bravery on 7 Jan. 1915, at Spina Khaisora (Tochi Valley). During operations against the Khostwal tribesmen, Capt. Jotham, who was commanding a party of about a dozen of the North Waziristan Militia, was attacked in a nullah, and almost surrounded by an overwhelming force of some 1,500 tribesmen. He gave the order to retire, and could have himself escaped, but most gallantly sacrificed his own life by attempting to effect the rescue of one of his men who had lost his horse."

The Victoria Cross was presented to Mr. F. C. Jotham by H.M. King George V. at Buckingham Palace, 29 Nov. 1916.

Capt. Jotham's father received the following, among many other, letters after his son's death. The first is from Lieut.-Colonel Sir George Roos-Keppel, G.C.I.E., K.C.S.I., etc., etc. :

" Chief Commissioner's Camp, N.W. Frontier Provinces,
" 1 August, 1915.

" Dear Mr. Jotham,

" I hope you will excuse my writing to you to tell you how glad I am that your son's services have been recognized by the grant of the V.C. No V.C. can have been more nobly won. Your son having miraculously cut his way through hundreds of fanatical tribesmen, deliberately turned back and went in again to save one of his sowars who was down in the mêlée, although he knew that he was practically certainly sacrificing his life. He killed seven of the enemy before his death, and his gallantry has made a deep impression, not only on the men of the North Waziristan Militia, but even on the enemy. We are all proud of him, and grateful to him for setting such a magnificent example, which is specially valuable in a critical time like the present one.

" Believe me,
" Yours very truly,
" G. Roos-Keppel."

The second letter is from Major St. Hill :

" Balgonie, Branksome Park Road, Camberley,
" 20 March, 1915.

" Dear Mr. Jotham,

" Thank you for your kind letter with particulars of your gallant son's death, and for the enclosures which I read with the greatest possible interest. Our acquaintance only lasted for six hours, but in that time I summed your son up as one of the most striking *men* that I had ever met, and I took a sincere liking for him, which I had hoped later might have developed into sincere friendship, but this was not to be. On the morning of the 1st–2nd Sept. 1913, I was in the rear coach of the Glasgow express which was telescoped by the Edinburgh express at Aisgill Junction. I was one of those who escaped practically unscathed from the coach. This coach at once caught fire, and I was working with others against time to extricate the unfortunate passengers before the coach was burnt. I noticed a man working with ceaseless energy and pluck and always in the right directions. He was on the top of the compartment, already a mass of flames, handing out the poor people as we could extricate them. The while talking to them as if nothing was at stake and cheering them with kind words. He actually, to my certain knowledge, handed out four himself, his hair singed, his coat and cap on fire, working quite unconcernedly to the last. This was your boy ! We travelled together to Leeds, and during this short journey I took to him in a way that I think I have never done to any man before. We wrote to each other at Christmas, 1913, and on the 12th Dec. I received a regimental card from him, on which he wrote that ' it was hard to be shut up in a mud (?), sun-baked fort when he longed to be in France, where he hoped I now was.' I at once replied, and to my sincere regret the letter was returned to me marked, ' Deceased, killed in action.' Hearing of his photograph in the ' Illustrated London News,' I wrote the letter which was forwarded to you, and to which you have kindly replied. Had he died with less honour to himself and glory to his country, I should have been surprised. I requested the Commandant of the R.M.C., after August, to record his great work at the fire with the War Office. This was done, and I told the Commandant then that I had never met a man who filled me with greater confidence in his personality and strength of character. He was just one of those Englishmen who for centuries have made the country famous, and who have made and extended our vast Empire without thought for himself and with no blowing of trumpets. I am proud and glad to have met him, and I shall carry his memory with me until my death. I then hope that I shall again meet him. If you have a photograph of him and can spare one, I shall be most truly thankful to you. It is hard to condole with you on your loss, when he died as we all hope that we may die when our time comes, but I am deeply sorry for you, as I am for the country, that his time was so short.

" Sincerely yours,
" Walter St. Hill,
" Major, Royal Fusiliers.
" Royal Military College, Camberley."

MOOR, GEORGE RAYMOND DALLAS, Lieut., was born in Melbourne 22 Oct. 1896, son of William Henry Moor (educated at Sandhurst, joined the South African Civil Service ; Auditor-General, Transvaal, retired) and

G. R. Dallas Moor.

Eva Moor (née Pender); and nephew of the late Sir Ralph Moor, formerly High Commissioner for Southern Nigeria. He was educated at Cheltenham College, and was commissioned into the 3rd Battn. Hampshire Regt. He had been destined for the Royal Engineers, and when he joined the Hampshire Regt. was not quite eighteen years of age. After six months' training in Egypt and England, he went with his regiment to the Dardanelles, and was at the landing at V Beach, etc., at Gallipoli. The following is an extract from a narrative by Lieut.-General Sir Beauvoir de Lisle, K.C.B., K.C.M.G., D.S.O. : " 5 June, 1915.—In the midst of this confusion the Irish counter-attacked and regained six hundred yards of our front line. Two adjacent battalions, owing to heavy casualties, were then commanded by Second Lieutenants. The battalion attacked fell back, and it was a rout. Seeing this, the commander of the battalion on the right ran across the open to rally them. To do so he had to shoot the leading four men, and the remainder came to their senses. As they were without officers, he collected them under cover, and leading them forward, regained the trenches which had been lost. It was a very remarkable performance, the more so as Second Lieut. Moor, of the 3rd Battn. Hampshire Regt., had left Cheltenham College only nine months before. I have often quoted this young officer as being one of the bravest men I have met in this war. For this act he was awarded the Victoria Cross. . . . Later in the war he was A.D.C. to Major-General W. Williams, commanding the 30th Division, and his favourite amusement, when not on duty, was to visit the front-line trenches and organize small enterprises. For leading these trench raids he gained the M.C. and bar. Unfortunately this gallant officer died in France from pneumonia, the result of Spanish influenza, just before the conclusion of hostilities, on 3 Nov. 1918." His decoration was gazetted 24 July, 1915, when he was only eighteen years of age: " George Raymond Dallas Moor, Second Lieut., 3rd Battn. Hampshire Regt. Date of Act of Bravery: 5 June, 1915. For most conspicuous bravery and resource on the 5th June, 1915, during operations south of Krithia, Dardanelles. When a detachment of a battalion on his left, which had lost all its officers, was rapidly retiring before a heavy Turkish attack, Second Lieut. Moor, immediately grasping the danger to the remainder of the line, dashed back some two hundred yards, stemmed the retirement, led back the men, and recaptured the lost trench. This young officer, who only joined the Army in Oct. 1914, by his personal bravery and presence of mind saved a dangerous situation." He was invalided home soon afterwards, suffering from dysentery. After recovering, he joined his regiment, the 1st Hampshires, in France, and was badly wounded in the arm. He returned to England, and—before regaining the use of his arm—was appointed A.D.C. to Major-General Williams, C.M.G., D.S.O., and went to France, where he won the M.C. His Military Cross was gazetted 6 Dec. 1919: " George Raymond Dallas Moor, Lieut., 1st Battn. The Hampshire Regt. For conspicuous gallantry and skill. He carried out a daylight reconnaissance all along the divisional front, in face of heavy machine-gun fire at close range, in many places well in front of our foremost posts." Lieut. G. R. Dallas Moor died of influenza at Mouveaux on the 3rd Nov. 1918. General Williams said of him: " This officer has a positive contempt for danger, and distinguishes himself on every occasion."

Major-General W. L. Williams also wrote of Lieut. Dallas Moor: " I first met Moor on 4 June, 1915, in a Turkish trench at Helles, Gallipoli—a tall, wild-looking, dark-haired boy of 18. My battalion, the 2nd Hampshires, had been ' over the top ' and gained their objectives; Moor, myself, and one other were the only officers left untouched. I said to him: ' Well done, boy! hold what you've got.' An hour afterwards I was hit, and a week afterwards I heard that Moor had been recommended for the V.C. for holding on to his trenches with magnificent gallantry, being himself the life and soul of the defence—you probably have the official account of the incident. On 17 April I was promoted to command of a division, and entitled to an A.D.C.—my first thought was for young Moor. I wrote to his Battalion Commander asking for him, saying that ' the boy has been at it so long he must want a rest.' His C.O. wrote back that he could not spare him. Early in 1918 I heard from him that he was wounded and in England, and though he could not get passed as fit he could come to me as A.D.C. He joined me 20 March, 1918, during our retreat before the German main attack. He remained with me until his death a few days before the Armistice. Whilst with me he won both the M.C. and a bar to it, and very thoroughly did he earn both. In the open fighting of the last few weeks of the war he was invaluable, day after day reconnoitring well out in front of our most advanced troops. A fine character and as fearless a soldier as ever lived. He got influenza about 4 Nov., and died a few days afterwards."

Albert Jacka.

JACKA, ALBERT, L.-Corpl., was born at Geelong, Victoria, son of Nathaniel and Elizabeth Jacka. He was educated at the State School in Victoria, which is a wonderful education, and joined the 14th Australian Infantry 7 Aug. 1914; served in the European War, taking part in the historic landing at Anzac on 25 April, 1915. He remained unwounded on the Peninsula until the evacuation of Gallipoli, and worked his way through the non-commissioned grades to commissioned rank. " At the time when he won his Victoria Cross Jacka was a Lance-Corporal of the 14th Battn., then commanded by Colonel Courtney, and he took part in the defence of Courtney's Post. On the 18th May, after three weeks of continuous fighting, Sanders Pasha made his great effort to drive the Anzacs into the sea. At this time the 14th Battn. had lost seventy-five per cent. of its effectives. Sanders threw the Turks against the war-worn, weakened Anzacs in overwhelming numbers, and the line from Quinn's Post to Courtney's bore the brunt of the attack. The Anzacs' resistance was marvellous and most successful. Not a Turk got through their lines. But at Courtney's a number of them got into a small communication trench and overcame the two or three men who held it. A wounded officer managed to give warning of the danger, and Jacka rushed into the trench alone with fixed bayonet, sheltered behind the traverse and kept the Turks from advancing. Some of his comrades came up to his assistance, but the first of them, Private Howard, was shot down as he entered into the trench. Jacka said to Lieut. Crabbe: ' You keep them here and I will take them at the other end of the trench.' He ran round and fell on the astounded Turks from their rear, shooting down five and killing two more with his bayonet, and driving three more into the hands of the men who were guarding the entrance under Lieut. Crabbe." His Victoria Cross was gazetted 24 July, 1915: " Albert Jacka, No. 435, L.-Corpl., 14th Battn. Australian Imperial Force. For most conspicuous bravery in the night of the 19th-20th May, 1915, at Courtney's Post, Gallipoli. L.-Corpl. Jacka, while holding a portion of our trench with four other men, was heavily attacked. When all except himself were killed or wounded, the trench was rushed and occupied by seven Turks. L.-Corpl. Jacka at once most gallantly attacked them single-handed and killed the whole party, five by rifle fire and two with bayonet." L.-Corpl. Jacka's was the first Victoria Cross awarded in the European War to a soldier of the Australian and New Zealand Army Corps, and until the Battle for Lone Pine, in Aug. 1915, it was the only Cross won by an Australian on Gallipoli. He was promoted to Sergeant and Company Sergt.-Major while at the Dardanelles. After the evacuation of the Peninsula he went to Egypt, and was promoted Second Lieutenant in March, 1916. He served on the Western Front from 7 July, 1917. " On the night of 5 Aug. Lieut. Jacka, with fourteen men of the 14th Battn., was sent to relieve the Anzacs who were holding an advanced trench to the north-east of the village of Pozières. It was not so much a trench really as a collection of shell-holes, joined by some shallow excavations. They had been there about half an hour when the Germans began the kind of bombardment which goes before a counter-attack, but they kept it up for hours. Seven of the forty-seven Australians were killed and four more wounded, as it was; but in an ordinary trench more damage would have been done. Very early in the morning the enemy attacked; perhaps there were about six hundred of them. The Anzacs stood up and fought hard to stem the tide of rushing Germans, but the latter went right over them. There were only seven sound Australians left, in addition to Lieut. Jacka, who was wounded. The Germans halted behind the Anzacs and formed up in a somewhat unusual manner. They seemed to gather in groups, then took a turn half left and went for our reserves. At this time Jacka managed to send back a message asking for help. The greater numbers had prevailed, and the Germans were beginning to make their way back with a considerable number of Anzac prisoners. They were evidently anxious to pick up any men who might have been left alive in the trench they had rushed. Lieut. Jacka told his seven men to fix bayonets, himself taking the rifle of one of his dead men. ' If we stay here they are bound to capture us,' he said, ' and I would sooner be dead than a prisoner. The supports cannot be long in coming up, let's go for them.' The seven were quite of the same mind, and at his word of command they went for the hundreds of the enemy, firing their rifles from the hip as they ran. Some of the Germans at once threw up their hands, but others began to fire at the Australians at very close range. These Germans were attacked with the bayonet, and some of them were killed. Then the front line of the Germans began te circle round the devoted band of Anzacs with the object of surrounding them. There was much bayonet fighting, and some of the Australian prisoners joined in the conflict. Jacka had been twice hit, but had been too busy to think about it, and the ring of enemies began to close in on the Anzacs. Just in time the supports came up; the fifty Australian prisoners were released and fifty Germans taken, while the rest of the Germans were shot down as they fled." For these services Lieut. Jacka was awarded the Military Cross. The " British Australasian " said in 1915: " An Australian patient at Woodcote Hill with an interesting experience is Private Howard, of Bendigo (14th Battn.), who was a mate of Jacka, the man who won the V.C. at Courtney's Post on 19 May. ' There were four of us Bendigo boys,' Private Howard said, ' in the 14th: Jacka, De Aruga, Poliness and myself. We were all mates together. Jacka was a Bendigo boy, though he really came from Wedderburn. But he was well known in Bendigo; I think he enlisted there. On the 19th May word came to us that the Turks had rushed a communication trench, and that Bert Jacka was holding them single-handed. There was a call for volunteers, and we three went. When we got near the trench we saw Jacka with his fixed bayonet, guarding the outlet of the communication trench, and when he saw us coming he rushed in. We rushed after him as fast as we could. I was unlucky enough to stop an expanding bullet as I entered the trench, and down I went. When the two others got in the work had been done by Jacka, single-handed. He had shot five Turks and bayoneted two more, seven altogether. As I was lying wounded in the dug-out he came to see me, and I said I was glad he had done a big thing He only said, " I think I lost my nut." ' "

TOMBS, JOSEPH, L.-Corpl., enlisted and was promoted to Lance-Corporal; served in the European War, and was awarded the Victoria Cross [London Gazette, 24 July, 1915]: " Joseph Tombs, No. 10073, L.-Corpl., 1st Battn. The King's (Liverpool Regt.). Date of Act of Bravery: 16 June, 1915. For most conspicuous gallantry near Rue du Bois, on the 16th June, 1915. On his own initiative he crawled out repeatedly under a very heavy shell and machine-gun fire, to bring in wounded men who were lying about one hundred yards in front of our trenches. He rescued four men, one of whom he dragged back by means of a rifle sling placed round his own neck and the man's body. This man was so severely wounded that unless he had been immediately attended to he must have died."

London Gazette, 16 Aug. 1915.—" Admiralty, 16 Aug. 1915. The King has been graciously pleased to approve of the grant of the Victoria Cross to the undermentioned Officers and Men for the conspicuous acts of bravery mentioned in the foregoing despatch."

UNWIN, EDWARD, Commander, was born at Forest Lodge, Hythe, Hampshire, on 17 March, 1864, son of Edward Wilberforce Unwin, M.A., J.P., and Henrietta Jane Unwin, daughter of Capt. and Mrs. Carmac. He was educated at Miss Hill's School, Cheltenham, Mr. Gedge's School, Malvern Wells, and on the Conway Training Ship. He served in Donald Currie's sailing ships and in the P. and O. Line, and in the Egyptian Navy, before joining the Royal Navy as Lieutenant on 16 Oct. 1895. He was promoted Lieut.-Commander in Oct. 1903, and Commander on retiring; was called up 29 July, 1914, and appointed Fleet Coaling Officer on Iron Duke, on Admiral Jellicoe's Staff; then in command of Hussar Feb. 1915 He was given the acting rank of Captain for the River Clyde landing. He was in charge of the lighters at the landing at Suvla on 7 Aug., and was in naval charge at Suvla Beach for the evacuation; he had charge of the Amethyst from March to Oct. on the south-east coast of America, and was in Jan. 1917, appointed Principal Naval Transport Officer, Egypt, and in Jan. 1918, P.N.T.O. Eastern Mediterranean; promoted Commodore Jan. 1919; Honours: C.M.G. for Suvla, March, 1916; Order of the Nile, 1918; C.B., 28 May, 1919. He was married on 21 April, 1897, at St. Mary's, Southampton, to Evelyn, daughter of General W. D. Carey, Royal Artillery, and they have two sons: Edward Harold Milford, born on 16 March, 1898, and John Leslie William, born 8 Aug. 1904; and two daughters: Thelma, born 25 Sept. 1902, and Enid Lorna Mary, born 3 Feb. 1906. He served in the punitive naval expedition to Benin in 1897, for which he has a Medal and clasp, and in South Africa, for which he has the Queen's Medal. He served in the European War. He was in command of the River Clyde, the converted collier which was used in the attempted landing on V Beach, Gallipoli, and his name appeared in the London Gazette of 16 Aug. 1915, as a recipient of the Victoria Cross: "Edward Unwin, Commander, Royal Navy." In General Sir Ian Hamilton's Despatch, which was published in the same Gazette, in bringing him to notice, he said: "While in River Clyde, observing that the lighters which were to form the bridge to the shore had broken adrift, Commander Unwin left the ship, and under a murderous fire attempted to get the lighters into position. He worked on, until suffering from the effects of cold and immersion, he was obliged to return to the ship, where he was wrapped up in blankets. Having in some degree recovered, he returned to his work against the doctor's order and completed it. He was later again attended by the doctor for three abrasions caused by bullets, after which he once more left the ship, this time in a lifeboat, to save some wounded men who were lying in shallow water near the beach. He continued at this heroic labour under continuous fire, until forced to stop through pure physical exhaustion." The following is taken from "Deeds that thrill the Empire": "Few more desperate adventures are recorded in history than the beaching of the tramp steamer River Clyde—the modern 'Horse of Troy'—at Sedd-el-Bahr, during the first landing of the British Expeditionary Force on the Gallipoli Peninsula. The whole operations called for the closest sympathy and co-operation between the Navy and the Army, and never have the two forces worked together in such perfect harmony. Unfortunately, the enemy had been warned of our intentions so long in advance that his defences were as nearly perfect as they could be, and where a foothold was obtained the loss of life was appalling. The River Clyde was selected to be cast ashore on the extremity of the peninsula with a living freight of about two thousand troops, an exploit without parallel in history. Under the guidance of Commander Edward Unwin, R.N., the vessel was prepared at Tenedos for her daring mission. Large holes were cut in the side level with the decks, and sloping gangways suspended by wire hawsers were run out so that the men could rush down them as soon as the ship touched the ground, while battlements of sandbags and steel plating were erected in the bows and on the bridge to shelter the machine guns by which the landing was to be covered. It was early on Sunday, 25 April, 1915, a lovely spring morning, that the River Clyde left the covering squadron of warships and headed for the beach. The heavy guns of the battleships boomed out from behind, their great shells hurtling over the steamer and crashing into the Turkish positions ashore; but not a gun was fired in reply. Barges had been made fast to the sides of the steamer, so that a floating bridge might be formed from them if she grounded too far from the beach, and alongside were five 'tows' of five boats each, packed with men of the Dublin Fusiliers, who were to land first and cover the disembarkation of the troops from the River Clyde. Unhappily, the scheme did not work as it was intended. As the flotilla drew nearer and nearer to the beach there was still no sign of opposition ashore, and everyone had begun to think the landing would be accomplished without opposition. Vain hope! The open boats and the River Clyde touched ground almost at the same moment, and no sooner had the first of them grated on the bottom than a terrific fire was opened from the whole of the surrounding hills that dominated the beach. The Turks had bided their time and chosen the moment well. For a considerable distance to seaward the bottom had been strewn with barbed wire, and as the men who escaped the first tornado of fire leapt into the water to rush ashore, they found themselves entangled in the wire, and were shot down as they stood. Only a handful of men succeeded in getting ashore and gaining the protection of a small ridge of sand on the beach. As for the boats, they were held fast, and their naval crews were wiped out in the pitiless hail of fire that was directed on them. There were some in which no soldier lived to reach the shore and no sailor to get back to his ship. On board the River Clyde the machine guns were busy, but the enemy's positions were so well concealed that they could do little, nor did the heavy guns from the fleet in the rear have much effect. As the vessels grounded, the lighters that were to form the bridge were run out ahead, and the men began to pour out of the holes in her sides and down the gangways; but the lighters failed to reach their proper stations. A gap was left between two of them which it was impossible for the men to cross, and scores were shot down as they stood helpless on the uncompleted bridge or tried to scramble ashore through the unseen wire entanglements below. All the time the steamer was the target of innumerable machine guns and pom-poms. Fortunately, she had been so strengthened that these had little effect; but if the Turks had had a few heavier weapons available, she would assuredly have been battered to pieces and the whole of her crowded human freight sent to destruction. As it was, three howitzer shells fired from the Asiatic side of the Dardanelles crashed into her, but luckily failed to explode. It was while the vessel lay thus helpless that the valour of the Navy came gloriously to the front. Commander Unwin and Able Seaman William Williams made a line fast to one of the drifting lighters, and, dropping over the side, waded through the water and towed the barge towards a spit of rock that gave direct access to the shore. Midshipman George Drewry, of the Royal Naval Reserve, was already in the water wading ashore to make a land end for the towing rope; but he met a wounded soldier in the water, and, with the assistance of another soldier, tried to carry him to land. The unfortunate man was shot dead in the arms of his would-be rescuers. In the meantime, Commander Unwin and Seaman Williams had nearly reached the rock with the lighter in tow, when they found that the rope they had was not long enough. Drewry at once went back to the ship to get another length, and while the other two were waiting fifty minutes, Williams was shot as he stood breast-deep in the water. The Commander carried him back to the lighter; but the brave fellow was dead. It was, indeed, nothing short of a miracle that brought any of that gallant band alive through the unceasing torrent of fire that was poured upon them. When Drewry returned with the rope it did not take long to make the lighter fast, and then the troops began at once to pour across the shot-swept bridge. They were mown down in scores, and the barges soon became piled with the dead and wounded. Those who succeeded in reaching the shore were little better off, for the enemy's fire commanded the beach almost as effectively as it did the water. Presently a shot severed the lashing rope, and again the lighters went adrift. Lieut. Morse and Midshipman Drewry were on board the inshore barge, and the latter was struck in the head by a fragment of the shell; but he hastily bound his wound with a soldier's scarf, and, jumping overboard with a line between his teeth, swam towards the other lighter; but for the second time that day a vital rope proved too short, and the plucky midshipman's strength was failing. With a fresh line, Midshipman Wilfred Malleson rushed into the breach, and, throwing himself over the side, succeeded in making the connection again; but once more it was broken, and although Malleson made two further efforts to carry a rope he was unsuccessful. In the meantime, Commander Unwin had been working like a Trojan, nearly all the time above his waist in water. By no means a young man—he had passed his fifty-first year—the physical strain began to tell, and he was obliged to return to the River Clyde, where the doctor ordered him at once to bed. Before long, however, he was up and doing again, defying the doctor's orders. He took charge of a boat and made several journeys, picking up wounded men as they lay helpless in the shallow water, and it was not until he was overcome by sheer physical exhaustion that he finally gave up. He had worked for many hours under the heaviest fire and the most trying conditions it is possible to imagine, but although he was hit three times, he was not seriously hurt. Another hero of this very costly but glorious exploit was Seaman George Samson, of the Naval Reserve, who remained on the lighters the whole of the day, busying himself among the wounded and giving all the assistance he could to the officers as they carried the lines from lighter to lighter. He was hit over and over again, but nothing could drive him from his post; and when he returned later to England he still had a dozen pieces of metal in his body. There is yet another series of heroic deeds to be recorded in connection with this ever-memorable landing, and they are the more remarkable because nearly a year elapsed before the authorities were able to discover the identity of the officer principally concerned in them. It has already been mentioned that the soldiers who succeeded in reaching the beach were exposed to a fire almost as deadly as when they were in the water or on the bridge of barges, and large numbers were struck down by Turkish shot and shell. The River Clyde lay not far away from them, and their cries drifted out to the ship with appalling clearness. Yet it seemed impossible to do anything to help them; but there was one group of men at any rate to whom the word 'impossible' did not occur. On board the River Clyde was Sub-Lieut. Arthur Waldene St. Clair Tisdall, a twenty-four-year-old officer of the Royal Naval Volunteers, who had been given his commission less than six months before. Unable to resist the heart-rending appeals from the beach, he jumped into the water, and pushed a boat before him as he endeavoured to wade ashore, in order to bring off as many of the wounded men as he could. It was more than one man's job, however, and Tisdall was compelled to call for assistance. It was immediately forthcoming. Leading Seaman James Malia joined him at once, and the two succeeded in getting the boat to the beach and loading it with wounded men, whom they carried back to the River Clyde. Twice did these two make this perilous, shot-swept journey, and then other men insisted on joining in. These were Chief Petty Officer William Perring and Leading Seaman Fred Curtis and James Parkinson, who, with Sub-Lieut. Tisdall still in command, made three more journeys to the shore and brought off as many wounded men as they could reach and their boat would carry. Those on board the stranded collier watched in mute admiration; but darkness fell before the work was done, and the young officer dropped out of sight as quickly and completely as if he had disappeared, and no one seemed to know who it was that had done this

Edward Unwin.

great work. Unfortunately, the gallant Tisdall fell in action a fortnight later, intrepidly facing the enemy on a spit of rock which made him the target of a hundred rifles. For close upon a year his extraordinary bravery passed without any sign of official recognition, and then, on 1 April, 1916, it was announced that the King had been pleased to confer on him the posthumous award of the Victoria Cross for 'most conspicuous bravery and devotion to duty.' Chief Petty Officer Perring, subsequently given a commission in the Royal Naval Volunteer Reserve, was awarded the Conspicuous Gallantry Medal, as also were Leading Seamen Malia and Parkinson, and there is no doubt that a similar honour would have been conferred on Leading Seaman Curtis had he not unfortunately been placed among the missing on 4 June, 1915. Sub-Lieut. Tisdall had had a most brilliant career at Cambridge, where he took double first-class Classical Honours and won the Chancellor's Gold Medal in 1913. He rowed in the First Trinity boat, and a volume of his poems had been published. There has not very often been a more remarkable instance of the combination of scholarship with courage on the battle-field. The rest of the immortal story of the River Clyde belongs to the Army, but the two Services had nobly shared the terrible glories of that awful day. In his Despatch dealing with the Gallipoli landing, General Sir Ian Hamilton wrote : ' Throughout the events I have chronicled the Royal Navy has been father and mother to the Army. Not one of us but realizes how much he owes to Vice-Admiral de Robeck (the Naval Commander-in-Chief) ; to the warships, French and British ; to the destroyers, mine-sweepers, picket boats, and to all their dauntless crews, who took no thought of themselves, but risked everything to give their soldier comrades a fair run at the enemy.' The services of the heroes of the River Clyde were rewarded by the King with a just generosity. Commander Unwin, Midshipman Drewry, Midshipman Malleson, Able Seaman Williams (killed in the action), and Seaman Samson, as well as Sub-Lieut. Tisdall, all received the Victoria Cross, while Lieut. Morse was appointed to the Distinguished Service Order. Many other officers and men received the D.S.C. and the D.S.M. respectively. No previous event had been signalized by the granting of so many Victoria Crosses ; but no other in the history of the Cross had so well merited them." His Victoria Cross was gazetted 16 Aug. 1915 : " Edward Unwin, Commander, Royal Navy. While in River Clyde, observing that the lighters which were to form the bridge to the shore had broken adrift, Commander Unwin left the ship, and under a murderous fire attempted to get the lighters into position. He worked on until, suffering from the effects of cold and immersion, he was obliged to return to the ship, where he was wrapped up in blankets. Having in some degree recovered, he returned to his work against the doctor's order and completed it. He was later again attended by the doctor for three abrasions caused by bullets, after which he once more left the ship, this time in a lifeboat, to save some wounded men who were lying in shallow water near the beach. He continued at this heroic labour under continuous fire, until forced to stop through pure physical exhaustion." On his recovery he again resumed, and worked throughout the night of 25 April, during which his voice could always be heard giving orders above the terrific din going on at the bows of the ship and on the beach. He left V Beach on 9 May, being sent home ill. He was operated on in Haslar Hospital, but appeared in Mudros Harbour on 1 July in command of the Endymion, and was later beach master during the whole of the landing at Suvla Bay. He controlled the beaches during the evacuation and was the last man to leave. As he boarded the ship that took him away, a soldier went overboard, and Capt. Unwin went after him and rescued him. For his services at the landing and evacuation of Suvla Bay Commander Unwin was mentioned in Despatches by Admiral de Robeck and General Munro (for the Suvla actions). He next assumed command of the Amethyst. His favourite recreation is yachting, and he holds a cup for the best cruise for three successive years. He belongs to a motor yacht club. He is also fond of croquet and tennis.

DREWRY, GEORGE LESLIE, Midshipman, was born 3 Nov. 1894, at 58, Claremont Road, Forest Gate, London, son of Thomas Drewry, Works Manager, Peninsular and Oriental Steam Navigation Company, and Mary Drewry, daughter of James and Naomi Kendall, of Intax Farm, Weelsby, Lincolnshire. He was educated at Merchant Taylors' School, Blackheath. Young Drewry began his adventurous career quite early, for when a boy he was knocked down and rendered unconscious by a motor, and his parents did not know what had become of him till he was brought home. When he left school he joined the Mercantile Marine, and was apprenticed on board the Indian Empire. It was whilst he was serving his early sea training that he fell from a mast of the ship into the sea and nearly lost his life. This, however, was a most everyday adventure in comparison with the one he had later on. Whilst sailing round Cape Horn in the Indian Empire, a large London sailing ship, a storm arose, and the vessel was wrecked upon a desert island. Fortunately the crew, including George Drewry, managed to get ashore with a very small supply of provisions, but during the night their boat was smashed up by heavy seas, and they were stranded on their island as castaways. For fourteen days they lived somehow, on edible roots and shell fish which they found upon the island, and they managed to hold out until they were rescued by a gunboat, a Chilian man-of-war. The whole ship's crew were saved. After this Drewry came back to England, and in 1912 he joined the P. and O. Service as an officer. From that time onwards he travelled all over the world. He joined the Royal Naval Reserve on 1 July, 1913, and he was at Port Said when he was called up for active service on 3 Aug. 1914, as a midshipman on H.M.S. Hussar. He served in the Dardanelles. The following admirable account of how Drewry won the V.C. is given by the courteous permission of the proprietors of the " Daily Chronicle " : " It was about ten o'clock on the evening of 23 April that the River Clyde, towing three lighters and a steamboat on her port side and a steam hopper on her starboard side, started on her perilous mission. She anchored for the night off Tenedos, but the weather changed, and in the morning a strong wind and rough sea led to fears for the success of the expedition. At about four o'clock in the afternoon sweepers came alongside with the troops, and orders were given to proceed at midnight. As the Clyde sheered towards the Turkish searchlights, on a calm night, just making headway against the current, visions of mines and submarines rose before the watchers on the boats as they thought of the two thousand troops in the hold. Soon after daybreak Midshipman Drewry was ordered to take charge of the hopper, and then came an anxious time as the vessels sheered towards Cape Helles. In a few minutes the bombardment commenced. Battleships, cruisers and destroyers thundered away, and the land seemed to be a mass of fire and smoke, as the ships raked it with shell. Straight through the line of battleships we went, and shell began to fall thick. The River Clyde got to within half a mile of the beach, but was told to wait. At last the signal was given, and in they dashed. At 6.10 the River Clyde struck, and the hopper went ahead and grounded on the port bow. Then the serious business commenced. Picket boats towed lifeboats full of troops inshore, and slipped them as the water shoaled. The soldiers jumped out as the boats beached ; but they were almost immediately wiped out, together with the boats' crews. There was a line from the stern of the hopper to the lighters, and this the crew of the River Clyde tried to haul in. Then the commander appeared on the lighters, and the steam pinnace took hold of them and plucked them in until she could go no closer. Instead of joining up to the hopper, the captain decided to make the connection with a spit of rock on the other bow. Midshipman Drewry jumped over the bow and waded ashore. Meeting a soldier wounded in the water, he tried to carry him ashore, with the assistance of another soldier, but he was again shot in the arms of his rescuers. Drewry then ran along the spit, throwing away his revolver, coat and hat. By this time Commander Unwin was in the water with a man named Williams, wading and towing the lighters towards the spit. Drewry waded out, gave a pull for a few minutes, and then climbed aboard the lighters. Capt. Unwin, still in the water, called out for more rope. A member of the crew, Ellard, with Midshipman Drewry, brought down the rope. By this time Williams had been hit, and the captain was carrying him towards the lighter. Ellard seized Williams and took him on board. Williams, however, was dead. A rope was then secured to the spit, and the daring operation had succeeded. Capt. Unwin was by this time exhausted, and it was only with considerable difficulty that he was hauled on to one of the lighters. All this time shells were falling all round the River Clyde and the lighters. Two shells dropped into one of the holds, killing several men, while the boiler was hit but not damaged. Meanwhile the men who were landing from the lighters were suffering severely. The first lighter was soon covered with dead and wounded. When the men of the landing party got ashore, they were little better off than in the lighters, for they were picked off before they could dig themselves in. In the meantime the lighters had drifted away from the spit, one of them with Lieut. Morse and Midshipman Drewry on it. The shower of shrapnel continued, and one fragment struck Drewry on the head, knocking him down and covering him with blood. In spite of his wound, however, he, with Lieut. Morse, succeeded in making the lighter fast again. He had his wound bound up with a soldier's scarf, and proceeded pluckily to the completion of his task, effecting a connection with the other lighters. Jumping overboard with a rope, he swam towards them, but when halfway across found that the rope was not long enough, and had to remain in the water until Lieut. Morse and Midshipman Malleson arrived with a picket boat and completed the operation. Commander Unwin distinguished himself by an heroic effort to remove the wounded from the lighters to the River Clyde. With the assistance of one or two volunteers he succeeded in taking off seven boat-loads of them, and placing them safely in No. 4 hold of the ship, a dangerous and difficult operation, that won for him the unstinted praise of all who witnessed it. The landing of the troops from the lighters of the River Clyde was suspended in the afternoon, and it was not till 8 p.m., when dusk had fallen, that the operation was resumed. At the same time the wounded on the lighters and the hopper were removed and transferred to a trawler. At about 11.30 almost all the troops were ashore. The Turks poured out a shower of shells, shrapnel, and every other death-dealing missile, but everyone lay low, and little harm was done. They ceased firing at about two in the morning. All through the night the village was burning, giving too much light to be agreeable to the British forces. Early in the morning our people worked up to the right, captured the port, entered the village, and took it slowly, house by house. Then Colonel Doughty-Wylie headed a charge up the ridge, and was killed just as he led his men into the old fort at the top of the ridge. It was not till the next day, however, that all the snipers were cleared from the village and the ridge. Samson, one of the hopper men, did very well on the Sunday afternoon. Two or three times he took wounded from the beach to his hopper. On the second day he was very severely wounded while sniping from the fore deck." (" Daily Chronicle," 17 Aug. 1915.) Midshipman Drewry was mentioned by Admiral Sir Michael de Robeck in his Despatch (dated 1 July, 1915) concerning the landing of the Mediterranean Expeditionary Force on the Gallipoli Peninsula, and the proceedings of the River Clyde : " He assisted Commander Unwin at the work of securing the lighters under heavy rifle and Maxim fire. He was wounded in the head, but continued his work, and twice subsequently attempted to swim from lighter to lighter with a line." For these services Midshipman Drewry was awarded the Victoria Cross [London Gazette,

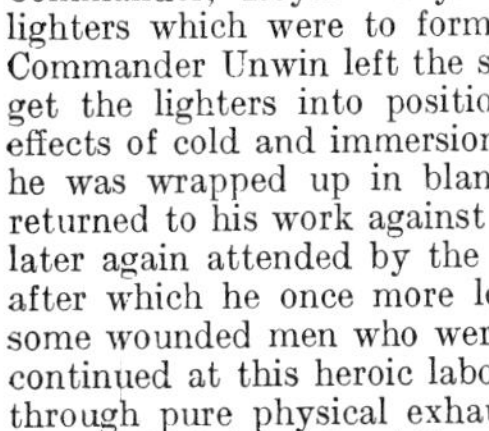

George Leslie Drewry.

16 Aug. 1915]: "George Leslie Drewry, Midshipman, Royal Naval Reserve, H.M.S. Hussar. Dates of Acts of Bravery: 25 and 26 April, 1915. Assisted Commander Unwin at the work of securing the lighters under heavy rifle and Maxim fire. He was wounded in the head, but continued his work, and twice subsequently attempted to swim from lighter to lighter with a line." Midshipman Drewry was promoted to Acting Lieutenant, R.N.R., H.M.S. Conqueror, 2 Sept. 1916. The Imperial Merchant Service Guild presented him with a sword of honour, as the first officer in the R.N.R. and in the Merchant Service to win the Victoria Cross. Lieut. Drewry was fatally injured on Friday evening, the 2nd Aug. 1918, at sea, on active service, when in command of H.M.T. William Jackson, on the Northern Patrol. A block fell from the end of a derrick and struck him heavily on the head, fracturing his skull and breaking his left arm. He died shortly afterwards. His brother officers of the Northern Patrol erected a beautiful memorial window to him in All Saints' Church, Forest Gate. One of his brothers is also in the Navy, Engineer-Lieut. Harry K. Drewry. The following is an extract from the diary of his friend, Surgeon P. Burrowes-Kelly, R.N., D.S.O.: "Midshipman Drewry (now Lieut.), R.N.R., V.C., was executive officer of the River Clyde. When the time arrived to run ship ashore was placed in command of the 'Greek Hopper' which accompanied us, and ran ashore on our port side. On his way through the water to the shore picked up a dangerously wounded Munster Fusilier in the shallow foreshore water, and endeavoured to carry him to safety. The man was shot dead in his arms. After lighters, etc., broke adrift, Drewry, though laid out from wounds of the head on a drifting lighter, succeeded in effecting to make lighter fast again, and then jumping overboard, he was seen to swim with rope or hauling line round his neck to the other part of his task. Shortly afterwards he was brought into the River Clyde in an exhausted and delirious condition. Has had a most adventurous career. As a small boy was run over in London traffic. Fell from aloft into a big sea, but was rescued. Later was marooned on a Southern Pacific island. After his term in Gallipoli, he returned to his ship, H.M.S. Hussar, and on completion of commission proceeded to the North Sea." Surgeon Burrowes-Kelly writes: "I have carefully gone through all my diaries, and I don't think I can find anything I can add about my friend Drewry. I consider the 'Daily Chronicle' account a very good one, indeed, and thought so when it first appeared. Drewry was of medium height, but powerfully built. He was a very good-looking, modest and charming young man. He was devoted to his captain, and was considered by all the Naval officers who knew him to have been an exceedingly brave fellow. Three days after the landing he and I were in Sedd-al-Bahr village, which was heaped with Turkish and British dead, and Drewry, V.C., was so overcome with the sight that he fainted, and never afterwards would he photograph anywhere near Sedd-al-Bahr. This could only happen to a gentle soul. I cannot tell you what a blow the news of Drewry's end was to me."

MALLESON, WILFRED ST. AUBYN, Midshipman, served in the Dardanelles, 1914–15, and during the landing of the Expeditionary Force swam with a line from lighter to lighter. Midshipman Malleson's gallantry has been described in two of the preceding biographies. He was awarded the Victoria Cross [London Gazette, 16 Aug. 1915]: "Wilfred St. Aubyn Malleson, Midshipman, Royal Navy. Also assisted Commander Unwin, and after Midshipman Drewry had failed from exhaustion to get a line from lighter to lighter, he swam with it himself and succeeded. The line subsequently broke, and he afterwards made two further but unsuccessful attempts at his self-imposed task." He became Acting Sub-Lieutenant, Royal Navy, H.M.S. Cornwallis.

WILLIAMS, WILLIAM CHARLES, Able Seaman, Royal Navy, served in the European War, in the Dardanelles. Surgeon P. Burrowes-Kelly, R.N., D.S.O., writes of him in his diary: "Saved the day on 25 April by holding on to a rope for over an hour, standing chest-deep in the sea and under continuous fire. Eventually dangerously wounded by a shell, and later killed by a shell, whilst his rescue was being effected by Commander Unwin. He was the pride of our ship's company, and described by Commander Unwin as the bravest sailor he had ever met." He was awarded the Victoria Cross [London Gazette, 16 Aug. 1915]: "William Charles Williams, Able Seaman, O.N. 186774 (R.F.R., B. 3766). Held on to a line in the water for over an hour and under heavy fire, until killed." An extract from a newspaper says: "Presiding at Chepstow Council, Mr. Lawrence presented a bronze war medallion to Mrs. F. M. Smith, as the next-of-kin of the late Seaman W. C. Williams, V.C., who participated in a gallant act on the River Clyde at the Gallipoli landing."

SAMSON, GEORGE MACKENZIE, Seaman, was born at Carnoustie, N.B.; joined the Royal Navy, serving in the European War. He was on the River Clyde, the converted collier which assisted at the attempted landing on V Beach, Gallipoli, on 25 and 26 April, 1915, and there won the Victoria Cross. The award was announced in the London Gazette of 16 Aug. 1915. In this Gazette Vice-Admiral de Robeck's Despatch was published with regard to the landing on the Peninsula on 25 and 26 April, 1915, and in it he named Seaman Samson, who was then one of the crew of H.M.S. Hussar, as one of four who helped Commander Unwin to get the lighters from the River Clyde to the shore in position (all five being given the Victoria Cross). The recommendation was: "Seaman, Royal Naval Reserve, George Mackenzie Samson, O.N. 2408A. Worked on a lighter all day under fire, attending wounded and getting out lines; he was eventually dangerously wounded by Maxim fire." The following is taken from the diary of Surgeon P. Burrowes-Kelly, D.S.O., R.N., with reference to Seaman Samson: "Was most prominent through 25 and 26 April. He effected many daring rescues of the wounded, stowed them carefully away in the hopper, and treated them himself until medical assistance was forthcoming. In the intervals he devoted his time to attending to snipers. Was prominent in the close fighting on V Beach on the night of 25th April. He was eventually covered by a Maxim and wounded in nineteen distinct places. Had the unique experience of being presented with a white feather (many months afterwards) about three hours before his public reception on his return to his native town of Carnoustie, N.B."

London Gazette, 16 Aug. 1915.—"Admiralty, 16 Aug. 1915. The following awards have been made in recognition of services during the operations in the vicinity of the Dardanelles prior to 25–26 April."

ROBINSON, ERIC GASCOIGNE, Lieut.-Commander, Royal Navy, served in the European War, and was awarded the Victoria Cross [London Gazette, 16 Aug. 1915]: "Eric Gascoigne, Robinson, Lieut.-Commander, Royal Navy. Date of Act of Bravery: 26 Feb. 1915. Lieut.-Commander Robinson on the 26th Feb. advanced alone, under heavy fire, into an enemy's gun position, which might well have been occupied, and, destroying a four-inch gun, returned to his party for another charge with which the second gun was destroyed. Lieut.-Commander Robinson would not allow members of his demolition party to accompany him, as their white uniforms rendered them very conspicuous. Lieut.-Commander Robinson took part in four attacks on the mine-fields, always under heavy fire." Another exploit of Lieut.-Commander Robinson's is related in "Deeds that thrill the Empire" (pages 393–401): "The splendid work of our submarines in the Sea of Marmora, where they sank, drove ashore or damaged over two hundred enemy ships in eight months of 1915, was carried out in the teeth of great and incessant dangers, and both we and our Allies, the French, lost a number of boats in the narrow and closely-guarded passage of the Dardanelles. It was the loss of one of these vessels, the E15, which led to a most brilliant exploit on the part of two little steam picket-boats belonging to the Fleet. On the night of 16 April, 1915, the E15 was detached from the flotilla lying at Tenedos, and sent into the Straits to reconnoitre a newly-laid mine-field about eleven miles up. The Turks, however, were keeping a very vigilant watch, and it was not long before the submarine was compelled to dive in order to escape their searchlights. Thus submerged, she continued to creep steadily up the Straits; but the strong head current gradually threw her off her course, and just off Kephez Point, where the land shelves out and the navigable channel is greatly reduced in width, she unfortunately ran aground. The water shallowed so imperceptibly that she was hard and fast, with her conning tower well out of the water, almost before her danger was realized; and the forts ashore at once opened a fire which demolished the conning tower, killed the Commander (Lieut.-Commander T. S. Brodie) and a number of men, and left the survivors no alternativ but to surrender. When our ships outside the Straits heard the firing, it was at once realized that something had gone wrong, and a seaplane was sent in next day to investigate. What had happened was clear enough to the observers aloft, and it was apparent, too, that the Turks had already set about trying to get the submarine afloat again with the object of using it against us. Steps were immediately taken to frustrate this intention. Aircraft tried to drop bombs on the stranded vessel; submarines went in and endeavoured to torpedo her; battleships entered the Straits and fired two score rounds from their heavy guns, but all to no purpose. When darkness fell, destroyers were sent in to see if they could get within range, but they were discovered and driven out by the heavy fire that was concentrated on them. Apart from the fact that the submarine and its secrets might be used against us, it was regarded by the Navy as a point of honour that E15 should not be left in the hands of an enemy, and especially of the Turks. Next morning Admiral de Robeck made a signal to the effect that two small steamboats, one from the Triumph and one from the Majestic, were to be fitted with outrigger torpedoes, manned by volunteer crews, and sent in that night to accomplish what aircraft, submarines, battleships and destroyers had failed in. It should be mentioned that an outrigger torpedo is one which is not fired from a tube, but carried in slings or clips that hang over the side of the boat. When the weapon is pointing towards the target the clips are opened, and the torpedo's engines come into action as she strikes the water. Throughout the fleet there was very little expectation that those who ventured on this exploit would ever return; but there was no lack of volunteers, and lots had to be cast to choose the boats' crews from among them. By nightfall all was ready, and at ten o'clock the little boats—less than fifty feet long, and with sides easily penetrable by a rifle bullet—got under way. Lieut.-Commander Eric G. Robinson, in the Triumph's boat, was in command, supported by Lieut. A. C. Brooke-Webb, of the Royal Naval Reserve, and Midshipman John B. Woolley, while Lieut. Claud Godwin had command of the Majestic's boat. The whole enterprise was fraught with the greatest danger, seeing that the boats had to steam ten or eleven miles through a narrow channel, dominated by the Turks on both sides, and that the enemy had been well warned the previous day of our intention to destroy the submarine by some means or another. For some time, however, all went well; and then, while they were still three or four miles from their goal, they were suddenly lit up by the glare of a searchlight. Instantly a torrent of fire was opened on them, and the sea, now brilliantly lit, seemed as though it were lashed by a terrific hailstorm. As if by a miracle, the boats remained unscathed,

E. Gascoigne Robinson.

forging their perilous way ahead against the strong current, the centre always of a dazzling blaze of light and the target of guns that increased in number as they advanced. As they got nearer and nearer to the stranded submarine fresh searchlights came into action from directly ahead, the enemy hoping by this means to blind the helmsmen and conceal the whereabouts of the E15. Presently, however, one of the Turks made a slip and threw his light directly on to the submarine. It was all our men wanted. The Majestic's boat was then no more than three hundred yards distant from it, and Lieut. Godwin put her end on to the target, slowed her down, and dropped his first torpedo. Unfortunately the glare of the searchlights confused his aim, and the weapon missed; and a few seconds afterwards the Turkish gunners scored their one and only hit of the night with a shot that carried away part of the boat's stern. She instantly began to fill, but Lieut. Godwin still had another torpedo in its slings, and he was determined to use it. Putting on steam, he again approached the submarine, and, taking careful aim, was rewarded after a few seconds by a great explosion, which occurred well under water, just forward of her conning tower. After such an attack no submarine would have any remaining value save as waste metal. In the meantime the Triumph's boat had observed the misfortune of her consort and hurriedly steamed up alongside. All the men of the damaged craft were taken aboard, including one—the only casualty—who had been mortally wounded. The forts and batteries ashore had redoubled their efforts when the torpedo struck home, but not another shot found its intended billet, and when the Triumph, now doubly loaded, set off down stream, the enemy gunners, for some reason best known to themselves, concentrated their fire on the drifting and tenantless wreck of the Majestic's boat. So this puny little attack succeeded where battleships, destroyers and airships had failed, and despite the furious cannonade to which the boats had been subjected, only one man was hit. Vice-Admiral de Robeck congratulated those concerned in a general signal, and the Admiralty telegraphed Lieut. Robinson's promotion to Commander for his services. The Distinguished Service Order was awarded to Lieut. Godwin, and the Distinguished Service Cross to Lieut. Brooke-Webb and Midshipman Woolley, while the boats' crews all received the Distinguished Service Medal. Commander Robinson had already performed in Gallipoli a deed of gallantry for which he was later awarded the Victoria Cross." The following extract with regard to Lieut.-Commander Robinson is taken from the diary of Surgeon Burrowes-Kelly, R.N., D.S.O.: "Did many good things during Dardanelles campaign. Amongst other gallant acts he advanced alone into a gun emplacement and blew up the guns quite close to the Tomb of Achilles over the Mendere bridge. He refused to allow any of his party to accompany him on his mission, as he feared that the white dress would expose them. On 17 April, on her passage to Sea of Marmora, E15 ran ashore off Kephez Point. Battleships could not operate to assist her owing to darkness. T.B.D.'s endeavoured to do so, but failed. As result of this, on the evening of 18 April, Robinson set out in command of two picket boats, one from the Majestic and one from Triumph. After exciting experiences he endeavoured to fire a torpedo from about three hundred yards' range from Majestic's picket boat, and this struck E15 between the bows and conning tower and exploded. This act of daring was carried out under a very heavy fire from the enemy, which fire sank the picket boat shortly after the discharge of torpedo. Triumph's picket, however, saved all, and Robinson returned with her dangerously overloaded in a choppy sea, having carried out his mission. He was promoted Commander for this work. On four occasions Robinson took part in mining operations in a fishing trawler under heavy enemy fire." He was mentioned in Despatches by General Sir Archibald Murray for his work on one of H.M. Monitors. The newspapers of Friday, 10 Oct. 1919, announced that Commodore Norris had cleared the Caspian Sea of Bolshevik ships, Commander Robinson leading the motor-boats: "In the far-off Caspian Sea a comparatively small group of British naval officers and men have nobly upheld the traditions of the forces. Rear-Admiral Seymour, Commanding in the Black Sea, tells the story of the operations, and bestows great praise on Commodore David T. Norris, C.B., in command of the British flotilla, who succeeded in driving the superior enemy from the Caspian. Altogether twelve enemy ships were sunk in Alexandrovsk harbour. News was received that the Bolshevik naval authorities at Astrakhan intended to carry out an attack on Petrovsk or Baku, with the object of obtaining oil, of which they were in urgent need. A preliminary to that was the occupation of Fort Alexandrovsk. Reinforcements reached Commodore Norris, and in an encounter some days later the flotilla had a severe fight with an enemy force, which included a destroyer and various armed barges. The destroyer was hit by a shot from the British ship Venture, and appeared to run ashore. The British ship, Emile Nobel, was hit in the engine-room, five men being killed and seven wounded. The vessel drew out of the line, but continued to fight. Five British ships followed the enemy into the harbour, and did great damage before drawing off in the direction of Astrakhan, as Commodore Norris intended, if possible, to remain on the enemy's line of retreat. During the next few days the operations of a seaplane provided the chief incidents. In the second raid on Fort Alexandrovsk one bomb hit an armed merchant cruiser and a large destroyer was sunk. On one occasion the seaplane ran into a fog and fell into the sea. The officers were not picked up until thirty-two hours later. Three or four days later a close reconnaissance of Fort Alexandrovsk was made. The coastal motor-boats proceeded up harbour under the command of Commander Eric G. Robinson, V.C. On their way up harbour they torpedoed a large barge, and on arrival up harbour a white flag was hoisted ashore, and a deputation came off. From these men full details of the Bolshevik occupation were obtained. Admiral Seymour specially mentions several officers and men, among them Acting-Capt. Basil G. Washington, C.M.G., who commanded the Windsor Castle, on which he was the only British officer, and Commander Kenneth A. F. Guy, who handled the crippled Emile Nobel with great ability."

London Gazette, 23 Aug. 1915.—"The King has been graciously pleased to award the Victoria Cross to the undermentioned Officers and Non-commissioned Officers in recognition of their most conspicuous bravery and devotion to duty."

BUTLER, JOHN FITZHARDINGE PAUL, Capt., was born at Berkeley, Gloucestershire, on 20 Dec. 1888, son of Lieut.-Colonel F. J. P. Butler, of Wyck Hill, Gloucestershire, and his wife, the late Honourable Elspeth Fitzhardinge, daughter of the 2nd Lord Gifford. He was educated at Wellington (Mr. Kempthorne's House), and at the Royal Military College, Sandhurst, where he gained the Military History Prize. He was given a commission in the King's Royal Rifle Corps in Feb. 1907, and was promoted to Lieutenant in Aug. 1909. He served in India till 1913, when he was seconded for service with the Gold Coast Regt. in West Africa. He served in the European War in the Togoland and Cameroons Expeditions and during the latter, in 1914, gained the Victoria Cross, which was gazetted 23 Aug. 1915: "John Fitzhardinge Paul Butler, Capt., King's Royal Rifle Corps, attached Pioneer Coy. Z, Gold Coast Regt., West African Frontier Force. For most conspicuous bravery in the Cameroons, West Africa, on 17 Nov. 1914. With a party of 13 men he went into the thick bush, and at once attacked the enemy, in strength about 100, including several Europeans; defeated them, and captured their machine gun and many loads of ammunition. On 27 Dec. 1914, when on patrol duty with a few men, he swam the Ekam River, which was held by the enemy, alone and in face of a brisk fire; completed his reconnaissance on the further bank and returned in safety. Two of his men were wounded while he was actually in the water." Lieut. Butler had been promoted to Captain in March, 1915. He was invested with the Victoria Cross at Buckingham Palace by the King on 24 Aug. 1915. Capt. Butler was several times mentioned in Despatches, and was created a, Companion of the Distinguished Service Order [London Gazette, 5 June, 1916]: "John Fitzhardinge Paul Butler, Capt., King's Royal Rifle Corps." He proceeded to South Africa with the Gold Coast Regt. in July, 1916, and died of wounds on 5 Sept. 1916.

John F. P. Butler.

FOSS, CHARLES CALVELEY, Capt., was born 9 March, 1885, at Kobe, Japan, son of the Right Rev. Hugh James Foss, D.D., Bishop of Osaka, and Janet (who died in 1894), daughter of Dr. William M'Ewen, M.D. of Chester. He was at Marlborough College (1899–1902, C.3), and entered the Army on 2 March, 1904, becoming Captain on 20 Nov. 1912. He served in the European War from 1914, to 11 Nov. 1918; was created a Companion of the Distinguished Service Order [London Gazette, 1 Jan. 1915]: "Charles Calveley Foss, Capt., 2nd Battn. Bedfordshire Regt." He was awarded the Victoria Cross [London Gazette, 23 Aug. 1915]: "Charles Calveley Foss, D.S.O., Capt., 2nd Battn. Bedfordshire Regt. Date of Act of Bravery: 12 March, 1915. For most conspicuous bravery at Neuve Chapelle, on the 12th March, 1915. After the enemy had captured a part of one of our trenches, and our counter-attack made with one officer and twenty men having failed (all but two of the party being killed or wounded in the attempt), Capt. Foss, on his own initiative, dashed forward with eight men, under heavy fire attacked the enemy with bombs, and captured the position, including the fifty-two Germans occupying it. The capture of this position from the enemy was of the greatest importance, and the utmost bravery was displayed in essaying the task with so very few men." He was later given the Brevets of Major and Lieutenant-Colonel. He served on the Staff as Brigade-Major of 20th Infantry Brigade, 7th Division; G.S.O.2 of the 2nd and 1st Canadian Divisions and Canadian and XXII. Corps, and as G.S.O.1 of the 57th Division. Major Foss married on 6 June, 1915, Vere Katharine, widow of Capt. Collard, 90th Punjabis, and 3rd daughter of the late J. Lambert Ovans.

LIDDELL, JOHN AIDAN, Capt., was born 3 Aug. 1888, at Benwell Hall, Newcastle-on-Tyne, Northumberland, eldest son of John Liddell, of Sherfield Manor, Basingstoke, J.P. for Northumberland, and Emily Catherine, second daughter of the late Major Henry A. Berry, of the Cameronians. He was educated at Mrs. Ware's Preparatory School, Frognal Hall, Hampstead; Stonyhurst (1900–1908), and at Balliol College, Oxford, where he greatly distinguished himself. At Stonyhurst the boys called him "Oozy" Liddell, because he was "always messing about with chemicals and engines." With a love of all things scientific, he was particularly interested in astronomy, and often assisted Father Cortie in the Observatory, where he became so useful that when the latter went to Vinaroz, Spain, in 1905, to observe the total solar eclipse of 30 Aug., he took Liddell, a boy of seventeen, with him as his chief assistant. He secured some remarkable photographs of the total eclipse of the sun. The boy's health had always been delicate, and in the following year his father and mother were anxious about him, and took him on a long sea voyage to the Cape of Good Hope, where he visited the late Sir David Gill at the Royal Observatory. That eminent astronomer

John Aidan Liddell.

was so struck with young Liddell that he wrote home and recommended that the boy should take up his own profession. On his return Aidan Liddell was elected a Member of the British Astronomical Association on 27 Feb. 1907. At Oxford he took the Honours Course in Zoology, and was the only man of his year who gained the Honours Degree in the First Class in this subject. " Not wishing to be a slacker," he joined the Special Reserve of Officers in the 3rd Battn. of the Argyll and Sutherland Highlanders on 1 June, 1912, and was promoted to Lieutenant in July, 1914. He later on took to flying, and secured his certificate as pilot at Brooklands in June, 1914. Thus soon after the outbreak of war (28 Aug.) he accompanied his battalion to the front with the rank of Acting Captain, and was placed in command of the Machine Gun Section of the battalion. He was at one time for forty-three consecutive days in the trenches without rest or change, and for his services as Commander of the Machine Gun Section he was mentioned in Despatches and given the Military Cross [London Gazette, 18 Feb. 1915]. He was promoted to Captain 2 Feb. 1915, and attached to the 2nd Battn. He was, however, invalided home, but as soon as he was well enough he joined the Royal Flying Corps in May, and returned again to the front on 23 July, where within eight days he had gained immortal fame and a mortal injury. He was awarded the Victoria Cross [London Gazette, 23 Aug. 1915] : " John Aidan Liddell, Capt., 3rd Battn. Argyll and Sutherland Highlanders. For most conspicuous bravery and devotion to duty on 31 July, 1915. When on a flying reconnaissance over Ostend–Bruges–Ghent he was severely wounded (his right thigh being broken), which caused momentary unconsciousness, but by a great effort he recovered partial control after his machine had dropped nearly 3,000 feet, and, notwithstanding his collapsed state, succeeded, although continually fired at, in completing his course, and brought the aeroplane into our lines half an hour after he had been wounded. The difficulties experienced by this officer in saving his machine and the life of his observer cannot be readily expressed, but as the control wheel and throttle control were smashed, and also one of the under-carriage struts, it would seem incredible that he could have accomplished his task." The official account leaves nothing more to be said respecting one of those deeds which now and again set the whole world agape with wonder and admiration. " Devotion to duty " was indeed one of Aidan Liddell's most marked characteristics. He was taken to the hospital at La Panne, Belgium, and at first it was hoped that he might recover and even that his leg might be saved. Eventually, however, septic poisoning set in and amputation was found necessary. He was not to live, however, and the intrepid airman—who had prepared himself equally well for this world and the next—faced death as unflinchingly as he had faced life. He had his mother with him, and fortified by the last rites of his Church, he died almost suddenly on 31 Aug. 1915, the Feast of his patron Saint, Aidan. His Colonel wrote: "We were very proud of our V.C., and he will always be affectionately remembered, not only for the honour he has gained for us, but also for his great abilities and delightful disposition. There has certainly been no more splendid instance of devotion to duty throughout this war, and no brighter example of all a soldier could wish to be or to do." One of his senior officers wrote : " I cannot write much, but we all feel as if the light had gone out, the light of our battalion. You see, he was always bright. In snow, in muddy trenches, or ante-room, he kept us laughing, and his influence will last. Soldiering had little to teach or give to him. His, by instinct, was the great gift a soldier can possess, and he gave it freely together with his life—to soldiering."

CAMPBELL, FREDERICK WILLIAM, Capt., was born in Oxford County, Ontario, 15 June, 1868. The son of Mr. and Mrs. Ephraim B. Campbell, he came of a long line of fighting military stock, his great-grandfather being Capt. Ames, who died about a century ago, and who helped to repel the United States invaders from Canada in the War of 1812. He was educated at Mount Forest School, and began his military career about 1894 in No. 5 Coy., 13th Wellington Rifles. He went out to the South African War, and was specially mentioned for having repaired the wheel of a gun carriage with legs from a table taken from a Boer house, the identical wheel being now in the Museum in Quebec Citadel (South African Queen's Medal and four clasps). He became Lieutenant in 1902. He was married on 25 Nov. 1903, at Mount Forest, Ontario, to Margaret Annie, daughter of the late Mr. and Mrs. MacGillivray, of Mount Forest, and had three children : Arthur Clive, born 1 Aug. 1904, and two daughters born later, Jean Margaret and Freda MacGillivray. On the outbreak of the European War he left Canada with the First Contingent as Lieutenant and Officer-in-Command of the Machine Gun Section, 1st Battn, 1st Brigade. On his forty-seventh birthday (15 June, 1915) Capt. Campbell, after leading his men with the greatest bravery and coolness, was mortally wounded in the hip. He lingered in hospital at Boulogne till the 19th. He was posthumously awarded the Victoria Cross [London Gazette, 23 Aug. 1915] : " Frederick William Campbell, Lieut., 1st Canadian Battn. Date of Act of Bravery : 15 June, 1915. For most conspicuous bravery on 15 June, 1915, during the action at Givenchy. Lieut. Campbell took two machine guns over the parapet, arrived at the German first line with one gun, and maintained his position there, under very heavy rifle, machine-gun and bomb fire, notwithstanding the fact that almost the whole of his detachment had then been killed or wounded. When our supply of bombs had become exhausted this officer advanced his gun still farther to an exposed position,

Frederick W. Campbell.

and firing about 1,000 rounds, succeeded in holding back the enemy's counter-attack. This very gallant officer was subsequently wounded, and has since died." He was gazetted Captain in France.

The following are some extracts from a pamphlet about Capt. Campbell :
" With the four-barred service medal, won in South Africa at Johannesburg, Dreifontein, Paardeberg and Cape Colony, the Victoria Cross, won at the Battle of Givenchy in the greatest war of all time, will take its place as a priceless treasure amongst present and future generations of Capt. Frederick William Campbell's family. . . .

" He was sent to the hospital at Boulogne, and there, on the 19th, his soul went forth to enter a higher service.

" The doctor wrote to Mrs. Campbell : ' He was wounded through the right thigh, close to the hip joint, which fractured the thigh bone. He felt very weak for the three days he was here, but he had practically no pain. At twelve noon, on the 19th, he became quite unconscious and passed very peacefully into rest at 3 p.m. His wound was beginning to heal and showed signs of improvement that day, but he died from weakness and heart failure, caused by the wound being, as all these cases are, so septic. I shall ever remember his sweet smile, his gratitude and cheerfulness, and how he was looking forward to getting better and returning to his home.'

" Capt. Campbell's Commanding Officer wrote as follows : ' I want to tell you how much we mourn the death of our gallant comrade-in-arms, your beloved husband. He was an example of bravery and good cheer —capable and resourceful. I had twice before recommended him for promotion and honours, and have again done so. This time I feel his name will be found in the list, as it richly deserves to be. He was so kindly— we will ever keep his memory in affectionate recollection.'

" The Colonel's recommendation went through, and Capt. Campbell was awarded posthumously the supreme award for bravery in battle and self-sacrificing devotion on the field of conflict. . . .

" Capt. Campbell had spent about eighteen months in the United States, and was present in London at the Coronation of King George V. He was a public school trustee of No. 15 S. S. at Normanby, his home in Canada, and was also a director of the Mount Forest Agricultural Society.

" In civilian life he was known and respected for his innate manliness, and in military circles the same qualities earned for him the love and respect of all ranks.

" After a strenuous life spent in the service of his country, all that is mortal of Capt. Campbell rests in a soldier's grave at Boulogne. Those who love him and mourn his death may well echo the words of that tribute to ' England's Dead ' :

" ' . . . They, in God's completed aims,
    Bear each his part ; unseen of bounded sight,
Down the vast firmament there floats and flames,
    Crested with stars and panoplied in light,

" ' Of strenuous clean souls a long array,
    With lambent lance and white, bright blinding sword,
All riding upon horses—what are they ?
    They are the dead which died in Christ their Lord

" ' For England, from old time. . . .'

" IN MEMORIAM

" Of Capt. Frederick William Campbell, V.C., farmer, of the township of Normanby, Ontario, Captain of E Coy., Mount Forest, 30th Wellington Regt., and Commander of the Machine Gun Section of the 1st Battn., 1st Brigade, First Canadian Contingent, who, after many gallant acts in which he fearlessly exposed himself for the safety of others, was wounded at the Battle of Givenchy on 15 June, 1915 ; died in hospital at La Toquet, France, on 19 June, and was awarded the posthumous honour of the Victoria Cross. Sir Max Aitken, concluding his graphic account of Capt. Campbell's gallant conduct, pays this tribute : In the words of Kinglake, ' And no man died that night with more glory, yet many died and there was much glory.'

" ' Fair Canada, our country dear,
    And Britain, mother of the free,
Have all to hope and naught to fear
    With sons as true and brave as he.
The cross that was the Empire's meed
    Will to his children's children tell
The glory of his knightly deed
    When gentle, valiant Campbell fell.
            —" ' A. W. WRIGHT.' "

The following is taken from " Thirty Canadian V.C.'s," published by Messrs. Skeffington :

" On the afternoon of the 15th of June, 1915, the 1st Canadian Infantry Battalion moved up to a jumping-off position in our front line, with two other battalions of the same brigade on its right, and a third in support. The 7th Division (British) was about to make an attempt to drive the Germans out of an important and formidable position known to our troops as ' Stony Mountain,' and the 1st Canadian Battalion had been told off to the task of covering and securing that division's right flank of attack. This meant the conquest and occupation of one hundred and fifty yards of the enemy's front line running southwards from ' Stony Mountain ' to another German stronghold called ' Dorchester.' It was too big a job to be undertaken in a casual, slap-dash manner or a happy-go-lucky spirit. Experts prepared it, and the artillery and the engineers took a hand in it. We know that our gunners are always eager to fight at pistol range. Major

George Ralston, C.F.A., had two guns of his battery dug into place and sandbagged at a point in our fire-trench called ' Duck's Bill ' by the morning of the 15th. These guns had been brought up to and through Givenchy during the night, in the usual way, and from the forward edge of the village they had been ' man-handled ' into the places prepared for them. One was commanded by Lieutenant C. S. Craig and the other by Lieutenant L. S. Kelly. All was ready before daybreak. The German line opposite was only seventy-five yards away. During the afternoon our batteries, firing from normal positions in the rear, bombarded selected points of the hostile front. At 5.45 the field of fire of our two entrenched guns was uncovered by knocking away the parapet in front of them. They immediately opened fire ; and in fifteen minutes they levelled the German parapet opposite for a distance of nearly two hundred yards, slashed the wire along the same frontage and disposed of six machine-gun emplacements. Then we sprang a mine close in to the German trench ; and then our infantry went over. The leading company of the 1st Battalion charged across the open ground through the smoke and flying earth of the explosion. They were met and swung slightly from their course by withering machine-gun fire from Stony Mountain ; but the unhit ran onwards, entered the hostile trench and took and occupied that system of defences called Dorchester. They fought to the left along the trench ; but Stony Mountain itself held them off. With the second wave of the attack came Lieutenant Campbell, his two Colt's machine-guns and their crews. On the way, before reaching the shelter of the captured trench, all the members of one of his gun-crews were wiped out. He got into the trench with only one of his guns and a few unwounded men. He immediately moved to the left towards Stony Mountain, until he was halted by a block in the trench. By this time one Private Vincent was the only man of his two crews still standing and unhit. All the others lay dead or wounded behind him. Vincent, who had been a lumberjack in the woods of Ontario in the days of peace, was as strong of body as of heart and a cool hand into the bargain. When his officer failed to find a suitable base for his gun in that particular position, Vincent saved time by offering his own broad back. So Campbell straddled Vincent's back with the tripod of the gun, and opened fire on the enemy. By this time our supply of bombs had given out and our attack was weakening. The Germans massed for a counter-attack. Campbell fired over a thousand rounds from his gun, from Vincent's back, dispersed the enemy's initial counter-attack, and afterwards maintained his position until the trench was entered by German bombers and he was seriously wounded. Then Vincent abandoned the tripod and dragged the gun away to safety. Campbell crawled back towards his friends. He was met and lifted by Sergeant-Major Owen and carried into our jumping-off trench, where he died."

COSGROVE, WILLIAM, Corpl., No. 8980, enlisted in the Royal Munster Fusiliers ; was promoted to Corporal, and served in the European War. In Gallipoli the Royal Munster Fusiliers served under Sir Ian Hamilton, and landed on V beach, near Sedd-el-Bahr, from the River Clyde under heavy covering fire from the fleet. The Turks made no sign until the boats began to beach, and then a tornado of fire swept the shore. When the River Clyde ran her nose ashore and her human freight disembarked, it was a company of the Munsters who led the way into the dense fire, followed by a second company, then a third. The fire was deadly, and Brigadier-General Napier was killed, and the Munsters lost heavily. How the survivors clung to that strip of beach is one of the most glorious tales of the Dardanelles. Capt. G. W. Geddes was again mentioned twice, as well as Capts. E. L. H. Henderson, G. W. Nightingale and C. R. Prendergast, and Corpl. William Cosgrove received the Victoria Cross [London Gazette, 23 Aug. 1915] : " William Cosgrove, No. 8980, Corpl., 1st Battn. Royal Munster Fusiliers. Date of Act of Bravery : 26 April, 1915. For most conspicuous bravery in the leading of his section with great dash during our attack from the beach to the east of Cape Helles, on the Turkish positions on the 26th April, 1915. Corpl. Cosgrove on this occasion pulled down the posts of the enemy's high wire entanglements single-handed, notwithstanding a terrific fire from both front and flanks, thereby greatly contributing to the successful clearing of the heights." Surgeon P. Burrowes Kelly, R.N., D.S.O., thus describes the event in his diary : " An Irish Giant. With his officers and brother Tommies dying and dead around him, continued a task he had set himself of clearing a way through the Turkish wire. Though under heavy fire he continued at his task, and eventually, aided by his exceptional strength, succeeded in wrenching a stanchion out of the ground. The others had failed to cut the wire. The manner in which the man worked out in the open will never be forgotten by those who were fortunate enough to witness it."

SMITH, ISSY, Acting-Corpl., served in the European War. The authors of " The Indian Corps in France," in describing the part taken by the 1st Manchesters in the Second Battle of Ypres, say that they came under a perfect inferno of shot and shell. " The Manchesters at once began to feel the effects of the fire, officers and men falling everywhere." Corpl. Issy Smith won the Victoria Cross, and Sergt. J. Bates, Corpl. Dervin and Private F. Richardson the Distinguished Conduct Medal. The Manchesters are described as being " as stubborn and superb here as at Givenchy." He was awarded the Victoria Cross [London Gazette, 23 Aug. 1915] : " Issy Smith, Acting Corpl., 1st Battn. The Manchester Regt. Date of Act of Bravery : 26 April, 1915. For most conspicuous bravery on the 26th April, 1915, near Ypres, when he

Issy Smith.

left his company on his own initiative and went well forward towards the enemy's position to assist a severely wounded man, whom he carried a distance of 250 yards into safety, whilst exposed the whole time to heavy machine-gun and rifle fire. Subsequently Corpl. Smith displayed great gallantry, when the casualties were very heavy, in voluntarily assisting to bring in many more wounded men throughout the day, and attending to them with the greatest devotion to duty, regardless of personal risk."

WILLIS, RICHARD RAYMOND, Capt., was born 13 Oct. 1876, son of R. A. Willis. He was educated at Harrow (Home Boarder, 1890–93) and Sandhurst, and was gazetted to the Lancashire Fusiliers on 20 Feb. 1897, becoming Lieutenant 20 July, 1898, and serving in the Nile Expedition in 1898 ; Battle of Khartum (Medal and clasp and Egyptian Medal). He was promoted to Captain 31 July, 1900. Capt. Willis served in the European War in the Dardanelles, 1914–15, and in France, 1915–19. He was awarded the Victoria Cross [London Gazette, 24 Aug. 1915] : " Richard Raymond Willis, Capt., Alfred Richards, No. 1293, Sergt., William Keneally, No. 1809, Private, 1st Battn. The Lancashire Fusiliers. Date of Act of Bravery : 25 April, 1915. On the 25th April, 1915, three companies and the Head-quarters of the 1st Battn. Lancashire Fusiliers, in effecting a landing on the Gallipoli Peninsula to the west of Cape Helles, were met by a very deadly fire from hidden machine guns which caused a great number of casualties. The survivors, however, rushed up and cut the wire entanglements, notwithstanding the terrific fire from the enemy, and after overcoming supreme difficulties, the cliffs were gained and the position maintained. Amongst the very gallant officers and men engaged in this most hazardous undertaking, Capt. Willis, Sergt. Richards and Private Keneally have been selected by their comrades as having performed the most signal acts of bravery and devotion to duty." In General Hamilton's first Despatch dated 20 May, 1915, the exploit of the Lancashire Fusiliers for which Capt. Willis and others received the Victoria Cross is described. We append some extracts from it : " So strong . . . were the defences of ' W ' Beach that the Turks may well have considered them impregnable, and it is my firm conviction that no finer feat of arms has ever been achieved by the British soldier—or any other soldier—than the storming of these trenches from open boats on the morning of 25 April. The landing at ' W ' had been entrusted to the 1st Battn. Lancashire Fusiliers (Major Bishop), and it was to the complete lack of the senses of danger or of fear of this daring battalion that we owed our astonishing success. . . . While the troops were approaching the shore no shot had been fired from the enemy's trenches, but as soon as the first boat touched the ground a hurricane of lead swept over the battalion. Gallantly led by their officers, the Fusiliers literally hurled themselves ashore, and, fired at from right, left and centre, commenced hacking their way through the wire. A long line of men was at once mown down as by a scythe, but the remainder were not to be denied. Covered by the fire of the warships, which had now closed right in to the shore, helped by the flanking fire of the company on the extreme left, they broke through the entanglements and collected under the cliffs on either side of the beach. Here the companies were rapidly re-formed, and set forth to storm the enemy's entrenchments wherever they could find them." Capt. Willis was wounded on 4 June, 1915 ; he was promoted Major in Aug. 1915, and after recovery served in France with the 2nd Lancashire Fusiliers, 1st Royal Inniskilling Fusiliers (Temporary Lieut.-Colonel Commanding), 8th West Riding Regt., 6th York and Lancaster Regt., and as Commandant Reinforcement Depôt and Officers' Training School, 11th Division. Whilst in command of the 1st Royal Inniskilling Fusiliers, Acting Lieut.-Colonel Willis received congratulatory telegrams from the Commander-in-Chief, Corps and Divisional Commanders for the distinguished services of the regiment under his command at Transloy and Beaumont Hamel, and the regiment was specially mentioned in telegraphic Despatch dated 1 Feb. 1917. As Commandant, Reinforcement Camp, in March, 1918, Major Willis organized all units for defence, and his services on this occasion were recognized in the following memorandum from the Commander 1st Corps, under date 13 April, 1918 : " The Corps Commander wishes to express his appreciation of the work done by the men of the Reinforcement Camp, Allouagne, under Major Willis, on the Bethune-Hinges Switch yesterday. This work was of the highest importance, and the loyal and energetic way in which it has been tackled reflects the greatest credit on all concerned." In 1919 Major Willis was appointed Second-in-Command, and temporarily in command of the 2nd Battn. Lancashire Fusiliers. Major Willis married, in 1907, Maude, daughter of Colonel J. A. Temple and niece of the late Sir R Temple, Bart., and they have two sons.

Richard Raymond Willis.

HAWKER, LANOE GEORGE, Capt., came of a famous fighting stock. He was born in Dec. 1890 ; son of the late Lieut. H. C. Hawker, of Home Croft, Longparish, Hants. He was educated at the Royal Naval College, Dartmouth, and the Royal Military Academy, Woolwich ; joined the Royal Engineers in

Lanoe George Hawker.

July, 1911, and transferred to the Royal Flying Corps in Oct. 1914. He served in the European War, first as Flight Commander and then as Squadron Commander of the Royal Flying Corps, with the rank of Major. On 19 April, 1915, the feat that secured for him the Companionship of the Distinguished Service Order was the dropping of bombs on the German airship shed at Gontrode. This was done from a height of only 200 feet in circumstances of the greatest risk. By great ingenuity he contrived to get shelter for his work from an unmanned enemy captive balloon. He was awarded the Victoria Cross [London Gazette, 24 Aug. 1915]: "Lanoe George Hawker, Capt., R.E. and R.F.C. Date of Act of Bravery: 25 July, 1915. For most conspicuous bravery and very great ability on the 25th July, 1915. When flying alone he attacked three German aeroplanes in succession. The first managed eventually to escape, the second was driven to ground damaged, and the third, which he attacked at a height of about 10,000 feet, was driven to earth in our lines, the pilot and observer being killed. The personal bravery shown by this officer was of the very highest order, as the enemy's aircraft were armed with machine guns, and all carried a passenger as well as the pilot." He was at first reported as missing, and afterwards as killed in Nov. 1916. The "Times" of 26 July, 1917, says that Major Hawker's death in the preceding Nov. is officially announced. An obituary notice says that Major Hawker was the son of the late Lieut. Henry Colley Hawker, R.N., and Mrs. Hawker, and the grandson of the late Peter William Lanoe Hawker, of Longparish House, Hants. The date of his promotion to Lieutenant is given as Oct. 1913, and to Squadron Commander as Feb. 1916. Lieut. Hawker was received by the King and decorated with the D.S.O. in October, 1915, and later received the Victoria Cross also at the hands of His Majesty.

RICHARDS, ALFRED JOSEPH, Sergt., was born 21 June, 1879, at Plymouth, Devon, son of Charles N. Richards (late Colour-Sergt., 2nd Battn. 20th Lancashire Fusiliers), and of Bridget Frances, his wife. He

was educated at St. Dominic's Priory School, near Byker Bridge, Newcastle-on-Tyne. He entered the Army 4 July, 1895, joining the ranks of the 1st Lancashire Fusiliers, and served in Ireland, England, Gibraltar, Malta, Crete, Egypt and India, in all seeing 20 years and six days of service. He served in the European War; was mentioned in Despatches [see Sir Ian Hamilton's Report], and received the Victoria Cross, by the vote of his comrades, for gallantry against the Turks during the Gallipoli landing—one of the three V.C.'s awarded on that occasion [London Gazette, 24 Aug. 1915]: "Richard Raymond Willis, Capt.; Alfred Richards, No. 1293, Sergt.; William Keneally, No. 1809, Private, 1st Battn. The Lancashire Fusiliers. Date of Acts

Alfred Joseph Richards.

of Bravery: 25 April, 1915. On the 25th April, 1915, three companies and the Headquarters of the 1st Battn. Lancashire Fusiliers, in effecting a landing on the Gallipoli Peninsula to the west of Cape Helles, were met by a very deadly fire from hidden machine guns which caused a great number of casualties. The survivors, however, rushed up to and cut the wire entanglements, notwithstanding the terrific fire from the enemy, and after overcoming supreme difficulties, the cliffs were gained and the position maintained. Amongst the very gallant officers and men engaged in this most hazardous undertaking, Capt. Willis, Sergt. Richards and Private Keneally have been selected by their comrades as having performed the most signal acts of bravery and devotion to duty." He married, 30 Sept. 1916, at Weybridge, Miss Dora Coombs, a young lady whom he first met when he was recovering from his wounds in a local hospital. At his wedding wounded soldiers formed a Guard of Honour inside the church. Sergt. Richards later became associated with Lord Roberts's scheme for the employment of disabled soldiers. He was discharged from the Army through the amputation of his right leg, from wounds received in the Gallipoli Landing. He was also awarded the Good Conduct Medal.

KENEALLY, WILLIAM, Private, was born at 38, Parnell Street, Wexford, Ireland, on 26 Dec. 1886, son of John

Keneally, ex-Colour-Sergt. in the Royal Irish Regt., and for twenty-five years a Colliery Weighman. He was educated at St. John's School, Wigan, and at St. Oswald's, Ashton-in-Makerfield, three and a half miles from Wigan, and enlisted in the Army in Sept. 1909. He served for about six years in India in the 1st Battn. Lancashire Fusiliers, and returned home, landing early in 1915. He served in the European War, being sent to France, and afterwards to the Dardanelles. Private Keneally was awarded the Victoria Cross [London Gazette, 24 Aug. 1915]: "William Keneally, Private, 1st Battn. The Lancashire Fusiliers. On the 25th April, 1915, three companies and the Headquarters of the 1st Battn. Lancashire Fusiliers, in

William Keneally.

effecting a landing on the Gallipoli Peninsula to the west of Cape Helles, were met by a deadly fire from hidden machine guns which caused a great number of casualties. The survivors, however, rushed up to and cut the wire entanglements, notwithstanding the terrific fire from the enemy, and after overcoming supreme difficulties, the cliffs were gained and the position maintained. Amongst the very gallant officers and men engaged in this most hazardous undertaking, Capt. Willis, Sergt. Richards and Private Keneally have been selected by their comrades as having performed the most signal acts of bravery and devotion to duty." He was promoted Sergeant. He was killed in action about the 26th June, 1916, at the Gallipoli "Lancashire" Landing.

London Gazette, 1 Sept. 1915.—"War Office, 1 Sept. 1915. His Majesty the King has been graciously pleased to approve of the grant of the Victoria Cross to the undermentioned Officers and Non-commissioned Officer for most conspicuous bravery and devotion to duty."

WHEELER, GEORGE GODFREY MASSY, Major, was born on 31 Jan. 1873, at Chakrata, India, son of General Wheeler and grandson of General Sir Hugh Massy Wheeler, of Indian Mutiny Fame. He was

educated at Bedford Modern School, and joined the Army on 20 May, 1893, in the 1st Wiltshire Regt.; on 13 Oct. 1897, transferred to the Indian Army, 7th Hariana Lancers; in May, 1902, he got his Captaincy, and from 1908 to 1912 was Commandant of 50th Camel Corps. In 1911 he became Major. In 1908 he served in the operations on the North-West Frontier, for which he received a Medal with clasp. Major Massy Wheeler was a keen sportsman in every sense of the word; a good polo player, and a most devoted Regimental Officer, and a great favourite in the regiment. Major Massy Wheeler was married. Major Massy Wheeler was awarded the Victoria Cross

G. G. Massy Wheeler.

[London Gazette, 1 Sept. 1915]: "George Godfrey Massy Wheeler, Major, late 7th Hariana Lancers. Dates of Acts of Bravery: 12 and 13 April, 1915. For most conspicuous bravery at Shaiba, Mesopotamia. On the 12th April, 1915, Major Wheeler asked permission to take out his squadron and attempt to capture a flag, which was the centre-point of a group of the enemy who were firing on one of our picquets. He advanced and attacked the enemy's infantry with the lance, doing considerable execution among them. He then retired, while the enemy swarmed out of hidden ground and formed an excellent target to our Royal Horse Artillery guns. On the 13th April, 1915, Major Massy Wheeler led his squadron to the attack of the 'North Mound.' He was seen far ahead of his men, riding single-handed straight for the enemy's standards. This gallant officer was killed on the Mound."

O'SULLIVAN, GERALD ROBERT, Capt., was born on 8 Nov. 1888, at Frankfield, Douglas, County Cork, Ireland, son of the late Lieut.-Colonel George Lidwill O'Sullivan, formerly of the 91st Argyll and Sutherland

Highlanders, and his wife, Charlotte Hiddingh, of Rowan House, Dorchester, daughter of the late W. H. Hiddingh, of Hope House, Cape Town, South Africa. He was educated at Wimbledon College, by private tutors, and at the Royal Military College, Sandhurst, from which he obtained a commission on 9 May, 1909, and joined the 2nd Battn. Royal Inniskilling Fusiliers in Dublin. He left England on 15 Sept. of the same year for Tientsin, North China, where he served with the 1st Battn. of his regiment for three years, and was present during the Chinese Rebellion of 1911 and 1912. The British troops, however, took no part in the fighting. In the autumn of 1912 he left China with his

Gerald Robert O'Sullivan.

regiment for Secunderabad, Central India. He served in the European War. His regiment formed part of the 29th Division, which went from India to England, and thence to the Dardanelles, landing there on 25 April, 1915. He fought with his regiment before Krithia, until he was severely wounded on 1 July, 1915, and there won the Victoria Cross. He had already been recommended in June, and had been wounded on that occasion, though not severely enough to go off duty. The award was announced in the London Gazette of 1 Sept. 1915: "Gerald Robert O'Sullivan, Capt., 27th Battn. Royal Inniskilling Fusiliers. For most conspicuous bravery during operations south-west of Krithia, on the Gallipoli Peninsula. On the night of the 1st–2nd July, 1915, when it was essential that a portion of a trench should be regained, Capt. O'Sullivan, although not belonging to the troops at this point, volunteered to lead a party of bomb-throwers to effect the recapture. He advanced in the open, under a very heavy fire, and in order to throw his bombs with greater effect, got up on the parapet, where he was completely exposed to the fire of the enemy occupying the trench. He was finally wounded, but not before his inspiring example had led on his party to make further efforts, which resulted in the recapture of the trench. On the night of the 18th–19th June, 1915, Capt. O'Sullivan saved a critical situation in the same locality by his great personal gallantry and good leading." He was mentioned in Despatches by General Sir Ian Hamilton. After being in hospital at Alexandria for a little over a month he returned to Gallipoli, and soon afterwards went with the 29th Division to the new landing at Suvla. He was reported missing after leading his men to the attack on Hill 70 on 21 Aug. One of his brother officers wrote: "On this occasion, as on all others, he was a dashing leader and a real brave man."

BOYD ROCHFORT, GEORGE ARTHUR, Lieut., was born at Middleton Park, Castletown, County Westmeath, Ireland, on 1 Jan. 1880, son of the late Major R. H. Boyd Rochfort, 15th Hussars, and Mrs. Boyd Rochfort,

George A. Boyd Rochfort.

daughter of the late H. Hemming, Esq., D.L., of Bentley Manor, Worcester. He was educated at Eton and Trinity College, Cambridge, and was married in Dublin on 9 June, 1901, to Miss E. Ussher, of Eastwell, County Galway. He served in the European War, joining the Army on 1 March, 1915, as Second Lieutenant in the 1st Battn. Scots Guards. Of his two brothers, Major H. Boyd Rochfort, D.S.O., M.C., commanded a battalion of Tanks during the 1918 advance, and Capt. C. Boyd Rochfort, Croix de Guerre with Palms, was with the Scots Guards till July, 1916, then became Brigade-Major to the 4th Army, R.F.C. He was mentioned in Despatches, and awarded the Victoria Cross [London Gazette, 1 Sept. 1915]: "George Arthur Boyd Rochfort, Second Lieut. 1st Battn., Special Reserve, Scots Guards. Date of Act of Bravery · 3 Aug. 1915. For most conspicuous bravery in the trenches, between Cambrin and La Bassée, on the 3rd Aug. 1915. At 2 a.m. a German trench-mortar bomb landed on the side of the parapet of the communication trench in which he stood, close to a small working party of his battalion. He might easily have stepped back a few yards round the corner into perfect safety, but, shouting to his men to look out, he rushed at the bomb, seized it and hurled it over the parapet, where it at once exploded. There is no doubt that this splendid combination of presence of mind and courage saved the lives of many of the working party." He was promoted to Lieutenant and Acting Captain, and was Adjutant of the Guards' Division at the front. Lieut. Boyd Rochfort has travelled a lot, and done some big game shooting ; polo and racing are his favourite pursuits. He played polo in the winning team for his county, Westmeath, for some years ; won the Westmeath Gold Cup, riding his own mare, Old Times, and the National Hunt Cup at Punchestown, with Kilhugh, a horse he bred himself. Of his three cousins, Colonel H. Rochfort Boyd, D.S.O., R.H.A., after serving throughout the whole war at the front, was finally killed at Cambrai in Nov. 1917 ; Colonel H. Cheape, D.S.O., commanded the Warwickshire Yeomanry in their wonderful advance to Jerusalem, and was torpedoed and drowned in the Mediterranean in Aug. 1917, and Major Leslie Cheape, Worcestershire Yeomanry, the crack polo player, was killed in Egypt in Aug. 1915.

JAMES, HERBERT, 2nd Lieut., was born at Birmingham, in Oct. 1887, son of Mr. and Mrs. W. James, of Edgbaston, Birmingham. He served in the European War, landing in Gallipoli with the 4th Battn. The Worcestershire Regt. on 25 April, 1915, and was awarded the Victoria Cross [London Gazette, 1 Sept. 1915]: "Second Lieut. Herbert James, 4th Battn. The Worcestershire Regt. For most conspicuous bravery during the operations in the southern zone of the Gallipoli Peninsula on 28 June, 1915. When a portion of a regiment had been checked, owing to all the officers being put out of action, Second Lieut. James, who belonged to a neighbouring unit, entirely on his own initiative gathered together a body of men and led them forward under heavy shell and rifle fire.

Herbert James.

He then returned, organized a second party, and again advanced. His gallant example put fresh life into the attack. On the 3rd July, in the same locality, Second Lieut. James headed a party of bomb-throwers up a Turkish communication trench, and after nearly all his bomb-throwers had been killed or wounded he remained alone at the head of the trench, and kept back the enemy single-handed till a barrier had been built behind him and the trench secured. He was throughout exposed to a murderous fire." He was twice wounded, and left the Peninsula on 5 Sept. 1915. He was in hospital in Egypt and in England. He went to France with the 1st Battn. The Worcestershire Regt., 29th Division, in March, 1916, and was wounded at the Battle of the Somme 7 July, 1916. He was married on the 5th Sept. 1916, at Stoke Damerel Parish Church, Devonport, to Gladys Beatrice, eldest daughter of Lieut. F. W. Lillicrap, Royal Engineers, late Water Engineer to the Devonport Corporation.

SOMERS, JAMES, Sergt., was born at Beltarbet, County Cavan, son of Robert and Charlotte Somers. He joined the Army, and served in the European War. He was awarded the Victoria Cross [London Gazette, 1 Sept. 1915]: "James Somers, No. 10512, Sergt., 1st Battn. Royal Inniskilling Fusiliers. Date of Act of Bravery : 1-2 July, 1915. For most conspicuous bravery on the night of the 1st-2nd July, 1915, in the southern

James Somers.

zone of the Gallipoli Peninsula, when, owing to hostile bombing, some of our troops had retired from a sap, Sergt. Somers remained alone on the spot until a party brought up bombs. He then climbed over into the Turkish trench, and bombed the Turks with great effect. Later on he advanced into the open under very heavy fire, and held back the enemy by throwing bombs into their flank until a barricade had been established. During this period he frequently ran to and from our trenches to obtain fresh supplies of bombs. By his great gallantry and coolness Sergt. Somers was largely instrumental in effecting the recapture of a portion of our trench which had been lost." James Somers joined the Special Reserve, Royal Munster Fusiliers, 14 Jan. 1913 ; joined the Regular Army 16 July, 1913. He served in France 23 Aug. to 23 Oct. 1914 ; with the Mediterranean Expeditionary Force 17 March, 1915 to 12 March, 1916 ; in France 4 April to 4 Sept. 1916. He was transferred to the R.A.S.C. 1 April, 1917.

London Gazette, 6 Sept. 1915.—" The King has been graciously pleased to award the Victoria Cross to Sidney Clayton Woodroffe, Second Lieutenant (late) 8th Battn. The Rifle Brigade."

WOODROFFE, SIDNEY CLAYTON, Second Lieut., was born at Lewes, Sussex, on 17 Dec. 1895, fourth and youngest son of Henry Long Woodroffe, of Woodmoor, Branksome Avenue, Bournemouth, and Clara, daughter of the late Henry Clayton. He was educated at Marlborough College (where he was Senior Prefect, Captain of the O.T.C., winner of the Curzon-Wyllie Medal, and member of the football fifteen 1912-13-14, hockey eleven and cricket twenty-two. He gained a classical scholarship at Pembroke College, Cambridge. He was gazetted to the 8th Battn. The Rifle Brigade on 23 Dec. 1914, and went to France 25 May, 1915, and was killed in action at Hooge, Flanders, 30 July, 1915, aged nineteen. He was awarded the Victoria Cross posthumously [London Gazette, 6 Sept. 1915]: "Sidney Clayton Woodroffe, Second Lieut. (late) 8th Battn. The Rifle Brigade. Date of Act of Bravery : 30 July, 1915. For most conspicuous bravery on the 30th July, 1915, at Hooge.

Sidney C. Woodroffe.

The enemy having broken through the centre of our front trenches, consequent on the use of burning liquids, this officer's position was heavily attacked with bombs from the flank, and subsequently from the rear, but he managed to defend his post until all his bombs were exhausted, and then skilfully withdrew his remaining men. This very gallant officer immediately led his party forward in a counter-attack under an intense rifle and machine-gun fire, and was killed whilst in the act of cutting the wire obstacles in the open." Lieut.-Colonel R. C. Maclachlan wrote to his father : " Your younger boy was simply one of the bravest of the brave, and the work he did that day will stand out as a record hard to beat ; later I will try to get you a more or less definite account. When the line was attacked and broken on his right he still held his trench, and only when the Germans were discovered to be in the rear of him did he leave it. He then withdrew his remaining men very skilfully right away to a flank, and worked his way alone back to me to report. He finally brought his command back, and then took part in the counter-attack. He was killed out in front, in the open, cutting the wire to enable the attack to be continued. This is the bald statement of his part of that day's action. He risked his life for others right through the day and finally gave it for the sake of his men. He was a splendid type of young officer, always bold as a lion, confident and sure of himself too. The loss he is to me personally is very great, as I had learnt to appreciate what a sterling fine lad he was. His men would have followed him anywhere." Mr. and Mrs. Woodroffe lost their two elder sons also in the European War. Lieut. K. H. C. Woodroffe, 6th Battn. Rifle Brigade, was killed in action on 9 May, 1915. He was also Senior Prefect at Marlborough and Captain (1912) of the cricket team. He took six wickets for Cambridge in his first (1913) Oxford and Cambridge Match at Lord's ; played cricket as a fast bowler for Hants C.C.C. in 1912 v. South Africans (5 wickets), and for Sussex C.C.C. in 1913. Capt. Leslie Woodroffe, M.C., 8th Battn. Rifle Brigade, was, while at Marlborough College, head of the school, and was in the cricket eleven and football fifteen. At Oxford he took a first class in Mods. and a second class in Lit. Hum. He was severely wounded in July, 1915, at Hooge, when his brother Sidney was killed, and was only able to return to his regiment 1 June, 1916 ; was again wounded on the day of his arrival, and died of these wounds three days later.

London Gazette, 7 Sept. 1915.—" The King has been graciously pleased to award the Victoria Cross to the undermentioned Officer."

FORSHAW, WILLIAM THOMAS, Lieut., was educated at Barrow Secondary School and Westminster Training College, and was a Master at North Manchester School. He volunteered for service with the Territorials, serving in Gallipoli in 1915 ; was mentioned in Despatches, and awarded the Victoria Cross [London Gazette, 7 Sept. 1915]: "William Thomas Forshaw, Lieut., 1/9th Battn. Manchester Regt. (Territorial Force). Date of Act of Bravery : 7th to 9th Aug. 1915. For most conspicuous bravery and determination in the Gallipoli Peninsula from the 7th to 9th Aug. 1915. When holding the north-west corner of the ' Vineyard,' he was attacked and heavily bombed by Turks, who advanced time after time by three trenches which converged at this point, but he held his own, not only directing his men and encouraging them by exposing himself with the utmost disregard to danger, but personally throwing bombs continuously for forty-one hours. When his detachment was relieved after twenty-four hours he volunteered to continue the direction of operations. Three times during the night of the 8th–9th Aug. he was heavily attacked, and once the Turks got over the barricade, but after shooting three with his revolver, he led his men forward and recaptured it. When he rejoined his battalion he was choked and sickened by bomb fumes, badly bruised by a fragment of shrapnel, and could barely lift his arm from continuous bomb-throwing. It was due to his personal example, magnificent courage, and endurance, that this very important corner was held." Mr. H. W. Nevison, in "The Dardanelles Campaign" (page 230), says: "Here, as in other places, it is impossible to record individual acts of courage, but the services of Lieut. W. T. Forshaw (9th Manchesters) became almost a legend on the Peninsula." After a vivid description of the fight for the Vineyard, Mr. Nevison remarks: "The actual territory gained was not much—barely 200 yards—but the Vineyard will always remain a memory in Lancastrian annals." He was promoted to Captain. Capt. Forshaw is a Freeman of Ashton-under-Lyne.

London Gazette, 1 Oct. 1915.—"The King has been graciously pleased to award the Victoria Cross to the undermentioned Officer and Man."

HANSEN, PERCY HOWARD, Capt., was born 26 Oct. 1890, in London, son of Vigo Hansen, Esq., and of E. Hansen. He was educated at Eton and Sandhurst, and was gazetted to the Lincolnshire Regt. as Second-Lieutenant 4 March, 1911, becoming Lieutenant 3 Aug. 1912. He served in the European War; was Adjutant and temporary Captain, 4 Sept. 1914, to 10 Aug. 1915. He was awarded the Victoria Cross [London Gazette, 1 Oct. 1915]: "Percy Howard Hansen, Capt., Adjutant, 6th (Service) Battn. The Lincolnshire Regt. Date of Act of Bravery: 9th Aug. 1915: For most conspicuous bravery on the 9th of Aug. 1915, at Yilghin Burnu, Gallipoli Peninsula. After the second capture of the 'Green Knoll' his battalion was forced to retire, leaving some wounded behind, owing to the intense heat from the scrub, which had been set on fire. When the retirement was effected, Capt. Hansen, with three or four volunteers, on his own initiative, dashed forward several times some 300 to 400 yards over open scrub under a terrific fire, and succeeded in rescuing from inevitable death from burning no less than six wounded men." He was promoted to Major. "Deeds that thrill the Empire" (pages 414 to 425) says: "On the night of 6th–7th Aug. 1915, our Mediterranean Expeditionary Force effected an important new landing of troops at Suvla Bay, Gallipoli, the scene of the most desperate fighting at the first landing in the previous April. This new landing formed part of a great offensive movement, which, it was hoped, would give us possession of the western end of the Peninsula. While a pretence of a disembarkation at Karachali, at the head of the Gulf of Saros, and an advance in force against Achi Baba were to be made, with the object of inducing the Turks to send their reserves to Krithia, the left of the Anzac Corps would attempt to gain the heights of Koja Chernen and the seaward ridges, and the newly arrived troops, having successfully effected their disembarkation at Suvla Bay, for which it was believed the Turks would be wholly unprepared, would endeavour to carry the Anafarta Hills and link up with the left of the Australasians. Thus, the British would hold the central crest of the spine of upland which runs through the western end of the Peninsula, and, with any reasonable good fortune, the reduction of the European defences of the Narrows could only be a matter of time. The force destined for Suvla Bay comprised two divisions of our new Army—the 10th (Irish), less one brigade, and the 11th (Northern)—and two Territorial Divisions, the 53rd and the 54th, and was under the command of Major-General Sir F. W. Stopford. The transports carrying the 11th Division, which had embarked at Kephalos Bay, in Imbros, entered the bay between nine and ten o'clock on the night of the 6th, and so successful had been the movements of which we have spoken in diverting the attention of the enemy elsewhere, that the landing was effected with practically no opposition, and by dawn on the 7th the whole division was ashore and in possession of both sides of the bay and the neck of land between them. Shortly after daybreak the greater part of the 11th Division arrived from Mitylene, and was soon followed by the remaining battalions, who came from Mudros, and by two o'clock in the afternoon the two divisions had deployed into the plain and held a line east of the Salt Lake, running from Karakol Dagh on the north to near the butt-end of the ridge called Yilghin Burnu. In the course of the afternoon we advanced our front a short distance in the face of a violent but comparatively innocuous shelling from the Turkish guns on the Anafarta slopes, and late that night, on our right, two battalions of the 11th Division, the 6th Lincolns and the 6th Border Regt., succeeded in capturing Yilghin Burnu, which we called Chocolate Hill, while to the northward the Irish carried the parallel position of Karakol Dagh, after a fight in which the 6th Munster Fusiliers particularly distinguished themselves. Thus our flanks were effectually safeguarded. But it was imperative to push on at once, otherwise all the advantages of the surprise landing must be nullified. This, most unfortunately, was not done. Our two divisions amounted to some twenty-five thousand men, and on the morning of the 8th the Turks on the Anafarta heights probably did not exceed four thousand, so that an attack resolutely pressed forward must have carried the position. The day, however, was intensely hot, and as water had to be brought from the beach, and the measures taken for its conveyance and distribution proved to be inadequate, our men soon began to suffer torments from thirst; while the Turkish commander, by pushing a thick screen of riflemen into the patches of scrub which covered the edge of the slopes, cleverly succeeded in conveying the impression that we were faced with a much larger force than was actually the case. General Stopford urged his divisional commanders to advance. But the latter objected that their men were exhausted by their efforts on the night of the 6th–7th, and by the fighting on the 7th, and that the want of water was telling cruelly on the new troops; and General Stopford did not insist. The fact that he considered he was insufficiently supported by artillery appears to have overcome his resolution. And so during the priceless daylight hours of the 8th nothing was attempted beyond sporadic attacks, in which we lost heavily and gained but little ground. About five o'clock in the afternoon, Sir Ian Hamilton, our Commander-in-Chief, arrived from Imbros and boarded H.M.S. Jonquil, where he saw General Stopford. Sir Ian informed him that he had received intelligence that considerable Turkish reinforcements were on the march from Suvla, and urged that the 11th Division should without delay make a concerted attack on the hills. 'I was met,' he writes in his Despatch of 11 Nov. 1915, the fullest and most luminous account which we possess of any of the operations of the Great War, 'by a *non possumus*. The objections of the morning were no longer valid; the men were well rested, watered and fed. But the divisional commanders disliked the idea of an advance at night, and General Stopford did not care, it seems, to force their hands.' At the same time the General declared that he was as eager as the Commander-in-Chief could be to advance, and that if the latter could see his way to overcome the objections of the divisional commanders, no one would be more pleased than himself. The Commander-in-Chief thereupon landed and proceeded to the headquarters of the 11th Division, where he represented to Major-General Hammersley that the sands were fast running out, and that by dawn the high ground to his front might very likely be occupied in force by the enemy. General Hammersley recognized the danger of delay, but declared that 'it was a physical impossibility at so late an hour (6 p.m.) to get out orders for a night attack, the troops being very much scattered.' One brigade, however—the 32nd—was, so General Hammersley admitted, more or less concentrated and ready to move; and Sir Ian Hamilton issued directions that, even if it were only with this brigade, the advance should begin at the earliest possible moment, so that a portion at least of the 11th Division should anticipate the arrival of the Turkish reinforcements on the heights, and dig themselves in in some good tactical position. It was not, however, until 4 a.m. on the morning of the 9th that the 32nd Brigade advanced to the attack, and made a gallant attempt to carry the main Anafarta ridge. But by this time the Turks had been strongly reinforced, and though one company of the East Yorks (Pioneers) actually succeeded in gaining the crest, they were unable to hold it, and the 32nd Brigade, fiercely assailed on both flanks, was obliged to fall back. At 5 a.m. the 33rd Brigade advanced up the slopes of Ismail Oglu Tepe, a gorse-covered hill, which our troops had named the Green Knoll, against which an unsuccessful attempt had been made the previous day, when the position had been captured and subsequently abandoned. Our men advanced with great courage in the face of a heavy shell and rifle fire, and in a quarter of an hour the crest was carried at the point of the bayonet. But to hold on to the ground thus gained was a far more difficult undertaking. It was a scorching day, and as the morning advanced the heat became more and more trying, and the troops suffered cruelly from want of water. The Turks kept up a ceaseless rifle fire and enfiladed us with shrapnel, the shells bursting low and all along our front. Presently our centre began to give way, though whether this was a result of the shrapnel fire, or whether, as some say, an order to retire came up from the rear, has never been clearly established. The 6th Border Regt. and the 6th Lincolns on the flanks, however, gallantly stood their ground, though both had sustained severe losses, until about midday an event occurred which obliged them to retire. The scrub on Hill 70, to the north of the Green Knoll, was set alight by shell fire, and the parched grass and bracken were so readily kindled that, aided by the wind which was blowing from this direction, a wall thirty feet high leaped up and swept right across our front. Compelled to abandon the ground which they had so gallantly won, and held, the remnant of the two battalions then fell back, with the rest of the brigade, to a trench four hundred yards below. The 6th Lincolns had suffered terribly. They had gone into action seven hundred strong; they came out a company of one hundred and twenty men, and those who reached the protection of the trench knew that hundreds of their comrades lay wounded and at the mercy of the flames. It was now that a most heroic action was performed. The adjutant of the battalion, Capt. Howard Percy Hansen, determined that an attempt must be made to rescue as many as possible, and called for volunteers to help him to bring them in. Lance-Corpl. Breese and two other brave men at once offered their services, and, with Capt. Hansen, they climbed up out of the trench, and, amidst a storm of bullets, ran up the hill and dashed into the blazing scrub. One by one, six of the wounded men were snatched from inevitable death and carried down the hill. More it was impossible to save, for by the time the last of the six had been brought in a barrier of fire and of dense black clouds of suffocating smoke had intervened, and the helpless men whom it enveloped would have been past all human aid, even if the rescuers could have contrived to reach them. No further attack could have been attempted that day, and by the morning of the 10th the enemy had been so strongly reinforced that our chance had gone for good. In the course of the day the 53rd Territorial Division, under General Lindley, which had now arrived, attacked the main Anafarta ridge, but failed to reach it. Our casualties from 6 Aug. to 10 Aug. amounted to at least thirty thousand men. Capt. Hansen's most heroic conduct was appropriately recognized by the Victoria Cross being conferred upon him; while L.-Corpl. Breese was awarded the Distinguished Conduct Medal 'for conspicuous bravery and devotion to duty.'"

Percy Howard Hansen.

POTTS, FREDERICK WILLIAM OWEN, Private, worked before the war for the Pulsometer Engineering Company, Reading. He joined the Army, and served in the European War He was the first Yeoman to win the V.C. in the European War. In a letter home he describes as follows the incident for which he had received the Victoria Cross: "It was in the charge on Hill 70, on 21 Aug., in which the Berkshire Yeomanry led a brilliant charge. When about a quarter of a mile from the summit we were told to get ready to charge. Not a man faltered, and, when the order was given to charge, over we went. About twenty yards from the other side I received a wound in the thigh, which completely knocked me off my feet, and I had to lie there. Presently another of our chaps crawled to where I was. He had been shot in the groin. There we lay all that night suffering from thirst, but it was much worse the next day. It seemed as though we should go mad for want of a drink. When the second night came, we decided to move if possible. It was no light job, as firing had been going on all around us. One bullet actually grazed my ear. However, we managed it somehow. Thus we were able to get some water from the water-bottles of men who had been killed, rather a painful job, but one of necessity. We found a hiding-place for the remainder of the night and next day. We dare not show ourselves during the day for fear of snipers; and oh, the thirst! I crawled from one body to another, getting water. It was like wine, though it was nearly boiling. At nightfall we decided that anything was better than death from thirst, so we tried to crawl to where we thought we could find the British lines. The other chap could hardly move, and after a few yards had to give up, so I laid him on a shovel and dragged him down the hill bit by bit, for about three-quarters of a mile. Before we started I prayed as I have never prayed before for strength, help and guidance, and I felt confident we should win through all right. On reaching the foot of the hill we came to a wood, and had not gone more than twenty yards when I received the command to halt. By good luck I had struck a British trench. I soon told my tale, and it was not long before they found the stretchers for both of us and took us through their trenches, where we were received with every kindness. From here we were conveyed to a field ambulance." He was awarded the Victoria Cross [London Gazette, 18 Oct. 1915]: "Frederick William Owen Potts, No. 1300, Private, 1/1st Berkshire Yeomanry (Territorial Force). Date of Act of Bravery: 21 Aug. 1915. For most conspicuous bravery and devotion to a wounded comrade in the Gallipoli Peninsula. Although himself severely wounded in the thigh in the attack on Hill 70 on the 21st Aug. 1915, he remained out over forty-eight hours under the Turkish trenches with a private of his regiment who was severely wounded and unable to move, although he could himself have returned to safety. Finally he fixed a shovel to the equipment of his wounded comrade, and using this as a sledge, he dragged him back over six hundred yards to our lines, though fired at by the Turks on the way. He reached our trenches at about 9.30 p.m. on the 23rd Aug." "Amendment: The Christian names of No. 1300, Private Potts, V.C., 1/1st Berkshire Yeomanry, Territorial Force, are Frederick William Owen,and not as stated in the London Gazette, dated 1 Oct. 1915, page 9641." (Extract from the London Gazette, dated 18 Oct. 1915.) "Deeds that thrill the Empire" (pages 830–845) says: "After the gallant but unsuccessful assaults on the Anafarta heights, which followed the landing of the 10th and 11th Divisions at Suvla Bay, at the beginning of Aug. 1915, our men employed themselves in consolidating what ground they had won, and the Suvla operations languished for some days. But, meantime, we were preparing for a second effort, and fresh troops, consisting of the famous 29th Division and the 2nd Mounted Division of Yeomanry (organized as dismounted troopers) were brought to the scene of action, and placed under the command of General de Lisle. The objective was the encircling hills behind the Suvla plain, extending from Hill 70 to Hill 100. The task before our men was one of the greatest difficulty, since, as all the advantage of surprise had long since been lost, the only tactics left to us were those of a frontal attack, and that against a strong position held in at least equal force by the enemy. The afternoon of 21 Aug. was the time chosen for the attack. After a heavy bombardment of the Turkish position from both land and sea, at 3 p.m. the 34th Brigade of the 11th Division, on the right of our line, rushed the Turkish trenches between Hetman Chair and the communication trench connecting it with the south-west corner of Hill 100, but failed to make good their point, through mistaking the direction and attacking from the north-east instead of the east, and the 33rd Brigade, sent up in haste, with orders to capture this communication trench at all costs, fell into precisely the same error. Meanwhile the 87th Brigade of the 29th Division, whose advance had been planned for 3.30 p.m., had attacked Hill 70 with great dash and carried some of the Turkish trenches there, though the enemy's artillery and machine-gun fire was too heavy to allow them to gain the crest. At the same time, the 80th Brigade, though they had been at first thrown into disorder by the scrub on Chocolate Hill catching fire, and had been unable to advance up the valley between the two spurs, owing to the failure of the 11th Division on their right, were making repeated and most gallant efforts to carry Hill 100 from the east. But they were decimated by a terrible cross-fire of shell and musketry, which simply swept the leading troops off the top of the spur, and were eventually obliged to fall back to a ledge to the south-west of Hill 70, where they found a little cover. About five o'clock, whilst the fighting was still in progress, the Yeomanry moved out from below the knoll of Lala Baba, where they had been held in reserve, to take up a position of readiness between Hill 70 and Hill 100. Their advance lay across a mile and a half of open country, where they were exposed to a devastating fire of shrapnel; but they moved forward in perfect order as if on parade. Sir Ian Hamilton has described this scene in his Despatch of 11 Dec. 1915: 'The advance of these English Yeomen was a sight calculated to send a thrill of pride through anyone with a drop of English blood running in his veins. Such superb martial spectacles are rare in modern war. Ordinarily it should always be possible to bring up reserves under some sort of cover from shrapnel fire. Here, for a mile and a half, there was nothing to conceal a mouse, much less some of the most stalwart soldiers England has ever sent from her shores. Despite the critical events in other parts of the field, I could hardly take my glasses from the Yeomen; they moved like men marching on parade. Here and there a shell would take toll of a cluster; there they lay. There was no straggling, the others moved steadily on; not a man was there who hung back or hurried.' At last the Yeomanry reached the foot of Chocolate Hill, where they rested for half an hour. Here they were comparatively safe from shell fire, but were much annoyed by the Turkish snipers, by whom they had lost a number of men, some of whom fell wounded and were immediately afterwards hit again and killed outright. After they had been a short while in the reserve trenches, the Yeomanry received the order to advance, and, making their way up the slopes by short rushes, they reached the foremost lines of the 29th Division, the Berkshire Yeomanry finally halting in a gully which was occupied by the Bucks and the Dorsets. As darkness was falling, the brigade was launched to the attack, in the hope that they might retrieve the fortunes of the day. All that valour could do they certainly did, and their right flank succeeded in carrying the trenches on a knoll so near the summit of Hill 100 that from the plain it looked as though the crest itself had been won. But this the Turks still held, and as our men were too exhausted, and had lost too heavily to undertake a second immediate assault, and as it was clear that when daylight came the knoll would be swept by fire, there was nothing for it but to fall back. Meanwhile, on the left the Berkshire Yeomanry had, with splendid courage and resolution, fought their way to the third Turkish trench, but by this time, so terrible had been their losses, they were reduced to a mere handful, and since it would have been impossible to hold the ground that they had won against a counter-attack in any force, they had no alternative but to retire also. Private Potts was not one of those who assisted to carry the enemy's trenches, since, before he had advanced thirty yards, he was hit at the top of the left thigh, the bullet going clean through, and, as he was subsequently told in hospital, only missing the artery by the fraction of an an inch. He fell to the ground and lay there helpless, while his comrades rushed on to the attack. Fortunately, he had fallen amidst a cluster of scrub, which, if it did not afford much protection from bullets, at any rate screened him from the view of the Turks, so long as he did not move. He had been lying there about half an hour when he heard a noise, and, looking round, saw a man whom he recognized as Private Andrews of the Berkshires, who, by a singular coincidence, hailed, like Potts himself, from Reading, crawling painfully towards him. Andrews had a bullet in the groin—a very dangerous wound—and he was suffering terribly and losing a great deal of blood. The two men had been together only a few minutes when a third man—a stranger to both of them—who had a wound in the leg, crawled up to their hiding-place. So cramped were they for room amid the scrub that Andrews, though in great pain, shifted his position a little, in order that the new-comer might find shelter also. The simple act of kindness probably saved his life, as not ten minutes afterwards the stranger was mortally wounded by a bullet which passed through both his legs. The night passed, and was succeeded by a day of scorching heat; the cries of the dying man for water were pitiful, but they had not a drop between the three of them, and could do nothing to quench his raging thirst. Potts and Andrews suffered terribly from the same cause, and from hunger as well, and it seemed as though the day would never end. The sun went down at last, but night brought them no relief, though it was bitterly cold, and there was a full moon, which made the countryside as light as day, so that they dared not move for fear of attracting the attention of the Turkish snipers. Their unfortunate comrade became delirious, and kept tossing from side to side, which added greatly to the dangers of their situation, since every time he moved the Turks fired at the clump of bushes. Potts lay as flat as he could, face to the ground, for the bullets were pattering all around them; but, even in that position he had a very narrow escape, one actually grazing the tip of his left ear and covering his face with blood. Towards morning death put an end to the sufferings of their hapless companion, who had kept on moaning almost to the last for the water which it was impossible for them to give him. His dead body had to remain with them, since they could neither move it nor get away themselves. During the whole of the next day the two men remained in their hiding-place, suffering indescribably from hunger, thirst, the scorching sun, and the pain of their wounds. In desperation, they plucked bits of the stalk of the scrub and tried to suck them, in the hope of moistening their parched throats a little, but they got no relief in that way. The day seemed interminable, for, though so exhausted, the pain they were enduring, and the noise of the fighting, which was still proceeding, prevented them from obtaining any sleep. They could not see any of their comrades, and they knew that it was impossible for any stretcher-bearers to get through to them, since they were too far up the hill, and the terrible fire kept up by the enemy rendered it hopeless for any stretcher-parties to venture out. When darkness fell, they decided that, as it would be certain death from hunger and thirst to remain where they were, even if they escaped the Turkish bullets, there was nothing for it but to make a move and endeavour to regain the British lines. They accordingly started to crawl down the hill, and though their progress was, of course, terribly slow, for every movement caused them intense pain, they succeeded, after several hours, in reaching the shelter of another patch of scrub, about three hundred yards away, where

Frederick W. O. Potts.

they passed the rest of the night, covering themselves with some empty sandbags that they found lying there, as they were nearly frozen. When morning came, they were able, for the first time in nearly thirty-six hours, to obtain water, by taking the water-bottles from some dead men who were lying near them. This afforded them immense relief. They crept back to their shelter, and Potts dressed his comrade's wound, which was bleeding badly, with his field-dressing, and afterwards Andrews performed the same service for him. All that day they lay concealed, but as soon as it grew dark, they started off again, though they did not for a moment suppose that they would live to reach the British lines. Every movement was torment, on account of the thorns from the scrub, and after going a few yards, they gave up the attempt, as Andrews was too exhausted to go any farther. He unselfishly urged Potts to leave him and look after himself, but this the other would not hear of; and, lifting Andrews up, he made a brave effort to carry him, but found himself far too weak. It began to look as though they were doomed to perish in this terrible place, when suddenly like an inspiration, a means of escape presented itself to them. Casting his eyes about him, Potts caught sight of an entrenching shovel, which had been dropped during the attack of the 21st, lying a little way off. He saw at once that the shovel might be used as a kind of sledge to draw his helpless comrade into safety, and, crawling up to it, brought it to where Andrews lay, placed him upon it, and began to drag him down the hill. Andrews sat on the shovel as best he could, with his legs crossed, the wounded one over the sound one, and, putting his hands behind his back, clasped Potts's wrists as he sat on the ground behind and hauled away at the handle. 'I prayed,' says Potts, 'as I never prayed before for strength, help and guidance, and I felt confident that we should win through all right.' As soon as they began to move, they were spotted by the Turks, who opened fire upon them; but, careless of the risk of being hit, Potts stood up, for the first time since he had been wounded, and tugged away desperately at the handle of the shovel. However, after going a few yards, he was forced to lie down and rest, and decided to wait until nightfall before continuing his journey. Then he started off again, and yard by yard dragged his burden down the hill, stopping every few paces to rest, for he was very weak and his wounded leg was causing him intense pain. Bullets from the Turkish snipers hummed continually past him, but, happily, none hit him, and at last, after three hours' toil and suffering, he reached a little wood, where he was in comparative safety and was able to stand upright. A little further on he was challenged by a British sentry, and found that he was close to one of our advanced trenches. He explained matters to the sentry, who summoned some of his comrades, and they brought a blanket, and, lifting Andrews on to it, carried him into the trench. There everything that kindness could suggest was done for him and his gallant rescuer, and when the two had rested a little, they were placed on stretchers and carried to the nearest dressing-station, from which they were afterwards sent to hospital at Malta. Private Frederick William Owen Potts, who for this amazing feat of heroism and endurance, in its way the most extraordinary in the war, was awarded the Victoria Cross," was at the time twenty-two years of age, and had joined the Berkshire Yeomanry four years previously. "At the time of his enlistment Potts could claim the distinction of being the youngest trooper in the Yeomanry, and he can now claim that of being the first of that splendid force to win the Victoria Cross. Before the war he was employed in the Pulsometer Engineering Company's Works at Reading."

London Gazette, 15 Oct. 1915.—"The King has been graciously pleased to award the Decoration of the Victoria Cross to the undermentioned Officers, Non-commissioned Officers and Men."

SHOUT, ALFRED JOHN, Capt., served with the Australian Expeditionary Force in the European War, and was awarded the Victoria Cross [London Gazette, 15 Oct. 1915]: "Alfred John Shout, Capt., 1st Battn. Australian Imperial Force. For most conspicuous bravery at Lone Pine trenches in the Gallipoli Peninsula. On the morning of the 9th Aug. 1915, with a very small party, Capt. Shout charged down the trenches strongly occupied by the enemy, and personally threw four bombs among them, killing eight and routing the remainder. In the afternoon of the same day, from the position gained in the morning, he captured a further length of trench, under similar conditions, and continued personally to bomb the enemy at close range under very heavy fire until he was severely wounded, losing his right hand and left eye. This most gallant officer has since succumbed to his injuries."

Alfred John Shout.

An Australian newspaper says: "After nearly three complete days' fighting in the Lone Pine trenches, during the longest and fiercest hand-to-hand struggle which had yet occurred in the Peninsula, the Turks still held a big communication trench winding almost directly to the point which was at first chosen for the headquarters. While Brigadier Smythe was standing outside the office, the Turks had come up to the trench, marching calmly three abreast, round the last elbow into the full view of some who were standing with the headquarters' party. Only a few barricades, breast-high separated them. Lieut. Howell Price, subsequently commanding the 3rd Battn., shot two with his revolver. The 1st Battn. was coming in shortly after to relieve a part of the garrison, and Capt. Sass, of that battalion, decided it was worth while to see how much of this sap could be captured. Accordingly he took his rifle and called for three men to follow him, carrying no rifles but only sandbags, and started. His method was

for himself to run forward to the next bend of the trench and fire round it fiercely, whether the Turks were there or no. The men placed their sandbags in front of him, making a low parapet. Then he ran on to the next bend and repeated the process. He shot about twelve Turks and won about twenty yards of trench before stopping. Early that afternoon Capt. Shout came along and joined his friends. They had a talk and started together, Capt. Sass with his rifle and Capt. Shout with bombs. Capt. Shout had a good look round to see the position, and then pushed the barricade down. The two went forward abreast, Capt. Sass shooting and Capt. Shout bombing. As Capt. Shout's bombs fell those following could hear the bustle of accoutrements and scrambling cries round the next corner. They finally reached the point where it was decided it would be suitable to build the last barricade. Capt. Shout all the time was laughing and joking, and cheering the men immensely by his example. He resolved to make a big throw before the final dash. He tried to light three bombs at once, so that they might be quickly thrown, and the Turks prevented from hindering the building of the barricade. He ignited all the three and threw one, then either the second or the third exploded as it was leaving his hand, shattered one hand and most of the other, destroyed one eye and laid open his cheek, and scored his breast and leg. Capt. Shout was, nevertheless, conscious and talked cheerfully. He drank tea and sent a message to his wife. Since the day of his arrival he had been the heart and soul of the firing line. His invincible buoyancy and cheerfulness were a great help to the men. He succumbed to his injuries." The following is an extract from the "British Australasian": "Wounded soldiers who have returned to the Commonwealth have been singing the praises of Capt. Shout, one of the nine Australians who were awarded the Victoria Cross a week or two ago. They say that soon after the landing at Gaba Tepe he was one of the only officers left in their battalion. Capt. Shout, though himself wounded, carried more than a dozen wounded men out of the firing line. His arm was then shattered, but he still refused to go to the rear, declaring that he would remain with the boys to the finish. At that time the Turks were attacking in thousands. The Australians were not properly entrenched and were hopelessly outnumbered. A little later Capt. Shout was again wounded, but struggled and struggled till he got to his feet, refusing all entreaties to go to the rear. Then he fell and tried to rise, but was carried away, still protesting. Imperial officers said they had never seen such gallantry."

SYMONS, WILLIAM JOHN, Second Lieut., was born on 10 July, 1889, at Eaglehawk, Bendigo, Victoria, Australia, eldest son of the late William Samson Symons, and his wife, Mary, both of whom were born in

William John Symons.

Australia. His father's parents migrated from Cornwall, and his mother's from Sheffield and America. He was educated at Eaglehawk State School. He joined the Army on 15 Aug. 1914, as a Private in the Australian Imperial Force, and two days later was promoted Colour-Sergeant. He served in the European War in the Gallipoli Peninsula and Egypt. He was promoted to a commission as Second Lieutenant on 26 April, 1915, after landing in Gallipoli. On the night of 8–9 Aug. 1915, he won the Victoria Cross at Lone Pine trenches. This was announced in the London Gazette of 15 Oct. 1915: "William John Symons, Second Lieut., 7th Battn. Australian Imperial Force.

For most conspicuous bravery on the night of 8–9 Aug. 1915, at Lone Pine trenches in the Gallipoli Peninsula. He was in command of the right section of the newly-captured trenches held by his battalion, and repelled several counter-attacks with great coolness. At about 5 a.m. on 9 Aug. a series of determined attacks were made by the enemy on an isolated sap, and six officers were in succession killed or severely wounded, a portion of the sap being lost. Lieut. Symons then led a charge and retook the lost sap, shooting two Turks with his revolver. The sap was under hostile fire from three sides, and Lieut. Symons withdrew some fifteen yards to a spot where some overhead cover could be obtained, and in the face of heavy fire built up a sand barricade. The enemy succeeded in setting fire to the fascines and woodwork of the head-cover, but Lieut. Symons extinguished the fire and rebuilt the barricade. His coolness and determination finally compelled the enemy to relinquish their attack." He was promoted Lieutenant in Aug. 1915, and Captain on 1 May, 1916. He was discharged, suffering from the effects of wounds and gas, on 17 Dec. 1918. He was mentioned in

Frederick Harold Tubb.

Despatches for conducting 250 men on a raid on 17 Feb. 1917, and was twice mentioned in Divisional Routine Orders for repelling raids. He was married on 15 Aug. 1918, at St. Mary's, Hayling Island, Hampshire, to Isabel Anna, daughter of H. E. and Mrs. Hockley, of Kenton, Hayling, and granddaughter of the late Chevalier de Montezuma. A daughter was born, Isabel Evelyn, at Armadale, Australia, on 21 May, 1919.

TUBB, FREDERICK HAROLD, Lieut., was born at St. Helena, Longwood, Victoria, Australia, son of Harry Tubb, Esq., and Mrs. Emma Tubb (née Abbott). Both of his parents were born in England, his father in Hampshire, and his mother in Wiltshire.

Mr. Harry Tubb came of a very old family from Cornwall, and at St. Neots there is still a window in the church put in by his ancestors in 1620. The Tubb family were always Loyalists. Their coat-of-arms was granted to the family by Charles II. In an old Cornish book from St. Neots the name is spelt "Tubbe." Major Tubb's mother came of an old family also. There is a legend about an elopement in 1826. His grandfather was a mining engineer; he erected some of the first gold-mining plants in Australia. Mr. Harry Tubb came to Australia in 1854 and his wife in 1855. Major Tubb wrote about 1916: "I have three brothers. All are fighting, or have been. One, Sapper A. C. Tubb, discharged lately in Australia, from wounds and fever in Gallipoli and Egypt; one, Capt. F. R. Tubb, 7th Battn., still going; got his M.C. at Pozières; the other, Lieut. Tubb, served in France with the 60th Battn. Australian Expeditionary Force. I am single. I am the 4th son; am five feet, six inches high—the smallest of the family. I have four sisters. I was educated at the school at No. 2707, Longwood; have played all games since I was able, and at 16 played senior football. Very keen and fond of sport, and have always taken a prominent part in Victoria in same. Very fond of shooting, and have a good record for rifle, game and trap-shooting (at pigeons, starlings, etc.). Have been on the land all my life, on my father's property, St. Helena, Longwood, well known in the north-eastern district of Victoria; also have landed interest myself in the same place. Have always been keen on military matters. On 20 June, 1900, I joined the Victorian Mounted Rifles, Lieut.-Colonel Tom Price in command. In the V.M.R., which was one of the first founded in Victoria, we supplied all our own horses, outfit, uniforms, etc. No pay of any sort. Then the Commonwealth Light Horse was founded. After the Federation of the States it incorporated with the V.M.R., now called the Australian Light Horse. I joined as a Private, after going through all the grades to Sergeant. When the Australian Compulsory Service came into force I transferred to the 60th Battn. of Infantry (Nov. 1911), because I was then in that area. As the Citizen Force grew our area was strong enough to form a battalion (the 58th), under Lieut.-Colonel H. E. Elliott. He was the C.O. of the 58th when I got my commission and transferred to the 7th Battn. Australian Imperial Force. He had a D.C.M. He is now Brigadier-General Elliott, C.M.G., commanding the 15th Brigade over here. Colonel Elliott was in command of the 7th Battn. when I got my Cross at Lone Pine. I am writing this under difficulties, as there is much doing in my battalion at present.—F. H. TUBB, Captain, 7th Australian Infantry, 2nd Brigade, 1st Australian Imperial Force.—Please send to my mother at St. Helena, Longwood, Victoria." He was awarded the Victoria Cross [London Gazette, 15 Oct. 1915]: "Harold Frederick Tubb, Lieut., 7th Battalion, Australian Imperial Force. For most conspicuous bravery and devotion to duty at Lone Pine trenches on the Gallipoli Peninsula, on 8 Aug. 1915. In the early morning the enemy made a determined counter-attack on the centre of the newly-captured trench held by Lieut. Tubb. They advanced up a sap and blew in a sandbag barricade, leaving only one foot of it standing, but Lieut. Tubb led his men back, repulsed the enemy and rebuilt the barricade, supported by strong bombing parties in the barricades, but on each occasion Lieut. Tubb, although wounded in the hand and arm, held his ground with the greatest coolness, and finally succeeded in maintaining his position under very heavy bomb fire." A newspaper correspondent wrote in 1917: "Major Frederick Harold Tubb, V.C., Australian Infantry, whose death from wounds is officially announced to-day, won the Victoria Cross at Lone Pine trenches in Gallipoli on 8 Aug. 1915. He then held the rank of Lieutenant. He was mortally wounded during the fighting on the Ypres front on Saturday. The gallant officer had been wounded, and was being carried back on a stretcher when he was struck by a shell. This was the second time the Victoria Cross has been won by a resident of Longwood. Lieut.-Colonel Maygar, V.C., who won the decoration in the South African War, having come from the same place." Lady Clementine Waring writes:

"I am more than happy to be given this opportunity of writing a few lines about my friend, Fred Tubb. Although I only knew him originally as a patient in my convalescent home, he always used to come back here for leave, ending by regarding Lennel as his British Home. 'Tubby!'—I can see him now, his whole personality radiating vitality and energy. I first met him at this convalescent home. He came with two other Australians, all three of whom had been wounded at Gallipoli. On that first evening it was whispered to me that he had been recommended for the V.C. . . . I can see his wrathful face and blazing eyes as he turned to refute the statement: he was ever modest. As I search my memory for facts, for figures, for things that happened during those weeks of his convalescence here, I can recall little that is concrete. The life of the convalescent is necessarily uneventful, yet it is in a hospital that one so speedily realizes and appreciates those whose characters, like 'Tubby's,' were cheerful, helpful, resourceful. But his character is revealed very truly in the following incidents, small in themselves, but large in their help to an understanding of him. The official announcement that Capt. F. H. Tubb had been awarded the V.C. for conspicuous bravery (defending Lone Pine Trench) appeared one morning in the 'Scotsman.' He had been staying the night at Berwick with the officers of the K.O.S.B.'s, and was soon expected back. Quickly we hurried to Coldstream and arranged with the Provost a reception, against his return, at Coldstream Bridge. When the transport car with himself and half a dozen friends eventually arrived, the people of Coldstream were assembled in goodly numbers. The car was stopped; a bewildered and angry hero emerged. The Provost in a few phrases said just what we all wanted to tell him. A huge bouquet was presented by the Belgian officers. 'Tubby' remained speechless, overwhelmed. Finally in a broken voice he murmured a few incoherent words of thanks, and, espying my small two-seater car near by, leaped in with an imploring 'For God's sake get me out of this!' and whirled off through the gates. I also remember taking him to a recruiting meeting over in England. (How proud we were of being on the Scottish side of the Tweed!) A neighbouring schoolmaster, filled with the enthusiasm which bubbled so easily in those days, asked for officers to speak at his out-of-the-way school-house in the Cheviots. I said I would bring three Australians, one of whom was a V.C. I never thought for one moment that all my persuasive powers would fail to get 'Tubby' on the platform. The other two spoke, and well; but he, he wandered round to the back of the hall and talked and talked to the collection of farm lads he found there. The speeches done, recruits were called for. None came. After the meeting, 'Tubby,' who, by this time, was boiling with indignation at the lethargy displayed, was conversing with little groups outside, begging, cajoling, arguing, but with no apparent avail. I can see him yet, dejected, dispirited, bitterly disappointed, climbing into our car, to go home full of disillusionment. A few days later, meeting the village schoolmaster, 'Tubby' was stopped. 'Splendid meeting, sir! You had a wonderful effect, scarcely a chap left of military age round our parts now. They are all gone.' It was with a proud and glittering eye that he returned home to us to tell the tale. He had a burning affection for his homeland—Britain is ever 'Home' to the Australian—his pride had sustained a cruel shock when he discovered the apparent slackness of her sons. With men like 'Tubby' to lead, the Briton must always follow. The last time 'Tubby' came home on leave he spent part of it here, and although his health was far from good, he was still the same dear cheerful companion we had always known, the splendid sportsman and the loyal friend. The manner of his death came as no surprise to those who knew his gallant spirit, and I, for one, feel certain it is the death 'Tubby' would have desired. . . . 'Tubby' was the first word I wrote in this short souvenir of a friend, and I have called him 'Tubby' throughout. But that was another thing about him—'Captain Tubb' would have hurt him as much as it would have seemed strange for us to say it."

THROSSELL, HUGO VIVIAN HOPE, Second Lieut., was born 27 Oct. 1884, at Fermoy, Northam, West Australia, youngest son of the late Hon. George Throssell, C.M.G., formerly Premier of Western Australia, and Mrs. Throssell. He was educated at Prince Alfred College, Adelaide, and was for some years engaged in agricultural pursuits in the back blocks of Western Australia. He is keen on football, boxing and all-round athletics. "On the outbreak of the European War he enlisted in the ranks of the 10th Light Horse; was promoted Sergeant, then gained a commission before the regiment left for Egypt. When the regiment went to Gallipoli dismounted, Throssell was left in Cairo in charge of the horses, but rejoined his unit on the Peninsula in time to take part in the famous charge of the Light Horse Brigade at Walker's Ridge on 7 Aug. 1915. Through this he passed unharmed, and three weeks later had another go at Hill 60, where he was severely wounded," and for his services on this occasion was awarded the Victoria Cross [London Gazette, 15 Oct. 1915]: "Hugo Vivian Hope Throssell, Second Lieut., 10th Light Horse Regt., Australian Imperial Force. For most conspicuous bravery and devotion to duty during operations on the Kaiakij Aghala (Hill 60) in the Gallipoli Peninsula, on 29 and 30 Aug. 1915. Although severely wounded in several places during a counter-attack, he refused to leave his post, or to obtain medical assistance, till all danger was passed, when he had his wounds dressed and returned to the firing line until ordered out of action by the medical officer. By his personal courage and example he kept up the spirits of his party and was largely instrumental in saving the situation at a critical period." "Deeds that thrill the Empire" (pages 408-413) says: "In the latter part of the August of 1915 a brilliant movement was carried out on the Gallipoli Peninsula by the troops under General Birdwood's command. Operations for the capture of Hill 60 had been begun by Major-General Cox on 21 Aug., and to complete this task another attack was planned. Hill 60, which lies to the north of the Kaiakij Aghala, overlooks the Birjuk Anafarta valley, and was tactically of great importance. The attack was again conducted by Major-General Cox, and under his command there were placed detachments from the 4th and 5th Australian Brigades, the New Zealand Mounted Rifles Brigade, and the 5th Connaught Rangers. It was decided that the advance should begin at 5 p.m. on 27 Aug., after being preceded by a very heavy artillery bombardment. The moment, however, that the British left the cover of their trenches a very hot fire was opened on them from field guns, rifles and machine guns, and this was followed before long by a storm of heavy shell. On the right of the attack the detachment from the 4th and 5th Australian Brigades was opposed by a battery of machine guns, and against this merciless fire the men could make no headway. In the centre, however, by a most determined assault the New Zealanders had carried one side of the topmost knoll. On the left a charge by two hundred and fifty men of the 5th Connaught Rangers broke the Turkish resistance by the suddenness of the attack and the compactness of its mass. In five minutes the Irishmen had carried the northern Turkish communication trenches, and they at once fought their way along the trenches with bombs, opposing strong parties which hurried up in turn from the enemy supports and the reserves. At midnight fresh troops were to have consolidated the hold of the British on the hill, but unfortunately the Irishmen were outbombed before then, and the 9th Australian Light Horse were driven back, after making a gallant attempt to recapture the lost communication trench. Nothing, however, could move the New Zealand Mounted Rifles. All through the night and all the next day they were subjected to bombing, bayonet charges, rifle, shrapnel, and heavy shell fire. But they clung to their one hundred and fifty yards of

Hugo V. H. Throssell.

trench with the greatest gallantry, with only a sandbag barricade separating them from the Turks. At 1 a.m. on the morning of 29 Aug. the 10th Australian Light Horse made their memorable advance to recapture the lost communication trenches on the left. Having rushed into the trench held by the New Zealanders, they dashed across the sandbag barricade amid the cheers of the Maorilanders ; and then, by shooting, bombing and bayoneting, they drove the Turks in headlong flight down the trench for about three hundred yards to the right. When the advance first began Second Lieut. Throssell was in the second line, in charge of the digging party, and under his supervision the men now set to work to build up another sandbag barricade. To give his men some protection in their work, Second Lieut. Throssell stood by them with a rifle, and every Turk who attempted to come round the traverse was shot down. Finding that these methods of attack were costing them dear, the Turks massed round the right angle of the traverse and began to attack the barricaders with bombs. The rest of the trench was also hotly engaged. The Turks opened a heavy rifle fire, and by continuous bomb attacks advanced as near as possible to the whole line of the trench. The trench was a veritable inferno, but the men were most hotly engaged on the extreme right, where, with Capt. Fry, Second Lieut. Throssell had tried hard to raise some covering as a shelter against the bombs. This task was of the utmost danger, for the bombs were lobbed with deadly accuracy into the trench, and were actually caught and thrown back by Second Lieut. Throssell, with Corporals Ferrier and McNee and Troopers Macmahon and Renton. When a bomb fell into the trench and could not be traced in the darkness, Second Lieut. Throssell shouted the order ' Down ! ' They at once flung themselves full-length on the ground, and waited for the explosion a second or two later. Men, however, were falling fast, but though Capt. Fry was killed, Second Lieut. Throssell never failed in directing his men. He had been three times wounded, and Ferrier, who was an expert in bomb-throwing, had had his arm shattered by a bursting bomb. Nearly every man in the trench had suffered some injury, but the gallant and dogged defence of the 10th Light Horse was still kept up. The overwhelming onslaughts of the Turks, who in numbers were superior, necessitated two retirements, and once again Second Lieut. Throssell stood by his men, rifle in hand, while they raised the sandbag barricades. The long-drawn-out fight against desperate odds continued into the second day, and at the height of the struggle the Turks rushed forward in a furious counter-attack, which tried the courage and endurance of the men to their uttermost limits. Reinforcements at length came, and Second Lieut. Throssell retired to have his wounds dressed. But he insisted on returning to the trench afterwards. This trench, which Second Lieut. Throssell and the men of the 10th Australian Light Horse had so gallantly captured and held, gave the British possession of Hill 60. Second Lieut (now Lieut.) Throssell had been promoted from the ranks, and much credit is due to him for his strong leadership and unflagging energy in so trying a struggle." Mr. Throssell was invalided to England and Australia after an attack of meningitis, rejoining his regiment and serving in Egypt and Palestine. He was promoted to Lieutenant. Since his return to Australia he has become a leading light in the Discharged Soldiers' Association in Western Australia. He married Katharine Susannah Prichard, author of a prize novel dealing with Australian life, " The Pioneers," published by Messrs. Hodder and Stoughton.

BASSETT, CYRIL, Corpl., comes from Mount Eden, Auckland. He joined the New Zealand Military Forces and served in Gallipoli in the European War. He was awarded the Victoria Cross [London Gazette, 15 Oct. 1915]: " Cyril Royston Guyton Bassett, No. 4/515, Corpl., New Zealand Divisional Signal Company. For most conspicuous bravery and devotion to duty on the Chunuk Bair ridge in the Gallipoli Peninsula on 7 Aug. 1915. After the New Zealand Infantry Brigade had attacked and established itself on the ridge, Corpl. Bassett, in full daylight and under a continuous fire, succeeded in laying a telephone line from the old position to the new one on Chunuk Bair. He has subsequently been brought to notice for further excellent and most gallant work connected with the repair of telephone lines by day and night under heavy fire." Cyril Bassett is said to have told a friend that he didn't know what he got his Victoria Cross for. He saw his mates doing things every day that he couldn't aspire to. The " British Australasian " for 9 Dec. 1915, says : " Last week a very human little scene was enacted in the establishment of a big outfitting firm in Victoria Street. It began with the entry of six stalwart New Zealand soldiers, who were escorting that modest young hero, Corpl. Bassett, V.C. Once inside the shop, each of the six men produced twopence, and the resultant shilling was applied to the purchase of the simple clip that carries the V.C. ribbon. Then, amid hearty congratulations, the ribbon was pinned on his breast, and all shook hands with him in turn. This simple tribute from his comrades was paid to the New Zealand V.C. man in the establishment of Berkeley's, which is one of the best-known shops in London to the men of Anzac."

Cyril Bassett.

BURTON, ALEXANDER STEWART, Corpl., joined the Australian Imperial Force, served in Gallipoli, and in company with his equally gallant comrades, Lieut. Tubb and Corpl. Dunstan, won the Victoria Cross. Corpl. Burton's decoration was gazetted posthumously, 15 Oct. 1915 : " Alexander Stewart Burton, No. 384, Corpl. ; William Dunstan, No. 2130, Corpl., 7th Battn. Australian Imperial Force. For most conspicuous bravery at Lone Pine trenches in the Gallipoli Peninsula

on the 9th Aug. 1915. In the early morning the enemy made a desperate counter-attack on the centre of the newly-captured trench held by Lieut. Tubb, Corpls. Burton and Dunstan, and a few men. They advanced up the sap and blew in a sandbag barricade, leaving only one foot of it standing, but Lieut. Tubb, with the two corporals, repulsed the enemy and rebuilt the barricade. Supported by strong bombing parties, the enemy twice again succeeded in blowing in the barricade, but on each occasion they were repulsed and the barricade rebuilt, although Lieut. Tubb was wounded in the head and arm, and Corpl. Burton was killed by a bomb while most gallantly building up the parapet under a hail of bullets."

Alexander S. Burton.

William Dunstan.

DUNSTAN, WILLIAM, Corpl., was born on 8 March, 1895, at 7, Cameron Street, Ballarat East, Victoria, son of William John Dunstan and Henrietta Dunstan. He was educated at Golden Point, Ballarat, joined the Australian Military Forces at the beginning of compulsory training, and rose to the rank of Captain in the Senior Cadets. He was transferred to the Citizen Forces as Lieutenant, and went into camp at the beginning of the war with the 70th Infantry, Ballarat Regt., at Queenscliff. Not being old enough to obtain a commission in the Australian Imperial Force, he enlisted on 1 June, 1915. He served in the European War ; was sent to Gallipoli 17 June, 1915, and was awarded the Victoria Cross, his name being joined with that of Corpl. Burton [London Gazette, 15 Oct. 1915]; " Alexander Stewart Burton, No. 384, Corpl. ; William Dunstan, No. 2130, Corpl., 7th Battn. Australian Imperial Force (Victoria). For most conspicuous bravery at Lone Pine trenches in the Gallipoli Peninsula on 9 Aug. 1915. In the early morning the enemy made a determined counter-attack on the centre of the newly-captured trench, held by Lieut. Tubb, Corpls. Burton and Dunstan, and a few men. They advanced up a sap and blew in a sandbag barricade, leaving only one foot of it standing, but Lieut. Tubb, with the two corporals, repulsed the enemy and rebuilt the barricade. Supported by strong bombing parties, the enemy twice again succeeded in blowing in the barricade, but on each occasion they were repulsed and the barricade rebuilt, although Lieut. Tubb was wounded in the head and arm, and Corpl. Burton was killed by a bomb while most gallantly building up the parapet under a hail of bombs." He was mentioned in Despatches for his services on this occasion. He rose to the rank of Company Sergeant-Major, and was given a commission on 2 Feb. 1916, and later promoted to Lieutenant.

HAMILTON, JOHN, Private, joined the Australian Imperial Forces, served in the European War, and was awarded the Victoria Cross [London Gazette, 18 Oct. 1915] : " John Hamilton, No. 943, Private, 1st Battn. Australian Imperial Force. For most conspicuous bravery on 9 Aug. 1915, in the Gallipoli Peninsula. During a heavy bomb attack by the enemy on the newly-captured position at Lone Pine, Private Hamilton, with utter disregard to personal safety, exposed himself under heavy fire on the parapet, in order to secure a better fire position against the enemy's bomb-throwers. His coolness and daring example had an immediate effect. The defence was encouraged and the enemy driven off with heavy loss." " Deeds that thrill the Empire " (pages 31–32), says : " Private J. Hamilton, of the 3rd Battn. Australian Infantry, won his V.C. on 9 Aug. 1915, at the immortal ' Lone Pine ' trenches on the Gallipoli Peninsula. The Turks had lost that all-important position, and started at daybreak to recapture it by bombing up the communication trenches. It was absolutely necessary that their approach should be watched. Hamilton climbed up on top of the parapet, arranged the sandbags to form a rough shelter, and kept a sharp look-out for the enemy. Thus for hours Hamilton remained in this dangerous position, exposed to Turkish guns, rifles and bombs under the open sky. He shot many Turks himself, and observed their movements, so that every time they attempted to work their way up the communication trench they were ignominiously driven out. He was helped by comrades for some part of the time, but he never left his post until immediate danger was over."

John Hamilton.

KEYSOR, LEONARD, Private, was born in London ; spent several years in Canada, and went to New South Wales three years before he won his Victoria Cross. " Deeds that thrill the Empire " (page 12) says : " At the beginning of Aug. 1915, the line held by the Australasian Corps at Gaba Tepe lay in a semicircle, with the enemy's trenches close up to it, in some places as near as fifteen or twenty yards, except in that part adjoining the shore, where the guns of our warships kept the Turks at a distance. Bomb fighting between them and the Anzacs was, therefore, of almost daily occurrence. One of the best bomb throwers among the latter was Private Leonard Keysor, of the 1st Battn. Australian Imperial Force. On 7–8 Aug. there was some fierce fighting of this description in the south-eastern corner of the Lone Pine trenches, where our men were so hard pressed that a section of the outer trench had to be abandoned, though they continued to prevent the Turks from establishing themselves there. During these encounters Keysor was in his element, not only throwing bombs, but constantly smothering with his coat or sandbags those of the enemy which had fallen into the trench and often throwing them back. Finally, when the enemy cut down the time of the fuses, he caught several bombs in the air just as if they were cricket balls, and hurled them back before they burst.

Leonard Keysor.

In the course of these feats of heroism Keysor was twice wounded and marked for hospital; but he declined to give in, and volunteered to throw bombs for another company which had lost all its bomb-throwers. Altogether he was throwing bombs for fifty hours almost continuously." He was awarded the Victoria Cross [London Gazette, 15 Oct. 1915]: "Leonard Keysor, No. 958, Private, 1st Battn. Australian Imperial Force. For most conspicuous bravery and devotion to duty at Lone Pine trenches in the Gallipoli Peninsula. On 7 Aug. 1915, he was in a trench which was being heavily bombed by the enemy. He picked up two live bombs and threw them back at the enemy at great risk to his own life, and continued throwing bombs, although himself wounded, thereby saving a portion of the trench which it was most important to hold. On 8 Aug., at the same place, Private Keysor successfully bombed the enemy out of a position, from which a temporary mastery over his own trench had been obtained, and was again wounded. Although marked for hospital, he declined to leave, and volunteered to throw bombs for another party which had lost its bomb-throwers. He continued to bomb the enemy till the situation was relieved." Private Keysor was at the time thirty years of age.

GEARY, BENJAMIN HANDLEY, Second Lieut., was born in London, S.W., 29 June, 1891, son of the late Rev. Henry Geary, Vicar of St. Thomas's Church, Portman Square, and Mrs. Geary (*née* Miss Alport, of Hornchurch, Essex). He was trained in St. Edmund's School, Canterbury, O.T.C., and afterwards in the Oxford O.T.C., and was commissioned 15 Aug. 1914, into the 4th East Surreys, then stationed in South Raglan Barracks, Devonport. He sailed from Southampton 26 Sept. 1914, to Havre; was one week at the base at St. Nazaire, and was then posted to the 1st Battn. East Surreys for service in the field. In Nov. 1914, he stole a German bayonet at night from occupied German trenches, for which he received thanks from Divisional Headquarters. The following is an account of Hill 60 which was dictated by Second Lieut. Geary while lying in bed only a day or two after recovering consciousness after a bullet through the head. He says that on this account his mind "may not have been working quite normally," and so his amanuensis had difficulty in getting the proper sequence. "I do not feel satisfied with the account, for there were many fine things unnoted which would put my share in the shade. As it stands now, however, it gives the impression I had shortly after the event. The decoration which came along five months later was a complete surprise."

Benjamin Handley Geary.

"19 April to 21 April on Hill 60.

"Note.—Saturday, 17 April.—The British, after exploding mines, took Hill 60 and improved position, which was a bit insecure.

"Saturday, 17 April.—Previously on each occasion when our guns started bombarding we were removed from barracks where we were billeted at Ypres, and sent out into trenches close by as a precautionary measure.

"On returning to barracks a dozen German prisoners were brought in, including one officer, who, on being questioned as to the whereabouts of the other officers, stated that 'they had just gone back for some supper when the explosions occurred.' Sunday.—After 'standing to' in readiness all Sunday, 18 April, two companies had to go up in support to the Hill, our guns being massed and directed upon the enemy's trenches. While we, i.e., the remaining two companies, were still out in the emergency trenches as before, we were told that we should also be wanted to reinforce (the battalion being put at the disposal of another brigade). Started to go up in darkness (Sunday night, 18 April). Our guide had only been that way once before, and at one point took us within a few yards of one of our own batteries. No harm was done, fortunately, as their firing soon informed us where we were. It was the most colossal noise ever heard. (I must not report what the Major in charge of the battery said.)

"Shortly after, during a lull, we tried to put in a little siesta on a bank, but suddenly had orders to move on. It was very slow work, and we had to move up the railway cutting, where for an hour or so we met a continuous procession of stretchers. There was something in the atmosphere (probably the gases of vitriol) which made everybody's eyes smart as painfully when they were shut as opened—it was almost like hot acid. Just after dawn we arrived in the Hill 60 section, and took over the trenches. It took us some hours to settle down, when one of the first persons I saw was a German with a wounded arm walking down the trench and crying, 'Kamarades!' He had crept up the communication trench to throw bombs, and had been shot by one of our men and fetched in. I mention this, as in trench warfare it was rather unique to take a single prisoner. We started at once improving our parapets, wherever possible to try and do so in daylight.

"About 5 p.m. of 19 April, the enemy started bombarding our trenches (which were on and about Hill 60), but our communication was all right, and the threefold reply of our guns seemed to shut them up. That night we spent improving communication trenches and trying to extend the trench on the Hill. (Sergt. Piper and Corpl. Hands did excellent work with their sections, as they always had done on digging parties. No. II. Platoon, to which they belonged, had had a particularly hard time, for being in a semi-support trench they had been working in reliefs on the communication trenches most of the day, and were all kept at it till dawn.) It was while helping me to extend the trench on the Hill that Capt. Huth, who was, as always, personally superintending, was killed. (I also seem to remember the above two N.C.O.'s, or, at any rate, Sergt. Piper, on the Hill the next night.) The next day—Tuesday, 20 April—as on the previous day, the Germans started putting over heavy shells, which continued all day, only on this occasion they seemed to have got the range exactly. Our adjutant was blown to bits, a parapet was blown in over me and the men next to me. I got free fairly easily, but the men required helping out, though only one was wounded. (Norton, a little further down the trench, was working hard at the spot where Wynyard was killed, digging away and trying to give the poor fellow something of a burial, which was a very unpleasant job and almost impossible.) We then started filling up the gaps, a rather difficult task, as the Germans were firing through these gaps from the front, and even from the rear, on the left where the trenches curved round. I got a snatch of food after this and tried to get a nap; soon disturbed; had to go and visit officers in the company on the Hill (A Coy.), to reconnoitre best way up, and discuss what to do in case of emergency. Came back and tried to get a bit more rest. Forward again to show Capt. Winter way up to A Coy.

"The Germans began to bombard about the same time as the previous day. Then news was brought that the Commanding Officer (Major Patterson) was hit; and later I heard that he had died a minute or two afterwards. Communication with nearly all our batteries being cut off, although we had a gunnery officer in the trench observing for them, our guns failed to reply as they had previously done, and when they did, it was ineffective. Very soon after a messenger came to our dug-out and said reinforcements were wanted on Hill 60, so I rushed along and collected my men and led them up in that direction.

"The communication trenches were so knocked about that it was almost impossible to find the ordinary way up. I looked through a gap and saw several men of the Bedfords holding the left crater, although there was no trench dug there. I rushed through and told the men to follow, and we were greeted with great cheers from the men already there, as they were so pleased at the sight of reinforcements. This was the left crater of the three. I placed the men round the inside of the rim of the crater, and then we hung on for the next few hours; the Germans were shelling all round us, but seemed unable to put shells inside the crater itself. As far as I know we lost no one from the shell fire actually in the crater. Next to me, at this time, was an officer (Kennedy) with a wound in the head, which I hastily bound up as best I could, who, with superb fortitude and pluck insisted on remaining with me until I begged him to be taken back. The enemy's trenches were not far in front, and they were pouring grenades over; they also had a machine gun trained on the only way our reinforcements could come up. One of our poor men who had been bowled over and killed blocked the mouth of this gap, which made it doubly hard to those attempting to creep through, as they had to expose themselves in getting over his body. Any reinforcements that with almost incredible pluck and in face of tremendous odds struggled through were accorded a hearty welcome, until we found that our cheering attracted the German fire. At the moment our crater was fast filling up with wounded and dead, till eventually you could hardly see the ground. The middle crater was held by no one; in fact, it would have been untenable, for shells and grenades were pouring in to it day and night. Officers continually coming up with reinforcements of both Surreys and Bedfords were with alarming regularity being shot down either wounded or killed, until at one time I discovered I was the only officer untouched on that part of the Hill, and was the only one who lasted the whole time from 5 p.m. till nearly dawn.

"The trouble was, I did not know how our men were holding out on the right of the Hill, and as I looked back the country was completely shell-swept to the town (Ypres), and it looked as though we must be completely cut off. I had no orders the whole night, and naturally the tension caused by the complete responsibility for our men on the Hill was very severe.

"Meanwhile, the Germans had started coming up their old communication trenches, one of which led up to the left crater, and, with the assistance of another man, I fired into them, the man next to me (Private White, C Coy.) loading my rifles as fast as he could. It was impossible to miss hitting them, as they had to come up single file and the nearest was hardly 10 yards off. At last they had had enough and had to abandon the attempt. Another communication trench led to the right of the middle crater, and the enemy also came up this, and were firing right into the backs of some of my men on the left.

"I then thought it advisable to dash across to the right and discover what was happening there. But first I sent a corporal and (I think) two men to try and get into touch with the officer in command of the trench to the left of the Hill (Clark), and find out how it went with them, but I did not see them again and do not know if they ever got there.

"On reaching the right I found that although the Germans had pushed into their extreme left, which they had succeeded in doing by working their way up the second of the aforesaid communication trenches, they were still hanging on like bull-dogs to most of the trench. With relief I discovered there were two officers left in this trench, one of my regiment (Davies) and one of the Bedfords; they likewise had received no orders, and we discussed the situation. We thought it might be advisable to make sure of holding the old line behind the Hill, lest we should be cut off and the enemy break right through, but we decided we must simply hang on as long as possible and not think of sacrificing the Hill until we had made sure that there was no one behind us. Davies was stronger than myself on this point and I owe my decision to him. As I went back I met a Major Lee bringing up another regiment, with orders to rush the part of the trench already occupied by the enemy; he asked me to explain the situation as he had not seen the position by daylight, and wished me to gather what men I could, and at a given signal (two or three flare lights instantaneously) to rush across the middle crater in combination with his charge on the right. I then gathered some men and started them digging a trench in rear of and commanding the middle crater. They naturally did not relish the job as they would be terribly exposed to a pitiless fire, but after an appeal they buckled to, and then I was going to sit down for a short rest as I was a bit done. Just then a German flare light went up, and looking round a corner I found an excellent view of the part of the trench which the Germans had taken, and where they had not much cover on our side, and so I got a fellow to load for me and so enjoyed a little more snap shooting at a target which could hardly be missed. I then left the men to carry on with this, and put another man in a prepared position, firing down the continuation of the communication trench down which these Germans would have to retire. They were rather crowded together, and I distinctly saw one fat Hun wearing glasses.

"On my return I found some Q.V.R.'s carrying up ammunition, not knowing where to take it. So I directed them and revisited the men in the left crater; the men were hanging on most gallantly and in most urgent need of this ammunition. On returning to Major Lee I told him I had not yet seen his signal. He informed me that no rush was necessary, for on easing off to the left they had found that the Germans had already evacuated the portions of the trench they had previously occupied, but were still very close up in their communication trench, and were throwing grenades at that spot at a great pace, making that part of the trench very difficult to hold. When I again returned to the left crater I thought that the men there could not possibly hold the position by themselves for very much longer. Therefore I thought that unless they got strongly reinforced they would be compelled to come back and dig themselves in in rear of the left crater, as the other men had done behind the middle crater. Again I went back to try to find Major Lee to inform him of the necessity of doing this as soon as possible, as the dawn was in view.

"Before I found him I was hit. I recollect, as I fell, trying to get this message out, but don't know to this moment if I succeeded.

"I would like to add one incident: I saw one man bowled clean over with a shot in the head, while firing over the brim of the crater. His comrade, who was crouching just by him, jumped straight up to the spot where the first had been marked, to use his rifle and retaliate. The night was full of such incidents. I remember at one time stopping for a moment and literally nearly weeping with pride to watch how these Englishmen were behaving. They were all simply grand."

He was awarded the Victoria Cross [London Gazette, 15 Oct. 1915]: "Benjamin Handley Geary, 4th Battn. (attached 1st Battn) The East Surrey Regt. For most conspicuous bravery and determination on Hill 60, near Ypres, on 20 and 21 April, 1915, when he held the left crater with his platoon, some men of the Bedfordshire Regt. and a few reinforcements which came up during the evening and night. The crater was first exposed to a very heavy artillery fire which broke down the defences, and afterwards, during the night, to repeated bomb attacks, which filled it with dead and wounded. Each attack was, however, repulsed, mainly owing to the splendid personal gallantry and example of Second Lieut. Geary. At one time he used a rifle with great effect, at another threw hand grenades, and exposed himself with entire disregard to danger in order to see by the light of the flares where the enemy were coming on. In the intervals between the attacks he spent his whole time arranging for the ammunition supply and for reinforcements. He was severely wounded just before daylight on 21 April." Lieut. Geary was promoted to Captain.

London Gazette, 28 Oct. 1915.—"War Office, 28 Oct. 1915. The King has been graciously pleased to award the Victoria Cross to No. 6738, L.-Sergt, Oliver Brooks, 3rd Battn. Coldstream Guards."

BROOKS, OLIVER, L.-Sergt., served in the European War, and was awarded the Victoria Cross [London Gazette, 28 Oct. 1915]: "Oliver Brooks, No. 6738, L.-Sergt., 3rd Battn. Coldstream Guards. For most conspicuous bravery near Loos 8 Oct. 1915. A strong party of the enemy having captured 200 yards of our trenches, L.-Sergt. Brooks, on his own initiative, led a party of bombers in the most determined manner, and succeeded in regaining possession of the lost ground. The signal bravery displayed by this non-commissioned officer in the midst of a hail of bullets from

Oliver Brooks.

the Germans was of the very first order, and the complete success attained in a very dangerous undertaking was entirely due to his absolute fearlessness, presence of mind and promptitude."

London Gazette, 18 Nov. 1915.—"The King has been graciously pleased to approve of the grant of the Victoria Cross to the undermentioned Officers, Non-commissioned Officers and Men in recognition of most conspicuous bravery and devotion to duty in the field."

DOUGLAS-HAMILTON, ANGUS FALCONER, Lieut.-Colonel, was born at Brighton, 20 Aug. 1863, son of Major-General Octavius Douglas-Hamilton, Second Bengal European Cavalry, who served in the Punjaub

A. F. Douglas-Hamilton.

Campaign in 1848 and 1849, and at the Siege of Delhi in 1857, and the actions at Hindon and Basil-Ka-Serai; and of Katherine A. W. Douglas-Hamilton. He was educated at Foster's Naval Preparatory School, and afterwards by Army Tutors, and at the Royal Military College, Sandhurst; entered the Army on 23 Aug. 1884, as a Lieutenant in the Queen's Own Cameron Highlanders, and was promoted Major in 1901. He served with the 1st Battn. of his regiment during the latter part of the Nile Expedition in 1885, and had a Medal and clasp, and the Khedive's Star, and throughout the operations of the Sudan Frontier Field Force in 1885 and 1886, being present at Kosheh during its investment and at the engagement at Ginniss. He became Captain 7 Dec. 1892.
From 1894 to 1899 he was Adjutant of the 6th Battn. Gordon Highlanders, and on vacating that appointment rejoined his regiment, and served with the 2nd Battn. in Gibraltar, Malta, South Africa, North China and India, until 24 Aug. 1912, when he retired. He rejoined for service in the European War, and was in the first instance employed as a transport officer on the Embarkation Staff at Southampton, and on 1 Oct. 1914, was appointed to command the 6th Battn. Cameron Highlanders, with the temporary rank of Lieutenant-Colonel. This gallant soldier died at the head of his men on Hill 70. In the action in which he was killed he won the Victoria Cross, which was gazetted on 18 Nov. 1915: "Angus Falconer Douglas-Hamilton, Major (temporary Lieutenant-Colonel), 6th Battn. Queen's Own Cameron Highlanders. For most conspicuous bravery and devotion to duty when commanding his battalion during operations on 25 and 26 Sept. 1915, on Hill 70. On the 26th, when the battalions on his right and left had retired, he rallied his own battalion again and again, and led his men forward four times. The last time he led all that remained, consisting of about 50 men, in a most gallant manner, and was killed at their head. It was mainly due to his bravery, untiring energy, and splendid leadership that the line at this point was enabled to check the enemy's advance." He was married on 1 Aug. 1894, at the Episcopalian Church, Highfield, Muir of Ord, Ross-shire, to Anna Watson, younger daughter of Capt. Alexander Watson Mackenzie, of Ord, Muir of Ord, Ross-shire, and left one daughter, Camilla Beatrice. His widow received from the King personally the Victoria Cross, which her husband had won.

READ, ANKETELL MOUTRAY, Capt., was born 27 Oct. 1884, at Bampton; youngest son of the late Colonel J. Moutray Read. He was educated at Glengarth Cheltenham, and the United Service College, West-

Anketell Moutray Read.

ward Ho! and was an officer of the college cadet corps. He passed direct into Sandhurst in 1901, and on 21 Nov. 1903, was gazetted to the Gloucestershire Regt., with which he served three years in India. After a transfer to the 7th Hariana Lancers, Indian Army, 12 July, 1907, he exchanged into the Northamptons in 1911. He joined the Royal Flying Corps in 1912, and went to France with the first Expeditionary Force on 11 Aug. 1914, being present at Maubeuge and Mons, and during the retreat to the Marne. Capt. Read was then attached to the 9th Lancers, and while with them was severely injured during the fighting on the Aisne in Sept. 1914. He rejoined the Northamptons in the trenches six months before his death, and was in temporary command owing to casualties.
Capt. Read was well known as an Army athlete. He won the heavyweight championship in India eight times, and the middleweight twice, winning both at the same meetings. He also won the Army and Navy Heavyweight Championship three times at Aldershot and Plymouth, making an unequalled record in service boxing. One of his judges said: "Read wins because he never accepts defeat, and never knows when he is beaten." Capt. Read was killed in France on the night of 24–25 Sept. 1915. He was awarded a posthumous Victoria Cross [London Gazette, 18 Nov. 1915]: "Anketell Moutray Read, Capt., 1st Battn. Northamptonshire Regt. For most conspicuous bravery during the first attack near Hulloch on the morning of 25 Sept. 1915. Although partially gassed, Capt. Read went out several times in order to rally parties of different units which were disorganized and retiring. He led them back into the firing line, and, utterly regardless of danger, moved freely about, encouraging them under a withering fire. He was mortally wounded while carrying out this gallant work. Capt. Read had previously shown conspicuous bravery during digging operations on 29, 30 and 31 Aug. 1915,

and on the night of 29–30 July he carried out of action an officer who was mortally wounded, under a hot fire of rifles and grenades." A local newspaper says : " The Victoria Cross has been conferred on the late Capt. Anketell Moutray Read, 1st Battn. Northamptonshire Regt., a native of Bampton, for an act of gallantry and devotion to duty. . . . Capt. Anketell Moutray Read was a son of Mrs. Moutray Read, who formerly resided at Little Breancamp, Washfield, and subsequently at Castle Grove, Bampton, the residence now " (at the time of Capt. A. Moutray Read's death) " of her eldest son, Major Moutray Read, who is away with his wife as a Commissioner in West Africa. Capt. Moutray Read was a tall, smart, well-built officer, and frequently visited Bampton during his mother's stay at Castle Grove. He was most keen on keeping up his athletic abilities, and used to practise boxing with the captain of the local football club, Private John Salisbury, who is at present with the 4th Devons at Ferozepore, India." " Baily's Magazine " for Nov. 1915, says : " Capt. A. M. Read won the heavyweight boxing championship of India eight times, and the middleweight twice. He also won the Army and Navy heavyweight title thrice."

MALING, GEORGE ALLAN, Lieut., was born 6 Oct. 1888, at Sunderland, son of Edwin Allan Maling, J.P.,

M.R.C.S., etc., and Maria Jane Maling. He was educated at Uppingham ; Oxford, and St. Thomas's Hospital (Degrees, M.A., M.B., B.Ch. Oxon., M.R.C.S., L.R.C.P.), and was commissioned as Lieutenant, R.A.M.C., 18 Jan. 1915. For his services at the Battle of Loos, while attached to the 12th Battn. Rifle Brigade, he was awarded the Victoria Cross [London Gazette, 18 Nov. 1915] : " George Allan Maling, M.B., Temporary Lieut., Royal Army Medical Corps. Date of Act of Bravery : 25 Sept. 1915. For most conspicuous bravery and devotion to duty during the heavy fighting near Fauquissart on 25 Sept. 1915. Lieut. Maling worked incessantly with untiring energy from

George Allan Maling.

6.25 a.m. on the 25th till 8 a.m. on the 26th, collecting and treating in the open, under heavy shell fire, more than 300 men. At about 11 a.m. on the 25th, he was flung down and temporarily stunned by the bursting of a large high-explosive shell, which wounded his only assistant and killed several of his patients. A second shell soon after covered him and his instruments with debris, but his high courage and zeal never failed him, and he continued his gallant work single-handed." He was mentioned in Despatches, and promoted to Captain in 1916. Subsequently served at the Military Hospital, Grantham, and for two years with 34th Field Ambulance, 11th Division. On May 5, 1917, at Sutton, Surrey, Capt. Maling married Daisy Wolmer, daughter of G. S. Wolmer, Esq., of Winnipeg, Canada. He is a keen fisherman and tennis player. When asked to amplify the above account, Capt. Maling said he had nothing to add to it. He had led a blameless life.

FLEMING-SANDES, ALFRED JAMES TERENCE, Temporary Second Lieut., was born at Northstead

Road, Tulse Hill Park, London, S.E., on 24 June, 1894, son of the late Alfred Fleming-Sandes and Grace Fleming-Sandes. He was educated at Dulwich College Preparatory School, and at King's School, Canterbury, where he was a School Monitor and Captain of Mr. Evan's House. He entered the Army as a Private in the Artists' Rifles on 5 Aug. 1914, and went to the front with the 1st Battn. 26 Oct. 1914. He had a commission given him in France on 9 May, 1915, and served with his new battalion, the 2nd East Surrey Regt., until wounded on 29 Sept. 1915, at Loos. He was awarded the Victoria Cross [London Gazette, 18 Nov. 1915] : " Alfred James

A. J. T. Fleming-Sandes.

Terence Fleming-Sandes, Temporary Second Lieut., East Surrey Regt. For most conspicuous bravery at Hohenzollern Redoubt on 29 Sept. 1915. Second Lieut. Fleming-Sandes was sent to command a company which at the time was in a very critical position. The troops on his right were retiring, and his own men, who were much shaken by continual bombing and machine-gun fire, were also beginning to retire, owing to shortage of bombs. Taking in the situation at a glance, he collected a few bombs, jumped on the parapet in full view of the Germans, who were only 20 yards away, and threw them. Although very severely wounded almost at once by a bomb, he struggled to his feet and continued to advance and throw bombs till he was again severely wounded. This most gallant act put new heart into his men, rallied them, and saved the situation." Needless to say, Lieut. Fleming-Sandes had a great reception when later he paid a visit to his old school. He was promoted Temporary Lieutenant, and was mentioned in Despatches.

HALLOWES, RUPERT PRICE, Second Lieut., was born on 5 May, 1881, at Redhill, Surrey, youngest son of Frederic Blackburn Hallowes, F.R.C.S., and Mary Anne Taylor, daughter of the Rev. W. Hutchinson, Rector of Checkly, Staffordshire. He was educated at Conyngham House, Ramsgate (C. Rose, Esq.), and at Haileybury College, and enlisted in the Artists' Rifles 5 Aug. 1914, to which corps he had belonged many

years, having been gazetted Second Lieut. 17 Nov. 1909, so that he re-enlisted as a private. He was a keen shot, and shot for Haileybury at Bisley for the Ashburton Shield in 1896 and 1897. He had

been appointed Assistant Manager of the Mansel Tin-Plate Works at Aberavon. He went out to France 27 Dec. 1915, and received a commission to the 4th Battn. Middlesex Regt. (Temporary Second Lieutenant) in April, 1915, and gained the Military Cross 19 July, 1915, at Loos. [London Gazette, 6 Sept. 1915] : " Rupert Price Hallowes, Temporary Second Lieut., 4th Battn. Middlesex Regt. For conspicuous gallantry on the night of 19 July, at Hooge, when, owing to the shortage of bombs the enemy was advancing down the communication trench. He got out of his trench, exposing himself fearlessly, and fired at the enemy in the open, hitting several. He also assisted in making

Rupert Price Hallowes.

a block dug-out in a communication trench, and under heavy shell fire rebuilt a parapet that had been blown in. Throughout the night he assisted in keeping touch and supplying bombs." He was killed in action 1 Oct. 1915, at Hooge, and was posthumously awarded the Victoria Cross. His Victoria Cross was gazetted 18 Nov. 1915 : " Rupert Price Hallowes, Temporary Second Lieut., 4th Battn. The Middlesex Regt. Dates of Acts of Bravery : between 25 Sept. and 1 Oct. 1915. For most conspicuous bravery and devotion to duty during the fighting at Hooge between 25 Sept. and 1 Oct. 1915. Second Lieut. Hallowes displayed throughout these days the greatest bravery and untiring energy, and set a magnificent example to his men during four heavy and prolonged bombardments. On more than one occasion he climbed up on the parapet, utterly regardless of danger, in order to put fresh heart into his men. He made daring reconnaissances of the German positions in our lines. When the supply of bombs was running short he went back under very heavy shell fire and brought up a fresh supply. Even after he was mortally wounded he continued to cheer those around him and to inspire them with fresh courage." He was twice mentioned in Despatches. The following are some extracts from letters : From Corpl. A. Raymond, 10 Nov. 1915 : " I was in the same trench when Lieut. Hallowes when he was killed. I do hope that he will get the V.C., for he deserved it as much as any one, as I know quite well, for I was in his company." From Private Bennett : " Lieut. Hallowes' first and foremost thoughts were of the trench. Some were in a dangerous part of the trench, and he went to see if they were all right, and as soon as he reached them the shell hit him. He knew no fear and never sent a man where he would not go himself. I am not certain how he won the V.C., but he earned it on several occasions. I saw him fetch in one wounded man under heavy fire, and then he went out again." From Private W. Corner, No. 11153, B Company, 4th Middlesex Regt. : " I would like to make a few remarks on the conduct of Lieut. Hallowes, who is, in my opinion, worthy of the highest honours for his brave conduct in the field. On Sunday, 26 Sept. (night), when we were in our advanced trench, we came across two wounded Royal Scots, and Lieut. Hallowes at once got out into the open and saw that the wounded men were got into safety. Just after they were rescued, the Germans started a severe bombardment. We had to get in the firing line, and there was Lieut. Hallowes standing on the parapet, encouraging his men. I am sure he was the means of saving these men's lives. He seemed to be everywhere, giving encouragement to everyone, and we all deeply regret the loss of such a brave officer. He was leading Platoon No. 8." " Deeds that thrill the Empire " (pages 386–393) says : " The summer campaign of 1915 in the West, on the British section of the Allied front, made comparatively little difference to the contours of our line as marked upon the map. Nevertheless, if, measured by the gain or loss of ground, the fighting was of slight importance, it was often of a desperate character and productive of heavy casualties. This was particularly the case in the Hooge area, lying on either side of the Menin-Ypres road, where fighting of a fierce and sanguinary character went on intermittently all through the summer months. Thus, on the last day of May we captured the outbuildings of the château, and, after being driven out, recaptured them again on the night of 3 June. On the 16th we attacked with some success south of Hooge, and carried one thousand yards of German front trenches and part of their second line, and afterwards repulsed a strong counter-attack. On the 18th of the same month we made some further progress north of the Menin-Ypres road ; while on 19 July an enemy redoubt at the western end of the Hooge defences was successfully mined and destroyed, and a small portion of their trenches was captured. In this action an officer of the 4th Middlesex, one of the battalions of the 3rd Division, Lieut. Rupert Price Hallowes, won the Military Cross by the daring bravery he displayed when the Germans delivered their counter-attack. Perceiving that owing to our shortage of bombs the enemy were approaching down the communication trench, he left his own trench, and, with the most perfect indifference to the risk to which he was exposing himself, went out into the open and fired at them, killing or wounding several. Later, he assisted in the repair of a communication trench, and in rebuilding a parapet that had been blown in by a shell, both under very heavy fire ; while throughout the night he rendered great assistance in keeping in touch with our supports and in supplying bombs. Fierce fighting again occurred at Hooge between 30 July and 9 Aug., but after that there was relative quiet along this part of our front until the last week in September, when a strong offensive movement was undertaken by us, with the object of detaining the left wing of the Duke of Würtemberg's command, and preventing the Germans from sending reinforcements southwards to the La Bassée district, where the main British advance was about to begin. At four o'clock on the morning of the 25th our artillery preparation began, and soon after 4.30 the British infantry advanced to the attack, the 14th Division on the left against the Bellewaarde Farm, and the 3rd Division, which included the 4th Middlesex, against the enemy's position north of Sanctuary Wood, on the south side of the Menin–Ypres road. The charge of our infantry carried all before it, and the whole of the German front-line trenches were soon in our hands. But the enemy had concentrated a mass of artillery behind their lines, and our new front was subjected to so heavy a bombardment that the gains on our left could not be held, though south of the highway the 3rd Division still clung to some of the ground it had won, and managed to consolidate its position. Between that day and 1 Oct., during which time the trenches held by the 4th Middlesex were subjected to four heavy and prolonged bombardments and repeated counter-attacks, Second Lieut. Hallowes again most brilliantly distinguished himself, 'displaying' in the words of the Gazette, 'the greatest bravery and untiring energy and setting a magnificent example to his men.' On the night of 26–27 Sept., perceiving two wounded men of the Royal Scots lying out in the open, he left his trench, and, under a fierce rifle fire, coolly superintended their removal to a place of safety. Scarcely had he returned to the trenches than the Germans started another severe bombardment, and shells of every description came raining down. The range was very accurate, and fearing that some of the men might begin to flinch, Lieut. Hallowes, utterly regardless of his own danger, climbed on to the parapet to put fresh heart into them. 'He seemed to be everywhere, giving encouragement to everyone,' wrote a private of his battalion. Lieut. Hallowes also made more than one daring reconnaissance of the German position, and when the supply of bombs was ruuning short, he went back, under very heavy shell fire, and brought up a fresh supply. For six days this most heroic officer braved death successfully, but such entire disregard of danger as he displayed cannot long be continued with impunity, and on the seventh (1 Oct.) he met his inevitable end. He was a hero to the last, for we are told that 'even after he was mortally wounded he continued to cheer those around him and to inspire them with fresh courage.' The Victoria Cross, for which he appears to have been recommended after the fighting on 25 Sept., was awarded to him posthumously, 'for most conspicuous bravery and devotion to duty,' and no one will be inclined to dispute his right to a foremost place on our most glorious roll of honour. . . . Like so many very brave men, he appears to have been a singularly modest one, and even after winning the Military Cross could not be persuaded by his relatives to tell them anything of the gallant action for which it had been awarded." The staff and employees of the Mansel Tin-Plate Works at Aberavon bore the entire cost (£400) of a new receiving ward and X-ray room at the Aberavon General Hospital to the memory of this gallant officer, and the Boy Scouts' Association, of which he was for many years assistant secretary, installed a complete X-ray apparatus. We reprint the following by permission of the editor of the "Morning Post": "The Duke of Cambridge's Own, otherwise the Middlesex Regt., is known everywhere as 'The Die Hards.' This is no boastful phrase or idle nickname, but is a sobriquet earned in one of the most terrific combats of the Peninsula. It was at Albuhera that they died hard, for out of twenty-five officers twenty-two fell, and of 570 men, 425 became casualties. The King's Colour was riddled with bullet holes, but no effort of the enemy could break the 57th Foot, who kept closing their ranks as their brave commander, Colonel Inglis, called out: 'Die hard, my men, die hard!' They did, and the whole Army proclaimed them. At Inkerman, when the soldier's battle was in progress, the old regiment again heard its colonel calling the historic phrase, 'Die Hards, remember Albuhera!' This is only one piece of history from a glorious record, which began at Mysore and the 2nd Battn., the old 77th Foot, also made honour for the colours by being one of the three regiments which stormed the breach at Ciudad Rodrigo. When raised in 1755 the regiment was formed chiefly of Londoners from the Middlesex Militia, and on the Somme it is still the London man who fills the ranks. The regiment was, in 1914, one of the few still possessing four battalions, as they were not included in the reduction folly of previous years. When mobilization began the 1st Battn. was at Woolwich and not allotted to any brigade; the 2nd was at Malta under Brigadier-General F. A. Adam; the 3rd lay at Cawnpore; and the 4th was at Devonport under orders for Bordon. The battalions were therefore so placed that they followed one another at intervals of time into the field. The 1st Battn. began on the lines of communication as defence troops, and the 4th was in the famous 8th Infantry Brigade of the 3rd Division, under B. J. Doran and Hubert Hamilton. The battalion at Malta came later into the force in France, and the Indian unit left Wheeler's Entrenchments for France under Willcocks. The Middlesex men were involved in the Great Retreat, and the commanding officers of the 1st and 4th Battns. were both mentioned in Despatches. In the big battle of Ypres-Armentières, which began on 11 Oct. 1914, the 4th Battn. was most distinguished, and its commander won for himself a brigade. The 2nd Corps was heavily engaged, and the 8th Brigade found itself opposed to heavy masses of the enemy. The pressure caused the 1st Gordon Highlanders to be driven from their trenches, and the 4th Middlesex, under Lieut.-Colonel Hull, coming to the rescue, retook the lost position in most gallant style. On another occasion in the same combat the Middlesex lost part of their trenches, but holding firmly to what remained, they retook the line with the assistance of the A. and S.H. Every German was either bayoneted or captured, and later information showed that no less than twelve battalions of the enemy had been in the front of the brigade. These two units were again associated in a trench exploit which occurred when the most severe pressure was being directed against the line held by the Highlanders and Middlesex. So grandly did these men fight that the German masses were not only driven off with great loss, but withdrew from the combat altogether. All four commanding officers were mentioned by Lord French—Lieut.-Colonels F. G. M. Rowley, R. H. Hayes, C. P. A. Hull, and B. E. Ward (who died from wounds). If the 'Die Hards' died hard in the Great Retreat, they also knew how to face odds at Neuve Chapelle. Soon after the battle had opened the 8th Division was heavily engaged, and, just as at Albuhera, the Middlesex men were faced with heavy losses and bore them without flinching. Amid a storm of bullets the men passed on into Neuve Chapelle, and took it. It was a glorious battle for the Middlesex Regt., for nearly thirty officers and men were specially mentioned, including Lieut.-Colonel R. H. Hayes once again, and Lieut.-Colonel E. Stephenson, the gallant commander of the 3rd Battn., who fell. The Second Battle of Ypres added further laurels to the regiment's record, and in this action the 3rd Battn., from India, took part in a glorious counter-attack in aid of the hard-pressed Canadians. The assault was magnificently delivered, and, although held up, it attracted force from harassed points, and it was at this place that one of the old Middlesex Volunteer Rifle Corps, the present Rangers of the London Regt., succeeded at great cost in reaching the original trench line. Loos offered new opportunities to the 'Die Hards,' and considering the determined character of the regiment's fighting, it was no surprise to read in the Report prepared by the Historical Section of the Committee of Imperial Defence that the Middlesex men performed great deeds near the Hohenzollern Redoubt. When the left attack was checked, the 1st Middlesex and their old comrades, the Argylls, were fighting valiantly against uncut wire and trying to force a way through. The 'Die Hards' hung on stubbornly, taking cover in the shell craters close to the German lines. It was a great day also for all the old Middlesex Volunteer Rifle Corps, who covered both the Counties of London and Middlesex with honour. At Hooge the 4th Battn. was engaged in a brilliant failure, and stubbornly aided the Gordons against a concentrated fire. It had thus been a case of holding on and dying hard on several occasions, and never once did a unit of the old regiment fail in the hour of danger. Always taught to remember Albuhera, they have done so with success throughout. In the early fighting of 1916 Sir Douglas Haig specially mentioned the 1st and 2nd Battns., but whether Regulars, Kitcheners, or Territorials the record has been just the same, and the latter units opened the offensive of 1 July with most brilliant work. The Middlesex Regt. is one which has grown to vast dimensions, and to it are allied the Peterborough Rangers and the Wentworth Regt. of Canada (a happy alliance, remembering Ypres), and also the Taranaki Rifles, of New Zealand. It has a Public Schools battalion, two Footballers battalions, three Public Works battalions, and one from Shoreditch and one from Islington. On many occasions the regiment has fought with distinction when outnumbered, and the present war is no exception to the regimental tradition. On one such occasion, at El-Bodon, the Duke of Wellington commended the 2nd Battn. for 'steadiness, discipline, and confidence,' and the same unit was thanked by Lord French in identical words after its fine work at Neuve Chapelle. He also said: 'Men of the 2nd Middlesex, I am proud of you. In all the annals of British warfare no regiment ever upheld its traditions more worthily. . . . I am proud to stand in the midst of you.' The wearers of the lemon yellow facings made history when the 57th and 77th were the West and East Middlesex. The old number of 77 is linked up with the Montgomery and the Atholl Highlanders, and it was with the Argylls and Gordons in Flanders and France that new associations were made. The Royal Elthorne Militia and the Royal East Middlesex Militia and the depot at Mill Hill have reinforced the battalions magnificently, and the New Army units, following tradition, have fought well, lost heavily, and died hard. But they have taken their toll of the enemy in the Battle of the Somme, have won victory, and crowned with imperishable fame the record of a grand old regiment, and not the least of the new men is Rupert Price Hallowes, V.C."—"Morning Post," 13 Oct. 1916.

JOHNSON, FREDERICK HENRY, Second Lieut., was born 15 Aug. 1890, at 13, Bedford Row (now High Road), Streatham, S.W., son of Samuel Roger Johnson and Emily, daughter of Henry White, of Ewell. He was educated at Middle Whitgift School, Croydon, and at St. Dunstan's College, Catford, and at Battersea Polytechnic (day scholar), and joined the London University O.T.C. in Aug. 1914; served in the European War, and won the Victoria Cross. The "Brixton Free Press" for 26 Nov. 1915, gives an interesting account of Second Lieut. Johnson and two other Londoners who have won the Victoria Cross: "Brixton, which has so many heroes in the war, has now secured the great distinction of having its own V.C., thanks to the courageous pertinacity of Lieut. Frederick Henry Johnson, whose home is in Cranworth Gardens, Brixton Road. He is not in the local battalion, but that matters not, for since the war the great majority of Brixton men have joined regiments which are 'foreign.' He is attached to the Royal Engineers, being in the 73rd Field Company, which has seen much active service since the war began. He is, moreover, a real Londoner, having been born at Streatham some twenty-five years ago. He won the Victoria Cross in the attack on Hill 70. On 25 Sept. he was with a section of his company, and, although wounded in the leg, he stuck to his post throughout the furious fighting and led several charges against one of the German redoubts. When things were very critical he repeatedly, although under very heavy fire, rallied his men, and by his splendid example and cool courage was mainly instrumental in saving the situation and establishing firmly his part of the position which had been captured from the enemy. He remained at his post until relieved in the evening. The gallant lieu-

Frederick H. Johnson.

tenant is a distinguished scholar as well as a brave warrior. He is a Whitworth Exhibitioner and obtained the B.Sc (engineering) degree with honours at the London University. He was once a student at the Battersea Polytechnic, and though so many Poly men have joined the Colours, he is the first of them to secure the coveted V.C. Nor does Lieut. Johnson stand alone in adding glorious lustre to our thousands of citizen soldiers. News comes that yet another local fighting lad has secured the V.C., namely, Second Lieut. A. T. Fleming-Sandes, who was born at Tulse Hill, and whose grandparents have lived for very many years at Clapham Road. Fleming-Sandes was educated at Dulwich College Preparatory School and at King's College, Canterbury. He was a brilliant scholar and won a couple of scholarships. When war broke out he was being coached for the Civil Service, but promptly abandoned this to join the Army. He joined the Artists' Rifles O.T.C. and obtained his commission in May, being attached to the 2nd East Surrey Regt. He was wounded in the 'big push,' in which he won the V.C., and is now home again, after a sojourn in the Castle Hospital, Dublin. His wounds included a broken arm, and this is still in a sling. He has recently been assisting in recruiting, and hopes to be fit enough to return to the front early in the New Year. A third V.C. hero, also of the East Surreys, is Capt. Geary, of Palace Road, Streatham Hill, whose plucky exploits we recorded some weeks ago." Lieut. Johnson's Victoria Cross was gazetted 18 Nov. 1915: "Frederick Henry Johnson, Temporary Second Lieut., 73rd Field Company, Royal Engineers: For most conspicuous bravery and devotion to duty in the attack on Hill 70 on 25 Sept. 1915. Second Lieut. Johnson was with a section of his company of the Royal Engineers. Although wounded in the leg, he stuck to his duty throughout the attack, led several charges on the German redoubt, and at a very critical time, under very heavy fire, repeatedly rallied the men who were near him. By his splendid example and cool courage he was mainly instrumental in saving the situation and in establishing firmly his part of the position which had been taken. He remained at his post until relieved in the evening." The "South Western Star" for 12 May, 1916, says: "A tremendous welcome was accorded Second Lieut. F. H. Johnson, R.E., V.C., at Battersea Polytechnic on Friday afternoon. Lieut. Johnson was an engineering student at the Polytechnic, and one of the most distinguished that institution has had. At the outbreak of war he offered his services to the country, and was soon afterwards given a commission in the Royal Engineers. The Victoria Cross was awarded him for most conspicuous bravery and devotion to duty in the attack on Hill 70 on 25 Sept. 1915. Although wounded in the leg he led several charges on the German redoubt, and at a very critical time, under very heavy fire, repeatedly rallied the men who were near him. By his splendid example and cool courage he was mainly instrumental in saving the situation. Friday's function opened with a procession in the Great Hall of the Polytechnic. At the head walked Lieut. Johnson and Canon Curtis to the organ accompaniment of 'See the Conquering Hero comes,' and resounding cheers from the Polytechnic students and the pupils of the Secondary Day School. The Mayor and Mayoress of Battersea and several of the governors of the Polytechnic were in the procession. Canon Curtis afterwards recounted the hero's splendid record at the institute, where he was one of the best students they had had, and read the official account of the deed that brought him glory. Courage in the battlefield was not always or chiefly a mere physical matter. Rather, it was born of devotion to duty, high purpose, and unselfish ambition. Lieut. Johnson's parents and his grandmother were on the platform. Canon Curtis associated himself with them in the pride and joy they must feel. He trusted that after the war Lieut. Johnson would return to the civil duties for which he was so well qualified. The Mayor of Battersea (Mr. W. J. Moore) said Lieut. Johnson's conduct was typical. With such men we need never fear for our country or doubt the issue of the war. Speaking with emotion, he made a reference to his own sons at the front. Mr. Gilbert, chairman of the London County Council Education Committee, said he honoured Lieut. Johnson as one of the first London scholars to obtain the V.C. His record and example were a reply to critics who spoke slightingly of the educational work of London. The war showed that our educational system had done more than most people had anticipated. Five Victoria Crosses had been won by old pupils of the London schools. More than 2,000 masters were serving with the Colours. The roll of one elementary school contained 400 names, and 32 commissions had been gained. Canon Curtis then asked Lieut. Johnson to accept the portrait of himself, which had been subscribed for by the governors, staff, and students of the Polytechnic. The Mayor led the deafening cheers that followed. Lieut. Johnson modestly said it was one thing to do something in action and another to come down and be applauded and looked at. A duplicate of the portrait was presented to the Polytechnic as a memorial of Lieut. Johnson's heroic deeds. Dr. Newman, the principal, said it would give future students some conception of the lieutenant's ideals and of the Polytechnic's appreciation of his merits. It would be a reminder that in England's great crisis the students, the staff, and the governors of the Polytechnic played their part. The proceedings closed with the singing of the National Anthem." Second Lieut. Johnson won quick promotion, and was a Major when officially reported, on 11 Dec. 1917, as killed in action.

Alexander Buller Turner.

TURNER, ALEXANDER BULLER, Second Lieut., was the son of Major Charles Turner, late Royal Berkshire Regt., of Thatcham, near Newbury, Berkshire. He joined the 1st Battn. 22 June, 1915, and was wounded on 15 Aug. He was awarded the Victoria Cross [London Gazette, 18 Nov. 1915]: "Alexander Buller Turner, Second Lieut., 3rd Battn., attached 1st Battn., Royal Berkshire Regt. Date of Act of Bravery: 28 Sept. 1915. For most conspicuous bravery, on the 28th Sept. 1915, at Fosse 8, near Vermelles. When the regimental bombers could make no headway in Slag Alley, Second Lieut. Turner volunteered to lead a new bombing attack. He pressed down the communication trench practically alone, throwing bombs incessantly with such dash and determination that he drove back the Germans about 150 yards without a check. His action enabled the reserves to advance with very little loss, and subsequently covered the flank of his regiment in its retirement, thus probably averting a loss of some hundreds of men. This most gallant officer has since died of wounds received in this action." Second Lieut. A. B. Turner died in hospital on the 30th Sept. 1915. Extract from Commanding Officer's letter: "The most gallant act I ever saw."

VICKERS, CHARLES GEOFFREY, Lieut. (Temporary Capt.), was born on 13 Oct. 1894, son of Charles Henry Vickers, Lace Manufacturer, Nottingham, and Jessie Anna Vickers (*née* Lomas), of Leicester. He was educated at Sidney House, Oundle School, and Merton College, Oxford. Between his school and University careers he visited Germany from Jan. to April, 1913, studying the language. He entered Merton College in Oct. 1913, winning a Classical Exhibition, and was reading for Honour Moderations and "Greats." He represented Oundle School and Merton College at Rugby football. He did five years' service in the Officers' Training Corps, obtaining Certificate "A" and being promoted Sergt. He obtained his commission in the 7th (Robin Hood) Battn. The Sherwood Foresters on the 2nd Sept. 1914, from the Oxford University Officers' Training Corps. He served in the European War, leaving England on the 25th Feb. 1915. He fought in Belgium, mostly at Ypres, until Sept. 1915, then in the Battle of Loos. He was awarded the Victoria Cross. Sir A. Conan Doyle says, in "The British Campaign in France and Flanders" (page 238): "At three o'clock there was a fresh infantry advance, the 7th Sherwood Foresters of the reserve 139th Brigade endeavouring to get forward, but losing so many in crossing the redoubt that they were unable to sally out from the farther side. The redoubt was soon so crowded with mixed units, all under heavy fire, that there might have been a Spion Kop but for the steadiness of all concerned. At one time the men, finding themselves practically without officers, began to fall back, but were splendidly rallied by Colonel Evill of the 1st Monmouths, and a few other survivors. The advent of two companies of the 5th Leicesters, retaining their disciplined order, helped to avert the danger, and the line was formed once again along the western face of the redoubt. During this movement the 7th Sherwood Foresters, who remained in the north-east of the redoubt were cut off, but with splendid pertinacity they held their ground, and made their way back when darkness fell. In the early morning of the 14th, Capt. Checkland, with a company of the 5th Sherwood Foresters, pushed an advance up to the place where their comrades of the 7th Battn. had been, and found Capt. Vickers of that regiment, who, with a bravery which deserves to be classic, defended almost single-handed a barrier, while he ordered a second one to be built up behind him, cutting him off from all succour. He was desperately wounded, but was brought back by his comrades." London Gazette, 18 Nov. 1915: "Charles Geoffrey Vickers, Second Lieut. (Temporary Capt.), 1/7th (Robin Hood) Battn. The Sherwood Foresters (Nottinghamshire and Derbyshire Regt.), Territorial Force. For most conspicuous bravery on the 14th Oct. in the Hohenzollern Redoubt. When nearly all his men had been killed or wounded, and with only two men available to hand him bombs, Capt. Vickers held a barrier for some hours against heavy German bomb attacks from front and flank. Regardless of the fact that his own retreat would be cut off, he had ordered a second barrier to be built behind him in order to ensure the safety of the trench. Finally, he was severely wounded, but not before his magnificent courage and determination had enabled the second barrier to be completed. A critical situation was thus saved." His Colonel's report was as follows: "Capt. Charles Geoffrey Vickers came into the British front-line trench at about 4 a.m. 13 Oct., and his company was detailed to hold this trench from 5th Brigade on the left to 138th Brigade on the right. About 4 p.m., 14 Oct., Capt. C. G. Vickers was ordered to take up a party to relieve Capt. Warren of this battalion in the Hohenzollern Redoubt. This he successfully accomplished, and himself took charge of the bomb fighting at the barricade at the north-west end of the redoubt. Having but few bomb-throwers, and these being quickly wounded, he continued to hold the barricade single-handed against a violent enemy's bombing attack whilst another barricade was constructed behind him, the original one being practically destroyed by the enemy's consistent bombing. Great difficulty was experienced in getting sandbags and material for the new barricade, and Capt. Vickers was alone for a long time. Meantime reinforcements had been sent for, and arrived just as Capt. Vickers fell wounded between the old and new barriers. His work in holding the barricade single-handed whilst another barricade was being built in his rear, rendering his return when the barricade was completed very uncertain, cannot be too highly estimated, and it is beyond doubt that had it not been for his real bravery and untiring exertions we could not possibly have hoped to retain our hold on the Hohenzollern Redoubt, for the retention of which he was, during his occupancy, personally and solely responsible." He returned to England, and on 1 June, 1916, joined the Reserve Battn. for light duty. He was passed as fit on 15 Sept.

Charles G. Vickers.

1916. On the 23rd Sept. he left England again and rejoined his former battalion. On 20 Feb. 1917, he was recalled from France as Instructor, and later Company Commander, in the 19th Officer Cadet Battn. He was promoted Captain 29 Aug. 1915. On 5 April, 1918, he returned to France a third time, was promoted Major, and appointed Second in Command of the 1st Lincolnshire Regt. He served in this capacity until the end of the war, fighting at Kemmel, on the Aisne, and throughout the 3rd Army advance from Aug. until Nov. 1918. He was again wounded; was mentioned in Despatches, and won the Croix de Guerre whilst commanding a composite battalion in the defence of the Marne in June of that year. Capt. Vickers is fond of tennis and literary pursuits. On 21 March, 1918, he married Miss Helen Tregoning Newton, daughter of Mr. and Mrs. A. H. Newton, of Harpenden, Herts, at St. Andrew's Church, Malden Road, London, N.W. His rank on disembodiment was Captain (Acting Major).

WELLS, HARRY, Sergt., served in the European War, and was awarded the Victoria Cross [London Gazette, 18 Nov. 1915]: " Harry Wells, No. 8088, Sergt., 2nd Battn. Royal Sussex Regt. For most conspicuous bravery near Le Tutoire on 25 Sept. 1915. When his platoon officer had been killed he took command and led his men forward to within fifteen yards of the German wire. Nearly half the platoon were killed or wounded, and the remainder were much shaken, but with the utmost coolness and bravery Sergt. Wells rallied them and led them forward. Finally, when very few were left, he stood up and urged them forward once more, but while doing this he was killed. He gave a magnificent display of courage and determination." Major F. W. B. Willett, Royal Sussex Regt., writes : 14 Oct. 1919, from the Barracks, Chichester : " I was present at the engagement at which Sergt. Wells was killed and subsequently received the V.C. I can therefore give you more or less the circumstances under which the award was made : At Loos, on the 25th Sept. 1919, the 2nd Royal Sussex assaulted the German lines about 6 a.m. Owing to the wire being entirely uncut the assault failed, the battalion losing 19 officers and nearly 600 men in less than 15 minutes. Numerous efforts to cut their way through were made by individuals, conspicuous among them being Sergt. Wells, who, after his platoon officer was killed, took command and three times rallied his men and led them against the wire under close and continuous machine-gun fire. During the third attempt Sergt. Wells and practically all the survivors of his platoon were killed."

RAYNES, JOHN CRAWSHAW, Sergt., was born about 10 April, 1886, at Ecclesall, Sheffield, Yorkshire, son of Stephen Raynes and Mrs. Stephen Raynes. He joined the R.H. and R.F.A. 10 Oct. 1904. He served in the European War, and was awarded the Victoria Cross [London Gazette, 18 Nov. 1915]: " John Crawshaw Raynes, No. 36830, Acting Sergt., A Battery, 71st Brigade, R.F.A. Date of Act of Bravery : 11 Oct. 1915. For conspicuous bravery and devotion to duty. On 11 Oct. 1915, at Fosse 7 de Bethune, his battery was being heavily bombarded by armour-piercing and gas shells. On ' Cease fire ' being ordered, Sergt. Raynes went out under an intense shell fire to assist Sergt. Ayres, who was lying wounded forty yards away. He bandaged him and returned to his gun when it was again ordered into action. A few minutes later ' Cease fire ' was again ordered, owing to the intensity of the enemy's fire, and Sergt. Raynes,

John Crawshaw Raynes.

calling on two gunners to help him—both of whom were killed shortly afterwards—went out and carried Sergt. Ayres into a dug-out. A gas shell burst at the mouth of the dug-out, and Sergt. Raynes once more ran across the open, fetched his own smoke-helmet, put it on Sergt. Ayres, and then, himself badly gassed, staggered back to serve his gun. On 12 Oct. 1915, at Quality Street, a house was knocked down by a heavy shell, four men being buried in the house and four in the cellar. The first man rescued was Sergt. Raynes, wounded in the head and leg, but he insisted on remaining under heavy shell fire to assist in the rescue of all the other men. Then, after having his wounds dressed, he reported himself immediately for duty with his battery, which was again being heavily shelled." He was promoted to Battery Sergeant-Major, and was discharged 11 Dec. 1918, " physically unfit." Battery Sergt.-Major Raynes married on 24 April, 1907, at the Registry Office, Leeds, Miss Mabel Dawson, and they have one son, John Kenneth, born 30 Jan. 1912.

POLLOCK, JAMES DALGLEISH, Corpl., served in the European War, and was awarded the Victoria Cross [London Gazette, 18 Nov. 1915]: " James Dalgleish Pollock, No. 12087, Corpl., 5th Battn. Queen's Own Cameron Highlanders. For most conspicuous bravery near the Hohenzollern Redoubt on 27 Sept. 1915. At about 12 noon, when the enemy's bombers in superior numbers were successfully working up the ' Little Willie ' trench towards Hohenzollern Redoubt, Corpl. Pollock, after obtaining permission, got out of the trench alone, walked along the top edge with the utmost coolness and disregard of danger, and compelled the enemy's bombers to retire by bombing them from above. He was under heavy machine-gun fire the whole time, but contrived to hold up the progress of the

Jas. Dalgleish Pollock.

Germans for an hour, when he was at length wounded."

WYATT, GEORGE HARRY, L.-Corpl., served in the European War, and was awarded the Victoria Cross [London Gazette, 18 Nov. 1914]: " George Harry Wyatt, No. 5854, L.-Corpl., 3rd Battn. Coldstream Guards. Date of Act of Bravery : 25–26 Aug. 1914. For most conspicuous bravery and devotion to duty. At Landrecies, on the night of the 25th–26th Aug. 1914, when a part of his battalion was hotly engaged at the end of a street, close to some farm buildings, the enemy, by means of incendiary bombs, set light to some straw stacks in the farmyard. L.-Corpl. Wyatt twice dashed out of the line under very heavy fire from the enemy, who were only twenty-five yards distant, and extinguished the burning straw. If the fire had spread it would have been quite impossible to have held our position. Also at Villers Cotteret, after having been wounded in the head, L.-Corpl. Wyatt continued firing until he could no longer see, owing to the blood which was pouring down his face. The Medical Officer bound up his wound, and told him to go to the rear, but he at once returned to the firing-line and continued to fight."

DUNSIRE, ROBERT, Private, served in the European War, and was awarded the Victoria Cross [London Gazette, 18 Nov. 1915]: " Robert Dunsire, No. 18274, Private, 13th Battn. Royal Scots (Lothian Regt.). For most conspicuous bravery on Hill 70 on 26 Sept. 1915. Private Dunsire went out under very heavy fire and rescued a wounded man from between the firing-lines. Later, when another man considerably nearer the German lines was heard shouting for help, he crawled out again with utter disregard to the enemy's fire and carried him in also. Shortly afterwards the Germans attacked over this ground."

HARVEY, SAMUEL, Private, served in the European War, and was awarded the Victoria Cross [London Gazette, 18 Nov. 1915]: " Samuel Harvey, No. 8273, Private, 1st Battn. Northumberland Fusiliers. Date of Act of Bravery : 29 Sept. 1915. For most conspicuous bravery in ' Big Willie ' trench on the 29th Sept. 1915. During a heavy bombing attack by the enemy, and when more bombs were urgently required for our front, Private Harvey volunteered to fetch them. The communication trench was blocked with wounded and reinforcements, and he went backwards and forwards across the open under intense fire, and succeeded in bringing up no less than thirty boxes of bombs before he was wounded in the head. It was mainly due

Samuel Harvey.

to Private Harvey's cool bravery in supplying bombs that the enemy was eventually driven back." Private Harvey was transferred to the 3rd (H.S.) G Battn. Northumberland Fusiliers on 7 Oct. 1916, as No. 31198.

LAIDLAW, DANIEL, Piper, was born 26 July, 1875, at Little Swinton, Berwickshire, the eldest surviving son of the late Robert Laidlaw, of Coldingham, Berwickshire, and Margaret, daughter of Robert Logan, of Jedburgh. He was educated at Berwick-upon-Tweed National Schools, and Lesbury, Northumberland. He joined the Army 11 April, 1896, and served in India in the 2nd Durham Light Infantry till June, 1898. He was claimed out of the D.L.I. by his eldest brother in 1898, and served in the K.O.S.B. as a piper until 11 April, 1912. On the walls of his cottage hangs a framed certificate stating that he was " employed on plague duty in Bombay from 22 March to 1 May, 1898," signed by the Secretary to the Governor, the late A. Woodburn, Esq. After returning from India he went to the Reserve, and was employed as canteen manager at Alexandria, Alnwick Co-operative Stores, and Messrs. D. and D. H. Porter, of South Doddington, the well-known horse breeders. When in Alnwick he was Assistant Scout-master to his brother-in-law, Scoutmaster Goodman. On the outbreak of war in Europe, Piper Laidlaw re-enlisted in the Army 1 Sept. 1915, in the King's Own Scottish Borderers, and went to France in the following June. The following account of the brave deed for which he was awarded the Victoria Cross was given by Piper Laidlaw himself to Press representatives who visited him in Lord Derby's Hospital at Winwick, near Warrington, where he was lying wounded : " We were waiting in the trenches as patiently as we could while our artillery gave the enemy a thorough bombardment—a task that took more than a day, I can tell you. On Saturday morning—a day I am not likely to forget—we got the order to raid the German trenches. At 6.30 in the morning the bugles sounded the advance, and I got over the parapet with Lieut. Young (who I am sorry to say has since been killed). I at once set the pipes going, and the laddies gave a cheer as they started off for the enemy's lines. As soon as they showed themselves over the trench top they began to fall fast, but they never wavered, but dashed straight on as I played the old air they all knew, ' Blue Bonnets over the Border.' My, but there's some fire in that old tune. I ran forward with them, piping for all I knew, and just as we were getting near the German lines I was wounded by shrapnel in the left ankle and leg. I was too excited to feel the pain just then, but scrambled along as best I could. I changed my tune to ' The Standard on the Braes o' Mar,' a grand tune for charging on. I kept on piping and piping, and hobbling after the laddies until I could go no farther, and then, seeing that the boys had won the position,

I began to get back as best I could to our own trenches. I got there somehow, and it is as much as I can remember." Piper Laidlaw has equalled the world-famous V.C. feat of Piper Findlater, Gordon Highlanders, in the Tirah Expedition. His bagpipes put heart into his comrades at a critical time in the advance of 25 Sept. Thus the trenches in France, like the Heights at Dargai, have produced a piper who exposed himself at considerable risk in order that he might hearten his comrades with the music of his pipes. Piper Laidlaw was promoted Corporal 25 Sept. 1915, for distinguished service in the field,and awarded the Victoria Cross [London Gazette, 18 Nov. 1915]: " Daniel Laidlaw, No. 15851, Piper, 7th Battn. King's Own Scottish Borderers. For most conspicuous bravery prior to an assault on German trenches near Loos and Hill 70 on 25 Sept. 1915. During the worst of the bombardment, Piper, Laidlaw, seeing that his company was shaken from the effects of gas, with absolute coolness and disregard of danger, mounted the parapet, marched up and down and played his company out of the trench. The effect of his splendid example was immediate, and the company dashed out to the assault. Piper Laidlaw continued playing his pipes until he was wounded." He was also given the French Croix de Guerre with Palms, and received the 1914-15 Star. What the sound of the pipes meant to our soldiers is given in the following extracts from a letter in " The Clarion " by Private J. McAnulty: " The Camerons had three pipers when I was with them, many a night when on our way to the trenches. Suddenly a note echoed through the air, and then the pipers would play their wizards' march. Everything seemed to become transformed ; your pack and your sticks fell by the roadside, and you no longer carried your rifle, but were dancing and singing through space, every man keeping in step with the music. The war happened before you were born, nobody ever died, but always sang and danced uproariously, made faces, stood on their heads and shook hands with everybody they met. Andrew and I, with our kilts and our bare legs, no longer looked out of place. All colours were different and mixed up, but everything which (by accident or design) got into the picture only made it more perfect." Piper Laidlaw also received King George's Coronation Medal in 1911. He married, on 11 April, 1906, at the Baptist Church, Alnwick, Northumberland, Georgina Mary, daughter of Robert Harvie, of Kilburnie, Ayrshire, and they have two sons : Andrew Robert, born 3 Feb. 1907, and John, born 26 July, 1910, and two daughters : Margaret, born 21 Aug. 1911, and Georgina, born 10 Dec. 1913. His three brothers also served in the Army, two of them serving in the European War. He was promoted Sergeant-Piper 12 Oct. 1917 ; demobilized 3 April, 1919 ; total service 20 years, 6 months. His eldest brother, Pipe-Major Laidlaw, served in the K.O.S.B. 21 years. Decorations, Egyptian Medal and Star, Chitral Medal with clasp, Indian Frontier, 1897–98, Tirah Expedition, 1897–98, Long Service and Good Conduct Medal. James, another brother, served in the present war, 1914–15 (Star) ; served in R.F.A. George, his youngest brother, served in the present war in R.E. (1914–15 Star).

PEACHMENT, GEORGE, Private, served in the European War, and was awarded the Victoria Cross [London Gazette, 18 Nov. 1915]: " George Peachment, No. 11941, Private, 2nd Battn. King's Royal Rifle Corps. Date of Act of Bravery : 25 Sept. 1915. For most conspicuous bravery near Hulluch on the 25th Sept. 1915. During very heavy fighting, when our front line was compelled to retire in order to reorganize, Private Peachment, seeing his Company Commander, Capt. Dubs, lying wounded, crawled to assist him. The enemy's fire was intense, but, though there was a shell-hole quite close, in which a few men had taken cover, Private Peachment never thought of saving himself. He knelt in the open by his officer and tried to help him, but while doing this he was first wounded by a bomb and a minute later mortally wounded by a rifle bullet. He was one of the youngest men in his battalion, and gave this splendid example of courage and self-sacrifice."

VICKERS, ARTHUR, Private, served in the European War, and was awarded the Victoria Cross [London Gazette, 18 Nov. 1915]: " Arthur Vickers, No. 3719, Private, 2nd Battn. Royal Warwickshire Regt. Date of Act of Bravery : 25 Sept. 1915. For most conspicuous bravery on the 25th Sept. 1915, during operations before Hulluch. During an attack by his battalion on the first-line German trenches, Private Vickers, on his own initiative and with the utmost bravery, went forward in front of his company under very heavy shell, rifle and machine-gun fire, and cut the wires which were holding up a great part of the battalion. Although it was broad daylight at the time, he carried out this work standing up. His gallant action contributed largely to the success of the assault."

THAPA, KULBIR, Rifleman, served with the Indian Corps in France in the European War, and was awarded the Victoria Cross [London Gazette, 18 Nov. 1915]: " Kulbir Thapa, No. 2129, Rifleman, 2nd Battn. 3rd (Queen Alexandra's Own) Gurkha Rifles, Indian Army. Date of Act of Bravery : 25 Sept. 1915. For most conspicuous bravery during operations against the German trenches south of Mauquissart. When himself wounded, on the 25th Sept. 1915, he found a badly wounded soldier of the 2nd Leicestershire Regt. behind the first-line German trench, and, though urged by the British soldier to save himself, he remained with him all day and night. In the early morning of the 26th Sept., in misty weather, he brought him out through the German wire, and, leaving him in a place of comparative safety, returned and brought in two wounded Gurkhas one after the other. He then went back in broad daylight for the British soldier, and brought him in also, carrying him most of the way

Kulbir Thapa.

and being at most points under the enemy's fire." The authors of " With the Indian Corps in France," in describing the Battle of Loos, say on pages 410–411 : " A deed which could hardly be surpassed for sheer bravery was performed by Rifleman Kulbir Thapa. He is the exception noted above, as having entered the German trench and escaped alive. Kulbir succeeded, after being wounded, in getting through the wire in some extraordinary way, and charged straight through to the German trench. In rear of it he found a badly injured man of the 2nd Leicesters. The wounded man begged Kulbir Thapa to leave him and save himself, but the Gurkha refused to do so, and remained by his side throughout the day and the following night. Luckily there was a heavy mist on the morning of the 26th Sept., of which Kulbir took advantage to bring the man out through the German wire. He succeeded, after hairbreadth escapes, in doing this unobserved, and put the wounded man in a place of safety. Not content with this, he returned and rescued, one after the other, two wounded Gurkhas. He then went back again and brought in the British soldier in broad daylight, carrying him most of the way under fire from the enemy. For these successive acts of extreme bravery Rifleman Kulbir Thapa received the Victoria Cross, and it will be agreed that seldom, if ever, has this supreme reward of valour been more splendidly won. The deaths of officers and men who won the V.C. have so often been recorded in this history, that it is pleasant to mention that Kulbir Thapa survived his wound, proceeded to Egypt with his regiment, and eventually returned to India. The barbarity of the Germans has seldom been more vividly illustrated than during this action. . . . It is on record that on the morning of the 26th Sept., during the dense fog which enabled Kulbir Thapa to perform his deeds of heroism, numbers of Germans left their trenches for the express purpose of shooting and bayoneting our wounded."

DAWSON, JAMES LENNOX, Corpl. served in the European War, and was awarded the Victoria Cross [London Gazette, 7 Dec. 1915]: " James Lennox Dawson, No. 91608, Corpl., 187th Company, Royal Engineers. For most conspicuous bravery and devotion to duty on 13 Oct. 1915, at Hohenzollern Redoubt. During a gas attack, when the trenches were full of men, he walked backwards and forwards along the parados, fully exposed to a very heavy fire, in order to be the better able to give directions to his own sappers, and to clear the infantry out of the sections of the trench that were full of gas. Finding three leaking gas cylinders, he rolled them some sixteen yards away from the trench, again under very heavy fire, and then fired rifle bullets into them to let the gas escape. There is no doubt that the cool gallantry of Corpl. Dawson on this occasion saved many men from being gassed."

James Lennox Dawson.

KENNY, THOMAS, Private, served in the European War, and was awarded the Victoria Cross [London Gazette, 7 Dec. 1915]: " Thomas Kenny, No. 17424, Private, 13th (Service) Battn. Durham Light Infantry. For most conspicuous bravery and devotion to duty on the night of the 4th Nov. 1915, near La Houssoie. When on patrol in a thick fog with Lieut. Brown, 13th Battn. Durham Light Infantry, some Germans, who were lying out in a ditch in front of their parapet, opened fire and shot Lieut. Brown through both thighs. Private Kenny, although heavily and repeatedly fired upon, crawled about for more than an hour with his wounded officer on his back, trying to find his way through the fog to our trenches. He refused more than once to go on alone, although told by Lieut. Brown to do so. At last, when utterly exhausted, he came to a ditch which he recognized, placed Lieut. Brown in it, and went to look for help. He found an officer and a few men of his battalion at a listening-post, and after guiding them back, with their assistance Lieut. Brown was brought in, although the Germans again opened heavy fire with rifles and machine guns, and threw bombs at thirty yards' distance. Private Kenny's pluck, endurance, and devotion to duty were beyond praise."

DARTNELL, WILBUR, Temporary Lieut., was born in Australia, and joined the Army in 1914. He served in the European War, 1914–15, and was awarded the Victoria Cross [London Gazette, 23 Dec. 1915]: " Wilbur Dartnell, Temporary Lieut., late 25th (Service) Battn. (Frontiersmen) The Royal Fusiliers (City of London Regt.). For most conspicuous bravery near Maktau (East Africa) on 3 Sept. 1915. During a mounted infantry engagement the enemy got within a few yards of our men, and it was found impossible to get the more severely wounded away. Lieut. Dartnell, who was himself being carried away wounded in the leg, seeing the situation, and knowing that the enemy's black troops murdered the wounded, insisted on being left behind in the hopes of being able to save the lives of the other wounded men. He gave his own life in the gallant attempt to save others."

Wilbur Dartnell.

INSALL, GILBERT STUART MARTIN, Capt., was born at Avenue Mozart, Paris, on 14 May, 1894, son of Gilbert Jenkins Insall, Honorary Professor at Ecole Odontotechnique, Paris, and Mary Stuart, daughter of the late John Read, of Tunbridge Wells. He was educated at the Anglo-Saxon School, Paris, and at the Paris University. He entered the Army in Sept. 1914, in the University and Public Schools Brigade of the Royal Fusiliers. He went to Brooklands in March, 1915, joining the Royal Flying Corps as Second Lieutenant, and left for the Western Front in July, 1915. He was awarded the Victoria Cross [London Gazette, 23 Dec. 1915]: "Gilbert Insall, Second Lieut., Royal Flying Corps. For most conspicuous bravery, skill and determination. He was patrolling in a Vickers fighting machine with First Class Air Mechanic T. H. Donald as Gunner, when a German machine was sighted, pursued and attacked. The German pilot led the Vickers machine over a rocket battery, but with great skill Lieut. Insall dived and got to close range, when Donald fired a drum of cartridges into the German machine, stopping the engine. The German pilot then dived through a cloud, followed by Lieut. Insall. Fire was again opened, and the German machine was brought down heavily in a ploughed field. On seeing the Germans scramble out of their machine and prepare to fire, Lieut. Insall dived to five hundred feet, thus enabling Donald to open heavy fire on them. The Germans then fled, one helping the other, who was apparently wounded. Other Germans then commenced heavy fire, but in spite of this Lieut. Insall turned again, and an incendiary bomb was dropped on the German machine, which was last seen wreathed in smoke. Lieut. Insall then headed west, in order to get back over the German trenches, but as he was only at two thousand feet altitude he dived across them for greater speed, Donald firing into the trenches as he passed over. The German fire, however, damaged the petrol tank, and with great coolness Lieut. Insall landed under cover of a wood five hundred yards inside our lines. The Germans fired some hundred and fifty shells at our machine, but without causing material damage. Much damage had, however, been caused by rifle fire, but during the night it was repaired behind screened lights, and at dawn Lieut. Insall flew his machine home with First Class Air Mechanic T. H. Donald as passenger." The action for which the Victoria Cross was awarded was performed on 7 Nov. 1915. On 14 Dec. 1915, while on patrol, he sighted and pursued far into the enemy's lines a German machine. In the course of the ensuing engagement his gunner, Corpl. Donald, was shot in the leg and his petrol tank perforated by bullets. The machine having made off, he tried to reach the British lines, but an anti-aircraft shell burst just beneath his machine, a large fragment penetrating his seat and lodging itself at the base of the spine. Although temporarily losing consciousness he was able to effect a correct landing, and was captured immediately. He was at once operated on, and the fragment of shell extracted. He was taken to hospital at Cologne, and later to Fort Prinz Karl, at Ingolstadt, and thence to Constance for two days, being sent from there to Heidelberg. He escaped from Heidelberg by means of a tunnel, with two companions. The tunnel took six months to make. All three were recaptured in heavy snow in the Black Forest five days later. He was awarded a month's "cells" punishment, plus five months' solitary confinement "as a reprisal." Moved to Crefeld. With a companion, escaped in a cart in daylight, to be recaptured a few hours later, after a lively chase across the fields. Received a further 15 days' "cells," and was removed to Ströhen, near Hannover. In Aug. 1917, escaped with two companions, covering 150 miles on foot in nine nights, and crossed the frontier into Holland. Was summoned to Buckingham Palace a fortnight after his return to England. Resumed flying duties as Instructor, and later joined a Defence of London Night Flying Squadron as Flight Commander. In June, 1919, he was attached to Inter-Allied Aeronautical Commission of Control (Germany).

Gilbert Stuart M. Insall.

DAVIES, RICHARD BELL, Squadron-Commander, Royal Navy, served in the European War, and was created a Companion of the Distinguished Service Order [London Gazette, 10 April, 1915]: "Admiralty, 10 April, 1915.—The King has been graciously pleased to give orders for the following appointments to the Distinguished Service Order . . . to the undermentioned Officers in recognition of services as mentioned. To be Companions of the Distinguished Service Order. For services rendered in the aerial attack on Dunkirk, 23 Jan. 1915: Richard Bell Davies, Squadron-Commander; Richard Edmund Charles Peirse, Flight Lieut. These officers have repeatedly attacked the German submarine station at Ostend and Zeebrugge, being subjected on each occasion to heavy and accurate fire, their machines being frequently hit. In particular, on 23 Jan., they each discharged eight bombs in an attack upon submarines alongside the Mole at Zeebrugge, flying down to close range. At the outset of this flight Lieut. Davies was severely wounded by a bullet in the thigh, but nevertheless he accomplished his task, handling his machine for an hour with great skill in spite of pain and loss of blood." He served in the Dardanelles; was twice mentioned in Despatches, and was awarded the Victoria Cross [London Gazette, 1 Jan. 1916]: "Richard Bell Davies, D.S.O., Squadron-Commander, Royal Navy. The King has been graciously pleased to approve of the grant of the Victoria Cross to Squadron-Commander Richard Bell Davies, D.S.O., R.N., and of the Distinguished Service Cross to Flight Sub-Lieut. Gilbert Formby Smylie, R.N., in recognition of their behaviour in the following circumstances. On the 19th Nov. these two officers carried out an air attack on Ferrijik Junction. Flight Sub-Lieut. Smylie's machine was received by very heavy fire and brought down. The pilot planed down over the station, releasing all his bombs except one, which failed to drop, simultaneously at the station from a very low altitude. Thence he continued his descent into the marsh. On alighting he saw the one unexploded bomb, and set fire to his machine, knowing that the bomb would ensure its destruction. He then proceeded towards Turkish territory. At this moment he perceived Squadron-Commander Davies descending, and fearing that he would come down near the burning machine, and thus risk destruction from the bomb, Flight Sub-Lieut. Smylie ran back, and from a short distance exploded the bomb by means of a pistol bullet. Squadron-Commander Davies descended at a safe distance from the burning machine, took up Sub-Lieut. Smylie, in spite of the near approach of a party of the enemy, and returned to the aerodrome, a feat of airmanship that can seldom have been equalled for skill and gallantry." He was promoted to Wing Commander, and in 1919 was awarded the Air Force Cross. He is Chevalier, Legion of Honour.

Richard Bell Davies.

London Gazette, 21 Jan. 1916.—"The King has been graciously pleased to approve of the grant of the Victoria Cross to Lieut.-Commander Edgar Christopher Cookson, D.S.O., R.N., in recognition of the following act of most conspicuous gallantry during the advance on Kut-el-Amara."

COOKSON, EDGAR CHRISTOPHER, Lieut.-Commander, Royal Navy, was born at Rock Ferry, Cheshire, 13 Dec. 1883, younger son of the late Capt. William Edgar Cookson, R.N., and Mrs. W. E. Cookson. He was first educated at Hazelhurst, Frant; entered the Britannia in Sept. 1887, and served in H.M.S. Dido on the China Station during the Boxer Rebellion in 1902, receiving a Medal. He served in the European War in 1914 and 1915, and was mentioned in Despatches [London Gazette, 5 April, 1915], by General Nixon, and was created a Companion of the Distinguished Service Order [London Gazette, 13 Sept. 1915]: "Admiralty, S.W., 13 Sept. 1915.—The King has been graciously pleased to give orders for the appointment of the following Officers to the Distinguished Service Order in recognition of the services mentioned. Edgar Christopher Cookson, Lieut.-Commander, Royal Navy. Lieut.-Commander Cookson was conducting a reconnaissance up a creek of the Eupharates, west of Qurnah, in the armed launch Shushan on 9 May, 1915, when he was heavily attacked by Arabs concealed in the reeds. Although severely wounded early in the action, he resumed command after his wounds had been temporarily dressed, and succeeded in most ably extricating the vessel from a most perilous position under heavy rifle fire." He was killed in action near Kut-el-Amara 28 Sept. 1915, and was posthumously awarded the Victoria Cross [London Gazette, 21 Jan. 1916]: "The King has been graciously pleased to approve of the grant of the Victoria Cross to Lieut.-Commander Edgar Christopher Cookson, D.S.O., R.N., in recognition of the following act of most conspicuous gallantry during the advance on Kut-el-Amara: On the 28th Sept. 1915, the river gunboat Comet had been ordered with other gunboats to examine, and if possible destroy, an obstruction placed across the river by the Turks. When the gunboats were approaching the obstruction, a very heavy rifle and machine-gun fire was opened on them from both banks. An attempt to sink the centre dhow of the obstruction by gun-fire having failed, Lieut.-Commander Cookson ordered the Comet to be placed alongside, and himself jumped on to the dhow with an axe and tried to cut the wire hawsers connecting it with the two other craft forming the obstruction. He was immediately shot in several places, and died within a very few minutes." "Deeds that thrill the Empire" (pages 214–222) says: "On the outer edges of the war the close co-operation between the Navy and the Army was at all times conspicuous, but it was in the strenuous campaign against the Turks in Persia that it was seen in its most striking form. By the very nature of the country the fighting was practically confined to the valleys of those great rivers, the Tigris and Euphrates, and of the Shatt-el-Arab, which is the name of the single outlet by which they reach the Persian Gulf after joining at Qurnah, and the officers and men of the Navy in those distant parts, who at first thought the war was going to end without giving them a chance of striking a blow at the enemy, threw themselves with tremendous enthusiasm into the opportunity which the Persian Campaign afforded them. It was in Nov. 1914, that the advanced parties of the British invading force were landed at Fao, and from that time onwards the Navy spared no effort to help them along by every means in its power. It is true that the Navy in those parts bore not the remotest resemblance—save for its men—to the squadrons of giants with which Sir John Jellicoe kept watch and ward over the North Sea; but it is equally true that such ships as his would have been altogether useless in such work as had to be done on those ancient Persian rivers. In the early stages of the advance into the heart of the enemy's country excellent work was done by the Clio and Espiegle, little sloops of just over one thousand tons, and armed with six 4-inch and four 3-pounder guns. Their respective commanding officers were Commander Colin MacKenzie, D.S.O., who was specially promoted for his services, and Capt. Wilfrid Nunn, who was awarded the D.S.O. The advance had not been long in progress, however, before these vessels had to be left behind owing to the shallowness of the waters that had to be navigated. Then it was that the men of the fleet set to work and fashioned a new fleet out of whatever material they could find, and this is how the result was described by Colonel Sir Mark Sykes: 'There are paddle steamers which once plied with passengers and now waddle along with a barge on either side, one perhaps containing a portable wireless station, and the other bullocks for heavy guns ashore; there are once respectable tugs which stagger along under a weight of boiler plating—to protect them from the enemy's fire—and are armed with guns of varying calibre;

there is a launch which pants indignantly between batteries of 4.7's, looking like a sardine between two cigarette-boxes; there is a steamer with a Christmas-tree growing amidships, in the branches of which its officers fondly imagine they are invisible to friend or foe. There is also a ship which is said to have started life as an aeroplane in Singapore, shed its wings, but kept its aerial propeller, took to water, and became a hospital. And this fleet is the cavalry screen, advance guard, rear guard, flank guard, railway, general headquarters, heavy artillery, line of communication, supply depôt, police force, field ambulance, aerial hangar and base of supply of the Mesopotamian Expedition. It was in one of these improvised warships—if that is not too dignified a term—that Lieut.-Commander Edgar Christopher Cookson was serving when he won the D.S.O. It was in the early days of the advance on Kut-el-Amara, when the advanced sections of our forces had reached the junction of the Tigris and Euphrates; and before pushing on along the valley of the former river, it was necessary to ascertain whether any considerable body of enemy troops had withdrawn up the Euphrates with the intention of coming down upon our lines of communication after the main force had passed on. The task of carrying out the reconnaissance fell to Lieut.-Commander Cookson and his armed launch, the Shushan. The little steamer plugged her way up the Euphrates for some distance, a sharp look-out being kept on either side; but no sign of the enemy was discovered. Presently Cookson came to a tributary branching off to the left, and, impelled more by instinct than anything else, slackened the speed of the lumbering launch and steered her out of the main stream between the closer banks of the creek. On either side the tributary was flanked by a dense growth of rushes, which gently swayed in the wash of a passing vessel. For some distance the Shushan pushed on, the men on deck scanning every yard of the banks as they passed, still without finding a trace of a living soul. The Lieutenant-Commander was about to give up this particular part of his search as useless, and had already given orders preparatory to putting the vessel about for the return journey, when suddenly from among the rushes on both sides of the creek there burst forth a furious fusillade of rifle-fire. The Arabs, lying concealed amidst and behind the dense-growing rushes, could not be seen; but the guns, machine guns and rifles on board the Shushan instantly got to work and rained a steady stream of bullets along the banks. With all possible haste, but still all too slowly, the cumbersome Shushan was turned round in mid-stream, and off she set at the best of her poor speed to break out of the hornet's nest into which she had stumbled. The enemy had disposed themselves well, but fortunately the launch had been well fitted up for the work she had to do, and rifle-fire had little effect upon her. Two or three small guns in the hands of the enemy might easily have meant her complete destruction. Lieut.-Commander Cookson had the misfortune to be severely wounded early in the fight, receiving an injury that should have kept him under cover until a place of safety had been reached; but as soon as his wound had been roughly dressed he insisted on taking personal charge of the vessel again. Going up-stream the Shushan had been able to pick her way carefully; now she was running for life in strange waters, where the slightest error in navigation would probably have thrown her, helpless, into the hands of the enemy. But Cookson handled his craft with admirable coolness and skill, pausing where a favourable opportunity offered for a round from one of the "big" guns, and running ahead with a burst of speed when discretion dictated. After a most exciting dash, a bend in the stream brought the freer and friendlier waters of the Euphrates into view again, and the little Shushan, her sides and upper works riddled with bullet-holes, ambled leisurely down to her base with as much dignity as such a quaint craft could command. Lieut.-Commander Cookson's D.S.O. was awarded for "most ably extricating the vessel from a perilous position under heavy rifle fire;" and besides that he had, though at considerable risk, secured valuable information regarding the position and strength of the enemy. The country was destined before many months were passed to lose the services of this gallant and distinguished young officer, though not before he had crowned his career with a deed that earned the highest of all the awards a fighting man can win. It was on 9 May, 1915, that he won the D.S.O.; and after a short spell of rest to recover from his wound, he was appointed to command the Comet, one of the largest boats in the river flotilla. On 28 Sept. 1915, when our forces were advancing successfully towards Kut, the Comet, which was in advance of the army, sighted a large enemy camp ahead, whereupon she signalled the news to those behind and prepared to wait until morning, when it was decided that the attack should be made. At daybreak the gunboats—there were others in company with the Comet—began to shell the enemy's camp, edging up closer and closer all the time. One by one the enemy's big guns were knocked out, but there was one that would not be silenced. Its position was concealed by a bend in the river, and every time the Comet put her nose round the corner in order to get a better target, the Turkish gunners, knowing the range of the bend "to a T," opened such an accurate fire that there was nothing for Lieut.-Commander Cookson to do but to get back again. The Comet was hit several times, and one shell went through the funnel; but no one on board was hurt. Presently, however, the field artillery ashore got to work, and after an exchange that did not end until five in the afternoon, the Turkish gun was finally silenced. After that the enemy cleared off as fast as they could: but one of our aeroplanes reported that they had placed a formidable obstruction across the river in order to prevent the advance of our armed steamers, and so delay the pursuit. As soon as it was dark, three boats, the Comet leading, set out to remove the obstruction. A number of Turks, however, had been left behind in concealed positions to protect it, armed with rifles and hand-bombs, and began to attack the small flotilla as soon as it came within reach. An answering fire was promptly opened from our boats, while some of the guns were trained on the boom in an attempt to destroy it that way. The obstruction consisted of three large dhows securely strung together and to the shore by means of strong wire hawsers. Gun-fire was quite useless against such a structure, and after but a little delay Cookson ordered the Comet to be placed alongside the central dhow. As the gunboat approached, the fire from the shore increased in intensity; but when the two boats were close enough together, the Lieutenant-Commander, hatchet in hand, sprang on board the dhow and began to hack at the hawsers. Exposure to the enemy's fire was inevitable, but with a little good fortune the task might have been carried through. Unhappily, there was no good fortune for Cookson that night. A score of Turkish marksmen turned their rifles on to him, and before his work was well begun he fell, shot in seven places. Ready hands dragged him back on board the Comet; but he was within a minute of death. His last words were: "I am done. It's a failure. Get back at full speed." Next day by the irony of fate the Turks had gone, and the boom was removed in perfect safety.' Four months after his death the Victoria Cross was awarded to him."

London Gazette, 22 Jan. 1916.—"His Majesty the King has been graciously pleased to award the Victoria Cross to the undermentioned Non-commissioned Officers and Man."

BURT, ALFRED ALEXANDER, Corpl., No. 1665, served in the European War, and was awarded the Victoria Cross [London Gazette, 22 Jan. 1916]: "Alfred Alexander Burt, No. 1665, Corpl., 1st Battn. Hertfordshire Regt. (Territorial Force). For most conspicuous bravery at Cuinchy on 27 Sept. 1915. His company had lined the front trench preparatory to an attack, when a large minenwerfer bomb fell into the trench. Corpl. Burt, who well knew the destructive power of this class of bomb, might easily have got under cover behind a traverse, but he immediately went forward, put his foot on the fuse, wrenched it out of the bomb and threw it over the parapet, thus rendering the bomb innocuous. His presence of mind and great pluck saved the lives of others in the traverse."

CAFFREY, JOHN, Private, was born at Birr, King's County, Ireland. He is the son of the late John Caffrey; was educated at St. Mary's Roman Catholic School, Nottingham, and is an old member of the 12th Nottingham Company, The Boys' Brigade. He enlisted on 9 Feb. 1910, when he was 18 years and 3 months old, in the 2nd Battn. York and Lancaster Regt.; served in the European War, and was in the Retreat from Mons, for which he holds the Star. He was awarded the Victoria Cross [London Gazette, 22 Jan. 1916]: "John Caffrey, No. 9730, Private, 2nd Battn. York and Lancaster Regt. Date of Act of Bravery: 16 Nov. 1915. For most conspicuous bravery on 16 Nov. 1915, near La Brique. A man of the West Yorkshire Regt. had been badly wounded and was lying in the open, unable to move, in full view of and about 300 to 400 yards from the enemy's trenches. Corpl. Stirk, Royal Army Medical Corps, and Private Caffrey at once started out to rescue him, but at the first attempt they were driven back by shrapnel fire. Soon afterwards they started again under close sniping and machine-gun fire, and succeeded in reaching and bandaging the wounded man, but just as Corpl. Stirk had lifted him on Private Caffrey's back, he himself was shot in the head. Private Caffrey put down the wounded man, bandaged Corpl. Stirk, and helped him back into safety. He then returned and brought in the man of the West Yorkshire Regt. He had made three journeys across the open under close and accurate fire, and had risked his own life to save others with the utmost coolness and bravery." He also holds the Cross of the Order of St. George, Fourth Class (Russia), for bringing in under heavy fire a superior officer who was seriously wounded. He was married on 24 March, 1917, at St. Barnabas' Church, Cambridge, to Florence, daughter of Mr. and Mrs. Avey. Private Caffrey holds two medals for the Cross-Country Championship of the Irish Army, and one medal for the Aldershot Cross-Country Championship.

John Caffrey.

DRAKE, ALFRED GEORGE, Corpl., served in the European War, and was awarded the Victoria Cross [London Gazette, 22 Jan. 1916]: "Alfred George Drake, No. S/107, Corpl., 8th Battn., Rifle Brigade. For most conspicuous bravery on the night of 23 Nov. 1915, near La Brique, France. He was one of a patrol of four which was reconnoitring towards the German lines. The patrol was discovered when close to the enemy, who opened heavy fire with rifles and a machine gun, wounding the officer and one man. The latter was carried back by the last remaining man. Corpl. Drake remained with his officer, and was last seen kneeling beside him and bandaging his wounds, regardless of the enemy's fire. Later a rescue party, crawling near the German lines, found the officer and corporal—the former unconscious, but alive and bandaged; Corpl. Drake beside him dead and riddled with bullets. He had given his life and saved his officer."

MEEKOSHA, SAMUEL, Corpl., served in the European War, and was awarded the Victoria Cross [London Gazette, 22 Jan. 1916]: "Samuel Meekosha, No. 1147, Corpl., 1/6th Battn. West Yorkshire Regt. (Territorial Force). For most conspicuous bravery near the Yser, on the 19th Nov. 1915. He was with a platoon of about twenty non-commissioned officers and men, who were holding an isolated trench. During a very heavy bombardment by the enemy, six of the platoon were killed and seven wounded, while all the remainder were more or less buried. When the senior non-commissioned officers had been either killed or wounded, Corpl. Meekosha at once took command, sent a runner for assistance, and in spite of no less than ten more big shells falling within twenty yards of him, continued to dig out the wounded and buried men in full view of the enemy and at close range from the German trenches. By his promptness and magnificent courage and determination he saved at least four lives." Privates Johnson, Sayers and Wilkinson, of the same battalion, received the D.C.M. for helping him.

London Gazette, 3 March, 1916—" His Majesty the King has been graciously pleased to award the Victoria Cross to the undermentioned Officer and Men."

SMITH, ALFRED VICTOR, Second Lieut., was born 22 July, 1891, at Guildford, Surrey, son of William Henry Smith, Chief Constable of Burnley, and Louisa, daughter of Jonathan Green, of Great Malvern. He

Alfred Victor Smith.

was educated at Hatfield School, St. Albans, and the Grammar School, Burnley, and joined the Army 10 Oct. 1914. He served in the European War in Gallipoli, and was awarded the Victoria Cross [London Gazette, 3 March, 1916]: " Alfred Victor Smith, Second Lieut., 5th Battn. East Lancashire Regt. Date of Act of Bravery : 23 Dec. 1915. For most conspicuous bravery. He was in the act of throwing a grenade, when it slipped from his hand and fell to the bottom of the trench, close to several of our officers and men. He immediately shouted out a warning, and himself jumped clear into safety ; but seeing that the officers and men were unable to get into cover, and knowing well that the grenade was due to explode, he returned without any hesitation and flung himself

down upon it. He was instantly killed by the explosion. His magnificent act of self-sacrifice undoubtedly saved many lives." This deed excited universal admiration, and the Keeper of the Privy Purse wrote to Lieut. Smith's parents :

" His Majesty has read with feelings of admiration the record of Lieut. Smith's noble conduct and self-sacrifice, and cannot but feel that the manifestations of admiration on the part of all classes of the community will in some degree lighten your burden and prove a lasting solace in the years to come."

Lieut.-Colonel Acton, his Commanding Officer, wrote :

" The Military History of no nation can tell of any finer deed, and to lose him in this way must leave his parents the proudest in the universe."

Brigadier-General A. W. Tufnell, Commanding 126th Infantry Brigade, wrote :

" His act was one of bravery I have never heard surpassed, and must make his parents the proudest in England, when everyone reads the story and couples his name with that old and honoured phrase, ' A Soldier and a Gentleman.' "

General V. d'Urbal, Commanding the Xth French Army Corps, published to his troops a General Order, of which the following is a translation :

" Xth French Army Staff,
" Headquarters,
" 7 March, 1916.

" A splendid example of self-sacrifice has been shown by an officer of the British Army, Lieut. A. Victor Smith, 5th Battn. East Lancashire Regt.

" This officer, having let fall a grenade in the trench, and perceiving that, in spite of his shout of warning, the officers and men in the vicinity were unable to take cover, did not hesitate to throw himself flat on the grenade. He was killed by the explosion, but this saved the lives of his comrades. The General Commanding the Xth Army considers that this act of sacrifice performed by one of our brave Allies is well worthy of being brought to the notice of all.

" (Signed) V. d'Urbal.
" J. Buficus, Chief of Staff."

The Croix de Guerre was afterwards awarded by the French President. A tribute to his personal character came from Blackpool, in a letter from the Lieutenant's old chief, the Chief Constable, who wrote to his (the Lieutenant's) parents :

" He was such a lovable lad ; all the men are upset. He was our pride. We shall not try to forget this affliction, but shall cherish his memory. We shall think so tenderly of him, his charming ways, indicative of the virtues of gentleness which endeared him to us all."

The officers of the regiment placed a brass memorial tablet, in honour of the Lieutenant's memory, in St. Catherine's Church, Burnley. The Magistrates and Watch Committee of Blackpool placed a bronze memorial tablet in St. John's Church, Blackpool. A large portrait in oils has been placed by public subscription in the Corporation Art Gallery at Burnley, and framed portraits as a chorister and an officer have been placed in St. Albans Cathedral.

HULL, CHARLES, Private (Shoeing-Smith), is the son of a Harrogate Corporation employé. He joined the Army, and served in the European War, on the North-West Frontier of India. He was awarded the Victoria Cross [London Gazette, 3 March, 1916]: " Charles Hull, No. 1053, Private (Shoeing-Smith), 21st Lancers. For most conspicuous bravery. When under close fire of the enemy, who were within a few yards, he rescued Capt. G. E. D. Learoyd, whose horse had been shot, by taking him up behind him and galloping into safety. Shoeing-Smith Hull acted entirely on his own initiative, and saved his officer's life at the imminent risk of his own." He also received the French Croix de Guerre.

CHRISTIAN, HARRY, Private, served in the European War, and was awarded the Victoria Cross [London Gazette, 3 March, 1916], for his bravery at Cuinchy, France, on 18 Oct. 1915 : " Harry Christian, No. 10210, Private, 2nd Battn. Royal Lancaster Regt. For most conspicuous bravery. He was holding a crater with five or six men in front of our trenches. The enemy commenced a very heavy bombardment of the position with heavy ' Minenwerfer ' bombs, forcing a temporary withdrawal. When he found that three men were missing, Private Christian at once returned alone to the crater, and although bombs were continually bursting actually on the edge of the crater, he found, dug out, and carried, one by one, into safety all three men, thereby undoubtedly saving their lives. Later he placed himself where he could see the bombs coming, and directed his comrades when and where to seek cover."

London Gazette, 30 March, 1916.—" His Majesty the King has been graciously pleased to award the Victoria Cross to the undermentioned Officers, Non-commissioned Officers and Men."

KILBY, ARTHUR FORBES GORDON, Capt., the only son of Sandford James Kilby, Esq., Bengal Police, Customs and Salt Department (retired), of Skelton House, Leamington, and of Alice Flora, his wife,

Arthur F. G. Kilby.

daughter of the late H. E. Scott, of Bevelaw, Midlothian ; was born at East Hayes, Cheltenham, on the 3rd Feb. 1885. He was educated at Bilton Grange, near Rugby, and at Winchester College, and was prepared for the Royal Military College, Sandhurst, by Alfred Geidt, at Frankfurt-am-Main. After the two years' course at Sandhurst, he joined the 1st Battn. of the South Staffordshire Regt. in Aug. 1905, being promoted Lieutenant in Oct. 1907, and Captain 1 April, 1910, at the early age of twenty-five. In Dec. of that year he was transferred to the 2nd Battn., which had just returned from South Africa. Among all those who, during the Great War of 1914-19, made good their claim to the title of hero there were few, if any, who, in the unanimous opinion of all who were in a position to judge, whether superiors, equals, or subordinates, did so more completely and incontestably than Capt. Arthur Kilby. Many a man, moved thereto by some sudden and evanescent impulse of enthusiasm, may on a particular occasion rise to a height of self-forgetfulness and contempt of danger that carries him on to the achievement of some exceptionally gallant deed which gains for him, and rightly so, the admiration of his fellows. Such displays of outstanding courage are the monopoly of no particular race of men or stage of civilization, and are at least as common among the backward peoples as they are among those in the forefront of enlightenment. This admitted, how much more deserving of honour is the man who, besides possessing this quality of mere physical bravery in fullest measure, combines with it equally rare gifts of mind and character and a high degree of moral courage that triumph over all difficulties and discouragements, not only under the exhilarating influences of the battlefield but also during long periods of wearisome inaction and uncertainty. It is a fine thing to perform some isolated outstanding act of individual bravery during the heat of the combat, but what of him who, through weeks and months in the trenches with the menace of death ever confronting him, not only constantly maintains his courage and his spirits at a level which evokes the wonderment of those around him, brave as they also are, but actually deliberately plans to excel in achievement whenever occasion offers or can be made, and knows intuitively, and causes his comrades to understand it too, that he will unerringly do so. All this, however, it can be said without hyperbole, is what Capt. Kilby did, according to the consensus of evidence offered by his general, his commanding officer, his brother officers, and the men who were so proud and glad to serve under him, as the following extracts from some among a large number of letters abundantly prove. Thus Major Morgan, of his battalion, writes : " His wonderful keenness and his absolute fearlessness animated his whole company with a spirit which will never be forgotten. The men of his company almost worshipped him. Personally knowing him as I did for so long, I feel I have lost a very gallant comrade and a very true friend, and I, of course, knew that he would behave just as he actually did." Capt. Wansbrough eulogized Capt. Kilby in the following words : " There is a particular kind of affection that can be inspired in one man by another, and as I came to know your son more intimately during the time I served under him, I felt this more and more. During the long monotonous days on the Aisne he was the life of our little company ; crowded together as we were in a cleft in the hillside, he would fascinate us for hours together with his knowledge—unique in my experience—of the enemy countries and of countless other themes. It is no exaggeration to say that we all came to love him then. I know I echo the feelings of the others when I say that I would gladly have followed him anywhere. Such trust and confidence did he inspire by his courage, tact, and soldierlike skill, it was a great privilege to serve under him while he had command of C Company. We felt absolute confidence in all he said and did." A retired officer under whom he had served as a junior subaltern, wrote of him as possessing " many moral and mental qualities not commonly found in the youth of to-day," and has pointed to his career as " eloquent proof of the fact that magnificent physical courage can go hand-in-hand with refinement of nature and a seriousness of mind which lead the possessors to turn to the higher side of things." Remarkable as he subsequently proved to be for the exceptional degree of personal courage, which characterized him, young Kilby was likewise exceptional in many other respects. He was far from being the "sealed pattern" sub. Of a serious, thoughtful turn of mind, and refined in his predilections, he had, notwithstanding his love of an open-air life, but little inclination towards games, but found his recreation in music, the culture of flowers, and in such subjects as the ornithology of British birds, on which he was quite an authority. From the moment of joining his regiment, realizing that knowledge is power, he devoted himself, *inter alia*, to the serious study of foreign languages, becoming an interpreter in German and in Hungarian, being the only officer in the Army to attain to the latter distinction prior to the war. Shortly before the outbreak of hostilities he was in Spain studying Spanish, and, as an officially accepted candidate, was also preparing himself for the Staff College entrance examination. As is the case with most men of intelligence and imagination, Kilby felt but little enthusiasm for the trivial round and the busy idleness of ordinary regimental service in time of peace—a fact which, combined with his reserve and his retiring modesty, which were in reality the mark of the self-contained man of character, prevented almost all of those in whose hands his destiny then lay from discerning the great promise that was latent within him and which needed only the incentive of adequate occasion to ensure its blossoming into achievement. That opportunity presented itself in the tragedy which overwhelmed Europe in Aug. 1914, which same month found Kilby participating in all the early operations in North-East France, including the Retreat from Mons. Already at this early stage this quiet, confident young man began to evince in prominent degree a soldierly self-sacrificing devotion to duty and spirit of helpfulness, notably in connection with the withdrawal on the 26th Aug. from Maroilles of the brigade of which his battalion formed part, when, on the evacuation of that place by the main body, he was sent back to instruct the rear-guard to fall back. In fulfilling this duty he came under the concentrated fire of the German artillery, and was knocked flat down by the concussion of the high explosives. The fatigues and privations to which he was subjected while wandering for hours alone and without food led to physical collapse a few days later, which necessitated his being sent to the base, whereby he missed being present at the Battle of the Marne; but he rejoined his battalion on the 24th Sept. 1914. While the British were holding the line of the Aisne, he voluntarily went out on many solitary sniping expeditions, on two occasions penetrating into the German lines and bringing back valuable information. During this wearisome phase of the war his good spirits and his well-informed conversation, the outcome of his peace-time reading, constituted him the life and soul of his brother officers. An exploit of which he sent home an interesting and amusing account, took place at the First Battle of Ypres under the following circumstances: The British line being reported to be broken, Capt. Kilby was sent with his company to the point of danger. Although this report proved to be premature, the troops to the right of Kilby's new position did subsequently fall back from their trenches, which the Germans thereupon occupied. Kilby at once took action as effective as it was gallant, executing "a brilliant counter-attack, in which, by rapid fire, he bluffed the enemy, whose force was several times the strength of his own, and turned them out of the reoccupied trenches and a wood which they had just taken." This action gained immediate recognition, the following message being passed down the lines to him: "Bravo, Kilby! Your colonel is proud of you and your company. Hearty congratulations on good work." A week later occurred the specific act for which he was awarded the Military Cross:

Extract from a Report by Major-General C. C. Monro, Commanding 2nd Division:

"On the 12th and 13th Nov. 1914, there was severe fighting round the position held by the 6th Infantry Brigade. A critical situation arose owing to the retreat of the French troops on the left flank of this brigade, and which eventually resulted in the 6th Brigade fighting facing north, east and south.

"The gap that was caused by the retirement of the French formed a gap between the trenches held by the South Staffordshire Regt. and the new line taken up by the French. This gap was filled by a portion of the South Staffords, and this exposed line was held by a portion of this regiment all day. This manœuvre was supervised by Capt. A. F. Kilby and Capt. S. G. Johnson, both of the South Staffords. Both these officers were wounded on this occasion."

For the above services Capt. Kilby was awarded the Military Cross. He was wounded in the right arm and lung by a rifle bullet, and was brought to England; but although he never fully recovered the strength of his right hand, he rejoined his battalion in May, 1915, and in Sept. of that year was recommended for the D.S.O., for performing during the months of Aug. and Sept., while his battalion was holding A2 Section of the front line, "consistent good work, making some very useful reconnaissances, imbuing all ranks with keenness by his example." An instance is cited as follows: "Capt. A. F. G. Kilby, on the night of 5–6 Sept., went out along the canal tow-path under cover of darkness, accompanied by Lieut. Thompson, 1st King's, and closely reconnoitred the German position on the embankment redoubt and brought back most useful information. The reconnaissance was a very dangerous one, as the canal bank is a hot-bed of snipers, and it required the greatest skill and courage to get right up to the German position as Capt. Kilby did. This is only one specific instance. This officer constantly made night reconnaissances of this nature." The distinction of the Distinguished Service Order was, however, not awarded to him. Closely following upon this came the supreme glory of his short life, which was recorded in the London Gazette of 30 March, 1916, as follows: "Capt. Kilby was specially selected at his own request, and on account of the gallantry he had previously displayed on many occasions, to attack with his company a strong enemy redoubt. The company charged along the narrow tow-path headed by Capt. Kilby, who, though wounded at the outset, continued to lead his men right up to the enemy wire under a devastating machine-gun fire and a shower of bombs Here he was shot down, but although his foot had been blown off, he continued to cheer on his men and to use a rifle. Capt. Kilby has been missing since this great act of valour, and his death has now to be presumed." Accounts furnished by certain of his brother officers and men serve to amplify this brief official statement. His brigadier wrote to his parents as follows: "He had such a sound military instinct, serene courage and unbounded confidence. It was a great and bitter blow when he was missing, and I kept hoping against hope that the search parties would find him. No men could have done more; they all loved him, and they all risked their lives in the search. . . . In all the losses of friends one has, there has hardly been a day since 25 Sept. that your son has not been in my thoughts. Amongst the many gallant officers in this brigade he and Colonel Moss always stood out. . . . Before the big fight your son's company was often in that part of the trenches just opposite the railway embankment immediately south of La Bassée Canal. He asked me himself if ever there was a serious attack to let him attack at that point. It was a very tough nut, but he was convinced it could be done. He knew the ground so well, and had all his plans cut and dried. I used to go up there with him and examine the German position and talk it all out. If anybody could have done it your son was the man. When the orders came for the big attack, I made him promise me that he would not go over until at least half the company had gone; it was so essential to have his brain and judgment to direct the men and not get knocked out at once. On the actual day, as you know, things went wrong with the gas, and my own idea is that your son realized that it was going to be a failure, and went in front to lead what he considered was a forlorn hope, for he was leading the men when last seen." Colonel Moss, commanding the 2nd South Staffordshires, gave the following additional details in a letter to Capt. Kilby's father: "The regiment had to attack the very strongest section of the German line. We started under very unfavourable conditions, as everyone was suffering badly from gas before we charged. Your son led his company against the embankment redoubt with the most magnificent gallantry. He was wounded at the very start, but still insisted on cheering his men right up to the German wire, which our guns had been unable to destroy. He was again wounded, but still continued to cheer on his men. This is the last we know of him. . . . As soon as it got dark men went out to look for the wounded. . . . The Germans kept up an intermittent fire along the embankment. The ground, however, was searched all night, but no trace of your son could be found. The next night search was again made among the dead, but without result. His loss was a terrible blow to me. He was beloved by the men and absolutely fearless." Company Quartermaster-Sergt. Allen, of Capt. Kilby's company, wrote: "He was worshipped by the men of the company. It was proved in the afternoon, when we were drawn out of these trenches. I called for volunteers to go in front with me and search for him. I had no less than forty out of the forty-seven left." The above and many other communications received by his parents from all ranks bear eloquent testimony to the admiration universally called forth by Kilby's splendid heroism on this occasion, and to the respect and affection which his consistent display of high qualities both as a soldier and as a man had inspired in all who knew him, so that a feeling of consternation seized the whole regiment when it became known that, as a sequel to that fateful though for him so glorious day, Capt. Kilby was missing. It necessarily followed that a recommendation for the award of a posthumous Victoria Cross to Capt. Kilby was forwarded to the proper authority, and this highest reward of individual gallantry was duly bestowed upon him. A few weeks after the Battle of Loos the Germans offered generous testimony to their admiration of his splendid bravery by erecting a cross with inscription bearing his name, on the tow-path outside their redoubt, and the commander of the battalion which had found his body wrote: "The Kilby family may think of their son with pride, as we remember him with respect." Thus ended this young and promising life—ended, that is to say, so far as the bodily presence of Capt. Kilby among his comrades is concerned; but it is safe to assert that as long as men continue to be inspired by the display of gallantry, self-abnegation and devotion to duty, the memory and the influence of this heroic young officer will infallibly live on and serve as an incentive to others to follow his fine example. Among the many hobbies with which Capt. Kilby occupied his versatile mind was the study of architecture, and this led him, when serving as a subaltern with his battalion at Strensall, to make visits to York Minster, and the noble outlines of this venerable edifice so strongly impressed him that he was wont to declare it to be one of the most beautiful of the English cathedrals. In addition to this, his family had in the past been closely associated with the city of York, and therefore it was deemed appropriate on these double grounds that the Minster should contain a memorial of him. Consequently a beautiful tablet has been erected in it to his memory, and will serve to inspire towards him in the generations to come the admiration and affection which animate those with whom he came into contact during his useful and blameless life.

Eric Archibald McNair.

McNAIR, ERIC ARCHIBALD, Capt., was born on 16 June, 1894, at Calcutta, India, second son of George B. McNair, Senior Partner in the firm of Morgan & Co., Solicitors, Calcutta, and Isabelle Frederica McNair, daughter of George McAllan Gow, of Jessore, Bengal. He was educated at Branksome, Godalming (Mr. Sylvester's); at Charterhouse, where he was a member of the Officers' Training Corps and head of the school, and at Magdalen College, Oxford, where he had a Demyship. He joined the Army on 14 Oct. 1914, as a Second Lieutenant in the 10th Battn. Royal Sussex Regt., and was transferred in Aug. 1915, to the 9th Battn., and was Lieutenant on 22 Dec. 1914. He served in the European War, going to the front in Sept. 1915. He was awarded the Victoria Cross [London Gazette, 30 March, 1916]: " Eric Archibald McNair, Lieut., Royal Sussex Regt. When the enemy exploded a mine, Lieut. McNair and many men of two platoons were hoisted into the air, and many men were buried. But, though much shaken, he at once organized a party with a machine gun to man the near edge of the crater, and opened rapid fire on a large party of the enemy who were advancing. The enemy were driven back, leaving many dead. Lieut. McNair then ran back for reinforcements, and sent to another unit for bombs, ammunition and tools to replace those buried. The communication trench being blocked, he went across the open under heavy fire, and led up the reinforcements the same way. His prompt and plucky action undoubtedly saved the situation." He commanded a company in Flanders and France from Oct. 1915, to Aug. 1916, and was promoted Captain in Oct. 1915, though he is described in the Gazette of his V.C. as a Lieutenant. He was severely wounded on 18 Aug. 1916, and was not passed fit for service until early in 1917, and was then put on probation for Staff work, and subsequently went through a special Staff course. After serving at home for some months, he went to the Italian front in the early part of 1918, attached to the Staff, but was invalided to the Genoa Base Hospital, and died on 12 Aug. 1918.

Arthur F. Saunders.

SAUNDERS, ARTHUR FREDERICK, Sergt., served in the European War, and was awarded the Victoria Cross [London Gazette, 30 March, 1916]: " Arthur Frederick Saunders, No. 3/10133, Sergt., 9th (Service) Battn. Suffolk Regt. For most conspicuous bravery. When his officer had been wounded in the attack, he took charge of two machine guns and a few men, and although severely wounded in the thigh, closely followed the last four charges of another battalion, and rendered every possible support. Later, when the remains of the battalion which he had been supporting had been forced to retire, he stuck to one of his guns, continued to give clear orders, and by continuous firing did his best to cover the retirement."

COTTER, WILLIAM RICHARD, Corpl., served in the European War, and was awarded the Victoria Cross [London Gazette, 30 March, 1916]: " William Richard Cotter, No. 6707, L.-Corpl. (Acting Corpl.), 6th Battn. East Kent Regt. For most conspicuous bravery and devotion to duty. When his right leg had been blown off at the knee, and he had also been wounded in both arms, he made his way unaided for 50 yards to a crater, steadied the men who were holding it, controlled their fire, issued orders, and altered the dispositions of his men to meet a fresh counter-attack by the enemy. For two hours he held his position, and only allowed his wounds to be roughly dressed when the attack had quieted down. He could not be moved back for 14 hours, and during all this time had a cheery word for all who passed him. There is no doubt that his magnificent courage helped greatly to save a critical situation."

KENNY, HENRY, Private, served in the European War, and was awarded the Victoria Cross [London Gazette, 30 March, 1916]: " Henry Kenny, No. 8655, 1st Battn. Loyal North Lancashire Regt. For most conspicuous bravery. Private Kenny went out on six different occasions on one day under a very heavy shell, rifle and machine-gun fire, and each time succeeded in carrying to a place of safety a wounded man who had been lying in the open. He was himself wounded in the neck whilst handing the last man over the parapet."

YOUNG, WILLIAM, Private, No. 5938, was born on 1 Jan. 1876, at Maryhill, Glasgow. He was the son of Samuel Young, Contractor's Labourer, and of Mary Ellen Young (née Simmonds). He was educated at an elementary school, and joined the Army at the age of 15 years. Before he was called up on the outbreak of the European War, Private Young was employed as a Labourer at gas works. He served in the European War, and displayed the utmost gallantry in saving the life of Sergt. Allan (golf professional), as described below. He was awarded the Victoria Cross [London Gazette, 30 March, 1916], for his bravery at Trench 5, east of Fouquevillers, France, 22 Dec. 1915: " William Young, No. 5938, Private, 8th (Service) Battn. East Lancashire Regt. For most conspicuous bravery. On seeing that his sergeant had been wounded, he left his trench to attend to him under very heavy fire. The wounded non-commissioned officer requested Private Young to

William Young.

get under cover, but he refused, and was almost immediately very seriously wounded by having both jaws shattered. Notwithstanding his terrible injuries, Private Young continued endeavouring to effect the rescue upon which he had set his mind, and eventually succeeded with the aid of another soldier. He then went unaided to the dressing-station, where it was discovered that he had also been wounded by a rifle bullet in the chest. The great fortitude, determination, courage and devotion to duty displayed by this soldier could hardly be sur-

passed." He died at Aldershot after an operation 28 Aug. 1916. His wife writes : " I could never draw from my husband an account of how he won his V.C., only what you already know, but I want to tell you that he was a 1st Battn. man with 17½ years' service. I do not want him to be published as a Kitchener man, as he was a Reservist at the outbreak of war." He is married and he and his wife have eight children : William, aged 15 ; John, aged 14 ; Mary Ellen, aged 12 ; Margaret, aged 10 ; Elizabeth, aged 9 ; Thomas, aged 7 ; Samuel, aged 5, and Frederick, aged 4. Mr. J. T. Kendall, of the " Lancashire Daily Post," kindly supplied the following facts : " At the time of joining up as a Reservist of the East Lancashires, he was living at 7, Heysham Street, Preston, with his wife and eight children. Like all heroes, he was extremely modest about his achievement, and even his wife knew nothing about it until congratulations began to shower upon her after the Gazette publication of 30 March, 1916. He later stated that he was in the trenches practically for the first time after leaving hospital for trouble with his eyes through being gassed, when he saw his sergeant fall. He volunteered to fetch him in, and had got him as far as the parapet when he was struck by a bullet in the jaw. They tried to get him in, but he refused to budge until the sergeant was safe. Private Young was brought to England for treatment, and was accorded a civic reception at Preston. A fund of £560 was raised for the benefit of his family. Unfortunately Private Young did not long live to enjoy the honour, and, as a matter of fact, he never received personally the award from His Majesty, as he died in Cambridge Hospital, Aldershot, the last Sunday in Aug. 1916, under an operation for his jaw. He was buried at Preston, the townspeople giving him one of the most magnificent funerals ever remembered."

London Gazette, 31 March, 1916.—" The King has been graciously pleased to approve of the grant of the Victoria Cross to the undermentioned Officer in recognition of his most conspicuous bravery and devotion to duty."

TISDALL, ARTHUR WALDERNE ST. CLAIR, Sub-Lieut., R.N.V.R. was born on 21 July, 1890, in Bombay, India. He was the second son of the Rev. William St. Clair Tisdall, (see Tisdalls of Charlesfort, " Burke's Landed Gentry of Ireland "), M.A., D.D., Vicar of St. George's, Deal, and his second wife, Marian Louisa, daughter of Rev. William Gray, M.A. He was educated at Bedford School, and was a member there of the O.T.C. Afterwards he went to Trinity College, Cambridge (Scholar), where he was also a member of the O.T.C., and rowed in the First Trinity boat. He graduated B.A. with Double First Classical Honours, gaining in 1913 the Chancellor's Gold Medal. He passed the combined examination for the Indian and Home Civil Services, also in 1913 accepted a post in the Home Civil Service. He joined the Royal Naval Volunteer Reserve in May, 1914. He served in the European War, taking part in the Antwerp Expedition, and got a commission as Sub-Lieutenant 1 Oct. of the same year. He served in Gallipoli from April, taking part in the landing there 25 April. He was killed on 6 May, 1915, at Achi Baba. He was awarded the Victoria Cross [London Gazette, 31 March, 1916]: " Arthur Walderne St. Clair Tisdall, Sub-Lieut., R.N.V.R. During the landing from the S.S. River Clyde at " V " Beach, in the Gallipoli Peninsula, 25 April, 1915, Sub-Lieut. Tisdall, hearing wounded men on the beach calling for assistance, jumped into the water, and pushing a boat in front of him, went to their rescue. He was, however, obliged to obtain help, and took with him on two trips Leading Seaman Malia, and on other trips Chief Petty Officer Perring and Leading Seamen Curtis and Parkinson. In all, Sub-Lieut. Tisdall made four or five trips between the ship and the shore, and was thus responsible for rescuing several wounded men under heavy and accurate fire. Owing to the fact that Sub-Lieut. Tisdall and the platoon under his orders were on detached service at the time, and that this officer was killed in action on 6 May, it has only now been possible to obtain complete information as to the individuals who took part in this gallant act." After describing the landing from the River Clyde, " Deeds that thrill the Empire " (pages 337–342) says : " There is yet another series of heroic deeds to be recorded in connection with this ever-memorable landing, and they are the more remarkable because nearly a year elapsed before the authorities were able to discover the identity of the officer principally concerned in them. It has already been mentioned that the soldiers who succeeded in reaching the beach were exposed to a fire almost as deadly as when they were in the water or on the bridge of barges, and large numbers were struck down by Turkish shot and shell. The River Clyde lay not far away from them, and their cries drifted out to the ship with appalling clearness. Yet it seemed impossible to do anything to help them ; but there was one group of men, at any rate, to whom the word ' impossible ' did not occur. On board the River Clyde was Sub-Lieut. Arthur Walderne St. Clair Tisdall, a twenty-four-year-old officer of the Royal Naval Volunteers, who had been given his commission less than six months before. Unable to resist the heart-rending appeals from the beach, he jumped into the water, and pushed a boat before him as he endeavoured to wade ashore, in order to bring off as many of the wounded men as he could. It was more than one man's job, however, and Tisdall was compelled to call for assistance. It was immediately forthcoming. Leading Seaman James Malia joined him at once, and the two succeeded in getting the boat to the beach and loading it with wounded men, whom they carried back to the River Clyde. Twice

Arthur W. St. C. Tisdall.

did these two make their perilous, shot-swept journey, and then other men insisted on joining in. These were Chief Petty Officer William Perring and Leading Seamen Fred Curtis and James Parkinson, who, with Sub-Lieut. Tisdall still in command, made three more journeys to the shore, and brought off as many men as they could reach and their boat would carry. Those on board the stranded collier watched in mute admiration; but darkness fell ere the work was done, and the young officer dropped out of sight as quickly and completely as if he had disappeared, and no one seemed to know who it was that had done this great work. Unfortunately the gallant Tisdall fell in action a fortnight later, intrepidly facing the enemy on a spit of rock that made him the target of a hundred rifles. For close upon a year his extraordinary bravery passed without any sign of official recognition, and then, on 31 March, 1916, it was announced that the King had been pleased to confer on him the posthumous award of the Victoria Cross for 'most conspicuous bravery and devotion to duty.' Chief Petty Officer Perring, subsequently given a commission in the Royal Naval Volunteer Reserve, was awarded the Conspicuous Gallantry Medal, as also were Leading Seamen Malia and Parkinson, and there is no doubt that a similar honour would have been conferred on Leading Seaman Curtis had he not, unfortunately, been placed among the missing on 4 June, 1915. Sub-Lieut. Tisdall had a most brilliant career at Cambridge, where he took Double First Class Classical Honours and won the Chancellor's Gold Medal in 1913. He rowed in the First Trinity Boat, and a volume of his poems has been published. There has seldom been a more remarkable instance of the combination of scholarship with courage on the battlefield. The rest of the immortal story of the River Clyde belongs to the Army, but the two services had nobly shared the terrible glories of that awful day. In his despatch dealing with the Gallipoli landing, General Sir Ian Hamilton wrote: 'Throughout the events I have chronicled the Royal Navy has been father and mother to the Army. Not one of us but realizes how much he owes to Vice-Admiral de Robeck (the Naval Commander-in-Chief); to the warships, French and British; to the destroyers, mine-sweepers, picket-boats, and to all their dauntless crews, who took no thought for themselves, but risked everything to give their soldier comrades a fair run at the enemy.' The services of the heroes of the River Clyde were rewarded by the King with a just generosity. Commander Unwin, Midshipman Drewry, Midshipman Malleson, Able Seaman Williams (killed in action), and Seaman Samson, as well as Sub-Lieut. Tisdall, all received the Victoria Cross, while Lieut. Morse was appointed to the Distinguished Service Order. Many other officers and men received the D.S.C. and the D.S.M. respectively. No previous event had been signalized by the granting of so many Victoria Crosses, but no other in the history of the Cross had so well merited them." The "Memoir and Poems of Sub-Lieut. A. W. St. Clair Tisdall, V.C." was published in 1916 by Messrs. Sidgwick and Jackson The following are two of Arthur Tisdall's poems:

"WHITE HANDS

" Your hands are white, my lady, white and clean,
    But I have looked and seen
The chapt and grimy hands that keep them so.
    You do not know.

" Your hands are white like Pilate's, white and clean;
    For others come between
To shed the innocent blood that gemmed them so.
    What did you know?

" With your white hands, my lady, stop your ear,
    Lest you may chance to hear
Your reckless slaves that curse you in their woe.
    Why should you know?"

" NORFOLK

" I'll go to Norfolk at the summer's close,
    And see again the hillsides gilt with grain,
The glassy fords, the woods, the turnip rows,
    The dim sad purple of the marsh again.

" I'll see the great farms and small villages,
    The towerless churches where few people pray,
The ruined abbeys in whose quires the breeze
    Sings sadly of an unreturning day.

" And there I'll walk long miles and swim and run,
    And look for hours on the flowers that grow
Purple on the sea-crowned marshes in the sun,
    And hope to change the world; it needs it so."

London Gazette, 20 April, 1915.—" His Majesty the King has been graciously pleased to confer the Victoria Cross on the Rev. Edward Noel Mellish, Temporary Chaplain to the Forces."

MELLISH, THE REV. EDWARD NOEL, Capt., was born on the 24th Dec. 1880, at Oakleigh Park, Barnet, North London, son of the late Edward Mellish and Mary Mellish. He was educated at Saffron Walden Grammar School, and served in the South African War as a Trooper in Baden-Powell's Police from Dec. 1900, to the end of the war. Mr. Mellish was ordained in 1912, and became Curate of St. Paul's, Deptford. He served in the European War as Acting Army Chaplain from May, 1915, to Feb. 1919, and was awarded the Victoria Cross 20 April, 1916: " Edward Noel Mellish, Capt. The Reverend, Temporary Chaplain to

the Forces. During heavy fighting on three consecutive days he repeatedly went backwards and forwards under continuous and heavy shell and machine-gun fire, between our original trenches and those captured from the enemy, in order to tend and rescue wounded men. He brought in ten badly-wounded men on the first day from ground swept by machine-gun fire. The battalion to which he was attached was relieved on the second day, but he went back and brought in twelve more wounded men. On the night of the third day he took charge of a party of volunteers, and once more returned to the trenches to rescue the remaining wounded This splendid work was quite voluntary, and outside the scope of his ordinary duties." " Deeds that thrill the Empire " (pages 766–778) says: " On 14–15 March, 1915, the village of St. Eloi, which lies along the Ypres-Armentières road, a little to the north of Wytschaete, was the scene of desperate fighting, when the Germans, after a tremendous artillery preparation, followed by the explosion of mines and a determined infantry attack in great force, succeeded in capturing the greater part of our first-line trenches, only to be driven out of them again by a dashing counter-attack in the early hours of the following morning. A little more than a year later, on 27 March, 1916, and the two following days, St. Eloi was again the scene of a fierce and sanguinary struggle; but on this occasion it was the British who were the aggressors, and, moreover, they succeeded in holding the ground that they had won. The main burden of this struggle was borne by the 1st Northumberland Fusiliers—the famous ' Fighting Fifth '—the 4th Royal Fusiliers, and some Canadian battalions. But it was the Fighting Fifth who were entitled to the lion's share of the victory which the British achieved. Supported by the Royal Fusiliers, they carried the first and second lines of German trenches on a front of some six hundred yards, capturing many prisoners and causing great loss to the enemy. Seldom, even in the present war, have soldiers been called upon to undertake a tougher job than that allotted to the Northumberland Fusiliers. The enemy's trenches were so ingeniously and elaborately protected by wire entanglements that it seemed almost impossible to reach them. But the Fusiliers were not to be discouraged by obstacles which no longer have any terror for the British. It was a painfully slow and dangerous task to cut through the wire, especially as our men were in full view of the enemy's guns, which belched forth a constant hurricane of shells. At last, however, an opening was effected, and then, says a Canadian officer who was present, ' the Fusiliers went for the first line of German trenches for all the world as though they were a football team rushing a goal at a Crystal Palace Cup Tie final.' A large number of the brave fellows fell, for their bodies were an easy target for the German machine guns and riflemen. They had to make a dash over a stretch of ground which afforded absolutely no cover; there was nothing between them and death but the breeze of an early morning—that is the only word to describe it— and like a wave they swept over the German trenches. The Huns, contrary to their usual practice, did not flinch before the British steel, and a desperate hand-to-hand struggle ensued. Finally, the superior bayonet work of our men gave them the upper hand, but not until the trenches were choked with corpses and slippery with blood. Subsequently the trenches captured by the Northumberland and Royal Fusiliers were taken over by the Canadians, who gained further ground. After exploding five mines in a direct line, which completely shattered the German defences, the Dominion troops advanced under cover of a heavy artillery fire, and though the enemy outnumbered them by at least five to two, carried the position at the point of the bayonet. Nor would they yield an inch of the ground which they had won, though, as the position was of vital importance to the Huns, they made desperate and repeated efforts to dislodge them. Many acts of signal heroism were performed during the Battle of St. Eloi. When the telephone wires were cut, one man traversed two hundred yards of open country under terrific shell fire, not once but three times, to link up his battery. Cut off from his comrades in an isolated trench, another man refused to leave a wounded comrade, though the trench was being so heavily shelled that he expected every minute to be his last, and finally succeeded in dragging the wounded man back to comparative safety. A young Staff officer, with the most complete indifference to the shells which were falling all round about him, reconnoitred the enemy's position and obtained information which contributed materially to ensure the success of the attack, and Canadians on several occasions crawled out under a heavy machine-gun fire to bring in wounded Germans, one of whom—an officer— showed his appreciation of his rescuer's courage and humanity by endeavouring to shoot him! But one of the bravest deeds of all—or rather series of deeds—was that performed by an Army Chaplain and former London curate, the Rev. Edward Noel Mellish, attached to the Royal Fusiliers, which was most deservedly recognized by the Victoria Cross being awarded him. During the three days' fighting this heroic ' padre ' went repeatedly under heavy and continuous shell and machine-gun fire between our original trenches and those captured from the enemy to tend and rescue wounded men. He brought in ten badly-wounded men on the first day from ground which was literally swept by the fire of the enemy's machine guns, and the danger which he ran may be gauged from the fact that three were actually killed while he was dressing their wounds. The Royal Fusiliers were relieved on the second day, but he went back and brought in twelve more wounded men. Nor did he desist from his efforts until the end of the battle, for on the night of the third day he took charge of a party of volunteers who went out to rescue the remaining wounded.

Rev. Edward N. Mellish.

'Nothing could be finer,' says an officer of the Northumberland Fusiliers, 'than the way Chaplain Mellish did his duty, and more than his duty, during the time he was stationed near us. Immediately the troops captured the trenches, and while the wounded men were picking their way painfully back, the enemy's guns were turned on full blast, and the intervening ground was deluged with shell fire and machine-gun bullets, not to mention shells or grenades that came from a portion of trench still in the enemy's hands. Into this tempest of fire the brave parson walked, a prayer-book under his arm, as though he were going on church parade in peace time. He reached the first batch of wounded, and knelt down to do what he could for them. The first few men he brought in himself without any aid, and it made us think a bit more of parsons to see how he walked quietly under fire, assisting the slow-moving wounded, and thinking more of saving them from discomfort than of his own safety. It was only when the ambulance parties were able to get out during a lull in the fighting that he took a rest. Next day he was out on the job as unconcerned as ever, and some men of my regiment had reason to be grateful for his attentions to them at critical moments. Some of the men would never have survived the ordeal had it not been for the prompt assistance rendered them by Mr. Mellish. One story of a Cockney soldier who was aided by the parson is worth repeating, because it is the best tribute to the parson that could be put on record. When the wounded man, who had hitherto been noted for his anti-religious bias, was safe in the base hospital, he told his mates how he had been saved and asked : " What religion is 'e ? " He was told, and made the answer : " Well, I'm the same as 'im now, and the bloke as sez a word agen our Church will 'ave 'is —— 'ead bashed in." ' When the Rev. Noel Mellish, who is thirty-four years of age, was gazetted Chaplain to the Forces it was a case of ' back to the Army again,' since he was a soldier before he became a clergyman, and, needless to say, a brave one. He went out to South Africa in Dec. 1900, and was among the first recruits for Baden-Powell's Police, with whom he did a good deal of blockhouse and frontier work. Before leaving England he had been in the Artists' Rifles, and so was well acquainted with military discipline and procedure. One who served with him in the South African War speaks of him as the bravest man he knew. On one occasion a party of Baden-Powell's Police were surrounded by Boers in a farmhouse, and there was practically no chance for them. Mr. Mellish was sent on what seemed a forlorn hope for assistance. He got safely through and delivered his message ; but though his duty ended there, he made his way back to his comrades in the besieged farmhouse, to tell them that relief was on the way and to do all he could to help them to hold out. At the close of the war he returned to England, but not long afterwards went to South Africa again and took an important post in the diamond mines at Jagersfontein, and there was no man more esteemed and honoured all over the mine. During the years he was at Jagersfontein he assisted at a church and native mission, reading the lessons at the mission in the somewhat fearsome language understood by the natives. Despite long and arduous days in the mine, he made light of sitting up all night by the bedside of a sick friend, and his life generally at Jagersfontein was such as to justify the remark of one of its inhabitants : ' It is such men as Mr. Mellish who restore one's faith in mankind.' Returning to England, he studied at King's College, London, and in 1912 took Holy Orders, and became one of the curates at St. Paul's Church, Deptford, a parish with a population of over twelve thousand, mostly poor people. In his parish he was just as strenuous a worker as he has proved himself on the field of battle. His chief activities were in connection with the Church Lads' Brigade, and week in and week out he laboured to perfect the boys in their drill and other duties. A fine specimen of a man himself—he stands over six feet in height and is broad and muscular—he taught his little band the value of discipline and to ' play the game.' He took over an old public-house at the back of the Empire Music Hall, Deptford, and converted it into a boys' club. The youngsters insisted on naming it after their captain, and the place is known as the Noel Club. Mr. Mellish is only the second clergyman to win the Victoria Cross. The first was an Irishman, the Rev. James Williams Adams, who won it as far back as 1879, during the Afghan War. Mr. Adams, who was known as the ' Fighting Parson,' shared all the hardships of Lord Roberts's famous march from Kabul to Kandahar, but it was at an earlier stage of the war that he gained the much-coveted distinction. The Afghans were pressing on the British force at the village of Bhagwana, when two troopers of the 9th Lancers, during a charge, were hurled with their horses into a deep and wide nullah. Adams, without hesitation, went to their assistance, plunged into the nullah, and, being an unusually powerful man, dragged the men, one after another, from under the struggling animals. The Afghans were close upon them and were keeping up a hot fire ; but Adams paid no heed to his own safety till he had pulled the almost exhausted lancers to the top of the slippery bank. The same day he rescued another of the lancers from the Afghan horsemen. Lord Roberts mentions the ' Fighting Parson ' and these incidents in his memoirs. Mr. Adams died in 1903, when Rector of Ashwell, Rutland. Early in the war the Rev. Noel Mellish, whose parents reside at Lewisham, lost a brother, Lieut. Coppin Mellish, who came back from Canada to join the Army." Mr. Mellish married, 3 Dec. 1918, at St. Paul's, Deptford, Elizabeth Wallace, daughter of L. T. Molesworth. He became Vicar of St. Mark's Church, Lewisham.

London Gazette, 13 May, 1916.—"His Majesty the King has been graciously pleased to confer the Victoria Cross on No. 501, Lance-Naik Lala, 41st Dogras, Indian Army, for most conspicuous bravery."

LALA, Lance-Naik, was born in the village of Parol in the district of Hamirpur, Kangra, Punjab, India, son of Dinga (Maila caste), Zamindar, First Grade. He had no schooling, but can read and write Hindi. He joined the Indian Army on 21 Feb. 1901. He served in the European War from 1914 ; "was in the first

batch of Indians that came to France, and returned in 1915 ; guarded the Suez Canal for three months, and then moved to Mesopotamia, and there got my V.C., beyond Sheikh Said, and then returned to India with the regiment in 1917. Kept fit all through, except got trench feet in France, and came to England to the Brighton Hospital, but soon rejoined my regiment. I am in the first eleven regimental football team. I have no newspapers here. I won my V.C. on 21 Jan. 1916. Indian papers would contain required accounts." He was awarded the Victoria Cross [London Gazette, 13 May, 1916]: "Lala, No. 501, Naik, 41st Dogras, Indian Army."

Lance-Naik Lala.

London Gazette, 21 June, 1916.—" His Majesty the King has been graciously pleased to award the Victoria Cross to the undermentioned Officer and Man."

SINTON, JOHN ALEXANDER, Capt., was born 2 Dec. 1884, and educated at Queen's College, Belfast (First place Honours and Exhibitioner) ; Liverpool School of Tropical Medicine ; Riddell Demonstrator in Pathology, Queen's University ; late House Surgeon and House Physician, Royal Victoria Hospital ; late Pathologist, Ulster Eye, Throat and Ear Hospital, and Clinical Pathologist, Mater Infirmorum Hospital, Belfast ; is M.B., D.P.H., Cantab. and Belfast ; D.T.M., Liverpool ; Indian Medical Service, B.Ch., B.A.O., R.U.I. He served in the European War, and was awarded the Victoria Cross [London Gazette, 21 June, 1916]: "John Alexander Sinton, M.B., Capt., Indian Medical Service. For most conspicuous bravery and devotion to duty. Although shot through both arms and through the side, he refused to go to the hospital, and remained as long as daylight lasted, attending to his duties under very heavy fire. In three previous actions Capt. Sinton displayed the utmost bravery."

SINGH, CHATTA, Sepoy, was born at Tilsanda, Cawnpore, India, in 1887, son of Ishu Singh, cultivator. He was educated at Tilsanda Village School, and joined the Army on 5 July, 1911, as a Sepoy in the 9th Bhopal Infantry. He served in the European War, and was awarded the Victoria Cross [London Gazette, 21 June, 1916]: "Chatta Singh, No. 3398, Sepoy, 9th Bhopal Infantry, Indian Army. For most conspicuous bravery and devotion to duty in leaving cover to assist his commanding officer, who was lying wounded and helpless in the open. Sepoy Chatta Singh bound up the officer's wound, and then dug cover for him with his entrenching tool, being exposed all the time to very heavy rifle fire. For five hours until nightfall he remained beside the wounded officer, shielding him with his own body on the exposed side. He then, under cover of darkness, went back for assistance, and brought the officer into safety." Capt.

Chatta Singh.

B. W. Browning, 9th Bhopal Infantry, writes : " I was not actually with the regiment in Mesopotamia when Chatta Singh did his deed for which he was awarded the V.C. He was awarded his V.C. for the Battle of the Wadi 13 Jan. 1916. As far as my memory serves me, the story is this : The regiment attacked the Turkish position and was driven back, leaving among the wounded in No Man's Land the Colonel (Colonel Thomas), wounded in the thigh. The Colonel of the regiment on our left was also left wounded in No Man's Land. Chatta Singh remained with these two officers for over 24 hours—I'm not sure of the length of time—dug a small parapet round each to protect them as much as possible, and fed them, all the time under heavy fire. They were subsequently brought in, and Colonel Thomas died later at Amara from shock and exposure."

London Gazette, 5 Aug. 1916.—" His Majesty the King has been graciously pleased to award the Victoria Cross to the undermentioned Officers, Non-commissioned Officer and Men for most conspicuous bravery and devotion to duty."

BATTEN-POOLL, ARTHUR HUGH HENRY, Lieut., was born 25 Oct. 1891, at Knightsbridge, London, S.W., son of R. P. H. Batten-Pooll. He was educated at Eton College, and joined the Army on 1 June, 1911. He served in the European War in France and was awarded the Victoria Cross [London Gazette, 5 Aug. 1916]: "Arthur Hugh Henry Batten-Pooll, Lieut., 3rd Royal Munster Fusiliers. For most conspicuous bravery whilst in command of a raiding party. At the moment of entry into the enemy's lines he was severely wounded by a bomb, which broke and mutilated all the fingers of his right hand. In spite of this he continued to direct operations with unflinching courage, his voice being clearly heard cheering on and directing his men. He was urged, but refused, to retire. Half an hour later, during the withdrawal, whilst personally assisting in the rescue of other wounded men, he received two further wounds. Still refusing assistance, he walked unaided to within one hundred yards of our lines, when he fainted, and was carried in by the covering party." He was promoted Captain 28 Feb. 1916. Capt. Batten-Pooll's Military Cross was gazetted in July, 1917, and he was mentioned in Despatches [London Gazette, in July, 1917]. His pursuits are scientific, and his favourite sport is Fives.

GREEN, JOHN LESLIE, Capt., was the son of Mr. J. G. and Mrs. Green, of Birchdene, Houghton, Huntingdonshire. He was educated at Felsted School; Downing College, Cambridge, and St. Bartholomew's Hospital. While at Cambridge he obtained Honours in Part I. of the Natural Sciences Tripos (1910), and was a keen boating man, rowing in many races for his college. He became medically qualified (M.R.C.S., L.R.C.P.) in 1913, but had not quite completed his course at Cambridge when, on the outbreak of war, he was commissioned in the R.A.M.C. He was at first attached to the 5th South Staffordshire Regt., then to a field ambulance in France, and lastly to the Sherwood Foresters, with whom he was serving when he met his death. He was posthumously awarded the Victoria Cross [London Gazette, 5 Aug. 1916]: "John Leslie Green, Capt., late Royal Army Medical Corps. For most conspicuous devotion to duty. Although himself wounded, he went to the assistance of an officer who had been wounded and was hung up in the enemy's wire entanglements, and succeeded in dragging him to a shell-hole, where he dressed his wounds, notwithstanding that bombs and rifle grenades were thrown at him the whole time. Capt. Green then endeavoured to bring the wounded officer into safe cover, and had nearly succeeded in doing so when he was himself killed." His Victoria Cross was given to his widow. Capt. Green was born 4 Dec. 1888. He was House Surgeon at Huntingdon County Hospital. He married, 1 Jan. 1916, Miss E. M. Moss, M.B., B.S., daughter of the late F. J. Moss, of Stainfield Hall, Lincolnshire. He was a keen all-round sportsman, a first-rate oar, equally good at golf and tennis, and always very popular at school and college.

JONES, RICHARD BASIL BRANDRAM, Lieut., was the elder son of Mr. and Mrs. H. T. B. Jones, of 2, Thicket Road, Anerley. After being at Dulwich College Preparatory School, he entered Dulwich College in 1909, and passed the London Matriculation when just sixteen years of age. He was a keen member of the O.T.C., and in 1913 won the Lane Challenge Cup (given for the highest score in the Dulwich team shooting for the Ashburton Shield at Bisley), and the Hamilton Challenge Cup, which he held again in 1914. He was also in the Dulwich Gymnastic Team, holding the post of gymnasium captain when he left. He left school for the Army in Sept. 1914, receiving a commission as Second Lieut. He was promoted Lieutenant in Dec., and later was appointed sniping officer to the battalion. He left for the front in Sept. 1915, and was there till his death, and was awarded the Victoria Cross [London Gazette, 5 Aug. 1916]: "Richard Basil Brandram Jones, Temporary Lieut., 8th Battn. North Lancashire Regt. Lieut. Jones was in charge of a platoon which was holding a crater recently captured from the enemy. Forty yards away the enemy exploded a mine, and isolated the British platoon by a heavy barrage fire. Attacking in overwhelming numbers, the platoon was in great danger; but, organizing his men, Lieut. Jones set a fine example by shooting no fewer than 15 of the enemy as they advanced, and counting off his victims as they fell. When all his ammunition was used, he was about to throw a bomb, and was shot through the head. The platoon continued to resist the enemy attack until they had used all their ammunition, and then resorted to throwing stones and ammunition boxes. When only nine of the platoon were left the men retired." The King handed the Victoria Cross to Mr. H. T. B. Jones, father of the late Lieut. R. B. Brandram Jones, of the Loyal North Lancashire Regt. In bestowing this and another posthumous Cross, he spoke most sympathetically to the parents of the gallant officers, and expressed both his warm sympathy for them and his admiration of the pluck of their boys.

A newspaper says:

"News of the death of another local hero has been received. He was Sniping Officer Lieut. Richard Basil Jones, son of Mr. and Mrs. H. T. B. Jones, of 2, Thicket Road, Anerley, and in a letter to Mr. Jones the Commanding Officer of the regiment writes: 'It is with very great regret that I have to write you of the death of your son. He was killed instantaneously by a bullet on the night of 21 and 22 May, when defending a crater against an attack by the Germans. He behaved in the most gallant manner, holding on with a few men till the last moment, and himself shot 15 Germans before he was killed. . . . Your son's death is a great loss to the regiment. He was my sniping officer, and a very gallant fellow.'

"A lieutenant in the same regiment has written, 'Nothing could have been finer than the fight he and his men put up against the Germans. . . . He was always cheerful, always ready to do daring deeds, and a good comrade. . . . Jonesie (his popular name) hung on to the last with his men, and as the Huns attacked he shot them down one by one. . . . Hero he was alive and hero he remained till death. We are all intensely sorrowful.'

"In another letter the same officer wrote: 'Jonesie kept his men in this crater, which was well in advance of our line. . . . He was a first-class shot, and coolly showed himself above the parapet and fought to the last. . . . Once wounded in the head he picked himself up and carried on—fine fellow that he was. He died a hero's death. Ever since I have been in the regiment we have been together in the same company. He was a topping pal.'

"A sergeant in the same regiment has written: 'It was a very strong attack, and the men under his command were outnumbered, but they stuck to their post and fought to the last, for they knew that they had a great leader with them, one who could cheer and give them courage. His memory will live for ever with the men of the —— Regiment. Before he was shot he accounted for no less than 15 of the enemy, which was a very brave act, for the position he held was sure death. He died a hero. No one in the battalion will miss him more than the men of his platoon and battalion snipers, for he was a gentleman, and was loved by everyone. . . . The men would have gone anywhere with him. Many a time have I heard his cheerful voice while passing through the trenches, joking and cheering the men when they were a little downhearted.'

"Much sympathy will be felt in Anerley with the relatives of this splendid type of a true and brave English soldier."

Lieut. R. B. Jones was born at Honor Oak Rise 30 April, 1897.

REES, LIONEL WILMOT BRABAZON, Major, was born on 31 July, 1884, son of Charles Herbert Rees, solicitor, of Carnarvon, and Leonora Maria Rees. He was educated at Colwall, at Eastbourne College, and at the Royal Military Academy (Tombs Memorial Prize, Dec. 1903), from which he had a commission in the Royal Garrison Artillery on 23 Dec. 1903. He was Lieutenant on 23 Dec. 1906; Captain 30 Oct. 1914, and Major and Brevet Lieut.-Colonel on 4 April, 1918. He served in the European War. He was seconded to the Royal Flying Corps on 10 Aug. 1914, and became a Flight Commander in Jan. 1915. He was an instructor at the Central Flying School in 1915. He was mentioned in Despatches [London Gazette, 5 Aug. 1915] for fighting and reconnaissance, and won the Military Cross [London Gazette of Sept. 1915] for taking a series of photographs under heavy fire, and after they were completed, attacking and bringing down a two-engined machine—his observer receiving the Distinguished Conduct Medal. He became a Squadron Commander on 1 Dec. 1915. He won the Victoria Cross on 1 July, 1916, as the result of the brilliant manner in which he took advantage of his own mistake [London Gazette, 5 Aug. 1916]: "Lionel Wilmot Brabazon Rees, Captain, Royal Artillery and Royal Flying Corps. For conspicuous gallantry and devotion to duty. Whilst on flying duties, Major Rees sighted what he thought to be a bombing party of our own machines returning home. He went up to escort them, but on getting nearer discovered they were a party of enemy machines, about ten in all. Major Rees was immediately attacked by one of the machines, and after a short encounter it disappeared behind the enemy lines, damaged. Five others then attacked him at long range, but these he dispersed on coming to close quarters; after seriously damaging two of the machines, seeing two others going westwards, he gave chase to them, but on coming nearer, he was wounded in the thigh, causing him to lose temporary control of his machine. He soon righted it, and immediately closed with the enemy, firing at a close-contact range of only a few yards, until all his ammunition was used up. He then returned home, landing his machine safely in our lines." He formed one of the War Office delegates of the Balfour Mission to America in 1917, and was rewarded for his work there by receiving the Brevet of Lieutenant-Colonel. He became a Wing Commander in the Royal Flying Corps on 1 May, 1917, and in the Royal Air Force on 1 April, 1918.

Lionel W. B. Rees.

CHAFER, GEORGE WILLIAM, Private, served in the European War, and was awarded the Victoria Cross [London Gazette, 5 Aug. 1916]: "George William Chafer, Private, No. 19384, East Yorkshire Regt. For most conspicuous bravery. During a very heavy hostile bombardment and attack on our trenches a man carrying an important written message to his company commander was half buried and rendered unconscious by a shell. Private Chafer, at once grasping the situation, on his own initiative took the message from the man's pocket, and, although severely wounded in three places, ran along the ruined parapet under heavy shell and machine-gun fire, and just succeeded in delivering it before he collapsed from the effect of his wounds. He displayed great initiative and a splendid devotion to duty at a critical moment." He was invested by the King at Buckingham Palace on 4 Nov. 1916. He was born at Rotherham in 1897; is an orphan, and his aunt, Mrs. Brooks, of Ravenfield Common, Rotherham, brought him up. He was educated at Rotherham, and joined the Army 2 June, 1915. Some particulars have been sent as to how he won his Victoria Cross: "C Coy., 1st Battn. East Yorkshire Regt., was subjected to very trying experience. Our trench had been almost levelled by enfilade shell fire and enemy trench mortars. It was being swept by deadly machine-gun fire, and the air was poisoned by gas fumes. Chafer was lying seriously wounded in hand and leg, bruised and dazed by the concussion, choking and blinded by gas, when he saw a man coming along with a written message. Another shell burst and partially buried this orderly, who shouted: 'Someone take this message for the Captain.' There was no one within hearing but Chafer; only dead and mortally wounded in sight. He took the message from the soldier, and, as the trench had been knocked in so badly, crawled on to the parapet in spite of excruciating pain, while big shells, small shells, bullets from machine guns and rifles were raining round, without further injury. The first living occupant of our trench Chafer reached was a corporal, and, his left hand shot through and bleeding profusely, yet clutching his rifle, he dragged himself painfully along the parapet with one leg torn by shell wounds, crying out, 'A message for the Captain.' After handing it over, Chafer collapsed."

ERSKINE, JOHN, Sergt., served in the European War, and was awarded the Victoria Cross [London Gazette, 5 Aug. 1916], for his bravery at Givenchy, France, on 22 June, 1916: "John Erskine, Acting Sergt., Scottish Rifles, Territorial Force. For most conspicuous bravery whilst the near lip of a crater, caused by the explosion of a large enemy mine, was being consolidated, Acting Sergt. Erskine rushed out under continuous fire with utter disregard of danger, and rescued a wounded sergeant and a private. Later, seeing his officer, who was believed to be dead, show signs of movement, he ran to him, bandaged his head, and remained with him for fully an hour, though repeatedly fired at, whilst a shallow trench was being dug to them. He then assisted in bringing in his officer, shielding him with his own body in order to lessen the chance of his being hit again."

HACKETT, WILLIAM, Sapper, was born at Nottingham on 11 June, 1873, son of John and Harriet Hackett. He married Alice Tooby on 16 April, 1900, and left a daughter and a son, who had his right foot amputated two months after his father

William Hackett.

enlisted. He worked as a miner for several years, living at Mexborough, Yorkshire. On the outbreak of war, though above the military age, he tried to enlist in the York and Lancaster Regt., but was three times rejected. He then joined the Tunnelling Corps, and proceeded to France with the 254th Tunnelling Company, Royal Engineers. He met his death in June, 1916, and was posthumously awarded the Victoria Cross, which was given to his widow by H.M. the King at Buckingham Palace on 29 Nov. 1916. His Victoria Cross was gazetted 5 Aug. 1916 : " William Hackett, Sapper, late Royal Engineers. For most conspicuous bravery when entombed with four others in a gallery owing to the explosion of an enemy mine. After working for twenty hours a hole was made through fallen earth and broken timber, and the outside party was met. Sapper Hackett helped three of the men through the hole, and could easily have followed, but refused to leave the fourth, who had been seriously injured, saying : ' I am a tunneller, and must look after the others first.' Meantime the hole was getting smaller, yet he still refused to leave his injured comrade. Finally the gallery collapsed, and though the rescue party worked desperately for four days, the attempt to reach the two men failed. Sapper Hackett, well knowing the nature of sliding earth and the chances against him, deliberately gave his life for his comrade." Capt. G. M. Edwards, R.E., Officer Commanding the 254th Tunnelling Company, wrote : " I find it very difficult to express to you adequately the admiration I and all my officers have for the heroic manner in which your husband, Sapper Hackett, met his death. Sad as his loss must be to his own people, yet his fearless conduct and his wonderful self-sacrifice must always be a source of pride and comfort to you all. Your husband deliberately sacrificed his own life to save his comrades, and even when three of the four were saved he refused to save himself because the remaining man was too injured to help himself. He has been recommended for the V.C., that simple medal which represents all that is brave and noble." The following tribute was also paid to him by the late Field-Marshal Sir E. Wood, V.C. : " The most divine-like act of self-sacrifice of which I have read was that of the late Sapper William Hackett, R.E., awarded posthumously the Victoria Cross."

PROCTOR, ARTHUR HERBERT, Rifleman, was born on 11 Aug. 1890, at Bootle, son of Arthur R. Proctor and Mrs. E. Proctor, daughter of Mr. E. Cumpsty. He was educated at Exeter Training College and Port Sunlight Schools, and joined the Army on 30 Nov. 1914, as a Rifleman in the 5th Battn. King's (Liverpool) Regt. (Territorial Force). He married Hilda M., daughter of Mr. and Mrs. Codd, of Birkenhead, and they have one son, Arthur Reginald, born 3 April, 1919. He served in the European War in France, from Feb. 1915, and was present at the battles of Neuve Chapelle, Festubert, Givenchy, the Somme and Arras. He was awarded the Victoria Cross [London Gazette, 5 Aug. 1916] : " Arthur Herbert Proctor, No. 3156, Private, King's (Liverpool) Regt. (Territorial Force). For most conspicuous bravery. Private Proctor,

Arthur Herbert Proctor.

noticing some movement on the part of two wounded men who were lying in the open in full view of the enemy at about 75 yards in front of our trenches, went out on his own initiative, and, though heavily fired at, ran and crawled to the two men, got them under cover of a small bank, dressed their wounds, and, after cheering them with a promise of rescue after dark, and leaving with them some of his clothing for warmth, regained our trenches, again being heavily fired at. At dusk both men were brought out alive" Rifleman Proctor received the Victoria Cross from the King at British Headquarters, France. When he arrived home he received an enthusiastic welcome at the Territorial Headquarters in Liverpool. After being congratulated by the Lord Mayor, he was marched through the streets by his comrades to the Produce Exchange, where he was employed at the outbreak of the war. Here he was presented with a gold watch and chain, a cheque for one hundred guineas, and £100 War Loan, 4½ per cent. Scrip, subscribed by members of the Exchange. Rifleman Proctor said that others equally deserved similar recognition, but were not equally fortunate in coming under the eyes of the powers that be.

STRINGER, GEORGE, Private, served in the European War in Mesopotamia. He was awarded the Victoria Cross [London Gazette 5 Aug. 1916] : " George Stringer, No. 15818, Private, 1st Battn. Manchester Regt. For most conspicuous bravery and determination. After the capture of an enemy position he was posted on the extreme right of his battalion to guard against any hostile attack. His battalion was subsequently forced back by an enemy counter-attack, but Private Stringer held his ground single-handed and kept back the enemy till all his grenades were expended. His very gallant stand saved the flank of his battalion and rendered a steady withdrawal possible."

London Gazette, 9 Sept. 1916.—" War Office, 9 Sept. 1916. The King has been graciously pleased to award the Victoria Cross to the undermentioned Officers, Non-Commissioned Officers and Men."

LOUDOUN-SHAND, STEWART WALTER, Temporary Major, was born in Ceylon, the second son of Mr. and Mrs. J. Loudoun-Shand, of Craigelle, Alleyn Park, Dulwich, S.E., and one of five brothers, all with the forces at the time when Stewart won his Victoria Cross and met his death. The youngest of these, Capt. E. G. Loudoun-Shand, the brilliant Oxford Rugby three-quarter and Scottish International, was lately wounded for the third time, but is happily recovering. Major Loudoun-Shand was an old boy of Dulwich College, and is the second scholar of that famous school to be given a posthumous V.C. in this war. When at school he was as fond of sport as was his more famous (in sporting circles) brother, E. G. Loudoun-Shand. He, however, left school too early to build up a great reputation as an athlete. He was a rare cricketer, a keen golfer and a strong swimmer. He had begun a business career in Williams

S. W. Loudoun-Shand.

Deacon's Bank when the South African War broke out, and was in the London Scottish. He sought eagerly for active service, but the way was barred by his youth, so far as that Regiment was concerned. He managed to enlist in the Pembrokeshire Yeomanry, and went all through the Boer War, and on his return home he was offered and accepted a mercantile appointment at Port Elizabeth. He stayed two or three years there, and later went to Ceylon, where his father had lived for twenty years and had secured an important appointment. As soon as the present war broke out Stewart Loudoun-Shand came home and at once offered his services. He was gazetted to the 10th Battn. Yorkshire Regt., and soon given his company. He got his Majority after his Colonel and both Majors had been killed in action. The story of his Victoria Cross is told in the London Gazette of 9 Sept. 1916 : " Stewart Walter Loudoun-Shand, temporary Major, late Yorkshire Regt. For most conspicuous bravery. When his company attempted to climb over the parapet to attack the enemy's trenches, they were met by very fierce machine-gun fire, which temporarily stopped their progress. Major Loudoun-Shand immediately leapt on the parapet, helped the men over it, and encouraged them in every way until he fell mortally wounded. Even then he insisted on being propped up in the trench, and went on encouraging the non-commissioned officers and men until he died."

CARTON DE WIART, ADRIAN, Capt. (Temporary Lieut.-Colonel), was born 5 May, 1880, at Brussels, and is the eldest son of the late Leon Carton de Wiart, barrister (of Brussels and Cairo). His uncle is the Belgian Minister of Justice. He was educated at the Oratory School, Edgbaston, and Balliol College, Oxford, where he studied for the law. At the outbreak of the South African War in 1899 he gave up studying and enlisted as a private, serving as a trooper in the Middlesex Yeomanry (Duke of Cambridge's Hussars), and was twice wounded, and received the Queen's Medal with three clasps. He afterwards obtained a commission in the 4th Dragoon Guards, 14 Sept. 1901, becoming Lieutenant 16 July, 1904, and Captain 1910. He became well known as a polo player and steeplechase rider. He was A.D.C. to Lieutenant-General, South Africa, 29 July, 1905, to 21 Oct. 1905, and A.D.C. to the G.O.C. in Chief, South Africa, 1 Nov. 1905, to 18 March, 1908. He was promoted to Captain 6 Feb. 1910 ; was Adjutant, Gloucestershire Yeomanry, 1 Jan. 1912, to 22 July, 1914 ; employed with the Somaliland Camel Force 22 July, 1914, to 7 March, 1915, during which operations he lost an eye. He was mentioned in Despatches, and awarded the Distinguished Service Order 5 May, 1914. Later he went to Flanders, where he was severely wounded several times, and lost his left hand at Zonnebeke. In spite of this he commanded a Gloucestershire Regiment which took La Boiselle. He received from the King of the Belgians the Order of Leopold and the Belgian War Medal. He was awarded the Victoria Cross [London Gazette, 9 Sept. 1916], for his behaviour at La Boiselle, France, 2-3 July, 1916 : " Adrian Carton de Wiart, Captain (Temporary Lieutenant-Colonel), D.S.O., 4th Dragoon Guards. . For most conspicuous bravery, coolness and determination during severe operations of a prolonged nature. It was owing in a great measure to his dauntless courage and inspiring example that a serious reverse was averted. He displayed the utmost energy and courage in forcing our attack home. After three other battalion commanders had become casualties, he controlled their commands, and ensured that the ground won was maintained at all

Geoffrey St. G. S. Cather.

costs. He frequently exposed himself in the organization of positions and of supplies, passing unflinchingly through fire barrage of the most intense nature. His gallantry was inspiring to all." In 1918 he was made a Companion of St. Michael and George. He was no less than eight times wounded during the Great War, and received the Croix d'Officier de l'Ordre de la Couronne and the Croix de Guerre. In 1908, he married the Countess Frederica, eldest daughter of Prince Fugger-Babenhausen and Nora, Princess Hohenlohe, and has two daughters.

CATHER, GEOFFREY ST. GEORGE SHILLINGTON, Temporary Lieut., was born on 11 Oct. 1890, at Christchurch Road, Streatham Hill, S.W. He was the son of the late R. G. Cather, of Limpsfield, Surrey, and of Mrs. Cather, of 26, Priory Road, West Hampstead N.W. He was educated at Hazelwood, Limpsfield, Surrey, and at Rugby School, and joined the Army in the University and Public Schools Corps in Sept. 1914, getting his commission in the 9th Battn. Royal Irish Fusiliers in May, 1915. He was Adjutant at the time he was killed. He served in the European War, and was awarded the Victoria Cross [London Gazette, 9 Sept. 1916], for his courage near Hamel, France, on 1 July, 1916 : " Geoffrey St. George Shillington Cather, Temporary Lieutenant, 9th Battn. Royal Irish Fusiliers. For most conspicuous bravery. From 7 p.m. till midnight he searched ' No Man's Land ' and brought in three wounded men. Next morning at 8 a.m. he continued his search, brought in another wounded man, and gave water to others, arranging for their rescue later. Finally, at 10.30 a.m. he took out water to another man, and was proceeding further on when he was himself killed. All this was carried out in full view of the enemy, and under direct machine-gun fire and intermittent artillery fire. He set a splendid example of courage and self-sacrifice."

BLACKBURN, ARTHUR SEAFORTH, Second Lieut., was, on the outbreak of the European War, a solicitor in South Australia. He joined up at once, served in France and was awarded the Victoria Cross [London Gazette, 9 Sept. 1916], for bravery at Pozières, France, 23 July, 1916 : " Arthur Seaforth Blackburn, Second Lieut., 10th Battn. Australian Infantry. For most conspicuous bravery. He was directed, with fifty men, to drive the enemy from a strong point. By dogged determination, he eventually captured their trench, after personally leading four separate parties of bombers against it, many of whom became casualties. In face of fierce opposition he captured 250 yards of trench. Then, after crawling forward with a sergeant to reconnoitre, he returned, attacked and seized another 120 yards of trench, establishing communication with the battalion on his left."

Arthur S. Blackburn.

BELL, DONALD SIMPSON, Second Lieut., was born 3 Dec. 1890, at Harrogate. He was the youngest son of Mr. and Mrs. Smith Bell, of East Parade, Harrogate. He was educated at St. Peter's School, Harrogate, where he gained a scholarship, and afterwards at Knaresborough Grammar School, and Westminster College, London. While at Westminster College he was very successful in the sports field, and won his colours for Soccer, Rugby and cricket. He was one of the school's fastest forwards, and did the 100-yards sprint in 10⅗ seconds from scratch. He gained an important position in the Association Football world, and played for the Bradford Club up to the time of his enlistment. Mr. T. E. Maley, Secretary of that Club, wrote of him : " He played many a fine game for both our teams. . . . A cheery, big chap, he took great interest in his men. He has triumphed, and if blameless life and unselfish and willing sacrifice have the virtue attached with which they are credited, Donald is in the possession of eternal happiness, and in his glorious record and great reward there is much to be envied." He was associated with Newcastle United as an amateur when he left for Bradford in the season 1912–13. In Bradford he played first as an amateur and afterwards as a professional. He had previously also played for Starbeck, Mirfield, and Bishop Auckland. He was a member of the Harrogate Claro Tent of the Independent Order of Rechabites. In 1911 he won the 100 yards at the Royal Polytechnic, London. He was an assistant master at the Starbeck Council School, near Harrogate, before he joined the West Yorkshire Regt. as a Private in Nov. 1914, and obtained his commission in 1915 (June). He was married at Kirkby Stephen, 5 June, 1916, to Rhoda Margaret Bonson, daughter of the late James Bonson, Esq., and Mrs. Bonson, of Kirkby Stephen. The following is an account of his action on 5 July, 1916, during the British advance on the Somme, Horseshoe Trench, sent by the Brigadier-General to the Mayor of Bradford : " At 4 a.m. an attack was made by the —th and —th, but the success was nullified by a heavy counter-attack by the enemy, which drove our advanced posts back to their original line. Up to midday little advance had been made. The objective of the brigade was strongly held by the enemy. During the afternoon parties of the —th and —th again gradually pushed back the enemy on our right. On the left the —th continued to gain ground slowly by bombing. The —th, who previously had done much work carrying stories, etc., were now ordered forward to reinforce and gradually relieve the —th, but the latter remained continuously in action during the day. After a long day's heavy fighting, our artillery fire and the exertions of the infantry began to have their effect. About 5.45 p.m. over 80 Germans surrendered to the battalion on the right. Almost simultaneously at 6 p.m. a very gallant assault across the open by the —th completed the German demoralization. Over 100 more wounded prisoners and two machine guns were captured, and the trench occupied. Pushing on patrols and small parties, a further line of trenches was taken, and from here a good view could be obtained." It was during the advance of the —th at 6 p.m. that Second Lieut. Bell performed his gallant act, for which he received the Victoria Cross [London

Donald Simpson Bell.

Gazette, 9 Sept. 1916] : " Donald Simpson Bell, Temporary Second Lieut., 9th Battn. Yorkshire Regt. Date of Act of Bravery : 5 July, 1916. For most conspicuous bravery. During an attack a very heavy enfilade fire was opened on the attacking company by a hostile machine gun. Second Lieut. Bell immediately, and on his own initiative, crept up a communication trench, and then, followed by Corpl. Colwill and Private Batey, rushed across the open under very heavy fire and attacked the machine gun, shooting the firer with his revolver, and destroying gun and personnel with bombs. This very brave act saved many lives and ensured the success of the attack. Five days later this gallant officer lost his life performing a very similar act of bravery." It was at Contalmaison that he lost his life on 10 July, 1916.

The following is an extract from the letter of Brigadier-General T. S. Lambert, Commanding the 69th Infantry Brigade, dated 16 Sept. 1916 :

" DEAR MR. BELL,
" In asking you and all your family to accept our deep sympathy in the loss of your son, may I say how glad we all are to have learnt of the recognition of his life's work given by His Majesty in the award of the V.C. Others will have told you how well he deserved the honour, both in the act which won it, at the capture of Horseshoe Trench, and at Contalmaison, when he lost his life. His was a great example, given at a time when it was most needed, and in his honour the spot where he now lies, and which is now a redoubt, has been officially called ' Bell's Redoubt.' Not only his own battalion but the whole brigade mourned his loss, but his memory will always remain with us while the 69th Brigade or any of its members who fought there remain. It is given to few to stand out among their comrades as he did, but in leading others his life was not given in vain."

Extract from the letter of Colonel H. G. Holmes, dated 12 Sept. 1916 :

" DEAR MRS. BELL,
" I am writing to say how very pleased I was to see in the Gazette yesterday that the V.C. had been given to your husband for his two very gallant actions of the 5th and 10th of July last. Everyone in the 9th Yorkshires will, I know, be delighted to see the announcement in the Gazette, and will be proud to know that your husband belonged to our battalion. I am extremely pleased that his gallantry has been recognized, and hope that this may be some little consolation to you."

Extract from the letter of Major H. A. S. Prior (afterwards Lieutenant-Colonel), dated 13 Sept. 1916 :

" DEAR MRS. BELL,
" On behalf of the officers, non-commissioned officers and men of this battalion, I write to offer you our most heartfelt congratulations on the honour which your gallant husband has won, both for those near and dear to him and also for this battalion. We are proud to have had him amongst us. During that short time he earned the love and respect of all who knew him and we join with you in deeply mourning his loss. The action which earned him the V.C. was one of noble self-denying, unflinching courage, and by that noble deed he saved many lives and assured the success of the attack."

CARTER, NELSON VICTOR, Sergt.-Major, was born at Eastbourne, 9 April, 1887, son of Richard and Rhoda Carter, of Harebeating, Hailsham, Sussex (who have six other sons serving, or who have served, in the Army). He was educated at Hailsham, and, when a lad of sixteen, joined the Royal Field Artillery, attaining later the rank of Bombardier. After three years' service he was invalided home from the East, and underwent a serious operation, which rendered him unfit for some time to serve in the army, or, as he wished to do, in the police force. In Oct. 1911, he married Kathleen Camfield (of Rotherfield), at St. Mary's Church, Old Town, Eastbourne. There is one daughter, Jessie Olive. At the time of the outbreak of the Great War he was employed as a cinema door-keeper, but enlisted in Lowther's Own on the 14 Sept. 1914, and was made Corporal the day he joined. In due time he was promoted Sergeant, and subsequently Company Sergeant-Major, second class warrant officer. On 4 March, 1916, he went over to France with A Company of the 12th Battn. of the Royal Sussex Regt., and at Boar's Head, Richebourg l'Avoué, his bravery won him the Victoria Cross [London Gazette, 9 Sept. 1916] : " Nelson Victor Carter, Company Sergt.-Major, 4th Company, 12th Battn. Royal Sussex Regt. Date of Act of Bravery : 30 June, 1916. For most conspicuous bravery. During an attack he was in command of the fourth wave of the assault. Under intense shell and machine-gun fire he penetrated, with a few men, into the enemy's second line and inflicted heavy casualties with bombs. When forced to retire to the enemy's first line, he captured a machine gun and shot the gunner with his revolver. Finally, after carrying several wounded men into safety, he was himself mortally wounded, and died in a few minutes. His conduct throughout the day was magnificent." The following is a letter from the captain of his company : " I take the earliest opportunity of offering you my heartiest congratulations on the great honour that has been bestowed upon your late husband, whose memory I shall always cherish as a good and great soldier. We served together for eighteen months, and for the four months preceding his death he was my right-hand man. On 30 June, he was in

Nelson Victor Carter.

command of the last platoon to go over the parapet. When I last saw him he was close to the German line, acting as leader to a small party of four or five men. I was afterwards told that he had entered the German second line, and had brought back an enemy machine gun, having put the gun team out of action. I heard that he shot one of them with his revolver. I next saw him about an hour later (I had been wounded in the meanwhile, and was lying in our trench). Your husband repeatedly went over the parapet. I saw him going over alone, and carrying in our wounded men from 'No Man's Land.' He brought them in on his back, and he could not have done this had he not possessed exceptional physical strength as well as courage. It was in going over for the sixth or seventh time that he was shot through the chest. I saw him fall just inside our trench. Somebody told me that he got back just inside our trench, but I do not know for certain. At ——— about a month previously your husband carried a man about 400 yards across the open under machine-gun fire and brought him safely into our trench. For this act I recommended him for the Military Cross. On every occasion, no matter how tight the hole we were in, he was always cheerful and hopeful, and never spared any pains to make the men comfortable and keep them cheery. In fact, it would be difficult to imagine a man better qualified to lead his comrades into action under the dangerous conditions." The following is a further tribute to him from the Quartermaster-Sergeant of A Company : " Your husband was a man beloved by all, and a splendid soldier, and it is a little consoling to know that he did his duty even to the last moment." Sergt.-Major Carter was a fine athlete, and won a Medal and a Silver Cup for boxing in 1915. The Medal was for the Regimental Championship and the Cup for the Heavyweight Championship.

The following are also letters written to Mrs. Carter :

"Kye Lami, The Greys, Eastbourne,
"16 July, 1916.
"MY DEAR MRS. CARTER,
" I have hesitated to write to you because I could get no news of your husband, but I now hear that there is no doubt, and I have to write and tell you how deeply I sympathize with you in your loss. I should like to say how much I admired him, and how much I appreciated the work he did during the time I commanded A Company. When the time came for them to do their job, the men rose to the occasion very fairly, and I consider that it was in no small degree due to the fine example always set by Sergt.-Major Carter. Always cheerful, and working with unceasing energy through the long months, of training and the trials in the trenches, he endeared himself to all, and the men would, I know, have gone anywhere with him. I personally feel that I have lost a very great friend, and one of the finest I ever knew. It was with pleasure that I was able to put forward his name with a recommendation for the Military Cross about a fortnight before he died, and I have no hesitation in saying that I should most certainly recommend him for further decoration for gallantry this time had he come through. At present I am unable to get about much, but I hope to get over to see you soon.
" With deepest sympathy and kind regards,
" Believe me,
" Yours very truly,
" HAROLD C. T. ROBINSON,
" Lieut., 12th Royal Sussex Regt."

" A Company, 12th Royal Sussex Regt.,
" B.E.F., France,
" 2 July, 1916.
" DEAR MRS. CARTER,
" I am very grieved to inform you that your husband, Company Sergeant-Major N. V. Carter was killed in action on the 30th June, whilst gallantly doing his duty for his King and country. The officers of A Company held a very high opinion of your husband, and fully sympathize with you in your sad bereavement.
" Yours very sincerely,
" W. E. C. SPENCER."

" A Company, 12th Royal Sussex Regt.,
" B.E.F., France,
" 2 July, 1916.
" DEAR MRS. CARTER,
" I am greatly grieved to inform you that your husband, Company Sergeant-Major Carter, was killed in action on the 30th June, whilst gallantly performing his duty to his King and country. As Company Quartermaster-Sergt. of A Company I express the heartfelt grief of his fellow non-commissioned officers and men. Your husband was a man beloved by all, and a splendid soldier, and it is a little consoling to know that he did his duty even to the last moment. His fellow men always had the highest esteem for him, and looked upon him as their leader. There has been caused in A Company a big loss and a big gap by the loss of your dear husband—a loss which is irreparable.
" May it somewhat help you to bear the burden to know that your husband's death was instantaneous.
" Please accept the sincere sympathy of A Company, one and all.
" Yours very respectfully,
" T. G. D. GRIGG,
" Company Quartermaster-Sergeant,
" A Company, 12th Royal Sussex Regt."

SANDERS, GEORGE, Corpl., was born on 8 July, 1894, at New Wortley, Leeds, son of Thomas Sanders, of 3, Shand Grove, Holbeck, and Mrs. Amy Sanders (*née* Hargreaves), who died 16 Feb. 1904. He was educated at Little Holbeck School, and later worked at the Airedale Foundry as a fitter's apprentice. He joined the West Yorkshire Regt. on 9 Nov. 1914, and served in the European War in France. He was awarded the Victoria

Cross [London Gazette, 9 Sept. 1916]: George Sanders, No. 3203, Sergt. (then Corpl.), The Prince of Wales's Own (West Yorkshire Regt.). For most conspicuous bravery. After an advance into the enemy's trenches

George Sanders.

he found himself isolated with a party of thirty men. He organized his defences, detailed a bombing party, and impressed on his men that his and their duty was to hold the position at all costs. Next morning he drove off an attack by the enemy and rescued some prisoners who had fallen into their hands. Later, two strong bombing attacks were driven off. On the following day he was relieved, after showing the greatest courage, determination and good leadership during thirty-six hours under very trying conditions. All the time his party was without food and water, having given all their water to the wounded during the first night. After the relieving force was firmly established, he brought his party, nineteen strong, back to our trenches."

He was invested by the King at Buckingham Palace on 15 Nov. 1916. On 27 June, 1917, he was given a commission, and was gazetted to the 2nd Prince of Wales's Own (West Yorkshire Regt.), attached 1/6th Battn. He was promoted Acting Captain 15 Dec. 1917. He was a prominent figure in the hard fighting during the German attack in April, 1918, and was taken prisoner at Kemmel Hill 25 April, 1918. He was posted as wounded and missing, being last seen wounded in the leg and in the right arm, but carrying on with his revolver in his left hand. In July following, however, his parents received a letter from him stating that he was a prisoner of war at Limburg. Capt. Sanders was repatriated on 26 Dec. 1918. For his services at Kemmel Hill he was awarded the Military Cross. He was demobilized 20 March, 1919.

COOKE, THOMAS, Private, No. 3055, was born 5 July, 1881, at Kaikoura, Marlborough, New Zealand, son of Tom and Caroline Ann Cooke ; was educated at Kaikoura D.H.S., New Zealand ; came as a youth to Wellington, where he lived until, a few

Thomas Cooke.

years before the war, he went to Melbourne. He was a builder. On 4 June, 1902, in Wellington, he married Maud Elizabeth, daughter of Richard Thomas and Sarah Elliott, and there are three children, Ethel Maud ; Reginald Thomas Arthur, born 1 Nov. 1904, and Florence Mildred. He joined the Australian Imperial Force 16 Feb. 1915, in Melbourne, and went with the Main Body to the Western Front, in the 8th Battn. Australian Infantry. In the late summer of 1916 the inhabitants of his birthplace, Kaikoura, and his friends in Wellington and New Zealand were delighted to hear that he had been awarded the Victoria Cross [London Gazette, 9 Sept. 1916]: " No. 3055, Private Thomas Cooke, New Zealand Imperial Force. For most conspicuous bravery. After a Lewis gun had been disabled, he was ordered to take his gun and gun-team to a dangerous part of the line. Here he did fine work, but came under very heavy fire, with the result that finally he was the only man left. He still stuck to his post, and continued to fire his gun. When assistance came he was found dead beside his gun. He set a splendid example of determination and devotion to duty." The above was promulgated in the Commonwealth of Australia Gazette, No. 184, of 14 Dec. 1916. A suggestion was made that the city of Wellington should do something to show Mrs. Cooke that her husband's gallant deed is not to pass unhonoured by the people of the city in which he spent most of his adult life. The Mayor stated that he had been in communication with Mrs. Cooke, and also with the late Private Cooke's mother. . . . He had done everything that was possible up to that time to show that the city was ready to do honour to the widow and the mother of a man who had done such gallant service for his country. Private Cooke was a great bandsman. He was always in a leading band and played first cornet.

FAULDS, WILLIAM FREDERICK, Private, was born at Cradock, Cape Province, South Africa, in 1895. His mother is Wilhelmina Faulds, of 34, Market Street, Cradock. He enlisted for the duration of the war, at Potchefstroom, South Africa, on 23 Aug. 1915, joining the 1st Battn. South African Infantry, and served throughout the campaign in German South-West Africa, 1914–15. He proceeded to France, and was awarded the Victoria Cross [London Gazette, 9 Sept. 1916]: " William Frederick Faulds, No. 4073, Private, South African Infantry. For most conspicuous bravery and devotion to duty. A bombing party under Lieut. Craig attempted to rush over 40 yards of ground which lay between the British and enemy trenches. Coming under very heavy rifle and machine-gun fire the officer and the majority of the party were killed or wounded. Unable to move, Lieut. Craig lay midway between the two lines of trench, the ground being quite open. In full daylight Private Faulds, accompanied by two other men, climbed over the parapet, ran out, picked up the officer, and carried him back, one man being severely wounded in so doing. Two days later Private Faulds again showed most conspicuous bravery in going out alone to bring in a wounded man, and carrying him nearly half a mile to a dressing station, subsequently rejoining his platoon. The artillery fire was at the time so intense that stretcher-bearers and others considered that any attempt to bring in the wounded men meant certain death. This risk Private Faulds faced unflinchingly, and his bravery was crowned with success." A cable from Johannesburg said that this award of the V.C. had sent a thrill of pride throughout the country. He was promoted Lance-Corporal 20 Aug. 1916, Corporal 18 Oct. 1916, Lance-Sergeant 18 Oct. 1916, Sergeant 12 April, 1917, Temporary Second Lieutenant 19 May, 1917. Lieut. Faulds was reported wounded and a prisoner of war in German hands 24 March, 1918. He was promoted to Temporary Lieutenant 9 Nov. 1918, and was repatriated to England 19 Nov. 1918 ; promoted to Lieutenant 16 March, 1919, and proceeded to South Africa, where he was demobilized.

HUTCHINSON, JAMES, Private, was born at 18, Bank Top, Radcliffe, on 9 July, 1895, son of Samuel Hutchinson and Ann Hutchinson. He was educated at Radcliffe Parish Church Schools, and joined the Army on 28 Sept. 1914, as a private in the 2/5th Battn. Lancashire Fusiliers. He served in the European War. On 28 June, 1916, a party of 63 N.C.O.'s and men and four officers were ordered to undertake a bombing raid. They reached their trench at 5 p.m., where they waited in dug-outs until gas and smoke-bombs were sent across to cover their whereabouts. This was done, and at 5.20 they made their way to an appointed spot. They then advanced 180 yards, at a walking pace, under cover of the smoke-bombs, until they came in view of the enemy, who began machine-gun and rifle fire, but failed to stop them, and they reached the wire, which had already been cut by artillery fire. They were then attacked by bombs. Private Hutchinson, as first bayonet man, entered the trench, and shot a man who was manipulating a machine gun through the head. He bayoneted a second and shot a third. On entering the second traverse he shot and bayoneted two more, and on entering the third, bayoneted and shot three more. In the fourth traverse he finished his ammunition, and was fortunate enough to escape unhurt, as the enemy were too upset to shoot straight. After the object was gained and retirement ordered he undertook the task, a very dangerous one, of covering the retirement, and then, on retiring himself, bandaged some of the wounded and led them back to the dressing station. During all this time this gallant soldier was exposed to fierce fire from machine guns and rifles at close quarters. He then carried a message from one end to the other of his battalion's lines to the Major of the Loyal North Lancashire Regt. He unfortunately lost his brother in this raid. He was told by the Major-General of the Division, who came to inspect them the following day, that he should have something to wear on his breast, and in the London Gazette of 9 Sept. 1916, his name appeared as having been awarded the Victoria Cross : " James Hutchinson, Private (now Corporal), No. 2579, Lancashire Fusiliers. For most conspicuous bravery. During an attack on the enemy's position this soldier was the leading man, and, entering their trench, shot two sentries and cleared two of the traverses. After our object had been gained and retirement ordered, Private Hutchinson, on his own initiative, undertook the dangerous task of covering the retirement, and he did this with such gallantry and determination that the wounded were removed into safety. During all this time this gallant soldier was exposed to fierce fire from machine guns and rifles at close quarters." He was always ready for any sport. He used to play football for his Sunday school team before the war.

JACKSON, WILLIAM, Private, No. 588, joined the Army in New South Wales, where he was a Labourer. He served in the European War, and was awarded the Victoria Cross [London Gazette, 9 Sept. 1916] : " William Jackson, No. 588, Private, 17th Battn. Australian Infantry. For most conspicuous bravery. On the return from a successful raid, several members of the raiding party were seriously wounded in ' No Man's Land ' by shell fire. Private Jackson got back safely, and after handing over a prisoner whom he had brought in, immediately went out again under a heavy shell fire and assisted in bringing in a wounded man. He then went out again, and with a sergeant was bringing in another wounded man, when his arm was blown off by a shell, and the sergeant was rendered unconscious. He then returned to our trenches, obtained assistance, and went out again to look for his two wounded comrades. He set a splendid example of pluck and determination. His work has always been marked by the greatest coolness and bravery." This took place near Armentières, France, 25–26 June, 1916.

William Jackson.

LEAK, JOHN, Private, joined the Army in Queensland, where he was a Teamster. He was awarded the Victoria Cross [London Gazette, 9 Sept. 1916] : " John Leak, No. 2053, Private, 9th Battn. Australian Infantry. For most conspicuous bravery. He was one of a party which finally captured an enemy strong point. At one assault, when the enemy's bombs were outranging ours, Private Leak rushed out of the trench, ran forward under heavy machine-gun fire at close range, and threw bombs into the enemy's bombing post. He then jumped into the post and bayoneted three unwounded enemy bombers. Later, when the enemy in overwhelming numbers was driving his party back, he was always the last to withdraw at each stage, and kept on throwing bombs. His courage and energy had

John Leak.

such an effect on the enemy that, on the arrival of reinforcements, the whole trench was recaptured." This was at Pozières, France, 23 July, 1916.

McFADZEAN, WILLIAM FREDERICK, Private, was born 9 Oct. 1895, at Lurgan, County Armagh, eldest son of William McFadzean and Mrs. McFadzean, of Rubicon, Cregagh, Belfast. He was educated at

William F. McFadzean.

Mountpottinger Boys' School and the Trade Preparatory School of the Municipal Technical Institute, Belfast, and subsequently became an apprentice in the firm of Spence, Brysin and Co. Ltd., 41, Great Victoria Street. An enthusiastic member of the Ulster Volunteer Force, No. 1 Battn. Ballynafeigh and Newtownbreda, East Belfast Regt., he joined on 22 Sept. 1914, as a private, the 14th (S.) Battn. Royal Irish Rifles (Y.C.V.'s). He was stationed at Finner Camp, Prandalstown, Seaford, and Liphook, and finally went to France with his battalion in Oct. 1915, and was killed in action 1 July, 1916. He was awarded the Victoria Cross [London Gazette, 9 Sept. 1916] : " William Frederick McFadzean, No. 14/18278, Private, late Royal Irish Rifles. For most

conspicuous bravery. While in a concentration trench and opening a box of bombs for distribution prior to an attack, when the box slipped down into the trench, which was crowded with men, and two of the safety pins fell out. Private McFadzean, instantly realizing the danger to his comrades, with heroic courage threw himself on the top of the bombs. The bombs exploded, blowing him to pieces, but only one other man was injured. He well knew the danger, being himself a bomber, but without a moment's hesitation gave his life for his comrades." The award was presented to his father by His Majesty the King, at Buckingham Palace, 28 Feb. 1917, who said : " I have very great pleasure in presenting to you the Victoria Cross for your son, the late Private McFadzean. I deeply regret that he did not live to receive it personally, but I am sure you are proud of your son ; nothing finer has been done in this war for which I have yet given the Victoria Cross, than the act performed by your son in giving his life so heroically to save the lives of his comrades." The Victoria Cross won by Private McFadzean was said to be the first awarded to the Royal Irish Rifles since the Crimean War, and the first Victoria Cross awarded to the 36th Ulster Division.

The following is a copy of a letter received from His Majesty the King :

" Buckingham Palace,
" 18 Dec. 1916.

" It is a matter of sincere regret to me that the death of Private McFadzean deprived me of the pride of personally conferring upon him the Victoria Cross, the greatest of all rewards for valour and devotion to duty.
(Signed) " GEORGE R.I.

" Mr. William McFadzean,
" Rubicon, Cregagh, Belfast."

Copy of letter received from Lieut.-Colonel F. C. Bowen, Officer Commanding 14th (Service) Battn. Royal Irish Rifles (Young Citizen Volunteers) :

" B.E.F.,
" 16 Sept. 1916.

" DEAR MR. McFADZEAN,
" It was with feelings of deep pride that I read the announcement of the granting of the V.C. to your gallant son, and my only regret is that he was not spared to us to wear his well-earned decoration. It was one of the very finest deeds of a war that is so full of big things, and I can assure you that the whole battalion rejoiced when they heard it.
" Your gallant boy, though gone from us, his deeds will for ever live in our memories, and the record will go down for all time in the ' Regimental History,' which he has added fresh and great lustre to.
" Yours sincerely,
" F. C. BOWEN,
" Lieutenant-Colonel Commanding
" 14th Battn. Royal Irish Rifles."

Copy of letter received from Lieut.-Colonel R. D. Spencer Chichester, who raised the 14th (S.) Battn. Royal Irish Rifles (Y.C.V.'s) :

" Eden Lodge,
" Dungiven,
" County Londonderry,
" 15 Sept. 1916.

" DEAR MRS. McFADZEAN,
" I feel that I must write to express to you my feeling of admiration for your son's splendid bravery.
" I was greatly grieved to hear of his death at the time that I heard of his magnificent and heroic deed. I did not write you then as I knew he was recommended for the Victoria Cross, and I waited to do so till it should have been definitely conferred on him.
" You must indeed be proud of such a son, and the thought of what he did must be a great consolation to you in your grief. I want to let you know that I am very proud of the fact that he served under me, and that he has added to the honour which his battalion has already won.
" It is not only his battalion which has every right to be proud of him, but the whole Ulster Division.
" No man could have died a nobler death.
" Believe me,
" Yours truly,
" R. SPENCER CHICHESTER,
" Lieutenant-Colonel."

Private W. F. McFadzean was a fine type of healthy young Ulsterman, standing six feet high, straight as a lath, and about 13 stone in weight. He was an enthusiastic junior player of the Collegians' Rugby Football Club, and was engaged in the linen business before enlisting in the famous Ulster Division, the 14th (Service) Battn. Royal Irish Rifles, which was locally, if not also officially, known as the Young Citizen Volunteers (Y.C.V.'s). He was most popular with his comrades, and many of them have expressed their regret at his loss and testified to his never failing cheerfulness under every circumstance. Only a few minutes before he made the great sacrifice he was singing his favourite song, "My Little Grey Home in the West." One who witnessed the occurrence says that on the way down from billets to the assembly trenches the late Private McFadzean was never in better spirits, keeping his platoon in laughter all the way. The trenches were about seven feet deep, and the bombs were being distributed to the bombers previous to the famous advance from Thiépval Wood (1 July, 1916). When Private McFadzean lifted a box (containing 12 Mills grenades) by the handle the box overturned, spilling the 12 bombs into the trench. He immediately threw himself flat on the bombs; two of them exploded, killing him and wounding the man on his left (Private George Gillespie), who had to have his left leg amputated above the knee. This happened early on the morning of the 1st July, about 1 o'clock. It was dark, and the trenches were under a terrific bombardment by the Germans, who had got news that the attack was to be made in the early hours of that morning. It appears that the ropes tying the boxes of bombs had all been cut across the front, possibly to facilitate distribution, but the men had not been told about it. It seems strange that the safety pins should drop out so easily in such a short distance, but these things will happen. A General wrote of Private McFadzean: "I know that his battalion, the 14th Royal Irish Rifles (the Y.C.V.'s), are immensely proud of his memory, and I am sure you must find consolation in the fact that he died so magnificently in saving the lives of his comrades and friends. Indeed I shall always be proud to remember that such a brave and heroic man was a soldier of the Brigade."

MILLER, JAMES, Private, was born at Taylor's Farm, Hoghton, near Preston, on 13 March, 1890, son of George Miller, and the late Mary Miller, of 1, Ollerton Terrace, Withnell, near Chorley. He entered the Army as a Private in the 7th Battn. Royal Lancaster Regt. He served in the European War, leaving for France on 18 July, 1915. "Taking part in the advanced fighting on 30 July, 1916, he was dispatched by his Battalion Commander for an important message to another part of the line. His journey was fraught with extreme peril, as he had to pass through a zone of terrific fire. He was mortally wounded, being shot through the stomach before he had proceeded very far, but pluckily continued his journey. He dropped down exhausted, but insisted on returning with the communication. He safely delivered his message, and after saying 'good-bye' to his comrades, he expired at his officer's feet. He gave his life with a supreme devotion to duty." He was awarded the

James Miller.

Victoria Cross [London Gazette, 9 Sept. 1916]: "James Miller, Private, late Royal Lancaster Regt. For most conspicuous bravery. His battalion was consolidating a position after its capture by assault, and Private Miller was ordered to taken an important message under heavy shell and rifle fire, and to bring back a reply at all costs. He was compelled to cross the open, and on leaving the trench was shot almost immediately in the back, the bullet coming out through his abdomen. In spite of this, with heroic courage and self-sacrifice he compressed with his hand the gaping wound in his adbomen, delivered his message, staggered back with the answer, and fell at the feet of the officer to whom he delivered it. He gave his life with a supreme devotion to duty." His Victoria Cross was given to his father, Mr. George Miller. A newspaper says: "Private James Miller, Royal Lancaster Regt., who 'gave his life with a supreme devotion to duty,' belonged to the little moorland village of Withnell, near Blackburn. He was 26 years of age, and six of his brothers are serving with the Colours. During his last furlough he told his sister that he had a presentiment that his end was near, adding that he would like to die a hero. Before the war Private Miller, who worked in a paper mill, was a popular local footballer."

O'MEARA, MARTIN, Private, No. 3970, was born in County Tipperary, and joined the Army in Western Australia, where he had been occupied as Sleeper Layer on the Railway. He served in the European War, and was awarded the Victoria Cross [London Gazette, 9 Sept. 1916, for his courage at Pozières, France, 9–12 Aug. 1916]: "Martin O'Meara, No. 3970, Private, 16th Battn. Australian Infantry. For most conspicuous bravery. During four days of very heavy fighting he repeatedly went out and brought in wounded officers and men from 'No Man's Land' under intense artillery and machine-gun fire. He also volunteered and carried up ammunition and bombs through a heavy barrage to a portion of the trenches which was being heavily shelled at the time. He showed throughout an utter contempt of danger, and undoubtedly saved many lives."

Martin O'Meara.

QUIGG, ROBERT, Private, is the son of Robert Quigg, of Giant's Causeway, Ireland, and of Mrs. Quigg. He worked on a farm before the war, and joined the Army in Sept. 1914, as a Private in the Royal Irish Rifles. He served in the European War, and was awarded the Victoria Cross [London Gazette, 9 Sept. 1916]: "Robert Quigg, No. 12/18645, Private, Royal Irish Rifles. For most conspicuous bravery. He advanced to the assault with his platoon three times. Early next morning, hearing a rumour that his platoon officer was lying out wounded, he went out seven times to look for him under heavy shell and machine-gun fire, each time bringing back a wounded man. The last man he dragged in on a waterproof sheet from within a few yards of the enemy's wire. He was seven hours engaged in this most gallant work, and finally was so exhausted that he had to give it up." The officer that Private Quigg sought to rescue was Sir Harry Macnaghten, who lives in the same district of North Antrim.

RITCHIE, WALTER POTTER, Drummer, was born in March, 1892, at 81, Hopehill Road, Glasgow, son of Walter Ritchie and Helen Monteith Ritchie, daughter of Mr. Murphy. He was formerly a Blacksmith's Apprentice, and an ardent member of the Episcopal Church, Troon, Glasgow. He joined the Army as a Drummer in the 8th Battn. Royal Scottish Rifles when under age. He was only sixteen when he joined the 2nd Battn. Seaforth Highlanders in Aug. 1908. There was some discussion on the question of getting him out of the Army in his family, but he had the last word. He served in the European War, and was at Mons and the Battle of the Aisne. He was awarded the Victoria Cross [London Gazette, 9 Sept. 1916]: "Walter Ritchie, No. 68, Drummer, Seaforth Highlanders.

Walter Potter Ritchie.

For most conspicuous bravery and resource, when on his own initiative he stood on the parapet of an enemy trench, and under heavy machine-gun fire and bomb attacks repeatedly sounded the 'Charge,' thereby rallying many men of various units, who, having lost their leaders, were wavering and beginning to retire. This action showed the highest type of courage and personal initiative. Throughout the day Drummer Ritchie carried messages over fire-swept ground, showing the greatest devotion to duty." He has been twice gassed and twice wounded (Oct. 1914, and July, 1916). He has also the French Croix de Guerre.

SHORT, WILLIAM, Private, was born at Eston, Middlesbrough, in Feb. 1901. His parents are both dead. He served in the European War as a Private in the 8th Battn. Alexandra, Princess of Wales's Own Yorkshire Regt. He died of wounds received in action on 7 Aug. 1916. He was posthumously awarded the Victoria Cross [London Gazette, 9 Sept. 1916]: "William Short, Private, late Yorkshire Regt. For most conspicuous bravery. He was foremost in the attack, bombing the enemy with great gallantry when he was severely wounded in the foot. He was urged to go back, but refused and continued to throw bombs. Later his leg was shattered by a shell, and he was unable to stand, so he lay in the trench adjusting detonators, and straightening the pins of bombs for his comrades. He died before he could be carried out of the trench. For the last eleven months he has always volunteered for dangerous enterprises, and has always set a magnificent example of bravery and devotion to duty." The Victoria Cross was awarded at an Investiture on 29 Nov. 1916, to his son, Mr. J. Short.

TURRALL, THOMAS GEORGE, Private, is the son of Mr. and Mrs. Turrall, of 23, Oakley Road, Small Heath, Birmingham. He joined the Army, and served in the European War, and was awarded the Victoria Cross [London Gazette, 9 Sept. 1916]: "Thomas George Turrall, No. 15888, Private, 10th Battn. Worcestershire Regt. For most conspicuous bravery and devotion to duty. During a bombing attack by a small party against the enemy, the officer in charge was badly wounded, and the party having penetrated the portion to a great depth, was compelled eventually to retire. Private Turrall remained with the wounded officer for three hours under continuous and very heavy fire from machine guns and bombs, and notwithstanding that both himself and the officer were at one time completely cut off from our troops, he held to his ground with determination, and finally carried the officer into our lines after our counter-attack had made this possible." The Lord Mayor of Birmingham (Alderman Neville Chamberlain) wrote to the parents of Private Turrall, who was the third Birmingham man to gain this distinction, expressing the pride with which the citizens had read of his gallant exploits: "I congratulate you upon having a son who has gained this distinction, so seldom awarded even in this war, in which heroism and courage are of daily occurrence." The first two Birmingham citizens to win the Victoria Cross were Lieut. James, of the Worcestershire Regt., and L.-Corpl. Vickers, of the Warwickshire Regt.

Theodore W. H. Veale.

VEALE, THEODORE WILLIAM HENRY, Private, was born in Clarence Street, Dartmouth, 11 Nov. 1893, eldest son of Henry Veale, Builder, and Ada Veale (Professional Pianist), of 12, Mansard Terrace, Dartmouth. He was educated at Dartmouth Council Schools, and joined the

Army on 4 Sept. 1914, as a Private in the 8th Devonshire Regt. (Buller's Own). He served in the European War, and won the Victoria Cross at Mametz Wood on 20 July, 1916, for rescuing a wounded officer under heavy shell fire. The award was announced in the London Gazette of 9 Sept. 1916 : " Theodore William Henry Veale, No. 10799, Private, Devon Regt. For most conspicuous bravery. Hearing that a wounded officer was lying out in front, Private Veale went out in search, and found him lying amidst growing corn within fifty yards of the enemy. He dragged the officer to a shell hole, returned for water, and took it out. Finding he could not single-handed carry in the officer, he returned for assistance, and took out two volunteers. One of the party was killed when carrying the officer, and heavy fire necessitated leaving the officer in a shell hole. At dusk Private Veale went out again with volunteers to bring in the officer. Whilst doing this an enemy patrol was observed approaching. Private Veale at once went back and procured a Lewis gun, and with the fire of the gun he covered the party, and the officer was finally carried to safety. The courage and determination displayed was of the highest order." He first heard of the high honour that he had won when the London papers reached the trenches. In a letter home he gave an account of the rescue. He stated that while he was in the trenches a cry for help was heard in front. A few minutes previously a man had been seen waving his hand, and it was thought that a German wanted to give himself up. On hearing the cry, however, he got out of the trench, went across the open under fire, and was surprised to find a wounded British officer close to the Germans. After describing the earlier part of his adventure, he said : " I crawled back again and got two more men and a corporal to come out with a waterproof sheet, which we put him on. We got about 80 yards, and when going over a bit of a bridge they shot the corporal through the head. I made the officer comfortable in a hole. I went back for a team and also for water. When evening came I led the way for our Chaplain, Rev. Crosse, D.S.O., Captain Duff, M.C., and Sergt. Smith, D.C.M. We reached him just before dark, and as we were about to carry him in we ' spotted' the Germans creeping up. I, not thinking, stood up and ran like hell about 150 yards to the trenches for my gun. I raced out again and covered him (the wounded officer) and the others while they got in with him." When he returned home the Mayor of Dartmouth presented him with a town's gift, consisting of an illuminated address and a silver coffee service and salver suitably inscribed. He was promoted Corporal in France on the same day he won the V.C., and his decoration was given him by the King at Buckingham Palace 5 Feb. 1917. During the time he was in Raglan Barracks he was being trained for the regimental sports by Lieut. Savill, whom he afterwards rescued. In the sports Private Veale was first in the mile race, first in the two-mile race, and second in the half-mile, in which last race Lieut. Savill was first.

A Dartmouth paper says :

" There was a considerable amount of excitement and quiet rejoicing in Dartmouth on Saturday when the news leaked through from unofficial quarters that Corpl. Theodore William Henry Veale, Devon Regt., had been awarded the Victoria Cross. Little knots of people gathered in the streets, clubs, hotels and cafés and eagerly discussed the good news, and lively satisfaction was expressed at the signal honour which young Veale has brought to his native town.

" He is well known in Dartmouth, for he is one of the best all-round athletes in the town. As a footballer he was a member of the Dartmouth United Football Association, and also the Dartmouth Athletic Reserves. At swimming, jumping and running he was continually to the fore, and his mother on Saturday with pride and pleasure showed ' The Western Morning News ' representative many trophies which he had won.

" The new V.C. is the eldest son of Mr. Henry Veale, a well-known Dartmouth builder, residing at 12, Mansard Terrace, in the Victoria Road, and the family has been in the town for many years. Mrs. Veale, Theodore's mother, is, however, a native of Plymouth. The gallant young corporal also holds the distinction of having been the very first in Dartmouth to respond to the call to arms. This was at the first of a series of meetings held in the town immediately after the outbreak of war. The meeting was presided over by Mr. Alderman Peek, who was at that time Mayor of Dartmouth, and so impressed was young Veale by the speeches that he led the way in responding to the invitation to enlist. As he sprang on the platform he was loudly applauded by his friends. That little incident is vividly remembered in Dartmouth to-day.

" Young Veale (who, by the way, is a teetotaler and non-smoker) was born in Clarence Street, Dartmouth, on 11 Nov. 1893. His brother, Sergt. Lawrence Veale, is serving with the Devons (Cyclist Battn.).

" A little while ago young Theodore wrote to his mother an account of the incident which won him the Cross. He wrote :

" ' Just a line to let you know I am now out for a rest, and am quite well. We have had a hot time. You will have seen in the papers about Somme Woods and the other places we have captured. I was in all that, and have come through without a scratch. I think a few of our Dartmouth lads have been wounded, and one I think is taken prisoner. I and Jimmy Bowers (another Dartmouth lad) are altogether all the time now. We have come a long way back by train. I took your parcel in action and ate what it contained under shell fire.

" ' I did a bit of rescue work whilst under heavy shell fire and rifle fire. Whilst we were in the trenches a company corporal said someone in front was waving his hand to come in. He said it was a German wanting to give himself up. Anyhow, we waited, and he didn't come. About twenty minutes afterwards I heard someone crying, " Help ! help ! " and I said to them, " Give me a rifle and a bomb," and out I went. I had only gone about 50 yards in the open when several shots went by me. I flopped down on the ground, but got up again and ran on until I got to the spot where the man had been seen waving. To my surprise it was one of our wounded officers. I laid down and did all I could for him, and I was well

fired at whilst I was there. He being so close to Germans, I pulled him back about 15 yards, for I found to my surprise that I was only about 10 yards from the Germans. I pulled him back, thinking they were going to pull him in. I went back to get some water, and I took it out to him. They fired at me again, and it is surprising how it was I was not hit. But I meant to save him at all costs ; so off I crawled back again, because it was all open, and I got two more men and a corporal to come out with a waterproof sheet, which we put him on.

" ' We tried to pull him back. We got about 80 yards back, and then had a rest, for you know how one's back aches after stooping. Well, the corporal stood up like on his knees, and we saw five Germans pop up out of the grass about 100 yards away. We had to go over a bit of a bridge, and they shot the corporal through the head. That made the other two with me nervous, and they wanted to get back. So I said, " Get back, and I'll manage." So they went, and I pulled the wounded officer into a hole, and left him comfortable, and went back. Then I sent a team out to cover any of them that might try to fire at him, and tracked out to him myself with water.

" ' When evening came I led the way for our Chaplain, who was also acting stretcher-bearer, Lieut. (now Capt.) Duff, and Sergt. Smith. We reached him just before dark, and as we were about to carry him in, we spotted Germans creeping up. Capt. Duff turned around and kept his eye on them with his revolver, and I, not thinking, stood up and ran like h— about 150 yards to the trench for my gun. I raced out again and covered him and the others while they ran in, and then, together with Mr Duff, got in safely. Don't you think I am lucky ? '

" It is freely rumoured in Dartmouth that the wounded officer whom Corpl Veale rescued was Lieut. Savill, a relative of Lord French."

Another cutting says :

" Corpl. Theodore W. H. Veale, V.C., has sent home to his father and mother, at Dartmouth, the following letter, which he has received from Mr. Edwin Savill, father of Lieut. Savill, the young officer whom the Dartmouth V.C. rescued from his perilous position in front of the German lines :

" ' 23, Leicester Terrace, Lancaster Gate,
" ' London, W.
" ' Dear Private Veale,   " ' 18 Sept. 1916.

" ' I was delighted to see your name among the list of V.C.'s last week. My son had told me of all you had done, and how persistent you had been in risking your life to save him. It was, therefore, very gratifying to see that your brave action had been recognized. I congratulate you upon earning an honour which is the most coveted in the British Army, but far more I congratulate myself in that one with your wonderful bravery was present—and thus my son is alive to-day. It must be a great thing to know that you have saved a son to his father and mother, and that but for the noble deed which you did they would for the rest of their lives be mourning his loss.

" ' I can assure you you have earned our unending gratitude. I hope you will let me have the pleasure of seeing you when you are in London, and that you will always let me hear from you if at any time I can be of service to you.   " ' Yours very truly,
" ' Edwin Savill.' "

" The following letter has also been received by Mr. Henry Veale from Colonel Burn, M.P. :

" ' 77, Cadogan Square, S.W.,
" ' Dear Mr. Veale,   " ' 19 Sept. 1916.

" ' I have just returned from the front, and take this, the first, opportunity of writing to offer you my most cordial congratulations on the heroism of your son, which has been recognized by the bestowal of the grandest of all distinctions—the V.C.

" ' Long may he live to wear it, and be an honour to Devon and Great Britain.

" ' Yours obediently,
" ' C. R. Burn.' "

London Gazette, 15 Sept. 1916.—" The King has been graciously pleased to approve the grant of the Victoria Cross to the undermentioned Officers in recognition of their bravery and devotion to duty as described in the foregoing despatch."

BINGHAM, EDWARD BARRY STEWART, Commander the Honourable, R.N., was born 26 July, 1881, at Bangor Castle, Bangor, Ireland. He is the third son of the 5th Baron Clanmorris and Lady Clanmorris. He was educated at Arnold House, and in H.M.S. Britannia, and joined

Edward B. S. Bingham.

the Navy as a Midshipman in 1897 He served as Lieutenant-Commander in H.M.S. Invincible in the Battle of the Bight of Heligoland, and later in the same ship in the Falkland Island victory, for which he was promoted to Commander. He took part in the Jutland Battle, and was awarded the Victoria Cross [London Gazette, 15 Sept. 1916] : " For the extremely gallant way in which he led his division in their attack, first on enemy destroyers and then on their battle cruisers. He finally sighted the enemy battle-fleet, and, followed by the one remaining destroyer of his division (Nicator), with dauntless courage he closed to within 3,000 yards of the enemy, in order to attain a favourable position for firin the torpedoes. While making this attack Nestor and Nicator were under concentrated fire of the secondary batteries of the High Sea Fleet. Nestor was subsequently sunk." The following account of the Battle of Jutland occurs in "Deeds that thrill the Empire" (pages 853–873): "It is not always realized by 'the man in the street' that in the exercise of sea-power, actual fighting plays a relatively small part. In land warfare, under modern conditions, the opposing forces are in absolutely continuous contact, and the ebb and flow of battle never ceases until one side is annihilated or driven to surrender. Naval war has never been like that. The ultimate object of the superior fleet is to control the seas—that is, to close the ocean highways completely to the enemy—and whether that control is secured either by the destruction of the hostile fleet or by instilling in it a healthy dread of putting its fate to the test of battle in the open is a matter of relative indifference. These few general remarks are necessary to preface the story of the greatest naval action of the first two years of war—and one, further, of the fiercest and most costly of which history has any record. In the early afternoon of 31 May, 1916, the light-cruiser scouts of the British Grand Fleet encountered off the north-western coast of Denmark some similar vessels belonging to the German navy. It transpired later that the German High Sea Fleet was 'out' in its full available strength, though with what object it had put to sea has not even yet been divulged. It is unlikely that the intention of its Commander-in-Chief, Admiral von Scheer, was to throw down the gage of battle to Sir John Jellicoe, nor, if he knew anything of the organization of our North Sea patrol, could he have hoped to cut off any appreciable part of our forces before reinforcements came up sufficient to deal comfortably with the German Navy. Speculation on these points is not of very much use. The facts—which are all that we have to deal with—are that when the advanced flotillas of the German fleet were somewhere near the Skagerrak—the first gateway into the Baltic—they found themselves engaged with the light craft standing out ahead of Vice-Admiral Sir David Beatty's Battle-Cruiser Division. It was at 2.20 in the afternoon that the curtain went up on a drama that was to prove to the hilt the valour and the efficiency of the British seaman of the twentieth century. At that hour the light cruiser Galatea, Commodore E. S. Alexander-Sinclair, senior ship in the fringe of scouts, wirelessed to the battle-cruisers astern that enemy ships were in sight. It was not a very uncommon message—indeed, it had been heard so often before without any sequel of importance that at first it quite failed to arouse any excitement. This time, however, events developed rapidly. As our scouts pushed on and extended their formation, they discovered the enemy to be in greater and still greater strength. From the seaplane-carrier Engadine an aerial scout was sent up, with Lieut. F. J. Rutland (an officer promoted from the ranks) as pilot, and Assistant Paymaster G. S. Trewin as observer; and although the clouds were so low that they had to fly at a height of only 900 feet, they were able to send back a message to the effect that the enemy was out in considerable force. Meantime, Sir David Beatty was bringing down his battle-cruisers, so that they could not get back to their bases in the Bight of Heligoland without a battle. Shortly after 3.30 he sighted five German battle-cruisers steaming full speed in a south-easterly direction —i.e., towards home—but the range of 23,000 yards was too great for effective gun-fire. He closed in towards the enemy, which was none other than the battle-cruiser squadron of the High Sea Fleet, under the command of Rear-Admiral Hipper, and in a quarter of an hour, when the distance between them had been reduced to 18,500 yards, the battle began. Before going any further, let it be said that there are two versions of this phase of the fight. One is that the Germans, finding themselves intercepted by superior forces, fled for their home waters for all they were worth. The other is that their intention was not so much to get home as to entice Beatty's ships down under the guns of the battle squadrons of the High Sea Fleet, which were coming up from the south under Von Scheer. Whatever the intentions were, however, it is the battle that matters. Sir David Beatty's flagship was the Lion, and with him were the Queen Mary, Princess Royal, Tiger, Indefatigable and New Zealand. Bringing up the rear, at a distance—unfortunately—of from 10,000 to 20,000 yards, was a division of fast battleships of the Queen Elizabeth class, under Rear-Admiral H. Evan-Thomas. The exact composition of the German battle-cruiser force is not certain, but it consisted of five ships which are believed to have been the Lützow, Derfflinger, Seydlitz, Moltke and Von der Tann. In any case, Sir David Beatty, even without the fast battleship division, had a very appreciable superiority, whether measured by numbers, the size of his ships, or the calibre of his guns. As the two forces ran south they fought with ever-increasing intensity. Our own ships had the superiority in gun-power, but the Germans were stoutly built and thickly armoured, and the high state of perfection to which their gunnery implements had been brought enabled them to inflict serious damage before our own gunnery began to tell upon their moral. The battle-cruisers Queen Mary (Capt. C. I. Prowse) and Indefatigable (Capt. C. F. Sowerby) were destroyed. That the Germans suffered heavily need not be emphasized. Time after time our salvos were seen to strike the enemy's ships, and although at this stage none was seen actually to sink, a vessel cannot sustain the impact of a number of 850, 1,250 or 1,400 lb. shells without severe damage. Our admirals were exceedingly reserved in their estimates of the injury inflicted on the enemy, and made no claim to have sunk a German ship unless it was actually seen to go down. It is obvious, however, that when a battle is being fought at the pace of twenty-eight miles an hour in a gathering, patchy mist, it is quite possible for an enemy ship reported as having been 'seen to leave the line' to have sunk a few minutes after without its last moments coming under the observation of the vessels responsible. Some of our destroyers, too, had a busy and fruitful time during this run south. Nominally, they accompanied the battle-cruisers in order to protect them against submarine attack (in which they succeeded to perfection), but opportunity came to them for still more effective work. At 4.15 a division of these vessels, under the command of Commander The Hon. E. B. S. Bingham, in the Nestor, moved out towards the enemy with the object of delivering a torpedo attack. On the way they met a flotilla of hostile destroyers setting out towards our own battle line with a similar object, and a fierce fight ensued between the opposing craft, in which two of the enemy's vessels were sunk without loss to us. The hostile attempt to attack our battle-cruisers was thus frustrated, and our boats pressed on with their original plan. The Nestor, Nomad and Nicator rushed in at the enemy under a terrific fire and discharged torpedoes at them. By all the rules of the game they should have been sunk with every man on board, and, as it was, the only one of the three to escape was the Nicator, whose commanding officer, Lieut. Jack Mocatta, was rewarded with the D.S.O. The Nestor and Nomad were both disabled within easy reach of the enemy's guns, and neither of them survived the experience, although, happily, many of those on board were saved by the enemy. These included Lieut.-Commander Paul Whitfield, in command of the Nomad, who was specially promoted to the rank of Commander, and Commander Bingham, of the Nestor, who was awarded the Victoria Cross for 'the extremely gallant way in which he led his division in their attack, first on the enemy destroyers, and then on their battle-cruisers. He finally sighted the enemy battle fleet, and, followed by the one remaining destroyer of his division (Nicator), with dauntless courage he closed to within 3,000 yards of the enemy in order to attain a favourable position for firing the torpedoes. While making this attack, Nestor and Nicator were under concentrated fire of the secondary batteries of the High Sea Fleet. Nestor was subsequently sunk.' In the meantime, our battle-cruisers, with the light cruisers of Commodore W. E. Goodenough's squadron spread out ahead, were still hotly engaged with Hipper's force. The battle was still travelling south at a high speed, and the German admiral doubtless thought he was leading Beatty on into a trap from which he would be unable to extricate himself. Soon after 4.35, however, the Southampton—Goodenough's flagship in the scouting squadron—signalled the approach from the south of the German battle fleet. It was one of the crucial moments of the fight. If Beatty, who now had the enemy battle-cruisers well in hand, had gone on, he would certainly have been annihilated; but he obviously had nothing to gain by throwing his ships away. He might have turned off sharp to the right —to the west—making for England and safety; but that was not the game. From the British point of view the battle was only beginning. Our battle-cruisers turned a complete half-circle. Where they had been running almost due south, they turned almost to due north. Where they had been steaming down into the jaws of the High Sea Fleet's battle squadrons they now began to play a game of their own—to lead the Germans back to the main divisions of the Grand Fleet. When the battle began Sir John Jellicoe with his battle squadrons had not been very far behind the battle-cruisers, but the high speed of the latter had widened the gap by many miles. It was 4.42 when Sir David Beatty turned his squadron about to avoid the German battle fleet, and another hour and a quarter passed, with hot fighting every inch of the way, before the leading battle-ships of the Grand Fleet were sighted five miles to the north. The action was now reaching its real culminating point. In spite of the loss of two of his ships, Sir David Beatty was gradually driving the enemy further and further towards the Danish coast, and when our battleships were sighted he saw that the supreme moment had arrived. He put on speed, and, turning sharp to the east, drove straight across the head of the enemy's line. As he did so, a fresh division of battle-cruisers, led by Rear-Admiral the Hon. Horace Hood in the Invincible, took station ahead of Beatty's division, and although the Invincible was destroyed in the close-range mêlée that followed, the German force was thrown into the utmost confusion by our tactics. So completely were they demoralized that two of our most lightly-armed cruisers, the Yarmouth and the Falmouth, carrying only eight 6-inch guns apiece, stood in towards the leading ships of the enemy, which carried 11 and 12-inch guns, and fired their guns and torpedoes at them for some time without sustaining any injury themselves. For some time now the weather had been growing unfavourable. Before the Grand Fleet came in sight the sea was covered with a patchy fog that enabled our ships to get only an occasional glimpse of the enemy, and as our battleships came down from the north they found it difficult to tell friend from foe—for one ship is very much like another in a mist at 20,000 yards. Nevertheless, the Grand Fleet came into action magnificently, and it was only robbed by the fortune of war from reaping the full harvest of Sir David Beatty's gallantry and skill. The latter officer had himself escaped from the trap the Germans had prepared for him. More than that, he had led the Germans on into such a position that, with ordinary luck on our side—or with an absence of luck on either side—the enemy could have looked for little short of annihilation. Then it was that Nature had her say. The mists deepened. Our leading battleships had not been in action more than a few minutes before the sea became so obscured that the battle degenerated into a sort of blind-man's buff. By this time it is beyond the slightest doubt that the enemy had no other thought than to escape the overwhelming force arrayed against him—and the circumstances were all in his favour. From the easterly course on to which he had been driven by Sir David Beatty, he turned first to the south and then to the south-west, and when, towards nine o'clock at night, our main squadrons caught their last glimpse of the enemy, he was apparently heading for the open sea. Throughout the night there were occasional bursts of fighting as opposing groups or single ships sighted each other for a few minutes in the darkness, but under such conditions there could be no approach to organized battle. In the misty night the enemy—or what remained of him—succeeded in getting back to his ports, and although our ships scoured the scene of action until well past noon on 1 June, no trace of a hostile ship was found. If, therefore, it had been the intention of the enemy to challenge our command of the sea, he had suffered a signal defeat, for he had been pulled up within two hundred miles of his bases—and on his own side of the North Sea—and compelled to abandon all pretence of commanding even the immediate neighbourhood of his own waters. It is still too early to say what were the material results of the action. On our own side we lost the battle-cruisers Queen Mary, Indefatigable and Invincible, the armoured cruisers Defence, Black Prince and Warrior, and the destroyers Ardent, Fortune, Nomad, Nestor, Shark, Sparrowhawk, Tipperary and Turbulent. Sir John Jellicoe's estimate of the German losses was as follows: Two battleships of the Dreadnought type and one pre-Dreadnought were seen to sink, and another Dreadnought was so severely damaged that her survival was doubtful. One battle-cruiser (the Lützow) was sunk, and another probably sunk. Five light cruisers were sent to the bottom, six destroyers were seen to sink, and three more were so damaged that they could hardly have survived the drubbing. Finally, one submarine was sunk. When it is realized that practically the whole of the first-line fighting strength of the British and German navies was engaged in this action, it will be understood that it is impossible to chronicle here even the names of those who were rewarded for their distinguished service. The incident which appealed most strongly to the nation was one in which the hero was one of the most junior ratings in the Fleet. This lad, 'Boy (First Class) John Travers Cornwell,' was the only person, other than an officer, mentioned in the original dispatches of Admiral Sir John Jellicoe and Vice-Admiral Sir David Beatty, and these were the words that were used: 'The fortitude of the wounded was admirable. A report from the commanding officer of the Chester' (a light cruiser) 'gives a splendid instance of devotion to duty. Boy (First Class) John Travers Cornwell, of the Chester, was mortally wounded early in the action. He, nevertheless, remained standing alone at a most exposed post, quietly awaiting orders until the end of the action, with the gun's crew dead and wounded all round him. His age was under sixteen and a half years. I regret that he has since died,' wrote Admiral Beatty, 'but I recommend his case for special recognition in justice to his memory, and as an acknowledgment of the high example set by him.' The posthumous award of the Victoria Cross was made, and various projects were set on foot whereby the lad's example could be preserved for all time. A third award of the V.C. was made in the case of Major F. J. W. Harvey, Royal Marine Light Infantry, of H.M.S. Lion, who, 'whilst mortally wounded and almost the only survivor after the explosion of an enemy shell in "Q" gunhouse with great presence of mind and devotion to duty ordered the magazine to be flooded, thereby saving the ship. He died shortly afterwards.' It is not the custom of the Admiralty to publish themselves, or to allow anyone else to publish, details of incidents in which petty officers and men of the Fleet have distinguished themselves. For their work in the Jutland Bank battle—by which name this action is officially known—Sir John Jellicoe was made a member of the Order of Merit, Sir David Beatty was promoted from K.C.B. to G.C.B., and Knighthoods of the Bath were bestowed upon Rear-Admiral Evan-Thomas and Rear-Admiral W. C. Pakenham, the latter being second in command of the Battle-Cruiser Squadron under Beatty. A large number of officers were promoted, and others were appointed C.B., D.S.O. or D.S.C., while the rewards for the rank and file included (besides the V.C. already mentioned) fifteen Conspicuous Gallantry Medals and 196 Distinguished Service Medals, while one petty officer received a bar to a D.S.M. already won. One particular incident may be mentioned as showing how much a D.S.M. may mean in the Navy. When writing on the Jutland Battle at the invitation of the Admiralty, Mr. Rudyard Kipling, describing the experiences of a destroyer, said: 'There were also three wise men who saved the ship, whose names must not be forgotten. They were Chief Engine-Room Artificer Lee, Stoker Petty Officer Gardiner and Stoker Elvins. When the funnel carried away, it was touch and go whether the foremost boiler would not explode. These three "put on respirators, and kept the fans going until all fumes, etc., were cleared away." To each man, you will observe, his own particular Hell, which he entered of his own particular initiative.' These three men, it will be seen, saved a ship between them. They also shared a single Distinguished Service Medal between them, Stoker Elvins being the recipient. If three men who save a warship share one D.S.M., one is left to imagine what was done by the other 195 winners of the D.S.M. in the battle of Jutland Bank. The full story of the Jutland honours and how they were won would occupy a volume in itself, and one is compelled to mention only a few, and those in the briefest possible terms. Mention has already been made of Flight-Lieut. Rutland, who went up in a seaplane to observe the enemy's strength before the action began. He was awarded the D.S.C. for this, but he was to win a second distinction. When the action was at its height the armoured cruiser Warrior was caught by the concentrated fire of the enemy and completely disabled, though, fortunately, she was not sunk. She drifted about for some time, perfectly helpless, until at last the seaplane-carrier Engadine came up and took her in tow. It was thought then that the cruiser would last out, but she made but slow progress towards England, and at last it was decided to abandon and sink her. In darkness and a rough sea the bulk of the crew were transferred in safety, but while a wounded seaman was being passed across to the Engadine in a stretcher the rolling of the ships threw him into the water. Two or three men in the Engadine immediately asked permission to go over the side to rescue him, but the captain refused. The ships were bumping together, and it certainly seemed madness to attempt a rescue. But Lieut. Rutland, who saw the whole incident, happened not to be near any superior officer. He therefore asked no one's permission, but jumped overboard at once. Thanks to his aid, the wounded man was hoisted on board the Engadine; but unfortunately he had been so badly crushed between the rolling ships that life was already extinct. Lieut. Rutland was awarded the Albert Medal for this gallant action. For the rest, one can only take a few typical cases from the official report: Capt. E. M. Phillpotts (H.M.S. Warspite): 'At a critical time, when the Fifth Battle Squadron was turning to form astern of the battle fleet, under a heavy fire, the Warspite, owing to a breakdown in her steering gear, turned towards the enemy, and got into a very dangerous position. She was splendidly handled, however, and got away to the northward clear of the enemy's fire. Also, when nearing the Firth of Forth, much damaged, she was attacked by three submarines, and was handled in such a manner as to get her safely into port.' Capt. Phillpotts was awarded the C.B. Fleet-Surgeon Alexander Maclean (H.M.S. Lion): 'Performed his exhausting duties with the greatest zeal and courage. The medical staff was seriously depleted by casualties; the wounded and dying had to be dressed under very difficult conditions on the mess-deck, which was flooded with a foot of water from damaged fire mains.' Awarded the D.S.O. Boatswain W. H. Fenn (H.M.S. Barham): 'Specially recommended. Was in charge of the after repair party and worked in fumes until he was overcome and removed. He returned again to the same work as soon as he had regained consciousness, and rendered invaluable services. Mr. Fenn had only returned from hospital the day before the action.' Noted for early promotion. Chief Gunner Alexander Grant (H.M.S. Lion): 'With the greatest zeal and coolness went from magazine to magazine to encourage the crews in maintaining a rapid supply of ammunition, also in taking charge of fire parties and extinguishing several extensive fires.' Promoted to Lieutenant. Lieut. R. M. Porter, Royal Naval Reserve (H.M.S. Barham): 'After having been severely burned in the cordite explosion at No. 2 starboard 6-inch gun, Lieut. Porter personally superintended the extinction of the fire and removal of wounded, and remained at his post for two hours after, when swelling from burns had closed his eyes and rendered his hands useless. His condition when he reached the medical party was critical.' Promoted to Lieutenant-Commander. These must be taken as typical of the Navy's work in the Jutland Battle, the first really great naval action of the war, from which the enemy escaped only because of the failing daylight and the rising fog. Its effect is to be measured not by the losses sustained on either side, the full extent of which we cannot yet know, but by the interval which elapses between 1 June, 1916, and the next (or should we say the first?) attempt on the part of the High Sea Fleet to challenge the supremacy of the Grand Fleet." Commander the Hon. E. B. S. Bingham was also twice mentioned in Despatches by Admiral Beatty 24 Aug. 1916. He was taken prisoner by the Germans on this occasion. In 1915 he married Vera, only child of Edward Temple Patterson, Esq. A keen lover of sport, he captained the Navy Polo Team for some years at Malta with success, and has ridden winners in various countries.

HARVEY, FRANCIS JOHN WILLIAM, Major, was born 29 April, 1873, and joined the Royal Marines 1 Sept. 1892, as Second Lieutenant, becoming Lieutenant 1 July, 1895, Captain 16 Jan. 1900, and Major 22 Jan. 1911. He served in the European War, and was present at the Jutland Battle, where he won the Victoria Cross [London Gazette, 15 Sept. 1916]: "Francis John William Harvey, Major, R.M.L.I. Whilst mortally wounded and almost the only survivor after the explosion of an enemy shell in a gunhouse, with great presence of mind and devotion to duty, ordered the magazine to be flooded, thereby saving the ship. He died shortly afterwards."

CORNWELL, JOHN TRAVERS, Boy, First Class, Royal Navy, was born on 8 Jan. 1900, at Leyton, son of Eli and Alice Cornwell. He was educated at Walton Road School, Manor Park. He wished to be a sailor when he left school, but his parents could not bear the thought of losing him so soon, so he bravely turned to the work that lay to his hand, and became a boy on a Brooke Bond's tea van. He was also a keen Boy Scout, and held two certificates. When the European War broke out his father promptly joined the Army, and Jack Cornwell was given his chance to join the Navy. He went through preliminary training at Devonport from 27 July, 1915, and became a First Class Boy on H.M.S. Chester for active service in Admiral Beatty's North Sea Squadron. A few months after Jack Cornwell joined his ship, Admiral Beatty came to grips with the German High Seas Fleet near Jutland, 31 May, 1916; he was mortally wounded in action, and died two days later in Grimsby hospital. He was posthumously awarded the Victoria Cross [London Gazette, 15 Sept. 1916]: "John Travers Cornwell, Boy (First Class), O.N.J. 42563. Mortally wounded early in the action, Boy, First Class, John Travers Cornwell remained standing alone at a most exposed post, quietly awaiting orders, until the end of the action, with the gun's crew dead and wounded around him. His age was under sixteen and a half years."

John Travers Cornwell.

The story of his brave deed was told in the following letter, written to his mother by the Captain of his ship:

"I know you would wish to hear of the splendid fortitude and courage shown by your son during the action of 31 May. His devotion to duty was an example for all of us. The wounds which resulted in his death within a short time were received in the first few minutes of the action. He remained steady at his most exposed post at the gun, waiting for orders. His gun would not bear on the enemy; all but two of the ten crew were killed or wounded, and he was the only one who was in such an exposed position. But he felt he might be needed, and, indeed, he might have been; so he stayed there, standing and waiting, under heavy fire, with just his own brave heart and God's help to support him. I cannot express to you my admiration of the son you have lost from this world. No other comfort would I attempt to give to the mother of so brave a lad, but to assure her of what he was, and what he did, and what an example he gave. I hope to place in the boys' mess a plate with his name on and the date, and the words, 'Faithful unto Death.' I hope some day you may be able to come and see it there. I have not failed to bring his name prominently before my Admiral."

Admiral Sir David Beatty himself, in his official Despatch describing the battle, wrote :

"Boy (First Class) John Travers Cornwell, of the Chester, was mortally wounded early in the action. He, nevertheless, remained standing alone at a most exposed post, quietly awaiting orders till the end of the action, with the gun's crew dead and wounded all round him. His age was under 16½ years. I regret that he has since died, but I recommend his case for special recognition in justice to his memory, and as an acknowledgment of the high example set by him."

The following article appeared in the "Daily Telegraph," 26 Nov. 1919 :

"Admiral of the Fleet Earl Beatty was the guest of the Cheshire Society in London at a dinner given in his honour at the Princes Restaurant last night. The Duke of Westminster presided, and among others present were the Lord Chancellor and Lady Birkenhead, the Countess Beatty, and the Lord Mayor and the Lady Mayoress. The Duke of Westminster, proposing the health of Earl Beatty, said that as Cheshire men they claimed him as their own. The manner in which he had carried out his duty had been the wonder of the whole world. Earl Beatty, in responding, said his connections with Cheshire were those of youth. He came to Cheshire when he was one year old. (Laughter.) He was an Irishman, and he was proud of it, but he was prouder still that an Irishman should be honoured by the glorious heart of Cheshire. Cheshire might well be proud of the record of the ship Chester, to which its county town had contributed, and which had worthily upheld the great tradition of the Service. The story was in the minds of the whole Empire how a boy showed what a boy could do in the way of making history, and giving an example of how English boys should live and how English boys should die. The story of the boy Cornwell, of his Majesty's ship Chester, was a record which added to the glorious pages of England. (Cheers.) The Lord Chancellor, in proposing 'The Visitors,' remarked that it would have been more creditable to those who controlled the early movements of Lord Beatty if he had appeared in Cheshire before he was a year old. (Laughter.) Nevertheless, despite the misfortune of his birth—(laughter)—they gave him a sincere welcome. Cheshire had three associations with naval history—the ancestor of Lord Howard of Effingham was a Cheshire woman ; Lady Hamilton also was a Cheshire woman ; and Lord Beatty was nearly a Cheshire man (Laughter.) The Lord Mayor responded. Cheshire, he said, was noted for its cheese. Cheese fed mice, mice fed cats, and the cat made Whittington Lord Mayor of London. (Laughter.)"

The "Times History of the War" says, in Vol. II., page 189, of Jack Cornwell:

"He was only a boy, under sixteen and a half years of age ; yet no record of the Cross was more impressive than that of his behaviour in the Jutland battle : Mortally wounded early in the action, he remained standing alone at a most exposed post, quietly awaiting orders, until the end of the action, with the gun's crew dead and wounded all round him. Some time elapsed before the steadfast courage of the boy was made known. Meanwhile he had been brought ashore, he had died at Grimsby of his wounds, and through one of the stupid blunders which are inseparable from officialdom he had been buried in what was no better than a pauper's grave. No sooner was the truth known of the lad's last hours of life and the manner of his death than public opinion demanded a befitting reinterment. Accordingly the body was exhumed, and there was an impressive funeral in Manor Park Cemetery. A few months afterwards the boy's father, Eli Cornwell, who had joined the Army, was buried in the same grave." . . . A committee was formed to organize a national memorial to Jack Cornwell. and £21,849 13s. 11½d. was raised. "A picture of the boy, standing by his gun, with Admiral Sir David Beatty's report of the incident, occupies a position of honour in more than 12,000 schools. At Buckingham Palace, on 9 February, 1917, the Queen received the members of the Jack Cornwell Memorial Fund Committee, who presented to her the first instalment of the proceeds of the appeal. Admiral Lord Beresford presented an address explaining the objects of the fund and the means adopted to carry them out. One form of the memorial was a contribution of £18,000 collected in the schools and by scholars of the United Kingdom to the 'Star and Garter' Fund, and it was proposed as another part of the scheme to place a portrait of Cornwell in each of the contributing schools. In accepting a cheque for £18,000, the Queen said : 'I am glad to know that in every school where the scholars have contributed to this memorial a picture of Jack Cornwell will be placed, which will serve to remind future generations of scholars in those schools of the lasting glory that attaches to the performance of duty.' On 23 March, 1917, a large company witnessed at the Mansion House the presentation to the Board of Admiralty of Mr. Frank O. Salisbury's picture, 'John Cornwell, V.C., on H.M.S. Chester.' Sir Edward Carson, the First Lord, received the picture on behalf of the Admiralty. The picture showed the lad standing by the side of a gun, which had just been fired. The inscription gave the official details of Cornwell's act. The artist unveiled the picture, and in formally presenting it to the Admiralty, said that the studies were taken on board the Chester. Cornwell's brother sat for the portrait. The captain, on being asked for a title for the picture, replied that he knew of none which was more appropriate than this : 'Thou hast set my feet in a large place.' In accepting the gift on behalf of the Admiralty, Sir Edward Carson paid a high tribute to the dead lad's courage and example. 'I ask people who grumble,' he said, 'if they ever heard the story of John Travers Cornwell. . . . I feel that this boy, who died at the post of duty, sends this message through me as First Lord of the Admiralty for the moment to the people of the Empire : "Obey your orders, cling to your post, don't grumble, stick it out." ' "

London Gazette, 26 Sept. 1916.—"His Majesty the King has been graciously pleased to award the Victoria Cross to the undermentioned Officers, Non-commissioned Officers and Men."

ADDISON, THE REV. WILLIAM ROBERT FOUNTAINE, was the son of the late W. G. Addison, of Goudhurst, and Alice Addison, of Cranbrook, Kent. He was educated at Salisbury Theological College, and was ordained and became curate of St. Edmund's, Salisbury, in 1913. During his curacy at Salisbury he acted as assistant chaplain to the Church Lads' Brigade. He had some years previously had experience of work in a Canadian lumber camp, work which fitted him in a particular sense for that of an Army Chaplain. He joined the Army as a Fourth Class Chaplain to the Forces, and served in the European War in Mesopotamia. He was awarded the Victoria Cross [London Gazette, 26 Sept. 1916] : "The Reverend William Robert Fountaine Addison, Chaplain. For most conspicuous bravery at Sannaiyat, Mesopotamia. He carried a wounded man to the cover of a trench, and assisted several others to the same cover, after binding up their wounds under heavy rifle and machine-gun fire. In addition to these unaided efforts, by his splendid example and utter disregard of personal danger, he encouraged the stretcher-bearers to go forward under heavy fire and collect the wounded." He was awarded the Order of St. George of Russia. Mr. Addison was married, at Christ Church, Brighton, to Marjorie, daughter of the late W. E. Wallis, of Caterham.

BAXTER, EDWARD FELIX, Second Lieut., served in the European War, and was awarded the Victoria Cross [London Gazette, 26 Sept. 1916, for his bravery near Blairville, France, 17–18 April, 1916 : "Edward Felix Baxter, Second Lieut., 1/8th Battn. King's Liverpool Regt. (Territorial Force). For most conspicuous bravery. Prior to a raid on the hostile line he was engaged during two nights in cutting wire close to the enemy's trenches. The enemy could be heard on the other side of the parapet. Second Lieut. Baxter, while assisting in the wire-cutting, held a bomb in his hand with the pin withdrawn ready to throw. On one occasion the bomb slipped and fell to the ground, but he instantly picked it up, unscrewed the base plug, and took out the detonator, which he smothered in the ground, thereby preventing the alarm being given and undoubtedly saving many casualties. Later he led the left storming party with the greatest gallantry, and was the first man into the trench, shooting the sentry with his revolver. He then assisted to bomb dug-outs, and finally climbed out of the trench and assisted the last man over the parapet. After this he was not seen again, though search parties went out at once to look for him. There seems no doubt that he lost his life in his great devotion to duty."

BELL, ERIC NORMAN FRANKLAND, Temporary Capt., was the son of Capt. E. H. Bell. On the outbreak of the European War was assistant to Professor Riley in the School of Architecture, Liverpool University. He joined the Army, served in the European War, and was awarded the Victoria Cross [London Gazette, 26 Sept. 1916] : "Eric Norman Frankland Bell, Temporary Capt., 9th Battn. Royal Inniskilling Fusiliers. For most conspicuous bravery. He was in command of a Trench Mortar Battery, and advanced with the infantry in the attack. When our front line was hung up by enfilading machine-gun fire, Capt. Bell crept forward and shot the machine gunner. Later, on no less than three occasions, when our bombing parties, which were clearing the enemy's trenches, were unable to advance, he went forward alone and threw trench-mortar bombs among the enemy. When he had no more bombs available, he stood on the parapet, under intense fire, and used a rifle with great coolness and effect on the enemy advancing to counter-attack. Finally, he was killed rallying and reorganizing infantry parties which had lost their officers. All this was outside the scope of his normal duties with his battery. He gave his life in his supreme devotion to duty." This took place at Thiépval, France 1 July, 1916.

BUCHANAN, ANGUS, Capt., was born 11 Aug. 1894, at The Old Bank House, Coleford, Gloucestershire. He is the son of Dr. Peter Buchanan, M.B., C.M., J.P., V.D., Deputy Coroner for the Forest of Dean, Major 2nd (Volunteer) Battn. Gloucestershire Regt. He was educated first at St. John's Boys' School, and in 1905 went to Monmouth Grammar School. Here he became captain of the school and captain of the football. He was also in the cricket team and rowing crew, and was Colour-Sergeant of the School Cadet Corps. He beat the school record (which had stood for thirty-two years) for putting the weight (1912). Added to his athletic prowess, he was studiously inclined, and for three years running carried off the essay prize. On leaving Monmouth in 1913, he obtained a scholarship at Jesus College, Oxford. He played in Oxford University Rugby Freshmen's Trials and in Oxford University A team 1913–14, and he was also in the Officers' Training Corps. His golf handicap was four. Directly the Great War broke out he applied for a commission, and was gazetted Second Lieutenant in the South Wales Borderers (4th Battn.) on 25 Nov. 1914. He went to Gallipoli in June, 1915, and was wounded on 7 Aug. of the same year at Suvla Bay and sent to Cairo to hospital. In Jan. 1916, he was promoted Temporary Captain when he won the Military Cross for his bravery at Helles on 7 Jan. [London Gazette, 3 June, 1916]. He was on this occasion twice mentioned in Despatches [London Gazette, 15 May, 1917] for his gallant conduct. He took part in the evacuation of the Dardanelles, and after a month's rest went to Mesopotamia. Here at Falaniyah Lines he won the Victoria Cross [London Gazette, 26 Sept. 1916] : "Angus Buchanan, Lieut. (Temporary Capt.), 4th Battn. South Wales Borderers. Date of Act of Bravery : 5 April, 1916. During an attack an officer was lying out in the open severely wounded about 150 yards from cover. Two men went to his assistance and one of them was hit at once. Capt. Buchanan, on seeing this, imme-

Angus Buchanan.

diately went out and, with the help of the other man, carried the wounded officer to cover under heavy machine-gun fire. He then returned and brought in the wounded man, again under heavy fire." He was wounded again in the evening of the same day. For some months he was in India recovering from his second wound, and when he returned to the front was wounded again 13 Feb. 1917, losing the sight of both eyes as a result. On 2 Sept. 1917, he relinquished his commission on account of wounds, retaining the rank of Captain. He was mentioned also in Mespotamia Despatches [London Gazette, 17 Oct. 1916], and he holds the Order of St. Vladimir, Fourth Class (with Swords). "The Dean Forest Guardian," 29 Sept. 1916, says: "It was our great pleasure to announce in 'The Guardian' of 9 June last that Lieut. (Temporary Capt.) Angus Buchanan, elder son of Dr. and Mrs. Buchanan, of Old Bank House, Coleford, had been awarded the Military Cross for gallant conduct in the field, and now has come to hand the news of an even greater honour which has been conferred upon him, no less than that of winning the Victoria Cross. That Coleford has been stirred by the announcement can readily be imagined; the inhabitants are, indeed, proud of the gallant young officer, as they have every reason to be. We feel sure that a brief biography of Capt. Buchanan will be read with interest by our readers. He was born at Coleford on the 11th Aug. 1894, so that he has recently entered upon his twenty-third year. He received his early education at the St. John's Boys' School, and in 1905 went to the Monmouth Grammar School, where he was held in much esteem by the head master (Mr. Lionel James), the other members of the staff and his fellow-scholars. He was naturally studiously inclined, and rapidly made headway, and for the last two years of his stay was head of the school, for three years in succession carrying off the essay prize. At the same time, he did not disregard the pleasure and benefit to be derived from participating in games, and was one of the best all-round athletes the Monmouth School has turned out. He gained his colours at cricket and Rugby football, besides being a member of the rowing crew, and he gained his first knowledge of drill in the Cadet Corps, in which he attained the rank of Colour-Sergeant. In 1912 he beat the school record (which had stood for thirty-two years) of putting the weight, exceeding the previous best by two feet three inches. Upon leaving Monmouth at the close of the summer term in 1913, he obtained a scholarship at Jesus College, Oxford, where he was in residence at the time war was declared. He immediately applied for a commission, chafing under the delay which ensued before he was appointed to a Second Lieutenancy in the South Wales Borderers. In the early summer of last year he proceeded with his regiment to Gallipoli, and in Aug. was wounded at Suvla Bay, being sent into hospital at Cairo, where he remained for some time. Soon after rejoining his regiment he was recommended for distinguished conduct at Helles on 7 Jan., for which he was subsequently awarded the Military Cross, his name appearing in the last King's Birthday Honours List. Later he took part in the evacuation of the Dardanelles, and after a month's rest, saw service in Mesopotamia. It was on 5 April, on this front, that he gained the coveted honour which has now been bestowed upon him, and some weeks later Dr. Buchanan received the following letter from the Lieut.-Colonel commanding the battalion:

"'8 April, 1916.

"'DEAR DR. BUCHANAN,

"'I regret to say that your son Angus was wounded in the arm on the evening of 5 April, when we were attacking and driving back the Turks, but I am very glad to tell you that the wound was only a slight one. The real reason for my letter is a far more pleasant one. During our advance in the morning we came under very heavy machine-gun fire, and suffered rather heavily. One of our officers, Lieut. Hemingway, was badly wounded, and lying in the open about 150 yards from cover. Your son, seeing his condition, and that the effort on the part of two men to carry him in had ended in one of them being shot, himself left his trench, and with the help of the unwounded man, brought Hemingway into the trench under a heavy fire. During the journey the man with him was wounded in the foot, but got into the trench. Angus then went back and fetched in the other man who had been wounded. I have forwarded a recommendation in his case for the Victoria Cross, and the Brigadier has sent in one and supported it. We sincerely hope he may be awarded it, but there is always a chance that he may only be awarded an honour of a lesser degree.

"'I should like to tell you that I have previously brought his name to the notice of the General for gallant conduct at Helles on 7 Jan.

"'Yours sincerely,

"'————————,

"'Lieut.-Colonel Commanding — South Wales Borderers.'"

"For some four months Capt. Buchanan was in India recovering from his second wound, and the last news is that he is once more in the fighting line. It is the sincere hope of his many friends that he will long be spared to enjoy his well-merited reward. The information that he had been gazetted for the V.C. was received with great elation in Coleford, and also by the masters and boys of his old school at Monmouth. When the news was announced on the screen at Coleford Cinema on Tuesday evening, the large audience assembled to witness the official film of 'The Battle of the Somme,' cheered vociferously. After the announcement had appeared in Wednesday morning's paper the bell in the old church tower was rung in honour of 'Coleford's V.C.' Capt. Buchanan's father was for some twenty-five years in the 'G' (Coleford) Company of Rifle Volunteers, for a considerable part of the time being officer in command, and retiring with the rank of Major. Dr. and Mrs. Buchanan have been the recipients of many congratulations on their son's notable achievement." A Bristol newspaper describes the investiture and the scene on Durdham Down: "For the investiture a large square had been barricaded off near the Reservoir, on the Westbury side of the Stoke Road. At the King's special wish, the troops on parade were marshalled in such a way as to give the largest possible number of civilians a clear view of the ceremony. The Royal daïs was draped in Imperial purple bearing in relief gilded lions' heads. A battalion of the Inland Waterways and Docks Transports, R.E., 800 strong, was drawn up inside that part of the square nearest to the city. On the opposite side of the square was the Bristol Volunteer Regt., while at that side of the square which faced the daïs were Bristol University O.T.C., Clifton College O.T.C., and the Bristol Grammar School contingent of the O.T.C. Also facing the daïs, but very much nearer to it, was a smart Guard of Honour of the 3rd Officer Cadet Battn., at the rear of which had been placed the band of the I.W. and D.T., R.E. Between the Guard of Honour and the daïs had been provided seats for the 127 recipients of decorations and medals, and on each side of that group were accommodated large parties of wounded soldiers. Soldiers and police had been placed at intervals along the inside of the barricade. Two Victoria Cross winners who had already been decorated were present—Sergt. T. E. Rendle, D.C.L.I., Bristol's first V.C. of this war, and Sergt. Cator. The path leading to the daïs was lined by members of the 3rd Officer Cadet Battn. Heralded by tremendous cheering, the Royal car arrived punctually at 2.45. On the appearance of the King in the square the Royal Standard was broken, and as their Majesties mounted the daïs, Col. C. Y. Crommelin, officer commanding troops in Bristol, who was in command of the parade, ordered the Royal Salute, and the band played the National Anthem. The Lord Mayor and Lady Mayoress, the Sheriff, and the party who are accompanying the King and Queen during their visit to the West were upon the daïs. The first to be decorated was Colonel Duncan Carter, C.B., of the Army Remount Depot, Shirehampton, who was invested as a Companion of the Order of St. Michael and St. George. The third investiture was that of a hero who has been sorely stricken in performing deeds of the utmost gallantry. This was Capt. Angus Buchanan of the South Wales Borderers, whom the King decorated with the Victoria Cross and the Military Cross. Unhappily, Capt. Buchanan is now blind, and had to be led on to the daïs. After decorating him, His Majesty kept him for some time in sympathetic conversation. The huge assembly also showed their sympathy with the gallant officer by according him a special ovation. Capt. Buchanan is a son of Dr. Buchanan, of Old Bank House, Coleford, Gloucestershire. Prior to the loss of his sight he had been wounded on three occasions in the present war. The next hero to be decorated also received a tribute of ringing cheers, for he was L.-Corpl. F. G. Room, a young Bristol soldier, who won the V.C. for an extraordinary act of bravery, which has already been described in our columns. His Majesty distributed the decorations and medals in a most gracious manner, sparing time to say a few kindly words to each of the recipients. The Rev. and Mrs. J. Ash Parsons, of Bristol, received the V.C. won recently by their son, Second Lieut. Hardy Parsons, who, unfortunately, succumbed to the wounds he suffered during the splendid deed for which the Cross was awarded. Undergraduates of the University of Bristol were also present to pay a tribute to the memory of Second Lieut. Parsons, who was a member of the University. Indeed, the distribution of decorations to the next-of-kin of fallen heroes was a pathetic feature of the investiture. The Rev. C. H. B. Hudson received the Military Cross won by his son, the late Second Lieut. Alban Hudson, of the Worcesters; Mr. H. King, the Military Cross awarded to his son, the late Second Lieut. Leonard King, of the Gloucesters; Mrs. Goode, the Military Medal won by her husband, the late Corpl. Sidney Goode, of the Gloucesters. Mrs. Lund received the Distinguished Conduct Medal won by her husband, the late Company Sergt.-Major Geoffrey Lund, Hants Regt."

MYLES, EDGAR KINGHORN, Capt., was born on 23 July, 1894, at Wanstead, Essex, son of Andrew Kinghorn Myles and Agnes Jane Myles, daughter of John Bain. His parents live at Wanstead, Essex. He joined the Army on 14 Aug. 1914, as a Private in the 9th Battn. Worcestershire Regt., and in Oct. 1914, was given a temporary commission as Second Lieutenant. He obtained a commission in the Regular Army in Aug. 1915, and was transferred to the Welsh Regt., to be reposted to the Worcestershire Regt. almost immediately. He served in Gallipoli and Mesopotamia. He was rearguard officer at the evacuations of Suvla Bay and Helles in 1915 and 1916. He was promoted Lieutenant in Sept. 1915. He was awarded the Victoria Cross [London Gazette, 26 Sept. 1916], whilst trying to relieve Kut under Lieut.-General Sir Stanley Maude, 9 April, 1916: "Edgar Kinghorn Myles, Lieut., Welsh Regt. For most conspicuous bravery. He went out alone on several occasions in front of our advanced trenches and under heavy rifle fire, and at great personal risk assisted wounded men lying in the open. On one occasion he carried a wounded officer to a place of safety under circumstances of great danger." He was promoted Temporary Capt. in Aug. 1916, and was created a Companion of the Distinguished Service Order [London Gazette, 25 Jan. 1917]: "Edgar Kinghorn Myles, Temporary Capt., Worcestershire Regt. When all the officers except two had become casualties, he, for five hours, inspired confidence in the defence against two counter-attacks, and sent back most accurate and valuable reports of the situation. His courage and fine example were largely responsible for the steadiness of all ranks under him." He is now employed in the Intelligence Department, War Office. His chief recreations are polo and golf.

Edgar Kinghorn Myles.

WILKINSON, THOMAS ORDE LAWDER, Temporary Lieut., was the son of C. E. O. Wilkinson. He served in the European War, and was awarded the Victoria Cross [London Gazette, 26 Sept. 1916], for his courage at La Boiselle, France, 5 July, 1916 : " Thomas Orde Lawder Wilkinson, Temporary Lieut., 7th Battn. North Lancashire Regt. During an attack, when a party of another unit was retiring without their machine gun, Lieut. Wilkinson rushed forward, and, with two of his men, got the gun int) action, and held up the enemy till they were relieved. Later, when the advance was checked during a bombing attack, he forced his way forward and found four or five men of different units stopped by a solid block of earth, over which the enemy was throwing bombs. With great pluck and promptness he mounted a machine gun on the top of the parapet and dispersed the enemy bombers. Subsequently he made two most gallant attempts to bring in a wounded man, but at the second attempt he was shot through the heart just before reaching the man. Throughout the day he set a magnificent example of courage and self-sacrifice."

CASTLETON, CLAUDE CHARLES, Sergt., No. 1352, was born at Lowestoft, England, son of J. C. Castleton. He joined the Australian Expeditionary Force on 10 March, 1915, and at the time of his enlistment was twenty-two years of age. He served in the European War, and was awarded the Victoria Cross [London Gazette, 26 Sept. 1916]: " Claude Charles Castleton, No. 1352, Sergt., 5th Battn. Australian Machine Gun Corps. During an attack on the enemy's trenches the infantry was temporarily driven back by the intense machine-gun fire opened by the enemy. Many wounded were left in ' No Man's Land ' lying in shell holes. Sergt. Castleton went out twice in face of this intense fire and each time brought in a wounded man on his back. He went out a third time, and was bringing in another wounded man when he was himself hit in the back and killed instantly. He set a splendid example of courage and self-sacrifice." This took place near Pozières, France, 28 July, 1916.

Claude Charles Castleton.

DAVIES, JOSEPH, Corpl., was born at Tipton, Staffordshire, on 28 April, 1889, son of Mr. John Davies and Mrs. Annie Davies of 48, Cross Street, Wednesbury. He entered the Army on 19 Aug. 1909, in the 1st Welsh Regt.; came from India and got into action in 1915, and received wounds. After rejoining above regiment was transferred to the 10th Battn. Royal Welsh Fusiliers, and served in the European War, and was promoted to Corporal. Sergt. Davies writes : " On 20 July we received orders that we were to take a position called Delville Wood at all costs. The Germans occupied the left flank, also the front of the wood. We started from Montauban at 10 p.m. on the night of the 19th, and reached and filed into the wood at about 2.45. After we had got on half way into the wood we found a party of Germans advancing on to us in two lines ; it being night, unfortunately we were between the two lines. Our company—being the leading company—of course had to take cover, and by throwing bombs and rapid fire caused them to retire. I was with eight men, detached from our company, and we saw a party of men attacking towards our right. I at once took charge and met them, killing part of them with bombs and rapid fire. The remainder that was left of them we killed with the bayonet. Then all went quiet again. We deployed to make the attack, at this stage being very near the Germans. Here we lost all our officers before making the attack. I took charge of the men and led them forward, losing my first lot of men, being fired on from all directions. I ran back and got together a party of stragglers and took them into the attack. At this point we occupied a position about fifty yards from the Germans gaining about 200 yards of the wood. Fire being so heavy, we had to retire back another 150 yards, but reserve troops coming to our assistance, we dug in, making a loop trench, and we had captured ground. I also took charge of the reserves in the trenches and kept them to their post. Also, I, with my Captain, named Follitt, D.S.O., M.C., made a reconnaissance before the attack on the 14th July, which proved a success. I and Capt. Follitt, D.S.O., M.C., brought back valuable information on several occasions, we being, the picked party for this work from the battalion. I, with the above Captain, also led the platoons over the top on the 18th Aug., when we captured two lines of trenches. On this occasion I got wounded. I was also at the Second Battle of Ypres with the 1st Welsh Regt." He was awarded the Victoria Cross [London Gazette, 26 Sept. 1916]: " Joseph Davies, Corpl., No. 34314, Royal Welsh Fusiliers. For most conspicuous bravery. Prior to an attack on the enemy in a wood he became separated with eight men from the rest of his company. When the enemy delivered their second counter-attack his party was completely surrounded, but he got them into a shell-hole, and by throwing bombs and opening rapid fire succeeded in routing them. Not content with this, he followed them up in their retreat, and bayoneted several of them. Corpl. Davies set a magnificent example of pluck and determination. He has done very gallant work, and was badly wounded in the Second Battle of Ypres." The action for which the Victoria Cross was awarded was performed on the 20th July, 1916, and the investiture took place on 7 Oct.

Joseph Davies.

1916. He was later promoted Sergeant. Sergt. Davies was informed of the bestowal on him of the Russian Order of St. George, First Class.

WARE, SIDNEY WILLIAM, Corpl., No. 920, was born on 11 Nov. 1892, at Whatcombe, in the parish of Whitechurch, Dorsetshire. He was the son of Mr. and Mrs. W. Ware. He was educated at the Church of England Boys' School, Whitechurch, and joined the Army 29 Nov. 1911. He served in the European War from 1914 to 16 April, 1916. He came over from India with the Indian Expeditionary Force on the outbreak of war ; was wounded in France 11 Nov. 1914. After ten days' leave from hospital he returned to France again. Later, he was sent from France to Mesopotamia, where he was wounded again 7 Jan. 1916. On recovering he rejoined his regiment, and won his V.C. 6 April, 1916. On 10 April, 1916, he was seriously wounded, and brought back to the Persian Gulf, where he died in the Rawal Pindi Hospital, Persian Gulf, on 16 April. He was always a very steady and trustworthy man, very fond of football and reading. Two more brothers were also killed in this war : Sergt. A. C. Ware, Dorset Regt., 1 July, 1916 ; Private A. Ware, Wiltshire Regt., 11 March, 1915. Two more brothers returned home safely, five serving in all. He was awarded the Victoria Cross, [London Gazette, 26 Sept. 1916], for his courage at Sannaiyat, Mesopotamia, 6 April, 1916 : " Sidney William Ware, No. 920, Corpl., 1st Battn. Seaforth Highlanders. For most conspicuous bravery. An order was given to withdraw to the cover of a communication trench. Corpl Ware, whose cool gallantry had been very marked during the advance, was one of a few men remaining unwounded. He picked up a wounded man and carried him some 200 yards to cover, and then returned for others, moving to and fro under very heavy fire for more than two hours until he had brought in all the wounded and was completely exhausted."

Sidney William Ware.

FYNN, JAMES HENRY, Private, No. 1/11220, is the son of Private John Fynn and of Mrs. John Fynn. He served in the European War, and was awarded the Victoria Cross [London Gazette, 26 Sept. 1916]: " James Henry Fynn, No. 1/11220, Private, 4th Battn. South Wales Borderers. After a night attack he was one of a small party which dug in in front of our advanced line and about 300 yards from the enemy's trenches. Seeing several wounded men lying out in front, he went out and bandaged them all under heavy fire, making several journeys in order to do so. He then went back to our advanced trench for a stretcher, and, being unable to get one, he himself carried on his back a badly wounded man into safety. He then returned, and, aided by another man, who was wounded during the act, carried in another badly wounded man. He was under continuous fire while performing this gallant work." This was at Sannaiyat, Mesopotamia, 9 April, 1916.

HILL, ALBERT, Private, was born on 24 May, 1895, at Manchester, and was educated at Trinity Wesleyan School, Denton, near Manchester. He joined the Army 3 Sept. 1914, as a Private. He served in the European War in France, and was awarded the Victoria Cross [London Gazette, 26 Sept. 1916]: " No. 15280, Albert Hill, Private, 10th Battn. Royal Welsh Fusiliers. When his battalion had deployed under very heavy fire for an attack on the enemy in a wood, he dashed forward when the order to charge was given, and, meeting two of the enemy suddenly, bayoneted them both. He was sent later by his platoon sergeant to get into touch with the company, and, finding himself cut off and almost surrounded by some twenty of the enemy, attacked them with bombs, killing and wounding many and scattering the remainder. He then joined a sergeant of his company, and helped him to fight the way back to the lines. When he got back, hearing that his company officer and a scout were lying out wounded, he went out and assisted to bring in the wounded officer, two other men bringing in the scout. Finally, he himself captured and brought in as prisoners two of the enemy. His conduct throughout was magnificent." He arrived home straight from the trenches to Denton, near Manchester, on the 11th Oct. 1916, and was met by thousands of people, who sang, " See the Conquering Hero comes." He was received by the Mayor at the Town Hall, and was then carried shoulder-high to his home, where his old mother waited for him with tears in her eyes. A crowd of children were at the door, and out of these he chose his little niece, and carried her inside and held her on his knee, while he talked to his friends. No doubt his little niece was delighted. He had the reputation of being, at that time, the youngest and smallest Victoria Cross winner.

Albert Hill.

Shahamad Khan.

SHAHAMAD KHAN, Naik, served in the European War, in Mesopotamia, and was awarded the Victoria Cross [London Gazette, 26 Sept. 1916]: "Shahamad Khan, Naik, No. 1605, 89th Punjabis." (See Appendix.) He was born about 1879, at the village of Takti, near Rawalpindi, son of Fayal Khan. He joined the Army 1 Dec. 1904, serving in the European War at Shaik Sa'id, Arabia, in Nov. 1914; in Egypt, the Dardanelles, France, Mesopotamia, the Mohmand Blockade, Salonika and the Caucasus. Shahamad Khan has now been promoted to Jemadar (Jan. 1920).

London Gazette, 26 Oct. 1916.—" The King has been graciously pleased to award the Victoria Cross to the undermentioned Officers, Non-commissioned Officers and Men."

CAMPBELL, JOHN VAUGHAN, D.S.O., Brevet Lieut.-Colonel, was born in London 31 Oct. 1876, son of the Hon. Ronald Campbell and Katherine, daughter of Bishop Claughton, and joined the Coldstream Guards 5 Sept. 1896, becoming Lieutenant 6 April, 1898. He was Adjutant, Coldstream Guards, 29 Dec. 1900, to 13 July, 1903. He served in the South African War, 1899–1902, as Acting Assistant Provost-Marshal; afterwards Station Staff Officer. He served as Adjutant, 2nd Battn. Coldstream Guards, from 30 Nov. 1900, to 31 May, 1902, and took part in the advance on Kimberley, including the actions at Belmont, Enslin, Modder River and Magersfontein; operations in the Orange Free State, Feb. to May, 1900, including actions at Poplar Grove, Dreifontein, Vet River and Zand River. He was mentioned in Despatches [London Gazette, 10 Sept. 1901, and 29 July, 1902]; operations in the Transvaal in May and June, 1900, including actions near Johannesburg, Pretoria and Diamond Hill; operations in the Transvaal, west of Pretoria, July to October, 1900, including action at Belfast; operations in the Transvaal, west of Pretoria, Nov. 1900; operations in Cape Colony, south of Orange River, 1900; operations in the Transvaal, Nov. to Dec. 1900; operations in Cape Colony, Dec. 1900, to 31 May, 1902. He received the Queen's Medal with six clasps, the King's Medal with two clasps, and was created a Companion of the Distinguished Service Order [London Gazette, 27 Sept. 1901]: " John Vaughan Campbell, Lieut., Coldstream Guards. In recognition of services in South Africa." He became Captain 27 June, 1903, and Major 21 June, 1913. Major Campbell served in the European War from 1914–18; became Temporary Lieut.-Colonel 29 July, 1915, and was given the Brevet of Lieut.-Colonel 1 Jan. 1916. He was awarded the Victoria Cross [London Gazette, 26 Oct. 1916], for his gallantry at Ginchy, France, 15 Sept. 1916: " John Vaughan Campbell, Major and Brevet Lieut.-Colonel (Temporary Lieut.-Colonel), Coldstream Guards. For most conspicuous bravery and able leading in an attack. Seeing that the first two waves of his battalion had been decimated by machine-gun and rifle fire, he took personal command of the third line, rallied his men with the utmost gallantry, and led them against the enemy machine guns, capturing the guns and killing the personnel. Later in the day, after consultation with other unit commanders, he again rallied the survivors of his battalion, and at a critical moment led them through a very heavy hostile fire barrage against the objective. He was one of the first to enter the enemy trench. His personal gallantry and initiative at a very critical moment turned the fortunes of the day and enabled the division to press on and capture objectives of the highest tactical importance." A newspaper cutting says: " The news, officially confirmed, was received with feelings of delight in Oswestry and the Welsh border district yesterday that Colonel John Vaughan Campbell, commanding the Coldstream Guards, had been awarded the Victoria Cross, and Capt. Francis Longueville, his fellow-townsman, the Distinguished Service Order, for gallantry in the recent historic charge of the Coldstreamers. The story will form an epic in the history of the war. Colonel Campbell, who is Master of Tanat Side Harriers, and resides at Broomhall, Oswestry, rallied his command to the sound of a huntsman's horn. Grandson of the second Earl Cawdor, Colonel Campbell served in the South African War, where he gained the Distinguished Service Order and the Queen's and King's Medals. His father, the Hon. Ronald Campbell, also held a commission in the Coldstream Guards, and fell in the Zulu War of 1879, after distinguished service." He was created a C.M.G. 1 Jan. 1918. He was Brigadier-General, commanding the 137th Brigade, Nov. 1916 to Nov. 1918; commanding the 3rd Guards Brigade, Nov. 1918, to March, 1919; subsequently commanding a Brigade. He was mentioned in Despatches 30 Nov. 1915 [London Gazette, 31 Dec. 1915]; 7 Nov. 1917 [London Gazette, 7 Dec. 1917]; 16 March, 1919 [London Gazette, 5 July, 1919]; was given the Brevet of Colonel and appointed A.D.C. to the King 5 June, 1919 [London Gazette, 9 June, 1919]; was awarded the Croix de Guerre 26 Oct. 1919; the Légion d'Honneur (Officier) [London Gazette, 19 Aug. 1919]; the Croix de Guerre with Palm [London Gazette, 19 Aug. 1919]. He is well-known as a rider to hounds, and has ridden in many steeplechases. He married, 18 July, 1904, in Wellington Barracks Chapel, Dorothy, elder daughter of the late John Penn, M.P., and their children are: John Ronald, born 18 Sept. 1905, and Diana.

John Vaughan Campbell.

CONGREVE, WILLIAM LA TOUCHE, Major, was born 22 March, 1891, at Burton Hall, Cheshire. He was the son of Lieut.-General Sir Walter Congreve, V.C., K.C.B., M.V.O., etc., and Lady Congreve, and was educated at Eton and Sandhurst. On 1 June, 1916, at St. Martin's-in-the-Fields, London, he married Pamela, daughter of Cyril Maude, Esq., and his wife, "Miss Winifred Emery," both well known on the stage. A daughter, Mary Gloria Congreve Congreve, was born after her father's death. As early as 20 Nov. 1914, he was mentioned in Field-Marshal Sir John French's Despatches [London Gazette, 17 Feb. 1915]; again in the Despatch dated 15 Oct. 1915 [London Gazette, 1 Jan. 1916]. In General Sir Douglas Haig's Despatches of 30 April, 1916 [London Gazette, 15 June, 1916], and in that of 13 Nov. 1916 [London Gazette, 4 Jan. 1917], for gallant and distinguished service in the field. He won the Victoria Cross in France [London Gazette, 26 Oct. 1916]: " William La Touche Congreve, Brevet Major, D.S.O., M.C., Rifle Brigade. Date of Acts of Bravery: 6–20 July, 1916. For most conspicuous bravery during a period of fourteen days preceding his death in action. This officer constantly performed acts of gallantry, and showed the greatest devotion to duty, and by his personal example inspired all those around him with confidence at critical periods of the operations. During preliminary preparations for the attack he carried out personal reconnaissances of the enemy lines, taking out parties of officers and non-commissioned officers for over 1,000 yards in front of our line, in order to acquaint them with the ground. All these preparations were made under fire. Later, by night, Major Congreve conducted a battalion to its position of employment, afterwards returning to it to ascertain the situation after assault. He established himself in an exposed forward position from whence he successfully observed the enemy, and gave orders necessary to drive them from their position. Two days later, when Brigade Headquarters was heavily shelled and many casualties resulted, he went out and assisted the medical officer to remove the wounded to places of safety, although he was himself suffering severely from gas and other shell effects. He again on a subsequent occasion showed supreme courage in tending wounded under heavy shell fire. He finally returned to the front line to ascertain the situation after an unsuccessful attack, and whilst in the act of writing his report was shot and killed instantly." He had been already recommended for the V.C. when at St. Eloi he had captured, practically single-handed, two officers and 72 men, but he had been given the D.S.O. instead. No other officer had previously been given the V.C., the D.S.O. and the M.C. At the time of his death he was Brigade Major. He was awarded the Legion of Honour by the French. Major William Congreve's father also holds the Victoria Cross, won in South Africa at Colenso, and his mother was in the Great War awarded the French Croix de Guerre (an honour rarely conferred upon women) in recognition of her courage and coolness when the hospital area of Nancy, where she was nursing, was under shell fire and attacks from bombing aeroplanes. A newspaper says: " There are two precedents for the award of the V.C. to both father and son. The first was the case of the late Lord Roberts, who won the honour in India in 1858, and his son, Lieut. F. H. S. Roberts, K.R.R.C., to whom it was awarded for his share in the gallant attempt to save the guns at Colenso on 15 Dec. 1899. It is a remarkable coincidence that General (then Captain) Congreve, whose son is now awarded the Cross, also won the honour for his bravery at Colenso, and it was he who, after being wounded and reaching shelter, saw Lieut. Roberts on the ground (he had been mortally wounded by a shell which burst under his horse), went out under heavy fire and brought him in. The other precedent is that of the late General Sir Charles Gough, who, like his brother, the late General Sir Hugh Gough, won the V.C. for exploits in India in 1857–58, and his son, Brigadier-General Sir John Edmond Gough, who received the decoration for conspicuous bravery in Somaliland in 1903, and lost his life in the Great War in Feb. 1915."

ALLEN, WILLIAM BARNSLEY, R.A.M.C., Capt., was born at Sheffield 8 June, 1892, and is the only son of Percy Edwin Allen and Edith Allen (*née* Barnsley). He was educated at Worksop College and Sheffield University. He gained the Gold Medal for Pathology in 1913, and has also won three bronze medals; M.B., Ch.B., Kaye Scholarship, and Second Class Honours. He joined the Army on 8 Aug. 1914, being gazetted Lieutenant on that date, and was promoted Captain 1 April, 1915 (T.F.). In May, 1916, at Gainsborough, he married Mary Young ("Mollie"), younger daughter of W. Y. Mercer, Esq., of Gainsborough. In August of that year he gained the Military Cross. Near Mesmil, Somme, France, on 3 Sept. 1916, his splendid behaviour under fire in the circumstances mentioned below gained him the Victoria Cross [London Gazette, 26, Oct. 1916]: " William Barnsley Allen, M.C., M.B., Capt., Royal Army Medical Corps. Date of Act of Bravery: 3 Sept. 1916. For most conspicuous bravery and devotion to duty. When gun detachments were unloading high-explosive ammunition from wagons which had just come up, the enemy suddenly began to shell the battery position. The first shell fell on one of the limbers, exploded the ammunition and caused several casualties. Capt. Allen saw the occurrence and at once, with utter disregard of danger, ran straight across the open, under heavy shell fire, commenced dressing the wounded, and undoubtedly by his promptness saved many of them from bleeding to death. He was himself hit four times during the first hour by pieces of shells, one of which fractured two of his ribs, but he never even mentioned this at the time, and coolly went on with his work till the last man was dressed and safely removed. He then went over to another battery and tended a wounded officer. It was only when this was done that he returned to his dug-out and reported his own injury." In July, 1917, he was awarded the Bar to the Military Cross, and was invalided to England on 22 July. On 4 Jan. 1918, he was made Acting Major. On 17 Oct. 1918, he was wounded for the third time, and invalided for the second time to England, and awarded D.S.O. on this date. He has served in France three years and two months; was transferred to Regular R.A.M.C., and dated back to Captain 8 Feb. 1918, which rank he held at the conclusion of the war.

William Barnsley Allen.

CHAVASSE, NOEL GODFREY, M.B., Capt., was born at Oxford, on 9 Nov. 1884, son of the Right Rev. The Lord Bishop of Liverpool, and of Edith Jane Chavasse, daughter of Canon Maude, Rector of Chirk. He was twin brother to the Rev. C. M. Chavasse, M.C., Temporary Chaplain to the Forces. He was educated at Magdalen College School (1896–1900); Liverpool College School (1900–1904); and at Trinity College, Oxford (1904–1908), and was a well-known athlete. He ran in the sports for Oxford against Cambridge, in 1907 and 1908. In the former year he ran a dead-heat in the 100 yards with K. G. Macleod, in 10½ seconds, and was second to his twin brother, C. M. Chavasse, in the quarter mile. He was not so successful in 1908, rupturing a thigh muscle in the hundred yards. He represented Oxford at Lacrosse, 1904–5 and 1905–6. Capt. Chavasse was a Medical Officer at the Royal Southern Hospital, Liverpool, before the war. He joined the

Noel Godfrey Chavasse.

Royal Army Medical Corps in 1913, being attached to the 10th (Liverpool Scottish) King's Own, and served with them in the European War in France. He was awarded the Military Cross. After he had been at the front two years he was awarded the Victoria Cross for gallantry at Guillemont [London Gazette, 26 Oct. 1916]: "Noel Godfrey Chavasse, M.C., M.B., Royal Army Medical Corps." He was awarded a Bar to the Victoria Cross [London Gazette, 14 Sept. 1917]: "His Majesty the King has been graciously pleased to approve of the award of the Victoria Cross to Capt. Noel Godfrey Chavasse, V.C., M.C., late R.A.M.C., attached Liverpool Regt. Though severely wounded early in the action whilst carrying a wounded soldier to the dressing station he refused to leave his post, and for two days not only continued to perform his duties but in addition went out repeatedly under heavy fire to search for and attend to the wounded who were lying out. During these searches, although practically without food during this period, worn with fatigue and faint with his wound, he assisted to carry in a number of badly wounded men over heavy and difficult ground. By his extraordinary energy and inspiring example he was instrumental in rescuing many wounded who would have otherwise undoubtedly succumbed under the bad weather conditions. This devoted and gallant officer subsequently died of his wounds." A memorial service for the officers and men of the King's (Liverpool) Regt. who have "laid down their lives for King, country and righteousness," was held in St. Nicholas Church, Liverpool. There was a crowded congregation, including the Lord Mayor (Mr. M. Muspratt), the Bishop of Liverpool (Dr. Chavasse), Lieut.-General Sir W. Pitcairn Campbell (Western Command), Brigadier-General Edwards, Rear-Admiral Stileman, Colonel Forbes Bell, Colonel G. Blair, Lieut.-Colonel A. Fairrie, and many officers and men of the regiment. The north aisle of the church was occupied by the wives and relatives of dead soldiers. The service was conducted by Archdeacon Spooner. Canon Lancelot gave an address. Alluding to the late Capt. Noel Chavasse, V.C., he said it was no wonder that the King felt that the whole Army would mourn the death of so brave and distinguished a brother, that his Brigadier declared him to have been the most gallant and modest man he had ever met, that the Major-General commanding the Division should say that his devotion was magnificent, or that the whole battalion, smothered in mud as they were, and ready to drop from exhaustion, paraded for his funeral. Capt. Chavasse might have been a great surgeon, or a really great clergyman and medical missionary. Such was the vision that floated before his mind from boyhood, but he was already a great Christian, with the sympathy of mind and loyalty of heart which were characteristic of all true greatness. Over him, and others like him, it might be said, with quivering heart and trembling lips, they would rejoice and give thanks. Capt. Chavasse was engaged to his cousin, Miss Gladys Chavasse, a daughter of the late Sir Thomas Chavasse, of Birmingham.

WHITE, ARCHIE CECIL THOMAS, Capt., was born at Boroughbridge, an old Yorkshire market town, which at one time sent two members to Parliament, and is the only son of the late Thomas White and Mrs. Thomas White, who lives at Norwood House, Langthorpe, Boroughbridge. He was educated at King's College, London, of which he is a fellow, and he joined the Yorkshire Regt. (the "Green Howards") as a Second Lieut., serving in the European War. The late Major-General Capper said of his regiment: "I knew it was a regiment I could hang my hat on at any time of the day or night, and Lieut. White was a very adequate peg." He went out to the Dardanelles and was wounded. His only brother, who had a commission in the same regiment, after enlisting as a Private, was killed. He went to France, and was awarded the Military Cross. He was awarded the Victoria Cross [London Gazette, 26 Oct. 1916]: "Archie Cecil Thomas White, Temporary Capt., 6th Battn. Yorkshire Regt. Dates of Acts of Bravery: 27 Sept. and 1 Oct. 1916. For most conspicuous bravery. He was in command of the troops that held the southern and western faces of a redoubt. For four days and nights by his indomitable spirit, great personal courage, and skilful dispositions, he held his position under heavy fire of all kinds and against several counter-attacks. Though short of supplies and ammuni-

Archie Cecil T. White.

tion, his determination never wavered. When the enemy attacked in greatly superior numbers and had almost ejected our troops from the redoubt, he personally led a counter-attack, which finally cleared the enemy out of the southern and western faces. He risked his life continually, and was the life and soul of the defence." Capt. White won his Victoria Cross at Stuff Redoubt, France. He later served as Brigade Major.

HOLLAND, JOHN VINCENT, Lieut., was born in July, 1889, at Athy, County Kildare, Ireland, eldest son of John Holland, M.R.C.V.S., of the Model Farm, Athy. He was educated at Clongowes Wood College, and at Liverpool University. Later he travelled extensively in South America (Brazil, Argentine, Chili and Bolivia), where he was engaged in ranching, railway engineering and hunting. He returned to England at the outbreak of war, and enlisted in the 2nd Life Guards on 2 Sept. 1914. He was gazetted Second Lieutenant in the 3rd Battn. Leinster Regt. in Feb. 1915. He served in the European War; went to France, and was attached to the 2nd Battn. Royal Dublin Fusiliers. He was wounded at the Second Battle of Ypres. After recovery from his wound, he went back to France, and was attached to the 7th Battn. Leinster Regt. as Battalion Bombing Officer. He saw service at Loos, Hulluch and the Somme in 1916. He was awarded the Victoria Cross [London Gazette, 26 Oct. 1916]: "John Vincent Holland, Lieut., 3rd Battn. Leinster Regt., attached 7th Battn. Date of Act of Bravery: 3 Sept. 1916. For most conspicuous bravery during a heavy engagement when, not content with bombing hostile dug-outs within the objective, he fearlessly led his bombers through our own artillery barrage and cleared a great part of the village in front. He started out with 26 bombers and finished up with only five, after capturing some 50 prisoners. By this very gallant action he undoubtedly broke the spirit of the enemy, and thus saved us many casualties when the battalion made a further advance. He was far from well at the time, and later had to go to hospital." A. C. T. White and his only brother, Second Lieut. J. F. White, went out to the Dardanelles with the same regiment, and both were wounded. His brother died of his wounds in Aug. 1915. Lieut. Holland won his Victoria Cross at Guillemont. He was later promoted to Captain. He was mentioned in Despatches, and awarded the Parchment of the 16th Irish Division. He was appointed Staff Instructor, Number Sixteen, Officer Cadet Battn., Kinnel Park, Rhyl. He married Frances, youngest daughter of Joseph Grogan, J.P., and Mrs. Grogan, of the Manor House, Queenstown, and Rossleague. Capt. Holland has hunted a good deal with the Kildare, Queen's County and County Carlow fox-hounds, and has shot big game abroad. He is also fond of tennis and cricket. It may have been remarked by readers of this book that a large number of Victoria Crosses in the European War and in other wars since (and including) the Crimea, have been won by Irishmen.

COURY, GABRIEL GEORGE, Lieut., was born on 13 June, 1896, at Sefton Park, Liverpool, son of the late Raphael and Marie Coury, of Liverpool. His father was a cotton merchant. He was educated at

Stonyhurst College, where he won many prizes for sports, and was then apprenticed to a cotton firm. He joined the Army in Aug. 1914, as a Private in the 6th Battn. The King's (Liverpool Regt.), and was given a commission in the 3rd Battn. The Prince of Wales's Volunteers (South Lancashire Regt.) in April, 1915; served in the European War, in France, in 4th Battn. South Lancashire Regt. until Aug. 1916; joined the R.F.C. as an Observer in France, and returned to England in May, 1917. Promoted Lieut. 8 Aug. 1916, and Capt. Sept. 1918. He was awarded the Victoria Cross [London Gazette, 26 Oct. 1916]: "Gabriel George Coury, Lieut. (then Second Lieut.), 3rd Battn. The Prince of Wales's Volunteers (South Lancashire Regt.). For most

Gabriel George Coury.

conspicuous bravery. During an advance he was in command of two platoons ordered to dig a communication trench from the old firing line to the position won. By his fine example and utter contempt of danger he kept up the spirits of his men, and completed his task under intense fire. Later, after his battalion had suffered severe casualties and the commanding officer had been wounded, he went out in front of the advanced position in broad daylight, and in full view of the enemy found his commanding officer and brought him back to the new advanced trench over ground swept by machine-gun fire. He not only carried out his original task, and saved his commanding officer, but also assisted in rallying the attacking troops when they were shaken and in leading them forward." He was invested at Buckingham Palace on 15 Nov. 1916, whilst he was attached to the Royal Flying Corps. He was married on 7 Jan. 1918, at St. Mary's, Clapham, to Katherine Mary, only daughter of the late Stuart Lovell and Mary Lovell, who lives at Clapham Common, London, S.W., and they have a daughter, Joan, born 11 Dec. 1918.

BOULTER, WILLIAM EWART, Sergt., was born on 14 Oct. 1892, at Wigston, Leicestershire. He is the son of Fred Boulter and of Mary Ann Boulter. He was educated at Wigston Council Schools, and joined the Army in Sept. 1914, and was promoted to Sergeant in May, 1915; embarked for France in July, 1915, with

William Ewart Boulter.

the 18th Division, and was engaged in trench warfare on the Somme, and later in the Battle of the Somme, July, 1916; was wounded on 14 July, 1916, and transferred to hospital in England on the 18th July, 1916; he was transferred to Ampthill Command Depot, under the command of His Grace the Duke of Bedford in Nov. 1916, being convalescent till March, 1917, and on being recommended for a commission, was sent to the 13th O.C.B. Newmarket. He was decorated with the Victoria Cross by His Majesty the King at an investiture held at Buckingham Palace on St. Patrick's Day, 1917. Gazetted Second Lieutenant on 27 June, 1917, he proceeded to France again in Aug. 1917, and served with the 7th Battn. Northamptonshire Regt. until contracting an attack of trench fever in Oct. 1917, which prevented him from being of any further use for active service. Promoted Lieutenant 27 Dec. 1918. Demobilized 24 April, 1919. Lieut. Boulter was a keen sportsman, taking part in football, cricket and tennis. He was awarded the Victoria Cross [London Gazette, 26 Oct. 1916] for his bravery at Trônes Wood, France, on 14 July, 1916: "William Ewart Boulter, No. 14603, Sergeant, 6th Battn. Northamptonshire Regt. For most conspicuous bravery. When one company and part of another were held up in the attack on a wood by a hostile machine gun, which was causing heavy casualties, Sergt. Boulter, with utter contempt of danger, and in spite of being severely wounded in the shoulder, advanced alone over the open under heavy fire in front of the gun, and bombed the gun team from their position. This very gallant act not only saved many casualties, but was of great military value, as it materially expedited the operation of clearing the enemy out of the wood, and thus covering the flank of the whole attacking force." He was the first man in his regiment to win the Victoria Cross. The Co-operative Society of Northampton gave him a clock to commemorate his deed, and twenty thousand people were present at Abingdon Park, Northampton, when he was presented with a gold wrist watch and a congratulatory address from the Corporation of Northampton.

GILL, ALFRED, Sergt., was born at Hospital Street, Birmingham, in the year 1880, son of Henry and Sophia Gill, of Dugdale Street, Birmingham. He served in the European War with the King's Royal Rifles, and was awarded the Victoria Cross [London Gazette, 26 Oct. 1916]: "Alfred Gill, Sergt., King's Royal Rifle Corps. For most conspicuous bravery. The enemy made a very strong counter-attack on the right flank of the battalion, and rushed the bombing post, after killing all the company bombers. Sergt. Gill rallied the remnants of his platoon, none of whom were skilled bombers, and reorganized his defences, a most difficult and dangerous task, the trench being very shallow and much damaged. Soon afterwards the enemy nearly surrounded his men by creeping up through the thick undergrowth, and commenced sniping at about 20 yards' range. Although it was almost certain death, Sergt. Gill stood boldly up in order to direct the fire of his men. He was killed almost at once, but not before he had shown his men where the enemy were, and thus enabled them to hold up their advance. By his supreme devotion to duty and self-sacrifice he saved a very dangerous situation." The following is quoted from a letter written to Mrs. Rosetta Gill by Sergt. Gill's Commanding Officer, dated 16 Aug. 1916: "The Adjutant has handed to me your letter of 8 Aug., as I was your late husband's Company Commander. I am afraid that it is quite true that your husband was killed in action on 7 July. He was shot through the head, and must have died at once. He could have known nothing about it. I would have written to you before had I known your address, as your husband was one of the most valued men in my company—a man whom anyone would be proud to call friend. He was killed when rallying his men under a terrible fire, and had he lived he would most certainly have got the D.C.M. I was quite close to him, and he was quite cool, despite the very trying circumstances. The battalion had just taken a wood, and the Germans were counter-attacking heavily. I am glad to say we drove them back, and we have since received the thanks of everyone, from Sir Douglas Haig down. It was entirely owing to the heroic example and self-sacrifice of men like your husband that we did so well. He was loved by his platoon, of which I am sorry to say only four or five remain. That day's work will always remain fixed in my memory as the one in which I lost so many gallant comrades. I lost all the officers and sergeants in my company, and very many of the men. You should justly be proud of your husband in his life and death. He had one of the finest natures I have ever known. No words of mine can express my sympathy with you in your terrible sorrow. May the memory of his heroic end support you."

Alfred Gill.

JONES, DAVID, Sergt., No. 14951, was born on 10 Jan. 1891. He was the son of David and Jessie Jones. He was educated at Heyworth Street Council School, Everton, where two tablets perpetuating his memory have been erected, a brass tablet inside the school and a marble one outside. He joined the Army 29 Aug. 1914, and was married on 27 May, 1915, to Elizabeth Dorothea Doyle, and went out to France in June, 1915; came home on leave in the following Nov., and was killed on 7 Oct. 1916. He was awarded the Victoria Cross [London Gazette, 26 Oct. 1916], for his bravery at Guillemont, France, 3 Sept. 1916: "David Jones, No. 14951, Sergt., 12th Battn. Liverpool Regt. For most conspicuous bravery, devotion to duty, and ability displayed in the handling of his platoon. The platoon to which he belonged was ordered to a forward position, and during the advance came under heavy machine-gun fire, the officer being killed and the platoon suffering heavy losses. Sergt. Jones led forward the remainder, occupied the position, and held it for two days and two nights without food or water, until relieved. On the second day he drove back three counter-attacks, inflicting heavy losses. His coolness was most praiseworthy. It was due entirely to his resource and example that his men retained confidence and held their post."

David Jones.

An officer wrote to Mrs. Jones:

"I have seen your advertisement about Sergt. Jones, V.C., in the 'Echo,' and though I am not able to throw much light on the subject, I feel sure you will not mind a line of condolence and congratulation from one who has known him since November, 1914, and has therefore been able to appreciate the magnificent qualities your husband possessed. It was on active service that his merits came out so strongly. He was a wonderful scout, and did some magnificent patrol work, which combined brain and bravery to a high degree. His fearlessness had a very great influence for good on the men of his platoon and company. Capt. Ballantyne more than any other officer was able to appreciate this, being for so long his Platoon Commander. Eventually, after being a bombing officer for several months, I returned to command my own Company, and to find Sergt. Jones the Sergeant of my old platoon, No. 12. I am so proud to think it was my old platoon that was with him at the time. When a Lewis Gun Sergeant became necessary, I chose him, and a better choice could not have been made. I am so proud, if very sad. And, Mrs. Jones, your great sorrow will, I am sure, be tempered by your great pride, though you will always say it would have been easier to bear if he had only known. I was in the attack on 7 Oct., and, as Senior Officer, became a little anxious as to what were the casualties. I remember asking my orderly about 8 p.m., I think, and his first words were: 'Sergt. Jones, he that did so well at Ginchy, has been killed.' I felt very cut up, as I had known him so long. Alas, many another brave man fell that day. Among them Sergt. Andy White, also in No. 10, fell. But the battalion, yes, the whole Division, did wonderfully well. I know you will excuse this writing when you know my right arm is all bound up (not badly hurt), and I have to use my left hand. Mr. Fred Austin, 75, Bagot Street, Wavertree, Sign Writer, knew your husband I believe, both being connected with coach-building. He is a great friend of mine. Accept my deepest sympathy for yourself in your irreparable loss of as brave and upright a man as one could wish for."

A newspaper cutting says:

"'Sergt. Jones was the right man in the right place at the right moment,' was how a fellow non-commissioned officer of the Liverpool Regt. summed him up. 'We walked right into hell by the back door, and suffered terribly. All our officers bowled out. The men were like sheep without a shepherd. Things were all in a muddle. Nobody seemed to know what to do. Sergt. Jones sprang forward and gave orders. The men quickly recovered their temporary dismay, and under his directions they resumed the rush on the enemy's position. The machine guns played hell with us, but the Sergeant led us straight to the goal. We carried the position with a rush, though we were greatly outnumbered. The enemy fled in panic, and we lost no time in making ourselves at home in the position. All night long the enemy deluged us with shell fire, and twice they attacked with great fury. They were determined to overwhelm us by sheer weight of numbers, but under the orders of Sergt. Jones we put our backs into it and drove off the Huns each time. We had neither food nor water, and the circumstances were about as depressing as they could be, but Jones never despaired. He was so cheerful himself that everybody felt ashamed to be anything else. So we held on like grim death for two days. We smashed the enemy up every time they tried to overwhelm us. It was very hard fighting indeed, but the boys stuck it well until relief came. We had been given up for lost. Nobody ever expected to see us again. That we had come through the ordeal safe and with honour was due entirely to Sergt. Jones's handling of the men, and nobody will begrudge him the honour he has won.'

"'He ought to be an officer,' was the remark of a private who served under Sergt. Jones during the two days' siege. 'He led us with great skill, and completely baffled the foe at every turn. Nothing could dismay him. At times there was enough to make one's heart sink to the boots, but Sergt. Jones was as chirpy as could be, and his cheeriness was infectious. We all felt sure that nothing could go wrong with us under his leadership, and we were right.'"

Another newspaper says:

"The Lord Mayor of Liverpool attended the unveiling ceremony, yesterday, of two memorials to Liverpool's schoolboy hero, Sergt. David Jones, V.C. The memorials erected by the school children of the Heyworth Street Council School were a brass tablet and framed photograph of Sergt. Jones in the interior of the school, and a marble tablet setting forth his heroic deed, which is placed on the exterior wall.

"The Lord Mayor, addressing the schoolboys, said Sergt. Jones performed a deed of which the city and Empire were proud. Sergt. Jones would always remain a shining example to them, and would teach them to do their duty.

"The unveiling ceremony in the school-yard was witnessed by a large section of the public, and was of a most impressive character. The Royal Welsh Fusiliers led the singing of two hymns, and after the unveiling of the tablet sounded the 'Last Post.' Those present included the wife and relatives of the V.C."

McNESS, FRED, L.-Sergt., was born 22 Jan. 1892, at Bramley, near Leeds, Yorkshire, son of John McNess, born at Perth, "tall, with many years' foreign service in the Royal Engineers, who died about 13 years ago."

Sergt. Fred McNess's mother, Mary McNess, is described as being "short, rather stout, very good-natured and the best of mothers." He himself "when a child was very delicate, but always to the front and leading when mischief was brewing: boyish pranks, such as apple and pear pouching, etc. Later, when in my teens, a great walker and lover of the country, my friend and self often doing 25 miles through the Wharfedale valleys on Sundays. A great lover of animals, especially horses and dogs. Carrier's assistant and well known in the city of Leeds." He received telegrams of congratulation from the Colonel, officers, N.C.O.'s and men of the 1st, 2nd and 3rd Reserve Battns. Scots Guards, from his former employers, Mr. J. H. Bowan and Councillor Charles Gibson, of Bramley, and from his old schoolmaster and scholars. L.-Sergt. McNess was educated at Bramley National School,and joined the Scots Guards about the 10th of Jan.1915. He was awarded the Victoria Cross [London Gazette, 26 Oct. 1916]: "Fred McNess, No. 13301, L.-Sergt., Scots Guards. For most conspicuous bravery. During a severe engagement he led his men on with the greatest dash in face of heavy shell and machine-gun fire. When the first line of enemy trenches was reached it was found that the left flank was exposed, and that the enemy was bombing down the trench. Sergt. McNess thereupon organized a counter-attack and led it in person. He was very severely wounded in the neck and jaw, but went on, passing through the barrage of hostile bombs, in order to bring up fresh supplies of bombs to his own men. Finally he established a 'block,' and continued encouraging his men and throwing bombs till utterly exhausted by loss of blood." While Lieut. Powell with other officers and men began working along a trench, it was suddenly discovered that the left flank had become exposed, and that the enemy was bombing down the trench. L.-Sergt. McNess rose to the occasion, gathering together a party of his own, and at once began working up to the communication trench. The Germans at home there in their own trenches, fought like furies. For an hour and a half the terrific contest raged, the brunt of which was borne by Sergt. McNess and a Corporal. Gradually the Germans were being driven back, but the Guardsmen were running short of bombs. In the nick of time, however, they discovered a supply of German bombs, found out how to use them, and the Huns were paid back in their own coin. Sergt. McNess was already badly wounded when, as he told a friend: "One of the men of my platoon was shot through the lungs, or some such place. He gasped terribly for breath, and fell behind me. Easing his head with my left hand, I threw bombs with the right, also saying a few cheering words to the boys. Presently I felt his head drop back—his fight was over. I was just preparing another bomb, with the upper part of my head and chest well above the parapet, when a German bomb burst near my neck, blowing away the left side of same and part of jaw, lower teeth and gum and upper teeth. Left arm was blown round my neck, and the biceps muscle was contracted like a ball on the top of left shoulder. Jugular vein, windpipe and carotid artery were fully exposed, and shoulder-blade badly out of place. My head lay helplessly on my arm, and sometimes almost rolled on my back. For a moment I was dazed, as I had already been hit three times with shrapnel in the early part of the morning while organizing men of some other unit, who had lost their officers and N.C.O.'s, but I was soon clear again; still, what with loss of blood and almost blinded with it, I had to leave the boys, but I did not go far, only to the first line, where I lay in a shell-hole and watched how things progressed. But feeling myself becoming weaker and weaker, I set off to find a doctor. I had not gone far when I met the remnants of a carrying party. I wrote on a piece of paper asking for a dressing station, and they asked for the direction the boys had advanced. They were carrying bombs and the boys wanted them, so, staggering away, I took them up through the barrage. Five parties I led back, but the last one never got there, for a shell came over, killed three of them, and broke my jaw in another two places, so, almost blinded with blood and falling at every three or four steps, I left the field." L.-Sergt. McNess was promoted Sergeant on the 4th of Sept. 1916.

Fred McNess.

CLARKE, LEO, Private (Acting Corpl.), was born on 1 Dec. 1892, in Hamilton, Ontario, and enlisted in the 27th Canadian Battn. 25 Feb. 1915, at Winnipeg, and proceeded to France 13 Oct. 1915, where he served with the 2nd Canadian Battn. until his death from wounds on 6 Aug. 1916. He was promoted to the rank of Acting Corporal on 6 Aug. 1916. He was awarded the Victoria Cross [London Gazette, 26 Oct. 1916]: Leo Clarke, No. 73132, Private (Acting Corporal), Canadian Infantry. For most conspicuous bravery. He was detailed with his section of bombers to clear the continuation of a newly-captured trench and cover the construction of a 'block.' After most of his party had become casualties, he was building a 'block,' when about 20 of the enemy with two officers counter-attacked. He boldly advanced against them, emptied his revolver into them, and afterwards two enemy rifles which he picked up in the trench. One of the officers then attacked him with the bayonet, wounding him in the leg, but he shot him dead. The enemy then ran away, pursued by Acting Corporal Clarke, who shot four more and captured a fifth. Later he was ordered to the dressing station, but returned next day to duty."

The following is taken from "Thirty Canadian V.C.'s," published by Messrs. Skeffington:

"Twice veterans of Ypres, the 1st Canadian Division moved southward to the Somme on the first day of September, 1916, and established headquarters near the battered town of Albert. A few days later they marched up the Bapaume Road, under heavy enemy shelling, and entered trenches behind Mouquet Farm, to the south of Courcelette, where they relieved the 4th Australian Division. This time the Headquarters were in the shaky shelters of Tara Hill. As soon as the division arrived in the new position the German artillery began to plaster the trenches with every variety of explosive missile, hoping to shake the nerve of the men from Ypres. About half-past two on the afternoon of the 9th of September the 2nd Battalion relieved the 4th Battalion in a trench on the right of the Canadian position. The 2nd had been chosen to attack a salient of German trench about 550 yards long, near the north end of Walker Avenue. This salient lay between the Canadians and Courcelette. Before they could attack the village, which was about a mile behind the German trench, the danger of the salient had to be swept from their path. The attack began that afternoon at a quarter to five. Only the first three companies of the battalion made the assault, the fourth being held in reserve; but when the attackers reached the German line they found that our barrage had not reduced the resistance of the enemy to the extent hoped for. Crowds of Germans were waiting to repel them. Corporal Leo Clarke was detailed by Lieutenant Hoey to take a section of the bombing platoon and clear out the Germans on the left flank. When the trench was captured, Clarke was to join up with Sergeant Nichols at a block which the latter was to build in the meantime. Clarke was the first of his party to enter the trench, which was found to be strongly garrisoned. His followers came close on his heels. They bombed their way along the trench from bay to bay, and forced a passage with bayonets and clubbed rifles whenever the need arose. But the odds were heavy against the Canadians, and at length, with his supply of bombs exhausted, Clarke found himself supported only by his dead and wounded. He decided to build a temporary barricade to the left of where Nichols was erecting the permanent block. As he was working at this, a party of Germans, including two officers, advanced cautiously towards him along the trench. The officers urged forward their reluctant men, who had already experienced more than they liked of Clarke's offensive methods. Clarke left his work of construction and advanced to meet them, determined to keep them at bay until Nichols had finished the job on the permanent block. His only weapon was a revolver. He emptied its contents into the mob, picked up a German rifle and exhausted its magazine in the same target, flung that aside, snatched up another and continued his hot fire. As Clarke was thus employed, the senior German officer took a rifle from one of his own men and lunged wildly at the Canadian. The point of the bayonet caught Clarke just below the knee; but that was the officer's last act in the war, for Clarke shot him dead where he stood. There were still five Germans left. They turned and ran—and Clarke dropped four of them as they dashed along the trench. The survivor, shouting in excellent English, begged so hard for his life that he was spared. Clarke had killed two officers and sixteen other ranks. But for Clarke's action, Sergeant Nichols could not have erected the permanent block, which was of vital importance to the security of the Canadian position. Though wounded in the back and the knee, Clarke refused to leave the trench until ordered to do so by Lieutenant Hoey. Next day he returned to his platoon in billets."

HUGHES, THOMAS, Private, was born in County Monaghan, Ireland, on the 30th May, 1885, son of Mr. and Mrs. Hughes, of County Monaghan, Ireland. He served in the European War, and was wounded. He was awarded the Victoria Cross [London Gazette, 26 Oct. 1916]: "Thomas Hughes, No. 3/5027, Private, Connaught Rangers. For most conspicuous bravery and determination. He was wounded in an attack, but returned at once to the firing line after having his wounds dressed. Later, seeing a hostile machine gun, he dashed out in front of his company, shot the gunner, and single-handed captured the gun. Though again wounded he brought back three or four prisoners." His own account is as follows: "On the 3rd of September we went over the top. After being hit in four different places, I noticed a machine gun firing in the German lines. So I rushed up, shot both the chaps on the gun and brought it back. I remember no more until I found myself down in the dressing station. P.S.—I forgot to mention I brought four German prisoners with the gun."

JONES, THOMAS ALFRED, Private, was born 25 Dec. 1880, at 39, Princess Street, Runcorn, Cheshire, son of Edward Jones. He was educated at the National School, Runcorn, serving in the Runcorn Volunteers for 14 years. He joined the Army. 5 Aug 1914, as Private, 1st Cheshire Regt., being the second man to be enlisted at the Drill Hall, Runcorn, at the commencement of the war. He took part in the operations at Hill 60 (for four months and two weeks), "and never once did the Germans break through their lines, and on being sent to another part of the line the General told them they were all heroes." He was present in several other engagements, and his extraordinary gallantry on 25 Sept. 1916, was subsequently recognized by the award of the Victoria Cross. He entered the German trenches alone, and at the point of the bayonet compelled 102 German soldiers and officers of the General Staff to surrender, after bombing them with their own bombs, with the aid of four comrades who followed him. He afterwards marched them to the British lines. He was recommended for the Victoria Cross by eleven officers of other regiments who witnessed the incident through field-glasses. Private Jones's father, describing the deed of valour for which his son won the Victoria Cross, writes: "On the morning of the 25th Sept. 1916, the company our son was in had taken a village from the Germans and had lost nearly all their officers, and it was in the afternoon, while digging, to entrench against the enemy, that bullets came so fast. Tom felt that

Thomas Alfred Jones.

he would be hit, and when his nearest comrade fell wounded, he dropped his spade and picked up his rifle, saying, 'If I am to be killed, I'll be killed fighting, not digging.' He set out to sight the sniper who had been so busy firing at them, and while on his way four bullets went through his tunic and one through his helmet (the helmet we have at home), and as soon as he got sight of him, he fired and killed him. He then killed two of the enemy who had been misusing the white flag. He then went into the trenches, after killing two officers; the rest surrendered. Soon afterwards four comrades joined him and helped to bring them in." Private Jones was also awarded the Distinguished Conduct Medal, 28 Sept. 1918, "For his utter fearlessness of danger and carrying messages safely through intense barrage fire, also guiding his comrades to their proper positions." He has also a long-service ribbon. He is an engineer, and was employed by the Salt Union before the war. A comrade who, until wounded, was with Jones, stated that he won the V.C. over and over again. He told the following story of Jones's coolness at Hill 60: "The Germans were coming across, and our rifles got too hot to fire, when Jones said, 'We will have a drum up' (make tea). We made tea, and gave a drink to all the boys who were firing into the enemy." On another occasion Jones led a party of sappers in an attack and blew up German saps. He won his Victoria Cross at Morval, and was gazetted 26 Oct. 1916: "Thomas Alfred Jones, No. 11000, Private, Cheshire Regt. For most conspicuous bravery. He was with his company consolidating the defences in front of a village, and noticing an enemy sniper at 200 yards' distance, he went out, and though one bullet went through his helmet and another through his coat, he returned the sniper's fire and killed him. He then saw two more of the enemy firing at him, although displaying a white flag. Both of these he also shot. On reaching the enemy trench he found several occupied dug-outs, and, single-handed, disarmed 102 of the enemy, including three or four officers, and marched them back to our lines through a heavy barrage. He had been warned of the misuse of the white flag by the enemy, but insisted on going out after them."

KERR, JOHN CHIPMAN, Private, No. 101465, joined the Canadian Military Forces and served in the European War. He was awarded the Victoria Cross for his bravery at Courcelette, France.

The following account of how he won his decoration is taken from "Thirty Canadian V.C.'s," published by Messrs. Skeffington:

"The war was no new thing, many Canadians were veteran soldiers and many were in Flanders graves, when Kerr decided that his services were more urgently required on the field of battle than on his own new acres in the Province of Alberta. He had gone north and west shortly before the outbreak of war, from the home of his family in Cumberland County, Nova Scotia, to virgin land on Spirit River, fifty miles from the nearest railway. Kerr found other 'homesteaders' on Spirit River who saw eye to eye with him in this matter—a dozen patriotic adventurers who were determined to exchange safe establishments in life for the prospects of violent deaths. Together they 'footed' the fifty miles to the railway. In Edmonton they enlisted in a body in the 66th Battalion. Early in June, 1916, four hundred officers and other ranks were drafted from the 66th, then training in England, to the 49th, then fighting in France. Private J. C. Kerr was a more or less unconsidered unit in that draft. These reinforcements, with others, reached France shortly after the Battle of Sanctuary Wood, an engagement in which the Germans attacked with so crushing a superiority of men and metal and the Canadians fought so stubbornly as to necessitate the withdrawal of fragments of battalions of a whole division for reorganization. The 49th Battalion was represented by one of these indomitable fragments. The Canadians marched from the Salient to the Somme in the autumn of that year. The 49th, up to strength once more and with its old spirit renewed, reached Albert on the 13th of September. Forty hours later it took up a battle position at a point near the Sunken Road, before and to the left of the village of Courcelette, with other battalions of the same brigade. In the great Canadian advance of September the 15th, in which our morning and evening attacks drove the Germans from the Sugar Refinery, Courcelette, and many more strongholds and intricate systems of defence, the 49th Battalion supported the Princess Patricia's and the 42nd Battalion on the extreme left of our frontage of aggressive operations. These battalions advanced the line to the left of Courcelette, keeping abreast of the units that assaulted and occupied the village and mopped up its crowded dug-outs and fortified houses. Their activities were devoted entirely to the subjection and occupation of strong trenches and trench machine-gun posts. They moved irresistibly forward, cleaning things up as they went. They reached and occupied their final objectives—with the exception of a length of trench about 250 yards in extent, which remained in the hands of the enemy until the following day. But the defenders of that isolated section of trench could not retreat, for the head of their communicating trench was blocked, they dared not attempt a rearward flight on the surface, and they were flanked right and left by the Canadians. So the matter rested for the night, with no more stir than an occasional exchange of bombs across the flanking barricades. On the afternoon of the 16th, a party of bombers from the 49th Battalion undertook to clear this offending piece of trench and so make possible the consolidation of the entire frontage gained in the previous day's offensives. Here is where the ex-homesteader from Spirit River steps into that high light which illuminates more frequently and glaringly the feeble activities of the music-hall stage than the grim heroics of the battle-field. Private John Chipman Kerr, as first bayonet-man, moved forward well in advance of his party. He twitched himself over the block in the communicating trench in less time than he had ever taken to negotiate a pasture fence on the home-farm. He advanced about thirty yards into the hostile position before a sentry took alarm and hurled a grenade. Kerr saw the grenade coming and, in the fraction of a second at his disposal, attempted to protect himself with his arm. He was partially successful in this, for when the bomb exploded it did no more than blow off the upper joint of his right fore-finger and wound him slightly in the right side. By this time the other members of the assaulting party were close to his heels. The exchange of bombs between the defenders and attackers now became general, though an angle in the trench hid each party from view of the other. Good throwing was done by our men, who were all experts; but Kerr felt that the affair promised to settle into a stationary action unless something new and sudden happened. So he clambered out of the trench and the shocks of that blind fight and moved along the parados until he came into close contact with, and full view of, the enemy. He was still armed with his rifle and two grenades; and, despite loss of blood, he was still full of enterprise and fight. He tossed the grenades among the crowded defenders beneath him and then opened fire into them with his rifle. Mud jambed the bolt of his rifle, whereupon he replaced it with the weapon of the second bayonet-man, Private Frank Long, who had followed him out of the trench and had just then caught up with him. While Kerr pumped lead into the massed enemy beneath his feet he directed the fire of his bombers so effectively, by voice and gesture, that the defenders were forced back to the shelter of the nearest bay. He immediately jumped down into the trench and went after them, with all the Canadian bombers and bayonet-men at his heels. A dug-out was reached; and while this was being investigated Kerr went on alone, rounded a bay and once again joined battle with the defenders of the trench. But the spirit of combat, even of resistance, had gone out of them. Up went their hands! Before having his wounds dressed, Private Kerr escorted the 62 Germans across open ground under heavy fire to a support trench, and then returned and reported himself for duty to his Company Commander. The official recommendation says: 'The action of this man at this juncture undoubtedly resulted in the capture of 62 prisoners and the taking of 250 yards of enemy trench.' This seems to be a conservative statement of the case. It takes no account of the other Germans who were involved in that brisk affair. They have been dead a long time." His Victoria Cross was gazetted 26 Oct. 1916: "John Chipman Kerr, No. 101465, Private, 49th Battn. Canadian Infantry. For most conspicuous bravery. During a bombing attack he was acting as bayonet man, and, knowing that bombs were running short, he ran along the parados under heavy fire until he was in close contact with the enemy, when he opened fire on them at point-blank range, and inflicted heavy loss. The enemy, thinking they were surrounded, surrendered. Sixty-two prisoners were taken, and 250 yards of enemy trench captured. Before carrying out this very plucky act, one of Private Kerr's fingers had been blown off by a bomb. Later, with two other men, he escorted back the prisoners under fire, and then returned to report himself for duty before having his wound dressed."

London Gazette, 25 Nov. 1916.—"His Majesty the King has been graciously pleased to confer the Victoria Cross on the undermentioned Officers, Non-Commissioned Officers and Men."

BRADFORD, ROLAND BOYS, M.C., Lieut. (Temporary Lieut.-Colonel), was born in 1892, and was educated at the Royal Naval School, Eltham, as were his brothers, Capt. T. A. Bradford, D.S.O., and Lieut. G. R. Bradford, V.C., R.N. He joined the Army, and was awarded the Military Cross. He was awarded the Victoria Cross [London Gazette, 25 Nov. 1916], for his fine behaviour at Eaucourt l'Abbaye, France: "Roland Boys Bradford, Lieut. (Temporary Lieut.-Colonel), M.C., 9th Battn. Durham Light Infantry. Date of Act of Bravery: 1 Oct. 1916. For most conspicuous bravery and good leadership in attack, whereby he saved the situation on the right flank of his Brigade and of the Division. Lieut.-Colonel Bradford's battalion was in support. A leading battalion having suffered very severe casualties and the Commander wounded, its flank became dangerously exposed at close quarters to the enemy. Raked by machine-gun fire, the situation of the battalion was critical. At the request of the wounded Commander, Lieut.-Colonel Bradford asked permission to command the exposed battalion in addition to his own. Permission granted, he at once proceeded to the foremost lines. By his fearless energy under fire of all descriptions, and his skilful leadership of the two battalions, regardless of all danger, he succeeded in rallying the attack, captured and defended the objective, and so secured the flank." He was afterwards promoted Captain and then made Brevet Major, and was one of the youngest Battalion Commanders in the Army. He became Temporary Brigadier-General. Brigadier-General R. B. Bradford was killed in action in Nov. 1917.

Roland Boys Bradford.

Tom Edwin Adlam.

ADLAM, TOM EDWIN, Second Lieut., was born at Waterloo Gardens, Salisbury, on 21 Oct. 1893. He is the son of John and Evangeline Adlam, and was educated at Bishop Wordsworth's School, Salisbury. In Sept. 1912, he joined the Territorial Force, and on 16 Nov. 1915, was given a commission as Second Lieutenant. From April, 1916, to Jan. 1919, he served as Instructor at No. 2 Officer Cadet Battn., Cambridge. On 21 June, 1916, at St. Mark's Church, South Farnborough, he married Ivy Annette, daughter of Mr. and Mrs. W. H. Mace, of Farnborough, Hants. There is one daughter,

Josephine. He was awarded the Victoria Cross for his behaviour at Thiépval and Swaben Reboubt, France [London Gazette, 25 Nov. 1916]: "Tom Edwin Adlam, Second Lieut., 7th Battn. Bedfordshire Regt. Date of Act of Bravery: 27–28 Sept. 1916. For most conspicuous bravery. A portion of a village which had defied capture had to be taken at all costs, to permit subsequent operations to develop. This minor operation came under very heavy machine-gun and rifle fire. Second Lieut. Adlam, realizing that time was all-important, rushed from shell-hole to shell-hole under heavy fire, collecting men for a sudden rush, and for this purpose also collected many enemy grenades. At this stage he was wounded in the leg, but nevertheless he was able to out-throw the enemy, and then, seizing his opportunity, and in spite of his wound, he led a rush, captured the position, and killed the occupants. Throughout the day he continued to lead his men in bombing attacks. On the following day he again displayed courage of the highest order, and, though again wounded and unable to throw bombs, he continued to lead his men. His magnificent example of valour, coupled with the skilful handling of the situation, produced far-reaching results." Lieut. Adlam also received the Italian Silver Medal for Military Valour. He became Acting Captain.

KELLY, HENRY, Temporary Second Lieut., was born on 10 July, 1887, at Moston, Manchester, son of Charles Kelly, of Dublin, and Jane Kelly (*née* McGarry), of Manchester. He was educated at St. Patrick's School, Manchester, and Xaverian Brothers' College, Victoria Park, Manchester, and joined the Army on 5 Sept. 1914, as Private. The following are his promotions: Temp. Second Lieutenant, 12 May, 1915; Temp. Lieutenant, 11 Sept. 1916; Temp. Captain, 21 Sept. 1917; Temp. Major, 19 July, 1919. He served in the European War in France, Belgium and Italy. Proceeded overseas to France in May, 1916; was present at the battles of the Somme, 1916; of the Ypres salient, 1917 (Messines Ridge, 7 June, 1917, and Menin Road, 20 Sept. 1917). Asiago Plateau, Italy, 15 June, 1918, and Piave, 27 Oct. 1918. He was awarded the Victoria Cross [London Gazette, 25 Nov. 1916]: "Henry Kelly, Temporary Second Lieut., 10th Battn. West Riding Regt. He showed the utmost valour in an attack on Flers line, immediately south-west of Le Sars, on the 4th Oct. 1916. He twice rallied his company under the heaviest fire, and eventually led the only three available men of his company into the enemy's trench, remaining there bombing until two of his men became casualties and enemy reinforcements arrived from the rear. He then carried his wounded Company Sergeant-Major back to our trenches, a distance of 70 yards, and subsequently three others." He was awarded the Military Cross [London Gazette, 24 Sept. 1918]: "Henry Kelly, Capt., V.C. On the night of 21–22 June, 1918, in a raid on the enemy trenches, this officer, who was commanding a raiding party of two companies, showed the utmost ability in assembling his party, in spite of a very bright moon, and carrying out the attack, which resulted in the capture of 51 prisoners and two machine guns. A large number of the enemy were killed. His gallantry under fire and fine leadership were undoubtedly largely responsible for the success of the raid." [London Gazette, 3 April, 1919]: Bar to Military Cross. "On 27 Oct. 1918, in an attack on the Austrian positions across the Piave, this officer led his company with the greatest dash and gallantry, to the capture of all its objectives. His coolness and utter disregard of danger under heavy fire of every description inspired all ranks, and by his skilful leadership his company succeeded in taking many machine guns and several hundreds of prisoners."

DOWNIE, ROBERT, Sergt., was born at Springburn, Glasgow, on 5 Jan. 1894, son of Mr. Francis Downie (deceased) and of Mrs. Elizabeth Jane Downie, who had 16 children. Five sons served in His Majesty's Forces, and two were killed. He was educated at St. Aloysius' School, Springburn, and joined the Army on 8 Feb. 1912, as a Private; served in the European War, in the 2nd Battn. Royal Dublin Fusiliers, from Aug. 1914, to March, 1919, and was five times wounded. He was awarded the Victoria Cross [London Gazette, 25 Nov. 1916]: "Robert Downie, No. 11213, Sergt., 2nd Battn. Royal Dublin Fusiliers. For most conspicuous bravery and devotion to duty in attack. When most of the officers had become casualties, this non-commissioned officer, utterly regardless of personal danger, moved about under heavy fire and reorganized the attack, which had been temporarily checked. At the critical moment he rushed forward alone, shouting: 'Come on, the Dubs!' This stirring appeal met with immediate response, and the line rushed forward at his call. Sergt. Downie accounted for several of the enemy, and in addition captured a machine gun, killing the team. Though wounded early in the fight, he remained with his company, and gave valuable assistance whilst the position was being consolidated. It was owing to Sergt. Downie's courage and initiative that this important position, which had resisted four or five previous attacks, was won." A public welcome was accorded him on 4 Jan. 1917, at the Springburn Town Hall, Glasgow, where the Lord Provost presided, and the Rev. Father M'Brierty was amongst those present; and in the evening of the same day he was present at a reception given in his honour by the United Irish League, at which he was presented with a gold watch, given him by his old school, and a purse containing treasury notes, by the Springburn Branch of the United Irish League. He has the Russian Order of St. George, the Military Medal and the Mons Medal, and has been twice mentioned in Despatches. Sergt. Downie married, on 4 April, 1914, at Gravesend, Kent, Ivy Sparks, daughter of Charles and Mrs Charles Sparks, and they have a son, Robert, born 18 April, 1915, and a daughter, Annie. Another daughter, Elizabeth, died 16 April, 1919.

Robert Downie.

The "Weekly Record" for 19 May, 1917, gives the following account of Sergt. Downie:

"'Come on, the Dubs!' High and clear above the battle-thunder rose the cheerful clarion-cry. The Dublins heard it and wondered. Like some siren voice it seemed to call them, and with a hoarse, responsive yell they rushed impetuously forward to the achievement of a glorious victory! Whence had come that magic call, and why? Ah! strange and wonderful is the answer to those questions. For the story of it we must go back to a certain day of the Great Push which commenced in the midsummer of last year, and is yet raging furiously along the Western Front. What day it was, or even in which month it fell, the official notice does not state, but it is sufficient for our purpose to know that to the Dublin Fusiliers, with whom our narrative is concerned, it was a day of terrible possibilities and of extremest peril. An attack had been organized upon one of those numerous bastions which the Hun, now fearful lest his greedy grip upon the fair lands of France might be loosened for ever, had strung up along his already trembling line. Hornet-nests of gunners, bombers and snipers were those bastions, and the pulling of the stings of them was the supremest test of soldierly ability and courage. To the Dublin Fusiliers that test had come on this fateful day, and right gallantly did they accept it. No easy task would be theirs. Well they knew that. But when the signal came—'Over you go!'—those brave lads, their hearts aflame, their blood a-tingling, swept forward with all their proverbial dash and élan. Soon, it seemed, they would be atop the hornet's nest itself. Already they were within measurable distance of it, when, from out its well-concealed emplacements, there tore blast upon blast of that ghastly machine-gun fire which knows not mercy nor respite. Rat-tat-tat! had it sounded, faintly and afar off, when first the Fusiliers ran out. Now, as they approached, it had merged into one low, sullen, ugly scream—the scream which tells of death and devastation. Mortal man could never face that suffocating simoon of lead. One by one the Fusiliers began to drop, and amongst the first of them to fall were the brave and splendid officers. A crisis had come. The men would soon be leaderless! Suddenly, and even as the men were wavering, a sturdy figure was observed to emerge, dominating upon the scene. It was that of a non-commissioned officer, Sergt. Robert Downie. He had glimpsed and grasped the situation with all its terrible and momentous possibilities—the officers down and out; the ranks thinning, and those remaining becoming more and more uncertain what to do, how to act; the attack temporarily held up; and, worst of all—— No, there would be no disaster, no defeat, if it were humanly possible to avert it. Such were the thoughts which flashed across the gallant Sergeant's mind as he cast a sweeping glance around. And with those thoughts came another thought. It was a risk, a great risk, but never venture never win! If only the boys would answer his call the situation might yet be saved. And so—— 'Come on, the Dubs!' The Sergeant's voice rose piercingly above the terrorizing din. Already he had been encouraging the wavering line by word and deed, and now, at the most critical moment of all, when the least of things might turn the scales for victory or defeat, his rousing slogan sounded. 'Come on, the Dubs!' The cry was an inspiration. Limbs that had sunk in weariness straightened into pulsing life again, muscles that had slackened grew taut, eyes brightened, jaws became firm and set, and the boys, with swelling breasts and deep, respondent shouts, surged out behind the Sergeant as he bounded towards the grim Hun bastion which had held them up. 'Come on, the Dubs!' And the Dubs, the lust of the fight now full upon them, charged savagely across the intervening space. In a trice their bayonets were reddening through the swirling smoke of battle. And the bold and intrepid Downie, we may be sure, was not the most idle of the stalwarts in that awful mêlée. First at the enemy's throat, as it were, he was soon raining his hefty blows about him, and to quote the plain but convincing words of the official intimation, he had quickly 'accounted for several of the enemy.' But, apart from the Huns themselves, there was one item in their armoury which he had determined to destroy, and that was a particularly troublesome machine gun. It he would have, or perish in the attempt, for with that keen, soldierly intelligence which he had always displayed, he saw that but for its power for mischief the 'Dubs' might have been at their goal long before. With a wild, impetuous rush he had cleared the ground, and, like a terrier amongst rats, he was soon scattering the crew right and left. A brief, fierce struggle, a few smothered cries of rage and pain, and the Huns lay quiet and still on the ensanguined ground. The gun was in our hero's hands, and the bastion was won! But it had yet to be held. The 'Dubs' had achieved a great victory, but not yet could they plume themselves upon ultimate triumph. The Huns, enraged at losing their fortress to the Irishmen, would be certain to counter-attack in the hope of regaining the position. And so, quick on the heels of that hot and irresistible charge of theirs, the men, grim and untiring, feverishly set themselves to the task of holding what they had gained. And a nerve-racking, appalling task it was. On every side were they being threatened with death. Through the air hurtled the 'heavies,' and with them came the vicious, venomous splutter of machine-gun bullets. But valiantly, resolutely, they worked on. Gradually, bit by bit, the defences were thrown up, the position consolidated, and the Huns, baulked and broken, fell back. The final triumph was with the gallant Dublins. Not without cost, however, had that bastion been taken. Four or five times before had it resisted assault, but the British, with that implacable determination which never knows defeat, had rushed it yet again and had secured it at last. The heroic Downie, in the holding of the position as in the taking of it, was the master-spirit of the day. He was everywhere, directing, counselling, and cheering on the men whom he had led so bravely forward. Time and again he cheated death as by a miracle, and even although wounded in the first wild rush for the stronghold itself, he kept firm to his purpose, and carried bravely on until the ground had not only been won but made strong and secure against any counter-attacks the Huns cared to deliver. Thus, by his wonderful courage, and still more wonderful initiative, he earned the right to wear the soldier's proudest laurel. There is a fine postscript to the tale of Sergt. Downie's heorism. Glasgow claims him as her son, and when he arrived in the city some time ago and was interviewed on the subject of his great deed he modestly refused to admit that he had done more than any of his brave companions on that fateful, fearful day. 'Every man in the battalion,' he said, 'won the Victoria Cross that day. I'm only one of the lucky ones. We had many casualties among the officers, and the company and regimental sergeant-majors deserve recognition for what they did.' Of the stirring and eventful circumstances of the glorious episode itself, the charge through that withering fire, the carrying of that supposedly impregnable bastion, the fight for, and the capture of, that pestilential machine gun, and, final act in the whole marvellous drama, the holding of the Hun fortress until victory was achieved—of these things he would say nothing. He had done but his duty, he thought, and, like a good soldier, he left it at that. But if Sergt. Downie, with soldierly modesty, refused to speak of either his deeds or of himself, some interesting facts were ascertained from other sources. The gallant fellow, it appears, is only in his twenty-third year, and is one of a family of sixteen, of whom thirteen are alive. His father, the late Mr. Frank Downie, was employed for thirty years in the Hydepark Locomotive Works, Glasgow, as an oiler and beltman. His mother resides in Springburn Road, in which district of the city Sergt. Downie was born. After leaving school he was employed in the same works as his father, but at the age of eighteen he joined the Army, in which he has served nearly five years. He went to France with the Expeditionary Force, and except for two periods on leave, he has been at the front since August, 1914. Up till the time of the performance of the act of bravery which gained for him the V.C. he had escaped unwounded, but he suffered on one occasion from the effects of gas poisoning. The intimation of her husband's triumph came to Mrs. Downie in a somewhat interesting way. In a letter immediately preceding the official announcement, the Sergeant simply wrote that he had good news for her, but he would not let her know what it was, he said, just yet. A few nights later Mrs. Downie had gone to her work in a certain munition factory, where she is engaged as a shell-inspector, when a telegram arrived at her home. She did not get it until her return next morning. 'I was afraid to open it,' she said. 'I was so excited, because telegrams never bring very good news!' Her sense of relief and joy when she did open it may be imagined. For here is the remarkable part of the whole story. When the Sergeant was leaving for the front, he had parted from his friends with the jocular remark: 'Good-bye; and next time I see you I'll bring the V.C.!' The joke had become a splendid fact! Mrs. Downie spoke with great pride of her husband. Pointing to a silver cup and a medal, she said he had won them for boxing, and when asked if he had done much boxing, Mrs. Downie replied: 'Oh, he's a great, daring boy, Robert!' and proceeded to describe the winning of the medal. It was at a fair in England. 'When he saw the names of two men put up at a booth to box, he said to me, "Wait a minute, Ivy, till I see this." The next thing I saw was Robert coming out with his medal and a black eye.' Three of Sergt. Downie's brothers, it may be added, are serving in the Army, and another brother was in the Navy, but was discharged on medical grounds. Sergt. David Downie, Royal Scots Fusiliers, the oldest member of the family, has twenty-three years' service to his credit, and he is the holder of the Military Medal. Mrs. Downie, the wife of the winner of the V.C., has two brothers serving. Her husband was promoted to his present rank on the field. One of the Sergeant's brothers relates a remarkable fact, one which probably cannot be equalled in any other part of the United Kingdom. Carleston Street, where the Sergeant's home is, is a comparatively short street of humble dwellings, and yet over two hundred have gone from it to the Army, sixteen have been killed, three have lost legs, and two have lost arms. Now the little thoroughfare can claim, as it does with unbounded pride, that it has a Victoria Cross hero of its very own."

TURNBULL, JAMES YOUNG, Sergt., served in the European War, and was awarded the Victoria Cross [London Gazette, 25 Nov. 1916]: "James Young Turnbull, No. 15888, Sergt., late 17th Battn. Highland Light Infantry. For most conspicuous bravery and devotion to duty, when, having with his party captured a post apparently of great importance to the enemy, he was subjected to severe counter-attacks, which were continuous throughout the whole day. Although his party was wiped out and replaced several times during the day, Sergt. Turnbull never wavered in his determination to hold the post, the loss of which would have been very serious. Almost single-handed he maintained his position, and displayed the highest degree of valour and skill in the performance of his duties. Later in the day this very gallant soldier was killed whilst bombing a counter-attack from the parados of our trench." His father and sister were given the Victoria Cross so gallantly won by Sergt. Turnbull.

Frederick J. Edwards.

EDWARDS, FREDERICK JEREMIAH, Private, was born at Queenstown, County Cork, son of the late Quartermaster-Sergt. Henry J. Edwards, Royal Garrison Artillery, and Mrs. Anne Edwards. He was educated at the Royal Hibernian Military School, and joined the Army on the 30th Oct. 1908. He served in the European War in France, and was awarded the Victoria Cross [London Gazette, 25 Nov. 1916]: "Frederick Jeremiah Edwards, No. 2442, Private, 12th (Service) Battn. Middlesex Regt. For most conspicuous bravery and resource. His part of the line was held up by machine-gun fire, and all officers had become casualties. There was confusion and indication of retirement. Private Edwards, grasping the situation, on his own initiative dashed out alone towards the gun, which he knocked out with bombs. This very gallant act, coupled with great presence of mind and a total disregard of personal danger, made further advance possible and cleared up a dangerous situation." Corpl. Edwards writes: "I was taken prisoner in April, 1918, just off Amiens. Previous to the war I served in the R.G.A. three years in Hong-Kong, finally finishing my service in the Middlesex Regt. I have got two brothers still serving: Sergt. H. Edwards, Norfolk Regt., and Gunner M. P. Edwards, R.G.A. Sergt. H. Edwards was taken prisoner in the Siege of Kut-el-Amara. I think this a good record for Regiment and Company: Private R. Ryder and myself were both in the same battalion, regiment and company, and both won the V.C. on the same day, and in the same Battle of Thiépval 26 Sept. 1916. I was recommended for the V.C. by the late Brigadier-General Maxwell, V.C., etc., who was then my Colonel. I was demobilized 20 March, 1919."

Lieut.-General Sir Ivor Maxse, K.C.B., C.V.O., D.S.O., Commanding 18th Division, wrote: "I have read with great pleasure the report of your Regimental Commander and Brigade Commander regarding your gallant conduct and devotion to duty in the field on 26 Sept. 1916, at the capture of Thiépval."

The following is an extract from a newspaper: "Corpl. F. J. Edwards, V.C., Middlesex Regt., a former boy in the Hibernian Military School, Phœnix Park, was presented yesterday, on behalf of the Governors, staff, students and boys, with a solid silver flask and cheque to be invested for him in the War Loan. The presentation had to be postponed from Saturday, as the boat on which the V.C. travelled was delayed. He is the second boy of the school to gain the distinction, the first being won in the Crimean War. The deed which won the award for Corpl. Edwards was the bombing of a German machine-gun party which had caused considerable damage. The Lord Lieutenant, who was accompanied by Sir Bryan Mahon and Major-General Foy, made the presentation in the gymnasium of the school, in the presence of the boys under Colonel M'Donnell, Commandant. His Excellency said they were all proud of Corpl. Edwards's distinction, and it would be a great encouragement to the boys to emulate his achievements."

RYDER, ROBERT, Private, served in the European War in France. He was awarded the Victoria Cross [London Gazette, 25 Nov. 1916]: "Robert Ryder, No. 3281, Private, 12th Battn. Middlesex Regt. For most conspicuous bravery and initiative during an attack. His company was held up by heavy rifle fire, and all his officers had become casualties. For want of leadership the attack was flagging. Private Ryder, realizing the situation, without a moment's thought for his own safety, dashed absolutely alone at the enemy trench, and by skilful manipulation of his Lewis gun, succeeded in clearing the trench. This very gallant act not only made possible but also greatly inspired the subsequent advance of his comrades, and turned possible failure into success."

London Gazette, 15 Dec. 1916.—"War Office, 15 Dec. 1916. His Majesty the King has been graciously pleased to confer the Victoria Cross on the undermentioned Officer and Man."

FREYBERG, BERNARD CYRIL, Capt. and Brevet Lieut.-Colonel, was born on 21 March, 1889, in London, son of the late J. Freyberg, Esq., of Wellington, New Zealand. He was educated at Wellington College, and New Zealand University, New Zealand, and joined the Army in Nov. 1909, as a Second Lieutenant in the 6th Hauraki Regt., New Zealand Military Forces, and transferred to the British Regular Army later; promoted Captain in May, 1916, and made Brevet Major in June, 1917; Brevet Lieutenant-Colonel in Jan. 1918. He served in the European War, and had a very distinguished record. He was a Company Commander in the Hood Battn. Royal Naval Division in 1914 and 1915, and from 1915 to 1917 commanded the Hood Battn. of the Royal Naval Division. He was in the retreat from Antwerp; was then stationed at the Suez Canal Defences for three weeks, and later took part in the operations on the Gallipoli Peninsula from the landing until the evacuation. He was created a Companion of the Distinguished Service Order [London Gazette]: "For most conspicuous gallantry and devotion to duty during the landing on the Peninsula the night of 24–25 April, 1915, when he swam ashore at night, alone, and lit flares on the beach to distract attention from the landing operations which were happening elsewhere. He was several hours in the water before being picked up. He was transferred to France, and there took part in the battles of the Somme (1916), the Ancre (1916), Arras (1917), Bullecourt (1917), Third Battle of Ypres, Passchendaele (1917–18), the First Battle of the Lys and of the Forêt de Nieppe (1918), Battle of Hill 63 and Ploegsteert Wood, Fourth Battle of Ypres, Gheluvelt, Battle of Ledingham, Second Battle of Lys, Crossings of the Scheldt and Dendre. He was awarded the Victoria Cross [London Gazette, 16 Dec. 1917]: "Bernard Cyril Freyberg, Lieut.-Colonel, Grenadier Guards. For most conspicuous bravery and brilliant leading as a battalion commander. By his splendid personal bravery he carried the initial attack straight through the enemy's front system of trenches. Owing to mist and heavy fire of all descriptions, Lieut.-Colonel Freyberg's command was much disorganized after the capture of the first objective. He personally rallied and reformed his men, including men from other units who had become intermixed. He inspired all with his own contempt of danger. At the appointed time he led his men forward to the successful assault of the second objective, many prisoners being captured. During this

Bernard Cyril Freyberg.

advance he was twice wounded. He again rallied and reformed all who were with him, and although unsupported in a very advanced position, he held his ground throughout the day and the following night under heavy artillery and machine-gun fire. When reinforced on the following morning he organized the attack on a strongly-fortified village, and showed a fine example of dash in personally leading the assault, capturing the village and 500 prisoners. In this operation he was again wounded. Later in the afternoon he was again wounded severely, but refused to leave the line till he had issued his final instructions. The personality, valour and utter contempt of danger on the part of this single officer enabled the furthermost objective of the corps to be permanently held, and on this point d'appui the line was eventually formed." He commanded the 173rd Infantry Brigade in the 58th Division in 1917, and the 88th Infantry Brigade in the 29th Division in 1918 and 1919. He was awarded a Bar to the Distinguished Service Order [London Gazette, Oct. 1918], for most conspicuous bravery and devotion to duty in the attacks which led up to the capture of Gheluvelt on 28 Sept. 1918, where the success of the operations was greatly due to his dash and leading power. Wherever the fighting was thickest, he was always to be found leading and encouraging his troops. He gained a second Bar to the Distinguished Service Order in the last five minutes of the war. In an action at Lessines he led the cavalry in a dash to save the bridge over the river Dendre, and with nine men only he rushed a village on horseback, and captured a village and 104 prisoners two minutes before the beginning of the armistice. The award of the Bar so dramatically gained was announced in the London Gazette of March, 1919. Brigadier-General Freyberg went later to the Rhine with the Army of Occupation. He was mentioned in Despatches no less than seven times, and was awarded the Croix de Guerre by the French Government. He was wounded nine times, and was awarded the C.M.G. in the Peace Gazette for services in the later stages of the war. He won the New Zealand Swimming Championships from 100 yards to a mile in 1905–6, and the 100 yards in 1909; played Rugby, and is a keen yachtsman.

LEWIS, HERBERT WILLIAM, Private, served in the European War, in Salonika, and was awarded the Victoria Cross [London Gazette, 15 Dec. 1916]: "Herbert William Lewis, No. 16224, Private, 11th Battn. Welsh Regt. For most conspicuous bravery and devotion to duty during a raid. On reaching the enemy trenches Private Lewis was twice wounded, but refused to be attended to, and showed great gallantry in searching enemy dug-outs. He was again wounded, and again refused attendance. At this point three of the enemy were observed to be approaching, and Private Lewis immediately attacked them single-handed, capturing all. Subsequently, during the retirement, he went to the assistance of a wounded man, and under heavy shell and rifle fire brought him to our lines, on reaching which he collapsed. Private Lewis showed throughout a brilliant example of courage, endurance, and devotion to duty."

London Gazette, 30 Dec. 1916.—"War Office, 30 Dec. 1916. His Majesty the King has been graciously pleased to confer the Victoria Cross on the undermentioned Officers.

BLOOMFIELD, WILLIAM ANDERSON, Capt., served in the European War in East Africa. He was awarded the Victoria Cross [London Gazette, 30 Dec. 1916]: "William Anderson Bloomfield, Capt., Scouts Corps, South African Mounted Brigade. For most conspicuous bravery. Finding that, after being heavily attacked in an advanced and isolated position, the enemy were working round his flanks, Capt. Bloomfield evacuated his wounded, and subsequently withdrew his command to a new position, he himself being amongst the last to retire. On arrival at the new position he found that one of the wounded—No. 2475, Corpl. D. M. P. Bowker—had been left behind. Owing to very heavy fire he experienced difficulties in having the wounded corporal brought in. Rescue meant passing over some 400 yards of open ground, swept by heavy fire, in full view of the enemy. This task Capt. Bloomfield determined to face himself, and, unmindful of personal danger, he succeeded in reaching Corpl. Bowker and carrying him back, subjected throughout the double journey to heavy machine-gun and rifle fire. This act showed the highest degree of valour and endurance."

BENNETT, EUGENE PAUL, Capt., was born at Stroud, Gloucestershire, on 4 June, 1892, and is the son of Charles Bennett, Accountant, and Florence Emma Sophia Bennett. He was educated at the Marling School, Stroud, Gloucestershire, and later became a Member of the Staff of the Bank of England. He joined the Artists' Rifles as Private in Oct. 1913, and when the Great War broke out went with the 1st Battn. to France in Oct. 1914. He was gazetted to the 2nd Battn. of the Worcester Regt. 1 Jan. 1915, and remained with them up to 5 Nov. 1916. He was awarded the Military Cross for work in a counter-attack on 26 Sept. 1915. He was again mentioned in Despatches, and awarded the Victoria Cross [London Gazette, 30 Dec. 1916]: "Eugene Paul Bennett, Temporary Lieut., 2nd Battn. Worcester Regt. Date of Act of Bravery: 5 Nov. 1916. For most conspicuous bravery in action when in command of the second wave of the attack. Finding that the first wave had suffered heavy casualties, its commander killed and the line wavering, Lieut. Bennett advanced at the head of the second wave, and by his personal example of valour and resolution reached his objective with but sixty men. Isolated with his small party, he at once took steps to consolidate his position under heavy rifle and machine-gun fire from both flanks, and, although wounded, he remained in command directing and controlling. He set an example of cheerfulness and resolution beyond all praise, and there is little doubt that but for his personal example of courage the attack would have been checked at the outset." This happened near Le Transloy, France. His wounds necessitated his return to England. The Bank of England presented him with a Sword of Honour. His hobbies are golf, Rugby football and swimming.

Eugene Paul Bennett.

London Gazette, 13 Jan. 1917.—"War Office, 13 Jan. 1917. His Majesty the King has been graciously pleased to confer the Victoria Cross on the undermentioned Men."

CUNNINGHAM, JOHN, Private, No. 12/21, East Yorkshire Regt. He served in the European War in France, and was awarded the Victoria Cross [London Gazette, 13 Jan. 1917]: "No. 12/21, John Cunningham, Private, 12th Battn. East Yorkshire Regt. For most conspicuous bravery and resource during operations. After the enemy's front line had been captured, Private Cunningham proceeded with a bombing section up a communication trench. Much opposition was encountered, and the rest of the section became casualties. Collecting all the bombs from the casualties, this gallant soldier went on alone. Having expended all his bombs, he returned for a fresh supply, and again proceeded to the communication trench, where he met a party of ten of the enemy. These he killed, and cleared the trench up to the enemy line. His conduct throughout the day was magnificent." The Lord Mayor of Hull presented Private Cunningham with an illuminated address on behalf of the city. He was the first Hull man to win the Victoria Cross. He is married, his wife's name being Ena Cunningham.

LAUDER, DAVID ROSS, Private, was born at Dalry, Scotland, and was employed as a Carter in his native town. He joined the 1/4th Battn. Royal Scots Fusiliers as Private, and served in the European War. His battalion after a short period of training went to the Dardanelles, and it was there that Private Lauder performed the brave action for which he was awarded the Victoria Cross [London Gazette, 13 Jan. 1917]: "David Ross Lauder, No. 7709, Private, Royal Scots Fusiliers. For most conspicuous bravery when with a bombing party retaking a sap. Private Lauder threw a bomb, which failed to clear the parapet and fell amongst the bombing party. There was no time to smother the bomb and Private Lauder at once put his foot on it, thereby localizing the explosion. His foot was blown off, but the remainder of the party through this act of sacrifice escaped unhurt." After thus heroically redeeming his own mistake, he was sent to a hospital in Malta, and then to England. He is now able to walk with only a slight limp, as he has been provided with an artificial leg. His Commanding Officer described his action as the pluckiest thing he had seen in Gallipoli—a land of brave deeds. The Serbians also awarded him the Serbian Medal for bravery. He obtained a position in a munition factory at Parkhead, Scotland, on being discharged from the Army.

London Gazette, 2 Feb. 1917.—"Admiralty, 2 Feb. 1917. The King has been graciously pleased to approve the posthumous grant of the Victoria Cross to the undermentioned Officers in recognition of their conspicuous gallantry in an attempt to reprovision the force besieged in Kut-el-Amara."

FIRMAN, HUMPHREY OSBALDESTON BROOKE, Lieut., was the son of H. B. Firman and of Mrs. H. B. Firman. He served in the European War, and was awarded the Victoria Cross posthumously [London Gazette, 2 Feb. 1917]: "Humphrey Osbaldeston Brooke Firman, Lieut., Royal Navy. In recognition of his conspicuous gallantry in an attempt to reprovision the force besieged in Kut-el-Amara." The General Officer Commanding Indian Expeditionary Force D reported on this attempt in the following words: "At 8 p.m. on 24 April, 1916, with a crew from the Royal Navy, under Lieut. Firman, R.N., assisted by Lieut.-Commander Cowley, R.N.V.R., the Julnar, carrying 270 tons of supplies, left Falahiyah in an attempt to reach Kut. Her departure was covered by all the artillery and machine-gun fire that could be brought to bear, in the hope of distracting the enemy's attention. She was, however, discovered, and shelled on her passage up the river. At 1 a.m. on the 25th General Townshend reported that she had not arrived, and that at midnight a burst of heavy firing had been heard at Magisis (some eight and a half miles from Kut by the river) which had suddenly ceased. There could be but little doubt that the enterprise had failed, and the next day the Air Service reported the Julnar in the hands of the Turks at Magisis. The leader of this brave attempt, Lieut. H. O. B. Firman, R.N., and his assistant, Lieut.-Commander C. H. Cowley, R.N.V.R., the latter of whom, throughout the campaign in Mesopotamia, performed magnificent service in command of the Mejideh, have been reported by the Turks to have been killed. The remainder of the gallant crew, including five wounded, are prisoners of war. Knowing well the chances against them, all the gallant officers and men who manned the Julnar for the occasion were volunteers. I trust that the services in this connection of Lieut. H. O. B. Firman, R.N., and Lieut.-Commander C. H. Cowley, R.N.V.R., his assistant, both of whom were unfortunately killed, may be recognized by the posthumous grant of some suitable honour." His father was received by the King at Buckingham Palace, and presented with the Victoria Cross.

Major E. W. C. Sandes, M.C., R.E., says in "Kut and Captivity" (pages 245–246): "The only chance of saving the garrison seemed to be in bringing to Kut a sufficient supply of food to keep the troops alive until the floods had subsided and a very large Relief Force had assembled—say for another two months. The Army Commander decided that an attempt should be made to run a ship up the Tigris laden with selected provisions for the garrison of Kut, and the fine twin-screw steamer Julnar was selected for this desperate venture. She was inspected by Admiral Wemyss, at Falahiyeh, on the evening of 8 April, to see if she was suitable for the attempt, and then, having unloaded all cargo, she was sent downstream to Amareh. There her cabins, saloons and upper-deck stanchions were removed, her masts cut down, and her bridge and engine-room protected by thin armour-plating. She was then loaded with about 270 tons of selected stores for the starving garrison of Kut. While at Amareh, volunteers were called for, and three officers and eleven men were selected. No married man was allowed to volunteer for the attempt to reach Kut. The three officers were Lieut.-Commander C. H. Cowley, R.N.V.R. (formerly of Messrs. Lynch Brothers), Lieut. H. O. B. Firman, R.N., and Engineer-Lieut. Lewis Reed, R.N.V.R. (also formerly of Messrs. Lynch Brothers). The eleven men belonged mostly to the Royal Navy. To this small band of heroes was given the task of running the Julnar through the Turkish position to Kut. The ship arrived at Falahiyeh on 23 April, but did not start for Kut till the following night. Every arrangement was made with all secrecy in Kut itself to unload the stores from the Julnar on her arrival near No. 12 Picquet (usually known as No. 3 Picquet), not far above the fort, where she was expected to run alongside the bank at about 4 a.m. on 25 April." Major Sandes was—as all readers of his fascinating book are, of course, aware—himself in Kut, and he continues: "Alas for our hopes! the Julnar failed to reach Kut. In the early morning of 25 April we could see her at the Magasis Ferry, aground and captured. It appears that the ship started at 8 p.m. from Falahiyeh, where the Relief Force flotilla was moored, and in half an hour had been discovered by the Turks by the aid of star shell. She ran through a hellish rifle fire from both banks in the Es-Sin position, and safely crossed the steel cable of a flying-bridge in that position. It is said that the cable broke. About fifteen minutes before reaching Fort Magasis, however, the ship was shelled at point-blank range by Turkish field guns brought down to the water's edge. A shell hit the bridge and killed Lieut. Firman, R.N., and others raked the ship, while bullets riddled her hull. At length, opposite Magasis, the Julnar fouled another steel cable, and was held up by it. The gallant crew then surrendered. The survivors, including five wounded, were removed to the shore, and later were sent up country, but Commander Cowley disappeared. There is no doubt that he was secretly murdered by the Turks. With the capture of the Julnar, the last hope of the relief of the garrison of Kut failed." It seems absurd to talk about the "dark ages" when one reads about the crimes perpetrated by present-day Germans and their unspeakable allies; and the yet more degraded, if more ignorant, Bolshevists. One cannot, fortunately, always judge a nation by its leaders, but it is well to remember that—even in this age of culture and civilization, when super-men and Socialists are peacocking about upon the earth—there is still a God in His Heaven, worshipped after their fashion by Christian and Mohammedan alike. "'Vengeance is mine, and I will repay,' saith the Lord." It is not lists of wanted criminals or Leagues of Nations alone that can regenerate the earth by the light of culture. "The Lord sitteth above the water-floods, be the earth never so unquiet."

COWLEY, CHARLES HENRY, Lieut.-Commander, joined the Royal Naval Volunteer Reserve, and served in the European War. He was awarded the Victoria Cross posthumously [London Gazette, 2 Feb. 1917]: "Charles Henry Cowley, Lieut.-Commander, Royal Naval Volunteer Reserve. In recognition of his conspicuous gallantry in an attempt to reprovision the force besieged in Kut-el-Amara." The General Officer Commanding Indian Expeditionary Force D reported on this attempt in the following words: "At 8 p.m. on 24 April, 1916, with a crew from the Royal Navy, under Lieut. Firman, R.N., assisted by Lieut.-Commander Cowley, R.N.V.R., the Julnar, carrying 270 tons of supplies, left Falahiyeh, in an attempt to reach Kut. Her departure was covered by all the artillery and machine-gun fire that could be brought to bear in the hope of distracting the enemy's attention. She was, however, discovered, and shelled on her passage up the river. At 1 a.m. on the 25th General Townshend reported that she had not arrived, and that at midnight a burst of heavy firing had been heard at Magisis (some eight and a half miles from Kut by the river) which had suddenly ceased. There could be but little doubt that the enterprise had failed, and the next day the Air Service reported the Julnar in the hands of the Turks at Magisis. The leader of this brave attempt, Lieut. H. O. B. Firman, R.N., and his assistant, Lieut.-Commander C. H. Cowley, R.N.V.R., the latter of whom, throughout the campaign in Mesopotamia, performed magnificent service in command of the Mejideh, have been reported by the Turks to have been killed. The remainder of the gallant crew, including five wounded, are prisoners of war. Knowing well the chances against them, all the gallant officers and men who manned the Julnar for the occasion were volunteers. I trust that the services in this connection of Lieut. H. O. B. Firman, R.N., and Lieut.-Commander C. H. Cowley, R.N.V.R., his assistant, both of whom were unfortunately killed, may be recognized by the posthumous grant of some suitable honour."

London Gazette, 12 Feb. 1917.—"War Office, 12 Feb. 1917. His Majesty the King has been graciously pleased to award the Victoria Cross to Thomas Mottershead, No. 1396, Sergt., late Royal Flying Corps."

MOTTERSHEAD, THOMAS, Sergt., served in the European War, and was awarded the Victoria Cross [London Gazette, 12 Feb. 1917]: "Thomas Mottershead, No. 1396, Sergt., late Royal Flying Corps. For most conspicuous bravery, endurance and skill when, attacked at an altitude of 9,000 feet, the petrol tank was pierced and the machine set on fire. Enveloped in flames, which his observer, Lieut. Gower, was unable to subdue, this very gallant soldier succeeded in bringing his aeroplane back to our lines, and though he made a successful landing, the machine collapsed on touching the ground, pinning him beneath wreckage from which he was subsequently rescued. Though suffering extreme torture from burns, Sergt. Mottershead showed the most conspicuous presence of mind in the careful selection of a landing-place, and his wonderful endurance and fortitude undoubtedly saved the life of his observer. He has since succumbed to his injuries." Sergt. Mottershead was married, his wife's name being Lilian Mottershead.

London Gazette, 6 March, 1917.—"Admiralty, 6 March, 1917. The King has been graciously pleased to approve of the posthumous grant of the Victoria Cross to the undermentioned Officer in recognition of his most conspicuous bravery and devotion to duty in the course of the Battle of Jutland. The full facts have now been ascertained: Commander L. W. Jones, R.N. (killed in action)."

JONES, LOFTUS WILLIAM, Commander, served in the European War, and was awarded the Victoria Cross [London Gazette, 6 March, 1917]: "In recognition of his most conspicuous bravery and devotion to duty in the course of the Battle of Jutland. On the afternoon of the 31st May, 1916, during the action, Commander Jones, in H.M.S. Shark, Torpedo Boat Destroyer, led a division of destroyers to attack the enemy Battle Cruiser Squadron. In the course of this attack a shell hit the Shark's bridge, putting the steering gear out of order, and very shortly afterwards another shell disabled the main engines, leaving the vessel helpless. The Commanding Officer of another destroyer, seeing the Shark's plight, came between her and the enemy and offered assistance, but was warned by Commander Jones not to risk being almost certainly sunk in trying to help. Commander Jones, though wounded in the leg, went up to help connect and man the after wheel. Meanwhile the forecastle gun with its crew had been blown away, and the same fate soon afterwards befell the after gun and crew. Commander Jones then went to the midship and only remaining gun, and personally assisted in keeping it in action. All this time the Shark was subjected to very heavy fire from enemy light cruisers and destroyers at short range. The gun's crew of the midship gun was reduced to three, of whom an Able Seaman was soon badly wounded in the leg. A few minutes later Commander Jones was hit by a shell, which took off his leg above the knee, but he continued to give orders to his gun's crew, while a Chief Stoker improvised a tourniquet round his thigh. Noticing that the ensign was not properly hoisted, he gave orders for another to be hoisted. Soon afterwards, seeing that the ship could not survive much longer, and as a German destroyer was closing, he gave orders for the surviving members of the crew to put on life-belts. Almost immediately this order had been given, the Shark was struck by a torpedo and sank. Commander Jones was unfortunately not among the survivors from the Shark, who were picked up by a neutral vessel in the night." The Victoria Cross won by Commander Jones was given by the King to his wife.

London Gazette, 10 March, 1917.—"The King has been graciously pleased to approve of the grant of the Victoria Cross to the undermentioned Non-commissioned Officer and Officer."

MOTT, EDWARD JOHN, Sergt., was born at Drayton, near Abingdon, Berkshire, on the 4th July, 1893, son of John Mott, Labourer. He was educated at Abingdon Council School. He joined the Army on the 31st Dec. 1910, enlisting in the 1st Battn. The Border Regt. He served in the European War, and was present at the Landing at the Dardanelles in April, 1915. He won the Distinguished Conduct Medal on 28 April, 1915. He was present at the Evacuation in Jan. 1916, and went to Egypt in Jan. 1916, and in March, 1916, to France. He was awarded the Victoria Cross for the attack on the Kaiser's birthday [London Gazette, 10 March, 1917]: "Edward John Mott, No. 9887, Sergt., The Border Regt. For most conspicuous gallantry and initiative when in an attack the company to which he belonged was held up at a strong point by machine-gun fire. Although severely wounded in the eye, Sergt. Mott made a rush for the gun, and after a fierce struggle seized the gunner and took him prisoner, capturing the gun. It was due to the dash and initiative of this non-commissioned officer that the left flank attack succeeded."

MURRAY, HENRY, Capt., served in the European War in France, and was awarded the D.C.M.; created a Companion of the Distinguished Service Order, and was awarded the Victoria Cross [London Gazette, 10 March, 1917]: "Henry Murray, D.S.O., D.C.M., Capt., 13th Battn. Australian Infantry, Australian Imperial Force. For most conspicuous bravery when in command of the right flank company in attack. He led his company to the assault with great skill and courage, and the position was quickly captured. Fighting of a very severe nature followed, and three heavy counter-attacks were beaten back, these successes being due to Capt. Murray's wonderful work. Throughout the night his company suffered heavy casualties through concentrated enemy shell fire, and on one occasion gave ground for a short way. This gallant officer rallied his command and saved the situation by sheer valour. He made his presence felt throughout the line, encouraging his men, heading bombing parties, leading bayonet charges, and carrying wounded to places of safety. His magnificent example inspired his men throughout."

Henry Murray.

London Gazette, 15 March, 1917.—"War Office, 15 March, 1917. His Majesty the King has been graciously pleased to approve of the award of the Victoria Cross to the undermentioned Officer and Non-commissioned Officers of the 1st Battn. Lancashire Fusiliers, in recognition of most conspicuous bravery displayed: Capt. (Temporary Major) Cuthbert Bromley (since drowned); No. 1506, Sergt. Frank Edward Stubbs (since died of wounds); No. 2609, Corpl. (now Sergt.) John Grimshaw. On the 25th April, 1915, Headquarters and three companies of the 1st Battn. Lancashire Fusiliers, in effecting a landing on the Gallipoli Peninsula to the west of Cape Helles, were met by very deadly fire from hidden machine guns, which caused a great number of casualties. The survivors, however, rushed up to and cut the wire entanglements, notwithstanding the terrific fire from the enemy, and after overcoming supreme difficulties, the cliffs were gained and the position maintained. Amongst the many very gallant officers and men engaged in this most hazardous undertaking, Capt. Bromley, Sergt. Stubbs, and Corpl. Grimshaw have been selected by their comrades as having performed the most signal acts of bravery and devotion to duty. The above awards of the Victoria Cross are to be read in conjunction with these conferred on the undermentioned for most conspicuous bravery on the same occasion, and notified in the Gazette of 24 Aug. 1915: Capt. Richard Raymond Willis, 1st Battn. Lancashire Fusiliers; No. 1293, Sergt. Alfred Richards, 1st Battn. Lancashire Fusiliers; No. 1809, Private William Keneally, 1st Battn. Lancashire Fusiliers. Note.—Consequent on the award of the Victoria Cross the award of the Distinguished Conduct Medal to No. 2609, Sergt. John Grimshaw, 1st Battn. Lancashire Fusiliers, which was published in the London Gazette dated 16 Nov. 1915, is hereby cancelled.

BROMLEY, CUTHBERT, Capt. (Temporary Major), was born on 19 Sept. 1878, and was the second son of Sir John Bromley and Lady Bromley, of Sutton Corner, Seaford, Sussex. He was educated at St. Paul's School. He joined the Army in May, 1898, in the Lancashire Fusiliers; was promoted Lieutenant in the 20th Regt. in Dec. 1898; Captain in June, 1901; Adjutant in May, 1914; was employed with the West African Frontier Force from July, 1901, to May, 1903; West African Medals (Southern Nigeria) 1901–2; Aro Expedition Medal with clasp; West African (Southern Nigeria), 1902, clasp; was Transport Officer while in India; Superintendent of Gymnasia (Irish Command) Sept. 1906, to Feb. 1907. He was awarded the Victoria Cross for his bravery at Gallipoli [London Gazette, 15 March, 1917]: "Cuthbert Bromley, Capt. (Temporary Major), 1st Battn. Lancashire Fusiliers. Date of Act of Bravery: 25 April, 1915. In effecting a landing of the Gallipoli Peninsula, Headquarters and three companies of the Lancashire Fusiliers were met by very deadly fire from hidden machine guns, which caused a great number of casualties. The survivors, however, rushed up to and cut the wire entanglements, notwithstanding the terrific fire from the enemy, and after overcoming supreme difficulties the cliffs were gained and the position maintained. Amongst the many very gallant officers and men engaged in this most hazardous undertaking, Major Bromley, Sergt. Stubbs and Sergt. Grimshaw have been selected by their comrades as having performed the most signal acts of bravery and devotion to duty." An extract from a newspaper says: "It was the wonderful spirit fostered by Bromley during years of camaraderie and fine example in the regiment which brought success at Cape Helles on the early morning of 25 April, 1915. His personal influence was immeasurable. He had made the Lancashire Fusiliers the champions in all India in military training, boxing, football and cross-country running. Those men who followed him ashore under hellish fire had true discipline. Bromley was with the men a leader and a comrade. Nothing that the enemy could do would have stopped the effort of any individual to win while it was possible for him to go on. And half the battalion won through that morning. The others died or fell wounded in the boats, in the water, on the beach, on the cliffs, or on the high ground gained and held while reinforcements were landed to push the advantage won." Mr. Henry W. Nevinson says in "The Dardanelles Campaign" (pages 100–102): "At V Beach, in spite of the incalculable courage and skill of the Irish Regulars and the sailors combined, the landing on the 25th had failed. At W Beach, not much more than half a mile north-west, over the cliff of Cape Helles, where the lighthouse and Fort I. had stood, the English covering party displayed equal heroism and gained greater success. W Beach is a shallower but longer arc of sandy shore, curving between Cape Helles and Cape Tekke, the two extreme points of the Peninsula. Between the two inaccessible cliffs and the fallen rocks which the sea washes, a gully has been cut by a short watercourse, draining the extremity of the high and slightly undulating plateau in which the Peninsula ends. Except after heavy rains, the gully is dry, but its occasional stream, working upon the sandstone formation, and aided by the north-east wind blowing dust over the plateau's surface, has piled up low heaps of sand dune, at that time covered with bent grass, spring flowers and the aromatic herbs which flourish upon the dry sea coasts of the Near East. Along its gentle curve the actual beach is rather more than a quarter of a mile in length, and its broadest part, where the gully runs out, is some forty yards across. Hidden in the shallows a strong wire entanglement had been laid, and another protected the whole length of the beach from end to end of the water's edge. To check communication with V Beach, two redoubts had been constructed upon the plateau south-east, and from them thick entanglements ran down to the cliff's edge at Cape Helles. Other entanglements on the north-west cut off communication with the more distant X Beach. The top rows, as it were, of the threatre, broken near the centre of the gully, were strongly entrenched; machine guns commanding the beach by converging fire were lodged in caves upon the cliffs on both sides; and the land and sea were planted with mines. In his Despatch, Sir Ian Hamilton justly says: 'So strong, in fact, were the defences of W Beach, that the Turks may well have considered them impregnable, and it is my firm conviction that no finer feat of arms has ever been achieved by the British soldier—or any other soldier—than the storming of these trenches from open boats.' These unsurpassed soldiers were men of the 1st Lancashire Fusiliers (86th Brigade), and in their honour W Beach was afterwards generally known as 'Lancashire Landing.'" "Three days after the Lancashire Landing, on 28 April, when the Brigade Major of the 86th Brigade led the attack on the Krithia Wood, Bromley went forward with him. Another brigade had had to withdraw; Bromley and the men who loved him went forward and won. When the successful survivors reorganized under cover, Bromley went forward to reconnoitre with the Brigade Major and three other ranks, up to the ground rising to the outskirts of Krithia itself, when he was wounded in the knee. He was got back by Sergt. Burtchell, of the Lancashire Fusiliers, and his wound was dressed; it was then discovered that he had also a bullet in his back which he had received three days before and never spoken of except to the man who had bandaged the wound. Before his wounds were really healed Bromley was back, and found himself in command of the battalion, fresh from the fierce fighting on 4 June. How he was welcomed! The battalion shook itself and readjusted those surviving to make the fighting machine efficient. The spirit of the regiment was infused into the reinforcements. Bromley made them feel that these events were those their ambition had desired, they were fighting on the same glorious plane as their ancestors at Minden. The battalion looked and behaved as if it was thoroughly happy, and it was happy. Then came 28 June. The battalion was ordered to leave the trenches in daylight and attack across the open. Bromley led it. He was hit in the foot just over the parapet. Two stretcher-bearers—bandsmen, only lately band boys—jumped to him. He made them carry him on to direct the attack, and when it failed, against all chances, he was carried back alive. Only 10 of the original battalion were left unwounded. The wound was serious, and Bromley was sent to Alexandria. When able to hobble he begged his way on board the Royal Edward to come back to the Peninsula. She was torpedoed, and it was like Bromley to stay on board and go down with her while any men remained unplaced in the boats. Fine swimmer as he was—he had once swum from Gozo to Malta—he was drowned before he could be picked up; it is believed that he was struck by a piece of wreckage. Thus he died; to live now in the memory of England, placed among the great men who have deserved, and won, the Cross of a soldier's self-sacrifice."

Cuthbert Bromley.

A newspaper cutting says:

"Sergt. Grimshaw was considerably affected when our correspondent told him that his honour was bracketed with that of Major Bromley and Sergt. Stubbs. 'Major Bromley,' he said, 'was the Adjutant of the battalion, and his bravery was superb. He set an example which was unequalled by anyone. He was wounded on 28 April, three days after the landing, and rejoined us three days afterwards, before he was really fit enough to do so. On 28 June he was again wounded. We had a big attack that day, and he refused to be taken away until he saw we were all right. He was hobbling about with two Turkish rifles as crutches, and was afterwards removed on a stretcher. He went to Egypt to recuperate, and was returning to the Peninsula on the Royal Edward when that ship was torpedoed, and unfortunately he was one of the drowned. He was admired by everyone in the battalion. I remember seeing him once in the landing, and he was one of the first men to reach the top of the cliffs.'"

STUBBS, FRANK EDWARD, Sergt., enlisted in the 1st Battn. Lancashire Fusiliers, and served in the European War. He was awarded the Victoria Cross, which he did not live to receive, his name appearing in the London Gazette of 15 March, 1917, together with the names of Capt. Bromley and Sergt. Grimshaw: "Edward Stubbs, No. 1506, Sergt. (since died of wounds). On 25 April, 1915, Headquarters and three companies of the 1st Battn. Lancashire Fusiliers, in effecting a landing on the Gallipoli Peninsula to the west of Cape Helles, were met by very deadly fire from hidden machine guns, which caused a great number of casualties. The survivors, however, rushed up to and cut the wire entanglements, notwithstanding the terrific fire from the enemy, and after overcoming supreme difficulties the cliffs were gained and the position maintained. Amongst the many very gallant officers and men engaged in this most hazardous undertaking, Capt. Bromley, Sergt. Stubbs and Corpl. Grimshaw have been selected by their comrades as having performed the most signal acts of bravery and devotion to duty. The above awards of the Victoria Cross are to be read in conjunction with those conferred on the undermentioned for most conspicuous bravery on the same occasion." The Victoria Cross was presented to his mother. Mr. Nevinson says in a note to page 103 in "The Dardanelles Campaign": "Excellent personal accounts of W Beach Landing by three 1st Lancashire officers are given in 'With the Twenty-ninth Division' (pages 57–63). It is hard to choose between the three; but I give some sentences from Major Adams, who had been twenty-five years in the regiment, and was killed a few days later, as were the other two: 'As the boats touched the shore a very heavy and brisk fire was poured into us, several officers and men being killed and wounded in the entanglements through which we were trying to cut a way. Several of my company were with me under the wire, one of my subalterns was killed next to me, and also the wire-cutter who was lying the other side of me. I seized his cutter and cut a small lane myself, through which a few of us broke and lined up under the only available cover procurable—a small sand ridge covered with bluffs of grass. I then ordered fire to be opened on the crests, but owing to submersion in the water and dragging rifles through the sand, the breech mechanism was clogged, thereby rendering the rifles ineffective. The only thing left to do was to fix bayonets and charge up the crests, which was done in a very gallant manner, though we suffered greatly in doing so. However, this had the effect of driving the enemy from his trenches, which we immediately occupied. . . . In my company alone I had 95 casualties out of 205 men.' A still more detailed account of the

Lancashire Landing, specially describing the services of Major Frankland (killed while trying to take assistance to V Beach about 8.30 am.) and of Capts. Willis, Shaw, Cunliffe and Haworth, is given in an additional chapter by Major Farmer (Lancashire Fusiliers) at the end of the same book (pages 175–191)."

GRIMSHAW, JOHN ELISHA, Corpl., was born at Abram, near Wigan, 20 Jan. 1893, son of John Grimshaw, Carpenter. He was educated at St. John's School, Abram, and joined the Army 13 Aug. 1912, in the Lancashire Fusiliers. He was in India at the outbreak of the Great War, and proceeded thence to Gallipoli. For his bravery and coolness during the landing of the Lancashire Fusiliers on Gallipoli Peninsula, he was awarded the Distinguished Conduct Medal, but was voted the Victoria Cross by his comrades [London Gazette, 15 March, 1917]: "John Grimshaw, Corpl., 1st Battn. Lancashire Fusiliers. Date of Act of Bravery: 25 April, 1915. On 25 April, 1915, Headquarters and three companies of the 1st Battn. Lancashire Fusiliers, in effecting a landing on the Gallipoli Peninsula to the west of Cape Helles, were met by very deadly fire from hidden machine guns, which caused a great number of casualties. The survivors, however, rushed up to and cut the wire entanglements, notwithstanding the terrific fire from the enemy, and after overcoming supreme difficulties, the cliffs were gained and the position maintained. Amongst the many very gallant officers and men engaged in this most hazardous undertaking, Capt. Bromley, Sergt. Stubbs and Corpl. Grimshaw have been selected by their comrades as having performed the most signal acts of bravery and devotion to duty." He was mentioned in Sir Ian Hamilton's Despatch. His own brief account of the adventure is as follows: "In boats we got within 200 or 300 yards from the shore when the Turks opened a terrible fire. Sailors were shot dead at their oars. With rifles held over our heads we struggled through the barbed wire in the water to the beach and fought a way to the foot of the cliffs, leaving the biggest part of our men dead and wounded." He would say nothing of his own experiences. The first intimation he received of his new honour was through the Hull representative of the "Daily Dispatch." He was content with his D.C.M., and had not the least inkling that his comrades had voted him the V.C. "Whose leg are you pulling?" he asked, and he took a great deal of convincing. Of the 800 men of the battalion who made the super-heroic Lancashire Landing, he is one of the 32 survivors. The people of Abram and district presented him with a gold watch and chain as a sign of their pride in their hero. After recovering from severe frost-bite, Sergt. Grimshaw was subsequently sent to Hull, where he became Musketry Instructor. At Hull he met Miss Margaret Stout, to whom he was married at All Saints', Hull, 26 Aug. 1916.

John Elisha Grimshaw.

London Gazette, 3 April, 1917.—"War Office, 3 April, 1917. His Majesty the King has been graciously pleased to approve of the award of the Victoria Cross to No. 731, L.-Sergt. (now Second Lieut.) Frederick William Palmer, Royal Fusiliers."

PALMER, FREDERICK WILLIAM, Second Lieut., served in the European War, and was awarded the Victoria Cross [London Gazette, 3 April, 1917]: "Frederick William Palmer, No. 731, L.-Sergt. (now Second Lieut.), Royal Fusiliers. For most conspicuous bravery, control and determination. During the progress of certain operations, all the officers of his company having been shot down, Sergt. Palmer assumed command, and, having cut his way under point-blank machine-gun fire, through the wire entanglements, he rushed the enemy's trench with six of his men, dislodged the hostile machine gun which had been hampering our advance, and established a block. He then collected men detached from other regiments, and held the barricade for nearly three hours against seven determined counter-attacks, under an incessant barrage of bombs and rifle grenades from his flank and front. During his temporary absence in search of more bombs an eighth counter-attack was delivered by the enemy, who succeeded in driving in his party and threatened the defences of the whole flank. At this critical moment, although he had been blown off his feet by a bomb and was greatly exhausted, he rallied his men, drove back the enemy and maintained his position. The very conspicuous bravery displayed by this Non-commissioned Officer cannot be overstated, and his splendid determination and devotion to duty undoubtedly averted what might have proved a serious disaster in this sector of the line."

London Gazette, 21 April, 1917.—"Admiralty, S.W., 21 April, 1917. The King has been graciously pleased to approve of the grant of the Victoria Cross to Commander Gordon Campbell, D.S.O., R.N."

CAMPBELL, GORDON, Commander, was born on 6 Jan. 1886, son of Colonel Frederick Campbell, C.B., J.P., V.D., R.A., Commanding the Argyll and Bute Territorial Artillery, and Mrs. Frederick Campbell. His elder brother is Commander James D. Campbell, O.B.E., and he is a cousin of Sir John Bruce Stuart Campbell, Bart., of Ardnamurchan, who is a Major in the Royal Scots. Gordon Campbell joined the Britannia in Sept. 1900; became a Cadet on 15 Jan. 1902, and was promoted to Midshipman on 15 Feb. of the same year. He became a Sub-Lieutenant 15 April, 1905; Lieutenant 1 Oct. 1907, and Lieutenant-Commander 1 Oct. 1915. His first ship was the Prince George in the Channel Fleet, then the Irresistible, in which he served in the Mediterranean as a Midshipman. He was on 8 Oct. 1903, appointed a Midshipman in the Flora, which commissioned at Devonport for service on the Pacific Station on 11 Nov. 1902. On promotion to Sub-Lieutenant he was appointed to the Royal Naval College, Greenwich, for a course of study, and on 7 May, 1906, was appointed to the Arun. After promotion to Lieutenant he was appointed to H.M.S. King Alfred, Flagship of Sir Hedworth Meux (then Lambton), on the China Station. From 5 Aug. 1910, until Oct. 1912, he served in H.M.S. Impregnable, boys' training ship at Devonport, and on 18 Oct. 1912, was appointed Lieutenant and Commander of the Ranger, of the Devonport Destroyer Flotilla. Until he commenced his brilliant exploits in the Q boats, he was in command of the destroyer Bittern, which was lost at sea a few months ago, and to which he was appointed in April, 1913. His war honours and promotions are as follows: Specially promoted Commander 29 March, 1916; received D.S.O. 31 May, 1916; decorated with V.C. 17 March, 1917; V.C. gazetted 21 April, 1917; specially promoted Captain 17 June, 1917; Bar to D.S.O. 27 July, 1917; second Bar to D.S.O. 2 Nov. 1917. Capt. Campbell has also received the Croix de Guerre with Palms, and was an Officier Légion d'Honneur. When advanced to Commander he passed over the heads of over 700 Lieutenant-Commanders, and when promoted to Captain he passed over more than 500 Commanders. There is nothing known to exceed these jumps in promotion either during the war or before it. A newspaper said: "When the war comes to an end the public will no doubt learn the precise nature of the acts of gallantry for which Commander Gordon Campbell, R.N., has been awarded first the D.S.O., and recently the V.C. For refraining from announcing the circumstances under which the gallant officer won these coveted decorations the authorities have no doubt good reason, and it is equally certain that the distinctions were thoroughly deserved." Commander Campbell's D.S.O. and V.C. were merely gazetted, the announcement of the award of his Victoria Cross reading as follows: London Gazette, 21 April, 1917.—"Admiralty, S.W., 21 April, 1917. The King has been graciously pleased to approve of the grant of the Victoria Cross to Commander Gordon Campbell, D.S.O., R.N. In recognition of his conspicuous gallantry, consummate coolness and skill in command of one of H.M. Ships in action." In a later Gazette fuller details were given, when the secrets concerning the award of the Victoria Cross to six naval officers and two men were revealed. When the awards were made only the names of the recipients were published, and the descriptions now given of the deeds show that they were all connected with the actions against enemy submarines of our "mystery" ships, whose business it was to lure submarines into positions in which they could be destroyed by guns or other means which were concealed to the latest possible moment. Capt. Gordon Campbell, V.C., D.S.O., R.N., was the leader of several of these actions. For one, in which he was in command of H.M.S. Q5, he was awarded the Victoria Cross, and for another, when he was on the Pargust, the Cross was awarded to the ship and worn by a Lieutenant and a Petty Officer who were selected by the vote of the ship's company. On another occasion, when he was in command of the Dunraven, the V.C. was awarded to a Lieutenant and to one of the gun's crew, and worn by a selected Petty Officer. A newspaper article says: "'I think nothing more inspiring could be written about the gallantry of officers and men on land or sea than the story of the officers and men of Q ships.'—Sir Eric Geddes at the Lord Mayor's Banquet. The Q boats referred to by the First Lord were the famous anti-U boat 'mystery' ships, for the most part tramp steamers fitted with cunningly-screened guns. On board of them were officers and men of the fighting Navy, so got up that they looked anything but what they actually were. Of the various Q ship Commanders, almost the only one of whom the public has heard is Capt. Gordon Campbell, the 'mystery' V.C. It is now possible to tell the story, hitherto known to very few, of how this officer won the coveted honour. Early in Feb. 1917, Gordon Campbell was navigating his U-boat 'strafer' through a certain part of the Irish Sea. At 9.45 a.m. a torpedo fired by a hidden submarine struck the vessel. A big hole was knocked in her side near the engine-room, and some of the bulkheads gave way. Gun crews were called to their fighting stations, and, by way of deceiving the enemy, certain boats were lowered, and a part of the crew, jumping into them, pulled away from the ship, which was in a sinking condition. The submarine's periscope showed up on the starboard side about 200 yards away. The gunners on board the Q boat pointed their weapons and watched their enemy. Passing across the bows, the submarine came to the surface on the port side about 300 yards away. Then destruction smote it swiftly and relentlessly. The ensign was hoisted. 'Fire,' came the order as every gun was brought to bear at point-blank range. The first shot from a 6-pounder struck the U boat's conning tower, and blew off the Commanding Officer's head. Quick-firing guns and maxims barked and rattled, beating the submarine's hull into scrap-iron. Finally the shattered hulk of the U boat reeled over and sank. 'Cease fire,' ordered Capt. Campbell as he sent away boats to pick up survivors. Of these only two were found—an officer and a man. Boats were recalled to the victorious ship, herself a maimed and stricken thing, slowly sinking by the stern, and help was signalled for. While the fight was on, the chief engineer and his staff remained in the flooded engine-room, and kept the dynamos and machinery going until driven from their posts by the inrushing water. They then crept on to the engines, and hid there until the fight ended. Even after friendly warships had come to their aid, the dangers of Campbell and his crew were not over. Time after time it seemed as if the sea would claim their vessel, but at 9.30 p.m. on the day following the action she was beached to prevent her from sinking." Capt. Campbell married, on 14 Jan. 1911, Mary Jeanne, daughter of H. V. S. Davids,

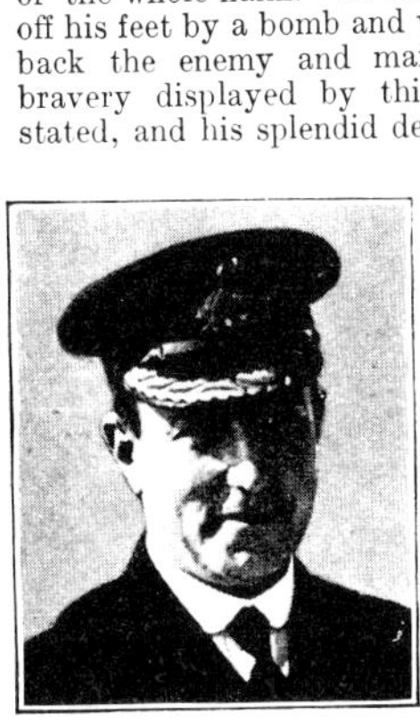

Gordon Campbell.

Esq., for many years British Consul in Java, and has a son, Frederick David Gordon, born on 8 Jan. 1915. His mother was Emilie Guilleaumena, daughter of the late Maclaine of Lochbuie.

Lieut.-Commander H. Auten, V.C., says in "Q Boat Adventures" (published by Herbert Jenkins): "The ideal Q boat commander should combine in his own person something of the qualities of Horatius Cocles and a successful impresario. Capt. Gordon Campbell seemed to be imbued with both these qualities. As an impresario he possessed a wonderful eye for detail. It is said of him that he caused one of his crew to dress as a girl and sit in a prominent position on the poop on a deck chair, with a view to attracting the Hun to his ship. On another occasion one of his officers, whose duty it was to go off with the 'panic party,' constructed a parrot, which he fastened inside a cage. This he proposed taking with him into the boat, thus lending local colour to the 'panic party.' Possibly it was these qualities that attracted to Capt. Campbell the attention of those gods who controlled the dramatic in warfare. No commander in the Q boat service was the centre of so many dramatic incidents as he."

London Gazette, 11 May, 1917.—"War Office, 11 May, 1917. His Majesty the King has been graciously pleased to approve of the award of the Victoria Cross to the undermentioned Officers and Man."

CHERRY, PERCY HERBERT, Capt., was born at Murradoc, Drysdale, Victoria, Australia, 4 June, 1895. He was the son of Mr. John G. Cherry and of Elizabeth Cherry, and was educated at Cradoc, Huon, Tasmania, whither he had come with his parents at the age of seven, and where they have since resided. He was at the Cradoc State School till he was thirteen years of age, and afterwards was privately educated almost up to the time of his enlistment. At the age of fourteen he accepted and won a challenge to make thirty-five apple-cases in an hour. This feat he subsequently surpassed, as he won the open case-making championship at Franklin, and later in the same year won a similar championship against all comers at the Launceston Fruit Show, being champion at the time of his death. He played the cornet in the Franklin Brass Band; was a member of the Franklin Rowing Club, and sang in the Church of England Choir. He was always ready and willing to help in anything for a good cause. At the age of thirteen he was a school cadet, and on the introduction of compulsory training was soon promoted to the rank of Sergeant and then Second Lieutenant, and used to drill the Cadets of four different districts. At the age of sixteen he won the President's trophy, Gold Medal, for the best shot at Franklin Rifle Range, being at the time the youngest member in the club. On the outbreak of the European War he entered the Claremont Camp, and was quickly promoted a Drill Instructor. He qualified as an Infantry Officer, but refused a commission as he was considered too young (twenty). His Commanding Officer at Claremont at the beginning of his military career wrote in glowing terms of his devotion to duty, honesty and truthfulness, and the excellent manner in which he performed his work. He subsequently left Tasmania as Quartermaster-Sergeant, and was Regimental Sergeant-Major at Gallipoli. Owing to the number of casualties among the officers in his battalion, Cherry was selected as an Acting Second Lieutenant, and soon after was severely wounded, and evacuated to Egypt. He got his commission as Second Lieutenant, and when he rejoined the battalion he attended a machine-gun course, and later did service with the Machine Gun Company when it was sent to France. He fought in France until dangerously wounded at Pozières, where he was mentioned in Despatches, and about this time was given his second Star. After recovering from his wounds he was appointed Adjutant at a camp in England, but ultimately managed to get to the front once more, and rejoined his unit in the middle of the winter with the rank of Captain, C Coy., 26th Battn. Australian Imperial Force. We cannot do better than quote in full General Birdwood's letter to Mrs. Cherry describing the events which won Capt. Cherry the Military Cross, and later the Victoria Cross: "I feel I must write to tell you how deeply and sincerely I sympathize with you in the death of your gallant son, and at the same time express to you our extreme admiration for him, and regret that he should have lost his life while fighting so bravely. As you will have heard, he was awarded the Military Cross for his fine work on the 1st March, when he led his company with such dash and courage in an attack on a trench near the village of Warlencourt. The wire where he led his men was not well cut, when he at once ran along the edge of the entanglements until he found an opening, through which he took his men. He met with fierce opposition from the Germans on entering a trench, but rallying his men he cleared it, and by his gallant and inspiring conduct ensured success. Even though wounded, he refused to leave his men, and later captured two hostile machine guns, which he turned on the enemy. As soon as his good work was reported, I recommended him for the Military Cross, which was immediately awarded, but, alas, I am sorry to say, news of it came only on the day he was killed, so to my regret he never heard of his decoration. On that day you know that he won the Victoria Cross, when he again displayed conspicuous bravery, determination and leadership. His battalion formed part of a force which captured the village of Lagnicourt, and when other senior officers became casualties in his company he carried on the fighting in face of the most determined opposition, and cleared the village. Having done this he took charge of the situation, and beat off a most resolute and heavy counter-attack made by the enemy. I am sorry to say he was wounded early in

Percy Herbert Cherry.

the morning, but refused to leave his post, where he remained encouraging (his men) all round him until towards the evening he was, to the great regret of all of us, killed by a German shell. I know that no words of mine can be of any real comfort to you in your great trouble, but I trust it will be some consolation to you to know how deeply his loss is regretted here by all his comrades, and to realize how bravely he died for his King and country, and for all that we hold dear." The official account of the bravery which won him the Victoria Cross is as follows [London Gazette, 11 May, 1917]: "Percy Herbert Cherry, Lieut. (Captaincy confirmed), M.C., Australian Imperial Force (7th Machine Gun Coy.). Date of Act of Bravery: 26 March, 1917. For most conspicuous bravery, determination and leadership when in command of a company detailed to storm and clear a village. After all the officers of this company had become casualties he carried on with care and determination in the face of fierce opposition, and cleared the village of the enemy. He sent frequent reports of progress made, and when held up for some time by an enemy strong point, he organized machine-gun and bomb parties and captured the position. His leadership, coolness and bravery set a wonderful example to his men. Having cleared the village, he took charge of the situation and beat off the most resolute and heavy counter-attacks made by the enemy. Wounded about 6.30 a.m., he refused to leave his post, and there remained, encouraging all to hold out at all costs, until, about 4.30 p.m., this very gallant officer was killed by an enemy shell." It is difficult to make a choice among the many letters of praise of their son received by his parents, but we give a few extracts from letters of brother officers: "Everybody knows that he earned it (the Victoria Cross) over and over again on the day he was killed, and I, as well as many others, know that he earned it by the work for which he has since got the Military Cross. Capt. Percy Cherry was the bravest man I have ever met. A man absolutely fearless, quick to decide, and quicker still to execute, it is no wonder that his Commanding Officer regarded him as the best Company Commander the battalion had ever had. When he first took over his company he was rather unpopular, for he was a little martinet on parade, and it speaks well for his character that at the finish they simply adored him, and would have followed him anywhere—to the next world if need be, as indeed many of them did." "Cherry enlisted when I was at Claremont, and not long ago his Colonel told me that he was absolutely the most brilliant young officer he had ever had under him."

CATES, GEORGE EDWARD, Second Lieut., served in the European War in France, and was awarded the Victoria Cross [London Gazette, 11 May, 1917]: "George Edward Cates, Second Lieut., 2nd Battn. Rifle Brigade. For most conspicuous gallantry and self-sacrifice. When engaged with some other men in deepening a captured trench, this officer struck with his spade a buried bomb, which immediately started to burn. Second Lieut. Cates, in order to save the lives of his comrades, placed his foot on the bomb, which immediately exploded. He showed the most conspicuous gallantry and devotion to duty in performing the act which cost him his life but saved the lives of others."

COX, CHRISTOPHER, Private, served in the European War in France. He was awarded the Victoria Cross [London Gazette, 11 May, 1917]: "Christopher Cox, Private, No. 13909, 7th Battn. Bedfordshire Regt. For most conspicuous bravery and continuous devotion to duty when acting as a stretcher-bearer. During the attack of his battalion the front wave was checked by the severity of the enemy artillery and machine-gun fire, and the whole line had to take cover in shell holes to avoid annihilation. Private Cox, utterly regardless of personal safety, went out over fire-swept ground, and single-handed rescued four men. Having collected the wounded of his own battalion, he then assisted to bring in the wounded of an adjoining battalion. On the two subsequent days he carried out similar rescue work with the same disregard of his own safety. He has on all occasions displayed the same high example of unselfishness and valour."

London Gazette, 8 June, 1917.—"War Office, 8 June, 1917. His Majesty the King has been graciously pleased to approve of the award of the Victoria Cross to the undermentioned Officers, Non-commissioned Officers and Men."

HENDERSON, EDWARD ELERS DELAVEL, Major (Acting Lieut.-Colonel), was born 2 Oct. 1878, and joined the West India Regt. as Second Lieut. from the Militia 13 Dec. 1900, serving in West Africa (Northern Nigeria) in 1901, and taking part in the operations against the forces of Bida and Kontagora (Medal with clasp). He became Lieutenant 10 Feb. 1902, and in that year served in West Africa (Northern Nigeria), being present at the operations at Argungu (clasp). In 1903 he saw active service in Northern Nigeria, taking part in the Kano-Sokuto Campaign (Medal with clasp). He was transferred to the North Staffordshire Regt. on 20 May, 1908, and became Captain 17 March, 1909. He was altogether employed with the West African Frontier Force from 13 Dec. 1900, to 28 June, 1905, and from 16 Feb. 1907, to 10 Sept. 1911. He served in the European War; was promoted to Major 1 Sept. 1915, and later became Acting Lieut.-Colonel. He was killed in action at the Shumran Bond, Mesopotamia, while gallantly leading his battalion to victory, for which he was posthumously awarded the Victoria Cross [London Gazette, 8 June, 1917]: "Edward Elers Delavel Henderson, Major (Acting Lieut.-Colonel), late North Staffordshire Regt. For

E. E. D. Henderson.

most conspicuous bravery, leadership and personal example when in command of his battalion. Lieut.-Colonel Henderson brought his battalion up to our two front-line trenches, which were under intense fire, and his battalion had suffered heavy casualties when the enemy made a heavy counter-attack, and succeeded in penetrating our line in several places, the situation becoming critical. Although shot through the arm, Lieut.-Colonel Henderson jumped on to the parapet, and advanced alone some distance in front of his battalion, cheering them on under the most intense fire over 500 yards of open ground. Again wounded, he nevertheless continued to lead his men on in the most gallant manner, finally capturing the position by a bayonet charge. He was again twice wounded, and died when he was eventually brought in."

LUMSDEN, FREDERICK WILLIAM, Lieut.-Colonel, was born 14 Dec. 1872, at Frizabad, India, son of the late John James Foote Lumsden, Indian Civil Service, and of Marguerite Lumsden (*née* White). He was educated at Bristol Grammar School, and joined the Army as a Second Lieutenant in the Royal Marine Artillery 1 Sept. 1890, becoming Lieutenant 1 July, 1891, and Captain 16 June, 1897. He distinguished himself in signalling and naval gunnery, and in the musketry course at Hythe he won a first-class certificate, passing out second among 120 officers. He was a graduate of the Staff College in 1907, and after studying the language in Germany for six months, he obtained a first-class interpreter's certificate in German. On 4 June, 1910, he was appointed General Staff Officer, Second Grade, in the Straits Settlements, and after holding the appointment at Singapore for four years until 3 June, 1914, he returned to England a few months before the outbreak of war. He had been given the Brevet of Major 1 Sept. 1911. He married the second daughter of the late Lieut.-General Harward, Royal Artillery, and his only daughter, Violet, married Capt. A. K. North, of the Oxfordshire and Buckinghamshire Light Infantry. He served in the European War; was G.S.O.3, 28 July, 1915; Brigade Major 21 Nov. 1915, to 26 Jan. 1916; G.S.O.2, 27 Jan. 1916. He was promoted to Lieut.-Colonel, and was created a Companion of the Distinguished Service Order, the award being gazetted in the New Year's Honours List [London Gazette, 1 Jan. 1917]. He further distinguished himself by winning the Distinguished Service Order no less than three times more, the Victoria Cross, and the Belgian Croix de Guerre, and was also created a Companion of the Order of the Bath—an uncommon record. The award of the two bars to the Distinguished Service Order was gazetted on the same day, 11 April, 1917—this must be almost unique— and were both for conspicuous gallantry and devotion to duty in reconnaissances. The following is the official account of the deed for which the Victoria Cross was awarded [London Gazette, 8 June, 1917]: "Major Frederick William Lumsden, D.S.O., R.M.A. For most conspicuous bravery, determination and devotion to duty. Six enemy field guns having been captured, it was necessary to leave them in dug-in positions, 300 yards in advance of the position held by our troops. The enemy kept the captured guns under heavy fire. Major Lumsden undertook the duty of bringing the guns into our lines. In order to effect this, he personally led four artillery teams and a party of infantry through the hostile barrage. As one of these teams sustained casualties, he left the remaining teams in a covered position, and, through very heavy rifle, machine-gun and shrapnel fire, led the infantry to the guns. By force of example and inspiring energy he succeeded in sending back two teams with guns, going through the barrage with the teams of the third gun. He then returned to the guns to await further teams, and these he succeeded in attaching to two of the three remaining guns, despite rifle fire, which had become intense at short range, and removed the guns to safety. By this time the enemy, in considerable strength, had driven through the infantry covering points, and blown up the breach of the remaining gun. Major Lumsden then returned, drove off the enemy, attached the gun to a team and got it away." On 23 April, 1918, the third bar to the Distinguished Service Order was gazetted, for conspicuous gallantry and disregard of danger during a large raid on the enemy's lines. He was awarded the Companionship of the Order of the Bath on 1 June, 1918. He was killed in action in June, 1918. An alarm was raised, and Brigadier-General Lumsden, as he had then become, going out in his usual fearless way to see what the trouble was, was shot through the head and killed instantly. A brother officer wrote: "He was without exception the finest leader I have ever met. I have worked with him now for a year and a half, and we all feel his loss to the division is irreparable. All the honours he gained, during the last year even, in every case were won over and over again, as there was hardly a day when he did not expose himself to danger in a way which was an example to all. His brigade became the finest in the division, solely owing to his fine influence and example. I can't express to you how much every soldier in this division admired him and how much we all feel his loss."

Frederick W. Lumsden.

WHEELER, GEORGE CAMPBELL, Major, was born 7 April, 1880, and joined the Army on 20 Jan. 1900, as Second Lieutenant, Unattached, and the Indian Staff Corps on 18 April, 1901. He became Lieutenant, Indian Army, 20 April, 1902, and Captain, 20 Jan. 1909. He served in the European War, and was awarded the Victoria Cross [London Gazette, 8 June, 1917]: "George Campbell Wheeler, Major, 2/9th Gurkha Rifles, Indian Army. For the most conspicuous bravery and determination. This officer, together with one Gurkha officer and eight men, crossed a river and immediately rushed the enemy's trench under heavy bombing, rifle, machine-gun and artillery fire. Having obtained a footing on the river bank, he was almost immediately afterwards counter-attacked by a strong enemy party with bombers. Major Campbell Wheeler at once led a charge with another officer and three men, receiving a severe bayonet wound in the head, but managed, in spite of this, to disperse the enemy. This bold action on his part undoubtedly saved the situation. In spite of his wound, he continued to consolidate his position." Major Wheeler was Temporary Lieutenant-Colonel, Indian Army, 24 Dec. 1916, to 18 June. 1917. He is married and has a son.

MACDOWELL, THAIN WENDELL, Capt., was born 16 Sept. 1890, at Lachute, Quebec, Canada, son of Rev. J. V. MacDowell and Mrs. MacDowell, now wife of J. F. Richardson. He was educated at Brockville Collegiate Institute and the University of Toronto, where he graduated B.A. 1915. He joined the Army 17 Sept. 1914, as a Lieutenant, 38th Battn. Canadian Expeditionary Force. He served during the European War in France and Belgium. He was awarded the Victoria Cross [London Gazette, 8 June, 1917]: "Thain Wendell MacDowell, Capt., 38th Battn. Canadians. For most conspicuous bravery and indomitable resolution in face of heavy machine-gun and shell fire. By his initiative and courage this officer, with the assistance of two runners, was enabled, in the face of great difficulties, to capture two machine guns, besides two officers and seventy-five men. Although wounded in the hand, he continued for five days to hold the position gained, in spite of heavy shell fire, until eventually relieved by his battalion. By his bravery and prompt action he undoubtedly succeeded in rounding up a very strong enemy machine post." He was awarded the Distinguished Service Order [London Gazette, Jan. 1917], for services at the Battle of the Somme 18 Nov. 1916. He was promoted Lieutenant 17 Sept. 1914, Captain 1 Aug. 1915, and Major 28 Feb. 1917. The following is taken from "Thirty Canadian V.C.'s," published by Messrs. Skeffington (pages 19–23): "Major MacDowell won his D.S.O. on 18 Nov. 1916, for his quick decision and determined action in an attack made by his battalion—the 38th, from Ottawa—on the British front, south of the Ancre, against Desire Trench and Desire Support Trench. With B Company, of which he was Captain, he advanced to within throwing distance, and bombed three German machine guns which had been holding up the advance, capturing, after severe hand-to-hand fighting, three officers and fifty of the enemy crews. It was this enterprise which cleared the way for the advance to the final objective. The same qualities of courage and swift decision were manifested on the occasion on which he won the Victoria Cross during the action of Vimy Ridge on the 9th April, 1917. MacDowell delights in battle detail. He wants to know just where he is going when he enters an engagement, and before the big attack on Vimy he studied all the available Intelligence Reports and aeroplane maps, even selecting the particular German dug-out in which he intended to establish his headquarters after the position was won. The 38th, having been reorganized after the battle on the Somme, had moved up to the trenches at Vimy just after Christmas Day, 1916. For four long winter months the battalion remained in front of the famous ridge until, on that day in April, it went up, in conjunction with other Canadian units, in full battle array and snatched the position from the enemy. It is impossible to over-estimate the strategic value of Vimy Ridge. Its two spurs, flung out west and south-west in a series of heights which dominated the western plain, were regarded by military experts as the backbone of the whole German position in France. The Ridge was not only a naturally strong position made as impregnable as German skill could make it; it was more than that. Upon it, it was argued, hinged —and still hinges—the entire strategy of the enemy's retreat in the west. The enemy had held the heights since the third month of the war. They were the great bastion of his lines. Four times had the Allies attacked the position, biting deep into the German line; but still the enemy held the Ridge, though the holding of it had cost him sixty thousand men. It was to obtain possession of this famous series of hills that the Canadian battalions climbed out of their trenches at 5.30 a.m. on that April day. Few men slept soundly on the night before the great attack. The stern, hard training for the operation which had been in process for some weeks had tightened and toughened every link in the chain from the highest rank to the lowest, and the last few hours dragged fitfully. All watches had been synchronized, and immediately 5.30 o'clock ticked a roar of artillery, awe-inspiring and stupendous, burst from the batteries, the hiding-places of which were only revealed by the short, sharp flashes; and Vimy Ridge was all afire with cataclysmic death and destruction. Behind the barrage, driving through No Man's Land towards their objective, went the Canadian battalions. Capt. MacDowell reached the German line about fifty yards to the right of the point for which he was aiming; but most of his men, having worked slightly farther to the right, became separated from their leader, who found himself alone with two runners. The German dug-out where he aimed at establishing himself could be seen in the shell-torn line, but there was no time to collect a party to clean the place up. But on the way to his destination MacDowell captured two enemy machine guns as an aside. He bombed one out of action, then attacked the other. The second gunner did not wait, but ran for shelter to a dug-out whither MacDowell followed and got him. Working their way along to the big dug-out the three Canadians saw that the place was more formidable than they had anticipated. It stretched far underground. MacDowell bawled down the deep passage, summoning the German occupants to surrender. No answer

Thain Wendell MacDowell.

came from out the depths to his demand ; but that Germans were down in the underground there seemed no doubt. The captain decided to go down and find out. It was a gigantic game of bluff he was playing, and it succeeded by reason of its very audacity. A flight of fifty-two steps led to the earthen floor below, and down those fifty-two steps went Capt. MacDowell. Along a narrow passage he went, and then, suddenly, as he turned a corner, which led into the main room of this subterranean fortress, he found himself face to face with a large group of the enemy. There were seventy-seven of them—though he did not know the exact number till afterwards, when they were counted—mostly Prussian Guards. Now, by all the laws of arithmetic and logic Capt. MacDowell ought to have been taken prisoner or killed. But he was not out to be governed by the laws of arithmetic or logic. He was out to capture Boches and to kill those he could not capture. Quick as a flash he turned and began to shout orders to an imaginary force behind him—and up went the hands of the seventy-seven stalwart Guards. ' Kamerad ! ' they said. It was one thing, however, to accept the surrender of this large party and quite another to get them out of the dug-out, for there was more than a chance that when they discovered there were but three Canadians to look after them they would try to overwhelm their captors. The captain decided to send the Germans up in batches of twelve, and the two runners, Kebus and Hay, marshalled them in the open at the top. Among the prisoners were two officers. What had been expected, once the Germans were marched up into the daylight, occurred. Some of them were furious at the trick which had been played on them, and one of them caught up a rifle and shot at one of the Canadians. The rebellion did not last long, for it was checked by quick, drastic measures. That afternoon, when the riot of the attack had quietened somewhat, MacDowell and his two men made a thorough exploration of the dug-out and a report on the position was sent back to headquarters. Here is the report in his own hurried words, written with a stump of pencil, with his note-book on his knee, as the German shells were crashing all around the entrance to the dug-out : ' While exploring this dug-out we discovered a large store of what we believe to be explosives in a room. There is also an old sap leading down underground in the direction of No. — Crater. This was explored . . . we have cut all the wires, for fear of possible destructive posts. The dug-out has three entries, and will accommodate easily 250 or 300 men, with the sap to spare. It is seventy-five feet underground and very comfortable. The cigars are very choice and my supply of Perrier water is very large. . . . They are firing at us all the time with their heavy guns from the south-east, but I have no casualties to report since coming in here, except being half scared to death myself by a " big brute." . . . We have taken two machine guns that I know of, and a third and possibly a fourth will be taken to-night. This post was a machine-gun post and was held by a machine-gun company. I believe they are the Prussian Guards ; all big, strong men who came in last night. They had plenty of rations ; but we had a great time taking them prisoners. It is a great story. My two runners, Kebus and Hay, did invaluable work getting them out of the dug-out. . . . There is a large number of wounded in front of here, as I can see by the rifles stuck in the ground. We are using German rifles, as ours are out of commission.' Five days later, when the enemy artillery slackened, reinforcements were sent up and succeeded in reaching the captain ; and when, finally, he was relieved from the position and reported himself at his battalion headquarters, one can imagine that his brother officers—those who were left—were glad to see him."

NEWLAND, JAMES ERNEST, Capt., served in the European War, and was awarded the Victoria Cross [London Gazette, 8 June, 1917] : " James Ernest Newland, Capt., 12th Battn. Australian Imperial Force. For most conspicuous bravery and devotion to duty in the face of heavy odds on three separate occasions. On the first occasion he organized the attack by his company on a most important objective, and led personally, under heavy fire, a bombing attack. He then rallied his company, which had suffered heavy casualties, and he was one of the first to reach the objective. On the following night his company, holding the captured position, was heavily counter-attacked. By personal exertion, utter disregard of fire and judicious use of reserves, he suc-

James Ernest Newland.

ceeded in dispersing the enemy and regaining the position. On a subsequent occasion, when the company on his left was overpowered and his own company attacked from the rear, he drove off a combined attack which had developed from these directions. These attacks were renewed three or four times, and it was Capt. Newland's tenacity and disregard for his own safety that encouraged the men to hold out. The stand made by this officer was of the greatest importance, and produced far-reaching results."

REID, OSWALD AUSTIN, Capt., was born at Johannesburg on 2 Nov. 1893. His father is Harry Austin Reid, a pioneer of Johannesburg, and formerly a Captain in the Commander-in-Chief's Bodyguard Regt. (Lord Roberts's Regt.). He has the medals for the South African Wars of 1877, 1881 and 1899–1902. His mother, Alice Gertrude Reid, is a pioneer lady of both Johannesburg and Kimberley, daughter of George Bottomley, J.P., Mayor of Kimberley and a Member of the Legislative Council for Griqualand West. He was educated at the Diocesan College, Cape Town, at St. John's College, Johannesburg, and at Radley College. At St. John's College he was captain of football and cricket and senior prefect. At Radley he was captain of cricket,

Rugby football, racquets and fives, and senior prefect, and in 1913, at Lord's, he captained the Public Schools Eleven in their match against the M.C.C. He joined the Army on 14 Aug. 1914, as a Second Lieutenant

Oswald Austin Reid.

in the 4th Battn. King's (Liverpool Regt.). He served in the European War, and the following are the particulars of his service : He was in France with the 4th Battn. of his regiment until wounded in April, 1915, and after another period of service with the 1st Battn., he was again wounded a year later. He was to have been mentioned in Despatches on two occasions, but the death of his commanding officer before leaving the fighting line prevented this. He then went to Peshawar with the 2nd Battn., and took part in the Mohmand operations. He was attached to the 6th Loyal North Lancashire Regt. when the Mesopotamian Expeditionary Force was formed. He took part in the operations at Kut, Bagdad and Samarrah, and was wounded again in Oct. 1917. He won the Victoria Cross at the battle of Dialah River [London Gazette, 8 June, 1917] : " Oswald Austin Reid, 1st Battn. King's (Liverpool Regt.), attached 1st Battn. Loyal North Lancashire Regt. For most conspicuous bravery in the face of desperate circumstances. By his dauntless courage and gallant leadership he was able to consolidate a small post with the advanced troops on the opposite side of a river to the main body, after his line of communications had been cut by the sinking of the pontoons. He maintained this position for thirty hours against constant attacks by bombs, machine-gun and shell fire, with the full knowledge that repeated attempts at relief had failed, and that his ammunition was all but exhausted. It was greatly due to his tenacity that the passage of the river was effected on the following night. During the operations he was wounded." He was mentioned by Lieut.-General Sir F. S. Maude in his Despatch on the capture of Bagdad, Dec. 1917. He went out to the Russian front in April, 1919. During his absence on active service the public of Johannesburg presented his father with a sword of honour to be given to him. He is the first Radleian to win the Victoria Cross. He also has the King of Italy's Silver Medal for Military Valour.

BALL, ALBERT, Capt., was born at Lenton, Nottingham , 14 Aug. 1896, son of Alderman Albert Ball J.P., of Sedgley House, The Park, Nottingham, and was educated at the Nottingham High School and at Trent

Albert Ball.

College. He was always busy as a young boy ; he would purchase internal combustion engines and dynamos and experiment with them. Wireless apparatus and motor-cycles were his chief hobbies when he joined up at the outbreak of the war as a Private in the 2/7th Sherwood Foresters. He became Second Lieutenant on 28 Oct. 1914, Lieutenant 10 Aug. 1916, Captain and Flight Commander 13 Sept. 1916. When he was with the Sherwood Foresters he would get up at 3 a.m., motor from Luton to Hendon and back—sixty miles—in order to learn to fly, do his day's work with the land army, and again go off on his motor-cycle for another lesson in flying in the evening. Albert Ball had an extraordinary sense of the nearness and protecting fatherhood of God. Ball took great care to be always fit. He gave up smoking and went to bed in good time. " No vice had ever made his vision blurred or his hand shake, and he practised and worked, using to the uttermost the gifts of God which he had not marred by evil thinking or living." After he joined the Royal Flying Corps, he " used to spend most of his time when on the ground looking after his machine or his gun, and when for any reason his particular machine was out of action he used to look quite miserable." A competent judge said of him : " He was by no means an exceptionally good pilot at first, but he was always practising and improving himself." One of his brother officers said that Ball " never was for one moment what flying men called a ' star ' performer ; he never ' swanked ' in the air. He was never a fancy pilot, but always a very great man. It was grit and fight, fight and grit, first, last, and all the time." Yet with all this strenuous training, spiritual and mental, for the race which was set before him, Albert Ball remained a boy, full of beans, ready to tackle anyone or anything, on the earth or above it. " I always sing," he wrote, " when up in the clouds ; it is very nice. But I am always happy, so it is not strange." And elsewhere he says " All my machines and officers are at last ready for war. We hope to have a smack in a day or two. . . . All is perfectly ready ; so you bet I am very happy." " It makes me laugh when you say it is dangerous to fly. I felt just ripping." After a long air duel with a German aeroplane, when neither could outwit the other and their ammunition was used up, Ball says : " There was nothing more to do after that, so we both burst out laughing. We couldn't help it ; it was so ridiculous. We flew side by side, laughing at each other for a few seconds, and then we waved adieu to each other and went off. He was a real sport, was that Hun." Of Albert Ball might it have been said as of Wordsworth's hero :

> " This is the Happy Warrior ; this is he
> Whom every man-at-arms would wish to be.

If he be called upon to face
Some awful moment to which Heaven has joined
Great issues, good or bad for human kind,
Is happy as a lover, and attired
With sudden brightness, like a man inspired."

During the early battles on the Somme he would be aloft from 2.30 a.m. till 9.30 at night. From the front he wrote home for some seeds for a garden he had out there : " You will think this idea strange, but, you see, it will be a good thing to take my mind off my work ; also I shall like it." He was awarded the Military Cross [London Gazette, 27 June, 1916] : " Albert Ball, Second Lieutenant, Nottinghamshire and Derbyshire Regt. and Royal Flying Corps. For conspicuous skill and gallantry on many occasions, notably when, after failing to destroy an enemy kite balloon with bombs, he returned for a fresh supply, went back and brought it down in flames. He has done great execution among the enemy aeroplanes. On one occasion he attacked six in one fight, forced down two and drove the others off. This occurred several miles over the enemy's lines." After this he could have remained in England as an instructor of air pilots, but he wrote to his mother : " I have offered, dear, to go out again and have another smack. I don't offer because I want to go, but because every boy who has loving people and a good home should go out and stand up for it. You think I have done enough, but, oh, no, there is not, or at least should not be, such a thought in such a war as this. . . . It is an honour to be able to fight and do one's best for such a country as this and for such dear people. I shall fight for you and come home for you, and God always looks after me and makes me strong ; may He look after you also." " I only scrap because it is my duty, and I do not think anything bad about the Hun. He is just a good chap with very little guts, trying to do his best. Nothing makes me feel more rotten than to see them go down ; but, you see, it is either them or me, so I must do my best to make it a case of *them*." " I am, indeed, looked after by God ; but oh, I do get tired of always living to kill. I am beginning to feel like a murderer. I shall be pleased when I have finished." " Oh, won't it be nice when all this beastly killing is over, and we can just enjoy ourselves and not hurt anyone. I hate this game, but it is the only thing one must do just now." He was created a Companion of the Distinguished Service Order [London Gazette, 22 Sept. 1916] : " Albert Ball, M.C., Second Lieut. (Temporary Lieut.), Nottinghamshire and Derbyshire Regt. and Royal Flying Corps. For conspicuous gallantry and skill. Observing seven enemy machines in formation, he immediately attacked one of them, and shot it down at fifteen yards' range. The remaining machines retired. Immediately afterwards, seeing five more hostile machines, he attacked one at about ten yards' range, and shot it down, flames coming out of the fuselage. He then attacked another of the machines which had been firing at him, and shot it down into a village, where it landed on the top of a house. He then went to the nearest aerodrome for more ammunition, and, returning, attacked three more machines, causing them to dive and get out of control. Being then short of petrol he came home. His own machine was badly shot about in these fights." He was promoted Lieutenant, and in the same Gazette his name again appears as the recipient of a Bar to his Distinguished Service Order, for subsequent acts of conspicuous gallantry : " Albert Ball, M.C., D.S.O., Nottinghamshire and Derbyshire Regt. and Royal Flying Corps. For conspicuous skill and gallantry. When on escort duty in a bombing raid, he saw four enemy machines in formation ; he dived on to them and broke up their formation, and then shot down the nearest one, which fell on its nose. He came down to about 500 feet to make certain it was wrecked. On another occasion, observing twelve enemy machines in formation, he dived in among them and fired a drum into the nearest machine, which went down out of control. Several more hostile machines then approached, and he fired three more drums at them, driving down another out of control. He then returned, crossing the lines at a low altitude, with his machine very much damaged." Lieut. Ball was invested with the insignia of the Distinguished Service Order by the King on the 18th Nov. 1916. He was promoted to Captain, and in Nov. 1916, received a Second Bar to his Distinguished Service Order [London Gazette, 25 Nov. 1916] : " Albert Ball, D.S.O., M.C., Second Lieut., Nottinghamshire and Derbyshire Regt. For conspicuous gallantry in action. He attacked three hostile machines, and brought one down, displaying great courage. He brought down eight hostile machines in a short period and forced many others to land." None of the honours which were showered upon him could make the boy conceited. When twenty years of age he was presented with the honorary freedom of his native city, Nottingham. Capt. Ball was reported missing on 8 May, 1917. His father writes : " I had a letter from his C.O. stating that when last seen Capt. Ball was fighting with his usual success, and was lost sight of flying into a cloud perfectly straight. I have since had information from people in Annoeullin who saw his last fight, and from the Commandant and others, that Capt. Ball's last fight was over the village next to Annoeullin. They saw three German machines over the village which were attacked by Capt. Ball, who crashed two down and then the third flew away. Capt. Ball was by this time flying very low, and was brought down by anti-aircraft guns. His machine planed down into Annoeullin, and the first person to get to the machine who saw the fight was Madame Sieppe Coulon, who has since shown the greatest respect to his memory by keeping his grave in order in the German cemetery at Annoeullin, where the officers and men of the 207th Squadron have erected a beautiful cross. He was buried with every respect by the Germans, interred in a coffin, and his personal effects and cash that were on him were returned to me." General Sir Hugh Trenchard, in writing to his father on 8 May, 1917, said : " As you know, he was the most daring, skilful and successful pilot the Royal Flying Corps has ever had. Everyone in the Royal Flying Corps looked upon him as their own personal asset, and he was a most popular officer. His good spirit was infectious, as whatever squadron he was with, the officers of it

tried to work up to his level and reputation. I have never met a man who has been so successful as he was in such a short time, and who was so modest and so reliable." The Adjutant of Capt. Ball's squadron wrote : " Like everyone else who knew him, I loved him." One in the ranks wrote : " I would have gone through anything for Capt. Ball, my superior officer. England has lost her best aviator. He was loved by all." Sir Douglas Haig said : " By his unrivalled courage and brilliant ability as an airman, Capt. Ball won for himself a prominent place in a most gallant service. His loss was a great one, but the splendid spirit which he typified and did so much to foster lives after him. The record of his deeds will ever stir the pride and imagination of his countrymen, and act as an example and incentive to those who have taken up his work." Capt. Ball was in well over a hundred fights. In his last eleven days actually twenty-six, and though the precise number of enemy machines he brought down in his short career is not known, there are records of forty-seven aeroplanes and one kite balloon. He was only twenty at the time of his death. The Germans put up a wooden cross over his grave, on which they carved a laurel wreath, and beneath it the words : " He gave his life for his Fatherland." At the risk of death one of their air scouts crossed the lines to drop a cylinder conveying tidings of the manner of Ball's death. With the news of his death came the announcement that the French Government had conferred upon him the Cross of a Chevalier of the Legion of Honour. The Russian Order of St. George had been given to him in Aug. 1916. He was posthumously awarded the Victoria Cross [London Gazette, 3 June, 1917] : " Albert Ball, Capt., Nottinghamshire and Derbyshire Regt. and Royal Flying Corps. For most conspicuous and consistent bravery, from the 25th April to the 6th May, 1917, during which period Capt. Ball took part in twenty-six combats in the air and destroyed eleven hostile aeroplanes, drove down two out of control and forced several others to land." He had more honours when killed at twenty years of age than any other man in the British Army at his age ever had, and was the first officer to receive the D.S.O. three times ; also the first British officer to receive the American Aero Club Diploma and Medal. His full honours were the Victoria Cross, the Distinguished Service Order with two Bars, the Military Cross, the Russian Order of St. George, the Legion of Honour, the Medal and Diploma of the Aero Club of America, and Honorary Freeman of the City of Nottingham. A very fine bronze statue is being erected to his memory in Nottingham by public subscription. Poole is the sculptor. His father and mother are also building and endowing a block of homes, designed by Lieut.-Colonel Brewill, D.S.O., for soldiers' wives and mothers, in memory of Capt. Albert Ball, V.C. A " Life of Capt. Ball, V.C.," by Walter A. Briscoe and H. Russell Stannard, has been published by Herbert Jenkins. He was mentioned many times in Despatches and in Parliament.

HARVEY, FREDERICK MAURICE WATSON, Lieut., was the son of the late Rev. Alfred Harvey and of Mrs. Alfred Harvey. He was educated at Portora Royal School, Enniskillen. He is an excellent Rugby footballer. He joined the Canadian Military Forces ; served in the European War, and was awarded the Victoria Cross [London Gazette, 8 June, 1917] : " Frederick Maurice Watson Harvey, Lieut., Canadian Force. For most conspicuous bravery and devotion to duty. During an attack by his regiment on a village, a party of the enemy ran forward to a wired trench just in front of the village, and opened rapid rifle and machine-gun fire at a very close range, causing heavy casualties in the leading troop. At this critical moment, when the enemy showed no intention whatever of retiring, and fire was still intense, Lieut. Harvey, who was in command of the leading troops, ran forward well ahead of his men and dashed at the trench, still fully manned, jumped the wire, shot the machine gunner, and captured the gun. His most courageous act undoubtedly had a decisive effect on the success of the operations." He was awarded the Military Cross [London Gazette, 26 June, 1918] : " For conspicuous gallantry and devotion to duty. In the attack, by his fearless leading, he overcame the resistance of the enemy, although the latter were in greatly superior numbers. He engaged many of the enemy single-handed, and although wounded and suffering from a considerable loss of blood, continued to fight his way forward until he effected a junction with another mounted party, thus contributing in a great degree to the success of the attack. He commanded his men with magnificent gallantry, skill and determination." The following is taken from " Thirty Canadian V.C.'s " : " The first Canadian cavalryman to win the Victoria Cross in this war is Lieut. Harvey, of Lord Strathcona's Horse. The Strathconas, raised for service in South Africa and originally recruited largely from the Royal North-West Mounted Police, distinguished themselves in the Boer War, and afterwards were established as a unit of the Canadian Permanent Militia. Along with the other regiments of our cavalry brigade, they fought as infantry in the trenches throughout the autumn and winter of 1915-16. The brigade was then withdrawn from the line, re-horsed and embarked upon a long course of training and waiting. March, 1917, found the Canadian Cavalry Brigade serving with the 15th Army Corps, north of Peronne on the Somme. At this time the brigade consisted of the Royal Canadian Dragoons, Lord Strathcona's Horse, the Fort Garry Horse, the Royal Canadian Horse Artillery, the Canadian Cavalry Machine Gun Squadron and a field ambulance. On the morning of 24 March the brigade received orders to form on a twelve-mile frontage, with Nurlu as its centre, and from there to advance beyond our infantry positions. By the evening of the same day the Royal Canadian Dragoons were in possession of several hostile positions, including the woods to the south-west of Lieramont ; and during the night the Fort Garry Horse, on the left of the advance, took the villages of Ytres and Etricourt. On the afternoon of the 25th, Capt. Sharpe with his squadron of F.G.H., dislodged the Germans from the smaller of two woods that they held in strength. From this first wood he launched an attack upon the second and larger, in open order at the gallop, and drove the enemy through and out of that cover and into the shelter of a trench beyond. This was the first instance, in more than two years, of cavalry riding straight at a position held by rifles and machine guns. At six o'clock of the following day (26 March) the Strathconas gained a wood south-east of Equancourt, where they dismounted, and from which they advanced upon and captured the village at the point of the bayonet. At the same time the Fort Garry Horse, attacking from the north, made their objectives in spite of heavy machine-gun fire. The admirable shooting of the R.C.H.A. had much to do with the success of the operation. During the night, and early in the morning of the 27th, the R.C.D.'s occupied the villages of Longasvesnes and Lieramont. They handed the defence of the former over to the infantry ; but they remained in the latter and there repulsed a strong counter-attack. High ground about the village of Guyencourt and Grebaussart Wood was the final objective of a series of attacks made by the Lord Strathcona's Horse and the Fort Garry Horse on the evening of the 27th. A heavy snowstorm delayed the initial stroke until 5.15 ; but then, the moment the air was clear enough for the leaders to see the way, a squadron of the Fort Garry Horse galloped forward to Hill 140, and there established two machine guns in commanding positions. This squadron then pushed around the hill into Grebaussart Wood, Jean Copse and Chauffeurs Wood, and successfully posted three more machine guns. Other squadrons of this regiment rode straight at the village of Saulcourt, and penetrated its outskirts. The Germans, retiring before them, were caught by our machine-gun fire. The Strathconas, with Guyencourt in view, charged on to a ridge on the left front of that village, where they were confronted by machine guns and strongly-wired positions ; so they swung to the right, rode at the north-west corner of she village and won to the partial shelter of its walls. It was at this stage of the swift action that Lieut. Harvey performed the conspicuous deed of valour that was recognized by the highest award. He commanded the leading troop of the charging Strathconas and rode well in front of his men. He was close to the edge of the village, when, by the failing light, he discovered a deadly menace to his command set fairly across his course—a wired trench containing a machine gun and a strong garrison. He swung from his saddle and sprinted straight at the gun, firing his revolver as he ran. He reached the triple entanglement and hurdled it, shot the machine gunner and jumped on to the gun. The man at the gun must have lost his nerve and his wits in the face of that amazing, swift frontal assault ; his hands must have fumbled, misguided by his flinching brain : we know that his gun jammed and that he died a violent death. Thus the trench became ours, the Strathconas took Guyencourt, and Harvey won the Cross."

McNAMARA, FRANK HUBERT, Lieut., served in the Great War, and for his services in Egypt on 20 March, 1917, was awarded the Victoria Cross [London Gazette, 8 June, 1917] : "Frank Hubert McNamara, Lieut., Australian Forces, Royal Flying Corps. For most conspicuous bravery and devotion to duty during an aerial bomb attack upon a hostile construction train, when one of our pilots was forced to land behind the enemy's lines. Lieut. McNamara, observing the pilot's predicament and the fact that hostile cavalry were approaching, descended to his rescue. He did this under heavy rifle fire, and in spite of the fact that he himself had been severely wounded in the thigh. He landed about 200 yards from the damaged machine, the pilot of which climbed into Lieut. McNamara's machine, and an attempt was made to rise. Owing, however, to his disabled leg, Lieut. McNamara was unable to keep his machine straight, and it turned over. The two officers, having extricated themselves, immediately set fire to the machine and made their way across to the damaged machine, which they succeeded in starting. Finally Lieut. McNamara, although weak from the loss of blood, flew the machine back to the aerodrome, a distance of 70 miles, and thus completed his comrade's rescue." "It may be of interest in connection with Lieut. McNamara's winning of the Victoria Cross—the first Victoria Cross won by the Australian Flying Corps—to give a short account of the history of the beginning and start of the Australian Flying Corps. The 'Bristol' Aviation Company sent out to Australia in 1911 one of their—then experimental—biplanes, for exhibition purposes. It was named a B.E/2 machine. It was most simple in its construction. The pilot sat in front on the lower plane ; his feet rested on a board fixed in front of it. There was no fusilage : the engine was fixed on the same plane at his back, with the propeller working in rear of the engine. In this machine General J. M. Gordon, who at this time was commandant of the Commonwealth Military Forces of New South Wales, made the first flight over Sydney, piloted by quite a lad, young Macdonald, who afterwards, on the breaking out of the World's War, was drowned in the Thames, his machine unfortunately failing him and falling into the river. Early in 1913 General Gordon, who had then become Chief of the Staff of the Australian Military Forces, founded the first Aviation School in Australia. A most suitable locality was chosen by him at 'Point Cook,' on a property belonging to Mr. E. Chirnside, on the shores of Hobson's Bay, Victoria, about 15 miles from Melbourne. There were many good reasons for the selection of this site. In the first place, for several miles round the land was level, further, the waters of Hobson's Bay were smooth, and from its shores planes could well be launched. Consequently the Flying School established there would meet the military and naval flying requirements. Having decided on the site, General Gordon lost no time in starting the school, while the plans and specifications for the permanent buildings were being considered. Canvas hangars, mechanics' shops, and quarters for all concerned were quickly erected. It was quite a comfortable camp. General Gordon had taken considerable trouble in obtaining from the War Office two reliable instructors. The first officer suggested to him from the War Office was the late Colonel Coddy. As the one object in view was the teaching of young Australians to fly, General Gordon felt that to adequately 'fill the job,' younger men than Coddy should be chosen. His representations on the point were favourably considered by the War Office, and two first-rate young officers, Mr. Eric Harrison and Mr. Petre, were selected, and duly arrived in Melbourne. It is due to the Australian Flying Corps, now as good as any in the world, to remember the names of these two young officers, who were their original instructors. It is needless to emphasize here the glorious work done by the Australian Flying Corps in every theatre of the Great War. To those like McNamara and his pals the thanks of the Empire are greatly due." Australian military history began when Colonel Johnston landed in New South Wales as commandant of the Military Forces. Portraits of this remarkable man are in the Sydney Art Gallery, and there are legends of his performances. His deposition of Governor Bligh, however, ended in a court martial at Chelsea Hospital, when Johnston was cashiered and returned to Sydney to die of a broken heart before the military authorities at home had relented and sent him out his sword. Colonel Johnston once rode out with 20 soldiers from Sydney towards Parramatta to suppress 500 desperate and rebellious men armed with guns, spades or any handy weapons. Johnston was better mounted than most of his troopers, and he left 17 and rode on with three men. With these he drove the 500 rebels from Parramatta to Sydney, where they were probably suitably punished, and the Commandant received a grant of useful land at Dapto. Australians serving in the Sudan brought back "The Sudan Goat." It is said that when he died in the Sydney Zoo a native-born imposter assumed his foreign title. Sailors served in China under Sir O'Moore Creagh and were "simply admirable." Except for some gunners and a half battalion of infantry, they were the only white troops available for various duties for which native troops could not be used. They dealt with numerous non-ticket holders on the railways, and were so useful that many were engaged by the Chinese Government when Sir O'Moore was thanked by the Australian Government for his arangements for their return tickets and general welfare. Australians served in South Africa and their doings come into this book. In the Great War, serving under General Birdwood ("Birdie"), who "charmed Kitchener and the Australians," Ian Hamilton, General Monash and others, they won for themselves a reputation second to none in the field. They sometimes got a bit out of hand when "resting," and some one said of them that their proper place was the front-line trenches or Australia, and a revue actor in London divided mankind into three classes, married, single and Australians.

PHILLIPS, ROBERT EDWIN, Temporary Lieut. and Adjutant, was born at Hill Top, West Bromwich, on 11 April, 1895, son of Alfred Phillips. His parents live at Hill Top, West Bromwich. He was educated at King Edward VI.'s Grammar School, Aston, Birmingham. He joined the Army on 17 March, 1914, as a Private in the 1/15th Coy. of the London Regt., and was given a commission in the 9th Battn. Royal Warwickshire Regt. on 3 Dec. 1914. He served in the European War. He arrived at Suvla Bay, Gallipoli, on 6 Oct. 1915, and served there until wounded on 17 Nov. 1915. He rejoined his regiment in Mesopotamia at the time of the fall of Kut-el-Amara, and served with them until 9 May, 1918. He was promoted Lieutenant on 10 April, 1916. He was awarded the Victoria Cross, the award being announced in the London Gazette of 8 June, 1917 : "Robert Edwin Phillips, Temporary Lieut. and Adjutant, Royal Warwickshire Regt. For most conspicuous bravery and devotion to duty. After his Commanding Officer had been mortally wounded in leading a counter-attack, Lieut. Phillips went out under the most intense fire to his assistance, and eventually, with the help of a comrade, succeeded in bringing him back to our lines. Lieut. Phillips had in the first instance tried to get a telephone wire across the open, following the battalion in their counter-attack. This was impossible when the signallers were killed. His Commanding Officer lay wounded in the open, and as the counter-attack had succeeded, he turned all his energies on getting him in. He showed sustained courage in its very highest form, and throughout he had but little chance of ever getting back alive." The action took place near Kut on 25 Jan. 1917. His Commanding Officer, Lieut.-Colonel E. E. D. Henderson, whom he brought in, but who died shortly afterwards, was also awarded the Victoria Cross, and the comrade who helped Lieut. Phillips, Corpl. Scott, was given the Distinguished Conduct Medal. He was promoted Captain on 26 Jan. 1917, and was Adjutant from 9 July, 1917, to 9 May, 1918. He obtained a transfer to the Royal Air Force on 9 May, 1918, to train for a pilot's certificate, but this was interrupted by leave home in Oct. 1918, and the subsequent signing of the Armistice. He was demobilized on 13 Feb. 1919. He was mentioned in Lieut.-General Maude's Despatch of 31 March, 1917, and in Lieut.-General Marshall's of 31 March, 1918, for distinguished service in Mesopotamia. On visiting his old school he was presented with a silver casket "as a small token of our thankfulness for what you and others have done, and as a token of our intense pride that one of our body should have risen to the greatest heights of courage and self-sacrifice."

POPE, CHARLES, Lieut., served in the European War, and was awarded the Victoria Cross [London Gazette, 8 June, 1917] : "Charles Pope, Lieut., late 11th Infantry Battn. Australian Imperial Force. For most conspicuous bravery and devotion to duty when in command of a very important picquet post in the sector held by his battalion, his orders being to hold this post at all costs. After the picquet post had been heavily attacked, the enemy in greatly superior numbers surrounded the post. Lieut. Pope, finding that he was running short of ammunition, sent back for further supplies. But the situation culminated before it could arrive, and in the hope of saving the position this very gallant officer was seen to charge with his picquet into a superior force, by which it was overpowered. By his sacrifice Lieut. Pope not only inflicted heavy loss on the enemy, but obeyed his order to hold the position to the last. His body, together with those of most of his men, was found in close proximity to eighty enemy dead—a sure proof of the gallant resistance which had been made."

HAINE, REGINALD LEONARD, Second Lieut. His father is at Scotland Yard. He served in the European War, and was awarded the Victoria Cross [London Gazette, 8 June, 1917]: "Reginald Leonard Haine, Second Lieut., H.A.C. For most conspicuous bravery and determination when our troops, occupying a pronounced salient, were repeatedly counter-attacked. There was an ever-present danger that if the enemy attack succeeded the garrison of the salient would be surrounded. Second Lieut. Haine organized and led with the utmost gallantry six bombing attacks against a strong point which

dangerously threatened our communication, capturing the position, together with fifty prisoners and two machine guns. The enemy then counter-attacked with a battalion of the Guard, succeeded in regaining his position, and the situation appeared critical. Second Lieut. Haine at once formed a block in his trench, and for the whole of the following night maintained his position against repeated determined attacks. Reorganizing his men on the following morning, he again attacked and captured the strong point, pressing the enemy back for several hundred yards, and thus relieving the situation. Throughout these operations this officer's superb courage, quick decision, and sound judgment were beyond praise, and it was his

Reginald L. Haine.

splendid personal example which inspired his men to continue their efforts during more than thirty hours of continuous fighting." He was presented by the Mayor of Richmond with an illuminated address, congratulating him on being the first Richmond man to win the Victoria Cross. Before enlisting he was a Boy Scout. He joined the H.A.C. a few days later than Pollard, on 24 Aug. 1914, and, like him, went abroad with the battalion in Sept. 1914. In Dec. 1916, he became Second Lieutenant. He was awarded the Military Cross, and a notice in the " Times " for 11 March, 1920, says that Capt. Haine, V.C., M.C., attached to Sikhs, Indian Army. was present at the Investiture at Buckingham Palace, and received the M.C. and Bar. When he enlisted, a lad in his teens, he was articled with a firm of chartered accountants. At the time when he received his Victoria Cross he was only 20 years of age.

The following is quoted by permission of the editor of " The City Press," from the issue for Saturday, 28 July, 1917 : " The investiture of V.C. heroes at Buckingham Palace on Saturday was followed by a rousing welcome at the Armoury House to the two recipients belonging to the H.A.C.—Capt. Alfred Oliver Pollard and Second Lieut. Reginald Leonard Haine. The regimental flag was broken in line with the Union Jack and the Stars and Stripes, and all the available artillery and infantry mounted a guard of honour. Preceded by the regimental band, playing ' See the Conquering Hero comes ' and the Regimental March, the two officers walked through cheering lines to a platform in the middle of the drill ground, where they were accompanied by their parents and a group of distinguished officers, including General Sir Henry Mackinnon, of C.I.V. fame, and Colonel the Earl of Denbigh, commanding the H.A.C. When the cheers had subsided, Lord Denbigh said that, during the many years he had had the honour of commanding the regiment, that day was one which made him feel more proud of it than any other event. He had seen various notable gatherings on that old ground, and the regiment when he first entered it 25 years ago was very different from what it was to-day. One never thought in those days that the H.A.C. would become the magnificent fighting force it had now developed into, and that the regiment would have an opportunity of congratulating two of its officers on having won the most desired honour for bravery in the British Army. (Hear, hear.) He had just come away from a most remarkable investiture by the King, and had heard recited the brave deeds which merited the honours bestowed by His Majesty. He did not wish to distinguish one from another, but when the Corps considered what those two H.A.C. boys—for he would call them boys—had done, it had reason to be proud of them, not merely on account of their pluck and bravery shown on the field, but because of the coolness and initiative they showed, and owed to the valuable training they had acquired. (Applause.) It was one thing to be able to follow in the field, and quite another thing to organize and lead men in a difficult situation, to keep up discipline, and to save the situation. The two winners were up against the Prussian Guard. Capt. Pollard had won the V.C. and the M.C. Bar for conspicuous bravery and determination at a place he was not allowed to mention. Troops of various units had become disorganized by shell fire, and Capt. Pollard dashed up to stop the retirement. With only four men, he started a counter-attack with bombs, and regained, not only the ground that had been lost, but more besides. He had already won the D.C.M. and the M.C. (Applause.) Second-Lieut. Haine organized with the utmost gallantry six bombing attacks against a strong point which dangerously threatened our communications, and he captured many prisoners and guns. The enemy regained the situation, and the position was critical. Reorganizing his men the next morning, he again attacked, captured a strong point, and relieved the situation. (Applause.) Those feats gave some idea of the fighting that some of the H.A.C. battalions had been doing in France for a long time. The two officers were to be congratulated on having come safely through, and on having been able to receive the honours they had won so well. One must not forget the men who were with and followed them, and those who followed and had not come back. (Hear, hear.) Fortunately, the losses on that occasion were small, compared with the importance of the gains, and the small losses were undoubtedly attributable to the excellent discipline and splendid training of the officers and men who took part in the fight. That showed the value of discipline and training. They were all very proud of being members of the old regiment, which had expanded during the war to an extent they never dreamt of. Whereas at the beginning of the war the H.A.C. consisted of two horse batteries and half a battalion of infantry, it now contained four mounted batteries in the field, a siege battery, and two infantry battalions that had done some of the hottest fighting which had taken place

on the fronts. In that connection he would like to read an extract from an address given to the H.A.C. Battalion in question by the Commander of the Army Corps to which they belonged. ' The fighting recently has been very severe, and, sitting behind, as I have to do, I admit that at times I was anxious, as it appeared that our position might possibly be worse than it was at the beginning. Then word came through that the H.A.C. were bombing up the Hun trench, and afterwards further word that the H.A.C had driven the enemy out of the front line. That was indeed a great relief to me. Nobody hates the Bosche more than I do, but I admire him as a very fine soldier. You had against you the finest troops of the German Army—the Prussian Guard—and you beat them. That is enough. Your regiment has a very fine record in history, and you have now added a page which is worthy of any previous page in that history. To thank you and to congratulate you, and to tell you how proud I am of you, is what I have come here for to-day.' The honours they had won had been numerous. Besides the two V.C.'s, he would like to mention the C.M.G. conferred on Colonel Treffry, and the C.B. on Colonel Reece. Nine officers had won the D.S.O. and 36 officers the M.C.—one with a Bar. Of other ranks, 15 had received the D.C.M., and 39 the M.M.—two with Bars. There were foreign distinctions as well. The regiment had sent at least 3,500 men for commissions in the Army. Of those many had won distinctions, and many had suffered casualties. (Applause.) He had heard on all sides the very best accounts from general officers of the behaviour of members of the corps in the field in France and elsewhere. The officers spoke of the men's steadiness, excellent behaviour, discipline, training, and coolness under fire, while in sheer hard fighting they had been hard to beat. (Applause.) The King told him that morning to let the officers and men know how proud he was to be connected with the regiment as Captain-General and Colonel, and to decorate those two officers. His Majesty sent to them all words of encouragement, and felt confident that they would do everything they possibly could to maintain the record of the H.A.C. (Applause.) With the utmost enthusiasm the assembled officers and men gave the H.A.C. fire—Zay, Zay, Zay—for the two V.C.'s, the King, and General Sir Henry Mackinnon."

POLLARD, ALFRED OLIVER, Lieut., joined the Honourable Artillery Company, and served in the European War. He was awarded the Distinguished Conduct Medal, and later the Military Cross ; was awarded

the Victoria Cross [London Gazette, 8 June, 1917]: " Alfred Oliver Pollard, M.C., Second Lieut., Honourable Artillery Company. For most conspicuous bravery and determination. The troops of various units on the left of this officer's battalion had become disorganized owing to the heavy casualties from shell fire ; and a subsequent determined enemy attack with very strong forces caused further confusion and retirement, closely pressed by hostile forces. Second Lieut. Pollard at once realized the seriousness of the situation, and dashed up to stop the retirement. With only four men he started a counter-attack with bombs, and pressed it home till he had broken the enemy attack, and regained all that had been lost and much ground in addition. The enemy retired

Alfred Oliver Pollard.

in disorder, sustaining many casualties. By his force of will, dash and splendid example, coupled with an utter contempt of danger, this officer, who has already won the D.C.M. and M.C., infused courage into every man who saw him." He joined the H.A.C. (Infantry) 8 Aug. 1914, and a month later went to France as a Sergeant ; he was awarded the D.C.M. for bravery near Ypres in Sept. 1915. In Jan. 1916, he was given a commission, and he later won the Military Cross, and subsequently a Bar to the M.C. Lieut. Pollard married, in 1918, Mary, daughter of Mr. Ainsley, of Trefilan, Purley.

BOOTH, FREDERICK CHARLES, Sergt., was born in March, 1890, son of Thomas Charles Booth. He was educated at Cheltenham College, where he was a boarder at Hazelwell. He served in the European War, and was awarded the Victoria Cross [London Gazette, 8 June, 1917]: " Frederick Charles Booth, No. 1630, Sergt., South African Forces, attached Rhodesia Native Regt. For most conspicuous bravery during an attack in thick bush on the enemy position. Under very heavy rifle fire Sergt. Booth went forward alone, and brought in a man who was dangerously wounded. Later he rallied native troops, who were badly disorganized, and brought them to the firing line. This N.C.O. has on many previous occasions displayed the greatest bravery, coolness and resource in action, and has set a splendid example of pluck, endurance and determination."

CATOR, HARRY, Sergt., was born at Drayton, Norfolk, on 24 Jan. 1894, son of Robert and Laura Cator. He was educated at Drayton School. He married 2 Sept. 1914, Rose Alice, only daughter of Mr. and Mrs. W. J. Morriss, of Great Yarmouth. He enlisted 3 Sept. 1914. He received the Military Medal for rescuing wounded 3 July, 1916, during the Somme offensive. The Victoria Cross was awarded for services on Easter Monday, 9 April, 1917 (Arras Battle). He was wounded on 12 April, three days later, by high-explosive shrapnel, breaking both upper and lower jaws. He was admitted to

Harry Cator.

Beaufort Hospital, Bristol. Service in France—twenty-two months. He was also presented with the Croix de Guerre 14 July, 1917. His Victoria Cross was gazetted 8 June, 1917: "Harry Cator, No. 5190, Sergt., East Surrey Regt. Date of Act of Bravery: 9 April, 1917. For most conspicuous bravery and devotion to duty. Whilst consolidating the first-line captured system his platoon suffered severe casualties from hostile machine-gun and rifle fire. In full view of the enemy and under heavy fire, Sergt. Cator with one man advanced across the open to attack the hostile machine gun. The man accompanying him was killed after going a short distance, but Sergt. Cator continued on, and picking up a Lewis gun and some drums on his way, succeeded in reaching the northern end of the hostile trench. Meanwhile, one of our bombing parties was seen to be held up by a machine gun. Sergt. Cator took up a position from which he sighted this gun, and killed the entire team and the officer, whose papers he brought in. He continued to hold that end of the trench with the Lewis gun with such effect that the bombing squad was enabled to work along, the result being that 100 prisoners and five machine guns were captured." The following letters of congratulation were received by Sergt. Cator: "Allow me to offer you my heartiest congratulations in winning the most coveted honour it is possible to win. I am certain no one in the Army has been more entitled to the Victoria Cross than yourself. Every time you have been in the line you have always inspired the men by your personal bravery, and when you were with me in B and C Company, I always knew things were all right when you were about. I was extremely sorry to hear you were wounded, and trust it is not of a serious nature. I must conclude now, trusting you are going on very nicely and sincerely hoping you will be spared to come through safely and live long to enjoy the proud distinction of the Victoria Cross." Another extract: "— tells me you are giving Sergt. Cator, V.C., a welcome home and presenting him with a watch to commemorate his earning the Victoria Cross. Sergt. Cator is a man who has done persistent good work throughout the war, and all of us in the Brigade are justly proud of him. In offering him your congratulations, will you add mine and the whole of my brigade. The act for which he was awarded the Victoria Cross was magnificent. It is only deeds of simply colossal heroism which get a Victoria Cross, so you can imagine how proud and delighted we were when Sergt. Cator was awarded the most coveted honour."

The "Surrey Comet," in a special note on the award of the Victoria Cross to Sergt. Harry Cator, of Great Yarmouth, says:

"The gallant East Surreys have covered themselves with glory in this war, and have a record for the highest honours of which any regiment might be proud and which few, if any, can rival. To its proud Honours' Roll there is added now a fifth Victoria Cross, won by Sergt. Harry Cator, for the performance of deeds of gallantry which will fill everyone who reads of them with admiration. Sergt. Cator is a New Army man and his home is in Great Yarmouth. In full view of the enemy this brave and devoted soldier went out, under heavy fire, with one man, to attack a hostile machine gun, which had waspishly inflicted severe casualties on his platoon. The man accompanying him was killed, but Sergt. Cator continued his advance alone, and picking up a Lewis machine gun on his way, succeeded in reaching the end of the enemy trench. Finding one of our bombing parties laid up by a machine gun, Sergt. Cator wiped out the whole gun team, including the officer, whose papers he brought in. Continuing his hold of the enemy trench, he enabled a bombing party to work along, the result being that a hundred prisoners and five machine guns were captured. This is indeed a glorious episode, for which the name and fame of Sergt. Harry Cator, of the East Surreys, will be enshrined for ever in the hearts of his countrymen and in the annals of the regiment, which is proud of him. Performed in contempt of death and of great odds, such deeds are as if inspired. Was ever the Victoria Cross bestowed more worthily?"

ORMSBY, JOHN WILLIAM, Sergt., served in the European War, and was awarded the Victoria Cross [London Gazette, 8 June, 1917]: "John William Ormsby, Sergt., No. 1836, King's Own Yorkshire Light Infantry. For most conspicuous bravery and devotion to duty, during operations which culminated in the capture of an important position. Acting as Company Sergeant-Major, he showed throughout the attack absolute indifference to the heavy machine-gun and rifle fire, and set a fine example. After clearing the village he pushed on and drove out many snipers from localities further forward. When the only surviving officer was wounded he took command of the company and led them forward, under heavy fire, for 400 yards to a new position. He organized his new position with great skill, and held his line with determination until relieved of his command. His conduct throughout was admirable, and inspired confidence in every man under his command." After leaving the Army, Sergt. Ormsby was presented with a cart and horse, and £500 was invested for him to restart life as a greengrocer.

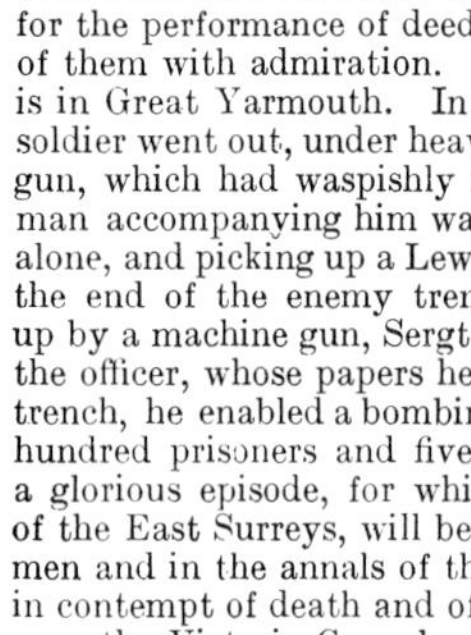
John Woods Whittle.

WHITTLE, JOHN WOODS, Sergt., served in the European War, and was awarded the Victoria Cross [London Gazette, 8 June, 1917]: "John Woods Whittle, No. 2902, Sergt., 12th Battn. Infantry, Australian Imperial Force. For conspicuous bravery and devotion to duty on two occasions. When in command of a platoon, the enemy, under cover of an intense artillery barrage, attacked the small trench he was holding. Owing to weight of numbers, the enemy succeeded in entering the trench, and it was owing to Sergt. Whittle personally collecting all available men and charging the enemy that the position was regained. On a second occasion when the enemy broke through the left of our line, Sergt. Whittle's own splendid example was the means of keeping the men well in hand. His platoon were suffering heavy casualties, and the enemy endeavoured to bring up a machine gun to enfilade the position. Grasping the situation, he rushed alone across the fire-swept ground and attacked the hostile gun crew with bombs before the gun could be got into action. He succeeded in killing the whole crew, and in bringing back the machine gun to our position."

SIFTON, ELLIS WELWOOD, L.-Sergt., No. 53730, served in the European War in France. He was awarded the Victoria Cross 8 June, 1919: "Ellis Melwood Sifton, No. 53730, L.-Sergt., late Canadian Infantry Battn. For most conspicuous bravery and devotion to duty. During the attack on enemy trenches, Sergt. Sifton's company was held up by machine gun fire, which inflicted many casualties. Having located the gun, he charged it single-handed, killing all the crew. A small enemy party advanced down the trench, but he succeeded in keeping these off till our men had gained the position. In carrying out this gallant act he was killed, but his conspicuous valour undoubtedly saved many lives and contributed largely to the success of the operation." "Thirty Canadian V.C.'s" (published by Messrs. Skeffington) says (pages 28–31): "On Easter Monday (9 April), 1917, in a mixture of recurrent rain and driving sleet, the Canadian troops took Vimy Ridge from the Germans. When it is said that the Canadians 'took' this ridge, the literally correct phrase is used. No other word expresses the historic incident so well. The Canadian battalions took Vimy Ridge; and L.-Sergt. Ellis Welwood Sifton, of the 18th Battn., from Ontario, was one of a few men whose deeds on that tremendous day won for them the highest mark of admiration their fellows could offer for valour. He gave his life for the award. The taking of Vimy Ridge was an operation which involved practically every Canadian unit. It was a scheme the authors of which hardly dared to hope would be so completely carried out, for the ridge was the pivot of the German millions on the whole Western front. It was an eight-thousand-yards-long fortress, deemed by its occupants to be impregnable, a bastion of inestimable strength and importance, an inland Gibraltar. British and French armies had tried several times to wrest it from the German grasp. The Germans had met their smashing blows, had quivered under them—but had continued to hold the ridge. On the morning of that Easter Monday they held it, arrogant as ever. In the evening they were gone! The slopes of Vimy were a maze of trenches of superb construction, fashioned to withstand the pounding of any artillery. The dug-outs were vast fortified underground chambers—some capable of sheltering entire battalions—where enemy shells could not find the occupants. Its machine-gun fortresses were formidable as miniature battleships. To familiarize themselves with the difficulties which an attack on this ridge would involve, the Canadian Divisions went into strict training for weeks behind the lines. Battalion commanders were called in conference to the headquarters of their brigades, brigadiers to their divisions, divisional commanders to corps; the results of these deliberations were made known to regimental officers; officers lectured the non-commissioned officers, the non-commissioned officers passed it on, as non-commissioned officers do, to the rank and file. All ranks trained. At 5.30 on the fateful morning the 18th Battn. was in position on the right wing of the 4th Brigade front. The dawn was dull, uncertain, depressing. Heavy clouds lay over the battlefield and a biting north-west wind scudded across the waste lands. With the first crash of the barrage which fell on the German front the waves of assaulting troops rose out of their trenches like gnomes of the night and started for the enemy lines. The 18th Battn. assaulted on a three-platoon frontage in four waves. Before them the fire-edged barrage swept on, destroying with the completeness of a flaming guillotine. The first German line was gained and captured with very small loss to the attackers. The Germans were stunned and demoralized by the hurricane of explosives which was being hurled at them. They called 'Kamerad!' and were dispatched, still meek and submissive, to a safer place. But at the second line, after the barrage had swept over it, the first opposition of importance was met. Here small parties of machine-gunners, tucked away in their concrete fortresses, had escaped the terrible shelling, and as the Canadians advanced they enfiladed the waves of men as they passed. One such nest stemmed the advance of 'C' Company. Men began to fall, hit by the unseen enemy. The others peered around in the gloom, trying to discover the nest. L.-Sergt. Sifton saw it first. The barrel of the gun showed over a parapet. Sifton did not wait to work out an elaborate attack, for there was no time to lose. He rushed ahead, leaped into the trench, charged into the crew, overthrew the gun and turned on the gunners with his bayonet. Before they had time to resist every one of the Germans was out of business. With the demolition of the machine gun, the advance of the 18th Battn. moved on. Sifton's men hurried up to support him, but before they reached the position a party of Germans advanced on him from down the trench. He attacked them with bayonet and clubbed rifle, and held them off till his comrades jumped into the trench and ended the unequal fight. But none noticed a dying German, one of Sifton's victims, who rolled over to the edge of the trench, picked up a rifle and took careful aim. That was how he died—the man from Ontario, of whom it was stated in official phraseology that 'his conspicuous valour undoubtedly saved many lives and contributed largely to the success of the operation.'"

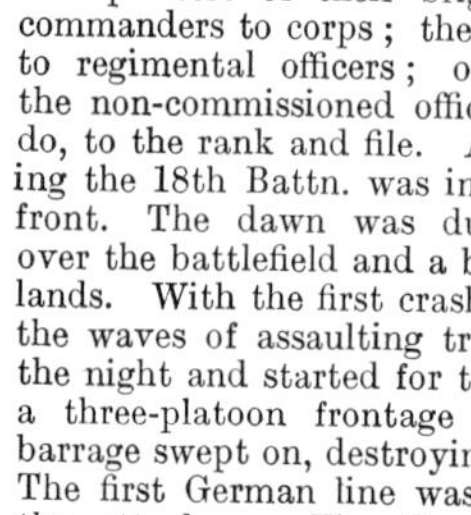
Thomas Steele.

STEELE, THOMAS, Sergt., was born on 6 Feb. 1891, at Claytons, Springhead, Oldham, son of Harry Steele, Motor Carrier,

and Elizabeth Steele, daughter of Mrs. Mitchell. The parents live at a village called Springhead, near Oldham, just within the borders of the West Riding of Yorkshire. He was educated at Austerlands, Yorkshire, and on leaving school entered the Rome Mill, near his home, as a Bobbin Carrier. Factory life, however, did not suit him, and on 22 Aug. 1911, he joined the Army as a Private in the Seaforth Highlanders. He served in the European War. He was stationed in India at the outbreak. His battalion was at once transferred to the Western front, and he took part in most of the earlier engagements, including the Retreat from Mons. They were sent to Mesopotamia in Nov. 1915, as part of the force which endeavoured to relieve General Townshend at Kut. He more than once distinguished himself before being "recommended for something," which was his way of telling his people at home about the possibility of his being awarded the Victoria Cross. The announcement of the award of the Victoria Cross was in the London Gazette of 8 June, 1917: "Thomas Steele, Sergt., No. 811, Seaforth Highlanders. For most conspicuous bravery and devotion to duty. At a critical moment, when a strong enemy counter-attack had temporarily regained some of the captured trenches, Sergt. Steele rushed forward and assisted a comrade to carry a machine gun into position. He kept the gun in action till relieved, being mainly instrumental in keeping the remainder of the line intact. Some hours later another strong attack enabled the enemy to reoccupy a portion of the captured trenches. Again Sergt. Steele showed the greatest bravery, and by personal valour and example was able to rally troops who were wavering. He encouraged them to remain in their trenches, and led a number of them forward, thus greatly helping to re-establish our line. On this occasion he was severely wounded. These acts of valour were performed under heavy artillery and rifle fire." He was appointed Lance-Corporal 31 Dec. 1913; promoted Corporal 1 June, 1915; Lance-Sergeant 10 Oct. 1915; Sergt. 7 Jan. 1917; gazetted 6 June, 1917; mentioned in Despatches by General Sir Stanley Maude in Aug. 1917; demobilized in Feb. 1919.

CUNNINGHAM, JOHN, Corpl., served in the European War in France. He died in hospital from the effect of wounds received in the action during which he won the Victoria Cross [London Gazette, 8 June, 1917]: "John Cunningham, No. 3916, Corpl., late 2nd Battn. Leinster Regt. For most conspicuous bravery and devotion to duty when in command of a Lewis Gun Section on the most exposed flank of the attack. His section came under heavy enfilade fire and suffered severely. Although wounded he succeeded almost alone in reaching his objective with his gun, which he got into action in spite of much opposition. When counter-attacked by a party of twenty of the enemy he exhausted his ammunition against them, then, standing in full view, he commenced throwing bombs. He was wounded again, and fell, but picked himself up and continued to fight single-handed with the enemy until his bombs were exhausted. He then made his way back to our lines with a fractured arm and other wounds. There is little doubt that the superb courage of this N.C.O. cleared up a most critical situation on the left flank of the attack. Corpl. Cunningham died in hospital from the effects of his wounds."

JARRATT, GEORGE, Corpl., served in the European War, and was awarded the Victoria Cross [London Gazette, 8 June, 1917]: "George Jarratt, No. 55295, Corpl., late Royal Fusiliers. For most conspicuous bravery and devotion in deliberately sacrificing his life to save others. He had, together with some wounded men, been taken prisoner and placed under guard in a dug-out. The same evening the enemy were driven back by our troops, the leading infantrymen of which commenced to bomb the dug-outs. A grenade fell in the dug-out, and without hesitation Corpl. Jarratt placed both feet on the grenade, the subsequent explosion blowing off both his legs. The wounded were later safely removed to our lines, but Corpl. Jarratt died before he could be removed. By this supreme act of self-sacrifice the lives of these wounded were saved."

BRYAN, THOMAS, L.-Corpl., served in the European War, and was awarded the Victoria Cross [London Gazette, 8 June, 1917]: "Thomas Bryan, No. 22040, L.-Corpl., 25th Battn. Northumberland Fusiliers. For most conspicuous bravery during an attack. Although wounded, this Non-commissioned Officer went forward alone, with a view to silencing a machine gun which was inflicting much damage. He worked up most skilfully along a communication trench, approached the gun from behind, disabled it and killed two of the team as they were abandoning the gun. As this machine gun had been a serious obstacle in the advance to the second objective, the results obtained by L.-Corpl. Bryan's gallant action were very far-reaching."

HEAVISIDE, MICHAEL, Private, was born at Durham City on 28 Oct. 1880, son of John Wilson Heaviside and of Annie Heaviside (née Fawell). He was educated at Kimblesworth Colliery, co. Durham, and joined the Army on 7 Sept. 1914. He served in the European War in the 10th and 15th Battns. The Durham Light Infantry. He was awarded the Victoria Cross [London Gazette, 8 June, 1917]: "Michael Heaviside, No. 4/9720, Private, 15th Battn. Durham Light Infantry. For most conspicuous bravery and devotion to duty. When the battalion was holding a block in the line, a wounded man was observed about 2 p.m. in a shell hole some sixty yards in advance of our block and about forty yards from the enemy line. He was making signals of distress and holding up an empty water bottle. Owing to snipers and machine-gun

Michael Heaviside.

fire it was impossible, during daylight, to send out a stretcher party. But Private Heaviside at once volunteered to carry water and food to the wounded man, despite the enemy fire. This he succeeded in doing and found the man to be badly wounded and nearly demented with thirst. He had lain out for four days and three nights, and the arrival of the water undoubtedly saved his life. Private Heaviside, who is a stretcher-bearer, succeeded the same evening, with the assistance of two comrades, in rescuing the wounded man."

JENSEN, JORGAN CHRISTIAN, Private, served in the European War, and was awarded the Victoria Cross [London Gazette, 8 June, 1917]: "Jorgan Christian Jensen, No. 2389, Private, 50th Battn. Australian Imperial Force. For most conspicuous bravery and initiative when, with five comrades, he attacked a barricade behind which were about 45 of the enemy and a machine gun. One of his party shot the gunner, and Private Jensen, single-handed, rushed the post and threw in a bomb. He had still a bomb in one hand, but taking another from his pocket with the other hand, he drew the pin with his teeth, and by threatening the enemy with two bombs and by telling them that they were surrounded, he induced them to surrender. Private Jensen then sent one of his prisoners to order a neighbouring enemy party to surrender, which they did. This latter party were then fired on

Jorgan Christian Jensen.

by another party of our troops, whereupon Private Jensen, utterly regardless of personal danger, stood on the barricade, waved his helmet, caused firing to cease, and sent his prisoners back to our lines. Private Jensen's conduct throughout was marked by extraordinary bravery and determination."

KENNY, THOMAS JAMES BEDE, Private, joined the Australian Imperial Forces, and served in the European War. He was awarded the Victoria Cross [London Gazette, 8 June, 1917]: "Thomas James Bede Kenny, No. 4195, Private, 2nd Battn. Australian Expeditionary Force. For most conspicuous bravery and devotion to duty when his platoon was held up by an enemy strong point and severe casualties prevented progress. Private Kenny, under very heavy fire at close range, dashed alone towards the enemy's position, killed one man in advance of the strong point who endeavoured to bar his way. He then bombed the position, captured the gun crew, all of whom he had wounded, killed an officer who showed fight, and seized the gun. Private Kenny's gallant action enabled his platoon to occupy the position, which was of great local importance."

Thomas J. B. Kenny.

MILNE, WILLIAM JOHNSTONE, Private, served in the European War, and was awarded the Victoria Cross [London Gazette, 8 June, 1917]: William Johnstone Milne, No. 427586, Private, 16th Battn. (Canadian Scottish). For most conspicuous bravery and devotion to duty in attack. On approaching the first objective, Private Milne observed an enemy machine gun firing on our advancing troops. Crawling on hands and knees, he succeeded in reaching the gun, killing the crew with bombs, and capturing the gun. On the line reforming, he again located a machine gun in the support line, and stalking this second gun as he had done the first, he succeeded in putting the crew out of action and capturing the gun. His wonderful bravery and resource on these two occasions undoubtedly saved the lives of many of his comrades. Private Milne was killed shortly after capturing the second gun." The account of how Private Milne won the Victoria Cross is quoted from "Thirty Canadian V.C.'s," published by Messrs. Skeffington (pages 26–28): "The 16th Canadian Battn. (the Canadian Scottish) occupied the left sub-sector of the 3rd Brigade front in the attack on Vimy Ridge on 9 April, 1917. On the left of the 16th was the 18th Battn., and on the right was the 14th Battn. Private W. J. Milne was of the 16th. In due time the important and detailed story of the attack on the ridge will be given to the outside world, and in that day the victory of the Canadian troops will be seen in its true perspective. The enormous amount of preliminary work required before the attack took place has been hinted at elsewhere in these pages. The 16th Battn. had its share in these preparations and also in the glory of conquest. The 2nd and the 3rd Brigades were appointed to capture the first two objectives, namely, Zwolfe Graben and Zwischen Stellung. After taking these two positions they were to consolidate and allow the 1st Brigade to pass through on their way to capture the farther objectives. Every unit was reported assembled and ready well ahead of 'Zero' hour, which was 5.30 a.m. Two minutes after our barrage opened on the enemy front our infantry climbed out of their trenches and went forward. As they went over No Man's Land a rising north-westerly wind blew up a storm of snow and sleet, which continued for several hours. As the 16th Battn. approached the first objective an enemy machine gun opened heavy fire on them, causing many casualties. Milne located the gun, and, crouching on his hands and knees, began to work his way forward. Over his shoulder was slung his bag of bombs. Several times he was fired at, but he continued to crawl till he was within bombing distance, then leaping to his feet, he hurled his bombs into the midst of the gun crew. Every German went down, dead or wounded. Milne rushed forward and captured the gun. The Canadian line reformed and the battalion continued its advance. They swarmed over the Zwolfe Graben, bundled out as prisoners those Germans who still crouched in the deep dug-outs, killed those who still offered resistance ; and then went ahead to the second position. Here again the hidden German machine gunners gave considerable trouble. Many of those nests of machine guns were concealed in pockets near or in dug-outs, and as our men advanced they were met by unexpected bursts of fire. Just before reaching Zwischen Stellung the battalion was again held up by a concrete emplacement hidden in a hay-stack near Terry Trench. Milne undertook to clear out this nest as before. He repeated his tactics, stalking the gun in the same way. He was again successful. This time he knocked out the weapon, causing the garrison to surrender. The second objective of the battalion was taken soon afterwards. Milne, however, did not live to know his bravery had won him the Victoria Cross. He was killed not many hours afterwards ; but his contribution towards the Vimy Ridge victory was officially recognized when the dust of conflict had settled down."

SYKES, ERNEST, Private, was before the war a Platelayer on the Railway at Micklehurst. He is married, and he and Mrs. Sykes have two children. On the outbreak of the European War he enlisted, served in France, and was awarded the Victoria Cross [London Gazette, 8 June, 1917] : " Ernest Sykes, No. 40989, Private, 27th (S.) Battn. Northumberland Fusiliers. For most conspicuous bravery and devotion to duty when his battalion in attack was held up about 350 yards in advance of our lines by intense fire from front and flank, and suffered heavy casualties. Private Sykes, despite this heavy fire, went forward and brought back four wounded—he made a fifth journey and remained out under conditions which appeared to be certain death, until he had bandaged all those who were too badly wounded to be moved. These gallant actions, performed under incessant machine-gun and rifle fire, showed an utter contempt of danger."

WALLER, HORACE, Private, was born on 23 Sept. 1897, at Batley Carr, Dewsbury, son of John Edward Waller, of Upper Road, Batley Carr, and Esther, daughter of John Myers, of Bradford. He was educated

at Purlwell Council School and Batley Grammar School, and joined the Army on 30 May, 1916, as Private, after being twice rejected on medical grounds, and then only in Grade C3. He served in the European War in France, and was awarded the Victoria Cross [London Gazette, 8 June, 1917] : " Horace Waller, No. 30144, Private, late King's Own Yorkshire Light Infantry. For most conspicuous bravery when with a bombing section forming a block in the enemy line. A very violent counter-attack was made by the enemy on this post, and although five of the garrison were killed, Private Waller continued for more than an hour to throw bombs, and finally repulsed the attack. In the evening the enemy again counter-attacked the post, and all the garrison became casualties

Horace Waller.

except Private Waller, who, although wounded later, continued to throw bombs for another half an hour, until he was killed. Throughout these attacks he showed the utmost valour, and it was due to his determination that the attacks on this important post were repulsed." Private H. Waller was reported missing, and is now believed to be dead. The following is an extract from a letter received from Brigadier-General H. R. Headlam, Commanding the 64th Infantry Brigade : " I command the brigade in which is the battalion to which he belonged, and consequently know very well the situation during which Private Waller performed his magnificent act of bravery. His fearless conduct and splendid bravery on that occasion were deciding factors at a critical period, and no man ever won the Victoria Cross more deservedly."

The " Batley Grammar School Magazine " says of him :

" When Waller was a member of that Fifth which worked on a trestle-table in the Staff room, what time joiners raised sweet melody in Big School, few of his chums suspected that his staid and peaceful frame concealed the spirit of the man who should bring the School its greatest honour on the field.

" The dry official notice is expanded by the more intimate touch of the letter from his Company Officer :

" ' DEAR MR. WALLER,

" ' It is with infinite regret I have to report that your son is " missing," believed killed. Words cannot describe the glorious fight he and his comrades made in certainly the most violent hand-to-hand fighting I ever witnessed. For an hour and a half in the first counter-attack he stood and bombed, and finally won. In the second and more violent attack he still held his post for an hour, fighting for half an hour after being wounded, until finally hit. I think the bravest boy I ever knew is this son of yours. Many of my company are gone, but the loss of none goes more to my heart than the loss of Horace. Perhaps in the opinion of the higher command I have asked too much in asking for the highest of all honours for him. I fervently hope not. My Colonel has endorsed the recommendation, but rewards are only a tithe of the gratification you can feel for having produced so fine, so courageous, so British a man. So long as this company holds together the glory of his deeds will never die.

" ' Believe me, faithfully yours,

" ' L. MARCH,

" ' Captain, C Company.'

" Horace Waller came to us with a Free Scholarship from Purlwell in 1909. In his first year he won a County Minor ; he went through from the Second to the Fifth, and left us in 1913. His anxiety to be playing the big game led him to make repeated attempts to join up, and after two medical rejections he was grouped in C. We have had Blues, but they were fearless tacklers, even in the playground ; our F.R.S. and present-day dons we knew as ' swots ' in days gone by ; but that the quiet boy in blue Norfolk, who never biffed his opponent at football, and whose chief delight was a steady Saturday ride and swim with the autocrat of the test-tube—that this apparently untypical Batley boy should face what for such a sensitive nature must have been the fires of hell, and having once felt its heat, should go down again to the flame—this must be beyond measure wonderful to those of us who worked along with him. And yet, when one remembers his persistence and his absolute loathing of an unfinished bit of work, the wonder fades into an understanding that the dogged perseverance which drove him to repeat an unsuccessful experiment urged him to finish his work in that last hot corner. I remember chaffing him one day on his reputation as the only subdued member of a none too law-abiding Fifth, and can see the whimsical twinkle in his eye as I suggested possible deeds of violence, just to show he had faults like ours. He was too sensitive to adopt my advice, yet mischievous enough to query what might be my feelings in case he made his first trial on me. Others may find lessons in the removal of Waller from our midst ; we, who worked with him, can but dimly express our sorrow and our sympathy for his family. But there is no dimmest shadow on the gleam of hope and pride that cuts athwart the sorrow, and reminds us that one of us, who gave no earnest of daring deeds, has won the bit of bronze, unobtrusive as his own life and personality, that is the soldier's highest tangible reward.

" G. McC. K."

London Gazette, 14 June, 1917.—" War Office, 14 June, 1917. His Majesty the King has been graciously pleased to approve of the award of the Victoria Cross to the undermentioned Officers and Non-commissioned Officers."

MOON, RUPERT THOMAS VANCE, Lieut., was born 14 Aug. 1892, at Bacchus Marsh, Victoria, Australia, son of Mr. and Mrs. Arthur Moon, of Kinaird, Toorak, Victoria, Australia. Mr. Arthur Moon is an Inspector

of the National Bank of Australasia, Ltd. Rupert Moon was educated at Kyneton Grammar School, Kyneton, Victoria, and joined the Australian Military Forces in the ranks, on 21 Aug. 1914. He sailed with the 1st Australian Division in the 4th Light Horse Regt. in Oct. 1914, and served from May to Dec. in the Gallipoli Campaign at Anzac. He went to France in May, 1916, and was gazetted as Second Lieutenant in the 58th Australian Infantry Battalion 9 Sept. 1916. He was awarded the Victoria Cross [London Gazette, 14 June, 1917] : " Rupert Vance Moon, Lieut., 58th Infantry Battn. Australian Imperial Force. For most conspicuous bravery during an attack on an enemy

Rupert Thomas V. Moon.

strong point. His own immediate objective was a position in advance of the hostile trench itself, and thence against the hostile trench, after the capture of which it was intended that his men should co-operate in a further assault on a strong point further in rear. Although wounded in the initial advance, he reached his first objective. Leading his men against the trench itself, he was again badly wounded and incapacitated for the moment. He nevertheless inspired and encouraged his men and captured the trench. Lieut. Moon continued to lead his much diminished command in the general attack with the utmost valour, being again wounded, and the attack was successfully pressed home. During the consolidation of the position, this officer was again badly wounded, and it was only after this fourth and severe wound through the face that he consented to retire from the fight. His bravery was magnificent, and was largely instrumental in the successful issue against superior numbers, the safeguarding of the flank of the attack and the capture of many prisoners and machine guns."

HIRSCH, DAVID PHILIP, Second Lieut. (Acting Capt.), was born on 28 Dec. 1896, at Leeds, elder son of Harry Hirsch and Edith Hirsch, of Weetwood, Leeds. He was educated at Willaston School, Nantwich, where he took a prominent part in all departments of school lfe, and was head of the school in his last year. He won an open exhibition at Worcester College, Oxford, in Dec. 1914, and then joined the Leeds University Officers' Training Corps. In April, 1915, he had a commission in the Yorkshire Regt. He served in the European War in France, went to the front in the early part of 1916, and was wounded in Sept., and at the same time was promoted Lieutenant and mentioned in Despatches. He was gazetted Captain in March, 1917, the promotion dating back to Nov. 1916. He was killed in action

David Philip Hirsch.

on 23 April, 1917, and was posthumously awarded the Victoria Cross [London Gazette, 14 June, 1917] : " David Philip Hirsch, Second

Lieut. (Acting Capt.), 4th Battn. Yorkshire Regt. For most conspicuous bravery and devotion to duty in attack. Having arrived at the first objective, Capt. Hirsch, although already wounded, returned over fire-swept slopes to satisfy himself that the defensive flank was being established. Machine-gun fire was so intense that it was necessary for him to be continuously up and down the line, encouraging his men to dig and hold the position. He continued to encourage his men by standing on the parapet and steadying them in the face of machine-gun fire and counter-attack until he was killed. His conduct throughout was a magnificent example of the greatest devotion to duty."

HARRISON, JOHN, Second Lieut., served in the European War, and was awarded the Victoria Cross [London Gazette, 14 June, 1917]: "John Harrison, Temporary Second Lieut., M.C., 11th (S.) Battn. East Yorkshire Regt. For most conspicuous bravery and self-sacrifice in an attack. Owing to darkness and to smoke from the enemy barrage, and from our own, and to the fact that our objective was in a dark wood, it was impossible to see when our barrage had lifted off the enemy front line. Nevertheless, Second Lieut. Harrison led his company against the enemy trench under heavy rifle and machine-gun fire, but was repulsed. Reorganizing his command as best he could in No Man's Land, he again attacked in darkness under terrific fire, but with no success. Then, turning round, this gallant officer single-handed made a dash at the machine-gun, hoping to knock out the gun and so save the lives of many of his company. His self-sacrifice and absolute disregard of danger was an inspiring example to all. (He is reported missing, believed killed.)"

BROWN, DONALD FORRESTER, Sergt., served in the European War, and was awarded the Victoria Cross [London Gazette, 14 June, 1917]: "Donald Forrester Brown, No. 8/3504, Sergt., 2nd Infantry Battn. New Zealand Forces. For most conspicuous bravery and determination in attack when the company to which he belonged suffered very heavy casualties in officers and men from machine-gun fire. At great personal risk this N.C.O. advanced with a comrade and succeeded in reaching a point within thirty yards of the enemy guns. Four of the gun crew were killed and the gun captured. The advance of the company was continued till it was again held up by machine-gun fire. Again Sergt. Brown and his comrade with great gallantry rushed the gun and killed the crew. After this second position had been won, the company came under very heavy shell fire, and the utter contempt for danger and coolness under fire of this N.C.O. did much to keep up the spirit of his men. On a subsequent occasion in attack, Sergt. Brown showed most conspicuous gallantry. He attacked single-handed a machine gun which was holding up the attack, killed the gun crew and captured the gun. Later, whilst sniping the retreating enemy, this very gallant soldier was killed." He was born at Dunedin, New Zealand, on 23 Feb. 1890, and was the son of Robert Brown, Draper, of Oamaru, New Zealand, and Jessie Brown, his wife. He was educated at South School, Oamaru, and Waitaki Boys' High School, Oamaru, and joined the Army 19 Oct. 1915.

Donald Forrester Brown.

The following is taken from "The Waitakian," the magazine of the Waitaki Boys' High School, where Lieut. D. F. Brown was educated:

"For three years he had been cultivating his farm at Totara, when his country's call to arms rang in his ears, and he could find no rest of mind until he had answered the summons, and enlisted as a private in the 9th Reinforcements. He sold his farm, and proceeded to Trentham at the close of 1915. After training he finally sailed by the transport Warrimoo, on Saturday, 9 Jan. 1916, having been promoted to the rank of Corporal. A further period of training followed his arrival in Egypt, and his letters at this time show how much he was interested in the country and the people. On 12 April, 1916, he writes: 'At present we are on board the Llandary, a 12,000-ton passenger boat, somewhere in the Mediterranean, and between Egypt and France, with a destroyer as escort. We have a splendid boat, and everything is all right.' In a letter dated 11 May, 1916, he announces his arrival in Marseilles as follows: 'On arrival we had to wait about 24 hours before disembarking, but once off we entrained straight away for our place in the north. We passed through some great country, and were altogether some 55 hours in the train, and as we were all in great mood, styled ourselves Massey's tourists. We reached our destination about 10.30 p.m., and found to our disgust that we had ten miles to march to reach our billets. That perhaps might not have been so bad, but it was as cold as cold could be, and raining cats and dogs, and after the heat of Egypt we were feeling it pretty bad. Well, on we marched in full pack, then the Colonel lost his way, and we had to retrace our steps, and arrived at our destination at 4.30 a.m. Some were so beat that they lay down by the way, not caring what became of them. Where we are now we can see the cannon sending their shells to the enemy lines. Aeroplanes of all sorts and sizes fly about.' His next letter is headed: 'My little dug-out, France, 20 May, 1916.' He had now been promoted to Sergeant. 'Here I am,' he writes. 'We have been trying conclusions for about a week, and are on the British front, in the north of France, near a town which sounds like Arm-tieres. We have the furthest advanced trench of the whole British front, and have constantly to be on the outlook for eventualities. The Germans have some great snipers—it has been my great joy to get one of the beggars located and to give him his deserts. The aeroplanes here are great, and seem to make a point of keeping the Germans busy: they fire and fire away, but it seems all waste.' On 19 June he writes again: 'The past week has been the hardest experienced at all parts of the Colonial lines. We have been giving Fritz a lot to think about, and he is learning not to hold us so cheaply as he has done. From where we are you can hear all the big bombardment at Ypres and St. Eloi. Soon we ourselves may shift that way, then it may be that the big offensive, so much talked about, will take place.' On 7 July he writes again: 'Here we are, still alive and well, although I must admit fairly well shaken up with explosive shells, and after 38 days in the trenches we have been relieved at last. Quite a big lot of wounded leave every day. Several attacks have been made on our trenches, but each time Fritz has had to shy off with his wounded and dead.' On 28 Aug. he reports a new location: 'We have been relieved from the trenches, and are now further south, just behind where the fighting is going on. This country is a great place, and travelling down to here was as good as a month by the sea. The crops all over are just lovely, and France can well hold her own for beauty. Shortly you will be hearing of us New Zealanders making an attack, as from what has been said and done, and the solid training we have been putting in, all leads to our making an attack shortly.' His last letter is ten days later: 'Just where we are at present things are going "Somme." We expect to get up very soon, and the noise is something deadly, and just here divisions go in and come out in a day or two reduced to less than company strength; so don't be surprised if I manage a trip. We are all in great spirits at being able to have a hand in this big push.'

"The following letter, written by Private J. Baxter, of his battalion, gives an account of his end:

"'N.Z. Convalescent Camp, Greytowers,
"'Hornchurch, Essex, England,
"'Nov. 16, 1916.

"'Dear Sir,

"'I have a very difficult letter to write, also a very sad one. You see, it is like this, your son was Sergeant of our platoon, and as I come from the same district, and knew him in civil life, I think it my duty to tell you how he died for his country. We advanced on the 15th Sept., and to me it looked as though the men in our platoon would have followed him anywhere, for the simple reason that he would never ask a man to go anywhere, or do anything, that he wouldn't do himself. Even when in the trenches at Armentières during a bombardment he would constantly go up and down the trenches seeing to the safety of his men, seemingly unconscious of any danger to himself. To go on with my narrative of our advance between High Wood and Flores on the Somme, we took our objective, which was the German front-line trench, and hung on from seven in the morning until we were relieved at two next morning; but what a roll-call the next day, only 57 remained out of an overstrength company. From the 16th till the 21st, when I got a slight wound, we were losing a lot of men carrying ammunition to the front line, with no officers, and the sergeants in charge of the company. I was not at the next advance, on the 1st Oct., but had a full account of the fight from a mate whom I met in hospital. The platoon had been reinforced by that time, so that it was nearly up to its original strength, but when they hopped the parapet one of Fritz's machine guns held them up, so the Sergeant ordered the men to stay where they were, while he tackled the gun crew by himself. He shot the lot with one of their own pistols which he was carrying, and still remained unhurt, when the rest of the men caught up on him. To reach their objective they had to go still further, and that is where one of the best men I ever saw met his death; he was the first to get on the parapet, and got sniped. The mate that I got the account from saw him fall, but he told them that morning that he would not come back. He was recommended for a V.C., and he well deserved it, as by his act he saved the lives of most of his men. The man who told me all about it was severely wounded, and he completely broke down when he was speaking to me about it. I can tell you the most of us have seen some sights during that advance which we are not likely to forget. I will now close by expressing my deepest sympathy for your bereavement.'

"The O.C. of his company, Capt. P. H. Ferguson, wrote as follows:

"'As O.C., 10th (North Otago) Company, when your son, Sergt. D. F. Brown, was serving with us, I feel it my duty to write and inform you of the high esteem in which he was held by the C.O. of the battalion, and by the officers and men, not only of his own platoon, but of the whole company. He was platoon sergeant of No. 12 platoon from the time of the formation of the 2nd Brigade in March last, and was always unsparing in his efforts to do his duty, and to do all he could for the welfare of those under him. Owing to the shortage of officers during the three months we were in the trenches at Armentières, your son virtually had command of the platoon for a considerable period, and I must say that he kept the platoon up to a high standard of efficiency. He was steady and reliable under fire, and in positions of danger, and by his example kept his men steady. He was in his element when in charge of a patrol in No Man's Land, and could always be relied upon to obtain any information required. He did most excellent work at the Somme, and I am told that he was instrumental in effecting the capture of a German machine gun and detachment. Unfortunately he was shot shortly after effecting this brave deed. I was with him during the initial stages of the attack on the Switch trench on the 15th Sept., but I was wounded before reaching the trench, and did not see him again. Your son was killed during a second attack on the 1st Oct., in the vicinity of Eaucourt l'Abbé, and, I believe, was buried where he fell. His loss is felt by all who knew him. The Army cannot afford to lose such men as he, but unfortunately on account of their bravery, and the risks they take in the execution of their duty, these men are frequently the first to fall. I can assure you, sir, that you and your family have the sincere sympathy of all the members of this battalion who were acquainted with your son. You have the consolation of knowing that he did his duty, and died nobly fighting for a just cause.'

" His Colonel wrote as follows :

" B.E.F., 3 Nov. 1916.

" 'DEAR MR. BROWN,

" I want to write and tell you how much we all regret the gallant death of your son, Donald Forrester ; he did some great work on 15 Sept., and again on 1 Oct., during our most successful attack on the German trenches, and he took a German machine gun, after killing five men ; if he had lived I had hoped to recommend him, at least for the D.C.M., and he might have got a Victoria Cross. He was an excellent N.C.O., and much liked by his men. I cannot speak too highly of him ; he is a great loss to the battalion. His name will never be forgotten, and is now added to that long list of noble men who have made the supreme sacrifice.

" 'With deep sympathy,

" 'G. S. SMITH, Lieut.-Colonel.'

" Hidden behind the meagre announcement of those ' Killed in action,' are many deeds that remain untold, for in the severe losses sustained often very few remain to chronicle them. A letter received by the last mail from Sergt. Donald Forrester Brown, written two days before his death, describes the offensive on the Somme, and how a few days before the letter was written, he was one of a party who went into action 200 strong and of whom only 35 returned. Private Connors, of Ardgowan, writing of this engagement, mentions that all the officers were killed, and that Sergts. J. Rodgers, D. F. Brown, and Corpl. R. Douglas (of Ardgowan), all from the Oamaru district, and two of them Waitakians, took command of the detachment, captured a trench, and consolidated the position, holding it against counter-attacks. As no other officer was present, no official recognition of their action may be made. Private Connors states later that the loss of Sergt. Brown was a keen personal one to him, as well as to his company. He commanded his men magnificently, and was strikingly cool when under fire.

" Capt. W. G. A. Gibson-Bishop, M.C., 10th (N.O.) Company, writes as follows to Sergt. Brown's parents :

" ' It is my painful duty to inform you that your son, Sergt. D. F. Brown, was killed in action on the 1st instant. I had known your gallant son only a few days before he died for his King and country, but it was quite long enough for me to judge of the many great qualities he possessed. He died while leading his men in a charge across " No Man's Land " with his usual dash and gallantry, when he was fatally wounded in the head. His end was sudden and he suffered no pain. Thus died a gallant soldier and a gentleman. In the first trench we took he did some very good work, and I sent forward a recommendation for a D.C.M. to Headquarters. I enclose a copy of my recommendation, but I regret that owing to his untimely end nothing further came of it. You have our heartfelt sympathy, and we trust the gallant way your son died will be of some consolation to you in your loss.'

" The following is a copy of the official recommendation referred to :

" ' 8/3504 Sergt. Brown, Donald Forrester.—For Bravery. He rushed a machine gun which was fully manned and killed four of the crew himself. I regret to state he was killed half an hour later.' "

GOSLING, WILLIAM, Sergt., served in the European War, and was awarded the Victoria Cross [London Gazette, 14 June, 1917] : " William Gosling, No. 645112, Sergt., 3rd Wessex Brigade, Royal Field Artillery (Territorial Force). For most conspicuous bravery when in charge of a heavy trench mortar. Owing to a faulty cartridge the bomb, after discharge, fell 10 yards from the mortar. Sergt. Gosling sprang out, lifted the nose of the bomb, which had sunk into the ground, unscrewed the fuse and threw it on the ground, where it immediately exploded. This very gallant and prompt action undoubtedly saved the lives of the whole detachment."

London Gazette, 22 June, 1917.—" Admiralty, 22 June, 1917. The King has been graciously pleased to approve of the award of the Victoria Cross to the undermentioned."

SANDERS, WILLIAM EDWARD, Lieut., was the eldest son of E. H. C. Sanders, and of Mrs. E. H. C. Sanders, who live at Auckland, New Zealand. His first seafaring experience was in small steamers on the New Zealand Coast, where he was serving as Mate in the barque Joseph Craig when she became a total wreck inside the Kaipara bar. He managed to get ashore in one of the boats, but had a narrow escape from drowning. When he passed for extra master he joined the service of the Union Steamship Company of New Zealand, and on the outbreak of war offered his services to the Admiralty. He was called up eighteen months later, when he came to England, and was commissioned Sub-Lieutenant in the Royal Naval Reserve on 19 April, 1916. He served in the European War. He was in command of the Prize, a topsail schooner, one of the now well-known " mystery " ships, which lured a German submarine to its doom by sending out a " panic party " and exhibiting other signs of distress, and then, when the submarine had come near enough, sank her within four minutes of the beginning of the action. The Prize herself was so badly damaged in her show of " harmlessness " that she was only able to reach harbour 120 miles away with great difficulty, being towed the last five miles by a motor launch. Lieut. Sanders was awarded the Victoria Cross for this action, but owing to the necessity at that time of keeping certain matters private, the London Gazette of 22 June, 1917, had only the announcement that the Victoria Cross had been awarded to " Acting Lieut. (now Lieut.- Commander) William Edward Sanders, Royal Naval Reserve. In recognition of his conspicuous gallantry, consummate coolness and skill in command of one of His Majesty's ships in action." He was promoted from Sub-Lieutenant to Lieutenant-Commander in a little over a year, one of the most remarkable cases of rapid promotion in the history of the Navy. He was drowned in 1916, when his ship, the Prize, was lost with

all hands, as the result of an engagement with one or more enemy submarines, while doing his duty in one of the most perilous enterprises that the Navy has ever undertaken. More details were given later on of the action for which Lieut.-Commander Sanders won the Victoria Cross.

A newspaper says :

" Lieut. William Edward Sanders, R.N.R., was awarded the Cross for an action of H.M.S. Prize on 30 April last year. The Prize, a topsail schooner of 200 tons, sighted an enemy submarine, which opened fire at three miles' range and approached slowly astern. The ' panic party,' in charge of Skipper William Henry Brewer, R.N.R. (Trawler Section), immediately abandoned ship. Ship's head was put into the wind, and the guns' crews concealed themselves by lying face downwards on the deck. The enemy continued deliberately shelling the schooner, inflicting severe damage and wounding a number of men. For twenty minutes she continued to approach, firing as she came, but at length, apparently satisfied that no one remained on board, she drew out on the schooner's quarter 70 yards away. The White Ensign was immediately hoisted, the screens dropped, and all guns opened fire. A shell struck the foremost gun of the submarine, blowing it to atoms and annihilating the crew. Another shot demolished the conning tower, and at the same time a Lewis gun raked the survivors off the submarine's deck. She sank four minutes after the commencement of the action in clouds of smoke, the glare of an internal fire being visible through the rents in her hull. The captain of the submarine, a warrant officer and one man were picked up and brought on board the Prize, which was then herself sinking fast. Captors and prisoners, however, succeeded in plugging the shot-holes and keeping the water under with the pumps. The Prize then set sail for the land, 120 miles distant. They were finally picked up two days later by a motor-launch and towed the remaining five miles into harbour. In another official statement not given in the Gazette, it is announced that the Prize, still under Lieut.-Commander Sanders, was lost with all hands, presumably as the result of an engagement with one or more enemy submarines."

Lieut.-Commander H. Auten, V.C., R.N.R., in " Q Boat Adventures " (published by Herbert Jenkins), says : " The Hun having become accustomed to tramp steamers of varying tonnage, it was thought that he might be less suspicious of a sailing craft. Consequently H.M.S. Prize, a topsail schooner of 200 tons, was fitted up as a Q boat, and placed under the command of Lieut. William Edward Sanders, R.N.R. The young Lieutenant had come home from New Zealand to join the Royal Naval Reserve on the outbreak of war, and when he was given command of a Q boat he was very keen to sink a submarine. About this period, the spring of 1917, the U boats had been very partial to coming to the surface and shelling out of existence any little sailing craft they came across. . . . The German has never heard of Queensberry rules." The Prize succeeded in sinking a submarine as is related in this delightful book. " The action of the Prize called for the utmost bravery on the part of the men lying concealed on board. Though badly shelled, with many wounded lying about, they lay absolutely still, prepared to wait until their commanding officer considered the moment opportune to open fire." Later on, when working in conjunction with a British submarine, H.M.S. Prize was herself sunk by a German submarine, with her heroic commander and all hands.

PARKER, WALTER RICHARD, L.-Corpl., was born on 20 Sept. 1881, at 5, Agnes Street, Grantham, Lincolnshire, son of Richard and Kate Parker, of Grantham. He was educated at Kentish Town, London, and

joined the Navy on 7 Sept. 1914. Prior to this he was working as Coremaker at the Stanton Ironworks new factory. He served in the European War in the Royal Marines in Gallipoli, and was awarded the Victoria Cross [London Gazette, 22 June, 1917] : " Walter Richard Parker, L.-Corpl., Royal Marine Light Infantry, No. Po./5229, Royal Naval Division. In recognition of his most conspicuous bravery and devotion to duty in the course of the Dardanelles operations. On the night of 30 April–1 May, 1915, a message asking for ammunition, water and medical stores was received from an isolated fire trench at Gaba Tepe. A party of non-commissioned officers and men were detailed to carry water and ammunition, and, in response to

Walter Richard Parker.

a call for a volunteer from among the stretcher-bearers, Parker at once came forward ; he had during the previous three days displayed conspicuous bravery and energy under fire whilst in charge of the battalion stretcher-bearers. Several men had already been killed in a previous attempt to bring assistance to the men holding the fire trench. To reach this trench it was necessary to traverse an area at least of four hundred yards wide, which was completely exposed and swept by rifle fire. It was already daylight when the party emerged from shelter, and at once one of the men was wounded ; Parker organized a stretcher party, and then going on alone succeeded in reaching the fire trench, all the water and ammunition carriers being either killed or wounded. After his arrival he rendered assistance to the wounded in the trench, displaying extreme courage and remaining cool and collected in very trying circumstances. The trench had finally to be evacuated, and Parker helped to remove and attend the wounded, although he himself was seriously wounded during this operation."

The following are extracts from the " Nottingham Evening Post," 23 June, 1917 :

" The Royal Marines supported the memorable landing at Gaba Tepe Beach by the Australian and British Forces, and were engaged with the hospital staff, under Surgeon Playne, D.S.O. Night and day they attended to the wounded, rendering first aid, and it was whilst doing so that Colonel Luard, Capt. Syson and Capt. Morton entered the hospital and called for a volunteer to go down to one of his companies of Marines which was enfiladed. It was recognized that the task was one involving the gravest peril, but L.-Corpl. Parker, who was the senior non-commissioned officer on duty, volunteered. Describing his performance himself, Corpl. Parker says that as soon as the time for the attempt to take relief to his comrades arrived he began to work his way from trench to trench for some considerable distance. He was suddenly confronted by an Australian officer, who threatened that if he did not go back he would shoot him, but notwithstanding this he proceeded. To reach his objective he had to pass an open space upon which day and night Turkish machine guns were ceaselessly firing. Corpl. Parker made a dash for the trap, and was immediately shot in two places, but in running on down the hill into a place called the Valley of Death he fell into a pond at the bottom. He was revived by the tremendous cheers from the officers and men from his own battalion. He remained with the troops throughout the night—a night which gained for Lieut. Alcock the Distinguished Service Cross, and during which Lieut. Hampson was killed. The Turks made a desperate charge, and Parker was shot again in several places. Crawling to the top of the hill almost exhausted he was ultimately carried to safety by the stretcher-bearers of his own division. He was taken in the hospital ship Gondola to Alexandria and transferred to another vessel, which, whilst proceeding through the Mediterranean, collided with an Italian ship during a fog. Ultimately he reached Southampton, and from there was sent to Netley Hospital. He recovered, and upon being discharged went back to barracks. Later, however, he was seized with illness, which resulted in brain fever, and this left his sight badly affected. He received his discharge 17 June, 1916. Corpl. Parker has received a number of letters from officers congratulating him on that night's work, but he declares that he was only doing his duty."

The "Hampshire County Times," for 12 Oct. 1917, says: "Another Notts man, L.-Corpl. Walter Richard Parker, Royal Marine Light Infantry, who has lived at Stapleford 18 years, has been awarded the Victoria Cross. It is over two years ago since he performed the acts which brought him the distinction, and it is understood that the delay has been occasioned owing to difficulties in communicating with the officers under whom Parker was serving at the time, but that the honour is thoroughly deserved will be admitted by everybody. Parker, who is 35 years of age, was born at 5, Agnes Street, Grantham, and has resided at Brookhill Terrace, Stapleford, for 18 years. He is the eldest son of Mr. Richard Parker and the late Mrs. Richard Parker, of Lime Grove, Stapleford. He enlisted in the Royal Marine Light Infantry as early as 7 Sept. 1914, and was attached to the Portsmouth Division, R.M.L.I., under the command of Colonel Luard, Capt. Morton and Capt. Syson. After a period of training the men were reviewed by the King, who was accompanied by Mr Winston Churchill, then First Lord of the Admiralty. They sailed on the Gloucester Castle from a West Coast port on the last day of Feb. 1915, calling at Malta, Lemnos, Alexandria and Port Said, and later they took part in the great review held in the Egyptian desert by General Sir Ian Hamilton just prior to the embarkation of the Dardanelles landing forces. L.-Corpl. Parker married Olive, the daughter of the late Mr. Joseph Orchard, who for many years held the position of Station Master at Stapleford. Prior to joining in Sept. 1914, he was working at the Stanton Ironworks new foundry, as a Coremaker, and he is now engaged on munition work.

"Other local V.C.'s are:—Capt. Albert Ball, V.C., D.S.O., M.C., late Royal Flying Corps (Nottingham); Capt. C. G. Vickers, V.C., Sherwood Foresters (Nottingham); Private Samuel Harvey, V.C., York and Lancaster Regt. (Nottingham); Private John Caffrey, V.C., York and Lancaster Regt. (Nottingham); Sapper William Hackett, V.C., late Royal Engineers (Nottingham); L.-Corpl. W. D. Fuller, V.C., Grenadier Guards (Mansfield)."

"There was a pleasing variation of the usual official routine at Forton Barracks on Wednesday, when Corpl. W. R. Parker, V.C., R.M.L.I., was presented with a handsome marble and gilt clock, together with a cheque, and a gold regimental brooch for Mrs. Parker. The inscription on the clock stated that it was 'presented to Corpl. W. R. Parker, V.C., by the Portsmouth Division R.M.L.I. (all ranks), as a mark of appreciation of his gallant conduct at Gallipoli, 1915.' The ceremony, which was performed by Brigadier-General C. N. Trotman, C.B. (Commandant), who himself fought with distinction in the Dardanelles operations, was made the occasion of a ceremonial parade. A hollow square was formed, the fourth side of which was occupied by the band of the division, the cadets and school children, together with civilians, while in the centre was a table, from which the presentations were made. Corpl. Parker, V.C., was accompanied by his father. Brigadier-General Trotman, who was supported by his full staff, said they were all proud of Corpl. Parker. He recalled that the landing at the Gallipoli Peninsula took place on the 25th April, 1915. The 29th Division and Plymouth Battalion of the R.M.L.I. landed at Cape Helles, and, of course, they all knew the story of that wonderful landing. At 3 p.m. on the 28th April, he (the speaker) received orders to land the Portsmouth Battn., to take the place of an Australian Brigade, which had been fighting since the original landing on the 25th April. The country was very difficult, and the Australians were hanging on to several ridges, as they were bound to do all through the 25th, 26th and 27th. They themselves did not know where they were. The different companies were mixed up, and it was nearly dark when the Portsmouth Battn. came up the gulley, which was about a mile from the sea. They saw the so-called trenches which they had to hold, and which were about a foot and a half deep. They could not get information of any sort, because no map had been made by those they relieved. The whole thing was done in the dark. Three companies were kept up in the front line, one being held behind in reserve. The Turks were only from 30 to 50 yards distant, just over the ridge. The whole situation was involved, for it was very difficult to get water or ammunition to anyone, but the men hung on all through the 29th and 30th. On that date the Portsmouth Battn. moved up to some trenches on the extreme left, where they were right amongst the Turks. There was a small trench which a platoon occupied on the first night, where they had maintained themselves all through, and which was 400 yards from the trench behind it. That was where Parker distinguished himself. Every man was at the front. There were no officers' servants of any kind left behind, and the casualties were very heavy. On the 1st May, when the Australian Battn. they had relieved came up and took their places, the men of the Portsmouth Battn. were absolutely exhausted, having been in the front line the whole time. About the middle of the night they were again called up, and made to go to the other end of the Anzac lines, where they were mixed up in a big battle. Then followed a week of incessant fighting, until they were relieved, and the battalion went down to Cape Helles to carry on the work at Gallipoli. Parker himself joined the Division soon after the war, but owing to some difficulty about his eyes was put into the medical unit of the Battalion, and was one of the men allowed the surgeons in addition to stretcher-bearers. The latter and the surgeons of the Brigade did extraordinarily good work from beginning to end. The surgeons were good, and everyone was good. Indeed, their work was beyond all praise. The speaker then read the official account of the circumstances under which Parker was awarded the V.C., which appeared in the London Gazette dated 22 June, 1917, as follows: 'The King has been pleased to approve of the award of the V.C. to L.-Corpl. Walter Richard Parker, R.M.L.I., Royal Naval Division, in recognition of his most conspicuous bravery and devotion to duty in the course of the Dardanelles operations. On the night of 30 April–1 May, 1915, a message asking for ammunition, water and medical stores was received from an isolated fire trench at Gaba Tepe. A party of non-commissioned officers and men were detailed to carry water and ammunition, and in repsonse to a call for volunteers from amongst the stretcher-bearers, Parker at once came forward. He had during the previous three days displayed conspicuous bravery and energy under fire while in charge of the Battalion stretcher-bearers. Several men had already been killed in a previous attempt to bring assistance to the men holding the fire trench. To reach this trench it was necessary to traverse an area of at least 400 yards which was completely exposed. It was already daylight when the party emerged from shelter, and at once one of the men was wounded. Parker organized the stretcher party, and then, going on alone, succeeded in reaching the fire trench. All the water and ammunition carriers had either been killed or wounded. After his arrival he rendered assistance to the wounded in the trench, displaying extreme courage, and remaining cool and collected under very trying circumstances. The trench had finally to be evacuated, and Parker helped to remove and attend the wounded, although he himself was seriously wounded during the operations.' Brigadier General Trotman said that spoke for itself. He then made the presentation, and called for three cheers for 'Parker, V.C.,' and these were given with enthusiasm. On behalf of the V.C., who was not well enough to make a speech, Brigadier-General Trotman expressed his thanks. Following a short selection of music by the band, the parade was dismissed."

London Gazette, 27 June, 1917.—"War Office, 27 June, 1917. His Majesty the King has been graciously pleased to approve of the award of the Victoria Cross to the undermentioned Officers, Warrant Officers, Non-commissioned Officers and Men."

COMBE, ROBERT GRIERSON, Lieut., served in the European War, and was awarded the Victoria Cross [London Gazette, 27 June, 1917]: "Robert Grierson Combe, Lieut., late 27th Battn. Canadian Infantry. For most conspicuous bravery and example. He steadied his company under intense fire, and led them through the enemy barrage, reaching the objective with only five men. With great coolness and courage, Lieut. Combe proceeded to bomb the enemy, and inflicted heavy casualties. He collected small groups of men, and succeeded in capturing the company objective, together with eighty prisoners. He repeatedly charged the enemy, driving them before him, and whilst personally leading his bombers, was killed by an enemy sniper. His conduct inspired all ranks, and it was entirely due to his magnificent courage that the position was carried, secured and held." "Thirty Canadian V.C.'s" (published by Messrs. Skeffington) says (pages 31–34): "When Capt. Stinson, of the 27th Canadian Battn., received a message from a breathless runner during the darkness of early morning on 3 May, 1917, to the effect that Lieut. R. G. Combe had but five men left out of his entire company, he realized that matters were serious on the right wing of the attacking formations. How serious he did not know until later. By the time he had sent reinforcements and investigated the situation, Lieut. Combe had lost his life and won the Victoria Cross. It had been planned by Headquarters that the attack on the German front-line system in the vicinity of Acreville should take place before dawn. But Lieut. Combe and a handful of followers were the only men of the 27th Battn. (City of Winnipeg) who reached their objective. Darkness and the enemy's concentration of artillery were responsible for the hold-up of the other sections of the advance. The battalion was in the ridge line with headquarters at Thelus Cave just prior to the attack, and they relieved troops who were already weary after a strenuous spell in the trenches. The attack began at 3.45 a.m. on the 3rd May; but the Germans had guessed very accurately the time of the intended assault, and two hours before our barrage opened they began to shell the assembly area with determined severity. So heavy was the fire that the attacking forces sustained many casualties before they were in the jumping-off trenches, and it was plain to the leaders that the problem of maintaining any kind of formation would be a difficult one. The 31st Battn. worked on the left of the 27th. It was still dark when the first waves of infantry went over the top and forward behind our barrage. They left in perfect order, walking into a darkness as intense as that of the Pit, save for the fitful flash of exploding shells. Terrible gaps were torn in their ranks as they advanced; whole groups of men were blown out of the line, and those who continued to stumble on soon lost touch with their fellows. The fears of the battalion commanders were fulfilled. Formation was impossible, and it was only with small groups that touch could be kept. The leading companies were forced to take cover at a distance of seven hundred yards from the German front line. They lay down in shell-holes and on the torn, trembling earth, scratching feebly at the hard surface to secure cover while they got their second wind. In a short time they were up and stumbling forward again; but they had only gone two hundred yards when the German artillery shortened range and the full force of the barrage fell on them. Under that staggering blow men collapsed in dozens, crushed by the weight of uptorn earth or blown to fragments. In the right company, Lieut. Combe was the only officer who had survived so far. His company was but a tattered remnant of what it had been a few moments before; but Combe had his orders surging at the back of his head, and he meant to carry them out. Collecting the handful of men left to him he began to work his way through the German barrage. He managed it. He brought his followers safely through that terrible curtain of fire, only to find that if he would reach the German line he must also get through the barrage of our own guns. He steadied his men and accomplished the second journey also. Just how he piloted them through the hail of shells it is impossible to explain; these things can only be guessed at. But he did it; and he had only five men left when he reached the German trenches. Back in the rear, Capt. Stinson, of the supporting company, saw the advance checked on the right; but there was no sign of failure on the left. He concluded that the latter wing had reached its objective. With a runner he scrambled forward towards the German line. When he was within twenty yards of the enemy trench he stopped, amazed, for the Germans were lining their parapet, waiting to meet the assaulting battalions. That was how Capt. Stinson discovered that the 31st Battn. had not reached its objective. He retired with the information. It was then that he received the message from Lieut. Combe, asking for reinforcements and stating his position. Capt. Stinson ordered Sergt. Boddington, of A Coy., to send forward twenty men to help Combe. The Captain himself went forward in advance, with a runner. He found Combe in the act of winning his posthumous decoration. Combe and his men had entered the German trench after a terrible struggle, aided by a few men of another company whom they had picked up. They bombed the Germans along the trench with German bombs, having exhausted their own long before. Eighty prisoners had been captured and were on their way back to our lines, and 250 yards of trench were in the hands of the invaders. Again and again the gallant little band charged the enemy, Combe always at their head, leading them around traverses and into dugouts. Along the whole of that 250 yards of trench lay dead and dying Germans. Combe was killed by a rifle bullet as he was leading his gallant bombers up the trench in the climax of his triumph."

BROOKS, EDWARD, Company Sergt.-Major, served in the European War, and was awarded the Victoria Cross [London Gazette, 27 June, 1917]: "Edward Brooks, No. 201154, Company Sergt.-Major, Oxford and Bucks Light Infantry. For most conspicuous bravery. This Warrant Officer, while taking part in a raid on the enemy's trenches, saw that the front wave was checked by an enemy machine gun at close quarters. On his own initiative, and regardless of personal danger, he rushed forward from the second wave with the object of capturing the gun, killing one of the gunners with his revolver and bayoneting another. The remainder of the gun's crew then made off, leaving the gun in his possession. Company Sergt.-Major Brooks then turned the machine gun on to the retreating enemy, after which he carried it back into our lines. By his courage and initiative he undoubtedly prevented many casualties, and greatly added to the success of the operations."

WHITE, ALBERT, Sergt., served in the European War, and was awarded the Victoria Cross [London Gazette, 27 June, 1917]: "Albert White, No. 24866, Sergt., late 2nd Battn. South Wales Borderers. For most conspicuous bravery and devotion to duty. Realizing during an attack that one of the enemy's machine guns, which had previously been located, would probably hold up the whole advance of his company, Sergt. White, without the slightest hesitation, and regardless of all personal danger, dashed ahead of his company to capture the gun. When within a few yards of the gun he fell riddled with bullets, having thus willingly sacrificed his life in order that he might secure the success of the operations and the welfare of his comrades."

FOSTER, EDWARD, Corpl., served in the European War in France, and was awarded the Victoria Cross [London Gazette, 27 June, 1917]: "Edward Foster, No. 13290, Corpl., 13th Battn. East Surrey Regt. For most conspicuous bravery and initiative. During an attack the advance was held up in a portion of a village by two enemy machine guns, which were entrenched and strongly covered by wire entanglements. Corpl. Foster, who was in charge of two Lewis guns, succeeded in entering the trench and engaged the enemy guns. One of the Lewis guns was lost, but Corpl. Foster, with reckless courage, rushed forward and bombed the enemy, thereby recovering the gun. Then, getting his two guns into action, he killed the enemy gun team and captured their guns, thereby enabling the advance to continue successfully."

HOWELL, GEORGE JULIAN, Corpl., served in the European War in France. He was awarded the Victoria Cross

George Julian Howell.

[London Gazette, 27 June, 1917]: "George Julian Howell, No. 2445, Corpl. 1st Infantry Battn. Australian Imperial Force. For most conspicuous bravery. Seeing a party of the enemy were likely to outflank his battalion, Corpl. Howell, on his own initiative, single-handed and exposed to heavy bomb and rifle fire, climbed on to the top of the parapet and proceeded to bomb the enemy, pressing them back along the trench. Having exhausted his stock of bombs, he continued to attack the enemy with his bayonet. He was then severely wounded. The prompt action and gallant conduct of this N.C.O. in the face of superior numbers was witnessed by the whole battalion, and greatly inspired them in the subsequent successful counter-attack."

WELCH, JAMES, L.-Corpl., was born on 7 July, 1889, at Strathfieldsaye,

James Welch.

son of Mr. and Mrs. D. Welch. He was educated at Strathfieldsaye, and joined the Army as a Private on 25 Jan. 1908. He served in the European War in France and Belgium from 1914, and was awarded the Victoria Cross [London Gazette, 27 June, 1917]: "James Welch, No. 8763, L.-Corpl., 1st Battn. Royal Berkshire Regt. For most conspicuous bravery. On entering the enemy trench he killed one man after a severe hand-to-hand struggle. Armed only with an empty revolver, L.-Corpl. Welch then chased four of the enemy across the open and captured them single-handed. He handled his machine gun with the utmost fearlessness, and more than once went into the open fully exposed to heavy fire at short range to search for and collect ammunition and spare parts, in order to keep his guns in action, which he succeeded in doing for over five hours till wounded by a shell. He showed throughout the utmost valour and initiative." He was promoted Corporal 21 April, 1917, and Sergeant in Aug. 1918. His service was 11 years, 4 months. Sergt. Welch was discharged unfit on 24 April, 1919. He was thanked by Brigade, Divisional and Battalion Commanders for service rendered. He took part in all kinds of sports. Sergt. Welch is married, and has a child, Daisy Victoria Welch.

DRESSER, TOM, Private, was born at Middlesbrough. He served in the European War, and was awarded the Victoria Cross [London Gazette, 27 June, 1917]: "Tom Dresser, No. 24297, Private, 7th Battn. Yorkshire Regt. For most conspicuous bravery and devotion to duty. Private Dresser, in spite of being twice wounded on the way and suffering great pain, succeeded in conveying an important message from battalion headquarters to the front line of trenches, which he eventually reached in an exhausted condition. His fearlessness and determination to deliver this message at any cost proved of the greatest value to his battalion at a critical period." Private Dresser was the first native of Middlesbrough to be awarded the Victoria Cross, and the townspeople gave him a hundred guineas and a gold watch and chain to commemorate it. He was also presented by the Committee of the Hull Soldiers' Club with a silver watch and chain.

WHITE, JACK, Private, served in the European War. He was awarded the Victoria Cross [London Gazette, 27 June, 1917]: "Jack White, No. 18105, Private, 6th Battn. Royal Lancaster Regt. For most conspicuous bravery and resource. This signaller during an attempt to cross a river saw the two pontoons ahead of him come under heavy machine-gun fire, with disastrous results. When his own pontoon had reached midstream, with every man except himself either dead or wounded, finding that he was unable to control the pontoon, Private White promptly tied a telephone wire to the pontoon, jumped overboard and towed it to the shore, thereby saving an officer's life and bringing to land the rifles and equipment of the other men in the boat, who were either dead or dying."

London Gazette, 5 July, 1917.—"War Office, 5 July, 1917. His Majesty the King has been graciously pleased to approve of the award of the Victoria Cross to the undermentioned Officer and Man."

HENDERSON, ARTHUR, Capt., was born 6 May, 1893, at Paisley, son of George Henderson, Retired Builder, and of Elizabeth Purdie, his wife (deceased). He was educated at Neilson Institution, Paisley, and in civil life was an Accountant and Stockbroker, being employed with Messrs. R. Easton & Company, in Glasgow. A prominent member of Ferguslie Cricket Club, he would have been appointed captain of the first eleven had there been no war. He enlisted in the local Argylls in Aug. 1914, and in April of the following year he was gazetted Second Lieutenant in the Special Reserve, being afterwards sent to France; he was attached to the 2nd Argyll and Sutherland Highlanders (old 93rd—the Thin Red Line of the Crimea). In the fighting on the Somme in 1916 he so distinguished himself that he was promoted to the rank of Captain in recognition of his gallantry and initiative, and showed the possession of high qualities as a leader. The fighting which won him the Military Cross took place on the Somme. His battalion had advanced through a veritable valley of death. Many of the wounded refused to fall out. Suddenly a gap was reported on the right of the attacking line, and

Arthur Henderson.

immediately the Germans, seeing their opportunity, threw a battalion of their best and freshest troops into it. Seizing a section of trench lightly held, the enemy used it as a jumping-off place from which to deliver what was meant to be a crushing blow at the right flank of the Argylls. It was necessary that this attack should continue the advance towards their objective. Two companies of the regiment were mustered to meet the new attack. " They did not wait for it," the narrator states, " for, led by an officer who was the idol of his men, this detachment left the trenches, and advanced across the open to meet the oncoming foe. The enemy were taken aback at this method of meeting an attack, and before they had time to recover the Argylls were on them with the bayonet. The German line held fast for only the fraction of a minute. The charge of the Highlanders was irresistible. The German attack was shattered with bayonet and bomb, and in a few minutes the battalion of picked troops was little more than a panic-stricken mob. Then the Argylls returned to their position and proceeded with their attack." This was in July, 1916. The following is an account by a " Times " War Correspondent of how Capt. Henderson won the Victoria Cross: " In one section of the battle-front, south of the Scarpe, a very gallant achievement has to be recorded of certain small bodies of Argyll and Sutherland Highlanders, and the Middlesex Regt., which, having taken part in and won to the farthest point of the line, had taken prisoners some 14 men and two officers. A counter-attack drove the greater part of the line back, but these troops held on and stayed, isolated and surrounded, fighting on all sides, till our men swept on again and relieved them. Through it all they kept their prisoners, whom they finally brought triumphantly home." Another account reads as follows: " The thrilling war annals of the Argyll and Sutherland Highlanders contain no more glorious episode than the historic stand made by Capt. Henderson's company against ten times their number, nor does the dazzling list of their regimental heroes contain a more honoured name than that of this brave leader. There is something incredibly fine about the whole picture, something reminiscent of the ' thin red line ' of immortal fame in the additional lustre won for the old 93rd by this gallant officer. Visualize, for a moment, the terrible scene. The Highlanders, isolated and alone, are almost surrounded by hordes of infuriated Huns; they are assailed on every side by over-whelming numbers; they are weary and exhausted with the terror and strain of the protracted battle; yet they stand there, resolute, grim, defiant, a wall of rock against which the sea of field-greys dashes itself in vain. Visualize, too, the leader in this tremendous conflict. He is wounded and spent; he suffers agony of body and anguish of mind, for he realizes, none better, the awful predicament of his men. At any moment, at any of the sides on which they are being assailed, the break-through may come, and the Highlanders will be swept away. Yet he conquers his bodily pain, he hides his mental misgivings; he leads like a lion; he cheers his Highland heroes, and by the sheer force of his personality carries them on to victory. It was not the first time that the Germans had tested the mettle of Scotia's sons, but it proved a time they are less likely to forget than others. And for this reason. They themselves were in numbers sufficient to swamp the Highlanders; they had all the advantages of the battle-ground; the defenders were alone and unsupported; they looked an easy prey. But, try as they might, they could not dislodge them. Faithfully and sternly the brave Scots stood their ground. Against them nought could prevail. Their victory, when it came, was splendid and complete. The official notice is reticent as to the date and place of this marvellous stand, but this we know, that it took place during one of the hottest phases of this year's offensive, and was itself one of the hottest, as it will ever remain one of the most memorable, incidents in it. The Argylls had been marked out to take a certain objective. When the word came to ' go,' they were up and away with all their proverbial zest and élan, and before them kept their leader, who was destined to perform such prodigies of valour ere the fateful day had closed. A charge by the Highlanders! What, in the great panorama of war, can compare with it? These sturdy Northmen are irresistible, and well the Germans know it. When the Argylls spread out on this occasion they were met by such a blast of lead as might have daunted the most hardened veterans. Men fell here, there, everywhere, yet on they kept, their eyes fixed on the distant prize, their one thought that of victory, never of defeat. But as they carried on, that merciless shower increased in its intensity. Others of the heroic attackers fell. It seemed impossible for human beings to face that blast and live. Capt. Henderson was the very soul of that great charge. He was out beyond his men, and it was inevitable that a drop from that furious leaden shower should get him. He pitched forward, but rose again, and though his arm hung limp he disdained to stay behind. Onward he ran, his voice cheerily sounding through the din and uproar of the fight and encouraging the Highlanders to keep up their conquering pace. A terrible ordeal for a wounded man, but bravely he accepted it. He was out to win. And it was no mere haphazard guidance that he gave them. His able brain was marking every phase of the fast-developing battle, his quick eye was detecting every contour of the ground. When the whirl of bullets became more dense than ever, he saw to it that the men took advantage of every little shelter; he was husbanding his resources for the final effort. Soon the Highlanders were at the enemy's very gates, and with a roar and a crash they were atop of them. The impact was terrific. The Huns, depending all the time upon their vicious machine guns, were literally overawed by the strength and fierceness of the Argylls' descent. In the forefront, too, a wounded leader! Not long did they wait as the Scotsmen hurled through their first line. A short and sharp struggle, and they had scattered. The Highlanders still swept on to their objective. This, too, was soon reached, and the gallant Argylls, sadly depleted in numbers, and almost exhausted though they were, captured a portion of the great Hindenburg tunnel trench and won their final objective. But the prize was yet to be held, and it was in the holding of it that the real test came. The Germans, never slow to counter-attack, had their guns trained on the spot almost in a trice, and before the victors could realize it, the shot and shell were pouring thick and fast upon them once again. It was a dreadful predicament. They were out beyond the succour of their comrades, the Huns were rapidly massing for the charge, and in that isolated spot it seemed as if their doom would speedily be sealed. A further rain of shells, a convergence of the field-greys from every side, and all would be over! Capt. Henderson, however, was of the true Scottish type. What he had gained he would hold. Retire? Never! Coolly and resolutely he set about the arduous work of consolidating, and by the time the first smashing run of the German infantry came, he had his little force ready to repel them. The struggle which ensued was bitter in the extreme. The Huns, estimated at ten times the number of the Highlanders, rushed furiously to the attack, but in vain. As they came down, withering showers of bombs and bullets spat through their ranks, and they fell back. The German tactics were obvious. Having the little company of Highlanders to themselves as it were, they endeavoured to surround them. From all sides the attacks came, but so splendidly did Capt. Henderson dispose his forces, so vigorously did he set up his defences, that, try as they might, the onrushing hordes could not break through. Long and fierce the miniature battle raged, and through it all the gallant leader kept ever in the forefront, directing, encouraging, until at last the joyful news came that help was at hand, and final victory was assured. Even then the tireless commander refused to quit his post. He continued to guide and to cheer his men to the last, and in the very moment of his ultimate triumph he fell." One who took part in that battle writes: " He always showed himself to be a born leader of men, and the type of officer who is appreciated in action; and if ever a man earned the V.C. he did that day. I went out at the beginning of the war and came through some battles before this one, but I never saw such leadership before. He carried everything in front of him, and all the time he was from ten to twenty paces in front of the attacking line. God knows how he managed to get us rushed through; but had the Captain not done so, I am afraid we would all have been lost." A remarkably vivid description of the onslaught, of the stand of the Argylls, and of the part taken by Capt. Henderson is also given by a Private in the regiment: " When we went over," he writes, " the Captain was in command. He was absolutely fearless. He led us like a lion, and he never seemed to mind anything. The ordeal we had to go through was the worst I have experienced. It is no reflection on the men to say that they were tried very severely, and it required all their courage to carry them through. Several times the attack was held up, and the position seemed hopeless. Never more so than when Capt. Henderson was hit and fell. He was on his feet at once, and without having his wounded arm attended to, he was in the thick of the fight again, urging the men forward and anticipating every possible move of the Huns. If there was a piece of ground ahead that offered the least prospect of cover, it was Capt. Henderson who ordered the men to rush it, and the men soon got that confidence which comes with the knowledge that one is being led by a born leader of men. Very soon we forgot all else but the task before us, and, led in person by Capt. Henderson, we swept over the enemy parapet, carrying all before us. The Germans fled in terror before the fierce officer with the winged arm, though he had not got a weapon with him, and they could easily have knocked him over had they made a stand. The excitement and the pain of his wound had tried Capt. Henderson greatly, but he refused to retire, and immediately set about getting the position ready to withstand the strong counter-attacks that the enemy were preparing. The position was not very bright. Against our company of Argylls the enemy were now massing the best troops they could get hold of, and were pushing a strong cordon around the position in the hope of cutting us off. Capt. Henderson foresaw these moves, and prepared for them as much as it was possible for a man in charge of a single company to dispose of his forces to meet the attacks of an enemy at least ten times as strong. He did not spare himself. His white, drawn face was always about among us, trying to inspire us with some of his own courage, and there was not a man of the battalion who would not have followed him anywhere. He stood up under heavy fire, directing the defence when the first enemy attack was launched. He was as cool as they make them, and did not seem to pay the slightest heed to the heavy hail of bullets. I saw him amid one party of our men who were attacked by eight times their own number. The Captain was encouraging his men, unmindful of the fact that the Germans were firing at him almost point-blank. The Germans launched their last attack just as assistance was on its way to us. They were met with a stubborn resistance, Capt. Henderson handling his men with great skill and courageously sticking at his post until the attack was smashed. After that attack failed the enemy let us have a bit of a rest. Capt. Henderson might then have claimed the right to leave the line, but he refused to do so. He remained about looking after the wounded, and it was while moving about to see what could be done to assist the troops advancing to our assistance that he was hit the last time. He sank to earth without a word, and we buried him behind the line with the honours due to a brave Highlander." Capt. Henderson was the first Paisley soldier to win the Victoria Cross. Capt. Henderson's Victoria Cross was gazetted 5 July, 1917: " Arthur Henderson, M.C., Second Lieut. (Acting Capt.), late Argyll and Sutherland Highlanders. For most conspicuous bravery. During an attack on the enemy trenches this officer, although almost immediately wounded in the left arm, led his company through the front enemy line until he gained his final objective. He then proceeded to consolidate his position, which, owing to heavy gun and machine-gun fire, and bombing attacks, was in danger of being isolated. By his cheerful courage and coolness he was enabled to maintain the spirit of his men under most trying conditions. Capt, Henderson was killed after he had successfully accomplished his task." A newspaper says at the time: " General regret will be felt that he was not spared to receive the honour in person from His Majesty, and it will devolve on his father to proceed to Buckingham Palace in due time to receive the Military Cross and the Victoria Cross, won in July, 1916, and April, 1917, respectively. Such a double distinction stamps the late Capt. Henderson as a man high above the average. It is known that he was one of the ablest and, at the same time, most popular officers in his division, esteemed and respected, not only by his brother officers, but also by the rank and file. A fellow officer, writing to the father of deceased, mentions that everyone, from the commanding officer downwards, in the battalion was anxiously waiting a decision regarding the V.C. recommendation, and adds: 'His conduct and courage on the 23rd would entitle him to higher honour if such were possible. He has won imperishable fame.'" The same newspaper says: "Paisley has sent many thousands of soldiers to the front; she has suffered severely by the sacrifice of her sons, and she has participated in all the honours of war—the M.M., D.C.M., M.C. and D.S.O. having up to the present been awarded to many young men from our town. The most coveted of all—the V.C.—has now been added, crowning our honours list, and the gallant soldier who has brought this high distinction to Paisley is Capt. Arthur Henderson, younger son of Bailie Henderson." A local newspaper says: "A fortnight ago we published the painful intelligence that Bailie Henderson had lost his only sons in the war—one being reported missing, and the other wounded, believed dead. He has now received official intimation that they are assumed to have been killed in action—Private George Henderson, Canadians, on 9 April, and Capt. Arthur Henderson, Argyll and Sutherland Highlanders, on 24 April. Much sympathy is expressed for Mrs. Henderson and the Bailie, who is the fourth Town Councillor to suffer a double bereavement in the war. Private George Henderson formerly in the building trade with his father, left Paisley early in 1911 for Lytton, British Columbia, where he was employed in the Civil Engineering Department of the Canadian North Pacific Railway. He was 32 years of age, and enlisted in the Expeditionary Force in March, 1916. After training at Vernon, British Columbia, he came to this country last Oct. In Nov. he visited his father at Riccartsbar Avenue, and, by a strange coincidence, Capt. Henderson, his brother, who had arrived from France, also reached home on a visit. The two brothers met for the first time for nearly six years. They arrived within an hour of each other. The names of both soldiers are on the roll of honour of the Oakshaw West United Free Church (Rev. James Cables)." The following copy of an interesting document is lent by Bailie George Henderson: "This parchment, subscribed by the Members of the Town Council of Paisley, in Common Council assembled, is a tribute of sympathy to their colleague, Bailie George Henderson, and of respect to the memory of his son, Capt. Arthur Henderson, V.C., M.C., who fell mortally wounded fighting in France for King and country on 24 April, 1917. Capt. Henderson enlisted in the local Territorial Force on the outbreak of war in Aug. 1914, and in April, 1915, received his commission as Second Lieutenant in the Argyll and Sutherland Highlanders (Special Reserve). In Sept. following he was sent to France with the 2nd Argyll and Sutherland Highlanders (93rd Highlanders). During the Battle of the Somme in July, 1916, he was promoted to be Captain in command of his company, and was awarded the Military Cross, in connection with which the following appeared in the London Gazette: 'For conspicuous gallantry in action. He led his company in the attack with great courage and determination, advancing our lines and consolidating the position won with great skill. He has previously done fine work.' He continued in command of his company until the day of his death, showing the possession of the highest qualities as a leader, winning the respect, admiration and devotion of his subordinates, and the complete confidence of his superiors. During severe fighting on 23 and 24 April, 1917, he conducted a remarkable attack on the German front (Hindenburg trench), described as one of the greatest achievements of the war, converting an apprehended defeat into a splendid success. Several times the attack was held up by numerically superior forces, and the position appeared quite hopeless, his company being surrounded, communications cut off, and himself badly wounded. On restoration of communications, it was suggested that he should retire with his company, but he refused, declaring that they would fight on until they had gained their final objective. This he did, handling his men with great skill, animating them with his own courage, and, amid a hail of bullets, maintaining his position until the enemy was beaten back. Having accomplished his purpose, forgetful of his wound, he set himself to aid his injured men, when he was again hit and fell without a word. So passed a gallant soldier and a trusted leader, whose name is written imperishably in the annals of Paisley, with that of his only brother, George, who also gave his life for his country on the battlefield of France. For these heroic deeds of bravery Capt. Henderson was posthumously awarded the coveted honour of the Victoria Cross. The official award appeared in the London Gazette of 5 July, 1917, as follows: 'His Majesty the King has been graciously pleased to approve of the award of the Victoria Cross to the undernoted officer: Second Lieut. (Acting Capt.) Arthur Henderson, M.C., late Argyll and Sutherland Highlanders, for most conspicuous bravery. During an attack on the enemy trenches this officer, although almost immediately wounded in the left arm, led his company through the front enemy line until he gained his final objective. He then proceeded to consolidate his position, which, owing to heavy gun and machine-gun fire, and bombing attacks, was in danger of being isolated. By his cheerful courage and coolness he was enabled to maintain the spirit of his men under most trying conditions. Capt. Henderson was killed after he had successfully accomplished his task.' He was 24 years of age. The decorations—V.C. and M.C.—won by his son were bestowed on Bailie Henderson by the King at an open-air investiture held at Buckingham Palace in presence of a large assemblage of spectators on 21 July, 1917.—Dated at Paisley, this eleventh day of Sept. 1917."

REACHITT, JOHN, Private, served in the European War. He was awarded the Victoria Cross [London Gazette, 5 July, 1917]: "John Reachitt, No. 18233, Private, 6th Battn. South Lancashire Regt. For most conspicuous bravery and devotion to duty when working down a broad, deep water-course. Five times he went forward in the face of very heavy machine-gun fire at very close range, being the sole survivor on each occasion. These advances drove back the enemy machine guns, and about 300 yards of water-course was made good in an hour. After his officer had been killed Private Reachitt, on his own initiative, organized and made several more advances. On reaching the enemy barricade, he was forced by a counter-attack to retire, giving ground slowly and continuing to throw bombs. On supports reaching him, he held a forward bend by bombing until the position was consolidated. The action of this gallant soldier saved the left flank and enabled his battalion to maintain its position.

London Gazette, 20 July, 1917.—"Admiralty, 20 July, 1917. The King has been graciously pleased to approve of the award of the following Honours, Decorations and Medals to Officers and Men for services in action with enemy submarines. To receive the Victoria Cross: Lieut. Ronald Neil Stuart, R.N.R., D.S.O.; W. Williams, Seaman, R.N.R."

London Gazette, 20 July, 1917.—"Admiralty, 20 July, 1917. Lieut Stuart and Seaman Williams were selected by the Officers and Ship's Company respectively of one of H.M. Ships to receive the Victoria Cross under Rule 13 of the Royal Warrant dated the 29th Jan. 1856."

STUART, RONALD NEIL, D.S.O., Lieut., Royal Naval Reserve, is the son of the late Capt. Stuart, of Prince Edward Island, Canada, and Mrs. Stuart. An only son, he has five sisters, one of whom was in charge of a hospital in France during the European War. Lieut. Stuart comes of an old seafaring family, his ancestors for generations having been captains in the Merchant Service. He was educated at Shaw Street College, Liverpool, and began his sea career on the barque Kirkhill, owned by Messrs. Steele & Co. During the third year of his apprenticeship on board the Kirkhill he was wrecked off the Falkland Islands. For many years he was associated with the Allan Line, and when it was taken over by the Canadian Pacific Railway Company his services were retained. The holder of a Board of Trade proficiency certificate when war broke out, the young sailor fell into his new duties almost automatically. His rapid promotion proved his keenness and capability. Probationary Sub-Lieutenant in Oct. 1914, he was confirmed in that rank in May of the following year, and was promoted full Lieutenant in Sept. 1916. He was created a Companion of the Distinguished Service Order in March, 1917. He was awarded the Victoria Cross [London Gazette, 20 July, 1917]: "Ronald Neil Stuart, D.S.O., Lieut., Royal Naval Reservè. Lieut. Stuart and a seaman were selected by the officers and ship's company respectively of one of His Majesty's ships to receive the Victoria Cross under Rule 13 of the Royal Warrant dated 29 Jan. 1856."

An extract from "Canada" says:

"The great honour of being the first Anglo-Canadian in the Imperial Forces to receive the Victoria Cross has fallen to a Prince Edward Island sailor, Lieut. Ronald Neil Stuart, D.S.O., R.N.R., who was decorated with the coveted bronze cross on Saturday at Buckingham Palace. The deed for which Lieut. Stuart won the honour has not been disclosed, but it is officially stated that it was for services in action with enemy submarines."

A newspaper says:

"Lieut. R. N. Stuart, V.C., D.S.O., R.N.R., was married at St. Clement's Church, Toxteth, Liverpool, last week to Miss E. Wright. Lieut. Stuart, who is a Prince Edward Islander, was formerly in the employ of the C.P.O.S."

WILLIAMS, W., Seaman, Royal Naval Reserve, served in the Dardanelles, was mentioned by Vice-Admiral de Robeck in his Despatch, and was awarded the Victoria Cross [London Gazette, 20 July, 1917]: "W. Williams, O.N/6224A, Seaman, Royal Naval Reserve, Royal Navy." Surgeon P. Burrowes Kelly, R.N., D.S.O., writes of him in his "Diary": "Saved the day on 25 April by holding on to a rope for over an hour standing chest-deep in the sea and under continuous fire. Eventually dangerously wounded by a shell, and later killed by a pom-pom whilst his rescue was being effected by Commander Unwin. He was the pride of our ship's company, and described by Commander Unwin as 'the bravest sailor he had ever met.'"

London Gazette, 2 Aug. 1917.—"War Office, 2 Aug. 1917. His Majesty the King has been graciously pleased to approve of the award of the Victoria Cross to the undermentioned Officers, Non-commissioned Officers and Men."

GRIEVE, ROBERT CUTHBERT, Capt., was born at Brighton, Melbourne, Victoria, Australia, on 19 June, 1889, son of John and Annie Deas Grieve. He was educated at Caulfield Grammar School, and at Wesley College, Victoria, and enlisted on 9 June, 1915, as a Private in the Australian Imperial Forces, and was given a commission in Jan. 1916, in the 37th Battn. A.I.F., being promoted Lieutenant in May, 1916, and Captain in Feb. 1917. He served in the European War, and was present at Armentières, Bois Grenier, L'Epinette, Ploegsteert Wood, Messines, La Basse Ville and Warneton. He was awarded the Victoria Cross for his gallantry during an attack on the German third-line system at Messines on 7 June, 1917. The award was announced in the London Gazette, 1 Aug. 1917: "Capt. Robert Cuthbert Grieve, Australian Infantry. For most conspicuous bravery. During an attack on the enemy's position in the face of heavy artillery and machine-

Robert Cuthbert Grieve.

gun fire, and after all his officers had been wounded and his company had suffered very heavy casualties, Capt. Grieve located two hostile machine guns which were holding up his advance. He then, single-handed, under continuous fire from these two machine guns, succeeded in bombing and killing the two crews, reorganized the remnants of his company, and gained his original objective. Capt. Grieve, by his utter disregard of danger and his coolness in mastering a very difficult position, set a splendid example, and when he finally fell wounded the position had been secured and the few remaining enemy were in full flight." Eighty-eight N.C.O.'s and men of his company, in writing to congratulate him on winning the first Victoria Cross for their battalion, said : " We, as men of your company, will cherish with pride your deeds of heroism and devotion which stimulated us to go forward in the face of all danger, and at critical moments gave the right guidance that won the day and added to the banner of Australia a name which time will never obliterate. We trust that your recovery may be a speedy one, and we can assure you that there awaits you on your return to the boys a very hearty welcome." Capt. Grieve was married at Scots Church, Sydney, on 7 Aug. 1918, to May Isobel, daughter of A. C. M. and C. Bowman, of Plinlimmon, Kurrajong, New South Wales. His wife served as a sister for three years with the Australian Imperial Force, and had nursed him through a serious illness, after meeting him at a casualty clearing station. He is fond of cricket and football, and played the former game for Brighton and the latter for the Collegian Club. He is a member of the firm of Grieve, Gardner & Co. He was discharged from the Australian Imperial Forces as medically unfit on 28 June, 1918, and holds the rank of Captain in the Australian Army Reserve.

CRAIG, JOHN MANSON, Second Lieut., was born on 5 March, 1896, at Innergeldie Comrie, Perthshire, son of the late John Craig, of Craigdarroch, Ayrshire, and of M. E. McCosh or Craig. He was educated at

John Manson Craig.

Morrison's Academy, Crieff, and joined the Army on 6 April, 1915. He served in the European War, in France, Egypt and Palestine, and gained the Victoria Cross in Palestine He was awarded the Victoria Cross [London Gazette, 1 Aug. 1917] : " John Manson Craig, Second Lieut., 1st/4th Battn., attached 1st/5th Battn., Royal Scots Fusiliers. For most conspicuous bravery on the occasion of an advanced post being rushed by a large party of the enemy. This officer immediately organized a rescue party, and the enemy was tracked over broken country back to his trenches. Second Lieut. Craig then set his party to work removing the dead and wounded. During the course of this operation his men came under heavy rifle and machine-gun fire. An N.C.O. was wounded, and the medical officer who went out to his aid was also severely wounded. Second Lieut. Craig at once went to their assistance, and succeeded in taking the N.C.O. under cover. He then returned for the medical officer, and whilst taking him to shelter was himself wounded. Nevertheless, by great perseverance, he succeeded in rescuing him also. As the enemy continued a heavy fire, and, in addition, turned on shrapnel and high explosives, Second Lieut. Craig scooped cover for the wounded, and thus was the means of saving their lives. These latter acts of bravery occurred in broad daylight, under full observation of the enemy and within close range. On three previous occasions this officer has behaved in a conspicuously brave manner, and has shown an exceptional example of courage and resource."

DUNVILLE, JOHN SPENCER, Second Lieut., was born on 7 May, 1896, at 46, Portland Place, London, son of Wing Commander John Dunville, C.B.E., Royal Air Force, and of Violet Dunville. He was educated

John Spencer Dunville.

at Ludgrove School and Eton College, and joined the Army, gazetted Second Lieutenant Special Reserve D., 16 Sept. 1914, and Second Lieutenant 1st Royal Dragoons 4 Jan. 1916. He served in the European War, in France and Flanders, from 6 June, 1915, to 19 April, 1916 (invalided to England sick for eight months), and from 22 Dec. 1916, to date of his death, 26 June, 1917. He was awarded the Victoria Cross [London Gazette, 1 Aug. 1917] : " John Spencer Dunville, Second Lieut., late 1st Royal Dragoons. For most conspicuous bravery. When in charge of a party consisting of scouts and Royal Engineers engaged in the demolition of the enemy's wire, this officer displayed great gallantry and disregard of all personal danger. In order to ensure the absolute success of the work entrusted to him, Second Lieut. Dunville placed himself between an N.C.O. of the Royal Engineers and the enemy's fire, and, thus protected, this N.C.O. was enabled to complete a work of great importance. Second Lieut. Dunville, although severely wounded, continued to direct his men in the wire-cutting and general operations until the raid was successfully completed, thereby setting a magnificent example of courage, determination and devotion to duty to all ranks under his command. This gallant officer has since succumbed to his wounds." The following are letters received by Capt. and Mrs. Dunville :

From Lord Hamilton of Dalziel :

" 16.8.17. " Fourth Army,
" B.E.F.,
" France.

" DEAR DUNVILLE,
" I am sending you under separate cover a copy of Army Routine Orders, such as is sent to all those who gain rewards for gallantry in action in this Army. It contains an account of your son's action for which he was given the Victoria Cross.
" Sir Henry Rawlinson wishes me to express his deep sympathy with Mrs. Dunville and yourself, and his regret that your son's gallant and self-sacrificing action should have cost him his life.
" All these cases pass through my hands, and I have never come across such an instance of deliberate and cold-blooded valour among all the cases I have had to deal with since I have been acting as Assistant Military Secretary to this Army.
" These official accounts are necessarily brief, and the whole story of what your son did is not told. The cavalry was then holding the line on the front of this Army north of St. Quentin. Your son was in command of a raiding party. He crawled up with the Corporal of Engineers who was to push the Bangalore torpedo under the wire. This is a long jointed tube filled with explosive, which is pushed under the wire and then exploded so as to make a passage. In carrying it across No Man's Land the joints became disunited, and it had to be repaired before being pushed under the wire. While this was being done, your son and the sapper were spotted by the enemy. The raiding party was waiting close by, and the whole success of the operation depended on the wire being cut quickly. The Corporal of Engineers was the expert who alone could repair the torpedo. To protect him while this was being done, your son lay in front of him, and enabled him to do what was wanted and blow up the wire successfully. This ensured the success of the raid.
" It was a magnificent thing to do, and all the more so that there was no excitement and ' go ' about it. He simply thought what was the best thing he could do to help his side and did it.
" I am very sorry that so gallant a life should have been sacrificed. But it was a most splendid death, and I hope it may be some consolation to you and his mother to know that he achieved his purpose.
" Yours sincerely,
(Signed) " HAMILTON OF DALZIEL."

From Colonel Wormald, Royal Dragoons :

" Saturday,
" June 30th, 1917.

" DEAR MRS. DUNVILLE,
" I feel I must write to you to express my deep sympathy, and that of all ranks of the regiment, to you and your husband in your irreparable loss.
" Since writing first to your husband the sad news, much has come to light to emphasize your boy's gallantry and devotion to duty. We, his brother officers, whilst we shall always mourn the loss of a cheerful companion and friend whom we could ill afford to lose, are justly proud of the gallant way in which a brother officer met his death. The record of his daring and devotion must always remain an incident in the history of the regiment of which all connected with it will look back with pride.
" All this is, I am afraid, small consolation to you and his father, and I can only add that you have my whole-hearted sympathy in your sorrow.
" I must give you an account of what happened to enable you to appreciate his bravery.
" A raid was ordered to be undertaken on the German lines about 800 yards in front of our outposts, and ' The Royals ' were detailed to carry it out. Two parties, each consisting of 50 Royals and two parties of three Sappers carrying torpedoes for destroying the enemy's wire, were told off. The right party consisted of men of Johnnie's squadron and were under command of Ronnie Henderson. The left party of similar numbers consisted of men of ' B ' Squadron under Barnard Helme. Each party had to march on a compass bearing to the point in the wire to be attacked. The parties moved through our lines at one a.m. on the morning of the 25th, and under cover of our artillery barrage moved on their objectives. Johnnie, who was Scout Officer, had the direction of the right party, and brought them right up to the place to be attacked, arriving there punctually at the scheduled time. Having got to the wire, it was his duty to direct the Sappers where they were to place the torpedo, and lay a tape to the gap made by the explosion to show the assaulting party the way through the gap. Just before reaching the main wire the advanced party came upon a narrow belt of low wire, which Johnnie and his scouts cut by hand. Johnnie then ran forward with the three Sappers, and when they reached the main wire they found that one of the joints of the torpedo had got bent in some way, and it could not be put together and had to be repaired. This occasioned some delay, and the operation, which in practice had taken under two minutes, took them over five minutes. Meantime the enemy had detected our intentions, and opened fire with rifles and hand grenades. The Sapper Corporal, a very gallant boy, states that during the whole of this time Johnnie was urging him to keep cool and kept assuring him that he was in no danger. He further stated that Johnnie deliberately interposed his own body between the enemy and himself, and that by his example and bravery he gave him the necessary confidence to carry out his task. The whole party then withdrew until the torpedo exploded, when Johnnie told them they could go back. The assaulting party then advanced, but, owing to increase in the enemy's fire, were unable to get through the gap. As the leading men got up to the gap Johnnie was wounded, his left arm being badly shattered by a bomb, it is thought. He then had to be taken back. And despite a dreadful wound, he walked

back the whole distance—to the outposts. A man of less grit could not have accomplished it. He was quite calm when he reached my head-quarters, and talked cheerfully to the doctor who attended to his wounds, and apologized to me for not having been able to get into the trenches. I saw him that morning again in hospital about three miles back ; the doctors held out very little hope of his recovery, so I got the division to send a wire to your husband. The doctor told me that he had another wound in his chest, which might have been caused by a fragment of the bomb which wounded him in the arm, or might have been from another bullet. Capt. Miles saw Johnnie that evening ; he was quite conscious, and the doctors were more hopeful. That night a clever surgeon called Lockwood was called in. The poor boy passed away at three a.m. on the morning of the 26th, quite painlessly. I don't think he suffered much pain at any time ; and when I last saw him, only complained of not being able to get his breath. This discomfort passed off during the afternoon and he slept peacefully for some time.

"I won't go into details of what happened to the other party. They got through the wire and killed some Germans, and obtained valuable identifications, but poor Barnard Helme was killed.

"Poor little Johnnie, I feel his death very deeply. I had seen a great deal of him lately, and realized what a splendid boy he was. Quite apart from his gallant end, he had been working indefatigably with his scouts in ' No Man's Land ' for a week before the raid, and was out nearly every night making himself acquainted with the ground over which the raid was to take place. He did everything that human power could do to make a success of the raid, and I cannot put into words the admiration which we all feel for him, and the respect in which we shall always retain him in memory.

"I can only repeat how truly sorry I am for you and his father.
"Yours very sympathetically,
(Signed) " F. W. WORMALD."

MAUFE, THOMAS HAROLD BROADBENT, Second Lieut., served in the European War, and was awarded the Victoria Cross [London Gazette. 2 Aug. 1917] : " Thomas Harold Broadbent Maufe, Second Lieut., R.G.A, For most conspicuous bravery and initiative. Under intense artillery fire this officer on his own initiative repaired, unaided, the telephone line between the forward and rear positions, thereby enabling his battery to immediately open fire on the enemy. Second Lieut. Maufe further saved what might have proved a most disastrous occurrence by extinguishing a fire in an advanced ammunition dump, caused by a heavy explosion, regardless of the risk he ran from the effects of gas shells which he knew were in the dump. By this great promptitude, resource and entire dis-regard of his own personal safety, he set an exceptionally fine example to all ranks."

WEARNE, FRANK BERNARD, Second Lieut., Essex Regt., served in the European War, and was awarded the Victoria Cross [London Gazette, 2 Aug. 1917] : " Frank Bernard Wearne, Second Lieut., Essex Regt. For most conspicuous bravery when in command of a small party on the left of a raid on the enemy's trenches. He gained his objective in the face of much opposition, and by his magnificent example and daring was able to maintain this position for a considerable time, according to in-structions. During this period Second Lieut. Wearne and his small party were repeatedly counter-attacked. Grasping the fact that if the left flank was lost his men would have to give way, Second Lieut. Wearne, at a moment when the enemy's attack was being heavily pressed and when matters were most critical, leapt on the parapet, and, followed by his left section, ran along the top of the trench, firing and throwing bombs. This unexpected and daring manœuvre threw the enemy off his guard and back in disorder. Whilst on the top of the trench Second Lieut. Wearne was severely wounded, but refused to leave his men. Afterwards he remained in the trench directing operations, consolidating his position and en-couraging all ranks. Just before the order to withdraw was given, this gallant officer was again severely hit for the second time, and while being carried away was mortally wounded. By his tenacity in remaining at his post, though severely wounded, and his magnificent fighting spirit, he was enabled to hold on to the flank."

YOUENS FREDERICK, Second Lieut., was born 14 Aug. 1893, at High Wycombe, Buckinghamshire, son of Vincent and Lizzie Youens. He was educated at the National School ; gained a scholarship, and entered the Royal Grammar School, High Wycombe. " The Wycombiensian " for Dec. 1917, says of Frederick Youens : " Few of us will forget the thrill of emotion and pride with which we heard the simple and moving story of Freddie Youe , s gallant sacrifice. He died as he had lived, a man of the highest ideals, of indomitable courage, and with a total disregard of self. The story of his life and his heroic death have been recounted in many places. Youen's school career was one of con-siderable distinction, a record of achieve-ments in the many-sided life of the school. He passed in succession the Junior and Senior Oxford Locals with Honours in both. In 1910 he passed the London Matriculation in the first division. In 1914, while teaching at Rochester, he gained a scholarship tenable at Oxford University. He was a prefect and a member of the O.T.C. He will be best remembered for his activities in the debating society. He was easily the best debater the school ever had, and an inspiring leader of his party. He possessed, too, a nice touch

Frederick Youens.

as an actor, and always took a lead in the school productions, his last and best character being ' Mrs. Malaprop.' We quote tributes to his memory by those who were at school with him. One of these old schoolfellows, who was a close friend of Youens in school days, says how all looked upon Youens as one of the best of idealists, one who would distinguish him-self in anything he undertook. ' I can well imagine how his men at the front would look up to him, and how much they will feel his loss. I find some consolation in reading of the magnificent way in which he sacrificed himself for others.' Youens was a member of the Medway Swimming Club, and he passed in life-saving at High Wycombe. In 1912 he went to Rochester, and was assistant schoolmaster at St. Peter's School, Rochester, until Aug. 1914, when he joined up. He was very fond of sport and taught the boys of the school in his spare time. He enlisted as a Private in the Royal Army Medical Corps, and in 1915 was transferred to the 7th Battn. East Surreys, and was severely wounded in the arm whilst doing voluntary R.A.M.C. work in the field all night after the battle, doing first-aid and setting the wounded under cover, for which he was com-mended by his captain. It was about a year before he was sufficiently recovered to rejoin his depôt at Kingston-on-Thames, and he was after-wards stationed at Dover and Hertford. He refused many posts in clerical capacities, whereby he could have had promotion, but went in for active work to gain promotion in order to gain a commission. He was gazetted Second Lieut. 13th Battn. Durham Light Infantry in Feb. 1917, and left in the same month for France. It was at Messines that he received the wounds from which he died two days afterwards, on 7 July, 1917." He was awarded the Victoria Cross [London Gazette, 2 Aug. 1917] : " Frederick Youens, Second Lieut. 13th Battn. Durham Light Infantry. For most conspicuous bravery and devotion to duty. While out on patrol this officer was wounded, and had to return to his trenches to have his wounds dressed. Shortly afterwards a report came in that the enemy were preparing to raid our trenches. Second Lieut. Youens, regardless of his wounds, immediately set out to rally the team of a Lewis gun, which had become disorganized owing to heavy shell fire. During this process an enemy's bomb fell on the Lewis gun position without exploding. Second Lieut. Youens immediately picked it up and hurled it over the parapet. Shortly afterwards another bomb fell near the same place ; again Second Lieut. Youens picked it up with the intention of throwing it away, when it exploded in his hand, severely wounding him and also some of his men. There is little doubt that the prompt and gallant action of Second Lieut. Youens saved several of his men's lives, and that by his energy and resource the enemy's raid was completely repulsed. This gallant officer has since succumbed to his wounds." The story of his heroism in this action is told by one of his brother officers in a letter to his mother : " He was an excellent fellow, and admired by everyone for his great bravery. He did one of the finest acts of bravery that has been done in this war, and I only hope you will be awarded wha the deserved. He was on a patrol, and was wounded. While he was being dressed in a dug-out, with his tunic and shirt off, the word came down that his company was being attacked. He immediately rushed out as he was, and rallied a Lewis gun team, and commenced firing at the Boche. They threw a bomb into the middle of the team, and he picked it up and threw it away. The Boche threw another in the same place, and your son picked it up and threw it away again. Unfortunately, the bomb burst very near to your son and severely wounded him. He died two days later. He undoubtedly save the situation by his display of coolness and disregard for danger." The Major of his battalion writes : " He was an ideal soldier, keen, efficient and brave, and was earmarked for early pro-motion. On several occasions his gallant work has been noted, and I sincerely hope that his last feat will be duly recognized. He was exceed-ingly popular with his men, who would cheerfully follow him anywhere." The Chaplain, writing, said : " As I wished him good luck, one of the senior officers said to me, ' That's a fine chap, just the sort of fellow we want in the battalion.' The first and almost only thing taken from him after his wound was a little diary, and in it a card bearing the words : ' Christ is risen.' I felt, as I conducted the service, surely death had no terrors for him."

FRICKLETON, SAMUEL, L.-Corpl., served in the European War in France. He was awarded the Victoria Cross [London Gazette, 2 Aug. 1917] : " No. 6/2133, Samuel Frickleton, L.-Corpl. 3rd Battn. New Zea-land Infantry. For most conspicuous bravery and determination when with attacking troops which came under heavy fire and were checked. Although slightly wounded, Corpl. Frickleton dashed forward at the head of his section, pushed into our barrage, and personally destroyed with bombs an enemy machine gun and crew which was causing heavy casualties. He then attacked a second gun, killing the whole of the crew of twelve. By the destruction of these two guns, he undoubtedly saved his own and other units from very severe casualties, and his magnificent courage and gallantry ensured the capture of the objective. During the consolidation of this position he received a second severe wound. He set throughout a great example of heroism." He was pro-moted Sergeant, and was given a com-mission in the 3rd Battn. New Zealand Rifle Brigade. He was appointed Assistant Provost-Marshal of the Wellington Military District (New Zealand) with the temporary rank of Lieutenant. He was presented with a sum of money in Treasury notes.

CARROLL, JOHN, Private, joined the Australian Military Forces and served in the European War. He was awarded the Victoria Cross [London Gazette, 2 Aug.

John Carroll.

1917]: " No. 1804, John Carroll, 3rd Battn. Australian Imperial Force. For most conspicuous bravery. During an attack immediately the barrage lifted, Private John Carroll rushed the enemy's trench and bayoneted four of the enemy. He then noticed a comrade in difficulties, and at once proceeded to his comrade's assistance, and killed one of the enemy. He continued working ahead with great determination until he came across a machine gun and team of four men in a shell-hole. Single-handed he attacked the entire team, killing three of the men and capturing the gun. Later on two of his comrades were buried by a shell, and, in spite of very heavy shell and machine-gun fire, he managed to extricate them. During the ninety-six hours the battalion was in the line Private Carroll displayed most wonderful courage and fearlessness. His magnificent example of gallantry and devotion to duty inspired all ranks in his battalion."

PATTISON, JOHN GEORGE, Private, was born at Woolwich, son of Henry Pattison, of Deptford, and his wife. He served in the European War, and was awarded the Victoria Cross [London Gazette, 1 Aug. 1917]: " John George Pattison, No. 808887, Private, 50th Canadian Infantry Battn. For most conspicuous bravery in attack. When the advance of our troops was held up by an enemy machine gun, which was inflicting severe casualties, Private Pattison, with utter disregard of his own safety, sprang forward, and, jumping from shell-hole to shell-hole, reached cover within thirty yards of the enemy gun. From this point, in face of heavy fire, he hurled bombs, killing and wounding some of the crew, then rushed forward, overcoming and bayoneting the surviving five gunners. His valour and initiative undoubtedly saved the situation and made possible the further advance to the objective." Private J. G. Pattison was killed in action on 3 June, 1917. A newspaper says: " The Mayor of Deptford unveiled a roll of honour in the Town Hall on Saturday, commemorating the valour and heroism of Private John George Pattison, Canadian Infantry, who was awarded the Victoria Cross for most conspicuous bravery in the attack at Vimy Ridge on 10 April, 1917. He was unfortunately killed in the following June, and the Victoria Cross was forwarded to his widow, who is resident in Calgary, Canada, to which he emigrated some years ago. At the invitation of the Mayor, his father, who has been resident in Deptford upwards of fifty years, signed the borough roll of honour, and Private Pattison's son, who has also seen service at the front, was presented with an illuminated record of his father's gallant deed, inscribed on the honours board in the council chamber. The ceremony was witnessed by a large audience, among whom were the Right. Hon. C. W. Bowerman, M.P., and Major Theodore Prestige, L.C.C., and Colonel the Hon. Rupert Carington, D.S.O." " Thirty Canadian V.C.'s " (published by Messrs. Skeffington) gives on pages 40–43 the following account of Private J. G. Pattison: " During the morning of 10 April, 1917, the 44th and 50th Battns. were instructed to capture and consolidate, as an outpost line, the eastern edge of Vimy Ridge, lying beyond Hill 145. The men of the 10th Brigade had been in reserve while their comrades swept over Vimy on the previous day, and were anxious to get in some good work with the rest of the corps. There is no doubt that they succeeded. The men of the 50th made their way to Beer Trench, and at zero hour, 3.15 p.m., went forward with a rush. Opposition was immediate and severe. From every broken tree and battered piece of cover machine-gun fire swept the attack, and casualties were extremely heavy; but the men continued to push forward. On the right ' C ' Company attacked, with ' D ' Company in close support; on the left ' A ' Company, with ' B ' Company in support. The leading companies found the ' going ' extremely hard, but for a time all went well, and though the advance was slow, steady progress was made. As the incessant fire thinned the waves of attacking troops, greater difficulty was encountered in enveloping the machine-gun nests that barred our progress. In the first stage of an attack made by determined troops the resistance close at hand is easily swamped; but as the men continue to push forward the innumerable obstructions and perils of the battlefield gather against their weakening impact, fatigue slows them, their front is broken and their connecting files are shot down; and so a steady enveloping movement becomes a series of bitterly contested little battles, where small parties in twos and threes fight strategic engagements with isolated strong points of the enemy. Finally a series of partial checks culminates in an abrupt cessation of the advance—and a gathering company finds itself held up before an embattled fortification whose point of vantage covers the whole local zone of attack. Then the real trouble begins. Time and again in the history of the war one hostile fortification left in otherwise captured territory has changed or materially affected the final issue of the engagement. It may serve as a rallying-point for a determined counter-attack, or by its wide zones of fire hamper the advance of reinforcements on the flanks, or prevent the supply of vital munitions to a new and precarious front line; its effectiveness is limited only by its natural position, and as this has been selected with care and forethought by an efficient enemy, one small but actively hostile strong-point may prove a very capable thorn in the side of a harassed general. On that April afternoon the 50th Battn. encountered just such a check. It was on the left of the battalion attacking zone, and the men of ' A ' Company, gradually gathering in the nearest cover, had organized and carried out several gallant attempts to rush the position. Each time they had been beaten back with heavy losses. Now ' B ' Company arrived to reinforce the assault. Another attack was organized, with no more success than the last; and then, as so often occurs, a critical situation was relieved by the clear-headed bravery of a single soldier. Private Pattison, an engineer from Calgary, proceeded to deal with the situation. He advanced single-handed towards the machine-gun post in a series of short rapid dashes, taking cover on the way in available shell-holes while deciding his next point of vantage. In a few moments he had reached a shell-hole within thirty yards of the vital strong-point. He stood up in full view of the machine gunners and under their point-blank fire threw three bombs with such good aim that the guns were put out of action and the crews temporarily demoralized. This was Pattison's opportunity, and he took it without hesitation. As his last bomb exploded amidst the Germans he rushed across the intervening space, and in a moment was using his bayonet upon the unhappy enemy. He had killed them all before his companions had caught him up. Twenty minutes later all objectives were gained and the Canadians busy consolidating the captured line. Pattison came unscathed through the day's fighting and through the successful attack on the Pimple on the following day; but he never wore his V.C., though he was aware that he had been recommended for that honour. He was killed on 2 June in the attack upon the Generating Station. Very few men of Pattison's age now reach the honour of the Victoria Cross, as this war has set almost too high a standard for their physical activity. Pattison was forty-two years old, a smart soldier and a good fellow. His son, a young soldier in his father's battalion, wears the ribbon upon his right breast, and probably will wear it on his left side, too, before this war is over."

John George Pattison.

Some further particulars sent by the Mayor of Deptford (who has himself been knighted for his services during the war) are here given: John George Pattison was born at Woolwich in 1874, son of Henry Alfred Pattison and Mrs. Pattison, daughter of John Wisking. He came to Deptford when he was four years of age, and was educated at Clifton Hill School, going to Canada in 1906. He married Sophia A. Allen, daughter of John Allen, and their children are: Ethel Mary; Henry John; Helena Margaret, and George Alfred. He joined the 137th Battn. Canadian Infantry in Calgary (where his wife and children live at 1622, West Avenue, Westmount); was drafted to the 50th Battn. in England, and went to France in Jan. 1917.

The following letter was written to Private Pattison's father, now residing at New Cross, London, S.E.:

" France,
" 7 Aug. 1917.

" Dear Mr. Pattison,

" Your letter regarding your son, J. G. Pattison, was sent to me for an answer, as I was his officer on 2nd June, when he was killed.

" It is with very great regret that I tell you this, as I have been his officer ever since he and his son joined the 137th Battn. in Calgary, and I knew him not only as the finest type of soldier but also as a friend. You are probably now aware that he has been awarded the greatest of honours, the Victoria Cross, for bravery. What a great pity he cannot be here to receive it!

" Personally I feel very badly in the matter, as we cannot afford to lose such men, but he died as he would have wished, in action, and while we were administering a severe defeat to the enemy.

" If you wish further particulars, please write me.

" You and Mrs. Pattison have the sincere sympathy of this battalion, who regret the loss of a brave soldier.

" Yours sincerely,
" Thomas H. Prescott, Lieutenant,
" 50th Battn. Canadians."

RATCLIFFE, WILLIAM, Private, served in the European War in France. He was awarded the Victoria Cross [London Gazette, 2 Aug. 1917]: " William Ratcliffe, No. 2251, Private, 2nd Battn. South Lancashire Regt. For most conspicuous bravery. After an enemy's trench had been captured, Private Ratcliffe located an enemy machine gun which was firing on his comrades from the rear, whereupon, single-handed and on his own initiative, he immediately rushed the machine-gun position and bayoneted the crew. He then brought the gun back into action in the front line. This very gallant soldier has displayed great resource on previous occasions, and has set an exceptionally fine example of devotion to duty." The " Observer " of 14 Oct. 1917, said: " Lord Derby was present yesterday evening at a dinner and presentation given at Liverpool by the National Union of Dock Labourers to one of their members, Private Ratcliffe, of the South Lancashire Regt., who had won the Victoria Cross for brave and distinguished conduct in the Messines Ridge fighting. Lord Derby, responding to the toast of the ' Navy and Army,' said that he was glad to find the proposed monetary presentation to Private Ratcliffe was not to take place, as it was against the military regulations to reward a man with money for doing his duty. But he cordially approved, as everyone else would, of the proposal to recognize their hero's bravery by making the presentation when he returned to civil life. He ventured to hope that at the present time there were no social grades. They were all British, fighting for a good cause. Many honours carried little weight in foreign countries, but the Victoria Cross was a soldier's honour known throughout the world as one which carried real merit, and if he could do anything by granting extra leave to enable Private Ratcliffe to earn the suggested Bar by matrimony, he would be pleased to do so. (Laughter.)"

London Gazette, 11 Aug. 1917.—" War Office, 11 Aug. 1917. His Majesty the King has been graciously pleased to approve of the award of the Victoria Cross to the undermentioned Officer."

BISHOP, WILLIAM AVERY, Capt., was born at Owen Sound, Ontario, Canada, 8 Feb. 1894, son of William Avery Bishop, Esq., Registrar of Grey County, Ontario. He was educated at the Royal Military College,

Kingston, Canada, and joined the Canadian Militia on 26 Aug. 1911. The writers of " Thirty Canadian V.C.'s " (published by Messrs. Skeffington) say on page 35: " This stripling received a commission in the Canadian Cavalry in March, 1915, and went to France with a Cavalry unit. He was in the trenches in those days when our Cavalry Brigade held a section of the line as infantry. Later, after only one experience of fighting Germans from horseback, he decided that he wanted more excitement, and joined the increasing host of airmen. . . . His headquarters in France as a flying man were until recently in the cosiest of aerodromes, cuddled close up against a small bunch of cool trees, which looked innocent enough from the air. An ancient farm is in the vicinity, and the title of the young airman's hut was ' The Abode of Love.' It is a fitting answer to the Hymn of Hate. Commanding this squadron of airmen, he brought it to perfection, and none disputed that he was a fitting successor to Capt. Ball, the famous English V.C. hero, who was the leader until his death. Every man of the squadron has brought down at least ten Germans, and the cheerful group is reputed to have the greatest percentage of flying nerve on the Western Front. His best and most daring work, however, has been done when he has been ' solo flying.' It is true that he attributes most of his success to ' luck,' but his comrades know that more than luck is needed to bring an airman safely out of some of the awkward situations in which he has been placed." He was awarded the Military Cross in 1917, and the Distinguished Service Order in 1917; also a Bar to the D.S.O. " Wing Adjutant " says: " Whilst the writer was at Netheravon in the latter part of 1915, Bishop was sent down to train as an observer. He at once acquired a certain amount of local celebrity by reason of his indignation at not being allowed to become a pilot. Someone in authority had decided that he had not the requisite qualities to fly; either his nerves were not quite good enough, or he had not enough ' go ' in him, or some other fault was found. The observer's course, with its hours of wireless and photography, bored him; the only hours which aroused his enthusiasm were those devoted to gunnery. All his spare time was spent on the ranges or in the gun-room, and by the time he had finished his course he was probably the best aerial shot on the station. Eventually he left for overseas with his squadron, still breathing out curses on those who condemned him to go as a passenger instead of piloting his own machine. He intended to apply again for permission to take his ticket and graduate as a pilot, and he amused us all by telling how, when his chance arrived, he would show them the mistake they had made. Even in those days he was fully confident of winning the Victoria Cross when the time came. It is highly probable that those days overseas as an observer were of great use to Bishop afterwards. He was able to perfect his gunnery and observe the habits and tactics of the Huns. This knowledge he afterwards turned to good account, being, in addition to a finished pilot, skilled in all the tricks of the air, a marvellous shot, who reserved his fire until sure of hitting the target and securing a victim." Rowland Hill, War Correspondent, gives the following vivid account of his V.C. adventure: " Once he dived into Hunland to find, twelve miles behind a line, a brand new nickel-plated, quite-the-latest-Potsdam-style aerodrome, with right nice, new Albatross machines on a nicely-plotted lawn. His sudden appearance upset the Huns' luncheon, so he politely spiralled up behind the airsheds, and when the first machine started up, swooped down on its tail at about fifty feet through a spray of machine-gun bullets, and sent it crashing down completely wrecked, its pilot killed. Turning again, he swept the second Albatross as it was just starting up, and saw it catch fire. Climbing up once more, he just managed to clear the sheds of the aerodrome. Reaching about a thousand feet, every kind of gun popping away at him, he found the third machine getting under way and swiftly raced after it. One little scrap in the air, and he caught it with the full blast of his machine gun, and sent it side-slipping into a clump of trees. The fourth machine, by this time, was climbing to get the advantage of height, so he followed suit, and three or four minutes' chase in the air resulted. The Hun turned to give battle when the fifth machine was also well under way, and they seemed to have our man sandwiched. But the British airman kept at number four until he had the satisfaction of seeing him flutter down completely out of control. He was just in a favourable position to grab the fifth Albatross when his ammunition gave out, so he waved the Hun a farewell with the empty drum and started an over-the-hundred mile clip for home." It is not easy to choose from the many exciting adventures and deeds of daring performed by this " Canadian Captain Ball," as he is called, but here is one more: " He once met three Albatross scouts who tried to surround him. The bullets were swishing and whining through his machine, past his ears, and all around. Then by good luck one of the Germans came across his line of fire; Bishop let the trigger of his gun go, and down crashed the Hun, while the victorious airman flew homewards." Another exploit which rejoiced his soul was his finding his equally youthful C.O. having a fearful scrap with five Germans in new machines. Out of the clouds dashed Bishop, with his Lewis gun clattering away for all it was worth. The first Hun crashed, a stream of bullets catching both pilot and observer from the rear. The next machine soon followed it, and the remaining three made off without more ado, so Bishop and his juvenile commander did " stunts " all the way home. His favourite method was to sweep like a hawk from the sky, spray a column of German troops marching along a road with his machine gun, and dash off again before they could collect their scattered nerves enough to realize what was happening. He gained the V.C. for an astounding feat which caused the Germans to put a price on his head. This is the story in his own words: " Went over one morning by myself to find Hun aerodrome. Nothing doing there; nobody at home. Flew off to find another; plenty of shrapnel buzzing around. Discovered fine, big 'drome; seven Hun machines lined up waiting to move off. Swooped down, gave them dose from Lewis gun. One Hun started his 'plane; gave him broadside, and saw him crash. Another Hun made a move; let him have ten rounds, and watched him crash into a big tree. Two more rose, I with them. Gave one remainder of tray of cartridges; he disappeared. Put fresh tray on, fired it all at fourth Hun; saw him crash; flew home." The official account of the exploit which took place near Cambrai, France, is very thrilling, and reads as follows [London Gazette, 11 Aug. 1917]: " William Avery Bishop, Capt., D.S.O., M.C., Canadian Cavalry and Royal Flying Corps. For most conspicuous bravery, determination and skill. Capt. Bishop, who had been sent out to work independently, flew, first of all, to an enemy aerodrome; finding no machine about, he flew on to another aerodrome about three miles south-east, which was at least twelve miles the other side of the line. Seven machines, some with their engines running, were on the ground. He attacked these from about fifty feet, and a mechanic, who was starting one of the engines, was seen to fall. One of the machines got off the ground, but at a height of sixty feet Capt. Bishop fired fifteen rounds into it at very close range, and it crashed to the ground. A second machine got off the ground, into which he fired thirty rounds at 150 yards' range, and it fell into a tree. Two more machines then rose from the aerodrome. One of these he engaged at the height of 1,000 feet, emptying the rest of his drum of ammunition. This machine crashed 300 yards from the aerodrome, after which Capt. Bishop emptied a whole drum into the fourth hostile machine, and then flew back to his station. Four hostile scouts were about 1,000 feet above him for about a mile of his return journey, but they would not attack. His machine was very badly shot about by machine-gun fire from the ground." " Thirty Canadian V.C.'s " says: " ' Give me the aeroplane I want,' said Capt. W. A. Bishop, ' and I'll go over to Berlin any night—or day—and come back too, with any luck.' It was during a discussion in the mess on the question of air reprisals that Canada's champion airman slipped in the quiet remark; and when a man who has won the V.C., the M.C., and the D.S.O., with a Bar, says he could bomb the German capital, it may be taken that he means what he says. He had then brought down nearly fifty German flyers, besides a few balloons. There is no trick of aircraft that this young Canadian does not know, though he is not a showy flyer. The number of his exploits is endless, and as his squadron moved from one part of the line to another he constantly found new pastures for adventure, new opponents to defeat, more Germans to kill. He has fought German airmen high over the waves of advancing battalions, and has heard as a faint whisper coming up to him the cheers of his fellow-countrymen when he shot down his enemies at their feet. He has chased a German Staff automobile along a dusty road, and opened fire on it, so that the driver lost his nerve and ditched the car, and the occupants threw their massive dignity to the winds and scrambled for shelter into a dug-out." He was promoted Major 28 Aug. 1917, and on 17 Oct. of the same year he married, at Toronto, Margaret Eaton, daughter of Mr. and Mrs. C. E. Burdon, and niece of Sir John C. Eaton. On 5 Aug. 1918, he was promoted Temporary Lieut.-Colonel, and appointed General Staff Officer, First Grade, Canadian Force. In addition to the previously mentioned decorations, Lieut.-Colonel Bishop holds also the Distinguished Flying Cross, has been made Chevalier of the Legion of Honour, First Class, and has been awarded the Croix de Guerre (with palm leaf) for distinguished service in the zone of the French armies. He was also mentioned three times in Despatches. He has written two books: " Winged Warfare " and " Hunting the Hun in the Air." At the time when Major Bishop was sent to Canada, a newspaper said: " A curious sequence of fatalities appears to overtake all the crack fighting pilots when their ' bag ' reaches the neighbourhood of fifty. Capt. Guynemer, the most famous of the Frenchmen, is dead with fifty-three Huns to his credit. Capt. Ball was killed with forty-seven, and Boelcke, Immelmann, Baron von Richthofen and Voss, the best pilots the Germans have possessed, all went under when they had accounted for fifty machines. The whole nation will rejoice that Major Bishop has been given the opportunity to rest on his laurels for a time."

William Avery Bishop.

London Gazette, 29 Aug. 1917.—" Admiralty, 29 Aug. 1917. Honours for service in the action in the Straits of Otranto on the 15th May, 1917. The King has been graciously pleased to approve of the award of the Victoria Cross to the undermentioned Officer."

WATT, JOSEPH, Skipper, Royal Naval Reserve, served in the European War, and was awarded the Victoria Cross [London Gazette, 29 Aug. 1917]: " Joseph Watt, Skipper, Royal Naval Reserve, 1206 W.S.A. For most conspicuous gallantry when the Allied drifter line in the Straits of Otranto was attacked by Austrian light cruisers on the morning of the 15th May, 1917. When hailed by an Austrian cruiser at about 100 yards' range and ordered to stop and abandon his drifter the Gowan Lea, Skipper Watt ordered full speed ahead, and called upon his crew to give three cheers and fight to the finish. The cruiser was then engaged, but after one round had been fired, a shot from the enemy disabled the breech of the drifter's gun. The gun's crew, however, stuck to the gun, endeavouring to make it work, being under heavy fire all the time. After the cruiser had passed on, Skipper Watt took the Gowan Lea alongside the badly-damaged drifter Floandi and assisted to remove the dead and wounded." A newspaper says: " Skipper Watt, V.C., Fraserburgh, was presented from the public of Fraserburgh with a purse of Treasury notes in celebration of the high distinction he has won for bravery." Mr. George Walker, managing owner of Skipper Watt's vessel, the Gowan Lea, presented him with a gold hunting watch and chain.

London Gazette, 6 Sept. 1917.—" War Office, 6 Sept. 1917. His Majesty the King has been graciously pleased to approve of the award of the Victoria Cross to the undermentioned Officers, Non-commissioned Officers and Men."

ACKROYD, HAROLD, Capt., served in the European War in France. He was awarded the Victoria Cross [London Gazette, 6 Sept. 1917: " Harold Ackroyd, M.C., M.D., Temporary Capt., Royal Army Medical Corps, attached 6th Battn. Royal Berkshire Regt. For most conspicuous bravery. During recent operations Capt. Ackroyd displayed the greatest gallantry and devotion to duty. Utterly regardless of danger, he worked continuously for many hours up and down and in front of the line tending the wounded and saving the lives of officers and men. In so doing he had to move across the open under heavy machine-gun, rifle and shell fire. He carried a wounded officer to a place of safety under very heavy fire. On another occasion he went some way in front of our advanced line and brought in a wounded man under continuous sniping and machine-gun fire. His heroism was the means of saving many lives, and provided a magnificent example of courage, cheerfulness and determination to the fighting men in whose midst he was carrying out his splendid work. This gallant officer has since been killed in action."

BEST-DUNKLEY, BERTRAM, Capt., served in the European War, and was awarded the Victoria Cross [London Gazette, 6 Sept. 1917]: " Bertram Best-Dunkley, Capt. (Temporary Lieut.-Colonel), late Lancashire Fusiliers. For most conspicuous bravery and devotion to duty when in command of his battalion, the leading waves of which, during an attack, became disorganized by reason of rifle and machine-gun fire at close range from positions which were believed to be in our hands. Lieut.-Colonel Best-Dunkley dashed forward, rallied his leading waves, and personally led them to the assault of these positions, which, despite heavy losses, were carried. He continued to lead his battalion until all their objectives had been gained. Had it not been for this officer's gallant qnd determined action it is doubtful if the left of the brigade would have reached its objectives. Later in the day, when our position was threatened, he collected his battalion headquarters, led them to the attack, and beat off the advancing enemy. This gallant officer has since died of wounds."

COLYER-FERGUSSON, THOMAS RIVERSDALE, Second Lieut. (Acting Capt.), served in the European War in Flanders, and was awarded the Victoria Cross [London Gazette, 6 Sept. 1917]: " Thomas Riversdale Colyer-Fergusson, Second Lieut. (Acting Capt.), 2nd Battn. Northamptonshire Regt. For most conspicuous bravery, skilful leading and determination in attack. The tactical situation having developed contrary to expectation, it was not possible for his company to adhere to the original plan of deployment, and, owing to the difficulties of the ground and to enemy wire, Capt. Colyer-Fergusson found himself with a Sergeant and five men only. He carried out the attack, nevertheless, and succeeded in capturing the enemy trench and disposing of the garrison. His party was then threatened by a heavy counter-attack from the left front, but this attack he successfully resisted. During this operation, assisted by his Orderly only, he attacked and captured an enemy machine gun and turned it on the assailants, many of whom were killed and a large number were driven into the hands of an adjoining British unit. Later, assisted only by his Sergeant, he again attacked and captured a second enemy machine gun, by which time he had been joined by other portions of his company, and was enabled to consolidate his position. The conduct of this officer throughout forms an amazing record of dash, gallantry and skill, for which no reward can be too great having regard to the importance of the position won. This gallant officer was shortly afterwards killed by a sniper."

BYE, ROBERT, Sergt., served in the European War, and was awarded the Victoria Cross [London Gazette, 6 Sept. 1917]: " Robert Bye, No. 939, Sergt., 1st Battn. Welsh Guards. For most conspicuous bravery. Sergt. Bye displayed the utmost courage and devotion to duty during an attack on the enemy's position. Seeing that the leading waves were being troubled by two enemy blockhouses, he, on his own initiative, rushed at one of them and put the garrison out of action. He then rejoined his company and went forward to the assault of the second objective. When the troops had gone forward to the attack on the third objective, a party was detailed to clear up a line of blockhouses which had been passed. Sergt. Bye volunteered to take charge of this party, accomplished his object, and took many prisoners. He subsequently advanced to the third objective, capturing a number of prisoners, thus rendering invaluable assistance to the assaulting companies. He displayed throughout the most remarkable initiative."

ANDREW, LESLIE WILTON, Sergt., 2nd Battn. Wellington Regt., New Zealand Infantry, was born at Ashurst, New Zealand, on 23 March, 1897, son of William Jeffrey Andrew, afterwards Head Master of the Wanganui East School, and Frances Hannah, his wife. He was educated at Wanganui Boys' High School and Wanganui Collegiate School. He was for some time in a lawyer's office, and then entered the service of the Railway Department in Wellington. He was a Sergeant in the No. 7 Company of Railway Engineers. He enlisted on 25 Oct. 1915, and proceeded to Egypt, landing there in June, 1916. He proceeded to France in Aug. 1916. He received his promotion to Sergeant on 1 Aug. 1917. Sergt. Andrew has been twice wounded, and three times buried in the debris caused by high-explosive shells. He was present at the battles of the Somme, Messines and La Basse Ville. He was awarded the Victoria Cross [London Gazette, 6 Sept. 1918]: " Leslie Wilton Andrew, Sergt., 2nd Battn. Wellington Regt., New Zealand Infantry. For most conspicuous bravery when in charge of a small party in an attack on the enemy's position. His objective was a machine-gun post, which had been located in an isolated building. On leading his men forward he encountered unexpectedly a machine-gun post which was holding up the advance of another company; he immediately attacked, capturing the machine gun and killing several of the crew. He then continued the attack on the machine-gun post which had been his original objective. He displayed great skill and determination in his disposition, finally capturing the post, killing several of the enemy, and putting the remainder to flight. Sergt. Andrew's conduct throughout was unexampled for cool daring, initiative and fine leadership, and his magnificent example was a great stimulant to his comrades."

Leslie Wilton Andrew.

A newspaper correspondent writes:

" Sergt. Leslie Wilton Andrew, whose winning of the V.C. was described in yesterday's cables, is a Wanganui boy, son of Mr. W. J. Andrew, Head Master of the Wanganui East School. Sergt. Andrew, who is an old boy of the Wanganui Collegiate School, was formerly in the service of the Railway Department in Wellington. He had his first instruction in the art of soldiering as a member of the Avenue School Cadets, under the present Head Master, Mr. James Aitken. In a telegram to Mr. Andrew, Sir James Allen (Minister of Defence) states that official advice has not yet come to hand regarding the announcement of the award of the Victoria Cross to Leslie Wilton Andrew, but there is little doubt that it refers to Mr. Andrew's son, and the Minister heartily congratulates Mr. Andrew on the high honour gained by his son, not alone for himself, but for his family and for the New Zealand Expeditionary Force. Sir James Allen adds: ' All New Zealanders must read with quickened pulse the story of Sergt. Andrew's fine achievement, and I am sure you must be very proud of having such a gallant son. I earnestly hope he may be spared and restored to you safely later on.' Sergt. Andrew is but twenty years of age. He enlisted and went into the non-coms. camp of the 11th Reinforcements, and passed for a commission before he was 19. He was kept back a month, and again sat for a commission, succeeding in passing a second time, and then went away with the 12ths, receiving only his certificate. He held marksman's and signaller's badges, and the Star for the best shot in his company. Sergt. Andrew has been twice wounded, and has three times been buried in the debris caused by high-explosive shells. He was wounded last Sept. in the Somme fighting, and received another wound later on. The gallant sergeant's friends will hear of his distinction with great pleasure, and will join in congratulations both to himself and to his family on his being awarded the much-coveted decoration of the little bronze cross ' for Valour.' Under date, 13 Aug., the official New Zealand correspondent thus describes the feat by which Sergt. Andrew won his V.C.:—' In all the recent fighting in which New Zealanders took part there was nothing finer than the heroism and leadership of a Wellington Regiment sergeant, detailed to attack and capture an enemy machine-gun position in an isolated estaminet. He led his men forward, only to come unexpectedly upon another gun that was sending out a continuous stream of bullets and stopping the advance on the left. He immediately attacked this position, killed several of the crew, and put the rest to flight. After this adventure he was able to get only three of his men together. With these three he proceeded to gain his ultimate objective. Observing that a frontal attack would mean the destruction of his little band, he led the party through some thistles and attacked from the rear. As soon as they were close enough the intrepid four threw bombs at the crew and rushed upon the Germans, killing four, putting the rest to flight, and capturing the gun and the position. Leaving two men behind to remove the gun, the sergeant took the remaining man with him and advanced on a reconnoitring expedition as far as the British barrage would permit. He brought back valuable information. Throughout the whole of these operations enemy shells were pounding into the position, and there was much machine-gun and rifle fire.' "

DAVIES, JAMES LLEWELLYN, Corpl., served in the European War, and was awarded the Victoria Cross [London Gazette, 6 Sept. 1915]: " James Llewellyn Davies, No. 31161, Corpl., late Royal Welsh Fusiliers (Nantymoel, Glamorgan). For most conspicuous bravery. During an attack on the enemy's line, this non-commissioned officer pushed through our own barrage and, single-handed, attacked a machine-gun emplacement after several men had been killed in attempting to take it. He bayoneted one of the machine-gun crew and brought in another man, together with the captured gun. Corpl. Davies, although wounded, then led a bombing party to the assault of a defended house, and killed a sniper who was harassing his platoon. This gallant non-commissioned officer has since died of wounds received during the attack."

BARRATT, THOMAS, Private, served in the European War, and was awarded the Victoria Cross [London Gazette, 6 Sept. 1917]: " No. 17114, Private Thomas Barratt, late South Staffordshire Regt. (Tipton). For most conspicuous bravery when as Scout to a patrol he worked his way towards the enemy line with the greatest gallantry and determination, in spite of continuous fire from hostile snipers at close range. These snipers he stalked and killed. Later his patrol was similarly held up, and again he disposed of the snipers. When during the subsequent withdrawal of the patrol it was observed that a party of the enemy were endeavouring to outflank them, Private Barratt at once volunteered to cover the retirement, and this he succeeded in accomplishing. His accurate shooting caused many casualties to the enemy, and prevented their advance. Throughout the enterprise he was under heavy machine-gun and rifle fire, and his splendid example of coolness and daring was beyond all praise. After safely regaining our lines, this very gallant soldier was killed by a shell."

McINTOSH, GEORGE, Private, served in the European War, and was awarded the Victoria Cross [London Gazette, 6 Sept. 1917]: " No. 265579, George McIntosh, Private, 1/6th Battn. Gordon Highlanders (Buckie, Banffshire). For most conspicuous bravery when, during the consolidation of a position, his company came under machine-gun fire at close range. Private McIntosh immediately rushed forward under heavy fire, and reaching the emplacement, he threw a Mills grenade into it, killing two of the enemy and wounding a third. Subsequently, entering the dug-out, he found two light machine guns, which he carried back with him. His quick grasp of the situation and the utter fearlessness and rapidity with which he acted undoubtedly saved many of his comrades, and enabled the consolidation to proceed unhindered by machine-gun fire. Throughout the day the cheerfulness and courage of Private McIntosh was indomitable, and to his fine example in a great measure was due the success which attended his company."

WHITHAM, THOMAS, Private, served in the European War, and was awarded the Victoria Cross [London Gazette, 6 Sept. 1917]: " Thomas Witham, Private, 1st Battn. Coldstream Guards. For most conspicuous bravery when during an attack an enemy machine gun was seen to be enfilading the battalion on the right. Private Witham, on his own initiative, immediately worked his way from shell hole to shell hole through our own barrage, rushed the machine gun, and although under a very heavy fire, captured it, together with an officer and two other ranks. The bold action on the part of Private Witham was of great assistance to the battalion on the right, and undoubtedly saved many lives and enabled the whole line to advance." An amendment in the London Gazette of 26 Sept. 1917, reads as follows : " No. 15067, Private Thomas Whitham, V.C., Coldstream Guards, is now correctly described. The surname was incorrectly published in Gazette of 6th instant (award Victoria Cross)."

London Gazette, 14 Sept. 1917.—" His Majesty the King has been graciously pleased to approve of the award of a Bar to the Victoria Cross to Capt. Noel Godfrey Chavasse, V.C., M.C., late R.A.M.C., attached Liverpool Regt."

Bar to V.C. :—Though severely wounded early in the action whilst carrying a wounded soldier to the dressing station, he refused to leave his post, and for two days not only continued to perform his duties, but in addition went out repeatedly under heavy fire to search for and attend to the wounded who were lying out. During these searches, although practically without food during this period, worn with fatigue and faint with his wound, he assisted to carry in a number of badly wounded men over heavy and difficult ground. By his extraordinary energy and inspiring example he was instrumental in rescuing many wounded who would have otherwise undoubtedly succumbed under the bad weather conditions. This devoted and gallant officer subsequently died of his wounds. Capt. Chavasse was formerly on the staff of the Royal Southern Hospital, Liverpool. He joined the R.A.M.C. on the outbreak of war, and shortly after proceeding to the front was awarded the Military Cross. His V.C. award was gazetted in Oct. last. He was born in 1884, and was educated at Liverpool and Oxford Universities. His twin brother is serving with the forces as a Chaplain.

London Gazette, 14 Sept. 1917.—" War Office, 14 Sept. 1917. His Majesty the King has been graciously pleased to approve of the award of the Victoria Cross to the undermentioned Officers, Non-commissioned Officers and Men."

COFFIN, CLIFFORD, Lieut.-Colonel (Temporary Brigadier-General), was born on 10 Feb. 1870, at Blackheath, son of Lieut.-General Sir Isaac Campbell Coffin, K.C.S.I., and of Catherine Eliza, daughter of Major Shepherd, H.E.I.C.S. He was educated at Haileybury College and Royal Military Academy, Woolwich, and joined the Army on 17 Feb. 1888, as Second Lieutenant, Royal Engineers. He served in the European War in Flanders. He was created a Companion of the Distinguished Service Order, his name appearing in the New Year's Honours List [London Gazette, 1 Jan. 1917]. He was awarded the Victoria Cross [London Gazette, 14 Sept. 1917. Date of Act of Bravery : 31 July, 1917]: " Clifford Coffin, D.S.O., Lieut.-Colonel (Temporary Brigadier-General), Royal Engineers. For most conspicuous bravery and devotion to duty. When his command was held up in attack owing to heavy machine-gun and rifle fire from front and right flank, and was establishing itself in a forward shell-hole line, he went forward and made an inspection of his front posts. Though under the heaviest fire from both machine guns and rifles, and in full view of the enemy, he showed an utter disregard of personal danger, walking quietly from shell hole to shell hole, giving advice generally and cheering the men by his presence. His very gallant conduct had the greatest effect on all ranks, and it was largely owing to his personal courage and example that the shell-hole line was held in spite of the very heaviest fire. Throughout the day his calm courage and cheerfulness exercised the greatest influence over all with whom he came in contact, and it is generally agreed that Brigadier-General Coffin's splendid example saved the situation, and had it not been for his action the line would certainly have been driven back." He was awarded a Bar to the Distinguished Service Order [London Gazette, 26 July, 1918] " for his work as a Brigade Commander in covering the withdrawal of the remainder of the division, and on one occasion commanding the infantry of the division with marked success, and on all occasions inspiring all ranks with his own courage and example." The Bar to the D.S.O. was chiefly awarded for services in March, 1918.

GRAHAM, JOHN REGINALD NOBLE, Capt., was born at 1, Alipore Lane, Calcutta, 17 Sept. 1892, son of John Frederick Noble Graham (East India Merchant), and his wife, Irene Maud Graham (née Campbell) : and grandson of Sir J. H. N. Graham, 1st Baronet. He was educated at Cheam School ; Eton, and Trinity College, Cambridge, and steered the Trial Eights at Eton (1910) and Cambridge (1911). He

John R. N. Graham.

joined the 9th Battn. Argyll and Sutherland Highlanders 15 Jan. 1915 ; was seconded to the Machine Gun Corps 22 June, 1916, after two years with the 9th Battn. Argyll and Sutherland Highlanders at home ; became Captain, 9th Argyll and Sutherland Highlanders, 13 July, 1916, and sailed for Mesopotamia in Sept. 1916, serving there till wounded on 22 April, 1917, with the 136th Machine Gun Coy. He was awarded the Victoria Cross for his service at Istabulat, Mesopotamia, whilst operating with the 56th Rifles (Frontier Force), Indian Army, in command of a section, 136th Coy. Machine Gun Corps. The decoration was gazetted 14 Sept. 1917 : " John Reginald Noble Graham, Capt., Machine Gun Corps. For most conspicuous bravery, coolness and resource when in command of a Machine Gun Section. Lieut. Graham accompanied his gun across open ground under very heavy rifle and machine-gun fire, and when his men became casualties he assisted in carrying the ammunition. Although twice wounded he continued during the advance to control his guns, and was able with one gun to open an accurate fire on the enemy, who were massing for a counter-attack. This gun was put out of action by the enemy's rifle fire, and he was again wounded. The advancing enemy forced him to retire, but before doing so he further disabled his gun, rendering it useless. He then brought a Lewis gun into action with excellent effect till all the ammunition was expended. He was again severely wounded, and forced, through loss of blood, to retire. His valour and skilful handling of his guns held up a strong counter-attack, which threatened to roll up the left flank of the brigade, and thus averted what might have been a critical situation." This took place on 22 April, 1917, on the second day of the fighting near Istabulat, the culminating point in the operations which led to the fall of Samana, the railhead about 70 miles north of Baghdad. The brigade found the Turks hastily but fairly securely dug in about three or four miles from the position from which they had been driven out the previous day. The enemy's left rested on the Tigris, and their right stretched beyond the Baghdad–Samana Railway. It was from the railway embankment that they developed the counter-attack about five o'clock in the evening. He was wounded, and sent to India ; returned to Mesopotamia 7 Oct. 1917. In Jan. 1918, he was transferred to Palestine from the 136th Coy., of which he afterwards got command with the rank of Major (16 Feb. 1918), commanding this company till Oct. 1918, when he came home, and was demobilized.

HEWITT, DENIS GEORGE WYLDBORE, Lieut., served in the European War, and was awarded the Victoria Cross [London Gazette, 14 Sept. 1917]: " Denis George Wyldbore Hewitt, Second Lieut., late Hampshire Regt. When his first objective had been captured he reorganized his company, and moved forward towards his objective. While waiting for the barrage to lift he was hit by a piece of shell, which exploded the signal lights in his haversack and set fire to his equipment and clothes. Having extinguished the flames, in spite of his wound and the severe pain he was suffering, he led forward the remains of the company under very heavy machine-gun fire and captured and consolidated his objective. He was subsequently killed by a sniper while inspecting the consolidation and encouraging his men."

COOPER, EDWARD, Sergt., No. 2794, was born 4 May, 1896, at Stockton-on-Tees, and is the son of William Edward Cooper, and his wife, Annie. He was educated at Bailey Street Council Schools, and played football for the school team for two years, and in local teams on leaving school. He is also fond of swimming. He was occupied as Assistant on a distributing fruit cart of the local Co-operative Society on the outbreak of the European War, but on 3 Sept. 1914, enlisted in the Army, and in the following July was drafted to France with the 12th King's Royal Rifle Corps. He was promoted Sergeant 13 March, 1917. Langemarck, Flanders, was the scene of the brave action which gained him the Victoria Cross [London Gazette, 14 Sept. 1917]: " Edward Cooper, No. R.2794, Sergt., King's Royal Rifle Corps. Date of Act of Bravery : 16 Aug. 1917. For most conspicuous bravery and initiative in attack. Enemy machine guns from a concrete blockhouse, 250 yards away,

Edward Cooper.

were holding up the advance of the battalion on his left, and were also causing heavy casualties to his own battalion. Sergt. Cooper, with four men, immediately rushed towards the blockhouse, though heavily fired on. About 100 yards distant he ordered his men to lie down and fire at the blockhouse. Finding this did not silence the machine guns, he immediately rushed forward, straight at them, and fired his revolver into an opening in the blockhouse. The machine guns ceased firing and the garrison surrendered. Seven machine guns and forty-five prisoners were captured in this blockhouse. By this magnificent act of courage he undoubtedly saved what might have been a serious check to the whole advance, at the same time saving a great number of lives." His own account is as follows : " When the advance was held up by concrete blockhouses in the village of Langemarck, I, along with a Lance-Corporal, who was wounded on reaching the blockhouse, rushed forward a distance of about

250 yards, and forced the garrison of forty-four men and an officer to surrender, along with seven machine guns ; and came out of the attack uninjured, after being buried on the 17 Aug. 1917, along with five men, one of whom was dead when dug out." Major-General W. Douglas-Smith, C.B., wrote as follows : " The Major-General 20th (Light) Division has received a report of the gallant conduct of R.2794, Sergt. E. Cooper, 12th Battn. K.R.R.C., on 16 Aug. 1917, in silencing the enemy machine guns and helping to capture seven machine guns and forty prisoners near Langemarck, and he wishes to congratulate him on his fine behaviour." On the announcement of the award, Sergt. Cooper's mother was asked if he had told her anything about his doings. " Oh, no," she said, " he would never do that. He is not that kind of boy ; he would be too much afraid that anyone would make a fuss about it. He writes regularly, but all we get to know from him is that he has been very busy." He is a good son and brother, conscientious and a lover of his home, and is very popular among his friends. He was decorated by His Majesty the King 26 Sept. 1917 ; commissioned 25 June, 1918, as a Second Lieutenant, 12th King's Royal Rifle Corps ; returned to France 4 Sept. 1918 ; demobilized 27 Jan. 1919. Lieut. Cooper was awarded the Médaille Militaire (French) 10 Sept. 1918. A local newspaper says : " Stockton is proud of its V.C. It is claimed that in no part of the country has any particular locality responded more loyally to the call of the King than has the district of Portrack, Stockton, where there are whole streets of households represented in either the Army or Navy—more particularly the Navy—and it is, therefore, most fitting that this high distinction should come to that part of the town." Nine out of the twelve V.C.'s awarded in this Honours List fell to Northcountrymen.

EDWARDS, ALEXANDER, Sergt., comes from Lossiemouth. He served in the European War, and was awarded the Victoria Cross [London Gazette, 14 Sept. 1917] : " No. 265473, Alexander Edwards, Sergt., 1/6th Battn. Seaforth Highlanders (Lossiemouth). For most conspicuous bravery in attack, when, having located a hostile machine gun in a wood, he, with great dash and courage, led some men against it, killed all the team and captured the gun. Later, when a sniper was causing casualties, he crawled out to stalk him, and although badly wounded in the arm, went on and killed him. One officer only was now left with the company, and realizing that the success of the operations depended on the capture of the furthest objective, Sergt. Edwards, regardless of his wound, led his men on till his objective was captured. He subsequently showed great skill in consolidating his position, and very great daring in personal reconnaissance. Although again twice wounded on the following day, this very gallant N.C.O. maintained throughout a complete disregard for personal safety, and his high example of coolness and determination engendered a fine fighting spirit in his men."

GRIMBALDESTON, WILLIAM HENRY, Sergt. (Acting Company Quartermaster-Sergt.), was born on 19 Sept. 1889, at Blackburn, Lancashire, son of Thomas and Isabella Grimbaldeston. He was educated at St. Alban's School, Blackburn, and joined the Army on 3 Sept. 1914. He served in the European War in Flanders, and was awarded the Victoria Cross [London Gazette, 14 Sept. 1917] : " No. 13531, William Henry Grimbaldeston, Sergt. (Acting Company Quartermaster-Sergt.), 1st Battn. King's Own Scottish Borderers. For most conspicuous bravery in attack. Noticing that the unit on his left was held up by enemy machine-gun fire from a blockhouse, though wounded he collected a small party to fire rifle grenades on this blockhouse. He then got a volunteer to assist him with rifle fire. In spite of very heavy fire from the blockhouse he pushed on towards it, and made for the entrance, from which he threatened with a hand grenade the machine-gun teams inside the blockhouse. These he forced to surrender one after another. The extraordinary courage and boldness of Company Quartermaster-Sergt. Grimbaldeston resulted in his capturing thirty-six prisoners, six machine guns and one trench mortar, and enabled the whole line to continue its advance." Sergt. Grimbaldeston enlisted for duration of war, and has since been demobilized (19 Jan. 1919). He was awarded the Croix de Guerre in Sept. 1917. He is married, and has a son, William Grimbaldeston.

Wm. H. Grimbaldeston.

REES, IVOR, Sergt., comes from Llanelly. He served in the European War, and was awarded the Victoria Cross [London Gazette, 14 Sept. 1917] : " No. 20002, Sergt. Ivor Rees, South Wales Borderers (Llanelly). A hostile machine gun opened fire at close range, inflicting many casualties. Leading his platoon forward by short rushes, Sergt. Rees gradually worked his way round the right flank to the rear of the gun position. When he was about 20 yards from the machine gun he rushed forward towards the team, shot one and bayoneted another. He then bombed the large concrete emplacement, killing five and capturing 30 prisoners, of whom two were officers, in addition to an undamaged machine gun."

SKINNER, JOHN, Company Sergt.-Major, comes from Pollokshields, Glasgow. He served in the European War, and was awarded the Victoria Cross [London Gazette, 14 Sept. 1917] : " John Skinner, Sergt. (Acting Company Sergt.-Major,) King's Own Scottish Borderers. While his company was attacking machine-gun fire opened on the left flank, delaying the advance. Although Company Sergt.-Major Skinner was wounded in the head, he collected six men and with great courage and determination worked round the left flank of three blockhouses from which the machine-gun fire was coming, and succeeded in bombing and taking the first blockhouse single-handed ; then, leading his six men towards the other two

blockhouses, he skilfully cleared them, taking 60 prisoners, three machine guns and two trench mortars. Skinner is a native of Glasgow, who joined the Army when 16, and has seen 17 years' service. He was wounded three times in the South African War, and has been wounded six times in the present war. He took part in the heavy fighting of the early days. When the King last visited Glasgow Skinner was decorated with the D.C.M."

MAYSON, TOM FLETCHER, Corpl. (L.-Sergt.), Royal Lancaster Regt., is the son of Mrs. Mayson, who keeps the village inn at Silecroft, Cumberland. He was formerly employed on a farm, and joined the Army as a Private in the Royal Lancaster Regt. He served in the European War, and was awarded the Victoria Cross [London Gazette, 14 Sept. 1917] : " No. 200717, Corpl. (L.-Sergt.) Tom Fletcher Mayson, Royal Lancaster Regt. For most conspicuous bravery and devotion to duty, when, with the leading wave of the attack his platoon was held up by machine-gun fire from a flank. Without waiting for orders, L.-Sergt. Mayson at once made for the gun, which he put out of action with bombs, wounding four of the team. The remaining three of the team fled, pursued by L.-Sergt. Mayson, to a dug-out, into which he followed them, and disposed of them with his bayonet. Later, when clearing up a strong point, this non-commissioned officer again tackled a machine gun single-handed, killing six of the team. Finally, during an enemy counter-attack, he took charge of an isolated post, and successfully held it until ordered to withdraw, as his ammunition was exhausted. He displayed throughout the most remarkable valour and initiative." In writing to his mother about a fortnight before the award of the Victoria Cross, he modestly said : " I have been recommended for great honour, but I leave you to guess what it is."

EDWARDS, WILFRID, Private, comes from Leeds. He served in the European War in Flanders, and was awarded the Victoria Cross [London Gazette, 14 Sept. 1917] : " No. 13303, Private Wilfrid Edwards, 7th Battn. King's Own Yorkshire Light Infantry (Leeds). For most conspicuous bravery when under heavy machine-gun and rifle fire from a strong concrete fort. Having lost all his company officers, without hesitation he dashed forward at great personal risk, bombed through the loopholes, surmounted the fort, and waved to his company to advance. By his splendid example he saved a most critical situation at a time when the whole battalion was held up and a leader urgently needed. Three officers and thirty other ranks were taken prisoners by him in the fort. Later Private Edwards did most valuable work as a runner, and he eventually guided most of the battalion out through very difficult ground. Throughout he set a splendid personal example to all, and was utterly regardless of danger."

LOOSEMORE, ARNOLD, Sergt., comes from Sheffield. He served in the European War, and was awarded the Victoria Cross [London Gazette, 14 Sept. 1917] : " Arnold Loosemore, No. 15805, Sergt., 8th Battn. West Riding Regt. For most conspicuous bravery and initiative during the attack on a strongly-held enemy position. His platoon having been checked by heavy machine-gun fire, he crawled through partially-cut wire, dragging his Lewis gun with him, and single-handed dealt with a strong party of the enemy, killing about twenty of them, and thus covering the consolidation of the position taken up by his platoon. Immediately afterwards his Lewis gun was blown up by a bomb, and three enemy rushed for him, but he shot them all with his revolver. Later he shot several enemy snipers, exposing himself to heavy fire each time. On returning to the original post he also brought back a wounded comrade under heavy fire at the risk of his life. He displayed throughout an utter disregard of danger." He was welcomed by Alderman A. Cattell, Lord Mayor of Sheffield, in the Town Hall on his return.

London Gazette, 17 Oct. 1917.—" War Office, 17 Oct. 1917. His Majesty the King has been graciously pleased to approve of the award of the Victoria Cross to the undermentioned Officer, Non-commissioned Officers and Men."

PARSONS, HARDY FALCONER, Second Lieut., was born near Leicester. He was the eldest son of the Rev. J. A. Ash Parsons, Pastor of Old King Street Wesleyan Chapel, Bristol, and was killed in action on 21 Aug. 1917, at the age of 20. Before joining the Army he was a student in the Bristol University, taking the medical course with a view to becoming a Medical Missionary. He had just come on the circuit plan, and had had but one opportunity of preaching. His text was " The Second Mile ; " his own career was a noble exposition of it. He never shirked a duty, nor (says an intimate friend) turned away from a call to service. He deliberately chose a commission in an infantry regiment, because it meant the utmost in the way of sacrifice. The gallant young officer came West when his father left Arnside, in Westmorland, for Bristol, and commenced his educational career at Kingswood School, later going to Bristol University, where he joined the O.T.C., and later he was in the 6th Officer Cadet Battn. at Oxford. To him this war was hateful, as all war was hateful, but he conceived it to be his duty to obey the summons of the Crown. With no illusions, but with a full sense of duty, he set about his military training. Like so many others of his generation, he was led to enlist by motives of the purest patriotism and chivalry. To his refined, gentle spirit, the idea of war was utterly repellent. Nevertheless, though assured on high medical authority of his unfitness for military service, so eager was he to take his share in the

Hardy Falconer Parsons.

struggle for right that he insisted on offering himself to the recruiting authorities, by whom, to his own great relief, he was at once accepted. Second Lieut. Parsons won the Victoria Cross for his heroic self-sacrifice. The award was announced in the London Gazette of 17 Oct. 1917: "Temporary Second Lieut. Hardy Falconer Parsons, late Gloucester Regt. For most conspicuous bravery during a night attack by a strong party of the enemy on a bombing post held by his command. The bombers holding the block were forced back, but Second Lieut. Parsons remained at his post, and single-handed, and although severely scorched and burnt by liquid fire, he continued to hold up the enemy with bombs until severely wounded. This very gallant act of self-sacrifice and devotion to duty undoubtedly delayed the enemy long enough to allow of the organization of a bombing party, which succeeded in driving back the enemy before they could enter any portion of the trenches. This gallant officer succumbed to his wounds."

CARMICHAEL, JOHN, Sergt., served in the European War, and was awarded the Victoria Cross [London Gazette, 17 Oct. 1917]: "No. 34795, John Carmichael, Sergt., North Staffordshire Regt. (Glasgow). For most conspicuous bravery. When excavating a trench, Sergt. Carmichael saw that a grenade had been unearthed and had started to burn. He immediately rushed to the spot, and shouting to his men to get clear, placed his steel helmet over the grenade and stood on the helmet. The grenade exploded and blew him out of the trench. Sergt. Carmichael could have thrown the bomb out of this trench, but he realized that by doing so he would have endangered the lives of the men working on the top. By this splendid act of resource and self-sacrifice Sergt. Carmichael undoubtedly saved many men from injury, but it resulted in serious injury to himself."

HOBSON, FREDERICK, Sergt., served in the European War, and was awarded the Victoria Cross [London Gazette, 17 Oct. 1917]: "No. 57113, Frederick Hobson, Sergt., late 20th Battn. Canadian Infantry. During a strong enemy counter-attack a Lewis gun in a forward post in a communication trench leading to the enemy lines was buried by a shell, and the crew, with the exception of one man, killed. Sergt. Hobson, though not a gunner, grasping the great importance of the post, rushed from his trench, dug out the gun, and got it into action against the enemy, who were now advancing down the trench and across the open. A jamb caused the gun to stop firing. Though wounded, he left the gunner to correct the stoppage, rushed forward at the advancing enemy, and with bayonet and clubbed rifle, single-handed held them back until he himself was killed by a rifle shot. By this time, however, the Lewis gun was again in action, and, reinforcements shortly afterwards arriving, the enemy were beaten off. The valour and devotion to duty displayed by this non-commissioned officer gave the gunner the time required to again get the gun into action, and saved a most serious situation." "Thirty Canadian V.C.'s" (published by Messrs. Skeffington) is written by Capt. Theodore Goodridge Roberts, New Brunswick Regt., late Headquarters, Canadian Army Corps, British Expeditionary Force; Private Robin Richards, late of the Princess Patricia's Canadian Light Infantry, British Expeditionary Force, and Private Stuart Martin, late No. 5 Canadian General Hospital, Salonika. They all three belong to the Canadian War Records Office. Their account of Private F. Hobson on pages 50–53 of their book is as follows: "The men of the 20th Canadian Battn. lay down in their trenches before Hill 70, on the night of the 14th Aug. 1917, in a soft drizzle of rain. They were to take part in the attack on the hill early next morning, and the artillerymen behind had already trained their guns on the enemy trenches, ready to let loose the bellow of destruction when the word was passed. Hill 70 lies near the La Bassée–Lens road, in the vicinity of Loos, the village of Cité St. Auguste on its right, Bois Hugo and Chalk Pit on its left. Its sides and crest are scarred with trenches and bruised by much shelling. The Allies have taken it from the Germans, and have been pushed out of it by the Germans more than once. On the 14th Aug., 1917, it was in German hands. Precisely at 4.25 o'clock on the morning of the 15th, just as a red streak smeared the horizon, the word for which the Canadians had been waiting was given, and the artillery barrage fell like a hammer-stroke on the German front line. For six minutes it pounded the trenches into pulp, then lifted to a hundred yards farther on, tore a line of devastation there for another six minutes, lifted again in another hundred yards' stride, and so continued its work of destruction at similar intervals. As the curtain of our shells rose from the German front line, the men of the 20th Battn., with other units, leaped from their jumping-off trenches and waded across No Man's Land. They found the Germans—all who remained of the front-line garrison—shaken, bruised, more or less subdued. Where they surrendered they were taken prisoners; where they resisted they were killed. In Cowley trench only one enemy machine gun was working and soon it was out-flanked and captured. In Commotion trench an emplacement was in action. It was smothered. Sergt. Frederick Hobson and some men of A company went forward up the enemy trench known as Nabob Alley. They bombed their way along, beating back the Germans, who retreated slowly and grudgingly; and, having conquered about seventy yards of the trench, they established a post at that point. The objectives of the battalion elsewhere were also gained and the position was consolidated. The attack was a success. All this happened on the 15th Aug. But to take a position is one thing: to hold it is another. For three days the Germans kept probing various parts of the line, hoping to find a spot which would yield. At 1.40 a.m. on the 18th, their artillery opened a heavy bombardment on the whole Canadian Corps front and for half an hour shells were rained on every part of the line. The general bombardment slackened for a short time, during which the village of St. Pierre received an avalanche of gas-shells; and at twelve minutes past four o'clock every gun the enemy could muster opened again on the front. The concentration of artillery was nerve-racking. It was almost demoralizing. Up in the advance posts the majority of the Lewis gun positions were obliterated, men and

guns being buried in the vast upheavals. Twenty minutes after the shelling began the headquarters of the 20th Battn. was hit by a heavy shell and vanished. Every wire leading to the posts was cut, every light extinguished. And in the darkness and confusion came word from the battalion stationed on the right of the 20th to the effect that the Germans were out in No Man's Land, coming to attack. Sergt. Hobson in his trench saw the grey figures swarming across the open ground. The Lewis guns had all been wiped out except one—and as this one was being brought into action a German shell landed beside it. When the smoke cleared, only one man of the crew remained alive, and he and the gun were buried in the debris. Hobson was no gunner, but he knew the importance of the position. He raced forward, seized an entrenching tool and hauled the dazed survivor out of the mud. 'Guess that was a close call,' said the survivor, Private A. G. Fuller. 'Guess so: let's get the gun out,' replied Hobson. They began to dig. Across the open ground came the Germans, firing at the two men as they advanced. A bullet hit Hobson, but he took no notice of his wound. Together he and Fuller got the gun into position and opened up on the Germans, who were now pouring down the trench. They were holding the enemy well when the gun jammed. Hobson picked up his rifle. 'I'll keep them back,' he said to Fuller, 'if you fix the gun!' He ran towards the advancing enemy, a lonely, wounded, desperate man against many, and with bayonet and clubbed rifle barred their passage. No man knows how many Germans were killed by Sergt. Hobson in that fierce encounter; dead and wounded were heaped in front of him when a shout from Fuller intimated that the gun was again ready for action. And just at that moment a German pushed his rifle forward and fired point-blank at the Canadian Horatius. As Hobson fell Gunner Fuller pressed the trigger of his Lewis gun and threw a stream of death into the German mob. A few minutes later reinforcements from B company took the enemy in the flank, and chased them back across No Man's Land; and the machine guns of B Company cleaned them up as they ran. They found Sergt. Frederick Hobson where he had fallen, still grasping his deadly rifle. His enemies were sprawled around him, silent witnesses to his prowess. His heroism had saved the situation—and he had fought his last fight."

MOYNEY, JOHN, L.-Sergt., was born 8 Jan. 1895, at Rathdowney, son of James Moyney and Bridget Moyney (née Butler). He was educated at Rathdowney, and joined the Army on 6 April, 1915, as a Private in the Irish Guards. He served in the European War, and was awarded the Victoria Cross [London Gazette, 17 Oct. 1917]: "John Moyney, No. 7708, L.-Sergt., 2nd Battn. Irish Guards. For most conspicuous bravery when in command of fifteen men forming two advanced posts. In spite of being surrounded by the enemy, he held his post for ninety-six hours, having no water and little food. On the morning of the fifth day a large force of the enemy advanced to dislodge him. He ordered his men out of their shell holes, and taking the initiative, attacked the advancing enemy with bombs, while he used his Lewis gun with great

John Moyney.

effect from a flank. Finding himself surrounded by superior numbers, he led back his men in a charge through the enemy, and reached a stream which lay between the posts and the line. Here he instructed his party to cross at once, while he and Private Woodcock remained to cover their retirement. When the whole of his force had gained the south-west bank unscathed, he himself crossed under a shower of bombs. It was due to endurance, skill and devotion to duty shown by this non-commissioned officer that he was able to bring his entire force safely out of action." Private John Moyney left England for France 5 Oct. 1915; was made Lance-Corporal 20 Dec. 1915; promoted Lance-Sergeant 8 Oct. 1916, and Sergeant 27 Sept. 1917, after he had won the V.C. He is married, and his wife's name is Bridget, and they have one child named Mary.

The following are some letters received by Sergt. Moyney:

"War Office,
"Whitehall, S.W.,
"19 Oct. 1917.

"DEAR SERGT. MOYNEY,

"I don't know you personally, and don't suppose you know me, but I want to send you a line just to offer you my very heartiest congratulations on your Victoria Cross, and on the splendid gallantry by which you won it, and to tell you how very proud I am to be serving in the same regiment as yourself. Wishing you all sorts of good luck, and again my most sincere congratulations,

"Faithfully yours,
"P. S. LONG-INNES, Major,
"1st Battn. Irish Guards."

"Regimental Headquarters,
"Irish Guards,
"Buckingham Gate,
"London, S.W.1.
"31 Oct. 1917.

"DEAR SERGT. MOYNEY,

"I am writing to offer you my hearty congratulations and best wishes on your being awarded the Victoria Cross.

"Yours was a splendid as well as being a most gallant action, and you have brought very great credit on the Irish Guards, as well as on yourself.

"Naturally I am especially glad about it as you are a Queen's County man.

"I only hope you will have the best of good luck, and will live long to enjoy your well-deserved reward. With best wishes,

"Yours faithfully,
"DE VESCI, Major,
"Regimental Adjutant, Irish Guards."

"Dunraven Castle,
"St. Brides Major,
"Glamorgan,
"19 Oct. 1917.

"SERGT. MOYNEY,
"I *must* write to congratulate you on your glorious achievements. I feel prouder than ever of being Irish and belonging to the Irish Guards. Deeds like yours and Private Woodcock's keep one's courage and spirits up here at home. It is hard sitting at home reading and waiting.

"God keep you.
"Yours,
"AILEEN ARDEE."

"2nd Battn. Royal Inniskilling Fusiliers,
"36th (Ulster) Base Depot,
"Camp 19,
"Havre,
"B.E.F.,
"18 Oct. 1917.

"MY DEAR MOYNEY,
"Congratulations, old man, on your V.C. Judging by how you worked under me as a Private and Lance-Corporal in No. 12 Platoon, I knew you would do well. There is nothing to lick the Irish, especially the Irish Guards. May you live long to enjoy it, and I wish you further success and the very best of luck.

"Yours sincerely,
"M. KENNEDY."

DAY, SIDNEY JAMES, Corpl., served in the European War, and was awarded the Victoria Cross [London Gazette, 17 Oct. 1917]: "No. 15092, Sidney James Day, Corpl., 11th Battn. Suffolk Regt. (Norwich). For most conspicuous bravery. Corpl. Day was in command of a bombing section detailed to clear a maze of trenches still held by the enemy; this he did, killing two machine-gunners and taking four prisoners. On reaching a point where the trench had been levelled, he went alone and bombed his way through to the left, in order to gain touch with the neighbouring troops. Immediately on his return to his section a stick bomb fell into a trench occupied by two officers (one badly wounded) and three other ranks. Corpl. Day seized the bomb and threw it over the trench, where it immediately exploded. This prompt action undoubtedly saved the lives of those in the trench. He afterwards completed the clearing of the trench, and establishing himself in an advanced position, remained for 66 hours at his post, which came under intense hostile shell and rifle-grenade fire. Throughout the whole operations his conduct was an inspiration to all."

ROOM, FREDERICK G., Private, served in the European War, and was awarded the Victoria Cross [London Gazette, 17 Oct. 1917]: "No. 8614, Private (Acting L.-Corpl.) Frederick G. Room, Royal Irish Regt. (Bristol). For most conspicuous bravery when in charge of his company stretcher-bearers. During the day the company had many casualties, principally from enemy machine guns and snipers. The company was holding a line of shell-holes and short trenches. L.-Corpl. Room worked continuously under intense fire, dressing the wounded and helping to evacuate them. Throughout this period, with complete disregard for his own life, he showed unremitting devotion to his duties. By his courage and fearlessness he was the means of saving many of his comrades' lives."

BROWN, HARRY, Private, served in the European War, and was awarded the Victoria Cross [London Gazette, 17 Oct. 1917]: "Harry Brown, Private, No. 226353, late Canadian Infantry Battn. For most conspicuous bravery, courage and devotion to duty. After the capture of a position, the enemy massed in force and counter-attacked. The situation became very critical, all wires being cut. It was of the utmost importance to get word back to Headquarters. This soldier and one other were given the message with orders to deliver the same at all costs. The other messenger was killed. Private Brown had his arm shattered, but continued on through an intense barrage until he arrived at the close support lines and found an officer. He was so spent that he fell down the dug-out steps, but retained consciousness long enough to hand over his message, saying, 'Important message.' He then became unconscious, and died in the dressing station a few hours later. His devotion to duty was of the highest possible degree imaginable, and his successful delivery of the message undoubtedly saved the loss of the position for the time and prevented many casualties." "Thirty Canadian V.C.'s" (published by Messrs. Skeffington) thus describes (pages 43–46) Private Harry Brown's heroic death: "Most men who have won the Victoria Cross have gained it by some act of violent, passionate valour. Private Harry Brown, No. 226353, of the 10th Battn., won it by suppressing the impulse to violence. Whilst others on the same field of battle were earning the decoration in the impetuous fury of assault Harry Brown was earning it by the terrible, pitiless restraint which he imposed on his emotions. His was the supreme courage of self-control, the silent valour of abnegation. The 10th Battn. took part in the attack on Hill 70, near Loos, which began on the 15th Aug. 1917, and lasted for several days. Before midnight of the 14th the battalion was in position, and at 4.25 a.m. the attack began.

The first German line was captured in face of fierce opposition, the fighting continuing intermittently throughout the day; but the position was held. During the night, attempts were made to consolidate the new line; but the 7th and the 8th Battns. were in difficulties, and the 10th Battn. was ordered next morning to move to their assistance. This second attack began at four o'clock on the afternoon of the 15th. Chalk Pit, the redoubt on the left of Hill 70, was assaulted by 'A,' 'B' and 'C' Companies. 'A' Company encountered terrible enemy machine-gun fire when within two hundred yards of the pit, and were forced to take cover in shell-holes for a time. After a short rest the position was captured in a rush, the waves of attackers, carried forward by the impetus of the advance, reaching a trench seventy-five yards beyond Chalk Pit. The German occupants were all either killed or captured. The position was being consolidated when Sergt. J. Wennevold and a party of men of 'C' Company went out to reinforce a post to the right of the new battalion front in order to protect the flank from a counter-attack. Consolidation of that position was terrible work. To the men who tried to dig into the hard, chalky soil that attempt must always remain a nightmare. They could make little impression on the earth. In one part of the front the result of the previous night's labour was a trench scarcely two feet deep, blunted tools and aching hands and backs. While the work was in progress the Germans poured a hurricane of fire from machine guns and field guns on the position. Men were killed and wounded faster than others could take their places. The crisis of that day and night of endurance and agony came at a quarter to five o'clock in the afternoon, when the Germans were seen massing for an attack on the right. By this time every wire to headquarters was cut by the enemy artillery. If they were allowed to attack, the companies in the trench would be annihilated and the hard-earned position lost. The situation was desperate. Only one chance of averting disaster remained. A runner must get through with a message to our artillery asking them to smash the German attack. Private Harry Brown and another runner undertook to deliver the message. When they set out on their desperate mission a hostile barrage was raking the open behind the newly occupied ground, the enemy's intention being to prevent supports coming up. The messengers had to get through this curtain of fire, a curtain under which nearly every yard of ground was being churned into a mess or torn up savagely in tons and tossed on high as if by some unseen Brobdingnagian hand. They had gone but a little way on their adventurous journey when one was killed and Brown was left, the only link between his isolated battalion and its hope of succour. If he failed to get through his comrades would be wiped out to a man. He continued to stumble along, sinking into new, smoking craters, now and then up to the waist, dragging himself out and crawling through the debris, lying still for short intervals till the shock of the explosions had passed. Flying missiles hit him and shattered an arm. He was bleeding and exhausted. He sat down, dazed and uncomprehendingly. But his will forced him to his feet again. He staggered onward towards the support lines, walking like a man in a dream, his brain in constant dark motion, his thoughts in a flux even as the ground on which he strove for a footing. It was a pained, dreary thing, sore and weary, that kept doggedly crawling and staggering on through the intensity of the shrapnel and the high explosive. His strength ran from him with the blood from his mangled arm. His steps were automatic. The last part of the journey was the worst. It was his *Via Dolorosa*. . . . An officer standing in a dug-out in the support line was peering out at the devastation which the enemy artillery was spreading so prodigally. Shells rained on every side, the earth shuddered and shrank at every blow. But the telephone to headquarters was working. A dark form crawled out of the ruin and stumbled towards the dug-out. It was a soldier—hatless, pale, dirty, haggard, one arm hanging limp and bloody by his side, his clothing torn and stained. He reached the steps of the dug-out, and seeing the officer, tried to descend. But his strength was gone, his limbs refused to act. He fell down the short stairway, spent—utterly spent and dying. The officer lifted him gently and brought him into the dug-out and laid him down. Then Brown handed over his precious slip of paper. 'Important message,' he whispered. And Private Harry Brown lay back and drifted into unconsciousness. He died a few hours later in the dressing station."

BUTLER, WILLIAM BOYNTON, Private, lives with his parents at Royal Terrace, Royal Road, Hunslet Carr, Leeds. He was educated at St. Oswald's School, Hunslet Carr, and joined the Army on 9 Jan. 1915, as a Private in the 17th Battn. West Yorkshire Regt. (Bantams). He received his training at Ilkley. He was attached to the 106th Trench Mortar Battery. For his services in the European War he was awarded the Victoria Cross [London Gazette, 17 Oct. 1917]: "William Boynton Butler, No. 17/1280, Private, West Yorkshire Regt. For most conspicuous bravery when in charge of a Stokes gun in trenches which were being heavily shelled. Suddenly one of the fly-off levers of a Stokes shell came off and fired the shell in the emplacement. Private Butler picked up the shell and jumped to the entrance of the emplacement, which at that moment a party of infantry were passing. He shouted to them to hurry past, as the shell was going off, and, turning round, placed himself between the party of men and the live shell, and so held it till they were out of danger. He then threw the shell on to the parados, and took cover in the bottom of the trench. The shell exploded almost on leaving his hand, greatly damaging the trench. By extreme good luck Private Butler was contused only. Undoubtedly his great presence of mind and disregard of his own life saved the lives of the officer and men in the emplacement and the party which was passing at the time." He was invested by the King at Buckingham Palace on 5 Dec. 1917. He had visited his home on the previous day, but his parents had gone up to London for the investiture, and, owing to a misunderstanding, this Victoria Cross hero found his house locked up and had to sit on the doorstep until recognized. He was given a civic reception at Leeds on the day after the investiture. He was awarded the French Croix de Guerre.

WOODCOCK, THOMAS, Private, was born at Wigan; was educated at St. Patrick's Roman Catholic School, Wigan, and later was employed in a colliery. He enlisted in the Irish Guards on 26 May, 1915. He served in the European War in France from 1915, and was awarded the Victoria Cross [London Gazette, 17 Oct. 1917]: "Thomas Woodcock, No. 8387, Private, 2nd Battn. Irish Guards. For most conspicuous bravery and determination. He was one of a post commanded by L.-Sergt. Moyney, which was surrounded. The post held out for ninety-six hours, but after that time was attacked from all sides in overwhelming numbers and was forced to retire. Private Woodcock covered the retirement with a Lewis gun, and only retired when the enemy had moved round and up to his post, and were only a few yards away. He then crossed the river, but hearing cries for help behind him, returned and waded into the stream amid a shower of bombs from the enemy, and rescued another member of the party. The latter he then carried across the open ground in broad daylight towards our front line regardless of machine-gun fire that was opened on him." The Mayor and citizens of Wigan accorded him a public welcome, and he was presented with a sum of over £200, the result of a public subscription, and with an illuminated address. Private Woodcock married and had three children. Private Woodcock, V.C., was killed in action on 27 March, 1918.

London Gazette, 2 Nov. 1917.—"Admiralty, 2 Nov. 1917. The King has been graciously pleased to approve of the award of the following Honours, Decorations and Medals for services in action with enemy submarines. To receive the Victoria Cross."

BONNER, CHARLES GEORGE, Lieut., was born on 29 Dec. 1884, in Shuttington, Warwickshire, youngest son of Samuel Bonner, J.P., Farmer, of Aldridge, near Walsall, and Jane Bonner, daughter of Charles Hellaby, of Bramcote Hall, Warwickshire.

Charles George Bonner.

He was educated at Sutton Coldfield and Coleshill Grammar Schools, and on H.M. Training Ship Conway. He served his apprenticeship in the Invermark of Aberdeen, and at twenty-one was awarded a Master Mariner's certificate. He visited every part of the globe, and was in the Incemore when she collided with the Kaiser Wilhelm off the Isle of Wight. At the outbreak of war he was in Antwerp, but succeeded in reaching England. He entered the Royal Naval Division as an able-bodied seaman in Sept. 1914, and in Dec. 1914, was transferred to the Royal Naval Reserve with the rank of Sub-Lieutenant. He served in the European War, and won great distinction in actions with submarines. For these he was awarded the Distinguished Service Cross in July, 1917, and later was awarded the highest honour of all—the Victoria Cross. This was announced in the "Court Circular" issued from York Cottage, Sandringham, on Sunday, 8 Oct 1917: "Lieut. Charles George Bonner, R.N.R., had the honour of being received by the King, when His Majesty conferred on him the Victoria Cross in recognition of his conspicuous gallantry and consummate coolness and skill in action with an enemy submarine." This was the second occasion on which the conferring of the Victoria Cross has been made known through the "Court Circular" before the award was officially announced in the London Gazette, and Lieut. Bonner is probably the only man who has received the Victoria Cross from the hands of the Sovereign on a Sunday. The award was announced in the London Gazette of 2 Nov. 1917: "To receive the Victoria Cross. Charles George Bonner, Lieut., D.S.C., R.N." Lieut. Bonner was married on 17 June, 1917, at Walsall Parish Church, to Alice Mabel, daughter of the late Thomas Partridge, of Walsall. His chief recreations are shooting and riding.

PITCHER, ERNEST, Petty Officer, Royal Navy, was born on 31 Dec. 1887, at Mullion, Cornwall, son of Mr. George Pitcher and of Mrs. Sarah Pitcher. He was educated at Swanage Board School, and joined the Royal Navy on 22 July, 1903; promoted Petty Officer 1 Aug. 1915. He served in the European War in H.M. ships King George V., Q 5, Parkhurst and Dunraven. He was awarded the Victoria Cross [London Gazette, 2 Nov. 1917]: "Ernest Pitcher, Petty Officer, O.N. 227029 (Po.)." Petty Officer Pitcher was selected by the crew of a gun of one of His Majesty's ships to receive the Victoria Cross under Rule 13 of the Royal Warrant dated the 29th Jan. 1856. Lieut.-Commander H. Auten says in "'Q' Boat Adventures" (published by Herbert Jenkins), when describing this encounter: "Although the submarine escaped, this was undoubtedly Capt. Campbell's greatest action—in fact, the greatest action of any 'Q' boat against a submarine. It was

Ernest Pitcher.

fought by a ship's company of heroes who had entire confidence in their commander, and the conduct of Lieut. Bonner was worthy of the V.C. he afterwards received from the King. For four hours he had been in the thick of the fighting, twice he had been blown up, and each time he rose, if not smiling, at least with a pluck and determination that must have had a very considerable influence upon the crew. A second V.C.

was awarded to Petty Officer Ernest Pitcher, the gunlayer of the after-gun. In his report to the Admiralty, Capt. Campbell wrote of his officers and men, ' Surely such bravery is hard to equal,' and he concluded with the words, ' We desired nothing better, not only to destroy the enemy and save the ship, but also to show ourselves worthy of the Victoria Cross which was recently bestowed upon the ship.'"

CRISP, THOMAS, Skipper, was born on 28 April, 1875, at Lowestoft, son of Mr. William Crisp and of Mrs. M. A. Crisp. He was educated at St. John's School, Lowestoft, and joined the Royal Naval Reserve. He

Thomas Crisp.

served in the European War, in Special Service Ships known as Armed Smacks. He was awarded the Victoria Cross [London Gazette, 8 Nov 1917]: "Posthumous award of the Victoria Cross. Skipper Thomas Crisp, R.N.R., 10055, D.A. (killed in action)." The following account of his heroic death is taken from a newspaper cutting: "Never was the Victoria Cross more fittingly awarded than to Skipper Crisp. Here is the story of the sinking of his smack, the Nelson, from an authoritative source: On an August afternoon, at about a quarter to three, the trawl was shot from the Nelson, and the smack was on the port tack. The skipper was below packing fish, one hand was on deck cleaning fish for the next morning's breakfast, and then the skipper came on deck, saw an object on the horizon, examined it closely, and sent for his glasses. Almost directly he sang out : ' Clear for action. Submarine.' He had scarcely spoken when a shot fell about a hundred yards away on the port bow. The motor-man got to his motor ; the deck hand dropped his fish and went to the ammunition room ; the other hands, at the skipper's orders, ' Let go your gear ; let go the warp, and put a dan on one end of it.' Meanwhile the gunlayer held his fire until the skipper said, ' It is no use waiting any longer ; we will have to let them have it.' Away in the distance the submarine sent shell after shell at the smack, and about the fourth shot the shell went through the port bow just below the water-line, before we fired, and then the skipper shoved her round. There was no confusion on board, not even when the seventh shell struck the skipper, passed through his side, through the deck, and out through the side of the ship. The second hand at once took charge of the tiller, and the firing continued. All the time water was pouring into the ship, and she was sinking. One man, the gunlayer, went to the skipper to see if he could render first aid, but it was obvious that he was mortally wounded. ' It's all right, boy ; do your best,' said the skipper, and then, to the second hand : ' Send a message off.' This was the message : ' Nelson being attacked by submarine. Skipper killed. Send assistance at once.' All this time the smack was sinking, and only five rounds of ammunition were left. The second hand went to the skipper lying there on the deck, and heard him say, ' Abandon ship. Throw the books overboard.' He was asked by his son then if they should lift him into the boat, but his answer was : ' Tom, I'm done ; throw me overboard.' He was too badly injured to be moved, and they left him there on his deck, with a smile on his lips, though with both legs hanging off, and took to the small boat, and about a quarter of an hour afterwards the Nelson went down by the head. It was just drawing into dusk and the crew of the boat pulled all that night. Towards morning the wind freshened and blew them out of their course. They pulled all that day, and had a pair of trousers and a large piece of oilskin fastened to two oars to attract attention, and once a vessel was sighted and once a group of mine-sweepers, but they passed out of sight. At night the weather became finer, and through that night they pulled until daybreak, when, at 10.30 a.m., they found a buoy and made fast to it. By afternoon they were sighted and rescued. The second hand, who took charge of the tiller after the skipper had been shot down, was his son, and so the great tradition goes on." Lieut.-Commander H. Auten, V.C., tells in "'Q' Boat Adventures" the marvellous story of the great fight put up by the Nelson and the death of her heroic skipper.

London Gazette, 8 Nov. 1917.—"War Office, 8 Nov. 1917. His Majesty the King has been graciously pleased to approve of the award of the Victoria Cross to the undermentioned Officers and Non-commissioned Officers and Men."

LEARMONTH, OKILL MASSEY, M.C., Major, served in the European War. He was promoted a non-commissioned officer on the field, and later was given a commission ; was awarded the Military Cross ; was promoted to Captain and to Acting Major. He was awarded the Victoria Cross [London Gazette, 8 Nov. 1917]: "Okill Massey Learmonth, M.C., Capt. (Acting Major), late 2nd Battn. Canadian Infantry. For most conspicuous bravery and exceptional devotion to duty. During a determined counter-attack on our new positions, this officer, when his company was momentarily surprised, instantly charged and personally disposed of the attackers. Later, he carried on a tremendous fight with the advancing enemy. Although under intense barrage fire and mortally wounded, he stood on the parapet of the trench, bombed the enemy continuously and directed the defence in such a manner as to infuse a spirit of utmost resistance into his men. On several occasions this very brave officer actually caught bombs thrown at him by the enemy and threw them back. When he was unable by reason of his wounds to carry on the fight, he still refused to be carried out of the line, and continued to give instructions and invaluable advice to his junior officers, finally handing over all his duties before he was evacuated from the front line to the hospital where he died." A newspaper cutting says : " There is a poignant romance connected with the late Capt. Learmonth, of the Canadian Forces, who came from Quebec, and whose award of the Victoria Cross was in the Gazette published yesterday. Capt. Learmonth went to France as a ranker with the Canadians, and was promoted a non-com. on the field. He received his commission just over twelve months ago, and about the same time married Miss S. W. Tamarche, who belonged to his own province, and was attached to the Canadian Nursing Service. Mrs. Learmonth was invalided back to Canada some time back, and her gallant husband died of wounds three months ago. Capt. Learmonth also held the Military Cross. He was in the Canadian Government service prior to the war." " Thirty Canadian V.C.'s " (published by Messrs. Skeffington) says (pages 55–57) : " With the Military Cross already in his possession, Capt. O. M. Learmonth, of the 2nd Battn., was one of that small number of Canadians who won the highest decoration during the capture of Hill 70 in Aug. 1917. The weather in which that attack began on the 15th of the month was unsettled and sultry. The weather in which the fighting ended on the 18th of the month was clear and sunny. It was during the fighting on the latter date that Learmonth died. On the 15th, the 2nd, 3rd, 4th and 5th Canadian Brigades attacked the hill, and the German defences about Cité St. Laurent. For the next two days they held the new trenches against constant counter-attacks and under incessant bombardment from every gun the Germans could bring to bear on the position. At midnight on the 16th the 2nd Battn. relieved the troops of the 3rd Brigade in the trenches from Chalk Pit down Hugo Trench to Hurray Alley. During the whole of the 17th the German bombardment continued with an even intensity which made the position one pandemonium for the men of the 2nd Battn. The line was very thinly held. The whole strength of the battalion was only 614 souls when day broke on the 18th. That was the day which knew the climax of the situation. At four o'clock in the morning the German artillery opened a terrific fire on the whole battalion front line and supports. For forty minutes the bombardment continued at full pressure. Then it lifted and the German troops attacked, using liquid fire. On the left wing the Germans succeeded in entering the trenches held by No. 4 Company ; but a bombing party was at once organized, and they were driven out again, leaving behind a Flammenwerfer and a considerable number of dead. Learmonth (who was then Acting Major) was in command of Nos. 2 and 3 Companies. He saw that a number of the Germans, after their advance had been checked within a few yards of our trenches, had found shelter to some extent in a small wood ; and to rout them out of the wood a bombing party from No. 3 Company was sent forward. They bombed the Germans out of the wood and down a trench named Horse Alley, driving them into the open, where our snipers and machine-gunners engaged them and cleaned them up. Throughout the whole of the attack Learmonth showed what his Commanding Officer has named a ' wonderful spirit.' Absolutely fearless, he so conducted himself that he imbued those with whom he came into contact with some of his personality. When the barrage started he was continually with his men and officers, encouraging them and making sure that no loophole was left through which the enemy could gain a footing. When the attack was launched against the thin Canadian line, Learmonth seemed to be everywhere at once. When the situation was critical, he took his turn at throwing bombs. He was wounded twice, but carried on as if he were perfectly fit and whole. He was wounded a third time, his leg this time being broken, but still he showed the same indomitable spirit. Lying in the trench, he continued to direct his men, encouraging them, cheering them, advising them. At a quarter past six that morning the battalion headquarters received word that Learmonth was badly wounded and was being carried out of the line on a stretcher ; but the enemy attack had been repulsed. He had waited till he saw the finish. They brought him down to headquarters, and, lying on his stretcher, he gave valuable information to the officers there before he was taken to hospital. He died shortly afterwards—the man who would not give in."

REYNOLDS, HENRY, Capt., was born on 16 Aug. 1881, at Whilton, Northamptonshire, son of the late Thomas Henry Reynolds and Tryphena, only daughter of Thomas Godsden. He joined the Army on 5 Oct. 1914, as Second Lieutenant. He was promoted to Lieutenant 4 May, 1917, and to Captain 2 July, 1917. He served in the European War in France, and was awarded the Military Cross [London Gazette, June, 1917] : " For a series of actions on 12 April, 1917, which meant being under artillery, machine-gun and rifle fire for a considerable time." He was awarded the Victoria Cross [London Gazette, 8 Nov. 1917] : " Henry Reynolds, M.C., Temporary Capt., 12th Battn. Royal Scots. For most conspicuous bravery when his company, in attack and approaching their final objective, suffered heavy casualties from enemy machine guns and from an enemy ' pillbox,' which had been passed by the first wave. Capt. Reynolds reorganized his men who were scattered, and then proceeded alone by rushes from shellhole to shell-hole, all the time being under heavy machine-gun fire. When near the ' pill-box ' he threw a grenade, intending that it should go inside but the enemy had blocked the entrance. He then crawled to the entrance and forced a phosphorous grenade inside. This set the place on fire and caused the death of three of the enemy, while the remainder, seven or eight, surrendered with two machine guns. Afterwards, though wounded, he continued to lead his company against another objective, and captured

Henry Reynolds.

it, taking seventy prisoners and two more machine guns. During the whole attack the company was under heavy machine-gun fire from the flanks, but, despite this, Capt. Reynolds kept complete control of his men."

The following is a letter from his Commanding Officer :

" Capt. H. Reynolds served under my command in France during the greater part of 1917.

" He is one of the most capable and conscientious officers that I have ever had under my command ; he is attentive to every detail in connection with his company ; has a sound knowledge of training and interior economy, and his company was always clean, smart, well-turned-out, thoroughly trained and efficient, and always willing and ready to take part in any action.

" Capt. Reynolds is physically a powerful man, capable of standing any amount of strain, and his unusual sense of duty was so pronounced that in action he was invaluable.

" He was awarded the Victoria Cross for a series of actions on 20 Sept. 1917, at Zonnebeke, everyone of which meant facing a terrible fire for a considerable period, and the Military Cross for a similar series on 12 April, 1917.

" I can confidently recommend him for a commission in the Regular Army, and suggest that a special preference be given to him, so that his commission may be dated back as early as possible.

(Signed) " J. A. S. RITSON,
" Lieut.-Colonel,
" 12th Battn. The Royal Scots,
" 7 March, 1919."

He married, 3 Oct. 1905, Gwendolen, third daughter of William Jones, and has three children : Thomas Henry William, Gwendolen Tryphena and Velia Rosemary.

BIRKS, FREDERICK, Second Lieut., served in the European War in France, and was awarded the Victoria Cross [London Gazette, 8 Nov. 1917] : " Frederick Birks, Second Lieut., late 6th Battn. Australian Imperial Force. For most conspicuous bravery in attack when, accompanied by only a corporal, he rushed a strong point which was holding up the advance. The corporal was wounded by a bomb, but Second Lieut. Birks went on by himself, killed the remainder of the enemy occupying the position, and captured a machine gun. Shortly afterwards he organized a small party, and attacked another strong point which was occupied by about twenty-five of the enemy, of whom many were killed and an officer and fifteen men captured. During the consolidation this officer did magnificent work in reorganizing parties of other units which had been disorganized during the operations. By his wonderful coolness and personal bravery Second Lieut. Birks kept his men in splendid spirits throughout. He was killed at his post by a shell whilst endeavouring to extricate some of his men who had been buried by a shell."

Frederick Birks.

COLVIN, HUGH, Second Lieut., was born on 18 March, 1887, at Burnley, Lancashire, son of Hugh Colvin, of Aberdeenshire. He was educated at Hatherlow Day School, Cheshire, and joined the Army as Private in Sept. 1908, in the 8th (King's Royal Irish) Hussars ; served one year in England, and in India with the regiment till 1914 ; served in France with the regiment till 1917, gaining the rank of Lance-Sergeant ; commissioned April, 1917, on the field to 2nd Battn. The Cheshire Regt., attached 9th (Service) Battn. ; Company Commander March, 1918. He was awarded the Victoria Cross [London Gazette, 8 Nov. 1917] : " Hugh Colvin, Second Lieut., Cheshire Regt., attached 9th Battn. For most conspicuous bravery in attack. When all the officers of his company except himself—and all but one in the leading company—had become casualties and losses were heavy, he assumed command of both companies and led them forward under heavy machine-gun fire with great dash and success. He saw the battalion on his right held up by machine-gun fire, and led a platoon to their assistance. Second Lieut. Colvin went on with only two men to a dug-out. Leaving the men on top, he entered it alone and brought up fourteen prisoners. He then proceeded with his two men to another dug-out, which had been holding up the attack by rifle and machine-gun fire and bombs. This he reached, and, killing or making prisoners of the crew, captured the machine gun. Being then attacked from another dug-out by fifteen of the enemy under an officer, one of his men was killed and the other wounded. Seizing a rifle, he shot five of the enemy, and, using another as a shield, he forced most of the survivors to surrender. This officer cleared several other dug-outs alone or with one man, taking about fifty prisoners in all. Later, he consolidated his position with great skill, and personally wired his front under heavy close-range sniping in broad daylight, when all others had failed to do so. The complete success of the attack in this part of the line was mainly due to Second

Hugh Colvin.

Lieut. Colvin's leadership and courage." Second Lieut. Colvin received a civic welcome at Chester, and later in the same day was entertained at the Depôt of the Cheshire Regt. He was appointed Supervisor of Physical Training Army Gymnastic Staff; Assistant Superintendent Jan. 1919, and Chief Instructor School of Physical Training, Army of the Rhine, with the rank of Major, May, 1919. He is an all-round athlete, good at distance running and gymnastics.

MOORE, MONTAGUE SHADWORTH SEYMOUR, Second Lieut. served in the European War in France. He was awarded the Victoria Cross [London Gazette, 8 Nov. 1917]: "Montague Shadworth Seymour Moore, Second Lieut., attached 15th Battn. Hampshire Regt. For most conspicuous bravery in operations necessitating a fresh attack on a final objective which had not been captured. Second Lieut. Moore at once volunteered for this duty, and dashed forward at the head of some seventy men. They were met with heavy machine-gun fire from a flank which caused severe casualties, with the result that he arrived at his objective—some 500 yards on—with only a sergeant and four men. Nothing daunted, he at once bombed a large dug-out and took twenty-eight prisoners, two machine guns and a light field gun. Gradually more officers and men arrived, to the number of about sixty. His position was entirely isolated, as the troops on the right had not advanced, but he dug a trench and repelled bombing attacks throughout the night. The next morning he was forced to retire a short distance. When opportunity offered he at once reoccupied his position, re-armed his men with enemy rifles and bombs, most of theirs being smashed, and beat off more than one counter-attack. Second Lieut. Moore held this post under continual shell fire for thirty-six hours, until his force was reduced to ten men, out of six officers and 130 men who had started the operation. He eventually got away his wounded, and withdrew under cover of a thick mist. As an example of dashing gallantry and cool determination this young officer's exploit would be difficult to surpass."

HANNA, ROBERT, Company Sergt.-Major, joined the Canadian Military Forces, and served in the European War in France. He was awarded the Victoria Cross [London Gazette, 8 Nov. 1917]: "Robert Hanna, Company Sergt.-Major, No. 75361, 29th Battn. Canadian Infantry. For most conspicuous bravery in attack, when his company met with most severe enemy resistance and all the company officers became casualties. A strong point, heavily protected by wire and held by a machine gun, had beaten off three assaults of the company with heavy casualties. This Warrant Officer, under heavy machine-gun and rifle fire, coolly collected a party of men, and leading them against this strong point, rushed through the wire and personally bayoneted three of the enemy and brained the fourth, capturing the position and silencing the machine gun. This most courageous action displaying courage and personal bravery of the highest order at this most critical moment of the attack, was responsible for the capture of a most important tactical point, and but for his daring action and determined handling of a desperate situation the attack would not have succeeded. Company Sergt.-Major Hanna's outstanding gallantry, personal courage and determined leading of his company is deserving of the highest possible reward." "Thirty Canadian V.C.'s" (published by Messrs. Skeffington) says of Hanna (pages 47–49): "When the first big attack was made by the Canadian troops on Hill 70 on the 15th Aug. 1917, the 29th (Vancouver) Battn. moved forward to the support of the 5th Brigade, remaining in the area for three days while the battle raged in the forward lines. The first stage of the attack ended on the 18th; and that night, under severe shelling, the 29th Battn. took over Commotion trench from the junction of Caliper and Conductor trenches to the junction of Nabob Alley and Commotion trench. On the morning of the 21st Aug. the second stage of the offensive was resumed. It was then the battalion took an active part in the struggle. The opening of the second phase was timed for 4.35 a.m. At 1 a.m. the companies began to move into the assembly positions. At 3.15 a.m. the scouts reported that the tapes had been laid, the companies were getting into position uneventfully and none of the enemy was to be seen. But about 4.10 a.m. the German artillery began to plump shells along the front of the parapet, increasing the intensity of the barrage towards 4.30, when a sudden deluge of 'fish-tails' descended on the trenches. Accompanying this bombardment was a curious kind of bomb, square in shape, which exploded with a great flame and sent out a dense, suffocating smoke. One of these dropped in the trench occupied by 'D' Company, wounding practically every man in a platoon. While attempts were being made to clear the debris, Sergt. Croll, who was stationed near the corner of Nun's Alley and Commotion trench, heard the word passed along: 'Heine has broken through the 25th and is coming down the trench.' Croll collected five unwounded men and kept the advancing Germans at bay by bombing them till reinforcements arrived from the 28th Battn. and drove the enemy out. Major Grimmett, who was in command of 'A' Company in support, hearing the bombing and concluding that something had gone wrong with 'D' Company, sent forward a platoon under Capt. Abbott. Our opening barrage by this time had begun and was moving forward. Abbott's platoon took up the fight, carried it into Nun's Alley and established a block there. The other companies—'B,' 'C' and the remainder of 'D'—had gone forward behind the barrage. One platoon of 'D' Company, which attempted an overland attack on Nun's Alley, was wiped out almost to a man by machine-gun fire. 'C' Company, attacking in the centre, was badly mauled. The left platoon was swept away by German machine-gun fire before it reached its objective. The right platoon had almost reached its objective—Cinnebar trench—when it ran into a strong enemy machine-gun post surrounded by barbed wire. Lieut. Carter, who had already been wounded, was killed in an attempt to drive the Germans out of this stronghold. Lieut. Sutherland, on the extreme right, got into Cinnebar trench and gave the order for rapid fire on a party of Germans who were advancing overland. In the act of picking up a rifle he was mortally hit by a sniper's bullet. Sergt. Stevens, who then took command, was lifting Sutherland's rifle when he, too, was shot through the head. A corporal took the sergeant's place. A moment later he also was killed. The remainder of the men fought on desperately till a platoon of the 28th Battn. came to their aid. In the meantime 'B' Company, to which Sergt.-Major Hanna belonged, had reached the objective in Cinnebar trench. Believing that all was well with 'C' Company, Lieut. Gordon, the commander, was about to send off the prearranged signal when it was discovered that the signal cartridges were wet. Before a substitute could be found word was brought that 'C' Company, on the left, was being badly smashed, all the officers having been killed. Lieut. McKinnon was sent along with a bombing party to aid 'C' Company. He was killed just as he joined the fight. Gordon then went along to the relief of the company on his left, after ordering Lieut. Montgomery to get a party of snipers outside the trench so that they could take toll of the enemy. Gordon was badly wounded in the arm. Lieut. Montgomery was soon afterwards killed by a German sniper. The leadership fell upon Sergt.-Major Hanna. Hanna saw that the crux of the position was a German post protected by a heavy wire and armed with a machine gun. He collected a party of his men and led them against the post amid a hail of rifle and machine-gun fire. Rushing through the wire he bayoneted three of the Germans, brained a fourth, and overthrew the machine gun. The redoubt was captured. The Germans arrived in force and counter-attacked. Hanna, who was now short of bombs, built a block. Again and again the enemy tried to rush his position; but he and his handful of men held it until they were relieved later that day. Next day the battalion frontage was taken over by another Canadian unit, and the 29th went back to a well-earned rest."

KNIGHT, ALFRED JOSEPH, Sergt., was born on 24 Aug. 1888, at Ladywood, Birmingham, son of Joseph Knight and of Annie Knight. He was educated at St. Philip's Grammar School, Edgbaston, Birmingham, and joined the Army on 26 Oct. 1914, in 2/8th Battn. London Regt. (The Post Office Rifles). He served in the European War in France, and was awarded the Victoria Cross [London Gazette, 8 Nov. 1917]: "Alfred Joseph Knight, No. 370995, Sergt., 2/8th Battn. London Regt. (Post Office Rifles). For most conspicuous bravery and devotion to duty during the operations against the enemy positions. Sergt. Knight did extraordinarily good work, and showed exceptional bravery and initiative when his platoon was attacking an enemy strong point and came under very heavy fire from an enemy machine gun. He rushed through our own barrage, bayoneted the enemy gunner, and captured the position single-handed. Later, twelve of the enemy, with a machine gun, were encountered in a shell-hole. He again rushed forward by himself bayoneted two and shot a third and caused the remainder to scatter. Subsequently, during the attack on a fortified farm, when entangled up to his waist in mud and seeing a number of the enemy firing on our troops, he immediately opened fire on them without waiting to extricate himself from the mud, killing six of the enemy. Again, noticing the company on his right flank being held up in their attack on another farm, Sergt. Knight collected some men and took up a position on the flank of this farm, from where he brought a heavy fire to bear on the farm, as a result of which the farm was captured. All the platoon officers of the company had become casualties before the first objective was reached, and this gallant N.C.O. took command of all the men of his own platoon and of the platoons without officers. His energy in consolidating and reorganizing was untiring. His several single-handed actions showed exceptional bravery, and saved a great number of casualties in the company. They were performed under heavy machine-gun and rifle fire, and without regard to personal risk, and were the direct cause of the objectives being captured." After dispersal (5 Feb. 1919) Sergt. Knight was gazetted Second Lieutenant Nottinghamshire and Derbyshire Regt. 17 March, 1919 [London Gazette, 26 July, 1919].

Alfred Joseph Knight.

OCKENDON, JAMES, Sergt., was born at Portsmouth on 10 Dec. 1889, son of Alfred Robert Ockendon, Plasterer, and Mary Ann Ockendon, daughter of Charles Verrall, of Portsmouth. He was educated at St. Agatha's School, Portsmouth, and joined the Army on 22 May, 1909, as a Private in the 1st Battn. Royal Dublin Fusiliers. He served in the European War. He landed in Gallipoli with his battalion on 25 April, 1915, and served continuously from then until 30 April, 1918, in Gallipoli and France. He was recommended for bravery on many occasions; was awarded the Military Medal 6–7 Aug. 1917, for services in France; awarded the Belgian Croix de Guerre in Jan. 1918, and was awarded the Victoria Cross [London Gazette, 10 Nov. 1917]: "James Ockendon, Sergt., No. 10605, Royal Dublin Fusiliers (Southsea). For most conspicuous bravery in attack. When acting as Company Sergeant-Major and seeing the platoon on the right held up by an enemy machine gun, he immediately rushed the machine gun, regardless

James Ockendon.

of his personal safety, and captured it. He killed the crew with the exception of one man, who made his escape. Sergt. Ockendon, however, followed him, and when well in front of the whole line, killed him and returned to his company. He then led a section to the attack on a farm. Under very heavy fire he rushed forward and called upon the garrison to surrender. As the enemy continued to fire on him, he opened fire, killing four, whereupon the remaining sixteen surrendered." The following is a rather more detailed description than the official notice of how Sergt. Ockendon won the Victoria Cross: In the attack on the morning of 4 Oct. 1917, east of Langemarck (Flanders) Sergt. James Ockendon was acting Company Sergeant-Major. Noticing the right platoon held up by an enemy machine gun which was causing many casualties, he, with absolute disregard for his personal safety, immediately rushed the gun, killed two of the gunners, and followed a third, who had made his escape, right across "No Man's Land," eventually killing him. He then led a party to the attack of T' Gord Ter Vesten Farm, which was heavily fired on as it advanced. He dashed ahead calling upon the garrison to surrender. They, however, continued to fire, and with great boldness he then opened fire himself, and having killed four of the enemy, forced the remainder, sixteen in number, to surrender to him. During the remainder of the day Sergt. Ockendon displayed the greatest gallantry, making many dangerous patrols and bringing back most valuable information as to the disposition and intentions of the enemy. He had the distinction of being the first Portsmouth V.C. He was married on 20 Aug. 1917, at Portsmouth, to Caroline Annie, daughter of Richard Harriss Green, of 15, Warwick Street, Southsea.

O'ROURKE, MICHAEL JAMES, Private, served in the European War in France, and was awarded the Victoria Cross [London Gazette, 8 Nov. 1917]: "Michael James O'Rourke, No. 428545, 7th Battn. Canadian Infantry. For most conspicuous bravery and devotion to duty during prolonged operations. For three days and nights Private O'Rourke, who is a stretcher-bearer, worked unceasingly in bringing the wounded into safety, dressing them and getting them food and water. During the whole of this period the area in which he worked was subjected to very severe shelling, and swept by heavy machine-gun and rifle fire. On several occasions he was knocked down and partially buried by enemy shells. Seeing a comrade who had been blinded stumbling around ahead of our trench, in full view of the enemy, who were sniping him, Private O'Rourke jumped out of his trench and brought the man back, being himself heavily sniped at while doing so. Again he went forward about 50 yards in front of our barrage, under very heavy and accurate fire from enemy machine guns and snipers, and brought in a comrade. On a subsequent occasion, when the line of advanced posts was retired to the line to be consolidated, he went forward under very heavy enemy fire of every description, and brought back a wounded man who had been left behind. He showed throughout an absolute disregard for his own safety, going wherever there were wounded to succour, and his magnificent courage and devotion in continuing his rescue work, in spite of exhaustion and the incessant heavy enemy fire of every description, inspired all ranks and undoubtedly saved many lives." The following is taken from "Thirty Canadian V.C.'s" (published by Messrs. Skeffington): "Down by the docks of the city of Victoria, British Columbia, you may observe a man who keeps a fruit stall and wears about an inch of dark red ribbon on his left breast. That fruit vendor is Michael James O'Rourke, late of the 7th Canadian Battn.; and the inch of dark red ribbon means that he has won the Victoria Cross. O'Rourke gained the decoration when he was a stretcher-bearer in the 7th Battn. during the big attack on the German positions near Lens, which began on the 15th Aug. 1917, and continued for several days. At 4.25 on that morning the 2nd, 3rd, 4th and 5th Canadian Brigades attacked and captured Hill 70 and the German defences about Cité St. Laurent. In conjunction with this operation a gas attack was successfully launched in the Avion sector and a subsidiary attack west of Lens. The opening of the main operation was no surprise to the enemy. Prisoners taken during the attack admitted that they had expected it and had been 'standing-to' for a fortnight in anticipation; and orders which were captured confirmed this statement, for they contained elaborate instructions in the method of procedure to be adopted when the attack was launched. Two hours before the advance began that summer morning the Germans were sending streams of gas shells into the district around Maroc and the Lens–Bethune road, while a 5.9 howitzer was playing on Loos at intervals of five minutes. When our barrage opened the 7th Battn. went forward and formed up in No Man's Land in the rear of the 10th Battn., which was to capture the front German line. At first there was a slight mix-up of battalions owing to enemy fire, but before long, though only after heavy fighting, the objectives were gained with the exception of the centre, where our men were held up by machine-gun fire from Cité St. Auguste and the brickworks. In time, however, reinforcements arrived and that obstacle was removed. For three days the fighting was the fiercest the Canadian battalions had up till then experienced. The Germans were in no mood to give up their positions without stubborn resistance, and the struggle ebbed and flowed day and night with bitter violence. On the front on which the 2nd Division attacked many Germans held out in small parties hidden in ruined houses and in deep cellars until cleared out by bomb and bayonet, while counter-attack after counter-attack was thrown against the battalions which had succeeded in clearing the German trenches. With the 7th Battn. were sixteen stretcher-bearers, including O'Rourke. Out of that sixteen, two were killed and eleven were wounded, for the Germans sniped at them as they worked to carry the wounded from the field. During those three days and nights O'Rourke worked unceasingly under fire, bringing food and water to them. The area in which he worked was continually subjected to the severest shelling, and was frequently swept by machine-gun and rifle fire. Several times he was knocked down and partially buried by shell-bursts. Once, seeing a comrade who had been blinded stumbling along in full view of the enemy, who were sniping at him, O'Rourke jumped out of the trench and brought him in, being himself heavily sniped at while doing so. Again he went forward about fifty yards in front of our barrage, under very heavy fire from machine guns and snipers, and brought in another wounded man; and later, when the advanced posts retired to the line, he braved a storm of enemy fire of every description and brought in a wounded man who had been left behind. It was for these acts, in which he showed an absolute disregard for his own safety, that O'Rourke gained the highest award—one of the comparatively few men who have been given the Victoria Cross in this war for saving life under fire."

London Gazette, 26 Nov. 1917.—"War Office, 26 Nov. 1917. His Majesty the King has been graciously pleased to approve of the award of the Victoria Cross to the undermentioned Officers, Non-commissioned Officers and Men."

EVANS, LEWIS PUGH, Major (Acting Lieut.-Colonel), was born on 3 Jan. 1881, at Abermaed, Aberystwith, second son of the late Sir Griffith Evans, K.C.I.E., D.L., J.P., and Lady Evans, of Lovesgrove, Aberystwith. He was educated at Eton College, and the Royal Military College, Sandhurst, and joined the Army on 23 Dec. 1899, as Second Lieutenant in the 2nd Battn. The Black Watch, becoming Lieutenant 1 May, 1901, and Captain 27 Oct. 1906. He was promoted Captain in 1906; passed out of the Staff College, Camberley, in Aug. 1914, and became a General Staff Officer, Third Grade, at the War Office in 1914. He served in the European War in France from 16 Sept. 1914, joining No. 3 Squadron of the Royal Flying Corps, on the Aisne, on the 22nd Sept. as an Observer. He served with them until 23 Dec. 1914, on which date he joined the 1st Battn. of his regiment, the Black Watch, as a Company Commander, and served with them until the 1st May, 1915, on which date he was appointed Brigade Major to the 7th Infantry Brigade, 3rd Division. He was created a Companion of the Distinguished Service Order [London Gazette, 24 July 1915] for his services in the action at Hooge on 16 June, 1915. The Gazette notice reads: "For conspicuous gallantry and devotion to duty on 16 June, 1915, at Hooge, when, after troops had become much mixed up, he continually moved up and down the firing line under heavy fire from 10 a.m. till midnight reorganizing units and bringing back their reports." In March, 1916, he was appointed G.S.O. Second Grade, with the 6th Division, and served with them in this capacity until March, 1917. In March, 1917, he was appointed Acting Lieutenant-Colonel in command of the 1st Lincolnshire Regt., 62nd Brugade, 21st Division, and was made an Officier of the Order of Leopold, with Croix de Guerre, in June, 1917. He saw service in South Africa from 1899–1902, taking part in the operations in the Orange Free State, Feb. to May, 1900, including the actions at Poplar Grove, Dreifontein and Vet River. Operations in the Transvaal in May and June, 1900, including actions near Johannesburg, Pretoria and Diamond Hill. Operations in the Transvaal, east of Pretoria, July to 29 Nov. 1900, including action at Belfast. Operations in Orange River Colony. Later, operations in Orange River Colony, Nov. 1900, to Jan. 1902 (Queen's Medal with five clasps; King's Medal with two clasps). He was awarded the Victoria Cross [London Gazette, 26 Nov. 1917] for services rendered on the 4th Oct.: "Lewis Pugh Evans, D.S.O., Major (Acting Lieut.-Colonel), Royal Highlanders, Commanding 1st Battn. Lincolnshire Regt. For most conspicuous bravery and leadership. Lieut.-Colonel Evans took his battalion in perfect order through a terrific enemy barrage, personally formed up all units, and led them to the assault. While a strong machine-gun emplacement was causing casualties and the troops were working round the flank, Lieut.-Colonel Evans rushed at it himself, and, by firing his revolver through the loophole, forced the garrison to capitulate. After capturing the first objective he was severely wounded in the shoulder, but refused to be bandaged, and reformed the troops, pointed out all future objectives, and again led his battalion forward. Again badly wounded, he nevertheless continued to command until the second objective was won, and, after consolidation, collapsed from loss of blood. As there were numerous casualties he refused assistance, and by his own efforts ultimately reached the dressing station. His example of cool bravery stimulated in all ranks the highest valour and determination to win." He was admitted to hospital wounded; evacuated to the United Kingdom, and returned to command the 1st Battn. The Lincolnshire Regt. on the 4th Jan. 1918. On the 23rd Jan. 1918, he was transferred to command the 1st Battn. The Black Watch. He was awarded a Bar to the Distinguished Service Order [London Gazette, 16 Sept. 1918], for conspicuous gallantry and devotion to duty in a three days' battle at Givenchy in April, 1918: "On the first day he was moving about everywhere in his forward area directing operations, the next day he personally conducted a reconnaissance for a counter-attack, which was carried out on the third day. It was largely due to his untiring energy and method that the enemy were checked and finally driven out of our forward system." On 10 June, 1918, he was appointed to the command of the 14th Infantry Brigade, 32nd Division, with the temporary rank of Brigadier-General. He was awarded the C.M.G. in May, 1919, for services rendered whilst in command of the 14th Infantry Brigade, in operations covering the period 8 Aug. to 11 Nov. He was married at Holy Trinity Church, Sloane Street, London, S.W., on 10 Oct. 1918, to Margaret Dorothea Segrave, eldest daughter of

Lewis Pugh Evans.

John Carbery Pryse-Rice and Dame Margaret Pryse-Rice, D.B.E., of Llwyn-y-Brain, Llandovery, Carmarthenshire. In Feb. 1919, he was transferred from the command of the 14th Infantry Brigade on the Rhine to Base Commandant of the British Base at Rotterdam.

BURMAN, WILLIAM FRANCIS, Sergt., was born at 5, Baker Street, Stepney, E., on 30 Aug. 1897, son of George Burman (deceased) and Agnes E. Burman. He was educated at Stepney Red Coat School, and joined the Army on 23 March, 1915. He served in the European War, and was awarded the Victoria Cross [London Gazette, 26 Nov. 1917]: " No. P/649, William Francis Burman, Sergt., 16th Battn. Rifle Brigade. When the advance of his company in attack was held up by machine-gun firing at point-blank range, he shouted to the men next to him to wait a few minutes, and going forward alone to what seemed certain death, killed the enemy gunner and carried the gun to the company's objective, where he used it with great effect. By this exceptionally gallant deed the progress of the attack was assured.

William Francis Burman.

About 15 minutes later it was observed that the battalion on the right was being impeded by about 40 enemy, who were enfilading them. Sergt. Burman with two others, ran forward and got behind the enemy, killing six and capturing two officers and 29 other ranks." He was promoted Sergeant 20 April, 1916 (on the field). Sergt. Burman was presented with a testimonial on 2 Aug. 1918, by the Mayor of Stepney. He was demobilized 7 March, 1919.

DWYER, JOHN JAMES, Sergt., was born at Port Sygnet, Tasmania, Australia, 9 March, 1890, son of Charles Dwyer and Mrs. Charles Dwyer. His parents live at Allonah, South Bruny, Tasmania. He was educated at the State School, Allonah, and joined the Australian Imperial Force as a Private in the Machine Gun Corps on 4 Feb. 1915. He served in the European War, and was awarded the Victoria Cross [London Gazette, 26 Nov. 1917]: " No. 2060, Sergt. John James Dwyer, Australian Machine Gun Corps, Australian Imperial Force. For most conspicuous bravery when in attack. Sergt. Dwyer, in charge of a Vickers machine gun, went forward with the first wave of the brigade. On reaching the final objective this non-commissioned officer rushed his gun forward in advance of the captured position, in

John James Dwyer.

order to obtain a commanding spot. Whilst advancing he noticed an enemy machine gun firing on the troops on our right flank and causing casualties. Unhesitatingly he rushed his gun forward to within 30 yards of the enemy gun and fired point-blank at it, putting it out of action and killing the gun crew. He then seized the gun, and totally ignoring the snipers from the rear of the enemy position, carried it back across the shell-swept ground to our front line, and established both it and his Vickers gun on the right flank of our brigade. Sergt. Dwyer commanded these guns with great coolness, and when the enemy counter-attacked our positions he rendered great assistance in repulsing them. On the following day, when the position was heavily shelled, this non-commissioned officer took up successive positions. On one occasion his Vickers gun was blown up by shell fire, but he conducted his gun team back to Headquarters through the enemy barrage, secured one of the reserve guns, and rushed it back to our position in the shortest possible time. During the whole of the attack his contempt of danger, cheerfulness and courage raised the spirits of all who were in his sector of the line." He was given a commission in the field.

LISTER, JOSEPH, Sergt., served in the European War in France. He was awarded the Victoria Cross [London Gazette, 26 Nov. 1917]: " Joseph Lister, No. 8133, 1st Battn. Lancashire Fusiliers. For most conspicuous bravery in attack. When advancing to the first objective, his company came under machine-gun fire from the direction of two ' pill-boxes.' Seeing that the galling fire would hold up our advance and prevent our troops keeping up with the barrage, Sergt. Lister dashed ahead of his men and found a machine gun firing from a shell-hole in front of the ' pill-box.' He shot two of the enemy gunners, and the remainder surrendered to him. He then went on to the ' pill-box ' and shouted to the occupants to surrender. They did so with the exception of one man, whom Sergt. Lister shot dead ; whereupon about 100 of the enemy emerged from shell-holes farther to the rear and surrendered. This non-commissioned officer's prompt act of courage enabled our line to advance with hardly a check and to keep up with the barrage, the loss of which might have jeopardized the whole course of the local battle."

McGEE, LEWIS, Sergt., served in the European War in France, and was posthumously awarded the Victoria Cross [London Gazette, 26 Nov. 1917]: " Lewis McGee, No. 456, Sergt., late 40th Battn. Australian Imperial Force. For most conspicuous bravery. When in the

advance to the final objective, Sergt. McGee led his platoon with great dash and bravery, though strongly opposed and under heavy shell fire. His platoon was suffering severely and the advance of the company was stopped by machine-gun fire from a ' pill-box ' post. Single-handed Sergt. McGee rushed the post armed only with a revolver. He shot some of the crew and captured the rest, and thus enabled the advance to proceed. He reorganized the remnants of his platoon, and was foremost in the remainder of the advance, and during consolidation of the position he did splendid work. This non-commissioned officer's coolness and bravery were conspicuous, and contributed largely to the success of the company's operations. Sergt. McGee was subsequently killed in action."

Lewis McGee.

MOLYNEUX, JOHN, Sergt., was born on 22 Nov. 1890, at 3, Marshall's Cross Road, Peasley Cross, St. Helens, Lancashire, son of Joseph and Minnie Jane Molyneux. He writes : " I was educated at Holy Trinity Church of England Schools, St. Helens, and joined the Army on 7 Sept. 1914, as a Private, and from home I was despatched to Dover to go into training. Before I joined the Colours I was a Miner, under the Sutton Heath and Lea Green Colliery Company. I served in the European War at Gallipoli, with the 29th Division at Suvla Bay, and got a slight wound and frost-bite after the storm on the 26th Nov. ; from there I was taken to Malta, and during my stay in hospital they evacuated the Peninsula, so I rejoined my unit in Egypt, and from there we sailed to France. I arrived at the latter end of March, and went through the Somme battles up to Nov. 1916. I got wounded again in the left forearm, which brought me to England." Sergt. Molyneux was awarded the

John Molyneux.

Victoria Cross [London Gazette, 26 Nov. 1917]: " John Molyneux, No. 1817, Sergt., 2nd Battn. Royal Fusiliers. For most conspicuous bravery and devotion to duty. During an attack, which was held up by machine-gun fire which caused many casualties, Sergt. Molyneux instantly organized a bombing party to clear the trench in front of a house. Many enemy were killed and a machine gun captured. Having cleared this obstacle, he immediately jumped out of the trench and called for someone to follow him, and rushed for the house. By the time the men arrived he was in the thick of a hand-to-hand fight ; this only lasted a short time, and the enemy surrendered, and, in addition to the dead and wounded, between 20 and 30 prisoners were taken. Apart from the personal bravery of this non-commissioned officer, his initiative and dash prevented a slight check from becoming a serious block in the advance, and undoubtedly prevented many casualties." Sergt. Molyneux writes : " I was awarded the Victoria Cross in the Ypres sector after the Battle of Poelcapelle, which was one of the worst I ever experienced, owing to the bad conditions of the ground, and also many blockhouses which we had to clear. I got through this battle without any wounds and none the worse after my experiences."

The following is an extract from Major-General De Lisle, Commanding 29th Division :

" No. 1817, Sergt. John Molyneux, V.C., 2nd Battn. Royal Fusiliers.

" Accept my congratulations on your Act of Gallantry and Devotion to Duty on the 9th of Oct. 1917, which has been brought to my notice by your Commanding Officer."

Sergt. Molyneux again writes : " Please note this was signed by his own hand. I would have forwarded same had it not been framed. I was also awarded the Belgian Croix de Guerre in Feb. 1918. I am a married man without children, my wife's name being Mary Agnes Molyneux. I came home in Dec. 1917, and received the Victoria Cross from His Majesty the King on the 12th of the same month, after having a nice month's leave. I rejoined my unit and stayed with them till I was demobilized on the 5th Jan. this year, at Cologne, after being with the 29th Division three years and a half."

RHODES, JOHN HAROLD, L.-Sergt., was born on 17 May, 1891, at Mellor Street, Packmoor, son of Ernest and Sarah Rhodes. He was educated at Church Schools, Newchapel, and joined the Grenadier Guards on 17 Feb. 1911, serving three years in the ranks, and rejoined his regiment as a Reservist on the outbreak of war, serving in France, and was wounded in July, 1915. He was awarded the D.C.M. and Bar, for gallantry on two occasions, and later at Cambrai the V.C. He was killed in action 27 Nov. 1917. He was married on 11 Dec. 1915, to Lizzie, daughter of Aaron and Elizabeth Meir, and leaves a widow, and a son named John. His Victoria Cross was awarded posthumously, and was gazetted 26 Nov. 1918 : " John Harold Rhodes, No. 15122, L.-Sergt.,

John Harold Rhodes.

3rd Battn. Grenadier Guards. For most conspicuous bravery when in charge of a Lewis gun section covering the consolidation of the right front company. He accounted for several enemy with his rifle, as well as by Lewis-gun fire, and upon seeing three enemy leave a ' pill-box,' he went out single-handed through our own barrage and hostile machine-gun fire, and effected an entry into the ' pill-box.' He there captured nine of the enemy, including a forward observation officer connected by telephone with his battery. These prisoners he brought back with him, together with valuable information."

Ernest Alfred Egerton.

EGERTON, ERNEST ALFRED, Corpl., was born on 10 Nov. 1897, at Mier Lane, Longton, Staffordshire, son of Mr. and Mrs. T. H. Egerton, of Mier Lane, The Mier, near Longton, Staffordshire. He was educated at Blurton Church School, Blurton, near Longton ; employed at the Florence Colliery, Longton, Staffordshire, prior to joining His Majesty's Forces on the 10th Nov. 1915, as Private in the 3rd North Stafford Regt. He transferred to the 16th Battn. Notts and Derby Regt. in Oct. 1916, in France, serving from 16 Oct. 1916, until 20 Aug. 1918. He was discharged from the Army 25 April, 1919, permanently unfit for further military service on account of tuberculosis of the lungs. He was promoted to Lance-Corporal 21 Feb. 1917 ; Corporal 23 Aug. 1917 ; Sergeant 11 May, 1918. Corpl. Egerton married, 1 Sept. 1918, Miss Elsie May Gimbert, at Forsbrooke Parish Church.

The following is an extract from a letter received from the Duke of Devonshire, Governor-General of Canada :

> " Government House,
> " Ottawa,
> " 2 March, 1918.

" To Corpl. Egerton, V.C.,
" I hope you will accept my most hearty congratulations for your gallant conduct, and for the well-merited reward of the Victoria Cross. I have always taken the greatest interest in the battalion since it was first raised, and I am very proud of the great work which it has done. You have added new glory to it, and I trust you will come through this trouble safe and sound, and will be long spared to enjoy the honour which you so well deserve.

> " Believe me,
> " Yours truly,
> (Signed) " DEVONSHIRE."

His Victoria Cross was gazetted 26 Nov. 1917 : " No. 71130, Ernest Albert Egerton, Corpl., 16th Battn. Nottinghamshire and Derbyshire Regt. (Longton). For most conspicuous bravery, initiative and devotion to duty when, during attack, owing to fog and smoke, visibility was obscured, and, in consequence thereof, the two leading waves of the attack passed over certain hostile dug-outs without clearing them. Enemy rifles, assisted by a machine gun, were from these dug-outs inflicting severe casualties on the advancing waves. When volunteers were called for to assist in clearing up the situation, Corpl. Egerton at once jumped up and dashed for the dug-outs under heavy fire at short range. He shot in succession a rifleman, a bomber and a gunner, by which time he was supported, and 29 of the enemy surrendered. The reckless bravery of the N.C.O. relieved in less than 30 seconds an extremely difficult situation. His gallantry is beyond all praise."

GREAVES, FRED, Acting Corpl., was born on 16 May, 1890, at Killamarsh, Derbyshire, son of Mr. Jude Greaves and of Mrs. Edith L. Greaves. He was educated at Bonds Main Council School, and joined the Army on the 26th Feb. 1915, serving in the European War in France, the Dardanelles and Egypt. He was awarded the Victoria Cross [London Gazette, 26 Nov. 1917] : " No. 23715, Fred Greaves, Acting Corporal, 9th Battn. Nottinghamshire and Derbyshire Regt. For most conspicuous bravery, initiative and leadership when his platoon was temporarily held up by machine-gun fire from a concrete stronghold. Seeing that his platoon commander and sergeant were casualties, and realizing that unless this post was taken quickly his men would lose the barrage, Corpl. Greaves, followed by another non-commissioned officer, rushed forward, regardless of his personal safety, reached the rear of the building and bombed the occupants, killing or capturing the garrison, and taking four enemy machine guns. It was solely due to the personal pluck, dash and initiative of this non-commissioned officer that the assaulting line at this point was not held up, and that our troops escaped serious casualties. Later in the afternoon, at a most critical period of the battle, when the troops of a flank brigade had given way temporarily under a heavy counter-attack, and when all the officers in his company were casualties, this gallant non-commissioned officer quickly grasped the situation. He collected his men, threw out extra posts on the threatened flank, and opened up rifle and machine-gun fire to enfilade the advance. The effect of Corpl.

Fred Greaves.

Greaves's conduct on his men throughout the battle cannot be over-estimated, and those under his command responded gallantly to his example."

The full story of how the Victoria Cross was won by Corpl. Greaves is told by a brother non-commissioned officer who was wounded in the same fight. To a special correspondent of the " Nottingham Guardian," this soldier said :

" The general opinion of the men who served with him is that Corpl. Greaves richly deserved the honour conferred on him. He displayed on that day qualities of leadership that were highly praised by the general officer commanding the division. It was an exceedingly critical position we were in. Our force ran into one of the enemy blockhouses or ' pill boxes,' and we were also caught between the fire of two groups of machine-gun posts. The officers and non-coms. went down with the exception of Greaves. The men suffered most severely, and, left without a leader, they were wavering. Greaves saw what was required. Shouting to the men not to mind, he went forward with some bombs in his hand. Another non-commissioned officer who was only slightly wounded went after them. Both were fired on by the enemy and had hairbreadth escapes. They seemed to be running through showers of bullets. Greaves got round the pill box, after dodging death from the snipers many times. He hurled in a couple of bombs and the fire from the pill boxes ceased. He made his way inside and brought out four machine guns in succession. That saved the day for us. Our men were no longer galled. They were able to consolidate the position, and they pushed on to the next objective. The effect of our advance was felt all over the field of battle, and our troops were able to gain their objectives with comparatively trifling losses. Later in the day the position was once more critical. Greaves had joined his company, which was heavily engaged with the Huns. The officers were knocked out, and the command fell to Greaves. He proved equal to the responsibility, which was greatly increased by the fact that a sudden enemy counter-attack swept away the infantry holding the adjoining lines. The Foresters were hard pressed, and were on the point of being forced back in their turn when Greaves saved the day once more. Calling to his men to hold on, he went forward into the thick of it, posting men here, moving a machine gun there, and generally making it clear to both our chaps and the enemy that there was a chap on the job who knew enough of the business to make it impossible for the enemy to get the best of us. The enemy attacked in masses. Greaves went about among the men, encouraging them and spurring them on by his example of cheerfulness and courage. Again and again the enemy attacked. Each time they were flung back, in spite of the overwhelming forces they had at their disposal. The example of Greaves and his band of Sherwoods was infectious. Our men gradually recovered the ground given up, and the enemy was sent rolling back in disorder once more. That this result was achieved was due entirely to the brilliant leadership and fine courage of Greaves. We all think highly of him, and hope he will get the commission for which the Colonel is willing to recommend him. He is one of the most modest chaps in the battalion, and the men all like him. He is a fine comrade, ready to do anything for his mates, and never thinking of himself at all. Before the acts that won him the Cross, Greaves had already come under the notice of his superiors for his coolness and dash under the most trying circumstances. On one occasion before he rushed a machine-gun post single-handed, and on another occasion he risked his life to bring a comrade out of action. How he kept going on the day he won the Cross I do not know. He was everywhere, and seemed to know just what to do at the proper time. The men soon gained confidence in his leadership, and would have been content to follow him anywhere he chose. In spite of the terrible ordeal we went through that day our casualties were comparatively light, and that was due entirely to the skilful way in which Greaves handled us and steered us through the dangerous parts of the day's operations. Good luck and long life to him is what we all say."

Second-Lieut. Harry Greaves, D.S.O., M.C., of the Nottinghamshire and Derbyshire Regt., brother of Sergt. Greaves, was recently awarded a second Bar to his Military Cross.

KONOWAL, PHILIP, Corpl., is the son of a Russian farmer, Miron Konowal, and of his wife, Eudkice, and was born in Russia on 15 Sept. 1888, and was educated in Ukrainia, Russia. He married on 25 July, 1909, Anna Stanka, of Russian parentage, and they have a daughter, May. He joined the Canadian Military Forces 12 July, 1915, and served in the European War. He was awarded the Victoria Cross [London Gazette, 26 Nov. 1917] : " Filip Konowal, Acting Corpl., 47th Infantry Battn. Canadian Expeditionary Force. For most conspicuous bravery and leadership when in charge of a section in attack. His section had the difficult task of mopping up cellars, craters and machine-gun emplacements. Under his able direction all resistance was overcome successfully, and heavy casualties were inflicted on the enemy. In one cellar he himself bayoneted three enemy and attacked single-handed seven others in a crater, killing them all. On reaching the objective, a machine gun was holding up the right flank, causing many casualties. Corpl. Konowal rushed forward and entered the emplacement, killed the crew, and brought the gun back to our lines. The next day he again attacked single-handed another machine-gun emplacement, killed three of the crew, and destroyed the gun and emplacement with explosives. This non-commissioned officer alone killed at least 16 of the enemy, and during the two days' actual fighting carried on continuously his good work until severely wounded."

The following account of Corpl. Konowal's heroism is given in " Thirty Canadian V.C.'s (published by Messrs. Skeffington) (pages 58–60) : " The fighting about Lens in Aug. 1917, called for more individual dash and initiative on the part of the troops engaged than had been required before. The house-to-house fighting, the repeatedly isolated and difficult positions, the many knotty problems which required instant solution—all these combined to make leadership, whether of a section or a battalion, more arduous and responsible, and, with it all, much more fascinating. Such fighting is after the hearts of most Canadians. As was expected, our men did well at it. After the successful attack on Hill 70, incessant fighting was forced upon our troops to maintain the new positions. The enemy's bombardment was constant and intense. It was decided to continue the offensive and improve our line. The 10th Brigade was instructed to capture Green Crassier and the enemy's defences about this point, and accordingly the attack was arranged for the 21st, with two battalions each of the 50th, 46th and 47th Battns., the 47th Battn. on the right to attack through Cité du Moulin to the Lens–Arras Road and Alpaca trench. At 4.35 a.m. our men went forward, penetrating the immediate German barrage without hesitation, and moving as if on parade. The morning was bright and sunny, and our fellows got away in splendid style, though they were badly harassed by machine-gun fire from Green Crassier, a barren expanse of slag heaps and broken railway tracks on the right front. However, our smoke barrage was most effective, and the drums of blazing oil thrown upon the enemy's communication lines and attempted formations did much to take the heart out of his resistance. Crossing the Lens–Arras Road, the troops plunged into the ruined houses beyond, and stiff fighting, in cellars, long dark tunnels, and comparatively deserted out-houses, ensued. Many were the isolated heroic combats that took place, and many men were reported missing after the battle who had fought out their lives in some underground chamber. Corpl. Konowal was in charge of a mopping-up section. In fighting of this description it is an undecided point whether the original assailants or the moppers-up get most excitement. The main attack sweeps on ; but in such a rabbit-warren of broken houses and tunnelled foundations many Germans and frequent machine guns are left to be eliminated at some cost by our following waves. The buildings about the Lens–Arras Road proved difficult enough to clear. The main body of our troops had passed through and continued to the objectives beyond, but a couple of buildings still held Germans and German machine guns, and there was heavy firing upon the rear of our advancing men. Entering one of these houses Konowal searched for the Germans, and finding no living traces of their occupation, dropped daringly into the cellar. Three men fired at him as he landed, but this he escaped unharmed. Then ensued a sanguinary battle in the dark, a mêlée of rifle fire and bayonets, with the odds three to one. Finally the scuffling ceased and Konowal emerged into the daylight—he had bayoneted the whole crew of the gun ! But this is all taken for granted in the business of mopping-up, and the corporal and his section continued their way along the road, every sense alert to locate the close rifle-crack that might betray the wily sniper. There was a large crater to the east of the road, and from the bodies of our good men before the edge it seemed obvious that a German machine gun had been in position there. Halting his men, Konowal advanced alone. Upon reaching the lip of the crater he saw seven Germans endeavouring to move the ubiquitous machine gun into a dug-out. He opened fire at once, killing three, and then, charging down upon them, accounted for the rest with the bayonet. These drastic methods rapidly concluded the clearing of their section of the line, and the coporal and his men moved on up to our new front, where the enemy was delivering heavy and incessant counter-attacks. Heavy fighting continued throughout the night, and in the morning troops of the 44th Battn., who were making an attack upon the Green Crassier, requested the aid of a party of the 47th in a raid upon a machine-gun emplacement in a tunnel about Fosse 4. Corpl. Konowal was an expert in this subterranean fighting, and his party succeeded in entering the tunnel. Two charges of ammonal, successfully exploded, somewhat demoralized the German garrison, and then Konowal, dashing forward in the darkness with the utter disregard of his own safety he had displayed all through the fighting, engaged the machine-gun crew with the bayonet, overcoming and killing them all. Altogether this good fighting man killed sixteen men in the two days of the actual battle, and continued his splendid work until he was very severely wounded."

HEWITT, WILLIAM HENRY, L.-Corpl., served in the European War in France. He was awarded the Victoria Cross [London Gazette, 26 Nov. 1917]: " No. 8162, William Henry Hewitt, L.-Corpl., 2nd Battn. South African Light Infantry. For most conspicuous bravery during operations. L.-Corpl. Hewitt attacked a ' pill-box ' with his section, and tried to rush the doorway. The garrison, however, proved very stubborn, and in the attempt this non-commissioned officer received a severe wound. Nevertheless, he proceeded to the loophole of the ' pill-box ' where, in his attempts to put a bomb into it, he was again wounded in the arm. Undeterred, however, he eventually managed to get a bomb inside, which caused the occupants to dislodge, and they were successfully and speedily dealt with by the remainder of the section."

MUGFORD, HAROLD, L.-Corpl., served in the European War in France, and was awarded the Victoria Cross [London Gazette, 26 Nov. 1917]: " Harold Mugford, No. 51507, L.-Corpl., 8th Machine Gun Squadron, Machine Gun Corps. For most conspicuous bravery and devotion to duty when, under intense shell and machine-gun fire, L.-Corpl. Mugford succeeded in getting his machine gun into a forward and very exposed position. From this point he was able to deal most effectively with the enemy, who were massing for counter-attack. His No. 2 was killed almost immediately, and at the same moment he himself was severely wounded. He was then ordered to a new position, and told to go to a dressing station as soon as the position was occupied. He refused to go to the dressing station, but continued on duty with his gun, inflicting severe loss on the enemy. Soon after he was again wounded, a shell breaking both of his legs. He still remained with his gun, begging his comrades to leave him and take cover. Shortly afterwards this non-commissioned officer was removed to the dressing-station, where he was again wounded in the arm. The valour and initiative displayed by L.-Corpl. Mugford was instrumental in breaking up the impending counter-attack of the enemy."

PEELER, WALTER, L.-Corpl., joined the Australian Military Forces, and served in the European War in France. He was awarded the Victoria Cross [London Gazette, 26 Nov. 1917]: " Walter Peeler, No. 114, L.-Corpl., 3rd Australian Pioneer Battn. Australian Expeditionary Force. For most conspicuous bravery when, with a Lewis gun accompanying the first wave of the assault, he encountered an enemy party sniping the advancing troops from a shell-hole. L.-Corpl. Peeler immediately rushed the position and accounted for nine of the enemy, and cleared the way for the advance. On two subsequent occasions he performed similar acts of valour, and each time accounted for a number of the enemy. During operations he was directed to a position from which an enemy machine gun was being fired on our troops. He located and killed the gunner, and the remainder of the enemy party ran into a dug-out close by. From this shelter they were dislodged by a bomb, and 10 of them ran out. These he disposed of. This non-commissioned officer actually accounted for over thirty of the enemy. He displayed an absolute fearlessness in making his way ahead of the first wave of the assault, and the fine example which he set ensured the success of the attack against most determined opposition."

Walter Peeler.

BUGDEN, PATRICK, Private, joined the Australian Military Forces, and served in the European War. He was posthumously awarded the Victoria Cross [London Gazette, 26 Nov. 1917]: " Patrick Bugden, No. 3774, Private, late Australian Imperial Force. For most conspicuous bravery and devotion to duty when on two occasions our advance was temporarily held up by strongly-defended ' pill-boxes.' Private Bugden, in the face of devastating fire from machine guns, gallantly led small parties to attack these strong points, and, successfully silencing the machine guns with bombs, captured the garrison at the point of the bayonet. On another occasion, when a Corporal, who had become detached from his company, had been captured and was being taken to the rear by the enemy, Private Bugden, single-handed, rushed to the rescue of his comrade, shot one enemy and bayoneted the remaining two, thus releasing the Corporal. On five occasions he rescued wounded men under intense shell and machine-gun fire, showing an utter contempt and disregard for danger. Always foremost in volunteering for any dangerous mission, it was in the execution of one of these missions that this gallant soldier was killed."

Patrick Bugden.

DANCOX, FREDERICK GEORGE, Private, was employed as a Hay Trusser before the War. He joined the Army, served in the European War in France, and was awarded the Victoria Cross [London Gazette, 26 Nov. 1917]: " No. 21654, Frederick George Dancox, Private, 4th Battn. Worcestershire Regt. For most conspicuous bravery and devotion to duty in attack. After the first objective had been captured and consolidation had been started, work was considerably hampered and numerous casualties were caused by an enemy machine gun firing from a concrete emplacement situated on the edge of our protective barrage. Private Dancox was one of a party of about 10 men detailed as moppers-up. Owing to the position of the machine-gun emplacement, it was extremely difficult to work round a flank. However, this man with great gallantry worked his way round through the barrage and entered the ' pill-box ' from the rear, threatening the garrison with a Mills bomb. Shortly afterwards he reappeared with a machine gun under his arm, followed by about 40 enemy. The machine gun was brought back to our position by Private Dancox, and he kept it in action throughout the day. By his resolution, absolute disregard of danger and cheerful disposition, the moral of his comrades was maintained at a very high standard under extremely trying circumstances." He is married, and has five children.

HATTON, ALBERT, Private, was born on 1 May, 1893, at Mill Head, Warton, near Carnforth, son of Jonathan Hatton, Blast Furnace Man, and one of the oldest employees at the Carnforth Ironworks, and Sarah Hatton. He was educated at Carnforth National School, and on leaving at thirteen was employed at various farms. He worked for a short period on the London and North Western Railway, and then entered the service of a contractor at Carnforth, leaving his employment to join the Army. He became a Private in the 5th King's Own Royal Lancaster Regt. on 15 Aug. 1915, and served in the European War ; was wounded on the Somme 22 Oct. 1916, and was in hospital at Aberdeen. He joined his regiment on 1 March, 1917, and on returning to the front was drafted to the 1st Battn. He was awarded the Victoria Cross [London Gazette, 26 Nov. 1917]: " No. 241475, Albert Hatton, Private, King's Own Royal Lancaster Regt. For most conspicuous bravery in attack. After the objective had been reached, Private Hatton rushed forward about three hundred yards under very heavy rifle and shell fire, and captured a machine gun and its crew, which was causing many losses to our men. He then went out again and brought in about twelve prisoners, showing the greatest disregard of his own safety and setting a very fine example to those around him." He had a great reception when he returned to his home in Carnforth, a procession formed of members of the Council, Volunteers, brass bands, residents and school children escorting him to his home three-quarters of a mile from the station.

HAMILTON, JOHN BROWN, Private (Acting L.-Corpl.), joined the Army, and served in the European War in France. He was awarded the Victoria Cross [London Gazette, 26 Nov. 1917]: "No. 331958, John Brown Hamilton, Private (Acting L.-Corpl.), 1/9th Battn. Highland Light Infantry. For most conspicuous bravery and devotion to duty during the enemy's attack on the line held by our brigades. The greatest difficulty was experienced in keeping the front and support lines supplied with small-arm ammunition, owing to the intense and continuous belt of artillery fire placed systematically by the enemy between our various lines and battalion headquarters. It was of vital importance for the successful maintenance of the defence of the position that ammunition should be got forward. At a time when

John Brown Hamilton.

this ammunition supply had reached a seriously low ebb, L.-Corpl. Hamilton on several occasions, on his own initiative, carried bandoliers of ammunition through the enemy's belts of fire to the front and support line, and then, passing along these lines in full view of the enemy's snipers and machine guns—who were lying out in front of our line at close range—distributed the ammunition to the men. In so doing he not only ensured the steady continuance of the defence by rifle fire, but by his splendid example of fearlessness and devotion to duty inspired all who saw him with fresh confidence and renewed their determination to hold on at all costs."

HUTT, ARTHUR, Private, served in the European War in France, and was awarded the Victoria Cross [London Gazette, 26 Nov. 1917]: "Arthur Hutt, Private, No. 267110, Royal Warwickshire Regt. (Earlsdon, Coventry). For most conspicuous bravery and initiative in attack, when all the officers and non-commissioned officers of No. 2 platoon having become casualties, Private Hutt took command of and led forward the platoon. He was held up by a strong post on his right, but immediately ran forward alone in front of the platoon and shot the officer and three men in the post, causing between forty and fifty others to surrender. Later, realizing that he had pushed too far, he withdrew his party. He personally covered the withdrawal by sniping the enemy, killing a number, and then carried back a badly wounded man and put him under shelter. Private Hutt then organized and consolidated his position, and learning that some wounded men were lying out and likely to become prisoners if left there, no stretcher-bearers being available, he went out and carried in four wounded men under heavy fire."

INWOOD, REGINALD ROY, Private, served in the European War in France, and was awarded the Victoria Cross [London Gazette, 26 Nov. 1917]: "No. 6506, Reginald Roy Inwood, Private 10th Battn. Australian Imperial Force. For most conspicuous bravery and devotion to duty during the advance to the second objective. He moved forward, through our barrage alone to an enemy strong post and captured it, together with nine prisoners, killing several of the enemy. During the evening he volunteered for a special all-night patrol, which went out 600 yards in front of our line, and there—by his coolness and sound judgment—obtained and sent back very valuable information as to the enemy's movements. In the early morning of 21 Sept. Private Inwood located a machine gun which was causing several casualties. He went out

Reginald Roy Inwood.

alone and bombed the gun and team, killing all but one, whom he brought in as a prisoner with the gun."

MELVIN, CHARLES, Private, served in the European War, and was awarded the Victoria Cross [London Gazette, 26 Nov. 1917]: "Charles Melvin, No. 871, Private, Royal Highlanders. For most conspicuous bravery, coolness and resource in action. Private Melvin's company had advanced to within fifty yards of the front-line trench of a redoubt, where, owing to the intensity of the enemy's fire, the men were obliged to lie down and wait for reinforcements. Private Melvin, however, rushed on by himself, over ground swept from end to end by rifle and machine-gun fire. On reaching the enemy trench, he halted and fired two or three shots into it, killing one or two enemy, but as the others in the trench continued to fire at him, he jumped into it, and attacked them with his bayonet in his hand, as owing to his rifle being damaged it was not 'fixed.' On being attacked in this resolute manner most of the enemy fled to their second line, but not before Private Melvin had killed two more and succeeded in disarming eight unwounded and one wounded. Private Melvin bound up the wounds of the wounded man, and, then driving his eight unwounded prisoners before him and supporting the wounded one, he hustled them out of the trench, marched them in and delivered them over to an officer. He then provided himself with a load of ammunition, and returned to the firing line, where he reported himself to his platoon sergeant. All this was done, not only under intense fire and machine-gun fire, but the whole way back Private Melvin and his party were exposed to a very heavy artillery

barrage fire. Throughout the day Private Melvin greatly inspired those near him with confidence and courage." "Some of us would almost rather that Thrums had a V.C. than any other place whatever, and the fitting thing has happened. Charles Melvin, of the Black Watch, seems to be in other ways quite characteristic of the place. 'Ye see,' said his mother in an interview, 'he never tells me onything in his letters, and onything I heard about this was through some of his chums.' Thrums itself took the event with no less reticence. It hung out no flags ; it rang no bells. And it probably thinks that Sir James Barrie, in sending a telegram to congratulate the hero, betrays an emotion only extenuated by his long residence in South Britain." One may note that the adjectival form of Kirriemuir is "Kirriemarian," not "Kirriemuiran," as the London papers print it. At least, the "Dundee Advertiser," which ought to be the better authority, gives the former spelling to Sir James Barrie's telegram.

London Gazette, 18 Dec. 1917.—"War Office, 18 Dec. 1917. His Majesty the King has been graciously pleased to approve of the award of the Victoria Cross to the undermentioned Officers, Non-commissioned Officers and Men."

BORTON, ARTHUR DRUMMOND, Lieut.-Colonel, was born on 1 July, 1883, son of Lieut.-Colonel A. C. Borton, J.P., and Mrs. A. C. Borton, of Cheveney, Kent, and grandson of the late Sir Arthur Borton, G.C.B., G.C.M.G. He was educated at Eton, and at the Royal Military College, Sandhurst, from which he passed into the 60th Rifles as Second Lieutenant. He served in the South African War in 1902, taking part in the operations in the Transvaal March to 31 May, 1902, and receiving the Queen's Medal with three clasps. He became Lieutenant 9 May, 1906, and retired from the Army in 1910, rejoining on the outbreak of the European War. He was connected in turn with the Royal Flying Corps, the Royal Naval Volunteer Reserve, and the 2/22nd Battn. London Regt. He was created a Companion of the Distinguished Service Order in 1915, for services in Gallipoli. He was awarded the Victoria Cross [London Gazette, 18 Dec. 1917]: "Arthur Drummond Borton, Lieut.-Colonel, D.S.O., London Regt. For most conspicuous bravery and leadership. Under most difficult conditions in darkness and in an unknown country, he deployed his battalion for attack, and at dawn led his attacking companies against a strongly held position. When the leading waves were checked by a withering machine-gun fire, Lieut.-Colonel Borton showed an utter contempt of danger, and moved freely up and down his lines under heavy fire. Reorganizing his command, he led his men forward, and captured the position. At a later stage of the fight he led a party of volunteers against a battery of field guns in action at point-blank range, capturing the guns and the detachments. His fearless leadership was an inspiring example to the whole brigade." Lieut.-Colonel Borton received a most enthusiastic welcome when he returned from Palestine, at the village of Yardley, where the further progress of his motor-car was stopped for speech-making and general congratulations, and Cheveney, where he was received by a guard of honour, by the Boy Scouts, and the wounded soldiers from Cheveney Hospital. A week later he received the Victoria Cross and the Distinguished Service Order at Buckingham Palace. He married in 1915, Lorna Stewart, daughter of Robert Stewart Lockhart.

LAFONE, ALEXANDER MALINS, Major, was born 19 Aug. 1870, at Cressfield Waterloo, near Liverpool, the younger son of the late Henry Lafone, of Knockholt, Kent, and Lucy, daughter of David Malins, of Edgbaston, Birmingham, his brother being Archdeacon of Furness. He was educated at Dulwich College, and passed for Cooper's Hill. After studying for two years at the Engineering Electrical Institute, South Kensington, and spending a year and a half at Messrs. Marshall & Sons, Gainsborough (in the workshops), he was appointed Assistant Manager and Engineer to the Jokai Tea Company, Assam, in 1894, and three years later, joined his father in business at Butler's Wharf, Limited. He was a director of several companies, and a few years ago became a partner in the firm of F. A. Roberts & Co. Leadenhall Street. He joined, 28 Dec. 1899, the Montgomeryshire Yeomanry, and served in South Africa, 1900, during operations in the Transvaal,

Alexander M. Lafone.

west of Pretoria ; was wounded in the right eye 18 Aug. 1900, and sailed for England 12 Dec. 1900. He received the Queen's Medal and three clasps. He was given a commission in the 1st County of London Middlesex Yeomanry 14 Aug. 1901, and promoted Captain 14 July, 1902, Major 22 Aug. 1911. He had previously held a commission as Second Lieutenant in the Hertfordshire Imperial Yeomanry from 25 April, 1901, till 19 June, 1901 when he resigned. On the outbreak of the European War he served with his regiment in Egypt, Dardanelles, the Balkans and Palestine. He was killed in action 27 Oct. 1917, and posthumously awarded the Victoria Cross [London Gazette, 18 Dec. 1917]: "Alexander Malins Lafone, Major, late 1st County of London (Middlesex Yeomanry). For most conspicuous bravery, leadership and self-sacrifice, when holding a position for over seven hours against vastly superior forces. All this time the enemy were shelling his position heavily, making it very difficult to see. In one attack, when the enemy cavalry charged his flank, he drove them back with heavy losses. In another charge they left fifteen casualties within twenty yards of his trench, one man, who reached his trench, being bayoneted by Major Lafone himself. When all his men, with the exception of three, had been hit, and the trench which he was holding was so full of wounded that it was difficult to move and fire, he ordered those who could walk to move to a trench slightly in the rear, and from his own position maintained a most heroic resistance. When finally surrounded and charged by the enemy, he stepped into the open and continued the fight until he was mortally wounded and fell unconscious. His cheerfulness and courage were a splendid inspiration to his men, and by his leadership and devotion he was enabled to maintain his position, which he had been ordered to hold at all costs." His Colonel, in a letter home, wrote: "He held a post until only three unwounded men remained against vastly superior odds, and was one of the last to fall, but not before he had shown such a magnificent example that he was enabled to hold his post from 3.45 in the morning until 11.30. . . . He is deeply mourned by officers and men, and his squadron is inconsolable. Everybody loved him, and his loss is one it is quite impossible to replace." One who knew him intimately says: "He was one of the most selfless men that ever lived, and had his life not been what it was he would not have been able to show the enduring bravery and absolute self-sacrifice which won for him the Victoria Cross. It was not won by one swift deed of courage in the heart of a charge."

JEFFRIES, CLARENCE SMITH, Capt., served in the European War, and for his gallantry while serving in France was awarded a posthumous Victoria Cross [London Gazette, 18 Dec. 1917]: "Clarence Smith Jeffries, Capt., late 34th Battn. Australian Imperial Force. For most conspicuous bravery in attack, when his company was held up by enemy machine-gun fire from concrete emplacements. Organizing a party, he rushed one emplacement, capturing four machine guns and thirty-five prisoners. He then led his company forward under extremely heavy enemy artillery barrage and enfilade machine-gun fire to the objective. Later, he again organized a successful attack on a machine-gun emplacement, capturing two machine guns and thirty more prisoners. This gallant officer was killed during the attack, but it was entirely due to his bravery and initiative that the centre of the attack was not held up for a lengthy period. His example had a most inspiring influence."

Clarence Smith Jeffries.

Clarence Smith Jeffries was born at Wallsend, Newcastle, New South Wales, son of Joshua and Barbara Jeffries. He was educated at Newcastle High School, and served in the Citizen Forces from the age of fourteen to the time of enlistment for active service, 8 Aug. 1914. He left Australia 27 May, 1916, as Provisional Lieutenant, and was confirmed in this rank at Salisbury in July, 1916. He proceeded to France, was present at the Battles of Messines (where he was wounded and promoted to Captain) and Passchendaele, when he was killed in action.

SHANKLAND, ROBERT, Lieut., was born at Ayr, only son of William Shankland, railway guard for forty years in the service of the Glasgow and South Western Railway Company. His parents live at 68, Church Street, Ayr. He was educated at Smith's Institution, and at Russell Street School, Ayr, and was a member of the local battalion of the Boys' Brigade. For two years he was in an accountant's office, and subsequently for seven years was clerk at Ayr passenger station. He emigrated to Canada in 1911, and when war broke out he was assistant cashier of the Crece Creamery Company, Winnipeg. He joined the Army as a Private in the Canadian Infantry. He served in the European War, and went through all non-commissioned ranks to that of Regimental Sergt.-Major, and while holding this rank was awarded the Distinguished Conduct Medal. He was given a commission as Second Lieutenant and was promoted Lieutenant. He was awarded the Victoria Cross [London Gazette, 18 Dec. 1917]: "Robert Shankland, Lieut.. Canadian Infantry. For most conspicuous bravery and resource in action under critical and adverse conditions. Having gained a position, he rallied the remnant of his own platoon and men of other companies, disposed them to command the ground in front, and inflicted heavy casualties upon the retreating enemy. Later, he dispersed a counter-attack, thus enabling supporting troops to come up unmolested. He then personally communicated to Headquarters an accurate and valuable report as to the position on the brigade frontage, and, after doing so, rejoined his command and carried on until relieved. His courage and splendid example inspired all ranks, and, coupled with his great gallantry and skill, undoubtedly saved a very critical situation." Lieut. Shankland was, on his return home, made a Freeman of the Borough of Ayr, and, in addition, received a presentation from the Boys' Brigade. "Thirty Canadian V.C.'s" says (pages 70–73): "The attack made by the 3rd and 4th Canadian Divisions on 26 Oct. formed an essential preliminary to the capture of the whole Passchendaele Ridge and town. It was necessary to establish a good jumping-off line for the attack on the village itself, and this was accomplished, though our men went through some very stiff fighting indeed before the position was won. The troops of the 9th Brigade had as their objectives Bellevue Spur and the high ground above it, and after the fighting a captured German officer remarked that the spur was considered to be the key of Passchendaele town, and that its capture by the Canadians was a notable feat of arms, considering the efforts made by the German Higher Command to ensure its successful defence. One does not know if the officer was merely endeavouring to alleviate the mild rigours of his captivity, but, in any case, the fighting was most difficult and critical, and too much praise cannot be given to the scattered parties of men who hung on to isolated positions in shell-holes and ditches along the crest of the hill, under the most intense shell fire, and held back the enemy until reinforcements arrived and consolidated the line. The 43rd Battn. held the centre of the 3rd Divisional front, on the left of the Gravenstafel–Bellevue Road, with the 58th Battn. on the right and the 4th Canadian Mounted Rifles on the left. At 5.40 a.m. the troops went forward in the steady rain, advancing splendidly over the muddy, wet ground, and by half-past six men of the 43rd were seen against the sky-line going over the crest of Bellevue Spur. The German artillery fire had been immediate and heavy, and formidable pill-boxes on the top and flanks of the hill maintained steady fire upon our troops causing many gaps in the waves of infantry stumbling and slipping upon the muddy slopes. 'D' Company, led by Capt. Galt and Lieut. Shankland, made good progress up the hill, until checked by the heavy fire of a machine gun in a strong emplacement to the right front. Collecting a few men, Capt. Galt attempted its capture, while Lieut. Shankland continued the advance with the remainder of the company. He gained the crest of the hill, and here close fighting won our men more ground. The pill-boxes were captured, but a trench some fifty yards beyond them checked the advance, and the weary survivors of the attack dug themselves in as well as possible. In the meantime the battle was going badly enough. On the right the troops of the 58th Battn., held up by determined resistance and the concentrated fire of many machine guns at Snipe Hall, had been unable to make good their objective, and were drifting back in twos and threes to the comparative shelter of the jumping-off line. But a few parties of men held out with Shankland's company on the crest, and maintained a rough and disjointed line of shell-holes, of which there were many, across the hill-top. Upon this line the Germans poured a relentless stream of lead. At no time previously had our men experienced such shelling. The mud and water dispersed by the bursting shells clogged the weapons of the Canadians, and, in spite of instant attention, in many cases rendered them temporarily useless. The going was terribly hard, but Lieut. Shankland held his battered line for four hours along the crest of the Spur, keeping his men together and in good spirits, recruiting those soldiers of other companies who had gained the hill but were left without officers, and maintaining against heavy counter-attack the Canadian position that had cost so much to win. But here a new danger asserted itself. On his left Shankland had established rough connection with the 8th Brigade, but now these troops were forced to withdraw, while on the right his flank was completely exposed, and German troops were advancing from the direction of Snipe Hall, enfilading his line, and threatening to cut him off altogether. After a careful survey of the whole position, he handed over the command to the machine-gun officer, who, though wounded, had refused to leave the line while his guns were in action, and making the best of his way back to Headquarters, handed in a very valuable report, giving a clear summary of a critical situation, and enabling steps to be taken that previous lack of information had rendered unwise. While the men of the 52nd and 58th Battns. drove back the enemy on the flanks, the lieutenant got back through the mud and shell fire to his own company on the hill-top. The Germans had attempted to rush this precarious position, and had been beaten back by our machine-gun fire with heavy losses. They had continued to lose, for the 52nd Battn., advancing in splendid style, drove many of them back across the fire of Shankland's company of the 43rd upon the crest of the Spur. Finally, the flanks were firmly established, and our troops consolidated the new line, with the object of our attack accomplished, though they had not penetrated as far into enemy country as they had hoped."

STRACHAN, HARCUS, Lieut., was born in 1889, at Bo'ness, Scotland, third son of the late William Strachan, Sheriff-Clark of Linlithgowshire, and of Mrs. William Strachan. He was educated at Bo'ness Academy, at the Royal High School, Edinburgh, and at Edinburgh University. He played Rugby football when at the Royal High School, Edinburgh. In 1905 he bought a ranch in Alberta, Canada. At the outbreak of war he set out for England, after failing to pass an eyesight test in Canada, intending to join the London Scottish; but when he arrived in England he was admitted, after much perseverance, to the Fort Garry Horse, Canadian Cavalry, as a Trooper. He served in the European War, was given a commission in the field, and in May, 1917, was awarded the Military Cross for bold conception, swift movement and courageous leading, resulting in the destruction of the enemy's defensive organization. He was awarded the Victoria Cross [London Gazette, 18 Dec. 1917]: "Harcus Strachan, M.C., Fort Garry Horse, Canadian Cavalry. For most conspicuous bravery and leadership during operations. He took command of the squadron of his regiment when the squadron leader, approaching the enemy front line at a gallop, was killed. Lieut. Strachan led the squadron through the enemy line of machine-gun posts, and then, with the surviving men, led the charge on the enemy battery, killing seven gunners with his sword. All the gunners having been killed and the battery silenced, he rallied his men and fought his way back at night through the enemy's line, bringing all unwounded men safely in, together with fifteen prisoners. The operation—which resulted in the silencing of an enemy battery, the killing of the whole battery personnel and many infantry, and the cutting of three main lines of telephone communication two miles in rear of the enemy's front line—was only rendered possible by the outstanding gallantry and fearless leading of this officer." He was presented with a sword of honour by his native town, Bo'ness, at a public reception, at which Lord Rosebery was present, and further honour was done to him when he was asked to sit for his portrait in oils, which is to hang in the Parliament House at Ottawa. He was promoted Major. He was released from the Canadian Forces in order to go with the British troops to Archangel. "Thirty Canadian V.C.'s" says (pages 88–93): "It is generally admitted that initiative and an aggressive spirit are very necessary concomitants of the successful cavalry leader. Their possession does not prove an infallible rule—cavalrymen claim no monopoly of these qualities—yet on occasion a cavalry officer's possession of them to a degree marks an exploit abnormal in its exceptional dash and daring. Such an exploit was that of Lieut. Strachan, of the Fort Garry Horse, in Nov. 1917, at Cambrai. During the morning of 20 Nov. the Canadian Cavalry Brigade moved forward to the outskirts of Masnieres, and there the troopers halted, awaiting word from the G.O.C. 88th Brigade, whose men were preparing the way for the cavalry. The British infantry and Tanks had broken the enemy's line between Gonnelieu and Hermies, and it was the intention of the Higher Command to push the cavalry forward through the gap, and with the mounted men to seize Bourlon Wood and Cambrai, to hold the passages across the Sensee River, and to cut off the enemy's troops between Havrincourt and the Sensee. Riding forward into Masnieres, General Seely received word that the attacking troops had secured their objectives, and accordingly the brigade advance guard, the Fort Garry Horse, entered the town and managed to get across the river bridge in the main street. The canal bridge beyond, however, had been broken down, either by the weight of a tank or blown up by the enemy during the crossing of one of these machines. At any rate, one of our tanks had plunged through into the canal beneath, and, without very radical repair, the bridge was impassable to mounted men. Another bridge, in a rather better condition, was discovered to the south-west, and Major Walker, of the Machine Gun Squadron, commandeered the help of every available man, including civilians and German prisoners, and by three o'clock the bridge was strong and practicable. This work was accomplished under very heavy fire. Upon the completion of the bridge, ' B ' Squadron of the Fort Garry Horse, under the command of Capt. Campbell, pushed forward across the canal and attacked the enemy's line upon the ridge, while the remainder of the regiment prepared to follow. But conflicting statements arrived from the infantry—there had been a check—and before the rest of the mounted men could advance, Colonel Patterson, commanding the Fort Garry Horse, received orders instructing him not only to remain west of the canal, but to withdraw any of his troops that might have crossed. Colonel Patterson immediately sent messengers after ' B ' Squadron, but the orderlies were unable to deliver their instructions. The Canadian troopers had wasted no time—opportunity had been denied them too long—and there had been little delay in getting to grips with the enemy. They were well away. Capt. Campbell's men came under machine-gun fire directly they left Masnieres, and for a few minutes the horses were hard put to it in the marshy ground about the canal. Before them the infantry had cut a gap in the German wire, and winning through the swamp they charged for this at the gallop, taking little heed of the heavy fire. Casualties were rather heavy at the gap. Capt. Campbell went down, and command was taken by Lieut. Strachan. There was no delay. Sweeping through the gap, Strachan led his men north towards Rumilly, and soon encountered the camouflaged road just south-east of the town. This obstacle was negotiated successfully enough, with some slight damage to the screens and an occasional telephone wire, and, forming in line of troop columns, the men went forward at the gallop to an objective dear to any cavalryman's heart. A battery of field guns lay before them. A good horse, firm ground and guns to be taken—a cavalryman wants no more. The Canadians charged down upon them, and in a moment were among the guns, riding the gunners down or sabreing them as they stood. Two of the guns were deserted by their crews as our fellows came thundering down, the third was blown up by its gunners, and the crew of the fourth fired a hasty round point-blank at the advancing troopers. This shot might have seriously disorganized the mounted men, but fortunately the gunners were much too demoralized to train their weapon surely. The shell went wide. There was a brief mêlée of plunging horses and stumbling artillerymen. Then the business was finished, and the men hoped for a breathing-space. But there was no rest for a while. Behind the guns a body of German infantry appeared, and, swinging his men about, Strachan led the troopers on into the thick of them. A few saddles were emptied, but the firing was vague and ragged. The Germans were not accustomed to this kind of thing and would not stand. They fled, our fellows cutting them down as they ran. Strachan gathered his men and continued towards Rumilly, under constant fire from blockhouses on the outskirts of the town. A sunken road crossed his line about half a mile east of the town, and here the troopers halted and prepared a hasty stronghold. All this time Lieut. Strachan had been anxiously waiting for news or sight of the main body of the Cavalry Brigade, and as the day passed and there was no sign of his regiment, he realized that something had gone wrong. He could not face the German Army with less than a hundred cavalrymen, however determined, but he decided to hold on awhile in the rough cover of the sunken road until it became obvious that no supports were coming to his assistance that night. The enemy had collected what troops he could, and the land of dismounted troopers were surrounded on three sides. Several tentative rushes had been made, but the steady fire of the Canadians had driven these back in disorder. Still, without rapid support it was impossible for the party to hold out much longer. Only five horses remained unwounded, and the strength of the squadron was under fifty men. Ammunition was none too plentiful, and Strachan called for two volunteers to carry messages back to Headquarters in Masnieres. The job was risky enough, but there was more difficulty in selecting applicants than procuring them. Two troopers, Privates Morrell and Vanwilderode, were dispatched, and in the meantime the lieutenant set his men to cutting three main telephone cables that ran along the side of the sunken road. This small operation in itself should have caused the enemy some slight annoyance. The light was going fast, and Strachan decided to abandon his horses and cut his way through to Masnieres. He imagined, shrewdly enough, that though the Germans were in no manner of doubt as to his presence, they were very vague about the strength of his party, and were by no means anxious to try for a definite conclusion until their numbers were assuredly overwhelming. The light was just strong enough to distinguish the church tower of Rumilly, and taking a compass bearing from the building, Strachan started off to fight his way back to the brigade. First he collected his horses, and with some commotion stampeded them to the eastwards. This manœuvre drew the fire of every machine-gun in the vicinity upon the unfortunate animals, for the Germans thought that, not content with the havoc that they had already created behind their lines, the irrepressible cavalrymen were starting off again upon their destructive mission. With the mêlée at its height, Strachan gathered his men, and led them off quietly towards the British lines. The journey back was hardly less eventful than the outgoing trip, though it was a great deal slower. Leading his men through the dark, Strachan made as straight a line as possible for the town where he had left the brigade. One might have imagined that the military ardour which had fired these troopers throughout the day would have been temporarily damped, but there was no sign of it. No less than four parties of Germans were encountered on the homeward route, and each time attacked and dispersed. On two occasions the enemy was numerically a great deal stronger, but disregarding the obvious, the dismounted troopers went forward with the bayonet, routed the unsuspecting Germans and captured more prisoners than they could conveniently handle. However, most of them were brought along, and after an hour of somewhat nervous travelling the remainder of the squadron reached the wire. At this point there was some slight difficulty in finding a gap that would admit the passage of the men, and in the search in the darkness the party became separated. Lieut. Cowen with the prisoners and half the men made the best of his way back to Masnieres, while Strachan sought another road with the rest of his squadron. Both parties were successful and came in without a further casualty. Comment on the day's action would be superfluous. Strachan had destroyed a battery, inflicted well over a hundred casualties, most effectively tangled German communications over a wide radius, and captured or caused the surrender of a number of the enemy exceeding the original strength of his squadron. Had conditions been favourable for the use of cavalry upon a larger scale a very great victory might have been won."

ROBERTSON, CLEMENT, Capt., served in the European War, and was awarded the Victoria Cross [London Gazette, 18 Dec. 1917]: " Clement Robertson, Temporary Lieut. (Acting Capt.), Special Reserve, late Royal West Surrey Regt., Tank Corps. Date of Act of Bravery: 4 Oct. 1917. For most conspicuous bravery in leading his Tanks in attack under heavy shell, machine-gun and rifle fire, over ground which had been heavily ploughed by shell fire. Capt. Robertson, knowing the risk of the Tanks missing the way, continued to lead them on foot, guiding them carefully and patiently towards their objective, although he must have known that his action would almost inevitably cost him his life. This gallant officer was killed after his objective had been reached, but his skilful leading had already ensured successful action. His utter disregard of danger and devotion to duty afford an example of outstanding valour."

COVERDALE, HARRY, Sergt., was born on 22 April, 1889, at Old Trafford, Manchester, son of John Coverdale and of Emily Coverdale. He was educated at Bangor Street Board School, and joined the Army on 7 Sept. 1914. He served in the European War in Gallipoli, Egypt and France, 1915 to 1918. He was awarded the Victoria Cross [London Gazette, 18 Dec. 1917]: " No 4926, Harry Coverdale, Sergt., Manchester Regt. (Old Trafford, Manchester). For most conspicuous bravery in attack on enemy strong points. He showed the utmost gallantry in approaching his objective, and when close to it, disposed of an enemy officer and two men who were sniping our flank, killing the officer and taking the two men prisoners. He then rushed two machine guns, killing or wounding the teams. He subsequently reorganized his platoon in order to capture another position, but after getting within a hundred yards of it, he was held up by our own barrage, and was obliged to return, having sustained nine casualties. Later, this gallant non-commissioned officer again went out with five men to capture this position, and when he had gone some distance he saw a considerable number of the enemy advancing. He thereupon withdrew his detachment man by man, he himself being the last to retire, when he was able to report that the enemy were forming for a counter-attack. By his gallant leadership and utter disregard of danger throughout the attack, he set a splendid example of fearlessness to his men, and inspired all with a spirit of emulation which undoubtedly contributed largely to the success of the operations." Lieut. Coverdale writes: " I have filled up particulars desired. I enlisted in the Engineers in 1914; was told that I would have to wait; didn't wish to wait, so asked to be put in the infantry, and was put in the Manchester Regt.; went in training at Riby with 4th Battn. I had the Military Medal presented in Aug. 1917, for carrying on and holding the objective after all officers had been killed or wounded. I had the D.C.M. ribbon presented to me on the field, and after wearing the ribbon for a fortnight, it was taken off me through a clerical error, and had the Military Medal presented instead. I had the honour of gaining my commission in my own regiment in Oct. 1918; remained with them until March, 1919; was then demobilized. I returned to my duties in civil life as an engineer. I am sorry I am unable to relate anything about sport which is very interesting. I was always taking part in all the regimental sports, being the goalkeeper and stumper for the team, always playing in those positions with our local team at home. I am still single; lost my father while I was at Gallipoli, and am living at home with my mother and sisters."

Harry Coverdale.

CLAMP, WILLIAM, Corpl., served in the European War in France, and was awarded the Victoria Cross [London Gazette, 18 Dec. 1917]: " No. 43537, William Clamp, Corpl., late 6th Battn. Yorkshire Regt. For most conspicuous bravery when an advance was being checked by intense machine-gun fire from concrete blockhouses and by snipers in ruined buildings. Corporal Clamp dashed forward with two men and attempted to rush the largest blockhouse. His first attempt failed owing to the two men with him being knocked out; but he at once collected some bombs, and, calling upon two men to follow him, again dashed forward. He was first to reach the blockhouse and hurled his bombs, killing many of the occupants. He then entered and brought out a machine gun and about twenty prisoners, whom he brought back under heavy fire from neighbouring snipers. This non-commissioned officer then again went forward encouraging and cheering the men, and succeeded in rushing several sniper's posts. He continued to display the greatest heroism until he was killed by a sniper. His magnificent courage and self-sacrifice was of the greatest value, and relieved what was undoubtedly a very critical situation."

COLLINS, JOHN, Corpl., was born in Nov. 1877. at West Hatch. Somerset, son of Tom Collins and Mary Ann Collins, of 54, High Street, Penydarren, Tydfil, South Wales. He was educated at West Hatch, in the county of Somerset, and joined the Army on 18 Nov. 1895, as a Driver in the R.H.A. He was seventeen when he first became a soldier, and he took part in the South African War, and was among the first of the troops to enter Ladysmith on its relief. He has the South African Queen's and King's Medals with seven clasps. Three of his brothers also served in that war, and his parents received congratulations from Queen Victoria, which gained for the Collins' family the name of "the fighting family of Penydarren." After the South African War he settled in Penydarren, and for some years worked at the Bedling Collieries. He was married at St. Illtyd's Church, Dowlais, on 17 March, 1910, to Mary Ellen O'Brien, daughter of John and Mary O'Brien.

John Collins.

He rejoined the Army at the outbreak of war, being the second of hundreds of Penydarren men recruited. He was transferred from the Welsh Horse, in which he re-enlisted, to the Royal Welsh Fusiliers. He served in the European War in Palestine. He was awarded the Victoria Cross [London Gazette, 18 Dec. 1917]: "No. 355652, John Collins, Acting Corpl., Royal Welsh Fusiliers. For most conspicuous bravery, resource and leadership, when, after deployment, prior to an attack, his battalion was forced to lie out in the open under heavy shell and machine-gun fire, which caused many casualties. This gallant non-commissioned officer repeatedly went out under heavy fire and brought wounded back to cover, thus saving many lives. In subsequent operations throughout the day Corpl. Collins was conspicuous in rallying and leading his command. He led the final assault with the utmost skill, in spite of heavy fire at close range and uncut wire. He bayoneted 15 of the enemy, and with a Lewis gun section pressed on beyond the objective and covered the reorganization and consolidation most effectively, although isolated and under fire from snipers and guns. He showed throughout a magnificent example of initiative and fearlessness." He was promoted to Sergeant 31 Oct. 1917. He was awarded the Distinguished Conduct Medal [London Gazette, 30 Nov. 1917]. He was wounded on 8 Oct. 1918 in France.

SAGE, THOMAS H., Private, served in the European War in France, and was awarded the Victoria Cross [London Gazette, 18 Dec. 1917]: "Thomas H. Sage, No. 33316, Private, 8th Battn. Somerset Light Infantry (Tiverton). For most conspicuous bravery during an attack on an enemy strong post. He was in a shell-hole with eight other men, one of whom was shot with a bomb. The live bomb fell into the shell-hole, and Private Sage, with great courage and presence of mind, immediately threw himself on it, thereby undoubtedly saving the lives of several of his comrades though he himself sustained very severe wounds."

London Gazette, 11 Jan. 1918.—" War Office, 11 Jan. 1918. His Majesty the King has been graciously pleased to approve of the award of the Victoria Cross to the undermentioned Officers, Non-commissioned Officers and Men, for most conspicuous bravery."

SHERWOOD-KELLY, JOHN, C.M.G., D.S.O., Major (Acting Lieut.-Colonel), served in the European War. He was created a Companion of the Distinguished Service Order, and was created a Companion of the Order of St. Michael and St. George. He was awarded the Victoria Cross [London Gazette, 11 Jan. 1918]: "John Sherwood-Kelly, C.M.G., D.S.O., Major (Acting Lieut.-Colonel), Norfolk Regt., Commanding a Battalion, Royal Inniskilling Fusiliers. For most conspicuous bravery and fearless leading when a party of men of another unit detailed to cover the passage of the canal by his battalion were held up on the near side of the canal by heavy rifle fire directed on the bridge. Lieut.-Colonel Sherwood-Kelly at once ordered covering fire, personally led the leading company of his battalion across the canal, and, after crossing, reconnoitred under heavy rifle and machine-gun fire the high ground held by the enemy. The left flank of his battalion advancing to the assault of this objective was held up by a thick belt of wire, whereupon he crossed to that flank, and with a Lewis gun team forced his way under heavy fire through obstacles, got the gun into position on the far side, and covered the advance of his battalion through the wire, thereby enabling them to capture the position. Later, he personally led a charge against some pits, from which a heavy fire was being directed on his men, captured the pits, together with five machine guns and 46 prisoners, and killed a large number of the enemy. The great gallantry displayed by this officer throughout the day inspired

the greatest confidence in his men, and it was mainly due to his example and devotion to duty that his battalion was enabled to capture and hold their objective." He served in Russia.

PEARKES, GEORGE RANDOLPH, Capt. (Acting Major), joined the Canadian Military Forces, and served in the European War in France. He was awarded the Military Cross, and was awarded the Victoria Cross [London Gazette, 11 Jan. 1918]: "George Randolph Pearkes, M.C., Capt. (Acting Major), 5th Battn. Canadian Mounted Rifles. For most conspicuous bravery and skilful handling of the troops under his command during the capture and consolidation of considerably more than the objectives allotted to him in an attack. Just before the advance, Major Pearkes was wounded in the left thigh. Regardless of his wound, he continued to lead his men with the utmost gallantry, despite many obstacles. At a particular stage of the attack his further advance was threatened by a strong point which was an objective of the battalion on his left, but which they had not succeeded in capturing. Quickly appreciating the situation, he captured and held this point,

George R. Pearkes.

thus enabling his further advance to be successfully pushed forward. It was entirely due to his determination and fearless personality that he was able to maintain his objective with the small number of men at his command against repeated enemy counter-attacks, both his flanks being unprotected for a considerable depth meanwhile. His appreciation of the situation throughout, and the reports rendered by him were invaluable to his Commanding Officer in making dispositions of troops to hold the position captured. He showed throughout a supreme contempt of danger and wonderful powers of control and leading." He was promoted to Lieut.-Colonel, and was later wounded for the fifth time during the war. The following is quoted from "Thirty Canadian V.C.'s," edited by Capt. Roberts, and published by Messrs. Skeffington (pages 67–70): "There are many wonderful deeds recorded in the history of the Canadian Corps at Passchendaele, but for stubborn endurance carried far beyond previous standards of physical limitations, for cool pluck and pertinacity under very terrible conditions, the story of the 5th Canadian Mounted Rifle Battn. on 30 Oct. 1917, is remarkable. The night of the 29th was clear and fine, and the moon was nearly full, the light helping our men to pick their way through to the assembly on the comparatively firm ground between the flooded shell-holes. Soon after 5 o'clock on the morning of the 30th the troops were in position, and at ten minutes to six A and C Companies went over the top and forward to the attack on Vapour Farm and the outlying defences of Passchendaele. The ground immediately before the 5th C.M.R. was very swampy, and owing to this it had been previously found impossible to send troops straight through Woodland Plantation. Accordingly the waves of our attacking infantry divided, and A Company went forward and round the south of the Plantation, while B Company attacked on the north. For nearly an hour the smoke covering the plantation prevented any observation of our progress, but soon a wounded runner stumbled into Headquarters with a report that the left of our attack had reached the intermediate objective. On the right the men of A Company had encountered the enemy south of the wood and fierce hand-to-hand fighting was still going on, with the Canadians steadily making their way forward. In this bayonet work, with the opponents waist-deep in mud and water, our men won the advantage, for the knowledge that a mis-step or a disabling wound meant a peculiarly unpleasant death in suffocating mud was an incentive to desperate fighting, and the Germans hated it from the start. By the time the smoke had cleared our troops had won their way around the copse, and the two companies, now barely half their original strength, had joined and were resting while our barrage hammered the line of the intermediate objective. But this halt was a mistake. The Germans, retreating before our advance, were given time to reform, and in a moment or two machine-gun and rifle fire became terribly heavy from the high ground to the east. However, led by Major Pearkes and reinforced by the remaining companies, the 5th C.M.R. went forward again, until our observers lost sight of them as they went over the ridge. Then occurred a time of anxious suspense for the men at Headquarters, until half an hour later a message came through from Major Pearkes saying that he was holding a line near to his final objectives with some fifty men, that the fighting was close and desperate, and that help was required. Major Pearkes was in a very difficult situation. He had taken his men forward, fighting his way through obstacle after obstacle until he had reached his objective, and now he was holding a hastily improvised line with both his flanks exposed to any German attack. The troops attacking with him on each side had been unable to make any headway, and only the well-directed and aggressive shooting of his men prevented a flanking move that might have cut him off completely. On his left the Artists' Rifles had been unable to capture Source Farm, and from this point heavy enfilading fire was poured upon his exposed line. It was impossible to maintain any position under such fire, and the Major realized that the only hope of holding his ground lay in the capture of this strong point. With the few men at his command he organized and led an attack, and the gallant recklessness of the assaulting party carried the place by storm. Now he could get forward again, and he did so, only halting to establish his line when it became obvious that his handful of men, though willing enough, could hardly fight their way through an entire army corps. He withdrew his men from Vanity House, consolidated a line of shell-holes from Source Farm to Vapour Farm and prepared to meet a strong counter-attack. His fighting strength was now twenty men. It is hard to conceive how so small a party may hold a previously unprepared position against a determined attack, but these men did so, and beat the Germans back in disorder. However, it was scarcely possible to withstand another such attack—ammunition was running short, the rate of casualties was much too high for so slight a garrison, and a flanking attack by the enemy could hardly fail to be successful—but Major Pearkes and his men held on, praying for reinforcements and determined to see it through. A company of the 2nd C.M.R. had been sent forward to reinforce the original assailants, and finally, as the fresh troops advanced, they came within sight of the weary garrison. Most of the ground behind the latter was low and swampy, and all of it was swept by the enemy's machine-gun fire, but the supporting company came over the heavy ground in splendid style. The men in the shell-holes could see the casualties occurring in the wave of men, but never for a moment was there any hesitation, and at last the reinforcements tumbled into Pearkes' rough line of defence. Affairs were still in a serious condition. The shell-fire was very heavy and counter-attacks were imminent, and it was not until after dusk that sufficient supports were available to cover the flanks and enable the successful consolidation of our new line."

RUSSELL, JOHN FOX, Capt., served in the European War. He was awarded the Military Cross [London Gazette, 16 Aug. 1917]. For his services in Palestine he was awarded the Victoria Cross [London Gazette, 11 Jan. 1918]: "John Fox Russell, M.C., Capt., late Royal Army Medical Corps, attached 116th Battn. Royal Welsh Fusiliers. For most conspicuous bravery displayed in action until he was killed. Capt. Russell repeatedly went out to attend the wounded under murderous fire from snipers and machine guns, and in many cases where no other means were at hand carried them in himself, although almost exhausted. He showed the highest possible degree of valour."

GEE, ROBERT, Capt., was born at Leicester on 7 May, 1876, son of Robert Gee and of Amy Gee, daughter of Robert Foulds, of Newark-on-Trent. He was apprenticed at the age of 16 to Mr. Shaw, Ornamental Metal and Iron Worker, of Aylestone, Leicestershire. He left his position before ending his apprenticeship, and joined the Army, enlisting in the Royal Fusiliers. He rose to non-commissioned rank, and studied military history, and was appointed a lecturer in that subject. He was given a commission in the Royal Fusiliers, and posted to the 2nd Battn. 31 May, 1915; proceeded to Gallipoli, and commanded a company; appointed Staff Captain, 86th Brigade, 15 March, 1916; was wounded 1 July, 1916, and was awarded the Military Cross in 1916. He served in Egypt in 1916, and in 1916 and 1917 he served on the Somme, and was present at the battles of Ypres and at Cambrai in 1917, and at Arras; in fact, was with the 29th Division, on the Staff, from 1916 till 24 June, 1917, and on the Staff, 86th Brigade, from 26 June, 1917. He was wounded in Aug. 1917; rejoined Staff in Sept. 1917; was wounded 30 Nov. 1917, and rejoined in Jan. 1918. Capt. Gee was mentioned in Despatches in Sept. 1916; Dec. 1917, and Jan, 1918. He was awarded the greatest of all decorations, the Victoria Cross, for the part he took in the great counter-attack at Cambrai with the 2nd Battn. of his regiment at Les Rives Vertes, Marcoing and Masnieres on 30 Nov. The award was announced in the London Gazette, 11 Jan. 1918: "Robert Gee, M.C., Lieut. (Temporary Capt.), 2nd Battn. Royal Fusiliers. For most conspicuous bravery, initiative and determination when an attack by a strong enemy force pierced our line and captured a brigade headquarters and ammunition dump. Capt. Gee, finding himself a prisoner, killed one of the enemy with his spiked stick, and succeeded in escaping. He then organized a party of the brigade staff, with which he attacked the enemy fiercely, closely followed and supported by two companies of infantry. By his own personal bravery and prompt action he, aided by his orderlies, cleared the locality. Capt. Gee established a defensive flank on the outskirts of the village, then finding that an enemy machine gun was still in action, with a revolver in each hand, and followed by one man, he rushed and captured the gun, killing eight of the crew. At this time he was wounded, but refused to have the wound dressed until he was satisfied that the defence was organized.". He was appointed Staff Captain, Tees Garrison, Middlesbrough. Capt. Gee is a fluent speaker, and took part in several patriotic efforts in Nottingham in the summer of 1918, also at Hartlepool and Middlesbrough. He has served 23 years with the Royal Fusiliers; was a first-class all-round sportsman, principally in hockey and cross-country running.

Robert Gee.

O'KELLY, CHRISTOPHER PATRICK JOHN, M.C., Capt., served in the European War; was awarded the Military Cross, and the Victoria Cross [London Gazette, 11 Jan. 1918]: "Christopher Patrick John O'Kelly, M.C., Lieut. (Acting Capt.), Canadian Infantry. For most conspicuous bravery in an action in which he led his company with extraordinary skill and determination. After the original attack had failed and two companies of his unit had launched a new attack, Capt. O'Kelly advanced his command over 1,000 yards under heavy fire without any artillery barrage, took the enemy positions on the crest of the hill by storm, and then personally organized and led a series of attacks against 'pill-boxes,' his company alone capturing six of them, with 100 prisoners and 10 machine guns. Later on in the afternoon, under the leadership of this gallant officer, his company repelled a strong counter-attack, taking more prisoners, and subsequently during the night captured a hostile raiding party consisting of one officer, ten men, and a machine gun. The whole of these achievements were chiefly due to the magnificent courage, daring and ability of Capt. O'Kelly." "Thirty Canadian V.C.'s" (edited by Capt. Roberts, and published by Messrs. Skeffington; pages 63–67) says: "When the Canadians went up to take the ridges before Passchendaele the men of the 52nd Battn. were in support, and were not pleased with their minor share in the preliminary offensive. Their fears were not justified, however, for no battalion engaged played a larger or more gallant part in the attack. The 9th Brigade attacked at 'zero' hour with the 43rd and 58th Battns., and at first reports were good, and the Canadians appeared to be making excellent progress up the difficult slopes of Bellevue Spur. But by 8.30 a.m. the news had changed, weary parties of survivors came straggling back in twos and threes to the jumping-off line, and the 52nd Battn. troops were aware that their services would be required in short order. Colonel Foster, the Commanding Officer, went forward to the front line and returned with news of a critical situation. On the right the 58th had encountered terrible machine-gun fire and had been unable to make any progress, while some forty men of Lieut. Shankland's company of the 43rd had managed to fight their way to the crest of the spur, had roughly entrenched themselves, being able to advance no more, and were still holding out after four hours of steady fighting, under heavy close-range fire from pill-boxes on the ridge, and in constant danger of a flanking move by the enemy on either hand. Lieut. O'Kelly, in charge of A company, was ordered to move at once to their assistance, advancing on the left flank of the 43rd Battn. post upon the hill, and filling the gap between the 8th and 9th Brigades. Drenched by the steady rain and pounded by the enemy's shells, the men of the 52nd were very bored indeed with inaction. They went forward strongly, penetrating the German barrage on the flank without losing very heavily, and making good progress up the low northern slope towards the crest of the spur, where their comrades of the 43rd were not only doing most effective shooting on their own account, but were preventing the Germans from paying very much attention to the manœuvres of the 52nd. The top of the hill was defended by numerous concrete machine-gun forts, and these fired spasmodically upon the advancing troops, causing a number of casualties but no delays. Lieut. O'Kelly had brought his men up well, and sweeping over the brow, they caught the flank of the enemy advancing against the 43rd Battn. post, driving the Germans before them and shooting them down as they ran. For a moment it was a most successful rout, but then the fire from the pill-boxes grew heavier, and there ensued a series of gallant attacks upon the strong points before them. Our troops rushed pill-box after pill-box, small parties of men striving to win close to the walls of each fort, while sections to the rear bombarded every opening and loophole with bullets and rifle-grenades. This made it very difficult indeed for the Germans to take aim, and allowed the actual assailants an opportunity of gaining the dead ground close beneath the walls and hurling their bombs inside through any aperture. The effect of quite a small bomb upon the mass of men in the confined space of a pill-box is very terrible, and usually the treatment requires no second application before the surrender of the garrison. However, the reduction of these forts is a very costly business, and many a time the attacking section would be caught within the zone of fire of a machine gun and practically wiped out, though on more than one occasion the attack was carried to a successful conclusion by two or three survivors, who would compel the garrison of thirty or forty men to surrender to them. Through all this fighting Lieut. O'Kelly led his men with wonderful judgment, selecting the point and method of attack with cool precision, and never losing sight of his main object—to gain ground and consolidate the ridge. Finally his force was joined by B Company, and the two companies of the 52nd set out to advance their line. The buildings of Bellevue Farm proved excellent cover for the retiring Germans, and there was stubborn fighting about the ruined outhouses before our fellows got through. A clear half-mile of ground was captured and consolidated, our men reaching the Wallemolen–Bellevue Road and driving the enemy before them from the country west of it. For a time the hostile bombardment was vague and uncertain, though on occasion a barrage would be placed before our advancing men, the enemy's gunners appearing to be supremely indifferent to the scattered parties of their own troops who were still holding out bravely enough before the Canadians. But directly our new line was in process of formation the German shelling became intense. For an hour the countryside was hammered and pounded, and then the inevitable counter-attack developed at two points of our thinly-held line. However, O'Kelly's men felt that they had saved the situation, his pluck and initiative had pulled a victory from a defeat, and the men of the 52nd had no intention of giving up a foot of the ground they had won. So heavy a fire was developed upon the attacking enemy that the counter-attack was shrivelled and dispersed two hundred yards from our line. The shelling began again, but our position was strong and clear, and consolidation was continued, while during the night Lieut. O'Kelly's men went forward again, and raided several strong points that might have hampered the advance of our men in the next phase of the offensive. The men of the 52nd Battn. have great reason to be pleased with themselves for that day's work, for they captured 9 officers and 275 men, no less than 21 machine guns, and more important still, saved a very critical situation indeed."

BENT, PHILIP ERIC, Lieut.-Colonel, joined the Army as Second Lieutenant, and served in the European War; was created a Companion of the Distinguished Service Order; became Temporary Lieutenant-Colonel, and was awarded the Victoria Cross [London Gazette, 11 Jan. 1918]: "Philip Eric Bent, D.S.O., Second Lieut. (Temporary Lieut.-Colonel), Leicestershire Regt. For most conspicuous bravery when, during a heavy hostile attack, the right of his own command and the battalion on his right were forced back. The situation was critical owing to the confusion caused by the attack and the intense artillery fire. Lieut.-Colonel Bent personally collected a platoon that was in reserve, and together with men from other companies and various regimental details, he organized and led them forward to the counter-attack, after issuing orders to other officers as to the further defence of the line. The counter-attack was successful and the enemy were checked. The coolness and magnificent example shown to all ranks by Lieut.-Colonel Bent resulted in the securing of a portion of the line which was of essential importance for subsequent operations. This very gallant officer was killed whilst leading a charge, which he inspired with the call of, 'Come on, the Tigers.'" At an investiture held at Buckingham Palace, Mrs. Sophy Bent, mother of Lieut.-Colonel Philip Bent, Leicestershire Regt., received both the D.S.O. and the Victoria Cross awarded to her son, who, though only a Second Lieutenant, was an Acting Lieutenant-Colonel.

LASCELLES, ARTHUR MOORE, Capt., 15th Durham Light Infantry, son of John Lascelles and the late Mary Elizabeth Lascelles. His father lives at Penmaen, Dyfi, Merionethshire, Wales. He was educated at Uppingham School, and joined the Cape Mounted Rifles; had 13 years' service in South Africa, which he left to help his country here. He served in the South African War. He went through the Rebellion and the Campaign in West Africa. Shortly after the outbreak of the war he joined the 3rd Durham Light Infantry, and was wounded on the Somme in 1916, where he won the Military Cross for determined gallantry and saving a critical situation. He was severely wounded at Masnieres, France, 3 Dec. 1917, and it was there that he won the Victoria Cross. The award of the Victoria Cross was announced in the London Gazette of 11 Jan. 1918: "Arthur Moore Lascelles, Capt., 3rd Durham Light Infantry. For most conspicuous bravery, initiative and devotion to duty when in command of his company in a very exposed position. After a very heavy bombardment, during which Capt. Lascelles was wounded, the enemy attacked in strong force, but was driven off, success being due in a great degree to the fine example set by this officer, who, refusing to allow his wound to be dressed, continued to encourage his men and organize the defence. Shortly afterwards the enemy again attacked and captured the trench, taking several of his men prisoners. Capt. Lascelles at once jumped on to the parapet, and followed by the remainder of his company, 12 men only, rushed across under very heavy machine-gun fire and drove over 60 of the enemy back, thereby saving a most critical situation. He was untiring in reorganizing the position, but shortly afterwards the enemy again attacked and captured the trench and Capt. Lascelles, who escaped later. The remarkable determination and gallantry of this officer in the course of operations, during which he received two further wounds, afforded an inspiring example to all."

Arthur Moore Lascelles.

The "Western Mail" (14 Jan. 1918) says:

"Capt. Lascelles is the younger surviving son of Mr. John Lascelles and of the late Mrs. Lascelles, of Penmaen, Dyfi, Merionethshire, where he was born about 36 years ago. He was educated at Uppingham School, and was in South Africa when the war commenced. He immediately joined the 1st Cape Mounted Rifles, which afterwards became known as the 1st Regiment of South African Mounted Infantry, as a Trooper, and served under General Botha until the conclusion of the successful campaign in German South-West Africa, attaining the rank of Quartermaster-Sergeant. Obtaining his discharge, he came over to this country two years last Nov., and obtained a commission in the Durham Light Infantry (Special Reserves), a regiment in which one of his brothers, Mr. Reginald Lascelles, served in the South African war, being subsequently drowned in India. Capt. Lascelles has been overseas for a considerable time, and was first wounded by shrapnel on the Somme in 1916. He is a married man with a boy of nine years, and his wife is doing her 'bit' by attending to the munition workers in canteens in the Midlands. He comes of a Welsh family who have been associated for many years with the naval and military forces of the Crown. His grandfather was serving on the St. Joseph when she brought Napoleon into Plymouth, whilst his great-grandfather was General Lascelles, of the Dragoon Guards. His cousin was the late Flight-Commander E. R. Mackenzie, D.S.O., of the Royal Navy, who was killed in an air fight in Jan. of last year."

With the use of his left arm only he again went out to France, attached to the 15th Durham Light Infantry, and was killed in action at Fontaine on 7 Nov. 1918.

Another account in the same newspaper says:

"Capt. Arthur Moore Lascelles, V.C., M.C., Durham Light Infantry, is another Welsh officer attached to an English regiment who has brought the supreme military honour to the Principality. To South Wales, apart from the decoration which the King has conferred upon Capt. Lascelles, there is a special interest in the honour, for almost side by side with his company, when they were attacked, was a Welsh regiment, whose position, like that of Capt. Lascelles' own company, would have been precarious, if not untenable, but for the initiative of this gallant officer. Capt. Lascelles, who has a brother employed at Messrs. Spillers and Bakers' at Cardiff, is now in a London hospital, and to-day he related to me the story of how a body of miners only about 60 strong withstood the attack of an overwhelmingly stronger force of the enemy. His company was in a very exposed position when, about ten o'clock at night, the Germans opened a heavy bombardment with trench mortars and aerial darts. Early on Capt. Lascelles was wounded, and in a matter of 25 minutes or so his company sustained heavy casualties, but he declined to allow his wounds to be dressed, preferring to continue to encourage his men—a fine example which so encouraged these miners that he was able to organize his defence successfully. 'My company,' remarked Capt. Lascelles, 'was on the right of my battalion, and the position had become so precarious that had my company given way it would have meant that the whole of the battalion would have been enfiladed and the Bosches enabled to get round to the rear. That would have resulted in seriously jeopardizing the position, and near by was a Welsh regiment, who, let me add, have done notable work in that particular part of the front. Shortly afterwards the enemy renewed the attack, and there ensued a period of bitter fighting. There was no question of retiring—it could not be done. Very soon the Bosche smashed my right bombing post, which enabled him to enfilade the whole of the trench occupied by my company. Two machine guns were in action, and at eleven o'clock, after an hour's fighting, the trench for a distance on the right of 250 yards was non-existent. The trench, of a depth of only about three feet, which forced us to keep our heads under the parapet, was soon reached, and several of my men were captured. By this time there were only about a dozen of us left. So it meant neck or nothing. About 50 yards to my rear I saw a number of Germans approaching. I sent a corporal and three men to try and hold them, or otherwise the company on my left would have been attacked in the rear. Meanwhile, what now remained of my company had a go at the Bosches. I at once jumped on the parapet, and, followed by only 12 men, rushed across under heavy machine-gun fire and drove about 60 of the enemy back. I was, unfortunately, wounded again, being hit in the elbow just as I went over the top; but I was able to reorganize the defence. Soon afterwards the enemy again attacked and captured the trench and myself. I was in their hands for a couple of hours, and when I recovered consciousness, after exhaustion, a big Hun took possession of my glasses and all I had, struck me with his fist, and kicked me. I escaped later as a result of a counter-attack by the rear, but it was due to the untiring devotion of a body of miners, mostly from the North, with a number from the South, that we were able to hold the ground. A more heroic company of men no officer would wish to command.'"

Another newspaper notice reads as follows:

"On the 7th Nov. 1918, at Fontaine, France, of wounds, Capt. Arthur Moore Lascelles, V.C. and M.C., 15th Battn. Durham Light Infantry, dearly-loved husband of Sophie Lascelles, and son of John Lascelles and the late Mrs. M. E. Lascelles, of Penmaen, Dyfi, Merionethshire, 38 years of age."

McAULAY, JOHN, Sergt., was born 27 Dec. 1888, at Kinghorn, Fife, eldest son of the late John McAulay, and Isabella, his wife. He was educated at Plean, Stirlingshire, and started life in working as a Miner, but, tiring of this occupation, became a member of the Glasgow Northern Police Force, and when war broke out in Europe he was a Police Sergeant. He joined the Army 3 Sept. 1914, as a Private in the Scots Guards, and served with distinction on the Western Front. He was awarded the Distinguished Conduct Medal, "For clearing pill-boxes at Ypres on 31 July, 1917, accounting for several snipers single-handed, and taking charge of his platoon after his officer was killed." A few months later Sergt. McAulay was awarded the Victoria Cross for self-sacrificing heroism, daring and initiative. He carried his wounded Commander, Lieut. Kinnaird, 500 yards to a place of safety. Seeing him lying out under a hail of bullets, Sergt. McAulay determined to bring him back. This he accomplished in the face of a most withering fire from snipers and machine guns. Knowing that his end was near, Lieut. Kinnaird whispered to the Sergeant to carry a last message to his mother, Lady Kinnaird. Sergt. McAulay, after having reached the haven with his burden, returned, resumed command of his company, and consolidated the position gained. The official account appeared in the London Gazette, 11 Jan. 1918: "John McAulay, Sergt., D.C.M., Scots Guards. For most conspicuous bravery and initiative in attack. When all his officers had become casualties, Sergt. McAulay assumed command of the company, and under shell and machine-gun fire successfully held and consolidated the objectives gained. He reorganized the company, cheered on and encouraged his men, and under heavy fire at close quarters, showed disregard of danger. Noticing a counter-attack developing in his exposed left flank, he successfully repulsed it by the skilful and bold use of machine guns, aided by his men only, causing heavy enemy casualties. Sergt. McAulay also carried his Company Commander, who was mortally wounded, a long distance to a place of safety under a very heavy fire. Twice he was knocked down by the concussion of a bursting shell, but, nothing daunting, he continued on his way until his objective was achieved, killing two of the enemy who endeavoured to intercept him. Throughout the day this very gallant non-commissioned officer displayed the highest courage, tactical skill and coolness under exceptionally trying circumstances." Sergt. McAulay holds the proud distinction of being the only Scottish Policeman who has won the Victoria Cross. He has also been mentioned twice in Despatches. A comrade, writing of Sergt. McAulay's soldierly ability, says: "Jack McAulay doesn't need me to sing his praises; in fact, like the rest of us in the Scots Guards, we are not keen on spreading about what we consider our duty. But I am simply echoing Major Sir Victor Mackenzie's words about him when I say Sergt. McAulay is an ideal soldier. Both of us hail from the same town, we have both been miners, and we are both in the Scots Guards.

John McAulay.

I saw the great deed he did, and know what the regiment thinks of it. But it is only one of many great deeds my comrades have done. He has won the V.C. not once, but several times." After winning the Victoria Cross, Sergt. McAulay was presented on behalf of the Sergeants' Mess of the Scots Guards, Wellington Barracks, with a silver cigarette case, by the Major Earl of Stair; he also received gifts from his former colleagues in the Police Force, and from the people of Plean. He married, 22 April, 1918, at Glasgow. Sergt. McAulay was a keen boxer, winning the heavyweight championship, Police Force, Glasgow, in 1912 at Glasgow.

MULLIN, GEORGE HARRY, Lieut., M.M., was born on 15 Aug. 1892, at Portland, Oregon, U.S.A., son of Mr. and Mrs. Harry Mullin. He was educated at Moosomin, Saskatchewan, Canada, and joined the Army on 11 Nov. 1914, as a Private. He served in the European War in Princess Patricia's Canadian Light Infantry; served as a Private in a company for 11 months, then joined the Snipers. He was wounded in the Third Battle of Ypres 2 June, 1916; was invalided to England, and rejoined the regiment the end of Sept. 1916. He was made Corporal, and put in charge of the Snipers in Nov. 1916. He was made Sergeant in April, 1917; had charge of Snipers and Scouts till March, 1918, when he returned to England for a commission. He received a commission 6 Aug. 1918, at the Canadian Officers' Training School, Bexhill; joined depot of the 6th Canadian Reserve 1 Sept., and held position of Bombing Officer of the 6th Canadian Reserve till the Armistice. In the spring of 1919 he was put in charge of baseball for the 6th Canadian Reserve, and played with the team and trained the players till June, when he returned to Canada with his wife, Mrs. B. D. Mullin, of Heaton Chapel, Stockport, England, where he was married 13 April, 1918. He received the Military Medal, and was awarded the Victoria Cross [London Gazette, 11 Jan. 1918]: "George Harry Mullin, M.M., No. 51339, Sergt., Canadian Infantry. For most conspicuous bravery in attack, when, single-handed, he captured a commanding 'pill-box' which had withstood the heavy bombardment and was causing heavy casualties to our forces and holding up the attack. He rushed a sniper's post in front, destroyed the garrison with bombs, and, crawling on to the top of the 'pill-box,' he shot the two machine gunners with his revolver. Sergt. Mullin then rushed to another entrance, and compelled the garrison of 10 to surrender. His gallantry and fearlessness were witnessed by many, and although rapid fire was directed upon him and his clothes riddled by bullets, he never faltered in his purpose, and he not only helped to save the situation but also indirectly saved many lives."

George Harry Mullin.

SPACKMAN, C. E., Sergt, comes from Fulham. He served in the European War, and was awarded the Victoria Cross [London Gazette, 11 Jan. 1918]: "C. E. Spackman, No. 9522, Sergt., 1st Battn. Border Regt. For most conspicuous bravery when, in action, the leading company was checked by the heavy fire of a machine gun mounted in a position which covered the approaches. The ground was absolutely devoid of cover of any description. Sergt. Spackman, realizing the position, and seeing that it would be impossible for troops to advance, went through the fire to attack the gun. Working forward gradually, he succeeded in killing all but one of the gun crew. He then rushed the gun and captured it single-handed, thereby enabling the company to advance. The behaviour of this non-commissioned officer was gallant in the extreme, and he set a fine example of courage and devotion to his men."

BARRON, COLIN, Corpl., born 20 Sept. 1895, at Baldavie, Boyndie, Banffshire, Scotland, is the son of Mr. Joseph Barron, and Mrs. Joseph Barron (deceased). He was educated at Blairmaud, Boyndie, Banffshire, and joined the Army on the 11th Oct. 1914, in the 3rd Canadian Battn. of the 1st Central Ontario Regt. Passchendale Ridge, France, was the scene of the exploit for which he was awarded the Victoria Cross [London Gazette, 11 Jan. 1918]: "Colin Barron, No. 404017, Corpl., 3rd Canadian Battn., 1st Central Ontario Regt. Date of Act of Bravery: 6 Nov. 1917. For conspicuous bravery when in attack his unit was held up by three machine guns. Corpl. Barron opened on them from a flank at point-blank range, rushed the enemy guns single-handed, killed four of the crew, and captured the remainder. He then, with remarkable initiative and skill, turned one of the captured guns on the retiring enemy, causing them severe casualties. The remarkable dash and determination displayed by this N.C.O. in rushing the guns produced far-reaching results, and enabled the advance to be continued." In March, 1918, the Duke of Richmond and Gordon presented him at Whitehills with a gold watch and a wallet of Treasury notes on behalf of the public in the parish and other friends. Sergt. Barron was invalided back to Toronto on account of his wounds. "Thirty Canadian V.C.'s" (edited by Capt. Roberts and published by Messrs. Skeffington), says on pages 85–88: "The two preliminary assaults on the high ground before Passchendaele had secured the Canadians an excellent jumping-off position for the attack on the village itself. The capture of Crest Farm on 30 Oct. by the 4th Division gave our men almost direct observation into the town, and the consequent concentrated fire of our riflemen and machine gunners rendered the position of the German garrison most uncomfortable. The 6th Nov. was the date chosen to justify the costly operations of 26 and 30 Oct., and at 6 a.m. the Canadians resumed the offensive, the 2nd Division troops on the right going forward to the capture of Passchendaele town, while on the left the 1st Division occupied the hills to the north. The 1st Division had difficult country to manage. Not only were there many pill-boxes to occupy, but ways and means of progress were terribly limited and clearly defined by the areas of swampy and impassable ground that lay before our advance. In view of the fact that we had so recently driven the Germans from the ground we were to cover, it was too much to hope that they were unaware of our limited attacking fronts, and the subsequent machine-gun barrages that swept our lines of progress proved the contrary. The 3rd Battn. attacked on the extreme left of the Canadian Corps front, with the intention of reaching the Goudberg Spur. But between our line and the Spur there lay a very formidable strong point indeed, the pill-box at Vine Cottage. Now the pill-box itself was a standing testimonial to the thoroughness of German defensive works, but, in addition to its 18-inch walls of reinforced concrete and its appropriate armament, no less than six machine guns had been placed in positions commanding every approach to this *chef-d'œuvre*. Our fellows had attempted the reduction of this minor fortress a week before Corpl. Barron and his section of the 3rd Battn. took the matter in hand, and had gained no appreciable results beyond a somewhat depressing casualty list and a raised estimation of German defensive ingenuity. However, its capture was imperative, and a special plan of attack was arranged. At zero hour, Lieut. Lord's platoon jumped off towards the south-east, intending to capture Vine Cottage and swing round northwards to the final objective. Advancing through the rain, our men got near the strong point and were met at once by heavy fire. Vine Cottage itself, though hardly justifying its name, was a pleasant building enough in its Belgian way, and it was not until the observer had approached it nearly that he could define German handiwork behind the crumbling bricks. The enemy, with simple cunning, had raised a concrete building within the broken walls, with such successful camouflage that our scouting aeroplanes had not reported it as a pill-box for some time, while the easy unconcern with which the building received a direct hit by an 18–pounder shell had caused our gunners anxiety to a degree. As the Canadians drew near they extended and attacked the position from three sides. Their advance was slow over the sodden ground. It was impossible to win close enough to the building or gun positions to throw bombs with good effect. Time and again our fellows charged, but from every point machine-gun fire drove them back, and finally they were forced to take whatever cover they could find, while a fresh scheme of attack was planned. The going was very heavy, and the mud and constant rain made the condition of the wounded terrible beyond description. Our men started to attack once more, and as they rose to their feet a diversion occurred to the front. Corpl. Barron, a Lewis gunner, had worked round the flank with his weapon, and was knocking out the German crews one after the other with his well-directed fire. Completely exposed, he directed his gun undisturbed by the point-blank shooting of the enemy, until he had silenced two of the opposing batteries. Then without waiting for his comrades, he charged the remaining position with the bayonet, getting in among the gunners and killing four of them before the rest of his platoon could arrive. The slackening of the heavy fire gave the Canadians a chance to get well forward and in a moment they were about the position. The guns Barron had been unable to reach kept up a heavy fire until our fellows were on top of them, when most of the crews surrendered, while others attempted to escape to the rear. But the Canadians had lost too many of their comrades to feel merciful, and they were infuriated at the general morale of men who would maintain murderous shooting until imminent danger pressed and then calmly sue for mercy. They took few prisoners. Corpl. Barron, however, had not finished his good work. Turning the enemy's guns about, he opened fire upon the retreating Germans, catching the groups upon the hillside, and shooting them down with such good effect that hardly a man escaped. That was a job well done, and the remaining men of the platoon moved northwards to the consolidation of Goudberg Spur with the capture of six machine guns and a strong pill-box to their credit, and the satisfying knowledge that the German losses were double the number of their own."

Colin Barron.

McBEATH, ROBERT, L.-Corpl., was born 22 Dec. 1897, at Kinlochbervie, Sutherlandshire, Scotland, son of the late Mr. and Mrs. McBeath. He was educated at Inshegan School, Kinlochbervie. He joined the Army 12 Aug. 1914, as a Private in the 1/5th Seaforth Highlanders, and was promoted Lance-Corporal 24 July, 1917. He was awarded the Victoria Cross [London Gazette, 11 Jan. 1918]: "Robert McBeath, No. 240171, L.-Corpl., 1/5th Battn. Seaforth Highlanders. For most conspicuous bravery on 20 Nov. 1917, when with his company in attack and approaching final objective, a nest of enemy machine guns in the western outskirts of a village opened fire both on his own unit and on the unit to the right. The advance was checked and heavy casualties resulted. When a Lewis gun was called for to deal with these machine guns, L.-Corpl McBeath volunteered for the duty, and immediately moved off alone with a Lewis gun and his revolver. He located one of the machine guns in action, and worked his way towards it, shooting the gunner with his revolver. Finding several of the hostile machine guns in action, he, with the assistance of a tank, attacked them and drove the gunners to ground in a deep dug-out. L.-Corpl. McBeath, regardless of all danger, rushed in after them, shot an enemy who opposed him on the steps, and drove the remainder of the garrison out of the dug-out, capturing three officers and 30 men. There were in all five machine guns mounted round the dug-out, and by putting them out of action he cleared the way for the advance of both units. The conduct of L.-Corpl. McBeath throughout three days of severe fighting was beyond praise." L.-Corpl. McBeath married, 19 Feb. 1918, at Edinburgh, Barbara, daughter of John McKay.

CLARE, GEORGE WILLIAM, Private, served in the European War in France, and was awarded the Victoria Cross [London Gazette, 11 Jan. 1918 : " No. 6657, George William Clare, Private, 5th Lancers. For most conspicuous bravery and devotion to duty when, acting as stretcher-bearer during most intense and continuous enemy bombing. Private Clare dressed and conducted wounded in the open to the dressing station about 500 yards away. At one period, when all the garrison of a detached post, which was lying out in the open about 150 yards to the left of the line occupied, had become casualties, he crossed the intervening space, which was continually swept by heavy rifle and machine-gun fire, and, having dressed all the cases, manned the post single-handed till a relief could be sent. Private Clare then carried a seriously wounded man through intense fire to cover, and later succeeded in getting him to the dressing station. At the dressing station he was told that the enemy was using gas shells to a large extent in the valley below, and as the wind was blowing the gas towards the line of trenches and shell-holes occupied, he started on the right of the line and personally warned every company post of the danger, the whole time under shell and rifle fire. This very gallant soldier was subsequently killed by a shell."

HOLMES, THOMAS WILLIAM, Private, served in the European War in France, and won the Victoria Cross at the age of 19. The award was announced in the London Gazette of 11 Jan. 1918 : " No. 838301, Thomas William Holmes, Private, 4th Battn. Canadian Mounted Rifles. For most conspicuous bravery and resource when the right flank of our attack was held up by heavy machine-gun and rifle fire from a ' pill-box ' strong point. Heavy casualties were producing a critical situation when Private Holmes, on his own initiative and single-handed, ran forward and threw two bombs, killing and wounding the crews of two machine guns. He then returned to his comrades, secured another bomb, and again rushed forward alone under heavy fire, and threw the bomb into the entrance of the ' pill-box,' causing the 19 occupants to surrender. By this act of valour at a very critical moment Private Holmes undoubtedly cleared the way for the advance of our troops and saved the lives of many of his comrades." Private Holmes attended at Buckingham Palace, and was decorated by the King. " Thirty Canadian V.C.'s " (edited by Capt. Roberts and published by Messrs. Skeffington) says on page 61 and following pages : " Heavy rain had been falling on the Passchendaele country for two days before the 4th Canadian Mounted Rifles waded up to their positions in the front line, between Wallemolen and Bellevue. All the dykes and ditches of the low country were full and overflowing, and even in that short space of time ground that was firm and solid had become dangerous swamp. However, the men pushed on through the darkness, and the slipping and splashing, the long halts, the interminable discussions with somewhat vague guides, all came to an end at last, and at five o'clock on the morning of 25 Oct. the regiment had arrived at its battered line. Through the day the weather cleared, the sun and wind considerably improved the ground, and the men were able to discern their objectives for the following day's attack—occasionally with mild misgiving, for there seemed entirely too much water about the low hills and copses they had to traverse. The C.M.R. were on the extreme left of the Canadian Corps front, with the Hood Battn. of the Royal Naval Division on their left, and the 43rd Battn. on the right. Their objectives were Woodland Copse and Source Farm, and it was hoped to consolidate a strong line upon Walle-molen Ridge, all with a view to the establishment of a good jumping-off line for the capture of Passchendaele town itself. Though the clearing of the weather had greatly improved the ground, it also improved the visibility, and the German artillery and riflemen made very effective shooting upon our hastily improvised communication lines. The persistent bombardment was very severe indeed, and while many gallant attempts were made to supply the soldiers in the front line with munitions, time after time the men of the carrying party were wiped out and the supplies dispersed by the incessant shells. Ammunition was plentiful, however, but the men went into action the following day with practically empty water-bottles. Soon after five o'clock on the 26th the troops were assembled in the jumping-off positions, ' C ' and ' D ' Companies in advance of the front line, and ' A ' and ' B ' Companies in close support. As our barrage opened at twenty minutes to six, the heavy rain began again, making the ground very difficult and slippery as our fellows went forward. Heavy fighting occurred at once, a line of pill-boxes across the flanks of the low hills maintaining concentrated machine-gun fire, and all these small fortresses had to be stormed with the bayonet. But they did not take long to clear, and after a few minutes of close bayonet work our troops swept through and on to the stubborn resistance of the Wallemolen-Bellevue line. Here was a serious check. North-east of Wolf Copse a German pill-box was situated, its own strong defences supplemented by a machine gun mounted close to the building on each side, and against their fire our men advanced, at times up to their waists in water. It was not possible to advance quickly, and man after man of our small attacking force went down into the mud. Reinforcements from ' A ' Company came up on the right, and a series of gallant attempts were made to rush the enemy's position, which was holding up our entire local advance. Each time our men failed to get home, and eventually they were forced to take whatever cover was possible some 50 yards from the pill-box. At this moment Private Holmes advanced alone. Making his way forward, indifferent to the concentrated fire of the two guns, Holmes reached a point from which he could throw his bombs. Then, with marvellous coolness, he hurled his missiles, with such precision that he succeeded in knocking out each gun, one after the other, killing and wounding every man about them. But this result was not sufficient for him, and he returned to his comrades for more ammunition. Securing another bomb from a friend, once more Holmes ran forward alone, this

time getting close to the pill-box itself. Landing his bomb within the entrance of the concrete fort, he caused such an explosion in the confined space that the unhappy survivors of the garrison crawled out and surrendered. One does not know how Private Holmes escaped the sweeping fire that was poured upon him, but there is no doubt that his gallant action saved a critical situation, and allowed our men to push forward and establish a strong line in advance of their immediate objective. Here they held back counter-attack after counter-attack, subjected to intense bombardment and heavy machine-gun fire on the right, until later in the day the gallant capture of Bellevue Spur by the 43rd and 52nd Battns. cleared the situation and permitted the consolidation of a strong line."

KINROSS, CECIL JOHN, Private, served in the European War, and was awarded the Victoria Cross [London Gazette, 11 Jan. 1918] : " Cecil John Kinross, No. 437793, Private, Canadian Infantry. For most conspicuous bravery in action during prolonged and severe operations. Shortly after the attack was launched, the company to which he belonged came under intense artillery fire, and further advance was held up by a very severe fire from an enemy machine gun. Private Kinross, making a careful survey of the situation, deliberately divested himself of all his equipment save his rifle and bandolier, and, regardless of his personal safety, advanced alone over the open ground in the broad daylight, charged the enemy machine gun, killing the crew of six, and seized and destroyed the gun. His superb example and courage instilled the greatest confidence in his company, and enabled a further advance of 300 yards to be made and a highly important position to be established. Throughout the day he showed marvellous coolness and courage, fighting with the utmost aggressiveness against heavy odds until severely wounded." The following is taken from " Thirty Canadian V.C.'s " (published by Messrs. Skeffington) : " On 28 Oct. 1917, the 49th Canadian Infantry Battn., under Lieut.-Colonel R. H. Palmer, moved from Wieltje area and relieved three companies of the 116th Battn. in the front line south-east of Wolf Copse, on the left of the Gravenstafel-Bellevue Road, the P.P.C.L.I. relieving the remaining company on the right of the road. The strength of the battalion consisted of twenty-one officers and 567 other ranks. The relief was a difficult business, the enemy very alert, and the bad weather and heavy going rendering the operation exceedingly arduous. However, by 1.50 a.m. on the 29th the relief was effected, and preparations for the morrow's offensive were immediately undertaken. The 3rd and 4th Canadian Divisions were to continue the attack on the outlying defences of Passchendaele ; to capture Vapour Farm, Vanity House, Meetcheele, Friesland, the high ground about Crest Farm, and other strong points ; and to establish a line approximately from Goudberg Copse in the north to the railway line just south of Vienna Cottages in the south. Six battalions were to attack at zero hour, 5.50 a.m. on the 30th, the 5th Canadian Mounted Rifles, the 49th Battn. P.P.C.L.I., 72nd, 78th and 85th Battns. in order from left to right. The troops of the 49th Battn. had as their objective Furst Farm and the pill-boxes about and beyond, and the strong points to the north of Meetcheele. Late in the afternoon the barrage maps were received at Battalion Headquarters, and Colonel Palmer found it would be necessary to evacuate the front-line positions occupied by ' A ' and ' D ' Companies, and establish a jumping-off line to the rear, as the conformation of the ground rendered the establishment of a really effective barrage a most delicate task. Of late the enemy had developed a mischievous habit of keeping very close indeed to our front line, making his way inside our barrage at the moment of its inception, and so being enabled to meet our attacking troops with a volume of fire quite unmitigated by the curtain of lead designed to eliminate such resistance. About midnight, 29–30 Oct. the troops moved to the assembly, the evacuation of the forward positions being postponed until the very last possible moment. The night was very clear, and as it was possible to discern almost any movement from a distance of two hundred yards, it is probable that German patrols were aware of the gathering. At any rate, about 4.30 a.m. two green flares went up near Furst Farm, were repeated in a moment from the rear, and at once the hostile shelling became more local and intense. By a quarter past five assembly was complete, and at 5.48 a.m., two minutes before zero hour, our barrage opened on the right and the troops went forward. The morning was clear and bright, a strong wind drying the ground somewhat during the night and making better foothold possible for the men ; but such a hurricane of fire encountered the troops as they advanced that only slow progress was possible. ' B ' Company, on the right, lost most of its effective strength before crossing the Wallemolen-Bellevue Road. ' B ' and ' C ' Companies, forming the first wave, were met at once by intense rifle, machine-gun and artillery fire, and progressed in a series of rushes, going forward indomitably in spite of their heavy losses. The supporting waves, ' A ' and ' D ' Companies, fared little better, and it was painfully evident that the advance would be brought to an early conclusion through sheer lack of the men to force a passage. Considering the resistance, however, good progress was made, the men taking no heed of their losses and fighting every inch of the way. Near Furst Farm the first real check occurred, a well-mounted machine gun covering our whole local advance and holding up the assailants, who took what cover the torn ground afforded, continuing to reply as well as might be to the heavy fire, until the situation was lightened by the heroic action of a private soldier. Private Kinross, completely indifferent to the bullets directed upon him, surveyed the whole position coolly and carefully, deciding upon a plan of action that pleased him thoroughly. Returning for a moment to cover, he cleared himself of all unnecessary equipment and made his way by devious courses to a point as near as possible to the vicious machine gun. Arrived there, he rushed the position, against point-blank fire, alone and in broad daylight, killing the six men of the crew and finally destroying the gun. It is impossible to tell properly of such deeds, but the daring of it, and the complete success, so heartened our men that in their immediate advance our line was carried forward a full three hundred yards and two strong positions stormed without a halt. This brought our men to the intermediate objectives, where the line was cleared of the enemy, held and consolidated. By this time the strength of the battalion had decreased to four officers and 125 men, and no further advance was possible, incessant fighting being necessary to maintain the position already gained. Throughout the day and night the troops held on, several platoons of the Royal Canadian Regt. reinforcing the sadly depleted ranks of the 49th and assisting in the defeat of three strong counter-attacks. By the evening of the 31st all our wounded had been removed from the forward area and the tired troops were relieved by the 42nd Battn. In the fighting of 30 Oct. the 49th Battn. gained more glory than German ground, yet a great deal of German ground was captured."

NICHOLAS, HENRY JAMES, Private, served in the European War, and was awarded the Victoria Cross [London Gazette, 11 Jan. 1918]: "Henry James Nicholas, No. 24213, Private, 1st Battn. New Zealand Infantry (Canterbury Regt.). For most conspicuous bravery and devotion to duty in attack. Private Nicholas, who was one of a Lewis gun section, had orders to form a defensive flank to the right of the advance, which was subsequently checked by heavy machine-gun and rifle fire from an enemy strong point. Whereupon, followed by the remainder of his section at an interval of about twenty-five yards, Private Nicholas rushed forward alone, shot the officer in command of the strong point, and overcame the remainder of the garrison of sixteen by means of bombs and bayonets, capturing four wounded prisoners and a machine gun. He captured this strong point practically single-handed, and thereby saved many casualties. Subsequently, when the advance had reached its limit, Private Nicholas collected ammunition under heavy machine-gun and rifle fire. His exceptional valour and coolness throughout the operations afforded an inspiring example to all." He was promoted Sergeant. Sergt. H. J. Nicholas, V.C., was killed in action.

ROBERTSON, JAMES PETER, Private, No. 552665, was born on 20 Nov. 1883, at Stellarton, Pictou, Nova Scotia, son of Alexander Robertson and of Janet Robertson. He was educated at Springhill, Nova Scotia, and joined the Army in April, 1915. He was awarded the Victoria Cross [London Gazette, 11 Jan. 1918]: James Peter Robertson, No. 552665, Private, 27th Battn. Canadian Infantry. For most conspicuous bravery and outstanding devotion to duty in attack. When his platoon was held up by uncut wire and a machine gun causing many casualties, Private Robertson dashed to an opening on the flank, rushed the machine gun, and after a desperate struggle with the crew, killed four and then turned the gun on the remainder, who, overcome by the fierceness of his onslaught, were running towards their own lines. His gallant work enabled the platoon to advance. He inflicted many more casualties among the enemy, and then, carrying the captured machine gun, he led his platoon to the final position, and got the gun into action, firing on the retreating enemy, who by this time were quite demoralized by the fire brought to bear on them. During the consolidation. Private Robertson's most determined use of the machine gun kept down the fire of the enemy's snipers. His courage and his coolness cheered his comrades and inspired them to the finest efforts. Later, when two of our snipers were badly wounded in front of our trench, he went out and carried one of them in under very severe fire. He was killed just as he returned with the second man." A newspaper says: "'For conspicuous and outstanding devotion to duty on 6 Nov. 1917, at Passchendaele. Private Robertson, during the attack, and just about 200 yards from the final objective, when his platoon was held by uncut wire and machine-gun fire causing many casualties, dashed to an opening on the flank, rushed the machine gun and, after a desperate struggle with the crew, killed four and then turned the gun on the remainder, who, filled with fear by the fierceness of his onslaught, were running towards their own lines. His gallant work enabled the platoon to advance. He inflicted many more casualties among the enemy, and then, carrying the machine gun, he led his platoon to the final objective. He then selected an excellent position and got the gun into action, firing on the retreating Germans, who by this time were quite demoralized by the fire brought to bear on them by their own captured gun. During the consolidation, Private Robertson's most determined use of the machine gun kept down the fire of the enemy snipers; his courage and his coolness cheered his comrades and inspired them to the finest efforts. Later, when two of our snipers were badly wounded in front of our trench, he went out to them and carried them in one after the other. This was done under very severe fire, and just as he returned with the second man he was killed.'—From official Gazette. 'Singing Pete,' he was called in Alberta, where he was a railway engineer, before the great call of the British Empire was heard across our land. Railroad men called him 'Singing Pete' because, day or night, in the cab or the road-house, his song could be heard. Every railroad man up and down the lines knew 'Singing Pete,' and many a time his sunny disposition cheered them and enlivened their hours of hard toil or recreation. In a great gathering of locomotive engineers in Cleveland, after Private Robertson's gallant deed and his fate became known, that gathering of 77,000 strong men from Canada and the United States rose and by a standing vote honoured the memory of the first Locomotive Engineer V.C. Every soldier who knew him and every friend bears testimony to the unfailing cheeriness of the disposition of Private Peter Robertson under every circumstance. 'We all lost in Pete a good pal and friend. He was very popular with both officers and men. In fact, he refused promotion to be with the boys as plain "Private," instead of an N.C.O. He was a good soldier. On behalf of his chums and friends, I extend to you our deepest sympathy in your loss and bereavement and share with you in both.' So wrote one of 'Pete's' comrades. His officer said: 'A better soldier and truer comrade never stepped in uniform.' Another officer: 'He was a dandy soldier and so cheerful and optimistic at all times, that he kept the boys in good spirits under even the most trying conditions.' In the Passchendaele offensive Robertson's battalion was receiving many casualties. A machine gun was proving very annoying. The commander of the battalion called for volunteers to go out and put the machine gun out of business. Pete, as usual, was first to volunteer, and first to reach the gun. How he killed four of the gun crew single-handed and then turned the gun on the fleeing enemy is told in the official record. This was not enough for 'Singing Pete.' He pushed forward, taking the captured gun with him, and finding a place of advantage, turned the gun again on the enemy. It was two days later that Private Robertson saw two Canadian snipers badly wounded out in front of the trench. He did not wait for orders. With a leap he was over the parapet and brought in one man. Again he scaled the parapet, but at that moment a German shell fell on No Man's Land. When the smoke cleared away the gallant rescuer was no more. He was killed instantly. Not the highest honour can make up for the loss of such a man; but Canada and the British Empire have done all in their power to recognize his great valour. Private Robertson's mother lives at Medicine Hat. She is a brave and courageous mother of a brave and courageous son, and to her there was given the Victoria Cross, the highest token of respect for deeds of merit which it is in the power of the British Empire to give. Here is what a near friend of Peter Robertson, V.C., said of him: 'Peter had four brothers and six sisters, and a happier, jollier family it would be difficult to find. As a boy he was noted for his winning manner and inherent chivalry, and had that cheerful happy nature that endeared him to all. The family moved to Springhill, N.S., and there his brother Dan is remembered well, for when a boy of fourteen he was presented by Sir Charles Tupper with a gold cross for saving life in the Springhill colliery disaster. While working in the Springhill mines, though wounded himself in a mine explosion, he went back at great risk and carried out a fellow-worker. The family in 1898 came out to Medicine Hat to join the father, who preceded them by some few months, and Peter, after a time, became an engineer on the Canadian Pacific Railway. As a fireman he was always most popular with the older engineers, who were sorry to see him later transferred to Lethbridge. They tell many stories of his jokes among them. It was from Lethbridge that he wrote his mother early in 1915, telling her he was enlisting with the 13th C.M.R.'s. In his letter he said, "The Empire needs the very best that's in us." In another letter he said: "I am writing this on 'Mothers' Day' to the best mother in the world," and you would think so too,' continues our informant, 'if you could have read, as I did, a letter from that mother to Peter, which was found in the pocket of an old uniform after the battalion had left Lethbridge. It was the most inspiring letter I ever read, every word poignant with the great self-sacrificing spirit we read of in all the great records of Scottish history. It is no marvel to me that he gave "the best that was in him," and gloried in the doing of it. Late in 1915 the 13th C.M.R.'s were moved down to Medicine Hat, where they waited impatiently to get away, and on one occasion mutinied over the delay. A story is told by Rev. H. Morrow, Knox Church, who witnessed the scene of several C.M.R.'s, who were standing near the depot one day, during this time of waiting, when a sneering pro-German bystander asked: "Are you fellows wearing that uniform for a meal ticket?" The narrator of the story said: "I saw Peter's fist double up, and the next moment the man was sprawling on the platform, holding his head in his hands. In fact, he did it just a little better than I would have done it myself," he added. Eventually the 13th C.M.R.'s got overseas, and after some training in England, some of the men, including Robertson, were transferred to the 27th Battn. Peter had many narrow escapes,' says our informant. 'On one occasion he and two others were buried alive in a dug-out all day, until dark, when their comrades dug them out, one boy having his hips badly squeezed. Another time, after the battalion, in an attack, suffered 1,000 casualties and as Pete's comrades in a shell-hole began to lose hope, and were saying that Pete, too, was one of the "missing," there was a rush of something coming, and all held their breath to find the next moment he had, with a mighty leap, landed right in their midst. There were fewer than 200 to answer the roll-call after that day, but next morning they were congratulated in person by Field-Marshal Sir Douglas Haig for their gallant fighting against overwhelming odds. Private Bolton, of the same battalion, paid great tribute to Pete, telling how he was always out where he could get the most Huns, on one occasion, in great wrath, killing more than fifty with the bayonet. Whenever a volunteer party was asked for, he was always the first to volunteer, and it is interesting to note that, in his greatest hour he acted on his own initiative, the captain having refused him permission to make the attempt, probably considering the attainment of his object an utter impossibility.' A British correspondent describing the winning of the V.C. by Peter Robertson, tells how his comrades saw him suddenly rise from the ground, near the German battery, to his full height and swoop down upon the surprised and terrified Germans, killing four, single-handed, and turning the machine gun to a better position, fired on the remainder, who were in retreat, thus saving the position and turning what might have been a German victory into retreat. Private Peter Robertson, V.C., was born in Pictou, N.S., the parents of both his father and mother being early settlers there from the Scottish Highlands. He was 34 years old and of perfect build, standing six feet three inches, says a friend of the V.C. He always had a song or a joke for everyone. In a letter from France he said: 'I met a fine French girl when I was up the lines. She couldn't talk English and I couldn't talk French, but we got along fine, just looking at each other.' Three of Peter Robertson's

James Peter Robertson.

brothers volunteered for service, two joining the 175th Battn., Alex. and Dave, John being rejected as unfit for military service. Alex. was wounded by shrapnel and was ten months in the hospital and then back to France. Dave, who was in the transport service, and Alex. were both in France when the armistice was signed. The Victoria Cross was presented to Private Robertson's mother, Mrs. J. Robertson, Medicine Hat, by Lieut.-Governor Brett, Alberta, at Medicine Hat, 25 April, 1918. In the presentation address the lieutenant-governor said : ' This cross is only a small thing, its cost is very little, but it has engraved on it the words : " For Valour," which mean a great deal. Money can do much—with money titles can be bought, but money cannot buy the Victoria Cross. It must be won by valour and service.' "

SINGH, GOBIND, Lance-Dafadar, is a Rahtor Rajput, the tribe to which the Maharajah Sir Pertab Singhji belongs. He joined the Jodhpur Lancers; was transferred to the 28th Cavalry, with which he served in the European War. He was awarded the Victoria Cross [London Gazette, 11 Jan. 1918] : " No. 2008, Gobind Singh, Lance-Dafadar, Indian Cavalry. For most conspicuous bravery and devotion to duty in thrice volunteering to carry messages between the regiment and Brigade Headquarters, a distance of one and a half miles over open ground, which was under the observation and heavy fire of the enemy. He succeeded each time in delivering his message, although on each occasion his horse was shot and he was compelled to finish his journey on foot." Dafadar Gobind Singh was present at Buckingham Palace at an Investiture, and on the same day that he received his Decoration was given a reception, together with two Indian cavalry officers who were visiting London as guests of the nation, and was presented with a piece of silver plate and a gold watch. At this reception General Sir O'Moore Creagh, V.C., late Commander-in-Chief in India, was present, and so was Lieut.-General Sir Pertab Singhji, that distinguished soldier who has fought in so many campaigns, and lately in the Great War. He was promoted Jemadar in the 28th Cavalry.

Gobind Singh.

London Gazette, 13 Feb. 1918.—" War Office, 13 Feb. 1918. His Majesty the King has been graciously pleased to approve of the award of the Victoria Cross to the undermentioned Officers, Non-commissioned Officers and Men."

ELLIOTT-COOPER, NEVILLE BOWES, Lieut.-Colonel, was born on 22 Jan. 1889, at 81, Lancaster Gate, London, W., youngest son of Sir Robert Elliott-Cooper, K.C.B., and of Lady Elliott-Cooper, of 44, Prince's Gate, S.W. He was educated at Eton and Sandhurst, and joined the Army on 9 Oct. 1908, as Second Lieutenant, in the Royal Fusiliers. He served in South Africa, Mauritius and India. He served in the European War in France. He was fatally wounded at the battle of Cambrai and taken prisoner on 30 Nov. 1917. He was awarded the V.C., D.S.O. and M.C. He was awarded the Military Cross [London Gazette, 14 May, 1916], for conspicuous ability in organizing an attack and consolidating craters subsequently gained. He has shown great ability in many difficult situations. He was created a Companion of the Distinguished Service Order [London Gazette, 18 July, 1917], for rallying his battalion when it had become temporarily disorganized, and for leading forward a patrol of twenty men under very heavy fire and returning to his brigadier with twenty prisoners and very valuable information. He was awarded the Victoria Cross [London Gazette, 13 Feb. 1918] : " Neville Bowes Elliott-Cooper, D.S.O., M.C., Capt. (Acting Lieut.-Colonel), 8th Battn. Royal Fusiliers. For most conspicuous bravery and devotion to duty. Hearing that the enemy had broken through our outpost line, he rushed out of his dug-out, and, on seeing them advancing across the open, he mounted the parapet and dashed forward, calling upon the Reserve Company and details of Battalion Headquarters to follow. Absolutely unarmed, he made straight for the advancing enemy, and under his direction our men forced them back 600 yards. While still some forty yards in front he was severely wounded. Realizing that his men were greatly outnumbered, and suffering heavy casualties, he signalled to them to withdraw, regardless of the fact that he himself must be taken prisoner. By his prompt and gallant leading he gained time for the reserves to move up and occupy the line of defence." He died on 11 Feb. 1918, of wounds received at Cambrai on 30 Nov. 1917. At the time of his death he was a prisoner of war at No. 1 Reserve Lazaret, Hanover. A service in his memory was held at St. Paul's, Knightsbridge, on the 15th March, 1918, which was attended by his relations and friends, and a detachment of the Royal Fusiliers, who lined the aisle during the service.

N. B. Elliott-Cooper.

The following is an extract from a letter received from his tutor at Eton : " He has been the very best, and has won the best thing in life here, and if he did not know it on earth, at least he knows it now. He has been most happy in life, and he has laid down his life, crowded with every earthly honour, for his country."

The following is a quotation from a letter received from a fellow officer : " His life will always be a shining example to all who knew him. Absolutely fearless, he never for one moment considered his own safety. Always happy and cheerful, his spirit was never daunted by hardship or danger. He was universally loved and admired, and his influence was enormous on those serving with him."

MACKENZIE, HUGH, Lieut., served in the European War, won the D.C.M., and was awarded the Victoria Cross [London Gazette, 13 Feb. 1918] : " Hugh MacKenzie, D.C.M., Lieut., late 7th Canadian Machine Gun Company, Canadian Machine Gun Corps. For most conspicuous bravery and leading when in charge of a section of four machine guns accompanying the infantry in an attack. Seeing that all the officers and most of the non-commissioned officers of an infantry company had become casualties, and that the men were hesitating before a nest of enemy machine guns, which were on commanding ground and causing them severe casualties, he handed over command of his guns to an N.C.O., rallied the infantry, organized an attack, and captured the strong point. Finding that the position was swept by machine-gun fire from a ' pill-box ' which dominated all the ground over which the troops were advancing, Lieut. MacKenzie made a reconnaissance and detailed flanking and frontal attacking parties, which captured the ' pill-box,' he himself being killed while leading the frontal attack. By his valour and leadership this gallant officer ensured the capture of these strong points, and so saved the lives of many men and enabled the objectives to be attained." " Thirty Canadian V.C.'s " (edited by Capt. Roberts and published by Messrs. Skeffington) says on page 76 and following pages : " The 7th Machine Gun Company had been in the line for eight days before the second phase of the Canadian operations against Passchendaele, and the continual heavy rain that had fallen before the 30th Oct. made offensive preparations very difficult indeed. But on the 29th, the day before the attack, the weather cleared, and a strong west wind made footing somewhat easier upon the higher ground—the lower ground was all flooded, or consisted of almost impenetrable swamp. The night was very clear and the moon full, and our fellows blessed the welcome light as they moved their guns to the forward positions ; the enemy, too, took advantage of the change in the weather, and there was some fairly heavy shelling of our lines and communications, though few casualties were caused among the machine gunners. Lieut. MacKenzie, in charge of the four guns of his company, was covering the 7th Brigade in the attack upon the difficult country about Friesland, Meetcheele and Graf. With his gun-positions on the high ground, he was prepared to bring direct fire upon the enemy as our troops advanced, and to lay an effective barrage before our line upon the occupation of the objectives. At ten minutes to six on the morning of the 30th, the P.P.C.L.I. and the 49th Battn. attacked, the troops for a time keeping close to our barrage and going forward wonderfully well, in spite of the terribly heavy hostile fire. But soon after zero our communications were cut by the intense shelling, and then came the usual anxious time in the support areas, when news is vague and contradictory, and there is no information available save that afforded by some wounded soldier stumbling back to safety. At last at seven o'clock a message came through saying that all was going well, and subsequent communications were fairly regular. Lieut. MacKenzie took forward his guns, two behind the Princess Pat's and two with the 49th Battn., finding many opportunities for effective fire. The casualties amongst his men were pretty heavy as they advanced, but they stuck close to the infantry, and took advantage of every piece of rising ground from which direct fire might be delivered. But the critical point of the attack was still to come. About the intermediate objective before Meetcheele the rising ground supplied much natural cover to the German riflemen and machine gunners retreating before our men. In addition to the enemy's supplementary defences of pill-boxes and concrete emplacements, the difficulties of the assailants were enhanced by the swampy ground on each side of the spur, limiting the field of attack to a narrow strip of ground, every foot of which was exposed to the fire of the machine guns upon the slope. One pill-box in particular on the crest of the hill maintained such a murderous fire that the attacking company of the Princess Pat's was brought to a halt upon the slope of the hill, with every officer and N.C.O. shot down, and the men remaining seeking what cover they could, unable to advance and unwilling to retreat. All this time MacKenzie had been ploughing forward with his guns, seeking good positions and finding them, rendering a German emplacement untenable, wiping out some hostile formation that threatened a sudden counter-attack, and endeavouring to keep down the heavy fire of the Germans immediately before our advancing infantry. Noting the hesitation of our men on the slope of the hill, he left a corporal in charge of his guns, and made his way through the heavy fire to our fellows in their terribly exposed position. The company had been very hard hit, two-thirds of its effectives were gone, but still the men were determined enough. Taking command of the company, he cheered them by his good spirits, and instantly set about arranging a plan for the downfall of the pill-box above them. Not only was there the pill-box to deal with, but the upper hill was a veritable nest of machine guns, and MacKenzie had to make a daring reconnaissance before he could effect a suitable scheme of attack. Detailing small parties, he sent them off to work their way round the flanks, overcoming any hostile resistance they might encounter, and to be prepared at a given moment to make an attack from the rear upon the pill-box that was holding up the advance. Then he arranged the frontal attack, choosing himself to lead a small party of men directly up the slope to the fort, while the remainder of his men attacked the same front from a different angle. At the word they went forward, MacKenzie leading the forlorn hope on the most exposed front of the attack. It was not possible to win through such fire unharmed, and he was shot through the head and killed at the moment of the capture of the pill-box by the flanking parties he had detailed. One may hope that he saw his object attained. This pill-box, in its dominating position upon the crest of the hill, commanded the lines of our attack for many hundred yards. By its capture Lieut. MacKenzie and his men saved the lives of many soldiers, and enabled the successful consolidation of our objectives upon the whole local front."

PATON, GEORGE HENRY TATHAM, Capt., was born 3 Oct. 1895, at Innellan, Argyllshire, and was a son of George William Paton, Deputy Chairman and Managing Director of Messrs Bryant and May, Limited, and of Mrs. Etta Tatham Paton, of 3 Whitehall Court, S.W. He was educated at Rottingdean School and at Clifton College. He entered the army in Sept. 1914, and was gazetted Second Lieutenant 1 Oct. 1914, to the 17th County of London Regt., and promoted Lieutenant 3 Oct. 1915. He transferred in Jan. 1916, to the Grenadier Guards; was gazetted Second Lieutenant 28 Jan. 1916, and became Acting Captain 4 June, 1917. He was awarded the Military Cross Aug. 1917, and was awarded the Victoria Cross [London Gazette, 13 Feb. 1918]: "George Henry Tatham Paton, M.C., Lieut. (Acting Capt.), Grenadier Guards. For most conspicuous bravery and self-sacrifice.

George Henry T. Paton.

When a unit on his left was driven back, thus leaving his flank in the air and his company practically surrounded, he fearlessly exposed himself to readjust the line, walking up and down within fifty yards of the enemy under a withering fire. He personally removed several wounded men and was the last to leave the village. Later, he again readjusted the line, exposing himself regardless of all danger the whole time, and when the enemy four times counter-attacked he sprang each time upon the parapet, deliberately risking his life, and being eventually mortally wounded, in order to stimulate his command. After the enemy had broken through on his left, he again mounted the parapet, and with a few men—who were inspired by his great example—forced them once more to withdraw, thereby undoubtedly saving the left flank." He was killed in action. The following are extracts from letters: From Colonel Sir Henry Streatfield, K.C.V.O., Commanding Grenadiers, dated 7 Dec. 1917: "Amongst all who have laid down their lives upon the field of Honour, there is no one that I regret the loss of more than your son. He was a born soldier and leader of men, beloved by his brother officers and esteemed and respected by his men, and his loss to the regiment is a great one. We, his old comrades, will long remember him with affection." From Lieut.-Colonel the Right Hon. Viscount Gort, M.V.O., D.S.O., dated 14 Dec. 1917: "His loss was a great personal grief to me, as he was extremely popular with everybody, both officers and men; always cheerful in difficulties, and, above all, an officer who had a wonderful natural aptitude for soldiering which I am confident would have carried him a long way had he been spared to develop it. I only write because I feel I should like to express to you my feelings of gratitude and admiration for the loyal and unselfish way your son carried out his duty, which was in every way worthy of the best traditions of the regiment." From Lieut.-Colonel the Right Hon. Viscount Gort, M.V.O., D.S.O., M.C., dated 16 Feb. 1918: "I need hardly tell you how proud I am about it, as he is the first Grenadier officer to gain the V.C. this war, or, indeed, since the Crimea."

STONE, WALTER NAPLETON, Lieut. (Acting Capt.), served in the European War in France. He was awarded the Victoria Cross [London Gazette, 13 Feb. 1918]: "Walter Napleton Stone, Lieut. (Acting Capt.), 3rd, attached 17th (Service), Battn. Royal Fusiliers. For most conspicuous bravery when in command of a company in an isolated position 1,000 yards in front of the main line, and overlooking the enemy's position. He observed the enemy massing for an attack, and afforded invaluable information to battalion headquarters. He was ordered to withdraw his company, leaving a rearguard to cover the withdrawal. The attack developing with unexpected speed, Capt. Stone sent three platoons back and remained with the rearguard himself. He stood on the parapet with the telephone under a tremendous bombardment, observing the enemy, and continued to send back valuable information until the wire was cut by his orders. The rearguard was eventually surrounded and cut to pieces, and Capt. Stone was seen fighting to the last, till he was shot through the head. The extraordinary coolness of this heroic officer and the accuracy of his information enabled dispositions to be made just in time to save the line and avert disaster."

WAIN, RICHARD WILLIAM LESLIE, Lieut. (Acting Capt.), was born on the 5th Dec. 1896, at Penarth, in the county of Glamorgan, son of Mr. Harris Wain, of 4, The Avenue, Llandaff, and Florence Emily, daughter of William Tucker, of Abergavenny, Monmouthshire. He was educated at Llandaff Cathedral School and St. Bees College, Cumberland, where he was the holder of a House Scholarship and gained the higher certificate of the Oxford and Cambridge Joint Board. He was one of the first to volunteer, and joined the Public Schools Corps, Middlesex Regt., from which he was gazetted to a commission as Second Lieutenant on 16 July, 1915, in the Manchester Regt.; Lieutenant 12 July, 1916, and Acting Captain 12 Nov. 1916. Taking a deep interest in mechanics and engineering, he qualified himself for work with the tanks. He served in the European War in France and Flanders, and was wounded during the battle on the Somme, in the glorious charge of the

Richard William L. Wain.

Manchesters on the 1st July, 1916, and again in Sept. 1917, while serving with the Tank Corps at Messines. He was posthumously awarded the Victoria Cross [London Gazette, 13 Feb. 1918]: "Richard William Leslie Wain, Temporary Lieut. (Acting Capt.), late Tank Corps. For most conspicuous bravery in command of a section of Tanks. During an attack the Tank in which he was, was disabled by a direct hit near an enemy strong point which was holding up the attack. Capt. Wain and one man, both seriously wounded, were the only survivors. Though bleeding profusely from his wounds, he refused the attention of stretcher-bearers, rushed out from behind the Tank with a Lewis gun, and captured the strong point, taking about half the garrison prisoners. Although his wounds were very serious, he picked up a rifle and continued to fire at the retiring enemy until he received a fatal wound in the head. It was due to the valour displayed by Capt. Wain that the infantry were able to advance." This was near Marcoing. A senior officer wrote: "Your son had been in my company since last Christmas (1916), and saw the whole of this year's (1917) fighting with it. He had already distinguished himself on several occasions, and always showed the very greatest gallantry. On 20 Nov., after passing the Hindenburg Line, the Tank in which he was, attacked a trench mortar battery and three machine guns. It received five hits from T.M. shells. The fifth shell stopped it and killed everyone except your son, who leapt from the car with a Lewis gun and engaged the three machine guns and T.M.'s in the open. He succeeded in putting them all out of action, but was afterwards killed by a sniper. He is buried on the Hindenburg line by his Tank, with a Lieutenant, whose commander he was, and the crew. . . . In conclusion I will only say that you have the heartfelt sympathy of every officer and man in the company, for the loss of so gallant a man. He was extremely popular with everyone in the battalion, and his loss is keenly felt both at work and play."

WALLACE, SAMUEL THOMAS DICKSON, Temporary Lieut., was born on 7 March, 1892, at Holmhill, Thornhill, Dumfriesshire, son of J. W. Wallace and Mrs. Wallace, of Ford, Thornhill, Dumfriesshire. He was educated at Dumfries Academy, and Edinburgh University; was a Member of Edinburgh University O.T.C. from 1911 to 1914; graduated B.Sc. in Agriculture in March, 1914, and joined the Army on 13 Oct. 1914, as Temporary Second Lieutenant, Royal Field Artillery. He served in the European War in France from May, 1915, to Jan. 1919, with the 63rd Brigade, Royal Field Artillery, 12th Division, and was in every engagement in which the above unit took part. He was awarded the Victoria Cross [London Gazette, 13 Feb. 1918]: "Samuel Thomas Dickson Wallace, Temporary Lieut., Royal Field Artillery. For most conspicuous bravery and devoted services in action in command of a section. When the personnel of the

Samuel T. D. Wallace.

battery was reduced to five by the fire of the artillery, machine guns, infantry and aeroplanes; had lost its Commander and five of the sergeants, and was surrounded by enemy infantry on the front right flank, and finally in rear, he maintained the fire of the guns by swinging the trails round close together, the men running and loading from gun to gun. He thereby not only covered other battery positions, but also materially assisted some small infantry detachments to maintain a position against great odds. He was in action for eight hours, firing the whole time, and inflicting severe casualties on the enemy. Then, owing to the exhausted state of his personnel, he withdrew when infantry supports arrived, taking with him the essential gun parts and all wounded men. His guns were eventually recovered." Lieut. Wallace was promoted to Captain in Aug. 1915. He was appointed Deputy Director of Agriculture, Central Provinces of India, in Feb. 1919.

BOUGHEY, STANLEY HENRY PARRY, Second Lieut., served in the European War in Palestine, and was awarded the Victoria Cross posthumously [London Gazette, 13 Feb. 1918]: "Stanley Henry Parry Boughey, Second Lieut., late 1/4th Battn. Royal Scots Fusiliers (Territorial Forces). For most conspicuous bravery. When the enemy in large numbers had managed to crawl up to within 30 yards of our firing lines, and with bombs and automatic rifles were keeping down the fire of our machine guns, he rushed forward alone with bombs right up to the enemy, doing great execution and causing the surrender of a party of 30. As he turned to go back for more bombs he was mortally wounded at the moment when the enemy were surrendering." On the announcement of the award, the Ayrshire County Territorial Association sent a congratulatory message to Mrs. Boughey, expressing the hope that the great honour might help to alleviate the loss of her gallant son.

EMERSON, JAMES SAMUEL, Temporary Second Lieut., was born on 3 Aug. 1895, at Collon, County Louth, son of the late John Emerson and Mrs. Emerson, of Seven Oaks, Collon, County Louth, Ireland; and a younger brother of Mr. W. A. W. Emerson, Indian Revenue Officer, of Palace Row, Armagh. He was educated at Mountjoy School, Dublin, and joined the Army on 15 Sept. 1914, as a Private in the 3rd Battn. Royal Irish Rifles. He served in the European War in France; was wounded in action at

James Samuel Emerson.

Hooge, and spent eight months in hospital. He went to France for the second time in July, 1916, and was gazetted to the Royal Inniskilling Fusiliers 1 Aug. 1917. He was awarded the Victoria Cross [London Gazette, 13 Feb. 1918]: "James Samuel Emerson, Temporary Second Lieut., late 9th Battn. Royal Inniskilling Fusiliers. For repeated acts of most conspicuous bravery. He led his company in an attack and cleared 400 yards of trench. Though wounded when the enemy attacked in superior numbers, he sprang out of the trench with eight men and met the attack in the open, killing many and taking six prisoners. For three hours after this, all other officers having become casualties, he remained with his company, and repeatedly repelled bombing attacks. Later, when the enemy again attacked in superior numbers, he led his men to repel the attack, and was mortally wounded."

A newspaper cutting says:

"This gallant young officer was the youngest son of the late Mr. John Emerson and Mrs. Emerson, Sevenoaks, Collon, Drogheda, and was 22 years of age. He was educated at Mountjoy School, Dublin, and joined the Royal Irish Rifles on the outbreak of the war. Wounded in action at Hooge, he then spent eight months in hospital. He was one of the guard on the Bank of Ireland, Dublin, during the Rebellion. He went to France for the second time in July, 1916, and was gazetted to the Royal Inniskilling Fusiliers at Finner, 1 Aug. 1917, from a cadet unit. He was killed in action on 6 Dec. 1917, after leading his men for twenty-four hours against a counter-attack, though severely wounded. At that time he was serving in the Tyrone Battn.

"Lieut.-Colonel Peacocke, D.S.O., his commanding officer, wrote to Mrs. Emerson at the time of his death: 'I am afraid before you receive this letter you will have heard of the death of your son. I am so sorry I could not write to you before, but I have only just got back to a place where it is possible to write. He was one of the most gallant officers I have ever seen, and his death was one of the biggest blows I have had since I have been out here. He was shot through the body whilst defending a most vital spot in our line—had he lost it a most critical situation would have arisen. He led his men for twenty-four hours in the hardest fighting I have yet seen, and he was calm, cool and collected the whole time. I cannot possibly say too much for his behaviour—he was quite wonderful. I saw him a very few minutes after being hit, and he was suffering no pain, and he died about fifteen minutes afterwards. My very deepest sympathy in your great loss, and I can't tell you how much I shall miss him as one of the best officers I have ever had.'

"Capt. T. W. G. Johnson, the Medical Officer, writes: 'It is with the greatest sympathy that I am now carrying out your late son's last request before he passed away. I am the battalion medical officer, and knew your son very well. As you know, he had only been with us a short time, but during that time we all saw how absolutely fearless he was, and how very much his men admired him. He was in command of his company when he fell, and it was owing to his magnificent courage and devotion to duty that the battalion line was able to hold fast. He had had his steel helmet torn with a bullet and been hit in the hand, but refused to leave his men. An enemy sniper eventually shot him, and before he passed away he asked me to write to you and let you know that he did his duty. We all miss him very much, and his place will never be filled in the battalion, as far as I am personally concerned. His death was quite quiet, and he suffered very little pain, and the padre and myself were with him in his last moments. We lost a lot of fine officers the same day, and, believe me, my heart is torn for every one of their parents. Please again accept my heartfelt sympathy in your sad bereavement.'

"This was the fifth V.C. won by the Ulster Division, the others, which were awarded for the desperate struggle at Thiépval on 1 July, 1916, being:

Late Lieut. G. St. J. S. Cather, Royal Irish Fusiliers.
Late Capt. E. N. F. Bell, Royal Inniskilling Fusiliers.
Late Private William M'Fadzean, Royal Irish Rifles.
Private (now Sergt.) J. Quigg, Royal Irish Rifles."

Another newspaper says:

"An interesting ceremony took place in the Whitworth Hall, Drogheda, on Wednesday, when the Victoria Cross—that most coveted of all battle-field distinctions—was presented to Mrs. Emerson, mother of the Collon officer hero, Lieut. J. S. Emerson, of the Royal Inniskilling Fusiliers, who died a gallant death in France fighting for his King and country. The spacious hall was packed on the occasion by an audience representing the different classes of the Drogheda public. Amongst those present were: General and Mrs. Henry, Collon; Mrs. Daly, Collon; Mr. W. P. and Mrs. Cairnes, Stameen; Capt. W. E. P. and Mrs. Cairnes, Mr. B. R. and Mrs. Balfour, Townley Hall; Mr. C. and Mrs. McKenny, Rev. Chancellor Ledoux and Mrs. Ledoux, Rev. F. S. Aldhouse, M.A., Rev. F. H. Aldhouse, Rev. Alex. and Mrs. Cairns, Rev. Alex. and Mrs. Hall, Mrs. and Miss Smyth, Piperstown; Mr. G. H. and Mrs. Pentland, Blackhall; the Misses Smith Greenhills; Lieut. Thornhill, Castlebellingham; Mr. G. H. and Mrs. Daly, Mr. and Mrs. Shannon, Mr. G. N. Kelly, Mr. A. T. Mitchell, Mr. T. Gloster, Collon; Colonel and Mrs. Thornhill, Rev. T. R. and Mrs. Brunskil, Mr. G. F. Gradwell, Mr. R. H. and Mrs. Taylor, Mr. and Mrs. Inglis and Miss Baikie, Mr. H. Armstrong, Mr. J. McKeever, Alderman and Mrs. Elcock, Mr. R. Murdock, Mr. M. McCullen, Mr. T. Robinson, Mr. and Mrs. Pierson, Mr. P. P. Keeley, Mr. J. J. and Mrs. Grayson, Mr. W. J. D. and Mrs. Walker and Mrs. Hamley, Mrs. Shaw, Mr. Charles and Miss Creaser, Mr. W. H. and Mrs. Jordan, Mrs. Tallan, Mr. H. and Mrs. Macoun, Miss Leland, Miss Whitty, Mr. and Mrs. McElderry, Mr. H. W. Saville, Mr. J. Kirkpatrick, etc., etc. The Mayor (Mr. W. T. Skeffington) presided. On the platform with him were: Brigadier-General Hackett-Payne (who made the presentation), Lord Fingall, Capt. Thornhill, Capt. W. A. Doran, Chairman, Louth County Council; Mr. J. Davis, T.C.; Mr. B. R. Balfour, D.L., J.P.; and Mr. J. A. Carvery, D.I., R.I.C. A detachment of the Northumberland Fusiliers from Millmount Barracks were lined up on each side of the hall. The friends of Lieut. Emerson present were: Mrs. Emerson (mother), Messrs. W. A. Emerson, Alfred Emerson, and John Emerson (brothers), and Mr. Lennox R. Mercer, Rathmines (uncle). The Mayor said: 'Brigadier-General Hackett-Payne, ladies and gentlemen, the presentation that will be made to-day by General Payne is, I believe, unprecedented in the annals of this county. Lieut. Emerson, in last December, lost his life gallantly leading his men against the enemy. He joined as a Private at the outbreak of the war, and for a considerable time fought in France. He got his commission twelve months ago, and while fighting he displayed the usual heroism and gallantry of the Irish race' (applause). 'We all regret that he is not here to-day to receive the V.C., and had he been living he would have received the coveted distinction from the hands of his Majesty the King; but inasmuch as he has passed away, the presentation will be made to-day to his mother, to whom we all tender our profound sorrow in her great trouble. The circumstances under which Lieut. Emerson lost his life and won the V.C. will be told you by General Payne.' Brigadier-General Hackett-Payne, C.B., in making the presentation, said: 'Ladies and gentlemen, we are assembled here to-day for the purpose of witnessing the presentation of two decorations to the friends of men, both of whom have lost their lives in gallantly doing their duty to their country' (applause) 'One of them is the V.C., a decoration which is not lightly won, and is only given to those who display conspicuous gallantry and bravery. The recipient of this much coveted distinction, had he been living, would be invested with it by the King himself, but he gave up his life gallantly leading his men. The distinction was awarded Lieut. Emerson for acts of the most conspicuous bravery. Leading his company in an attack on the enemy, he cleared four hundred yards of trench, and though wounded and with the enemy attacking in superior numbers, sprang out of the trench with eight men and met the attack in the open, killing many and taking prisoners. He remained with his company, refusing to go to the dressing station, and repeatedly repelled the German attacks. Later on, when the enemy attacked in greater numbers, he again led his men, but was mortally wounded. His heroism and bravery inspired his men to hold out until reinforcements arrived. Lieut. Emerson's acts, in face of the enemy, were gallant, praiseworthy and remarkable, and worthy of the coveted distinction now being presented to his mother' (applause). Mrs. Emerson accompanied by her son, Mr. W. A. Emerson, then ascended the platform, and amidst applause received the V.C. The wife of a Dundalk hero belonging to the R.F.A., Sergt. Brogan, was also presented with a Military Medal won by her husband for great valour."

GOURLEY, CYRIL EDWARD, Sergt., was born on 19 Jan. 1893, at Wavertree, Liverpool, son of Galbraith Gourley, Merchant, and Cissie Gourley, daughter of Edward Ashcroft, of Wavertree. He was educated at Calday Grange Grammar School, and at Liverpool University, where he graduated with the degree of Bachelor of Commercial Science, and would probably have sat for the M.A. degree but for mobilization orders. He would normally have followed a commercial career, and before mobilization he entered the offices of Messrs. Alfred Holt and Co., of the Blue Funnel Line. He joined the Army as a Private in the Royal Field Artillery, Territorial Forces, on 19 May, 1914. He served in the European War, being mobilized on 4 Aug. 1914, and going to France on 28 Sept. 1915. He won the Military Medal [London Gazette, 1917] for conspicuous gallantry in extinguishing a fire caused by an enemy shell in the vicinity of one of our munition dumps. He was awarded the Victoria Cross [London Gazette, 13 Feb. 1918]: "Cyril Edward Gourley, Sergt., Royal Field Artillery (Territorial Force). For most conspicuous bravery when in command of a section of howitzers. Though the enemy advanced in force, getting within four hundred yards in front, between three hundred and four hundred yards to one flank, and with snipers in rear, Sergt. Gourley managed to keep one gun in action practically throughout the day. Though frequently driven off he always returned, carrying ammunition, laying and firing the gun himself, taking first one and then another of the detachment to assist him. When the enemy advanced he pulled his gun out of the pit and engaged a machine gun at five hundred yards, knocking it out with a direct hit. All day he held the enemy in check, firing with open sights on enemy parties in full view at three hundred to eight hundred yards, and thereby saved his guns, which were withdrawn at nightfall." On 5 Jan. 1918, he was given a commission as Second Lieutenant in the Royal Field Artillery. Lieut. Gourley remained with the 55th Division until its disbandment in the spring of 1919, at Brusssels. He was appointed Acting Captain 19 May, 1919, and proceeded home for demobilization with the cadre of the 276th Brigade, Royal Field Artillery, in June, 1919.

Cyril Edward Gourley.

MILLS, W., Private, served in the European War, and was awarded the Victoria Cross [London Gazette, 13 Feb. 1918]: "W. Mills, No. 375499, Private, 1/10th Battn. Manchester Regt. (Territorial Force). For most conspicuous bravery and self-sacrifice. When, after an intense gas attack, a strong enemy patrol endeavoured to rush our posts, the garrisons of which had been overcome, and though badly gassed himself, he met the attack single-handed and continued to throw bombs until the arrival of reinforcements, and remained at his post until the enemy's attacks had been finally driven off. While being carried away he died from gas poisoning. It was solely due to his exertions, when his only chance of personal safety lay in remaining motionless, that the enemy was defeated and the line retained intact."

SHEPHERD, ALBERT EDWARD, Private, was born at Royston, near Barnsley, Yorkshire, on 11 Jan. 1897 son of Noah Shepherd, Miner, and of Mrs. Laura Shepherd, who died on 7 Nov. 1911, daughter of Mr. Joseph Darwin. He was educated at Royston West Riding School, and for three years before enlisting was a Pony Driver in the New Monckton Colliery. He joined the Army on 4 Aug. 1915, as a Private in the King's Royal Rifles Corps (12th Battn.). He served in the European War in France and Belgium. His service was from 4 Aug. 1915, to 1 Jan. 1919, and he was promoted to Lance-Corporal 28 Aug. 1918, and Corporal 28 Sept. 1918. He won the Victoria Cross on the morning of 20 Nov. 1917, at Cambrai, for taking charge of his company when it was without leaders, and capturing machine guns, and reaching the Hindenburg front line, and then going back under heavy enfilade fire to get the assistance of tanks, and returning six hundred yards and consolidating [London Gazette, 13 Feb. 1918]: "No. R.15089, Albert Edward Shepherd, Private, King's Royal Rifle Corps. For most conspicuous bravery as a company runner. When his company was held up by a machine gun at point-blank range, he volunteered to rush the gun, and though ordered not to, rushed forward and threw a Mills bomb, killing two gunners and capturing the gun. The company, on continuing its advance, came under heavy enfilade machine-gun fire. When the last officer and the last non-commissioned officer had become casualties, he took command of the company, ordered the men to lie down, and himself went back some seventy yards under severe fire to obtain the help of a tank. He then returned to his company, and finally led them to their last objective. He showed throughout conspicuous determination and resource." Private Shepherd hinted that it was probable that he would receive some decoration "for something he had done out yonder," but his friends never imagined that he was to receive the highest of military decorations. He was invested by the King at Buckingham Palace, and on returning to his home at Royston he was met at the station by thousands of people, and at the Royston Palace was presented with a gold watch and chain by the Patriotic Fund, and with a Bible by the scholars of the Primitive Methodist Chapel, with which he was formerly connected. A fund was begun to present him with War Bonds. He was twice gassed, and twice wounded (in the arm) during the war. His chief recreations are boxing and running. Since he joined the Army he has developed into quite a useful boxer, and has won all but one of the eleven contests he has engaged in. His wife's name is Mrs. Rosezillah Shepherd, and their child is Mildred Shepherd.

Albert Edward Shepherd.

THOMAS, JOHN, L.-Corpl., was born on 10 May, 1886, at Openshaw, Manchester, son of Edward Thomas, Boot and Shoe Maker, and Elizabeth Thomas, Nurse. He was educated at St. Barnabas, Openshaw, Manchester, and joined the Army on 7 June, 1909, as Private in the 2/5th North Staffordshire Regt., and was promoted Corporal 10 Nov. 1918, and Sergeant 21 March, 1919, serving in the European War in France. He was awarded the Victoria Cross [London Gazette, 13 Feb. 1918]: "John Thomas, Private, No. 50842, L.-Corpl., North Staffordshire Regt. (East Manchester). For most conspicuous bravery and initiative in action. He saw the enemy making preparations for a counter-attack, and with a comrade, on his own initiative, decided to make a close reconnaissance. These two went out in broad daylight in full view of the enemy and under heavy machine-gun fire. His comrade was hit within a few yards of the trench, but, undeterred, L.-Corpl. Thomas went on alone. Working round a small copse, he shot three snipers, and then pushed on to a building used by the enemy as a night post. From here he saw whence the enemy were bringing up their troops and where they were congregating. He stayed in this position for an hour, sniping the enemy the whole time and doing great execution. He returned to our lines, after being away three hours, with information of the utmost value, which enabled definite plans to be made and artillery fire to be brought on the enemy's concentration, so that when the attack took place it was broken up." Corpl. Thomas, describing the incident of how he won the V.C., writes: "I wish to mention how I got so close to the enemy was by crawling on my stomach for about 800 yards of open country. I was sniped at by enemy snipers, but I bluffed them by pretending that they had hit me, but I again crawled on and gained the village of Fontaine, which was then in German occupation, and worked my way from house to house, so that I got valuable information as regards his movements, and that is how I spent the three hours away from our lines." He married, on the 11th June, 1919, at the Parish Church of St. Matthew's, Douglas, Isle of Man, Amelia, eldest daughter of Mr. and Mrs. Wood, of Hulme, Manchester.

He writes: "I am working very hard for a living. I suffer from the effects of shell concussion, through being blown up at Bullecourt, March, 1918. I receive the . . . Partial Disablement Pension of 9/4 per week."

London Gazette, 27 Feb. 1918.—"War Office, 27 Feb. 1918. His Majesty the King has been graciously pleased to approve of the award of the Victoria Cross to the undermentioned Non-commissioned Officers and Man."

TRAIN, C. W., Corpl., is the son of Mr. and Mrs. Train, of 58, Chatterton Road, Finsbury Park, N., and has lived in Islington all his life. He was educated at the Gillespie Road London County Council Schools, attended St. Thomas's Church Sunday School, and joined the church football team there. He was employed as a Solicitor's Clerk at Messrs. Walker, Martineau and Co., of Gray's Inn. He comes of a fighting stock, for his father, a native of Midlothian, who came to London 30 years ago, was for many years a member of the old Volunteers and considered a crack shot. Corpl. Train has a brother, Private G. F. Train, of the Royal Field Artillery, who has been twice at the French front and also in Salonika, and was wounded. He joined the London Scottish about 10 years before he won his Victoria Cross. He served in the European War in France, and is entitled to the Mons Star. He received his first stripe; was twice invalided home, and after the second time was sent to Salonika, where he was later promoted Corporal. For his subsequent services in Palestine he was awarded the Victoria Cross [London Gazette, 27 Feb. 1918]: "C. W. Train, No. 510051, Corpl., 2/14th Battn. London Regt. For most conspicuous bravery, dash and initiative displayed under heavy fire when his company was unexpectedly engaged at close range by a party of the enemy with two machine guns and brought to a standstill. Corpl. Train, on his own initiative, rushed forward and engaged the enemy with rifle grenades, and succeeded in putting some of the team out of action with a direct hit. He then shot at and wounded an officer in command, and with bomb and rifle killed and wounded the remainder of the team. After this he went to the assistance of a comrade who was bombing the enemy from their front, and shot at and killed one of the enemy who was carrying the second gun out of action. His courage and devotion to duty undoubtedly saved his battalion heavy casualties and enabled them to advance to their objective at a time when the situation seemed critical."

The following extract, taken from a comrade's letter, gives a vivid description of the incident in which Corpl. Train took such a leading part:

"We just lay there and pelted each other for about three quarters of an hour, when a chap in our platoon named Train made a dart forward of about twenty yards, and gradually crept up to their barricade, let off one or two rifle grenades on the way, and dodged their bullets. He worked right up to the end of their barricade and enfiladed it with his own rifle fire. A German officer in charge of the barricade let fire at Train with his revolver. Train flopped, and shot him, wounding him severely. That finished it! They all scooted out of the other end of the barricade, and as they came out so we brought them down. One of them cleared out of the back way, and tried to get his machine gun away, and had got it on his shoulders and gone about fifty yards, but Train got him tapped and brought down with a beauty between the shoulders, so, as you will see, it was his day out, as at the finish he had practically drove the Turks out of the trench on his own, and captured two macbine guns, which would undoubtedly have caused many casualties in our ranks later in the day. The sight at the barricade I shall never forget. The Turks were lying all over the shop, not one escaped, and they were nearly all dead. The German officer was dancing about holding his trousers and offering an orange for a field dressing. That was the finish of the spasm, and ''ot' is not the word."

A newspaper says:

"Major-General Sir Newton Moore attended a meeting of the Islington Borough Council yesterday evening, at which an Islington V.C., Sergt. Train, was presented with an illuminated address and a parcel of War Bonds and Treasury Notes of the value of £216, as a tribute to his heroism, and the General added his warm congratulations to those of the Council."

Sergt. C. W. Train was also presented with a gold-knobbed walking-stick by Mr. E. Smallwood, M.P., on behalf of the Highbury Patriotic Meeting. Sergt. Train was twice offered a commission, which he refused, preferring to stay in the ranks.

CHRISTIE, JOHN ALEXANDER, L.-Corpl., was the son of the late Andrew Christie and Sarah Christie, of 35, Fairbridge Road, Upper Holloway, N. He was Scotch by parentage. He spent some time in the Midlands before going to live at Islington, where he was engaged as a Clerk on the London and North Western Railway. He joined the Army as a Rifleman in the 1/4th Battn. London Regt., and served in the European War; went out with his regiment to Gallipoli; was present at the landing at Suvla Bay, and was wounded at Chocolate Hill. He returned home, and later was sent to Egypt, and then to Palestine. He took part in the famous hundred-mile march across the Arabian desert. He was present at the first and second battles of Gaza, and at this place he had an attack of sun-stroke. He was awarded the Victoria Cross for an act which was thus described by an officer (the scene of the achievement was a hill before Jerusalem): "At a critical time in the darkness and confusion, L.-Corpl. Christie filled his pockets with bombs, and quite alone got out of the trenches, and following the Turkish trench in the open, rained bombs on the Turkish bombers. We afterwards counted twenty-six dead Austrians in that particular trench." He was sent for and congratulated in the presence of all officers in the section. The award was announced in the London Gazette, 27 Feb. 1918: "No. 450685, John Alexander Christie, Rifleman (L.-Corpl.), London Regt. For most conspicuous bravery, when, after a position had been captured, the enemy immediately made counter and bombing attacks up communication trenches. L.-Corpl. Christie realizing the position, took a supply of bombs over the top, proceeding alone about 50 yards in the open along the communication trench, and bombed the enemy. He continued to do this alone, in spite of very heavy opposition, until a block had been established. Returning towards our lines, he heard voices behind him; he at once turned back and bombed another party moving up the trench, entirely breaking up a further bombing attack. By his prompt and effective action he undoubtedly cleared a difficult position at a most critical time and saved many lives. Throughout he was subjected to heavy machine-gun fire and shell fire. He showed the greatest coolness and a total disregard for his own safety." He was an enthusiastic athlete, and played for St. John's Football Club, Holloway, and was also a keen scholar at the Working Men's College at Holloway. He was killed in action in France between the 21st and 29th March, 1918.

James Duffy.

DUFFY, JAMES, Private, was born at Bonagee, Letterkenny, County Donegal, son of Peter and Kate Duffy. He was educated at Drumlodge, near Letterkenny, and joined the Army 1 Dec. 1914, serving in the European War in Palestine. He was awarded the Victoria Cross [London Gazette, 27 Feb. 1918]: "James Duffy, No. 6/17978, Private, Royal Inniskilling Fusiliers. For most conspicuous bravery displayed whilst his company was holding a very exposed position. Private Duffy (a stretcher-bearer) and another stretcher-bearer went out to bring in a seriously-wounded comrade; when the other stretcher-bearer was wounded he returned to get another man; when again going forward the relief stretcher-bearer was killed. Private Duffy then went forward alone, and under heavy fire succeeded in bringing both wounded men under cover and attended to their injuries. His gallantry undoubtedly saved both men's lives." On his first visit to Bonagee, Letterkenny, after he was awarded the Victoria Cross, Private James Duffy received a hearty reception. His wife's maiden name was Maggie Hegarty.

London Gazette, 15 March, 1918.—"War Office, 15 March, 1918. His Majesty the King has been graciously pleased to approve of the award of the Victoria Cross to the undermentioned Officer."

DIARMID, ALLASTAIR MALCOLM CLUNY McREADY-, Temporary Lieutenant (Acting Capt.), served in the European War in France, and was awarded the Victoria Cross [London Gazette, 15 March, 1918]: "Allastair Malcolm Cluny McReady-Diarmid (formerly Arthur Malcolm McReady-Drew), Temporary Lieut. (Acting Capt.), late 17th (Service) Battn. Middlesex Regt. For most conspicuous bravery and brilliant leadership. When the enemy penetrated some distance into our position and the situation was extremely critical, Capt. McReady-Diarmid at once led his company forward through a heavy barrage. He immediately engaged the enemy, with such success that he drove them back at least 300 yards, causing numerous casualties and capturing 27 prisoners. The following day the enemy again attacked and drove back another company which had lost all its officers. This gallant officer at once called for volunteers and attacked. He drove them back again for 300 yards, with heavy casualties. Throughout this attack Capt. McReady-Diarmid led the way himself, and it was absolutely and entirely due to his marvellous throwing of bombs that the ground was regained. His absolute disregard for danger, his cheerfulness and coolness at a most trying time inspired all who saw him. This gallant officer was eventually killed by a bomb when the enemy had been driven right back to their original starting-point."

The "Middlesex County Times," 27 April, 1918, says: "On Saturday last, at Windsor Castle, His Majesty the King presented to Mrs. McReady-Diarmid the V.C. won by her husband, Lieut. (Acting Capt.) Allastair McReady-Diarmid, of the Middlesex Regt., whose parents live at Goldsmith Avenue, Acton."

His wife is a native of Dursley, and from the outbreak of war Capt. McReady-Diarmid had made his home in that town.

London Gazette, 2 April, 1918.—"War Office, 2 April, 1918. His Majesty the King has been graciously pleased to approve of the award of the Victoria Cross to the undermentioned Officer."

McCUDDEN, JAMES BYFORD, Second Lieut., was born on 28 March, 1895, at Gillingham, Kent, son of Quartermaster-Sergt. W. H. McCudden, Royal Engineers, and subsequently Warrant Officer R.E., and of Gillingham, Kent. His parents are Scotch and Irish respectively. He was educated at the R.E. School, Brompton Barracks, Gillingham, Kent. He joined the Royal Flying Corps as mechanic from the Royal Engineers in May, 1913, and served in the European War with such extraordinary distinction that he became known as the leading British airman. He was awarded the Croix de Guerre on the 21st Jan. 1916, which was pinned on his breast by General Joffre at Lillers the same day (see "Illustrated War News," 16 Feb. 1916, page 3). He won the Military Medal [London Gazette, 1 Oct. 1916] for consistent gallantry, courage and dash, during the month of Sept. 1916, in attacking and destroying an enemy machine and forcing two others to land. He held at this time the rank of Flight-Sergeant in the R.F.C. on 1 Jan. 1917, and subsequently won all the Decorations open to British Army officers for valour—two of them twice over. The Military Cross was awarded [London Gazette, 16 Feb. 1917] for following a hostile machine to a height of 300 feet and driving it to the ground. A Bar was awarded [London Gazette, 5 Oct. 1917] for his work during the period 15 Aug. to 28 Sept. 1917, when he took part in many offensive patrols and destroyed five enemy machines, driving three others down out of control. He was created a Companion of the Distinguished Service Order [London Gazette, 14 Dec. 1917] for conspicuous gallantry on 29 and 30 Nov. 1917, in attacking and bringing down within the British lines an enemy two-seater, both occupants being taken prisoners, and destroying another machine in very bad weather. A Bar to the Distinguished Service Order was awarded [London Gazette, 3 Jan. 1918] for skill and gallantry on 23

James Byford McCudden.

Nov. 1917, when he destroyed four enemy machines, three of which fell within the British lines, and also drove his patrol against six enemy machines and drove them off. He was awarded the Victoria Cross [London Gazette, 2 April, 1918]: "James Byford McCudden, D.S.O., M.C., M.M., Second Lieut. (Temporary Capt.), General List and Royal Flying Corps. For conspicuous bravery, exceptional perseverance, and a very high devotion to duty. Capt. McCudden has at the present time accounted for 54 enemy aeroplanes. Of these, 42 have been definitely destroyed, 19 of them on our side of the lines. Only 12 out of the 54 have been driven out of control. On two occasions he has totally destroyed four two-seater enemy aeroplanes on the same day, and on the last occasion all four machines were destroyed in the space of one hour and thirty minutes. While in his present squadron he has participated in 78 offensive patrols, and in nearly every case has been the leader. On at least 30 other occasions, whilst with the same squadron, he has crossed the lines alone, either in pursuit or in quest of enemy aeroplanes. The following incidents are examples of the work he has done recently: On 23 Dec. 1917, when leading his patrol, eight enemy aeroplanes were attacked between 2.30 p.m. and 3.50 p.m. Of these, two were shot down by Capt. McCudden in our lines. On the morning of the same day he left the ground at 10.50, and encountered four enemy aeroplanes; of these he shot two down. On 30 Jan. 1918, he, single-handed, attacked five enemy scouts, as a result of which two were destroyed. On this occasion he only returned home when the enemy scouts had been driven far east; his Lewis gun ammunition was all finished, and the belt of his Vickers gun had broken. As a patrol leader, he has at all times shown the utmost gallantry and skill, not only in the manner in which he has attacked and destroyed the enemy, but in the way he has during several aerial fights protected the newer members of his flight, thus keeping down their casualties to a minimum. This officer is considered, by the record which he has made, by his fearlessness, and by the great service which he has rendered to his country, deserving of the very highest honour." The award of the Victoria Cross was announced, without details (such a record must have taken time to compile), at an earlier date. He was promoted Temporary Major in July, 1918. He was killed on leaving Marquiz to take over his new squadron. The crack German pilot Immelmann was a deadly rival of his. They had three duels, but the fight was broken off on each occasion without either man being able to claim an advantage. Two of his brothers were killed after making their names as airmen, and the youngest brother is now in the Royal Air Force. His native town, Gillingham, intended to make him a Freeman, but his death prevented that, and the Certificate of Freedom was presented to his mother in a silver casket, which bore the borough arms of Gillingham, and the arms of the Royal Flying Corps, together with the following inscription: "Presented to Capt. James Byford McCudden, a native of Gillingham in recognition of the great services rendered by him to his country, and as a mark of appreciation of his fellow-townsmen of his bravery in the face of the enemy." Accompanying the Certificate of Freedom was a bundle of War Bonds and Treasury notes of the value of £114. Mr. and Mrs. McCudden also received from the Aero Club of America the Medal of Honour and Merit awarded to their son.

London Gazette, 9 April, 1918.—"War Office, 9 April, 1918. His Majesty the King has been graciously pleased to approve of the award of the Victoria Cross to the undermentioned Non-commissioned Officer."

ROBERTSON, CHARLES GRAHAM, L.-Corpl., was born on 4 July, 1879, only son of James and Catherine Robertson, and was a native of Penrith, Cumberland. He was educated at Dorking High School; was a booking clerk at Dorking, and took a prominent part in local sport. For some time he played football with Dorking Second XI. He served in the South African War as a Trooper in the Middlesex Yeomanry. He served in the European War, and was awarded the Military Medal, and was awarded the Victoria Cross [London Gazette, 9 April, 1918]: "Charles Graham Robertson, M.M., No. G. 58769, L.-Corpl., 10th Battn. Royal Fusiliers. For most conspicuous bravery and devotion to duty in repelling a strong attack by the enemy on our position. On realizing that he was being cut off, L.-Corpl. Robertson sent back two men to get reinforcements, and remained at his post (with only one other man) firing his Lewis gun and killing large numbers of the enemy, who were in range on his right. No reinforcements came up, and, realizing that he was being completely cut off, he withdrew, with the only survivor of the garrison of the post, to a point about ten yards further back, where he successfully held his position. Here he again stayed for some considerable time, firing his Lewis gun and inflicting casualties on the enemy. The position was, however, made impossible for him by the heavy hostile bombing and machine-gun fire, so he was forced again to withdraw, and arrived at a defended post. At this post he got on top of the parapet with a comrade, mounted his gun in a shell-hole and continued firing at the enemy, who were pouring across the top and down an adjacent trench. He had not been firing long when his comrade was killed and he himself severely wounded. He managed to crawl back, bringing his gun with him, but could no longer fire it, as he had exhausted all his ammunition. L.-Corpl. Robertson was alone throughout these operations, except for the presence of one other man, who later was killed, and the most determined resistance and the fine fight which he put up undoubtedly prevented the enemy from making a more rapid advance. His initiative, resource and the magnificent fighting spirit are worthy of the highest praise."

Charles G. Robertson.

The Victoria Cross

277

London Gazette, 24 April, 1918.—" War Office, 24 April, 1918. His Majesty the King has been graciously pleased to approve of the award of the Victoria Cross to the undermentioned Officers."

COLLINGS-WELLS, JOHN STANHOPE, Capt. (Acting Lieut.-Colonel), was born on 19 July, 1880, eldest son of Arthur and Caroline Mary Collings-Wells, of Caddington Hall, Hertfordshire. He was educated at Uppingham School, and at Christ Church, Oxford, and joined the Army in 1903, and served for fifteen years in the Hertfordshire Militia. He served in the European War in France, and was created a Companion of the Distinguished Service Order [London Gazette, 18 July, 1917] for conspicuous gallantry in command of a battalion in holding its objective against heavy counter-attacks, and later for his leadership and bravery in forming and commanding a composite battalion, which achieved its object under very adverse circumstances." He was awarded the Victoria Cross posthumously [London Gazette, 24 April, 1918] : " John Stanhope Collings-Wells, Capt. (Acting Lieut.-Colonel), late Bedfordshire Regt. For most conspicuous bravery, skilful leading

John S. Collings-Wells.

and handling of his battalion in very critical situations during a withdrawal. When the rearguard was almost surrounded and in great danger of being captured, Lieut.-Colonel Collings-Wells, realizing the situation, called for volunteers to remain behind and hold up the enemy whilst the remainder of the rearguard withdrew, and with his small body of volunteers held them up for one and a half hours until they had expended every round of ammunition. During this time he moved freely amongst his men guiding and encouraging them, and by his great courage undoubtedly saved the situation. On a subsequent occasion, when his battalion was ordered to carry out a counter-attack, he showed the greatest bravery. Knowing that his men were extremely tired after six days' fighting, he placed himself in front and led the attack, and even when twice wounded refused to leave them, but continued to lead and encourage his men until he was killed at the moment of gaining their objective. The successful results of the operation were, without doubt, due to the undaunted courage exhibited by this officer." He was killed on 27 March, 1918, at Albert.

HAYWARD, REGINALD FREDERICK JOHNSON, Capt., was born at Beersheba, East Griqualand, South Africa, 17 June, 1891, eldest son of Frederick Johnson Hayward, a well-known East Griqualand Stock Breeder, and of Gertrude Hayward, his wife, and grandson of the late Mr. J. F. Hayward and of Mrs. Hayward, of Aroona, Limpley Stoke, Wiltshire. He was educated at Hilton College, Natal, South Africa, where he was in the football fifteen for the last three years, and in the cricket eleven for the last two, and was also Regimental Sergt.-Major of Cadets in 1907 and 1908. After leaving school, he went to the Business College in Durban, and played football for Natal against English Rugby teams, and in the Currie Cup Competition of 1911. He is a keen shot and fond of all games, riding, motoring, etc. In May, 1912, he went to England and entered the Royal Veterinary College of Surgeons, and while there captained the Rugby Fifteen in 1913–14.

Reginald F. J. Hayward.

He always represented the Rosslyn Park Club in their first fifteen, and also played several games for the Middlesex first fifteen. When war broke out, he at once joined up, and was gazetted Second Lieutenant in the 6th Wiltshires 29 Sept. 1914 ; was promoted Lieutenant 24 Dec. 1914, and transferred to the 1st Wiltshires in March, 1915. He received the Military Cross [London Gazette, 8 Oct. 1916] for conspicuous gallantry and initiative at Stuff Redoubt, Somme. He was awarded the Bar to his Military Cross [London Gazette, 18 Sept. 1917] during the Battle of Messines, 7 June, 1917. He was promoted to Acting Captain 19 Dec. 1916. Capt. Hayward was awarded the Victoria Cross [London Gazette, 24 April, 1918] : " Reginald Frederick Johnson Hayward, Lieut. (Acting Capt.), M.C., Wiltshire Regt. For most conspicuous bravery in action. This officer, while in command of a company, displayed almost superhuman powers of endurance and consistent courage of the rarest nature. In spite of the fact that he was buried, wounded in the head, and rendered deaf on the first day of operations, and had his arm shattered two days later, he refused to leave his men (even though he received a third serious injury to his head) until he collapsed from sheer physical exhaustion. Throughout the whole of this period the enemy were attacking his company's front without cessation ; but Capt. Hayward continued to move across the open from one trench to another with absolute disregard of his own personal safety, concentrating entirely on reorganizing his defences and encouraging his men. It was almost entirely due to the magnificent example of ceaseless energy of this officer that many most determined attacks upon his portion of the trench system failed entirely." Capt. Hayward became Adjutant 3rd Battn. The Wiltshire Regt. 1 May, 1919. An extract from a newspaper says : " On several previous occasions we have referred to the glorious record which Rugby football has gained through the valour of those who played or still play the game, and in this connection it has of late frequently

been pointed out that Durban Rugby men have not been in the least behind their confrères of other parts of the world. Now Durban claims its V.C. In last week's issue of this paper it was conjectured that the Lieut. R. F. Hayward, of the Wilts, to whom the V.C. had been awarded was the R. F. J. Hayward of local Wanderers and Natal Rugby fame. Such has proved the case. The story of his extraordinary valour will bear re-telling. The London Gazette records it in the following terms : ' Lieut. Hayward, although buried by a shell, wounded in the head and rendered deaf, during the first day's operations, and his arm shattered two days later, and subsequently again seriously wounded in the head, refused to leave his men until he collapsed. Although the enemy were incessantly attacking, he continued to move in the open from trench to trench, absolutely regardless of his own safety, concentrating himself entirely on reorganizing the defences and encouraging his men. The complete failure of many very determined attacks on his trenches were almost entirely due to his magnificent example and ceaseless energy.' I think I can say without exaggeration that few men have figured more prominently in this war than has Lieut. R. F. J. Hayward. It does not seem very long since I last saw him, yet it must be over three years. It was just prior to his departure for Europe, and I remember thinking, as, standing by the Natal Bank, I bade him adieu, what a fine man he had grown into, for I remember Hayward as a youngster fresh from Hilton College. Since then his name has cropped up frequently. First of all, as a Military Cross winner. Then that he had been badly wounded. Again, as having won a Bar to his Military Cross. Then more wounds. And now, greatest honour of all—the Victoria Cross. I am not surprised. Though in some respects I have had to pay heavily for it, I shall never regret having become an enthusiast of sport, and for having retained my interest after the days of my active participation therein had passed. It has enabled me to meet many very fine characters, and in the days that I knew Hayward he appealed to me as one of the finest sportsmen I had met. In those days—1909 I think it was—I was hon. secretary of the local Wanderers Rugby Football Club, and Hayward, who had just left Hilton College and was finishing his education at the Business College, joined the club. He was a tall, hefty youngster. Just the type to train into a first-class Rugby forward, as he subsequently did. I forget how it came about, but after playing one or two matches for the Wanderers, the Selection Committee in their wisdom decided to leave him out. He was as keen as mustard, and the unpleasant duty of advising him that he had not been picked for the following match fell on me. I remember there was considerable competition for places amongst the forwards that year, and I explained as sympathetically as I could that that was the reason. I could see he was bitterly disappointed, and I felt it the more because in my own mind I considered a mistake was being made. But what impressed me was the sporting way Hayward took his disappointment. It impressed me so much that I vowed to myself that as long as I had any say in the administration of the club, young Hayward would never be dropped again. And he never was, but that was not due to my influence. It was his own good play. I had one season in the Wanderers pack with him, and so could judge to a nicety what his value to the side was. The following season I was home in England. It was in that season that Smythe's British team visited South Africa. Hayward had improved to such an extent that he played for Natal against the visitors in the match at Maritzburg, and, on the testimony of Capt. H. Ramsay Rae, I have it that he played a storming good game. That match was played on a Wednesday. On the following Saturday the return fixture was played in Durban, and Hayward was left out—because of his youth. That was what Capt. Ramsay Rae told me, and he was on the Selection Committee. I will not repeat what I said when I heard the explanation. Lead melts at a comparatively low temperature. The following year Hayward walked into the Natal team. I was on the Selection Committee this year, but I did not need to use my persuasive powers on behalf of the young forward. The Currie Cup was held at Cape Town, and the team we chose is published below, with a few interesting remarks opposite the names of some of the players :

M. Anderson (killed in action).
G. Ballenden.
W. J. Christopher (killed in action).
H. Daniell.
J. Dent.
H. F. Dowling.
J. R. English.
B. Flack (killed in action).
A. J. Fletcher (killed in action).
C. E. Gilson.
F. H. Harkness.
R. F. J. Hayward (V.C., M.C. and Bar).
F. T. Janion (killed in action).
J. Laughton.
R. H. Lazarus (wounded).
H. T. Lee.
R. G. Miller (killed in action).
J. Oberle.
H. Perfect (died, natural causes).
L. R. Randles.
K. O. Siedle (mentioned in Despatches).
L. B. Siedle.
H. W. Stockdale.
H. W. Taylor (Military Cross).
T. Worthington.

What a fine lot of fellows they were ! They were nearly all youngsters, and just the stamp that an English public school would take a pride in. I remember thinking this and remarking on it to someone at the luncheon which Mr. Otto Siedle (chairman of the Natal Rugby Union) gave to the team at the Durban Club just prior to its embarking on the mail boat for

Cape Town. Little did we think in those days that at least six of the twenty-five players would die fighting valiantly for their country. Probably there are more than six. Indeed, I am afraid there are, but in cases where I am not quite certain I have left a blank. Only twenty-four of the twenty-five sailed, for at the very last moment Miller was taken ill with appendicitis, and his kit had to be taken off the boat. This loss handicapped Natal considerably, but that was only one of the misfortunes the team encountered. On arriving at Cape Town, Hayward injured his back in a practice match, and was unable to participate in the first two matches, but after that, although suffering from his injury, he played in the remaining five games, viz., against the Western Province, North Eastern, Transvaal, Free State, and Border. On returning to Durban Mr. D. O. Allardyce, the manager of the team, in relating to me the salient features of the tournament, referred particularly to Hayward, Laughton and Lazarus, speaking of them in the highest terms. And praise from Mr. Allardyce means something. I am writing the above recollections more or less from memory, my records having got somewhat scattered the last few months. In 1912 I was absent from Durban, and cannot recollect if Hayward played for the Wanderers that year. I do not think so. Whether he did or not he played quite long enough in Durban to justify himself, as one of the best forwards we have had. It goes without saying he was never deficient in pluck. He had, in addition, strength, endurance and skill. He was a scrupulously clean player, and I never met a more modest one. Originally, Hayward hailed from East Griqualand, and I believe he returned there after leaving Durban. He never lost his interest and affection for the Wanderers Club, but now it is doubtful if the poor old Wanderers will ever be resuscitated to take a pride in her children; but if the Wanderers does not survive the war, Durban and Natal Rugby will, and Durban and Natal Rugby will always point with pride to the name of R. F. J. Hayward, V.C., and twice M.C."

FLOWERDEW, GORDON MURIEL, Lieut., served in the European War in France. He was awarded the Victoria Cross [London Gazette, 24 April, 1918]: "Gordon Muriel Flowerdew, Lieut., late Lord Strathcona's Horse, Canadian Cavalry. For most conspicuous bravery and dash when in command of a squadron detailed for special service of a very important nature. On reaching the first objective, Lieut. Flowerdew saw two lines of the enemy, each about sixty strong, with machine guns in the centre and flanks, one line being about two hundred yards behind the other. Realizing the critical nature of the operation, and how much depended upon it, Lieut. Flowerdew ordered a troop under Lieut. Harvey, V.C., to dismount and carry out a special movement while he led the remaining three troops to the charge. The squadron (less one troop) passed over the lines, killing many of the enemy with the sword, and, wheeling about, galloped at them again. Although the squadron had then lost about seventy per cent. of its numbers, killed and wounded, from rifle and machine-gun fire directed on it from the front and both flanks, the enemy broke and retired. The survivors of the squadron then established themselves in a position where they were joined, after much hand-to-hand fighting, by Lieut. Harvey's party. Lieut. Flowerdew was dangerously wounded through both thighs during the operations, but continued to cheer on his men. There can be no doubt that this officer's great valour was the prime factor in the capture of the position." "Thirty Canadian V.C.'s" (published by Messrs. Skeffington) says (pages 94–96): "March 30th, 1918, dawned full of menace for the Allied line. Early that morning the Canadian Cavalry Brigade received information that the Germans had captured Mézières and were advancing on Amiens. The brigade was ordered to cut across country and arrest the advance. Already the Germans had occupied the Bois de Moreuil, the strategic importance of which could hardly be over-estimated. From the wood they could overlook the whole of the valley leading up to Amiens and to the main railroad to Paris. The cavalry decided to attack. Reaching the north-east edge of the wood, headquarters were established in a small wood adjoining the large one. The smaller wood had not then been occupied by the Germans, but they were sending bursts of rifle and machine-gun fire at the cavalry from their cover, and it was imperative that the attack should not be postponed. The Royal Canadian Dragoons, who were leading, sent an advance-guard squadron, commanded by Capt. Nordheimer, around the north-east corner at a gallop. A second squadron, under Capt. Newcomen, rode at the south-east face, intending to get into touch with Nordheimer's squadron. A third squadron, under Major Timmis, followed in support of Capt. Nordheimer. Though raked by a heavy fire, Nordheimer's squadron charged into the north-east corner of the wood, and came to grips with the enemy in a hand-to-hand combat. Many of the enemy were killed, for they refused to surrender; but at last a large party, of about three hundred, driven from cover, retired from the wood south of the point at which the cavalry had entered. It was then that Lord Strathcona's Horse received the order to advance, Lieut. Flowerdew's squadron in support of Nordheimer, while the remainder of the regiment moved, dismounted, against the southern front of the wood. The mounted squadron rounded the corner of the wood at a gallop, to cut off the retreat of the enemy on the eastern side. They were nearly at the destination when suddenly in front of them they saw, from the top of a road in a cut bank, two lines of Germans facing them. There were about sixty Germans in each line, and machine guns were posted in the centre and on the flanks of both, the rear line about two hundred yards behind the first. Immediately the enemy saw the horsemen they opened fire. Flowerdew quickly ordered a troop under Lieut. Harvey, V.C., to dismount and carry out a special movement. With the remaining men he charged the German lines. From the enemy machine guns came a concentrated stream of fire on the rushing cavalry. There is little need to describe that charge. It was a return to the days when battles were decided by the strength of men's arms. It was the charge of the Light Brigade over again, on a smaller scale—smaller in physical weight of onslaught and

opposition, but equal in spirit. The Germans stood up boldly to the attack. They never expected that the horsemen would penetrate into their midst. There was no question of surrender, nor much time for it. Through the first line went the squadron, across the intervening space and through the second line, cutting down the enemy as they passed. Behind the second line they wheeled and rode through again full tilt. Over seventy per cent. of the attackers were casualties, but the fury of the charge was more than the Germans could face. They broke and fled. Nor was this all, for the enemy who were still fighting in the wood, hearing the clatter of hoofs behind them, believed themselves surrounded and their resistance to our dismounted troops weakened. The survivors of Lieut. Flowerdew's men established themselves in a position in which they were joined later by Harvey and those of his force who were left. Both leaders had been wounded, Flowerdew having been shot through both thighs. Only after the action was the full importance of the victory realized, and of Flowerdew it is written in official language that 'there can be no doubt that this officer's great valour was the prime factor in the capture of the position.'"

London Gazette, 1 May, 1918.—"Air Ministry, 1 May, 1918. His Majesty the King has been graciously pleased to award the Victoria Cross to the undermentioned Officers of the Royal Air Force, for services displaying outstanding bravery."

JERRARD, ALAN, Lieut., served in the European War in Italy. He received his training in flying at a Lincolnshire aerodrome. He was awarded the Victoria Cross [London Gazette, 1 May, 1918]: "Alan Jerrard, Lieut., Royal Air Force, formerly South Staffordshire Regt. When on an offensive patrol with two other officers he attacked five enemy aeroplanes, and shot down one in flames, following it down to within one hundred feet of the ground. He then attacked an enemy aerodrome from a height of only fifty feet from the ground, and, engaging single-handed some nineteen machines, which were either landing or attempting to take off, succeeded in destroying one of them, which crashed on the aerodrome. A large number of machines then attacked him, and whilst thus fully occupied, he observed that one of the pilots of his patrol was in difficulties. He went immediately to his assistance, regardless of his own personal safety, and destroyed a third enemy machine. Fresh enemy aeroplanes continued to rise from the aerodrome, which he attacked one after another, and only retreated, still engaged with five enemy machines, when ordered to do so by his patrol leader. Although apparently wounded, this very gallant officer turned repeatedly and attacked single-handed the pursuing machines, until he was eventually overwhelmed by numbers and driven to the ground. Lieut. Jerrard had greatly distinguished himself on four previous occasions, within a period of twenty-three days, in destroying enemy machines, displaying bravery and ability of the very highest order."

McLEOD, ALAN ARNETT, Second Lieut., served in the European War, and was awarded the Victoria Cross [London Gazette, 1 May, 1918]: "Alan Arnett McLeod, Second Lieut., Royal Air Force. Whilst flying with his observer (Lieut. A. W. Hammond, M.C.), attacking hostile formations by bombs and machine-gun fire, he was assailed at a height of five thousand feet by eight enemy triplanes, which dived at him from all directions, firing from their front guns. By skilful manoeuvring he enabled his observer to fire bursts at each machine in turn, shooting three of them down out of control. By this time Lieut. McLeod had received five wounds, and whilst continuing the engagement a bullet penetrated his petrol

Alan Arnett McLeod.

tank and set the machine on fire. He then climbed out on to the left bottom plane, controlling his machine from the side of the fuselage, and by side-slipping steeply, kept the flames to one side, thus enabling the observer to continue firing until the ground was reached. The observer had been wounded six times when the machine crashed in 'No Man's Land,' and Second Lieut. McLeod, notwithstanding his own wounds, dragged him away from the burning wreckage at great personal risk from heavy machine-gun fire from the enemy's lines. This very gallant pilot was again wounded by a bomb whilst engaged in this act of rescue, but he persevered until he had placed Lieut. Hammond in comparative safety before falling himself from exhaustion and loss of blood." He returned to Stonewall, Manitoba, Canada, his home, on leave, when convalescent. He died of wounds.

London Gazette, 3 May, 1918.—"War Office, 3 May, 1918. His Majesty the King has been graciously pleased to approve of the award of the Victoria Cross to the undermentioned Officers, Non-commissioned Officers and Man."

BUSHELL, CHRISTOPHER, Capt. (Temporary Lieut.-Colonel), was born 31 Oct. 1888, at Hinderton Lodge, Neston, Cheshire, younger son of the late Reginald Bushell and Mrs. Bushell, Hillside, St. Margaret's-at-Cliffe. He was educated at Moorland House, Heswall, Cheshire; Rugby; and Corpus Christi College, Oxford.

Christopher Bushell.

He always kept in touch with his school, and devoted much of his time and energy to the Rugby clubs, Notting Dale. At Oxford he was captain of his College boat; also at Henley. He was called to the Bar in 1912, and joined the Army in 1912, in the Special Reserve of Officers, as Second Lieutenant in 1st Battn. Royal West Surrey Regt. He served in the European War in France; in the Retreat from Mons; was severely wounded 14 Sept. 1914; returned to France in Nov. 1915, and served there until his death in action 8 Aug. 1918. Was A.D.C. to 33rd Division Nov. 1915, to June, 1916; Staff Captain, 100th Brigade, through Battle of the Somme; Temporary Commander 7th Queen's, Dec. 1916, with whom he served as C.O., Second in Command, and finally permanent C.O. until 8 Aug. 1918. He fell near Morlancourt, leading his men in the opening attack of the last great offensive. He was created a Companion of the Distinguished Service Order, New Year's List, Jan. 1918: "For continued gallantry and devotion to duty on numerous occasions." He was awarded the Victoria Cross [London Gazette, 3 May, 1918]: "Christopher Bushell, D.S.O., Capt. (Temporary Lieut.-Colonel), 7th Battn. Royal West Surrey Regt. For most conspicuous bravery and devotion to duty when in command of his battalion. Lieut.-Colonel Bushell personally led C Company of his battalion, who were co-operating with an Allied regiment in a counter-attack, in face of very heavy machine-gun fire. In the course of this attack he was severely wounded in the head, but he continued to carry on, walking about in front of both English and Allied troops, encouraging and reorganizing them. He refused even to have his wound attended to until he had placed the whole line in a sound position, and formed a defensive flank to meet a turning movement by the enemy. He then went to Brigade Headquarters and reported the situation, had his wound dressed, and returned to the firing line, which had come back a short distance. He visited every portion of the line, both English and Allied, in the face of terrific machine-gun and rifle fire, exhorting the troops to remain where they were and to kill the enemy. In spite of the wounds, this gallant officer refused to go to the rear, and had eventually to be removed to the dressing station in a fainting condition. To the magnificent example of energy, devotion and courage shown by their commanding officer is attributed the fine spirit displayed and the keen fight put up by his battalion, not only on the day in question, but on each succeeding day of the withdrawal." In Aug. 1915, he married Rachel, daughter of the Rev. E. Lambert, Wye, Kent, and leaves one daughter, born in 1916.

ANDERSON, WILLIAM HERBERT, Lieut.-Colonel, was born 29 Dec. 1881, at Glasgow. He was the son of William James Anderson, C.B.E., J.P., Chartered Accountant and Stockbroker, of Glasgow, and of Eleanora

William H. Anderson.

Kay, daughter of Alexander Kay, of Cornhill, Biggar, Lanarkshire. He was educated at Glasgow Academy, Fettes College, and Tours, France. On 4 July, 1909, at Tullichawan, Alexandria, Dumbartonshire, he married Gertrude Campbell Gilmour, daughter of William Ewing Gilmour, of Rosehall, Sutherlandshire, and Gertrude Campbell, daughter of James Campbell, of Tullichawan, Alexandria, Dumbartonshire. Two sons were born to them: William Allan Campbell Anderson, 4 May, 1911, and Charles Patrick Anderson, 4 Aug. 1913. Lieut.-Colonel W. H. Anderson joined the 1st Lanark Rifle Volunteers (afterwards the 5th Scottish Rifles) in 1900, and retired in 1908 with the rank of Lieutenant on becoming a partner in his father's business of Messrs. Kerr, Andersons & MacLeod, Chartered Accountants and Stockbrokers, Glasgow. Colonel Anderson took a keen interest in politics, and when war broke out he was holding for the second time the office of President of the Junior Imperial Unionists. On the outbreak of war he offered his services to his country, and in Sept. 1914, joined the 17th Highland Light Infantry (the Chamber of Commerce Battn.) with the rank of Captain. In Nov. 1915, he was appointed Second in Command of the 19th Highland Light Infantry with the rank of Major, and remained in that position till he went to France in Sept. 1916, being attached Second in Command to the 9th East Surreys in Oct. of that year. He was invalided home in March, 1917, and on returning to France in June was appointed Second in Command of the 12th Highland Light Infantry. He commanded the battalion from Dec. of that year, and was promoted Lieut.-Colonel in Feb. 1918. He was awarded the Victoria Cross [London Gazette, 3 May, 1918]: "William Herbert Anderson, Temporary Major (Acting Lieut.-Colonel), Highland Light Infantry. For most conspicuous bravery, determination and gallant leading of his command. The enemy attacked on the right of the battalion frontage, and succeeded in penetrating the wood held by our men. Owing to successive lines of the enemy following on closely, there was the gravest danger that the flank of the whole position would be turned. Grasping the seriousness of the situation, Colonel Anderson made his way across the open in full view of the enemy, now holding the wood on the right, and after much effort succeeded in gathering the remainder of the two right companies. He personally led the counter-attack, and drove the enemy from the wood, capturing twelve machine guns and seventy prisoners, and restoring the original line. His conduct in leading the charge was quite fearless, and his most splendid example was the means of rallying and inspiring the men during a most critical hour. Later on the same day, in another position, the enemy had penetrated to within three hundred yards of the village, and were holding a timber yard in force. Colonel Anderson reorganized his men after they had been driven in, and brought them forward to a position of readiness for a counter-attack. He led the attack in person, and throughout showed the utmost disregard for his own

safety. The counter-attack drove the enemy from his position, but resulted in this very gallant officer losing his life. He died fighting within the enemy's lines, setting a magnificent example to all who were privileged to serve under him." The following are extracts from letters referring to Lieut.-Colonel W. H. Anderson, V.C., 12th H.L.I.:

Brigadier-General ———— :

"I am extremely proud of the announcement in this morning's papers 'For Valour.' It is something great, indeed, to know that his actions have been recognized by those over him, and there is no higher prize to be won than that. May I express my gratification at the Gazette, and particularly the last paragraph of the description—and may I add to those words, 'and to those whom he served under,' of whom I am proud to have been one."

Brigadier-General ———— :

"His heroic death and its recognition will, I trust, be a great consolation to you and yours. Never was a V.C. more splendidly won, and the account of such absolute disregard of danger and devotion to duty crowned by such magnificent success, will send a thrill of pride through all who read it. It is what I would have expected he would do from my knowledge of him when he served in the 46th Brigade under me."

Lieut.-Colonel ———— :

"I shall always remember him as the best of friends, the most loyal of officers, and one of the best types of an upright gentleman. Of course, it's all just what we would have expected him to do. My only consolation is—he died as he would have wished with the battalion he loved, and with the battalion which loved him."

Lieut.-Colonel ———— :

"It is with the greatest of pride that I read the announcement of your husband's V.C. and his most noble deeds. It means the greatest of human courage to lead a counter-attack once, but to do it twice is the utmost of human endurance. I feel so proud of having known him. I know the whole of the 9th East Surreys join me in this."

An officer of a neighbouring battalion writes:

"If you could have seen Colonel Anderson last week before he was killed, counter-attacking thousands of Germans with a mere handful of men, you would believe in the British Army for all time. If ever a man won the V.C. it was Colonel Anderson, and I do hope he gets it."

A Staff Captain:

"As you probably know, we have come through some of the hardest fighting ever yet known. The last week has been simply terrible, but we stopped the Hun all right, though at the cost of some fine fellows. Poor Anderson did magnificently commanding the battalion, and everybody who witnessed his gallant act of self-sacrifice spoke highly of him. He certainly deserved the Victoria Cross."

Captain ———— :

"I was with Colonel Anderson in the capacity of Adjutant all through the show, and I never wish to serve under a more gallant officer. If I were allowed, I would give you ever so many details of the splendid way in which he led two counter-attacks, of the way he held a position all day against masses of the Bosches, and finally, being outflanked, of the way in which we all fought our way out, all under his immediate command. Of the way he died I cannot express too highly the admiration I feel. He was at the head of his men and died in the enemy's lines leading a counter-attack, which drove them back and enabled the village to be evacuated. I wish to say how much we grieve over the loss of our gallant C.O., in whom the men and officers had absolute trust, and I only speak the truth when I say that he cannot be replaced."

CASSIDY, BERNARD MATTHEW, Second Lieut., served in the European War in France. He was awarded the Victoria Cross [London Gazette, 3 May, 1918]: "Bernard Matthew Cassidy, Second Lieut., late 2nd Battn. Lancashire Fusiliers. For most conspicuous bravery, self-sacrifice and exceptional devotion to duty during a hostile attack. At a time when the flank of the division was in danger, Lieut. Cassidy was in command of the left company of his battalion, which was in close support. He was given orders prior to the attack that he must hold on to his position to the last. He most nobly carried this out to the letter. The enemy came on in overwhelming numbers and endeavoured to turn the flank. He, however, continually rallied his men under a terrific bombardment. The enemy were several times cleared out of the trench by his personal leadership. His company was eventually surrounded, but Lieut. Cassidy still fought on, encouraging and exhorting his men until eventually killed. By his most gallant conduct the whole line was held up at this point, and the left flank was undoubtedly saved from what might have been a disaster."
"The Times History of the War" says (30 July, 1919):
"The details of Cassidy's 'exceptional devotion' called to mind the terribly significant order which had been issued by Field-Marshal Sir Douglas Haig—that there was to be no retirement, and that the British Army was to hold on to the last. A hostile attack was being made and the flank of a division was in danger. Cassidy was in command of the left company

of his battalion, which was in support. ' He was given orders prior to the attack that he must hold on to his position to the last. He most nobly carried this out to the letter.' In overwhelming numbers the enemy came on and tried to turn the flank ; but Cassidy, in spite of a terrific bombardment, continually rallied his men, and as the result of his personal leadership the enemy were several times cleared out of a trench. The Lieutenant's company was eventually surrounded, but still the undaunted subaltern fought on, exhorting his men until at last he was killed. Cassidy had made his last stand, but his heroism held up the whole attack at this point and undoubtedly saved the left flank from what might have been a disaster. This episode of sheer valour and stern obedience to the very letter of a stern order was known to be but one of many such episodes at this particular period."

McDOUGALL, STANLEY ROBERT, Sergt., son of John McDougall. His parents live at Hobart, Tasmania. He served in the European War, and was awarded the Victoria Cross [London Gazette, 3 May, 1918] : " No. 4061, Sergt. Stanley Robert McDougall, 47th Battn. Australian Imperial Force. For most conspicuous bravery and devotion to duty when the enemy attacked our line and his first wave succeeded in gaining an entry. Sergt. McDougall, who was at a post in a flank company, realized the situation and at once charged the enemy's second wave single-handed with rifle and bayonet, killing seven and capturing a machine gun which they had. This he turned on to them, firing from the hip, causing many casualties and routing that wave. He then turned his attention to those who had entered, until his ammunition ran out, all the time firing at close quarters, when he seized a bayonet and charged again, killing three men and an enemy officer, who was just about to kill one of our officers. He used a Lewis gun on the enemy, killing many and enabling us to capture 33 prisoners. The prompt action of this non-commissioned officer saved the line and enabled the enemy's advance to be stopped."

Stanley R. McDougall.

COLUMBINE, HERBERT GEORGE, Private, No. 50720, was born on the 28th Nov. 1893, in London, son of Herbert Columbine (killed in action on the 11th July, 1900, in South Africa), and Emma Columbine. He was educated at Melvin Road Council Schools, Penge, and joined the Army in 1911, as a Private in the 19th Hussars, and later transferred to the Machine Gun Corps. He served in the European War in France from Aug. 1914, being killed in action 22 March, 1918. He was awarded the Victoria Cross [London Gazette, 3 May, 1918] : " Herbert George Columbine, No. 50720, Private, 9th Squadron, Machine Gun Corps. For most conspicuous bravery and self-sacrifice displayed when, owing to casualties, Private Columbine took over command of a gun and kept it firing from 9 a.m. till 1 p.m. in an isolated position with no wire in front. During this time wave after wave of the enemy failed to get up to him. Owing to his being attacked by a low-flying aeroplane, the enemy at last

Herbert G. Columbine.

gained a strong footing in the trench on either side. The position being untenable, he ordered the two remaining men to get away, and, though being bombed from either side, he kept his gun firing and inflicted tremendous losses. He was eventually killed by a bomb which blew up him and his gun. He showed throughout the highest valour, determination and self-sacrifice."

The deed is thus described by Dr. P. G. C. Atkinson, who was an eye-witness :

" Nothing I have seen or heard of could be finer than the heroism of this soldier. The enemy attacked suddenly in great force. They made considerable headway, and from 'vantage ground on either side they started to enfilade our trenches, causing very severe casualties among the men. Part of our defence system included a machine-gun post somewhat in advance of the main trench. The men working this were all knocked out. Running the gauntlet of very heavy fire, Private Columbine rushed forward and took charge of this gun. He was followed by some comrades, and, in spite of the fact that the whole of the enemy machine guns in the immediate neighbourhood concentrated their heaviest fire against the post, which was almost unprotected by any of the devices commonly used, Columbine kept the machine gun going for over four hours. All that time the enemy had been working round the position with strong forces, and actually had the post cut off save for one narrow gap, by which it was still possible to communicate with the main position. For the whole of the time, save when he went across the fire-swept ground to bring ammunition, the brave chap remained at his post, and despite repeated rushes, he kept the enemy at bay. In the course of the fight a German officer appeared and repeatedly urged his men to the attack on the isolated post, but every rush of the Germans was stopped in a few yards by the deadly fire from this brave gunner, who was actually wounded, but continued to work his gun in spite of that. Early in the afternoon it became obvious that the position was hopeless, and Columbine told the only two unwounded comrades left that it was folly for them to remain

there. ' Save yourselves ; I'll carry on,' was what he said. They were reluctant to go, but he insisted, and in the end they came to see the force of his contention that there was no point in sacrificing three lives where one was enough. He shouted a few words of farewell, and that was the last his comrades heard from him. From where we lay we could see the fight going on, the swarms of grey-blue infantry around the position, the machine gun, manned by the wounded hero, spitting out death. In the course of the hour, from noon to one, the enemy made eight attempts to rush the post. Each one was brought to a standstill. Therefore new tactics were necessary. Retiring to their position the enemy concentrated heavy rifle and machine-gun fire on the hero and his gun. At the same time a number of hostile aeroplanes appeared overhead. They were promptly engaged by our machines, but one detached itself from the fighting group and came down to about a hundred feet or so above the machine-gun position, circling above for a few seconds like a great vulture ready to pounce on its prey. We saw Columbine elevate his gun to attack his new enemy. The fight could only have one ending. A bomb was launched from the aeroplane, and there was a sharp report, gun and gunner blown up. The heroic fight of Columbine was not without its value, for the way in which he delayed the enemy attack gave us time to consolidate our position in the immediate neighbourhood, and when the enemy attacked they found that the four hours' stand made by this one man had put the German plans hopelessly out of gear so far as the capture of that series of positions was concerned. The comrades of the dead hero speak highly of him."

In a letter to the deceased soldier's mother, Capt. MacAndrews, commanding the 9th Machine Gun Squadron, wrote :

" The news reached this Brigade last night that the King has the pleasure of granting your son the Victoria Cross. He nobly earned the honour, his bravery and determination on 22 March are beyond words. This is the only V.C. which this Brigade has had ; in fact, I think it is the only one the Division has had. I had a full parade of the Squadron this morning to read out the account of his action and also the letter of congratulation which we received from the General ' on behalf of the whole Brigade on the bestowal of this very distinguished honour.' In your loss of such a gallant son you have the very deepest sympathy of everyone in this Squadron, where he used to be so extremely popular. We all sincerely trust that your great sorrow may be to some extent lessened by your pride of his noble death, so noble that the King has honoured him with the very highest award."

Lieut. Eade, 9th Machine Gun Squadron, wrote :

" You will no doubt have been informed by the War Office that No. 50720, Private Columbine, H. G., is wounded and missing. He was in my sub-section, and although I had not the luck to be with him on the 22nd March, I heard what happened from those who were. He kept his gun firing to the last, although the Germans had got into the trench on both sides of him and were throwing bombs at him. In the end he was seen to be hit by a bomb and very badly wounded. He was one of my best gun numbers, and is a great loss to the squadron. I deeply sympathize with you, but it may be some consolation to you to know that he has been recommended for a medal in token of his bravery. It was the bravest deed I have ever heard of."

London Gazette, 8 May, 1918.—" War Office, 8 May, 1918. His Majesty the King has been graciously pleased to approve of the award of the Victoria Cross to the undermentioned Officers, Non-commissioned Officers and Men."

WATSON, OLIVER CYRIL SPENCER, Major (Acting Lieut.-Colonel), D.S.O., was born on 7 Sept. 1876, in London, youngest son of the late Mr. William Spencer Watson, M.B., F.R.C.S., of London. He was educated at St. Paul's School and Sandhurst, and was gazetted to the Yorkshire Regt. in 1897. He took part in the Tirah and China campaigns. He served in the European War in Gallipoli and France, and was created a Companion of the Distinguished Service Order [London Gazette, 20 May, 1917] : " Oliver Cyril Spencer Watson, for the following action : On 3 May, during the attack near Bullecourt, Lieut.-Colonel W. Watson, commanding the battalion, was killed. Major O. C. S. Watson was sent up to take his place. On arriving at the railway cutting he found men of all units of the brigade, who had returned there after the first unsuccessful attack. Displaying the highest soldierly qualities, he organized these men, inspired them with his own

Oliver C. S. Watson.

coolness and confidence and personally led them forward to a second attack. This attack was eventually brought to nothing by machine-gun fire, but Major Watson continued to advance alone, in an endeavour to reach the men still holding on in front, until he was badly wounded. All units of the brigade were talking about his great gallantry and fine leadership." Lieut.-Colonel Watson was awarded the Victoria Cross [London Gazette, 8 May, 1918] : " Oliver Cyril Spencer Watson, D.S.O., (R. of O.), Major (Acting, Lieut.-Colonel) late King's Own (Yorkshire Light Infantry). For most conspicuous bravery, self-sacrificing devotion to duty, and exceptionally gallant leading during a critical period of operations. His command was at a point where continual attacks were made by the enemy in order to pierce the line, and an intricate system of old trenches in front, coupled with the fact that his position was under constant rifle and machine-gun fire, rendered the situation still more dangerous. A counter-attack had been made against the enemy position, which at first achieved its object, but as they were holding out in two improvised strong points, Lieut.-Colonel Watson saw that immediate action was necessary, and he led his remaining small reserve to the attack, organizing bombing parties and leading attacks under intense rifle and machine-gun fire. Outnumbered, he finally ordered his men to retire, remaining himself in a communication trench to cover the retirement, though he faced almost certain death by so doing. The assault he led was at a critical moment, and without doubt saved the line. Both in the assault and in covering his men's retirement he held his life as nothing, and his splendid bravery inspired all troops in the vicinity to rise to the occasion and save a breach being made in a hardly tried and attenuated line. Lieut.-Colonel Watson was killed while covering the withdrawal."

ROBERTS, FRANK CROWTHER, Capt. (Acting Lieut.-Colonel), was born 2 June, 1891, son of the Rev. Frank Roberts, Vicar of St. John's, Southall, and of Mrs. Frank Roberts ; and nephew of the Rev. Canon and Mrs. Parr, of Milton Bryan, Bedfordshire. He joined the Army in 1911, serving in the European War in France ; he was created a Companion of the Distinguished Service Order in 1915 ; awarded the Military Cross in 1917, and was awarded the Victoria Cross [London Gazette, 8 May, 1918] : " Frank Crowther Roberts, D.S.O., M.C., Capt., Acting Lieut.-Colonel), 1st Battn. The Worcester Regt. During continuous operations which covered over twelve days Lieut.-Colonel Roberts showed most conspicuous bravery, exceptional military skill in dealing with the many very difficult situations of the retirement, and amazing endurance and energy in encouraging and inspiring all ranks under his command. On one occasion the enemy attacked a village and had practically cleared it of our troops, when this officer got together an improvised party and led a counter-attack which temporarily drove the enemy out of the village, thus covering the retirement of troops on their flanks, who would otherwise have been cut off. The success of this action was entirely due to his personal valour and skill."

TOYE, A. MAURICE, Second Lieut. (Acting Capt.), served in the European War in France ; was awarded the Military Cross, and was awarded the Victoria Cross [London Gazette, 8 May, 1918] : " A. Maurice Toye, M.C., Second Lieut. (Acting Capt.), 2nd Battn. Middlesex Regt. For most conspicuous bravery and fine leadership displayed in extremely critical circumstances. When the enemy captured the trench at a bridgehead, he three times re-established the post, which was eventually recaptured by fresh enemy attacks. After ascertaining that his three other posts were cut off, he fought his way through the enemy with one officer and six men of his company. Finding 70 men of the battalion on his left retiring, he collected them, counter-attacked, and took up a line which he maintained until reinforcements arrived. Without this action the defence of the bridge must have been turned. In two subsequent operations, when in command of a composite company, he covered the retirement of his battalion with skill and courage. Later, with a party of battalion headquarters, he pressed through the enemy in the village, firing at them in the streets, thus covering the left flank of the battalion retirement. Finally, on a still later occasion, when in command of a mixed force of the brigade, he re-established, after hard fighting, a line that had been abandoned before his arrival. He was twice wounded within ten days, but remained at duty. His valour and skilful leading throughout this prolonged period of intense operations were most conspicuous."

JACKSON, HAROLD, Sergt., became a well-known amateur boxer, and in 1910 he knocked out Private Grooby and " Dido " Fossit. He left his home in 1912 to work on the railway at Nottingham, and later become a Bricklayer in the employment of Messrs. MacAlpine. He joined the Army in April, 1915, as a Trooper in the 18th Hussars, and a few months later was transferred to the East Yorkshire Regt. He served in the European War, and was awarded the Victoria Cross [London Gazette, 8 May, 1918] : " No. 18474, Harold Jackson, Sergt., East Yorkshire Regt. (Kirton, near Boston, Lincolnshire). For most conspicuous bravery and devotion to duty. Sergt. Jackson volunteered and went out through the hostile barrage and brought back valuable information regarding the enemy's movements. Later, when the enemy had established themselves in our line, this N.C.O. rushed at them, and, single-handed, bombed them out into the open. Shortly afterwards, again single-handed, he stalked an enemy machine gun, threw Mills bombs at the detachment, and put the gun out of action. On a subsequent occasion, when all his officers had become casualties, this very gallant N.C.O. led his company in the attack, and when ordered to retire, he withdrew the company successfully under heavy fire. He then went out repeatedly under heavy fire and carried in wounded."

MASTERS, RICHARD GEORGE, Private, served in the European War in France, and was awarded the Victoria Cross [London Gazette, 8 May, 1918] : " Richard George Masters, Private, Army Service Corps (Motor Transport), attached 141st Field Ambulance. For most conspicuous bravery and devotion to duty. Owing to an enemy attack, communications were cut off and wounded could not be evacuated. The road was reported impassable, but Private Masters volunteered to try to get through, and after the greatest difficulty succeeded, although he had to clear the road of all sorts of debris. He made journey after journey throughout the afternoon, over a road consistently shelled and swept by machine-gun fire, and was on one occasion bombed by an aeroplane. The greater part of the wounded cleared from this area were evacuated by Private Masters, as his was the only car that got through during this particular time."

WHITFIELD, HAROLD, Private, was born at Oswestry, Shrewsbury. He served in the European War, and was promoted Sergeant. He was awarded the Victoria Cross [London Gazette, 8 May, 1918] : " Harold Whitfield, No. 230199, Private, 10th Yeomanry Battn. King's Shropshire

Light Infantry. For most conspicuous bravery, initiative and absolute disregard of personal safety. During the first and heaviest of three counter-attacks made by the enemy on the position which had just been captured by his battalion, Private Whitfield, single-handed, charged and captured a Lewis gun which was harassing his company at short range. He bayoneted or shot the whole gun team, and turning the gun on the enemy, drove them back with heavy casualties, thereby completely restoring the whole situation in his part of the line. Later he organized and led a bombing attack on the enemy who had established themselves in an advanced position close to our lines, and from which they were enfilading his company. He drove the enemy back with great loss, and by establishing his party in their position saved many lives, and materially assisted in the defeat of the counter-attack." Sergt. Harold Whitfield was personally decorated and congratulated by the King on 31 May, 1918, at an Investiture held at Leeds.

London Gazette, 17 May, 1918.—" Admiralty, 17 May, 1918. Honours for miscellaneous service. The King has been graciously pleased to approve of the award of the following honours, decorations and medals to the undermentioned Officers and Men. Action in Heligoland Bight on the 17 Nov. 1917. Posthumous award of the Victoria Cross. Ordinary Seaman John Carless."

CARLESS, JOHN HENRY, Ordinary Seaman, was born on 11 Nov. 1896, at Walsall, son of John Thomas and Elizabeth Carless. He was educated at St. Mary's the Mount Roman Catholic School, and joined the Army on 1 Sept. 1915. He served in the European War on H.M.S. Caledon, and was posthumously awarded the Victoria Cross for conspicuous bravery in the Battle of Heligoland Bight in Nov. 1917 [London Gazette, 17 May, 1918] : " John Henry Carless, Ordinary Seaman, O.N.J. 43703 (Po.) (killed in action). Although mortally wounded in the abdomen, he still went on serving the gun at which he was acting as rammer, lifting a projectile and helping to clear away the other casualties. He collapsed once, but got up, tried again, and served on the new gun's crew. He then fell and died. He not only set a very inspiring and

John Henry Carless.

memorable example, but he also, whilst mortally wounded, continued to do effective work against the King's enemies."

London Gazette, 23 May, 1918.—" War Office, 23 May, 1918. His Majesty the King has been graciously pleased to approve of the award of the Victoria Cross to the undermentioned Officers, Non-commissioned Officers and Men."

FORBES-ROBERTSON, JAMES, Capt. (Acting Lieut.-Colonel), was born 7 July, 1884, younger son of the late Farquhar Forbes-Robertson and Mrs. Farquhar Forbes-Robertson. He was educated at Cheltenham College (1897–1902) ; was commissioned in the Border Regt. 2 March, 1904, and became Lieutenant 31 Aug. 1906. He served in the European War from 1914 ; as Temporary Captain, Border Regt. (30 Oct. 1914, to 2 Nov. 1914) ; was promoted to Captain 3 Nov. 1914, and appointed Staff Captain 28 Nov. 1914. Capt. Forbes-Robertson was awarded the Military Cross ; created a Companion of the Distinguished Service Order, and was awarded the Victoria Cross [London Gazette, 23 May, 1918] : " James Forbes-Robertson, D.S.O., M.C., Capt. (Acting Lieut.-Colonel), Border Regt. For most conspicuous bravery whilst commanding his battalion during the heavy fighting. Through his quick judgment, resource, untiring energy and magnificent example, Lieut.-Colonel Forbes-Robertson on four separate occasions saved the line from breaking, and averted a situation which might have had the most serious and far-reaching results. On the first occasion, when troops in front were falling back, he made a rapid reconnaissance on horseback, in full view of the enemy, under heavy machine-gun and close-range shell fire. He then organized and, still mounted, led a counter-attack, which completely successful in re-establishing our line. When his horse was shot under him he continued on foot. Later on the same day, when troops to the left of his line were giving way, he went to that flank and checked and steadied the line, inspiring confidence by his splendid coolness and disregard of personal danger. His horse was wounded three times, and he was thrown five times. The following day when the troops on both his flanks were forced to retire, he formed a post at battalion headquarters, and with his battalion still held his ground, thereby covering the retreat of troops on his flanks. Under the heaviest fire this gallant officer fearlessly exposed himself when collecting parties, organizing and encouraging. On a subsequent occasion, when troops were retiring on his left, and the condition of things on his right was obscure, he again saved the situation by his magnificent example and cool judgment. Losing a second horse, he continued alone on foot until he had established a line to which his own troops could withdraw and so conform to the general situation." He was appointed to the command of a brigade, with the temporary rank of Brigadier-General.

J. Forbes-Robertson.

PRYCE, THOMAS TANNATT, Capt., Grenadier Guards, was born at The Hague, Holland, on 17 Jan. 1886, only son of the late Thomas Pryce, of Pentreheylin Hall, Montgomery, and Rosalie Susannah Pryce, daughter of Mr. Van Motman. He was educated at Mr. Deedes's Preparatory School, Shrewsbury; at Shrewsbury School, and at the Royal Agricultural College, Cirencester. He joined the Army on 25 Aug. 1914, as a Private in the Honourable Artillery Company. He served in the European War; was given a commission in the 6th Battn. Gloucestershire Regt. 11 Oct. 1915, and was promoted Captain in 1916. He was transferred to the 4th Battn. Grenadier Guards 11 Sept. 1916, and promoted Captain in April, 1918. He was awarded the Military Cross [London Gazette, 23 Dec. 1915]: "For conspicuous gallantry at Gommecourt on the night of 25-26 Nov. 1915. When in charge of an assaulting column he suc-

Thomas Tannatt Pryce.

ceeded in entering the German trenches unobserved, clearing them and bombing large parties of the enemy who were crowded in deep dug-outs. Although wounded himself, he subsequently extracted his men successfully in face of superior numbers." He was awarded a Bar to the Military Cross [London Gazette, 19 July, 1916]: "For conspicuous gallantry in action. He commanded the leading platoon in the assault with great dash and determination, right up to the enemy's trenches, under very heavy fire of all kinds. He set a fine example." He was awarded the Victoria Cross [London Gazette, 23 May, 1918]: "Thomas Tannatt Pryce, Lieut. (Acting Capt.), M.C., 4th Battn. Grenadier Guards. For most conspicuous bravery, devotion to duty and self-sacrifice when in command of a flank on the left of the Grenadier Guards. Having been ordered to attack a village, he personally led forward two platoons, working from house to house, killing some thirty of the enemy, seven of whom he killed himself. The next day he was occupying a position with some thirty to forty men, the remainder of his company having become casualties. As early as 8.15 a.m. his left flank was surrounded and the enemy was enfilading him. He was attacked no less than four times during the day, and each time beat off the hostile attack, killing many of the enemy. Meanwhile, the enemy brought up three field guns to within 300 yards of his line, and were firing over open sights and knocking his trench in. At 6.15 p.m. the enemy had worked to within sixty yards of his trench. He then called on his men, telling them to cheer, and charge the enemy and fight to the last. Led by Capt. Pryce, they left their trench and drove back the enemy with the bayonet some 100 yards. Half an hour later the enemy had again approached in stronger force. By this time Capt. Pryce had only 17 men left and every round of his ammunition had been fired. Determined that there should be no surrender, he once again led his men in a bayonet charge, and was last seen engaged in a fierce hand-to-hand struggle with overwhelming numbers of the enemy. With some forty men he had held back at least one enemy battalion for over ten hours. His company undoubtedly stopped the advance through the British line, and thus had great influence on the battle." He was reported missing from 13 April, 1918, and later it was learnt that he was killed on that date. He was mentioned in Despatches, by Field-Marshal Sir Douglas Haig [London Gazette, 7 April, 1918]: "For gallant and distinguished services in the field." His Colonel wrote: "Your husband was perfectly splendid, and his record will be one of the finest episodes of the war." The Army Commander wrote: "There is no finer stand made in the history of the British Army." He was married, on 11 March, 1908, at Ashwell, Hertfordshire, to Margaret Sybil, daughter of E. S. Fordham, Metropolitan Police Magistrate, and Annie Fordham, and there are three daughters: Rosalie Doreen Margaret; Violet Rita, and Pauline Leonora Evelyn. Capt. Pryce was formerly a member of the Stock Exchange. He was fond of shooting, long-distance running (for which he won three silver cups) and tennis.

HORSFALL, BASIL ARTHUR, Second Lieut., was the youngest of the four sons of C. W. F. and Mrs. Horsfall, of Colombo, Ceylon. He was educated at Borlase School, Marlow. At Borlase he was in the cricket eleven for three years, heading the batting averages in 1905: played in the football eleven for two years, and was runner-up for the fives cup, and was a member of the Games Committee. He returned to Ceylon, and entered the Public Works Department as an Accountant, and was acting as Financial Assistant when the war broke out. He had joined the Ceylon Engineer Volunteers, and this unit was mobilized on the outbreak of war. He applied at once for leave to come to England to enlist in the Regular Army, but although he was released from his civil appointment, he was not allowed to leave the Ceylon Engineers, who were carrying out important work. He received permission to come to England in the autumn of 1916, and was gazetted to the East Lancashire Regt. on 19 Dec. 1916. He went to the front in the spring of 1917, and was wounded. Two of his four brothers, all of whom enlisted at the outbreak of war, were wounded on the same day. He returned to the front in the winter. He was killed in action, just after giving an example of grit and tenacity, which won for him the Victoria Cross [London Gazette, 23 May, 1918]: "Basil Arthur Horsfall, Second Lieut., late East Lancashire Regt. For most conspicuous bravery and devotion to duty. Second Lieut. Horsfall was in command of the centre platoon during an attack on our positions. When the enemy first attacked his three forward sections were driven back and he was wounded in the head. Nevertheless, he immediately organized the remainder of his men and made a counter-attack, which recovered his original positions. On hearing that out of the remaining three officers

of his company two were killed and one wounded, he refused to go to the dressing station, although his wound was severe. Later his platoon had to be withdrawn to escape very heavy shell fire, but immediately the shelling lifted he made a second counter-attack and again recovered his positions. When the order to withdraw was given he was the last to leave his position, and, although exhausted, said he could have held on if it had been necessary. His conduct was a splendid example to his men, and he showed throughout the utmost disregard of danger. This very gallant officer was killed when retiring to the positions in rear."

BUCHAN, JOHN CRAWFORD, Lieut., was born on 10 Oct. 1892, at Alloa, third son of David Buchan, Esq., Editor of the "Alloa Advertiser." He was 24 years of age. He was educated at Alloa Academy, and was a Reporter on the "Alloa Advertiser." Before the war he was a worker in the Scottish camps of the Y.M.C.A., as was his elder brother, the late Lieut. David Buchan, of the Gordon Highlanders, who was killed in action in France on 9 April, 1917. The brothers died under almost similar circumstances. John Buchan was in Switzerland when the war broke out, and he came home and joined the ranks of the R.A.M.C., afterwards receiving a commission in the local Territorial Regiment. He was awarded the Victoria Cross [London Gazette, 17 May, 1918]:

John Crawford Buchan.

"John Crawford Buchan, Second Lieut., Argyll and Sutherland Highlanders. For most conspicuous bravery and devotion to duty. When fighting with his platoon in the forward position of the battle zone, Second Lieut. Buchan, although wounded early in the day, insisted on remaining with his men, and continually visited all his posts, encouraging and cheering his men, in spite of most severe shell fire, from which his platoon was suffering heavy casualties. Later, when the enemy were creeping closer and heavy machine-gun fire was raking his position, Second Lieut. Buchan, with utter disregard of his personal safety, continued to visit his posts, and though still further injured accidentally, he continued to encourage his men and visit his posts. Eventually, when he saw the enemy had practically surrounded his command, he collected his men and prepared to fight his way back to the supporting line. At this point the enemy, who had crept round his right flank, rushed towards him, shouting out 'Surrender.' 'To hell with surrender,' he replied, and shooting the foremost of the enemy, he finally repelled this advance with his platoon. He then fought his way back to the supporting line of the forward position, where he held out till dusk. At dusk he fell back as ordered, but in spite of his injuries again refused to go to the aid post, saying his place was beside his men. Owing to the unexpected withdrawal of troops on the left flank, it was impossible to send orders to Second Lieut. Buchan to withdraw, as he was already cut off, and he was last seen holding out against overwhelming odds. The gallantry, self-sacrifice and utter disregard of personal safety displayed by this officer during these two days of most severe fighting is in keeping with the best traditions of the British Army." His father, Mr. D. Buchan, writes: "I have been on holiday, and if not too late I herewith send photograph of my missing boy, John C. Buchan, V.C. The sketch you give is quite accurate. None of my boys were married. My youngest boy, Second Lieut. Francis H. Buchan, 11th Rifle Brigade, was killed by a shell, near Bethune, in August last."

DAVIES, JOHN THOMAS, Corpl., was born on 29 Sept. 1896, at Rockferry, Cheshire, son of John Davies, of Birkenhead, and of Margaret Davies, of Mostyn, North Wales. He was educated at Arthur Street School, St. Helens, and before becoming a soldier was a Brick Worker employed at the Ravenhead Brick and Tile Works, St. Helens. He joined the Army as a Private in the South Lancashire Regt., being one of the St. Helens "Pals." He served in the European War in France from 6 Nov. 1915, until 24 March, 1918, when he was taken prisoner of war at St. Quentin. He was repatriated 1 Jan. 1919. He was twice wounded in 1916, and was reported "probably killed at his gun" in performing the act of bravery for which he was awarded the Victoria Cross. Fortunately this was not so.

John Thomas Davies.

He wrote later to tell his parents that he was a prisoner of war in Germany. The award of the Victoria Cross was announced in the London Gazette of 23 May, 1918: "No. 20765, John Thomas Davies, 11th (Service) Battn. South Lancashire Regt. (St. Helens). For most conspicuous bravery and devotion to duty under heavy rifle and machine-gun fire. When his company—outflanked on both sides—received orders to withdraw, Corpl. Davies knew that the only line of withdrawal lay through a deep stream lined with a belt of barbed wire, and that it was imperative to hold up the enemy as long as possible. He mounted the parapet, fully exposing himself, in order to get a more effective field of fire, and kept his Lewis gun in action to the last, causing the enemy many casualties and checking their advance. By his very great devotion to duty he enabled part of his company to get across the river, which they would otherwise have been unable to do, thus undoubtedly saving the lives of many of his comrades. When last seen this gallant N.C.O. was still firing his gun, with the enemy close on the top of him, and was in all probability killed at his gun."

STONE, CHARLES EDWIN, Gunner, has lived all his life in the neighbourhood of Belper. Like his father, who formerly resided at Sutton-in-Ashfield, and later at Huthwaite, he was a Miner. He is one of a family of 13 children, and one of his brothers was killed in action in the European War in 1917. He served in the European War, and was awarded the Military Medal. He was awarded the Victoria Cross [London Gazette, 23 May, 1918]: Date of Act of Bravery: 21 March, 1918: "Charles Edwin Stone, No. 34328, M.M., Gunner, C Battery, 83rd Brigade, Royal Field Artillery. For most conspicuous bravery, initiative and devotion to duty. After working hard at his gun for six hours under heavy gas and shell fire, Gunner Stone was sent back to the rear section with an order. He delivered the order, and voluntarily, under a very heavy barrage, returned with a rifle to the forward position to assist in holding up the enemy on a sunken road. Lying in the open, about 100 yards from the enemy, under very heavy machine-gun fire, he calmly and effectively shot the enemy until ordered to retire. He then took up a position on the right flank of the two rear guns, and held the enemy at bay, though they again and again attempted to outflank the guns. During this period one of the enemy managed to break through, and, regardless of fierce machine-gun fire raging at the time, Gunner Stone rushed after him and killed him, thereby saving the flank of the guns. Later he was one of the party which captured the machine gun and four prisoners who, in the dusk, had got round to the rear of the gun position. This most gallant act undoubtedly saved the detachment serving the guns. Gunner Stone's behaviour throughout the whole day was beyond all praise, and his magnificent example and fine work through these critical periods undoubtedly kept the guns in action, thereby holding up the enemy on the battle zone at the most crucial moment."

COUNTER, JACK THOMAS, Private, was born on 3 Nov. 1898, at Blandford, Dorsetshire, son of Frank and Rosina Counter. He was educated at Blandford National School; was apprenticed to the International Stores, but did not complete his apprenticeship, and joined the Army in Feb. 1917, as a Private. He was awarded the Victoria Cross [London Gazette, 23 May, 1918]: "No. 94081, Jack Thomas Counter, Private, King's Liverpool Regt. For most conspicuous gallantry and devotion to duty. It was necessary for information to be obtained from the front line, in which the enemy had effected a lodgment. The only way was from the support line along a sunken road, and thence down a forward slope for about 250 yards with no cover, in full view of the enemy, and swept by their machine-gun and rifle fire. After a small party had tried unsuccessfully (the leader having been killed and another wounded before leaving the sunken road), it was thought that a single man had more chance of getting through. This was attempted five times, but on each occasion the runner was killed in full view of the position from which he had started. Private Counter, who was near his officer at the time, and had seen the five runners killed one after the other, then volunteered to carry the message. He went out under terrific fire and succeeded in getting through. He then returned, carrying with him the vital information with regard to the estimated number of enemy in our line, the exact position of our flank, and the remaining strength of our troops. This information enabled his commanding officer to organize and launch the final counter-attack, which succeeded in regaining the whole of our position. Subsequently this man carried back five messages across the open under a heavy artillery barrage to company headquarters. Private Counter's extraordinary courage in facing almost certain death, because he knew that it was vital that the message should be carried, produced a most excellent impression on his young and untried companions."

Jack Thomas Counter.

The following is quoted from the "Western Gazette," Friday, 28 June, 1918:

"Saturday last was a memorable day in the history of Blandford Forum in that its burgesses had the honour of giving an official welcome to the first of its sons to be awarded the coveted military decoration of the Victoria Cross. It will be a day, too, long to be remembered by the central figure of the occasion—Private Jack Thomas Counter, of the King's Liverpool Regt., and a native of this old Dorset Borough. Earlier in the day, Private Counter, who was accompanied by his father, had attended the Investiture at Buckingham Palace, where the King had pinned the medal on his breast. His Majesty entered into conversation with the lad and warmly congratulated him upon the bravery of his action, and the large crowd who had assembled at the Palace and within its precincts gave him a hearty and enthusiastic reception. On returning home later in the day Private Counter had to undergo what was perhaps a still greater ordeal in the reception, speeches and presentations, given to him by the townspeople by whom he is so well known. The modest and unassuming manner in which the lad accepted these tributes was very marked, and gained for him a still greater degree of respect and appreciation from the large crowds who had assembled. Private Counter, V.C., arrived at Blandford by the 7.21 p.m. train, which entered the station amid the explosions of detonators. The young hero was met by the Mayor (Alderman J. J. Lamperd), attended by the mace-bearers, and the Town Clerk (Mr. W. H. Wilson), and escorted to the station entrance, where a huge crowd had assembled. Immediately opposite the doors a landau, decorated with flags, was in waiting, and on Counter taking his seat he was given an enthusiastic reception. The procession to the Market Place was headed by the Town Band, following which came the Blandford Detachment of Volunteers, who acted as a guard of honour. Lieut. J. Higgens was in command of the detachment, whilst Sergt.-Major Mead was in charge of the section detailed to pull the landau through the streets. The members of the Corporation, wearing their robes, and the Borough officials followed, and the procession made its way through the crowded streets to the Market Place, where a large platform had been erected opposite the Municipal Buildings. The Market Place was crowded, and many hundreds of men from the Royal Air Force Camp were present, and enthusiastically cheered their brave comrade. In addition to the Mayor and members and officials of the Corporation, on the platform were Mr. F. Counter (father of the V.C.), the Revs. Father Hegarty (Mayor's chaplain), F. E. Overton (rector), M. E. R. Brockman, C.F., and Gomer Evans. The National Anthem having been sung, the Mayor said they would agree with him that never since the war began had they been assembled for any purpose that gave them as much pleasure as the object of their meeting that day. Proceeding, he read the official account of Private Counter's exploit, and added that while Englishmen all over the world might rejoice to read such exploits they in Blandford had special reason to do so, for Private Counter was a Blandfordian from head to toe. He was born in Blandford, he lived and worked there till he joined up, and they had every hope of seeing him back there safe and sound when the war was over. The winning of an honour like that was the only thing wanting in Blandford's contribution to the war. Everything else possible they had done. Right from the start they had sent to the Colours their bravest and best in numbers that compared favourably with any town of the same size. Those of them who were too old or too useless to make soldiers came forward in other necessary ways to do their bit. They knew that in helping every war charity Blandford had taken a leading part. Of this they had an example in the recent Red Cross collection, when Blandford had the happy distinction of contributing more than any other town in the county. Their ladies also did their share in helping in every way to provide comforts for the soldiers. In the honours of war, too, when their Blandford boys had been in competition with men from all parts of their mighty Empire, they had taken their full share. In addition to this honour won by Private Counter, the following honours had been gained by Blandfordians: Croix de Guerre, Valentine Watts; Military Cross, Bertram George; D.C.M., Harold Edwin Kerley and William Cole; D.S.M., Charles Carter; M.M., Edwin Hunt, Jack Hunt, Robert James Snelling, Willie Nesbitt, Cecil Nesbitt and Gerald George A. Gibbs. Now they might say the splendid bravery of Private Counter, and the honour which followed it, came to add a crowning link to an already good record. They had set on foot a public contribution and he had great pleasure in presenting Private Counter with a War Savings Certificate for £100 and the freedom of the Borough of his old and native town. The lists were still open at both banks, and many places in the town, and they sincerely hoped they would be able to make it another hundred or even two hundred pounds. He deserved it, both for his bravery and also for the credit which his bravery and the honour had brought on the town. (Applause.) Proceeding, the Mayor said those who had seen the subscription list would have observed that the International Tea Co. had contributed ten guineas to the fund. He was delighted to say that on the previous day the company sent him a beautiful 18-carat gold English lever with an inscription on it, that he might present it to Private Counter on that occasion. On his mentioning this to Councillor Best, he suggested that the amount collected in the boxes on the occasion of the concert organized by the officers and men of the R.F.C. (and which realized over £40) should be spent in purchasing a chain to accompany the watch, which they had accordingly done. The International Tea Company wrote: 'We hear with very great pleasure of the honour that has been conferred upon Jack Thomas Counter, and we are pleased to join in the public testimonial that is being presented to him to commemorate his gallant deed. As prior to the war he was in the service of this company, we desire to present him with the accompanying gold watch as a recognition of his bravery, and shall be very glad if you will be so good as to present it to him with our best wishes for his future.' In conclusion, the Mayor said he hoped the feelings they showed that day would be lasting, and that when Private Counter returned to them at the dawn of peace they would always remember that when the whole Empire was in its agony he was one of those who came forward to convince a new and powerful enemy that 'Britons never will be slaves.' (Cheers.) Private Counter, who was heartily cheered, replied: 'Mr. Mayor and fellow citizens,—It is with great pleasure I receive the honorary freedom of the Borough of my native town; also the War Savings Certificate and the watch and chain. I may say that in what I was able to accomplish I was only doing my duty as a soldier of the King. I thank you one and all for your kindness to me this evening.' (Cheers.) The Rev. M. E. R. Brockman, C.F., on behalf of the clergy of the town and district, and of the chaplains of the adjoining camp, offered their united congratulations to Private Counter on having won the most coveted honour any soldier or servant of the King could wish to win, and expressed the hope that for many years he would live to enjoy the honour. Carlyle had said, 'a brave man must be ready to give his life away,' and this young man had been ready to do so. In the performance of a great deed, there were three things every Englishman was proud of possessing—a fine courage, resourcefulness, and a fine spirit of sacrifice—and Private Counter had displayed all these. This boy was the son of poor parents, and because of that he was particularly glad to be associated with the Mayor and those who had worked with him in doing their utmost to give him the greatest honour possible. (Applause.) In conclusion, the reverend gentleman saluted and congratulated Private Counter in the names of the clergy, and wished him long life and happiness. (Cheers.)—The salute was given, and acknowledged by Private Counter amidst great cheering. Further hearty cheers having been given at the call of the Mayor, the National Anthem was again sung, and cheers were accorded the Mayor for his efforts in connection with the reception. The procession was then reformed, and Private Counter was taken to his home in Dorset Street, where innumerable admirers crowded round to shake his hand. Before the crowd had dispersed hearty cheers were given for Percy Counter, an elder brother, who has had the misfortune to lose a leg in the war. These were acknowledged by the young man concerned, and the V.C. appeared to be greatly pleased at the recognition accorded his brother. During the present week Mr. George Best has been making an interesting war display in his office window. The exhibits include Jack Counter's Victoria Cross and the gold watch and chain ; a Military Medal won by a local man named Snelling ; a replica of the German medal struck in honour of the Lusitania ' Victory ' ; a German watch picked up on the battlefield in France, and a dagger snatched from a German at Messines Ridge by a Blandford lad. In addition there is a local ' Roll of Honour ' containing the names of 83 Blandfordians who have given their lives in the war, and a list of the local men who have gained naval and military honours. The greatest interest has been displayed in the exhibits, particularly in the Victoria Cross."

London Gazette, 4 June, 1918.—" War Office, 4 June, 1918. His Majesty the King has been graciously pleased to approve of the award of the Victoria Cross to the undermentioned Officers and Men."

DOUGALL, ERIC STUART, Lieut. (Acting Major), was born on 13 April, 1886, at Brookside, Tunbridge Wells, only son of Andrew and Emily E. Dougall, who live at 13, Mount Ephraim, Tunbridge Wells. Mr. A.

Eric Stuart Dougall.

Dougall was formerly Engineer to the Tunbridge Wells Gas Company. He was educated at Tonbridge School, and at Pembroke College, Cambridge, of which he was also an exhibitioner. He was also an athletic " blue." After leaving Cambridge he became Assistant Engineer to the Bombay Port Trust. He came to England on leave in Jan. 1916, and applied for and was granted a commission in the Royal Field Artillery. He served in the European War in France and Flanders. He was awarded the Military Cross [London Gazette, Aug. 1917] for bravery during the Battle of Messines. He was gazetted Major on 4 April, 1918, and was continuously in action during the early stages of the German offensive in March and April, 1918, and was killed on 14 April at Mont Kemmel, only four days after performing a deed for which he was awarded the Victoria Cross [London Gazette, 4 June, 1918] : " Eric Stuart Dougall, Lieut. (Acting Capt.), Special Reserve, attached A Battery, 88th Brigade, Royal Field Artillery. For most conspicuous bravery and skilful leadership in the field when in command of his battery. Capt. Dougall maintained his guns in action from early morning throughout a heavy concentration of gas and high-explosive shell. Finding that he could not clear the crest, owing to the withdrawal of our line, Capt. Dougall ran his guns on to the top of the ridge to fire over open sights. By this time our infantry had been pressed back in line with the guns. Capt. Dougall at once assumed command of the situation, rallied and organized the infantry, supplied them with Lewis guns, and armed as many gunners as he could spare with rifles. With these he formed a line in front of his battery, which during this period was harassing the advancing enemy with a rapid rate of fire. Although exposed to both rifle and machine-gun fire, this officer fearlessly walked about as though on parade, calmly giving orders and encouraging everybody. He inspired the infantry with his assurance that ' so long as you stick to your trenches I will keep my guns here.' This line was maintained throughout the day, thereby delaying the enemy's advance for over 12 hours. In the evening, having expended all ammunition, the battery received orders to withdraw. This was done by man-handling the guns over a distance of about 800 yards of shell-cratered country, an almost impossible feat considering the ground and the intense machine-gun fire. Owing to Capt. Dougall's personality and skilful leadership throughout this trying day, there is no doubt that a serious breach in our line was averted. This gallant officer was killed four days later whilst directing the fire of his battery." The Adjutant wrote : " A finer man never breathed, and his place in the brigade can never be filled. He was in command of his battery at the time of his death, and for the past week had been performing most gallant work." Capt. Dougall's Victoria Cross was given to Miss Dougall privately by the King, as his parents were unavoidably prevented from being present.

KNOX, CECIL LEONARD, Second Lieut., a cousin of Mr. E. Knox, of Kilmersdon, Chairman of the Frome Rural District Council, was by profession a Civil Engineer. He served in the European War, and for his services in France was awarded the Victoria Cross [London Gazette, 4 June, 1918] : " Cecil Leonard Knox, Temporary Second Lieut., 150th Field Company, Royal Engineers. For most conspicuous bravery and devotion to duty. Twelve bridges were entrusted to this officer for demolition, and all of them were successfully destroyed. In the case of one steel girder bridge, the destruction of which he personally supervised, the time fuse failed to act. Without hesitation, Second Lieut. Knox ran to the bridge, under heavy fire and machine-gun fire, and when the enemy were actually on the bridge he tore away the time fuse and lit the instantaneous fuse, to do which he had to get under the bridge. This was an act of the highest devotion to duty, entailing the gravest risks, which, as a practical civil engineer, he fully realized."

BEAL, ERNEST FREDERICK, Second Lieut., was the son of Mr. and Mrs. J. J. W. Beal, of Brighton. He served in the European War, and for his services in France was awarded the Victoria Cross [London Gazette,

Ernest Frederick Beal.

4 June, 1918] : " Ernest Frederick Beal, Second Lieut., 13th (Service) Battn. Yorkshire Regt. For most conspicuous bravery and determined leading when in command of a company detailed to occupy a certain section of trench. When the company was established, it was found that a considerable gap of about 400 yards existed between the left flank of the company and the neighbouring unit, and that this gap was strongly held by the enemy. It was of vital importance that the gap should be cleared, but no troops were then available. Organizing a small party of less than a dozen men, he led them against the enemy. On reaching an enemy machine gun, Second Lieut. Beal immediately sprang forward, and with his revolver killed the team and captured the gun. Continuing along the trench he encountered and dealt with another machine gun in the same manner—and in all captured four enemy guns, and inflicted severe casualties. Later in the evening, when a wounded man had been left in the open under heavy enemy fire, he, regardless of danger, walked up close to an enemy machine gun and brought in the wounded man on his back. Second Lieut. Beal was killed by a shell on the following morning." In the Council Chamber at Brighton, in the presence of a large attendance of members of the Corporation, the Mayor presented to Mr. and Mrs. J. J. W. Beal, parents of the late Second Lieut. E. F. Beal, V.C., an illuminated address, recording the congratulations and sympathy of the Town Council. It was pointed out that the gallant officer was the first inhabitant of Brighton to earn that coveted award. For many years previous to the war he was a zealous officer of the local Boys' Brigade, and originally enlisted in the Sussex Yeomanry. Mr. J. J. W. Beal, in acknowledging the presentation, expressed appreciation of the kindly feeling his fellow citizens had shown in the matter.

CROSS, ARTHUR HENRY, L.-Corpl., is the son of Mr. Cross, Farmer, of Norwich. He went to live in Camberwell, and was employed on the Great Eastern Railway, and afterwards at Woolwich Dockyard. He joined the Army under the Derby Scheme as a Private in the 21st London Regt. He served in the European War, and for his services in France was awarded the Victoria Cross [London Gazette, 4 June, 1918] : " No. 62995, Arthur Henry Cross, L.-Corpl., 40th Battn. Machine Gun Corps. For most conspicuous bravery and initiative. L.-Corpl. Cross volunteered to make a reconnaissance of the position of two machine guns which had been captured by the enemy. He advanced single-handed to the enemy trench, and with his revolver forced seven of the enemy to surrender and carry the machine guns with their tripods and ammunition to our lines. He then handed over his prisoners, collected teams for his guns, which he brought into action with exceptional dash and skill, annihilating a very heavy attack by the enemy. It is impossible to speak too highly of the extreme gallantry, initiative and dash displayed by this N.C.O., who showed throughout four days of operations supreme devotion to duty." His wife is Mrs. Frances Grace Cross.

YOUNG, T., Private, served in the European War, and for his services in France was awarded the Victoria Cross [London Gazette, 4 June, 1918] : " T. Young, No. 203590, Private, 9th Battn. Durham Light Infantry. For most conspicuous bravery in face of the enemy when acting as a stretcher-bearer. He showed throughout the whole course of the operations a most magnificent example of courage and devotion to duty. On nine different occasions he went out in front of our line in broad daylight under heavy rifle, machine-gun and shell fire, which was directed on him, and brought back wounded to safety, those too badly wounded to be moved before dressing he dressed under this harassing fire, and carried them unaided to our lines and safety ; he rescued and saved nine lives in this manner. His untiring energy, coupled with an absolute disregard of personal danger, and the great skill he showed in dealing with casualties, is beyond all praise. For five days Private Young worked unceasingly, evacuating wounded from seemingly impossible places."

London Gazette, 7 June, 1918.—" War Office, 7 June, 1918. His Majesty the King has been graciously pleased to approve of the award of the Victoria Cross to the undermentioned Officers and Non-commissioned Officer."

STORKEY, PERCY VALENTINE, Lieut., served in the European War in France, and was awarded the Victoria Cross [London Gazette, 7 June,

Percy Valentine Storkey.

1918] : " Percy Valentine Storkey, Lieut., 19th Battn. Australian Imperial Force. For most conspicuous bravery, leadership and devotion to duty when in charge of a platoon in attack. On emerging from the wood the enemy trench line was encountered, and Lieut. Storkey found himself with six men. While continuing his move forward a large enemy party —about 80 to 100 strong—armed with several machine guns, was noticed to be holding up the advance of the troops on the right. Lieut. Storkey immediately decided to attack this party from the flank and rear, and while moving forward in the attack was joined by Lieut. Lipscomb and four men. Under the leadership of Lieut. Storkey, this small party of two officers and 10 other ranks charged the enemy position with fixed bayonets, driving the enemy out, killing and wounding about 30, and capturing three officers and 50 men, also one machine gun. The splendid courage shown by this officer in quickly deciding his course of action, and his skilful method of attacking against such great odds, removed a dangerous obstacle to the advance of the troops on the right, and inspired the remainder of our small party with the utmost confidence when advancing to the objective line." He was promoted to Captain. Capt. Storkey was decorated by the King at Buckingham Palace.

HERRING, ALFRED CECIL, Second Lieut., was born on 26 Oct. 1888,

Alfred Cecil Herring.

at Tottenham, Middlesex, son of George Edward and Cecilia Emily Herring. He was educated at Tottenham County School; captain of school at cricket and football, and in civil life is a Chartered Accountant; served Articles under Daniel Steuart Fripp, Esq., F.C.A., and passed final examination as a Chartered Accountant in Dec. 1912. He joined the Army on 10 Dec. 1914, as a Paymaster. Later he obtained a commission in the Army Service Corps as Second Lieutenant. He served in the European War. After serving for a year in France with the Army Service Corps, he was attached to the 6th (Service) Battn. Northamptonshire Regt. He was awarded the Victoria Cross for holding up the enemy for eleven hours on 22 Jan. 1918, at St. Quentin [London Gazette, 7 June, 1918]: " Alfred Cecil Herring, Temporary Second Lieut. For most conspicuous bravery, initiative and devotion to duty when, after severe fighting, the enemy gained a position on the south bank of the canal. His post was cut off from the troops on both flanks and surrounded. Second Lieut. Herring, however, immediately counterattacked, and recaptured the position, together with 20 prisoners and six machine guns. During the night the post was continually attacked, but all attacks were beaten off. This was largely due to the splendid heroism displayed by Second Lieut. Herring, who continually visited his men and cheered them up. It was entirely due to the bravery and initiative of this officer that the enemy advance was held up for 11 hours at an exceedingly critical period. His magnificent heroism, coupled with the skilful handling of his troops, were most important factors leading to success." He became a prisoner of war on 23 March, 1918; repatriated in Dec. 1918; promoted Lieutenant 26 April, 1918; promoted Major 27 Jan. 1919, as a Group Accountant with the Cost Accounting Committee.

MOUNTAIN, ALBERT, Sergt., served in the European War, and took part in operations at Hamelincourt, for which he was awarded the Victoria Cross [London Gazette, 7 June, 1918]: " No. 19/11, Albert Mountain, Sergt., 15 17th Battn. West Yorkshire Regt. For most conspicuous bravery and devotion to duty during an enemy attack, when his company was in an exposed position on a sunken road, having hastily dug themselves in. Owing to the intense artillery fire, they were obliged to vacate the road and fall back. The enemy in the meantime was advancing in mass preceded by an advanced patrol about 200 strong. The situation was critical, and volunteers for a counter-attack were called for. Sergt. Mountain immediately stepped forward, and his party of ten men followed him. He then advanced on the flank with a Lewis gun, and brought enfilade fire to bear on the enemy patrol, killing about 100. In the meantime the remainder of the company made a frontal attack, and the entire enemy patrol was cut up and thirty prisoners taken. At this time the enemy main body appeared, and the men, who were numerically many times weaker than the enemy, began to waver. Sergt. Mountain rallied and organized his party and formed a defensive position from which to cover the retirement of the rest of the company and the prisoners. With this party of one Non-commissioned Officer and four men he successfully held at bay 600 of the enemy for half an hour, eventually retiring and rejoining his company. He then took command of the flank post of the battalion which was ' in the air,' and held on there for 27 hours until finally surrounded by the enemy. Sergt. Mountain was one of the few who managed to fight their way back. His supreme fearlessness and initiative undoubtedly saved the whole situation."

London Gazette, 21 June, 1918.—" War Office, 21 June, 1918. His Majesty the King has been graciously pleased to approve of the award of the Victoria Cross to the undermentioned men."

CRUICKSHANK, ROBERT EDWARD, Private, was born on 17 June, 1888, at

Robert E. Cruickshank.

Winnipeg, Canada, son of Robert and Mary Cruickshank. He was educated at Central Foundation School, Cowper Street, E.C., and Bancroft School, Woodford Wells, Essex, and joined the Army on 9 Nov. 1915, first in the Royal Flying Corps; transferred at own request to London Scottish; served in the City of London Yeomanry (Rough Riders) 1908–1911. He served in the European War in Egypt, Salonika, Palestine and France. He was wounded first at Leuze Wood, Somme, 10 Sept. 1916. He was awarded the Victoria Cross [London Gazette, 21 June, 1918]: " No. 511828, Robert Edward Cruickshank, Private,

2/14th Battn. London Regt. (London Scottish) (Territorial Forces). For most conspicuous bravery and devotion to duty in attack. The platoon to which Private Cruickshank belonged came under very heavy rifle and machine-gun fire at short range, and was led down a steep bank into a wadi, most of the men being hit before they reached the bottom. Immediately after reaching the bottom of the wadi the officer in command was shot dead, and the Sergeant who then took over command sent a runner back to Company Headquarters asking for support, but was mortally wounded almost immediately after; the Sergeant having in the meantime been killed, the only remaining N.C.O. (a Lance-Corporal), believing the first messenger to have been killed, called for a volunteer to take a second message back. Private Cruickshank immediately responded and rushed up the slope, but was hit and rolled back into the wadi bottom. He again rose and rushed up the slope, but being again wounded, rolled back into the wadi. After his wounds had been dressed he rushed a third time up the slope and again fell badly wounded. Being now unable to stand, he rolled himself back amid a hail of bullets. His wounds were now of such a nature as to preclude him making any further attempt, and he lay all day in a dangerous position, being sniped at and again wounded where he lay. He displayed the utmost valour and endurance, and was cheerful and uncomplaining throughout." Lieut.-General Sir Robert Baden-Powell was present at a fête at Wood Green, Tottenham, at which Private Cruickshank was presented with a gold watch by Messrs. Lipton, in whose employ he was many years before he joined the Army. The fête was held in aid of a fund by which he was presented with a £200 War Bond and a cheque for £50. Before joining he was in the employ of Messrs. Lever Brothers, Limited, and he was presented with a £100 War Bond by Lord Leverhulme. Private Cruickshank was formerly an Assistant Scoutmaster. He is a well-known organizer and speaker in the Liberal interests. He is a member of the Ancient Order of Druids and of the Royal Antediluvian Order of Buffaloes. He married, 22 March, 1919, Miss Gwendoline May Mansell, of Bush Hill Park, N.

KARANBAHADUR RANA, Rifleman, Gurkha Rifles, served in the European War, and was awarded the Victoria Cross [London Gazette, 21 June, 1918]: " Karanbahadur Rana, No. 4146, Rifleman, 2/3rd Battn.

Karanbahadur Rana.

Queen Alexandra's Own Gurkha Rifles. For most conspicuous bravery, resource in action under adverse conditions, and utter contempt for danger. During an attack he, with a few other men, succeeded under intense fire in creeping forward with a Lewis gun, in order to engage an enemy machine gun which had caused severe casualties to officers and other ranks who had attempted to put it out of action. No. 1 of the Lewis gun opened fire, and was shot immediately. Without a moment's hesitation Rifleman Karanbahadur pushed the dead man off the gun, and in spite of bombs thrown at him and heavy fire from both flanks, he opened fire and knocked out the enemy machine-gun crew; then, switching his fire on to the enemy bombers and riflemen in front of him, he silenced their fire. He kept his gun in action and showed the greatest coolness in removing defects which on two occasions prevented the gun from firing. During the remainder of the day he did magnificent work, and when a withdrawal was ordered he assisted with covering fire until the enemy were close on him; he displayed throughout a very high standard of valour and devotion to duty." Naik Karanbahadur Rana came to England to take part in the Procession of Indian Troops through London on Saturday, 2 Aug. 1919. They were received at Buckingham Palace by His Majesty the King-Emperor, who thus addressed his Indian soldiers : " It is with feelings of pride and gratification that I welcome here in my home this representative contingent of British and Indian officers and men of my Army in India, and I am especially glad that this meeting should take place when we are celebrating peace after victory. I deeply regret that unavoidable circumstances prevented your joining the troops of the Empire and of our Allies in the Victory Procession on 19 July. I thank the British troops for their magnificent services in the field. I gratefully recognize the prompt and cheerful response of the Territorials to their country's call, their patient endurance of a prolonged separation from their homes, and the sacrifices they made in giving up their occupations in civil life. When temporary trouble arose in India they, in common with their comrades from Mesopotamia, who were on their way home, of their free will remained at their posts (though their home-coming was at hand). The exemplary conduct of all has filled me and their countrymen with admiration. I heartily thank all my Indian soldiers for their loyal devotion to me and to my Empire, for their sufferings, cheerfully borne, in the various campaigns in which they have served in lands and climates so different from their own. At times their hearts must have been sad at the long separation from their homes; but they have fought and died bravely. They have rivalled the deeds of their ancestors ; they have established new and glorious traditions which they can hand on to their children for ever. I am glad to see among you representatives of the Imperial Service Troops, and I thank the Princes of the native States of India and their subjects for their noble response to the call made by me for the defence of the Empire and for the cause in which the Allies have fought and conquered. I know you will all unite with me in gratitude to God for the victory we have achieved. I trust you will enjoy your visit to England. May you return in safety, and take with you to your homes and villages my personal message of thanks and goodwill." At the Investiture held at Buckingham Palace on the same occasion, Naik Karanbahadur Rana was personally decorated with the Victoria Cross by His Majesty the King-Emperor.

London Gazette, 28 June, 1918.—"War Office, 28 June, 1918. His Majesty the King has been graciously pleased to approve of the award of the Victoria Cross to the undermentioned Officers, Non-commissioned Officers and Men."

GRIBBLE, JULIAN ROYDS, Lieut. (Temporary Capt.), was born on 5 Jan. 1897, in London. He was educated at Eton College and the R.M.C., Sandhurst, and joined the Army on 15 May, 1915, as Second Lieutenant Royal Warwickshire Regt. He served in the European War in France, and was awarded the Victoria Cross [London Gazette, 28 June, 1918]: "Julian Royds Gribble, Lieut. (Temporary Capt.), 10th (Service) Battn. Royal Warwickshire Regt. For most conspicuous bravery and devotion to duty. Capt. Gribble was in command of the right company of the battalion when the enemy attacked, and his orders were to hold on to the last. His company was eventually entirely isolated, though he could easily have withdrawn them at one period, when the rest of the battalion on his left were driven back to a secondary position. His right flank was 'in the air' owing to the withdrawal of all troops of a neighbouring division. By means of a runner to the company on his left, he intimated his determination to hold on till other orders were received from Battalion Headquarters, and this he inspired his command to accomplish. His company was eventually surrounded by the enemy at close range, and he was seen fighting to the last. By his splendid example of grit, Capt. Gribble was materially instrumental in preventing for some hours the enemy obtaining a complete mastery of the crest of the ridge, and by his magnificent self-sacrifice he enabled the remainder of his own brigade to be withdrawn, as well as another garrison and three batteries of field artillery." Capt. Gribble was eventually wounded and taken prisoner by the Huns, and died in captivity on Armistice day.

Julian Royds Gribble.

JAMES, MANLEY ANGELL, Capt., was born on 12 July, 1896, at Odiham, Hampshire, son of John Angell James, M.R.C.S., L.R.C.P., Medical Practitioner, and Emily Cornwell James, of 43, Nevil Road, Bishopston, Bristol. He was educated at Bristol Grammar School; passed for a proficiency certificate as a cadet in the O.T.C., and rose to be a Sergeant; gained his First Fifteen colours for Rugby football and First Eleven colours for hockey and cricket. Later, he played cricket for the Bristol Nomads Club, of which his father was captain, and football at three-quarter for the famous Bristol Rugby Football Club. He joined the Army on 1 Dec. 1914, as a Second Lieutenant in the Gloucestershire Regt. (8th Battn.), and was promoted Lieutenant on 28 June, 1915, and Captain 22 Feb. 1917. He served in the European War; went to France with the 19th Division in 1915, and in the battle of the Somme (1916) was severely wounded at La Boiselle, with the result that he had to spend five months in England. He returned to the 8th Gloucesters in France in Dec. 1916, and was slightly wounded in the spring of 1917. Later he was for a time on the headquarters staff of the 57th Brigade, but he was anxious to get back to his battalion, and rejoined it in June, 1917. He was mentioned in Despatches in June, 1917, and was present at the fierce fighting at Wytschaete and Messines Ridge. He was awarded the Military Cross [London Gazette, July, 1917]. Previous to a British attack he took up a forward position under heavy hostile barrage, in order to obtain accurate information as to the progress of the advance. Afterwards he assisted to capture a strong point, and made a very daring personal reconnaissance. The London Gazette stated: "His total disregard of danger and brilliant initiative throughout the action was largely responsible for its success." He was awarded the Victoria Cross [London Gazette, 28 June, 1918]: "Manley Angell James, M.C., Capt., Gloucester Regt. For most conspicuous bravery and devotion to duty in attack at Vélu Wood. Capt. James led his company forward with magnificent determination and courage, inflicting severe losses on the enemy and capturing twenty-seven prisoners and two machine guns. He was wounded, but refused to leave his company, and repulsed three hostile onslaughts the next day. Two days later, although the enemy had broken through on his right flank, he refused to withdraw, and made a most determined stand, inflicting very heavy losses on the enemy and gaining valuable time for the withdrawal of guns. He was ordered by the senior officer on the spot to hold on 'to the last,' in order to enable the brigade to be extricated. He then led his company forward in a local counter-attack on his own initiative, and was again wounded. He was last seen working a machine gun single-handed, after having been wounded a third time. No praise can be too high for the gallant stand made by this company, and Capt. James, by his dauntless courage and magnificent example, undoubtedly enabled the battalion to be withdrawn before being completely cut off." After the operations on the 3rd Army front at Cambrai, during March, 1918, Capt. James was reported wounded and missing from 23 March, and no news was received by his family until early in May, when his father received a field postcard to tell him that he was alive though very seriously wounded. He had been wounded in the neck, shoulder and jaw, and another bullet had passed through his stomach. He was in hospital as a prisoner of war at Stralkowo Camp, near Posen, on the borders of Poland, from where he went to Rastatt, and Schweidnitz in Silesia. He reached home after the Armistice on Christmas Day, 1918.

Manley Angell James.

McKEAN, GEORGE BURDON, Lieut., served in the European War in France. He was awarded the Military Medal, and was promoted Lieutenant. He was awarded the Victoria Cross [London Gazette, 28 June, 1918]: "George Burdon McKean, Lieut., 14th Canadian Infantry Battn. (Quebec Regt.). For most conspicuous bravery and devotion to duty during a raid on the enemy's trenches. Lieut. McKean's party, which was operating on the right flank, was held up at a block in the communication trench by most intense fire from hand grenades and machine guns. This block, which was too close to our trenches to have been engaged by the preliminary bombardment, was well protected by wire and covered by a well-protected machine gun thirty yards behind it. Realizing that if this block were not destroyed the success of the whole operation might be marred, he ran into the open to the right flank of the block, and with utter disregard of danger, leaped over the block head first on top of the enemy. Whilst lying on the ground on top of one of the enemy, another rushed at him with fixed bayonet. Lieut. McKean shot him through the body and then shot the enemy underneath him, who was struggling violently. This very gallant action enabled this position to be captured. Lieut. McKean's supply of bombs ran out at this time, and he sent back to our front line for a fresh supply. Whilst waiting for them, he engaged the enemy single-handed. When the bombs arrived, he fearlessly rushed the second block, killing two of the enemy, captured four others, and drove the remaining garrison, including a hostile machine-gun section, into a dug-out. The dug-out, with its occupants and machine gun, was destroyed. This officer's splendid bravery and dash undoubtedly saved many lives, for had not this position been captured the whole of the raiding party would have been exposed to dangerous enfilading fire during the withdrawal. His leadership at all times has been beyond praise.'

COLLIN, JOSEPH HENRY, Second Lieut., was the second son of Joseph Collin, Railway Worker, of 8, Petterie Terrace, Harraby, Carlisle. He was educated at St. Patrick's School, Carlisle, and later took up a position as assistant in the Carlisle branch of Messrs. Joseph Hepworth & Son, Limited, Clothiers, Leeds. He joined the Army as a Private in the Argyll and Sutherland Highlanders in 1915, and during his training in England was promoted Sergeant. He served in the European War, and took part in the battles of the Somme and the Ancre, and was given a commission. After his training course in England, he returned to France in Oct. 1917. He was awarded the Victoria Cross [London Gazette, 28 June, 1918]: "Joseph Henry Collin, Second Lieut., 1/4th Battn. Royal Lancashire Regt. For most conspicuous bravery, devotion to duty and self-sacrifice in action. After offering a long and gallant resistance against heavy odds in the Keep held by his platoon, this officer, with only five of his men remaining, slowly withdrew in the face of superior numbers, contesting every inch of the ground. The enemy were pressing him hard with bombs and machine-gun fire from close range. Single-handed, Second Lieut. Collin attacked the machine gun and team. After firing his revolver into the enemy, he seized a Mills grenade and threw it into the hostile team, putting the gun out of action, killing four of the team and wounding two others. Observing a second hostile machine gun firing, he took a Lewis gun, and selecting a high point of vantage on the parapet whence he could engage the gun, he, unaided, kept the enemy at bay until he fell mortally wounded. The heroic self-sacrifice of Second Lieut. Collin was a magnificent example to all." He was killed in action on 9 April, 1918. Lieut. Collin in his youth was an enthusiastic footballer, and he had won prizes for sprinting.

SCHOFIELD, JOHN, Second Lieut., served in the European War in France, and was awarded the Victoria Cross [London Gazette, 28 June, 1918]: "John Schofield, Temporary Second Lieut., Lancashire Fusiliers, attached 2/5th Battn. (T.F.). For most conspicuous bravery and devotion to duty in operations. Second Lieut. Schofield led a party of nine men against a strong point which was reported strongly held by the enemy, and was attacked by about one hundred of the enemy with bombs. He disposed his men so skilfully and made such good use of rifle and Lewis-gun fire that the enemy took cover in dug-outs. This officer himself then held up and captured a party of twenty. With the help of other parties this position was then cleared of the enemy, who were all killed or captured. He then collected the remainder of his men, made his party up to ten, and proceeded towards the front line, previously informing his commanding officer as to the position, and that he was proceeding to retake the front line. He met large numbers of the enemy in a communication trench in front of him and in a drain on his right and left. His party opened rapid rifle fire, and he climbed out on to the parapet under point-blank machine-gun fire, and by his fearless demeanour and bravery forced the enemy to surrender. As a result, 123 of the enemy, including several officers, were captured by Second Lieut. Schofield and his party. This very gallant officer was killed a few minutes later."

CROWE, JOHN, Second Lieut., is an excellent rifle shot and an all-round athlete. He has won many prizes and spoons at Bisley. He gained the Inter-Colonial Rifle Cup; he was the holder for two years in succession of the Henry Whitbread Cup, competed for in connection with the Army Rifle Association; he was one of three winners of the Colonial Cup, the last ever presented by Lord Roberts at the Bisley meeting, and also received from him a walking-stick, one of his most treasured possessions; he won the Shooting Cup at Dover three years in succession, and he has a number of prizes won in hockey, running and obstacle competitions. He joined the Army in the Worcestershire Regt., and served for many years in India. He was married and went to live in Brighton, and has four children. He served in the European War, and was awarded the Victoria Cross [London Gazette, 28 June, 1918]: "For most conspicuous bravery, determination and skilful leading when the enemy, for the third time having attacked a post in a village, broke past on to the high ground, and established a machine gun and snipers in the broken ground at the back of the village. Second Lieut. Crowe twice went forward with two N.C.O.'s and seven men to engage the enemy, both times in face of active machine-gun fire and sniping. His action was so daring that on each occasion the enemy withdrew from the high ground into the village, where Second Lieut. Crowe followed them, and himself opened fire upon the enemy as they collected in the doorways of the houses. On the second occasion, taking with him only two men of his party, he attacked two enemy machine guns which were sweeping the post, killed both the gunners with his rifle, and prevented any others from reaching the guns and bringing them in action again. He then turned upon a party of the enemy who were lined up in front of him, killed several, and the remainder withdrew at once. He captured both the guns, one of which was the battalion Lewis gun, which had been captured by the enemy on the previous day. Throughout the seven days of operations Second Lieut. Crowe showed an utter disregard of danger and was recklessly brave. His personal example and cheerfulness contributed largely to the determination of the garrison of the post to hold out. It may safely be said that but for his coolness and skill at the last moment, when he personally placed the covering party in close proximity to the enemy, who were again closing round, and were also forming up in fours near by, the garrison of the post could never have effected its escape. The valour and zeal displayed by Second Lieut. Crowe were of the highest order." He was promoted Captain at the same time that he was awarded the Victoria Cross. He was one of those who recognized the possibilities of horticulture on the battlefield, when there was an urgent demand for vegetables in the early part of the war, and the neighbourhood of his quarters was quickly transformed into a garden. The French Government, as a reward for his horticultural efforts, awarded him the Diploma d'Honneur de l'Encouragement.

GREGG, WILLIAM, Sergt., was born at Heanor, Derbyshire, on 27 Jan. 1890, son of Mr. and Mrs. William Gregg, of 97, Yorke Street, Mansfield Woodhouse, Derbyshire. He was educated at Heanor Mundy Street School; before the war was a Miner in the Shipley Colliery. He joined the Army on 24 Nov. 1914, as a Private in the Rifle Brigade. He served in the European War. He was wounded during the course of the Somme offensive. He was awarded the Military Medal for a daring daylight patrol on the 4th Feb. 1917, and getting very useful information. And the Distinguished Conduct Medal for most conspicuous bravery on the 30th Nov. 1917. The enemy attacked in large numbers, and seeing the battalion on the left being hard pressed, this brave N.C.O. carried several messages across a road swept by machine-gun fire, being cut off from his company; he led a counter-attack, killing and driving off the enemy.

William Gregg.

He was awarded the Victoria Cross, which was announced in the London Gazette of 28 June, 1918: "William Gregg, D.C.M., M.M., No. S. 6522, Sergt., Rifle Brigade (Heanor). For most conspicuous bravery and brilliant leadership in action. Two companies of his unit attacked the enemy's outpost position without artillery preparation. Sergt. Gregg was with the right company, which came under heavy fire from the right flank as it advanced. All the officers with the company were hit. He at once took command of the attack. He rushed an enemy post and personally killed an entire machine-gun team, and captured the gun and four men in a dug-out near by. He then rushed another post, killed two men and captured another. In spite of heavy casualties, he reached his objective, and started consolidating the position. By his prompt and effective action this gallant N.C.O. saved the situation at a critical time and ensured the success of the attack. Later, Sergt. Gregg's party was driven back by an enemy counter-attack, but reinforcements coming up, he led a charge, personally bombed a hostile machine gun, killed the crew and captured the gun. Once again he was driven back. He led another successful attack, and hung on to the position until ordered by his company commander to withdraw. Although under very heavy rifle and machine-gun fire for several hours, Sergt. Gregg displayed throughout the greatest coolness and contempt of danger, walking about encouraging his men and setting a magnificent example." He was made Acting Corporal on the 7th Jan. 1917, Corporal 2 March, 1917, Acting Sergeant 5 June, 1917, and Sergt. 12 Dec. 1917. He was married on 25 June, 1910, at Heanor Church, to Sarah Hardy, daughter of Mr. and Mrs. William Hardy.

WOODALL, JOSEPH EDWARD, Corpl. (L.-Sergt.), served in the European War, and for his services in France was awarded the Victoria Cross [London Gazette, 28 June, 1918]: "Joseph Edward Woodall, No. Z. 1030, Corpl. (L.-Sergt.), 1st Battn. Rifle Brigade. For most conspicuous bravery and fine leadership during an attack. Sergt. Woodall was in command of a platoon which, during the advance, was held up by a machine gun. On his own initiative he rushed forward, and, single-handed, captured the gun and eight men. After the objective had been gained, heavy fire was encountered from a farmhouse some two hundred yards in front. Sergt. Woodall collected ten men, and with great dash and gallantry rushed the farm and took thirty prisoners. Shortly afterwards, when the officer in charge was killed, he took entire command, reorganized the two platoons, and disposed them most skilfully. Throughout the day,

in spite of intense shelling and machine-gun fire, this gallant N.C.O. was constantly on the move, encouraging the men and finding out and sending back invaluable information. The example set by Sergt. Woodall was simply magnificent, and had a marked effect on the troops. The success of the operation on this portion of the front is attributed almost entirely to his coolness, courage and utter disregard for his own personal safety."

HEWITSON, JAMES, L.-Corpl., was born on 15 Oct. 1892, at Thwaite Farm, Coniston, Lancashire, son of Matthew and Margaret Hewitson. He was educated at Coniston Church of England School, and joined the Army on 17 Nov. 1914, serving in the European War in France. He was awarded the Victoria Cross [London Gazette, 28 June, 1918]: "No. 15883, James Hewitson, L.-Corpl., 1/4th Battn. Royal Lancaster Regt. (Territorial Forces) (Coniston). For most conspicuous bravery, initiative and daring in action. In a daylight attack on a series of crater posts, L.-Corpl. Hewitson led his party to their objective with dash and vigour, clearing the enemy from both trench and dug-outs, killing in one dug-out six of the enemy who would not surrender. After capturing the final objective, he observed a hostile machine-gun team coming into action against his men. Working his way round the edge of the crater, he attacked the team, killing four and capturing one. Shortly afterwards he engaged a hostile bombing party which was attacking a Lewis-gun post. He routed the party, killing six of them. The extraordinary feats of daring performed by this gallant N.C.O. crushed the hostile opposition at this point." He writes: "I have been promoted Corporal since I won the V.C., and I have a wife they call Elizabeth Hewitson."

James Hewitson.

BEESLEY, WILLIAM, Private, served in the European War in France, and was awarded the Victoria Cross [London Gazette, 28 June, 1918]: "William Beesley, No. B. 203174, Private, Rifle Brigade. For most conspicuous bravery. The enemy's outpost position was attacked by two companies of his unit without artillery preparation. Private Beesley was in the leading wave of the left company, which came under heavy fire as it approached the enemy's front line. His platoon sergeant and all the section commanders were killed. This young soldier, realizing the situation at once, took command and led the assault. Single-handed, he rushed a post, and with his revolver killed two of the enemy at a machine gun. He then shot dead an officer who ran across from a dug-out to take their place at the machine gun. Three more officers appeared from the dug-out. These he called on to surrender; seeing one of them trying to get rid of a map, he shot him and obtained the map. He took four more prisoners from a dug-out and two others from a shelter close by, disarmed them and sent them back to our lines. At this moment his Lewis gun was brought up by a comrade who was acting as a carrier. Private Beesley at once brought it into action, and used it with great effect against the enemy as they bolted towards their support line, inflicting many casualties. For four hours Private Beesley and his comrade held on to the position under very heavy machine-gun and rifle fire. The enemy then advanced to counter-attack and the other soldier was wounded. Private Beesley carried on by himself, and actually maintained his position until 10 p.m., long after the posts on his right and left had been practically wiped out and the survivors had fallen back. It was mainly due to his action that the enemy were prevented from rushing the position, and that the remnants of his company, when compelled to withdraw, were able to do so without further loss. When darkness set in, Private Beesley made his way back to the original line from which the attack had started, bringing with him the wounded carrier and the Lewis gun. He at once mounted the Lewis gun in the trench and remained in action until things quietened down. The indomitable pluck, skilful shooting and good judgment in economizing ammunition displayed by Private Beesley stamp the incident as one of the most brilliant actions in recent operations."

POULTER, ARTHUR, Private, served in the European War in France, and was awarded the Victoria Cross [London Gazette, 28 June, 1918]: "Arthur Poulter, No. 24066, Private, 1/4th Battn. West Riding Regt." The following is an account of a presentation to Private Poulter: "In the Hospital Square of the Stamford Road Military Hospital, Norbury, London, yesterday, Mr. H. T. Kemp, K.C. Recorder of Hull, who is chairman of the Society of Yorkshiremen in London, presented, on behalf of that institution, a silver watch to Private Arthur Poulter, V.C., 1/4th West Riding Regt. Private Poulter, whose home is at Wortley, Leeds, is one of nine sons, all of whom have seen service in the war. He joined the West Riding Regt. as a volunteer in 1916. The Victoria Cross was conferred on him for gallantry in saving life in the face of the enemy. The official report of his heroism has already appeared in 'The Yorkshire Post.' The watch was engraved with the arms of the society and bore a suitable inscription, and Mr. Kemp, in making the presentation on behalf of the society and congratulating Private Poulter on the great honour he had obtained, remarked that he was the eighth Leeds

Arthur Poulter.

man upon whom the coveted distinction had been conferred. He had proved himself a true Yorkshireman."

"War Office, 11 July, 1918. His Majesty the King has been graciously pleased to approve of the award of the Victoria Cross to the undermentioned Officers and Non-commissioned Officer."

HUDSON, CHARLES EDWARD, Capt., served in the European War, as Second Lieutenant, in Italy; was promoted Lieutenant, and Captain, 11th Battn. Nottinghamshire and Derbyshire Regt., and became Temporary Lieut.-Colonel. He was awarded the Military Cross, created a Companion of the Distinguished Service Order, and awarded the Victoria Cross [London Gazette, 11 July, 1918]: "Charles Edward Hudson, Capt., Temporary Lieut.-Colonel, D.S.O., M.C., Nottinghamshire and Derbyshire Regt. For most conspicuous bravery and devotion to duty when his battalion was holding the right front sector during an attack on the British front. The shelling had been very heavy on the right, the trench destroyed, and considerable casualties had occurred, and all the officers on the spot were killed or wounded. This enabled the enemy to penetrate our front line. The enemy pushed their advance as far as the support line which was the key to our right flank. The situation demanded immediate action. Lieut.-Colonel Hudson, recognizing its gravity, at once collected various headquarter details, such as orderlies, servants, runners, etc., and, together with some Allies, personally led them up the hill. Driving the enemy down the hill towards our front line, he again led a party of about five up the trench, where there were about 200 enemy, in order to attack them from the flank. He then with two men got out of the trench and rushed the position, shouting to the enemy to surrender, some of whom did. He was then severely wounded by a bomb which exploded on his foot. Although in great pain, he gave directions for the counter-attack to be continued, and this was done successfully, about 100 prisoners and six machine guns being taken. Without doubt the high courage and determination displayed by Lieut.-Colonel Hudson saved a serious situation, and had it not been for his quick determination in organizing the counter-attack a large number of the enemy would have dribbled through, and counter-attack on a larger scale would have been necessary to restore the situation." Capt. Hudson was born 29 May, 1892, at Derby, the son of Lieut.-Colonel H. E. Hudson, Sherwood Foresters, and of Mrs. Hudson. He was educated at Sherborne School, Dorset, and at Sandhurst, and entered the Army in Nov. 1914. He went to Italy in Nov. 1918, and was wounded in June, 1919, in the Austrian attack at Assiago, Western Italy. He returned to France in Sept. 1919, as Lieutenant-Colonel Commanding the 2nd Battn. Sherwood Foresters; came home from Cologne and went to Russia in April, 1919, as Captain and Brevet Major. He was Brigade Major to the Vlozda Force, North Russia, until 30 Aug. 1919. He was three times mentioned in Despatches; received a Bar to his D.S.O., the Croix de Guerre and the Italian Croce de Valore.

HARDY, THE REV. THEODORE BAYLEY, C.F., 4th Class, was born at Exeter 20 Oct. 1863, son of George and Sarah Richardson Hardy, both of Exeter, and members of an old Devonshire family. He was educated at the City of London School and London University (B.A. 1889). He was ordained Deacon in the diocese of Southwell in 1898, and Priest the following year, and was a master at the Nottingham High School from 1891 to 1907, when he was appointed Head Master of Bentham Grammar School, which post he held until 1913, when he accepted the living at Hutton Roof. There he remained until he volunteered for service, and proceeded to the front as a Temporary Chaplain. While at Nottingham he was curate of Burton Joyce-with-Bulcote from 1898 to 1902, and afterwards held the curacy at St. Augustine's, New Basford, for five years. He married at Belfast, 13 Sept. 1888, Florence Elizabeth, third daughter of William Hastings, Civil Engineer,

The Rev. T. B. Hardy.

Belfast. They had one son, William Hastings Hardy, born in 1892 (M.B., R.A.M.C., who served during the Great War in the Eastern Mediterranean, attaining the rank of Major), and one daughter, Mary Elizabeth Hardy (B.A., who was for nearly two years with the Red Cross at Dunkirk, in France). He was created a Companion of the Distinguished Service Order [London Gazette, Sept. 1917]: "Theodore Bayley Hardy, Chaplain to the Forces, 4th Class. For conspicuous bravery and devotion to duty. He went out into the open to help to bring in wounded; on discovering a man buried in mud, whom it was impossible to extricate, he remained under fire ministering to his spiritual and bodily comfort till he died." On 16 Sept. 1916, he became a Temporary Chaplain of the Fourth Class. He was awarded the Military Cross [London Gazette, Oct. 1917], for repeatedly going out under heavy fire to help the stretcher-bearers during an attack. Mr. Hardy was awarded the Victoria Cross [London Gazette, 11 July, 1918]: "Rev. Theodore Bayley Hardy, D.S.O., M.C., Temporary Chaplain to the Forces, 4th Class, 'A' Chaplain Department, attached 8th Lincolnshire Regt. For most conspicuous bravery and devotion to duty on many occasions. Although over fifty years of age, he has, by his fearlessness, devotion to men of his battalion, and quiet, unobtrusive manner, won the respect and admiration of the whole division. His marvellous energy and endurance would be remarkable even in a very much younger man, and his valour and devotion are exemplified in the following incidents: An infantry patrol had gone out to attack a previously located enemy post in the ruins of a village, the Rev. T. B. Hardy (C.F.) being then at company headquarters. Hearing firing, he followed the patrol, and about four hundred yards beyond our front line of posts found an officer of the patrol dangerously wounded. He remained with the officer until he was able to get assistance to bring him in. During this time there was a great deal of firing, and an enemy patrol actually penetrated between the spot at which the officer was lying and our front line and captured three of our men. On a second occasion, when an enemy shell exploded in the middle of one of our posts, the Rev. T. B. Hardy at once made his way to the spot, despite the shell and trench-mortar fire which was going on at the time, and set to work to extricate the buried men. He succeeded in getting out one man who had been completely buried. He then set to work to extricate a second man, who was found to be dead. During the whole of this time that he was digging out the men this chaplain was in great danger, not only from shell fire, but also because of the dangerous condition of the wall of the building which had been hit by the shell which buried the men. On a third occasion he displayed the greatest devotion to duty when our infantry, after a successful attack, were gradually forced back to their starting trench. After it was believed that all our men had withdrawn from the wood, Chaplain Hardy came out of it, and on reaching an advanced post, asked the men to help him to get in a wounded man. Accompanied by a sergeant, he made his way to the spot where the man lay, within ten yards of a pill-box which had been captured in the morning, but was subsequently recaptured and occupied by the enemy. The wounded man was too weak to stand, but between them the Chaplain and the sergeant eventually succeeded in getting him to our lines. Throughout the day the enemy's artillery, machine-gun and trench-mortar fire was continuous, and caused many casualties. Notwithstanding, this very gallant chaplain was seen moving quietly amongst the men and tending the wounded, absolutely regardless of his personal safety." The following is a copy of a telegram received by his daughter, Miss M. E. Hardy: "The King is deeply grieved to hear of the death from wounds of your dear father, whose bravery and self-sacrifice had won for him the love and respect of all who served with him. His Majesty heartily sympathizes with you and yours in your sorrow.—STAMFORDHAM." Mr. Hardy was killed in action 18 Oct. 1918. Colonel Hitch, O.C., 8th Lincolnshire Regt., writing to a member of the family, says: "He appealed to us all, both officers and men, by his absolute fearlessness, physical and moral, and by his simple sincerity and lack of cant or humbug. We loved him for his self-effacing devotion to duty, and we respected him for his fearless denunciation of the coarse word or picture. . . . His gallantry in action won him distinction which will make his name famous in history, and yet his retiring nature made it almost a penance to wear those ribbons which most of us would give our right arm for. . . . We had a short memorial service, which the Corps Chaplain, Hales, conducted, and it was the most moving and sincere service I have ever attended. . . . The service was voluntary, and officers and men of nearly all the units with whom he had come into contact were there. What his loss has meant to us is more than I can express, but his name will always be recalled with reverence, and to those of us who knew him really intimately a great blank has appeared in our daily lives, though, thank God, we shall meet him again under happier surroundings." Throughout his life Mr. Hardy was devoted to outdoor sport of all kinds, especially boating, swimming, riding and walking. In cricket and football he was handicapped by his extreme short sight. He was always very keen on physical culture.

SADLIER, CLIFFORD WILLIAM KING, Lieut., served in the European War, and for his services in France was awarded the Victoria Cross [London Gazette, 11 July, 1918]: "Clifford William King Sadlier, 51st Battn. Australian Imperial Force. For conspicuous bravery during a counter-attack by his battalion on strong enemy positions. Lieut. Sadlier's platoon, which was on the left of the battalion, had to advance through a wood when a strong enemy machine-gun post caused casualties and prevented the platoon from advancing. Although himself wounded, he at once collected his bombing section, led them against the machine guns, and succeeded in killing the crews and capturing two of the guns. By this time Lieut. Sadlier's party were all casualties, and he alone attacked a third enemy machine gun with his revolver, killing the crew of four and taking the gun. In doing so, he was again wounded. The very gallant conduct of this officer was the means of clearing the flank and allowing the battalion to move forward, thereby saving a most critical situation. His coolness and utter disregard of danger inspired all."

Clifford W. K. Sadlier.

RUTHVEN, WILLIAM, Sergt., joined the Australian Military Forces, and served in the European War, and for his services in France was awarded the Victoria Cross [London Gazette, 11 July, 1918]: "William Ruthven, No. 1946, Sergt., 22nd Battn. Australian Imperial Forces. For most conspicuous bravery and initiative in action. During the advance Sergt. Ruthven's company suffered numerous casualties, and his company commander was severely wounded. He thereupon assumed com-

William Ruthven

mand of this portion of the assault, took charge of the company headquarters, and rallied the section in his vicinity. As the leading wave approached its objective, it was subjected to heavy fire from an enemy machine-gun at close range. Without hesitation he at once sprang out, threw a bomb which landed beside the post, and rushed the position, bayoneting one of the crew and capturing the gun. He then encountered some of the enemy coming out of a shelter. He wounded two, captured six others in the same position, and handed them over to an escort from the leading wave, which had now reached the objective. Sergt. Ruthven then reorganized the men in his vicinity and established a post in the second objective. Observing enemy movement in a sunken road near by, he, without hesitation and armed only with a revolver, went over the open alone and rushed the position, shooting two enemy who refused to come out of their dug-outs. He then, single-handed, mopped up this post and captured the whole of the garrison, amounting in all to thirty-two, and kept them until assistance arrived to escort them back to our lines. During the remainder of the day this gallant non-commissioned officer set a splendid example of leadership, moving up and down his position under fire, supervising consolidation and encouraging his men. Throughout the whole operation he showed the most magnificent courage and determination, inspiring everyone by his fine fighting spirit, his remarkable courage and his dashing action." He was promoted to Second Lieutenant on 16 Aug. 1918. The King held a private Investiture at Buckingham Palace, and conferred the Victoria Cross upon Second Lieut. (formerly Sergt.) William Ruthven, A.I.F.

London Gazette, 22 July, 1918.—" Admiralty, 22 July, 1918. Honours for services in the operations against Zeebrugge and Ostend on the night of the 22nd and 23rd April, 1918."

" Admiralty, 22 July, 1918. The King has been graciously pleased to approve of the award of the Victoria Cross to the undermentioned Officers and Men."

CARPENTER, ALFRED, Commander, Royal Navy, served in the European War, and was awarded the Victoria Cross [London Gazette 22 July, 1918]: " Alfred Carpenter, Commander, Royal Navy. For most conspicuous gallantry. This officer was in command of Vindictive. He set a magnificent example to all those under his command by his calm composure when navigating mined waters, bringing his ship alongside the Mole in darkness. When Vindictive was within a few yards of the Mole, the enemy started and maintained a heavy fire from batteries, machine guns and rifles on to the bridge. He showed most conspicuous bravery, and did much to encourage similar behaviour on the part of the crew, supervising the landing from the Vindictive on to the Mole, and walking round the decks directing operations and encouraging the men in the most dangerous and exposed positions. By his encouragement to those under him, his power of command and personal bearing, he undoubtedly contributed greatly to the success of the operation. Capt. Carpenter was selected by the officers of the Vindictive, Iris II. and Daffodil, and of the naval assaulting force to receive the Victoria Cross under Rule 13 of the Royal Warrant dated the 29th Jan. 1856."

SANDFORD, RICHARD DOUGLAS, Lieut., Royal Navy, born 11 May, 1891, was the youngest son of the late Venerable E. G. Sandford, Archdeacon of Exeter, and of Mrs. Sandford, 15, The Beacon, Exmouth, whose sons have greatly distinguished themselves in the war. R. D. Sandford was one of those who received the Victoria Cross for conspicuous gallantry at Zeebrugge on St. George's Day. He entered the Navy on the 15th Jan. 1904, and between Sept. 1908, and Dec. 1913, served in several of His Majesty's ships. In Jan. 1914, he was appointed to the Submarine Service, and served in it until the day of his death, 23 Nov. 1918. Perhaps the best proof of what he was is the smile that lights up the faces of any who speak of him. As a child he was the " friend of all the world." It was " Hullo, Dick ! " wherever he went. It was as natural for the Bishop to give the " grubby little imp " a lift in his carriage as it was for the groundsman of the County Cricket ground to share his bread-and-cheese lunch with him. He never lost this simple friendliness. He was an almost perfect companion, happy, interested in everything, simple-hearted, faithful and wonderfully understanding. But " he was very undemonstrative: he expressed himself in the things he did, such simple kind things." In hospital he discovered that one of the men who was wounded and not doing very well could not be moved to the verandah because there was some difficulty about getting his bed there from the particular ward he was in. For Dick it was the most natural thing in the world to ask and insist on changing beds with him. And when picked up shot through the thigh and hand, after blowing up the Mole, " he was simple as ever, and thinking of the other fellows hurt; and when it came to doing anything, he was full of helping himself along, with his sense of humour still strong, even when it became a question as to whether we could get him over the side of the Phœbe." Indeed, one can hardly imagine him any way else but with a large grin upon his face. There never can have been anyone whose sense of the ridiculous was so spontaneous, or so explosive, or so infectious. And he had no ordinary powers of description either—not that it came out in his letters, which were usually a few lines of apology for his delay in writing, or maybe for his nib " having a cold and sneezing over the paper." He was too busy living. If the submarine in which he was gained the reputation amongst friends of being the " most cheery and most piratical of her flotilla," one may be sure that " Baldy's " laugh and joy in life had something to do with it. In one of his few short leaves from duty in the North Sea he wanted to see what life in France was like. Everything rose to the occasion. Wherever he went he was followed by every kind of missile. The quietest spots became infernos. Everybody laughed, of course. " Do you remember when Dick was with us ? " followed by loud laughter, became a sort of proverb with the battery whose guest he was. But he was a great deal more than just a cheerful companion possessed with an irrepressible sense of humour. He could be the quietest person on earth listening to music or reading a book. And in the give-and-take of conversation it was as easy for him to listen as talk himself; and he could be serious as easily as laugh. He was most uncritical, and " was a pattern in the way he said and thought good of other people." But he was entirely unself-conscious about it. He never did or said an unkind thing in his life. True, when things did not go quite right, there were moments in which he was by no means placid or serene, and such moments were most electrical; but he was incapable of saying anything that could leave any sense of bitterness. He had, behind everything, an absolutely unquestioned sense of duty, so clear that I doubt if it ever caused him a moment's thought. He could not bear to see things badly done or shirked. His indignant remark, " I couldn't do a thing like that myself," when a junior went away to time and left his job for somebody else to finish, was as true as it was surprising to hear him say it. He trusted others and liked to be trusted himself, and could not bear to be interfered with in his own job. " A most competent officer," " An almost ideal officer," are phrases that might mean less than they do. But it is not by accident that a man carries out " one of the finest feats of the whole war." He may have been right when he said, " We only got there at all because every bally thing went wrong," and it was like him, when reading the account of some of the Victoria Crosses won in France, to say in his quiet way, " What a child it makes one feel ! " But the story of C3 will be immortal all the same. In the words of the Gazette of his Victoria Cross [22 July, 1918]: " Lieutenant Richard Douglas Sandford, R.N., was in command of C3, and most skilfully placed that vessel in between the piles of the viaduct before lighting his fuse and abandoning her. He eagerly undertook this hazardous enterprise, although well aware (as were all his crew) that if the means of rescue failed, and he or any of his crew were in the water at the moment of the explosion, they would be killed outright by the force of such explosion. Yet Lieutenant Sandford disdained to use the gyro steering, which would have enabled him and his crew to abandon the submarine at a safe distance, and preferred to make sure, as far as was humanly possible, of the accomplishment of his duty." Three months later, just after he came out of hospital, appeared the list of Zeebrugge and Ostend honours. His was one of the six Victoria Crosses. He was also awarded the Legion of Honour (Chevalier) by the French Government. It snowed telegrams. That was only natural. But they were not ordinary telegrams at all. They came from his friends' little brothers and sisters, " Well done, Uncle Baldy " ; from his friends—nearly all of them quite mad ; from his old friends who had known him as a small boy—a perfectly delightful collection, such as could only have been sent to Dick. And surely there are few who have worn a V.C. more simply or more happily. It is the story of a short life ; in some ways it was wonderfully complete, but with him has gone much sunshine. Lieut. Sandford died on Saturday, 23 Nov. 1918, of typhoid fever at Cleveland Hospital, Grangetown.

Richard D. Sandford.

BAMFORD, EDWARD, Capt., was born 28 May, 1887, at Highgate, N., son of the Rev. Robert Bamford, B.A., Church of England (deceased), and Mrs. Myers, of Elmtree, St. Mary Church, Torquay. He was educated at Sherborne, and afterwards by R. H. Hammond, Esq., at Malvern House, Kearsney, near Dover. He joined the Royal Marine Light Infantry in July, 1905, as Second Lieutenant, and a year later was promoted Lieutenant. As Subaltern he served in H.M.S. Bulwark, H.M.S. Magnificent and H.M.S. Britannia. He served in H.M.S. Britannia for the first 15 months of the war (Third Battle Squadron); was in H.M.S. Britannia when she ran aground near Inch Keith, after going out to support the Battle Cruiser Squadron in the Dogger Bank fight (Britannia did not take part in the fight). He was shelled in the Ypres salient in April, 1916, when attached to the Guards Brigade as a spectator; commissioned the Chester 2 May, 1916, and was commanding the Royal Marine detachment of that ship at Jutland 31 May, 1916. He witnessed the blowing up of H.M.S. Invincible at Jutland; was on board the Chester, next astern of the Falmouth, when that ship was torpedoed in Aug. 1916, and witnessed the torpedoing of the Nottingham on the same day. In May, 1916, he was promoted Temporary Captain, and for his services in H.M.S. Chester in the Battle of Jutland 31 May, 1916, he was created a Companion of the Distinguished Service Order [London Gazette, 15 Sept. 1916], and mentioned in Admiral Jellicoe's Despatch of that date: " Remarks of Vice-Admiral Sir David Beatty: Capt. Edward Bamford, R.M.L.I. In after control when it was blown to pieces by a shell-burst. Slightly burnt in face and slightly wounded in leg. Then assisted to work one gun with a much reduced crew, and controlled another gun. Assisted in extinguishing a fire, and in general showed great coolness, power of command, judgment and courage when exposed to a very heavy fire." For his services in the Battle of Jutland he was also awarded the Russian Order of St. Anne (with Swords). He was promoted Captain, Sept. 1916, and was relieved for special service in Feb. 1918, and given command of the Portsmouth Company of the 4th Royal Marine Battn., and led them on to the Mole

Edward Bamford.

at Zeebrugge from H.M.S. Vindictive 23 April, 1918 (*vide* Sir Roger Keyes' Despatches), being specially disembarked from H.M.S. Chester for these operations. He received the Brevet of Major 23 April, 1918, as a reward for the part he took in the Zeebrugge operations. He was further awarded the Victoria Cross [London Gazette, 22 July, 1918]: "Edward Bamford, Capt., D.S.O., Royal Marine Light Infantry. Date of Act of Bravery: night of 22–23 April, 1918. For most conspicuous gallantry. This officer landed on the Mole from Vindictive with numbers 5, 7 and 8 platoons of the Marines storming force, in the face of great difficulties. When on the Mole, and under heavy fire, he displayed the greatest initiative in the command of his company, and by his total disregard of danger, showed a magnificent example to his men. He first established a strong point on the right of the disembarkation, and, when satisfied that that was safe, led an assault on a battery to the left with the utmost coolness and valour. Capt. Bamford was selected by the officers of the R.M.A. and R.M.L.I. detachments to receive the Victoria Cross under Rule 13 of the Royal Warrant, dated 29 Jan. 1856." He has since been made an officer of the Legion of Honour by the President of the French Republic (for Zeebrugge). Major Bamford writes: "It is difficult to give further particulars of Zeebrugge, as Admiral Keyes' Despatch is so full of details. I landed at the head of the 5th Platoon (Lieut., now Brevet Major, T. F. V. Cooke, D.S.O.). With Lieut. Cooke's platoon I moved along the upper promenade of the Mole, to quiet some snipers who were disturbing the landing of the remainder. We came abreast the spot where the Iris was trying to get alongside, and hailed her. She replied with loud cheers, but it was clear she would never get close enough to the Mole to land her men, and when I last saw her she had shoved off and was being badly shelled with tracer shell. Lieut. Cooke was shot in the head at my side, just before 12.15 a.m., when the submarine blew up the shore end of the Mole. The blockships could now be seen stealing across the harbour towards the canal entrance, and did not appear to be receiving much attention from the Huns. I climbed down the scaling ladders abreast Vindictive, having withdrawn the men from the right, and, crossing the Mole, collected men of the 7th and 8th Platoons, and with a few of the 5th started an assault against the batteries at the seaward end of the Mole. This was interrupted by the general recall (Ks on the syren), and we returned to the ship, crossing the Mole in small parties, so as not to clog the ladders, which were under heavy fire from the shore batteries." He embarked in H.M.S. Royal Sovereign in Aug. 1918: was present in that ship at the surrender of the High Seas Fleet in the Firth of Forth. His favourite recreations are golf, hockey, tennis, boat-sailing and fishing.

FINCH, NORMAN AUGUSTUS, Sergt., was born on 26 Dec. 1890, at 42, Ninevah Road, Handsworth, Birmingham, son of Richard William John and Emma Amelia Finch, of 37, Gosforth Road, Southport, Lancashire. He was educated at Benson Road Board School, and at Grove Lane Council School. He joined the Royal Marine Artillery as a Private in Jan. 1908. He was awarded the Victoria Cross for his services in the foretop of H.M.S. Vindictive at Zeebrugge on the night of 22–23 April, 1918 [London Gazette, 22 July, 1918]: "Norman Augustus Finch, Sergt., No. R.M.A. /12150, Royal Marine Artillery. For most conspicuous gallantry. Sergt. Finch was second in command of the pom-poms and Lewis guns in the foretop of the Vindictive, under Lieut. Charles N. B. Rigley, R.M.A. At one period Vindictive was being hit every few seconds, chiefly in the upper works, from which splinters caused many casualties. It was difficult to locate the guns which were doing the most damage, but Lieut. Rigley, Sergt. Finch and the Marines' foretop kept up a continuous fire with pom-poms and Lewis guns, changing rapidly from one target to another, thus keeping the enemy's fire down to some considerable extent. Unfortunately two heavy shells made direct hits on the foretop, which was completely exposed to enemy concentration of fire. All in the top were killed or disabled except Sergt. Finch, who was, however, severely wounded; nevertheless, he showed consummate bravery, remaining in his battered and exposed position. He once more got a Lewis gun in action, and kept up a continuous fire, harassing the enemy on the Mole, until the foretop received another direct hit, the remainder of the armament being then put completely out of action. Before the top was destroyed Sergt. Finch had done invaluable work, and by his bravery undoubtedly saved many lives. This very gallant Sergeant of the Royal Marine Artillery was selected by the 4th Battn. of Royal Marines, who were mostly Royal Marine Light Infantry, to receive the Victoria Cross under Rule 13 of the Royal Warrant dated 29 Jan. 1856." He has the 1915 Star.

McKENZIE, ALBERT EDWARD, Able Seaman, Royal Navy, was born on 23 Oct. 1898, at 10, Alice Street, Bermondsey, S.E., son of Alexander McKenzie (deceased) and Eliza McKenzie, daughter of Richard and Eliza Marks. He lived most of his life at 1, Shorncliffe Road, Old Kent Road, S.E., with his widowed mother. He was educated at Webb Street, Bermondsey, and Mina Road, Southwark, London County Council Schools, and went to St. Mark's, Camberwell, Sunday School. He joined the Navy in 1913 as First-Class Boy. Whilst in the Navy he distinguished himself at boxing and football. For boxing he gained two medals on the Arethusa, two on the Neptune, and one during Harwich training. He was "runner-up" in the light-weight boxing competition, and won the boxing championship of the 4th Battle Squadron, besides four other medals. He served in the European War in various capacities and centres, including mine-sweeping, and was latterly attached to H.M.S. Neptune, from which he volunteered for the Zeebrugge expedition after training at Chatham. He is the youngest of a large and patriotic family, several of whom bore arms in the war, another of them laying down his life. He was the most distinguished member of what was known in South London as "St. Mark's Little Army," being the 4,286 men from the parish of St. Mark's, Camberwell (the largest number from any ecclesiastical parish in London), who joined the Forces; it gained 81 War Honours, and 518 members laid down their lives. He was awarded the Victoria Cross for bravery at Zeebrugge [London Gazette, 22 July, 1918]: "Albert Edward McKenzie, Able Seaman, O.N. J31736, Royal Navy. For most conspicuous gallantry. This rating belonged to B Company of seaman storming party. On the night of the operation he landed on the Mole with his machine gun in the face of great difficulties, and did very good work, using his gun to the utmost advantage. He advanced down the Mole with Lieut.-Commander Harrison, who, with most of his party, was killed, and accounted for several of the enemy running from a shelter to a destroyer alongside the Mole. This very gallant seaman was severely wounded whilst working his gun in an exposed position. Able Seaman McKenzie was selected by the men of the Vindictive, Iris II. and Daffodil, and of the naval assaulting force, to receive the Victoria Cross under Rule 13 of the Royal Warrant, dated the 29th Jan. 1856." In the postscript (characteristic modesty) to a letter to one of his brothers, full of graphic details, concluding with a eulogy of a chum, Able Seaman McKenzie described the part he took in the attack on the Mole thus: "Well, we got within about fifteen minutes' run of the Mole, when some marines got excited and fired their rifles. Up went four big star shells, and they spotted us. That caused it. They hit us with the first two shells and killed seven marines. They were still hitting us when we got alongside. There was a heavy swell on, which smashed all our gangways bar two, one aft and one forward. I tucked the old Lewis gun under my arm and nipped over the gangway aft. There were two of my gun's crew killed inboard, so I only had two left—with myself, three. I turned to my left and advanced about fifty yards, then lay down. There was a spiral staircase which led down into the Mole, and Commander Brock fired his revolver down and dropped Mills'. You ought to have seen them nip out and try to get across to the destroyer tied up against the Mole, but this little chicken met them half way with the box of tricks, and I ticked about a dozen off before I clicked. My Lewis gun was shot spinning out of my hands, and all I had left was the stock and pistol grip which I kindly took a bloke's photo with who looked too business-like for me with a rifle and a bayonet. It half stunned him, and gave me time to get out my pistol and finish him off. Then I found a rifle and bayonet, and joined up our crowd who had just come off the destroyer. All I remember was pushing, kicking and kneeing every German who got in the way. When I was finished I couldn't climb the ladder, so a mate of mine lifted me up and carried me up the ladder, and then I crawled on my hands and knees inboard." He was invested by the King at Buckingham Palace, and on his return was given a civic reception in the Borough of Southwark, on the doorsteps of his home in Shorncliffe Road, which was a blaze of colour of flags and bunting, to welcome its hero home—on crutches—and the Mayor mentioned that Able Seaman McKenzie's honour was unique in a double sense, in that he was the first London sailor to receive the Victoria Cross, and also the first to be awarded it by the votes of his comrades. Able Seaman McKenzie, V.C., did not live to enjoy the honours that he had so magnificently earned. After almost complete recovery from his wounds he succumbed to influenza, 3 Nov. 1918. A present of War Bonds and a most touching Presentation Address from his many friends in the Parish of St. Mark's, Camberwell, was given to his widowed mother. "We are prouder of you than we can say," was the way the subscribers summed up their admiration of their fellow parishioner. He was buried at Camberwell Cemetery, 9 Nov. 1918. The Right Honourable T. J. Macnamara, M.P., Financial Secretary to the Admiralty, and Capt. Carpenter, V.C., of the Vindictive, were present at his funeral, and the following message from the King and Queen to Canon Veasey, Vicar of the Church of St. Mark's, Camberwell, of which McKenzie was a member and where the first part of the funeral service was held, was read: "In the special circumstances of Able Seaman Albert Edward McKenzie's lamentable death, and the fact of his being a V.C., and the first London sailor to receive that most honourable reward, you are authorized to express at the public funeral at St. Mark's, Camberwell, the sympathy of their Majesties with the widowed mother and family. Their Majesties were grieved to hear of his untimely death, and to think that he had been spared so short a time to wear the proud decoration which he so nobly won." Proud, indeed, must his widowed mother have been to receive this message and the following tribute from the hero of the Vindictive, Capt. Carpenter, V.C.: "The splendid example which your boy set at Zeebrugge will be accorded a high place of honour in the naval records of the British Empire." And the closing words of Dr. Macnamara when he presented to her the Presentation Address intended for her heroic son: "Mrs. McKenzie has lost a son, but the nation has found a hero." A memorial in the form of a monument of honour over his grave was unveiled and dedicated, 4 Oct. 1918, at Camberwell Cemetery. The Mayor of Southwark, at the time of the exploit, unveiled the memorial and concluded a stirring address with the words: "Albert E. McKenzie died nobly; we perpetuate his name; God bless him!" His portrait was painted by the order of the Head of the Department of Naval Publicity, to be hung in the Imperial War Museum.

Albert Edward McKenzie.

London Gazette, 25 July, 1918.—"His Majesty the King has been graciously pleased to approve of the award of the Victoria Cross to the undermentioned Officers and Non-commissioned Officer."

GROGAN, GEORGE WILLIAM ST. GEORGE, Lieut.-Colonel (Temporary Brigadier-General), was born 1 Sept. 1875, in Fifeshire, N.B. He was gazetted to the West India Regt. as Second Lieutenant 5 Sept. 1896; became Lieutenant 22 Dec. 1897; served in Sierra Leone, 1898, and West

Africa 1898–99 (Medal); became Captain, West India Regt. 22 Dec. 1897. Capt. Grogan was employed with the Egyptian Army 9 May, 1902, to 10 May, 1907. He was transferred to the Yorkshire Light Infantry 27 March, 1907, and to the Worcestershire Regt. 18 Jan. 1908. He served in the European War from 1914; was promoted to Major 28 Sept. 1914; temporary Lieutenant-Colonel 22 March, 1915; was mentioned in Despatches, and created a C.M.G. (1916); created a Companion of the Distinguished Service Order. He became temporary Brigadier-General, and was awarded the Victoria Cross [London Gazette, 25 July, 1918]: " George William St. George Grogan, Major and Brevet Lieut.-Colonel (Temp. Brigadier-General), C.M.G., D.S.O., Worcestershire Regt. For most conspicuous bravery and leadership throughout three days of intense fighting. Brigadier-General Grogan was, except for a few hours, in command of the remnants of the infantry of a Division and various attached troops. His actions during the whole battle can only be described as magnificent. The utter disregard for his personal safety, combined with sound practical ability which he displayed, materially helped to stay the onward thrust of the enemy masses. Throughout the third day of operations, a most critical day, he spent his time under artillery, trench mortar, rifle and machine-gun fire, riding up and down the front line encouraging his troops, reorganizing those who had fallen into disorder, leading back into the line those who were beginning to retire, and setting such a wonderful example that he inspired with his enthusiasm not only his own men, but also the Allied troops who were alongside. As a result the line held and repeated enemy attacks were repulsed. He had one horse shot under him, but nevertheless continued on foot to encourage his men until another horse was brought. He displayed throughout the highest valour, powers of command and leadership." Two days after gaining the V.C. he was awarded a Bar to the Distinguished Service Order. He was given the command of the 1st Brigade of the Russian Relief Force, and was created a C.B. in 1919.

YOULL, JOHN SCOTT, Second Lieut., youngest son of Richard and Margaret Youll, was born on 6 June, 1897, at Thornley, County Durham. His parents live at Thorncroft, Thornley. He was educated at Thornley

John Scott Youll.

Council School, and later was a student at the technical classes held by the Durham County Council at Wingate. When he was about fifteen years old he began work at Thornley Colliery as an apprentice electrician. He joined the Army on reaching military age, on 1 July, 1916, as a Sapper in the Royal Engineers (Durham Territorials), and trained for a year in England. He served in the European War. He went to France in July, 1916, and did such good service for six months as a sapper that he was recommended for a commission. In June, 1917, he was gazetted to the Northumberland Fusiliers, and went back almost immediately to France. He was mentioned in Despatches for the part he took in the fierce fighting at Polygon Wood. He was transferred with his battalion to the Italian front in Oct. 1917, where he gained the Victoria Cross and the Italian Silver Medal for Valour. He was the first officer of his regiment to win the Victoria Cross since the Siege of Lucknow. The award was announced in the London Gazette of 25 July, 1918: " John Scott Youll Second Lieut., 11th Battn. Northumberland Fusiliers. For most conspicuous bravery and devotion to duty during enemy attacks when in command of a patrol, which came under the hostile barrage. Sending his men back to safety, he remained to observe the situation. Unable subsequently to rejoin his company, Second Lieut. Youll reported to a neighbouring unit, and when the enemy attacked he maintained his position with several men of different units until the troops on his left had given way and an enemy machine gun had opened fire from behind him. He rushed the gun, and, having killed most of the team, opened fire on the enemy with the captured gun, inflicting heavy casualties. Then, finding that the enemy had gained a footing in a portion of the front line, he organized and carried out with a few men three separate counter-attacks. On each occasion he drove back the enemy, but was unable to maintain his position by reason of reverse fire. Throughout the fighting his complete disregard of personal safety and very gallant leading set a magnificent example to all." He was killed in action on 27 Oct. 1918, at the crossing of the Piave.

HALLIWELL, JOEL, L.-Corpl., was born at Middleton, Lancashire. He was educated at Parkfield Church of England School, and before becoming a soldier was employed as a foreman in a Middleton Cotton Mill. He joined the Army and served in the European War. He was awarded the Victoria Cross [London Gazette, 25 July, 1918]: " No. 9860, Joel Halliwell, L.-Corpl., 11th Battn. Lancashire Fusiliers. For most conspicuous bravery and determination displayed during the withdrawal of the remnants of the battalion, when closely engaged with the enemy. L.-Corpl. Halliwell, having captured a stray enemy horse, rode out under heavy rifle and machine-gun fire and rescued a man from No Man's Land. He repeated this performance several times, and succeeded in rescuing one officer and nine other ranks. He made another effort to reach a wounded man, but was driven back by the very close advance of the enemy. His conduct was magnificent throughout, and was a splendid and inspiring example to all who saw him." He received an enthusiastic welcome when he came home on leave from the Mayor and Mayoress and the Council of Middleton, the children of his old school, and the general townsfolk of Middleton, and later a gold watch and chain and War Bonds were presented to him.

London Gazette, 17 Aug. 1918.—" War Office, 17 Aug. 1918. The King has been graciously pleased to approve of the award of the Victoria Cross to the following Non-commissioned Officers and Man."

DAVEY, PHILIP, Corpl., served in the European War. He was awarded

Philip Davey.

the Victoria Cross [London Gazette, 17 Aug. 1918]: " No. 1377, Philip Davey, M.M., Corpl., 10th Battn. Australian Imperial Force. For most conspicuous bravery and initiative in attack. In a daylight operation against the enemy position his platoon advanced 200 yards, capturing part of the enemy line, and whilst the platoon was consolidating the enemy pushed a machine gun forward under cover of a hedge and opened fire from close range, inflicting heavy casualties and hampering work. Alone Corpl. Davey moved forward in the face of a fierce point-blank fire, and attacked the gun with hand grenades, putting half the crew out of action. Having used all available grenades, he returned to the original jumping-off trench, secured a further supply, and again attacked the gun, the crew of which had, in the meantime, been reinforced. He killed the crew, eight in all, and captured the gun. This very gallant N.C.O. then mounted the gun in the new post, and used it in repelling a determined counter-attack, during which he was severely wounded. By his determination Corpl. Davey saved the platoon from annihilation, and made it possible to consolidate and hold a position of vital importance to the success of the whole operation."

BROWN, WALTER ERNEST, Corpl., served in the European War, and was awarded the D.C.M. He was awarded the Victoria Cross [London Gazette, 17 Aug. 1918]: " Walter Ernest Brown, D.C.M., No. 1689A, Corpl., 20th Battn. Australian Imperial Force. For most conspicuous bravery and determination when with an advance party from his battalion which was going into the line in relief. The company to which he was attached carried out during the night a minor operation resulting in the capture of a small system of enemy trench. Early on the following morning an enemy strong post about seventy yards distant caused the occupants of the newly captured trench great inconvenience by persistent sniping. Hearing that it had been decided to rush this post, Corpl. Brown, on his own initiative, crept out along the shallow trench and made a dash towards the post. An enemy machine gun opened fire from another trench, and forced him to take cover. Later he again dashed forward and reached his objective. With a Mills grenade in his hand he stood at the door of a dug-out and called on the occupants to surrender. One of the enemy rushed out, a scuffle ensued, and Corpl. Brown knocked him down with his fist. Loud cries of ' Kamerad ! ' were then heard, and from the dug-out an officer and eleven other ranks appeared. This party Corpl. Brown brought back as prisoners to our line, the enemy meanwhile from other positions bringing heavy machine-gun fire to bear on the party."

AXFORD, THOMAS LESLIE, L.-Corpl., served in the European War, and was awarded the Victoria Cross [London Gazette, 17 Aug. 1918]: " Thomas

Thomas Leslie Axford.

Leslie Axford, L.-Corpl., No. 3399, M.M., A.I.F. For most conspicuous bravery and initiative during operations. When the barrage lifted and the infantry advance commenced, his platoon was able to reach the first enemy defences through gaps which had been cut in the wire. The adjoining platoon being delayed in uncut wire, enemy machine guns got into action and inflicted many casualties, including the Company Commander. L.-Corpl. Axford, with great initiative and magnificent courage, at once dashed to the flank, threw his bombs amongst the machine-gun crews, jumped into the trench, and charged with his bayonet. Unaided he killed ten of the enemy and took six prisoners; he threw the machine guns over the parapet, and called out to the delayed platoon to come on. He then rejoined his own platoon, and fought with it during the remainder of the operations. Prior to the incidents above mentioned, he had assisted in the laying out of the tapes for the jumping-off position, which was within 100 yards of the enemy. When the tapes were laid he remained out as a special patrol to ensure that the enemy did not discover any unusual movement on our side. His initiative and gallantry undoubtedly saved many casualties, and most materially assisted towards the complete success of his company in the task assigned to it."

DALZIEL, HENRY, Driver, served in the European War. He was awarded the Victoria Cross [London Gazette, 17 Aug. 1918]: " No. 1936, Henry Dalziel, Driver, Australian Imperial Force. For most conspicuous bravery and devotion to duty when in action with a Lewis gun section. His company met with determined resistance from a strong point which was strongly garrisoned, manned by numerous machine-guns, and undamaged by our artillery fire, also protected by strong wire entanglements. A heavy concentration of machine-gun fire caused many casualties, and held up our advance. His Lewis gun having come into action and silenced enemy guns in one direction, an enemy gun opened fire from another direction. Private Dalziel dashed at it, and with his revolver killed or captured the entire crew and gun, and allowed our advance to continue. He was severely wounded in the hand, but carried on and took part in the capture of the final objective. He twice went over open ground under heavy enemy artillery and machine-gun fire to secure ammunition, and though suffering from considerable loss of blood, he filled magazines and served his gun until severely wounded through the head. His magnificent bravery and devotion to duty was an inspiring example to all his comrades, and his dash and unselfish courage at a most critical time undoubtedly saved many lives and turned what would have been a severe check into a splendid success."

Henry Dalziel.

Driver Dalziel was born 18 Feb. 1893, at Irvinebank, North Queensland, son of James and Eliza Maggie Dalziel, both Australians; the father, who is a miner, is a Victorian, and the mother a Queenslander. Henry Dalziel was educated at different State Schools in Queensland, Victoria and Western Australia, and was a fireman on the Cairns-Atherton Railway when he enlisted. He is fond of sport, and is above the average in the country district to which he belongs as a swimmer, footballer and boxer, although he never entered into competitions. Henry Dalziel fought in Gallipoli in the 15th Battn., and was in the August charge, when 850 went out to draw the fire, so that the unspeakable Turk could be attacked on the left flank. The 15th Battn. drove the Turks out of the trenches, but, unfortunately, the 15th was mowed down like a field of wheat, and returned with 250 men. Henry Dalziel's mate was shot dead by his shoulder.

The following is an extract from the " Northern Herald " for 19 Dec. 1918:

" The 'People's Journal,' a well-known Home paper, has the following description of how the Cairns district V.C., Harry Dalziel, won his great distinction: 'Harry Dalziel, of the A.I.F., won the V.C. thrice over. It was the most brilliant single-handed effort of the war, and how he escaped being riddled through and blown to pieces is a miracle. Our company was getting it hot from Fritz. His machine guns were beating a continuous tattoo, and our casualties were rapidly growing. The enemy was strongly fortified. Earthworks, barbed wire, and his guns. Our advance was held up by the strafe, and our reserves were crowding upon us. And what was most maddening was the thought of our helplessness. Made the teeth grit. The worst strafe was coming from a spot on our left, about 100 yards distant. We couldn't fix that machine gun nohow, and first thing I saw through the smother was Harry rushing straight at death with a five-barrelled Colt in his hand. It seemed suicide, and how he escaped that hurricane of lead nobody on this earth will ever tell me. Dalziel got them, and single-handed he sailed into the Germans. He laid out four, and the others threw up their hands? One of his hands was almost shot away, but he stuck to it like a hero. " Come on, lads; we've got 'em guessing! " he shouted, and we had. It was a walk-over after that. But Dalziel, shot hand and all, was not finished for the day. We ran short of ammunition, and Harry had another two dashes across No Man's Land to bring it up. Every kind of missile was banging, bursting, whizzing, and pinging round him! Yet he came through it, and no man ever more worthily won the coveted Victoria Cross. He got another severe head wound, but refused to lie down. Covered with blood and one hand useless, he kept his gun going. I'm proud to be a comrade of Harry Dalziel's, one of the best and bravest in His Majesty's uniform.' The official notice in the London Gazette reads as follows: 'The dash and unselfish courage of Driver Henry Dalziel, A.I.F., at a most critical time undoubtedly saved many lives, and turned what would have been a severe check into a splendid success.' "

Gunner Dalziel's hand was useless for some time, until the wound was healed, but he still has it intact. We give an account of an Australian " Diggers' Backsheesh Feed " from the " Barron Valley Advocate " of 17 May, 1919:

" On Thursday evening the members of the Atherton Sub-branch of the Sailors' and Soldiers' Imperial League of Australia entertained their old 'cobber' and gallant V.C. to dinner at Markham's B. V. Hotel. There was a large attendance, including a few civilians, and some apologies were received from members unable to attend, but forwarding their sincere wishes for a happy reunion and long life to the hero guest. The menu cards, printed in gold, and adorned with the colours of his battalion, were typical of the occasion. These were in much demand, and as each card bore the V.C.'s autograph, a souvenir of this unique gathering—to do honour to the Tableland's V.C.—was carefully treasured by those lucky enough to get one. Host 'Monsieur Markham' provided a capital spread, much enjoyed by all, and conviviality was general until 10.30, when the call for 'sick parade' was sounded. At the invitation of the Ladies' League, the V.C. and all returned soldiers adjourned to the Shire Hall, where a euchre party and dance was being held in aid of the Anzac Memorial Fund. Here the Diggers further enjoyed themselves, their presence also adding to the success of the dance, which was continued till an early hour. The arrangements for the dinner were admirably carried out, thanks to the foresight of Capt. Nye, Sergt. Brown and Driver Cloutier, the greater burden of the work falling on the latter's shoulders as secretary, and needless to say was carried out in his usual energetic fashion. Capt. Nye (president of the Atherton Sub-branch of the Returned Sailors' and Soldiers' League) presided, the vice-chair being held by Driver C. E. W. Hyde. The room was very beautifully decorated, and as one looked at the faces of the Diggers assembled (grave and gay) came the realization of all that it meant. 'Home, Country, Empire,' all symbolistic and characteristic of our own beloved ones were the reminders of the days that had passed, on the menu list, each item bearing some significance to the Digger which he laughed at, and which he alone is privileged to enjoy to the full, having lived through the time. At the head of the table was the guest of the evening, and looking on his quiet unassuming bearing, one is filled with pride to think that Australia can produce such sons. Silent, yet cheerful, his face showing that he was among his best friends, and who knew all about it, untrammelled by the conventions of civil functions—he was 'At Home.' An extensive toast list was commenced with the 'The King' by Captain Nye. 'Fallen Comrades,' by Capt. Nye, was drunk in a silence that brought to our mind our loved ones far away, and in fancy we saw their beloved faces and heard their familiar voices, 'Still with you, Boys, have a good time.' The toast of the evening 'Our Guest,' was then proposed by the president as follows: 'Gentlemen, it gives me great honour to propose this toast, but before asking you to drink it, I feel it only right to briefly refer to the deeds of our hero, which won him the high distinction. Most of us have been in stunts of some kind or other, while on service; many had taken place up till 4 July, 1918. On that date the Australians were engaged on a very serious stunt, making a dash across country; in the vicinity of Hamel, shortly after the battle of Villers Bretonneux, where the Australians distinguished themselves, and which I consider was the crisis of the war. Their advance was seriously delayed by the fire of a machine gun which was holding up a big section of the line. Fired by a determination to carry on, Driver Dalziel ran forward alone to the machine gun, which was manned by six Germans. Armed with his revolver, he rapidly disposed of five of the enemy; the sixth proved a tougher proposition and seriously wounded Dalziel, causing him to drop his revolver in a hand-to-hand encounter. His opponent was disposed of by his remaining weapon, the service dagger. Though wounded in the hand, Driver Dalziel was still eager to keep things going, so arming himself he went further forward and met a party of 13 Germans, who promptly surrendered. Hurrying them back to the line, he took possession of the machine gun and used it to good advantage again on the enemy, who had now concentrated their fire on the section in an endeavour to stop the advance. Twice during the day Driver Dalziel made his way through the fire-swept section to secure ammunition, though again wounded, and in his own words, had got on really well with his gun. It was only on returning to the line, still with the captured gun, that he realized the wound he had received in his head had earned him a " Blighty." Such were the deeds that had brought him the highest honour that a soldier can win, and to say that I am proud to stand here and have the privilege to ask you to drink his health but feebly expresses my thoughts. Gentlemen, " Our Guest, our hero, our cobber." The room rang with applause, hearty and deep, the gallant guest, covered with confusion at the recital which he would wish forgotten. As the long applause died away it was redoubled when the V.C. rose, each Digger seeming to experience a delight on making a bigger noise than his companion, to express his delight on seeing their comrade rise to the occasion. A few words, short, manly and sincere, the tone, more than the words, full of feeling, expressing his thanks, was the signal for a further storm of delight. Frederica de Browning, then being in a reminiscent mood, related to the company happenings in his own career, refreshing his memory from 'His Diary.' The item was much appreciated. The next toast, 'Our Allies,' was very ably dealt with by Sergt. D. G. Brown, who showed that he had studied the subject closely. Specially he called attention to the whole-hearted assistance of France. The Frenchman loved his country, and cannot conceive any man not being willing to die for it. May the same spirit be fostered in our boys. May the years and teachings of those who would belittle this spirit be cast into oblivion, for without it no people can become a nation. Dr. J. I. M. Jamieson (Herberton), responded in a matter of great characteristic manner, paying special attention to the sufferings of Service. He confessed to having a down on the Belgians because they used to take the handles off the pumps. As one looked at the humorous twinkle in Dr. Jim's eye as he said this, it conjured up visions of a very different Dr. Jim in Belgium, looking for a wash. The toast was drunk with musical honours. Mr. J. Agnew then roused the boys with a song 'Boys of the Dardenelles,' so much so that the Captain insisted on the chorus again and everybody 'gave it a hiding.' Gunner Watson then proposed the 'The Navy,' and as he pictured the busy handy man, always in a job on his tub, failing at nothing, one realized he had given a great deal of thought to the subject. His picture of the North Sea, ice, sleet, fog and through it all the tireless watchdogs of our Navy going back and forth, first we shivered then we got hot with enthusiasm for the ones who had never failed—The Navy. Private Wallace responded, endorsing all Gunner Watson's remarks, and looking into the future, hoped for the day to come when Australia's Navy, with the glorious traditions of the Mother Navy as a mark, would endeavour to emulate it in the manner of a daughter worthy of such a mother. Gunner Bardon proposed 'The Army,' and opened with the remarks: 'The Army, I don't know why I should be asked to propose the toast of " The Army," with all you blokes here. However, here goes. I've got nothing to say against the army, and I've got a lot to say for it; it kept me for three years, fed and clothed me, and I could say a lot more if only I could just remember. I could say a bit against it also, but not in here amongst you boys. I'd prefer to say it outside. Anyhow, I've got a real good man coming up on the " second wave " and he'll tell you all about it.' (Loud and much applause.) Vice-chairman Driver Hyde responded. His remarks dealing with the vast organization that had grown so rapidly, showing a knowledge of detail, though arising from his personal experience, and which made him forget the petty incidents which were very real and big at the time, but at which they all now laughed. His speech was that of the matured thinker who recognized that success was the one thing that counted, everything else was secondary. 'All Patriotic Workers,' was proposed by Sergt. G. Bott, whose remarks proved that the earnest endeavours of those at home for the welfare of the boys had been keenly appreciated. He felt that he would never be able to express his thanks to the kind hearts of those who had worked and for the spirit that had prompted them. Gunner West responded, and related personal experiences. He specially signalled out the work done by the Salvation Army.

It had been his experience that no matter where the trouble was, no matter how deep the mud, the good old Salvation Army were there—always something clean and hot, and if you couldn't pay, ' Never mind, Digger, wire in.' He felt that he must in addition to responding propose a special toast : ' The Salvation Army.' The toast was drunk with musical honours, and ably responded to by Driver Hyde. Frederica de Browning then rendered that pathetic song : ' Me ! Me ! Me ! ', giving as an encore, ' The Green Eye of the Little Yellow God.' Calling the company to attention, the Captain here presented to the guest an illuminated testimonial, headed with the official despatch, commending the V.C., and the Soldiers of the Tableland, whose names were inscribed. The reading was as follows :

" ' From Returned Soldiers to
DRIVER HARRY DALZIEL, V.C.,
15th Battalion, Machine Gun Section,
4th Division, A.I.F.

" ' An enemy strong-point, manned by numerous guns, strongly resisted our advance of the Lewis Gun Section, to which Driver Dalziel was attached. He dashed, with his revolver, at one gun and captured and killed the crew of the gun. He was severely wounded in the hand, but carried on. He traversed open ground twice under heavy artillery and machine-gun fire to secure ammunition.—Official Despatch.'

" ' This Testimonial is presented by the Atherton Sub-Branch of the Returned Sailors' and Soldiers' Imperial League of Australia, as a mark of esteem and admiration for his gallant conduct in the Field of France, where he won the Highest Military Honour.

" ' We wish you a long life to wear the honour so gallantly won.
" ' Capt. (Dr.) NYE, President.
" ' Sergt. D. G. BROWN, Treasurer.
" ' Driver L. M. CLOUTIER, Secretary.
" ' And 60 names of Members of the Atherton Sub-Branch.'

" In addition to the address, a cheque from Mr. C. Harding for £25, also £10 from Mr. W. C. Abbott, were presented. Almost overcome by his feelings, Driver Dalziel suitably responded. Trooper Rossiter proposed ' The Atherton Tableland,' and expressed surprise that such a large number of Chinamen had been allowed to get hold of the land. Personally, he had never met a Chinaman yet that he was afraid of. His holding at Tolga had Chinamen around it, and he had never seen a Chinaman out before him, or after him, while working the block. He'd back a returned soldier against a Chinaman any day. ' I know a lot of people will say I'm mad, but that doesn't affect me in the slightest. I've been considered mad since the age of two years. Since then I've travelled over a lot of Australia, and my settling down at Atherton speaks for itself so far as I'm concerned. Anyhow, I've beaten the Chink, and so can you chaps. Everything about the Tableland is good ; it will do me, though I must confess that there is one matter in which I seem never to make any progress, that is the Tableland ladies, they seem to side-step me. I don't know why. However, I compliment them on their good looks, and trust that some kind friend will enlighten me as to why they look at me askance.' The speaker caused much amusement. Councillor G. E. Martin (Chairman, Tinaroo Shire Council), responded, welcoming all returned soldiers to the Tableland, and pointing out that his council had been instrumental in first calling attention to the suitability of the Tableland for ' Our Boys.' Councillor E. S. Williams (Chairman, Eacham Shire Council) supported, endorsing Councillor Martin's remarks. He referred to the splendid work done by our womenfolk in the battle against the hardships of conquering the dense jungle of fifteen years ago. He could see the day when the whole of the Tableland from Atherton to the coast range would be peopled by a really prosperous people, who would play a very important part in the affairs of our nation. ' The Ladies,' proposed by Private G. Currie, was very good, a solid little talk on our fairer sex, and breathing the spirit of appreciation and admiration of our helpmates in all the struggles of life. Corpl. M. de la Sollaye, in his very admirable manner, supported the toast, and gave some good advice to Trooper Rossiter, whom he was very much afraid lacked tact. You know, asking the mater to ' Beat it ' is not tact. (Loud applause.) Mr. J. Agnew rendered ' The Bandolero,' for the enjoyment of the company. Private Treloar proposed ' The Press,' and was seconded by Trooper Rossiter, who spoke in eulogistic terms of the Atherton press. Messrs. W. Morris, ' Barron Valley Advocate,' F. H. Browning ' Tableland Examiner,' and J. T. McMahon ' Cairns Post,' responded, and each offered to do a line of matrimonial advertisements for half-rates. The ' B.V.A.' offered it ' free,' as it considered Trooper Rossiter too good a man to lose. Secretary Driver Cloutier proposed ' The Chairman ' (Capt. Nye), and in a few manly words conveyed the feelings of his fellow members to the president. He was quite sure that while Capt. Nye remained at the head of affairs matters with the League would be ' Très bon.' (Musical honours.) The Diggers' War Cry was a roaring one :

" ' Shall we attacka da Ma Moselle ? No ! no ! '
" ' Shall we pincha da bottle a whisk ? Wee ! wee ! '
" ' What shall we do then ? Boota da Bolshevik, boota da Bolshevik, Chuck'er him out ! '

" The evening closed with ' God save the King,' and as one left the room, he realized that perhaps never again would it be his privilege to attend such a unique gathering, realizing that in that room had been seated men who had helped to save the Empire and Australia, and who were the nucleus of a nation and breed that would produce like for a glorious future. ' All honour to our Returned Diggers.' "

London Gazette, 28 Aug. 1918.—" Admiralty, S.W., 28 Aug. 1918. The King has been graciously pleased to approve of the award of the Victoria Cross to the undermentioned Officers, in recognition of their gallantry and devotion to duty."

DRUMMOND, GEOFFREY HENEAGE, Lieut.-Commander, joined the Royal Naval Volunteer Reserve and served in the European War. He was awarded the Victoria Cross for conspicuous gallantry during the second raid on Ostend [London Gazette, 28 Aug. 1918] : " Geoffrey Heneage Drummond, Lieut.-Commander, Royal Naval Volunteer Reserve. Volunteered for rescue work in command of M.L. 254. Following Vindictive to Ostend, when off the piers a shell burst on board, killing Lieut. Gordon Ross and Deckhand J. Thomas, wounding the coxswain, and also severely wounding Lieut. Drummond in three places. Notwithstanding his wounds, he remained on the bridge, navigated his vessel, which was already seriously damaged by shell fire, into Ostend harbour, placed her alongside Vindictive, and took off two officers and thirty-eight men, some of whom were killed and many wounded while embarking. When informed that there was no one alive left on board, he backed his vessel out clear of the piers before sinking exhausted from his wounds. When H.M.S. Warwick fell in with M.L. 254 off Ostend half an hour later the latter was in a sinking condition. It was due to the indomitable courage of this gallant officer that the majority of the crew of the Vindictive were rescued."

BOURKE, ROWLAND, Lieut., Royal Naval Volunteer Reserve, was born 28 Nov. 1885, in London, son of the late Isidore McWilliam Bourke, M.D., of Curraleagh, County Mayo, Ireland, retired Surgeon Major, 72nd Highlanders, and of his wife, Marianna (née Carozzi), of London, England. He lived in Canada from 1902, mining in Klondyke and fruit-growing in British Columbia. He joined the Royal Naval Volunteer Reserve as Sub-Lieutenant 7 Jan. 1916, and served in the European War, becoming Lieutenant 7 Jan. 1917. He was in command M.L. 276, stand-by M.L. for rescue of Blocksby's crews. Rescue M.L. 532 was very badly damaged. Succeeded in M.L. 276 in rescuing 38 officers and men from Brilliant, and then towing M.L. 532 to within five miles of Dunkirk, where she proceeded under her own power. For these services he was subsequently created a Companion of the Distinguished Service Order. On 23 Nov. 1918, he was made Chevalier, Legion of Honour.

Rowland Bourke.

He was promoted to Lieutenant-Commander 23 April, 1918. On the 9th and 10th of May he was in command of 276, again stand-by M.L. for rescue. After the rescue M.L. had rescued Vindictive's crew from Ostend they entered the harbour in case anyone had been overlooked, and after about ten minutes' search found Lieut. Sir John Alleyne and two seamen, whom they rescued. Lieut.-Commander R. Bourke was awarded the Victoria Cross [London Gazette, 28 Aug. 1918] : " Volunteered for rescue work in command of M.L. 276, and followed Vindictive into Ostend, engaging the enemy's machine guns on both piers with Lewis guns. After M.L. 254 had backed out, Lieut. Bourke laid his vessel alongside Vindictive to make further search. Finding no one, he withdrew, but hearing cries in the water he again entered the harbour, and after a prolonged search eventually found Lieut. Sir John Alleyne and two ratings, all badly wounded, in the water, clinging to an up-ended skiff, and rescued them. During all this time the motor launch was under a very heavy fire at close range, being hit in fifty-five places, once by a six-inch shell, two of her small crew being killed and others wounded. The vessel was seriously damaged and speed greatly reduced. Lieut. Bourke, however, managed to bring her out and carry on until he fell in with a monitor, which took him in tow. This episode displayed daring and skill of a very high order, and Lieut. Bourke's bravery and perseverance undoubtedly saved the lives of Lieut. Alleyne and two of the Vindictive's crew."

CRUTCHLEY, VICTOR ALEXANDER CHARLES, Lieut., served in the European War. He was awarded the Distinguished Service Cross, and was awarded the Victoria Cross [London Gazette, 28 Aug. 1918] : " Victor Alexander Charles Crutchley, D.S.C., Lieut. Royal Navy. This officer was in Brilliant in the unsuccessful attempt to block Ostend on the night of 22–23 April, and at once volunteered for further effort. He acted as First Lieutenant of Vindictive, and worked with untiring energy fitting out that ship for further service. On the night of 9–10 May, after his commanding officer had been killed and the second in command severely wounded, Lieut. Crutchley took command of the Vindictive and did his utmost by manœuvring the engines to place that ship in an effective position. He displayed great bravery both in the Vindictive and in M.L. 254, which rescued the crew after the charges had been blown out and the former vessel sunk between the piers of Ostend harbour, and did not himself leave the Vindictive until he had made a thorough search with an electric torch for survivors under a heavy fire. Lieut. Crutchley took command of M.L. 254, when the commanding officer sank exhausted with his wounds, the second in command having been killed. The vessel was full of wounded and very seriously damaged by shell fire, the fore part being flooded. With indomitable energy and by dint of baling with buckets and shifting weight aft, Lieut. Crutchley and the unwounded kept her afloat, but the leaks could not be kept under, and she was in a sinking condition, with her forecastle nearly awash, when picked up by H.M.S. Warwick. The bearing of this very gallant officer and fine seaman throughout these operations off the Belgian coast was altogether admirable and an inspiring example to all thrown in contact with him."

London Gazette, 14 Sept. 1918.—" Admiralty, 14 Sept. 1918. Honours for services in action with enemy submarines. The King has been graciously pleased to approve of the grant of the following Honours, Decorations and Medals to the undermentioned Officers and Men for services in action with enemy submarines. To receive the Victoria Cross."

AUTEN, HAROLD, D.S.C., Lieut., R.N.R., served in the European War. He was awarded the Distinguished Service Cross, and was awarded the Victoria Cross [London Gazette, 14 Sept. 1918]: " Harold Auten, D.S.C., Lieut., Royal Naval Reserve." This official statement, unlike the great majority of official statements of the award of the Victoria Cross, is unaccompanied by details. The reason for this was that Lieut. Auten was in command of a " hush " ship, and it was necessary to the existence of these vessels that their methods of warfare should be kept secret. When he was presented with his Victoria Cross in the Quadrangle of Buckingham Palace, the band played, " Hush, hush, hush! Here comes the Bogey Man," greatly to the amusement of the King and the spectators. Lieut.-Commander Harold Auten, V.C., R.N.R., describes his first ' Q ' Boat in his thrilling book, " ' Q ' Boat Adventures." He says that in the summer of 1915 he was on the staff of the Captain of the Devonport Dockyard, when he was told there was an appointment for him to a ship called the Zylpha, in which a lieutenant-commander named McLeod was to be captain. When he reached her, " she was a dirty old tramp of some 2,000 tons. . . . From end to end she was absolutely filthy, added to which she was no longer in her teens. . . . I returned to the barracks, where I met my captain. I asked him what on earth the ship was going to do. ' Well,' he said, ' it's a great secret. We're going to put some guns on board, disguise them, and put to sea after German submarines.' " Lieut.-Commander Auten describes the fitting out of the mystery ship, and " To me fell the task of purchasing civilian clothes for the whole of the crew. It must be remembered that the crew had to appear as if they belonged to a merchant ship, consequently nondescript clothing was essential. One evening I went ashore, and in a back street of Portsmouth made the acquaintance of a second-hand clothes dealer, a child of Abraham. We proceeded to bargain for two suits of plain clothes for each member of the crew, numbering about forty; one had to be fairly new and the other half worn. The old clothes dealer rubbed his hands with delight. Such orders did not come his way every day. Next day he came aboard and solemnly measured the men, as if he had been doing business in Savile Row. Later, there came aboard huge bundles that smelt most evilly, and the second lieutenant was sent to the paymaster for the sum of sixty pounds. It is never an easy task extracting money from a paymaster; but when you tell him it is for secondhand clothing you are liable to be convicted of fraud. Every paymaster in His Majesty's Navy knows that the Board of Admiralty does not deal in secondhand clothing. However, the second lieutenant managed to get the sixty pounds; but how he did it no one knew. He now wears the ribbon of the D.S.C.; probably he got it for that action. Then the bundles were opened, and the crew proceeded to get into their new garments. Never have I seen such a ruffianly crew in my life as they looked when they had changed their smart uniforms for the garments brought by Shylock. One tall stoker was rigged in a parson's coat and a bowler hat; there was nothing else to fit his manly form. He excited the admiration of his messmates; but, personally, I thought the bowler hat was rather an anachronism. However, he seemed satisfied. Perhaps I should mention that the parson's suit was supplied as part of the shore-going bundle. At last the Zylpha was ready for sea, and we left Portsmouth on the twelfth day after we had taken her over. Then began the training of the crew in their theatrical ' stunt.' The men threw themselves into the business with whole-hearted zest. The ' panic party ' was the prize item, and although there was much laughter and now and again a little horseplay, the men quickly grasped the idea and proved an astonishing success. One thing that probably helped was that we were all, officers and men, new to the game, consequently we could make allowances for each other. One of the things that struck me in particular was that some of the smartest men in uniform looked the most dishevelled and untidy objects in their civilian clothes. Never was there a stronger proof that clothes make the man than was shown by the crew of the Zylpha. When I regarded myself in the looking-glass for the first time after donning my ' Q ' boat clothes, I had to confess that I had fallen in my own estimation. I had hitherto thought that I was a much better-looking fellow." Of the adventures of the Zylpha and other ' Q ' boats one may read at length in " ' Q ' Boat Adventures."

Harold Auten.

London Gazette, 16 Sept. 1918.—" War Office, 16 Sept. 1918. The King has been graciously pleased to approve of the award of the Victoria Cross to the undermentioned Officer and Non-commissioned Officers."

BORELLA, ALBERT, Lieut., served in the European War, and was awarded the Military Medal. He was awarded the Victoria Cross [London Gazette, 16 Sept. 1918]: " Albert Borella, M.M., Lieut., 26th Battn. Australian Imperial Force. For most conspicuous bravery in attack. Whilst leading his platoon with the first wave, Lieut. Borella marked an enemy machine gun firing through our barrage. He ran out ahead of his men into the barrage, shot two German machine gunners with his revolver, and captured the gun. He then led his party, now reduced to ten men and two Lewis guns, against a very strongly-held trench, using his revolver and later a rifle, with great effect, causing many enemy casualties. His leading and splendid example resulted in the garrison being quickly shot or captured. Two large dug-outs were also bombed and thirty prisoners taken. Subsequently the enemy twice counter-attacked in strong force, on the second occasion outnumbering Lieut. Borella's platoon by ten to one, but his cool determination inspired his men to resist heroically, and the enemy were repulsed with very heavy loss."

MEIKLE, JOHN, Sergt., served in the European War, and was awarded the Military Medal. He was awarded the Victoria Cross [London Gazette, 16 Sept. 1918]: " John Meikle, M.M., No. 200854, Sergt., late 4th Battn. Seaforth Highlanders. (Nitshill). For most conspicuous bravery and initiative when his company, having been held up by machine-gun fire, he rushed single-handed a machine-gun nest. He emptied his revolver into the crews of the two guns, and put the remainder out of action with a heavy stick. Then, standing up, he waved his comrades on. Very shortly afterwards another hostile machine gun checked progress and threatened also the success of the company on the right. Most of his platoon having become casualties, Sergt. Meikle seized the rifle and bayonet of a fallen comrade, and again rushed forward against the gun crew, but was killed almost on the gun position. His bravery allowed two other men who followed him to put this gun out of action. This gallant non-commissioned officer's valour, devotion to duty and utter disregard for his personal safety was an inspiring example to all."

KAEBLE, JOSEPH, Corpl., served in the European War, and was awarded the Military Medal. He was posthumously awarded the Victoria Cross [London Gazette, 16 Sept. 1918]: " Joseph Kaeble, M.M., No. 889958, Corpl., late Quebec Regt. For most conspicuous bravery and extraordinary devotion to duty when in charge of a Lewis-gun section in the front-line trenches, on which a strong enemy raid was attempted. During an intense bombardment Corpl. Kaeble remained at the parapet with his Lewis gun shouldered ready for action, the field of fire being very short. As soon as the barrage lifted from the front line, about fifty of the enemy advanced towards his post. By this time the whole of his section except one had become casualties. Corpl. Kaeble jumped over the parapet, and holding his Lewis gun at the hip, emptied one magazine after another into the advancing enemy, and, although wounded several times by fragments of shells and bombs, he continued to fire, and entirely blocked the enemy by his determined stand. Finally, firing all the time, he fell backwards into the trench, mortally wounded. While lying on his back in the trench he fired his last cartridges over the parapet at the retreating Germans, and before losing consciousness shouted to the wounded about him: ' Keep it up, boys; do not let them get through! We must stop them!' The complete repulse of the enemy attack at this point was due to the remarkable personal bravery and self-sacrifice of this gallant non-commissioned officer, who died of his wounds shortly afterwards."

TAIT, JAMES EDWARD, Lieut., served in the European War, and was awarded the Military Cross. He was posthumously awarded the Victoria Cross [London Gazette, 27 Sept. 1918]: " James Edward Tait, M.C., Lieut., late 78th Battn. Manitoba Regt. For most conspicuous bravery and initiative in attack. The advance having been checked by intense machine-gun fire, Lieut. Tait rallied his company and led it forward with consummate skill and dash under a hail of bullets. A concealed machine gun, however, continued to cause many casualties. Taking a rifle and bayonet, Lieut. Tait dashed forward alone and killed the enemy gunner. Inspired by his example, his men rushed the position, capturing twelve machine guns and twenty prisoners. His valorous action cleared the way for his battalion to advance. Later, when the enemy counter-attacked our positions under intense artillery bombardment, this gallant officer displayed outstanding courage and leadership, and, though mortally wounded by a shell, continued to direct and aid his men until his death." Lieut. J. E. Tait was the author of an article entitled " The Vimy Ridge," descriptive of the beginning of the battle, which appeared in " Canada," of 28 July, 1917, from which the following extracts are taken: " We spent the day in preparation for the battle. We were in support lines, and all night long the enemy ' crumps ' had whined overhead, searching, groping for our batteries, and we had lain and listened with a smile in our hearts, for to-night was Y.Z. night, and to-morrow at dawn would begin what might possibly be the world's biggest battle, and at last we would get to grips with the enemy—that mysterious enemy whom we never saw, yet who daily took toll of our bravest and best. The Canadians were to take the ridge—that great, black, sinister-looking mass from which the grass, if it had ever grown there, had long since disappeared, battered and riven by shell fire until it looked as though every yard of it had come under the plough; the whole ridge was a morass of mud and water-filled shell and crater holes. Vimy Ridge! Magic name! For two years a black, forbidding sentinel of the Powers of Darkness, to-morrow a bulwark of civilization. Vimy Ridge, of tragic memory, sepulchre of thousands of the bravest sons of France and England, was to be taken to-morrow. Thoughts of home! Surely it were no sign of weakness to think of home at this time. Canoes, guns, trails, the camp on the river, the smell of wood smoke at twilight, the sunset on the lake. Oh! sweet memories: the bitter cold, the snow-clad trail, the yelp of the Husky, the howl of the Indian dog, how far away it all seemed, that old world which we left so long ago, and how different to that in which we live now: a world of mud and many-coloured star-shells, of continual thunder and lightning, a world of endless days and restless nights; of

James Edward Tait.

' runyars ' and ' crumps,' a world of death and devastation, and unspeakable misery and desolation. Superfluous kit was packed for return to the transport lines, iron rations were made up, ammunition and bombs distributed, and at dusk we moved off in sections at 25 yards' interval, a battalion of English troops preceding us silently down the communication trench towards the front line. It was quite dark when we reached the valley, and Fritz was shelling it heavily. He had an unpleasant way of finding the communication trenches. Arrangements had been made to cross overland. Guides had been placed at certain points, and a white tape laid across the valley for our guidance. We stumbled across in the dark, falling into shell-holes and over boulders, the big, ominous-looking ridge ahead of us, occasionally thrown into faint relief by the enemy starshells on the other side of the crest, and eventually the tape led us to the mouth of the tunnel, where the battalion was to be accommodated for the night. At 4.30 a.m. the command was passed down to file out by sections. It could be heard coming along while it was still far down the tunnel : ' Move out by sections ; pass it along.' We filed out from the quiet of the tunnel into the darkness and turmoil of the world above, and moved silently into the assembly trenches. A cold wind was blowing and it was still quite dark. We could just see the shadowy forms of the battalion in front of us, who were to take the enemy first and second line trenches. Our artillery was pounding Fritz's lines, while he was sending over one or two ; he was evidently unaware of the mighty storm which was gathering around him, or the forces which were silently mustering only a short distance away. It was now 5 a.m., and in half an hour we would be ' over the top.' At 5.15 a.m. a whisper comes down the trench, ' Fix bayonets ; pass it along.' Bayonets are silently fixed, and everything is ready. Five minutes ! Our artillery suddenly ceases, and a strange, uncanny silence seems to brood over the land, broken only by an occasional shell from the enemy's lines, who is still all unsuspecting of the terrible cataclysm so soon to envelop him. ' One minute more, boys.' It was the cheery voice of our Company Commander—alas ! among this glorious company of the unreturning brave. Another minute of strange, uncanny silence, then, just as the eastern sky began to lighten, with a soul-shattering crash every gun in the world opened fire on the German lines, and we climbed the parapet and moved across No Man's Land under a curtain of fire such as even this present war had not seen. We consolidated our newly-won positions in preparation for the counterattack, but it did not materialize. Fritz had no stomach for a fight, and contented himself with sniping and spraying our line with machine guns. About midday the weather improved, and the afternoon was fine. We were on the extreme end of the ridge, and the flat country to the north lay below us, with the red buildings of Givenchy and Lens gleaming in the sun. With the improvement in the weather conditions the rival aircraft got busy, and as a result Fritz shelled our new positions heavily. We spent the afternoon in consolidating, and by nightfall had made our positions fairly secure. One of the most impressive features of the day's operations was the old German front line when darkness had fallen. Here, where the Very lights were wont to hiss, and splutter and the machine guns spit suspiciously into the gloom of No Man's Land, everything was still, and silence reigned over the deserted ridge, save for the ghostly passage of the stretcher-bearers."

BRILLANT, JOHN, M.C., Lieut., served in the European War, and was awarded the Military Cross. He was awarded the Victoria Cross posthumously, for his services in France [London Gazette, 27 Sept. 1918] :

John Brillant.

" John Brillant, M.C., Lieut., 22nd Battn. Quebec Regt. For most conspicuous bravery and outstanding devotion to duty when in charge of a company which he led in attack during two days with absolute fearlessness and extraordinary ability and initiative, the extent of the advance being twelve miles. On the first day of operations, shortly after the attack began, his company's left flank was held up by an enemy machine gun. Lieut. Brillant rushed and captured the machine gun, personally killing two of the enemy crew. While doing this he was wounded, but refused to leave his command. Later on the same day his company was held up by heavy machine-gun fire. He reconnoitred the ground personally, organized a party of two platoons, and rushed straight for the machine-gun nest. Here 150 enemy and fifteen machine guns were captured, Lieut. Brillant personally killing five of the enemy, and being wounded a second time. He had this wound dressed immediately, and again refused to leave his company. Subsequently this gallant officer detected a field gun firing on his men over open sights. He immediately organized and led a ' rushing ' party towards the gun. After progressing about 600 yards he was again seriously wounded. In spite of this third wound he continued to advance for some 200 yards more, when he fell unconscious from exhaustion and loss of blood. Lieut. Brillant's wonderful example throughout the day inspired his men with an enthusiasm and dash which largely contributed towards the success of the operations."

ZENGEL, RAPHAEL LOUIS, Sergt., served in the European War, and was awarded the Military Medal. For his services in France he was posthumously awarded the Victoria Cross [London Gazette, 27 Sept. 1918] : " Raphael Louis Zengel, No. 424252, Sergt., Saskatchewan Regt., Canadian Expeditionary Force. For most conspicuous bravery and devotion to duty when protecting the battalion right flank. He was leading his platoon gallantly forward to the attack, but had not gone far when he realized that a gap had occurred on his flank, and that an enemy machine gun was firing at close range into the advancing line. Grasping the situation, he rushed forward some 200 yards ahead of the platoon, tackled the machine-gunemplacement, killed the officer and operator of the gun, and dispersed the crew. By his boldness and prompt action he undoubtedly saved the lives of many of his comrades. Later, when the battalion was held up by very heavy machine-gun fire, he displayed much tactical skill and directed his fire with destructive results. Shortly afterwards he was rendered unconscious for a few minutes by an enemy shell, but on recovering consciousness he at once continued to direct harassing fire on the enemy. Sergt. Zengel's work throughout the attack was excellent, and his utter disregard for personal safety, and the confidence he inspired in all ranks, greatly assisted in bringing the attack to a successful end."

Raphael Louis Zengel.

GOOD, HERMAN JAMES, Corpl., was born on 29 Nov. 1887, at Bathhurst, N.B., son of Walter Good, South Bathurst, Gloucester County, N.B. He was educated at Big River School, Gloucester County, and joined the Army on 29 June, 1915, as Private, No. 445120, and served in the European War in the 55th, 2nd Pioneer and 13th Battns. He was awarded the Victoria Cross [London Gazette, 27 Sept. 1918] : " No. 445120, Herman James Good, Corpl., 13th Battn. Quebec Regt. For most conspicuous bravery and leading when in attack his company was held up by heavy fire from three machine guns, which were seriously delaying the advance. Realizing the gravity of the situation, this N.C.O. dashed forward alone, killing several of the garrison and capturing the remainder. Later on Corpl. Good, while alone, encountered a battery of 5.9-inch guns, which were in action at the time. Collecting three men of his section, he charged the battery under point-blank fire and captured the entire crews of three guns." A newspaper correspondent writes : " Among the returning men on the Olympic was L.-Sergt. Herman Good, V.C., a native of Bathurst, N.B., who went overseas with the 55th New Brunswick Regt. L.-Sergt Good was met by his parents and Mayor Burns, of Bathurst, at Pier Two, and left yesterday afternoon for his home. He is a splendid type of young Canadian, standing a good six feet, and wearing the familiar bonnet of the Highland Brigade. Sergt. Good may agree with his name in all that exemplifies young Canada and soldiery in general, but it is doubtful if he is considered ' good ' by the gunners of the three machine guns of a small German garrison ; in fact, it is safe to assume that those Germans whose lives he spared and whom he took prisoners, considered him not good, but horrid. He was born in Bathurst not so many years ago, and has six brothers and eight sisters. In June, 1915, he enlisted, and went overseas in Oct. of the same year. He has been gassed, shell-shocked and wounded on three separate occasions, and wears on his coat three gold wound-stripes. Of his action that made him the winner of the Victoria Cross, he has very little to say, and it was necessary for ' The Daily Echo ' representative to obtain the official document, which notified him of the awarding of the highest honour the British Government can bestow, in order to get information. It was on 8 Aug. 1918, after three years of fighting, that he showed ' most conspicuous bravery,' his company being held up by heavy machine fire from three machine guns, which were seriously delaying the advance. Realizing the gravity of the situation, this N.C.O. dashed forward, killing several of the garrison and capturing the remainder.' Not content with this, L.-Sergt. Good, the report says, ' later alone encountered a battery of 5.9-inch guns which were in action at the time. Collecting three of his section, he charged the battery under point-blank fire and captured the crew and guns.' ' What did you think when you put those guns out of action ? ' the reporter asked. ' That somebody had to put them out,' said Sergt. Good, V.C., simply. The little purple-red ribbon with its small bronze cross is on the tunic of the young Canadian, and yesterday he had with him the Victoria Cross itself, which was presented to him on 29 March at Buckingham Palace by the King. He was the only Canadian at this celebration. His parents, in company with Mayor Burns, arrived in the city on Sunday to meet their son, and they are two very charming and proud old people. Mrs. Good told the reporter of the anxiety when the news came of her son having been gassed on the day following his gallant action. ' I can't say that Victoria Crosses meant a great deal just then,' she confided. ' You see we had lost another son in France a few months before that. ' It was an anxious time, too, when we heard about the riots at Rhyl and Kinmel Camps,' said Mr. Good. ' The papers said that a Victoria Cross man was killed, and we feared that it might be our boy. But this happened seventeen days before he arrived in England.' The party will arrive in Bathurst to-night, where a royal welcome awaits the V.C. man from his fellow-townsmen."

Herman James Good.

COPPINS, FREDERICK GEORGE, Corpl., was born in London. He joined the Canadian Military Forces and served in the European War. For his services in France he was awarded the Victoria Cross [London Gazette, 27 Sept. 1918] : " No. 1987, Frederick George

Coppins, Corpl., Manitoba Regt. For conspicuous bravery and devotion to duty when, during an attack his platoon came unexpectedly under fire of numerous machine guns. It was not possible to advance or retire, and no cover was available.

Frederick G. Coppins.

It became apparent that the platoon would be annihilated unless the enemy machine guns were silenced immediately. Corpl. Coppins, without hesitation and on his own initiative, called on four men to follow him, and leaped forward in the face of intense machine-gun fire. With his comrades he rushed straight for the machine guns. The four men with him were killed and Corpl. Coppins wounded. Despite his wounds, he reached the hostile machine guns alone, killed the operator of the first gun and three of the crew, and made prisoners of four others, who surrendered. Corpl. Coppins, by this act of outstanding valour, was the means of saving many lives of the men of his platoon, and enabled the advance to be continued. Despite his wound, this gallant N.C.O. continued with his platoon to the final objective, and only left the line when it had been made secure and when ordered to do so." During a collision between strikers and police in Winnipeg, Corpl. Coppins, who was a special constable, was dragged from his horse and kicked, being seriously injured.

BRERETON, ALEXANDER, Private (Acting Corpl.), was born at Alexander, Manitoba, on 13 Nov. 1892, son of C. P. Brereton, Esq., of McConnell, Manitoba; has three brothers and two sisters, one brother serving with Medical Corps; was educated at Hamiota, and joined the Army on 31 Jan. 1916. He served in the European War, and was awarded the Victoria Cross [London Gazette, 27 Sept. 1918]: "No. 830651, Alexander Brereton, Private (Acting Corpl.), 8th Battn. Manitoba Regt. For most conspicuous bravery during an attack, when a line of hostile machine guns opened fire suddenly on his platoon, which was in an exposed position and no cover available. This gallant N.C.O. at once appreciated the critical situation, and realized that unless something was done at once his platoon would be annihilated.

Alexander Brereton.

On his own initiative, without a moment's delay and alone, he sprang forward and reached one of the hostile machine-gun posts, where he shot the man operating the machine gun and bayoneted the next one who attempted to operate it, whereupon nine others surrendered to him. Corpl. Brereton's action was a splendid example of resource and bravery, and not only undoubtedly saved many of his comrades' lives, but also inspired his platoon to charge and capture the five remaining posts."

CROAK, JOHN BERNARD, Private, served in the European War, and for his services in France was posthumously awarded the Victoria Cross [London Gazette, 27 Sept. 1918]: "No. 445312, John Bernard Croak, Private, late 13th Battn. Quebec Regt. For most conspicuous bravery in attack when, having become separated from his section, he encountered a machine-gun nest, which he bombed and silenced, taking the gun and crew prisoners. Shortly afterwards he was severely wounded, but refused to desist. Having rejoined his platoon, a very strong point, containing several machine guns, was encountered. Private Croak, however, seeing an opportunity, dashed forward alone, and was almost immediately followed by the remainder of the platoon in a brilliant charge. He was the first to arrive at the trench line, into which he led his men, capturing three machine guns and bayoneting or capturing the entire garrison. The perseverance and valour of this gallant soldier, who was again severely wounded and died of his wounds, were an inspiring example to all."

STATTON, PERCY CLYDE, Sergt., joined the Army, serving in the European War; was awarded the Military Medal, and for his services in France was awarded the Victoria Cross [London Gazette, 27 Sept. 1918]: "Percy Clyde Statton, Sergt., M.M., No. 506, 40th Battn. Australian Expeditionary Force. For most conspicuous bravery and initiative in action when in command of a platoon which reached its objective, the remainder of the battalion being held up by heavy machine-gun fire. He skilfully engaged two machine-gun posts with Lewis-gun fire, enabling the remainder of his battalion to advance The advance of his battalion on his left had been brought to a standstill by heavy machine-gun fire, and the first of our assaulting detachments to reach the machine-gun posts were put out of action in taking the first gun. Armed only with a revolver, in broad daylight, Sergt. Statton at once rushed four enemy machine-gun posts in succession, disposing of two of them, and killing five of the enemy. The remaining two posts retired and were wiped out by Lewis-gun fire. Later in the evening, under heavy machine-gun fire, he went out again and brought in two badly-wounded men. Sergt. Statton set a magnificent example of quick decision, and the success of the attacking troops was largely due to his determined gallantry."

TRAVIS, RICHARD CHARLES, Sergt., served in the European War; was awarded the Distinguished Conduct Medal, the Military Medal, and was posthumously awarded the Victoria Cross for his services in France [London Gazette, 27 Sept. 1918]: "Richard Charles Travis, Sergt., No.

9/523, D.C.M., M.M., late Otago Regt., New Zealand Force. For most conspicuous bravery and devotion to duty. During surprise operations it was necessary to destroy an impassable wire block. Sergt. Travis, regardless of all personal danger, volunteered for this duty. Before zero hour, in broad daylight, and in close proximity to enemy posts, he crawled out and successfully destroyed the block with bombs, thus enabling the attacking parties to pass through. A few minutes later a bombing party on the right of the attack was held up by two enemy machine guns, and the success of the operation was in danger. Perceiving this, Sergt. Travis with great gallantry and utter disregard of danger, rushed the position, and killed the crew and captured the guns. An enemy officer and three men immediately rushed at him from a bend in the trench and attempted to retake the guns. These four he killed single-handed, thus allowing the bombing party, on which much depended, to advance. The success of the operation was almost entirely due to the heroic work of this gallant N.C.O., and to the vigour with which he made and used opportunities for inflicting casualties on the enemy. He was killed twenty-four hours later when, under a most intense bombardment prior to an enemy counter-attack, he was going from post to post encouraging the men."

London Gazette, 22 Oct. 1918.—"War Office, 22 Oct. 1918. His Majesty the King has been graciously pleased to approve of the award of the Victoria Cross to the undermentioned Non-commissioned Officers and Men."

HARRIS, THOMAS JAMES, Sergt., No. 358, served in the European War, and was awarded the Victoria Cross [London Gazette, 22 Oct. 1918]: "Thomas James Harris, Sergt., No. 358, M.M., late Royal West Kent Regt.) (Lower Halling, Kent). For most conspicuous bravery and devotion to duty in attack when the advance was much impeded by hostile machine guns concealed in crops and shell-holes. Sergt. Harris led his section against one of these, capturing it and killing seven of the enemy. Later, on two successive occasions, he attacked single-handed two enemy machine guns which were causing heavy casualties and holding up the advance. He captured the first gun and killed the crew, but was himself killed when attacking the second one. It was largely due to the great courage and initiative of this gallant N.C.O. that the advance of the battalion was continued without delay and undue casualties. Throughout the operations he showed a total disregard for his own personal safety, and set a magnificent example to all ranks."

FORSYTH, SAMUEL, Sergt., served in the European War, and for his services in France was awarded the Victoria Cross [London Gazette, 22 Oct. 1918]: "No. 4/400, Samuel Forsyth, Sergt., late New Zealand Engineers, attached 2nd Battn. Auckland Regt. For most conspicuous bravery and devotion to duty in attack. On nearing the objective, his company came under heavy machine-gun fire. Through Sergt. Forsyth's dashing leadership and total disregard of danger, three machine-gun positions were rushed, and the crews taken prisoner before they could inflict many casualties on our troops. During subsequent advance his company came under heavy fire from several machine guns, two of which he located by a daring reconnaissance. In his endeavour to gain support from a Tank, he was wounded, but after having the wound bandaged, he again got in touch with the Tank, which, in the face of very heavy fire from machine guns and anti-Tank guns, he endeavoured to lead with magnificent coolness to a favourable position. The Tank, however, was put out of action. Sergt. Forsyth then organized the Tank crew and several of his men into a section, and led them to a position where the machine guns could be out-flanked. Always under heavy fire, he directed them into positions which brought about a retirement of the enemy machine guns and enabled the advance to continue. This gallant N.C.O. was at that moment killed by a sniper. From the commencement of the attack until the time of his

Edward Benn Smith.

death Sergt. Forsyth's courage and coolness, combined with great power of initiative, proved an invaluable incentive to all who were with him, and he undoubtedly saved many casualties among his comrades."

SMITH, EDWARD BENN, L.-Sergt., was born on 10 Nov. 1898, at 1, North Quay, Maryport, son of Charles Henry Smith, Seaman, Royal Naval Reserve, and Martha Smith, daughter of John Benn, R.N.R. He comes of a family with a notable record for bravery on both sides of the house. His father fought in the Navy at the Dardanelles, while on his mother's side he can claim two generations of gallant lifeboatmen at Maryport, Cumberland. He was educated at the National School, Maryport. He joined the Army on 4 May, 1917, as a Private in the Lancashire Fusiliers, serving in the European War, in the 42nd Division in France. He was awarded the Distinguished Conduct Medal.

[Copy of Commanding Officer's Report.]

"On 10 Aug. 1918, south-east of Hébuterne, this N.C.O. led a daylight patrol. By skilful handling and use of cover he examined two points of the enemy line about which information was required. This information he obtained. When on the point of returning, Sergt. Smith noticed a party of forty of the enemy coming forward from their main line of resistance, obviously to take up night outpost dispositions. Sergt. Smith decided to wait for the enemy, and engage them, though outnumbered. He inflicted heavy casualties on the enemy, who at once scattered. His initiative and determination to inflict casualties on the enemy was a fine example.   (Signed) "A. SOLLY-FORD.
                "Major-General Commanding Division."

He was further honoured by being awarded the Victoria Cross, the announcement being made in the London Gazette, 22 Oct. 1918: "No. 51396, Edward Benn Smith, D.C.M., Corpl. (L.-Sergt.), Lancashire Fusiliers. For most conspicuous bravery, leadership and personal example during an attack and in subsequent operations. Sergt. Smith, while in command of a platoon, personally took a machine-gun post, rushing the garrison with his rifle and bayonet. The enemy, on seeing him advance, scattered, to throw hand grenades at him. Regardless of all danger, and almost without halting in his rush on the post, this N.C.O. shot and killed at least six of the enemy. Later, seeing another platoon requiring assistance, he led his men to them, took command of the situation, and captured the objective. During the enemy counter-attack on the following day he led a section forward and restored a portion of the line. His personal bravery, skill and initiative were outstanding, and his conduct throughout exemplified magnificent courage and skill, and was an inspiring example to all." He won the Decoration at the age of nineteen, and is said to be the youngest V.C. in the Service. He was given a magnificent civic welcome on his return home to his native town, Maryport, and complimentary speeches were made in the market-place, one speaker pointing out how Sergt. Smith gave point to the old saying, "Canny old Cummerlan' caps them aw still." The military authorities offered him a commission, but wished him to remain and make the Army his career, a course which at the time he did not feel disposed to adopt, though he later changed his mind. Certainly, judging from the description given of him by a local paper, he would be a great asset to the Army. It said: "Sergt. Smith is not only a V.C., but looks it. He is a British soldier every inch of him. He is an A1 man from the crown of his head to the soles of his feet. There is not a C3 part about him. He has not only won the V.C., but he has a chest on which to display it." He re-enlisted in the Cameron Highlanders 5 May, 1919. He received as presents a clock (long case, oak), silver tea set, £200 in War Bonds, gold watch and chain (albert), gold brooch, and pipe (meerschaum), all given to mother and father. Sergt. Smith is unmarried.

COLLEY, HAROLD JOHN, Private (Acting Sergt.), was born on 26 May, 1894, at Winson Street, Dudley Road, Birmingham, son of John Colley and Mrs. John Colley. He was educated at Dudley Road Council School, and joined the Army on 1 Sept. 1914, as Private in the Duke of Cornwall's Light Infantry. Shortly after, being a cyclist, he was made a despatch rider. He served in the European War in France. He went to France in the early part of 1915 as despatch rider, and was in all the great events up to the time of his death on 30 March, 1917, at Cambrai, when rescuing his mate who was buried by a shell. He was also wounded, and recommended three times up to that period; then sent to England for a few weeks, and then sent back; joined 10th Lancashire Fusiliers. In the first engagement after he went back was awarded Special Certificate of Merit for rescuing two men under H.M. trench-mortar bomb. He was awarded the Victoria Cross [London Gazette, 22 Oct. 1918]: "Harold John Colley, M.M., Private Acting Sergt.), late 10th Battn. Lancashire Fusiliers. On 25 Aug., in front of Martinpuich, shortly after its capture, a very strong counter-attack was delivered by the enemy. Sergt. Colley's company was holding an advanced position, with two platoons in advance and two in support. The forward platoons were ordered to hold on at all costs. This N.C.O. rushed forward without orders to help the two forward platoons. He rallied the men, and threatened to shoot anyone who went back. The enemy were advancing quickly, and had already obtained a footing in this trench. Sergt. Colley then formed a defensive flank and held it. Out of the two platoons only three men remained unwounded, and he himself was dangerously wounded in the stomach. It was entirely due to Sergt. Colley's action that the enemy were prevented from breaking through, and were eventually driven off. His courage and tenacity saved a very critical situation." He was up till then L.-Corpl. Colley; won the M.M. on 4 June, 1918, and was made full Sergeant on the battle-field, for holding an outpost after the sergeant had been wounded, with four comrades; he captured it, killing five Germans, capturing eight, and driving the remainder off.

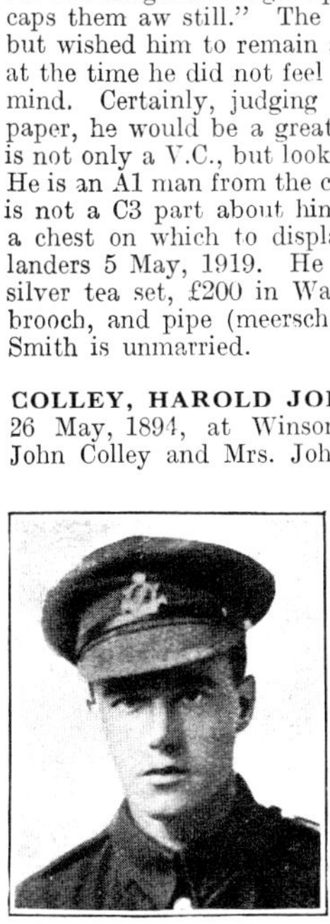

Harold John Colley.

RICHARDSON, JAMES, Private, was born on 25 Nov. 1897, at Bellshill, Lanarkshire, Scotland, son of David Richardson, Chief of Police, Chilliwack, B.C., and of Mary Prosser Richardson. He was educated at John Street Public School, Bridgeton, Glasgow, and joined the Canadian Military Forces in Aug. 1914, at Vancouver, B.C., serving in the European War in France and Belgium. He was awarded the Victoria Cross [London Gazette, 22 Oct. 1918]: "James Richardson, No. 28930, Private (Piper), late Manitoba, Regt., Canadian Expeditionary Force. For most conspicuous bravery and devotion to duty when, prior to attack, he obtained permission from his commanding officer to play his company 'over the top.' As the company approached the objective, it was held up by very strong wire, and came under intense fire, which caused heavy casualties and demoralized the formation for the moment. Realizing the situation, Piper Richardson strode up and down outside the wire playing his pipes with the greatest coolness. The effect was instantaneous. Inspired by his splendid example, the company rushed the wire with such fury and determination that the obstacle was overcome and the position captured. Later, after participating in bombing operations, he was detailed to take back a wounded comrade and prisoners. After proceeding about two hundred yards, Piper Richardson remembered that he had left his pipes behind. Although strongly urged not to do so, he insisted on returning to recover his pipes. He has never been seen since, and death has been presumed accordingly, owing to lapse of time." The following appreciation of Piper Richardson is by Carolyn Cornell in "The Tribune Junior," Winnipeg, 11 Jan. 1919: "How the skirl of the pipes led the Canadian Scottish to victory in the awful Battle of the Somme, Oct. 1916, has only recently been fully told when the Victoria Cross was granted posthumously to Piper James Richardson, who performed this heroic act. It was between 8 Oct. and 9 Oct. 1916, that the action took place in which Piper Richardson led the attack over the top and with the wild music of the hills of Scotland fired his followers to show the world what a Scotsman can do. The attack was victorious. Canada was honoured, but the young piper has gone. Only his spirit remains to the country which strives to do him honour—a memory which thrills every Canadian boy and makes him proud of this land of mountains and plains and of the motherland across the sea, of brave and valorous men, whose history is full of such deeds as the one performed by Piper James Richardson, of the Canadian Scottish, in the valley of the Somme. Piper Richardson was the son of Chief of Police and Mrs. D. Richardson, of Chilliwack, B.C. He was born at Bellshill, Lanarkshire, Scotland. While residing in Rutherglen, Scotland, he was a member of the corps of Boy Scouts. The Richardson family came to Canada about five years ago. James enlisted at the age of seventeen years in the 72nd Seaforth Highlanders, at Vancouver, in Aug. 1914, and went to France with the first contingent. He was attached to the 16th Canadian Scottish, and was through all the big engagements with the Canadians during the first two years of the war, including the memorable stand made at St. Julien in April, 1915, which placed Canada's name in the histories of the world for ever. Previous to enlisting, James Richardson was working in Vancouver, where he was well known for his piping. He competed in the piping contests at the Caledonian sports in Vancouver, North Vancouver and Victoria, and won valuable prizes. His father is in possession of three gold medals which he won in contests. David Richardson, a brother of the V.C., is also in the Navy. That young Richardson was not lacking in daring and physical courage before he went overseas is shown in an incident which happened in Vancouver, where he was working, in the year 1914. The factory where he was employed is situated near False Creek, Vancouver. One day, while he was working, the alarm was given that a boy was drowned in the creek. James Richardson at once ran to the spot, dived under the water and brought up the body, but life was extinct. It is now more than two years since Piper Richardson 'played his men over the top' in his last gallant attack, and Lieut.-Colonel C. W. Peck, then Major Peck, recommended him for the V.C. at that time. Through some technicality the award was not gazetted, however, until last fall. With three other pipers Richardson played the men over at the beginning of the Battle of the Somme, and continued to play as the troops advanced in a murderous fire. He came back safely, but suddenly remembered that he had left behind his beloved pipes. He had been helping to carry in wounded. He went back for the pipes and has never been seen since. Lieut.-Colonel Peck, now Officer Commanding the 16th Battn., who recommended the Decoration for the heroic young piper, has since then been given the V.C. himself. An officer of the battalion, telling the story of Piper Richardson's deed, said: 'Volunteers were asked for, one from each of the four companies. The first four who came were taken. It was the first time any piper had gone out with the Canadian Scottish, or, perhaps, with any Canadian battalions. It was a wonderful thing to hear these men playing away at their pipes while the attacking party were cutting the wire, and it had a wonderful effect on them. The skirl of the pipes continued until the men got through. Then the pipers went forward with the men. Richardson was seen walking strongly towards the German trench, playing his pipes.' We are fortunate in having several letters of the brave young piper, which speak volumes themselves of his high spirits, his cheeriness, his good-humour and bravery. He had many narrow escapes. The fact that one of the most hair-raising escapes only came out by chance leads one to believe that he probably had them every day, but did not mention them. In the very first engagement in which he took part, the taking of the little wood near St. Julien, in April, 1915, he performed a feat of daring worthy of decoration itself. Through his nerve the battalion was able to secure 's position. He did not mention this event for more than a year, and then only on the request of his father, who had had an imperfect account of it from a returned soldier. In writing to his father, in June, 1916, Piper Richardson said of this experience: 'I would like very much to know the name of the man who related my experience to you. There were only three men in the battalion to my knowledge who knew of my experience, and only one man saw me actually go through it. It is now over a year since this incident happened during the Germans' second attempt to take Ypres, and it seems funny to start to relate the story so long after, but I suppose I will have to do so. Well, you will remember we made a charge at St. Julien on the 22nd April, 1915, and took a wood from the Germans. After we had carried the wood some of us kept going on Fritz's heels, and after advancing about thirty yards on the other side of the woods, the party, about fifty men, started to dig in, but I kept going on my own, although the thing was ridiculous. Well, I may tell you I didn't get very far ahead, about forty yards, before I landed at a farmhouse, and, sure enough, the Fritzies were all clustered round it sheltering from the flying bullets. When I saw what I was up

James Richardson.

against I didn't know what to do, but, believe me, my brain worked like lightning. As it was dark save for the moonlight, I " flopped " to see if I was spotted, and I really thought that while I was lying there they would hear my heart beating. Lying motionless, I saw an officer (judging by his voice and actions) coming towards me and waving his arms, as if letting his men know to follow on. My brain told me that I had two alternatives, namely, to shoot the nearest man I saw (which was the officer) and make a dash for my pals, or give myself up as a prisoner. I risked the former and aimed as quick and true as I could at my man, who rolled over like a log. Then you talk about running—there isn't a man who could have covered the ground quicker than I did, and nobody could be more thankful than I was when I found myself amongst my own kith and kin. I told the sergeant-major that the farmhouse in front was full of Germans, and that they would have to be cleared out if we intended to hold our portion through the next day. Well, as the farmhouse was an ideal sniping post for the Huns, the matter was reported to the artillery, which, needless to say, put the farmhouse out of business.' That the young piper had a keen sense of humour is shown in many little stories that he related. Especially in letters to his mother does he tell these stories. In the following one he concludes with the promise that he will not frequent the more dangerous route any more. The letter was dated May, 1916. He says : ' Well, I had a nice little spin on the bicycle down to brigade headquarters with a message. By the way, I have got a bicycle here for my own use, that is, for carrying messages, etc., and it is certainly a very handy asset when moving from one billet to another. On two occasions last week I got messages to take up to the firing line, and, without thinking, I started off on the bike and delivered the goods. On both occa- sions I was told that I did the trip very quickly, and, of course, I just said that I hit the high spots only, when doing daylight trips up there. Well, there was nothing more said until a couple of days after, when I was detailed as guide for an officer going to the trenches. The officer asked me how far we had to go by my route, so I said about three miles each way, and this fairly tickled the officer, as he was told he would have six miles to walk each way. Well, we got about half-way and turned into my road, as I call it, and the officer looked at me as much as to say, " Are you sure of the road ? " He stopped, and we went into a shell-hole by the side of the road, where he took out a plan of the country which he studied care- fully. After a pause he informed me the road we were on was exposed the whole way to the Germans, and therefore we couldn't proceed further. Well, when we got on to the main road we started off through woods, across fields, over ditches, etc., and at last, after about six miles' walk, we got to the trenches. Leaving the officer there, I thought I would risk the road, once more at the double, ' knees up.' Well, I got back safely, but, believe me, the road seemed very long with my new information, and I had a great yarn to tell my pals. They said, " I bet Jimmy won't take that road again," and I don't intend to, either. You would have laughed at this little incident if you had been here. While we were busy unloading the wagons a stray bullet came over and " strafed " a chap right through the hips, whereupon he shouted, " I've got a blighty." He just lay down where he was and laughed like to burst his sides, passing remarks that he would soon be having a good time in Scotland, while we were still " carrying on " out here.' In a letter to his brother and sister, after telling about pushing up the line, he says : ' I was at a town yesterday on pass, where we were billeted over a year ago, and I went to a house there which I used to go to, and the family knew me right away. The old lady has a fine daughter there whom I get on well with. I was asking her if she would come to Canada with me (Ha ! ha !), but she said her fiancé was at the war, so that finished me. I am with my old company, but I am sorry to say very few old faces. Of course I am with them with the pipes when in billets only, then when we move back to the line I go back on the ration job, and only see the trenches once a week. Father asks me about the cooking job. Well, I think I told you that I got fed up with it, and as it is optional duty, I quit. I had to cook for eighteen men and had no help, so it was no soft job. You must remember that one hasn't things fixed up out here to make such a job easy. It is a case of getting bricks together for a fireplace, chasing after water, which is sometimes hard to find, and then nothing but grousing if you put salt instead of sugar in the tea (some good reason for a grouse, eh ?). You would have laughed here one morning at such an incident. The morning was very cold, and here was " Your Humble " sitting on a box, frying bacon, while the water boiled for tea. There was a wind blowing, and, of course, the dixie was taking extra long to boil, so the men started to gather round the fire as a hint for me to hurry up the grub. Well, the pot at last came to the boil, and I put in the tea, taking the dixie off. I then asked one of them to " sling " me over the sugar, with the result that he passed me the salt, and I, like a silly clown, dumped the salt in before noticing the mistake. The language that followed made another dixie of water boil right away. I have not com- posed a tune yet. The old ones are sufficient for me yet. We are going to strafe Fritz some of these fine days, and I sure mean to let him hear the " Braes o' Mar " if I get the chance. I can assure you if I get the pipes going Fritz will get it on his neck. This mob of ours takes no prisoners. Fritz can be big and fat if he likes, but he hasn't the nerve ; therefore I would rather face him in a charge than be a Hun and have to face this mob. Well, I think I'll stop bletherin' in the meantime, so, So long——' Major Gavin H. Davies, of the 16th Canadian Scottish, when he heard of the con- ferring of the Victoria Cross for the brave deed of Piper Richardson, wrote the young hero's father as follows : ' It was with the greatest pleasure in the world that I saw this photo, and read the good news about your " Bonny Boy " had at last been awarded the greatest medal of all. He was a delightful chap, and in my company from when we left Vancouver. Never tired, however long the march was, and always ready with a willing hand to do anything and give the boys a tune, and always anxious to lead his company " over the top." He was a great loss to the battalion, and I am sure greater to you. I had always hoped that he would receive the V.C.

I was in the fight when " Jimmy " went back for his pipes, but never returned. You have my deep sympathy in his loss and best of congratula- tions on the great award.' John Stephen, of Hamilton, Ontario, composed the following lines on Piper Richardson's heroic deed, which were printed in a Toronto paper with an account of his award and his death :

" ' Over the top and awa', awa'.
Come, Piper, gie us a blaw, a blaw.'
The piper played as he forward strode,
A merry old tune for a rough old road.

" He played the lads through the mud and fire.
When the men were held by the ugly wire,
He played and strutted up and down
As if on parade in his old home town.

" The day was won and the men were proud.
' Where is the piper ? ' called the crowd ;
The wounded he tended back to light,
But he has gone into the night.

" The pipes are lost and the piper's gone,
The men are forlorn without his song ;
But forever floats his brave old tune
Where seas are murmuring to the moon.

" Where the crowds are jostling in the street,
Where brave men march with rhythmic beat ;
At set of sun you can hear his note
Like a far song from a wee bird's throat.

" Tune up your pipes for the way is long ;
Tune up ! for we cannot spare your song.
Over the top and awa', awa'.
Tune up for a blaw, a blaw."

A newspaper lately gave the words of " Blue Bonnets over the Border," and of Piper Richardson's favourite, " Braes o' Mar," both of which Piper Laidlaw played at the time he won his Victoria Cross :

" BLUE BONNETS OVER THE BORDER

" March, march, Ettrick and Teviotdale,
Why, my lads, dinna ye march forward in order ?
March, march, Eskdale and Liddesdale,
All the Blue Bonnets are over the Border.

" Many a banner spread, flutters above your head,
Many a crest that is famous in story,
Mount and make ready then, sons of the mountain glen,
Fight for your Queen and the old Scottish glory."

When wounded Laidlaw changed to " The Standard on the Braes o' Mar " :

" The Standard on the Braes o' Mar
Is up and streaming rarely,
The gathering pipes on Lochnagar
Are sounding long and clearly.

" The Highland men frae hill and glen,
Wi' belted plaids and glittering blades,
Wi' bonnets blue and hearts so true,
Are coming late and early."

London Gazette, 23 Oct. 1918.—" War Office, 23 Oct. 1918. His Majesty the King has been graciously pleased to approve of the award of the Victoria Cross to the undermentioned Non-commissioned Officer."

HUNTER, DAVID FERGUSON, Corpl., served in the European War, and was awarded the Victoria Cross [London Gazette, 23 Oct. 1918] : " David Ferguson Hunter, Corpl., 1/5th Battn. Highland Light Infantry. For most conspicuous bravery, deter- mination and devotion to duty. When the battalion to which he belonged relieved another unit in the front line, Corpl. Hunter was detailed to take on an advanced post which was established in shell holes close to the enemy. Relief was carried out in darkness, and there was no oppor- tunity for reconnoitring the adjacent ground. On the following afternoon the enemy drove back the posts on Corpl. Hunter's flanks, and established posts in close proximity to and around him, thus completely isolating his command. Despite the fact that he was exceedingly short of rations and of water, this gallant N.C.O. determined to hold on to his post to the last. On the evening of the second day he endeavoured to communicate with

David F. Hunter.

his company without result. Nevertheless, he maintained his position, and repelled frequent attacks until the evening of the third day, when a counter-attack relieved him. Without food and water he had held on to his post for over forty-eight hours. Not only did he withstand constant attacks, but he had also to undergo the barrage fire of the enemy and of our own attacks, which came right across his post. The outstanding bravery, coupled with the determination, fortitude and endurance, displayed by Corpl. Hunter is beyond all praise, and is a magnificent example to all."

London Gazette, 26 Oct. 1918.—" War Office, 26 Oct. 1918. The King has been graciously pleased to approve of the award of the Victoria Cross to the following Officer, Non-commissioned Officers and Man."

MACINTYRE, DAVID LOWE, Lieut., was born on 18 June, 1895, at Portnahaven, Islay, second son of the Rev. Archibald Stewart MacIntyre, of 25, Downie Terrace, Corstorphine Road, Edinburgh, United Free

David Lowe MacIntyre.

Church Minister, and his wife, Elizabeth daughter of the late David Lowe, Horticultural Builder, of Gilmore Park, Edinburgh. He was educated at George Watson's College, where he was in the Cadets, and Edinburgh University, where he joined the O.T.C. ; and was gazetted to the Argyll and Sutherland Highlanders on 6 May, 1915. He embarked for active service in Jan. 1916, and was attached to the 6th Battn. Highland Light Infantry. He served in the War in Egypt, Palestine and Syria from 16 Jan. 1916, to 2 April, 1918, and in France from 10 April, 1918, to 27 Sept. 1918, on which date he was wounded at Moeuvres, in France. Promoted from Second Lieutenant to Lieutenant 1 July, 1917. Adjutant of the Battn. (6th H.L.I.) June to Sept. 1918.

He was awarded the Victoria Cross [London Gazette, 26 Oct. 1918]: " David Lowe MacIntyre, Lieut., Argyll and Sutherland Highlanders. For most conspicuous bravery in attack when, acting as Adjutant of his battalion, he was constantly in evidence in the firing line, and by his coolness under most heavy shell and machine-gun fire inspired the confidence of all ranks. Three days later he was in command of the firing line during an attack, and showed throughout most courageous and skilful leading in face of heavy machine-gun fire. When barbed wire was encountered, he personally reconnoitred it before leading his men forward. On one occasion, when extra strong entanglements were reached, he organized and took forward a party of men, and under heavy machine-gun fire supervised the making of gaps. Later, when the greater part of our line was definitely held up, Lieut. MacIntyre rallied a small party, pushed forward through the enemy barrage in pursuit of an enemy machine-gun detachment, and ran them to earth in a ' pill-box,' a short distance ahead, killing three and capturing an officer, ten other ranks, and five machine-guns. In this redoubt he and his party raided three ' pill-boxes ' and disposed of the occupants, thus enabling the battalion to capture the redoubt." When the battalion was ordered to take up a defensive position, Lieut. MacIntyre, after he had been relieved of command of the firing line, reconnoitred the right flank, which was exposed. When doing this an enemy machine gun opened fire close to him. Without any hesitation he rushed it single-handed, put the team to flight, and brought in the gun. On returning to the redoubt he continued to show splendid spirit while supervising consolidation. The success of the advance was largely due to Lieut. MacIntyre's fine leadership and initiative, and his gallantry and leading was an inspiring example to all." His two brothers are in the Scottish Horse and Black Watch respectively.

SPALL, ROBERT, Sergt., served in the European War, and for his services in France was awarded the Victoria Cross [London Gazette, 26 Oct. 1918]: " Robert Spall, Sergt., No. 475212, late Eastern Ontario Regt. (P.P.C.L.I.). For most conspicuous bravery and self-sacrifice when, during an enemy counter-attack, his platoon was isolated. Thereupon Sergt. Spall took a Lewis gun, and standing on the parapet, fired upon the advancing enemy, inflicting severe casualties. He then came down from the trench, directing the men into a sap seventy-five yards from the enemy. Picking up another Lewis gun, this gallant N.C.O. again climbed the parapet, and by his fire held up the enemy. It was while holding up the enemy at this point he was killed. Sergt. Spall deliberately gave his life in order to extricate his platoon from a most difficult situation, and it was owing to his bravery that the platoon was saved."

MINER, HARRY GARNET, Corpl., served in the European War, and was awarded the Victoria Cross for his services in France [London Gazette, 26 Oct. 1918]: " Harry Garnet Miner, No. 823828, Corpl., late 58th Battn.

Harry Garnet Miner.

2nd Central Ontario Regt. For most conspicuous bravery and devotion to duty in attack, when, despite severe wounds, he refused to withdraw. He rushed an enemy machine-gun post single-handed, killed the entire crew and turned the gun on the enemy. Later, with two others, he attacked another enemy machine-gun post, and succeeded in putting the gun out of action. Corpl. Miner then rushed single-handed an enemy bombing post, bayoneting two of the garrison and putting the remainder to flight. He was mortally wounded in the performance of this gallant deed." He was born at Chatham, Ontario, 24 June, 1890, son of John and Orpha Miner. He was educated at Highgate, Ontario, and joined the Army on 1 Dec. 1915. He sailed for overseas 25 Oct.

1916, with 161st Battn., and after six weeks' training in England was transferred to 58th Battn. in France, and served until his death. Private Miner was promoted to Lance-Corporal 1 Oct. 1916, and Corporal 1 Jan. 1918. The following is an extract from a letter :

" DEAR MR. AND MRS. MINER,
" Please accept the sincere sympathy of the 58th Canadian Infantry Battn. and myself upon the loss of your son, Corpl. H. Miner, late of our B Company, this unit. As you have no doubt heard, he has been awarded the Victoria Cross for valour in the field. Our battalion is more than proud of having had such a man as a non-commissioned officer in our unit, and no words can express the tremendous loss both you at home and his country have suffered. The Canadian Corps have covered themselves with honour during the past year with their successes, but these have only been made possible by the wonderful courage and deeds of such men as your son. I shall not repeat here the gallant deeds performed by him, as they are already known throughout the British Empire, but all ranks of the battalion join me in congratulating you upon the great distinction won by your son. Again I deeply sympathize with you on our great loss. He was an admirable soldier (never a braver one served), and was dutifully followed by all men under his command.
    " R. L. SMYTHE, Major,
    " Officer Commanding 58th Canadian
    " Infantry Battn."

Mr. and Mrs. Miner have received the following letters from officers of his unit. Lieut. W. W. Johnson writes : " Just a line to tell you a little about the work of your son Harry. During the last six months I have been his company commander and he was one of my best N.C.O.'s. He was awarded the French Croix de Guerre for very valuable wiring north of Lens last January. On the 8th Aug. the first day of the big advance for the Canadians, he went forward with the first wave in charge of half a platoon of men. Soon they came up against a nest of German machine guns and he went forward and captured them, and in doing so was mortally wounded. Everything possible was done for him, but the wounds were too severe and he passed away at the rear. No finer or more daring work has ever been done in the war than was accomplished by your son, and our only regret is that he was unable to recover from his wounds." Lieut. F. G. Dykes writes referring to Corpl.

Thomas Dinesen.

Miner : " Though he has since died, you can perhaps take consolation from the fact that he contributed very materially to our company's success in breaking through the enemy line, and ours was the leading company at what was admitted to be one of the most difficult points in the line then being attacked."

DINESEN, THOMAS, Private, served in the European War, and for his services in France was awarded the Victoria Cross [London Gazette, 26 Oct. 1918]: " Thomas Dinesen, No. 2075467, Private, 42nd Battn. Quebec Regt. For most conspicuous and continuous bravery displayed during ten hours of hand-to-hand fighting, which resulted in the capture of over a mile of strongly garrisoned and stubbornly defended enemy trenches. Five times in succession he rushed forward alone, and single-handed put hostile guns out of action, accounting for twelve of the enemy with bomb and bayonet. His sustained valour and resourcefulness inspired his comrades at a very critical stage of the action, and were an example to all." He became Lieutenant.

London Gazette, 30 Oct. 1918.—" War Office, 30 Oct. 1918. His Majesty the King has been graciously pleased to approve of the award of the Victoria Cross to the undermentioned Officers, Chief Petty Officer, Non-Commissioned Officers and Man."

WEST, RICHARD ANNESLEY, Lieut.-Colonel, was born 26 Sept. 1878, at 1, Oxford Street, Cheltenham, fourth son of the late Augustus George West, Esq., of White Park, County Fermanagh, formerly Lieutenant,

Richard Annesley West.

76th Hindoostan Regt., and of Sara, daughter of the Rev. Canon Richard Booth Eyre, M.A., Rector of Eyre Court, County Galway. He was educated at Channel View School, Clevedon, and at Monkton Combe School, Bath. He served in the South African War, 1900-1902, as a Trooper, 45th Irish Hunt Coy., Imperial Yeomanry, and later as Trooper, N.C.O. and Lieutenant in the 2nd Battn. Kitchener's Fighting Scouts, being promoted Lieutenant in that Corps in Nov. 1901. He was afterwards a Superintendent in the Transvaal Repatriation Department. In Jan. 1904, he was appointed Lieutenant and Assistant Adjutant of the Transvaal Horse Artillery Volunteers, serving with that regiment till 1912, when he went on to the Transvaal Reserve of Officers. For his services in the South African War he received the Queen's and King's Medals with clasps. On the outbreak of the European War he joined the North Irish Horse, Cavalry Special Reserve, and was gazetted Lieutenant 11 Aug. 1914, and Captain 18 Nov. 1915, prior to which latter date he had become attached to the North Somerset Yeomanry with the temporary rank of Major in July, 1915. He became an Acting Major in the Tank Corps 18 Jan. 1918, and Acting Lieutenant-Colonel in the same corps 22 Aug. 1918, being in command of the 6th Light Tank Battn. For his services with the North Somerset Yeomanry at Monchy-le-Preux in April, 1917, he was created a Companion of the Distinguished Service Order [London Gazette, 1 Jan. 1918]: "On 11 April, 1917, at Monchy-le-Preux, his squadron was sent forward to reinforce the right flank of the Brigade under very heavy shell and machine-gun fire. By his excellent example, rapid grasp of the situation and skilful disposition of his squadron, he did much to avert an impending German counter-attack. He had shown great ability in command of a squadron since July, 1915." He was awarded the Military Cross (Immediate Reward) [London Gazette of Nov. 1918]: "During the advance on 8 Aug. at Guillencourt, in command of a company of Light Tanks, he displayed magnificent leadership and personal bravery. He was able to point out many targets to his Tanks that they would not otherwise have seen. During the day he had two horses shot under him, while he and his orderly between them killed five of the enemy and took seven prisoners. On the 10th he rendered great services to the Cavalry by personally reconnoitring the ground in front of Le Quesnoy, and later in the day, under very heavy machine-gun fire, rallied and organized the crews of Tanks that had been ditched, withdrawing them after dark." He was awarded a Bar to the D.S.O. [London Gazette, 7 Nov. 1918]: "For conspicuous gallantry near Courcelles on 21 Aug. 1918. In consequence of this action being fought in a thick mist, this officer decided to accompany the attack to assist in maintaining direction and cohesion. This he did mounted, until his horse was shot under him, then on foot until the final objective was reached. During the advance, in addition to directing his Tanks, he rallied and led forward small bodies of Infantry lost in the mist, showing throughout a fine example of leadership and a total disregard of personal safety, and materially contributed to the success of the operations. Major West was in command of the battalion most of the time, his Commanding Officer having been killed early in the action. The consistent gallantry displayed by this officer throughout the operations since 8 Aug. has been remarkable." He was awarded the Victoria Cross [London Gazette, 30 Oct. 1918]: "Richard Annesley West, D.S.O., M.C., Capt. (Acting Lieut.-Colonel), late North Irish Horse (Cavalry Special Reserve) and Tank Corps. For most conspicuous bravery and leadership on 21 Aug. at Courcelles, and self-sacrifice 2 Sept. 1918. During an attack, the infantry having lost their bearings in the dense fog, this officer at once collected and reorganized any men he could find, and led them to their objective in face of heavy machine-gun fire. Throughout the whole action he displayed the most utter disregard of danger, and the capture of the objective was in a great part due to his initiative and gallantry. On a subsequent occasion it was intended that a battalion of Light Tanks, under the command of this officer, should exploit the initial Infantry and Heavy Tank attack. He therefore went forward in order to keep in touch with the progress of the battle, and arrived at the front line when the enemy were in process of delivering a local counter-attack. The Infantry Battalion had suffered heavy officer casualties, and its flanks were exposed. Realizing that there was a danger of this battalion giving way, he at once rode out in front of them under extremely heavy machine-gun and rifle fire and rallied the men. In spite of the fact that the enemy were close upon him, he took charge of the situation and detailed non-commissioned officers to replace officer casualties. He then rode up and down in front of them in face of certain death, encouraging the men and calling to them, 'Stick it, men; show them fight, and for God's sake put up a good fight.' He fell riddled by machine-gun bullets. The magnificent bravery of this very gallant officer at the critical moment inspired the infantry to redoubled efforts, and the hostile attack was defeated." Another and fuller account speaks of his "brilliant leadership" on the first, and his "amazing self-sacrifice" on the second occasion, which undoubtedly saved the situation. Lieut.-Colonel Richard Annesley West, V.C., D.S.O., M.C., was killed in action on 2 Sept. 1918, and was buried the same evening in the Abbey at Mory, four miles north of Bapaume. He married, on 16 July, 1909, at Pretoria, Transvaal, Maude Ethel, daughter of Henry Willian Cushing, of London, and a posthumous daughter, Gertrude Annesley, was born at Hove, Sussex, on Sunday, 17 Nov. 1918. He was mentioned in General Sir J. French's first Despatch of 7 Sept. 1914; in Sir Douglas Haig's Despatch of 7 Nov. 1917, and in Sir Douglas Haig's Despatch of 8 Nov. 1918, for gallant and distinguished service in the field.

SEWELL, CECIL HAROLD, Lieut., served in the European War, and was awarded the Victoria Cross [London Gazette, 30 Oct. 1918]: "Cecil Harold Sewell, Lieut., late Royal West Kent Regt (attached 3rd (Light) Battn. Tank Corps). When in command of a section of whippet light tanks in action this officer displayed most conspicuous bravery and initiative in getting out of his own tank and crossing open ground under heavy shell and machine-gun fire to rescue the crew of another whippet of his section which had side-slipped into a large shell hole, overturned, and taken fire. The door of the tank having become jammed against the side of the shell hole, Lieut. Sewell, by his own unaided efforts, dug away the entrance to the door and released the crew."

GABY, A. E., Lieut., was born at Scottsdale, Tasmania, and enlisted in the Australian Expeditionary Force as a Private in Western Australia on 6 Jan. 1916, being at that time 24 years old. He served in the European War, and for his services in France was awarded the Victoria Cross [London Gazette, 30 Oct. 1918]: "A. E. Gaby, Lieut., late 28th Battn. Australian Imperial Force. During the attack east of Villers Bretonneux, near Amiens, on the morning of 8 Aug. 1918, this officer led his company with great dash, being well in front. On reaching the wire in front of the enemy trench, strong opposition was encountered. The enemy were holding a strong point in force about 40 yards beyond the wire, and commanded the gap with four machine guns and rifles. The advance was at once checked. Lieut. Gaby found another gap in the wire, and entirely by himself approached the strong point, while machine guns and rifles were still being fired from it. Running along the parapet, still alone, and at point-blank range, he emptied his revolver into the garrison, drove the crews from their guns, and compelled the surrender of 50 of the enemy, with four machine guns. He then quickly reorganized his men and led them on to his final objective, which he captured and consolidated. On the morning of the 11th Aug. 1918, during an attack east of Framerville, near Amiens, Lieut. Gaby again led his company with great dash on to the objective. The enemy brought heavy rifle and machine-gun fire to bear upon the line, but in the face of this heavy fire Lieut. Gaby walked along his line of posts, encouraging his men to quickly consolidate the line. While engaged on this duty he was killed by an enemy sniper."

A. E. Gaby.

PROWSE, GEORGE, Chief Petty Officer, Royal Naval Volunteer Reserve, formerly worked as a Collier at the Mountain Colliery, Gorseinon, South Wales. He married a girl who was engaged at a West Wales War Factory. He joined the Royal Naval Volunteer Reserve, and served in the European War. He distinguished himself many times in action, and was recommended for the Distinguished Conduct Medal. He was twice wounded. He was awarded the Victoria Cross [London Gazette, 30 Oct. 1918]: "No. W2/424, George Prowse, Chief Petty Officer, Royal Naval Volunteer Reserve (Landore). For most conspicuous bravery and devotion to duty when, during an advance, a portion of his company became disorganized by heavy machine-gun fire from an enemy strong point. Collecting what men were available, he led them with great coolness and bravery against this strong point, capturing it, together with 28 prisoners and five machine guns. Later he took a patrol forward in face of much enemy opposition and established it on important high ground. On another occasion he displayed great heroism by attacking single-handed an ammunition limber which was trying to recover ammunition, killing three men who accompanied it and capturing the limber. Two days later he rendered valuable services when covering the advance of his company with a Lewis gun section, and located later on two machine-gun positions in a concrete emplacement, which were holding up the advance of the battalion on the right. With complete disregard of personal danger he rushed forward with a small party and attacked and captured these posts, killing six enemy and taking thirteen prisoners and two machine guns. He was the only survivor of this gallant party, but by this daring and heroic action he enabled the battalion on the right to push forward without further machine-gun fire from the village. Throughout the whole operations his magnificent example and leadership were an inspiration to all, and his courage was superb." He was killed in action. He was a good football player and was a member of the Gorseinon Football Club.

SIMPSON, WALTER, Corpl. (L.-Sergt.), served in the European War, and for his services in France was awarded the Victoria Cross [London Gazette, 30 Oct. 1918]: "Walter Simpson, No. 41788, Corpl. (L.-Sergt.), 6th Battn. Lincolnshire Regt. For most conspicuous bravery and initiative when with a daylight patrol sent out to reconnoitre and to gain touch with a neighbouring division. When on the west bank of a river an enemy machine-gun post was sighted on the east bank. The river being too deep to force, Sergt. Simpson volunteered to swim across, and, having done so, crept up alone in rear of the machine-gun post. He shot the sentry and also a second enemy who ran out; he then turned and caused four to surrender. A crossing over the river was subsequently found, and the officer and one man of his patrol joined him, and reconnaissance was continued along the river bank. After proceeding some distance machine-gun and rifle fire was opened on the patrol, and the officer was wounded. In spite of the fact that no cover was available, Sergt. Simpson succeeded in covering the withdrawal of the wounded officer under most dangerous and difficult conditions, and under heavy fire. The success of the patrol, which cleared up a machine-gun post on the flank of the attacking troops of a neighbouring division and obtained an identification, was greatly due to the very gallant conduct of Sergt. Simpson."

JUDSON, REGINALD STANLEY, Sergt., served in the European War, and was awarded the D.C.M., the M.M. and the Victoria Cross [London Gazette, 30 Oct. 1918]: "Reginald Stanley Judson, D.C.M., M.M., No. 24/1699, Sergt., 1st Battn. Auckland Regt., New Zealand Force. For most conspicuous bravery and devotion to duty when, in an attack on enemy positions, he led a small bombing party under heavy fire and captured an enemy machine gun. He then proceeded up the sap alone, bombing three machine-gun crews before him. Jumping out of the trench, he ran ahead of the enemy. Then, standing on the parapet, he ordered the party, consisting of two officers and ten men, to surrender. They instantly fired on him, but he threw a bomb and jumped amongst them, killed two and put the rest to flight, and so captured two machine guns. This prompt and gallant action not only saved many lives, but also enabled the advance to be continued unopposed."

NEEDHAM, SAMUEL, Private, Bedfordshire Regt., was born at Great Limber, North Lincolnshire, on 16 Aug. 1885, son of the late Septimus and Mary Needham. He was educated at Grimsby, and joined the Army at the outbreak of the European War, on 14 Dec. 1914, as a Private in the Army Service Corps. He served in the European War. He served for twenty months with the Army Service Corps, and was then transferred to the Bedfordshire Regt. He went out to Egypt in Jan. 1917. He was awarded the Victoria Cross [London Gazette, 28 Oct. 1918]:

"On the night of 10–11 Sept. 1918, near Kefr Kasim, Palestine, one of our strong patrols was attacked by enemy in considerable force, supported by heavy and field artillery, also machine-gun fire. At a critical moment, when the patrol had been overcome by superior numbers, forced back and thrown into confusion, Private Needham showed extraordinary bravery. A fresh body of enemy were coming on when he ran back, faced alone and fired rapidly at about 40 Turks at only 30 yards' range. His action checked the enemy, and just gave the patrol commander time to get together his men after the shaking they had in the first encounter. Even then, had he not been ordered back, it is thought Private Needham would have remained where he was and deliberately sacrificed his life to save his comrades.

Samuel Needham.

The patrol had twenty-five casualties out of a total of fifty, but successfully got back all their wounded, and it was only by the action of individuals, of which this one is the most outstanding of all, that the whole lot were not cut off by the enemy and either killed or made prisoners. Apart from what he actually effected in holding up the enemy single-handed, Private Needham's example was of greatest value at a critical moment, when men were somewhat shaken, owing to enemy swarming round them, and the fact of this man standing up to the enemy by himself did more than anything to instil confidence in the men, and undoubtedly saved a critical situation." He died at Palestine on 4 Nov. 1918, and is buried at Kantara Military Cemetery, about 27 miles from Port Said, on the east bank of the Suez Canal, Egypt.

London Gazette, 8 Nov. 1918.—" Air Ministry, 8 Nov. 1918. His Majesty the King has been graciously pleased to approve of the award of the Victoria Cross to Lieut. (Acting Capt.) F. M. F. West, M.C., R.A.F. (formerly of the Special Reserve, Royal Munster Fusiliers).

WEST, FERDINAND MAURICE FELIX, Lieut. (Acting Capt.), served in the European War, and was awarded the Military Cross [London Gazette, 26 July, 1918]. He was awarded the Victoria Cross [London Gazette, 8 Nov. 1918]: "Ferdinand Maurice Felix West, Lieut. (Acting Capt.), Royal Air Force (formerly of the Special Reserve, Royal Munster Fusiliers). Capt. West, while engaging hostile troops at a low altitude far over the enemy lines, was attacked by seven aircraft. Early in the engagement one of his legs was partially severed by an explosive bullet, and fell powerless into the controls, rendering the machine for the time unmanageable. Lifting his disabled leg, he regained control of the machine, and although wounded in the other leg, he, with surpassing bravery and devotion to duty, manœuvred his machine so skilfully that his observer was enabled to get several good bursts into the enemy machines, which drove them away. Capt. West then, with rare courage and determination, desperately wounded as he was, brought his machine over our lines and landed safely. Exhausted by his exertions, he fainted, but on regaining consciousness insisted on writing his report."

London Gazette, 15 Nov. 1918.—" War Office, 15 Nov. 1918. His Majesty the King has been graciously pleased to approve of the award of the Victoria Cross to the undermentioned Officers, Non-commissioned Officers and Men."

PECK, CYRUS WESLEY, Lieut.-Colonel. A newspaper cutting says: "A comfortably-built, middle-aged man, in 1914, living in British Columbia, where he represented Skeena in the Canadian Parliament, was Mr. Cyrus Wesley Peck. The day the war broke out he enlisted, and he has just received at the hands of the King the V.C. he won while in command of a Canadian Highland Battn. at Vimy Ridge. Not so bad for a comfortably-built, middle-aged man." He was created a Companion of the Distinguished Service Order. His Victoria Cross was gazetted 15 Nov. 1918 : "Cyrus Wesley Peck, D.S.O., Lieut.-Colonel, 16th Battn. Manitoba Regt. For most conspicuous bravery and skilful leading when in attack under intense fire. His command quickly captured the first objective, but progress to the further objective was held up by enemy machine-gun fire on his right flank. The situation being critical in the extreme, Colonel Peck pushed forward, and made a personal

Cyrus Wesley Peck.

reconnaissance under heavy machine-gun and sniping fire across a stretch of ground which was heavily swept by fire. Having reconnoitred the position, he returned, reorganized his battalion, and, acting upon the knowledge personally gained, pushed them forward and arranged to protect his flanks. He then went out under the most intense artillery and machine-gun fire, intercepted the Tanks, gave them the necessary directions, pointing out where they were to make for, and thus pave the way for a Canadian infantry battalion to push forward. To this battalion he subsequently gave requisite support. His magnificent display of courage and fine qualities of leadership enabled the advance to be continued, although always under heavy artillery and machine-gun fire, and contributed largely to the success of the brigade attack."

BEAK, DANIEL MARCUS WILLIAM, D.S.O., M.C., Temporary Commander, Royal Naval Volunteer Reserve, was born on 27 Jan. 1891, at Southampton, son of Mr. and Mrs. W. H. Beak, formerly of West End House, Donhead St. Mary, Wiltshire. He was educated at Taunton's School, Southampton, and joined the R.N.V.R. on 26 Jan. 1915. Joined the ranks, rose to be Petty Officer, and later gazetted, on 8 May, 1915, a Sub-Lieutenant in the Royal Naval Volunteer Reserve for duty with Royal Naval Division, serving in France in the European War. Also served in Gallipoli ; present at the evacuation. He was awarded the Military Cross [London Gazette, 26 Jan. 1917]. He was awarded a Bar to the Military Cross [London Gazette, 17 July, 1917 ; appeared in second supplement Wednesday, 18 July, 1917]. He was created a Companion of the Distinguished Service Order.

Daniel Marcus W. Beak

He was awarded the Victoria Cross [London Gazette, 15 Nov. 1918]: "Daniel Marcus William Beak, D.S.O., M.C., Temporary Commander, Drake Battn. Royal Naval Volunteer Reserve. For most conspicuous bravery, courageous leadership and devotion to duty during a prolonged period of operations. He led his men in attack, and, despite heavy machine-gun fire, four enemy positions were captured. His skilful and fearless leadership resulted in the complete success of this operation and enabled other battalions to reach their objectives. Four days later, though gazed by a shell fragment, in the absence of the brigade commander, he reorganized the whole brigade under extremely heavy gun fire and led his men with splendid courage to their objective. An attack having been held up, he rushed forward, accompanied by only one runner, and succeeded in breaking up a nest of machine guns, personally bringing back nine or ten prisoners. His fearless example instilled courage and confidence in his men, who then quickly resumed the advance under his leadership. On a subsequent occasion he displayed great courage and powers of leadership in attack, and his initiative, coupled with the confidence with which he inspired all ranks, not only enabled his own and a neighbouring unit to advance, but contributed very materially to the success of the Naval Division in these operations." Mentions : 1. Mentioned in Despatch of Sir Douglas Haig's, dated 7 April, 1918. 2. Mentioned in a subsequent Despatch of Sir Douglas Haig's [Papers of 21 Dec. 1918]. Promotions and Appointments : 1. Appointed Adjutant Drake Battn. 12 Dec. 1916. 2. Promoted from Sub-Lieutenant to Acting Commander to command Drake Battn. on 19 March, 1917. Reverted to Sub-Lieutenant on 3 April, 1917. 3. On same day, 3 April 1917, promoted to Temporary Lieut.-Commander as Second-in-Command of Drake Battn. 4. Promoted Temporary Commander to command Howe Battn. on 31 Dec. 1917. Remained with Howe Battn. until its disbandment in Feb. 1918. Then transferred to command temporarily the Anson Battn. On 12 March, 1918, transferred to command permanently the Drake Battn., and remained with them until demobilization of Royal Naval Division in June, 1919. The Freedom of the County Borough of Southampton was conferred upon him on 2 April, 1919.

RUTHERFORD, CHARLES SMITH, Lieut., was born in 1892, at Colborne, son of Mrs. Mabella Rutherford, of the Post Office, Colborne. He joined the Canadian Military Forces, 83rd Battn., March 1916, as Private, at Toronto, and served in the European War, and was awarded the Military Medal and the Military Cross, and was awarded the Victoria Cross [London Gazette, 15 Nov. 1918]: "Charles Smith Rutherford, M.C., M.M., Lieut., Quebec Regt., Canadian Imperial Forces. For most conspicuous bravery, initiative and devotion to duty. When in command of an assaulting party, Lieut. Rutherford found himself a considerable distance ahead of his men, and at the same moment observed a fully-armed strong enemy party outside a 'pill-box' ahead of him. He beckoned to them with his revolver to come to him ; in return, they waved to him to come to them. This he boldly did, and informed them that they were prisoners. This fact

Charles S. Rutherford.

an enemy officer disputed, and invited Lieut. Rutherford to enter the 'pill-box,' an invitation he discreetly declined. By masterly bluff, however, he persuaded the enemy that they were surrounded, and the whole party of forty-five, including two officers and three machine guns, surrendered to him. Subsequently he induced the enemy officer to stop the fire of an enemy machine gun close by, and Lieut. Rutherford took advantage of the opportunity to hasten the advance of his men to his support. Lieut. Rutherford then observed that the right assaulting party was held up by heavy machine-gun fire from another 'pill-box.' Indicating an objective to the remainder of his party, he attacked the 'pill-box' with a Lewis gun section, and captured a further thirty-five prisoners with machine guns, thus enabling the party to continue their advance. The bold and gallant action of this officer contributed very materially to the capture of the main objective, and was a wonderful inspiration to all ranks in pressing home the attack on a very strong position."

WHITE, WILLIAM ALLISON, Second Lieut., was born on 19 Oct. 1894, at Mitcham, Surrey, son of Samuel and Elizabeth White. He was educated at Salter's Hill School, West Norwood, S.E., and Barrow-in-Furness, Lancashire, Technical School, and joined the Army on 22 Feb. 1910, as a Private in 4th Battn. King's Own (Royal Lancaster) Regt. Discharged on termination of engagement (as a Machine-Gun Sergt.) 22 Feb. 1916. Joined the M.G.C. as a Staff Sergt.-Instructor at the Machine Gun School. He was commissioned 26 June, 1917; promoted Lieutenant 26 Dec. 1918. He served in the European War in 1917 and 1918 in France and Belgium, and was awarded the Victoria Cross [London Gazette, 15 Nov. 1918]: "William Allison White, Temporary Second Lieut., Machine Gun Corps. For most conspicuous bravery and initiative in attack. When the advance of the infantry was being delayed by an enemy machine gun, he rushed the gun position single-handed, shot the three gunners and captured the gun. Later, in similar circumstances, he attacked a gun accompanied by two men, but both of the latter were immediately shot down. He went on alone to the gun position, and bayoneted or shot the team of five men and captured the gun. On a third occasion, when the advance was held up by hostile fire from an enemy position, he collected a small party and rushed the position, inflicting heavy losses on the garrison. Subsequently, in consolidating the position by the skilful use of captured enemy and his own machine guns, he inflicted severe casualties on the enemy. His example of fearless and unhesitating devotion to duty under circumstances of great personal danger greatly inspired the neighbouring troops, and his action had a marked effect on the operations." Lieut. W. A. White, V.C., was decorated by the King at Buckingham Palace on 27 March, 1919.

CALVERT, LAURENCE, Sergt., was born 16 Feb. 1892, at Hunslet, Leeds, son of George Calvert (Tinsmith), deceased, and Beatrice Calvert, widow. He was educated at Rowland Road Board School and Cockburn High School, and joined the Territorials 17 April, 1914, serving in the European War. He was awarded the Military Medal for bravery during the attack at Vaulx, Vaulxcourt, on 2 Sept. 1918. Sergt. Calvert writes : "I like all outdoor sports, such as football, running, etc." Of his V.C. he says that it was awarded for the attack on Havrincourt, when "my company were held up by machine-gun fire at a place called Boggart's Hole. I attacked the guns single-handed, killed the crew of seven Germans and captured the guns ; was recommended for the V.C., and was lucky to get it ; was in action for four days after, during many counter-attacks, but my battalion refused to give ground, and held the village of Havrincourt all the time during heavy shell fire."

Laurence Calvert.

He was awarded the Victoria Cross [London Gazette, 15 Nov. 1918]: "Laurence Calvert, M.M., Sergt., No. 240194, 5th Battn. King's Own (Yorkshire Light Infantry) (Territorial Forces). For most conspicuous bravery and devotion to duty in attack when the success of the operation was rendered doubtful owing to severe enfilade machine-gun fire. Alone and single-handed, Sergt. Calvert, rushing forward against the machine-gun team, bayoneted three and shot four. His valour and determination in capturing single-handed two machine guns and killing the crews thereof enabled the ultimate objective to be won. His personal gallantry inspired all ranks." Sergt. Calvert was created Chevalier de l'Ordre de Léopold II. (Belgium) for his fighting record during the latter months of the war. The award appeared in Part II. Orders, dated 2 Feb. 1919

LAURENT, HARRY JOHN, Sergt., served in the European War, and for his services in France was awarded the Victoria Cross [London Gazette, 15 Nov. 1918]: "Harry John Laurent, No. 24/214, Sergt., New Zealand Rifle Brigade. For most conspicuous bravery, skill and enterprise when during an attack he was detailed to exploit an initial success and keep in touch with the enemy. With a party of twelve he located the enemy support line very strongly held, at once charged the position, followed by his men, and completely disorganized the enemy by his sudden onslaught. In the subsequent hand-to-hand fighting which ensued, he showed great resourcefulness in controlling and encouraging his men, and 30 of the enemy having been killed, the remainder surrendered, a total of one officer and 111 other ranks in all. The success of this daring venture, which caused his party four casualties only, was due to his gallantry and enterprise."

KNIGHT, ARTHUR GEORGE, Sergt., served in the European War, and for his services in France was awarded the Victoria Cross [London Gazette, 15 Nov. 1918]: "Arthur George Knight, No. 426402, Sergt., late 10th Battn. Canadian Infantry. For most conspicuous bravery, initiative and devotion to duty when, after an unsuccessful attack, Sergt. Knight led a bombing section forward, under very heavy fire of all descriptions, and engaged the enemy at close quarters. Seeing that his party continued to be held up, he dashed forward alone, bayoneting several of the enemy machine gunners and trench-mortar crews, and forcing the remainder to retire in confusion. He then brought forward a Lewis gun and directed his fire on the retreating enemy, inflicting

Arthur George Knight.

many casualties. In the subsequent advance of his platoon in pursuit, Sergt. Knight saw a party of about thirty of the enemy go into a deep tunnel which led off the trench. He again dashed forward alone, and, having killed one officer and two N.C.O.'s, captured twenty other ranks. Subsequently he routed, single-handed, another enemy party which was opposing the advance of his platoon. On each occasion he displayed the greatest valour under fire at very close range, and by his example of courage, gallantry and initiative was a wonderful inspiration to all. This very gallant N.C.O. was subsequently fatally wounded." A newspaper cutting says : "The late Sergt. Knight joined the 46th Battn. at Regina in Dec. 1914, and was with the 10th Battn. when he won the distinction. He was killed on 3 Sept. last. He was a carpenter by trade, and was born at Haywards Heath, Sussex, in 1886. He was awarded the Croix de Guerre in July of this year."

McNAMARA, JOHN, Corpl., served in the European War, and for gallantry in France was awarded the Victoria Cross [London Gazette, 15 Nov. 1918]: "John McNamara, No. 28939, Corpl., 9th Battn. East Surrey Regt. (Preston). For conspicuous bravery, initiative and devotion to duty. When operating a telephone in evacuated enemy trenches occupied by his battalion, Corpl. McNamara realized that a determined enemy counter-attack was gaining ground. Rushing to join the nearest post, he made the most effective use of a revolver taken from a wounded officer. Then seizing a Lewis gun, he continued to fire it till it jammed. By this time he was alone in the post. Having destroyed his telephone, he joined the nearest post, and again displayed great courage and initiative in maintaining Lewis-gun fire until reinforcements arrived. It was undoubtedly due to the magnificent courage and determination of Private McNamara that

John McNamara.

the other posts were enabled to hold on, and his fine example of devotion is worthy of the highest praise." The following is an extract from the "Daily Telegraph," 21 Nov. 1919 : "Kingston welcomed home yesterday the 9th East Surrey Regt., 'The Gallants,' who have been at the front since Aug. 1915, serving in France, Flanders and Germany. Earl Haig telegraphed his best wishes, adding his thanks to the regiment for all they did in the Great War. The battalion are at present stationed at Clipstone, but a representative party came to Kingston on Wednesday evening, and were quartered at the regimental depôt. Headed by the band of the 2nd Battn., the men yesterday marched into the town, amid the ringing of bells from the parish church and the cheers of crowds. Colonel Cameron, the commanding officer, was at the head of the troops, who were formed up on a platform in the market place, where they were greeted by the Mayor and Mayoress, and Colonel Brettell, who took the battalion to France in 1915. At the head of the battalion was the Colour party and officers, and on the left, in the leading ranks, the battalion's mascot, a little French boy, Vignolle Serge, aged thirteen years, who wore on his uniform the 1914–15 general service and Victory ribbons, and one red and three blue chevrons. The lad, whose home was within the war area of France, attached himself to the battalion, and refused to leave them. He was sent five times under escort to his home, but each time made his way back to the battalion, on one occasion getting back before the escort. The Mayoress attached a laurel wreath to the Colours, which were presented to the battalion by the King at Tournai. The whole parade stood at the salute. A speech of welcome was given by the Mayor, who stated that 'The Gallants' were the first to enter Lens and also Cambrai. Colonel Cameron replied on behalf of the regiment. During the proceedings the fine record of the regiment in the way of decorations was mentioned, including the winning of the Victoria Cross by Private McNamara, who subsequently laid down his life. Afterwards the troops were entertained at luncheon."

WEALE, HENRY, L.-Corpl., served in the European War in France, and was awarded the Victoria Cross [London Gazette, 15 Nov. 1918]: "Henry Weale, No. 5046, L.-Corpl., 14th Battn. Royal Welsh Fusiliers. For most conspicuous bravery and initiative in attack. The adjacent battalion having been held up by enemy machine guns, L.-Corpl. Weale was ordered to deal with the hostile posts. When his Lewis gun failed him, on his own initiative he rushed the nearest post and killed the crew, then went for the others, the crews of which fled on his approach, this gallant N.C.O. pursuing them. His very dashing deed cleared the way for the advance, inspired his comrades, and resulted in the capture of all the machine guns."

WILCOX, ALFRED, L.-Corpl., was born at Aston, near Birmingham, 16 Dec. 1884, son of William and Sarah Wilcox, both of Birmingham. He was educated at Burlington Street School, Aston, Birmingham. He writes : "I first joined as a volunteer in the 1st Royal Warwickshire Vol. Battn. After serving four years, my business took me to Liverpool, where I still served as a Territorial another three years, making in all seven years' pre-war service —retiring full Corporal." He joined the Royal Bucks Hussars on the 25th March, 1915, and later was dismounted and

Alfred Wilcox.

attached to the 2/4th Oxfordshire and Buckinghamshire Light Infantry, and went to the front in Dec. 1917. He received his first promotion in April, 1918 ; was Corporal Sept. 1918, and was awarded the Victoria Cross [London Gazette, 15 Nov. 1918]: " Alfred Wilcox, No. 285242, L.-Corpl., 2/4th Battn. Oxfordshire and Buckinghamshire Light Infantry. For most conspicuous bravery and initiative in attack when his company was held up by heavy and persistent machine-gun fire at close range. On his own initiative with four men he rushed forward to the nearest enemy gun, bombed it and killed the gunner. Being then attacked by an enemy bombing party, Corpl. Wilcox picked up enemy stick bombs, and led his company against the next gun, finally capturing and destroying it. Although left with only one man, he continued bombing and captured a third gun. He again bombed up the trench, captured a fourth gun, and then rejoined his platoon. Corpl. Wilcox displayed in this series of successful individual enterprises exceptional valour, judgment and initiative." Corpl. Wilcox wrote : " My battalion was ordered to take what was known as Junction Post—believed to be strongly held by machine guns. I was in charge of the leading section ; my duty was to cut through the wire and locate the posts. Having got to the wire and successfully cut it, I went back for my section, which I had left in a shell hole a hundred yards to the rear, only to find all but one wounded. That one I told to follow me. Getting through the gap I had already cut, and making my way in the trench the enemy was holding, I got into it, and, bombing my way, captured my first gun. Being quite safe from the enemy fire, I still proceeded up the trench, capturing a second gun after a hand-to-hand struggle, in which I bayoneted my man ; then bombing a third post, killing five. My own rifle by this time being clogged with mud, I had to resort to German stick bombs, which accounted for a fourth post with its gun. I carried on, driving the remainder of the post right away, leaving behind them about twelve dead in all and four guns (one light, three heavy). I then returned to the guns. Finding I could not remove the three latter, I put them out of action, and had to withdraw owing to lack of support and no fire-arms, my own gun having been dumped for the free use of German stick bombs." He received congratulations from Colonel Flanagan, who said : " Such acts are a credit to himself and all the battalion," and from the Divisional General and General Birdwood, Commanding the Fifth Army. He was wounded 2 Nov. 1918, and was discharged on 2 May, 1919. He married on 6 Sept. 1913, Ellen Louisa, daughter of Mr. Frederick and Mrs. Elizabeth Clarke, and they have a son, Leonard, born on 3 April, 1916, and a daughter, Doris, born 10 Sept. 1914. He is fond of sport, and is a cyclist (road racing). He also goes in for swimming, football, long-distance walking, and is still a member of the Birchfield Harriers.

The following is an extract from the " Daily Telegraph," Saturday, 8 May, 1920:

" There was a very happy reunion at the Cannon Street Hotel last night, when all ranks of the 2nd Regt. of the 1st Bucks Hussars met at a most successful smoking concert. Old friendships were renewed, old battles were fought over again, plans for future meetings were laid, and the whole very large company enjoyed itself immensely. The programme was as good as could be, and included songs from Messrs. W. C. Neal, J. L. Philip, E. J. Goode, C. J. Abbott, V. L. Kebble, and F. Lansley, humour from Messrs. H. J. Byron, W. L. Dunning, and Dan George, ventriloquial sketches from Mr. Claude Chandler, and pianoforte solos from Messrs. H. Miles and D. Dyer. Colonel the Hon. W. A. W. Lawson, D.S.O., was in the chair, and spoke of his delight in the glory they had won. One of the pleasantest features of the evening was the health of the regiment's V.C., L.-Corpl. Alfred Wilcox, proposed by Major Mackinnon, and that hero's reply. He modestly described his deed thus : ' I saw a lot of square-heads, as I call 'em, in front of me, and I was after 'em. If I hadn't been after 'em they'd have been after me, and I used more language than the British Army ever learnt.' He further regretted that, having received his training under Colonel Lawson, he was not able to win his V.C. under him."

SEAMAN, ERNEST, L.-Corpl., was born on 16 Aug. 1893, at 9, Derby Street, Heigham, Norwich, Norfolk, son of the late Henry Seaman and Mrs. Palmer, of The King's Inn, Bungay Road, Scole, Norfolk, daughter of William March, of Horsford, Norfolk. He was educated at the Council School, Scole, and joined the Army in Dec. 1915, as a Private in the Expeditionary Force Canteens. He served in the European War in France from the 24th Dec. 1915, till his death. He saw considerable service around the Ypres sector, where he was killed, and also around Passchendaele Ridge. He was promoted to L.-Corpl. about fourteen days before he was killed. He was awarded the Victoria Cross [London Gazette, 15 Nov. 1918]: " Ernest Seaman, L.-Corpl., No. 42364, late 2nd Battn. Royal Inniskilling Fusiliers. For most conspicuous bravery and devotion to duty. When the right flank of his company was held up by a nest of enemy machine guns, he, with great courage and

Ernest Seaman.

initiative, rushed forward under heavy fire with his Lewis gun, and engaged the position single-handed, capturing two machine guns and twelve prisoners, and killing one officer and two men. Later in the day he again rushed another enemy machine-gun post, capturing the gun under heavy fire. He was killed immediately after. His courage and dash were beyond all praise, and it was entirely due to the very gallant conduct of L.-Corpl. Seaman that his company was enabled to push forward to its objective and capture many prisoners." " He was one of the best soldiers whom

I had ever met, an excellent soldier in every sense of the word, and very keen in his duties. He always volunteered to help in any extra work that had to be done, no matter how dangerous and difficult, and for his constant devotion to duty and gallantry in voluntarily attending his wounded comrades under heavy fire, I recommended his being awarded the Military Medal.—V. E. S. Mattocks, Capt., Officer Commanding A Company."

METCALF, WILLIAM HENRY, M.M., L.-Corpl., was born at Waige, Walsh County, Maine, U.S.A., in Jan. 1885. He enlisted at Valcartier, and was wounded in Sept. 1918—on the occasion when he won the V.C. He is a Barber by trade. He served in the European War in France, and was awarded the Military Medal. He was awarded the Victoria Cross for gallantry in France [London Gazette, 15 Nov. 1918]: " William Henry Metcalf, No. 22614, L.-Corpl., 16th Battn. Canadian Infantry, Manitoba Regt. For most conspicuous bravery, initiative and devotion to duty in attack, when, the right flank of the battalion being held up, he realized the situation and rushed forward under intense machine-gun fire to a passing Tank on the left. With his signal flag he walked in front of the Tank, directing it along the trench in a perfect hail of bullets and bombs. The machine-gun strong points were overcome, very heavy casualties were inflicted on the enemy, and a very critical situation was relieved. Later, although wounded, he continued to advance until ordered to get into a shell hole and have his wounds dressed. His valour throughout was of the highest standard."

William Henry Metcalf.

McIVER, HUGH, Private, was born on 21 June, 1890, at Linwood, Kilbarchan, Renfrewshire, Scotland, son of Hugh McIver and of Mary McIver (née Flynn). He was educated at St. Charles' Roman Catholic Schools, Newton, Lanarkshire, Scotland. He joined the Army on 18 Aug. 1914, and served in the European War in France in the 2nd Royal Scots from 11 May, 1915, to 19 Oct. 1917, and from 12 Feb. 1918, to 2 Sept. 1918, and was killed in action 2 Sept. 1918. He was awarded the Military Medal [London Gazette, 19 Sept. 1916], and a Bar to the Military Medal [London Gazette, 21 Oct. 1918]. He was awarded the Victoria Cross [London Gazette, 15 Nov. 1918]: " Hugh McIver, No. 12311, Private, late 2nd Battn. The Royal Scots. For most conspicuous bravery and devotion to duty when employed as a company-runner east of Courcelles-le-Comte on 23 Aug. 1918. In spite of heavy artillery and machine-gun fire, he carried messages regardless of his own safety. Single-handed, he pursued an enemy scout into a machine-gun post, and having killed six of the garrison, captured twenty prisoners with two machine guns. This gallant action enabled the company to advance unchecked. Later, he succeeded at great personal risk in stopping the fire of a British tank which was directed in error against our own troops at close range. By this very gallant action Private McIver undoubtedly saved many lives." Mr. and Mrs. McIver, his father and mother, were received by the King at Buckingham Palace on 13 Feb. 1919, when the Victoria Cross was handed to them. He was also entitled to the Mons Star, 1914-15. Private McIver is buried at Vraucourt Copse British Cemetery, four and three-quarter miles north-east of Bapaume. He was not married.

Hugh McIver.

The following is a copy of a personal letter from the Officer Commanding the company to which deceased belonged :

" 2nd Battn. The Royal Scots,
" 8 Sept. 1918.

" My dear Mrs. McIver,

" I am writing these few lines to you to try to express, both on my own behalf and also for the men of my company, our greatest sympathy for you in the loss of your son Hugh in the recent fighting.

" It came as a great blow to me, as he was my personal orderly, and he was quite close to me when he was killed. We were going up a hill, attacking some machine guns, when he was killed by a bullet, and it may soften your blow a little to know he never felt it.

" It is only about ten days since I recommended him for the Victoria Cross, and it is quite likely that it will be awarded to you, and if ever a man deserved the V.C., Hugh did, as he was one of the best and bravest boys in the battalion ; in fact, the bravest I have ever known.

" I am sending on to you his Military Medal and rose, which I cut off his breast for you. His other personal effects will follow later.

" I can only say, Mrs. McIver, that your son died a hero's death, and he has left a record in the battalion second to none. Again expressing my deepest sympathy to you and yours,

" I am,
" Yours very sincerely,
(Signed) " Alick Gordon, Capt.,
" Officer Commanding, C Company,
" 2nd Battn. The Royal Scots."

HARVEY, JACK, Private, was born at 2, Curral Grove, Old Kent Road, Peckham, 24 Aug. 1891, son of W. Harvey, Yard Foreman. He was educated at Ruby Street School, Old Kent Road, Peckham, S.E.; joined the Army 26 Nov. 1914, at Bermondsey, as a Private in the 1/22nd Battn. London Regt. (The Queen's) (T.F.). He served in the European War on the Western Front, his period of active service extending over three and a half years. The following is a list of the engagements in which he was present: Loos, 30 Dec. 1915; the Hairpin, 30 Dec. 1915; raid near Bully Grenay, 9 July, 1916; High Wood, 15 Sept. 1916; Butte de Morlencourt, 7 Oct. 1916; Messines Ridge, 7 June, 1917; Bourlon Wood, 30 Nov. 1917; resistance to the German offensive, 21 March, 1918; Aveluy Wood, 30 March, 1918; Happy Valley, 30 March, 1918; Ardela Wood 30 Aug. 1918; Bouchevesnes (where he won the V.C.), 2 Sept. 1918; the march through Lille, 28 Oct. 1918; outpost line at Monstier, 10–11 Nov. 1918. He was awarded the Victoria Cross [London Gazette, 15 Nov. 1918]: "No. 631139, Jack Harvey, 1/22nd Battn. London Regt. (The Queen's). For most conspicuous gallantry and disregard of personal danger on the 2nd Sept. 1918, during the advance north of Péronne. The advance of his company was held up by intense machine-gun fire; this man at once dashed forward a distance of fifty yards alone through our barrage and in the face of heavy enemy fire, and rushed a machine-gun post, shooting two of the team and bayoneting another. He then destroyed the gun, and continued to work his way along the enemy trench, and going forward alone for about two hundred yards, single-handed rushed an enemy dug-out, which contained thirty-seven Germans, and compelled them to surrender. By these two acts of great gallantry he saved the company heavy casualties, and enabled the whole of the attacking line to advance. Throughout the entire operation he showed the most magnificent courage and determination, and by the splendid example he set to all ranks materially assisted in the success of the operation." This official account, which appeared in the Gazette, appeared originally in Battalion Orders, and concluded: "The Commanding Officer heartily congratulates the recipient on his well-deserved honour. The Army, Corps, Division and Brigade Commanders request that their congratulations be conveyed to Private Jack Harvey." General Sir H. Rawlinson wrote from the Headquarters of the Fourth Army: "I congratulate you on the gallantry and devotion to duty for which you have been awarded the Victoria Cross." He was discharged 10 Jan. 1919. Corpl. Jack Harvey's wife is Rose Harvey, and they have no children.

CRICHTON, JAMES, Private, served in the European War, and for his services in France was awarded the Victoria Cross [London Gazette, 15 Nov. 1918]: "James Crichton, No. 14/131, Private, 2nd Battn. Auckland Regt., New Zealand Force. For most conspicuous bravery and devotion to duty, when, although wounded in the foot, he continued with the advancing troops, despite difficult canal and river obstacles. When his platoon was subsequently forced back by a counter-attack he succeeded in carrying a message which involved swimming a river and crossing an area swept by machine-gun fire, subsequently rejoining his platoon. Later he undertook on his own initiative to save a bridge which had been mined, and though under close fire of machine guns and snipers, he succeeded in removing the charges, returning with the fuses and detonators. Though suffering from a painful wound, he displayed the highest degree of valour and devotion to duty."

London Gazette, 20 Nov. 1918.—"Admiralty, 20 Nov. 1918. With reference to the announcements of the award of the Victoria Cross to Naval Officers and Men for services in action with enemy submarines, the following are the accounts of the actions for which these awards were made:

"(1) Action of H.M.S. Q5 on the 17th Feb. 1917.

"On the 17th Feb. 1917, H.M.S. Q5, under the command of Commander Campbell, D.S.O., R.N., was struck by a torpedo abreast of No. 3 hold. Action stations were sounded and the 'panic party' abandoned ship. The engineer officer reported that the engine-room was flooding, and was ordered to remain at his post as long as possible, which he and his staff, several of whom were severely wounded, most gallantly did. The submarine was observed on the starboard quarter 200 yards distant, watching the proceedings through his periscope. He ran past the ship on the starboard side so closely that the whole hull was visible beneath the surface, finally emerging about 300 yards on the port bow. The enemy came down the port side of the ship, and fire was withheld until all guns could bear at point-blank range. The first shot beheaded the captain of the submarine as he was climbing out of the conning tower, and the submarine finally sank with conning tower open and crew pouring out. One officer and one man were rescued on the surface and taken prisoner, after which the boats were recalled and all hands proceeded to do their utmost to keep the ship afloat. A wireless signal for assistance had been sent out when (but not until) the fate of the submarine was assured, and a destroyer and sloop arrived a couple of hours later and took Q5 in tow. She was finally beached in safety the following evening. The action may be regarded as the supreme test of naval discipline. The chief engineer and engine-room watch remained at their posts to keep the dynamo working until driven out by the water, then remaining concealed on top of the cylinders. The guns' crews had to remain concealed in their gun houses for nearly half an hour, while the ship slowly sank lower in the water.

"(The award of the Victoria Cross to Commander Gordon Campbell, D.S.O., R.N., was announced in London Gazette No. 30029, dated the 21st April, 1917.)

"(2) Action of H.M.S. Prize on the 30th April, 1917.

"H.M.S. Prize, a topsail schooner of 200 tons, under command of Lieut. William Edward Sanders, R.N.R., sighted an enemy submarine on the 30th April, 1917. The enemy opened fire at three miles range and approached slowly astern. The 'panic party,' in charge of Skipper William Henry Brewer, R.N.R. (Trawler Section), immediately abandoned ship. Ship's head was put into the wind, and the guns' crews concealed themselves by lying face downwards on the deck. The enemy continued deliberately shelling the schooner, inflicting severe damage and wounding a number of men. For 20 minutes she continued to approach, firing as she came, but at length, apparently satisfied that no one remained on board, she drew out on the schooner's quarter 70 yards away. The White Ensign was immediately hoisted, the screens dropped, and all guns opened fire. A shell struck the foremost gun of the submarine, blowing it to atoms and annihilating the crew. Another shot demolished the conning tower, and at the same time a Lewis gun raked the survivors off the submarine's deck. She sank four minutes after the commencement of the action in clouds of smoke, the glare of an internal fire being visible through the rents in her hull. The captain of the submarine, a warrant officer and one man were picked up and brought on board the Prize, which was then herself sinking fast. Captors and prisoners, however, succeeded in plugging the shot holes and keeping the water under with the pumps. The Prize then set sail for the land, 120 miles distant. They were finally picked up two days later by a motor-launch and towed the remaining five miles into harbour.

"(The award of the Victoria Cross to Acting Lieut. William Edward Sanders, R.N.R., was announced in London Gazette No. 30147, dated the 22nd June, 1917.)

"(3) Action of H.M.S. Pargust on the 7th June, 1917.

"On the 7th June, 1917, while disguised as a British merchant vessel with a dummy gun mounted aft, H.M.S. Pargust was torpedoed at very close range. Her boiler-room, engine-room, and No. 5 hold were immediately flooded, and the starboard lifeboat was blown to pieces. The weather was misty at the time, fresh breeze and a choppy sea. The 'panic party,' under the command of Lieut. F. R. Hereford, D.S.C., R.N.R., abandoned ship, and as the last boat was shoving off, the periscope of the submarine was observed close before the port beam about 400 yards distant. The enemy then submerged, and periscope reappeared directly astern, passing to the starboard quarter, and then round to the port beam, when it turned again towards the ship, breaking surface about 50 yards away. The lifeboat, acting as a lure, commenced to pull round the stern; submarine followed closely, and Lieut. Hereford, with complete disregard of the danger incurred from fire of either ship or submarine (who had trained a maxim on the lifeboat), continued to decoy her to within 50 yards of the ship. The Pargust then opened fire with all guns, and the submarine, with oil squirting from her side and the crew pouring out of the conning tower, steamed slowly across the bows with a heavy list. The enemy crew held up their hands in token of surrender, whereupon fire immediately ceased. The submarine then began to move away at a gradually increasing speed, apparently endeavouring to escape in the mist. Fire was reopened until she sank, one man clinging to the bow as she went down. The boats, after a severe pull to windward, succeeded in saving one officer and one man. American destroyers and a British sloop arrived shortly afterwards, and the Pargust was towed back to port. As on the previous occasions, officers and men displayed the utmost courage and confidence in their captain, and the action serves as an example of what perfect discipline, when coupled with such confidence, can achieve.

"(The award of the Victoria Cross to Lieut. Ronald Neil Stuart, D.S.O., R.N.R., and Seaman William Williams, R.N.R., O.N., 6224A., was announced in London Gazette No. 30194, dated the 20th July, 1917.)

"(4) Action of H.M.S. Dunraven on the 8th Aug. 1917.

"On the 8th Aug. 1917, H.M.S. Dunraven, under the command of Capt. Gordon Campbell, V.C., D.S.O., R.N., sighted an enemy submarine on the horizon. In her rôle of armed British merchant ship, the Dunraven continued her zigzag course, whereupon the submarine closed, remaining submerged to within 5,000 yards, and then, rising to the surface, opened fire. The Dunraven returned the fire with her merchant-ship gun, at the same time reducing speed to enable the enemy to overtake her. Wireless signals were also sent out for the benefit of the submarine: 'Help! come quickly—submarine chasing and shelling me.' Finally, when the shells began falling close, the Dunraven stopped and abandoned ship by the 'panic party.' The ship was then being heavily shelled, and on fire aft. In the meantime the submarine closed to 400 yards distant, partly obscured from view by the dense clouds of smoke issuing from the Dunraven's stern. Despite the knowledge that the after magazine must inevitably explode if he waited, and, further, that a gun and gun's crew lay concealed over the magazine, Capt. Campbell decided to reserve his fire until the submarine had passed clear of the smoke. A moment later, however, a heavy explosion occurred aft, blowing the gun and gun's crew into the air, and accidentally starting the fire-gongs at the remaining gun positions; screens were immediately dropped, and the only gun that would bear opened fire, but the submarine, apparently frightened by the explosion, had already commenced to submerge. Realizing that a torpedo must inevitably follow, Capt. Campbell ordered the surgeon to remove all wounded and conceal them in cabins; hoses were also turned on the poop, which was a mass of flames. A signal was sent out warning men-of-war to divert all traffic below the horizon in order that nothing should interrupt the final phase of the action. Twenty minutes later a torpedo again struck the ship abaft the engine-room. An additional party of men were again sent away as a 'panic party,' and left the ship to outward appearances completely abandoned, with the White Ensign flying and guns unmasked. For the succeeding fifty minutes the submarine examined the ship through her periscope. During this period boxes of cordite and shells exploded every few minutes, and the fire on the poop still blazed furiously. Capt. Campbell and the handful of officers and men who remained on board lay hidden during this ordeal. The submarine then rose to the surface astern, where no guns could bear and shelled the ship closely for twenty minutes. The enemy then submerged and steamed past the ship 150 yards off, examining her through the periscope. Capt. Campbell decided then to fire one of his torpedoes, but missed by a few inches. The submarine crossed the bows and came slowly down the other side, whereupon a second torpedo was fired and missed again. The enemy observed it and immediately submerged. Urgent signals for assistance were immediately sent out, but pending arrival of assistance Capt. Campbell arranged for a third 'panic party' to jump overboard if necessary and leave one gun's crew on board for a final attempt to destroy the enemy, should he again attack. Almost immediately afterwards, however, British and American destroyers arrived on the scene, the wounded were transferred, boats were recalled and the fire extinguished. The Dunraven, although her stern was awash, was taken in tow, but the weather grew worse, and early the following morning she sank with colours flying.

"(The award of the Victoria Cross to Lieut. Charles George Bonner, D.S.C., R.N.R., and P.O. Ernest Pitcher, O.N. 227029 (Po.), was announced in London Gazette No. 30363, dated the 2nd Nov. 1917.)

"(5) Action of H.M. Armed Smack Nelson, on the 15th Aug. 1917.

"On the 15th Aug. 1917, the Smack Nelson was engaged in fishing when she was attacked by gunfire from an enemy submarine. The gear was let go and the submarine's fire was returned. The submarine's fourth shot went through the port bow just below the water line, and the seventh shell struck the skipper, Thomas Crisp, partially disembowelling him, and passed through the deck and out through the side of the ship. In spite of the terrible nature of his wound, Skipper Crisp retained consciousness, and his first thought was to send off a message that he was being attacked and giving his position. He continued to command his ship until the ammunition was almost exhausted and the smack was sinking. He refused to be moved into the small boat when the rest of the crew were obliged to abandon the vessel as she sank, his last request being that he might be thrown overboard.

"(The posthumous award of the Victoria Cross to Skipper Thomas Crisp, D.S.C., R.N.R., 10055 D.A., was announced in London Gazette No. 30363, dated the 2nd Nov. 1917.)

"(6) Action of H.M.S. Stock Force, on the 30th July, 1918.

"H.M.S. Stock Force, under the command of Lieut. Harold Auten, D.S.C., R.N.R., was torpedoed by an enemy submarine at 5 p.m. on the 30th July, 1918. The torpedo struck the ship abreast No. 1 hatch, entirely wrecking the fore part of the ship, including the bridge, and wounding three ratings. A tremendous shower of planks, unexploded shells, hatches and other debris followed the explosion, wounding the first lieutenant (Lieut. E. J. Grey, R.N.R.) and the navigating officer (Lieut. L. E. Workman, R.N.R.) and adding to the injuries of the foremost gun's crew and a number of other ratings. The ship settled down forward, flooding the foremost magazine and between decks to the depth of about three feet. 'Panic party,' in charge of Lieut. Workman, R.N.R., immediately abandoned ship, and the wounded were removed to the lower deck, where the surgeon (Surgeon Probationer G. E. Strahan, R.N.V.R.), working up to his waist in water, attended to their injuries. The captain, two guns' crews and the engine-room staff remained at their posts. The submarine then came to the surface ahead of the ship half a mile distant, and remained there a quarter of an hour, apparently watching the ship for any doubtful movement. The 'panic party' in the boat accordingly commenced to row back towards the ship in an endeavour to decoy the submarine within range of the hidden guns. The submarine followed, coming slowly down the port side of the Stock Force, about three hundred yards away. Lieut. Auten, however, withheld his fire until she was abeam, when both of his guns could bear. Fire was opened at 5.40 p.m.; the first shot carried away one of the periscopes, the second round hit the conning tower, blowing it away and throwing the occupant high into the air. The next round struck the submarine on the water-line, tearing her open and blowing out a number of the crew. The enemy then subsided several feet into the water and her bows rose. She thus presented a large and immobile target, into which the Stock Force poured shell after shell until the submarine sank by the stern, leaving a quantity of debris on the water. During the whole of the action one man (Officer's Steward, Second Class, R. J. Starling) remained pinned down under the foremost gun after the explosion of the torpedo, and remained there cheerfully and without complaint, although the ship was apparently sinking, until the end of the action. The Stock Force was a vessel of 360 tons, and despite the severity of the shock sustained by the officers and men wher she was torpedoed, and the fact that her bows were almost obliterated, she was kept afloat by the exertions of her ship's company until 9.25 p.m. She then sank with colours flying, and the officers and men were taken off by two torpedo boats and a trawler. The action was cited as one of the finest examples of coolness, discipline and good organization in the history of Q ships.

"(The award of the Victoria Cross to Lieut. Harold Auten, D.S.C., R.N.R., was announced in London Gazette No. 30900, dated the 14th Sept. 1918.)"

London Gazette, 27 Nov. 1918.—"War Office, 27 Nov. 1918. His Majesty the King has been graciously pleased to approve of the award of the Victoria Cross to the undermentioned Officers, Non-commissioned Officers and Men."

GORT, THE RIGHT HONOURABLE LIEUT.-COLONEL JOHN STANDISH SURTEES PRENDERGAST, Viscount, and Baron Kiltarton, was born in July, 1886, son of the fifth Viscount Gort and Eleanor, daughter of R. S. Surtees. His mother, the Dowager Lady Gort, married Colonel S. M. Benson in 1908. He was educated at Harrow School, and at the Royal Military College, Sandhurst, and entered the Army on 16 Aug. 1905, as a Second Lieutenant in the Grenadier Guards, becoming Lieutenant 1 April, 1907. He was married, in 1910, to Connie, daughter of George Medlicott Vereker, and they have a son, the Honourable Charles Standish Vereker, born on 23 Feb. 1912, and a daughter. He was A.D.C. to the G.O.C., London District, 3 Sept. 1913, to 4 Aug. 1914, and was promoted to Captain 5 Aug. 1914, serving in the European War. He was awarded the Military Cross [London Gazette, 23 June, 1915], and was created a Companion of the Distinguished Service Order, his name appearing in the Birthday Honours List on 4 June, 1917. He was awarded a Bar to the Distinguished Service Order for the following services [London Gazette, 25 Aug. 1917]: "Although hit in two places in the shoulder by the bursting of a shell early in the day, and in great pain, he refused to leave his battalion, and personally superintended the consolidation subsequent to a successful attack. He remained with them until 5 p.m. on the following day, when he was ordered to come out and have his wounds dressed. His conduct set a very fine example of self-sacrifice, and was of great value in maintaining the high morale and offensive spirit of his battalion." He was awarded the Victoria Cross [London Gazette, 27 Nov. 1918]: "Capt. and Brevet Major (Acting Lieut.-Colonel) John Standish Surtees Prendergast Vereker, Viscount Gort, D.S.O., M.V.O., M.C., 1st Battn. Grenadier Guards. For most conspicuous bravery, skilful leading and devotion to duty during the attack of the Guards Division on 27 Sept. 1918, across the Canal Du Nord, near Flesquieres, when in command of the 1st Battn. Grenadier Guards, the leading battalion of the 3rd Guards Brigade. Under heavy artillery and machine-gun fire he led his battalion with great skill and determination to the 'forming-up' ground, where very severe fire from artillery and machine guns was again encountered. Although wounded, he quickly grasped the situation, directed a platoon to proceed down a sunken road to make a flanking attack, and, under terrific fire, went across open ground to obtain the assistance of a Tank, which he personally led and directed to the best possible advantage. While thus fearlessly exposing himself, he was again severely wounded by a shell. Notwithstanding considerable loss of blood, after lying on a stretcher for awhile, he insisted on getting up and personally directing the further attack. By his magnificent example of devotion to duty and utter disregard of personal safety all ranks were inspired to exert themselves to the utmost, and the attack resulted in the capture of over 200 prisoners, two batteries of field guns and numerous machine guns. Lieut.-Colonel Viscount Gort then proceeded to organize the defence of the captured position until he collapsed; even then he refused to leave the field until he had seen the 'success signal' go up on the final objective. The successful advance of the battalion was mainly due to the valour, devotion and leadership of this very gallant officer." Viscount Gort was created a Member of the Victorian Order in 1910.

FRISBY, CYRIL HUBERT, Lieut. (Acting Capt.), was born on 17 Sept. 1885, at New Barnet, son of Henry and Zoë Pauline Frisby. He was educated at Haileybury College, and joined the Army on 26 Oct. 1916, as a Private in the Hampshire Regt., going to No. 5 Officer Cadet Battn. at Cambridge in Dec. of the same year. He was given a commission on 28 March, 1917, as a Second Lieutenant in the Coldstream Guards. He served in the European War in France. The following extract is taken from the "Times History of the War" Capt. Frisby and Corpl. Jackson were together in the desperate affair which won for them the Cross. The officer was in command of a company detailed to capture the canal crossing on the Demicourt–Graincourt Road. When the canal was reached the leading platoon came under annihilating machine-gun fire from a strong post under the old iron bridge on the far side of the canal, and in spite of reinforcing waves the platoon was unable to advance Seeing that unless this machine-gun post was captured the whole of the advance in this area would fail, Capt. Frisby determined on taking what he might well have looked upon as the measure of a forlorn hope. Calling for volunteers to follow him, he dashed forward with three other ranks, the first to offer being the gallant Jackson, who was a young non-commissioned officer, and had shown a glorious spirit of bravery and duty ever since the battle opened. These four Coldstream Guardsmen climbed down into the canal under an intense point-blank machine-gun fire, and by their dash, recklessness and resolution, captured the post with a dozen men and two machine guns. In this swift successful enterprise Capt. Frisby was wounded in the leg by a bayonet, but he remained at duty, and having restored the situation, enabled the attacking companies to advance. After reaching and consolidating his objective, he gave timely support to the company on his right, which had lost all its officers and sergeants—an illustration of the fury of the fight—organized its defences and beat off a heavy hostile attack." He was awarded the Victoria Cross [London Gazette, 27 Nov 1918]: "Cyril Hubert Frisby, Lieut. (Acting Capt.), Coldstream Guards (Special Reserve), attached 1st Battn. For conspicuous bravery, leadership and devotion to duty in action on 27 Sept. 1918, across the Canal Du Nord, near Graincourt, when in command of a company detailed to capture the canal crossing on the Demicourt–Graincourt Road. On reaching the canal, the leading platoon came under annihilating machine-gun fire from a strong machine-gun post under the old iron bridge on the far side of the canal, and was unable to advance,

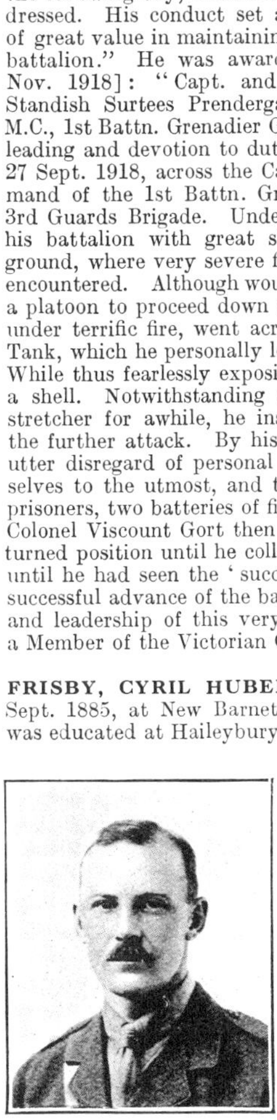

Cyril Hubert Frisby.

despite reinforcing waves. Capt. Frisby realized at once that unless this post was captured the whole advance in this area would fail. Calling for volunteers to follow him, he dashed forward, and with three other ranks, he climbed down into the canal under an intense point-blank machine-gun fire, and succeeded in capturing the post with two machine guns and twelve men. By his personal valour and initiative he restored the situation and enabled the attacking companies to continue the advance. Having reached and consolidated his objective, he gave timely support to the company on his right, which had lost all its officers and sergeants, organized its defences, and beat off a heavy hostile counter-attack. He was wounded in the leg by a bayonet in the attack on the machine-gun post, but remained at duty throughout, thereby setting a splendid example to all ranks." He was married, in London, on 18 April, 1911, to Audrey, youngest daughter of the late John Ogilvie-Grant and of Lucy Ogilvie-Grant, and they have a son, Henry Julian Fellowes, born on 20 May, 1913. Capt. Frisby is a member of the London Stock Exchange ; he has played Rugby football for Surrey County, and is a member of the Guards' Club, and of two golf clubs, Rye and Worplesdon.

JOYNT, WILLIAM DONOVAN, Lieut., was born at Elsterwick, Melbourne, Victoria, 19 March, 1899, son of Edward Kelly Joynt, late of Ballina, County Mayo, Ireland, and his wife, Alice Joynt, daughter of

William Donovan Joynt.

W. J. Woolcott, late of Exeter, Devon-shire, Solicitor, one of the leading lawyers of early Melbourne. He was educated at Melbourne Grammar School, and joined the Army as a Ranker 5 May, 1915, relinquishing the farming pursuits in which he had previously been engaged. He was given a commission 24 Dec. 1915, and was promoted Lieutenant 31 Dec. 1916, in the 8th Australian Infantry Battn. In the European War he was engaged in every large operation, with the exception of one, undertaken by his battalion in France. He fought on the Somme in 1916, the Ypres raid at the "Ravine," near the "Bluff," in which he was wounded and for which he received a mention in Divisional Orders ; the advance to the Hindenburg line, Bapaume,

n the early part of 1917 ; Lagnicourt, Bullecourt, the Third Battle of Ypres, Polygon Wood, Broadsende Ridge and Passchendaele Ridge in 1917. He was awarded the Victoria Cross [London Gazette, 27 Nov. 1918] : " William Donovan Joynt, Lieut., 8th Battn. Australian Imperial Force. For most conspicuous bravery and devotion to duty during the attack on Herleville Wood, near Chuignes, Peronne, on the 23rd Aug. 1918. His company commander having been killed early in the advance, he immediately took charge of the company, which he led with courage and skill. On approaching Herleville Wood, the troops of the leading battalion, which his battalion was supporting, suffered very heavy casualties and were much shaken. Lieut. Joynt, grasping the situation, rushed forward under very heavy machine-gun and artillery fire, collected and reorganized the remnant of the battalion, and kept them under cover, pending the arrival of his own company. He then made a personal reconnaissance, and found that the fire from the wood was checking the whole advance and causing heavy casualties to troops on his flanks. Dashing out in front of his men, he inspired and led a magnificent frontal bayonet attack on the wood. The enemy were staggered by this sudden onslaught and a very critical situation was saved. Later, at Plateau Wood, this very gallant officer again, with a small party of volunteers, rendered invaluable service, and after severe hand-to-hand fighting turned a stubborn defence into an abject surrender. His valour and determination was conspicuous throughout, and he continued to do magnificent work until badly wounded by a shell." In the last year of the war he took part in the battles in the Lys salient, in Nieppe Forest, at Nerris, and the final British offensive from Amiens in Aug., being wounded again near Peronne 26 Aug. 1918, and was promoted Captain 28 Oct. 1918.

GRANT, J. G., Sergt., served in the European War, and for his services in France was awarded the Victoria Cross [London Gazette, 27 Nov. 1918] : " J. G. Grant, No. 10/2850, Sergt., 1st Battn. Wellington Regt., New Zealand Forces. For most conspicuous bravery and devotion to duty near Bancourt on the 1st Sept. 1918, when sergeant in command of a platoon forming part of the leading waves of the battalion attacking the high ground to the east of Bancourt. On reaching the crest, it was found that a line of five enemy machine-gun posts offered a serious obstacle to further advance. Under point-blank fire, however, the company advanced against these posts. When about twenty yards from the posts, Sergt. Grant, closely followed by a comrade, rushed forward ahead of his platoon, and with great dash and bravery entered the centre post, demoralizing the garrison and enabling the men of his platoon to mop up the position. In the same manner he then rushed the post on the left, and the remaining posts were quickly occupied and cleared by his company. Throughout the whole operation on this and the two previous days, Sergt. Grant displayed coolness, determination and valour of the highest order, and set a splendid example to all."

JACKSON, THOMAS NORMAN, Private (L.-Corpl.), served in the European War, and for his services in France was awarded the Victoria Cross [London Gazette, 27 Nov. 1918] : " Thomas Norman Jackson, No. 20810, Private (L.-Corpl.), late 1st Battn. Coldstream Guards (Swinton). For most conspicuous bravery and self-sacrifice in the attack across the Canal Du Nord, near Graincourt. On the morning

Thomas Norman Jackson.

of the 27th Sept. 1918, L.-Corpl. Jackson was the first to volunteer to follow Capt. C. H. Frisby, Coldstream Guards, across the Canal Du Nord in his rush against an enemy machine-gun post. With two comrades he followed his officer across the canal, rushed the post, captured the two machine guns, and so enabled the companies to advance. Later in the morning, L.-Corpl. Jackson was the first to jump into a German trench which his platoon had to clear, and after doing further excellent work he was unfortunately killed. Throughout the whole day until he was killed this young N.C.O. showed the greatest valour and devotion to duty, and set an inspiring example to all."

L.-Corpl. Jackson's mother writes : " Capt Frisby, who was with my son when he won his V.C., came to Swinton to unveil a photo in oils of him. In his address to the public he told them how Corpl. Jackson had distinguished himself in the attack on the Canal du Nord. Capt. Frisby said : ' The official story in the London Gazette does not really tell you what he did that day on the 27th Sept. A big attack was to take place on the Hindenburg line. Our jumping-off place was about 50 yards from the Canal du Nord. The canal had no water in it. It was about 50 feet across and 15 feet deep. Its walls were nearly vertical, and were made of brick, faced here and there with concrete. The Germans had festooned these walls with barbed wire, so that it was impossible to slide down them ; one of my platoons was detailed to capture the crossing and hold it, and enable the rest of the battalion to cross. There was no-where else to cross. I sent two sections of Lewis gunners and bombers, 16 men in all, and Corpl. Jackson was of that number of the 16 men. Only two returned, Corpl. Jackson and Sergt. Smith, another Yorkshire man. The rest became casualties as soon as they got into the wire. The Germans were bombarding us with trench mortars. Corpl. Jackson actually got into the bed of the canal, and located the German strong post underneath the iron bridge. When volunteers were called for, to make another effort, someone said, " Here we are, sir." " Come on," I said. " Who is it ? " " Corpl. Jackson, sir." That small party got across ; the post was taken, and the battalion were enabled to get across and carry on the attack. Later on Corpl. Jackson's platoon was detailed to go to a certain German trench. I was told by one of the officers that as soon as they got into the trench Corpl. Jackson called out, " Come on, boys." He was first in the trench. I am told that he killed two Boches and was then killed.' "

WOOD, WILFRED, Private, served in the European War, and for his services in Italy was awarded the Victoria Cross [London Gazette, 27 Nov. 1918] : " Wilfred Wood, No. 59812, Private, 10th Battn. North-umberland Fusiliers (Stockport). For most conspicuous bravery and initiative on 28 Oct. 1918, near Casa Van, Italy, when a unit on the right flank having been held up by hostile machine guns and snipers, Private Wood, on his own initiative, worked forward with his Lewis gun, enfiladed the enemy machine-gun nest, and caused 140 enemy to surrender. The advance was continued till a hidden machine gun opened fire at point-blank range. Without a moment's hesitation, Private Wood charged the machine gun, firing his Lewis gun from the hip at the same time. He killed the machine-gun crew, and without further orders pushed on and enfiladed a ditch from which three officers and 160 men subsequently surrendered. The conspicuous valour and initiative of this gallant soldier. in the face of intense rifle and machine-gun fire was beyond all praise."

BADLU, SINGH, Ressaidar, served in the European War, and for his gallantry in Palestine was posthumously awarded the Victoria Cross [London Gazette, 27 Nov. 1918] : " Badlu Singh, Ressaidar, late 14th Lancers, Indian Army, attached 29th Lancers. For most conspicuous bravery and self-sacrifice on the morning of the 23rd Sept. 1918, when his squadron charged a strong enemy position on the west bank of the River Jordan, between the river and Kh. es Samariveh Village. On nearing the position Ressaidar Badlu Singh realized that the squadron was suffering casualties from a small hill on the left front occupied by machine guns and 200 infantry. Without the slightest hesitation he collected six other ranks and with the greatest dash and an entire disregard of danger charged and captured the position, thereby saving very heavy casualties to the squadron. He was mortally wounded on the very top of the hill when capturing one of the machine guns single-handed, but all the machine guns and infantry had surrendered to him before he died. His valour and initiative were of the highest order."

London Gazette, 30 Nov. 1918.—" Air Ministry, 30 Nov. 1918. His Majesty the King has been graciously pleased to confer the Victoria Cross on the undermentioned Officers of the Royal Air Force, in re-cognition of bravery of the highest possible order."

BARKER, WILLIAM GEORGE, Major, was born on 3 Nov. 1894, at Dauphin, Manitoba, Canada, son of G. W. J. Barker, of Winnipeg, Manitoba, Canada. He was educated at Dauphin College, and joined the Army for service in the Great War 1 Nov. 1914, in the Manitoba Regt. ; was attached to the Royal Air Force.

William George Barker.

The value of his services may be measured by the number of decorations he received—no less than eight—including the Victoria Cross, and French and Italian ones. He began by obtaining the Military Cross for contact patrol at the capture of Beaumont Hamel 20 Nov. 1916. At the capture of Bullecourt he obtained a Bar to the Military Cross 9 April, 1917, again for contact patrol. He then received the Companionship of the Distinguished Service Order, for destroying enemy aircraft on 5 Jan. 1918. He was awarded a Second Bar to the Military Cross, for destroying enemy aircraft on 24 April, 1918; a Bar to the Distinguished Service Order for destroying enemy aircraft, 20 July, 1918; the French Croix de Guerre for destroying enemy aircraft on the French Front, 26 May, 1918; the Italian Silver Medal for valour, for destroying aircraft on the Italian Front. This magnificent record was crowned by the award of the Victoria Cross [London Gazette, 30 Nov. 1918]: "William George Barker, D.S.O., M.C., Capt. (Acting Major), 201st Squadron, Royal Air Force. On the morning of the 27th Oct., 1918, this officer observed an enemy two-seater over the Fôret de Mormal. He attacked this machine, and after a short burst it broke up in the air. At the same time a Fokker biplane attacked him, and he was wounded in the right thigh, but managed, despite this, to shoot down the enemy aeroplane in flames. He then found himself in the middle of a large formation of Fokkers, who attacked him from all directions, and was again severely wounded in the left thigh, but succeeded in driving down two of the enemy in a spin. He lost consciousness after this, and his machine fell out of control. On recovery he found himself being again attacked heavily by a large formation, and singling out one machine, he deliberately charged and drove it down in flames. During this fight his left elbow was shattered and he again fainted, and on regaining consciousness he found himself still being attacked, but, notwithstanding that he was now severely wounded in both legs and his left arm shattered, he dived on the nearest machine and shot it down in flames. Being greatly exhausted, he dived out of the fight to regain our lines, but was met by another formation, which attacked and endeavoured to cut him off, but after a hard fight he succeeded in breaking up this formation and reached our lines, where he crashed on landing. This combat, in which Major Barker destroyed four enemy machines (three of them in flames), brought his total successes up to fifty enemy machines destroyed, and is a notable example of the exceptional bravery and disregard of danger which this very gallant officer has always displayed throughout his distinguished career." The 1914–15 Star and the various war decorations complete what must be an almost unique collection of rewards for service in the Great War. Major Barker gives the following as the duties which he undertook in his fighting career with the Royal Air Force: Artillery observation, reconnaissance and photography, contact patrol, day and night bombing of the enemy, ground targets, sky dropping from Capron aeroplanes in Italy, and aerial fighting, with a confirmed record of fifty-two enemy aircraft destroyed. He was three times mentioned in British Despatches. Major Barker, in conjunction with another V.C., Colonel Bishop, is floating in Toronto a private company to be known as the Bishop-Barker Aviation Company, Limited, to promote civil aviation in Canada and the United States.

BEAUCHAMP-PROCTOR, ANDREW WEATHERBY, Lieut. (Acting Capt.), served in the European War, and was awarded the M.C. and the D.F.C.; was created a Companion of the Distinguished Service Order, and was awarded the Victoria Cross [London Gazette, 30 Nov. 1918]: "Andrew Weatherby Beauchamp-Proctor, Lieut. (Acting Capt.), D.S.O., M.C., D.F.C., No. 84 Squadron, Royal Air Force. Between 8 Aug. 1918, and 8 Oct. 1918, this officer proved himself victor in twenty-six decisive combats, destroying twelve enemy kite balloons, ten enemy aircraft, and driving down four other enemy aircraft completely out of control. Between 1 Oct. 1918, and 5 Oct. 1918, he destroyed two enemy scouts, burnt three enemy kite balloons, and drove down one enemy scout completely out of control. On 1 Oct. 1918, in a general engagement with about twenty-eight machines, he crashed one Fokker biplane near Fontaine, and a second near Ramicourt; on 2 Oct. he burnt a hostile balloon near Selvigny; on 3 Oct. he drove down, completely out of control, an enemy scout near Mont d'Origny, and burnt a hostile balloon; on 5 Oct. the third hostile balloon near Bohain. On 8 Oct. 1918, while flying home at a low altitude, after destroying an enemy two-seater near Maretz, he was painfully wounded in the arm by machine-gun fire, but, continuing, he landed safely at his aerodrome, and after making his report was admitted to hospital. In all he has proved himself conqueror over fifty-four foes, destroying twenty-two enemy machines, sixteen enemy kite balloons, and driving down sixteen enemy aircraft completely out of control. Capt. Beauchamp-Proctor's work in attacking enemy troops on the ground and in reconnaissance during the withdrawl following on the Battle of St. Quentin from 21 March, 1918, and during the victorious advance of our Armies commencing on 8 Aug., has been almost unsurpassed in its brilliancy, and as such has made an impression on those serving in his squadron and those around him that will not be easily forgotten. Capt. Beauchamp-Proctor was awarded the Military Cross on 22 June, 1918; D.F. Cross on 2 July, 1918; Bar to M.C. on 16 Sept. 1918, and Distinguished Service Order on 2 Nov. 1918."

London Gazette, 14 Dec. 1918.—"War Office, 14 Dec. 1918. His Majesty the King has been graciously pleased to approve of the award of the Victoria Cross to the undermentioned Officers, Warrant Officer, Non-commissioned Officers and Men."

CLARK-KENNEDY, WILLIAM HEW, Lieut.-Colonel, was born on 3 March, 1879, at Dunskey, Wigtownshire, Scotland, second son of the late Capt. Clark-Kennedy, of Knockgray, Carsphairn, Galloway, Scotland, late Coldstream Guards, and the Hon. Mrs. Clark-Kennedy. He was educated at Westminster, and entered the service of the Standard Life Assurance Company in London in 1897. He joined "Paget's Horse" in 1899, and served with distinction in the South African War, being mentioned in Despatches and receiving the Queen's Medal with four clasps. He went to Canada in 1903 as an official of the Standard Life Assurance Company, and became later assistant manager for Canada. He served in the European War. He came overseas with the First Canadian Contingent as a Company Commander of the 13th Battn. Montreal Royal Highlanders. He was reported killed at the Second Battle of Ypres in April, 1915, being three times knocked over by shells, the third time being entirely buried and rendered unconscious, the men either side of him being killed. He eventually managed to dig himself out, although the Germans were close by. For this battle he was awarded the Croix de Guerre avec Palme. He was created a Companion of the Distinguished Service Order [London Gazette, 18 Jan. 1916], awarded for the Battle of Festubert, May, 1915. He was created a Companion of the Order of St. Michael and St. George in June, 1918, and was awarded a Bar to the Distinguished Service Order [London Gazette, 11 Jan. 1919] for 8 Aug. 1918, the advance on the Somme. He was promoted Major in 1915, Brigade Capt. in 1915–16, Brigade-Major in 1916, and Lieut.-Colonel in 1917, and was mentioned in Despatches seven times. He won the Victoria Cross on 27–28 Aug. 1918, between Wancourt and Fresnes–Rouvroy line (near Chérisy) [London Gazette, 14 Dec. 1918]: "William Hew Clark-Kennedy, C.M.G., D.S.O., Lieut.-Colonel, 24th Battn. Quebec Regt. For most conspicuous bravery, initiative and skilful leading on the 27th and 28th Aug. 1918, when in command of his battalion. On the 27th he led his battalion with great bravery and skill from Crow and Aigrette trenches in front of Wancourt to the attack on the Fresnes–Rouvroy line. From the outset the brigade, of which the 24th Battn. was a central unit, came under very heavy shell and machine-gun fire, suffering many casualties, especially amongst leaders. Units became partially disorganized, and the advance was checked. Appreciating the vital importance to the brigade front of a lead by the centre, and undismayed by annihilating fire, Lieut.-Colonel Clark-Kennedy, by sheer personality and initiative, inspired his men and led them forward. On several occasions he set an outstanding example by leading parties straight at the machine-gun nests which were holding up the advance and overcame these obstacles. By controlling the direction of neighbouring units and collecting men who had lost their leaders, he rendered valuable services in strengthening the line, and enabled the whole brigade to move forward. By the afternoon, very largely due to the determined leadership of this officer and disregard for his own life, his battalion, despite heavy losses, had made good the maze of trenches west of Cherisy and Cherisy Village, had crossed the Sensee River bed, and had occupied Occident Trench in front of the heavy wire of the Fresnes-Rouvroy line; under continuous fire he then went up and down his line until far into the night, improving the position, giving wonderful encouragement to his men, and sent back very clear reports. On the next day he again showed valorous leadership in the attack on the Fresnes–Rouvroy line and Upton Wood. Though severely wounded soon after the start, he refused aid, and dragged himself to a shell hole, from which he could observe. Realizing that his exhausted troops could advance no further, he established a strong line of defence, and thereby prevented the loss of most important ground. Despite intense pain and serious loss of blood, he refused to be evacuated for over five hours, by which time he had established the line in a position from which it was possible for the relieving troops to continue the advance. It is impossible to overestimate the results achieved by the valour and leadership of this officer." He married, on 5 Sept. 1914, Kate, elder daughter of the late Robert Reford, Esq., Montreal, Canada. Lieut.-Colonel W. H. Clark-Kennedy is a keen sportsman, both fishing and shooting, and is an excellent shot. He is now the manager of the Standard Life Assurance Company in Canada.

W. H. Clark-Kennedy.

BURGES, DAN, Lieut.-Colonel, was born 1 July, 1873, in London, son of the late Daniel Travers Burges, Town Clerk of Bristol, and the late Alice Sarah, eldest daughter of the late Benjamin Travers. He was educated at Winchester, and the Royal Military College, Camberley, and passed into the Army 21 Oct. 1893, as Second Lieutenant, Gloucestershire Regt.; was promoted Lieutenant 8 July, 1897. He served in South Africa, 1899–1902, as Lieutenant, 2nd Gloucestershire Regt. with the 6th Division (General Kelly-Kenny), up to the occupation of Bloemfontein; commanded Mounted Signallers Company, Army Headquarters, till 31 July, 1900; was Signalling Officer successively to Colonel Hickman's Column and General Plumer's Column; Chief Staff Officer to Colonel Vialls' Column; Signalling Officer to General W. Kitchener to end of war. He took part in the Relief of Kimberley, and was present during operations in the Orange Free State, Feb. to May, 1900, including operations at Paardeberg (17 to 26 Feb.); during actions at Poplar Grove, Dreifontein, Vet River (5 and 6 May), and Zand River; during operations in the Transvaal, east of Pretoria, July to 29 Nov. 1900, including action at Rhenoster Kop; during operations in Orange River Colony, May to 29 Nov. 1900; during operations in Cape Colony, south of Orange River, 1899–1900; in the operations in Cape Colony, north of Orange River; during operations in the Transvaal, 30 Nov. 1900, to Feb. 1901, and March, 1901, to 31 May, 1902; during operations in Orange River Colony, March, 1901; during operations in Cape Colony, Feb. to March, 1901. He received the Queen's Medal with four clasps, and the King's Medal with two clasps. He was promoted Captain 25 Oct. 1903; was Adjutant Indian Volunteers, 1908–13.

He served during the European War, 1914–18, as Company Commander, 2nd Gloucestershire Regt., until severely wounded in the Second Battle of Ypres (9 May, 1915), and was promoted Major 1 Sept. 1915. Commanded 10th East Yorkshire Regt. in Egypt and France from 9 Nov. 1915, to 30 June, 1916. He was Instructor, Senior Officers' School, Aldershot, Oct. 1916, to March, 1917 ; he served with 2nd Gloucestershire Regt., Struma Front, July and Aug. 1917. He was given the rank of Temporary Lieut.-Colonel, and commanded the 7th South Wales Borderers on the Doiran Front, Sept. 1917, to Sept. 1918, when he was severely wounded and lost his left leg. He was created a Companion of the Distinguished Service Order [London Gazette, 3 June, 1918]. A newspaper says : " Probably the most striking feature of the Despatch is the allusion made to the heroic work of the 7th Battn. of the South Wales Borderers during their attack between ' Pip ' Ridge and Grand Couronne. This battalion (a new service battalion of the old 24th Foot) was commanded by Lieut.-Colonel D. Burges, V.C., D.S.O., who was taken prisoner by the Bulgars during the attack, but was abandoned in a dug-out with one of his legs severely shattered. The gallant commanding officer gained his V.C. during this fight, out of which the 7th S.W.B. came with only nineteen unwounded men and one wounded officer. It is another stirring episode in the great fighting career of the S.W.B., and reflects the standard of the new armies. Equally commendable was the fight made by another battalion of this famous regiment the 8th S.W.B., commanded by Lieut.-Colonel R. C. Dobbs, D.S.O." He received the Victoria Cross [London Gazette, 14 Dec. 1918] : " Daniel Burges, Major (Temporary Lieut.-Colonel), D.S.O., Gloucestershire Regt., Commanding 7th Battn. South Wales Borderers. For most conspicuous bravery, skilful leading and devotion to duty in the operations at Jumeaux (Balkans) on 18 Sept. 1918. His valuable reconnaissance of the enemy first-line trenches enabled him to bring his battalion without casualties to the assembly point, and from thence he maintained direction with great skill, though every known landmark was completely obscured by smoke and dust. When still some distance from its objective, the battalion came under severe machine-gun fire, which caused casualties amongst company leaders. Lieut.-Colonel Burges, though himself wounded, quite regardless of his own safety, kept moving to and fro through his command, encouraging his men and assisting them to maintain formation and direction. Finally, as they neared the enemy's position, he led them forward through a decimating fire until he was again hit twice and fell unconscious. His coolness and courage were most marked throughout, and afforded magnificent example to all ranks." He was given the Brevet of Lieut.-Colonel 1 Jan. 1919. Lieut.-Colonel Burges received the Croix de Guerre avec Palme, Greek Military Cross (Second Class), and was thrice mentioned in Despatches [London Gazettes, 12 June, 1915 ; 11 June, 1918, and 21 Jan. 1919] ; also mentioned in French General Orders, Salonica Nov. 1917. He married 5 Oct. 1905, at St. Bartholomew's, Southsea, Katharine Blanche, second daughter of the late Capt. Edmund Fortescue, Rifle Brigade. They have no children.

VANN, BERNARD WILLIAM, Capt. (Acting Lieut.-Colonel), was born 9 July, 1887, at Rushden, Northamptonshire, son of Alfred George Collins Vann, M.A., Head Master of Chichele College, Higham Ferrers, and of Hannah Elizabeth Vann. He was educated at Chichele College, Higham Ferrers, and at Jesus College, Cambridge, where he was a Hockey Blue, and he also played for several Association league teams. He took his degree in 1910 ; was ordained deacon in 1912 ; was a curate for two years, and at the time of the outbreak of war was chaplain and assistant master at Wellingborough School. He applied for an Army Chaplaincy, but, impatient of delay, joined the Sherwood Foresters in Aug. 1914 · was Second Lieutenant, 1 Sept. 1914 ; Captain, 1 June, 1916 ; acting Major, 20 June, 1916, and Lieut.-Colonel, 6 Oct. 1917. He was awarded the Military Cross 15 Aug. 1915 ; a Bar to the Military Cross, 14 Nov. 1916 ; the Croix de Guerre with Palm, Feb. 1917, and the Victoria

Bernard William Vann.

Cross [London Gazette, 14 Dec. 1918] (posthumous) : " Bernard William Vann, M.C., Capt. (Acting Lieut.-Colonel), late 1/8th Battn., attached 1/6th Battn., Nottinghamshire and Derbyshire Regt. (Territorial Force). For most conspicuous bravery, devotion to duty and fine leadership during the attack at Bellenglise and Lehaucourt on 29 Sept. 1918. He led his battalion with great skill across the Canal du Nord through a very thick fog and under heavy fire from field and machine guns. On reaching the high ground above Bellenglise, the whole attack was held up by fire of all descriptions from the front and right flank. Realizing that everything depended on the advance going forward with the barrage, Lieut.-Colonel Vann rushed up to the firing line, and with the greatest gallantry led the line forward. By his prompt action and absolute contempt for danger the whole situation was changed, the men were encouraged and the line swept forward. Later, he rushed a field gun single-handed, and knocked out three of the detachment. The success of the day was in no small degree due to the splendid gallantry and fine leadership displayed by this officer. Lieut.-Colonel Vann, who had on all occasions set the highest example of valour, was killed near Ramicourt on 3 Oct., when leading his battalion in attack." The " Times " published the following appreciation by " A. H.," of Capt. (Acting Lieut.-Colonel) Bernard William Vann, V.C., M.C., 1/8th, attached 1/6th Battn. Nottinghamshire and Derbyshire Regt. (T.F.), who fell near Ramicourt on 3 Oct., and to whom the award of the Victoria Cross was announced on 16 Dec. : " The posthumous award of the Victoria Cross to Bernard Vann affords a brother officer an opportunity to put on

record a few reminiscences of a very gallant officer. If I cannot speak from any personal knowledge of his life before the war, one knows that his wonderful influence over men and boys with whom he worked as a clergyman will live long in the memory of those with whom he came in contact. He had no hesitation at the outbreak of war in deciding to join as a combatant. I can think of him only as a fighter, not merely against the enemy in the field, but a fighter against everything and everybody that was not an influence for good to his men. Sometimes the strength of his personality and the force of his convictions drove him up against ' authority,' but he had no fear for himself, and nothing on earth would have moved him to do what he felt to be wrong. I remember an occasion when as a subaltern his outspoken expressions led to something like a heated argument with his Army Commander, General Allenby, who, however, never forgot him, and always inquired kindly about him. It was his extraordinary courage and tenacity which will be remembered by all who knew him ; where danger was Bernard Vann must inevitably be. Buried and badly bruised by a trench mortar in May, 1915, he just dug himself out, and set to work to organize the defence, and help to dig out others. He was in bed for days afterwards, but refused to go down the line. When, shortly afterwards, a neighbouring unit recently arrived in France was temporarily confused and out of hand under a first experience of liquid fire, it was Vann who, revolver in hand, saved a serious situation, and, by pure personal example, restored confidence at a critical moment. Wounded severely at the Hohenzollern Redoubt in Oct. 1915, he continued to carry on an incessant bombing fight for several hours until ordered by the Brigadier to come away. In Sept. 1916, although suffering continuous agony for days beforehand from neuritis, caused by one of his many wounds, he insisted on leading his company on a raid, and himself killed or captured several Germans. He was so bad that the next day he had to be taken away, and was ill in England for several months. Vann's physical strength and his prowess at football, at which he almost invariably led his battalion team to victory, were a byword in his brigade. He had no use for ' slackers,' whether in games or in the line—but ' slackers ' in his platoon, his company, or his battalion were few, for he inspired all by his wonderful example of courage and energy. His death was typical of his life. A difficult operation had to be carried out at a few hours' notice in face of strong opposition. Heavy machine-gun fire held up a portion of the line, and there, as a matter of course, was Bernard Vann, leading and encouraging his men—to be killed instantaneously by a sniper's bullet at the moment of victory. He had been wounded seven or eight times, and had been awarded the Military Cross and Bar and the Croix de Guerre with Palm. His many friends will rejoice with his young Canadian widow that the constant gallantry and magnificent example of this fine Christian gentleman can be recognized by the highest award the country can bestow." Lieut.-Colonel (Rev.) B. W. Vann was married, 27 Dec. 1917, at St. Paul's, Knightsbridge, to Doris Victoria, daughter of Geoffrey Strange Beck, of Port Arthur, and their son Bernard Geoffrey, was born 2 June, 1919. Mrs. Vann received from the King the Victoria Cross awarded to her late husband.

HUTCHESON, BELLENDEN SEYMOUR, Capt., was born on 16 Dec. 1883, at Mount Carmel, Illinois, U.S.A., son of Mr. Bellenden Hutcheson, of Mound City, Illinois, and Luella Bellenden Hutcheson. He graduated in medicine at the North-Western University, Chicago, Illinois, and later practised as a physician and surgeon at Mound City, Illinois. He served in the European War, joining the 97th Battn. on 14 Dec. 1915, and serving as M.O. to that unit. He afterwards served in France as M.O. of 75th Battn. He was awarded the Military Cross for work on 8 Aug. 1918, and was awarded the Victoria Cross [London Gazette, 14 Dec 1918] : " Bellenden Seymour Hutcheson, Capt., Canadian Army Medical Corps, attached 75th Battn., 1st Central Ontario Regt. For most conspicuous bravery and devotion to duty on 2 Sept., when, under most intense shell, machine-gun and rifle fire, he went through the Quéant-Drocourt

Bellenden S. Hutcheson.

Support Line with the battalion. Without hesitation and with utter disregard of personal safety, he remained on the field until every wounded man had been attended to. He dressed the wounds of a seriously wounded officer under terrific machine-gun and shell fire, and, with the assistance of prisoners and of his own men, succeeded in evacuating him to safety, despite the fact that the bearer party suffered heavy casualties." Capt. Hutcheson is unmarried.

McGREGOR, DAVID STUART, Lieut., was born at Edinburgh 16 Oct. 1895, son of David McGregor, Clothier, Edinburgh, and of Annie McDonald, or McGregor, his wife. He was educated at George Watson's College, and George Heriot's School, Edinburgh. He was an apprentice of the Commercial Bank of Scotland, and had joined the Midlothian R.F.A. (T.F.) in 1913. Prior to mobilization he had made satisfactory progress in his professional studies, and was an associate of the Scottish Bankers' Institute. He had also passed most of the examinations for the full membership When war broke out, volunteering for

David Stuart McGregor.

service abroad, he was posted with commission to the 6th Royal Scots in 1915 ; sent to Egypt in May, 1916, but was immediately transferred to France, where he took part in the severe fighting of that summer on the Somme. Responding to a call to young officers for volunteers for machine-gun work, he was trained for that service ; posted to the 29th Battn., with whom he served till he was killed, under circumstances officially narrated in the London Gazette, 14 Dec. 1918. He was awarded the Victoria Cross [London Gazette, 14 Dec. 1918] : " David Stuart McGregor, Lieut., late 6th Battn. Royal Scots (Territorial Force), and 29th Battn. Machine Gun Corps." The following is a copy of the original recommendation which led to the award of the Victoria Cross (posthumous) to Lieut. David Stuart McGregor, 6th Royal Scots, attached Machine Gun Corps : " For the most conspicuous gallantry and devotion to duty near Hoogmolen on 22 Oct. 1918, when in command of a section of machine guns attached to the right flank platoon of the assaulting battalion. In the assembly position he concealed his guns on a limber under the bank of a sunken road. Immediately the troops advanced at zero they were subjected to intense enfilade machine-gun fire from Hill 66 on the right flank. Lieut. McGregor fearlessly went forward into the open to locate the enemy guns, and having done so, realized that it was impossible to get his guns carried forward either by pack or by hand without great delay, as the ground was absolutely bare and swept by a hail of bullets. Ordering the teams to follow by a more covered route, he went to the limber, got on to it, and, lying flat, told the driver to leave cover and gallop forward. This the driver did, gallop-ing down about six hundred yards of absolutely open road under the heaviest machine-gun fire into cover beyond. The driver, horses and limber were all hit, but Lieut. McGregor succeeded in getting the guns into action, effectively engaging the enemy, subduing their fire and enabling the advance to be resumed. With the utmost gallantry he continued to expose himself in order to direct and control the fire of his guns, until, about an hour later, this very gallant officer was killed whilst observing fire effect for the Trench Mortar Battery. His great gallantry and supreme devotion to duty were the admiration of all ranks, and especially the officers and men of the 1st Border Regt., who witnessed this extraordinary action." For the rest it may be added that Lieut. McGregor was inter-ested in sport generally ; was an expert swimmer, and, as such, the holder of trophies of his powers in the natatory art. He was also a good golfer, and no mean Rugby player.

BARRETT, JOHN CRIDLAN, Lieut., was born on 10 Aug. 1897, at 30, Regent Street, Royal Leamington Spa, son of Josephus Teague Barrett and Fanny Ada Barrett (née Cridlan). He was educated at the Merchant

John Cridlan Barrett.

Taylors' School, and joined the Army on 27 Jan. 1916, being posted to 3/5th Battn. Leicestershire Regt. at Bulwell, Notts. Trained there, and at Chesterfield and Catterick Bridge. Proceeded overseas on 1 July, 1916, and served uninterruptedly until 1 Oct. 1918. Held the post of Sig-nalling Officer to the 1/5th Battn. Leicester-shire Regt. from Feb. 1917, to May, 1918. Wounded at Gommecourt in Feb. 1917. Present at German retreat in Feb. 1917, fighting round Lens during summer, 1917 ; German retreat from La Bassée salient in Aug. 1918. Gassed at Gorre in May, 1918. Present in Hindenburg Line battle on 27 Sept. 1918, when awarded the V.C. Promoted to Lieutenant 27 July, 1917. Lieut. Barrett was awarded the Victoria Cross [London Gazette, 14 Dec. 1918] : " John Cridlan Barrett, Lieut., 1/5th Battn. Leicestershire Regt. (Terri-torial Force). For most conspicuous bravery and devotion to duty on 24 Sept. 1918, during the attack on Partruet. Owing to the darkness and smoke barrage, a considerable number of men lost direction, and Lieut. Barrett found himself advancing towards Fagan's trench—a trench of great strength, containing numerous machine guns. Without hesitation he collected all available men and charged the nearest group of machine guns, being wounded on the way. In spite of this he gained the trench and vigorously attacked the garrison, personally disposing of two machine guns and inflicting many casualties. He was again severely wounded, but, nevertheless, climbed out of the trench in order to fix his position and locate the enemy. This he succeeded in doing, and, despite exhaustion from wounds, gave detailed orders to his men to cut their way back to the battalion, which they did. He was again wounded so seriously that he had to be carried out. In spite of his wounds he had managed to fight on, and his spirit was magnificent throughout. It was due to his coolness and grasp of the situation that any of his party were able to get out alive."

A cutting from a newspaper in April, 1920, reads as follows :
" Lieut. J. C. Barrett, Paddington's second V.C., was presented by local people with a cheque for £330 and other gifts, as a mark of appreciation of his bravery. General Sir Ian Hamilton, in making the presentation, said : We are inclined to envy those who are born with a silver spoon in their mouth, but when we come across a young man starting his career with the V.C. on his breast we do not envy—we admire. The silver spoon is a freak of fortune which might just as well—or better—have happened to us ; the other, the V.C., means a reputation sought and carried off from the cannon's mouth. It is all very well for Shakespeare to talk of the ' Bubble ' reputa-tion—in Paddington the ' bubble ' becomes ' brass.' "

LYALL, GRAHAM THOMSON, Lieut., was born at Manchester 8 March, 1892, son of the Rev. Robert Henry Lyall, M.A., of Turncroft Lane, Darwen, Lancashire, and the late Agnes Lisette Lyall, whose maiden

name was Wells. He was educated at Nelson Municipal Secondary School, later qualifying as a Mechanical Engineer, and some time before the war emigrated to Welland, Canada, where he took a position

Graham Thomson Lyall.

in the plant of the Canadian Steel Foun-dries, afterwards accepting a position with the Canadian Niagara Power Com-pany, Niagara Falls, Ontario. He was active in social and Church circles in his new home, and being of genial disposition, was immensely popular. When the Euro-pean War broke out, he enlisted in the Canal Guard, Sept. 1914, and after serving for some months on Lock Seven, joined (in Sept. 1915) the 81st Infantry Battn., and was soon promoted to the rank of Corporal. In England he reverted to the ranks to proceed (in June, 1916) to France with the 4th Canadian Mounted Rifles, where he received rapid promotion through the non-commissioned ranks, and being granted a commission for conspicuous bravery in action, was gazetted 28 April, 1917, after a short course at the Canadian Officers' Training School, Bexhill, under the command of Brigadier-General Critchley, C.M.G., D.S.O., as a Lieutenant. He was awarded the Victoria Cross for supreme courage and devotion to duty during the operations north of Cambrai in Sept. 1918 [London Gazette, 14 Dec. 1918] : " Graham Thomson Lyall, Lieut., 102nd Battn. 2nd Central Ontario Regt. For most conspicuous bravery and skilful leading during the operation north of Cambrai. On 27 Sept. 1918, whilst leading his platoon against Bourlon Wood, he rendered invaluable support to the leading company, which was held up by a strong point, which he captured by a flank movement, together with thirteen prisoners, one field gun and four machine guns. Later, his platoon, now much weakened by casualties, was held up by machine guns at the southern end of Bourlon Wood. Collect-ing any men available, he led them towards the strong point, and, springing forward alone, rushed the position single-handed and killed the officer in charge, subsequently capturing at this point forty-five prisoners and five machine guns. Having made good his final objective, with a further capture of forty-seven prisoners, he consolidated his position and thus protected the remainder of the company. On 1 Oct., in the neighbourhood of Blecourt, when in command of a weak company, by skilful dispositions he captured a strongly-defended position, which yielded sixty prisoners and seventeen machine guns. During two days of operations Lieut. Lyall captured in all three officers, 182 other ranks, twenty-six machine guns, and one field gun, exclusive of heavy casualties inflicted. He showed throughout the utmost valour and high powers of command." The recom-mendation for this the greatest of military honours, signed by the com-manding officers of the 11th Canadian Infantry Brigade, the 4th Canadian Division, and the Canadian Corps, has little to add to the Gazette account of the award beyond the additional statement that during both operations, on the attainment of the objective, he tended wounded under fire. The local Canadian paper commented on his feat thus : " This most remarkable record is probably unexcelled in all the annals of war. His feat required not only courage and resource, but also the very highest type of military intelligence ; a thorough understanding of military technique, and a per-sonality of the most inspiring character." He was personally decorated by the King at the Investiture at Buckingham Palace on 15 March, 1919. The inhabitants of Darwen presented him with a French bronze clock and ornaments, in recognition of his achievement. He was married, 24 April, 1919, in the High United Free Church, Airdrie, Lanarkshire, his father taking part of the service, to Elizabeth Moffatt, eldest daughter of Alex-ander Frew, Provost of Airdrie, and Elizabeth Moffatt Frew, of Meadowside House, Airdrie. At present manager of Drumbathie Brickworks (Alex-ander Frew & Co.), he is now resident at Forrest Park, Drumgelloch, Airdrie. That he is a keen sportsman may be gathered from the fact that he goes in for tennis, swimming, shooting, rowing, canoeing, cricket and hockey. In his schooldays he was a very proficient swimmer, having won many prizes and accomplishing some remarkable feats, including swimming across the River Clyde from the Clock Lighthouse to Dunoon at the age of four-teen ; thus becoming champion long-distance swimmer of his age and period.

TOWNER, EDGAR THOMAS, Lieut., served in the European War, and won the Military Cross. He was awarded the Victoria Cross [London Gazette, 14 Dec. 1918] : " Edgar Thomas Towner, M.C., Lieut., 2nd Battn. Austra-lian Machine Gun Corps. For most conspicuous bravery, initiative and devo-tion to duty on 1 Sept. 1918, in the attack on Mont St. Quentin, near Peronne, when in charge of four Vickers guns. During the early stages of the advance he located and captured, single-handed, an enemy machine gun which was causing casualties, and by turning it on the enemy inflicted severe losses. Subsequently, by the skil-full tactical handling of his guns, he cut off and captured twenty-five of the enemy. Later, by fearless reconnaissance under heavy fire, and by the energy, foresight and promptitude with which he brought

Edgar Thomas Towner.

fire to bear on various enemy groups, he gave valuable support to the infantry advance. Again, when short of ammunition, he secured an enemy machine gun, which he mounted and fired in full view of the enemy, causing the enemy to retire further, and enabling our infantry to advance. Under intense fire, although wounded, he maintained the fire of this gun at a very critical period. During the following night he steadied and gave valuable support to a small detached post, and by his coolness and cheerfulness inspirited the men in a great degree. Throughout the night he kept close watch by personal reconnaissance on the enemy movements, and was evacuated exhausted thirty hours after being wounded. The valour and resourcefulness of Lieut. Towner undoubtedly saved a very critical situation, and contributed largely to the success of the attack."

GORLE, ROBERT VAUGHAN, Lieut., served in the European War, and for his services in France was awarded the Victoria Cross [London Gazette, 14 Dec. 1918]: "Robert Vaughan Gorle, Temporary Lieut., A Battery, 50th Brigade, Royal Field Artillery. For most conspicuous bravery, initiative and devotion to duty during the attack on Ledeghem on 1 Oct. 1918, when in command of an 18-pounder gun working in close conjunction with infantry. He brought his gun into action in the most exposed positions on four separate occasions, and disposed of enemy machine guns by firing over open sights under direct machine-gun fire at 500 to 600 yards' range. Later, seeing that the infantry were being driven back by intense hostile fire, he, without hesitation, galloped his gun in front of the leading infantry, and on two occasions knocked out enemy machine guns which were causing the trouble. His disregard of personal safety and dash were a magnificent example to the wavering line, which rallied and retook the northern end of the village." Lieut. Gorle was born at Southsea 6 May, 1896, son of Major Harry Vaughan Gorle, D.S.O., retired, late A.S.C., and Ethel Catharine (who died in 1904), eldest daughter of the Rev. Canon Archdall, Rector of Glanmire, County Cork. He was educated at The Wells House, Malvern Wells, and at Rugby, and, before the war, was farming in the Transvaal. After the cessation of hostilities he thought of farming still in South Africa, but this time in North-Eastern Rhodesia. His favourite recreations are shooting and tennis.

DEAN, DONALD JOHN, Temporary Lieut., was born on 19 April, 1897, at Herne Hill, S.E., son of John H. Dean, Esq., and Grace Dean. He was educated at Quernmore College, and joined the Army on 19 April, 1915, as a Private in the 28th London Regt.

Donald John Dean.

(Artists' Rifles). He served in the European War in France, and was awarded the Victoria Cross [London Gazette, 14 Dec. 1918]: "Donald John Dean, Lieut., 8th Battn. Royal West Kent Regt. For most conspicuous bravery, skilful command, and devotion to duty during the period 24 to 26 Sept. 1918, when holding, with his platoon, an advance post established in a newly-captured enemy trench north-west of Lens. The left flank of the position was insecure, and the post, when taken over on the night of 24 Sept., was ill-prepared for defence. Shortly after the post was occupied the enemy attempted, without success, to recapture it. Under heavy machine-gun fire consolidation was continued, and shortly after midnight another determined enemy attack was driven off. Throughout the night Lieut. Dean worked unceasingly with his men, and about 6 a.m. on 25 Sept. a resolute enemy attack, supported by heavy shell and trench mortar fire, developed. Again, owing to the masterly handling of his command, Lieut. Dean repulsed the attack, causing heavy enemy casualties. Throughout the 25th and the night of 25-26 Sept. consolidation was continued under heavy fire, which culminated in intense artillery fire on the morning of the 26th, when the enemy again attacked and was finally repulsed with loss. Five times in all (thrice heavily) was this post attacked, and on each occasion the attack was driven back. Throughout the period Lieut. Dean inspired his command with his own contempt of danger, and all fought with the greatest bravery. He set an example of valour, leadership and devotion to duty of the very highest order."

McCARTHY, LAWRENCE DOMINIC, Lieut., comes from York, Western Australia. He served in the European War, and for his services in France was awarded the Victoria Cross [London Gazette, 14 Dec. 1918]: "Lawrence Dominic McCarthy, 16th Battn. Australian Imperial Force. For most conspicuous bravery, initiative, and leadership on the morning of 23 Aug. 1918, in attack near Madame Wood, east of Vermandovillers (north of Chaulnes). Although the objectives of his battalion were attained without serious opposition, the battalion on the left flank was heavily opposed by well-posted machine guns. Lieut. McCarthy, realizing the position, at once engaged the nearest machine-gun post, but still the attacking troops failed to get forward. This officer then determined to attack the nearest post. Leaving

Lawrence D. McCarthy.

his men to continue the fire fight, he, with two others, dashed across the open and succeeded in reaching the block. Although single-handed, as he had out-distanced his comrades, and despite serious opposition and obstacles, he captured the gun and continued to fight his way down the trench, inflicting heavy casualties and capturing three more machine guns. At this stage, being some 700 yards from his starting-point, he was joined

by one of his men, and together they continued to bomb up the trench until touch was established with an adjoining unit. Lieutenant McCarthy, during this most daring advance, single-handed killed 20 of the enemy and captured in addition five machine-guns and 50 prisoners. By his gallant and determined action he saved a critical situation, prevented many casualties, and was mainly, if not entirely, responsible for the final objective being taken."

YOUNG, FRANK EDWARD, Second Lieut., was born on 2 Oct. 1895, at Cherat, North-Western Provinces, India, son of Sergt. (now Capt.) F. Young and Mrs. Young. He was educated at the Regimental Schools and Kempston County School, and joined the Army as a Bugler in the Hertfordshire Territorials 15 Nov. 1909, serving in the European War in France from 20 Jan. 1915, to May, 1916, and Sept. 5 1918. He was promoted to Sergeant in Dec. 1914, and to Second Lieutenant 26 April, 1916. He was awarded the Victoria Cross [London Gazette, 14 Dec. 1918]: "Frank Edward Young, Second Lieut., late 1st Battn. Hertfordshire Regt. (Territorial Force). For most conspicuous bravery, determination, and exceptional devotion to duty on 18 Sept. 1918, south-east of Havrincourt, when during an enemy counter-attack and throughout an extremely intense enemy barrage he visited all posts, warned the garrisons, and encouraged the men.

Frank Edward Young.

In the early stages of the attack he rescued two of his men who had been captured, and bombed and silenced an enemy machine gun. Although surrounded by the enemy, Second Lieut. Young fought his way back to the main barricade and drove out a party of the enemy who were assembling there. By his further exertions the battalion was able to maintain a line of great tactical value, the loss of which would have meant serious delay to future operations. Throughout four hours of intense hand-to-hand fighting Second Lieut. Young displayed the utmost valour and devotion to duty, and set an example to which the company gallantly responded. He was last seen fighting hand-to-hand against a considerable number of the enemy." He was at first reported missing, but was afterwards found to have been killed at the close of his great day's work.

The "Hertfordshire Express" says :

"One of the most striking tributes is that of the second in command of the battalion, Major Clerk, D.S.O., M.C. Writing on 19 Sept. the day after the affair in which Second Lieut. Young fell, Major Clerk says : 'Yesterday afternoon the enemy attacked the battalion in force. Your son was largely instrumental in saving No. 4 Company's front. The enemy came down one trench. Frank bombed them out himself. A little later he rescued one of our men who had been taken prisoner. He knocked down with his fist one of this lot of the enemy, and scattered the rest, and got our man away. Later he was captured, but got away. Later, again, he was found to be missing. . . . He was magnificent.' Another remarkable account is given by Major Barber, Quartermaster of the Battalion. This officer writes : ' We were in a part of the line that was heavily shelled by the enemy, and a portion of our line was temporarily taken. It was here that Frank particularly distinguished himself by his extraordinary gallantry and courage. For he is reported to have gone in practically single-handed and to have knocked out several of the enemy with his fists, and then to have bombed right up the trench, practically clearing it single-handed. His name was on everyone's lips for his wonderful work and extraordinary skill and courage. I have just seen Capt. —— (another officer of the Battalion), and he says he seemed to be everywhere where most wanted.' We may further quote the remarkable tribute of the officer in command of the Battalion (Lieut.-Colonel Heselton) after the heroic young officer's body was found : ' I did so hope that he was alive and a prisoner. Unfortunately, I only saw him for a few minutes, just when he came up (to join the battalion), and we were going into the line. He really was the most gallant boy I ever met, and I only wish he had been spared, because he was just the priceless fellow one wants out here. The whole battalion mourns him, and the men who fought with him thought the world of him.' Apart from the actual allusions in these letters to the circumstances in which the Victoria Cross was won by Lieut. Young, nothing is more remarkable than the glimpse they give of a personality which gained the utmost respect and esteem among officers and men in course of the few days he was among them before his death in battle. We quote below some of the more personal tributes from his brother officers and from these and what has been given above, it is evident that in addition to great endowments for the most critical tasks of war the young subaltern from Hitchin had qualities which made the readiest sort of appeal to the friendship and admiration of those among whom he might bear, for however short a time, the stress of war. A brief record of Lieut. Young's life may be given here as that of a youthful hero about whom more than this generation of the people of the district may be eager to learn something. He was born in India when his father was serving on the North-West Frontier—the scene of so many of our ' little wars ' of the years before the Great War. He was in India up to the age of 7, when Capt. Young, then Colour-Sergeant, was posted to the 3rd Battn. of the Bedfordshires— a unit of the old Militia—with headquarters at Bedford. At Bedford the boy attended the Kempston Council School. His people were in Bedford for the next seven years. Young Frank had just finished his schooling when the family came to Hitchin on Capt. Young's transfer to the Hitchin Company of the 1st Hertfordshire Regt. as instructor. This was in 1909, and the lad made his first start in life shortly after the family's removal to Hitchin by entering the establishment of Messrs. W. B. Moss & Sons, Ltd.

He was in this firm's employ for twelve months, and then took a place on the staff of the Orleans Club in St. James's Street, London. There he remained for about a year, when, returning to Hitchin, he made a beginning in what looked like being his life's work. He started at the Hitchin Electric Power Station with the intention of following up electrical engineering. There he remained up to the outbreak of war, and then found himself summoned to another sort of destiny, with death and much honour at the end of it. Doubtless inheriting the military tastes of his father, the lad had already joined the 1st Herts Regt. Hitchin Company, as a boy. This was in Nov. 1909, at the age of 14. He joined as bugler, and having maintained his connection with the Regiment during his stay in London, he was private at the start of the war, and, along with his father, was mobilized for war service. He was then in his nineteenth year, and was showing great promise as a young soldier, having already been made one of the battalion scouts. Private Young, as he then was, volunteered for foreign service, but medical disability prevented him from going abroad with the 1st Battn. in Nov. 1914, when the Herts Regt. earned early distinction as one of the first Territorial units to appear in the field. As a matter of fact, the lad had to undergo an operation before he could be passed fit. This he cheerfully did, and on his recovery he joined the newly formed 2nd Battn. Herts Regt. with headquarters at Stowlangtoft, near Bury St. Edmunds. There he was promoted Sergeant before the end of 1914, and in Jan. 1915, he was sent to France with the first reinforcing draft for the 1st Battn. It is interesting to note that Capt. Young was then Sergeant-Major with the battalion in France, and his son reached the unit in the trenches on a stiff sector of the front opposite La Bassée, a name which figured so often in the war news of that time. Father and son were therefore together for a time in the unending warfare of the trenches. The battalion was in the big Festubert fighting of the summer of 1915, and in the Battle of Loos of Sept. of that year. Earlier even than these big ' shows,' however—in fact, within a week of his arrival at the front—the future V.C. participated in the big affair at the brickfields in front of La Bassée in which O'Leary of the Irish Guards won the V.C.—one of the most notable of the early awards. Having completed five years' Territorial service in the autumn of 1915, Young had the usual month's leave home on re-engaging. His leave was spent in Hitchin, and when he returned to France he remained with the battalion till Jan. 1916. Then there was a call for bombing instructors, and, having already some reputation as a bomber, Sergt. Young—he was one of the platoon sergeants of his company—was sent to Rouen to be attached to the central training staff as an instructor in bombing. He continued on this duty for three months, until invalided home with sickness. He was in hospital in Cardiff from May to July, 1916, and was then attached to the 3/1st Herts Regt. at Halton Camp, near Tring. It was while at this camp that Sergt. Young was recommended for and obtained admission to an Officers' Cadet Battalion with a view to a commission. His father, Capt. Young, it may be noted, had meantime himself been commissioned. The son began his cadet training at Oxford in Jan. 1917, having just previously set up a record in a bombing course, a special certificate being awarded him. He was commissioned on April 26, 1917, and was posted as Second Lieutenant to the 3/1st Battn. of his old Regiment, the Hertfordshires, at Halton, where, also, his father was an officer. This battalion was, however, broken up, and the whole of the officers went to Luton, where they were attached to the 25th Reserve Training Battn. Here Lieut. Young was Battalion Bombing Officer, but in Dec. of last year this unit was also broken up, and Lieut. Young was now sent to the 5th Reserve Battn. Bedfordshire Regt., at Crowborough. In the spring of the present year, Second Lieut. Young, attracted, like many of the best young officers, to the Flying Corps, applied for admission to that arm of the service. He went through the ' ground course '—training in the engineering and other technical phases of the service—at Reading. This lasted six weeks, and he then proceeded to Sleaford, Lincs, for the flying course. Unfortunately, one of his flights ended in a somewhat awkward crash, by which the young officer was badly shaken. The effects of this accident remaining with him, Young, thinking it probable that he would not be able to do justice to himself or to the service, asked to be returned to his own regiment. He thus rejoined the 5th Reserve Battn. Bedfordshire Regt. at Crowborough, in July of this year. Then he came to Hitchin for the last time at the beginning of Sept. on forty-eight hours' leave, before proceeding to France to join his old Regiment, the Hertfordshires, in the firing line. Capt. Young saw his son embark at Folkestone on 5 Sept. He appears to have been detained some days—as is usual —at the base. It was on 12 Sept. that he joined his old unit, and six days afterwards, on 18 Sept., he was reported missing. The last communication received at his home from Second Lieut. Young, reporting that he was well, was a field postcard, dated 17 Sept. It was on the 18th that he got partly through a day of splendid action by which he gained the Victoria Cross, and in which, though at first reported missing, he was in fact killed. A short memorial service was held at St. Saviour's Church, Hitchin, in memory of the gallant V.C. hero. The Rev. G. B. Gainsford conducted the service. Capt. and Mrs. Young and family and Miss Dennis were present. The opening hymn was ' There is a blessed home,' which was followed by prayers and Psalms 121, 130 and 138. The impressive service closed with the hymn, ' On the Resurrection morning.' As the congregation left the church, the organist (Mr. J. H. White, A.R.C.O.) played ' O rest in the Lord ' (' Elijah '). The Rev. J. G. Williams (St. Saviour's, Hitchin) writes : ' It was my privilege to know Frank Young fairly intimately. He was not a man given to much speech, especially in the matter of his deepest feelings. What impressed me most in him was a certain quality of simplicity and directness. He seemed to be a man who would be able to act with promptness and decision. Those who really knew him would not be surprised when they heard of his valiant and distinguished end on the battlefield. I remember, in the first week of the war, meeting him loaded with his kit and equipment preparatory to going out, and I could not but admire his outlook on things. He said, " This is war. We are now in for the real thing. We have been playing at soldiers " (referring to his Territorial experiences) : " now we must go and *be* soldiers." That was the purport of his conversation. There was in him no sign of regret that it had come to that. He showed no impetuous eagerness to go out and do great things, but only a quiet determination to " face the music " and do his duty. He spoke gravely, but at the same time cheerfully, and did not appear to be anything but glad that the Herts Territorials had at last a chance of proving their metal. How well they have done so will remain one of the priceless memories of Hitchin town. I think that the foundation of his soldierly character was not so much his physical as his moral courage.' "

WILLIAMS, JOHN HENRY, Company Sergt.-Major, was born on 29 Sept. 1886, at Nantyglo, Monmouthshire, son of Henry and Elizabeth Williams. He was educated at Brierly Hill School, Ebbw Vale, and joined the Army on 12 Nov. 1914, as a Private, and was promoted Sergeant on 1 Jan. 1915, and Company Sergeant-Major on 2 Oct. 1917. He served in the European War in France and Belgium. He received the Distinguished Conduct Medal for continued and sustained coolness and gallantry in the Battle of Mametz Wood from 10 to 12 July, 1916. He subsequently again distinguished himself, and was rewarded with the Military Medal for bravery at Pilkem Ridge on 31 July, 1917, at the beginning of the battle for Passchendaele Heights, and a Bar to it, which was awarded to him for bravery in a raid in the Armentières sector into the enemy's line on 30 Oct. 1918, when he brought back a wounded comrade. He was awarded the Victoria Cross [London Gazette, 14 Dec. 1918] : " John Henry Williams, D.C.M., M.M. and Bar, No. 20408, Company Sergt.-Major, 10th Battn. South Wales Borderers. For most conspicuous bravery, initiative, and devotion to duty on the night of 7–8 Oct. 1918, during the attack on Villers Outreaux, when, observing that his company was suffering heavy casualties from an enemy machine gun, he ordered a Lewis gun to engage it, and went forward under heavy fire to the flank of the enemy post, which he rushed single-handed, capturing 15 of the enemy. These prisoners, realizing that Company Sergt.-Major Williams was alone, turned on him, and one of them gripped his rifle. He succeeded in breaking away and bayoneting five enemy, whereupon the remainder again surrendered. By his gallant action and total disregard of personal danger he was the means of enabling not only his own company, but also those on the flanks, to advance." He was decorated by the King at Buckingham Palace on 22 Feb. 1919, with all four decorations, being the first to receive the four decorations at the same time from His Majesty. The Lieutenant-Colonel commanding the 10th Battn. South Wales Borderers wrote : " I am writing to wish you my most heartiest congratulations on your being awarded the V.C. All ranks of the Battalion are delighted and send their heartiest congratulations. I thank you also for bringing to the Battalion and the Regiment such a glorious honour. Those of us who know you know full well how much you deserved winning the Victoria Cross. I hope you are recovering from your wound, and will have a long and happy life to enjoy your well-deserved honour. . . . Again wishing you all the best and many congratulations. . . ." He received other letters of a like nature from officers in the 10th Battn. South Wales Borderers, expressing their delight at his success, and on the distinction which he had brought to his battalion. He was discharged from the Army through wounds received in action on 17 Oct. 1918. His wife's name is Gertrude Williams, and they have three sons : Ivor, Edgar and Harry, and a daughter, Mary.

McNALLY, WILLIAM, Sergt., served in the European War, and was awarded the Military Medal. He was awarded the Victoria Cross [London Gazette, 14 Dec. 1918] : " William McNally, No. 13820, Sergt., M.M., 8th Battn. Yorkshire Regt. (Murton Colliery, Co. Durham). For most conspicuous bravery and skilful leading during the operations on 27 Oct. 1918, across the Piave, when his company was most seriously hindered in its advance by heavy machine-gun fire from the vicinity of some buildings on a flank ; utterly regardless of personal safety, he rushed the machine-gun post single-handed, killing the team and capturing the gun. Later, at Vazzola, on 29 Oct. 1918, when his company, having crossed the Monticano River, came under heavy rifle and machine-gun fire, Sergt. McNally immediately directed the fire of his platoon against the danger point, while he himself crept to the rear of the enemy position. Realizing that a frontal attack would mean heavy losses, he, unaided, rushed the position, killing or putting to flight the garrison, and capturing a machine gun. On the same day, when holding a newly-captured ditch, he was strongly counter-attacked from both flanks. By his coolness and skill in controlling the fire of his party, he frustrated the attack, inflicting heavy casualties on the enemy. Throughout the whole operations his innumerable acts of gallantry set a high example to his men, and his leading was beyond all praise."

LOWERSON, ALBERT DAVID, Sergt., was born at Myrtleford, Bogong, Victoria. He enlisted in the Australian Imperial Force on 12 July, 1915, and was at that time 19 years of age, and was residing with his parents at the town aforementioned. He served in the European War, and was awarded the Victoria Cross [London Gazette, 14 Dec. 1918] : " Albert David Lowerson, No. 2358, Sergt., 21st Battn. Australian Imperial Force. For most conspicuous bravery and tactical skill, on the 1st Sept. 1918, during the attack on Mont St. Quentin, north of Peronne when very strong opposition was met with early in the attack, and every foot of ground was stubbornly contested by the enemy. Regardless of heavy enemy machine-gun fire, Sergt. Lowerson moved about fearlessly directing his men, encouraging them to still greater effort, and finally led them

Albert D. Lowerson.

ing business as an iron and steel merchant and manufacturers' agent. Since demobilization he has been appointed as manager for an important firm of ironmasters and merchants. He was married on 31 Aug. 1907, at St. Paul's, Brisbane, Queensland, Australia, to Florence McFarlane, daughter of the late Alexander Donaldson and Christina Donaldson, of Brisbane, and they have a son, George Zac, born 2 Nov. 1909. Previous to joining the Army on 5 Sept. 1914, he resided at Edgbaston, Birmingham ; he moved to Sale, Cheshire, in 1915, an I is now residing in Northumberland. When the war broke out he enlisted in the 3rd (King's Own) Hussars on 5 Sept. 1914, and transferred to the Devonshire Regt. 14 April, 1917. He served in the European War and Irish Rebellion (1916). He was awarded the Victoria Cross for capturing (with a comrade) as many as two hundred German prisoners [London Gazette, 14 Dec. 1918] : " No. 63514, George Onions, L.-Corpl., 1st Battn. Devonshire Regt. Having been sent out with one man at Achiet-le-Petit on 22 Aug. 1918, to get touch with the battalion on the right flank, he observed the enemy advancing in large numbers. Realizing his opportunity he boldly placed himself with his comrade on the flank of the advancing enemy, and opened rapid fire when the target was most favourable. When the enemy were about 100 yards from him, the line wavered and some hands were seen to be thrown up. L.-Corpl. Onions then rushed forward, and with the assistance of his comrade took about 2C0 of the enemy prisoners, and marched them back to his company commander." L.-Corpl. Onions was wounded and severely gassed on the same day, and went into hospital at Liverpool. He was demobilized on 14 Feb. 1919. He has the 1914–15 Star. He served with the 3rd Hussars Reserve Regt. (the 9th Reserve Regt. of Cavalry) in the Irish Rebellion in Dublin, Easter, 1916, and with the 3rd (King's Own) Hussars and 1st Battn. The Devonshire Regt. in Belgium and France 1915–1918. Trooper A. R. F. Onions, his only brother of military age, enlisted in the Dragoon Guards in Aug. 1914, and served in France 1915–1918 in the 4th and 7th Dragoon Guards. He gained the D.C.M.

LESTER, FRANK, Corpl., was born 18 Feb. 1896, at West View, Huyton, son of John Lester, Market Gardener, and Ellen, his wife. He was educated at Hoylake National School, and joined up in March, 1916 ; was put in the 10th South Lancashire Regt., and soon promoted to Sergeant-Instructor, training troops at Prees Heath and Kinmel Park. He was sent to France in March, 1916, and reverted to Private, as is usual on going out. He was transferred to the 10th Lancashire Fusiliers before going out to France. He was slightly wounded on 21 March, and was in hospital at Rouen. He regained two stripes, and came to England soon after ; was stationed at Cromer, and was drafted out again in Sept. Corpl. Frank Lester was killed in action on 12 Oct. by a sniper. His Lieutenant, who was with him when it happened, forwarded particulars and later called to tell his parents that Frank had behaved very gallantly during the morning, and he had brought his bravery to the notice of his Colonel. By his last action he had been the means, at least, of saving six lives. He was so bright and cheerful and a good soldier. Corpl. Frank Lester was awarded the Victoria Cross [London Gazette, 14 Dec. 1918] : " Frank Lester, No. 51674, Private, late 10th Battn. Lancashire Fusiliers. Date of Act of Bravery : 12 Oct. 1918. For most conspicuous bravery and self-sacrifice during the clearing of the village of Neuville on 12 Oct. 1918, when with a party of about seven men under an officer, he was the first to enter a house from the back door, and shot two Germans as they attempted to get out by the front door. A minute later a fall of masonry blocked the door by which the party had entered. The only exit into the street was under fire at point-blank range. The street was also swept by the fire of machine guns at close range. Observing that an enemy sniper was causing heavy casualties to a party in a house across the street, Private Lester exclaimed, ' I'll settle him,' and, dashing out into the street, shot the sniper at close quarters, falling mortally wounded at the same instant. This gallant man well knew it was certain death to go into the street, and the party opposite was faced with the alternative of crossing the fire-swept street or staying where it was and being shot one by one. To save their lives he sacrificed his own." One of Lester's friends says of him, " He was an old Boys' Brigade boy, who was very bright and cheerful, helped his father with his market garden, and was a true soldier."

The following are letters from officers :

" DEAR MR. LESTER,

" I have only just got your address, or I would have written to you before to condole with you in the death of your brave son. It will be, I'm sure, a consolation to you to know that he won the Victoria Cross.

" I was commanding the gallant 10th Battn. Lancashire Fusiliers at the time, and am now at the above address for a few weeks.

" Your son's superb action is one of the bravest acts I can recall in this terrible war. He has added one more V.C. to the record of the Regiment, which has more V.C.'s to its credit than any Regiment in the British Army.

" I have seen the spot where the gallant deed was done in the village of Neuville, north of Le Cateau. It was a day of gallant deeds, and two Military Crosses, one Distinguished Conduct Medal, and three Military Medals were gained that day (12th October) by the Battalion.

" His Majesty the King afterwards visited the village and the Divisional General showed him the battlefield and explained the part taken by the Battalions engaged.

" This is the second Victoria Cross gained by the Battalion I had the honour to command during the final battles that resulted in the present Armistice. We are all proud of your son."

" DEAR MR. LESTER,

" I have been meaning to write to you for some time past to tell you how proud the Battalion are and the Regiment will be of the great honour your son has brought to us.

" We bitterly regret that such a very gallant man should not be with us to share it, but I trust it will be of some small consolation to you to know that he will always be affectionately remembered.

" On behalf of the officers and men I would like to express our deep sympathy to you and all his people."

Two accounts of Corpl. Lester from a local newspaper are given below :

" Another well-known and popular Port Sunlight soldier has made the great sacrifice in the fight for freedom, Corpl. George Hall falling at the same time as Corpl. Frank Lester, the latter having been awarded the V.C. Corpl. Hall and Corpl. Lester had been the very best of pals since joining the Army. They had been together all the time. They came home on leave together, were transferred from one battalion to another, and still kept the best of pals. Corpl. Hall enlisted 4 Dec. 1916 in the Royal Welsh Fusiliers. He was in training at Prees Heath camp, and in June, 1917, was transferred along with Corpl. Lester, V.C., to the Lancashire Fusiliers. He came home on draft leave on 6 Dec. 1917, and was married on the 8th, to Miss Edith Jolley, daughter of Mr. and Mrs. Jolley, of 222, New Chester Road, Port Sunlight. He proceeded to France on 13 Dec. of the same year, and was slightly wounded on 21 March, 1918. He came home to England in July, for the Battalion to be reformed, and went back to France in Sept., and on the 12 Oct. was reported wounded. It was not until the 27th of last month that official news came that he was killed in action. Formerly employed at Messrs. Lever Brothers, in No. 1 Stamping Room, he was the only son of Mr. Walter Hall, of New Chester Road, Port Sunlight. He was in his 21st year, and made his home with his young wife at 222, New Chester Road, Port Sunlight. The greatest sympathy will go to the bereaved families, in the great loss they have sustained. A sad feature of these heroes' death is they both arranged with their respective families that in the event of anything happening to either of them, the other would write home and inform his people, but as fate would have it both fell in the same action."

The second account says :

" ' Remember me to all at home, and tell them I did my best,' was the dying message of Corpl. Frank Lester, whose heroic deeds on the 12th of Oct. led to the posthumous award of the V.C. And what a best it had been ! Truly he had given his life for others. Born at Huyton, in Lancashire, he was brought as a baby in arms to Hoylake, by his parents, Mr. and Mrs. John Lester. When school-age arrived, he was sent to the Church of England Schools, first in the infants' department, and later in the boys. There, as also in the ranks of the Boys' Brigade, which he joined later, his character was moulded into one possessing, among other qualities, quiet determination and the spirit of self-sacrifice and devotion to duty. After leaving school in 1910, he started to learn joinering, but on the family removing to Irby in 1912, the rest of his time (before freely and voluntarily joining the Army) was spent in assisting his father on his market garden. The whole family is musical, Mr. and Mrs. Lester both being good vocalists, who assisted the Hoylake Temperance choir, and the Congregational Church choir before their removal. Frank shone as an instrumentalist, becoming organist of the little chapel on Irby Mill Hill. After joining up, his previous knowledge of drill and discipline, grounded in him while at school and in the Boys' Brigade, enabled him to make rapid progress. He became Sergeant-Instructor, but had to relinquish his rank on being drafted out to the front. He had again reached the rank of Corporal before he did the deed which will cause his name and memory to be treasured for all time in the annals of Hoylake and Irby."

TANDEY, H., D.C.M., M.M., Private, served in the European War, and was awarded the Distinguished Conduct Medal and the Military Medal. He was awarded the Victoria Cross for his services in France [London Gazette, 14 Dec. 1918] : " H. Tandey, D.C.M., M.M., No. 34506, Private, 5th Battn. West Riding Regt. (Territorial Force) (Leamington). For most conspicuous bravery and initiative during the capture of the village and the crossings at Marcoing, and the subsequent counter-attack on 28 Sept. 1918. When, during the advance on Marcoing, his platoon was held up by machine-gun fire, he at once crawled forward, located the machine gun, and with a Lewis gun team knocked it out. On arrival at the crossings he restored the plank bridge under a hail of bullets, thus enabling the first crossing to be made at this vital spot. Later in the evening, during an attack, he, with eight comrades, was surrounded by an overwhelming number of Germans, and though the position was apparently hopeless, he led a bayonet charge through them, fighting so fiercely that 37 of the enemy were driven into the hands of the remainder of his company. Although twice wounded, he refused to leave till the fight was won."

Robert Mactier

MACTIER, ROBERT, Private, came from Tatura, Victoria, Australia. He served in the European War, and for his services in France was posthumously awarded the Victoria Cross [London Gazette, 14 Dec. 1918] : " Robert Mactier, Private, late 23rd Battn. Australian Imperial Force. For most conspicuous bravery and devotion to duty on the morning of the 1st Sept. 1918, during the attack on the village of Mont St. Quentin. Prior to the advance of the battalion, it was necessary to clear up several enemy strong points close to our line. This the bombing patrols sent forward failed to effect, and the battalion was unable to move. Private Mactier single-handed, and in daylight, thereupon jumped out of the trench, rushed past the block, closed with and killed the machine-gun garrison of eight men with his revolver and bombs, and threw the enemy machine gun over the parapet. Then, rushing forward about 20 yards, he jumped into another strong point held by a garrison of six men, who immediately surrendered. Continuing to the next block through the trench, he disposed of an enemy machine gun which had been enfilading our flank advancing troops, and was then killed by another machine gun at close range. It was entirely due to this exceptional valour and determination of Private Mactier that the battalion was able to move on to its ' jumping-off ' trench and carry out the successful operation of capturing the village of Mont St. Quentin a few hours later." Private Mactier was born 17 May, 1890, at Tatura, son of Robert and Christina Mactier, and was educated at the State School (No. 1441), Tatura. He joined the Australian Imperial Force on 27 Feb. 1917, and was killed in action at Mont St. Quentin 1 Sept. 1918.

YOUNG, JOHN FRANCIS, Private, was born on 14 Jan. 1893, at Kidderminster ; went to Canada, and was a Tobacco Packer in Montreal, where he enlisted on 20 Oct. 1915, in the 87th Battn. Quebec Regt., being one of the few " originals " of that unit. He served in the European War ; was wounded, and for services in France was awarded the Victoria Cross [London Gazette, 14 Dec. 1918] : " John Francis Young, No. 177239, Private, 87th Battn. Quebec Regt. For most conspicuous bravery and devotion to duty in attack at Dury Arras sector on 2 Sept. 1918, when acting as a stretcher-bearer attached to D Company of the 87th Battn. Quebec Regt. This company in the advance over the ridge suffered heavy casualties from shell and machine-gun fire. Private Young, in spite of the complete absence of cover, without the least hesitation went out and in the open, fire-swept ground dressed the wounded. Having exhausted his stock of dressings, on more than one occasion he returned, under intense fire, to his company headquarters for a further supply. This work he continued for over an hour, displaying throughout the most absolute fearlessness. To his courageous conduct must be ascribed the saving of the lives of many of his comrades. Later, when the fire had somewhat slackened, he organized and led stretcher parties to bring in the wounded whom he had dressed. All through the operations of 2, 3 and 4 Sept. Private Young continued to show the greatest valour and devotion to duty."

RAYFIELD, WALTER LEIGH, Private, No. 2204279, was born on 7 Oct. 1879, at Richmond-on-Thames. He was educated at a private school in London ; went to Canada at the age of 10, his education being finished in Canada and America. He joined the Army on 10 July, 1917 at Victoria, British Columbia. He joined up in May, 1917, at the British Recruiting Office at Los Angeles, California, after being rejected twice. He served in the European War, and was awarded the Victoria Cross, [London Gazette, 12 Dec. 1918] : " Walter Leigh Rayfield, No. 2204279, Private, 7th Battn. British Columbia Regt. For most conspicuous bravery, devotion to duty and initiative during operations east of Arras from 2 to 4 Sept. 1918. Ahead of his company he rushed a trench occupied by a large party of the enemy, personally bayoneting two and taking 10 prisoners. Later, he located and engaged with great skill, under constant rifle fire, an enemy sniper who was causing many casualties. He then rushed the section trench from which the sniper had been operating, and so demoralized the enemy by his coolness and daring that 30 others surrendered to him. Again, regardless of his personal safety, he left cover under heavy machine-gun fire and carried in a badly wounded comrade. His indomitable courage, cool foresight and daring reconnaissance were invaluable to his company commander and an inspiration to all ranks." He was Invested at Buckingham Palace 8 March, 1919, by H.M. the King. He was promoted Corporal 27 Sept. 1918, and Acting Sergeant 7 Jan. 1919. He was discharged at Vancouver, British Columbia, 25 April, 1919. Sergt. Rayfield is not married.

Walter Leigh Rayfield.

BEATHAM, ROBERT MATTHEW, Private, was born in the county of Cumberland, England. He went out to Australia, and joined the Australian Military Forces, serving in the European War in France. He was posthumously awarded the Victoria Cross [London Gazette, 14 Dec. 1918] : " Robert Matthew Beatham, No. 2742, Private, late 8th Battn. Australian Imperial Force. For most conspicuous bravery and self-sacrifice during the attack north of Rosières, east of Amiens, on 9 Aug. 1918. When the advance was held up by heavy machine-gun fire, Private Beatham dashed forward, and, assisted by one man, bombed and fought the crews of four enemy machine guns, killing 10 of them and capturing 10 others, thus facilitating the advance and saving many casualties. When the final objective was reached, although previously wounded, he again dashed forward and bombed a machine gun, being riddled with bullets and killed in doing so. The valour displayed by this gallant soldier inspired all ranks in a wonderful manner."

Robert M. Beatham.

George Cartwright.

CARTWRIGHT, GEORGE, Private, is a Londoner who went out to Australia and joined the Australian Military Forces, serving in the European War. For his services in France he was awarded the Victoria Cross [London Gazette, 14 Dec. 1918] : " George Cartwright, Private, 33rd Battn. Australian Expeditionary Force. For most conspicuous bravery and devotion to duty on the morning of the 31st Aug. 1918, during the attack on Road Wood, south-west of Bouchavesnes, near Peronne. When two companies were held up by machine-gun fire from the south-western edge of the wood, without hesitation Private Cartwright moved against the gun in a most deliberate manner under intense fire. He shot three of the team, and, having bombed the post, captured the gun and nine enemy. This gallant deed had a most inspiring effect on the whole line, which immediately rushed forward. Throughout the operation Private Cartwright displayed wonderful dash, grim determination and courage of the highest order."

CURREY, WILLIAM MATTHEW, Private, comes from New South Wales. He served in the European War, and for his services in France was awarded the Victoria Cross [London Gazette, 14 Dec. 1918] : " William Matthew Currey, No. 1584A, Private, 53rd Battn. Australian Imperial Force. For most conspicuous bravery and daring in the attack on Peronne on the morning of 1 Sept. 1918. When the battalion was suffering heavy casualties from a 77mm. field gun at very close range, Private Currey, without hesitation, rushed forward under intense machine-gun fire and succeeded in capturing the gun single-handed after killing the entire crew. Later, when the advance of the left flank was checked by an enemy strong point, Private Currey crept around the flank and engaged the post with a Lewis gun. Finally, he rushed the post single-handed, causing many casualties. It was entirely owing to his gallant conduct that the situation was relieved and the advance enabled to continue. Subsequently he volunteered to carry orders for the withdrawal of an isolated company, and this he succeeded in doing despite shell and rifle fire, returning later with valuable information. Throughout the operations his striking example of coolness, determination and utter disregard of danger had a most inspiring effect on his comrades, and his gallant work contributed largely to the success of the operations."

William M. Currey.

NUNNEY, CLAUDE JOSEPH PATRICK, D.C.M., M.M., Private served in the European War, and won the Distinguished Conduct Medal and the Military Medal, and for his services in France was awarded the Victoria Cross [London Gazette, 14 Dec. 1918] : " Claude Joseph Patrick Nunney, D.C.M., M.M., No. 410935, Private, 38th Battn. Eastern Ontario Regt. For most conspicuous bravery during the operations against the Drocourt–Quéant line on 1 and 2 Sept. 1918. On 1 Sept., when his battalion was in the vicinity of Vis-en-Artois, preparatory to the advance, the enemy laid down a heavy barrage and counter-attacked. Private Nunney, who was at this time at company headquarters, immediately on his own initiative proceeded through the barrage to the company outpost lines, going from post to post and encouraging the men by his own fearless example. The enemy were repulsed and a critical situation was saved. During the attack on 2 Sept. his dash continually placed him in advance of his companions, and his fearless example undoubtedly helped greatly to carry the company forward to its objectives. He displayed throughout the highest degree of valour until severely wounded."

London Gazette, 26 Dec. 1918.—" War Office, 26 Dec. 1918. His Majesty the King has been graciously pleased to approve of the award of the Victoria Cross to the undermentioned Officers, Non-commissioned Officers and Men."

GREENWOOD, HARRY, D.S.O., M.C., Major (Acting Lieut.-Colonel), served in the European War ; was created a Companion of the Distinguished Service Order and awarded the Military Cross. For his services near Ovillers, 23–24 Oct. 1918, he was awarded the Victoria Cross [London Gazette, 26 Dec. 1918] : " Harry Greenwood, D.S.O., M.C., Temporary Major (Acting Lieut.-Colonel), 9th Battn. Yorkshire Light Infantry. For most conspicuous bravery, devotion to duty and fine leadership on the 23rd–24th Oct. 1918. When the advance of his battalion on the 23rd Oct. was checked, and many casualties caused by an enemy machine-gun post, Lieut.-Colonel Greenwood single-handed rushed the post and killed the crew. At the entrance to the village of Ovillers, accompanied by two battalion runners, he again rushed a machine-gun post and killed the occupants. On reaching the objective west of Duke's Wood his command was almost surrounded by hostile machine-gun posts, and the enemy at once attacked his isolated force. The attack was repulsed, and, led by Lieut.-Colonel Greenwood, his troops swept forward and captured the last objective, with 150 prisoners, eight machine guns and one field gun. During the attack on the Green Line, south of Poix Du Nord, on 24 Oct., he again displayed the greatest gallantry in rushing a machine-gun post, and he showed conspicuously good leadership in the handling of his command in the face of heavy fire. He inspired his men in the highest degree, with the result that the objective was captured, and, in spite of heavy casualties, the line was held. During the further advance on Grand Gay Farm Road, on the afternoon of 24 Oct., the skilful and bold handling of his battalion was productive of most important results, not only in securing the flank of his brigade, but also in safeguarding the flank of the division. His valour and leading during two days of fighting were beyond all praise."

WARK, BLAIR ANDERSON, D.S.O., Major, served in the European War, and was created a Companion of the Distinguished Service Order. For his services in France, south-east of Bellicourt, from 29 Sept. to 1 Oct. 1918, Major Wark was awarded the Victoria Cross [London Gazette, 26 Dec. 1918]: " Blair Anderson Wark, D.S.O., Major, 32nd Battn. Australian Imperial Force. For most conspicuous bravery, initiative and control during the period 29 Sept. to 1 Oct. 1918, in the operations against the Hindenburg line at Bellicourt, and the advance through Nauroy, Etricourt, Magny La Fosse and Joncourt. On 29 Sept., after personal reconnaissance under heavy fire, he led his command forward at a critical period and restored the situation. Moving fear-lessly at the head of, and at times far in advance of, his troops, he cheered his men on through Nauroy, thence towards Etricourt. Still leading his assaulting companies, he observed a battery of 77mm. guns firing on his rear com-panies and causing heavy casualties. Collecting a few of his men, he rushed the battery, capturing four guns and ten of the crew. Then, moving rapidly forward with only two N.C.O.'s, he surprised and captured 50 Germans near Magny La Fosse. On 1 Oct. 1918, he again showed fearless leading and gallantry in attack, and without hesitation, and regardless of personal risk, dashed forward and silenced machine guns which were causing heavy casualties. Throughout he displayed the greatest courage, skilful leading and devotion to duty, and his work was invaluable." An Army Order by General Sir H. S. Rawlinson, Commanding the 4th Army, shows that the gallant deeds for which he won his V.C. extended over a period of twelve days. The Order concludes with the remark : " It is beyond doubt that the success achieved by the Brigade during the heavy fighting was due to this officer's (Major Wark's) gallantry, determination, skill and great courage." Major B. A. Wark, V.C., D.S.O., married, at St. George's Church, Worthing, Miss Phyllis Marquiss-Munro, daughter of Mr. Marquiss-Munro, of Eardley House, Worthing, and 16, Norfolk Mansions, Prince of Wales Road, London, S.W.

Blair Anderson Wark.

JOHNSON, JAMES, Second Lieut., served in the European War, and for his services in France, south-west of Wez Macquart, on 14 Oct. 1918, was awarded the Victoria Cross [London Gazette, 26 Dec. 1918]: " James Johnson, Second Lieut., 2nd, attached 36th, Battn. Northumberland Fusiliers. For most conspicuous bravery and devotion to duty south-west of Wez Macquart on the morning of 14 Oct. 1918, during operations by strong patrols. He repelled frequent counter-attacks, and for six hours under heavy fire he held back the enemy. When at length he was ordered to retire he was the last to leave the advanced position, carrying a wounded man. Three times subsequently this officer returned and brought in badly wounded men under intense enemy machine-gun fire. His valour, cheerfulness and utter disregard of danger inspired all."

HUFFAM, JAMES PALMER, Second Lieut., was born 31 March, 1897, at Dunblane, Perthshire, son of Edward Valentine and Dorothy Huffam. He was educated at Berwick-upon-Tweed. He joined the Army 21 Feb. 1915, as a Private, in the 2/7th Northumberland Fusiliers volunteered and went to France 6 June, 1915, and served with the 1/7th North-umberland Fusiliers, with two of his brothers : was promoted Corporal in Sept. 1915, and Sergeant in May, 1916. He returned to England to join the Officers' Training Corps at Oxford on 26 Aug. 1917 ; was given a commission 30 Jan. 1918, as Second Lieutenant, in the same battalion as his eldest brother, Lieut. A. M. Huffam, 5th, attached 1/6th, Duke of Wellington's West Riding Regt. He was awarded the Victoria Cross [London Gazette, 26 Dec. 1918]: " James Palmer Huffam, Second Lieut., 5th, attached 2nd, Battn. Duke of Welling-ton's West Riding Regt. For most conspicuous bravery and devotion to duty on the 31st Aug. 1918. With three men he rushed an enemy machine-gun post and put it out of action. His post was then heavily attacked, and he withdrew fighting, carrying back a wounded comrade. Again, in the night of 31 Aug. 1918, at Saint Servin's Farm, accompanied by two men only, he rushed an enemy machine gun, capturing eight prisoners and enabling the advance to continue. Throughout the whole fighting from 29 Aug. to 1 Sept. 1918, he showed the utmost gallantry." Lieut. Huffam was the first Berwick man to win the V C. He is a good all-round sportsman. Second Lieut. James Palmer Huffam, V.C., was presented with a gold watch and a cheque by the inhabitants of Berwick and district in recognition of the honour he has brought to the town.

James Palmer Huffam.

O'NIELL, JOHN, M.M., Sergt., served in the European War, won the Military Medal, and for his gallantry in France, near Moorseele, 14 Oct. 1918, was awarded the Victoria Cross [London Gazette, 26 Dec. 1918]: " John O'Niell, M.M., No. 4119, Sergt., 2nd Battn. Leinster Regt. For most conspicuous bravery and devotion to duty near Moorseele on 14 Oct. 1918, when the advance of his com-pany was checked by two machine guns and an enemy field battery firing over open sights. At the head of eleven men only he charged the battery, capturing four field guns, two machine guns and sixteen prisoners. Again, on the morning of the 20th Oct. 1918, Sergt. O'Niell, with one man, rushed an enemy machine-gun position, routing about 100 enemy and causing many casualties. Through-out the operations he displayed the most remarkable courage and powers of leadership."

John O'Niell.

ELCOCK, ROLAND EDWARD, M.M., L.-Corpl. (Acting Corpl.), served in the European War, won the Military Medal, and for gallantry in France, south-east of Capelle Ste. Catherine, 15 Oct. 1918, was awarded the Victoria Cross [London Gazette, 26 Dec. 1918]: " Roland Edward Elcock, M.M., No. 271410, L.-Corpl. (Acting Corpl.), 11th Battn. Royal Scots (Wolverhampton). For most conspicuous bravery and initiative south-east of Capelle Ste. Catherine on the 15th Oct. 1918, when in charge of a Lewis gun team. Entirely on his own initiative, Corpl. Elcock rushed his gun up to within ten yards of enemy guns, which were causing heavy casualties and holding up the advance. He put both guns out of action, captured five prisoners, and undoubtedly saved the whole attack from being held up. Later, near the River Lys, this non-commissioned officer again attacked an enemy machine gun and captured the crew. His behaviour throughout the day was absolutely fearless."

WEATHERS, LAWRENCE CARTHAGE, L.-Corpl. (Temporary Corpl.), comes from Te Koparu, New Zealand. He served in the European War, and for his gallantry in France, north of Peronne, 2 Sept. 1918, was awarded the Victoria Cross [London Gazette, 26 Dec. 1918]: " Lawrence Carthage Weathers, No. 1153, L.-Corpl. (Temporary Corpl.), 43rd Battn. Australian Imperial Force. For most conspicuous bravery and devotion to duty on 2 Sept. 1918, north of Peronne, when with an advanced bombing party. The attack having been held up by a strongly-held enemy trench, Corpl. Weathers went forward alone under heavy fire, and attacked the enemy with bombs. Then, returning to our lines for a further supply of bombs, he again went forward with three comrades, and attacked under very heavy fire. Regardless of personal danger, he mounted the enemy parapet and bombed the trench, and with the support of his comrades, captured 180 prisoners and three machine guns. His valour and determination resulted in the successful capture of the final objective, and saved the lives of many of his comrades."

Lawrence C. Weathers.

GORDON, BERNARD SIDNEY, M.M., L.-Corpl., comes from Beacons-field, Tasmania. He served in the European War, won the Military Medal, and for his gallantry in France, east of Bray, was awarded the Victoria Cross [London Gazette, 26 Dec. 1918]: " No. 23, Bernard Sidney Gordon, M.M., L.-Corpl., 41st Battn. Australian Imperial Force. For most conspicuous bravery and de-votion to duty on 26–27 Aug. 1918, east of Bray. He led his section through heavy shell fire to the objective, which he con-solidated. Single-handed he attacked an enemy machine gun which was enfilading his company, killed the man on the gun and captured the post, which contained one officer and ten men. He then cleared up a trench, capturing twenty-nine prisoners and two machine guns. In clearing up further trenches he captured twenty-two prisoners, including one officer, and three machine guns. Practically unaided he captured, in the course of these operations, two officers and sixty-one other ranks, together with six machine guns, and displayed throughout a wonderful example of fearless initiative."

Bernard Sidney Gordon.

HOLMES, WILLIAM EDGAR, Private, was born on 26 June, 1895 at Wood Stanway, son of Edward Holmes, Timber Feller, and Ellen Elizabeth Holmes, daughter of Mr. and Mrs. Stanley. He was educated at Church Stanway, and later worked as a Groom, and subsequently helped his father, who worked on the Stanway Estate. He joined the Army in July, 1915, as a Private in the Gloucestershire Regt., and was transferred to the 2nd Battn. Grenadier Guards, serving in the

European War. He went out to France at its outbreak, and took part in the Retreat from Mons and the Battle of Ypres. He had frost-bite so severely that he had to have two of his toes amputated.   He went out

William Edgar Holmes.

to France again in 1915. He was twice wounded before 9 Oct. 1918, when he was killed in action while winning the Victoria Cross. The award of this, the greatest of war decorations, was announced in the [London Gazette, 26 Dec. 1918] : "William Edgar Holmes, Private 2nd Battn. Grenadier Guards. For most conspicuous bravery and devotion to duty at Cattenières on 9 Oct. 1918. He carried in two men under the most intense fire, and while he was attending to a third case he was severely wounded.   In spite of this he continued to carry wounded, and was shortly afterwards again wounded with fatal results. By his self-sacrifice he was the means of saving the lives of several of his comrades." The Commanding Officer of his company wrote : " . . . It really was a most extremely gallant act to go on carrying when he was already wounded ; unfortunately he only got another twenty yards. I cannot say how sorry I am, not only for his own sake, but also because the company loses such a gallant man, who always, both in and out of the line, showed such a good example." Second Lieut. B. R. Osborne, in a letter to Private Holmes's mother, states that Private Holmes was acting as a stretcher-bearer in his platoon, and was hit in the throat while trying to get a wounded man back to the aid post. He wrote : "May I add that he was one of the best men in my platoon, always cheerful, and loved by everybody." Two of Private Holmes's friends in the platoon wrote : "In your loss it will be a great comfort to you to know that Edgar died the bravest of deaths whilst trying to save a wounded comrade. His loss to us will be very great, as we have been close comrades for the last four years. He was always the life and soul of our platoon. We cannot really express the depths of our sympathy for you in your great bereavement, but we hope you will be able to seek consolation in the fact that he died a hero's death."

MOFFAT, MARTIN, Private, No. 18321, comes from Sligo. He joined

Martin Moffat.

the Army as a Private in the 2nd Battn. Leinster Regt., and served in the European War. For his gallantry near Ledeghem, 14 Oct. 1918, he was awarded the Victoria Cross [London Gazette, 26 Dec. 1918]: "Martin Moffat, No. 18321, Private, 2nd Battn. Leinster Regt. For most conspicuous bravery and devotion to duty on 14 Oct. 1918, near Ledeghem, when, advancing with five comrades across the open, the party suddenly came under heavy rifle fire at close range from a strongly held house. Rushing towards the house through a hail of bullets, Private Moffat threw bombs, and then working to the back of the house, rushed the door single-handed, killing two and capturing 30 of the enemy. He displayed the greatest valour and initiative throughout."

RYAN, JOHN, Private, comes from Tumut, New South Wales. He served in the European War, and for his ser-

John Ryan.

vices in France in the attack on the Hindenburg defences on 30 Sept. 1918, was awarded the Victoria Cross [London Gazette, 26 Dec. 1918]: "No. 1717, Private John Ryan, 55th Battn. Australian Imperial Force. For most conspicuous bravery and devotion to duty during an attack against the Hindenburg defences on 30 Sept. 1918. In the initial assault on the enemy's positions Private Ryan went forward with great dash and determination, and was one of the first to reach the enemy trench. His exceptional skill and daring inspired his comrades, and despite heavy fire, the hostile garrison was soon overcome and the trench occupied. The enemy then counter-attacked, and succeeded in establishing a bombing party in the rear of the position.   Under fire from front and rear, the position was critical, and necessitated prompt action. Quickly appreciating the situation, he organized and led the men near him with bomb and bayonet against the enemy bombers, finally reaching the position with only three men. By skilful bayonet work, his small party succeeded in killing the first three Germans on the enemy's flank, then, moving along the embankment, Private Ryan alone rushed the remainder with bombs. He fell wounded after he had driven back the enemy, who suffered heavily as they retired across No Man's Land. A particularly dangerous situation had been saved by this gallant soldier, whose example of determined bravery and initiative was an inspiration to all."

WOODS, JAMES PARK, Private, comes from Perth, Western Australia.

James Park Woods.

He served in the European War, and for his services near Le Verguier, north-west of St. Quentin, on 18 Sept. 1918, was awarded the Victoria Cross [London Gazette, 26 Dec. 1918] : "James Park Woods, No. 3244A, Private, 48th Battn. Australian Imperial Force. For conspicuous bravery and devotion to duty near Le Verguier, north-west of St. Quentin, on 18 Sept. 1918, when, with a weak patrol, he attacked and captured a very formidable enemy post, and subsequently, with two comrades, held the same against heavy enemy counter-attacks. Although exposed to heavy fire of all descriptions, he fearlessly jumped on the parapet and opened fire on the attacking enemy, inflicting severe casualties. He kept up his fire and held up the enemy until help arrived, and throughout the operations displayed a splendid example of valour, determination and initiative."

London Gazette, 6 Jan. 1919.—" War Office, 6 Jan. 1919.   His Majesty the King has been graciously pleased to approve of the award of the Victoria Cross to the undermentioned Officers, Non-commissioned Officers and Men."

JOHNSON, DUDLEY GRAHAM, Major (Temporary Lieut.-Colonel), was born on 13 Feb. 1884, at Rockliffe, Bourton-on-the-Water, Gloucestershire, younger son of the late Capt. William Johnson, Inniskilling

Dudley Graham Johnson.

Dragoons, and Mrs. Rosina Johnson, of Oddington, Moreton-in-Marsh, Gloucestershire. He was educated at Bradfield College, and joined the Militia (3rd Wiltshire Regt.) in 1901, and the Regular Army, as Second Lieutenant in the 24th Regt. (South Wales Borderers), in July, 1903 ; promoted Lieutenant in 1907 ; Captain in March, 1914 ; Major in Dec. 1917, and was Adjutant of the 2nd Battn. 1909-12. He was married on 12 June, 1912, at Daylesford, to Marjorie, only daughter of the late Rev. Arthur George Grisewood, Rector of Daylesford, Chipping Norton, and they have a son, Peter John Dudley, born on 3 Aug. 1914, and a daughter, Patience Mary, born on 6 April, 1917. He served in the Great War : at Tsingtau, China, with the 2nd Battn. South Wales Borderers, 1914 ; at Gallipoli, with the 2nd Battn. South Wales Borderers, 1915 (wounded 25 April). Home Service from then till 1916. In France with the 19th Division (Nov. and Dec.) 1916. In France with the 1st Division, as D.A.A.G., 1917-18. In France, Commanding the 1st Battn. South Wales Borderers (Jan. to March), 1918. Commanding the 2nd Battn. Royal Sussex Regt. (April, May and Aug. to Dec.), 1918 (wounded 27 May). In Germany, Commanding the 2nd Battn. Royal Sussex Regt. 1919. He was created a Companion of the Distinguished Service Order for his services at Tsingtau in 1914 [London Gazette, 12 March, 1915]. He was awarded a Bar to the Distinguished Service Order for his services in the action near Pontruet, in France, in Sept. 1918 [London Gazette, 6 Jan. 1919]. He was promoted from General Staff Officer, 3rd Grade, to Brigade Major, on 25 May, 1916, and appointed D.A.A.G. 5 Jan. 1917. He was awarded the Military Cross [London Gazette, 1 Jan. 1918]. He was awarded the Victoria Cross [London Gazette, 6 Jan. 1919]: " Dudley Graham Johnson, D.S.O., M.C., South Wales Borderers, attached 2nd Battn. Royal Sussex Regt. For most conspicuous bravery and leadership during the forcing of the Sambre Canal on the 4th Nov. 1918. The 2nd Infantry Brigade, of which the 2nd Battn. Royal Sussex Regt. formed part, was ordered to cross by the lock south of Catillon. The position was strong, and before the bridge could be thrown a steep bank leading up to the lock and a waterway about 100 yards short of the canal had to be crossed. The assaulting platoons and bridging parties, Royal Engineers, on their arrival at the waterway were thrown into confusion by a heavy barrage and machine-gun fire, and heavy casualties were caused. At this moment Lieut.-Colonel Johnson arrived, and, realizing the situation, at once collected men to man the bridges and assist the Royal Engineers, and personally led the assault. In spite of his efforts heavy enemy fire again broke up the assaulting and bridging parties. Without any hesitation, he again reorganized the platoons and bridging parties, and led them at the lock, this time succeeding in effecting a crossing, after which all went well. During all this time Lieut.-Colonel Johnson was under a very heavy fire, which, though it nearly decimated the assaulting columns, left him untouched. His conduct was a fine example of great valour, coolness and intrepidity, which, added to his splendid leadership and the offensive spirit that he had inspired in his battalion, were entirely responsible for the successful crossing."

MACGREGOR, JOHN, Capt., was born in 1888, at Nairn, Scotland, emigrating to Canada in 1909. He joined the Canadian Army as a Private in the 11th C.M.R. at Vancouver in March, 1915 (after snow-shoeing 120 miles across country). He served in France from 22 Sept. 1915, being promoted to Sergeant in Sept. 1916 ; was gazetted Lieutenant 12 May, 1917, and promoted Captain, 2nd Canadian Mounted Rifles, 5 Feb. 1918. He was awarded the D.C.M., the Military Cross with Bar, and the Victoria Cross [London Gazette, 6 Jan. 1919]: " John Macgregor, M.C., D.C.M., Temporary Captain, 2nd

John Macgregor.

C.M.R. Battn. 1st Central Ontario Regt. For most conspicuous bravery, leadership and self-sacrificing devotion to duty near Cambrai from 29 Sept. to 3 Oct. 1918. He led his company under intense fire, and when the advance was checked by machine guns, although wounded, pushed on and located the enemy's guns. He then ran forward in broad daylight, in face of heavy fire from all directions, and, with rifle and bayonet, single-handed put the enemy's crews out of action, killing four and taking eight prisoners. His prompt action saved many casualties and enabled the advance to continue. After reorganizing his command under heavy fire he rendered most useful support to neighbouring troops. When the enemy were showing stubborn resistance he went along the line, regardless of danger, organized platoons, took command of the leading waves and continued the advance. Later, after a personal daylight reconnaissance under heavy fire, he established his company in Neuville St Remy, thereby greatly assisting the advance into Tilloy. Throughout the operations Capt. Macgregor displayed bravery and heroic leadership."

BISSETT, WILLIAM DAVIDSON, Lieut., was born in the Parish of St. Martin, Perthshire, 7 Aug. 1893. He is the son of Mr. and Mrs. John Bissett, of Ewing Cottage, Crieff, Perthshire, N.B. He was educated at

William Davidson Bissett.

Taylor's Institution, Crieff, and enlisted on 29 April, 1912, as a Private in the 6th (T.F.) Battn. Argyll and Sutherland Highlanders. At the outbreak of war he mobilized with his regiment, which was a unit of the 51st Division, and after training went with his regiment to France 1 May, 1915. He was promoted Lance-Corporal 25 July, 1915, and Corporal, 24 Oct. of the same year (for services as a Bomber in the trenches), by Brigadier-General Ross, G.O.C., 152nd Brigade, 51st Division. Promoted Battalion Bombing Sergeant 1 May, 1916, he was in Sept. of that year selected by his Commanding Officer as suitable for a commission, and was gazetted Second Lieutenant on 19 Dec. following. He rejoined his regiment in France 12 May, 1917, and was awarded the Victoria Cross [London Gazette, 6 Jan. 1919]: " William Davidson Bissett, Lieut., 1/6th Battn. Argyll and Sutherland Highlanders (T.F.). East of Maing, on 25 Oct., in command of the company, after a determined enemy counter-attack had turned his left flank, he withdrew to the railway. The enemy continued to advance in force after his men had exhausted their ammunition. Under heavy fire he mounted the railway embankment, and calling upon his men to charge with the bayonet, drove back the enemy with heavy loss, and later, again charging forward, established his line." The following is an account of a public presentation to Lieut. Bissett: " Lieut. W. D. Bissett, of the 6th Argyll and Sutherland Highlanders (Paisley), who has been awarded the Victoria Cross for conspicuous service in France on 25 Oct. last, was last night honoured in his native town of Crieff by an enthusiastic demonstration in the Porteous Hall. When the news of Lieut. Bissett's honour was received in Crieff, where he has spent most of his life with his parents, the Town Council at once took steps to mark the auspicious occasion. In a short time a handsome sum was collected, and last night the Lieutenant was presented with a handsome gold watch, suitably inscribed, along with War Bonds. A large and representative company were on the platform, including the father and mother of Lieut. Bissett. Provost Mungall, who has taken a specially active interest in the recognition of the gallant officer, presided, and made the presentation. In the course of his remarks he mentioned that Crieff had already a long list of honours won on the field of battle. The list contained two D.S.O.'s, three M.C.'s, one M.S.M., twelve M.M.'s, one Belgian Croix de Guerre, and three 'Mentions in Despatches.' To that they now added a V.C. So far as he knew this was the second V.C. that had come to Perthshire—Comrie claimed the other, and Strathearn claimed them both. (Cheers.) Lieut. Bissett, in acknowledging, said he would always remember that occasion and the wonderful night he spent with the Crieff people. Referring to the 25th Oct., he said that the men of his company were absolutely confident. He was proud of his men, and he himself felt as happy as a schoolboy. His servant, Private M'Neil, M.M., an old soldier, was also confident of success, and when they had men like these the V.C. was easily won. Major Gardiner and Major M'Kean, Argyll and Sutherland Highlanders, paid great tribute to the many excellent qualities of Lieut. Bissett. Mr. J. Gardiner, M.P. for West Perth, in proposing a vote of thanks to Provost Mungall, said that Lieut. Bissett had added lustre to the fair town of Crieff." Lieutenant W. D. Bissett was married to Miss Hilda Heywood, at Emmanuel Parish Church, West Hampstead. Mrs. Bissett was a nursing sister (T.F.N.S.). Lieut. Bissett writes: " I have served since the outbreak of war, and have been over two years on Active Service. I was invested by the King on 10 July, and on 11 July received a civic reception from Paisley, at which my wife was

present. It is interesting to note that my chum, Lieut. J. Buchan, Argyll and Sutherland Highlanders, was also awarded the V.C. Also Capt. A. Henderson, V.C., Argyll and Sutherland Highlanders, was a Private with me in the same company, 1/6th Argyll and Sutherland Highlanders, at the outbreak of war." In Dec. 1918, he proceeded to Italy to the Piave Front. Four months later he left Italy for France.

KERR, GEORGE FRASER, M.C., M.M., Lieut., was born in 1894, at Deseronto. He joined the Army in Sept. 1914, as a Private in the 3rd Battn. 1st

George Fraser Kerr.

Central Ontario Regt., being gazetted Lieutenant in 1917. He served in the European War in France, and was awarded the Military Medal, and the Military Cross for his gallantry on 27 Sept. 1918, at Bourlon Wood. He was awarded the Victoria Cross [London Gazette, 6 Jan. 1919]: " George Fraser Kerr, M.C., M.M., Lieut., 3rd Battn. 1st Central Ontario Regt. For most conspicuous bravery and leadership during the Bourlon Wood operations on 27 Sept. 1918, when in command of the left support company in attack. He handled his company with great skill, and gave timely support by outflanking a machine gun which was impeding the advance. Later, near the Arras-Cambrai road, the advance was again held up by a strong point. Lieut. Kerr, far in advance of his company, rushed this strong point single-handed and captured four machine guns and thirty-one prisoners. His valour throughout this engagement was an inspiring example to all."

GREGG, MILTON FOWLER, M.C., Lieut., is another of the Canadian-born recipients, being a native of Mountain Dale, New Brunswick, and he is 26 years old. He, too, is a former " ranker," having served with the 13th

Milton Fowler Gregg.

Battn. in France before taking a commission in the K.O.R.L. Regt. of the Imperial Army. He afterwards transferred to the 40th Canadian Battn. Before the war he was a School Teacher. He served in the European War, and was awarded the Military Cross. For his gallantry near Cambrai, from 27 Sept. 1918, to 1 Oct. 1918, he was awarded the Victoria Cross [London Gazette, 6 Jan. 1919]: " Milton Fowler Gregg, M.C., Lieut., Royal Canadian Regiment, Nova Scotia Regt. For most conspicuous bravery and initiative during operations near Cambrai 27 Sept. to 1 Oct. 1918. On 28 Sept., when the advance of the brigade was held up by fire from both flanks and by thick uncut wire, he crawled forward alone and explored the wire until he found a small gap, through which he subsequently led his men, and forced an entry into the enemy trench. The enemy counter-attacked in force, and through lack of bombs the situation became critical. Although wounded, Lieut. Gregg returned alone under terrific fire and collected a further supply. Then, rejoining his party, which by this time was much reduced in numbers, and, in spite of a second wound, he reorganized his men and led them with the greatest determination against the enemy trenches, which he finally cleared. He personally killed or wounded 11 of the enemy, and took 25 prisoners, in addition to 12 machine guns captured in this trench. Remaining with his company in spite of wounds, he again on the 30th Sept. led his men in attack until severely wounded. The outstanding valour of this officer saved many casualties and enabled the advance to continue."

HONEY, SAMUEL LEWIS, Lieut., was born at Conn, Wellington County, Ontario, 9 Feb. 1894, son of the Rev. George E. Honey, Methodist Minister, of the Hamilton Conference, and Metta Honey, whose maiden name was Blaisdell, and who is a native of Boston, Massachusetts, U.S.A., where she lived before her marriage. He was educated at Walkerton High School, where he passed the Honour Matriculation Examinations with first-class honours in English and French and second-class honours in Latin and German, and graduated in June, 1914. He joined the Army in Jan. 1915, as a Private in the 34th Battn. (Walkerton). He served in the European War; was a Sergeant when he won the Military Medal for his service in a trench raid a few weeks before the Battle of Vimy Ridge, and also when he was awarded the Distinguished Conduct Medal for services during the progress of that battle. He was given a commission in the 78th Battn. Manitoba Regt., on 9 April, 1917, at Vimy Ridge, and was promoted Lieutenant. He was awarded the Victoria Cross for bravery in action during the Bourlon Wood operations from 27 Sept. to 2 Oct. 1918 [London Gazette, 6 Jan. 1919]: " Samuel Lewis Honey, Lieut., late 78th Battn. Manitoba Regt. On 27 Sept., when his company commander and all other officers of his company became casualties, Lieut Honey took command and skilfully reorganized under most severe enemy shelling and machine-gun fire. He continued the advance with great dash and gained the objective, but finding his company was suffering casualties from enfilade machine-gun fire, he made a personal reconnaissance, and locating the machine-gun nest, he rushed it single-handed, capturing the guns and ten prisoners. Having organized his position, he repelled four enemy counter-attacks, and when darkness fell he again went out himself alone, and having located an enemy post, he led out a party and captured the post of three guns by stealth. He immediately advanced his line, and his new position proved of great value in the jump off the following morning. On 29 Sept. he led his company against a strong enemy position with great initiative and daring, and continued on the succeeding days of the battle to display the same wonderful example of leadership and bravery. He died of wounds received during the last day of the attack by his battalion."

INGRAM, GEORGE MORBY, M.M., Lieut., comes from South Yarra, Victoria. He served in the European War; won the Military Medal, and for services in France was awarded the Victoria Cross [London Gazette, 6 Jan. 1919]: "George Morby Ingram, M.M., Lieut., 24th Battn. Australian Imperial Force. For most conspicuous bravery and initiative during the attack on Montbréhain, east of Peronne, on 3 Oct. 1918. When early in the advance his platoon was held up by a strong point, Lieut. Ingram, without hesitation, dashed out and rushed the post, at the head of his men, capturing nine machine guns, and killing 42 enemy after stubborn resistance. Later, when the company had suffered severe casualties from enemy posts, and many leaders had fallen, he at once took control of the situation, rallied his men under intense fire and led them forward. He himself rushed the first post, shot six of the enemy and captured a machine gun, thus overcoming serious resistance. On two subsequent occasions he again displayed great dash and resource in the capture of enemy posts, inflicting many casualties and taking 62 prisoners. Throughout the whole day he showed the most inspiring example of courage and leadership, and freely exposed himself, regardless of danger."

George Morby Ingram.

MAXWELL, JOSEPH, M.C., D.C.M., Lieut., comes from Sydney, New South Wales. He served in the European War, and was awarded the Distinguished Conduct Medal and the Military Cross. For gallantry in France, north of St. Quentin, on 3 Oct. 1918, he was awarded the Victoria Cross [London Gazette, 6 Jan. 1919]: "Joseph Maxwell, M.C., D.C.M., Lieut., 18th Battn. Australian Imperial Force. For most conspicuous bravery and leadership in attack on the Beaurevoir–Fonsomme line, near Estrées, north of St. Quentin, on the 3rd Oct. 1918. His company commander was severely wounded early in the advance, and Lieut. Maxwell at once took charge. The enemy wire, when reached under intense fire, was found to be exceptionally strong and closely supported by machine guns, whereupon Lieut. Maxwell pushed forward single-handed through the wire, and captured the most dangerous gun, killing three and capturing four enemy. He thus enabled his company to penetrate the wire and reach the objective. Later he again dashed forward and silenced, single-handed, a gun which was holding up a flank company. Subsequently, when with two men only he attempted to capture a strong party of the enemy, he handled a most involved situation very skilfully, and it was due to his resource that he and his comrades escaped. Throughout the day Lieut. Maxwell set a high example of personal bravery, coupled with excellent judgment and quick decision."

Joseph Maxwell.

KIRK, JAMES, Second Lieut., was born at Willow Bank, Adswood, Cheadle Hulme, Cheshire, son of James and Rachel Kirk. He was educated at Miss Chadwick's, Cheadle Hulme, and at Brentnall Street, Stockport, and was well known in Ashton and district as a sportsman. He played for the Seymour Old Boys' Association Football Team, being honorary secretary in the season 1912–13, when the club went right through their competition without sustaining a single defeat. His position in the team as a centre-half was always assured. He was also a well-known member of the Edge Lane Cricket Club. He joined the Army at the age of seventeen, 10 Oct. 1914, in the 6th Battn. Manchester Regt., as a Private, and after doing part of his training at Southport and part at Crowborough, left England for the Dardanelles in July, 1915, and was present at the storming of Achi Baba in Sept. 1915. In Nov. 1915, he was invalided from Gallipoli to Egypt with frost-bite, and spent six weeks in hospital at Cairo, and then when convalescent joined the 1st Camel Corps; was promoted Quartermaster-Sergeant 5 Jan. 1916, and remained with it until Jan. 1917. He happened to be on a trek over the desert and came in contact with his old regiment, the Manchester, which he rejoined, and went with the vanguard to France in Feb. 1917. He was promoted Sergeant in April, 1917; left France with a recommendation for a commission in Dec. 1917; was gazetted Second Lieutenant in June, 1918, and returned to France in Oct. He was killed in action a week before the end of the war, after performing an act of bravery for which he was posthumously awarded the Victoria Cross [London Gazette, 6 Jan. 1919]: "James Kirk, Second Lieutenant, late 10th, attached 2nd, Battn. Man-

James Kirk.

chester Regt. For most conspicuous bravery and devotion to duty north of Ors on 4 Nov. 1918, whilst attempting to bridge the Oise Canal. To cover the bridging of the canal he took a Lewis gun, and under intense machine-gun fire paddled across the canal in a raft, and at a range of 10 yards expended all his ammunition. Further ammunition was paddled across to him, and he continuously maintained covering fire for the bridging party from a most exposed position till killed at his gun. The supreme contempt of danger and magnificent self-sacrifice displayed by this gallant officer prevented many casualties and enabled two platoons to cross the bridge before it was destroyed." The following extract from the recommendation for this award amplifies the official account somewhat: "In order to cover the bridging of the canal he took a Lewis gun and four magazines and paddled across the canal on a raft under a most intense machine-gun barrage. The bank bristled with machine guns. He set up his Lewis gun at ten yards' range, and fired off the whole of his ammunition. Further ammunition was paddled across to him on the raft, and he continued firing, covering the Royal Engineers in their task. He was wounded in the arm and the face, but still fired continuously from a most exposed position until he was shot through the head and fell dead. . . . It was a conscious death to save the men of his platoon and to inspire all who saw him with an example of most magnificent devotion." Major-General Lambert, Commanding the 32nd Division, wrote to his father: "May I on behalf of the 32nd Division say how much pleasure we have felt in the announcement that His Majesty has awarded the Victoria Cross to your son, the late Second Lieut. J. Kirk, for his great gallantry at Ors on 4 Nov. No doubt others have told you with what great personal bravery he crossed the canal in the face of machine-gun and rifle fire, and, after doing most invaluable work with a Lewis gun in keeping down enemy fire, was shot through the head after a display of the most outstanding courage and high example. May I at the same time offer to you and to all his relatives our deepest sorrow and sympathy in his loss. I hope it may be some consolation to you to know that his young life was not given in vain, and that he is and always will be to us, his comrades, an example of the highest devotion and courage which will not be forgotten. The great victory which ended the war was due to the spirit which he gave his life to encourage, and which his regiment and the nation will, I hope, ever be proud to remember." On behalf of his battalion the Commanding Officer, Lieut.-Colonel Robertson, wrote: "If we may be allowed, we would like to share the grief you feel in that he did not live to wear the Victoria Cross, and tell you how proud we all are that we had the honour of serving as comrades with such a soldier, and respect the glory and honour which he has brought to the battalion, an honour for which, I know, he if anyone would have gladly died to obtain. My sincere respects, sir, always."

CALDWELL, THOMAS, Sergt., served in the European War, and for his gallantry in France, near Oudenarde, on 31 Oct. 1918, was awarded the Victoria Cross [London Gazette, 6 Jan. 1919]: "Thomas Caldwell, Sergt., No. 295536, 12th Battn. Royal Scots Fusiliers. For most conspicuous bravery and initiative in attack near Oudenarde on the 31st Oct. 1918, when in command of a Lewis gun section engaged in clearing a farmhouse. When his section came under intense fire at close range from another farm, Sergt. Caldwell rushed towards the farm, and, in spite of very heavy fire, reached the enemy position, which he captured single-handed, together with 18 prisoners. This gallant and determined exploit removed a serious obstacle from the line of advance, saved many casualties, and led to the capture by his section of about 70 prisoners, eight machine guns and one trench mortar."

CLARKE, JAMES, Sergt., was born on 6 April, 1894, at High Street, Winsford, Cheshire. He is the son of Mr. and Mrs. John Clarke. He was educated at St. John's Schools, Over Winsford, Cheshire, and joined the Army on 10 Oct. 1915, and was discharged on 13 May, 1919. He served in the European War, and was awarded the Victoria Cross [London Gazette, 6 Jan. 1919]: "James Clarke, No. 37721, Sergt., 15th Battn. Lancashire Fusiliers (Rochdale). For most conspicuous bravery and initiative during the attack at Happegarbe on 2 Nov. 1918, when in command of a platoon. He led his men forward with great determination, and on being held up by heavy machine-gun fire, rushed forward through a thick, strongly-held ridge, captured in succession four machine guns, and single-handed bayoneted the crews. Later he led the remnants of his platoon to the capture of three machine guns and many prisoners. In the later stages of the attack on the same day, when his platoon was held up by enemy machine guns, he successfully led a Tank against them over very exposed ground. Continuing the attack on 3 Nov., after capturing many prisoners and gaining his objective, he organized his line most skilfully and held up the enemy. On 4 Nov., in the attack on the Oise-Sambre Canal, under heavy fire from the canal bank, he rushed forward with a Lewis-gun team in the face of an intense barrage, brought the gun into action, and effectively silenced the enemy's fire, thus enabling his company to advance and gain their objectives. Throughout the whole of these operations Sergt. Clarke acted with magnificent bravery and total disregard of personal safety, and by his gallantry and high sense of duty set an inspiring example to all ranks."

CURTIS, HORACE AUGUSTUS, Sergt., served in the European War, and for services in France, east of Le Cateau, on 18 Oct. 1918, was awarded the Victoria Cross [London Gazette, 6 Jan. 1919]: "Horace Augustus Curtis, Sergt., No. 14107, 2nd Battn. Royal Dublin Fusiliers. For most conspicuous bravery and devotion to duty east of Le Cateau on the morning of the 18th Oct. 1918, when in attack his platoon came unexpectedly under intense machine-gun fire. Realizing that the attack would fail unless the enemy guns were silenced, Sergt. Curtis, without hesitation, rushed forward through our own barrage and the enemy fire, and killed and wounded the teams of two of the guns, whereupon the remaining four guns surrendered. Then, turning his attention to a trainload of reinforcements, he succeeded in capturing over 100 enemy before his comrades joined him. His valour and disregard of danger inspired all."

RIGGS, FREDERICK CHARLES, Sergt., was the adopted son of Mrs. Burgam, of 39, Capstone Road, Bournemouth. He was adopted when five years old. He was educated at the Malmesbury Park Council School, Bournemouth, and before the war worked for Messrs. Pickford & Sons, Carriers. He joined the Army as a Private in the 15th Hussars on 4 Sept. 1914. He was transferred to the York and Lancaster Regt. (6th Battn.), and went to France in 1915. From there he was sent to Gallipoli until the evacuation, when he was for some time in Egypt. He was sent back to France, and was severely wounded in the head in the Battle of the Somme. After a short period of convalescence in England he again went to France, and was killed on 1 Oct. 1918, near Epinoy, while winning the Victoria Cross. The award was announced in the London Gazette of 6 Jan. 1919 : " Frederick Charles Riggs, M.M., Sergt., No. 20695, late 6th Battn. York and Lancaster Regt. (Bournemouth). For most conspicuous bravery and self-sacrifice on the morning of 1 Oct. 1918, near Epinoy, when, having led his platoon through strong uncut wire under severe fire, he continued straight on, and although losing heavily from flanking fire, succeeded in reaching his objective, where he handled and captured a machine gun. He later handled two captured guns with great effect and caused the surrender of 50 enemy. Subsequently, when the enemy again advanced in force, Sergt. Riggs cheerfully encouraged his men to resist, and while exhorting his men to resist to the last, this very gallant soldier was killed." He had won the Military Medal.

Frederick Charles Riggs.

MERRIFIELD, WILLIAM, Sergt., was born in 1890, at Brentwood, Essex, and was, prior to enlisting, employed for a year and a half as a Fireman on the Canadian Pacific Railway. He served in the European War, and for gallantry near Abancourt 1 Oct. 1918, was awarded the Victoria Cross [London Gazette, 6 Jan. 1919] : " William Merrifield, No. 8000, Sergt., 4th Battn. Central Ontario Regt. For most conspicuous bravery and devotion to duty during the attack near Abancourt on the 1st Oct. 1918. When his men were held up by an intense fire from two machine-gun emplacements, he attacked them both single-handed. Dashing from shell-hole to shell-hole he killed the occupants of the first post, and, although wounded, continued to attack the second post, and with a bomb killed the occupants. He refused to be evacuated, and led his platoon until again severely wounded. Sergt. Merrifield has served with exceptional distinction on many former occasions, and throughout the action of the 1st Oct. showed the highest qualities of valour and leadership." A newspaper correspondent says : " When the special train carrying the Prince of Wales westwards was near Oba yesterday, Sergt. W. Merrifield, of Sault Ste. Marie, went on board and was invested with the Victoria Cross by the Prince. Sergt. Merrifield won the V.C. at Cambrai in Oct. 1918, when he rushed two German machine-gun emplacements single-handed, killed the crews and then led his platoon forward until he was wounded twice and disabled."

William Merrifield.

DAYKINS, JOHN BRUNTON, Corpl. (Acting Sergt.), served in the European War in France, and for services at Solèsmes on 20 Oct. 1918, was awarded the Victoria Cross [London Gazette, 6 Jan. 1919] : " John Brunton Daykins, Corpl. (Acting Sergt.), No. 205353, 2/4th Battn. York and Lancaster Regt. (Territorial Force). For most conspicuous bravery and initiative at Solèsmes on 20 Oct. 1918, when, with twelve remaining men of his platoon, he worked his way most skilfully, in face of heavy opposition, towards the church. By prompt action he enabled his party to rush a machine gun, and during subsequent severe hand-to-hand fighting he himself disposed of many of the enemy and secured his objective, his party, in addition to heavy casualties inflicted, taking 30 prisoners. He then located another machine gun which was holding up a portion of his company. Under heavy fire he worked his way alone to the post, and shortly afterwards returned with 25 prisoners and an enemy machine gun, which he mounted at his post. His magnificent fighting spirit and example inspired his men, saved many casualties, and contributed very largely to the success of the attack."

COLTMAN, WILLIAM HAROLD, Private (L.-Corpl), is one of five brothers in the Army. His home is at Burton-on-Trent. He served in the European War ; won the D.C.M. and M.M., and for gallantry north-east of Sequehart 3–4 Oct. 1918, was awarded the Victoria Cross [London Gazette, 6 Jan. 1919] : " William Harold Coltman, D.C.M., M.M., Private (L.-Corpl)., No. 241028, 1/6th Battn. North Staffordshire Regt. (Territorial Force). For most conspicuous bravery, initiative and devotion to duty. During the operations at Mannequin Hill, north-east of Sequehart on the 3rd and 4th Oct. 1918, L.-Corpl. Coltman, a stretcher bearer, hearing that wounded had been left behind during a retirement, on his own initiative went forward alone in the face of fierce enfilade fire, found the wounded, dressed them, and on three successive occasions carried comrades on his back to safety, thus saving their lives. This very gallant N.C.O. tended the wounded unceasingly for 48 hours."

ARCHIBALD, ADAM, Sapper, was born 14 Jan. 1879, at Leith, Scotland, and is the son of Rennie and Christina Anderson Archibald, of Leith. He was educated at Leith Walk Public School, Edinburgh. He is " a successful amateur gardener, an enthusiastic bowler, and a humble disciple of Izaak Walton." On 6 June, 1902, at Edinburgh, he married Margaret Lander Sinclair, daughter of William and Elizabeth Murray Sinclair, and they have four children : Elizabeth, Christina, Margaret, and Rennie (born 1915). He was outside foreman over Messrs. Stuart's Granolithic Works, Duff Street, Edinburgh. On the outbreak of the European War he joined the Army under Lord Derby's Scheme 4 Nov. 1915, and went to Chatham 10 Nov. 1916. He went to France in Sept. 1917, and for services near Ors was awarded the Victoria Cross [London Gazette, 6 Jan 1919] : " Adam Archibald, No. 213078, Sapper, 218th Field Company, Royal Engineers. Date of Act of Bravery : 4 Nov. 1918. For most conspicuous bravery and self-sacrifice on 4 Nov. 1918, near Ors, when with a party building a floating bridge across the canal. He was foremost in the work under a very heavy artillery barrage and machine-gun fire. The latter was directed at him from a few yards' distance while he was working on the cork floats ; nevertheless, he persevered in his task, and his example and efforts were such that the bridge, which was essential to the success of the operations, was very quickly completed. The supreme devotion to duty of this gallant sapper, who collapsed from gas-poisoning on completion of his work, was beyond all praise."

Adam Archibald.

HARVEY, NORMAN, Private, was born 6 April, 1899, at Newton-le-Willows, son of Charles William and Mary Harvey. He was educated at St. Peter's School, Newton-le-Willows, and joined the Army in Nov. 1914 (at the age of 15 years). He was at that time working at Messrs. Caulfield's, at Newton. He was sent to France, and was slightly wounded when only 16 years old, and again severely wounded at 18 years ; for a short period Private Harvey was retained in England, being still unde overseas age, where he was given a course of instruction in physical and bayonet work at Portsmouth, and passed with excellent qualifications. During the shortage of men at the following Easter, this gallant lad begged to be allowed to return to France, and was transferred to the Royal Inniskilling Fusiliers. He was awarded the Victoria Cross [London Gazette, 6 Jan. 1919] : " Norman Harvey, Private, No. 42954, 1st Battn. The Royal Inniskilling Fusiliers. For most conspicuous bravery and devotion to duty near Ingoyghen on 20 Oct. 1918, when his battalion was held up and suffered heavy casualties from enemy machine guns. On his own initiative he rushed forward and engaged the enemy single-handed, disposing of 20 enemy and capturing two guns. Later, when his company was checked by another enemy strong point, he again rushed forward alone and put the enemy to flight. Subsequently, after dark he voluntarily carried out single-handed an important reconnaissance and gained valuable information. Private Harvey throughout the day displayed the greatest valour, and his several actions enabled the line to advance, saved many casualties, and inspired all." Sergt. Couch, who recommended Private Harvey for the Victoria Cross, writes : " On the 25th Oct. 1918, my platoon was attacking. Suddenly very heavy machine-gun fire was opened on us from a farm about forty yards to my left front. It held my platoon up, and we all got down to fire. Five of my men were wounded, and I saw Private Harvey rush forward under heavy machine-gun fire and go round the left of the farm. Later, I heard a few rifle shots, and the machine gun stopped firing, and then I saw Private Harvey bring about a dozen Bosches from the farm I went forward to the farm and found two dead Bosches and one badly wounded with the bayonet There were two machine guns there. He was doing awfully fine work all day, and seemed to bear a charmed life, because he was running about under heavy machine-gun fire all the time He went forward to another farmhouse where machine-gun fire was coming from, and was away about fifteen minutes, and when he came back he was laughing, and told me the Bosches ' beat it' when he went for them Second Lieut. Savage afterwards told me he volunteered to go to this farm. I don't know how he stuck it, because he was limping about all day with a sprained ankle, which has since made him go sick.' He holds a certificate as Instructor, and has the 1915 Star. Private Harvey is keen on football and gymnastics.

The " Earlestown Guardian " for 10 Jan. 1919, says :
" Newton-le-Willows has been very much in the lime-light this week, and gentlemen of the Press have bestowed much of their valuable time within its boundaries, and they have been surprised to find how far those boundaries extend. The reason is not far to seek, for, as all the world knows, a Newton lad has been awarded the Victoria Cross, and thus put a grand finishing-touch to the long list of decorations which have been won by lads from the town. The news did not come altogether as a surprise to some few who were in the know, for a letter written by a comrade of Private Harvey had revealed the fact that there was something in the wind.

Norman Harvey.

Private Harvey himself had very considerable doubts as to whether he would ever have the good fortune to gain the award, though he knew that he had been recommended for it, and it was owing to these doubts that, in telling his parents, he asked them to keep the news quiet, and ' not let the " Earlestown Guardian " get hold of it.' Knowing that the local picture halls had offered awards to any local lad gaining the V.C., and that —as apparently none had been fortunate enough to do so—the money was likely to be distributed, the fact that a recommendation for the same had been made, was known to the proprietors. Then Mrs. Harvey received a letter from her son saying that the ribbon of the cross had been sent him, and he was to receive the decoration when he came across. Even that, however, did not satisfy her, and she determined that she would not count upon the news as true until she saw it gazetted. It was, therefore, with much pleasure that we perused a telegram which we received from London on Monday, acquainting us with the fact that Tuesday's Gazette contained the news of the award, and our representative set out to find where Private Harvey lived and to take the news along. He found that the home of the new V.C. was situated in just about the most inaccessible point of the township of Newton that it was possible to find. Rumour had it that he resided by the ' Bull,' at Lowton, but fact showed that he had lived there, but that his people had since moved into Parkside Old Station Buildings, a row of perhaps half a dozen houses alongside the railway of the Main line to Manchester, which at one time comprised the historic station near the spot where Mr. Huskisson was killed on the day that the Manchester to Liverpool line was opened, and near where the memorial stands at this day. Here, just within the Newton boundaries, he found Mrs. Harvey, who was naturally delighted to hear that the news was at last gazetted, and was very pleased to receive his congratulations. He learned that Private Norman Harvey enlisted in Nov. of 1914, at the early age of 15, in the South Lancashire Regt. He was at that time working at Messrs. Caulfield's, Newton, and had previously been for a short time with Messrs. Randall, of High Street. He was sent across the water in . . ., and was wounded slightly when 16 years of age, and more severely when 18. As he was still under the overseas age, some attempt was then made to have him retained in this country, and he was put in for a course of instruction at physical and bayonet work, finishing up at Portsmouth with excellent qualifications. During the shortage of men last Easter, however, he asked to be sent overseas again, and was put in the Royal Inniskilling Fusiliers, with whom he served so brilliantly as to add to the lustre of the deeds which already shine in the records of this heroic regiment."

MILES, FRANCIS GEORGE, Private, joined the Army as a Private in the 1/5th Battn. Gloucestershire Regt. (Territorial Force), and served in the European War, and for gallantry in France, near Bois l'Evêque, was awarded the Victoria Cross [London Gazette, 6 Jan. 1919]: " No. 17324, Private Francis George Miles, 1/5th Battn. Gloucester Regt. (T.F.). For most conspicuous bravery and initiative in attack on 23 Oct. 1918, during the advance against the Bois l'Evêque, when his company was held up by a line of enemy machine guns in the sunken road near the Moulin J. Jacques. Private Miles alone, and on his own initiative, went forward under exceptionally heavy fire, located a machine gun, shot the gunner, and put the gun out of action. Observing another gun near by, he again advanced alone, shot the gunner, rushed the gun, and captured the team of eight. Finally, he stood up and beckoned to his company, who, acting on his signals, were enabled to work round the rear of the line and to capture 16 machine guns, one officer and 50 other ranks. It was due to the courage, initiative and entire disregard of personal safety shown by this very gallant soldier that the company was enabled to advance at a time when any delay would have jeopardized seriously the whole operation." He was invested at Buckingham Palace, and two days later returned to his home, the village of Clearwell, near Coleford, Gloucestershire. After being welcomed at Gloucester by the Mayor and Mayoress and the City High Sheriff, he went on to Coleford, where the inhabitants were so enthusiastic that they carried him two and a half miles to his home. The little Gloucestershire village was gay with flowers and flags.

Francis George Miles.

A newspaper correspondent writes :

" Private Francis G. Miles, V.C., No. 17324, 1/5th Gloucester Regt., was born 22 years ago in the village of Clearwell, near Coleford, and is the son of the late Christopher George Miles and of Mrs. Frederick Clack. He is an old scholar of the Clearwell Church of England School, and after leaving was employed by the Princess Royal Colliery Company. During that time he attended the evening classes organized at the school by Mr. S. Evans. On 28 Dec. 1914, he enlisted with his stepfather in the 9th Gloucesters, then training at Cheltenham, and in April, 1915, he went with them to Fovant, near Salisbury, for four months' training with the 26th Division. On 21 Sept. 1915, he was sent to France, where he received his first baptism of fire, and continued with the regiment until he contracted a poisoned foot and had to go to hospital. During his stay there his battalion was ordered to Salonika, so when he got well he was attached to the 8th Gloucesters, and then attached to the Royal Engineers, with whom his trade as a miner proved very useful in tunnelling operations. In July, 1917, he was wounded, having been blown up and buried by a mine, being the only one who escaped alive out of 50. He was sent back to Halifax Hospital (Yorkshire). When he recovered he was keen for active service, and was sent to the 5th Gloucesters in Italy, in Nov. 1917, where he stayed until Aug. 1918. His regiment was then sent back to reinforce the 25th Division in France, and with that division he distinguished himself on 23 Oct. 1918. He fought on the Somme, at Albert, Peronne and Ypres with the 48th Division, but gained the V.C. with the 25th Division. The news of his distinction has been known in Clearwell for several days being first announced by Major Vereker at a meeting which was taking place at Clearwell Castle, and naturally has caused much rejoicing. Private Miles was home on leave at the time, and he and his family have received many congratulations. The villagers intend to make him a handsome present, and he will be fêted upon returning from his visit to the King. There are now two V.C. men residing in adjoining parishes, the first to obtain the honour being Capt Angus Buchanan, V.C., M.C., of Coleford. Clearwell is one of the most patriotic villages in the country, having contributed one or more soldiers from every house. It boasts the record of having sent more soldiers in proportion to the population than any village in England. The whole village is overjoyed with Miles's meritorious performance."

TOWERS, JAMES, Private, lives at Church House Farm, Broughton Preston. He served in the European War, and for his gallantry in France, at Méricourt near Lens, was awarded the Victoria Cross [London Gazette, 6 Jan. 1919] : " James Towers, No 30245, 2nd Battn. Scottish Rifles. For most conspicuous bravery and devotion to duty at Méricourt on 6 Oct. 1918, when, under heavy fire, five runners having failed to deliver an important message, Private Towers, well aware of the fate of the runners who had already attempted the task, volunteered for the duty. In spite of heavy fire opened on him as soon as he moved, he went straight through from cover to cover and eventually delivered the message. His valour, determination, and utter disregard of danger were an inspiring example to all." A newspaper says :

James Towers.

" An Historic Regiment.—An interesting pamphlet dealing with the history of the Cameronians (Scottish Rifles) has been written by the Rev. D. Ferrier, of Bothwell, with a foreword by Lieut.-Colonel C. B. Vandeleur, commanding the depôt of the Cameronians at Hamilton. It gives an account of the part taken by Richard Cameron in Covenanting days, and of the formation of the regiment at Douglas Dale, Lanarkshire, by his followers under the leadership of Lieut.-Colonel William Cleland and Colonel the Earl of Angus to support King William. They won their first great victory at Killiecrankie, fought at Blenheim, in the American War of Independence, and under Sir John Moore at Corunna (where they were commanded by Sir William Maxwell of Monreith). The Cameronians were the 26th Regiment of the Line. In 1881 the 90th, the Perthshire Light Infantry, known as ' The Perthshire Greybreeks,' were linked with them as second battalion. In the present war the 1st Battn. was on the left of the line at the Battle of Mons, and took part also in the Battle of Le Cateau and the artillery fight at Nery. The 2nd Battn was almost wiped out at Neuve Chapelle. Other battalions have also done great service—the 6th Battn. at Festubert, the 10th at Arras, and the 11th in operations in Macedonia. The badge of the regiment consists of the Douglas Star (in honour of Lord Angus, the first Colonel) and the bugle of the 90th Regt. It is the custom of the regiment to go on church parade armed, a memento of the days when the persecuted Covenanters carried their weapons to conventicles."

WILKINSON, ALFRED, Private, was born at Inverness. He joined the Royal Scots Greys in 1914, and was transferred to the 2nd Seaforths in 1915. He served in the European War, and won the Victoria Cross for services described below by a newspaper correspondent :

" On 20 Oct. 1918, he was carrying a message just on the battle-line at Daours, near Corbie, on the Somme, due east of Amiens, when the last coach of a hospital train, just as it passed him, was hit by a bomb from a German aeroplane. Private Wilkinson himself was hit on the face by shrapnel from the explosion, with the result that he had afterwards to get 14 teeth extracted. In spite of this wound, he remained on the scene of the explosion, and found that an Australian soldier—a despatch rider, who had been going in the opposite direction—had got his motor cycle completely wrecked, and had himself been very seriously wounded. Wilkinson carried the Australian back to the Casualty Clearing Station, and the medical officer who made the examination found that the Australian—whose name is Day, and who has already returned to Australia demobilized —was in danger of losing his life, and that a transfusion of blood was immediately necessary. The gallant Seaforth offered to give his blood to save the Australian's life, and the necessary amount of blood was withdrawn from his veins. The Australian authorities regard Wilkinson's double act of heroism as one of the most outstanding examples of grit that the war has produced."

Private A. Wilkinson's Victoria Cross was gazetted 6 Jan. 1919 : " Alfred Wilkinson, No. 43839, Private, 1/5th Battn. Manchester Regt. (Territorial Force). For most conspicuous bravery and devotion to duty on 20 Oct. 1918, during the attack on Marou, when four runners in succession having been killed in an endeavour to deliver a message to the supporting company, Private Wilkinson volunteered for the duty. He succeeded in delivering the message, though the journey involved exposure to extremely heavy machine-gun and shell fire for 600 yards. He showed magnificent courage and complete indifference to danger, thinking only of the needs of his company, and entirely disregarding any consideration for personal safety. Throughout the remainder of the day Private Wilkinson continued to do splendid work." Three brothers of Private Wilkinson have been killed in action in the European War. He was given a gold watch by his fellow members of the St. Joseph's Boys' and Young Men's Society, and the directors of the Mather Lane Spinning Company, where he worked as a Piecer, have presented him with an illuminated address and £50.

Thomas Ricketts.

RICKETTS, THOMAS, Private, was born on 15 April, 1901, at Middle Arm, Newfoundland, son of John Ricketts, a Fisherman, and Amelia Ricketts. When only a schoolboy of 15 he joined the Army in Sept. 1916, declaring himself 18, and served in the European War in France. He was awarded the D.C.M., and the French Croix de Guerre (with Golden Star). He was awarded the Victoria Cross [London Gazette, 6 Jan. 1919]: " Thomas Ricketts, No. 3102, Private, 1st Battn. Royal Newfoundland Regt. (Canadians). Near Ledeghem, on 14 Oct. he volunteered to go with his section commander and a Lewis gun to attempt to outflank a battery causing casualties at point-blank range. Their ammunition was exhausted when still 300 yards from the battery. The enemy began to bring up their gun teams. Private Ricketts doubled back 100 yards under the heaviest machine-gun fire, procured ammunition, dashed back again to the Lewis gun, and by very accurate fire drove the enemy and the gun teams into a farm. His platoon then advanced and captured the four field guns, four machine guns and eight prisoners A fifth field gun was subsequently intercepted by fire and captured." " This is the youngest V.C. in my Army," said the King, introducing Private Ricketts to a Bishop who happened to be in the room at York Cottage, Sandringham, where the Investiture took place.

London Gazette, 31 Jan. 1919.—" War Office, 31 Jan. 1919. His Majesty the King has been graciously pleased to approve of the award of the Victoria Cross to the undermentioned Officers and Non-commissioned Officers."

CLOUTMAN, BRETT MACKAY, M.C., Lieut. (Acting Major), of Marsden House, Colney Hatch Lane, Muswell Hill, N., was born 7 Nov. 1891, in London, and is the son of Alfred Benjamin Cloutman (Governor of Maple and Co.), and stepson of Alice Mary Cloutman, of The Old Hall, Highgate. This well-known house, with its old-time portico, happens to be in the parish of St. Pancras, but the residents of Hornsey will feel a genuine pride in the honour accorded to Major Cloutman, for the family lived for some years at Hill Crest, Waverley Road, Crouch End, N., and are known to many in the borough on account of their long association with Ferme Park Baptist Church, Mr. Cloutman still being the chairman of the Brotherhood there. This V.C. is the last awarded in the Great War, marking a brave deed performed only five days before the signing of the Armistice. Major Cloutman was educated at Berkhamsted School, Stanley House School, Margate ; Bishop's Stortford College, and graduated at the London University in 1913, B.A. with honours (Modern Languages). He was in the London University Officers' Training Corps (Royal Engineers' Contingent), 1909–12. He joined the Army 2 Sept. 1914, enlisting in the 12th Battn. of the County of London Regt. (The Rangers). He had tried previously to get a commission but was unable owing to his eyesight. However, in March, 1915, he obtained one in the Kent (Fortress) Royal Engineers at Gillingham. He was promoted Acting Captain 2 July, 1915, and first went into action in June, 1917, at Vimy Ridge. From Oct. to Nov. 1917, he was in the Ypres district and took part in the fierce fighting at Passchendale Ridge. In Dec. he was sent to Italy, where he spent the winter on the Piave with the Italian Army. In the spring of 1918 he returned to France, to Nieppe Forest, and in the following Aug. took part in the brilliant advance of the Third Army from the Somme to the Sambre. For his conduct on 30 Sept. 1918, he was subsequently awarded the Military Cross : " For conspicuous gallantry and devotion to duty at Banteaux on the morning of 30 Sept. 1918. He made a personal reconnaissance under heavy machine-gun fire to ascertain the possibility of bridging the Canal d'Escaut." In Nov. he gained the highest honour, the Victoria Cross [London Gazette, 31 Jan. 1919] : " Brett Mackay Cloutman, M.C., Lieut. (Acting Major), 59th Field Company, Royal Engineers. Date of Act of Bravery : 6 Nov. 1918. On the 6th Nov. 1918, at Pont-sur-Sambre, Major Cloutman, after reconnoitring the river crossings, found the Quartes Bridge almost intact, but prepared for demolition. Leaving his party under cover, he went forward alone, swam across the river, and having cut the ' leads ' from the charges, returned the same way, despite the fact that the bridge and all approaches thereto were swept by enemy shells and machine-gun fire at close range. Although the bridge was blown up later in the day by other means, the abutments remained intact." This bald official account gives but a slight idea of the incident. The bridge was a single-span structure on stone abutments, situated in quiet country surroundings. Close by was a cottage, and a lock and another building just beyond. The infantry were to advance after the retiring Germans, and it was most desirable to save this bridge from the destruction which would have hindered the

Brett Mackay Cloutman.

progress of our men. The enemy had placed charges at his end, and Major Cloutman made it his business to destroy these. The cottage was full of machine-gunners and the banks of the river also concealed some of the enemy. Major Cloutman managed to reach the river unseen, swam across, and crept along the bank, taking cover as best he could towards the bridge, where he accomplished his object on one side. On his way to the other side, however, the enemy in the lock-keeper's cottage perceived him and directed machine-gun fire at him. He managed to complete his work and set out by the way he had come. He succeeded in dodging the fire which was directed at the bank by which the enemy knew he must return, and swam across the river once more, but on landing and making his way back to the British the lock-house gunners once more did their best to hit him. He reached our lines in safety, nevertheless. The Directors and Staff of Maple and Co., Limited, presented Major Cloutman with a handsome writing table in token of their admiration of his bravery. On 17 Feb. 1916, he married, at Chiswick, Margaret Hunter, daughter of Walter Hunter and the late Mrs. Hunter, of Bedford Park, W., and they have one daughter, Mary Reeve. Major B. M. Cloutman's elder brother, Lieut. W. R. Cloutman, was killed in action on 21 Aug. 1915, while serving with the 178th Tunnelling Company, Royal Engineers. He was overcome by the poisonous fumes in some old trench working near Albert, in an heroic attempt to rescue an N.C.O. under his command who had fallen a victim to the same deadly peril.

HEDGES, FREDERICK WILLIAM, Capt., served in the European War in France, and for services north-east of Bonsies 24 Oct. 1918, was awarded the Victoria Cross [London Gazette, 31 Jan. 1919] : " Frederick William Hedges, Lieut., Bedford Regt., attached 6th Battn. Northamptonshire Regt. For most conspicuous bravery and initiative during the operations north-east of Bonsies on the 24th Oct. 1918. He led his company with great skill towards the final objective, maintaining direction under the most difficult conditions. When the advance was held up by machine-gun posts, accompanied by one sergeant and followed at some considerable distance by a Lewis-gun section, he again advanced and displayed the greatest determination, capturing six machine guns and 14 prisoners. His gallantry and initiative enabled the whole line to advance, and tended largely to the success of subsequent operations." Capt. Hedges was decorated by the King at Buckingham Palace.

MITCHELL, COULSON NORMAN, M.C., Capt., served in the European War, and was awarded the Military Cross. For gallantry in France at the Canal de l'Escaut, north-east of Cambria, 8–9 Oct. 1918, he was awarded the Victoria Cross [London Gazette, 31 Jan. 1919] : " Coulson Norman Mitchell, M.C., Capt., 4th Battn. Canadian Engineers. For most conspicuous bravery and devotion to duty on the night of 8–9 Oct. 1918, at the Canal de l'Escaut, north-east of Cambrai. He led a small party ahead of the first wave of infantry in order to examine the various bridges on the line of approach, and, if possible, to prevent their demolition. On reaching the canal he found the bridge already blown up. Under a heavy barrage he crossed to the next bridge, where he cut a number of ' lead ' wires. Then, in total darkness, and unaware of the position or strength of the enemy at the bridgehead, he dashed across the main bridge over the canal. This bridge was found to be heavily charged for demolition, and whilst Capt. Mitchell, assisted by his N.C.O., was cutting the wires, the enemy attempted to rush the bridge, in order to blow the charges, whereupon he at once dashed to the assistance of his sentry, who had been wounded, killed three of the enemy, captured 12, and maintained the bridgehead until reinforced. Then, under heavy fire, he continued his task of cutting wires and removing charges, which he well knew might at any moment have been fired by the enemy. It was entirely due to his valour and decisive action that this important bridge across the canal was saved from destruction."

Coulson N. Mitchell.

DOYLE, MARTIN, Company Sergt.-Major, was born at New Ross, County Wexford, Ireland, on 25 Oct. 1891. He was in the thick of some of the heaviest fighting in the early part of the war, and was promoted Sergeant. In March, 1918, he was awarded the Military Medal, and received the following letter from the 24th Divisional Commander, Major-General A. L. Daly : " I am very pleased to see that your gallant conduct has been rewarded by the award of the Military Medal, and I offer you my personal congratulations." At about the same time he was captured by the Germans, and was very cruelly treated while in captivity, but regained his liberty as the result of a counter-attack by his regiment. He had been recommended for the Victoria Cross, as he just mentioned to his parents in letters home, but when he came home on leave could not be induced to expand on his military achievements. Eventually the recommendation was passed, and he sent home the following letter to his parents :

Martin Doyle.

" MY DEAR PARENTS,

" By now you will have had my telegram. At last my V.C. has come through. I received the glad tidings to-day (Friday). I will be home in about a fortnight. I am all in a whirl of joy.

" Your loving son,

" MARTIN."

The award which so delighted him was announced in the London Gazette of 31 Jan. 1919 : " Martin Doyle, M.M., Company Sergt.-Major, No. 10864, 1st Battn. Munster Fusiliers (New Ross, County Wexford). On the 2nd Sept. 1918, near Riencourt, as Acting Company Sergeant-Major, command of the company devolved upon him consequent on officer casualties. Observing that some of our men were surrounded by the enemy, he led a party to their assistance, and by skill and leadership worked his way along the trenches, killed several of the enemy and extricated the party, carrying back under heavy fire a wounded officer to a place of safety. Later, seeing a Tank in difficulties, he rushed forward under intense fire, routed the enemy who were attempting to get into it, and prevented the advance of another enemy party collecting for a further attack on the Tank. An enemy machine gun now opened on the Tank at close range, rendering it impossible to get the wounded away, whereupon Company Sergt.-Major Doyle, with great gallantry, rushed forward, and, single-handed, silenced the machine gun, capturing it with three prisoners. He then carried a wounded man to safety under a very heavy fire. Later in the day, when the enemy counter-attacked his position, he showed great power of command, driving back the enemy and capturing many prisoners. Throughout the whole of these operations Company Sergt.-Major Doyle set the very highest example to all ranks by his courage and total disregard of danger." He is fond of most sports. He competed for and won the mile race open to the 57th Division in France in 1918, and won the novice boxing (light-weight) match of his regiment in 1913.

CAIRNS, HUGH, Sergt., D.C.M., served in the European War, and for gallantry in France was awarded the Victoria Cross [London Gazette, 31 Jan. 1919] : " Hugh Cairns, D.C.M., Sergt., No. 472168, late 46th Battn. Saskatchewan Regt. For most conspicuous bravery before Valenciennes on 1 Nov. 1918, when a machine gun opened on his platoon. Without a moment's hesitation Sergt. Cairns seized a Lewis gun and single-handed, in face of direct fire, rushed the post, killed the crew of five, and captured the gun. Later, when the line was held up by machine-gun fire, he again rushed forward, killing 12 enemy and capturing 18 and two guns. Subsequently, when the advance was held up by machine guns and field guns, although wounded he led a small party to outflank them, killing many and capturing all the guns. After consolidation he went with a battle patrol to exploit Marly, and forced 60 enemy to surrender. Whilst disarming this party he was severely wounded. Nevertheless, he opened fire and inflicted heavy losses. Finally he was rushed by about 20 enemy, and collapsed from weakness and loss of blood. Throughout the operation he showed the highest degree of valour, and his leadership greatly contributed to the success of the attack. He died on the 2nd Nov. from wounds."

Hugh Cairns.

WARING, WILLIAM, Corpl. (L.-Sergt.), was born on 13 Oct. 1885, at Welshpool, son of Richard and Annie Waring. He was educated at the National School, Welshpool, and joined the Army in the Montgomeryshire Yeomanry in 1904. His father writes : " He was mobilized on 4 Aug. 1914, as Sergeant, and transferred in April, 1916, to the 25th (S.) Battn. Royal Welsh Fusiliers, in which corps he was serving when he won the M.M. and V.C. Sergt. Waring was in possession of the Territorial Long Service Medal. He had the distinction of winning a silver watch for being the best shot in his squadron (1913). In May, 1914, his troop was awarded a silver cup for being the best troop in the squadron. Sergt. Waring won many distinctions on the local football field, and played for many of the best local football teams in Montgomeryshire. The late Sergt. Waring was a single man. I am sorry no account of his death has reached us." He served in the European War in Egypt and France ; was awarded the Military Medal [London Gazette, November, 1917], and for gallantry in France was awarded the Victoria Cross [London Gazette, 31 Jan. 1919] : " William Waring, M.M., No. 355014, Corpl. (L.-Sergt.), late 25th Battn. Royal Welsh Fusiliers (Territorial Force). For most conspicuous bravery and devotion to duty at Ronssoy on 18 Sept. 1918. He led an attack against enemy machine guns which were holding up the advance of neighbouring troops, and, in the face of devastating fire from flank and front, single-handed, rushed a strong point, bayoneting four of the garrison and capturing 20 with their guns. L.-Sergt. Waring then, under heavy shell and machine-gun fire, reorganized his men, and led and inspired them for another 400 yards, when he fell mortally wounded. His valour, determination and leadership were conspicuous throughout."

William Waring.

McPHIE, JAMES, Corpl., was born at 21, Salisbury Place, Edinburgh, 18 Dec. 1894, son of Allan McPhie (deceased) and Elizabeth McPhie. He was educated at South Bridge School, and joined the Territorial Force in the beginning of 1912. He served in the European War, and was awarded the Victoria Cross [London Gazette, 31 Jan. 1919] : " No. 422047, James McPhie, Corpl., late 416th Field Company, Royal Engineers (Territorial Force). For most conspicuous bravery on 14 Oct. 1918, when with a party of sappers maintaining a cork float bridge across the Canal de la Sensée, near Aubencheul-au-Bac. The farther end of the bridge was under close machine-gun fire and within reach of hand grenades. When infantry, just before dawn, were crossing it, closing up resulted and the bridge began to sink and break. Accompanied by a sapper, he jumped into the water and endeavoured to hold the cork and timbers together, but this they failed to do. Corpl. McPhie then swam back, and, having reported the broken bridge, immediately started to collect material for repair. It was now daylight. Fully aware that the bridge was under close fire and that the far bank was almost entirely in the hands of the enemy, with the inspiring words, ' It is death or glory work which must be done for the sake of our patrol on the other side,' he led the way, axe in hand, on to the bridge, and was at once severely wounded, falling partly into the water, and died after receiving several further wounds. It was due to the magnificent example set by Corpl. McPhie that touch was maintained with the patrol on the enemy bank at a most critical period."

James McPhie.

A newspaper says :

" A sum of £744 was raised by the public of Edinburgh for Mrs. McPhie, mother of Corpl. McPhie, posthumously awarded the V.C. An annuity bond bringing a weekly income of 22s. 3d. was purchased, and this, along with the balance of £14, was presented to Mrs. McPhie at Edinburgh yesterday by the Lord Provost."

AMEY, WILLIAM L., Corpl., served in the European War, and for his gallantry in France, at Landrecies, was awarded the Victoria Cross [London Gazette, 31 Jan. 1919] : " William L. Amey, Corpl., No. 307817, 1/8th Battn. Royal Warwickshire Regt. (T.F.) (Birmingham). For most conspicuous bravery on 4 Nov. 1918, during the attack on Landrecies, when owing to fog many hostile machine-gun nests were missed by the leading troops. On his own initiative he led his section against a machine-gun nest, under heavy fire, drove the garrison into a neighbouring farm, and finally captured about 50 prisoners and several machine guns. Later, single-handed, and under heavy fire, he attacked a machine-gun post in a farmhouse, killed two of the garrison and drove the remainder into a cellar until assistance arrived. Subsequently, single-handed, he rushed a strongly-held post, capturing 20 prisoners. He displayed throughout the day the highest degree of valour and determination."

LEWIS, ALLAN LEONARD, L.-Corpl., was born 28 Feb. 1895, at Wood Villa, Whitney-on-Wye, son of Mr. and Mrs. George Lewis. He was educated at Whitney-on-Wye School, and joined the Army in March, 1915, as a Private in the Mechanical Transport Section, the Royal Army Service Corps. He was for some time with the School of Instruction, British Expeditionary Force, France. While in France he was taken ill with jaundice, returning to England ; on his recovery he was transferred to No. 8 Platoon, Northamptonshire Regt., at Sheerness. He returned to France, and was posthumously awarded the Victoria Cross [London Gazette, 31 Jan. 1919] ; " Allan Leonard Lewis, L.-Corpl., 6th Battn. Northamptonshire Regt. For most conspicuous bravery at Ronssoy on 18 Sept. 1918, when in command of a section on the night of an attacking line held up by intense machine-gun fire. L.-Corpl. Lewis, seeing that two enemy machine guns were enfilading the line, crawled forward, single-handed, and successfully bombed the guns, and by rifle fire later caused the whole team to surrender, thereby enabling the whole line to advance. On 21 Sept. 1918, he again displayed great powers of command, and having rushed his company through the enemy barrage, was killed while getting his men under cover from heavy machine-gun fire. Throughout he showed a splendid disregard of danger, and his leadership at a critical period was beyond praise." L.-Corpl. Lewis was a handsome, well-built young man ; high principled and steadfast, he was of an amiable disposition that attached friendships. " As a lad he indulged in outdoor games with much zest, and as a youth proved a good shot and a lucky angler ; having a natural fondness for acquiring knowledge."

Allan Leonard Lewis.

A correspondent in the " Hereford Times," 8 Feb. 1919, writes :

" Seven new V.C.'s were announced by the War Office last week, and among them was a Herefordshire soldier, L.-Corpl. Allan Leonard Lewis, 6th Battn. Northamptonshire Regt., of Wyeside, Brilley Whitney-on-Wye, to whom it has been awarded, alas, posthumously ! It was bestowed ' For most conspicuous bravery at Ronssoy on 18 Sept. 1918, when in command of a section on the right of an attacking line held up by intense machine-gun fire. L.-Corpl. Lewis, seeing that two enemy machine guns were enfilading the line, crawled forward, single-handed, and successfully bombed the guns, and by rifle fire later caused the whole team to surrender, thereby enabling the whole line to advance. On 21 Sept. 1918, he again displayed great powers of command, and, having rushed his company through the enemy barrage, was killed while getting his men under cover from heavy machine-gun fire. Throughout he showed a splendid disregard of danger, and his leadership at a critical period was beyond all praise.'

"It was in Oct. last that news reached Whitney of L.-Corpl. Lewis's death in action, and a month later a comrade in the Australian Forces wrote giving brief details. The V.C. was struck on the head by shrapnel, which penetrated the temple, death obviously being instantaneous. But not till nine days afterwards was the body found. On discovering it on 30 Sept., north-west of St. Quentin, the Australian, carrying out the unwritten compact of comrades facing the enemy in the field, took from it the deceased's pay book and forwarded it to his mother. Information since received shows the V.C. was buried east of Lempire, south-west of Le Catelet. The first incident described in the official record unquestionably ranks as one of the most valorous deeds even in this war of unexampled bravery, and it will assuredly provoke feelings of patriotic pride in the breast of every Herefordshire resident to reflect that a 'son of the soil' from a humble rural home should have won immortal fame on the battlefield in what happily proved to be the closing stages of the most gigantic struggle in the world's history. The natural gratification afforded by the achievement is, unfortunately, saddened by the fact that three days later this Herefordshire hero fell in battle, so that there will be no opportunity for his friends and fellow-countrymen to demonstrate their feelings of admiration for him in a glad home-coming, such as they would have delighted to give him had he survived. He died as hundreds of thousands of Britain's best have died—that we might live—and the conspicuous glory he achieved is imperishable, constituting a shining example for future generations of Herefordshire boys to emulate. In the phraseology of the King's message of sympathy to the bereaved parents—'He whose death we mourn died in the noblest of causes. His country will be ever grateful to him for the sacrifice he has made for freedom and justice.'

"L.-Corpl. Lewis was the second son of Mr. and Mrs. George Lewis, whose little cottage stands on the left bank of the Wye, in the parish of Brilley, within three-quarters of a mile of Whitney-on-Wye Station, on the main road from Hereford to Glasbury. From a height which gives an excellent view of a beautiful landscape of fertile meadows and wooded hills, the garden, in a setting of fruit trees, slopes away so precipitately that a stone, if started from the door of the house (the only entrance), would roll sheer into the river. The V.C., who was born at Wood Villa, Whitney-on-Wye, was one of a family of nine children—five boys and four girls. He was only 23 years of age; had he lived he would have been 24 on the 28th inst. A brother, the eldest son, Frank, is a Private in the Brecknockshire Regt., now stationed in India. Though their home is in the civil parish of Brilley, the family are in all their associations Whitney-on-Wye people, inasmuch as their home is nearer the latter village than the former. Allan and all his brothers and sisters have in turn attended Whitney-on-Wye School; the two younger boys and one little girl are still scholars there. In Allan's time the late Mr. Pickering was schoolmaster. Two of the elder sisters are employed at the 'Queen's Arms,' Hereford, and an aunt, Mrs. Carpenter, also resides in the city, in Widemarsh Street. Allan's father is a native of Brilley, and has lived in that neighbourhood all his life, following the occupation of a jobbing carpenter. His mother is a Dorsetshire woman, whose bright disposition irradiates the home, where obviously the virtue of thrift is not neglected. She was born at Lyme Regis, and came to Herefordshire nearly thirty years ago as lady's maid at Cabalva, then the residence of the late Mr. and Mrs. Heaton. Allan, when he left school at the age of 13, went to work on the land, first for Mr. Tom Prosser, The Wern Farm, Brilley, and afterwards for Mr. Price, at Penalt, near Hay. But agricultural work and prospects had no attraction for him, and, like many other Herefordshire sons of the soil, he soon migrated to South Wales. Here he obtained a situation as gardener to Mr. J. Picton, Truscod, Llandilo, in Carmarthenshire. Allan was, however, of a mechanical turn of mind and hankered after something different from gardening. Motors were more to his liking, and after a period of conductorship and training he was employed as a motor-'bus driver at Neath, on the G.W.R. Pontardawe road service. It was while on this work that he answered, voluntarily, the call of his country, and exchanged overalls for khaki. This was in March, 1915, and his brother followed suit two months later. Both said they would not 'stay to be fetched,' and both vowed that whatever else might happen to them they would not allow themselves to be taken prisoners alive by the Germans. Curiously enough, Frank is now guarding Mesopotamian prisoners of war in India. The future V.C. joined the Mechanical Transport Section of the Royal Army Service Corps, but fate decreed that he should eventually be transferred to the infantry; and it was in the infantry that he distinguished himself so magnificently, proving not only a valiant soldier, but a gallant and daring leader of men. He was last home on leave in Aug. 1918, and having a natural fondness for acquiring knowledge, reflected that he had learnt something of Welsh in Wales and something of French in France. Up to the day he made the supreme sacrifice L.-Corpl. Lewis went though much fighting without a scratch, but in the early part of last year he suffered from jaundice, for which he was under treatment in a Red Cross Hospital at Longleat, Wiltshire, the residence of Lord and Lady Bath, both of whom, and also Lady Kathleen, displayed more than an ordinary interest in him."

London Gazette, 13 Feb. 1919.—"War Office, 13 Feb. 1919. His Majesty the King has been graciously pleased to approve of the award of the Victoria Cross to the undermentioned Officers."

WATERS, ARNOLD HORACE SANTO, Temporary Capt. (Acting Major), was born on 23 Sept. 1886, at Plymouth, son of the Rev. Richard Waters, Minister of the United Methodist Free Church, and Abigail Waters.

Arnold H. S. Waters.

He was educated at the Hoe Grammar School, Plymouth. He is an Engineer, and for two years before the war was engaged on important work in the Rhymney Valley and Eastern Valleys, South Wales, for his firm, Messrs. Wilcox and Raikes, Consulting Engineers, of Birmingham and Westminster. He joined the Army on 30 Jan. 1915, as a Second Lieutenant in the Royal Engineers. He served in the European War, and succeeded in winning the Military Cross, the Distinguished Service Order, and the Victoria Cross. The Military Cross was won in July, 1917. He was created a Companion of the Distinguished Service Order [London Gazette, 3 June, 1918]: "Arnold Horace Santo Waters, M.C., Lieut. (Acting Major), Royal Engineers." He was mentioned in Despatches in June, 1918, and was awarded the Victoria Cross [London Gazette, 13 Feb. 1919]: "Arnold Horace Santo Waters, D.S.O., M.C., Temporary Captain (Acting Major), 218th Field Company, Royal Engineers. For most conspicuous bravery and devotion to duty on the 4th Nov. 1918, near Ors, when bridging with his Field Company the Oise–Sambre Canal. From the outset the task was under artillery and machine-gun fire at close range, the bridge being damaged and the building party suffering severe casualties. Major Waters, hearing that all his officers had been killed or wounded, at once went forward and personally supervised the completion of the bridge, working on cork floats while under fire at point-blank range. So intense was the fire that it seemed impossible that he could escape being killed. The success of the operation was due entirely to his valour and example."

A newspaper correspondent says:

"The Mayor moved a resolution that an illuminated address should be presented to Major Waters, V.C., D.S.O., M.C., congratulating him upon his distinguished and gallant services in the war, and remarked that although not strictly a Plymouth man, Major Waters was in sentiment and upbringing. He was educated in the town, and lived here until about 19 years of age, and his father was a highly esteemed minister in the town. They would like to put into permanent form their appreciation of his gallantry. When he went to the King, he had been recommended for a further bar to the D.S.O., but the King decided, on seeing his record, that it was not a case for a further bar to the D.S.O., and awarded him the V.C. He moved that they should present Major Waters with the following address:

"'That we, the Mayor, aldermen, and burgesses of the borough of Plymouth in Council assembled, having heard with great satisfaction that His Majesty the King has been pleased to confer the V.C., the D.S.O., and the M.C. upon Major Arnold Horace Santo Waters, of the Royal Engineers (who was born and educated at Plymouth), desire to place on record our profound admiration of the gallant conduct of Major Waters with H.M. Forces in the Great War, and to offer him hearty congratulations on the well-deserved honours which have been bestowed upon him."

MARSHALL, JOHN NEVILLE, M.C., Lieut. (Acting Lieut.-Colonel), served in the European War and was awarded the Military Cross. He was awarded the Victoria Cross [London Gazette, 13 Feb. 1919] for services in France: "John Neville Marshall, M.C., Lieut. (Acting Lieut.-Colonel), late Irish Guards (Special Reserve), attached 16th Battn. Lancashire Fusiliers. For most conspicuous bravery, determination and leadership in the attack on the Sambre–Oise Canal, near Catillon, on the 4th Nov. 1918, when a partly-constructed bridge came under concentrated fire and was broken before the advanced troops of his battalion could cross. Lieut.-Colonel Marshall at once went forward and organized parties to repair the bridge. The first party were soon killed or wounded, but by personal example he inspired his command, and volunteers were instantly forthcoming. Under intense fire and with complete disregard of his own safety, he stood on the bank encouraging his men and assisting in the work, and when the bridge was repaired attempted to rush across at the head of his battalion, and was killed while so doing. The passage of the canal was of vital importance, and the gallantry displayed by all ranks was largely due to the inspiring example set by Lieut.-Colonel Marshall."

London Gazette, 17 March, 1919.—"Admiralty, 17 March, 1919. The King has been graciously pleased to approve of the posthumous award of the Victoria Cross to the undermentioned Officers."

BRADFORD, G. N., Lieut.-Commander, Royal Navy, served in the European War, and was awarded the Victoria Cross [London Gazette, 17 March, 1919]: "G. N. Bradford, Lieut.-Commander, Royal Navy. For most conspicuous gallantry at Zeebrugge on the night of the 22nd–23rd April, 1918. This officer was in command of the Naval storming parties embarked in Iris II. When Iris II. proceeded alongside the Mole great difficulty was experienced in placing the parapet anchors owing to the motion of the ship. An attempt was made to land by the scaling ladders before the ship was secured. Lieut. Claude E. K. Hawkings (late Erin) managed to get one of the ladders in position and actually reached the parapet, the ladder being crashed to pieces just as he stepped off it. This very gallant young officer was last seen defending himself with his revolver. He was killed on the parapet. Though securing the ship was not part of his duties, Lieut.-Commander Bradford climbed up the derrick which carried a large parapet anchor and was rigged out over the port side; during this climb the ship was surging up and down and the derrick crashing on the Mole. Waiting his opportunity, he jumped with the parapet anchor on to the Mole and placed it in position. Immediately after hooking on the parapet anchor, Lieut.-Commander Bradford was riddled with bullets from machine guns, and fell into the sea between the Mole and the ship. Attempts to recover his body failed. Lieut.-Commander Bradford's action was one of absolute self-sacrifice. Without a moment's hesitation he went to certain death, realizing that in such action lay the only possible chance of securing Iris II. and enabling her storming parties to land." Lieut.-Commander Bradford's brother, Brigadier-General Bradford, had also won the Victoria Cross.

HARRISON, ARTHUR LEYLAND, Lieut.-Commander, was born on 3 Feb. 1886, at Torquay, Devonshire, son of the late Lieut.-Colonel A. J. Harrison, of the 7th Royal Fusiliers, and of Mrs. A. J. Harrison, of Waddon Cottage, Durham Road, Wimbledon, S.W. He was educated at Dover College, and joined the Navy as a cadet in Sept. 1902. He was promoted Lieutenant in Oct. 1908, and Lieutenant-Commander in Oct. 1916. He was a member of the United Services Rugby Football team, and gained two international caps in the season 1913–1914, playing against Ireland and France. He was one of the players who took part in one of the finest games played by the Royal Navy and Army officers' teams at Queen's Club in March, 1914, when the teams were presented to the King after the match. He served in the European War. He took part in the battles of Heligoland Bight (1914), Dogger Bank (1915), and Jutland (1916), and was mentioned in Despatches for his services in the last-mentioned action [London Gazette, 15 Sept. 1916]. He was awarded the Victoria Cross [London Gazette, 17 March, 1919]: "Lieut.-Commander Arthur Leyland Harrison, R.N. For most conspicuous gallantry at Zeebrugge on the night of the 22nd–23rd April, 1918. This officer was in immediate command of the Naval Storming parties embarked in Vindictive. Immediately before coming alongside the Mole, Lieut.-Commander Harrison was struck on the head by a fragment of a shell which broke his jaw and knocked him senseless. Recovering consciousness, he proceeded on to the Mole and took over command of his party, who were attacking the seaward end of the Mole. The silencing of the guns on the Mole head was of the first importance, and though in a position fully exposed to the enemy's machine-gun fire, Lieut.-Commander Harrison gathered his men together and led them to the attack. He was killed at the head of his men, all of whom were either killed or wounded. Lieut.-Commander Harrison, though already severely wounded and undoubtedly in great pain, displayed indomitable resolution and courage of the highest order in pressing his attack, knowing as he did that any delay in silencing the guns might jeopardize the main object of the expedition, i.e., the blocking of the Zeebrugge-Bruges Canal."

Arthur L. Harrison.

London Gazette, 15 May, 1919.—"War Office, 15 May, 1919. His Majesty the King has been graciously pleased to approve of the award of the Victoria Cross to the undermentioned Officers."

FINDLAY, GEORGE DE CARDONNEL ELMSALL, Capt. (Acting Major), Royal Engineers, was born on 20 Aug. 1889, in Dumbartonshire, son of Robert Elmsall Findlay, of Boturich, Balloch, and Jane Cecilia Louise Findlay. He was educated at St. Ninian's, Moffat (captain football Eleven and Fifteen), and Harrow School (won Spencer Cup, 1907 Bisley; captain, winning school, shooting Eight, 1908 Bisley), and Royal Military Academy, Woolwich (won revolver shooting, 1908 and 1909), and joined the Army on 30 Jan. 1910, serving in the 5th Field Troop, Royal Engineers (sick leave 10 months as result of riding accident breaking both legs); and Assistant Adjutant for Musketry at Chatham. He served in the European War training recruits in musketry till Feb. 1915; works on Lines of Communication till May, 1916; Staff Officer to C.E. Vth Corps May 1916, to June, 1917; O.C. 409th Lowland Field Company, Royal Engineers (T.F.) June, 1917, to Sept. 1919. He was mentioned in Despatches 9 April, 1917, and 16 March, 1919. Awarded the Military Cross for work during the Passchendaele Battle (immediate award in Nov. 1917) [London Gazette, 15 Jan. 1918]. Awarded Bar to Military Cross (immediate award Oct. 1918) for work in offensives culminating in taking of the Hindenburg Line [London Gazette, Jan. 1919]. Awarded the Victoria Cross [London Gazette, 15 May, 1919]: "George de Cardonnel Elmsall Findlay, D.S.O., M.C., Capt. (Acting Major), 409th (Lowland) Field Company, Royal Engineers (T.F.) For most conspicuous bravery and devotion to duty during the forcing of the Sambre–Oise Canal at the Lock, two miles south of Catillon, on 4 Nov. 1918, when in charge of the bridging operations at this crossing. Major Findlay was with the leading bridging and assaulting parties which came under heavy fire while trying to cross the dyke between the forming-up line and the Lock. The casualties were severe, and the advance was stopped. Nevertheless, under heavy and incessant fire he collected what men he could and repaired the bridges, in spite of heavy casualties in officers and other ranks.

George de C. E. Findlay.

Although wounded, Major Findlay continued his task and after two unsuccessful efforts, owing to his men being swept down, he eventually placed the bridge in position across the Lock, and was the first man across, subsequently remaining at this post of danger till further work was completed. His cool and gallant behaviour inspired volunteers from different units at a critical time when men became casualties almost as soon as they joined him in the fire-swept zone, and it was due to Major Findlay's gallantry and devotion to duty that this most important crossing was effected." Major Findlay's favourite sports are game shooting and rifle shooting, also riding and outdoor games.

BELLEW, EDWARD DONALD, Capt., joined the Canadian Military Forces, serving in the European War. He was awarded the Victoria Cross [London Gazette, 15 May, 1919]: "Edward Donald Bellew, Capt., 7th Canadian Infantry Battn. (British Columbia Regt.). For most conspicuous bravery and devotion to duty near Keerselaere on 24 April, 1915, during the German attack on the Ypres salient. The enemy's attack broke in full force against the front and right flank of the battalion, the latter being exposed owing to a gap in the line. The advance was temporarily stayed by Capt. Bellew, who had sited his guns on the left of the right company. Reinforcements were sent forward, but were surrounded and destroyed. With the enemy in strength less than 100 yards from him, with no further assistance in sight, and with his rear threatened, Capt. Bellew and Sergt. Peerless, each operating a gun, decided to stay where they were and fight it out. Sergt. Peerless was killed and Capt. Bellew was wounded and fell. Nevertheless he got up and maintained his fire till ammunition failed and the enemy rushed the position. Capt. Bellew then seized a rifle, smashed his machine gun, and, fighting to the last, was taken prisoner."

Edward Donald Bellew.

The following particulars have lately been sent to us:—Capt. E. D. Bellew is the son of Major Patrick Francis Bellew, H.E.I.C.S., and of Letitia Frances Bellew. His grandfather, Major Walter Henry Bellew, was one of the last three men with Dr. Brydon, the only survivor of the Kabul Army of 1842, a force of 16,000 men. E. D. Bellew was born 28 Oct. 1882, at Malabar Hill, Bombay, India; was educated at Blundell's School; Clifton College, and at the Royal Military College, Sandhurst, in 1900 (Heavy-weight Boxing, also Rugby Football Cup). He joined the 18th Royal Irish Regt. in May, 1901, and retired with the rank of Lieutenant. He married in London, England, on 24 Aug. 1901, Charlotte Muriel Rees, and went out to Canada, where he became an engineer of harbour construction in the Dominion of Canada Civil Service. He joined the Canadian Military Forces, and served in the European War in the British Columbia Regt., 17th Canadian Infantry, as a Lieutenant, from 10 Aug. 1914, being promoted to Capt. 10 Jan. 1916. He has the Victoria Cross, 1914–15 Star, War Decoration and Victory Medal, and was mentioned for work in the Second Battle of Ypres (first gas attack).

The following is an extract from "The Civilian," July, 1919 (the Civil Service Monthly of Canada):

"CIVIL SERVANTS UNDER ARMS

"THROUGH DEATH TO THE VICTORIA CROSS

"Never was the world so full of the heroes of gallant deeds and marvellous escapes from death as it is to-day, and it is indeed a remarkable record that stands out from among the thousands that render fiction colourless and tame. Such is the story of Capt. E. D. Bellew, whose winning of the Victoria Cross was briefly reported in the last issue of 'The Civilian.' Capt. Bellew is the only living man who went to the front from the Canadian Civil Service, won the greatest reward of a British soldier, and returned to Canada with his honours. Lieut. J. E. Tait, of Winnipeg, who won the V.C., paid the supreme sacrifice on the field of battle, and Lieut. Milton F. Gregg, V.C., joined the Civil Service after his return from the war. Edward Donald Bellew was born in 1882, at Malabar Hill, Bombay; his father, Major Patrick Bellew, formerly of the Indian Army, being Assay Master of the Bombay Mint. His grandfather, Major Walter Henry Bellew, who was Assistant Quartermaster-General of the Forces in India, lost his life in the retreat from Cabul in the First Afghan War of 1842, while his great-grandfather, Sir Patrick Bellew, a Major-General, was Military Governor at Quebec in 1798. The coming V.C. was thus born of fighting blood, and inherited as well, perhaps, an interest in Britain's Empire overseas. He received his primary education at Clifton College, near Bristol, and wound up at Sandhurst. Passing that famous Military School, he became a Subaltern in the 18th Royal Irish Regt., then in India, but eventually decided to follow a civilian occupation, and so resigned his commission. Young Bellew came to Canada in 1907; spent three years in Northern British Columbia, and then joined the Provincial Forestry Service. In 1912 he entered the Dominion Civil Service as Assistant to the District Engineer of Public Works at Vancouver. When the war broke out he immediately volunteered for service overseas, and applied for a commission in the 11th Irish Fusiliers of Canada. In the organization of the First Canadian Expeditionary Force at Valcartier, he was made Machine Gun Officer of the 7th Battn., and in that capacity he endured the miseries of Salisbury Plain, and finally went to France in Feb. 1915. On the 10th of the following month he was engaged, with his battalion, in the action of Neuve-Chapelle. It was at the ever-memorable Second Battle of Ypres—sometimes called 'St. Julien,' and erroneously 'Langemarck '—that Lieut. Bellew experienced a whole lifetime of warfare crowded into a few hours. Sir John French said that, in that action, the Canadians saved the situation, and it might be said with truth that the 7th and 8th Battns. once saved the Canadian position—as it was saved by other battalions at other critical moments. These two units held the Gravenstafel ridge. The London ' Times ' said : ' Had the Gravenstafel position gone, the enemy in an hour would have pushed behind the 28th Division and the whole of the Eastern section.' Out of that struggle the 7th Battn. brought but a skeleton of its rank and file, and but five officers. Lieut. Bellew was not one of the five. Of his part in the fight we have two official reports. ' The Canadian Eye-Witness ' wrote : ' Lieut. E. D. Bellew, Machine Gun Officer of the 7th Battn., hoisted a loaf, stuck on the point of his bayonet, in defiance of the enemy, which drew upon him a perfect fury of fire ; he fought his gun until it was smashed to atoms, and then continued to use relays of loaded rifles until he was wounded and taken prisoner.' Major P. Byng Hall, D.S.O., of the 7th Battn., wrote to the Officer Commanding from Germany : ' Lieut. Bellew acted with the greatest coolness, courage and judgment, protecting first my flank, then moving to my rear again and covering my retirement. If he had not been stunned by a shell he would have got his gun into action again.' While his detachment was covering the retirement of the battalion to a new position, a heavy shell burst among them, and Lieut. Bellew alone survived to carry on. Snatching up rifle after rifle, he gave the Huns an amazing exhibition of rapid fire, though the gas fumes were rapidly overcoming him. Then another shell exploded close by, and when he came to himself he was in the hands of the enemy. His captors conveyed him to Staden, and there he was placed on trial and convicted of an infraction of the laws of war in that he continued fire after part of his unit had been forced, by exhaustion of their ammunition, to surrender ! Sentence of death was pronounced, and the Huns prepared to wreak their montrous punishment upon the man who had dared to withstand them. The prisoner was placed before the wall of Staden Church, and a firing-party drawn up before him. Inside the Church many Canadian wounded, knowing of the scene outside, waited with bated breath for the volley. But Lieut. Bellew was determined to fight to the last, even if only words were available, and he vigorously protested and warned the Huns that their crime would be learned of and that certain reprisal would follow. At the last moment the officer in charge ordered the prisoner returned to custody. A new trial was ordered. It took place at Roulers, and the death sentence was not again pronounced. Lieut. Bellew was then sent with a large party of wounded Canadians to a prison camp in Saxony. They were crowded into fourth-class Belgian railway carriages, and a wounded and gassed Algerian or Senegalese soldier was placed in each compartment. ' You English gentlemen can enjoy the company of your black friends during your trip to Germany,' said the exulting Huns. The presence of the wounded Africans was no annoyance in comparison with the insults and indignities heaped upon the prisoners at every point along the trip, the German Red Cross women especially distinguishing themselves in tormenting the helpless wounded men. For two years and eight months Lieut. Bellew languished in the hands of the Huns, being an inmate of six different camps in that time. Pigs'-blood soup, mangold-wurzels and bread that was sixty per cent. sawdust were features of the usual diet. The parcels of food sent in by the British and Canadian Red Cross were frequently plundered by the guards, but enough of the contents reached the prisoners to save them from the hideous diseases that follow such foul diet as the Huns provided, with death as the only probable relief. Thousands of friendless Serbians and Russians died of dropsy because they had no alternative food. Such sufferings break down the strongest, and even the physique that had made Lieut. Bellew a champion amateur boxer began to yield to this inhumanity, following gas and shell-shock. At length a Swiss medical commission selected him as fit only for internment in a neutral land, and he was transferred to the little mountain republic. There he spent eleven months, and with good medical attention and the ministrations of his wife, who was able to join him, regained so much of his strength that he was able to go to England after the signing of the Armistice, and to return to Canada early in April of this year. During his long imprisonment the details of his splendid conduct at Ypres had become a matter of official record, and it had been determined to award him the Victoria Cross. This decision had to be kept a profound secret, for, if it had leaked out and the news of it had reached Germany, additional tortures would doubtless have been inflicted on the prisoner and his chances of surviving the close of the war would have been very slim. The announcement was deferred until a few weeks ago, when Capt. Bellew (for a promotion had been given him) was back in Canada and all the formalities complied with. His friends in many lands rejoice at the news, and the Civil Service of Canada proudly places his name at the head of its Roll of Honour."

Herewith the record of the 7th Canadian Battn. British Columbia Regt., taken from "The Daily Sun," Vancouver, British Columbia, Monday, 22 Sept. 1919 : " While the long and valuable services of such a battalion as the 7th cannot very well be measured in terms of honours won, and the early months of the war were particularly notorious for a multitude of deeds done for which the authorities could not be expected to adequately reward the heroes concerned, the long list of decorations won by the battalion speaks of one of the finest careers in all the British Armies. The honours won in the 7th cover all ranks, from the senior officers to the rank and file, and are conspicuous because of the possession of no less than three Victoria Cross winners in the battalion. The supreme award in the British service is held by Capt. Bellew, V.C., Sergt. Rayfield, V.C., and Private M. J. O'Rourke, V.C., all of whom have returned to Vancouver, and two of whom—Capt. Bellew and Private O'Rourke—are residents of this city. The C.M.G. was conferred upon Brigadier-General Odlum, long the commanding officer of the 7th in the line, and Lieut.-Colonel Gardner, the gallant commander who was evacuated to England, and who returned to his battalion in the later days of the war for the third time, and met his death on the field. The Distinguished Service Order, with two Bars, is held by Lieut.-Colonel Gilson, who brought the battalion back to Vancouver after serving at the front from Feb. of 1915 ; and the D.S.O., with one Bar, by Major D. Philpot, who came back as Second-in-Command, after serving with the unit from the Valcartier days to the day of demobilization. Seven officers of the battalion hold the Distinguished Service Order, and 34 have been decorated with the Military Cross for gallantry in action, while 46 Distinguished Conduct Medals have been given to the non-commissioned officers and men of the 7th. The Military Medal and Bar is held by 11 N.C.O.'s and men, and 167 other ranks hold the Military Medal. The Meritorious Service Medal is held by four members of the battalion, and the late Lieut.-Colonel Gardner received, in addition to other honours, the distinction of the Légion d'Honneur of France, a decoration seldom conferred upon foreign officers, and a signal honour to any battalion chosen for such a donation. The French Médaille Militaire was presented to Coy. Sergt.-Major Ward, who already had the Distinguished Conduct Medal, and Major Philpot, D.S.O., and Major Gibson, D.S.O., wear the ribbon of the French Croix de Guerre as a recognition by the French Army command of their brilliant services in the field. Five non-commissioned officers and men hold the Belgian Croix de Guerre, and there are the Médaille d'Honneur of France, the Décoration Militaire of Belgium, and two Russian Medals of St. George in the battalion. In addition to the winners of the numerous British and foreign decorations, 35 of the 7th officers, non-commissioned officers and men were mentioned in Despatches for exceptional work in the field, making a grand total of honours and decorations won that will bear comparison with any unit in the Army."

DE WIND, EDMUND, Second Lieut., was born 11 Dec. 1883, at Comber, County Down, Ireland, youngest son of Arthur Hughes De Wind (who died in 1917), and Margaret Jane De Wind, of Kinvara, Comber. He was educated at Campbell College, Belfast ; and afterwards became a clerk in the Bank of Ireland at Cavan, and in 1911 emigrated to Edmonton, Canada, where he was employed in the Bank of Commerce. He took a keen interest in the Ulster Volunteer Force while living in Canada. He joined the Army in 1915, as a Private in the 31st Battn. Second Canadian Contingent, and served in the European War ; was with his battalion in the machine-gun section from 1915 to 1917, and took part in the battles of St. Eloi, Ypres, and the Somme. He qualified for a commission, and was posted to the 17th Battn. Royal Irish Rifles on 26 Sept. 1917, at Dundalk. He went back to the front in the following Dec., and joined the 15th (North Belfast) Battn. of his regiment, and served in the St. Quentin area with the Ulster Division until the great Retreat, in which his battalion suffered very heavily. He was killed in action, and was posthumously awarded the Victoria Cross [London Gazette, 15 May, 1919] : " Edmund De Wind, Second Lieut., 15th Battn. Royal Irish Rifles (North Belfast Volunteers). For most conspicuous bravery and self-sacrifice on 21 March, 1918, at the Race-course Redoubt, near Groagie. For seven hours he held this most important post, and, though twice wounded and practically single-handed, he maintained his position until another section could be got to his help. On two occasions with two N.C.O.'s only he got out on top under heavy machine-gun and rifle fire, and cleared the enemy out of the trench, killing many. He continued to repel attack after attack, until he was mortally wounded and collapsed. His valour, self-sacrifice and example were of the highest order." Lieut. De Wind was engaged to be married. He was extremely popular, and made friends wherever he went. He played a good deal of hockey and cricket when living in Ireland, and was also an enthusiastic yachtsman, rifleman, angler and tennis player.

London Gazette, 24 May, 1919.—" Admiralty, S.W., 24 May, 1919. The King has been graciously pleased to approve of the posthumous award of the Victoria Cross to the undermentioned Officers."

SAXTON-WHITE, GEOFFREY, Lieut.-Commander, Royal Navy, was born on 2 July, 1886, at Bromley, Kent, son of Mr. and Mrs. W. H. White. He was educated at Parkfield, Haywards Heath, and Bradfield College, and joined the Royal Navy through Britannia College in 1901. He served in the European War ; in H.M.S. Monarch in 1914, when war broke out, for 18 months. Back to submarines in 1915, D6 at Harwich ; E14 in 1916 at Malta. He was posthumously awarded the Victoria Cross [London Gazette 24 May, 1919] : " Geoffrey Saxton-White, Lieut.-Commander, Royal Navy. For gallantry and devotion to duty as Commanding Officer of H.M. Submarine E14 on 27 Jan. 1918. E14 left Mudros on the 27th Jan. under instructions to force the Narrows and attack the Goeben, which was reported aground off Nagara Point, after being damaged during her sortie from the Dardanelles. The latter vessel was not found, and E14 turned back. At about 8.45 a.m. on 28 Jan. a torpedo was fired from E 14 at an enemy ship ; eleven seconds after the torpedo left the tube a heavy explosion took place, causing all lights to go out, and sprang the fore hatch. Leaking badly, the boat was blown to 15 feet, and at once a heavy fire came from the forts, but the hull was not hit. E14 then dived and proceeded on her way out. Soon afterwards the boat became out of control, and as the air supply was nearly exhausted, Lieut.-Commander White decided to run the risk of proceeding on the surface. Heavy fire was immediately opened from both sides, and, after running the gauntlet for half an hour, being

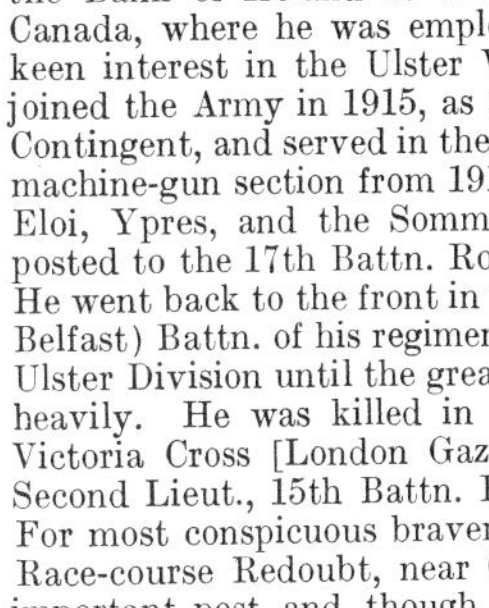

Geoffrey Saxton-White.

steered from below, E14 was so badly damaged that Lieut.-Commander White turned towards the shore in order to give the crew a chance of being saved. He remained on deck the whole time himself until he was killed by a shell." He leaves a widow, Sibyl White, daughter of Mrs. H. S. Thomas, Penshurst, Grand Parade, Plymouth, and three little children: Peter, aged 7 years; Anthony, aged 6 years; Sheila, aged two years.

PARSLOW, FREDERICK, Lieut., Royal Naval Reserve, served in the European War He was awarded the Victoria Cross [London Gazette, 24 May, 1919]: "Frederick Parslow, Lieut., Royal Naval Reserve. For gallantry and devotion to duty when in command of the horse transport Anglo-Californian on 4 July, 1915. At 8 a.m. on 4 July, 1915, a large submarine was sighted on the port beam at a distance of about one mile. The ship, which was entirely unarmed, was immediately manœuvred to bring the submarine astern, every effort being made to increase speed, and an S.O.S. call was sent out by wireless, an answer being received from a man-of-war. At 9 a.m. the submarine opened fire, and maintained a steady fire, making occasional hits, until 10.30 a.m.; meanwhile Lieut. Parslow constantly altered course and kept the submarine astern. At 10.30 a.m. the enemy hoisted the signal to 'abandon the vessel as fast as possible,' and in order to save life Lieut. Parslow decided to obey, and stopped engines to give as many of the crew as wished an opportunity to get away in the boats. On receiving a wireless message from a destroyer, however, urging him to hold on as long as possible, he decided to get way on the ship again. The submarine then opened a heavy fire on the bridge and boats with guns and rifles, wrecking the upper bridge, killing Lieut. Parslow, and carrying away one of the port davits, causing the boat to drop into the sea and throwing its occupants into the water. Throughout the attack Lieut. Parslow remained on the bridge, on which the enemy fire was concentrated, entirely without protection, and by his magnificent heroism succeeded, at the cost of his own life, in saving a valuable ship and cargo for the country. He set a splendid example to the officers and men of the Mercantile Marine."

BISSETT SMITH, ARCHIBALD, Lieut., Royal Naval Reserve, served in the European War, and was awarded the Victoria Cross [London Gazette, 24 May, 1919]: "Archibald Bissett Smith, Lieut., Royal Naval Reserve. For most conspicuous gallantry and devotion to duty when in command of the S.S. Otaki, on the 10th March, 1917. At about 2.30 p.m. on 10 March, 1917, the S.S. Otaki, whose armament consisted of one 4.7-in. gun for defensive purposes, sighted the disguised German raider Moewe, which was armed with four 5.9-inch, one 4.1-inch and two 22-pdr. guns, and two torpedo tubes. The Moewe kept the Otaki under observation for some time and finally called upon her to stop. This Lieut. Smith refused to do, and a duel ensued at ranges of 1,900–2,000 yards, and lasted for about 20 minutes. During this action the Otaki scored several hits on the Moewe, causing considerable damage, and starting a fire, which lasted for three days. She sustained several casualties and received much damage herself, and was heavily on fire. Lieut. Smith, therefore, gave orders for the boats to be lowered to allow the crew to be rescued. He remained on the ship himself and went down with her when she sank with the British colours still flying, after what was described in an enemy account as 'a duel as gallant as naval history can relate.'"

London Gazette, 9 June, 1919.—"War Office, 9 June, 1919. His Majesty the King has been graciously pleased to approve of the award of the Victoria Cross to the undermentioned Officer and Non-commissioned Officer."

ELSTOB, WILFRITH, D.S.O., M.C., Lieut.-Colonel, was the son of the Rev. Canon and Mrs. Elstob. He served in the European War, was awarded the Military Cross, created a Companion of the Distinguished Service Order, and awarded the Victoria Cross [London Gazette, 9 June, 1919]: "Wilfrith Elstob, D.S.O., M.C., the late, Temporary Lieut.-Colonel, 16th Battn. Manchester Regt. For most conspicuous bravery, devotion to duty and self-sacrifice during operations at Manchester Redoubt, near St. Quentin, on the 21st March, 1918. During the preliminary bombardment he encouraged his men in the posts in the Redoubt by frequent visits, and when repeated attacks developed controlled the defence at the points threatened, giving personal support with revolver, rifle and bombs. Single-handed he repulsed one bombing assault, driving back the enemy and inflicting severe casualties. Later, when ammunition was required, he made several journeys under severe fire in order to replenish the supply. Throughout the day Lieut.-Colonel Elstob, although twice wounded, showed the most fearless disregard of his own safety, and by his encouragement and noble example inspired his command to the fullest degree. The Manchester Redoubt was surrounded in the first wave of the enemy attack, but by means of the buried cable Lieut.-Colonel Elstob was able to assure his Brigade Commander that 'The Manchester Regiment will defend Manchester Hill to the last.' Some time after this post was overcome by vastly superior forces, and this very gallant officer was killed in the final assault, having maintained to the end the duty which he had impressed on his men—namely, 'Here we fight and here we die.' He set throughout the highest example of valour, determination, endurance and fine soldierly bearing."

SAYER, JOHN WILLIAM, L.-Corpl., was born on 12 April, 1879, at Ilford, Essex, son of Samuel Sayer, Farmer, and Margaret Sayer. The family of Sayer have lived in Essex and farmed (Chadwell Heath) for generations. His father and mother are still living at Wangye Hall Farm, Chadwell Heath, Essex. He was educated at Ilford, Essex, and joined the Army on 25 July, 1916. He served in the European War in France from Dec. 1916, until he was

John William Sayer.

wounded and died in 1918. He was always fond of all outdoor sports, and was from boyhood known to possess a dauntless and fearless disposition. It was no surprise to his friends and relatives that he should gain so great an honour. He was formerly, before living at Cricklewood, an Ilford tradesman (Corn and Seed Merchant). He was awarded a posthumous Victoria Cross [London Gazette, 9 June, 1919]: "John William Sayer (the late), No. G/14498, L.-Corpl., 8th Battn. Royal West Surrey Regt. For most conspicuous bravery, determination, and ability displayed on 31 March 1918, at Le Vergoier, when holding for two hours, in face of incessant attacks, the flank of a small isolated post. Owing to mist the enemy approached the post from both sides to within thirty yards before being discovered. L.-Corpl. Sayer, however, on his own initiative and without assistance, beat off a succession of flank attacks and inflicted heavy casualties on the enemy. Though attacked by rifle and machine-gun fire, bayonet, and bombs, he repulsed all attacks, killing many and wounding others. During the whole time he was continuously exposed to rifle and machine-gun fire, but he showed the utmost contempt of danger, and his conduct was an inspiration to all. His skilful use of fire of all descriptions enabled the post to hold out till nearly all the garrison had been killed and himself wounded and captured. He subsequently died as a result of wounds at Le Cateau." L.-Corpl. Sayer was married on 15 Aug. 1904, at Ilford Parish Church. His wife's name is Edith Louise, daughter of Henry and Louise Maynard (deceased), and the names of their children are: Olive Edith, born 15 Aug. 1905; Eric Maynard, born 24 March, 1907; Ivy Louise, born 18 Dec. 1908; Dorothy Margaret, born 27 Aug. 1910; William John, born 17 Sept. 1912, and Joyce Madeline, born 13 Oct. 1918 (posthumous). The King handed to Mrs. Sayer, at an Investiture at Buckingham Palace, the Victoria Cross won by her late husband.

London Gazette, 18 July, 1919.—"Air Ministry. The King has been graciously pleased to approve of the award of the Victoria Cross to the undermentioned Officer."

MANNOCK, EDWARD, Major, R.E., served during the European War, and was awarded the D.S.O. with two Bars, M.C. with Bar, and the Victoria Cross [London Gazette, 18 July, 1919]: "Capt. (Acting Major) Edward

Edward Mannock.

Mannock, D.S.O., M.C., 85th Squadron, R.F.C. On the 17th June, 1918, he attacked a Halberstadt machine near Armentières and destroyed it from a height of 8,000 feet. On the 7th July, 1918, near Doulieu, he attacked and destroyed one Fokker (red-bodied) machine, which went vertically into the ground from a height of 1,500 feet. Shortly afterwards he ascended 1,000 feet and attacked another Fokker biplane, firing 60 rounds into it, which resulted in an immediate spin, resulting, it is believed, in a crash. On the 14th July, 1918, near Merville, he attacked and crashed a Fokker from 7,000 feet and brought a two-seater down damaged. On the 19th July, 1918, near Merville, he fired 80 rounds into an Albatross two-seater, which went to the ground in flames. On the 20th July, 1918, east of La Bassée, he attacked and crashed an enemy two-seater from a height of 10,000 feet. About an hour afterwards he attacked at 8,000 feet a Fokker biplane, near Steenwercke, and drove it down out of control, emitting smoke. On the 22nd July, 1918, near Armentières, he destroyed an enemy triplane from a height of 10,000 feet." H.M. the King presented, at Buckingham Palace, to Mr. Mannock, the V.C., D.S.O. with two Bars, and M.C. with Bar, which had been awarded to his son, the late Major Mannock. Major Mannock was awarded the undermentioned distinctions for his previous combats in the air in France and Flanders: Military Cross, gazetted 17 Sept. 1917; Bar to Military Cross, gazetted 16 Sept. 1918; Distinguished Service Order, gazetted 3 Aug. 1918; Bar to Distinguished Service Order (2nd), gazetted 16 Sept. 1918. This highly distinguished officer, during the whole of his career in the Royal Air Force, was an outstanding example of fearless courage, remarkable skill, devotion to duty and self-sacrifice, which has never been surpassed. The total number of machines definitely accounted for by Major Mannock up to the date of his death in France (26 July, 1918) is 50—the total specified in the Gazette of 3 Aug. 1918, was incorrectly given as 48, instead of 41.

London Gazette, 22 Aug. 1919.—"Admiralty, S.W., 22 Aug. 1919. The King has been graciously pleased to approve of the award of the Victoria Cross to Lieut. Augustine Willington Shelton Agar, R.N., in recognition of his conspicuous gallantry, coolness and skill under extremely difficult conditions in action."

Augustine W. S. Agar.

AGAR, AUGUSTINE WILLINGTON SHELTON, Lieut., Royal Navy, served in the European War, and was awarded the Victoria Cross [London Gazette, 22 Aug. 1919]: "Augustine Willington Shelton Agar, Lieut., Royal Navy, In recognition of his conspicuous gallantry, coolness and skill under extremely difficult conditions in action." Lieut. Agar was also created a Companion of the Distinguished Service Order. A newspaper says: "The King decorated Lieut. Agar with the Victoria Cross and conferred the D.S.O. on him at Buckingham Palace, engaging in quite half an hour's talk with the naval hero, who took part in the torpedoing of the Bolshevist Baltic fleet." Lieut. Agar was born 4 Jan. 1890, at Kandy, Ceylon, son of John Shelton Agar, Planter, Ceylon, and Emily Cruille Agar. He was educated at Framlingham College, Suffolk, and at Eastman's Naval Academy, and entered the Royal Navy in May, 1905, becoming Lieutenant 30 June, 1912. Lieut. Agar served with the Grand Fleet in 1914 and 1915, in H.M.S. Hibernia; in Gallipoli in 1915, and was present at the evacuation in 1915; in North Russia in 1917 and 1918 in H.M.S. Iphigenia. In 1918 he was employed by the Admiralty for special service in coastal motor-boats, and in 1919 he served in the Baltic on special service in coastal motor-boats under the Foreign Office. He was, as has been related in the Gazette, awarded the Victoria Cross for the sinking of the Bolshevist Cruiser Olig, on the night of 12 June, 1919, in H.M. Coastal Motor Boat No. 4. He was awarded the Distinguished Service Order for the attack on Kronstadt Naval Harbour on the night of 18 Aug. 1919, when in command of H.M. Coastal Motor Boat No. 7.

London Gazette, 4 Sept. 1919.—" War Office, 4 Sept. 1919. His Majesty the King has been graciously pleased to approve of the award of the Victoria Cross to the undermentioned Officers."

KER, ALLAN EBENEZER, Lieut., 3rd Battn. Gordon Highlanders. He served during the European War, and was awarded the Victoria Cross [London Gazette, 4 Sept. 1919]: " Allan Ebenezer Ker, Lieut. For most

conspicuous bravery and devotion to duty. On the 21st March, 1918, near St. Quentin, after a heavy bombardment, the enemy penetrated our line, and the flank of the 61st Division became exposed. Lieut. Ker, with one Vickers gun, succeeded in engaging the enemy's infantry, approaching under cover of dead ground, and held up the attack, inflicting many casualties. He then sent back word to his Battalion Headquarters that he had determined to stop with his Sergeant and several men who had been badly wounded, and fight until a counter-attack could be launched to relieve him. Just as ammunition failed his party were attacked from behind with bombs, machine guns, and with the bayonet. Several bayonet attacks were delivered, but each time they were repulsed

Allan Ebenezer Ker.

by Lieut. Ker and his companions with their revolvers, the Vickers gun having by this time been destroyed. The wounded were collected into a small shelter, and it was decided to defend them to the last and to hold the enemy as long as possible. In one of the many hand-to-hand encounters a German rifle and bayonet and a small supply of ammunition was secured, and subsequently used with good effect against the enemy. Although Lieut. Ker was very exhausted from want of food and gas poisoning, and from the supreme exertions he had made during ten hours of the most severe bombardment, fighting and attending to the wounded, he refused to surrender until all his ammunition was exhausted and his position was rushed by large numbers of the enemy. His behaviour throughout the day was absolutely cool and fearless, and by his determination he was materially instrumental in engaging and holding up for three hours more than 500 of the enemy."

BRUCE, WILLIAM ARTHUR McCRAE, Lieut., 59th Scinde Rifles, Indian Army. He served during the European War, and was posthumously awarded the Victoria Cross [London Gazette, 4 Sept. 1919]: " William Arthur McCrae Bruce, Lieut. (the late), 59th Scinde Rifles (Frontier Force), Indian Army. For most conspicuous bravery and devotion to duty. On the 19th Dec. 1914, near Givenchy, during a night attack, Lieut. Bruce was in command of a small party, which captured one of the enemy trenches. In spite of being severely wounded in the neck, he walked up and down the trench encouraging his men to hold on against several counter-attacks for some hours, until killed. The fire from rifles and bombs was very heavy all day, and it was due to the skilful disposition made and the example and encouragement shown by Lieut. Bruce that his men were able to hold out until dusk, when the trench was finally captured by the enemy." A newspaper correspondent wrote: " The Gazette narrates the incidents of extreme bravery which gained the V.C. for Lieut. Allan Ker, of the 3rd Gordon Highlanders, and (posthumously) for Lieut. W. Bruce, 59th Scinde Rifles. Lieut. Ker's exploit occurred in March of last year, near St. Quentin, where, with a handful of men, he defended an isolated post, and held up 500 of the enemy for three hours. Lieut. Bruce's service dates as far back as December, 1914. He captured a trench at Givenchy, and, although wounded in the neck, kept his men resisting counter-attacks until he was killed."

London Gazette, 29 Sept. 1919.—" War Office, 29 Sept. 1919. His Majesty the King has been graciously pleased to approve of the grant of the Victoria Cross to the undermentioned Non-commissioned Officer."

SULLIVAN, ARTHUR PERCY, Corpl., comes from Crystal Brook, South Australia. He served in the European War and was awarded the Victoria Cross [London Gazette, 29 Sept. 1919]; " Arthur Percy Sullivan, No. 133003, Corpl., 45th Battn. Royal Fusiliers For most conspicuous bravery and devotion to duty on the 10th Aug. 1919, at the Sheika River, North Russia. The platoon to which he belonged, after fighting a rearguard covering action, had to cross the river by means of a narrow plank, and during the passage an officer and three men fell into a deep swamp. Without hesitation, under intense fire, Corpl. Sullivan jumped into the river and rescued all four, bringing them out singly. But for this gallant action his

comrades would undoubtedly have been drowned. It was a splendid example of heroism, as all ranks were on the point of exhaustion and the enemy less than 100 yards distant."

London Gazette, 23 Oct. 1919.—" War Office, 23 Oct. 1919. His Majesty the King has been graciously pleased to approve of the award of the Victoria Cross to the undermentioned Non-commissioned Officer."

PEARSE, SAMUEL GEORGE, M.M., Sergt., came from Mildura, Australia. He served in the European War, won the Military Medal, and was awarded the Victoria Cross [London Gazette, 23 Oct. 1919]: " North Russia. The late Samuel George Pearse, M.M., No. 133002, Sergt., 45th Battn. Royal Fusiliers. For most conspicuous bravery, devotion to duty and self-sacrifice during the operation against the enemy battery position north of Emtsa (North Russia) on the 29th Aug. 1919. Sergt. Pearse cut his way through the enemy barbed wire under very heavy machine-gun and rifle fire and cleared a way for the troops to enter the battery position. Seeing that a blockhouse was harassing our advance and causing us casualties, he charged the blockhouse single-handed, killing the occupants with bombs. This gallant non-commissioned

Samuel George Pearse.

officer met his death a minute later, and it was due to him that the position was carried with so few casualties. His magnificent bravery and utter disregard for personal danger won for him the admiration of all troops." Sergt. Pearse was the son of George Pearse, of Koorlong, Mildura, Australia. He joined the Australian Military Forces in 1915, serving in the A.I.F.; was demobilized 18 July, 1919; re-enlisted in the 45th Battn. Royal Fusiliers, and served in the Russian Relief Force. He was killed in action as related above.

London Gazette.—" Admiralty, S.W., 11 Nov. 1919. The King has been graciously pleased to approve of the award of the Victoria Cross to the undermentioned Officers."

DOBSON, CLAUDE CONGREVE, Commander, Royal Navy. He served during the European War, and was awarded the D.S.O., and awarded the Victoria Cross [London Gazette, 11 Nov. 1919]: " Claude Congreve Dobson, D.S.O., Commander, Royal Navy. For most conspicuous gallantry, skill and devotion to duty on the occasion of the attack on Kronstadt Harbour on the 18th Aug. 1919. Commander Dobson organized and was in command of the Coastal Motor Boat Flotilla. He led the flotilla through the chain of forts to the entrance of the harbour. Coastal Motor Boat No. 31, from which he directed the general operations, then passed in under a very heavy machine-gun fire, and torpedoed the Bolshevik battleship Andrei Pervozanni, subsequently returning through the heavy fire of the forts and batteries to the open

Claude Congreve Dobson.

sea." Simultaneously with his visit to the Palace to receive his V.C., Commander Claude Dobson, the hero of the C.M.B.'s at Kronstadt, has been appointed to the Osea for the C.M.B. flotilla. He is the second V.C. attached to the Osea, the other being his comrade of the flotilla, Lieut. Augustine Agar, who attacked the Bolshevist cruiser Oleg.

STEELE, GORDON CHARLES, Lieut., Royal Navy, served during the European War, and was awarded the Victoria Cross [London Gazette, 11 Nov. 1919]: " Gordon Charles Steele, Lieut., Royal Navy. For most conspicuous gallantry, skill and devotion to duty on the occasion of the attack on Kronstadt Harbour on the 18th Aug. 1919. Lieut. Steele was second-in-command of H.M. Coastal Motor Boat No. 88. After this boat had entered the harbour the commanding officer, Lieut. Dayrell-Reed, was shot through the head, and the boat was thrown off her course. Lieut. Steele took the wheel, steadied the boat, lifted Lieut. Dayrell-Reed away from the steering and firing position, and torpedoed the Bolshevik battleship Andrei Pervozanni at a hundred yards' range. He had then a difficult manœuvre to perform to get a clear view of the battleship Petropavlovsk, which was overlapped by the Andrei

Gordon Charles Steele.

Pervozanni, and obscured by smoke coming from the ship. The evolution, however, was skilfully carried out, and the Petropavlovsk torpedoed. This left Lieut. Steele with only just room to turn, in order to regain the entrance to the harbour, but he effected the movement with success, and firing his machine guns along the wall on his way, passed under the line of forts through a heavy fire out of the harbour." Lieut. Steele was born 1 Nov. 1892, at Exeter, son of the late Capt. H. W. Steele, R.N., and of Mrs. Selina May Steele, daughter of the late Major-General Symonds, R.M.L.I. He was educated at Vale College (Preparatory), Ramsgate, and in H.M.S. Worcester, Nautical Training College, and his early sea service was on the P. and O. Steam Navigation Company's ships, in which he was Master Mariner, and he entered the R.N.R. 12 Aug. 1909. He was serving in H.M.S. Conqueror as Acting Sub-Lieutenant, R.N.V.R., when war broke out, and was appointed to the Submarine Service in Oct. 1914, serving in D8 and E22. He served in the first Q boat commissioned, and was mentioned in Despatches for sinking an enemy submarine in Aug. 1915. He was transferred from the Royal Naval Reserve to the Royal Navy for distinguished service in action 17 Aug. 1915, being the first officer so transferred. He served in H.M.S. Royal Oak at the Battle of Jutland, and later in the Iron Duke. He was appointed in command H.M.S. P.C.63 in 1917, and H.M.S. Cornflower in 1918. If ever a Victoria Cross was well earned, it was this one, given for sinking a Bolshevist cruiser. One can only wonder how even one or two men from civilized countries can be so deluded as to have any truck with that bloodthirsty and debased ruffian Lenin, who holds rule by violence in a so-called "free" country, where labour is conscripted, where it literally is a crime punishable with death to have moderately clean hands, where men and women alike have sunk far below the level of the beasts of the field, and where not only the aristocracy but the middle and working classes are at the peril of their lives, ground under the heel of a criminal lunatic or worse. The following is the latest, though doubtless not the worst, published account of the doings of this monster and his horde of devils. It is taken from the "Daily Telegraph" of 7 April, 1920:

"Reuter's Agency has received communication of a letter written by a British officer serving in South Russia. It contains a terrible account of the treatment of two British officers by the Bolsheviks. The writer says:

"'One of them I know slightly' (the name is given, but is omitted for obvious reasons). 'The two officers, who were captured at Rostoff, were stripped naked and their arms were broken. They were marched in this condition through the main streets of the town. On arrival at the public square they were tied to posts and passing officers drew their revolvers and fired at them, only aiming at their arms and legs. They were not killed then, but were later taken away to be shot, and because they would not kneel down, but preferred to die standing, like soldiers, their legs were broken. They were then shot and their miseries ended.

"'I can tell you another pleasant thing the Bolsheviks did in Rostoff when they captured it. There was a big hospital there, containing about 500 wounded officers of the Volunteer Army. There was no time to get them away, and they were left. The Bolsheviks placed inflammable materials in the basement of the building, set fire to it, and placed a cordon of sentries all round to prevent anyone escaping. All the wounded were either killed by the sentries or burned to death.'"

London Gazette, 31 Jan. 1920.—"War Office, 31 Jan. 1920. The King has been pleased to approve of the award of the Victoria Cross to the following Warrant Officer."

George Evans.

EVANS, GEORGE, Company Sergt.-Major, was born in Kensington in 1876. He is six feet and half an inch in height, and enlisted in March, 1894, in the Scots Guards. He served in the South African War of 1899–1902, going out with the 1st Battn. Scots Guards, and serving for six months in the Orange Free State. He was present at the actions of Belmont and Modder River. During the war he was for some time on the strength of the Imperial Representative Corps which accompanied King George V. and Queen Mary (then Duke and Duchess of Cornwall and York) in their tour, when they visited Australia for the Commonwealth Celebrations. Evans afterwards returned to South Africa, and served in the latter part of the Boer War. He was an Instructor in the Scots Guards, and left the Regiment in Aug. 1902. Evans became an Inspector at Manchester of the National Society for the Prevention of Cruelty to Children. This Society, which is under the patronage of Their Most Gracious Majesties the King and Queen, says in its Annual Report that, "The sole object of the Society is that every child in the land shall live an endurable life." The Society, so far as one can gather from its Report, seeks not only to rescue children from cruelty and neglect, but to set matters right as far as possible. Its object is not necessarily to take the children away from their homes, but where it is feasible to help their parents—even the erring ones—to look after them properly. The Annual Report for 1918–19 says: "The records of the Inspectors who went to the war are exceptionally good, as might have been expected; indeed, it is impossible to read them without a feeling of profound satisfaction that they have been spared to return to duties which demand of them the same spirit of initiative and pluck that distinguished their services on sea and land. In different parts of the world, and in every battle area, these brave men have won distinction of which they and the Society to which they belong may well be very proud. It is proposed in due course to prepare an account of what has been done, that it may be a permanent tribute to the value of what the Society's officers were able to do." And now this account will contain a record of the gallantry of "The Children's V.C.," as the "Daily Sketch" called the N.S.P.C.C. Inspector, ex-Company Sergt.-Major George Evans. Inspector George Evans, who has an excellent record in the Society, joined the 18th Battn. Manchester Regt. on 4 Jan. 1915; was promoted Second-Class Warrant Officer, Company Sergeant-Major, 15 March, 1915, and went to France 8 Nov. 1915. He was wounded in the arm during the Somme offensive in July, 1916, and taken prisoner. On 6 June, 1918, he was exchanged into Holland, where he remained from June to 19 Nov. 1918, and he was demobilized on 20 Feb. 1919. He was awarded the Victoria Cross [London Gazette, 31 Jan. 1920]: "George Evans, No. 10947, Company Sergt.-Major, 18th Manchester Regt. For most conspicuous bravery and devotion to duty during the attack at Guillemont on 30 July, 1916, when under heavy rifle and machine-gun fire he volunteered to take back an important message after five runners had been killed in attempting to do so. He had to cover about 700 yards, the whole of which was under observation from the enemy. Company Sergt.-Major Evans, however, succeeded in delivering the message, and although wounded, rejoined his company, although advised to go to the dressing station. The return journey to the company again meant a journey of 700 yards under severe rifle and machine-gun fire, but by dodging from shell-hole to shell-hole he was able to do so, and was taken prisoner some hours later. On previous occasions at Montauban and Trônes Wood this gallant Warrant Officer displayed great bravery and devotion to duty, and has always been a splendid example to his men." A few more particulars have been obtained from Sergt. Evans. He was born 16 Feb. 1876, son of Daniel Jones Evans and Georgina Evans, at Kensington, London, W. He has had a varied career. He was educated at various schools in London. His mother died when he was six weeks old and his father when he was thirteen, since when he kept himself. He enlisted in the Scots Guards 5 March, 1894; served in the South African War, as related above, and was selected as a member of the Imperial Representative Corps which visited Australia at the inauguration of the Australian Commonwealth. He re-enlisted 4 Jan. 1915, in the 18th Manchester Regt. (3rd City Pals), and was a prisoner of war from 30 July, 1916; "was in various camps in Germany treated like a criminal," and was exchanged into Holland 10 June, 1918. His wife's name is Clara Evans (*née* Bates), and their children are Daniel Jones, Constance, Violet May and George.

London Gazette, 10 Sept. 1920.—"War Office, 10 Sept. 1920. The King has approved the award of the Victoria Cross to the undermentioned Officers for acts of gallantry in India, where both sacrificed their lives in their country's cause."

ANDREWS, HENRY JOHN, Temporary Capt., was an officer in the Salvation Army for over thirty years. Commissioner Blowers, who was in charge of the Salvation Army's work in India at the time of the doctor's death, writes: "From the day of his arrival in India he was armed with a medicine chest, and prescribed for many a member of the Army's Bombay Staff in those days of thirty years ago. The Salvation Army owes to him the commencement of its medical work in India. He was the pioneer of this branch of the Army's work in Nagercoil—commencing with a good penknife and razor for surgical instruments. His first building for medical purposes was a bath-room, converted into a medical room. From that beginning he brought into existence a creditable hospital. From Nagercoil he went to Anand, in Guzerat, and commenced medical work there. At this point of his career he and his leaders thought he ought to qualify, and he came out with Honours. He again returned to India to bring into existence yet another medical centre, that at Moradabad, one of the finest hospitals that exist in India to-day. The military authorities took in many ways Dr. Andrews's hospital as a model, especially with the administration and handling of Indian troops." His Victoria Cross was gazetted 10 Sept. 1920: "The late Temporary Capt. Henry John Andrews, M.B.E., Indian Medical Service. For most conspicuous bravery and devotion to duty on 22 Oct. 1919, when as Senior Medical Officer in charge of Khajuri Post (Waziristan) he heard that a convoy had been attacked in the vicinity of the post, and that men had been wounded. He at once took out an Aid Post to the scene of action, and, approaching under heavy fire, established an Aid Post under conditions which afforded some protection to the wounded but not to himself. Subsequently he was compelled to move his Aid Post to another position, and continued most devotedly to attend to the wounded. Finally, when a Ford van was available to remove the wounded, he showed the utmost disregard of danger in collecting the wounded under fire and in placing them in the van, and was eventually killed whilst himself stepping into the van on the completion of his task."

KENNY, WILLIAM DAVID, Lieut., was awarded the Victoria Cross [London Gazette, 10 Sept. 1920]: "The late Lieut. William David Kenny, 4/39th Garhwal Rifles, Indian Army. For most conspicuous bravery and devotion to duty near Kot Kai (Waziristan) on 2 Jan. 1920, when in command of a company holding an advanced covering position, which was repeatedly attacked by the Mahsuds in greatly superior numbers. For over four hours this officer maintained his position, repulsing three determined attacks, being foremost in the hand-to-hand fighting which took place, and repeatedly engaging the enemy with bomb and bayonet. His gallant leadership undoubtedly saved the situation and kept intact the right flank, on which depended the success of the operations and the safety of the troops in rear. In the subsequent withdrawal, recognizing that a diversion was necessary to enable the withdrawal of the company, which was impeded by their wounded, with a handful of his men he turned back and counter-attacked the pursuing enemy, and, with the rest of his party, was killed fighting to the last. This very gallant act of self-sacrifice not only enabled the wounded to be withdrawn, but also averted a situation which must have resulted in considerable loss of life."

London Gazette, 29 Oct. 1920.—"War Office, 29 Oct. 1920. The King has been pleased to approve of the award of the Victoria Cross to the late Capt. George Stuart Henderson, D.S.O., M.C., 2nd Battn. Manchester Regt."

HENDERSON, GEORGE STUART, Capt., was born 5 Dec. 1893. He was gazetted to the Manchester Regt. 24 Jan. 1914; became Lieutenant 9 Nov. 1914; Captain 24 July, 1916; was mentioned in Despatches; awarded the Military Cross; created a Companion of the Distinguished

Service Order, and awarded the Victoria Cross [London Gazette, 29 Oct. 1920]: " George Stuart Henderson, D.S.O., M.C., late Capt., 2nd Battn. Manchester Regt. On the evening of 24 July, 1920, when about fifteen miles from Hillah (Mesopotamia), the company under his command was ordered to retire. After proceeding about 500 yards a large party of Arabs suddenly opened fire from the flank, causing the company to split up and waver. Regardless of all danger, Capt. Henderson at once re-organized the company, led them gallantly to the attack and drove off the enemy. On two further occasions this officer led his men to charge the Arabs with the bayonet and forced them to retire. At one time, when the situation was extremely critical and the troops and transport were getting out of hand, Capt. Henderson, by sheer pluck and coolness, steadied his command, prevented the company from being cut up, and saved the situation. During the second charge he fell wounded, but refused to leave his command, and just as the company reached the trench they were making for he was again wounded. Realizing that he could do no more, he asked one of his N.C.O.'s to hold him up on the embankment, saying, 'I'm done now, don't let them beat you.' He died fighting."

SUPPLEMENTARY DETAILS

London Gazette, 13 May, 1916.—" War Office, 13 May, 1916. His Majesty the King has been graciously pleased to confer the Victoria Cross on No. 501 Lance-Naik Lala, 41st Dogras, Indian Army, for most conspicuous bravery. Finding a British officer of another regiment lying close to the enemy, he dragged him into a temporary shelter, which he himself had made, and in which he had already bandaged four wounded men. After bandaging his wounds he heard calls from the Adjutant of his own regiment, who was lying in the open severely wounded. The enemy were not more than one hundred yards distant, and it seemed certain death to go out in that direction, but Lance-Naik Lala insisted on going out to his Adjutant, and offered to crawl back with him on his back at once. When this was not permitted, he stripped off his own clothing to keep the wounded officer warmer, and stayed with him till just before dark, when he returned to the shelter. After dark he carried the first wounded officer back to the main trenches, and then, returning with a stretcher, carried back his Adjutant. He set a magnificent example of courage and devotion to his officers."—(For Lance-Naik Lala, see page 208.)

London Gazette, 26 Sept. 1916.—" War Office, 26 Sept. 1916. His Majesty the King has been graciously pleased to confer the Victoria Cross on No. 1605 Naik Shahamad Khan, Punjabis, for most conspicuous bravery. He was in charge of a machine gun section in an exposed position in front of and covering a gap in our new line within 150 yards of the enemy's entrenched position. He beat off three counter-attacks, and worked his gun single-handed after all his men, except two belt-fillers, had become casualties. For three hours he held the gap under very heavy fire while it was being made secure. When his gun was knocked out by hostile fire he and his two belt-fillers held their ground with rifles till ordered to withdraw. With three men sent to assist him he then brought back his gun, ammunition, and one severely wounded man unable to walk. Finally he himself returned and removed all remaining arms and equipment except two shovels. But for his great gallantry and determination our line must have been penetrated by the enemy."—(For Naik Shahamad Khan, see page 220.)

Capt. J. G. Smyth, V C., writes as follows :
" Office of the 1/55th Coke's Rifles, F.F., Ambala, India, 14 Feb. 1920. To General Sir O'Moore Creagh, V.C., G.C.B., G.C.S.I. Sir,—I have the honour to forward herewith the biographical record of Subadar Mir Dast. V.C., I.O.M., of this battalion. The delay in submission, due to the regiment being on field service, is regretted. Please acknowledge receipt. I have the honour to be, sir, your obedient servant, J. Smyth, Captain, Commanding Depot 1/55th Coke's Rifles, F.F."

DAST, MIR, Subadar, Bahadur, I.O.M., 1/55th Coke's Rifles, F.F., was born in 1874, at Maidan, Tirah, son of Mada Mir, Kambar Khel, Afridi, of Maidan, Tirah, India. He enlisted in 1/55th Coke's Rifles, F.F., 3 Dec. 1894; promoted Naik 15 Sept. 1901; Havildar 29 Sept. 1904; Jemadar 3 March, 1909; Subadar 27 April, 1915; went on pension 22 Sept. 1917; was awarded the Victoria Cross [London Gazette, 29 June, 1915]. He served in the European War in France from 19 Jan. 1915, being attached to 57th (Wilde's) Rifles, F.F., and took part in the actions of Neuve Chapelle and the Second Battle of Ypres, April and May, 1915. He was gassed, but continued to carry out his duties until June, 1915, when he was wounded and sent to England. During his convalescence the effects of gas-poisoning became more marked, and he was sent back to India 19 Oct. 1915, when he rejoined the regiment. He never recovered his health, and was transferred to the pension establishment on 22 Sept. 1917. He received the Order of British India 3 June, 1916. He was awarded the I.O.M. in 1908, for gallantry in action at Khan Khor Beg during the Mohmand campaign. He also received the Cross of the Order of Saint George, 3rd Class, for his distinguished services whilst in France. He served in the following campaigns : North-West Frontier of India, 1897–98 (Tochi ; Medal and clasp); North-West Frontier of India, 1901–2 (Waziristan ; clasp); North-West Frontier of India, 1908 (Mohmand ; Medal and clasp); European War, Expeditionary Force " A."—(For Subadar Mir Dast, see page 176.)

NAMES OMITTED FROM CORRECT POSITIONS IN THIS VOLUME

London Gazette, 24 Dec. 1858.—" War Office, 24 Dec. 1858. The Queen has been graciously pleased to confirm the grant of the Decoration of the Victoria Cross to the undermentioned Officers, Non-commissioned Officers and Privates of Her Majesty's Forces and Indian Military Forces, which Decoration has been provisionally conferred upon them by the Commander-in-Chief in India, in accordance with the rules laid down in Her Majesty's Warrant instituting the same, on account of Acts of Bravery performed by them in that country, during operations under his command, as recorded against their several names."

BANKES, WILLIAM GEORGE HAWTREY, Cornet, son of the Right Hon. George Bankes, M.P., of Kingston Lacy and Corfe Castle ; an Old Westminster Boy ; joined the 7th Hussars in April, 1857. "On 19 March, 1858, a strong force of cavalry, horse artillery and some infantry, under Brigadier Campbell, of the Bays, was sent from Alumbagh in the direction of the Moosabagh to prevent the enemy escaping from that side of the city. Cornet Bankes was temporarily attached to ' H ' Troop, escorting the guns, and the force left its encampment about two a.m. They had some skirmishing here and there as they passed various villages where the ground was wooded and broken, and about one o'clock in the afternoon they halted for a rest and feed. Not far away was a small fort, or rezai, apparently unoccupied, but a vidette approaching it was fired upon. The brigadier sent Lieut.-Col. James Hagart, with ' H ' Troop—then not more than half its proper strength—some of Hodson's Horse, a few men of the 78th Highlanders, and two of Major Tomb's guns, to see about it. They unlimbered and fired a couple of shells, when, to everybody's astonishment, about fifty villagers, maddened with bhang or opium, and led by the daroga, or headman—an enormously tall fellow—rushed out straight upon the guns. Hagart ordered the 7th to charge, and one of the first men down was Capt. Slade of ' H ' Troop. With the greatest gallantry, Cornet Bankes led on the troop, and shot three of the rebels at the same moment that Lieut. Wilkin had his foot nearly cut through. Wilkin's horse, a stallion, would not leave the ranks, and everything devolved on the young cornet. Unhappily his bravery was unavailing. A young mutineer, a mere boy, dropped on his knee and hamstrung Bankes's horse with a slash of his tulwar, and, the cornet's revolver being empty, he went down at the mercy of the fiends, who did not know what mercy meant. Men who were there say that had he trusted to his sword he might have saved himself, but,

as it was, he lay to be hacked almost out of semblance to a human being." The Victoria Cross was provisionally conferred upon him by Sir Colin Campbell. He died on the 6th of April, after lingering eighteen days.

MEMORANDUM.

London Gazette, 24 Dec. 1858.—" Cornet William George Hawtrey Bankes, 7th Hussars, upon whom the Commander-in-Chief in India has reported that the Decoration of the Victoria Cross has been provisionally conferred, for conspicuous gallantry in thrice charging a body of infuriated fanatics who had rushed on the guns employed in shelling a small mud fort in the vicinity of Moosa-Bagh, Lucknow, on the 19th March, 1858—of the wounds he received on which occasion he subsequently died—would have been recommended to Her Majesty for confirmation in that distinction had he survived."

London Gazette, 8 June, 1917.—" War Office, 8 June, 1917. His Majesty the King has been graciously pleased to approve of the award of the Victoria Cross to the undermentioned Officers, Non-commissioned Officers and Men."

MACKINTOSH, DONALD, Lieut., was awarded the Victoria Cross [London Gazette, 8 June, 1917]: " Lieut. Donald Mackintosh, late Seaforth Highlanders. For most conspicuous bravery and resolution in the face of intense machine-gun fire. During the initial advance he was shot through the right leg, but, though crippled, he continued to lead his men and captured the trench. In the captured trench Lieut. Mackintosh collected men of another company who had lost their leader, and drove back a counter-attack. He was again wounded, and although unable to stand, he continued, nevertheless, to control the situation. With only fifteen men left he ordered his party to be ready to advance to final objective, and with great difficulty got out of the trench and encouraged his men to advance. He was again wounded and fell. The gallantry and devotion to duty of this officer were beyond all praise."

London Gazette, 22 July, 1918.—" Admiralty, 22 July, 1918. Honours for services in the operations against Zeebrugge and Ostend on the night of the 22nd and 23rd April, 1918. The King has been graciously pleased to approve of the award of the Victoria Cross to the undermentioned Officers and Men."

DEAN, PERCY THOMPSON, Lieut., Royal Naval Volunteer Reserve (of Bradford), was awarded the Victoria Cross [London Gazette, 22 July, 1918]: "Lieut. Percy Thompson Dean, Royal Naval Volunteer Reserve (Motor Launch 282). For most conspicuous gallantry. Lieut. Dean handled his boat in a most magnificent and heroic manner when embarking the officers and men from the blockships at Zeebrugge. He followed the blockships, and closed Intrepid and Iphigenia under a constant and deadly fire from machine and heavy guns at point-blank range, embarking over 100 officers and men. This completed, he was proceeding out of the canal, when he heard that an officer was in the water. He returned, rescued him, and then proceeded, handling his boat throughout as calmly as if engaged in a practice manœuvre. Three men were shot down at his side whilst he conned his ship. On clearing the entrance to the canal the steering gear broke down. He manœuvred his boat by the engines, and avoided complete destruction by steering so close in under the mole that the guns in the batteries could not depress sufficiently to fire on the boat. The whole of the operation was carried out under a constant machine-gun fire at a few yards' range. It was solely due to this officer's courage and daring that M.L. 282 succeeded in saving so many lives."

London Gazette, 14 Dec. 1918.—"War Office, 14 Dec. 1918. His Majesty the King has been graciously pleased to approve of the award of the Victoria Cross to the undermentioned Officers, Warrant Officer, Non-commissioned Officers and Men."

JOHNSON, WILLIAM HENRY, Sergt., served in the European War, and for services at Ramicourt 3 Oct. 1918, was awarded the Victoria Cross [London Gazette, 14 Dec. 1918]: "William Henry Johnson, Sergt., No. 306122, 1/5th Battn. Nottinghamshire and Derbyshire Regt. (T.F.) (Work-sop). For most conspicuous bravery at Ramicourt on the 3rd Oct. 1918. When his platoon was held up by a nest of machine guns at very close range, Sergt. Johnson worked his way forward under very heavy fire, and single-handed charged the post, bayoneting several gunners and capturing two machine guns. During his attack he was severely wounded by a bomb, but continued to lead forward his men. Shortly afterwards the line was once more held up by machine guns. Again he rushed forward and attacked the post single-handed. With wonderful courage he bombed the garrison, put the guns out of action and captured the teams. He showed throughout the most exceptional gallantry and devotion to duty."

London Gazette, 31 Jan. 1919.—"War Office, 31 Jan. 1919. His Majesty the King has been graciously pleased to approve of the award of the Victoria Cross to the undermentioned Officers and Non-commissioned Officers."

ALGIE, WALLACE LLOYD, Lieut., who was killed in action on the 10th Oct. 1918, was a native of Alton, Ontario, Canada, being by profession a banker. He enlisted at Toronto in April, 1916, and was drafted to the 98th Battn. from the Reserve of Officers in Canada, and was awarded the Victoria Cross [London Gazette, 31 Jan. 1919]: "Wallace Lloyd Algie, Lieut., late 20th Battn. 1st Central Ontario Regt. For most conspicuous bravery and self-sacrifice on the 11th Oct. 1918, north-east of Cambrai, when with attacking troops which came under heavy enfilade machine-gun fire from a neighbouring village. Rushing forward with nine volunteers, he shot the crew of an enemy machine gun, and, turning it on the enemy, enabled his party to reach the village. He then rushed another machine gun, killed the crew, captured an officer and ten enemy, and thereby cleared the end of the village. Lieut. Algie, having established his party, went back for reinforcements, but was killed when leading them forward. His valour and personal initiative in the face of intense fire saved many lives and enabled the position to be held."

INDEX

INDEX